KEY TO WORLD MAP PAGES

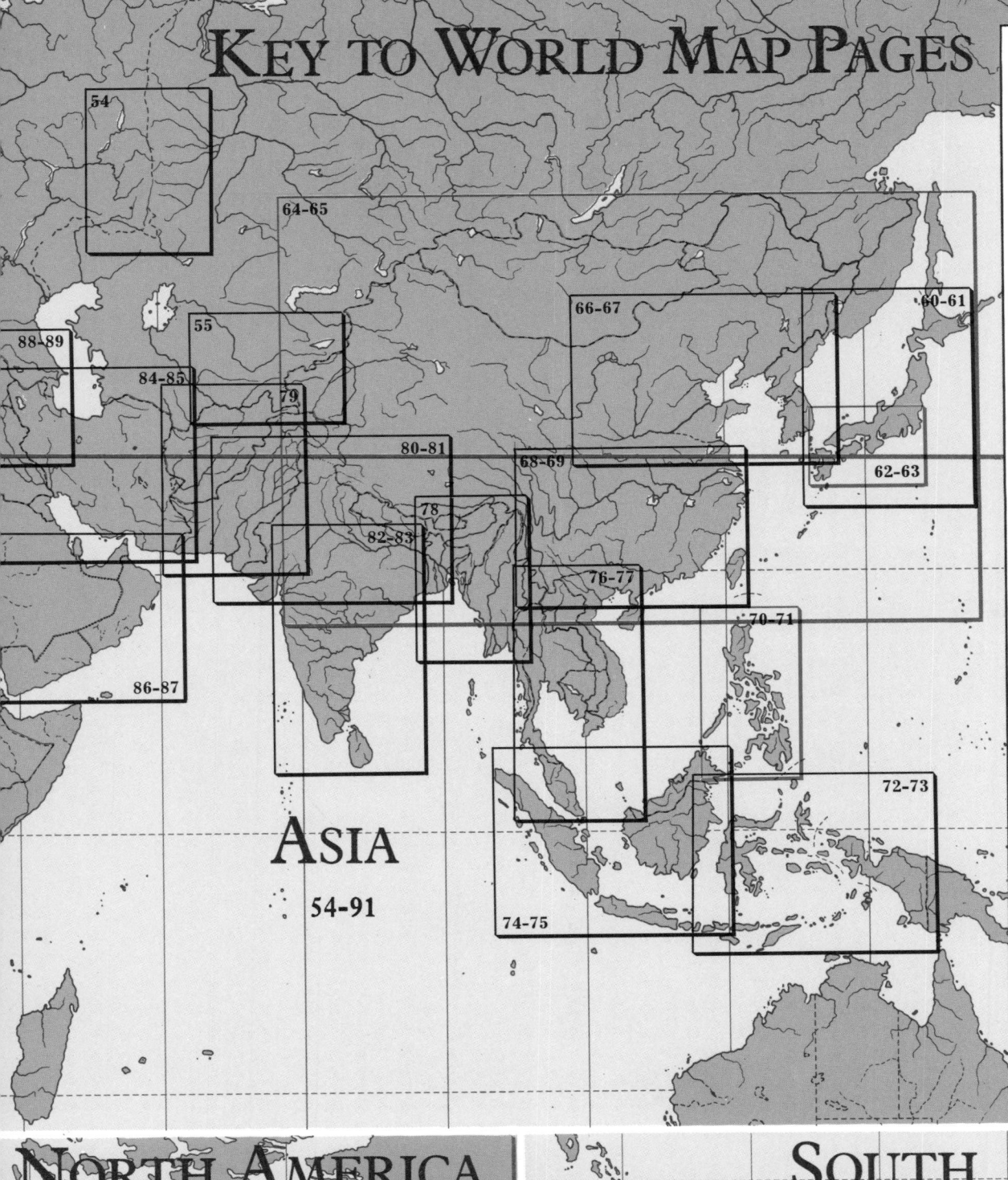

ASIA
54-91

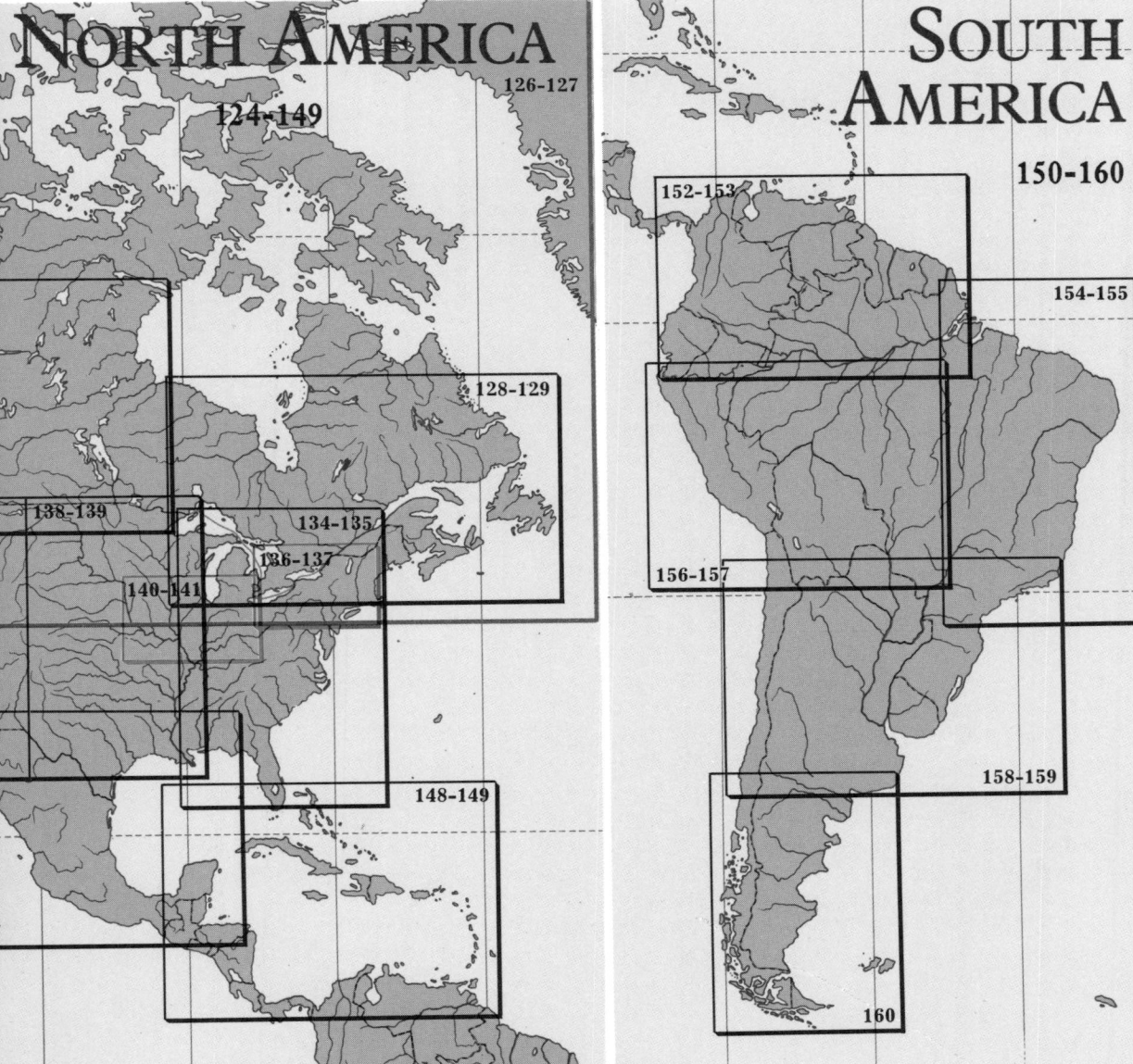

NORTH AMERICA
124-149

SOUTH AMERICA
150-160

COUNTRY INDEX

PHILIP'S

ATLAS
OF THE
WORLD

PHILIP'S

ATLAS
OF THE
WORLD

Published by George Philip Limited
59 Grosvenor Street, London W1X 9DA

ISBN 0-540-05632-4

Printed in Hong Kong

PHILIP'S WORLD MAPS

The reference maps which form the main body of this atlas have been prepared in accordance with the highest standards of international cartography to provide an accurate and detailed representation of the earth. The scales and projections used have been carefully chosen to give balanced coverage of the world, while emphasizing the most densely populated and economically significant regions. A hallmark of Philip's mapping is the use of hill shading and relief colouring to create a graphic impression of landforms: this makes the maps exceptionally easy to read. However, knowledge of the key features employed in the construction and presentation of the maps will enable the reader to derive the fullest benefit from the atlas.

Map sequence

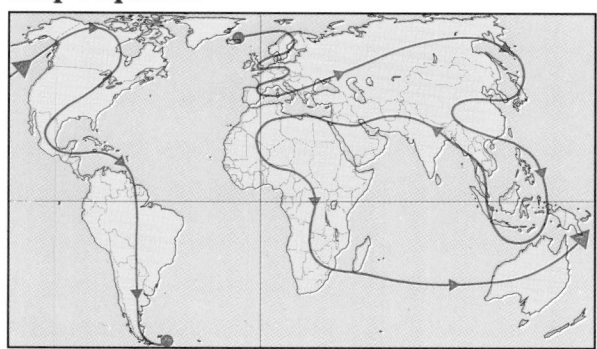

The atlas covers the earth continent by continent: first Europe; then its land neighbour Asia (mapped north before south, in a clockwise sequence), then Africa, Australia and Oceania, North America and South America. This is the classic arrangement adopted by most cartographers since the 16th century. For each continent, there are maps at a variety of scales. First, physical relief and political maps of the whole continent. Then a series of larger-scale maps of the regions within the continent, each followed, where required, by still larger-scale maps of the most important or densely populated areas. The governing principle is that by turning the pages of the atlas, the reader moves steadily from north to south through each continent, with each map overlapping its neighbours. A key map showing this sequence, and the area covered by each map, can be found on the endpapers of the atlas.

Map presentation

With very few exceptions (eg for the Arctic and Antarctic), the maps are drawn with north at the top, regardless of whether they are presented upright or sideways on the page. In the borders will be found the map title; a locator diagram showing the area covered and the page numbers for maps of adjacent areas; the scale; the projection used; the degrees of latitude and longitude; and the letters and figures used in the index for locating place names and geographical features. Physical relief maps also have a height reference panel identifying the colours used for each layer of contouring.

Map symbols

Each map contains a vast amount of detail which can only be conveyed clearly and accurately by the use of symbols. Points and circles of varying sizes locate and identify the relative importance of towns and cities; different styles of type are employed for administrative, geographical and regional place names. A variety of pictorial symbols denote landscape features such as glaciers, marshes and reefs, and man-made structures including roads, railways, airports, canals and dams. International borders are shown by red lines. Where neighbouring countries are in dispute, for example in the Middle East, the maps show the *de facto* boundary between nations, regardless of the legal or historical situation. The symbols are explained on the first page of the World Maps section of the atlas.

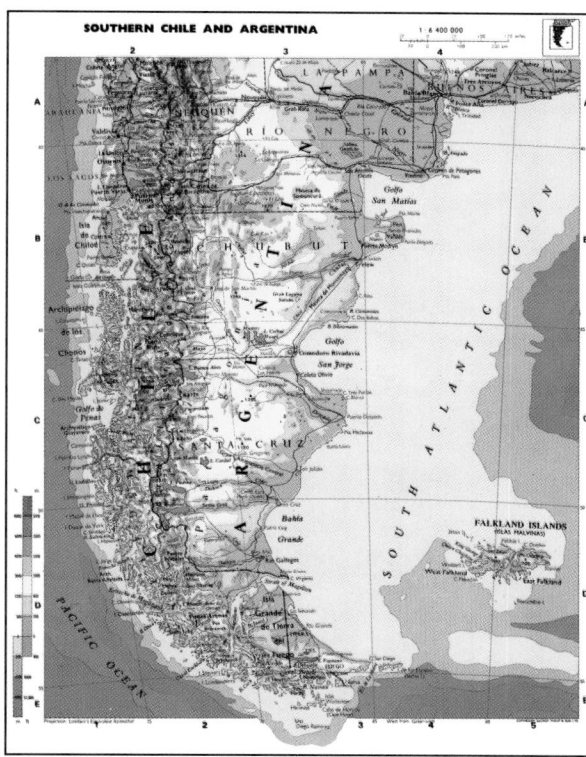

Map scales

1: 16 000 000
1 inch = 252 statute miles

The scale of each map is given in the numerical form known as the 'representative fraction'. The first figure is always one, signifying one unit of distance on the map; the second figure, usually in millions, is the number by which the map unit must be multiplied to give the equivalent distance on the earth's surface. Calculations can easily be made in centimetres and kilometres, by dividing the earth units figure by 100 000 (ie deleting the last five 0s). Thus 1:1 000 000 means 1 cm = 10 km. The calculation for inches and miles is more laborious, but 1 000 000 divided by 63 360 (the number of inches in a mile) shows that 1:1 000 000 means approximately 1 inch = 16 miles. The table below provides distance equivalents for scales down to 1:50 000 000.

LARGE SCALE		
1: 1 000 000	1 cm = 10 km	1 inch = 16 miles
1: 2 500 000	1 cm = 25 km	1 inch = 39.5 miles
1: 5 000 000	1 cm = 50 km	1 inch = 79 miles
1: 6 000 000	1 cm = 60 km	1 inch = 95 miles
1: 8 000 000	1 cm = 80 km	1 inch = 126 miles
1: 10 000 000	1 cm = 100 km	1 inch = 158 miles
1: 15 000 000	1 cm = 150 km	1 inch = 237 miles
1: 20 000 000	1 cm = 200 km	1 inch = 316 miles
1: 50 000 000	1 cm = 500 km	1 inch = 790 miles
SMALL SCALE		

Measuring distances

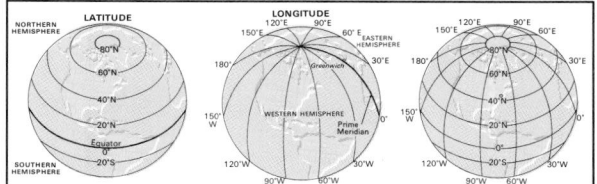

Although each map is accompanied by a scale bar, distances cannot always be measured with confidence because of the distortions involved in portraying the curved surface of the earth on a flat page. As a general rule, the larger the map scale (ie the lower the number of earth units in the representative fraction), the more accurate and reliable will be the distance measured. On small-scale maps such as those of the world and of entire continents, measurement may only be accurate along the 'standard parallels', or central axes, and should not be attempted without considering the map projection.

Map projections

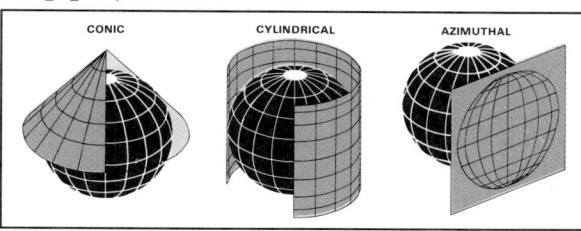

Unlike a globe, no flat map can give a true scale representation of the world in terms of area, shape and position of every region. Each of the numerous systems that have been devised for projecting the curved surface of the earth on to a flat page involves the sacrifice of accuracy in one or more of these elements. The variations in shape and position of landmasses such as Alaska, Greenland and Australia, for example, can be quite dramatic when different projections are compared.

For this atlas, the guiding principle has been to select projections that involve the least distortion of size and distance. The projection used for each map is noted in the border. Most fall into one of three categories - conic, cylindrical or azimuthal - whose basic concepts are shown above. Each involves plotting the forms of the earth's surface on a grid of latitude and longitude lines, which may be shown as parallels, curves or radiating spokes.

Latitude and longitude

Accurate positioning of individual points on the earth's surface is made possible by reference to the geometrical system of latitude and longitude. Latitude *parallels* are drawn west-east around the earth and numbered by degrees north and south of the Equator, which is designated 0° of latitude. Longitude *meridians* are drawn north-south and numbered by degrees east and west of the *prime meridian*, 0° of longitude, which passes through Greenwich in England. By referring to these co-ordinates and their sub-divisions of minutes (1/60th of a degree) and seconds (1/60th of a minute), any place on earth can be located to within a few hundred yards. Latitude and longitude are indicated by blue lines on the maps; they are straight or curved according to the projection employed. Reference to these lines is the easiest way of determining the relative positions of places on different maps, and for plotting compass directions.

Name forms

For ease of reference, both English and local name forms appear in the atlas. Oceans, seas and countries are shown in English throughout the atlas; country names may be abbreviated to their commonly accepted form (eg Germany, not Federal Republic of Germany). Conventional English forms are also used for place names on the smaller-scale maps of the continents. However, local name forms are used on all large-scale and regional maps, with the English form given in brackets only for important cities - the large-scale map of European Russia thus shows Moskva (Moscow). For countries which do not use a Roman script, place names have been transcribed according to the systems adopted by the British and US Geographic Names Authorities. For China, the Pin Yin system has been used, with some more widely known forms appearing in brackets, as with Beijing (Peking). Both English and local names appear in the index, the English form being cross-referenced to the local form.

CONTENTS

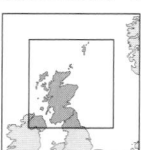
NOTE
The titles to the World Maps
list the main countries, states
and provinces covered by
each map. A name given in
italics indicates that only part
of the country is shown on
the map.

Netherlands, Belgium and Luxembourg
1:1 000 000

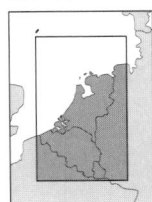

20-21

Northern France
1:2 000 000

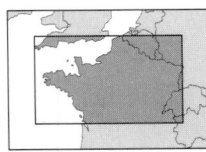

22-23

Southern France
1:2 000 000
Corsica, Monaco

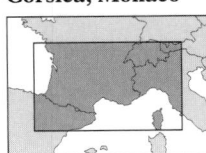

24-25

Germany 1:2 000 000

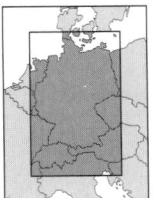

26-27

Switzerland 1:800 000
Liechtenstein

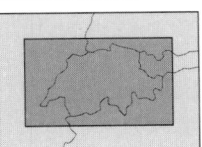

28-29

Austria, Czechoslovakia and Hungary 1:2 000 000
Poland

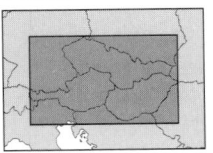

30-31

Malta, Crete, Corfu, Rhodes and Cyprus
1:800 000 - 1:1 040 000

32

Balearics, Canaries and Madeira 1:800 000 - 1:1 600 000
Mallorca, Menorca, Ibiza

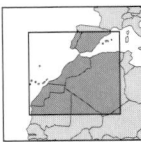

33

Eastern Spain 1:2 000 000
Andorra

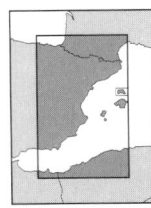

34-35

Western Spain and Portugal 1:2 000 000

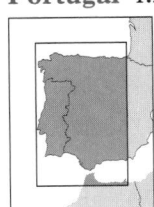

36-37

Northern Italy and Western Yugoslavia
1:2 000 000
San Marino

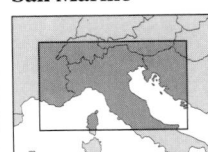

38-39

Southern Italy 1:2 000 000
Sardinia, Sicily

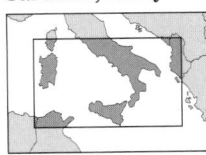

40-41

Eastern Yugoslavia and Bulgaria 1:2 000 000

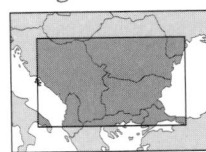

42-43

Greece and Albania
1:2 000 000

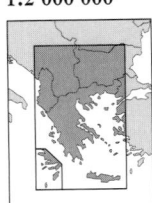

44-45

Romania 1:2 000 000

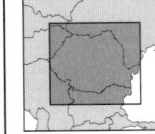

46

Poland 1:2 000 000

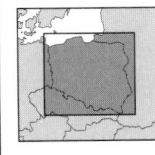

47

European Russia
1:8 000 000
Turkey

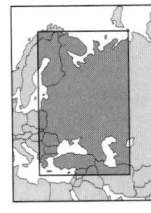

48-49

Central European Russia
1:4 000 000
Russian SFSR, Estonia, Latvia, Lithuania, Byelorussia, *Ukraine*

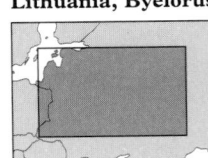

50-51

Southern European Russia 1:4 000 000
Russian SFSR, Ukraine, Georgia, Armenia, Azerbaijan, Moldavia

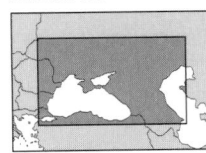

52-53

ASIA

Southern Urals 1:4 000 000
Russian SFSR

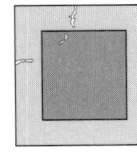

54

Tashkent Region 1:4 000 000
Kazakhstan, Kirgizia, Tadzhikistan, *Uzbekistan*

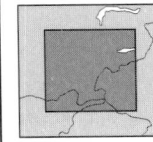

55

Union of Soviet Socialist Republics 1:16 000 000
Russian SFSR, Kazakhstan, Turkmenistan, Uzbekistan

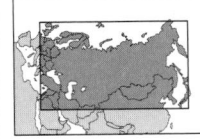

56-57

Asia: Physical
1:40 000 000
58

Asia: Political
1:40 000 000
59

Japan 1:4 000 000
Ryukyu Islands

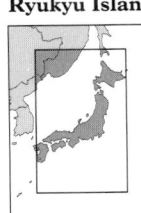

60-61

Southern Japan 1:2 000 000

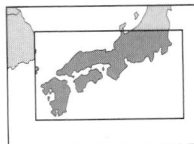

62-63

China 1:12 000 000
Mongolia

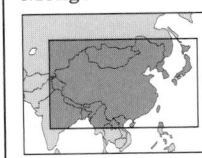

64-65

Northern China and Korea 1:4 800 000
North Korea, South Korea

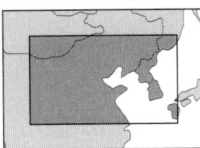

66-67

Southern China 1:4 800 000
Hong Kong, Taiwan, Macau

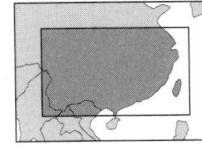

68-69

Philippines 1:3 200 000

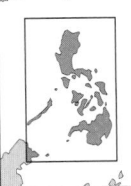

70-71

Eastern Indonesia
1:5 600 000

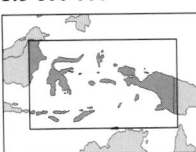

72-73

Western Indonesia
1:5 600 000
Malaysia, Singapore, Brunei

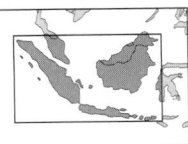

74-75

Mainland South-East Asia 1:4 800 000
Thailand, Vietnam, Cambodia, Laos

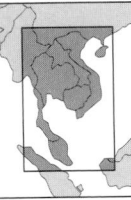

76-77

Bangladesh, North-Eastern India and Burma
1:4 800 000
Bhutan

78

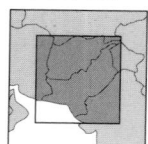
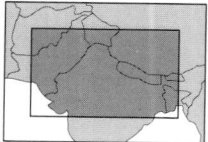
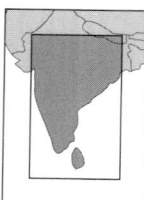
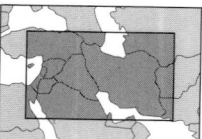
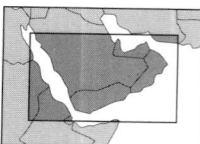
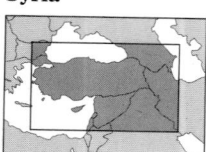
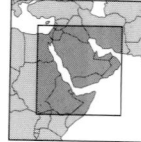
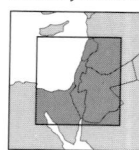
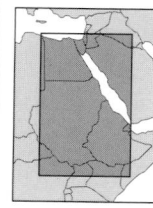
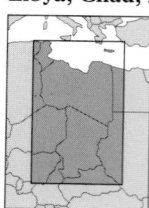
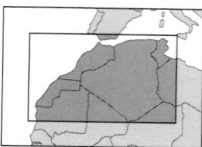
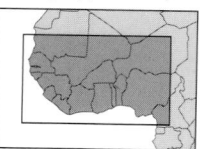
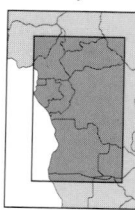
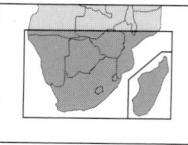
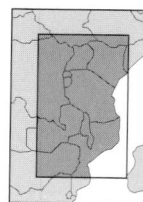
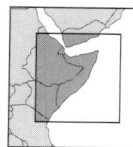
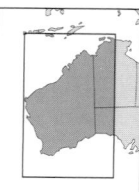

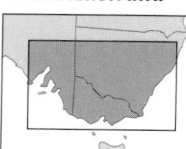

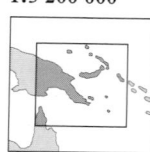

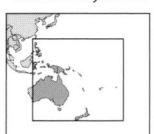
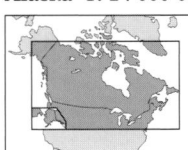

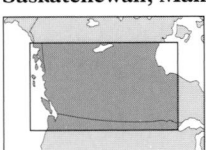
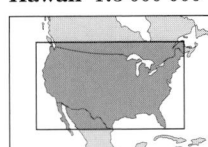

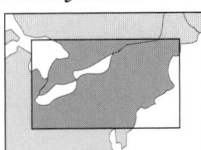
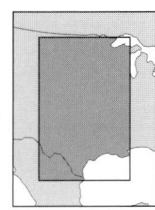
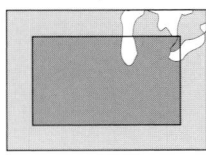
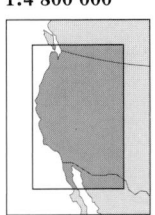

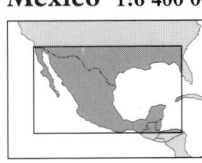
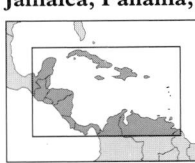
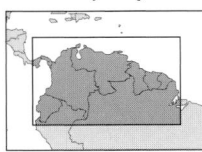
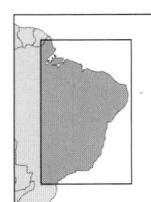
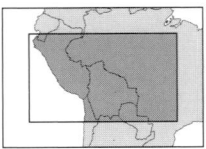
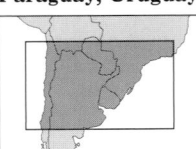
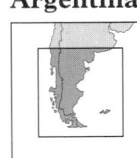
IX

WORLD STATISTICS: COUNTRIES

This alphabetical list includes all the countries and territories of the world. If a territory is not completely independent, then the country it is associated with is named. The area figures give the total area of land, inland water and ice. Units for areas and populations are thousands. The annual income is the Gross National Product per capita in US dollars. The figures are the latest available, usually 1989-90.

Country/Territory	Area km² Thousands	Area miles² Thousands	Population Thousands	Capital	Annual Income US $
Adélie Land (Fr)	432	167	0.03	-	
Afghanistan	652	25	15,814	Kabul	450
Albania	28.8	11.1	3,202	Tiranë	1,000
Algeria	2,382	920	24,597	Algiers	2,170
American Samoa (US)	0.20	0.08	40	Pago Pago	6,000
Amsterdam I. (Fr)	0.05	0.02	0.03	-	
Andorra (Fr/Spain)	0.45	0.17	50	Andorre-la-Vella	
Angola	1,247	481	9,747	Luanda	620
Anguilla (UK)	0.40	0.09	7	The Valley	
Antigua & Barbuda	0.44	0.17	80	St. John's	3,000
Argentina	2,767	1,068	31,929	Buenos Aires	2,160
Aruba (Neths)	0.19	0.07	63	Oranjestad	
Ascension I. (UK)	0.09	0.03	1.5	Georgetown	
Australia	7,687	2,968	16,807	Canberra	14,400
Austral.Antarc.Terr.	6,120	2,363	0	-	
Austria	83.9	32.4	7,618	Vienna	17,360
Azores (Port)	2.2	0.87	260	Ponta Delgada	
Bahamas	13.9	5.4	250	Nassau	11,370
Bahrain	0.68	0.26	489	Manama	6,500
Bangladesh	144	56	106,507	Dacca	180
Barbados	0.43	0.17	256	Bridgetown	6,370
Belau (US)	0.46	0.18	180	Koror	
Belgium	30.5	11.8	9,931	Brussels	16,390
Belize	23.0	8.9	180	Belmopan	1,600
Benin	113	43	4,591	Porto-Novo	380
Bermuda (UK)	0.05	0.02	58	Hamilton	25,000
Bhutan (India)	47.0	18.1	1,483	Thimphu	190
Bolivia	1,099	424	7,193	La Paz/Sucre	600
Botswana	582	225	1,256	Gaborone	960
Bouvet I. (Nor)	0.05	0.02	0.02	-	
Brazil	8,512	3,286	147,404	Brasilia	2,550
Brit. Antarctic Terr. (UK)	1,709	660	0.3	Stanley	
Brit. Ind. Oc. Terr (UK)	0.08	0.03	3	-	
Brunei	5.8	2.2	251	Bandar Seri Begawan	6,000
Bulgaria	111	43	9,003	Sofia	2,320
Burkina Faso	274	106	8,763	Ouagadougou	310
Burma (Myanmar)	677	261	40,810	Rangoon	500
Burundi	27.8	10.7	5,302	Bujumbura	220
Cambodia	181	70	8,055	Phnom Penh	300
Cameroon	475	184	11,540	Yaoundé	1,010
Canada	9,976	3,852	26,220	Ottawa	19,020
Canary Is. (Spain)	7.3	2.8	1,700	Las Palmas/S.Cruz	
Cape Verde Is.	4.0	1.6	368	Praia	760
Cayman Is. (UK)	0.26	0.10	21	Georgetown	
Cent. African Rep.	623	241	2,841	Bangui	390
Chad	1,284	496	5,538	Ndjamena	190
Chatham Is. (NZ)	0.96	0.37	0.05	Waitangi	
Chile	757	292	12,961	Santiago	1,770
China	9,597	3,682	1,119,700	Beijing	360
Christmas I. (Aus)	0.14	0.05	2	The Settlement	
Cocos (Keeling) Is. (Aus)	0.01	0.005	0.70	-	
Colombia	1,139	440	31,192	Bogotá	1,190
Comoros	2.2	0.86	503	Moroni	460
Congo	342	132	1,940	Brazzaville	930
Cook Is. (NZ)	0.24	0.11	20	Avarua	900
Costa Rica	51.1	19.7	2,960	San José	1,790
Crozet Is. (Fr)	0.51	0.19	35	-	
Cuba	111	43	10,520	Havana	3,000
Cyprus	9.3	3.6	694	Nicosia	10,320
Czechoslovakia	128	49	15,651	Prague	4,000
Denmark	43.1	16.6	5,135	Copenhagen	20,510
Djibouti	23.2	9.0	394	Djibouti	1,000
Dominica	0.75	0.29	80	Roseau	1,800
Dominican Rep.	48.7	18.8	7,018	Santo Domingo	790
Ecuador	284	109	10,490	Quito	1,040
Egypt	1,001	387	53,080	Cairo	630
El Salvador	21.0	8.1	5,207	San Salvador	1,040
Equatorial Guinea	28.1	10.8	341	Malabo	430
Ethiopia	1,222	472	50,774	Addis Ababa	120
Falkland Is. (UK)	12.2	4.7	2	Stanley	
Faroe Is. (Den)	1.4	0.54	47	Tórshavn	20,510
Fiji	18.3	7.1	740	Suva	1,640
Finland	338	131	4,962	Helsinki	22,060
France	552	213	56,160	Paris	17,830
French Guiana (Fr)	90.0	34.7	90	Cayenne	2,500
French Polynesia (Fr)	4.0	1.5	190	Papeete	6,000
Gabon	268	103	1,132	Libreville	2,770
Gambia, The	11.3	4.4	835	Banjul	230
Germany	357	138	78,620	Berlin/Bonn	16,500
Ghana	239	92	14,566	Accra	380
Gibraltar (UK)	0.007	0.003	31	-	4,000
Greece	132	51	10,031	Athens	5,340
Greenland (Den)	2,176	840	60	Godthåb	6,000
Grenada	0.34	0.13	100	St. George's	1,900
Guadeloupe (Fr)	1.7	0.66	340	Basse-Terre	7,000
Guam (US)	0.55	0.21	139	Agana	6,000
Guatemala	109	42	8,935	Guatemala City	920
Guinea	246	95	6,705	Conakry	430
Guinea-Bissau	36.1	13.9	966	Bissau	180
Guyana	215	83	1,023	Georgetown	310
Haiti	27.8	10.7	5,609	Port-au-Prince	400
Honduras	112	43	4,951	Tegucigalpa	900
Hong Kong (UK)	1.1	0.40	5,768	-	10,320
Hungary	93.0	35.9	10,563	Budapest	2,560
Iceland	103	40	251	Reykjavik	21,240
India	3,288	1,269	811,817	Delhi	350
Indonesia	1,905	735	179,136	Jakarta	490
Iran	1,648	636	54,203	Tehran	4,500
Iraq	438	169	18,279	Baghdad	2,000
Ireland	70.3	27.1	3,515	Dublin	8,500
Israel	27.0	10.4	4,566	Jerusalem	9,750
Italy	301	116	57,517	Rome	15,150
Ivory Coast	322	125	12,097	Abidjan	790
Jamaica	11.0	4.2	2,375	Kingston	1,260
Jan Mayen I. (Nor)	0.38	0.15	0.06	-	
Japan	378	146	123,120	Tokyo	23,730
Johnston I. (US)	0.002	0.0009	0.30	-	
Jordan	89.2	34.4	4,102	Amman	1,730
Kenya	580	224	24,872	Nairobi	380
Kerguelen Is. (Fr)	7.2	2.8	0	-	
Kermadec Is. (NZ)	0.03	0.01	0	-	
Kiribati	0.72	0.28	70	Tarawa	700
Korea, North	121	47	22,420	Pyongyang	900
Korea, South	99.0	38.2	42,380	Seoul	4,400
Kuwait	17.8	6.9	2,048	Kuwait City	16,380
Laos	237	91	3,972	Vientiane	170
Lebanon	10.4	4.0	2,897	Beirut	2,000
Lesotho	30.4	11.7	1,700	Maseru	470
Liberia	111	43	2,508	Monrovia	500
Libya	1,760	679	4,385	Tripoli	5,800
Liechtenstein	0.16	0.06	28	Vaduz	33,000
Luxembourg	2.6	1.0	378	Luxembourg	24,860
Macau (Port)	0.02	0.006	450	-	2,000
Madagascar	587	227	11,602	Antananarivo	230
Madeira (Port)	0.81	0.31	280	Funchal	
Malawi	118	46	8,022	Lilongwe	180
Malaysia	330	127	16,957	Kuala Lumpur	2,130
Maldives	0.30	0.12	206	Malé	
Mali	1,240	479	7,960	Bamako	260
Malta	0.32	0.12	350	Valletta	5,820
Mariana Is. (US)	0.48	0.18	22	Saipan	
Marshall Is. (US)	0.18	0.07	42	Majuro	
Martinique (Fr)	1.1	0.42	340	Fort-de-France	4,000
Mauritania	1,025	396	1,969	Nouakchott	490
Mauritius	1.9	0.72	1,068	Port Louis	1,950
Mayotte (Fr)	0.37	0.14	84	Mamoundzou	
Mexico	1,958	756	84,490	Mexico City	1,990
Micronesia, Fed. Stat (US)	0.70	0.27	103	Kolonia	
Midway Is. (US)	0.005	0.002	0.45	-	
Monaco	0.002	0.0001	28	-	20,000
Mongolia	1,567	605	2,070	Ulan Bator	400
Montserrat (UK)	0.10	0.04	10	Plymouth	
Morocco	447	172	24,521	Rabat	900
Mozambique	802	309	15,326	Maputo	80
Namibia	824	318	1,817	Windhoek	1,006
Nauru	0.02	0.008	9	Domaneab	
Nepal	141	54	18,442	Katmandu	170
Netherlands	41.9	16.2	14,891	Amsterdam	16,010
Neths. Antilles (Neths)	0.99	0.38	191	Willemstad	6,000
New Caledonia (Fr)	19.0	7.3	163	Nouméa	4,000
New Zealand	269	104	3,389	Wellington	11,800
Nicaragua	130	50	3,745	Managua	800
Niger	1,267	489	6,894	Niamey	290
Nigeria	924	357	109,175	Lagos (Abuja)	250
Niue (NZ)	0.26	0.10	4	Alofi	
Norfolk I. (Aus)	0.03	0.01	2	Kingston	
Norway	324	125	4,227	Oslo	21,850
Oman	212	82	1,422	Muscat	5,220
Pakistan	796	307	108,678	Islamabad	370
Panama	77.1	29.8	2,370	Panama City	1,780
Papua New Guinea	463	179	3,593	Port Moresby	900
Paraguay	407	157	4,157	Asunción	1,030
Peru	1,285	496	21,792	Lima	1,090
Peter 1st I. (Nor)	0.18	0.07	0	-	
Philippines	300	116	60,097	Manila	700
Pitcairn I. (UK)	0.03	0.01	0.05	Adamstown	
Poland	313	121	37,931	Warsaw	1,760
Portugal	92.4	35.7	10,467	Lisbon	4,260
Puerto Rico (US)	8.9	3.4	3,660	San Juan	6,010
Qatar	11.0	4.2	422	Doha	10,000
Queen Maud Land (Nor)	2,800	1,081	0	-	
Réunion (Fr)	2.5	0.97	585	St.-Denis	
Romania	238	92	23,512	Bucharest	2,500
Ross Dependency (NZ)	435	168	0	-	
Rwanda	26.3	10.2	6,989	Kigali	310
St. Christopher/Nevis	0.36	0.14	50	Basseterre	3,000
St. Helena (UK)	0.31	0.12	7	Jamestown	
St. Lucia	0.62	0.24	150	Castries	1,810
St. Paul I. (Fr)	0.007	0.003	0	-	
St. Pierre & Miquelon (Fr)	0.24	0.09	6	St. Pierre	
St. Vincent/Grenadines	0.39	0.15	110	Kingstown	1,300
San Marino	0.06	0.02	23	San Marino	
São Tomé & Príncipe	0.96	0.37	116	São Tomé	360
Saudi Arabia	2,150	830	14,435	Riyadh	6,230
Senegal	197	76	7,171	Dakar	650
Seychelles	0.28	0.11	67	Victoria	4,000
Sierra Leone	71.7	27.7	4,046	Freetown	200
Singapore	0.62	0.24	2,685	Singapore	10,450
Solomon Is.	28.9	11.2	325	Honiara	570
Somalia	638	246	7,339	Mogadishu	170
South Africa	1,221	471	34,492	Pretoria	2,460
South Georgia (UK)	3.8	1.4	0.05	-	
South Sandwich Is. (UK)	0.38	0.15	0	-	
Spain	505	195	38,811	Madrid	9,150
Sri Lanka	65.6	25.3	16,810	Colombo	430
Sudan	2,506	967	24,484	Khartoum	450
Surinam	163	63	400	Paramaribo	2,500
Svalbard (Nor)	62.0	23.9	4	Longyearbyen	
Swaziland	17.4	6.7	763	Mbabane	900
Sweden	450	174	8,541	Stockholm	21,710
Switzerland	41.3	15.9	6,647	Bern	30,270
Syria	185	71	11,719	Damascus	1,020
Taiwan	36.0	13.9	20,300	Taipei	6,600
Tanzania	945	365	24,802	Dar es Salaam	120
Thailand	513	198	55,448	Bangkok	1,170
Togo	56.8	21.9	3,349	Lome	390
Tokelau (NZ)	0.01	0.005	2	Nukunonu	
Tonga	0.75	0.29	120	Nuku'alofa	910
Trinidad & Tobago	5.1	2.0	1,263	Port of Spain	3,160
Tristan da Cunha (UK)	0.11	0.04	0.33	Edinburgh	
Tunisia	164	63	7,990	Tunis	1,260
Turkey	779	301	56,741	Ankara	1,360
Turks & Caicos Is. (UK)	0.43	0.17	9	Grand Turk	
Tuvalu	0.03	0.01	9	Funafuti	600
Uganda	236	91	17,804	Kampala	250
United Arab Emirates	83.6	32.3	1,546	Abu Dhabi	18,430
United Kingdom	244	94	57,405	London	14,570
United States	9,373	3,619	249,928	Washington	21,100
Uruguay	177	68	3,077	Montevideo	2,620
USSR	22,402	8,649	285,861	Moscow	3,000
Vanuatu	12.2	4.7	150	Port Vila	860
Vatican City	0.0004	0.0002	1.0	-	
Venezuela	912	352	19,246	Caracas	2,450
Vietnam	332	127	65,681	Hanoi	300
Virgin Is. (UK)	0.15	0.06	12	Road Town	
Virgin Is. (US)	0.34	0.13	111	Charlotte Amalie	
Wake Is.	0.008	0.003	0.30	-	
Wallis & Futuna Is. (Fr)	0.20	0.08	16	Mata-Utu	
Western Sahara (Mor)	266	103	190	El Aiun	
Western Samoa	2.8	1.1	185	Apia	720
Yemen	528	204	10,183	San'a	640
Yugoslavia	256	99	23,764	Belgrade	2,490
Zaïre	2,345	906	34,491	Kinshasa	260
Zambia	753	291	7,804	Lusaka	390
Zimbabwe	391	151	9,122	Harare	660

World Statistics: Cities

This list shows the principal cities with more than 500,000 inhabitants (for China only cities with more than 1 million are included). The figures are taken from the most recent census or estimate available, and as far as possible, are the population of the metropolitan area, eg greater New York, Mexico or London. All the figures are in thousands. The top twenty cities are indicated with their rank in brackets following the name.

Afghanistan	
Kabul	1,127
Algeria	
Algiers	1,722
Oran	664
Angola	
Luanda	1,200
Argentina	
Buenos Aires [8]	10,728
Cordoba	1,055
Rosario	1,016
Mendoza	668
La Plata	611
San Miguel de Tucuman	571
Australia	
Sydney	3,531
Melbourne	2,965
Brisbane	1,215
Perth	1,083
Adelaide	1,013
Austria	
Vienna	1,483
Bangladesh	
Dacca	4,770
Chittagong	1,840
Khulna	860
Rajshahi	430
Belgium	
Brussels	970
Antwerp	500
Bolivia	
La Paz	993
Brazil	
São Paulo [3]	16,832
Rio de Janeiro [7]	11,141
Belo Horizonte	3,446
Recife	2,945
Pôrto Alegre	2,924
Salvador	2,362
Fortaleza	2,169
Çuritiba	1,926
Brasilia	1,557
Nova Iguaçu	1,325
Belem	1,296
Santos	1,200
Goiâna	928
Campinas	845
Manaus	834
São Gonçalo	731
Guarulhos	718
Duque de Caxias	666
Santo Andre	637
Osasco	594
São Bernado do Campo	566
São Luis	564
Natal	512
Bulgaria	
Sofia	1,129
Burma	
Rangoon	2,459
Mandalay	533
Cambodia	
Phnom Penh	500
Cameroon	
Douala	1,030
Yaoundé	654
Central African Rep.	
Bangui	597
Chad	
Ndjamena	512
Canada	
Toronto	3,427
Montréal	2,921
Vancouver	1,381
Ottawa-Hull	819
Edmonton	785
Calgary	671
Winnipeg	623
Québec	603
Hamilton	557
Chile	
Santiago	4,858
China	
Shanghai [5]	12,320
Beijing [10]	9,750
Tianjin	5,459
Shenyang	4,285
Wuhan	3,493
Canton	3,359
Chongqing	2,832
Harbin	2,668
Chengdu	2,642
Xi'an	2,387
Zibo	2,329
Nanjing	2,290
Nanchang	2,289
Lupanshui	2,247
Taiyuan	1,929
Changchun	1,908
Dalian	1,682
Zhaozhuang	1,612
Zhengzhou	1,610
Kunming	1,516
Jinan	1,464
Tangshan	1,410
Guiyang	1,403
Lanzhou	1,391
Linyi	1,385
Pingxiang	1,305
Qiqihar	1,301
Anshan	1,298
Qingdao	1,273
Xintao	1,272
Hangzhou	1,271
Fushun	1,270
Yangcheng	1,265
Yulin	1,255
Dongguang	1,230
Chao'an	1,227
Xiaogan	1,219
Fuzhou	1,205
Suining	1,195
Changsha	1,193
Shijiazhuang	1,187
Jilin	1,169
Xintai	1,167
Puyang	1,125
Baotou	1,119
Bozhou	1,112
Zhongshan	1,073
Luoyang	1,063
Laiwu	1,054
Leshan	1,039
Urumchi	1,038
Ningbo	1,033
Datong	1,020
Huainan	1,019
Heze	1,017
Handan	1,014
Linhai	1,012
Macheng	1,010
Changshu	1,004
Colombia	
Bogotá	4,185
Medellin	1,506
Cali	1,397
Barranquilla	920
Cartagena	560
Congo	
Brazzaville	596
Cuba	
Havana	2,059
Czechoslovakia	
Prague	1,194
Denmark	
Copenhagen	1,339
Dominican Rep.	
Santo Domingo	1,313
Ecuador	
Guayaquil	1,301
Quito	1,110
Egypt	
Cairo [18]	6,325
Alexandria	2,893
El Giza	1,858
Shubra el Kheima	711
El Salvador	
San Salvador	973
Ethiopia	
Addis Ababa	1,686
Finland	
Helsinki	987
France	
Paris [13]	8,510
Lyons	1,170
Marseilles	1,080
Lille	935
Bordeaux	628
Toulouse	523
Germany	
Berlin	3,301
Hamburg	1,594
Munich	1,189
Cologne	928
Essen	623
Frankfurt	619
Dortmund	584
Düsseldorf	563
Stuttgart	552
Leipzig	545
Bremen	533
Duisburg	525
Dresden	518
Hanover	500
Ghana	
Accra	965
Greece	
Athens	3,027
Thessalonika	872
Guatemala	
Guatemala	2,000
Guinea	
Conakry	705
Haiti	
Port-au-Prince	1,144
Honduras	
Tegucigalpa	605
Hong Kong	
Kowloon	2,302
Hong Kong	1,176
Tsuen Wan	690
Hungary	
Budapest	2,115
India	
Calcutta [11]	9,194
Bombay [14]	8,243
Delhi	5,729
Madras	4,289
Bangalore	2,922
Ahmadabad	2,548
Hyderabad	2,546
Poona	1,686
Kanpur	1,639
Nagpur	1,302
Jaipur	1,015
Lucknow	1,008
Coimbatore	920
Patna	919
Surat	914
Madurai	908
Indore	829
Varanasi	797
Jabalpur	757
Agra	747
Vadodara	744
Cochin	686
Dhanbad	678
Bhopal	671
Jamshedpur	670
Allahabad	650
Ulhasnagar	649
Tiruchchirappalli	610
Ludhiana	606
Srinagar	606
Vishakhapatnam	604
Amritsar	595
Gwalior	556
Calicut	546
Vijayawada	543
Meerut	537
Dharwad	527
Trivandrum	520
Salem	519
Solapur	515
Jodhpur	506
Ranchi	503
Indonesia	
Jakarta [17]	7,348
Surabaya	2,224
Medan	1,806
Bandung	1,567
Semarang	1,026
Palembang	787
Ujung Pandang	709
Malang	512
Iran	
Tehran [19]	6,043
Mashhad	1,464
Esfahan	987
Tabriz	971
Shiraz	848
Ahvaz	580
Bakhtaran	561
Qom	543
Iraq	
Baghdad	4,649
Basra	617
Mosul	571
Ireland	
Dublin	921
Italy	
Rome	2,817
Milan	1,464
Naples	1,203
Turin	1,012
Palermo	731
Genoa	712
Ivory Coast	
Abidjan	1,850
Bouaké	640
Jamaica	
Kingston	525
Japan	
Tokyo [6]	11,829
Yokohama	2,993
Osaka	2,636
Nagoya	2,116
Sapporo	1,543
Kyoto	1,479
Kobe	1,411
Fukuoka	1,160
Kawasaki	1,089
Kitakyushu	1,056
Hiroshima	1,044
Sakai	818
Chiba	789
Sendai	700
Okayama	572
Kumamoto	556
Kagoshima	531
Higashiosaka	523
Hamamatsu	514
Amagasaki	509
Funabashi	507
Jordan	
Amman	1,160
Irbid	680
Kenya	
Nairobi	1,429
Mombasa	500
Korea, North	
Pyongyang	2,639
Hamhung	775
Chongjin	754
Chinnampo	691
Sinuiju	500
Korea South	
Seoul [9]	10,513
Pusan	3,754
Taegu	2,206
Inchon	1,604
Kwangju	1,165
Taejon	866
Ulsan	551
Lebanon	
Beirut	702
Libya	
Tripoli	980
Benghazi	650
Madagascar	
Antananarivo	703
Malaysia	
Kuala Lumpur	1,103
Mali	
Bamako	646
Mauritania	
Nouakchott	500
Mexico	
Mexico City [1]	18,748
Guadalajara	2,587
Monterrey	2,335
Puebla	1,218
León	947
Torreón	730
San Luis Potosi	602
Ciudad Juárez	596
Mérida	580
Culiacán Rosales	560
Mexicali	511
Mongolia	
Ulan Bator	500
Morocco	
Casablanca	2,158
Rabat-Salé	893
Fès	548
Mozambique	
Maputo	1,070
Netherlands	
Rotterdam	1,040
Amsterdam	1,038
The Hague	684
Utrecht	526
New Zealand	
Auckland	851
Nicaragua	
Managua	682
Nigeria	
Lagos	1,097
Ibadan	1,060
Ogbomosho	527
Norway	
Oslo	643
Pakistan	
Karachi	5,208
Lahore	2,953
Faisalabad	1,104
Rawalpindi	795
Hyderabad	752
Multan	722
Gujranwala	659
Peshawar	556
Panama	
Panama City	625
Paraguay	
Asunción	708
Peru	
Lima-Callao	4,605
Arequipa	592
Philippines	
Manila	1,728
Quezon City	1,326
Cebu	552
Caloocan	524
Poland	
Warsaw	1,671
Lodz	852
Krakow	744
Wroclaw	640
Poznan	586
Portugal	
Lisbon	1,612
Oporto	1,315
Puerto Rico	
San Juan	1,816
Romania	
Bucharest	2,014
Saudi Arabia	
Riyadh	2,000
Jedda	1,400
Mecca	618
Medina	500
Senegal	
Dakar	1,382
Singapore	
Singapore	2,600
Somali Rep.	
Mogadishu	1,000
South Africa	
Cape Town	1,912
Johannesburg	1,762
East Rand	1,038
Durban	982
Pretoria	823
Port Elizabeth	652
West Rand	647
Vereeniging	540
Spain	
Madrid	3,123
Barcelona	1,694
Valencia	739
Seville	668
Zaragoza	596
Malaga	595
Sri Lanka	
Colombo	1,412
Sudan	
Omdurman	600
Khartoum	510
Sweden	
Stockholm	1,471
Gothenburg	720
Malmö	500
Switzerland	
Zurich	839
Syria	
Damascus	1,361
Aleppo	1,308
Taiwan	
Taipei	2,680
Kaohsiung	1,343
Taichung	715
Tainan	657
Panchiao	506
Tanzania	
Dar es Salaam	1,100
Thailand	
Bangkok	5,609
Tunisia	
Tunis	774
Turkey	
Istanbul	5,495
Ankara	2,252
Izmir	1,490
Adana	776
Bursa	614
Uganda	
Kampala	500
United Kingdom	
London [17]	6,735
Birmingham	994
Leeds	710
Glasgow	703
Sheffield	528
Liverpool	500
Uruguay	
Montevideo	1,248
United States	
New York [2]	18,120
Los Angeles [4]	13,770
Chicago [15]	8,181
San Francisco [20]	6,042
Philadelphia	5,963
Detroit	4,620
Dallas	3,766
Boston	3,736
Washington	3,734
Houston	3,642
Miami	3,001
Cleveland	2,769
Atlanta	2,737
Saint Louis	2,467
Seattle	2,421
Minneapolis-SP.	2,388
San Diego	2,370
Baltimore	2,343
Pittsburgh	2,284
Phoenix	2,030
Tampa	1,995
Denver	1,858
Cincinnati	1,729
Kansas City	1,575
Milwaukee	1,572
Portland	1,414
Sacramento	1,385
Norfolk	1,380
Columbus	1,344
San Antonio	1,323
New Orleans	1,307
Indianapolis	1,237
Buffalo	1,176
Providence	1,118
Charlotte	1,112
Hartford	1,108
Salt Lake City	1,065
San Jose	712
Memphis	653
Jacksonville	610
USSR	
Moscow [12]	8,967
Leningrad	5,020
Kiev	2,587
Tashkent	2,073
Baku	1,757
Kharkhov	1,611
Minsk	1,589
Gorki	1,438
Novosibirsk	1,436
Sverdlovsk	1,367
Kuybyshev	1,257
Yerevan	1,199
Tbilisi	1,194
Dnepropetrovsk	1,179
Chelyabinsk	1,179
Omsk	1,148
Odessa	1,115
Donetsk	1,110
Alma-Ata	1,108
Kazan	1,094
Perm	1,091
Ufa	1,083
Rostov	1,020
Volgograd	999
Riga	915
Krasnoyarsk	912
Saratov	905
Voronezh	887
Zaporozhye	884
Lvov	790
Krivoy Rog	713
Vladivostok	648
Izhevsk	635
Yaroslavl	633
Togliatti	630
Irkutsk	626
Ulyanovsk	625
Krasnodar	620
Frunze	616
Karaganda	614
Barnaul	602
Khaborovsk	601
Novokuznetsk	600
Dushanbe	595
Vilnius	582
Kishinev	565
Orenburg	547
Penza	543
Tula	540
Mariupol	529
Kemerovo	520
Ryazan	515
Astrakhan	509
Lugansk	509
Nikolayev	503
Tomsk	502
Naberezhniye-Chelni	501
Gomel	500
Venezuela	
Caracas	3,247
Maracaibo	1,295
Valencia	1,135
Maracay	857
Barquisimeto	718
Vietnam	
Ho Chi Minh	3,900
Hanoi	3,100
Haiphong	1,279
Da-Nang	500
Yemen	
San'a	500
Yugoslavia	
Belgrade	1,470
Zagreb	1,175
Skopje	505
Zaïre	
Kinshasa	2,654
Lubumbashi	543
Zambia	
Lusaka	900
Zimbabwe	
Harare	681
Bulawayo	500

WORLD STATISTICS: DISTANCES

The table shows air distances in miles and kilometres between thirty major cities. Known as 'Great Circle' distances, these measure the shortest routes between the cities, which aircraft use where possible. The maps show the world centred on six individual cities, and illustrate, for example, why direct flights from Japan to northern America and Europe are across the Arctic regions, and Singapore is on the direct line route from Europe to Australia. The maps have been constructed on an Azimuthal Equidistant projection, on which all distances measured through the centre point are true to scale. The circular lines are drawn at 5,000, 10,000 and 15,000 km from the central city.

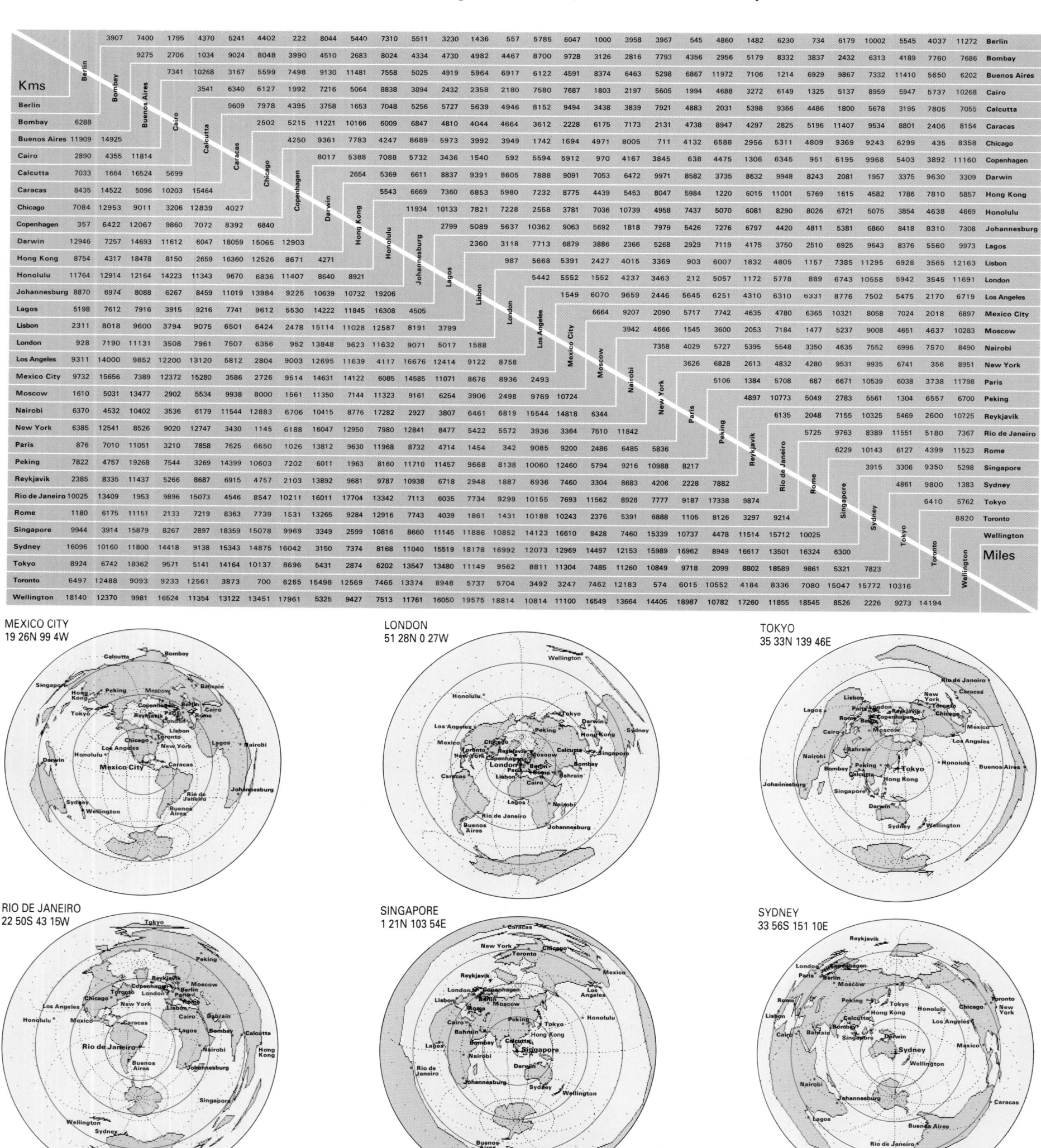

Distances in Kms (upper-right triangle), measured from each row city to the cities that follow it:

From	To cities (Kms)
Berlin	3907, 7400, 1795, 4370, 5241, 4402, 222, 8044, 5440, 7310, 5511, 3230, 1436, 557, 5785, 6047, 1000, 3958, 3967, 545, 4860, 1482, 6230, 734, 6179, 10002, 5545, 4037, 11272
Bombay	9275, 2706, 1034, 9024, 8048, 3990, 4510, 2683, 8024, 4334, 4730, 4982, 4467, 8700, 9728, 3126, 2816, 7793, 4356, 2956, 5179, 8332, 3837, 2432, 6313, 4189, 7760, 7686
Buenos Aires	7341, 10268, 3167, 5599, 7498, 9130, 11481, 7558, 5025, 4919, 5964, 6917, 6122, 4591, 8374, 6463, 5298, 6867, 11972, 7106, 1214, 6929, 9867, 7332, 11410, 5650, 6202
Cairo	3541, 6340, 6127, 1992, 7216, 5064, 8838, 3894, 2432, 2358, 2180, 7580, 7687, 1803, 2197, 5605, 1994, 4688, 3272, 6149, 1325, 5137, 8959, 5947, 5737, 10268
Calcutta	9609, 7978, 4395, 3758, 1653, 7048, 5256, 5727, 5639, 4946, 8152, 9494, 3438, 3839, 7921, 4883, 2031, 5398, 9366, 4486, 1800, 5678, 3195, 7805, 7055
Caracas	2502, 5215, 11221, 10166, 6009, 6847, 4810, 4044, 4664, 3612, 2228, 6175, 7173, 2131, 4738, 8947, 4297, 2825, 5196, 11407, 9534, 8801, 2406, 8154
Chicago	4250, 9361, 7783, 4247, 8689, 5973, 3992, 3949, 1742, 1694, 4971, 8005, 711, 4132, 6588, 2956, 5311, 4809, 9369, 9243, 6299, 435, 8358
Copenhagen	8017, 5388, 7088, 5732, 3436, 1540, 592, 5594, 5912, 970, 4167, 3845, 638, 4475, 1306, 6345, 951, 6195, 9968, 5403, 3892, 11160
Darwin	2654, 5369, 6611, 8837, 9391, 8605, 7888, 9091, 7053, 6472, 9971, 8582, 3735, 8632, 9948, 8243, 2081, 1957, 3375, 9630, 3309
Hong Kong	5543, 6669, 7360, 6853, 5980, 7232, 8775, 4439, 5453, 8047, 5984, 1220, 6015, 11001, 5769, 1615, 4582, 1786, 7810, 5857
Honolulu	11934, 10133, 7821, 7228, 2558, 3781, 7036, 10739, 4958, 7437, 5070, 6081, 8290, 8026, 6721, 5075, 3854, 4638, 4669
Johannesburg	2799, 5089, 5637, 10362, 9063, 5692, 1818, 7979, 5426, 7276, 6797, 4420, 4811, 5381, 6860, 8418, 8310, 7308
Lagos	2360, 3118, 7713, 6879, 3886, 2366, 5268, 2929, 7119, 4175, 3750, 2510, 6925, 9643, 8376, 5560, 9973
Lisbon	987, 5668, 5391, 2427, 4015, 3369, 903, 6007, 1832, 4805, 1157, 7385, 11295, 6928, 3565, 12163
London	5442, 5552, 1552, 4237, 3463, 212, 5057, 1172, 5778, 889, 6743, 10558, 5942, 3545, 11691
Los Angeles	1549, 6070, 9659, 2446, 5645, 6251, 4310, 6310, 6331, 8776, 7502, 5475, 2170, 6719
Mexico City	6664, 9207, 2090, 5717, 7742, 4635, 4780, 6365, 10321, 8058, 7024, 2018, 6897
Moscow	3942, 4666, 1545, 3600, 2053, 7184, 1477, 5237, 9008, 4651, 4637, 10283
Nairobi	7358, 4029, 5727, 5395, 5548, 3350, 4635, 7552, 6996, 7570, 8490
New York	3626, 6828, 2613, 4832, 4280, 9531, 9935, 6741, 356, 8951
Paris	5106, 1384, 5708, 687, 6671, 10539, 6038, 3738, 11798
Peking	4897, 10773, 5049, 2783, 5561, 1304, 6557, 6700
Reykjavik	6135, 2048, 7155, 10325, 5469, 2600, 10725
Rio de Janeiro	5725, 9763, 8389, 11551, 5180, 7367
Rome	6229, 10143, 6127, 4399, 11523
Singapore	3915, 3306, 9350, 5298
Sydney	4861, 9800, 1383
Tokyo	6410, 5762
Toronto	8820

Distances in Miles (lower-left triangle), measured from each row city to the cities listed before it (Berlin, Bombay, Buenos Aires, Cairo, ...):

From	To cities (Miles)
Bombay	6288
Buenos Aires	11909, 14925
Cairo	2890, 4355, 11814
Calcutta	7033, 1664, 16524, 5699
Caracas	8435, 14522, 5096, 10203, 15464
Chicago	7084, 12953, 9011, 3206, 12839, 4027
Copenhagen	357, 6422, 12067, 9860, 7072, 8392, 6840
Darwin	12946, 7257, 14693, 11612, 6047, 18059, 15065, 12903
Hong Kong	8754, 4317, 18478, 8150, 2659, 16360, 12526, 8921, 4271
Honolulu	11764, 12914, 12164, 14223, 11343, 9670, 6836, 11407, 8640, 8921
Johannesburg	8870, 6974, 8088, 6267, 8459, 11019, 13984, 9225, 10639, 10732, 19206
Lagos	5198, 7612, 7916, 3915, 9216, 7741, 9612, 5530, 14222, 11845, 16308, 4505
Lisbon	2311, 8018, 9600, 3794, 9075, 6501, 6424, 2478, 15114, 11028, 12587, 8191, 3799
London	928, 7190, 11131, 3508, 7961, 7507, 6356, 952, 13848, 9623, 11632, 9071, 5017, 1588
Los Angeles	9311, 14000, 9852, 12200, 13120, 5812, 2804, 9003, 12695, 11639, 4117, 16676, 12414, 9122, 8758
Mexico City	9732, 15656, 7389, 12372, 15280, 3586, 2726, 9514, 14631, 14122, 6085, 14585, 11071, 8676, 8936, 2493
Moscow	1610, 5031, 13477, 2902, 5534, 9938, 8000, 1561, 11350, 7144, 11323, 9161, 6254, 3906, 2498, 9769, 10724
Nairobi	6370, 4532, 10402, 3536, 6179, 11544, 6706, 10415, 8771, 17282, 2927, 3807, 6461, 6819, 15544, 14818, 6344
New York	6385, 12541, 8526, 9020, 12747, 3430, 1145, 6188, 16047, 12950, 7980, 12841, 8477, 5422, 5572, 3936, 3364, 7510, 11842
Paris	876, 7010, 11051, 3210, 7858, 7625, 6650, 1026, 13812, 9630, 11968, 8732, 4714, 1454, 342, 9085, 9200, 2486, 6485, 5836
Peking	7822, 4757, 19268, 7544, 3269, 14399, 10603, 7202, 6011, 1963, 8160, 11710, 11457, 9668, 8138, 10060, 12460, 5794, 9216, 10988, 8217
Reykjavik	2385, 8335, 11437, 5266, 8687, 6915, 4757, 2103, 13892, 9681, 9787, 10938, 6718, 2948, 1887, 6936, 7460, 3304, 8683, 4206, 2228, 7882
Rio de Janeiro	10025, 13409, 1953, 9896, 15073, 4546, 8547, 10211, 16011, 17704, 13342, 7113, 6035, 7734, 9299, 10155, 7693, 11562, 8928, 7777, 9187, 17338, 9874
Rome	1180, 6175, 11151, 2133, 7219, 8363, 7739, 1531, 13265, 9284, 12916, 7743, 4039, 1861, 1431, 10188, 10243, 2376, 5391, 6888, 1105, 8126, 3297, 9214
Singapore	9944, 3914, 15879, 8267, 2897, 18359, 15078, 9969, 3349, 2599, 10816, 8660, 11145, 11886, 10852, 14123, 16610, 8428, 7460, 15339, 10737, 4478, 11514, 15712, 10025
Sydney	16096, 10160, 11800, 14418, 9138, 15343, 16042, 3150, 7374, 8168, 11040, 15519, 18178, 16992, 12073, 12969, 14497, 12153, 15989, 16962, 8949, 16617, 13501, 16324, 6300
Tokyo	8924, 6742, 18362, 9571, 5141, 14164, 10137, 8696, 5431, 2874, 6202, 13547, 13480, 11149, 9562, 8811, 11304, 7485, 11260, 10849, 9718, 2099, 8802, 18589, 9861, 5321, 7823
Toronto	6497, 12488, 9093, 9233, 12561, 3873, 700, 6265, 15498, 12569, 7465, 13374, 8948, 5737, 5704, 3492, 3247, 7462, 12183, 574, 6015, 10552, 4184, 8336, 7080, 15047, 15772, 10316
Wellington	18140, 12370, 9981, 16524, 11354, 13122, 13451, 17961, 5325, 9427, 7513, 11761, 16050, 19575, 18814, 10814, 11100, 16549, 13664, 14405, 18987, 10782, 17260, 17855, 18545, 8526, 2226, 9273, 14194

Maps centred on six individual cities:

MEXICO CITY 19 26N 99 4W

LONDON 51 28N 0 27W

TOKYO 35 33N 139 46E

RIO DE JANEIRO 22 50S 43 15W

SINGAPORE 1 21N 103 54E

SYDNEY 33 56S 151 10E

World Statistics: Climate

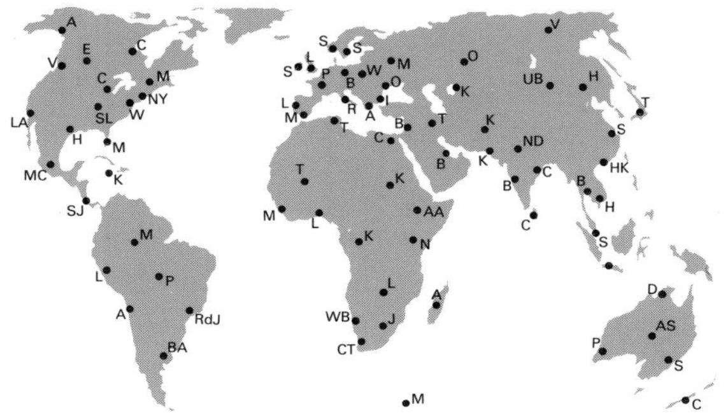

Rainfall and temperature figures are provided for more than seventy cities around the world. Since climate is affected by altitude, the height of each city is shown in metres beneath its name. For each month, the figures in red show average temperature in degrees Celsius or centigrade, and in blue the total rainfall or snow; the average annual temperature and total annual rainfall are given at the end of the rows.

	Jan.	Feb.	Mar.	Apr.	May	June	July	Aug.	Sept.	Oct.	Nov.	Dec.	Year
EUROPE AND USSR													
Athens, Greece	62	37	37	23	23	14	6	7	15	51	56	71	402
107 m	10	10	12	16	20	25	28	28	24	20	15	11	18
Berlin, Germany	46	40	33	42	49	65	73	69	48	49	46	43	603
55 m	-1	0	4	9	14	17	19	18	15	9	5	1	9
Istanbul, Turkey	109	92	72	46	38	34	34	30	58	81	103	119	816
114 m	5	6	7	11	16	20	23	23	20	16	12	8	14
Kazalinsk, USSR	10	10	13	13	15	5	5	8	8	10	13	15	125
63 m	-12	-11	-3	6	18	23	25	23	16	8	-1	-7	7
Lisbon, Portugal	111	76	109	54	44	16	3	4	33	62	93	103	708
77 m	11	12	14	16	17	20	22	23	21	18	14	12	17
London, UK	54	40	37	37	46	45	57	59	49	57	64	48	593
5 m	4	5	7	9	12	16	18	17	15	11	8	5	11
Málaga, Spain	61	51	62	46	26	5	1	3	29	64	64	62	474
33 m	12	13	16	17	19	29	25	26	23	20	16	13	18
Moscow, USSR	39	38	36	37	53	58	88	71	58	45	47	54	624
156 m	-13	-10	-4	6	13	16	18	17	12	6	-1	-7	4
Odessa, USSR	57	62	30	21	34	34	42	37	37	13	35	71	473
64 m	-3	-1	2	9	15	20	22	22	18	12	9	1	10
Omsk, USSR	15	8	8	13	31	51	51	51	28	25	18	20	318
85 m	-22	-19	-12	-1	10	16	18	16	10	1	-11	-18	-1
Paris, France	56	46	35	42	57	54	59	64	55	50	51	50	619
75 m	3	4	8	11	15	18	20	19	17	12	7	4	12
Rome, Italy	71	62	57	51	46	37	15	21	63	99	129	93	744
17 m	8	9	11	14	18	22	25	25	22	17	13	10	16
Shannon, Irish Republic	94	67	56	53	61	57	77	79	86	86	96	117	929
2 m	5	5	7	9	12	14	16	16	14	11	8	6	10
Stockholm, Sweden	43	30	25	31	34	45	61	76	60	48	53	48	554
44 m	-3	-3	-1	5	10	15	18	17	12	7	3	0	7
Verkhoyansk, USSR	5	5	3	5	8	23	28	25	13	8	8	5	134
100 m	-50	-45	-32	-15	0	12	14	9	2	-15	-38	-48	-17
ASIA													
Bahrain	8	18	13	8	<3	0	0	0	0	0	18	18	81
5 m	17	18	21	25	29	32	33	34	31	28	24	19	26
Bangkok, Thailand	8	20	36	58	198	160	160	175	305	206	66	5	1,397
2 m	26	28	29	30	29	29	28	28	28	28	26	25	28
Beirut, Lebanon	191	158	94	53	18	3	<3	<3	5	51	132	185	892
34 m	14	14	16	18	22	24	27	28	26	24	19	16	21
Bombay, India	3	3	3	<3	18	485	617	340	264	64	13	3	1,809
11 m	24	24	26	28	30	29	27	27	27	28	27	26	27
Calcutta, India	10	31	36	43	140	297	325	328	252	114	20	5	1,600
6 m	20	22	27	30	30	30	29	29	29	28	23	19	26
Colombo, Sri Lanka	89	69	147	231	371	224	135	109	160	348	315	147	2,365
7 m	26	26	27	28	28	27	27	27	27	27	26	26	27
Harbin, China	6	5	10	23	43	94	112	104	46	33	8	5	488
160 m	-18	-15	-5	6	13	19	22	21	14	4	-6	-16	3
Ho Chi Minh, Vietnam	15	3	13	43	221	330	315	269	335	269	114	56	1,984
9 m	26	27	29	30	29	28	28	28	27	27	27	26	28
Jakarta, Indonesia	300	300	211	147	114	97	64	43	66	112	142	203	1,798
8 m	26	26	27	27	27	27	27	27	27	27	27	26	27
Hong Kong	33	46	74	137	292	394	381	361	257	114	43	31	2,162
33 m	16	15	18	22	26	28	28	28	27	25	21	18	23
Kabul, Afghanistan	31	36	94	102	20	5	3	3	<3	15	20	10	338
1,815 m	-3	-1	6	13	18	22	25	24	20	14	7	3	12
Karachi, Pakistan	13	10	8	3	3	18	81	41	13	<3	3	5	196
4 m	19	20	24	28	30	31	30	29	28	28	24	20	26
New Delhi, India	23	18	13	8	13	74	180	172	117	10	3	10	640
218 m	14	17	23	28	33	34	31	30	29	26	20	15	25
Shanghai, China	48	58	84	94	94	180	147	142	130	71	51	36	1,135
7 m	4	5	9	14	20	24	28	28	23	19	12	7	16
Singapore	252	173	193	188	173	173	170	196	178	208	254	257	2,413
10 m	26	27	28	28	28	28	28	27	27	27	27	27	27
Tehran, Iran	46	38	46	36	13	3	3	3	3	8	20	31	246
1,220 m	2	5	9	16	21	26	30	29	25	18	12	6	17
Tokyo, Japan	48	74	107	135	147	165	142	152	234	208	97	56	1,565
6 m	3	4	7	13	17	21	25	26	23	17	11	6	14
Ulan Bator, Mongolia	<3	<3	3	5	10	28	76	51	23	5	5	3	208
1,325 m	-26	-21	-13	-1	6	14	16	14	8	-1	-13	-22	-3
AFRICA													
Addis Ababa, Ethiopia	<3	3	25	135	213	201	206	239	102	28	<3	0	1,151
2,450 m	19	20	20	20	19	18	18	19	21	22	21	20	20
Antananarivo, Madagas.	300	279	178	53	18	8	8	10	18	61	135	287	1,356
1,372 m	21	21	21	19	18	15	14	15	17	19	21	21	19
Cairo, Egypt	5	5	5	3	3	<3	0	0	<3	<3	3	5	28
116 m	13	15	18	21	25	28	28	28	26	24	20	15	22
Cape Town, South Africa	15	8	18	48	79	84	89	66	43	31	18	10	508
17 m	21	21	20	17	14	13	12	13	14	16	18	19	17
Johannesburg, S. Africa	114	109	89	38	25	8	8	8	23	56	107	125	709
1,665 m	20	20	18	16	13	10	11	13	16	18	19	20	16
Khartoum, Sudan	<3	<3	<3	<3	3	8	53	71	18	5	<3	0	158
390 m	24	25	28	31	33	34	32	31	32	32	28	25	29
Kinshasa, Zaïre	135	145	196	196	158	8	3	3	31	119	221	142	1,354
325 m	26	26	27	27	26	24	23	24	25	26	26	26	25
Lagos, Nigeria	28	46	102	150	269	460	279	64	140	206	69	25	1,836
3 m	27	28	29	28	28	26	26	25	26	26	28	28	27
Lusaka, Zambia	231	191	142	18	3	<3	<3	0	<3	10	91	150	836
1,277 m	21	22	21	21	19	16	16	18	22	24	23	22	21
Monrovia, Liberia	31	56	97	216	516	973	996	373	744	772	236	130	5,138
23 m	26	26	27	27	26	25	24	25	25	25	26	26	26
Nairobi, Kenya	38	64	125	211	158	46	15	23	31	53	109	86	958
1,820 m	19	19	19	19	18	16	16	16	18	19	18	18	18
Timbuktu, Mali	<3	<3	3	<3	5	23	79	81	38	3	<3	<3	231
301 m	22	24	28	32	34	35	32	30	32	31	28	23	29
Tunis, Tunisia	64	51	41	36	18	8	3	8	33	51	48	61	419
66 m	10	11	13	16	19	23	26	27	25	20	16	11	18
Walvis Bay, South Africa	<3	5	8	3	3	<3	<3	3	<3	<3	<3	<3	23
7 m	19	19	19	18	17	16	15	14	14	15	17	18	18
AUSTRALIA, NEW ZEALAND AND ANTARCTICA													
Alice Springs, Australia	43	33	28	10	15	13	8	8	8	18	31	38	252
579 m	29	28	25	20	15	12	12	14	18	23	26	28	21
Christchurch, N. Zealand	56	43	48	48	66	66	69	48	46	43	48	56	638
10 m	16	16	14	12	9	6	6	7	9	12	14	16	11
Darwin, Australia	386	312	254	97	15	3	<3	3	13	51	119	239	1,491
30 m	29	29	29	29	28	26	25	26	28	29	30	29	28
Mawson, Antarctica	11	30	20	10	44	180	4	40	3	20	0	0	362
14 m	0	-5	-10	-14	-15	-16	-18	-18	-19	-13	-5	-1	-11
Perth, Australia	8	10	20	43	130	180	170	149	86	56	20	13	881
60 m	23	23	22	19	16	14	13	13	15	16	19	22	18
Sydney, Australia	89	102	127	135	127	117	117	76	73	71	73	73	1,181
42 m	22	22	21	18	15	13	12	13	15	18	19	21	17
NORTH AMERICA													
Anchorage, Alaska, USA.	20	18	15	10	13	18	41	66	66	56	25	23	371
40 m	-11	-8	-5	2	7	12	14	13	9	2	-5	-11	2
Chicago, Ill., USA	51	51	66	71	86	89	84	81	79	66	61	51	836
251 m	-4	-3	2	9	14	20	23	22	19	12	5	-1	10
Churchill, Man., Canada	15	13	18	23	32	44	46	58	51	43	39	21	402
13 m	-28	-26	-20	-10	-2	6	12	11	5	-2	-12	-22	-7
Edmonton, Alta., Canada	25	19	19	22	43	77	89	78	39	17	16	25	466
676 m	-15	-10	-5	4	11	15	17	16	11	6	-4	-10	3
Honolulu, Hawaii, USA	104	66	79	48	25	18	23	28	36	48	64	104	643
12 m	23	18	19	20	22	24	25	26	26	24	22	19	22
Houston, Tex., USA,	89	76	84	91	119	117	99	99	104	94	89	109	1,171
12 m	12	13	17	21	24	27	28	29	26	22	16	12	21
Kingston, Jamaica	23	15	23	31	102	89	38	91	99	180	74	36	800
34 m	25	25	25	26	26	28	28	28	27	27	26	26	26
Los Angeles, Calif., USA	79	76	71	25	10	3	<3	<3	5	15	31	66	381
95 m	13	14	14	16	17	19	21	22	21	18	16	14	17
Mexico City, Mexico	13	5	10	20	53	119	170	152	130	51	18	8	747
2,309 m	12	13	16	18	19	19	17	18	18	16	14	13	16
Miami, Fla., USA	71	53	64	81	173	178	155	160	203	234	71	51	1,516
8 m	20	20	22	23	25	27	28	28	27	25	22	21	24
Montréal, Que., Canada	72	65	74	74	66	82	90	92	88	76	81	87	946
57 m	-10	-9	-3	-6	13	18	21	20	15	9	2	-7	6
New York, N.Y., USA	94	97	91	81	81	84	107	109	86	89	76	91	1,092
96 m	-1	-1	3	10	16	20	23	23	21	15	7	2	8
St Louis, Mo., USA	58	64	89	97	114	114	89	86	81	74	71	64	1,001
173 m	0	1	7	13	19	24	26	26	22	15	8	2	14
San José, Costa Rica	15	5	20	46	229	241	211	241	305	300	145	41	1,798
1,146 m	19	19	21	21	22	21	21	21	21	20	20	19	20
Vancouver, B.C., Canada	154	115	101	60	52	45	32	41	67	114	150	182	1,113
14 m	3	5	6	9	12	15	17	17	14	10	6	4	10
Washington, D.C., USA	86	76	91	84	94	99	112	109	94	74	66	79	1,064
22 m	1	2	7	12	18	23	25	24	20	14	8	3	13
SOUTH AMERICA													
Antofagasta, Chile	0	0	0	<3	<3	3	5	3	<3	3	<3	0	13
94 m	21	21	20	18	16	15	14	14	15	16	18	19	17
Buenos Aires, Argentina	79	71	109	89	76	61	56	61	79	86	84	99	950
27 m	23	23	21	17	13	9	10	11	13	15	19	22	16
Lima, Peru	3	<3	<3	<3	5	5	8	8	8	3	3	<3	41
120 m	23	24	24	22	19	17	17	16	17	18	19	21	20
Manaus, Brazil	249	231	262	221	170	84	58	38	46	107	142	203	1,811
44 m	28	28	28	27	28	28	28	28	29	29	29	28	28
Paraná, Brazil	287	236	239	102	13	<3	3	5	28	127	231	310	1,582
260 m	23	23	23	23	23	21	21	22	24	24	24	23	23
Rio de Janeiro, Brazil	125	122	130	107	79	53	41	43	66	79	104	137	1,082
61 m	26	26	25	24	22	21	21	21	21	22	23	25	23

WORLD STATISTICS: PHYSICAL DIMENSIONS

Each topic list is divided into continents and within a continent the items are listed in size order. The order of the continents is as in the atlas, Europe through to South America. Certain lists down to this mark > are complete; below they are selective. The world top ten are shown in square brackets; in the case of mountains this has not been done because the world top thirty are all in Asia. The figures are rounded as appropriate.

WORLD, CONTINENTS, OCEANS

	km²	miles²	%
The World	509,450,000	196,672,000	
Land	149,450,000	57,688,000	29.3
Water	360,000,000	138,984,000	70.7
Asia	44,500,000	17,177,000	29.8
Africa	30,302,000	11,697,000	20.3
North America	24,241,000	9,357,000	16.2
South America	17,793,000	6,868,000	11.9
Antarctica	14,100,000	5,443,000	9.4
Europe	9,957,000	3,843,000	6.7
Australia & Oceania	8,557,000	3,303,000	5.7
Pacific Ocean	179,679,000	69,356,000	49.9
Atlantic Ocean	92,373,000	35,657,000	25.7
Indian Ocean	73,917,000	28,532,000	20.5
Arctic Ocean	14,090,000	5,439,000	3.9

SEAS

Pacific	km²	miles²
South China Sea	2,318,000	895,000
Bering Sea	2,268,000	875,000
Sea of Okhotsk	1,528,000	590,000
East China & Yellow	1,249,000	482,000
Sea of Japan	1,008,000	389,000
Gulf of California	162,000	62,500
Bass Strait	75,000	29,000

Atlantic	km²	miles²
Caribbean Sea	2,766,000	1,068,000
Mediterranean Sea	2,516,000	971,000
Gulf of Mexico	1,543,000	596,000
Hudson Bay	1,232,000	476,000
North Sea	575,000	223,000
Black Sea	452,000	174,000
Baltic Sea	397,000	153,000
Gulf of St. Lawrence	238,000	92,000

Indian	km²	miles²
Red Sea	438,000	169,000
The Gulf	239,000	92,000

MOUNTAINS

Europe		m	ft
Mont Blanc	France/Italy	4,807	15,771
Monte Rosa	Italy/Switzerland	4,634	15,203
Dom	Switzerland	4,545	14,911
Weisshorn	Switzerland	4,505	14,780
Matterhorn/Cervino	Italy/Switzerland	4,478	14,691
Mt. Maudit	France/Italy	4,465	14,649
Finsteraarhorn	Switzerland	4,275	14,025
Aletschhorn	Switzerland	4,182	13,720
Jungfrau	Switzerland	4,158	13,642
Barre des Ecrins	France	4,103	13,461
Gran Paradiso	Italy	4,061	13,323
Piz Bernina	Italy/Switzerland	4,052	13,294
Ortles	Italy	3,899	12,792
Monte Viso	Italy	3,841	12,602
Grossglockner	Austria	3,797	12,457
Wildspitze	Austria	3,774	12,382
Weisskügel	Austria/Italy	3,736	12,257
Dammastock	Switzerland	3,640	11,942
Tödi	Switzerland	3,623	11,886
Presanella	Italy	3,556	11,667
Monte Adamello	Italy	3,554	11,660
Mulhacén	Spain	3,478	11,411
Pico de Aneto	Spain	3,404	11,168
Marmolada	Italy	3,342	10,964
Etna	Italy	3,340	10,958
> Musala	Bulgaria	2,925	9,596
Olympus	Greece	2,917	9,570
Gerlach	Czechoslovakia	2,655	8,711
Galdhöpiggen	Norway	2,469	8,100
Pietrosul	Romania	2,305	7,562
Hvannadalshnúkur	Iceland	2,119	6,952
Narodnaya	USSR	1,894	6,214
Ben Nevis	UK	1,343	4,406

Asia		m	ft
Everest	China/Nepal	8,848	29,029
Godwin Austen (K2)	China/Kashmir	8,611	28,251
Kanchenjunga	India/Nepal	8,598	28,208
Lhotse	China/Nepal	8,516	27,939
Makalu	China/Nepal	8,481	27,824
Cho Oyu	China/Nepal	8,201	26,906
Dhaulagiri	Nepal	8,172	26,811
Manaslu	Nepal	8,156	26,758
Nanga Parbat	Kashmir	8,126	26,660
Annapurna	Nepal	8,078	26,502
Gasherbrum	China/Kashmir	8,068	26,469
Broad Peak	India	8,051	26,414
Gosainthan	China	8,012	26,286
Disteghil Sar	Kashmir	7,885	25,869
Nuptse	Nepal	7,879	25,849
Masherbrum	Kashmir	7,826	25,676
Nanda Devi	India	7,817	25,646
Rakaposhi	Kashmir	7,788	25,551
Kamet	India	7,756	25,446
Namcha Barwa	China	7,756	25,446
Gurla Mandhata	China	7,728	25,354
Muztag	China	7,723	25,338
Kongur Shan	China	7,719	25,324
Tirich Mir	Pakistan	7,690	25,229
Saser	Kashmir	7,672	25,170
> Pik Kommunizma	USSR	7,495	24,590
Aling Gangri	China	7,315	23,999
Elbrus	USSR	5,633	18,481
Demavand	Iran	5,604	18,386
Ararat	Turkey	5,165	16,945
Gunong Kinabalu	Malaysia (Borneo)	4,101	13,455
Yu Shan	Taiwan	3,997	13,113
Fuji-san	Japan	3,776	12,388
Rinjani	Indonesia	3,726	12,224
Mt. Rajang	Philippines	3,364	11,037
Pidurutalagala	Sri Lanka	2,524	8,281

Africa		m	ft
Kilimanjaro	Tanzania	5,895	19,340
Mt. Kenya	Kenya	5,199	17,057
Ruwenzori	Uganda/Zaïre	5,109	16,762
Ras Dashan	Ethiopia	4,620	15,157
Meru	Tanzania	4,565	14,977
Karisimbi	Rwanda/Zaïre	4,507	14,787
Mt. Elgon	Kenya/Uganda	4,321	14,176
Batu	Ethiopia	4,307	14,130
Gughe	Ethiopia	4,200	13,779
Toubkal	Morocco	4,165	13,665
Irhil Mgoun	Morocco	4,071	13,356
Mt. Cameroon	Cameroon	4,070	13,353
Teide	Spain (Tenerife)	3,718	12,198
Thabana Ntlenyana	Lesotho	3,482	11,424
> Emi Kussi	Chad	3,415	11,204
Mt. aux Sources	Lesotho/S. Africa	3,282	10,768
Mt. Piton	Réunion	3,069	10,069

Oceania		m	ft
Puncak Jaya	Indonesia	5,029	16,499
Puncak Mandala	Indonesia	4,760	15,617
Puncak Trikora	Indonesia	4,750	15,584
Mt. Wilhelm	Papua New Guinea	4,508	14,790
> Mauna Kea	USA (Hawaii)	4,208	13,806
Mauna Loa	USA (Hawaii)	4,169	13,678
Mt. Cook	New Zealand	3,764	12,349
Mt. Balbi	Solomon Is.	2,743	8,999
Orohena	Tahiti	2,241	7,352
Kosciusko	Australia	2,230	7,316

North America		m	ft
Mt. McKinley	USA (Alaska)	6,194	20,321
Mt. Logan	Canada	6,050	19,849
Citlaltepetl	Mexico	5,700	18,701
Mt. St.Elias	USA/Canada	5,489	18,008
Popocatepetl	Mexico	5,452	17,887
Mt. Foraker	USA (Alaska)	5,304	17,401
Ixtaccihuatl	Mexico	5,286	17,342
Lucania	USA (Alaska)	5,226	17,145
Mt. Steele	Canada	5,011	16,440
Mt. Bona	USA (Alaska)	5,005	16,440
Mt. Blackburn	USA (Alaska)	4,996	16,391
Mt. Sanford	USA (Alaska)	4,949	16,237
Mt. Wood	Canada	4,848	15,905
Nev. de Toluca	Mexico	4,670	15,321
Mt. Fairweather	USA (Alaska)	4,663	15,298
Mt. Whitney	USA	4,418	14,495
Mt. Elbert	USA	4,399	14,432
Mt. Harvard	USA	4,395	14,419
Mt. Rainier	USA	4,392	14,409
Blanca Peak	USA	4,364	14,317
Long's Peak	USA	4,345	14,255
Nev. de Colima	Mexico	4,339	14,235
Mt. Shasta	USA	4,317	14,163
Tajumulco	Guatemala	4,217	13,835
Gannett Peak	USA	4,202	13,786
> Mt. Waddington	Canada	3,994	13,104
Mt. Robson	Canada	3,954	12,972
Ch. Grande	Costa Rica	3,837	12,589
Loma Tinta	Haiti	3,175	10,417

South America		m	ft
Aconcagua	Argentina	6,960	22,834
Illimani	Bolivia	6,882	22,578
Bonete	Argentina	6,872	22,546
Ojos del Salado	Argentina/Chile	6,863	22,516
Tupungato	Argentina/Chile	6,800	22,309
Pissis	Argentina	6,779	22,241
Mercedario	Argentina/Chile	6,770	22,211
Huascaran	Peru	6,768	22,204
Llullaillaco	Argentina/Chile	6,723	22,057
Nudo de Cachi	Argentina	6,720	22,047
Yerupaja	Peru	6,632	21,758
N. de Tres Cruces	Argentina/Chile	6,620	21,719
Incahuasi	Argentina/Chile	6,601	21,657
Ancohuma	Bolivia	6,550	21,489
Sajama	Bolivia	6,520	21,391
Coropuna	Peru	6,425	21,079
Ausangate	Peru	6,384	20,945
Cerro del Toro	Argentina	6,380	20,932
Ampato	Peru	6,310	20,702
Chimborasso	Ecuador	6,267	20,561
> Cotopaxi	Ecuador	5,897	19,347
Cayambe	Ecuador	5,796	19,016
S. Nev.de S. Marta	Colombia	5,775	18,947
Pico Bolivar	Venezuela	5,007	16,427

Antarctica		m	ft
Vinson Massif		4,897	16,066
Mt. Kirkpatrick		4,528	14,855
Mt. Markham		4,349	14,268

OCEAN DEPTHS

Atlantic Ocean	m	ft	
Puerto Rico (Milwaukee) Deep	9,200	30,183	[7]
Cayman Trench	7,680	25,197	[10]
Gulf of Mexico	5,203	17,070	
Mediterranean	5,121	16,801	
Black Sea	2,211	7,254	
North Sea	310	1,017	
Baltic Sea	294	965	
Hudson Bay	111	364	

Indian Ocean	m	ft
Java Trench	7,450	24,442
Red Sea	2,266	7,434
Persian Gulf	73	239

Pacific Ocean	m	ft	
Mariana Trench	11,022	36,161	[1]
Tonga Trench	10,822	35,505	[2]
Japan Trench	10,554	34,626	[3]
Kuril Trench	10,542	34,586	[4]
Mindanao Trench	10,497	34,439	[5]
Kermadec Trench	10,047	32,962	[6]
Peru-Chile Trench	8,050	26,410	[8]
Aleutian Trench	7,822	25,662	[9]
Middle American Trench	6,662	21,857	

Arctic Ocean	m	ft
Molloy Deep	5,608	18,399

LAND LOWS

		m	ft
Caspian Sea	Europe	-28	-92
Dead Sea	Asia	-400	-1,312
Lake Assal	Africa	-156	-512
Lake Eyre North	Oceania	-16	-52
Death Valley	N. America	-86	-282
Valdés Peninsula	S. America	-40	-131

Rivers

Europe

		km	miles	
Volga	Caspian Sea	3,700	2,300	
Danube	Black Sea	2,850	1,770	
Ural	Caspian Sea	2,535	1,574	
Dnieper	Volga	2,285	1,420	
Kama	Volga	2,030	1,260	
Don	Volga	1,990	1,240	
Petchora	Arctic	1,790	1,110	
Oka	Volga	1,480	920	
Belaya	Kama	1,420	880	
Dniester	Black Sea	1,400	870	
Vyatka	Kama	1,370	850	
Rhine	North Sea	1,320	820	
N. Dvina	Arctic	1,290	800	
Desna	Dnieper	1,190	740	
Elbe	North Sea	1,145	710	
Vistula	Baltic Sea	1,090	675	
Loire	Atlantic	1,020	635	
Thames	North Sea	335	210	

Asia

		km	miles	
Yangtse	Pacific	6,380	3,960	[3]
Yenisei-Angara	Arctic	5,550	3,445	[5]
Ob-Irtysh	Arctic	5,410	3,360	[6]
Hwang Ho	Pacific	4,840	3,005	[7]
Amur	Pacific	4,510	2,800	[9]
Mekong	Pacific	4,500	2,795	[10]
Lena	Arctic	4,400	2,730	
Irtysh	Ob	4,250	2,640	
Yenisei	Arctic	4,090	2,540	
Ob	Arctic	3,680	2,285	
Indus	Indian	3,100	1,925	
Brahmaputra	Indian	2,900	1,800	
Syr Darya	Aral Sea	2,860	1,775	
Salween	Indian	2,800	1,740	
Euphrates	Indian	2,700	1,675	
Vilyuy	Lena	2,650	1,645	
Kolyma	Arctic	2,600	1,615	
Amu Darya	Aral Sea	2,540	1,575	
Ural	Caspian Sea	2,535	1,575	
Ganges	Indian	2,510	1,560	
Si Kiang	Pacific	2,100	1,305	
Irrawaddy	Indian	2,010	1,250	
Tarim-Yarkand	Lop Nor	2,000	1,240	
Tigris	Indian	1,900	1,180	
Angara	Yenisei	1,830	1,135	
Godavari	Indian	1,470	915	
Sutlej	Indian	1,450	900	
Yamuna	Indian	1,400	870	

Africa

		km	miles	
Nile	Mediterranean	6,670	4,140	[1]
Zaïre/Congo	Atlantic	4,670	2,900	[8]
Niger	Atlantic	4,180	2,595	
Zambezi	Indian	2,740	1,700	
Oubangi/Uele	Zaïre	2,250	1,400	
Kasai	Zaïre	1,950	1,210	
Shaballe	Indian	1,930	1,200	
Orange	Atlantic	1,860	1,155	
Cubango	Okavango Swamps	1,800	1,120	
Limpopo	Indian	1,600	995	
Senegal	Atlantic	1,600	995	
Volta	Atlantic	1,500	930	
Benue	Niger	1,350	840	

Australia

		km	miles	
Murray-Darling	Indian	3,720	2,310	
Darling	Murray	3,070	1,905	
Murray	Indian	2,575	1,600	
Murrumbidgee	Murray	1,690	1,050	

North America

		km	miles	
Mississippi-Missouri	Gulf of Mexico	6,020	3,740	[4]
Mackenzie	Arctic	4,240	2,630	
Mississippi	Gulf of Mexico	3,780	2,350	
Missouri	Mississippi	3,725	2,310	
Yukon	Pacific	3,185	1,980	
Rio Grande	Gulf of Mexico	3,030	1,880	
Arkansas	Mississippi	2,340	1,450	
Colorado	Pacific	2,330	1,445	
Red	Mississippi	2,040	1,270	
Columbia	Pacific	1,950	1,210	
Saskatchewan	L Winnipeg	1,940	1,205	
Snake	Columbia	1,670	1,040	
Churchill	Hudson Bay	1,600	990	
Ohio	Mississippi	1,580	980	
Brazos	Gulf of Mexico	1,400	870	
St Lawrence	Atlantic	1,170	730	

South America

		km	miles	
Amazon	Atlantic	6,430	3,990	[2]
Paraná-Plate	Atlantic	4,000	2,480	
Purus	Amazon	3,350	2,080	
Madeira	Amazon	3,200	1,990	
São Francisco	Atlantic	2,900	1,800	
Paraná	Plate	2,800	1,740	
Tocantins	Atlantic	2,640	1,640	
Paraguay	Paraná	2,550	1,580	
Orinoco	Atlantic	2,500	1,550	
Pilcomayo	Paraná	2,500	1,550	
Araguaia	Tocantins	2,250	1,400	
Juruá	Amazon	2,000	1,240	
Xingu	Amazon	1,980	1,230	
Ucayali	Amazon	1,900	1,180	
Marañón	Amazon	1,600	990	
Uruguay	Plate	1,600	990	
Magdalena	Caribbean	1,540	960	

Lakes

Europe

		km²	miles²	
Lake Ladoga	USSR	18,400	7,100	
Lake Onega	USSR	9,700	3,700	
Saimaa system	Finland	8,000	3,100	
Vänern	Sweden	5,500	2,100	
Rybinsk Res.	USSR	4,700	1,800	

Asia

		km²	miles²	
Caspian Sea	Iran/USSR	371,000	143,000	[1]
Aral Sea	USSR	36,000	13,900	[6]
Lake Baikal	USSR	31,500	12,200	[9]
Tonlé Sap	Cambodia	20,000	7,700	
Lake Balkhash	USSR	18,500	7,100	
Dongting Hu	China	12,000	4,600	
Issyk Kul	USSR	6,200	2,400	
Lake Urmia	Iran	5,900	2,300	
Koko Nur	China	5,700	2,200	
Poyang Hu	China	5,000	1,900	
Lake Khanka	China/USSR	4,400	1,700	
Lake Van	Turkey	3,500	1,400	
Ubsa Nur	China	3,400	1,300	

Africa

		km²	miles²	
Lake Victoria	E. Africa	68,000	26,000	[3]
Lake Tanganyika	C. Africa	33,000	13,000	[7]
Lake Malawi/Nyasa	E. Africa	29,000	11,000	[10]
Lake Chad	C. Africa	25,000	9,700	
Lake Turkana	Ethiopia/Kenya	8,500	3,300	
Lake Volta	Ghana	8,500	3,300	
Lake Bangweulu	Zambia	8,000	3,100	
Lake Rukwa	Tanzania	7,000	2,700	
Lake Mai-Ndombe	Zaïre	6,500	2,500	
Lake Kariba	Zambia/Zimbabwe	5,300	2,000	
Lake Mobutu	Uganda/Zaïre	5,300	2,000	
Lake Nasser	Egypt/Sudan	5,200	2,000	
Lake Mweru	Zambia/Zaïre	4,900	1,900	
Lake Cabora Bassa	S. Africa	4,500	1,700	
Lake Kyoga	Uganda	4,400	1,700	
Lake Tana	Ethiopia	3,630	1,400	
Lake Kivu	Rwanda/Zaïre	2,650	1,000	
Lake Edward	Uganda/Zaïre	2,200	850	

Australia

		km²	miles²	
Lake Eyre	Australia	9,000	3,500	
Lake Torrens	Australia	5,800	2,200	
Lake Gairdner	Australia	4,800	1,900	

North America

		km²	miles²	
Lake Superior	Canada/USA	82,200	31,700	[2]
Lake Huron	Canada/USA	59,600	23,000	[4]
Lake Michigan	USA	58,000	22,400	[5]
Great Bear Lake	Canada	31,500	12,200	[8]
Great Slave Lake	Canada	28,700	11,100	
Lake Erie	Canada/USA	25,700	9,900	
Lake Winnipeg	Canada	24,400	9,400	
Lake Ontario	Canada/USA	19,500	7,500	
Lake Nicaragua	Nicaragua	8,200	3,200	
Lake Athabasca	Canada	8,000	3,100	
Smallwood Res.	Canada	6,530	2,520	
Reindeer Lake	Canada	6,400	2,500	
Lake Winnipegosis	Canada	5,400	2,100	
Nettilling Lake	Canada	5,500	2,100	
Lake Nipigon	Canada	4,850	1,900	
Lake Manitoba	Canada	4,700	1,800	

South America

		km²	miles²	
Lake Titicaca	Bolivia/Peru	8,200	3,200	
Lake Poopo	Peru	2,800	1,100	

Islands

Europe

		km²	miles²	
Great Britain	UK	229,880	88,700	[8]
Iceland	Atlantic Ocean	103,000	39,800	
Ireland	Ireland/UK	84,400	32,600	
Novaya Zemlya (N)	USSR	48,200	18,600	
W. Spitzbergen	Norway	39,000	15,100	
Novaya Zemlya (S)	USSR	33,200	12,800	
Sicily	Italy	25,500	9,800	
Sardinia	Italy	24,000	9,300	
NE.Spitzbergen	Norway	15,000	5,600	
Corsica	France	8,700	3,400	
Crete	Greece	8,350	3,200	
Zealand	Denmark	6,850	2,600	

Asia

		km²	miles²	
Borneo	S E. Asia	737,000	284,000	[3]
Sumatra	Indonesia	425,000	164,000	[6]
Honshu	Japan	230,000	88,800	[7]
Celebes	Indonesia	189,000	73,000	
Java	Indonesia	126,700	48,900	
Luzon	Philippines	104,700	40,400	
Mindanao	Philippines	95,000	36,700	
Hokkaido	Japan	78,400	30,300	
Sakhalin	USSR	76,400	29,500	
Sri Lanka	Indian Ocean	65,600	25,300	
Taiwan	Pacific Ocean	36,000	13,900	
Kyushu	Japan	35,700	13,800	
Hainan	China	34,000	13,100	
Timor	Indonesia	33,600	13,000	
Shikoku	Japan	18,800	7,300	
Halmahera	Indonesia	18,000	6,900	
Ceram	Indonesia	17,150	6,600	
Sumbawa	Indonesia	15,450	6,000	
Flores	Indonesia	15,200	5,900	
Samar	Philippines	13,100	5,100	
Negros	Philippines	12,700	4,900	
Bangka	Indonesia	12,000	4,600	
Palawan	Philippines	12,000	4,600	
Panay	Philippines	11,500	4,400	
Sumba	Indonesia	11,100	4,300	
Mindoro	Philippines	9,750	3,800	
Buru	Indonesia	9,500	3,700	
Bali	Indonesia	5,600	2,200	
Cyprus	Mediterranean	3,570	1,400	
Wrangel I.	USSR	2,800	1,000	

Africa

		km²	miles²	
Madagascar	Indian Ocean	587,000	226,600	[4]
Socotra	Indian Ocean	3,600	1,400	
Réunion	Indian Ocean	2,500	965	
Tenerife	Atlantic Ocean	2,350	900	
Mauritius	Indian Ocean	1,865	720	

Oceania

		km²	miles²	
New Guinea	Indon./Pap. NG	780,000	301,080	[2]
New Zealand (S)	New Zealand	150,500	58,100	
New Zealand (N)	New Zealand	114,400	44,200	
Tasmania	Australia	67,800	26,200	
New Britain	Papua NG	37,800	14,600	
New Caledonia	Pacific Ocean	16,100	6,200	
Viti Levu	Fiji	10,500	4,100	
Hawaii	Pacific Ocean	10,450	4,000	
Bougainville	Papua NG	9,600	3,700	
Guadalcanal	Solomon Is	6,500	2,500	
Vanua Levu	Fiji	5,550	2,100	
New Ireland	Papua NG	3,200	1,200	

North America

		km²	miles²	
Greenland	Greenland	2,175,600	839,800	[1]
Baffin I.	Canada	508,000	196,100	[5]
Victoria I.	Canada	212,200	81,900	[9]
Ellesmere I.	Canada	212,000	81,800	[10]
Cuba	Cuba	114,500	44,200	
Newfoundland	Canada	96,000	37,100	
Hispaniola	Atlantic Ocean	76,200	29,400	
Banks I.	Canada	67,000	25,900	
Devon I.	Canada	54,500	21,000	
Melville I.	Canada	42,400	16,400	
Vancouver I.	Canada	32,150	12,400	
Somerset I.	Canada	24,300	9,400	
Jamaica	Caribbean	11,400	4,400	
Puerto Rico	Atlantic Ocean	8,900	3,400	
Cape Breton I.	Canada	4,000	1,500	

South America

		km²	miles²	
Tierra del Fuego	Argentina/Chile	47,000	18,100	
Falkland I. (E.)	Atlantic Ocean	6,800	2,600	
South Georgia	Atlantic Ocean	4,200	1,600	
Galapagos (Isabela)	Pacific Ocean	2,250	870	

INTRODUCTION TO WORLD GEOGRAPHY

THE UNIVERSE

About 15 billion years ago, time and space began with the most colossal explosion in cosmic history: the 'Big Bang' that initiated the universe. According to current theory, in the first millionth of a second of its existence it expanded from a dimensionless point of infinite mass and density into a fireball about 30 billion kilometres across; and it has been expanding ever since.

It took almost a million years for the primal fireball to cool enough for atoms to form. They were mostly hydrogen, still the most abundant material in the universe. But the new matter was not evenly distributed around the young universe, and a few billion years later atoms in relatively dense regions began to cling together under the influence of gravity, forming distinct masses of gas separated by vast expanses of empty space. These first proto-galaxies, to begin with, were dark places: the universe had cooled. But gravitational attraction continued its work, condensing matter into coherent lumps inside the galactic gas clouds. About three billion years later, some of these masses had contracted so much that internal pressure produced the high temperatures necessary to bring about nuclear fusion: the first stars were born.

There were several generations of stars, each feeding on the wreckage of its extinct predecessors as well as the original galactic gas swirls. With each new generation, progressively larger atoms were forged in stellar furnaces and the galaxy's range of elements, once restricted to hydrogen, grew larger. About ten billion years after the Big Bang, a star formed on the outskirts of our galaxy with enough matter left over to create a retinue of planets. Some 4.7 billion years after that, a few planetary atoms had evolved into structures of complex molecules that lived, breathed and eventually pointed telescopes at the sky.

They found that their Sun is just one of more than 100 billion stars in the home galaxy alone. Our galaxy, in turn, forms part of a local group of 25 or so similar structures, some much larger than our own; there are at least 100 million other galaxies in the universe as a whole. The most distant ever observed, a highly energetic galactic core known only as Quasar PKS 2000-330, lies about 15 billion light-years away.

LIFE OF A STAR

For most of its existence, a star produces energy by the nuclear fusion of hydrogen into helium at its core. The duration of this hydrogen-burning period – known as the main sequence – depends on the star's mass; the greater the mass, the higher the core temperatures and the sooner the star's supply of hydrogen is exhausted. Dim, dwarf stars consume their hydrogen slowly, eking it out over a thousand billion years or more. The Sun, like other stars of its mass, should spend about 10 billion years on the main sequence; since it was formed less than five billion years ago, it still has half its life left.

Once all a star's core hydrogen has been fused into helium, nuclear activity moves outward into layers of unconsumed hydrogen. For a time, energy production sharply increases: the star grows hotter and expands enormously, turning into a so-called red giant. Its energy output will increase a thousandfold, and it will swell to a hundred times its present diameter.

After a few hundred million years, helium in the core will become sufficiently compressed to initiate a new cycle of nuclear fusion: from helium to carbon. The star will contract somewhat, before beginning its last expansion, in the Sun's case engulfing the Earth and perhaps Mars. In this bloated condition, the Sun's outer layers will break off into space, leaving a tiny inner core, mainly of carbon, that shrinks progressively under the force of its own gravity: dwarf stars can attain a density more than 10,000 times that of normal matter, with crushing surface gravities to match. Gradually, the nuclear fires will die down, and the Sun will reach its terminal stage: a black dwarf, emitting insignificant amounts of energy.

However, stars more massive than the Sun may undergo another transformation. The additional mass allows gravitational collapse to continue indefinitely: eventually, all the star's remaining matter shrinks to a point, and its density approaches infinity – a state that will not permit even sub-atomic structures to survive.

The star has become a black hole: an anomalous 'singularity' in the fabric of space and time. Although vast coruscations of radiation will be emitted by any matter falling into its grasp, the singularity itself has an escape velocity that exceeds the speed of light, and nothing can ever be released from it. Within the boundaries of the black hole, the laws of physics are suspended, but no physicist can ever observe the extraordinary events that may occur.

THE END OF THE UNIVERSE

The likely fate of the universe is disputed. One theory (top) dictates that the expansion begun at the time of the Big Bang will continue 'indefinitely', with ageing galaxies moving farther and farther apart in an immense, dark graveyard. Alternately, (bottom) gravity may overcome the expansion. Galaxies will fall back together until everything is again concentrated at a single point, followed by a new Big Bang and a new expansion, in an endlessly repeated cycle. The first theory is supported by the amount of visible matter in the universe; the second assumes there is enough dark material to bring about the gravitational collapse.

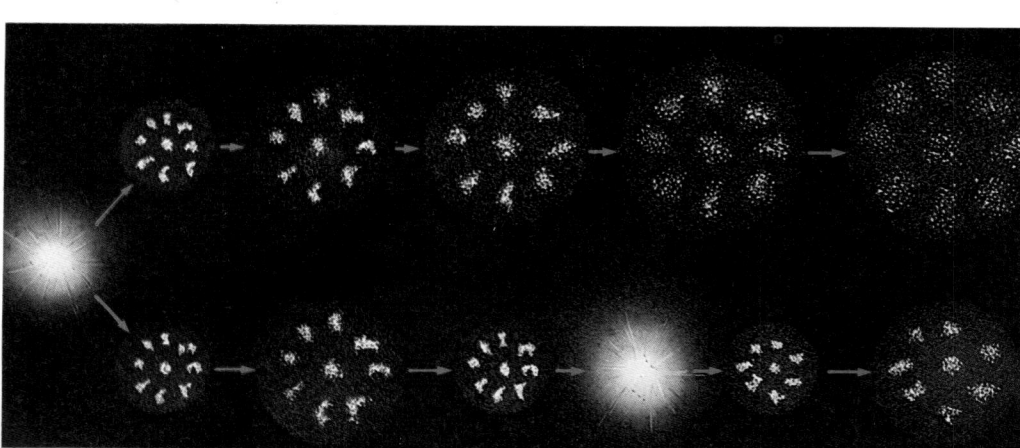

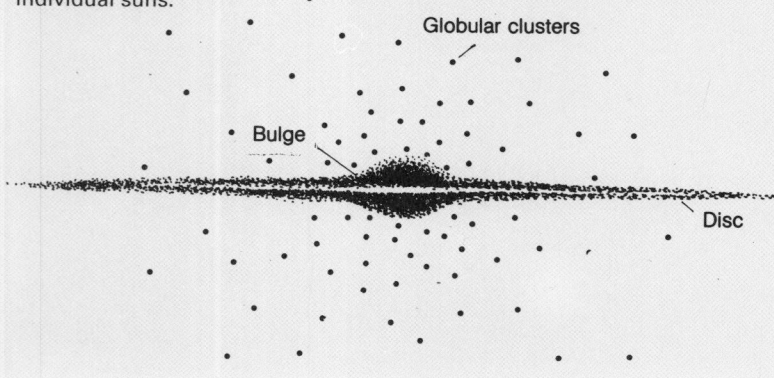

GALACTIC STRUCTURES

The universe's 100 million galaxies show clear structural patterns, originally classified by the American astronomer Edwin Hubble in 1925. Spiral galaxies like our own (top row) have a central, almost spherical bulge and a surrounding disc composed of spiral arms. Barred spirals (bottom row) have a central bar of stars across the nucleus, with spiral arms trailing from the ends of the bar. Elliptical galaxies (far left) have a uniform appearance, ranging from a flattened disc to a near sphere. So-called SO galaxies (left row, right) have a central bulge, but no spiral arms. A few have no discernible structure at all. Galaxies also vary enormously in size, from dwarfs only 2,000 light-years across to great assemblies of stars 80 or more times larger.

THE HOME GALAXY

The Sun and its planets are located in one of the spiral arms, a little less than 30,000 light-years from the galactic centre and orbiting around it in a period of more than 200 million years. The centre is invisible from the Earth, masked by vast, light-absorbing clouds of interstellar dust. The galaxy is probably around 12 billion years old and, like other spiral galaxies, has three distinct regions. The central bulge is about 30,000 light-years in diameter. The disc in which the Sun is located is not much more than 1,000 light-years thick but 100,000 light-years from end to end. Around the galaxy is the halo, a spherical zone 150,000 light-years across studded with globular star-clusters and sprinkled with individual suns.

Globular clusters

Bulge

Disc

Solar System

Star charts are drawn as projections of a vast, hollow sphere with the observer in the middle. Each circle below represents one hemisphere, centred on the north and south celestial poles respectively – projections of the Earth's poles in the heavens. At the present era, the north pole is marked by the star Polaris; the south pole has no such convenient reference point. The rectangular map shows the stars immediately above and below the celestial equator.

Astronomical coordinates are normally given in terms of 'Right Ascension' for longitude and 'Declination' for latitude or altitude. Since the stars appear to rotate around the Earth once every 24 hours, Right Ascension is measured eastward – anti-clockwise – in hours and minutes. One hour is equivalent to 15 angular degrees; zero on the scale is the point at which the Sun crosses the celestial equator at the spring equinox, known to astronomers as the First Point in Aries. Unlike the Sun, stars always rise and set at the same point on the horizon. Declination measures (in degrees) a star's angular distance above or below the celestial equator.

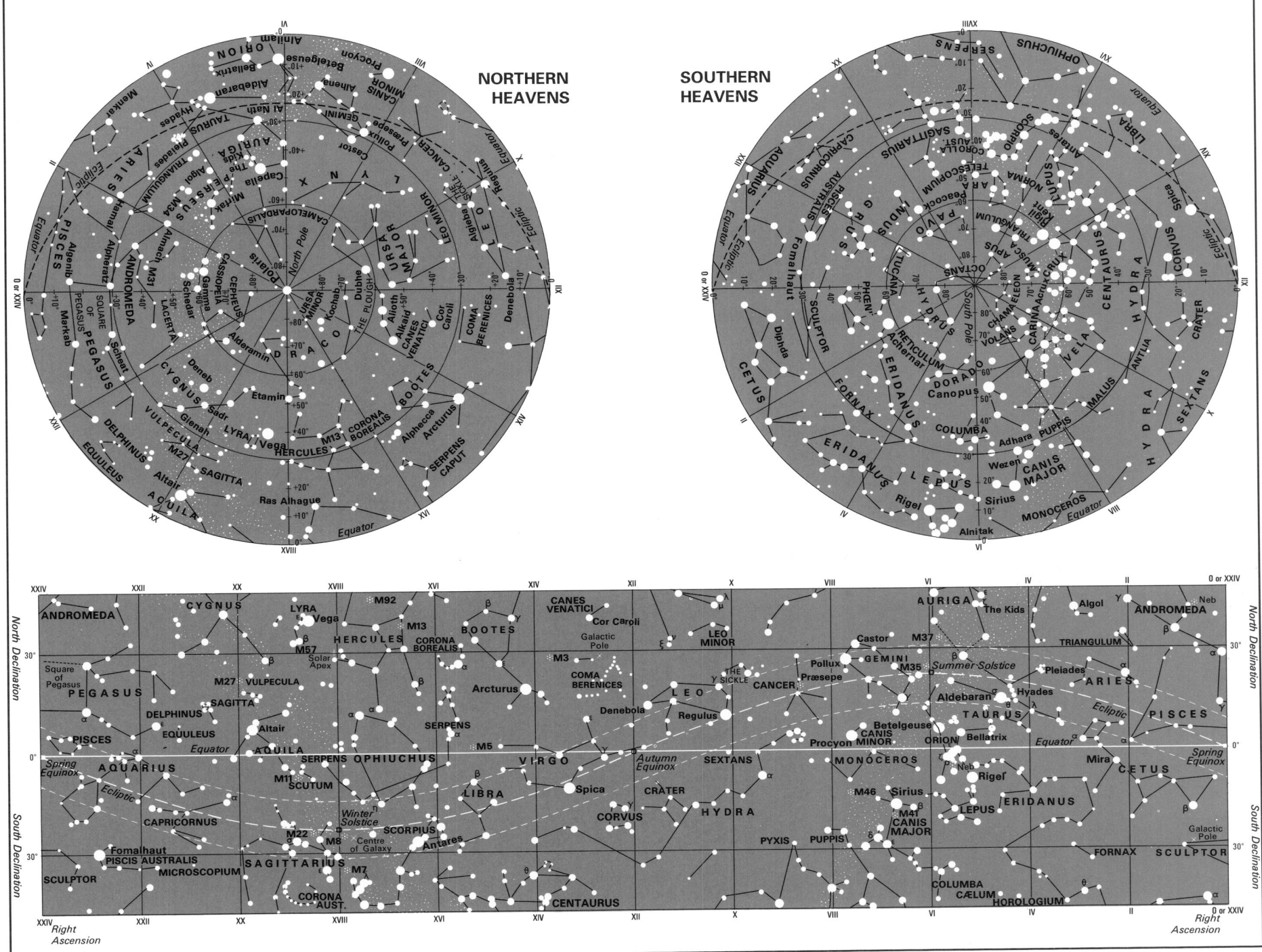

THE CONSTELLATIONS

The constellations and their English names

Andromeda	Andromeda	Circinus	Compasses	Lacerta	Lizard
Antila	Air Pump	Columba	Dove	Leo	Lion
Apus	Bird of Paradise	Coma Berenices	Berenice's Hair	Leo Minor	Little Lion
Aquarius	Water-carrier	Corona Australis	Southern Crown	Lepus	Hare
Aquila	Eagle	Corona Borealis	Northern Crown	Libra	Scales
Ara	Altar	Corvus	Crow	Lupus	Wolf
Aries	Ram	Crater	Cup	Lynx	Lynx
Auriga	Charioteer	Crux	Southern Cross	Lyra	Harp
Boötes	Herdsman	Cygnus	Swan	Mensa	Table
Caelum	Chisel	Delphinus	Dolphin	Microscopium	Microscope
Camelopardalis	Giraffe	Dorado	Swordfish	Monoceros	Unicorn
Cancer	Crab	Draco	Dragon	Musca	Fly
Canes Venatici	Hunting Dogs	Equuleus	Little House	Norma	Level
Canis Major	Great Dog	Eridanus	Eridanus	Octans	Octant
Canis Minor	Little Dog	Fornax	Furnace	Ophiuchus	Serpent Bearer
Capricornus	Goat	Gemini	Twins	Orion	Orion
Carina	Keel	Grus	Crane	Pavo	Peacock
Cassiopeia	Cassiopeia	Hercules	Hercules	Pegasus	Winged Horse
Centaurus	Centaur	Horologium	Clock	Perseus	Perseus
Cepheus	Cepheus	Hydra	Water Snake	Phoenix	Phoenix
Cetus	Whale	Hydrus	Sea Serpent	Pictor	Easel
Chamaeleon	Chameleon	Indus	Indian	Pisces	Fishes

Piscis Austrinus	Southern Fish
Puppis	Ship's Stern
Pyxis	Mariner's Compass
Reticulum	Net
Sagitta	Arrow
Sagittarius	Archer
Scorpius	Scorpion
Sculptor	Sculptor
Scutum	Shield
Serpens	Serpent
Sextans	Sextant
Taurus	Bull
Telescopium	Telescope
Triangulum	Triangle
Triangulum Australe	Southern Triangle
Tucana	Toucan
Ursa Major	Great Bear
Ursa Minor	Little Bear
Vela	Sails
Virgo	Virgin
Volans	Flying Fish
Vulpecula	Fox

THE NEAREST STARS

The 20 nearest stars, excluding the Sun, with their distance from Earth in light-years*

Proxima Centauri	4.3
Alpha Centauri A	4.3
Alpha Centauri B	4.3
Barnard's Star	6.0
Wolf 359	8.1
Lal 21185	8.2
Sirius A	8.7
Sirius B	8.7
UV Ceti A	9.0
UV Citi B	9.0
Ross 154	9.3
Ross 248	10.3
Epsilon Eridani	10.8
L 789-6	11.1
Ross 128	11.1
61 Cygni A	11.2
61 Cygni B	11.2
Procyon A	11.3
Procyon B	11.3
Epsilon Indi	11.4

Many of the nearest stars, like Alpha Centauri A and B, are doubles, orbiting about the common centre of gravity and to all intents and purposes equidistant from Earth. Many of them are dim objects, with no name other than the designation given by the astronomers who investigated them. However, they include Sirius, the brightest star in the sky, and Procyon, the seventh brightest. Both are far larger than the Sun: of the nearest stars only Epsilon Eridani is similar in size and luminosity.

* A light-year equals approx. 9,500,000,000,000 kilometres

THE SOLAR SYSTEM

Lying 27,000 light years from the centre of one of billions of galaxies that comprise the observable universe, our solar system contains nine planets and their moons, innumerable asteroids and comets and a miscellany of dust and gas, all tethered by the immense gravitational field of the Sun, the middling-sized star whose thermonuclear furnaces provide them all with heat and light. The solar system was probably formed about 4.6 billion years ago, when a spinning cloud of gas, mostly hydrogen but seeded with other, heavier elements, condensed enough to ignite a nuclear reaction and create a star. The Sun still accounts for almost 99.9% of the system's total mass; one planet, Jupiter, contains most of the remainder.

By composition as well as distance, the planetary array divides quite neatly in two: an inner system of four small, solid planets, including the Earth, and an outer system, from Jupiter to Neptune, of four huge gas giants. Between the two groups lies a scattering of asteroids, perhaps as many as 40,000; possibly the remains of a planet destroyed by some unexplained catastrophe, they are more likely to be debris left over from the solar system's formation, prevented by the gravity of massive Jupiter from coalescing into a larger body. The ninth planet, Pluto, seems to be a world of the inner system type: small, rocky and something of an anomaly.

By the 1990s, the solar system also included some newer anomalies: several thousand spacecraft. Most were in orbit around the Earth, but some had probed far and wide around the system. The information beamed back by these robotic investigators has transformed our knowledge of our celestial environment.

Much of the early history of science is the story of people trying to make sense of the errant points of light that were all they knew of the planets. Now, men have themselves stood on the Earth's Moon; probes have landed on Mars and Venus and orbiting radars have mapped far distant landscapes with astonishing accuracy. In the 1980s, the US Voyagers skimmed all four major planets of the outer system, bringing new revelations with each close approach. Only Pluto, inscrutably distant in an orbit that takes it 50 times the Earth's distance from the Sun, remains unvisited by our messengers.

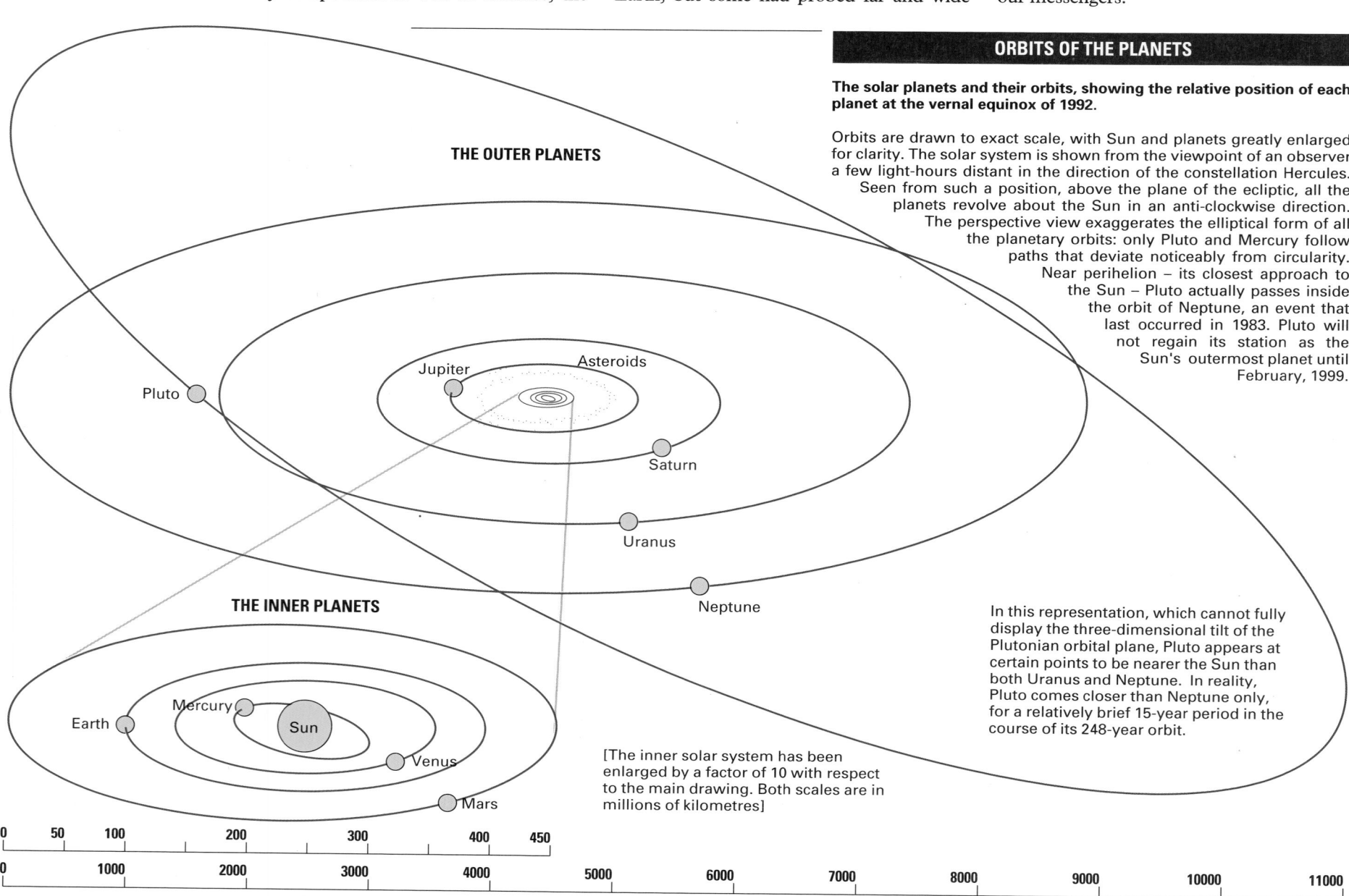

ORBITS OF THE PLANETS

The solar planets and their orbits, showing the relative position of each planet at the vernal equinox of 1992.

Orbits are drawn to exact scale, with Sun and planets greatly enlarged for clarity. The solar system is shown from the viewpoint of an observer a few light-hours distant in the direction of the constellation Hercules. Seen from such a position, above the plane of the ecliptic, all the planets revolve about the Sun in an anti-clockwise direction. The perspective view exaggerates the elliptical form of all the planetary orbits: only Pluto and Mercury follow paths that deviate noticeably from circularity. Near perihelion – its closest approach to the Sun – Pluto actually passes inside the orbit of Neptune, an event that last occurred in 1983. Pluto will not regain its station as the Sun's outermost planet until February, 1999.

THE OUTER PLANETS

THE INNER PLANETS

In this representation, which cannot fully display the three-dimensional tilt of the Plutonian orbital plane, Pluto appears at certain points to be nearer the Sun than both Uranus and Neptune. In reality, Pluto comes closer than Neptune only, for a relatively brief 15-year period in the course of its 248-year orbit.

[The inner solar system has been enlarged by a factor of 10 with respect to the main drawing. Both scales are in millions of kilometres]

PLANETARY DATA

	Mean distance from Sun (million km)	Mass (Earth = 1)	Period of orbit (Earth years)	Period of rotation (Earth days)	Equatorial diameter (km)	Average density (water = 1)	Surface gravity (Earth = 1)	Escape velocity (km/sec)	Number of known satellites
Sun	-	*332,946*	-	*25.38*	*1,392,000*	*1.41*	*27.9*	*617.5*	-
Mercury	58.3	0.06	0.241	58.67	4,878	5.5	0.38	4.27	0
Venus	107.7	0.8	0.615	243	12,104	5.25	0.90	10.36	0
Earth	149.6	1.0	1.00	0.99	12,756	5.52	1.00	11.18	1
Mars	227.3	0.1	1.88	1.02	6,794	3.94	0.38	5.03	2
Jupiter	777.9	317.8	11.86	0.41	142,800	1.33	2.64	60.22	16
Saturn	1,427.1	95.2	29.63	0.42	120,000	0.706	1.16	36.25	17
Uranus	2,872.3	14.5	83.97	0.45	52,000	1.70	1.11	22.4	15
Neptune	4,502.7	17.2	164.8	0.67	48,400	1.77	1.21	23.9	8
Pluto	5,894.2	0.002	248.63	6.38	3,000	5.50	0.47	5.1	1

Planetary days are given in sidereal time -- that is, with respect to the stars rather than the Sun. Most of the information in the table was confirmed by spacecraft and often obtained from photographs and other data transmitted back to the Earth. In the case of Pluto, however, only earthbound observations have been made, and no spacecraft can hope to encounter it until well into the next century. Given the planet's small size and great distance, figures for its diameter and rotation period cannot be definitive.

Since Pluto does not appear to be massive enough to account for the perturbations in the orbits of Uranus and Neptune that led to its 1930 discovery, it is quite possible that a tenth and even more distant planet may exist. Once Pluto's own 248-year orbit has been observed for long enough, further discrepancies may give a clue as to any tenth planet's whereabouts. Even so, distance alone would make it very difficult to locate, especially since telescopes powerful enough to find it are normally engaged in galactic study.

THE PLANETS

Mercury is the closest planet to the Sun and hence the fastest-moving. It has no significant atmosphere and a cratered, wrinkled surface very similar to that of Earth's moon.

Venus has much the same physical dimensions as Earth. However, its carbon dioxide atmosphere is 90 times as dense, accounting for a runaway greenhouse effect that makes the Venusian surface, at 475°C, the hottest of all the planets. Radar mapping shows relatively level land with volcanic regions whose sulphurous discharges explain the sulphuric acid rains reported by soft-landing space probes before they succumbed to Venus's fierce climate.

Earth seen from space is easily the most beautiful of the inner planets; it is also, and more objectively, the largest, as well the only home of known life. Living things are the main reason why the Earth is able to retain a substantial proportion of corrosive and highly reactive oxygen in its atmosphere, a state of affairs that contradicts the laws of chemical equilibrium; the oxygen in turn supports the life that constantly regenerates it.

Mars was once considered the likeliest of the other planets to share Earth's cargo of life: seasonal expansion of dark patches strongly suggested vegetation and the planet's apparent icecaps indicated the vital presence of water. But close inspection by spacecraft brought disappointment: chemical reactions account for the seeming vegetation, the icecaps are mainly frozen carbon dioxide and whatever oxygen the planet once possessed is now locked up in the iron-bearing rock that covers its cratered surface and gives it its characteristic red hue.

Jupiter masses almost three times as much as all the other planets together; had it scooped up a little more matter during its formation, it might have evolved into a small companion star for the Sun. The planet is mostly gas, under intense pressure in the lower atmosphere above a core of fiercely compressed hydogen and helium. The upper layers form strikingly-coloured rotating belts, the outward sign of the intense storms created by Jupiter's rapid diurnal rotation. Close approaches by spacecraft have shown an orbiting ring system, and discovered several previously unknown moons: Jupiter has at least 16.

Saturn is structurally similar to Jupiter, rotating fast enough to produce an obvious bulge at its equator. Ever since the invention of the telescope, however, Saturn's rings have been the feature that has attracted most observers. Voyager probes in 1980 and 1981 sent back detailed pictures that showed them to be composed of thousands of separate ringlets, each in turn made up of tiny icy particles, interacting in a complex dance that may serve as a model for the study of galactic and even larger structures.

Uranus was unknown to the ancients: although it is faintly visible to the naked eye, it was not discovered until 1781. Its composition is broadly similar to Jupiter and Saturn, though its distance from the Sun ensures an even colder surface temperature. Observations in 1977 suggested the presence of a faint ring system, amply confirmed when Voyager 2 swung past the planet in 1986.

Neptune is always more than 4,000 million Km from Earth, and despite its diameter of almost 50,000 km it can only be seen by telescope. Its 1846 discovery was the result of mathematical predictions by astronomers seeking to explain irregularities in the orbit of Uranus, but until Voyager 2 closed with the planet in 1989 little was known of it. Like Uranus, it has a ring system; Voyager's photographs revealed a total of eight moons.

Pluto is the most mysterious of the solar planets, if only because even the most powerful telescopes can scarcely resolve it from a point of light to a disc. It was discovered as recently as 1930, like Neptune as the result of perturbations in the orbits of the two then outermost planets. Its small size as well as its eccentric and highly tilted orbit have led to suggestions that it is a former satellite of Neptune, somehow liberated from its primary. In 1978 Pluto was found to have a moon of its own, Charon, apparently half the size of Pluto itself.

Mean distance from Sun in million kilometres

Mercury	58.3
Venus	107.7
Earth	149.6
Mars	227.9
Jupiter	777.9
Saturn	1,427.1
Uranus	2,872.3
Neptune	4,502.7
Pluto	5,894.2

THE EARTH: TIME & MOTION

The basic unit of time measurement is the day, one rotation of the Earth on its axis. The subdivision of the day into hours, minutes and seconds is arbitrary and simply for our convenience. Our present calendar is based on the solar year of 365.24 days, the time taken by the Earth to orbit the Sun. As the Earth rotates from west to east, the Sun appears to rise in the east and set in the west. When the Sun is setting in Shanghai, on the opposite side of the world New York is just emerging into sunlight. Noon, when the sun is directly overhead, is coincident at all places on the same meridian, with shadows pointing directly toward the poles.

Calendars based on the movements of the Sun and Moon have been used since ancient times. The Julian Calendar, with its leap year, introduced by Julius Caesar, fixed the average length of the year at 365.25 days, which was about 11 minutes too long (the Earth completes its orbit in 365 days, 5 hours, 48 minutes and 46 seconds of mean solar time). The cumulative error was rectified by the Gregorian Calendar, introduced by Pope Gregory XIII in 1582, when he decreed that the day following October 4 was October 15, and that century years do not count as leap years unless divisible by 400. England did not adopt the reformed calendar until 1752, when she found herself 11 days behind the continent.

Britain imposed the Gregorian Calendar on all its possessions, including the American colonies. All dates preceding September 2 were marked O.S., for Old Style.

EARTH DATA

Maximum distance from the Sun (Aphelion): 152,007,016 km.
Minimum distance from Sun (Perihelion): 147,000,830 km.
Obliquity of the ecliptic: 23° 27' 08".
Length of year - solar tropical (equinox to equinox): 365.24 days
Length of year - sidereal (fixed star to fixed star): 365.26 days
Length of day - mean solar day: 24h, 03m, 56s.
Length of day - mean sidereal day: 23h, 56m, 04s.

Superficial area: 510,000,000 sq. km.
Land surface: 149,000,000 sq. km. (29.2%)
Water surface: 361,000,000 sq. km. (70.8%)
Equatorial circumference: 40,077 km.
Meridional circumference: 40,009 km.
Equatorial diameter: 12,756.8 km.
Polar diameter: 12,713.8 km.
Equatorial radius: 6,378.4 km.
Polar radius: 6,356.9 km.
Volume of the Earth: 1,083,230 x 10^6 cu. km.
Mass of the Earth: 5.9 x 10^{21} tonnes

THE SEASONS

The Earth revolves around the Sun once a year in an 'anti-clockwise' direction, tilted at a constant angle, 66½°. In June, the northern hemisphere is tilted towards the Sun: as a result it receives more hours of sunshine in a day and therefore has its warmest season, summer. By December, the Earth has rotated halfway round the Sun so that the southern hemisphere that is tilted towards the Sun and has its summer; the hemisphere that is tilted away from the Sun has winter. On 21 June the Sun is directly overhead at the Tropic of Cancer (23½° N), and this is midsummer in the northern hemisphere. Midsummer in the southern hemisphere occurs on 21 December, when the Sun is overhead at the Tropic of Capricorn (23½° S).

DAY & NIGHT

The Sun appears to rise in the east, reach its highest point at noon, and then set in the west, to be followed by night. In reality it is not the Sun that is moving but the Earth revolving from west to east.

At the summer solstice in the northern hemisphere (21 June), the Arctic has total daylight and the Antarctic total darkness. The opposite occurs at the winter solstice (21 December). At the equator, the length of day and night are almost equal all year.

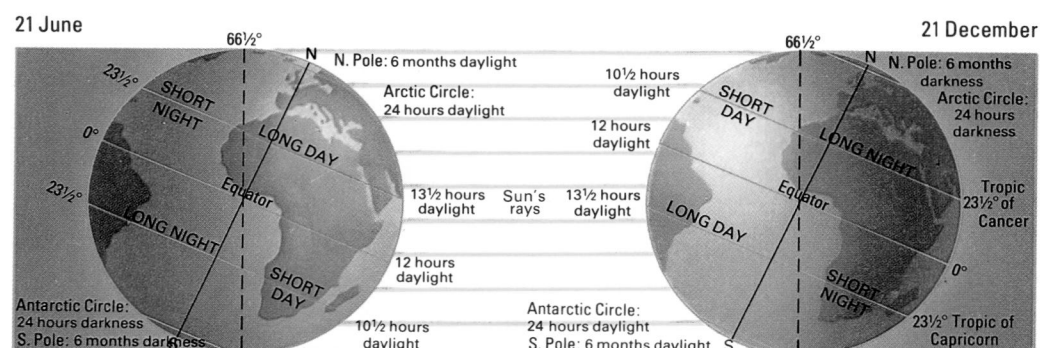

THE SUN'S PATH

The diagrams on the left illustrate the apparent path of the Sun at (A) the equator, (B) in mid-latitude (45°), (C) at the Arctic Circle (66½°) and (D) at the North Pole, where there is six months of continuous daylight and six months of continuous night.

MEASUREMENTS OF TIME

Astronomers distinguish between solar time and sidereal time. Solar time derives from the period taken by the Earth to rotate on its axis: one rotation defines a solar day. But the speed of the Earth along its orbit around the Sun is not constant. The length of day - or 'apparent solar day' - as defined by the apparent successive transits of the Sun - is irregular because the Earth must complete more than one rotation before the Sun returns to the same meridian. The constant sidereal day is defined as the interval between two successive apparent transits of a star, or the first point of Aries, across the same meridian. If the Sun is at the equinox and overhead at a meridian one day, then the next day it will be to the east by approximately 1°. Thus the Sun will not cross the meridian until four minutes after the sidereal noon.

From the diagrams on the right it is possible to discover the time of sunrise or sunset on a given date and for latitudes between 60°N and 60°S.

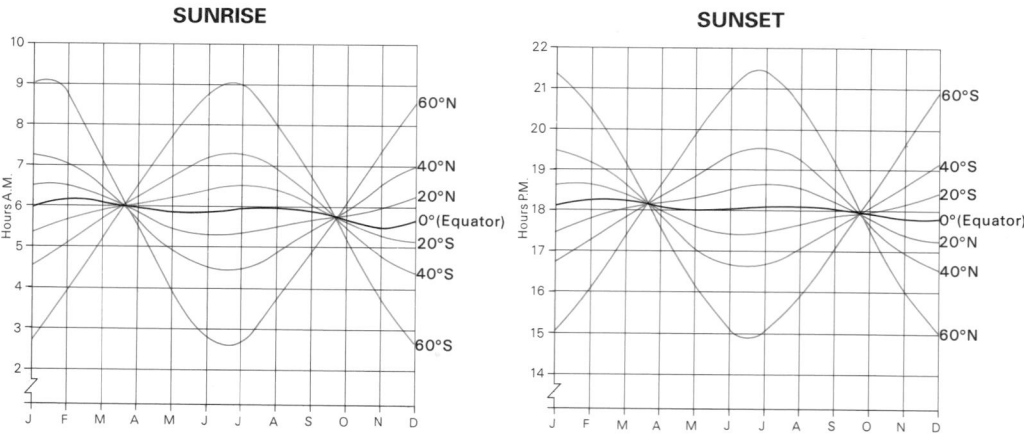

THE MOON

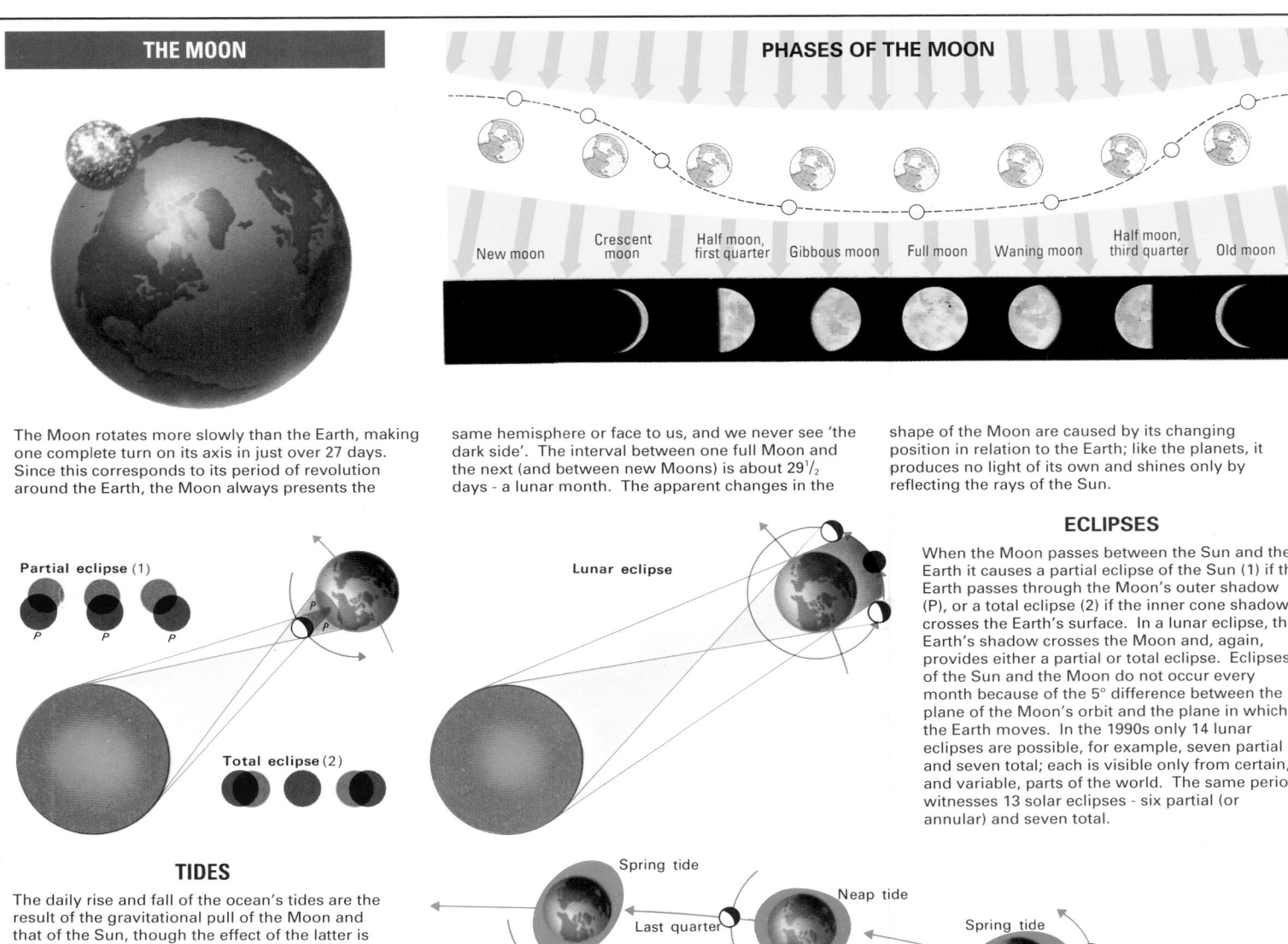

PHASES OF THE MOON

New moon | Crescent moon | Half moon, first quarter | Gibbous moon | Full moon | Waning moon | Half moon, third quarter | Old moon

MOON DATA

Distance from Earth: The Moon orbits at a mean distance of 384,199.1 km, at an average speed of 3,683 km/h in relation to the Earth.

Size & mass: The average diameter of the Moon is 3,475.1 km. It is 400 times smaller than the Sun but is about 400 times closer to the Earth, so we see them as the same size. The Moon has a mass of 7,348 x 10^{19} tonnes, with a density 3.344 times that of water.

Visibility: Only 59% of the Moon's surface is directly visible from Earth. Reflected light takes 1.25 seconds to reach Earth - compared to 8 minutes 27.3 seconds for light from the Sun.

Temperature: With the Sun overhead the temperature on the lunar equator can reach 117.2°C [243°F]. At night it can sink to -162.7°C [-261°F].

The Moon rotates more slowly than the Earth, making one complete turn on its axis in just over 27 days. Since this corresponds to its period of revolution around the Earth, the Moon always presents the same hemisphere or face to us, and we never see 'the dark side'. The interval between one full Moon and the next (and between new Moons) is about 29½ days - a lunar month. The apparent changes in the shape of the Moon are caused by its changing position in relation to the Earth; like the planets, it produces no light of its own and shines only by reflecting the rays of the Sun.

Partial eclipse (1)

Lunar eclipse

Total eclipse (2)

ECLIPSES

When the Moon passes between the Sun and the Earth it causes a partial eclipse of the Sun (1) if the Earth passes through the Moon's outer shadow (P), or a total eclipse (2) if the inner cone shadow crosses the Earth's surface. In a lunar eclipse, the Earth's shadow crosses the Moon and, again, provides either a partial or total eclipse. Eclipses of the Sun and the Moon do not occur every month because of the 5° difference between the plane of the Moon's orbit and the plane in which the Earth moves. In the 1990s only 14 lunar eclipses are possible, for example, seven partial and seven total; each is visible only from certain, and variable, parts of the world. The same period witnesses 13 solar eclipses - six partial (or annular) and seven total.

TIDES

The daily rise and fall of the ocean's tides are the result of the gravitational pull of the Moon and that of the Sun, though the effect of the latter is only 46.6% as strong as that of the Moon. This effect is greatest on the hemisphere facing the Moon and causes a tidal 'bulge'. When lunar and solar forces pull together, with Sun, Earth and Moon in line (near new and full Moons), higher 'spring tides' (and lower low tides) occur; when lunar and solar forces are least coincidental with the Sun and Moon at an angle (near the Moon's first and third quarters), 'neap tides' occur, which have a small tidal range.

Spring tide — Neap tide — Spring tide — Full moon — Last quarter — New moon — Neap tide — First quarter

Gravitational pull by Sun and Moon

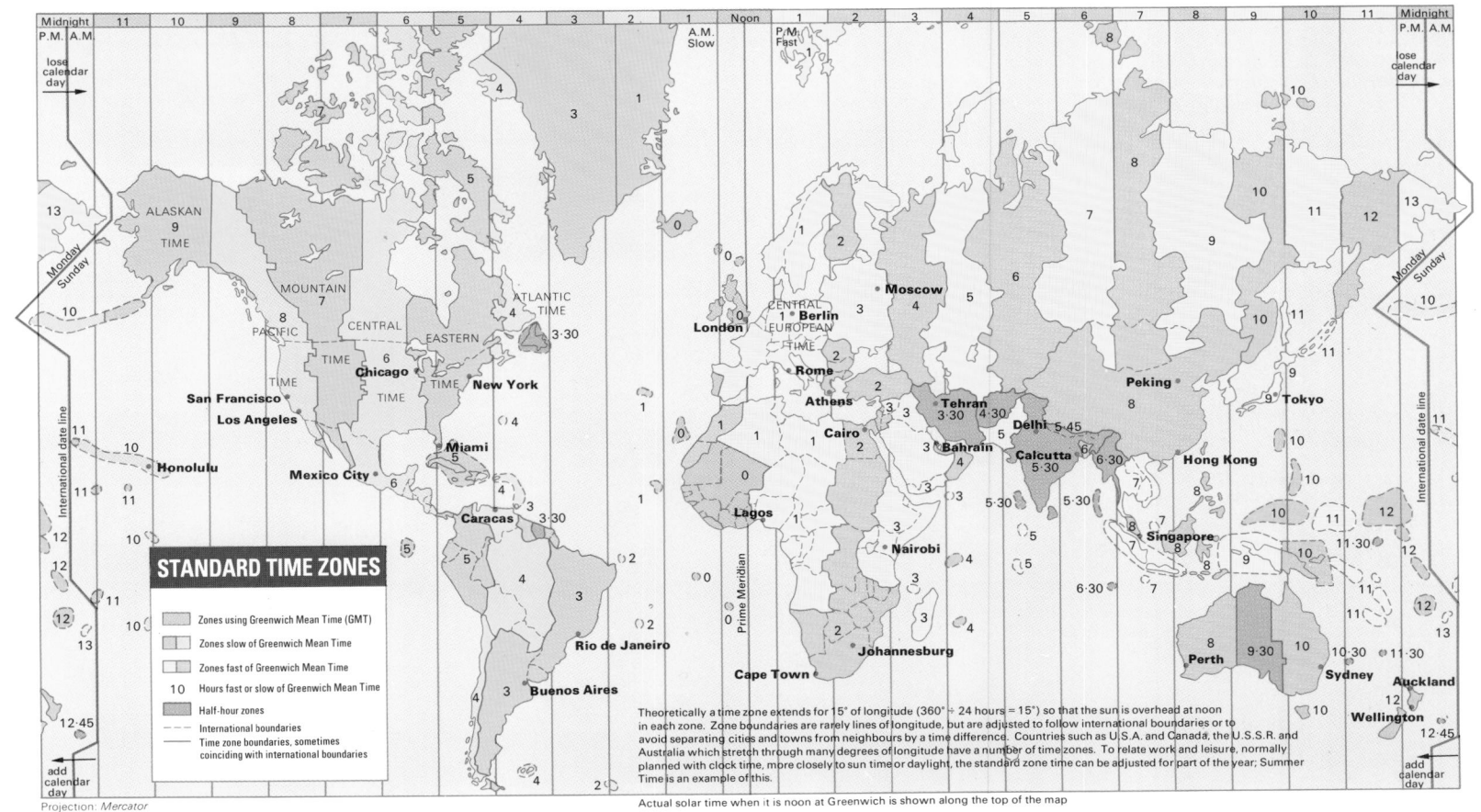

TIME ZONES

The Earth rotates through 360° in 24 hours, and therefore it moves 15° every hour. The world is divided into 24 standard time zones, each centred on lines of longitude at 15° intervals, so that every country falls within one or more agreed zones. The Greenwich meridian, based on the location of the Royal Observatory in London, lies at the centre of the first zone. All places to the west of Greenwich are one hour behind for every 15° of longitude; places to the east are ahead by one hour for every 15°.
When it is 12 noon at the Greenwich meridian, 180° east it is midnight of the same day – while 180° west the day is only just beginning. To overcome this the International Date Line was established, approximately following the 180° meridian. Thus if you travelled eastwards from Japan (140° East) to Samoa (170° West) you would pass from Sunday night into Sunday morning.

STANDARD TIME ZONES

- Zones using Greenwich Mean Time (GMT)
- Zones slow of Greenwich Mean Time
- Zones fast of Greenwich Mean Time
- **10** Hours fast or slow of Greenwich Mean Time
- Half-hour zones
- International boundaries
- Time zone boundaries, sometimes coinciding with international boundaries

Theoretically a time zone extends for 15° of longitude (360° ÷ 24 hours = 15°) so that the sun is overhead at noon in each zone. Zone boundaries are rarely lines of longitude, but are adjusted to follow international boundaries or to avoid separating cities and towns from neighbours by a time difference. Countries such as U.S.A. and Canada, the U.S.S.R. and Australia which stretch through many degrees of longitude have a number of time zones. To relate work and leisure, normally planned with clock time, more closely to sun time or daylight, the standard zone time can be adjusted for part of the year; Summer Time is an example of this.

Actual solar time when it is noon at Greenwich is shown along the top of the map

Projection: Mercator

THE EARTH: GEOLOGY

The complementary, almost jigsaw-puzzle fit of the Atlantic coasts led to Alfred Wegener's proposition of continental drift in Germany (1915). His theory suggested that an ancient super-continent, which he called Pangaea, incorporating all the Earth's land masses, gradually split up to form the continents we know today. By 180 million years ago Pangaea had divided into two major groups and the southern part, Gondwanaland, had itself begun to break up with India and Antarctica-Australia becoming isolated. By 135 million years ago the widening of the splits in the North Atlantic and Indian Oceans persisted, a South Atlantic gap had appeared and India continued to move 'north' towards Asia. By 65 million years ago South America had completely split from Africa.
To form today's pattern India 'collided' with Asia (crumpling up sediments to form the Himalayas); South America rotated and moved west to connect with North America; Australia separated from Antarctica and moved north; and the familiar gap developed between Greenland and Europe.

The origin of the Earth is still open to conjecture, although the most widely accepted theory is that it was formed from a solar cloud consisting mainly of hydrogen 4,600 million years ago. The cloud condensed, forming the planets. The lighter elements floated to the surface of the Earth, where they cooled to form a crust; the inner material remained hot and molten. The first rocks were formed over 3,500 million years ago, but the Earth's surface has since been constantly altered.

The crust consists of a brittle, low-density material varying from 5 to 50 kilometres deep beneath the continents, consisting predominately of silica and aluminium: hence its name, sial. Below the sial is a basaltic layer known as sima, comprising mainly silica and magnesium. The crust accounts for only 1.5 per cent of the Earth s volume.

Immediately below the crust the mantle begins, with a distinct change in density and chemical properties. The rock is rich in iron and magnesium silicates, and temperatures reach 1,600°C. The rigid upper mantle extends down to a depth of about 1,000 kilometres, below which is a more viscous lower mantle about 1,900 kilometres thick.

The outer core, measuring about 2,100 kilometres thick, consists of molten iron and nickel at 2,100°C to 5,000°C, possibly separated from the less dense mantle by an oxidized shell. About 5,000 kilometres below the surface is a liquid transition zone, below which is the solid inner core, a sphere of about 2,700 kilometres diameter where rock is three times as dense as in the crust. The temperature at the centre of the Earth is probably about 5,000°C.

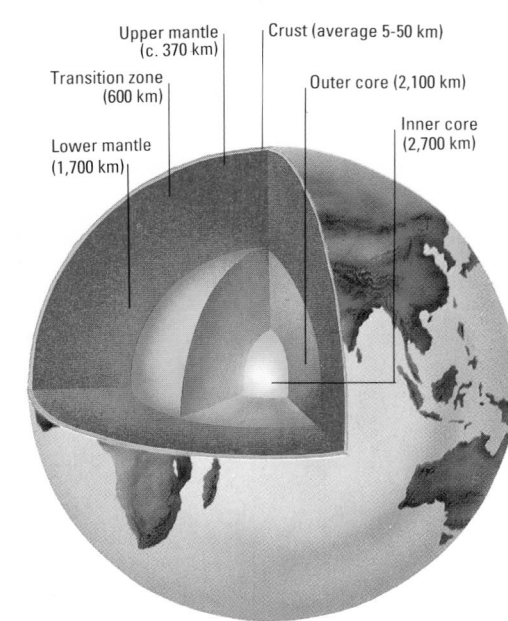

Upper mantle (c. 370 km)
Crust (average 5-50 km)
Transition zone (600 km)
Outer core (2,100 km)
Lower mantle (1,700 km)
Inner core (2,700 km)

CONTINENTAL DRIFT

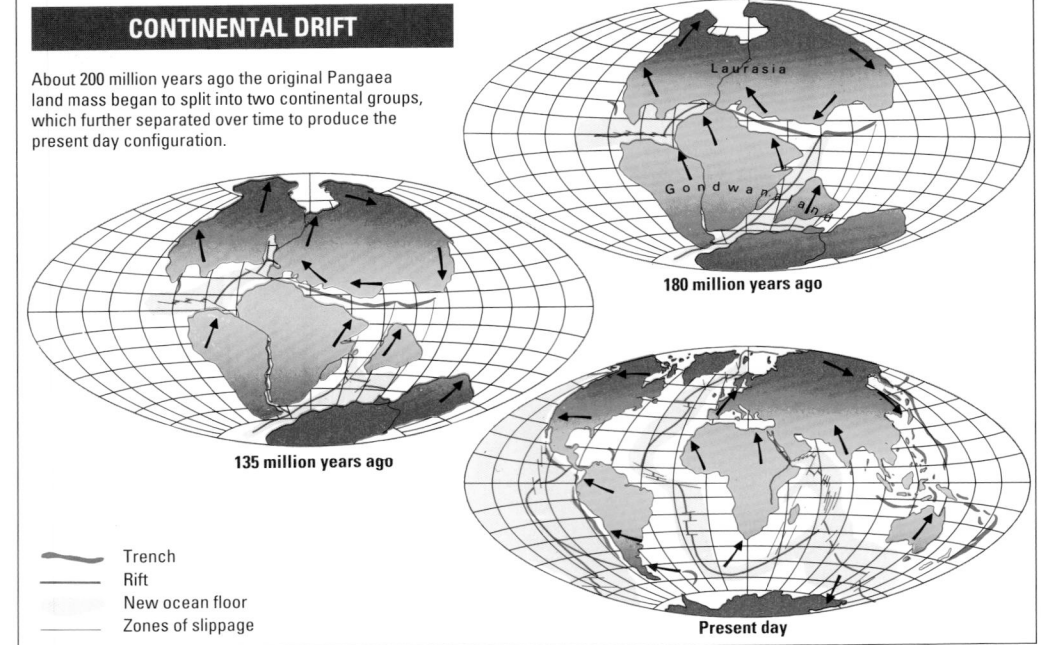

About 200 million years ago the original Pangaea land mass began to split into two continental groups, which further separated over time to produce the present day configuration.

Laurasia
Gondwanaland

180 million years ago

135 million years ago

Present day

- ～～～ Trench
- ──── Rift
- New ocean floor
- Zones of slippage

PLATE TECTONICS

The original debate about the drift theory of Wegener and others formed a long prelude to a more radical idea: plate tectonics. The discovery that the continents are carried along on the top of slowly-moving crustal plates (which float on heavier liquid material – the lower mantle – much as icebergs do on water) provided the mechanism for the drift theories to work. The plates converge and diverge along margins marked by seismic and volcanic activity. Plates diverge from mid-ocean ridges where molten lava pushes up and forces the plates apart at a rate of up to 40 mm a year; converging plates form either a trench (where the oceanic plates sink below the lighter continental rock) or mountain ranges (where two continents collide).

The debate about plate tectonics is not over, however. In addition to abiding questions such as what force actually moves the plates (massive convection currents in the Earth's interior is the most popular explanation), and why many volcanoes and earthquakes occur in mid-plate (such as Hawaii and central China), evidence began to emerge in the early 1990s that, with more sophisticated equipment and models, the whole theory might be in doubt.

EARTHQUAKES

Earthquake magnitude is usually rated according to either the Richter or the Modified Mercalli scale, both devised by seismologists in the 1930s. The Richter scale measures absolute earthquake power with mathematical precision: each step upwards represents a ten-fold increase in shockwave amplitude. Theoretically, there is no upper limit, but the largest earthquakes measured have been rated at between 8.8 and 8.9. The 12–point Mercalli scale, based on observed effects, is often more meaningful, ranging from I (earthquakes noticed only by seismographs) to XII (total destruction); intermediate points include V (people awakened at night; unstable objects overturned), VII (collapse of ordinary buildings; chimneys and monuments fall); and IX (conspicuous cracks in ground; serious damage to reservoirs).

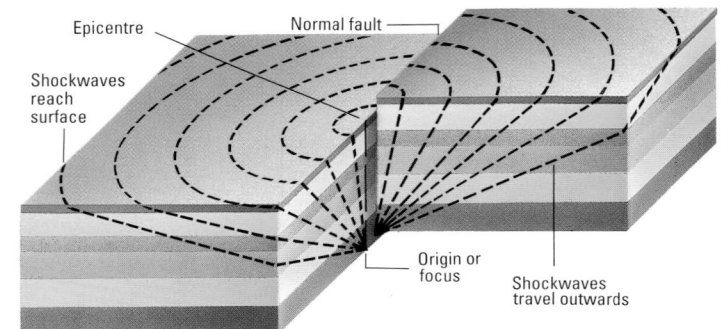

Epicentre
Normal fault
Shockwaves reach surface
Origin or focus
Shockwaves travel outwards

DISTRIBUTION

NOTABLE EARTHQUAKES SINCE 1900

Year	Location	Mag.	Deaths
1906	San Francisco, USA	8.3	503
1906	Valparaiso, Chile	8.6	22,000
1908	Messina, Italy	7.5	83,000
1915	Avezzano, Italy	7.5	30,000
1920	Gansu, China	8.6	180,000
1923	Yokohama, Japan	8.3	143,000
1927	Nan Shan, China	8.3	200,000
1932	Gansu, China	7.6	70,000
1934	Bihar, India/Nepal	8.4	10,700
1935	Quetta, India*	7.5	60,000
1939	Chillan, Chile	8.3	28,000
1939	Erzincan, Turkey	7.9	30,000
1960	Agadir, Morocco	5.8	12,000
1962	Khorasan, Iran	7.1	12,230
1963	Skopje, Yugoslavia	6.0	1,000
1964	Anchorage, Alaska	8.4	131
1968	N. E. Iran	7.4	12,000
1970	N. Peru	7.7	66,794
1972	Managua, Nicaragua	6.2	5,000
1974	N. Pakistan	6.3	5,200
1976	Guatemala	7.5	22,778
1976	Tangshan, China	8.2	650,000
1978	Tabas, Iran	7.7	25,000
1980	El Asnam, Algeria	7.3	20,000
1980	S. Italy	7.2	4,800
1985	Mexico City, Mexico	8.1	4,200
1988	N.W. Armenia, USSR	6.8	55,000
1990	N. Iran	7.7	36,000

The highest magnitude recorded on the Richter scale is 8.9, in Japan on 2 March 1933 (2,990 deaths). The most devastating quake ever was at Shaanxi (Shensi), central China, on 24 January 1566, when an estimated 830,000 people were killed.

* now Pakistan

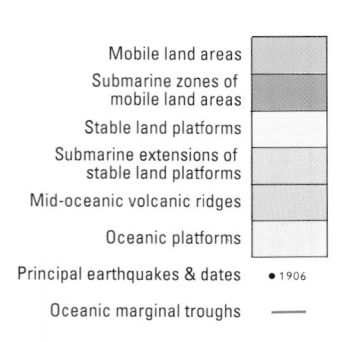

- Mobile land areas
- Submarine zones of mobile land areas
- Stable land platforms
- Submarine extensions of stable land platforms
- Mid-oceanic volcanic ridges
- Oceanic platforms
- Principal earthquakes & dates •1906
- Oceanic marginal troughs ───

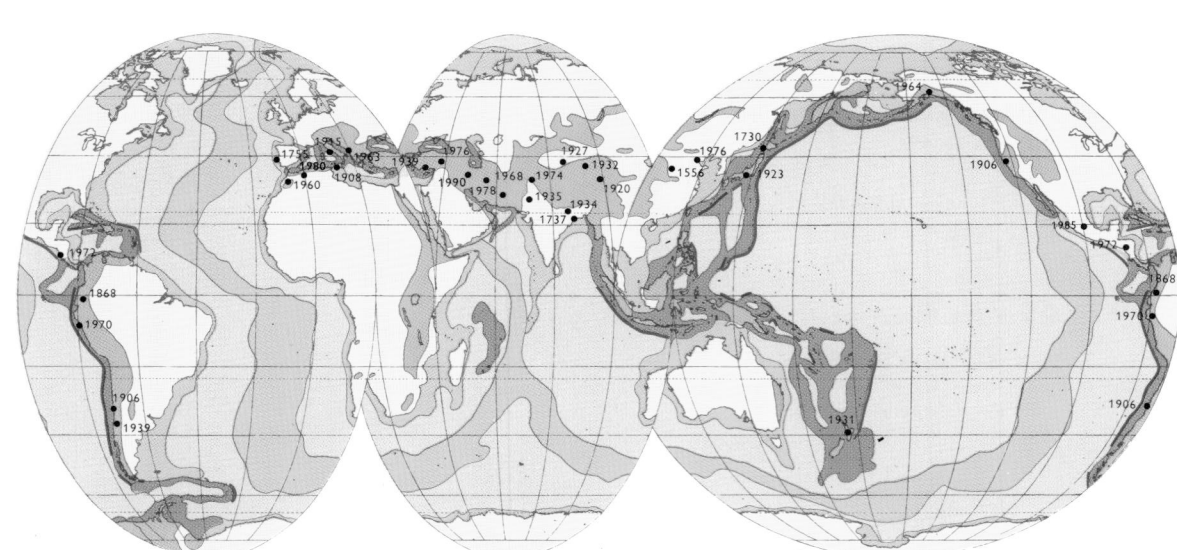

Earthquakes are a series of rapid vibrations originating from the the slipping or faulting of parts of the Earth's crust when stresses within build to breaking point, and usually occur at depths between 8 and 30 kilometres.

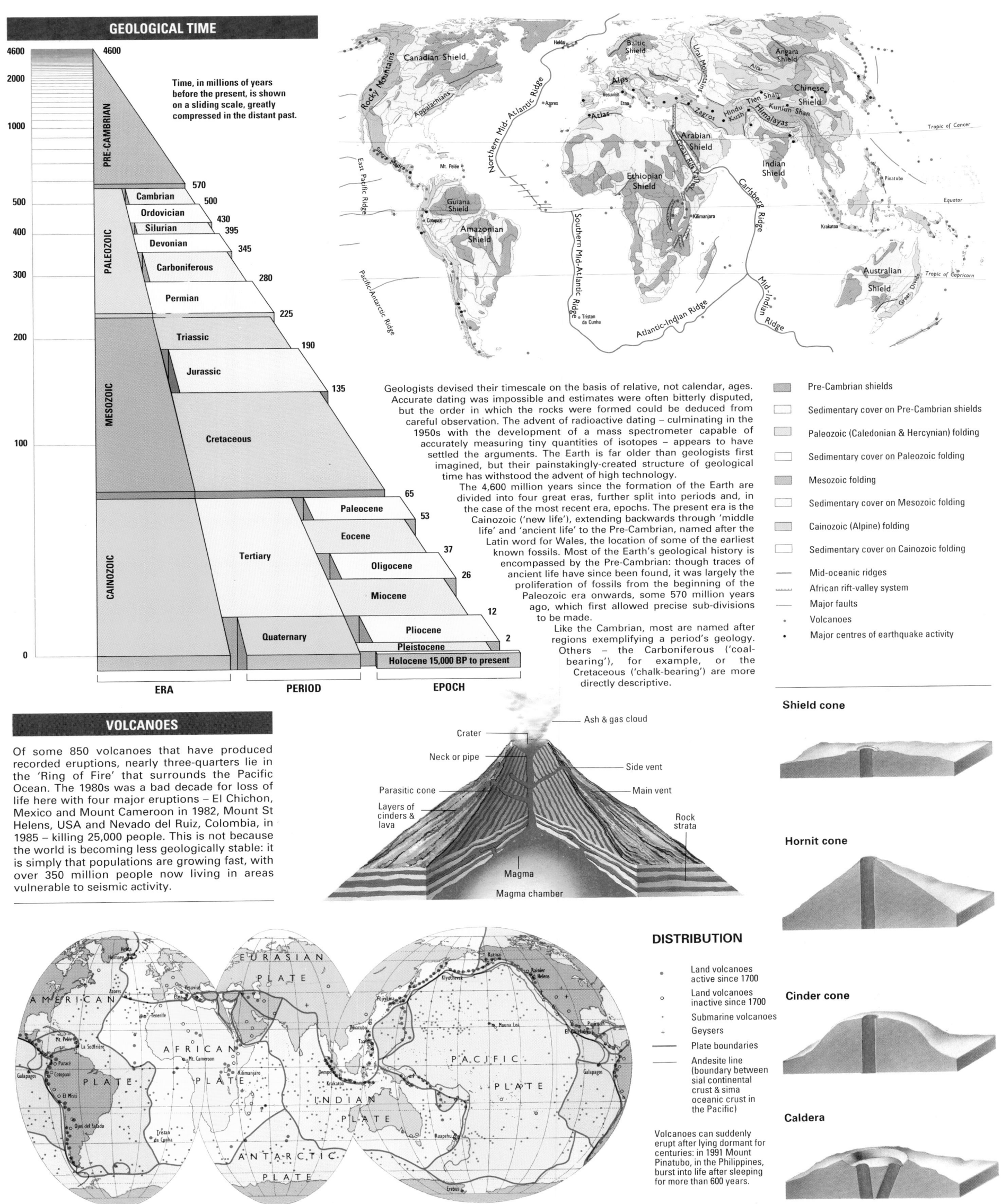

GEOLOGICAL TIME

Time, in millions of years before the present, is shown on a sliding scale, greatly compressed in the distant past.

Scale (millions of years): 4600, 2000, 1000, 500, 400, 300, 200, 100, 0

PRE-CAMBRIAN — 4600

PALEOZOIC
- Cambrian — 570
- Ordovician — 500
- Silurian — 430
- Devonian — 395
- Carboniferous — 345
- Permian — 280

MESOZOIC
- Triassic — 225
- Jurassic — 190
- Cretaceous — 135

CAINOZOIC
- Tertiary
  - Paleocene — 65
  - Eocene — 53
  - Oligocene — 37
  - Miocene — 26
  - Pliocene — 12
- Quaternary
  - Pleistocene — 2
  - Holocene 15,000 BP to present

ERA	PERIOD	EPOCH

Geologists devised their timescale on the basis of relative, not calendar, ages. Accurate dating was impossible and estimates were often bitterly disputed, but the order in which the rocks were formed could be deduced from careful observation. The advent of radioactive dating – culminating in the 1950s with the development of a mass spectrometer capable of accurately measuring tiny quantities of isotopes – appears to have settled the arguments. The Earth is far older than geologists first imagined, but their painstakingly-created structure of geological time has withstood the advent of high technology.

The 4,600 million years since the formation of the Earth are divided into four great eras, further split into periods and, in the case of the most recent era, epochs. The present era is the Cainozoic ('new life'), extending backwards through 'middle life' and 'ancient life' to the Pre-Cambrian, named after the Latin word for Wales, the location of some of the earliest known fossils. Most of the Earth's geological history is encompassed by the Pre-Cambrian: though traces of ancient life have since been found, it was largely the proliferation of fossils from the beginning of the Paleozoic era onwards, some 570 million years ago, which first allowed precise sub-divisions to be made.

Like the Cambrian, most are named after regions exemplifying a period's geology. Others – the Carboniferous ('coal-bearing'), for example, or the Cretaceous ('chalk-bearing') are more directly descriptive.

Legend:
- Pre-Cambrian shields
- Sedimentary cover on Pre-Cambrian shields
- Paleozoic (Caledonian & Hercynian) folding
- Sedimentary cover on Paleozoic folding
- Mesozoic folding
- Sedimentary cover on Mesozoic folding
- Cainozoic (Alpine) folding
- Sedimentary cover on Cainozoic folding
- Mid-oceanic ridges
- African rift-valley system
- Major faults
- Volcanoes
- Major centres of earthquake activity

VOLCANOES

Of some 850 volcanoes that have produced recorded eruptions, nearly three-quarters lie in the 'Ring of Fire' that surrounds the Pacific Ocean. The 1980s was a bad decade for loss of life here with four major eruptions – El Chichon, Mexico and Mount Cameroon in 1982, Mount St Helens, USA and Nevado del Ruiz, Colombia, in 1985 – killing 25,000 people. This is not because the world is becoming less geologically stable: it is simply that populations are growing fast, with over 350 million people now living in areas vulnerable to seismic activity.

Volcano diagram labels:
- Ash & gas cloud
- Crater
- Neck or pipe
- Parasitic cone
- Layers of cinders & lava
- Side vent
- Main vent
- Rock strata
- Magma
- Magma chamber

Cone types:
- Shield cone
- Hornit cone
- Cinder cone
- Caldera

DISTRIBUTION

- Land volcanoes active since 1700
- Land volcanoes inactive since 1700
- Submarine volcanoes
- Geysers
- Plate boundaries
- Andesite line (boundary between sial continental crust & sima oceanic crust in the Pacific)

Volcanoes can suddenly erupt after lying dormant for centuries: in 1991 Mount Pinatubo, in the Philippines, burst into life after sleeping for more than 600 years.

THE EARTH: OCEANS

The Earth is a misnamed planet: almost 71% of its total surface area – 360,059,000 square kilometres – is covered by its oceans and seas. This great cloak of liquid water gives the planet its characteristic blue appearance from space, and is one of two obvious differences between the Earth and its near-neighbours in space, Mars and Venus. The other difference is the presence of life, and the two are closely linked.

In a strict geographical sense, the Earth has only three oceans: the Atlantic, the Pacific and the Indian. Sub-divided vertically instead of horizontally, however, there are many more. The most active is the sunlit upper layer, home of most sea-life and the vital interface between air and water. In this surface zone, huge energies are exchanged between the oceans and the atmosphere above; it is also a kind of membrane through which the ocean breathes, absorbing enormous quantities of carbon dioxide and partially exchanging them for oxygen, largely through the phytoplankton, tiny plants that photosynthesize solar energy and provide the food base for all other marine life.

As depth increases, light and colour fade away, the longer wavelengths dying first. At 50 metres, the ocean is a world of green and blue and violet; at 100 metres, only blue remains; by 200 metres, there is only a dim twilight. The temperature falls away with the light until some time before 1,000 metres – the precise depth varies – there occurs a temperature change almost as abrupt as the transition between air and water far above.

Below this thermocline, at a near-stable 3°C, the waters are forever unmoved by the winds of the upper world and are stirred only by the slow action of deep ocean currents. The pressure is crushing, touching 1,000 atmospheres in the deepest trenches: a force of one tonne bearing down on every square centimetre.

Yet even here the oceans support life, and not only the handful of strange, deep-sea creatures that find a living in the near-empty abyss. The deep ocean serves as a gigantic storehouse both for heat and for assorted atmospheric chemicals, regulating and balancing the proportions of various trace compounds and elements and ensuring a large measure of stability for both the climate and the ecology that depend on it.

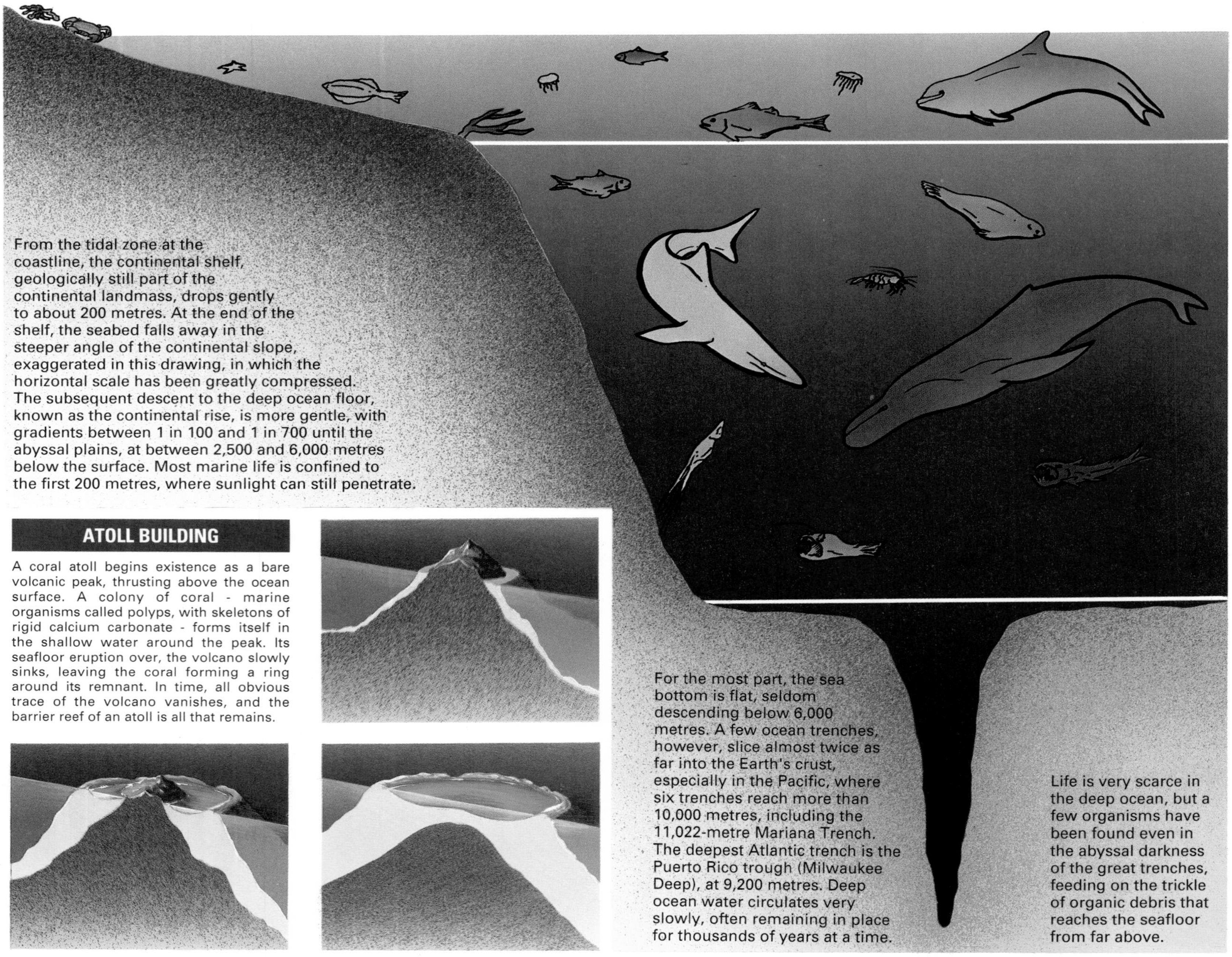

From the tidal zone at the coastline, the continental shelf, geologically still part of the continental landmass, drops gently to about 200 metres. At the end of the shelf, the seabed falls away in the steeper angle of the continental slope, exaggerated in this drawing, in which the horizontal scale has been greatly compressed. The subsequent descent to the deep ocean floor, known as the continental rise, is more gentle, with gradients between 1 in 100 and 1 in 700 until the abyssal plains, at between 2,500 and 6,000 metres below the surface. Most marine life is confined to the first 200 metres, where sunlight can still penetrate.

- Sea level
- 200 metres
- 500 metres
- 1,000 metres
- 1,500 metres
- 2,000 metres
- 6,000 metres
- 11,000 metres

For the most part, the sea bottom is flat, seldom descending below 6,000 metres. A few ocean trenches, however, slice almost twice as far into the Earth's crust, especially in the Pacific, where six trenches reach more than 10,000 metres, including the 11,022-metre Mariana Trench. The deepest Atlantic trench is the Puerto Rico trough (Milwaukee Deep), at 9,200 metres. Deep ocean water circulates very slowly, often remaining in place for thousands of years at a time.

Life is very scarce in the deep ocean, but a few organisms have been found even in the abyssal darkness of the great trenches, feeding on the trickle of organic debris that reaches the seafloor from far above.

ATOLL BUILDING

A coral atoll begins existence as a bare volcanic peak, thrusting above the ocean surface. A colony of coral - marine organisms called polyps, with skeletons of rigid calcium carbonate - forms itself in the shallow water around the peak. Its seafloor eruption over, the volcano slowly sinks, leaving the coral forming a ring around its remnant. In time, all obvious trace of the volcano vanishes, and the barrier reef of an atoll is all that remains.

PROFILE OF AN OCEAN

The deep ocean floor is no more uniform than the surface of the continents, although it was not until the development of effective sonar equipment that it was possible to examine submarine contours in detail. The Atlantic (right) and the Pacific show similar patterns. Off-shore comes the continental shelf, sliding downwards to the continental slope and the steeper continental rise, after which the seabed rolls onward into the abyssal plains. In the wide Pacific, these are interrupted by gently-rising abyssal hills; in both oceans, the plains extend all the way to the mid-oceanic ridges, where the upwelling of new crustal material is constantly forcing the oceans wider. Volcanic activity is responsible for the formation of seamounts and tablemounts or guyots, their flat-topped equivalents. In this cross-section, only the Azores are high enough to break the surface and become islands.

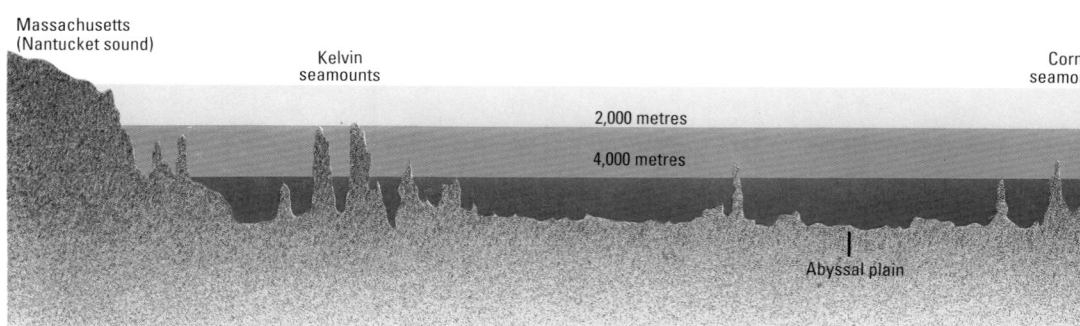

Massachusetts (Nantucket sound)

Kelvin seamounts

2,000 metres

4,000 metres

Corner seamounts

Abyssal plain

10

OCEAN CURRENTS

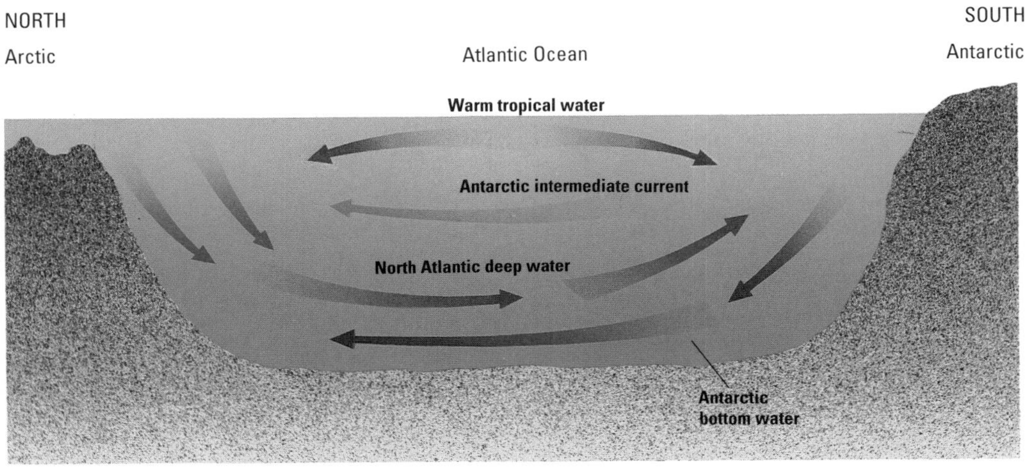

NORTH		SOUTH
Arctic	Atlantic Ocean	Antarctic

Warm tropical water

Antarctic intermediate current

North Atlantic deep water

Antarctic bottom water

Moving immense quantities of energy as well as billions of tonnes of water every hour, the ocean currents are a vital part of the great heat engine that drives the Earth's climate. They themselves are produced by a twofold mechanism. At the surface, winds push huge masses of water before them; in the deep ocean, below an abrupt temperature gradient that separates the churning surface waters from the still depths, density variations cause slow vertical movements.

The pattern of circulation of the great surface currents is determined by the displacement known as the Coriolis effect. As the Earth turns beneath a moving object - whether it is a tennis ball or a vast mass of water - it appears to be deflected to one side. The deflection is most obvious near the equator, where the Earth's surface is spinning eastward at 1700 km/h; currents moving poleward are curved clockwise in the northern hemisphere and anti-clockwise in the southern.

The result is a system of spinning circles known as gyres. The Coriolis effect piles up water on the left of each gyre, creating a narrow, fast-moving stream that is matched by a slower, broader returning current on the right. North and south of the equator, the fastest currents are located in the west and in the east respectively. In each case, warm water moves from the equator and cold water returns to it. Cold currents often bring an upwelling of nutrients with them, supporting the world's most economically important fisheries.

Depending on the prevailing winds, some currents on or near the equator may reverse their direction in the course of the year - a seasonal variation on which Asian monsoon rains depend, and whose occasional failure can bring disaster to millions of people.

CURRENTS & TEMPERATURES

(Northern Hemisphere: winter)

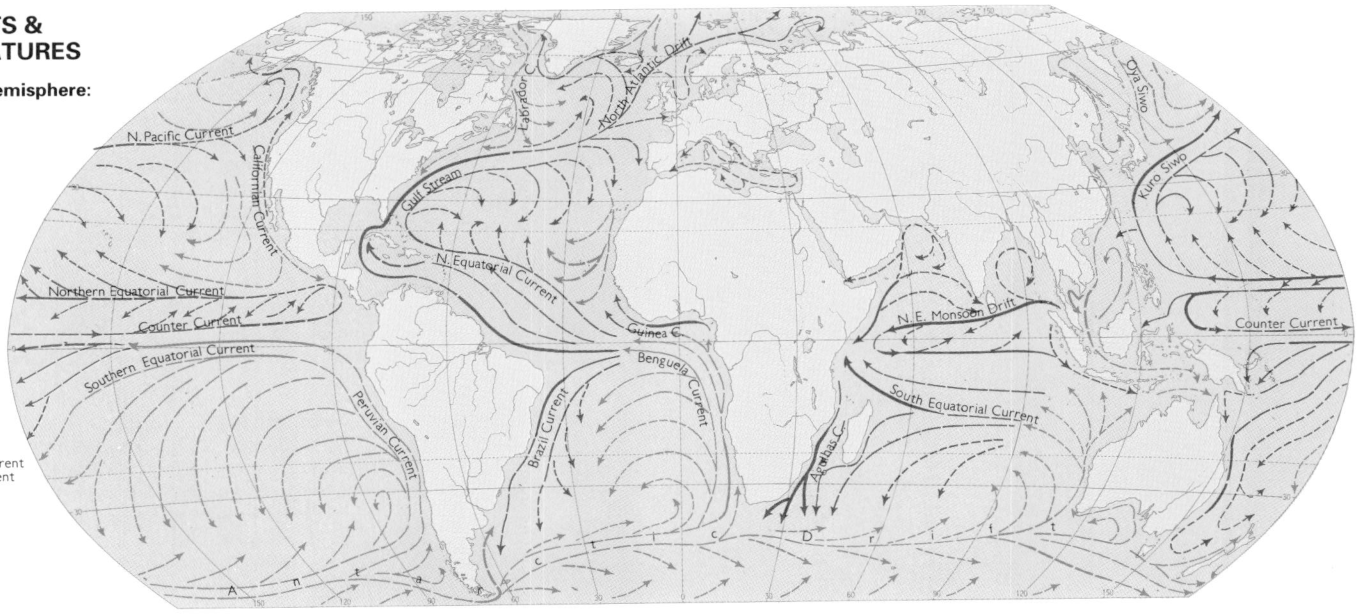

→ Warm Current
→ Cold Current

CURRENTS & TEMPERATURES

(Northern Hemisphere: summer)

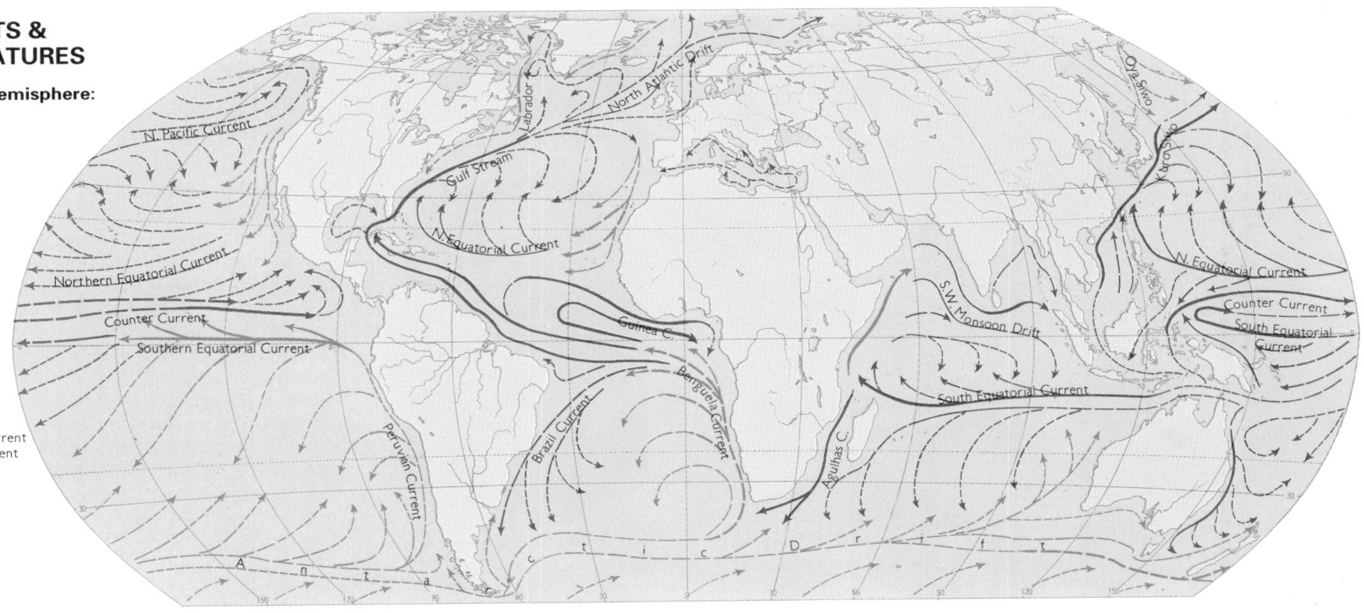

→ Warm Current
→ Cold Current

SEAWATER

The chemical composition of the sea, in grams per tonne of seawater, excluding the elements of water itself

Chlorine	19400
Sodium	10800
Magnesium	1290
Sulphur	904
Calcium	411
Potassium	392
Bromine	67
Strontium	8.1
Boron	4.5
Fluorine	1.3
Lithium	0.17
Rubidium	0.12
Phosphorus	0.09
Iodine	0.06
Barium	0.02
Arsenic	0.003
Cesium	0.0003

Seawater also contains virtually every other element, although the quantities involved are too small for reliable measurement. In natural conditions, its composition is broadly consistent across the world's seas and oceans; but especially in coastal areas, variations, sometimes substantial, may be caused by the presence of industrial waste and sewage sludge.

Mid-Atlantic ridge   Atlantic seamount   Azores   Josephine seamounts   Gettysburg seamounts   Gibraltar

THE EARTH: ATMOSPHERE

Extending from the surface far into space, the atmosphere is a meteor shield, a radiation deflector, a thermal blanket and a source of chemical energy for the Earth's diverse inhabitants. Five-sixths of its mass is found in the first 15 kilometres, the troposphere, no thicker in relative terms than the skin of an onion. Clouds, cyclonic winds, precipitation and virtually all the phenomena we call weather occur in this narrow layer. Above, a thin layer of ozone blocks ultra-violet radiation. Beyond 100 kilometres, atmospheric density is lower than most laboratory vacuums, yet these tenuous outer reaches, composed largely of hydrogen and helium, trap cosmic debris and incoming high-energy particles alike.

CIRCULATION OF THE AIR

30°N

Equator

30°S

STRUCTURE OF ATMOSPHERE

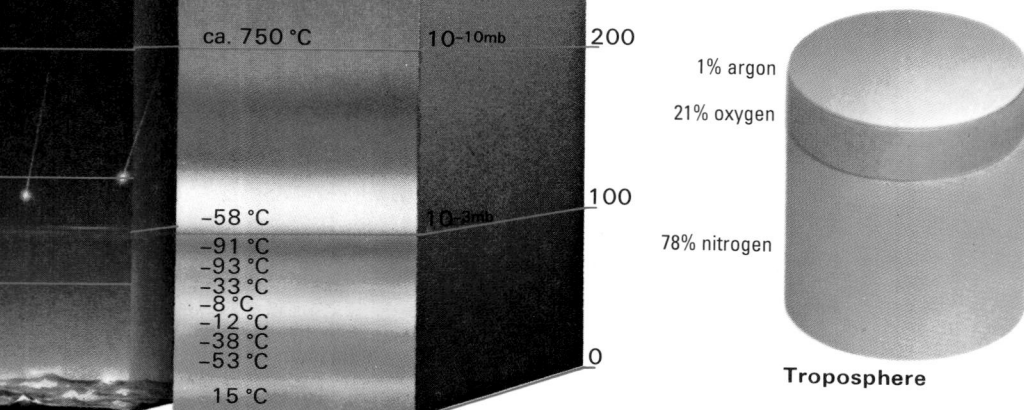

F2

F1

E

D

Mesosphere
Ozone layer
Tropopause

TEMPERATURE

ca. 2 200 °C

ca. 1 500 °C

ca. 750 °C

−58 °C
−91 °C
−93 °C
−33 °C
−8 °C
−12 °C
−38 °C
−53 °C

15 °C

PRESSURE

$10^{-53}mb$

$10^{-47}mb$ 900 km

$10^{-41}mb$ 800

$10^{-35}mb$ 700

                600

$10^{-28}mb$ 500

$10^{-22}mb$ 400

$10^{-16}mb$ 300

$10^{-10}mb$ 200

                100

$10^{-3}mb$

                0

$10^{3}mb$

CHEMICAL STRUCTURE

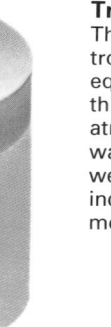

Inner:
50% helium
50% hydrogen

Middle:
25% helium
75% hydrogen

Outer:
100% hydrogen

Exosphere

15% helium

15% oxygen
& atomic
oxygen

70% nitrogen

Ionosphere

1% ozone
1% argon

18% oxygen

80% nitrogen

Stratosphere

1% argon

21% oxygen

78% nitrogen

Troposphere

Exosphere
The atmosphere's upper layer has no clear outer boundary, merging imperceptibly with interplanetary space. Its lower boundary, at an altitude of approximately 600 kilometres, is almost equally vague. The exosphere is mainly composed of hydrogen and helium in changing proportions, with a small quantity of atomic oxygen up to 600 kilometres. Helium vanishes with increasing altitude, and above 2,400 kilometres the exosphere is almost entirely hydrogen.

Ionosphere
Gas molecules in the ionosphere, mainly helium, oxygen and nitrogen, are electrically charged - ionized - by the Sun's radiation. Within the ionosphere's range of 50 to 600 kilometres in altitude, they group themselves into four layers, known conventionally as D, E, F1 and F2, all of which can reflect radio waves of differing frequencies. The high energy of ionospheric gas gives it a notional temperature of more than 2,000°C, although its density is negligible. The auroras - *aurora borealis* and its southern counterpart, *aurora australis* - occur in the ionosphere when charged particles from the Sun interact with the Earth's magnetic fields, at their strongest near the poles.

Stratosphere
Separated at its upper and lower limits by the distinct thresholds of the stratopause and the tropopause, the stratosphere is a remarkably stable layer between 50 kilometres and about 15 kilometres. Its temperature rises from -55°C at its lower extent to approximately 0°C near the stratopause, where a thin layer of ozone absorbs ultra-violet radiation. "Mother-of-pearl" or nacreous cloud occurs at about 25 kilometres' altitude. Stratospheric air contains enough ozone to make it poisonous, although it is in any case far too rarified to breathe.

Troposphere
The narrowest of all the atmospheric layers, the troposphere extends up to 15 kilometres at the equator but only 8 kilometres at the poles. Since this thin region contains about 85% of the atmosphere's total mass and almost all of its water vapour, it is also the realm of the Earth's weather. Temperatures fall steadily with increasing height by about 1°C for every 100 metres above sea level.

Heated by the relatively high surface temperatures near the Earth's equator, air expands and rises to create a belt of low pressure. Moving northward towards the poles, it gradually cools, sinking once more and producing high pressure belts at about latitudes 30° North and South. Water vapour carried with the air falls as rain, releasing vast quantities of energy as well as liquid water when it condenses.

The high and low pressure belts are both areas of comparative calm, but between them, blowing from high to low pressure areas, are the prevailing winds. The atmospheric circulatory system is enormously complicated by the Coriolis effect brought about by the spinning Earth: winds are deflected to the right in the northern hemisphere and to the left in the southern, giving rise to the typically cyclonic pattern of swirling clouds carried by the moving masses of air.

Although clouds appear in an almost infinite variety of shapes and sizes, there are recognizable features that form the basis of a classification first put forward by Luke Howard, a London chemist, in 1803 and later modified by the World Meteorological Organization. The system derives from the altitude of clouds and whether they form hairlike filaments ('cirrus'), heaps or piles ('cumulus') or layers ('stratus'). Each characteristic carries some kind of message – not always a clear one – to forecasters about the weather to come.

CLASSIFICATION OF CLOUDS

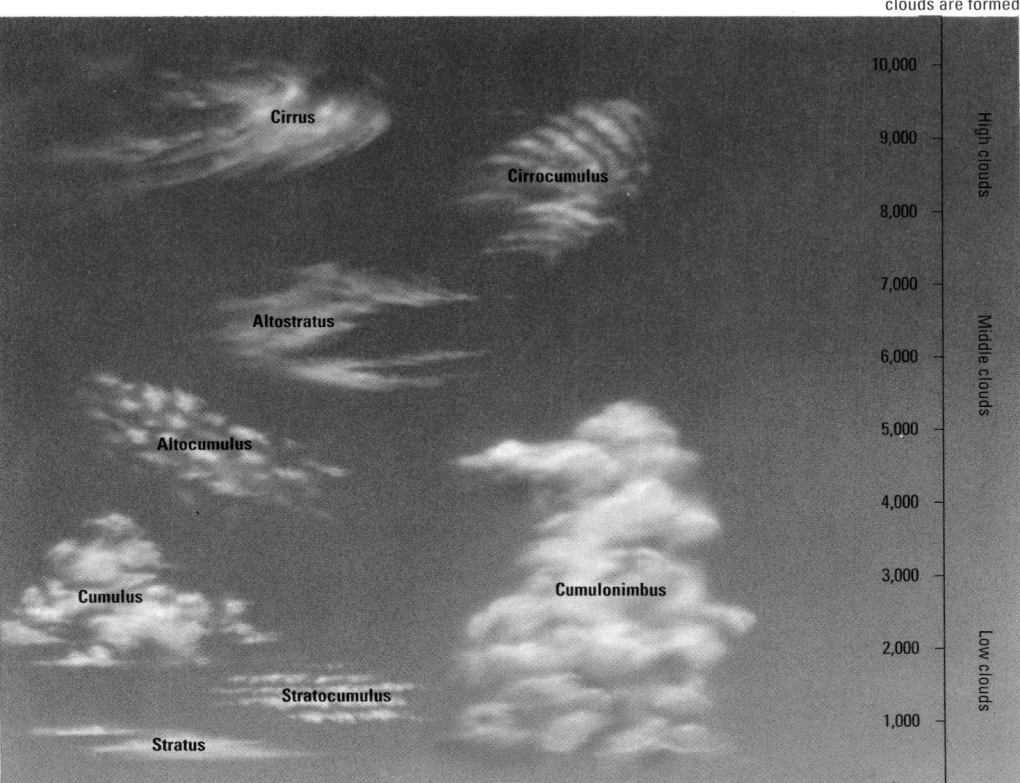

Altitude at which clouds are formed

Clouds form when damp, usually rising, air is cooled. Thus they form when a wind rises to cross hills or mountains; when a mass of air rises over, or is pushed up by, another mass of denser air; or when local heating of the ground causes convection currents. The types of clouds are classified according to altitude as high, middle, or low. The high ones, composed of ice crystals, are cirrus, cirrostratus and cirrocumulus. The middle clouds are altostratus, a grey or bluish striated, fibrous, or uniform sheet producing light drizzle, and altocumulus, a thicker and fluffier version of cirrocumulus. The low clouds include nimbostratus, a dark grey layer that brings almost continuous rain or snow; cumulus, a detached 'heap' – brilliant white in sunlight but dark and flat at the base; and stratus, which forms dull, overcast skies at low altitudes. Cumulonimbus, associated with storms and rains, heavy and dense with flat base and a high, fluffy outline, can be tall enough to occupy middle as well as low altitudes.

PRESSURE & WINDS

January

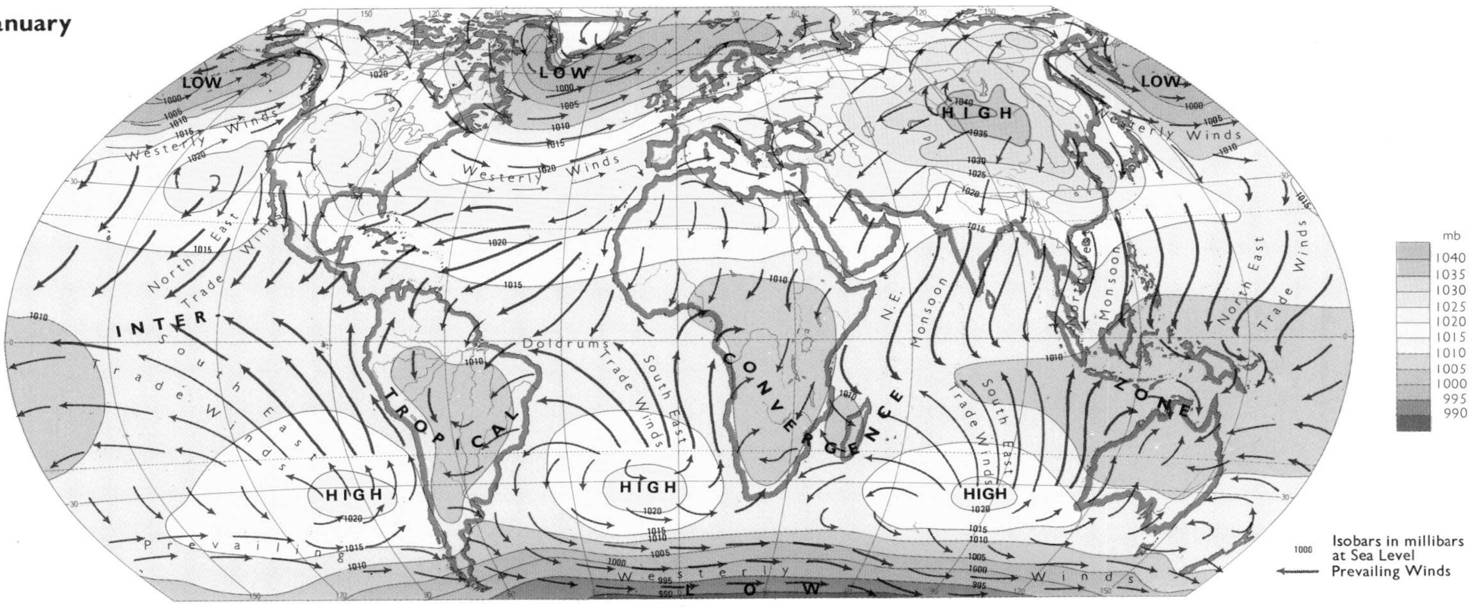

July

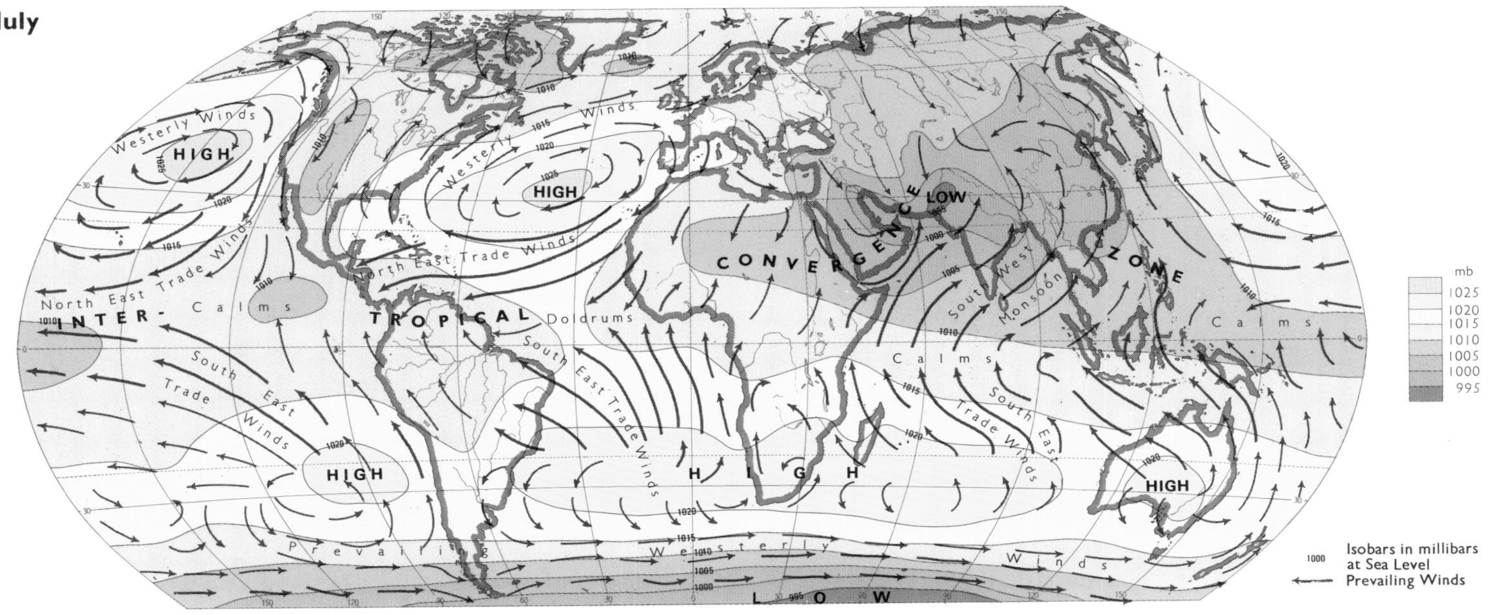

Isobars in millibars at Sea Level
← Prevailing Winds

THE EARTH: CLIMATE

Climate is weather in the long term: the seasonal pattern of hot and cold, wet and dry, averaged over time. At the simplest level, it is caused by the uneven heating of the Earth. Surplus heat at the equator passes towards the poles, levelling out the energy differential. Its passage is marked by a ceaseless churning of the atmosphere and the oceans, further agitated by the the Earth's diurnal spin and the motion it imparts to moving air and water. The heat's means of transport – by winds and ocean currents, by the continual evaporation and recondensation of water molecules – is the weather itself.

There are four basic types of climate, each open to considerable sub-division: tropical, desert, temperate and polar. But although latitude is obviously a critical factor, it is not the only determinant. The differential heating of land and sea, the funnelling and interruption of winds and ocean currents by landmasses and mountain ranges, and the transpiration of vegetation: all combine to add complexity. New York, Naples and the Gobi Desert share almost the same latitude, for example, but their climates are very different. And although the sheer intricacy of the weather system often defies day-to-day prediction in these or any other places – despite the satellites and number-crunching supercomputers with which present-day meteorologists are equipped – their climatic patterns retain a year-on-year stability.

They are not indefinitely stable, however. The planet regularly passes through long, cool periods of around 100,000 years: these are the ice ages, probably caused by recurring long-term oscillations in the Earth's orbital path and fluctuations in the Sun's energy output. In the present era, the Earth is nearest to the Sun in the middle of the northern hemisphere's winter; 11,000 years ago, at the end of the last ice age, the northern winter fell with the Sun at its most distant.

Left to its own devices, the climate even now should be drifting towards another glacial period. But global warming caused by increasing carbon dioxide levels in the atmosphere, largely the result of 20th-century fuel-burning and deforestation, may well precipitate change far faster than the great, slow cycles of the solar system.

CLIMATE REGIONS

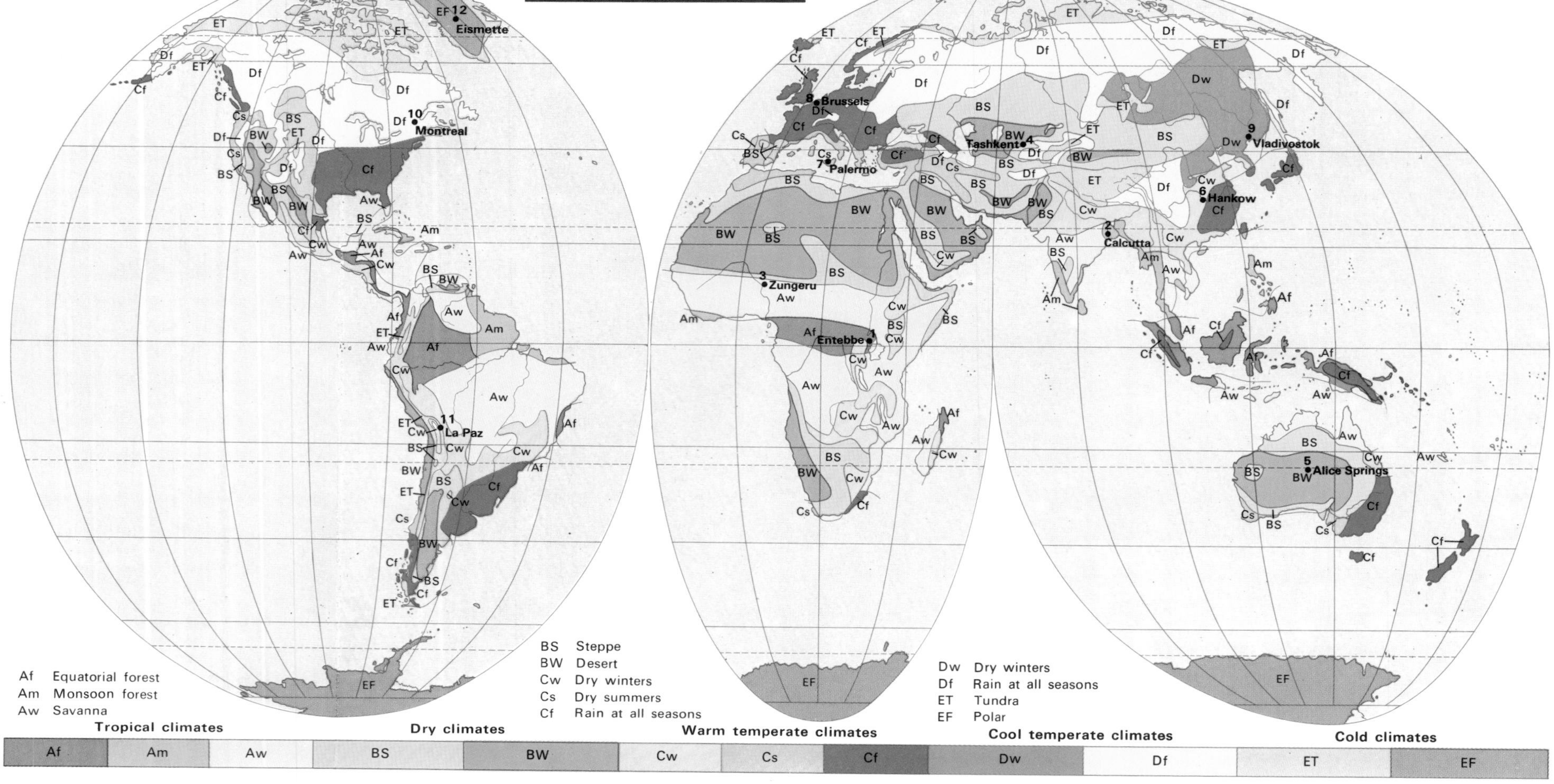

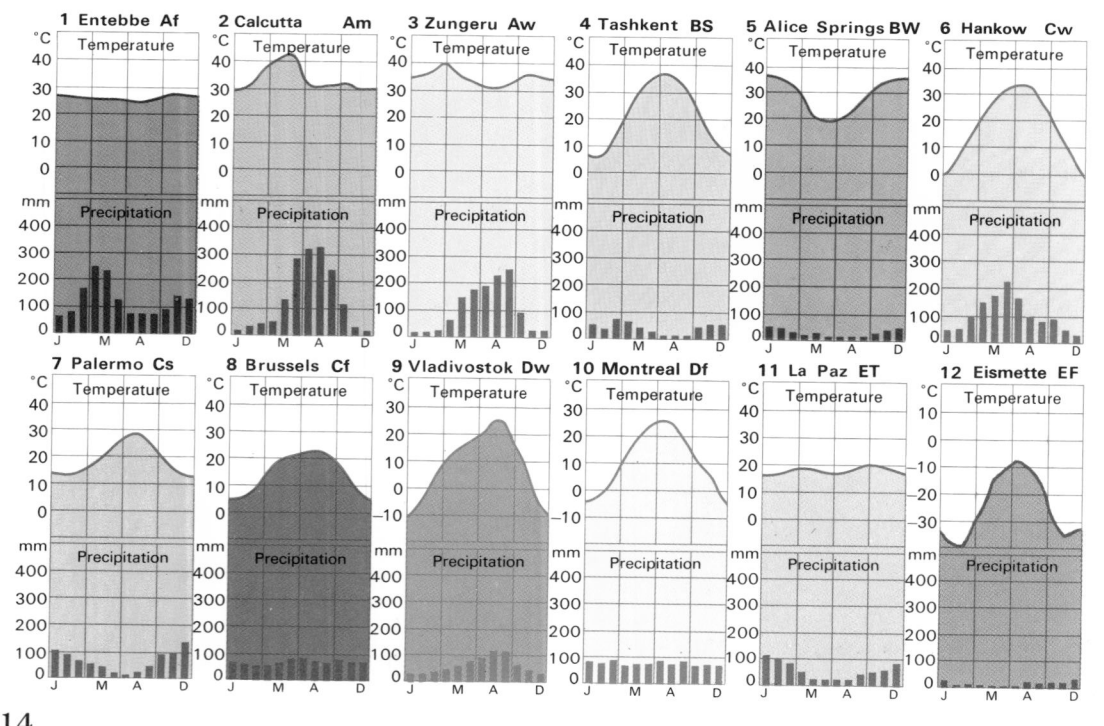

Af	Equatorial forest
Am	Monsoon forest
Aw	Savanna
Tropical climates	

BS	Steppe
BW	Desert
Cw	Dry winters
Cs	Dry summers
Cf	Rain at all seasons

Dw	Dry winters
Df	Rain at all seasons
ET	Tundra
EF	Polar

Af	Am	Aw	BS	BW	Cw	Cs	Cf	Dw	Df	ET	EF
Tropical climates			Dry climates		Warm temperate climates			Cool temperate climates			Cold climates

Climate graphs (temperature °C and precipitation mm, months J M A D):
1 Entebbe Af · 2 Calcutta Am · 3 Zungeru Aw · 4 Tashkent BS · 5 Alice Springs BW · 6 Hankow Cw · 7 Palermo Cs · 8 Brussels Cf · 9 Vladivostok Dw · 10 Montreal Df · 11 La Paz ET · 12 Eismette EF

CLIMATE & WEATHER TERMS

Absolute humidity: amount of water vapour contained in a given volume of air.
Cloud cover: amount of cloud in the sky; measured in oktas (from 1 - 8), with 0 clear, & 8 total cover.
Condensation: the conversion of water vapour, or moisture in the air into liquid.
Cyclone: violent storm resulting from counter clockwise rotation of winds in the northern hemisphere & clockwise in the southern: called hurricane in N. America, typhoon in the Far East.
Depression: approximately circular area of low pressure.
Dew: water droplets condensed out of the air after the ground has cooled at night.
Dew point: temperature at which air becomes saturated (reaches a relative humidity of 100%) at a constant pressure.
Drizzle: precipitation where drops are less than 0.5 mm (0.02 in) in diameter.
Evaporation: conversion of water from liquid into vapour, or moisture in the air.
Frost: dew that has frozen when the air temperature falls below freezing point.
Hail: frozen rain; small balls of ice, often falling during thunder storms.
Hoar frost: formed on objects when the dew point is below freezing point.
Humidity: amount of moisture in the air.
Isobar: cartographic line connecting places of equal atmospheric pressure.
Isotherm: cartographic line connecting places of equal temperature.
Lightning: massive electrical discharge released in thunderstorm from cloud to cloud or cloud to ground, the result of the tip becoming positively charged & the bottom negatively charged.
Precipitation: measurable rain, snow, sleet or hail.
Prevailing wind: most common direction of wind at a given location.
Rain: precipitation of liquid particles with diameter larger than 0.5 mm (0.02 in).
Relative humidity: amount of water vapour contained in a given volume of air at a given temperature.
Sleet: translucent or transparent ice-pellets (partially melted snow).
Snow: formed when water vapour condenses below freezing point.
Thunder: sound produced by the rapid expansion of air heated by lightning.
Tidal wave: giant ocean wave generated by earthquakes (tsunami) or cyclonic winds.
Tornado: severe funnel-shaped storm that twists as hot air spins vertically (waterspout at sea).
Whirlwind: rapidly rotating column of air, only a few metres across made visible by dust.

14

WINDCHILL FACTOR

In sub-zero weather, even moderate winds significantly reduce effective temperatures. The chart below shows the windchill effect across a range of speeds. Figures in the pink zone are not dangerous to well-clad people; in the blue zone, the risk of serious frostbite is acute.

	Wind speed (km/h)				
	16	32	48	64	80
0°C	-8	-14	-17	-19	-20
-5°C	-14	-21	-25	-27	-28
-10°C	-20	-28	-33	-35	-36
-15°C	-26	-36	-40	-43	-44
-20°C	-32	-42	-48	-51	-52
-25°C	-38	-49	-56	-59	-60
-30°C	-44	-57	-63	-66	-68
-35°C	-51	-64	-72	-74	-76
-40°C	-57	-71	-78	-82	-84
-45°C	-63	-78	-86	-90	-92
-50°C	-69	-85	-94	-98	-100

BEAUFORT WIND SCALE

Named for the 19th-century British naval officer who devised it, the Beaufort Scale assesses wind speed according to its effects. It was originally designed as an aid for sailors, but has since been adapted for use on land.

Scale	Wind speed kph	mph	Effect
0	0-1	0-1	**Calm** Smoke rises vertically
1	1-5	1-3	**Light air** Wind direction shown only by smoke drift
2	6-11	4-7	**Light breeze** Wind felt on face; leaves rustle; vanes moved by wind
3	12-19	8-12	**Gentle breeze** Leaves and small twigs in constant motion; wind extend small flag
4	20-28	13-18	**Moderate** Raises dust and loose paper; small branches move
5	29-38	19-24	**Fresh** Small trees in leaf sway; crested wavelets on inland waters
6	39-49	25-31	**Strong** Large branches move; difficult to use umbrellas; overhead wires whistle
7	50-61	32-38	**Near gale** Whole trees in motion; difficult to walk against wind
8	62-74	39-46	**Gale** Twigs break from trees; walking very difficult
9	75-88	47-54	**Strong gale** Slight structural damage
10	89-102	55-63	**Storm** Trees uprooted; serious structural damage
11	103-117	64-72	**Violent Storm** Widespread damage
12	118+	73+	**Hurricane**

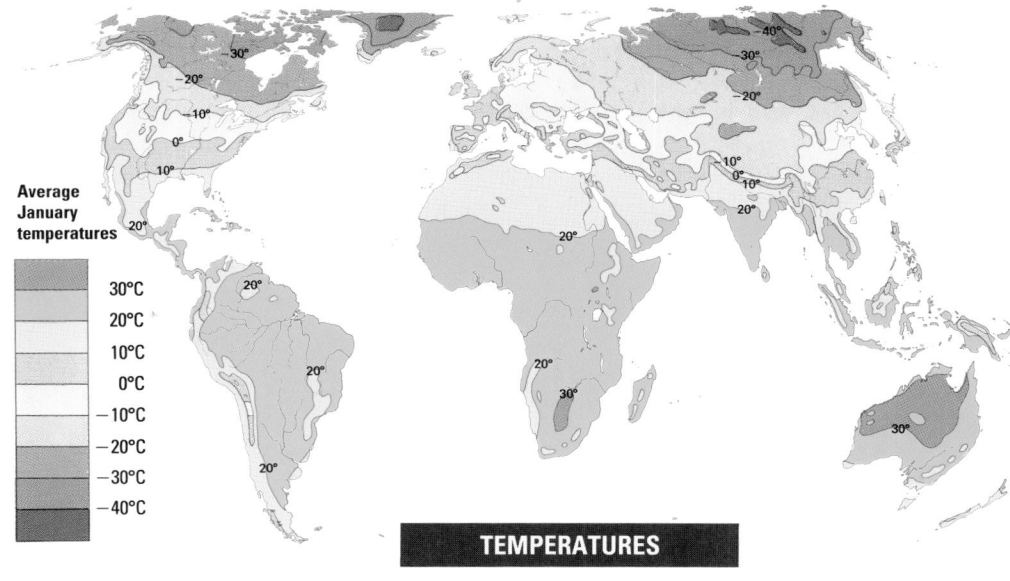

Average January temperatures

30°C
20°C
10°C
0°C
-10°C
-20°C
-30°C
-40°C

TEMPERATURES

Average July temperatures

30°C
20°C
10°C
0°C
-10°C

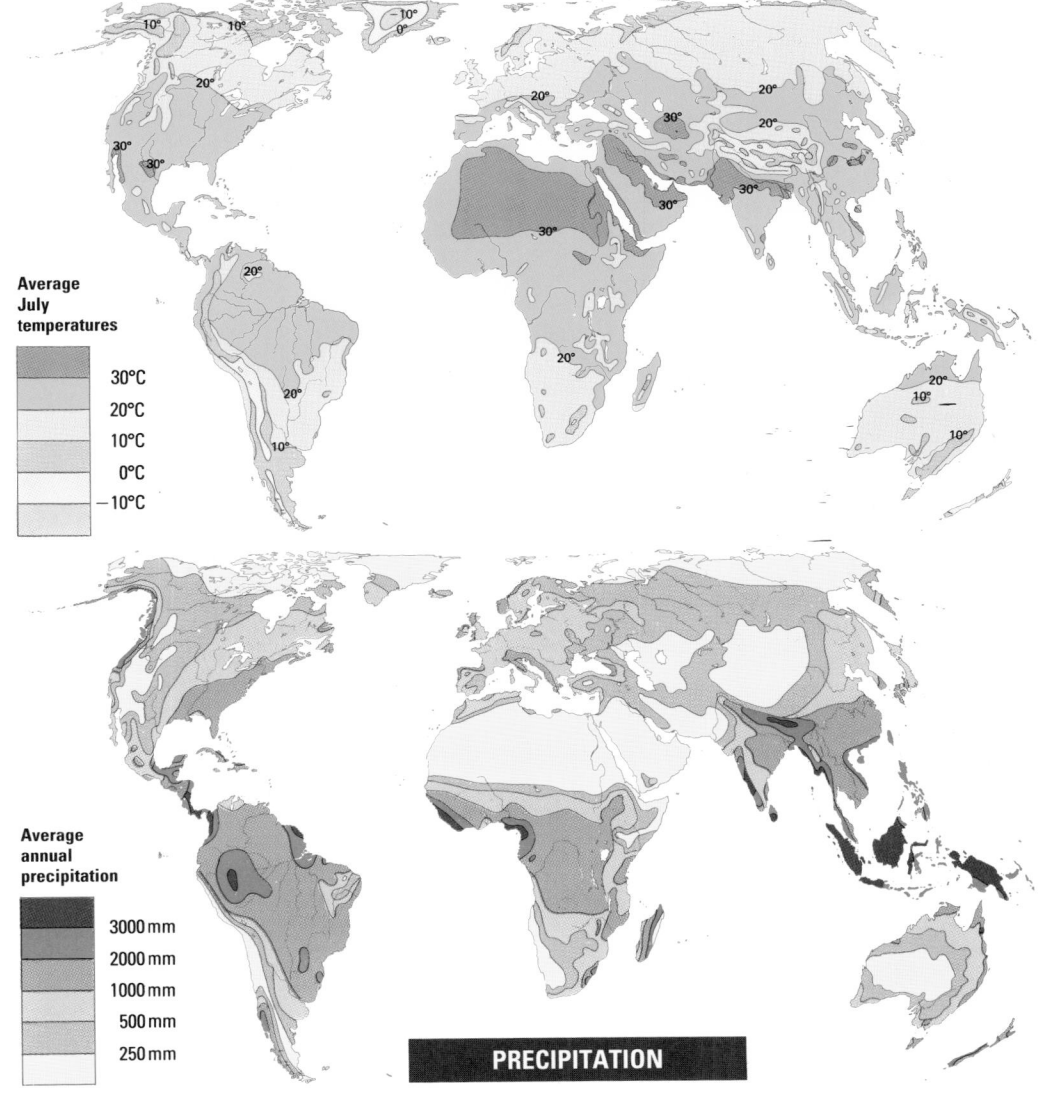

Average annual precipitation

3000 mm
2000 mm
1000 mm
500 mm
250 mm

PRECIPITATION

CLIMATE RECORDS

Temperature

Highest recorded temperature: Al Aziziyah, Libya, 58°C [136.4°F], 13 Sep. 1922.

Highest mean annual temperature: Dallol, Ethiopia, 34.4°C [94°F], 1960-66.

Longest heatwave: Marble Bar, W. Australia, 162 days over 38°C [100°F], 23 Oct. 1923 - 7 Apr. 1924.

Lowest recorded temperature (outside poles): Verkhoyansk, Siberia, USSR -68°C [-90°F], 6 Feb. 1933. Verkhoyansk also registered the greatest annual range of temperature: - 70°C to 37°C [-94°F to 98°F].

Lowest mean annual temperature: Polus Nedostupnosti, Pole of Cold, Antarctica, -57.8°C [-72°F].

Precipitation

Driest place: Arica, N. Chile, 0.8mm [0.3 in] per year (60-year average).

Longest drought: Calama, N. Chile: no recorded rainfall in 400 years to 1971.

Wettest place (average): Tututendo, Colombia: mean annual rainfall 11,770 mm [463.4 in].

Wettest place (12 months): Cherrapunji, Meghalaya, N.E. India, 26,470 mm [1,040 in], Aug. 1860 to Aug. 1861. Cherrapunji also holds the record for rainfall in one month: 930 mm [37 in] July 1861.

Wettest place (24 hours): Cilaos, Réunion, Indian Ocean, 1,870 mm [73.6 in], 15-16 Mar. 1952.

Heaviest hailstones: Gopalganj, Bangladesh, up to 1.02 kg [2.25 lb], 14 Apr. 1986 (killed 92 people).

Heaviest snowfall (continuous): Bessans, Savoie, France, 1730 mm [68 in] in 19 hours, 5-6 Apr. 1969.

Heaviest snowfall (season/year): Paradise Ranger Station, Mt Rainier, Washington, USA, 31,102 mm [1,224.5 in], 19 Feb. 1971 to 18 Feb. 1972.

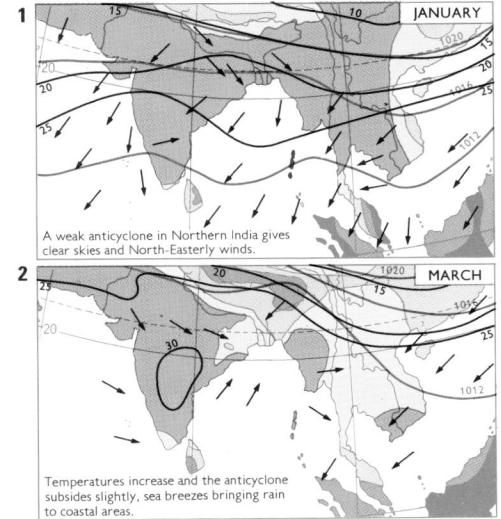

1 JANUARY

A weak anticyclone in Northern India gives clear skies and North-Easterly winds.

2 MARCH

Temperatures increase and the anticyclone subsides slightly, sea breezes bringing rain to coastal areas.

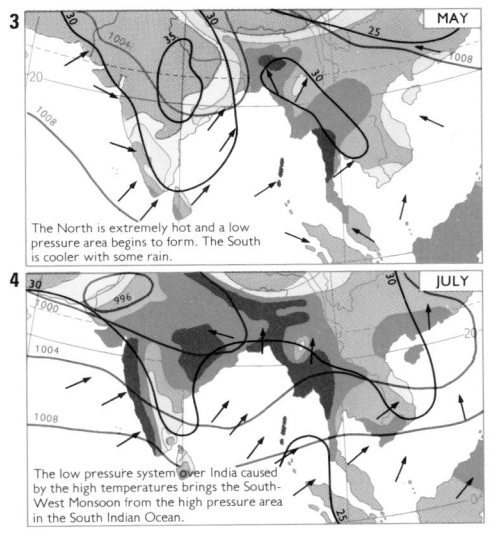

3 MAY

The North is extremely hot and a low pressure area begins to form. The South is cooler with some rain.

4 JULY

The low pressure system over India caused by the high temperatures brings the South-West Monsoon from the high pressure area in the South Indian Ocean.

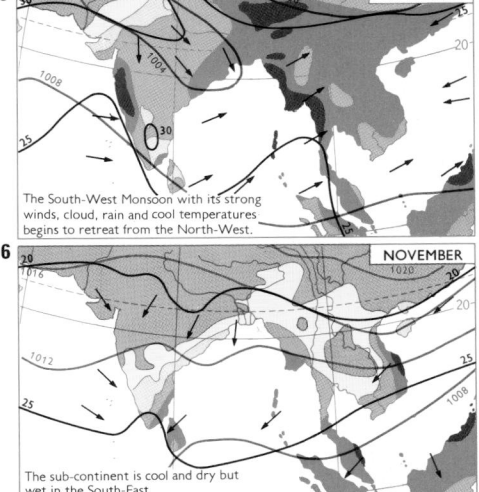

5 SEPTEMBER

The South-West Monsoon with its strong winds, cloud, rain and cool temperatures begins to retreat from the North-West.

6 NOVEMBER

The sub-continent is cool and dry but wet in the South-East.

COPYRIGHT. GEORGE PHILIP & SON. LTD.

THE MONSOON

While it is crucial to the agriculture of South Asia, the monsoon that follows the dry months is unpredictable - in duration as well as intensity. A season of very heavy rainfall, causing disastrous floods, can be succeeded by years of low precipitation, leading to serious drought.

Monthly rainfall

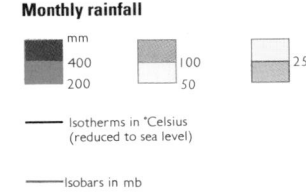

mm
400
200

100
50

25

Isotherms in °Celsius (reduced to sea level)

Isobars in mb

Prevailing winds

COPYRIGHT. GEORGE PHILIP LTD.

15

THE EARTH: WATER

Fresh water is essential to all terrestrial life, from the humblest bacterium to the most advanced technological society. Yet freshwater resources form a minute fraction of the Earth's 1.41 billion cubic kilometres of water: most human needs must be met from the 2,000 cubic kilometres circulating in rivers at any one time. Agriculture accounts for huge quantities: without large-scale irrigation, most of the world's people would starve. And since fresh water is just as essential for most industrial processes – smelting a tonne of nickel, for example, requires about 4,000 tonnes of water – the combination of growing population and advancing industry has put water supplies under strain.

Fortunately water is seldom used up: the planet's hydrological cycle circulates it with benign efficiency, at least on a global scale. More locally, though, human activity can cause severe shortages: water for industry and agriculture is being withdrawn from many river basins and underground aquifers faster than natural recirculation can replace it.

THE HYDROLOGICAL CYCLE

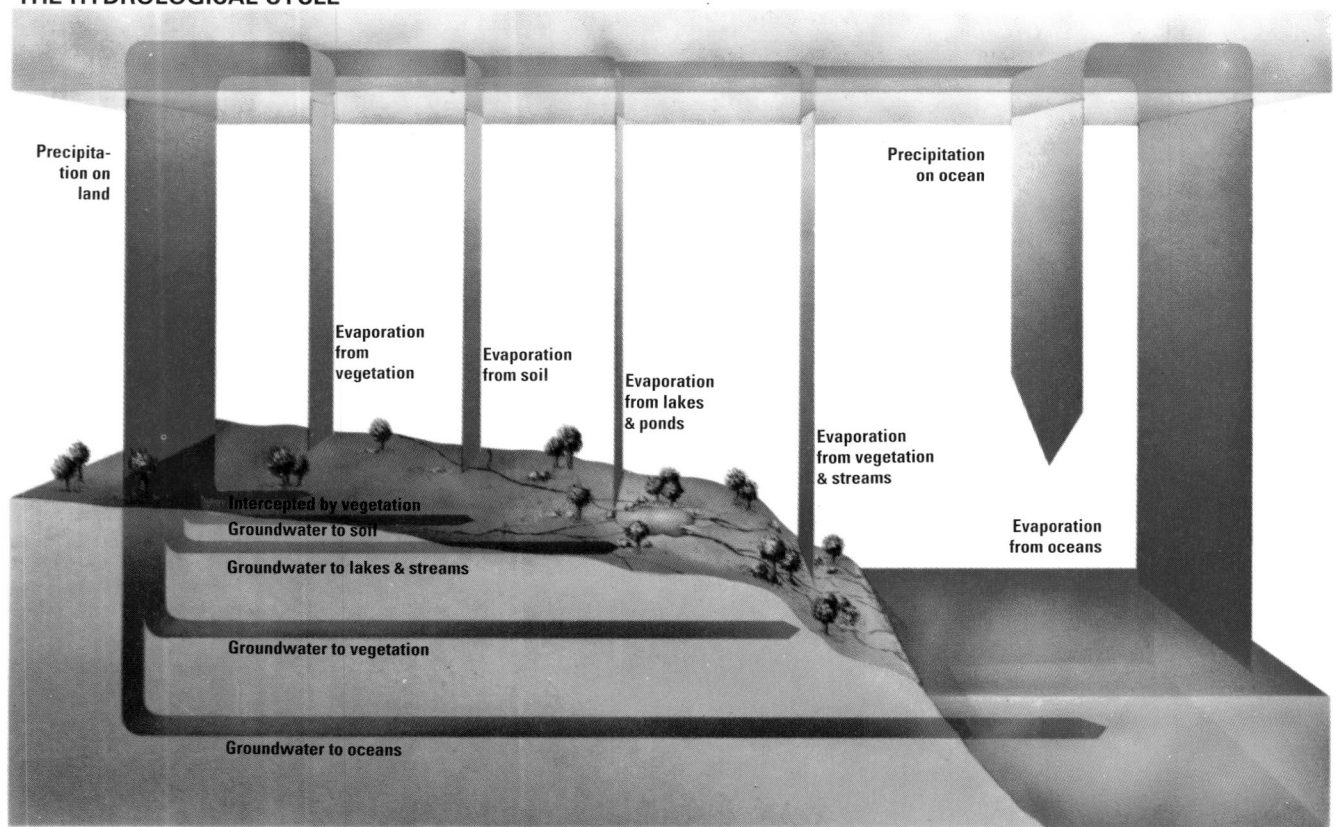

Water vapour is constantly drawn into the air from the Earth's rivers, lakes, seas and plant transpiration. In the atmosphere, it circulates around the planet, transporting energy as well as water itself. When the vapour cools it falls as rain or snow, and returns to the surface to evaporate once more. The whole cycle is driven by the Sun.

WATER DISTRIBUTION

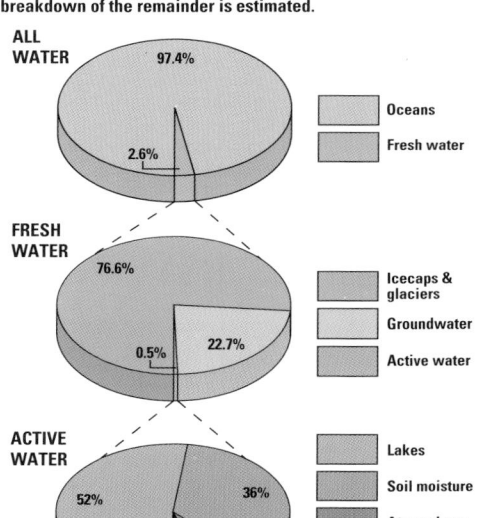

The distribution of planetary water, by percentage. Oceans and icecaps together account for more than 99% of the total; the breakdown of the remainder is estimated.

ALL WATER — Oceans, Fresh water
FRESH WATER — Icecaps & glaciers, Groundwater, Active water
ACTIVE WATER — Lakes, Soil moisture, Atmosphere, Rivers, Living things

Almost all the world's water is 3,000 million years old, and all of it cycles endlessly through the hydrosphere, though at different rates. Water vapour circulates over days, even hours, deep ocean water circulates over millenia and ice-cap water remains solid for millions of years.

WATER RUNOFF

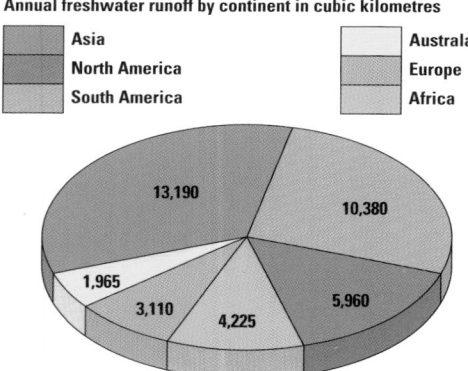

Annual freshwater runoff by continent in cubic kilometres

Asia | Australasia
North America | Europe
South America | Africa

WATER UTILIZATION

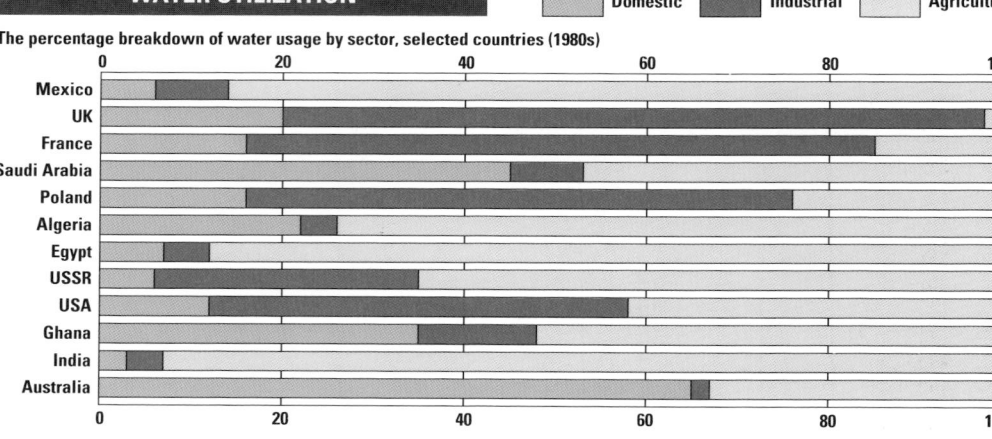

The percentage breakdown of water usage by sector, selected countries (1980s)

Domestic | Industrial | Agriculture

Mexico, UK, France, Saudi Arabia, Poland, Algeria, Egypt, USSR, USA, Ghana, India, Australia

WATER SUPPLY

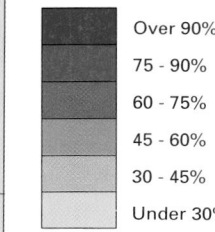

Percentage of total population with access to safe drinking water (latest available year, 1980s)

- Over 90%
- 75 - 90%
- 60 - 75%
- 45 - 60%
- 30 - 45%
- Under 30%

Least well provided countries (rural areas only):

Paraguay	8%	Guinea	15%
Mozambique	12%	Mauritania	17%
Uganda	12%	Malawi	17%
Angola	15%	Morocco	17%

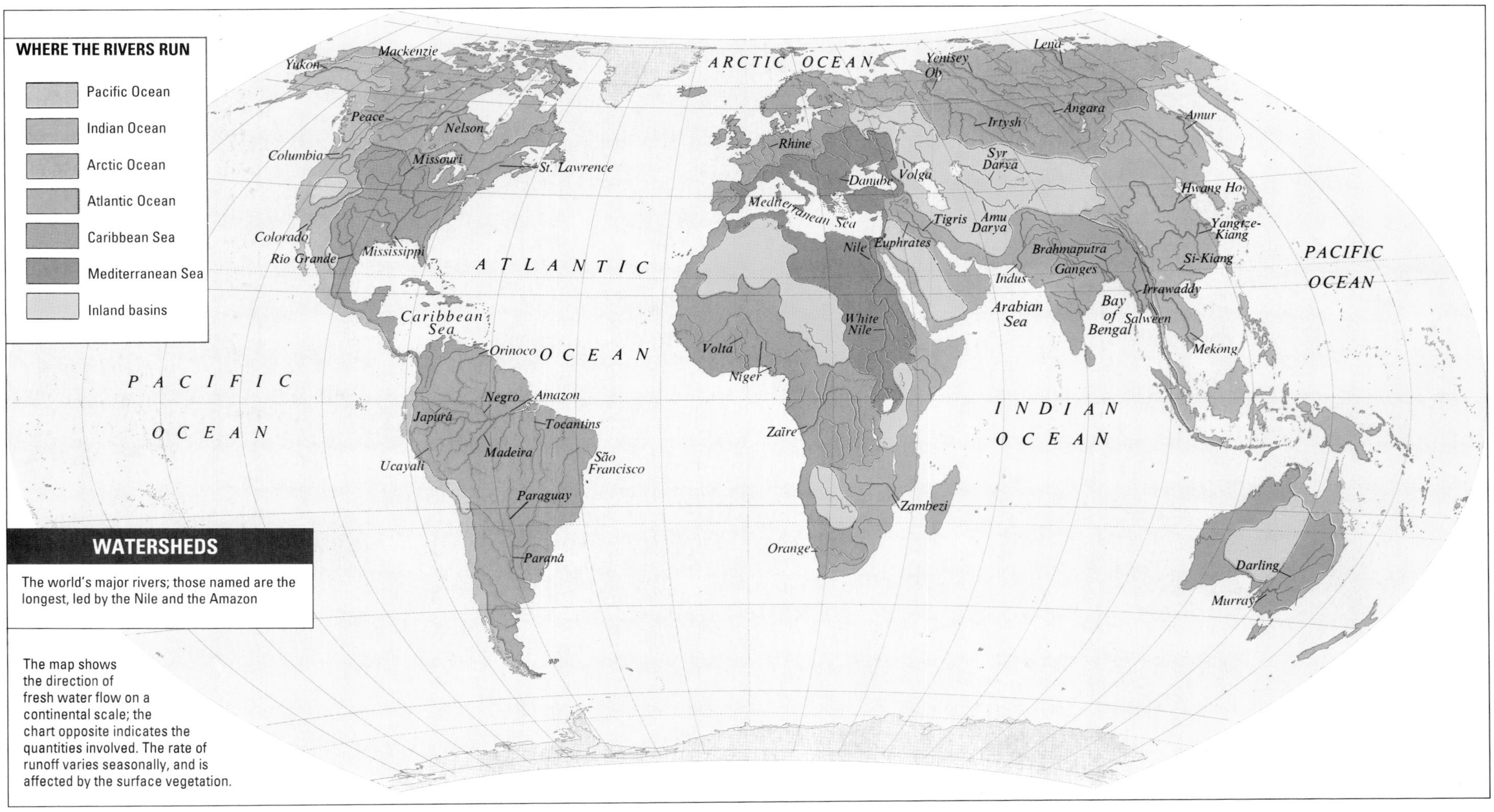

WHERE THE RIVERS RUN

- Pacific Ocean
- Indian Ocean
- Arctic Ocean
- Atlantic Ocean
- Caribbean Sea
- Mediterranean Sea
- Inland basins

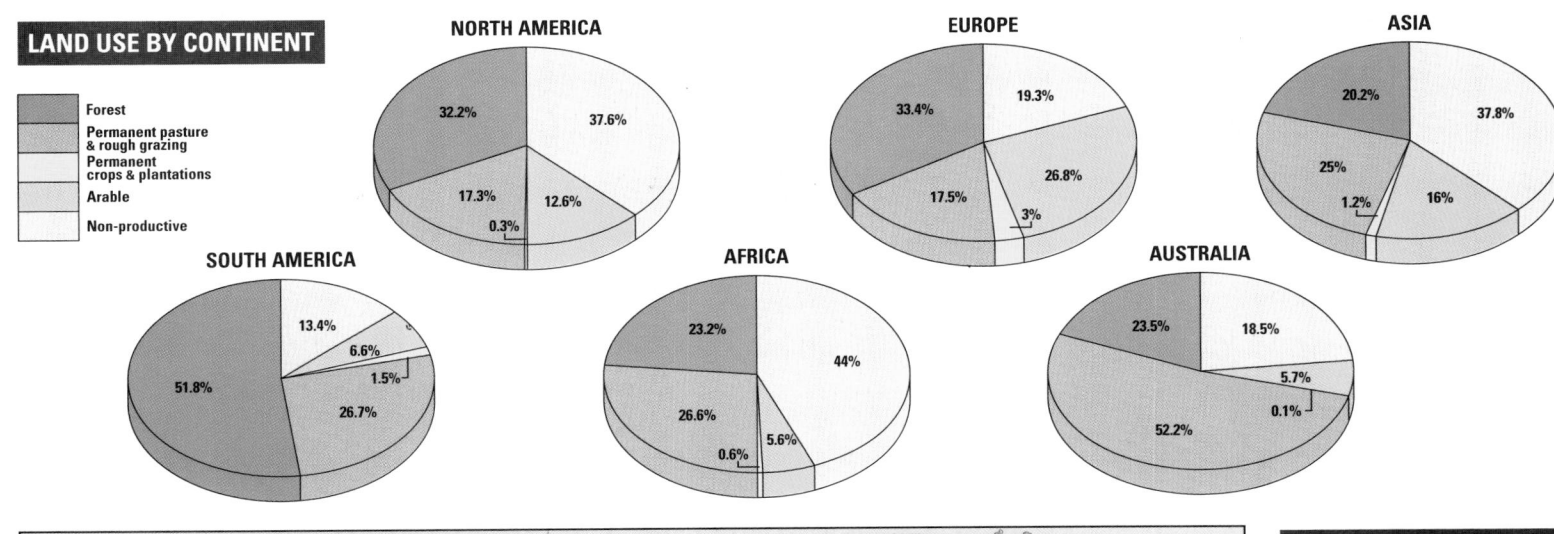

Yukon *Mackenzie* ARCTIC OCEAN *Yenisey* *Ob* *Lena*

Peace *Nelson* *Irtysh* *Angara* *Amur*

Columbia *Missouri* *Rhine* *Syr Darya* *Hwang Ho*

Colorado *St. Lawrence* *Danube* *Volga* *Amu Darya* *Yangtze-Kiang*

Rio Grande *Mississippi* *Mediterranean Sea* *Tigris* *Euphrates* *Si-Kiang* PACIFIC OCEAN

ATLANTIC OCEAN *Nile* *Indus* *Ganges* *Brahmaputra* *Irrawaddy*

Caribbean Sea *White Nile* *Arabian Sea* *Bay of Bengal* *Salween*

Orinoco *Volta* *Niger* *Mekong*

Negro *Amazon* INDIAN OCEAN

PACIFIC OCEAN *Japurá* *Tocantins* *Zaïre*

Ucayali *Madeira* *São Francisco*

Paraguay *Zambezi*

Orange *Darling*

Paraná *Murray*

WATERSHEDS

The world's major rivers; those named are the longest, led by the Nile and the Amazon

The map shows the direction of fresh water flow on a continental scale; the chart opposite indicates the quantities involved. The rate of runoff varies seasonally, and is affected by the surface vegetation.

LAND USE BY CONTINENT

- Forest
- Permanent pasture & rough grazing
- Permanent crops & plantations
- Arable
- Non-productive

NORTH AMERICA
32.2% / 37.6% / 17.3% / 12.6% / 0.3%

EUROPE
33.4% / 19.3% / 17.5% / 26.8% / 3%

ASIA
20.2% / 37.8% / 25% / 16% / 1.2%

SOUTH AMERICA
13.4% / 6.6% / 1.5% / 51.8% / 26.7%

AFRICA
23.2% / 44% / 26.6% / 5.6% / 0.6%

AUSTRALIA
23.5% / 18.5% / 5.7% / 52.2% / 0.1%

The proportion of productive land has reached its upper limit in Europe, and in Asia more than 80% of potential cropland is already under cultivation. Elsewhere, any increase is often matched by corresponding losses due to desertification and erosion; projections for 2025 show a decline in cropland per capita for all continents, most notably in Africa.

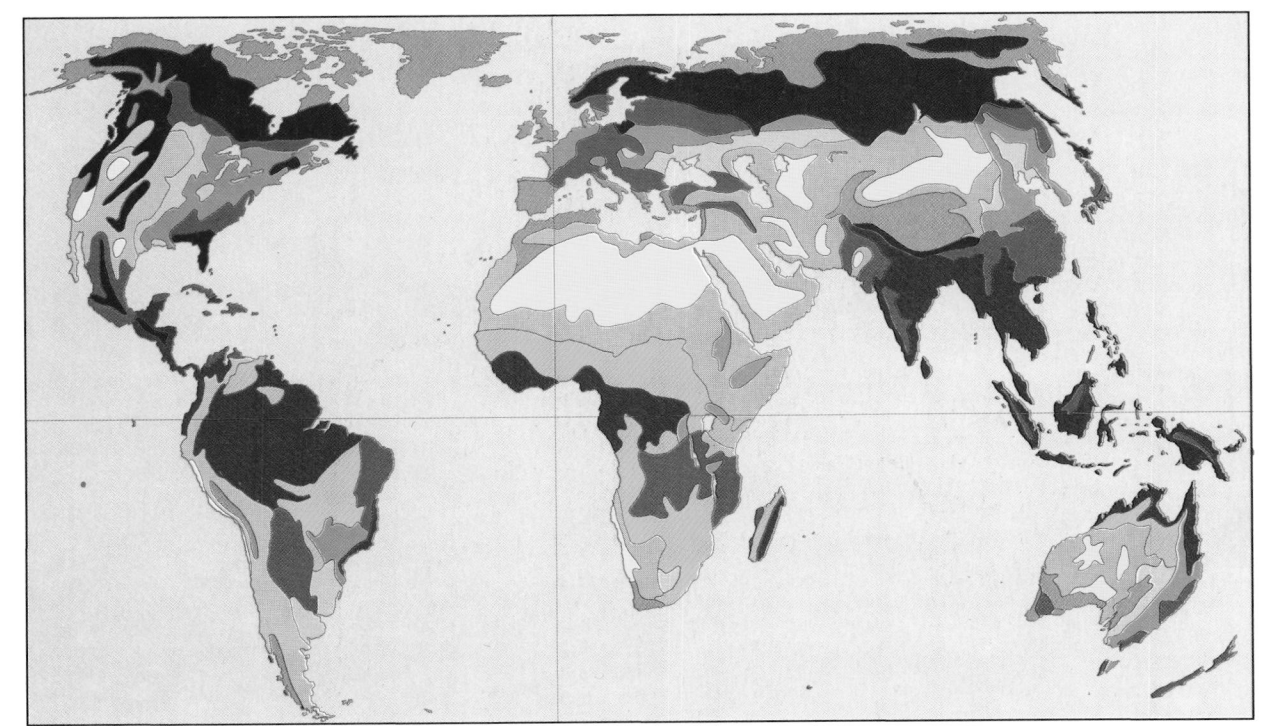

NATURAL VEGETATION

Regional variation in vegetation

- Tundra & mountain vegetation
- Needleleaf evergreen forest
- Mixed needleleaf evergreen & broadleaf deciduous trees
- Broadleaf deciduous woodland
- Mid-latitude grassland
- Evergreen broadleaf & deciduous trees & shrubs
- Semi-desert scrub
- Desert
- Tropical grassland (savanna)
- Tropical broadleaf rainforest & monsoon forest
- Sub-tropical broadleaf & needleleaf forest

The map illustrates the natural climax vegetation of a region, as dictated by its climate and topography. In most cases, human agricultural activity has drastically altered the vegetation pattern. Western Europe, for example, lost most of its broadleaf forest many centuries ago, and irrigation has turned some natural semi-desert into productive land.

COPYRIGHT GEORGE PHILIP LTD.

THE EARTH: LANDSCAPE

Above and below the surface of the oceans, the features of the Earth's crust are constantly changing. The phenomenal forces generated by convection currents in the molten core of our planet carry the vast segments or 'plates' of the crust across the globe in an endless cycle of creation and destruction. New crust emerges along the central depths of the oceans, where molten magma flows from the margins of neighbouring plates to form the massive mid-ocean ridges. The sea floor spreads, and where ocean plates meet continental plates, they dip back into the earth's core to melt once again into magma.

Less dense, the continental plates 'float' among the oceans, drifting into and apart from each other at a rate which is almost imperceptibly slow. A continent may travel little more than 25 millimetres per year – in an average lifetime, Europe will move no more than a man's height – yet in the vast span of geological time, this process throws up giant mountain ranges and opens massive rifts in the land's surface.

The world's greatest mountain ranges have been formed in this way – the Himalayas by the collision of the Indo-Australian and Eurasian plates, the Andes by the meeting of the Nazca and South American plates. The Himalayas are a classic example of 'fold mountains', formed by the crumpling of the Earth's surface where two land masses have been driven together. The coastal range of the Andes, by contrast, was formed by the upsurge of molten volcanic rock created by the friction of the continent 'overriding' the ocean plate.

Destruction of the landscape, however, begins as soon as it is formed. Wind, water, ice and sea, the main agents of erosion, mount a constant assault that even the hardest rocks cannot withstand. Mountain peaks may dwindle by as little as a few millimetres each year, but if they are not uplifted by further movements of the crust they will eventually be reduced to rubble. Water is the most powerful destroyer – it has been estimated that 100 billion tonnes of rock is washed into the oceans every year.

When water freezes, its volume increases by about nine per cent, and no rock is strong enough to resist this pressure. Where water has penetrated tiny fissures or seeped into softer rock, a severe freeze followed by a thaw may result in rockfalls or earth-slides, creating major destruction in a few minutes. Over much longer periods, acidity in rainwater breaks down the chemical composition of porous rocks like limestone, eating away the rock to form deep caves and tunnels. Chemical decomposition also occurs in riverbeds and glacier valleys, hastening the process of mechanical erosion.

Rivers and glaciers, like the sea itself, generate much of their effect through abrasion – pounding the landscape with the debris they carry with them. But as well as destroying they also create new landscapes, many of them spectacular : vast deltas, as at the mouth of the Mississippi or the Nile; cliffs, rock arches and stacks, as on the south coast of Australia; and the fjords cut by long-melted glaciers in British Columbia, Norway and New Zealand.

The vast ridges that divide the Earth's crust beneath each of the world's major oceans mark the boundaries between tectonic plates which are moving very gradually in opposite directions. As the plates shift apart, molten magma rises from the Earth's core to seal the rift and the sea floor slowly spreads towards the continental landmasses. The rate of sea floor spreading has been calculated by magnetic analysis of the rock – at about 40 mm [1.5 in] a year in the North Atlantic. Near the ocean shore, underwater volcanoes mark the line where the continental rise begins. As the plates meet, much of the denser ocean crust dips beneath the continental plate and is melted back into the magma.

THE SPREADING EARTH

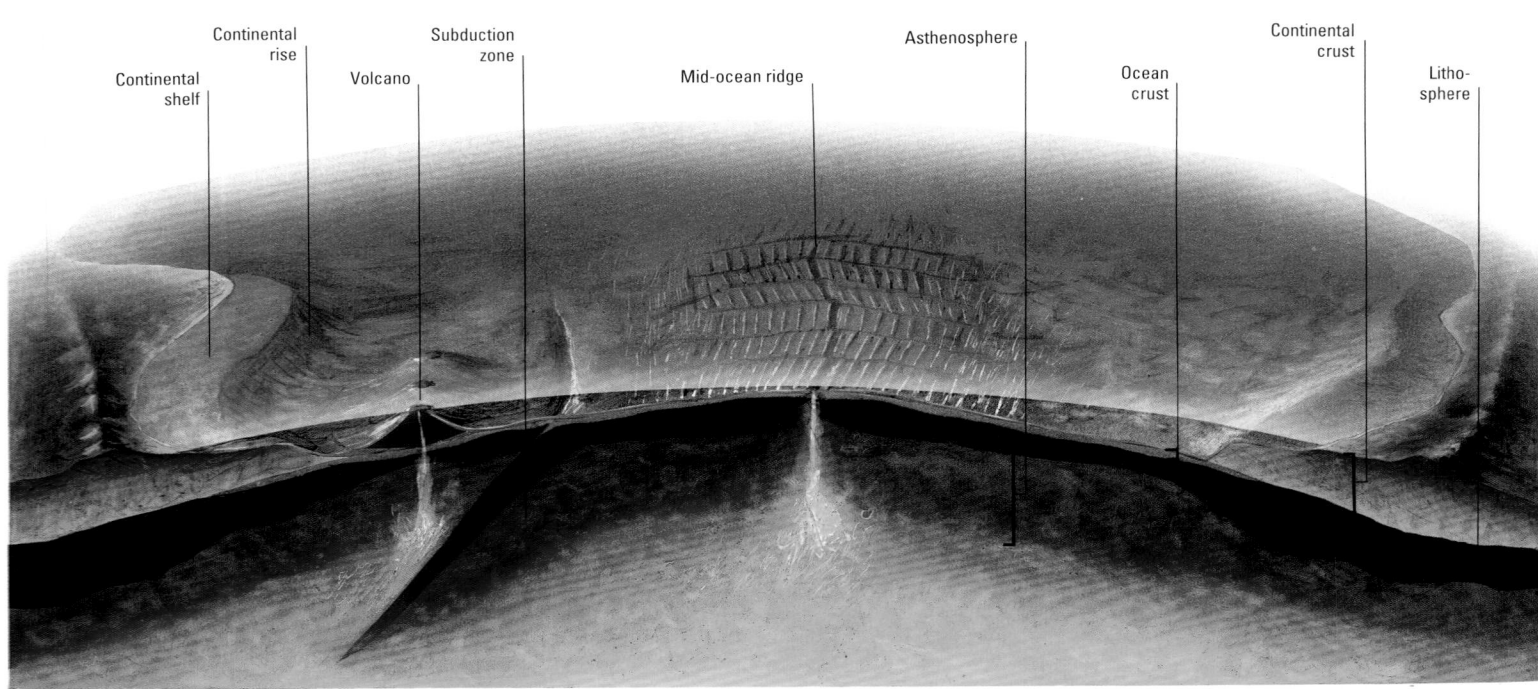

Continental shelf · Continental rise · Volcano · Subduction zone · Mid-ocean ridge · Asthenosphere · Ocean crust · Continental crust · Litho-sphere

TYPES OF ROCK

Rocks are divided into three types, according to the way in which they are formed:

Igneous rocks, including granite and basalt, are formed by the cooling of magma from within the Earth's crust.

Metamorphic rocks, such as slate, marble and quartzite, are formed below the Earth's surface by the compression or baking of existing rocks.

Sedimentary rocks, like sandstone and limestone, are formed on the surface of the Earth from the remains of living organisms and eroded fragments of older rocks.

MOUNTAIN BUILDING

Mountains are formed when pressures on the Earth's crust caused by continental drift become so intense that the surface buckles or cracks. This happens most dramatically where two tectonic plates collide : the Rockies, Andes, Alps, Urals and Himalayas resulted from such impacts. These are all known as fold mountains, because they were formed by the compression of the rocks, forcing the surface to bend and fold like a crumpled rug.

The other main building process is when the crust fractures to create faults, allowing rock to be forced upwards in large blocks; or when the pressure of magma within the crust forces the surface to bulge into a dome, or erupts to form a volcano. Large mountain ranges may reveal a combination of those features; the Alps, for example, have been compressed so violently that the folds are fragmented by numerous faults and intrusions of molten rock.

Over millions of years, even the greatest mountain ranges can be reduced by erosion to a landscape known as a peneplain.

Types of fold: Geographers give different names to the degrees of fold that result from continuing pressure on the rock strata. A simple fold may be symmetric, with even slopes on either side, but as the pressure builds up, one slope becomes steeper and the fold becomes asymmetric. Later, the ridge or 'anticline' at the top of the fold may slide over the lower ground or 'syncline' to form a recumbent fold. Eventually, the rock strata may break under the pressure to form an overthrust and finally a nappe fold.

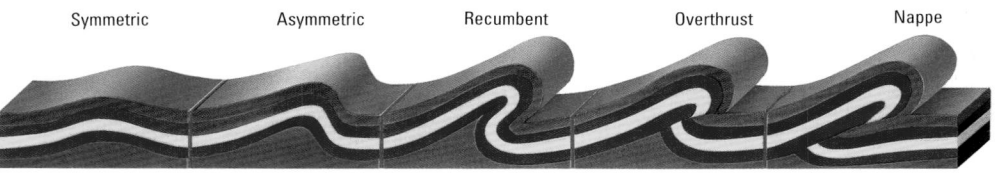

Symmetric · Asymmetric · Recumbent · Overthrust · Nappe

Types of fault: Faults are classified by the direction in which the blocks of rock have moved. A normal fault results when a vertical movement causes the surface to break apart; compression causes a reverse fault. Sideways movement causes shearing, known as a strike-slip fault. When the rock breaks in two places, the central block may be pushed up in a horst fault, or sink in a graben fault.

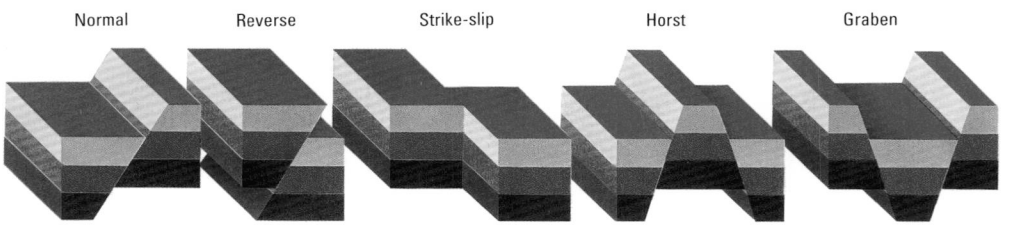

Normal · Reverse · Strike-slip · Horst · Graben

MOULDING THE LAND

While hidden forces of extraordinary power are moving the continents from below the Earth's crust, the more familiar elements of wind and water, heat and cold combine to sculpt the surface of the landscape. Erosion by weathering is seen in desert regions, where rocks degrade imperceptibly into sand through the effects of changing temperatures and strong winds.

The power of water is fiercer still. Coastlines change faster than most landscape features, both by erosion and by the build-up of sand and pebbles carried by the sea. In severe storms, giant waves pound the shoreline with rocks and boulders, and frequently destroy concrete coastal defences; but even in quieter conditions, the sea steadily erodes cliffs and headlands and creates new land in the form of sand-dunes, spits and salt-marshes.

Rivers, too, are incessantly at work shaping the landscape on their way to join the sea. In highland regions, where the flow is rapid, they cut deep gorges and V-shaped valleys. As they reach more gentle slopes, rivers release some of the debris they have carried downstream, broadening out and raising levees along their banks by depositing mud and sand. In the lowland plains, they may drift into meanders, depositing more sediment and even building deltas when they finally approach the sea.

Ice has created some of the world's dramatic landscapes. As glaciers move slowly downhill, they scrape away rock from the mountains and valley sides, creating spectacular landscape features.

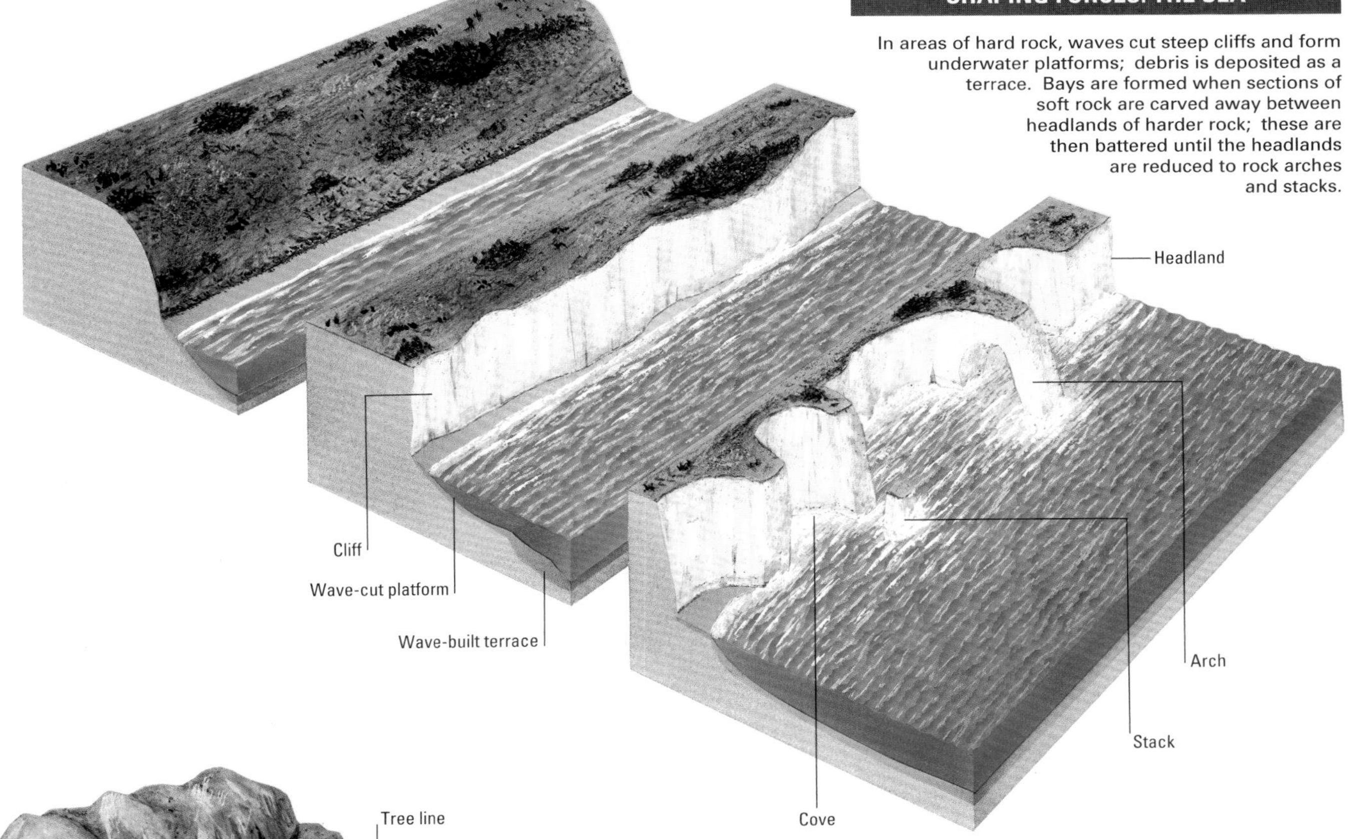

SHAPING FORCES: RIVERS

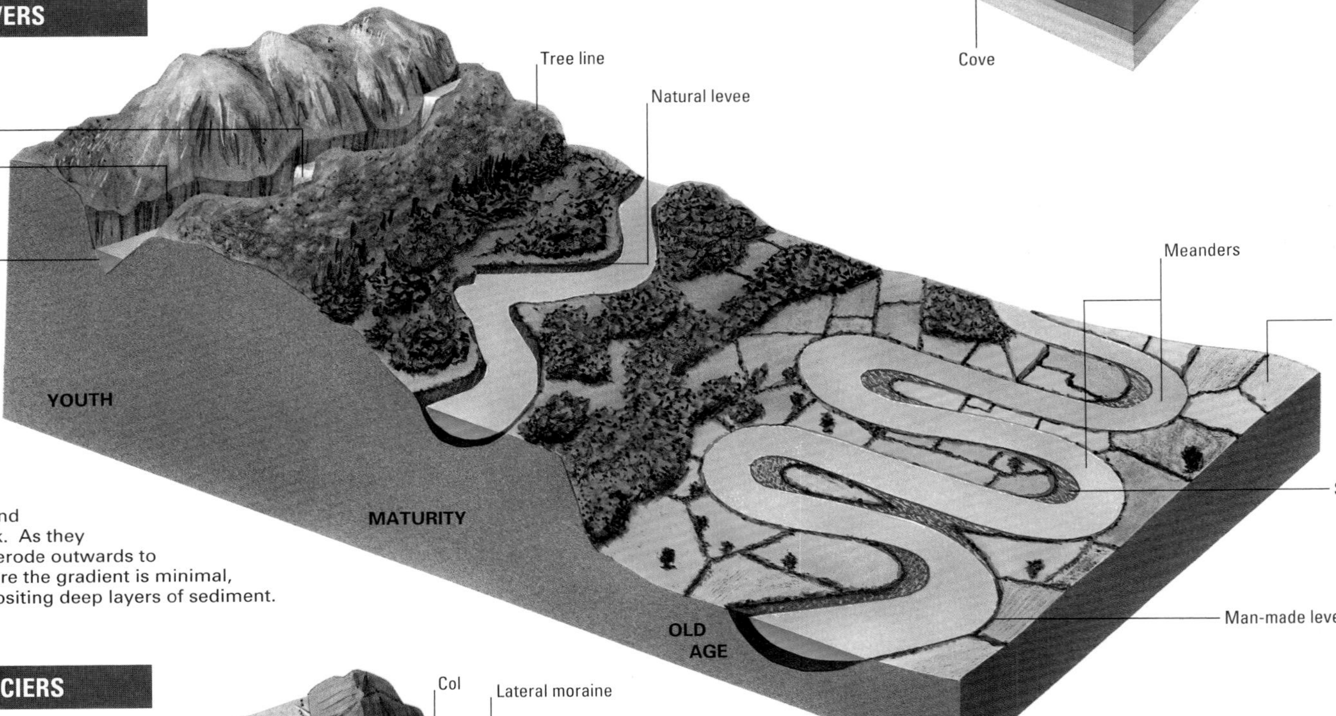

Rivers shape the landscape according to the speed of their flow. In their youthful, upland stage they erode soft rocks quickly, cutting steep narrow valleys and tumbling in waterfalls over harder rock. As they mature they deposit some debris and erode outwards to widen the valley. In their old age, where the gradient is minimal, they meander across wide plains, depositing deep layers of sediment.

SHAPING FORCES: THE SEA

In areas of hard rock, waves cut steep cliffs and form underwater platforms; debris is deposited as a terrace. Bays are formed when sections of soft rock are carved away between headlands of harder rock; these are then battered until the headlands are reduced to rock arches and stacks.

Headland

Cliff

Wave-cut platform

Wave-built terrace

Arch

Stack

Cove

Tree line

Natural levee

Waterfall

Gorge

V-shaped valley

YOUTH

MATURITY

OLD AGE

Meanders

Floodplain

Sediment

Man-made levee

SHAPING FORCES: GLACIERS

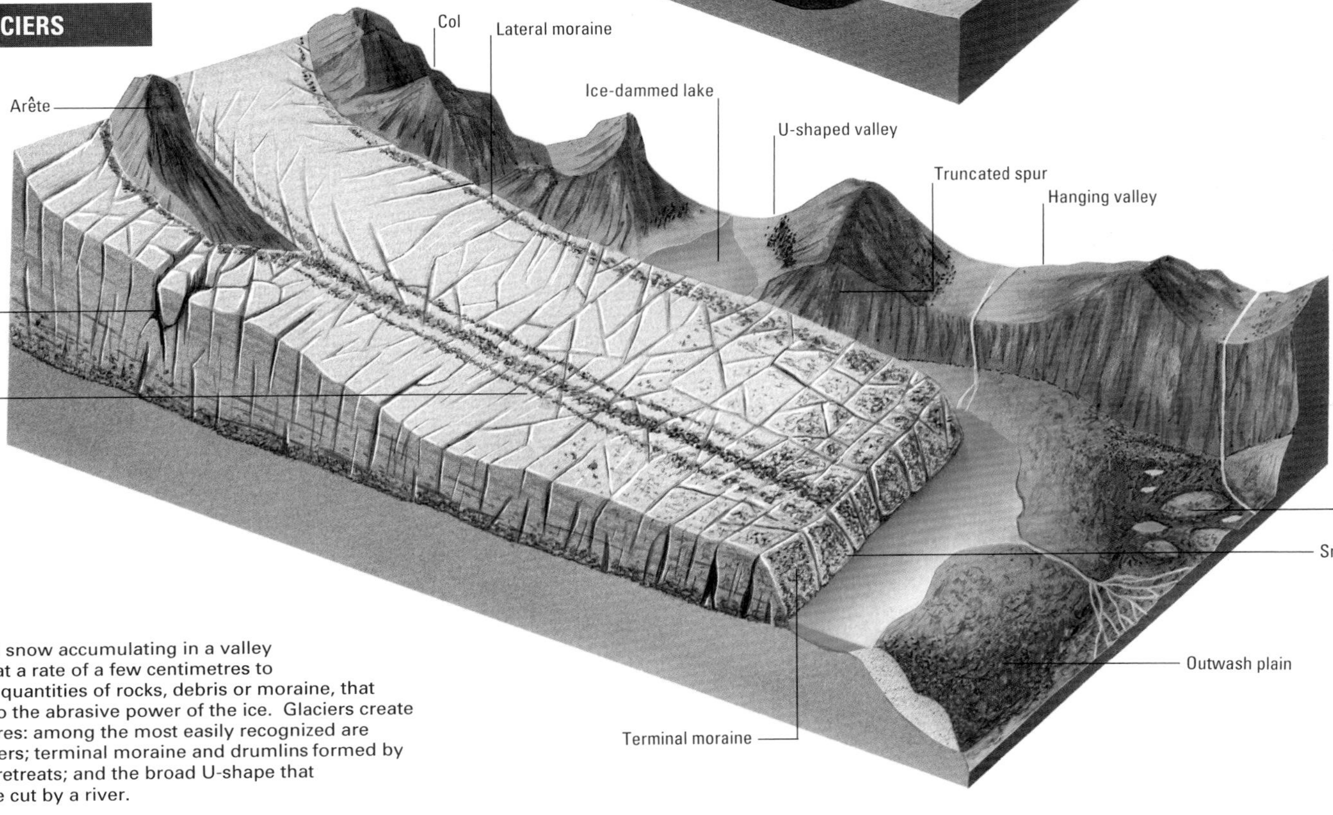

Col

Lateral moraine

Ice-dammed lake

U-shaped valley

Truncated spur

Hanging valley

Arête

Crevasse

Medial moraine

Drumlins

Snout

Outwash plain

Terminal moraine

Glaciers are formed from compressed snow accumulating in a valley head or cirque. They move downhill at a rate of a few centimetres to several metres per day, eroding large quantities of rocks, debris or moraine, that is caught up by the glacier and adds to the abrasive power of the ice. Glaciers create numerous distinctive landscape features: among the most easily recognized are hanging valleys, cut by tributary glaciers; terminal moraine and drumlins formed by rock debris deposited when a glacier retreats; and the broad U-shape that distinguishes a glacial valley from one cut by a river.

THE EARTH: ENVIRONMENT

Unique among the planets, the Earth has been the home of living creatures for most of its existence. Precisely how these improbable assemblies of self-replicating chemicals ever began remains a matter of conjecture, but the planet and its passengers have matured together for a very long time. Over three billion years, life has not only adapted to its environment: it has also slowly changed that environment to suit itself.

The planet and its biosphere – the entirety of its living things – function like a single organism. The British scientist James Lovelock, who first stated this 'Gaia hypothesis' in the 1970s, went further: the planet, he declared, actually was a living organism, equipped on a colossal scale with the same sort of stability-seeking mechanisms used by lesser lifeforms like bacteria and humans to keep themselves running at optimum efficiency.

Lovelock's theory was inspired by a study of the Earth's atmosphere, whose constituents he noted are very far from the state of chemical equilibrium observed elsewhere in the solar system. The atmosphere has contained a substantial amount of free oxygen for the last two billion years; yet without constant renewal, the oxygen molecules would soon be locked permanently in oxides. The nitrogen, too, would find chemical stability, probably in nitrates (accounting for some of the oxygen). Without living plants and algae to remove it, carbon dioxide would steadily increase from its present-day 0.03%; in a few million years, it would form a thick blanket similar to the atmosphere of lifeless Venus, where surface temperatures reach 475°C.

It is not enough, however, for the biosphere simply to produce oxygen. While falling concentrations would be first uncomfortable and ultimately fatal for most contemporary life, at levels above the current 21% even moist vegetation is highly inflammable, and a massive conflagration becomes almost inevitable – a violent form of negative feedback to set the atmosphere on the path back to sterile equilibrium.

Fortunately, the biosphere has evolved over eons into a subtle and complex control system, sensing changes and reacting to them quickly but gently, tending always to maintain the balance it has achieved.

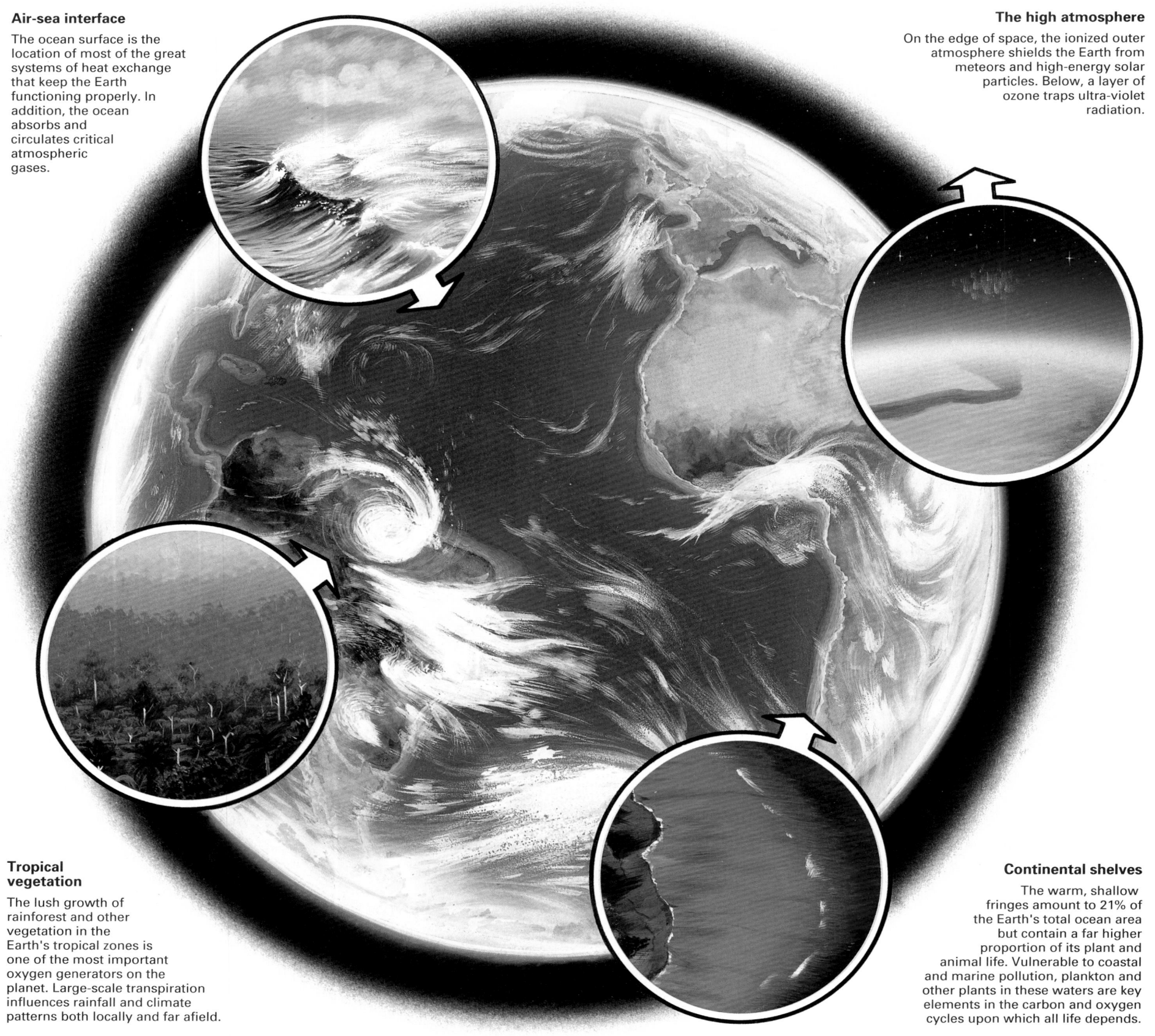

Air-sea interface

The ocean surface is the location of most of the great systems of heat exchange that keep the Earth functioning properly. In addition, the ocean absorbs and circulates critical atmospheric gases.

The high atmosphere

On the edge of space, the ionized outer atmosphere shields the Earth from meteors and high-energy solar particles. Below, a layer of ozone traps ultra-violet radiation.

Tropical vegetation

The lush growth of rainforest and other vegetation in the Earth's tropical zones is one of the most important oxygen generators on the planet. Large-scale transpiration influences rainfall and climate patterns both locally and far afield.

Continental shelves

The warm, shallow fringes amount to 21% of the Earth's total ocean area but contain a far higher proportion of its plant and animal life. Vulnerable to coastal and marine pollution, plankton and other plants in these waters are key elements in the carbon and oxygen cycles upon which all life depends.

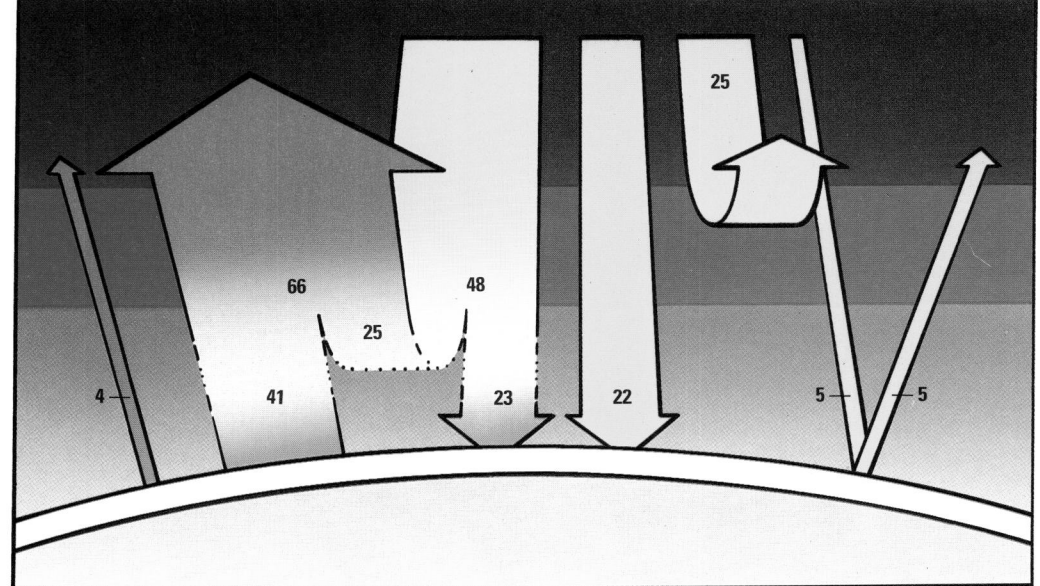

THE EARTH'S ENERGY BALANCE

Apart from a modest quantity of internal heat from its molten core, the Earth receives all its energy from the Sun. If the planet is to remain at a constant temperature, it must re-radiate exactly as much as it receives. Even a minute surplus would lead to a warmer Earth, a deficit to a cooler one; because the planetary energy budget is constantly audited by the laws of physics, which do not permit juggling, it must balance with absolute precision. The temperature at which thermal equilibrium is reached depends on a multitude of interconnected factors. Two of the most important are the relative brightness of the Earth – its index of reflectivity, called the albedo – and the heat-trapping capacity of the atmosphere – the celebrated 'greenhouse effect'.

Because the Sun is very hot, most of its energy arrives in the form of relatively short-wave radiation: the shorter the waves, the more energy they carry. Some of the incoming energy is reflected straight back into space, exactly as it arrived; some is absorbed by the atmosphere on its way towards the surface; some is absorbed by the earth itself. Absorbed energy heats the Earth and its atmosphere alike. But since its temperature is very much lower that that of the Sun, outgoing energy is emitted at much longer infra-red wavelengths. Some of the outgoing radiation escapes directly into outer space; some of it is reabsorbed by the atmosphere. Atmospheric energy eventually finds its way back into space, too, after a complex series of interactions. These include the air movements we call the weather and, almost incidentally, the maintenance of life on Earth.

This diagram does not attempt to illustrate the actual mechanisms of heat exchange, but gives a reasonable account (in percentages) of what happens to 100 energy 'units'. Short-wave radiation is shown in yellow, long-wave in red.

THE CARBON CYCLE

Most of the constituents of the atmosphere are kept in constant balance by complex cycles in which life plays an essential and indeed a dominant part. The control of carbon dioxide, which left to its own devices would be the dominant atmospheric gas, is possibly the most important, although since all the Earth's biological and geophysical cycles interact and interlock, it is hard to separate them even in theory and quite impossible in practice.

The Earth has a huge supply of carbon, only a small quantity of which is in the form of carbon dioxide. Of that, around 98% is dissolved in the sea; the fraction circulating in the air amounts to only 340 parts per million of the atmosphere, where its capacity as a greenhouse gas is the key regulator of the planetary temperature. In turn, life regulates the regulator, keeping carbon dioxide concentrations below danger level.

If all life were to vanish tomorrow from the Earth, the atmosphere would begin the process of change immediately, although it might take several million years to achieve a new, inorganic stability. First, the oxygen content would begin to fall away; with no more assistance than a little solar radiation, a few electrical storms and its own high chemical potential, oxygen would steadily combine with atmospheric nitrogen and volcanic outgassing. In doing so, it would yield sufficient acid to react with carbonaceous rocks such as limestone, releasing carbon dioxide. Once carbon dioxide levels exceeded about 1%, its greenhouse power would increase disproportionately. Rising temperatures – well above the boiling point of water would speed chemical reactions; in time, the Earth's atmosphere would consist of little more than carbon dioxide and superheated water vapour.

Living things, however, circulate carbon. They do so first by simply existing: after all, the carbon atom is the basic building block of living matter. During life, plants absorb atmospheric carbon dioxide, incorporating the carbon itself into their structure – leaves and trunks in the case of land plants, shells

in the case of plankton and the tiny creatures that feed on it. The oxygen thereby freed is added to the atmosphere, at least for a time. Most plant carbon is returned to circulation when the plants die and decay, combining once more with the oxygen released during life. However, a small proportion – about one part in 1000 – is removed almost permanently, buried beneath mud on land, at sea sinking as dead matter to the ocean floor. In time, it is slowly compressed into sedimentary rocks such as limestone and chalk.

But in the evolution of the Earth, nothing is quite permanent. On an even longer timescale, the planet's crustal movements force new rock upward in mid-ocean ridges. Limestone deposits are

moved, and sea levels change; ancient limestone is exposed to weathering, and a little of its carbon is released to be fixed in turn by the current generation of plants.

The carbon cycle has continued quietly for an immensely long time, and without gross disturbance there is no reason why it would not continue almost indefinitely in the future. However, human beings have found a way to release fixed carbon at a rate far faster than existing global systems can recirculate it. Oil and coal deposits represent the work of millions of years of carbon accumulation; but it has taken only a few human generations of high-energy scavenging to endanger the entire complex regulatory cycle.

Organic decay, animal respiration & burning

AIR

Plankton photosynthesis

Absorbtion by living plants

Plankton respiration

Mineral washout

LAND

SEA

Sea shells to sedimentary rock

[98% of existing carbon dioxide held in solution in the sea]

THE GREENHOUSE EFFECT

Constituting barely 0.03% of the atmosphere, carbon dioxide has a hugely disproportionate effect on the Earth's climate and even its habitability. Like the glass panes in a greenhouse, it is transparent to most incoming short-wave radiation, which passes freely to heat the planet beneath. But when the warmed earth re-transmits that energy, in the form of longer-wave infra-red radiation, the carbon dioxide functions as an opaque shield, so that the planetary surface (like the interior of a greenhouse) stays relatively hot.

Recent increases in CO_2 levels are causing alarm: global warming associated with a runaway greenhouse effect could bring disaster. But a serious reduction would be just as damaging, with surface temperatures falling dramatically; during the last ice age, for example, the carbon dioxide concentration was around 180 parts per million, and a total absence of the gas would likely leave the planet a ball of ice, or at best frozen tundra.

The diagram shows incoming sunlight as yellow; high-energy ultra-violet (blue) is trapped by the ozone layer while outgoing heat from the warmed Earth (red) is partially retained by carbon dioxide.

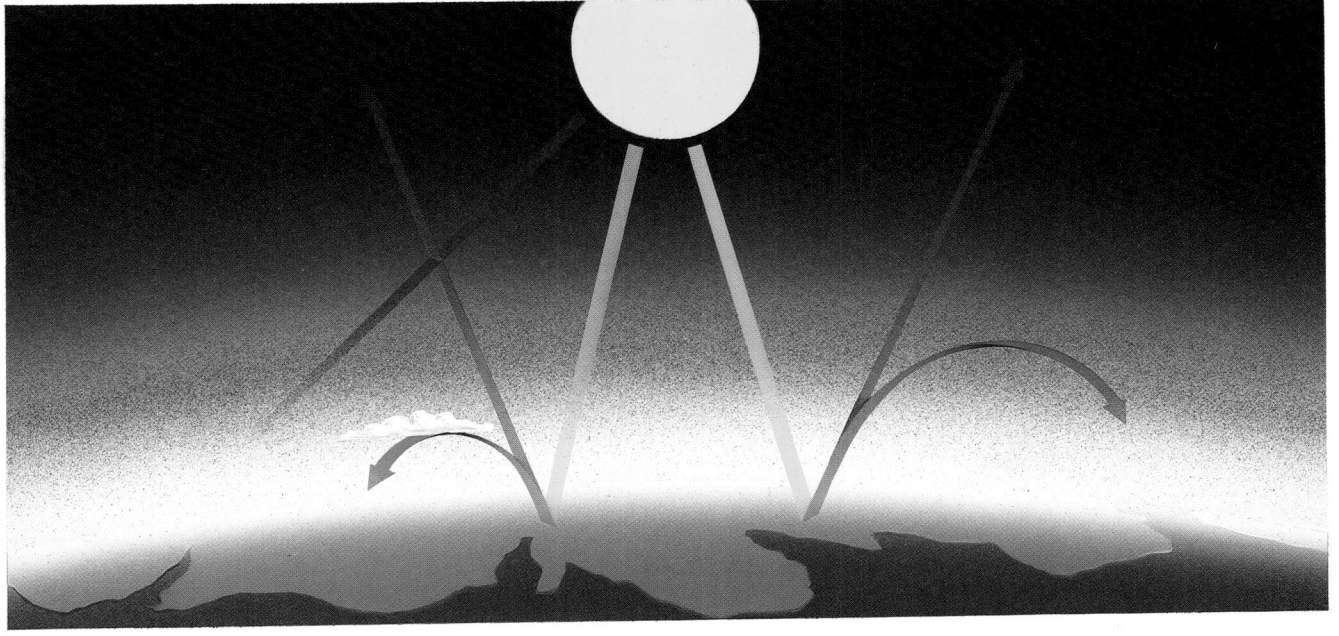

PEOPLE: DEMOGRAPHY

As the 20th century draws to its close, the Earth's population increases by nearly 10,000 every hour – enough to fill a new major city every week. The growth is almost entirely confined to the developing world, which accounted for 67% of total population in 1950 and is set to reach 84% by 2025. In developed countries, populations are almost static, and in some places, such as Germany, are actually falling. In fact, there is a clear correlation between wealth and low fertility: as incomes rise, reproduction rates drop.

The decline is already apparent. With the exception of Africa, the actual rates of increase are falling nearly everywhere. The structure of populations, however, ensures that human numbers will continue to rise even as fertility diminishes. Developed nations, like the UK, have an even spread across ages, and usually a growing proportion of elderly people: the over-75s often outnumber the under-5s, and women of child-bearing age form only a modest part of the total. Developing nations fall into a pattern somewhere between that of Kenya and Brazil: the great majority of their people are in the younger age groups, about to enter their most fertile years. In time, even Kenya's population profile should resemble the developed model, but the transition will come about only after a few more generations' growth.

It remains to be seen whether the planet will tolerate the population growth that seems inevitable before stability is reached. More people consume more resources, increasing the strain on an already troubled environment. However, more people should mean a greater supply of human ingenuity – the only commodity likely to resolve the crisis .

LARGEST NATIONS

The world's most populous nations, in millions (1989)

1.	China	1120
2.	India	812
3.	USSR	286
4.	USA	250
5.	Indonesia	179
6.	Brazil	147
7.	Japan	123
8.	Nigeria	109
9.	Pakistan	109
10.	Bangladesh	107
11.	Mexico	84
12.	Germany	79
13.	Vietnam	66
14.	Philippines	60
15.	Italy	58
16.	UK	57
17.	Turkey	57
18.	France	56
19.	Thailand	55
20.	Iran	55
21.	Egypt	53
22.	Ethiopia	51
23.	S. Korea	43
24.	Burma	41
25.	Spain	39

CROWDED NATIONS

Population per square kilometre (1989), exc. nations of less than one million

1.	Hong Kong	5826.2
2.	Singapore	4401.6
3.	Bangladesh	795.4
4.	Mauritius	577.3
5.	Taiwan	554.2
6.	Netherlands	439.0
7.	S. Korea	432.3
8.	Puerto Rico	412.9
9.	Belgium	328.5
10.	Japan	327.0
11.	Lebanon	283.2
12.	Rwanda	280.1
13.	India	273.1
14.	Sri Lanka	259.6
15.	El Salvador	251.3
16.	Trinidad & Tobago	246.2
17.	UK	236.8
18.	Germany	224.9
19.	Israel	224.6
20.	Jamaica	219.3

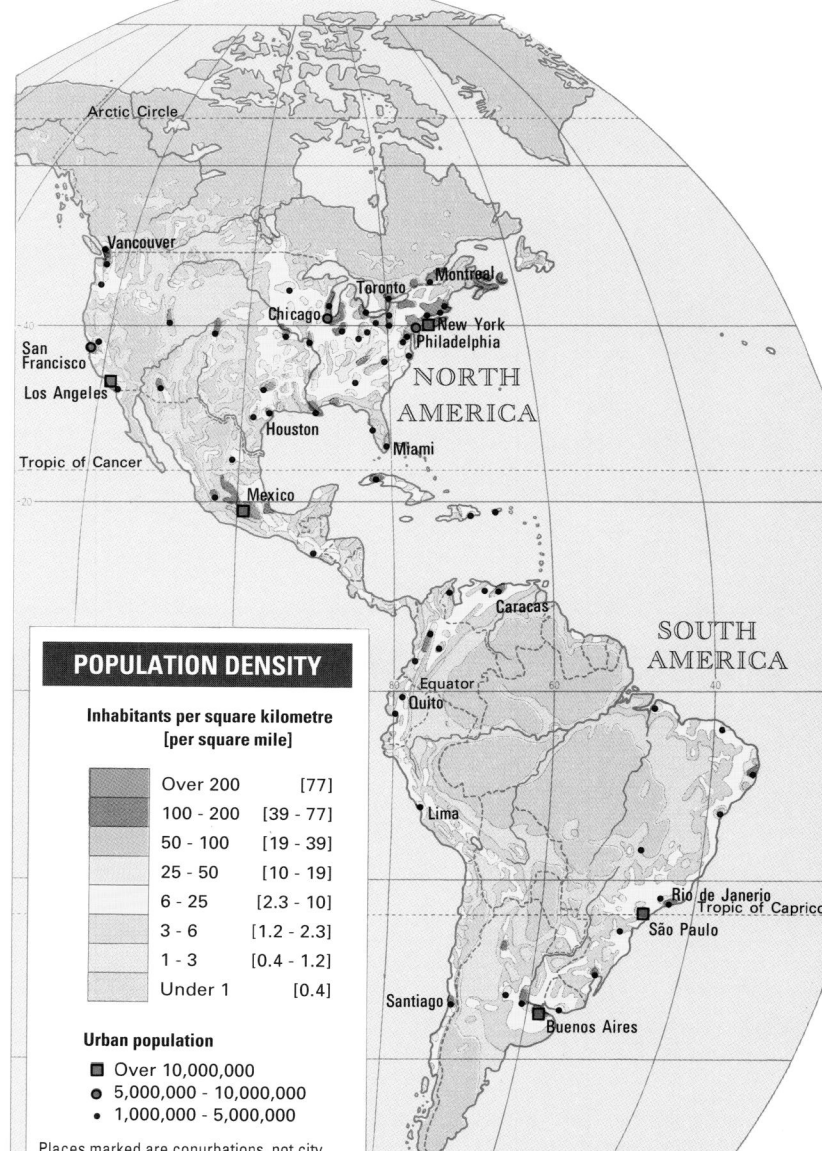

POPULATION DENSITY

Inhabitants per square kilometre [per square mile]

	Over 200	[77]
	100 - 200	[39 - 77]
	50 - 100	[19 - 39]
	25 - 50	[10 - 19]
	6 - 25	[2.3 - 10]
	3 - 6	[1.2 - 2.3]
	1 - 3	[0.4 - 1.2]
	Under 1	[0.4]

Urban population
- ■ Over 10,000,000
- ● 5,000,000 - 10,000,000
- • 1,000,000 - 5,000,000

Places marked are conurbations, not city limits; San Francisco itself, for example, has an official population of less than a million.

Projection : Mollweide's Interrupted Homolographic

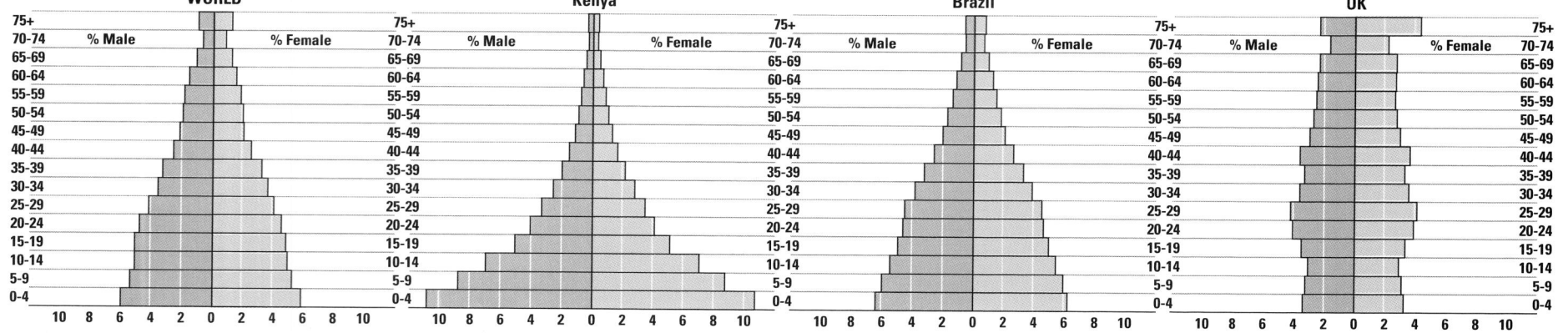

RATES OF GROWTH

Apparently small rates of population growth lead to dramatic increases over two or three generations. The table below translates annual percentage growth into the number of years required to double a population.

% change	Doubling time
0.5	139.0
1.0	69.7
1.5	46.6
2.0	35.0
2.5	28.1
3.0	23.4
3.5	20.1
4.0	17.7

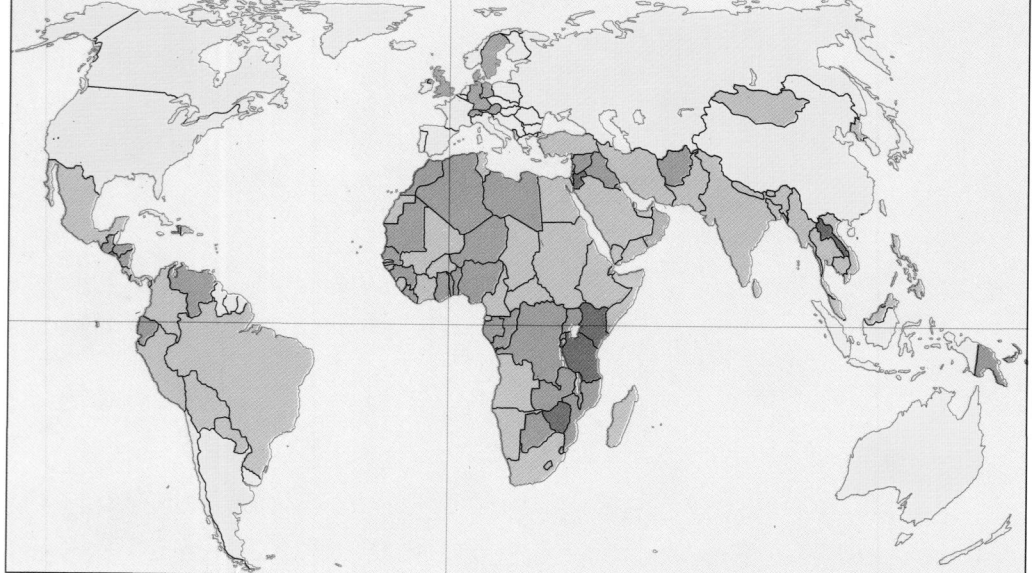

POPULATION CHANGE

Estimated percentage change in total population, 1988-2000

	Over 60%
	40 - 60%
	20 - 40%
	0 - 20% [USA 0.8%]
	[UK 0.3%]
	Loss or no change

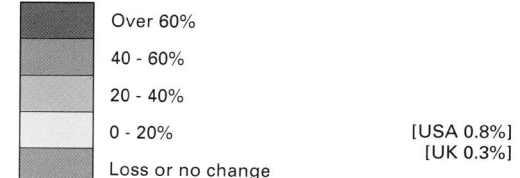

Highest expected gain*		Lowest expected gain	
Haiti	+84%	Andorra	-15%
Kenya	+82%	Switzerland	-10%
El Salvador	+77%	Oman	-5%
Jordan	+75%	Sweden	-4%
Tanzania	+74%	Germany (W)	-2%

* India (191 million), China (187), Nigeria (49), Pakistan (48), Indonesia (38), Bangladesh (36) & Brazil (34) are expected to gain most in total population over the same period

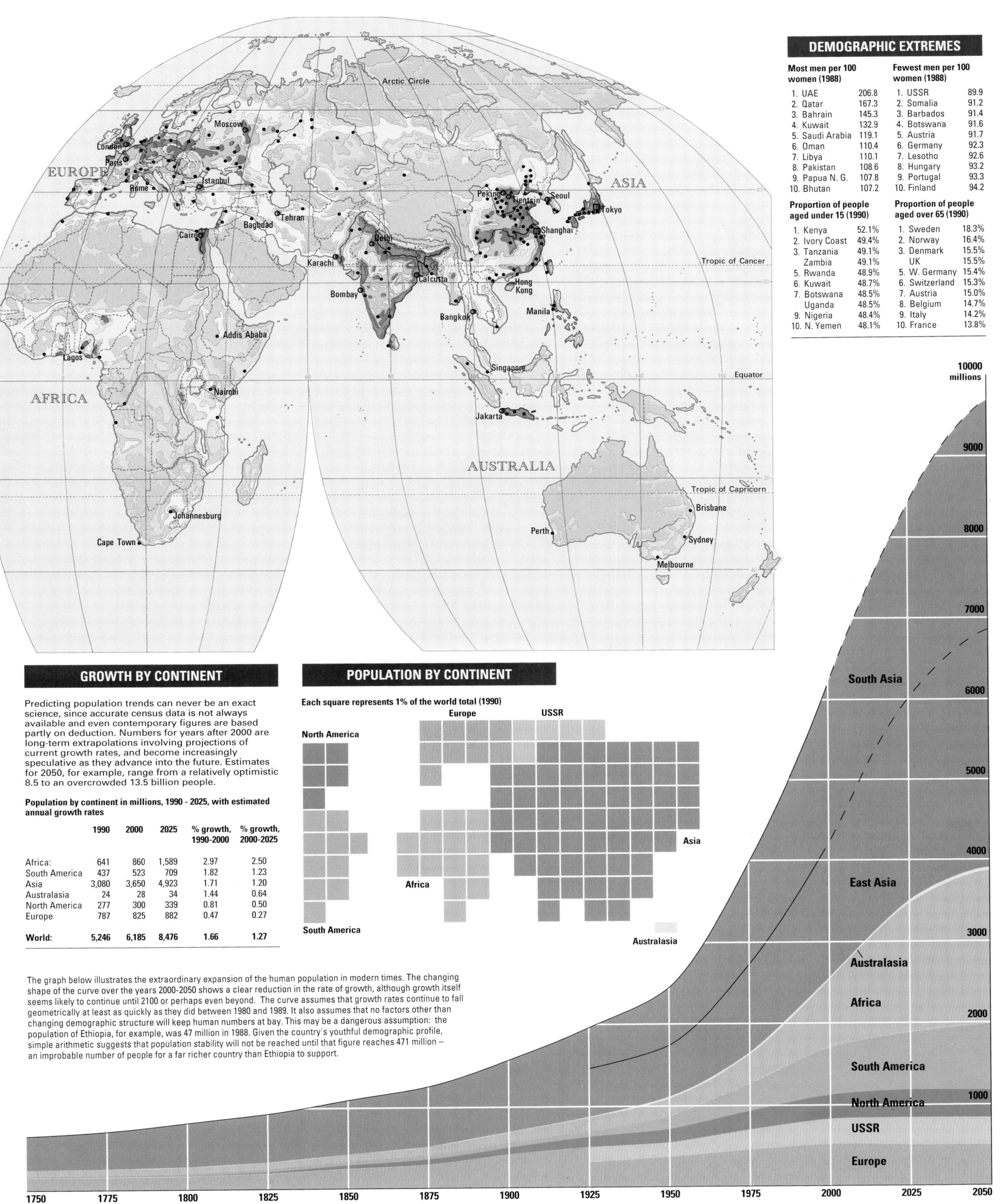

DEMOGRAPHIC EXTREMES

Most men per 100 women (1988)		Fewest men per 100 women (1988)	
1. UAE	206.8	1. USSR	89.9
2. Qatar	167.3	2. Somalia	91.2
3. Bahrain	145.3	3. Barbados	91.4
4. Kuwait	132.9	4. Botswana	91.6
5. Saudi Arabia	119.1	5. Austria	91.7
6. Oman	110.4	6. Germany	92.3
7. Libya	110.1	7. Lesotho	92.6
8. Pakistan	108.6	8. Hungary	93.2
9. Papua N. G.	107.8	9. Portugal	93.3
10. Bhutan	107.2	10. Finland	94.2

Proportion of people aged under 15 (1990)		Proportion of people aged over 65 (1990)	
1. Kenya	52.1%	1. Sweden	18.3%
2. Ivory Coast	49.4%	2. Norway	16.4%
3. Tanzania	49.1%	3. Denmark	15.5%
Zambia	49.1%	UK	15.5%
5. Rwanda	48.9%	5. W. Germany	15.4%
6. Kuwait	48.7%	6. Switzerland	15.3%
7. Botswana	48.5%	7. Austria	15.0%
Uganda	48.5%	8. Belgium	14.7%
9. Nigeria	48.4%	9. Italy	14.2%
10. N. Yemen	48.1%	10. France	13.8%

GROWTH BY CONTINENT

Predicting population trends can never be an exact science, since accurate census data is not always available and even contemporary figures are based partly on deduction. Numbers for years after 2000 are long-term extrapolations involving projections of current growth rates, and become increasingly speculative as they advance into the future. Estimates for 2050, for example, range from a relatively optimistic 8.5 to an overcrowded 13.5 billion people.

Population by continent in millions, 1990 - 2025, with estimated annual growth rates

	1990	2000	2025	% growth, 1990-2000	% growth, 2000-2025
Africa:	641	860	1,589	2.97	2.50
South America	437	523	709	1.82	1.23
Asia	3,080	3,650	4,923	1.71	1.20
Australasia	24	28	34	1.44	0.64
North America	277	300	339	0.81	0.50
Europe	787	825	882	0.47	0.27
World:	**5,246**	**6,185**	**8,476**	**1.66**	**1.27**

POPULATION BY CONTINENT

Each square represents 1% of the world total (1990)

North America
Europe
USSR
Asia
Africa
South America
Australasia

The graph below illustrates the extraordinary expansion of the human population in modern times. The changing shape of the curve over the years 2000-2050 shows a clear reduction in the rate of growth, although growth itself seems likely to continue until 2100 or perhaps even beyond. The curve assumes that growth rates continue to fall geometrically at least as quickly as they did between 1980 and 1989. It also assumes that no factors other than changing demographic structure will keep human numbers at bay. This may be a dangerous assumption: the population of Ethiopia, for example, was 47 million in 1988. Given the country's youthful demographic profile, simple arithmetic suggests that population stability will not be reached until that figure reaches 471 million – an improbable number of people for a far richer country than Ethiopia to support.

23

PEOPLE: CITIES

In 1750, barely three humans in every hundred lived in a city; by 2000, more than half of a vastly greater world population will find a home in some kind of urban area. In 1850, only London and Paris had more than a million inhabitants; by 2000, at least 24 cities will each contain over ten million people. The increase is concentrated in the Third World, if only because levels of urbanization in most developed countries - more than 90% in the UK and Belgium, and almost 75% in the USA, despite that country's great open spaces - has already reached practical limits.

Such large-scale concentration is relatively new to the human race. Although city life has always attracted country-dwellers in search of trade, employment or simply human contact, until modern times they paid a high price. Crowding and poor sanitation ensured high death rates, and until about 1850, most cities needed a steady flow of incomers simply to maintain their populations: there were 600,000 more deaths than births in 18th-century London, for example, and some other large cities showed an even worse imbalance.

With improved public health, cities could grow from their own human resources, and large-scale urban living became a commonplace in the developed world. Since about 1950, the pattern has been global. Like their counterparts in 19th-century Europe and the USA, the great new cities are driven into rapid growth by a kind of push-pull mechanism. The push is generated by agricultural overcrowding: only so many people can live from a single plot of land, and population pressure drives many into towns; The pull comes from the possibilities of economic improvement, an irresistible lure to the world's rural hopefuls.

Such improvement is not always obvious: the typical Third World city, with millions of people living (often illegally) in shanty towns and many thousands existing homelessly on the ill-made streets, does not present a great image of prosperity. Yet modern shanty towns are healthier than industrializing Pittsburgh or Manchester in the last century, and these

human ant-hills teem with industry as well as squalor: throughout the world, above-average rates of urbanization have gone hand-in-hand with above-average economic growth. Surveys consistently demonstrate that Third World city-dwellers are generally better off than their rural counterparts, whose poverty is less concentrated but often more desperate. This only serves to increase the attraction of the city for the rural poor.

However, the sheer speed of the urbanization process threatens to overwhelm the limited abilities of city authorities to provide even rudimentary services and administration. The 24 million people expected to live in Mexico City by 2000, for example, would swamp a more efficient local government than Mexico can provide. Improvements are often swallowed up by the relentless rise in urban population: although safe drinking water should reach 75% of Third World city-dwellers by the end of the century - a considerable achievement - population growth will add 100 million to the list of those without it.

THE URBANIZATION OF THE EARTH

City-building, 1850-2000; each white spot represents a city of at least one million inhabitants.

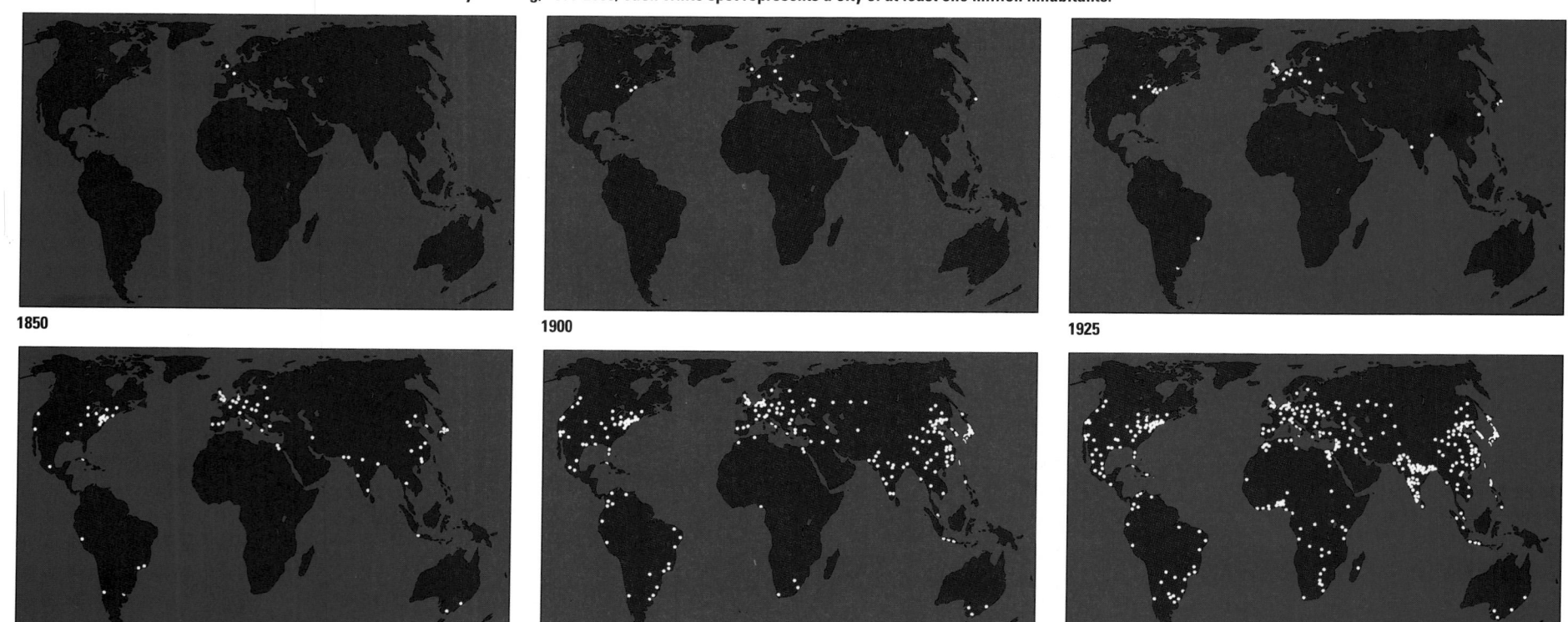

1850 | 1900 | 1925

1950 | 1975 | 2000

URBAN POPULATION

Percentage of total population living in towns & cities (1990)

[UK 92.5%]

[USA 74.0 %]

Over 75%	
50 - 75%	
25 - 50%	
10 - 25%	
Under 10%	

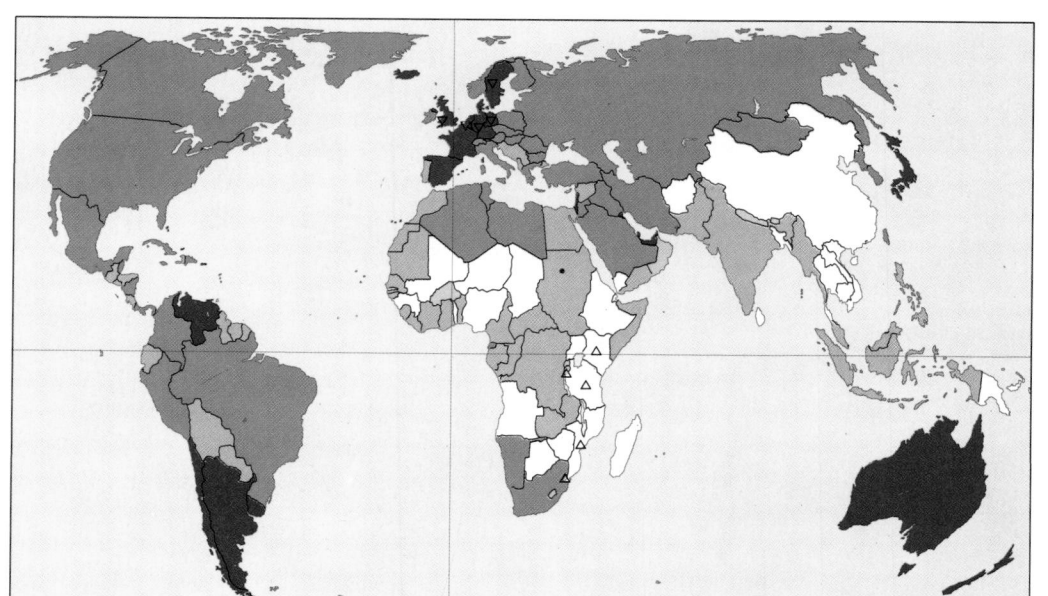

Highest urban population*		Lowest urban population	
Macau	98.7%	Bhutan	5.3%
Belgium	96.9%	Burundi	7.3%
Kuwait	95.6%	Rwanda	7.7%
Hong Kong	93.2%	Burkina Faso	9.0%
UK	92.5%	Nepal	9.6%
Israel	91.6%	Uganda	10.4%
Iceland	90.5%	Oman	10.0%

* Several countries, including Bermuda, Monaco, Singapore & Vatican City, are designated as '100% urban'

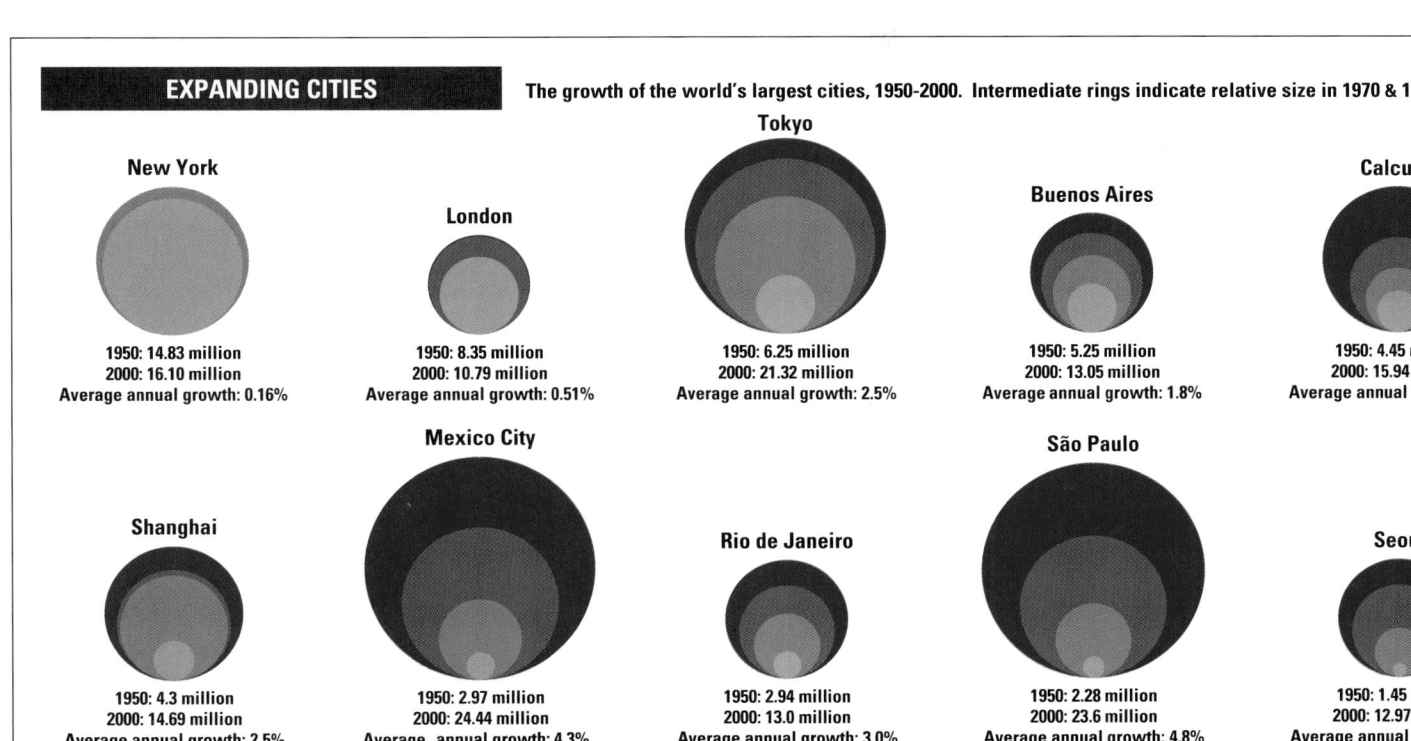

EXPANDING CITIES

The growth of the world's largest cities, 1950-2000. Intermediate rings indicate relative size in 1970 & 1985.

New York
1950: 14.83 million
2000: 16.10 million
Average annual growth: 0.16%

London
1950: 8.35 million
2000: 10.79 million
Average annual growth: 0.51%

Tokyo
1950: 6.25 million
2000: 21.32 million
Average annual growth: 2.5%

Buenos Aires
1950: 5.25 million
2000: 13.05 million
Average annual growth: 1.8%

Calcutta
1950: 4.45 million
2000: 15.94 million
Average annual growth: 2.6%

Shanghai
1950: 4.3 million
2000: 14.69 million
Average annual growth: 2.5%

Mexico City
1950: 2.97 million
2000: 24.44 million
Average annual growth: 4.3%

Rio de Janeiro
1950: 2.94 million
2000: 13.0 million
Average annual growth: 3.0%

São Paulo
1950: 2.28 million
2000: 23.6 million
Average annual growth: 4.8%

Seoul
1950: 1.45 million
2000: 12.97 million
Average annual growth: 4.5%

Each set of circles illustrates a city's size in 1950, 1970, 1985 and 2000. In most cases, expansion has been steady and, often, explosive. New York and London, however, went through patches of negative growth during the period. In New York, the world's largest city in 1950, population reached a peak around 1970. London shrank slightly between 1970 and 1985 before resuming a very modest rate of increase. In both cases, the divergence from world trends can be explained in part by counting methods: each is at the centre of a great agglomeration, and definitions of where 'city limits' lie may vary over time. But their relative decline also matches a pattern often seen in mature cities in the developed world, where urbanization, already at a very high level, has reached a plateau.

CITIES IN DANGER

As the 1980s advanced, most industrial countries, alarmed by acid rain and urban smog, took significant steps to limit air pollution. These controls, however, are expensive to install and difficult to enforce, and clean air remains a luxury most developed as well as developing cities must live without.

Those taking part in the United Nations' Global Environment Monitoring System (right) frequently show dangerous levels of pollutants ranging from soot to sulphur dioxide and photochemical smog; air in the majority of cities without such sampling equipment is likely to be at least as bad.

URBAN AIR POLLUTION

The world's most polluted cities: number of days each year when sulphur dioxide levels exceeded the WHO threshold of 150 micrograms per cubic metre (average over 4 to 15 years, 1970s - 1980s)

Sulphur dioxide is the main pollutant associated with industrial cities. According to the World Health Organization, more than seven days in a year above 150 µg per cubic metre bring a serious risk of respiratory disease: at least 600 million people live in urban areas where SO_2 concentrations regularly reach damaging levels.

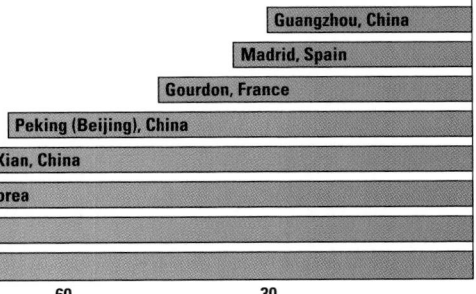

Manila, Philippines
Calcutta, India
Milan, Italy
Zagreb, Yugoslavia
Guangzhou, China
Madrid, Spain
Gourdon, France
Peking (Beijing), China
Xian, China
Seoul, South Korea
Tehran, Iran
Shenyang, China

120   90   60   30

INFORMAL CITIZENS

Proportion of population living in squatter settlements, selected cities in the developing world (1980s)

Urbanization in most Third World countries has been coming about far faster than local governments can provide services and accommodation for the new city-dwellers. Many – in some cities, most – find their homes in improvised squatter settlements, often unconnected to power, water and sanitation networks. Yet despite their ramshackle housing and marginal legality, these communities are often the most dynamic part of a city economy. They are also growing in size; and given the squatters' reluctance to be counted by tax-demanding authorities, the percentages shown here are likely to be underestimates.

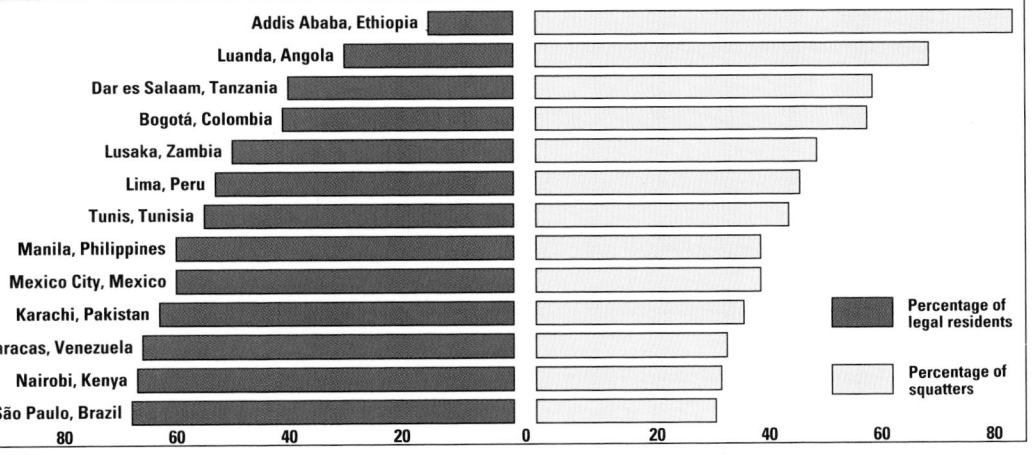

Addis Ababa, Ethiopia
Luanda, Angola
Dar es Salaam, Tanzania
Bogotá, Colombia
Lusaka, Zambia
Lima, Peru
Tunis, Tunisia
Manila, Philippines
Mexico City, Mexico
Karachi, Pakistan
Caracas, Venezuela
Nairobi, Kenya
São Paulo, Brazil

80   60   40   20   0   20   40   60   80

Percentage of legal residents
Percentage of squatters

LARGEST CITIES

The world's most populous cities, in millions of inhabitants, based on estimates for the year 2000*

1. Mexico City — 24.4
2. São Paulo — 23.6
3. Tokyo-Yokohama — 21.3
4. New York — 16.1
5. Calcutta — 15.9
6. Bombay — 15.4
7. Shanghai — 14.7
8. Tehran — 13.7
9. Jakarta — 13.2
10. Buenos Aires — 13.1
11. Rio de Janeiro — 13.0
12. Seoul — 13.0
13. Delhi — 12.8
14. Lagos — 12.4
15. Cairo-Giza — 11.8
16. Karachi — 11.6
17. Manila-Quezon — 11.5
18. Peking (Beijing) — 11.5
19. Dhaka — 11.3
20. Osaka-Kobe — 11.2
21. Los Angeles — 10.9
22. London — 10.8
23. Bangkok — 10.3
24. Moscow — 10.1
25. Tientsin (Tianjin) — 10.0
26. Lima-Callao — 8.8
27. Paris — 8.8
28. Milan — 8.7
29. Madras — 7.8
30. Baghdad — 7.7
31. Chicago — 7.0
32. Bogotá — 6.9
33. Hong Kong — 6.1
34. Leningrad — 5.8
35. Pusan — 5.8
36. Santiago — 5.6
37. Shenyang — 5.5
38. Madrid — 5.4
39. Naples — 4.5
40. Philadelphia — 4.3

[City populations are based on urban agglomerations rather than legal city limits. In some cases, such as Tokyo-Yokohama and Cairo-Giza, where two adjacent cities have merged into one concentration, they have been regarded as a single unit]

* For list of largest cities in 1990, see page XI

URBAN ADVANTAGES

Despite overcrowding and poor housing, living standards in the developing world's cities are almost invariably better than in the surrounding countryside. Resources - financial, material and administrative - are concentrated in the towns, which are usually also the centres of political activity and pressure. Governments - frequently unstable, and rarely established on a solid democratic base - are usually more responsive to urban discontent than rural misery. In many countries, especially in Africa, food prices are often kept artificially low, appeasing underemployed urban masses at the expense of agricultural development. The imbalance encourages further cityward migration, helping to account for the astonishing rate of post-1950 urbanization and putting great strain on the ability of many nations to provide even modest improvements for their people.

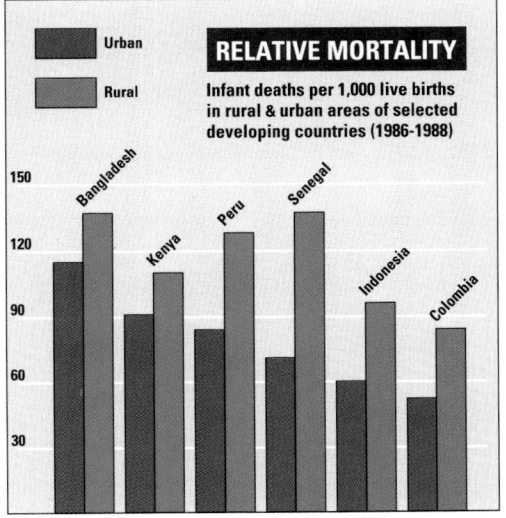

RELATIVE MORTALITY
Infant deaths per 1,000 live births in rural & urban areas of selected developing countries (1986-1988)

Urban
Rural

Bangladesh, Kenya, Peru, Senegal, Indonesia, Colombia

150   120   90   60   30

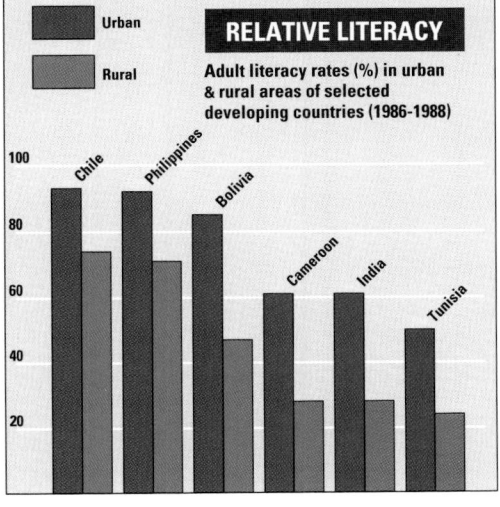

RELATIVE LITERACY
Adult literacy rates (%) in urban & rural areas of selected developing countries (1986-1988)

Urban
Rural

Chile, Philippines, Bolivia, Cameroon, India, Tunisia

100   80   60   40   20

COPYRIGHT GEORGE PHILIP LTD.

25

PEOPLE: THE HUMAN FAMILY

Strictly speaking, all human beings belong to a single race: *Homo sapiens* has no sub-species. But although all humans are inter-fertile, anthropologists and geneticists distinguish three main racial types, whose differences reflect not so much evolutionary origin as long periods of separation.

Racial affinities are not always obvious. The Caucasoid group stems from Europe, North Africa and India, but still includes Australian aboriginals within its broad type; Mongoloid peoples comprise American Indians and Eskimos as well as most Chinese, central Asians and Malays; Negroids are mostly of African origin, but also include the Papuan peoples of New Guinea.

Migration in modern times has mingled racial groups to an unprecedented extent, and most nations now have some degree of racially mixed population.

Language is almost the definition of a particular human culture; the world has well over 5,000, most of them with only a few hundred thousand speakers. In one important sense, all languages are equal: although different vocabularies and linguistic structures greatly influence patterns of thought, all true human languages can carry virtually unlimited information. But even if there is no theoretical difference in the communicative power of English and one of the 500 or more tribal languages of Papua New Guinea, for example, an English speaker has access to very much more of the global culture than a Papuan who knows no other tongue.

Like language, religion encourages the internal cohesion of a single human group at the expense of creating gulfs of incomprehension between different groups. All religions satisfy a deep-seated human need, assigning men and women to a comprehensible place in what most of them still consider a divinely ordered world. But religion is also a means by which a culture can assert its individuality: the startling rise of Islam in the late 20th century is partly a response by large sections of the developing world to the secular, Western-inspired world order from which many non-Western peoples feel excluded. Like uncounted millions of human beings before them, they find in their religion not only a personal faith but a powerful group identity.

RACE

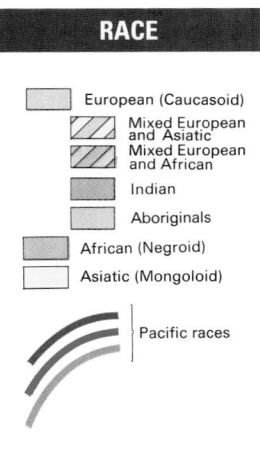

- European (Caucasoid)
- Mixed European and Asiatic
- Mixed European and African
- Indian
- Aboriginals
- African (Negroid)
- Asiatic (Mongoloid)

Pacific races

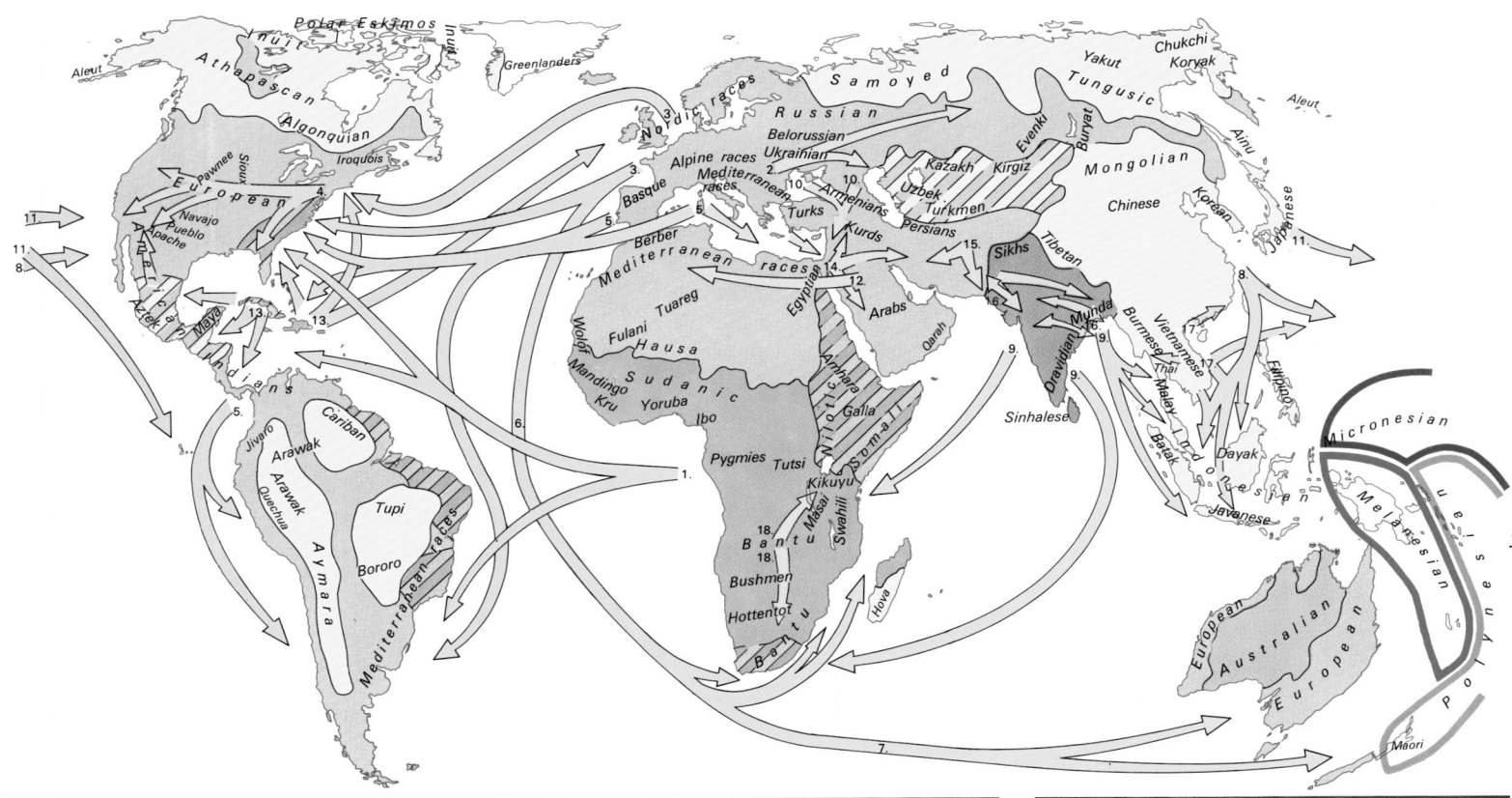

MOVEMENTS OF POPULATION

1. Africa to America (slaves), c. 1500-1860
2. Western Russia to Siberia, c. 1850-1950
3. W., E. & N. Europe to N. America, c. 1850-1900
4. From East Coast N. America, c. 1860-1960
5. Southern Europe to America, c. 1880-1920
6. Europe to S., E. & Central Africa, c. 1880-1950
7. Europe to Australia & N. Zealand, c. 1840-1950
8. China to S-E Asia & N. America, c. 1900-1950
9. India to Africa & South-East Asia, c. 1860-1910

Major migrations of peoples since 600 AD

10. European & N. American Jews to Israel, 1948-
11. Japan to N. & S. America, c. 1870-1910
12. Arabs to North Africa, 7th-9th centuries
13. C. America to N. America & Europe, c. 1950-1970
14. Migration in the Middle East, c. 1950-
15. Refugees from Afghanistan, 1979-
16. Migration in India, 1946-
17. Migration in & from South-East Asia, c. 1960-
18. Spread of the Bantu peoples, c. 1700-1900

BUILDING THE USA

U.S. Immigration 1820-1990

'Give me your tired, your poor/Your huddled masses yearning to breathe free....'

So starts Emma Lazarus's poem *The New Colossus*, inscribed on the Statue of Liberty. For decades the USA was the magnet that attracted millions of immigrants, notably from Central and Eastern Europe, the flow peaking in the early years of this century.

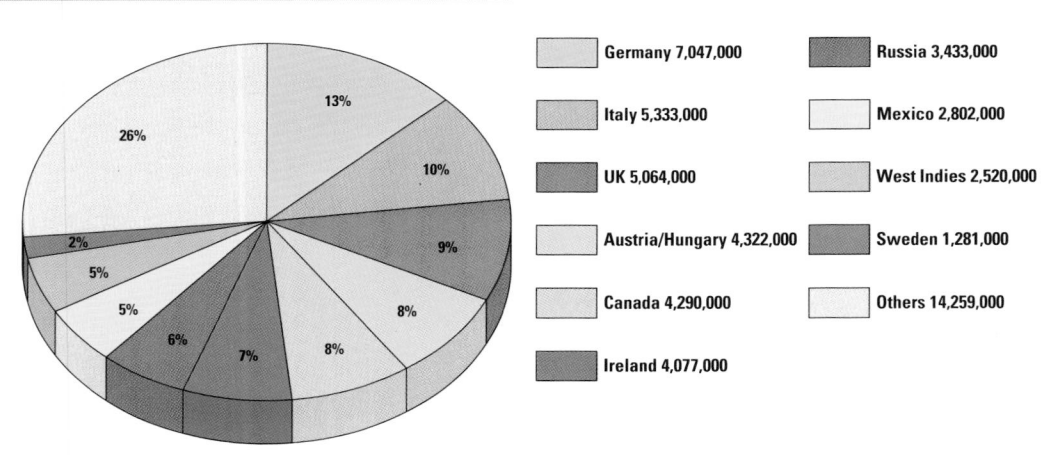

- Germany 7,047,000
- Italy 5,333,000
- UK 5,064,000
- Austria/Hungary 4,322,000
- Canada 4,290,000
- Ireland 4,077,000
- Russia 3,433,000
- Mexico 2,802,000
- West Indies 2,520,000
- Sweden 1,281,000
- Others 14,259,000

MIGRATION

The movement of migrants in thousands (1985-1990)

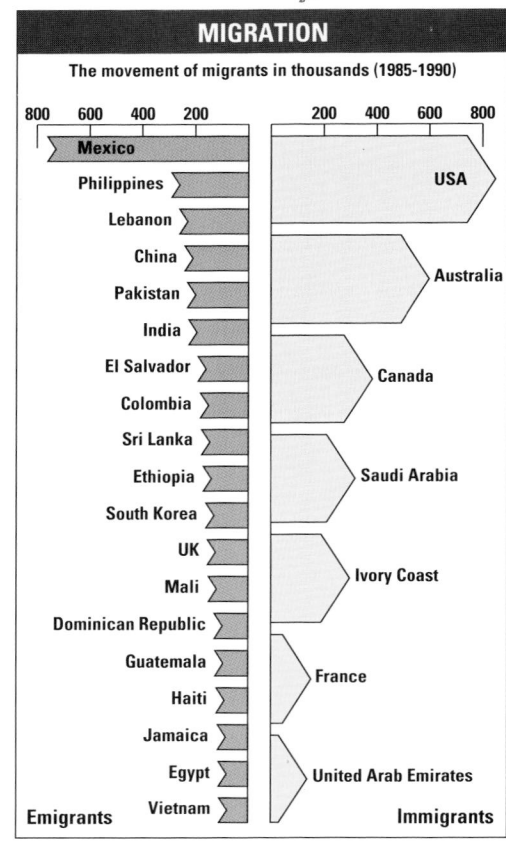

Emigrants — Immigrants

Mexico, Philippines, Lebanon, China, Pakistan, India, El Salvador, Colombia, Sri Lanka, Ethiopia, South Korea, UK, Mali, Dominican Republic, Guatemala, Haiti, Jamaica, Egypt, Vietnam

USA, Australia, Canada, Saudi Arabia, Ivory Coast, France, United Arab Emirates

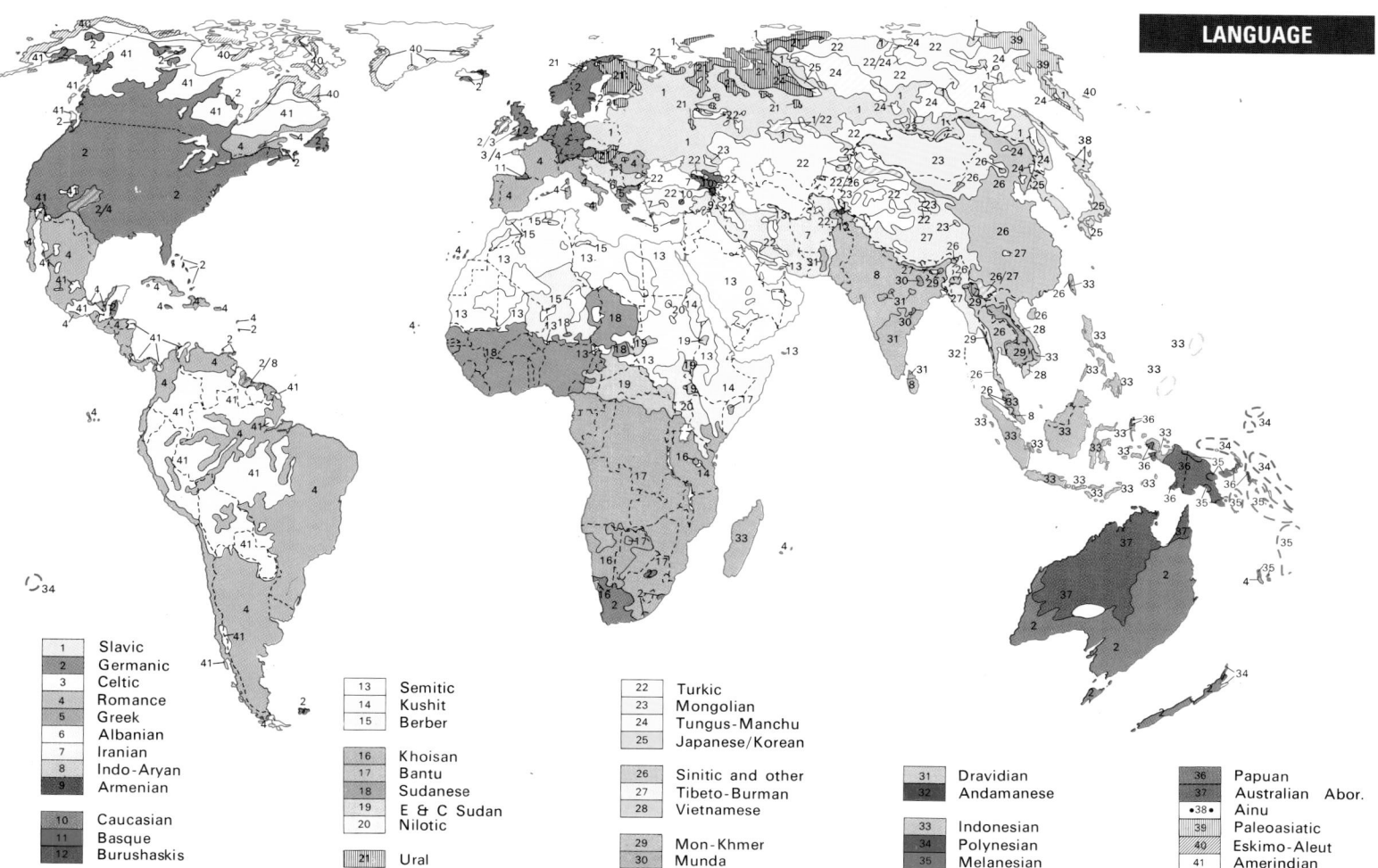

LANGUAGE

OFFICIAL LANGUAGES

Language	Total population	World %
English	1400m	27.0%
Chinese	1070m	19.1%
Hindi	700m	13.5%
Spanish	280m	5.4%
Russian	270m	5.2%
French	220m	4.2%
Arabic	170m	3.3%
Portuguese	160m	3.0%
Malay	160m	3.0%
Bengali	150m	2.9%
Japanese	120m	2.3%

1	Slavic
2	Germanic
3	Celtic
4	Romance
5	Greek
6	Albanian
7	Iranian
8	Indo-Aryan
9	Armenian
10	Caucasian
11	Basque
12	Burushaskis
13	Semitic
14	Kushit
15	Berber
16	Khoisan
17	Bantu
18	Sudanese
19	E & C Sudan
20	Nilotic
21	Ural
22	Turkic
23	Mongolian
24	Tungus-Manchu
25	Japanese/Korean
26	Sinitic and other
27	Tibeto-Burman
28	Vietnamese
29	Mon-Khmer
30	Munda
31	Dravidian
32	Andamanese
33	Indonesian
34	Polynesian
35	Melanesian
36	Papuan
37	Australian Abor.
38	Ainu
39	Paleoasiatic
40	Eskimo-Aleut
41	Amerindian

Languages form a kind of tree of development, splitting from a few ancient proto-tongues into branches that have grown apart and further divided with the passage of time. English and Hindi, for example, both belong to the great Indo-European family, although the relationship is only apparent after much analysis and comparison with non-Indo-European languages such as Chinese or Arabic; Hindi is part of the Indo-Aryan subgroup; English is a member of Indo-European's Germanic branch; French, another Indo-European tongue, traces its descent through the Latin, or Romance, branch. A few languages – Basque is one example – have no apparent links with any other, living or dead. Most modern languages, of course, have acquired enormous quantities of vocabulary from each other.

MOTHER TONGUES

Native speakers of the major languages, in millions (1989)

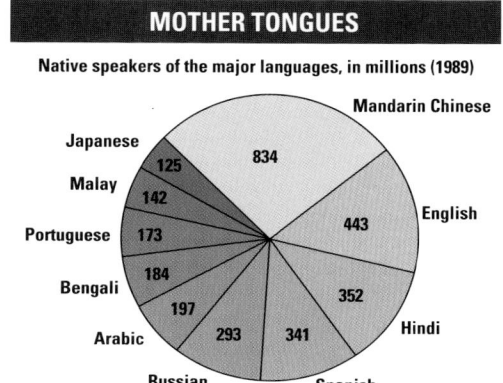

Mandarin Chinese 834, English 443, Hindi 352, Spanish 341, Russian 293, Arabic 197, Bengali 184, Portuguese 173, Malay 142, Japanese 125

Religions are not as easily mapped as the physical contours of landscape. Divisions are often blurred and frequently overlapping: most nations include people of many different faiths – or no faith at all. Some religions, like Islam and Christianity, have proselytes worldwide; others, like Hinduism and Confucianism, are restricted to a particular area, though modern migrations have taken some Indians and Chinese very far from their cultural origins. It is also difficult to show the degree to which religion exercises control over daily life: Christian Western Europe, for example, is nowadays far less dominated by its religion than are the Islamic nations of the Middle East. Similarly, figures for the major faiths' adherents make no distinction between nominal believers enrolled at birth and those for whom religion is a vital part of existence.

RELIGION

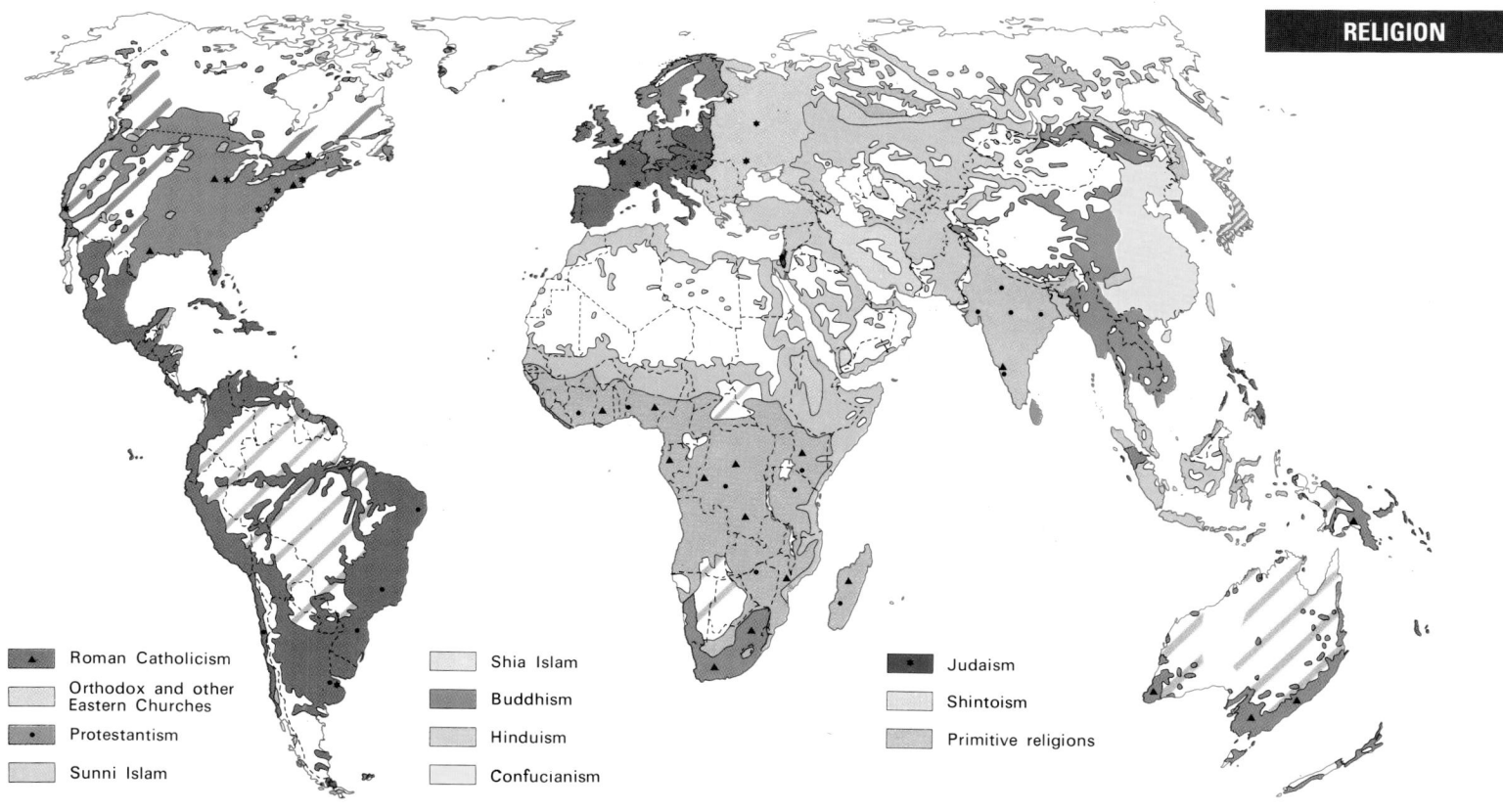

RELIGIOUS ADHERENTS

Christian	1667m
Roman Catholic	952m
Protestant	337m
Orthodox	162m
Anglican	70m
Other Christian	148m
Muslim	881m
Sunni	841m
Shia	40m
Hindu	663m
Buddhist	312m
Chinese folk	172m
Tribal	92m
Jewish	18m
Sikhs	17m

- Roman Catholicism
- Orthodox and other Eastern Churches
- Protestantism
- Sunni Islam
- Shia Islam
- Buddhism
- Hinduism
- Confucianism
- Judaism
- Shintoism
- Primitive religions

PEOPLE: CONFLICT & COOPERATION

Humans are social animals, rarely functioning well except in groups. Evolution has made them so: hunter-gatherers in cooperative bands were far more effective than animals that prowled alone. Agriculture, the building of cities and industrialization are all developments that depended on human cooperative ability – and in turn increased the need for it.

Unfortunately, human groups do not always cooperate so well with other human groups, and friction between them sometimes leads to cooperatively organized violence. War is itself a very human activity, with no real equivalent in any other species. Always murderous, it is sometimes purposeful and may even be very effective. The colonization of the Americas and Australia, for example, was in effect the waging of aggressive war by well-armed Europeans against indigenous peoples incapable of offering a serious defence.

More often, war achieves little but death and ruin. However, the great 20th-century wars appear to have cured the notoriously aggressive Europeans of their previous bad habits, although at the cost of between 50 and 100 million dead. The relative peace in the postwar developed world is at least partly due to the nuclear weapons with which rival powers have armed themselves – weapons so powerful that their use would leave a scarcely habitable planet with no meaningful distinction between victor and vanquished.

Yet warfare remains endemic: the second half of the 20th century was one of the bloodiest periods in history, and death by organized violence remains unhappily common. The map below attempts to show the serious conflicts that have scarred the Earth since 1945. Most are civil wars in poor countries, rather than international conflicts between rich ones; some of them are still unresolved, while others, like apparently extinct volcanoes, may erupt again at intervals, adding to the world's miserable population of refugees.

THE WORLD'S REFUGEES

Refugees and their national origin; the host nations and the relative size of their refugee populations (1991)

▨ Refugees in millions

◔ Refugees as a proportion of host country's population

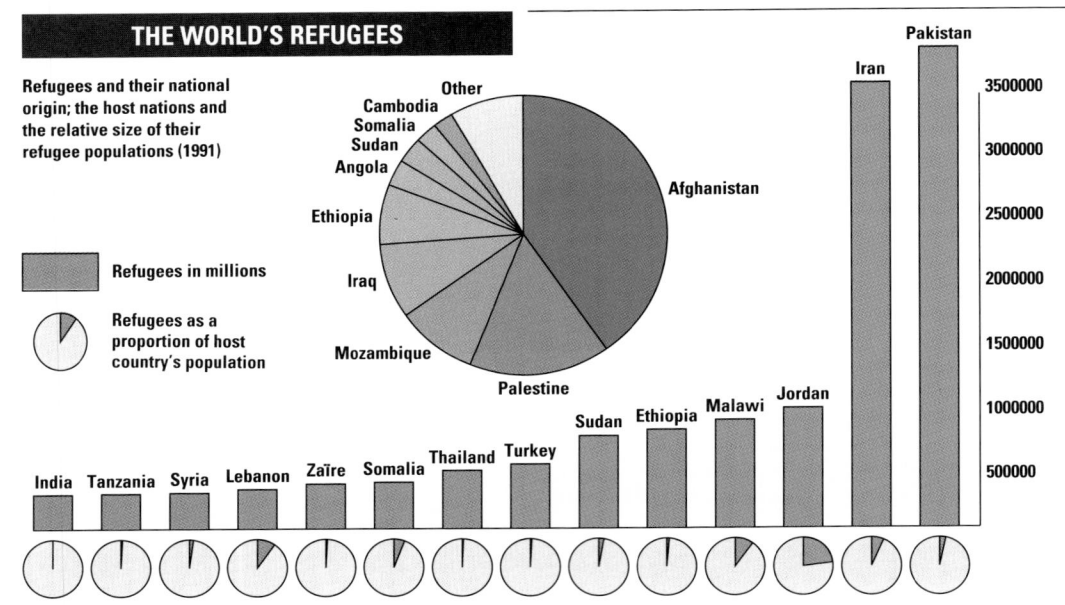

The pie-chart shows the origins of the world's refugees, the bar-chart their destinations. According to the United Nations High Commissioner for Refugees in 1990, there were almost 15 million of them, a number that continued to increase and was almost certain to be amplified during the decade. Some have fled from climatic change, some from economic disaster and others from political persecution; the great majority are the victims of war.
All but a few who make it overseas seek asylum in neighbouring countries, which are often the least equipped to deal with them and where they are rarely welcome. Lacking any rights or power, they frequently become an embarrassment and a burden to their reluctant hosts.
Usually, the best any refugee can hope for is rudimentary food and shelter in temporary camps that all to often become semi-permanent, with little prospect of assimilation by host populations: many Palestinians, for example, have been forced to live in camps since 1948.

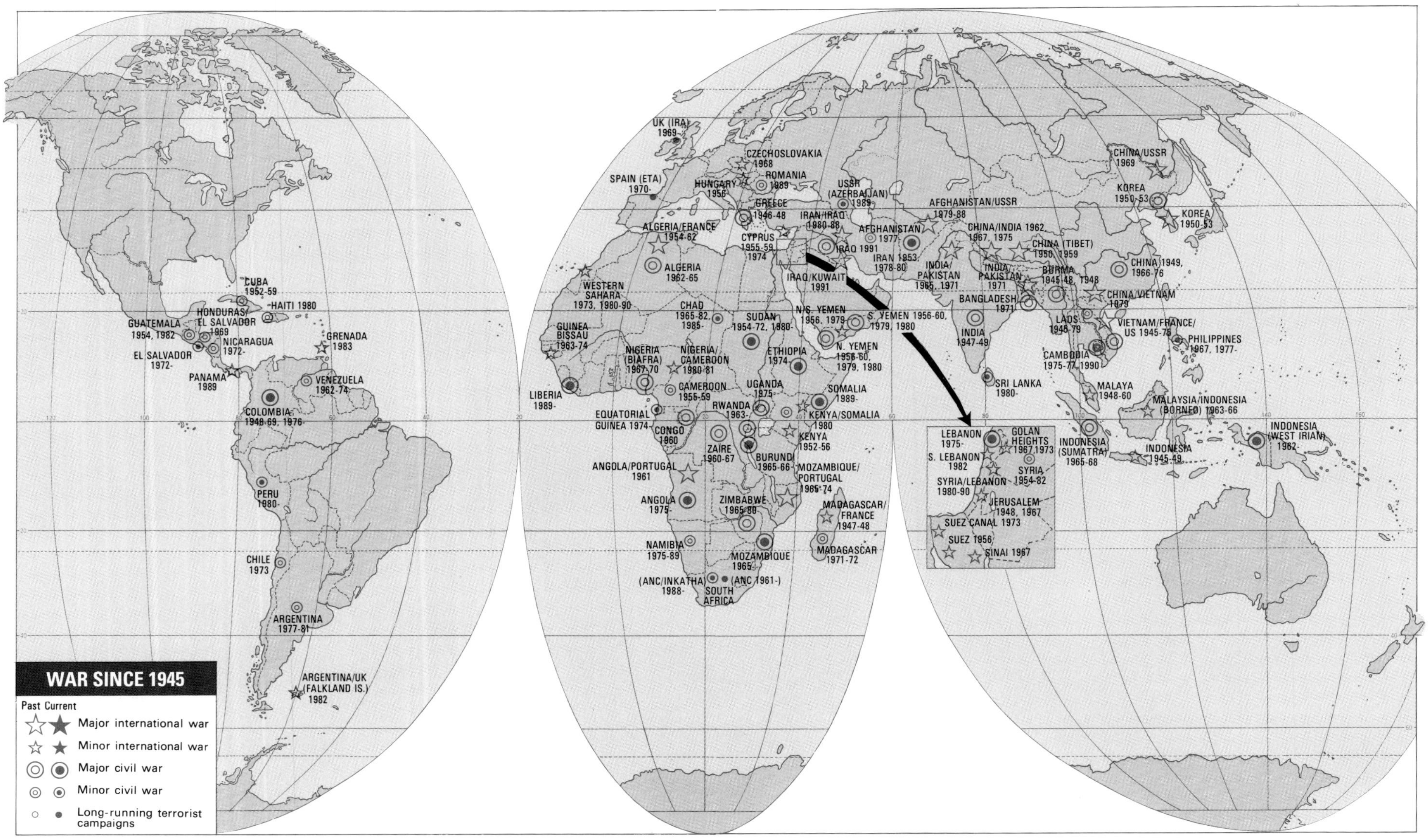

WAR SINCE 1945

Past Current
☆ ★ Major international war
☆ ★ Minor international war
◎ ● Major civil war
◎ ● Minor civil war
○ ● Long-running terrorist campaigns

28

COPYRIGHT GEORGE PHILIP LTD.

The United Nations Organization was born as World War II drew to its conclusion. Six years of strife had strengthened the world's desire for peace, but an effective international organization was needed to help achieve it. That body would replace the League of Nations which, since its inception in 1920, had signally failed to curb the aggression of at least some of its member nations. At the United Nations Conference on International Organization held in San Francisco, the United Nations Charter was drawn up. Ratified by the Security Council and signed by 51 nations, it came into effect on 24 October 1945.

The Charter set out the aims of the organization: to maintain peace and security, and develop friendly relations between nations; to achieve international cooperation in solving economic, social, cultural and humanitarian problems; to promote respect for human rights and fundamental freedoms; and to harmonize the activities of nations in order to achieve these common goals.

By 1991, the UN had expanded to 159 member countries; it is the largest international political organization, employing 23,000 people worldwide; its headquarters in New York accounts for 7,000 staff and it also has major offices in Rome, Geneva and Vienna.

The United Nations has six principal organs:

The General Assembly
The forum at which member nations discuss moral and political issues affecting world development, peace and security meets annually in September, under a newly-elected President whose tenure lasts one year. Any member can bring business to the agenda, and each member nation has one vote. Decisions are made by simple majority, save for matters of very great importance, when a two-thirds majority is required. While the General Assembly has no powers of enforcement, its recommendations to member nations are regarded as persuasive and it is empowered to instruct UN organs or agencies to implement its decisions.

The Security Council
A legislative and executive body, the Security Council is the primary instrument for establishing and maintaining international peace by attempting to settle disputes between nations. It has the power to dispatch UN forces to stop aggression, and member nations undertake to make armed forces, assistance and facilities available as required. The Security Council has ten temporary members elected by the General Assembly for two-year terms, and five permanent members - China, France, USSR, UK and USA. On questions of substance, the vote of each of the permanent members is required within the necessary nine-vote majority.

The Economic and Social Council
By far the largest United Nations executive, the Council operates as a conduit between the General Assembly and the many United Nations agencies it instructs to implement Assembly decisions, and whose work it coordinates. The Council also sets up commissions to examine economic conditions, collects data and issues studies and reports, and may make recommendations to the Assembly. The Council's overall aim is to help the peoples of the world with education, health and human rights. It has 54 member countries, elected by the General Assembly to three-year terms.

The Secretariat
This is the staff of the United Nations, and its task is to administer the policies and programmes of the UN and its organs, and assist and advise the Head of the Secretariat, the Secretary-General – a full-time, non-political, appointment made by the General Assembly.

The Trusteeship Council
The Council administers trust territories with the aim of promoting their advancement. Only one remains - the Trust Territory of the Pacific Is. (Palau), administered by the USA.

The International Court of Justice (the World Court)
The World Court is the judicial organ of the United Nations. It deals only with United Nations disputes and all members are subject to its jurisdiction, which includes both cases submitted to it by member nations and matters especially provided for in the Charter or in treaties. The Court's decisions are only binding in respect of a particular dispute; failure to heed a judgement may involve recourse to the Security Council. There are 15 judges, elected for nine-year terms by the General Assembly and the Security Council. The Court sits in The Hague.

United Nations agencies and programmes, and inter-governmental agencies coordinated by the UN, contribute to harmonious world development. Social and humanitarian operations include:

United Nations Development Programme (UNDP): plans and funds projects to help developing countries make better use of resources. Voluntary pledges of $1.3 billion were made for 1990, to fund almost 7,000 projects in 152 countries.

United Nations International Childrens' Fund (UNICEF): created at the General Assembly's first session in 1945 to help children in the aftermath of World War II, it now provides basic healthcare and aid worldwide. Voluntarily funded, three-quarters of its income is derived from government donations.

United Nations Fund for Population Activities (UNFPA): promotes awareness of population issues and family planning, providing appropriate assistance.

Food & Agriculture Organization (FAO): aims to raise living standards and nutrition levels in rural areas by improving food production and distribution.

United Nations Educational, Scientific & Cultural Organization (UNESCO): promotes international cooperation through broader and better education.

World Health Organization (WHO): promotes and provides for better health care, public and environmental health and medical research.

Membership: There are 13 independent states who are not members of the UN – Andorra, Kiribati, Liechtenstein, N. Korea, S. Korea, Monaco, Nauru, San Marino, Switzerland, Taiwan, Tonga, Tuvalu and Vatican City. The UN's 159 members include two who are not independent nations – the Soviet republics of Byelorussia and Ukraine. There were 51 members in 1945. Official languages are Chinese, English, French, Russian, Spanish and (a recent addition) Arabic.

Funding: The UN budget for 1988-1989 was US $ 1,788,746,000. Contributions are assessed by members' ability to pay, with the maximum 25% of the total, the minimum 0.01%. Contributions for 1988-1989 were: USA 25%, Japan 11.38%, USSR 9.99%, W. Germany 8.08%, France 6.25%, UK 4.86%, Italy 3.99%, Canada 3.09%, Spain 1.95%, Netherlands 1.65% (others 23.75%).

Peacekeeping: The UN has been involved in 18 peacekeeping operations worldwide since 1945, five of which (Afghanistan/Pakistan, Iran/Iraq, Angola, Namibia and Honduras) were initiated in 1988-1989. In June 1991 UN personnel totalling over 11,000 were working in eight separate areas.

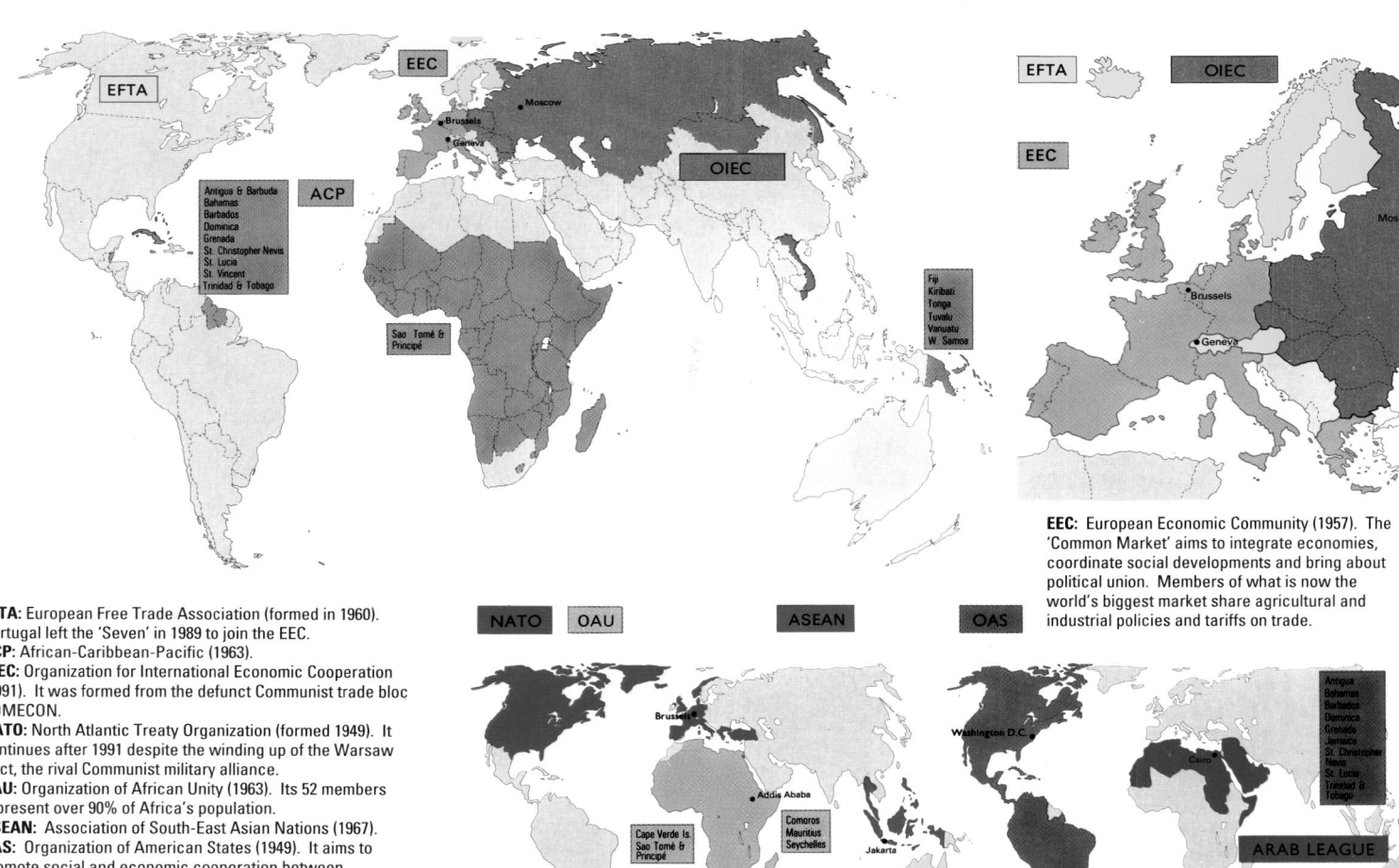

EFTA: European Free Trade Association (formed in 1960). Portugal left the 'Seven' in 1989 to join the EEC.
ACP: African-Caribbean-Pacific (1963).
OIEC: Organization for International Economic Cooperation (1991). It was formed from the defunct Communist trade bloc COMECON.
NATO: North Atlantic Treaty Organization (formed 1949). It continues after 1991 despite the winding up of the Warsaw Pact, the rival Communist military alliance.
OAU: Organization of African Unity (1963). Its 52 members represent over 90% of Africa's population.
ASEAN: Association of South-East Asian Nations (1967).
OAS: Organization of American States (1949). It aims to promote social and economic cooperation between developed countries of North America and developing nations of Latin America.
LAIA: Latin American Integration Association (1980).

United Nations agencies are involved in many aspects of international trade, safety and security:
General Agreement on Tariffs and Trade (GATT): sponsors international trade negotiations and advocates a common code of conduct.
International Maritime Organization (IMO): promotes unity amongst merchant shipping, especially in regard to safety, marine pollution and standardization.
International Labour Organization (ILO): seeks to improve labour conditions and promote productive employment to raise living standards.
World Meteorological Organization (WMO): promotes cooperation in weather observation, reporting and forecasting.
World Intellectual Property Organization (WIPO): seeks to protect intellectual property such as artistic copyright, scientific patents and trademarks.
Disarmament Commission: considers and makes recommendations to the General Assembly on disarmament issues.
International Atomic Energy Agency (IAEA): fosters development of peaceful uses for nuclear energy, establishes safety standards and monitors the destruction of nuclear material designed for military use.

EEC: European Economic Community (1957). The 'Common Market' aims to integrate economies, coordinate social developments and bring about political union. Members of what is now the world's biggest market share agricultural and industrial policies and tariffs on trade.

The World Bank comprises three United Nations agencies:
International Monetary Fund (IMF): cultivates international monetary cooperation and expansion of trade.
International Bank for Reconstruction & Development (IBRD): provides funds and technical assistance to developing countries.
International Finance Corporation (IFC): Encourages the growth of productive private enterprise in less developed countries.

OECD: Organization for Economic Cooperation and Development (1961). The 24 major Western free-market economies plus Yugoslavia as an associate member. 'G7' is its 'inner group' of USA, Canada, Japan, UK, Germany, Italy and France.
COMMONWEALTH: The Commonwealth of Nations evolved from the British Empire; it comprises 18 nations recognizing the British monarch as head of state and 32 nations with their own heads of state.
OPEC: Organization of Petroleum Exporting Countries (1960). It controls three-quarters of the world's oil supply.

PRODUCTION: AGRICULTURE

The invention of agriculture transformed human existence more than any other development, though it may not have seemed much of an improvement to its first practitioners. Primitive farming required brutally hard work, and it tied men and women to a patch of land, highly vulnerable to local weather patterns and to predators, especially human predators – drawbacks still apparent in much of the world today. It is difficult to imagine early humans being interested in such an existence while there were still animals around to hunt and wild seeds and berries to gather. Probably the spur was population pressure, with consequent overhunting and scarcity.

Despite its difficulties, the new life-style had a few overwhelming advantages. It supported far larger populations, eventually including substantial cities, with all the varied cultural and economic activities they allowed. Later still, it furnished the surpluses that allowed industrialization, another enormous step in human development.

Machines relieved many farmers of their burden of endless toil, and made it possible for relatively small numbers to provide food for more than five billion people.

Then as now, the whole business of farming involves the creation of a severely simplified ecology, under the tutelage and for the benefit of the farmer. Natural plant life is divided into crops, to be protected and nurtured, and weeds, the rest, to be destroyed. From the earliest days, crops were selectively bred to increase their food yield, usually at the expense of their ability to survive, which became the farmer's responsibility; 20th-century plant geneticists have carried the technique to highly productive extremes. Due mainly to new varieties of rice and wheat, world grain production has increased by 70% since 1965, more than doubling in the developing countries, although such high yields demand equally high consumption of fertilizers and pesticides to maintain them. Mechanized farmers in North America and Europe continue to turn out huge surpluses, although not without environmental costs.

Where production is inadequate, the reasons are as likely to be political as agricultural. The Soviet Union, with a high proportion of the world's best farmland at its disposal, continues to record dismal harvests. Africa, the only continent where food production per capita is actually falling, suffers even more acutely from economic mismanagement, as well as from the traditional enemies of war and banditry.

There are other limits to progress. Increasing population puts relentless pressure on farmers not only to maintain high yields but also to increase them. Most of the world's potential cropland is already under the plough. The over-working of marginal land is one of the prime causes of desertification; new farmlands burned out of former rainforests are seldom fertile for long. Human numbers may yet outrun the land's ability to feed them, as they did almost 10,000 years ago.

SELF-SUFFICIENCY IN FOOD

Balance of trade in food products as a percentage of total trade in food products (1988)

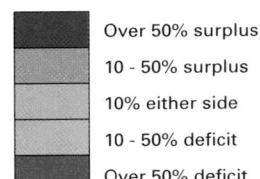

- Over 50% surplus
- 10 - 50% surplus
- 10% either side
- 10 - 50% deficit
- Over 50% deficit

Most self-sufficient		Least self-sufficient	
Uganda	93%	Algeria	-97%
Argentina	92%	Saudi Arabia	-95%
Burma	86%	Czechoslovakia	-92%
Chile	82%	Venezuela	-92%
Iceland	82%	Gabon	-88%
Uruguay	82%	Oman	-88%
Kenya	80%	Syria	-88%
New Zealand	80%	Egypt	-86%
Costa Rica	79%	Japan	-85%

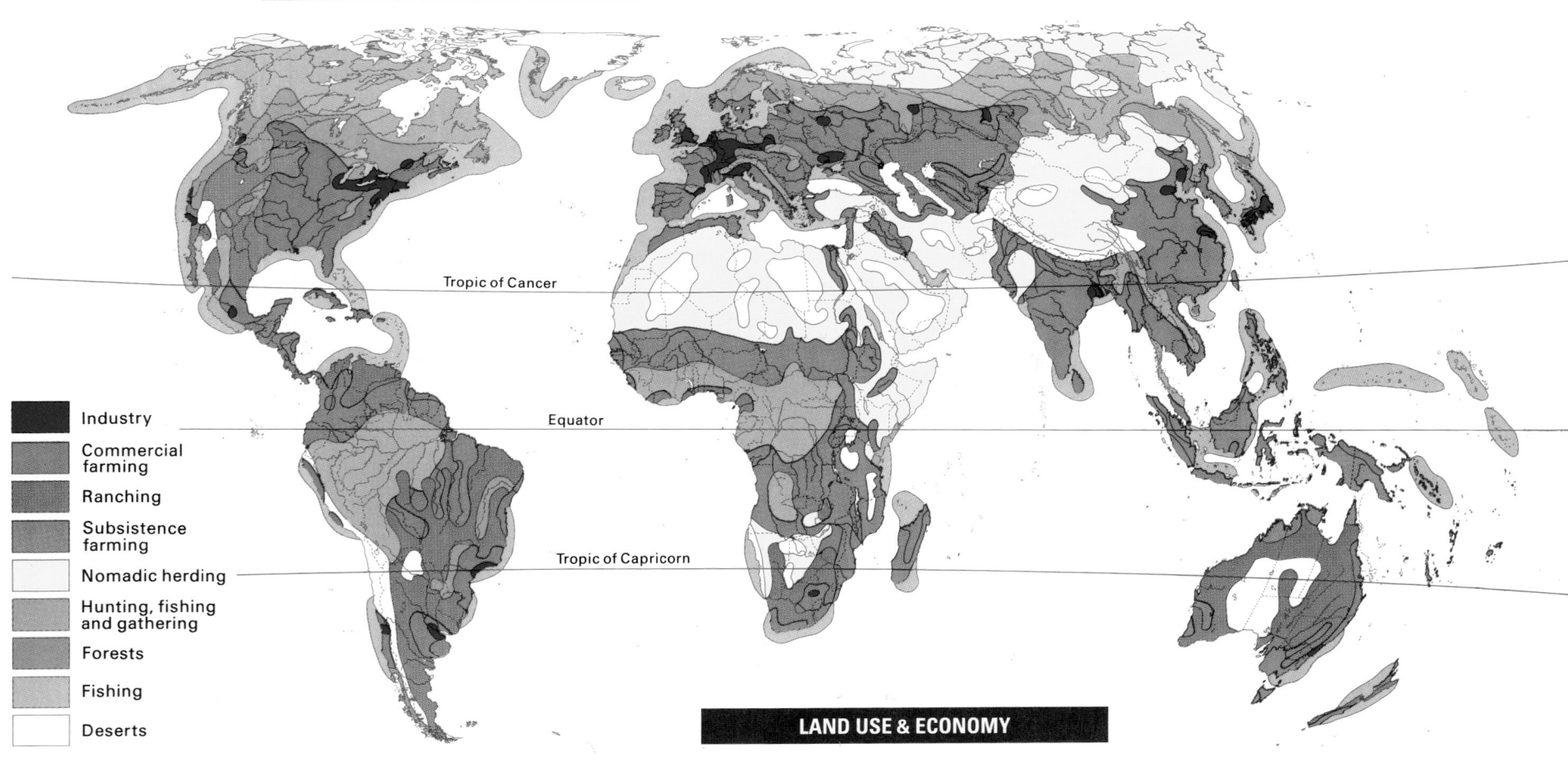

- Industry
- Commercial farming
- Ranching
- Subsistence farming
- Nomadic herding
- Hunting, fishing and gathering
- Forests
- Fishing
- Deserts

Tropic of Cancer

Equator

Tropic of Capricorn

LAND USE & ECONOMY

STAPLE CROPS

Wheat: Grown in a range of climates, with most varieties - including the highest-quality bread wheats - requiring temperate conditions. Mainly used in baking, it is also used for pasta and breakfast cereals.

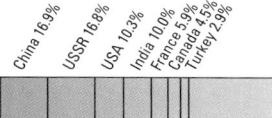

World total (1989): 538,056,000 tonnes

Maize: Originating in the New World and still an important human food in Africa and Latin America, in the developed world it is processed into breakfast cereals, oil, starches and adhesives. It is also used for animal feed.

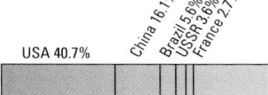

World total (1989): 470,318,000 tonnes

Oats: Most widely used to feed livestock, but eaten by humans as oatmeal or porridge. Oats have a beneficial effect on the cardio-vascular system, and human consumption is likely to increase.

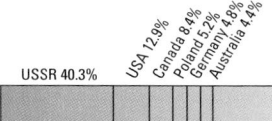

World total (1989): 42,197,000 tonnes

Millet: The name covers a number of small grained cereals, members of the grass family with a short growing season. Used to produce flour and meal, animal feed and fermented to make beer, especially in Africa.

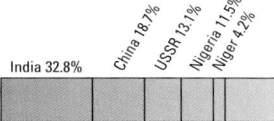

World total (1989): 30,512,000 tonnes

Cassava: A tropical shrub that needs high rainfall (over 1000 mm annually) and a 10 - 30 month growing season to produce its large, edible tubers. Used as flour by humans, as cattle feed and in industrial starches.

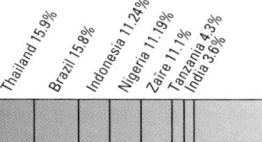

World total (1989): 147,500,000 tonnes

Cereals are grasses with starchy, edible seeds; every important civilization has depended on them as a source of food. The major cereal grains contain about 10% protein and 75% carbohydrate; grain is easy to store, handle and transport, and contributes more than any other group of foods to the energy and protein content of human diet. If all the cereals were consumed directly by man, there would be no shortage of food in the world, but a considerable proportion of the total output is used as animal feed.

Starchy tuber crops or root crops, represented here by potatoes and cassava, are second in importance only to cereals as staple foods; easily cultivated, they provide high yields for little effort and store well – potatoes for up to six months, cassava for up to a year in the ground. Protein content is low (2% or less), starch content high, with some minerals and vitamins present, but populations that rely heavily on these crops may suffer from malnutrition.

Rice: Thrives on the high humidity and temperatures of the Far East, where it is the traditional staple food of half the human race. Usually grown standing in water, rice responds well to continuous cultivation, with three or four crops annually.

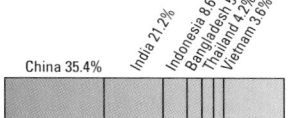

World total (1989): 506,291,000 tonnes

Barley: Primarily used as animal feed, but widely eaten by humans in Africa and Asia. Elsewhere, malted barley furnishes beer and spirits. Able to withstand the dry heat of sub-arid tropics, its growing season is only 80 days.

World total (1989): 168,964,000 tonnes

Rye: Hardy and tolerant of poor and sandy soils, it is an important foodstuff and animal feed in Central and Eastern Europe and the USSR. Rye produces a dark, heavy bread as well as alcoholic drinks.

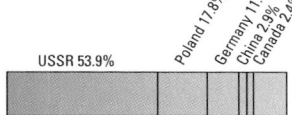

World total (1989): 34,893,000 tonnes

Potatoes: The most important of the edible tubers, potatoes grow in well-watered, temperate areas. Weight for weight less nutritious than grain, they are a human staple as well as an important animal feed.

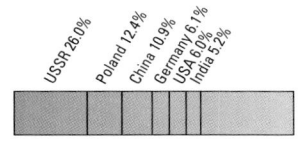

World total (1989): 276,740,000 tonnes

Soya: Beans from soya bushes are very high - 30-40% - in protein. Most are processed into oil and proprietary protein foods. Consumption since 1950 has tripled, mainly due to the health-conscious developed world.

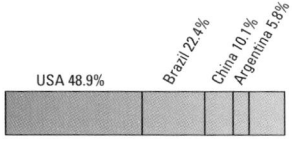

World total (1989): 107,350,000 tonnes

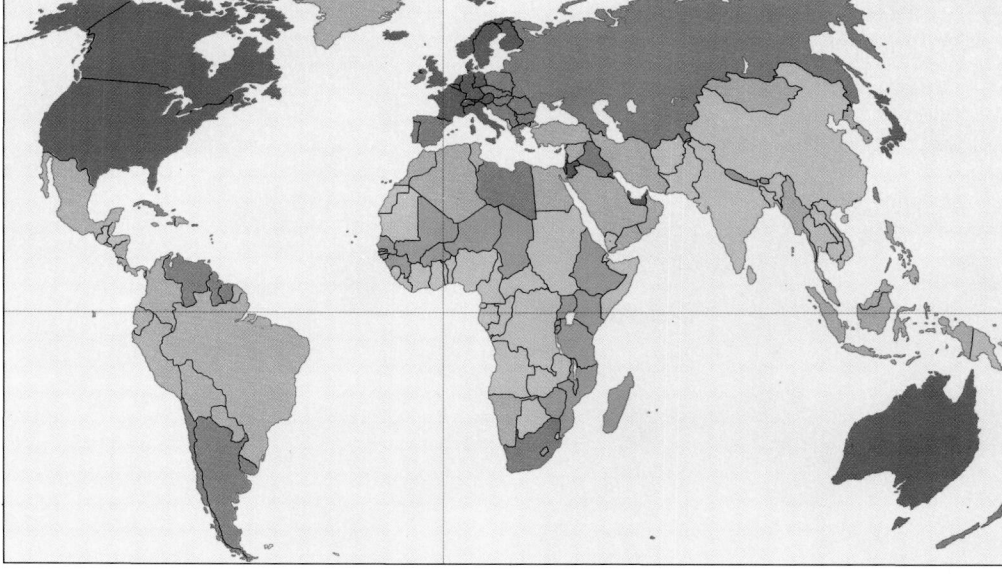

IMPORTANCE OF AGRICULTURE

Percentage of the total population dependent on agriculture (1989)

- Over 75%
- 50 - 75%
- 25 - 50%
- 10 - 25%
- Under 10%

Most dependent		Least dependent	
Nepal	91.5%	Singapore	1.0%
Burundi	91.4%	Hong Kong	1.3%
Bhutan	90.9%	Bahrain	1.8%
Niger	87.7%	Belgium¹	1.9%
Burkina Faso	84.6%	UK	2.0%
Mozambique	81.9%	USA	2.4%
Mali	81.4%	UAE	2.7%
Tanzania	81.4%	Puerto Rico	3.0%

¹ includes Luxembourg

FOOD & POPULATION

Comparison of food production and population by continent (1989). The left column indicates percentage shares of total world food production; the right shows population in proportion.

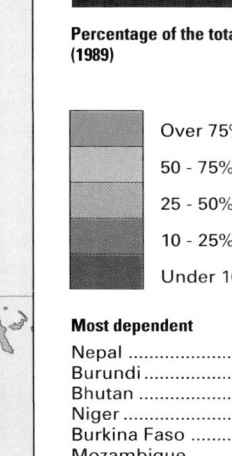

Australasia 1.2% / 0.4%
Europe 27.6% / 15.5%
Asia 44.5% / 58.3%
S. America 6.5% / 6.7%
N. America 13.8% / 7.1%
Africa 6.7% / 12.0%

FOOD — POPULATION

ANIMAL PRODUCTS

Traditionally, food animals subsisted on land unsuitable for cultivation, supporting agricultural production with their fertilizing dung. But free-ranging animals grow slowly and yield less meat than those more intensively reared; the demands of urban markets in the developed world have encouraged the growth of factory-like production methods. A large proportion of staple crops, especially cereals, are fed to animals, an inefficient way to produce protein but one likely to continue as long as people value meat and dairy products in their diet.

Cheese: Least perishable of all dairy products, cheese is milk fermented with selected bacterial strains to produce a foodstuff with a potentially immense range of flavours and textures. The vast majority of cheeses are made from cow's milk, although sheep and goat cheeses are highly prized.

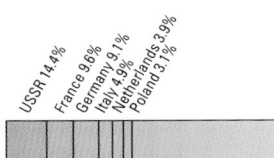

World total (1989): 14,475,276 tonnes

Lamb & Mutton: Sheep are the least demanding of domestic animals. Although unsuited to intensive rearing, they can thrive on marginal pastureland incapable of supporting beef cattle on a commercial scale. Sheep are raised as much for their valuable wool as for the meat that they provide, with Australia the world leader.

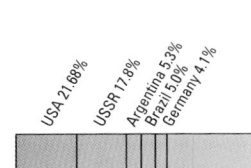

World total (1989): 6,473,000 tonnes

Beef & Veal: Most beef and veal is reared for home markets, and the top five producers are also the biggest consumers. The USA produces nearly a quarter of the world's beef and eats even more. Australia, with its small domestic market, is by far the largest exporter.

World total (1989): 49,436,000 tonnes

Sugar cane: Confined to tropical regions, cane sugar accounts for the bulk of international trade in the commodity. Most is produced as a foodstuff, but some countries, notably Brazil and South Africa, distill sugar cane and use the resulting ethyl alcohol to make motor fuels.

World total (1989): 1,007,184,000 tonnes

SUGARS

Milk: Many human groups, including most Asians, find raw milk indigestible after infancy, and it is often only the starting point for other dairy products such as butter, cheese and yoghurt. Most world milk production comes from cows, but sheep's milk and goats' milk are also important.

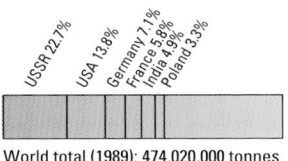

World total (1989): 474,020,000 tonnes

Butter: A traditional source of vitamin A as well as calories, butter has lost much popularity in the developed world for health reasons, although it remains a valuable food. Most butter from India, the world's second-largest producer, is clarified into ghee, which has religious as well as nutritional importance.

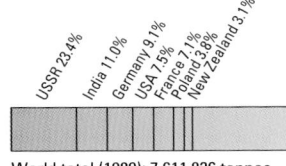

World total (1989): 7,611,826 tonnes

Pork: Although pork is forbidden to many millions, notably Muslims, on religious grounds, more is produced than any other meat in the world, mainly because it is the cheapest. It accounts for about 90% of China's meat output, although per capita meat consumption is relatively low.

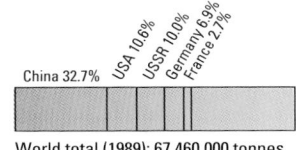

World total (1989): 67,460,000 tonnes

Fish: Commercial fishing requires large shoals of fish, of only one species, within easy reach of markets. Although the great majority are caught wild in the sea, fish-farming of both marine and freshwater species is assuming increasing importance, especially as natural stocks become depleted.

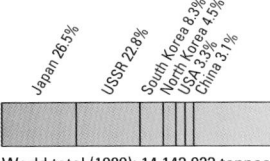

World total (1989): 14,143,923 tonnes

Sugar beet: A temperate crop closely related to the humble beetroot, sugar beet's yield after processing is indistinguishable from cane sugar. Sugar beet is steadily replacing sugar cane imports in Europe, to the detriment of the developing countries that rely on it as a major cash crop.

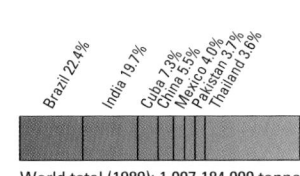

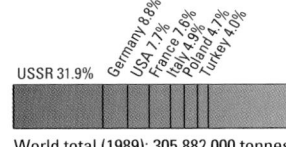

World total (1989): 305,882,000 tonnes

PRODUCTION: ENERGY

We live in a high-energy civilization. While vast discrepancies exist between rich and poor – a North American consumes 13 times as much energy as a Chinese, for example – even developing nations have more power at their disposal than was imaginable a century ago. Abundant energy supplies keep us warm or cool, fuel our industries and our transport systems, even feed us: high-intensity agriculture, with its fertilizers, pesticides and machinery, is heavily energy-dependent.

Unfortunately, most of the world's energy comes from fossil fuels: coal, oil and gas deposits laid down over many millions of years. These are the Earth's capital, not its income, and we are consuming that capital at an alarming rate (see box, opposite). New discoveries have persistently extended the known reserves: in 1989, the reserves-to-production ratio for oil assured over 45 years' supply, an improvement of almost a decade on the 1970 situation. But despite the effort and ingenuity of prospectors, stocks are clearly limited. They are also very unequally distributed, with the Middle East accounting for most oil reserves, and the USSR possessing an even higher proportion of the world's natural gas. Coal reserves are more evenly shared, and also more plentiful: coal should outlast oil and gas by a very wide margin.

It is possible to reduce energy demand by improving efficiency: most industrial nations have dramatically increased output since the 1970s without a matching rise in energy consumption. But as fossil stocks continue to diminish, renewable energy sources – solar, wave and wind power, as well as more conventional hydro-electricity – must take on steadily greater importance.

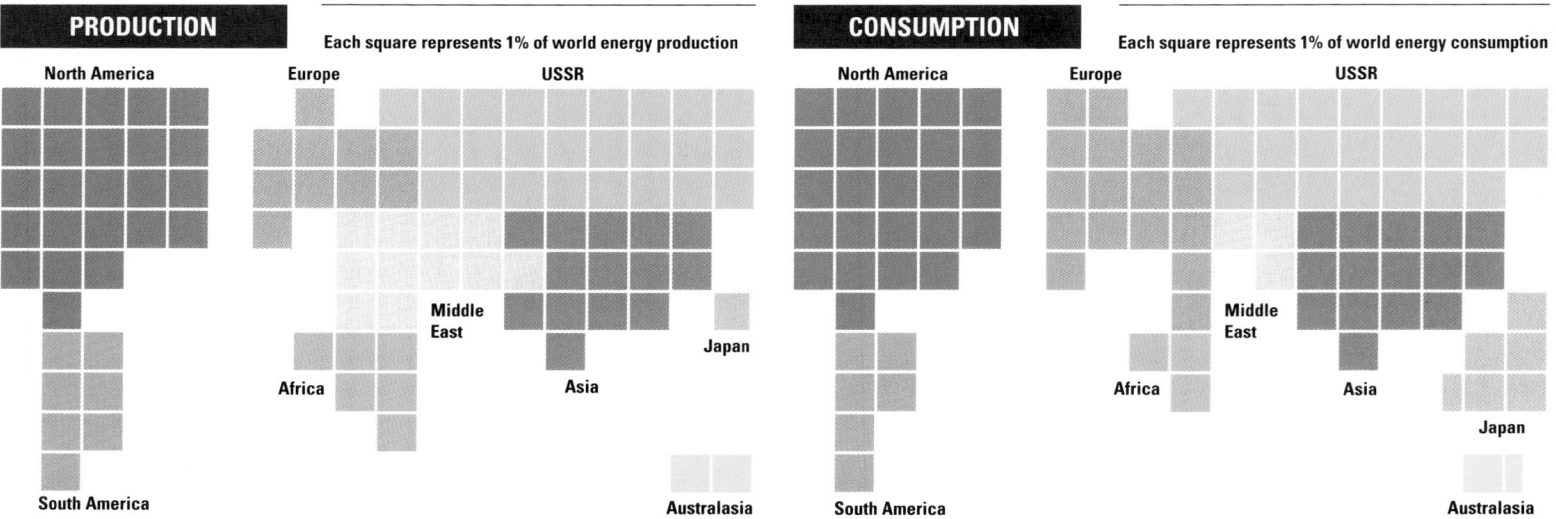

PRODUCTION
Each square represents 1% of world energy production

North America · Europe · USSR · Middle East · Japan · Africa · Asia · South America · Australasia

CONSUMPTION
Each square represents 1% of world energy consumption

North America · Europe · USSR · Middle East · Africa · Asia · Japan · South America · Australasia

CONVERSIONS

For historical reasons, oil is still traded in 'barrels'. The weight and volume equivalents shown below are all based on average density 'Arabian light' crude oil, and should be considered approximate.

The energy equivalents given for a tonne of oil are also somewhat imprecise: oil and coal of different qualities will have varying energy contents, a fact usually reflected in their price on world markets.

1 barrel:
   0.136 tonnes
   159 litres
   35 Imperial gallons
   42 US gallons

1 tonne:
   7.33 barrels
   1185 litres
   256 Imperial gallons
   261 US gallons

1 tonne oil:
   1.5 tonnes hard coal
   3.0 tonnes lignite
   12,000 kWh

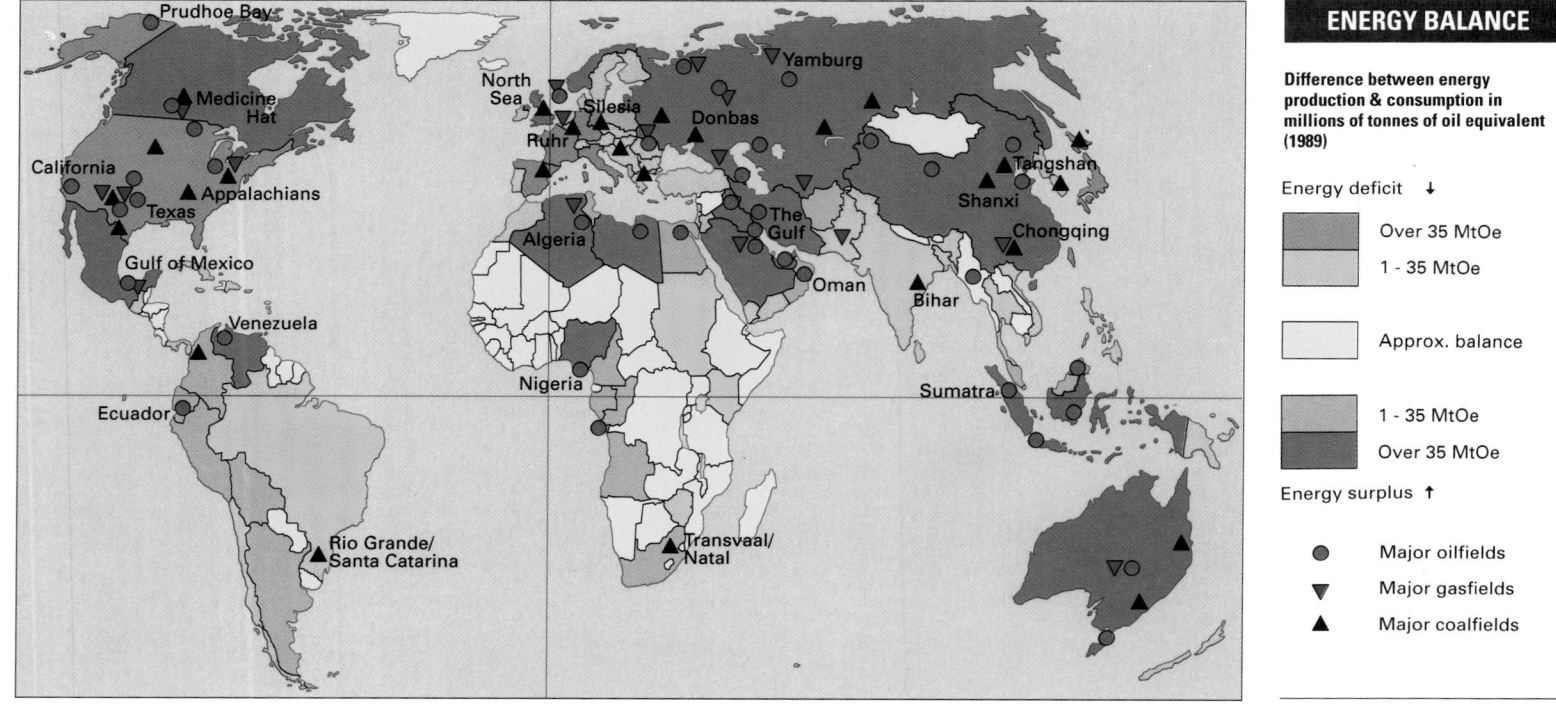

Prudhoe Bay · Medicine Hat · California · Appalachians · Texas · Gulf of Mexico · Venezuela · Ecuador · Rio Grande/Santa Catarina · North Sea · Ruhr · Silesia · Donbas · Yamburg · Algeria · The Gulf · Oman · Nigeria · Transvaal/Natal · Tangshan · Shanxi · Chongqing · Bihar · Sumatra

ENERGY BALANCE

Difference between energy production & consumption in millions of tonnes of oil equivalent (1989)

Energy deficit ↓
- Over 35 MtOe
- 1 - 35 MtOe

- Approx. balance

- 1 - 35 MtOe
- Over 35 MtOe

Energy surplus ↑

- ● Major oilfields
- ▽ Major gasfields
- ▲ Major coalfields

SOURCES OF WORLD ENERGY

Oil · Gas · Coal · Nuclear · Hydro

Australasia · Africa · Latin America · Western Europe · Middle East · Asia · North America · USSR & Eastern Europe

Energy produced by all world regions, measured in million tonnes of oil equivalent (1989): total world production was 8019 MtOe. Only energy from oil, gas, coal, nuclear and hydro-electric sources is included: wind, solar and geothermal power together met only 0.025% of the global demand.

Pie chart: 6.6% · 38.5% · 21.5% · 27.8% · 5.6%

FOSSIL FUEL RESERVES

Known world reserves in years as a multiple of annual production, 1970, 1980 and 1989

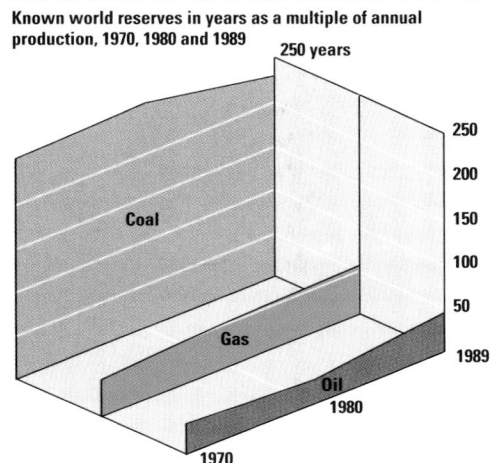

250 years

Coal

Gas

Oil

1989
1980
1970

250
200
150
100
50

ENERGY AND OUTPUT

Tonnes of oil equivalent consumed to produce US $1000 of GDP, four industrial nations (1973-89)

Intensity of energy use is a rough indicator of efficiency: the 1973-4 oil crisis caused a dramatic improvement in each of the countries illustrated, though the USA remains relatively profligate. Exactly comparable figures for communist economies are not available, but estimates suggest that for equivalent production, the USSR and China use between two and four times as much energy as the USA.

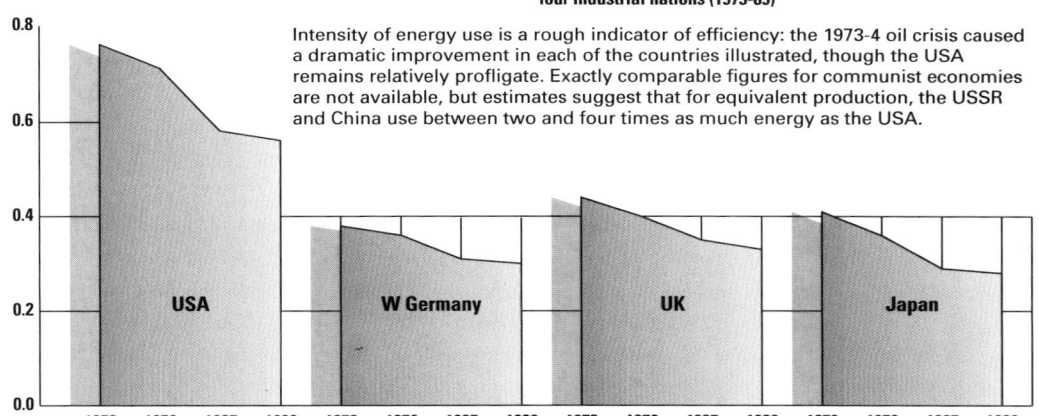

USA   W Germany   UK   Japan

1973 1979 1985 1989 | 1973 1979 1985 1989 | 1973 1979 1985 1989 | 1973 1979 1985 1989

COAL RESERVES

World coal reserves by region & country, thousand million tonnes (1988)

EG: E. Germany
Co: Colombia

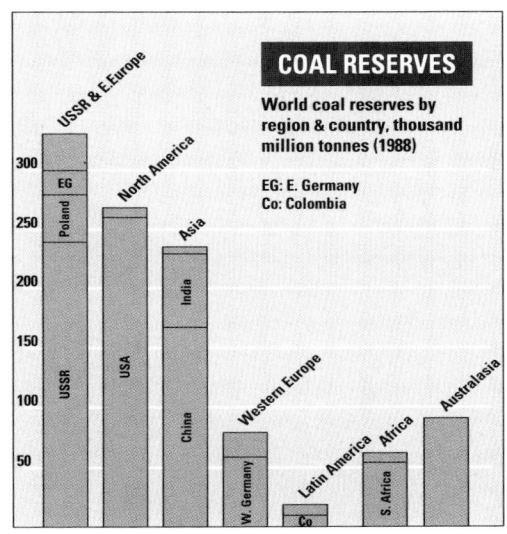

GAS RESERVES

World natural gas reserves by region & country, thousand million tonnes (1988)

Ca: Canada
In: Indonesia
Ma: Malaysia
AD: Abu Dhabi
SA: Saudi Arabia
Qa: Qatar
Iq: Iraq
No: Norway
Ne: Netherlands
Ve: Venezuela
Mx: Mexico
Al: Algeria
Ni: Nigeria

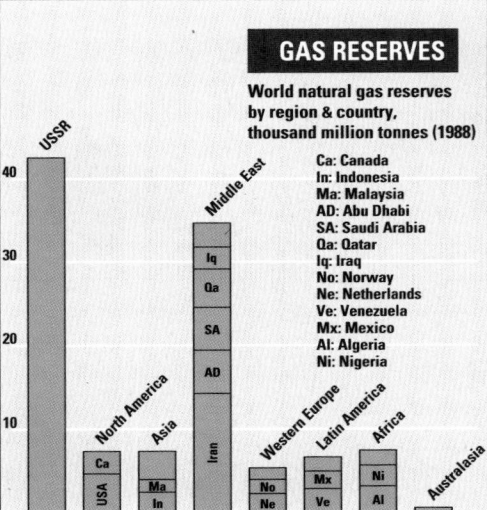

OIL RESERVES

World oil reserves by region & country, thousand million tonnes (1988)

AD: Abu Dhabi
Ve: Venezuela
Mx: Mexico

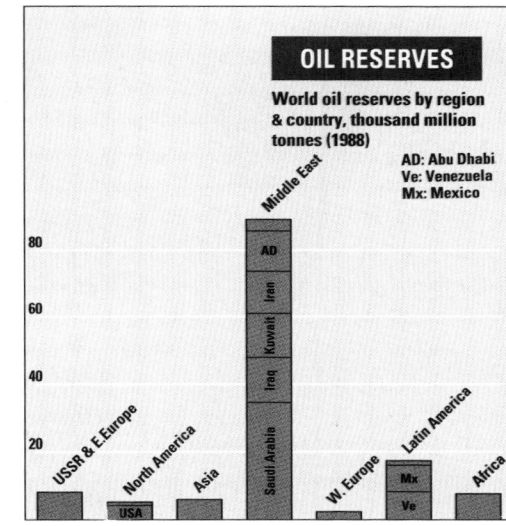

OIL MOVEMENTS

Major world movements of oil in millions of tonnes (1989)

Middle East to Western Europe	195.5
Middle East to Japan	150.0
Middle East to Asia (exc. Japan and China)	127.5
Latin America to USA	126.1
Middle East to USA	94.1
USSR to Western Europe	78.1
North Africa to Western Europe	93.5
West Africa to Western Europe	39.6
West Africa to USA	59.8
Canada to USA	45.0
South-East Asia to Japan	42.2
Latin America to Western Europe	28.7
Western Europe to USA	28.7
Middle East to Latin America	20.5

Total world movements: 1577 million tonnes

Only inter-regional movements in excess of 20 million tonnes are shown. Other Middle Eastern oil shipments throughout the world totalled 47.4 million tonnes; miscellaneous USSR oil exports amounted to 88.8 million tonnes.

FUEL EXPORTS

Fuels as a percentage of total value of all exports (1986)

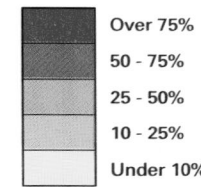

Over 75%
50 - 75%
25 - 50%
10 - 25%
Under 10%

Direction of trade

Coal
Oil

Arrows show the major trade direction of selected fuels, & are proportional to export value

NUCLEAR POWER

Percentage of electricity generated by nuclear power stations, leading nations (1988)

1.	France	70%	11. W. Germany	34%
2.	Belgium	66%	12. Japan	28%
3.	Hungary	49%	13. Czechoslovakia	27%
4.	South Korea	47%	14. UK	18%
5.	Sweden	46%	15. USA	17%
6.	Taiwan	41%	16. Canada	16%
7.	Switzerland	37%	17. Argentina	12%
8.	Finland	36%	18. USSR	11%
9.	Spain	36%	19. Yugoslavia	6%
10.	Bulgaria	36%	20. Netherlands	5%

The decade 1980-1990 was a bad time for the nuclear power industry. Major projects regularly ran vastly over-budget, and fears of long-term environmental damage were heavily reinforced by the 1986 Soviet disaster at Chernobyl. Although the number of reactors in service continued to increase throughout the period, orders for new plant shrank dramatically, and most countries cut back on their nuclear programmes.

HYDRO-ELECTRICITY

Percentage of electricity generated by hydro-electrical power stations, leading nations (1988)

1.	Paraguay	99.9%	11. Laos	95.5%
2.	Zambia	99.6%	12. Nepal	95.2%
3.	Norway	99.5%	13. Iceland	94.0%
4.	Congo	99.1%	14. Uruguay	93.0%
5.	Costa Rica	98.3%	15. Brazil	91.7%
6.	Uganda	98.3%	16. Albania	87.2%
7.	Rwanda	97.7%	17. Fiji	81.4%
8.	Malawi	97.6%	18. Ecuador	80.7%
9.	Zaïre	97.4%	19. C. African Rep.	80.4%
10.	Cameroon	97.2%	20. Sri Lanka	80.4%

Countries heavily reliant on hydro-electricity are usually small and non-industrial: a high proportion of hydro-electric power more often reflects a modest energy budget than vast hydro-electric resources. The USA, for instance, produces only 8% of power requirements from hydro-electricity; yet that 8% amounts to more than three times the hydro-power generated by all of Africa.

ALTERNATIVE ENERGY SOURCES

Solar: Each year the sun bestows upon the Earth almost a million times as much energy as is locked up in all the planet's oil reserves, but only an insignificant fraction is trapped and used commercially. In some experimental installations, mirrors focus the sun's rays on to boilers, whose steam generates electricity by spinning turbines. Solar cells turn the sunlight into electricity directly, and although efficiencies are still low, advancing technology offers some prospect of using the sun as the main world electricity source by 2100.

Wind: Caused by uneven heating of the Earth, winds are themselves a form of solar energy. Windmills have been used for centuries to turn wind power into mechanical work; recent models, often arranged in banks on gust-swept high ground, usually generate electricity.

Tidal: The energy from tides is potentially enormous, although only a few installations have been built to exploit it. In theory at least, waves and currents could also provide almost unimaginable power, and the thermal differences in the ocean depths are another huge well of potential energy. But work on extracting it is still in the experimental stage.

Geothermal: The Earth's temperature rises by 1°C for every 30 metres' descent, with much steeper temperature gradients in geologically active areas. El Salvador, for example, produces 39% of its electricity from geothermal power stations. More than 130 are operating worldwide.

Biomass: The oldest of human fuels ranges from animal dung, still burned in cooking fires in much of North Africa and elsewhere, to sugar cane plantations feeding high-technology distilleries to produce ethanol for motor vehicle engines. In Brazil and South Africa, plant ethanol provides up to 25% of motor fuel. Throughout the developing world most biomass energy comes from firewood: although accurate figures are impossible to obtain, it may yield as much as 10% of the world's total energy consumption.

PRODUCTION: MINERALS

Even during the Stone Age, when humans often settled near the outcrops of flint on which their technology depended, mineral resources have attracted human exploiters. Their descendants have learned how to make use of almost every known element. These elements can be found, in one form or another, somewhere in the Earth's bountiful crust. Iron remains the most important, but modern industrial civilization has a voracious appetite for virtually all of them.

Mineral deposits once dictated the site of new industries; today, most industrial countries are heavily dependent on imports for many of their key materials. Most mining, and much refining of raw ores, is done in developing countries, where labour is cheap.

The main map below shows the richest sources of the most important minerals at present; some reserves – lead and mercury, for example – are running very low. The map takes no account of undersea deposits, most of which are considered inaccessible. Growing shortages, though, may encourage submarine mining: plans have already been made to recover the nodules of manganese found widely scattered on ocean floors.

MINERAL EXPORTS

Minerals & metals as a percentage of total exports (1986)

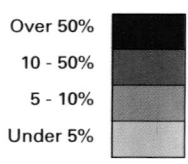

- Over 50%
- 10 - 50%
- 5 - 10%
- Under 5%

Direction of trade

- Copper
- Iron
- Bauxite (Aluminium)

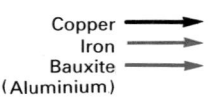

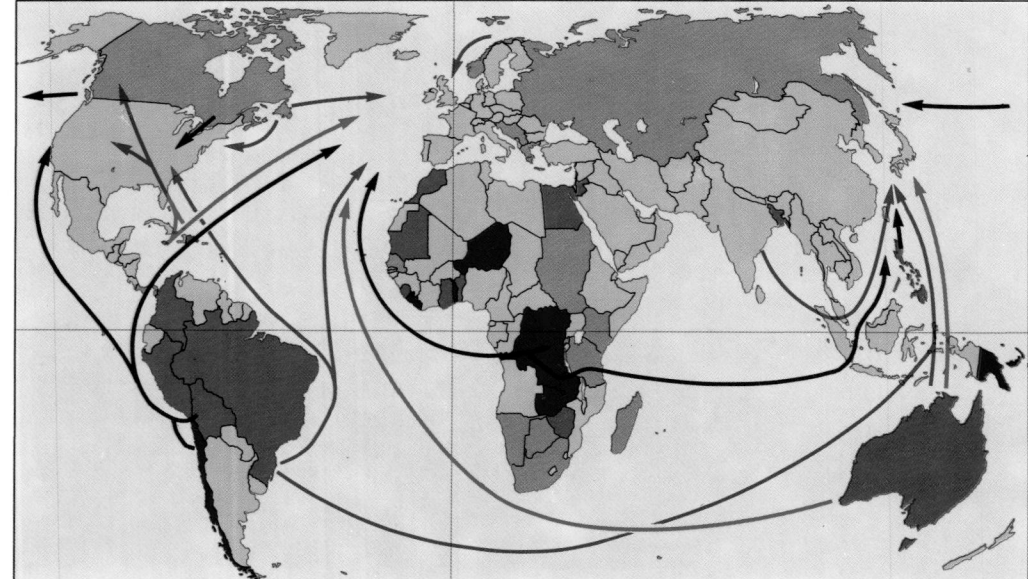

URANIUM

In its pure state, uranium is an immensely heavy, white metal; but although spent uranium is employed as projectiles in anti-missile cannon, where its mass ensures a lethal punch, its main use is as a fuel in nuclear reactors, and in nuclear weaponry. Uranium is very scarce: the main source is the rare ore pitchblende, which itself contains only 0.2% uranium oxide. Only a minute fraction of that is the radioactive U^{235} isotope, though so-called breeder reactors can transmute the more common U^{238} into highly radioactive plutonium. The USSR is known to have large reserves.

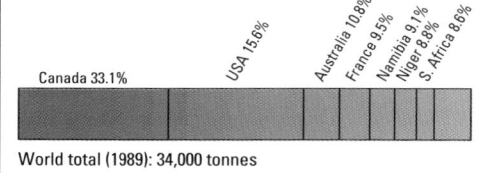

Canada 33.1% | USA 15.6% | Australia 10.8% | France 9.5% | Namibia 9.1% | Niger 8.8% | S. Africa 8.6%

World total (1989): 34,000 tonnes

Aluminium: Produced mainly from its oxide, bauxite, which yields 25% of its weight in aluminium. The cost of refining and production is often too high for producer-countries to bear, so bauxite is largely exported. Lightweight and corrosion resistant, aluminium alloys are widely used in aircraft, vehicles, cans and packaging.

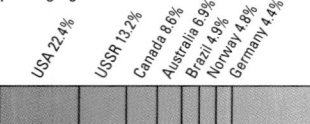

USA 22.4% | USSR 13.2% | Canada 8.6% | Australia 6.9% | Brazil 4.9% | Norway 4.8% | Germany 4.4%

World total (1989): 18,000,000 tonnes *

Copper: Derived from low-yielding sulphide ores, copper is an important export for several developing countries. An excellent conductor of heat and electricity, it forms part of most electrical items, and is used in the manufacture of brass and bronze. Major importers include Japan and Germany.

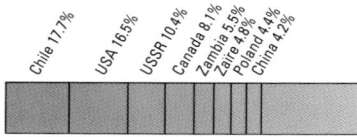

Chile 17.7% | USA 16.5% | USSR 10.4% | Canada 8.1% | Zambia 5.5% | Zaïre 4.8% | Poland 4.4% | China 4.2%

World total (1989): 9,100,000 tonnes *

Lead: A soft metal, obtained mainly from galena (lead sulphide), which occurs in veins associated with iron, zinc and silver sulphides. Its use in vehicle batteries accounts for the USA's prime consumer status; lead is also made into sheeting and piping. Its use as an additive to paints and petrol is decreasing.

USSR 14.7% | Australia 14.6% | USA 12.3% | China 10.1% | Canada 8.1% | Peru 5.7% | Mexico 4.9%

World total (1989): 3,400,000 tonnes *

Mercury: The only metal that is liquid at normal temperatures, most is derived from its sulphide, cinnabar, found only in small quantities in volcanic areas. Apart from its value in thermometers and other instruments, most mercury production is used in anti-fungal and anti-fouling preparations, and to make detonators.

USSR 27.3% | China 18.2% | Spain 17.6% | Algeria 12.7% | USA 7.8% | Mexico 6.3% | Turkey 3.7%

World total (1989): 5,500,000 kilograms *

DIAMOND

Most diamond is found in kimberlite, or "blue ground", a basic peridotite rock; erosion may wash the diamond from its kimerlite matrix and deposit it with sand or gravel on river beds. Only a small proportion of the world's diamond, the most flawless, is cut into gemstones - "diamonds"; most is used in industry, where the material's remarkable hardness and abrasion resistance finds a use in cutting tools, drills and dies, as well as in styluses. Australia, not among the top 12 producers at the beginning of the 1980s, had by 1986 become world leader and by 1989 was the source of 37.5% of world production. The other main producers were Zaïre (18.9%), Botswana (16.3%), the USSR (11.8%) and South Africa (9.7%). Between them, these five nations accounted for over 94% of the world total of 96,600,000 carats - at 0.2 grams per carat, almost one tonne.

Tin: Soft, pliable and non-toxic, used to coat 'tin' (tin-plated steel) cans, in the manufacture of foils and in alloys. The principal tin-bearing mineral is cassiterite (SnO_2), found in ore formed from molten rock. Producers and refiners were hit by a price collapse in 1991.

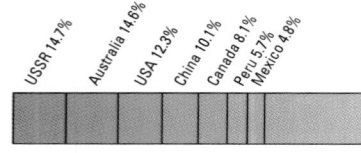

Brazil 22.5% | China 14.8% | Malaysia 14.4% | Indonesia 14.2% | Bolivia 7.1% | Thailand 6.6% | USSR 6.3%

World total (1989): 223,000 tonnes *

Zinc: Often found in association with lead ores, zinc is highly resistant to corrosion, and about 40% of the refined metal is used to plate sheet steel, particularly vehicle bodies – a process known as galvanizing. Zinc is also used in dry batteries, paints and dyes.

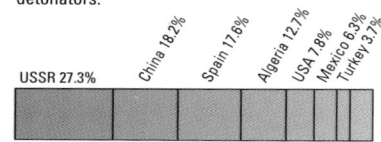

Canada 16.6% | USSR 12.9% | Australia 11.0% | China 8.5% | Peru 9.2% | USA 4.0% | Mexico 3.9%

World total (1989): 7,300,000 tonnes *

Gold: Regarded for centuries as the most valuable metal in the world and used to make coins, gold is still recognized as the monetary standard. A soft metal, it is alloyed to make jewellery; the electronics industry values its corrosion resistance and conductivity.

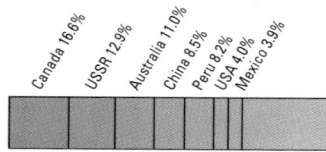

S. Africa 29.9% | USSR 14.1% | USA 13.1% | Australia 10.0% | Canada 3.9% | China 4.2% | Brazil 2.4%

World total (1989): 2,026,000 kilograms *

Silver: Most silver comes from ores mined and processed for other metals (including lead and copper). Pure or alloyed with harder metals, it is used for jewellery and ornaments. Industrial use includes dentistry, electronics, photography and as a chemical catalyst.

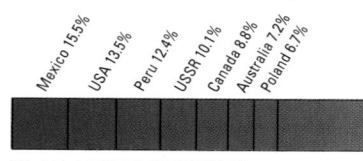

Mexico 15.5% | USA 13.5% | Peru 12.4% | USSR 10.1% | Canada 8.8% | Australia 7.2% | Poland 6.7%

World total (1989): 14,896,000 kilograms *

* Figures for aluminium are for refined metal, all other figures refer to ore production.

STRUCTURAL REGIONS

- Pre-Cambrian shields
- Sedimentary cover on Pre-Cambrian shields
- Palæozoic (Caledonian and Hercynian) folding
- Sedimentary cover on Palæozoic folding
- Mesozoic folding
- Sedimentary cover on Mesozoic folding
- Cainozoic (Alpine) folding
- Sedimentary cover on Cainozoic folding

Sullivan
Sudbury
Great Lakes
Asbestos
Bingham
Arizona
Florida
Tropic of Cancer
Jamaica
Carajas
Rondonia
Minas Gerais

IRON & FERRO-ALLOYS

Ever since the art of high-temperature smelting was discovered, some time in the second millennium BC, iron has been by far the most important metal known to man. The earliest iron ploughs transformed primitive agriculture and led to the first human population explosion, while iron weapons - or the lack of them - ensured the rise or fall of entire cultures.

Widely distributed around the world, iron ores usually contain 25-60% iron; blast furnaces process the raw product into pig-iron, which is then alloyed with carbon other minerals to produce steels of various qualities. From the time of the Industrial Revolution steel has been almost literally the backbone of modern civilization, the prime structural material on which all else is built.

Iron-smelting usually developed close to sources of ore and, later, to the coalfields that fueled the furnaces. Today, most ore comes from a few richly-endowed locations where large-scale mining is possible. Iron and steel plants are generally built at coastal sites so that giant ore carriers, which account for a sizeable proportion of the world's merchant fleet, can easily discharge their cargoes.

World production of pig iron and ferro-alloys (1988). All countries with an annual output of more than one million tonnes are shown

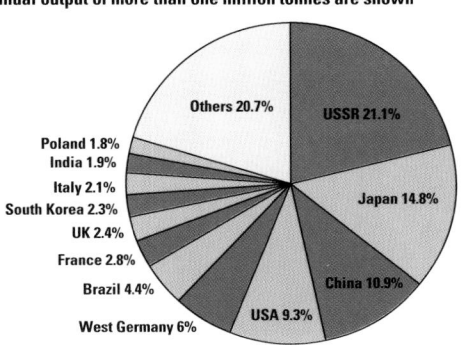

Others 20.7%
USSR 21.1%
Japan 14.8%
China 10.9%
USA 9.3%
West Germany 6%
Brazil 4.4%
France 2.8%
UK 2.4%
South Korea 2.3%
Italy 2.1%
India 1.9%
Poland 1.8%

Total world production: 545 million tonnes

Development of world production of pig iron and ferro-alloys (1945-1988) in million tonnes

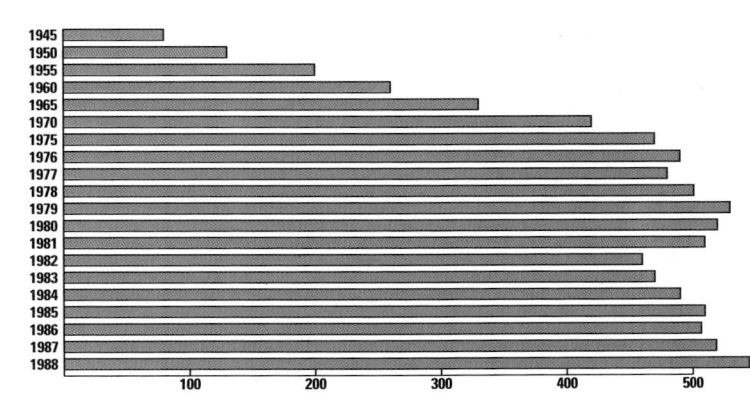

Chromium: Most of the world's chromium production is alloyed with iron and other metals to produce steels with various different properties. Combined with iron, nickel, cobalt and tungsten, chromium produces an exceptionally hard steel, resistant to heat; chrome steels are used for many household items where utility must be matched with appearance - cutlery, for example. Chromium is also used in production of refractory bricks, and its salts for tanning and dyeing leather and cloth.

Manganese: In its pure state, manganese is a hard, brittle metal. Alloyed with chrome, iron and nickel, it produces abrasion-resistant steels; manganese-aluminium alloys are light but tough. Found in batteries and inks, manganese is also used in glass production. Manganese ores are frequently found in the same location as sedimentary iron ores. Pyrolusite (MnO₂) and psilomelane are the main economically-exploitable sources.

Nickel: Combined with chrome and iron, nickel produces stainless and high-strength steels; similar alloys go to make magnets and electrical heating elements. Nickel combined with copper is widely used to make coins; cupro-nickel alloy is very resistant to corrosion. Its ores yield only modest quantities of nickel - 0.5 to 3.0% - but also contain copper, iron and small amounts of precious metals. Japan, the USA, the UK, Germany and France are the principal importers.

USSR 24.4% | China 17.2% | Brazil 15.5% | Australia 10.7% | USA 5.8% | India 5.2% | Canada 4.1% | South Africa 3.0% | Sweden 2.2%

World total production of iron ore (1989): 989,000,000 tonnes

S. Africa 33.7% | USSR 29.9% | India 7.9% | Turkey 6.7% | Albania 5.5% | Zimbabwe 4.9% | Finland 3.9%

World total (1989): 12,700,000 tonnes

USSR 36.7% | S. Africa 15.1% | China 11.3% | Gabon 9.7% | Australia 8.9% | India 5.6%

World total (1989): 24,000,000 tonnes

USSR 23.1% | Canada 22.3% | New Caledonia 10.6% | Australia 7.1% | Indonesia 6.6% | Cuba 4.9% | S. Africa 3.7%

World total (1989): 910,000 tonnes

DISTRIBUTION

Murmansk
Norilsk
Mirnyy
Urals
Nikepol
Krivoy Rog
Kounradskiy
Almaden
Hebei
Central Morocco
Yunnan
Agadez
Bihar
Philippines
Goa
Malaysia
Guinea
Belitung
Equator
Bakwanga
Ok Tedi
Rössing
Gove
Weipa
Copperbelt
Argyle
Great Dyke
Hamersley Range
Mt. Isa
New Caledonia
Orapa
Tropic of Capricorn
Witwatersrand
Kimberley
Kalgoorlie
Broken Hill
Roxby Downs

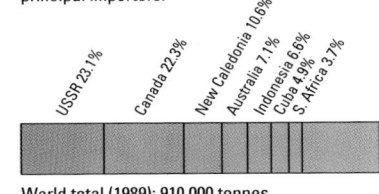

Base metals
□ Copper
▲ Lead
▽ Mercury
▽ Tin
◇ Zinc

Iron and ferro-alloys
● Iron
◖ Chrome
▣ Nickel
▲ Manganese

Light metals
● Bauxite

Rare metals
◇ Uranium

Precious metals
▽ Gold
◓ Silver

Precious stones
◆ Diamonds

Mineral fertilizers
◖ Phosphates

Industrial minerals
◉ Asbestos

PRODUCTION: MANUFACTURING

In its broadest sense, manufacturing is the application of energy, labour and skill to raw materials in order to transform them into finished goods with a higher value than the various elements used in production.

Since the early days of the Industrial Revolution, manufacturing has implied the use of an organized workforce harnessed to some form of machine. The tendency has consistently been for increasingly expensive human labour to be replaced by increasingly complex machinery, which has evolved over time from water-powered looms to fully-integrated robotic plants.

Obviously, not all industries – or manufacturing countries - have reached the same level. Textiles, for example, the foundation of the early industrial revolution in the West, can be mass-produced with fairly modest technology; today, they are usually produced in developing countries, mostly in Asia, where low labour costs compensate for the large workforce the relatively simple machinery requires. Nevertheless, the trend towards high-technology production, however uneven, seems inexorable. Gains in efficiency make up for the staggering cost of the equipment itself, and the outcome is that fewer and fewer people are employed to produce more and more goods.

One paradoxical result of the increase in industrial efficiency is a relative decline in the importance of the industrial sector of a nation's economy. The economy has already passed through one transition, generations past, when workers were drawn from the land into factories. The second transition releases labour into what is called the service sector of the economy: a diffuse but vital concept that includes not only such obvious services as transport and administration, but also finance, insurance and activities as diverse as fashion design or the writing of computer software.

The process is far advanced in the mature economies of the West, with Japan not far behind. Almost two-thirds of US wealth, for example, is now generated in the service sector, and less than half of Japanese Gross National Product comes from industry. The shrinkage, though, is only relative: between them, these two industrial giants produce almost twice as much manufactured goods as the rest of the world put together. And it is on the solid base of production that the rest of their prosperity rests.

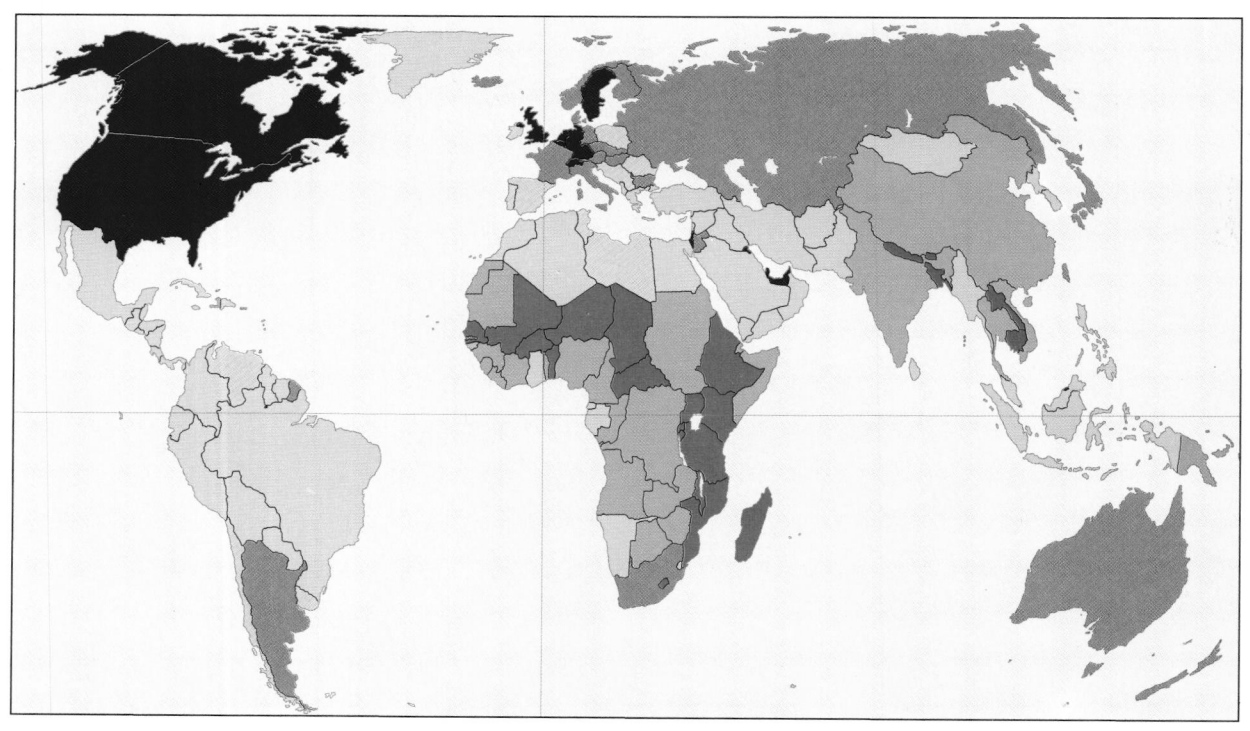

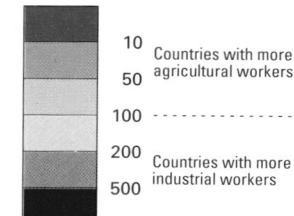

EMPLOYMENT

The number of workers employed in manufacturing for every 100 workers engaged in agriculture

10	Countries with more agricultural workers
50	
100	- - - - - - - -
200	Countries with more industrial workers
500	

Selected countries
(latest available figure, 1986-1989)

Singapore	6,166
Hong Kong	2,632
UK	912
Belgium	751
West Germany	749
USA	641
Sweden	615
France	331
Japan	320
Czechoslovakia	286

DIVISION OF EMPLOYMENT

Distribution of workers between agriculture, industry and services, selected countries (late 1980s)

The six countries selected illustrate the usual stages of economic development, from dependence on agriculture through industrial growth to the expansion of the services sector.

- ■ Agriculture
- ■ Industry
- □ Services

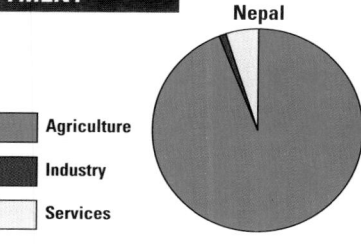
Nepal

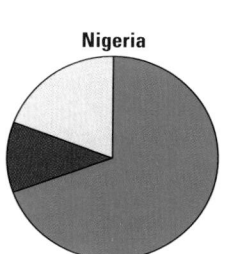
Nigeria

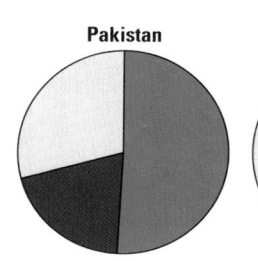
Pakistan

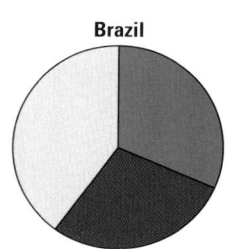
Brazil

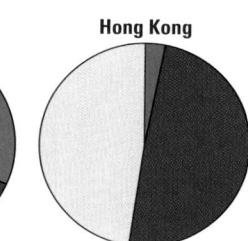
Hong Kong

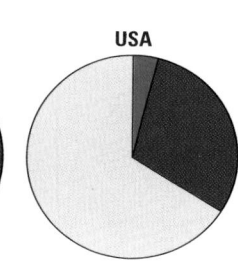
USA

THE WORKFORCE

Percentages of men and women between 15 and 64 in employment, selected countries (late 1980s)

The figures include employees and self-employed, who in developing countries are often subsistence farmers. People in full-time education are excluded. Because of the population age structure in developing countries, the employed population has to support a far larger number of non-workers than its industrial equivalent. For example, more than 52% of Kenya's people are under 15, an age group that makes up less than a tenth of the UK population.

- □ Men
- □ Women

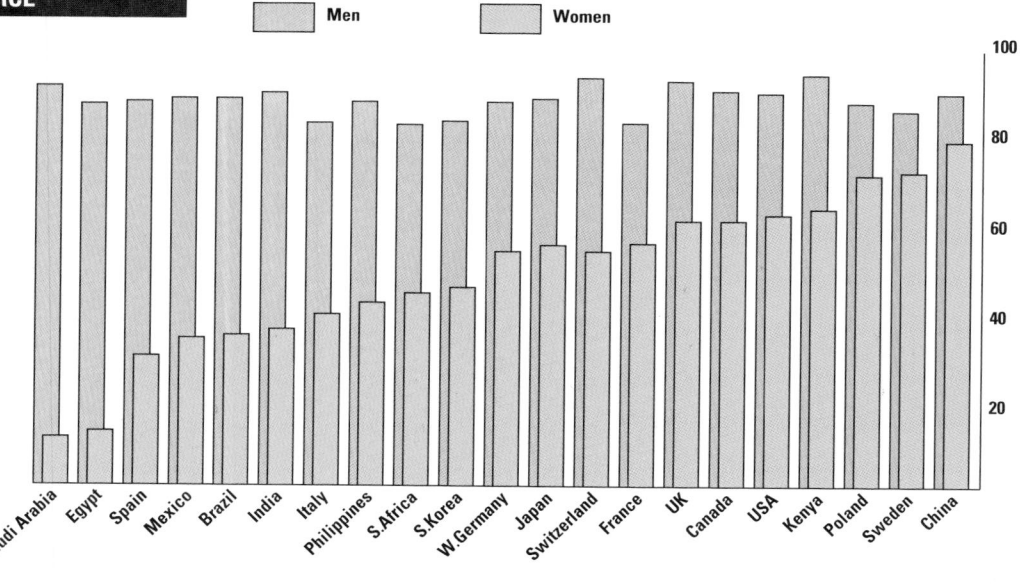

WEALTH CREATION

The Gross National Product (GNP) of the world's largest economies, US $ billion (1989)

1.	USA	5,237,707	21.	Denmark	105,263
2.	Japan	2,920,310	22.	Norway	92,097
3.	Germany	1,272,959	23.	Saudi Arabia	89,986
4.	France	1,000,866	24.	Indonesia	87,936
5.	Italy	871,955	25.	South Africa	86,029
6.	UK	834,166	26.	Turkey	74,731
7.	Canada	500,337	27.	Argentina	68,780
8.	China	393,006	28.	Poland	66,974
9.	Brazil	375,146	29.	Thailand	64,437
10.	Spain	358,352	30.	Hong Kong	59,202
11.	India	287,383	31.	Yugoslavia	59,080
12.	Australia	242,131	32.	Greece	53,626
13.	Netherlands	237,451	33.	Algeria	53,116
14.	Switzerland	197,984	34.	Venezuela	47,164
15.	South Korea	186,467	35.	Israel	44,131
16.	Sweden	184,230	36.	Portugal	44,058
17.	Mexico	170,053	37.	Philippines	42,754
18.	Belgium	162,026	38.	Pakistan	40,134
19.	Austria	131,899	39.	New Zealand	39,437
20.	Finland	109,705	40.	Colombia	38,607

Accurate figures for the USSR and other Communist nations were impossible to obtain.

PATTERNS OF PRODUCTION

Breakdown of industrial output by value, selected countries (1987)

	Food & agriculture	Textiles & clothing	Machinery & transport	Chemicals	Other
Algeria	26%	20%	11%	1%	41%
Argentina	24%	10%	16%	12%	37%
Australia	18%	7%	21%	8%	45%
Austria	17%	8%	25%	6%	43%
Belgium	19%	8%	23%	13%	36%
Brazil	15%	12%	24%	9%	40%
Burkina Faso	62%	18%	2%	1%	17%
Canada	15%	7%	25%	9%	44%
Denmark	22%	6%	23%	10%	39%
Egypt	20%	27%	13%	10%	31%
Finland	13%	6%	24%	7%	50%
France	18%	7%	33%	9%	33%
Greece	20%	22%	14%	7%	38%
Hong Kong	6%	40%	20%	2%	33%
Hungary	6%	11%	37%	11%	35%
India	11%	16%	26%	15%	32%
Indonesia	23%	11%	10%	10%	47%
Iran	13%	22%	22%	7%	36%
Israel	13%	10%	28%	8%	42%
Ireland	28%	7%	20%	15%	28%
Italy	7%	13%	32%	10%	38%
Japan	10%	6%	38%	10%	37%
Kenya	35%	12%	14%	9%	29%
Malaysia	21%	5%	23%	14%	37%
Mexico	24%	12%	14%	12%	39%
Netherlands	19%	4%	28%	11%	38%
New Zealand	26%	10%	16%	6%	43%
Norway	21%	3%	26%	7%	44%
Pakistan	34%	21%	8%	12%	25%
Philippines	40%	7%	7%	10%	35%
Poland	15%	16%	30%	6%	33%
Portugal	17%	22%	16%	8%	38%
Singapore	6%	5%	46%	8%	36%
South Africa	14%	8%	17%	11%	49%
South Korea	15%	17%	24%	9%	35%
Spain	17%	9%	22%	9%	43%
Sweden	10%	2%	35%	8%	44%
Thailand	30%	17%	14%	6%	33%
Turkey	20%	14%	15%	8%	43%
UK	14%	6%	32%	11%	36%
USA	12%	5%	35%	10%	38%
Venezuela	23%	8%	9%	11%	49%
W.Germany	12%	5%	38%	10%	36%
Yugoslavia	13%	17%	25%	6%	39%

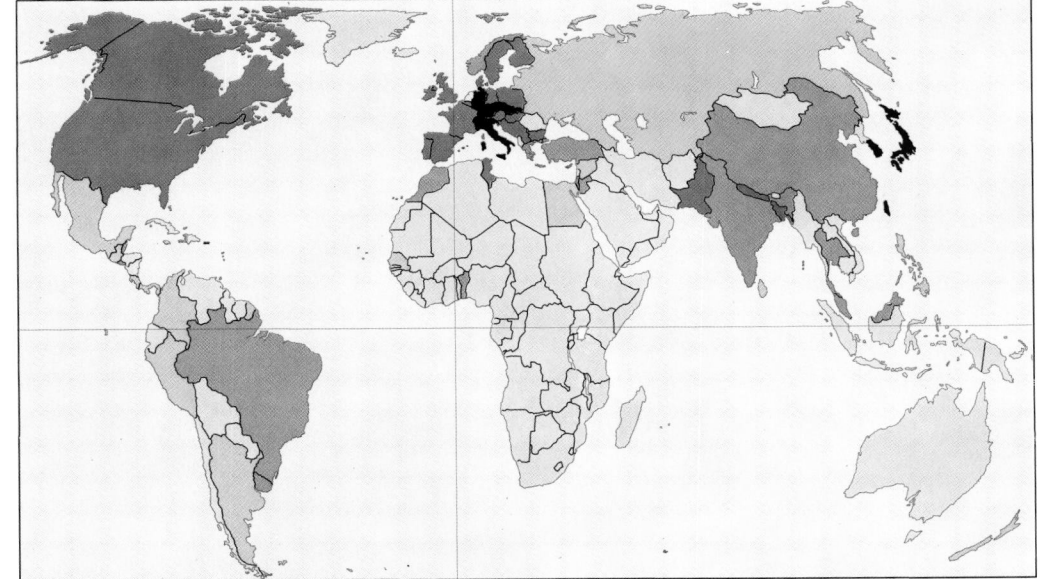

INDUSTRY & TRADE

Maunfactured goods as a percentage of total exports (1989)

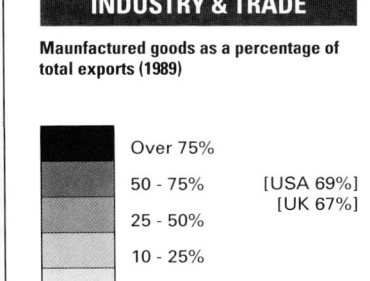

- Over 75%
- 50 - 75%   [USA 69%]
- 25 - 50%   [UK 67%]
- 10 - 25%
- Under 10%

The Far East & South-East Asia (Japan 99.5%, Macau 98.5%, Taiwan 96.8%, Hong Kong 96.1%, S. Korea 95.9%) is most dominant, but many countries in Europe (eg Austria 98.4%) & the Caribbean (eg Cuba 96.9%) are also heavily dependent on manufactured goods.

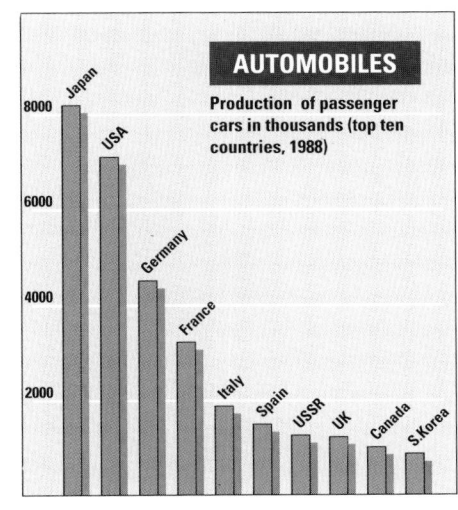

AUTOMOBILES

Production of passenger cars in thousands (top ten countries, 1988)

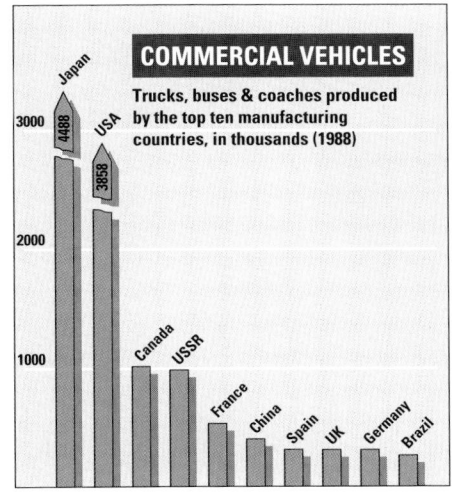

COMMERCIAL VEHICLES

Trucks, buses & coaches produced by the top ten manufacturing countries, in thousands (1988)

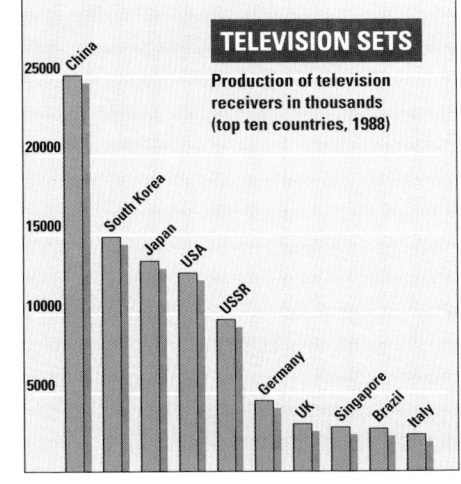

TELEVISION SETS

Production of television receivers in thousands (top ten countries, 1988)

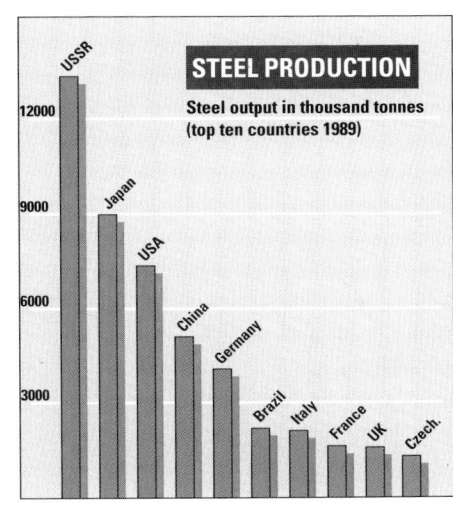

STEEL PRODUCTION

Steel output in thousand tonnes (top ten countries 1989)

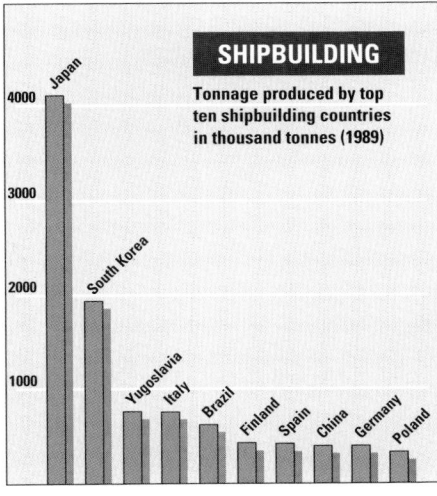

SHIPBUILDING

Tonnage produced by top ten shipbuilding countries in thousand tonnes (1989)

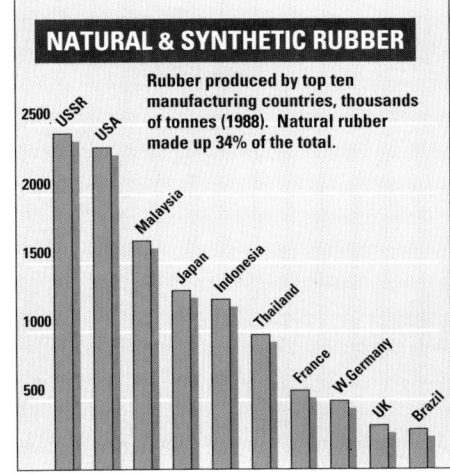

NATURAL & SYNTHETIC RUBBER

Rubber produced by top ten manufacturing countries, thousands of tonnes (1988). Natural rubber made up 34% of the total.

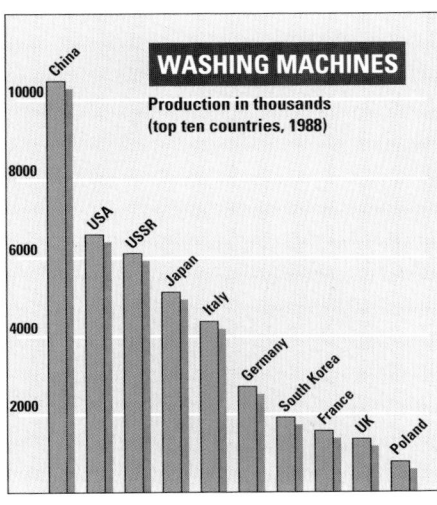

WASHING MACHINES

Production in thousands (top ten countries, 1988)

INDUSTRIAL POWER

Industrial output (mining, manufacturing, construction, energy & water production), top 40 nations, US $ billion (1988)

1. USA	1,249.54		21. Austria	50.63
2. Japan	1,155.41		22. Belgium	46.88
3. Germany	479.69		23. Poland	39.52
4. USSR	326.54		24. Finland	35.50
5. France	304.95		25. South Africa	35.46
6. UK	295.00		26. Saudi Arabia	33.36
7. Italy	286.00		27. Denmark	30.79
8. China	174.05		28. Iraq	30.27
9. Canada	171.06		29. Czechoslovakia	30.18
10. Spain	126.60		30. Yugoslavia	29.32
11. Brazil	116.13		31. Indonesia	29.03
12. Netherlands	76.48		32. Norway	28.74
13. Sweden	75.17		33. Argentina	26.27
14. South Korea	74.00		34. Turkey	26.07
15. India	72.69		35. Israel	24.15
16. Australia	72.63		36. Algeria	22.88
17. E. Germany	64.66		37. Venezuela	22.70
18. Switzerland	63.37		38. Romania	22.19
19. Mexico	61.57		39. Iran	19.90
20. Taiwan	54.81		40. Thailand	18.62

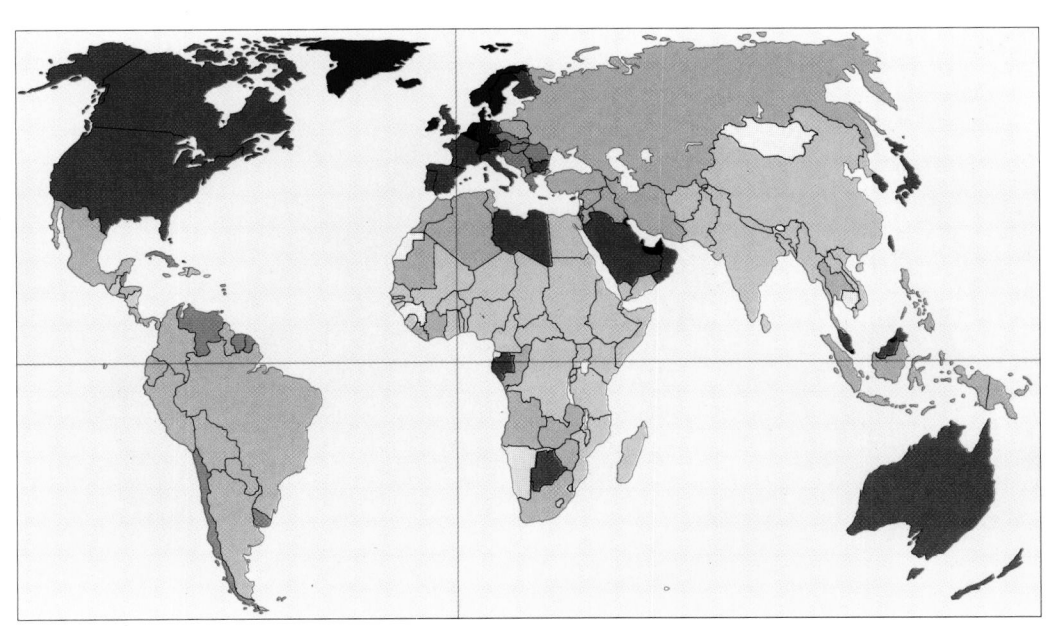

EXPORTS PER CAPITA

Value of exports in US $, divided by total population (1988)

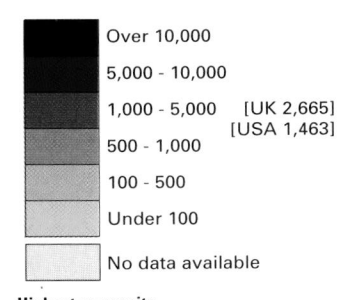

- Over 10,000
- 5,000 - 10,000
- 1,000 - 5,000   [UK 2,665]
- 500 - 1,000   [USA 1,463]
- 100 - 500
- Under 100
- No data available

Highest per capita

Singapore	16,671
Hong Kong	12,676
UAE	10,217
Belgium	10,200
Bahamas	8,580
Qatar	8,431

PRODUCTION: TRADE

Thriving international trade is the outward sign of a healthy world economy – the obvious indicator that some countries have goods to sell and others the wherewithal to buy them. Despite local fluctuations, trade throughout the 1980s grew consistently faster than output, increasing in value by almost 50% in the decade 1979-89. It remains dominated by the wealthy, industrialized countries of the Organization for Economic Development: between them, the 24 OECD members account for almost 75% of world imports and exports in most years. OECD dominance is just as marked in the trade in 'invisibles' - a column in the balance sheet that includes, among other headings, the export of services, interest payments on overseas investments, tourism and even remittances from migrant workers abroad. In the UK, 'invisibles' account for more than half all trading income.

However, the size of these great trading economies means that imports and exports usually comprise a fraction of their total wealth: in the case of the famously export-conscious Japanese, trade in goods and services amounts to less than 18% of GDP. In poorer countries, trade - often in a single commodity - may amount to 50% GDP or more. And there are oddities: import-export figures for the entrepôt economy of Singapore, for example, the transit point for much Asian trade, are almost double that small nation's total earnings.

WORLD TRADE

Percentage of total world exports by value (1989)

- Over 10%
- 5 - 10%
- 1 - 5%
- 0.5 - 1%
- 0.25 - 0.5%
- Under 0.25%

[USA 15.7%]   [UK 6.3%]

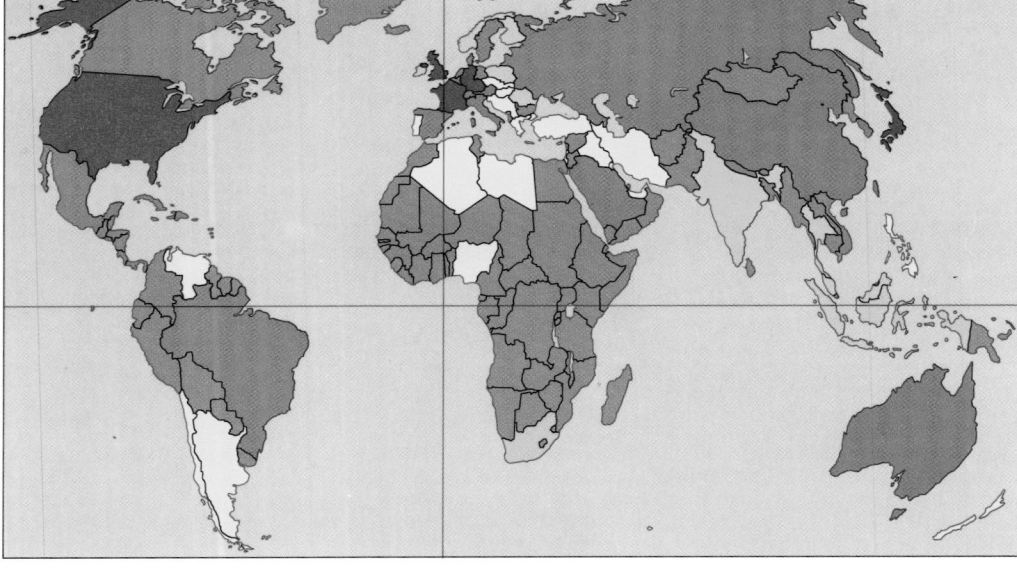

THE GREAT TRADING NATIONS

The imports and exports of the top ten trading nations as a percentage of world trade (1989). Each country's trade in manufactured goods is shown in orange.

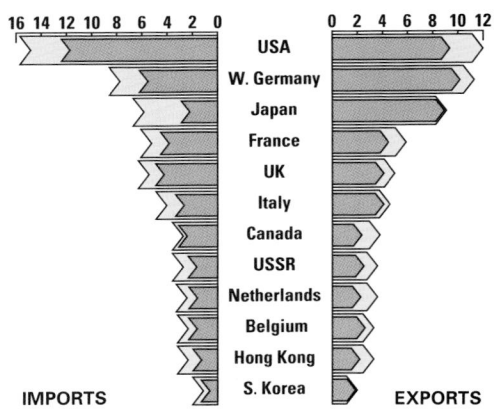

IMPORTS   EXPORTS

USA
W. Germany
Japan
France
UK
Italy
Canada
USSR
Netherlands
Belgium
Hong Kong
S. Korea

MAJOR EXPORTS

Leading manufactured items and their exporters, by percentage of world total in US dollars (late 1980s)

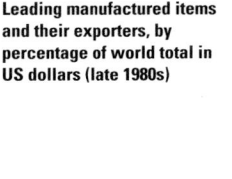

AIRCRAFT
- USA 51%
- UK 13%
- W. Germany 9%
- France 8%
- Canada 5%
- Italy 3%
- Other 11%

TELECOMMUNICATIONS GEAR
- Japan 33%
- USA 14%
- W. Germany 9%
- France 5%
- UK 5%
- Sweden 4%
- Hong Kong 4%
- Canada 4%
- Italy 3%
- Other 19%

DATA PROCESSING EQUIPMENT
- USA 24%
- Japan 22%
- W. Germany 11%
- UK 6%
- France 6%
- Ireland 5%
- Canada 4%
- Italy 4%
- Singapore 4%
- Other 14%

AUTOMOBILES
- Japan 31.5%
- W. Germany 24%
- Canada 12%
- Belgium 7%
- France 7.5%
- USA 6%
- Spain 3%
- Italy 3%
- Sweden 3%
- Other 3%

PAPER & BOARD
- Canada 19%
- Finland 14%
- Sweden 13%
- W. Germany 12%
- USA 8%
- France 5%
- Netherlands 4%
- Japan 4%
- Italy 3%
- UK 3%
- Other 15%

ELECTRICAL MACHINERY
- Japan 22%
- W. Germany 19%
- USA 14%
- UK 8%
- France 7%
- Netherlands 6%
- Italy 4%
- Switzerland 4%
- Belgium 4%
- Other

TRADED PRODUCTS

Top ten manufactures traded, by value in billions of US $ (late 1980s)

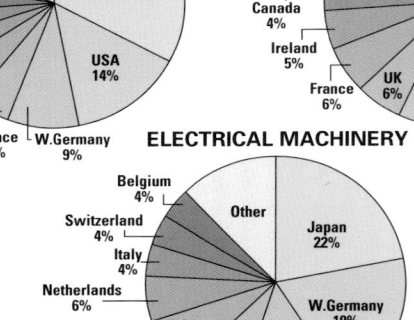

- Automobiles
- Engines & vehicle parts
- Data processing equipment
- Telecommunications
- Transistors etc
- Aircraft
- Paper & board
- Trucks
- Meas. & control instruments
- Electrical machinery

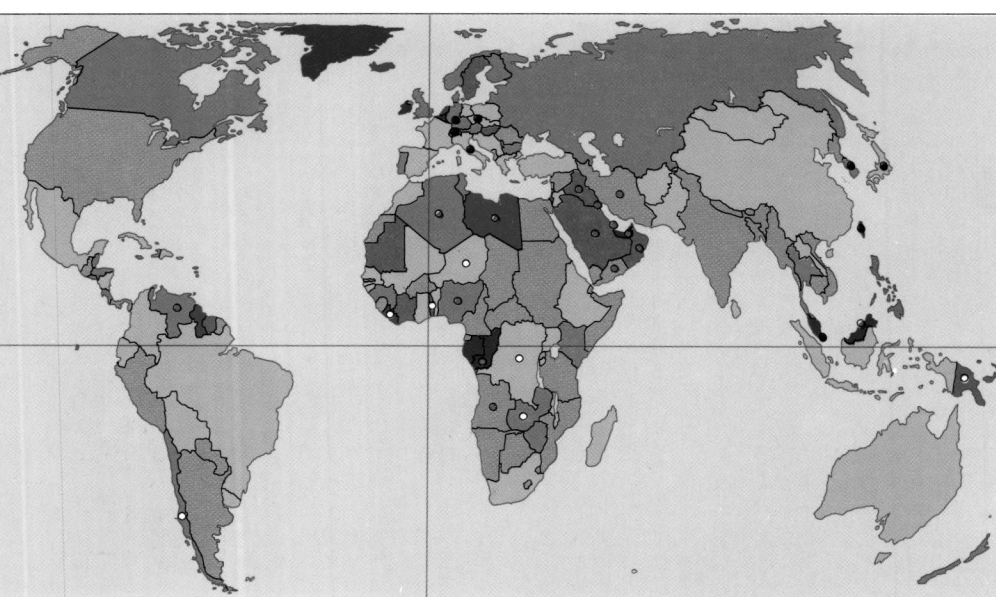

DEPENDENCE ON TRADE

Value of exports as a percentage of Gross Domestic Product (1988)

- Over 50%
- 40 - 50%
- 30 - 40%
- 20 - 30%   [UK 21%]
- 10 - 20%   [USA 6.5%]
- Under 10%

- ● Most dependent on industrial exports (over 75% of total exports)
- ● Most dependent on fuel exports (over 75% of total exports)
- ○ Most dependent on mineral & metal exports (over 75% of total exports)

WORLD SHIPPING

While ocean passenger traffic is now relatively modest, sea transport still carries most of world trade. Oil and bulk carriers make up the majority of the world fleet, although the general cargo category was the fastest growing in 1989, a year in which total tonnage increased by 1.5%.

Almost 30% of world shipping sails under a 'flag of convenience', whereby owners take advantage of low taxes by registering their vessels in a foreign country the ships will never see, notably Panama and Liberia.

MERCHANT FLEETS

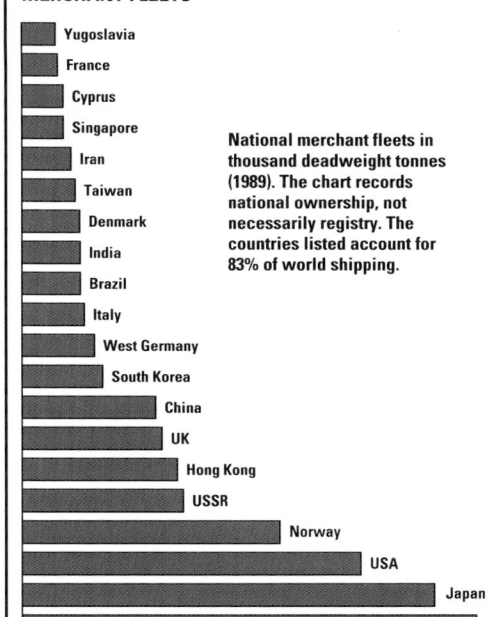

Yugoslavia
France
Cyprus
Singapore
Iran
Taiwan
Denmark
India
Brazil
Italy
West Germany
South Korea
China
UK
Hong Kong
USSR
Norway
USA
Japan
Greece

20,000   40,000   60,000   80,000

National merchant fleets in thousand deadweight tonnes (1989). The chart records national ownership, not necessarily registry. The countries listed account for 83% of world shipping.

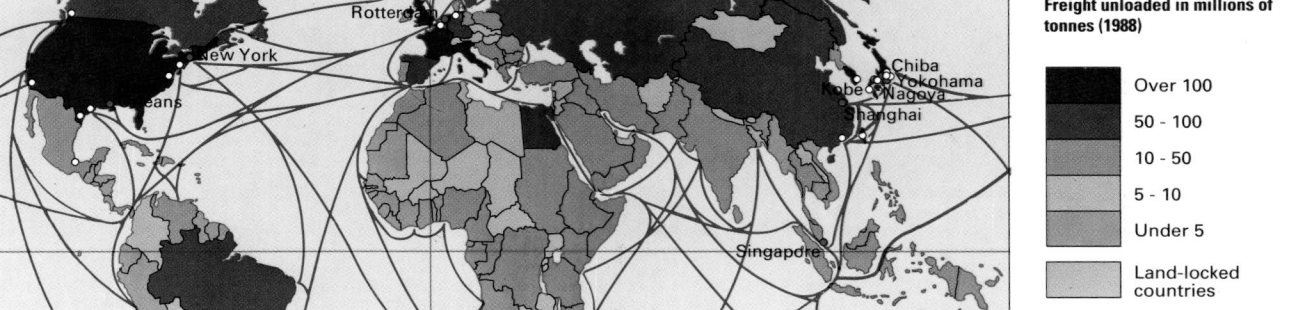

Rotterdam
New York
Orleans
Chiba
Yokohama
Kobe Nagoya
Shanghai
Singapore

Types of vessel by deadweight tonnage (1989)

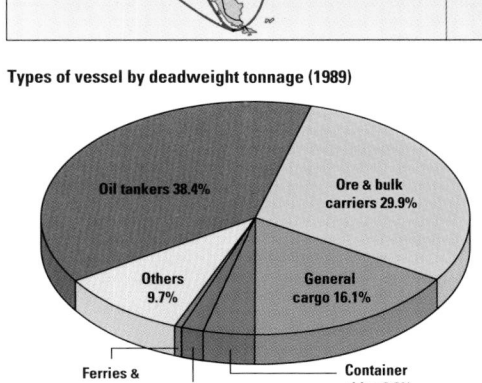

Oil tankers 38.4%
Ore & bulk carriers 29.9%
Others 9.7%
General cargo 16.1%
Ferries & passenger ships 0.5%
Liquid gas carriers 1.6%
Container ships 3.8%

THE GREAT PORTS

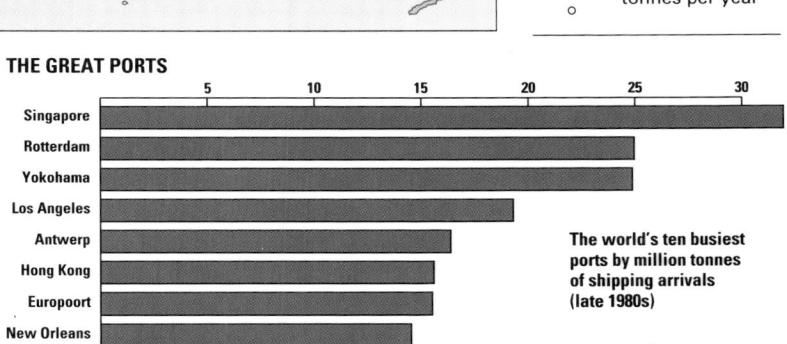

5   10   15   20   25   30

Singapore
Rotterdam
Yokohama
Los Angeles
Antwerp
Hong Kong
Europoort
New Orleans
Hamburg
Kobe

The world's ten busiest ports by million tonnes of shipping arrivals (late 1980s)

FREIGHT

Freight unloaded in millions of tonnes (1988)

- Over 100
- 50 - 100
- 10 - 50
- 5 - 10
- Under 5
- Land-locked countries

Major seaports

- Over 100 million tonnes per year
- 50-100 million tonnes per year

TRADE IN PRIMARY PRODUCTS

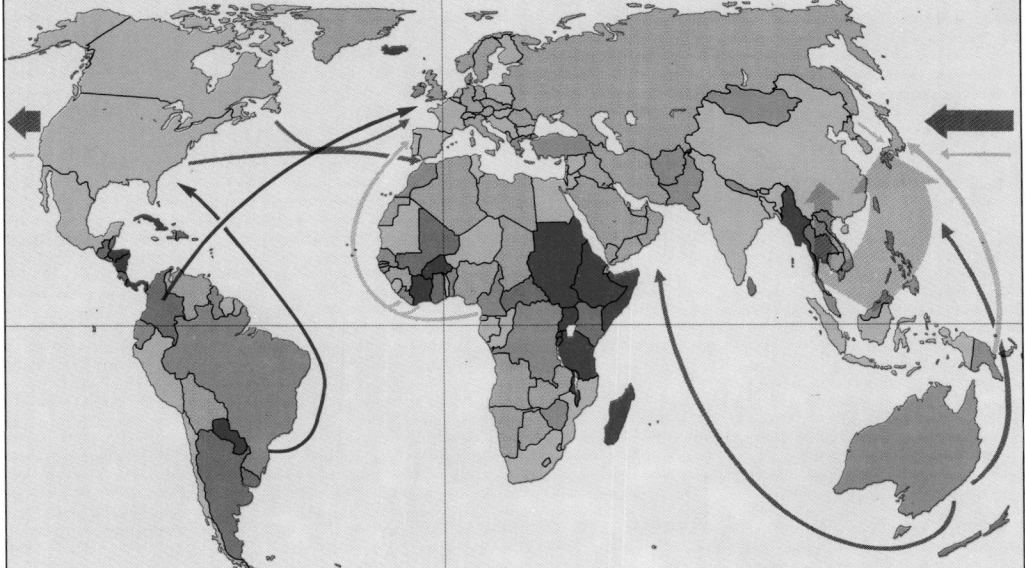

Exports in primary products (excluding fuels, minerals & metals) as a percentage of total exports (1988)

- Over 75%
- 50 - 75%
- 25 - 50%
- 10 - 25%   [USA 17.6%]
- Under 10%   [UK 9%]

Direction of trade

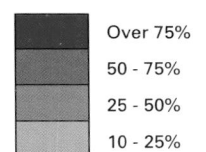

Major movements of wheat

Major movements of coffee

Major movements of hardwoods

Arrows show the major trade direction of selected primary products, & are proportional to export value

BALANCE OF TRADE

Value of exports in proportion to the value of imports (1988)

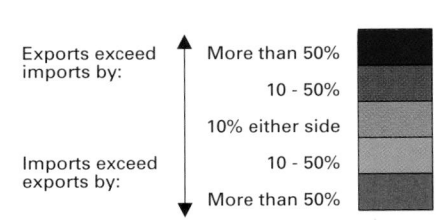

Exports exceed imports by:
- More than 50%
- 10 - 50%

10% either side

Imports exceed exports by:
- 10 - 50%
- More than 50%

The total world trade balance should amount to zero, since exports must equal imports on a global scale. In practice, at least $100 billions in exports go unrecorded, leaving the world with an apparent deficit and many countries in a better position than public accounting reveals. However, a favourable trade balance is not necessarily a sign of prosperity: many poorer countries must maintain a high surplus in order to service debts, and do so by restricting imports below their real requirements.

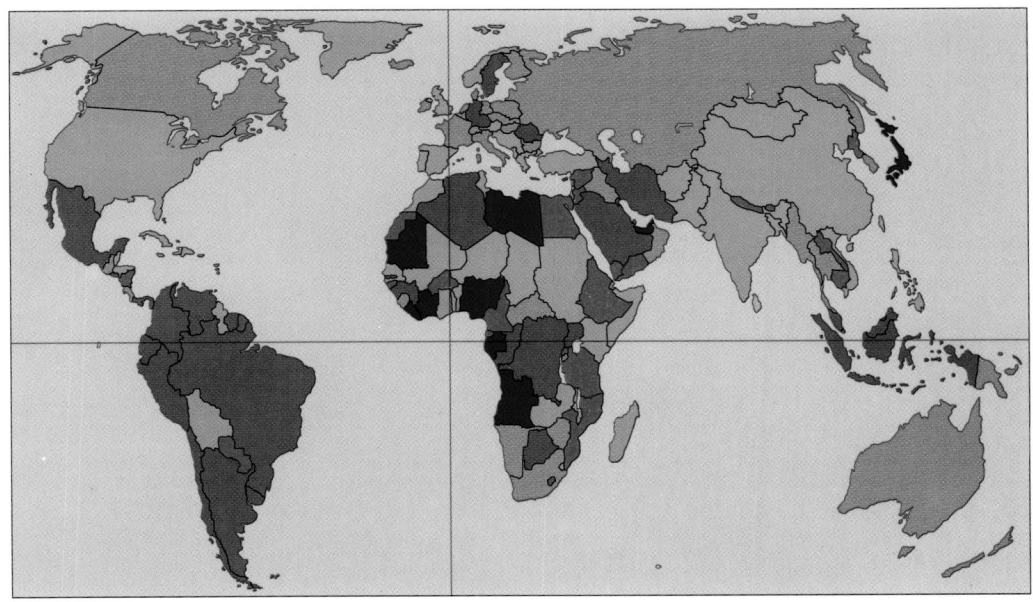

QUALITY OF LIFE: WEALTH

Throughout the 1980s, most of the world became at least slightly richer. There were exceptions: in Africa, the poorest of the continents, many incomes actually fell, and the upheavals in Eastern Europe in 1989 left whole populations awash with political freedom but worse off financially in economies still teetering towards capitalism.

Most of the improvements, however, came to those who were already, in world terms, extremely affluent: the gap between rich and poor grew steadily wider. And in those developing countries that showed significant statistical progress, advances were often confined to a few favoured areas while conditions in other, usually rural, districts went from bad to worse.

The pattern of world poverty varies from region to region. In most of Asia, the process of recognized development is generally under way, with production increases outpacing population growth. By 2000, less than 10% of the Chinese population should be officially rated 'poor': without the means to buy either adequate food or the basic necessities required to take a full part in everyday life. Even India's lower growth rate should be enough to reduce the burden of poverty for at least some of its people. In Latin America, average per capita production is high enough for most countries to be considered 'middle income' in world rankings. But although adequate resources exist, Latin American wealth is distributed with startling inequality. According to a 1990 World Bank report, a tax of only 2% on the richest fifth would raise enough money to pull every one of the continent's 437 million people above the poverty line.

In Africa, solutions will be harder to find. The bane of high population growth has often been aggravated by incompetent administration, a succession of natural disasters and war. Population is the crux of the problem: numbers are growing anything up to twice as fast as the economies that try to support them. Aid from the developed world is only a partial solution; although Africa receives more than any other continent, much has been wasted on over-ambitious projects or lost in webs of inexperienced or corrupt bureaucracy. Yet without aid, Africa seems doomed to permanent crisis.

The rich countries can afford to increase their spending. The 24 members of the Organisation for Economic Cooperation and Development comprise only 16% of the world's population, yet between them the nations accounted for almost 80% of total world production in 1988, a share that is likely to increase as 2000 approaches.

CURRENCIES

Currency units of the world's most powerful economies

1. USA: US Dollar($,US$) = 100 cents
2. Japan: Yen (Y,¥) = 100 sen
3. Germany: Deutsche Mark (DM) = 100 Pfennige
4. France: French Franc (Fr) = 100 centimes
5. Italy: Italian Lira (L, £, Lit)
6. UK: Pound Sterling (£) = 100 pence
7. Canada: Canadian Dollar (C$, Can$) = 100 cents
8. China: Renminbi Yuan (RMBY, $, Y) = 10 jiao = 100 fen
9. Brazil: Cruzado (Cr$) = 100 centavos
10. Spain: Peseta (Pta, Pa) = 100 céntimos
11. India: Indian Rupee (Re, Rs) = 100 paisa
12. Australia: Australian Dollar ($A) = 100 cents
13. Netherlands: Guilder, Florin (Gld, f) = 100 centimes
14. Switzerland: Swiss Franc (SFr, SwF) = 100 centimes
15. South Korea: Won (W) = 100 Chon
16. Sweden: Swedish Krona (SKr) = 100 ore
17. Mexico: Mexican Pesos (Mex$) = 100 centavos
18. Belgium: Belgian Franc (BFr) = 100 centimes
19. Austria: Schilling (S, Sch) = 100 groschen
20. Finland: Markka (FMk) = 100 penni
21. Denmark: Danish Krone (DKr) = 100 ore
22. Norway: Norwegian Krone (NKr) = 100 ore
23. Saudi Arabia: Riyal (SAR, SRI$) = 100 halalah
24. Indonesia: Rupiah (Rp) = 100 sen
25. South Africa: Rand (R) = 100 cents

CONTINENTAL SHARES

Shares of population and of wealth (GNP) by continent

Generalized continental figures show the startling difference between rich and poor but mask the successes or failures of individual countries. Japan, for example, with less than 4% of Asia's population, produces almost 70% of the continent's output.

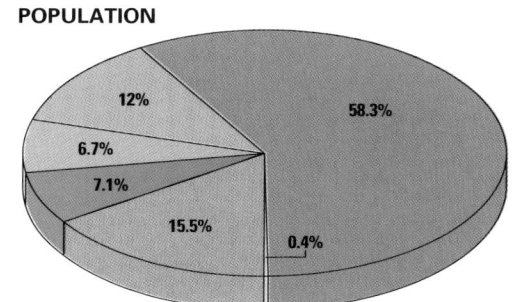

POPULATION

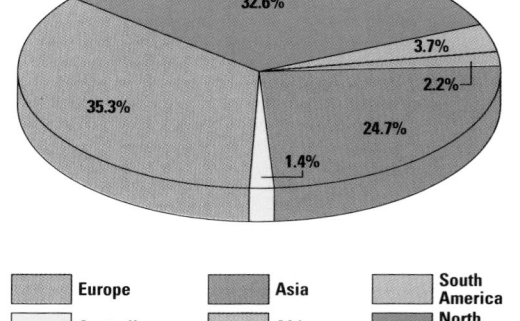

GNP

Europe — Australia — Asia — Africa — South America — North America

LEVELS OF INCOME

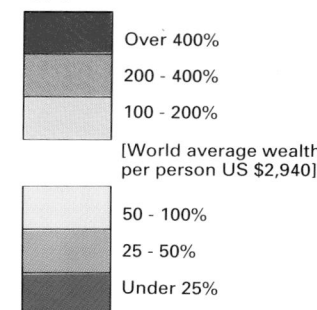

Gross National Product per capita: the value of total production divided by population (1986)

Over 400%
200 - 400%
100 - 200%

[World average wealth per person US $2,940]

50 - 100%
25 - 50%
Under 25%

[Gross National Product (GNP) is the value of a nation's total production plus or minus the net balance of foreign financial transactions – including investments, banking and insurance]

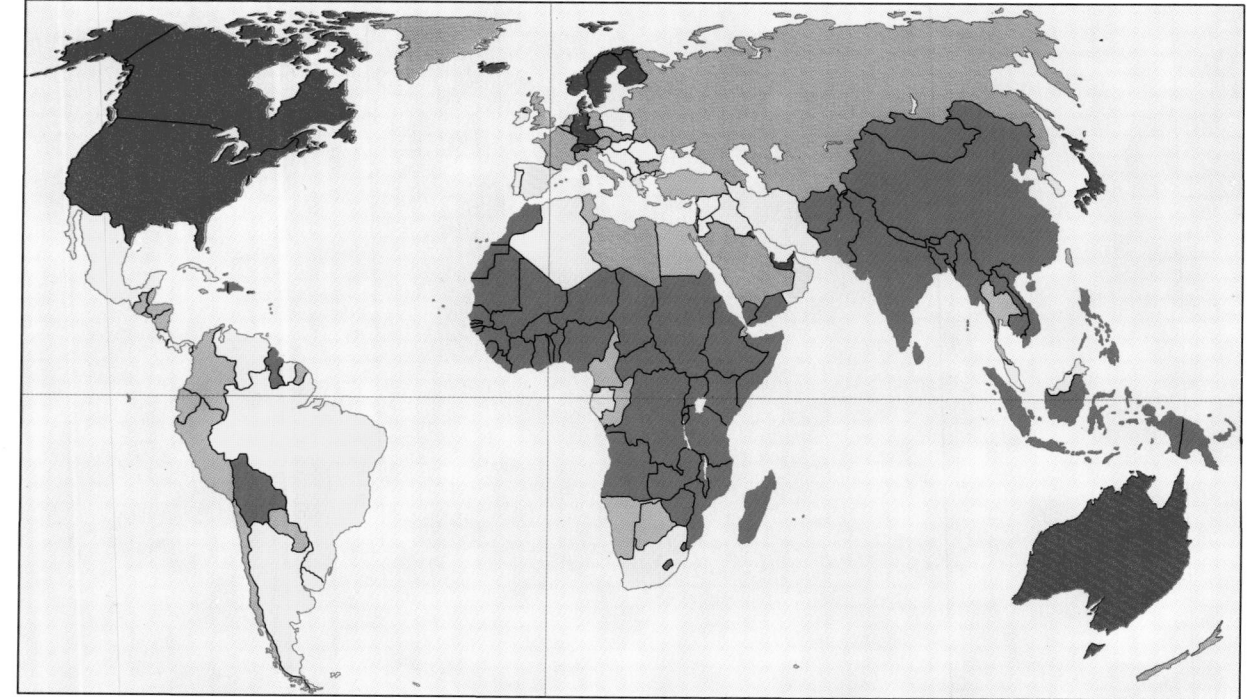

INDICATORS

The gap between the world's rich and poor is now so great that it is difficult to illustrate it on a single graph. Car ownership in the USA, for example, is almost 2,000 times as common as it is in Bangladesh. Within each income group, however, comparisons have some meaning: the affluent Japanese on their overcrowded island have far fewer cars than the Americans; the Chinese, perhaps because of propaganda value, have more television sets than the Indians, whose per capita income is similar, while Nigerians prefer to spend their money on vehicles.

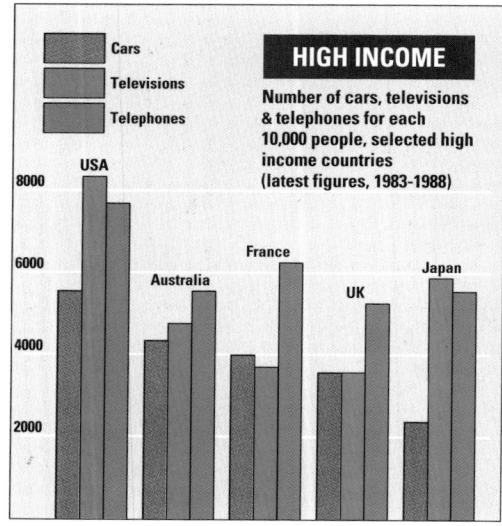

HIGH INCOME

Number of cars, televisions & telephones for each 10,000 people, selected high income countries (latest figures, 1983-1988)

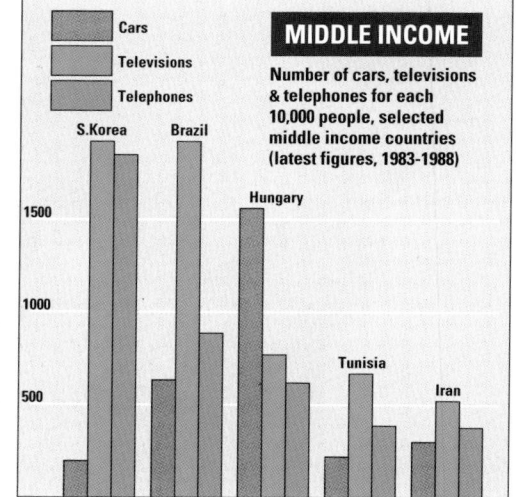

MIDDLE INCOME

Number of cars, televisions & telephones for each 10,000 people, selected middle income countries (latest figures, 1983-1988)

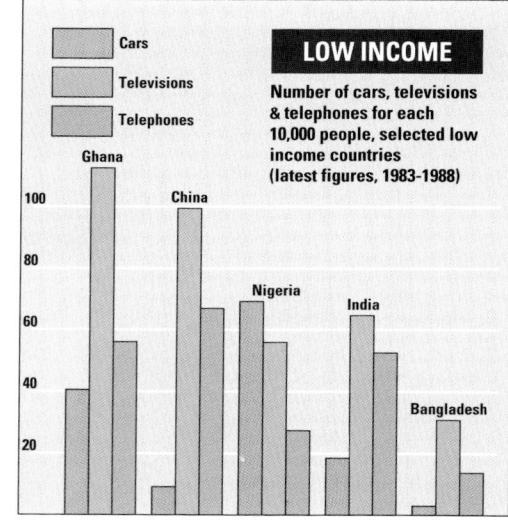

LOW INCOME

Number of cars, televisions & telephones for each 10,000 people, selected low income countries (latest figures, 1983-1988)

40

DEBT & AID

International debtors and the development aid they receive (1989)

■ Debt, $ per capita

■ Aid, $ per capita

Although aid grants make a vital contribution to many of the world's poorer countries, they are usually dwarfed by the burden of debt that developing economies are expected to repay. In the case of Mozambique, aid amounted to more than 70% of GNP. In 1990, the World Bank rated Mozambique as the world's poorest country; yet debt interest payments came to almost 75 times its entire export earnings.

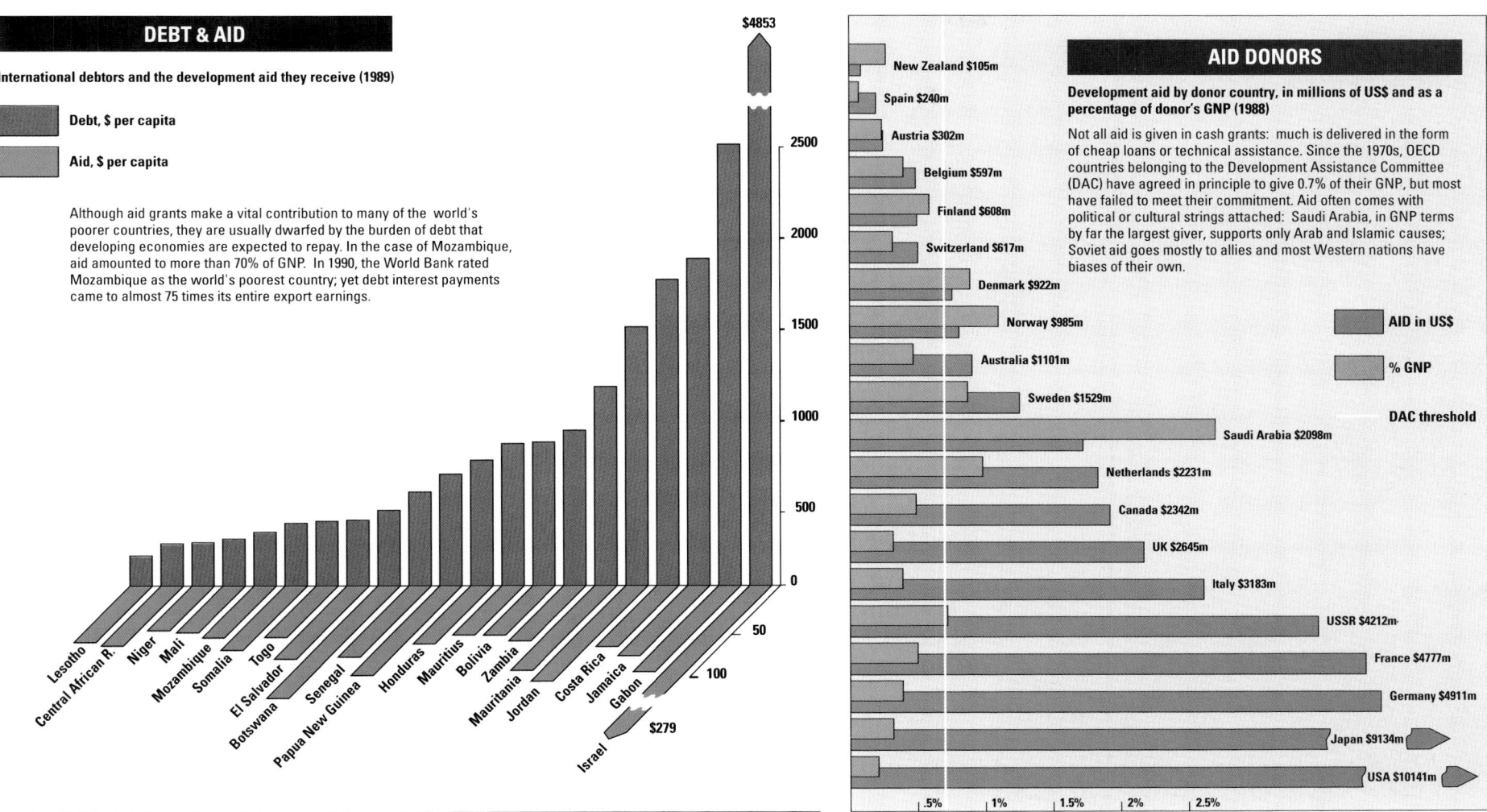

$4853

Lesotho, Central African R., Niger, Mali, Mozambique, Somalia, Togo, El Salvador, Botswana, Senegal, Papua New Guinea, Honduras, Mauritius, Bolivia, Zambia, Mauritania, Jordan, Costa Rica, Jamaica, Gabon, Israel $279

AID DONORS

Development aid by donor country, in millions of US$ and as a percentage of donor's GNP (1988)

Not all aid is given in cash grants: much is delivered in the form of cheap loans or technical assistance. Since the 1970s, OECD countries belonging to the Development Assistance Committee (DAC) have agreed in principle to give 0.7% of their GNP, but most have failed to meet their commitment. Aid often comes with political or cultural strings attached: Saudi Arabia, in GNP terms by far the largest giver, supports only Arab and Islamic causes; Soviet aid goes mostly to allies and most Western nations have biases of their own.

■ AID in US$

■ % GNP

DAC threshold

New Zealand $105m, Spain $240m, Austria $302m, Belgium $597m, Finland $608m, Switzerland $617m, Denmark $922m, Norway $985m, Australia $1101m, Sweden $1529m, Saudi Arabia $2098m, Netherlands $2231m, Canada $2342m, UK $2645m, Italy $3183m, USSR $4212m, France $4777m, Germany $4911m, Japan $9134m, USA $10141m

Inflation (right) is an excellent index of a country's financial stability, and usually its prosperity or at least its prospects. Inflation rates above 20% are generally matched by slow or even negative growth; above 50%, an economy is left reeling. Most advanced countries during the 1980s had to wrestle with inflation that occasionally touched or even exceeded 10%; in Japan, the growth leader, price increases averaged only 1.8% between 1980 and 1988.

Government spending (below right) is more difficult to interpret. Obviously, very low levels indicate a weak state, and high levels a strong one; but in poor countries, the 10-20% absorbed by the government may well amount to most of the liquid cash available, whereas in rich countries most of the 35-50% typically in government hands is returned in services. GNP per capita figures (below) should also be compared with caution. They do not reveal the vast differences in living costs between different countries: the equivalent of US $100 is worth considerably more in poorer nations than it is in the USA itself.

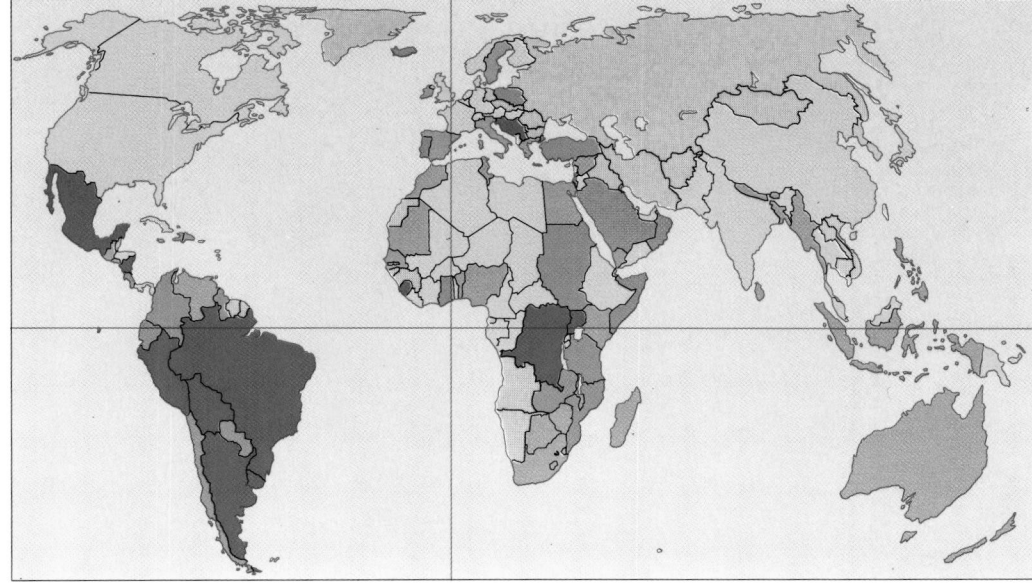

INFLATION

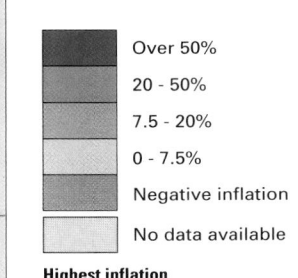

Average annual rate of inflation (1980-1988)

- Over 50%
- 20 - 50%
- 7.5 - 20%
- 0 - 7.5%
- Negative inflation
- No data available

Highest inflation
Bolivia 483%
Argentina 291%
Brazil 189%

Lowest inflation
Oman .... -6.5%
Saudi Arabia .... -4.2%
Kuwait .... -3.9%

[UK 5.7%] [USA 4.0%]

THE WEALTH GAP

The world's richest & poorest countries, by Gross National Product per capita in US $ (1989)

1.	Liechtenstein	33,000	1.	Mozambique	80
2.	Switzerland	30,270	2.	Ethiopia	120
3.	Bermuda	25,000	3.	Tanzania	120
4.	Luxembourg	24,860	4.	Laos	170
5.	Japan	23,730	5.	Nepal	170
6.	Finland	22,060	6.	Somalia	170
7.	Norway	21,850	7.	Bangladesh	180
8.	Sweden	21,710	8.	Malawi	180
9.	Iceland	21,240	9.	Bhutan	190
10.	USA	21,100	10.	Chad	190
11.	Denmark	20,510	11.	Sierra Leone	200
12.	Canada	19,020	12.	Burundi	220
13.	UAE	18,430	13.	Gambia	230
14.	France	17,830	14.	Madagascar	230
15.	Austria	17,360	15.	Nigeria	250
16.	Germany	16,500	16.	Uganda	250
17.	Belgium	16,390	17.	Mali	260
18.	Kuwait	16,380	18.	Zaïre	260
19.	Netherlands	16,010	19.	Niger	290
20.	Italy	15,150	20.	Burkina Faso	310

GNP per capita is calculated by dividing a country's Gross National Product by its population. The UK ranks 21st, with US $14,570.

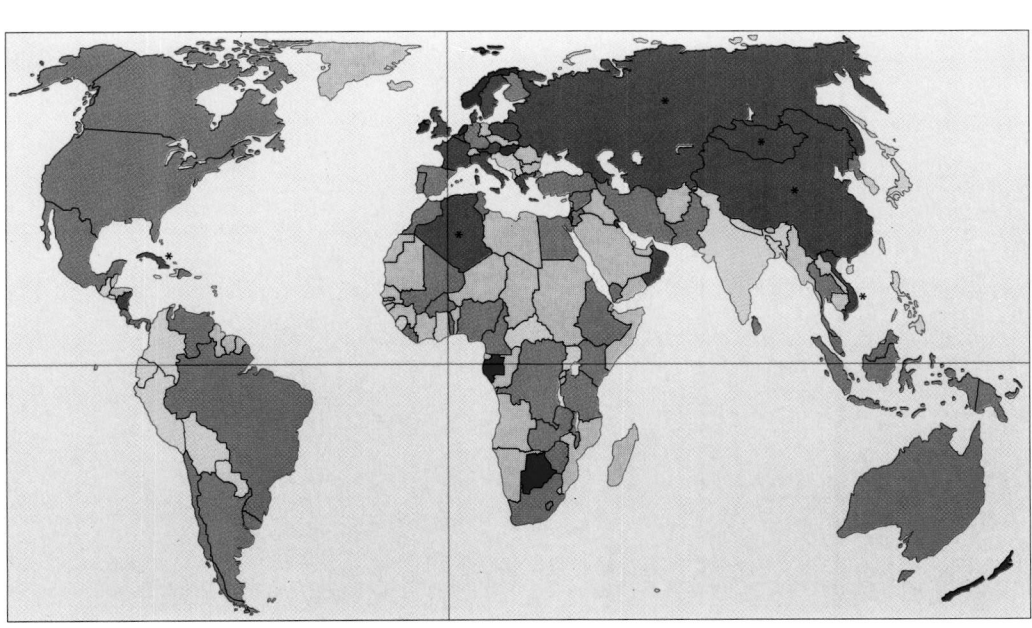

STATE REVENUE

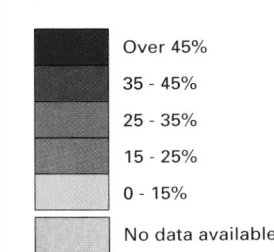

Central government revenue as a percentage of GNP (1988) [* estimate]

- Over 45%
- 35 - 45%
- 25 - 35%
- 15 - 25%
- 0 - 15%
- No data available

Highest proportion
Botswana 74%
Hungary 58%
Kuwait 52%
Netherlands 51%
Gabon 47%

[UK 36.4%] [USA 19.7%]

QUALITY OF LIFE: STANDARDS

At first sight, most international contrasts are swamped by differences in wealth. The rich not only have more money, they have more of everything, including years of life. Those with only a little money are obliged to spend most of it on food and clothing, the basic maintenance costs of existence; air travel and tourism are unlikely to feature on the lists of their expenditure. However, poverty and wealth are both relative: slum-dwellers living on social security payments in an affluent industrial country have far more resources at their disposal than an average African peasant, but feel their own poverty none the less acutely. A middle-class Indian lawyer cannot command a fraction of the earnings of a counterpart in New York, London or Rome; nevertheless, he rightly sees himself as prosperous.

In 1990 the United Nations Development Programme published its first Human Development Index, an attempt to construct a comparative scale by which at least a simplified form of well-being might be measured. The index, running from 1 to 100, combined figures for life expectancy and literacy with a wealth scale that matched incomes against the official poverty lines of a group of industrialized nations. National scores ranged from a startling 98.7 for Sweden to a miserable 11.6 for Niger, reflecting the all too familiar gap between rich and poor.

Comparisons between nations with similar incomes are more interesting, showing the effect of government policies. For example, Sri Lanka was awarded 78.9 against 43.9 for its only slightly poorer neighbour, India; Zimbabwe, at 57.6, had more than double the score of Senegal, despite no apparent disparities in average income. Some development indicators may be interpreted in two ways. There is a very clear correlation, for example, between the wealth of a nation and the level of education that its people enjoy. Education helps create wealth, of course; but are rich countries wealthy because they are educated, or well-educated because they are rich? Women's fertility rates appear to fall almost in direct proportion to the amount of secondary education they receive; but high levels of female education are associated with rich countries, where fertility is already low.

Not everything, though, is married to wealth. The countries cited on these pages have been chosen, representatively, to give a range covering different cultures as well as different economic power, revealing disparities among rich and among poor as well as between the two obvious groups.

Income distribution, for example, shows that in Brazil (following the general pattern of Latin America) most national wealth is concentrated in a few hands; Bangladesh is much poorer, but what little wealth there is is more evenly spread.

Among the developed countries the USA, with its poorest 20% sharing less than 5% of the national cake, has a noticeably less even distribution than Japan, where despite massive industrialization traditional values act as a brake against poverty. Hungary, still enmeshed in Communism when these statistics were compiled, shows the most even distribution of all, which certainly matches with Socialist theory. However, the inequalities in Communist societies, a contributing factor in the demise of most of them in the late 1980s, are not easily measured in money terms: Communist élites are less often rewarded with cash than with power and privilege, commodities not easily expressed statistically.

There are other limits to statistical analysis. Even without taking account of such imponderables as personal satisfaction, it will always be more difficult to measure a reasonable standard of living than a nation's income or its productivity. Lack of money certainly brings misery, but its presence does not guarantee contentment.

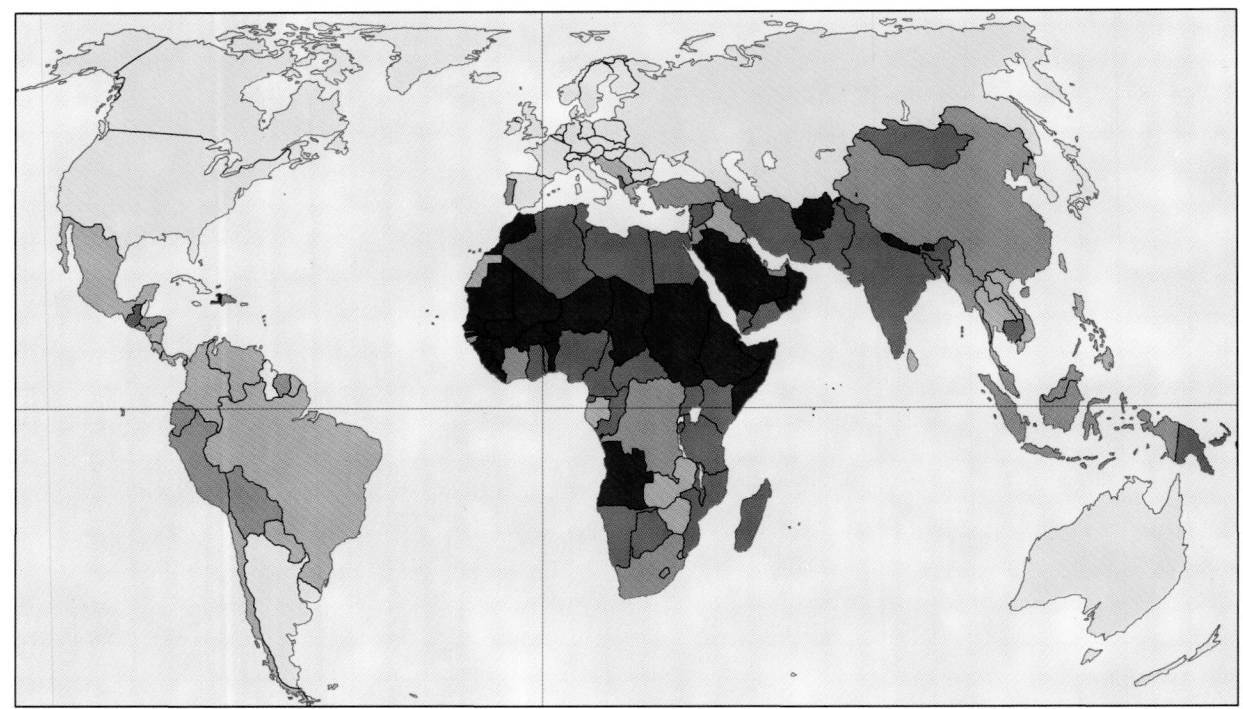

LITERACY

Percentage of adult population unable to read or write (1988)

- Over 75%
- 50 - 75%
- 25 - 50%
- 10 - 15%
- Under 10%

Highest rates of illiteracy

Somalia	88%
Burkina Faso	87%
Niger	86%
Mali	83%
Mauritania	83%
Chad	78%
Benin	76%
Nepal	76%
Guinea	75%

[UK 4.86%] [USA 4%]

EDUCATION

The developing countries made great efforts in the 1970s and 1980s to bring at least a basic education to their people. Primary school enrolments rose above 60% in all but the poorest nations. Figures often include teenagers or young adults, however, and there are still an estimated 300 million children worldwide who receive no schooling at all. Secondary and higher education are expanding far more slowly, and the gap between rich and poor is probably even larger than it appears from the charts here, while the bare statistics provide no real reflection of educational quality.

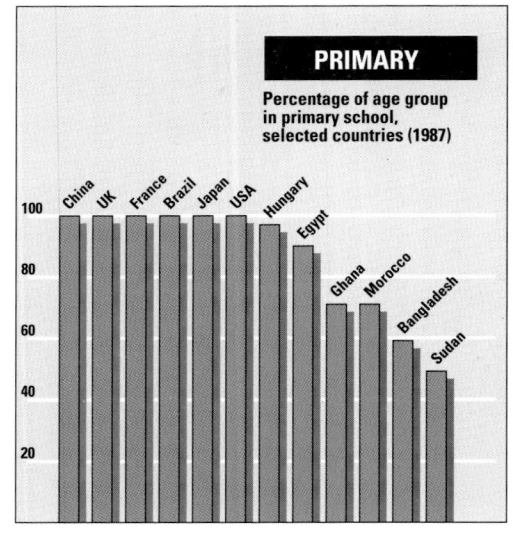

PRIMARY
Percentage of age group in primary school, selected countries (1987)

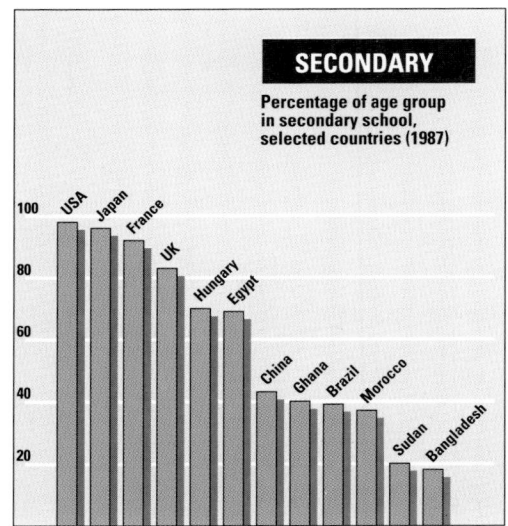

SECONDARY
Percentage of age group in secondary school, selected countries (1987)

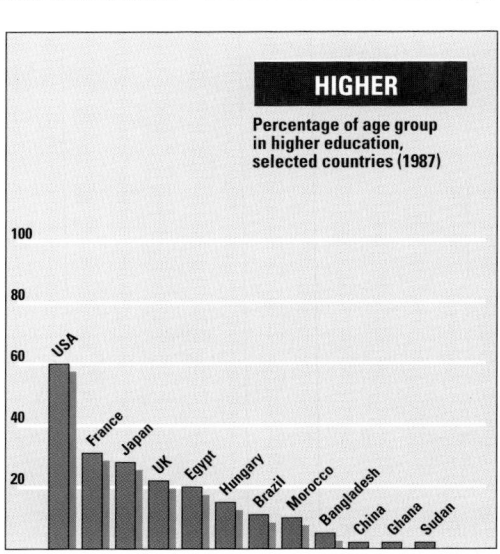

HIGHER
Percentage of age group in higher education, selected countries (1987)

DISTRIBUTION OF SPENDING

Percentage share of household spending, (1989)

- Food
- Clothing
- Energy & Housing
- Medicine & Education
- Transport
- Other

UK USA Japan Hungary Brazil Egypt Nigeria B'desh

DISTRIBUTION OF INCOME

Percentage share of household income from poorest fifth to richest fifth, selected countries (1989)

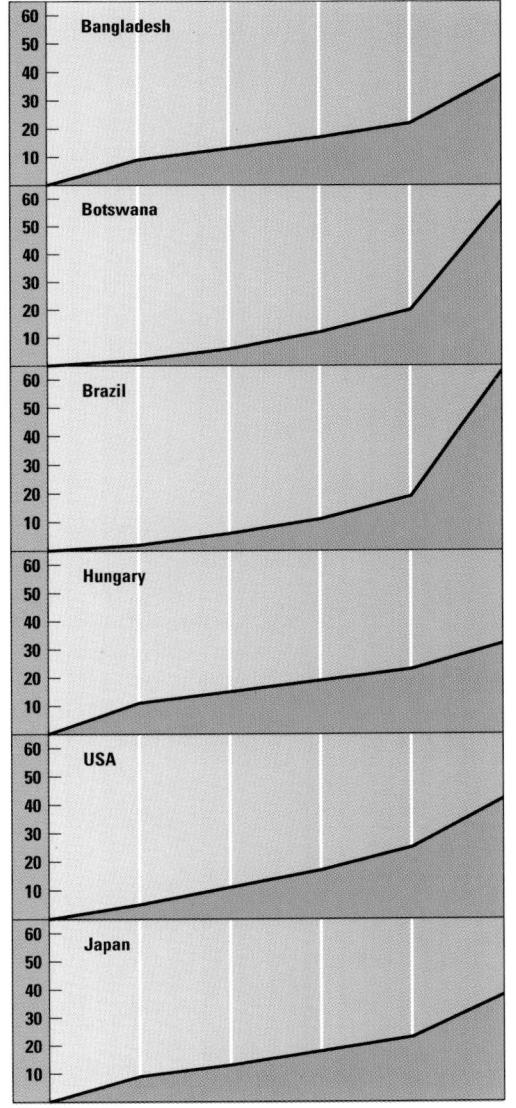

Bangladesh

Botswana

Brazil

Hungary

USA

Japan

FERTILITY & EDUCATION

- **Fertility rate: average number of children borne per woman**
- **Percentage of female age group in secondary education**

Fertility rates compared with female education, selected countries (1988)

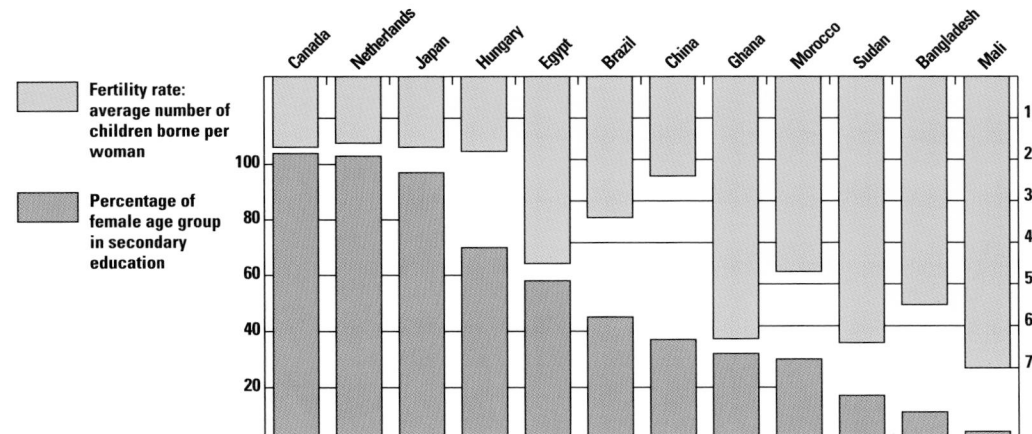

Canada Netherlands Japan Hungary Egypt Brazil China Ghana Morocco Sudan Bangladesh Mali

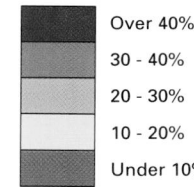

Since the age group for secondary schooling is usually defined as 12 to 17 years, percentages for countries with a significant number of 11- or 18-year-olds in secondary school may actually exceed 100. A high proportion of employed women may indicate either an advanced, industrial economy where female opportunities are high, or a poor country where many women's lives are dominated by agricultural toil. The lowest rates are found in Islamic nations, whose religious precepts often exclude women even from field-work.

WOMEN AT WORK

Women in paid employment as a percentage of the total workforce (1989)

- Over 40%
- 30 - 40%
- 20 - 30%
- 10 - 20%
- Under 10%

Highest proportion
Burundi	53%
Ghana	51%
Mozambique	48%

Lowest proportion
UAE	6%
Saudi Arabia	7%
Bangladesh	7%

[UK 42%] [USA 44%]

TOURIST SPENDING

Countries spending the most on overseas tourism US $ million (1987)

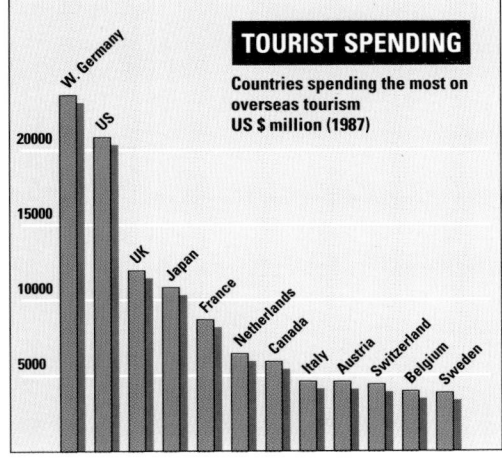

W. Germany US UK Japan France Netherlands Canada Italy Austria Switzerland Belgium Sweden

TOURIST EARNING

Countries receiving the most from overseas tourism US $ million (1987)

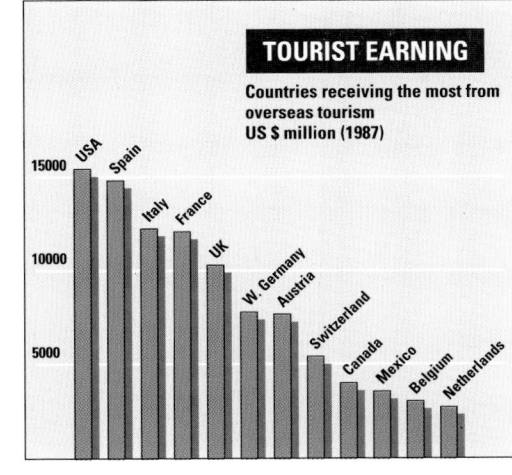

USA Spain Italy France UK W. Germany Austria Switzerland Canada Mexico Belgium Netherlands

Small economies in attractive areas are often completely dominated by tourism: in some West Indian islands, tourist spending provides over 90% of total income. In cash terms the USA is the world leader: its 1987 earnings exceeded 15 billion dollars, though that sum amounted to only 0.4% of its GDP.

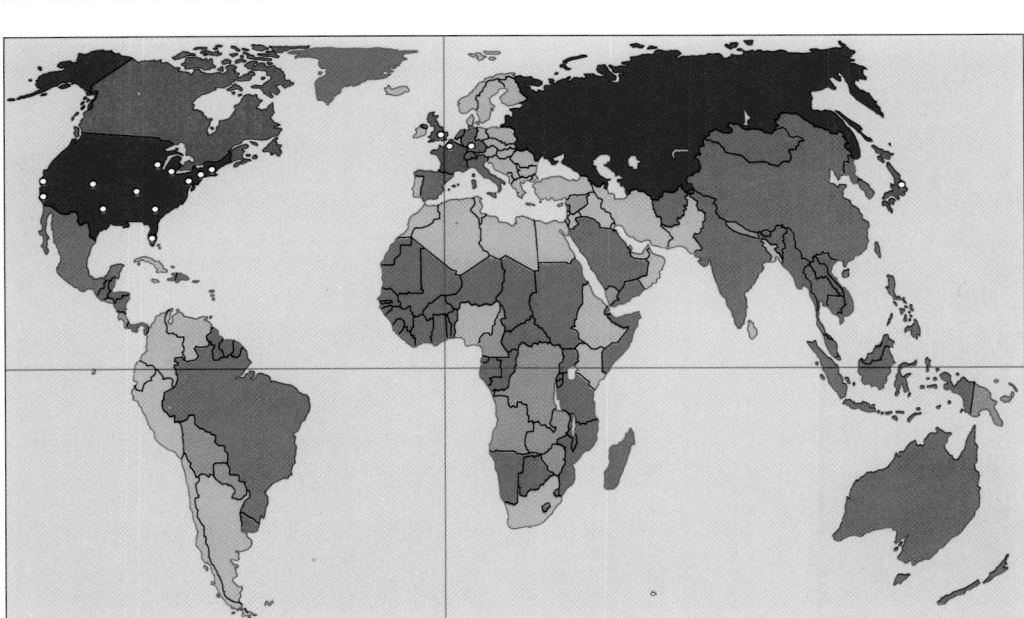

AIR TRAVEL

Millions of passenger km [number carried, international & domestic, multiplied by distance flown by each from airport of origin] (1988)

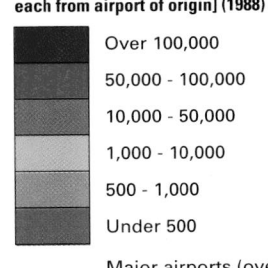

- Over 100,000
- 50,000 - 100,000
- 10,000 - 50,000
- 1,000 - 10,000
- 500 - 1,000
- Under 500

○ Major airports (over 20 million passengers a year)

The world's busiest airport in terms of total passengers is Chicago's O'Hare; the busiest international airport is Heathrow, the largest of London's airports.

43

QUALITY OF LIFE: HEALTH

According to statistics gathered in the late 1980s and early 1990s, a third of the world's population has no access to safe drinking water: malaria is on the increase; cholera, thought vanquished, is reappearing in South America; an epidemic of the terrifying AIDS virus is gathering force in Africa; and few developing countries can stretch their health care budgets beyond US $2 per person per year.

Yet human beings, by every statistical index, have never been healthier. In the richest nations, where food is plentiful, the demands of daily work are rarely onerous and medical care is both readily available and highly advanced, the average life expectancy is often more than 75 years – approaching the perceived limits for human longevity. In middle-income nations such as Brazil and the Philippines, life expectancy usually extends at least to the mid-60s; in China, it has already reached 70. Even in poverty-stricken Ethiopia and Chad, lifespans are close to 50. Despite economic crisis, drought, famine and even war, every country in the world reported an increase between 1965 and 1990.

It was not always so, even in countries then considered rich. By comparison, in 1880 the life expectancy of an average Berliner was under 30 years and infant mortality in the United Kingdom, then the wealthiest nation, stood at 144 per thousand births – a grim toll exceeded today only by three of the poorest African countries (Mali, Sierra Leone and Guinea). Even by 1910, European death rates were almost twice as high as the world average less than 80 years later; infant mortality in Norway, Europe's healthiest country, was then higher than in present-day Indonesia. In far less than a century, human prospects have improved beyond recognition.

In global terms, the transformation is less the result of high technology medicine – still too expensive for all but a minority, even in rich countries – than of improvements in agriculture and hence nutrition, matched by the widespread diffusion of the basic concepts of disease and public health. One obvious consequence, as death rates everywhere continue to fall, is sustained population growth. Another is the rising expectation of continued improvement felt by both rich and poor nations alike.

In some ways, the task is easier for developing countries, striving with limited resources to attain health levels to which the industrialized world has only recently become accustomed. As the tables below illustrate, infectious disease is rare among the richer nations, while ailments such as cancer, which tend to kill in advanced years, do not seriously impinge on populations with shorter lifespans.

Yet infectious disease is relatively cheap to eliminate, or at least reduce, and it is likely to be easier to raise life expectancy from 60 to 70 than from 75 to 85. The ills of the developed world and its ageing population are more expensive to treat – though most poor countries would be happy to suffer from the problems of the affluent. Western nations regularly spend more money on campaigns to educate their citizens out of over-eating and other bad habits than many developing countries can devote to an entire health budget – an irony that marks the dimensions of the rich-poor divide.

Indeed, wealth itself may be the most reliable indicator of longevity. Harmful habits are usually the province of the rich; yet curiously, though the dangerous effects of tobacco have been proved beyond doubt, the affluent Japanese combine very high cigarette consumption with the longest life expectancy of all the major nations. Similarly, heavy alcohol consumption seems to have no effect on longevity: the French, world leaders in 1988 and in most previous surveys, outlive the more moderate British by a year, and the abstemious Indians by almost two decades.

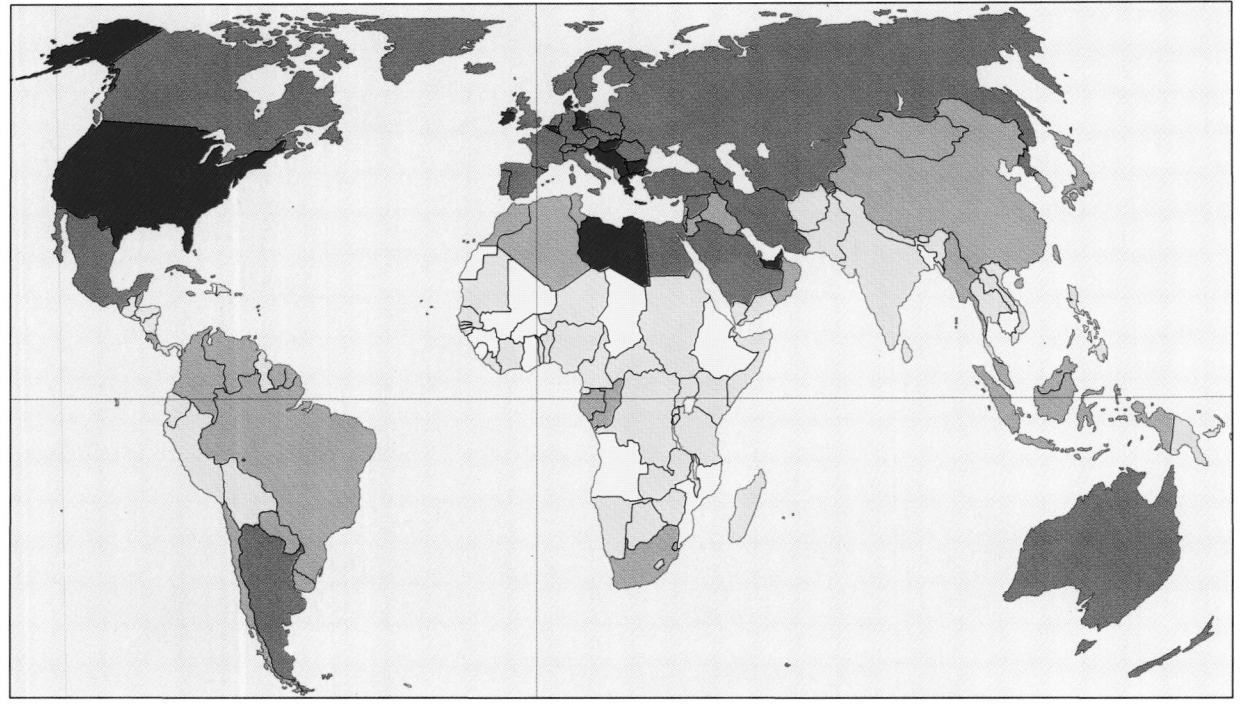

FOOD CONSUMPTION

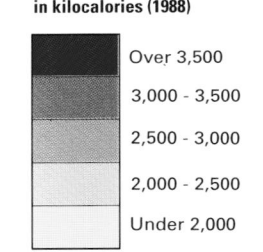

Average daily food intake per person in kilocalories (1988)

- Over 3,500
- 3,000 - 3,500
- 2,500 - 3,000
- 2,000 - 2,500
- Under 2,000

Highest intake

East Germany	3,814
UAE	3,733
Greece	3,688
USA	3,645
Bulgaria	3,642

Lowest intake

Mozambique	1,595
Chad	1,717
Ethiopia	1,749
Ghana	1,759
Guinea	1,776

[USA 3,645] [UK 3,256]

CAUSES OF DEATH

The rich not only live longer, on average, than the poor; they also die from different causes. Infectious and parasitic diseases, all but eliminated in the developed world, remain a scourge in poorer countries. On the other hand, more than two-thirds of the populations of OECD nations eventually succumb to cancer or circulatory disease; the proportion in Latin America is only about 45%. In addition to the three major diseases shown here, respiratory infection and injury also claim more lives in developing nations, which lack the drugs and medical skills required to treat them.

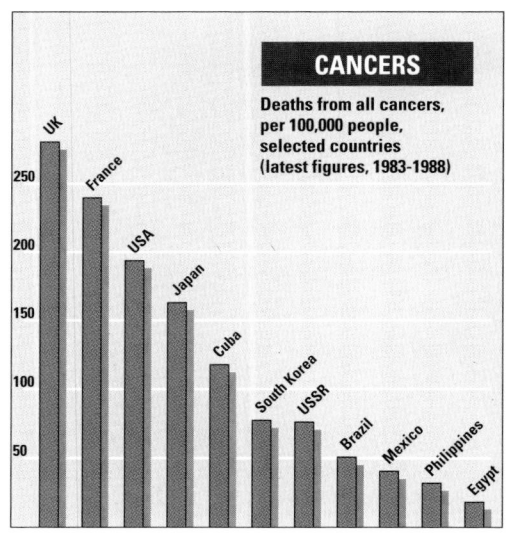

CANCERS

Deaths from all cancers, per 100,000 people, selected countries (latest figures, 1983-1988)

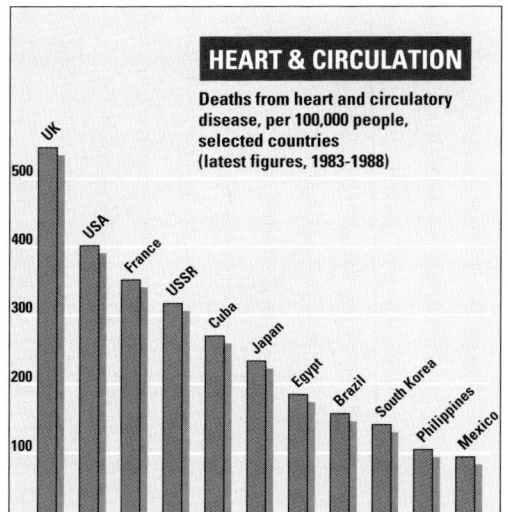

HEART & CIRCULATION

Deaths from heart and circulatory disease, per 100,000 people, selected countries (latest figures, 1983-1988)

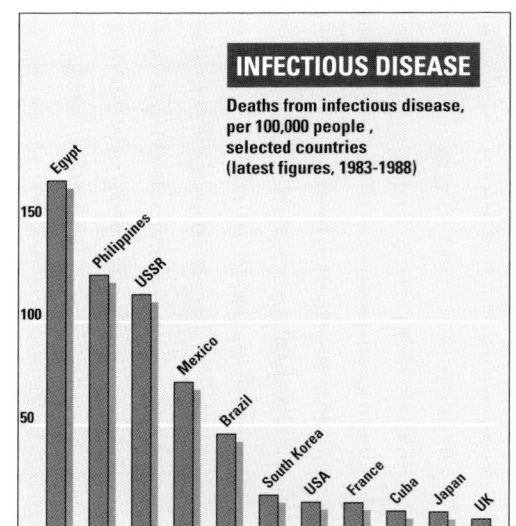

INFECTIOUS DISEASE

Deaths from infectious disease, per 100,000 people, selected countries (latest figures, 1983-1988)

LIFE EXPECTANCY

Years of life expectancy at birth, selected countries (1988-1989)

The chart shows combined data for both sexes. On average, women live longer than men worldwide, even in developing countries with high maternal mortality rates. Overall, life expectancy is steadily rising, though the difference between rich and poor nations remains dramatic.

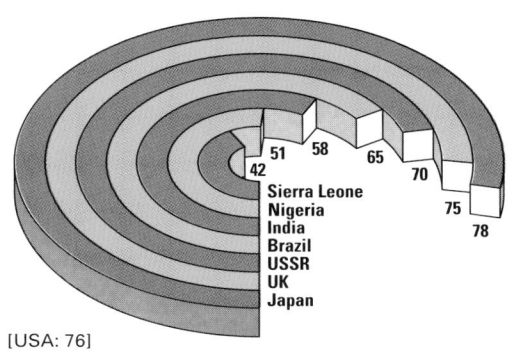

51 58 65 70 75 78
42
Sierra Leone
Nigeria
India
Brazil
USSR
UK
Japan

[USA: 76]

INFANT MORTALITY

Number of babies who die before the age of one year, per thousand live births (1988)

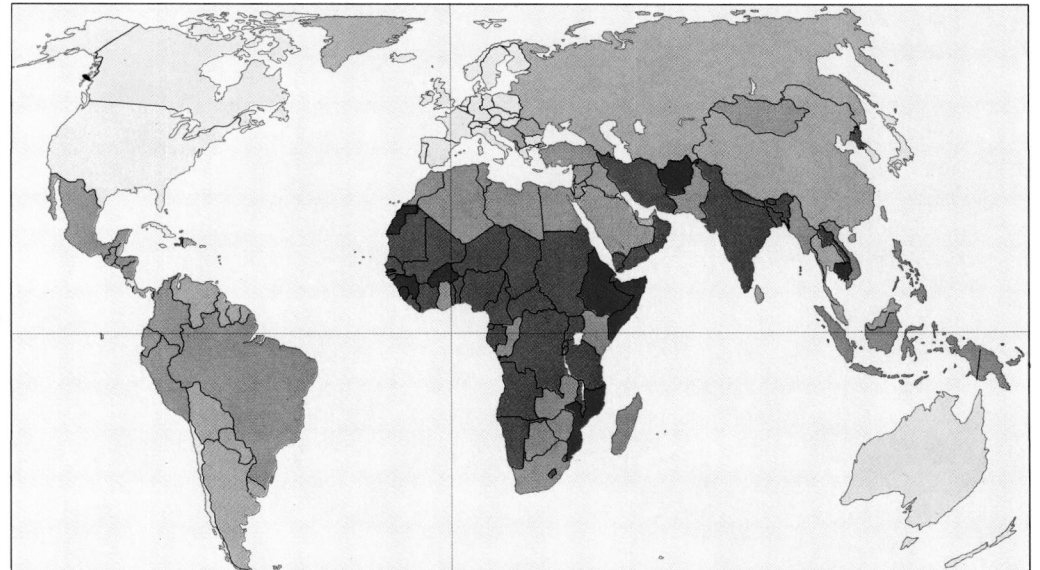
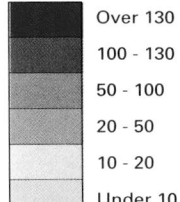

	Over 130
	100 - 130
	50 - 100
	20 - 50
	10 - 20
	Under 10

Highest infant mortality
Afghanistan 172
Ethiopia 154

Lowest infant mortality
Iceland 3
Japan 5

[USA 10] [UK 9]

HOSPITAL CAPACITY

Hospital beds available for each 1,000 people (1983-1988)

Highest capacity		Lowest capacity	
Finland	14.9	Bangladesh	0.2
Sweden	13.2	Nepal	0.2
France	12.9	Ethiopia	0.3
USSR	12.8	Mauritania	0.4
Netherlands	12.0	Mali	0.5
North Korea	11.7	Burkina Faso	0.6
Switzerland	11.3	Pakistan	0.6
Austria	10.4	Niger	0.7
Czechoslovakia	10.1	Haiti	0.8
Hungary	9.1	Chad	0.8

[UK 8] [USA 5.9]

The availability of a bed can mean anything from a private room in a well-equipped Californian teaching hospital to a place in the overcrowded annexe of a rural African clinic. In the Third World especially, quality of treatment can vary enormously from place to place within the same country.

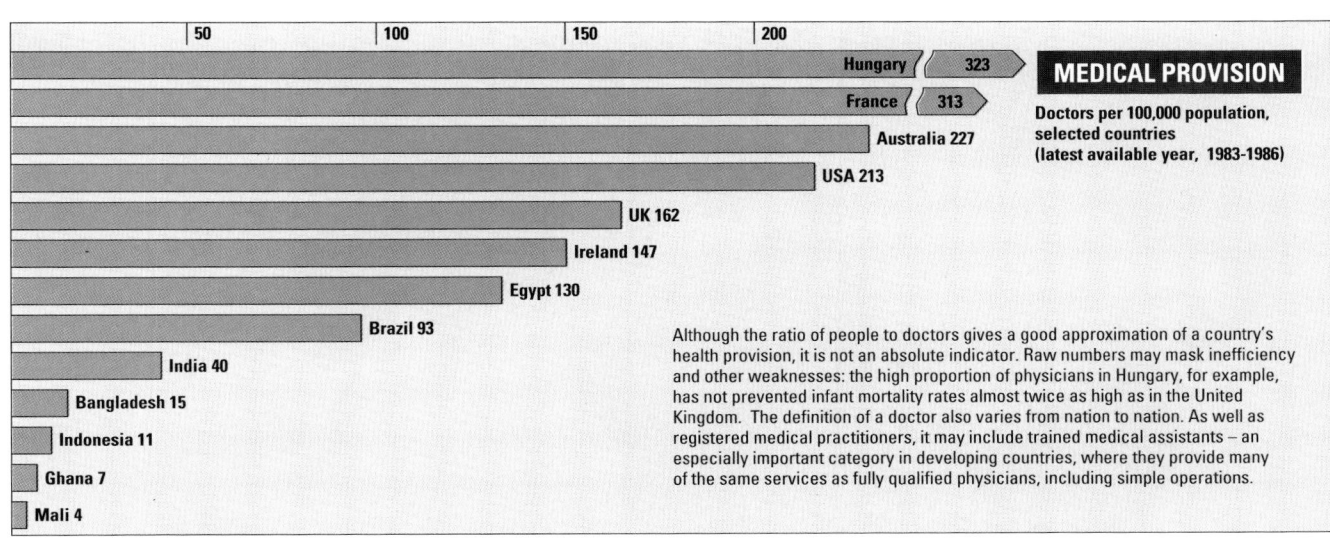

50 100 150 200
Hungary 323
France 313
Australia 227
USA 213
UK 162
Ireland 147
Egypt 130
Brazil 93
India 40
Bangladesh 15
Indonesia 11
Ghana 7
Mali 4

MEDICAL PROVISION

Doctors per 100,000 population, selected countries (latest available year, 1983-1986)

Although the ratio of people to doctors gives a good approximation of a country's health provision, it is not an absolute indicator. Raw numbers may mask inefficiency and other weaknesses: the high proportion of physicians in Hungary, for example, has not prevented infant mortality rates almost twice as high as in the United Kingdom. The definition of a doctor also varies from nation to nation. As well as registered medical practitioners, it may include trained medical assistants – an especially important category in developing countries, where they provide many of the same services as fully qualified physicians, including simple operations.

THE AIDS CRISIS

The Acquired Immune Deficiency Syndrome was first identified in 1981, when American doctors found otherwise healthy young men succumbing to rare infections. By 1984, the cause had been traced to the Human Immunodeficiency Virus (HIV), which can remain dormant for many years and perhaps indefinitely: only half of those known to carry the virus in 1981 had developed AIDS ten years later.

By 1991 the World Health Organization knew of more than 250,000 AIDS cases worldwide and suspected the true number to be at least four times as high. In Western countries in the early 1990s, most AIDS deaths were among male homosexuals or needle-sharing drug-users. However, the disease is spreading fastest among heterosexual men and women, which is its usual vector in the Third World, where most of its victims live. Africa is the most severely hit: the Ugandan authorities, for example, estimate that as many as 25% of the under-5s in some districts have been infected.

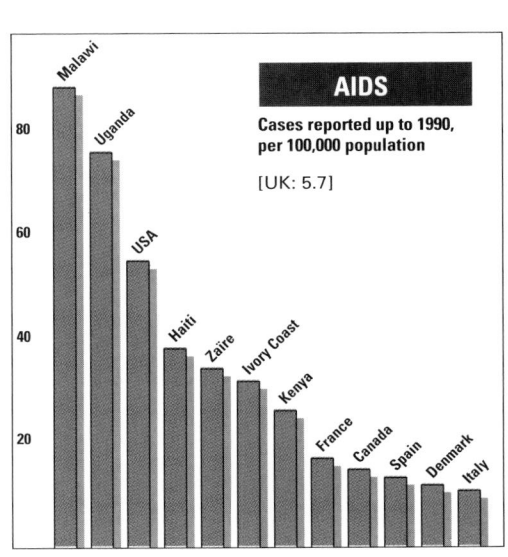

AIDS

Cases reported up to 1990, per 100,000 population

[UK: 5.7]

Malawi
Uganda
USA
Haiti
Zaire
Ivory Coast
Kenya
France
Canada
Spain
Denmark
Italy

80
60
40
20

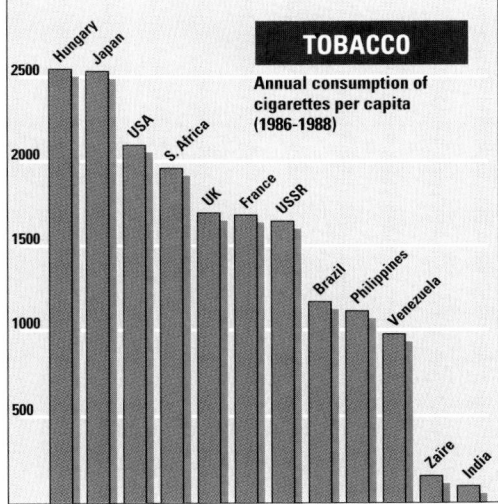

TOBACCO

Annual consumption of cigarettes per capita (1986-1988)

Hungary
Japan
USA
S. Africa
UK
France
USSR
Brazil
Philippines
Venezuela
Zaire
India

2500
2000
1500
1000
500

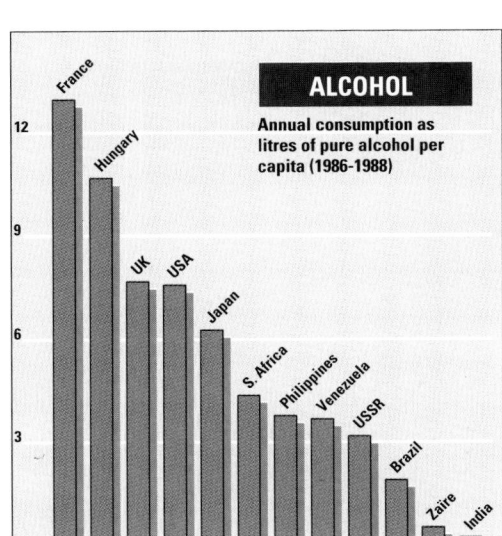

ALCOHOL

Annual consumption as litres of pure alcohol per capita (1986-1988)

France
Hungary
UK
USA
Japan
S. Africa
Philippines
Venezuela
USSR
Brazil
Zaire
India

12
9
6
3

CRIME & PUNISHMENT

MURDER RATES

Murders per 100,000 population, selected countries (1986)

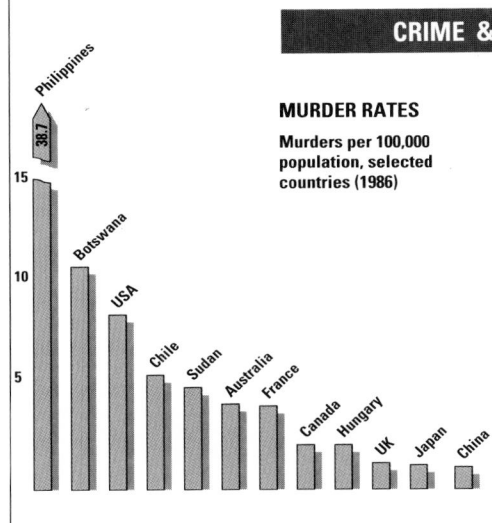

Philippines 38.7
Botswana
USA
Chile
Sudan
Australia
France
Canada
Hungary
UK
Japan
China

15
10
5

Crime rates are difficult to compare internationally. Standards of reporting and detection vary greatly, as do the definitions of many types of crime. Murder is probably the best detected as well as the most heinous, but different legal systems make different distinctions between murder and manslaughter or other forms of culpable homicide. By any reckoning, however, the USA's high murder rate stands out against otherwise similar Western countries, although it is dwarfed by the killings recorded in the very different culture of the Philippines.

PRISON POPULATIONS

Prisoners per 100,000 population, selected developed countries (1988)

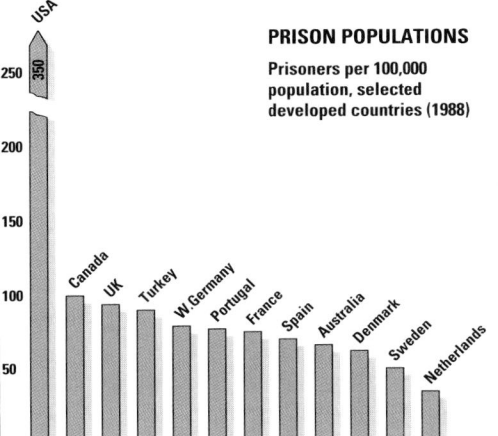

USA 350
Canada
UK
Turkey
W.Germany
Portugal
France
Spain
Australia
Denmark
Sweden
Netherlands

250
200
150
100
50

Differences in prison population reflect penal policies as much as the relative honesty or otherwise of different nations, and by no means all governments publish accurate figures. In more than 50 countries, people are still regularly imprisoned without trial, in 60 torture is a normal part of interrogation, and some 130 retain the death penalty, often administered for political crimes and in secret. Over 2,000 executions were recorded in 1990 by the civil rights organization Amnesty International; the real figure, as Amnesty itself maintains, was almost certainly much higher.

QUALITY OF LIFE: ENVIRONMENT

Humans have always had a dramatic effect on their environment, at least since the invention of agriculture almost 10,000 years ago. Generally, the Earth has accepted human interference without obvious ill effects: the complex systems that regulate the global environment have absorbed substantial damage while maintaining a stable and comfortable home for the planet's trillions of lifeforms. But advancing human technology and the rapidly expanding populations it supports are now threatening to overwhelm the Earth's ability to cope.

Industrial wastes, acid rainfall, expanding deserts and large-scale deforestation all combine to create environmental change at a rate far faster than the Earth can accommodate. Equipped with chain-saws and flame-throwers, humans can now destroy more forest in a day than their ancestors could in a century, upsetting the balance between plant and animal, carbon dioxide and oxygen, on which all life ultimately depends. The fossil fuels that power industrial civilization have pumped enough carbon dioxide and other green~house gases into the atmosphere to make climatic change a near-certainty. Chlorofluorocarbons (CFCs) and other man-made chemicals are rapidly eroding the ozone layer, the planet's screen against ultra-violet radiation.

As a result, the Earth's average temperature has risen by approximately 0.5°C since the beginning of this century. Further rises seem inevitable, with 1990 marked as the hottest year worldwide since records began. A warmer Earth probably means a wetter Earth, with melting icecaps raising sea levels and causing severe flooding in some of the world's most densely populated regions. Other climatic models suggest an alternative doom: rising temperatures could increase cloud cover, reflecting more solar energy back into space and causing a new ice age.

Either way, the consequences for humans could be disastrous – perhaps the Earth's own way of restoring ecological balance over the next few thousand years. Fortunately, there is a far faster mechanism available. Human ingenuity has provoked the present crisis; but human ingenuity, inspired if need be by fear, can respond to it. Production of CFCs is already almost at a standstill, and the first faltering steps towards stabilization and ultimately reduction of carbon dioxide have been taken, with Denmark pioneering the way by taxing emissions in 1991.

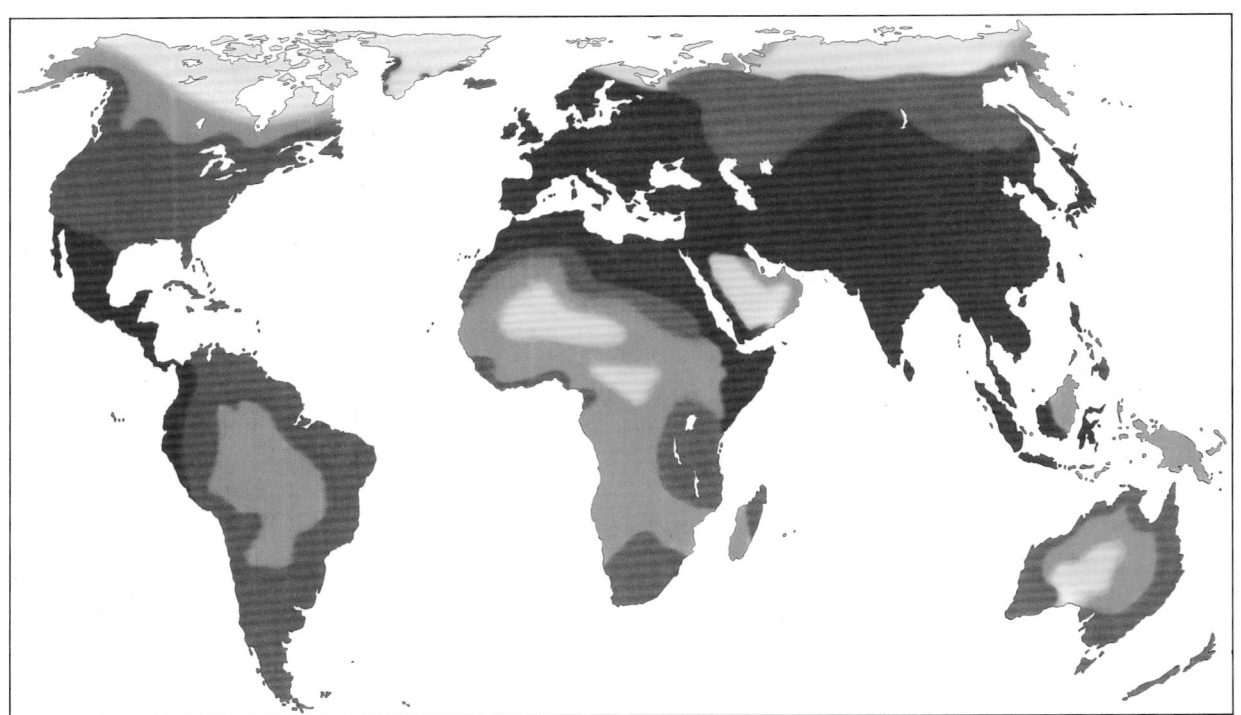

THE HISTORY OF HUMAN EXPANSION

The growth of ecological control: areas where human activity dominates the environment, from primitive times to the year 2000

- By 1500 AD
- By 1900 AD
- By 2000 AD
- Areas not dominated by human activity

THE RISE IN CARBON DIOXIDE

Emissions of carbon dioxide in millions of tonnes, 1950-1991

Atmospheric concentration of carbon dioxide, parts per million, 1750-2000. Pre-1950 data were obtained from air samples trapped in Antarctic ice.

Since the beginning of the Industrial Revolution, human activity has pumped steadily more carbon dioxide into the atmosphere. Most was quietly absorbed by the oceans, whose immense 'sink' capacity meant that 170 years were needed for levels to increase from the pre-industrial 280 parts per million to 300 (inset graph). But the vast increase in fuel-burning since 1950 (main graph) has overwhelmed even the oceanic sink. Atmospheric concentrations are now rising almost as steeply as carbon dioxide emissions themselves.

GREENHOUSE POWER

Relative contributions to the greenhouse effect by the major heat-absorbing gases in the atmosphere

The chart combines greenhouse potency and volume. Carbon dioxide has a greenhouse potential of only 1 but its concentration of 350 parts per million, makes it predominate. CFC 12, with 25,000 times the absorption capacity of CO_2, is present only as 0.00044 ppm.

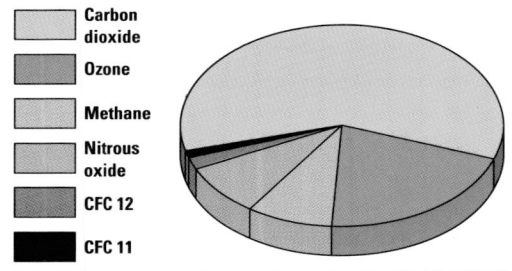

- Carbon dioxide
- Ozone
- Methane
- Nitrous oxide
- CFC 12
- CFC 11

CARBON DIOXIDE

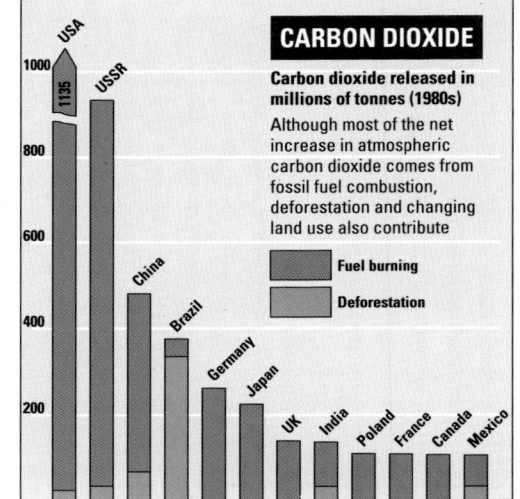

Carbon dioxide released in millions of tonnes (1980s)

Although most of the net increase in atmospheric carbon dioxide comes from fossil fuel combustion, deforestation and changing land use also contribute

- Fuel burning
- Deforestation

GLOBAL WARMING

The rise in average temperatures caused by carbon dioxide and other greenhouse gases (1960-2020)

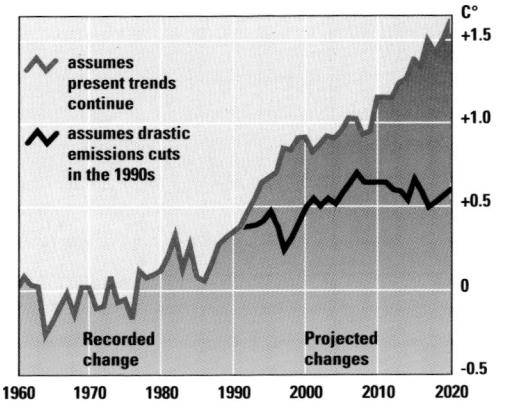

- assumes present trends continue
- assumes drastic emissions cuts in the 1990s

Recorded change

Projected changes

ACID RAIN

Acid rainfall & sources of acidic emissions (1980s)

Acid rain is caused when sulphur & nitrogen oxides in the air combine with water vapour to form sulphuric, nitric & other acids.

Regions where sulphur and nitrogen oxides are released in high concentrations, mainly from fossil fuel combustion.

• Major cities with high levels of air pollution (including nitrogen & sulphur emissions)

Areas of heavy acid deposition

pH numbers indicate acidity, decreasing from a neutral 7. Normal rain, slightly acid from dissolved carbon dioxide, never exceeds a pH of 5.6.

pH less than 4.0 (most acidic)
pH 4.0 to 4.5
pH 4.5 to 5.0

Areas where acid rain is a potential danger

THE ANTARCTIC

The vast Antarctic ice-sheet, containing some 70% of the Earth's fresh water, plays a crucial role in the circulation of atmosphere and oceans and hence in determining the planetary climate. The frozen southern continent is also the last remaining wilderness – the largest area to remain free from human colonization.

Ever since Amundsen and Scott raced for the South Pole in 1911, various countries have pressed territorial claims over sections of Antarctica, spurred in recent years by its known and suspected mineral wealth: enough iron ore to supply the world at present levels for 200 years, large oil reserves and, probably, the biggest coal deposits on Earth.

However, the 1961 Antarctic Treaty set aside the area for peaceful uses only, guaranteeing freedom of scientific investigation, banning waste disposal and nuclear testing, and suspending the issue of territorial rights. By 1990, the original 12 signatories had grown to 25, with a further 15 nations granted observer status in subsequent deliberations. However, the Treaty itself was threatened by wrangles between different countries, government agencies and international pressure groups.

Finally, in July, 1991, the belated agreement of the UK and the US assured unanimity on a new accord to ban all mineral exploration for a further 50 years. The ban can only be rescinded if all present signatories, plus a majority of any future adherents, agree. While the treaty has always lacked a formal mechanism for enforcement, it is firmly underwritten by public concern generated by the efforts of environmental pressure groups such as Greenpeace, foremost in the campaign to have Antarctica declared a 'World Park'.

It seems likely that the virtually uninhabited continent will remain untouched by tourism, nuclear-free and dedicated to peaceful scientific research.

DESERTIFICATION

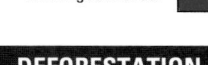

Existing deserts
Areas with a high risk of desertification
Areas with a moderate risk of desertification
Former areas of rainforest
Existing rainforest

DEFORESTATION

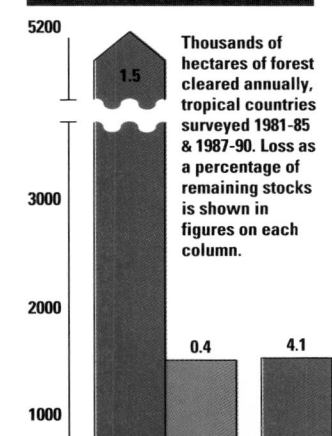

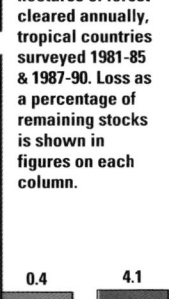

Thousands of hectares of forest cleared annually, tropical countries surveyed 1981-85 & 1987-90. Loss as a percentage of remaining stocks is shown in figures on each column.

5200

1.5

3000

2000

1000

0

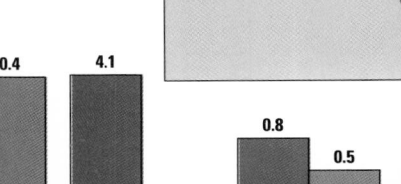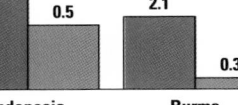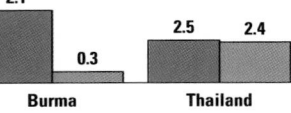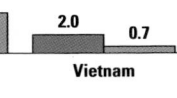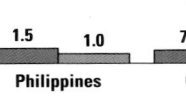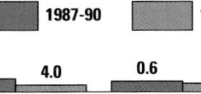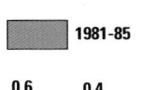

	Brazil	India	Indonesia	Burma	Thailand	Vietnam	Philippines	Costa Rica	Cameroon
1987-90	1.5 / 0.4	4.1	0.8	2.1	2.5	2.0	1.5	7.6	0.6
1981-85		0.3	0.5	0.3	2.4	0.7	1.0	4.0	0.4

1987-90   1981-85

WATER POLLUTION

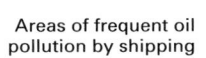

Severely polluted sea areas & lakes
Less polluted sea areas & lakes
Areas of frequent oil pollution by shipping

▶ Major oil tanker spills
▲ Major oil rig blow outs
▼ Offshore dumpsites for industrial & municipal waste
— Severely polluted rivers & estuaries

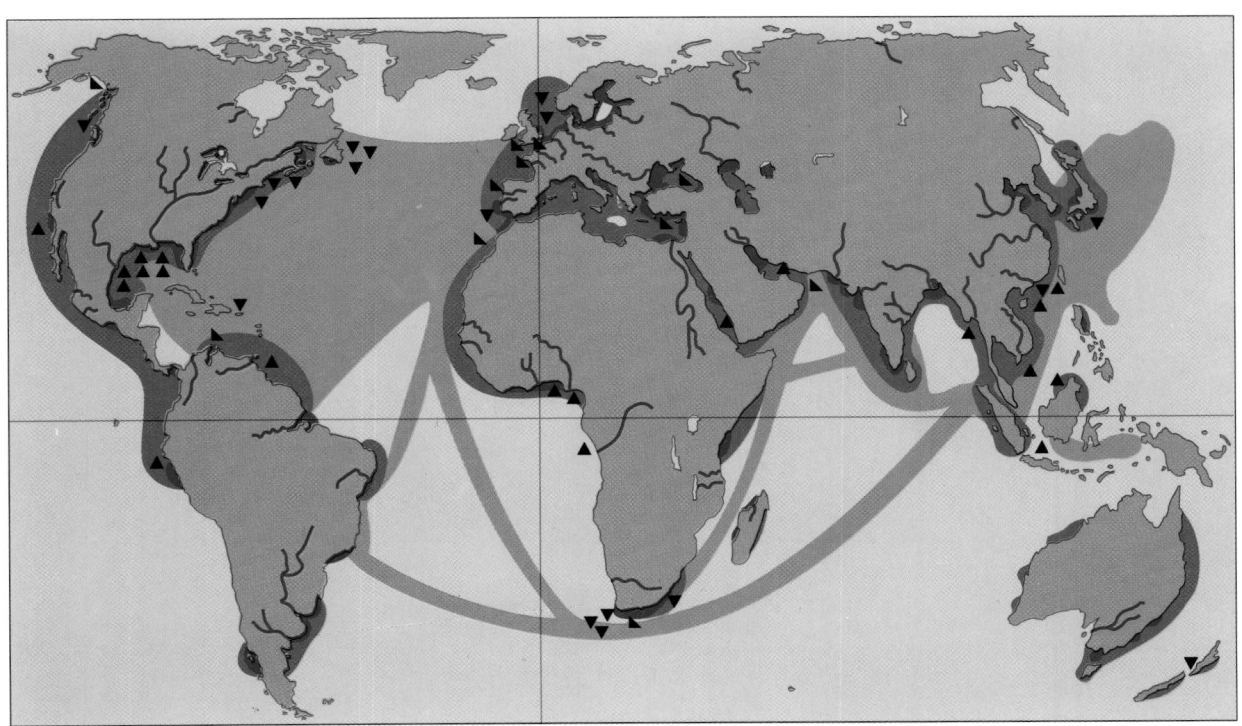

Poisoned rivers, domestic sewage and oil spillage have combined in recent years to reduce the world's oceans to a sorry state of contamination, notably near the crowded coasts of industrialized nations. Shipping routes, too, are constantly affected by tanker discharges. Oil spills of all kinds, however, declined significantly during the 1980s, from a peak of 750,000 tonnes in 1979 to under 50,000 tonnes in 1990. The most notorious tanker spill of that period – when the *Exxon Valdez* (94,999 gross registered tonnes) ran aground in Prince William Sound, Alaska, in March 1989 – released only 267,000 barrels, a relatively small amount compared to the results of blow-outs and war damage (see table). The worst tanker accident in history occurred in July 1979, when the *Atlantic Empress* and the *Aegean Captain* collided off Trinidad.

CITY MAPS

Oslo, Copenhagen 2, Helsinki, Stockholm 3, London 4, Paris 5, The Ruhr 6, Berlin, Hamburg, Munich 7, Madrid, Barcelona, Lisbon, Athens 8, Turin, Milan, Rome, Naples 9, Prague, Warsaw, Vienna, Budapest 10, Moscow, Leningrad 11, Osaka, Hong Kong, Seoul 12, Tokyo 13, Peking, Shanghai, Tientsin, Canton 14, Bangkok, Manila, Singapore, Jakarta 15, Delhi, Bombay, Calcutta 16, Istanbul, Tehran, Baghdad, Karachi 17, Lagos, Cairo, Johannesburg 18, Sydney, Melbourne 19, Montreal, Toronto 20, Boston 21, New York 22, Philadelphia 24, Washington, Baltimore 25, Chicago 26, San Francisco 27, Los Angeles 28, Mexico City 29, Havana, Caracas, Lima, Santiago 30, Rio de Janeiro, São Paulo 31, Buenos Aires 32

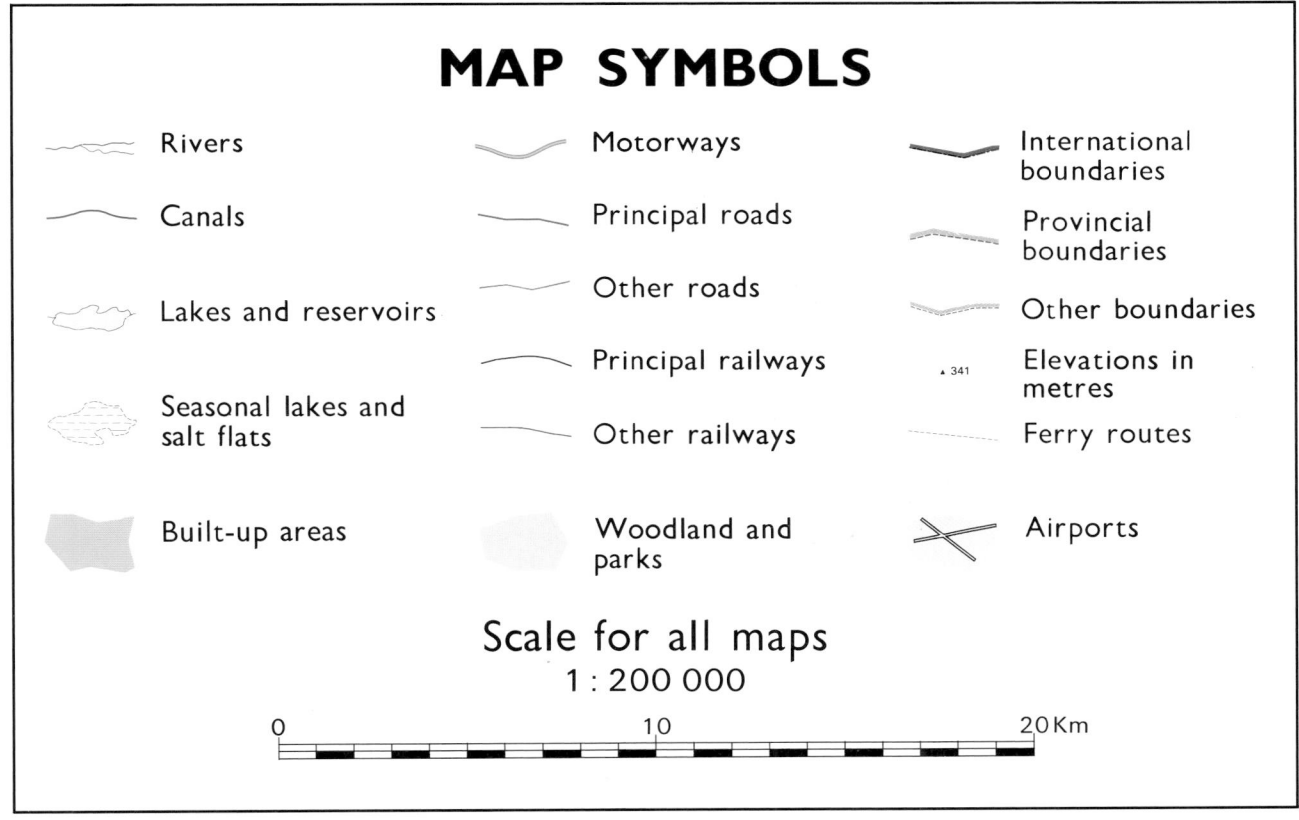

MAP SYMBOLS

Rivers	Motorways	International boundaries
Canals	Principal roads	Provincial boundaries
Lakes and reservoirs	Other roads	Other boundaries
	Principal railways	.341 Elevations in metres
Seasonal lakes and salt flats	Other railways	Ferry routes
Built-up areas	Woodland and parks	Airports

Scale for all maps
1 : 200 000

0   10   20 Km

1: 200 000

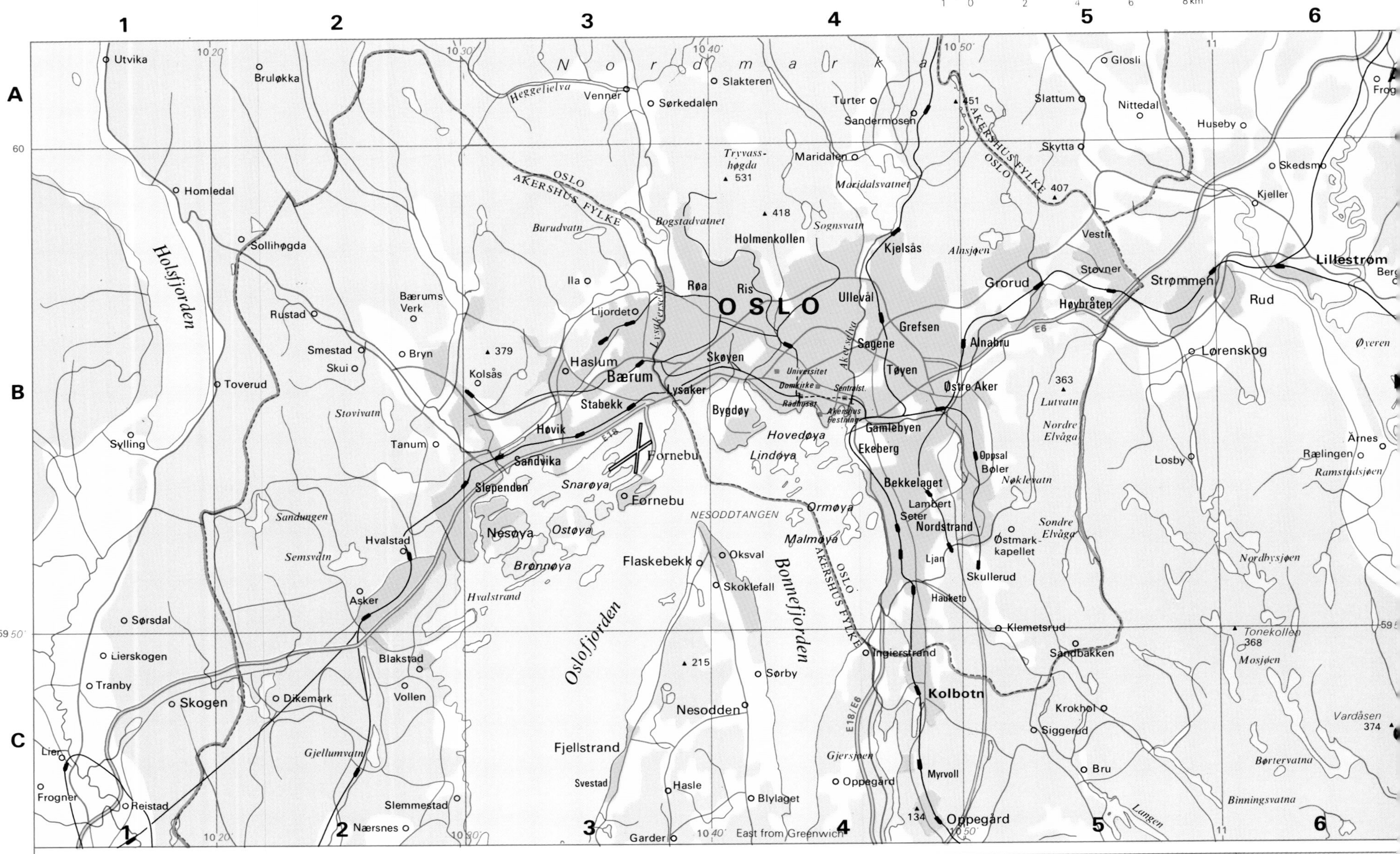

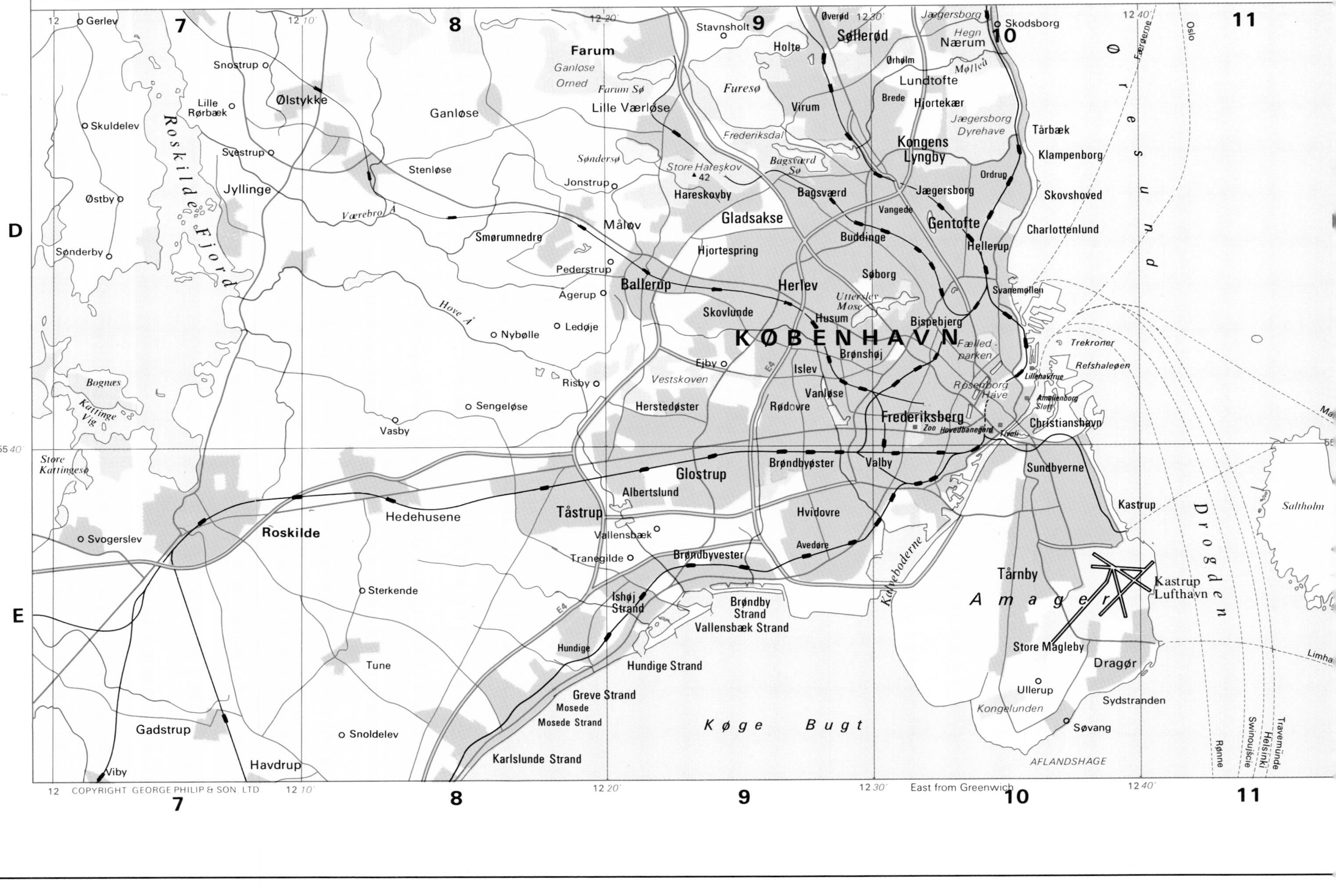

5 miles
8 km

1 2 3 4 5 6

A

Utvika
Bruløkka
Heggelielva
Venner
Sørkedalen
Slakteren
Turter
Sandermosen
Slattum
Nittedal
Huseby
Frogn
Glosli

60
Homledal
OSLO AKERSHUS FYLKE
Tryvass-høgda
▲ 531
Maridalen
Maridalsvatnet
Skytta
407
Skedsmo
Kjeller

Sollihøgda
Burudvatn
Bogstadvatnet
▲ 418
Holmenkollen
Sognsvatn
Kjelsås
Alnsjøen
Vestli
Stovner
Høybråten
Strømmen
Lillestrøm
Berg

Bærums Verk
Rustad
Ila
Røa
Ris
Ullevål
OSLO
Grorud
Rud
Øyeren

B
Smestad
Bryn
379
Haslum
Skøyen
Sagene
Grefsen
Alnabru
E6
Lørenskog

Skui
Kolsås
Bærum
Universitet
Domkirke
Sentralst
Tøyen
Østre Aker
363
Lutvatn

Toverud
Lysaker
Rådhuset
Akershus festning
Gamlebyen
Oppsal
Bøler
Nøklevatn
Losby

Sylling
Stovivatn
Stabekk
Bygdøy
Hovedøya
Lindøya
Ekeberg
Lambert Seter
Nordstrand
Sondre Elvåga
Årnes
Rælingen

Tanum
Hovik
Fornebu
Bekkelaget
Østmark-kapellet
Ramstadsjøen

Sandvika
Snarøya
Førnebu
Ormøya
Malmøya
Ljan
Nordbysjøen

Slependen
Sandungen
Semsvatn
Nesøya
Ostøya
NESODDTANGEN
Hauketo

Hvalstad
Brønnøya
Flaskebekk
Oksvall
Skullerud
Tonekollen
368
Mosjøen

Sørsdal
Asker
Hvalstrand
Skoklefall
Klemetsrud
Sandbakken
59 50

C
Lierskogen
Blakstad
▲ 215
Sørby
Ingierstrand
Kolbotn
Krokhøl
Vardåsen
374

Tranby
Dikemark
Vollen
Nesodden
Gjersjøen
E18/E6
Siggerud
Bru
Børtervatna

Skogen
Gjellumvatn
Fjellstrand
Svestad
Hasle
Oppegård
Myrvoll
Binningsvatna

Lier
Frogner
Reistad
Slemmestad
Næsnes
Blylaget
134
Oppegård
Langen

10 20   10 30   10 40   East from Greenwich   10 50

7 8 9 10 11

Gerlev
Stavnsholt
Øverød 12 30
Jægersborg
Skodsborg
Oslo
Faxinge

Snostrup
Holte
Søllerød
Hegn
Nærum
12 40

Lille Rørbæk
Ølstykke
Farum
Ganlose Orned
Furesø
Ørholm
Møllea
Skuldelev
Ganløse
Lille Værløse
Virum
Brede
Hjortekær
Jægersborg Dyrehave
Tårbæk

Svestrup
Stenløse
Frederiksdal
Bagsværd Sø
Kongens Lyngby
Ordrup
Klampenborg

D
Østby
Jyllinge
Jonstrup
Søndersø
Store Hareskov
42
Hareskovby
Bagsværd
Jægersborg
Skovshoved

Sønderby
Værebro Å
Målov
Gladsakse
Vangede
Gentofte
Charlottenlund

Smørumnedre
Pederstrup
Ågerup
Ballerup
Hjortespring
Buddinge
Søborg
Hellerup

Hove Å
Nybølle
Ledøje
Skovlunde
Herlev
Husum
Utterslev Mose
Svanemøllen

Bognæs
Kattinge Vig
Risby
Ejby
Islev
Brønshøj
Bispebjerg
Fælledparken
Trekroner
Refshaleøen

KØBENHAVN
Lillegrund
Sengeløse
Vestskoven
Vanløse
Rosenborg Have

55 40
Store Kattingesø
Vasby
Herstedøster
Rødovre
Frederiksberg
Zoo
Hovedbanegård
Christianshavn

Glostrup
Brøndbyøster
Valby
Sundbyerne

Svogerslev
Roskilde
Hedehusene
Albertslund
Tåstrup
Hvidovre
Kastrup

Sterkende
Vallensbæk
Avedøre
Kalveboderne
Drogden
Saltholm

Tranegilde
Brøndbyvester
Tårnby
Kastrup Lufthavn
Amager

E
Ishøj Strand
Brøndby Strand
Vallensbæk Strand
Store Magleby
Dragør

Tune
Hundige
Hundige Strand
Ullerup
Sydstranden

Gadstrup
Snoldelev
Greve Strand
Mosede
Mosede Strand
Kongelunden
Søvang

Viby
Havdrup
Karlslunde Strand
Køge Bugt
AFLANDSHAGE
Travemünde Helsinki Swinoujscie
Rønne

12   12 10   12 20   12 30   East from Greenwich   12 40

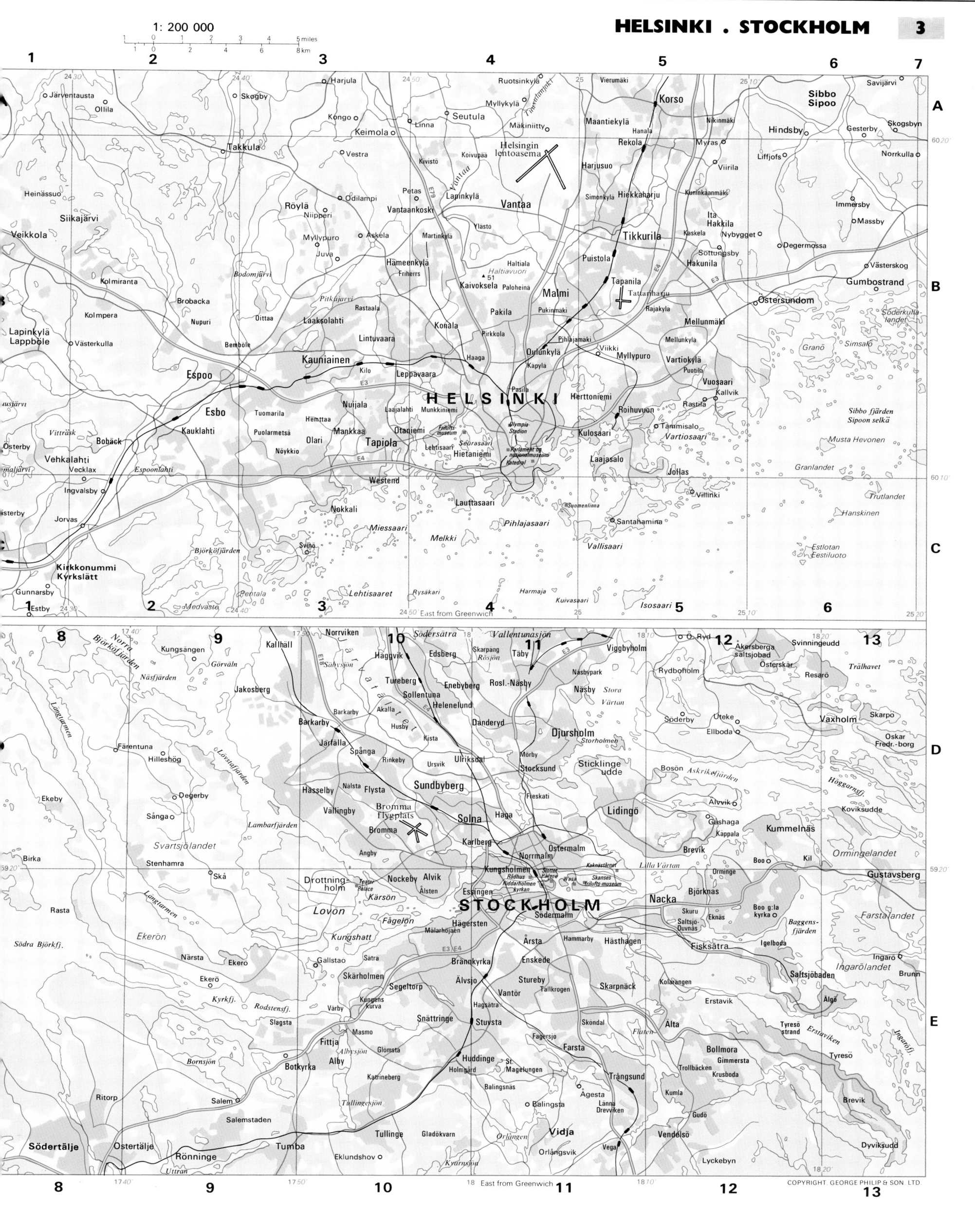

1:200 000

0 1 2 3 4 5 miles
0 1 2 3 4 5 6 7 8 km

A B C D

7 6 5 4 3 2 1

East from Greenwich

West from Greenwich

GREATER LONDON

River Thames

Epping Forest

Heathrow Airport

Blackmore · Heybridge · Doddinghurst · Mountnessing · Shenfield · Brentwood · Ingrave · Herongate · Bulphan · Orsett · Chadwell St. Mary · Little Thurrock · Tilbury · Northfleet · Singlewell · Istead Rise · Meopham · New Ash Green · Culverstone Green · Stansted · Trottiscliffe · Borough Green · Wrotham

Chipping Ongar · Toot Hill · Pilgrims Hatch · Weald Park · Brook Street · Kelvedon Hatch · Harold Hill · Harold Wood · Gallows Corner · Squirrel's Heath · Emerson Park · Cranham · Upminster · South Ockendon · North Stifford · South Stifford · Aveley · West Thurrock · Purfleet · Greenhithe · Stone · Swanscombe · Dartford · Wilmington · Hextable · Swanley · West Kingsdown · Hartley · Farningham · Eynsford · Shoreham · Otford · Dunton Green · Riverhead · Sevenoaks · Kemsing

Theydon Bois · Stapleford Abbotts · Abridge · Chigwell Row · Collier Row · Romford · Havering-atte-Bower · Gidea Park · Hornchurch · Rainham · Wennington · Belvedere · Erith · Northumberland Heath · Slade Green · Crayford · Bexleyheath · Welling · East Wickham · Bexley · Sidcup · North Cray · St Paul's Cray · St Mary Cray · Crockenhill · Chelsfield · Badgers Mount · Knockholt Pound · Halstead · Pratts Bottom

Epping · Loughton · High Beach · Waltham Abbey · Cheshunt · Enfield · Chingford · Woodford · Woodford Green · Buckhurst Hill · Chigwell · Grange Hill · Hainault · Barkingside · Clayhall · Gants Hill · Ilford · Redbridge · Wanstead · Forest Gate · Manor Park · East Ham · West Ham · Stratford · Newham · Barking · Beckton · North Woolwich · Silvertown · Woolwich · Plumstead · Abbey Wood · West Heath · Thamesmead · Creekmouth · Shooters Hill · Eltham · Chislehurst · Mottingham · Grove Park · Orpington · Southborough · Green Street Green · Downe · Cudham · Biggin Hill · Tatsfield · Westerham

Cuffley · Potters Bar · Northaw · Barnet · New Barnet · East Barnet · Hadley Wood · Cockfosters · Southgate · Palmers Green · Winchmore Hill · Enfield Lock · Enfield Wash · Ponders End · Lower Edmonton · Upper Edmonton · Edmonton · Tottenham · Wood Green · Hornsey · Crouch End · Muswell Hill · Finchley · Friern Barnet · Whetstone · North Finchley · Totteridge · Arkley · Mill Hill · Hendon · Colindale · Burnt Oak · Edgware · Stone Grove · Stanmore · Belmont · Harrow Weald · Wealdstone · Kenton · Wembley · Kingsbury · Neasden · Willesden · Cricklewood · Golders Green · Hampstead Garden Suburb · Highgate · Kentish Town · Camden · Islington · Stoke Newington · Hackney · Bethnal Green · Stepney · Tower Hamlets · City · Shoreditch · Whitechapel · Wapping · Bermondsey · Rotherhithe · Deptford · Greenwich · Blackheath · Lewisham · Catford · Lee · Hither Green · Grove Park · Bellingham · Beckenham · Penge · Sydenham · Forest Hill · Dulwich · East Dulwich · Peckham · Camberwell · Brixton · Clapham · Battersea · Wandsworth · Tooting · Streatham · Mitcham · Wimbledon · Merton · Morden · St Helier · Carshalton · Wallington · Beddington · Croydon · Addiscombe · Shirley · Selsdon · Sanderstead · Warlingham · Woldingham · Caterham · Whyteleafe · Kenley · Coulsdon · Old Coulsdon · Purley · Waddington

Radlett · Bricket Wood · Shenley · Green Street · Borehamwood · Elstree · Bushey · South Oxhey · Stanmore · Pinner · Northwood · Ruislip · Eastcote · Rayners Lane · North Harrow · West Harrow · Harrow · Harrow on the Hill · Roxeth · South Harrow · Greenford · Perivale · Wembley · Alperton · Ealing · Acton · Chiswick · Brentford · Kew · Richmond · Twickenham · Teddington · Hampton · Sunbury · Walton on Thames · Weybridge · Esher · Claygate · Oxshott · Cobham · Stoke D'Abernon · Leatherhead · Fetcham · Great Bookham · Ashtead · Epsom · Ewell · Cheam · Sutton · Banstead · Burgh Heath · Kingswood · Tadworth · Walton on the Hill · Headley

Chipperfield · Abbots Langley · Watford · Cassiobury Park · Croxley Green · Chorleywood · Rickmansworth · Denham Green · Harefield · Ickenham · Uxbridge · Cowley · Yiewsley · West Drayton · Hillingdon · Hayes · Hayes End · Iver · Denham · Hounslow · Isleworth · Heston · Cranford · Harlington · Harmondsworth · East Bedfont · Feltham · Ashford · Staines · Egham · Thorpe · Laleham · Chertsey · Shepperton · Sunbury · Hanworth · Hampton · East Molesey · Thames Ditton · Long Ditton · Surbiton · Kingston upon Thames · Hook · Chessington · Malden · New Malden · Raynes Park · Wimbledon · Roehampton · Putney · Fulham · Hammersmith · Kensington · Chelsea · Westminster · Lambeth · Southwark · Paddington · Marylebone · Maida Vale · Kilburn · Brondesbury · Bayswater · Notting Hill · Shepherds Bush

River Lea · River Roding · River Ingrebourne · River Darent · River Cray · River Crane · River Mole · River Wey · River Wandle · Grand Union Canal · Watling Street · Grand Junction Canal

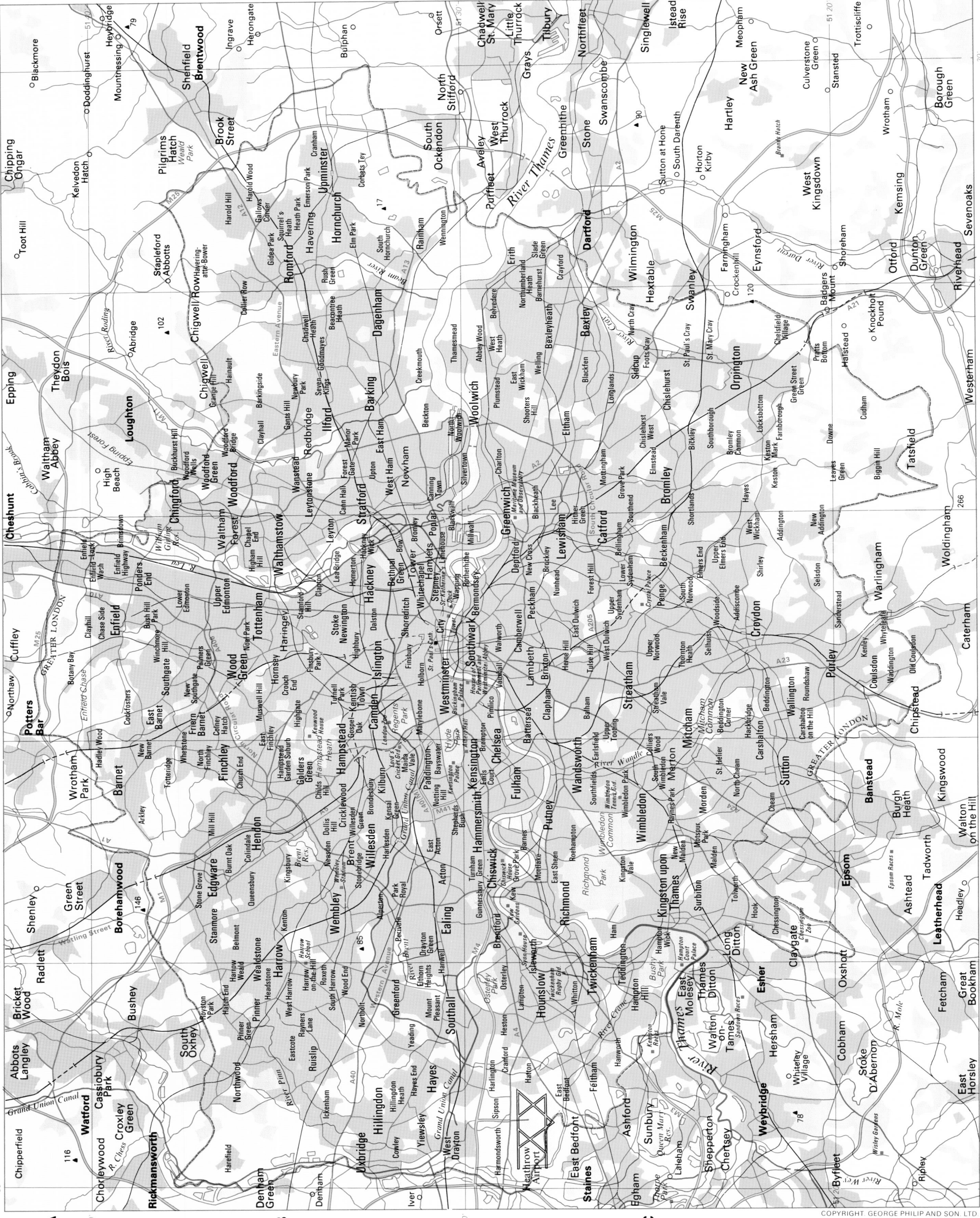

COPYRIGHT GEORGE PHILIP AND SON, LTD.

1:200 000

5 miles
8 km

PARIS

East from Greenwich

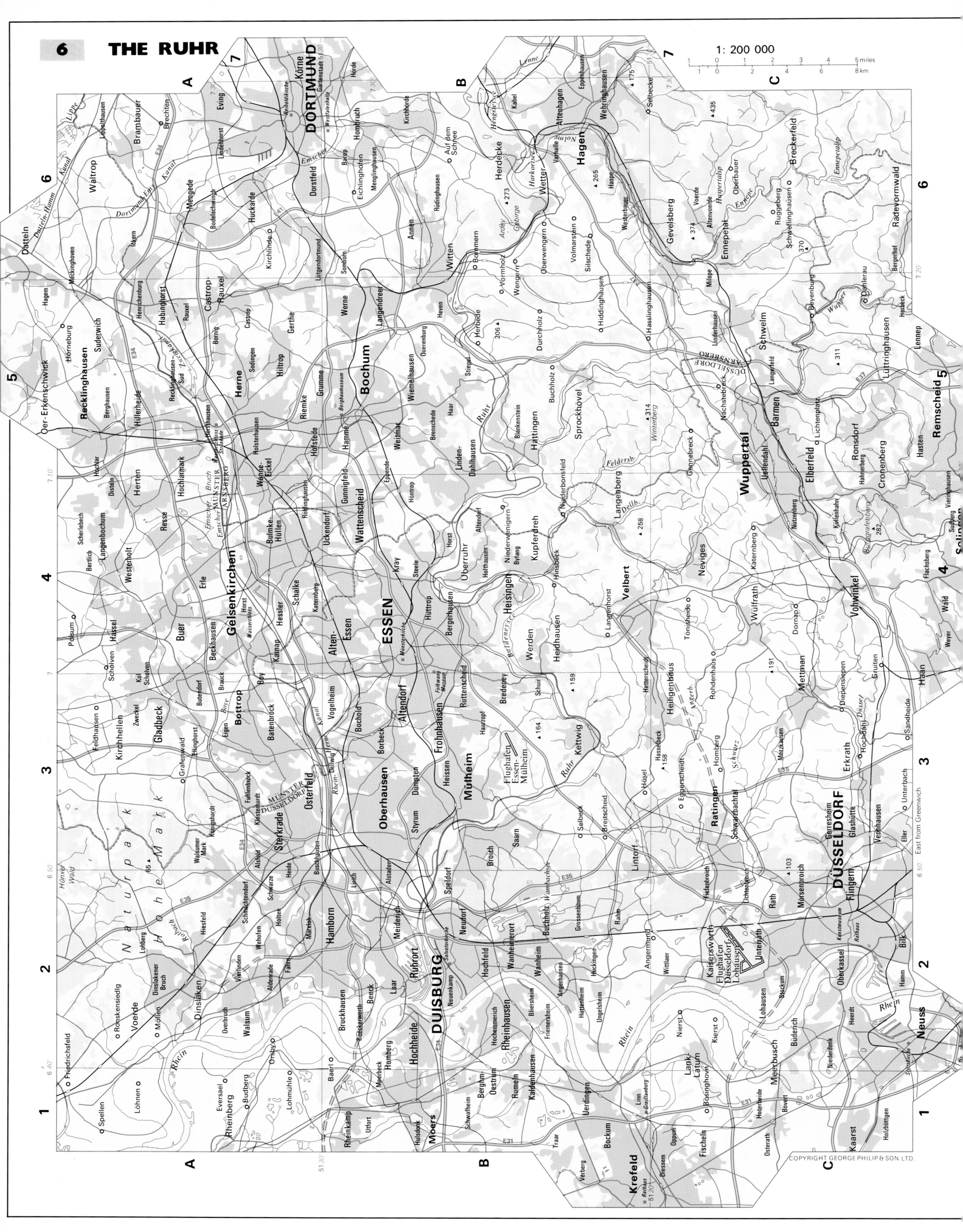

1: 200 000

COPYRIGHT GEORGE PHILIP & SON LTD.

1 : 200 000

0 1 2 3 4 5 miles
0 2 4 6 8 km

1 2 3 4 5

Berlin (upper map)

Pausin · Wansdorf · Botzow · Frohnau · Glienicke · Schildow · Röntgental · Zepernick · Birkenhöhe · Elisenau · Stienitzsee
Hennigsdorf · Stolpe-Süd · Hermsdorf · Lübars · Blankenfelde · Buch · Schwanebeck · Birkholzaue · Werneuchen
Schönwalde · Nieder Neuendorf · Schulzendorf · Waidmannslust · Karow · Neu Buch · Birkholz · Löhme · Rudolfshöhe
Alter Finkenkrug · Siedlung Schönwalde · Heiligensee · Buchholz · Lindenberg · Blumberg · Krummensee · Wegendorf · Neuhonow
Waldheim · Falkensee · Falkenhagen · Johannesstift · Tegeler See · Scharfenberg · Flughafen Tegel · Rosenthal · Niederschönhausen · Blankenburg · Malchow · Ahrensfelde · Trappenfelde · Paulshof · Altlandsberg Nord
Finkenkrug · Seegefeld · Spandau · Haselhorst · Reinickendorf · Pankow · Weissensee · Heinersdorf · Wartenberg · Falkenberg · Eiche · Mehrow · Seeberg · Altlandsberg
Döberitz · Dallgow · Staaken · Siemensstadt · Wedding · Prenzlauerberg · Mitte · Hohenschönhausen · Marzahn · Eiche Süd · Honow · Friedrichslust · Fredersdorf Nord
Seeburg · Charlottenburg · Schloss Charlottenburg · Tiergarten · Hellersdorf · Neuenhagen · Fredersdorf
Gatow · Teufelsberg · Spree · Deutsche Oper · Zoo Station · Brandenburg Gate · **BERLIN** · Kreuzberg · Friedrichshain · Biesdorf · Wuhlgarten · Birkenstein · Bollensdorf · Dahlwitz-Hoppegarten · Vogelsdorf
Grunewald · Olympic Stadium · Rathaus · Schöneberg · Treptow · Friedrichsfelde · Kaulsdorf · Mahlsdorf · Münchehofe
Gross Glienicke · Krampnitz · Kladow · Schmargendorf · Friedenau · Neukölln · Flughafen Tempelhof · Karlshorst · Heidemühle · Kleinschönebeck · Schöneiche
Neu Fahrland · Sacrow · Schwanenwerder · Dahlem · Tempelhof · Oberschöneweide · Waldesruh · Fichtenau · Schönblick
Nedlitz · Krumme Lanke · Steglitz · Niederschöneweide · Johannisthal · Aldershof · Köpenick · Grosse Müggelsee · Wilhelmshagen · Woltersdorf
Wannsee · Nikolassee · Zehlendorf · Lichterfelde · Lankwitz · Mariendorf · Britz · Telton-kanal · Grünau · Müggelberge · Rahnsdorf · Springeberg · Erkner
Potsdam · Klein Gleinicke · Dreilinden · Kleinmachnow · Seehof · Marienfelde · Buckow · Altglienicke · Wendenschloss · Müggelheim · Neu Buchhorst · Gosen
Babelsberg · Kienwerder · Stahnsdorf · Teltow · Ruhlsdorf · Heinersdorf · Lichtenrade · Grossziethen · Rudow · Bohnsdorf · Karolinenhof · Dahmic · Schmöckwitz · Neu Zittau
Friederikenhof · Kleinziethen · Schönefeld · Flughafen Schönefeld · Eichwalde

Hamburg (lower left map)

6 7 8

Quickborn · Harksheide · Tangstedter Forst · Duvenstedter Brook · Ost Rantzau · Renzel · Norderstedt · Glasmoor · Wulksfelde
Höhenraden · Wulfsmühle · Hasloh · Haslohfeld · Moorbek · Duvenstedt · Ammersbek
Pinneberg · Tangstedt · Winzeldorf · Ochsenzoll · Glashütte · Lemsahl · Wohldorf-Ohlstedt
Rellingen · Ellerbek · Egenbüttel · Bönningstedt · Garstedt · Hummelsbüttel · Mellingstedt · Bergstedt · Volksdorf
Halstenbeck · Neuegenbüttel · Schnelsen · Langenhorn · Poppenbüttel · Sasel · Berne
Brande · Krupunder · Niendorf · Flughafen Hamburg · Fuhlsbüttel · Wellingsbüttel · Meiendorf · Farmsen
Friedrichshulde · Eidelstedt · Gross Borstel · Alsterdorf · Ohlsdorf · Steilshoop · Brämfeld · Rahlstedt
Schenefeld · Lurup · Lokstedt · Stellingen · Winterhude · Hinschenfelde · Wandsbek · Tonndorf · Jenfeld
Sülldorf · Osdorf · Bahrenfeld · Eimsbüttel · Harvestehude · Barmbek · Uhlenhorst · Marienthal · Horn
Iserbrook · Gross-Flottbek · St. Pauli · Rotherbaum · Eilbek · Höhenfelde · Billstedt
Blankenese · Nienstedten · Othmarschen · Ottensen · Altona · Hamm · Hammerbrook · Kirchsteinbek
Finkenwerder · Waltershof · Steinwerder · Kl. Grasbrook · Rothenburgsort · Billbrook · Boberg
Rosengarten · Neuenfelde · Altenwerder · Veddel · Georgswerder · Billwärder · Billwerder
Nincop · Vierzigstücken · Francop · Wilhelmsburg · Goetjensort · Moorfleet · Bf. Mittlerer Landweg
Neugraben-Fischbek · Neuwiedenthal · Moorburg · Kirchdorf · Tatenberg · Spadenland · Allermöhe
Neu Wulmstorf · Hausbruch · Heimfeld · Harburg · Neuland · Funfhausen · Moorwerder · Ochsenwerder · Reithbrook · Marschlande
Schwarze Berge · Eissendorf

München (lower right map)

9 10 11

Etzenhausen · Riedmoos · Unterschleissheim
Dachau · Mittenheim · Oberschleissheim · Garching · Carlshof
Udlding · Dachau Ost · Badersfeld · Hochbrück · Lustheim
Obermoos Schwaige · Rothschwaige · Olympia-Ruderregattastrecke · Neuherberg · Ismaning
Gröbenried · Karlsfeld · Dirnismaning · Speichersee
Eschenried · Ludwigsfeld · Feldmoching · Am Hasenbergl · Freimann · Unterföhring
Gerberau · Moosach · Milbertshofen · Johanneskirchen · Aschheim
Allach · Untermenzing · Gross-Lappen · Schwabing · Oberföhring
Langwald · Obermenzing · Bogenhausen · Dornach · Feldkirchen
Lockhausen · Blutenberg · Nymphenburg · Neuhausen · Schloss Nymphenburg · Zamdorf · Haidhausen · Dagfling · Riem · Flughafen München-Riem
Aubing · Neu Aubing · Freiham · Pasing · Laim · **MÜNCHEN** · Ramersdorf · Salmdorf
Freimann · Locham · Gräfelfing · Klein-Hadern · Gross-Hadern · Sendling · Berg am Laim · Strassrudering · Gronsdorf
Planegg · Martinsried · Thalkirchen · Giessing · Neuperlach · Haar · Keferloh
Krailling · Neuried · Fürstenried · Fasangarten · Perlach · Solalinden · Oden-Stockach
Forstenried · Solln · Harlaching · Unterbiberg · Waldperlach · Putzbrunn · Neubiberg
Maxhof · Warnberg · Grosshesselohe · Geiselgasteig · Perlacher Forst · Ottobrunn · Hohenbrunn
Pullach · Am Wald · Taufkirchen · Winning · Bergham · Wachterhof
Höllriegelskreuth · Forstenrieder Park · Grünwalder Forst · Furth · Kirchstockbach
Buchenhain · Grünwald · Unterhaching · Westerham · Höhenkirchen
Baierbrunn · Laufzorn · Oberhaching · Deisenhofen · Brunnthal · Strasslach

East from Greenwich

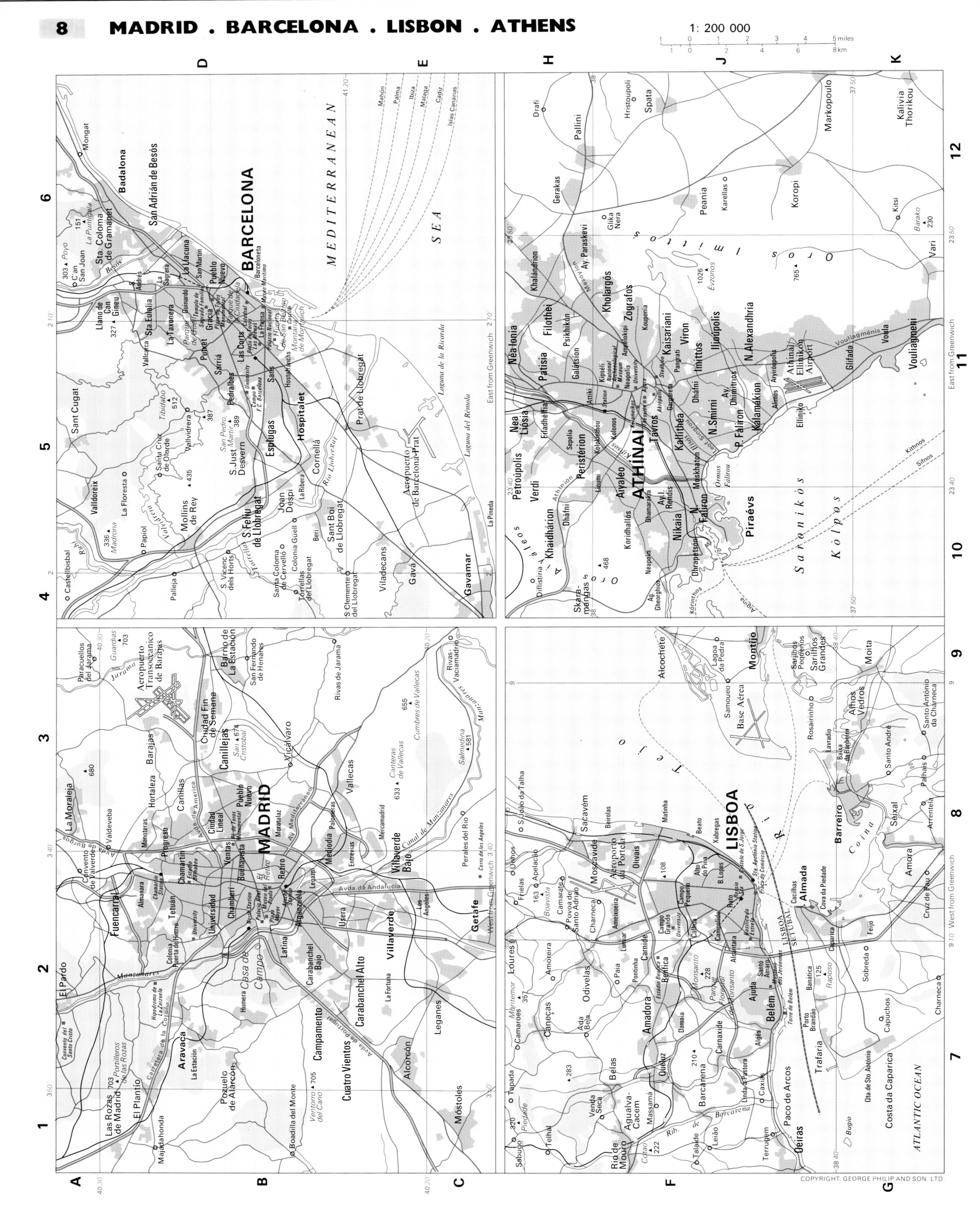

1 : 200 000

5 miles
8 km

MILANO

Monza
Lissone
Desio
Cinisello Bálsamo
Sesto S. Giovanni
Lambrate
Bresso
Baldinasco
Córsico
Rho

TORINO

Séttimo Tor.
Chieri
Volpiano
Moncalieri
Nichelino
Mirafiori
Grugliasco
Pianezza
Rívoli
Alpignano
Caselle Tor.
Venaria

NÁPOLI

Acerra
Afragola
Casória
Arzano
Caivano
Frattamaggiore
Giugliano in Camp.
Pórtici
Torre del Greco
Torre Annunziata
Bosco-trecase
Ercolano
Golfo di Nápoli
Vesúvio

ROMA

CITTÀ DEL VATICANO
E.U.R.
Cinecittà
Centocelle
Ostiense
Acilia
Via Appia Antica
Agro Romano

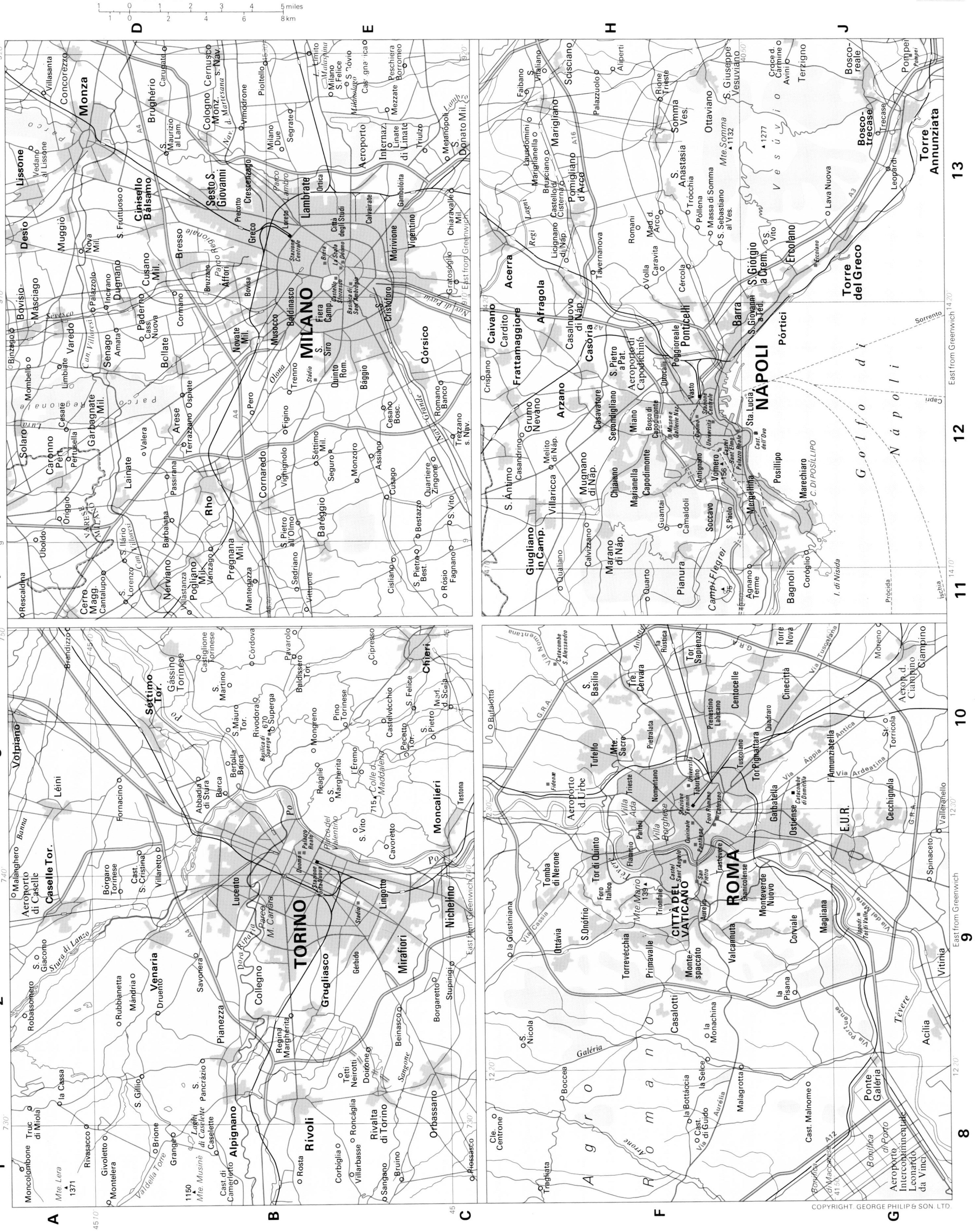

COPYRIGHT GEORGE PHILIP & SON LTD

1 : 200 000

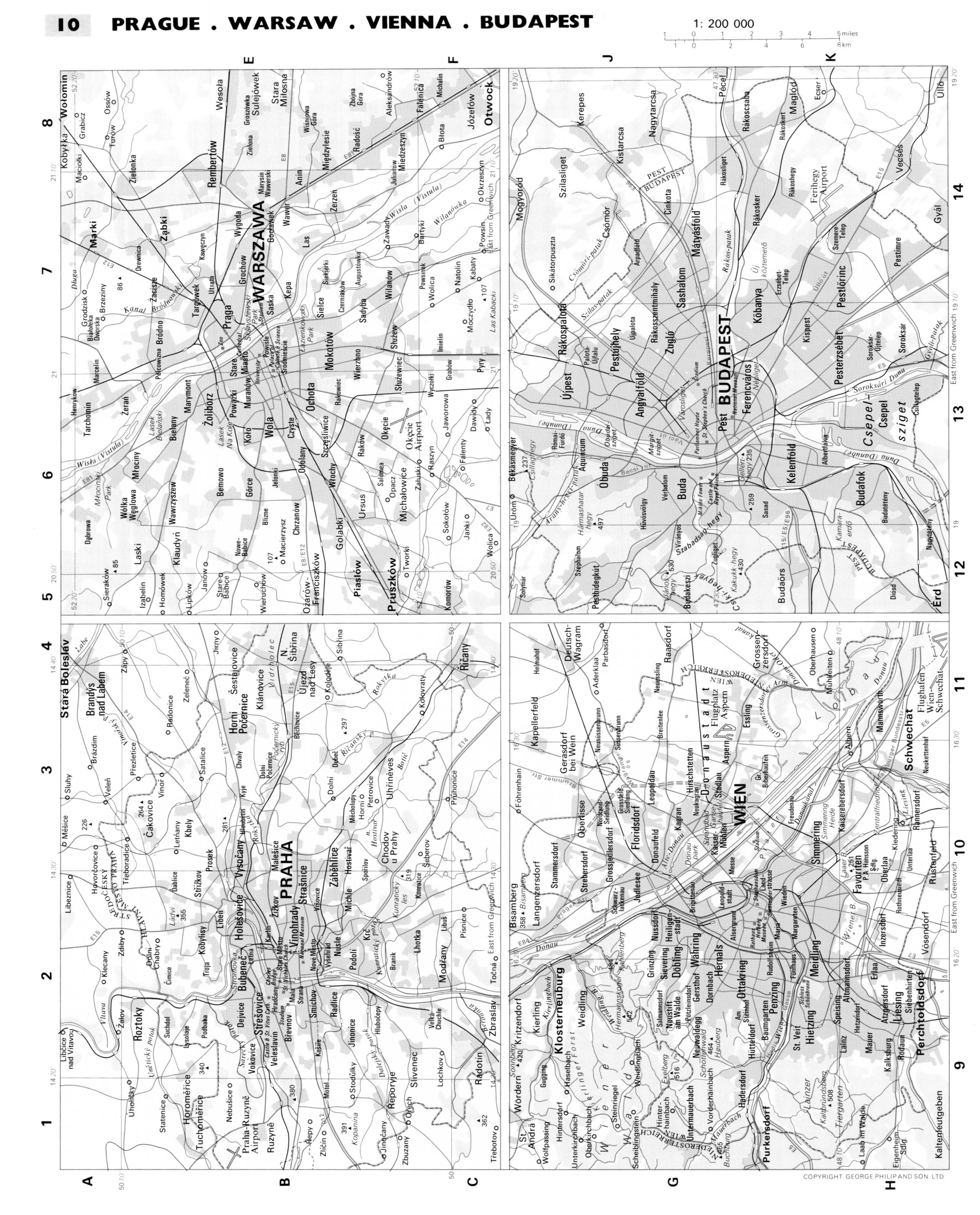

1: 200 000

miles / km scale

Leningrad map (top)

Lisiy Nos, Olgino, Kolomyagi, Novaya Derevnya, Udelnaya, Ruchyi, Gorelny, Vsevolozhsk, Lesnoy, Grazhdanka, Rybatskaya, Berngardovka, Kalytino, Noyoye Kovalyova, Krasnaya Gorka, Primorskoye Prospekt, O. Verperluda, Bobylyskaya, Lakhtinskiy, Oz. Lakhtinskiy Razliv, Staraya Derevnya, Balshaya Neva, O. Trudyashchikhsya, Kirov Stadium, Ostrova Kirovskiye, Apterkarskiy Ostrov, Petrogradskaya Storona, Vyborgskaya Storona, Finland Station, Polyustrovo, Rzhevka, Selytsy, Khirvosti, Koltushi, Pavlovo, O. Volynyy, O. Dekabristov, Malaya Neva, Fortress of St. Peter & St. Paul, Admiralteyskaya Storona, Bolshaya-Okhta, Zanevka, Yanino, Staraya, Ostrov Vasilyevskiy, Hermitage & Winter Palace, Old Admiralty, St. Isaac's Cathedral, Moskva Station, Alexander Nevsky Abbey, Malaya-Okhta, Kudrovo, Novosergiyevka, Oz. Korkinskoye, Tavry, Razmitelevo, **LENINGRAD**, Vitebsk Station, Fontanka, Obvodnyy kanal, Baltic Station, Warszawa Station, Volodarskoye, Myaglovo, Ozerki, Ostrov Kanonerskiy, Ostrov Gutuyevskiy, Volynkina-Derevnya, Obukhovo, Vesolyy Posolok, Khaboye, GOROD LENINGRAD, Avtovo, Moskovskiy Prospekt, Farforovskaya, Lesnozavodskaya, Novosaratovka, Aleksandrovskoye, Novoaleksandrovskoye, Rybatskoye, Strelyna, Posolok Lenina, Uritsk, Ulyanka, Ligovo, Dakhnoye, Airport, Srednyaya Rogatka, Kupchino, Ust-Slavyanka, Sosnovaya, Posolok Lenina

Gulf of Finland

59 50, 30 40' East from Greenwich

Moscow map (bottom)

Sheremetyevo Airport, Khimki, Kolytsevaya, Moskovskaya, Automobilnaya Doroga, Chelobityevo, Mytishchi, Zhegalovo, Saburovo, Kurkino, Lianozovo, Taynka, Tsentralnyy, Oboldino, Maryino, Putilkovo, Novokhovrino, Beskudnikovo, Medvedkovo, Vatutino, Druzhba, Medvezhiy Ozyora, Medvezhiy Ozyora, Mitino, Bratsevo, Degunino, Vladykino, Babushkin, Pekhra-Pokrovskoye, Almazovo, Novonikolyskoye, Chernyovo, Penyagino, Khimki-Khovrino, Nikolskiy, Likhoborka, 157, Abramtsevo, Vostochnyy, Tushino, Timiryazev Park, Petrovsko-Razumovskoye, Dzerzhinskiy Park, Ostankino, Sokolniki Park, Bogorodskoye, Sosenka, Galyanovo, 140, Balashikha, Novaya, Krasnogorsk, Pavshino, Myakinino, Strogino, Pokrovsko-Sresnevo, Petrovskiy Park, Riga Station, Sokolniki, Izmaylovo, Gorenki, Pekhra-Yakovievskaya, Vishnyaki, Golyevo, Troitse-Lykovo, Frunze, Dzerzhinskiy, **MOSKVA**, Leningrad Station, Izmayloskiy Shosse, Nikolyskoye, Serebryanka, Pekhorka, Arkhangelyskoye, Zakharkovo, Rublovo, Khorosovo, Sverdlov, Kazan Station, Leportovo, 150, Entuziastov, Reutov, Saltykovka, Kutsino, Tatarovo, Mnevniki, Krasno-Presnenskaya, Bolshoi Theatre, Red Square, St. Basil's Cathedral, Lenin Mausoleum, Bauman, Novogireyevo, Zheleznodorozhnyy, Razdory, Cherepkovo, Krylatskoye, Kremlin, Tretyakov Art Gallery, Zhdanov, Perovo, Kuskovo, Plyushchevo, Veshnyaki, Serebryanka, Fenino, Temnikovo, Barvikha, Romashkovo, Fili-Mazilovo, Kiev Stn., Gorkiy Park, Pavelets Station, Vykhino, Kosino, Kozhukhovo, Mikhelysona, Marusino, Poduskino, Nemchinovka, Kuntsevo, Davydkovo, Luzhniki Sports Centre Lenin Stadium, Lenin, Moskvoretskiy, Tekstilyshchik, Kuzyminki, Zhulebino, 94, Nekrasovka, Koreneyo, Novoivanovskoye, Lochino, Mamonovo, Bakovka, Aminyevo, Ochakovo, Lomonosov University, Leninskiye Gory, 150, Oktyabrskiy, Nogatino, Kolomenskoye, Lyublino, Lyubertsy, Tomilino, Odintsovo, Zarechye, Meshcherskiy, Nikulino, Ramenki, Yugo-Zarad, Cheryomushki, Maryino, Kuryanovo, Kapotnya, Kotelyniki, Kraskovo, Malakhovka, Choboty, Peredelkino, Solntsevo, Orlovo, Rumyantsevo, Zyuzino, Volkhonka-Zil, Dyapkino, Lenino, Borisovo, Besedy, Chkalova, Tokarevo, Udelynaya, Dzerzhinskiy, Rasskazovka, Salaryevo, Belyayevo Bogorodskoye, 250, Certanovo, Certanovka, Uzkoye, Pokrovskoye, Yasenevo, Brateyevo, Mamonovo, Ostrov, Petrovskoye, Lytkarino, Vereya, Vnukovo, Vnukovo Airport, Teplyy Star, Kr. Stroitel, Biryulyovo, Gorod Moskva, Ashcherino, Oktyabrskiy, Srednevo, Peredelytsy, Valuyevo, Letovo, Baturino, Kommunarka, Mikhaylovskoye, Bitsa, Molokovo, Zaozerye, Ostrovtsy, 38

37 40' East from Greenwich

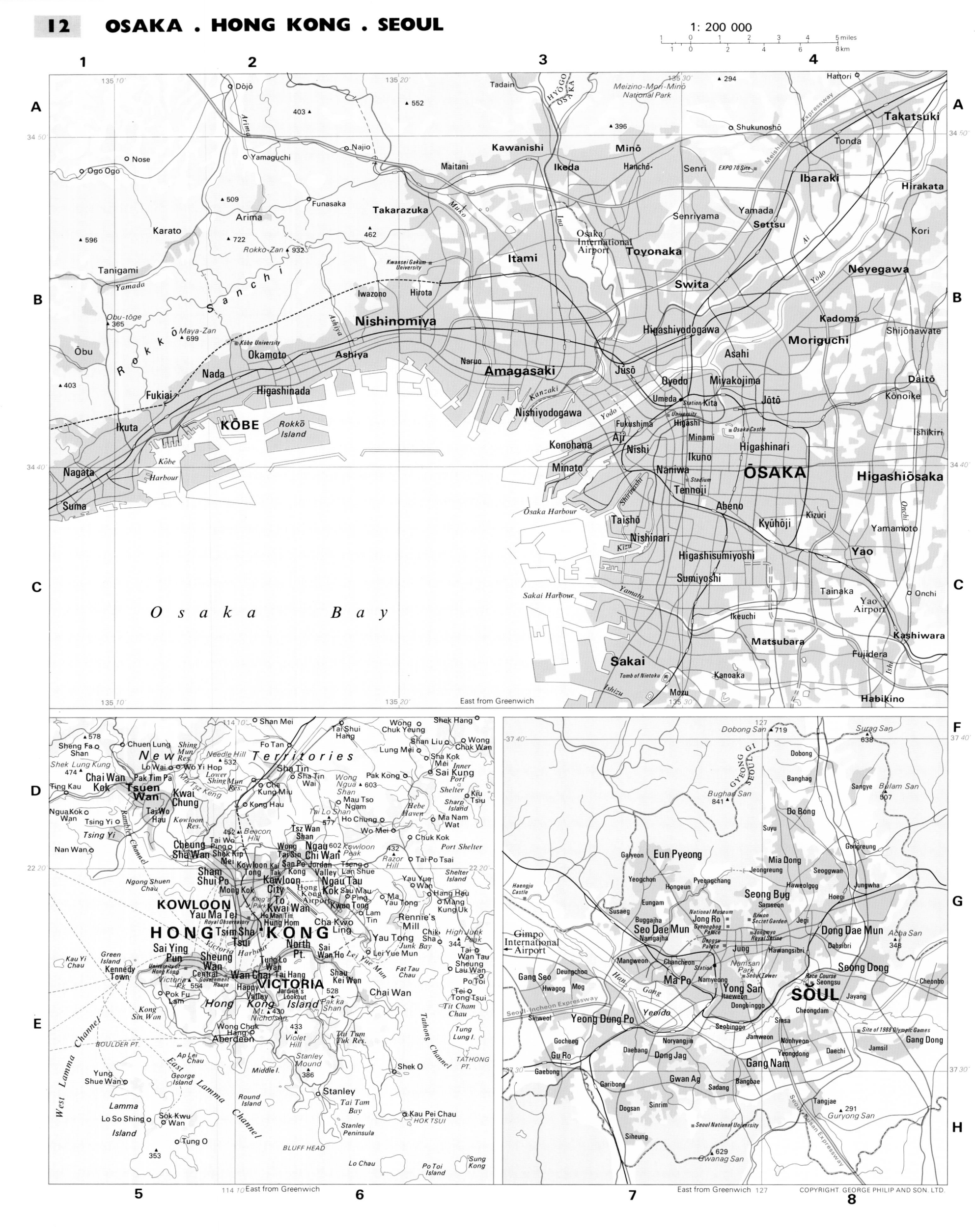

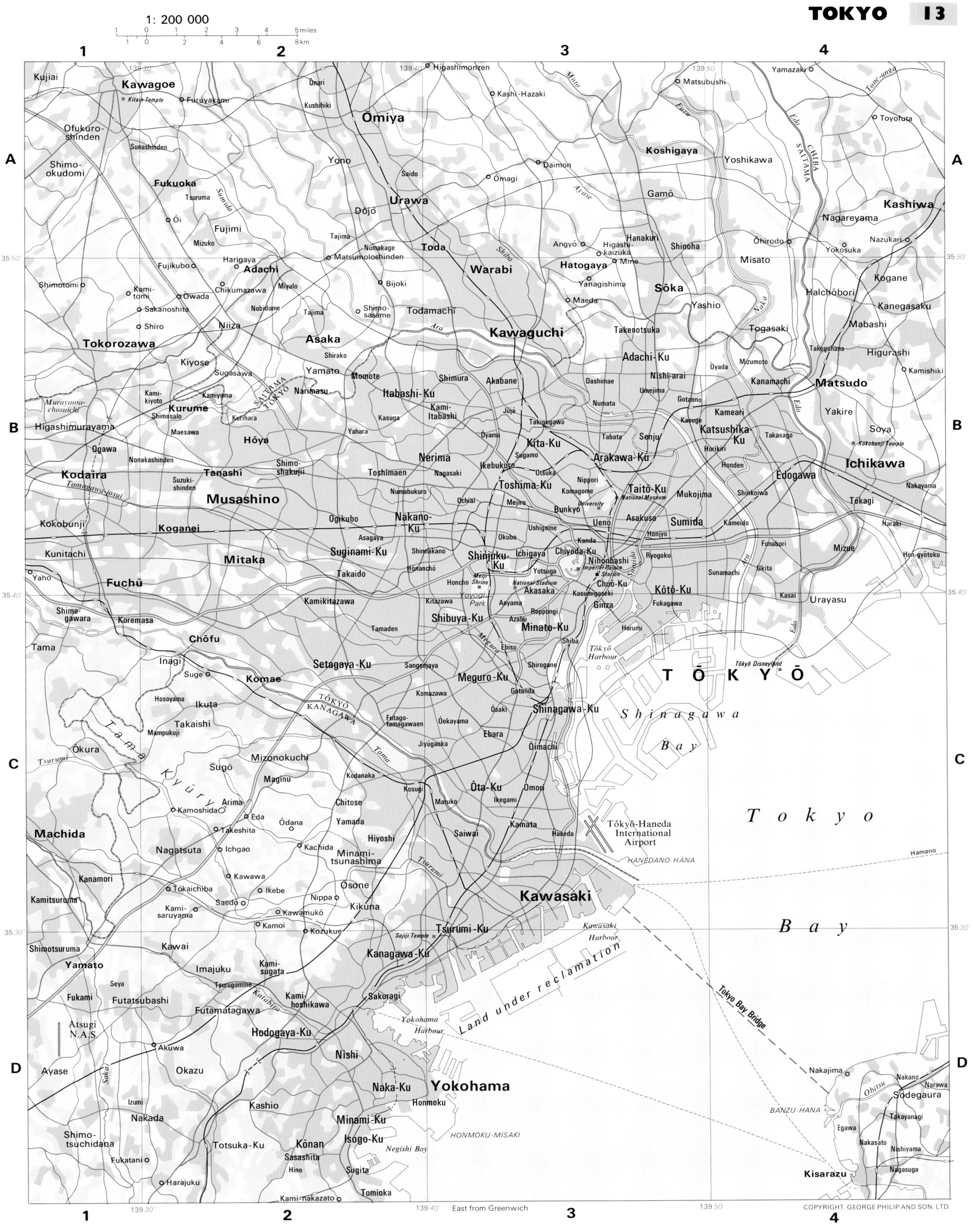

1: 200 000

1   0   1   2   3   4   5 miles
1   0   2   4   6   8 km

1

Kujiai
Kawagoe
Kitain Temple
Furuyakami
139 30'
Ōnari
Kushihiki
Higashimonzen
139 40'
Kashi-Hazaki
Yamazaki
139 50'
Matsubushi
Toyofuta
Tone-ringa
3
4

Ōmiya
Koshigaya
Yoshikawa
Gamō
CHIBA
SAITAMA
Kashiwa

A
Ofukuro-shinden
Shimo-okudomi
Yono
Saido
Ōmagi
Daimon
Nagareyama
Nazukari
A

Fukuoka
Tsuruma
Sumida
Urawa
Dōjō
Ara
Ayase
Ōhirodo
Yokosuka
Kogane

Ōi
Fujimi
Mizuko
Tajima
Numakage
Matsumoloshinden
Toda
Angyō
Higashi-kaizuka
Mine
Shinoha
Misato
Hachōbori
35 50'
35 50'

Shimotomi
Harigaya
Fujikubo
Adachi
Bijoki
Warabi
Hatogaya
Yanagishima
Maeda
Sōka
Yashio
Togasaki
Kanegasaku
Mabashi
Higurashi

Kami-tomi
Sakanoshita
Ōwada
Chikumazawa
Miyalo
Nobidome
Shiro
Niiza
Shimo-sasame
Todamachi
Kawaguchi
Takenotsuka
Ōyada
Mizumoto
Kamanachi
Matsudo
Takegahana
Kamishiki

Tokorozawa
Kiyose
Sugasawa
Asaka
Shirako
Yamato
Todachō
Adachi-Ku
Dashimae
Nishi-arai
Umejima
Gotanno
Yakire
Soya

Higashimurayama
Kami-kiyoto
Kamiyama
Kurume
Shimosalo
Maesawa
Kurihara
Hōya
Narimasu
Itabashi-Ku
Kasuga
Yahara
Ōyama
Jūjō
Takinegawa
Tabata
Senju
Kasuge
Kasago
Katsushika-Ku
Takasago
Kokubunji Temple
B
Murayama-chosuichi
Kokubunji Temple
B

Ogawa
Nonakashinden
Suzuki-shinden
Shimo-shakujii
Kami-Itabashi
Kita-Ku
Sugamo
Ōtsuka
Arakawa-Ku
Hōriki
Honden
Ichikawa

Kodaira
Tanashi
Nerima
Nagasaki
Toshima-Ku
Nippori
Komagome
Taitō-Ku
Mukojima
Shinkoiwa
Edogawa

Tumagawa-losui
Musashino
Toshimaen
Numabukuro
Ochiai
Mejiro
Bunkyō
University
National Museum
Sumida
Kameido
Haraki
Nakayama

Kokobunji
Koganei
Ogikubo
Nakano-Ku
Asagaya
Shinnakano
Okubo
Ushigome
Ueno
Asakusa
Honjo
Tōkagi

Kunitachi
Suginami-Ku
Hōnanchō
Shinjuku-Ku
Ichigaya
Kanda
Nihonbashi
Ryogoku
Funahori
Mizue
Hon-gyōtoku

Yaho
Mitaka
Takaido
Meiji Shrine
Honcho
Yotsuya
Chiyoda-Ku
Imperial Palace
Station
Chūo-Ku
Kōtō-Ku
Sunamachi
Ukita
Kasai
Urayasu
35 40'
35 40'

Fuchū
Kamikitazawa
National Stadium
Akasaka
Kasumigaseki
Ginza
Fukagawa

Shimo-gawara
Koremasa
Kitazawa
Yoyogi Park
Anyama
Roppongi
Ōyama
Azabu
Harumi

Tama
Chōfu
Tamaden
Shibuya-Ku
Minato-Ku
Shiba
Tōkyō Harbour
Tōkyō Disneyland

Inagi
Suge
Komae
Setagaya-Ku
Sangenjaya
Ebisu
Shirogane
TŌKYŌ

Hosoyama
Ikuta
Meguro-Ku
Komazawa
Gotanda
Shinagawa-Ku

Takaishi
Mampukuji
TŌKYŌ KANAGAWA
Futago-tamagawaen
Ōokayama
Ōsaki
Shinagawa Bay

Ōkura
Tsurumi
Kyūryū
Sugō
Mizonokuchi
Jiyūgaoka
Ebara
Ōimachi
C
C

Kamoshida
Arima
Maginu
Kōdanaka
Ōta-Ku
Ōmori
Tokyo

Machida
Takeshita
Ōdana
Chitose
Kosugi
Matuko
Ikegami
Bay

Nagatsuta
Ichgao
Eda
Yamada
Saiwai
Kamata
Haneda
Tōkyō-Haneda International Airport
Hamano

Kanamori
Tōkaichiba
Kawawa
Ikebe
Hiyoshi
Minami-tsunashima
HANEDANO-HANA

Kamitsuruma
Kami-saruyama
Saedo
Kawamukō
Nippa
Ōsone
Kikuna
Kawasaki
Kawasaki Harbour

Kamoi
Kozukue
Tsurumi-Ku
35 30'
35 30'

Shimotsuruma
Kawai
Kami-sugata
Kanagawa-Ku
Tokyo Bay Bridge

Yamato
Imajuku
Tsurugamine
Karabifro
Kami-hoshikawa
Sakuragi
Land under reclamation

Seya
Futatsubashi
Futamatagawa
Yokohama Harbour
Nakajima
Nakano
Narawa

Fukami
Sakai
Hodogaya-Ku
Obitsu
Sodegaura
Takayanagi

Atsugi N.A.S.
Akuwa
Nishi
BANZU-HANA
Egawa
D
Ayase
Okazu
Naka-Ku
Yokohama
Nakasato
Nishiyama
D

Izumi
Kashio
Honmoku
HONMOKU-MISAKI
Kisarazu
Nagasuga

Nakada
Minami-Ku
Isogo-Ku
Negishi Bay

Shimo-tsuchidana
Fukatani
Totsuka-Ku
Kōnan
Sasashita
Hino
Sugita

Harajuku
Kami-nakazato
Tomioka

1
139 30'
2
139 40'
East from Greenwich
3
139 50'
COPYRIGHT. GEORGE PHILIP AND SON. LTD
4

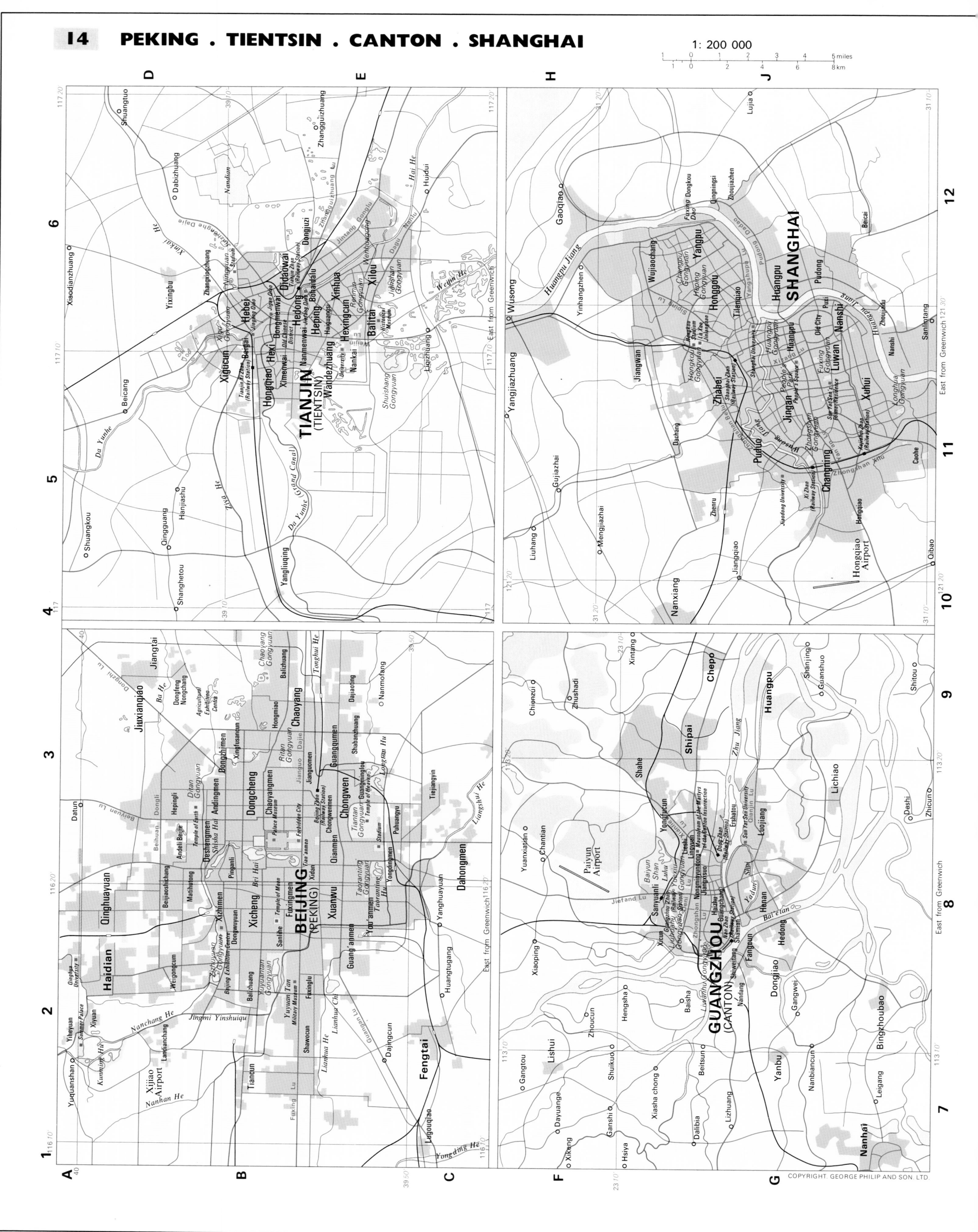

1: 200 000

COPYRIGHT. GEORGE PHILIP AND SON. LTD.

1: 200 000

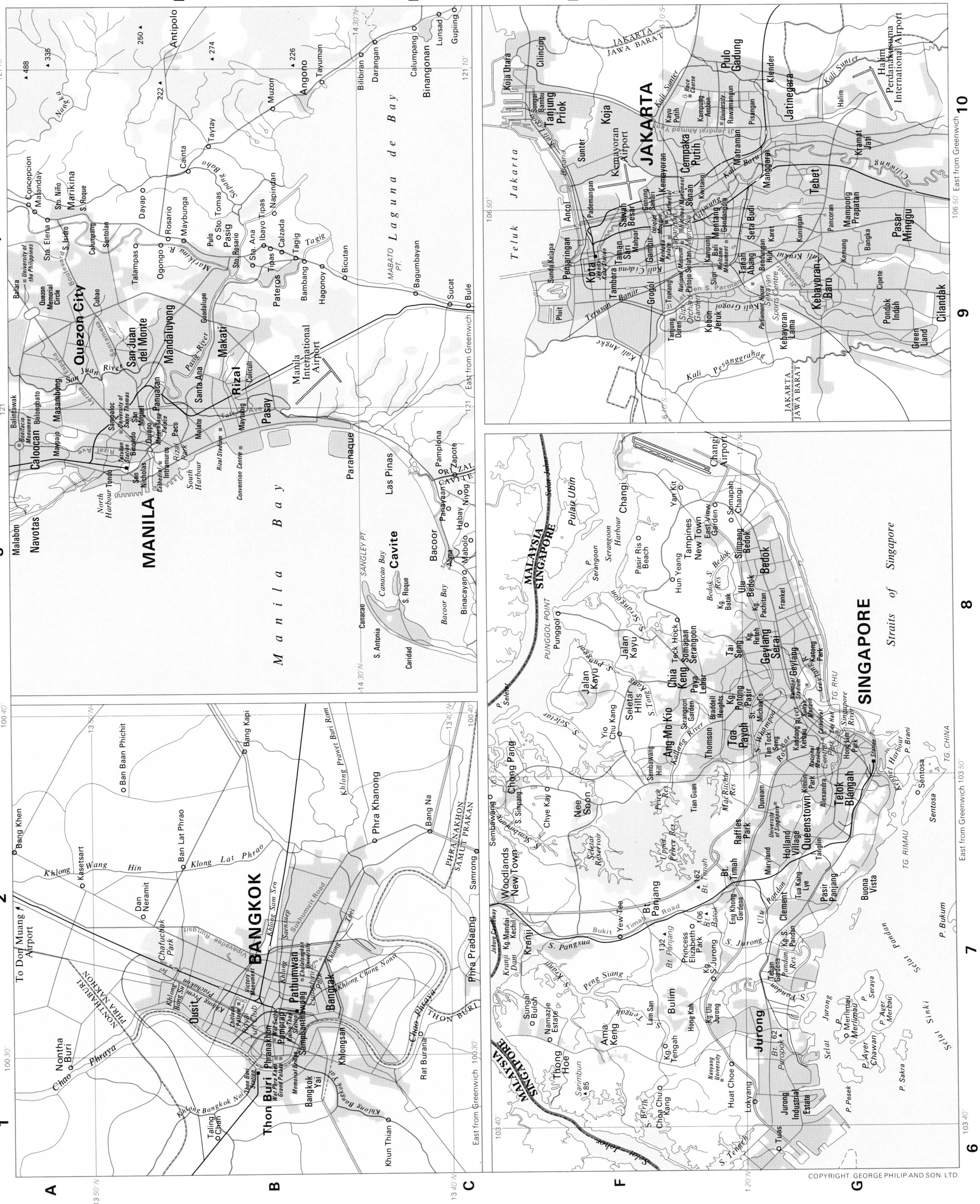

5 miles
8 km

MANILA

Antipolo
250
335
488
222
Concepcion
Malanday
Marikina
S. Roque
Sta. Elena
S. Isidro
Calumpang
Santolan
Dayap
Rosario
Maybunga
Napindan
Sto. Tomas
Ibayo Tipas
Ska. Ana
Calzada
Pasig
Tipas
Tagig
Bicutan
Bambang
Hagonoy
Sucat
Bule
Bagumbayan

University of the Philippines
Bahra
Quezon Memorial Circle
Cubao
Cainta
Taytay
Muzon
Angono
Tayuman
Binangonan
Bilibiran
Darangan
Lunsad
Guping
226
274

Quezon City
San Juan del Monte
Mandaluyong
Makati
Rizal
Santa Ana
Pasay
Manila International Airport

Laguna de Bay
MABATO PT.

Balintawak
Bonifacio Monument
Maypajo
Balonghato
Masambong
Sampaloc
University of Santo Tomas
San Miguel
Malacanang Palace
Paco
Pandacan
Ermita
Intramuros
Malate
Maytubig
Rizal Park
Rizal Stadium
Convention Centre

Caloocan
Malabon
Navotas
Tonda
North Harbour
San Nicholas
South Harbour

Manila Bay

SANGLEY PT.
Canacao Bay
Bacoor Bay
S. Antonia
Caridad
Canaoan
S. Roque
Binacayan
Mabolo
Alma
Bacoor
Cavite

Paranaque
Las Pinas
Zapote
Pamplona
CAVITE
RIZAL
Niyog
Habay

East from Greenwich

BANGKOK

To Don Muang Airport
Ban Baan Phichit
Bang Kapi
Bang Khen
Kasetsart
Wang Hin
Dan Neramit
Ban Lat Phrao
Klong Lat Phrao

Khlong Prawet Buri Rom
Phra Khanong
Bang Na

NONTHABURI
PHRA NAKHON
SAMUT PRAKAN
PHRA NAKHON
THON BURI
Samrong

Nontha Buri
Thon Buri
Phranakhon
Dusit
Pathumwan
Pomprap
Samphanthawong
Bangrak
Bangkok Yai
Phra Pradaeng
Phra Padaeng

Chatuchak Park
Lumpini Park
Chitlada
Grand Palace
Victory Monument
Sukhumvit Road

Chao Phraya
Khlong Bangkok Noi
Khlong Bangkok Yai
Khun Thian
Rat Burana
Taling Chan

JAKARTA

JAKARTA BARAT
JAWA BARAT
Cilincing
Pulo Gadung
Klender
Halim Perdanakusuma International Airport

JAKARTA
Tanjung Priok
Koja Utara
Koja
Kemayoran Airport
Kemayoran
Cempaka Putih
Jatinegara
Kramat Jati

Sunter
Ancol
Pademangan
Gunung Sahari
Senen
Matraman
Tebet
Kota
Sawah Besar
Tambra
Sari
Gambir
Bali
Menteng
Setu Budi
Pasar Minggu
Grogol
Kebon Jeruk
Tanah Abang
Kebayoran Baru
Pondok Indah
Green Land
Cilandak

Teluk Jakarta
Kali Sunter
Kali Cideng
Kali Krukut
Kali Pesanggrahan
Kali Angke

JAKARTA JAWA BARAT

SINGAPORE

MALAYSIA
SINGAPORE

Changi Airport
Pulau Ubin
Serangoon Harbour
Pasir Ris
Tampines New Town
Changi
Yan Kit

SINGAPORE
Straits of Singapore
Punggol
Yio Chu Kang
Seletar Hills
Ang Mo Kio
Bedok
Simpang Bedok
Geylang Serai
Jalan Kayu
Chia Keng
Teck Hock
Paya Lebar
Katong
Toa Payoh
Thomson
Serangoon
Bradell Heights
Raffles Park
Holland Village
Queenstown
Telok Blangah
Sentosa

Woodlands New Town
Kranji
Bt. Panjang
Bukit Timah
Bt. Timah
Jurong
Bulim
Nee Soon
Sembawang
Chye Kay
Clementi
Pasir Panjang
Buona Vista

MacRitchie Res.
Peirce Res.
Seletar Reservoir

Jurong Industrial Estate
TG CHINA
TG RIMAU
Sentosa

East from Greenwich

1: 200 000

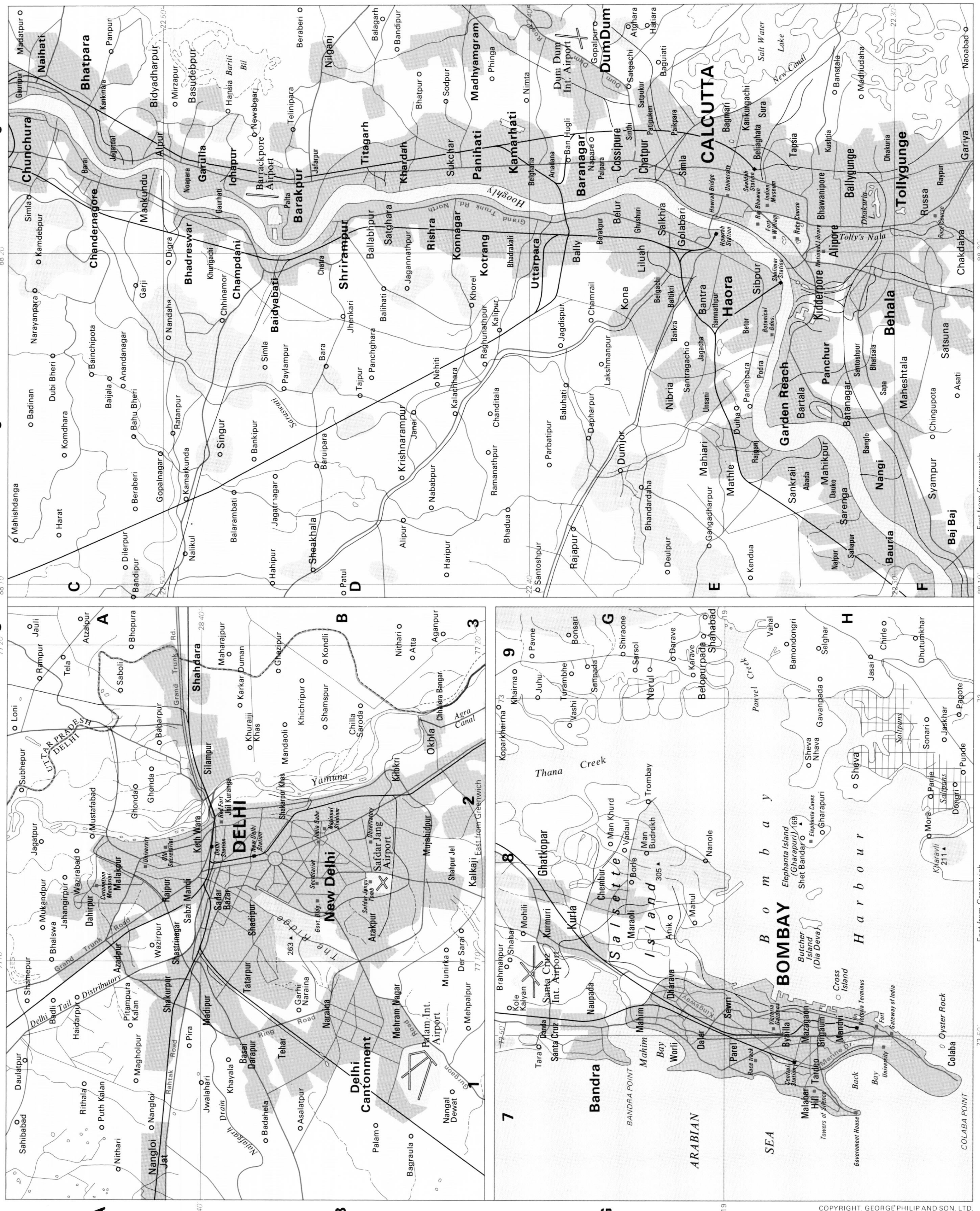

0 1 2 3 4 5 miles
1 2 4 6 8 km

CALCUTTA (North section)

Naihati, Bhatpara, Gaurpur, Madatpur, Panpur, Bidyadharpur, Basudebpur, Mirzapur, Balagarh, Berabari, Niiganj, Bandipur, Balagarh, Chunchura, Chandernagore, Makundu, Ajpur, Garulta, Ichapur, Barrackpore Airport, Jagtdal, Newabganj, Telinipara, Titagarh, Khardah, Sukchar, Bhatpur, Sodpur, Madhyamgram, Phinga, Nimta, Dum Dum Int. Airport, Gopalpur, Atghara, Hatiara, Baguiati, DumDum, Naobad, Madhjudaha, Banstala, Sura, Kankinara, Barri, Noapara, Pelta, Jafalpa, Panihati, Kamarhati, Belghoria, Baranagar, Cossipure, Chatpur, Simla, Bagmari, Kankungachi, Tapsia, Kushtia, Dhakuria, Gariya

CALCUTTA, Howrah, Haora, Sibpur, Kidderpore, Behala, Tollygunge, Russa, Ballygunge, Bhawanipore, Aliport, University, Sealdah Station, Bantra, Garden Reach, Panchur, Santoshpur, Bartala, Maheshtala, Nangi, Syampur, Baj Baj, Bauria

Hooghly, North Trunk Rd, Grand Trunk Rd, Tolly's Nala, New Canal, Salt Water Lake, East from Greenwich

DELHI / NEW DELHI (lower-left section)

Daulatpur, Sahibabad, Nithari, Rampur, Jauli, Atzalpur, Bhopura, Shahdara, Maharajpur, Nithari, Atta, Aganpur, Loni, Tela, Saboli, Bakhtawarpur, Karkar Duman, Ghazipur, Kondli, Subhepur, Mukandpur, Ghonda, Khichripur, Shamspur, Chilla Saroda, Chhalera Bangar, Agra Canal, Silampur, Shakurpur Khas, Mandaoli, Okhla, Kilokri, Bhalswa, Jahangirpuri, Wazirabad, Yamuna, Kalkaji, Mustafabad, Ghondai, **DELHI**, Red Fort, Jhil Kuranja, **New Delhi**, Keshwara, Delhi Station, New Delhi Station, Secretariat, Safdar Jang Airport, Munirudpur, Shahpur Jat, Shakurbasti, Sadar Bazar, Sahzi Mandi, Shahdurpur, Arakpur, Der Sarai, Malakpur, Rajpur, Wazirpur, Azadpur, Tatarpur, Garhi Narnia, Mehpalpur, Palam Int. Airport, Delhi Cantonment, Mehram Nagar, Nangal Dewat, Palam, Bagraula, Nangloi Jat, Rithala, Puth Kalan, Khayala, Badahela, Asalatpur

Grand Trunk Road, Ring Road, Rohtak Road, Gurgaon Road, The Ridge, Najafgarh Drain, Delhi Tail Distributary, UTTAR PRADESH / DELHI, 263, 77 10, 77 20, 28 40, East from Greenwich

BOMBAY (lower-right section)

Koparkherria, Khairna, Juhu, Turambhe, Bonsari, Shiraone, Darave, Karave, Shahabad, Vahal, Chirle, Dhutumkhar, Pavne, Sempada, Sarsol, Belopurpada, Bamondongri, Selghar, Vashi, Nerul, Thana Creek, Panvel Creek, Jasai, Pagote, Ghatkopar, Man Khurd, Vadaul, Trombay, Gavanpada, Sheva Nhava, Sonari, Jaskar, Pupde, Brahmanpur, Shabar, Kurmuri, Kurla, Chembur, Mora, Panje, Saltpans, Dongri, Kole Kalyan, Mohili, Maraoli, Salsette Island, Elephanta Island (Gharapuri) 169, 305, Butcher Island, Cross Island, Khaprali, 211, Santa Cruz Int. Airport, Dharavi, Anik, Mahul, Sewri, Elephanta Caves, Gharapuri, Sheva, **BOMBAY**, Bandra, Bandra Point, Mahim Bay, Worli, Dadar, Parel, Mazagaon, Byculla, Girgaum, Marine Dr, Malabar Hill, Back Bay, Tardeo, Fort, Gateway of India, Colaba, Colaba Point, Victoria Terminus, Towers of Silence, University, Government House, Oyster Rock, Kingsway

Bombay Harbour, ARABIAN SEA, Thana Creek, 72 50, 79 50, 73, East from Greenwich

COPYRIGHT. GEORGE PHILIP AND SON. LTD.

1: 200 000

1 0 1 2 3 4 5 miles
1 0 2 4 6 8 km

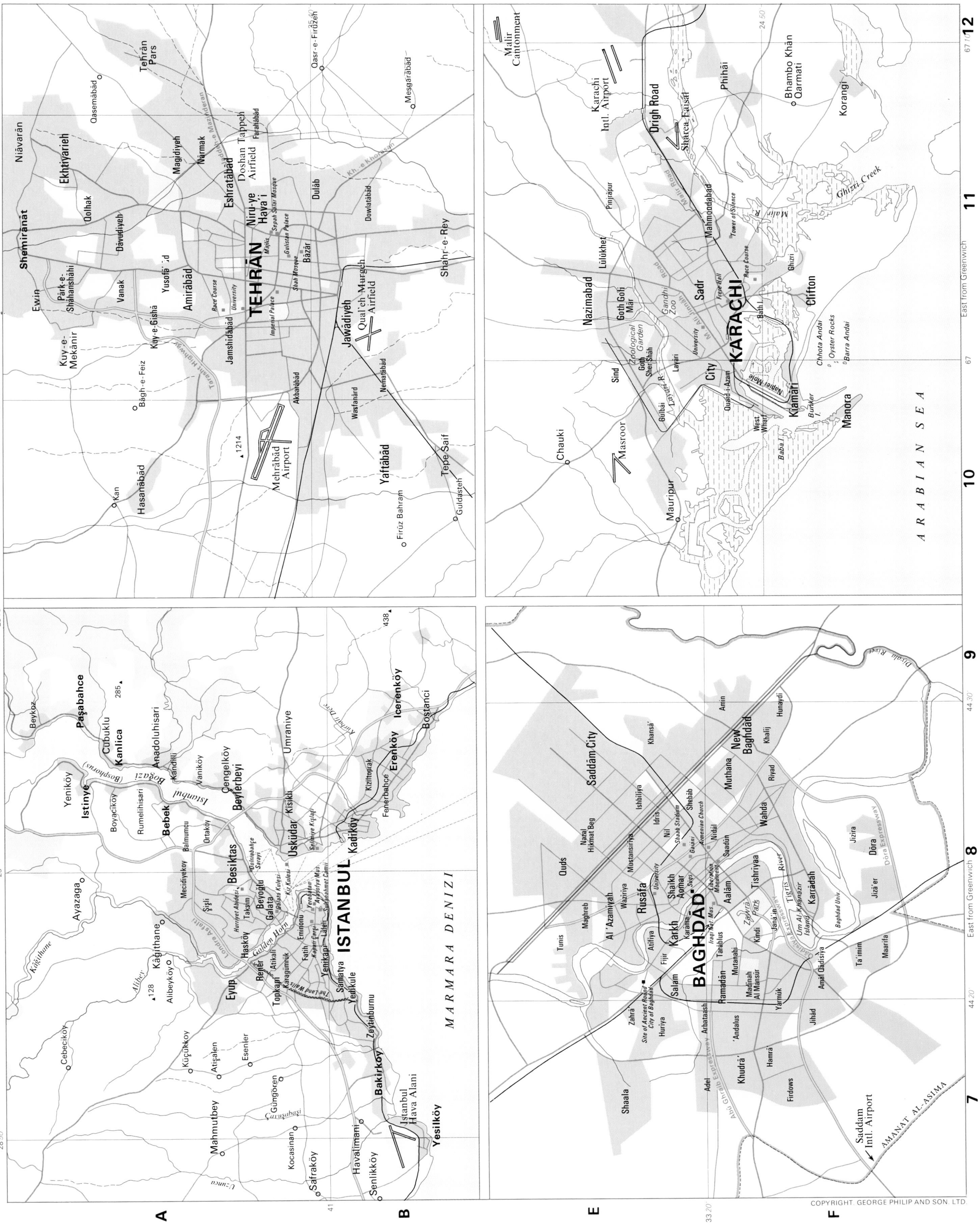

ISTANBUL

Beykoz
Paşabahçe
Kanlıca
Çubuklu
Anadoluhisarı
Yeniköy
İstinye
Kandilli
Vaniköy
Çengelköy
Beylerbeyi
Bebek
Rumelihisarı
Boyacıköy
Ortaköy
Üsküdar
Kısıklı
Fenerbahçe
Erenköy
İçerenköy
Bostancı
Ümraniye
Kızıltoprak
Kadıköy
Mecidiyeköy
Şişli
Taksim
Beşiktaş
Beyoğlu
Galata
Haskoy
Eyüp
Fatih
Eminönü
Kağıthane
Alibeyköy
Ayazağa
Cebeciköy
Küçükköy
Atışalen
Esenler
Topkapı
Samatya
Yenikule
Bakırköy
Zeytinburnu
Yeşilköy
İstanbul Hava Alanı
Mahmutbey
Havalimanı
Kocasinan
Safraköy
Şenliköy
Çırçırbaşı
Güngören

MARMARA DENIZI

Boğaziçi (Bosphorus)
İstanbul Boğazı
Golden Horn

TEHRĀN

Tehrān Pars
Qasemābād
Qasr-e-Firūzeh
Niāvarān
Ekhtiyārieh
Shemirānāt
Magidiyeh
Narmak
Eshratābād
Doshan Tappeh Airfield
Farahābād
Dulāb
Dowlatābād
Mesgarābād
Qolhak
Davūdiyeh
Niru-ye Hava i
Bāzār
Shahr-e-Rey
Ewin
Park-e-Shāhanshāhi
Vanak
Amirābād
Yusofābād
Kuy-e-Gisha
Jamshidābād
Kuy-e-Mekānir
Bāgh-e-Feiz
Akbarābād
Wastīabād
Nematābād
Qual'eh Murgh Airfield
Jawādiyeh
Hasanābād
Kan
Mehrābād Airport
Yaftābād
Tepe Saif
Guldasteh
Firūz Bahram

Mahmūdābād

BAGHDAD

Saddām City
Khansā
New Baghdad
Amin
Khalij
Hunaydi
Istabliyya
Idris
Riyad
Muthana
Wahda
Nazal Hikmat Beg
Nil
Shebab
Nidai
Ouds
Maghreb
Al 'Azamiyah
Mustansiriya
Shaikh 'Aqmar
Saadun
Jizira
Dōra
Tunis
Wazīriya
Rusāfa
Aalām
Karrādah
Fiir
Karkh
Zahrā
Atfiya
Karaimat
Zahrā
Pātis
Kindi
Ta'mim
Salam
Mutanabi
Yarmuk
Ja'uūn
Ma'arifa
Huriya
Abhateasb
Madinah Al Mansūr
Ramadān
'Andalus
Jihad
Khudrā
Hamrā
Firdows
Shaala
Adel
Saddam Intl. Airport
AMANAT AL-ASIMA

Tigris River
Diyala River

KARACHI

Malir Cantonment
Karachi Intl. Airport
Drigh Road
Phihāi
Bhambo Khān
Qarmati
Korangi
Sharea Faisal
Mahmoodabad
Nazimabad
Lūlūkhet
Goth Goli Mār
Sadr
Ghizri
Clifton
Sind
Lyāri R.
University
Lakhi
Gandhi
Zoo
Tower of Silence
Goth Sher Shah
City
Quaid-i-Azam
Kiamari
Chhota Andai
Oyster Rocks
Barra Andai
Bhihai
Masroor
Mauripur
West Wharf
Baba I.
Manora
Chauki

Ghizri Creek
Malir R.
ARABIAN SEA

East from Greenwich

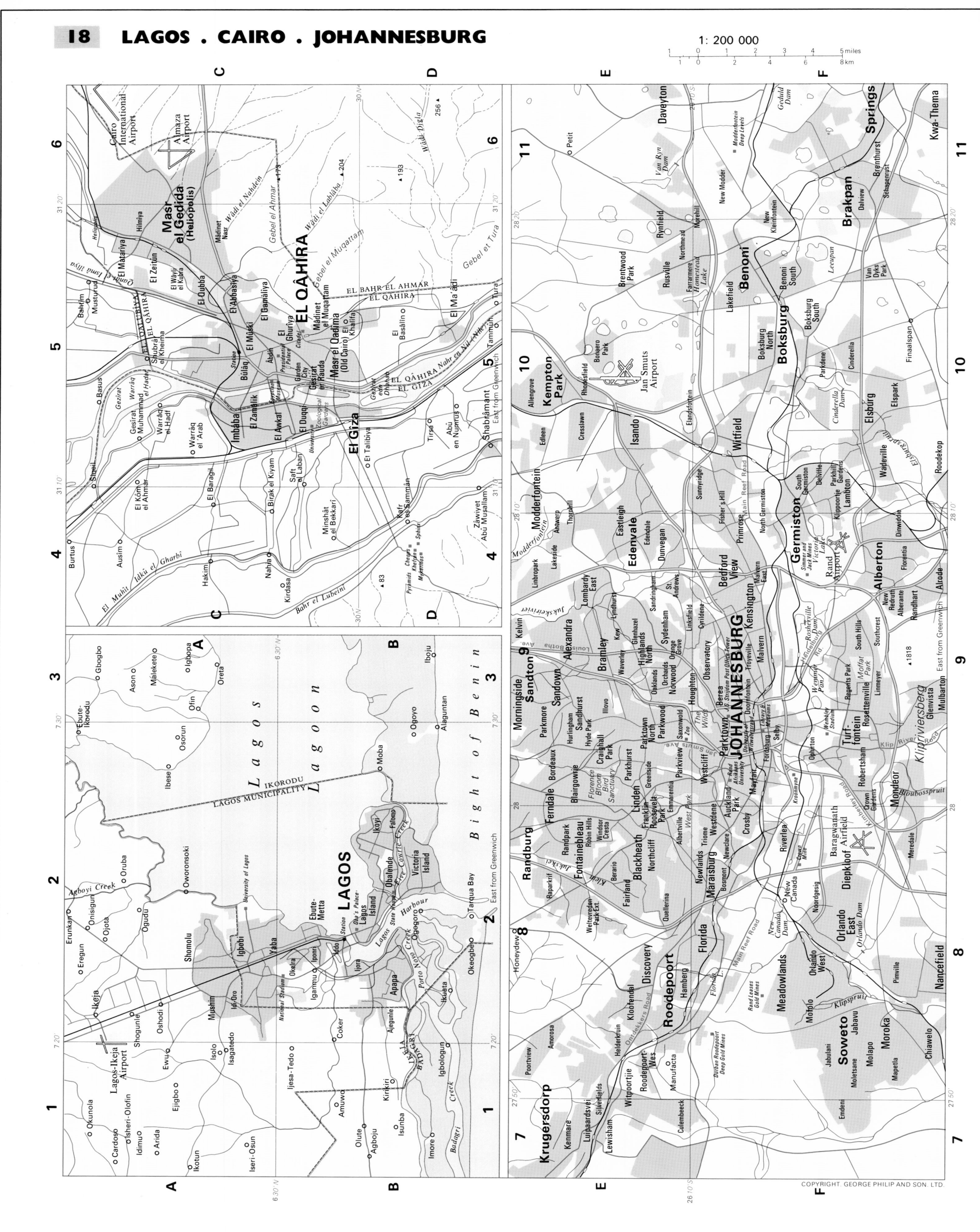

1: 200 000

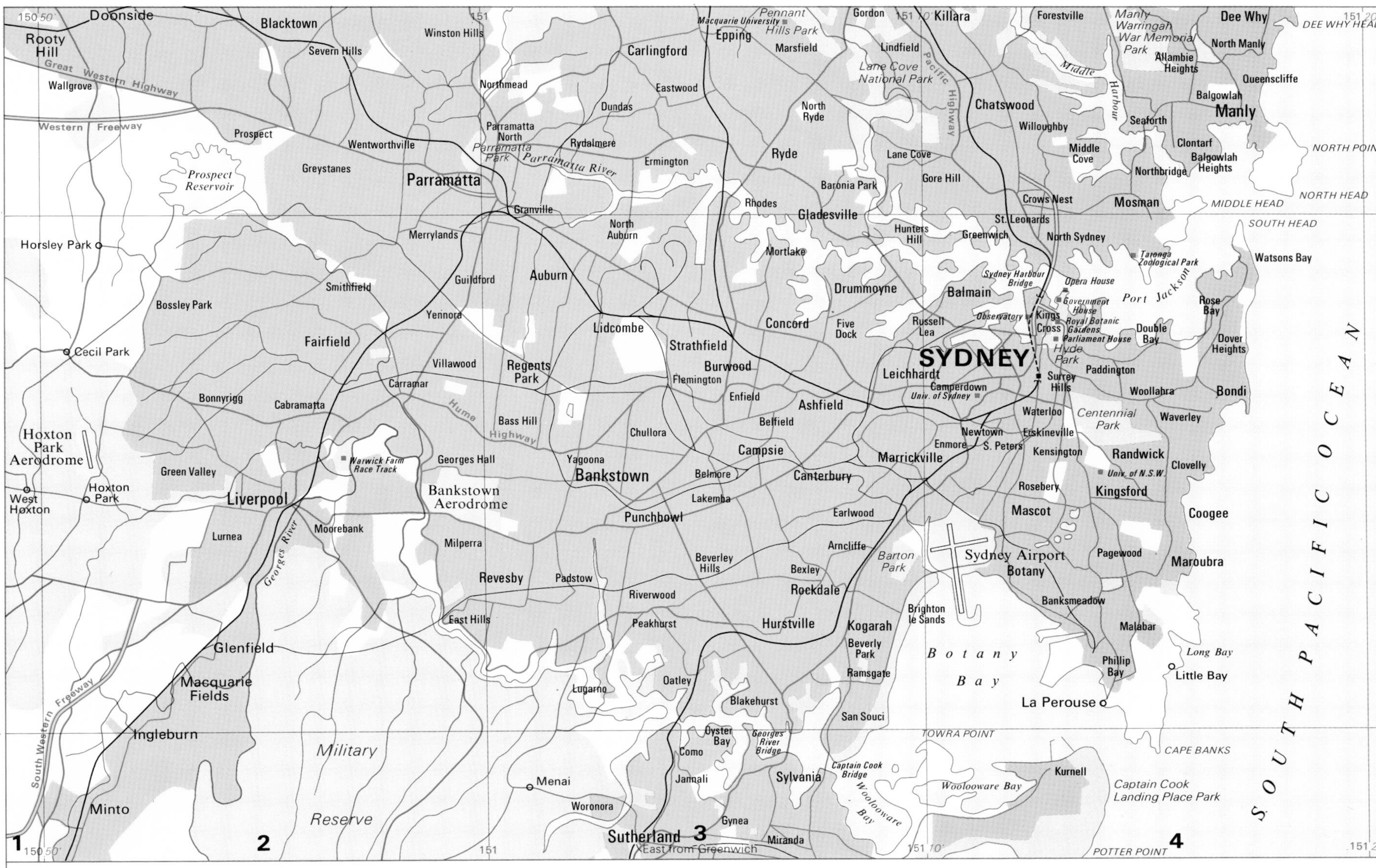

1   0   1   2   3   4   5 miles
1   0   2   4   6   8 km

1   2   3   4

Sydney map

Doonside
Rooty Hill
Wallgrove
Great Western Highway
Western Freeway
Blacktown
Severn Hills
Winston Hills
Northmead
Carlingford
Epping
Macquarie University
Pennant Hills Park
Gordon
Killara
Forestville
Manly Warringah War Memorial Park
Dee Why
North Manly
DEE WHY HEAD
Prospect
Wentworthville
Parramatta North
Parramatta Park
Parramatta River
Dundas
Rydalmere
Marsfield
Eastwood
Ermington
North Ryde
Ryde
Lane Cove National Park
Lindfield
Chatswood
Willoughby
Allambie Heights
Queenscliffe
Balgowlah
North Manly
Seaforth
Clontarf
Northbridge
Balgowlah Heights
Manly
NORTH POINT
Prospect Reservoir
Greystanes
Parramatta
Granville
North Auburn
Merrylands
Guildford
Villawood
Auburn
Lidcombe
Rhodes
Gladesville
Mortlake
Drummoyne
Concord
Five Dock
Baronia Park
Gore Hill
Lane Cove
Hunters Hill
Greenwich
St Leonards
Crows Nest
North Sydney
Mosman
MIDDLE HEAD
SOUTH HEAD
Horsley Park
Smithfield
Fairfield
Yennora
Carramar
Hume Highway
Bass Hill
Regents Park
Flemington
Burwood
Enfield
Ashfield
Strathfield
Russell Lea
Balmain
Sydney Harbour Bridge
Government House
Observatory
Kings Cross
Royal Botanic Gardens
Opera House
Parliament House
Taronga Zoological Park
Port Jackson
Watsons Bay
Rose Bay
Double Bay
Dover Heights
Bossley Park
Cecil Park
Bonnyrigg
Cabramatta
Hoxton Park Aerodrome
West Hoxton
Hoxton Park
Green Valley
Georges Hall
Warwick Farm Race Track
Bankstown
Yagoona
Belmore
Campsie
Canterbury
Chullora
Belfield
SYDNEY
Leichhardt
Camperdown
Univ. of Sydney
Newtown
S. Peters
Enmore
Marrickville
Hyde Park
Paddington
Woollahra
Bondi
Waverley
Georges River
Liverpool
Lurnea
Moorebank
Milperra
Revesby
Padstow
Punchbowl
Lakemba
Earlwood
Beverly Hills
Bexley
Riverwood
Rockdale
Arncliffe
Hurstville
Kogarah
Brighton le Sands
Roseberry
Mascot
Sydney Airport
Botany
Banksmeadow
Pagewood
Maroubra
Univ. of N.S.W.
Kingsford
Randwick
Clovelly
Coogee
South Western Freeway
Glenfield
Macquarie Fields
Ingleburn
Minto
East Hills
Peakhurst
Oatley
Lugarno
Beverly Park
Ramsgate
San Souci
Blakehurst
Georges River Bridge
Barton Park
Botany Bay
Malabar
Phillip Bay
Long Bay
Little Bay
La Perouse
Military Reserve
Menai
Woronora
Como
Jannali
Oyster Bay
Sylvania
Captain Cook Bridge
Woolooware Bay
TOWRA POINT
CAPE BANKS
Kurnell
Captain Cook Landing Place Park
Sutherland
Gynea
Miranda
East from Greenwich
POTTER POINT
SOUTH PACIFIC OCEAN

150 50'   151   151 10'   151 20'
33 50'   34

5   6   7   8   9

Melbourne map

Westmeadows
Broadmeadows
Epping
Lalor
Mill Park
Plenty
Wattle Glen
Diamond Creek
Watsons Creek
Little Sugarloaf
Melbourne Airport
Tullamarine
Campbellfield
Thomastown
Greensborough
Maroonda
Kangaroo Ground
Hume Highway
Keilor
Airport West
Glenroy
Fawkner
Bundoora
Bundoora Park
Reservoir
Watsonia
Research
Eltham
Diamond Ck.
Mt. Lofty
Aquaduct
Warrandyte
Warrandyte Park
Wonga Park
Essendon Airport
Pascoe Vale
Coburg
Preston
Latrobe Uni.
Heidelberg West
Macleod
Rosanna
View Bank
Lower Plenty
Yarra River
Warrandyte South
Keilor East
Niddrie
Essendon
Moonee Ponds
Moonee Valley Racecourse
Thornbury
Heidelberg
Warringal Park
Templestowe
Park Orchards
Warranwood
Chirnside Park
Lilydale
Avondale Heights
Brunswick
Northcote
Fairfield
Ivanhoe
Bullen Park
Bulleen
Banyule Flats Res.
Templestowe Lower
Doncaster East
Donvale
Croydon North
Mooroolbark
Braybrook
Ascot Vale
Flemington Racecourse
Royal Park
Zoo
Carlton
Melb. Uni.
Kew
Yarra Bend N.P.
Eastern Freeway
Balwyn North
Doncaster
Warrandyte
Maidstone
Western Highway
Sunshine
Tottenham
Footscray
Parl. House
Fitzroy Gdns
M.C.G.
Richmond
Balwyn
Box Hill
Blackburn
Mitcham
Ringwood
Croydon
Kilsyth
Brooklyn
Yarraville
MELBOURNE
Kew
Surrey Park
Box Hill South
Blackburn Lake
Nunawading
East Ringwood
Heathmont
Mt. Dandenong
Montrose
Newport
Spotswood
Fishermans Bend
Albert Park
Kings Domain
Middle Park
Sth Yarra
Toorak
Malvern
Glen Iris
Ashburton
Canterbury
Surrey Hills
Camberwell
Burwood
Burwood Hwy
Forest Hill
Vermont
Vermont Sth.
Wantirna
Boronia
Bayswater
Altona North
Williamstown
Altona Sports Park
Cherry Lake
St. Kilda
Armadale
Caulfield
Elsternwick
Ashwood
Chadstone
Mt. Waverley
Syndal
Burwood East
Glen Waverley
The Basin
Olinda
Altona
Altona Bay
Hobsons Bay
Port Melbourne
Brighton
Elwood
Glenhuntly
Ormond
Carnegie
Murrumbeena
Caulfield Racecourse
Ashwood
Jells Park
Wheelers Hill
Wattle Park
One Tree Hill
Sassafras
Ferntree Gully
Ferntree Gully N.P.
Knoxfield
Scoresby
Knox Park
Upper Ferntree Gully
Belgrave
Upwey
Tremont
Tecoma
McKinnon
Bentleigh
Bentleigh East
Oakleigh
Notting Hill
Monash Uni.
Caribbean Gardens
Mulgrave
Rowville
Puffing Billy Stn.
Clayton
Princes Hwy
East from Greenwich
Maribyrnong River
Marybyrnong
Moonee Ponds Ck.
Steele Ck.
Merri Ck.
Edgars Ck.
Darebin Ck.
Plenty River
Mullum Mullum Ck.
Dandenong Ck.

144 50'   145   145 10'   145 20'
37 40'   37 50'

COPYRIGHT GEORGE PHILIP AND SON LTD

1: 200 000

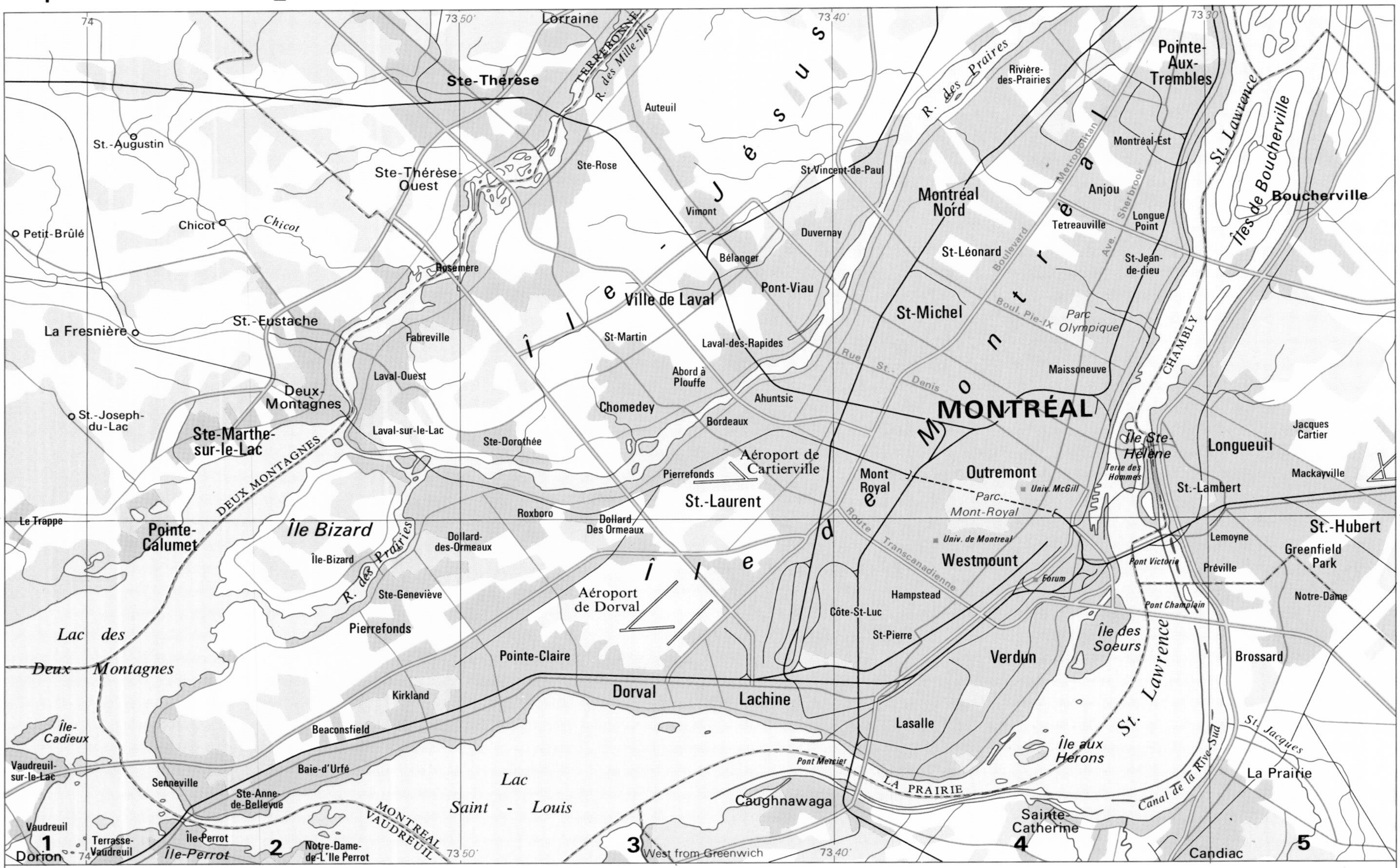

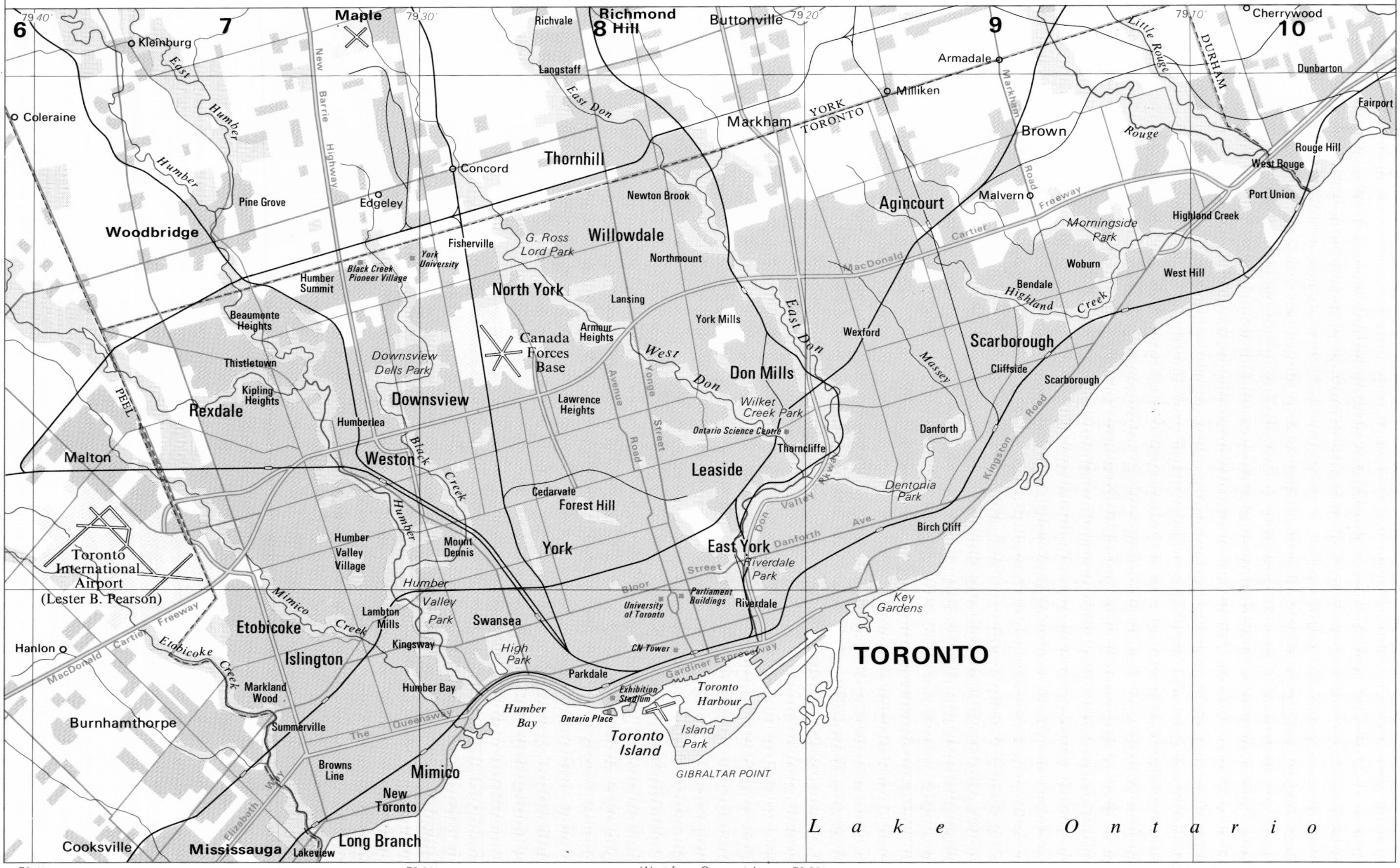

Lorraine
Ste-Thérèse
TERREBONNE
R. des Mille-Îles
Auteuil
St.-Augustin
Ste-Thérèse-Ouest
Ste-Rose
Petit-Brûlé
Chicot
Chicot
Vimont
Rosemère
Bélanger
Pont-Viau
Duvernay
St-Vincent-de-Paul
Île Jésus
Ville de Laval
La Fresnière
St.-Eustache
Fabreville
St-Martin
Laval-des-Rapides
Laval-Ouest
Abord à Plouffe
Deux-Montagnes
Chomedey
Ahuntsic
St.-Joseph-du-Lac
Ste-Marthe-sur-le-Lac
Laval-sur-le-Lac
Ste-Dorothée
Bordeaux
Aéroport de Cartierville
Pierrefonds
DEUX MONTAGNES
St.-Laurent
Mont Royal
Outremont
Univ. McGill
Parc Mont-Royal
Le Trappe
Pointe-Calumet
Île Bizard
Roxboro
Dollard Des Ormeaux
Dollard-des-Ormeaux
Île-Bizard
R. des Prairies
Ste-Geneviève
Pierrefonds
Aéroport de Dorval
Route Transcanadienne
Univ. de Montreal
Westmount
Forum
Hampstead
Côte-St-Luc
St-Pierre
Lac des Deux Montagnes
Pointe-Claire
Kirkland
Dorval
Lachine
Verdun
Île des Soeurs
Lasalle
Île-Cadieux
Beaconsfield
Vaudreuil-sur-le-Lac
Baie-d'Urfé
Senneville
Ste-Anne-de-Bellevue
Lac Saint-Louis
MONTREAL VAUDREUIL
Vaudreuil
Terrasse-Vaudreuil
Île-Perrot
Notre-Dame-de-L'Ile Perrot
Dorion
Caughnawaga
Pont Mercier
LA PRAIRIE
Sainte-Catherine
Île aux Herons
St. Lawrence
Canal de la Rive-Sud
La Prairie
St. Jacques
Candiac
Rivière-des-Prairies
R. des Prairies
Pointe-Aux-Trembles
Montréal-Est
Montréal Nord
Anjou
Longue Point
Tetreauville
St-Léonard
St-Jean-de-dieu
Boulevard Metropolitan
Ave. Sherbrooke
Boul. Pie-IX
Parc Olympique
St-Michel
Maisonneuve
Rue St. Denis
MONTRÉAL
Île de Montréal
Île Ste-Hélène
Terre des Hommes
CHAMBLY
St. Lawrence
Îles de Boucherville
Boucherville
Longueuil
Jacques Cartier
Mackayville
St.-Lambert
Lemoyne
Pont Victoria
Préville
St.-Hubert
Greenfield Park
Pont Champlain
Notre-Dame
Brossard
West from Greenwich

Maple
Richvale
Richmond Hill
Buttonville
Cherrywood
Kleinburg
East Humber
Langstaff
East Don
Armadale
Milliken
Little Rouge
DURHAM
Dunbarton
Coleraine
Humber
Markham
YORK
TORONTO
Brown
Rouge
Fairport
Concord
Thornhill
New Barrie Highway
Rouge Hill
West Rouge
Pine Grove
Edgeley
Newton Brook
Malvern
Agincourt
Port Union
Woodbridge
Fisherville
G. Ross Lord Park
Willowdale
Cartier Freeway
Highland Creek
Morningside Park
York University
Black Creek Pioneer Village
Northmount
MacDonald
Woburn
Humber Summit
North York
Lansing
Bendale
Highland Creek
West Hill
Beaumonte Heights
Canada Forces Base
Armour Heights
York Mills
East Don
Wexford
Scarborough
Thistletown
Downsview Dells Park
West Don
Don Mills
Massey
Cliffside
Scarborough
PEEL
Kipling Heights
Rexdale
Downsview
Lawrence Heights
Avenue Road
Yonge Street
Wilket Creek Park
Ontario Science Centre
Danforth
Humberlea
Thorncliffe
Kingston Road
Malton
Weston
Black Creek
Leaside
Dentonia Park
Cedarvale
Forest Hill
Don Valley Parkway
Danforth Ave.
Birch Cliff
Toronto International Airport (Lester B. Pearson)
Humber Valley Village
Mount Dennis
York
East York
Riverdale Park
Bloor Street
Humber
Parliament Buildings
Riverdale
Key Gardens
Mimico Creek
Lambton Mills
Valley Park
Swansea
University of Toronto
Etobicoke
Hanlon
MacDonald Cartier Freeway
Etobicoke Creek
Kingsway
Islington
CN Tower
TORONTO
High Park
Gardiner Expressway
Parkdale
Markland Wood
Humber Bay
Exhibition Stadium
Toronto Harbour
Burnhamthorpe
Humber Bay
Ontario Place
Summerville
The Queensway
Toronto Island
Island Park
Browns Line
Mimico
GIBRALTAR POINT
New Toronto
Elizabeth Way
Lake Ontario
Cooksville
Mississauga
Lakeview
Long Branch
West from Greenwich

1: 200 000

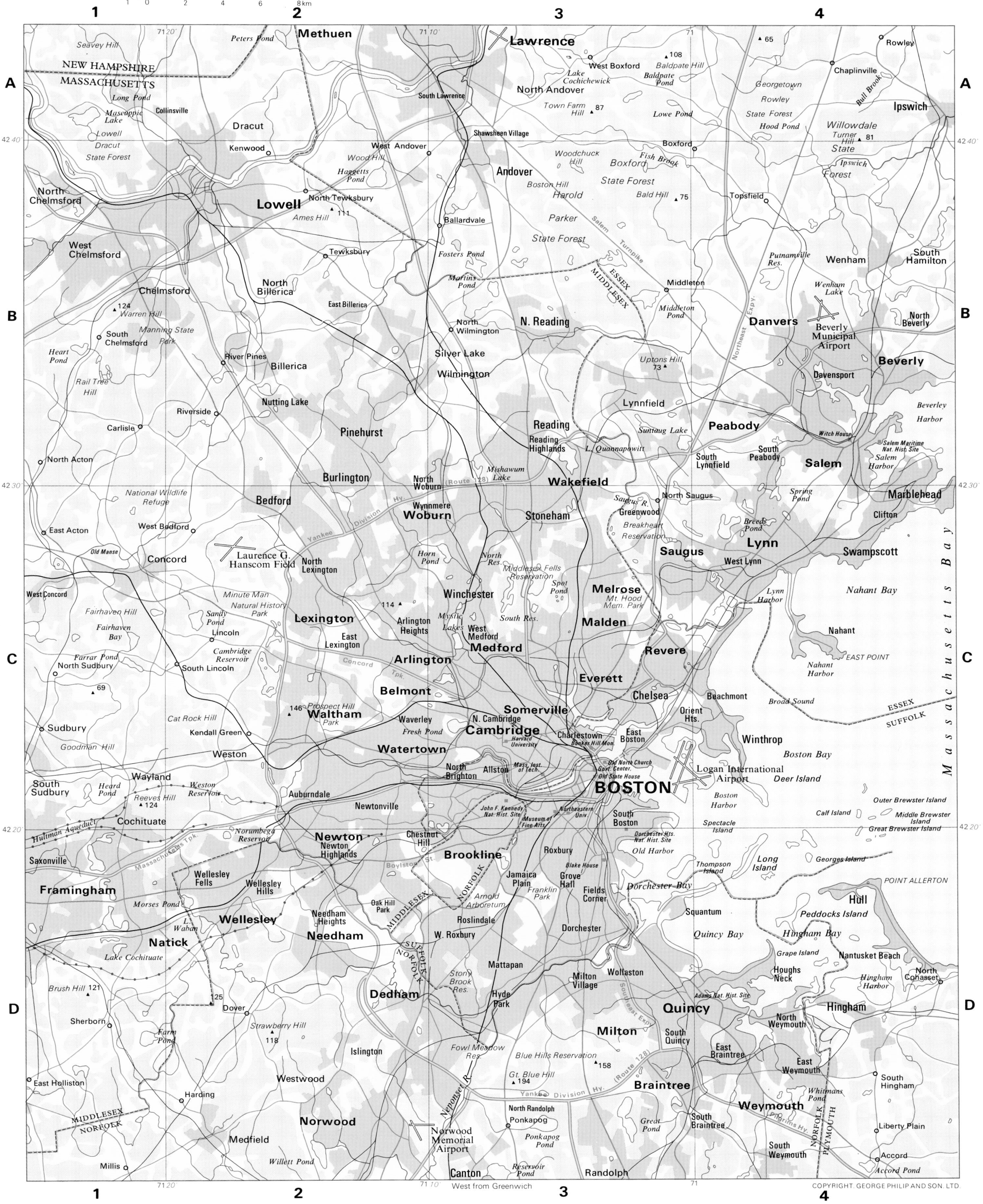

0 1 2 3 4 5 miles
0 1 2 4 6 8 km

1 **2** **3** **4**

71°20' 71°10' 71°

Seavey Hill
Peters Pond
Methuen
Lawrence
▲ 65
Rowley

West Boxford
Baldpate Hill
Chaplinville

NEW HAMPSHIRE
MASSACHUSETTS
Lake Cochichewick
North Andover
▲ 108
Baldpate Pond
Georgetown
Rowley
Ipswich

A Long Pond
Collinsville
Dracut
Town Farm Hill ▲ 87
Lowe Pond
State Forest
Hood Pond
Willowdale
Turner Hill ▲ 81
State **A**

Mascoppic Lake
Lowell Dracut State Forest
Kenwood
West Andover
Shawsheen Village
Andover
Woodchuck Hill
Boxford
Fish Brook
State Forest
Ipswich Forest

42°40' 42°40'

North Chelmsford
Lowell
North Tewksbury
North Billerica
Haggetts Pond
Boston Hill
Harold
Bald Hill ▲ 75
Topsfield
Putnamville Res.
Wenham
South Hamilton

West Chelmsford
Ames Hill ▲ 111
Wood Hill
Ballardvale
Parker State Forest
Salem Turnpike
Wenham Lake

B Chelmsford
Warren Hill ▲ 124
East Billerica
Tewksbury
Fosters Pond
Martins Pond
ESSEX MIDDLESEX
Middleton
Middleton Pond
Danvers
Beverly Municipal Airport
North Beverly **B**

South Chelmsford
Manning State Park
North Wilmington
N. Reading
Uptons Hill 73 ▲
Beverly

Heart Pond
River Pines
Billerica
Silver Lake
Lynnfield
Davensport
Beverley Harbor

Rail Tree Hill
Nutting Lake
Wilmington
Reading
Suntaug Lake
Peabody
Witch House
Salem Maritime Nat. Hist. Site

Riverside
Pinehurst
Reading Highlands
L. Quannapowitt
South Lynnfield
South Peabody
Salem
Salem Harbor

North Acton
Carlisle
Mishawum Lake
(Route 28)
Wakefield
North Saugus
Marblehead

42°30' **Burlington**
North Woburn
Saugus R.
Spring Pond
42°30'

East Acton
Bedford
West Bedford
Wynnmere
Stoneham
Greenwood
Breakheart Reservation
Breeds Pond
Clifton

National Wildlife Refuge
Yankee Division Hy.
Woburn
Horn Pond
North Res.
Middlesex Fells Reservation
Spot Pond
Saugus
West Lynn
Lynn
Swampscott

C Old Manse
Laurence G. Hanscom Field
North Lexington
Winchester
North Res.
South Res.
Melrose
Mt. Hood Mem. Park
Lynn Harbor
Nahant Bay **C**

West Concord
Fairhaven Hill
Minute Man Natural History Park
114 ▲
Mystic Lakes
Malden
Nahant

Fairhaven Bay
Sandy Pond
Lexington
Arlington Heights
West Medford
Medford
Nahant Harbor

Farrar Pond
North Sudbury ▲ 69
Lincoln
East Lexington
Cambridge Reservoir
Concord Tpk.
Arlington
Revere
EAST POINT

South Lincoln
Prospect Hill
Belmont
Everett
Chelsea
Beachmont
Broad Sound
ESSEX SUFFOLK

Cat Rock Hill
146 ▲
Waltham Park
Waverley
Fresh Pond
N. Cambridge
Somerville
Orient Hts.
Winthrop
Boston Bay

Sudbury
Goodman Hill
Kendall Green
Weston
Cambridge
Charlestown
Bunker Hill Mon.
East Boston
Logan International Airport
Deer Island

South Sudbury
Heard Pond
Reeves Hill ▲ 124
Weston Reservoir
Harvard University
Old North Church
Govt. Center
Old State House

42°20' Wayland
Auburndale
Newtonville
North Brighton
Allston
Mass. Inst. of Tech.
BOSTON
Boston Harbor
Outer Brewster Island
42°20'

Hultman Aqueduct
Cochituate
Norumbega Reservoir
Massachusetts Tpk.
John F. Kennedy Nat. Hist. Site
Northeastern Univ.
South Boston
Spectacle Island
Calf Island
Middle Brewster Island
Great Brewster Island

Saxonville
Newton
Newton Highlands
Chestnut Hill
Museum of Fine Arts
Dorchester Hts. Nat. Hist. Site
Old Harbor
Thompson Island
Long Island
Georges Island
POINT ALLERTON

D **Framingham**
Wellesley Fells
Wellesley Hills
Brookline
Roxbury
Blake House
Grove Hall
Franklin Park
Fields Corner
Dorchester Bay
Houghs Neck
Hull
Peddocks Island **D**

Morses Pond
Oak Hill Park
Jamaica Plain
Arnold Arboretum
Squantum
Grape Island
Nantasket Beach

Wellesley
Needham Heights
NORFOLK
Roslindale
W. Roxbury
Dorchester
Quincy Bay
Hingham Bay
North Cohasset

Natick
Boylston St.
Needham
MIDDLESEX NORFOLK
Mattapan
Wollaston
Milton Village
Adams Nat. Hist. Site
Hingham Harbor

Lake Cochituate
SUFFOLK NORFOLK
Stony Brook Res.
Hyde Park
Milton
Quincy
North Weymouth
Hingham
South Hingham

Brush Hill ▲ 121
25
Dover
Strawberry Hill
118
Fowl Meadow Res.
Blue Hills Reservation
▲ 158
Milton
South Quincy
East Braintree
East Weymouth

Sherborn
Islington
Gt. Blue Hill ▲ 194
Braintree
South Braintree
Whitmans Pond

East Holliston
Farm Pond
Westwood
Yankee Division Hy.
(Route 128)
Southeast Expy.
Weymouth
South Hingham

MIDDLESEX NORFOLK
Harding
Norwood
North Randolph
Ponkapog
Ponkapog Pond
Great Pond
South Braintree
NORFOLK PLYMOUTH
Liberty Plain

Millis
Medfield
Willett Pond
Norwood Memorial Airport
Reservoir Pond
South Weymouth
Accord
Accord Pond

1 **Canton** **2** **Randolph** **3** **4**

71°20' 71°10' West from Greenwich 71°

Massachusetts Bay

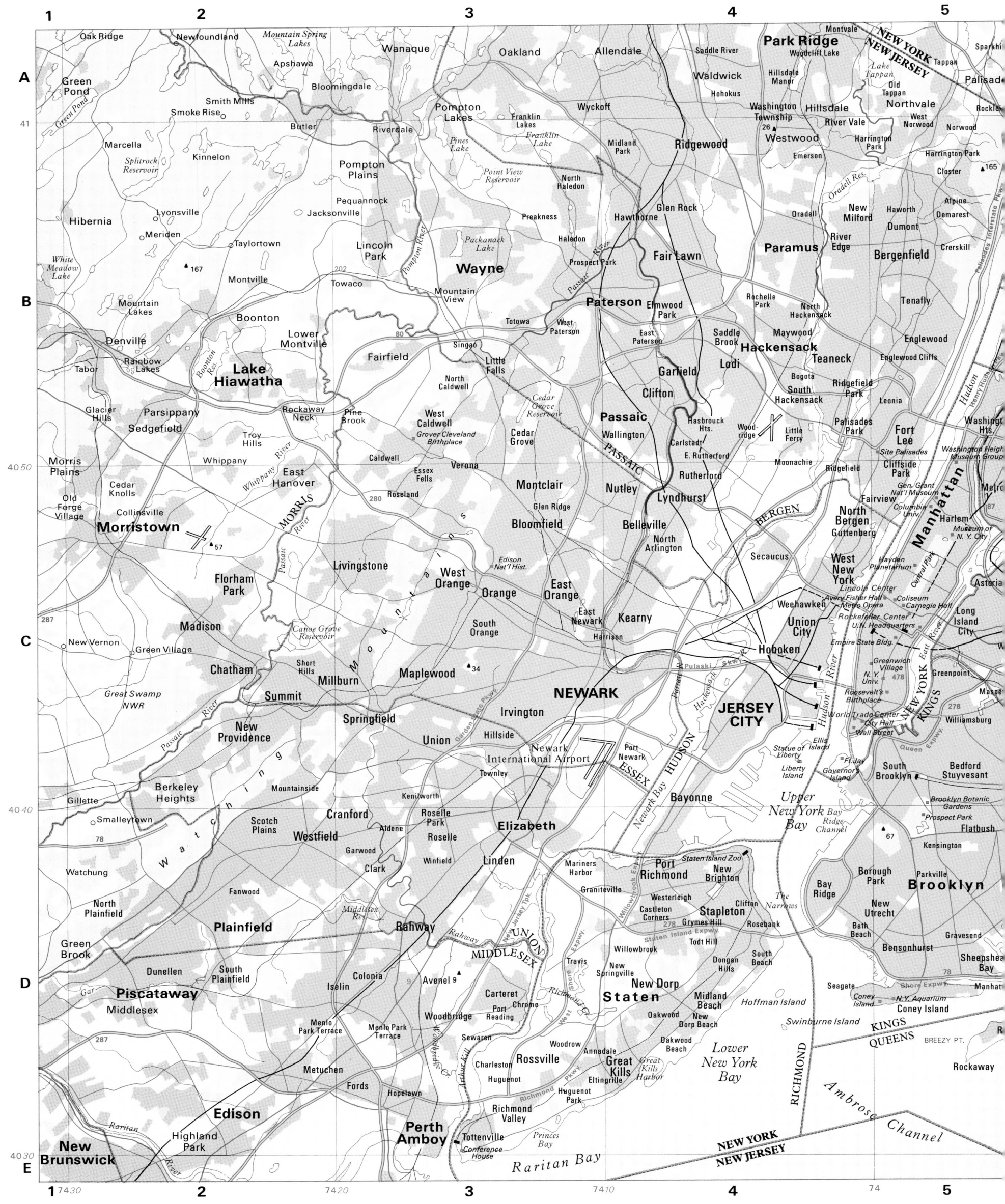

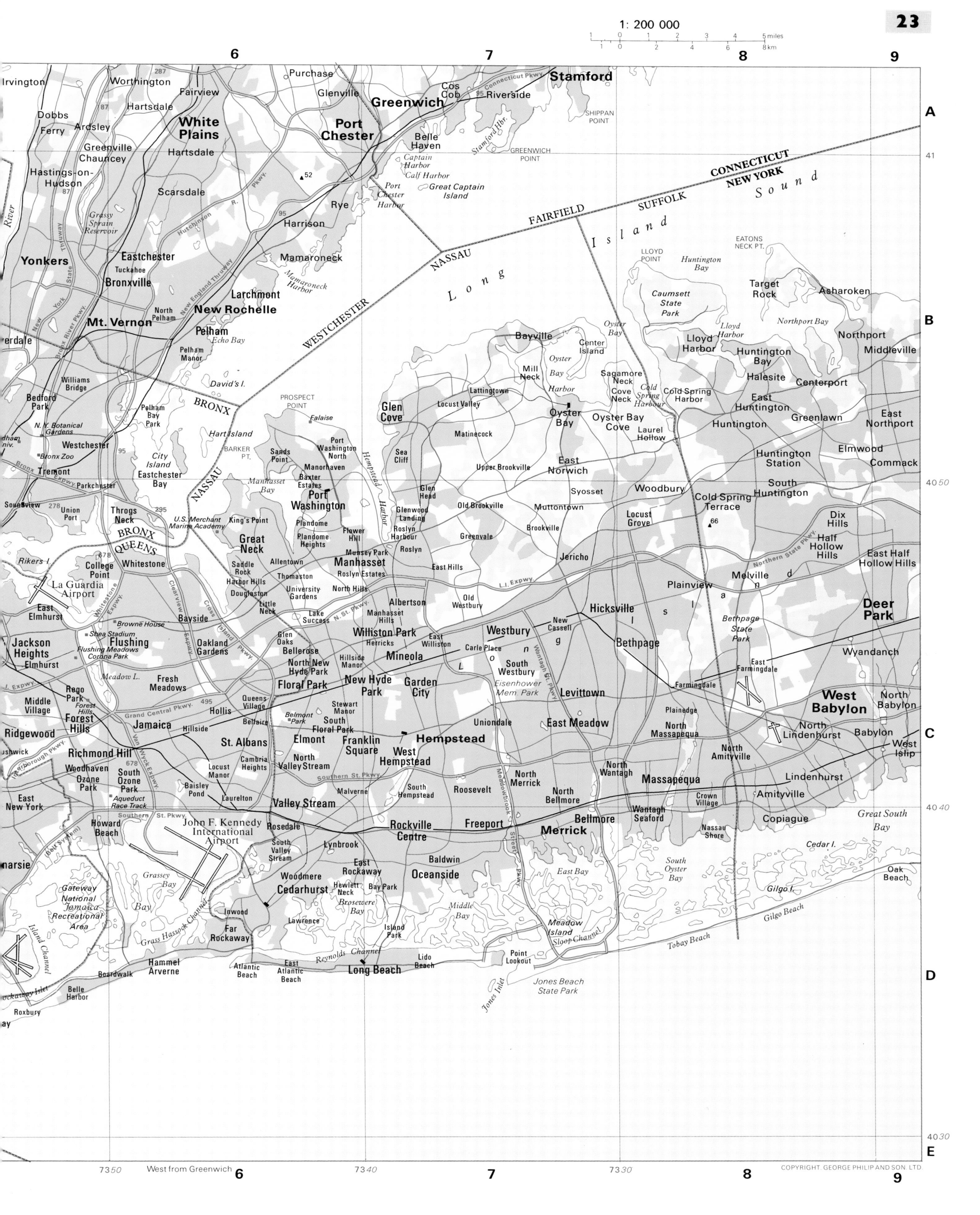

1: 200 000

5 miles
8 km

West from Greenwich

Irvington
Worthington
Fairview
Purchase
Glenville
Cos Cob
Riverside
Stamford
Greenwich
Dobbs Ferry
Hartsdale
87
Ardsley
Hartsdale
White Plains
Port Chester
Belle Haven
SHIPPAN POINT
Greenville
Chauncey
Hartsdale
Captain Harbor
Stamford Hbr.
GREENWICH POINT
Hastings-on-Hudson
87
Scarsdale
52
Calf Harbor
Great Captain Island
Port Chester Harbor
Rye
95
CONNECTICUT
NEW YORK
Sound
Harrison
FAIRFIELD
Long Island
SUFFOLK
NASSAU
Yonkers
Eastchester
Mamaroneck
Tuckahoe
Bronxville
Memaroneck Harbor
Larchmont
WESTCHESTER
LLOYD POINT
Huntington Bay
EATONS NECK PT.
North Pelham
New Rochelle
Bayville
Center Island
Caumsett State Park
Target Rock
Asharoken
Mt. Vernon
Pelham
Echo Bay
Oyster Bay
Lloyd Harbor
Northport Bay
rdale
Pelham Manor
David's I.
Mill Neck
Oyster Bay Harbor
Sagamore Neck
Cold Spring Harbor
Cold Spring Harbor
Lloyd Harbor
Huntington Bay
Northport
Middleville
Bedford Park
Williams Bridge
PROSPECT POINT
BRONX
Glen Cove
Lattingtown
Locust Valley
Cove Neck
Halesite
East Huntington
Centerport
N.Y. Botanical Gardens
Pelham Bay Park
Falaise
Laurel Hollow
Huntington
Greenlawn
East Northport
Westchester
Hart Island
BARKER PT.
Port Washington North
Matinecock
Upper Brookville
East Norwich
Huntington Station
Elmwood
Bronx Zoo
City Island
Sands Point
Manorhaven
Sea Cliff
Old Brookville
Woodbury
South Huntington
Commack
Tremont
95
Eastchester Bay
Baxter Estates
Glen Head
Syosset
Cold Spring Terrace
Dix Hills
Parkchester
Manhasset Bay
Port Washington
Glenwood Landing
Greenvale
Muttontown
Brookville
66
Half Hollow Hills
278
Plandome
Roslyn Harbour
Jericho
East Half Hollow Hills
Soundview
Union Port
295
U.S. Merchant Marine Academy
King's Point
Plandome Heights
Flower Hill
Mursey Park
Roslyn
Melville
Throgs Neck
BRONX QUEENS
Great Neck
Allentown
Roslyn Estates
East Hills
Plainview
Deer Park
Rikers I.
College Point
Whitestone
678
Saddle Rock
Harbor Hills
Thomaston
North Hills
Old Westbury
New Cassell
Hicksville
Bethpage State Park
East Farmingdale
Wyandanch
La Guardia Airport
Browne House
Bayside
University Gardens
Little Neck
Lake Success
Manhasset Hills
Albertson
Westbury
Bethpage
East Elmhurst
Douglaston
Glen Oaks
Williston Park
Herricks
East Williston
Carle Place
South Westbury
Farmingdale
West Babylon
Jackson Heights
Shea Stadium
Flushing
Oakland Gardens
Bellerose
Mineola
Levittown
North Babylon
Flushing Meadows Corona Park
North New Hyde Park
Hillside Manor
Eisenhower Mem. Park
Elmhurst
Meadow L.
Fresh Meadows
Floral Park
New Hyde Park
Garden City
Uniondale
East Meadow
Plainedge
North Massapequa
North Lindenhurst
Babylon
Rego Park
Forest Hills
495
Grand Central Pkwy
Queens Village
Stewart Manor
Roosevelt
North Merrick
North Wantagh
Massapequa
West Islip
Middle Village
Hollis
South Floral Park
Uniondale
North Bellmore
North Amityville
Lindenhurst
Forest Hills
Jamaica
Hillside
Belmont Park
South
Hempstead
Merrick
Wantagh
Crown Village
Amityville
Ridgewood
St. Albans
Elmont
Franklin Square
West Hempstead
South Hempstead
Seaford
Copiague
Richmond Hill
678
Cambria Heights
North Valley Stream
Malverne
Roosevelt
Bellmore
Nassau Shore
Great South Bay
Woodhaven Ozone Park
Locust Manor
Baisley Pond
Laurelton
Valley Stream
Freeport
East Bay
Cedar I.
East New York
Aqueduct Race Track
Rosedale
Rockville Centre
South Oyster Bay
Oak Beach
Howard Beach
St. Pkwy.
John F. Kennedy International Airport
Lynbrook
Baldwin
Gilgo I.
Gateway National Jamaica Recreational Area
South Valley Stream
Woodmere
East Rockaway
Oceanside
Gilgo Beach
narsie
Grassey Bay
Cedarhurst
Hewlett Neck
Bay Park
Middle Bay
Meadow Island Sloop Channel
Tobay Beach
Island Channel
Inwood
Lawrence
Broswere Bay
Island Park
Hammel Arverne
Atlantic Beach
East Atlantic Beach
Reynolds Channel
Long Beach
Lido Beach
Point Lookout
Jones Beach State Park
Boardwalk
Belle Harbor
Roxbury
Jones Inlet

1: 200 000

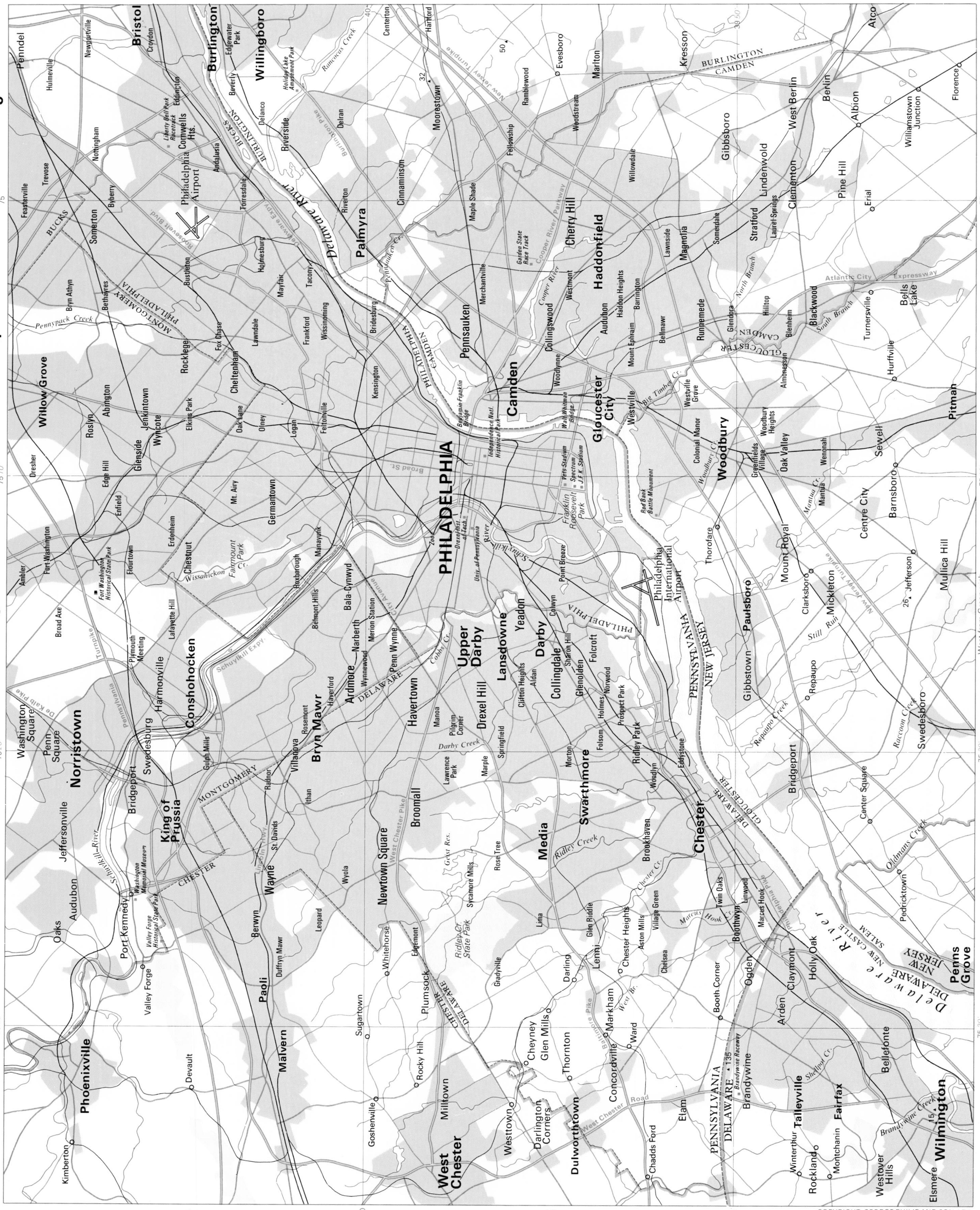

5 miles
8 km

PHILADELPHIA

Bristol
Burlington
Willingboro
Palmyra
Pennsauken
Camden
Gloucester City
Woodbury
Cherry Hill
Haddonfield
Berlin
Pitman

Willow Grove
Norristown
King of Prussia
Conshohocken
Bryn Mawr
Ardmore
Upper Darby
Darby
Lansdowne
Yeadon
Havertown
Drexel Hill
Collingdale
Swarthmore
Media
Broomall
Newtown Square
Wayne
Paoli
Malvern
Phoenixville

West Chester
Dulworthtown
Chester
Wilmington
Fairfax
Talleyville

Delaware River
Schuylkill River
Pennypack Creek
Darby Creek
Chester Creek
Ridley Creek
Brandywine Creek

PENNSYLVANIA
NEW JERSEY
DELAWARE

Philadelphia International Airport

COPYRIGHT GEORGE PHILIP AND SON LTD

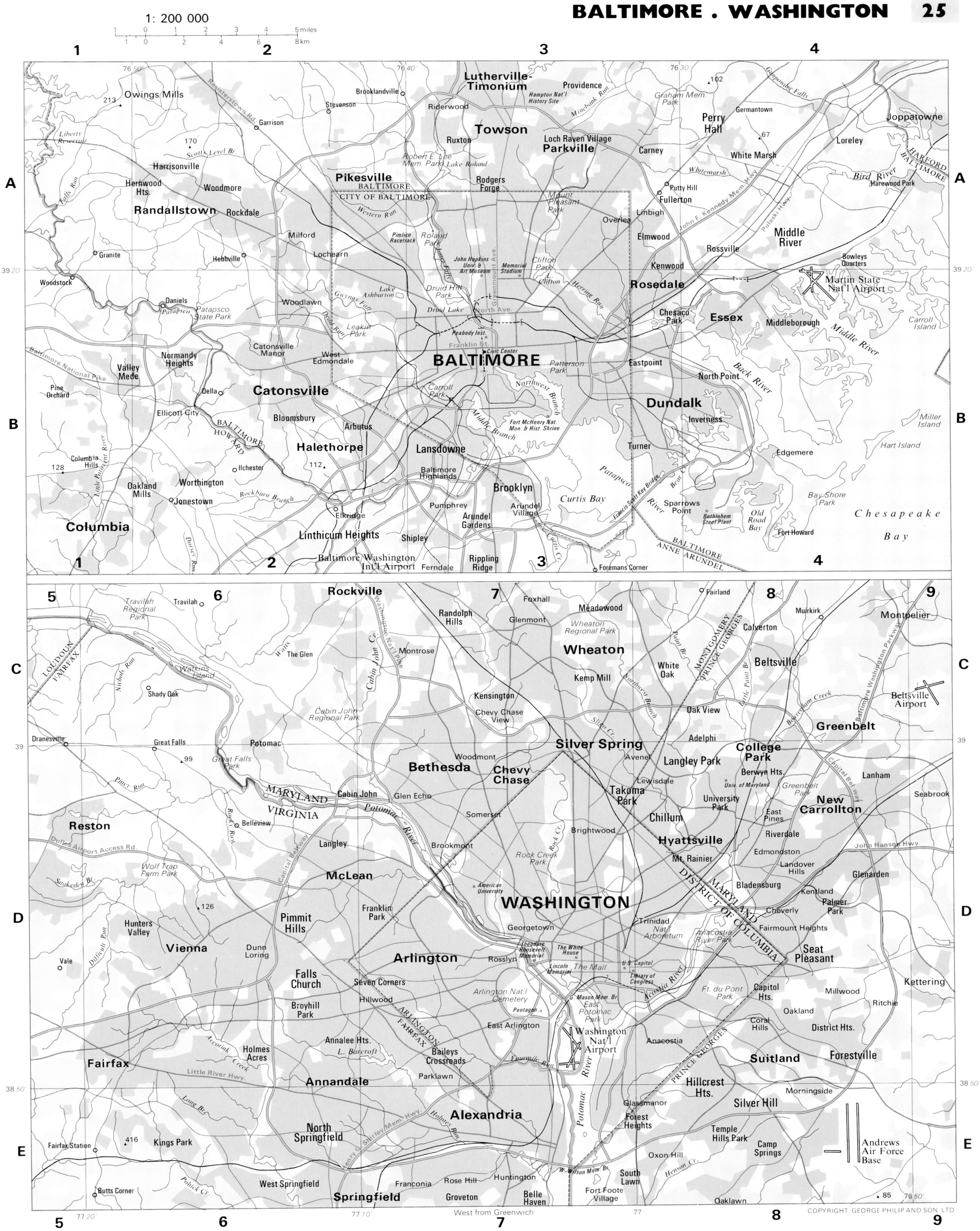

1:200 000

0 1 2 3 4 5 miles
0 1 2 3 4 5 6 7 8 km

1   2   3   4

Owings Mills
213
Liberty Reservoir
170
Scotts Level Br.
Reisterstown Rd.
Garrison
Brooklandville
Riderwood
Stevenson
Lutherville-Timonium
Providence
Hampton Nat'l History Site
Graham Mem. Park
Germantown
102
Perry Hall
67
White Marsh
Loreley
Joppatowne
HARFORD / BALTIMORE
Bird River
Harewood Park

A
Harrisonville
Hernwood Hts.
Woodmore
Pikesville
BALTIMORE CITY OF BALTIMORE
Western Run
Ruxton
Towson
Parkville
Carney
Loch Raven Village
Robert E. Lee Mem. Park/Lake Roland
Mount Pleasant Park
Linbigh
Overlea
Putty Hill
Fullerton
Rossville
Middle River
Bowleys Quarters
Carroll Island
A
39 20
Randallstown
Rockdale
Granite
Milford
Lochearn
Hebbville
Rodgers Forge
Pimlico Racetrack
Roland Park
Druid Hill Park
John Hopkins Univ & Art Museum
Memorial Stadium
Clifton Park
Clifton
Herring Run
Elmwood
Kenwood
Rosedale
Chesaco Park
Essex
Middleborough
Martin State Nat'l Airport
Carroll Island
39 20
Woodstock
Daniels Patapsco
Patapsco State Park
Woodlawn
Lake Ashburton
Gwynns Falls
Druid Lake
North Ave.
Peabody Inst.
Franklin St.
Civic Center
BALTIMORE
Patterson Park
Eastpoint
North Point
Dundalk
Inverness
Middle River
Miller Island
B
Baltimore National Pike
Valley Mede
Pine Orchard
Normandy Heights
Catonsville Manor
West Edmondale
Leakin Park
Carroll Park
Northwest Branch
Fort McHenry Nat. Mon. & Hist. Shrine
Turner
Edgemere
Hart Island
B
Columbia Hills
128
Oakland Mills
Worthington
Jonestown
Ellicott City
Oella
Catonsville
Bloomsbury
Arbutus
Halethorpe
112
Ilchester
Rockburn Branch
Lansdowne
Middle Branch
Baltimore Highlands
Pumphrey
Elkridge
Brooklyn
Arundel Village
Patapsco River
Francis Scott Key Bridge
Curtis Bay
Sparrows Point
Bethlehem Steel Plant
Bay Shore Park
Old Road Bay
Fort Howard
Chesapeake Bay
1   2
Columbia
Linthicum Heights
Shipley
Arundel Gardens
Rippling Ridge
Curtis Cr.
BALTIMORE / ANNE ARUNDEL
Foremans Corner
3   4
Baltimore Washington Int'l Airport
Ferndale

5   6   7   8   9

Rockville
Randolph Hills
Foxhall
Meadowood
Fairland
Muirkirk
Montpelier
Travilah Regional Park
Travilah
Glenmont
Wheaton Regional Park
Calverton
C
LOUDOUN / FAIRFAX
The Glen
Montrose
Cabin John Cr.
Seneca Nat'l Park
Wheaton
White Oak
Beltsville
Beltsville Airport
C
39
Shady Oak
Cabin John Regional Park
Kensington
Kemp Mill
Oak View
Adelphi
Greenbelt
39
Dranesville
Great Falls
99
Great Falls Park
Potomac
Chevy Chase View
Silver Spring
Avenel
Langley Park
Berwyn Hts.
College Park
Univ. of Maryland
Greenbelt Park
Lanham
Seabrook
D
Pimmit Run
MARYLAND VIRGINIA
Cabin John
Bethesda
Chevy Chase
Somerset
Glen Echo
Takoma Park
Lewisdale
Chillum
University Park
East Pines
New Carrollton
Reston
Langley
Brookmont
Rock Creek Park
Brightwood
Hyattsville
Mt. Rainier
Riverdale
Edmonston
Glenarden
D
Wolf Trap Farm Park
126
Hunters Valley
McLean
Franklin Park
American University
Georgetown
Trinidad Nat. Arboretum
Bladensburg
Landover Hills
Kentland
Palmer Park
Cheverly
Fairmount Heights
Vienna
Vale
Dunn Loring
Pimmit Hills
WASHINGTON
Theodore Roosevelt Memorial
The White House
Rosslyn
U.S. Capitol
The Mall
Lincoln Memorial
Library of Congress
Anacostia River Park
DISTRICT OF COLUMBIA
MARYLAND
Seat Pleasant
Kettering
Falls Church
Seven Corners
Hillwood
Arlington
Arlington Nat'l Cemetery
Pentagon
G. Mason Mem. Br.
East Potomac Park
Ft. du Pont Park
Capitol Hts.
Millwood
Ritchie
E
Fairfax
Broyhill Park
Annalee Hts.
Holmes Acres
L. Barcroft
Hillcrest Hts.
East Arlington
Baileys Crossroads
Parklawn
Washington Nat'l Airport
Anacostia
Oakland
Coral Hills
District Hts.
Suitland
Forestville
E
38 50
Accotink Creek
Little River Hwy.
Annandale
Fourmile Run
Glassmanor
Forest Heights
Hillcrest Hts.
Silver Hill
Morningside
38 50
Fairfax Station
416
Kings Park
North Springfield
Alexandria
Potomac River
Oxon Hill
South Lawn
Temple Hills Park
Camp Springs
Andrews Air Force Base
85
76 50
Butts Corner
Pohick Cr.
West Springfield
Springfield
Franconia
Rose Hill
Groveton
Huntington
Belle Haven
W. Wilson Mem. Br.
Fort Foote Village
Henson Cr.
Oaklawn

77 20   77 10   West from Greenwich   77   COPYRIGHT GEORGE PHILIP AND SON LTD

5   6   7   8   9

1 : 200 000

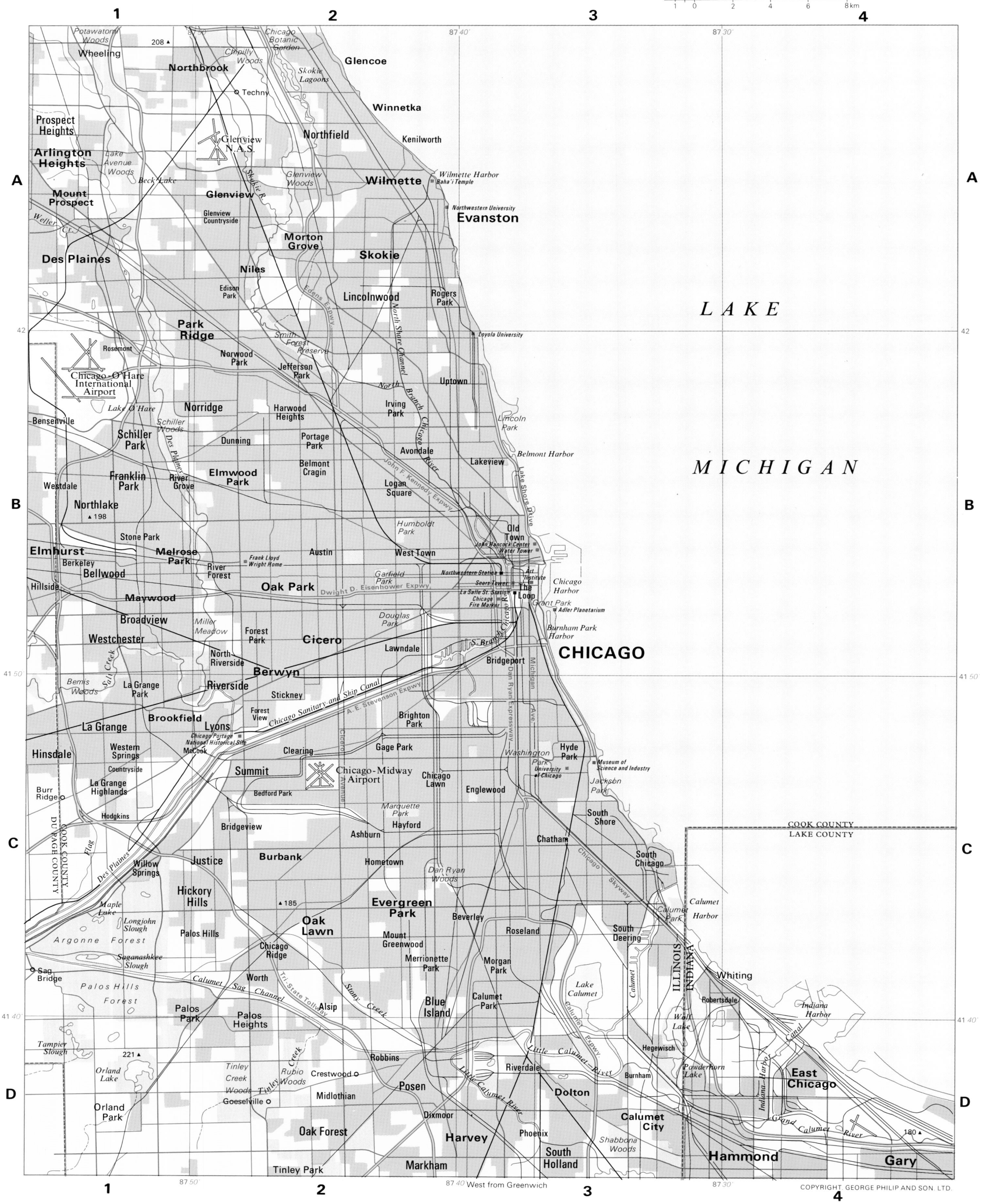

1 0 1 2 3 4 5 miles
1 0 2 4 6 8 km

1 **2** **3** **4**

Potawatomi Woods

208 ▲

Wheeling

Northbrook

Chbilly Woods

Glencoe

Chicago Botanic Garden

● Techny

Skokie Lagoons

Winnetka

Prospect Heights

Northfield

Glenview N.A.S.

Kenilworth

A Arlington Heights

Lake Avenue Woods

Beck Lake

Glenview Woods

Wilmette

Wilmette Harbor
● *Baha'i Temple*

A

Mount Prospect

Weller Cr.

Glenview

Glenview Countryside

Skokie R.

Edens Expwy.

● Northwestern University

Evanston

Des Plaines

Morton Grove

Niles

Skokie

Edison Park

Lincolnwood

Rogers Park

North Shore Channel

Park Ridge

Smith Forest Preserve

● Loyola University

42

Chicago-O'Hare International Airport

Rosemont

Norwood Park

Jefferson Park

Uptown

North Branch Chicago River

42

Lake O'Hare

Bensenville

Norridge

Harwood Heights

Irving Park

Lincoln Park

Schiller Woods

Dunning

Portage Park

Avondale

Lakeview

Belmont Harbor

Des Plaines R.

Schiller Park

Elmwood Park

Belmont Cragin

Lake Shore Drive

B Westdale

Franklin Park

River Grove

Logan Square

B

▲ 198

Northlake

Old Town

John Hancock Center
Water Tower

Stone Park

Humboldt Park

West Town

Elmhurst

Melrose Park

Austin

Northwestern Station

Art Institute

Berkeley

River Forest

Frank Lloyd Wright Home

Sears Tower

LaSalle St. Station
Chicago Fire Market

Chicago Harbor

Bellwood

Oak Park

Garfield Park

The Loop

Hillside

Dwight D. Eisenhower Expwy.

Grant Park
● *Adler Planetarium*

Maywood

Douglas Park

Burnham Park Harbor

Broadview

Miller Meadow

Forest Park

Cicero

Lawndale

S. Branch

CHICAGO

Westchester

North Riverside

41 50

Berwyn

Bridgeport

41 50

Bemis Woods

Salt Creek

La Grange Park

Riverside

Stickney

Dan Ryan Expressway

Brookfield

Lyons

Forest View

Brighton Park

Michigan Ave.

La Grange

Chicago Portage National Site

Chicago Sanitary and Ship Canal

A.E. Stevenson Expwy.

Hinsdale

Western Springs

McCook

Clearing

Gage Park

Washington Park

Hyde Park

Museum of Science and Industry

Countryside

Summit

Cicero Avenue

Chicago-Midway Airport

Chicago Lawn

University of Chicago

Jackson Park

Burr Ridge

La Grange Highlands

Bedford Park

Englewood

Hodgkins

Marquette Park

Ashburn

Hayford

South Shore

Bridgeview

C

Flag Cr.

Des Plaines R.

Justice

Burbank

Hometown

Dan Ryan Woods

Chatham

Chicago River

South Chicago

C

Willow Springs

Hickory Hills

Calumet Park

South Deering

Calumet Harbor

Maple Lake

Palos Hills

▲ 185

Oak Lawn

Evergreen Park

Beverley

Roseland

South Deering

Longjohn Slough

Argonne Forest

Mount Greenwood

Calumet River

Dan Ryan Woods

Lake Calumet

Suganashkee Slough

Chicago Ridge

Merrionette Park

Morgan Park

Calumet Sag Channel

Sag Bridge

Worth

Alsip

Blue Island

Calumet Park

Lake Calumet

ILLINOIS

INDIANA

Whiting

Palos Hills Forest

Palos Park

Palos Heights

Stony Creek

Little Calumet River

Hegewisch

Robertsdale

Indiana Harbor

41 40

Tampier Slough

221 ▲

Little Calumet River

Burnham

Wolf Lake

Powderhorn Lake

East Chicago

41 40

D

Orland Lake

Tinley Creek

Rubio Woods

Crestwood ●

Robbins

Riverdale

Dolton

Shabbona Woods

180 ▲

D

Orland Park

Tinley Creek Woods

● Goeselville

Midlothian

Dixmoor

Posen

Calumet City

Indiana Harbor Canal

Grand Calumet River

Oak Forest

Harvey

Phoenix

South Holland

Hammond

Gary

Tinley Park

Markham

1 **2** **3** **4**

COPYRIGHT GEORGE PHILIP AND SON LTD.

COOK COUNTY
LAKE COUNTY

DU PAGE COUNTY

COOK COUNTY

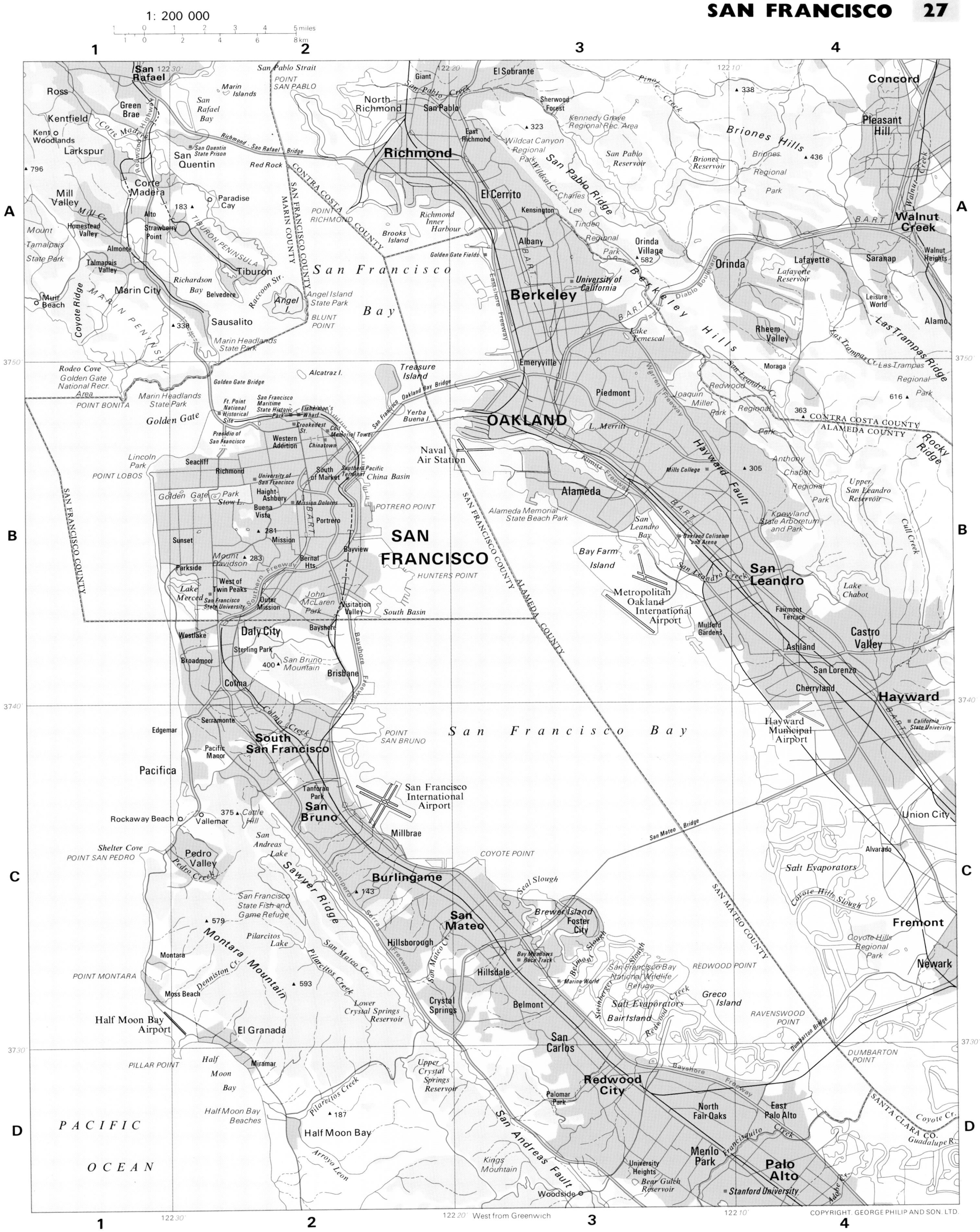

1: 200 000

5 miles
8 km

1 **2** **3** **4**

San Rafael   122 30'   San Pablo Strait   122 20'   Giant   El Sobrante   Pinole Creek   122 10'   338   Concord
Ross   POINT SAN PABLO   North Richmond   Sherwood Forest   Kennedy Grove Regional Rec. Area   Pleasant Hill
Kentfield   Marin Islands   San Pablo   323   Wildcat Canyon Regional Park   San Pablo Reservoir   Briones Hills   436
Green Brae   San Rafael Bay   East Richmond   St. Charles   Briones Reservoir   Briones Regional Park
Kent Woodlands   San Quentin State Prison   **Richmond**   Wildcat Cr.   Lee   San Pablo Ridge
Larkspur   Richmond – San Rafael Bridge   Richmond Inner Harbour   Kensington   Tilden   Walnut Creek
796   Corte Madera   Red Rock   El Cerrito   Regional Park   Orinda Village   582   Orinda   Lafayette   Saranap   Walnut Heights
A   San Quentin   Paradise Cay   Brooks Island   Albany   Lafayette Reservoir   Leisure World   Alamo   **A**
Mount Tamalpais State Park   Homestead Valley   183   Strawberry Point   Golden Gate Fields   Rheem Valley   Las Trampas Ridge   Las Trampas Regional Park
Almonte   University of California   616
Talmalpais Valley   Tiburon   **Berkeley**   Diablo Boulevard   Moraga   Redwood Regional Park   363   CONTRA COSTA COUNTY
Marin City   Richardson Bay   Belvedere   Angel Island State Park   Emeryville   Lake Temescal   San Leandro Cr.   ALAMEDA COUNTY
Muir Beach   Sausalito   Angel I.   BLUNT POINT   Piedmont   Joaquin Miller Park   Anthony Chabot Regional Park   Rocky Ridge
Coyote Ridge   338   Marin Headlands State Park   Treasure Island   **OAKLAND**   Mills College   305   Upper San Leandro Reservoir   Cull Creek
3750   Rodeo Cove   Golden Gate National Recr. Area   Alcatraz I.   Oakland Bay Bridge   L. Merritt   Knowland State Arboretum and Park   3750
POINT BONITA   Marin Headlands State Park   Ft. Point National Historical Site   San Francisco Maritime State Historic Park   Yerba Buena I.   **Alameda**   San Leandro Bay   Oakland Coliseum and Arena   **San Leandro**
Golden Gate   Fisherman's Wharf   Naval Air Station   Bay Farm Island   Lake Chabot
Presidio of San Francisco   Coit Memorial Tower   Alameda Memorial State Beach Park   Fairmont Terrace   Castro Valley
POINT LOBOS   Lincoln Park   Crookedest St.   Chinatown   China Basin   Metropolitan Oakland International Airport   Mulford Gardens   Ashland
B   Seacliff   Western Addition   South of Market   Metropolitan Oakland International Airport   San Lorenzo   **B**
Richmond   University of San Francisco   Southern Pacific Terminal   POTRERO POINT   Cherryland   **Hayward**
Golden Gate Park   Haight-Ashbury   Mission Dolores   **SAN FRANCISCO**   California State University
Stow L.   Buena Vista   Portrero   HUNTERS POINT   Hayward Municipal Airport
Sunset   281   Mission   Bayview   POINT SAN BRUNO
Parkside   Mount Davidson   283   Bernal Hts.   John McLaren Park   Visitacion Valley   South Basin
3740   Lake Merced   West of Twin Peaks   Outer Mission   Bayshore   3740
San Francisco State University   **Daly City**   San Francisco Bay
Westlake   Sterling Park   San Bruno Mountain   Union City
Broadmoor   400   Brisbane
Colma   San Mateo Bridge   Alvarado
Edgemar   Serramonte   *San Francisco Bay*   Salt Evaporators
Pacifica   **South San Francisco**   POINT SAN BRUNO   Coyote Hills Slough
Pacific Manor   375   Cattle Hill   Tanforan Park   **Fremont**
Rockaway Beach   Vallemar   **San Bruno**   San Francisco International Airport   Coyote Hills Regional Park   **Newark**
Shelter Cove   San Andreas Lake   Millbrae   COYOTE POINT
POINT SAN PEDRO   Pedro Valley   Sawyer Ridge   Seal Slough   Brewer Island   Foster City   REDWOOD POINT
C   Pedro Creek   San Francisco State Fish and Game Refuge   143   **Burlingame**   Bay Meadows Race Track   Marine World   San Francisco Bay National Wildlife Refuge   **C**
Montara   Pilarcitos Lake   579   Hillsborough   **San Mateo**   Belmont Slough   Greco Island
POINT MONTARA   Montara Mountain   **San Mateo**   Salt Evaporators
Moss Beach   Denniston Cr.   593   Hillsdale   Sketchworger Slough   Bairland   RAVENSWOOD POINT
Pilarcitos Creek   Lower Crystal Springs Reservoir   Crystal Springs   Redwood Cr.   Salt Evaporators   DUMBARTON POINT
Half Moon Bay Airport   El Granada   **San Carlos**   Dumbarton Bridge
3730   PILLAR POINT   Upper Crystal Springs Reservoir   Palomar Park   SANTA CLARA CO.   3730
Half Moon Bay   Miramar   187   Palomar   North Fair Oaks   East Palo Alto   Guadalupe R.
D   *PACIFIC*   Half Moon Bay Beaches   Kings Mountain   **Redwood City**   Bayshore Freeway   Coyote Cr.   **D**
Half Moon Bay   San Andreas Fault   Francisquito Cr.
OCEAN   Arroyo Leon   University Heights   **Menlo Park**   Adobe Cr.
Woodside   Bear Gulch Reservoir   **Palo Alto**
Stanford University

1   122 30'   **2**   122 20'   West from Greenwich   **3**   122 10'   **4**

1 : 200 000

5 miles
8 km

LOS ANGELES

Angeles National Forest

Waterman Mountain
Silver Mountain
San Gabriel River
Strawberry Peak 1879
Josephine Pk.
Mount Disappointment
San Gabriel Peak 1877
Mount Lowe
Mount Markham
Mt Wilson
Mt. Wilson Observatory
Mount Harvard
Echo Mountain

Azusa
Irwindale
Duarte
Las Lomas
Santa Fe Flood Control Basin
San Gabriel River
Baldwin Park
Bassett
La Puente
Rowland
Fallon
West Covina
La Habra Heights
LOS ANGELES / ORANGE
La Habra
Sunshine Acres
Fuller Park

Monrovia
Sierra Madre
Arcadia
Temple City
El Monte
Hilgrove District
Puente Hills
Hacienda Hts.
Whittier
Buena Park
Colorado Fwy.

Altadena
Pasadena
California Inst. of Tech
San Marino
South Pasadena
Rosemead
San Gabriel
San Bernardino Fwy.
South San Gabriel
Monterey Park
Montebello
Los Nietos
Santa Fe Springs
Rose Bowl
Pomona Fwy.
Rio Hondo

La Canada
Montrose
San Rafael Hills
El Sereno
California State University
Alhambra
Commerce
Pico Rivera
Rosemead Blvd.
Santa Ana Fwy.
San Gabriel River
Norwalk
Artesia

La Crescenta
Flint Peak 575
Eagle Rock
Highland Park
Garvanza
Lincoln Heights
Boyle Heights
East Los Angeles
Bell Gardens
Maywood
Downey
Bellflower
Clearwater
Hynes
Artesia Fwy.
Hollydale
North Long Beach

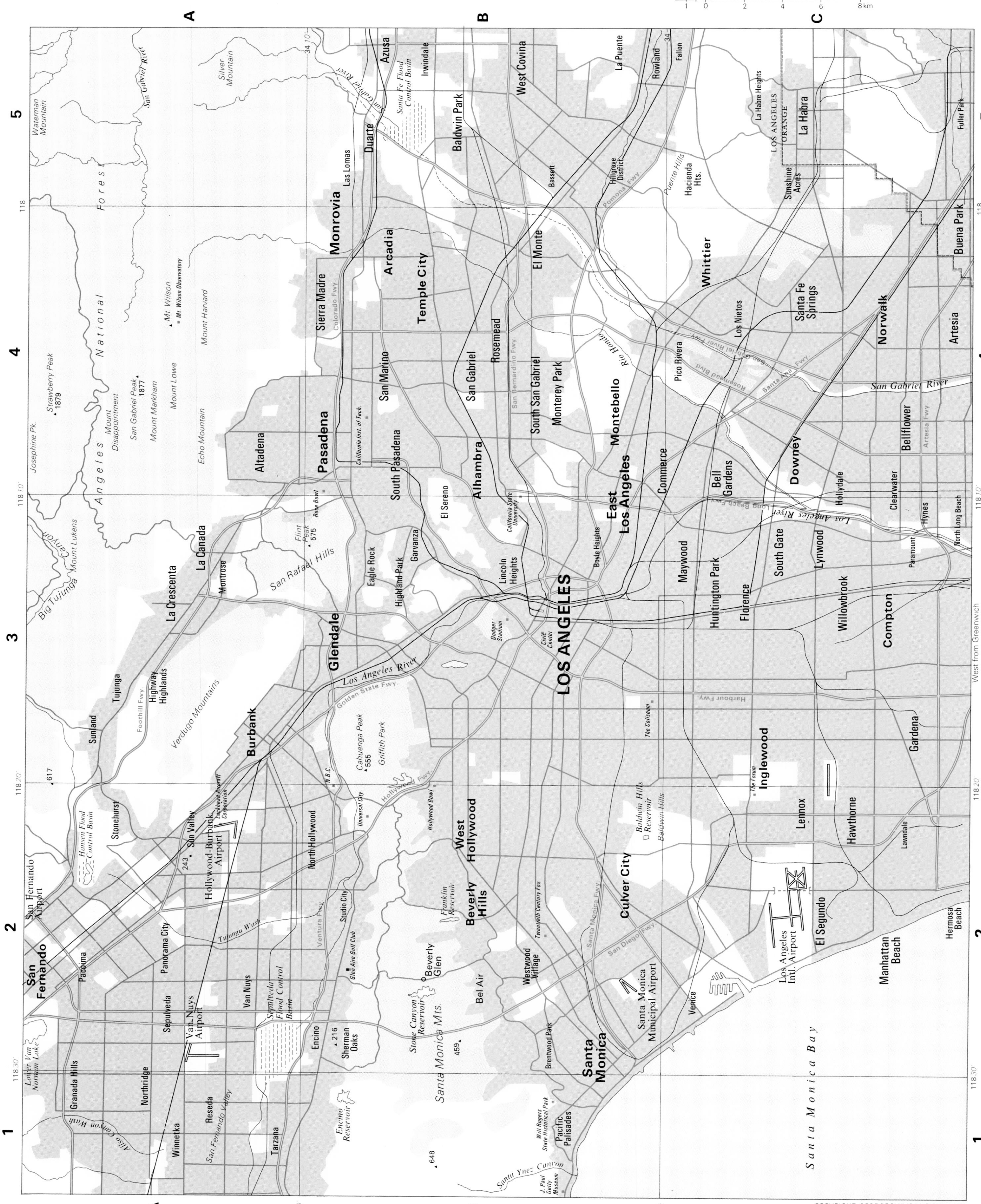

Tujunga
Highway Highlands
Glendale
Los Angeles River
Dodger Stadium
Civic Center
Huntington Park
South Gate
Lynwood
Willowbrook
Compton
Paramount

Foothill Fwy.
Verdugo Mountains
Golden State Fwy.
Cahuenga Peak 555
Griffith Park
Florence

Sunland
Burbank
N.B.C.
Harbour Fwy.
The Coliseum

617
Hollywood-Burbank Airport
Lockheed-Burbank Company
243
North Hollywood
Universal City
West Hollywood
Hollywood Fwy.
Hollywood Bowl
The Forum
Inglewood
Gardena

San Fernando Airport
Hansen Flood Control Basin
Sun Valley
Studio City
Franklin Reservoir
Baldwin Hills Reservoir
Baldwin Hills
Lennox
Hawthorne
Lawndale

San Fernando
Pacoima
Panorama City
Tujunga Wash
Ventura Fwy.
Beverly Hills
Beverly Glen
Bel Air
Westwood Village
Twentieth Century Fox
Culver City
Santa Monica Fwy.
Los Angeles Intl. Airport
El Segundo
Manhattan Beach
Hermosa Beach

Sepulveda
Van Nuys
Sepulveda Flood Control Basin
Santa Monica Mts.
Stone Canyon Reservoir
San Diego Fwy.
Santa Monica Municipal Airport
Venice

Granada Hills
Northridge
Reseda
Van Nuys Airport
216
Encino
Sherman Oaks
459
Glen Aire Golf Club
Brentwood Park
Santa Monica

Winnetka
Tarzana
Encino Reservoir
648
Will Rogers State Historical Park
Pacific Palisades
J. Paul Getty Museum
Santa Ynez Canyon

Lower Van Norman Lake
Aliso Canyon Wash
San Fernando Valley
Big Tujunga Canyon
Mount Lukens
Stonehurst

Santa Monica Bay

West from Greenwich

1 : 200 000

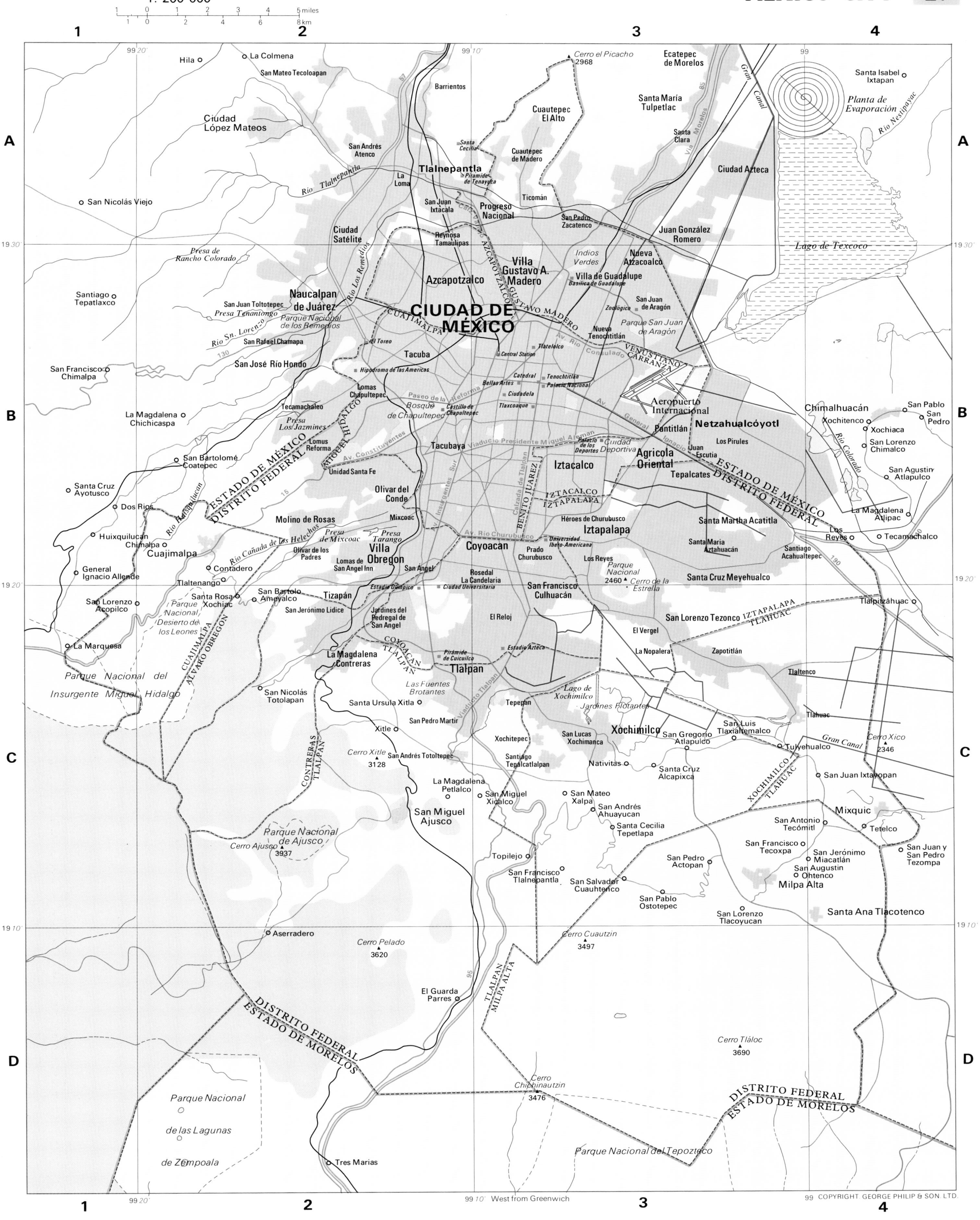

1 0 1 2 3 4 5 miles
1 0 2 4 6 8 km

1 **2** **3** **4**

99 20'

Hila
La Colmena
San Mateo Tecoloapan
Barrientos
Cerro el Picacho 2968
Ecatepec de Morelos
Santa Isabel Ixtapan

Ciudad López Mateos
Cuautepec El Alto
Santa María Tulpetlac
Santa Clara
Planta de Evaporación
Rio Nestipayac

A

San Andrés Atenco
Santa Cecilia
Cuautepec de Madero
Ciudad Azteca
Gran Canal
Via Morelos

San Nicolás Viejo
Rio Tlalnepantla
La Loma
Tlalnepantla
Pirámide de Tenayuca
Ticomán
Juan González Romero

19 30'
Presa de Rancho Colorado
Ciudad Satélite
San Juan Ixtácala
Progreso Nacional
San Pedro Zacatenco
Nueva Azcacoalco
Lago de Texcoco
19 30'

Santiago Tepatlaxco
San Juan Toltotepec
Reynosa Tamaulipas
Azcapotzalco
Villa Gustavo A. Madero
Indios Verdes
Villa de Guadalupe
Basílica de Guadalupe
San Juan de Aragón

Naucalpan de Juárez
Presa Tenantongo
Parque Nacional de los Remedios
Rio Sn. Lorenzo
CIUDAD DE MÉXICO
Zoológica
Nueva Tenochtitlán
Parque San Juan de Aragón

San Francisco Chimalpa
San Rafael Chamapa
130
Rio Los Remedios
CUAJIMALPA
El Toreo
Tacuba
la Central Station
Tlatelolco
Av. Rio Consulado
VENUSTIANO CARRANZA

B
La Magdalena Chichicaspa
San Bartolomé Coatepec
Tecamachaleo
Presa Los Jazmines
Hipódromo de las Americas
Lomas Chapultepec
Bosque de Chapultepec
Castillo de Chapultepec
Paseo de la Reforma
Bellas Artes
Catedral
Tenochtitlán
Palacio Nacional
Ciudadela
Tlaxcoaque
Chimalhuacán
Xochitenco
Xochiaca
San Pablo San Pedro
B

Lomas Reforma
Netzahualcóyotl
San Lorenzo Chimalco

Santa Cruz Ayotusco
Dos Rios
Lomas Reforma
Unidad Santa Fe
Av. Constituyentes
Tacubaya
Viaducto Presidente Miguel Aleman
Palacio de los Deportes
Ciudad Deportiva
Los Piriles
Juan Escutia
Agricola Oriental
San Agustín Atlapulco

Huixquilucan
Chimalpa
Cuajimalpa
Molino de Rosas
Mixcoac
Iztacalco
Tepalcates
ESTADO DE MÉXICO DISTRITO FEDERAL

Contadero
ESTADO DE MÉXICO DISTRITO FEDERAL
16
Olivar del Conde
Presa Mixcoac
Presa Tarango
IZTACALCO
IZTAPALAPA
Héroes de Churubusco
Santa Martha Acatitla
La Magdalena Atlipac

General Ignacio Allende
Rio Cañada de Los Helechos
Olivar de los Padres
Lomas de San Angel Inn
Villa Obregon
San Angel
Coyoacan
Prado Churubusco
Santa María Aztahuacán
Los Reyes
Tecamachalco

Tlaltenango
AV. ALVARO OBREGON
CUAJIMALPA
Universidad Ibero-Americana
Los Reyes
Santiago Acahualtepec
190

19 20'
San Lorenzo Acopilco
Parque Nacional Desierto de los Leones
Santa Rosa Xochiac
San Bartolo Ameyalco
Tizapán
Estadio Olímpico
Ciudad Universitaria
Rosedal La Candelaria
San Francisco Culhuacán
Parque Nacional 2460 Cerro de la Estrella
Santa Cruz Meyehualco
Tlalpitzáhuac
19 20'

La Marquesa
San Jerónimo Lidice
Jardines del Pedregal de San Angel
El Reloj
El Vergel
San Lorenzo Tezonco
IZTAPALAPA
TLAHUAC

Parque Nacional del Insurgente Miguel Hidalgo
CONTRERAS TLALPAN
COYOACAN TLALPAN
Pirámide de Cuicuilco
Estadio Azteca
La Nopalera
Zapotitlán
Tlaltenco

San Nicolás Totolapan
La Magdalena Contreras
Tlalpan
Las Fuentes Brotantes
Tepepan
Lago de Xochimilco
Jardines Flotantes
Tlahuac

C
Santa Ursula Xitla
San Pedro Martir
Xochitepec
San Lucas Xochimanca
Xochimilco
San Gregorio Atlapulco
Santa Cruz Alcapixca
Nativitas
San Luis Tlaxialtemalco
Tulyehualco
Gran Canal
Cerro Xico 2346
San Juan Ixtayopan
C

Xitle
Cerro Xitle 3128
San Andrés Totoltepec
Santiago Tepalcatlalpan
XOCHIMILCO TLAHUAC

La Magdalena Petlalco
San Miguel Xicalco
San Mateo Xalpa
San Antonio Tecómitl
Mixquic

San Miguel Ajusco
San Andrés Ahuayucan
Santa Cecilia Tepetlapa
San Jerónimo Miacatlán
Tetelco
San Juan y San Pedro Tezompa

Parque Nacional de Ajusco
Cerro Ajusco 3937
Topilejo
San Pedro Actopan
San Francisco Tecoxpa
San Augustín Ohtenco
Milpa Alta

San Francisco Tlalnepantla
San Salvador Cuauhtenco
San Pablo Ostotepec
San Lorenzo Tlacoyucan
Santa Ana Tlacotenco

19 10'
Aserradero
Cerro Pelado 3620
Cerro Cuautzin 3497
19 10'

D
Cerro Tláloc 3690
D

Parque Nacional
El Guarda Parres
TLALPAN MILPA ALTA
96
DISTRITO FEDERAL ESTADO DE MORELOS
Cerro Chichinautzin 3476
DISTRITO FEDERAL ESTADO DE MORELOS

de las Lagunas
de Zempoala
Tres Marias
Parque Nacional del Tepozteco

1 **2** **3** **4**

99 20'
99 10' West from Greenwich
99

1: 200 000

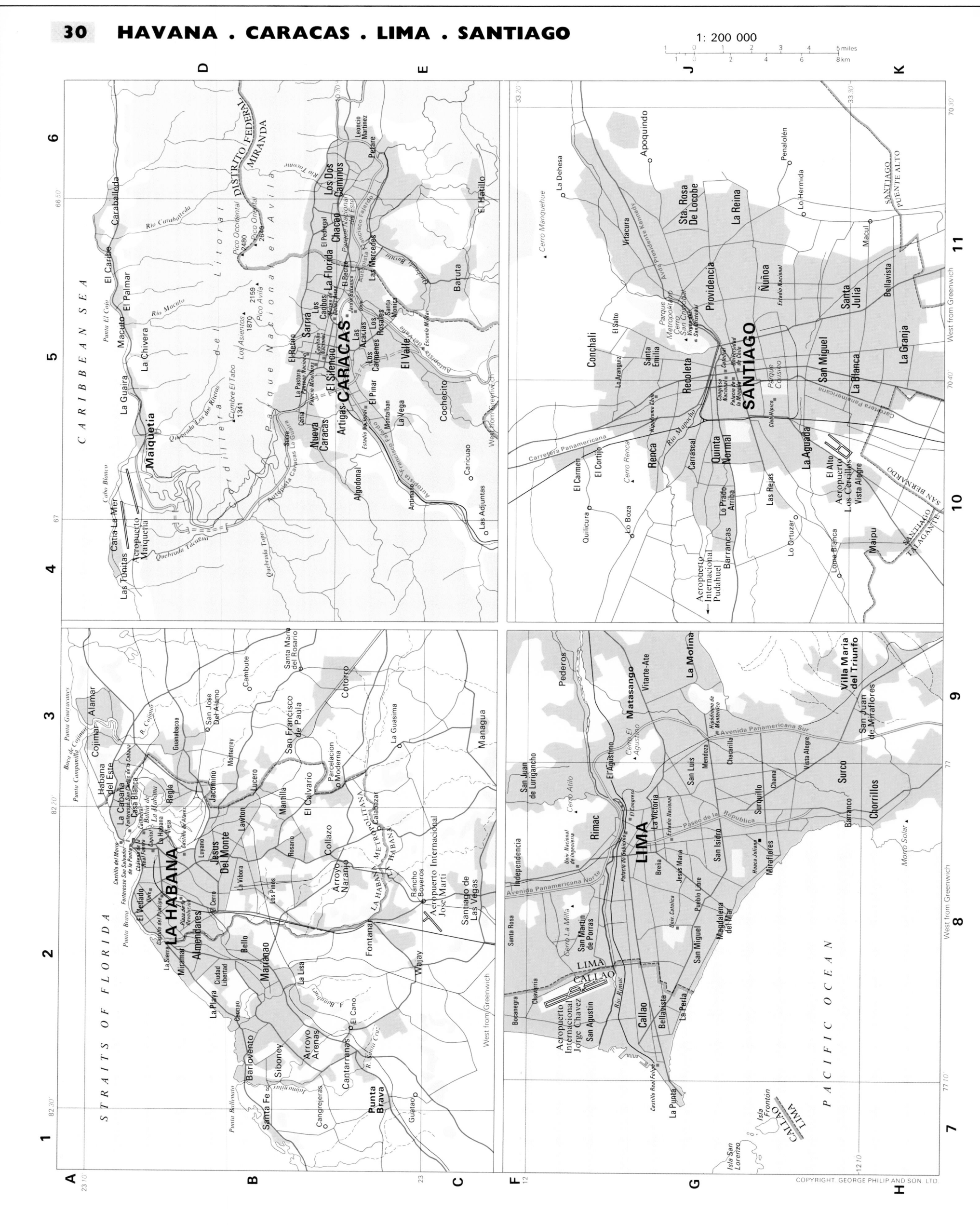

1: 200 000

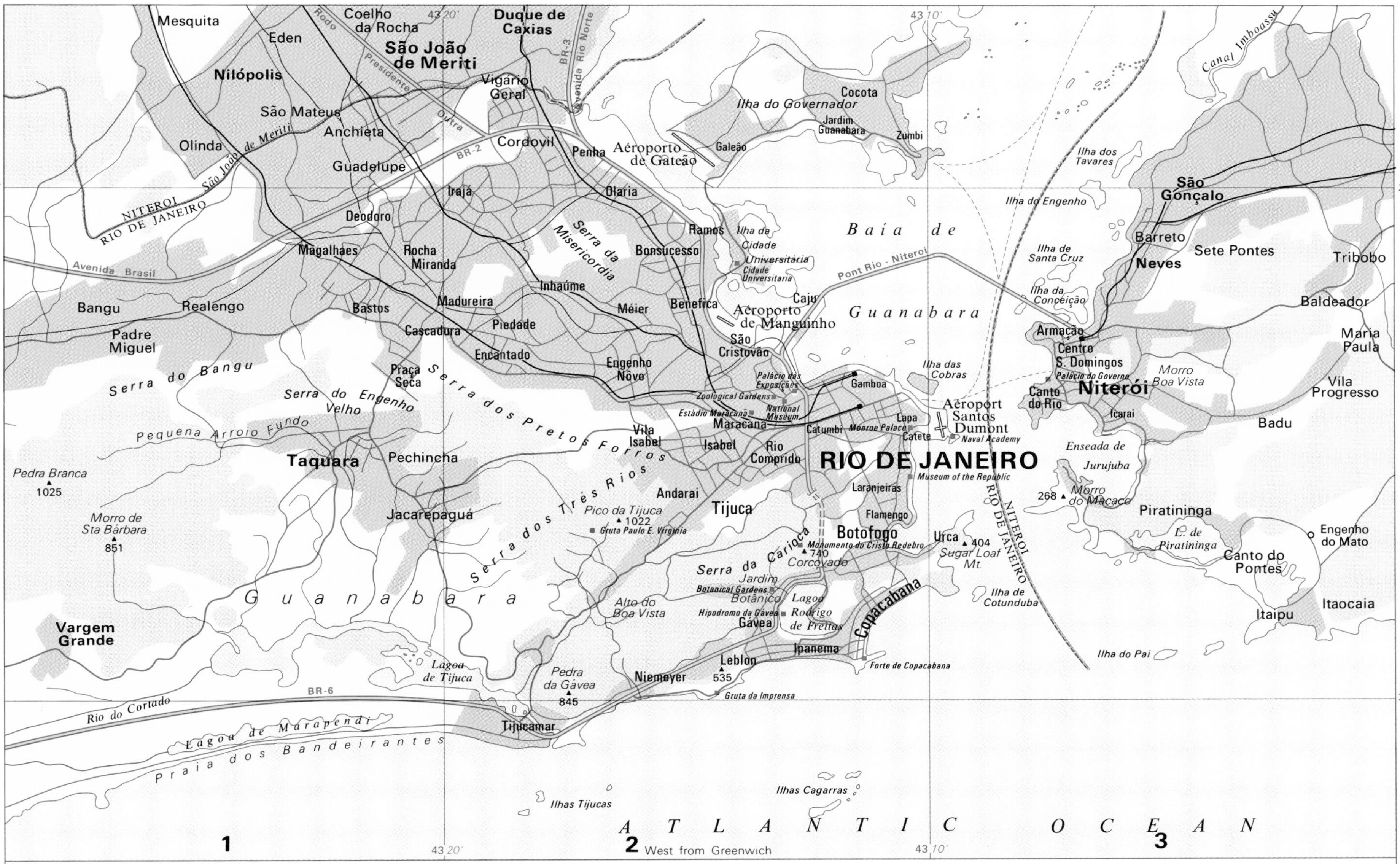

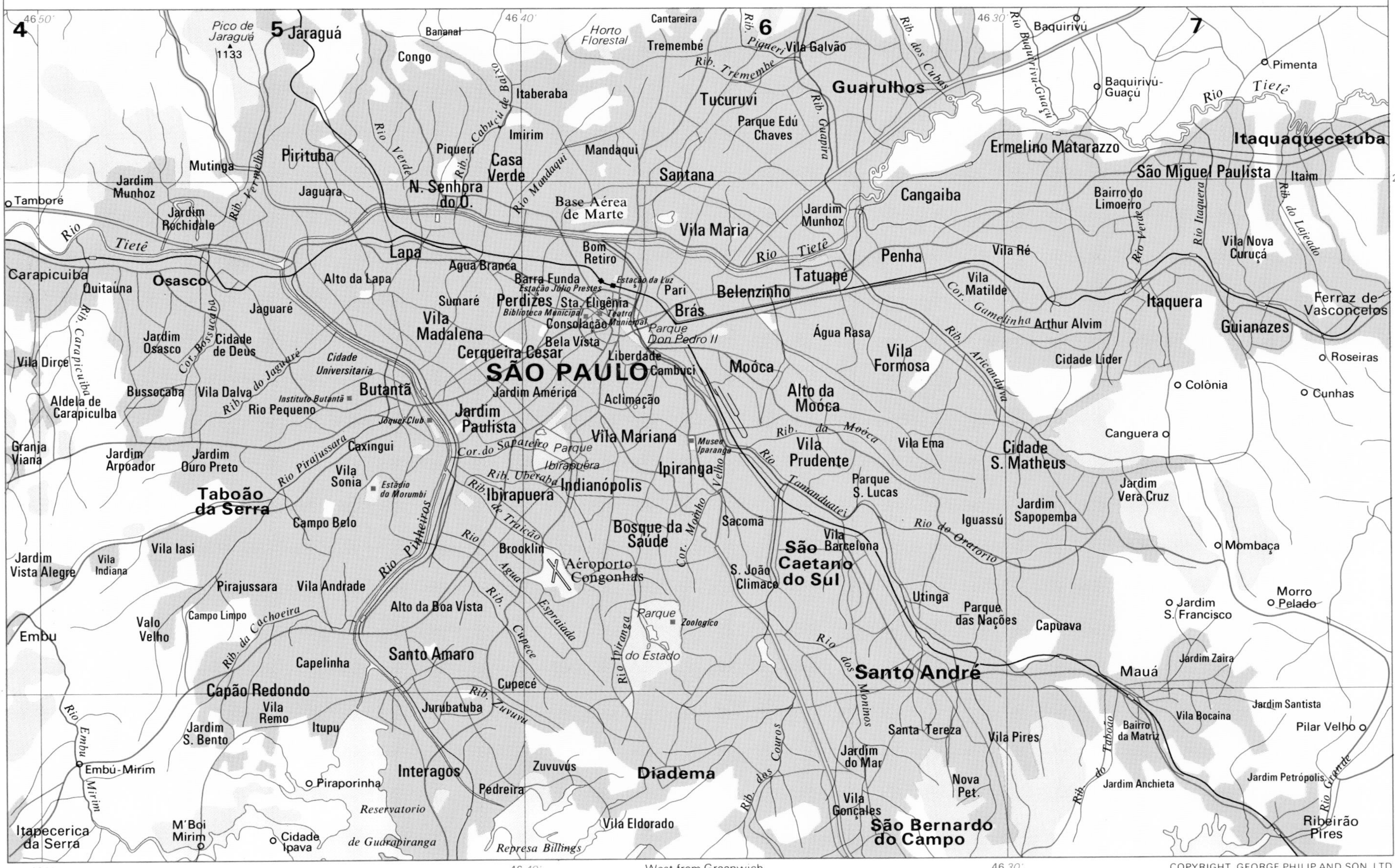

5 miles
8 km

RIO DE JANEIRO

Mesquita · Eden · Coelho da Rocha · Duque de Caxias · São João de Meriti · Vigario Geral · Cocota · Ilha do Governador · Jardim Guanabara · Zumbi · Ilha dos Tavares · São Gonçalo

Nilópolis · São Mateus · Anchieta · Cordovil · Penha · Aéroporto de Galeão · Galeão · Ilha do Engenho · Barreto · Sete Pontes · Tribobo

Olinda · Guadelupe · Irajá · Olaria · Baldeador · Maria Paula

Deodoro · Bonsucesso · Ramos · Ilha de Santa Cruz · Neves · Badu

Bangu · Magalhães · Rocha Miranda · Madureira · Inhaúme · Méier · Benefica · Caju · Ilha da Conceição · Armação · Centro · S. Domingos · Morro Boa Vista · Vila Progresso

Realengo · Bastos · Cascadura · Piedade · Encantado · Engenho Novo · São Cristovão · Aéroporto de Manguinho · Gamboa · Ilha das Cobras · Palacio das Exposições · Zoological Gardens · Aéroport Santos Dumont · Palacio do Governa · Niterói · Icarai

Padre Miguel · Praça Seca · Estádio Maracanã · Maracana · National Museum · Catumbi · Monroe Palace · Catete · Naval Academy · Canto do Rio

Serra do Bangu · Serra do Engenho · Serra do Engenho Velho · Vila Isabel · Isabel · Rio Comprido · **RIO DE JANEIRO** · Enseada de Jurujuba · Morro do Macaco · Piratininga

Pedra Branca 1025 · Taquara · Pechincha · Serra dos Três Rios · Serra dos Pretos Forros · Andarai · Laranjeiras · Museum of the Republic · 268

Morro de Sta Bárbara 851 · Jacarepaguá · Pico da Tijuca 1022 · Tijuca · Flamengo · Botofogo · Urca · I.e de Piratininga · Canto do Pontes · Engenho do Mato

Gruta Paulo E. Virginia · Serra da Carioca · Monumento do Cristo Redebro · 740 Corcovado · Sugar Loaf Mt. 404 · Ilha de Cotunduba · Itaipu

Vargem Grande · G u a n a b a r a · Jardim Botânico · Botanical Gardens · Alto do Boa Vista · Hipodromo da Gávea · Lagoa Rodrigo de Freitas · Ipanema · Copacabana · Itaocaia

Lagoa de Tijuca · Pedra da Gávea 845 · Gávea · Leblon 535 · Forte de Copacabana · Ilha do Pai

Rio do Cortado · BR-6 · Niemeyer · Tijucamar · Gruta da Imprensa

Lagoa de Marapendi · Praia dos Bandeirantes · Ilhas Tijucas · Ilhas Cagarras

A T L A N T I C   O C E A N

West from Greenwich

SÃO PAULO

Pico de Jaraguá 1133 · 5 Jaraguá · Bananal · Cantareira · Horto Florestal · Tremembé · 6 · Vila Galvão · Baquirivú · Pimenta · 7

Congo · Itaberaba · Tucuruvi · Guarulhos · Baquirivú-Guaçu · Rio Tietê

Jardim Munhoz · Piquerí · Imirim · Mandaqui · Parque Edu Chaves · Ermelino Matarazzo · Itaquaquecetuba

Mutinga · Pirituba · Jaguara · Casa Verde · Santana · Cangaiba · São Miguel Paulista · Itaim

Tamboré · Jardim Rochidale · N. Senhora do Ó · Base Aérea de Marte · Vila Maria · Jardim Munhoz · Vila Ré · Vila Nova Curuçá

Carapicuiba · Osasco · Lapa · Água Branca · Bom Retiro · Rio Tietê · Penha · Tatuapé · Itaquera · Ferraz de Vasconcelos

Quitaúna · Jaguaré · Alto da Lapa · Barra Funda · Estação da Luz · Pari · Belenzinho · Vila Matilde · Arthur Alvim · Guianazes

Vila Dirce · Jardim Osasco · Cidade de Deus · Sumaré · Perdizes · Sta. Efigênia · Brás · Água Rasa · Cidade Lider · Colônia · Roseiras

Bussocaba · Vila Dalva · Rio Pequeno · Instituto Butantã · Vila Madalena · Consolação · Liberdade · Cambuci · Moóca · Vila Formosa · Cunhas

Aldeia de Carapicuiba · Cidade Universitaria · Butantã · Cerqueira Cesar · **SÃO PAULO** · Alto da Moóca · Cidade S. Matheus · Canguera

Granja Viana · Jardim Arpoador · Jardim Ouro Preto · Cexingui · Jardim América · Aclimação · Vila Mariana · Museu Ipiranga · Vila Prudente · Parque S. Lucas · Jardim Vera Cruz

Taboão da Serra · Vila Sonia · Estádio do Morumbi · Jardim Paulista · Ibirapuera · Indianópolis · Ipiranga · Vila Ema · Jardim Sapopemba · Mombaça

Jardim Vista Alegre · Vila Indiana · Campo Belo · Brooklin · Bosque da Saúde · Sacomã · S. João Climaco · Vila Barcelona · São Caetano do Sul · Iguassú · Morro Pelado

Embu · Valo Velho · Campo Limpo · Vila Andrade · Alto da Boa Vista · Aéroporto Congonhas · Parque Zoologico · Parque das Nações · Capuava · Jardim S. Francisco

Pirajussara · Capelinha · Santo Amaro · Cupecé · Utinga · **Santo André** · Mauá · Jardim Zaira

Capão Redondo · Vila Remo · Jurubatuba · Santa Tereza · Vila Pires · Jardim Santista · Pilar Velho

Jardim S. Bento · Itupu · Interagos · Zuvuvus · Diadema · Jardim do Mar · Nova Pet. · Vila Bocaina · Jardim Petrópolis

Embú-Mirim · Piraporinha · Pédreira · Vila Gonçales · Jardim Anchieta

Itapecerica da Serra · M'Boi Mirim · Cidade Ipava · Vila Eldorado · **São Bernardo do Campo** · Ribeirão Pires

Reservatorio de Guarapiranga · Represa Billings

West from Greenwich

1: 200 000

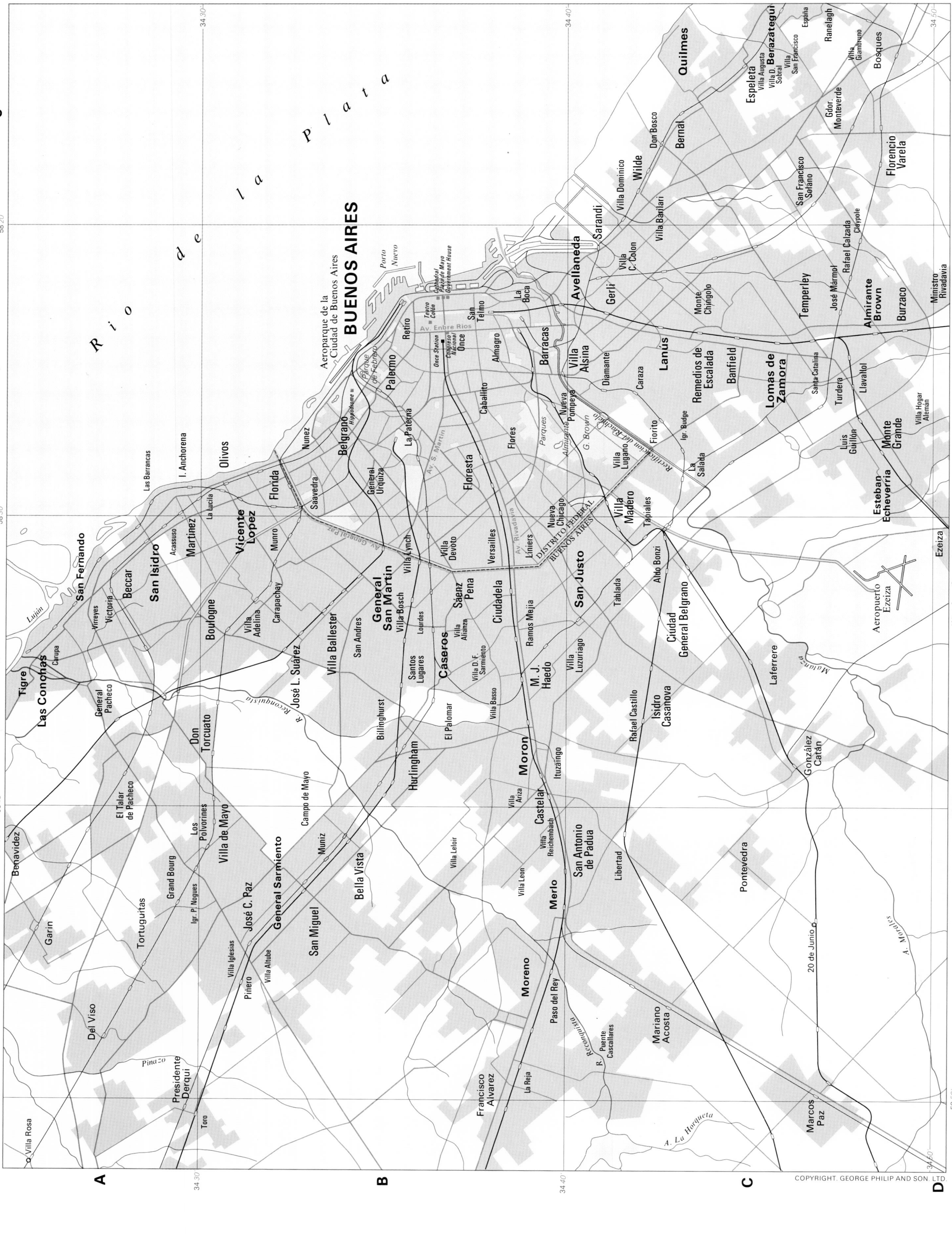

5 miles
8 km

A   B   C   D

BUENOS AIRES

Rio de la Plata

Aeroparque de la Ciudad de Buenos Aires

Porto Nuevo

Retiro

Palermo

Belgrano

Nunez

Olivos

I. Anchorena

Las Barrancas

La Lucila

Martinez

Acassuso

Beccar

San Isidro

San Fernando

Victoria

Virreyes

Lujan

Tigre

Las Conchas

Carupa

Benavidez

General Pacheco

Don Torcuato

El Talar de Pacheco

Los Polvorines

Garin

Del Viso

Presidente Derqui

Toro

Villa Rosa

Pinazo

Tortuguitas

Grand Bourg

Igr. P. Nogues

José C. Paz

General Sarmiento

San Miguel

Bella Vista

Muniz

Villa de Mayo

Campo de Mayo

Villa Iglesias

Piñero

Villa Altube

Moreno

Paso del Rey

Francisco Alvarez

La Reja

Merlo

Libertad

San Antonio de Padua

Villa Leon

Villa Leloir

Villa Reichembach

Castelar

Villa Ariza

Ituzaingo

Moron

M. J. Haedo

Ramos Mejia

Ciudadela

Sáenz Peña

Cáseros

Villa D. F. Sarmiento

Santos Lugares

Villa Bosch

San Andres

Villa Ballester

José L. Suárez

Villa Adelina

Boulogne

Carapachay

Munro

Florida

Vicente Lopez

Saavedra

General Urquiza

La Paterna

Villa Lynch

Villa Devoto

Versailles

Nueva Chicago

Villa Luzuriago

Villa Basso

Billinghurst

Hurlingham

El Palomar

Lourdes

San Justo

Tablada

Alto Bonzi

Tapiales

Villa Madero

Villa Lugano

DISTRITO FEDERAL BUENOS AIRES

Liniers

Nueva Pompeya

Parques

Flores

Floresta

Caballito

Almagro

Once

Congreso Nacional

Once Station

Av. Entre Rios

San Telmo

La Boca

Barracas

Villa Alsina

Diamante

Caraza

Fiorito

Igr. Budge

Villa Soldati

Rectification del Riachuelo

G. Brown

Riachuelo

Aeropuerto Ezeiza

Ezeiza

West from Greenwich

Rafael Castillo

Isidro Casanova

Laferrere

González Catán

Ciudad General Belgrano

Gerli

Sarandi

Avellaneda

Villa Dominico

Villa C. Colon

Wilde

Don Bosco

Bernal

Quilmes

Berazategui

Espeleta

Villa Augusta

Villa D. Sobral

Villa San Francisco

España

Ranelagh

Villa Giambuono

Bosques

Gdor Monteverde

Florencio Varela

San Francisco Solano

Villa Bariliari

Calpole

Rafael Calzada

Monte Chingolo

Lanús

Remedios de Escalada

Banfield

Santa Catalina

Lomas de Zamora

Temperley

José Mármol

Almirante Brown

Burzaco

Turdera

Llavallol

Luis Guillon

Monte Grande

Esteban Echeverria

Villa Hogar Alemán

Ministro Rivadavia

Marcos Paz

20 de Junio

Pontevedra

Mariano Acosta

Puente Cascallares

A. La Horqueta

A. Morales

A. Matanza

Teatro Colón

Catedral

Casa de Gobierno Government House

Hipodromo

Parque de Febrero

Av. S. Martin

Av. General Paz

Av. Rivadavia

Reconquista

COPYRIGHT. GEORGE PHILIP AND SON. LTD.

INDEX TO CITY MAPS

Place names in this index are given a letter-figure reference to a map square made from the lines of latitude and longitude that appear on the city maps. The full geographic reference is provided in the border of each map. The letter-figure reference will take the reader directly to the square, and by using the geographical co-ordinates the place sought can be pinpointed within that square.

The location given is the city or suburban centre, and not necessarily the name. Lakes, airports and other features having a large area are given co-ordinates for their centres. Rivers that enter the sea, lake or main stream within the map area have the co-ordinates of that entrance.

If the river flows through the map, then the co-ordinates are given to the name. The same rule applies to canals. A river carries the symbol → after its name.

As an aid to identification, every place name is followed by the city map name or its abbreviation; for example, Oakland in California will be followed by S.F. Some of the place names so described will be completely independent of the main city.

An explanation of the alphabetical order rules is to be found at the beginning of the World Map Index.

ABBREVIATIONS USED IN THE INDEX

Ath. - Athinai (Athens)
B. - Baie, Bahia, Bay, Bucht
B.A. - Buenos Aires
Bagd. - Baghdad
Balt. - Baltimore
Bangk. - Bangkok
Barc. - Barcelona
Beij. - Beijing (Peking)
Berl. - Berlin
Bomb. - Bombay
Bost. - Boston
Bud. - Budapest
C. - Cabo, Cap, Cape
Calc. - Calcutta
Car. - Caracas
Chan. - Channel
Chic. - Chicago
Cr. - Creek
E. - East
El Qâ. - El Qâhira (Cairo)
G. - Golfe, Golfo, Gulf, Guba
Gzh. - Guangzhou (Canton)
H.K. - Hong Kong
Hbg. - Hamburg
Hd. - Head
Hels. - Helsinki
Hts. - Heights
I.(s). - Île, Ilha, Insel, Isla, Island, Isle
Ist. - Istanbul
J. - Jabal, Jebel
Jak. - Jakarta
Jobg. - Johannesburg
K. - Kap, Kapp
Kar. - Karachi
Kep. - Kepulauan
Købn. - København (Copenhagen)
L. - Lac, Lacul, Lago, Lagoa, Lake
L.A. - Los Angeles
La Hab. - La Habana (Havana)
Len. - Leningrad
Lisb. - Lisboa (Lisbon)
Lon. - London
Mdrd. - Madrid
Melb. - Melbourne
Méx. - México
Mil. - Milano
Mos. - Moskva (Moscow)
Mt.(e). - Mont, Monte, Monti, Montaña, Mountain
Mtrl. - Montréal
Mün. - München (Munich)
N. - Nord, Norte, North, Northern, Nouveau
Nápl. - Nápoli (Naples)
N.Y. - New York City
Os. - Ostrov
Oz. - Ozero
Pen. - Peninsula, Peninsule
Phil. - Philadelphia
Pk. - Park, Peak
Pra. - Praha (Prague)
Pt. - Point
Pta. - Ponta, Punta
Pte. - Pointe
R. - Rio, River
Ra.(s). - Range(s)
Res. - Reserve, Reservoir
Rio J. - Rio de Janeiro
S. - San, South
S.F. - San Francisco
S. Pau. - São Paulo
Sa. - Serra, Sierra
Sd. - Sound
Shang. - Shanghai
Sing. - Singapore
St. - Saint, Sankt, Sint
Sta. - Santa, Station
Ste. - Sainte
Stgo. - Santiago
Sto. - Santo
Stock. - Stockholm
Str. - Strait, Stretto
Syd. - Sydney
Tehr. - Tehran
Tianj. - Tianjin (Tientsin)
Tori. - Torino (Turin)
Trto. - Toronto
W. - West
Wash. - Washington
Wsaw. - Warszawa (Warsaw)

A

Aalām, *Bagd.* **17 F8** 33 19N 44 23 E
Abada, *Calc.* **16 E5** 22 32N 88 13 E
Abbadia di Stura, *Tori.* **9 B3** 45 7N 7 44 E
Abbey Wood, *Lon.* **4 C5** 51 29N 0 7 E
Abbots Langley, *Lon.* **4 A2** 51 42N 0 25W
Abeno, *Ōsaka* **12 C4** 34 38N 135 31 E
Aberdeen, *H.K.* **12 E6** 22 14N 114 8 E
Abfanggraben, *Mün.* **7 F11** 48 10N 11 41 E
Abington, *Phil.* **24 A4** 40 7N 75 7W
Ablon-sur-Seine, *Paris* **5 C4** 48 43N 2 25 E
Abord à Plouffe, *Mtrl.* **20 A3** 43 32N 73 43W
Abramtsevo, *Mos.* **11 E10** 55 49N 37 49 E
Abridge, *Lon.* **4 B5** 51 38N 0 7 E
Abû en Numrus, *El Qâ.* **18 D5** 29 57N 31 12 E
Acassuso, *B.A.* **32 A3** 34 29 S 58 30W
Accord, *Bost.* **21 D4** 42 10N 70 52W
Accord Pond, *Bost.* **21 D4** 42 10N 70 53W
Accotink Cr. →, *Wash.* **25 D6** 38 51N 77 15W
Acerra, *Nápl.* **9 H13** 40 56N 14 22 E
Acha San, *Sŏul* **12 G8** 37 33N 127 5 E
Acheres, *Paris* **5 B2** 48 57N 2 3 E
Acília, *Rome* **9 G9** 41 47N 12 21 E
Aclimação, *S. Pau.* **31 E6** 23 34 S 46 37W
Acostia →, *Wash.* **25 D8** 38 51N 77 1W
Acton, *Lon.* **4 B3** 51 30N 0 16W
Açúcar, Pão de, *Rio J.* **31 B3** 22 56 S 43 9W
Ada Beja, *Lisb.* **8 F7** 38 47N 9 13W
Adabe Cr. →, *S.F.* **27 D4** 37 26N 122 6W
Adachi, *Tōkyō* **13 B2** 35 49N 139 34 E
Adachi-Ku, *Tōkyō* **13 B3** 35 47N 139 47 E
Adams Nat. Hist. Site, *Bost.* **21 D4** 42 15N 71 0W
Addington, *Lon.* **4 C4** 51 21N 0 1W
Addiscombe, *Lon.* **4 C4** 51 22N 0 4W
Adel, *Bagd.* **17 E7** 33 20N 44 17 E
Adelphi, *Wash.* **25 C8** 39 0N 76 58W
Aderklaa, *Wien* **10 G11** 48 17N 16 32 E
Admiralteyskaya Storona, *Len.* **11 B4** 59 56N 30 20 E
Áffori, *Mil.* **9 D6** 45 31N 9 10 E
Aflandshage, *Købn.* **2 E10** 55 33N 12 35 E
Afragola, *Nápl.* **9 H12** 40 55N 14 18 E
Aganpur, *Delhi* **16 B3** 28 33N 77 20 E
Agboju, *Lagos* **18 B1** 6 27N 7 16 E
Agboyi Cr. →, *Lagos* **18 A2** 6 33N 7 24 E
Ågerup, *Købn.* **2 D8** 55 43N 12 19 E
Agesta, *Stock.* **3 E11** 59 12N 18 6 E
Agincourt, *Trto.* **20 D9** 43 47N 79 16W
Agnano Terme, *Nápl.* **9 J12** 40 49N 14 10 E
Agora, *Ath.* **8 J11** 37 57N 23 43 E
Agra Canal, *Delhi* **16 B2** 28 33N 77 17 E
Agricola Oriental, *Méx.* **29 B3** 19 23N 99 4W
Agro Romano, *Rome* **9 F8** 41 56N 12 17 E
Agua Branca, *S. Pau.* **31 E5** 23 31 S 46 40W
Agua Espraiada →, *S. Pau.* **31 E6** 23 36 S 46 41W
Água Rasa, *S. Pau.* **31 E6** 23 32 S 46 33W
Agualva-Cacem, *Lisb.* **8 F7** 38 46N 9 15W
Agustino, Cerro El, *Lima* **30 G8** 12 3 S 76 59W
Ahrensfelde, *Berl.* **7 A4** 52 34N 13 34 E
Ahuntsic, *Mtrl.* **20 A3** 43 32N 73 41W
Ai →, *Ōsaka* **12 B4** 34 46N 135 35 E
Aigremont, *Paris* **5 B2** 48 54N 2 1 E
Airport West, *Melb.* **19 E6** 37 42 S 144 52 E
Aiyaleo, *Ath.* **8 J11** 37 59N 23 40 E
Ajegunle, *Lagos* **18 B2** 6 26N 7 20 E
Aji, *Ōsaka* **12 B3** 34 40N 135 27 E
Ajuda, *Lisb.* **8 F7** 38 42N 9 12W
Ajusco, Parque Nacional de, *Méx.* **29 C2** 19 12N 99 15W
Akabane, *Tōkyō* **13 B3** 35 46N 139 42 E
Akalla, *Stock.* **3 D10** 59 24N 17 55 E
Akasaka, *Tōkyō* **13 B3** 35 40N 139 43 E
Akbarābād, *Tehr.* **17 C5** 35 40N 51 20 E
Åkersberga Saltsjobad, *Stock.* **3 D12** 59 26N 18 15 E
Akerselva →, *Oslo* **2 B4** 59 54N 10 45 E
Akrópolis, *Ath.* **8 J11** 37 57N 23 43 E
Akuwa, *Tōkyō* **13 D2** 35 26N 139 30 E
Al 'Azamiyah, *Bagd.* **17 E8** 33 22N 44 22 E
Alaguntan, *Lagos* **18 B2** 6 25N 7 29 E
Alamar, *La Hab.* **30 B3** 23 9N 82 16W
Alameda, *S.F.* **27 B3** 37 46N 122 15W
Alameda Memorial State Beach Park, *S.F.* **27 B3** 37 45N 122 16W
Alamo, *S.F.* **27 A4** 37 51N 122 2W
Albany, *S.F.* **27 A3** 37 53N 122 17W
Alberante, *Jobg.* **18 F9** 26 16 S 28 7 E
Albern, *Wien* **10 H10** 48 9N 16 29 E
Albert Hall, *Lon.* **4 C3** 51 29N 0 10W
Albert Park, *Melb.* **19 F6** 37 51 S 144 58 E
Albertfalva, *Bud.* **10 K13** 47 26N 19 3 E
Alberton, *Jobg.* **18 F9** 26 15 S 28 7 E
Albertslund, *Købn.* **2 E9** 55 39N 12 21 E
Albertson, *N.Y.* **23 C7** 40 46N 73 38W
Albertville, *Jobg.* **18 E8** 26 9 S 27 58 E
Albion, *Phil.* **24 C5** 39 46N 74 57W
Alby, *Stock.* **3 E10** 59 14N 17 51 E
Albysjön, *Stock.* **3 E10** 59 14N 17 52 E
Alcantara, *Lisb.* **8 F7** 38 43N 9 10W
Alcatraz I., *S.F.* **27 B2** 37 49N 122 25W
Alcochete, *Lisb.* **8 F9** 38 45N 8 58W
Alcorcón, *Mdrd.* **8 B2** 40 20N 3 48W
Aldan, *Phil.* **24 B3** 39 55N 75 17W
Aldela de Carapiculba, *S. Pau.* **31 E5** 23 34 S 46 49W
Aldene, *N.Y.* **22 D3** 40 39N 74 17W
Aldenrade, *Ruhr* **6 A2** 51 31N 6 44 E
Alder Planetarium, *Chic.* **26 B3** 41 5N 87 36W
Aldershof, *Berl.* **7 B4** 52 26N 13 33 E
Aldo Bonzi, *B.A.* **32 C3** 34 42 S 58 31W
Aleksandrovskoye, *Len.* **11 B4** 59 51N 30 20 E
Aleksandrów, *Wsaw.* **10 E8** 52 10N 21 14 E
Alexander Nevsky Abbey, *Len.* **11 B4** 59 54N 30 23 E
Alexandra, *Jobg.* **18 E9** 26 6 S 28 5 E
Alexandra, *Sing.* **15 G7** 1 17N 103 49 E
Alexandria, *Wash.* **25 E7** 38 49N 77 5W
Alfortville, *Paris* **5 C4** 48 48N 2 24 E
Algés, *Lisb.* **8 F7** 38 42N 9 13W
Älgo, *Stock.* **3 E13** 59 16N 18 20 E
Algodonal, *Car.* **30 E5** 10 29N 66 58W
Alhambra, *L.A.* **28 B4** 34 5N 118 7W
Alhos Vedros, *Lisb.* **8 G8** 38 39N 9 1W
Alibey →, *Ist.* **17 A2** 41 3N 28 56 E
Alibeyköy, *Ist.* **17 A2** 41 4N 28 56 E
Alima, *Manila* **15 E3** 14 27N 120 55 E
Alimos, *Ath.* **8 J11** 37 52N 23 43 E
Aliperti, *Nápl.* **9 H13** 40 53N 14 28 E
Alipore, *Calc.* **16 E6** 22 31N 88 20 E
Alipur, *Calc.* **16 D5** 22 43N 88 12 E
Aliso Canyon Wash →, *L.A.* **28 A1** 34 15N 118 31W
Allach, *Mün.* **7 F9** 48 11N 11 27 E
Allambie Heights, *Syd.* **19 A4** 33 46 S 151 15 E
Allendale, *N.Y.* **22 A4** 41 1N 74 9W
Allengrove, *Jobg.* **18 E10** 26 5 S 28 14 E
Allentown, *N.Y.* **23 C6** 40 47N 73 43W
Allermohe, *Hbg.* **7 E8** 53 29N 10 7 E
Allerton, Pt., *Bost.* **21 D4** 42 18N 70 52W
Allston, *Bost.* **21 C3** 42 21N 71 7W
Alluets, Forêt des, *Paris* **5 B1** 48 56N 1 55 E
Almada, *Lisb.* **8 F8** 38 41N 9 8W
Almagro, *B.A.* **32 B4** 34 38 S 58 24W
Almanara, *Mdrd.* **8 B2** 40 28N 3 41W
Almaza Airport, *El Qâ.* **18 C6** 30 5N 31 21 E
Almazovo, *Mos.* **11 D12** 55 50N 38 3 E
Almendares, *La Hab.* **30 B2** 23 6N 82 23W
Almendares →, *La Hab.* **30 B2** 23 7N 82 24W
Almirante Brown, *B.A.* **32 C4** 34 48 S 58 23W
Almirante G. Brown, Parques, *B.A.* **32 C4** 34 40 S 58 28W
Almonesson, *Phil.* **24 C4** 39 48N 75 5W
Almonte, *S.F.* **27 A1** 37 53N 122 31W
Alnabru, *Oslo* **2 B5** 59 55N 10 50 E
Alnsjoen, *Oslo* **2 B5** 59 57N 10 51 E
Alperton, *Lon.* **4 B3** 51 32N 0 17W
Alpignano, *Tori.* **9 B1** 45 6N 7 31 E
Alpine, *N.Y.* **22 B5** 40 57N 73 57W
Alpur, *Calc.* **16 C6** 22 50N 88 23 E
Alrode, *Jobg.* **18 F9** 26 17 S 28 7 E
Alsergrund, *Wien* **10 G10** 48 13N 16 21 E
Alsfeld, *Ruhr* **6 A3** 51 31N 6 50 E
Alsip, *Chic.* **26 C2** 41 40N 87 44W
Alstaden, *Ruhr* **6 B2** 51 28N 6 49 E
Ålsten, *Stock.* **3 E10** 59 19N 17 57 E
Alster →, *Hbg.* **7 D8** 53 38N 10 4 E
Alsterdorf, *Hbg.* **7 D8** 53 36N 10 0 E
Älta, *Stock.* **3 E12** 59 15N 18 11 E
Altadena, *L.A.* **28 A4** 34 11N 118 8W
Alte-Donau →, *Wien* **10 G10** 48 14N 16 25 E
Alte Süderelbe, *Hbg.* **7 D7** 53 31N 9 52 E
Alten-Essen, *Ruhr* **6 B4** 51 29N 7 1 E
Altendorf, *Ruhr* **6 B3** 51 27N 6 58 E
Altenhagen, *Ruhr* **6 B6** 51 22N 7 27 E
Altenvoerde, *Ruhr* **6 C6** 51 18N 7 22 E
Altenwerder, *Hbg.* **7 D7** 53 30N 9 55 E
Alter Finkenkrug, *Berl.* **7 A1** 52 35N 13 3 E
Altglenicke, *Berl.* **7 B4** 52 25N 13 32 E
Altlandsberg Nord, *Berl.* **7 A5** 52 34N 13 43 E
Altmannsdorf, *Wien* **10 H9** 48 9N 16 18 E
Alto, *S.F.* **27 A1** 37 54N 122 30W
Alto da Boa Vista, *S. Pau.* **31 E5** 23 38 S 46 42W
Alto da Lapa, *S. Pau.* **31 E5** 23 31 S 46 43W
Alto da Moóca, *S. Pau.* **31 E6** 23 34 S 46 33W
Alto do Pina, *Lisb.* **8 F8** 38 44N 9 7W
Altona, *Hbg.* **7 D7** 53 32N 9 56 E
Altona, *Melb.* **19 F5** 37 51 S 144 49 E
Altona B., *Melb.* **19 F6** 37 52 S 144 51 E
Altona North, *Melb.* **19 F5** 37 50 S 144 49 E
Altona Sports Park, *Melb.* **19 F6** 37 51 S 144 51 E
Altstadt, *Hbg.* **7 D8** 53 32N 10 0 E
Alvarado, *S.F.* **27 C4** 37 35N 122 4W
Alvik, *Stock.* **3 E10** 59 19N 17 58 E
Älvsjo, *Stock.* **3 E11** 59 16N 18 0 E
Älvvik, *Stock.* **3 D12** 59 21N 18 15 E
Am Hasenbergl, *Mün.* **7 F10** 48 12N 11 33 E
Am Steinhof, *Wien* **10 G9** 48 12N 16 17 E
Am Wald, *Mün.* **7 G10** 48 3N 11 36 E
Ama Keng, *Sing.* **15 F7** 1 23N 103 41 E
Amadora, *Lisb.* **8 F7** 38 45N 9 13W
Amagasaki, *Ōsaka* **12 B3** 34 42N 135 23 E
Amager, *Købn.* **2 E10** 55 36N 12 35 E
Amāl Qādisiya, *Bagd.* **17 F8** 33 16N 44 20 E
Amalienborg Slott, *Købn.* **2 D10** 55 41N 12 35 E
Amata, *Mil.* **9 D5** 45 34N 9 8 E
Ambler, *Phil.* **24 A3** 40 9N 75 13W
Ambrose Channel, *N.Y.* **22 D5** 40 31N 73 50W
Ameixoeira, *Lisb.* **8 F8** 38 46N 9 8W
Ames Hill, *Bost.* **21 B2** 42 38N 71 13W
Amin, *Bagd.* **17 F8** 33 19N 44 29 E
Aminyevo, *Mos.* **11 E8** 55 41N 37 25 E
Amirābād, *Tehr.* **17 C5** 35 43N 51 24 E
Amityville, *N.Y.* **23 C8** 40 40N 73 23W
Ammersbek →, *Hbg.* **7 C8** 53 42N 10 7 E
Amora, *Lisb.* **8 G8** 38 37N 9 6W
Amoreira, *Lisb.* **8 F7** 38 48N 9 11W
Amorosa, *Jobg.* **18 E8** 26 5 S 27 52 E
Ampelokipi, *Ath.* **8 J11** 37 58N 23 47 E
Amper →, *Mün.* **7 F9** 48 14N 11 25 E
Amselhain, *Berl.* **7 A5** 52 38N 13 43 E
Amuwo, *Lagos* **18 B1** 6 28N 7 18 E
Anacostia, *Wash.* **25 D8** 38 51N 76 59W
Anacostia River Park, *Wash.* **25 D8** 38 54N 76 57W
Anadoluhisari, *Ist.* **17 A3** 41 4N 29 3 E
Anandanagar, *Calc.* **16 C5** 22 51N 88 16 E
Anchieta, *Rio J.* **31 A1** 22 48 S 43 21W
Ancol, *Jak.* **15 H9** 6 7 S 106 49 E
Andalus, *Bagd.* **17 F7** 33 19N 44 18 E
Andalusia, *Phil.* **24 A5** 40 4N 74 58W
Andarai, *Rio J.* **31 B2** 22 56 S 43 14W
Andeli Beijie, *Beij.* **14 B3** 39 57N 116 21 E
Anderson Cr. →, *Melb.* **19 E8** 37 44 S 145 12 E
Andilly, *Paris* **5 A3** 49 0N 2 17 E
Andingmen, *Beij.* **14 B3** 39 55N 116 23 E
Andover, *Bost.* **21 B3** 42 39N 71 7W
Andrésy, *Paris* **5 B2** 48 58N 2 3 E
Andrews Air Force Base, *Wash.* **25 E8** 38 48N 76 52W
Ang Mo Kio, *Sing.* **15 F8** 1 22N 103 50 E
Ångby, *Stock.* **3 D10** 59 20N 17 53 E
Angel I., *S.F.* **27 A2** 37 52N 122 25W
Angel Island State Park, *S.F.* **27 A2** 37 52N 122 25W
Angerbruch →, *Ruhr* **6 C3** 51 18N 6 59 E
Angerhausen, *Ruhr* **6 B2** 51 22N 6 43 E
Angermund, *Ruhr* **6 C2** 51 19N 6 46 E
Angke, Kali →, *Jak.* **15 H9** 6 6 S 106 46 E
Angono, *Manila* **15 D4** 14 31N 121 8 E
Angyalföld, *Bud.* **10 J13** 47 32N 19 5 E
Angyō, *Tōkyō* **13 A3** 35 50N 139 45 E
Aniene →, *Rome* **9 F10** 41 56N 12 35 E
Anik, *Bomb.* **16 G8** 19 1N 72 53 E
Anin, *Wsaw.* **10 E7** 52 13N 21 9 E
Anjou, *Mtrl.* **20 A4** 43 36N 73 33W
Annadale, *N.Y.* **22 D3** 40 32N 74 10W
Annalee Heights, *Wash.* **25 D6** 38 51N 77 10W
Annandale, *Wash.* **25 D6** 38 50N 77 11W
Annen, *Ruhr* **6 B6** 51 27N 7 22 E
Annet-sur-Marne, *Paris* **5 B6** 48 55N 2 43 E
Anthony Chabot Regional Park, *S.F.* **27 B4** 37 46N 122 7W
Antignano, *Nápl.* **9 H12** 40 51N 14 13 E
Antimano, *Car.* **30 E5** 10 27N 66 59W
Antipolo, *Manila* **15 D5** 14 35N 121 10 E
Antony, *Paris* **5 C3** 48 44N 2 17 E
Antwerp, *Jobg.* **18 E9** 26 5 S 28 9 E
Aoyama, *Tōkyō* **13 C3** 35 39N 139 42 E
Ap Lei Chau, *H.K.* **12 E5** 22 14N 114 9 E
Apapa, *Lagos* **18 B2** 6 26N 7 21 E
Apelacão, *Lisb.* **8 F8** 38 48N 9 7W
Apoquindo, *Stgo* **30 J11** 33 23 S 70 30W
Apshawa, *N.Y.* **22 A2** 41 1N 74 22W
Apterkarskiy Os., *Len.* **11 B4** 59 57N 30 20 E
Aquincum, *Bud.* **10 J13** 47 33N 19 3 E
Ara →, *Tōkyō* **13 B4** 35 41N 139 50 E
Arakawa-Ku, *Tōkyō* **13 B3** 35 44N 139 48 E
Arakpur, *Delhi* **16 B2** 28 35N 77 11 E
Arany-hegyi-patak →, *Bud.* **10 J13** 47 34N 19 4 E
Aravaca, *Mdrd.* **8 B2** 40 27N 3 47W
Arbataash, *Bagd.* **17 E7** 33 20N 44 19 E
Arbutus, *Balt.* **25 B2** 39 15N 76 41W
Arc de Triomphe, *Paris* **5 B3** 48 52N 2 17 E
Arcadia, *L.A.* **28 B4** 34 7N 118 1W
Arceuil, *Paris* **5 C3** 48 48N 2 19 E
Arden, *Phil.* **24 C2** 39 48N 75 29W
Ardey Gebirge, *Ruhr* **6 B6** 51 24N 7 23 E
Ardmore, *Phil.* **24 A3** 40 0N 75 17W
Ardsley, *N.Y.* **23 A5** 41 0N 73 50W
Arese, *Mil.* **9 D5** 45 32N 9 4 E
Arganzuela, *Mdrd.* **8 B2** 40 23N 3 42W
Argenteuil, *Paris* **5 B3** 48 56N 2 15 E
Argonne Forest, *Chic.* **26 C1** 41 42N 87 53W
Ariadana, *Calc.* **16 E6** 22 39N 88 22 E
Aricanduva →, *S. Pau.* **31 E6** 23 31 S 46 33W
Arida, *Lagos* **18 A1** 6 33N 7 16 E
Arima, *Ōsaka* **12 B2** 34 47N 135 15 E
Arima, *Tōkyō* **13 C2** 35 33N 139 33 E
Arima →, *Ōsaka* **12 A2** 34 50N 135 14 E
Arkhangelyskoye, *Mos.* **11 E7** 55 47N 37 17 E
Arkley, *Lon.* **4 B3** 51 38N 0 13W
Arlington, *Bost.* **21 C2** 42 24N 71 10W
Arlington, *Wash.* **25 D7** 38 53N 77 7W
Arlington Heights, *Bost.* **21 C2** 42 25N 71 10W
Arlington Heights, *Chic.* **26 A1** 42 5N 87 55W
Arlington Nat. Cemetery, *Wash.* **25 D7** 38 52N 77 4W
Armação, *Rio J.* **31 B3** 22 52 S 43 6W
Armadale, *Melb.* **19 F7** 37 51 S 145 0 E
Armadale, *Trto.* **20 C9** 43 50N 79 14W
Armainvilliers, Forêt d', *Paris* **5 C6** 48 46N 2 42 E
Armour Heights, *Trto.* **20 D8** 43 45N 79 25W
Arncliffe, *Syd.* **19 B3** 33 56 S 151 8 E
Arnold Arboretum, *Bost.* **21 D3** 42 18N 71 8W
Arnouville-les-Gonesse, *Paris* **5 B4** 48 59N 2 24 E
Arrentela, *Lisb.* **8 G8** 38 37N 9 6W
Arrone →, *Rome* **9 F8** 41 55N 12 16 E
Arroyo Arenas, *La Hab.* **30 B2** 23 3N 82 27W
Arroyo Cr. →, *S.F.* **26 D2** 37 27N 122 25W
Arroyo Naranjo, *La Hab.* **30 B2** 23 2N 82 21W
Årsta, *Stock.* **3 E11** 59 17N 18 3 E
Artesia, *L.A.* **28 C4** 33 51N 118 4W
Arthur Alvim, *S. Pau.* **31 E7** 23 32 S 46 28W
Arthur Kill →, *N.Y.* **22 D3** 40 32N 74 15W
Artigas, *Car.* **30 E5** 10 29N 66 56W
Arundel Gardens, *Balt.* **25 B3** 39 12N 76 37W
Arundel Village, *Balt.* **25 B3** 39 13N 76 35W
Aryiróupolis, *Ath.* **8 J11** 37 52N 23 44 E
Arzano, *Nápl.* **9 H12** 40 54N 14 16 E
Asagaya, *Tōkyō* **13 B2** 35 41N 139 38 E
Asahi, *Ōsaka* **12 B4** 34 43N 135 31 E
Asaka, *Tōkyō* **13 B2** 35 47N 139 35 E
Asakusa, *Tōkyō* **13 B3** 35 42N 139 47 E
Asalatpur, *Delhi* **16 B1** 28 37N 77 4 E
Asati, *Calc.* **16 F5** 22 28N 88 15 E
Aschheim, *Mün.* **7 F11** 48 10N 11 42 E
Ascot Vale, *Melb.* **19 E6** 37 46 S 144 53 E
Aserradero, *Méx.* **29 D2** 19 10N 99 16W

34 Asharoken

Asharoken, N.Y. 23 B8 40 55N 73 21W
Ashburn, Chic. 26 C2 41 45N 87 43W
Ashburton, Melb. 19 F7 37 51 S 145 4 E
Ashburton, L., Balt. 25 B2 39 19N 76 40W
Ashchherino, Mos. 11 F10 55 36N 37 46 E
Ashfield, Syd. 19 B3 33 53 S 151 7 E
Ashford, Lon. 4 C2 51 25N 0 26W
Ashiya, Ōsaka 12 B2 34 43N 135 18 E
Ashiya →, Ōsaka 12 B2 34 42N 135 18 E
Ashland, S.F. 27 B4 37 41N 122 7W
Ashstead, Lon. 4 D3 51 18N 0 17W
Ashwood, Melb. 19 F7 37 52 S 145 5 E
Askela, Hels. 3 B3 60 16N 24 47 E
Asker, Oslo 2 B2 59 50N 10 25 E
Askrikefjärden, Stock. 3 D12 59 22N 18 13 E
Asnieres, Paris 5 B3 48 54N 2 16 E
Ason, Lagos 18 A3 6 34N 7 31 E
Aspern, Wien 10 G10 48 13N 16 29 E
Aspern, Flugplatz, Wien 10 G11 48 13N 16 30 E
Assiano, Mil. 9 E5 45 27N 9 3 E
Aston Mills, Phil. 24 B2 39 52N 75 26W
Astoria, N.Y. 22 C5 40 46N 73 55W
Atares, Castillo de, La Hab. 30 B2 23 7N 82 21W
Atco, Phil. 24 C5 39 46N 74 53W
Atghara, Calc. 16 E6 22 37N 88 26 E
Athens = Athínai, Ath. 8 J11 37 58N 23 43 E
Athínai, Ath. 8 J11 37 58N 23 43 E
Athinai-Ellinikón Airport, Ath. 8 J2 37 51N 23 44 E
Athis-Mons, Paris 5 C4 48 42N 2 23 E
Atīfiya, Bagd. 17 E8 33 21N 44 21 E
Atikali, Ist. 17 A2 41 1N 28 56 E
Atilo, Cerro, Lima 30 G8 12 2 S 77 2W
Atişalen, Ist. 17 A2 41 3N 28 52 E
Atlandsberg, Berl. 7 A5 52 33N 13 43 E
Atlantic Beach, N.Y. 23 D6 40 35N 73 44W
Atta, Delhi 16 B2 28 34N 77 19 E
Attiki, Ath. 8 H11 38 0N 23 43 E
Atzalpur, Delhi 16 A3 28 43N 77 20 E
Atzgersdorf, Wien 10 H9 48 8N 16 18 E
Aubervilliers, Paris 5 B4 48 54N 2 22 E
Aubing, Mün. 7 G9 48 9N 11 25 E
Auburn, Syd. 19 B3 33 51 S 151 1 E
Auburndale, Bost. 21 C2 42 20N 71 14W
Auckland Park, Jobg. 18 F9 26 11 S 28 0 E
Audubon, Phil. 24 A2 40 7N 75 25W
Auf-dem-Schnee, Ruhr 6 B6 51 26N 7 25 E
Auffargis, Paris 5 C1 48 42N 1 53 E
Augustówka, Wsaw. 10 E7 52 11N 21 5 E
Aulnay-sous-Bois, Paris 5 B4 48 56N 2 29 E
Aurelio, Rome 9 F9 51 54N 12 26 E
Ausîm, El Qâ. 18 C4 30 7N 31 8 E
Aussen Alster, Hbg. 7 D8 53 33N 10 0 E
Austerlitz, Gare d', Paris 5 B4 48 50N 2 22 E
Austin, Chic. 26 B2 41 53N 87 45W
Auteuil, Mtrl. 20 A3 43 37N 73 44W
Avedøre, Købn. 2 E9 55 37N 12 27 E
Aveley, Lon. 4 C6 51 29N 0 15 E
Avellaneda, B.A. 32 C4 34 40 S 58 22W
Avenel, N.Y. 22 D3 40 34N 74 16W
Avenel, Wash. 25 D8 38 59N 76 59W
Avila, Parque National el, Car. 30 D5 10 31N 66 52W
Avila, Pico, Car. 30 D5 10 32N 66 52W
Avini, Nápl. 9 J13 40 48N 14 28 E
Avondale, Chic. 26 B2 41 56N 87 41W
Avondale Heights, Melb. 19 E6 37 45 S 144 52 E
Avtovo, Len. 11 B3 59 51N 30 16 E
Ayase, Tōkyō 13 D1 35 25N 139 26 E
Ayase →, Tōkyō 13 A3 35 52N 139 45 E
Ayazaga, Ist. 17 A2 41 6N 28 59 E
Ayer Chawan, P., Sing. 15 G7 1 16N 103 41 E
Ayer Merbau, P., Sing. 15 G7 1 16N 103 42 E
Ayía Paraskevi, Ath. 8 H11 38 1N 23 49 E
Áyios Dhimitrios, Ath. 8 J11 37 53N 23 44 E
Áyios Ioánnis Rendis, Ath. 8 J10 37 57N 23 39 E
Azabu, Tōkyō 13 C3 35 39N 139 43 E
Azadpur, Delhi 16 A2 28 42N 77 10 E
Azcapotzalco, Méx. 29 B2 19 28N 99 10W
Azteca, Estadia, Méx. 29 C3 19 8N 99 9W
Azusa, L.A. 28 B5 34 7N 117 54W

B

Ba He →, Beij. 14 B3 39 57N 116 27 E
Baba I., Kar. 17 H10 24 49N 66 57 E
Babarpur, Delhi 16 A2 28 41N 77 16 E
Babelsberg, Berl. 7 B1 52 22N 13 7 E
Babushkin, Mos. 11 D10 55 51N 37 42 E
Babylon, N.Y. 23 C9 40 42N 73 19W
Back →, Balt. 25 B4 39 17N 76 27W
Back B., Bomb. 16 H7 18 56N 72 48 E
Bacoor, Manila 15 E3 14 27N 120 56 E
Bacoor B., Manila 15 E3 14 27N 120 54 E
Badagri Cr. →, Lagos 18 B1 6 24N 7 17 E
Badahela, Delhi 16 B1 28 38N 77 4 E
Badalona, Barc. 8 D6 41 26N 2 14 E
Badersfeld, Mün. 7 F10 48 15N 11 31 E
Badgers Mt., Lon. 4 C5 51 20N 0 8 E
Badi, Delhi 16 A1 28 44N 77 8 E
Badinan, Calc. 16 C5 22 53N 88 14 E
Badu, Rio J. 31 B3 22 54 S 43 3W
Baerl, Ruhr 6 B2 51 29N 6 40 E
Bærum, Oslo 2 B3 59 54N 10 36 E
Bærums Verk, Oslo 2 B2 59 56N 10 28 E
Baggensfjärden, Stock. 3 E12 59 18N 18 19 E
Bággio, Mil. 9 E5 45 27N 9 6 E
Bāgh-e-Feiz, Tehr. 17 C4 35 44N 51 19 E
Baghdād, Bagd. 17 E8 33 20N 44 23 E
Bagmari, Calc. 16 E6 22 34N 88 23 E
Bagneux, Paris 5 C3 48 47N 2 18 E
Bagnolet, Paris 5 B4 48 52N 2 25 E
Bagnoli, Nápl. 9 J11 40 48N 14 9 E
Bagraula, Delhi 16 B1 28 34N 77 4 E
Bagsværd, Købn. 2 D9 55 45N 12 27 E
Bagsværd Sø, Købn. 2 D9 55 46N 12 28 E
Baguiati, Calc. 16 E6 22 36N 88 25 E
Bagumbayan, Manila 15 E4 14 28N 121 3 E
Baha'i Temple, Chic. 26 A2 42 4N 87 41W
Bahrenfeld, Hbg. 7 D7 53 34N 9 55 E
Bahtîm, El Qâ. 18 C5 30 8N 31 16 E
Bahu Bheri, Calc. 16 C5 22 50N 88 14 E
Baidyabati, Calc. 16 D5 22 46N 88 19 E
Baie-d'Urfé, Mtrl. 20 B2 43 25N 73 53W
Baierbrunn, Mün. 7 G10 48 1N 11 29 E
Baijala, Calc. 16 C5 22 51N 88 16 E
Baileys Crossroads, Wash. 25 D7 38 50N 77 6W
Bailly, Paris 5 B2 48 50N 2 4 E
Bainchipota, Calc. 16 C5 22 51N 88 16 E
Bair I., S.F. 27 C3 37 30N 122 13W
Bairro da Matriz, S. Pau. 31 F7 23 40 S 46 27W
Bairro do Limoeiro, S. Pau. 31 E7 23 30 S 46 27W
Baisha, Gzh. 14 G8 23 8N 113 11 E
Baisley Pond, N.Y. 23 C6 40 40N 73 47W
Baixa da Banheira, Lisb. 8 G8 38 39N 9 2W
Baiyun Shan, Gzh. 14 G8 23 8N 113 15 E
Baj Baj, Calc. 16 F5 22 28N 88 11 E
Bakirkoy, Ist. 17 B2 40 58N 28 52 E
Bakovka, Mos. 11 E8 55 40N 37 19 E
Bala-Cynwyd, Phil. 24 A3 40 0N 75 15W
Balagarh, Calc. 16 D6 22 44N 88 27 E
Balara, Manila 15 D4 14 39N 121 3 E
Balarambati, Calc. 16 D5 22 48N 88 12 E
Balashikha, Mos. 11 E11 55 48N 37 58 E
Bald Hill, Bost. 21 B3 42 38N 71 0W
Baldeador, Rio J. 31 B3 22 51 S 43 1W
Baldeneysee, Ruhr 6 B4 51 24N 7 1 E
Baldissero Torinese, Tori. 9 B3 45 4N 7 48 E
Baldpate Hill, Bost. 21 A3 42 42N 71 0W
Baldpate Pond, Bost. 21 A3 42 41N 71 0W
Baldwin, N.Y. 23 D7 40 38N 73 37W
Baldwin Hills, L.A. 28 B2 34 0N 118 21W
Baldwin Hills Res., L.A. 28 B2 34 0N 118 21W
Baldwin Park, L.A. 28 B5 34 5N 117 57W
Bal'etan →, Gzh. 14 G8 23 5N 113 14 E
Balgowlah, Syd. 19 A4 33 47 S 151 16 E
Balgowlah Heights, Syd. 19 A4 33 48 S 151 16 E
Balham, Lon. 4 C4 51 26N 0 8W
Balihati, Calc. 16 D5 22 44N 88 18 E
Balingsnäs, Stock. 3 E11 59 13N 18 0 E
Balingsta, Stock. 3 E11 59 12N 18 3 E
Balintawak, Manila 15 D3 14 39N 120 59 E
Balitai, Tianj. 14 E6 39 5N 117 11 E
Balizhuang, Beij. 14 B3 39 53N 116 28 E
Ballabhpur, Calc. 16 D6 22 44N 88 20 E
Ballainvilliers, Paris 5 C3 48 40N 2 17 E
Ballardvale, Bost. 21 B3 42 37N 71 9W
Ballenato, Pta., La Hab. 30 B2 23 55N 82 28W
Ballerup, Købn. 2 D9 55 43N 12 21 E
Bally, Calc. 16 E6 22 38N 88 20 E
Ballygunge, Calc. 16 E6 22 31N 88 21 E
Balmain, Syd. 19 B4 33 51 S 151 11 E
Balmumcu, Ist. 17 A3 41 3N 29 2 E
Balongbato, Manila 15 D3 14 39N 120 59 E
Baltikri, Calc. 16 E5 22 36N 88 18 E
Baltimore, Balt. 25 B3 39 17N 76 37W
Baltimore Highlands, Balt. 25 B3 39 14N 76 38W
Baltimore-Washington Int. Airport, Balt. 25 B3 39 11N 76 39W
Baluhati, Calc. 16 E5 22 39N 88 15 E
Balwyn, Melb. 19 E7 37 48 S 145 4 E
Balwyn North, Melb. 19 E7 37 47 S 145 4 E
Bambang, Manila 15 D4 14 31N 121 4 E
Bamondongri, Bomb. 16 H9 18 58N 73 1 E
Ban Baan Phichit, Bangk. 15 B2 13 49N 100 37 E
Ban Hugli, Calc. 16 E6 22 38N 88 22 E
Ban Lat Phrao, Bangk. 15 B2 13 47N 100 35 E
Banabuey →, La Hab. 30 B2 23 5N 82 27W
Bananal, S. Pau. 31 D5 23 27 S 46 41W
Banática, Lisb. 8 F7 38 40N 9 11W
Bandeirantes, Praia dos, Rio J. 31 C1 23 0 S 43 23W
Bandipur, Calc. 16 D6 22 43N 88 26 E
Bandipur, Calc. 16 C4 22 50N 88 9 E
Bandra, Bomb. 16 G7 19 3N 72 49 E
Bandra Pt., Bomb. 16 G7 19 2N 72 49 E
Banfield, B.A. 32 C4 34 44 S 58 24W
Bang Kapi, Bangk. 15 B2 13 45N 100 38 E
Bang Khen, Bangk. 15 A2 13 52N 100 35 E
Bang Na, Bangk. 15 B2 13 40N 100 36 E
Bang Su, Khlong →, Bangk. 15 B2 13 47N 100 31 E
Bangbae, Sŏul 12 H7 37 29N 126 59 E
Banghag, Sŏul 12 G8 37 38N 127 1 E
Bangka, Jak. 15 J9 6 15 S 106 48 E
Bangkok, Bangk. 15 B2 13 44N 100 30 E
Bangkok Noi, Khlong →, Bangk. 15 B1 13 45N 100 29 E
Bangkok Yai, Bangk. 15 B1 13 43N 100 29 E
Bangkok Yai, Khlong →, Bangk. 15 B1 13 44N 100 29 E
Banglo, Calc. 16 E5 22 31N 88 14 E
Bangrak, Bangk. 15 B2 13 43N 100 31 E
Bangu, Rio J. 31 B1 22 52 S 43 26W
Bangu, Sa. do, Rio J. 31 B1 22 53 S 43 24W
Bankipur, Calc. 16 D5 22 47N 88 13 E
Bankra, Calc. 16 E5 22 36N 88 17 E
Banks, C., Syd. 19 C4 34 0 S 151 16 E
Bankstown, Syd. 19 B3 33 55 S 151 2 E
Bankstown Aerodrome, Syd. 19 B2 33 55 S 150 59 E
Banna →, Tori. 9 A3 45 12N 7 42 E
Banstala, Calc. 16 E6 22 31N 88 24 E
Banstead, Lon. 4 D3 51 18N 0 12W
Bantra, Calc. 16 E5 22 35N 88 18 E
Banyule Flats Res., Melb. 19 E7 37 44 S 145 5 E
Baquirivú, S. Pau. 31 D7 23 26 S 46 28W
Baquirivú-Guaçu, S. Pau. 31 D7 23 28 S 46 28W
Bara, Calc. 16 D5 22 45N 88 16 E
Baragwanath Airfield, Jobg. 18 F8 26 14 S 27 58 E
Barai, Calc. 16 C6 22 52N 88 22 E
Barajas, Mdrd. 8 B3 40 28N 3 34W
Barajas, Aeropuerto Transoceanico de, Mdrd. 8 B3 40 28N 3 33W
Barakpur, Calc. 16 D6 22 47N 88 21 E
Baranagar, Calc. 16 E6 22 38N 88 22 E
Barbaiana, Mil. 9 D5 45 32N 9 1 E
Barca, Tori. 9 B3 45 6N 7 43 E
Barcarena, Lisb. 8 F7 38 43N 9 16W
Barcarena →, Lisb. 8 F7 38 41N 9 16W
Barcelona, Barc. 8 D6 41 22N 2 10 E
Barcelona-Prat, Aeropuerta de, Barc. 8 E5 41 17N 2 5 E
Barceloneta, Barc. 8 D6 41 22N 2 11 E
Barcroft, L., Wash. 25 D6 38 50N 77 9W
Baréggio, Mil. 9 E5 45 28N 9 0 E
Bariti Bil, Calc. 16 D6 22 48N 88 25 E
Barkarby, Stock. 3 D10 59 24N 17 52 E
Barker Pt., N.Y. 23 B6 40 50N 73 44W
Barking, Lon. 4 B5 51 32N 0 5 E
Barkingside, Lon. 4 B5 51 35N 0 4 E
Barlovento, La Hab. 30 B2 23 5N 82 28W
Barmbek, Hbg. 7 D8 53 34N 10 1 E
Barmen, Ruhr 6 C5 51 16N 7 12 E
Barneau, Paris 5 D6 48 38N 2 43 E
Barnes, Lon. 4 C3 51 28N 0 14W
Barnet, Lon. 4 B3 51 39N 0 11W
Barnsboro, Phil. 24 C4 39 45N 75 9W
Baronia Park, Syd. 19 A3 33 49 S 151 8 E
Barop, Ruhr 6 B6 51 29N 7 25 E
Barra, Nápl. 9 H12 40 50N 14 19 E
Barra Andai, Kar. 17 H11 24 47N 66 59 E
Barra Funda, S. Pau. 31 E6 23 31 S 46 39W
Barracas, B.A. 32 B4 34 39 S 58 24W
Barrackpore Airport, Calc. 16 D6 22 46N 88 21 E
Barrancas, Stgo 30 J10 33 26 S 70 44W
Barranco, Lima 30 G8 12 9 S 77 2W
Barreiro, Lisb. 8 G8 38 39N 9 5W
Barreto, Rio J. 31 B3 22 50 S 43 5W
Barrientos, Méx. 29 A2 19 34N 99 11W
Barrington, Phil. 24 B4 39 52N 75 3W
Barrio de La Estación, Mdrd. 8 B3 40 26N 3 32W
Bartala, Calc. 16 E5 22 32N 88 15 E
Barton Park, Syd. 19 B3 33 56 S 151 9 E
Bartyki, Wsaw. 10 F7 52 10N 21 6 E
Baru, Kali →, Jak. 15 J10 6 12 S 106 51 E
Baruipara, Calc. 16 D5 22 45N 88 13 E
Baruta, Car. 30 E5 10 26N 66 52W
Barvikha, Mos. 11 E7 55 44N 37 16 E
Basai Darapur, Delhi 16 B1 28 38N 77 6 E
Bass Hill, Syd. 19 B3 33 54 S 151 0 E
Bassett, L.A. 28 B5 34 3N 117 59W
Bastille, Place de la, Paris 5 B4 48 51N 2 22 E
Bastos, Rio J. 31 B1 22 52 S 43 21W
Basudebpur, Calc. 16 D6 22 49N 88 24 E
Basus, El Qâ. 18 C5 30 7N 31 12 E
Batanagar, Calc. 16 E5 22 31N 88 15 E
Batenbrock, Ruhr 6 A3 51 31N 6 57 E
Bath Beach, N.Y. 22 D4 40 36N 74 0W
Bath I., Kar. 17 H11 24 49N 67 1 E
Batok, Bukit, Sing. 15 F7 1 21N 103 46 E
Battersea, Lon. 4 C4 51 28N 0 9W
Baturino, Mos. 11 F9 55 35N 37 30 E
Bauman, Mos. 11 E10 55 45N 37 40 E
Baumgarten, Wien 10 G9 48 12N 16 17 E
Bauria, Calc. 16 E5 22 30N 88 10 E
Baxter Estates, N.Y. 23 B6 40 50N 73 42W
Bay Farm I., S.F. 27 B3 37 44N 122 14W
Bay Meadows Race Track, S.F. 27 C3 37 32N 122 17W
Bay Park, N.Y. 23 D7 40 37N 73 39W
Bay Ridge, N.Y. 22 D4 40 37N 74 1W
Bay Ridge Channel, N.Y. 22 D4 40 39N 74 1W
Bay Shore Park, Balt. 25 B4 39 13N 76 25W
Baykoz, Ist. 17 A3 41 7N 29 7 E
Bayonne, N.Y. 22 C4 40 40N 74 6W
Bayshore, S.F. 27 B3 37 42N 122 24W
Bayside, N.Y. 23 C6 40 45N 73 46W
Bayswater, Lon. 4 B3 51 30N 0 10W
Bayswater, Melb. 19 F8 37 50 S 145 17 E
Bayview, S.F. 27 B2 37 44N 122 23W
Bayville, N.Y. 23 B7 40 54N 73 33W
Bāzār, Tehr. 17 C5 35 40N 51 25 E
Beachmont, Bost. 21 C4 42 23N 70 59W
Beacon Hill, H.K. 12 D6 22 21N 114 10 E
Beaconsfield, Mtrl. 20 B2 43 25N 73 53W
Beacontree Heath, Lon. 4 B5 51 33N 0 9 E
Beam →, Lon. 4 B6 51 30N 0 10 E
Bear Cr. →, Balt. 25 B3 39 13N 76 30W
Bear Gulch Res., S.F. 27 D3 37 26N 122 13W
Beato, Lisb. 8 F8 38 44N 9 5W
Beauchamp, Paris 5 A3 49 0N 2 11 E
Beaumonte Heights, Trto. 20 D7 43 45N 79 34W
Beaverdam Cr. →, Wash. 25 C8 39 0N 76 5W
Bebek, Ist. 17 A3 41 4N 29 2 E
Beccar, B.A. 32 A3 34 27 S 58 32W
Běchovice, Pra. 10 B3 50 4N 14 36 E
Beck L., Chic. 26 A1 42 4N 87 52W
Beckenham, Lon. 4 C4 51 24N 0 1W
Beckhausen, Ruhr 6 A4 51 33N 7 1 E
Beckton, Lon. 4 B5 51 30N 0 4 E
Beddington, Lon. 4 C4 51 21N 0 8W
Beddington Corner, Lon. 4 C4 51 23N 0 9W
Bedford, Bost. 21 C2 42 27N 71 15W
Bedford Park, Chic. 26 C2 41 46N 87 46W
Bedford Park, N.Y. 23 B5 40 52N 73 52W
Bedford Stuyvesant, N.Y. 22 C5 40 41N 73 56W
Bedford View, Jobg. 18 F9 26 10 S 28 7 E
Bedok, Sing. 15 G8 1 19N 103 56 E
Beeck, Ruhr 6 B2 51 28N 6 44 E
Beeckerwerth, Ruhr 6 B2 51 28N 6 42 E
Behala, Calc. 16 E5 22 30N 88 18 E
Bei Hai, Beij. 14 B3 39 54N 116 21 E
Beicai, Shang. 14 J12 31 11N 121 32 E
Beicang, Tianj. 14 D5 39 13N 117 7 E
Beigai, Tianj. 14 E6 39 9N 117 10 E
Beijiaoshichang, Beij. 14 B2 39 57N 116 19 E
Beijing, Beij. 14 B2 39 53N 116 21 E
Beinasco, Tori. 9 B2 45 1N 7 34 E
Beirolas, Lisb. 8 F8 38 46N 9 5W
Beitsun, Gzh. 14 G8 23 7N 113 10 E
Békásmegyer, Bud. 10 J13 47 35N 19 3 E
Bekkelaget, Oslo 2 B4 59 53N 10 47 E
Bel Air, L.A. 28 B2 34 4N 118 27W
Bela Vista, S. Pau. 31 E6 23 33 S 46 38W
Bélanger, Mtrl. 20 A3 43 35N 73 42W
Belas, Lisb. 8 F7 38 46N 9 17W
Belém, Lisb. 8 F7 38 41N 9 12W
Belém, Torre de, Lisb. 8 F7 38 41N 9 12W
Belenzinho, S. Pau. 31 E6 23 32 S 46 34W
Belfield, Syd. 19 B3 33 53 S 151 6 E
Belgachi, Calc. 16 E5 22 36N 88 18 E
Belgharia, Calc. 16 E6 22 39N 88 22 E
Belgrano, B.A. 32 B4 34 33 S 58 27W
Belgrave, Melb. 19 F9 37 54 S 145 21 E
Bell Gardens, L.A. 28 C4 33 58N 118 9W
Bella Vista, B.A. 32 B2 34 34 S 58 41W
Bellaire, N.Y. 23 C6 40 42N 73 44W
Bellavista, Lima 30 G8 12 4 S 77 8W
Bellavista, Stgo 30 K11 33 31 S 70 35W
Belle Harbour, N.Y. 23 D5 40 34N 73 51W
Belle Haven, N.Y. 23 A7 41 0N 73 37W
Belle Haven, Wash. 25 E7 38 46N 77 3W
Bellefonte, Phil. 24 C1 39 45N 75 30W
Bellerose, N.Y. 23 C6 40 44N 73 42W
Belleview, Wash. 25 D6 38 57N 77 14W
Belleville, N.Y. 22 C4 40 48N 74 8W
Bellflower, L.A. 28 C4 33 53N 118 7W
Bellingham, Lon. 4 C4 51 25N 0 1W
Bellmawr, Phil. 24 B4 39 52N 75 5W
Bellmore, N.Y. 23 D7 40 39N 73 31W
Bello, La Hab. 30 B2 23 5N 82 24W
Bells Lake, Phil. 24 C4 39 45N 75 3W
Bellwood, Chic. 26 B1 41 52N 87 53W
Belmont, Bost. 21 C2 42 23N 71 10W
Belmont, Lon. 4 B3 51 36N 0 18W
Belmont, S.F. 27 C3 37 31N 122 17W
Belmont Cragin, Chic. 26 B2 41 56N 87 45W
Belmont Harbor, Chic. 26 B3 41 56N 87 38W
Belmont Hills, Phil. 24 A3 40 1N 75 15W
Belmont Slough, S.F. 27 C3 37 32N 122 15W
Belmore, Syd. 19 B3 33 55 S 151 5 E
Belopurpada, Bomb. 16 G9 19 0N 73 1 E
Beltsville, Wash. 25 C8 39 2N 76 54W
Beltsville Airport, Wash. 25 C9 39 1N 76 49W
Belur, Calc. 16 E6 22 37N 88 21 E
Belvedere, Lon. 4 C5 51 29N 0 9 E
Belvedere, S.F. 27 A2 37 52N 122 27W
Belyayevo Bogorodskoye, Mos. 11 F9 55 39N 37 31 E
Bemböle, Hels. 3 B2 60 13N 24 39 E
Bemis Woods, Chic. 26 C1 41 49N 87 54W
Bemowo, Wsaw. 10 E6 52 15N 20 53 E
Benavidez, B.A. 32 A2 34 24 S 58 41W
Bendale, Trto. 20 D9 43 45N 79 13W
Bendungan Hilir, Jak. 15 J9 6 12 S 106 48 E
Benefica, Rio J. 31 B2 22 52 S 43 14W
Benfica, Lisb. 8 F7 38 45N 9 11W
Benin B., Lagos 18 B2 6 24N 7 28 E
Benjamin Franklin Br., Phil. 24 B4 39 57N 75 8W
Benoni, Jobg. 18 F10 26 11 S 28 18 E
Benoni South, Jobg. 18 F10 26 12 S 28 17 E
Bensenville, Chic. 26 B1 41 57N 87 56W
Bensonhurst, N.Y. 22 D5 40 35N 73 59W
Bentleigh, Melb. 19 F7 37 54 S 145 2 E
Bentleigh East, Melb. 19 F7 37 54 S 145 4 E
Beraberi, Calc. 16 D6 22 46N 88 27 E
Berario, Jobg. 18 E8 26 7 S 27 57 E
Berazategui, B.A. 32 C5 34 45 S 58 15W
Berea, Jobg. 18 F9 26 10 S 28 3 E
Berg am Laim, Mün. 7 G10 48 7N 11 38 E
Bergbaumuseum, Ruhr 6 B5 51 29N 7 13 E
Bergenfield, N.Y. 22 B5 40 55N 73 59W
Berger, Oslo 2 B6 59 56N 11 7 E
Bergerhausen, Ruhr 6 B4 51 26N 7 2 E
Bergerhof, Ruhr 6 C6 51 12N 7 21 E
Bergham, Mün. 7 G10 48 2N 11 37 E
Berghausen, Ruhr 6 A5 51 36N 7 12 E
Berghm-Oestrum, Ruhr 6 B1 51 25N 6 39 E
Bergstedt, Hbg. 7 C8 53 40N 10 7 E
Beri, Barc. 8 D5 41 20N 2 1 E
Berih, Sungei →, Sing. 15 F7 1 22N 103 40 E
Berkeley, Chic. 26 B1 41 53N 87 54W
Berkeley, S.F. 27 A3 37 51N 122 16W
Berkeley Heights, N.Y. 22 C2 40 40N 74 26W
Berkeley Hills, S.F. 27 A3 37 51N 122 11W
Berlin, Berl. 7 A3 52 31N 13 23 E
Berlin, Phil. 24 C5 39 47N 74 55W
Bermondsey, Lon. 4 C4 51 29N 0 3W
Bernabeu, Estadio, Mdrd. 8 B2 40 27N 3 41W
Bernal, B.A. 32 C5 34 43 S 58 17W
Bernal Heights, S.F. 27 B2 37 44N 122 24W
Berne, Hbg. 7 D8 53 38N 10 8 E
Berngardovka, Len. 11 A5 60 0N 30 34 E
Berthpage, N.Y. 23 C8 40 45N 73 29W
Bertlich, Ruhr 6 A4 51 36N 7 4 E
Bertolla Barca, Tori. 9 B3 45 6N 7 44 E
Berwyn, Chic. 26 B2 41 50N 87 47W
Berwyn, Phil. 24 A2 40 2N 75 26W
Berwyn Heights, Wash. 25 D8 38 59N 76 55W
Besedy, Mos. 11 F10 55 38N 37 47 E
Besiktas, Ist. 17 A3 41 2N 29 0 E
Beskudnikovo, Mos. 11 D9 55 52N 37 34 E
Besós →, Barc. 8 D6 41 24N 2 13 E
Bessancourt, Paris 5 A3 49 2N 2 12 E
Bestazzo, Mil. 9 E5 45 25N 9 0 E
Bethayres, Phil. 24 A4 40 7N 75 3W
Bethesda, Wash. 25 D7 38 59N 77 6W
Bethlehem Steel Plant, Balt. 25 B4 39 13N 76 29W
Bethnal Green, Lon. 4 B4 51 31N 0 2W
Bethpage State Park, N.Y. 23 C8 40 45N 73 25W
Betor, Calc. 16 E5 22 34N 88 17 E
Beuvronne →, Paris 5 B6 48 59N 2 40 E
Beverley, Chic. 26 C3 41 42N 87 39W
Beverley Hills, Syd. 19 B3 33 56 S 151 5 E
Beverley Park, Syd. 19 B3 33 58 S 151 8 E
Beverly, Bost. 21 B4 42 34N 70 53W
Beverly, Phil. 24 A5 40 3N 74 55W
Beverly Glen, L.A. 28 B2 34 6N 118 26W
Beverly Harbor, Bost. 21 B4 42 32N 70 51W
Beverly Hills, L.A. 28 B2 34 5N 118 24W
Beverly Municipal Airport, Bost. 21 B4 42 36N 70 55W
Bexley, Lon. 4 C5 51 26N 0 8 E
Bexley, Syd. 19 B3 33 56 S 151 7 E
Bexleyheath, Lon. 4 C5 51 27N 0 8 E
Beyenburg, Ruhr 6 C5 51 15N 7 19 E
Beylerbeyi, Ist. 17 A3 41 2N 29 2 E
Beyoğlu, Ist. 17 A2 41 1N 28 58 E
Bezons, Paris 5 B3 48 56N 2 13 E
Bhadrakali, Calc. 16 D6 22 40N 88 20 E
Bhadreswar, Calc. 16 D5 22 49N 88 22 E
Bhadua, Calc. 16 D5 22 40N 88 12 E
Bhalswa, Delhi 16 A2 28 44N 77 10 E
Bhambo Khān Qarmati, Kar. 17 H11 24 49N 67 7 E
Bhandardaha, Calc. 16 E5 22 37N 88 12 E
Bhatpara, Calc. 16 C6 22 52N 88 25 E
Bhatpur, Calc. 16 D6 22 43N 88 25 E
Bhatsala, Calc. 16 E5 22 30N 88 16 E
Bhawanipore, Calc. 16 E6 22 32N 88 21 E
Bhopura, Delhi 16 A2 28 41N 77 19 E
Białołeka Dworska, Wsaw. 10 E7 52 19N 21 1 E
Bickley, Lon. 4 C5 51 23N 0 3 E
Bicutan, Manila 15 D4 14 30N 121 3 E
Bidyadharpur, Calc. 16 C6 22 50N 88 24 E
Bielany, Wsaw. 10 E6 52 17N 20 57 E
Biesdorf, Berl. 7 A4 52 30N 13 33 E
Bièvre →, Paris 5 C2 48 44N 2 9 E
Bièvres, Paris 5 C3 48 45N 2 13 E
Big Timber Cr. →, Phil. 24 B4 39 52N 75 7W
Big Tujunga Canyon →, L.A. 28 A3 34 16N 118 12W
Biggin Hill, Lon. 4 D5 51 18N 0 1 E
Bijoki, Tōkyō 13 B2 35 49N 139 38 E
Bilibiran, Manila 15 E5 14 29N 121 10 E
Bilk, Ruhr 6 C2 51 12N 6 46 E
Billbrook, Hbg. 7 D8 53 31N 10 4 E
Bille →, Hbg. 7 D8 53 32N 10 4 E
Billerica, Bost. 21 B2 42 33N 71 16W
Billinghurst, B.A. 32 B3 34 34 S 58 37W
Billings, Represa, S. Pau. 31 F6 23 42 S 46 39W
Billstedt, Hbg. 7 D8 53 32N 10 6 E
Billwerder, Hbg. 7 D8 53 30N 10 7 E
Billwerder B., Hbg. 7 D8 53 31N 10 3 E
Binacayan, Manila 15 E3 14 27N 120 55 E
Binangonan, Manila 15 E5 14 28N 121 10 E
Binaria, Jak. 15 H10 6 7 S 106 51 E
Bingzhoubao, Gzh. 14 G8 23 2N 113 11 E
Binningsvatna, Oslo 2 C6 50 46N 11 3 E
Binondo, Manila 15 D3 14 36N 120 58 E
Binzago, Mil. 9 D5 45 37N 9 8 E
Birak el Kiyam, El Qâ. 18 C4 30 2N 31 9 E
Birch Cliff, Trto. 20 D9 43 41N 79 16W
Bird →, Balt. 25 A4 39 22N 76 22W
Birka, Stock. 3 D8 59 20N 17 33 E
Birkenhöhe, Berl. 7 A4 52 38N 13 36 E
Birkenstein, Berl. 7 A5 52 31N 13 40 E
Birkholz, Berl. 7 A4 52 37N 13 34 E
Birkholzaue, Berl. 7 A4 52 38N 13 36 E
Biryulyovo, Mos. 11 F10 55 35N 37 40 E
Bisamberg, Wien 10 G10 48 19N 16 21 E
Bispebjerg, Købn. 2 D10 55 42N 12 31 E
Bitsa, Mos. 11 F9 55 35N 37 36 E
Biwon Secret Garden, Sŏul 12 G7 37 34N 126 59 E
Bizard, Î., Mtrl. 20 B2 43 29N 73 53W
Björknas, Stock. 3 E12 59 19N 18 12 E
Björköfjärden, Hels. 3 C2 60 7N 24 38 E
Black Cr. →, Trto. 20 D8 43 40N 79 30W
Blackburn, Melb. 19 E7 37 48 S 145 9 E
Blackburn L., Melb. 19 E7 37 49 S 145 9 E
Blackburn South, Melb. 19 F7 37 50 S 145 9 E
Blackfen, Lon. 4 C5 51 26N 0 6 E
Blackheath, Jobg. 18 E8 26 8 S 27 57 E
Blackheath, Lon. 4 C5 51 28N 0 0 E
Blackmore, Lon. 4 A6 51 41N 0 19 E
Blacktown, Syd. 19 A2 33 46 S 150 56 E
Blackwall, Lon. 4 B4 51 30N 0 0 E
Blackwood, Phil. 24 C4 39 47N 75 4W
Bladensburg, Wash. 25 D8 38 55N 76 55W
Blairgowrie, Jobg. 18 E9 26 6 S 28 0 E
Blakehurst, Syd. 19 B3 33 59 S 151 6 E
Blakstad, Oslo 2 C2 50 49N 10 28 E
Blanco, C., Car. 30 D5 10 36N 66 59W
Blankenburg, Berl. 7 A3 52 35N 13 27 E
Blankenese, Hbg. 7 D6 53 33N 9 48 E
Blankenfelde, Berl. 7 A3 52 37N 13 23 E
Blankenstein, Ruhr 6 B5 51 24N 7 11 E
Blenheim, Phil. 24 C4 39 48N 75 4W
Bliersheim, Ruhr 6 B2 51 23N 6 42 E
Blind Cr. →, Melb. 19 F8 37 53 S 145 12 E
Blizne, Wsaw. 10 E6 52 14N 20 52 E
Bloomfield, N.Y. 22 C3 40 48N 74 12W
Bloomingdale, N.Y. 22 A3 41 0N 74 19W
Bloomsbury, Balt. 25 B2 39 15N 76 44W
Błota, Wsaw. 10 F8 52 9N 21 11 E
Bloubosspruit →, Jobg. 18 F9 26 16 S 28 0 E
Blue Hills Reservation, Bost. 21 D3 42 13N 71 5W
Blue Island, Chic. 26 C2 41 40N 87 40W
Bluff Hd., H.K. 12 E6 22 11N 114 12 E
Blumberg, Berl. 7 A4 52 36N 13 39 E
Blunt Pt., S.F. 27 A2 37 51N 122 25W
Blutenberg, Mün. 7 G9 48 9N 11 27 E
Blylaget, Oslo 2 C4 59 46N 10 41 E
Boa Vista, Alto do, Rio J. 31 B2 22 58 S 43 16W
Boa Vista, Morro, Rio J. 31 B3 22 53 S 43 5W
Boadilla del Monte, Mdrd. 8 B1 40 24N 3 52W
Boardwalk, N.Y. 23 D6 40 34N 73 49W
Boavista, Lisb. 8 F8 38 48N 9 8W
Bobäck, Hels. 3 B2 60 10N 24 31 E
Boberg, Hbg. 7 D8 53 30N 10 9 E
Bobigny, Paris 5 B4 48 54N 2 26 E
Bobylyskaya, Len. 11 B3 59 59N 30 10 E
Bocanegra, Lima 30 F8 11 59 S 77 7W
Boccea, Rome 9 F8 41 57N 12 19 E
Bochold, Ruhr 6 B3 51 28N 6 57 E
Bochum, Ruhr 6 B5 51 28N 7 13 E
Bockum, Ruhr 6 B1 51 21N 6 37 E
Bodelschwingh, Ruhr 6 A6 51 33N 7 22 E
Bodomjarvi, Hels. 3 B3 60 15N 24 40 E
Bogenhausen, Mün. 7 G10 48 8N 11 36 E
Bognæs, Købn. 2 D7 55 41N 12 1 E
Bogorodskoye, Mos. 11 E10 55 48N 37 42 E
Bogota, N.Y. 22 B4 40 52N 74 2W
Bogstadvatnet, Oslo 2 B3 59 58N 10 37 E
Bohaidalu, Tianj. 14 E6 39 7N 117 12 E
Bohnsdorf, Berl. 7 B4 52 23N 13 34 E
Bois-Colombes, Paris 5 B3 48 55N 2 16 E
Bois-d'Arcy, Paris 5 C2 48 48N 2 1 E
Boisement, Paris 5 A2 49 1N 2 0 E
Boissy-St.-Léger, Paris 5 C5 48 44N 2 31 E
Boksburg, Jobg. 18 F10 26 12 S 28 15 E
Boksburg North, Jobg. 18 F10 26 12 S 28 15 E
Boksburg South, Jobg. 18 F10 26 13 S 28 16 E
Boldinasco, Mil. 9 E5 45 29N 9 8 E
Bøler, Oslo 2 B5 59 53N 10 50 E
Bollate, Mil. 9 D5 45 32N 9 7 E
Bollensdorf, Berl. 7 A5 52 30N 13 42 E
Bollmora, Stock. 3 E12 59 14N 18 14 E
Bolshaya Nevka, Len. 11 B3 59 58N 30 18 E
Bolshaya-Okhta, Len. 11 B4 59 56N 30 26 E
Bolshoi Theatre, Mos. 11 E9 55 45N 37 37 E
Bom Retiro, S. Pau. 31 E6 23 31 S 46 38W
Bombay, Bomb. 16 H8 18 56N 72 50 E
Bombay Harbour, Bomb. 16 H8 18 58N 72 55 E
Bombay Univ., Bomb. 16 H7 18 55N 72 49 E
Bommern, Ruhr 6 B6 51 25N 7 20 E
Bonaero Park, Jobg. 18 E10 26 7 S 28 15 E
Bondi, Syd. 19 B4 33 53 S 151 16 E
Bondoufle, Paris 5 D4 48 36N 2 22 E
Bondy, Paris 5 B4 48 54N 2 28 E
Bondy, Forêt de, Paris 5 B5 48 54N 2 33 E
Bonifacio Monument, Manila 15 D3 14 38N 120 58 E
Bonifica di Maccarese, Rome 9 F8 41 50N 12 15 E
Bonifica di Porto, Rome 9 G8 41 48N 12 16 E
Bonita, Pt., S.F. 27 B1 37 48N 122 31W
Bonnefjorden, Oslo 2 B4 59 50N 10 44 E
Bonnelles, Paris 5 D2 48 37N 2 1 E
Bonneuil-sur-Marne, Paris 5 C5 48 46N 2 30 E
Bönningstedt, Hbg. 7 C7 53 40N 9 54 E
Bonnyrigg, Syd. 19 B2 33 53 S 150 54 E
Bonsari, Bomb. 16 G9 19 4N 73 1 E
Bonsucesso, Rio J. 31 B2 22 51 S 43 15W
Boo, Stock. 3 D12 59 20N 18 16 E
Boonton, N.Y. 22 B2 40 54N 74 24W
Boonton Res., N.Y. 22 B2 40 53N 74 24W
Booth Corner, Phil. 24 B2 39 50N 75 29W
Boothwyn, Phil. 24 C2 39 49N 75 26W
Borbeck, Ruhr 6 B3 51 28N 6 56 E
Bordeaux, Jobg. 18 E9 26 5 S 28 1 E
Bordeaux, Mtrl. 20 A3 43 31N 73 43W
Borehamwood, Lon. 4 B3 51 39N 0 15W
Borgaretto, Tori. 9 B2 45 0N 7 35 E
Bórgaro Torinese, Tori. 9 B2 45 9N 7 39 E
Borghese, Villa, Rome 9 F9 41 54N 12 29 E
Borisovo, Mos. 11 F10 55 38N 37 44 E
Borle, Bomb. 16 G8 19 2N 72 54 E
Bornig, Ruhr 6 A5 51 33N 7 16 E
Bornsjön, Stock. 3 E9 59 14N 17 44 E
Boronia, Melb. 19 F8 37 51 S 145 17 E
Borough Green, Lon. 4 D6 51 17N 0 18 E
Borough Park, N.Y. 22 D5 40 38N 73 59W
Børtervatna, Oslo 2 C6 50 46N 11 3 E
Boscoreale, Nápl. 9 J13 40 46N 14 28 E
Boscotrecase, Nápl. 9 J13 40 46N 14 27 E
Bösinghovn, Ruhr 6 C1 51 18N 6 38 E
Bosmont, Jobg. 18 F8 26 10 S 27 57 E
Bosön, Stock. 3 D12 59 22N 18 11 E
Bosporus = Istanbul Boğazi, Ist. 17 A3 41 5N 29 3 E
Bosque da Saúde, S. Pau. 31 E6 23 36 S 46 37W
Bosques, B.A. 32 C5 34 48 S 58 15W
Bossley Park, Syd. 19 B2 33 51 S 150 53 E
Bossucaba →, S. Pau. 31 E5 23 31 S 46 46W
Bostanci, Ist. 17 B3 40 57N 29 5 E
Bostelbek, Hbg. 7 E7 53 28N 9 55 E
Boston, Bost. 21 C3 42 21N 71 3W
Boston B., Bost. 21 C4 42 22N 70 55W
Boston Harbor, Bost. 21 C4 42 20N 70 58W
Boston Hill, Bost. 21 B3 42 38N 71 5W
Botany, Syd. 19 B4 33 56 S 151 12 E
Botany B., Lon. 4 A4 51 40N 0 7W
Botany B., Syd. 19 B4 33 58 S 151 11 E
Botič →, Pra. 10 B3 50 4N 14 26 E
Botkyrka, Stock. 3 E9 59 15N 17 49 E
Botofogo, Rio J. 31 B2 22 56 S 43 10W
Bottrop, Ruhr 6 A3 51 32N 6 57 E
Bötzow, Berl. 7 A1 52 39N 13 8 E
Bouafle, Paris 5 B1 48 57N 1 54 E

Chodov u Prahy **35**

Boucherville, *Mtrl.* **20 A5** 43 36N 73 28W
Boucherville, Îs. de, *Mtrl.* **20 A5** 43 36N 73 28W
Bougival, *Paris* **5 B2** 48 51N 2 8 E
Boulder Pt., *H.K.* **12 E5** 22 14N 114 6 E
Boullay-les-Troux, *Paris* **5 C2** 48 40N 2 2 E
Boulogne, *B.A.* **32 B3** 34 30 S 58 33W
Boulogne, Bois de, *Paris* **5 B3** 48 51N 2 14 E
Boulogne-Billancourt, *Paris* **5 B3** 48 50N 2 14 E
Bouqueval, *Paris* **5 A4** 49 1N 2 25 E
Bourg-la-Reine, *Paris* **5 C3** 48 46N 2 19 E
Boussy-St.-Antoine, *Paris* **5 C5** 48 41N 2 33 E
Bouviers, *Paris* **5 C2** 48 46N 2 4 E
Bovert, *Ruhr* **6 C1** 51 16N 6 37 E
Bovisa, *Mil.* **9 D6** 45 30N 9 10 E
Bovísio-Masciago, *Mil.* **9 D5** 45 36N 9 8 E
Bow, *Lon.* **4 B4** 51 31N 0 1W
Bowleys Quarters, *Balt.* **25 A4** 39 20N 76 24W
Box Hill, *Melb.* **19 E7** 37 48 S 145 6 E
Boxford State Forest, *Bost.* **21 B3** 42 39N 71 2W
Boy, *Ruhr* **6 A3** 51 31N 7 0 E
Boyaciköy, *Ist.* **17 A3** 41 5N 29 2 E
Boye →, *Ruhr* **6 A3** 51 30N 6 59 E
Boyle Heights, *L.A.* **28 B3** 34 1N 118 12 E
Braddell Heights, *Sing.* **15 F8** 1 20N 103 51 E
Brahmanpur, *Bomb.* **16 G8** 19 5N 72 52 E
Braintree, *Bost.* **21 D3** 42 12N 71 0W
Brakpan, *Jobg.* **18 F11** 26 14 S 28 20 E
Brambauer, *Ruhr* **6 A6** 51 35N 7 26 E
Bramfeld, *Hbg.* **7 D8** 53 36N 10 5 E
Bramley, *Jobg.* **18 E9** 26 7 S 28 4 E
Brande, *Hbg.* **7 D6** 53 37N 9 49 E
Brandenburg Gate, *Berl.* **7 A3** 52 30N 13 21 E
Brandizzo, *Tori.* **9 A3** 45 10N 7 49 E
Brands Hatch, *Lon.* **4 C6** 51 21N 0 15 E
Brandýs nad Labem, *Pra.* **10 A3** 50 10N 14 39 E
Brandywine, *Phil.* **24 C1** 39 49N 75 32W
Brandywine Cr. →, *Phil.* **24 C1** 39 43N 75 31W
Brani, P., *Sing.* **15 G8** 1 15N 103 50 E
Branik, *Pra.* **10 B2** 50 1N 14 25 E
Brännkyrka, *Stock.* **3 E11** 59 17N 18 0 E
Brás, *S. Pau.* **31 E6** 23 32 S 46 36W
Brateyevo, *Mos.* **11 F10** 55 39N 37 45 E
Bratsevo, *Mos.* **11 D8** 55 51N 37 24 E
Brauck, *Ruhr* **6 A3** 51 32N 7 0 E
Brava, Pta., *La Hab.* **30 B2** 23 8N 82 23W
Braybrook, *Melb.* **19 E6** 37 46 S 144 51 E
Brázdim, *Pra.* **10 A3** 50 10N 14 35 E
Breakheart Reservation, *Bost.* **21 C3** 42 28N 71 1W
Brechten, *Ruhr* **6 A6** 51 34N 7 27 E
Breckerfeld, *Ruhr* **6 C6** 51 15N 7 28 E
Brede, *Købn.* **2 D10** 55 47N 12 30 E
Bredeney, *Ruhr* **6 B3** 51 24N 6 59 E
Breeds Pond, *Bost.* **21 C4** 42 28N 70 58W
Breezy Pt., *N.Y.* **22 D5** 40 33N 73 56W
Breitenlee, *Wien* **10 G11** 48 15N 16 30 E
Breitscheid, *Ruhr* **6 B3** 51 21N 6 51 E
Breña, *Lima* **30 G8** 12 3 S 77 3W
Brenschede, *Ruhr* **6 B5** 51 26N 7 12 E
Brent, *Lon.* **4 B3** 51 33N 0 15W
Brent →, *Lon.* **4 B2** 51 30N 0 20W
Brent Res., *Lon.* **4 B3** 51 34N 0 14W
Brentford, *Lon.* **4 C3** 51 28N 0 18W
Brenthurst, *Jobg.* **18 F11** 26 15 S 28 21 E
Brentwood, *Lon.* **4 B6** 51 36N 0 18 E
Brentwood Park, *Jobg.* **18 E10** 26 7 S 28 17 E
Brentwood Park, *L.A.* **28 B2** 34 3N 118 29W
Brera, *Mil.* **9 E6** 45 28N 9 11 E
Bresso, *Mil.* **9 D6** 45 32N 9 11 E
Brétigny-sur-Orge, *Paris* **5 D3** 48 36N 2 18 E
Brevik, *Stock.* **3 D12** 59 20N 18 12 E
Břevnov, *Pra.* **10 B2** 50 4N 14 22 E
Brewer I., *S.F.* **27 C3** 37 33N 122 16W
Bricket Wood, *Lon.* **4 A2** 51 42N 0 21W
Bridesburg, *Phil.* **24 B4** 39 59N 75 4W
Bridgeport, *Chic.* **26 B3** 41 50N 87 38W
Bridgeport, *Phil.* **24 A2** 40 6N 75 21W
Bridgeview, *Chic.* **26 C2** 41 45N 87 48W
Brie-Comte-Robert, *Paris* **5 C5** 48 41N 2 36 E
Brighton, *Melb.* **19 F6** 37 55 S 144 59 E
Brighton le Sands, *Syd.* **19 B3** 33 57 S 151 9 E
Brighton Park, *Chic.* **26 C2** 41 48N 87 41W
Brightwood, *Wash.* **25 D7** 38 57N 77 1W
Brigittenau, *Wien* **10 G10** 48 14N 16 22 E
Briis-sous-Forges, *Paris* **5 D2** 48 37N 2 7 E
Brimbank Park, *Melb.* **19 E6** 37 43 S 144 50 E
Brimsdown, *Lon.* **4 B4** 51 39N 0 0 E
Brione, *Tori.* **9 B1** 45 8N 7 28 E
Briones Hills, *S.F.* **27 A4** 37 56N 122 8W
Briones Regional Park, *S.F.* **27 A4** 37 55N 122 8W
Briones Res., *S.F.* **27 A3** 37 55N 122 11W
Brisbane, *S.F.* **27 B2** 37 40N 122 23W
Bristol, *Phil.* **24 A5** 40 6N 74 53W
Britz, *Berl.* **7 B3** 52 26N 13 27 E
Brixton, *Lon.* **4 C4** 51 27N 0 8W
Broad Axe, *Phil.* **24 A3** 40 8N 75 14W
Broad Sd., *Bost.* **21 C4** 42 23N 70 56W
Broadmeadows, *Melb.* **19 E6** 37 40 S 144 55 E
Broadmoor, *S.F.* **27 B2** 37 41N 122 29W
Broadview, *Chic.* **26 B1** 41 51N 87 52W
Brobacka, *Hels.* **3 B2** 60 15N 24 36 E
Brockley, *Lon.* **4 C4** 51 27N 0 2W
Bródno, *Wsaw.* **10 E7** 52 17N 21 1 E
Bródnowski, Kanal, *Wsaw.* **10 E7** 52 17N 21 3 E
Broich, *Ruhr* **6 B3** 51 25N 6 50 E
Bromley, *Lon.* **4 C5** 51 24N 0 0 E
Bromley-by-Bow, *Lon.* **4 B4** 51 31N 0 0 E
Bromley Common, *Lon.* **4 C5** 51 22N 0 2 E
Bromma, *Stock.* **3 D10** 59 21N 17 55 E
Bromma flygplats, *Stock.* **3 D10** 59 21N 17 56 E
Brompton, *Lon.* **4 C3** 51 29N 0 10W
Brøndby Strand, *Købn.* **2 E9** 55 36N 12 25 E
Brøndbyøster, *Købn.* **2 E9** 55 39N 12 26 E
Brøndbyvester, *Købn.* **2 E9** 55 37N 12 23 E
Brondesbury, *Lon.* **4 B3** 51 32N 0 12W
Brønnøya, *Oslo* **2 B3** 59 51N 10 32 E
Brønshøj, *Købn.* **2 D9** 55 41N 12 29 E
Bronx Zoo, *N.Y.* **23 B5** 40 50N 73 51W
Bronxville, *N.Y.* **23 B6** 40 56N 73 49W
Brook Street, *Lon.* **4 B6** 51 36N 0 17 E
Brookfield, *Chic.* **26 C1** 41 48N 87 50W
Brookhaven, *Phil.* **24 B2** 39 52N 75 23W
Brooklandville, *Balt.* **25 A2** 39 25N 76 40W
Brooklin, *S. Pau.* **31 E6** 23 37 S 46 39W
Brookline, *Bost.* **21 D3** 42 19N 71 8W
Brooklyn, *Balt.* **25 B3** 39 13N 76 36W
Brooklyn, *Melb.* **19 E5** 37 49 S 144 49 E
Brooklyn, *N.Y.* **22 D5** 40 37N 73 57W
Brookmont, *Wash.* **25 D7** 38 57N 77 7W
Brooks I., *S.F.* **27 A2** 37 53N 122 21W
Brookville, *N.Y.* **23 C7** 40 48N 73 33W
Broomall, *Phil.* **24 B2** 39 58N 75 22W
Brosewere B., *N.Y.* **23 D6** 40 37N 73 40W
Brossard, *Mtrl.* **20 B5** 43 27N 73 28W
Brou-sur-Chantereine, *Paris* **5 B5** 48 53N 2 37 E
Brown, *Trto.* **20 D9** 43 48N 79 14W
Browns Line, *Trto.* **20 E7** 43 36N 79 32W
Broyhill Park, *Wash.* **25 D6** 38 52N 77 12W
Bru, *Oslo* **2 C5** 59 47N 10 54 E
Bruckhausen, *Ruhr* **6 B2** 51 29N 6 43 E
Brughério, *Mil.* **9 D6** 45 33N 9 17 E
Bruino, *Tori.* **9 B1** 45 1N 7 27 E
Bruløkka, *Oslo* **2 A2** 60 1N 10 22 E
Brunn, *Stock.* **3 E13** 59 17N 18 25 E
Brunnthal, *Mün.* **7 G11** 48 0N 11 41 E
Brunoy, *Paris* **5 C4** 48 41N 2 29 E
Brunswick, *Melb.* **19 E6** 37 45 S 144 57 E
Brusciano, *Nápl.* **9 H13** 40 55N 14 25 E
Brush Hill, *Bost.* **21 D1** 42 15N 71 22W
Bruzzano, *Mil.* **9 D6** 45 31N 9 10 E
Bry-sur-Marne, *Paris* **5 B5** 48 50N 2 32 E
Bryn, *Oslo* **2 B2** 59 55N 10 27 E
Bryn Athyn, *Phil.* **24 A4** 40 8N 75 3W
Bryn Mawr, *Phil.* **24 A3** 40 1N 75 19W
Brzeziny, *Wsaw.* **10 E7** 52 19N 21 2 E
Bubeneč, *Pra.* **10 B2** 50 6N 14 24 E
Buc, *Paris* **5 C2** 48 46N 2 7 E
Buch, *Berl.* **7 A3** 52 38N 13 29 E
Buchburg, *Wien* **10 G9** 48 13N 16 11 E
Buchenhain, *Mün.* **7 G9** 48 1N 11 29 E
Buchholz, *Berl.* **7 A3** 52 36N 13 25 E
Buchholz, *Ruhr* **6 B2** 51 23N 6 46 E
Buckhurst Hill, *Lon.* **4 B5** 51 37N 0 2 E
Buckingham Palace, *Lon.* **4 B4** 51 30N 0 8W
Buckow, *Berl.* **7 B3** 52 25N 13 26 E
Buda, *Bud.* **10 J13** 47 30N 19 2 E
Budafok, *Bud.* **10 K13** 47 25N 19 2 E
Budakeszi, *Bud.* **10 J12** 47 30N 18 56 E
Budaörs, *Bud.* **10 K12** 47 27N 18 57 E
Budapest, *Bud.* **10 K13** 47 29N 19 3 E
Budatétény, *Bud.* **10 K13** 47 25N 19 1 E
Budberg, *Ruhr* **6 A1** 51 32N 6 38 E
Buddinge, *Købn.* **2 D10** 55 44N 12 30 E
Büderich, *Ruhr* **6 C2** 51 15N 6 41 E
Buena Park, *L.A.* **28 C4** 33 51N 118 1W
Buena Vista, *S.F.* **27 B2** 37 45N 122 26W
Buenavista, *Mdrd.* **8 B2** 40 25N 3 40W
Buenos Aires, *B.A.* **32 B4** 34 36 S 58 22W
Buenos Aires, Aeroparque de la Ciudad de, *B.A.* **32 B4** 34 34 S 58 25W
Buer, *Ruhr* **6 A4** 51 34N 7 2 E
Bufalotta, *Rome* **9 F10** 41 59N 12 33 E
Buggajha, *Sŏul* **12 G7** 37 34N 126 55 E
Bughan San, *Sŏul* **12 G7** 37 38N 126 58 E
Bugio, *Lisb.* **8 G7** 38 39N 9 18W
Bukit Panjang, *Sing.* **15 F7** 1 22N 103 45 E
Bukit Timah, *Sing.* **15 F7** 1 20N 103 47 E
Bulam San, *Sŏul* **12 G8** 37 38N 127 4 E
Bûlâq, *El Qâ.* **18 C5** 30 3N 31 14 E
Bule, *Manila* **15 E4** 14 26N 121 2 E
Bulim, *Sing.* **15 F7** 1 22N 103 43 E
Bull Brook →, *Bost.* **21 A4** 42 41N 70 52W
Bulleen, *Melb.* **19 E7** 37 46 S 145 4 E
Bullen Park, *Melb.* **19 E7** 37 46 S 145 4 E
Bullion, *Paris* **5 D1** 48 37N 1 59 E
Bulmke-Hüllen, *Ruhr* **6 A4** 51 31N 7 7 E
Bulphan, *Lon.* **4 B7** 51 32N 0 21 E
Bundoora, *Melb.* **19 E7** 37 41 S 145 2 E
Bundoora Park, *Melb.* **19 E7** 37 42 S 145 2 E
Bunker I., *Kar.* **17 H10** 24 48N 66 57 E
Bunkyo, *Tōkyō* **13 B3** 35 42N 139 45 E
Buona Vista, *Sing.* **15 G7** 1 16N 103 47 E
Buquirivú-Guaçu →, *S. Pau.* **31 D7** 23 28 S 46 28W
Burbank, *Chic.* **26 C2** 41 44N 87 46W
Burbank, *L.A.* **28 A3** 34 12N 118 18W
Bures, *Paris* **5 B1** 48 56N 1 57 E
Bures-sur-Yvette, *Paris* **5 C2** 48 41N 2 9 E
Burggrafenberg, *Ruhr* **6 C4** 51 13N 7 7 E
Burgh Heath, *Lon.* **4 D3** 51 18N 0 13W
Burlingame, *S.F.* **27 C2** 37 34N 122 20W
Burlington, *Bost.* **21 B2** 42 30N 71 13W
Burlington, *Phil.* **24 A5** 40 4N 74 53W
Burnham, *Chic.* **26 D3** 41 38N 87 33W
Burnham Park Harbor, *Chic.* **26 B3** 41 51N 87 36W
Burnhamthorpe, *Trto.* **20 E7** 43 37N 79 35W
Burnt Oak, *Lon.* **4 B3** 51 36N 0 15W
Burr Ridge, *Chic.* **26 C1** 41 46N 87 54W
Burtus, *El Qâ.* **18 C4** 30 8N 31 8 E
Burudvatn, *Oslo* **2 B3** 59 58N 10 35 E
Burwood, *Melb.* **19 F7** 37 50 S 145 6 E
Burwood, *Syd.* **19 B3** 33 52 S 151 5 E
Burwood East, *Melb.* **19 F7** 37 51 S 145 8 E
Burzaco, *B.A.* **32 C4** 34 49 S 58 23W
Buschhausen, *Ruhr* **6 A3** 51 30N 6 50 E
Bush Hill Park, *Lon.* **4 B4** 51 38N 0 4W
Bushey, *Lon.* **4 B2** 51 38N 0 22W
Bushwick, *N.Y.* **23 C5** 40 41N 73 54W
Bushy Cr. →, *Melb.* **19 E8** 37 42 S 145 17 E
Bushy Park, *Lon.* **4 C2** 51 24N 0 20W
Bussocaba, *S. Pau.* **31 E5** 23 34 S 46 47W
Bussy-St.-Georges, *Paris* **5 B6** 48 50N 2 41 E
Bussy-St.-Martin, *Paris* **5 B6** 48 50N 2 41 E
Bustleton, *Phil.* **24 A4** 40 4N 75 2W
Butantã, *S. Pau.* **31 E5** 23 34 S 46 42W
Butcher I., *Bomb.* **16 H8** 18 57N 72 53 E
Butendorf, *Ruhr* **6 A3** 51 33N 6 59 E
Butler, *N.Y.* **22 B2** 40 59N 74 20W
Buttonville, *Trto.* **20 C8** 43 51N 79 20W
Butts Corner, *Wash.* **25 E6** 38 46N 77 19W
Byailla, *Bomb.* **16 H8** 18 58N 72 50 E
Byberry, *Phil.* **24 A5** 40 6N 74 59W
Byfang, *Ruhr* **6 B4** 51 24N 7 5 E
Byfleet, *Lon.* **4 D2** 51 19N 0 28W
Bygdøy, *Oslo* **2 B4** 59 54N 10 40 E

C

C.N. Tower, *Trto.* **20 E8** 43 38N 79 23W
Caballito, *B.A.* **32 B4** 34 37 S 58 25W
Cabin John, *Wash.* **25 D6** 38 58N 77 10W
Cabin John Cr. →, *Wash.* **25 C7** 39 2N 77 8W
Cabin John Regional Park, *Wash.* **25 C6** 39 0N 77 10W
Cabramatta, *Syd.* **19 B2** 33 53 S 150 56 E
Cabuçú de Baixo →, *S. Pau.* **31 D5** 23 30 S 46 40W
Cachan, *Paris* **5 C3** 48 47N 2 19 E
Cachenka →, *Mos.* **11 E7** 55 46N 37 17 E
Cachoeira →, *S. Pau.* **31 E5** 23 38 S 46 43W
Cacilhas, *Lisb.* **8 F8** 38 41N 9 8W
Cadieux, Î., *Mtrl.* **20 B1** 43 25N 74 1W
Cagarras, Is., *Rio J.* **31 C2** 23 1 S 43 12W
Cahuenga Pk., *L.A.* **28 B3** 34 8N 118 19 E
Cainta, *Manila* **15 D4** 14 34N 121 6 E
Cairo = El Qâhira, *El Qâ.* **18 C5** 30 2N 31 13 E
Cairo Int. Airport, *El Qâ.* **18 C6** 30 7N 31 23 E
Caivano, *Nápl.* **9 H12** 40 57N 14 18 E
Caju, *Rio J.* **31 B2** 22 52 S 43 12W
Čakovice, *Pra.* **10 B3** 50 9N 14 31 E
Calabazar, *La Hab.* **30 B2** 23 1N 82 20W
Calcutta, *Calc.* **16 E6** 22 34N 88 21 E
Caldwell, *N.Y.* **22 B3** 40 50N 74 19W
Calf Harbour, *N.Y.* **23 B7** 40 59N 73 37W
Calf I., *Bost.* **21 C4** 42 20N 70 53W
Calhua, *Lisb.* **8 F8** 38 44N 9 9W
California, Univ. of, *S.F.* **27 A3** 37 52N 122 16W
California Inst. of Tech., *L.A.* **28 B4** 34 8N 118 8W
California State Univ., *L.A.* **28 B3** 34 4N 118 10W
California State Univ., *S.F.* **27 C4** 37 39N 122 6W
Callao, *Lima* **30 G8** 12 3 S 77 8W
Caloocan, *Manila* **15 D3** 14 39N 120 58 E
Calumet →, *Chic.* **26 C3** 41 43N 87 31W
Calumet, L., *Chic.* **26 C3** 41 40N 87 35W
Calumet City, *Chic.* **26 D3** 41 36N 87 32W
Calumet Harbor, *Chic.* **26 C3** 41 43N 87 30W
Calumet Park, *Chic.* **26 C3** 41 40N 87 39W
Calumet Sag Channel →, *Chic.* **26 C2** 41 40N 87 47W
Calumpang, *Manila* **15 D4** 14 37N 121 5 E
Calvairate, *Mil.* **9 E6** 45 27N 9 13 E
Calverton, *Wash.* **25 C8** 39 3N 76 56W
Calvizzano, *Nápl.* **9 H12** 40 54N 14 11 E
Calzada, *Manila* **15 D4** 14 32N 121 4 E
Camarate, *Lisb.* **8 F8** 38 48N 9 7W
Camaroes, *Lisb.* **8 F7** 38 49N 9 14W
Camberwell, *Lon.* **4 C4** 51 28N 0 5W
Camberwell, *Melb.* **19 F7** 37 50 S 145 5 E
Cambria Heights, *N.Y.* **23 C6** 40 41N 73 44W
Cambridge, *Bost.* **21 C3** 42 23N 71 7W
Cambridge Res., *Bost.* **21 C2** 42 24N 71 16W
Cambuci, *S. Pau.* **31 E6** 23 33 S 46 47W
Cambute, *La Hab.* **30 B3** 23 5N 82 16W
Camden, *Lon.* **4 B4** 51 32N 0 8W
Camden, *Phil.* **24 B4** 39 56N 75 7W
Camp Springs, *Wash.* **25 E8** 38 48N 76 55W
Campamento, *Mdrd.* **8 B2** 40 23N 3 46W
Campanilla, Pta., *La Hab.* **30 A3** 23 10N 82 18W
Campbellfield, *Melb.* **19 E6** 37 40 S 144 57 E
Camperdown, *Syd.* **19 B4** 33 53 S 151 11 E
Campi Flegrei, *Nápl.* **9 H11** 40 50N 14 9 E
Campo, Casa de, *Mdrd.* **8 B2** 40 25N 3 45W
Campo Belo, *S. Pau.* **31 E5** 23 36 S 46 44W
Campo de Mayo, *B.A.* **32 B2** 34 32 S 58 40W
Campo Grando, *Lisb.* **8 F8** 38 45N 9 9W
Campo Limpo, *S. Pau.* **31 E5** 23 38 S 46 46W
Campo Pequeño, *Lisb.* **8 F8** 38 44N 9 8W
Campolide, *Lisb.* **8 F8** 38 43N 9 9W
Campsie, *Syd.* **19 B3** 33 54 S 151 6 E
C'an San Joan, *Barc.* **8 D6** 41 28N 2 11 E
Canacao, *Manila* **15 E3** 14 29N 120 54 E
Canacao B., *Manila* **15 E3** 14 29N 120 54 E
Cañada de los Helechos →, *Méx.* **29 B2** 19 21N 99 15W
Canarsie, *N.Y.* **23 D5** 40 38N 73 53W
Candiac, *Mtrl.* **20 B5** 43 23N 73 29W
Caneças, *Lisb.* **8 F7** 38 48N 9 13W
Cangaiba, *S. Pau.* **31 E6** 23 30 S 46 31W
Cangrejeras, *La Hab.* **30 B1** 23 3N 82 30W
Canguera, *S. Pau.* **31 E7** 23 34 S 46 26W
Canillas, *Mdrd.* **8 B3** 40 27N 3 38W
Canillejas, *Mdrd.* **8 B3** 40 26N 3 36W
Cann Hall, *Lon.* **4 B5** 51 33N 0 0 E
Canning Town, *Lon.* **4 B5** 51 30N 0 1 E
Canoe Grove Res., *N.Y.* **22 C2** 40 45N 74 21W
Cantalupo, *Mil.* **9 D4** 45 34N 8 58 E
Cantareira, *S. Pau.* **31 D6** 23 26 S 46 36W
Cantarranas, *La Hab.* **30 B2** 23 2N 82 28W
Canteras de Vallecas, *Mdrd.* **8 B3** 40 20N 3 37W
Canterbury, *Melb.* **19 E7** 37 49 S 145 4 E
Canterbury, *Syd.* **19 B3** 33 55 S 151 7 E
Canto do Rio, *Rio J.* **31 B3** 22 54 S 43 7W
Canton, *Bost.* **21 D3** 42 10N 71 8W
Caohe, *Shang.* **14 J11** 31 10N 121 24 E
Caonao, *La Hab.* **30 B2** 23 5N 82 24W
Capão Redondo, *S. Pau.* **31 E5** 23 39 S 46 45W
Caparica, *Lisb.* **8 F8** 38 40N 9 9W
Caparica, Costa da, *Lisb.* **8 G7** 38 38N 9 15W
Capelinha, *S. Pau.* **31 E5** 23 39 S 46 44W
Capitol Heights, *Wash.* **25 D8** 38 52N 76 55W
Capodichino, Aeroporto di, *Nápl.* **9 H12** 40 52N 14 17 E
Capodimonte, *Nápl.* **9 H12** 40 52N 14 14 E
Capodimonte, Bosco di, *Nápl.* **9 H12** 40 52N 14 15 E
Captain Cook Bridge, *Syd.* **19 C3** 34 0 S 151 7 E
Captain Cook Landing Place Park, *Syd.* **19 C4** 34 1 S 151 14 E
Captain Harbour, *N.Y.* **23 B7** 40 59N 73 37W
Capuava, *S. Pau.* **31 E7** 23 38 S 46 28W
Capuchos, *Lisb.* **8 G7** 38 38N 9 16W
Caraballeda, *Car.* **30 D5** 10 36N 66 50W
Carabanchel Alto, *Mdrd.* **8 B2** 40 22N 3 44W
Carabanchel Bajo, *Mdrd.* **8 B2** 40 23N 3 44W
Carabatteda →, *Car.* **30 D5** 10 37N 66 51W
Caracas, *Car.* **30 E5** 10 30N 66 54W
Carapachay, *B.A.* **32 B3** 34 31 S 58 32W
Carapicuiba, *S. Pau.* **31 E5** 23 31 S 46 49W
Carapicuiba →, *S. Pau.* **31 E5** 23 31 S 46 49W
Caravita, *Nápl.* **9 H13** 40 52N 14 21 E
Caraza, *B.A.* **32 C4** 34 41 S 58 25W
Cardito, *Nápl.* **9 H12** 40 56N 14 17 E
Cardoso, *Lagos* **18 A1** 6 34N 7 16 E
Caribbean Gardens, *Melb.* **19 F8** 37 54 S 145 12 E
Caricuao, *Car.* **30 E5** 10 25N 66 58W
Caridad, *Manila* **15 E3** 14 28N 120 53 E
Carioca, Sa. da, *Rio J.* **31 B2** 22 57 S 43 13W
Carle Place, *N.Y.* **23 C7** 40 44N 73 35W
Carlingford, *Syd.* **19 A3** 33 46 S 151 3 E
Carlisle, *Bost.* **21 B1** 42 31N 71 20W
Carlshof, *Mün.* **7 F11** 48 15N 11 41 E
Carlstadt, *N.Y.* **22 B4** 40 50N 74 6W
Carlton, *Melb.* **19 E6** 37 47 S 144 57 E
Carnaxide, *Lisb.* **8 F7** 38 43N 9 14W
Carnegie, *Melb.* **19 F7** 37 53 S 145 3 E
Carnegie Hall, *N.Y.* **22 C5** 40 45N 73 59W
Carnetin, *Paris* **5 B6** 48 54N 2 42 E
Carney, *Balt.* **25 A3** 39 23N 76 31W
Carnide, *Lisb.* **8 F7** 38 45N 9 10W
Caronno Pert, *Mil.* **9 D5** 45 35N 9 2 E
Carramar, *Syd.* **19 B2** 33 51 S 150 58 E
Carrascal, *Stgo* **30 J10** 33 25 S 70 42W
Carrières-sous-Bois, *Paris* **5 B2** 48 55N 2 6 E
Carrières-sous-Poissy, *Paris* **5 B2** 48 56N 2 2 E
Carrières-sur-Seine, *Paris* **5 B3** 48 55N 2 11 E
Carroll I., *Balt.* **25 B4** 39 19N 76 20W
Carroll Park, *Balt.* **25 B3** 39 16N 76 38W
Carshalton, *Lon.* **4 C3** 51 22N 0 10W
Carshalton on the Hill, *Lon.* **4 C4** 51 20N 0 9W
Carteret, *N.Y.* **22 D3** 40 34N 74 13W
Cartierville, Aéroport de, *Mtrl.* **20 A3** 43 31N 73 42 E
Carugate, *Mil.* **9 D6** 45 32N 9 20 E
Carupa, *B.A.* **32 A3** 34 25 S 58 33W
Casa Blanca, *La Hab.* **30 B3** 23 8N 82 19W
Casa Verde, *S. Pau.* **31 D5** 23 29 S 46 40W
Casalnuovo di Nápoli, *Nápl.* **9 H12** 40 54N 14 20 E
Casalotti, *Rome* **9 F9** 41 54N 12 22 E
Casandrino, *Nápl.* **9 H12** 40 56N 14 15 E
Casavatore, *Nápl.* **9 H12** 40 53N 14 15 E
Cascadura, *Rio J.* **31 B2** 22 52 S 43 19W
Caselette, *Tori.* **9 B1** 45 6N 7 28 E
Caselette, Laghi di, *Tori.* **9 B1** 45 7N 7 29 E
Caselle Torinese, *Tori.* **9 A3** 45 10N 7 38 E
Caseros, *B.A.* **32 B3** 34 36 S 58 34W
Casória, *Nápl.* **9 H12** 40 54N 14 17 E
Cassignanica, *Mil.* **9 E7** 45 27N 9 20 E
Cassiobury Park, *Lon.* **4 B2** 51 39N 0 25W
Castel di Camerletto, *Tori.* **9 B1** 45 6N 7 27 E
Castel di Guido, *Rome* **9 F8** 41 53N 12 17 E
Castel Malnome, *Rome* **9 F8** 41 50N 12 19 E
Castel San Cristina, *Tori.* **9 B3** 45 8N 7 40 E
Castel Sant'Angelo, *Rome* **9 F9** 41 54N 12 27 E
Castelar, *B.A.* **32 B3** 34 39 S 58 39W
Castellbisbal, *Barc.* **8 D4** 41 28N 1 58 E
Castello di Cisterna, *Nápl.* **9 H13** 40 54N 14 24 E
Castelvécchio, *Tori.* **9 B3** 45 1N 7 46 E
Castiglione Torinese, *Tori.* **9 B3** 45 6N 7 48 E
Castleton Corners, *N.Y.* **22 D4** 40 36N 74 8W
Castro Valley, *S.F.* **27 B4** 37 41N 122 5W
Castrop, *Ruhr* **6 A5** 51 32N 7 18 E
Castrop-Rauxel, *Ruhr* **6 A5** 51 33N 7 18 E
Cat Rock Hill, *Bost.* **21 C2** 42 23N 71 18W
Caterham, *Lon.* **4 D4** 51 16N 0 5W
Catete, *Rio J.* **31 B2** 22 54 S 43 10W
Catford, *Lon.* **4 C4** 51 26N 0 1W
Catia, *Car.* **30 D5** 10 31N 66 56W
Catia La Mer, *Car.* **30 D4** 10 36N 67 0W
Catonsville, *Balt.* **25 B2** 39 16N 76 43W
Catonsville Manor, *Balt.* **25 B2** 39 17N 76 44W
Cattle Hill, *S.F.* **27 C2** 37 36N 122 27W
Catumbi, *Rio J.* **31 B2** 22 54 S 43 12W
Caughnawaga, *Mtrl.* **20 B3** 43 24N 73 40W
Caulfield, *Melb.* **19 F7** 37 52 S 145 1 E
Caulfield Racecourse, *Melb.* **19 F7** 37 53 S 145 4 E
Caumsett State Park, *N.Y.* **23 B8** 40 55N 73 27W
Cavite, *Manila* **15 E3** 14 29N 120 54 E
Cavoretto, *Tori.* **9 B3** 45 1N 7 41 E
Caxias, *Lisb.* **8 F7** 38 42N 9 16W
Caxingui, *S. Pau.* **31 E5** 23 35 S 46 43W
Cebeciköy, *Ist.* **17 A2** 41 7N 28 53 E
Cecchignola, *Rome* **9 G10** 41 48N 12 29 E
Cecil Park, *Syd.* **19 B2** 33 52 S 150 51 E
Cecilienhof, *Berl.* **7 B1** 52 35N 13 5 E
Cedar Grove, *N.Y.* **22 B3** 40 50N 74 13W
Cedar Grove Res., *N.Y.* **22 B3** 40 51N 74 12W
Cedar I., *N.Y.* **23 D8** 40 38N 73 22W
Cedar Knolls, *N.Y.* **22 C2** 40 49N 74 27W
Cedarhurst, *N.Y.* **23 D6** 40 37N 73 43W
Cedarvale, *Trto.* **20 D8** 43 41N 79 26W
Celle →, *Paris* **5 D1** 48 36N 1 59 E
Cempaka Putih, *Jak.* **15 J10** 6 10 S 106 51 E
Çengelköy, *Ist.* **17 A3** 41 2N 29 3 E
Centennial Park, *Syd.* **19 B4** 33 53 S 151 14 E
Center Square, *Phil.* **24 C2** 39 46N 75 22W
Centerport, *N.Y.* **23 B8** 40 53N 73 22W
Centerton, *Phil.* **24 B5** 39 59N 74 53W
Centocelle, *Rome* **9 F10** 41 52N 12 34 E
Central Park, *N.Y.* **22 C5** 40 47N 73 58W
Central Park, *Sing.* **15 G8** 1 17N 103 50 E
Centre City, *Phil.* **24 C3** 39 46N 75 11W
Centre I., *N.Y.* **23 B7** 40 54N 73 31W
Cércola, *Nápl.* **9 H13** 40 51N 14 21 E
Cergy-Pontoise, *Paris* **5 A2** 49 1N 2 4 E
Cernay-la-Ville, *Paris* **5 C1** 48 40N 1 58 E
Cernusco sul Navíglio, *Mil.* **9 D6** 45 31N 9 19 E
Cerqueira Cesar, *S. Pau.* **31 E5** 23 33 S 46 40W
Cerro Ajusco, *Méx.* **29 C2** 19 12N 99 15W
Cerro de la Estrella, *Méx.* **29 B3** 19 20N 99 5W
Cerro de los Angeles, *Mdrd.* **8 C2** 40 18N 3 41W
Cerro el Picacho, *Méx.* **29 A3** 19 35N 99 6W
Cerro Maggiore, *Mil.* **9 D4** 45 35N 8 57 E
Certanovka →, *Mos.* **11 F9** 55 38N 37 48 E
Certanovo, *Mos.* **11 F9** 55 38N 37 36 E
Cesano Boscone, *Mil.* **9 E5** 45 26N 9 5 E
Cesate, *Mil.* **9 D5** 45 35N 9 4 E
Cha Kwo Ling, *H.K.* **12 E6** 22 18N 114 13 E
Chabot, L., *S.F.* **27 B4** 37 43N 122 6W
Chacao, *Car.* **30 D5** 10 30N 66 50W
Chacarilla, *Lima* **30 G9** 12 6 S 76 59W
Chadds Ford, *Phil.* **24 B1** 39 52N 75 35W
Chadstone, *Melb.* **19 F7** 37 52 S 145 5 E
Chadwell Heath, *Lon.* **4 B5** 51 34N 0 8 E
Chadwell St. Mary, *Lon.* **4 C7** 51 29N 0 20 E
Chai Wan, *H.K.* **12 E6** 22 16N 114 14 E
Chai Wan Kok, *H.K.* **12 D5** 22 22N 114 6 E
Chakdaha, *Calc.* **16 F5** 22 28N 88 19 E
Chama, *Lima* **30 G8** 12 7 S 77 0W
Chamartin, *Mdrd.* **8 B2** 40 27N 3 40W
Chamberi, *Mdrd.* **8 B2** 40 26N 3 42W
Chambourcy, *Paris* **5 B2** 48 54N 2 2 E
Champdani, *Calc.* **16 D5** 22 48N 88 19 E
Champigny-sur-Marne, *Paris* **5 C5** 48 49N 2 30 E
Champlain, Pont, *Mtrl.* **20 B4** 43 28N 73 31W
Champlan, *Paris* **5 C3** 48 42N 2 16 E
Champrosay, *Paris* **5 D4** 48 39N 2 25 E
Champs-sur-Marne, *Paris* **5 B5** 48 50N 2 34 E
Chamrail, *Calc.* **16 E5** 22 38N 88 17 E
Chancheon, *Sŏul* **12 G7** 37 33N 126 56 E
Chandernagore, *Calc.* **16 C6** 22 51N 88 21 E
Chanditala, *Calc.* **16 D5** 22 41N 88 15 E
Changi, *Sing.* **15 F8** 1 23N 103 59 E
Changi Airport, *Sing.* **15 F8** 1 21N 103 59 E
Changning, *Shang.* **14 J11** 31 13N 121 24 E
Changpu Gongyuan, *Shang.* **14 J12** 31 17N 121 31 E
Chanteloup-les-Vignes, *Paris* **5 B2** 48 58N 2 1 E
Chantereine, *Paris* **5 B5** 48 53N 2 37 E
Chantian, *Gzh.* **14 F8** 23 12N 113 16 E
Chao Phraya →, *Bangk.* **15 B2** 13 40N 100 31 E
Chaoyang, *Beij.* **14 B3** 39 53N 116 26 E
Chaoyang Gongyuan, *Beij.* **14 B3** 39 54N 116 28 E
Chaoyangmen, *Beij.* **14 B3** 39 54N 116 23 E
Chapel End, *Lon.* **4 B4** 51 35N 0 1W
Chapet, *Paris* **5 B1** 48 58N 1 55 E
Chaplinville, *Bost.* **21 A4** 42 42N 70 54W
Chapultepec, Bosque de, *Méx.* **29 B2** 19 25N 99 11W
Chapultepec, Castillo de, *Méx.* **29 B2** 19 25N 99 10W
Charenton-le-Pont, *Paris* **5 C4** 48 49N 2 25 E
Charles-de-Gaulle, Aéroport, *Paris* **5 A5** 49 0N 2 33 E
Charles Lee Tinden Regional Park, *S.F.* **27 A3** 37 53N 122 14W
Charleston, *N.Y.* **22 D3** 40 32N 74 14W
Charlestown, *Bost.* **21 C3** 42 22N 71 4W
Charlottenburg, *Berl.* **7 A2** 52 31N 13 14 E
Charlottenburg, Schloss, *Berl.* **7 A2** 52 31N 13 18 E
Charlottenlund, *Købn.* **2 D10** 55 44N 12 35 E
Charlton, *Lon.* **4 C5** 51 29N 0 1 E
Charneca, *Lisb.* **8 F8** 38 47N 9 8W
Charneca, *Lisb.* **8 G7** 38 37N 9 12W
Chase Side, *Lon.* **4 B4** 51 39N 0 4W
Châteaufort, *Paris* **5 C2** 48 44N 2 5 E
Châtenay-Malabry, *Paris* **5 C3** 48 46N 2 16 E
Chatham, *Chic.* **26 C3** 41 45N 87 36W
Chatham, *N.Y.* **22 C2** 40 44N 74 23W
Châtillon, *Paris* **5 C3** 48 48N 2 17 E
Chatou, *Paris* **5 B2** 48 53N 2 9 E
Chatpur, *Calc.* **16 E6** 22 36N 88 22 E
Chatra, *Calc.* **16 D5** 22 45N 88 19 E
Chatswood, *Syd.* **19 A4** 33 47 S 151 11 E
Chauki, *Kar.* **17 G10** 24 55N 66 56 E
Chavarria, *Lima* **30 G8** 12 0 S 77 7W
Chavenay, *Paris* **5 B1** 48 51N 1 59 E
Chavenay-Villepreux, Aérodrôme de, *Paris* **5 B1** 48 50N 1 58 E
Chaville, *Paris* **5 C3** 48 48N 2 11 E
Che Kung Miu, *H.K.* **12 D6** 22 22N 114 10 E
Cheam, *Lon.* **4 C3** 51 21N 0 12W
Chelles, *Paris* **5 B5** 48 53N 2 35 E
Chelles, Canal de, *Paris* **5 B5** 48 51N 2 35 E
Chells-le-Pin, Aérodrome, *Paris* **5 B5** 48 53N 2 36 E
Chelmsford, *Bost.* **21 B1** 42 35N 71 20W
Chelobityevo, *Mos.* **11 D10** 55 54N 37 40 E
Chelsea, *Bost.* **21 C3** 42 23N 71 1W
Chelsea, *Lon.* **4 C3** 51 29N 0 10W
Chelsea, *Phil.* **24 B2** 39 51N 75 27W
Chelsfield Village, *Lon.* **4 C5** 51 21N 0 8 E
Cheltenham, *Phil.* **24 A4** 40 3N 75 6W
Chembur, *Bomb.* **16 G8** 19 3N 72 53 E
Chennevières, *Paris* **5 A2** 49 0N 2 6 E
Chennevières-sur-Marne, *Paris* **5 C5** 48 47N 2 31 E
Cheongdam, *Sŏul* **12 G8** 37 31N 127 2 E
Cheonho, *Sŏul* **12 G8** 37 32N 127 6 E
Cheops, *El Qâ.* **18 D4** 29 58N 31 8 E
Chepo, *Gzh.* **14 G9** 23 7N 113 23 E
Cherepkovo, *Mos.* **11 E8** 55 45N 37 21 E
Chernyovo, *Mos.* **11 D7** 55 50N 37 17 E
Cherry Hill, *Phil.* **24 B4** 39 54N 75 1W
Cherry L., *Melb.* **19 F5** 37 51 S 144 49 E
Cherryland, *S.F.* **27 B4** 37 40N 122 7W
Cherrywood, *Trto.* **20 C10** 43 51N 79 8W
Chertsey, *Lon.* **4 C2** 51 23N 0 29W
Cheryomushki, *Mos.* **11 E9** 55 40N 37 35 E
Chesaco Park, *Balt.* **25 B3** 39 18N 76 30W
Chesapeake B., *Balt.* **25 B4** 39 12N 76 22W
Cheshunt, *Lon.* **4 A4** 51 42N 0 0 E
Chess →, *Lon.* **4 B2** 51 38N 0 27W
Chessington, *Lon.* **4 C3** 51 21N 0 18W
Chessington Zoo, *Lon.* **4 C3** 51 20N 0 19W
Chester, *Phil.* **24 B2** 39 50N 75 23W
Chester Cr. →, *Phil.* **24 B2** 39 50N 75 21W
Chester Heights, *Phil.* **24 B2** 39 53N 75 27W
Chestnut, *Phil.* **24 A3** 40 4N 75 13W
Chestnut Hill, *Bost.* **21 D2** 42 19N 71 10W
Cheung Sha Wan, *H.K.* **12 D5** 22 20N 114 8 E
Cheverly, *Wash.* **25 D8** 38 55N 76 54W
Chevilly-Larue, *Paris* **5 C4** 48 46N 2 21 E
Chevreuse, *Paris* **5 C2** 48 42N 2 2 E
Chevry-Cossigny, *Paris* **5 C5** 48 43N 2 39 E
Chevy Chase, *Wash.* **25 D7** 38 59N 77 4W
Chevy Chase View, *Wash.* **25 C7** 39 0N 77 4W
Cheyney, *Phil.* **24 B1** 39 55N 75 31W
Chhalera Bangar, *Delhi* **16 B2** 28 33N 77 17 E
Chhinamor, *Calc.* **16 D5** 22 48N 88 17 E
Chhota Andai, *Kar.* **17 H11** 24 48N 66 59 E
Chia Keng, *Sing.* **15 F8** 1 21N 103 52 E
Chiaíano, *Nápl.* **9 H12** 40 53N 14 13 E
Chiaravalle Milanese, *Mil.* **9 E6** 45 24N 9 16 E
Chiawelo, *Jobg.* **18 F8** 26 17 S 27 51 E
Chicago, *Chic.* **26 B3** 41 52N 87 38W
Chicago, Univ. of, *Chic.* **26 C3** 41 47N 87 35W
Chicago Harbor, *Chic.* **26 B3** 41 52N 87 36W
Chicago Lawn, *Chic.* **26 C2** 41 47N 87 40W
Chicago-Midway Airport, *Chic.* **26 C2** 41 47N 87 45W
Chicago-O'Hare Int. Airport, *Chic.* **26 B1** 41 58N 87 53W
Chicago Ridge, *Chic.* **26 C2** 41 41N 87 46W
Chicago Sanitary and Ship Canal, *Chic.* **26 C2** 41 49N 87 45W
Chichinautzin, Cerro, *Méx.* **29 D3** 19 6N 99 8W
Chicot, *Mtrl.* **20 A2** 43 35N 73 56W
Chicot →, *Mtrl.* **20 A2** 43 34N 73 51W
Chienzui, *Gzh.* **14 F9** 23 12N 113 22 E
Chieri, *Tori.* **9 B3** 45 0N 7 49 E
Chigwell, *Lon.* **4 B5** 51 36N 0 6 E
Chigwell Row, *Lon.* **4 B5** 51 37N 0 7 E
Chik Sha, *H.K.* **12 E6** 22 17N 114 16 E
Chikumazawa, *Tōkyō* **13 B2** 35 49N 139 32 E
Childs Hill, *Lon.* **4 B3** 51 33N 0 12W
Chilla Saroda, *Delhi* **16 B2** 28 35N 77 18 E
Chillum, *Wash.* **25 D8** 38 57N 76 58W
Chilly-Mazarin, *Paris* **5 C3** 48 42N 2 17 E
Chimalhuacán, *Méx.* **29 B4** 19 25N 89 57 E
Chimalpa, *Méx.* **29 B2** 19 21N 99 19W
China, Tg., *Sing.* **15 G8** 1 14N 103 50 E
China Basin, *S.F.* **27 B2** 37 46N 122 22W
Chingford, *Lon.* **4 B5** 51 37N 0 0 E
Chingupota, *Calc.* **16 F5** 22 29N 88 14 E
Chipilly Woods, *Chic.* **26 A2** 42 8N 87 48W
Chipperfield, *Lon.* **4 A2** 51 42N 0 29W
Chipping Ongar, *Lon.* **4 A6** 51 41N 0 15 E
Chipstead, *Lon.* **4 D4** 51 17N 0 8W
Chirle, *Bomb.* **16 H9** 18 55N 73 2 E
Chirnside Park, *Melb.* **19 E8** 37 45 S 145 18 E
Chislehurst, *Lon.* **4 C5** 51 24N 0 6 E
Chislehurst West, *Lon.* **4 C5** 51 25N 0 3 E
Chiswick, *Lon.* **4 C3** 51 29N 0 16W
Chiswick House, *Lon.* **4 C3** 51 28N 0 15W
Chitlade Palace, *Bangk.* **15 B2** 13 45N 100 31 E
Chitose, *Tōkyō* **13 C2** 35 33N 139 37 E
Chiyoda-Ku, *Tōkyō* **13 B3** 35 41N 139 44 E
Chkalova, *Mos.* **11 F11** 55 39N 37 56 E
Choa Chu Kang, *Sing.* **15 F7** 1 22N 103 40 E
Choboty, *Mos.* **11 F8** 55 39N 37 21 E
Chodov u Prahy, *Pra.* **10 B3** 50 1N 14 30 E

36 Chōfu

Chōfu, Tōkyō 13 C2 35 38N 139 32 E
Choisel, Paris 5 C2 48 41N 2 1 E
Choisy-le-Roi, Paris 5 C4 48 46N 2 24 E
Chomedey, Mtrl. 20 A3 43 32N 73 45W
Chong Nonsi, Khlong →, Bangk. 15 B2 13 42N 100 32 E
Chong Pang, Sing. 15 F7 1 26N 103 49 E
Chongwen, Beij. 14 B3 39 52N 116 23 E
Chongwenmen, Beij. 14 B3 39 52N 116 22 E
Chorleywood, Lon. 4 B2 51 39N 0 29W
Chornaya →, Mos. 11 E12 55 41N 38 0 E
Chorrillos, Lima 30 H8 12 10 S 77 1W
Christianshavn, Købn. 2 D10 55 40N 12 35 E
Chrome, N.Y. 22 D3 40 34N 74 13W
Chrzanów, Wsaw. 10 E6 52 13N 20 53 E
Chuen Lung, H.K. 12 D5 22 23N 114 6 E
Chuk Kok, H.K. 12 D6 22 20N 114 15 E
Chulalongkon Univ., Bangk. 15 B2 13 44N 100 31 E
Chullora, Syd. 19 B3 33 54 S 151 5 E
Chunchura, Calc. 16 C6 22 53N 88 23 E
Chuō-Ku, Tōkyō 13 B3 35 40N 139 46 E
Church End, Lon. 4 B3 51 35N 0 11W
Chvaly, Pra. 10 B3 50 6N 14 35 E
Chye Kay, Sing. 15 F7 1 25N 103 49 E
Ciampino, Rome 9 G10 41 47N 12 36 E
Ciampino, Aeroporto di, Rome 9 G10 41 47N 12 35 E
Cicero, Chic. 26 B2 41 51N 87 44W
Cidade, I. da, Rio J. 31 B2 22 51 S 43 13W
Cidade de Deus, S. Pau. 31 E5 23 33 S 46 45W
Cidade Ipava, S. Pau. 31 F5 23 42 S 46 45W
Cidade Lider, S. Pau. 31 E7 23 33 S 46 27W
Cidade São Matheus, S. Pau. 31 E7 23 35 S 46 29W
Cidena, Kali →, Jak. 15 H9 6 9 S 106 48 E
Cilandak, Jak. 15 J9 6 17 S 106 47 E
Cilincing, Jak. 15 H10 6 6 S 106 54 E
Ciliwung →, Jak. 15 J10 6 6 S 106 47 E
Čimice, Pra. 10 B2 50 8N 14 25 E
Cinderella, Jobg. 18 F10 26 14 S 28 15 E
Cinderella Dam, Jobg. 18 F10 26 14 S 28 14 E
Cinecittà, Rome 9 F10 41 51N 12 34 E
Cinisello Bálsamo, Mil. 9 D6 45 33N 9 13 E
Cinkota, Bud. 10 J14 47 31N 19 14 E
Cinnaminson, Phil. 24 B5 39 59N 74 59W
Cipete, Jak. 15 J9 6 15 S 106 47 E
Cipresso, Tori. 9 B3 45 2N 7 48 E
Cisliano, Mil. 9 E4 45 26N 8 59 E
Città degli Studi, Mil. 9 E6 45 28N 9 12 E
Città del Vaticano, Rome 9 F9 41 54N 12 26 E
City I., N.Y. 23 B6 40 50N 73 47W
Ciudad Azteca, Méx. 29 A3 19 32N 99 1W
Ciudad Fin de Semana, Mdrd. 8 B3 40 26N 3 34W
Ciudad General Belgrano, B.A. 32 C3 34 43 S 58 33W
Ciudad Libertad, La Hab. 30 B2 23 5N 82 25W
Ciudad Lineál, Mdrd. 8 B3 40 26N 3 38W
Ciudad López Mateos, Méx. 29 A2 19 33N 99 16W
Ciudad Satélite, Méx. 29 A2 19 30N 99 13W
Ciudad Universitaria, Méx. 29 C2 19 9N 99 10W
Ciudadela, B.A. 32 B3 34 38 S 58 32W
Ciudadela, Parque de la, Barc. 8 D6 41 23N 2 11 E
Clairefontaine, Paris 5 D1 48 36N 1 54 E
Clamart, Paris 5 C3 48 48N 2 15 E
Clapham, Lon. 4 C4 51 27N 0 8W
Clapton, Lon. 4 B4 51 33N 0 3W
Clark, N.Y. 22 D3 40 38N 74 18W
Clarksboro, Phil. 24 C3 39 48N 75 13W
Claye-Souilly, Paris 5 B6 48 56N 2 41 E
Claygate, Lon. 4 C3 51 21N 0 19W
Clayhall, Lon. 4 B5 51 35N 0 3 E
Clayhill, Lon. 4 A4 51 40N 0 5W
Claymont, Phil. 24 C2 39 48N 75 27W
Claypole, B.A. 32 C4 34 48 S 58 20W
Clayton, Melb. 19 F7 37 55 S 145 7 E
Clearing, Chic. 26 C2 41 47N 87 45W
Clearwater, L.A. 28 C3 33 52N 118 10W
Clement, Sing. 15 G7 1 18N 103 46 E
Clementon, Phil. 24 C5 39 48N 74 59W
Clichy, Paris 5 B3 48 54N 2 18 E
Clichy-sous-Bois, Paris 5 B5 48 54N 2 32 E
Cliffside, Trto. 20 D9 43 44N 79 14W
Cliffside Park, N.Y. 22 C5 40 49N 73 59W
Clifton, Bost. 21 C4 42 29N 70 52W
Clifton, Kar. 17 H11 24 48N 67 1 E
Clifton, N.Y. 22 D4 40 37N 74 4W
Clifton, N.Y. 22 B4 40 51N 74 7W
Clifton, L., Balt. 25 B3 39 19N 76 35W
Clifton Heights, Phil. 24 B3 39 55N 75 17W
Clifton Park, Balt. 25 A3 39 20N 76 35W
Clontarf, Syd. 19 A4 33 48 S 151 16 E
Closter, N.Y. 22 B5 40 58N 73 57W
Clovelly, Syd. 19 B4 33 54 S 151 15 E
Cobbin's Brook →, Lon. 4 A5 51 40N 0 0 E
Cobbs Cr. →, Phil. 24 B3 39 58N 75 18W
Cobham, Lon. 4 D2 51 19N 0 23W
Cobras, I. das, Rio J. 31 B3 22 53 S 43 9W
Coburg, Melb. 19 E7 37 44 S 144 56 E
Cochecito, Car. 30 E5 10 26N 66 55W
Cochichewick, L., Bost. 21 A3 42 42N 71 5W
Cochituate, Bost. 21 C1 42 20N 71 21W
Cochituate, L., Bost. 21 D1 42 16N 71 21W
Cockfosters, Lon. 4 B4 51 39N 0 8W
Cocota, Rio J. 31 A2 22 48 S 43 11W
Coelho da Rocha, Rio J. 31 A1 22 46 S 43 21W
Cœuilly, Paris 5 C5 48 48N 2 32 E
Coignières, Paris 5 C1 48 44N 1 55 E
Coina, Lisb. 8 G8 38 39N 9 5W
Cojimar, La Hab. 30 B3 23 9N 82 17W
Cojimar →, La Hab. 30 B3 23 9N 82 17W
Cojimar, Boca de, La Hab. 30 A3 23 10N 82 17W
Coker, Lagos 18 B2 6 28N 7 20 E
Colaba, Bomb. 16 H7 18 53N 72 48 E
Colaba Pt., Bomb. 16 H7 18 53N 72 48 E
Cold Spring Harbor, N.Y. 23 B8 40 52N 73 27W
Cold Spring Terrace, N.Y. 23 C8 40 49N 73 25W
Coleraine, Trto. 20 D6 43 49N 79 40W
Colindale, Lon. 4 B3 51 35N 0 15W
Collazo, La Hab. 30 B2 23 2N 82 21W
College Park, Wash. 25 D8 38 59N 76 55W
College Point, N.Y. 23 C5 40 47N 73 50W
Collégien, Paris 5 B6 48 50N 2 41 E
Collegno, Tori. 9 B2 45 5N 7 34 E
Collier Row, Lon. 4 B5 51 35N 0 9 E
Colliers Wood, Lon. 4 C3 51 24N 0 10W
Collingdale, Phil. 24 B3 39 54N 75 17W
Collingswood, Phil. 24 B4 39 55N 75 4W
Collinsville, Bost. 21 A1 42 40N 71 23W
Collinsville, N.Y. 22 C2 40 48N 74 26W
Colma, S.F. 27 B2 37 40N 122 27W
Colma Cr. →, S.F. 27 C2 37 38N 122 23W
Colney Hatch, Lon. 4 B4 51 36N 0 9W
Cologno Monzese, Mil. 9 D6 45 31N 9 16 E
Colombes, Paris 5 B3 48 55N 2 15 E
Colonia, N.Y. 22 D3 40 35N 74 18W
Colônia, S. Pau. 31 E7 23 33 S 46 27W
Colonia Güell, Barc. 8 D5 41 21N 2 2 E
Colonia Puerta de Hierro, Mdrd. 8 B2 40 27N 3 43W
Colonial Manor, Phil. 24 B4 39 51N 75 9W
Colorado →, Méx. 29 B4 19 23N 89 58 E
Colosseo, Rome 9 F9 41 53N 12 29 E
Columbia, Balt. 25 B1 39 12N 76 50W
Columbia Hills, Balt. 25 B1 39 14N 76 51W
Columbia Univ., N.Y. 22 C5 40 48N 73 58W
Colwyn, Phil. 24 B3 39 54N 75 14W
Combault, Paris 5 C5 48 48N 2 37 E
Combs-la-Ville, Paris 5 D5 48 39N 2 33 E
Comércio, Praça do, Lisb. 8 F8 38 41N 9 9W
Commack, N.Y. 23 B9 40 50N 73 19W
Commerce, L.A. 28 B4 34 0N 118 9W
Como, Syd. 19 C3 34 0 S 151 4 E
Compans, Paris 5 A6 48 59N 2 39 E
Compton, L.A. 28 C3 33 53N 118 14W
Conceição, I. da, Rio J. 31 B3 22 52 S 43 6W
Concepcion, Manila 15 D4 14 39N 121 6 E
Conchali, Stgo 30 J11 33 22 S 70 39W
Concord, Bost. 21 C1 42 27N 71 20W
Concord, S.F. 27 A4 37 58N 122 3W
Concord, Syd. 19 B3 33 52 S 151 6 E
Concord, Trto. 20 D8 43 48N 79 29W
Concordville, Phil. 24 B1 39 53N 75 31W
Concorezzo, Mil. 9 D6 45 35N 9 19 E
Condécourt, Paris 5 A1 49 2N 1 56 E
Coney Island, N.Y. 22 D4 40 34N 74 0W
Conflans-Ste.-Honorine, Paris 5 B2 48 59N 2 5 E
Congo, S. Pau. 31 D5 23 27 S 46 42W
Congonhas, Aéroporto, S. Pau. 31 E6 23 38 S 46 39W
Conshohocken, Phil. 24 A3 40 4N 75 18W
Contadero, Méx. 29 B2 19 20N 99 17W
Convento de Valverde, Mdrd. 8 A2 40 30N 3 40W
Coogee, Syd. 19 B4 33 55 S 151 16 E
Cooksville, Trto. 20 E7 43 35N 79 38W
Cooper →, Phil. 24 B4 39 57N 75 6W
Copacabana, Rio J. 31 B2 22 58 S 43 11W
Copenhagen = København, Købn. 2 D9 55 40N 12 26 E
Copiague, N.Y. 23 D8 40 39N 73 23W
Coral Hills, Wash. 25 D8 38 51N 76 55W
Corbeil-Essonnes, Paris 5 D4 48 36N 2 29 E
Corbets Tey, Lon. 4 B6 51 32N 0 15 E
Corbiglia, Tori. 9 B1 45 3N 7 29 E
Corcovado, Rio J. 31 B2 22 57 S 43 12W
Cordon, Paris 5 D6 48 39N 2 41 E
Córdova, Tori. 9 B3 45 5N 7 48 E
Cordovil, Rio J. 31 A2 22 49 S 43 18W
Cormano, Mil. 9 D6 45 32N 9 10 E
Cormeilles-en-Parisis, Paris 5 B3 48 58N 2 11 E
Cornaredo, Mil. 9 D5 45 30N 9 1 E
Cornaya →, Len. 11 B5 59 53N 30 35 E
Cornellá, Barc. 8 D5 41 21N 2 4 E
Cornwells Heights, Phil. 24 A5 40 4N 74 57W
Coróglio, Nápl. 9 J12 40 48N 14 10 E
Coronation Memorial, Delhi 16 A2 28 42N 77 12 E
Córsico, Mil. 9 E5 45 25N 9 6 E
Corte Madera, S.F. 27 A1 37 55N 122 30W
Corte Madera →, S.F. 27 A1 37 55N 122 30W
Corviale, Rome 9 F9 41 51N 12 25 E
Cos Cob, N.Y. 23 A7 41 1N 73 36W
Cossigny, Paris 5 C6 48 43N 2 40 E
Cossipore, Calc. 16 E6 22 37N 88 22 E
Cotao, Lisb. 8 F7 38 45N 9 17W
Côte St.-Luc, Mtrl. 20 B4 43 28N 73 39W
Cotorro, La Hab. 30 B3 23 2N 82 15W
Cotunduba, I. de, Rio J. 31 B3 22 57 S 43 9W
Coubert, Paris 5 C6 48 40N 2 41 E
Coubron, Paris 5 B5 48 54N 2 34 E
Coulsdon, Lon. 4 D4 51 18N 0 7W
Countryside, Chic. 26 C1 41 47N 87 52W
Courbevoie, Paris 5 B3 48 53N 2 14 E
Courcouronnes, Paris 5 D4 48 37N 2 24 E
Courdimanche, Paris 5 A1 49 2N 2 0 E
Courcelle, Paris 5 C2 48 43N 2 7 E
Couros →, S. Pau. 31 F6 23 37 S 46 34W
Courtry, Paris 5 B5 48 55N 2 35 E
Cousino, Parque, Stgo 30 J11 33 27 S 70 40W
Cove Neck, N.Y. 23 B8 40 52N 73 29W
Cowley, Lon. 4 B2 51 31N 0 28W
Coyoacan, Méx. 29 B3 19 21N 99 9W
Coyote Cr. →, S.F. 27 D4 37 28N 122 4W
Coyote Hills Regional Park, S.F. 27 C4 37 32N 122 7W
Coyote Hills Slough, S.F. 27 C4 37 33N 122 7W
Coyote Pt., S.F. 27 C3 37 35N 122 18W
Coyote Ridge, S.F. 27 A1 37 51N 122 33W
Craighall Park, Jobg. 18 E9 26 7 S 28 1 E
Crane →, Lon. 4 C2 51 29N 0 29W
Cranford, Lon. 4 C2 51 29N 0 25W
Cranford, N.Y. 22 D3 40 39N 74 19W
Cranham, Lon. 4 B6 51 33N 0 16 E
Cray →, Lon. 4 C5 51 28N 0 8 E
Crayford, Lon. 4 C6 51 27N 0 11 E
Creekmouth, Lon. 4 B5 51 30N 0 6 E
Crerskill, N.Y. 22 B5 40 56N 73 57W
Crescenzago, Mil. 9 D6 45 30N 9 14 E
Crespières, Paris 5 B1 48 52N 1 55 E
Cressely, Paris 5 C2 48 44N 2 6 E
Cresslawn, Jobg. 18 E10 26 6 S 28 13 E
Crestwood, Chic. 26 D2 41 38N 87 43W
Creteil, Paris 5 C4 48 47N 2 27 E
Cricklewood, Lon. 4 B3 51 33N 0 13W
Crispano, Nápl. 9 H12 40 57N 14 17 E
Cristo Redebro, Monumento do, Rio J. 31 B2 22 56 S 43 12W
Crockenhill, Lon. 4 C5 51 22N 0 9 E
Croissy-Beaubourg, Paris 5 C5 48 49N 2 39 E
Croissy-sur-Seine, Paris 5 B2 48 52N 2 8 E
Cronenberg, Ruhr 6 C4 51 12N 7 9 E
Crosby, Jobg. 18 F8 26 11 S 27 59 E
Crosne, Paris 5 C4 48 43N 2 27 E
Cross I., Bomb. 16 H8 18 56N 72 51 E
Crouch End, Lon. 4 B4 51 34N 0 7W
Croud →, Paris 5 B4 48 57N 2 24 E
Crown Gardens, Jobg. 18 F9 26 15 S 28 0 E
Crown Mines, Jobg. 18 F8 26 12 S 27 57 E
Crown Village, N.Y. 23 C8 40 40N 73 26W
Crows Nest, Syd. 19 A4 33 49 S 151 12 E
Croxley Green, Lon. 4 B2 51 38N 0 26W
Croydon, Lon. 4 C4 51 22N 0 5W
Croydon, Melb. 19 E8 37 48 S 145 17 E
Croydon, Phil. 24 A5 40 5N 74 54W
Croydon North, Melb. 19 E8 37 46 S 145 16 E
Cruz de Pau, Lisb. 8 G8 38 37N 9 7W
Crystal Palace, Lon. 4 C4 51 25N 0 4W
Crystal Springs, S.F. 27 C2 37 31N 122 20W
Csepel, Bud. 10 K13 47 25N 19 4 E
Csepelsziget, Bud. 10 K13 47 25N 19 4 E
Csillaghegy, Bud. 10 J13 47 35N 19 2 E
Csillagtelep, Bud. 10 K13 47 24N 19 5 E
Cski-hegyek, Bud. 10 K12 47 30N 18 57 E
Csömör, Bud. 10 J14 47 33N 19 14 E
Cuajimalpa, Méx. 29 B2 19 21N 99 17W
Cuatro Vientos, Mdrd. 8 B2 40 22N 3 47W
Cuautepec de Madero, Méx. 29 A3 19 32N 99 8W
Cuautepec El Alto, Méx. 29 A3 19 33N 99 7W
Cuautzin, Cerro, Méx. 29 D3 19 10N 99 8W
Cubao, Manila 15 D4 14 37N 121 3 E
Cubas →, S. Pau. 31 D6 23 28 S 46 31W
Cubuklu, Ist. 17 A3 41 5N 29 4 E
Cudham, Lon. 4 D5 51 19N 0 4 E
Cuffley, Lon. 4 A4 51 42N 0 6W
Cuicuilco, Pirámido de, Méx. 29 C2 19 17N 99 10W
Culembeeck, Jobg. 18 E7 26 9 S 27 49 E
Culiculi, Manila 15 D4 14 33N 121 0 E
Cull Creek, S.F. 27 B4 37 45N 122 2W
Culver City, L.A. 28 B2 34 1N 118 24W
Culverstone Green, Lon. 4 C7 51 20N 0 20 E
Cumbre El Tabo, Car. 30 D5 10 33N 66 56W
Cumbres de Vallecas, Mdrd. 8 B3 40 20N 3 33W
Cunhas, S. Pau. 31 E7 23 34 S 46 23W
Cupecé, S. Pau. 31 E5 23 39 S 46 40W
Cupece →, S. Pau. 31 E6 23 37 S 46 42W
Curtis B., Balt. 25 B3 39 13N 76 34W
Curtis Cr. →, Balt. 25 B3 39 12N 76 34W
Cusago, Mil. 9 E5 45 26N 9 1 E
Cusano Milanese, Mil. 9 D6 45 33N 9 11 E
Çuvuşabaşi →, Ist. 17 A2 40 58N 28 51 E
Cyrildene, Jobg. 18 F9 26 10 S 28 6 E
Czernrakow, Wsaw. 10 E7 52 11N 21 3 E
Czyste, Wsaw. 10 E6 52 13N 20 57 E

D

Da Yunhe →, Tianj. 14 D5 39 19N 117 10 E
Dabizhuang, Tianj. 14 D6 39 11N 117 16 E
Ďáblice, Pra. 10 B2 50 8N 14 29 E
Dabsibri, Sŏul 12 G8 37 33N 127 2 E
Dachang, Shang. 14 J11 31 17N 121 24 E
Dachau, Mün. 7 F9 48 15N 11 27 E
Dachau-Ost, Mün. 7 F9 48 15N 11 27 E
Dachauer Moos, Mün. 7 F9 48 13N 11 27 E
Daebang, Sŏul 12 G7 37 30N 126 55 E
Daechi, Sŏul 12 G8 37 30N 127 2 E
Dagenham, Lon. 4 B5 51 32N 0 8 E
Daglfing, Mün. 7 G10 48 8N 11 39 E
Dahirpur, Delhi 16 A2 28 43N 77 11 E
Dahlem, Berl. 7 B2 52 27N 13 16 E
Dahlerau, Ruhr 6 C5 51 13N 7 18 E
Dahlwitz-Hoppegarten, Berl. 7 A5 52 30N 13 41 E
Dahongmen, Beij. 14 C3 39 48N 116 21 E
Daiman, Tōkyō 13 A3 35 53N 139 44 E
Daitō, Ōsaka 12 B4 34 42N 135 38 E
Dajiaoting, Beij. 14 B3 39 51N 116 27 E
Dajingcun, Beij. 14 B2 39 50N 116 13 E
Dakhnoye, Len. 11 C3 59 49N 30 15 E
Dalar, Bomb. 16 G7 19 0N 72 49 E
Dalejský →, Pra. 10 B2 50 2N 14 24 E
Dalibia, Gzh. 14 G7 23 2N 113 6 E
Dallgow, Berl. 7 A1 52 32N 13 5 E
Dalston, Lon. 4 B4 51 32N 0 4W
Dalview, Jobg. 18 F11 26 14 S 28 20 E
Daly City, S.F. 27 B2 37 42N 122 27W
Damaia, Lisb. 8 F7 38 44N 9 12W
Dämeritzsee, Berl. 7 B5 52 34N 13 43 E
Damiette, Paris 5 C2 48 41N 2 7 E
Dampierre, Paris 5 C1 48 42N 1 59 E
Dan Neramit, Bangk. 15 B2 13 48N 100 34 E
Dan Ryan Woods, Chic. 26 C2 41 44N 87 40W
Dandenong, Mt., Melb. 19 E9 37 49 S 145 21 E
Danderyd, Stock. 3 D11 59 24N 18 1 E
Danforth, Trto. 20 D9 43 43N 79 16W
Daniels, Balt. 25 B2 39 19N 76 49W
Danvers, Bost. 21 B4 42 34N 70 56W
Dapharpur, Calc. 16 E5 22 38N 88 14 E
Darangan, Manila 15 E5 14 29N 121 10 E
Darave, Bomb. 16 G9 19 1N 73 1 E
Darby, Phil. 24 B3 39 55N 75 15W
Darby Cr. →, Phil. 24 B3 39 54N 75 15W
Darent →, Lon. 4 C6 51 21N 0 12 E
Darling, Phil. 24 B2 39 54N 75 28W
Darlington Corners, Phil. 24 B1 39 55N 75 34W
Dartford, Lon. 4 C6 51 26N 0 13 E
Dashi, Gzh. 14 G8 23 1N 113 17 E
Dashimae, Tōkyō 13 B3 35 46N 139 46 E
Datteln, Ruhr 6 A6 51 39N 7 20 E
Datteln-Hamm Kanal, Ruhr 6 A6 51 38N 7 28 E
Datun, Beij. 14 A3 40 0N 116 23 E
Dauko, Calc. 16 E5 22 31N 88 12 E
Daulatpur, Delhi 16 A1 28 44N 77 6 E
Davenport, Bost. 21 B4 42 33N 70 54W
Daveyton, Jobg. 18 E11 26 9 S 28 24 E
Davidkovo, Mos. 11 E8 55 43N 37 29 E
David's I., N.Y. 23 C6 40 53N 73 46W
Davidson, Mt., S.F. 27 B2 37 44N 122 27W
Davron, Paris 5 B1 48 52N 1 56 E
Dāvudiyeh, Tehr. 17 C5 35 45N 51 25 E
Dawidy, Wsaw. 10 F6 52 8N 20 58 E
Dayap, Manila 15 D4 14 35N 121 4 E
Dayuange, Gzh. 14 F7 23 11N 113 7 E
Dead Run →, Balt. 25 B2 39 18N 76 41W
Dedham, Bost. 21 D2 42 14N 71 10W
Dee Why, Syd. 19 A4 33 46 S 151 17 E
Deer I., Bost. 21 C4 42 21N 70 57W
Deer Park, N.Y. 23 C9 40 46N 73 19W
Degerby, Stock. 3 D9 59 22N 17 42 E
Degermossa, Hels. 3 B6 60 17N 25 12 E
Degunino, Mos. 11 D9 55 52N 37 33 E
Deisenhofen, Mün. 7 G10 48 0N 11 35 E
Dejvice, Pra. 10 B2 50 6N 14 23 E
Dekabristov, Os., Len. 11 B3 59 56N 30 15 E
Del Viso, B.A. 32 A2 34 27 S 58 47W
Delanco, Phil. 24 A5 40 2N 74 57W
Delaware →, Phil. 24 A4 40 1N 75 0W
Delbruch, Ruhr 6 B4 51 22N 7 8 E
Delhi, Delhi 16 B2 28 39N 77 13 E
Delhi Cantonment, Delhi 16 B1 28 35N 77 7 E
Delhi Univ., Delhi 16 A2 28 41N 77 12 E
Dellwig, Ruhr 6 B3 51 29N 6 55 E
Delran, Phil. 24 A5 40 0N 74 57W
Delville, Jobg. 18 F10 26 11 S 28 13 E
Demarest, N.Y. 22 B5 40 57N 73 57W
Denham, Lon. 4 B1 51 35N 0 30W
Denham Green, Lon. 4 B2 51 34N 0 29W
Denniston Cr. →, S.F. 27 C2 37 30N 122 29W
Dentonia Park, Trto. 20 D9 43 42N 79 17W
Denville, N.Y. 22 B2 40 53N 74 28W
Deodoro, Rio J. 31 B1 22 50 S 43 21W
Depgsu Palace, Sŏul 12 G7 37 34N 126 58 E
Deptford, Lon. 4 C4 51 28N 0 1W
Der Sarai, Delhi 16 B2 28 33N 77 10 E
Des Plaines, Chic. 26 A1 42 2N 87 54W
Des Plaines →, Chic. 26 B1 41 48N 87 49W
Deshengmen, Beij. 14 B3 39 56N 116 21 E
Desierto de los Leones, Parque Nacional, Méx. 29 C2 19 18N 99 18W
Desio, Mil. 9 D6 45 36N 9 12 E
Deuil-la-Barre, Paris 5 B3 48 58N 2 19 E
Deulpur, Calc. 16 E5 22 36N 88 10 E
Deungchon, Sŏul 12 G7 37 33N 126 52 E
Deutsch-Wagram, Wien 10 G11 48 17N 16 33 E
Deutsche Oper, Berl. 7 A2 52 30N 13 19 E
Deutscher Museum, Mün. 7 G10 48 7N 11 35 E
Deux-Montagnes, Mtrl. 20 A2 43 32N 73 53W
Deux Montagnes, L. des, Mtrl. 20 B2 43 27N 73 59W
Devault, Phil. 24 A1 40 4N 75 32W
Dháfni, Ath. 8 J11 37 55N 23 44 E
Dhakuria, Calc. 16 E6 22 30N 88 22 E
Dhakuria L., Calc. 16 E6 22 30N 88 21 E
Dhamarakia, Ath. 8 J10 37 58N 23 39 E
Dharava, Bomb. 16 G8 19 1N 72 51 E
Dhrapersón, Ath. 8 J10 37 56N 23 37 E
Dhutumkhar, Bomb. 16 H9 18 54N 73 1 E
Dia Deva, Bomb. 16 H8 18 57N 72 53 E
Diadema, S. Pau. 31 F6 23 41 S 46 37W
Diamante, B.A. 32 C4 34 41 S 58 25W
Diamond Cr. →, Melb. 19 E7 37 44 S 145 9 E
Diamond Creek, Melb. 19 E8 37 40 S 145 10 E
Didaowai, Tianj. 14 E6 39 8N 117 12 E
Diepensiepen, Ruhr 6 C3 51 14N 6 58 E
Diepkloof, Jobg. 18 F8 26 14 S 27 57 E
Diessem, Ruhr 6 C1 51 19N 6 34 E
Difficult Run →, Wash. 25 D6 38 55N 77 18W
Digla, W. →, El Qâ. 18 D6 29 58N 31 22 E
Digra, Calc. 16 D5 22 49N 88 19 E
Dikemark, Oslo 2 C2 59 48N 10 22 E
Dilerpur, Calc. 16 C5 22 51N 88 10 E
Dinslaken, Ruhr 6 A2 51 33N 6 43 E
Dinslakener Bruch, Ruhr 6 A2 51 34N 6 44 E
Dinwiddie, Jobg. 18 F9 26 16 S 28 9 E
Diósd, Bud. 10 K12 47 24N 18 57 E
Dirnismaning, Mün. 7 F10 48 13N 11 38 E
Disappointment, Mt., L.A. 28 A4 34 15N 118 7W
Discovery, Jobg. 18 E8 26 8 S 27 54 E
Disteln, Ruhr 6 A4 51 36N 7 9 E
District Heights, Wash. 25 D8 38 51N 76 53W
Ditan Gongyuan, Beij. 14 B3 39 56N 116 23 E
Dix Hills, N.Y. 23 C8 40 48N 73 21W
Dixmoor, Chic. 26 D2 41 37N 87 40W
Diyala →, Bagd. 17 F9 33 13N 44 30 E
Djakarta = Jakarta, Jak. 15 H10 6 9 S 106 52 E
Djursholm, Stock. 3 D11 59 24N 18 5 E
Do Bong, Sŏul 12 G8 37 37N 127 1 E
Dobbs, N.Y. 23 A5 41 1N 73 52W
Döberitz, Berl. 7 A1 52 32N 13 3 E
Döbling, Wien 10 G10 48 14N 16 20 E
Dobong, Sŏul 12 G8 37 39N 127 2 E
Dobong San, Sŏul 12 F8 37 40N 127 0 E
Dōbrowa, Wsaw. 10 E6 52 19N 20 52 E
Doddinghurst, Lon. 4 A6 51 40N 0 18 E
Dodger Stadium, L.A. 28 B3 34 4N 118 14W
Dogsan, Sŏul 12 H7 37 28N 126 54 E
Doirone, Tori. 9 B2 45 3N 7 32 E
Dōjō, Ōsaka 12 A2 34 51N 135 14 E
Dōjō, Tōkyō 13 A2 35 51N 139 37 E
Dollard-des-Ormeaux, Mtrl. 20 B3 43 29N 73 49W
Dollis Hill, Lon. 4 B3 51 33N 0 13W
Dolni, Pra. 10 B3 50 3N 14 33 E
Dolni Chabry, Pra. 10 B2 50 8N 14 26 E
Dolni Počernice, Pra. 10 B3 50 5N 14 34 E
Dolton, Chic. 26 D3 41 37N 87 35W
Domont, Paris 5 A3 49 2N 2 19 E
Don Bosco, B.A. 32 C5 34 42 S 58 17W
Don Mills, Trto. 20 D8 43 44N 79 21W
Don Pedro II, Parque, S. Pau. 31 E6 23 33 S 46 36W
Don Torcuato, B.A. 32 A3 34 29 S 58 38W
Donau →, Bud. 10 J13 47 33N 19 4 E
Donau-Oder Kanal, Wien 10 G11 48 12N 16 32 E
Donaufeld, Wien 10 G10 48 15N 16 24 E
Donaukanal, Wien 10 G10 48 13N 16 27 E
Donaupark, Wien 10 G10 48 14N 16 24 E
Donaustadt, Wien 10 G10 48 13N 16 29 E
Doncaster, Melb. 19 E7 37 47 S 145 8 E
Doncaster East, Melb. 19 E7 37 46 S 145 8 E
Dong Dae Mun, Sŏul 12 G8 37 34N 127 2 E
Dong Jag, Sŏul 12 G7 37 30N 126 56 E
Dongala Forest Reserve, Melb. 19 F9 37 50 S 145 20 E
Dongan Hills, N.Y. 22 D4 40 35N 74 5W
Dongbinggo, Sŏul 12 G7 37 31N 126 58 E
Dongcheng, Beij. 14 B3 39 54N 116 23 E
Dongfeng Nongchang, Beij. 14 B3 39 57N 116 28 E
Dongjiao, Gzh. 14 G8 23 5N 113 12 E
Dongjuzi, Tianj. 14 E6 39 7N 117 14 E
Dongkou, Shang. 14 J12 31 17N 121 33 E
Dongmenwai, Tianj. 14 E6 39 8N 117 11 E
Dongri, Bomb. 16 H8 18 57N 72 50 E
Dongwuyuan, Beij. 14 B2 39 55N 116 18 E
Dongzhimen, Beij. 14 B3 39 55N 116 25 E
Donvale, Melb. 19 E8 37 47 S 145 11 E
Doonside, Syd. 19 A2 33 46 S 150 51 E
Doornfontein, Jobg. 18 F9 26 11 S 28 3 E
Dōra, Baghd. 17 F8 33 15N 44 25 E
Dora Riparia →, Tori. 9 B2 45 4N 7 38 E
Dorchester, Bost. 21 D3 42 17N 71 4W
Dorchester B., Bost. 21 D3 42 18N 71 1W
Dorchester Heights Nat. Hist. Site, Bost. 21 D3 42 19N 71 2W
Dorion, Mtrl. 20 B1 43 23N 74 1W
Dornach, Mün. 7 G11 48 9N 11 41 E
Dornap, Ruhr 6 C4 51 15N 7 3 E
Dornbach, Wien 10 G9 48 13N 16 18 E
Dorsey Run →, Balt. 25 B2 39 11N 76 47W
Dorstfeld, Ruhr 6 A6 51 30N 7 26 E
Dortmund, Ruhr 6 A6 51 30N 7 28 E
Dorval, Mtrl. 20 B3 43 26N 73 45W
Dorval, Aéroport de, Mtrl. 20 B3 43 28N 73 44W
Dos Rios, Méx. 29 B1 19 22N 99 20W
Doshan Tappeh Airport, Tehr. 17 C5 35 41N 51 28 E
Dotmund-Ems Kanal, Ruhr 6 A6 51 35N 7 24 E
Double B., Syd. 19 B4 33 52 S 151 15 E
Douglas Park, Chic. 26 B2 41 51N 87 42W
Douglaston, N.Y. 23 C6 40 46N 73 44W
Dove Elbe →, Hbg. 7 E8 53 28N 10 7 E
Dover, Bost. 21 D2 42 14N 71 16W
Dover Heights, Syd. 19 B4 33 52 S 151 16 E
Dowlatābād, Tehr. 17 D5 35 38N 51 27 E
Downe, Lon. 4 C5 51 20N 0 3 E
Downey, L.A. 28 C4 33 56N 118 9W
Downsview, Trto. 20 D7 43 43N 79 30W
Downsview Dells Park, Trto. 20 D7 43 44N 79 30W
Dracut, Bost. 21 A2 42 40N 71 17W
Dragør, Købn. 2 E10 55 35N 12 38 E
Drancy, Paris 5 B4 48 55N 2 26 E
Dranesville, Wash. 25 C5 39 0N 77 20W
Draveil, Paris 5 C4 48 41N 2 23 E
Drayton Green, Lon. 4 B3 51 30N 0 19W
Dreilinden, Berl. 7 B2 52 24N 13 10 E
Dresher, Phil. 24 A4 40 9N 75 9W
Drewnica, Wsaw. 10 E7 52 18N 21 6 E
Drexel Hill, Phil. 24 B3 39 56N 75 18W
Drexel Inst. of Technology, Phil. 24 B3 39 57N 75 11W
Drigh Road, Kar. 17 G11 24 52N 67 7 E
Drogden, Købn. 2 E11 55 37N 12 42 E
Drottningholm, Stock. 3 E10 59 19N 17 53 E
Druento, Tori. 9 B2 45 8N 7 34 E
Druid Hill Park, Balt. 25 B3 39 19N 76 38W
Druid Lake, Balt. 25 B3 39 19N 76 38W
Drummoyne, Syd. 19 B3 33 51 S 151 8 E
Druzhba, Mos. 11 D10 55 53N 37 44 E
Duarte, L.A. 28 B5 34 8N 117 57W
Dubeč, Pra. 10 B3 50 3N 14 35 E
Dubi Bheri, Calc. 16 E5 22 52N 88 16 E
Duffryn Mawr, Phil. 24 A2 40 2N 75 27W
Dugnano, Mil. 9 D6 45 33N 9 11 E
Dugny, Paris 5 B4 48 57N 2 24 E
Duiha, Calc. 16 E5 22 34N 88 15 E
Duisburg, Ruhr 6 B2 51 26N 6 45 E
Dulāb, Tehr. 17 D5 35 39N 51 27 E
Dulworthtown, Phil. 24 B1 39 54N 75 33W
Dum Dum, Calc. 16 E6 22 38N 88 25 E
Dum Dum Int. Airport, Calc. 16 E6 22 38N 88 26 E
Dumbarton Pt., S.F. 27 D4 37 29N 122 6W
Dumjor, Calc. 16 E5 22 37N 88 13 E
Dumont, N.Y. 22 B5 40 56N 73 59W
Dümpten, Ruhr 6 B3 51 27N 6 54 E
Duna →, Bud. 10 J13 47 33N 19 4 E
Dunbarton, Trto. 20 C10 43 50N 79 6W
Dundalk, Balt. 25 B3 39 17N 76 31W
Dundas, Syd. 19 A3 33 47 S 151 3 E
Dunearn, Sing. 15 G7 1 19N 103 49 E
Dunellen, N.Y. 22 D2 40 35N 74 26W
Dunn Loring, Wash. 25 D6 38 54N 77 13W
Dunning, Chic. 26 B2 41 56N 87 48W
Dunton Green, Lon. 4 D6 51 17N 0 11 E
Dunvegan, Jobg. 18 E9 26 9 S 28 8 E
Duomo, Mil. 9 E6 45 28N 9 11 E
Duomo, Nápl. 9 H12 40 51N 14 15 E
Duomo, Tori. 9 B3 45 4N 7 45 E
Duque de Caxias, Rio J. 31 A2 22 46 S 43 18W
Durban Roodepoort Deep Gold Mines, Jobg. 18 F8 26 11 S 27 52 E
Durchholz, Ruhr 6 B5 51 23N 7 18 E
Düssel →, Ruhr 6 C3 51 13N 6 58 E
Düsseldorf, Ruhr 6 C2 51 13N 6 46 E
Düsseldorf-Lohausen, Flughafen, Ruhr 6 C2 51 17N 6 45 E
Duvenstedt, Hbg. 7 C8 53 42N 10 6 E
Duvenstedter Brook, Hbg. 7 C8 53 43N 10 8 E
Duvernay, Mtrl. 20 A3 43 35N 73 40W
Dyakovo, Mos. 11 E9 55 40N 37 39 E
Dyviksudd, Stock. 3 E13 59 11N 18 23 E
Dzerzhinskiy, Mos. 11 F11 55 38N 37 51 E
Dzerzhinskiy, Mos. 11 E9 55 47N 37 37 E
Dzerzhinskiy Park, Mos. 11 E9 55 50N 37 37 E

E

Eagle Rock, L.A. 28 B3 34 8N 118 12 E
Ealing, Lon. 4 B3 51 30N 0 18W
Earls Court, Lon. 4 C3 51 29N 0 11W
Earlsfield, Lon. 4 C3 51 26N 0 10W
Earlwood, Syd. 19 B3 33 55 S 151 8 E
East Acton, Bost. 21 C1 42 28N 71 24W
East Acton, Lon. 4 B3 51 30N 0 14W
East Arlington, Wash. 25 D7 38 51N 77 4W
East Atlantic Beach, N.Y. 23 D6 40 35N 73 43W
East B., N.Y. 23 D7 40 38N 73 32W
East Barnet, Lon. 4 B4 51 38N 0 9W
East Bedfont, Lon. 4 C2 51 26N 0 28W
East Billerica, Bost. 21 B2 42 35N 71 13W
East Boston, Bost. 21 C3 42 22N 71 1W
East Braintree, Bost. 21 D4 42 13N 70 58W
East Chicago, Chic. 26 D4 41 38N 87 26W
East Don →, Trto. 20 D8 43 48N 79 25W
East Dulwich, Lon. 4 C4 51 26N 0 4W
East Elmhurst, N.Y. 23 C5 40 45N 73 52W
East Farmingdale, N.Y. 23 C8 40 44N 73 25W
East Finchley, Lon. 4 B3 51 35N 0 10W
East Half Hollow Hills, N.Y. 23 C9 40 47N 73 19W
East Ham, Lon. 4 B5 51 32N 0 3 E
East Hanover, N.Y. 22 C2 40 49N 74 21W
East Hills, N.Y. 23 C7 40 47N 73 37W
East Hills, Syd. 19 B2 33 57 S 150 59 E
East Holliston, Bost. 21 D1 42 12N 71 25W
East Horsley, Lon. 4 D2 51 16N 0 25W
East Humber →, Trto. 20 D7 43 47N 79 35W
East Huntington, N.Y. 23 B8 40 52N 73 24W
East Lamma Channel, H.K. 12 E5 22 13N 114 9 E
East Lexington, Bost. 21 C2 42 25N 71 12W
East Los Angeles, L.A. 28 B3 34 1N 118 10 E
East Meadow, N.Y. 23 C7 40 42N 73 31W
East Molesey, Lon. 4 C2 51 24N 0 21W
East New York, N.Y. 23 C5 40 40N 73 53W
East Newark, N.Y. 22 C4 40 45N 74 9W
East Northport, N.Y. 23 B9 40 52N 73 18W
East Norwich, N.Y. 23 B7 40 50N 73 31W
East Orange, N.Y. 22 C3 40 46N 74 11W
East Palo Alto, S.F. 27 D4 37 28N 122 8W
East Paterson, N.Y. 22 B4 40 53N 74 8W
East Pines, Wash. 25 D8 38 57N 76 54W
East Point, Bost. 21 C4 42 25N 70 54W
East Potomac Park, Wash. 25 D7 38 52N 77 1W
East Richmond, S.F. 27 A3 37 56N 122 19W
East Ringwood, Melb. 19 E8 37 48 S 145 15 E
East River →, N.Y. 22 C5 40 48N 73 54W
East Rockaway, N.Y. 23 D6 40 38N 73 40W
East Rutherford, N.Y. 22 B4 40 50N 74 5W
East Sheen, Lon. 4 C3 51 27N 0 16W
East View Garden, Sing. 15 F8 1 20N 103 57 E
East Weymouth, Bost. 21 D4 42 13N 70 55W
East Wickham, Lon. 4 C5 51 28N 0 5 E
East Williston, N.Y. 23 C7 40 45N 73 37W
East York, Trto. 20 D8 43 40N 79 22W
Eastchester, N.Y. 23 B6 40 56N 73 49W
Eastchester B., N.Y. 23 B6 40 50N 73 48W
Eastcote, Lon. 4 B2 51 34N 0 23W
Eastleigh, Jobg. 18 E9 26 7 S 28 9 E
Eastpoint, Balt. 25 B3 39 17N 76 34W
Eastwood, Syd. 19 A3 33 47 S 151 4 E
Eatons Neck Pt., N.Y. 23 B8 40 57N 73 24W
Eaubonne, Paris 5 B3 48 59N 2 16 E
Ebara, Tōkyō 13 C3 35 35N 139 42 E
Ebisu, Tōkyō 13 C3 35 38N 139 42 E

Gerthe 37

Ebute-Ikorodu, *Lagos* **18 A2** 6 35N 7 29 E
Ebute-Metta, *Lagos* **18 B2** 6 28N 7 23 E
Ecatepec de Morelos, *Méx.* **29 A3** 19 35N 99 2W
Echo B., *N.Y.* **23 B6** 40 54N 73 45W
Echo Mt., *L.A.* **28 A4** 34 12N 118 8W
Écouen, *Paris* **5 A4** 49 1N 2 22 E
Ecquevilly, *Paris* **5 B1** 48 57N 1 55 E
Ecsør, *Bud.* **10 K14** 47 26N 19 19 E
Eda, *Tōkyō* **13 C2** 35 33N 139 33 E
Eddington, *Phil.* **24 A5** 40 5N 74 55W
Eddystone, *Phil.* **24 B2** 39 51N 75 20W
Eden, *Rio J.* **31 A1** 22 47 S 43 23W
Edendale, *Jobg.* **18 E9** 26 8 S 28 9 E
Edenvale, *Jobg.* **18 E9** 26 8 S 28 9 E
Edgars Cr. →, *Melb.* **19 E6** 37 43 S 144 58 E
Edge Hill, *Phil.* **24 A4** 40 7N 75 9W
Edgeley, *Trto.* **20 D7** 43 47N 79 31W
Edgemar, *S.F.* **27 C2** 37 39N 122 29W
Edgemere, *Balt.* **25 B4** 39 14N 76 26W
Edgemont, *Phil.* **24 B2** 39 58N 75 26W
Edgewater Park, *Phil.* **24 A5** 40 3N 74 54W
Edgware, *Lon.* **4 B3** 51 36N 0 15W
Edison, *N.Y.* **22 D2** 40 31N 74 23W
Edison Park, *Chic.* **26 A2** 42 1N 87 48W
Edleen, *Jobg.* **18 E10** 26 5 S 28 12 E
Edmondston, *Wash.* **25 D8** 38 56N 76 54W
Edo →, *Tōkyō* **13 C4** 35 38N 139 52 E
Edogawa, *Tōkyō* **13 B4** 35 43N 139 52 E
Edsberg, *Stock.* **3 D10** 59 26N 17 57 E
Edwards L., *Melb.* **19 E6** 37 42 S 144 59 E
Eestiluoto, *Hels.* **3 C6** 60 7N 25 13 E
Egawa, *Tōkyō* **13 D4** 35 22N 139 54 E
Egenbüttel, *Hbg.* **7 D7** 53 39N 9 51 E
Eggerscheidt, *Ruhr* **6 C3** 51 19N 6 53 E
Egham, *Lon.* **4 C1** 51 25N 0 30W
Eiche, *Berl.* **7 A4** 52 33N 13 35 E
Eiche Sud, *Berl.* **7 A4** 52 33N 13 35 E
Eichlinghofen, *Ruhr* **6 B6** 51 29N 7 24 E
Eichwalde, *Berl.* **7 B4** 52 22N 13 37 E
Eidelstedt, *Hbg.* **7 D7** 53 36N 9 54 E
Eiffel, Tour, *Paris* **5 B3** 48 51N 2 17 E
Eigen, *Ruhr* **6 A3** 51 32N 6 56 E
Eilbek, *Hbg.* **7 D8** 53 34N 10 2 E
Eimsbüttel, *Hbg.* **7 D7** 53 34N 9 57 E
Eissendorf, *Hbg.* **7 E7** 53 27N 9 57 E
Ejby, *Købn.* **2 D9** 55 41N 12 24 E
Ejigbo, *Lagos* **18 A1** 6 33N 7 18 E
Ekeberg, *Oslo* **2 B4** 59 53N 10 46 E
Ekeby, *Stock.* **3 D8** 59 21N 17 35 E
Ekerö, *Stock.* **3 E9** 59 17N 17 46 E
Ekerön, *Stock.* **3 E9** 59 18N 17 41 E
Ekhtiyarieh, *Tehr.* **17 C5** 35 46N 51 28 E
Eklundshov, *Stock.* **3 E10** 59 11N 17 54 E
Eknäs, *Stock.* **3 E12** 59 18N 18 13 E
El 'Abbasiya, *El Qâ.* **18 C5** 30 3N 31 16 E
El Agustino, *Lima* **30 G8** 12 2 S 77 0W
El Alto, *Stgo* **30 J10** 33 29 S 70 42W
El Awkal, *El Qâ.* **18 C5** 30 2N 31 12 E
El Baragil, *El Qâ.* **18 C4** 30 4N 31 9 E
El Basâlîn, *El Qâ.* **18 D5** 29 58N 31 16 E
El Calvario, *La Hab.* **30 B3** 23 3N 82 19W
El Cano, *La Hab.* **30 B2** 23 2N 82 27W
El Caribe, *Car.* **30 D5** 10 36N 66 52W
El Carmen, *Stgo* **30 J10** 33 22 S 70 43W
El Cerrito, *S.F.* **27 A3** 37 54N 122 18W
El Cerro, *La Hab.* **30 B2** 23 6N 82 23W
El Cojo, Pta., *Car.* **30 D5** 10 36N 66 53W
El Cortijo, *Stgo* **30 J10** 33 22 S 70 42W
El Duqqi, *El Qâ.* **18 C5** 30 1N 31 12 E
El Gamâlîya, *El Qâ.* **18 C5** 30 2N 31 15 E
El Ghurîya, *El Qâ.* **18 C5** 30 2N 31 15 E
El Gîza, *El Qâ.* **18 C5** 30 0N 31 12 E
El Granada, *S.F.* **27 C2** 37 30N 122 27W
El Guarda Parres, *Méx.* **29 D2** 19 9N 99 11W
El Hatillo, *Car.* **30 E6** 10 25N 66 49W
El Khalîfa, *El Qâ.* **18 C5** 30 0N 31 15 E
El Kôm el Ahmar, *El Qâ.* **18 C5** 30 6N 31 10 E
El Ma'âdi, *El Qâ.* **18 D5** 29 57N 31 15 E
El Matarîya, *El Qâ.* **18 C5** 30 7N 31 18 E
El Monte, *L.A.* **28 B4** 34 3N 118 1W
El Muhît Idkû el Gharbî →, *El Qâ.* **18 C4** 30 6N 31 6 E
El Mûskî, *El Qâ.* **18 C5** 30 3N 31 15 E
El Palmar, *Car.* **30 D5** 10 36N 66 53W
El Palomar, *B.A.* **32 B3** 34 36 S 58 37W
El Pardo, *Mdrd.* **8 A2** 40 30N 3 46W
El Pedregal, *Car.* **30 D5** 10 30N 66 51W
El Pinar, *Car.* **30 E5** 10 28N 66 56W
El Plantio, *Mdrd.* **8 B1** 40 28N 3 51W
El Qâhira, *El Qâ.* **18 C5** 30 2N 31 13 E
El Qubba, *El Qâ.* **18 C5** 30 4N 31 16 E
El Recreo, *Car.* **30 E5** 10 29N 66 52W
El Reloj, *Méx.* **29 C3** 19 19N 99 9W
El Retiro, *Car.* **30 D5** 10 31N 66 54W
El Salto, *Stgo* **30 J11** 33 22 S 70 38W
El Segundo, *L.A.* **28 C2** 33 55N 118 24W
El Sereno, *L.A.* **28 B3** 34 6N 118 10 E
El Silencio, *Car.* **30 D5** 10 30N 66 55W
El Sobrante, *S.F.* **27 A3** 37 58N 122 17W
El Talar de Pacheco, *B.A.* **32 A3** 34 27 S 58 38W
El Talibîya, *El Qâ.* **18 D5** 29 59N 31 10 E
El Valle, *Car.* **30 E5** 10 29N 66 54W
El Vedado, *La Hab.* **30 B2** 23 8N 82 23W
El Vergel, *Méx.* **29 C3** 19 18N 99 5W
El Wâyli el Kubra, *El Qâ.* **18 C5** 30 5N 31 17 E
El Zamalik, *El Qâ.* **18 C5** 30 3N 31 12 E
Elam, *Phil.* **24 B1** 39 51N 75 32W
Élancourt, *Paris* **5 C1** 48 47N 1 57 E
Elandsfortein, *Jobg.* **18 E10** 26 9 S 28 13 E
Elbe →, *Hbg.* **7 D6** 53 32N 9 49 E
Elberfeld, *Ruhr* **6 C4** 51 15N 7 9 E
Elephanta Caves, *Bomb.* **16 H8** 18 57N 72 57 E
Elephanta I., *Bomb.* **16 H8** 18 57N 72 56 E
Elisenau, *Berl.* **7 A4** 52 38N 13 37 E
Elizabeth, *N.Y.* **22 D3** 40 39N 74 13W
Elkins Park, *Phil.* **24 A4** 40 4N 75 8W
Elkridge, *Balt.* **25 B2** 39 13N 76 42W
Ellboda, *Stock.* **3 D12** 59 24N 18 15 E
Eller, *Ruhr* **6 C3** 51 12N 6 51 E
Ellerbek, *Hbg.* **7 D7** 53 39N 9 52 E
Ellicott City, *Balt.* **25 B2** 39 15N 76 49W
Ellinghorst, *Ruhr* **6 A3** 51 33N 6 57 E
Ellinikón, *Ath.* **8 J11** 37 50N 23 45 E
Ellis I., *N.Y.* **22 C4** 40 41N 74 2W
Elm Park, *Lon.* **4 B6** 51 32N 0 12 E
Elmers End, *Lon.* **4 C4** 51 23N 0 2W
Elmhurst, *Chic.* **26 B1** 41 53N 87 55W
Elmhurst, *N.Y.* **23 C5** 40 44N 73 53W
Elmont, *N.Y.* **23 C6** 40 42N 73 42W
Elmstead, *Lon.* **4 C5** 51 24N 0 2 E
Elmwood, *Balt.* **25 A3** 39 20N 76 31W
Elmwood, *N.Y.* **23 B8** 40 51N 73 20W
Elmwood Park, *Chic.* **26 B2** 41 55N 87 48W
Elmwood Park, *N.Y.* **22 B4** 40 54N 74 7W
Elsburg, *Jobg.* **18 F10** 26 15 S 28 13 E
Elsburgspruit →, *Jobg.* **18 F10** 26 16 S 28 12 E
Elsmere, *Phil.* **24 C1** 39 44N 75 35W
Elspark, *Jobg.* **18 F10** 26 15 S 28 13 E
Elsternwick, *Melb.* **19 F7** 37 52 S 145 0 E
Eltham, *Lon.* **4 C5** 51 27N 0 3 E
Eltham, *Melb.* **19 E7** 37 42 S 145 9 E
Elthorn Heights, *Lon.* **4 B2** 51 31N 0 20W
Eltingrille, *N.Y.* **22 D4** 40 32N 74 9W
Elwood, *Melb.* **19 F6** 37 53 S 144 59 E
Élysée, *Paris* **5 B3** 48 52N 2 19 E
Embu, *S. Pau.* **31 E4** 23 38 S 46 50W
Embu-Mirim, *S. Pau.* **31 F5** 23 41 S 46 49W
Embu Mirim →, *S. Pau.* **31 F5** 23 43 S 46 47W
Emdeni, *Jobg.* **18 F7** 26 14 S 27 49 E
Émerainville, *Paris* **5 C5** 48 48N 2 37 E
Emerson, *N.Y.* **22 B4** 40 57N 74 2W
Emerson Park, *Lon.* **4 B6** 51 34N 0 13 E
Emeryville, *S.F.* **27 B3** 37 49N 122 17W
Eminonu, *Ist.* **17 A2** 41 0N 28 57 E
Emmarentia, *Jobg.* **18 E9** 26 9 S 28 0 E
Emperor's Palace, *Tōkyō* **13 B3** 35 40N 139 45 E
Empire State Building, *N.Y.* **22 C5** 40 44N 73 59W
Emscher →, *Ruhr* **6 A6** 51 30N 7 26 E
Emscher Bruch, *Ruhr* **6 A4** 51 33N 7 8 E
Emscher Zweigkanal, *Ruhr* **6 A4** 51 33N 7 9 E
Encantado, *Rio J.* **31 B2** 22 53 S 43 19W
Encino, *L.A.* **28 B2** 34 9N 118 28W
Encino Res., *L.A.* **28 B1** 34 8N 118 30W
Enebyberg, *Stock.* **3 D10** 59 25N 17 59 E
Enfield, *Lon.* **4 B4** 51 39N 0 4W
Enfield, *Phil.* **24 A3** 40 6N 75 11W
Enfield, *Syd.* **19 B3** 33 53 S 151 6 E
Enfield Chase, *Lon.* **4 A4** 51 40N 0 8W
Enfield Highway, *Lon.* **4 B4** 51 39N 0 2W
Enfield Lock, *Lon.* **4 A4** 51 40N 0 1W
Enfield Wash, *Lon.* **4 B4** 51 39N 0 2W
Eng Khong Gardens, *Sing.* **15 F7** 1 20N 103 46 E
Engenho, I. do, *Rio J.* **31 B3** 22 50 S 43 6W
Engenho Nôvo, *Rio J.* **31 B2** 22 53 S 43 17W
Engenho Velho, Sa. do, *Rio J.* **31 B1** 22 54 S 43 21W
Engenno do Mato, *Rio J.* **31 B3** 22 56 S 43 2W
Enghein-les-Bains, *Paris* **5 B3** 48 58N 2 18 E
Englewood, *Chic.* **26 C3** 41 46N 87 38W
Englewood, *N.Y.* **22 B5** 40 53N 73 58W
Englewood Cliffs, *N.Y.* **22 B5** 40 53N 73 59W
Englischer Garten, *Mün.* **7 G10** 48 9N 11 35 E
Enmore, *Syd.* **19 B4** 33 54 S 151 10 E
Ennepe →, *Ruhr* **6 C6** 51 17N 7 23 E
Ennepetal, *Ruhr* **6 C6** 51 17N 7 21 E
Ennepetalsp →, *Ruhr* **6 C6** 51 14N 7 24 E
Enskede, *Stock.* **3 E11** 59 17N 18 4 E
Entrevias, *Mdrd.* **8 B2** 40 22N 3 40W
Épiais-les-Louvres, *Paris* **5 A5** 49 1N 2 33 E
Epinay, *Paris* **5 B3** 48 57N 2 19 E
Epinay-sous-Sénart, *Paris* **5 C5** 48 41N 2 30 E
Epinay-sur-Orge, *Paris* **5 C3** 48 40N 2 19 E
Eppende, *Ruhr* **6 B4** 51 28N 7 9 E
Eppenhausen, *Ruhr* **6 B6** 51 22N 7 29 E
Epping, *Lon.* **4 A5** 51 41N 0 6 E
Epping, *Melb.* **19 D7** 37 39 S 145 1 E
Epping, *Syd.* **19 A3** 33 46 S 151 5 E
Epping Forest, *Lon.* **4 B5** 51 39N 0 2 E
Epsom, *Lon.* **4 D3** 51 19N 0 15W
Epsom Racecourse, *Lon.* **4 D3** 51 18N 0 15W
Éragny, *Paris* **5 A2** 49 1N 2 5 E
Ercolano, *Nápl.* **9 J13** 40 48N 14 21 E
Érd, *Bud.* **10 K12** 47 23N 18 56 E
Erdenheim, *Phil.* **24 A3** 40 5N 75 12W
Eregun, *Lagos* **18 A2** 6 35N 7 22 E
Erenköy, *Ist.* **17 B3** 40 58N 29 3 E
Ergal, *Paris* **5 C1** 48 47N 1 55 E
Erial, *Phil.* **24 C4** 39 46N 75 0W
Erith, *Lon.* **4 C6** 51 28N 0 11 E
Erkner, *Berl.* **7 B5** 52 25N 13 44 E
Erkrath, *Ruhr* **6 C3** 51 13N 6 54 E
Erlaa, *Wien* **10 H9** 48 9N 16 19 E
Erle, *Ruhr* **6 A4** 51 33N 7 4 E
Ermelino Matarazzo, *S. Pau.* **31 D7** 23 29 S 46 28W
Ermington, *Syd.* **19 A3** 33 48 S 151 4 E
Ermont, *Paris* **5 B3** 48 59N 2 15 E
Ersébet-Telep, *Bud.* **10 K14** 47 27N 19 10 E
Ershatou, *Gzh.* **14 G8** 23 6N 113 18 E
Erskineville, *Syd.* **19 B4** 33 54 S 151 12 E
Erstavik, *Stock.* **3 E12** 59 16N 18 14 E
Erstaviken, *Stock.* **3 E12** 59 16N 18 20 E
Erunkan, *Lagos* **18 A2** 6 36N 7 23 E
Eschenried, *Mün.* **7 F9** 48 13N 11 24 E
Esenler, *Ist.* **17 A2** 41 1N 28 52 E
Esher, *Lon.* **4 C2** 51 22N 0 20W
Eshratābād, *Tehr.* **17 C5** 35 42N 51 27 E
España, *B.A.* **32 C5** 34 46 S 58 14W
Espeleta, *B.A.* **32 C5** 34 45 S 58 15W
Esplugas, *Barc.* **8 D5** 41 22N 2 5 E
Espoo, *Hels.* **3 B2** 60 13N 24 38 E
Espoonlahti, *Hels.* **3 B2** 60 9N 24 31 E
Esposizione Univ. di Roma (E.U.R.), *Rome* **9 G9** 41 49N 12 28 E
Essen, *Ruhr* **6 B4** 51 27N 7 0 E
Essen-Mülheim, Flughafen, *Ruhr* **6 B3** 51 24N 6 56 E
Essendon, *Melb.* **19 E6** 37 44 S 144 55 E
Essendon Airport, *Melb.* **19 E6** 37 43 S 144 54 E
Essex, *Balt.* **25 B4** 39 18N 76 28W
Essex Falls, *N.Y.* **22 C3** 40 49N 74 16W
Essingen, *Stock.* **3 E10** 59 19N 17 59 E
Essling, *Wien* **10 G11** 48 12N 16 30 E
Est, Gare de l', *Paris* **5 B4** 48 52N 2 21 E
Estado, Parque do, *S. Pau.* **31 E6** 23 38 S 46 38W
Estby, *Hels.* **3 C1** 60 5N 24 27W
Este, Parque Nacional del, *Car.* **30 E5** 10 29N 66 50W
Esteban Echeverria, *B.A.* **32 C4** 34 48 S 58 29W
Estlotan, *Hels.* **3 C6** 60 7N 25 13 E
Estrela, Basilica da, *Lisb.* **8 F8** 38 42N 9 9W
Étiolles, *Paris* **5 D4** 48 38N 2 28 E
Etobicoke, *Trto.* **20 E7** 43 39N 79 34W
Etobicoke Cr. →, *Trto.* **20 E7** 43 35N 79 32W
Etzenhauzen, *Mün.* **7 F9** 48 16N 11 27 E
Eun Pyeong, *Sŏul* **12 G7** 37 36N 126 56 E
Eungam, *Sŏul* **12 G7** 37 34N 126 55 E
Evanston, *Chic.* **26 A2** 42 3N 87 40W
Évecquemont, *Paris* **5 A1** 49 0N 1 56 E
Everett, *Bost.* **21 C3** 42 24N 71 3W
Evergreen Park, *Chic.* **26 C2** 41 43N 87 42W
Eversael, *Ruhr* **6 A1** 51 32N 6 39 E
Evesboro, *Phil.* **24 B5** 39 54N 74 55W
Eving, *Ruhr* **6 A6** 51 33N 7 28 E
Evry, *Paris* **5 D4** 48 38N 2 26 E
Évry-les-Châteaux, *Paris* **5 D5** 48 39N 2 38 E
Évzonos, *Ath.* **8 J11** 37 55N 23 49 E
Ewin, *Tehr.* **17 C5** 35 47N 51 23 E
Ewu, *Lagos* **18 A1** 6 33N 7 19 E
Exelberg, *Wien* **10 G9** 48 14N 16 15 E
Eynsford, *Lon.* **4 C6** 51 21N 0 12 E
Eyup, *Ist.* **17 A2** 41 2N 28 55 E
Ez Zeitûn, *El Qâ.* **18 C5** 30 6N 31 18 E
Ézanville, *Paris* **5 A4** 49 1N 2 21 E
Ezeiza, *B.A.* **32 D3** 34 50 S 58 31W
Ezeiza, Aeropuerto, *B.A.* **32 C3** 34 48 S 58 32W

F

Fabreville, *Mtrl.* **20 A2** 43 33N 73 51W
Fælledparken, *Købn.* **2 D10** 55 42N 12 34 E
Fågelön, *Stock.* **3 E10** 59 18N 17 55 E
Fagersjo, *Stock.* **3 E11** 59 14N 18 4 E
Fagnano, *Mil.* **9 E4** 45 24N 8 59 E
Fahrn, *Ruhr* **6 A2** 51 30N 6 45 E
Faibano, *Nápl.* **9 H13** 40 55N 14 27 E
Fair Lawn, *N.Y.* **22 B4** 40 55N 74 7W
Fairfax, *Phil.* **24 C1** 39 47N 75 33W
Fairfax, *Wash.* **25 D6** 38 50N 77 19W
Fairfax Station, *Wash.* **25 E6** 38 48N 77 19W
Fairfield, *Melb.* **19 E7** 37 46 S 145 2 E
Fairfield, *N.Y.* **22 B3** 40 53N 74 17W
Fairfield, *Syd.* **19 B2** 33 52 S 150 56 E
Fairhaven B., *Bost.* **21 C1** 42 25N 71 21W
Fairhaven Hill, *Bost.* **21 C1** 42 26N 71 21W
Fairland, *Jobg.* **18 E8** 26 8 S 27 57 E
Fairland, *Wash.* **25 C8** 39 4N 76 57W
Fairmont Terrace, *S.F.* **27 B4** 37 42N 122 7W
Fairmount Heights, *Wash.* **25 D8** 38 54N 76 54W
Fairmount Park, *Phil.* **24 A3** 40 3N 75 13W
Fairport, *Trto.* **20 D10** 43 49N 79 4W
Fairview, *N.Y.* **22 C5** 40 48N 73 59W
Fairview, *N.Y.* **23 A6** 41 1N 73 46W
Falenica, *Wsaw.* **10 F8** 52 9N 21 12 E
Falenty, *Wsaw.* **10 F6** 52 8N 20 55 E
Falkenburg, *Berl.* **7 A4** 52 34N 13 32 E
Falkenhagen, *Berl.* **7 A1** 52 34N 13 5 E
Falkensee, *Berl.* **7 A1** 52 34N 13 4 E
Fallon, *L.A.* **28 C5** 33 59N 117 54W
Falls Church, *Wash.* **25 D6** 38 53N 77 12W
Falls Run →, *Balt.* **25 A1** 39 21N 76 52W
Falomo, *Lagos* **18 B2** 6 26N 7 26 E
Fangcun, *Gzh.* **14 G8** 23 6N 113 13 E
Fanwood, *N.Y.* **22 D2** 40 37N 74 23W
Far Rockaway, *N.Y.* **23 D6** 40 36N 73 45W
Farahābād, *Tehr.* **17 C5** 35 41N 51 29 E
Färentuna, *Stock.* **3 D8** 59 23N 17 39 E
Farforovskaya, *Len.* **11 B4** 59 52N 30 27 E
Farm Pond, *Bost.* **21 D2** 42 13N 71 20W
Farmingdale, *N.Y.* **23 C8** 40 43N 73 27W
Farmsen, *Hbg.* **7 D8** 53 36N 10 8 E
Farnborough, *Lon.* **4 C5** 51 21N 0 3 E
Farningham, *Lon.* **4 C6** 51 23N 0 12 E
Farrar Pond, *Bost.* **21 C1** 42 24N 71 21W
Farrarmere, *Jobg.* **18 E10** 26 9 S 28 18 E
Farsta, *Stock.* **3 E11** 59 14N 18 5 E
Farstalandet, *Stock.* **3 E13** 59 18N 18 23 E
Farum, *Købn.* **2 D8** 55 48N 12 21 E
Farum Sø, *Købn.* **2 D9** 55 48N 12 21 E
Fasanerie-Nord, *Mün.* **7 F10** 48 11N 11 32 E
Fasangarten, *Mün.* **7 G10** 48 5N 11 36 E
Fat Tau Chau, *H.K.* **12 E6** 22 16N 114 16 E
Fatih, *Ist.* **17 A2** 41 0N 28 56 E
Favoriten, *Wien* **10 H10** 48 9N 16 23 E
Fawkner, *Melb.* **19 E6** 37 42 S 144 56 E
Fawkner Park, *Melb.* **19 F6** 37 50 S 144 58 E
Feasterville, *Phil.* **24 A4** 40 9N 75 0W
Febrero, Parque de, *B.A.* **32 B4** 34 36 S 58 25W
Feijó, *Lisb.* **8 G8** 38 39N 9 9W
Feldersbruch →, *Ruhr* **6 B5** 51 23N 7 4 E
Feldhausen, *Ruhr* **6 A3** 51 36N 6 58 E
Feldkirchen, *Mün.* **7 G11** 48 8N 11 43 E
Feldmoching, *Mün.* **7 F10** 48 14N 11 32 E
Fellowship, *Phil.* **24 B5** 39 56N 74 57W
Feltham, *Lon.* **4 C2** 51 26N 0 24W
Feltonville, *Phil.* **24 A4** 40 1N 75 8W
Fenerbahce, *Ist.* **17 B3** 40 58N 29 2 E
Fengtai, *Beij.* **14 C2** 39 49N 116 14 E
Fenino, *Mos.* **11 E11** 55 43N 37 56 E
Ferencváros, *Bud.* **10 K13** 47 29N 19 5 E
Ferihegyi Airport, *Bud.* **10 K14** 47 26N 19 14 E
Ferndale, *Balt.* **25 B3** 39 11N 76 38W
Ferndale, *Jobg.* **18 E9** 26 5 S 28 0 E
Ferntree Gully, *Melb.* **19 F8** 37 52 S 145 17 E
Ferntree Gully Nat. Park, *Melb.* **19 F8** 37 52 S 145 19 E
Ferny Cr. →, *Melb.* **19 F8** 37 54 S 145 16 E
Férolles-Attilly, *Paris* **5 C5** 48 44N 2 37 E
Ferraz de Vasconcelos, *S. Pau.* **31 E7** 23 32 S 46 22W
Ferrières-en-Brie, *Paris* **5 C6** 48 49N 2 42 E
Ferry, *N.Y.* **23 A5** 41 0N 73 52W
Fetcham, *Lon.* **4 D2** 51 17N 0 21W
Feucherolles, *Paris* **5 B1** 48 52N 1 58 E
Fichtenau, *Berl.* **7 B5** 52 27N 13 42 E
Fields Corner, *Bost.* **21 D3** 42 18N 71 3W
Fiera Camp, *Mil.* **9 E5** 45 28N 9 9 E
Figino, *Mil.* **9 E5** 45 29N 9 4 E
Fijir, *Bagd.* **17 E8** 33 21N 44 21 E
Filadhélfia, *Ath.* **8 H11** 38 2N 23 43 E
Fili-Masilovo, *Mos.* **11 E8** 55 44N 37 29 E
Filothei, *Ath.* **8 H11** 38 2N 23 46 E
Finaalspan, *Jobg.* **18 F10** 26 16 S 28 16 E
Finchley, *Lon.* **4 B3** 51 36N 0 11W
Finkenkrug, *Berl.* **7 A1** 52 33N 13 3 E
Finkenwerder, *Hbg.* **7 D7** 53 32N 9 51 E
Finsbury, *Lon.* **4 B4** 51 31N 0 6W
Finsbury Park, *Lon.* **4 B4** 51 34N 0 6W
Fiorito, *B.A.* **32 C4** 34 42 S 58 26W
Firdows, *Bagd.* **17 F7** 33 17N 44 17 E
Firōz Bahram, *Tehr.* **17 D4** 35 37N 51 14 E
Fischeln, *Ruhr* **6 C1** 51 18N 6 35 E
Fish Brook →, *Bost.* **21 B3** 42 39N 71 1W
Fishermans Bend, *Melb.* **19 E6** 37 49 S 144 55 E
Fisher's Hill, *Jobg.* **18 F10** 26 10 S 28 10 E
Fisherville, *Trto.* **20 D8** 43 46N 79 28W
Fisksätra, *Stock.* **3 E12** 59 17N 18 13 E
Fittja, *Stock.* **3 E10** 59 14N 17 51 E
Fitzroy Gardens, *Melb.* **19 E6** 37 48 S 144 58 E
Five Cowrie Cr. →, *Lagos* **18 B2** 6 26N 7 25 E
Five Dock, *Syd.* **19 B3** 33 52 S 151 8 E
Fjellstrand, *Oslo* **2 C3** 59 47N 10 36 E
Flachsberg, *Ruhr* **6 C4** 51 11N 7 4 E
Flag →, *Chic.* **26 C1** 41 43N 87 55W
Flamengo, *Rio J.* **31 B2** 22 56 S 43 11W
Flaminio, *Rome* **9 F9** 41 55N 12 28 E
Flaskebekk, *Oslo* **2 B3** 59 51N 10 39 E
Flatbush, *N.Y.* **22 D5** 40 39N 73 56W
Flaten, *Stock.* **3 E11** 59 15N 18 9 E
Flemington, *Syd.* **19 B3** 33 53 S 151 4 E
Flemington Racecourse, *Melb.* **19 E6** 37 47 S 144 54 E
Fleury-Mérogis, *Paris* **5 D4** 48 37N 2 21 E
Flingern, *Ruhr* **6 C2** 51 13N 6 48 E
Flint Pk., *L.A.* **28 B3** 34 9N 118 11 E
Floral Park, *N.Y.* **23 C6** 40 43N 73 42W
Florence, *L.A.* **28 C3** 33 57N 118 13W
Florence, *Phil.* **24 C5** 39 44N 74 55W
Florence Bloom Bird Sanctuary, *Jobg.* **18 E9** 26 7 S 28 0 E
Florencio Varela, *B.A.* **32 C5** 34 49 S 58 18W
Florentia, *Jobg.* **18 F9** 26 16 S 28 8 E
Flores, *B.A.* **32 B4** 34 38 S 58 27W
Floresta, *B.A.* **32 B4** 34 37 S 58 27W
Florham Park, *N.Y.* **22 C2** 40 46N 74 23W
Florida, *B.A.* **32 B4** 34 31 S 58 28W
Florida, *Jobg.* **18 F8** 26 10 S 27 55 E
Florida L., *Jobg.* **18 F8** 26 10 S 27 54 E
Floridsdorf, *Wien* **10 G10** 48 15N 16 26 E
Flourtown, *Phil.* **24 A3** 40 6N 75 13W
Flower Hill, *N.Y.* **23 C6** 40 48N 73 40W
Flushing, *N.Y.* **23 C6** 40 45N 73 49W
Flushing Meadows Corona Park, *N.Y.* **23 C5** 40 44N 73 50W
Flysta, *Stock.* **3 D10** 59 22N 17 54 E
Fo Tan, *H.K.* **12 D6** 22 23N 114 11 E
Föhrenhain, *Wien* **10 G10** 48 19N 16 26 E
Folcroft, *Phil.* **24 B3** 39 53N 75 16W
Folsom, *Phil.* **24 B3** 39 53N 75 19W
Fontainebleau, *Jobg.* **18 E8** 26 6 S 27 57 E
Fontana, *La Hab.* **30 B2** 23 1N 82 24W
Fontanka, *Len.* **11 B3** 59 54N 30 16 E
Fontenay-aux-Roses, *Paris* **5 C3** 48 47N 2 17 E
Fontenay-le-Fleury, *Paris* **5 C2** 48 48N 2 2 E
Fontenay-lès-Briis, *Paris* **5 D2** 48 37N 2 9 E
Fontenay-sous-Bois, *Paris* **5 B4** 48 51N 2 28 E
Foots Cray, *Lon.* **4 C5** 51 24N 0 7 E
Footscray, *Melb.* **19 E6** 37 48 S 144 56 E
Forbidden City, *Beij.* **14 B3** 39 53N 116 21 E
Fordham Univ., *N.Y.* **23 B5** 40 51N 73 51W
Fords, *N.Y.* **22 D3** 40 31N 74 19W
Fordsburg, *Jobg.* **18 F9** 26 12 S 28 2 E
Foremans Corner, *Balt.* **25 B3** 39 11N 76 33W
Forest Gate, *Lon.* **4 B5** 51 32N 0 1 E
Forest Heights, *Wash.* **25 E7** 38 48N 77 0W
Forest Hill, *Lon.* **4 C4** 51 26N 0 2W
Forest Hill, *Melb.* **19 F8** 37 50 S 145 10 E
Forest Hill, *Trto.* **20 D8** 43 41N 79 25W
Forest Hills, *N.Y.* **23 C5** 40 42N 73 51W
Forest Park, *Chic.* **26 B2** 41 51N 87 47W
Forest View, *Chic.* **26 C2** 41 48N 87 47W
Forestville, *Syd.* **19 A4** 33 46 S 151 12 E
Forestville, *Wash.* **25 D8** 38 50N 76 52W
Forges-les-Bains, *Paris* **5 D2** 48 37N 2 5 E
Fornacino, *Tori.* **9 B3** 45 9N 7 44 E
Fornebu, *Oslo* **2 B3** 59 53N 10 36 E
Fornebu Airport, *Oslo* **2 B3** 59 56N 10 37 E
Foro Italico, *Rome* **9 F9** 41 56N 12 26 E
Foro Romano, *Rome* **9 F9** 41 53N 12 29 E
Forst Rantzau, *Hbg.* **7 C6** 53 43N 9 49 E
Forstenried, *Mün.* **7 G9** 48 5N 11 29 E
Forstenrieder Park, *Mün.* **7 G9** 48 3N 11 27 E
Fort du Pont Park, *Wash.* **25 D8** 38 52N 76 56W
Fort Foote Village, *Wash.* **25 E7** 38 46N 77 1W
Fort Howard, *Balt.* **25 B4** 39 12N 76 26W
Fort Lee, *N.Y.* **22 B5** 40 50N 73 58W
Fort McHenry Nat. Mon., *Balt.* **25 B3** 35 15N 76 35W
Fort Washington, *Phil.* **24 A3** 40 8N 75 13W
Fort William, *Calc.* **16 E6** 22 33N 88 20 E
Foster City, *S.F.* **27 C3** 37 33N 122 15W
Fosters Pond, *Bost.* **21 B3** 42 36N 71 8W
Fourcherolle, *Paris* **5 C1** 48 42N 1 58 E
Fourmile Run →, *Wash.* **25 D7** 38 50N 77 2W
Fourqueux, *Paris* **5 B2** 48 53N 2 3 E
Fowl Meadow Res., *Bost.* **21 D3** 42 13N 71 8W
Fox Chase, *Phil.* **24 A4** 40 4N 75 5W
Foxhall, *Wash.* **25 C7** 39 4N 77 3W
Framingham, *Bost.* **21 D1** 42 18N 71 24W
Francisco Alvarez, *B.A.* **32 B1** 34 38 S 58 50W
Francisquito Cr. →, *S.F.* **27 D4** 37 27N 122 9W
Franconia, *Wash.* **25 E7** 38 47N 77 7W
Franconville, *Paris* **5 B3** 48 59N 2 13 E
Francop, *Hbg.* **7 D7** 53 30N 9 51 E
Frankel, *Sing.* **15 G8** 1 18N 103 55 E
Frankford, *Phil.* **24 A4** 40 1N 75 5W
Franklin L., *N.Y.* **22 B3** 40 59N 74 13W
Franklin Lakes, *N.Y.* **22 B3** 40 59N 74 13W
Franklin Park, *Bost.* **21 D3** 42 18N 71 5W
Franklin Park, *Chic.* **26 B1** 41 55N 87 52W
Franklin Park, *Wash.* **25 D7** 38 55N 77 9W
Franklin Res., *L.A.* **28 B2** 34 5N 118 24W
Franklin Roosevelt Park, *Jobg.* **18 E8** 26 8 S 27 59 E
Franklin Roosevelt Park, *Phil.* **24 B3** 39 54N 75 10W
Franklin Square, *N.Y.* **23 C6** 40 42N 73 40W
Frattamaggiore, *Nápl.* **9 H12** 40 56N 14 16 E
Frauenkirche, *Mün.* **7 G10** 48 8N 11 34 E
Frederiksberg, *Købn.* **2 D10** 55 40N 12 33 E
Frederiksdal, *Købn.* **2 D9** 55 46N 12 25 E
Fredersdorf, *Berl.* **7 A5** 52 31N 13 45 E
Fredersdorf Nord, *Berl.* **7 A5** 52 32N 13 45 E
Freeport, *N.Y.* **23 D7** 40 39N 73 35W
Freidrichshain, Volkspark, *Berl.* **7 A3** 52 31N 13 25 E
Freiham, *Mün.* **7 G9** 48 8N 11 25 E
Freimann, *Mün.* **7 F10** 48 11N 11 37 E
Fremont, *S.F.* **27 C4** 37 33N 122 2W
Fresh Meadows, *N.Y.* **23 C6** 40 43N 73 47W
Fresh Pond, *Bost.* **21 C3** 42 22N 71 8W
Freskati, *Stock.* **3 D11** 59 22N 18 3 E
Fresnes, *Paris* **5 C3** 48 45N 2 18 E
Fretay, *Paris* **5 C3** 48 40N 2 12 E
Freudenau, *Wien* **10 G10** 48 11N 16 25 E
Friedenau, *Berl.* **7 B3** 52 28N 31 20 E
Friederikenhof, *Berl.* **7 B3** 52 23N 13 21 E
Friedrichsfeld, *Ruhr* **6 A1** 51 37N 6 39 E
Friedrichsfelde, *Berl.* **7 B4** 52 29N 13 33 E
Friedrichshagen, *Berl.* **7 B4** 52 27N 13 37 E
Friedrichshain, *Berl.* **7 A3** 52 31N 13 25 E
Friedrichshulde, *Hbg.* **7 D7** 53 36N 9 51 E
Friedrichslust, *Berl.* **7 A5** 52 33N 13 43 E
Frielas, *Lisb.* **8 F8** 38 49N 9 6W
Friemersheim, *Ruhr* **6 B2** 51 23N 6 42 E
Friern Barnet, *Lon.* **4 B4** 51 37N 0 9W
Friherrs, *Hels.* **3 B3** 60 16N 24 49 E
Frogner, *Oslo* **2 A6** 60 1N 11 6 E
Frohnau, *Berl.* **7 A2** 52 38N 13 16 E
Frohnhausen, *Ruhr* **6 B3** 51 26N 6 56 E
Frontón, I., *Lima* **30 G7** 12 7 S 77 11W
Frunze, *Mos.* **11 E9** 55 47N 37 33 E
Fuchź, *Tōkyō* **13 B1** 35 40N 139 29 E
Fuencarral, *Mdrd.* **8 B2** 40 29N 3 42W
Fuhlenbrock, *Ruhr* **6 A3** 51 32N 6 54 E
Fuhlsbüttel, *Hbg.* **7 D8** 53 37N 10 1 E
Fujidera, *Ōsaka* **12 C4** 34 34N 135 36 E
Fujikubo, *Tōkyō* **13 B2** 35 49N 139 31 E
Fujimi, *Tōkyō* **13 A2** 35 50N 139 33 E
Fukagawa, *Tōkyō* **13 C3** 35 39N 139 48 E
Fukami, *Tōkyō* **13 D1** 35 28N 139 27 E
Fukiai, *Ōsaka* **12 B2** 34 42N 135 12 E
Fukuoka, *Tōkyō* **13 A2** 35 52N 139 31 E
Fukushima, *Ōsaka* **12 B3** 34 41N 135 28 E
Fulatani, *Tōkyō* **13 D1** 35 22N 139 30 E
Fulham, *Lon.* **4 C3** 51 28N 0 12W
Fuller Park, *L.A.* **28 C5** 33 51N 117 56W
Fullerton, *Balt.* **25 A3** 39 22N 76 30W
Funabori, *Tōkyō* **13 B4** 35 41N 139 52 E
Funasaka, *Ōsaka* **12 B2** 34 48N 135 16 E
Fünfhaus, *Wien* **10 G10** 48 11N 16 20 E
Fünfhausen, *Hbg.* **7 E8** 53 27N 10 2 E
Furesø, *Købn.* **2 D9** 55 47N 12 25 E
Fürstenried, *Mün.* **7 G9** 48 5N 11 28 E
Furth, *Mün.* **7 G10** 48 2N 11 35 E
Furu →, *Tōkyō* **13 A3** 35 54N 139 49 E
Furuyakami, *Tōkyō* **13 A2** 35 54N 139 31 E
Futago-tamagawaen, *Tōkyō* **13 C2** 35 36N 139 39 E
Futamatagawa, *Tōkyō* **13 D2** 35 27N 139 31 E
Futatsubashi, *Tōkyō* **13 D1** 35 28N 139 29 E
Fuxing Dao, *Shang.* **14 J12** 31 16N 121 33 E
Fuxing Gongyuan, *Shang.* **14 J11** 31 13N 121 27 E
Fuxinglu, *Beij.* **14 B2** 39 52N 116 16 E
Fuxingmen, *Beij.* **14 B2** 39 53N 116 19 E

G

Gadstrup, *Købn.* **2 E7** 55 34N 12 5 E
Gaebong, *Sŏul* **12 H7** 37 29N 126 52 E
Gage Park, *Chic.* **26 C2** 41 47N 87 42W
Gagny, *Paris* **5 B5** 48 53N 2 32 E
Gaillon, *Paris* **5 A1** 49 1N 1 53 E
Galata, *Ist.* **17 A2** 41 1N 28 58 E
Galátsion, *Ath.* **8 H11** 38 1N 23 45 E
Galeâo, *Rio J.* **31 A2** 22 49 S 43 14W
Galéria →, *Rome* **9 F9** 41 57N 12 20 E
Gallows Corner, *Lon.* **4 B6** 51 35N 0 13 E
Gällstaö, *Stock.* **3 E10** 59 17N 17 51 E
Galyanovo, *Mos.* **11 E10** 55 48N 37 47 E
Galyeon, *Sŏul* **12 G7** 37 36N 126 55 E
Gambir, *Jak.* **15 H9** 6 9 S 106 48 E
Gamboa, *Rio J.* **31 B2** 22 53 S 43 11W
Gambolóita, *Mil.* **9 E6** 45 26N 9 13 E
Gamelinha →, *S. Pau.* **31 E6** 23 31 S 46 31W
Gamlebyen, *Oslo* **2 B4** 59 54N 10 46 E
Gamlebyen, *Shang.* **14 J11** 31 13N 121 29 E
Gamō, *Tōkyō* **13 A3** 35 52N 139 48 E
Gang Dong, *Sŏul* **12 G8** 37 30N 127 5 E
Gang Nam, *Sŏul* **12 G7** 37 30N 126 59 E
Gang Sea, *Sŏul* **12 G7** 37 32N 126 51 E
Gangadharpur, *Calc.* **16 E5** 22 35N 88 11 E
Gangtou, *Gzh.* **14 F7** 23 12N 113 8 E
Gangwei, *Gzh.* **14 G8** 23 4N 113 11 E
Ganløse, *Købn.* **2 D8** 55 47N 12 15 E
Ganløse Orned, *Købn.* **2 D8** 55 48N 12 18 E
Ganshi, *Gzh.* **14 F7** 23 10N 113 8 E
Gants Hill, *Lon.* **4 B5** 51 34N 0 4 E
Gaoqiao, *Shang.* **14 H12** 31 21N 121 34 E
Garbagnate Milanese, *Mil.* **9 D5** 45 34N 9 4 E
Garbatella, *Rome* **9 F10** 41 51N 12 30 E
Garches, *Paris* **5 B3** 48 50N 2 11 E
Garching, *Mün.* **7 F11** 48 14N 11 39 E
Garden City, *El Qâ.* **18 C5** 30 2N 31 14 E
Garden City, *N.Y.* **23 C7** 40 43N 73 37W
Garden Reach, *Calc.* **16 E5** 22 33N 88 15 E
Gardena, *L.A.* **28 C3** 33 53N 118 18W
Garder, *Oslo* **2 C3** 59 45N 10 38 E
Garfield, *N.Y.* **22 B4** 40 52N 74 7W
Garfield Park, *Chic.* **26 B2** 41 52N 87 42W
Gargareta, *Ath.* **8 J11** 37 57N 23 43 E
Garges-lès-Gonesse, *Paris* **5 B4** 48 58N 2 25 E
Garhi Naraina, *Delhi* **16 B1** 28 37N 77 8 E
Garibong, *Sŏul* **12 H7** 37 29N 126 54 E
Garin, *B.A.* **32 A2** 34 25 S 58 44W
Gariya, *Calc.* **16 F6** 22 28N 88 23 E
Garji, *Calc.* **16 C5** 22 50N 88 19 E
Garne, *Paris* **5 C1** 48 41N 1 58 E
Garrison, *Balt.* **25 A2** 39 24N 76 45W
Garstedt, *Hbg.* **7 C7** 53 40N 9 59 E
Gartenstadt, *Ruhr* **6 B6** 51 30N 7 30 E
Garulia, *Calc.* **16 D6** 22 48N 88 22 E
Garvanza, *L.A.* **28 B3** 34 6N 118 11 E
Garwood, *N.Y.* **22 D3** 40 38N 74 18W
Gary, *Chic.* **26 D4** 41 35N 87 23W
Gåshaga, *Stock.* **3 D12** 59 21N 18 13 E
Gássino Torinese, *Tori.* **9 B3** 45 7N 7 49 E
Gästerby, *Hels.* **3 C1** 60 8N 24 27 E
Gateão, Aéroporto de, *Rio J.* **31 A2** 22 49 S 43 15W
Gateway of India, *Bomb.* **16 H8** 18 55N 72 50 E
Gatow, *Berl.* **7 B1** 52 29N 13 11 E
Gaurhati, *Calc.* **16 D6** 22 48N 88 21 E
Gauripur, *Calc.* **16 C6** 22 53N 88 25 E
Gavá, *Barc.* **8 E5** 41 18N 2 0 E
Gavamar, *Barc.* **8 E4** 41 16N 1 58 E
Gavanpada, *Bomb.* **16 H9** 18 57N 73 0 E
Gávea, *Rio J.* **31 B2** 22 58 S 43 13W
Gávea, Pedra da, *Rio J.* **31 B2** 22 59 S 43 18W
Gbogbo, *Lagos* **18 A3** 6 35N 7 31 E
Gebel el Ahmar, *El Qâ.* **18 C5** 30 2N 31 19 E
Gebel el Muqattam, *El Qâ.* **18 C5** 30 1N 31 17 E
Gebel et Tura, *El Qâ.* **18 D5** 29 56N 31 15 E
Geduld Dam, *Jobg.* **18 F11** 26 12 S 28 24 E
Geiselgasteig, *Mün.* **7 G10** 48 3N 11 33 E
Geist Res., *Phil.* **24 B2** 39 57N 75 24W
Gellért hegy, *Bud.* **10 K13** 47 29N 19 3 E
Gelsenkirchen, *Ruhr* **6 A4** 51 32N 7 2 E
General Ignacio Allende, *Méx.* **29 B1** 19 20N 99 21W
General Pacheco, *B.A.* **32 A3** 34 27 S 58 36W
General San Martin, *B.A.* **32 B3** 34 35 S 58 32W
General Sarmiento, *B.A.* **32 B2** 34 32 S 58 43W
General Urquiza, *B.A.* **32 B4** 34 34 S 58 28W
Gennebreck, *Ruhr* **6 C5** 51 18N 7 12 E
Gennevilliers, *Paris* **5 B3** 48 56N 2 17 E
Gentilly, *Paris* **5 C4** 48 48N 2 21 E
Gentofte, *Købn.* **2 D10** 55 44N 12 32 E
Georges →, *Syd.* **19 B2** 33 56 S 150 55 E
Georges Hall, *Syd.* **19 B2** 33 54 S 150 59 E
Georges I., *Bost.* **21 D4** 42 19N 70 55W
Georges River Bridge, *Syd.* **19 C3** 34 0 S 151 6 E
Georgetown, *Wash.* **25 D7** 38 54N 77 3W
Georgetown Rowley State Forest, *Bost.* **21 A4** 42 41N 70 56W
Georgsweide, *Hbg.* **7 D8** 53 30N 10 1 E
Gerasdorf bei Wein, *Wien* **10 G10** 48 17N 16 28 E
Gerberau, *Mün.* **7 F9** 48 12N 11 27 E
Gérbido, *Tori.* **9 B2** 45 2N 7 36 E
Gerlev, *Købn.* **2 D7** 55 49N 12 0 E
Gerli, *B.A.* **32 C4** 34 41 S 58 22W
Germantown, *Balt.* **25 A4** 39 24N 76 28W
Germantown, *Phil.* **24 A3** 40 2N 75 11W
Germiston, *Jobg.* **18 F9** 26 13 S 28 10 E
Gerresheim, *Ruhr* **6 C3** 51 14N 6 51 E
Gersthof, *Wien* **10 G9** 48 14N 16 18 E
Gerthe, *Ruhr* **6 A5** 51 31N 7 16 E

38 Gesîrat el Rauda

Gesîrat el Rauda, *El Qâ.* **18 C5** 30 1N 31 13 E
Gesîrat Muhammad, *El Qâ.* **18 C5** 30 6N 31 11 E
Gesterby, *Hels.* **3 A6** 60 20N 25 17 E
Getafe, *Mdrd.* **8 C2** 40 18N 3 43W
Gevelsberg, *Ruhr* **6 C6** 51 19N 7 21 E
Geylang, *Sing.* **15 G8** 1 18N 103 53 E
Geylang →, *Sing.* **15 G8** 1 18N 103 52 E
Geylang Serai, *Sing.* **15 G8** 1 19N 103 53 E
Gezîrat edn Dhahab, *El Qâ.* **18 D5** 29 59N 31 13 E
Gezîrat Warrâq el Hadar, *El Qâ.* **18 C5** 30 6N 31 13 E
Gharapuri, *Bomb.* **16 H8** 18 57N 72 57 E
Ghatkopar, *Bomb.* **16 G8** 19 4N 72 54 E
Ghazipur, *Delhi* **16 B2** 28 37N 77 19 E
Ghizri, *Kar.* **17 H11** 24 49N 67 2 E
Ghizri Cr. →, *Kar.* **17 H11** 24 47N 67 5 E
Ghonda, *Delhi* **16 A2** 28 41N 77 16 E
Ghushuri, *Calc.* **16 E6** 22 37N 88 21 E
Gianicolense, *Rome* **9 F9** 51 53N 12 28 E
Giant, *S.F.* **27 A2** 37 58N 122 20W
Gibbsboro, *Phil.* **24 B5** 39 50N 74 57W
Gibbstown, *Phil.* **24 C3** 39 49N 75 17W
Gibraltar Pt., *Trto.* **20 E8** 43 36N 79 23W
Gidea Park, *Lon.* **4 B6** 51 35N 0 11 E
Giesing, *Mün.* **7 G10** 48 6N 11 35 E
Gif-sur-Yvette, *Paris* **5 C2** 48 42N 2 8 E
Gilgo Beach, *N.Y.* **23 D8** 40 36N 73 24W
Gilgo I., *N.Y.* **23 D8** 40 37N 73 23W
Gillette, *N.Y.* **22 C2** 40 40N 74 29W
Gimmersta, *Stock.* **3 E12** 59 14N 18 14 E
Ginza, *Tōkyō* **13 C3** 35 39N 139 46 E
Girgaum, *Bomb.* **16 H8** 18 57N 72 50 E
Giugliano in Campánia, *Nápl.* **9 H12** 40 55N 14 12 E
Givoletto, *Tori.* **9 B1** 45 9N 7 29 E
Gjellumvatn, *Oslo* **2 C2** 59 47N 10 26 E
Gjersjoen, *Oslo* **2 C4** 59 47N 10 47 E
Glacier Hills, *N.Y.* **22 B2** 40 51N 74 28W
Gladbeck, *Ruhr* **6 A3** 51 34N 6 58 E
Gladesville, *Syd.* **19 B3** 33 50 S 151 8 E
Gladökvarn, *Stock.* **3 E10** 59 11N 17 59 E
Gladsakse, *Købn.* **2 D9** 55 45N 12 25 E
Glashutte, *Hbg.* **7 C8** 53 41N 10 2 E
Glashütte, *Ruhr* **6 C3** 51 13N 6 51 E
Glasmoor, *Hbg.* **7 C8** 53 42N 10 1 E
Glassmanor, *Wash.* **25 E7** 38 49N 77 0W
Glen Cove, *N.Y.* **23 B7** 40 52N 73 38W
Glen Echo, *Wash.* **25 D7** 38 58N 77 8W
Glen Hd., *N.Y.* **23 C7** 40 49N 73 37W
Glen Iris, *Melb.* **19 F7** 37 51 S 145 3 E
Glen Mills, *Phil.* **24 B2** 39 55N 75 29W
Glen Oaks, *N.Y.* **23 C6** 40 45N 73 43W
Glen Riddle, *Phil.* **24 B2** 39 53N 75 26W
Glen Ridge, *N.Y.* **22 C3** 40 48N 74 12W
Glen Rock, *N.Y.* **22 B4** 40 57N 74 7W
Glen Waverley, *Melb.* **19 F8** 37 52 S 145 10 E
Glenardon, *Wash.* **25 D8** 38 56N 76 51W
Glencoe, *Chic.* **26 A2** 42 7N 87 44W
Glendale, *L.A.* **28 B3** 34 9N 118 15 E
Glendora, *Phil.* **24 B4** 39 50N 75 4W
Glenfield, *Syd.* **19 B2** 33 58 S 150 53 E
Glenhazel, *Jobg.* **18 E9** 26 8 S 28 6 E
Glenhuntly, *Melb.* **19 F7** 37 52 S 145 1 E
Glenmont, *Wash.* **25 C7** 39 3N 77 4W
Glenolden, *Phil.* **24 B3** 39 54N 75 17W
Glenroy, *Melb.* **19 E6** 37 42 S 144 55 E
Glenside, *Phil.* **24 A4** 40 6N 75 9W
Glenview, *Chic.* **26 A2** 42 3N 87 48W
Glenview Countryside, *Chic.* **26 A2** 42 3N 87 49W
Glenview Woods, *Chic.* **26 A2** 42 4N 87 46W
Glenville, *N.Y.* **23 A6** 41 1N 73 41W
Glenvista, *Jobg.* **18 F9** 26 17 S 28 3 E
Glenwood Landing, *N.Y.* **23 C7** 40 48N 73 38W
Glienicke, *Berl.* **7 A2** 52 38N 13 18 E
Glomsta, *Stock.* **3 E10** 59 14N 17 55 E
Glosli, *Oslo* **2 A5** 60 1N 10 55 E
Glostrup, *Købn.* **2 E9** 55 39N 12 23 E
Gloucester City, *Phil.* **24 B4** 39 53N 75 7W
Gocheog, *Sŏul* **12 G7** 37 30N 126 52 E
Gocławek, *Wsaw.* **10 E7** 52 14N 21 7 E
Goeselville, *Chic.* **26 D2** 41 37N 87 46W
Goetjensort, *Hbg.* **7 E8** 53 29N 10 2 E
Golabari, *Calc.* **16 E6** 22 35N 88 20 E
Golabki, *Wsaw.* **10 E6** 52 12N 20 52 E
Golden Gate, *S.F.* **27 B2** 37 48N 122 29W
Golden Gate Bridge, *S.F.* **27 B2** 37 49N 122 28W
Golden Gate National Recreation Area, *S.F.* **27 B1** 37 49N 122 31W
Golden Gate Park, *S.F.* **27 B2** 37 46N 122 28W
Golden Horn, *Ist.* **17 A2** 41 1N 28 57 E
Golders Green, *Lon.* **4 B3** 51 34N 0 11W
Golyevo, *Mos.* **11 E7** 55 48N 37 18 E
Gometz-la-Ville, *Paris* **5 C2** 48 40N 2 7 E
Gometz-le-Châtel, *Paris* **5 C2** 48 40N 2 8 E
Gondangdra, *Jak.* **15 J9** 6 11 S 106 49 E
Gonesse, *Paris* **5 B4** 48 59N 2 26 E
Gongreung, *Sŏul* **12 G8** 37 36N 127 3 E
González Catán, *B.A.* **32 C3** 34 46 S 58 38W
Goodman Hill, *Bost.* **21 C1** 42 22N 71 23W
Goodmayes, *Lon.* **4 B5** 51 33N 0 6 E
Gopalnagar, *Calc.* **16 C5** 22 50N 88 13 E
Gopalpur, *Calc.* **16 E6** 22 38N 88 26 E
Górce, *Wsaw.* **10 E6** 52 15N 20 55 E
Gordon, *Syd.* **19 A3** 33 46 S 151 8 E
Gore Hill, *Syd.* **19 A4** 33 49 S 151 10 E
Gorelyy →, *Len.* **11 A5** 60 1N 30 30 E
Gorenki, *Mos.* **11 E11** 55 47N 37 53 E
Gorkiy Park, *Mos.* **11 E9** 55 43N 37 36 E
Görväln, *Stock.* **3 D9** 59 26N 17 45 E
Gose Elbe →, *Hbg.* **7 E8** 53 28N 10 6 E
Gosen, *Berl.* **7 B5** 52 23N 13 43 E
Gosener kanal, *Berl.* **7 B5** 52 24N 13 42 E
Goshenville, *Phil.* **24 B1** 39 59N 75 32W
Gospel Oak, *Lon.* **4 B4** 51 32N 0 9W
Gotanda, *Tōkyō* **13 C3** 35 37N 139 43 E
Gotanno, *Tōkyō* **13 B3** 35 45N 139 49 E
Goth Goli Mār, *Kar.* **17 G11** 24 53N 67 1 E
Goth Sher Shāh, *Kar.* **17 G10** 24 53N 66 59 E
Gournay-sur-Marne, *Paris* **5 B5** 48 51N 2 34 E
Goussainville, *Paris* **5 A4** 49 1N 2 27 E
Gouvernes, *Paris* **5 B6** 48 51N 2 41 E
Governador, I. do, *Rio J.* **31 A2** 22 48 S 43 13W
Governor's I., *N.Y.* **22 C4** 40 41N 74 1W
Grabicz, *Wsaw.* **10 E8** 52 19N 21 12 E
Grabów, *Wsaw.* **10 F6** 52 8N 20 59 E
Gracia, *Barc.* **8 D6** 41 24N 2 10 E
Gradyville, *Phil.* **24 B2** 39 56N 75 27W
Gräfelfing, *Mün.* **7 G9** 48 7N 11 25 E
Grafenwald, *Ruhr* **6 A3** 51 34N 6 54 E
Graham Memorial Park, *Balt.* **25 A4** 39 25N 76 29W
Gran Canal, *Méx.* **29 A3** 19 34N 99 1W
Granada Hills, *L.A.* **28 A1** 34 16N 118 30W
Grand Bourg, *B.A.* **32 A2** 34 29 S 58 42W
Grand Calumet →, *Chic.* **26 D4** 41 37N 87 28W
Grand Union Canal, *Lon.* **4 A2** 51 42N 0 26W
Grande →, *S. Pau.* **31 F7** 23 43 S 46 24W
Grange, *Tori.* **9 B1** 45 7N 7 29 E
Grange Hill, *Lon.* **4 B5** 51 36N 0 5 E
Granite, *Balt.* **25 A1** 39 20N 76 51W
Graniteville, *N.Y.* **22 D3** 40 37N 74 10W
Granja Viana, *S. Pau.* **31 E4** 23 35 S 46 50W
Granlandet, *Hels.* **3 B6** 60 10N 25 15 E
Granö, *Hels.* **3 B6** 60 13N 25 14 E
Grant Park, *Chic.* **26 B3** 41 52N 87 37W
Granville, *Syd.* **19 A3** 33 49 S 151 1 E
Grape I., *Bost.* **21 D4** 42 16N 70 55W
Grass Hassock Channel, *N.Y.* **23 D6** 40 36N 73 47W
Grassey B., *N.Y.* **23 D6** 40 37N 73 47W
Grassy Sprain Res., *N.Y.* **23 B5** 40 58N 73 50W
Gratosóglio, *Mil.* **9 E6** 45 24N 9 1 E
Gratzwalde, *Berl.* **7 B5** 52 28N 13 42 E
Gravesend, *N.Y.* **22 D5** 40 36N 73 56W
Grays, *Lon.* **4 C6** 51 28N 0 19 E
Grazhdanka, *Len.* **11 B4** 59 59N 30 24 E
Great Blue Hill, *Bost.* **21 D3** 42 12N 71 4W
Great Bookham, *Lon.* **4 D2** 51 16N 0 21W
Great Brewster I., *Bost.* **21 C4** 42 19N 70 53W
Great Captain I., *N.Y.* **23 B7** 40 59N 73 37W
Great Falls, *Wash.* **25 D6** 38 59N 77 17W
Great Falls Park, *Wash.* **25 D6** 38 59N 77 14W
Great Kills, *N.Y.* **22 D4** 40 32N 74 9W
Great Kills Harbour, *N.Y.* **22 D4** 40 32N 74 8W
Great Neck, *N.Y.* **23 C6** 40 48N 73 44W
Great Pond, *Bost.* **21 D3** 42 11N 71 2W
Great South B., *N.Y.* **23 D9** 40 39N 73 19W
Greco, *Mil.* **9 D6** 45 30N 9 12 E
Greco I., *S.F.* **27 C3** 37 30N 122 10W
Green Brae, *S.F.* **27 A1** 37 57N 122 31W
Green Brook, *N.Y.* **22 D2** 40 35N 74 26W
Green I., *H.K.* **12 E5** 22 17N 114 6 E
Green Land, *Jak.* **15 J9** 6 17 S 106 46 E
Green Pond, *N.Y.* **22 A2** 41 1N 74 29W
Green Street, *Lon.* **4 A3** 51 40N 0 16W
Green Street Green, *Lon.* **4 C5** 51 21N 0 5 E
Green Valley, *Syd.* **19 B2** 33 54 S 150 53 E
Green Village, *N.Y.* **22 C2** 40 44N 74 27W
Greenbelt, *Wash.* **25 C8** 39 0N 76 52W
Greenbelt Park, *Wash.* **25 D8** 38 58N 76 53W
Greenfield Park, *Mtrl.* **20 B5** 43 29N 73 28W
Greenfields Village, *Phil.* **24 C4** 39 49N 75 9W
Greenford, *Lon.* **4 B2** 51 31N 0 21W
Greenhithe, *Lon.* **4 C6** 51 27N 0 17 E
Greenlawn, *N.Y.* **23 B8** 40 52N 73 22W
Greenpoint, *N.Y.* **22 C5** 40 43N 73 57W
Greensborough, *Melb.* **19 E7** 37 41 S 145 5 E
Greenside, *Jobg.* **18 E9** 26 8 S 28 1 E
Greenvale, *N.Y.* **23 C7** 40 48N 73 35W
Greenville Chauncey, *N.Y.* **23 B5** 40 59N 73 50W
Greenwich, *Lon.* **4 C4** 51 28N 0 0 E
Greenwich, *N.Y.* **23 A7** 41 1N 73 37W
Greenwich, *Syd.* **19 B4** 33 50 S 151 11 E
Greenwich Observatory, *Lon.* **4 C4** 51 28N 0 0 E
Greenwich Pt., *N.Y.* **23 A7** 41 0N 73 34W
Greenwich Village, *N.Y.* **22 C5** 40 44N 73 59W
Greenwood, *Bost.* **21 C3** 42 29N 71 2W
Grefsen, *Oslo* **2 B4** 59 56N 10 47 E
Grégy-sur-Yerres, *Paris* **5 C5** 48 40N 2 37 E
Greiffenburg, *Ruhr* **6 B1** 51 20N 6 37 E
Gressy, *Paris* **5 B6** 48 58N 2 40 E
Greve Strand, *Købn.* **2 E8** 55 34N 12 18 E
Greystanes, *Syd.* **19 A2** 33 49 S 150 58 E
Griebnitzsee, *Berl.* **7 B1** 52 23N 13 8 E
Griffith Park, *L.A.* **28 B3** 34 7N 118 18 E
Grignon, *Paris* **5 B1** 48 50N 1 56 E
Grigny, *Paris* **5 D4** 48 39N 2 23 E
Grinzing, *Wien* **10 G10** 48 15N 16 20 E
Grisy-Suisnes, *Paris* **5 C6** 48 41N 2 40 E
Gröbenried, *Mün.* **7 F9** 48 13N 11 25 E
Grochów, *Wsaw.* **10 E7** 52 15N 21 5 E
Grodzisk, *Wsaw.* **10 E7** 52 19N 21 4 E
Grogol, *Jak.* **15 H9** 6 9 S 106 47 E
Grogol, Kali →, *Jak.* **15 J9** 6 11 S 106 47 E
Gronsdorf, *Mün.* **7 G11** 48 7N 11 42 E
Grorud, *Oslo* **2 B5** 59 57N 10 52 E
Gross Borstel, *Hbg.* **7 D7** 53 36N 9 58 E
Gross Flottbek, *Hbg.* **7 D7** 53 33N 9 53 E
Gross Glienicke, *Berl.* **7 B1** 52 28N 13 6 E
Gross-Hadern, *Mün.* **7 G9** 48 6N 11 29 E
Gross-Lappen, *Mün.* **7 F10** 48 11N 11 35 E
Grosse Krampe, *Berl.* **7 B5** 52 23N 13 40 E
Grosse Müggelsee, *Berl.* **7 B4** 52 26N 13 38 E
Grossenbaum, *Ruhr* **6 B2** 51 22N 6 46 E
Grossenzersdorf, *Wien* **10 G11** 48 12N 16 33 E
Grossenzersdorfer Arm →, *Wien* **10 G11** 48 12N 16 31 E
Grosser Biberhaufen, *Wien* **10 G10** 48 12N 16 28 E
Grosser Wannsee, *Berl.* **7 B2** 52 25N 13 10 E
Grossfeld-Siedlung, *Wien* **10 G10** 48 16N 16 26 E
Grosshesselohe, *Mün.* **7 G10** 48 3N 11 32 E
Grossjedlersdorf, *Wien* **10 G10** 48 16N 16 23 E
Grossziethen, *Berl.* **7 B3** 52 23N 13 26 E
Groszówka, *Wsaw.* **10 E8** 52 14N 21 13 E
Grove Hall, *Bost.* **21 D3** 42 18N 71 4W
Grove Park, *Lon.* **4 C5** 51 25N 0 1 E
Grove Park, *Lon.* **4 C3** 51 28N 0 15W
Groveton, *Wash.* **25 E7** 38 46N 77 6W
Grugliasco, *Tori.* **9 B2** 45 5N 7 34 E
Gruiten, *Ruhr* **6 C4** 51 12N 7 0 E
Grumme, *Ruhr* **6 B5** 51 30N 7 15 E
Grumo Nevano, *Nápl.* **9 H12** 40 56N 14 15 E
Grünau, *Berl.* **7 B4** 52 25N 13 34 E
Grunewald, *Berl.* **7 B2** 52 28N 13 13 E
Grünwald, *Mün.* **7 G10** 48 2N 11 31 E
Grünwalder Forst, *Mün.* **7 G10** 48 2N 11 33 E
Grymes Hill, *N.Y.* **22 D4** 40 36N 74 6W
Gu Ro, *Sŏul* **12 G7** 37 30N 126 51 E
Guadalupe, *Manila* **15 D4** 14 34N 121 2 E
Guadalupe →, *S.F.* **27 D4** 37 28N 122 4W
Guadalupe, Basilica de, *Méx.* **29 B3** 19 29N 99 7W
Guadelupe, *Rio J.* **31 A1** 22 49 S 43 20W
Guanabacoa, *La Hab.* **30 B3** 23 7N 82 17W
Guanabara, *Rio J.* **31 B1** 22 57 S 43 20W
Guanabara, B. de, *Rio J.* **31 B2** 22 52 S 43 10W
Guanabara, Jardim, *Rio J.* **31 A2** 22 48 S 43 11W
Guang'anmen, *Beij.* **14 B2** 39 51N 116 18 E
Guangminglou, *Beij.* **14 B3** 39 51N 116 23 E
Guangqumen, *Beij.* **14 B3** 39 52N 116 25 E
Guangzhou, *Gzh.* **14 G8** 23 6N 113 13 E
Guanshuo, *Gzh.* **14 G9** 23 4N 113 22 E
Guantai, *Nápl.* **9 H12** 40 52N 14 11 E
Guapira →, *S. Pau.* **31 D6** 23 30 S 46 33W
Guarapiranga, Res. de, *S. Pau.* **31 F5** 23 42 S 46 43W
Guardias, *Mdrd.* **8 B3** 40 29N 3 31W
Guarulhos, *S. Pau.* **31 D6** 23 28 S 46 32W
Guatao, *La Hab.* **30 B2** 23 0N 82 29W
Guayacanes, Pta., *La Hab.* **30 A3** 23 10N 82 16W
Gubernador Monteverde, *B.A.* **32 C5** 34 47 S 58 16W
Gudö, *Stock.* **3 E12** 59 12N 18 12 E
Güell, Parque de, *Barc.* **8 D6** 41 24N 2 10 E
Guermantes, *Paris* **5 B6** 48 51N 2 42 E
Gugging, *Wien* **10 G9** 48 18N 16 15 E
Guianazes, *S. Pau.* **31 E7** 23 32 S 46 24W
Guildford, *Syd.* **19 B2** 33 51 S 150 59 E
Guinardó, *Barc.* **8 D6** 41 24N 2 10 E
Gujiazhai, *Shang.* **14 H11** 31 21N 121 23 E
Gulbāi, *Kar.* **17 G10** 24 52N 66 58 E
Guldasteh, *Tehr.* **17 D4** 35 36N 51 15 E
Gulistan Palace, *Tehr.* **17 C5** 35 40N 51 24 E
Gulph Mills, *Phil.* **24 A2** 40 4N 75 20W
Gumbostrand, *Hels.* **3 B6** 60 15N 25 17 E
Güngören, *Ist.* **17 A2** 41 1N 28 52 E
Gunnarsby, *Hels.* **3 C1** 60 6N 24 28W
Gunnersbury, *Lon.* **4 C3** 51 29N 0 17W
Gunnigfeld, *Ruhr* **6 B4** 51 29N 7 8 E
Gunpowder Falls →, *Balt.* **25 A4** 39 23N 76 36W
Gunung Sahari, *Jak.* **15 H9** 6 9 S 106 49 E
Gupiing, *Manila* **15 E5** 14 27N 121 11 E
Guryong San, *Sŏul* **12 H8** 37 28N 127 3 E
Gustavsberg, *Stock.* **3 E13** 59 19N 18 23 E
Guttenberg, *N.Y.* **22 C4** 40 48N 74 0W
Gutuyevskiy, Os., *Len.* **11 B3** 59 53N 30 15 E
Guyancourt, *Paris* **5 C2** 48 46N 2 4 E
Guyancourt, Aérodrome de, *Paris* **5 C2** 48 45N 2 3 E
Gvali-patak →, *Bud.* **10 K13** 47 23N 19 7 E
Gwan Ag, *Sŏul* **12 H7** 37 29N 126 57 E
Gwanag San, *Sŏul* **12 H7** 37 27N 126 58 E
Gwynns Falls →, *Balt.* **25 B2** 39 19N 76 42W
Gyál, *Bud.* **10 K14** 47 23N 19 13 E
Gyeongbong Palace, *Sŏul* **12 G7** 37 34N 126 58 E
Gynea, *Syd.* **19 C3** 34 1 S 151 5 E

H

Haaga, *Hels.* **3 B4** 60 13N 24 53 E
Haan, *Ruhr* **6 C3** 51 11N 6 59 E
Haar, *Mün.* **7 G11** 48 6N 11 43 E
Haar, *Ruhr* **6 B5** 51 26N 7 13 E
Haarzopf, *Ruhr* **6 B3** 51 25N 6 57 E
Habana del Este, *La Hab.* **30 B3** 23 9N 82 19W
Habay, *Manila* **15 E3** 14 27N 120 56 E
Habikino, *Ōsaka* **12 C4** 34 33N 135 36 E
Habinghorst, *Ruhr* **6 A5** 51 34N 7 18 E
Hacienda Heights, *L.A.* **28 C5** 33 59N 117 59W
Hackbridge, *Lon.* **4 C4** 51 23N 0 9W
Hackensack, *N.Y.* **22 B4** 40 52N 74 4W
Hackney, *Lon.* **4 B4** 51 32N 0 3W
Hackney Wick, *Lon.* **4 B4** 51 32N 0 1W
Haddon Heights, *Phil.* **24 B4** 39 53N 75 3W
Haddonfield, *Phil.* **24 B4** 39 53N 75 3W
Hadersdorf, *Wien* **10 G9** 48 12N 16 14 E
Hadley Wood, *Lon.* **4 B3** 51 39N 0 10W
Haga, *Stock.* **3 D11** 59 21N 18 1 E
Hagem, *Ruhr* **6 A5** 51 38N 7 19 E
Hagen, *Ruhr* **6 B6** 51 21N 7 27 E
Hägersten, *Stock.* **3 E10** 59 18N 17 59 E
Haggetts Pond, *Bost.* **21 B2** 42 39N 71 11W
Häggvik, *Stock.* **3 D10** 59 26N 17 56 E
Hagonoy, *Manila* **15 D4** 14 30N 121 4 E
Hagsätra, *Stock.* **3 E11** 59 15N 18 0 E
Hahipur, *Calc.* **16 D5** 22 47N 88 10 E
Hahnerberg, *Ruhr* **6 C4** 51 12N 7 9 E
Hai He →, *Tianj.* **14 E6** 39 4N 117 17 E
Haidarpur, *Delhi* **16 A1** 28 43N 77 8 E
Haidhausen, *Mün.* **7 G10** 48 7N 11 36 E
Haidian, *Beij.* **14 B2** 39 59N 116 16 E
Haight-Ashbury, *S.F.* **27 B2** 37 46N 122 26W
Haiguangsi, *Tianj.* **14 E6** 39 7N 117 11 E
Hainault, *Lon.* **4 B5** 51 36N 0 6 E
Haizhu Guangchang, *Gzh.* **14 G8** 23 6N 113 14 E
Hakim, *El Qâ.* **18 C4** 30 4N 31 7 E
Hakunila, *Hels.* **3 B5** 60 16N 25 6 E
Halchōbori, *Tōkyō* **13 B4** 35 48N 139 55 E
Haledon, *N.Y.* **22 B3** 40 57N 74 11W
Halesite, *N.Y.* **23 B8** 40 53N 73 24W
Halethorpe, *Balt.* **25 B2** 39 14N 76 41W
Half Hollow Hills, *N.Y.* **23 C8** 40 48N 73 21W
Half Moon B., *S.F.* **26 D2** 37 27N 122 25W
Half Moon Bay Airport, *S.F.* **27 C1** 37 31N 122 30W
Half Moon Bay Beaches, *S.F.* **26 D2** 37 28N 122 28W
Halim, *Jak.* **15 J10** 6 15 S 106 53 E
Halim Perdanakusuma Airport, *Jak.* **15 J10** 6 16 S 106 53 E
Halstead, *Lon.* **4 D5** 51 19N 0 8 E
Halstenbeck, *Hbg.* **7 D7** 53 38N 9 50 E
Haltiala, *Hels.* **3 B4** 60 16N 24 57 E
Haltiavuori, *Hels.* **3 B4** 60 16N 24 56 E
Ham, *Lon.* **4 C3** 51 25N 0 18W
Ham, *Paris* **5 A2** 49 1N 2 3 E
Hamberg, *Jobg.* **18 E8** 26 9 S 27 54 E
Hamborn, *Ruhr* **6 B2** 51 29N 6 46 E
Hamburg, *Hbg.* **7 D8** 53 33N 10 0 E
Hamburg Flughafen, *Hbg.* **7 D7** 53 38N 9 59 E
Hämeenkylä, *Hels.* **3 B3** 60 16N 24 48 E
Hamm, *Hbg.* **7 D8** 53 33N 10 2 E
Hamm, *Ruhr* **6 C2** 51 12N 6 44 E
Hammarby, *Stock.* **3 E11** 59 17N 18 5 E
Hamme, *Ruhr* **6 B5** 51 29N 7 12 E
Hammel Arverne, *N.Y.* **23 D6** 40 35N 73 48W
Hammerbrook, *Hbg.* **7 D8** 53 32N 10 1 E
Hammersmith, *Lon.* **4 C3** 51 29N 0 14W
Hammond, *Chic.* **26 D4** 41 36N 87 29W
Hampstead, *Lon.* **4 B3** 51 33N 0 10W
Hampstead, *Mtrl.* **20 B4** 43 28N 73 37W
Hampstead Garden Suburb, *Lon.* **4 B3** 51 34N 0 11W
Hampstead Heath, *Lon.* **4 B3** 51 33N 0 10W
Hampton Court Palace, *Lon.* **4 C2** 51 24N 0 20W
Hampton Hill, *Lon.* **4 C2** 51 25N 0 21W
Hampton Wick, *Lon.* **4 C3** 51 24N 0 18W
Hamrā, *Bagd.* **17 F7** 33 18N 44 18 E
Han Gang →, *Sŏul* **12 G7** 37 32N 126 55 E
Hanakuri, *Tōkyō* **13 A3** 35 50N 139 47 E
Hanala, *Hels.* **3 A5** 60 20N 25 4 E
Hancho, *Ōsaka* **12 B3** 34 48N 135 28 E
Haneda, *Tōkyō* **13 C3** 35 32N 139 44 E
Hang Hau, *H.K.* **12 E6** 22 19N 114 16 E
Hanjiashu, *Tianj.* **14 D5** 39 11N 117 4 E
Hanlon, *Trto.* **20 E7** 43 38N 79 39W
Hansen Flood Control Basin, *L.A.* **28 A2** 34 15N 118 23W
Hansia, *Calc.* **16 D6** 22 48N 88 24 E
Hanskinen, *Hels.* **3 C6** 60 8N 25 15 E
Hanwell, *Lon.* **4 B2** 51 30N 0 20W
Hanworth, *Lon.* **4 C2** 51 26N 0 23W
Haora, *Calc.* **16 E5** 22 34N 88 18 E
Happy Valley, *H.K.* **12 E6** 22 16N 114 10 E
Harajuku, *Tōkyō* **13 D2** 35 22N 139 30 E
Haraki, *Tōkyō* **13 B4** 35 42N 139 56 E
Harat, *Calc.* **16 C5** 22 52N 88 11 E
Harbor Hills, *N.Y.* **23 C6** 40 46N 73 44W
Harburg, *Hbg.* **7 E7** 53 27N 9 59 E
Harding, *Bost.* **21 D2** 42 12N 71 19W
Hardricourt, *Paris* **5 A1** 49 0N 1 53 E
Harefield, *Lon.* **4 B2** 51 36N 0 28W
Hareskovby, *Købn.* **2 D9** 55 45N 12 23 E
Harewood Park, *Balt.* **25 A4** 39 22N 76 21W
Harigaya, *Tōkyō* **13 B2** 35 49N 139 33 E
Haringey, *Lon.* **4 B4** 51 34N 0 4W
Haripur, *Calc.* **16 D5** 22 42N 88 10 E
Harjula, *Hels.* **3 A3** 60 21N 24 45 E
Harjusuo, *Hels.* **3 B5** 60 19N 25 0 E
Harkortsee, *Ruhr* **6 B6** 51 23N 7 24 E
Harksheide, *Hbg.* **7 C8** 53 43N 10 0 E
Harlaching, *Mün.* **7 G10** 48 5N 11 33 E
Harlem, *N.Y.* **22 C5** 40 48N 73 56W
Harlesden, *Lon.* **4 B3** 51 32N 0 14W
Harlington, *Lon.* **4 C2** 51 29N 0 25W
Harmaja, *Hels.* **3 C4** 60 6N 24 58 E
Harmashatar hegy, *Bud.* **10 J13** 47 33N 19 0 E
Harmondsworth, *Lon.* **4 C2** 51 29N 0 29W
Harmonville, *Phil.* **24 A3** 40 5N 75 18W
Harold Hill, *Lon.* **4 B6** 51 36N 0 14 E
Harold Parker State Forest, *Bost.* **21 B3** 42 37N 71 4W
Harold Wood, *Lon.* **4 B6** 51 35N 0 14 E
Harrington Park, *N.Y.* **22 B5** 40 59N 73 59W
Harrison, *N.Y.* **22 C4** 40 44N 74 9W
Harrison, *N.Y.* **23 B6** 40 57N 73 42W
Harrisonville, *Balt.* **25 A2** 39 22N 76 49W
Harrow, *Lon.* **4 B2** 51 34N 0 20W
Harrow on the Hill, *Lon.* **4 B2** 51 34N 0 21W
Harrow School, *Lon.* **4 B2** 51 34N 0 20W
Harrow Weald, *Lon.* **4 B2** 51 36N 0 20W
Hart I., *Balt.* **25 B4** 39 14N 76 23W
Hart I., *N.Y.* **23 B6** 40 51N 73 46W
Hartford, *Phil.* **24 B5** 39 58N 74 53W
Hartley, *Lon.* **4 C6** 51 22N 0 18 E
Hartsdale, *N.Y.* **23 A6** 41 1N 73 48W
Harumi, *Tōkyō* **13 C3** 35 38N 139 47 E
Harvard, Mt., *L.A.* **28 A4** 34 12N 118 4W
Harvard Univ., *Bost.* **21 C3** 42 23N 71 7W
Harvestehude, *Hbg.* **7 D7** 53 34N 9 58 E
Harvey, *Chic.* **26 D3** 41 36N 87 39W
Harwood Heights, *Chic.* **26 B2** 41 57N 87 46W
Hasanābād, *Tehr.* **17 C4** 35 44N 51 16 E
Hasbrouck Heights, *N.Y.* **22 B4** 40 51N 74 6W
Haselbach, *Wien* **10 G9** 48 18N 16 14 E
Haselhorst, *Berl.* **7 A2** 52 33N 13 14 E
Hasköy, *Ist.* **17 A2** 41 2N 28 57 E
Hasle, *Oslo* **2 C3** 59 46N 10 38 E
Hasloh, *Hbg.* **7 C7** 53 41N 9 54 E
Haslohfeld, *Hbg.* **7 C7** 53 41N 9 56 E
Haslum, *Oslo* **2 B3** 59 55N 10 34 E
Haspe, *Ruhr* **6 B6** 51 21N 7 25 E
Haspertalsp, *Ruhr* **6 C6** 51 17N 7 24 E
Hasselbeck, *Ruhr* **6 C3** 51 19N 6 56 E
Hässelby, *Stock.* **3 D10** 59 22N 17 50 E
Hasslinghausen, *Ruhr* **6 C5** 51 20N 7 16 E
Hasten, *Ruhr* **6 C5** 51 11N 7 11 E
Hästhagen, *Stock.* **3 E11** 59 18N 18 9 E
Hastings-on-Hudson, *N.Y.* **23 B5** 40 59N 73 51W
Hatch End, *Lon.* **4 B2** 51 36N 0 22W
Hatiara, *Calc.* **16 E6** 22 36N 88 26 E
Hatogaya, *Tōkyō* **13 B3** 35 49N 139 44 E
Hattingen, *Ruhr* **6 B5** 51 23N 7 11 E
Hatton, *Lon.* **4 C2** 51 28N 0 25W
Hattori, *Ōsaka* **12 A4** 34 51N 135 36 E
Hauketo, *Oslo* **2 B4** 59 50N 10 48 E
Hauldres →, *Paris* **5 D5** 48 37N 2 37 E
Hausbruch, *Hbg.* **7 E7** 53 28N 9 53 E
Havalimani, *Ist.* **17 B2** 40 59N 28 50 E
Havana = La Habana, *La Hab.* **30 B2** 23 7N 82 21W
Havdrup, *Købn.* **2 E7** 55 33N 12 7 E
Havel →, *Berl.* **7 A2** 52 37N 13 11 E
Havelkanal, *Berl.* **7 A2** 52 36N 13 10 E
Haverford, *Phil.* **24 A3** 40 0N 75 18W
Havering, *Lon.* **4 B6** 51 33N 0 12 E
Havering-atte-Bower, *Lon.* **4 B6** 51 37N 0 11 E
Havertown, *Phil.* **24 B3** 39 58N 75 18W
Hawangsibri, *Sŏul* **12 G8** 37 33N 127 1 E
Haweolgog, *Sŏul* **12 G8** 37 35N 127 1 E
Haworth, *N.Y.* **22 B5** 40 57N 73 59W
Hawthorne, *L.A.* **28 C2** 33 54N 118 21W
Hawthorne, *N.Y.* **22 B4** 40 57N 74 8W
Hayes, *Lon.* **4 C5** 51 22N 0 0 E
Hayes, *Lon.* **4 B2** 51 30N 0 25W
Hayes End, *Lon.* **4 B2** 51 31N 0 25W
Hayford, *Chic.* **26 C2** 41 45N 87 42W
Hayward, *S.F.* **27 B4** 37 40N 122 4W
Hayward Fault, *S.F.* **27 B3** 37 46N 122 10W
Haywood Municipal Airport, *S.F.* **27 C4** 32 39N 122 9W
Headley, *Lon.* **4 D3** 51 16N 0 16W
Headstone, *Lon.* **4 B2** 51 35N 0 21W
Heard Pond, *Bost.* **21 C1** 42 20N 71 23W
Heart Pond, *Bost.* **21 B1** 42 33N 71 23W
Heath Park, *Lon.* **4 B6** 51 34N 0 12 E
Heathmont, *Melb.* **19 E8** 37 49 S 145 14 E
Heathrow Airport, *Lon.* **4 C2** 51 28N 0 27W
Hebbville, *Balt.* **25 A2** 39 20N 76 45W
Hebe Haven, *H.K.* **12 D6** 22 21N 114 15 E
Hebei, *Tianj.* **14 E6** 39 9N 117 11 E
Hedehusene, *Købn.* **2 E8** 55 39N 12 11 E
Hedong, *Gzh.* **14 G8** 23 5N 113 14 E
Hedong, *Tianj.* **14 E6** 39 7N 117 11 E
Heerdt, *Ruhr* **6 C2** 51 13N 6 42 E
Hegewisch, *Chic.* **26 D3** 41 39N 87 32W
Heggelielva →, *Oslo* **2 A3** 60 1N 10 36 E
Heide, *Ruhr* **6 A3** 51 31N 6 50 E
Heidelberg, *Melb.* **19 E7** 37 45 S 145 4 E
Heidelberg West, *Melb.* **19 E7** 37 43 S 145 2 E
Heidemühle, *Berl.* **7 B5** 52 29N 13 40 E
Heidhausen, *Ruhr* **6 B4** 51 22N 7 1 E
Heiligenhaus, *Ruhr* **6 C3** 51 19N 6 57 E
Heiligensee, *Berl.* **7 A2** 52 36N 13 13 E
Heiligenstadt, *Wien* **10 G10** 48 14N 16 21 E
Heimfeld, *Hbg.* **7 E7** 53 28N 9 57 E
Heinässuo, *Hels.* **3 B1** 60 18N 24 27 E
Heinersdorf, *Berl.* **7 A3** 52 34N 13 26 E
Heisingen, *Ruhr* **6 B4** 51 24N 7 3 E
Heissen, *Ruhr* **6 B3** 51 26N 6 54 E
Helderkruin, *Jobg.* **18 E8** 26 7 S 27 51 E
Helenelund, *Stock.* **3 D10** 59 24N 17 58 E
Heliopolis, *El Qâ.* **18 C5** 30 5N 31 19 E
Hellersdorf, *Berl.* **7 A4** 52 32N 13 35 E
Hellerup, *Købn.* **2 D10** 55 44N 12 33 E
Helmahof, *Wien* **10 G11** 48 18N 16 34 E
Helsingfors, *Hels.* **3 B4** 60 10N 24 55 E
Helsinki, *Hels.* **3 B4** 60 10N 24 55 E
Helsinki Airport, *Hels.* **3 B4** 60 18N 24 58 E
Hempstead, *N.Y.* **23 C7** 40 42N 73 37W
Hempstead Harbor, *N.Y.* **23 B7** 40 50N 73 39W
Hemttaa, *Hels.* **3 B3** 60 11N 24 45 E
Henan, *Gzh.* **14 G8** 23 5N 113 14 E
Hendon, *Lon.* **4 B3** 51 35N 0 14W
Hengsha, *Gzh.* **14 G8** 23 9N 113 12 E
Hengsteysee, *Ruhr* **6 B6** 51 24N 7 27 E
Hennigsdorf, *Berl.* **7 A2** 52 38N 13 12 E
Henrichenburg, *Ruhr* **6 A5** 51 35N 7 19 E
Henriville, *Paris* **5 C1** 48 44N 1 56 E
Henrykow, *Wsaw.* **10 E6** 52 19N 20 58 E
Henson Cr. →, *Wash.* **25 E8** 38 47N 76 58W
Heping, *Tianj.* **14 E6** 39 7N 117 11 E
Heping Gongyuan, *Shang.* **14 J12** 31 16N 121 30 E
Hepingli, *Beij.* **14 B3** 39 57N 116 23 E
Herbeck, *Ruhr* **6 C5** 51 12N 7 18 E
Herbede, *Ruhr* **6 B5** 51 25N 7 16 E
Herblay, *Paris* **5 B2** 48 59N 2 9 E
Herdecke, *Ruhr* **6 B6** 51 24N 7 25 E
Herlev, *Købn.* **2 D9** 55 43N 12 27 E
Hermannskogel, *Wien* **10 G9** 48 16N 16 17 E
Hermitage and Winter Palace, *Len.* **11 B3** 59 55N 30 19 E
Hermosa Beach, *L.A.* **28 C2** 33 51N 118 23W
Hermsdorf, *Berl.* **7 A2** 52 37N 13 18 E
Hernals, *Wien* **10 G10** 48 13N 16 20 E
Herne, *Ruhr* **6 A5** 51 32N 7 13 E
Herne Hill, *Lon.* **4 C4** 51 27N 0 6W
Hernwood Heights, *Balt.* **25 A2** 39 22N 76 49W
Héroes de Churubusco, *Méx.* **29 B3** 19 21N 99 6W
Herongate, *Lon.* **4 B7** 51 35N 0 21 E
Herons, Î. aux, *Mtrl.* **20 B4** 43 25N 73 34W
Herricks, *N.Y.* **23 C7** 40 45N 73 39W
Herring Run →, *Balt.* **25 B3** 39 18N 76 30W
Hersham, *Lon.* **4 C2** 51 21N 0 22W
Herstedøster, *Købn.* **2 D9** 55 40N 12 22 E
Herten, *Ruhr* **6 A4** 51 35N 7 8 E
Herttoniemi, *Hels.* **3 B5** 60 12N 25 2 E
Hessler, *Ruhr* **6 A4** 51 31N 7 3 E
Heston, *Lon.* **4 C2** 51 28N 0 22W
Hetterscheidt, *Ruhr* **6 B3** 51 20N 6 59 E
Hetzendorf, *Wien* **10 H9** 48 9N 16 17 E
Heuberg, *Wien* **10 G9** 48 13N 16 16 E
Heven, *Ruhr* **6 B5** 51 26N 7 18 E
Hewlett Neck, *N.Y.* **23 D6** 40 37N 73 41W
Hexi, *Tianj.* **14 E5** 39 8N 117 9 E
Hexingcun, *Tianj.* **14 E6** 39 6N 117 10 E
Hextable, *Lon.* **4 C6** 51 24N 0 10 E
Heybridge, *Lon.* **4 B7** 51 39N 0 22 E
Hibernia, *N.Y.* **22 B2** 40 57N 74 29W
Hickory Hills, *Chic.* **26 C2** 41 43N 87 49W
Hicksville, *N.Y.* **23 C7** 40 46N 73 30W
Hiddinghausen, *Ruhr* **6 B5** 51 21N 7 17 E
Hiekkaharju, *Hels.* **3 B5** 60 18N 25 2 E
Hiesfeld, *Ruhr* **6 A2** 51 33N 6 46 E
Hietaniemi, *Hels.* **3 B4** 60 10N 24 54 E
Hietzing, *Wien* **10 G9** 48 10N 16 17 E
Higashi, *Ōsaka* **12 B4** 34 41N 135 30 E
Higashi-kaizuka, *Tōkyō* **13 A3** 35 50N 139 46 E
Higashimonzen, *Tōkyō* **13 A3** 35 55N 139 40 E
Higashimurayama, *Tōkyō* **13 B1** 35 45N 139 26 E
Higashinada, *Ōsaka* **12 B2** 34 42N 135 15 E
Higashinari, *Ōsaka* **12 B4** 34 40N 135 32 E
Higashiōsaka, *Ōsaka* **12 C4** 34 39N 135 37 E
Higashisumiyoshi, *Ōsaka* **12 C4** 34 37N 135 31 E
Higashiyodogawa, *Ōsaka* **12 B3** 34 44N 135 28 E
High Beach, *Lon.* **4 B5** 51 39N 0 1 E
High Junk Pk., *H.K.* **12 E6** 22 17N 114 17 E
High Park, *Trto.* **20 E8** 43 38N 79 27W
Higham Hill, *Lon.* **4 B4** 51 35N 0 2W
Highbury, *Lon.* **4 B4** 51 33N 0 6W
Highgate, *Lon.* **4 B4** 51 34N 0 8W
Highland Cr. →, *Trto.* **20 D9** 43 45N 79 13W
Highland Creek, *Trto.* **20 D9** 43 46N 79 8W
Highland Park, *L.A.* **28 B3** 34 7N 118 13 E
Highland Park, *N.Y.* **22 D2** 40 30N 74 25W
Highlands North, *Jobg.* **18 E9** 26 8 S 28 5 E
Highway Highlands, *L.A.* **28 A3** 34 14N 118 16W
Higurashi, *Tōkyō* **13 B4** 35 47N 139 55 E
Hila, *Méx.* **29 A2** 19 35N 99 17W
Hillcrest Heights, *Wash.* **25 E8** 38 49N 76 57W
Hillerheide, *Ruhr* **6 A5** 51 35N 7 12 E
Hilleshög, *Stock.* **3 D9** 59 23N 17 42 E
Hillgrove District, *L.A.* **28 B5** 34 1N 117 58W
Hillingdon, *Lon.* **4 B2** 51 32N 0 27W
Hillingdon Heath, *Lon.* **4 B2** 51 31N 0 26W
Hillsborough, *S.F.* **27 C2** 37 32N 122 21W
Hillsdale, *N.Y.* **22 A4** 41 0N 74 1W
Hillsdale, *S.F.* **27 C3** 37 32N 122 18W
Hillsdale Manor, *N.Y.* **22 A4** 41 1N 74 3W
Hillside, *Chic.* **26 B1** 41 52N 87 55W
Hillside, *N.Y.* **23 C6** 40 42N 73 46W
Hillside Manor, *N.Y.* **23 C6** 40 44N 73 40W
Hilltop, *Phil.* **24 C4** 39 49N 75 4W
Hillwood, *Wash.* **25 D7** 38 52N 77 9W
Hilmîya, *El Qâ.* **18 C5** 30 6N 31 19 E
Hiltrop, *Ruhr* **6 A5** 51 31N 7 15 E
Hindsby, *Hels.* **3 A6** 60 20N 25 13 E
Hingham, *Bost.* **21 D4** 42 14N 70 54W
Hingham B., *Bost.* **21 D4** 42 17N 70 56W
Hingham Harbor, *Bost.* **21 D4** 42 15N 70 53W
Hino, *Tōkyō* **13 D2** 35 23N 139 35 E
Hinsbeck, *Ruhr* **6 B4** 51 22N 7 4 E
Hinschenfelde, *Hbg.* **7 D8** 53 35N 10 0 E
Hinsdale, *Chic.* **26 C1** 41 47N 87 55W
Hinterhainbach, *Wien* **10 G9** 48 14N 16 13 E
Hintersdorf, *Wien* **10 G9** 48 18N 16 13 E
Hirakata, *Ōsaka* **12 B4** 34 48N 135 38 E
Hirota, *Ōsaka* **12 B3** 34 45N 135 20 E
Hirschstetten, *Wien* **10 G10** 48 14N 16 27 E
Hither Green, *Lon.* **4 C4** 51 26N 0 0 E
Hiyoshi, *Tōkyō* **13 C2** 35 32N 139 38 E
Hjortekær, *Købn.* **2 D10** 55 47N 12 32 E
Hjortespring, *Købn.* **2 D9** 55 44N 12 25 E
Hlubočepy, *Pra.* **10 B2** 50 2N 14 23 E
Ho Chung, *H.K.* **12 D6** 22 21N 114 14 E
Ho Man Tin, *H.K.* **12 E6** 22 18N 114 11 E
Hoboken, *N.Y.* **22 C4** 40 44N 74 3W
Hobsons B., *Melb.* **19 F6** 37 51 S 144 55 E
Hochbrück, *Mün.* **7 F10** 48 14N 11 37 E
Hochdahl, *Ruhr* **6 C3** 51 13N 6 55 E
Hochemmerich, *Ruhr* **6 B2** 51 24N 6 41 E
Hochfeld, *Ruhr* **6 B2** 51 25N 6 45 E
Hochheide, *Ruhr* **6 B2** 51 27N 6 40 E
Hochlar, *Ruhr* **6 A5** 51 36N 7 11 E
Hochlarmark, *Ruhr* **6 A4** 51 34N 7 11 E
Hodgkins, *Chic.* **26 C1** 41 46N 87 53W
Hodogaya-Ku, *Tōkyō* **13 D2** 35 26N 139 35 E
Hoegi, *Sŏul* **12 G8** 37 35N 127 3 E
Hofberg, *Wien* **10 G10** 48 12N 16 21 E
Hoffman I., *N.Y.* **22 D4** 40 34N 74 3W
Hofstede, *Ruhr* **6 A5** 51 30N 7 11 E
Höggarnsfjärden, *Stock.* **3 D13** 59 22N 18 22 E
Hohe Mark, Naturpark, *Ruhr* **6 A2** 51 35N 6 49 E
Hohe Schaar, *Hbg.* **7 E7** 53 29N 9 58 E
Hohenbrunn, *Mün.* **7 G11** 48 2N 11 42 E
Hohenfelde, *Hbg.* **7 D8** 53 33N 10 1 E
Höhenkirchen, *Mün.* **7 G11** 48 1N 11 42 E
Hohenraden, *Hbg.* **7 C6** 53 41N 9 49 E
Hohenschönhausen, *Berl.* **7 A4** 52 33N 13 30 E
Hohenwisch, *Hbg.* **7 E7** 53 29N 9 53 E
Hohokus, *N.Y.* **22 A4** 41 0N 74 5W
Hok Tsui, *H.K.* **12 E6** 22 12N 114 15 E

Kennedy Town 39

Holborn, *Lon.* 4 B4 51 31N 0 7W
Holečovice, *Pra.* 10 B2 50 6N 14 28 E
Holland Village, *Sing.* 15 G7 1 18N 103 47 E
Hollis, *N.Y.* 23 C6 40 42N 73 45W
Höllriegelskreuth, *Mün.* 7 G9 48 2N 11 30 E
Holly Oak, *Phil.* 24 C2 39 47N 75 27W
Hollydale, *L.A.* 28 C4 33 55N 118 10W
Hollywood Bowl, *L.A.* 28 B2 34 6N 118 21W
Hollywood-Burbank Airport, *L.A.* 28 A2 34 11N 118 21W
Holmenkollen, *Oslo* 2 B4 59 57N 10 41 E
Holmes, *Phil.* 24 B3 39 53N 75 18W
Holmes Acres, *Wash.* 25 D6 38 51N 77 13W
Holmes Run →, *Wash.* 25 E7 38 48N 77 6W
Holmesburg, *Phil.* 24 A4 40 2N 75 2W
Holmgård, *Stock.* 3 E10 59 14N 18 0 E
Holsfjorden, *Oslo* 2 B1 59 58N 10 17 E
Holsterhausen, *Ruhr* 6 A5 51 32N 7 11 E
Holte, *Købn.* 2 D9 55 48N 12 27 E
Holten, *Ruhr* 6 B4 51 31N 6 47 E
Holthausen, *Ruhr* 6 B4 51 25N 7 5 E
Holzbüttgen, *Ruhr* 6 C1 51 13N 6 37 E
Homberg, *Ruhr* 6 B2 51 27N 6 41 E
Hombruch, *Ruhr* 6 B6 51 28N 7 27 E
Homerton, *Lon.* 4 B4 51 32N 0 2W
Homestead Lake, *Jobg.* 18 F10 26 10 S 28 17 E
Homestead Valley, *S.F.* 27 A1 37 53N 122 32W
Hometown, *Chic.* 26 C2 41 44N 87 42W
Homledal, *Oslo* 2 B1 59 59N 10 18 E
Homówek, *Wsaw.* 10 E5 52 17N 20 48 E
Hon-gyōtoku, *Tōkyō* 13 B4 35 41N 139 57 E
Hōnanchō, *Tōkyō* 13 B2 35 40N 139 39 E
Honcho, *Tōkyō* 13 B3 35 40N 139 41 E
Honden, *Tōkyō* 13 B4 35 43N 139 50 E
Honeydew, *Jobg.* 18 E8 26 4 S 27 55 E
Hong Kah, *Sing.* 15 F7 1 21N 103 43 E
Hong Kong, *H.K.* 12 E5 22 17N 114 11 E
Hong Kong, Univ. of, *H.K.* 12 E5 22 16N 114 8 E
Hong Kong Airport, *H.K.* 12 E6 22 19N 114 11 E
Hong Kong I., *H.K.* 12 E6 22 16N 114 11 E
Hong Lim Park, *Sing.* 15 G8 1 17N 103 50 E
Hongeun, *Sŏul* 12 G7 37 35N 126 56 E
Honggiao, *Shang.* 14 J11 31 12N 121 22 E
Honggou, *Shang.* 14 J11 31 16N 121 29 E
Hongkou Gongyuan, *Shang.* 14 J11 31 17N 121 28 E
Hongmiao, *Beij.* 14 B3 39 54N 116 26 E
Hongqiao, *Tianj.* 14 E5 39 8N 117 9 E
Hongqiao Airport, *Shang.* 14 J10 31 12N 121 19 E
Honjyo, *Tōkyō* 13 B3 35 41N 139 48 E
Honmoku, *Tōkyō* 13 D2 35 24N 139 39 E
Hönow, *Berl.* 7 A4 52 32N 13 38 E
Höntrop, *Ruhr* 6 B4 51 27N 7 8 E
Hood Pond, *Bost.* 21 A4 42 40N 70 57W
Hooghly →, *Calc.* 16 D6 22 41N 88 21 E
Hook, *Lon.* 4 C3 51 22N 0 17W
Hopelawn, *N.Y.* 22 D3 40 31N 74 17W
Hörde, *Ruhr* 6 B7 51 29N 7 30 E
Horikiri, *Tōkyō* 13 B4 35 44N 139 50 E
Horn, *Hbg.* 7 D8 53 33N 10 5 E
Horn Pond, *Bost.* 21 C2 42 28N 71 9W
Hornchurch, *Lon.* 4 B6 51 33N 0 14 E
Horneburg, *Ruhr* 6 A5 51 37N 7 17 E
Horni, *Pra.* 10 B3 50 2N 14 33 E
Horni Počernice, *Pra.* 10 B3 50 6N 14 36 E
Hornsey, *Lon.* 4 B4 51 35N 0 7W
Horoměřice, *Pra.* 10 B1 50 8N 14 20 E
Horsley Park, *Syd.* 19 B2 33 50 S 150 51 E
Horst, *Ruhr* 6 B4 51 26N 7 6 E
Horsthausen, *Ruhr* 6 A5 51 33N 7 12 E
Hortaleza, *Mdrd.* 8 B3 40 28N 3 38W
Horto Florestal, *S. Pau.* 31 D6 23 27 S 46 38W
Horton Kirby, *Lon.* 4 C6 51 23N 0 14 E
Hösel, *Ruhr* 6 B3 51 20N 6 53 E
Hosoyama, *Tōkyō* 13 C2 35 36N 139 31 E
Hospitalet, *Barc.* 8 D5 41 21N 2 6 E
Hostafranchs, *Barc.* 8 D5 41 21N 2 8 E
Hoterheide, *Ruhr* 6 C1 51 16N 6 37 E
Houbetin, *Pra.* 10 B3 50 6N 14 33 E
Houghs Neck, *Bost.* 21 D4 42 15N 70 57W
Houghton, *Jobg.* 18 F9 26 10 S 28 3 E
Houilles, *Paris* 5 B3 48 56N 2 11 E
Hounslow, *Lon.* 4 C2 51 28N 0 21W
Houses of Parliament, *Lon.* 4 C4 51 29N 0 7W
Hove Å →, *Købn.* 2 D8 55 43N 12 7 E
Hovedøya, *Oslo* 2 B4 59 53N 10 43 E
Høvik, *Oslo* 2 B3 59 54N 10 34 E
Hovorčovice, *Pra.* 10 A3 50 10N 14 31 E
Howard Beach, *N.Y.* 23 D5 40 39N 73 50W
Hoxton Park, *Syd.* 19 B2 33 55 S 150 51 E
Hoxton Park Aerodrome, *Syd.* 19 B2 33 54 S 150 50 E
Hōya, *Tōkyō* 13 B2 35 44N 139 34 E
Høybråten, *Oslo* 2 B5 59 56N 10 55 E
Hradčany, *Pra.* 10 B2 50 5N 14 24 E
Hsiya, *Gzh.* 14 G7 23 9N 113 6 E
Huangpu, *Gzh.* 14 G9 23 5N 113 23 E
Huangpu, *Shang.* 14 J12 31 14N 121 30 E
Huangpu Gongyuan, *Shang.* 14 J11 31 14N 121 29 E
Huangpu Jiang →, *Shang.* 14 J11 31 11N 121 29 E
Huangtugang, *Beij.* 14 C2 39 49N 116 15 E
Huat Choe, *Sing.* 15 F7 1 20N 103 41 E
Huckarde, *Ruhr* 6 A6 51 32N 7 24 E
Huckingen, *Ruhr* 6 B2 51 21N 6 44 E
Huddinge, *Stock.* 3 E11 59 14N 18 0 E
Hudson →, *N.Y.* 22 B5 40 43N 73 6W
Huertas de San Beltran, *Barc.* 8 D5 41 22N 2 9 E
Huguenot, *N.Y.* 22 D3 40 32N 74 13W
Huguenot Park, *N.Y.* 22 D3 40 31N 74 12W
Huidui, *Tianj.* 14 E6 39 4N 117 16 E
Huisquilucan →, *Méx.* 29 B2 19 24N 99 17W
Huixquilucan, *Méx.* 29 B1 19 21N 99 21W
Hull, *Bost.* 21 D4 42 18N 70 54W
Hulman Aqueduct, *Bost.* 21 C1 42 20N 71 23W
Hulmeville, *Phil.* 24 A5 40 8N 74 55W
Hulsdonk, *Ruhr* 6 B1 51 27N 6 36 E
Humaljärvi, *Hels.* 3 B1 60 10N 24 26 E
Humber →, *Trto.* 20 D7 43 47N 79 38W
Humber B., *Trto.* 20 E8 43 37N 79 27W
Humber Bay, *Trto.* 20 E8 43 38N 79 29W
Humber Summit, *Trto.* 20 D7 43 45N 79 32W
Humber Valley Park, *Trto.* 20 E8 43 39N 79 29W
Humber Valley Village, *Trto.* 20 D7 43 40N 79 31W
Humberlea, *Trto.* 20 D7 43 43N 79 31W
Humboldt Park, *Chic.* 26 B2 41 54N 87 42W
Humera, *Mdrd.* 8 B2 40 25N 3 46W
Hummelsbüttel, *Hbg.* 7 D8 53 39N 10 4 E
Hun Yeang, *Sing.* 15 F8 1 21N 103 55 E
Hunaydi, *Bagd.* 17 F8 33 18N 44 29 E
Hundige, *Købn.* 2 E8 55 35N 12 18 E
Hundige Strand, *Købn.* 2 E9 55 35N 12 20 E
Hung Hom, *H.K.* 12 E6 22 18N 114 11 E
Hunters Hill, *Syd.* 19 B3 33 50 S 151 9 E
Hunters Pt., *S.F.* 27 B2 37 43N 122 21W
Hunters Valley, *Wash.* 25 D6 38 54N 77 17W
Huntington, *N.Y.* 23 B8 40 51N 73 25W
Huntington, *Wash.* 25 E7 38 47N 77 4W
Huntington B., *N.Y.* 23 B8 40 54N 73 24W
Huntington Bay, *N.Y.* 23 B8 40 56N 73 26W
Huntington Park, *L.A.* 28 C3 33 58N 118 13W
Huntington Station, *N.Y.* 23 B8 40 50N 73 23W
Hünxer Wald, *Ruhr* 6 A2 51 37N 6 49 E
Hurffville, *Phil.* 24 C4 39 45N 75 6W
Huriya, *Bagd.* 17 E7 33 21N 44 19 E
Hurlingham, *B.A.* 32 B3 34 35 S 58 37W
Hurlingham, *Jobg.* 18 E9 26 6 S 28 2 E
Hurstville, *Syd.* 19 B3 33 57 S 151 6 E
Husby, *Stock.* 3 D10 59 24N 17 56 E
Huseby, *Oslo* 2 A6 60 0N 11 1 E
Hostivař, *Pra.* 10 B3 50 3N 14 31 E
Husum, *Købn.* 2 D9 55 42N 12 27 E
Hütteldorf, *Wien* 10 G9 48 12N 16 15 E
Hüttenheim, *Ruhr* 6 B2 51 21N 6 43 E
Huttrop, *Ruhr* 6 B4 51 26N 7 3 E
Hüvösvölgy, *Bud.* 10 J13 47 32N 19 0 E
Hvalstad, *Oslo* 2 B2 59 51N 10 27 E
Hvalstrand, *Oslo* 2 B3 59 50N 10 30 E
Hvidovre, *Købn.* 2 E9 55 38N 12 27 E
Hwagog, *Sŏul* 12 G7 37 32N 126 51 E
Hyattsville, *Wash.* 25 D8 38 57N 76 57W
Hyde Park, *Bost.* 21 D3 42 15N 71 7W
Hyde Park, *Chic.* 26 C3 41 47N 87 35W
Hyde Park, *Jobg.* 18 E9 26 6 S 28 2 E
Hyde Park, *Lon.* 4 B3 51 30N 0 10W
Hyde Park, *Syd.* 19 B4 33 52 S 151 12 E
Hynes, *L.A.* 28 C3 33 52N 118 10W

I

Ibaraki, *Ōsaka* 12 B4 34 48N 135 34 E
Ibayo Tipas, *Manila* 15 D4 14 32N 121 4 E
Ibese, *Lagos* 18 A2 6 33N 7 28 E
Ibirapuera, *S. Pau.* 31 E5 23 36 S 46 40W
Ibirapuera, Parque, *S. Pau.* 31 E6 23 35 S 46 38W
Iboju, *Lagos* 18 B3 6 25N 7 31 E
Icarai, *Rio J.* 31 B3 22 54 S 43 6W
Icerenköy, *Ist.* 17 B3 40 58N 29 6 E
Ichapur, *Calc.* 16 D6 22 48N 88 22 E
Ichgao, *Tōkyō* 13 C2 35 32N 139 32 E
Ichigaya, *Tōkyō* 13 B3 35 41N 139 43 E
Ichikawa, *Tōkyō* 13 B4 35 43N 139 54 E
Ickenham, *Lon.* 4 B2 51 33N 0 26W
Ickern, *Ruhr* 6 A6 51 35N 7 21 E
Iddo, *Lagos* 18 B2 6 28N 7 22 E
Idi-Oro, *Lagos* 18 B2 6 31N 7 21 E
Idimu, *Lagos* 18 A1 6 34N 7 17 E
Idris, *Bagd.* 17 E8 33 22N 44 27 E
Iganmu, *Lagos* 18 B2 6 28N 7 22 E
Igbobi, *Lagos* 18 A2 6 31N 7 22 E
Igbologun, *Lagos* 18 B1 6 24N 7 19 E
Igbopa, *Lagos* 18 A3 6 32N 7 31 E
Igelboda, *Stock.* 3 E12 59 17N 18 17 E
Igny, *Paris* 5 C3 48 44N 2 13 E
Iguassú, *S. Pau.* 31 E6 23 36 S 46 30W
Ijesa-Tedo, *Lagos* 18 B2 6 29N 7 19 E
Ijora, *Lagos* 18 B2 6 27N 7 22 E
Ikebe, *Tōkyō* 13 C2 35 31N 139 34 E
Ikebukuro, *Tōkyō* 13 B3 35 43N 139 42 E
Ikeda, *Ōsaka* 12 B3 34 48N 135 25 E
Ikegami, *Tōkyō* 13 C3 35 33N 139 42 E
Ikeja, *Lagos* 18 A2 6 35N 7 20 E
Ikeuchi, *Ōsaka* 12 C4 34 35N 135 32 E
Ikotun, *Lagos* 18 A1 6 32N 7 16 E
Ikoyi, *Lagos* 18 B2 6 27N 7 26 E
Ikuata, *Lagos* 18 B2 6 24N 7 21 E
Ikuno, *Ōsaka* 12 B4 34 40N 135 30 E
Ikuta, *Ōsaka* 12 B4 34 41N 135 10 E
Ikuta, *Tōkyō* 13 C2 35 36N 139 32 E
Ila, *Oslo* 2 B3 59 57N 10 35 E
Ilchester, *Balt.* 25 B2 39 14N 76 46W
Ilford, *Lon.* 4 B5 51 33N 0 4 E
Ilioúpolis, *Ath.* 8 J11 37 54N 23 47 E
Illovo, *Jobg.* 18 E9 26 7S 28 3 E
Ilsós →, *Ath.* 8 J11 37 55N 23 41 E
Imajuku, *Tōkyō* 13 D2 35 28N 139 32 E
Imbāba, *El Qâ.* 18 C5 30 3N 31 12 E
Imielin, *Wsaw.* 10 F7 52 9N 21 0 E
Imirim, *S. Pau.* 31 D6 23 29 S 46 39W
Imittós, *Ath.* 8 J11 37 55N 23 45 E
Immersby, *Hels.* 3 B6 60 18N 25 16 E
Imore, *Lagos* 18 B1 6 25N 7 17 E
Imperial Palace, *Tōkyō* 13 B3 35 41N 139 45 E
Ina →, *Ōsaka* 12 B3 34 48N 135 27 E
Inagi, *Tōkyō* 13 C2 35 38N 139 31 E
Incirano, *Mil.* 9 D5 45 34N 9 9 E
Independencia, *Lima* 30 F8 11 59 S 77 3W
Indian Gabe, *Delhi* 16 B2 28 36N 77 13 E
Indian Museum, *Calc.* 16 E6 22 33N 88 21 E
Indiana Harbor, *Chic.* 26 C4 41 40N 87 26W
Indiana Harbor Canal, *Chic.* 26 D4 41 39N 87 26W
Indianópolis, *S. Pau.* 31 E6 23 35 S 46 38W
Indios Verdes, *Méx.* 29 B3 19 29N 99 6W
Ingarö, *Stock.* 3 E13 59 17N 18 24 E
Ingaröfjärden, *Stock.* 3 E13 59 14N 18 25 E
Ingarölandet, *Stock.* 3 E13 59 17N 18 22 E
Ingenieur Budge, *B.A.* 32 C4 34 43 S 58 27W
Ingierstrand, *Oslo* 2 C4 59 49N 10 46 E
Ingleburn, *Syd.* 19 C2 34 0 S 150 52 E
Inglewood, *L.A.* 28 C3 33 57N 118 19W
Ingrave, *Lon.* 4 B7 51 35N 0 20 E
Inqvalsby, *Hels.* 3 C2 60 9N 24 32 E
Inhaúme, *Rio J.* 31 B2 22 51 S 43 17W
Inner Port Shelter, *H.K.* 12 D6 22 22N 114 17 E
Interagos, *S. Pau.* 31 F5 23 41 S 46 42W
Intramuros, *Manila* 15 D3 14 35N 120 57 E
Invalides, *Paris* 5 B3 48 51N 2 18 E
Inverness, *Balt.* 25 B4 39 15N 76 29W
Inwood, *N.Y.* 23 D6 40 36N 73 45W
Inzersdorf, *Wien* 10 H10 48 8N 16 21 E
Ipanema, *Rio J.* 31 B2 22 59 S 43 12W
Ipiranga, *S. Pau.* 31 E6 23 35 S 46 36W
Ipiranga →, *S. Pau.* 31 E6 23 37 S 46 37W
Iponri, *Lagos* 18 B2 6 28N 7 22 E
Ipswich, *Bost.* 21 A4 42 41N 70 50W
Ipswich →, *Bost.* 21 A4 42 39N 70 53W
Irajá, *Rio J.* 31 B2 22 50 S 43 19W
Irving Park, *Chic.* 26 B2 41 57N 87 42W
Irvington, *N.Y.* 22 C3 40 43N 74 13W
Irwindale, *L.A.* 28 B5 34 6N 117 54W
Isabel, *Rio J.* 31 B2 22 55 S 43 14W
Isagatedo, *Lagos* 18 A1 6 31N 7 19 E
Isando, *Jobg.* 18 E10 26 8 S 28 12 E
Isar →, *Mün.* 7 F11 48 15N 11 41 E
Iselin, *N.Y.* 22 D3 40 34N 74 19W
Iserbrook, *Hbg.* 7 D7 53 34N 9 48 E
Iseri-Osun, *Lagos* 18 B1 6 29N 7 18 E
Ishbīlīya, *Bagd.* 17 E8 33 21N 44 26 E
Isheri-Olofin, *Lagos* 18 A1 6 34N 7 16 E
Ishi →, *Ōsaka* 12 C4 34 34N 135 37 E
Ishikiri, *Ōsaka* 12 B4 34 40N 135 38 E
Ishizu →, *Ōsaka* 12 C3 34 33N 135 26 E
Ishøj Strand, *Købn.* 2 E9 55 35N 12 20 E
Isidro Casanova, *B.A.* 32 C3 34 42 S 58 36W
Island Channel, *N.Y.* 23 D5 40 35N 73 52W
Island Park, *N.Y.* 23 D7 40 36N 73 38W
Island Park, *Trto.* 20 E8 43 37N 79 22W
Islev, *Købn.* 2 D9 55 41N 12 27 E
Isleworth, *Lon.* 4 C3 51 28N 0 19W
Islington, *Bost.* 21 D2 42 13N 71 13W
Islington, *Lon.* 4 B4 51 32N 0 6W
Islington, *Trto.* 20 E7 43 38N 79 30W
Ismaning, *Mün.* 7 F11 48 13N 11 40 E
Ismayloskiypark, *Mos.* 11 E10 55 46N 37 46 E
Isogo-Ku, *Tōkyō* 13 D2 35 23N 139 37 E
Isolo, *Lagos* 18 A1 6 31N 7 19 E
Isosaari, *Hels.* 3 C5 60 6N 25 3 E
Issy-les-Moulineaux, *Paris* 5 C3 48 49N 2 15 E
Istanbul, *Ist.* 17 B2 41 0N 28 58 E
Istanbul Boğazi, *Ist.* 17 A3 41 5N 29 3 E
Istanbul Hava Alani, *Ist.* 17 B2 40 58N 28 50 E
Istead Rise, *Lon.* 4 C7 51 24N 0 21 E
Istinye, *Ist.* 17 A3 41 6N 29 3 E
Isumba, *Lagos* 18 B1 6 25N 7 17 E
Ita Hakkila, *Hels.* 3 B5 60 17N 25 7 E
Itabashi-Ku, *Tōkyō* 13 B2 35 46N 139 38 E
Itaberaba, *S. Pau.* 31 D6 23 28 S 46 39W
Itaewon, *Sŏul* 12 G7 37 32N 126 58 E
Itaim, *S. Pau.* 31 D7 23 29 S 46 23W
Itaipu, *Rio J.* 31 B3 22 58 S 43 2W
Italie, Place d', *Paris* 5 C4 48 49N 2 22 E
Itami, *Ōsaka* 12 B3 34 46N 135 24 E
Itaocaia, *Rio J.* 31 B3 22 58 S 43 2W
Itapecerica da Serra, *S. Pau.* 31 F5 23 42 S 46 50W
Itaquaquecetuba, *S. Pau.* 31 D7 23 29 S 46 23W
Itaquera, *S. Pau.* 31 E7 23 32 S 46 27W
Itaquera →, *S. Pau.* 31 E7 23 28 S 46 26W
Ithan, *Phil.* 24 A2 40 1N 75 21W
Itupu, *S. Pau.* 31 F5 23 40 S 46 43W
Ituzaingo, *B.A.* 32 B3 34 39 S 58 38W
Ivanhoe, *Melb.* 19 E7 37 45 S 145 3 E
Iver, *Lon.* 4 B1 51 32N 0 30W
Ivry-sur-Seine, *Paris* 5 C4 48 49N 2 22 E
Iwazono, *Ōsaka* 12 B2 34 45N 135 18 E
Izabelin, *Wsaw.* 10 E5 52 17N 20 48 E
Izmaylovo, *Mos.* 11 E10 55 47N 37 47 E
Iztacalco, *Méx.* 29 B3 19 23N 99 6W
Iztapalapa, *Méx.* 29 B3 19 21N 99 6W
Izumi, *Tōkyō* 13 D1 35 25N 139 29 E

J

J. G. Strijdom Post Office Tower, *Jobg.* 18 F9 26 11 S 28 2 E
J. Paul Getty Museum, *L.A.* 28 B1 34 2N 118 33W
Jabavu, *Jobg.* 18 F8 26 14 S 27 52 E
Jabulani, *Jobg.* 18 F8 26 14 S 27 51 E
Jacarepaguá, *Rio J.* 31 B1 22 56 S 43 20W
Jackson Heights, *N.Y.* 23 C5 40 44N 73 53W
Jackson Park, *Chic.* 26 C3 41 46N 87 34W
Jacksonville, *N.Y.* 22 B3 40 57N 74 18W
Jacomino, *La Hab.* 30 B3 23 6N 82 19W
Jacques Cartier, *Mtrl.* 20 A5 43 31N 73 27W
Jægersborg, *Købn.* 2 D10 55 45N 12 31 E
Jægersborg Dyrehave, *Købn.* 2 D10 55 46N 12 33 E
Jægersborg Hegn, *Købn.* 2 D10 55 49N 12 33 E
Jafarpur, *Calc.* 16 D6 22 45N 88 22 E
Jagacha, *Calc.* 16 E5 22 35N 88 17 E
Jagannathpur, *Calc.* 16 D5 22 43N 88 18 E
Jagatdal, *Calc.* 16 C6 22 51N 88 23 E
Jagatmagar, *Calc.* 16 D5 22 46N 88 13 E
Jagatpur, *Delhi* 16 A2 28 44N 77 13 E
Jagdispur, *Calc.* 16 E5 22 39N 88 17 E
Jaguara, *S. Pau.* 31 E5 23 30 S 46 45W
Jaguaré, *S. Pau.* 31 E5 23 32 S 46 45W
Jaguaré →, *S. Pau.* 31 E5 23 32 S 46 45W
Jahangirpur, *Delhi* 16 A2 28 43N 77 12 E
Jaimanitas →, *La Hab.* 30 B2 23 5N 82 29W
Jakarta, *Jak.* 15 H10 6 9 S 106 52 E
Jakarta, Teluk, *Jak.* 15 H9 6 5 S 106 50 E
Jakosberg, *Stock.* 3 D9 59 25N 17 47 E
Jalan Kayu, *Sing.* 15 F8 1 24N 103 52 E
Jamaica, *N.Y.* 23 C6 40 42N 73 48W
Jamaica B., *N.Y.* 23 D6 40 36N 73 49W
Jamaica Plain, *Bost.* 21 D3 42 18N 71 6W
Jamshīdābād, *Tehr.* 17 C5 35 42N 51 22 E
Jamsil, *Sŏul* 12 G8 37 30N 127 4 E
Jamweon, *Sŏul* 12 G8 37 30N 127 0 E
Jan Smuts Airport, *Jobg.* 18 E10 26 7 S 28 14 E
Janai, *Calc.* 16 D5 22 43N 88 15 E
Janā'in, *Bagd.* 17 F8 33 18N 44 22 E
Janki, *Wsaw.* 10 F6 52 8N 20 52 E
Jannali, *Syd.* 19 C3 34 0 S 151 4 E
Jánoshegy, *Bud.* 10 J12 47 31N 18 57 E
Janów, *Wsaw.* 10 E6 52 16N 20 50 E
Janvry, *Paris* 5 D2 48 38N 2 9 E
Jaraguá, *S. Pau.* 31 D5 23 27 S 46 44W
Jaraguá, Pico de, *S. Pau.* 31 D5 23 27 S 46 46W
Jarama →, *Mdrd.* 8 B3 40 29N 3 32W
Jardim América, *S. Pau.* 31 E6 23 34 S 46 39W
Jardim Anchieta, *S. Pau.* 31 F7 23 41 S 46 27W
Jardim Arpoador, *S. Pau.* 31 E5 23 35 S 46 48W
Jardim do Mar, *S. Pau.* 31 F6 23 40 S 46 33W
Jardim Munhoz, *S. Pau.* 31 B6 23 30 S 46 33W
Jardim Osasco, *S. Pau.* 31 E5 23 33 S 46 47W
Jardim Ouro Preto, *S. Pau.* 31 E5 23 35 S 46 46W
Jardim Paulista, *S. Pau.* 31 E5 23 34 S 46 41W
Jardim Petrópolis, *S. Pau.* 31 F7 23 41 S 46 23W
Jardim Rochidale, *S. Pau.* 31 E5 23 30 S 46 46W
Jardim Santista, *S. Pau.* 31 F7 23 40 S 46 24W
Jardim São Bento, *S. Pau.* 31 E6 23 31 S 46 40W
Jardim São Francisco, *S. Pau.* 31 E7 23 38 S 46 26W
Jardim Sapopemba, *S. Pau.* 31 E7 23 36 S 46 29W
Jardim Vera Cruz, *S. Pau.* 31 E7 23 35 S 46 27W
Jardim Vista Alegre, *S. Pau.* 31 E5 23 37 S 46 49W
Jardim Zaira, *S. Pau.* 31 E7 23 39 S 46 25W
Jardines Flotantes, *Méx.* 29 C3 19 16N 99 6W
Jardine's Lookout, *H.K.* 12 E6 22 16N 114 11 E
Järfälla, *Stock.* 3 D10 59 23N 17 51 E
Järvafältet, *Stock.* 3 D10 59 25N 17 54 E
Järventausta, *Hels.* 3 A1 60 21N 24 28 E
Jasai, *Bomb.* 16 H9 18 56N 73 1 E
Jaskhar, *Bomb.* 16 H8 18 54N 72 58 E
Jatinegara, *Jak.* 15 J10 6 13 S 106 52 E
Jauli, *Delhi* 16 A3 28 44N 77 20 E
Jawādiyeh, *Tehr.* 17 D5 35 39N 51 22 E
Jaworowa, *Wsaw.* 10 F6 52 9N 20 56 E
Jayang, *Sŏul* 12 G8 37 32N 127 3 E
Jedlesee, *Wien* 10 G10 48 15N 16 23 E
Jefferson, *Phil.* 24 C3 39 45N 75 12W
Jefferson Park, *Chic.* 26 B2 41 58N 87 46W
Jeffersonville, *Phil.* 24 A2 40 8N 75 23W
Jegi, *Sŏul* 12 G8 37 34N 127 1 E
Jells Park, *Melb.* 19 F8 37 53 S 145 11 E
Jelonki, *Wsaw.* 10 E6 52 14N 20 54 E
Jenfeld, *Hbg.* 7 D8 53 34N 10 8 E
Jenkintown, *Phil.* 24 A4 40 6N 75 8W
Jeongreung, *Sŏul* 12 G8 37 35N 127 0 E
Jericho, *N.Y.* 23 C7 40 47N 73 32W
Jerónimes, Mosteiro dos, *Lisb.* 8 F7 38 41N 9 11W
Jersey City, *N.Y.* 22 C4 40 42N 74 4W
Jésus, Î., *Mtrl.* 20 A3 43 36N 73 44W
Jesus Del Monte, *La Hab.* 30 B2 23 6N 82 21W
Jesús Maria, *Lima* 30 G8 12 4 S 77 3W
Jhenkari, *Calc.* 16 D5 22 45N 88 18 E
Jhil Kuranga, *Delhi* 16 B2 28 39N 77 14 E
Jiangqiao, *Shang.* 14 J11 31 15N 121 20 E
Jiangtai, *Beij.* 14 B3 39 57N 116 28 E
Jianguomen, *Beij.* 14 B3 39 53N 116 24 E
Jiangwan, *Shang.* 14 J11 31 18N 121 28 E
Jianshan Gongyuan, *Tianj.* 14 E6 39 5N 117 12 E
Jihād, *Bagd.* 17 F7 33 17N 44 19 E
Jingan, *Shang.* 14 J11 31 14N 121 25 E
Jinočany, *Pra.* 10 B1 50 2N 14 16 E
Jinonice, *Pra.* 10 B2 50 3N 14 22 E
Jirny, *Pra.* 10 B4 50 7N 14 41 E
Jiuxianqiao, *Beij.* 14 B3 39 58N 116 28 E
Jiyūgaoka, *Tōkyō* 13 C3 35 35N 139 40 E
Jīzā'er, *Bagd.* 17 F8 33 15N 44 23 E
Jīzīra, *Bagd.* 17 F8 33 15N 44 25 E
Joan Despi, *Barc.* 8 D5 41 22N 2 2 E
Joaquin Miller Park, *S.F.* 27 B3 37 48N 122 11W
Johannesburg, *Jobg.* 18 F9 26 11 S 28 2 E
Johanneskirchen, *Mün.* 7 F10 48 10N 11 38 E
Johannesstift, *Berl.* 7 A2 52 34N 13 12 E
Johannisthal, *Berl.* 7 B4 52 26N 13 30 E
John F. Kennedy Int. Airport, *N.Y.* 23 D6 40 39N 73 45W
John F. Kennedy Nat. Hist. Site, *Bost.* 21 C3 42 20N 71 7W
John Hancock Center, *Chic.* 26 B3 41 53N 87 37W
John Hopkins Univ., *Balt.* 25 B3 39 19N 76 37W
John McLaren Park, *S.F.* 27 B2 37 43N 122 24W
Joinville-le-Pont, *Paris* 5 C4 48 49N 2 27 E
Jollas, *Hels.* 3 B5 60 10N 25 5 E
Jones Beach State Park, *N.Y.* 23 D7 40 35N 73 32W
Jones Falls →, *Balt.* 25 B3 39 20N 76 36W
Jones Inlet, *N.Y.* 23 D7 40 34N 73 34W
Jonestown, *Balt.* 25 B2 39 13N 76 48W
Jong Ro, *Sŏul* 12 G7 37 34N 126 58 E
Jongmyo Royal Shrine, *Sŏul* 12 G7 37 34N 126 59 E
Jonstrup, *Købn.* 2 D9 55 45N 12 20 E
Joppatowne, *Balt.* 25 A4 39 24N 76 20W
Jordan Valley, *H.K.* 12 D6 22 20N 114 12 E
Jorge Chavez, Aeropuerto Int., *Lima* 30 G8 12 2 S 77 8W
Jorvas, *Hels.* 3 C2 60 8N 24 30 E
José C. Paz, *B.A.* 32 B2 34 31 S 58 44W
José L. Suárez, *B.A.* 32 B3 34 32 S 58 34W
José Mármol, *B.A.* 32 C4 34 47 S 58 22W
Jose Marti, Aeropuerto Int., *La Hab.* 30 C2 22 59N 82 22W
Josephine Pk., *L.A.* 28 A4 34 17N 118 7W
Jōsō, *Ōsaka* 12 B3 34 42N 135 27 E
Jōtō, *Ōsaka* 12 B4 34 42N 135 33 E
Jouars-Pontchartrain, *Paris* 5 C1 48 47N 1 53 E
Jouy-en-Josas, *Paris* 5 C3 48 46N 2 10 E
Jouy-le-Moutier, *Paris* 5 A2 49 0N 2 2 E
Józefów, *Wsaw.* 10 F8 52 8N 21 13 E
Juan Escutia, *Méx.* 29 B3 19 23N 99 3W
Juan González Romero, *Méx.* 29 A3 19 30N 99 3W
Juhu, *Bomb.* 16 G9 19 5N 73 0 E
Juilly, *Paris* 5 A6 49 0N 2 42 E
Jūjā, *Tōkyō* 13 B3 35 45N 139 43 E
Jukskeirivier →, *Jobg.* 18 E9 26 5 S 28 6 E
Julianów, *Wsaw.* 10 E7 52 10N 21 9 E
Jung, *Sŏul* 12 G7 37 33N 126 59 E
Jungfernheide, Volkspark, *Berl.* 7 A2 52 32N 13 18 E
Jungfernsee, *Berl.* 7 B1 52 25N 13 6 E
Jungwha, *Sŏul* 12 G8 37 35N 127 3 E
Junk B., *H.K.* 12 E6 22 17N 114 15 E
Jurong, *Sing.* 15 G7 1 19N 103 40 E
Jurong, Selat, *Sing.* 15 G7 1 17N 103 42 E
Jurong, Sungei →, *Sing.* 15 G7 1 17N 103 45 E
Jurubatuba, *S. Pau.* 31 F5 23 40 S 46 41W
Jurujuba, Enseada de, *Rio J.* 31 B3 22 54 S 43 6W
Justice, *Chic.* 26 C2 41 44N 87 49W
Juusjärvi, *Hels.* 3 B1 60 12N 24 26 E
Juva, *Hels.* 3 B1 60 16N 24 45 E
Juvisy-sur-Orge, *Paris* 5 D4 48 41N 2 21 E
Jwalahari, *Delhi* 16 B1 28 40N 77 6 E
Jyllinge, *Købn.* 2 D7 55 45N 12 6 E

K

Kaarst, *Ruhr* 6 C1 51 13N 6 36 E
Kabaty, *Wsaw.* 10 F7 52 8N 21 4 E
Kabel, *Ruhr* 6 B6 51 24N 7 28 E
Kadiköy, *Ist.* 17 B3 40 59N 29 1 E
Kadoma, *Ōsaka* 12 B4 34 44N 135 35 E
Kafr es Sammân, *El Qâ.* 18 D4 29 58N 31 8 E
Kāğithane, *Ist.* 17 A2 41 4N 28 58 E
Kāğithane →, *Ist.* 17 A2 41 9N 28 56 E
Kagran, *Wien* 10 G10 48 14N 16 26 E
Kahlenberg, *Wien* 10 G9 48 16N 16 19 E
Kai Tak, *H.K.* 12 D6 22 20N 114 11 E
Kaisariani, *Ath.* 8 J11 37 57N 23 46 E
Kaiser-Mühlen, *Wien* 10 G10 48 13N 16 25 E
Kaiserebersdorf, *Wien* 10 H10 48 9N 16 26 E
Kaiserswerth, *Ruhr* 6 C2 51 18N 6 44 E
Kaivoksela, *Hels.* 3 B4 60 15N 24 53 E
Kakukk-hegy, *Bud.* 10 K12 47 29N 18 57 E
Kalachhara, *Calc.* 16 D5 22 48N 88 15 E
Kalamákion, *Ath.* 8 J11 37 52N 23 43 E
Kaldenhausen, *Ruhr* 6 B1 51 23N 6 39 E
Kalipur, *Calc.* 16 D5 22 40N 88 17 E
Kalkaji, *Delhi* 16 B2 28 32N 77 12 E
Kalksburg, *Wien* 10 H9 48 8N 16 15 E
Kallang →, *Sing.* 15 F8 1 21N 103 51 E
Kallhäll, *Stock.* 3 D9 59 26N 17 48 E
Kallithéa, *Ath.* 8 J11 37 56N 23 43 E
Kallvik, *Hels.* 3 B5 60 12N 25 8 E
Kaltbründsberg, *Wien* 10 G9 48 10N 16 13 E
Kaltenleutgeben, *Wien* 10 H9 48 7N 16 11 E
Kalveboderne, *Købn.* 2 E10 55 37N 12 31 E
Kalytino, *Len.* 11 B5 59 59N 30 39 E
Kamaraerdő, *Bud.* 10 K12 47 26N 18 59 E
Kamarhati, *Calc.* 16 D6 22 40N 88 23 E
Kamarkunda, *Calc.* 16 D5 22 49N 88 12 E
Kamata, *Tōkyō* 13 C3 35 33N 139 43 E
Kamdebpur, *Calc.* 16 C5 22 53N 88 19 E
Kameari, *Tōkyō* 13 B4 35 45N 139 50 E
Kameido, *Tōkyō* 13 B4 35 42N 139 50 E
Kami-hoshikawa, *Tōkyō* 13 D2 35 27N 139 35 E
Kami-Itabashi, *Tōkyō* 13 B3 35 45N 139 40 E
Kami-nakazato, *Tōkyō* 13 D2 35 22N 139 36 E
Kami-saruyama, *Tōkyō* 13 C2 35 30N 139 31 E
Kami-sugata, *Tōkyō* 13 D2 35 28N 139 34 E
Kami-tomi, *Tōkyō* 13 B1 35 48N 139 29 E
Kamikitazawa, *Tōkyō* 13 C2 35 39N 139 36 E
Kamikiyoto, *Tōkyō* 13 B2 35 45N 139 30 E
Kamishiki, *Tōkyō* 13 B4 35 46N 139 57 E
Kamitsuruma, *Tōkyō* 13 C1 35 30N 139 26 E
Kamiyama, *Tōkyō* 13 B2 35 46N 139 32 E
Kamoi, *Tōkyō* 13 C2 35 30N 139 34 E
Kamoshida, *Tōkyō* 13 C2 35 33N 139 31 E
Kampong Batak, *Sing.* 15 F8 1 20N 103 54 E
Kampong Mandai Kechil, *Sing.* 15 F7 1 26N 103 46 E
Kampong Pachitan, *Sing.* 15 G8 1 19N 103 54 E
Kampong Potong Pasir, *Sing.* 15 F8 1 20N 103 52 E
Kampong Reteh, *Sing.* 15 G8 1 19N 103 53 E
Kampong Tengah, *Sing.* 15 F7 1 22N 103 42 E
Kampong Ulu Jurong, *Sing.* 15 F7 1 20N 103 42 E
Kampung Ambon, *Jak.* 15 J10 6 11 S 106 53 E
Kampung Bali, *Jak.* 15 J9 6 11 S 106 48 E
Kan, *Tehr.* 17 C4 35 45N 51 16 E
Kanagawa-Ku, *Tōkyō* 13 D2 35 29N 139 38 E
Kanamachi, *Tōkyō* 13 B4 35 46N 139 52 E
Kanamori, *Tōkyō* 13 C1 35 31N 139 27 E
Kanda, *Tōkyō* 13 B3 35 41N 139 45 E
Kandang Kerbau, *Sing.* 15 G8 1 18N 103 51 E
Kandilli, *Ist.* 17 A3 41 4N 29 3 E
Kanegasaku, *Tōkyō* 13 B4 35 48N 139 56 E
Kangaroo Ground, *Melb.* 19 E8 37 41 S 145 13 E
Kankinara, *Calc.* 16 C6 22 51N 88 24 E
Kankurgachi, *Calc.* 16 E6 22 34N 88 23 E
Kanlica, *Ist.* 17 A3 41 5N 29 3 E
Kanoaka, *Ōsaka* 12 C4 34 33N 135 31 E
Kanonerskiy, Os., *Len.* 11 B3 59 53N 30 13 E
Kanzaki →, *Ōsaka* 12 B3 34 41N 135 24 E
Kapellerfeld, *Wien* 10 G10 48 18N 16 29 E
Kapotnya, *Mos.* 11 F10 55 38N 37 48 E
Käppala, *Stock.* 3 D12 59 21N 18 13 E
Käpylä, *Hels.* 3 B4 60 13N 24 57 E
Karachi, *Kar.* 17 G11 24 50N 67 0 E
Karachi Int. Airport, *Kar.* 17 G11 24 5N 67 9 E
Karachi Univ., *Kar.* 17 G11 24 51N 67 0 E
Karagümrük, *Ist.* 17 A2 41 1N 28 56 E
Karāma, *Bagd.* 17 E8 33 20N 44 22 E
Karato, *Ōsaka* 12 B2 34 46N 135 12 E
Karave, *Bomb.* 16 G9 19 0N 73 0 E
Karet, *Jak.* 15 J9 6 12 S 106 49 E
Karkar Duman, *Delhi* 16 A2 28 39N 77 18 E
Karkh, *Bagd.* 17 E8 33 20N 44 22 E
Karlberg, *Stock.* 3 D11 59 20N 18 1 E
Karlin, *Pra.* 10 B2 50 5N 14 26 E
Karlsfeld, *Mün.* 7 F9 48 13N 11 28 E
Karlshorst, *Berl.* 7 B4 52 29N 13 31 E
Karlslunde Strand, *Købn.* 2 E8 55 33N 12 15 E
Karnap, *Ruhr* 6 A4 51 31N 7 0 E
Karolinenhof, *Berl.* 7 B4 52 23N 13 38 E
Karow, *Berl.* 7 A3 52 36N 13 29 E
Karrādah, *Bagd.* 17 F8 33 17N 44 23 E
Kärsön, *Stock.* 3 E10 59 19N 17 54 E
Kasai, *Tōkyō* 13 C4 35 39N 139 52 E
Kasetsart, *Bangk.* 15 A2 13 50N 100 34 E
Kashi-Hazaki, *Tōkyō* 13 A3 35 54N 139 42 E
Kashio, *Tōkyō* 13 D2 35 23N 139 34 E
Kashiwa, *Tōkyō* 13 A4 35 51N 139 57 E
Kashiwara, *Ōsaka* 12 C4 34 34N 135 37 E
Kaskela, *Hels.* 3 B5 60 17N 25 6 E
Kastrup, *Købn.* 2 E10 55 38N 12 39 E
Kastrup Lufthavn, *Købn.* 2 E11 55 37N 12 14 E
Kasuga, *Tōkyō* 13 B2 35 45N 139 38 E
Kasuge, *Tōkyō* 13 B3 35 45N 139 49 E
Kasumigasek, *Tōkyō* 13 C3 35 40N 139 46 E
Katabira →, *Tōkyō* 13 D2 35 27N 139 38 E
Katernberg, *Ruhr* 6 A4 51 30N 7 4 E
Katong Park, *Sing.* 15 G8 1 18N 103 53 E
Katrineberg, *Stock.* 3 E10 59 18N 17 54 E
Katsushika-Ku, *Tōkyō* 13 B4 35 44N 139 51 E
Kattinge Vig, *Købn.* 2 D7 55 40N 12 1 E
Kau Pei Chau, *H.K.* 12 E6 22 12N 114 15 E
Kau Yi Chau, *H.K.* 12 E5 22 17N 114 4 E
Kauklahti, *Hels.* 3 B2 60 11N 24 36 E
Kaulsdorf, *Berl.* 7 B4 52 29N 13 34 E
Kauniainen, *Hels.* 3 B3 60 13N 24 44 E
Kawagoe, *Tōkyō* 13 A1 35 54N 139 29 E
Kawaguchi, *Tōkyō* 13 B3 35 47N 139 43 E
Kawai, *Tōkyō* 13 D2 35 29N 139 31 E
Kawamukō, *Tōkyō* 13 C2 35 30N 139 34 E
Kawanishi, *Ōsaka* 12 B3 34 49N 135 24 E
Kawasaki, *Tōkyō* 13 C3 35 31N 139 43 E
Kawasaki Harbour, *Tōkyō* 13 D3 35 30N 139 47 E
Kawawa, *Tōkyō* 13 C2 35 31N 139 33 E
Kawęczyn, *Wsaw.* 10 E7 52 16N 21 3 E
Kayu Putih, *Jak.* 15 J10 6 10 S 106 53 E
Kbely, *Pra.* 10 B3 50 8N 14 32 E
Kearny, *N.Y.* 22 C4 40 45N 74 8W
Kebayoran Baru, *Jak.* 15 J9 6 14 S 106 47 E
Kebayoran Lama, *Jak.* 15 J9 6 13 S 106 46 E
Kebon Jeruk, *Jak.* 15 J9 6 11 S 106 46 E
Keferloh, *Mün.* 7 G11 48 5N 11 43 E
Keilor, *Melb.* 19 E6 37 42 S 144 50 E
Keilor East, *Melb.* 19 E6 37 44 S 144 51 E
Keimola, *Hels.* 3 A3 60 20N 24 49 E
Kelenföld, *Bud.* 10 K13 47 27N 19 2 E
Kelvedon Hatch, *Lon.* 4 A6 51 40N 0 15 E
Kelvin, *Jobg.* 18 E9 26 4S 28 5 E
Kemang, *Jak.* 15 J9 6 15 S 106 48 E
Kemayoran, *Jak.* 15 J10 6 10 S 106 51 E
Kemayoran Airport, *Jak.* 15 H10 6 8 S 106 50 E
Kemp Mill, *Wash.* 25 C7 39 0N 77 1W
Kempton Park, *Jobg.* 18 E10 26 5 S 28 14 E
Kempton Racecourse, *Lon.* 4 C2 51 24N 0 23W
Kemsing, *Lon.* 4 D6 51 18N 0 12 E
Kendall Green, *Bost.* 21 C2 42 22N 71 16W
Kendua, *Calc.* 16 E5 22 34N 88 10 E
Keng Hau, *H.K.* 12 D6 22 22N 114 10 E
Kenilworth, *Chic.* 26 A2 42 5N 87 42W
Kenilworth, *N.Y.* 22 C3 40 40N 74 16W
Kenley, *Lon.* 4 D4 51 19N 0 6W
Kenmare, *Jobg.* 18 E7 26 6 S 27 48 E
Kennedy Grove Regional Rec. Area, *S.F.* 27 A3 37 56N 122 14W
Kennedy Town, *H.K.* 12 E5 22 16N 114 6 E

40 Kensal Green

Kensal Green, Lon. 4 B3 51 32N 0 13W
Kensington, Jobg. 18 F9 26 11 S 28 6 E
Kensington, Lon. 4 C3 51 29N 0 10W
Kensington, N.Y. 22 D5 40 38N 73 57W
Kensington, Phil. 24 B4 39 59N 75 6W
Kensington, S.F. 27 A3 37 54N 122 17W
Kensington, Syd. 19 B4 33 54 S 151 13 E
Kensington, Wash. 25 C7 39 1N 77 4W
Kensington Palace, Lon. 4 B3 51 30N 0 11W
Kent Woodlands, S.F. 27 A1 37 56N 122 34W
Kentfield, S.F. 27 A1 37 57N 122 33W
Kentish Town, Lon. 4 B4 51 32N 0 8W
Kentland, Wash. 25 D8 38 55N 76 53W
Kenton, Lon. 4 B3 51 34N 0 17W
Kenwood, Balt. 25 A4 39 20N 76 30W
Kenwood, Bost. 21 B2 42 40N 71 14W
Kenwood House, Lon. 4 B4 51 34N 0 9W
Kepa, Wsaw. 10 E7 52 13N 21 3 E
Keppel Harbour, Sing. 15 G7 1 15N 103 49 E
Kerameikos, Ath. 8 J11 37 58N 23 42 E
Kerepes, Bud. 10 J14 47 33N 19 17 E
Keston, Lon. 4 C5 51 21N 0 1 E
Keston Mark, Lon. 4 C5 51 21N 0 2 E
Keth Wara, Delhi 16 A2 28 40N 77 13 E
Kettering, Wash. 25 D9 38 53N 76 49W
Kettwig, Ruhr 6 B3 51 22N 6 56 E
Kew, Jobg. 18 E9 26 7 S 28 5 E
Kew, Lon. 4 C3 51 28N 0 17W
Kew, Melb. 19 E7 37 48 S 145 2 E
Kew Gardens, Lon. 4 C3 51 28N 0 17W
Key Gardens, Trto. 20 E9 43 39N 79 18W
Khaboye, Len. 11 B6 59 53N 30 44 E
Khaidhárion, Ath. 8 H10 38 2N 23 38 E
Khairna, Bomb. 16 G9 19 5N 73 0 E
Khalándrion, Ath. 8 H11 38 3N 23 48 E
Khalīj, Bagd. 17 F8 33 18N 44 28 E
Khansā, Bagd. 17 E8 33 21N 44 28 E
Kharavli, Bomb. 16 H8 18 54N 72 55 E
Khardah, Calc. 16 D6 22 43N 88 22 E
Khayala, Delhi 16 B1 28 39N 77 6 E
Khefren, El Qâ. 18 D4 29 58N 31 8 E
Khichripur, Delhi 16 B2 28 37N 77 18 E
Khimki, Mos. 11 D8 55 53N 37 24 E
Khimki-Khovrino, Mos. 11 D9 55 51N 37 31 E
Khimkinskoye Vdkr., Mos. 11 D8 55 51N 37 27 E
Khirvosti, Len. 11 B5 59 56N 30 37 E
Khlongsan, Bangk. 15 B1 13 43N 100 29 E
Kholargós, Ath. 8 J11 37 59N 23 48 E
Khorel, Calc. 16 D5 22 41N 88 18 E
Khorosovo, Mos. 11 E8 55 46N 37 27 E
Khudrā, Bagd. 17 F7 33 19N 44 17 E
Khun Thian, Bangk. 15 B1 13 41N 100 27 E
Khuraiji Khas, Delhi 16 B2 28 38N 77 16 E
Khurigachi, Calc. 16 D5 22 48N 88 21 E
Kiamari, Kar. 17 H10 24 49N 66 58 E
Kidderpore, Calc. 16 E5 22 32N 88 19 E
Kienwerder, Berl. 7 B2 52 22N 13 11 E
Kierling, Wien 10 G9 48 18N 16 16 E
Kierlingbach →, Wien 10 G9 48 18N 16 19 E
Kierlinger Forst, Wien 10 G9 48 17N 16 14 E
Kierst, Ruhr 6 C2 51 18N 6 42 E
Kifisós →, Ath. 8 J11 37 58N 23 42 E
Kikenka →, Len. 11 B2 59 50N 30 3 E
Kikuna, Tōkyō 13 C2 35 30N 139 37 E
Kil, Stock. 3 D12 59 20N 18 19 E
Kilburn, Lon. 4 B3 51 32N 0 11W
Killara, Syd. 19 A4 33 46 S 151 10 E
Kilo, Hels. 3 B3 60 13N 24 47 E
Kilokri, Delhi 16 B2 28 34N 77 15 E
Kilsyth, Melb. 19 E8 37 48 S 145 18 E
Kimberton, Phil. 24 A1 40 7N 75 34W
Kimlin Park, Sing. 15 G7 1 18N 103 49 E
Kindi, Bagd. 17 F8 33 18N 44 22 E
King of Prussia, Phil. 24 A2 40 5N 75 22W
Kings Cross, Syd. 19 B4 33 52 S 151 12 E
Kings Domain, Melb. 19 E6 37 49 S 144 58 E
Kings Mt., S.F. 27 D3 37 27N 122 19W
King's Park, H.K. 12 E6 22 18N 114 10 E
Kings Park, Wash. 25 E6 38 48N 77 17W
King's Point, N.Y. 23 C6 40 48N 73 45W
Kingsbury, Lon. 4 B3 51 34N 0 15W
Kingsford, Syd. 19 B4 33 55 S 151 14 E
Kingston upon Thames, Lon. 4 C3 51 24N 0 17W
Kingston Vale, Lon. 4 C3 51 25N 0 25W
Kingsway, Trto. 20 E7 43 38N 79 32W
Kingswood, Lon. 4 D3 51 17N 0 12W
Kinnelon, N.Y. 22 B2 40 59N 74 23W
Kipling Heights, Trto. 20 D7 43 43N 79 34W
Kipséli, Ath. 8 J11 37 59N 23 45 E
Kirchhellen, Ruhr 6 A3 51 36N 6 56 E
Kirchhörde, Ruhr 6 B6 51 27N 7 27 E
Kirchlinde, Ruhr 6 A6 51 31N 7 22 E
Kirchof, Hbg. 7 E8 53 29N 10 1 E
Kirchsteinbek, Hbg. 7 D8 53 31N 10 7 E
Kirchstockbach, Mün. 7 G11 48 1N 11 40 E
Kirchtrudering, Mün. 7 G11 48 7N 11 40 E
Kirdasa, El Qâ. 18 C4 30 2N 31 6 E
Kirikiri, Lagos 18 B1 6 26N 7 18 E
Kirkkonummi, Hels. 3 C1 60 6N 24 28W
Kirkland, Mtrl. 20 B2 43 26N 73 51W
Kirovskiye, Os., Len. 11 B3 59 57N 30 14 E
Kisarazu, Tōkyō 13 D4 35 21N 139 54 E
Kisikli, Ist. 17 A3 41 1N 29 2 E
Kispest, Bud. 10 K13 47 27N 19 8 E
Kista, Stock. 3 D10 59 24N 17 57 E
Kistarcsa, Bud. 10 J14 47 32N 19 16 E
Kita, Ōsaka 12 B4 34 41N 135 30 E
Kita-Ku, Tōkyō 13 B3 35 44N 139 44 E
Kitain-Temple, Tōkyō 13 A1 35 54N 139 29 E
Kitazawa, Tōkyō 13 C3 35 39N 139 40 E
Kiu Tsiu, H.K. 12 D6 22 22N 114 17 E
Kiuvasaari, Hels. 3 C5 60 6N 25 0 E
Kivistö, Hels. 3 B4 60 18N 24 50 E
Kiyose, Tōkyō 13 B2 35 46N 139 31 E
Kiziltoprak, Ist. 17 B3 40 58N 29 3 E
Kizu →, Ōsaka 12 C3 34 37N 135 27 E
Kizuri, Ōsaka 12 C4 34 38N 135 34 E
Kjeller, Oslo 2 B6 59 58N 11 1 E
Kjelsås, Oslo 2 B4 59 57N 10 47 E
Kladow, Berl. 7 B1 52 27N 13 9 E
Klampenborg, Købn. 2 D10 55 46N 12 35 E
Klánovice, Pra. 10 B3 50 5N 14 40 E
Klaudyń, Wsaw. 10 E6 52 17N 20 50 E
Klecany, Pra. 10 A2 50 10N 14 24 E
Kledering, Wien 10 H10 48 8N 16 26 E
Klein Gleinicke, Berl. 7 B1 52 23N 13 5 E
Klein-Hadern, Mün. 7 G9 48 7N 11 28 E
Klein Jukskei →, Jobg. 18 E8 26 6 S 27 57 E
Kleinburg, Trto. 20 C7 43 51N 79 37W
Kleine Grasbrook, Hbg. 7 D7 53 31N 9 59 E
Kleinmachnow, Berl. 7 B2 52 24N 13 14 E
Kleinschönebeck, Berl. 7 B5 52 29N 13 42 E
Kleinziethen, Berl. 7 B3 52 22N 13 26 E
Klemetsrud, Oslo 2 B5 59 50N 10 51 E
Klender, Jak. 15 J10 6 12 S 106 53 E
Klippoortje, Jobg. 18 F10 26 14 S 28 10 E
Klipriviersberg, Jobg. 18 F9 26 16 S 28 2 E
Klipspruit →, Jobg. 18 F8 26 14 S 27 53 E
Kloofendal, Jobg. 18 E8 26 8 S 27 52 E
Klosterhardt, Ruhr 6 A3 51 32N 6 52 E
Klosterneuburg, Wien 10 G9 48 18N 16 19 E
Knockholt Pound, Lon. 4 D5 51 18N 0 7 E
Knowland State Arboretum and Park, S.F. 27 B4 37 45N 122 7W
Knox Park, Melb. 19 F8 37 54 S 145 15 E
Knoxville, Melb. 19 F8 37 53 S 145 14 E
Köbanya, Bud. 10 K13 47 28N 19 9 E
Kobe, Ōsaka 12 B2 34 41N 135 13 E
Kōbe Harbour, Ōsaka 12 C2 34 39N 135 11 E
København, Købn. 2 D9 55 40N 12 26 E
Kobylisy, Pra. 10 B2 50 7N 14 26 E
Kobyłka, Wsaw. 10 D8 52 20N 21 10 E
Kocasinan, Ist. 17 A2 41 1N 28 50 E
Kočife, Pra. 10 B2 50 3N 14 21 E
Kodaira, Tōkyō 13 B1 35 43N 139 28 E
Kodanaka, Tōkyō 13 C2 35 34N 139 37 E
Kogane, Tōkyō 13 B4 35 49N 139 55 E
Koganei, Tōkyō 13 B2 35 42N 139 31 E
Kogarah, Syd. 19 B3 33 57 S 151 8 E
Køge Bugt, Købn. 2 E9 55 34N 12 24 E
Köhlbrand Rethe, Hbg. 7 D7 53 31N 9 56 E
Köhlfleet, Hbg. 7 D7 53 32N 9 53 E
Koivupää, Hels. 3 B4 60 18N 24 53 E
Koja, Jak. 15 H10 6 8 S 106 52 E
Koja Utara, Jak. 15 H10 6 5 S 106 53 E
Kokobunji, Tōkyō 13 B1 35 42N 139 27 E
Kokobunji-Temple, Tōkyō 13 B4 35 44N 139 55 E
Kol Scholven, Ruhr 6 A3 51 35N 6 59 E
Kolarängen, Stock. 3 E12 59 16N 18 10 E
Kolbotn, Oslo 2 C4 59 48N 10 48 E
Kole Kalyan, Bomb. 16 G8 19 5N 72 50 E
Kolmiranta, Hels. 3 B2 60 15N 24 31 E
Kolmpera, Hels. 3 B2 60 15N 24 32 E
Koło, Wsaw. 10 E6 52 14N 20 56 E
Kolodeje, Pra. 10 B3 50 3N 14 38 E
Kolokinthou, Ath. 8 J11 38 0N 23 42 E
Kolomenskoye, Mos. 11 E10 55 40N 37 40 E
Kolomyagi, Len. 11 A3 60 0N 30 19 E
Kolónos, Ath. 8 J11 37 59N 23 43 E
Kolovraty, Pra. 10 B3 50 0N 14 37 E
Kolsås, Oslo 2 B3 59 55N 10 30 E
Koltushi, Len. 11 B5 59 55N 30 38 E
Komae, Tōkyō 13 C2 35 37N 139 34 E
Komagome, Tōkyō 13 B3 35 43N 139 45 E
Komazawa, Tōkyō 13 C3 35 37N 139 40 E
Komdhara, Calc. 16 C5 22 52N 88 14 E
Kommunarka, Mos. 11 F8 55 35N 37 29 E
Komorów, Wsaw. 10 F5 52 9N 20 48 E
Kona, Calc. 16 E5 22 37N 88 18 E
Konala, Hels. 3 B4 60 14N 24 52 E
Kōnan, Tōkyō 13 D2 35 23N 139 35 E
Kondli, Delhi 16 B2 28 36N 77 19 E
Kong Sin Wan, H.K. 12 E5 22 15N 114 7 E
Kongelunden, Købn. 2 E10 55 34N 12 34 E
Kongens Lyngby, Købn. 2 D10 55 46N 12 30 E
Kongo, Hels. 3 A3 60 20N 24 47 E
Königshardt, Ruhr 6 A3 51 33N 6 51 E
Konnagar, Calc. 16 D6 22 42N 88 21 E
Konohana, Ōsaka 12 B3 34 40N 135 26 E
Kōnoike, Ōsaka 12 B4 34 42N 135 37 E
Konradshöhe, Berl. 7 A2 52 35N 13 13 E
Koonung Cr. →, Melb. 19 E7 37 46 S 145 4 E
Kopanina, Pra. 10 B1 50 3N 14 17 E
Koparkhairna, Bomb. 16 G8 19 6N 72 59 E
Köpenick, Berl. 7 B4 52 26N 13 35 E
Korangi, Kar. 17 H11 24 47N 67 8 E
Koremasa, Tōkyō 13 C1 35 39N 139 29 E
Korenevo, Mos. 11 E12 55 40N 38 0 E
Kori, Ōsaka 12 B4 34 47N 135 38 E
Koridhallós, Ath. 8 J10 37 59N 23 39 E
Korkinskoye, Oz., Len. 11 B6 59 55N 30 42 E
Körne, Ruhr 6 A7 51 30N 7 30 E
Korso, Hels. 3 A5 60 21N 25 5 E
Koshigaya, Tōkyō 13 A3 35 53N 139 47 E
Kosino, Mos. 11 E11 55 43N 37 50 E
Kosugi, Tōkyō 13 C2 35 34N 139 39 E
Kota, Jak. 15 H9 6 7 S 106 48 E
Kotelyniki, Mos. 11 F11 55 39N 37 52 E
Kōtō-Ku, Tōkyō 13 B3 35 40N 139 48 E
Kotrang, Calc. 16 D6 22 41N 88 20 E
Kouponia, Ath. 8 J11 37 57N 23 47 E
Koviksudde, Stock. 3 D13 59 21N 18 21 E
Kowloon, H.K. 12 E5 22 18N 114 10 E
Kowloon City, H.K. 12 E6 22 19N 114 11 E
Kowloon Pk., H.K. 12 D6 22 20N 114 13 E
Kowloon Res., H.K. 12 D5 22 21N 114 9 E
Kowloon Tong, H.K. 12 D6 22 20N 114 10 E
Kozhukhovo, Mos. 11 E11 55 43N 37 53 E
Kozukue, Tōkyō 13 C2 35 30N 139 35 E
Krailling, Mün. 7 G9 48 5N 11 25 E
Kramat Jati, Jak. 15 J10 6 15 S 106 51 E
Krampnitz, Berl. 7 B1 52 27N 13 3 E
Krampnitzsee, Berl. 7 B1 52 27N 13 3 E
Kranji, Sing. 15 F7 1 26N 103 45 E
Kranji, Sungei →, Sing. 15 F7 1 26N 103 44 E
Kranji Dam, Sing. 15 F7 1 26N 103 44 E
Kraskovo, Mos. 11 F11 55 39N 37 58 E
Krasnaya Gorka, Len. 11 B5 59 58N 30 38 E
Krasno-Presnenskaya, Mos. 11 E9 55 45N 37 32 E
Krasnogorsk, Mos. 11 E7 55 49N 37 18 E
Krasnyj Stroitel, Mos. 11 F9 55 36N 37 35 E
Kray, Ruhr 6 B4 51 27N 7 4 E
Krč, Pra. 10 B2 50 2N 14 26 E
Krefeld, Ruhr 6 B1 51 20N 6 33 E
Kremlin, Mos. 11 E9 55 45N 37 38 E
Kresson, Phil. 24 B5 39 51N 74 54W
Kreuzberg, Berl. 7 A3 52 30N 13 24 E
Krishnarampur, Calc. 16 D5 22 43N 88 13 E
Kritzendorf, Wien 10 G9 48 19N 16 18 E
Krokhol, Oslo 2 C5 59 48N 10 55 E
Krugersdorp, Jobg. 18 E7 26 6 S 27 48 E
Krukut, Kali →, Jak. 15 J9 6 13 S 106 48 E
Krumme Lanke, Berl. 7 B2 52 27N 13 14 E
Krummensee, Berl. 7 A5 52 35N 13 41 E
Krupunder, Hbg. 7 D7 53 37N 9 53 E
Krusboda, Stock. 3 E12 59 13N 18 14 E
Krylatskoye, Mos. 11 E8 55 44N 37 23 E
Küçúkkoy, Ist. 17 A2 41 3N 28 52 E
Kudrovo, Len. 11 B5 59 54N 30 30 E
Kujiai, Tōkyō 13 A1 35 57N 139 26 E
Küllenhahn, Ruhr 6 C4 51 14N 7 8 E
Kulosaari, Hels. 3 B5 60 11N 25 0 E
Kulturpalasset, Wsaw. 10 E7 52 14N 21 0 E
Kumla, Stock. 3 E12 59 13N 18 11 E
Kummelnäs, Stock. 3 D12 59 21N 18 16 E
Kungens kurva, Stock. 3 E10 59 15N 17 53 E
Kungsängen, Stock. 3 D9 59 26N 17 43 E
Kungshatt, Stock. 3 E10 59 17N 17 53 E
Kungsholmen, Stock. 3 D11 59 20N 18 2 E
Kuningan, Jak. 15 J9 6 13 S 106 49 E
Kuninkaanmäki, Hels. 3 B5 60 18N 25 7 E
Kunitachi, Tōkyō 13 B1 35 41N 139 27 E
Kunming Hu, Beij. 14 B2 39 59N 116 13 E
Kunratice, Pra. 10 B2 50 0N 14 28 E
Kunratický →, Pra. 10 B2 50 2N 14 24 E
Kunsthalle, Hbg. 7 D8 53 33N 10 0 E
Kuntsevo, Mos. 11 E8 55 43N 37 23 E
Kupchino, Len. 11 B4 59 50N 30 23 E
Kupferdreh, Ruhr 6 B4 51 23N 7 5 E
Kurbali Dere →, Ist. 17 B3 40 58N 29 1 E
Kurihara, Tōkyō 13 B2 35 45N 139 34 E
Kurkino, Mos. 11 D8 55 53N 37 22 E
Kurla, Bomb. 16 G8 19 4N 72 52 E
Kurmuri, Bomb. 16 G8 19 4N 72 53 E
Kurnell, Syd. 19 C4 34 0 S 151 10 E
Kurume, Tōkyō 13 B2 35 45N 139 31 E
Kuryanovo, Mos. 11 F10 55 39N 37 42 E
Kushihiki, Tōkyō 13 A2 35 54N 139 36 E
Kushtia, Calc. 16 E6 22 31N 88 23 E
Kuskovo, Mos. 11 E10 55 44N 37 48 E
Kutsino, Mos. 11 E11 55 44N 37 55 E
Kuy-e-Gishā, Tehr. 17 C5 35 44N 51 23 E
Kuy-e-Mekānir, Tehr. 17 C5 35 46N 51 22 E
Kuzyminki, Mos. 11 E10 55 42N 37 46 E
Kvarnsjön, Stock. 3 E10 59 11N 17 58 E
Kwa-Thema, Jobg. 18 F11 26 17 S 28 23 E
Kwai Chung, H.K. 12 D5 22 22N 114 7 E
Kwitang, Jak. 15 J10 6 11 S 106 50 E
Kwun Tong, H.K. 12 E6 22 18N 114 13 E
Kyje, Pra. 10 B3 50 6N 14 33 E
Kyōhōji, Ōsaka 12 C4 34 38N 135 33 E
Kyrkfjärden, Stock. 3 E9 59 16N 17 45 E
Kyrkslätt, Hels. 3 C1 60 6N 24 28W

L

La Aguada, Stgo 30 J10 33 28 S 70 40W
La Blanca, Stgo 30 K11 33 30 S 70 40W
La Boca, B.A. 32 B4 34 38 S 58 22W
La Bottáccia, Rome 9 F8 41 54N 12 18 E
La Bretèche, Paris 5 B2 48 51N 2 1 E
La Brosse, Paris 5 C1 48 43N 1 20 E
La Cabana, La Hab. 30 B3 23 8N 82 20W
La Canada, L.A. 28 A3 34 12N 118 12W
La Cassa, Tori. 9 A2 45 11N 7 30 E
La Celle-les-Bordes, Paris 5 D1 48 38N 1 57 E
La Celle-St.-Cloud, Paris 5 B2 48 50N 2 9 E
La Chivera, Car. 30 D5 10 35N 66 54W
La Colmena, Méx. 29 A2 19 35N 99 16W
La Courneuve, Paris 5 B4 48 55N 2 22 E
La Crescenta, L.A. 28 A3 34 13N 118 14W
La Défense, Paris 5 B3 48 53N 2 12 E
La Dehesa, Stgo 30 J11 33 21 S 70 33W
La Estación, Mdrd. 8 B2 40 27N 3 48W
La Floresta, Barc. 8 D5 41 26N 2 3 E
La Florida, Car. 30 D5 10 30N 66 52W
La Fortuna, Mdrd. 8 B2 40 21N 3 46W
La Fransa, Barc. 8 D5 41 22N 2 9 E
La Fresnière, Mtrl. 20 A2 43 33N 73 58W
La Frette-sur-Seine, Paris 5 B3 48 58N 2 11 E
La Garenne-Colombes, Paris 5 B3 48 54N 2 15 E
La Giustiniana, Rome 9 F9 41 59N 12 24 E
La Grange, Chic. 26 C1 41 48N 87 53W
La Grange des Noues, Paris 5 A4 49 1N 2 28 E
La Grange Highlands, Chic. 26 C1 41 46N 87 53W
La Grange Park, Chic. 26 C1 41 49N 87 51W
La Granja, Stgo 30 K11 33 31 S 70 38W
La Guaira, Car. 30 D5 10 36N 66 55W
La Guardia Airport, N.Y. 23 C5 40 46N 73 52W
La Guasima, La Hab. 30 B3 23 0N 82 17W
La Habana, La Hab. 30 B2 23 7N 82 21W
La habana, B. de, La Hab. 30 B3 23 7N 82 20W
La Habana Vieia, La Hab. 30 B2 23 7N 82 20W
La Habra, L.A. 28 C5 33 56N 117 57W
La Habre Heights, L.A. 28 C5 33 59N 117 56W
La Horqueta →, B.A. 32 C1 34 43 S 58 51W
La Lisa, La Hab. 30 B2 23 3N 82 25W
La Llacuna, Barc. 8 D6 41 24N 2 12 E
La Loma, Méx. 29 A2 19 31N 99 11W
La Lucila, B.A. 32 B4 34 30 S 58 29W
La Magdalena Atlipac, Méx. 29 B4 19 22N 89 56 E
La Magdalena Chichicaspa, Méx. 29 B2 19 24N 99 18W
La Magdalena Contreras, Méx. 29 C2 19 17N 99 13W
La Magdalena Petlalco, Méx. 29 C2 19 13N 99 10W
La Maison Blanche, Paris 5 C1 48 44N 1 54 E
La Maladrerie, Paris 5 B2 48 54N 2 1 E
La Marquesa, Méx. 29 C1 19 18N 99 22W
La Milla, Cerro, Lima 30 G8 12 2 S 77 5W
La Molina, Lima 30 G9 12 4 S 76 56W
La Monachina, Rome 9 F9 41 53N 12 21 E
La Moraleja, Mdrd. 8 A3 40 30N 30 38W
La Nopalera, Méx. 29 C3 19 18N 99 5W
La Pastora, Car. 30 D5 10 31N 66 55W
La Paterna, B.A. 32 B4 34 35 S 58 26W
La Patte-d'Oie, Paris 5 A3 49 0N 2 10 E
La Perla, Lima 30 G8 12 4 S 77 7W
La Perouse, Syd. 19 B4 33 59 S 151 14 E
La Pineda, Barc. 8 E5 41 15N 2 1 E
La Pisana, Rome 9 F9 41 51N 12 23 E
La Playa, La Hab. 30 B2 23 6N 82 26W
La Prairie, Mtrl. 20 B5 43 25N 73 29W
La Puente, L.A. 28 B5 34 1N 117 54W
La Punta, Lima 30 G7 12 4 S 77 10W
La Puntigala, Barc. 8 D6 41 27N 2 13 E
La Queue-en-Brie, Paris 5 C5 48 47N 2 34 E
La Reina, Stgo 30 J11 33 26 S 70 33W
La Reja, B.A. 32 B2 34 38 S 58 48W
La Ribera, Barc. 8 D5 41 21N 2 4 E
La Romanie, Paris 5 C1 48 43N 1 53 E
La Rústica, Rome 9 F10 41 54N 12 36 E
La Sagrera, Barc. 8 D6 41 25N 2 11 E
La Salada, B.A. 32 C4 34 43 S 58 28W
La Scala, Mil. 9 E6 45 28N 9 11 E
La Selce, Rome 9 F9 41 53N 12 20 E
La Sierra, La Hab. 30 B2 23 7N 82 24W
La Taxonera, Barc. 8 D6 41 25N 2 10 E
La Vega, Car. 30 E5 10 28N 66 56W
La Verrière, Paris 5 C1 48 45N 1 57 E
La Vibora, La Hab. 30 B2 23 5N 82 22W
La Victoria, Lima 30 G8 12 3 S 77 2W
La Ville-du-Bois, Paris 5 D3 48 39N 2 16 E
Laab im Walde, Wien 10 H9 48 9N 16 10 E
Laaer Berg, Wien 10 H10 48 9N 16 24 E
Laajalahti, Hels. 3 B3 60 11N 24 48 E
Laajasalo, Hels. 3 B5 60 10N 25 1 E
Laaksolahti, Hels. 3 B3 60 14N 24 45 E
Laar, Ruhr 6 B2 51 27N 6 44 E
Lablâba, W. el →, El Qâ. 18 C5 30 1N 31 19 E
Lachine, Mtrl. 20 B3 43 26N 73 42W
Ládvi, Pra. 10 B2 50 8N 14 27 E
Łady, Wsaw. 10 F6 52 8N 20 57 E
Lafayette, S.F. 27 A4 37 52N 122 6W
Lafayette Hill, Phil. 24 A3 40 5N 75 15W
Lafayette Res., S.F. 27 A4 37 52N 122 8W
Laferrere, B.A. 32 C3 34 45 S 58 35W
Lagny, Paris 5 B6 48 52N 2 42 E
Lagoa da Pedra, Lisb. 8 F9 38 43N 8 58W
Lagos, Lagos 18 B2 6 27N 7 23 E
Lagos Harbour, Lagos 18 B2 6 26N 7 23 E
Lagos-Ikeja Airport, Lagos 18 A1 6 34N 7 19 E
Lagos Island, Lagos 18 B2 6 26N 7 23 E
Lagos Lagoon, Lagos 18 B2 6 30N 7 28 E
Laguna de B., Manila 15 E4 14 29N 121 6 E
Laim, Mün. 7 G10 48 7N 11 30 E
Lainate, Mil. 9 D5 45 34N 9 1 E
Lainz, Wien 10 H9 48 10N 16 16 E
Lainzer Tiergarten, Wien 10 G9 48 10N 16 13 E
Lajeado →, S. Pau. 31 E7 23 28 S 46 24W
Lake Avenue Woods, Chic. 26 A1 42 4N 87 53W
Lake Hiawatha, N.Y. 22 B2 40 52N 74 23W
Lakefield, Jobg. 18 F10 26 11 S 28 17 E
Lakemba, Syd. 19 B3 33 55 S 151 5 E
Lakeside, Jobg. 18 E9 26 5 S 28 8 E
Lakeview, Chic. 26 B3 41 56N 87 38W
Lakeview, Trto. 20 E7 43 35N 79 32W
Lakhtinskiy, Len. 11 B2 59 59N 30 9 E
Lakhtinskiy Razliv, Oz., Len. 11 B3 59 59N 30 12 E
Lakshmanpur, Calc. 16 E5 22 38N 88 16 E
Laleham, Lon. 4 C2 51 24N 0 29W
Lâleli, Ist. 17 A2 41 0N 28 57 E
Lalor, Melb. 19 E6 37 40 S 144 59 E
Lam San, Sing. 15 F7 1 22N 103 43 E
Lam Tin, H.K. 12 E6 22 18N 114 14 E
Lambarfjärden, Stock. 3 D9 59 21N 17 48 E
Lambert, Oslo 2 B4 59 52N 10 48 E
Lambeth, Lon. 4 C4 51 28N 0 6W
Lambrate, Mil. 9 E6 45 28N 9 16 E
Lambro →, Mil. 9 E6 45 24N 9 17 E
Lambro, Parco, Mil. 9 E6 45 29N 9 14 E
Lambton, Jobg. 18 F10 26 14 S 28 10 E
Lambton Hills, Trto. 20 E7 43 39N 79 30W
Lamma I., H.K. 12 E5 22 12N 114 7 E
Lampton, Lon. 4 C2 51 28N 0 21W
Landianchang, Beij. 14 B2 39 57N 116 13 E
Landover Hills, Wash. 25 D8 38 56N 76 54W
Landstrasse, Wien 10 G10 48 12N 16 23 E
Landwehr kanal, Berl. 7 B3 52 29N 13 24 E
Lane Cove, Syd. 19 A3 33 48 S 151 9 E
Lane Cove National Park, Syd. 19 A3 33 47 S 151 8 E
Langen, Oslo 2 C5 59 44N 10 57 E
Langenberg, Ruhr 6 B4 51 20N 7 7 E
Langenbochum, Ruhr 6 A4 51 36N 7 7 E
Langendreer, Ruhr 6 B5 51 28N 7 18 E
Langenhorn, Hbg. 7 D7 53 39N 9 59 E
Langenhorst, Ruhr 6 B4 51 21N 7 1 E
Langenzersdorf, Wien 10 G10 48 18N 16 21 E
Langer See, Berl. 7 B4 52 24N 13 37 E
Langerfeld, Ruhr 6 C5 51 16N 7 14 E
Langley, Wash. 25 D6 38 57N 77 11W
Langley Park, Wash. 25 D8 38 59N 76 58W
Langstaff, Trto. 20 C8 43 50N 79 26W
Längtarmen, Stock. 3 E9 59 18N 17 43 E
Längtarmen, Stock. 3 D8 59 24N 17 36 E
Langwald, Mün. 7 F9 48 10N 11 25 E
Lanham, Wash. 25 D8 38 59N 76 51W
Lank-Latum, Ruhr 6 C2 51 18N 6 40 E
Lankwitz, Berl. 7 B3 52 25N 13 21 E
Länna Drevviken, Stock. 3 E11 59 12N 18 8 E
L'Annunziatella, Rome 9 G10 41 49N 12 33 E
Lansdowne, Balt. 25 B3 39 14N 76 38W
Lansdowne, Phil. 24 B3 39 56N 75 16W
Lansing, Trto. 20 D8 43 45N 79 24W
Lanús, B.A. 32 C4 34 42 S 58 23W
Lapa, Rio J. 31 B2 22 54 S 43 10W
Lapa, S. Pau. 31 E5 23 31 S 46 42W
Lapangan Merdeka, Jak. 15 J9 6 10 S 106 49 E
Lapinkylä, Hels. 3 B4 60 18N 24 51 E
Lapinkylä, Hels. 3 B1 60 13N 24 27 E
Lappböle, Hels. 3 B1 60 13N 24 27 E
Laranjeiras, Rio J. 31 B2 22 55 S 43 10W
Larchmont, N.Y. 23 B6 40 55N 73 44W
Larkspur, S.F. 27 A1 37 55N 122 31W
Las, Wsaw. 10 E7 52 13N 21 6 E
Las Acacias, Car. 30 E5 10 29N 66 54W
Las Adjuntas, Car. 30 E4 10 25N 67 0W
Las Barrancas, B.A. 32 A4 34 28 S 58 29W
Las Conchas, B.A. 32 A3 34 25 S 58 34W
Las Corts, Barc. 8 D5 41 23N 2 9 E
Las Fuentes Brotantes, Méx. 29 C2 19 16N 99 11W
Las Kabacki, Wsaw. 10 F7 52 7N 21 2 E
Las Lomas, L.A. 28 B5 34 8N 117 59W
Las Mercedes, Car. 30 E5 10 28N 66 51W
Las Pinas, Manila 15 E3 14 29N 120 58 E
Las Rejas, Stgo 30 J10 33 27 S 70 42W
Las Rozas de Madrid, Mdrd. 8 B1 40 29N 3 52W
Las Trampas Cr. →, S.F. 27 A4 37 53N 122 6W
Las Trampas Regional Park, S.F. 27 B4 37 49N 122 3W
Las Trampas Ridge, S.F. 27 A4 37 50N 122 3W
Las Tunitas, Car. 30 D4 10 36N 67 1W
Lasalle, Mtrl. 20 B4 43 26N 73 37W
Lasek Bielański, Wsaw. 10 E6 52 17N 20 57 E
Lasek Na Kole, Wsaw. 10 E6 52 15N 20 56 E
Laski, Wsaw. 10 E6 52 18N 20 50 E
Latina, Mdrd. 8 B2 40 24N 3 44W
Latrobe Univ., Melb. 19 E7 37 43 S 145 3 E
Lattingtown, N.Y. 23 B7 40 52N 73 34W
Laufzorn, Mün. 7 G10 48 0N 11 33 E
Laurel Hollow, N.Y. 23 B8 40 51N 73 28W
Laurel Springs, Phil. 24 C4 39 49N 75 0W
Laurelton, N.Y. 23 C6 40 40N 73 45W
Laurence Hanscom Field, Bost. 21 C2 42 28N 71 16W
Lausdomini, Nápl. 9 H13 40 55N 14 26 E
Lauttasaari, Hels. 3 C4 60 9N 24 53 E
Lava Nuova, Nápl. 9 J13 40 47N 14 23 E
Laval-des-Rapides, Mtrl. 20 A3 43 33N 73 41W
Laval-Ouest, Mtrl. 20 A2 43 32N 73 52W
Laval-sur-le-Lac, Mtrl. 20 A2 43 31N 73 52W
Lavradio, Lisb. 8 F8 38 40N 9 2W
Lawndale, Chic. 26 B2 41 50N 87 42W
Lawndale, L.A. 28 C2 33 52N 118 22W
Lawndale, Phil. 24 A4 40 3N 75 5W
Lawnside, Phil. 24 B4 39 51N 75 1W
Lawrence, Bost. 21 A3 42 43N 71 7W
Lawrence, N.Y. 23 D6 40 36N 73 43W
Lawrence Heights, Trto. 20 D8 43 43N 79 25W
Lawrence Park, Phil. 24 B2 39 57N 75 20W
Lawton, La Hab. 30 B2 23 5N 82 20W
Layāri, Kar. 17 G11 24 52N 67 0 E
Layāri →, Kar. 17 G10 24 52N 66 58 E
Lazienkowski Park, Wsaw. 10 E7 52 13N 21 1 E
Le Blanc-Mesnil, Paris 5 B4 48 56N 2 27 E
Le Bourget, Paris 5 B4 48 56N 2 25 E
Le Chesnay, Paris 5 C2 48 49N 2 8 E
Le Christ de Saclay, Paris 5 C3 48 43N 1 59 E
Le Kremlin-Bicêtre, Paris 5 C4 48 48N 2 21 E
Le Mesnil-Amelot, Paris 5 A5 49 1N 2 35 E
Le Mesnil-le-Roi, Paris 5 B2 48 56N 2 7 E
Le Mesnil-St.-Denis, Paris 5 C1 48 44N 1 57 E
Le Pecq, Paris 5 B2 48 53N 2 6 E
Le Perreux, Paris 5 B4 48 50N 2 29 E
Le Pin, Paris 5 B5 48 54N 2 37 E
Le Plessis-Bouchard, Paris 5 A3 49 0N 2 14 E
Le Plessis-Gassot, Paris 5 A4 49 2N 2 24 E
Le Plessis-Pâté, Paris 5 D3 48 36N 2 19 E
Le Plessis-Robinson, Paris 5 C3 48 47N 2 15 E
Le Plessis-Trévise, Paris 5 C5 48 48N 2 34 E
Le Port-Marly, Paris 5 B2 48 52N 2 6 E
Le Pré-St.-Gervais, Paris 5 B4 48 53N 2 23 E
Le Raincy, Paris 5 B5 48 53N 2 31 E
Le Thillay, Paris 5 A4 49 0N 2 28 E
Le Trappe, Mtrl. 20 B1 43 30N 74 1W
Le Val d'Enfer, Paris 5 C3 48 45N 2 11 E
Le Vésinet, Paris 5 B2 48 54N 2 8 E
Lea →, Lon. 4 B4 51 30N 0 2W
Lea Bridge, Lon. 4 B4 51 33N 0 2W
Leakin Park, Balt. 25 B2 39 18N 76 41W
Leaside, Trto. 20 D8 43 42N 79 22W
Leatherhead, Lon. 4 D3 51 17N 0 19W
Leaves Green, Lon. 4 D5 51 19N 0 1 E
Leblon, Rio J. 31 B2 22 59 S 43 14W
Léchelle, Forêt de la, Paris 5 C6 48 43N 2 41 E
Ledøje, Købn. 2 D8 55 42N 12 18 E
Lee, Lon. 4 C5 51 27N 0 0 E
Leeupan, Jobg. 18 F10 26 13 S 28 18 E
Leganes, Mdrd. 8 C2 40 19N 3 45W
Legazpi, Mdrd. 8 B2 40 23N 3 41W
Legoa, Kali →, Jak. 15 H10 6 6 S 106 52 E
Lehtisaaret, Hels. 3 C3 60 6N 24 46 E
Lehtisaari, Hels. 3 B4 60 10N 24 51 E
Lei Yue Mun, H.K. 12 E6 22 17N 114 14 E
Leião, Lisb. 8 F7 38 43N 9 17W
Leichhardt, Syd. 19 B3 33 53 S 151 9 E
Leigang, Gzh. 14 G7 23 2N 113 6 E
Léini, Tori. 9 A3 45 11N 7 42 E
Leisure World, S.F. 27 A4 37 51N 122 4W
Lemoyne, Mtrl. 20 B5 43 29N 73 29W
Lemsahl, Hbg. 7 C8 53 41N 10 5 E
Lenin, Mos. 11 E9 55 43N 37 34 E
Leningrad, Len. 11 B3 59 55N 30 15 E
Lenino, Mos. 11 F9 55 38N 37 39 E
Leninskiye Gory, Mos. 11 E9 55 41N 37 32 E
Lenne →, Ruhr 6 B7 51 25N 7 30 E
Lennep, Ruhr 6 C5 51 11N 7 15 E
Lenni, Phil. 24 B2 39 53N 75 27W
Lennox, L.A. 28 C2 33 56N 118 20W
Leonardo da Vinci, Aeroporto Int., Rome 9 G8 41 47N 12 15 E
Leoncio Martinez, Car. 30 E6 10 29N 66 48W
Leonia, N.Y. 22 B5 40 51N 73 59W
Leopard, Phil. 24 A2 40 1N 75 26W
Leopardi, Nápl. 9 J13 40 45N 14 24 E
Leopoldau, Wien 10 G10 48 15N 16 26 E
Leopoldstadt, Wien 10 G10 48 13N 16 22 E
Leportovo, Mos. 11 E10 55 46N 37 43 E
Leppävaara, Hels. 3 B3 60 13N 24 49 E
Lera, Mte., Tori. 9 A1 45 10N 7 27 E
L'Éremo, Tori. 9 B3 45 2N 7 44 E
Les Alluets-le-Roi, Paris 5 B1 48 54N 1 55 E
Les Clayes-sous-Bois, Paris 5 C1 48 49N 1 59 E
Les Essarts-le-Roi, Paris 5 C1 48 42N 1 53 E
Les Gâtines, Paris 5 C1 48 48N 1 58 E
Les Grésillons, Paris 5 B2 48 56N 2 1 E
Les Layes, Paris 5 C1 48 43N 1 55 E
Les Lilas, Paris 5 B4 48 52N 2 25 E
Les Loges-en-Josas, Paris 5 C2 48 45N 2 8 E
Les Molières, Paris 5 C2 48 40N 2 4 E
Les Mureaux, Paris 5 B1 48 59N 1 54 E
Les Pavillons-sous-Bois, Paris 5 B5 48 54N 2 30 E
Les Vaux de Cernay →, Paris 5 C1 48 41N 1 59 E
Lésigny, Paris 5 C5 48 44N 2 37 E
Lesnosavodskaya, Len. 11 B4 59 51N 30 29 E
Lesnoy, Len. 11 B4 59 59N 30 22 E
Lester B. Pearson Int. Airport, Trto. 20 D7 43 40N 79 38 E
L'Étang-la-Ville, Paris 5 B2 48 52N 2 4 E
Letná, Pra. 10 B2 50 0 S 14 26 E
Letňany, Pra. 10 B3 50 8N 14 30 E
Letovo, Mos. 11 F8 55 34N 37 24 E
Leuville-sur-Orge, Paris 5 D3 48 36N 2 15 E
Levallois-Perret, Paris 5 B3 48 53N 2 16 E
Lévis St.-Nom, Paris 5 C1 48 43N 1 57 E
Levittown, N.Y. 23 C7 40 43N 73 31W
Lewisdale, Wash. 25 D8 38 58N 76 59W
Lewisham, Jobg. 18 E7 26 7 S 27 49 E
Lewisham, Lon. 4 C4 51 27N 0 1W
Lexington, Bost. 21 C2 42 25N 71 12W
Leyton, Lon. 4 B4 51 33N 0 1W
Leytonstone, Lon. 4 B5 51 34N 0 0 E
L'Hautil, Paris 5 A2 49 0N 2 0 E
L'Hay-les-Roses, Paris 5 C4 48 46N 2 20 E
Lhotka, Pra. 10 B2 50 1N 14 26 E
Liangshui He →, Beij. 14 C3 39 48N 116 23 E
Lianhua Chi, Beij. 14 B2 39 52N 116 16 E
Lianhua He →, Beij. 14 B2 39 52N 116 13 E
Lianozovo, Mos. 11 D9 55 53N 37 34 E
Libčice nad Vitavou, Pra. 10 A2 50 11N 14 22 E
Liben, Pra. 10 B2 50 6N 14 27 E
Liberdade, S. Pau. 31 E6 23 33 S 46 37W
Libertad, B.A. 32 C2 34 41 S 58 41W
Liberty I., N.Y. 22 C4 40 41N 74 2W
Liberty Plain, Bost. 21 D4 42 11N 70 52W
Liberty Res., Balt. 25 A1 39 23N 76 52W
Libeznice, Pra. 10 A2 50 11N 14 29 E
Library of Congress, Wash. 25 D7 38 53N 77 0W
Libuč, Pra. 10 B2 50 0N 14 27 E
Lichiao, Gzh. 14 G8 23 3N 113 18 E
Lichtenbroich, Ruhr 6 C2 51 17N 6 49 E
Lichtenburg, Berl. 7 A4 52 31N 13 30 E
Lichtenplatz, Ruhr 6 C5 51 14N 7 11 E
Lichtenrade, Berl. 7 B3 52 23N 13 24 E
Lichterfelde, Berl. 7 B2 52 25N 13 19 E
Licignano di Nápoli, Nápl. 9 H13 40 54N 14 21 E
Lidcombe, Syd. 19 B3 33 52 S 151 3 E
Lidingö, Stock. 3 D11 59 21N 18 8 E
Lido Beach, N.Y. 23 D7 40 35N 73 37W
Lier, Oslo 2 C1 59 47N 10 13 E
Lierskogen, Oslo 2 C1 59 49N 10 15 E
Lieshi Lingyuan, Gzh. 14 G8 23 7N 113 16 E
Liesing, Wien 10 H9 48 8N 16 17 E
Liesing →, Wien 10 H10 48 8N 16 28 E
Lieusant, Paris 5 D5 48 38N 2 33 E
Liffjofs, Hels. 3 B6 60 19N 25 12 E
Ligovo, Len. 11 C3 59 49N 30 10 E
Lijordet, Oslo 2 B3 59 56N 10 36 E
Likhoborka →, Mos. 11 D9 55 50N 37 37 E
Likova →, Mos. 11 F8 55 36N 37 20 E
Lilla Värtan, Stock. 3 D12 59 20N 18 11 E
Lille Rørbæk, Købn. 2 D7 55 47N 12 6 E
Lille Værløse, Købn. 2 D9 55 47N 12 22 E
Lillehavfrue, Købn. 2 D10 55 42N 12 35 E
Lillestrøm, Oslo 2 B6 59 57N 11 3 E
Liluah, Calc. 16 E5 22 37N 88 19 E

Mikhaylovskoye 41

Lilydale, Melb. 19 E9 37 45 S 145 21 E
Lima, Lima 30 G8 12 3 S 77 2W
Lima, Phil. 24 B2 39 55N 75 26W
Limbiate, Mil. 9 D5 45 35N 9 7 E
Limehouse, Lon. 4 B4 51 30N 0 1W
Limeil-Brévannes, Paris 5 C4 48 44N 2 29 E
Limito, Mil. 9 E6 45 28N 9 19 E
Limoges-Fourches, Paris 5 D5 48 37N 2 39 E
Limours, Paris 5 D2 48 38N 2 4 E
Linas, Paris 5 D3 48 37N 2 16 E
Linate, Mil. 9 E6 45 26N 9 16 E
Linate, Aeroporto Internazionale di, Mil. 9 E6 45 26N 9 16 E
Linbigh, Balt. 25 A3 39 21N 76 31W
Linbropark, Jobg. 18 E9 26 5 S 28 7 E
Lincoln, Bost. 21 C2 42 25N 71 18W
Lincoln Center, N.Y. 22 C5 40 46N 43 59W
Lincoln Heights, L.A. 28 B3 34 4N 118 12 E
Lincoln Memorial, Wash. 25 D7 38 53N 77 2W
Lincoln Park, Chic. 26 B3 41 57N 87 38W
Lincoln Park, N.Y. 22 B3 40 56N 74 18W
Lincoln Park, S.F. 27 B1 37 47N 122 30W
Lincolnwood, Chic. 26 A2 42 1N 87 43W
Linda-a-Pastora, Lisb. 8 F7 38 42N 9 15W
Linden, Jobg. 18 E9 26 8 S 28 0 E
Linden, N.Y. 22 D3 40 38N 74 14W
Linden-Dahlhausen, Ruhr 6 B5 51 25N 7 10 E
Lindenberg, Berl. 7 A4 52 36N 13 31 E
Lindenhorst, Ruhr 6 A6 51 33N 7 27 E
Lindenhurst, N.Y. 23 C8 40 40N 73 22W
Lindenwold, Phil. 24 C5 39 49N 74 59W
Linderhausen, Ruhr 6 C6 51 17N 7 17 E
Lindfield, Syd. 19 A3 33 46 S 151 9 E
Lindøya, Oslo 2 B4 59 53N 10 42 E
Lingotto, Tori. 9 B2 45 1N 7 39 E
Liniers, B.A. 32 B3 34 39 S 58 30W
Linksfield, Jobg. 18 E9 26 9 S 28 6 E
Linmeyer, Jobg. 18 F9 26 15 S 28 4 E
Linn, Ruhr 6 B1 51 20N 6 38 E
Linna, Hels. 3 A4 60 20N 24 50 E
Linthicum Heights, Balt. 25 B2 39 12N 76 47W
Lintorf, Ruhr 6 B3 51 20N 6 50 E
Lintuvaara, Hels. 3 B3 60 14N 24 49 E
Linwood, Phil. 24 C2 39 49N 75 25W
Lioúmi, Ath. 8 J11 38 0N 23 40 E
Lipków, Wsaw. 10 E5 52 16N 20 48 E
Lippalthausen, Ruhr 6 A6 51 36N 7 26 E
Liqizhuang, Tianj. 14 E6 39 4N 117 10 E
Lirich, Ruhr 6 B2 51 29N 6 49 E
Lisboa, Lisb. 8 F8 38 42N 9 8W
Lisbon = Lisboa, Lisb. 8 F8 38 42N 9 8W
Lishui, Gzh. 14 F7 23 12N 113 9 E
Lisiy Nos, Len. 11 A2 60 1N 30 0 E
Lissone, Mil. 9 D6 45 36N 9 14 E
Lissy, Paris 5 D6 48 38N 2 42 E
Litoral, Cord. del, Car. 30 D5 10 33N 66 54W
Little B., Syd. 19 B4 33 58 S 151 15 E
Little Calumet →, Chic. 26 D3 41 39N 87 34W
Little Falls, N.Y. 22 B3 40 52N 74 14W
Little Ferry, N.Y. 22 B4 40 50N 74 2W
Little Neck, N.Y. 23 C6 40 46N 73 43W
Little Paint Br. →, Wash. 25 C8 39 0N 76 55W
Little Patuxent →, Balt. 25 B1 39 13N 76 51W
Little Rouge →, Trto. 20 C9 43 45N 79 11W
Little Sugarloaf, Melb. 19 E8 37 40 S 145 18 E
Little Thurrock, Lon. 4 C7 51 29N 0 20 E
Liuhang, Shang. 14 H11 31 21N 121 21 E
Liuhuahu Gongyuan, Gzh. 14 G8 23 8N 113 14 E
Liverpool, Syd. 19 B2 33 55 S 150 55 E
Livingstone, N.Y. 22 C3 40 47N 74 19W
Livry-Gargan, Paris 5 B5 48 55N 2 31 E
Liwanhu Gongyuan, Gzh. 14 G8 23 7N 113 13 E
Lizhuang, Gzh. 14 G7 23 6N 113 7 E
Ljan, Oslo 2 B4 59 51N 10 48 E
Llano de Can Gineu, Barc. 8 D6 41 27N 2 10 E
Llavallol, B.A. 32 C4 34 48 S 58 25W
Llobregat →, Barc. 8 D5 41 19N 2 5 E
Lloyd Harbor, N.Y. 23 B8 40 54N 73 26W
Lloyd Pt., N.Y. 23 B8 40 56N 73 29W
Lo Aranguiz, Stgo 30 J11 33 23 S 70 40W
Lo Boza, Stgo 30 J10 33 23 S 70 43W
Lo Chau, H.K. 12 E6 22 11N 114 15 E
Lo Hermida, Stgo 30 J11 33 28 S 70 33W
Lo Ortuzar, Stgo 30 J10 33 28 S 70 43W
Lo Prado Arriba, Stgo 30 J10 33 26 S 70 42W
Lo So Shing, H.K. 12 E5 22 12N 114 7 E
Lo Wai, H.K. 12 D5 22 22N 114 8 E
Lobau, Wien 10 G11 48 10N 16 31 E
Lobos, Pt., S.F. 27 B1 37 46N 122 30W
Loch Raven Village, Balt. 25 A3 39 23N 76 34W
Locham, Mün. 7 G9 48 7N 11 26 E
Lochearn, Balt. 25 A2 39 20N 76 43W
Lochino, Mos. 11 E7 55 41N 37 17 E
Lochkov, Pra. 10 B2 50 0N 14 21 E
Lockhausen, Mün. 7 F9 48 10N 11 24 E
Locksbottom, Lon. 4 C5 51 21N 0 3 E
Locust Grove, N.Y. 23 C8 40 48N 73 29W
Locust Manor, N.Y. 23 C6 40 41N 73 45W
Locust Valley, N.Y. 23 B7 40 52N 73 36W
Lodi, N.Y. 22 B4 40 52N 74 5W
Lofty, Mt., Melb. 19 E8 37 42 S 145 17 E
Logan, Phil. 24 A4 40 2N 75 8W
Logan Int. Airport, Bost. 21 C4 42 22N 71 0W
Logan Square, Chic. 26 B2 41 55N 87 42W
Lognes-Émerainville, Aérodrome de, Paris 5 C5 48 49N 2 37 E
Lohausen, Ruhr 6 C2 51 16N 6 44 E
Lohberg, Ruhr 6 A2 51 34N 6 45 E
Löhme, Berl. 7 A5 52 37N 13 40 E
Lohmühle, Ruhr 6 A1 51 30N 6 39 E
Löhnen, Ruhr 6 A1 51 35N 6 39 E
Lokstedt, Hbg. 7 D7 53 36N 9 56 E
Lokyang, Sing. 15 G7 1 19N 103 40 E
Lōlōkhet, Kar. 17 G11 24 54N 67 2 E
Loma Blanca, Stgo 30 J10 33 29 S 70 43W
Lomas Chapultepec, Méx. 29 B2 19 25N 99 12W
Lomas de San Angel Inn, Méx. 29 B2 19 20N 99 13W
Lomas de Zamora, B.A. 32 C4 34 45 S 58 24W
Lombardy East, Jobg. 18 E9 26 6 S 28 7 E
Lomonosov Univ., Mos. 11 E9 55 42N 37 31 E
Lomus Reforma, Méx. 29 B2 19 24N 99 14W
London, Lon. 4 B4 51 30N 0 6W
London, City of, Lon. 4 B4 51 30N 0 6W
London, Tower of, Lon. 4 B4 51 30N 0 4W
London Zoo, Lon. 4 B4 51 31N 0 9W
Long B., Syd. 19 B4 33 59 S 151 15 E
Long Beach, N.Y. 23 D7 40 35N 73 39W
Long Branch, Trto. 20 E7 43 35N 79 31W
Long Brook →, Wash. 25 E6 38 49N 77 15W
Long Ditton, Lon. 4 C3 51 22N 0 19W
Long I., Bost. 21 D4 42 19N 70 59W
Long I., N.Y. 23 C7 40 45N 73 30W
Long Island City, N.Y. 22 C5 40 45N 73 56W
Long Island Sd., N.Y. 23 B7 40 57N 73 30W
Long Pond, Bost. 21 A1 42 41N 71 22W
Longchamp, Hippodrôme de, Paris 5 B3 48 51N 2 13 E
Longchêne, Paris 5 D2 48 38N 2 0 E
Longhua Gongyuan, Shang. 14 J11 31 10N 121 26 E
Longjohn Slough, Chic. 26 C1 41 42N 87 52W
Longjumeau, Paris 5 C3 48 41N 2 17 E
Longlands, Lon. 4 C5 51 25N 0 5 E
Longpont-sur-Orge, Paris 5 D3 48 38N 2 17 E
Longtan Hu →, Beij. 14 B3 39 51N 116 24 E
Longue Point, Mtrl. 20 A4 43 35N 73 31W
Longueuil, Mtrl. 20 A5 43 31N 73 29W
Loni, Delhi 16 A2 28 45N 77 17 E
Lord's Cricket Ground, Lon. 4 B3 51 31N 0 10W
Loreley, Balt. 25 A4 39 23N 76 24W
Lørenskog, Oslo 2 B5 59 55N 10 59 E
Loreto, Mil. 9 E6 45 29N 9 12 E
Lorraine, Mtrl. 20 A3 43 39N 73 46W
Los Angeles, L.A. 28 B3 34 3N 118 14 E
Los Angeles, Mdrd. 8 B2 40 20N 3 41W
Los Angeles →, L.A. 28 C3 33 55N 118 10W
Los Angeles Int. Airport, L.A. 28 C2 33 56N 118 23W
Los Asientos, Car. 30 D5 10 32N 66 53W
Los Caobos, Car. 30 D5 10 30N 66 53W
Los Carmenes, Car. 30 E5 10 28N 66 54W
Los Cerrillas, Aeroporto, Stgo 30 J10 33 29 S 70 42W
Los Dos Caminos, Car. 30 D6 10 30N 66 49W
Los dos Riteras →, Car. 30 D5 10 35N 66 57W
Los Jazmines, Presa, Méx. 29 B2 19 25N 99 15W
Los Nietos, L.A. 28 C4 33 57N 118 4W
Los Pinos, La Hab. 30 B2 23 4N 82 22W
Los Pirules, Méx. 29 B3 19 24N 99 2W
Los Polvorines, B.A. 32 B2 34 30 S 58 41W
Los Remedios →, Méx. 29 B2 19 28N 99 13W
Los Remedios, Parque Nacional de, Méx. 29 B2 19 27N 99 15W
Los Reyes, Méx. 29 B4 19 21N 99 6W
Los Rosales, Car. 30 E5 10 28N 66 53W
Losby, Oslo 2 B5 59 53N 10 59 E
Loughton, Lon. 4 B5 51 38N 0 4 E
Loures, Lisb. 8 F7 38 49N 9 10W
Louveciennes, Paris 5 B2 48 51N 2 8 E
Louvres, Paris 5 A5 49 2N 2 30 E
Lovön, Stock. 3 E10 59 18N 17 51 E
Lövstafjärden, Stock. 3 D9 59 23N 17 46 E
Lowe, Mt., L.A. 28 A4 34 13N 118 5W
Lowe Pond, Bost. 21 A3 42 41N 71 0W
Lowell, Bost. 21 B2 42 38N 71 16W
Lowell Dracut State Forest, Bost. 21 B1 42 39N 71 22W
Lower Crystal Springs Res., S.F. 27 C2 37 31N 122 21W
Lower Edmonton, Lon. 4 B4 51 37N 0 3W
Lower Monteville, N.Y. 22 B2 40 53N 74 21W
Lower New York B., N.Y. 22 D4 40 32N 74 5W
Lower Plenty, Melb. 19 E7 37 44 S 145 7 E
Lower Shing Mun Res., H.K. 12 D5 22 22N 114 9 E
Lower Sydenham, Lon. 4 C4 51 25N 0 2W
Lower Van Norman L., L.A. 28 A2 34 17N 118 28W
Lübars, Berl. 7 A3 52 37N 13 21 E
Lubeinī, Bahr el →, El Qâ. 18 C4 30 1N 31 5 E
Lubya →, Len. 11 A5 60 1N 30 39 E
Lucento, Tori. 9 B2 45 5N 7 39 E
Lucero, La Hab. 30 B3 23 5N 82 19W
Ludwigsfeld, Mün. 7 F9 48 12N 11 27 E
Lugarno, Syd. 19 B3 33 59 S 151 2 E
Lugouqiao, Beij. 14 C2 39 49N 116 10 E
Luhu, Gzh. 14 G8 23 9N 113 16 E
Luipaardsvei, Jobg. 18 E7 26 6 S 27 49 E
Luis Guillón, B.A. 32 C4 34 48 S 58 26W
Lujia, Shang. 14 J12 31 15N 121 37 E
Lukens, Mt., L.A. 28 A3 34 16N 118 12W
Lumiar, Lisb. 8 F8 38 4N 9 10W
Lundtofte, Købn. 2 D10 55 47N 12 32 E
Lung Mei, H.K. 12 D6 22 23N 114 15 E
Lunsad, Manila 15 E5 14 27N 121 11 E
Luojiang, Gzh. 14 G8 23 5N 113 17 E
Lura →, Mil. 9 D5 45 34N 9 5 E
Lurnea, Syd. 19 B2 33 56 S 150 54 E
Lurup, Hbg. 7 D7 53 35N 9 54 E
Lustheim, Mün. 7 F10 48 14N 11 34 E
Lütgendortmund, Ruhr 6 A6 51 30N 7 20 E
Lutherville-Timonium, Balt. 25 A3 39 25N 76 36W
Lüttringhausen, Ruhr 6 C5 51 12N 7 14 E
Lutvatn, Oslo 2 B5 59 54N 10 52 E
Luwan, Shang. 14 J11 31 12N 121 27 E
Luyano, La Hab. 30 B2 23 6N 82 21W
Luzhniki Sports Centre, Mos. 11 E9 55 43N 37 31 E
Lyckebyn, Stock. 3 E12 59 11N 18 13 E
Lynbrook, N.Y. 23 D6 40 38N 73 41W
Lyndhurst, Jobg. 18 E9 26 7 S 28 6 E
Lyndhurst, N.Y. 22 C4 40 49N 74 7W
Lynn, Bost. 21 C4 42 28N 70 57W
Lynn Harbor, Bost. 21 C4 42 26N 70 56W
Lynnfield, Bost. 21 B3 42 32N 71 2W
Lynwood, L.A. 28 C3 33 55N 118 11W
Lyon, Gare de, Paris 5 B4 48 50N 2 22 E
Lyons, Chic. 26 C2 41 48N 87 49W
Lyonsville, N.Y. 22 B2 40 57N 74 26W
Lysaker, Oslo 2 B3 59 54N 10 38 E
Lysakerselva →, Oslo 2 B3 59 54N 10 38 E
Lysolaje, Pra. 10 B2 50 8N 14 22 E
Lytkarino, Mos. 11 F11 55 34N 37 55 E
Lyubertsy, Mos. 11 E11 55 40N 37 51 E
Lyublino, Mos. 11 E10 55 41N 37 44 E

M

Ma Nam Wat, H.K. 12 D6 22 21N 114 16 E
Ma Po, Sŏul 12 G7 37 32N 126 56 E
Ma Tsz Keng, H.K. 12 D5 22 23N 114 7 E
Ma Yau Tong, H.K. 12 E6 22 19N 114 14 E
Maantiekylä, Hels. 3 A5 60 20N 25 0 E
Maarifa, Bagd. 17 F8 33 15N 44 21 E
Mabashi, Tōkyō 13 B4 35 48N 139 55 E
Mabato Pt., Manila 15 E4 14 29N 121 3 E
Mabolo, Manila 15 E3 14 26N 120 56 E
Macaco, Morro do, Rio J. 31 B3 22 56 S 43 6W
McCook, Chic. 26 C2 41 47N 87 49W
McGill Univ., Mtrl. 20 A4 43 30N 73 35W
Machida, Tōkyō 13 C1 35 32N 139 26 E
Macierzysz, Wsaw. 10 E6 52 13N 20 50 E
Maciołki, Wsaw. 10 E7 52 19N 21 9 E
Mackayville, Mtrl. 20 A5 43 30N 73 26W
McKinnon, Melb. 19 F7 37 54 S 145 1 E
Mclean, Wash. 25 D6 38 56N 77 10W
Macleod, Melb. 19 E7 37 43 S 145 4 E
Macopocho →, Stgo 30 J10 33 24 S 70 40W
Macquarie Fields, Syd. 19 B2 33 59 S 150 53 E
Macquarie Univ., Syd. 19 A3 33 46 S 151 7 E
MacRitchie Res., Sing. 15 F7 1 20N 103 49 E
Macul, Stgo 30 K11 33 30 S 70 35W
Macuto, Car. 30 D5 10 36N 66 53W
Macuto →, Car. 30 D5 10 36N 66 53W
Madatpur, Calc. 16 C6 22 53N 88 27 E
Maddalena, Colle della, Tori. 9 B3 45 2N 7 43 E
Madhudaha, Calc. 16 E6 22 30N 88 24 E
Madhyamgram, Calc. 16 D6 22 41N 88 26 E
Madīnah Al Mansōr, Bagd. 17 F8 33 18N 44 20 E
Mâdînet el Muqattam, El Qâ. 18 C5 30 1N 31 15 E
Mâdînet Nasr, El Qâ. 18 C5 30 4N 31 18 E
Madipur, Delhi 16 B1 28 40N 77 8 E
Madison, N.Y. 22 C2 40 45N 74 24W
Madonna della Scala, Tori. 9 B3 44 59N 7 46 E
Madonna dell'Arco, Nápl. 9 H13 40 52N 14 23 E
Madrid, Mdrd. 8 B2 40 24N 3 42W
Madrona, Barc. 8 D5 41 27N 2 1 E
Madureira, Rio J. 31 B2 22 52 S 43 19W
Maeda, Tōkyō 13 B3 35 48N 139 45 E
Maesawa, Tōkyō 13 B2 35 44N 139 31 E
Magalhaes, Rio J. 31 B1 22 51 S 43 22W
Magdalena del Mar, Lima 30 G8 12 5 S 77 5W
Magholpur, Delhi 16 A1 28 41N 77 6 E
Maghreb, Bagd. 17 E8 33 23N 44 22 E
Magidiyeh, Tehr. 17 C5 35 43N 51 28 E
Maginu, Tōkyō 13 C2 35 34N 139 34 E
Magliana, Rome 9 F9 41 50N 12 26 E
Maglód, Bud. 10 K14 47 27N 19 18 E
Magnolia, Phil. 24 B4 39 51N 75 1W
Magny-les-Hameaux, Paris 5 C2 48 44N 2 3 E
Maharajpur, Delhi 16 B2 28 39N 77 19 E
Maheshtala, Calc. 16 F5 22 29N 88 15 E
Mahiari, Calc. 16 E5 22 35N 88 14 E
Mahikpur, Calc. 16 E5 22 32N 88 13 E
Mahim, Bomb. 16 G8 19 2N 72 50 E
Mahim B., Bomb. 16 G7 19 2N 72 49 E
Mahishdanga, Calc. 16 C5 22 53N 88 11 E
Mahlsdorf, Berl. 7 A4 52 30N 13 37 E
Mahmoodabad, Kar. 17 G11 24 51N 67 4 E
Mahmutbey, Ist. 17 A1 41 2N 28 49 E
Mahpar, Jak. 15 H9 6 9 S 106 49 E
Mahul, Bomb. 16 G8 19 0N 72 53 E
Maida Vale, Lon. 4 B3 51 31N 0 11W
Maidstone, Melb. 19 E6 37 47 S 144 52 E
Maincourt-sur-Yvette, Paris 5 C1 48 42N 1 58 E
Maipu, Stgo 30 K10 33 30 S 70 45W
Maiquetia, Car. 30 D5 10 35N 66 57W
Maiquetia Aeropuerto, Car. 30 D4 10 36N 67 0W
Maisons-Alfort, Paris 5 C4 48 48N 2 26 E
Maisons-Laffitte, Paris 5 B2 48 57N 2 8 E
Maissoneuve, Mtrl. 20 A4 43 32N 73 33W
Maitani, Ōsaka 12 B3 34 48N 135 22 E
Majadahonda, Mdrd. 8 B1 40 28N 3 52W
Majlis, Tehr. 17 C5 35 41N 51 25 E
Makati, Manila 15 D4 14 33N 121 7 E
Mäkiniitty, Hels. 3 A4 60 20N 24 58 E
Mala Straná, Pra. 10 B2 50 5N 14 24 E
Malabar, Syd. 19 B4 33 58 S 151 14 E
Malabar Hill, Bomb. 16 H7 18 57N 72 48 E
Malabon, Manila 15 D3 14 39N 120 56 E
Malacanang Palace, Manila 15 D3 14 35N 120 59 E
Malagrotta, Rome 9 F9 41 52N 12 20 E
Malakhovka, Mos. 11 F12 55 39N 38 0 E
Malakoff, Paris 5 C3 48 49N 2 18 E
Malakpur, Delhi 16 A2 28 42N 77 12 E
Malanday, Manila 15 D4 14 38N 121 5 E
Malanghero, Tori. 9 A2 45 12N 7 39 E
Mälarhöjaden, Stock. 3 E10 59 18N 17 58 E
Malaspina, L., Mil. 9 E6 45 28N 9 18 E
Malassis, Paris 5 D2 48 37N 2 3 E
Malate, Manila 15 D3 14 34N 120 59 E
Malaya Neva, Len. 11 B3 59 56N 30 16 E
Malaya-Okhta, Len. 11 B4 59 55N 30 25 E
Malchow, Berl. 7 A3 52 34N 13 29 E
Malden, Bost. 21 C3 42 26N 71 3W
Malden, Lon. 4 C3 51 23N 0 15W
Malešice, Pra. 10 B3 50 5N 14 30 E
Malekete, Lagos 18 A3 6 33N 7 32 E
Malir →, Kar. 17 H11 24 49N 67 4 E
Malir Cantonment, Kar. 17 G12 24 58N 67 10 E
Malmi, Hels. 3 B4 60 15N 24 59 E
Malmøya, Oslo 2 B4 59 52N 10 45 E
Måløv, Købn. 2 D9 55 44N 12 20 E
Malton, Trto. 20 D7 43 42N 79 38W
Malvern, Jobg. 18 F9 26 11 S 28 6 E
Malvern, Melb. 19 F7 37 50 S 145 2 E
Malvern, Phil. 24 A1 40 2N 75 31W
Malvern, Trto. 20 D9 43 47N 79 13W
Malvern East, Jobg. 18 F9 26 11 S 28 7 E
Malverne, N.Y. 23 C6 40 40N 73 40W
Mamaroneck, N.Y. 23 B6 40 56N 73 44W
Mamaroneck Harbour, N.Y. 23 B6 40 56N 73 42W
Mamonovo, Mos. 11 F10 55 36N 37 49 E
Mamonovo, Mos. 11 E8 55 41N 37 18 E
Mampong Prapatan, Jak. 15 J9 6 15 S 106 49 E
Mampukuji, Tōkyō 13 C2 35 36N 139 31 E
Man Budrukh, Bomb. 16 G8 19 2N 72 55 E
Man Khurd, Bomb. 16 G8 19 3N 72 55 E
Manacor, Manila 15 D3 14 37N 120 59 E
Managua, La Hab. 30 C3 22 58N 82 17W
Manayunk, Phil. 24 A3 40 1N 75 12W
Mandaluyong, Manila 15 D4 14 35N 121 1 E
Mandaoli, Delhi 16 B2 28 37N 77 17 E
Mandaqui, S. Pau. 31 D6 23 29 S 46 37W
Mandaqui →, S. Pau. 31 D6 23 30 S 46 40W
Mandres-les-Roses, Paris 5 C5 48 42N 2 32 E
Mandvi, Bomb. 16 H8 18 57N 72 50 E
Mang Kung Uk, H.K. 12 E6 22 18N 114 16 E
Manggarai, Jak. 15 J10 6 12 S 106 50 E
Manguinho, Aéroporto de, Rio J. 31 B2 22 52 S 43 14W
Mangweon, Sŏul 12 G7 37 33N 126 55 E
Manhasset, N.Y. 23 C6 40 47N 73 40W
Manhasset B., N.Y. 23 C6 40 49N 73 43W
Manhasset Hills, N.Y. 23 C7 40 45N 73 39W
Manhattan, N.Y. 22 C5 40 48N 73 57W
Manhattan Beach, L.A. 28 C2 33 53N 118 24W
Manhatten, N.Y. 22 D5 40 34N 73 56W
Manila, Manila 15 D3 14 35N 120 58 E
Manila B., Manila 15 D3 14 32N 120 58 E
Manila Int. Airport, Manila 15 D4 14 31N 121 0 E
Mankkaa, Hels. 3 B3 60 11N 24 47 E
Mankunda, Calc. 16 C6 22 50N 88 21 E
Manly, Syd. 19 A4 33 47 S 151 17 E
Manly Warringah War Memorial Park, Syd. 19 A4 33 46 S 151 15 E
Manning State Park, Bost. 21 B1 42 34N 71 20W
Mannsworth, Wien 10 H11 48 8N 16 30 E
Manoa, Phil. 24 B3 39 58N 75 18W
Manor Park, Lon. 4 B5 51 32N 0 1 E
Manora, Kar. 17 H10 24 47N 66 58 E
Manorhaven, N.Y. 23 B6 40 50N 73 41W
Manoteras, Mdrd. 8 B3 40 28N 3 39W
Manquehue, Cerro, Stgo 30 J11 33 21 S 70 35W
Mantegazza, Mil. 9 D4 45 30N 8 58 E
Mantilla, La Hab. 30 B3 23 4N 82 20W
Mantua, Phil. 24 C3 39 47N 75 10W
Mantua Cr. →, Phil. 24 C3 39 47N 75 13W
Manufacta, Jobg. 18 E8 26 9 S 27 51 E
Manzanares, Canal de, Mdrd. 8 C3 40 19N 3 38W
Mapetla, Jobg. 18 F8 26 16 S 27 51 E
Maple, Trto. 20 C7 43 51N 79 30W
Maple L., Chic. 26 C1 41 43N 87 53W
Maple Shade, Phil. 24 B4 39 57N 75 0W
Maplewood, N.Y. 22 C3 40 43N 74 16W
Maracana, Rio J. 31 B2 22 54 S 43 13W
Maraisburg, Jobg. 18 F8 26 10 S 27 57 E
Marano di Nápoli, Nápl. 9 H12 40 53N 14 11 E
Maraoli, Bomb. 16 G8 19 2N 72 53 E
Marapendi, L. de, Rio J. 31 C1 23 0 S 43 23W
Marblehead, Bost. 21 C4 42 29N 70 51W
Marcelin, Wsaw. 10 E6 52 19N 20 59 E
Marcella, N.Y. 22 B2 40 59N 74 29W
Marcos Paz, B.A. 32 C2 34 46 S 58 49W
Marcoussis, Paris 5 D3 48 38N 2 13 E
Marcus Hook, Phil. 24 C2 39 49N 75 25W
Marcus Hook Cr. →, Phil. 24 B2 39 49N 75 24W
Marechiaro, Nápl. 9 J12 40 48N 14 12 E
Mareil-Marly, Paris 5 B2 48 52N 2 4 E
Margareten, Wien 10 G10 48 11N 16 20 E
Margency, Paris 5 A3 49 0N 2 17 E
Margitsziget, Bud. 10 J13 47 31N 19 2 E
Maria, Wien 10 G10 48 11N 16 21 E
Maria Paula, Rio J. 31 B3 22 53 S 43 1W
Marianao, La Hab. 30 B2 23 4N 82 25W
Marianella, Nápl. 9 H12 40 53N 14 13 E
Mariano Acosta, B.A. 32 C2 34 42 S 58 47W
Mariano J. Haedo, B.A. 32 B3 34 39 S 58 35W
Maridalen, Oslo 2 B4 59 59N 10 45 E
Maridalsvatnet, Oslo 2 B4 59 59N 10 46 E
Mariendorf, Berl. 7 B3 52 26N 13 23 E
Marienfelde, Berl. 7 B3 52 24N 13 23 E
Marienthal, Hbg. 7 D8 53 34N 10 4 E
Mariglanella, Nápl. 9 H13 40 55N 14 26 E
Marigliano, Nápl. 9 H13 40 55N 14 27 E
Marikina, Manila 15 D4 14 38N 121 5 E
Marikina →, Manila 15 D4 14 33N 121 5 E
Marin City, S.F. 27 A1 37 52N 122 30W
Marin Headlands State Park, S.F. 27 A2 37 50N 122 28W
Marin Is., S.F. 27 A2 37 57N 122 27W
Marin Pen., S.F. 27 A1 37 50N 122 30W
Marine World, S.F. 27 C3 37 32N 122 16W
Mariners Harbour, N.Y. 22 D3 40 38N 74 10W
Mario, Mt., Rome 9 F9 41 55N 12 27 E
Markham, Chic. 26 D2 41 35N 87 40W
Markham, Phil. 24 B1 39 53N 75 30W
Markham, Trto. 20 D8 43 49N 79 22W
Markham, Mt., L.A. 28 A4 34 14N 118 6W
Marki, Wsaw. 10 E7 52 19N 21 6 E
Markland Wood, Trto. 20 E7 43 38N 79 34W
Marlton, Phil. 24 B5 39 53N 74 55W
Marly, Forêt de, Paris 5 B2 48 52N 2 2 E
Marly-le-Roi, Paris 5 B2 48 52N 2 5 E
Marne →, Paris 5 C4 48 47N 2 29 E
Marne-la-Vallée, Paris 5 B5 48 50N 2 37 E
Marolles-en-Brie, Paris 5 C5 48 44N 2 33 E
Maroondah Aquaduct, Melb. 19 E7 37 40 S 145 9 E
Maroubra, Syd. 19 B4 33 56 S 151 16 E
Marple, Phil. 24 B2 39 56N 75 20W
Marquette Park, Chic. 26 C2 41 46N 87 42W
Marrickville, Syd. 19 B3 33 54 S 151 9 E
Marschlande, Hbg. 7 E8 53 27N 10 9 E
Marsfield, Syd. 19 A3 33 46 S 151 7 E
Marte, Base Aérea de, S. Pau. 31 E6 23 30 S 46 38W
Martesana, Navíglio della, Mil. 9 D6 45 31N 9 17 E
Martin State Nat. Airport, Balt. 25 B4 39 19N 76 24W
Martinez, B.A. 32 A3 34 29 S 58 31W
Martinkylä, Hels. 3 B4 60 17N 24 51 E
Martins Pond, Bost. 21 B3 42 35N 71 7W
Martinsried, Mün. 7 G9 48 6N 11 27 E
Maruko, Tōkyō 13 C3 35 33N 139 40 E
Marusino, Mos. 11 E11 55 41N 37 58 E
Marxloh, Ruhr 6 A2 51 30N 6 47 E
Maryino, Mos. 11 E10 55 40N 37 45 E
Maryland, Sing. 15 G7 1 19N 103 47 E
Maryland, Univ. of, Wash. 25 D8 39 58N 76 56W
Marylebone, Lon. 4 B4 51 31N 0 9W
Marymont, Wsaw. 10 E6 52 16N 20 58 E
Marysin Wawerski, Wsaw. 10 E7 52 14N 21 9 E
Marzahn, Berl. 7 A4 52 32N 13 34 E
Masambong, Manila 15 D4 14 38N 121 0 E
Mascot, Syd. 19 B4 33 55 S 151 12 E
Mascuppic L., Bost. 21 A1 42 40N 71 23W
Masmo, Stock. 3 E10 59 15N 17 53 E
Maspeth, N.Y. 23 C5 40 43N 73 55W
Masr el Gedida, El Qâ. 18 C5 30 5N 31 19 E
Masr el Qadima, El Qâ. 18 C5 30 0N 31 14 E
Masroor Airport, Kar. 17 G10 24 53N 66 56 E
Massa di Somma, Nápl. 9 H13 40 50N 14 22 E
Massachusetts B., Bost. 21 C4 42 25N 70 50W
Massachusett's Inst. of Tech., Bost. 21 C3 42 22N 71 6W
Massamá, Lisb. 8 F7 38 45N 9 16W
Massapequa, N.Y. 23 C8 40 40N 73 28W
Massby, Hels. 3 B6 60 17N 25 16 E
Massey →, Trto. 20 D9 43 42N 79 19W
Massy, Paris 5 C3 48 43N 2 18 E
Matarza →, B.A. 32 C3 34 47 S 58 37W
Matasango, Lima 30 G9 12 3 S 76 58W
Mathle, Calc. 16 E5 22 34N 88 13 E
Matihutong, Beij. 14 B2 39 56N 116 19 E
Matinecock, N.Y. 23 B7 40 51N 73 36W
Matinha, Lisb. 8 F8 38 45N 9 6W
Matramam, Jak. 15 J10 6 12 S 106 51 E
Matsubara, Ōsaka 12 C4 34 34N 135 33 E
Matsubushi, Tōkyō 13 A3 35 55N 139 49 E
Matsudo, Tōkyō 13 B4 35 46N 139 54 E
Matsumoloshinden, Tōkyō 13 B2 35 50N 139 36 E
Mattapan, Bost. 21 D3 42 16N 71 6W
Mátyásföld, Bud. 10 J14 47 30N 19 12 E
Mau Tso Ngam, H.K. 12 D6 22 22N 114 13 E
Mauá, S. Pau. 31 E7 23 39 S 46 27W
Mauer, Wien 10 H9 48 9N 16 16 E
Mauerbach →, Wien 10 G9 48 12N 16 13 E
Mauldre, Paris 5 C1 48 56N 1 53 E
Maurecourt, Paris 5 B2 48 59N 2 3 E
Mauregard, Paris 5 A5 49 2N 2 34 E
Maurepas, Paris 5 C1 48 46N 1 55 E
Mauripur, Kar. 17 G10 24 52N 66 55 E
Maxhof, Mün. 7 G9 48 5N 11 29 E
Maya-Zan, Ōsaka 12 B2 34 43N 135 12 E
Maybunga, Manila 15 D4 14 34N 121 4 E
Mayfair, Jobg. 18 F9 26 11 S 28 0 E
Mayfair, Phil. 24 A4 40 2N 75 3W
Maypajo, Manila 15 D3 14 38N 120 58 E
Maytubig, Manila 15 D3 14 33N 120 59 E
Maywood, Chic. 26 B1 41 52N 87 51W
Maywood, L.A. 28 C3 33 59N 118 12W
Maywood, N.Y. 22 B4 40 53N 74 3W
Mazagaon, Bomb. 16 H8 18 57N 72 50 E
M'Boi Mirim, S. Pau. 31 F5 23 42 S 46 46W
Meadow I., N.Y. 23 D7 40 36N 73 32W
Meadow L., N.Y. 23 C5 40 44N 73 50W
Meadowlands, Jobg. 18 F8 26 12 S 27 53 E
Meadowood, Wash. 25 C7 39 4N 77 0W
Mecholupy, Pra. 10 B3 50 3N 14 32 E
Měčice, Pra. 10 A3 50 11N 14 31 E
Mecidiyekoy, Ist. 17 A3 41 4N 29 0 E
Meckinghoven, Ruhr 6 A5 51 37N 7 19 E
Médan, Paris 5 B1 48 57N 1 59 E
Medfield, Bost. 21 D2 42 11N 71 18W
Medford, Bost. 21 C3 42 25N 71 7W
Media, Phil. 24 B2 39 55N 75 23W
Mediodia, Mdrd. 8 B3 40 22N 3 39W
Medvasto, Hels. 3 C2 60 5N 24 38 E
Medvedkovo, Mos. 11 D9 55 52N 37 37 E
Medvezhiy Ozyora, Mos. 11 D11 55 52N 37 59 E
Meerbeck, Ruhr 6 B1 51 28N 6 38 E
Meerbusch, Ruhr 6 C2 51 16N 6 40 E
Meguro →, Tōkyō 13 C3 35 37N 139 45 E
Meguro-Ku, Tōkyō 13 C3 35 37N 139 42 E
Mehpalpur, Delhi 16 B1 28 32N 77 7 E
Mehrābād Airport, Tehr. 17 C4 35 41N 51 18 E
Mehram Nagar, Delhi 16 B1 28 34N 77 8 E
Mehrow, Berl. 7 A4 52 34N 13 37 E
Meiderich, Ruhr 6 B2 51 27N 6 47 E
Meidling, Wien 10 G10 48 10N 16 20 E
Meiendorf, Hbg. 7 D8 53 37N 10 8 E
Méier, Rio J. 31 B2 22 52 S 43 15W
Meiji Shrine, Tōkyō 13 B3 35 41N 139 41 E
Meizino-Mori-Minō National Park, Ōsaka 12 A3 34 51N 135 28 E
Mejiro, Tōkyō 13 B3 35 43N 139 43 E
Melbourne, Melb. 19 E6 37 48 S 144 58 E
Melbourne Airport, Melb. 19 E6 37 40 S 144 50 E
Melbourne Univ., Melb. 19 E6 37 47 S 144 57 E
Melito di Nápoli, Nápl. 9 H12 40 55N 14 13 E
Melkki, Hels. 3 C4 60 8N 24 53 E
Mellingstedt, Hbg. 7 C8 53 40N 10 6 E
Mellunkylä, Hels. 3 B5 60 14N 25 5 E
Mellunmäki, Hels. 3 B5 60 14N 25 6 E
Melrose, Bost. 21 C3 42 27N 71 2W
Melrose, N.Y. 22 C5 40 49N 73 55W
Melrose Park, Chic. 26 B1 41 53N 87 50W
Melun-Sénart, Paris 5 D5 48 3N 2 31 E
Melun-Villaroche, Aérodrome de, Paris 5 D6 48 37N 2 41 E
Melville, N.Y. 23 C8 40 47N 73 24W
Menai, Syd. 19 C3 34 1 S 151 1 E
Menandon, Paris 5 A2 49 2N 2 3 E
Mendoza, Lima 30 G9 12 5 S 76 59W
Mengede, Ruhr 6 A6 51 34N 7 23 E
Mengjiazhai, Shang. 14 J11 31 19N 121 21 E
Menglinghausen, Ruhr 6 B6 51 28N 7 25 E
Menlo Park, S.F. 27 D3 37 27N 122 11W
Menlo Park Terrace, N.Y. 22 D3 40 34N 74 18W
Mentang, Jak. 15 J9 6 11 S 106 49 E
Menucourt, Paris 5 A1 49 1N 1 59 E
Meopham, Lon. 4 C7 51 22N 0 21 E
Mérantaise →, Paris 5 C2 48 42N 2 8 E
Mercamadrid, Mdrd. 8 B3 40 21N 3 39W
Merced, L., S.F. 27 B2 37 43N 122 29W
Merchantville, Phil. 24 B4 39 56N 75 3W
Mercier, Pont, Mtrl. 20 B3 43 24N 73 39W
Merdeka Palace, Jak. 15 J9 6 10 S 106 49 E
Meredale, Jobg. 18 F8 26 16 S 27 58 E
Mergellina, Nápl. 9 J12 40 49N 14 14 E
Meriden, N.Y. 22 B2 40 56N 74 27W
Merion Station, Phil. 24 B3 39 59N 75 15W
Merlimau, Sing. 15 G7 1 17N 103 42 E
Merlimau, P., Sing. 15 G7 1 17N 103 42 E
Merlo, B.A. 32 B2 34 39 S 58 43W
Merri Cr. →, Melb. 19 E6 37 47 S 144 59 E
Merrick, N.Y. 23 D7 40 39N 73 32W
Merrionette Park, Chic. 26 C2 41 41N 87 40W
Merritt, L., S.F. 27 B3 37 48N 122 15W
Merrylands, Syd. 19 B2 33 50 S 150 59 E
Merton, Lon. 4 C3 51 24N 0 11W
Mesgarābād, Tehr. 17 D6 35 27N 51 30 E
Meshcherskiy, Mos. 11 E8 55 40N 37 23 E
Mesquita, Rio J. 31 A1 22 46 S 43 29W
Messe, Wien 10 G10 48 13N 16 24 E
Messy, Paris 5 B6 48 58N 2 42 E
Metanópoli, Mil. 9 E6 45 24N 9 15 E
Methuen, Bost. 21 A2 42 42N 71 12W
Metropolitan Opera, N.Y. 22 C5 40 46N 74 59W
Mettman, Ruhr 6 C3 51 15N 6 58 E
Metuchen, N.Y. 22 D2 40 32N 74 21W
Metzkausen, Ruhr 6 C3 51 16N 6 57 E
Meudon, Paris 5 C3 48 48N 2 14 E
Meulan, Paris 5 A1 49 0N 1 54 E
México, Aeropuerto Int. de, Méx. 29 B3 19 25N 99 4W
México, Ciudad de, Méx. 29 B2 19 25N 99 7W
Mezzate, Mil. 9 E6 45 26N 9 17 E
Mia Dong, Sŏul 12 G8 37 36N 127 0 E
Miano, Nápl. 9 H12 40 53N 14 15 E
Miasto, Wsaw. 10 E7 52 15N 21 0 E
Michalin, Wsaw. 10 F8 52 9N 21 13 E
Michalowice, Wsaw. 10 E6 52 10N 20 52 E
Michle, Pra. 10 B2 50 3N 14 28 E
Mickleton, Phil. 24 C3 39 47N 75 14W
Middle →, Balt. 25 B4 39 18N 76 24W
Middle B., N.Y. 23 D7 40 36N 73 36W
Middle Branch →, Balt. 25 B3 39 15N 76 37W
Middle Brewster I., Bost. 21 C4 42 20N 70 51W
Middle Cove, Syd. 19 A4 33 48 S 151 13 E
Middle Harbour, Syd. 19 A4 33 47 S 151 14 E
Middle Hd., Syd. 19 A4 33 49 S 151 15 E
Middle I., H.K. 12 E6 22 16N 114 10 E
Middle Park, Melb. 19 F6 37 50 S 144 57 E
Middle River, Balt. 25 A4 39 20N 76 26W
Middle Village, N.Y. 23 C5 40 43N 73 52W
Middleborough, Balt. 25 B4 39 18N 76 26W
Middlesex, N.Y. 22 D2 40 34N 74 27W
Middlesex Fells Reservation, Bost. 21 C3 42 27N 71 6W
Middlesex Res., N.Y. 22 D3 40 37N 74 19W
Middleton, Bost. 21 B3 42 35N 71 1W
Middleton Pond, Bost. 21 B3 42 35N 71 1W
Middleville, N.Y. 23 B9 40 54N 73 19W
Midland Beach, N.Y. 22 D4 40 34N 74 6W
Midland Park, N.Y. 22 B3 40 59N 74 9W
Midlothian, Chic. 26 D2 41 37N 87 43W
Miedzeszyn, Wsaw. 10 E8 52 10N 21 11 E
Międzylesie, Wsaw. 10 E8 52 12N 21 10 E
Miessaari, Hels. 3 C3 60 8N 24 47 E
Mikhaylovskoye, Mos. 11 F9 55 35N 37 35 E

42 Mikhelysona

Mikhelysona, Mos. 11 E11 55 42N 37 52 E
Milano, Mil. 9 E5 45 28N 9 10 E
Milano Due, Mil. 9 E6 45 29N 9 16 E
Milano San Felice, Mil. 9 E6 45 28N 9 18 E
Milanolago, Mil. 9 E6 45 27N 9 17 E
Milbertshofen, Mün. 7 F10 48 10N 11 34 E
Milburn, N.Y. 22 C3 40 43N 74 19W
Milford, Balt. 25 A2 39 21N 76 43W
Mill Cr. →, S.F. 27 A1 37 53N 122 31W
Mill Hill, Lon. 4 B3 51 37N 0 14W
Mill Neck, N.Y. 23 B7 40 53N 73 33W
Mill Park, Melb. 19 E7 37 40 S 145 3 E
Mill Valley, S.F. 27 A1 37 54N 122 33W
Millbrae, S.F. 27 C2 37 35N 122 22W
Mille-Iles, R. des →, Mtrl. 20 A3 43 39N 73 46W
Miller I., Balt. 25 B4 39 15N 76 21W
Miller Meadow, Chic. 26 B2 41 51N 87 49W
Milliken, Trto. 20 D9 43 49N 79 17W
Millis, Bost. 21 D1 42 10N 71 21W
Mills College, S.F. 27 B3 37 46N 122 10W
Milltown, Phil. 24 B1 39 57N 75 32W
Millwall, Lon. 4 C4 51 29N 0 0 E
Millwood, Wash. 25 D8 38 52N 76 52W
Milon-la-Chapelle, Paris 5 C2 48 43N 2 3 E
Milpa Alta, Méx. 29 C3 19 11N 99 0W
Milperra, Syd. 19 B2 33 56 S 150 59 E
Milspe, Ruhr 6 C5 51 18N 7 19 E
Milton, Bost. 21 D3 42 14N 71 2W
Milton Village, Bost. 21 D3 42 15N 71 4W
Mimico, Trto. 20 E8 43 36N 79 29W
Mimico Cr. →, Trto. 20 E7 43 37N 79 33W
Minami, Ōsaka 12 B4 34 40N 135 30 E
Minami-Ku, Tōkyō 13 D2 35 24N 139 37 E
Minami-tsunashima, Tōkyō 13 C2 35 32N 139 37 E
Minato, Ōsaka 12 C3 34 39N 135 25 E
Minato-Ku, Tōkyō 13 C3 35 39N 139 44 E
Mine, Tōkyō 13 B3 35 49N 139 46 E
Minebank Run →, Balt. 25 A3 39 24N 76 33W
Mineola, N.Y. 23 C7 40 44N 73 38W
Ministro Rivadavia, B.A. 32 D4 34 50 S 58 22W
Minō, Ōsaka 12 B3 34 49N 135 28 E
Minshât el Bekkarî, El Qâ. 18 C4 30 0N 31 8 E
Minto, Syd. 19 C2 34 1 S 150 51 E
Minute Man Nat. Hist. Park, Bost. 21 C2 42 25N 71 16W
Mirafiori, Tori. 9 B2 45 1N 7 36 E
Miraflores, Lima 30 G8 12 7 S 77 2W
Miramar, La Hab. 30 B2 23 7N 82 25W
Miramar, S.F. 27 D2 37 29N 122 27W
Miranda, Syd. 19 C3 34 2 S 151 6 E
Mirzapur, Calc. 16 D6 22 49N 88 24 E
Misato, Tōkyō 13 B4 35 49N 139 51 E
Misericordia, Sa. da, Rio J. 31 B2 22 51 S 43 17W
Mishawum L., Bost. 21 B3 42 30N 71 8W
Mission, S.F. 27 B2 37 44N 122 25W
Mississauga, Trto. 20 E7 43 35N 79 34W
Mitaka, Tōkyō 13 B2 35 41N 139 34 E
Mitcham, Lon. 4 C3 51 23N 0 10W
Mitcham, Melb. 19 E8 37 48 S 145 12 E
Mitcham Common, Lon. 4 C4 51 23N 0 8W
Mitino, Mos. 11 D8 55 51N 37 20 E
Mitry, Paris 5 B5 48 59N 2 36 E
Mitry-Mory, Paris 5 B5 48 59N 2 38 E
Mitry-Mory, Aérodrome de, Paris 5 B5 48 59N 2 37 E
Mitte, Berl. 7 A3 52 32N 13 24 E
Mittel Isarkanal, Mün. 7 F11 48 12N 11 40 E
Mittenheim, Mün. 7 F10 48 15N 11 33 E
Mixcoac, Presa de, Méx. 29 B2 19 21N 99 14W
Mixquic, Méx. 29 C4 19 13N 98 58W
Miyakojima, Ōsaka 12 B4 34 42N 135 31 E
Miyalo, Tōkyō 13 B2 35 49N 139 35 E
Mizonokuchi, Tōkyō 13 C2 35 35N 139 34 E
Mizue, Tōkyō 13 B4 35 41N 139 54 E
Mizuko, Tōkyō 13 A2 35 50N 139 32 E
Mizumoto, Tōkyō 13 B4 35 46N 139 52 E
Młocinski Park, Wsaw. 10 E6 52 19N 20 57 E
Młociny, Wsaw. 10 E6 52 18N 20 55 E
Mnevniki, Mos. 11 E8 55 45N 37 28 E
Moba, Lagos 18 B2 6 26N 7 28 E
Moczydło, Wsaw. 10 F7 52 8N 21 2 E
Modderfontein, Jobg. 18 E10 26 5 S 28 10 E
Modderfontein →, Jobg. 18 E9 26 5 S 28 10 E
Modřany, Pra. 10 B2 50 0N 14 24 E
Moers, Ruhr 6 B1 51 26N 6 37 E
Moffat Park, Jobg. 18 F9 26 15 S 28 4 E
Mofolo, Jobg. 18 F8 26 13 S 27 53 E
Mog, Sŏul 12 G7 37 32N 126 52 E
Mogyorod, Bud. 10 J14 47 35N 19 14 E
Mohili, Bomb. 16 G8 19 5N 72 52 E
Moinho Velho →, S. Pau. 31 E6 23 35 S 46 35W
Moissy-Cramayel, Paris 5 D5 48 37N 2 35 E
Moita, Lisb. 8 G9 38 39N 8 59W
Mokotów, Wsaw. 10 E7 52 12N 21 0 E
Molapo, Jobg. 18 F8 26 15 S 27 51 E
Mole →, Lon. 4 D2 51 14N 0 20W
Moletsane, Jobg. 18 F8 26 14 S 27 50 E
Molino de Rosas, Méx. 29 B2 19 21N 99 14W
Mølleå →, Købn. 2 D10 55 48N 12 35 E
Möllen, Ruhr 6 A2 51 35N 6 41 E
Mollins de Rey, Barc. 8 D5 41 24N 2 1 E
Molokovo, Mos. 11 F11 55 35N 37 53 E
Mombaça, S. Pau. 31 E7 23 37 S 46 25W
Mombello, Mil. 9 D5 45 36N 9 7 E
Momote, Tōkyō 13 B2 35 46N 139 37 E
Monash Univ., Melb. 19 F7 37 54 S 145 8 E
Monbulk Cr. →, Melb. 19 F8 37 55 S 145 12 E
Moncalieri, Tori. 9 B3 45 0N 7 41 E
Moncolombone, Tori. 9 A1 45 12N 7 28 E
Mondeor, Jobg. 18 F9 26 16 S 28 0 E
Moneda, Palacio de la, Stgo 30 J11 33 26 S 70 39W
Mong Kok, H.K. 12 E6 22 19N 114 10 E
Mongat, Barc. 8 D6 41 27N 2 16 E
Mongreno, Tori. 9 B3 45 3N 7 45 E
Moninos →, S. Pau. 31 F6 23 40 S 46 33W
Monrovia, L.A. 28 B4 34 9N 118 1W
Monsanto, Lisb. 8 F7 38 44N 9 12W
Monsanto, Parque Florestal de, Lisb. 8 F7 38 43N 9 11W
Mont Royal, Mtrl. 20 A4 43 30N 73 38W
Mont-Royal, Parc, Mtrl. 20 A4 43 30N 73 36W
Montalban, Car. 30 E5 10 28N 66 56W
Montana de Montjuich, Barc. 8 D5 41 21N 2 9 E
Montara, S.F. 27 C2 37 32N 122 30W
Montara, Pt., S.F. 27 C1 37 32N 122 31W
Montara Mt., S.F. 27 C2 37 32N 122 27W
Montchanin, Phil. 24 C1 39 47N 75 35W
Montclair, N.Y. 22 C3 40 49N 74 12W
Monte Chingolo, B.A. 32 C4 34 43 S 58 22W
Monte Grande, B.A. 32 C4 34 48 S 58 27W
Monte Sacro, Rome 9 F10 41 56N 12 32 E
Montebello, L.A. 28 B4 34 1N 118 8W
Montelera, Tori. 9 B1 45 9N 7 26 E
Montemor, Lisb. 8 F7 38 49N 9 12W
Monterey Park, L.A. 28 B4 34 3N 118 7W
Monterrey, La Hab. 30 B3 23 5N 82 18W
Montespaccato, Rome 9 F9 41 54N 12 23 E
Montesson, Paris 5 B2 48 54N 2 8 E
Monteverde Nuovo, Rome 9 F9 41 52N 12 26 E
Montfermeil, Paris 5 B5 48 54N 2 33 E
Montgeron, Paris 5 C4 48 42N 2 27 E
Montigny-le-Bretonneux, Paris 5 C2 48 46N 2 1 E
Montigny-les-Cormeilles, Paris 5 B3 48 59N 2 11 E
Montijo, Lisb. 8 F9 38 42N 8 58W
Montjay-la-Tour, Paris 5 B6 48 54N 2 40 E
Montlhéry, Paris 5 D3 48 38N 2 16 E
Montlignon, Paris 5 A3 49 0N 2 16 E
Montmagny, Paris 5 B4 48 58N 2 21 E
Montmorency, Paris 5 B3 48 59N 2 19 E
Montmorency, Forêt de, Paris 5 A3 49 2N 2 16 E
Montparnasse, Gare, Paris 5 B3 48 50N 2 19 E
Montpelier, Wash. 25 C8 39 3N 76 50W
Montréal, Mtrl. 20 A4 43 30N 73 33W
Montréal, Î. de, Mtrl. 20 A4 43 30N 73 40W
Montréal, Univ. de, Mtrl. 20 B4 43 29N 73 37W
Montréal-Est, Mtrl. 20 A4 43 37N 73 31W
Montréal Nord, Mtrl. 20 A4 43 36N 73 36W
Montreuil, Paris 5 B4 48 51N 2 27 E
Montrose, L.A. 28 A3 34 12N 118 12W
Montrose, Melb. 19 E8 37 49 S 145 19 E
Montrose, Wash. 25 C7 39 2N 77 7W
Montrouge, Paris 5 C3 48 48N 2 18 E
Montvale, N.Y. 22 A4 41 2N 74 1W
Montville, N.Y. 22 B2 40 55N 74 23W
Monza, Mil. 9 D6 45 35N 9 16 E
Monzoro, Mil. 9 E5 45 27N 9 2 E
Moóca, S. Pau. 31 E6 23 33 S 46 35W
Moóca →, S. Pau. 31 E6 23 35 S 46 35W
Moonachie, N.Y. 22 C4 40 50N 74 2W
Moonee Ponds, Melb. 19 E6 37 45 S 144 53 E
Moonee Valley Racecourse, Melb. 19 E6 37 45 S 144 55 E
Moorbek, Hbg. 7 C7 53 41N 9 58 E
Moorburg, Hbg. 7 E7 53 29N 9 55 E
Moorebank, Syd. 19 B2 33 56 S 150 56 E
Moorestown, Phil. 24 B5 39 58N 74 56W
Moorfleet, Hbg. 7 D8 53 30N 10 4 E
Mooroolbark, Melb. 19 E8 37 46 S 145 19 E
Moorwerder, Hbg. 7 E8 53 28N 10 3 E
Moosach, Mün. 7 F10 48 10N 11 30 E
Mora, Bomb. 16 H8 18 54N 72 55 E
Moraga, S.F. 27 B4 37 49N 122 7W
Morainvilliers, Paris 5 B1 48 55N 1 56 E
Morales →, B.A. 32 C2 34 47 S 58 35W
Morangis, Paris 5 C4 48 42N 2 20 E
Moratalaz, Mdrd. 8 B3 40 24N 3 39W
Morbras →, Paris 5 C5 48 46N 2 30 E
Mörby, Stock. 3 D11 59 23N 18 3 E
Morce →, Paris 5 B4 48 57N 2 25 E
Morden, Lon. 4 C3 51 24N 0 13W
Morehill, Jobg. 18 F11 26 10 S 28 20 E
Moreno, B.A. 32 B2 34 38 S 58 45W
Moreno, Rome 9 G10 41 48N 12 37 E
Morgan Park, Chic. 26 C3 41 41N 87 38W
Moriguchi, Ōsaka 12 B4 34 43N 135 34 E
Morivione, Mil. 9 E6 45 26N 9 12 E
Morningside, Jobg. 18 E9 26 4 S 28 3 E
Morningside, Wash. 25 E8 38 49N 76 53W
Morningside Park, Trto. 20 D9 43 46N 79 12W
Moroka, Jobg. 18 F8 26 15 S 27 52 E
Moron, B.A. 32 B3 34 39 S 58 37W
Morris Plains, N.Y. 22 C2 40 49N 74 29W
Morristown, N.Y. 22 C2 40 47N 74 28W
Morro, Castillo del, La Hab. 30 B2 23 8N 82 21W
Morro Pelado, S. Pau. 31 E7 23 38 S 46 24W
Morro Solar, Lima 30 H8 12 11 S 77 1W
Morsang-sur-Orge, Paris 5 D4 48 39N 2 21 E
Mörsenbroich, Ruhr 6 C2 51 15N 6 48 E
Morses Pond, Bost. 21 D2 42 17N 71 19W
Morte →, Paris 5 C3 48 40N 2 16 E
Mortlake, Lon. 4 C3 51 27N 0 15W
Mortlake, Syd. 19 B3 33 50 S 151 6 E
Morton, Phil. 24 B2 39 54N 75 20W
Morton Grove, Chic. 26 A2 42 2N 87 46W
Mory, Paris 5 B5 48 58N 2 37 E
Moscavide, Lisb. 8 F8 38 47N 9 6W
Moscow = Moskva, Mos. 11 E9 55 45N 37 37 E
Mosede, Købn. 2 E8 55 34N 12 17 E
Mosede Strand, Købn. 2 E8 55 34N 12 17 E
Mosjøen, Oslo 2 C6 50 49N 11 0 E
Moskhaton, Ath. 8 J11 37 55N 23 40 E
Moskva, Mos. 11 E9 55 45N 37 37 E
Moskvoretskiy, Mos. 11 E9 55 42N 37 37 E
Mosman, Syd. 19 A4 33 49 S 151 15 E
Moss Beach, S.F. 27 C2 37 31N 122 30W
Móstoles, Mdrd. 8 C1 40 18N 3 51W
Moto →, Tōkyō 13 A3 35 53N 139 45 E
Motol, Pra. 10 B1 50 3N 14 19 E
Motspur Park, Lon. 4 C3 51 23N 0 14W
Mottingham, Lon. 4 C5 51 26N 0 1 E
Mount Airy, Phil. 24 A3 40 3N 75 10W
Mount Dennis, Trto. 20 D8 43 40N 79 28W
Mount Ephraim, Phil. 24 B4 39 52N 75 5W
Mount Greenwood, Chic. 26 C2 41 42N 87 42W
Mount Hood Memorial Park, Bost. 21 C3 42 26N 71 1W
Mount Pleasant, Lon. 4 B2 51 30N 0 22W
Mount Pleasant Park, Balt. 25 A3 39 22N 76 34W
Mount Prospect, Chic. 26 A1 42 3N 87 54W
Mount Royal, Phil. 24 C3 39 48N 75 12W
Mount Tamalpais State Park, S.F. 27 A1 37 53N 122 34W
Mount Vernon, N.Y. 23 B6 40 54N 73 49W
Mount Waverley, Melb. 19 F7 37 52 S 145 7 E
Mount Wilson Observatory, L.A. 28 A4 34 13N 118 4W
Mountain Lakes, N.Y. 22 B2 40 54N 74 27W
Mountain Spring Ls., N.Y. 22 A2 41 2N 74 21W
Mountain View, N.Y. 22 B3 40 55N 74 15W
Mountainside, N.Y. 22 C2 40 40N 74 21W
Mountnessing, Lon. 4 B7 51 39N 0 21 E
Moûtiers, Paris 5 D1 48 36N 1 58 E
Mozu, Ōsaka 12 C3 34 33N 135 29 E
Müggelberge, Berl. 7 B4 52 25N 13 37 E
Müggelheim, Berl. 7 B5 52 24N 13 40 E
Muggiò, Mil. 9 D6 45 35N 9 13 E
Mugnano di Nápoli, Nápl. 9 H12 40 54N 14 12 E
Mühleiten, Wien 10 G11 48 10N 16 33 E
Mühlenau →, Hbg. 7 C7 53 41N 9 56 E
Mühlenfliess →, Berl. 7 A5 52 32N 13 42 E
Muir Beach, S.F. 27 A1 37 51N 122 34W
Muirkirk, Wash. 25 C8 39 3N 76 53W
Mujahidpur, Delhi 16 B2 28 33N 77 14 E
Mukandpur, Delhi 16 A2 28 44N 77 10 E
Muko →, Ōsaka 12 B3 34 48N 135 22 E
Mukojima, Tōkyō 13 B3 35 43N 139 49 E
Mulbarton, Jobg. 18 F9 26 17 S 28 3 E
Mulford Gardens, S.F. 27 B3 37 42N 122 10W
Mulgrave, Melb. 19 F8 37 55 S 145 12 E
Mülheim, Ruhr 6 B3 51 25N 6 53 E
Mullica Hill, Phil. 24 C3 39 44N 75 13W
Mullum Mullum Cr. →, Melb. 19 E8 37 44 S 145 10 E
Münchehofe, Berl. 7 B5 52 29N 13 40 E
München, Mün. 7 G10 48 8N 11 34 E
Munchen-Riem, Flughafen, Mün. 7 G11 48 7N 11 42 E
Munich = München, Mün. 7 G10 48 8N 11 34 E
Munirka, Delhi 16 B2 28 33N 77 10 E
Muniz, B.A. 32 B2 34 33 S 58 41W
Munkkiniemi, Hels. 3 B4 60 11N 24 52 E
Munro, B.A. 32 B3 34 31 S 58 31W
Munsey Park, N.Y. 23 C6 40 47N 73 40W
Münsterkirche, Ruhr 6 B4 51 27N 7 0 E
Muranów, Wsaw. 10 E6 52 14N 20 58 E
Murayama-chosuichi, Tōkyō 13 B1 35 45N 139 26 E
Murrumbeena, Melb. 19 F7 37 53 S 145 4 E
Musashino, Tōkyō 13 B2 35 42N 139 33 E
Mushin, Lagos 18 A2 6 31N 7 21 E
Musinè, Mte., Tori. 9 B1 45 7N 7 27 E
Musocco, Mil. 9 E5 45 29N 9 8 E
Musta Hevonen, Hels. 3 B6 60 11N 25 14 E
Mustafabad, Delhi 16 A2 28 43N 77 13 E
Mustansiriya, Bagd. 17 E8 33 22N 44 24 E
Musturud, El Qâ. 18 C5 30 8N 31 17 E
Muswell Hill, Lon. 4 B4 51 35N 0 8W
Mutanabi, Bagd. 17 F8 33 19N 44 21 E
Muthana, Bagd. 17 F8 33 19N 44 27 E
Mutinga, S. Pau. 31 D5 23 29 S 46 46W
Muttontown, N.Y. 23 C7 40 49N 73 32W
Muzon, Manila 15 D4 14 32N 121 8 E
Myaglovo, Len. 11 B5 59 53N 30 39 E
Myakinino, Mos. 11 E8 55 48N 37 22 E
Mykerinos, El Qâ. 18 D4 29 28N 31 8 E
Myllykylä, Hels. 3 A4 60 21N 24 57 E
Myllypuro, Hels. 3 B5 60 13N 25 3 E
Myras, Hels. 3 B5 60 19N 25 6 E
Myrvoll, Oslo 2 C4 59 47N 10 48 E
Mystic Lakes, Bost. 21 C3 42 26N 71 8W
Mytishchi, Mos. 11 D10 55 53N 37 44 E

N

Nababpur, Calc. 16 D5 22 42N 88 12 E
Nações, Parque das, S. Pau. 31 E6 23 38 S 46 30W
Nachstebreck, Ruhr 6 C5 51 17N 7 14 E
Nacka, Stock. 3 E12 59 19N 18 10 E
Nada, Ōsaka 12 B2 34 42N 135 13 E
Nærsnes, Oslo 2 C2 59 45N 10 27 E
Nærum, Købn. 2 D10 55 48N 12 33 E
Nagareyama, Tōkyō 13 A4 35 51N 139 54 E
Nagasaki, Tōkyō 13 B3 35 43N 139 40 E
Nagasuga, Tōkyō 13 D4 35 21N 139 57 E
Nagata, Ōsaka 12 C1 34 39N 135 8 E
Nagatsuta, Tōkyō 13 C2 35 32N 139 31 E
Nagytarcsa, Bud. 10 J14 47 31N 19 17 E
Nagytétény, Bud. 10 K12 47 23N 18 59 E
Nahant, Bost. 21 C4 42 25N 70 54W
Nahant B., Bost. 21 C4 42 26N 70 54W
Nahant Harbor, Bost. 21 C4 42 25N 70 55W
Nahdein, W. el →, El Qâ. 18 C5 30 3N 31 19 E
Nahia, El Qâ. 18 C4 30 2N 31 7 E
Naihati, Calc. 16 C6 22 53N 88 25 E
Najafgarh Drain →, Delhi 16 B1 28 39N 77 4 E
Najio, Ōsaka 12 B2 34 49N 135 18 E
Naka →, Tōkyō 13 B4 35 49N 139 52 E
Naka-Ku, Tōkyō 13 D2 35 25N 139 38 E
Nakada, Tōkyō 13 D2 35 24N 139 30 E
Nakajima, Tōkyō 13 D4 35 25N 139 54 E
Nakano, Tōkyō 13 D4 35 25N 139 56 E
Nakano-Ku, Tōkyō 13 B2 35 42N 139 39 E
Nakasato, Tōkyō 13 D4 35 22N 139 55 E
Nakayama, Tōkyō 13 B4 35 43N 139 57 E
Nalikul, Calc. 16 D5 22 49N 88 10 E
Nalpur, Calc. 16 E5 22 31N 88 10 E
Namazie Estate, Sing. 15 F7 1 25N 103 42 E
Namgajha, Sŏul 12 G7 37 33N 126 55 E
Namsan Park, Sŏul 12 G7 37 32N 126 59 E
Namyeong, Sŏul 12 G7 37 32N 126 57 E
Nan Wan, H.K. 12 D5 22 20N 114 5 E
Nanbiancun, Gzh. 14 G7 23 4N 113 10 E
Nancefield, Jobg. 18 F8 26 17 S 27 54 E
Nanchang He →, Beij. 14 B2 39 58N 116 14 E
Nandaha, Calc. 16 D5 22 49N 88 18 E
Nandang, Gzh. 14 G8 23 6N 113 12 E
Nandian, Tianj. 14 D6 39 10N 117 16 E
Nangal Dewat, Delhi 16 B1 28 33N 77 5 E
Nangi, Calc. 16 E5 22 30N 88 13 E
Nangka →, Manila 15 D4 14 38N 121 8 E
Nangloi, Delhi 16 A1 28 41N 77 4 E
Nangloi Jat, Delhi 16 A1 28 41N 77 3 E
Nanhai, Gzh. 14 G7 23 2N 113 6 E
Nanhan He →, Beij. 14 B2 39 57N 116 11 E
Naniwa, Ōsaka 12 C3 34 39N 135 29 E
Nankai, Tianj. 14 E5 39 7N 117 10 E
Nanmenwai, Tianj. 14 E6 39 8N 117 10 E
Nanole, Bomb. 16 G8 19 0N 72 55 E
Nanshi, Shang. 14 J11 31 12N 121 29 E
Nanterre, Paris 5 B3 48 53N 2 12 E
Nantouillet, Paris 5 A6 49 0N 2 42 E
Nantusket Beach, Bost. 21 D4 42 16N 70 52W
Nanxiang, Shang. 14 J10 31 17N 121 18 E
Naoabad, Calc. 16 F6 22 28N 88 26 E
Napara, Calc. 16 E6 22 38N 88 23 E
Napier Mole, Kar. 17 H10 24 49N 66 58 E
Napindan, Manila 15 D4 14 32N 121 5 E
Naples = Nápoli, Nápl. 9 J12 40 50N 14 14 E
Nápoli, Nápl. 9 J12 40 50N 14 14 E
Nápoli, G. di, Nápl. 9 J12 40 46N 14 15 E
Naraina, Delhi 16 B1 28 36N 77 8 E
Narawa, Tōkyō 13 D4 35 25N 139 58 E
Narayanpara, Calc. 16 C5 22 53N 88 18 E
Narberth, Phil. 24 A3 40 0N 75 16W
Narimasu, Tōkyō 13 B2 35 46N 139 35 E
Nārmak, Tehr. 17 C5 35 42N 51 28 E
Närsta, Stock. 3 E9 59 17N 17 43 E
Naruo, Ōsaka 12 B3 34 43N 135 22 E
Näsby, Stock. 3 D11 59 25N 18 5 E
Näsbypark, Stock. 3 D11 59 25N 18 5 E
Näsfjärden, Stock. 3 D9 59 25N 17 41 E
Nassau Shore, N.Y. 23 D8 40 39N 73 26W
Natick, Bost. 21 D2 42 16N 71 19W
Nation, Place de la, Paris 5 B4 48 51N 2 23 E
National Arboretum, Wash. 25 D8 39 54N 76 59W
Nativitas, Méx. 29 C3 19 15N 99 5W
Natolin, Wsaw. 10 F7 52 8N 21 4 E
Naucalpan de Juárez, Méx. 29 B2 19 28N 99 14W
Naupada, Bomb. 16 G8 19 3N 72 50 E
Navíglio di Pavia, Mil. 9 E5 45 24N 9 9 E
Navíglio Grande, Mil. 9 E5 45 25N 9 5 E
Navotas, Manila 15 D3 14 39N 120 56 E
Nazal Hikmat Beg, Bagd. 17 E8 33 23N 44 25 E
Nazimabad, Kar. 17 G11 24 54N 67 1 E
Nazukari, Tōkyō 13 A4 35 50N 139 57 E
Néa Alexandhria, Ath. 8 J11 37 52N 23 46 E
Néa Faliron, Ath. 8 J10 37 55N 23 39 E
Néa Ionía, Ath. 8 H11 38 3N 23 45 E
Néa Liósia, Ath. 8 H11 38 3N 23 43 E
Néa Smirni, Ath. 8 J11 37 54N 23 43 E
Neapolis, Ath. 8 J11 37 58N 23 45 E
Neasden, Lon. 4 B3 51 35N 0 16W
Neauphle-le-Château, Paris 5 C1 48 48N 1 53 E
Nebučice, Pra. 10 B1 50 6N 14 19 E
Nedlitz, Berl. 7 B1 52 25N 13 3 E
Nee Soon, Sing. 15 F7 1 24N 103 49 E
Needham, Bost. 21 D2 42 16N 71 13W
Needham Heights, Bost. 21 D2 42 17N 71 14W
Needle Hill, H.K. 12 D5 22 23N 114 9 E
Negishi B., Tōkyō 13 D2 35 23N 139 38 E
Nehiti, Calc. 16 D5 22 42N 88 16 E
Nekrasovka, Mos. 11 E11 55 41N 37 55 E
Nematābād, Tehr. 17 D5 35 38N 51 21 E
Nemchinovka, Mos. 11 E7 55 42N 37 19 E
Népliget, Bud. 10 K13 47 29N 19 7 E
Neponset →, Bost. 21 D3 42 12N 71 9W
Nerima, Tōkyō 13 B3 35 44N 139 40 E
Nerul, Bomb. 16 G9 19 2N 73 0 E
Nerviano, Mil. 9 D4 45 32N 8 58 E
Nesodden, Oslo 2 C4 59 48N 10 41 E
Nesoddtangen, Oslo 2 B4 59 52N 10 41 E
Nesøya, Oslo 2 B3 59 52N 10 31 E
Nestipayac →, Méx. 29 A4 19 33N 89 57W
Netzahualcóyotl, Méx. 29 B3 19 24N 99 2W
Neu Aubing, Mün. 7 G9 48 8N 11 25 E
Neu Buch, Berl. 7 A4 52 37N 13 31 E
Neu Buchhorst, Berl. 7 B5 52 24N 13 44 E
Neu Fahrland, Berl. 7 B1 52 26N 13 3 E
Neu Lindenberg, Berl. 7 A4 52 36N 13 33 E
Neu Wulmstorf, Hbg. 7 E6 53 27N 9 48 E
Neu Zittau, Berl. 7 B5 52 23N 13 44 E
Neubiberg, Mün. 7 G11 48 4N 11 40 E
Neudorf, Hbg. 7 E8 53 27N 10 4 E
Neudorf, Ruhr 6 B2 51 25N 6 47 E
Neuegenbüttel, Hbg. 7 D7 53 38N 9 54 E
Neuenfelde, Hbg. 7 D6 53 31N 9 48 E
Neuenhagen, Berl. 7 A4 52 32N 13 38 E
Neuenkamp, Ruhr 6 B2 51 26N 6 43 E
Neuessling, Wien 10 G11 48 15N 16 32 E
Neugraben-Fischbek, Hbg. 7 E6 53 28N 9 49 E
Neuhausen, Mün. 7 G10 48 9N 11 32 E
Neuherberg, Mün. 7 F10 48 13N 11 35 E
Neuhönow, Berl. 7 A5 52 34N 13 44 E
Neuilly-Plaisance, Paris 5 B5 48 51N 2 30 E
Neuilly-sur-Marne, Paris 5 B5 48 51N 2 31 E
Neuilly-sur-Seine, Paris 5 B3 48 53N 2 15 E
Neukagran, Wien 10 G10 48 14N 16 27 E
Neukettenhof, Wien 10 H10 48 7N 16 28 E
Neukölln, Berl. 7 B3 52 28N 13 25 E
Neuland, Hbg. 7 E8 53 27N 10 0 E
Neuperlach, Mün. 7 G10 48 6N 11 37 E
Neuried, Mün. 7 G9 48 5N 11 27 E
Neuss, Ruhr 6 C2 51 12N 6 42 E
Neustift am Walde, Wien 10 G9 48 14N 16 17 E
Neusüssenbrunn, Wien 10 G10 48 16N 16 29 E
Neuville-sur-Oise, Paris 5 A2 49 0N 2 3 E
Neuwaldegg, Wien 10 G9 48 14N 16 17 E
Neuwiedenthal, Hbg. 7 E7 53 28N 9 52 E
Neva →, Len. 11 B4 59 56N 30 20 E
Neves, Rio J. 31 B3 22 51 S 43 5W
Neviges, Ruhr 6 C4 51 18N 7 6 E
New Addington, Lon. 4 C4 51 20N 0 0 E
New Ash Green, Lon. 4 C6 51 22N 0 18 E
New Baghdād, Bagd. 17 F8 33 18N 44 28 E
New Barnet, Lon. 4 B3 51 38N 0 10W
New Brighton, N.Y. 22 D4 40 38N 74 5W
New Brunswick, N.Y. 22 D2 40 30N 74 29W
New Canada, Jobg. 18 F8 26 12 S 27 56 E
New Canada Dam, Jobg. 18 F8 26 12 S 27 56 E
New Canal →, Calc. 16 E6 22 33N 88 25 E
New Carrollton, Wash. 25 D8 38 58N 76 52W
New Cassell, N.Y. 23 C7 40 45N 73 32W
New Cross, Lon. 4 C4 51 28N 0 1W
New Delhi, Delhi 16 B2 28 36N 77 11 E
New Dorp, N.Y. 22 D4 40 34N 74 7W
New Dorp Beach, N.Y. 22 D4 40 33N 74 6W
New Hyde Park, N.Y. 23 C7 40 43N 73 39W
New Kleinfontein, Jobg. 18 F11 26 11 S 20 20 E
New Malden, Lon. 4 C3 51 24N 0 15W
New Milford, N.Y. 22 B4 40 56N 74 0W
New Modder, Jobg. 18 F11 26 10 S 28 21 E
New Providence, N.Y. 22 C2 40 42N 74 23W
New Redruth, Jobg. 18 F9 26 15 S 28 7 E
New Rochelle, N.Y. 23 B6 40 55N 73 45W
New South Wales, Univ. of, Syd. 19 B4 33 55 S 151 14 E
New Southgate, Lon. 4 B4 51 37N 0 7W
New Springville, N.Y. 22 D4 40 35N 74 9W
New Territories, H.K. 12 D5 22 23N 114 10 E
New Toronto, Trto. 20 E7 43 35N 79 30W
New Utrecht, N.Y. 22 D5 40 36N 73 59W
New Vernon, N.Y. 22 C2 40 44N 74 30W
New York Aquarium, N.Y. 22 D5 40 33N 73 59W
New York Botanical Gdns., N.Y. 23 B5 40 51N 73 51W
New York Univ., N.Y. 22 C5 40 43N 74 59W
Newabgarj, Calc. 16 D6 22 47N 88 23 E
Newark, N.Y. 22 C3 40 43N 74 10W
Newark, S.F. 27 C4 37 32N 122 2W
Newark B., N.Y. 22 C4 40 40N 74 8W
Newark Int. Airport, N.Y. 22 C3 40 41N 74 10W
Newbury Park, Lon. 4 B5 51 34N 0 5 E
Newclare, Jobg. 18 F8 26 11 S 27 58 E
Newfoundland, N.Y. 22 A2 41 2N 74 25W
Newham, Lon. 4 B5 51 31N 0 1 E
Newlands, Jobg. 18 F8 26 10 S 27 57 E
Newport, Melb. 19 F6 37 50 S 144 51 E
Newportville, Phil. 24 A5 40 7N 74 53W
Newton, Bost. 21 D2 42 19N 71 13W
Newton Brook, Trto. 20 D8 43 47N 79 24W
Newton Highlands, Bost. 21 D2 42 19N 71 13W
Newtonville, Bost. 21 C2 42 20N 71 11W
Newtown, Syd. 19 B4 33 54 S 151 11 E
Newtown Square, Phil. 24 B2 39 59N 75 24W
Neyegawa, Ōsaka 12 B4 34 45N 135 36 E
Ngau Chi Wan, H.K. 12 D6 22 20N 114 12 E
Ngau Tau Kok, H.K. 12 E6 22 19N 114 12 E
Ngong Shuen Chau, H.K. 12 E5 22 19N 114 8 E
Ngua Kok Wan, H.K. 12 D5 22 21N 114 5 E
Niāvarān, Tehr. 17 C5 35 47N 51 29 E
Nibria, Calc. 16 E5 22 36N 88 15 E
Nichelino, Tori. 9 C2 44 59N 7 38 E
Nichols Run →, Wash. 25 C6 39 2N 77 17W
Nicholson, Mt., H.K. 12 E6 22 15N 114 11 E
Nidāl, Bagd. 17 F8 33 19N 44 25 E
Niddrie, Melb. 19 E6 37 44 S 144 51 E
Nieder Neuendorf, Berl. 7 A2 52 36N 13 12 E
Niederbonsfeld, Ruhr 6 B4 51 22N 7 8 E
Niederdonk, Ruhr 6 C2 51 14N 6 41 E
Niederschöneweide, Berl. 7 B3 52 27N 13 30 E
Niederschönhausen, Berl. 7 A3 52 35N 13 25 E
Niederwenigern, Ruhr 6 B4 51 24N 7 8 E
Niemeyer, Rio J. 31 B2 22 59 S 43 16W
Niendorf, Hbg. 7 D7 53 37N 9 57 E
Nienstedten, Hbg. 7 D7 53 33N 9 51 E
Nierst, Ruhr 6 C2 51 19N 6 43 E
Nihonbashi, Tōkyō 13 B3 35 41N 139 46 E
Niipperi, Hels. 3 B3 60 18N 24 45 E
Niiza, Tōkyō 13 B2 35 48N 139 33 E
Nikaia, Ath. 8 J10 37 57N 23 38 E
Nikinmäki, Hels. 3 A5 60 20N 25 8 E
Nikolassee, Berl. 7 B2 52 25N 13 12 E
Nikolo-Khovanskoye, Mos. 11 F8 55 36N 37 27 E
Nikolskiy, Mos. 11 E8 55 49N 37 29 E
Nikolyskoye, Mos. 11 E11 55 46N 37 53 E
Nikulino, Mos. 11 E8 55 40N 37 25 E
Nil, Bagd. 17 E8 33 21N 44 25 E
Nil, Nahr en →, El Qâ. 18 D5 29 57N 31 14 E
Nile = Nil, Nahr en →, El Qâ. 18 D5 29 57N 31 14 E
Niles, Chic. 26 A2 42 1N 87 48W
Nilganj, Calc. 16 D6 22 45N 88 25 E
Nilópolis, Rio J. 31 A1 22 47 S 43 23W
Nimta, Calc. 16 D6 22 40N 88 24 E
Nincop, Hbg. 7 D6 53 30N 9 48 E
Ningyuan, Tianj. 14 E6 39 9N 117 12 E
Nippa, Tōkyō 13 C2 35 31N 139 36 E
Nippori, Tōkyō 13 B3 35 43N 139 45 E
Niru-ye-Hava'i, Tehr. 17 C5 35 41N 51 26 E
Nishi, Ōsaka 12 B3 34 40N 135 28 E
Nishi, Tōkyō 13 D2 35 26N 139 37 E
Nishi-arai, Tōkyō 13 B3 35 46N 139 48 E
Nishinari, Ōsaka 12 C3 34 37N 135 28 E
Nishinomiya, Ōsaka 12 B2 34 44N 135 18 E
Nishiyama, Tōkyō 13 D4 35 22N 139 57 E
Nishiyodogawa, Ōsaka 12 B3 34 41N 135 24 E
Nisida, I. di, Nápl. 9 J11 40 47N 14 10 E
Niterói, Rio J. 31 B3 22 53 S 43 7W
Nithari, Delhi 16 B3 28 34N 77 20 E
Nittedal, Oslo 2 A5 60 0N 10 57 E
Niyog, Manila 15 E3 14 27N 120 57 E
Noapara, Calc. 16 D6 22 49N 88 22 E
Nobidome, Tōkyō 13 B2 35 48N 139 34 E
Nockeby, Stock. 3 E10 59 19N 17 56 E
Noel Park, Lon. 4 B4 51 35N 0 5W
Nogatino, Mos. 11 E10 55 41N 37 41 E
Nogent-sur-Marne, Paris 5 B4 48 50N 2 28 E
Noiseau, Paris 5 C5 48 46N 2 32 E
Noisiel, Paris 5 B5 48 51N 2 37 E
Noisy-le-Grand, Paris 5 B5 48 50N 2 33 E
Noisy-le-Roi, Paris 5 B2 48 50N 2 3 E
Noisy-le-Sec, Paris 5 B4 48 53N 2 27 E
Nokkali, Hels. 3 C3 60 8N 24 45 E
Nøklevatn, Oslo 2 B5 59 52N 10 52 E
Nolme →, Ruhr 6 B6 51 23N 7 26 E
Nomentano, Rome 9 F10 41 55N 12 30 E
Nonakashinden, Tōkyō 13 B2 35 44N 139 30 E
Nongminyundong Jiangxisuo, Gzh. 14 G8 23 7N 113 15 E
Nonhyeon, Sŏul 12 G8 37 30N 127 1 E
Nontha Buri, Bangk. 15 A1 13 50N 100 29 E
Noordgesig, Jobg. 18 F8 26 13 S 27 56 E
Nord, Gare du, Paris 5 B4 48 52N 2 21 E
Nordbysjøen, Oslo 2 B6 59 51N 11 1 E
Nordereble, Hbg. 7 D7 53 32N 9 59 E
Norderelbe →, Hbg. 7 E8 53 29N 10 3 E
Norderstedt, Hbg. 7 C7 53 42N 9 59 E
Nordmarka, Oslo 2 A4 60 1N 10 38 E
Nordrand-Seidlung, Wien 10 G10 48 16N 16 26 E
Nordre Elvåga, Oslo 2 B5 59 53N 10 54 E
Nordstrand, Oslo 2 B4 59 52N 10 48 E
Normandy Heights, Balt. 25 B2 39 17N 76 48W
Norra Björköfjärden, Stock. 3 D8 59 26N 17 39 E
Norridge, Chic. 26 B2 41 57N 87 49W
Norristown, Phil. 24 A2 40 7N 75 20W
Norrkula, Hels. 3 B6 60 19N 25 20 E
Norrmalm, Stock. 3 D11 59 20N 18 3 E
Norrviken, Stock. 3 D10 59 27N 17 52 E
North Acton, Bost. 21 B1 42 30N 71 23W
North Amityville, N.Y. 23 C8 40 41N 73 25W
North Andover, Bost. 21 A3 42 41N 71 7W
North Arlington, N.Y. 22 C4 40 47N 74 7W
North Auburn, Syd. 19 B3 33 50 S 151 3 E
North Babylon, N.Y. 23 C9 40 43N 73 19W
North Bellmore, N.Y. 23 C7 40 40N 73 32W
North Bergen, N.Y. 22 C4 40 48N 74 0W
North Beverly, Bost. 21 B4 42 34N 70 51W
North Billerica, Bost. 21 B2 42 35N 71 16W
North Branch →, Phil. 24 C4 39 50N 75 5W
North Branch Chicago River →, Chic. 26 B2 41 53N 87 42W
North Brighton, Bost. 21 C3 42 21N 71 8W
North Caldwell, N.Y. 22 B3 40 52N 74 15W
North Cambridge, Bost. 21 C3 42 23N 71 7W
North Cheam, Lon. 4 C3 51 22N 0 11W
North Chelmsford, Bost. 21 B1 42 38N 71 23W
North Cohasset, Bost. 21 D4 42 15N 70 50W
North Cray, Lon. 4 C5 51 25N 0 8 E
North Fair Oaks, S.F. 27 D3 37 28N 122 11W
North Finchley, Lon. 4 B3 51 36N 0 10W
North Germiston, Jobg. 18 F9 26 12 S 28 9 E
North Hackensack, N.Y. 22 B4 40 54N 74 2W
North Haledon, N.Y. 22 B3 40 58N 74 11W
North Harbour, Manila 15 D3 14 37N 120 57 E
North Hd., Syd. 19 A4 33 49 S 151 18 E
North Hills, N.Y. 23 C6 40 46N 73 40W
North Hollywood, L.A. 28 B2 34 9N 118 22W
North Lexington, Bost. 21 C2 42 27N 71 14W
North Lindenhurst, N.Y. 23 C8 40 42N 73 22W
North Long Beach, L.A. 28 C3 33 53N 118 10W
North Manly, Syd. 19 A4 33 46 S 151 17 E
North Massapequa, N.Y. 23 C8 40 42N 73 27W
North Merrick, N.Y. 23 C7 40 41N 73 33W
North New Hyde Park, N.Y. 23 C6 40 44N 73 42W
North Pelham, N.Y. 23 B6 40 54N 73 46W
North Plainfield, N.Y. 22 D2 40 37N 74 27W
North Point, Balt. 25 B4 39 16N 76 29W
North Pt., H.K. 12 E6 22 17N 114 12 E
North Pt., Syd. 19 A4 33 48 S 151 18 E
North Randolph, Bost. 21 D3 42 11N 71 5W
North Reading, Bost. 21 B3 42 34N 71 5W
North Res., Bost. 21 C3 42 27N 71 6W
North Richmond, S.F. 27 A2 37 57N 122 22W
North Riverside, Chic. 26 B2 41 50N 87 48W
North Ryde, Syd. 19 A3 33 47 S 151 7 E
North Saugus, Bost. 21 C3 42 29N 71 0W
North Shore Channel →, Chic. 26 B2 41 58N 87 42W
North Springfield, Wash. 25 E6 38 48N 77 11W
North Stifford, Lon. 4 B6 51 30N 0 18 E

Pitampura Kalan 43

North Sudbury, *Bost.* **21 C1** 42 24N 71 24W
North Sydney, *Syd.* **19 B4** 33 50 S 151 13 E
North Tewksbury, *Bost.* **21 B2** 42 38N 71 14W
North Valley Stream, *N.Y.* **23 C6** 40 41N 73 42W
North Wantagh, *N.Y.* **23 C7** 40 41N 73 30W
North Weymouth, *Bost.* **21 D4** 42 14N 70 56W
North Wilmington, *Bost.* **21 B3** 42 34N 71 9W
North Woburn, *Bost.* **21 B2** 42 30N 71 10W
North Woolwich, *Lon.* **4 B5** 51 30N 0 3 E
North York, *Trto.* **20 D8** 43 45N 79 27W
Northaw, *Lon.* **4 A4** 51 42N 0 8W
Northbridge, *Syd.* **19 A4** 33 49 S 151 15 E
Northbrook, *Chic.* **26 A1** 42 7N 87 50W
Northcliff, *Jobg.* **18 E8** 26 8 S 27 58 E
Northcote, *Melb.* **19 E7** 37 46 S 145 0 E
Northeastern Univ., *Bost.* **21 C3** 42 20N 71 4W
Northfield, *Chic.* **26 A2** 42 5N 87 45W
Northfleet, *Lon.* **4 C7** 51 26N 0 21 E
Northlake, *Chic.* **26 B1** 41 54N 87 53W
Northmead, *Jobg.* **18 E10** 26 9 S 28 19 E
Northmead, *Syd.* **19 A3** 33 47 S 151 0 E
Northmount, *Trto.* **20 D8** 43 46N 79 23W
Northolt, *Lon.* **4 B2** 51 32N 0 22W
Northport, *N.Y.* **23 B8** 40 54N 73 20W
Northport B., *N.Y.* **23 B8** 40 54N 73 22W
Northridge, *L.A.* **28 A1** 34 14N 118 30W
Northumberland Heath, *Lon.* **4 C6** 51 28N 0 10 E
Northvale, *N.Y.* **22 A5** 41 0N 73 59W
Northwest Branch →, *Balt.* **25 B3** 39 16N 76 35W
Northwest Branch →, *Wash.* **25 C8** 39 2N 76 56W
Northwestern Univ., *Chic.* **26 A2** 42 3N 87 40W
Northwood, *Lon.* **4 B2** 51 36N 0 25W
Norumbega Res., *Bost.* **21 D2** 42 19N 71 17W
Norwalk, *L.A.* **28 C4** 33 53N 118 4W
Norwood, *Bost.* **21 D2** 42 11N 71 13W
Norwood, *Jobg.* **18 E9** 26 9 S 28 4 E
Norwood, *N.Y.* **22 B5** 40 59N 73 57W
Norwood, *Phil.* **24 B3** 39 53N 75 17W
Norwood Memorial Airport, *Bost.* **21 D3** 42 11N 71 9W
Norwood Park, *Chic.* **26 B2** 41 59N 87 48W
Noryangjin, *Sŏul* **12 G7** 37 30N 126 56 E
Nose, *Ōsaka* **12 B2** 34 49N 135 10 E
Nossa Senhora do Ó, *S. Pau.* **31 E5** 23 30 S 46 41W
Notre-Dame, *Mtrl.* **20 B5** 43 28N 73 28W
Notre-Dame, *Paris* **5 B4** 48 51N 2 21 E
Notre-Dame, Bois, *Paris* **5 C5** 48 45N 2 34 E
Notre Dame de L'Île Perrot, *Mtrl.* **20 B2** 43 23N 73 53W
Notting Hill, *Lon.* **4 B3** 51 30N 0 12W
Notting Hill, *Melb.* **19 F7** 37 54 S 145 9 E
Nottingham, *Phil.* **24 A5** 40 7N 74 58W
Nova Milanese, *Mil.* **9 D6** 45 35N 9 12 E
Novate Milanese, *Mil.* **9 D5** 45 30N 9 8 E
Novaya Derevnya, *Len.* **11 A3** 60 0N 30 19 E
Nové Mesto, *Pra.* **10 B2** 50 4N 14 25 E
Novoaleksandrovskoye, *Len.* **11 B4** 59 50N 30 31 E
Novogireyevo, *Mos.* **11 E10** 55 45N 37 46 E
Novoivanovskoye, *Mos.* **11 E7** 55 42N 37 21 E
Novokhovrino, *Mos.* **11 D8** 55 53N 37 27 E
Novonikolyskoye, *Mos.* **11 D7** 55 50N 37 14 E
Novosaratovka, *Len.* **11 B5** 59 50N 30 32 E
Novosergiyevka, *Len.* **11 B5** 59 54N 30 34 E
Nowe-Babice, *Wsaw.* **10 E6** 52 15N 20 51 E
Nöykkio, *Hels.* **3 B3** 60 10N 24 42 E
Noyoye Kovalyova, *Len.* **11 B5** 59 58N 30 34 E
Nozay, *Paris* **5 D3** 48 39N 2 14 E
Nueva Atzacoalco, *Méx.* **29 B3** 19 29N 99 4W
Nueva Caracas, *Car.* **30 D5** 10 30N 66 57W
Nueva Chicago, *B.A.* **32 B4** 34 39 S 58 29W
Nueva Pompeya, *B.A.* **32 C4** 34 40 S 58 25W
Nueva Tenochtitlán, *Méx.* **29 B3** 19 27N 99 5W
Nuijala, *Hels.* **3 B3** 60 12N 24 46 E
Numabukuro, *Tōkyō* **13 B2** 35 43N 139 39 E
Numakage, *Tōkyō* **13 A2** 35 50N 139 37 E
Numata, *Tōkyō* **13 B3** 35 45N 139 46 E
Nunawading, *Melb.* **19 E8** 37 49 S 145 10 E
Nunez, *B.A.* **32 B4** 34 32 S 58 27W
Nunhead, *Lon.* **4 C4** 51 27N 0 3W
Ñuñoa, *Stgo* **30 J11** 33 27 S 70 35W
Nupuri, *Hels.* **3 B2** 60 14N 24 36 E
Nusle, *Pra.* **10 B2** 50 3N 14 26 E
Nussdorf, *Wien* **10 G10** 48 15N 16 21 E
Nuthe →, *Berl.* **7 B1** 52 22N 13 5 E
Nutley, *N.Y.* **22 C4** 40 49N 74 9W
Nutting L., *Bost.* **21 B2** 42 32N 71 16W
Nützenberg, *Ruhr* **6 C4** 51 15N 7 8 E
Nybølle, *Købn.* **2 D8** 55 42N 12 15 E
Nybygget, *Hels.* **3 B6** 60 17N 25 11 E
Nymphenburg, *Mün.* **7 G10** 48 9N 11 30 E
Nymphenburg, Schloss, *Mün.* **7 G10** 48 9N 11 30 E

O

Oak Beach, *N.Y.* **23 D9** 40 38N 73 19W
Oak Forest, *Chic.* **26 D2** 41 36N 87 44W
Oak Hill Park, *Bost.* **21 D2** 42 17N 71 11W
Oak Lane, *Phil.* **24 A4** 40 3N 75 8W
Oak Lawn, *Chic.* **26 C2** 41 42N 87 45W
Oak Park, *Chic.* **26 B2** 41 52N 87 47W
Oak Ridge, *N.Y.* **22 A2** 41 2N 74 28W
Oak Valley, *Phil.* **24 C4** 39 48N 75 9W
Oak View, *Wash.* **25 C8** 39 1N 76 58W
Oakland, *N.Y.* **22 A3** 41 1N 74 13W
Oakland, *S.F.* **27 B3** 37 48N 122 18W
Oakland, *Wash.* **25 D8** 38 52N 76 54W
Oakland Coliseum, *S.F.* **27 B3** 37 44N 122 11W
Oakland Gardens, *N.Y.* **23 C6** 40 45N 73 46W
Oakland Int. Airport, *S.F.* **27 B3** 37 43N 122 12W
Oakland Mills, *Balt.* **25 B2** 39 13N 76 49W
Oakland Naval Air Station, *S.F.* **27 B3** 37 47N 122 19W
Oaklands, *Jobg.* **18 E9** 26 8 S 28 4 E
Oaklawn, *Wash.* **25 E8** 38 46N 76 56W
Oakleigh, *Melb.* **19 F7** 37 54 S 145 5 E
Oaks, *Phil.* **24 A2** 40 8N 75 26W
Oakwood, *N.Y.* **22 D4** 40 34N 74 7W
Oakwood Beach, *N.Y.* **22 D4** 40 33N 74 7W
Oatley, *Syd.* **19 B3** 33 59 S 151 4 E
Obalende, *Lagos* **18 B2** 6 26N 7 25 E
Oba's Palace, *Lagos* **18 B2** 6 26N 7 22 E
Oberbauer, *Ruhr* **6 C6** 51 17N 7 25 E
Oberföhring, *Mün.* **7 G10** 48 10N 11 37 E
Oberhaching, *Mün.* **7 G10** 48 1N 11 35 E
Oberhausen, *Ruhr* **6 B3** 51 28N 6 54 E
Oberhausen, *Wien* **10 G11** 48 10N 16 34 E
Oberkassel, *Ruhr* **6 C2** 51 14N 6 45 E
Oberkirchbach, *Wien* **10 G9** 48 17N 16 12 E
Oberlaa, *Wien* **10 H10** 48 8N 16 24 E
Oberlisse, *Wien* **10 G10** 48 17N 16 26 E
Obermenzing, *Mün.* **7 F9** 48 10N 11 28 E
Obermoos Schwaige, *Mün.* **7 F9** 48 14N 11 27 E
Oberschleissheim, *Mün.* **7 F10** 48 15N 11 33 E
Oberschöneweide, *Berl.* **7 B4** 52 27N 13 31 E
Oberwengern, *Ruhr* **6 B6** 51 23N 7 22 E
Obitsu →, *Tōkyō* **13 D4** 35 25N 139 56 E
Oboldino, *Mos.* **11 D11** 55 53N 37 56 E
Observatory, *Jobg.* **18 F9** 26 10 S 28 4 E
Ōbu, *Ōsaka* **12 B1** 34 43N 135 8 E
Obu-tōge, *Ōsaka* **12 B1** 34 44N 135 9 E
Óbuda, *Bud.* **10 J13** 47 33N 19 2 E
Obudaisziget, *Bud.* **10 J13** 47 33N 19 3 E
Obukhovo, *Len.* **11 B4** 59 53N 30 22 E
Occidental, Pico, *Car.* **30 D5** 10 32N 66 51W
Oceanside, *N.Y.* **23 D7** 40 38N 73 37W
Ochakovo, *Mos.* **11 E8** 55 41N 37 26 E
Ochiai, *Tōkyō* **13 B3** 35 43N 139 42 E
Ochota, *Wsaw.* **10 E6** 52 13N 20 58 E
Ochsenwerder, *Hbg.* **7 E8** 53 28N 10 4 E
Ochsenzoll, *Hbg.* **7 C8** 53 41N 10 0 E
Ōdana, *Tōkyō* **13 C2** 35 33N 139 35 E
Öden-Stockach, *Mün.* **7 G11** 48 5N 11 41 E
Odilampi, *Hels.* **3 B3** 60 18N 24 45 E
Odintsovo, *Mos.* **11 E7** 55 40N 37 16 E
Odivelas, *Lisb.* **8 F7** 38 47N 9 10W
Odolany, *Wsaw.* **10 E6** 52 13N 20 55 E
Oeiras, *Lisb.* **8 F7** 38 41N 9 18W
Oella, *Balt.* **25 B2** 39 16N 76 46W
Oer-Erkenschwick, *Ruhr* **6 A5** 51 38N 7 15 E
Oern, *Mün.* **7 G10** 48 10N 11 32 E
Ofin, *Lagos* **18 A3** 6 32N 7 30 E
Ofukuro-shinden, *Tōkyō* **13 A1** 35 53N 139 28 E
Ogawa, *Tōkyō* **13 B1** 35 44N 139 28 E
Ogden, *Phil.* **24 C2** 39 49N 75 27W
Ogikubo, *Tōkyō* **13 B2** 35 42N 139 37 E
Ogo Ogo, *Ōsaka* **12 B1** 34 49N 135 8 E
Ogogoro, *Lagos* **18 B2** 6 25N 7 24 E
Ogongo, *Manila* **15 D4** 14 35N 121 4 E
Ogoyo, *Lagos* **18 B2** 6 25N 7 29 E
Ogudu, *Lagos* **18 A2** 6 34N 7 24 E
O'Hare, L., *Chic.* **26 B1** 41 57N 87 53W
Ōhirodo, *Tōkyō* **13 A4** 35 50N 139 53 E
Ohlsdorf, *Hbg.* **7 D8** 53 37N 10 3 E
Ōi, *Tōkyō* **13 A2** 35 51N 139 31 E
Ōimachi, *Tōkyō* **13 C3** 35 35N 139 43 E
Oise →, *Paris* **5 A2** 49 2N 2 5 E
Oittaa, *Hels.* **3 B3** 60 15N 24 42 E
Ojota, *Lagos* **18 A2** 6 35N 7 23 E
Okamoto, *Ōsaka* **12 B2** 34 43N 135 15 E
Okazu, *Tōkyō* **13 D2** 35 25N 139 31 E
Okęcie, *Wsaw.* **10 E6** 52 11N 20 56 E
Okęcie Airport, *Wsaw.* **10 E6** 52 10N 20 57 E
Okelra, *Lagos* **18 B2** 6 29N 7 22 E
Okeogbe, *Lagos* **18 B2** 6 24N 7 23 E
Okhla, *Delhi* **16 B2** 28 33N 77 16 E
Okhta →, *Len.* **11 B4** 59 56N 30 25 E
Okkervil →, *Len.* **11 B4** 59 56N 30 30 E
Okrzeszyn, *Wsaw.* **10 F7** 52 8N 21 8 E
Oksval, *Oslo* **2 B4** 59 51N 10 40 E
Oktyabrskiy, *Mos.* **11 F11** 55 37N 37 58 E
Oktyabrskiy, *Mos.* **11 E9** 55 41N 37 35 E
Okubo, *Tōkyō* **13 B3** 35 41N 139 42 E
Okunola, *Lagos* **18 A1** 6 35N 7 17 E
Ōkura, *Tōkyō* **13 C1** 35 35N 139 27 E
Olari, *Hels.* **3 B3** 60 10N 24 44 E
Olaria, *Rio J.* **31 B2** 22 50 S 43 16W
Old Brookville, *N.Y.* **23 C7** 40 49N 73 35W
Old Cairo, *El Qâ.* **18 C5** 30 0N 31 14 E
Old Coulsdon, *Lon.* **4 D4** 51 17N 0 6W
Old Forge Village, *N.Y.* **22 C2** 40 48N 74 29W
Old Harbor, *Bost.* **21 D3** 42 19N 71 1W
Old Road B., *Balt.* **25 B4** 39 12N 76 27W
Old Tappan, *N.Y.* **22 A5** 41 0N 73 59W
Old Town, *Chic.* **26 B3** 41 54N 87 37W
Old Westbury, *N.Y.* **23 C7** 40 46N 73 35W
Oldmans Cr. →, *Phil.* **24 C2** 39 47N 75 26W
Olgino, *Len.* **11 A3** 60 0N 30 10 E
Olimpico, Estadio, *Méx.* **29 C2** 19 19N 99 11W
Olinda, *Melb.* **19 F9** 37 51 S 145 21 E
Olinda, *Rio J.* **31 A1** 22 49 S 43 25W
Olivais, *Lisb.* **8 F8** 38 45N 9 7W
Olivar de los Padres, *Méx.* **29 B2** 19 21N 99 14W
Olivar del Conde, *Méx.* **29 B2** 19 22N 99 12W
Olivos, *B.A.* **32 B4** 34 30 S 58 28W
Ollila, *Hels.* **3 A2** 60 20N 24 32 E
Olney, *Phil.* **24 A4** 40 2N 75 8W
Olona →, *Mil.* **9 E5** 45 29N 9 6 E
Ølstykke, *Købn.* **2 D7** 55 47N 12 8 E
Olute, *Lagos* **18 B1** 6 27N 7 17 E
Olympia-Stadion, *Hels.* **3 B4** 60 11N 24 55 E
Olympique Parc, *Mtrl.* **20 A4** 43 33N 73 33W
Ōmagi, *Tōkyō* **13 A3** 35 52N 139 43 E
Ōmiya, *Tōkyō* **13 A2** 35 54N 139 37 E
Ōmori, *Tōkyō* **13 C3** 35 34N 139 43 E
Ōnari, *Tōkyō* **13 A2** 35 55N 139 36 E
Once, *B.A.* **32 B4** 34 37 S 58 24W
Onchi, *Ōsaka* **12 C4** 34 36N 135 38 E
Onchi →, *Ōsaka* **12 C4** 34 38N 135 37 E
One Tree Hill, *Melb.* **19 F8** 37 52 S 145 19 E
Onisigun, *Lagos* **18 A2** 6 35N 7 24 E
Ōokayama, *Tōkyō* **13 C3** 35 36N 139 40 E
Opacz, *Wsaw.* **10 E6** 52 10N 20 53 E
Ophirton, *Jobg.* **18 F9** 26 13 S 28 1 E
Oppegård, *Oslo* **2 C4** 59 45N 10 49 E
Oppsal, *Oslo* **2 B5** 59 53N 10 50 E
Oppum, *Ruhr* **6 C1** 51 19N 6 36 E
Oradell, *N.Y.* **22 B4** 40 57N 74 2W
Oradell Res., *N.Y.* **22 B4** 40 58N 74 0W
Orange, *N.Y.* **22 C3** 40 46N 74 15W
Orange Grove, *Jobg.* **18 E9** 26 9 S 28 5 E
Oratorio →, *S. Pau.* **31 E6** 23 36 S 46 32W
Orbassano, *Tori.* **9 B2** 45 0N 7 31 E
Orchards, *Jobg.* **18 E9** 26 9 S 28 4 E
Ordrup, *Købn.* **2 D10** 55 45N 12 34 E
Orech, *Pra.* **10 B1** 50 1N 14 17 E
Oresund, *Købn.* **2 D11** 55 45N 12 40 E
Oreta, *Lagos* **18 A3** 6 31N 7 31 E
Orge →, *Paris* **5 D3** 48 36N 2 17 E
Orgeval, *Paris* **5 B1** 48 55N 1 58 E
Orhølm, *Købn.* **2 D10** 55 48N 12 30 E
Orient Heights, *Bost.* **21 C4** 42 23N 70 59W
Oriental, Pico, *Car.* **30 D5** 10 32N 66 51W
Origgio, *Mil.* **9 D5** 45 35N 9 1 E
Orinda, *S.F.* **27 A3** 37 52N 122 10W
Orinda Village, *S.F.* **27 A3** 37 53N 122 12W
Orland L., *Chic.* **26 D1** 41 38N 87 52W
Orland Park, *Chic.* **26 D1** 41 37N 87 52W
Orlando Dam, *Jobg.* **18 F8** 26 15 S 27 55 E
Orlando East, *Jobg.* **18 F8** 26 14 S 27 55 E
Orlando West, *Jobg.* **18 F8** 26 13 S 27 54 E
Orlången, *Stock.* **3 E11** 59 11N 18 2 E
Orlångsvik, *Stock.* **3 E11** 59 11N 18 3 E
Orlovo, *Mos.* **11 F8** 55 38N 37 22 E
Orly, *Paris* **5 C4** 48 45N 2 23 E
Ormesson-sur-Marne, *Paris* **5 C5** 48 47N 2 32 E
Orminge, *Stock.* **3 E12** 59 19N 18 14 E
Ormingelandet, *Stock.* **3 D13** 59 20N 18 22 E
Ormond, *Melb.* **19 F7** 37 54 S 145 1 E
Órmos Fálirou, *Ath.* **8 J11** 37 54N 23 40 E
Ormøya, *Oslo* **2 B4** 59 52N 10 45 E
Oros Aiyáleos, *Ath.* **8 J10** 38 0N 23 36 E
Oros Imittoś, *Ath.* **8 J11** 37 53N 23 48 E
Örpadfold, *Bud.* **10 J14** 47 32N 19 12 E
Orpington, *Lon.* **4 C5** 51 22N 0 6 E
Orsay, *Paris* **5 C3** 48 41N 2 11 E
Orsby, *Ruhr* **6 A2** 51 31N 6 41 E
Orsett, *Lon.* **4 B7** 51 30N 0 22 E
Ortaköy, *Ist.* **17 A3** 41 3N 29 1 E
Ortica, *Mil.* **9 E6** 45 28N 9 16 E
Oruba, *Lagos* **18 A2** 6 34N 7 24 E
Ōsaka, *Ōsaka* **12 C4** 34 42N 135 30 E
Ōsaka B., *Ōsaka* **12 C2** 34 35N 135 18 E
Ōsaka Castle, *Ōsaka* **12 B4** 34 41N 135 30 E
Ōsaka Harbour, *Ōsaka* **12 C3** 34 38N 135 25 E
Ōsaka Univ., *Ōsaka* **12 B3** 34 41N 135 29 E
Ōsaki, *Tōkyō* **13 C3** 35 36N 139 42 E
Osasco, *S. Pau.* **31 E5** 23 31 S 46 46W
Osdorf, *Berl.* **7 B3** 52 24N 13 20 E
Osdorf, *Hbg.* **7 D7** 53 34N 9 50 E
Oshodi, *Lagos* **18 A2** 6 33N 7 21 E
Oskar Frederikborg, *Stock.* **3 D13** 59 24N 18 24 E
Oslo, *Oslo* **2 B4** 59 54N 10 43 E
Oslofjorden, *Oslo* **2 C3** 59 40N 10 35 E
Ōsone, *Tōkyō* **13 C2** 35 31N 139 37 E
Osorun, *Lagos* **18 A2** 6 33N 7 29 E
Ospiate, *Mil.* **9 D5** 45 32N 9 6 E
Ossów, *Wsaw.* **10 E8** 52 18N 21 12 E
Ostankino, *Mos.* **11 E9** 55 49N 37 37 E
Østby, *Købn.* **2 D7** 55 45N 12 2 E
Osterath, *Ruhr* **6 C1** 51 16N 6 36 E
Österby, *Hels.* **3 B1** 60 10N 24 25 E
Osterfeld, *Ruhr* **6 A3** 51 30N 6 53 E
Osterley, *Lon.* **4 C2** 51 28N 0 21W
Osterley Park, *Lon.* **4 C2** 51 29N 0 21W
Östermalm, *Stock.* **3 D11** 59 20N 18 4 E
Österskär, *Stock.* **3 D12** 59 26N 18 16 E
Östersundom, *Hels.* **3 B6** 60 15N 25 10 E
Ostertälje, *Stock.* **3 E8** 59 11N 17 39 E
Ostiense, *Rome* **9 F9** 41 51N 12 29 E
Østmarkkapellet, *Oslo* **2 B5** 59 52N 10 51 E
Ostøya, *Oslo* **2 B3** 59 52N 10 34 E
Östra Ryd, *Stock.* **3 D12** 59 27N 18 11 E
Ostre Aker, *Oslo* **2 B4** 59 54N 10 49 E
Ostrov, *Mos.* **11 F11** 55 36N 37 50 E
Ostrovtsy, *Mos.* **11 F12** 55 36N 38 0 E
Ōta-Ku, *Tōkyō* **13 C3** 35 34N 139 41 E
Otaniemi, *Hels.* **3 B3** 60 11N 24 49 E
Otford, *Lon.* **4 D6** 51 18N 0 11 E
Othmarschen, *Hbg.* **7 D7** 53 33N 9 53 E
Otsuka, *Tōkyō* **13 B3** 35 43N 139 44 E
Ottakring, *Wien* **10 G9** 48 12N 16 18 E
Ottávia, *Rome* **9 F9** 41 57N 12 24 E
Ottaviano, *Nápl.* **9 H13** 40 50N 14 28 E
Ottensen, *Hbg.* **7 D7** 53 33N 9 55 E
Ottobrunn, *Mün.* **7 G11** 48 3N 11 40 E
Ottocalli, *Nápl.* **9 H12** 40 52N 14 17 E
Otwock, *Wsaw.* **10 F8** 52 8N 21 13 E
Ouerenburg, *Ruhr* **6 B5** 51 27N 7 16 E
Ouiapo, *Manila* **15 D3** 14 35N 120 59 E
Oulunkylä, *Hels.* **3 B4** 60 13N 24 58 E
Ourcq, Canal de l', *Paris* **5 B4** 48 54N 2 28 E
Ousit, *Bangk.* **15 B2** 13 47N 100 31 E
Outer Brewster I., *Bost.* **21 C4** 42 20N 70 52W
Outer Mission, *S.F.* **27 B2** 37 43N 122 26W
Outremont, *Mtrl.* **20 A4** 43 31N 73 36W
Overbruch, *Ruhr* **6 A2** 51 32N 6 43 E
Overlea, *Balt.* **25 A3** 39 21N 76 32W
Overod, *Købn.* **2 D9** 55 48N 12 28 E
Ōwada, *Tōkyō* **13 B2** 35 48N 139 31 E
Owings Mills, *Balt.* **25 A2** 39 25N 76 47W
Oworonsoki, *Lagos* **18 A2** 6 32N 7 24 E
Oxon Hill, *Wash.* **25 E8** 38 48N 76 59W
Oxshott, *Lon.* **4 D2** 51 19N 0 21W
Oyada, *Tōkyō* **13 B4** 35 46N 139 50 E
Ōyama, *Tōkyō* **13 B3** 35 44N 139 42 E
Øyeren, *Oslo* **2 B6** 59 55N 11 6 E
Oyodo, *Ōsaka* **12 B3** 34 42N 135 29 E
Oyster B., *N.Y.* **23 B7** 40 52N 73 31W
Oyster B., *Syd.* **19 C3** 34 0 S 151 5 E
Oyster Bay Cove, *N.Y.* **23 B8** 40 51N 73 29W
Oyster Bay Harbour, *N.Y.* **23 B7** 40 53N 73 32W
Oyster Rock, *Bomb.* **16 H7** 18 54N 72 49 E
Oyster Rocks, *Kar.* **17 H11** 24 48N 66 59 E
Ozarów-Franciszków, *Wsaw.* **10 E5** 52 13N 20 48 E
Ozerki, *Len.* **11 B6** 59 53N 30 42 E
Ozoir-la-Ferrière, *Paris* **5 C6** 48 46N 2 40 E
Ozone Park, *N.Y.* **23 C5** 40 40N 73 50W

P

Pacific Manor, *S.F.* **27 C2** 37 38N 122 27W
Pacific Palisades, *L.A.* **28 B1** 34 2N 118 32W
Pacifica, *S.F.* **27 C2** 37 37N 122 27W
Packanack L., *N.Y.* **22 B3** 40 56N 74 15W
Paco, *Manila* **15 D3** 14 35N 120 59 E
Paco de Arcos, *Lisb.* **8 F7** 38 41N 9 17W
Paddington, *Lon.* **4 B3** 51 30N 0 10W
Paddington, *Syd.* **19 B4** 33 53 S 151 14 E
Pademangan, *Jak.* **15 H9** 6 7 S 106 49 E
Paderno, *Mil.* **9 D5** 45 33N 9 9 E
Padre Miguel, *Rio J.* **31 B1** 22 52 S 43 25W
Padstow, *Syd.* **19 B3** 33 57 S 151 2 E
Pagewood, *Syd.* **19 B4** 33 56 S 151 14 E
Pagote, *Bomb.* **16 H8** 18 53N 72 59 E
Pai, I. do, *Rio J.* **31 B3** 22 59 S 43 5W
Paia, *Lisb.* **8 F7** 38 46N 9 11W
Paikpara, *Calc.* **16 E6** 22 36N 88 23 E
Paint Br. →, *Wash.* **25 C8** 38 57N 76 55W
Paiyun Airport, *Gzh.* **14 F8** 23 10N 113 15 E
Pak ka Shan, *H.K.* **12 E6** 22 16N 114 13 E
Pak Kong, *H.K.* **12 D6** 22 22N 114 15 E
Pak Tim Pa, *H.K.* **12 D5** 22 22N 114 7 E
Pakila, *Hels.* **3 B4** 60 15N 24 55 E
Palace Museum, *Beij.* **14 B3** 39 54N 116 21 E
Palaión Fáliron, *Ath.* **8 J11** 37 53N 23 42 E
Palaiseau, *Paris* **5 C3** 48 42N 2 14 E
Palam, *Delhi* **16 B1** 28 35N 77 4 E
Palam Int. Airport, *Delhi* **16 B1** 28 32N 77 8 E
Palazzo Reale, *Nápl.* **9 H12** 40 50N 14 15 E
Palazzo Reale, *Tori.* **9 B3** 45 4N 7 40 E
Palazzolo, *Mil.* **9 D5** 45 34N 9 9 E
Palazzuolo, *Nápl.* **9 H13** 40 54N 14 28 E
Palermo, *B.A.* **32 B4** 34 35 S 58 24W
Palhais, *Lisb.* **8 G8** 38 37N 9 2W
Palisades, *N.Y.* **22 A5** 41 1N 73 57W
Palisades Park, *N.Y.* **22 B4** 40 50N 74 1W
Palleja, *Barc.* **8 D5** 41 25N 2 0 E
Palmer Park, *Wash.* **25 D8** 38 55N 76 52W
Palmers Green, *Lon.* **4 B4** 51 36N 0 6W
Palmyra, *Phil.* **24 A4** 40 0N 75 1W
Palo Alto, *S.F.* **27 D4** 37 27N 122 8W
Paloheinä, *Hels.* **3 B4** 60 15N 24 56 E
Palomar Park, *S.F.* **27 D3** 37 29N 122 16W
Palomeras, *Mdrd.* **8 B3** 40 22N 3 39W
Palos Heights, *Chic.* **26 D2** 41 39N 87 47W
Palos Hills, *Chic.* **26 C2** 41 42N 87 49W
Palos Hills Forest, *Chic.* **26 C1** 41 40N 87 52W
Palos Park, *Chic.* **26 C1** 41 40N 87 50W
Palota-Üjfalu, *Bud.* **10 J13** 47 33N 19 7 E
Palpara, *Calc.* **16 E6** 22 38N 88 22 E
Palta, *Calc.* **16 D6** 22 46N 88 23 E
Pamplona, *Manila* **15 E3** 14 27N 120 58 E
Panayaan, *Manila* **15 E3** 14 27N 120 57 E
Panchghara, *Calc.* **16 D5** 22 44N 88 16 E
Panchur, *Calc.* **16 E5** 22 32N 88 16 E
Pancoran, *Jak.* **15 J9** 6 14 S 106 49 E
Pandan, Selat, *Sing.* **15 G7** 1 16N 103 45 E
Pandan, Sungei →, *Sing.* **15 G7** 1 18N 103 43 E
Pandan Res., *Sing.* **15 G7** 1 18N 103 44 E
Panehpara, *Calc.* **16 E5** 22 34N 88 15 E
Pangrati, *Ath.* **8 J11** 37 56N 23 45 E
Pangsua, Sungei →, *Sing.* **15 F7** 1 25N 103 45 E
Panihati, *Calc.* **16 D6** 22 41N 88 22 E
Panjang, Bukit, *Sing.* **15 F7** 1 22N 103 45 E
Panje, *Bomb.* **16 H8** 18 54N 72 57 E
Panke →, *Berl.* **7 A3** 52 31N 13 22 E
Pankow, *Berl.* **7 A3** 52 34N 13 23 E
Panorama City, *L.A.* **28 A2** 34 13N 118 26W
Panpur, *Calc.* **16 C6** 22 51N 88 26 E
Pantheon, *Rome* **9 F9** 41 53N 12 28 E
Pantin, *Paris* **5 B4** 48 53N 2 24 E
Pantitlán, *Méx.* **29 B3** 19 24N 99 4W
Panuacan, *Manila* **15 D4** 14 35N 121 0 E
Panvel Cr. →, *Bomb.* **16 H9** 18 59N 73 0 E
Paoli, *Phil.* **24 A2** 40 2N 75 28W
Papiol, *Barc.* **8 D5** 41 25N 2 0 E
Paracuellos del Jarama, *Mdrd.* **8 A3** 40 30N 3 31W
Paradise Cay, *S.F.* **27 A2** 37 54N 122 28W
Paramount, *L.A.* **28 C3** 33 53N 118 11W
Paramus, *N.Y.* **22 B4** 40 56N 74 2W
Paranaque, *Manila* **15 D3** 14 30N 120 59 E
Paray-Vieille-Poste, *Paris* **5 C4** 48 42N 2 20 E
Parbasdorf, *Wien* **10 G11** 48 16N 16 35 E
Parbatipur, *Calc.* **16 E5** 22 39N 88 13 E
Parcelacion Moderna, *La Hab.* **30 B3** 23 2N 82 19W
Parco Regionale, *Mil.* **9 D5** 45 35N 9 5 E
Parel, *Bomb.* **16 H7** 18 59N 72 49 E
Pari, *S. Pau.* **31 E6** 23 32 S 46 36W
Parioli, *Rome* **9 F9** 41 55N 12 29 E
Paris, *Paris* **5 B4** 48 53N 2 20 E
Paris-Le Bourget, Aéroport de, *Paris* **5 B4** 48 58N 2 26 E
Paris-Orly, Aéroport de, *Paris* **5 C4** 48 43N 2 22 E
Pārk-e-Shahānshāh, *Tehr.* **17 C5** 35 46N 51 24 E
Park Orchards, *Melb.* **19 E8** 37 46 S 145 13 E
Park Ridge, *Chic.* **26 A1** 42 0N 87 50W
Park Ridge, *N.Y.* **22 A4** 41 2N 74 2W
Park Royal, *Lon.* **4 B3** 51 31N 0 16W
Parkchester, *N.Y.* **23 C5** 40 49N 73 50W
Parkdale, *Trto.* **20 E8** 43 38N 79 25W
Parkdene, *Jobg.* **18 F10** 26 11 S 28 15 E
Parkhafen, *Hbg.* **7 D7** 53 32N 9 54 E
Parkhill Gardens, *Jobg.* **18 F10** 26 14 S 28 11 E
Parkhurst, *Jobg.* **18 E9** 26 8 S 28 1 E
Parklawn, *Wash.* **25 D7** 38 50N 77 7W
Parkmore, *Jobg.* **18 E9** 26 5 S 28 2 E
Parkside, *S.F.* **27 B2** 37 44N 122 29W
Parktown, *Jobg.* **18 F9** 26 10 S 28 2 E
Parktown North, *Jobg.* **18 E9** 26 8 S 28 2 E
Parkview, *Jobg.* **18 E9** 26 9 S 28 1 E
Parkville, *Balt.* **25 A3** 39 23N 76 34W
Parkville, *N.Y.* **22 D5** 40 38N 73 57W
Parkwood, *Jobg.* **18 E9** 26 9 S 28 2 E
Parque Edú Chaves, *S. Pau.* **31 D6** 23 29 S 46 34W
Parramatta, *Syd.* **19 A2** 33 49 S 150 59 E
Parramatta →, *Syd.* **19 A3** 33 49 S 151 3 E
Parramatta North, *Syd.* **19 A3** 33 48 S 151 0 E
Parramatta Park, *Syd.* **19 A3** 33 48 S 151 0 E
Parsippany, *N.Y.* **22 B2** 40 51N 74 26W
Paşabahce, *Ist.* **17 A3** 41 6N 29 5 E
Pasadena, *L.A.* **28 B4** 34 9N 118 8W
Pasar Minggu, *Jak.* **15 J9** 6 16 S 106 49 E
Pasay, *Manila* **15 D3** 14 32N 120 59 E
Pascoe Vale, *Melb.* **19 E6** 37 43 S 144 55 E
Pasig, *Manila* **15 D4** 14 33N 121 4 E
Pasig →, *Manila* **15 D4** 14 31N 121 6 E
Pasila, *Hels.* **3 B4** 60 12N 24 56 E
Pasing, *Mün.* **7 G9** 48 8N 11 28 E
Pasir Panjang, *Sing.* **15 G7** 1 17N 103 46 E
Pasir Ris Beach, *Sing.* **15 F8** 1 22N 103 56 E
Paso del Rey, *B.A.* **32 B2** 34 39 S 58 45W
Passaic, *N.Y.* **22 B4** 40 51N 74 9W
Passaic →, *N.Y.* **22 B3** 40 42N 74 10W
Passirana, *Mil.* **9 D5** 45 32N 9 2 E
Patapsco →, *Balt.* **25 B2** 39 19N 76 49W
Patapsco State Park, *Balt.* **25 B2** 39 18N 76 47W
Pateres, *Manila* **15 D4** 14 32N 121 3 E
Paterson, *N.Y.* **22 B4** 40 54N 74 9W
Pathumwan, *Bangk.* **15 B2** 13 44N 100 31 E
Patipukun, *Calc.* **16 E6** 22 36N 88 24 E
Patisia, *Ath.* **8 H11** 38 2N 23 45 E
Patterson Park, *Balt.* **25 B3** 39 17N 76 34W
Patul, *Calc.* **16 D4** 22 45N 88 9 E
Paulo E. Virginia, Gruta, *Rio J.* **31 B2** 22 56 S 43 16W
Paulsboro, *Phil.* **24 C3** 39 49N 75 14W
Paulshof, *Berl.* **7 A5** 52 34N 13 42 E
Pausin, *Berl.* **7 A1** 52 38N 13 2 E
Pavarolo, *Tori.* **9 B3** 45 4N 7 49 E
Pavlovo, *Len.* **11 B5** 59 55N 30 38 E
Pavne, *Bomb.* **16 G9** 19 5N 73 1 E
Pavshino, *Mos.* **11 E7** 55 49N 37 20 E
Paya Lebar, *Sing.* **15 F8** 1 21N 103 52 E
Paylampur, *Calc.* **16 D5** 22 46N 88 15 E
Peabody, *Bost.* **21 B4** 42 32N 70 57W
Peabody Inst., *Balt.* **25 B3** 39 17N 76 37W
Peakhurst, *Syd.* **19 B3** 33 57 S 151 3 E
Pécel, *Bud.* **10 K14** 47 29N 19 20 E
Pecetto Torinese, *Tori.* **9 B3** 45 1N 7 44 E
Pechincha, *Rio J.* **31 B1** 22 55 S 43 20W
Pechorka →, *Mos.* **11 F12** 55 37N 38 2 E
Peckham, *Lon.* **4 C4** 51 28N 0 3W
Pecqueuse, *Paris* **5 D2** 48 38N 2 3 E
Peddocks I., *Bost.* **21 D4** 42 17N 70 56W
Pederstrup, *Købn.* **2 D9** 55 44N 12 20 E
Pedra Branca, *Rio J.* **31 B1** 22 55 S 43 26W
Pedralbes, *Barc.* **8 D5** 41 23N 2 7 E
Pedregal de San Angel, Jardines del, *Méx.* **29 C2** 19 19N 99 12W
Pedreira, *S. Pau.* **31 F5** 23 41 S 46 40W
Pedreros, *Lima* **30 G8** 12 2 S 76 57W
Pedricktown, *Phil.* **24 C2** 39 45N 75 24W
Pedro Cr. →, *S.F.* **27 C2** 37 35N 122 31W
Pedro Valley, *S.F.* **27 C2** 37 35N 122 29W
Peirce Res., *Sing.* **15 F7** 1 22N 103 49 E
Pekhra-Pokrovskoye, *Mos.* **11 D11** 55 50N 37 56 E
Pekhra-Yakovievskaya, *Mos.* **11 E11** 55 47N 37 57 E
Peking = Beijing, *Beij.* **14 B2** 39 53N 116 21 E
Pelado, Cerro, *Méx.* **29 D2** 19 10N 99 14W
Pelcowizna, *Wsaw.* **10 E7** 52 17N 21 0 E
Pelham, *N.Y.* **23 B6** 40 54N 73 46W
Pelham B. Park, *N.Y.* **23 B6** 40 52N 73 48W
Pelham Manor, *N.Y.* **23 B6** 40 53N 73 46W
Penalolén, *Stgo* **30 J11** 33 28 S 70 30W
Peng Siang →, *Sing.* **15 F7** 1 24N 103 43 E
Penge, *Lon.* **4 C4** 51 24N 0 3W
Penha, *Rio J.* **31 A2** 22 49 S 43 17W
Penha, *S. Pau.* **31 E6** 23 31 S 46 32W
Penjaringan, *Jak.* **15 H9** 6 7 S 106 48 E
Penn Square, *Phil.* **24 A3** 40 8N 75 19W
Penn Wynne, *Phil.* **24 B3** 39 59N 75 16W
Pennant Hills Park, *Syd.* **19 A3** 33 46 S 151 6 E
Penndel, *Phil.* **24 A5** 40 9N 74 54W
Penns Grove, *Phil.* **24 C2** 39 44N 75 27W
Pennsauken, *Phil.* **24 B4** 39 57N 75 5W
Pennsauken Cr. →, *Phil.* **24 B4** 39 59N 75 3W
Pennsylvania, Univ. of, *Phil.* **24 B3** 39 51N 75 11W
Pennypack Cr. →, *Phil.* **24 A4** 40 0N 75 3W
Pentala, *Hels.* **3 C3** 60 6N 24 40 E
Penyagino, *Mos.* **11 D8** 55 50N 37 20 E
Penzing, *Wien* **10 G9** 48 11N 16 18 E
Pequannock, *N.Y.* **22 B3** 40 57N 74 17W
Pequena Arroio Fundo →, *Rio J.* **31 B1** 22 58 S 43 21W
Perales del Rio, *Mdrd.* **8 C3** 40 18N 3 38W
Perchtoldsdorf, *Wien* **10 H9** 48 7N 16 17 E
Perdizes, *S. Pau.* **31 E6** 23 32 S 46 39W
Peredelkino, *Mos.* **11 F8** 55 38N 37 20 E
Peredelytsy, *Mos.* **11 F8** 55 36N 37 21 E
Peristérion, *Ath.* **8 H11** 38 1N 23 42 E
Perivale, *Lon.* **4 B3** 51 31N 0 18W
Perlach, *Mün.* **7 G10** 48 5N 11 37 E
Perlacher Forst, *Mün.* **7 G10** 48 4N 11 34 E
Pero, *Mil.* **9 D5** 45 30N 9 5 E
Peropok, Bukit, *Sing.* **15 G7** 1 19N 103 42 E
Perovo, *Mos.* **11 E10** 55 44N 37 45 E
Perrot, Î., *Mtrl.* **20 B2** 43 23N 73 56W
Perry Hall, *Balt.* **25 A4** 39 24N 76 28W
Perth Amboy, *N.Y.* **22 D3** 40 30N 74 16W
Pertusella, *Mil.* **9 D5** 45 35N 9 3 E
Pesanggrahag, Kali →, *Jak.* **15 J9** 6 10 S 106 44 E
Peschiera Borromeo, *Mil.* **9 E6** 45 26N 9 19 E
Pesek, P., *Sing.* **15 G7** 1 17N 103 41 E
Pest, *Bud.* **10 K13** 47 29N 19 4 E
Pesterzsébet, *Bud.* **10 K13** 47 26N 19 6 E
Pesthidegkút, *Bud.* **10 J12** 47 33N 18 57 E
Pestimre, *Bud.* **10 K14** 47 24N 19 11 E
Pestlörinc, *Bud.* **10 K14** 47 26N 19 11 E
Pestujhely, *Bud.* **10 J13** 47 32N 19 7 E
Petare, *Car.* **30 E6** 10 29N 66 48W
Petas, *Hels.* **3 B4** 60 15N 24 50 E
Peters Pond, *Bost.* **21 A2** 42 43N 71 15W
Petit, *Jobg.* **18 E11** 26 6 S 28 22 E
Petit-Brûlé, *Mtrl.* **20 A1** 43 35N 74 2W
Petojo Selatan, *Jak.* **15 J9** 6 10 S 106 48 E
Petrograd = Leningrad, *Len.* **11 B3** 59 55N 30 15 E
Petrogradskaya Storona, *Len.* **11 B4** 59 56N 30 20 E
Petroúpolis, *Ath.* **8 H11** 38 3N 23 40 E
Petrovice, *Pra.* **10 B3** 50 2N 14 33 E
Petrovsko-Rasumovskoye, *Mos.* **11 E9** 55 49N 37 34 E
Petrovskoye, *Mos.* **11 F11** 55 36N 37 53 E
Petrovsky Park, *Mos.* **11 E9** 55 47N 37 34 E
Pfaueninsel, *Berl.* **7 B1** 52 26N 13 7 E
Phihāi, *Kar.* **17 G11** 24 50N 67 8 E
Philadelphia, *Phil.* **24 B3** 39 57N 75 11W
Philadelphia Airport, *Phil.* **24 A5** 40 4N 75 0W
Philadelphia Int. Airport, *Phil.* **24 B3** 39 52N 75 16W
Phillip B., *Syd.* **19 B4** 33 58 S 151 14 E
Phinga, *Calc.* **16 D6** 22 41N 88 25 E
Phoenix, *Chic.* **26 D3** 41 36N 87 37W
Phoenixville, *Phil.* **24 A1** 40 7N 75 31W
Phra Khanong, *Bangk.* **15 B2** 13 40N 100 36 E
Phra Pradaeng, *Bangk.* **15 C2** 13 39N 100 33 E
Phranakhon, *Bangk.* **15 B1** 13 44N 100 29 E
Pianezza, *Tori.* **9 B2** 45 6N 7 32 E
Pianura, *Nápl.* **9 H11** 40 51N 14 10 E
Piaslów, *Wsaw.* **10 E5** 52 11N 20 49 E
Pico Rivera, *L.A.* **28 C4** 33 59N 118 5W
Piedade, *Lisb.* **8 F7** 38 49N 9 16W
Piedade, *Rio J.* **31 B2** 22 52 S 43 18W
Piedade, Cova da, *Lisb.* **8 F8** 38 40N 9 8W
Piedmont, *S.F.* **27 B3** 37 49N 122 14W
Pierrefitte, *Paris* **5 B4** 48 58N 2 21 E
Pierrefonds, *Mtrl.* **20 B2** 43 27N 73 52W
Pierrelaye, *Paris* **5 A2** 49 1N 2 8 E
Pietralata, *Rome* **9 F10** 41 55N 12 33 E
Pihlajamäki, *Hels.* **3 B4** 60 14N 24 58 E
Pihlajasaari, *Hels.* **3 C4** 60 8N 24 55 E
Pikesville, *Balt.* **25 A2** 39 22N 76 42W
Pilar Velho, *S. Pau.* **31 F7** 23 40 S 46 22W
Pilarcitos Cr. →, *S.F.* **27 C2** 37 33N 122 24W
Pilarcitos L., *S.F.* **27 C2** 37 33N 122 25W
Pilgrim Corner, *Phil.* **24 B3** 39 57N 75 19W
Pilgrims Hatch, *Lon.* **4 B6** 51 37N 0 17 E
Pillar Pt., *S.F.* **26 D2** 37 29N 122 30W
Pimenta, *S. Pau.* **31 D7** 23 27 S 46 24W
Pimlico, *Lon.* **4 C4** 51 29N 0 8W
Pimmit Hills, *Wash.* **25 D6** 38 54N 77 12W
Pimville, *Jobg.* **18 F8** 26 16 S 27 54 E
Pinazo →, *B.A.* **32 A2** 34 29 S 58 49W
Pine Brook, *N.Y.* **22 B3** 40 51N 74 18W
Pine Grove, *Trto.* **20 D7** 43 47N 79 34W
Pine Hill, *Phil.* **24 C5** 39 47N 74 59W
Pine Orchard, *Balt.* **25 B1** 39 16N 76 52W
Pinehurst, *Bost.* **21 B2** 42 31N 71 12W
Piñero, *B.A.* **32 B2** 34 31 S 58 46W
Pines Lake, *N.Y.* **22 B3** 40 59N 74 15W
Piney Run →, *Wash.* **25 D6** 38 58N 77 14W
Pinganli, *Beij.* **14 B3** 39 56N 116 20 E
Pinheiros →, *S. Pau.* **31 E5** 23 37 S 46 44W
Pinjrāpur, *Kar.* **17 G11** 24 53N 67 4 E
Pinn →, *Lon.* **4 B2** 51 30N 0 28W
Pinnau →, *Hbg.* **7 C6** 53 40N 9 49 E
Pinneberg, *Hbg.* **7 C6** 53 40N 9 48 E
Pinner, *Lon.* **4 B2** 51 35N 0 22W
Pinner Green, *Lon.* **4 B2** 51 35N 0 23W
Pino Torinese, *Tori.* **9 B3** 45 2N 7 46 E
Pinole Cr. →, *S.F.* **27 A3** 37 58N 122 12W
Pioltello, *Mil.* **9 D6** 45 30N 9 19 E
Piossasco, *Tori.* **9 C1** 44 59N 7 27 E
Piqueri, *S. Pau.* **31 D5** 23 29 S 46 41W
Piqueri →, *S. Pau.* **31 D6** 23 27 S 46 34W
Pira, *Delhi* **16 A1** 28 40N 77 7 E
Piraévs, *Ath.* **8 J10** 37 54N 23 39 E
Pirajussara, *S. Pau.* **31 E5** 23 37 S 46 46W
Pirajussara →, *S. Pau.* **31 E5** 23 33 S 46 42W
Piraporinha, *S. Pau.* **31 F5** 23 41 S 46 44W
Piratininga, *Rio J.* **31 B3** 22 56 S 43 4W
Piratininga, L. de, *Rio J.* **31 B3** 22 56 S 43 4W
Pirituba, *S. Pau.* **31 D5** 23 29 S 46 44W
Pirkkola, *Hels.* **3 B4** 60 14N 24 55 E
Pisangan, *Jak.* **15 J10** 6 12 S 106 52 E
Piscataway, *N.Y.* **22 D2** 40 34N 74 27W
Pisnice, *Pra.* **10 C2** 49 59N 14 28 E
Pitampura Kalan, *Delhi* **16 A1** 28 41N 77 7 E

44 Pitkajarvi

Pitkajarvi, Hels. 3 B3 60 15N 24 45 E
Pitman, Phil. 24 C4 39 44N 75 7W
Plainedge, N.Y. 23 C8 40 43N 73 27W
Plainfield, N.Y. 22 D2 40 36N 74 23W
Plainview, N.Y. 23 C8 40 46N 73 27W
Plaisir, Paris 5 C1 48 49N 1 56 E
Plandome, N.Y. 23 C6 40 48N 73 42W
Plandome Heights, N.Y. 23 C6 40 48N 73 42W
Planegg, Mün. 7 G9 48 6N 11 25 E
Plazo Mayor, Mdrd. 8 B2 40 25N 3 43W
Pleasant Hill, S.F. 27 A4 37 56N 122 4W
Plenty, Melb. 19 E7 37 40 S 145 5 E
Pluit, Jak. 15 H9 6 7 S 106 47 E
Plumsock, Phil. 24 B2 39 58N 75 28W
Plumstead, Lon. 4 C5 51 29N 0 5 E
Plymouth Meeting, Phil. 24 A3 40 6N 75 16W
Plyushchevo, Mos. 11 E10 55 44N 37 45 E
Po →, Tori. 9 B3 45 7N 7 46 E
Po Toi, H.K. 12 E6 22 16N 114 17 E
Po Toi I., H.K. 12 E6 22 10N 114 15 E
Podbaba, Pra. 10 B2 50 7N 14 22 E
Podoli, Pra. 10 B2 50 2N 14 25 E
Podra, Calc. 16 E5 22 33N 88 16 E
Poduskino, Mos. 11 E7 55 43N 37 15 E
Poggioreale, Nápl. 9 H12 40 51N 14 17 E
Pogliano Milanese, Mil. 9 D4 45 32N 8 59 E
Pohick Cr. →, Wash. 25 E6 38 47N 77 16W
Point Breeze, Phil. 24 B3 39 54N 75 13W
Point Lookout, N.Y. 23 D7 40 35N 73 34W
Point View Res., N.Y. 22 B3 40 58N 74 14W
Pointe-Aux-Trembles, Mtrl. 20 A4 43 38N 73 30W
Pointe-Calumet, Mtrl. 20 B2 43 29N 73 58W
Pointe-Claire, Mtrl. 20 B3 43 27N 73 48W
Poissy, Paris 5 B2 48 55N 2 2 E
Pok Fu Lam, H.K. 12 E5 22 16N 114 7 E
Pokrovsko-Sresnevo, Mos. 11 E8 55 48N 37 27 E
Pokrovskoye, Mos. 11 F9 55 37N 37 36 E
Póllena, Nápl. 9 H13 40 51N 14 22 E
Polsum, Ruhr 6 A4 51 37N 7 2 E
Polyustrovo, Len. 11 B4 59 57N 30 25 E
Pomigliano d'Arco, Nápl. 9 H13 40 54N 14 23 E
Pompei, Nápl. 9 J13 40 45N 14 29 E
Pomponne, Paris 5 B6 48 52N 2 40 E
Pomprap, Bangk. 15 B2 13 44N 100 30 E
Pompton →, N.Y. 22 B3 40 53N 74 16W
Pompton Lakes, N.Y. 22 A3 41 0N 74 15W
Pompton Plains, N.Y. 22 B3 40 58N 74 18W
Ponders End, Lon. 4 B4 51 38N 0 2W
Pondok Indah, Jak. 15 J9 6 16 S 106 46 E
Ponkapog, Bost. 21 D3 42 11N 71 4W
Ponkapog Pond, Bost. 21 D3 42 11N 71 5W
Pont-Viau, Mtrl. 20 A3 43 34N 73 41W
Pontault-Combault, Paris 5 C5 48 47N 2 36 E
Pontcarré, Paris 5 C6 48 47N 2 42 E
Pontchartrain, Paris 5 C1 48 48N 1 54 E
Ponte Galéria, Rome 9 G8 41 48N 12 19 E
Pontes, Canto do, Rio J. 31 B3 22 56 S 43 3W
Pontevedra, B.A. 32 C2 34 44 S 58 41W
Ponticelli, Nápl. 9 H12 40 51N 14 19 E
Pontinha, Lisb. 8 F7 38 45N 9 11W
Pontoise, Paris 5 A2 49 2N 2 4 E
Poortview, Jobg. 18 E8 26 5 S 27 51 E
Poplar, Lon. 4 B4 51 30N 0 0 E
Poppenbüttel, Hbg. 7 D8 53 39N 10 4 E
Port Chester, N.Y. 23 A6 41 0N 73 40W
Port Chester Harbour, N.Y. 23 B7 40 58N 73 38W
Port Jackson, Syd. 19 B4 33 51 S 151 14 E
Port Kennedy, Phil. 24 A2 40 6N 75 25W
Port Melbourne, Melb. 19 F6 37 50 S 144 54 E
Port Newark, N.Y. 22 C4 40 41N 74 9W
Port Reading, N.Y. 22 D3 40 34N 74 13W
Port Richmond, N.Y. 22 D4 40 38N 74 7W
Port Shelter, H.K. 12 D6 22 20N 114 17 E
Port Union, Trto. 20 D10 43 47N 79 7W
Port Washington, N.Y. 23 C6 40 49N 73 42W
Port Washington North, N.Y. 23 B6 40 50N 73 41W
Portage Park, Chic. 26 B2 41 56N 87 45W
Portela, Aeroporto da, Lisb. 8 F8 38 46N 9 7W
Pórtici, Nápl. 9 J12 40 48N 14 19 E
Porto Brandão, Lisb. 8 F7 38 40N 9 12W
Porto Novo Cr. →, Lagos 18 B2 6 25N 7 22 E
Porto Nuevo, B.A. 32 B4 34 35 S 58 22W
Portrero, S.F. 27 B3 37 46N 122 25W
Posen, Chic. 26 D2 41 38N 87 41W
Posíllipo, Nápl. 9 J12 40 49N 14 13 E
Posíllipo, C. di, Nápl. 9 J12 40 48N 14 12 E
Posolok Lenina, Len. 11 C2 59 50N 30 5 E
Potawatomi Woods, Chic. 26 A1 42 8N 87 53W
Potomac, Wash. 25 D6 38 59N 77 13W
Potomac →, Wash. 25 D7 38 58N 77 9W
Potrero Pt., S.F. 27 B2 37 45N 122 22W
Potsdam, Berl. 7 B1 52 23N 13 3 E
Potter Pt., Syd. 19 C4 34 2 S 151 13 E
Potters Bar, Lon. 4 A4 51 41N 0 10W
Potzham, Mün. 7 G10 48 1N 11 36 E
Pötzleinsdorf, Wien 10 G9 48 14N 16 17 E
Povoa de Santo Adriao, Lisb. 8 F8 38 47N 9 9W
Powderhorn L., Chic. 26 D3 41 38N 87 31W
Powičle, Wsaw. 10 E7 52 14N 21 1 E
Powōzki, Wsaw. 10 E6 52 15N 20 58 E
Powsin, Wsaw. 10 F7 52 8N 21 6 E
Powsinek, Wsaw. 10 F7 52 9N 21 6 E
Poyo, Barc. 8 D6 41 28N 2 12 E
Pozuelo de Alarcón, Mdrd. 8 B2 40 25N 3 48W
Praça Seca, Rio J. 31 B1 22 53 S 43 20W
Prado, Museo del, Mdrd. 8 B2 40 25N 3 42W
Prado Churubusco, Méx. 29 B3 19 20N 99 8W
Praga, Wsaw. 10 E7 52 15N 21 2 E
Prague = Praha, Pra. 10 B2 50 4N 14 25 E
Praha, Pra. 10 B2 50 4N 14 25 E
Praha-Ruzyně Airport, Pra. 10 B1 50 6N 14 16 E
Praires, R. des →, Mtrl. 20 A4 43 38N 73 36W
Prat de Llobregat, Barc. 8 E5 41 19N 2 5 E
Prater, Wien 10 G10 48 12N 16 25 E
Pratts Bottom, Lon. 4 C5 51 20N 0 7 E
Prawet Buri Rom, Khlong →, Bangk. 15 B2 13 43N 100 38 E
Preakness, N.Y. 22 B3 40 56N 74 12W
Precotto, Mil. 9 D6 45 30N 9 13 E
Prédecelles →, Paris 5 D2 48 36N 2 7 E
Pregnana Milanese, Mil. 9 D4 45 30N 9 0 E
Prem Prachakan, Khlong →, Bangk. 15 B2 13 46N 100 35 E
Prenestino Labicano, Rome 9 F10 41 53N 12 33 E
Prenzlauerberg, Berl. 7 A3 52 32N 13 24 E
Presidente Derqui, B.A. 32 A1 34 29 S 58 50W
Presidente Outra, Rodo, Rio J. 31 A1 22 47 S 43 21W
Preston, Melb. 19 E6 37 44 S 144 59 E
Pretos Forros, Sa. dos, Rio J. 31 B2 22 54 S 43 17W
Préville, Mtrl. 20 B5 43 28N 73 29W
Přezletice, Pra. 10 B3 50 9N 14 34 E
Primavalle, Rome 9 F9 41 55N 12 25 E
Primrose, Jobg. 18 F9 26 11 S 28 9 E
Princes B., N.Y. 22 D3 40 30N 74 12W
Princess Elizabeth Park, Sing. 15 F7 1 21N 103 45 E
Progreso, Mdrd. 8 B3 40 27N 3 39W
Progreso Nacional, Méx. 29 A3 19 30N 99 9W
Prosek, Pra. 10 B3 50 7N 14 30 E
Prospect, Syd. 19 A2 33 48 S 150 55 E
Prospect Heights, Chic. 26 A1 42 5N 87 55W
Prospect Hill Park, Bost. 21 C2 42 23N 71 13W
Prospect Park, N.Y. 22 B3 40 55N 74 10W
Prospect Park, Phil. 24 B3 39 53N 75 18W
Prospect Pt., N.Y. 23 B6 40 52N 73 42W
Prospect Res., Syd. 19 A2 33 49 S 150 53 E
Providence, Balt. 25 A3 39 25N 76 34W
Providencia, Stgo 30 J11 33 25 S 70 36W
Průhonice, Pra. 10 C3 50 0N 14 33 E
Pruszków, Wsaw. 10 E5 52 10N 20 48 E
Psikhikón, Ath. 8 H11 38 1N 23 46 E
Pudong, Shang. 14 J12 31 13N 121 30 E
Puduo, Shang. 14 J11 31 15N 121 24 E
Pueblo Libre, Lima 30 G8 12 5 S 77 4W
Pueblo Nuevo, Barc. 8 D6 41 23N 2 11 E
Pueblo Nuevo, Mdrd. 8 B3 40 25N 3 37W
Puente Cascallares, B.A. 32 C2 34 41 S 58 48W
Puente Hills, L.A. 28 C5 33 59N 117 59W
Puffing Billy Station, Melb. 19 F9 37 54 S 145 20 E
Puhuangyu, Beij. 14 B3 39 50N 116 22 E
Puistola, Hels. 3 B5 60 16N 25 2 E
Pukinmäki, Hels. 3 B4 60 15N 24 57 E
Pullach, Mün. 7 G9 48 3N 11 31 E
Pulo, Manila 15 D4 14 34N 121 4 E
Pulo Gadung, Jak. 15 J10 6 11 S 106 54 E
Pumphrey, Balt. 25 B3 39 13N 76 39W
Punchbowl, Syd. 19 B3 33 55 S 151 3 E
Punde, Bomb. 16 H8 18 53N 72 57 E
Punggol, Sing. 15 F8 1 23N 103 54 E
Punggol, Sungei →, Sing. 15 F8 1 24N 103 54 E
Punggol Pt., Sing. 15 F8 1 24N 103 54 E
Punta Brava, La Hab. 30 B2 23 1N 82 29W
Puolarmetsä, Hels. 3 B3 60 11N 24 41 E
Puotila, Hels. 3 B5 60 13N 25 6 E
Purchase, N.Y. 23 A6 41 2N 73 43W
Purfleet, Lon. 4 C6 51 29N 0 14 E
Purkersdorf, Wien 10 G9 48 12N 16 11 E
Purley, Lon. 4 C4 51 20N 0 6W
Puteaux, Paris 5 B3 48 53N 2 14 E
Puth Kalan, Delhi 16 A1 28 42N 77 4 E
Putilkovo, Mos. 11 D8 55 51N 37 22 E
Putnamville Res., Bost. 21 B4 42 36N 70 56W
Putney, Lon. 4 C3 51 27N 0 13W
Putty Hill, Balt. 25 A3 39 22N 76 30W
Putxet, Barc. 8 D5 41 24N 2 8 E
Putzbrunn, Mün. 7 G11 48 4N 11 42 E
Pyeongchang, Sŏul 12 G7 37 35N 126 57 E
Pyramids, El Qâ. 18 D4 29 58N 31 7 E
Pyry, Wsaw. 10 F6 52 8N 21 0 E

Q

Qanât el Ismâilîya, El Qâ. 18 C5 30 7N 31 17 E
Qasemābād, Tehr. 17 C6 35 4N 51 3 E
Qasr-e-Firōzeh, Tehr. 17 D6 35 29N 51 31 E
Qianmen, Beij. 14 B3 39 51N 116 21 E
Qibao, Shang. 14 K11 31 9N 121 20 E
Qingguang, Tianj. 14 D5 39 11N 117 2 E
Qinghua Univ., Beij. 14 A2 40 0N 116 17 E
Qinghuayuan, Beij. 14 B2 39 59N 116 19 E
Qingningsi, Shang. 14 J12 31 16N 121 33 E
Qolhak, Tehr. 17 C5 35 45N 51 26 E
Quadraro, Rome 9 F10 41 51N 12 33 E
Quaid-i-Azam, Kar. 17 G10 24 50N 66 59 E
Qual'eh Murgeh Airport, Tehr. 17 D5 35 38N 51 22 E
Qualiano, Nápl. 9 H11 40 55N 14 9 E
Quannapowitt, L., Bost. 21 B3 42 30N 71 4W
Quartiere Zingone, Mil. 9 E5 45 25N 9 3 E
Quarto, Nápl. 9 H11 40 52N 14 8 E
Quds, Bagd. 17 E8 33 23N 44 24 E
Quebrada Baruta →, Car. 30 E5 10 29N 66 53W
Quebrada Tácagua →, Car. 30 D4 10 36N 67 1W
Quebrada Topo →, Car. 30 D4 10 32N 67 0W
Queen Mary Res., Lon. 4 C2 51 24N 0 27W
Queens Village, N.Y. 23 C6 40 43N 73 44W
Queensbury, Lon. 4 B3 51 35N 0 16W
Queenscliffe, Syd. 19 A4 33 47 S 151 17 E
Queenstown, Sing. 15 G7 1 18N 103 48 E
Quellerina, Jobg. 18 E8 26 9 S 27 56 E
Queluz, Lisb. 8 F7 38 45N 9 14W
Quezon City, Manila 15 D4 14 37N 121 2 E
Quickborn, Hbg. 7 C7 53 43N 9 54 E
Quilicura, Stgo 30 J10 33 22 S 70 43W
Quilmes, B.A. 32 C5 34 43 S 58 15W
Quincy, Bost. 21 D3 42 14N 71 0W
Quincy B., Bost. 21 D4 42 16N 70 59W
Quincy-sous-Sénart, Paris 5 C5 48 40N 2 32 E
Quinta Normal, Stgo 30 J10 33 26 S 70 40W
Quinto Romano, Mil. 9 E5 45 28N 9 7 E
Quirinale, Rome 9 F9 41 53N 12 29 E
Quitaúna, S. Pau. 31 E5 23 31 S 46 48W

R

Raasdorf, Wien 10 G11 48 14N 16 33 E
Raccoon Cr. →, Phil. 24 C3 39 48N 75 21W
Raccoon Str., S.F. 27 A2 37 52N 122 26W
Radevormwald, Ruhr 6 C6 51 12N 7 22 E
Radlett, Lon. 4 A3 51 41N 0 19W
Radlice, Pra. 10 B2 50 3N 14 23 E
Radnor, Phil. 24 A2 40 2N 75 21W
Radonice, Pra. 10 B3 50 8N 14 36 E
Radotin, Pra. 10 C2 49 59N 14 21 E
Rælingen, Oslo 2 B6 59 53N 11 5 E
Rafael Calzada, B.A. 32 C4 34 47 S 58 21W
Rafael Castillo, B.A. 32 C3 34 42 S 58 36W
Raffles Park, Sing. 15 G7 1 19N 103 48 E
Raghunathpur, Calc. 16 D5 22 41N 88 16 E
Rahlstedt, Hbg. 7 D8 53 35N 10 7 E
Rahm, Ruhr 6 B2 51 21N 6 47 E
Rahnsdorf, Berl. 7 B5 52 25N 13 41 E
Rahway, N.Y. 22 D3 40 36N 74 17W
Rail Tree Hill, Bost. 21 B1 42 32N 71 22W
Rainbow Lakes, N.Y. 22 B2 40 53N 74 27W
Rainham, Lon. 4 B6 51 31N 0 11 E
Rainier, Mt., Wash. 25 D8 38 56N 76 57W
Raj Bhawan, Calc. 16 E6 22 33N 88 20 E
Rajakylä, Hels. 3 B5 60 15N 25 5 E
Rajapur, Calc. 16 E5 22 39N 88 11 E
Rajganj, Calc. 16 E5 22 34N 88 14 E
Rajpur, Delhi 16 A2 28 41N 77 12 E
Rákos-patak →, Bud. 10 K14 47 29N 19 12 E
Rákoscsaba, Bud. 10 K14 47 28N 19 17 E
Rákoshegy, Bud. 10 K14 47 27N 19 14 E
Rákosker, Bud. 10 K14 47 28N 19 14 E
Rákoskert, Bud. 10 K14 47 27N 19 18 E
Rákosliget, Bud. 10 K14 47 29N 19 16 E
Rákospalota, Bud. 10 J13 47 34N 19 7 E
Rákosszentmihály, Bud. 10 J13 47 31N 19 8 E
Raków, Wsaw. 10 E6 52 11N 20 56 E
Rakowiec, Wsaw. 10 E6 52 12N 20 58 E
Ramadān, Bagd. 17 F8 33 19N 44 20 E
Ramanathpur, Calc. 16 D5 22 41N 88 14 E
Rambler Channel, H.K. 12 D5 22 21N 114 6 E
Ramblewood, Phil. 24 B5 39 55N 74 56W
Ramenki, Mos. 11 E8 55 41N 37 28 E
Ramersdorf, Mün. 7 G10 48 6N 11 35 E
Ramnathpur, Calc. 16 E5 22 35N 88 18 E
Ramos, Rio J. 31 B2 22 50 S 43 14W
Ramos Mejia, B.A. 32 B3 34 39 S 58 33W
Rampur, Delhi 16 A2 28 44N 77 18 E
Ramsgate, Syd. 19 B3 33 58 S 151 8 E
Ramstadjøen, Oslo 2 B6 59 53N 11 3 E
Rancho Boyeros, La Hab. 30 C2 22 59N 82 22W
Rancho Colorado, Presa de, Méx. 29 B2 19 29N 99 16W
Rancocas Cr. →, Phil. 24 A5 40 2N 74 58W
Rand Afrikaans Univ., Jobg. 18 F9 26 11 S 28 0 E
Rand Airport, Jobg. 18 F9 26 14 S 28 8 E
Randallstown, Balt. 25 A2 39 21N 76 46W
Randburg, Jobg. 18 E8 26 5 S 27 57 E
Randhart, Jobg. 18 F9 26 16 S 28 7 E
Randolph, Bost. 21 D3 42 10N 71 3W
Randolph Hills, Wash. 25 C7 39 3N 77 6W
Randpark, Jobg. 18 E8 26 6 S 27 58 E
Randwick, Syd. 19 B4 33 54 S 151 14 E
Ranelagh, B.A. 32 C5 34 47 S 58 14W
Rannersdorf, Wien 10 H10 48 7N 16 27 E
Raparkrif, Jobg. 18 E8 26 5 S 27 57 E
Raposo, Lisb. 8 F7 38 40N 9 11W
Raritan →, N.Y. 22 D2 40 30N 74 27W
Raritan B., N.Y. 22 E3 40 29N 74 12W
Rasskazovka, Mos. 11 F8 55 38N 37 20 E
Rasta, Stock. 3 E8 59 18N 17 37 E
Rastaala, Hels. 3 B3 60 15N 24 47 E
Rastila, Hels. 3 B5 60 12N 25 7 E
Raszyn, Wsaw. 10 F6 52 9N 20 54 E
Rat Burana, Bangk. 15 B2 13 40N 100 30 E
Ratanpur, Calc. 16 D5 22 49N 88 14 E
Rath, Ruhr 6 C2 51 16N 6 49 E
Ratingen, Ruhr 6 C3 51 18N 6 52 E
Rato, Lisb. 8 F8 38 43N 9 8W
Rauxel, Ruhr 6 A5 51 34N 7 18 E
Ravenswood Pt., S.F. 27 C4 37 30N 122 8W
Rawamangun, Jak. 15 J10 6 11 S 106 52 E
Rayners Lane, Lon. 4 B2 51 34N 0 23W
Raynes Park, Lon. 4 C3 51 24N 0 12W
Raypur, Calc. 16 F6 22 28N 88 22 E
Razdory, Mos. 11 E7 55 44N 37 17 E
Razmitelevo, Len. 11 B5 59 54N 30 39 E
Razor Hill, H.K. 12 D6 22 20N 114 15 E
Reading, Bost. 21 B3 42 31N 71 5W
Reading Highlands, Bost. 21 B3 42 31N 71 5W
Reáglie, Tori. 9 B3 45 3N 7 44 E
Real, Palacio, Mdrd. 8 B2 40 25N 3 43W
Real Felipe, Castillo, Lima 30 G8 12 4 S 77 9W
Real Fuerta, Château de la, La Hab. 30 B2 23 8N 82 20W
Realengo, Rio J. 31 B1 22 52 S 43 24W
Réau, Paris 5 D5 48 36N 2 37 E
Recklinghausen, Ruhr 6 A5 51 37N 7 12 E
Recklinghausen-Süd, Ruhr 6 A5 51 34N 7 14 E
Recoleta, Stgo 30 J11 33 25 S 70 40W
Reconquista →, B.A. 32 B3 34 35 S 58 35W
Red Bank Battle Mon., Phil. 24 B3 39 52N 75 11W
Red Fort, Delhi 16 B2 28 39N 77 14 E
Red Rock, S.F. 27 A2 37 55N 122 25W
Red Square, Mos. 11 E9 55 45N 37 37 E
Redbridge, Lon. 4 B5 51 34N 0 3 E
Redwood City, S.F. 27 D3 37 29N 122 14W
Redwood Cr. →, S.F. 27 C3 37 31N 122 11W
Redwood Pt., S.F. 27 C3 37 32N 122 11W
Redwood Regional Park, S.F. 27 B4 37 48N 122 8W
Reeves Hill, Bost. 21 C1 42 20N 71 20W
Refshaleøen, Købn. 2 D10 55 41N 12 36 E
Regents Park, Jobg. 18 F9 26 14 S 28 3 E
Regents Park, Lon. 4 B4 51 31N 0 9W
Regents Park, Syd. 19 B3 33 52 S 151 1 E
Regi Lagni →, Nápl. 9 H13 40 56N 14 23 E
Regina Margherita, Tori. 9 B2 45 4N 7 34 E
Regla, La Hab. 30 B3 23 7N 82 19W
Rego Park, N.Y. 23 C5 40 43N 73 51W
Reiherstieg, Hbg. 7 D7 53 30N 9 58 E
Reinickendorf, Berl. 7 A3 52 34N 13 22 E
Reinoldikirche, Ruhr 6 A6 51 30N 7 28 E
Reistad, Oslo 2 C1 59 46N 10 16 E
Reitbrook, Hbg. 7 E8 53 28N 10 8 E
Rekola, Hels. 3 B5 60 19N 25 4 E
Rellingen, Hbg. 7 D7 53 39N 9 50 E
Rembertów, Wsaw. 10 E7 52 15N 21 9 E
Remedios de Escalada, B.A. 32 C4 34 43 S 58 24W
Rémola, Laguna del, Barc. 8 E5 41 16N 2 4 E
Remscheid, Ruhr 6 C5 51 11N 7 11 E
Renca, Stgo 30 J10 33 24 S 70 42W
Renca, Cerro, Stgo 30 J10 33 23 S 70 40W
Rener, Ist. 17 A2 41 1N 28 56 E
Renmin Gongyuan, Tianj. 14 E6 39 6N 117 12 E
Rennemoulin, Paris 5 B2 48 50N 2 2 E
Rennie's Mill, H.K. 12 E6 22 18N 114 15 E
Renzel, Hbg. 7 C7 53 43N 9 52 E
Repaupo, Phil. 24 C3 39 48N 75 18W
Repaupo Cr. →, Phil. 24 C3 39 49N 75 20W
Řeporyje, Pra. 10 B1 50 1N 14 18 E
République, Place de la, Paris 5 B4 48 52N 2 22 E
Repy, Pra. 10 B1 50 4N 14 17 E
Resarö, Stock. 3 D13 59 25N 18 20 E
Rescaldna, Mil. 9 D4 45 36N 8 57 E
Research, Melb. 19 E8 37 42 S 145 10 E
Reseda, L.A. 28 A1 34 12N 118 31W
Reservoir, Melb. 19 E7 37 42 S 145 1 E
Reservoir Pond, Bost. 21 D3 42 10N 71 7W
Residenz, Mün. 7 G10 48 8N 11 34 E
Resse, Ruhr 6 A4 51 34N 7 6 E
Reston, Wash. 25 D6 38 57N 77 20W
Retiro, B.A. 32 B4 34 35 S 58 23W
Retiro, Mdrd. 8 B2 40 24N 3 40W
Reutov, Mos. 11 E11 55 45N 37 50 E
Réveillon →, Paris 5 C5 48 42N 2 30 E
Revere, Bost. 21 C3 42 25N 71 0W
Revesby, Syd. 19 B3 33 57 S 151 0 E
Revolucion, Plaza de la, La Hab. 30 B2 23 7N 82 23W
Rexdale, Trto. 20 D7 43 43N 79 35W
Reynolds Channel, N.Y. 23 D6 40 35N 73 41W
Reynosa Tamaulipas, Méx. 29 A2 19 30N 99 10W
Rheem Valley, S.F. 27 A4 37 50N 122 8W
Rhein-Herne Kanal, Ruhr 6 B3 51 29N 6 59 E
Rheinberg, Ruhr 6 A1 51 32N 6 37 E
Rheinhausen, Ruhr 6 B2 51 24N 6 43 E
Rheinkamp, Ruhr 6 B1 51 29N 6 36 E
Rho, Mil. 9 D5 45 31N 9 2 E
Rhodes, Syd. 19 A3 33 49 S 151 6 E
Rhodesfield, Jobg. 18 E10 26 6 S 28 14 E
Rhodon, Paris 5 C2 48 42N 2 3 E
Rhodon →, Paris 5 C2 48 42N 2 4 E
Rhu, Tg., Sing. 15 G8 1 17N 103 51 E
Ribeirão Pires, S. Pau. 31 F7 23 42 S 46 23W
Říčanský →, Pra. 10 B3 50 5N 14 36 E
Říčany, Pra. 10 C3 49 59N 14 39 E
Ricarda, Laguna de la, Barc. 8 E5 41 17N 2 6 E
Richardson B., S.F. 27 A2 37 52N 122 29W
Richmond, Lon. 4 C3 51 27N 0 17W
Richmond, Melb. 19 E7 37 48 S 145 0 E
Richmond, S.F. 27 B2 37 46N 122 27W
Richmond, S.F. 27 A2 37 56N 122 21W
Richmond →, N.Y. 22 D3 40 34N 74 11W
Richmond, Pt., S.F. 27 A2 37 54N 122 23W
Richmond Hill, N.Y. 23 C5 40 41N 73 51W
Richmond Hill, Trto. 20 C8 43 51N 79 24W
Richmond Inner Harbour, S.F. 27 A2 37 54N 122 20W
Richmond Park, Lon. 4 C3 51 26N 0 16W
Richmond Valley, N.Y. 22 D3 40 31N 74 13W
Richvale, Trto. 20 C8 43 51N 79 26W
Rickers I., N.Y. 23 C5 40 47N 73 53W
Rickmansworth, Lon. 4 B2 51 38N 0 28W
Riddel Cr. →, Melb. 19 F8 37 52 S 145 13 E
Riderwood, Balt. 25 A3 39 24N 76 37W
Ridgefield, N.Y. 22 C4 40 49N 74 0W
Ridgefield Park, N.Y. 22 B4 40 52N 74 1W
Ridgewood, N.Y. 23 C5 40 42N 73 53W
Ridley Cr. →, Phil. 24 B2 39 51N 75 20W
Ridley Creek State Park, Phil. 24 B2 39 57N 75 26W
Ridley Park, Phil. 24 B3 39 52N 75 19W
Riedmoos, Mün. 7 F10 48 16N 11 32 E
Riem, Mün. 7 G11 48 8N 11 41 E
Riemke, Ruhr 6 A5 51 30N 7 12 E
Rimac, Lima 30 G8 12 2 S 77 2W
Rimau, Tg., Sing. 15 G7 1 15N 103 48 E
Ringwood, Melb. 19 E8 37 48 S 145 4 E
Rinkeby, Stock. 3 D10 59 23N 17 55 E
Rio Comprido, Rio J. 31 B2 22 55 S 43 12W
Rio de Janeiro, Rio J. 31 B2 22 54 S 43 12W
Rio de Mouro, Lisb. 8 F7 38 46N 9 15W
Rio Hondo →, L.A. 28 B4 34 2N 118 15W
Rio Pequeno, S. Pau. 31 E5 23 34 S 46 44W
Rione Trieste, Nápl. 9 H13 40 52N 14 27 E
Ripley, Lon. 4 D2 51 17N 0 29W
Rippling Ridge, Balt. 25 B3 39 11N 76 37W
Ris, Oslo 2 B4 59 56N 10 41 E
Ris-Orangis, Paris 5 D4 48 38N 2 24 E
Risby, Købn. 2 D8 55 41N 12 19 E
Rishra, Calc. 16 D6 22 42N 88 20 E
Ritan Gongyuan, Beij. 14 B3 39 53N 116 24 E
Ritchie, Wash. 25 D8 38 52N 76 51W
Rithala, Delhi 16 A1 28 43N 77 6 E
Ritorp, Stock. 3 E8 59 12N 17 38 E
Rivalta di Torino, Tori. 9 B1 45 2N 7 31 E
Rivas de Jarama, Mdrd. 8 B3 40 22N 3 31W
Rivas-Vaciamadrio, Mdrd. 8 C3 40 19N 3 30W
Rivasacco, Tori. 9 A1 45 10N 7 29 E
Rive Sud, Canal de la, Mtrl. 20 B4 43 24N 73 31W
River Edge, N.Y. 22 B4 40 56N 74 1W
River Forest, Chic. 26 B2 41 53N 87 49W
River Grove, Chic. 26 B1 41 55N 87 50W
River Pinės, Bost. 21 B2 42 33N 71 17W
River Vale, N.Y. 22 B4 40 59N 74 1W
Riverdale, Chic. 26 D3 41 38N 87 37W
Riverdale, N.Y. 22 B3 40 59N 74 17W
Riverdale, Trto. 20 E8 43 39N 79 21W
Riverdale, Wash. 25 D8 38 57N 76 54W
Riverdale Park, Trto. 20 D8 43 40N 79 21W
Riverhead, Lon. 4 D6 51 16N 0 10 E
Riverlea, Jobg. 18 F8 26 12 S 27 58 E
Riverside, Bost. 21 B2 42 32N 71 18W
Riverside, Chic. 26 C2 41 49N 87 49W
Riverside, N.Y. 23 B5 40 54N 73 54W
Riverside, N.Y. 23 A7 41 1N 73 34W
Riverside, Phil. 24 A5 40 2N 74 57W
Riverton, Phil. 24 A4 40 0N 75 0W
Riverwood, Syd. 19 B3 33 57 S 151 3 E
Rivière-des-Praires, Mtrl. 20 A4 43 38N 73 34W
Rivodora, Tori. 9 B3 45 5N 7 47 E
Rivoli, Tori. 9 B1 45 4N 7 30 E
Riyad, Bagd. 17 F8 33 18N 44 27 E
Rizal, Manila 15 D4 14 33N 121 0 E
Rizal Park, Manila 15 D3 14 35N 120 58 E
Rizel Stadium, Manila 15 D3 14 34N 120 59 E
Røa, Oslo 2 B3 59 57N 10 39 E
Robassomero, Tori. 9 A2 45 11N 7 34 E
Robbins, Chic. 26 D2 41 38N 87 42W
Robert E. Lee Memorial Park, Balt. 25 A3 39 23N 76 40 E
Robertsdale, Chic. 26 C3 41 40N 87 30W
Robertsham, Jobg. 18 F9 26 15 S 28 1 E
Robin Hills, Jobg. 18 E8 26 6 S 27 58 E
Rocha Miranda, Rio J. 31 B1 22 51 S 43 20W
Rochar →, Sing. 15 G8 1 18N 103 52 E
Rochelle Park, N.Y. 22 B4 40 54N 74 4W
Rock Cr. →, Wash. 25 D7 38 54N 77 3W
Rock Creek Park, Wash. 25 D7 38 56N 77 2W
Rockaway, N.Y. 22 D5 40 32N 73 56W
Rockaway Beach, S.F. 27 C2 37 36N 122 29W
Rockaway Islet, N.Y. 23 D5 40 34N 73 53W
Rockaway Neck, N.Y. 22 B2 40 51N 74 21W
Rockaway Point, N.Y. 23 D5 40 33N 73 54W
Rockburn Branch →, Balt. 25 B2 39 13N 76 43W
Rockdale, Balt. 25 A2 39 21N 76 46W
Rockdale, Syd. 19 B3 33 57 S 151 8 E
Rockland, Phil. 24 C1 39 47N 75 34W
Rocklege, Phil. 24 A4 40 4N 75 5W
Rockleigh, N.Y. 22 A5 41 0N 73 55W
Rockville, Wash. 25 C6 39 4N 77 10W
Rockville Centre, N.Y. 23 D7 40 39N 73 38W
Rocky Hill, Phil. 24 B1 39 58N 75 32W
Rocky Ridge, S.F. 27 B4 37 47N 122 2W
Rocky Run →, Wash. 25 D6 38 58N 77 14W
Rodaon, Wien 10 H9 48 8N 16 16 E
Rodeo Cove, S.F. 27 B1 37 49N 122 32W
Rodgers Forge, Balt. 25 A3 39 22N 76 37W
Roding →, Lon. 4 B5 51 30N 0 5 E
Rodość, Wsaw. 10 E8 52 11N 21 11 E
Rødovre, Købn. 2 D9 55 40N 12 26 E
Rodrigo de Freitas, L., Rio J. 31 B2 22 58 S 43 12W
Rodstensfjärden, Stock. 3 E9 59 16N 17 48 E
Roehampton, Lon. 4 C3 51 27N 0 15W
Rogers Park, Chic. 26 A2 42 0N 87 40W
Rohdenhaus, Ruhr 6 C4 51 18N 7 0 E
Röhlinghausen, Ruhr 6 A4 51 30N 7 9 E
Roihuvuon, Hels. 3 B5 60 11N 25 2 E
Roissy, Paris 5 C5 48 47N 2 39 E
Roissy-en-France, Paris 5 A5 49 0N 2 30 E
Rokkō Sanchi, Ōsaka 12 B2 34 44N 135 13 E
Rokko-Zan, Ōsaka 12 B2 34 46N 135 16 E
Rokytka →, Pra. 10 B3 50 6N 14 27 E
Roland Lake, Balt. 25 A3 39 23N 76 38W
Roland Park, Balt. 25 A3 39 20N 76 39W
Roma, Rome 9 F9 41 54N 12 28 E
Római-Fürdö, Bud. 10 J13 47 34N 19 4 E
Romainville, Paris 5 B4 48 52N 2 26 E
Romani, Nápl. 9 H13 40 52N 14 22 E
Romano Banco, Mil. 9 E5 45 25N 9 6 E
Romashkovo, Mos. 11 E7 55 43N 37 19 E
Rome = Roma, Rome 9 F9 41 54N 12 28 E
Romford, Lon. 4 B6 51 34N 0 11 E
Roncáglia, Tori. 9 B1 45 2N 7 29 E
Rönninge, Stock. 3 E9 59 12N 17 45 E
Ronsdorf, Ruhr 6 C5 51 13N 7 11 E
Ronskensiedig, Ruhr 6 A2 51 36N 6 41 E
Rontgental, Berl. 7 A4 52 38N 13 31 E
Roodekop, Jobg. 18 F10 26 17 S 28 11 E
Roodepoort, Jobg. 18 E8 26 9 S 27 53 E
Roodepoort-Wes, Jobg. 18 E8 26 8 S 27 51 E
Roosevelt, N.Y. 23 C7 40 40N 73 35W
Rooty Hill, Syd. 19 A2 33 46 S 150 50 E
Roppongi, Tōkyō 13 C3 35 39N 139 44 E
Rosairinho, Lisb. 8 F8 38 40N 9 0W
Rosanna, Melb. 19 E7 37 44 S 145 4 E
Rosario, La Hab. 30 B2 23 3N 82 21W
Rosario, Manila 15 D4 14 35N 121 4 E
Rose B., Syd. 19 B4 33 51 S 151 16 E
Rose Hill, Wash. 25 E7 38 47N 77 6W
Rose Tree, Phil. 24 B2 39 56N 75 23W
Rosebank, N.Y. 22 D4 40 36N 74 4W
Rosebery, Syd. 19 B4 33 55 S 151 12 E
Rosedal La Candelaria, Méx. 29 B3 19 20N 99 10W
Rosedale, Balt. 25 B3 39 19N 76 31W
Rosedale, N.Y. 23 D6 40 39N 73 43W
Roseiras, S. Pau. 31 E7 23 33 S 46 23W
Roseland, Chic. 26 C3 41 42N 87 37W
Roseland, N.Y. 22 C3 40 49N 74 17W
Roselle, N.Y. 22 D3 40 39N 74 15W
Roselle Park, N.Y. 22 D3 40 39N 74 16W
Rosemead, L.A. 28 B4 34 4N 118 4W
Rosemere, Mtrl. 20 A2 43 34N 73 50W
Rosemont, Chic. 26 B1 41 59N 87 52W
Rosemont, Phil. 24 A3 40 1N 75 19W
Rosenborg Have, Købn. 2 D10 55 41N 12 33 E
Rosengarten, Hbg. 7 D6 53 31N 9 49 E
Rosenthal, Berl. 7 A3 52 35N 13 22 E
Rosettenville, Jobg. 18 F9 26 15 S 28 3 E
Rosherville Dam, Jobg. 18 F9 26 13 S 28 6 E
Rósio, Mil. 9 E4 45 25N 8 57 E
Rösjön, Stock. 3 D11 59 26N 18 0 E
Roskilde, Købn. 2 E7 55 38N 12 5 E
Roskilde Fjord, Købn. 2 D7 55 45N 12 4 E
Roslags-Näsby, Stock. 3 D11 59 25N 18 2 E
Roslindale, Bost. 21 D3 42 17N 71 7W
Roslyn, N.Y. 23 C7 40 47N 73 38W
Roslyn, Phil. 24 A4 40 7N 75 8W
Roslyn Estates, N.Y. 23 C6 40 47N 73 40W
Roslyn Harbour, N.Y. 23 C7 40 48N 73 38W
Rosne →, Paris 5 B4 48 58N 2 25 E
Rosny-sous-Bois, Paris 5 B5 48 52N 2 30 E
Ross, S.F. 27 A1 37 57N 122 33W
Rosslyn, Wash. 25 D7 38 53N 77 4W
Rossville, Balt. 25 A4 39 20N 76 28W
Rossville, N.Y. 22 D3 40 32N 74 12W
Rosta, Tori. 9 B1 45 4N 7 27 E
Rotbach →, Ruhr 6 A2 51 34N 6 41 E
Rothenburgsort, Hbg. 7 D8 53 32N 10 2 E
Rotherbaum, Hbg. 7 D7 53 33N 9 58 E
Rotherhithe, Lon. 4 C4 51 29N 0 2W
Rothneusiedl, Wien 10 H10 48 8N 16 23 E
Rothschmaige, Mün. 7 F9 48 14N 11 27 E
Rouge →, Trto. 20 D9 43 47N 79 12W
Rouge Hill, Trto. 20 D10 43 48N 79 6W
Round I., H.K. 12 E6 22 13N 114 11 E
Roundshaw, Lon. 4 C4 51 20N 0 7W
Roussigny, Paris 5 D2 48 38N 2 6 E
Rowland, L.A. 28 B5 34 0N 117 55W
Rowley, Bost. 21 A4 42 43N 70 52W
Rowville, Melb. 19 F8 37 55 S 145 14 E
Roxboro, Mtrl. 20 A3 43 30N 73 48W
Roxborough, Phil. 24 A3 40 1N 75 13W
Roxbury, Bost. 21 D3 42 19N 71 5W
Roxbury, N.Y. 23 D5 40 33N 73 53W
Roxeth, Lon. 4 B2 51 33N 0 20W
Royal Observatory, H.K. 12 E6 22 18N 114 10 E
Royal Park, Melb. 19 E6 37 46 S 144 57 E
Röylä, Hels. 3 B3 60 18N 24 42 E
Royston Park, Lon. 4 B2 51 36N 0 22W
Rozas, Portilleros de las, Mdrd. 8 B2 40 29N 3 49W
Roztoky, Pra. 10 B2 50 9N 14 23 E
Rubbianetta, Tori. 9 B2 45 9N 7 34 E
Rubi →, Barc. 8 D5 41 26N 2 0 E
Rubio Woods, Chic. 26 D2 41 38N 87 45W
Rublovo, Mos. 11 E8 55 47N 37 21 E
Ruchyi, Len. 11 A4 60 0N 30 25 E
Rud, Oslo 2 B6 59 56N 11 0 E
Rüdinghausen, Ruhr 6 B6 51 26N 7 22 E
Rudnevka →, Mos. 11 E11 55 43N 37 56 E
Rudolfsheim, Wien 10 G10 48 12N 16 20 E
Rudolfshöhe, Berl. 7 A5 52 37N 13 44 E
Rudow, Berl. 7 B3 52 24N 13 29 E
Rueil-Malmaison, Paris 5 B3 48 52N 2 11 E
Ruffys Cr. →, Melb. 19 E7 37 45 S 145 7 E
Ruggeberg, Ruhr 6 C6 51 16N 7 23 E
Ruhlsdorf, Berl. 7 B2 52 22N 13 15 E
Ruhr →, Ruhr 6 B3 51 27N 6 56 E
Ruhrort, Ruhr 6 B2 51 27N 6 44 E
Ruislip, Lon. 4 B2 51 34N 0 24W
Rumelihisari, Ist. 17 A3 41 4N 29 2 E
Rumeln, Ruhr 6 B1 51 24N 6 39 E
Rumyantsevo, Mos. 11 F8 55 38N 37 25 E
Rungis, Paris 5 C4 48 44N 2 20 E
Runnemede, Phil. 24 B4 39 50N 75 4W
Ruotsinkylä, Hels. 3 A4 60 21N 24 57 E
Rusāfa, Bagd. 17 E8 33 21N 44 23 E
Rush Green, Lon. 4 B6 51 33N 0 10 E
Russa, Calc. 16 F6 22 29N 88 21 E
Russell Lea, Syd. 19 B4 33 52 S 151 10 E
Rustad, Oslo 2 B2 59 56N 10 24 E
Rustenfeld, Wien 10 H10 48 7N 16 23 E
Rusville, Jobg. 18 E10 26 9 S 28 18 E
Rutherford, N.Y. 22 C4 40 49N 74 6W
Rüttenscheid, Ruhr 6 B3 51 25N 6 58 E
Ruxton, Balt. 25 A3 39 23N 76 38W
Ruzyně, Pra. 10 B1 50 5N 14 17 E
Rybatskaya, Len. 11 B4 59 59N 30 29 E
Rybatskoye, Len. 11 B4 59 50N 30 29 E
Rydalmere, Syd. 19 A3 33 48 S 151 2 E
Rydboholm, Stock. 3 D12 59 26N 18 12 E
Ryde, Syd. 19 A3 33 48 S 151 6 E
Rye, N.Y. 23 B6 40 58N 73 40W
Rynfield, Jobg. 18 E10 26 9 S 28 19 E
Ryogoku, Tōkyō 13 B3 35 40N 139 48 E
Rysäkari, Hels. 3 C4 60 6N 24 50 E
Rzhevka, Len. 11 B5 59 59N 30 31 E

Serangoon Garden 45

S

Saadōn, Bagd. 17 F8 33 19N 44 25 E
Saarn, Ruhr 6 B3 51 24N 6 51 E
Saavedra, B.A. 32 B4 34 33 S 58 29W
Saboli, Delhi 16 A2 28 42N 77 18 E
Sabugo, Lisb. 8 F7 38 49N 9 17W
Saburovo, Mos. 11 D7 55 53N 37 15 E
Säbysjön, Stock. 3 D10 59 26N 17 52 E
Sabzi Mandi, Delhi 16 A2 28 40N 77 12 E
Sacavém, Lisb. 8 F8 38 47N 9 5W
Saclay, Paris 5 C3 48 43N 2 10 E
Saclay, Étang de, Paris 5 C2 48 44N 2 9 E
Sacoma, S. Pau. 31 E6 23 36 S 46 35W
Sacré-Coeur, Paris 5 B4 48 53N 2 20 E
Sacrow, Berl. 7 B1 52 25N 13 6 E
Sacrower See, Berl. 7 B1 52 26N 13 6 E
Sadang, Sŏul 12 H7 37 29N 126 58 E
Sadar Bazar, Delhi 16 B2 28 39N 77 11 E
Saddām City, Bagd. 17 E8 33 23N 44 27 E
Saddle Brook, N.Y. 22 B4 40 53N 74 5W
Saddle River, N.Y. 22 A4 41 1N 74 6W
Saddle Rock, N.Y. 23 C6 40 47N 73 45W
Sadr, Kar. 17 G11 24 51N 67 2 E
Sadyba, Wsaw. 10 E7 52 11N 21 3 E
Saedo, Tōkyō 13 C2 35 30N 139 33 E
Saensaep, Khlong →, Bangk. 15 B2 13 44N 100 32 E
Sáenz Pena, B.A. 32 B3 34 37 S 58 32W
Safdar Jang Airport, Delhi 16 B2 28 35N 77 12 E
Safdar Jangs Tomb, Delhi 16 B2 28 35N 77 12 E
Safraköy, Ist. 17 A1 41 0N 28 48 E
Saft el Laban, El Qâ. 18 C5 30 1N 31 10 E
Sag Bridge, Chic. 26 C1 41 41N 87 55W
Sagamore Neck, N.Y. 23 B8 40 53N 73 29W
Saganashkee Slough, Chic. 26 C1 41 41N 87 53W
Sagene, Oslo 2 B4 59 55N 10 46 E
Sagrada Família, Temple de, Barc. 8 D6 41 24N 2 10 E
Sahapur, Calc. 16 E5 22 31N 88 11 E
Sahibabad, Delhi 16 A1 28 45N 77 4 E
Sai Kung, H.K. 12 D6 22 22N 114 16 E
Sai Wan Ho, H.K. 12 E6 22 17N 114 12 E
Sai Ying Pun, H.K. 12 E5 22 17N 114 8 E
Saido, Tōkyō 13 A2 35 52N 139 39 E
Sailmouille →, Paris 5 D3 48 37N 2 17 E
St. Albans, N.Y. 23 C6 40 42N 73 44W
St. Andrä, Wien 10 G9 48 19N 16 12 E
St. Andrews, Jobg. 18 E9 26 9 S 28 7 E
St. Aubin, Paris 5 C2 48 44N 2 8 E
St. Augustin, Mtrl. 20 A2 43 37N 73 58W
St. Basil's Cathedral, Mos. 11 E9 55 45N 37 38 E
St.-Benoit, Paris 5 C1 48 40N 1 54 E
St.-Brice-sous-Forêt, Paris 5 A4 49 0N 2 21 E
St.-Cloud, Paris 5 B3 48 50N 2 12 E
St.-Cyr-l'École, Paris 5 C2 48 47N 2 4 E
St.-Cyr-l'École, Aérodrome de, Paris 5 C2 48 48N 2 4 E
St. Davids, Phil. 24 A2 40 2N 75 23W
St.-Denis, Paris 5 B4 48 56N 2 20 E
St. Eustache, Mtrl. 20 A2 43 33N 73 54W
St.-Forget, Paris 5 C2 48 42N 2 0 E
St. Georg, Hbg. 7 D8 53 33N 10 1 E
St.-Germain, Forêt de, Paris 5 B2 48 57N 2 5 E
St. Germain-en-Laye, Paris 5 B2 48 53N 2 4 E
St.-Germain-lès-Corbeil, Paris 5 D4 48 37N 2 29 E
St.-Gratien, Paris 5 B3 48 58N 2 17 E
St. Helier, Lon. 4 C3 51 23N 0 11W
St.-Hubert, Mtrl. 20 B5 43 29N 73 25W
St. Isaac's Cathedral, Len. 11 B3 59 55N 30 19 E
St. Jacques →, Mtrl. 20 B5 43 26N 73 29W
St.-Jean-de-Beauregard, Paris 5 D3 48 39N 2 10 E
St.-Jean-de-dieu, Mtrl. 20 A4 43 34N 73 31W
St. Joseph-du-Lac, Mtrl. 20 A1 43 32N 74 0W
St. Katherine's Dock, Lon. 4 B4 51 30N 0 5W
St. Kilda, Melb. 19 F6 37 51 S 144 58 E
St. Lambert, Mtrl. 20 A5 43 30N 73 29W
St.-Lambert, Paris 5 C2 48 43N 2 1 E
St.-Laurent, Mtrl. 20 A3 43 30N 73 43W
St. Lawrence, Mtrl. 20 A5 43 26N 73 29W
St.-Lazare, Gare, Paris 5 B3 48 52N 2 19 E
St.-Léonard, Mtrl. 20 A4 43 35N 73 34W
St. Leonards, Syd. 19 B4 33 50 S 151 12 E
St. Leu-la-Forêt, Paris 5 A3 49 1N 2 14 E
St.-Louis, L., Mtrl. 20 B3 43 24N 73 48W
St. Magelungen, Stock. 3 E11 59 13N 18 4 E
St.-Mandé, Paris 5 B4 48 50N 2 24 E
St.-Mard, Paris 5 A6 49 2N 2 41 E
St.-Martin, Mtrl. 20 A3 43 33N 73 45W
St.-Martin, Bois, Paris 5 C5 48 48N 2 35 E
St. Mary Cray, Lon. 4 C5 51 23N 0 7 E
St.-Maur-des-Fossés, Paris 5 C4 48 48N 2 29 E
St.-Maurice, Paris 5 C4 48 49N 2 24 E
St.-Mesmes, Paris 5 B6 48 59N 2 41 E
St. Michaeliskirche, Hbg. 7 D7 53 32N 9 59 E
St. Michael's, Sing. 15 G8 1 19N 103 51 E
St.-Michel, Mtrl. 20 A4 43 34N 73 37W
St.-Michel-sur-Orge, Paris 5 D3 48 38N 2 18 E
St. Nikolaus-Kirken, Pra. 10 B2 50 5N 14 23 E
St. Nom-la-Bretèche, Paris 5 B2 48 51N 2 1 E
St.-Ouen, Paris 5 B4 48 56N 2 20 E
St. Ouen-l'Aumône, Paris 5 A2 49 2N 2 6 E
St. Pauli, Hbg. 7 D7 53 33N 9 57 E
St. Pauls Cathedral, Lon. 4 B4 51 30N 0 5W
St. Paul's Cray, Lon. 4 C5 51 23N 0 6 E
St. Petersburg = Leningrad, Len. 11 B3 59 55N 30 15 E
St.-Pierre, Mtrl. 20 B4 43 27N 73 38W
St. Prix, Paris 5 A3 49 0N 2 15 E
St.-Quentin, Étang de, Paris 5 C2 48 47N 2 0 E
St. Quentin-en-Yvelines, Paris 5 C1 48 46N 1 57 E
St.-Rémy-lès-Chevreuse, Paris 5 C2 48 42N 2 4 E
St.-Thibault-des-Vignes, Paris 5 B6 48 52N 2 41 E
St. Veit, Wien 10 G9 48 11N 16 16 E
St.-Vincent-de-Paul, Mtrl. 20 A4 43 36N 73 39W
Ste.-Anne-de-Bellevue, Mtrl. 20 B2 43 24N 73 55W
Ste.-Catherine, Mtrl. 20 B4 43 24N 73 34W
Ste.-Dorothée, Mtrl. 20 A3 43 31N 73 48W
Ste.-Gemme, Paris 5 B1 48 52N 1 59 E
Ste.-Geneviève, Mtrl. 20 B2 43 28N 73 51W
Ste.-Geneviève-des-Bois, Paris 5 D3 48 38N 2 19 E
Ste.-Hélène, Î., Mtrl. 20 A4 43 31N 73 32W
Ste. Marthe-sur-le-Lac, Mtrl. 20 A2 43 31N 73 56W
Ste.-Rose, Mtrl. 20 A3 43 37N 73 46W
Ste. Thérèse, Mtrl. 20 A3 43 38N 73 49W
Ste. Thérèse-Ouest, Mtrl. 20 A2 43 36N 73 50W
Saiwai, Tōkyō 13 C3 35 32N 139 41 E
Sakai, Ōsaka 12 C3 34 34N 135 27 E
Sakai →, Tōkyō 13 D1 35 27N 139 29 E
Sakai Harbour, Ōsaka 12 C3 34 36N 135 26 E
Sakanoshita, Tōkyō 13 B2 35 48N 139 30 E
Sakra, P., Sing. 15 G7 1 15N 103 41 E
Sakuragi, Tōkyō 13 D2 35 28N 139 38 E
Salam, Bagd. 17 E8 33 20N 44 20 E
Salaryevo, Mos. 11 F8 55 37N 37 25 E
Salem, Bost. 21 B4 42 30N 70 54W
Salem, Stock. 3 E9 59 13N 17 46 E
Salem Harbor, Bost. 21 B4 42 30N 70 52W
Salem Maritime Nat. Hist. Site, Bost. 21 B4 42 31N 70 52W
Salemstaden, Stock. 3 E9 59 13N 17 46 E
Salkhia, Calc. 16 E6 22 36N 88 21 E
Salmannsdorf, Wien 10 G9 48 14N 16 14 E
Salmdorf, Mün. 7 G11 48 7N 11 43 E
Salmedina, Mdrd. 8 C3 40 18N 3 35W
Salomea, Wsaw. 10 E6 52 11N 20 55 E
Salsette I., Bomb. 16 G8 19 2N 72 53 E
Salt Cr. →, Chic. 26 C1 41 51N 87 54W
Salt Cr. →, Melb. 19 E7 37 45 S 145 4 E
Salt Water L., Calc. 16 E6 22 33N 88 26 E
Saltholm, Købn. 2 E11 55 38N 12 46 E
Saltsjö-Duvnäs, Stock. 3 E12 59 18N 18 12 E
Saltsjöbaden, Stock. 3 E12 59 16N 18 18 E
Saltykovka, Mos. 11 E11 55 45N 37 54 E
Salvatorkirche, Ruhr 6 B2 51 26N 6 45 E
Sam Sen, Khlong →, Bangk. 15 B2 13 45N 100 33 E
Samatya, Ist. 17 B2 40 59N 28 55 E
Samoueo, Lisb. 8 F8 38 43N 8 59W
Sampaloc, Manila 15 D3 14 36N 120 59 E
Samphanthawong, Bangk. 15 B2 13 44N 100 31 E
Samrong, Bangk. 15 C2 13 39N 100 35 E
Samseon, Sŏul 12 G8 37 34N 127 0 E
San Agustin, Lima 30 G8 12 1 S 77 9W
San Agustin Atlapulco, Méx. 29 B4 19 23N 89 57 E
San Andreas Fault, S.F. 27 D3 37 27N 122 18W
San Andreas L., S.F. 27 C2 37 35N 122 25W
San Andres, B.A. 32 B3 34 34 S 58 33W
San Andrés, Barc. 8 D6 41 26N 2 11 E
San Andrés Ahuayucan, Méx. 29 C3 19 13N 99 7W
San Andrés Atenco, Méx. 29 A2 19 32N 99 13W
San Andrés Totoltepec, Méx. 29 C2 19 15N 99 10W
San Andrián de Besós, Barc. 8 D6 41 25N 2 13 E
San Angel, Méx. 29 B2 19 20N 99 11W
San Antonia, Manila 15 E3 14 29N 120 53 E
San Antonio de Padua, B.A. 32 C2 34 40 S 58 42W
San Augustin Ohtenco, Méx. 29 C3 19 12N 99 0W
San Bartolo Ameyalco, Méx. 29 C2 19 19N 99 16W
San Bartolomé Coatepec, Méx. 29 B2 19 23N 99 18W
San Basilio, Rome 9 F10 41 56N 12 35 E
San Bóvio, Mil. 9 E6 45 27N 9 18 E
San Bruno, S.F. 27 C2 37 36N 122 24W
San Bruno, Pt., S.F. 27 C2 37 39N 122 22W
San Bruno Mt., S.F. 27 B2 37 41N 122 26W
San Carlos, S.F. 27 C3 37 30N 122 16W
San Carlos de la Cabana, Forteresse, La Hab. 30 B2 23 8N 82 20W
San Clemente del Llobregat, Barc. 8 E4 41 19N 1 59 E
San Cristobal, Mdrd. 8 B3 40 25N 3 35W
San Cristobal, Cerro, Stgo 30 J11 33 25 S 70 38W
San Cristoforo, Mil. 9 E5 45 26N 9 9 E
San Donato Milanese, Mil. 9 E6 45 24N 9 16 E
San Felice, Tori. 9 B3 45 1N 7 46 E
San Feliu de Llobregat, Barc. 8 D5 41 22N 2 2 E
San Fernando, B.A. 32 A3 34 26 S 58 32W
San Fernando, L.A. 28 A2 34 17N 118 26W
San Fernando Airport, L.A. 28 A2 34 17N 118 25W
San Fernando de Henares, Mdrd. 8 B3 40 25N 3 31W
San Fernando Valley, L.A. 28 A1 34 12N 118 31W
San Francisco, S.F. 27 B2 37 46N 122 23W
San Francisco, Univ. of, S.F. 27 B2 37 47N 122 27W
San Francisco B., S.F. 27 C3 37 39N 122 14W
San Francisco Chimalpa, Méx. 29 B1 19 26N 99 20W
San Francisco Culhuacán, Méx. 29 C3 19 19N 99 8W
San Francisco de Paula, La Hab. 30 B3 23 3N 82 17W
San Francisco Int. Airport, S.F. 27 C2 37 37N 122 22W
San Francisco Solano, B.A. 32 C5 34 46 S 58 19W
San Francisco State Univ., S.F. 27 B2 37 43N 122 28W
San Francisco Tecoxpa, Méx. 29 C3 19 12N 99 0W
San Francisco Tlalnepantla, Méx. 29 C3 19 12N 99 8W
San Fruttuoso, Mil. 9 D6 45 34N 9 14 E
San Gabriel, L.A. 28 B4 34 5N 118 5W
San Gabriel →, L.A. 28 C4 33 53N 118 6W
San Gabriel Pk., L.A. 28 A4 34 14N 118 5W
San Giacomo, Tori. 9 A2 45 11N 7 36 E
San Gillio, Tori. 9 B2 45 8N 7 32 E
San Giórgio a Crem, Nápl. 9 J13 40 50N 14 20 E
San Giovanni a Teduccio, Nápl. 9 J12 40 49N 14 18 E
San Giuseppe Vesuviano, Nápl. 9 H13 40 50N 14 29 E
San Gregorio Atlapulco, Méx. 29 C3 19 15N 99 4W
San Isidro, B.A. 32 A3 34 28 S 58 30W
San Isidro, Lima 30 G8 12 5 S 77 2W
San Isidro, Manila 15 D4 14 38N 121 5 E
San Jerónimo Lidice, Méx. 29 C2 19 19N 99 14W
San Jerónimo Miacatlán, Méx. 29 C4 19 12N 98 59W
San Jorge, Castelo de, Lisb. 8 F8 38 42N 9 8W
San Jose Del Alamo, La Hab. 30 B3 23 6N 82 17W
San José Rio Hondo, Méx. 29 B2 19 26N 99 14W
San Juan →, Manila 15 D4 14 35N 121 0 E
San Juan de Aragón, Méx. 29 B3 19 28N 99 4W
San Juan de Aragón, Parque, Méx. 29 B3 19 27N 99 4W
San Juan de Lurigancho, Lima 30 F8 11 59 S 77 0W
San Juan de Miraflores, Lima 30 H9 12 10 S 76 58W
San Juan del Monte, Manila 15 D4 14 36N 121 1 E
San Juan Ixtacala, Méx. 29 A2 19 31N 99 10W
San Juan Ixtayopan, Méx. 29 C4 19 14N 98 59W
San Juan Toltotepec, Méx. 29 B2 19 28N 99 15W
San Juan y San Pedro Tezompa, Méx. 29 C4 19 12N 98 57W
San Just Desvern, Barc. 8 D5 41 22N 2 4 E
San Justo, B.A. 32 C3 34 40 S 58 33W
San Leandro, S.F. 27 B4 37 43N 122 9W
San Leandro B., S.F. 27 B3 37 45N 122 13W
San Leandro Cr. →, S.F. 27 B3 37 44N 122 12W
San Lorenzo, Mil. 9 D4 45 34N 8 57 E
San Lorenzo, S.F. 27 B4 37 41N 122 6W
San Lorenzo →, Méx. 29 B2 19 28N 99 17W
San Lorenzo, I., Lima 30 G7 12 6 S 77 12W
San Lorenzo Acopilco, Méx. 29 C1 19 19N 99 20 E
San Lorenzo Chimalco, Méx. 29 B4 19 24N 89 58 E
San Lorenzo Tezonco, Méx. 29 C3 19 19N 99 3W
San Lorenzo Tlacoyucan, Méx. 29 C3 19 10N 99 2W
San Lucas Xochimanca, Méx. 29 C3 19 15N 99 6W
San Luis, Lima 30 G8 12 4 S 77 0W
San Luis Tlaxialtemalco, Méx. 29 C3 19 16N 99 2W
San Marino, L.A. 28 B4 34 7N 118 5W
San Martin, Barc. 8 D6 41 24N 2 11 E
San Martin de Porras, Lima 30 G8 12 1 S 77 5W
San Martino, Tori. 9 B3 45 6N 7 47 E
San Mateo, S.F. 27 C3 37 33N 122 19W
San Mateo Cr. →, S.F. 27 C2 37 31N 122 22W
San Mateo Tecoloapan, Méx. 29 A2 19 35N 99 14W
San Mateo Xalpa, Méx. 29 C3 19 13N 99 8W
San Máuro Torinese, Tori. 9 B3 45 6N 7 45 E
San Miguel, B.A. 32 B2 34 32 S 58 43W
San Miguel, Lima 30 G8 12 5 S 77 6W
San Miguel, Manila 15 D3 14 36N 120 59 E
San Miguel, Stgo 30 J11 33 29 S 70 39W
San Miguel Ajusco, Méx. 29 C2 19 13N 99 11W
San Miguel Xicalco, Méx. 29 C3 19 13N 99 9W
San Nicholas, Manila 15 D3 14 36N 120 57 E
San Nicola, Rome 9 F9 41 58N 12 21 E
San Nicolás Totolapan, Méx. 29 C2 19 16N 99 16W
San Nicolás Viejo, Méx. 29 A1 19 31N 99 21W
San Onófrio, Rome 9 F9 41 57N 12 25 E
San Pablo, Méx. 29 B4 19 25N 89 56 E
San Pablo, S.F. 27 A2 37 57N 122 20W
San Pablo, Pt., S.F. 27 A2 37 57N 122 25W
San Pablo Cr. →, S.F. 27 A2 37 58N 122 22W
San Pablo Ostotepec, Méx. 29 C3 19 11N 99 5W
San Pablo Res., S.F. 27 A3 37 55N 122 14W
San Pablo Ridge, S.F. 27 A3 37 55N 122 15W
San Pablo Str., S.F. 27 A2 37 58N 122 25W
San Pancrázio, Tori. 9 B2 45 6N 7 32 E
San Pedro, Méx. 29 B4 19 24N 89 56 E
San Pedro, Pt., S.F. 27 C1 37 35N 122 31W
San Pedro Actopan, Méx. 29 C3 19 12N 99 4W
San Pedro Martir, Barc. 8 D5 41 23N 2 6 E
San Pedro Martir, Méx. 29 C2 19 16N 99 10W
San Pedro Zacatenco, Méx. 29 A3 19 30N 99 6W
San Pietro, Rome 9 F9 41 53N 12 27 E
San Pietro, Tori. 9 B3 45 1N 7 45 E
San Pietro a Patierno, Nápl. 9 H12 40 53N 14 17 E
San Pietro all'Olmo, Mil. 9 E5 45 29N 9 0 E
San Po Kong, H.K. 12 D6 22 20N 114 11 E
San Quentin, S.F. 27 A2 37 56N 122 27W
San Rafael, S.F. 27 A1 37 58N 122 30W
San Rafael B., S.F. 27 A2 37 57N 122 28W
San Rafael Chamapa, Méx. 29 B2 19 27N 99 15W
San Rafael Hills, L.A. 28 A3 34 10N 118 12W
San Roque, Manila 15 D4 14 37N 121 5 E
San Salvador Cuauhtenco, Méx. 29 C3 19 11N 99 8W
San Salvador de la Punta, Forteresse, La Hab. 30 B2 23 8N 82 21W
San Sebastiano al Vesúvio, Nápl. 9 H13 40 50N 14 22 E
San Siro, Mil. 9 E5 45 28N 9 7 E
San Souci, Syd. 19 B3 33 59 S 151 8 E
San Telmo, B.A. 32 B4 34 37 S 58 23W
San Vicenc dels Horts, Barc. 8 D5 41 23N 2 0 E
San Vitaliano, Nápl. 9 H13 40 55N 14 28 E
San Vito, Mil. 9 E5 45 24N 9 0 E
San Vito, Nápl. 9 J13 40 49N 14 22 E
San Vito, Tori. 9 B3 45 2N 7 41 E
Sandbakken, Oslo 2 C5 59 49N 10 54 E
Sandermosen, Oslo 2 A4 60 0N 10 48 E
Sanderstead, Lon. 4 D4 51 19N 0 4W
Sandheide, Ruhr 6 C3 51 12N 6 56 E
Sandhurst, Jobg. 18 E9 26 6 S 28 3 E
Sandown, Jobg. 18 E9 26 5 S 28 4 E
Sandown Racecourse, Lon. 4 C2 51 22N 0 21W
Sandringham, Jobg. 18 E9 26 8 S 28 6 E
Sands Point, N.Y. 23 B6 40 50N 73 43W
Sandton, Jobg. 18 E9 26 5 S 28 4 E
Sandungen, Oslo 2 B2 59 52N 10 21 E
Sandvika, Oslo 2 B3 59 53N 10 32 E
Sandy Pond, Bost. 21 C2 42 26N 71 18W
Sånga, Stock. 3 D9 59 21N 17 42 E
Sangano, Tori. 9 B1 45 1N 7 26 E
Sangenjaya, Tōkyō 13 C2 35 37N 139 39 E
Sangley Pt., Manila 15 E3 14 29N 120 54 E
Sangone →, Tori. 9 B2 45 1N 7 32 E
Sangye, Sŏul 12 G8 37 38N 127 3 E
Sankrail, Calc. 16 E5 22 33N 88 13 E
Sanlihe, Beij. 14 B2 39 53N 116 18 E
Sanlintang, Shang. 14 K11 31 9N 121 29 E
Sannois, Paris 5 B3 48 58N 2 15 E
Sanpada, Bomb. 16 G9 19 3N 73 0 E
Sans, Barc. 8 D5 41 22N 2 7 E
Sant Ambrogio, Basilica di, Mil. 9 E6 45 27N 9 10 E
Sant Boi de Llobregat, Barc. 8 D5 41 20N 2 2 E
Sant Cugat, Barc. 8 D5 41 28N 2 5 E
Santa Ana, Manila 15 D4 14 34N 121 0 E
Santa Ana Tlacotenco, Méx. 29 C4 19 11N 98 58W
Santa Bárbara, Morro de, Rio J. 31 B1 22 56 S 43 26W
Santa Catalina, B.A. 32 C4 34 47 S 58 24W
Santa Cecilia Tepetlapa, Méx. 29 C3 19 13N 99 5W
Santa Clara, Méx. 29 A3 19 33N 99 3W
Santa Coloma de Cervelló, Barc. 8 D5 41 21N 2 0 E
Santa Coloma de Gramanet, Barc. 8 D6 41 27N 2 12 E
Santa Cruz, Bomb. 16 G7 19 4N 72 51 E
Santa Cruz →, La Hab. 30 B2 23 4N 82 29W
Santa Cruz, Ilhe de, Rio J. 31 B3 22 51 S 43 7W
Santa Cruz Alcapixca, Méx. 29 C3 19 14N 99 4W
Santa Cruz Ayotusco, Méx. 29 B1 19 22N 99 21W
Santa Cruz de Olorde, Barc. 8 D5 41 25N 2 3 E
Santa Cruz Int. Airport, Bomb. 16 G8 19 5N 72 51 E
Santa Cruz Meyehualco, Méx. 29 B3 19 20N 99 2W
Santa Elena, Manila 15 D4 14 38N 121 5 E
Santa Eligênia Consolação, S. Pau. 31 E6 23 32 S 46 38W
Santa Emilia, Stgo 30 J11 33 23 S 70 39W
Santa Eulalia, Barc. 8 D6 41 25N 2 10 E
Santa Fe, La Hab. 30 B2 23 4N 82 30W
Santa Fe Flood Control Basin, L.A. 28 B5 34 7N 117 57W
Santa Fe Springs, L.A. 28 C4 33 56N 118 3W
Santa Isabel Ixtapan, Méx. 29 A4 19 35N 89 57W
Santa Julia, Stgo 30 K11 33 30 S 70 35W
Santa Lucia, Nápl. 9 J12 40 49N 14 15 E
Santa Margherita, Tori. 9 B3 45 3N 7 43 E
Santa Maria Aztahuacán, Méx. 29 B3 19 21N 99 2W
Santa Maria del Rosario, La Hab. 30 B3 23 3N 82 15W
Santa Maria Tulpetlac, Méx. 29 A3 19 34N 99 3W
Santa Martha Acatitla, Méx. 29 B3 19 21N 99 2W
Santa Monica, Car. 30 E5 10 28N 66 53W
Santa Monica, L.A. 28 B2 34 1N 118 29W
Santa Monica B., L.A. 28 C1 33 58N 118 30W
Santa Monica Mt., L.A. 28 B2 34 6N 118 29W
Santa Rosa, Lima 30 F8 11 59 S 77 5W
Santa Rosa De Locobe, Stgo 30 J11 33 25 S 70 33W
Santa Rosa Xochiac, Méx. 29 C2 19 19N 99 17W
Santa Tereza, S. Pau. 31 F6 23 40 S 46 33W
Santa Ursula Xitla, Méx. 29 C2 19 16N 99 11W
Santa Ynez Canyon →, L.A. 28 B1 34 2N 118 33W
Santahamina, Hels. 3 C5 60 8N 25 2 E
Santana, S. Pau. 31 D6 23 29 S 46 36W
Sant'Anastasia, Nápl. 9 H13 40 51N 14 24 E
Sant'Ántimo, Nápl. 9 H12 40 56N 14 14 E
Santeny, Paris 5 C5 48 43N 2 34 E
Santiago, Stgo 30 J11 33 26 S 70 40W
Santiago Acahualtepec, Méx. 29 B3 19 20N 99 0W
Santiago de Las Vegas, La Hab. 30 C2 22 58N 82 22W
Santiago Tepalcatlalpan, Méx. 29 C3 19 14N 99 8W
Santiago Tepatlaxco, Méx. 29 B1 19 28N 99 20W
Sant'Ilário, Mil. 9 D4 45 34N 8 59 E
Santo Amaro, Lisb. 8 F7 38 42N 9 11W
Santo Amaro, S. Pau. 31 E5 23 39 S 46 42W
Santo Andre, Lisb. 8 G8 38 38N 9 3W
Santo André, S. Pau. 31 E6 23 39 S 46 41W
Santo António, Qta. de, Lisb. 8 G7 38 39N 9 15W
Santo António da Charneca, Lisb. 8 G8 38 37N 9 1W
Santo Niño, Manila 15 D4 14 38N 121 5 E
Santo Rosario, Manila 15 D4 14 33N 121 4 E
Santo Thomas, Univ. of, Manila 15 D3 14 36N 120 59 E
Santo Tomas, Manila 15 D4 14 33N 121 4 E
Santolan, Manila 15 D4 14 36N 121 4 E
Santos Dumont, Aéroport, Rio J. 31 B3 22 54 S 43 9W
Santos Lugares, B.A. 32 B3 34 35 S 58 35W
Santoshpur, Calc. 16 E5 22 31N 88 16 E
Santragachi, Calc. 16 E5 22 35N 88 17 E
Sanyuanli, Gzh. 14 G8 23 8N 113 14 E
São Bernardo do Campo, S. Pau. 31 F6 23 42 S 46 32W
São Caetano do Sul, S. Pau. 31 E6 23 37 S 46 34W
São Cristovão, Rio J. 31 B2 22 53 S 43 13W
São Domingos, Centro, Rio J. 31 B3 22 53 S 43 6W
São Gonçalo, Rio J. 31 A3 22 49 S 43 4W
São João Climaco, S. Pau. 31 E6 23 37 S 46 35W
São João da Talha, Lisb. 8 F8 38 49N 9 5W
São João de Meriti, Rio J. 31 A1 22 47 S 43 18W
São Lucas, Parque, S. Pau. 31 E6 23 35 S 45 32W
São Mateus, Rio J. 31 A1 22 48 S 43 22W
São Miguel Paulista, S. Pau. 31 D7 23 29 S 46 26W
São Paulo, S. Pau. 31 E6 23 32 S 46 38W
Sapa, Calc. 16 E5 22 30N 88 15 E
Sapang Baho →, Manila 15 D4 14 33N 121 4 E
Sapateiro →, S. Pau. 31 E5 23 35 S 46 41W
Saranap, S.F. 27 A4 37 52N 122 4W
Sarandi, B.A. 32 C4 34 40 S 58 20W
Saraswati →, Calc. 16 D5 22 46N 88 15 E
Sarcelles, Paris 5 B4 48 59N 2 22 E
Sarecky →, Pra. 10 B2 50 7N 14 23 E
Sarenga, Calc. 16 E5 22 31N 88 12 E
Sarilhos Grandes, Lisb. 8 F9 38 40N 8 58W
Sarilhos Pequenos, Lisb. 8 F9 38 40N 8 58W
Sarimbun, Sing. 15 F7 1 24N 103 40 E
Saronikòs Kòlpos, Ath. 8 J10 37 52N 23 38 E
Sarriá, Barc. 8 D5 41 22N 2 8 E
Sarria, Car. 30 D5 10 30N 66 53W
Sarsol, Bomb. 16 G9 19 2N 73 0 E
Sartrouville, Paris 5 B3 48 56N 2 10 E
Sasad, Bud. 10 K13 47 28N 19 0 E
Sasashita, Tōkyō 13 D2 35 23N 139 35 E
Sasel, Hbg. 7 D8 53 39N 10 7 E
Sashalom, Bud. 10 J14 47 30N 19 10 E
Saska, Wsaw. 10 E7 52 14N 21 3 E
Sassafras, Melb. 19 F9 37 52 S 145 20 E
Satalice, Pra. 10 B3 50 7N 14 34 E
Satgachi, Calc. 16 E6 22 37N 88 25 E
Satghara, Calc. 16 D6 22 43N 88 21 E
Satpukur, Calc. 16 E6 22 37N 88 24 E
Sätra, Stock. 3 E10 59 17N 17 54 E
Satsuna, Calc. 16 F5 22 28N 88 17 E
Sau Mau Ping, H.K. 12 E6 22 19N 114 13 E
Saugus, Bost. 21 C3 42 28N 71 0W
Saugus →, Bost. 21 C3 42 27N 70 58W
Saulx-les-Chartreux, Paris 5 C3 48 41N 2 16 E
Sausalito, S.F. 27 A2 37 51N 122 28W
Sausset →, Paris 5 B5 48 56N 2 28 E
Savigny-sur-Orge, Paris 5 C4 48 40N 2 21 E
Savijärvi, Hels. 3 A6 60 21N 25 19 E
Savonera, Tori. 9 B2 45 7N 7 36 E
Sawah Besar, Jak. 15 H9 6 8 S 106 49 E
Sawyer Ridge, S.F. 27 C2 37 34N 122 24W
Saxonville, Bost. 21 D1 42 19N 71 24W
Saxonwold, Jobg. 18 E9 26 9 S 28 2 E
Scarborough, Trto. 20 D9 43 44N 79 14W
Scarsdale, N.Y. 23 B6 40 58N 73 47W
Sceaux, Paris 5 C3 48 46N 2 17 E
Schalke, Ruhr 6 A4 51 33N 7 4 E
Schapenrust, Jobg. 18 F11 26 15 S 28 21 E
Scharfenberg, Berl. 7 A2 52 35N 13 15 E
Scheiblingstein, Wien 10 G9 48 16N 16 13 E
Schenefeld, Hbg. 7 D7 53 36N 9 52 E
Scherlebech, Ruhr 6 A4 51 37N 7 8 E
Schildow, Berl. 7 A3 52 38N 13 22 E
Schiller Park, Chic. 26 B1 41 56N 87 52W
Schiller Woods, Chic. 26 B1 41 57N 87 51W
Schlachtensee, Berl. 7 B2 52 26N 13 13 E
Schlossgarten, Berl. 7 A2 52 31N 13 18 E
Schmachtendorf, Ruhr 6 A2 51 32N 6 48 E
Schmargendorf, Berl. 7 B2 52 28N 13 17 E
Schmöckwitz, Berl. 7 B5 52 22N 13 38 E
Schnelsen, Hbg. 7 D7 53 38N 9 54 E
Scholven, Ruhr 6 A4 51 36N 7 0 E
Schönblick, Berl. 7 B5 52 27N 13 43 E
Schönbrunn, Schloss, Wien 10 G9 48 10N 16 19 E
Schöneberg, Berl. 7 B3 52 28N 13 20 E
Schönefeld, Berl. 7 B4 52 23N 13 30 E
Schöneiche, Berl. 7 B5 52 28N 13 41 E
Schönwalde, Berl. 7 A1 52 37N 13 7 E
Schottenwald, Wien 10 G9 48 13N 16 16 E
Schuir, Ruhr 6 B3 51 23N 6 59 E
Schulzendorf, Berl. 7 A2 52 36N 13 16 E
Schuylkill →, Phil. 24 B3 39 53N 75 11W
Schwabing, Mün. 7 G10 48 10N 11 35 E
Schwafheim, Ruhr 6 B1 51 25N 6 36 E
Schwanebeck, Berl. 7 A4 52 37N 13 32 E
Schwanenwerder, Berl. 7 B2 52 26N 13 10 E
Schwarz →, Ruhr 6 C3 51 19N 6 44 E
Schwarzbachtal, Ruhr 6 C3 51 17N 6 51 E
Schwarze, Ruhr 6 A2 51 31N 6 48 E
Schwarze Berge, Hbg. 7 E7 53 27N 9 54 E
Schwarzlackenau, Wien 10 G10 48 16N 16 23 E
Schwechat, Wien 10 H10 48 8N 16 28 E
Schweflinghaüsen, Ruhr 6 C6 51 15N 7 24 E
Schwelm, Ruhr 6 C5 51 16N 7 16 E
Scisciano, Nápl. 9 H13 40 54N 14 28 E
Scoresby, Melb. 19 F8 37 54 S 145 14 E
Scotch Plains, N.Y. 22 D2 40 39N 74 22W
Scotts Level Br. →, Balt. 25 A2 39 23N 76 45W
Sea Cliff, N.Y. 23 B7 40 50N 73 38W
Seabrook, Wash. 25 D9 38 58N 76 49W
Seacliff, S.F. 27 B2 37 47N 122 28W
Seaforth, Syd. 19 A4 33 48 S 151 15 E
Seagate, N.Y. 22 D4 40 34N 74 0W
Seal Slough, S.F. 27 C3 37 34N 122 17W
Sears Tower, Chic. 26 B3 41 52N 87 38W
Seat Pleasant, Wash. 25 D8 38 53N 76 53W
Seavey Hill, Bost. 21 A1 42 42N 71 23W
Šeberov, Pra. 10 B3 50 0N 14 30 E
Secaucus, N.Y. 22 C4 40 47N 74 3W
Secondigliano, Nápl. 9 H12 40 53N 14 15 E
Seddinsee, Berl. 7 B5 52 23N 13 41 E
Sedgefield, N.Y. 22 B2 40 51N 74 26W
Sedriano, Mil. 9 E4 45 29N 8 58 E
Seeberg, Berl. 7 A5 52 33N 13 41 E
Seeburg, Berl. 7 A1 52 30N 13 7 E
Seefeld, Berl. 7 A5 52 37N 13 40 E
Seegefeld, Berl. 7 A1 52 33N 13 5 E
Seehof, Berl. 7 B2 52 24N 13 17 E
Segeltorp, Stock. 3 E10 59 16N 17 56 E
Segrate, Mil. 9 E6 45 29N 9 17 E
Seguro, Mil. 9 E5 45 28N 9 3 E
Seine →, Paris 5 C4 48 48N 2 25 E
Seixal, Lisb. 8 G8 38 38N 9 5W
Selbeck, Ruhr 6 B3 51 22N 6 51 E
Selbecke, Ruhr 6 C6 51 20N 7 28 E
Selby, Jobg. 18 F9 26 12 S 28 2 E
Seletar, P., Sing. 15 F8 1 26N 103 51 E
Seletar, Sungei →, Sing. 15 F8 1 25N 103 51 E
Seletar Hills, Sing. 15 F8 1 23N 103 52 E
Seletar Res., Sing. 15 F7 1 24N 103 48 E
Selghar, Bomb. 16 H9 18 57N 73 1 E
Selhurst, Lon. 4 C4 51 23N 0 5W
Selsdon, Lon. 4 C4 51 20N 0 3W
Selytsy, Len. 11 B6 59 56N 30 42 E
Sembawang, Sing. 15 F7 1 26N 103 49 E
Sembawang, Sungei →, Sing. 15 F7 1 26N 103 48 E
Sembawang Hill, Sing. 15 F7 1 22N 103 49 E
Semsvatn, Oslo 2 B2 59 51N 10 25 E
Senago, Mil. 9 D5 45 34N 9 7 E
Senan, Jak. 15 J10 6 10 S 106 50 E
Sénart, Forêt de, Paris 5 D4 48 40N 2 28 E
Senayan Sports Centre, Jak. 15 J9 6 12 S 106 47 E
Sendling, Mün. 7 G10 48 7N 11 31 E
Sengeløse, Købn. 2 D8 55 40N 12 14 E
Senju, Tōkyō 13 B3 35 44N 139 48 E
Senlikköy, Ist. 17 B1 40 58N 28 47 E
Senlisse, Paris 5 C1 48 41N 1 59 E
Senneville, Mtrl. 20 B2 43 24N 73 57W
Senri, Ōsaka 12 B4 34 49N 135 30 E
Senriyama, Ōsaka 12 B4 34 47N 135 30 E
Sentosa, Sing. 15 G7 1 15N 103 49 E
Sentosa, P., Sing. 15 G7 1 15N 103 49 E
Seo Dae Mun, Sŏul 12 G7 37 34N 126 55 E
Seobinngo, Sŏul 12 G7 37 31N 126 58 E
Seoggwan, Sŏul 12 G8 37 35N 127 2 E
Seong Bug, Sŏul 12 G8 37 35N 127 0 E
Seong Dong, Sŏul 12 G8 37 33N 127 3 E
Seongsu, Sŏul 12 G8 37 32N 127 2 E
Seoul = Sŏul, Sŏul 12 G8 37 34N 127 51 E
Seoul National Univ., Sŏul 12 H7 37 28N 126 57 E
Seoul Tower, Sŏul 12 G7 37 32N 126 59 E
Sepah Salar Mosque, Tehr. 17 C5 35 40N 51 25 E
Sepolia, Ath. 8 H11 38 1N 23 42 E
Sepulveda, L.A. 28 A2 34 13N 118 27W
Sepulveda Flood Control Basin, L.A. 28 A2 34 10N 118 28W
Serangoon, P., Sing. 15 F8 1 23N 103 55 E
Serangoon, Sungei →, Sing. 15 F8 1 23N 103 55 E
Serangoon Garden, Sing. 15 F8 1 21N 103 51 E

46 Serangoon Harbour

Serangoon Harbour, *Sing.* **15 F8** 1 23N 103 57 E
Seraya, P., *Sing.* **15 G7** 1 16N 103 43 E
Serebryanka, *Mos.* **11 E11** 55 44N 37 53 E
Serebryanka →, *Mos.* **11 E10** 55 47N 37 44 E
Serednevo, *Mos.* **11 F7** 55 35N 37 18 E
Serramonte, *S.F.* **27 C2** 37 39N 122 28W
Servon, *Paris* **5 C5** 48 43N 2 35 E
Šestajovice, *Pra.* **10 B3** 50 6N 14 40 E
Sesto San Giovanni, *Mil.* **9 D6** 45 31N 9 13 E
Seta Budi, *Jak.* **15 J9** 6 12 S 106 49 E
Setagaya-Ku, *Tōkyō* **13 C2** 35 37N 139 36 E
Sete Pontes, *Rio J.* **31 B3** 22 50 S 43 4W
Seter, *Oslo* **2 B4** 59 52N 10 47 E
Séttimo Milanese, *Mil.* **9 E5** 45 28N 9 3 E
Séttimo Torinese, *Tori.* **9 B3** 45 8N 7 46 E
Settsu, *Ōsaka* **12 B4** 34 47N 135 33 E
Setuny →, *Mos.* **11 E8** 55 43N 37 21 E
Seurasaari, *Hels.* **3 B4** 60 11N 24 53 E
Seutula, *Hels.* **3 A4** 60 20N 24 52 E
Seven Corners, *Wash.* **25 D7** 38 53N 77 9W
Seven Kings, *Lon.* **4 B5** 51 33N 0 5 E
Sevenoaks, *Lon.* **4 D6** 51 16N 0 11 E
Severn Hills, *Syd.* **19 A2** 33 46 S 150 57 E
Sévesco →, *Mil.* **9 D5** 45 35N 9 9 E
Sevran, *Paris* **5 B5** 48 56N 2 31 E
Sèvres, *Paris* **5 C3** 48 49N 2 13 E
Sewaren, *N.Y.* **22 D3** 40 33N 74 15W
Sewell, *Phil.* **24 C4** 39 46N 75 8W
Sewri, *Bomb.* **16 H8** 18 59N 72 50 E
Seya, *Tōkyō* **13 D1** 35 28N 139 28 E
Sforzesso, Castello, *Mil.* **9 E6** 45 28N 9 10 E
Sha Kok Mei, *H.K.* **12 D6** 22 23N 114 16 E
Sha Tin, *H.K.* **12 D6** 22 23N 114 11 E
Sha Tin Wai, *H.K.* **12 D6** 22 22N 114 11 E
Shaala, *Bagd.* **17 E7** 33 22N 44 16 E
Shabanzhuang, *Beij.* **14 B3** 39 51N 116 25 E
Shabbona Woods, *Chic.* **26 D3** 41 36N 87 33W
Shabrâmant, *El Qâ.* **18 D5** 29 56N 31 11 E
Shadipur, *Delhi* **16 B2** 28 38N 77 11 E
Shady Oak, *Wash.* **25 C6** 39 1N 77 17W
Shahabad, *Bomb.* **16 G9** 19 0N 73 2 E
Shahar, *Bomb.* **16 G8** 19 5N 72 52 E
Shahdara, *Delhi* **16 A2** 28 40N 77 18 E
Shahe, *Gzh.* **14 G8** 23 9N 113 19 E
Shahpur Jel, *Delhi* **16 B2** 28 33N 77 12 E
Shahr-e-Rey, *Tehr.* **17 D5** 35 36N 51 25 E
Shaikh Aomar, *Bagd.* **17 E8** 33 20N 44 23 E
Shakarpor Khas, *Delhi* **16 B2** 28 37N 77 14 E
Shakurpur, *Delhi* **16 A1** 28 40N 77 8 E
Sham Shui Po, *H.K.* **12 E5** 22 19N 114 9 E
Shamepur, *Delhi* **16 A1** 28 44N 77 8 E
Shamian, *Gzh.* **14 G8** 23 6N 113 13 E
Shamspur, *Delhi* **16 B2** 28 36N 77 17 E
Shan Liu, *H.K.* **12 D6** 22 23N 114 16 E
Shan Mei, *H.K.* **12 D6** 22 24N 114 10 E
Shanghai, *Shang.* **14 J12** 31 14N 121 28 E
Shanghetou, *Tianj.* **14 D5** 39 11N 117 0 E
Shanjing, *Gzh.* **14 G9** 23 4N 113 23 E
Sharea Faisal, *Kar.* **17 G11** 24 52N 67 8 E
Sharon Hill, *Phil.* **24 B3** 39 54N 75 16W
Sharp I., *H.K.* **12 D6** 22 21N 114 17 E
Sharp Park, *S.F.* **27 C2** 37 38N 122 29W
Shau Kei Wan, *H.K.* **12 E6** 22 16N 114 13 E
Shawocun, *Beij.* **14 B2** 39 53N 116 13 E
Shawsheen Village, *Bost.* **21 A3** 42 40N 71 7W
Shea Stadium, *N.Y.* **23 C5** 40 45N 73 50W
Sheakhala, *Calc.* **16 D5** 22 45N 88 10 E
Shebāb, *Bagd.* **17 E8** 33 20N 44 26 E
Sheepshead B., *N.Y.* **22 D5** 40 35N 73 55W
Shek Hang, *H.K.* **12 D6** 22 24N 114 17 E
Shek Kip Mei, *H.K.* **12 D5** 22 20N 114 9 E
Shek Lung Kung, *H.K.* **12 D5** 22 23N 114 5 E
Shek O, *H.K.* **12 E6** 22 13N 114 15 E
Shellpot Cr. →, *Phil.* **24 C1** 39 44N 75 30W
Shelter Cove, *S.F.* **27 C1** 37 35N 122 30W
Shelter I., *H.K.* **12 E6** 22 19N 114 17 E
Shemirānāt, *Tehr.* **17 C5** 35 47N 51 25 E
Shenfield, *Lon.* **4 B6** 51 37N 0 19 E
Sheng Fa Shan, *H.K.* **12 D5** 22 23N 114 5 E
Shenley, *Lon.* **4 A3** 51 41N 0 16W
Shepherds Bush, *Lon.* **4 B3** 51 30N 0 13W
Shepperton, *Lon.* **4 C2** 51 23N 0 26W
Sherborn, *Bost.* **21 D1** 42 14N 71 22W
Sherman Oaks, *L.A.* **28 B2** 34 8N 118 29W
Sherwood Forest, *S.F.* **27 A3** 37 57N 122 16W
Shet Bandar, *Bomb.* **16 H8** 18 57N 72 55 E
Sheung Lau Wan, *H.K.* **12 E6** 22 16N 114 16 E
Sheung Wan, *H.K.* **12 E5** 22 16N 114 9 E
Sheva, *Bomb.* **16 H8** 18 56N 72 57 E
Sheva Nhava, *Bomb.* **16 H8** 18 57N 72 57 E
Shiba, *Tōkyō* **13 C3** 35 38N 139 45 E
Shiba →, *Tōkyō* **13 A3** 35 50N 139 44 E
Shibuya-Ku, *Tōkyō* **13 C3** 35 39N 139 41 E
Shijōnawate, *Ōsaka* **12 B4** 34 44N 135 37 E
Shimo-okudomi, *Tōkyō* **13 A1** 35 52N 139 27 E
Shimo-tsuchidana, *Tōkyō* **13 D1** 35 24N 139 27 E
Shimogawara, *Tōkyō* **13 C1** 35 39N 139 27 E
Shimosalo, *Tōkyō* **13 B2** 35 45N 139 31 E
Shimosasame, *Tōkyō* **13 B2** 35 48N 139 37 E
Shimoshakujii, *Tōkyō* **13 B2** 35 43N 139 35 E
Shimotomi, *Tōkyō* **13 B1** 35 49N 139 27 E
Shimotsuruma, *Tōkyō* **13 D1** 35 29N 139 26 E
Shimura, *Tōkyō* **13 B3** 35 46N 139 41 E
Shinagawa B., *Tōkyō* **13 C3** 35 35N 139 48 E
Shinagawa-Ku, *Tōkyō* **13 C3** 35 36N 139 44 E
Shing Mun Res., *H.K.* **12 D5** 22 23N 114 8 E
Shinjuku-Ku, *Tōkyō* **13 B3** 35 41N 139 42 E
Shinkoiwa, *Tōkyō* **13 B4** 35 43N 139 51 E
Shinnakano, *Tōkyō* **13 B3** 35 41N 139 40 E
Shinoha, *Tōkyō* **13 A3** 35 50N 139 49 E
Shipai, *Gzh.* **14 G9** 23 8N 113 20 E
Shipley, *Balt.* **25 B3** 39 12N 76 39W
Shippan Pt., *N.Y.* **23 A7** 41 1N 73 31W
Shirako, *Tōkyō* **13 B2** 35 47N 139 36 E
Shiraone, *Bomb.* **16 G9** 19 2N 73 1 E
Shirinashi →, *Ōsaka* **12 C3** 34 38N 135 27 E
Shirley, *Lon.* **4 C4** 51 22N 0 2W
Shiro, *Tōkyō* **13 B2** 35 48N 139 30 E
Shirogane, *Tōkyō* **13 C3** 35 37N 139 44 E
Shisha Hai, *Beij.* **14 B3** 39 55N 116 21 E
Shitou, *Gzh.* **14 G9** 23 1N 113 23 E
Shiweitang, *Gzh.* **14 G8** 23 6N 113 12 E
Shogunle, *Lagos* **18 A2** 6 34N 7 20 E
Shomolu, *Lagos* **18 A2** 6 32N 7 22 E
Shooters Hill, *Lon.* **4 C5** 51 28N 0 4 E
Shoreditch, *Lon.* **4 B4** 51 31N 0 4W
Shoreham, *Lon.* **4 D6** 51 19N 0 10 E
Short Hills, *N.Y.* **22 C2** 40 44N 74 21W
Shortlands, *Lon.* **4 C5** 51 23N 0 0 E
Shrirampur, *Calc.* **16 D5** 22 45N 88 21 E
Shuangkou, *Tianj.* **14 D5** 39 14N 117 2 E
Shuangtuo, *Tianj.* **14 D6** 39 13N 117 19 E
Shubrâ el Kheima, *El Qâ.* **18 C5** 30 6N 31 14 E
Shuikuo, *Gzh.* **14 F8** 23 10N 113 10 E
Shuishang Gongyuan, *Tianj.* **14 E5** 39 5N 117 9 E
Shukunoshō, *Ōsaka* **12 A4** 34 50N 135 31 E
Sibbo, *Hels.* **3 A6** 60 21N 25 14 E
Sibbo fjärden, *Hels.* **3 B6** 60 11N 25 17 E
Siboney, *La Hab.* **30 B2** 23 4N 82 28W
Sibpur, *Calc.* **16 E5** 22 34N 88 19 E
Sibřina, *Pra.* **10 B4** 50 3N 14 40 E
Sidcup, *Lon.* **4 C5** 51 25N 0 6 E
Siebenhirten, *Wien* **10 H9** 48 8N 16 17 E
Siedlung, *Berl.* **7 A1** 52 35N 13 7 E
Siekierki, *Wsaw.* **10 E7** 52 12N 21 4 E
Sielce, *Wsaw.* **10 E7** 52 12N 21 2 E
Siemensstadt, *Berl.* **7 A2** 52 32N 13 16 E
Sieraków, *Wsaw.* **10 E5** 52 19N 20 48 E
Sierra Madre, *L.A.* **28 B4** 34 9N 118 3W
Sievering, *Wien* **10 G10** 48 15N 16 20 E
Siggerud, *Oslo* **2 C5** 59 47N 10 52 E
Siheung, *Sŏul* **12 H7** 37 28N 126 54 E
Siikajärvi, *Hels.* **3 B2** 60 17N 24 31 E
Sikátorpuszta, *Bud.* **10 J14** 47 34N 19 10 E
Silampur, *Delhi* **16 B2** 28 39N 77 16 E
Silschede, *Ruhr* **6 B6** 51 21N 7 22 E
Silver Hill, *Wash.* **25 E8** 38 49N 76 55W
Silver L., *Bost.* **21 B3** 42 33N 71 9W
Silver Mt., *L.A.* **28 A5** 34 12N 117 55W
Silver Spring, *Wash.* **25 D7** 38 59N 77 2W
Silverfields, *Jobg.* **18 E7** 26 7 S 27 49 E
Silvertown, *Lon.* **4 C5** 51 29N 0 1 E
Simla, *Calc.* **16 E6** 22 35N 88 22 E
Simmer and Jack Mines, *Jobg.* **18 F9** 26 12 S 28 8 E
Simmering, *Wien* **10 G10** 48 10N 16 24 E
Simmering Heide, *Wien* **10 G10** 48 10N 16 26 E
Simonkylä, *Hels.* **3 B5** 60 18N 25 1 E
Simpang Bedok, *Sing.* **15 G8** 1 19N 103 56 E
Simsalö, *Hels.* **3 B6** 60 14N 25 17 E
Singao, *N.Y.* **22 B3** 40 53N 74 14W
Singapore, *Sing.* **15 G8** 1 17N 103 51 E
Singapore →, *Sing.* **15 G8** 1 17N 103 51 E
Singapore, Univ. of, *Sing.* **15 G7** 1 19N 103 49 E
Singapore Airport, *Sing.* **15 F8** 1 21N 103 54 E
Singlewell, *Lon.* **4 C7** 51 25N 0 21 E
Singur, *Calc.* **16 D5** 22 48N 88 13 E
Sinicka →, *Mos.* **11 D7** 55 52N 37 18 E
Sinki, Selat, *Sing.* **15 G7** 1 15N 103 42 E
Sinrim, *Sŏul* **12 H7** 37 28N 126 56 E
Sinsa, *Sŏul* **12 G8** 37 31N 127 0 E
Sinthi, *Calc.* **16 E6** 22 37N 88 23 E
Sinweol, *Sŏul* **12 G7** 37 31N 126 51 E
Sipoo, *Hels.* **3 A6** 60 21N 25 14 E
Sipoon selkä, *Hels.* **3 B6** 60 11N 25 17 E
Sipson, *Lon.* **4 C2** 51 29N 0 26W
Siqeil, *El Qâ.* **18 C4** 30 7N 31 10 E
Şişli, *Ist.* **17 A2** 41 3N 28 58 E
Skå, *Stock.* **3 E9** 59 19N 17 44 E
Skärholmen, *Stock.* **3 E10** 59 16N 17 53 E
Skarpäng, *Stock.* **3 D11** 59 26N 18 0 E
Skarpnäck, *Stock.* **3 E11** 59 16N 18 7 E
Skarpö, *Stock.* **3 D13** 59 24N 18 22 E
Skedsmo, *Oslo* **2 B6** 59 59N 11 2 E
Skhodnya →, *Mos.* **11 D8** 55 53N 37 23 E
Skodsborg, *Købn.* **2 D10** 55 49N 12 34 E
Skogby, *Hels.* **3 A2** 60 21N 24 40 E
Skogen, *Oslo* **2 C1** 59 48N 10 18 E
Skogsbyn, *Hels.* **3 A6** 60 20N 25 18 E
Skokie, *Chic.* **26 A2** 42 2N 87 43W
Skokie →, *Chic.* **26 A2** 42 3N 87 46W
Skokie Lagoons, *Chic.* **26 A2** 42 7N 87 46W
Skoklefall, *Oslo* **2 B4** 59 50N 10 40 E
Sköndal, *Stock.* **3 E11** 59 15N 18 6 E
Skovlunde, *Købn.* **2 D9** 55 42N 12 25 E
Skovshoved, *Købn.* **2 D10** 55 45N 12 35 E
Skøyen, *Oslo* **2 B4** 59 55N 10 40 E
Skui, *Oslo* **2 B2** 59 55N 10 25 E
Skuldelev, *Købn.* **2 D7** 55 46N 12 1 E
Skullerud, *Oslo* **2 B5** 59 51N 10 50 E
Skuru, *Stock.* **3 E12** 59 18N 18 12 E
Skytta, *Oslo* **2 B5** 59 59N 10 54 E
Slade Green, *Lon.* **4 C6** 51 27N 0 11 E
Slagsta, *Stock.* **3 E9** 59 15N 17 48 E
Slakteren, *Oslo* **2 A4** 60 1N 10 40 E
Slattum, *Oslo* **2 A5** 60 0N 10 55 E
Slemmestad, *Oslo* **2 C2** 59 46N 10 29 E
Slependen, *Oslo* **2 B3** 59 52N 10 30 E
Sligo Cr. →, *Wash.* **25 C7** 39 0N 77 1W
Slipi, *Jak.* **15 J9** 6 11 S 106 47 E
Slipi Orchard Garden, *Jak.* **15 J9** 6 10 S 106 46 E
Slivenec, *Pra.* **10 B2** 50 1N 14 21 E
Slone Canyon Res., *L.A.* **28 B2** 34 6N 118 27W
Sloop Channel, *N.Y.* **23 D7** 40 36N 73 31W
Sluhy, *Pra.* **10 A3** 50 11N 14 33 E
Służew, *Wsaw.* **10 E7** 52 10N 21 1 E
Służewiec, *Wsaw.* **10 E7** 52 10N 21 0 E
Smalleytown, *N.Y.* **22 D2** 40 39N 74 28W
Smestad, *Oslo* **2 B2** 59 55N 10 25 E
Smichov, *Pra.* **10 B2** 50 4N 14 23 E
Smith Forest Preserve, *Chic.* **26 B2** 41 59N 87 45W
Smith Mills, *N.Y.* **22 A2** 41 0N 74 23W
Smithfield, *Syd.* **19 B2** 33 51 S 150 56 E
Smoke Rise, *N.Y.* **22 A2** 41 0N 74 24W
Smørumnedre, *Købn.* **2 D8** 55 44N 12 7 E
Snakeden Br. →, *Wash.* **25 D6** 38 58N 77 17W
Snarøya, *Oslo* **2 B3** 59 52N 10 33 E
Snättringe, *Stock.* **3 E10** 59 15N 17 58 E
Snoldelev, *Købn.* **2 E8** 55 33N 12 10 E
Snostrup, *Købn.* **2 D7** 55 48N 12 7 E
Søborg, *Købn.* **2 D9** 55 43N 12 29 E
Sobreda, *Lisb.* **8 G7** 38 39N 9 11W
Soccavo, *Nápl.* **9 H12** 40 50N 14 11 E
Sodegaura, *Tōkyō* **13 D4** 35 24N 139 57 E
Söderby, *Stock.* **3 D12** 59 24N 18 12 E
Söderkullalandet, *Hels.* **3 B6** 60 14N 25 19 E
Södermalm, *Stock.* **3 E11** 59 18N 18 4 E
Södersätra, *Stock.* **3 D10** 59 27N 17 56 E
Södertälje, *Stock.* **3 E8** 59 11N 17 36 E
Sodingen, *Ruhr* **6 A5** 51 32N 7 15 E
Sodpur, *Calc.* **16 D6** 22 42N 88 24 E
Södra Björkfjärden, *Stock.* **3 E8** 59 17N 17 34 E
Soeurs, Î. des, *Mtrl.* **20 B4** 43 27N 73 32W
Sognsvatn, *Oslo* **2 B4** 59 58N 10 43 E
Soignolles-en-Brie, *Paris* **5 D6** 48 39N 2 43 E
Soisy-sous-Montmorency, *Paris* **5 B3** 48 59N 2 17 E
Soisy-sur-Seine, *Paris* **5 D4** 48 39N 2 27 E
Sojiji Temple, *Tōkyō* **13 D3** 35 29N 139 40 E
Sok Kwu Wan, *H.K.* **12 E5** 22 12N 114 7 E
Sōka, *Tōkyō* **13 B3** 35 49N 139 48 E
Sokolniki, *Mos.* **11 E10** 55 47N 37 40 E
Sokolniki Park, *Mos.* **11 E10** 55 48N 37 40 E
Sokołów, *Wsaw.* **10 F6** 52 9N 20 51 E
Solalinden, *Mün.* **7 G11** 48 5N 11 42 E
Solaro, *Mil.* **9 D5** 45 36N 9 6 E
Solers, *Paris* **5 D6** 48 39N 2 43 E
Solingen, *Ruhr* **6 C4** 51 10N 7 5 E
Sollentuna, *Stock.* **3 D10** 59 25N 17 56 E
Søllerød, *Købn.* **2 D9** 55 48N 12 29 E
Sollihøgda, *Oslo* **2 B2** 59 58N 10 21 E
Solln, *Mün.* **7 G10** 48 4N 11 31 E
Solna, *Stock.* **3 D10** 59 21N 17 59 E
Solntsevo, *Mos.* **11 F8** 55 39N 37 24 E
Solymár, *Bud.* **10 J12** 47 35N 18 56 E
Somapah Changi, *Sing.* **15 F8** 1 20N 103 57 E
Somapan Serangoon, *Sing.* **15 F8** 1 21N 103 53 E
Somborn, *Ruhr* **6 B6** 51 29N 7 20 E
Somerdale, *Phil.* **24 B4** 39 50N 75 1W
Somerset, *Wash.* **25 D7** 38 57N 77 5W
Somerton, *Phil.* **24 A4** 40 7N 75 1W
Somerville, *Bost.* **21 C3** 42 22N 71 5W
Somma, Mte., *Nápl.* **9 H13** 40 50N 14 25 E
Somma Vesuviana, *Nápl.* **9 H13** 40 52N 14 26 E
Sonari, *Bomb.* **16 H8** 18 54N 72 59 E
Sønderby, *Købn.* **2 D7** 55 44N 12 2 E
Søndersø, *Købn.* **2 D9** 55 46N 12 21 E
Sondre Elvågo, *Oslo* **2 B5** 59 51N 10 54 E
Sonnberg, *Wien* **10 G9** 48 19N 16 15 E
Sørby, *Oslo* **2 C4** 59 49N 10 41 E
Sørkedalen, *Oslo* **2 A3** 60 1N 10 37 E
Soroksár, *Bud.* **10 K13** 47 24N 19 7 E
Soroksár-Újtelep, *Bud.* **10 K13** 47 25N 19 7 E
Soroksari Duna →, *Bud.* **10 K13** 47 25N 19 5 E
Sørsdal, *Oslo* **2 B1** 59 50N 10 16 E
Sosenka →, *Mos.* **11 E10** 55 46N 37 42 E
Sosnovaya, *Len.* **11 C2** 59 49N 30 8 E
Sottungsby, *Hels.* **3 B5** 60 16N 25 8 E
Sŏul, *Sŏul* **12 G8** 37 34N 127 51 E
Soundview, *N.Y.* **23 C5** 40 49N 73 53W
South Basin, *S.F.* **27 B2** 37 42N 122 22W
South Beach, *N.Y.* **22 D4** 40 35N 74 4W
South Boston, *Bost.* **21 C3** 42 20N 71 2W
South Braintree, *Bost.* **21 D4** 42 11N 70 59W
South Branch →, *Phil.* **24 C4** 39 50N 75 5W
South Brooklyn, *N.Y.* **22 C5** 40 41N 73 59W
South Chelmsford, *Bost.* **21 B1** 42 34N 71 22W
South Chicago, *Chic.* **26 C3** 41 44N 87 32W
South Darenth, *Lon.* **4 C6** 51 23N 0 15 E
South Deering, *Chic.* **26 C3** 41 42N 87 33W
South Floral Park, *N.Y.* **23 C6** 40 42N 73 41W
South Gate, *L.A.* **28 C3** 33 56N 118 12W
South Germiston, *Jobg.* **18 F10** 26 11 S 28 13 E
South Hackensack, *N.Y.* **22 B4** 40 51N 74 2W
South Hamilton, *Bost.* **21 B4** 42 36N 70 52W
South Harbour, *Manila* **15 D3** 14 34N 120 58 E
South Harrow, *Lon.* **4 B2** 51 33N 0 21W
South Hd., *Syd.* **19 B4** 33 50 S 151 16 E
South Hempstead, *N.Y.* **23 C7** 40 40N 73 37W
South Hills, *Jobg.* **18 F9** 26 14 S 28 5 E
South Hingham, *Bost.* **21 D4** 42 12N 70 53W
South Holland, *Chic.* **26 D3** 41 36N 87 35W
South Hornchurch, *Lon.* **4 B6** 51 32N 0 11 E
South Huntington, *N.Y.* **23 C8** 40 49N 73 23W
South Lawn, *Wash.* **25 E7** 38 47N 77 0W
South Lawrence, *Bost.* **21 A3** 42 41N 71 9W
South Lincoln, *Bost.* **21 C2** 42 24N 71 19W
South Lynnfield, *Bost.* **21 B4** 42 30N 70 59W
South Norwood, *Lon.* **4 C4** 51 23N 0 3W
South Ockendon, *Lon.* **4 B6** 51 30N 0 16 E
South of Market, *S.F.* **27 B2** 37 46N 122 24W
South Orange, *N.Y.* **22 C3** 40 45N 74 14W
South Oxley, *Lon.* **4 B2** 51 37N 0 23W
South Oyster B., *N.Y.* **23 D8** 40 38N 73 27W
South Ozone Park, *N.Y.* **23 C6** 40 41N 73 49W
South Pasadena, *L.A.* **28 B4** 34 7N 118 8W
South Peabody, *Bost.* **21 B4** 42 30N 70 57W
South Peters, *Syd.* **19 B4** 33 54 S 151 11 E
South Plainfield, *N.Y.* **22 D2** 40 35N 74 24W
South Quincy, *Bost.* **21 D3** 42 13N 71 0W
South Res., *Bost.* **21 C3** 42 26N 71 6W
South San Francisco, *S.F.* **27 C2** 37 38N 122 26W
South San Gabriel, *L.A.* **28 B4** 34 3N 118 6W
South Shore, *Chic.* **26 C3** 41 45N 87 34W
South Sudbury, *Bost.* **21 C1** 42 21N 71 24W
South Valley Stream, *N.Y.* **23 D6** 40 38N 73 43W
South Westbury, *N.Y.* **23 C7** 40 44N 73 34W
South Weymouth, *Bost.* **21 D4** 42 10N 70 56W
South Wimbledon, *Lon.* **4 C3** 51 24N 0 11W
South Yarra, *Melb.* **19 F6** 37 50 S 144 59 E
Southall, *Lon.* **4 B2** 51 30N 0 22W
Southborough, *Lon.* **4 C5** 51 23N 0 3 E
Southcrest, *Jobg.* **18 F9** 26 15 S 28 5 E
Southend, *Lon.* **4 C4** 51 25N 0 0 E
Southfields, *Lon.* **4 C3** 51 26N 0 11W
Southgate, *Lon.* **4 B4** 51 38N 0 7W
Southwark, *Lon.* **4 C4** 51 29N 0 5W
Søvang, *Købn.* **2 E10** 55 34N 12 37 E
Soweto, *Jobg.* **18 F8** 26 14 S 27 52 E
Soya, *Tōkyō* **13 B4** 35 44N 139 55 E
Spadenland, *Hbg.* **7 E8** 53 28N 10 3 E
Spandau, *Berl.* **7 A1** 52 33N 13 9 E
Spånga, *Stock.* **3 D10** 59 23N 17 53 E
Sparkhill, *N.Y.* **22 A5** 41 1N 73 55W
Sparrows Point, *Balt.* **25 B4** 39 13N 76 29W
Spectacle I., *Bost.* **21 C4** 42 19N 70 59W
Speicher-See, *Mün.* **7 F11** 48 12N 11 42 E
Speising, *Wien* **10 H9** 48 10N 16 17 E
Speldorf, *Ruhr* **6 B2** 51 26N 6 49 E
Spellen, *Ruhr* **6 A1** 51 36N 6 36 E
Sphinx, *El Qâ.* **18 D4** 29 58N 31 8 E
Spinaceto, *Rome* **9 G9** 41 47N 12 27 E
Splitrock Res., *N.Y.* **22 B2** 40 58N 74 26W
Spořilov, *Pra.* **10 B3** 50 2N 14 29 E
Spot Pond, *Bost.* **21 C3** 42 26N 71 4W
Spotswood, *Melb.* **19 F6** 37 50 S 144 52 E
Spree →, *Berl.* **7 A2** 52 32N 13 12 E
Spreehafen, *Hbg.* **7 D7** 53 31N 9 59 E
Spring Pond, *Bost.* **21 C4** 42 29N 70 56W
Springeberg, *Berl.* **7 B5** 52 26N 13 43 E
Springfield, *N.Y.* **22 C3** 40 42N 74 18W
Springfield, *Phil.* **24 B3** 39 56N 75 19W
Springfield, *Wash.* **25 E6** 38 46N 77 10W
Springs, *Jobg.* **18 F11** 26 15 S 28 23 E
Sprockhövel, *Ruhr* **6 B5** 51 22N 7 14 E
Squantum, *Bost.* **21 D3** 42 17N 71 0W
Squirrel's Heath, *Lon.* **4 B6** 51 34N 0 12 E
Srednaya Rogatka, *Len.* **11 C4** 59 49N 30 22 E
Śródmieście, *Wsaw.* **10 E7** 52 13N 21 0 E
Staaken, *Berl.* **7 A1** 52 31N 13 8 E
Staatsoper, *Wien* **10 G10** 48 12N 16 21 E
Stabekk, *Oslo* **2 B3** 59 54N 10 36 E
Stadlau, *Wien* **10 G10** 48 13N 16 27 E
Stahnsdorf, *Berl.* **7 B2** 52 23N 13 12 E
Staines, *Lon.* **4 C2** 51 26N 0 29W
Stains, *Paris* **5 B4** 48 57N 2 22 E
Stamford, *N.Y.* **23 A7** 41 2N 73 32W
Stamford Harbor, *N.Y.* **23 A7** 41 0N 73 34W
Stamford Hill, *Lon.* **4 B4** 51 34N 0 4W
Stammersdorf, *Wien* **10 G10** 48 18N 16 24 E
Stanford Univ., *S.F.* **27 D4** 37 26N 122 10W
Stanley, *H.K.* **12 E6** 22 13N 114 12 E
Stanley Mound, *H.K.* **12 E6** 22 13N 114 12 E
Stanley Pen., *H.K.* **12 E6** 22 12N 114 12 E
Stanmore, *Lon.* **4 B3** 51 37N 0 18W
Stansted, *Lon.* **4 C6** 51 20N 0 18 E
Stapleford Abbotts, *Lon.* **4 B6** 51 37N 0 10 E
Stapleton, *N.Y.* **22 D4** 40 36N 74 5W
Stará Boleslav, *Pra.* **10 A3** 50 11N 14 39 E
Stara Milosna, *Wsaw.* **10 E8** 52 15N 21 12 E
Staraya, *Len.* **11 B5** 59 55N 30 37 E
Staraya Derevnya, *Len.* **11 B3** 59 58N 30 15 E
Stare, *Wsaw.* **10 E7** 52 15N 21 0 E
Stare Babice, *Wsaw.* **10 E5** 52 15N 20 49 E
Staré Mesto, *Pra.* **10 B2** 50 5N 14 25 E
State House, *Lagos* **18 B2** 6 26N 7 24 E
Staten, *N.Y.* **22 D4** 40 34N 74 7W
Staten Island Zoo, *N.Y.* **22 D4** 40 38N 74 6W
Statenice, *Pra.* **10 B1** 50 9N 14 19 E
Stavnsholt, *Købn.* **2 D9** 55 48N 12 24 E
Steele, *Ruhr* **6 B4** 51 27N 7 4 E
Steele Creek, *Melb.* **19 E6** 37 44 S 144 52 E
Steglitz, *Berl.* **7 B2** 52 27N 13 19 E
Stehstücken, *Berl.* **7 B1** 52 23N 13 7 E
Steilshoop, *Hbg.* **7 D8** 53 36N 10 2 E
Steinberger Slough, *S.F.* **27 C3** 37 32N 122 13W
Steinriegel, *Wien* **10 G9** 48 16N 16 12 E
Steinstücken, *Berl.* **7 B1** 52 21N 13 7 E
Steinwerder, *Hbg.* **7 D7** 53 32N 9 57 E
Stellingen, *Hbg.* **7 D7** 53 35N 9 56 E
Stenhamra, *Stock.* **3 D9** 59 20N 17 40 E
Stenløse, *Købn.* **2 D8** 55 46N 12 11 E
Stephansdom, *Wien* **10 G10** 48 12N 16 21 E
Stepney, *Lon.* **4 B4** 51 30N 0 3W
Sterkende, *Købn.* **2 E8** 55 36N 12 10 E
Sterkrade, *Ruhr* **6 A3** 51 31N 6 52 E
Sterling Park, *S.F.* **27 B2** 37 41N 122 27W
Stevenson, *Balt.* **25 A2** 39 24N 76 42W
Stewart Manor, *N.Y.* **23 C6** 40 43N 73 40W
Sticklinge udde, *Stock.* **3 D11** 59 23N 18 6 E
Stickney, *Chic.* **26 C2** 41 49N 87 46W
Stienitzaue, *Berl.* **7 A5** 52 38N 13 44 E
Stiepel, *Ruhr* **6 B5** 51 25N 7 14 E
Stiftskirche, *Ruhr* **6 C2** 51 12N 6 41 E
Still Run →, *Phil.* **24 C3** 39 47N 75 16W
Stockholm, *Stock.* **3 E11** 59 19N 18 4 E
Stocksund, *Stock.* **3 D11** 59 23N 18 3 E
Stockum, *Ruhr* **6 C2** 51 16N 6 44 E
Stodůlky, *Pra.* **10 B1** 50 3N 14 19 E
Stoke D'Abernon, *Lon.* **4 D2** 51 19N 0 23W
Stoke Newington, *Lon.* **4 B4** 51 33N 0 4W
Stolpe-Süd, *Berl.* **7 A2** 52 37N 13 14 E
Stone, *Lon.* **4 C6** 51 26N 0 16 E
Stone Grove, *Lon.* **4 B3** 51 37N 0 16W
Stone Park, *Chic.* **26 B1** 41 53N 87 52W
Stonebridge, *Lon.* **4 B3** 51 32N 0 16W
Stoneham, *Bost.* **21 C3** 42 29N 71 5W
Stonehurst, *L.A.* **28 A2** 34 15N 118 21W
Stony Brook Res., *Bost.* **21 D3** 42 15N 71 8W
Stony Cr. →, *Chic.* **26 C2** 41 40N 87 45W
Stony Cr. →, *Melb.* **19 E6** 37 49 S 144 53 E
Stora Värtan, *Stock.* **3 D11** 59 25N 18 7 E
Store Hareskov, *Købn.* **2 D9** 55 46N 12 23 E
Store Kattingesø, *Købn.* **2 E7** 55 39N 12 0 E
Store Magleby, *Købn.* **2 E10** 55 35N 12 35 E
Storholmen, *Stock.* **3 D11** 59 23N 18 8 E
Stovivatn, *Oslo* **2 B2** 59 54N 10 26 E
Stovner, *Oslo* **2 B5** 59 57N 10 55 E
Stow L., *S.F.* **27 B2** 37 46N 122 28W
Stračnice, *Pra.* **10 B2** 50 4N 14 28 E
Strandbad Gansehäufe, *Wien* **10 G10** 48 13N 16 26 E
Strasslach, *Mün.* **7 G10** 48 0N 11 30 E
Strasstrudering, *Mün.* **7 G11** 48 6N 11 41 E
Stratford, *Lon.* **4 B5** 51 33N 0 0 E
Stratford, *Phil.* **24 C4** 39 49N 75 0W
Strathfield, *Syd.* **19 B3** 33 52 S 151 5 E
Strawberry Hill, *Bost.* **21 D2** 42 14N 71 15W
Strawberry Pk., *L.A.* **28 A4** 34 16N 118 7W
Strawberry Pt., *S.F.* **27 A1** 37 53N 122 30W
Streatham, *Lon.* **4 C4** 51 25N 0 7W
Streatham Vale, *Lon.* **4 C4** 51 24N 0 8W
Strebersdorf, *Wien* **10 G10** 48 17N 16 23 E
Střečovice, *Pra.* **10 B2** 50 5N 14 23 E
Strelyna, *Len.* **11 C1** 59 49N 30 0 E
Střížkov, *Pra.* **10 B2** 50 7N 14 28 E
Strogino, *Mos.* **11 E8** 55 48N 37 24 E
Strømmen, *Oslo* **2 B5** 59 56N 10 59 E
Stromovka, *Pra.* **10 B2** 50 6N 14 25 E
Strunkede Wasserschloss, *Ruhr* **6 A5** 51 33N 7 12 E
Studio City, *L.A.* **28 B2** 34 8N 118 24W
Stupinigi, *Tori.* **9 C2** 44 59N 7 36 E
Stura di Lanzo →, *Tori.* **9 A2** 45 11N 7 47 E
Stureby, *Stock.* **3 E11** 59 15N 18 4 E
Stuvsta, *Stock.* **3 E11** 59 15N 18 0 E
Styrum, *Ruhr* **6 B3** 51 27N 6 52 E
Subhepur, *Delhi* **16 A2** 28 44N 77 15 E
Sucat, *Manila* **15 E4** 14 27N 121 2 E
Success, L., *N.Y.* **23 C6** 40 45N 73 42W
Suchdol, *Pra.* **10 B2** 50 8N 14 22 E
Sucre, *Car.* **30 D5** 10 31N 66 57W
Sucy-en-Brie, *Paris* **5 C5** 48 46N 2 31 E
Sudberg, *Ruhr* **6 C4** 51 10N 7 6 E
Sudbury, *Bost.* **21 C1** 42 22N 71 24W
Suderelbe →, *Hbg.* **7 E7** 53 28N 9 58 E
Suderwich, *Ruhr* **6 A5** 51 36N 7 16 E
Sugamo, *Tōkyō* **13 B3** 35 44N 139 43 E
Sugar Loaf Mt. = Açúcar, Pão de, *Rio J.* **31 B3** 22 56 S 43 9W
Sugartown, *Phil.* **24 B1** 39 59N 75 30W
Sugasawa, *Tōkyō* **13 B2** 35 46N 139 32 E
Suge, *Tōkyō* **13 C2** 35 37N 139 32 E
Suginami-Ku, *Tōkyō* **13 B2** 35 41N 139 37 E
Sugita, *Tōkyō* **13 D2** 35 22N 139 37 E
Sugō, *Tōkyō* **13 C2** 35 34N 139 33 E
Suitland, *Wash.* **25 D8** 38 50N 76 55W
Sukchar, *Calc.* **16 D6** 22 42N 88 22 E
Sulejówek, *Wsaw.* **10 E8** 52 14N 21 14 E
Sulldorf, *Hbg.* **7 D6** 53 34N 9 49 E
Sultan Mosque, *Sing.* **15 G8** 1 18N 103 51 E
Suma, *Ōsaka* **12 C1** 34 38N 135 8 E
Sumaré, *S. Pau.* **31 E5** 23 32 S 46 41W
Sumida, *Tōkyō* **13 B3** 35 42N 139 49 E
Sumida →, *Tōkyō* **13 B3** 35 39N 139 45 E
Sumiyoshi, *Ōsaka* **12 C4** 34 36N 135 30 E
Summer Palace, *Beij.* **14 B2** 39 59N 116 13 E
Summerville, *Trto.* **20 E7** 43 37N 79 33W
Summit, *Chic.* **26 C2** 41 47N 87 47W
Summit, *N.Y.* **22 C2** 40 43N 74 22W
Sun Valley, *L.A.* **28 A2** 34 13N 118 21W
Sunamachi, *Tōkyō* **13 B4** 35 40N 139 50 E
Sunashinden, *Tōkyō* **13 A2** 35 53N 139 30 E
Sunbury, *Lon.* **4 C2** 51 25N 0 26W
Sunda Kelapa, *Jak.* **15 H9** 6 6 S 106 48 E
Sundbyberg, *Stock.* **3 D10** 59 22N 17 57 E
Sundbyerne, *Købn.* **2 E10** 55 39N 12 36 E
Sung Kong, *H.K.* **12 E6** 22 11N 114 17 E
Sungai Bambu, *Jak.* **15 H10** 6 6 S 106 53 E
Sungai Buloh, *Sing.* **15 F7** 1 25N 103 42 E
Sungei Simpang, *Sing.* **15 F7** 1 26N 103 49 E
Sunland, *L.A.* **28 A3** 34 15N 118 18W
Sunnyridge, *Jobg.* **18 F10** 26 10 S 28 10 E
Sunset, *S.F.* **27 B2** 37 44N 122 29W
Sunshine, *Melb.* **19 E5** 37 48 S 144 49 E
Sunshine Acres, *L.A.* **28 C5** 33 56N 117 59W
Suntaug L., *Bost.* **21 B3** 42 31N 71 0W
Sunter, *Jak.* **15 H10** 6 7 S 106 51 E
Sunter, Kali, *Jak.* **15 J10** 6 10 S 106 53 E
Suomenlinna, *Hels.* **3 C4** 60 9N 24 59 E
Superga, *Tori.* **9 B3** 45 4N 7 46 E
Superga, Basilica di, *Tori.* **9 B3** 45 5N 7 45 E
Sura, *Calc.* **16 E6** 22 33N 88 24 E
Surag San, *Sŏul* **12 F8** 37 40N 127 4 E
Surbiton, *Lon.* **4 C3** 51 23N 0 17W
Surco, *Lima* **30 G8** 12 9 S 77 0W
Suresnes, *Paris* **5 B3** 48 52N 2 13 E
Surquillo, *Lima* **30 G8** 12 6 S 77 1W
Surrey Hills, *Melb.* **19 F7** 37 50 S 145 5 E
Surrey Hills, *Syd.* **19 B4** 33 53 S 151 13 E
Surrey Park, *Melb.* **19 E7** 37 49 S 145 6 E
Susaeg, *Sŏul* **12 G7** 37 34N 126 54 E
Süssenbrunn, *Wien* **10 G10** 48 16N 16 29 E
Sutherland, *Syd.* **19 C3** 34 2 S 151 3 E
Sutton, *Lon.* **4 C3** 51 21N 0 11W
Sutton at Hone, *Lon.* **4 C6** 51 24N 0 14 E
Suyu, *Sŏul* **12 G8** 37 37N 127 0 E
Suzukishinden, *Tōkyō* **13 B2** 35 43N 139 31 E
Svanemøllen, *Købn.* **2 D10** 55 43N 12 34 E
Svartsjölandet, *Stock.* **3 D9** 59 20N 17 43 E
Sverdlov, *Mos.* **11 E9** 55 46N 37 36 E
Svestad, *Oslo* **2 C3** 59 46N 10 36 E
Svestrup, *Købn.* **2 D7** 55 46N 12 8 E
Svinningeudd, *Stock.* **3 D12** 59 26N 18 17 E
Svinö, *Hels.* **3 C3** 60 7N 24 44 E
Svogerslev, *Købn.* **2 E7** 55 38N 12 0 E
Swampscott, *Bost.* **21 C4** 42 28N 70 53W
Swanley, *Lon.* **4 C5** 51 23N 0 9 E
Swanscombe, *Lon.* **4 C6** 51 26N 0 18 E
Swansea, *Trto.* **20 E8** 43 39N 79 27W
Swarthmore, *Phil.* **24 B2** 39 54N 75 22W
Swedesboro, *Phil.* **24 C3** 39 45N 75 17W
Swedesburg, *Phil.* **24 A3** 40 5N 75 19W
Swinburne I., *N.Y.* **22 D4** 40 33N 74 3W
Swita, *Ōsaka* **12 B4** 34 45N 135 30 E
Syampur, *Calc.* **16 F5** 22 28N 88 12 E
Sycamore Mills, *Phil.* **24 B2** 39 57N 75 25W
Sydenham, *Jobg.* **18 E9** 26 9 S 28 5 E
Sydney, *Syd.* **19 B4** 33 52 S 151 12 E
Sydney, Univ. of, *Syd.* **19 B4** 33 54 S 151 11 E
Sydney Airport, *Syd.* **19 B4** 33 56 S 151 10 E
Sydney Harbour Bridge, *Syd.* **19 B4** 33 51 S 151 12 E
Sydstranden, *Købn.* **2 E10** 55 34N 12 38 E
Sylling, *Oslo* **2 B1** 59 54N 10 16 E
Sylvania, *Syd.* **19 C3** 34 0 S 151 7 E
Syndal, *Melb.* **19 F7** 37 52 S 145 9 E
Syon House, *Lon.* **4 C3** 51 28N 0 18W
Syosset, *N.Y.* **23 C7** 40 49N 73 30W
Szabadság-hegy, *Bud.* **10 J12** 47 30N 18 59 E
Szczęsliwice, *Wsaw.* **10 E6** 52 12N 20 57 E
Szemere-Telep, *Bud.* **10 K14** 47 26N 19 13 E
Sźephalom, *Bud.* **10 J12** 47 34N 18 57 E
Szilasliget, *Bud.* **10 J14** 47 34N 19 16 E

T

Tabata, *Tōkyō* **13 B3** 35 44N 139 46 E
Tablada, *B.A.* **32 C3** 34 41 S 58 32W
Taboão →, *S. Pau.* **31 F7** 23 40 S 46 27W
Taboão da Serra, *S. Pau.* **31 E5** 23 36 S 46 45W
Tabor, *N.Y.* **22 B2** 40 52N 74 28W
Täby, *Stock.* **3 D11** 59 26N 18 2 E
Tacony, *Phil.* **24 A4** 40 1N 75 2W
Tacuba, *Méx.* **29 B2** 19 26N 99 11W
Tacubaya, *Méx.* **29 B2** 19 24N 99 10W
Tadain, *Ōsaka* **12 A3** 34 51N 135 24 E
Tadworth, *Lon.* **4 D3** 51 17N 0 14W
Tagig, *Manila* **15 D4** 14 31N 121 4 E
Tagig →, *Manila* **15 D4** 14 31N 121 5 E
Tai Hang, *H.K.* **12 E6** 22 16N 114 11 E
Tai Lo Shan, *H.K.* **12 D6** 22 21N 114 13 E
Tai Po Tsai, *H.K.* **12 D6** 22 20N 114 15 E
Tai Seng, *Sing.* **15 F8** 1 20N 103 53 E
Tai Shui Hang, *H.K.* **12 D6** 22 24N 114 13 E
Tai Tam B., *H.K.* **12 E6** 22 12N 114 13 E
Tai Tam Tuk Res., *H.K.* **12 E6** 22 14N 114 13 E
Tai Wan Tau, *H.K.* **12 E6** 22 17N 114 17 E
Tai Wo Hau, *H.K.* **12 D5** 22 21N 114 7 E
Tai Wo Ping, *H.K.* **12 D5** 22 20N 114 9 E
Ta'imim, *Bagd.* **17 F8** 33 15N 44 21 E
Tainaka, *Ōsaka* **12 C4** 34 36N 135 35 E
Taishō, *Ōsaka* **12 C3** 34 38N 135 27 E
Taitō-Ku, *Tōkyō* **13 B3** 35 43N 139 47 E
Tajima, *Tōkyō* **13 B2** 35 48N 139 36 E
Tajpur, *Calc.* **16 D5** 22 44N 88 15 E
Takaido, *Tōkyō* **13 B2** 35 40N 139 37 E
Takaishi, *Tōkyō* **13 C2** 35 36N 139 31 E
Takarazuka, *Ōsaka* **12 B2** 34 47N 135 20 E
Takasago, *Tōkyō* **13 B4** 35 44N 139 52 E
Takatsuki, *Ōsaka* **12 A4** 34 50N 135 37 E
Takayanagi, *Tōkyō* **13 D4** 35 23N 139 57 E
Takegahana, *Tōkyō* **13 B4** 35 47N 139 54 E
Takenotsuka, *Tōkyō* **13 B3** 35 47N 139 47 E
Takeshita, *Tōkyō* **13 C2** 35 33N 139 32 E
Takinegawa, *Tōkyō* **13 B3** 35 45N 139 44 E
Takkula, *Hels.* **3 B2** 60 19N 24 38 E
Takoma Park, *Wash.* **25 D7** 38 58N 77 0W
Taksim, *Ist.* **17 A2** 41 2N 28 58 E
Talaide, *Lisb.* **8 F7** 38 44N 9 18W
Talampas, *Manila* **15 D4** 14 36N 121 4 E
Taling Chan, *Bangk.* **15 B1** 13 46N 100 27 E
Talleyville, *Phil.* **24 C1** 39 48N 75 32W
Tallkrogen, *Stock.* **3 E11** 59 16N 18 4 E
Talmapais Valley, *S.F.* **27 A1** 37 52N 122 32W
Tama, *Tōkyō* **13 C1** 35 38N 139 26 E
Tama →, *Tōkyō* **13 C2** 35 32N 139 39 E
Tama Kyźryō, *Tōkyō* **13 C2** 35 34N 139 30 E
Tamaden, *Tōkyō* **13 C2** 35 39N 139 38 E
Tamagawa-josui →, *Tōkyō* **13 B1** 35 41N 139 47 E
Taman Sari, *Jak.* **15 H9** 6 8 S 106 48 E
Tamanduatei →, *S. Pau.* **31 E6** 23 37 S 46 38W
Tambora, *Jak.* **15 H9** 6 8 S 106 47 E
Tamboré, *S. Pau.* **31 E4** 23 30 S 46 50W
Tammisalo, *Hels.* **3 B5** 60 11N 25 5 E
Tammûh, *El Qâ.* **18 D5** 29 55N 31 15 E
Tampier Slough, *Chic.* **26 D1** 41 39N 87 54W
Tan Tock Seng, *Sing.* **15 G8** 1 19N 103 50 E
Tanah Abang, *Jak.* **15 J9** 6 12 S 106 48 E
Tanashi, *Tōkyō* **13 B2** 35 43N 139 32 E
Tanforan Park, *S.F.* **27 C2** 37 37N 122 24W
Tangjae, *Sŏul* **12 H8** 37 29N 127 2 E
Tanglin, *Sing.* **15 G7** 1 18N 103 47 E
Tangstedt, *Hbg.* **7 C7** 53 40N 9 51 E
Tangstedter Forst, *Hbg.* **7 C8** 53 43N 10 3 E
Tanigami, *Ōsaka* **12 B2** 34 45N 135 10 E
Tanjung Duren, *Jak.* **15 J9** 6 10 S 106 46 E
Tanjung Priok, *Jak.* **15 H10** 6 6 S 106 52 E
Tanum, *Oslo* **2 B2** 59 53N 10 28 E
Taoranting Gongyuan, *Beij.* **14 B3** 39 51N 116 20 E
Taoranting Hu, *Beij.* **14 B3** 39 50N 116 20 E
Tapada, *Lisb.* **8 F7** 38 49N 9 16W
Tapanila, *Hels.* **3 B5** 60 15N 25 2 E
Tapiales, *B.A.* **32 C3** 34 42 S 58 30W
Tapiola, *Hels.* **3 B3** 60 10N 24 48 E
Tappan, *N.Y.* **22 A5** 41 1N 73 57W
Tappan, L., *N.Y.* **22 A5** 41 1N 73 59W
Tappeh, *Tehr.* **17 C5** 35 41N 51 29 E
Tapsia, *Calc.* **16 E6** 22 32N 88 23 E
Taquara, *Rio J.* **31 B1** 22 55 S 43 21W
Tara, *Bomb.* **16 G7** 19 5N 72 49 E
Tarāblus, *Bagd.* **17 F8** 33 19N 44 21 E
Tarango, Presa, *Méx.* **29 B2** 19 21N 99 12W
Tårbæk, *Købn.* **2 D10** 55 46N 12 35 E
Tarchomin, *Wsaw.* **10 E6** 52 19N 20 58 E
Tardeo, *Bomb.* **16 H7** 18 57N 72 48 E
Target Rock, *N.Y.* **23 B8** 40 55N 73 24W
Targówek, *Wsaw.* **10 E7** 52 16N 21 3 E
Tårnby, *Købn.* **2 E10** 55 37N 12 35 E
Taronga Zoo. Park, *Syd.* **19 B4** 33 50 S 151 14 E

Villejust 47

Tarqua B., *Lagos*	**18 B2**	6 24N	7 23 E
Tarzana, *L.A.*	**28 A1**	34 10N	118 32W
Tåstrup, *Købn.*	**2 E8**	55 39N	12 18 E
Tatarovo, *Mos.*	**11 E8**	55 45N	37 24 E
Tatarpur, *Delhi*	**16 B1**	28 38N	77 9 E
Tatenberg, *Hbg.*	**7 E8**	53 29N	10 3 E
Tathong Channel, *H.K.*	**12 E6**	22 15N	114 16 E
Tathong Pt., *H.K.*	**12 E6**	22 14N	114 17 E
Tatsfield, *Lon.*	**4 D5**	51 17N	0 1 E
Tattariharju, *Hels.*	**3 B5**	60 15N	25 2 E
Tatuapé, *S. Pau.*	**31 E6**	23 31 S	46 33W
Taufkirchen, *Mün.*	**7 G10**	48 2N	11 36 E
Tavares, I. dos, *Rio J.*	**31 A3**	22 49 S	43 6W
Tavernanova, *Nápl.*	**9 H13**	40 54N	14 21 E
Taverny, *Paris*	**5 A3**	49 1N	2 13 E
Távros, *Ath.*	**8 J11**	37 57N	23 43 E
Tavry, *Len.*	**11 B6**	59 54N	30 40 E
Taylortown, *N.Y.*	**22 B2**	40 56N	74 23W
Tayninka, *Mos.*	**11 D10**	55 53N	37 45 E
Taytay, *Manila*	**15 D4**	14 34N	121 7 E
Tayuman, *Manila*	**15 D4**	14 31N	121 9 E
Teaneck, *N.Y.*	**22 B4**	40 52N	74 1W
Teatro Colón, *B.A.*	**32 B4**	34 36 S	58 23 E
Teban Gardens, *Sing.*	**15 G7**	1 19N	103 44 E
Tebet, *Jak.*	**15 J10**	6 14 S	106 50 E
Tecamachaleo, *Méx.*	**29 B2**	19 25N	99 14W
Techny, *Chic.*	**26 A2**	42 6N	87 48W
Teck Hock, *Sing.*	**15 F8**	1 21N	103 54 E
Tecoma, *Melb.*	**19 F9**	37 54 S	145 20 E
Teddington, *Lon.*	**4 C2**	51 25N	0 20W
Tegel, *Berl.*	**7 A2**	52 34N	13 16 E
Tegel, Flughafen, *Berl.*	**7 A2**	52 35N	13 15 E
Tegeler Fliess →, *Berl.*	**7 A3**	52 37N	13 21 E
Tegeler See, *Berl.*	**7 A2**	52 34N	13 15 E
Tegelort, *Berl.*	**7 A2**	52 34N	13 13 E
Tehar, *Delhi*	**16 B1**	28 37N	77 7 E
Tehrān, *Tehr.*	**17 C5**	35 41N	51 25 E
Tehrān Pars, *Tehr.*	**17 C6**	35 44N	51 32 E
Tei Tong Tsui, *H.K.*	**12 E6**	22 16N	114 17 E
Tejo →, *Lisb.*	**8 F8**	38 45N	9 3W
Tekstilyshchik, *Mos.*	**11 E10**	55 42N	37 41 E
Tela, *Delhi*	**16 A2**	28 43N	77 19 E
Telhal, *Lisb.*	**8 F7**	38 48N	9 18W
Telinipara, *Calc.*	**16 D6**	22 46N	88 23 E
Telok Blangah, *Sing.*	**15 G7**	1 17N	103 49 E
Teltow, *Berl.*	**7 B2**	52 23N	13 17 E
Teltow kanal, *Berl.*	**7 B3**	52 26N	13 29 E
Temescal, L., *S.F.*	**27 A3**	37 50N	122 13W
Temnikovo, *Mos.*	**11 E12**	55 43N	38 1 E
Tempelhof, *Berl.*	**7 B3**	52 27N	13 23 E
Tempelhof, Flughafen, *Berl.*	**7 B3**	52 28N	13 27 E
Temperley, *B.A.*	**32 C4**	34 46 S	58 22W
Temple City, *L.A.*	**28 B4**	34 6N	118 3W
Temple Hills Park, *Wash.*	**25 E8**	38 48N	76 56W
Templestowe, *Melb.*	**19 E7**	37 45 S	145 8 E
Templestowe Lower, *Melb.*	**19 E7**	37 45 S	145 6 E
Tenafly, *N.Y.*	**22 B5**	40 54N	73 58W
Tenantongo, Presa, *Méx.*	**29 B2**	19 28N	99 15W
Tengah →, *Sing.*	**15 F7**	1 23N	103 43 E
Tengeh, Sungei →, *Sing.*	**15 F6**	1 20N	103 39 E
Tennoji, *Ōsaka*	**12 C4**	34 39N	135 30 E
Tenochtitlán, *Méx.*	**29 B3**	19 26N	99 7W
Tepalcates, *Méx.*	**29 B3**	19 23N	99 3W
Tepe Saif, *Tehr.*	**17 D4**	35 36N	51 17 E
Tepepan, *Méx.*	**29 C3**	19 16N	99 9W
Teplyy Star, *Mos.*	**11 F9**	55 37N	37 30 E
Tepozteco, Parque Nac. del, *Méx.*	**29 D3**	19 3N	99 5W
Terrasse Vaudreuil, *Mtrl.*	**20 B2**	43 23N	73 59W
Terrazzano, *Mil.*	**9 D5**	45 32N	9 4 E
Terrugem, *Lisb.*	**8 F7**	38 41N	9 17W
Terusan Banjir, *Jak.*	**15 H9**	6 7 S	106 46 E
Terzigno, *Nápl.*	**9 J13**	40 48N	14 29 E
Tessancourt-sur-Aubette, *Paris*	**5 A1**	49 1N	1 55 E
Testona, *Tori.*	**9 C3**	44 59N	7 42 E
Tetelco, *Méx.*	**29 C4**	19 12N	98 57W
Tetreauville, *Mtrl.*	**20 A4**	43 35N	73 32W
Tetti Neirotti, *Tori.*	**9 B2**	45 3N	7 32 E
Tetuán, *Mdrd.*	**8 B2**	40 27N	3 42W
Teufelsberg, *Berl.*	**7 B2**	52 29N	13 14 E
Tévere →, *Rome*	**9 F9**	41 56N	12 27 E
Tewksbury, *Bost.*	**21 B2**	42 37N	71 12W
Texcoco, L. de, *Méx.*	**29 B4**	19 30N	89 58 E
Thalkirchen, *Mün.*	**7 G10**	48 6N	11 32 E
Thames Ditton, *Lon.*	**4 C2**	51 23N	0 20W
Thamesmead, *Lon.*	**4 B5**	51 30N	0 7 E
Thana Cr. →, *Bomb.*	**16 G8**	19 4N	72 54 E
The Basin, *Melb.*	**19 F8**	37 51 S	145 19 E
The Glen, *Wash.*	**25 C6**	39 2N	77 12W
The Loop, *Chic.*	**26 B3**	41 52N	87 37W
The Narrows, *N.Y.*	**22 D4**	40 37N	74 3W
The Ridge, *Delhi*	**16 B2**	28 37N	77 10 E
The White House, *Wash.*	**25 D7**	38 53N	77 1W
The Wilds, *Jobg.*	**18 F9**	26 10 S	28 2 E
Theseión, *Ath.*	**8 J11**	37 57N	23 43 E
Theydon Bois, *Lon.*	**4 A5**	51 40N	0 6 E
Thiais, *Paris*	**5 C4**	48 46N	2 23 E
Thieux, *Paris*	**5 A6**	49 0N	2 40 E
Thistletown, *Trto.*	**20 D7**	43 44N	79 34W
Thiverval-Grignon, *Paris*	**5 B1**	48 51N	1 55 E
Thomaston, *N.Y.*	**23 C6**	40 47N	73 43W
Thomastown, *Melb.*	**19 E7**	37 40 S	145 2 E
Thompson I., *Bost.*	**21 D4**	42 19N	70 59W
Thomson, *Sing.*	**15 F8**	1 20N	103 50 E
Thon Buri, *Bangk.*	**15 B1**	13 45N	100 29 E
Thong Hoe, *Sing.*	**15 F7**	1 25N	103 42 E
Thorigny-sur-Marne, *Paris*	**5 B6**	48 53N	2 41 E
Thornbury, *Melb.*	**19 E7**	37 44 S	145 1 E
Thorncliffe, *Trto.*	**20 D8**	43 42N	79 20W
Thornhill, *Jobg.*	**18 E9**	26 6 S	28 9 E
Thornhill, *Trto.*	**20 D8**	43 48N	79 25W
Thornton, *Phil.*	**24 B1**	39 54N	75 31W
Thornton Heath, *Lon.*	**4 C4**	51 23N	0 6W
Thorofare, *Phil.*	**24 B3**	39 50N	75 11W
Throgs Neck, *N.Y.*	**23 C6**	40 48N	73 49W
Tian Guan, *Sing.*	**15 F7**	1 21N	103 49 E
Tian'anmen, *Beij.*	**14 B3**	39 53N	116 21 E
Tiancun, *Beij.*	**14 B2**	39 54N	116 12 E
Tianjin, *Tianj.*	**14 E5**	39 7N	117 12 E
Tiantan Gongyuan, *Beij.*	**14 B3**	39 51N	116 22 E
Tiateloco, *Méx.*	**29 B3**	19 27N	99 8W
Tibidabo, *Barc.*	**8 D5**	41 25N	2 6 E
Tiburon, *S.F.*	**27 A2**	37 52N	122 27W
Tiburon Pen., *S.F.*	**27 A2**	37 53N	122 28W
Tiburtino, *Rome*	**9 F10**	41 53N	12 30 E
Ticomán, *Méx.*	**29 A3**	19 31N	99 8W
Tiefenbroich, *Ruhr*	**6 C2**	51 18N	6 49 E
Tiefersee, *Berl.*	**7 B1**	52 24N	13 5 E
Tiejiangyin, *Beij.*	**14 C3**	39 49N	116 23 E
Tientsin = Tianjin, *Tianj.*	**14 E5**	39 7N	117 12 E
Tiergarten, *Berl.*	**7 A3**	52 31N	13 20 E
Tietê →, *S. Pau.*	**31 D7**	23 28 S	46 24W
Tigery, *Paris*	**5 D5**	48 38N	2 30 E
Tigre, *B.A.*	**32 A3**	34 25 S	58 34W
Tigris →, *Bagd.*	**17 F8**	33 17N	44 23 E
Tijuca, *Rio J.*	**31 B2**	22 56 S	43 13W
Tijuca, L. de, *Rio J.*	**31 B2**	22 59 S	43 20W
Tijuca, Pico da, *Rio J.*	**31 B2**	22 56 S	43 15W
Tijucamar, *Rio J.*	**31 C2**	23 0 S	43 18W
Tijucas, Is., *Rio J.*	**31 C2**	23 1 S	43 17W
Tikkurila, *Hels.*	**3 B5**	60 17N	25 2 E
Tilanqiao, *Shang.*	**14 J11**	31 15N	121 29 E
Tilbury, *Lon.*	**4 C7**	51 27N	0 21 E
Timah, Bukit, *Sing.*	**15 F7**	1 21N	103 46 E
Timiryazev Park, *Mos.*	**11 E9**	55 49N	37 33 E
Ting Kau, *H.K.*	**12 D5**	22 22N	114 4 E
Tinley Cr. →, *Chic.*	**26 D2**	41 39N	87 45W
Tinley Creek Woods, *Chic.*	**26 D2**	41 38N	87 48W
Tinley Park, *Chic.*	**26 D2**	41 35N	87 46W
Tipas, *Manila*	**15 D4**	14 32N	121 4 E
Tirsa, *El Qâ.*	**18 D5**	29 57N	31 12 E
Tishrīyaa, *Bagd.*	**17 F8**	33 18N	44 24 E
Tit Cham Chau, *H.K.*	**12 E6**	22 15N	114 17 E
Titagarh, *Calc.*	**16 D6**	22 44N	88 22 E
Tivoli, *Købn.*	**2 D10**	55 40N	12 35 E
Tizapán, *Méx.*	**29 C2**	19 19N	99 13W
Tlalnepantla, *Méx.*	**29 A2**	19 32N	99 11W
Tlalnepantla →, *Méx.*	**29 A2**	19 30N	99 18W
Tláloc, Cerro, *Méx.*	**29 D3**	19 7N	99 3W
Tlalpan, *Méx.*	**29 C2**	19 17N	99 10W
Tlalpitzáhuac, *Méx.*	**29 C4**	19 19N	98 56W
Tlaltenango, *Méx.*	**29 B2**	19 20N	99 17W
Tlaltenco, *Méx.*	**29 C3**	19 19N	99 0W
Tlaxcoaque, *Méx.*	**29 B3**	19 25N	99 8W
To Kwai Wan, *H.K.*	**12 E6**	22 18N	114 11 E
Toa Payoh, *Sing.*	**15 F8**	1 20N	103 50 E
Tobay Beach, *N.Y.*	**23 D8**	40 36N	73 26W
Točná, *Pra.*	**10 C2**	49 58N	14 25 E
Tocome →, *Car.*	**30 D6**	10 28N	66 49W
Toda, *Tōkyō*	**13 A3**	35 50N	139 40 E
Todamachī, *Tōkyō*	**13 B2**	35 48N	139 39 E
Todt Hill, *N.Y.*	**22 D4**	40 36N	74 6W
Toei, Khlong →, *Bangk.*	**15 B2**	13 43N	100 32 E
Togasaki, *Tōkyō*	**13 B4**	35 47N	139 51 E
Tōkagi, *Tōkyō*	**13 B4**	35 42N	139 55 E
Tōkaichiba, *Tōkyō*	**13 C2**	35 31N	139 30 E
Tokarevo, *Mos.*	**11 F11**	55 38N	37 54 E
Tokorozawa, *Tōkyō*	**13 B1**	35 47N	139 28 E
Tōkyō, *Tōkyō*	**13 C3**	35 43N	139 45 E
Tōkyō B., *Tōkyō*	**13 C4**	35 33N	139 53 E
Tōkyō-Haneda Int. Airport, *Tōkyō*	**13 C3**	35 33N	139 45 E
Tōkyō Harbour, *Tōkyō*	**13 C3**	35 38N	139 46 E
Tokyo Univ., *Tōkyō*	**13 B3**	35 42N	139 46 E
Tollygunge, *Calc.*	**16 F6**	22 29N	88 21 E
Tolly's Nala, *Calc.*	**16 E6**	22 33N	88 19 E
Tolworth, *Lon.*	**4 C3**	51 22N	0 17W
Tomang, *Jak.*	**15 J9**	6 10 S	106 47 E
Tomba di Nerone, *Rome*	**9 F9**	41 58N	12 26 E
Tomilino, *Mos.*	**11 F11**	55 39N	37 55 E
Tomioka, *Tōkyō*	**13 D2**	35 22N	139 37 E
Tonda, *Ōsaka*	**12 B4**	34 49N	135 35 E
Tondo, *Manila*	**15 D3**	14 36N	120 57 E
Tone-unga →, *Tōkyō*	**13 A4**	35 55N	139 56 E
Tonekollen, *Oslo*	**2 C6**	50 49N	11 0 E
Tong Kang, Sungei →, *Sing.*	**15 F8**	1 23N	103 53 E
Tonghui He →, *Beij.*	**14 B3**	39 53N	116 28 E
Tönisheide, *Ruhr*	**6 C4**	51 18N	7 3 E
Tonndorf, *Hbg.*	**7 D8**	53 35N	10 8 E
Toorak, *Melb.*	**19 F7**	37 50 S	145 1 E
Toot Hill, *Lon.*	**4 A6**	51 41N	0 11 E
Topilejo, *Méx.*	**29 C3**	19 12N	99 9W
Topkapi, *Ist.*	**17 A2**	41 1N	28 55 E
Topsfield, *Bost.*	**21 B4**	42 38N	70 57W
Tor di Quinto, *Rome*	**9 F9**	41 56N	12 27 E
Tor Pignattara, *Rome*	**9 F10**	41 52N	12 31 E
Tor Sapienza, *Rome*	**9 F10**	41 53N	12 35 E
Torcy, *Paris*	**5 B5**	48 51N	2 39 E
Torino, *Tori.*	**9 B2**	45 5N	7 39 E
Toro, *B.A.*	**32 B1**	34 30 S	58 50W
Toronto, *Trto.*	**20 E9**	43 39N	79 13W
Toronto, Univ. of, *Trto.*	**20 E8**	43 39N	79 23W
Toronto Harbour, *Trto.*	**20 E8**	43 38N	79 21W
Toronto I., *Trto.*	**20 E8**	43 37N	79 23W
Toronto Int. Airport, *Trto.*	**20 D7**	43 40N	79 38 E
Torre Annunziata, *Nápl.*	**9 J13**	40 45N	14 26 E
Torre Cervara, *Rome*	**9 F10**	41 55N	12 35 E
Torre del Greco, *Nápl.*	**9 J13**	40 47N	14 21 E
Torre Novo, *Rome*	**9 F10**	41 51N	12 36 E
Torrellas →, *Barc.*	**8 D5**	41 23N	2 1 E
Torrellas del Llobregat, *Barc.*	**8 D4**	41 20N	1 59 E
Torresdale, *Phil.*	**24 A5**	40 3N	74 59W
Torrevécchia, *Rome*	**9 F9**	41 55N	12 25 E
Tortuguitas, *B.A.*	**32 A2**	34 28 S	58 44W
Toshima-Ku, *Tōkyō*	**13 B3**	35 43N	139 43 E
Toshimaen, *Tōkyō*	**13 B2**	35 43N	139 38 E
Totowa, *N.Y.*	**22 B3**	40 54N	74 13W
Totsuka-Ku, *Tōkyō*	**13 D2**	35 23N	139 32 E
Tottenham, *Lon.*	**4 B4**	51 35N	0 4W
Tottenham, *Melb.*	**19 E6**	37 48 S	144 51 E
Tottenville, *N.Y.*	**22 D3**	40 30N	74 14W
Totteridge, *Lon.*	**4 B3**	51 37N	0 11W
Toussus-le-Noble, *Paris*	**5 C2**	48 44N	2 6 E
Toussus-le-Noble, Aérodrome de, *Paris*	**5 C2**	48 44N	2 6 E
Toverud, *Oslo*	**2 B2**	59 55N	10 20 E
Towaco, *N.Y.*	**22 B3**	40 55N	74 18W
Tower Hamlets, *Lon.*	**4 B4**	51 31N	0 2W
Town Farm Hill, *Bost.*	**21 A3**	42 40N	71 3W
Townley, *N.Y.*	**22 C3**	40 41N	74 14W
Towra Pt., *Syd.*	**19 C4**	34 0 S	151 10 E
Towson, *Balt.*	**25 A3**	39 24N	76 36W
Tøyen, *Oslo*	**2 B4**	59 55N	10 47 E
Toyofuta, *Tōkyō*	**13 A4**	35 54N	139 55 E
Toyonaka, *Ōsaka*	**12 B3**	34 46N	135 28 E
Traar, *Ruhr*	**6 B1**	51 22N	6 36 E
Trafaria, *Lisb.*	**8 F7**	38 40N	9 13W
Tragliata, *Rome*	**9 F8**	41 58N	12 14 E
Traicão →, *S. Pau.*	**31 E6**	23 35 S	46 41W
Trälhavet, *Stock.*	**3 D13**	59 26N	18 22 E
Tranby, *Oslo*	**2 C1**	59 49N	10 14 E
Tranegilde, *Købn.*	**2 E9**	55 37N	12 20 E
Trångsund, *Stock.*	**3 E11**	59 13N	18 8 E
Trappenfelde, *Berl.*	**7 A4**	52 34N	13 39 E
Trappes, *Paris*	**5 C1**	48 46N	1 59 E
Trastévere, *Rome*	**9 F9**	51 53N	12 28 E
Travilah, *Wash.*	**25 C6**	39 4N	77 15W
Travilah Regional Park, *Wash.*	**25 C6**	39 4N	77 17W
Travis, *N.Y.*	**22 D3**	40 35N	74 11W
Treasure I., *S.F.*	**27 B2**	37 49N	122 22W
Třeboradice, *Pra.*	**10 B3**	50 9N	14 31 E
Třebotov, *Pra.*	**10 C1**	49 58N	14 17 E
Trecase, *Nápl.*	**9 J13**	40 46N	14 26 E
Trekroner, *Købn.*	**2 D10**	55 42N	12 36 E
Tremblay-lès-Gonesse, *Paris*	**5 B5**	48 58N	2 30 E
Tremembé, *S. Pau.*	**31 D6**	23 27 S	46 36W
Tremembe →, *S. Pau.*	**31 D6**	23 27 S	46 34W
Tremont, *Melb.*	**19 F9**	37 53 S	145 20 E
Tremont, *N.Y.*	**23 B5**	40 50N	73 52W
Trenno, *Mil.*	**9 E5**	45 29N	9 6 E
Treptow, *Berl.*	**7 B3**	52 29N	13 27 E
Tres Marias, *Méx.*	**29 D2**	19 3N	99 15W
Trés Rios, Sa. dos, *Rio J.*	**31 B2**	22 56 S	43 17W
Tretiakov Art Gallery, *Mos.*	**11 E9**	55 44N	37 38 E
Trevose, *Phil.*	**24 A5**	40 8N	74 59W
Trezzano sul Navíglio, *Mil.*	**9 E5**	45 24N	9 4 E
Tribobo, *Rio J.*	**31 B3**	22 50 S	43 0W
Triel-sur-Seine, *Paris*	**5 B2**	48 58N	2 0 E
Trieste, *Rome*	**9 F10**	41 55N	12 30 E
Trinidad, *Wash.*	**25 D8**	38 54N	76 59W
Triome, *Jobg.*	**18 F8**	26 10 S	27 58 E
Trionfale, *Rome*	**9 F9**	41 54N	12 26 E
Triulzo, *Mil.*	**9 E6**	45 25N	9 16 E
Trócchia, *Nápl.*	**9 H13**	40 51N	14 23 E
Troitse-Lykovo, *Mos.*	**11 E8**	55 47N	37 23 E
Troja, *Pra.*	**10 B2**	50 7N	14 25 E
Trollbäcken, *Stock.*	**3 E12**	59 14N	18 12 E
Trombay, *Bomb.*	**16 G8**	19 2N	72 56 E
Troparevo, *Mos.*	**11 F8**	55 39N	37 29 E
Trottiscliffe, *Lon.*	**4 D7**	51 18N	0 21 E
Troy Hills, *N.Y.*	**22 B2**	40 50N	74 23W
Troyeville, *Jobg.*	**18 F9**	26 11 S	28 4 E
Truc di Miola, *Tori.*	**9 A2**	45 11N	7 30 E
Trudyashchikhsya, Os., *Len.*	**11 B3**	59 58N	30 18 E
Trutlandet, *Hels.*	**3 C6**	60 9N	25 17 E
Tryvasshøgda, *Oslo*	**2 B4**	59 59N	10 40 E
Tseng Lan Shue, *H.K.*	**12 D6**	22 20N	114 14 E
Tsentralynyy, *Mos.*	**11 D11**	55 53N	37 51 E
Tsim Sha Tsui, *H.K.*	**12 E6**	22 17N	114 10 E
Tsing Yi, *H.K.*	**12 D5**	22 21N	114 6 E
Tsuen Wan, *H.K.*	**12 D5**	22 22N	114 7 E
Tsurugamine, *Tōkyō*	**13 D2**	35 28N	139 33 E
Tsuruma, *Tōkyō*	**13 A2**	35 52N	139 31 E
Tsurumi →, *Tōkyō*	**13 C3**	35 32N	139 40 E
Tsurumi-Ku, *Tōkyō*	**13 D3**	35 30N	139 41 E
Tsz Wan Shan, *H.K.*	**12 D6**	22 20N	114 11 E
Tua Kang Lye, *Sing.*	**15 G7**	1 18N	103 46 E
Tuas, *Sing.*	**15 G6**	1 19N	103 39 E
Tuchoměřice, *Pra.*	**10 B1**	50 7N	14 16 E
Tuckahoe, *N.Y.*	**23 B6**	40 56N	73 49W
Tucuruvi, *S. Pau.*	**31 D6**	23 28 S	46 35W
Tufello, *Rome*	**9 F10**	41 56N	12 32 E
Tufnell Park, *Lon.*	**4 B4**	51 33N	0 8W
Tujunga, *L.A.*	**28 A3**	34 15N	118 16W
Tujunga Wash →, *L.A.*	**28 A2**	34 12N	118 23W
Tullamarine, *Melb.*	**19 E6**	37 41 S	144 50 E
Tullinge, *Stock.*	**3 E10**	59 12N	17 54 E
Tullingesjön, *Stock.*	**3 E10**	59 12N	17 52 E
Tulse Hill, *Lon.*	**4 C4**	51 26N	0 6W
Tulyehualco, *Méx.*	**29 C3**	19 15N	99 0W
Tumba, *Stock.*	**3 E9**	59 12N	17 49 E
Tune, *Købn.*	**2 E8**	55 35N	12 10 E
Tung Lo Wan, *H.K.*	**12 E6**	22 17N	114 11 E
Tung Lung I., *H.K.*	**12 E6**	22 15N	114 17 E
Tung O, *H.K.*	**12 E5**	22 11N	114 8 E
Tunis, *Bagd.*	**17 E8**	33 23N	44 21 E
Tuomarila, *Hels.*	**3 B3**	60 11N	24 41 E
Tura, *El Qâ.*	**18 D5**	29 55N	31 16 E
Turambhe, *Bomb.*	**16 G9**	19 4N	73 0 E
Turdera, *B.A.*	**32 C4**	34 48 S	58 26W
Tureberg, *Stock.*	**3 D10**	59 25N	17 55 E
Turffontein, *Jobg.*	**18 F9**	26 14 S	28 2 E
Turin = Torino, *Tori.*	**9 B2**	45 5N	7 39 E
Turner, *Balt.*	**25 B3**	39 14N	76 31W
Turner Hill, *Bost.*	**21 A4**	42 40N	70 53W
Turnersville, *Phil.*	**24 C4**	39 46N	75 3W
Turnham Green, *Lon.*	**4 C3**	51 29N	0 16W
Turów, *Wsaw.*	**10 E8**	52 19N	21 11 E
Turter, *Oslo*	**2 A4**	60 0N	10 46 E
Tuscolano, *Rome*	**9 F10**	41 52N	12 31 E
Tushino, *Mos.*	**11 D8**	55 50N	37 24 E
Tuusulanjoki →, *Hels.*	**3 A4**	60 20N	24 54 E
Twickenham, *Lon.*	**4 C2**	51 26N	0 20W
Twickenham Rugby Ground, *Lon.*	**4 C2**	51 27N	0 20W
Twin Oaks, *Phil.*	**24 B2**	39 50N	75 25W
Twórki, *Wsaw.*	**10 E5**	52 10N	20 49 E
Tyresö, *Stock.*	**3 E13**	59 14N	18 20 E
Tyresö strand, *Stock.*	**3 E12**	59 15N	18 17 E

U

Uberaba →, *S. Pau.*	**31 E6**	23 35 S	46 41W
Uberruhr, *Ruhr*	**6 B4**	51 25N	7 4 E
Ubin, P., *Sing.*	**15 F8**	1 24N	103 57 E
Uboldo, *Mil.*	**9 D5**	45 36N	9 0 E
Uckendorf, *Ruhr*	**6 B4**	51 29N	7 7 E
Udelnaya, *Len.*	**11 A4**	60 0N	30 21 E
Udelynaya, *Mos.*	**11 F11**	55 38N	37 59 E
Udlding, *Mün.*	**7 F9**	48 15N	11 25 E
Uellendahl, *Ruhr*	**6 C5**	51 16N	7 10 E
Ueno, *Tōkyō*	**13 B3**	35 42N	139 46 E
Uerdingen, *Ruhr*	**6 B1**	51 21N	6 38 E
Uhlenhorst, *Hbg.*	**7 D8**	53 34N	10 1 E
Üholičky, *Pra.*	**10 B1**	50 9N	14 19 E
Uhřiněves, *Pra.*	**10 B3**	50 2N	14 35 E
Üjezd nad Lesy, *Pra.*	**10 B3**	50 4N	14 39 E
Üjpalota, *Bud.*	**10 J13**	47 32N	19 8 E
Üjpest, *Bud.*	**10 J13**	47 35N	19 4 E
Ukita, *Tōkyō*	**13 B4**	35 40N	139 51 E
Ullerup, *Købn.*	**2 E10**	55 34N	12 36 E
Ullevål, *Oslo*	**2 B4**	59 56N	10 46 E
Üllo, *Bud.*	**10 K14**	47 23N	19 20 E
Ulriksdal, *Stock.*	**3 D10**	59 23N	17 59 E
Ulu Bedok, *Sing.*	**15 G8**	1 19N	103 55 E
Ulu Pandan →, *Sing.*	**15 G7**	1 19N	103 45 E
Ulyanka, *Len.*	**11 B3**	59 50N	30 14 E
Um Al-Khanazir, *Bagd.*	**17 F8**	33 17N	44 22 E
Umeda, *Ōsaka*	**12 B3**	34 41N	135 29 E
Umejima, *Tōkyō*	**13 B3**	35 46N	139 48 E
Umraniye, *Ist.*	**17 A3**	41 1N	29 4 E
Unětický →, *Pra.*	**10 B2**	50 9N	14 24 E
Ungelsheim, *Ruhr*	**6 B2**	51 21N	6 43 E
Unhos, *Lisb.*	**8 F8**	38 49N	9 7W
Unidad Santa Fe, *Méx.*	**29 B2**	19 23N	99 13W
Union, *N.Y.*	**22 C3**	40 42N	74 16W
Union City, *N.Y.*	**22 C4**	40 45N	74 2W
Union City, *S.F.*	**27 C4**	37 36N	122 2W
Union Port, *N.Y.*	**23 C5**	40 48N	73 51W
Uniondale, *N.Y.*	**23 C7**	40 42N	73 35W
United Nations H.Q., *N.Y.*	**22 C5**	40 45N	73 59W
Universal City, *L.A.*	**28 B2**	34 8N	118 21W
Universidad de Chila, *Stgo*	**30 J11**	33 26 S	70 39W
University Gardens, *N.Y.*	**23 C6**	40 46N	73 42W
University Heights, *S.F.*	**27 D3**	37 26N	122 13W
University Park, *Wash.*	**25 D8**	38 58N	76 56W
Unsani, *Calc.*	**16 E5**	22 35N	88 15 E
Unterbach, *Ruhr*	**6 C3**	51 12N	6 53 E
Unterbiberg, *Mün.*	**7 G10**	48 6N	11 38 E
Unterföhring, *Mün.*	**7 F11**	48 11N	11 38 E
Unterhaching, *Mün.*	**7 G10**	48 3N	11 37 E
Unterkirchbach, *Wien*	**10 G9**	48 17N	16 12 E
Unterlaa, *Wien*	**10 H10**	48 8N	16 24 E
Untermauerbach, *Wien*	**10 G9**	48 14N	16 11 E
Untermenzing, *Mün.*	**7 F9**	48 10N	11 28 E
Unterrath, *Ruhr*	**6 C2**	51 16N	6 45 E
Unterschleissheim, *Mün.*	**7 F10**	48 16N	11 35 E
Upminster, *Lon.*	**4 B6**	51 33N	0 14 E
Upper Brookville, *N.Y.*	**23 B7**	40 50N	73 35W
Upper Crystal Springs Res., *S.F.*	**26 D2**	37 28N	122 20W
Upper Darby, *Phil.*	**24 B3**	39 57N	75 16W
Upper Edmonton, *Lon.*	**4 B4**	51 36N	0 3W
Upper Elmers End, *Lon.*	**4 C4**	51 23N	0 1W
Upper Fern Tree Gully, *Melb.*	**19 F8**	37 53 S	145 18 E
Upper New York B., *N.Y.*	**22 D4**	40 39N	74 3W
Upper Norwood, *Lon.*	**4 C4**	51 24N	0 6W
Upper Peirce Res., *Sing.*	**15 F7**	1 22N	103 47 E
Upper San Leandro Res., *S.F.*	**27 B4**	37 46N	122 6W
Upper Sydenham, *Lon.*	**4 C4**	51 26N	0 4W
Upper Tooting, *Lon.*	**4 C4**	51 25N	0 9W
Upton, *Lon.*	**4 B5**	51 32N	0 1 E
Uptons Hill, *Bost.*	**21 B3**	42 33N	71 0W
Uptown, *Chic.*	**26 B2**	41 58N	87 40W
Upwey, *Melb.*	**19 F9**	37 53 S	145 20 E
Urawa, *Tōkyō*	**13 A2**	35 51N	139 39 E
Urayasu, *Tōkyō*	**13 C4**	35 39N	139 53 E
Urbe, Aeroporto d', *Rome*	**9 F10**	41 57N	12 30 E
Urca, *Rio J.*	**31 B3**	22 56 S	43 9W
Uritsk, *Len.*	**11 C3**	59 49N	30 10 E
Üröm, *Bud.*	**10 J13**	47 35N	19 1 E
Ursus, *Wsaw.*	**10 E6**	52 11N	20 52 E
Ursvik, *Stock.*	**3 D10**	59 23N	17 57 E
Usera, *Mdrd.*	**8 B2**	40 22N	3 42W
Ushigome, *Tōkyō*	**13 B3**	35 42N	139 44 E
Usküdar, *Ist.*	**17 A3**	41 1N	29 0 E
Ust-Slavyanka, *Len.*	**11 C5**	59 51N	30 32 E
Uteke, *Stock.*	**3 D12**	59 24N	18 15 E
Utfort, *Ruhr*	**6 B1**	51 28N	6 37 E
Utinga, *S. Pau.*	**31 E6**	23 38 S	46 31W
Utrata, *Wsaw.*	**10 E7**	52 15N	21 4 E
Uttarpara, *Calc.*	**16 E5**	22 39N	88 21 E
Utterslev Mose, *Købn.*	**2 D9**	55 42N	12 29 E
Uttran, *Stock.*	**3 E9**	59 12N	17 43 E
Utvika, *Oslo*	**2 A1**	60 2N	10 15 E
Uxbridge, *Lon.*	**4 B2**	51 32N	0 28W
Uzkoye, *Mos.*	**11 F9**	55 37N	37 32 E
Uzunca →, *Ist.*	**17 A1**	41 54N	28 50 E

V

Vadaul, *Bomb.*	**16 G8**	19 2N	72 55 E
Værebro Å →, *Købn.*	**2 D8**	55 47N	12 7 E
Vahal, *Bomb.*	**16 H9**	18 58N	73 2 E
Vaires-sur-Marne, *Paris*	**5 B5**	48 52N	2 38 E
Val della Torre, *Tori.*	**9 B1**	45 8N	7 27 E
Valby, *Købn.*	**2 E9**	55 39N	12 29 E
Valcannuta, *Rome*	**9 F9**	41 52N	12 25 E
Valdeveba, *Mdrd.*	**8 B3**	40 29N	3 39W
Vale, *Wash.*	**25 D5**	38 55N	77 20W
Valentino, Parco del, *Tori.*	**9 B3**	45 3N	7 41 E
Valenton, *Paris*	**5 C4**	48 44N	2 27 E
Valera, *Mil.*	**9 D5**	45 33N	9 3 E
Vallcarca, *Barc.*	**8 D5**	41 25N	2 9 E
Valldoreix, *Barc.*	**8 D5**	41 27N	2 3 E
Vallecas, *Mdrd.*	**8 B3**	40 22N	3 37W
Vallemar, *S.F.*	**27 C2**	37 36N	122 28W
Vallensbæk, *Købn.*	**2 E9**	55 38N	12 21 E
Vallensbæk Strand, *Købn.*	**2 E9**	55 36N	12 23 E
Vallentunasjön, *Stock.*	**3 D11**	59 27N	18 1 E
Valleranello, *Rome*	**9 G9**	41 46N	12 29 E
Valley Forge, *Phil.*	**24 A2**	40 5N	75 27W
Valley Forge Hist. State Park, *Phil.*	**24 A2**	40 5N	75 27W
Valley Mede, *Balt.*	**25 B1**	39 16N	76 50W
Valley Stream, *N.Y.*	**23 C6**	40 40N	73 43W
Vällingby, *Stock.*	**3 D10**	59 21N	17 52 E
Vallisaari, *Hels.*	**3 C5**	60 7N	25 0 E
Vallvidrera, *Barc.*	**8 D5**	41 24N	2 6 E
Valo Velho, *S. Pau.*	**31 E5**	23 38 S	46 47W
Valuyevo, *Mos.*	**11 F8**	55 30N	37 21 E
Valvidrera →, *Barc.*	**8 D5**	41 25N	2 0 E
Van Dyks Park, *Jobg.*	**18 F10**	26 15 S	28 18 E
Van Nuys, *L.A.*	**28 A2**	34 11N	118 27W
Van Nuys Airport, *L.A.*	**28 A2**	34 12N	118 29W
Van Ryn Dam, *Jobg.*	**18 E11**	26 8 S	28 21 E
Vanak, *Tehr.*	**17 C5**	35 45N	51 23 E
Vangede, *Købn.*	**2 D10**	55 45N	12 30 E
Vaniköy, *Ist.*	**17 A3**	41 3N	29 3 E
Vanløse, *Købn.*	**2 D9**	55 41N	12 28 E
Vantaa, *Hels.*	**3 B4**	60 18N	24 56 E
Vantaa →, *Hels.*	**3 B4**	60 13N	24 53 E
Vantaankoski, *Hels.*	**3 B4**	60 18N	24 50 E
Vantör, *Stock.*	**3 E11**	59 16N	18 2 E
Vanves, *Paris*	**5 C3**	48 49N	2 17 E
Vanzago, *Mil.*	**9 D4**	45 31N	8 59 E
Värby, *Stock.*	**3 E10**	59 15N	17 52 E
Vardåsen, *Oslo*	**2 C6**	50 48N	11 6 E
Varedo, *Mil.*	**9 D5**	45 35N	9 8 E
Varennes-Jarcy, *Paris*	**5 C5**	48 40N	2 33 E
Vargem Grande, *Rio J.*	**31 B1**	22 58 S	43 27W
Városliget, *Bud.*	**10 J13**	47 30N	19 5 E
Vartiokylä, *Hels.*	**3 B5**	60 13N	25 6 E
Vartiosaari, *Hels.*	**3 B5**	60 11N	25 5 E
Vasby, *Købn.*	**2 D8**	55 40N	12 12 E
Vashi, *Bomb.*	**16 G8**	19 4N	72 59 E
Vasilyevskiy, Os., *Len.*	**11 B3**	59 55N	30 16 E
Västerkulla, *Hels.*	**3 B2**	60 16N	24 31 E
Västerskog, *Hels.*	**3 B6**	60 16N	25 17 E
Vasto, *Nápl.*	**9 H12**	40 51N	14 16 E
Vatutino, *Mos.*	**11 D10**	55 52N	37 40 E
Vaucresson, *Paris*	**5 B2**	48 50N	2 9 E
Vaudreuil, *Mtrl.*	**20 B1**	43 24N	74 1W
Vaudreuil-sur-le Lac, *Mtrl.*	**20 B1**	43 25N	74 1W
Vauhallan, *Paris*	**5 C3**	48 44N	2 12 E
Vaujours, *Paris*	**5 B5**	48 56N	2 34 E
Vauréal, *Paris*	**5 A2**	49 2N	2 1 E
Vaux-sur-Seine, *Paris*	**5 A1**	49 0N	1 57 E
Vauxhall, *Lon.*	**4 C4**	51 29N	0 7W
Vaxholm, *Stock.*	**3 D13**	59 24N	18 20 E
Vecklax, *Hels.*	**3 B2**	60 10N	24 31 E
Vecsés, *Bud.*	**10 K14**	47 24N	19 16 E
Vedano al Lissone, *Mil.*	**9 D6**	45 36N	9 16 E
Veddel, *Hbg.*	**7 D8**	53 31N	10 2 E
Vega, *Stock.*	**3 E11**	59 11N	18 8 E
Vehkalahti, *Hels.*	**3 B2**	60 11N	24 30 E
Veikkola, *Hels.*	**3 B1**	60 17N	24 26 E
Velbert, *Ruhr*	**6 B4**	51 21N	7 1 E
Veleň, *Pra.*	**10 A3**	50 10N	14 33 E
Veleslavin, *Pra.*	**10 B2**	50 5N	14 21 E
Vélizy-Villacoublay, *Paris*	**5 C3**	48 47N	2 11 E
Velka-Chuchle, *Pra.*	**10 B2**	50 0N	14 23 E
Venaria, *Tori.*	**9 B2**	45 8N	7 37 E
Venda Seca, *Lisb.*	**8 F7**	38 46N	9 15W
Vendelsö, *Stock.*	**3 E12**	59 12N	18 11 E
Venice, *L.A.*	**28 C2**	33 59N	118 27W
Venner, *Oslo*	**2 A3**	60 1N	10 36 E
Vennhausen, *Ruhr*	**6 C3**	51 13N	6 51 E
Ventas, *Mdrd.*	**8 B2**	40 26N	3 40W
Ventorro del Cano, *Mdrd.*	**8 B2**	40 23N	3 49W
Verberg, *Ruhr*	**6 B1**	51 21N	6 34 E
Verde →, *S. Pau.*	**31 E7**	23 29 S	46 27W
Verdi, *Ath.*	**8 H11**	38 2N	23 40 E
Verdugo Mt., *L.A.*	**28 A3**	34 12N	118 17W
Verdun, *Mtrl.*	**20 B4**	43 27N	73 35W
Vereya, *Mos.*	**11 F12**	55 37N	38 2 E
Vérhalom, *Bud.*	**10 J13**	47 31N	19 1 E
Vermelho →, *S. Pau.*	**31 E5**	23 30 S	46 46W
Vermont, *Melb.*	**19 F8**	37 50 S	145 12 E
Vermont South, *Melb.*	**19 F8**	37 51 S	145 11 E
Verneuil-sur-Seine, *Paris*	**5 B1**	48 58N	1 59 E
Vernouillet, *Paris*	**5 B1**	48 58N	1 56 E
Verona, *N.Y.*	**22 C3**	40 49N	74 15W
Verperluda, Os., *Len.*	**11 B2**	59 59N	30 0 E
Verrières-le-Buisson, *Paris*	**5 C3**	48 44N	2 16 E
Versailles, *B.A.*	**32 B3**	34 38 S	58 31W
Versailles, *Paris*	**5 C2**	48 48N	2 7 E
Veshnyaki, *Mos.*	**11 E10**	55 43N	37 48 E
Vesolyy Posolok, *Len.*	**11 B4**	59 53N	30 28 E
Vestli, *Oslo*	**2 B5**	59 58N	10 55 E
Vestra, *Hels.*	**3 B3**	60 19N	24 46 E
Vestskoven, *Købn.*	**2 D9**	55 41N	12 23 E
Vesuvio, *Nápl.*	**9 J13**	40 49N	14 25 E
Vets Stadium, *Phil.*	**24 B3**	39 54N	75 10W
Viby, *Købn.*	**2 E7**	55 33N	12 1 E
Vicálvaro, *Mdrd.*	**8 B3**	40 24N	3 36W
Vicente Lopez, *B.A.*	**32 B4**	34 31 S	58 30W
Victoria, *B.A.*	**32 A3**	34 27 S	58 32W
Victoria, *H.K.*	**12 E6**	22 17N	114 11 E
Victoria, Pont, *Mtrl.*	**20 B4**	43 29N	73 32W
Victoria Gardens, *Bomb.*	**16 H8**	18 58N	72 50 E
Victoria Harbour, *H.K.*	**12 E5**	22 17N	114 10 E
Victoria Island, *Lagos*	**18 B2**	6 25N	7 25 E
Victoria L., *Jobg.*	**18 F9**	26 13 S	28 9 E
Victoria Lawn Tennis Courts, *Melb.*	**19 F7**	37 50 S	145 1 E
Victoria Park, *H.K.*	**12 E5**	22 16N	114 8 E
Vidja, *Stock.*	**3 E11**	59 12N	18 4 E
Vidrholec, *Pra.*	**10 B3**	50 5N	14 39 E
Vienna = Wien, *Wien*	**10 G10**	48 12N	16 22 E
Vienna, *Wash.*	**25 D6**	38 54N	77 16W
Vieringhausen, *Ruhr*	**6 C4**	51 10N	7 9 E
Vierlinden, *Ruhr*	**6 A2**	51 32N	6 45 E
Vierumäki, *Hels.*	**3 A5**	60 21N	25 2 E
Vierzigstücken, *Hbg.*	**7 D6**	53 30N	9 49 E
View Bank, *Melb.*	**19 E7**	37 43 S	145 6 E
Vigário Geral, *Rio J.*	**31 A2**	22 48 S	43 18W
Vigentino, *Mil.*	**9 E6**	45 26N	9 13 E
Viggbyholm, *Stock.*	**3 D11**	59 26N	18 7 E
Vighignolo, *Mil.*	**9 E5**	45 29N	9 2 E
Vigneux-sur-Seine, *Paris*	**5 C4**	48 42N	2 24 E
Viikki, *Hels.*	**3 B5**	60 13N	25 1 E
Viirila, *Hels.*	**3 B5**	60 19N	25 8 E
Vila Andrade, *S. Pau.*	**31 E5**	23 37 S	46 44W
Vila Barcelona, *S. Pau.*	**31 E6**	23 37 S	46 33W
Vila Bocaina, *S. Pau.*	**31 F7**	23 40 S	46 26W
Vila Dalva, *S. Pau.*	**31 E5**	23 34 S	46 46W
Vila Dirce, *S. Pau.*	**31 E4**	23 33 S	46 50W
Vila Eldorado, *S. Pau.*	**31 F6**	23 42 S	46 38W
Vila Ema, *S. Pau.*	**31 E6**	23 35 S	46 31W
Vila Formosa, *S. Pau.*	**31 E6**	23 36 S	46 44W
Vila Galvão, *S. Pau.*	**31 D6**	23 27 S	46 34W
Vila Gonçales, *S. Pau.*	**31 F6**	23 42 S	46 33W
Vila Iasi, *S. Pau.*	**31 E5**	23 37 S	46 47W
Vila Indiana, *S. Pau.*	**31 E5**	23 37 S	46 48W
Vila Isabel, *Rio J.*	**31 B2**	22 54 S	43 15W
Vila Madalena, *S. Pau.*	**31 E5**	23 32 S	46 41W
Vila Maria, *S. Pau.*	**31 E6**	23 31 S	46 36W
Vila Mariana, *S. Pau.*	**31 E6**	23 34 S	46 36W
Vila Matilde, *S. Pau.*	**31 E6**	23 31 S	46 30W
Vila Nova Curuçá, *S. Pau.*	**31 E7**	23 31 S	46 25W
Vila Pires, *S. Pau.*	**31 F6**	23 41 S	46 30W
Vila Progresso, *Rio J.*	**31 B3**	22 53 S	43 1W
Vila Prudente, *S. Pau.*	**31 E6**	23 35 S	46 33W
Vila Ré, *S. Pau.*	**31 E7**	23 31 S	46 29W
Vila Remo, *S. Pau.*	**31 F5**	23 40 S	46 45W
Vila Sonia, *S. Pau.*	**31 E5**	23 35 S	46 43W
Viladecans, *Barc.*	**8 E5**	41 18N	2 1 E
Villa Ada, *Rome*	**9 F10**	41 55N	12 30 E
Villa Adelina, *B.A.*	**32 B3**	34 31 S	58 33W
Villa Alianza, *B.A.*	**32 B3**	34 37 S	58 33W
Villa Alsina, *B.A.*	**32 C4**	34 40 S	58 24W
Villa Altube, *B.A.*	**32 B2**	34 31 S	58 45W
Villa Ariza, *B.A.*	**32 B3**	34 38 S	58 39W
Villa Augusta, *B.A.*	**32 C5**	34 45 S	58 15W
Villa Ballester, *B.A.*	**32 B3**	34 33 S	58 33W
Villa Barilari, *B.A.*	**32 C4**	34 42 S	58 20W
Villa Basso, *B.A.*	**32 B3**	34 38 S	58 36W
Villa Bosch, *B.A.*	**32 B3**	34 35 S	58 33W
Villa C. Colon, *B.A.*	**32 C4**	34 41 S	58 21W
Villa D. F. Sarmiento, *B.A.*	**32 B3**	34 38 S	58 35W
Villa D. Sobral, *B.A.*	**32 C5**	34 45 S	58 15W
Villa de Guadalupe, *Méx.*	**29 B3**	19 29N	99 6W
Villa de Mayo, *B.A.*	**32 B2**	34 30 S	58 40W
Villa Devoto, *B.A.*	**32 B3**	34 36 S	58 31W
Villa Dominico, *B.A.*	**32 C5**	34 41 S	58 19W
Villa Giambruno, *B.A.*	**32 C5**	34 48 S	58 15W
Villa Gustavo A. Madero, *Méx.*	**29 B3**	19 29N	99 8W
Villa Hogar Alemán, *B.A.*	**32 C4**	34 49 S	58 26W
Villa Iglesias, *B.A.*	**32 B2**	34 30 S	58 45W
Villa Leloir, *B.A.*	**32 B2**	34 36 S	58 41W
Villa Leon, *B.A.*	**32 B2**	34 38 S	58 41W
Villa Lugano, *B.A.*	**32 C4**	34 41 S	58 27W
Villa Luzuriago, *B.A.*	**32 C3**	34 40 S	58 34W
Villa Lynch, *B.A.*	**32 B3**	34 35 S	58 31W
Villa Madero, *B.A.*	**32 C3**	34 41 S	58 30W
Villa Maria del Triunfo, *Lima*	**30 G9**	12 9 S	76 57W
Villa Obregon, *Méx.*	**29 B2**	19 20N	99 12W
Villa Reichembach, *B.A.*	**32 B2**	34 39 S	58 40W
Villa Rosa, *B.A.*	**32 A1**	34 25 S	58 5W
Villa San Francisco, *B.A.*	**32 C5**	34 46 S	58 15W
Villacoublay, Aérodrome de, *Paris*	**5 C3**	48 46N	2 12 E
Village Green, *Phil.*	**24 B2**	39 52N	75 26W
Villanova, *Phil.*	**24 A2**	40 1N	75 20W
Villarbasse, *Tori.*	**9 B1**	45 2N	7 27 E
Villaretto, *Tori.*	**9 B3**	45 8N	7 41 E
Villaricca, *Nápl.*	**9 H12**	40 55N	14 11 E
Villaroche, *Paris*	**5 D5**	48 37N	2 39 E
Villaroy, *Paris*	**5 C2**	48 46N	2 5 E
Villasanta, *Mil.*	**9 D6**	45 36N	9 18 E
Villastanza, *Mil.*	**9 D4**	45 32N	8 57 E
Villaverde, *Mdrd.*	**8 B2**	40 21N	3 42W
Villaverde Bajo, *Mdrd.*	**8 B2**	40 20N	3 40W
Villawood, *Syd.*	**19 B2**	33 52 S	150 58 E
Ville-d'Avray, *Paris*	**5 C3**	48 49N	2 11 E
Ville de Laval, *Mtrl.*	**20 A3**	43 34N	73 43W
Villebon-sur-Yvette, *Paris*	**5 C3**	48 41N	2 14 E
Villecresnes, *Paris*	**5 C5**	48 43N	2 31 E
Villejuif, *Paris*	**5 C4**	48 47N	2 21 E
Villejust, *Paris*	**5 C3**	48 41N	2 15 E

48 Villemoisson-sur-Orge

Villemoisson-sur-Orge, *Paris* 5 C3 48 40N 2 19 E
Villemomble, *Paris* 5 B5 48 52N 2 30 E
Villeneuve-la-Garenne, *Paris* 5 B3 48 56N 2 19 E
Villeneuve-le-Roi, *Paris* 5 C4 48 43N 2 24 E
Villeneuve-St.-Georges, *Paris* 5 C4 48 43N 2 27 E
Villeneuve-sous-Dammartin, *Paris* 5 A5 49 2N 2 38 E
Villennes-sur-Seine, *Paris* 5 B1 48 56N 2 0 E
Villeparisis, *Paris* 5 B5 48 56N 2 36 E
Villepinte, *Paris* 5 B5 48 57N 2 30 E
Villepreux, *Paris* 5 C1 48 49N 1 59 E
Villevaudé, *Paris* 5 B5 48 55N 2 39 E
Villeziers, *Paris* 5 C3 48 40N 2 10 E
Villiers-le-Bâcle, *Paris* 5 C2 48 44N 2 8 E
Villiers-le-Bel, *Paris* 5 A4 49 0N 2 23 E
Villiers-St. Frédéric, *Paris* 5 C1 48 49N 1 53 E
Villiers-sur-Marne, *Paris* 5 C5 48 49N 2 32 E
Villiers-sur-Orge, *Paris* 5 D3 48 39N 2 18 E
Villinki, *Hels.* 3 C5 60 9N 25 6 E
Villoresi, Canale, *Mil.* 9 D4 45 33N 8 59 E
Vimodrone, *Mil.* 9 D6 45 30N 9 16 E
Vimont, *Mtrl.* 20 A3 43 36N 73 43W
Vincennes, *Paris* 5 B4 48 51N 2 26 E
Vincennes, Bois de, *Paris* 5 C4 48 49N 2 26 E
Vinohrady, *Pra.* 10 B2 50 4N 14 26 E
Vinoř, *Pra.* 10 B3 50 8N 14 34 E
Vinořský →, *Pra.* 10 A3 50 11N 14 39 E
Violet Hill, *H.K.* 12 E6 22 15N 114 11 E
Virányos, *Bud.* 10 J12 47 31N 18 59 E
Virgeo del San Cristóbal, *Stgo* 30 J11 33 25 S 70 38W
Viroflay, *Paris* 5 C3 48 48N 2 10 E
Viron, *Ath.* 8 J11 37 55N 23 46 E
Virreyes, *B.A.* 32 A3 34 27 S 58 33W
Virum, *Købn.* 2 D9 55 47N 12 27 E
Viry-Châtillon, *Paris* 5 C4 48 40N 2 21 E
Vishnyaki, *Mos.* 11 E11 55 46N 37 53 E
Visitacion Valley, *S.F.* 27 B2 37 42N 122 23W
Vista Alegre, *Lima* 30 G9 12 8 S 76 59W
Vista Alegre, *Stgo* 30 K10 33 30 S 70 43W
Vitacura, *Stgo* 30 J11 33 23 S 70 35W
Vitarte-Ate, *Lima* 30 G9 12 3 S 76 57W
Vitinia, *Rome* 9 G9 41 47N 12 24 E
Vitry-sur-Seine, *Paris* 5 C4 48 47N 2 23 E
Vitträsk, *Hels.* 3 B1 60 11N 24 29 E
Vittuone, *Mil.* 9 E4 45 28N 8 57 E
Vladykino, *Mos.* 11 D9 55 51N 37 35 E
Vltava →, *Pra.* 10 A2 50 10N 14 2 E
Vnukovo, *Mos.* 11 F7 55 37N 37 17 E
Voerde, *Ruhr* 6 C6 51 18N 7 23 E
Voerde, *Ruhr* 6 A2 51 35N 6 42 E
Vogelheim, *Ruhr* 6 B3 51 29N 6 59 E
Vohwinkel, *Ruhr* 6 C4 51 13N 7 4 E
Voisins-le-Bretonneux, *Paris* 5 C2 48 45N 2 3 E
Vokovice, *Pra.* 10 B2 50 5N 14 21 E
Volgelsdorf, *Berl.* 7 B5 52 30N 13 44 E
Volkhonka-Zil, *Mos.* 11 F9 55 39N 37 37 E
Volkovka →, *Len.* 11 B4 59 54N 30 25 E
Volksdorf, *Hbg.* 7 D8 53 39N 10 8 E
Volla, *Nápl.* 9 H13 40 52N 14 20 E
Vollen, *Oslo* 2 C2 59 48N 10 27 E
Volmarstein, *Ruhr* 6 B6 51 22N 7 22 E
Volodarskoye, *Len.* 11 B4 59 54N 30 23 E
Volpiano, *Tori.* 9 A3 45 12N 7 46 E
Volynkina-Derevnya, *Len.* 11 B3 59 53N 30 18 E
Volynyy, Os., *Len.* 11 B3 59 57N 30 14 E
Võmero, *Nápl.* 9 H12 40 50N 14 13 E
Vorderhainbach, *Wien* 10 G9 48 13N 16 12 E
Vorhalle, *Ruhr* 6 B6 51 23N 7 26 E
Vormholz, *Ruhr* 6 B5 51 24N 7 19 E
Vösendorf, *Wien* 10 H10 48 7N 16 20 E
Vostochnyy, *Mos.* 11 E11 55 49N 37 51 E
Vouliagmeni, *Ath.* 8 K11 37 50N 23 46 E
Vrčovice, *Pra.* 10 B2 50 4N 14 28 E
Vsevolozhsk, *Len.* 11 A5 60 0N 30 39 E
Vuosaari, *Hels.* 3 B5 60 13N 25 8 E
Vyborgskaya Storona, *Len.* 11 B4 59 57N 30 22 E
Vyčehrad, *Pra.* 10 B2 50 3N 14 25 E
Vykhino, *Mos.* 11 E10 55 42N 37 48 E
Vysočany, *Pra.* 10 B2 50 6N 14 29 E

W

Waban, L., *Bost.* 21 D2 42 17N 71 18W
Wachterhof, *Mün.* 7 G11 48 2N 11 42 E
Waddington, *Lon.* 4 D4 51 18N 0 7W
Wadeville, *Jobg.* 18 F10 26 15 S 28 11 E
Wahda, *Bagd.* 17 F8 33 18N 44 26 E
Währing, *Wien* 10 G10 48 14N 16 20 E
Waidmannslust, *Berl.* 7 A3 52 36N 13 20 E
Wajay, *La Hab.* 30 B2 23 0N 82 25W
Wakefield, *Bost.* 21 B3 42 30N 71 5W
Wald, *Ruhr* 6 C4 51 11N 7 3 E
Waldesruh, *Berl.* 7 B4 52 28N 13 37 E
Waldheim, *Berl.* 7 A1 52 34N 13 3 E
Waldperlach, *Mün.* 7 G11 48 4N 11 40 E
Waldtrudering, *Mün.* 7 G11 48 6N 11 42 E
Waldwick, *N.Y.* 22 A4 41 1N 74 5W
Wall Street, *N.Y.* 22 C4 40 42N 74 0W
Wallgrove, *Syd.* 19 A2 33 47 S 150 51 E
Wallington, *Lon.* 4 C4 51 21N 0 8W
Wallington, *N.Y.* 22 B4 40 50N 74 8W
Walnut Cr. →, *S.F.* 27 A4 37 55N 122 3W
Walnut Creek, *S.F.* 27 A4 37 53N 122 3W
Walnut Heights, *S.F.* 27 A4 37 52N 122 2W
Walsum, *Ruhr* 6 A2 51 32N 6 42 E
Walsumer Mark, *Ruhr* 6 A3 51 33N 6 50 E
Walt Whitman Br., *Phil.* 24 B4 39 4N 75 9W
Waltershof, *Hbg.* 7 D7 53 31N 9 54 E
Waltham, *Bost.* 21 C2 42 23N 71 14W
Waltham Abbey, *Lon.* 4 A5 51 41N 0 1 E
Waltham Forest, *Lon.* 4 B4 51 36N 0 0 E
Walthamstow, *Lon.* 4 B4 51 34N 0 1W
Walton on Thames, *Lon.* 4 C2 51 22N 0 23W
Walton on the Hill, *Lon.* 4 D3 51 16N 0 14W
Waltrop, *Ruhr* 6 A6 51 36N 7 25 E
Walworth, *Lon.* 4 C4 51 29N 0 5W
Wambachsee, *Ruhr* 6 B2 51 23N 6 47 E
Wan Chai, *H.K.* 12 E6 22 16N 114 10 E
Wanaque, *N.Y.* 22 A3 41 1N 74 17W
Wandezhuang, *Tianj.* 14 E5 39 6N 117 10 E
Wandle →, *Lon.* 4 C3 51 27N 0 11W
Wandsbek, *Hbg.* 7 D8 53 34N 10 4 E
Wandsworth, *Lon.* 4 C3 51 27N 0 11W
Wang Hin, Khlong →, *Bangk.* 15 A2 13 50N 100 35 E
Wanheim, *Ruhr* 6 B2 51 23N 6 45 E
Wanheimerort, *Ruhr* 6 B2 51 24N 6 45 E
Wanne-Eickel, *Ruhr* 6 A4 51 31N 7 9 E
Wannsee, *Berl.* 7 B1 52 25N 13 9 E
Wansdorf, *Berl.* 7 A1 52 38N 13 5 E
Wanstead, *Lon.* 4 B5 51 34N 0 1 E
Wantagh Seaford, *N.Y.* 23 D8 40 39N 73 28W
Wantirna, *Melb.* 19 F8 37 50 S 145 14 E
Wapping, *Lon.* 4 B4 51 30N 0 3W
Warabi, *Tōkyō* 13 B3 35 49N 139 42 E
Ward, *Phil.* 24 B1 39 52N 75 30W
Warlingham, *Lon.* 4 D4 51 18N 0 2W
Warnberg, *Mün.* 7 G10 48 4N 11 31 E
Warngal Park, *Melb.* 19 E7 37 45 S 145 4 E
Warrandyte, *Melb.* 19 E8 37 43 S 145 13 E
Warrandyte Park, *Melb.* 19 E8 37 44 S 145 14 E
Warrandyte South, *Melb.* 19 E8 37 44 S 145 14 E
Warranwood, *Melb.* 19 E8 37 46 S 145 14 E
Warrâq el 'Arab, *El Qâ.* 18 C5 30 4N 31 11 E
Warrâq el Hadf, *El Qâ.* 18 C5 30 5N 31 12 E
Warren Hill, *Bost.* 21 B1 42 35N 71 21W
Warsaw = Warszawa, *Wsaw.* 10 E7 52 14N 21 0 E
Warszawa, *Wsaw.* 10 E7 52 14N 21 0 E
Wartenberg, *Berl.* 7 A4 52 34N 13 31 E
Warwick Farm Racetrack, *Syd.* 19 B2 33 54 S 150 56 E
Wasa, *Stock.* 3 E11 59 19N 18 5 E
Wasfanārd, *Tehr.* 17 D5 35 38N 51 20 E
Washington, *Wash.* 25 D7 38 53N 77 2W
Washington Heights, *N.Y.* 22 B5 40 51N 73 56W
Washington Memorial Museum, *Phil.* 24 A2 40 5N 75 26W
Washington Nat. Airport, *Wash.* 25 D7 38 51N 77 2W
Washington Park, *Chic.* 26 C3 41 47N 87 36W
Washington Square, *Phil.* 24 A3 40 9N 75 19W
Washington Township, *N.Y.* 22 A4 41 0N 74 3W
Wasserschloss, *Ruhr* 6 A4 51 32N 7 1 E
Watching Mts., *N.Y.* 22 C2 40 43N 74 20W
Watchung, *N.Y.* 22 D2 40 38N 74 29W
Waterloo, *Syd.* 19 B4 33 53 S 151 12 E
Waterman Mt., *L.A.* 28 A5 34 14N 117 56W
Watertown, *Bost.* 21 C2 42 22N 71 10W
Watford, *Lon.* 4 A2 51 40N 0 27W
Watkins Island, *Wash.* 25 C6 39 2N 77 15W
Watsonia, *Melb.* 19 E7 37 43 S 145 6 E
Watsons B., *Syd.* 19 B4 33 50 S 151 18 E
Watsons Creek, *Melb.* 19 E8 37 40 S 145 13 E
Wattenscheid, *Ruhr* 6 B4 51 28N 7 8 E
Wattle Glen, *Melb.* 19 D8 37 39 S 145 11 E
Wattle Park, *Melb.* 19 F7 37 50 S 145 6 E
Watts →, *Wash.* 25 C6 39 2N 77 15W
Waverley, *Bost.* 21 C2 42 23N 71 10W
Waverley, *Jobg.* 18 E9 26 7 S 28 4 E
Waverley, *Syd.* 19 B4 33 53 S 151 15 E
Wawer, *Wsaw.* 10 E7 52 13N 21 8 E
Wawrzyszew, *Wsaw.* 10 E6 52 17N 20 53 E
Wayland, *Bost.* 21 C1 42 21N 71 20W
Wayne, *N.Y.* 22 B3 40 55N 74 15W
Wayne, *Phil.* 24 A2 40 2N 75 24W
Wazirabad, *Delhi* 16 A2 28 43N 77 13 E
Wazīrīya, *Bagd.* 17 E8 33 22N 44 23 E
Wazirpur, *Delhi* 16 A2 28 41N 77 10 E
Weald Park, *Lon.* 4 B6 51 37N 0 16 E
Wedding, *Berl.* 7 A3 52 32N 13 21 E
Weehawken, *N.Y.* 22 C4 40 45N 74 2W
Wegendorf, *Berl.* 7 A5 52 36N 13 45 E
Wehofen, *Ruhr* 6 A2 51 31N 6 46 E
Wehringhausen, *Ruhr* 6 B6 51 21N 7 28 E
Weidling, *Wien* 10 G9 48 17N 16 18 E
Weidling →, *Wien* 10 G9 48 17N 16 19 E
Weidlingbach, *Wien* 10 G9 48 16N 16 15 E
Weigongcum, *Beij.* 14 B2 39 57N 116 16 E
Weijin He →, *Tianj.* 14 E6 39 3N 117 12 E
Weissensee, *Berl.* 7 A3 52 33N 13 27 E
Weitmar, *Ruhr* 6 B5 51 27N 7 11 E
Welcome Monument, *Jak.* 15 J9 6 12N 106 49 E
Weller Creek, *Chic.* 26 A1 42 2N 87 52W
Wellesley, *Bost.* 21 D2 42 17N 71 17W
Wellesley Fells, *Bost.* 21 D2 42 18N 71 18W
Wellesley Hills, *Bost.* 21 D2 42 18N 71 16W
Welling, *Lon.* 4 C5 51 27N 0 6 E
Wellingsbüttel, *Hbg.* 7 D8 53 38N 10 6 E
Weltevreden Park Extension, *Jobg.* 18 E8 26 7 S 27 56 E
Wembley, *Lon.* 4 B3 51 33N 0 17W
Wembley Stadium, *Jobg.* 18 F9 26 13 S 28 1 E
Wembley Stadium, *Lon.* 4 B3 51 33N 0 16W
Wemmer Pan, *Jobg.* 18 F9 26 13 S 28 3 E
Wendenschloss, *Berl.* 7 B4 52 24N 13 35 E
Wengern, *Ruhr* 6 B6 51 24N 7 20 E
Wenham, *Bost.* 21 B4 42 36N 70 53W
Wenham L., *Bost.* 21 B4 42 35N 70 53W
Wenhuagong, *Tianj.* 14 E6 39 5N 117 14 E
Wennington, *Lon.* 4 B6 51 30N 0 12 E
Wenonah, *Phil.* 24 C4 39 47N 75 9W
Wentworthville, *Syd.* 19 A2 33 48 S 150 58 E
Werden, *Ruhr* 6 B4 51 23N 7 1 E
Werne, *Ruhr* 6 B5 51 29N 7 18 E
Werneuchen, *Berl.* 7 A5 52 38N 13 44 E
Wesoła, *Wsaw.* 10 E8 52 15N 21 13 E
West Andover, *Bost.* 21 B2 42 39N 71 10W
West Babylon, *N.Y.* 23 C8 40 43N 73 21W
West Bedford, *Bost.* 21 C2 42 28N 71 18W
West Berlin, *Phil.* 24 C5 39 48N 74 56W
West Boxford, *Bost.* 21 A3 42 42N 71 3W
West Caldwell, *N.Y.* 22 B3 40 51N 74 16W
West Chelmsford, *Bost.* 21 B1 42 36N 71 23W
West Chester, *Phil.* 24 B1 39 57N 75 35W
West Concord, *Bost.* 21 C1 42 27N 71 24W
West Covina, *L.A.* 28 B5 34 4N 117 55W
West Don →, *Trto.* 20 D8 43 44N 79 24W
West Drayton, *Lon.* 4 B2 51 30N 0 28W
West Dulwich, *Lon.* 4 C4 51 26N 0 5W
West Edmondale, *Balt.* 25 B2 39 17N 76 42W
West Ham, *Lon.* 4 B5 51 31N 0 1 E
West Harrow, *Lon.* 4 B2 51 34N 0 21W
West Heath, *Lon.* 4 C5 51 29N 0 7 E
West Hempstead, *N.Y.* 23 C7 40 41N 73 38W
West Hill, *Trto.* 20 D9 43 46N 79 10W
West Hollywood, *L.A.* 28 B2 34 5N 118 21W
West Hoxton, *Syd.* 19 B1 33 55 S 150 49 E
West Islip, *N.Y.* 23 C9 40 41N 73 18W
West Kingsdown, *Lon.* 4 C6 51 20N 0 15 E
West Lamma Channel, *H.K.* 12 E5 22 14N 114 4 E
West Lynn, *Bost.* 21 C4 42 27N 70 58W
West Medford, *Bost.* 21 C3 42 25N 71 7W
West New York, *N.Y.* 22 C4 40 46N 74 1W
West Norwood, *N.Y.* 22 B5 40 59N 73 58W
West of Twin Peaks, *S.F.* 27 B2 37 43N 122 27W
West Orange, *N.Y.* 22 C3 40 46N 74 15W
West Park, *Jobg.* 18 E8 26 9 S 27 59 E
West Paterson, *N.Y.* 22 B3 40 54N 74 11W
West Rouge, *Trto.* 20 D10 43 48N 79 7W
West Roxbury, *Bost.* 21 D3 42 16N 71 9W
West Springfield, *Wash.* 25 E6 38 47N 77 13W
West Thurrock, *Lon.* 4 C6 51 28N 0 16 E
West Town, *Chic.* 26 B2 41 53N 87 42W
West Wharf, *Kar.* 17 H10 24 49N 66 58 E
West Wickham, *Lon.* 4 C4 51 22N 0 0 E
Westbury, *N.Y.* 23 C7 40 45N 73 34W
Westchester, *Chic.* 26 B1 41 51N 87 53W
Westchester, *N.Y.* 23 B5 40 51N 73 51W
Westcliff, *Jobg.* 18 F9 26 10 S 28 1 E
Westdale, *Chic.* 26 B1 41 55N 87 54W
Westdene, *Jobg.* 18 F8 26 10 S 27 59 E
Westend, *Hels.* 3 C3 60 9N 24 48 E
Westerbauer, *Ruhr* 6 B6 51 20N 7 23 E
Westerham, *Lon.* 4 D5 51 16N 0 4 E
Westerham, *Mün.* 7 G10 48 3N 11 36 E
Westerholt, *Ruhr* 6 A4 51 36N 7 5 E
Westerleigh, *N.Y.* 22 D4 40 37N 74 7W
Western Addition, *S.F.* 27 B2 37 47N 122 25W
Western Run →, *Balt.* 25 A2 39 22N 76 39W
Western Springs, *Chic.* 26 C1 41 47N 87 52W
Westfalenhalle, *Ruhr* 6 B6 51 29N 7 27 E
Westfield, *N.Y.* 22 D2 40 39N 74 21W
Westlake, *S.F.* 27 B2 37 42N 122 29W
Westmeadows, *Melb.* 19 D6 37 39 S 144 55 E
Westminster, *Lon.* 4 B4 51 30N 0 7W
Westminster Abbey, *Lon.* 4 C4 51 29N 0 7W
Westmont, *Phil.* 24 B4 39 54N 75 3W
Westmount, *Mtrl.* 20 B4 43 29N 73 35W
Weston, *Bost.* 21 C2 42 22N 71 16W
Weston, *Trto.* 20 D7 43 42N 79 30W
Weston Res., *Bost.* 21 C2 42 20N 71 11W
Westover Hills, *Phil.* 24 C1 39 45N 75 35W
Westtown, *Phil.* 24 B1 39 56N 75 32W
Westville, *Phil.* 24 B4 39 52N 75 7W
Westville Grove, *Phil.* 24 B4 39 51N 75 7W
Westwood, *Bost.* 21 D2 42 12N 71 14W
Westwood, *N.Y.* 22 B4 40 59N 74 3W
Westwood Village, *L.A.* 28 B2 34 3N 118 26W
Wetter, *Ruhr* 6 B6 51 23N 7 23 E
Wexford, *Trto.* 20 D9 43 45N 79 18W
Wey →, *Lon.* 4 D2 51 18N 0 27W
Weybridge, *Lon.* 4 C2 51 22N 0 27W
Weyer, *Ruhr* 6 C4 51 10N 7 1 E
Weymouth, *Bost.* 21 D4 42 12N 70 57W
Whampoa, Sungei →, *Sing.* 15 G8 1 18N 103 52 E
Wheaton, *Wash.* 25 C7 39 2N 77 2W
Wheaton Regional Park, *Wash.* 25 C7 39 3N 77 1W
Wheelers Hill, *Melb.* 19 F8 37 53 S 145 10 E
Wheeling, *Chic.* 26 A1 42 8N 87 54W
Whetstone, *Lon.* 4 B3 51 37N 0 10W
Whippany, *N.Y.* 22 B2 40 49N 74 24W
Whippany →, *N.Y.* 22 B2 40 50N 74 20W
White Marsh, *Balt.* 25 A4 39 23N 76 28W
White Meadow L., *N.Y.* 22 B1 40 55N 74 30W
White Oak, *Wash.* 25 C8 39 2N 76 59W
White Plains, *N.Y.* 23 A6 41 0N 73 46W
Whitechapel, *Lon.* 4 B4 51 31N 0 3W
Whitehorse, *Phil.* 24 B2 39 59N 75 28W
Whiteley Village, *Lon.* 4 C2 51 21N 0 25W
Whitemarsh →, *Balt.* 25 A4 39 22N 76 29W
Whitestone, *N.Y.* 23 C6 40 47N 73 48W
Whiting, *Chic.* 26 C4 41 41N 87 30W
Whitmans Pond, *Bost.* 21 D4 42 12N 70 55W
Whittier, *L.A.* 28 C4 33 58N 118 2W
Whitton, *Lon.* 4 C2 51 27N 0 21W
Whyteleafe, *Lon.* 4 D4 51 18N 0 5W
Wieden, *Wien* 10 G10 48 11N 16 22 E
Wiemelhausen, *Ruhr* 6 B5 51 27N 7 13 E
Wien, *Wien* 10 G10 48 12N 16 22 E
Wien-Schwechat, Flughafen, *Wien* 10 H11 48 6N 16 34 E
Wiener Berg, *Wien* 10 H10 48 9N 16 21 E
Wiener Wald, *Wien* 10 G9 48 16N 16 14 E
Wieruchów, *Wsaw.* 10 E5 52 14N 20 49 E
Wierzbno, *Wsaw.* 10 E7 52 11N 21 1 E
Wilanów, *Wsaw.* 10 E7 52 10N 21 4 E
Wilanówka →, *Wsaw.* 10 F7 52 13N 21 6 E
Wildcat Canyon Regional Park, *S.F.* 27 A3 37 56N 122 17W
Wildcat Cr. →, *S.F.* 27 A3 37 57N 122 15W
Wilde, *B.A.* 32 C5 34 24 S 58 18W
Wilhelmsburg, *Hbg.* 7 E7 53 29N 9 59 E
Wilhelmshagen, *Berl.* 7 B5 52 26N 13 42 E
Wilket Creek Park, *Trto.* 20 D8 43 43N 79 21W
Willesden, *Lon.* 4 B3 51 32N 0 15W
Willesden Green, *Lon.* 4 B3 51 32N 0 13W
Willett Pond, *Bost.* 21 D2 42 10N 71 14W
William Girling Res., *Lon.* 4 B4 51 38N 0 1W
Williams Bridge, *N.Y.* 23 B5 40 52N 73 51W
Williamsburg, *N.Y.* 22 C5 40 42N 73 56W
Williamstown, *Melb.* 19 F6 37 51 S 144 52 E
Williamstown Junction, *Phil.* 24 C5 39 45N 74 56W
Willingboro, *Phil.* 24 A5 40 2N 74 53W
Williston Park, *N.Y.* 23 C7 40 45N 73 38W
Willoughby, *Syd.* 19 A4 33 48 S 151 12 E
Willow Grove, *Phil.* 24 A4 40 8N 75 7W
Willow Springs, *Chic.* 26 C1 41 44N 87 51W
Willowbrook, *L.A.* 28 C3 33 54N 118 13W
Willowbrook, *N.Y.* 22 D4 40 35N 74 8W
Willowdale, *Phil.* 24 B5 39 52N 74 58W
Willowdale, *Trto.* 20 D8 43 46N 79 25W
Willowdale State Forest, *Bost.* 21 B4 42 39N 70 54W
Wilmette, *Chic.* 26 A2 42 4N 87 42W
Wilmette Harbor, *Chic.* 26 A2 42 4N 87 41W
Wilmington, *Bost.* 21 B3 42 33N 71 9W
Wilmington, *Lon.* 4 C6 51 25N 0 12 E
Wilmington, *Phil.* 24 C1 39 44N 75 33W
Wilson, Mt., *L.A.* 28 A4 34 13N 118 4W
Wimbledon, *Lon.* 4 C3 51 25N 0 13W
Wimbledon Common, *Lon.* 4 C3 51 26N 0 14W
Wimbledon Park, *Lon.* 4 C3 51 25N 0 11W
Wimbledon Tennis Ground, *Lon.* 4 C3 51 25N 0 12W
Winchester, *Bost.* 21 C3 42 26N 71 8W
Winchmore Hill, *Lon.* 4 B4 51 38N 0 5W
Windsor Cresta, *Jobg.* 18 E8 26 7 S 27 59 E
Winfield, *N.Y.* 22 D3 40 38N 74 16W
Winnetka, *Chic.* 26 A2 42 6N 87 43W
Winnetka, *L.A.* 28 A1 34 10N 118 32W
Winning, *Mün.* 7 G10 48 2N 11 37 E
Winston Hills, *Syd.* 19 A2 33 46 S 150 57 E
Winterberg, *Ruhr* 6 C5 51 19N 7 12 E
Winterhude, *Hbg.* 7 D8 53 35N 10 0 E
Winterthur, *Phil.* 24 C1 39 48N 75 35W
Winthrop, *Bost.* 21 C4 42 22N 70 58W
Winzeldorf, *Hbg.* 7 C7 53 40N 9 54 E
Wisley Gardens, *Lon.* 4 D2 51 18N 0 28W
Wiśniowa Góra, *Wsaw.* 10 E8 52 13N 21 12 E
Wissahickon Cr. →, *Phil.* 24 A3 40 0N 75 12W
Wissinoming, *Phil.* 24 A4 40 1N 75 4W
Wissous, *Paris* 5 C3 48 44N 2 19 E
Witch House, *Bost.* 21 B4 42 31N 70 54W
Witfield, *Jobg.* 18 F10 26 11 S 28 12 E
Witpoortjie, *Jobg.* 18 E8 26 8 S 27 50 E
Witten, *Ruhr* 6 B6 51 26N 7 20 E
Wittenau, *Berl.* 7 A2 52 35N 13 19 E
Wittlaer, *Ruhr* 6 C2 51 19N 6 44 E
Witwatersrand, Univ. of, *Jobg.* 18 F9 26 11 S 28 1 E
Włochy, *Wsaw.* 10 E6 52 12N 20 54 E
Wo Mei, *H.K.* 12 D6 22 21N 114 15 E
Wo Yi Hop, *H.K.* 12 D5 22 23N 114 8 E
Woburn, *Bost.* 21 C3 42 29N 71 9W
Woburn, *Trto.* 20 D9 43 46N 79 12W
Wohldorf-Ohlstedt, *Hbg.* 7 C8 53 41N 10 7 E
Wola, *Wsaw.* 10 E6 52 14N 20 57 E
Woldingham, *Lon.* 4 D4 51 16N 0 1W
Wolf Lake, *Chic.* 26 D3 41 39N 87 31W
Wolf Trap Farm Park, *Wash.* 25 D6 38 56N 77 17W
Wolfpassing, *Wien* 10 G9 48 18N 16 10 E
Wolica, *Wsaw.* 10 F7 52 9N 21 3 E
Wolica, *Wsaw.* 10 F6 52 7N 20 51 E
Wólka Węglowa, *Wsaw.* 10 E6 52 18N 20 52 E
Wollaston, *Bost.* 21 D3 42 15N 71 2W
Wołomin, *Wsaw.* 10 D8 52 20N 21 12 E
Woltersdorf, *Berl.* 7 B5 52 27N 13 44 E
Wong Chuk Hang, *H.K.* 12 E6 22 15N 114 10 E
Wong Chuk Wan, *H.K.* 12 D6 22 23N 114 17 E
Wong Chuk Yeung, *H.K.* 12 D6 22 24N 114 15 E
Wong Ngua Shan, *H.K.* 12 D6 22 22N 114 14 E
Wong Tai Sin, *H.K.* 12 D6 22 20N 114 11 E
Wonga Park, *Melb.* 19 E8 37 44 S 145 17 E
Wood End, *Lon.* 4 B2 51 33N 0 21W
Wood Green, *Lon.* 4 B4 51 36N 0 6W
Wood Hill, *Bost.* 21 B2 42 39N 71 11W
Woodbridge, *N.Y.* 22 D3 40 33N 74 16W
Woodbridge, *Trto.* 20 D7 43 47N 79 35W
Woodbridge Cr. →, *N.Y.* 22 D3 40 32N 74 15W
Woodbury, *N.Y.* 23 C8 40 49N 73 28W
Woodbury, *Phil.* 24 B4 39 50N 75 9W
Woodbury Cr. →, *Phil.* 24 B4 39 51N 75 11W
Woodbury Heights, *Phil.* 24 C4 39 49N 75 7W
Woodchuck Hill, *Bost.* 21 B3 42 39N 71 4W
Woodcliff Lake, *N.Y.* 22 A4 41 1N 74 2W
Woodford, *Lon.* 4 B5 51 36N 0 1 E
Woodford Bridge, *Lon.* 4 B5 51 36N 0 3 E
Woodford Green, *Lon.* 4 B5 51 36N 0 1 E
Woodford Wells, *Lon.* 4 B5 51 37N 0 1 E
Woodhaven, *N.Y.* 23 C5 40 41N 73 51W
Woodlands, *Sing.* 15 F7 1 26N 103 46 E
Woodlawn, *Balt.* 25 B2 39 19N 76 44W
Woodlyn, *Phil.* 24 B2 39 52N 75 21W
Woodlynne, *Phil.* 24 B4 39 54N 75 6W
Woodmere, *N.Y.* 23 D6 40 38N 73 43W
Woodmont, *Wash.* 25 D7 38 59N 77 5W
Woodmore, *Balt.* 25 A2 39 22N 76 47W
Woodridge, *N.Y.* 22 B4 40 50N 74 4W
Woodrow, *N.Y.* 22 D3 40 32N 74 11W
Woodside, *Lon.* 4 C4 51 23N 0 4W
Woodside, *N.Y.* 23 C5 40 44N 73 54W
Woodside, *S.F.* 27 D3 37 26N 122 16W
Woodstock, *Balt.* 25 B1 39 19N 76 52W
Woodstream, *Phil.* 24 B5 39 54N 74 57W
Woollahra, *Syd.* 19 B4 33 53 S 151 15 E
Woolooware B., *Syd.* 19 C3 34 1 S 151 8 E
Woolwich, *Lon.* 4 C5 51 29N 0 4 E
Wördern, *Wien* 10 G9 48 19N 16 12 E
World Trade Center, *N.Y.* 22 C4 40 42N 74 0W
Worli, *Bomb.* 16 G7 19 1N 72 49 E
Woronora, *Syd.* 19 C3 34 1 S 151 2 E
Worth, *Chic.* 26 C2 41 41N 87 47W
Worthington, *Balt.* 25 B2 39 14N 76 47W
Worthington, *N.Y.* 23 A6 41 2N 73 49W
Wrotham, *Lon.* 4 D6 51 18N 0 18 E
Wrotham Park, *Lon.* 4 A3 51 40N 0 10W
Wuhlgarten, *Berl.* 7 A4 52 31N 13 34 E
Wujiaochang, *Shang.* 14 J12 31 18N 121 31 E
Wülfrath, *Ruhr* 6 C4 51 16N 7 2 E
Wulfsmühle, *Hbg.* 7 C7 53 41N 9 51 E
Wulksfelde, *Hbg.* 7 C8 53 42N 10 6 E
Wupper →, *Ruhr* 6 C5 51 14N 7 18 E
Wuppertal, *Ruhr* 6 C5 51 17N 7 10 E
Würm →, *Mün.* 7 G9 48 8N 11 27 E
Würm-kanal, *Mün.* 7 F9 48 13N 11 29 E
Wusong, *Shang.* 14 H11 31 22N 121 29 E
Wusong Jiang →, *Shang.* 14 J11 31 15N 121 29 E
Wyandanch, *N.Y.* 23 C8 40 44N 73 20W
Wyckoff, *N.Y.* 22 A3 41 0N 74 10W
Wyczółki, *Wsaw.* 10 F6 52 9N 20 59 E
Wygoda, *Wsaw.* 10 E7 52 15N 21 7 E
Wyncote, *Phil.* 24 A4 40 5N 75 8W
Wynnewood, *Phil.* 24 A3 40 0N 75 17W
Wynnmere, *Bost.* 21 C3 42 29N 71 9W
Wyola, *Phil.* 24 A2 40 0N 75 24W

X

Xabregas, *Lisb.* 8 F8 38 43N 9 6W
Xiaodianzhuang, *Tianj.* 14 D6 39 14N 117 14 E
Xiaoping, *Gzh.* 14 F8 23 12N 113 13 E
Xiasha chong, *Gzh.* 14 G7 23 8N 113 9 E
Xicheng, *Beij.* 14 B2 39 54N 116 19 E
Xico, Cerro, *Méx.* 29 C4 19 15N 98 56W
Xicun, *Gzh.* 14 G8 23 8N 113 13 E
Xidan, *Beij.* 14 B3 39 52N 116 20 E
Xigu Gongyuan, *Tianj.* 14 D6 39 10N 117 10 E
Xigucun, *Tianj.* 14 D5 39 10N 117 9 E
Xijiao Airport, *Beij.* 14 B2 39 57N 116 12 E
Xikeng, *Gzh.* 14 F7 23 11N 113 6 E
Xilou, *Tianj.* 14 E6 39 5N 117 12 E
Ximenwai, *Tianj.* 14 E5 39 8N 117 9 E
Xingfusancun, *Beij.* 14 B3 39 55N 116 25 E
Xinhua, *Tianj.* 14 E6 39 6N 117 12 E
Xinkai He →, *Tianj.* 14 D6 39 12N 117 15 E
Xintang, *Gzh.* 14 G9 23 9N 113 24 E
Xitle, *Méx.* 29 C2 19 15N 99 12W
Xitle, Cerro, *Méx.* 29 C2 19 14N 99 12W
Xiyuan, *Beij.* 14 B2 39 59N 116 14 E
Xizhimen, *Beij.* 14 B2 39 55N 116 19 E
Xochiaca, *Méx.* 29 B4 19 24N 89 58 E
Xochimilco, *Méx.* 29 C3 19 15N 99 5W
Xochimilco, L. de, *Méx.* 29 C3 19 16N 99 7W
Xochitenco, *Méx.* 29 B4 19 24N 89 58 E
Xochitepec, *Méx.* 29 C3 19 15N 99 9W
Xuanwu, *Beij.* 14 B2 39 52N 116 19 E
Xuhui, *Shang.* 14 J11 31 11N 121 26 E

Y

Yaba, *Lagos* 18 A2 6 30N 7 22 E
Yadun Shui, *Gzh.* 14 G8 23 5N 113 15 E
Yaftābād, *Tehr.* 17 D4 35 37N 51 17 E
Yagoona, *Syd.* 19 B3 33 54 S 151 2 E
Yahara, *Tōkyō* 13 B2 35 44N 139 37 E
Yaho, *Tōkyō* 13 B1 35 40N 139 26 E
Yakire, *Tōkyō* 13 B4 35 45N 139 54 E
Yamada, *Ōsaka* 12 B4 34 47N 135 32 E
Yamada, *Tōkyō* 13 C2 35 33N 139 37 E
Yamada →, *Ōsaka* 12 B2 34 45N 135 10 E
Yamaguchi, *Ōsaka* 12 B2 34 49N 135 14 E
Yamamoto, *Ōsaka* 12 C4 34 38N 135 37 E
Yamato, *Tōkyō* 13 B2 35 46N 139 36 E
Yamato, *Tōkyō* 13 D1 35 29N 139 27 E
Yamato →, *Ōsaka* 12 C3 34 36N 135 26 E
Yamazaki, *Tōkyō* 13 A4 35 55N 139 53 E
Yamuna →, *Delhi* 16 B2 28 37N 77 15 E
Yan Kit, *Sing.* 15 F8 1 21N 103 58 E
Yanagishima, *Tōkyō* 13 B3 35 49N 139 45 E
Yanbu, *Gzh.* 14 G7 23 5N 113 9 E
Yanghuayuan, *Beij.* 14 C2 39 49N 116 18 E
Yangjiazhuang, *Shang.* 14 H11 31 22N 121 25 E
Yangliuqing, *Tianj.* 14 E5 39 8N 117 0 E
Yangpu, *Shang.* 14 J12 31 16N 121 32 E
Yanino, *Len.* 11 B5 59 55N 30 36 E
Yao, *Ōsaka* 12 C4 34 37N 135 36 E
Yao Airport, *Ōsaka* 12 C4 34 35N 135 36 E
Yarmōk, *Bagd.* 17 F7 33 18N 44 19 E
Yarra →, *Melb.* 19 E6 37 51 S 144 53 E
Yarra Bend Nat. Park, *Melb.* 19 E7 37 47 S 145 0 E
Yarraville, *Melb.* 19 E6 37 48 S 144 53 E
Yasenevo, *Mos.* 11 F9 55 36N 37 21 E
Yashio, *Tōkyō* 13 B3 35 48N 139 49 E
Yau Ma Tei, *H.K.* 12 E5 22 18N 114 10 E
Yau Tong, *H.K.* 12 E6 22 17N 114 14 E
Yau Yue Wan, *H.K.* 12 E6 22 19N 114 15 E
Yauza →, *Mos.* 11 D10 55 54N 37 43 E
Yeading, *Lon.* 4 B2 51 31N 0 23W
Yeadon, *Phil.* 24 B3 39 55N 75 15W
Yedikule, *Ist.* 17 B2 40 59N 28 55 E
Yenikapi, *Ist.* 17 A2 41 0N 28 56 E
Yeniköy, *Ist.* 17 A3 41 6N 29 3 E
Yennora, *Syd.* 19 B2 33 51 S 150 58 E
Yeogchon, *Sŏul* 12 G7 37 35N 126 55 E
Yeoido, *Sŏul* 12 G7 37 31N 126 55 E
Yeong Dung Po, *Sŏul* 12 G7 37 31N 126 54 E
Yeongdong, *Sŏul* 12 G8 37 30N 127 1 E
Yerba Buena I., *S.F.* 27 B2 37 48N 122 21W
Yerres, *Paris* 5 C5 48 43N 2 30 E
Yerres →, *Paris* 5 C5 48 43N 2 26 E
Yesilköy, *Ist.* 17 B2 40 57N 28 50 E
Yew Tee, *Sing.* 15 F7 1 23N 103 45 E
Yiewsley, *Lon.* 4 B2 51 31N 0 27W
Yiheyuan, *Beij.* 14 A2 40 0N 116 14 E
Yinhangzhen, *Shang.* 14 H12 31 20N 121 31 E
Yio Chu Kang, *Sing.* 15 F8 1 23N 103 51 E
Yixingbu, *Tianj.* 14 D6 39 11N 117 12 E
Ylästö, *Hels.* 3 B4 60 17N 24 35 E
Yodo →, *Ōsaka* 12 B4 34 45N 135 35 E
Yokohama, *Tōkyō* 13 D3 35 26N 139 41 E
Yokohama Harbour, *Tōkyō* 13 D2 35 27N 139 39 E
Yokosuka, *Tōkyō* 13 A4 35 50N 139 54 E
Yong San, *Sŏul* 12 G7 37 32N 126 58 E
Yongding He →, *Beij.* 14 C1 39 49N 116 10 E
Yongdingmen, *Beij.* 14 B3 39 50N 116 20 E
Yongfucun, *Gzh.* 14 G8 23 8N 113 17 E
Yonkers, *N.Y.* 23 B5 40 56N 73 52W
Yono, *Tōkyō* 13 A2 35 52N 139 37 E
York, *Trto.* 20 D8 43 40N 79 26W
York Mills, *Trto.* 20 D8 43 45N 79 22W
Yoshikawa, *Tōkyō* 13 A4 35 53N 139 50 E
Yotsuga, *Tōkyō* 13 B3 35 40N 139 44 E
You'anmen, *Beij.* 14 B2 39 51N 116 19 E
Yoyogi Park, *Tōkyō* 13 C3 35 40N 139 41 E
Yuanxiatian, *Gzh.* 14 F8 23 12N 113 17 E
Yuexiu Gongyuan, *Gzh.* 14 G8 23 8N 113 16 E
Yugo-Zarad, *Mos.* 11 E9 55 40N 37 30 E
Yung Shue Wan, *H.K.* 12 E5 22 13N 114 6 E
Yuquanshan, *Beij.* 14 A2 40 0N 116 13 E
Yusofābād, *Tehr.* 17 C5 35 43N 51 24 E
Yuyuan Tan, *Beij.* 14 B2 39 53N 116 16 E
Yuyuantan Gongyuan, *Beij.* 14 B2 39 54N 116 16 E
Yvelines, Forêt des, *Paris* 5 D1 48 38N 1 53 E
Yvette →, *Paris* 5 C1 48 43N 1 57 E

Z

Záběhlice, *Pra.* 10 B2 50 3N 14 29 E
Żacisze, *Wsaw.* 10 E7 52 17N 21 4 E
Zahrā, *Bagd.* 17 E7 33 22N 44 19 E
Zakharkovo, *Mos.* 11 E7 55 46N 37 18 E
Žalov, *Pra.* 10 A2 50 10N 14 22 E
Załuski, *Wsaw.* 10 F6 52 9N 20 55 E
Zamdorf, *Mün.* 7 G10 48 8N 11 35 E
Zanevka, *Len.* 11 B5 59 55N 30 31 E
Zaozerye, *Mos.* 11 F12 55 35N 38 1 E
Zapote, *Manila* 15 E3 14 27N 120 56 E
Zapotitlán, *Méx.* 29 C3 19 18N 99 2W
Zápy, *Pra.* 10 B4 50 9N 14 40 E
Zarechye, *Mos.* 11 E8 55 41N 37 22 E
Zawady, *Wsaw.* 10 E7 52 10N 21 6 E
Zâwiyet Abû Musallam, *El Qâ.* 18 D4 29 56N 31 9 E
Zawrā Park, *Bagd.* 17 F8 33 18N 44 23 E
Zbójna Góra, *Wsaw.* 10 E8 52 11N 21 13 E
Zbraslav, *Pra.* 10 C2 49 58N 14 23 E
Zbuzany, *Pra.* 10 B1 50 1N 14 17 E
Zdiby, *Pra.* 10 B2 50 9N 14 27 E
Zehlendorf, *Berl.* 7 B2 52 26N 13 16 E
Zeleneč, *Pra.* 10 B3 50 8N 14 39 E
Zempoala, Parque Nac. de las Lagunas de, *Méx.* 29 D2 19 5N 99 18W
Zepernick, *Berl.* 7 A4 52 38N 13 33 E
Żerań, *Wsaw.* 10 E6 52 18N 20 58 E
Zerzeń, *Wsaw.* 10 E7 52 12N 21 7 E
Zeytinburnu, *Ist.* 17 B2 40 58N 28 53 E
Zhabei, *Shang.* 14 J11 31 16N 121 26 E
Zhangguizhuang, *Tianj.* 14 E6 39 7N 117 19 E
Zhangxingzhuang, *Tianj.* 14 D6 39 10N 117 12 E
Zhdanov, *Mos.* 11 E10 55 44N 37 41 E
Zhegalovo, *Mos.* 11 D11 55 54N 37 59 E
Zheleznodorozhnyy, *Mos.* 11 E12 55 45N 38 0 E
Zhenru, *Shang.* 14 J11 31 16N 121 22 E
Zhicun, *Gzh.* 14 G8 23 0N 113 18 E
Zhongshan Gongyuan, *Shang.* 14 J11 31 13N 121 24 E
Zhoucun, *Gzh.* 14 F8 23 11N 113 11 E
Zhoujiadu, *Shang.* 14 J11 31 11N 121 29 E
Zhoujiazhen, *Shang.* 14 J12 31 16N 121 33 E
Zhu Jiang →, *Gzh.* 14 G9 23 6N 113 20 E
Zhulebino, *Mos.* 11 E11 55 42N 37 50 E
Zhushadi, *Gzh.* 14 F9 23 11N 113 22 E
Zielona, *Wsaw.* 10 E8 52 14N 21 11 E
Zielonka, *Wsaw.* 10 E7 52 18N 21 9 E
Zitadella, *Berl.* 7 A2 52 31N 13 11 E
Zizhuyuan Gongyuan, *Beij.* 14 B2 39 55N 116 17 E
Žižkov, *Pra.* 10 B2 50 5N 14 28 E
Zličin, *Pra.* 10 B1 50 3N 14 17 E
Zōbki, *Wsaw.* 10 E7 52 17N 21 6 E
Zografos, *Ath.* 8 J11 37 58N 23 47 E
Żoliborz, *Wsaw.* 10 E6 52 16N 20 57 E
Zugliget, *Bud.* 10 K12 47 30N 18 59 E
Zugló, *Bud.* 10 J13 47 31N 19 8 E
Zumbi, *Rio J.* 31 A2 22 49 S 43 10W
Zuvuvu →, *S. Pau.* 31 F5 23 40 S 46 42W
Zuvuvus, *S. Pau.* 31 F6 23 41 S 46 39W
Zweckel, *Ruhr* 6 A3 51 35N 6 57 E
Zyuzino, *Mos.* 11 F9 55 39N 37 34 E

WORLD MAPS

MAP SYMBOLS

SETTLEMENTS

◻ PARIS   ■ Berne   ◉ Livorno   ◉ Brugge   ◉ Algeciras   ⊙ Fréjus   ○ Oberammergau   ₒThira

Settlement symbols and type styles vary according to the scale of each map and indicate the importance
of towns on the map rather than specific population figures

∴   Ruins or Archæological Sites   ˅   Wells in Desert

ADMINISTRATION

——— International Boundaries

— — — International Boundaries
(Undefined or Disputed)

·········· Internal Boundaries

        National Parks

        Country Names

        NICARAGUA

Administrative
Area Names

KENT

CALABRIA

International boundaries show the *de facto* situation where there are rival claims to territory

COMMUNICATIONS

——— Principal Roads

〜〜 Other Roads

-·-·- Trails and Seasonal Roads

⋈   Passes

✧   Airfields

━━ Principal Railways

⌐⌐ Railways
Under Construction

〜 Other Railways

╕--╞ Railway Tunnels

·········· Principal Canals

PHYSICAL FEATURES

〜 Perennial Streams

········ Intermittent Streams

⬭ Perennial Lakes

⬭ Intermittent Lakes

✳✳ Swamps and Marshes

▨ Permanent Ice
and Glaciers

▲ 8848   Elevations in metres

▾ 8050   Sea Depths in metres

1134   Height of Lake Surface
Above Sea Level
in metres

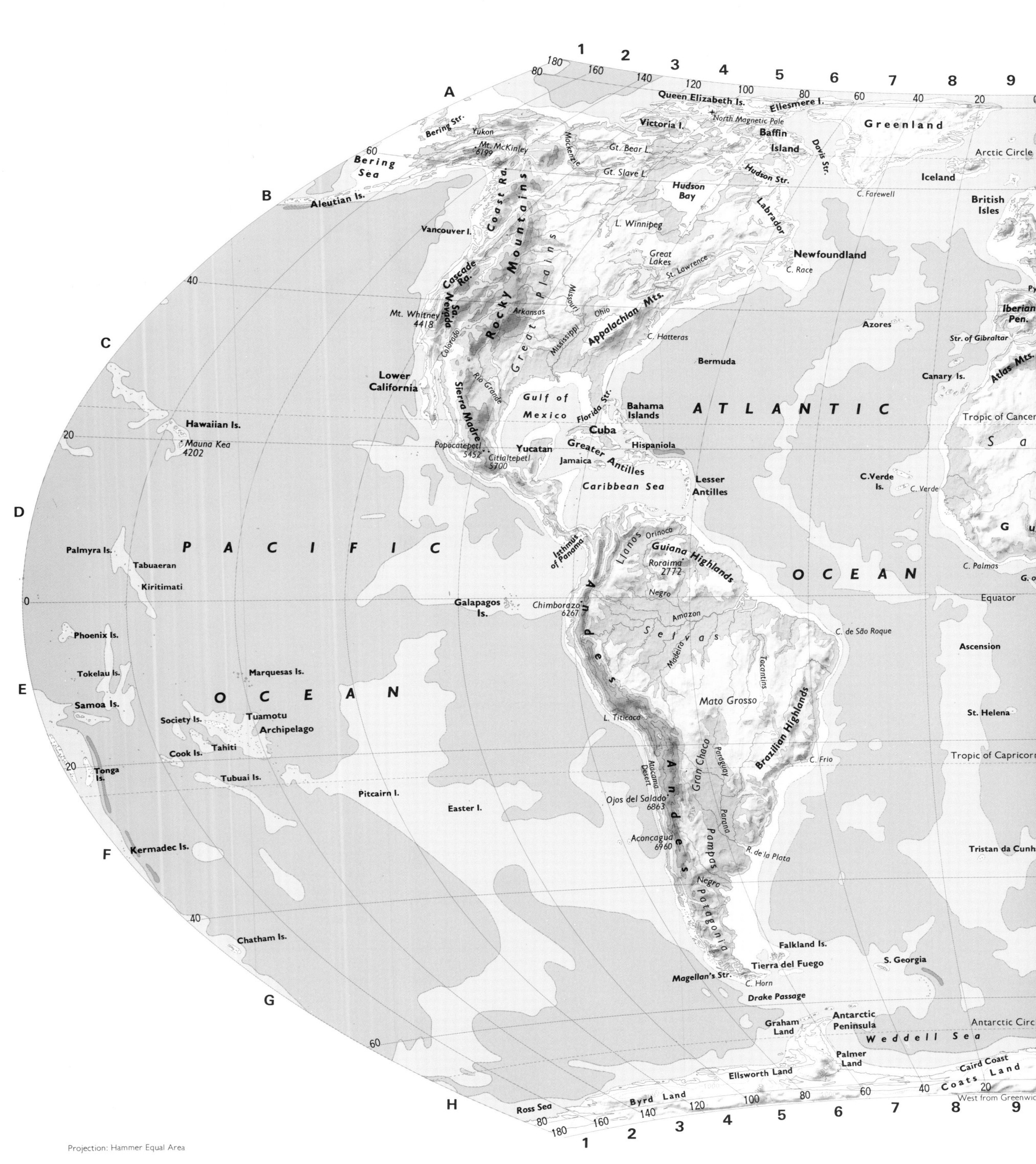

1 2 3 4 5 6 7 8 9

180 80 160 140 120 100 80 60 40 20

A

Queen Elizabeth Is. **Ellesmere I.** **G r e e n l a n d**

Bering Str. Yukon *North Magnetic Pole* Arctic Circle

**Bering
Sea** Mt. McKinley
6199 Gt. Bear L. **Victoria I.** **Baffin
Island** Davis Str.

Mackenzie Gt. Slave L. Hudson Str. C. Farewell **Iceland**

B **Aleutian Is.** **Hudson
Bay** Labrador **British
Isles**

Vancouver I. L. Winnipeg **Newfoundland** Py

Great
Lakes St. Lawrence C. Race

40 Mt. Whitney
4418 Arkansas Missouri Ohio **Appalachian Mts.** **Iberian
Pen.**

C Colorado Mississippi C. Hatteras **Azores** Str. of Gibraltar Atlas Mts.

**Lower
California** Rio Grande **Bermuda** **Canary Is.** Tropic of Cancer

20 **Hawaiian Is.** **Gulf of
Mexico** Florida Str. **Bahama
Islands** **A T L A N T I C** S a

*Mauna Kea
4202* Popocatepetl
5452 **Cuba** **Hispaniola** **C. Verde
Is.** C. Verde

Citlaltepetl
5700 **Yucatan** **Greater Antilles** Jamaica **Lesser
Antilles** C. o

Caribbean Sea

D **Palmyra Is.** Orinoco Llanos **Guiana Highlands** **O C E A N** **Gu**

Tabuaeran Isthmus
of Panama Roraima
2772 C. Palmas G. o

Kiritimati Negro

0 **P** **A** **C** **I** **F** **I** **C** **Galapagos
Is.** Chimborazo
6267 Amazon Equator

Phoenix Is. Selvas C. de São Roque **Ascension**

Madera

Tokelau Is. **Marquesas Is.** Tocantins

E **Samoa Is.** **O C E A N** **Mato Grosso** **St. Helena**

Society Is. **Tuamotu
Archipelago** L. Titicaca **Brazilian Highlands**

Cook Is. Tahiti Gran Chaco Paraguay C. Frio Tropic of Capricorn

20 **Tonga
Is.** **Tubuai Is.** Atacama
Desert Parana **Tristan da Cunha**

Pitcairn I. Ojos del Salado
6863

Kermadec Is. **Easter I.** Aconcagua
6960 Pampas

F

Negro

Patagonia

40 **Chatham Is.** Paraná R. de la Plata

Falkland Is. **S. Georgia**

G **Tierra del Fuego**

Magellan's Str. C. Horn

Drake Passage

**Graham
Land** **Antarctic
Peninsula** Antarctic Circle

60 **Palmer
Land** **W e d d e l l S e a**

Ellsworth Land Caird Coast

Ross Sea Byrd Land C o a t s   L a n d

West from Greenwich

H

80 120 100 80 60 40 20

180 160 140 5 6 7 8 9

1 2 3 4

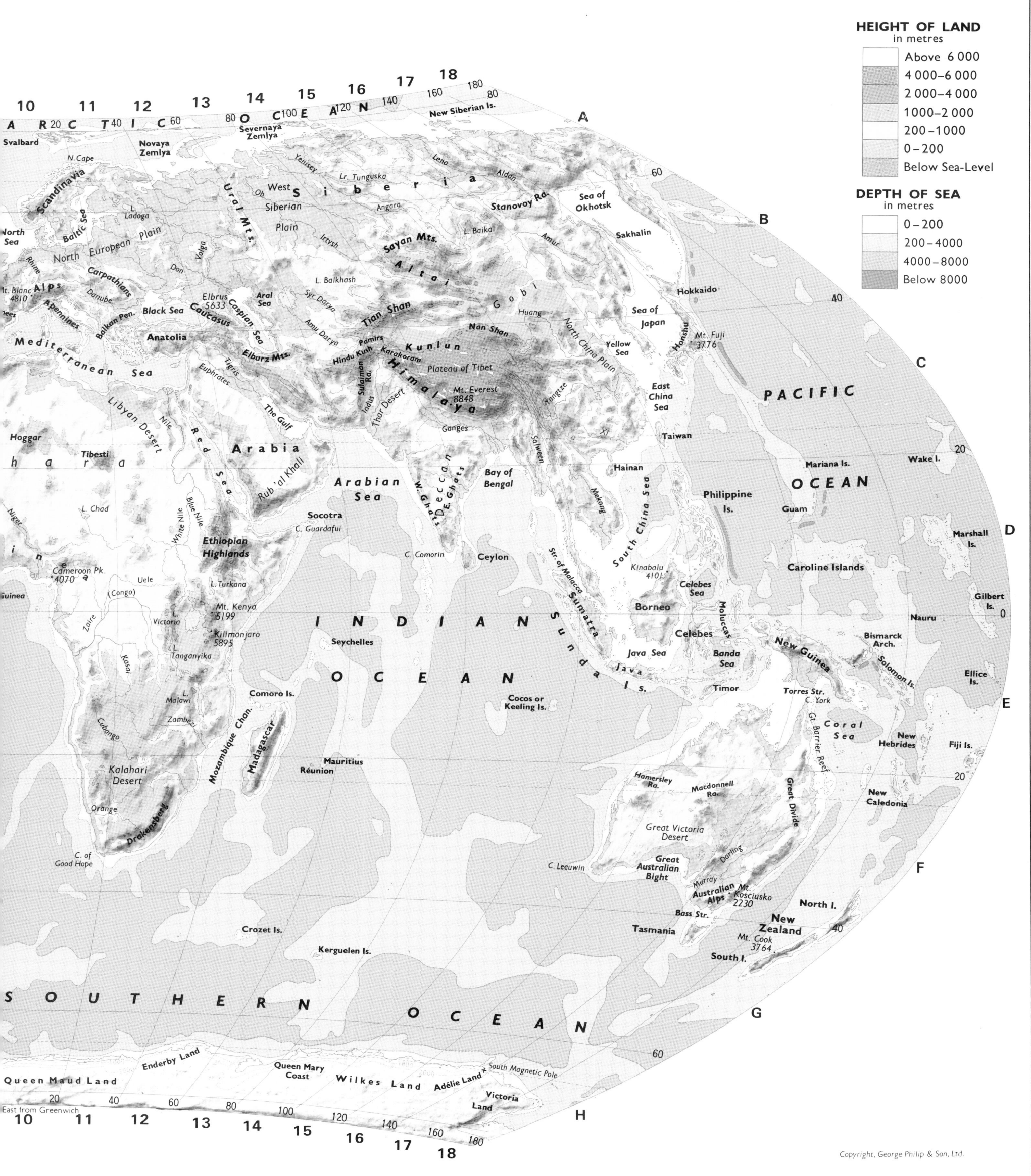

HEIGHT OF LAND
in metres

Above 6 000
4 000–6 000
2 000–4 000
1000–2 000
200–1000
0–200
Below Sea-Level

DEPTH OF SEA
in metres

0–200
200–4000
4000–8000
Below 8000

10   11   12   13   14   15   16   17   18
180
A R C T I C   O C E A N
20   40   60   80   100   E   A   120   N   140   160   180   80
Svalbard
N. Cape
Novaya
Zemlya
Severnaya
Zemlya
New Siberian Is.   A
Scandinavia
North
Sea
Baltic Sea
L. Ladoga
Ural Mts.
West Siberian Plain
Ob
Yenisey
Lr. Tunguska
S i b e r i a
Lena
Aldan
Angara
Stanovoy Ra.
Sea of Okhotsk
60
B
North European Plain
Rhine
Carpathians
Danube
Volga
Don
Irtysh
L. Balkhash
Sayan Mts.
Altai
L. Baikal
Amur
Sakhalin
Hokkaido
40
Mt. Blanc 4810
Alps
Apennines
Pyrenees
Black Sea
Balkan Pen.
Elbrus 5633
Caucasus
Caspian Sea
Aral Sea
Syr Darya
Amu Darya
Tian Shan
Pamirs
Kunlun
Nan Shan
Gobi
Huang
North China Plain
Yellow Sea
Sea of Japan
Honshu
Mt. Fuji 3776
Hokkaido   C
Anatolia
Elburz Mts.
Hindu Kush
Karakoram
Plateau of Tibet
Mt. Everest 8848
Himalaya
Yangtze
East China Sea
PACIFIC
Mediterranean Sea
Tigris
Euphrates
Sulaiman Ra.
Thar Desert
Indus
Ganges
Salween
Xi
Taiwan
20
Libyan Desert
Nile
Red Sea
Arabia
Rub 'al Khali
The Gulf
Deccan
W. Ghats
E. Ghats
Bay of Bengal
Mekong
Hainan
Mariana Is.
OCEAN
Wake I.
Hoggar
Tibesti
Sahara
L. Chad
Arabian Sea
Socotra
C. Guardafui
Philippine Is.
Guam
D
Niger
Cameroon Pk. 4070
Guinea
Ethiopian Highlands
C. Comorin
Ceylon
South China Sea
Kinabalu 4101
Celebes Sea
Caroline Islands
Marshall Is.
Gilbert Is.
0
Uele
(Congo)
Zaire
L. Turkana
Mt. Kenya 5199
Kilimanjaro 5895
I N D I A N
Sumatra
Sunda Is.
Borneo
Celebes
Moluccas
Banda Sea
New Guinea
Bismarck Arch.
Nauru
Ellice Is.
E
Kasai
Victoria
L. Tanganyika
Seychelles
O C E A N
Java Sea
Java
Timor
New Hebrides
Fiji Is.
L. Malawi
Zambezi
Comoro Is.
Cocos or Keeling Is.
Torres Str.
C. York
Coral Sea
20
Cubango
Mozambique Chan.
Madagascar
Mauritius
Réunion
Gt. Barrier Reef
New Caledonia
F
Kalahari Desert
Orange
Drakensberg
C. of Good Hope
Hamersley Ra.
Macdonnell Ra.
Great Victoria Desert
C. Leeuwin
Great Australian Bight
Murray
Darling
Australian Alps
Mt. Kosciusko 2230
Great Divide
North I.
40
Crozet Is.
Kerguelen Is.
Bass Str.
Tasmania
New Zealand
Mt. Cook 3764
South I.
G
S O U T H E R N   O C E A N
60
Queen Maud Land
Enderby Land
Queen Mary Coast
Wilkes Land
Adélie Land
South Magnetic Pole
Victoria Land   H
East from Greenwich
20   40   60   80   100   120   140   160   180
10   11   12   13   14   15   16   17   18

Copyright, George Philip & Son, Ltd.

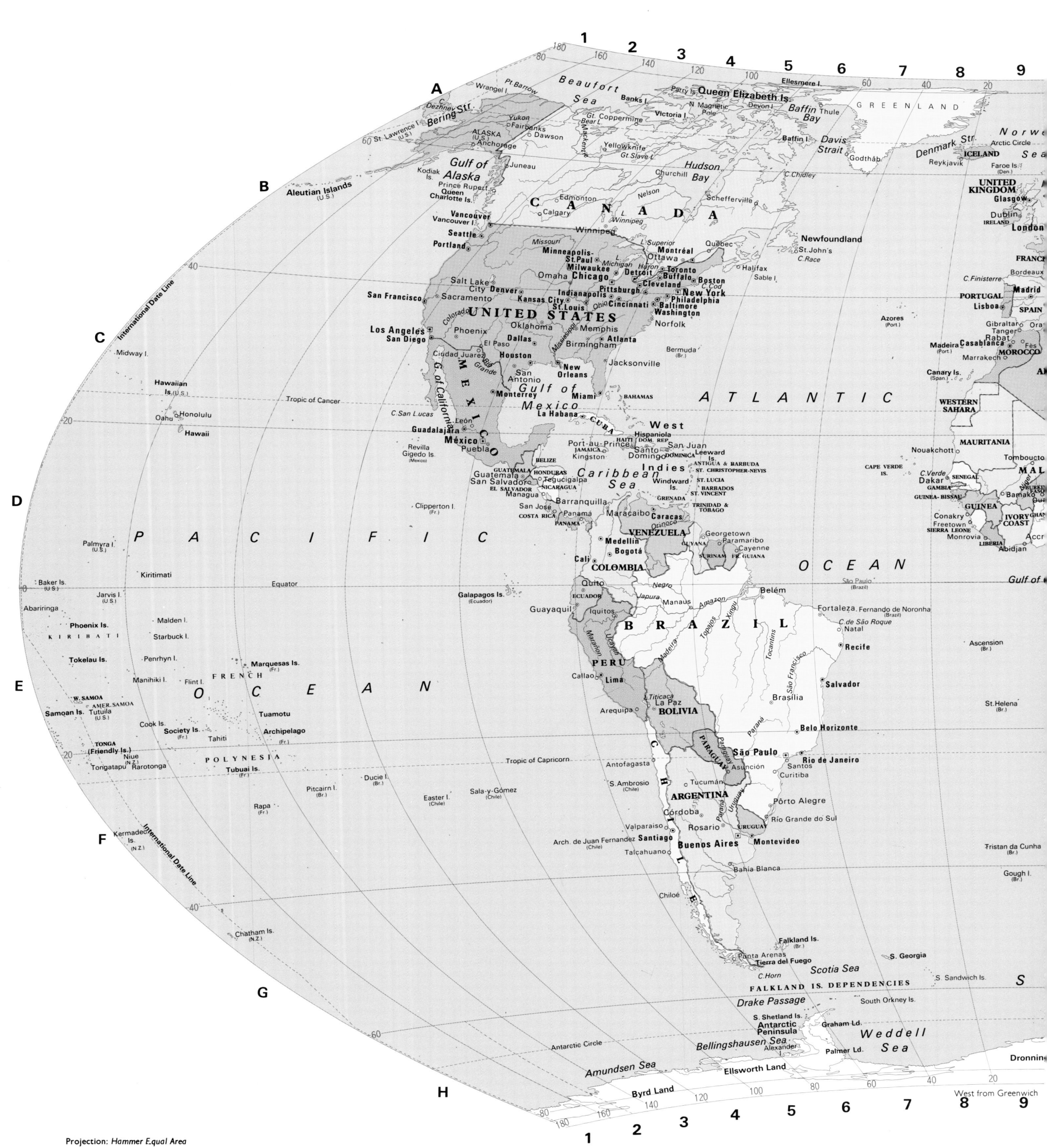

Projection: *Hammer Equal Area*

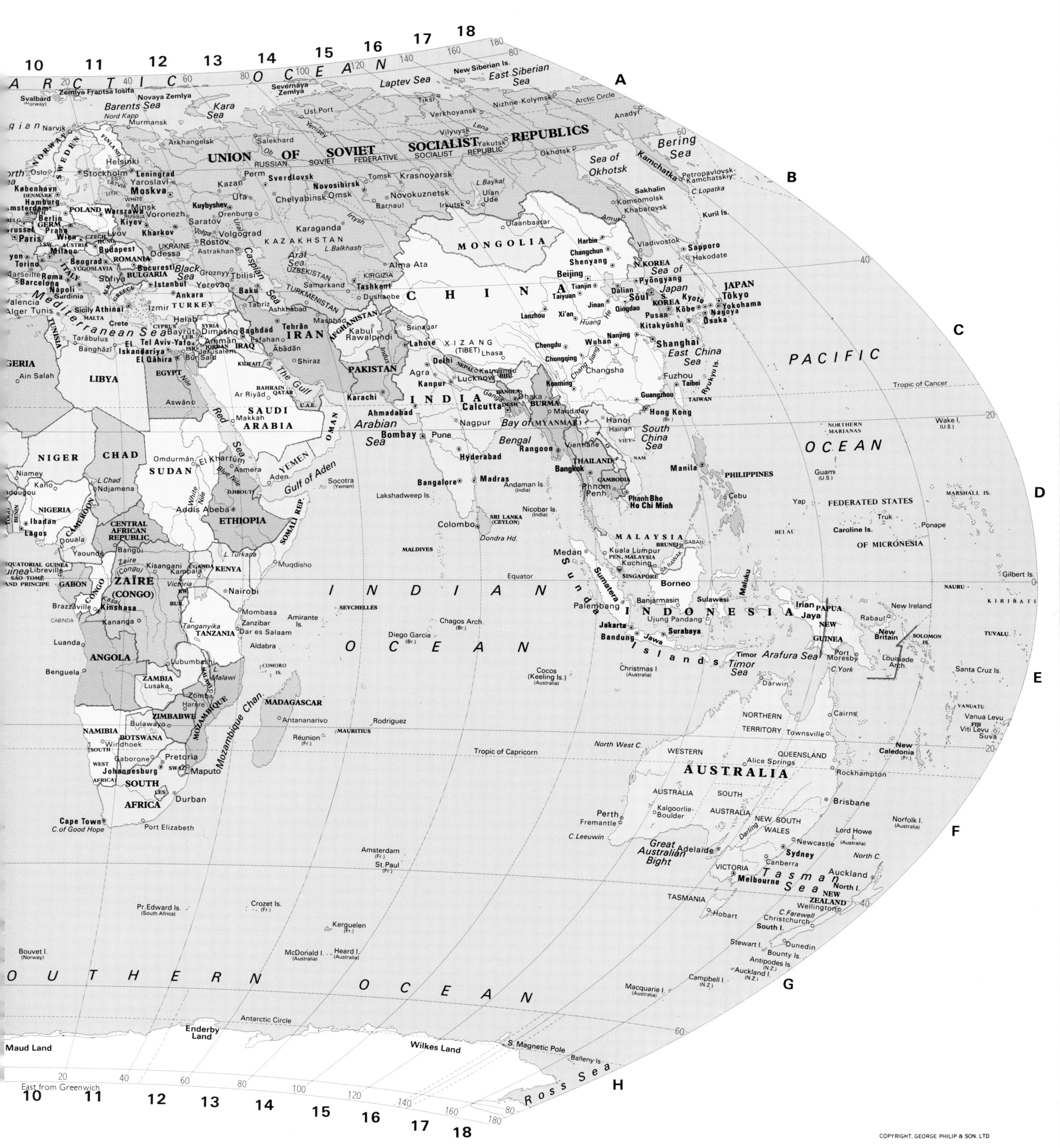

1 : 28 000 000

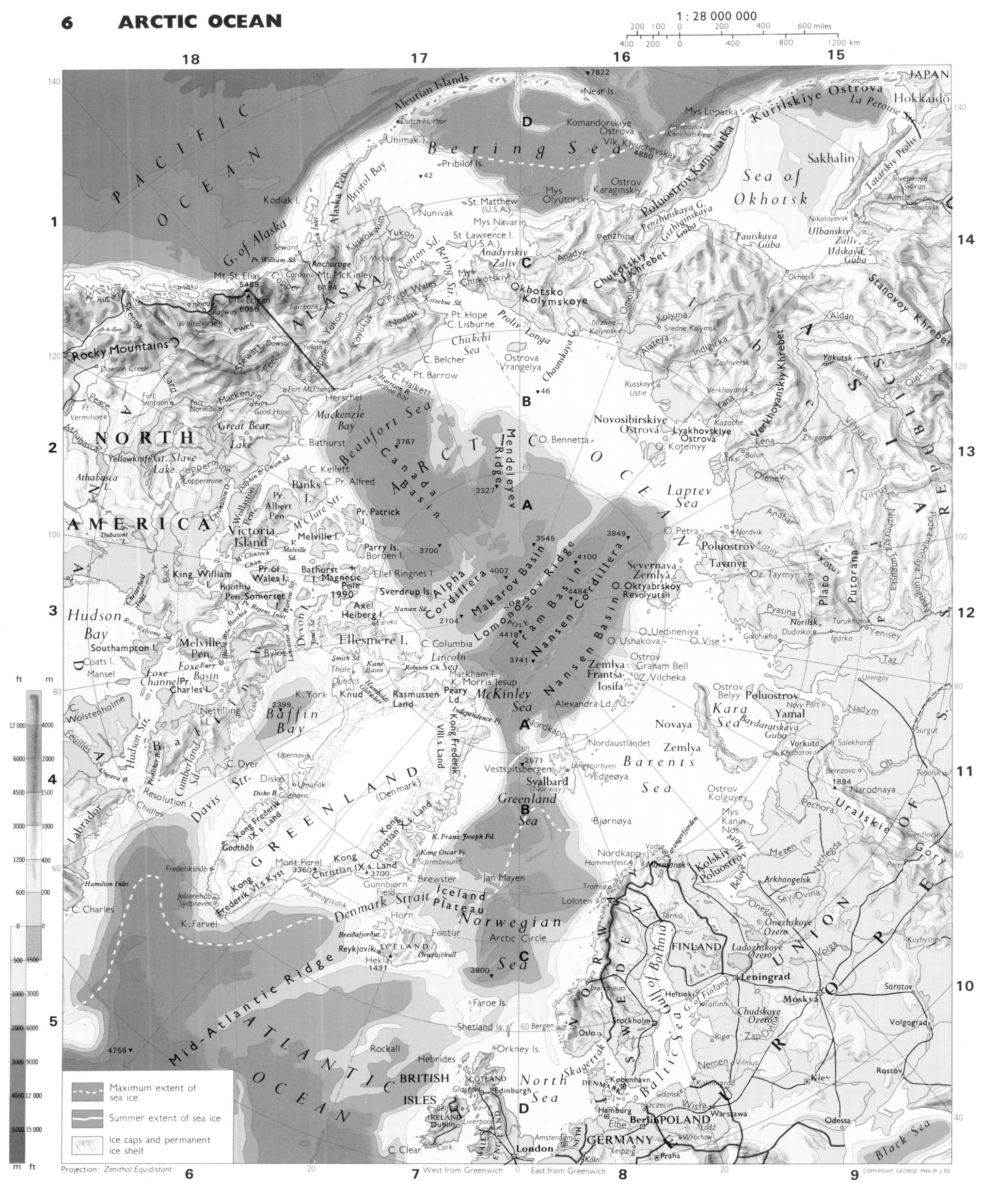

Maximum extent of sea ice

Summer extent of sea ice

Ice caps and permanent ice shelf

Projection: Zenithal Equidistant

COPYRIGHT GEORGE PHILIP LTD

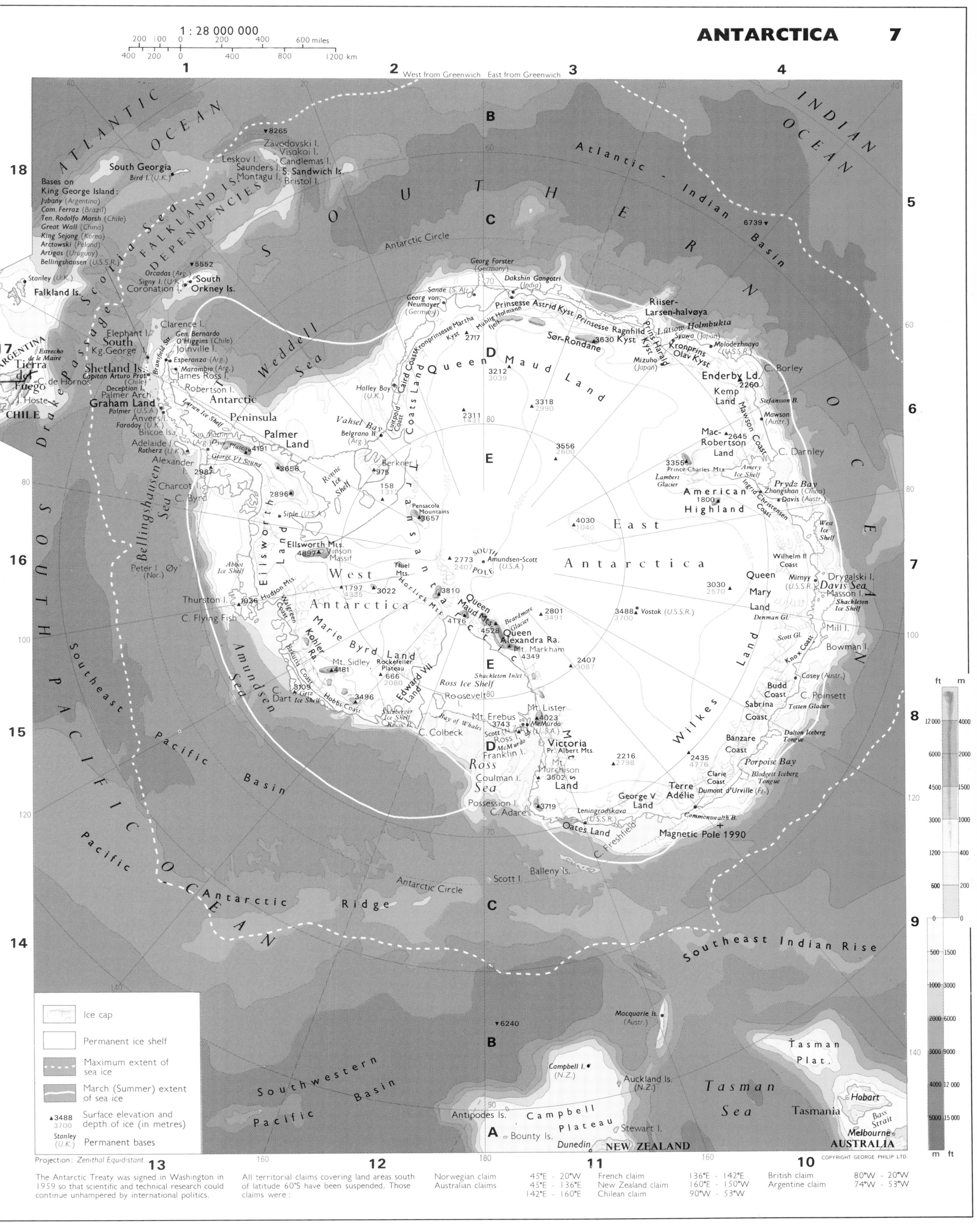

1 : 28 000 000

200 100 0 200 400 600 miles
400 200 0 400 800 1200 km

West from Greenwich East from Greenwich

ATLANTIC OCEAN

SOUTHERN

INDIAN OCEAN

Atlantic - Indian Basin

Bases on King George Island :
Jubany (Argentina)
Com. Ferraz (Brazil)
Ten. Rodolfo Marsh (Chile)
Great Wall (China)
King Sejong (Korea)
Arctowski (Poland)
Artigas (Uruguay)
Bellingshausen (U.S.S.R.)

Zavodovski I.
Visokoi I.
Leskov I. Candlemas I.
Saunders I. Montagu I.
S. Sandwich Is.
Bristol I.

South Georgia
Bird I. (U.K.)

Stanley (U.K.)
Falkland Is.

Antarctic Circle

Georg Forster (Germany)
Dakshin Gangotri (India)

Sanae (S. Afr.)
Georg von Neumayer (Germany)

Prinsesse Astrid Kyst
Prinsesse Ragnhild Kyst

Riiser-Larsen-halvøya

Lützow-Holmbukta
Syowa (Japan)
Molodezhnaya (U.S.S.R.)

Orcadas (Arg.)
Signy I. (U.K.) South Orkney Is.
Coronation I.

Clarence I.
Elephant I.
South Kg. George
Gen. Bernardo O'Higgins (Chile)
Joinville I.

Martha Kyst
Mühlig Hofmann fjell
2717

Sør-Rondane

Prins Harald Kyst
Kronprins Olav Kyst

Mizuho (Japan)
3630

Weddell Sea

Queen Maud Land

Enderby Ld.
2260

C. Borley

Kemp Land

Stefansson B.

Mawson (Austr.)

Esperanza (Arg.)
Marambio (Arg.)
Capitan Arturo Prat (Chile)
James Ross I.
Robertson I.

Halley Bay (U.K.)

3212
3039

3318
2990

Mac-Robertson Land
2645

C. Darnley

Deception I.
Palmer Arch.
Graham Land
Palmer

Anvers I.
Faraday (U.K.)
Biscoe Is.

Antarctic Peninsula

Palmer Land

Vahsel Bay
Belgrano II (Arg.)

Coats Land

Filchner Coast

2311
1431

80

3556

3355
2600

Prince Charles Mts.
Zhongshan (China)
Davis (Austr.)

Amery Ice Shelf

Prydz Bay

Lambert Glacier

Ingrid Christensen Coast

Adelaide I.
Rotherz (U.K.)

Alexander I.

Charcot I.

Plateau 4191

3658

George VI Sound

Berkner I.

975

158
1311

American Highland
1800

East Antarctica

West Ice Shelf

2987

C. Byrd

2896

Ronne Ice Shelf

Siple (U.S.A.)

Pensacola Mountains
3657

4030
1040

Peter I. Øy (Nor.)

Bellingshausen Sea

Ellsworth Land

Ellsworth Mts.
4897
Vinson Massif

2773
SOUTH POLE
Amundsen-Scott (U.S.A.)
2407
3039

Queen Mary Land

Wilhelm II Coast

Mirnyy (U.S.S.R.)

Drygalski I.
Davis Sea
Masson I.

Thurston I.
1036

Abbot Ice Shelf

West Antarctica

Thiel Mts.
3810

Queen Maud Mts.
4176

1797
4335

3022

Horlick Mts.

3030
2570

Shackleton Ice Shelf

C. Flying Fish

Amundsen Sea

Marie Byrd Land

Kohler Ra.

Beardmore Glacier
2801
3491

3488
3700 Vostok (U.S.S.R.)

Denman Gl.

4528

Queen Alexandra Ra.
Mt. Markham
4349

2407
3087

Scott Gl.
Knox Coast

Mill I.

Bowman I.

Mt. Sidley
4181

Rockefeller Plateau
666
2080

4176

Edward VII Land

Shackleton Inlet

Wilkes Land

Budd Coast

Casey (Austr.)

C. Poinsett

3109

Getz Ice Shelf

Dart Ice Shelf

3496

Shirberger Ice Shelf

Ross Ice Shelf

Roosevelt I.
80

Sabrina Coast

Totten Glacier

Dalton Iceberg Tongue

Hobbs Coast

Bay of Whales

Mt. Erebus
3743
McMurdo

Scott (N.Z.)
McMurdo (U.S.A.)

4023
Mt. Lister

Banzare Coast

C. Colbeck

Ross I.

Victoria Land

Pr. Albert Mts.

Porpoise Bay

2216
2798

2435
4776

Clarie Coast

Blodgett Iceberg Tongue

Franklin I.

Ross Sea

Coulman I.

Mt. Murchison
3502

George V Land

Terre Adélie

Dumont d'Urville (Fr.)

Possession I.
3719

Leningradskaya (U.S.S.R.)

Oates Land

Commonwealth B.

Magnetic Pole 1990

C. Adare

C. Freshfield

Scott I.

Antarctic Circle

Ballery Is.

Southeast Indian Rise

Southwestern Pacific Basin

Macquarie Is. (Austr.)

Tasman Plat.

Campbell I. (N.Z.)

Auckland Is. (N.Z.)

Tasman Sea

Tasmania

Hobart

Bass Strait

Antipodes Is.
Bounty Is.
Dunedin

Campbell Plateau
Stewart I.

Melbourne

NEW ZEALAND

AUSTRALIA

Legend:
- Ice cap
- Permanent ice shelf
- Maximum extent of sea ice
- March (Summer) extent of sea ice
- ▲3488 / 3700 Surface elevation and depth of ice (in metres)
- Stanley (U.K.) Permanent bases

Projection: Zenithal Equidistant

ft / m scale:
12 000 / 4000
9000 / 3000
6000 / 2000
4500 / 1500
3000 / 1000
1200 / 400
600 / 200
0 / 0
500 / 1500
1000 / 3000
2000 / 6000
3000 / 9000
4000 / 12 000
5000 / 15 000

COPYRIGHT GEORGE PHILIP LTD.

The Antarctic Treaty was signed in Washington in 1959 so that scientific and technical research could continue unhampered by international politics.

All territorial claims covering land areas south of latitude 60°S have been suspended. Those claims were :

Norwegian claim	45°E - 20°W	French claim	136°E - 142°E	British claim	80°W - 20°W
Australian claims	45°E - 136°E	New Zealand claim	160°E - 150°W	Argentine claim	74°W - 53°W
	142°E - 160°E	Chilean claim	90°W - 53°W		

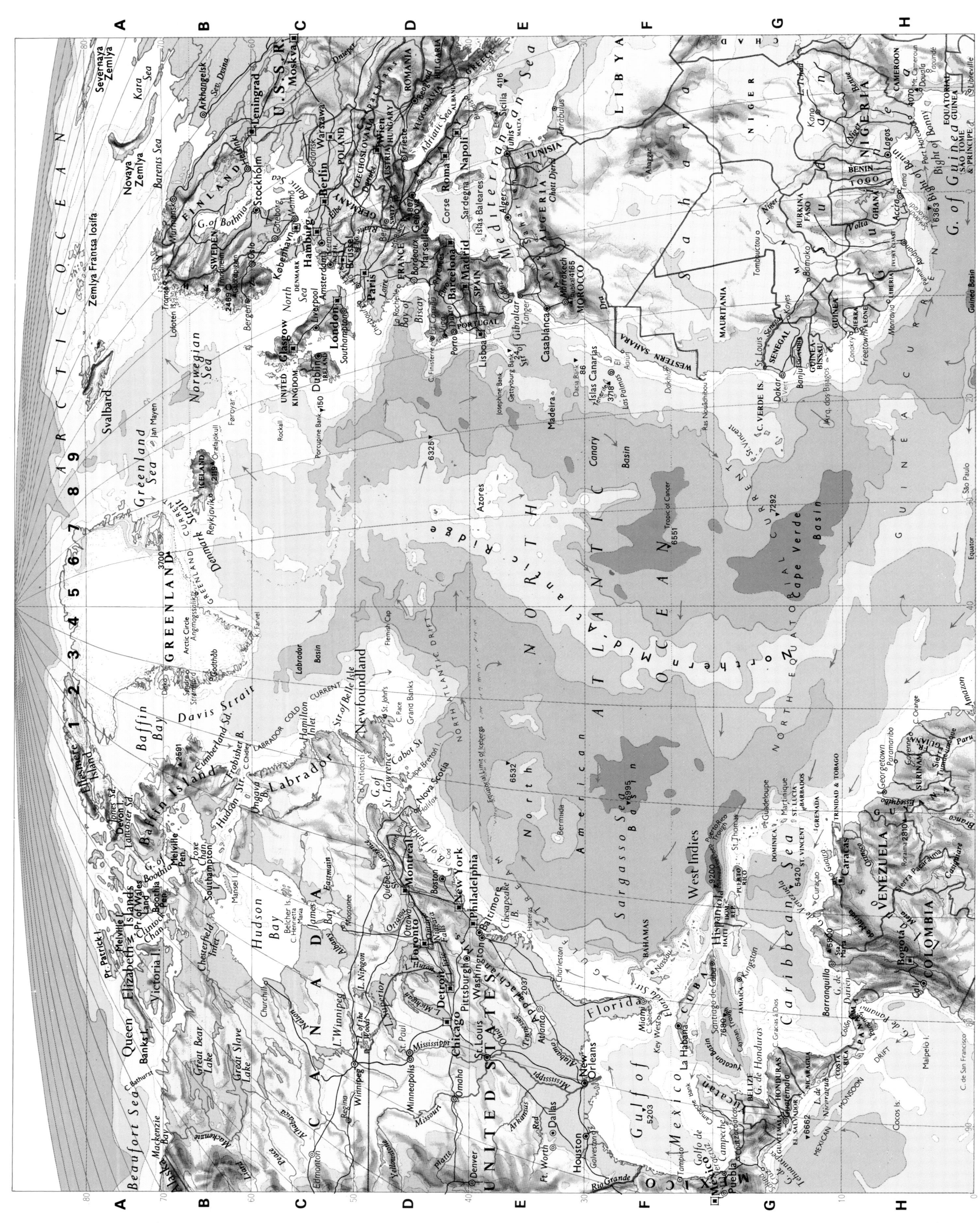

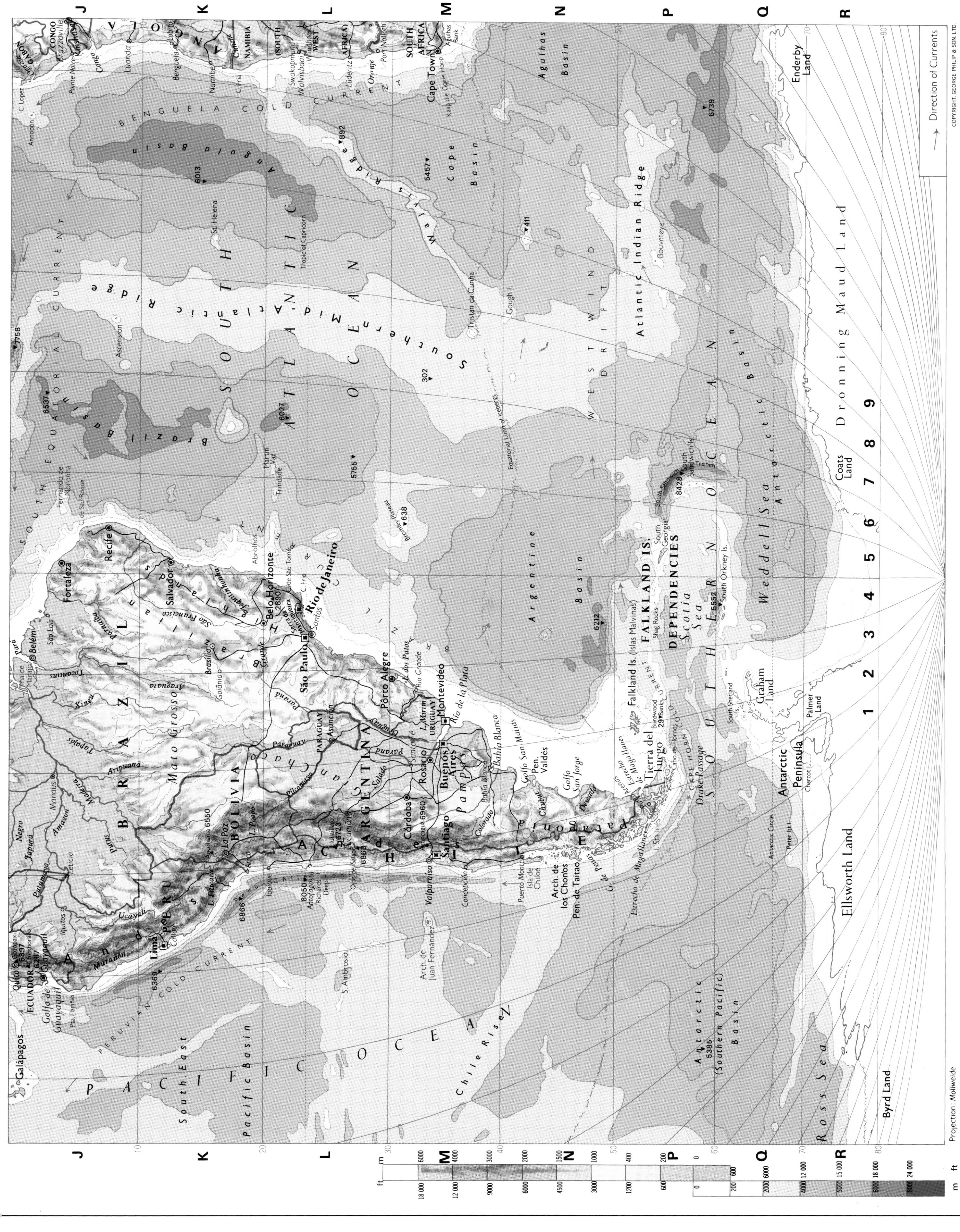

ATLANTIC

SOUTH

OCEAN

PACIFIC OCEAN

SOUTHERN OCEAN

BRAZIL

ARGENTINA

CHILE

BOLIVIA

PARAGUAY

URUGUAY

PERU

ECUADOR

ANGOLA

CONGO

GABON

NAMIBIA (SOUTH WEST AFRICA)

SOUTH AFRICA

Cape Town

Mid-Atlantic Ridge

Southern Antilles Ridge

South Equatorial Current

Brazil Basin

Angola Basin

Cape Basin

Agulhas Basin

Argentine Basin

Scotia Sea

Weddell Sea

Drake Passage

Ross Sea

Antarctic Peninsula

Dronning Maud Land

Enderby Land

Coats Land

Ellsworth Land

Byrd Land

Graham Land

Palmer Land

BENGUELA COLD CURRENT

PERUVIAN COLD CURRENT

BRAZIL CURRENT

SOUTH EAST DRIFT

WEST WIND DRIFT

ANTARCTIC DRIFT

Quito
Guayaquil
Lima
Callao
La Paz
Santiago
Valparaíso
Concepción
Córdoba
Rosario
Buenos Aires
Montevideo
Pôrto Alegre
São Paulo
Rio de Janeiro
Belo Horizonte
Salvador
Recife
Fortaleza
Belém
Manaus
Asunción

Galápagos
St. Helena
Ascension
Tristan da Cunha
Gough I.
Bouvetøya
South Georgia
South Sandwich Is.
South Orkney Is.
South Shetland Is.
Falkland Is. (Islas Malvinas)
FALKLAND IS. DEPENDENCIES

Río de la Plata
Tierra del Fuego
CAPE HORN
Pampas
Patagonia

Atlantic Indian Ridge
Chile Rise
Pacific Basin
Antarctic (Southern Pacific) Basin

Tropic of Capricorn
Equatorial Limit of Icebergs
Antarctic Circle

Direction of Currents

Projection: Mollweide

COPYRIGHT GEORGE PHILIP & SON LTD.

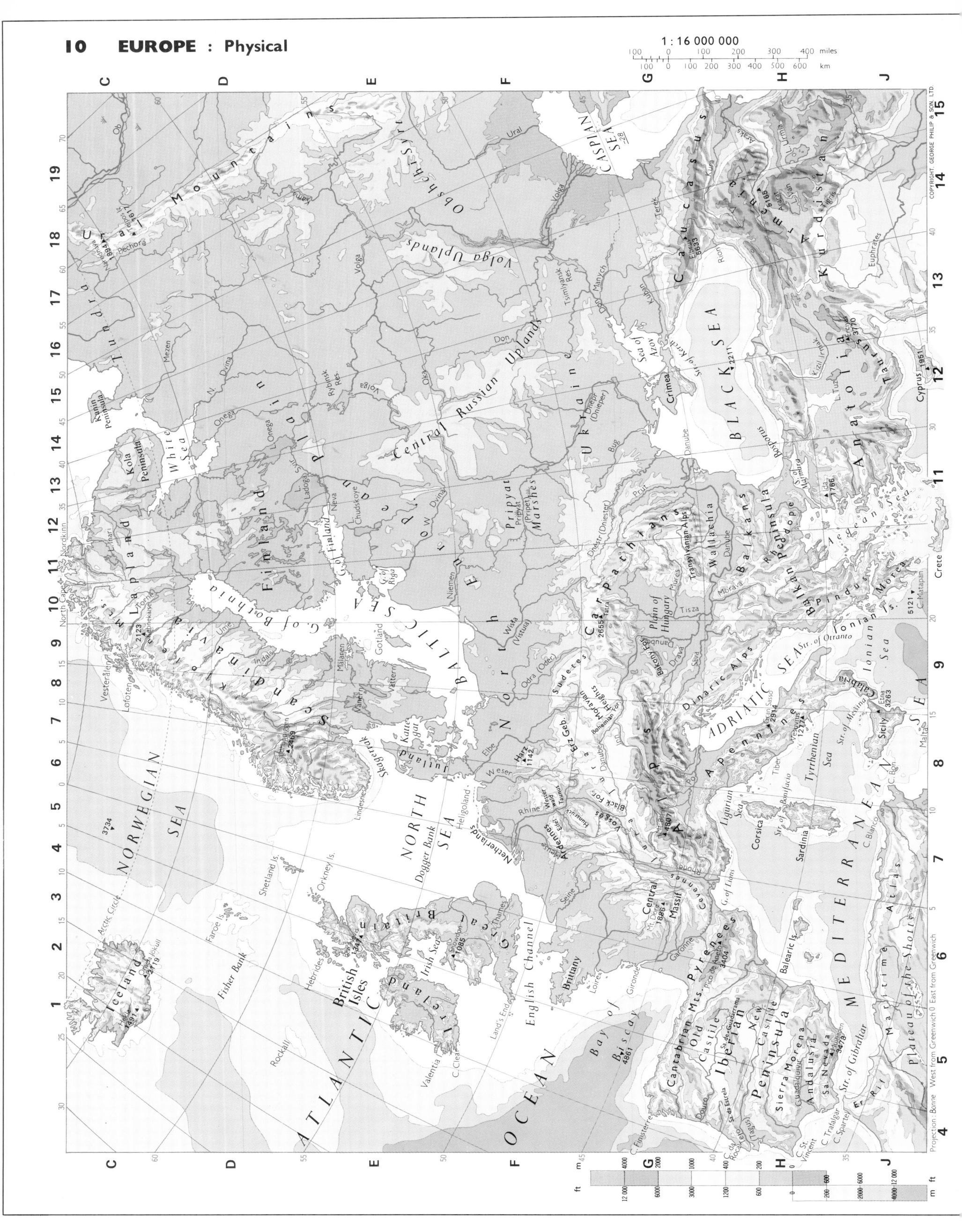

1 : 16 000 000

Projection : Bonne

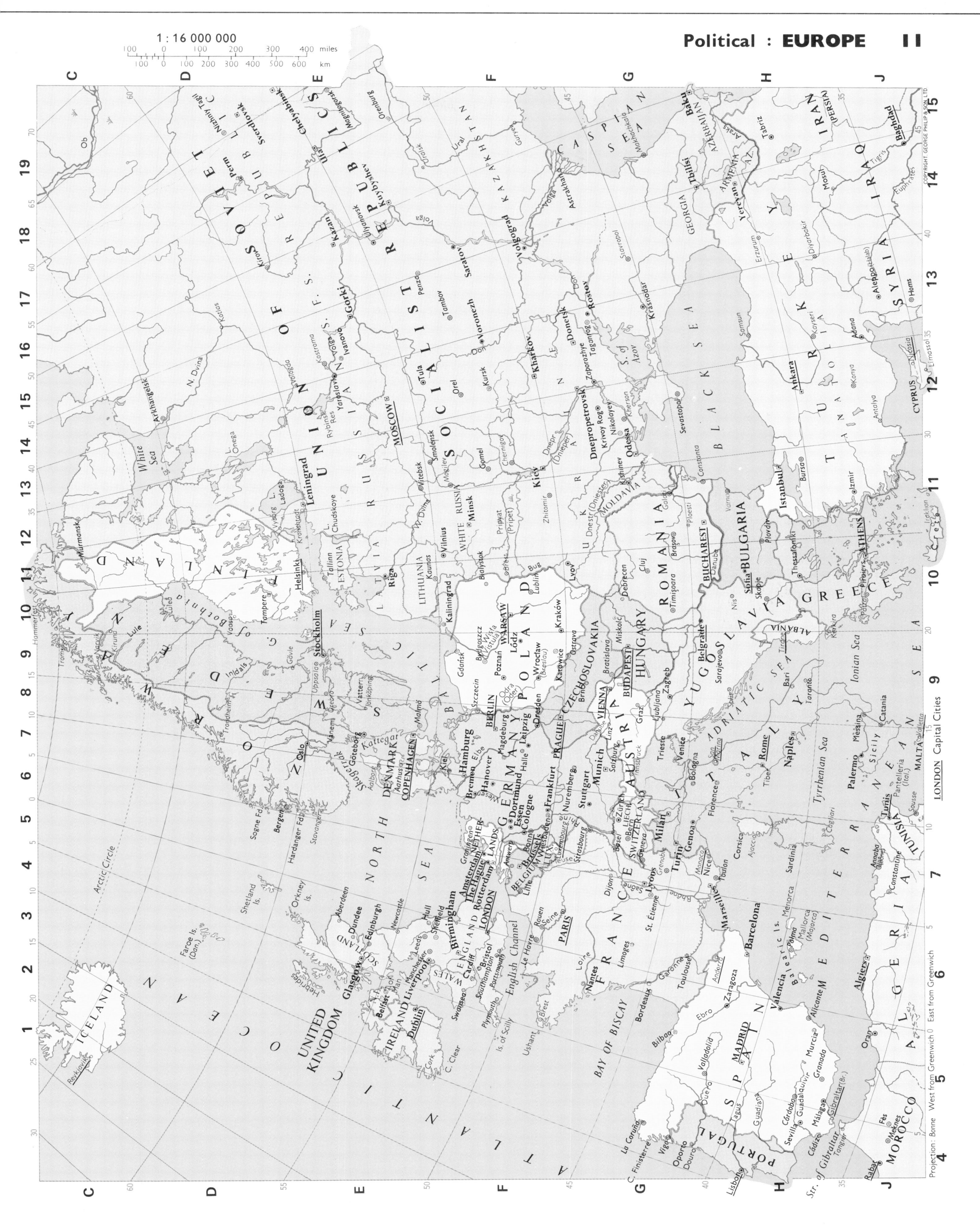

1 : 16 000 000

100   0   100   200   300   400 miles
100   0   200   300   400   500   600 km

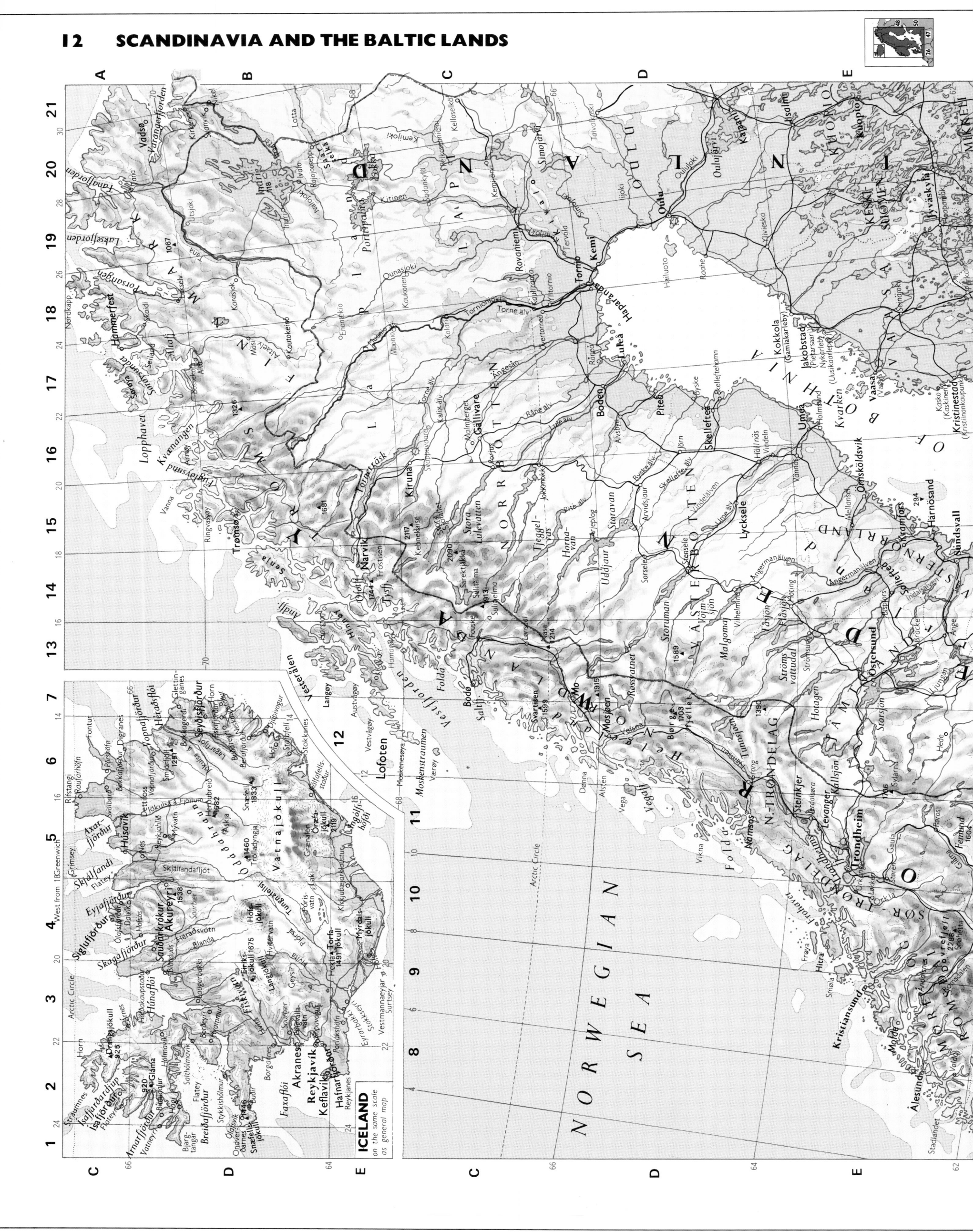

NORWEGIAN SEA

ICELAND
on the same scale
as general map

1 : 4 000 000

50   0   50   100 miles
50   0   50   100   150 km

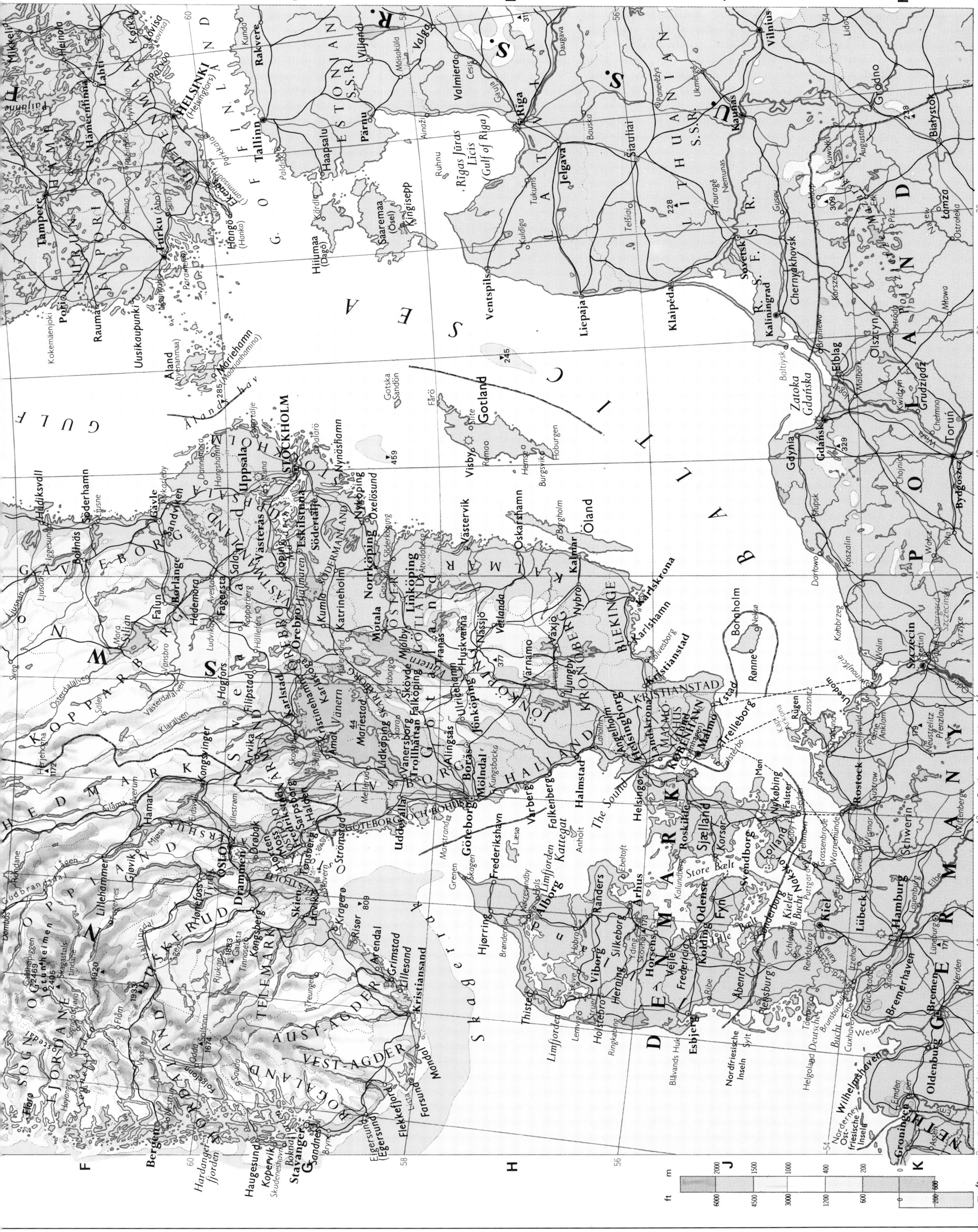

Mikkeli
Heinola
Lahti
Kotka
Lovisa
Hämeenlinna
HELSINKI (Helsingfors)
Rakvere
Kunda
Rakvere
ESTONIAN S.S.R.
Valga
Viljandi
Mõisaküla
311

Tampere
Pori
Rauma
Kenava
Turku (Åbo)
Ekenäs
GULF OF FINLAND
Tallinn
Haapsalu
Pärnu
Valmiera
Cēsis
Gauja
Riga
S.S.R.
Vilnius
228

Uusikaupunki
Hangö (Hanko)
Hiiumaa (Dagö)
Saaremaa (Ösel)
Kingisepp
Ruhnu
Rigas Jūras Līcis (Gulf of Riga)
Ainaži
Tukums
Jelgava
Bauska
Šiauliai
LATVIAN
Panevėžys
Ukmergė
Kaunas
LITHUANIAN
S.S.R.
Grodno
Białystok

Åland (Ahvenanmaa)
Mariehamn (Maarianhamina)
285
BALTIC SEA
Ventspils
Liepāja
Kuldīga
Telšiai
228
Klaipėda
R. S. F. S. R.
Kaliningrad
Chernyakhovsk
Gusev
Tauragė
Nemunas
Suwałki
Augustów
Łomża
Ostrołęka
308

GULF
Söderhamn
Hudiksvall
Gävle
Sandviken
Dalälven
Uppsala
STOCKHOLM
Nyköping
Nynäshamn
Gotska Sandön
Fårö
Gotland
Visby
Roma
Hemse
Burgsvik
Hoburgen
459
245

Gdynia
Gdańsk
Zatoka Gdańska
Elbląg
Malbork
Olsztyn
POLAND
Grudziądz
Chełmno
Toruń
Bydgoszcz

GÄVLEBORG
Bollnäs
Ljusdal
Falun
Mora
Siljan
Borlänge
Hedemora
Fagersta
Avesta
Köping
Västerås
Eskilstuna
Södertälje
SÖDERMANLAND
Katrineholm
Norrköping
Linköping
Motala
Vänern
ÖLAND
Oskarshamn
Västervik
Kalmar
Öland
Borgholm

KOPPARBERG
Ludvika
Örebro
VÄSTMANLAND
Kumla
Mjölby
ÖSTERGÖTLAND
Vadstena
Nässjö
Vetlanda
Karlskrona
Karlshamn
BLEKINGE
Bornholm
Rønne
Nexø
Szczecin (Stettin)
Świnoujście
Usedom
Wolin

Hagfors
Filipstad
Karlstad
VÄRMLAND
Kristinehamn
Karlskoga
ÖREBRO
Skövde
Falköping
Jönköping
Huskvarna
377
Växjö
Ljungby
KRONOBERG
JÖNKÖPING
Kristianstad
Rügen
Greifswald
Anklam
Neustrelitz
Prenzlau

Arvika
Kongsvinger
Lidköping
Skara
Vänersborg
Trollhättan
Alingsås
Borås
Ulricehamn
HALLAND
Halmstad
Laholm
Ängelholm
Helsingborg
Landskrona
MALMÖ
Ystad
Trelleborg
Rostock
Güstrow
Schwerin
Wittenberge

HEDMARK
OPPLAND
AKERSHUS
OSLO
Drammen
Hamar
Gjøvik
Lillehammer
Kongsberg
Skien
ÄLVSBORG
GÖTEBORGS OCH BOHUS
GÖTEBORG
Mölndal
Kungsbacka
Varberg
Falkenberg
Kattegat
Anholt
Læsø
The Sound
Helsingør
KØBENHAVN (Copenhagen)
Roskilde
SJÆLLAND
Korsør
Store Bælt
Nykøbing
Falster
Møn
Fehmarn
Lübeck
Hamburg
GERMANY

BERGEN
Hardangerfjorden
Haugesund
Kopervik
Stavanger
Sandnes
ROGALAND
VEST-AGDER
AUST-AGDER
TELEMARK
Arendal
Grimstad
Lillesand
Kristiansand
Mandal
Farsund
Flekkefjord
Egersund (Eggersund)
Frederikshavn
Hjørring
Skagen
Grenen
Aalborg
Randers
Århus
Viborg
Silkeborg
Herning
Horsens
Vejle
Fredericia
Kolding
Odense
Fyn
Svendborg
Langeland
Lolland
DENMARK
Skagerrak
Thisted
Limfjorden
Holstebro
Ringkøbing
Esbjerg
Ribe
Åbenrå
Sønderborg
Flensburg
Schleswig
Rendsburg
Kiel
Kieler Bucht
Neumünster
Itzehoe
Elbe
Glückstadt
Bremerhaven
Bremen
Oldenburg
Wilhelmshaven
Wesermünde
Cuxhaven
Nordfriesische Inseln
Sylt
Helgoland
Norderney Ostfriesische Inseln
Groningen
NETHERLANDS

Projection Conical with two standard parallels
East from Greenwich

ft m
6000 2000
4500 1500
3000 1000
1200 400
600   200
0
m ft

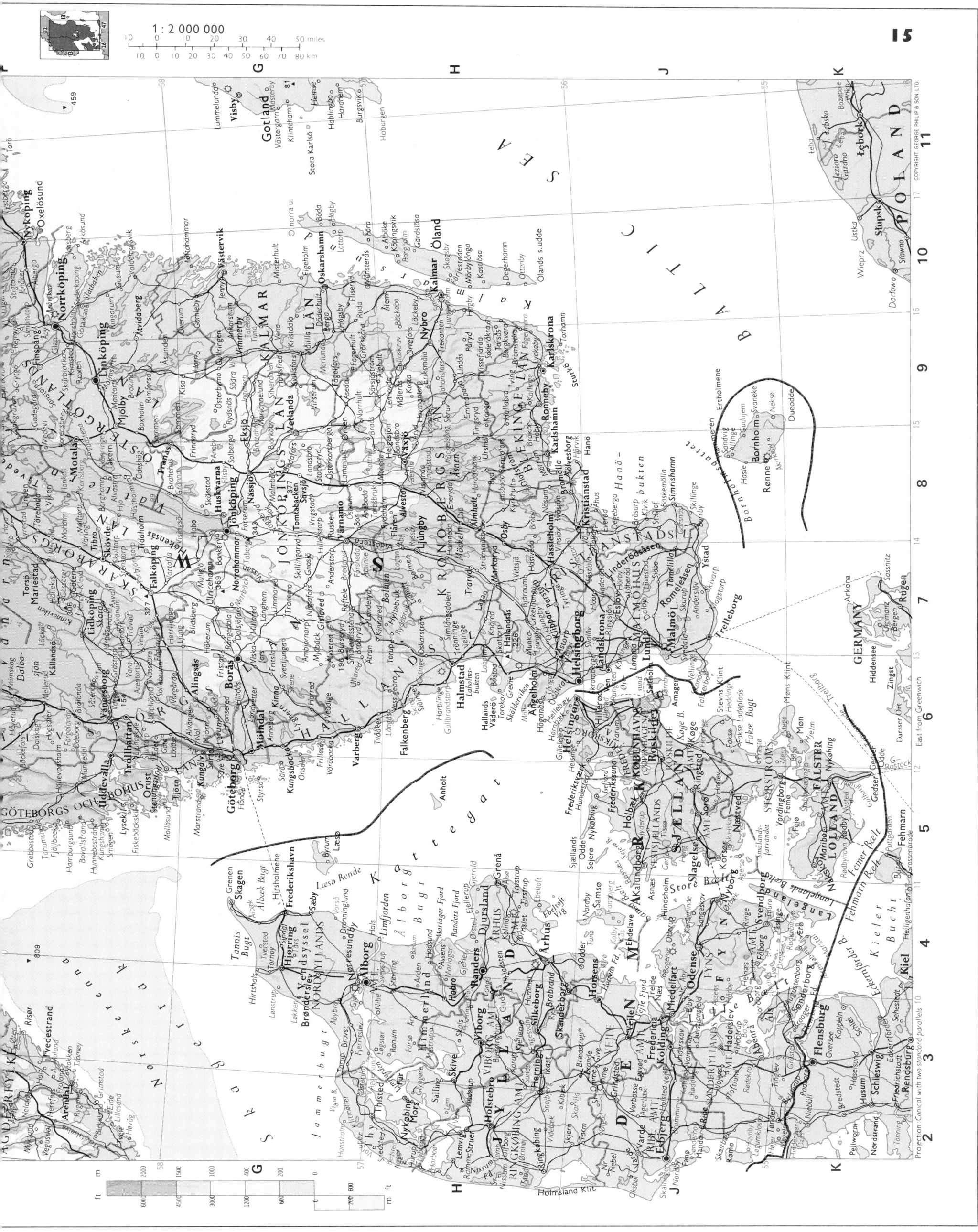

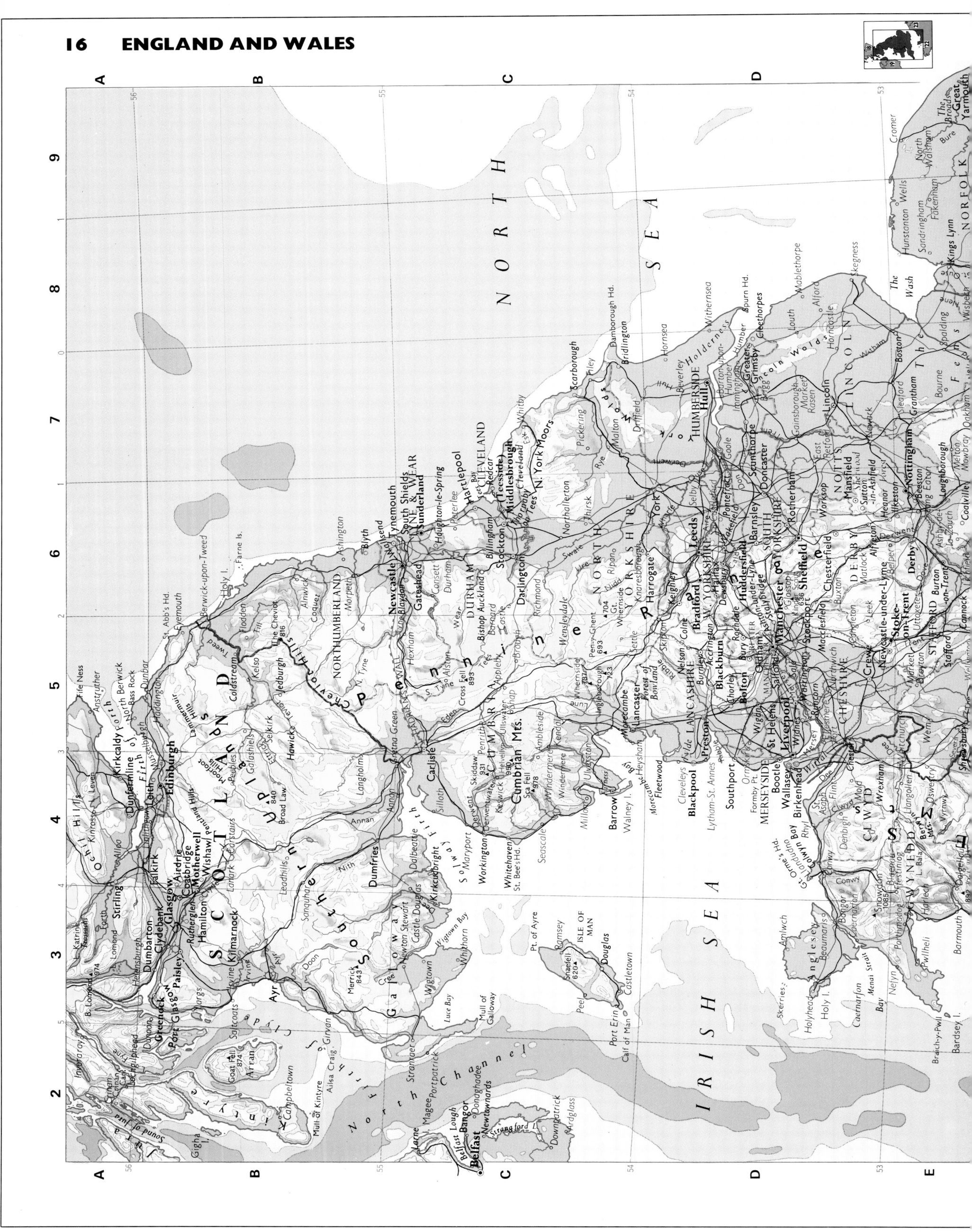

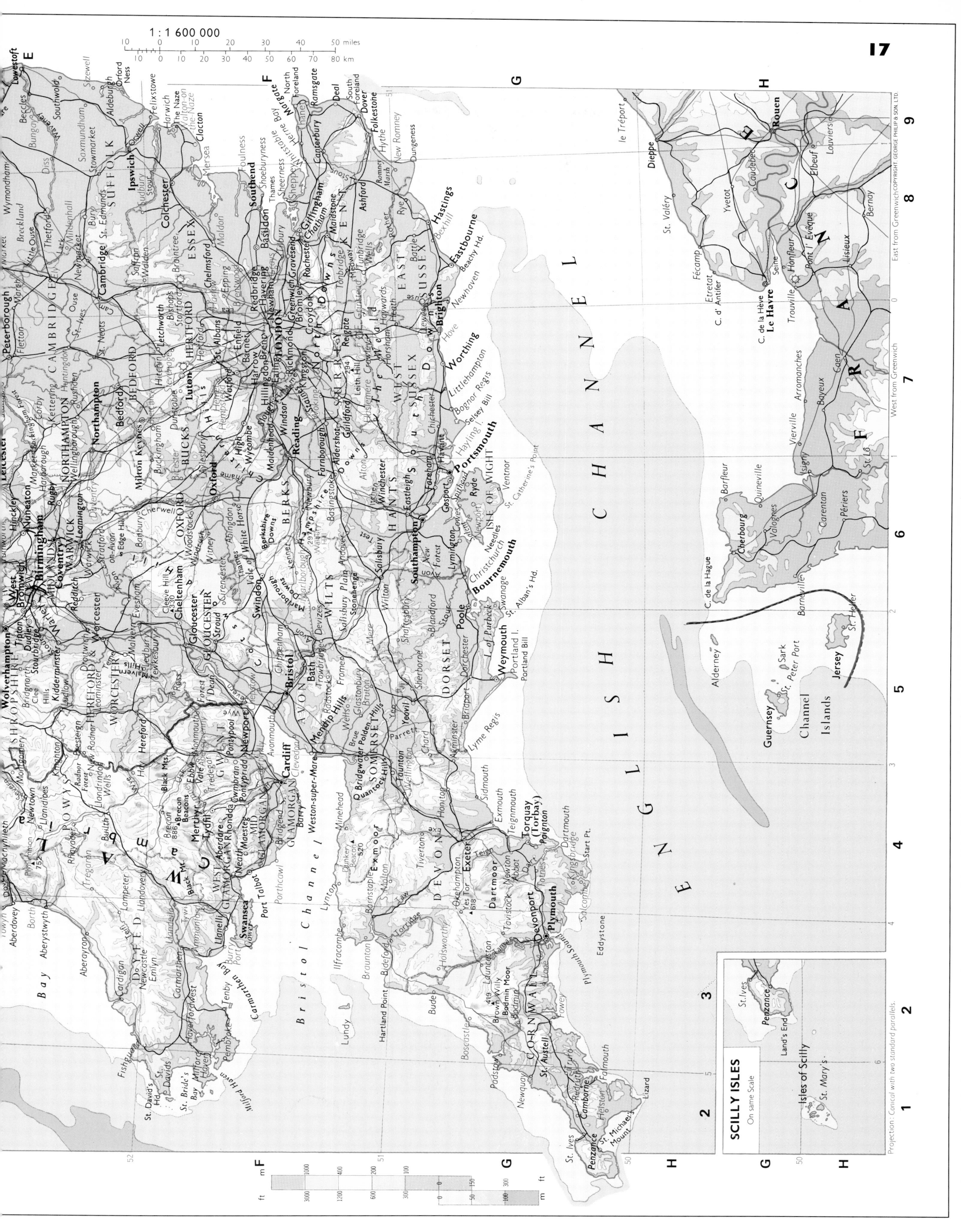

1 : 1 600 000

10   10   20   30   40   50 miles
10   0   10   20   30   40   50   60   70   80 km

E

F

G

H

9

8

7

6

5

4

3

2

1

SCILLY ISLES
On same Scale

Isles of Scilly

St. Mary's

St. Ives

Penzance

Land's End

G

H

Projection: Conical with two standard parallels.

East from Greenwich COPYRIGHT GEORGE PHILIP & SON LTD.

West from Greenwich

E N G L I S H   C H A N N E L

F R A N C E

Channel Islands

Guernsey

St. Peter Port

Sark

Jersey

St. Helier

Alderney

C. de la Hague

Cherbourg

Rouen

Dieppe

Le Havre

CORNWALL

DEVON

DORSET

SOMERSET

WILTS

HANTS

Plymouth

Exeter

Bristol

Cardiff

Swansea

LONDON

Brighton

Portsmouth

Southampton

Bournemouth

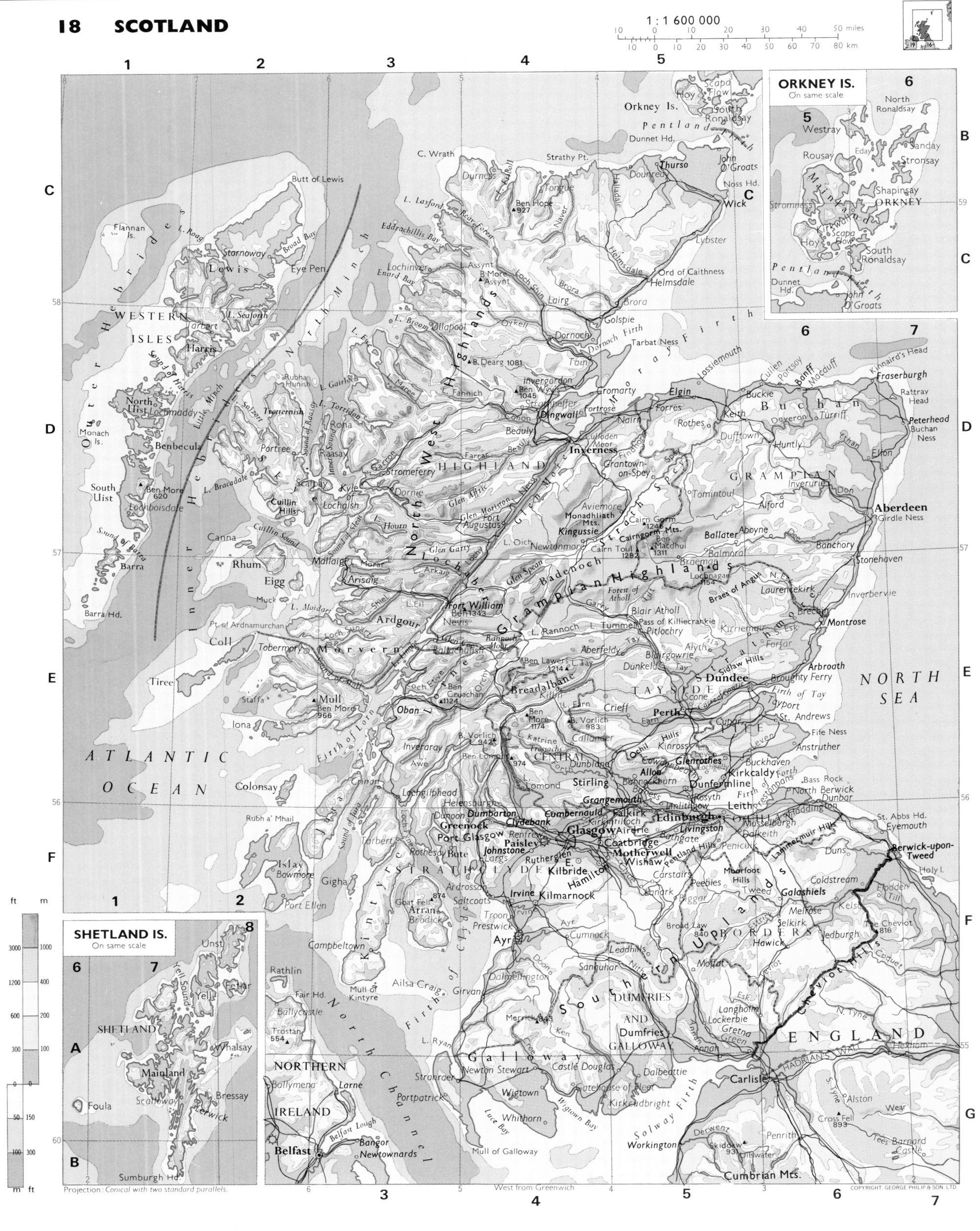

18 SCOTLAND

1 : 1 600 000

ORKNEY IS.
On same scale

SHETLAND IS.
On same scale

Projection: Conical with two standard parallels.

COPYRIGHT. GEORGE PHILIP & SON, LTD.

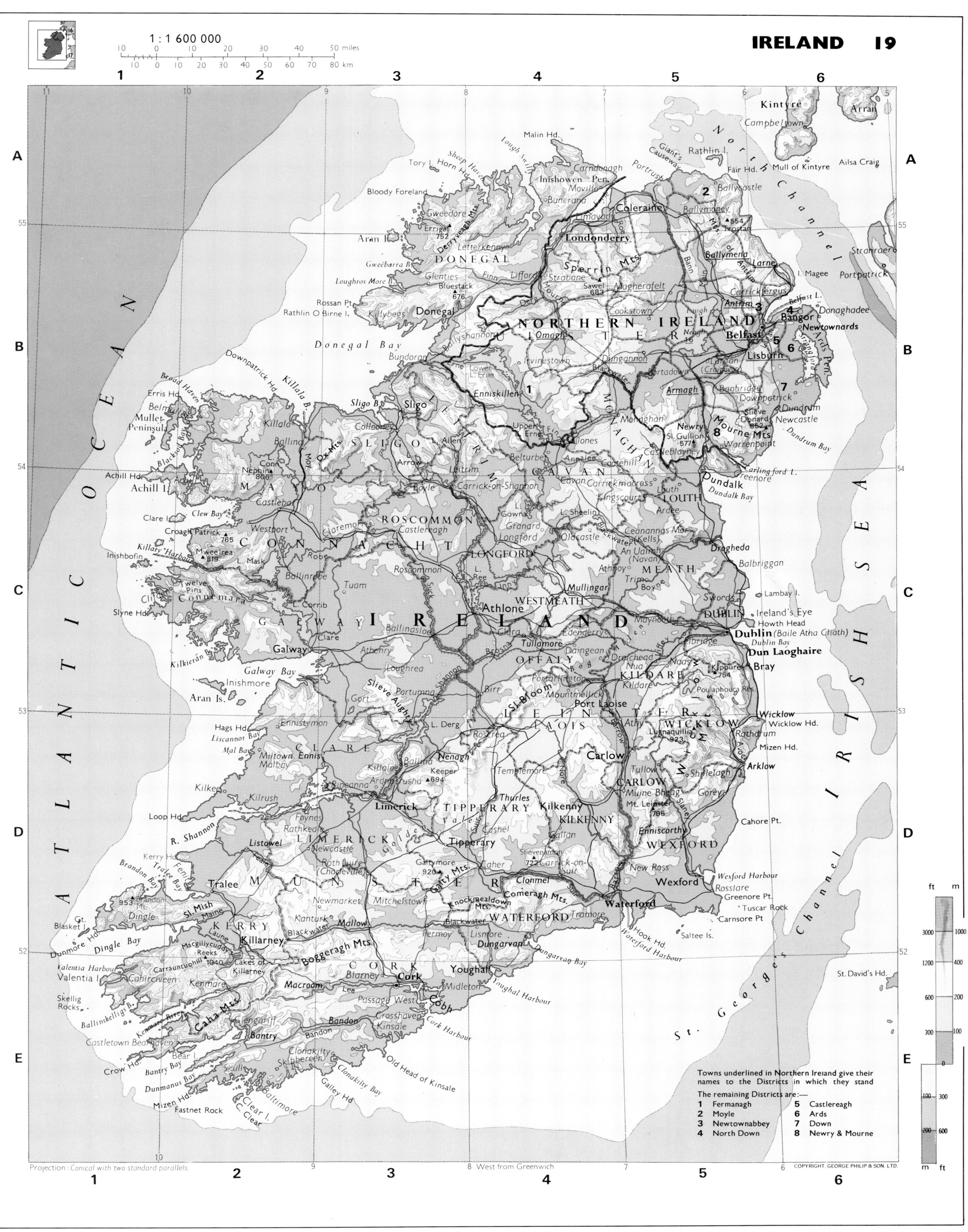

1 : 1 600 000

10   0   10   20   30   40   50 miles

10   0   10   20   30   40   50   60   70   80 km

NORTHERN IRELAND

ULSTER

DONEGAL

LEITRIM

SLIGO

MAYO

CONNACHT

ROSCOMMON

LONGFORD

CAVAN

MONAGHAN

LOUTH

MEATH

WESTMEATH

GALWAY

IRELAND

OFFALY

KILDARE

DUBLIN

Dun Laoghaire

WICKLOW

LEINSTER

LAOIS

CLARE

TIPPERARY

KILKENNY

CARLOW

WEXFORD

LIMERICK

MUNSTER

WATERFORD

KERRY

CORK

ATLANTIC OCEAN

IRISH SEA

St. Georges Channel

North Channel

Donegal Bay

Galway Bay

Dingle Bay

Bantry Bay

Towns underlined in Northern Ireland give their
names to the Districts in which they stand

The remaining Districts are:—

1	Fermanagh	5	Castlereagh
2	Moyle	6	Ards
3	Newtownabbey	7	Down
4	North Down	8	Newry & Mourne

Projection: Conical with two standard parallels.

West from Greenwich

COPYRIGHT. GEORGE PHILIP & SON. LTD.

ft	m
3000	1000
1200	400
600	200
300	100
100	300
200	600
m	ft

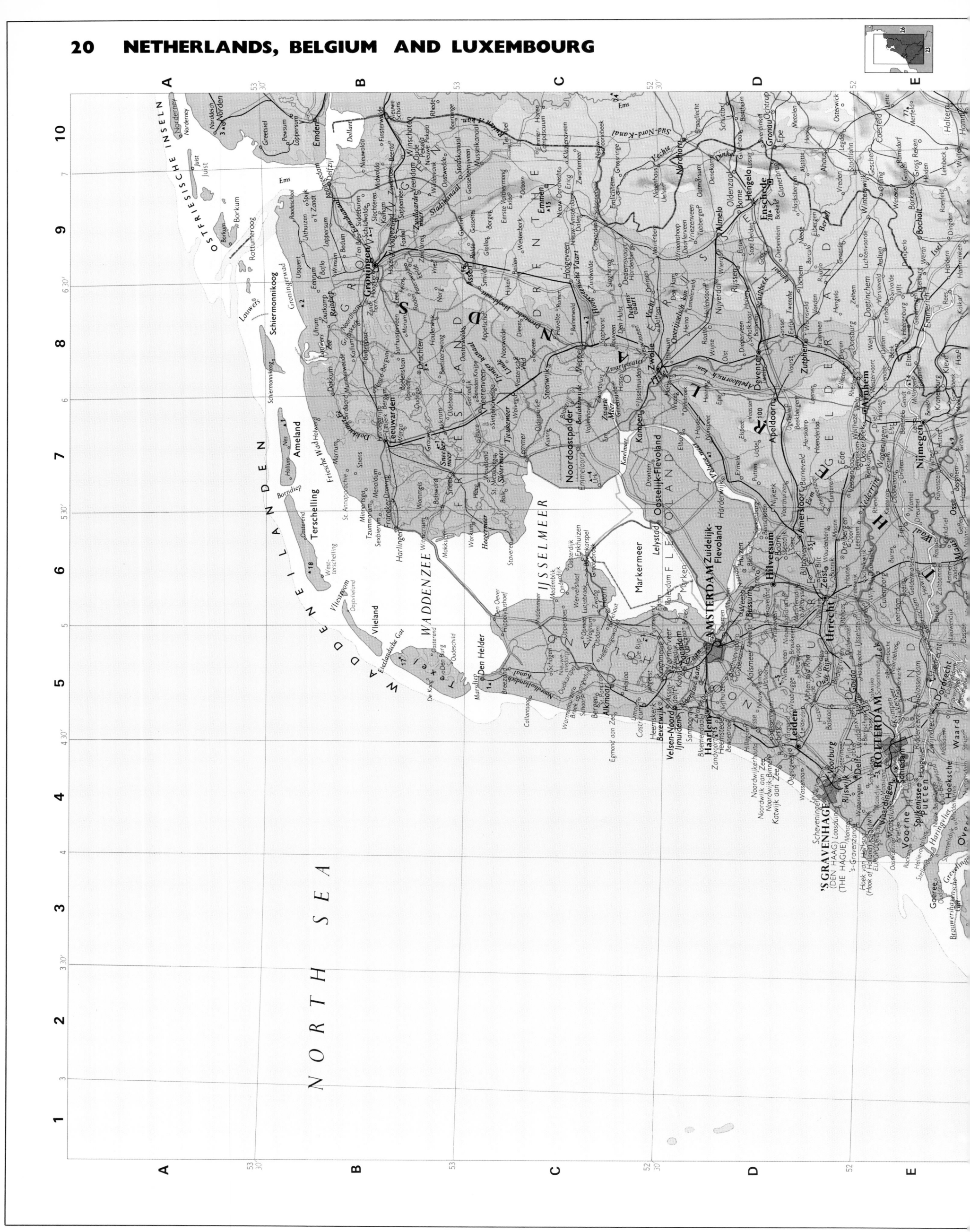

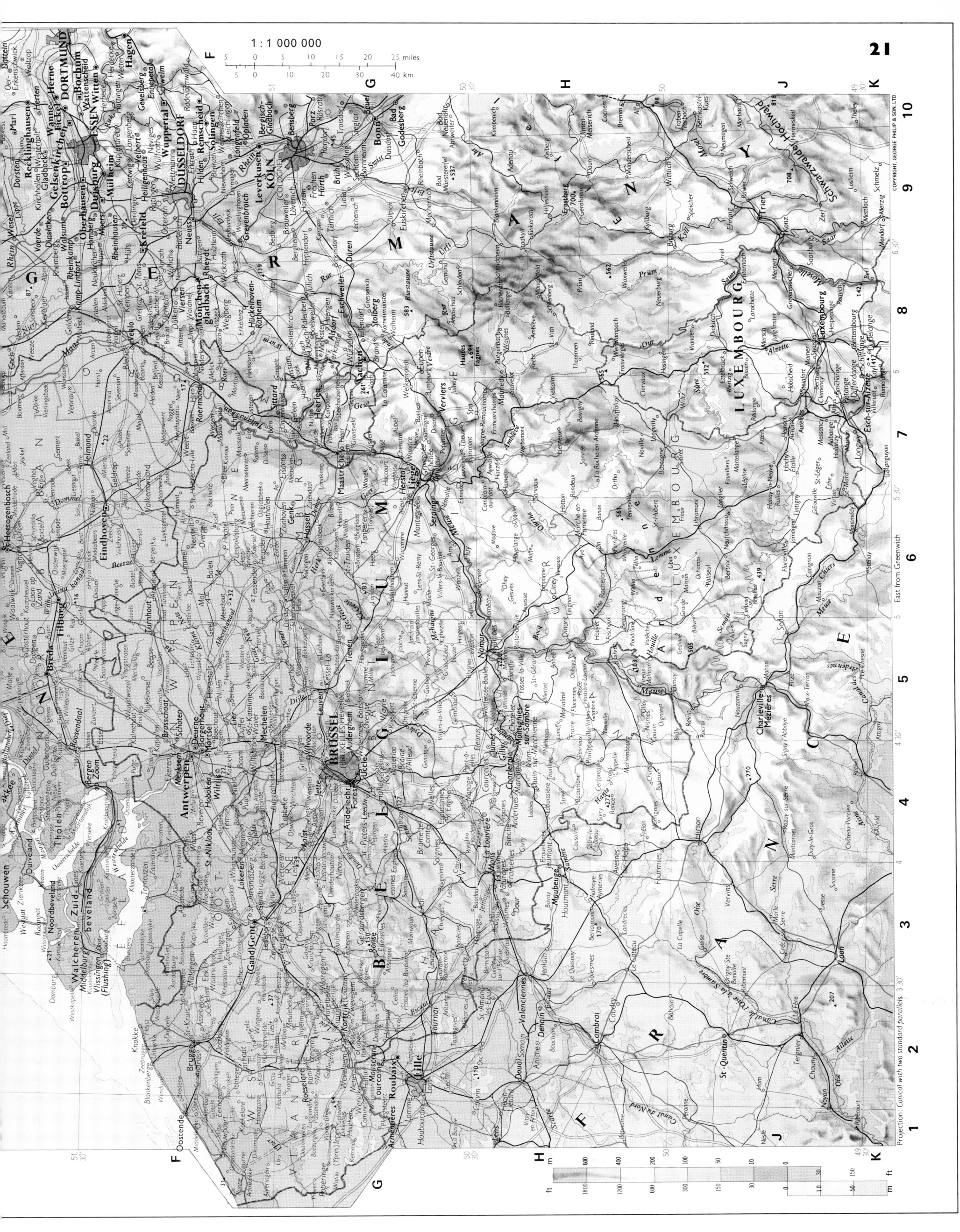

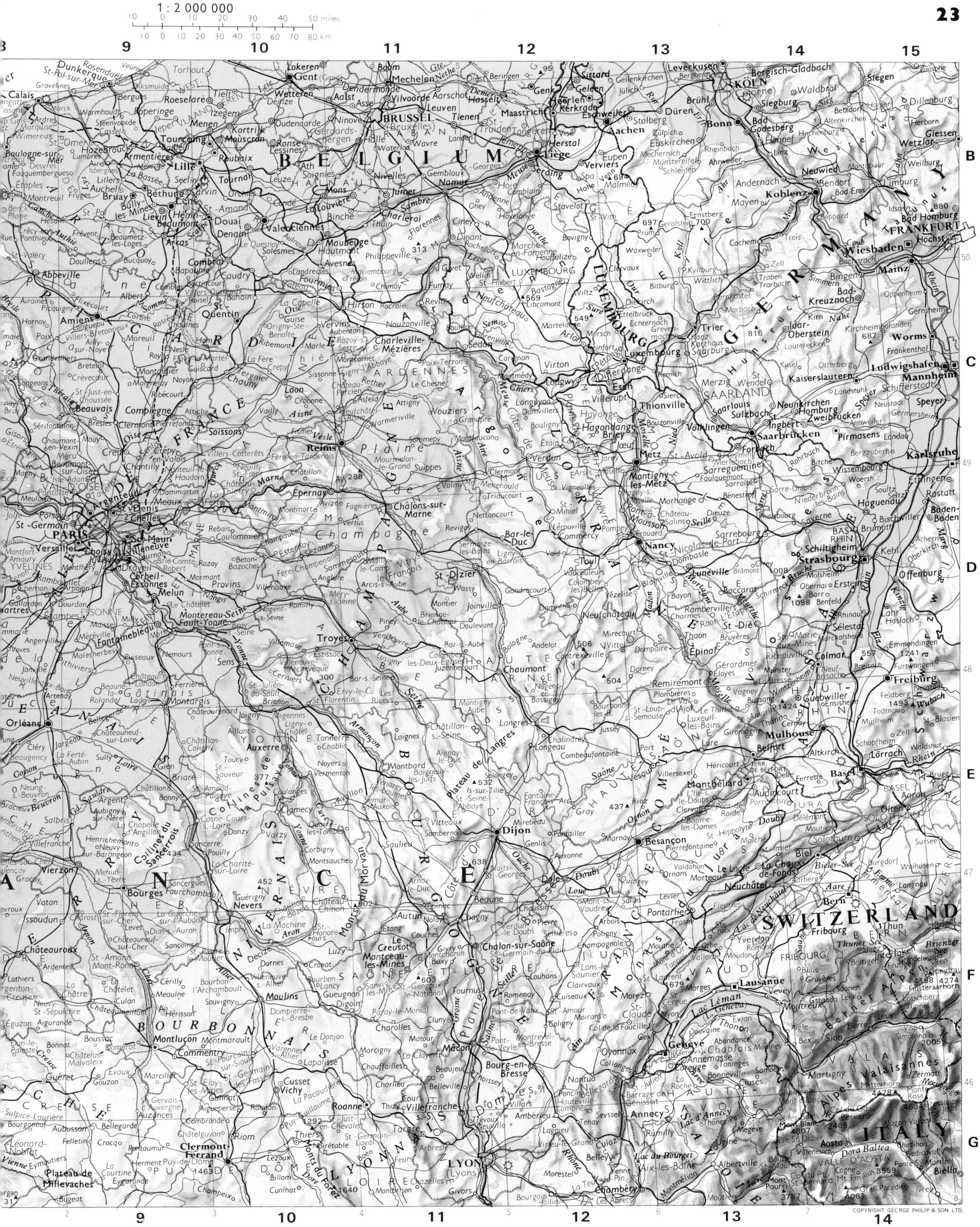
1: 2 000 000
50 miles
80 km
BELGIUM
LUXEMBOURG
GERMANY
SWITZERLAND
ITALY
FRANCE
PARIS
BRUSSEL (Bruxelles)
Luxembourg
Strasbourg
Reims
Dijon
Lyon (Lyons)
Genève
Lausanne
Bern
Basel
Frankfurt
Köln
Mannheim
Saarbrücken
Nancy
Metz
Troyes
Besançon
Orléans
Bourges
Clermont-Ferrand
Lille
Amiens
Liège
Aachen
Koblenz
Wiesbaden
Mainz
Ludwigshafen
Karlsruhe
Freiburg
Mulhouse
Annecy
Chambéry
Aosta
ARDENNES
CHAMPAGNE
LORRAINE
BOURGOGNE
FRANCHE-COMTÉ
BOURBONNAIS
NIVERNAIS
SAVOIE
JURA
VOSGES
SAARLAND
Lac Léman
Plateau de Langres
Côte d'Or
Alpes Valaisannes
Berner Alpen
Monts du Morvan
Monts du Forez
Plateau de Millevaches

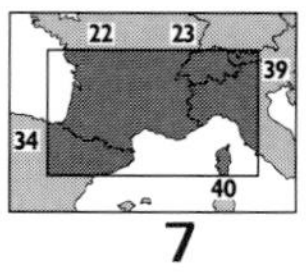

ATLANTIC OCEAN

Golfe de Gascogne

Projection: Conical with two standard parallels

West from Greenwich   East from Greenwich

ft   m
12,000 4000
9000   3000
6000   2000
4500   1500
3000   1000
1200   400
600   200
0
200   600
2000   6000
m   ft

1 : 2 000 000

10   0   10   20   30   40   50 miles
10   0   10 20 30 40 50 60 70 80 km

8   9   10   11   12   13   14

SWITZERLAND

Luzern · Zuger See · Glarus · Landquart · Rätikon · Nauders
La Chaux-de-Fonds · Le Locle · Biel · Bieler See · Burgdorf · Brunnen · Davos · 3244
Neuchâtel · Bern · Aare · Langnau · Schwyz · UNTER WALDEN · Klosters · 2899 · Malles Venosta
Fribourg · Thun · Thuner See · Interlaken · Brienz · Andermatt · GRAUBÜNDEN (GRISONS) · Zernez
FRIBOURG · Bulle · Gruyères · Grindelwald · Hinter Rhein · Splügenpass · Ortles
Lausanne · Vevey · Montreux · Berner Alpen · 4158 · Airolo · Bellinzona · Adamello · 3554
Lac Léman · Évian · Sierre · Sion · Simplonpass · 2055 · Locarno · Lugano · Breno
Genève · Annemasse · Martigny · VALAIS · Valaisannes · Matterhorn · Monte Rosa · 4634 · L. Maggiore · Como · Bergamo · Brescia
Annecy · Mont Blanc · Aosta · VAL D'AOSTA · Varese · Busto Arsizio · Monza · MILANO · Crema · Monticelli
Chambéry · Albertville · Gran Paradiso 4061 · Biella · Novara · Vigevano · Pavia · Cremona
Grenoble · SAVOIE · TORINO · Asti · Alessandria · Voghera · Parma
Valence · Briançon · Pinerolo · Cúneo · Mondovì · Savona · GENOVA · Rapallo · La Spezia · Carrara · Massa
ALPES-DE-HAUTE-PROVENCE · Digne · Imperia · Golfo di Génova · Livorno
Avignon · PROVENCE · ALPES-MARITIMES · San Remo · Menton · MONACO · Nice · Antibes · Cannes
Nîmes · Arles · Aix-en-Provence · Draguignan · Fréjus · St-Raphaël
MARSEILLE · Toulon · Hyères · ILES D'HYÈRES · **LIGURIAN SEA** · Gorgona · Elba
du Lion · Capraia · C. Corse · Bastia · Étang de Biguglia · Pianosa
CORSICA · HAUTE CORSE · Corte · 2710 · 1766
MEDITERRANEAN SEA · Ajaccio · CORSE DU SUD · G. de Valinco · Sartène · Bonifacio

8   5   9   6   10   7   11   8   12   13   14

COPYRIGHT GEORGE PHILIP & SON LTD.

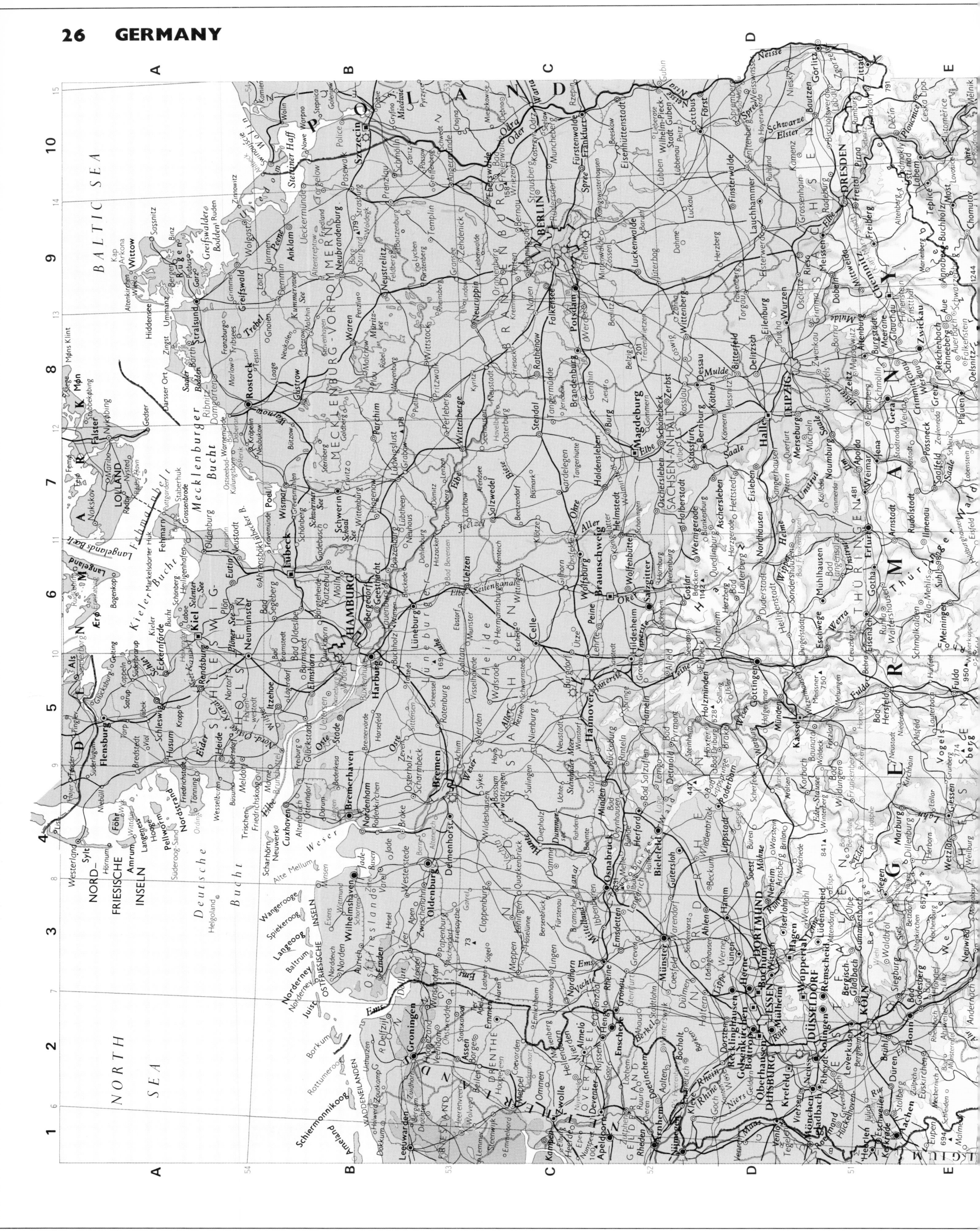

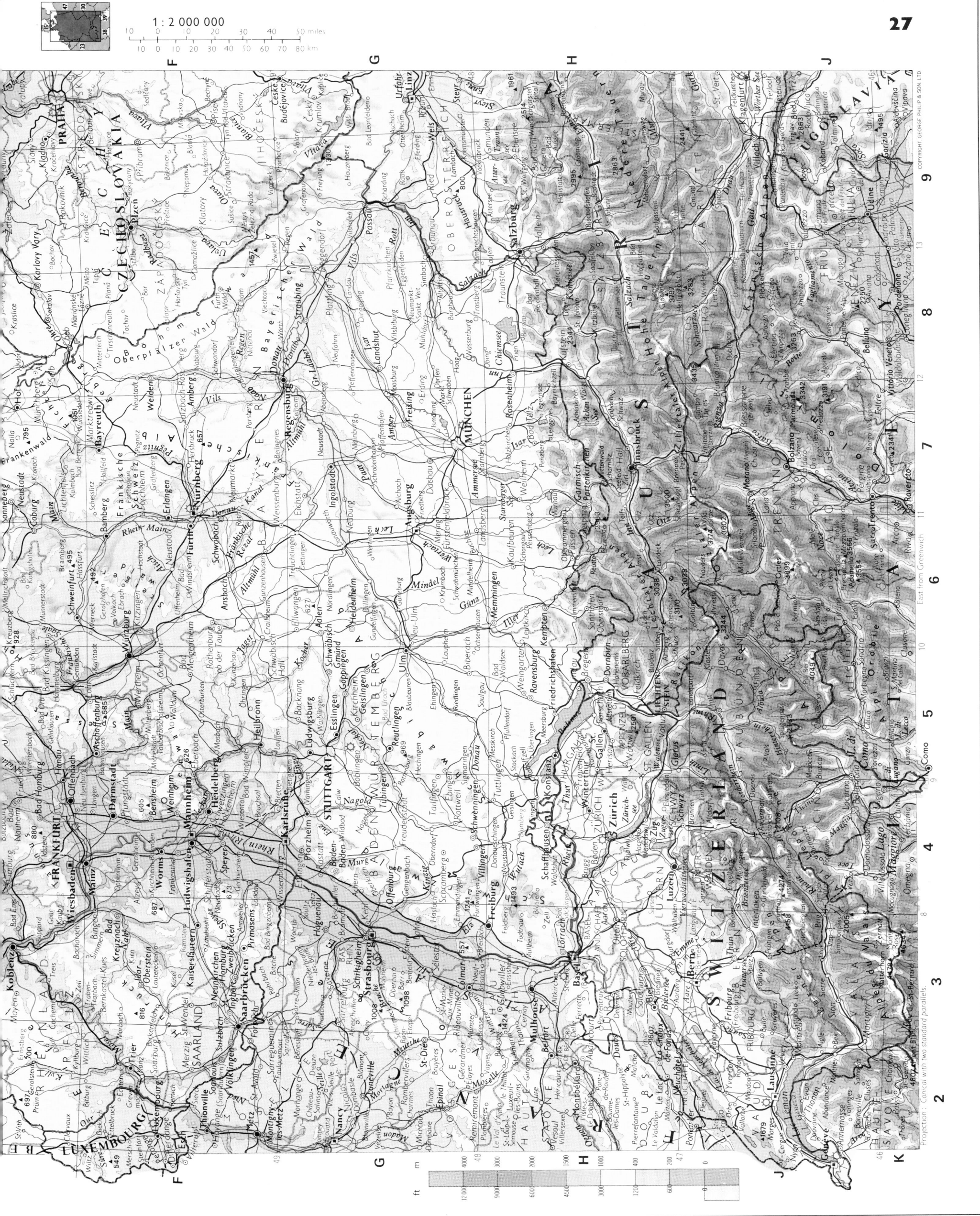

1 : 2 000 000

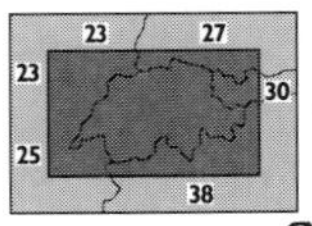

Grid columns: 1 2 3 4 5 6

A

B

C

D

E

FRANCE

HAUTE-SAÔNE

Vesoul
Belfort
Besançon
MULHOUSE
BASEL (BASLE)
Lörrach
B. Rheinfelden
Rheinfelden
Pratteln
Liestal
LANDSCHAFT
AARGAU
Aarau
Olten
Zofingen
Langenthal
Sursee
LUZERN

Montbéliard
Audincourt
Valentigney
Mandeure
Hérimoncourt
Porrentruy
Delémont
Moutier
Solothurn
Grenchen
Biel (Bienne)
Burgdorf

DOUBS
Morteau
Le Locle
La Chaux-de-Fonds
La Neuveville
NEUCHÂTEL
Neuchâtel
Bielersee
Lyss
Aarberg
BERN (BERNE)
Zollikofen
Ostermundigen
Worb
Langnau i. E.

Pontarlier
Les Verrières
Fleurier
Ste-Croix
Chasseron 1607
Grandson
Yverdon
Orbe
Estavayer-le-Lac
Payerne
Avenches
Murten
Düdingen
Fribourg (Freiburg)
Marly-le-Grand
Schwarzenburg
FRIBOURG
Thun
Steffisburg
Thunersee
Spiez
Interlaken
Brienz
Meiringen

Vallorbe
Le Pont
La Sarraz
Mt. Tendre 1679
Le Brassus
Morbier
Morez
Bussigny
LAUSANNE
Romont
Bulle
Gruyère
Molson
Châtel-St-Denis 2002
Château-d'Oex
Gstaad
Zweisimmen
Frutigen
Adelboden
Kandersteg
Grindelwald
OBERLAND
BERNER ALPEN

St-Claude
Divonne-les-Bains
Nyon
Morges
Rolle
Lutry
Léman (L. Geneva)
Vevey
Montreux
Villeneuve
Aigle
Leysin
Les Diablerets
Wildhorn
Wildstrubel
Montana
Leukerbad
Simplon

Oyonnax
GENÈVE (GENEVA)
Vernier
Chêne-Bourg
Annemasse
HAUTE-SAVOIE
Thonon-les-Bains
Évian-les-Bains
Monthey
St-Maurice
Bex
Sion
Sierre
Visp
Brig
VALAIS
Simplonpass
Mte. Leone 3553

Bellegarde-s.-V.
St-Julien-en-Genevois
Annecy
Bonneville
La Roche
Cluses
Sallanches
Chamonix-Mont-Blanc
Col du Gd.-St-Bernard
Martigny
Orsières
Matterhorn 4478
Monte Rosa
Dufourspitze 4634
Weisshorn
Zermatt
Saas-Fee

Belley
Aix-les-Bains
Lac du Bourget
Ugine
Albertville
Beaufort
Col du Petit-St-Bernard
VALLE D'AOSTA
Aosta
Mont Blanc 4807
Courmayeur

Projection: Conical with two standard parallels

1 : 800 000

5 0 5 10 15 20 25 miles
5 0 10 20 30 40 km

GERMANY

DEN WÜRTTEMBERG

Blumb'g.
Stockach
Baienfurt
Wolfegg
Leutkirch
Obergünzburg
Schongau
Engen
Sipplingen
Heiligenberg
Isny
Altusried
Wildpoldsried
Peiting
Bonndorf im Schwarzwald
Singen
Radolfzell
Überlingen
Weingarten
Wiggensbach
Buchenberg
Marktoberdorf
Stühlingen
Thayngen
Ravensburg
Kisslegg
Kempten
1125
St. Mang
Durach
SCHAFFHAUSEN
Gottmadingen
Meersburg
Meckenbeuren
Argen
Wangen i. A.
Sulzberg
Rettenberg
Nesselwang
Schwangau
Beringen
Konstanz 252 396
Tettnang
Wertnau
1243
Mittelberg
Pfronten
Füssen
Neuhausen a. Rh.
Steinach Rhein
Kreuzlingen
Friedrichshafen
Wangen i. A.
Immenstadt i. A.
Sonthofen
Hindelang
Tiengen
THURGAU
Weinfelden
Romanshorn
Langenargen
Lindenberg i. A.
Weiler Simmerberg
Blaichach
Balderschwang
Fischen i. A.
2594
Würenlingen
Bülach
Neftenbach
Sulgen
Amriswil
Lindau
Scheidegg
Oberstaufen
Oberstdorf
Hinterhornbach
Rhein (Rhine)
Frauenfeld
Arbon
Bregenzer Wald
2777
Winterthur
Elgg
Aadorf
Münchwilen
Rorschach
Rheineck
Bregenz
Imst
Baden
Kloten
Effretikon
Wil
Bischofszell
Goldach
Lustenau
Lermoos
Wettingen
Regensdorf
Wetzikon
Sirnach
St. Gallen
Gossau
St. Margrethen
Dornbirn
Hohenems
Götzis
Oberstdorf
2594
Nassereith
Dietikon
Dübendorf
Turbenthal
Flawil
Teufen
Hohe Ifen 2232
Mittelberg
Hoher Freschen 2004
ZÜRICH
Uster
Pfäffikon
Degersheim
A.R. HERISAU
APPENZELL
Rankweil
Damüls
Schröcken
3645
Madelegabel
Haselgehr
Kilchberg
Küsnacht
Hinwil
Wald
Wattwil
I.R.
Oberriet
Feldkirch
Frastanz
Rote Wand 2704
2974
Thalwil
Horgen
Meilen
Stäfa
Rüti
Rapperswil
Ebnat Kappel
Nesslau
Grabs
Buchs
VORARLBERG
Nenzing
Bludenz
Langen
St. Anton am Arlberg
Parseier Sp.
Landeck
Wädenswil
Zürichsee
Lachen
Speer 1950
Unterwasser
Sevelen
Schaan
Vaduz
Dalaas
Albergpass 1793
Kuchen Sp. 3148
Ischgl
Vesul Sp.
St. Leonhard i. Pitztal
Horw
Sins
Cham
Baar
Zug
Einsiedeln
Nesslau
Säntis 2501
Churfirsten
Walenstadt
LIECHTENSTEIN
Schesaplana 2964
Montafon
2817
Schruns
3036
2853
3294
Martina
Nauders
3602
Hochdorf
Zugersee
Arth
Goldau
Glarus
Walensee
Mels
Sargans
Rätikon
Schiers
St. Antönien
Klosters
Silvretta Gruppe
3399
3312
Scuol/Schuls
Samnaun
Weisskogel 3735
Luzern
Schwyz
Mythen 1899
SCHWYZ
Brunnen
Muotathal
Schwanden
Weisstannen
Pizol 2844
Bad Ragaz
Landquart
Langwies
Unterengadin
Schleins
3085
3089
3533
Vierwaldstättersee
434
Stans
NIDWALDEN
Altdorf
Bürglen
GLARUS Alpen
Linthal
Elm
2794
3247
Flims
Tamins
Chur
Domat/Ems
Arosa
Sertig
3063
Ardez
Zernez
National-Park
Sesvenna 3205
S. Valentino n. M. (St. Valentin)
Málles Venosta (Mals)
Engelberg
2928
Erstfeld
Tödi 3620
Disentis
Ilanz
Chur walden
Lenzerheide
Wiesen
Filisur
Susch
3154
Spóndigna (Spondinig)
Sluderns (Schluderns)
Sulden
Titlis 3239
Oberalpstock 3328
Oberalppass 2044
Sedrun
Vorderrhein
Thusis
Tiefencastel
Albula
3418
3063
P. Kesch
Samedan
Livigno
Sta. Maria
Spóndiga
Silandro (Schlanders)
Láces (Latsch)
Adige
3602
Gadmen
Dammastock 3630
Hospental
P. Medel 3210
3149
Vals
Thalkirch 3000
Splügen
Hinterrhein
Savognin
3339
P. d'Err
3378
La Punt
St. Moritz
Pontresina
Zernez
Reschen
Göschenen
Grimselpass 2165
Furkapass 2431
Gletsch
2108
2199
Rheinwald Gorge
Rheinwaldhorn 3402
2065
Prosto del S. Bernardino (S. Bernardino)
Splügenpass 2133
3209
P. Platta 2245
Mulegns
Julierpass 2284
Silvaplana
3392
Maloja
Pso. del Stelvio 2757
Ortles 3899
3283
Münster
Bedretto
Realp S. Gottardo
Airolo
Adula-Gruppe
Olivone
3063
Campodolcino
Pzo. Stella 3163
3131
Malojapass 1815
Pso. del Bernina 2328
P. Bernina 4049
Bormio
3006
Ponte di Legno
Vermiglio
Blinnenhorn 3374
Basodino 3273
Fusio 3072
Campo Tencia 3025
Mesocco
Rossa
Chiavenna
Mera
Vicosoprano
Poschiavo
Grósio
Sóndalo
Mte. Adamello 3554
Ca. Presanella 3556
Pinzolo
Fóppiano 2732
Fóppiano
TICINO
Biasca
Pte. Disgrázia 3678
Chiesa
S. Martino
Navate
Tirano
Vezza d'Oglio
2237
2322
Maggia
Sonogno
Botto
Morbegno
Adda
Pzo. di Coca 3052
Capo di Ponte
Dimaro
Tione di Trento
Locarno
Muralto
Bellinzona
Arbedo
Giubiasco
Gravedona
Morbegno
Valtellina
Cédegolo
Pieve di Bono
Intragna
Ascona
Cadenazzo
Dongo
Cólico
Delébio
Gera Lola
Sóndrio
Schilpário
Breno
Pso. di Gino 2245
Lago di Como
Mte. Legnone 2609
Alpi
Dezzo
Borno
Bienno
Vermiglio
Ca. Presanella
Domodóssola
Premosello
Cánnero
Maccagno
Porlezza
Menággio
199
Belláno
Varenna
Orobie
Vestone
Lago di Garda
Masera
Mergózzo
Lago Maggiore 193
Luino
Lago di Lugano
Griante
Bellágio
Introbio
S. Martino de Calvi
Clusone
Gandino
Pisogne
Toce
Lugano
277
Grantola
Orévola
Ornavasso
Gravellona Toce
Pallanza
Intra
Ponte Tresa
Melide
Mte. Generoso 1701
Mte. S. Primo 1686
Mandello del Lário
Bérbeno
S. Giovanni Bianco
Clusone
Gazzaniga
Mte. Colombine 2215
Ómegna
Stresa
Laveno
Mendrisio
Balerna
Neso
Canzo
Cassazza
Lóvere
Marone
Condino
Storo
Riva del Garda
Lago d'Orta
Varese
Malnate
Chiasso
Como
Erba
Oggióno
Calolziocorte
Zogno
Albino
Darfa
Breno
Vobarno
Varese
Lago di Varese
Olgiate Com.
Lecco
Brianza
Séveso
LOMBARDIA
Válle Seriana
Gándino
Lago d'Iseo
Sárnico
Gardone
Val Trómpia
Sarezzo
Arona
Borgosésia
Serravalle
Borgomanero
Somma Lombardo
Gallarate
Cassano Magnano
Saronno
Meda
Seregno
Carate Brianza
Merate
Ponte S. Pietro
Seriate
BERGAMO
Stezzano
Casazza
Iseo

East from Greenwich

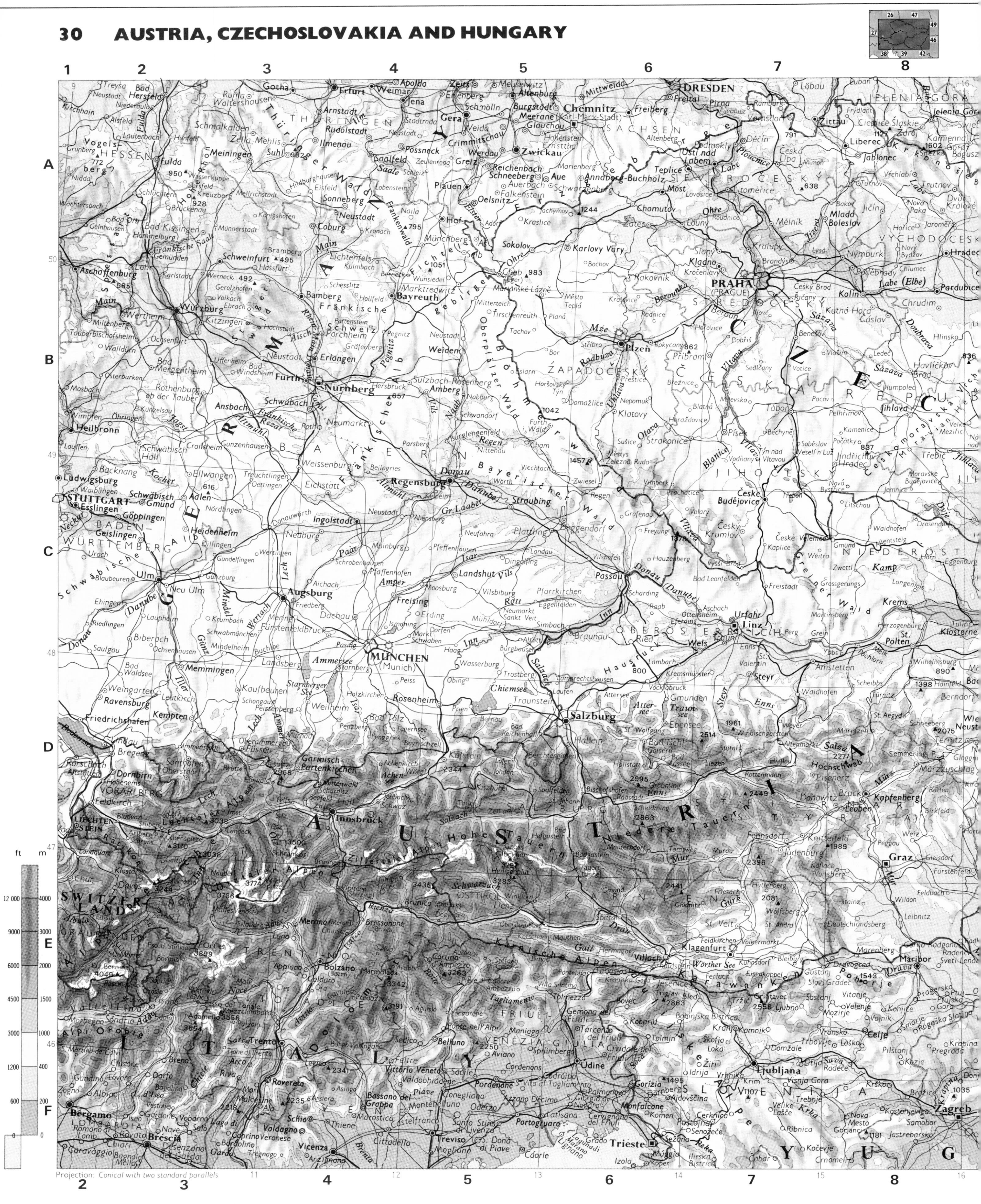

DRESDEN

PRAHA (PRAGUE)

 STUTTGART

MÜNCHEN (Munich)

Salzburg

Linz

Graz

Ljubljana

Zagreb

Trieste

AUSTRIA

SWITZERLAND

ITALY

BAYERN

HESSEN

THÜRINGEN

SACHSEN

BADEN-WÜRTTEMBERG

NIEDERÖSTERREICH

OBERÖSTERREICH

KÄRNTEN

SLOVENIA

ft m
12 000 4000
9000 3000
6000 2000
4500 1500
3000 1000
1200 400
600 200
0 0

Projection: Conical with two standard parallels

1 : 2 000 000

50 miles
80 km

East from Greenwich

COPYRIGHT. GEORGE PHILIP & SON. LTD

POLAND

CZECHOSLOVAKIA

HUNGARY

YUGOSLAVIA

ROMANIA

Wrocław (Breslau)

Częstochowa

Kraków

Katowice

Ostrava

Brno

Olomouc

WIEN (VIENNA)

Bratislava

BUDAPEST

Debrecen

Timişoara

Arad

Oradea

Miskolc

Košice

Uzhgorod

Szeged

Pécs

Subotica

Kikinda

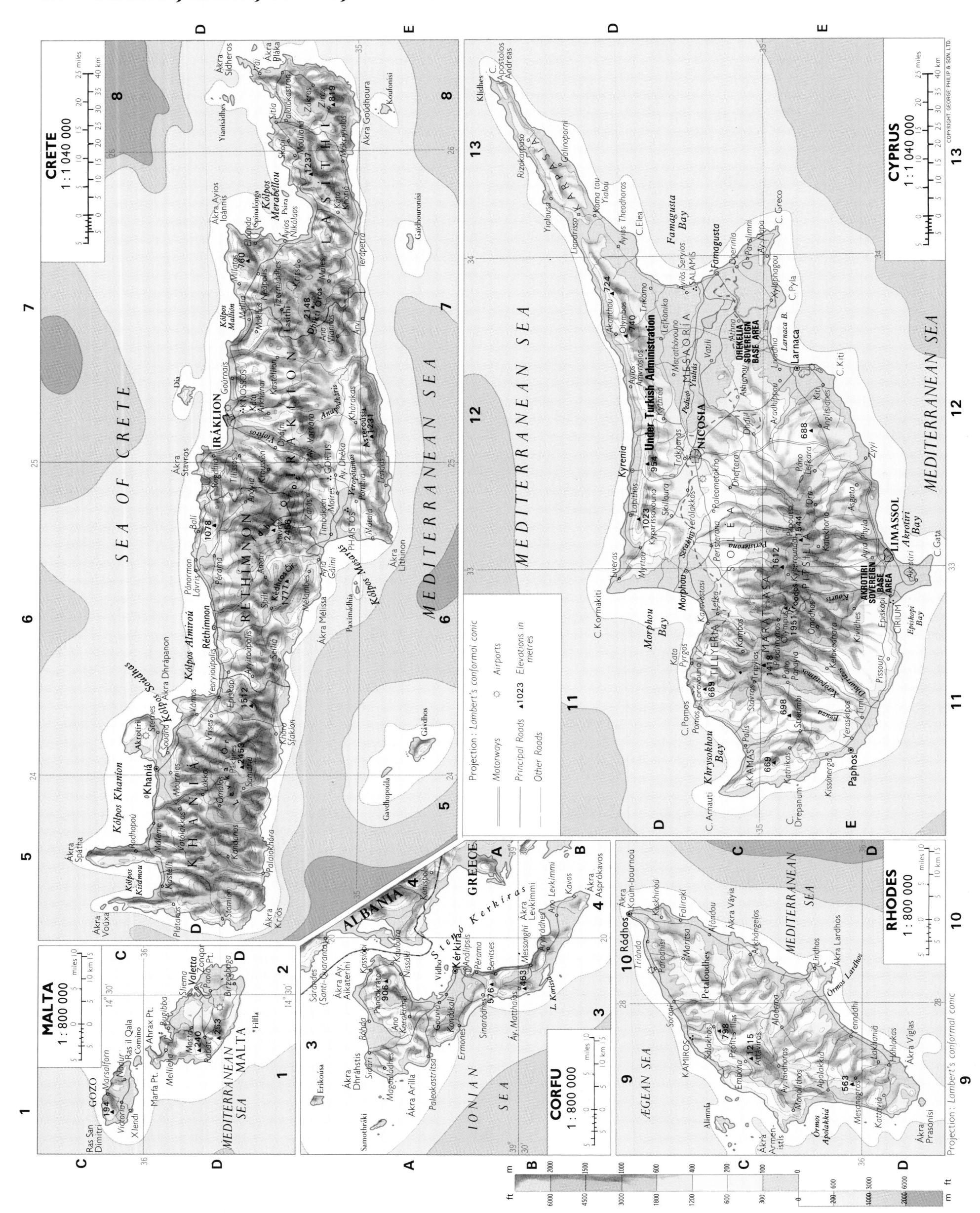

CRETE
1:1 040 000

MALTA
1:800 000

CORFU
1:800 000

RHODES
1:800 000

CYPRUS
1:1 040 000

Projection: Lambert's conformal conic

Motorways
Principal Roads
Other Roads
Airports
▲1023 Elevations in metres

SEA OF CRETE

MEDITERRANEAN SEA

MEDITERRANEAN SEA

IONIAN SEA

AEGEAN SEA

GREECE

ALBANIA

COPYRIGHT GEORGE PHILIP & SON LTD.

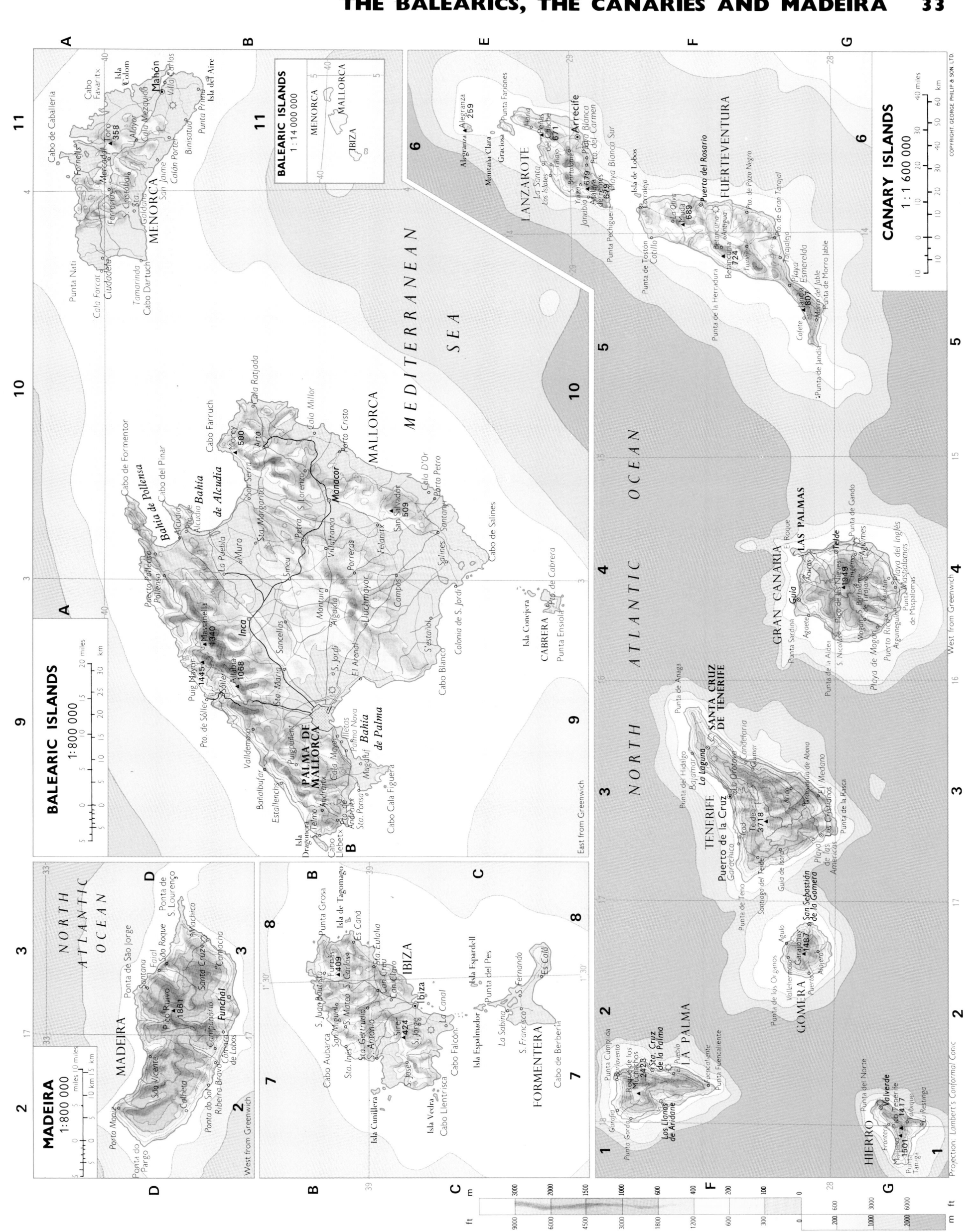

BALEARIC ISLANDS
1:14 000 000

MENORCA

MALLORCA

IBIZA

MEDITERRANEAN SEA

MENORCA

Cabo de Caballeria
Punta Nati
Cala Forcat
Ciudadela
Cabo Dartuch
Punta Prima
Cabo Favaritx
Isla Colom
Villa Carlos
Isla del Aire
Mahón
Mercadal
Toro 358

MALLORCA

Cabo de Formentor
Puerto Pollensa
Pollensa
Bahía de Pollensa
Cabo del Pinar
Bahía de Alcudia
Cabo Farruch
Morey 500
Artá
Cala Ratjada
Alcudia
Puig Mayor 1445
Massanella 1340
Alfabia 1068
Inca
La Puebla
Muro
Sta. Margarita
Petra
Sineu
Manacor
Porto Cristo
Cala Millor
S. Lorenzo
S. Salvador 509
Felanitx
Villafranca
Porreras
Porto Petro
Cabo Salines
PALMA DE MALLORCA
Bahía de Palma

MADEIRA
1:800 000

NORTH ATLANTIC OCEAN

MADEIRA

Ponta de Sao Jorge
Faial
Sao Roque
Camacha
Santana
Santa Cruz
Funchal
Pico Ruivo 1861
Campanario
Camara de Lobos
Calheta
Porto Moniz
Sao Vicente
Ponta do Sol
Ribeira Brava
Ponta de Pargo

IBIZA

Punta Grosa
Isla de Tagomago
Es Caná
Sta. Eulalia
S. Juan Bautista
Fornas 409
San Carlos
San Mateo
IBIZA
S. Antonio
Sirer 424
S. Jorge

FORMENTERA

La Sabina
S. Francisco
Es Caló
Cabo de Berberia

CANARY ISLANDS
1:1 600 000

COPYRIGHT GEORGE PHILIP & SON, LTD.

LANZAROTE

Alegranza 259
Montaña Clara
Graciosa
Punta Farrones
Arrecife
Pto. del Carmen
Playa Blanca

FUERTEVENTURA

La Oliva
Acud 689
Betancuria 724
Puerto del Rosario
Corralejo
Morro del Jable

GRAN CANARIA

LAS PALMAS
Teide 1949
Gáldar
Telde
Agaete
Playa del Inglés
Maspalomas

TENERIFE

SANTA CRUZ DE TENERIFE
La Laguna
Puerto de la Cruz
Teide 3718
Icod

LA PALMA

Sta. Cruz de la Palma
Los Llanos de Aridane 2423

GOMERA

San Sebastián de la Gomera 1487

HIERRO

Valverde 1501

NORTH ATLANTIC OCEAN

ft
9000
6000
4500
3000
1800
1200
600
300
0

m
3000
2000
1500
1000
600
400
200
100
0

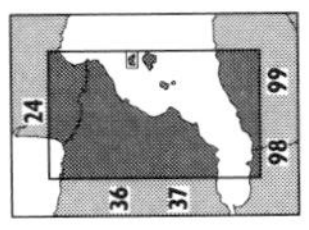

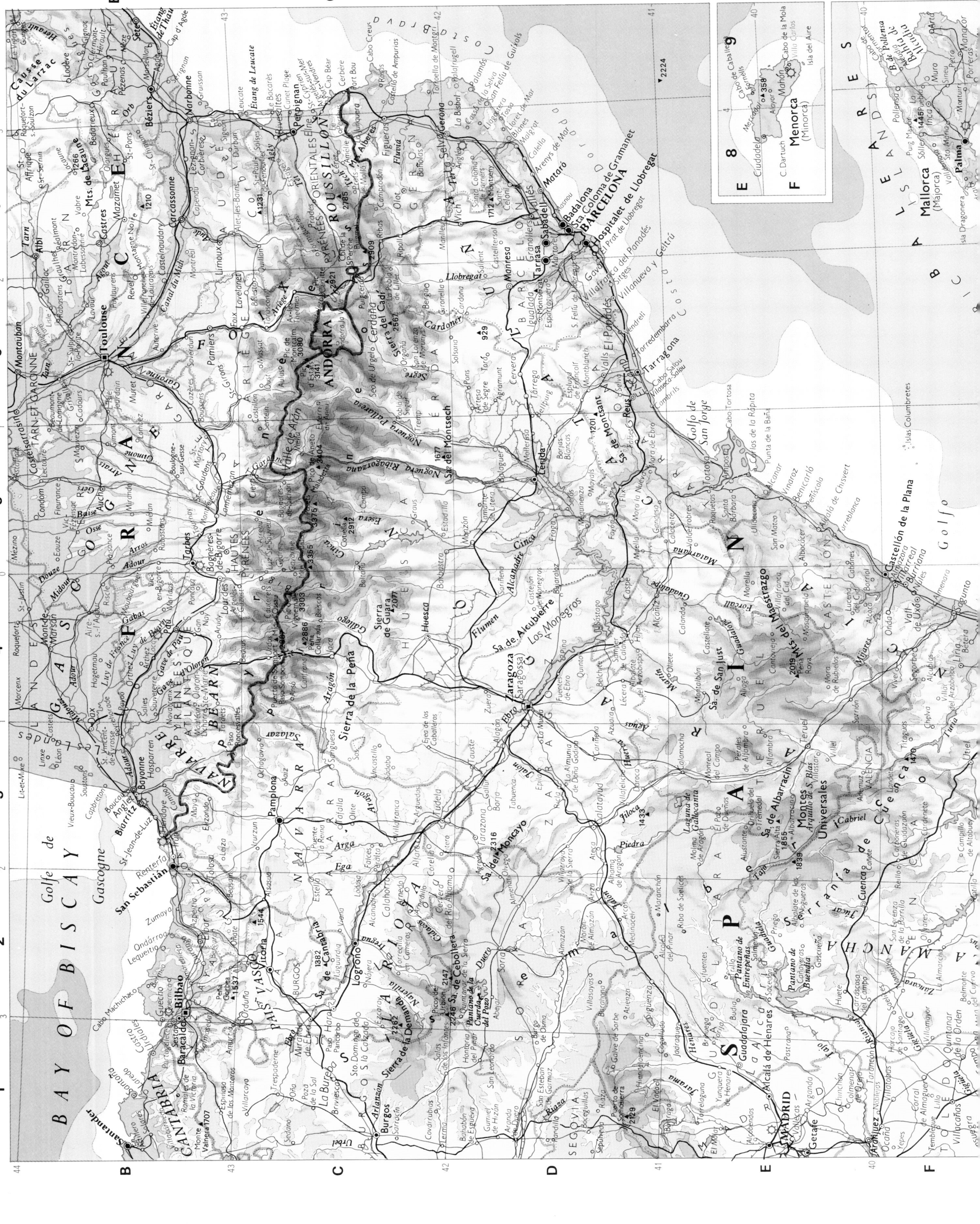

BAY OF BISCAY

Golfe de Gascogne

FRANCE

PYRÉNÉES

ANDORRA

ROUSSILLON

NAVARRA

ARAGÓN

CATALUÑA

BARCELONA

Zaragoza (Saragossa)

Pamplona

San Sebastián

Bilbao

Santander

Toulouse

Narbonne

Perpignan

Gerona

Tarragona

Lérida

Huesca

Teruel

VALENCIA

Castellón de la Plana

MADRID

Mallorca (Majorca)

Palma

Menorca (Minorca)

ISLANDS

BALEARES

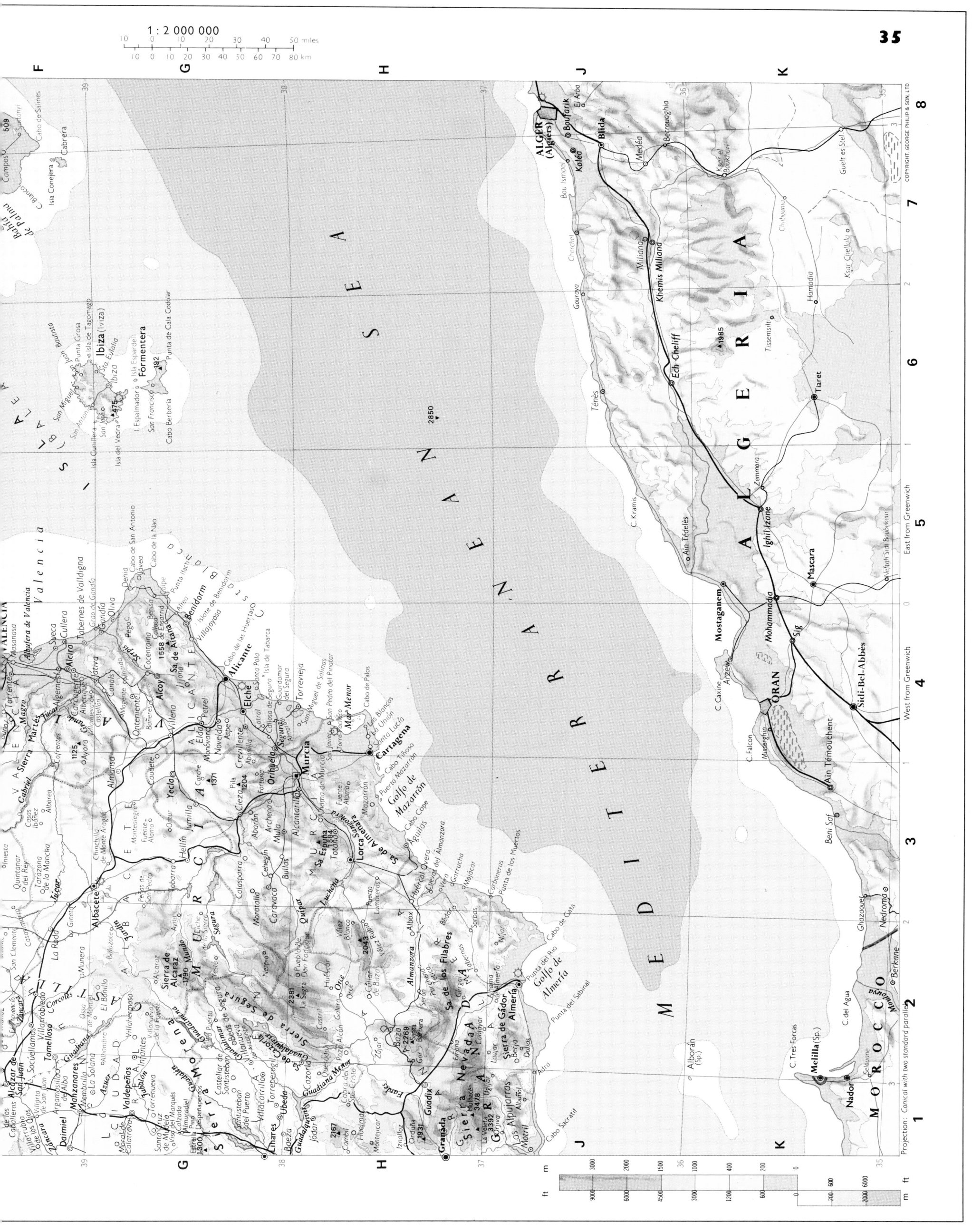

1 : 2 000 000

Projection: Conical with two standard parallels

East from Greenwich

West from Greenwich

COPYRIGHT GEORGE PHILIP & SON, LTD

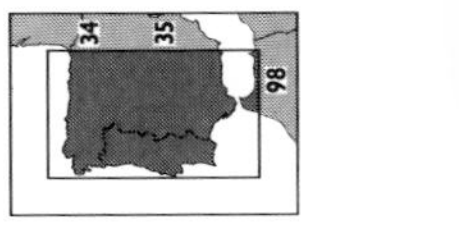

BAY OF BISCAY

ATLANTIC OCEAN

San Sebastián
Bilbao
Baracaldo
Santander
Gijón
Oviedo
Mieres
Sama de Langreo
PAÍS VASCO
Vitoria
Logroño
LA RIOJA
BURGOS
Burgos
CANTABRIA
Picos de Europa
ASTURIAS
León
Palencia
PALENCIA
Valladolid
VALLADOLID
Duero
MADRID
Segovia
Sierra de Guadarrama
Ávila
Salamanca
SALAMANCA
Zamora
ZAMORA
Sierra de la Culebra
LEÓN
Carrión
Astorga
Sa. de Gata
Sierra de Gredos
ORENSE
Orense
GALICIA
LUGO
Lugo
Santiago de Compostela
La Coruña
El Ferrol
Vigo
Pontevedra
Cabo Finisterre
Cabo Ortegal
Cabo de Peñas
PORTUGAL
Porto (Oporto)
Vila Nova de Gaia
Póvoa de Varzim
Matosinhos
Aveiro
Coimbra
Braga
Lamego
VILA REAL
Bragança
BRAGANÇA
GUARDA
Viseu
VISEU
Douro
Tajo
Ega
Ebro
Pisuerga
Esla
Tera
Tormes
Águeda
Duero

Ría de Santa Marta

1 : 2 000 000

10   0   10   20   30   40   50 miles
10   0   10   20   30   40   50   60   70   80 km

MEDITERRANEAN

SEA

MOROCCO

LISBOA

Badajoz

Sevilla

Córdoba

Jaén

Granada

Sierra Nevada

Málaga

Cádiz

Huelva

Gibraltar (Br.)

Ceuta (Sp.)

Tánger (Tangier)

Tétouan

Larache

Melilla (Sp.)

Golfo de Cádiz

Golfo de Almería

Strait of Gibraltar

Costa del Sol

Marbella

Algeciras

Almería

Ciudad Real

Mérida

Cáceres

Évora

Faro

A L G A R V E

PORTALEGRE

SETÚBAL

Montes de Toledo

Alborán (Sp.)

West from Greenwich

Projection: Conical with two standard parallels

ft   m
9000 3000
6000 2000
4500 1500
3000 1000
1200   400
600   200
0   0

Projection: Conical with two standard parallels

East from Greenwich

LIGURIAN SEA

Golfo di Génova

CORSE (CORSICA)

HAUTE CORSE

SWITZERLAND

1 : 2 000 000

HUNGARY

Graz

YUGOSLAVIA

Ljubljana

Zagreb

Klagenfurt

Villach

Maribor

BOSNA

HERCEGOVINA

DINARA PLANINA

Banja Luka

Trieste

Udine

Golfo di Venézia

Venézia (Venice)

Laguna Veneta

Chióggia

Pádova

Vicenza

Bologna

Ferrara

Ravenna

Forlì

Cesena

Rímini

SAN MARINO

Pesaro

Fano

Firenze (Florence)

Ancona

Senigállia

Iesi

Macerata

Arezzo

Perugia

UMBRIA

MARCHE

Terni

ABRUZZI

Pescara

Chieti

Ortona

Vasto

Térmoli

ROMA

LAZIO

Viterbo

MOLISE

Split

Brac

Vis

Korčula

Lastovo

Mljet

A D R I A T I C   S E A

ADRIATIC

Monte Sant'Ángelo

Gargano

COPYRIGHT GEORGE PHILIP & SON LTD

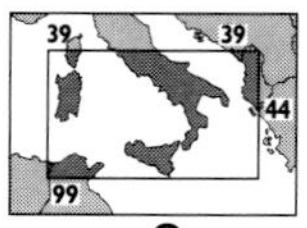

Grid columns
1 2 3 4 5 6

CORSE / CORSICA

Iles Sanguinaires
G. d'Ajaccio
Tavaro
C. di Muro
Petreto
2136 Zonza
Propriano
Levie
Favone
Solenzara
CORSE
CORSICA
G. de Valinco
Sartène
Porto-Vecchio
CORSE-DU-SUD
Iles Cerbicales
Bonifacio
I. de Cavallo
Bouches de Bonifacio
Maddalena
Santa Teresa Gallura
La Maddalena
Caprera
Punta dello Scorno
Costa Smeralda
Asinara
Golfo dell' Asinara
Pto. Cervo
Arzachena
Lischia
Golfo Aranci
Coghinas
Ággius
Calangiánus
G. di Ólbia
Porto Tórres
Témpio Pausania
1362
Ólbia
Tavolara
C. dell'Argentiera
Sorso
M. Limbara
Sássari
Sennori
Oschiri
Osilo
L. di Coghinas
Tanaunella
Ittiri
Ozieri
Posada
Féttilia
Pattada
Alghero
Villanova
Bonorva
1259
Bitti
Monteleone
Tirso
Orune
C. Comino
Bosa
Núoro
Temo
Oliena
Dorgali
Macomer
Golfo di Orosei
SARDEGNA
Ghilarza
L. del Tirso
Fonni
Monti del Gennargentu
1834
Cábras
Oristano
Sorgono
Baunei
C. di Monte Santu
Golfo di Oristano
M. Arci
812
SARDEGNA
Arbatax
Arborea
Terralba
Láconi
Lanusei
S. Gavino
Nurri
Tierzu
Monreale
Mándas
SARDINIA
Gúspini
Sanluri
Senorbi
Arbus
1236
Gonnosfanádiga
Villacidro
Serramanna
C. Pécora
M. Linas
Dolianova
Fluminimaggiore
Assémini
Sestu
Iglesias
Gonnesa
Sínnai
1069
Siliqua
Selárgius
Quartu Sant'Elena
Portoscuso
Carloforte
Carbonia
1116
Cágliari
San Pietro
Santadi
Golfo di Cágliari
Sant'Antioco
Porto Botte
Serpentara
Sant' Antíoco
Pula
C. Carbonara
Teulada
G. di Palmas
C. Spartivento

TYRRHENIAN SEA

3719

3589

Ustica

ROMA / Rome area
Iles Sanguinaires
Vatican City
ROMA (Rome)
Tivoli
Subiaco
Conca del Lúcino
Fregene
Palestrina
Fiascone
2283
Lido di Óstia (Lido di Roma)
Tevere (Tiber)
Velletri
Alatri
Véroli
Sora
Prática di Mare
Lazio
Frascati
Monte S. Giovanni
Ferentino
Ísola del Liri
Ánzio
Cisterna di Latina
Ceccano
Arpino
Nettuno
Aprilia
Priverno
Cassino
Latina
Sonnino
Fondi
Frosinone
Pontinia
1533
Monte Circeo
541
Terracina
Sessa
Sabáudio
Fórmia
Aurunca
Gaeta
Mintúrno
Garigliano
Zannone
Golfo di Gaeta
Palmarola
Mondragone
Casal di
Ísole Ponziane
Ponza
283
Volturno
Giugliano
Ventotene
Pozz
Procida
788
Íschia (Naples)

SICILY area
Castellammare del Golfo
G. di Castellammare
Favorotta
C. San Vito
Terrasini
C. Gallo
PALERMO
1110
Monreale
Bagheria
Levanzo
Trápani
Érice
Partinico
Misilmeri
Termini Imerese
Ísole Égadi
Alcamo
S. Giuseppe
Campa
Maréttimo
Paceco
Jato
Favignana
Stagnone
Calatafimi
Marineo
Camporeale
Salemi
1613
SICI
Carleone
Lercara
Mado
Marsala
Gibellina
Bisacquino
Prizzi
Alia
Castelvetrano
Partanna
Sambuca di Sicilia
Búrgio
Mazzara del Vallo
Menfi
Mussomeli
Caterin
Campobello di Mazara
Belice
Sciacca
Platani
San Cataldo
Ribera
Racalmuto
Caltaniss
Sicilian Channel
Cattólica Eraclea
Canicatti
Siculiana
Agrigento
Naro
Porto Empédocle
Favara
Licata
Palma di Montechiaro
Campobello di Lucano
Royanusa

TUNISIA area
Iles de la Galite
C. Blanc
Cani
Bizerte (Binzert)
Plane
C. Serrat
Menzel-Bourguiba
Zembra
El Kala
Mateur
Golfe de Tunis
C. Bon
ALGERIA
Tabarka
Tébourba
Kelibia
Medjerda
TUNIS
Halq el Oued
Menzel-Temime
Bou Salem
Béja
Soliman
Nabeul
TUNISIA
Téboursouk
Zaghouan
Hammamet

Sicilian Channel

Pantelleria
836 (It.)
Pantelleria

MEDITE (MEDITERRANEAN)
1319
Malta

East from Greenwich

Projection: Conical with two standard parallels

Elevation scale
ft	m
9000	3000
6000	2000
4500	1500
3000	1000
1200	400
600	200
0	0
200	600
2000	6000
4000	12.000

m   ft

1 : 2 000 000

10 0 10 20 30 40 50 miles
10 0 10 20 30 40 50 60 70 80 km

ADRIATIC SEA

IONIAN SEA

MEDITERRANEAN SEA

ALBANIA

TIRANA

Durrësi (Durazzo)

Vlorë (Valona)

Berati

Kérkira (Corfu)

Strait of Otranto

ABRUZZI
MOLISE
Campobasso
Isernia
Benevento
Avellino
NAPOLI
Salerno
G. di Salerno
Capri
Sorrento

Fóggia
Lucera
G. di Manfredónia
Manfredónia
Monte Sant'Ángelo
Testa del Gargano
Vieste
Barletta
Trani
Bisceglie
Molfetta
Bari
Cerignola
Canosa
Andria
Corato
Bitonto
Mola di Bari
Monopoli
Altamura
Gravina
Gióia del Colle
Fasano
Ostuni
Bríndisi
Francavilla Fontana
Mesagne
Lecce
Nardò
Galatina
Máglie
Otranto
Gallipoli
Ugento
Tricase
C. Santa Maria di Leuca

BASILICATA
Potenza
Matera
Táranto
Golfo di Táranto
Mandúria

POTENZA
Lagonegro
G. di Policastro
C. Palinuro

CALABRIA
Cosenza
Catanzaro
Golfo di Sant'Eufémia
Golfo di Squillace
Crotone
Rossano
Corigliano
Acri
Nicastro
Vibo Valéntia
Gióia Táuro
Palmi
Reggio di Calábria
Messina
Str. di Messina

Isole Eólie o Lípari (Aeolian Is.)
Strómboli
Salina
Lípari
Vulcano
Alicudi
Filicudi
Panarea

Milazzo
Barcellona
Patti
Monti Nébrodi
Taormina
Etna 3340
Acireale
Catánia
Golfo di Catánia
Paternò
Enna
Lentini
Augusta
Siracusa
Cómiso
Ragusa
Módica
Noto
G. di Noto
Pachino
C. Passero

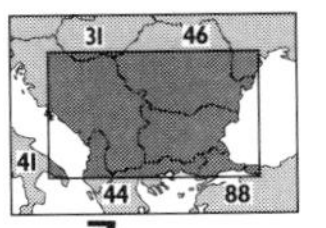

HUNGARY

YUGOSLAVIA

ROMANIA

BOSNA

HERCEGOVINA

CRNA GORA

MONTENEGRO

SRBIJA

ALBANIJA

MAKEDONIJA

ADRIATIC SEA

Beograd (Belgrade)

Sarajevo

Timişoara

Arad

Novi Sad

Skopje

Tirana (Tiranë)

Shkodra (Shkodër)

Durrës (Durazzo)

Dubrovnik

Autonomna Pokrajina Kosovo

Autonomna Pokrajina Vojvodina

Socijalistička

Danube

Danube (Dunav)

Drina

Sava

Morava

Vardar

ft   m
9000 3000
6000 2000
4500 1500
3000 1000
1200 400
600   200
0
200   600
2000 6000
m   ft

Projection: Conical with two standard parallels

East from Greenwich

1 : 2 000 000

10   0   10   20   30   40   50 miles
10   0   10 20 30 40 50 60 70 80 km

8   9   10   11   12   13   14

TRANSILVANIA

Turda · Cîmpia Turzii · Band · Sovata
Tele Mare · Iara · Ludus · Tîrgu Mures
1827 · Aries
Mures · Mures Mică
1438 · Mtii Trascău · Aiud · Tîrnava Mare · Tîrnăveni · Sighisoara
ALBA · Teius · Blaj · Dumbrăveni · 806 · Homorod · Baraolt
Alba-Iulia · Mediaş · Agnita
Orăştie · Cugir · Sebes · Seica Mare · Soars · Făgăras · Feldioara
Vintu de Jos · Daia-Sibiu · Nocrich · Avrig · Pasu de Jos
SIBIU · Sibiu · Olt
Grădistea de Munte · Tălmaciu · Cisnădie · Victoria · Muntii Făgăras
untii Sebesului · 2245 · 2543 · Negoiu · Moldoveanu · 2535
ceg · Petrila · Meridionali · 2507 · Omul · 2956
Petroşani · 2518 · Cîmpulung
Vulcan · Novaci · Horezu · Rîmnicu Vîlcea

R O M A N I A

P O R T ... C O R I

O L T · V A L A H I A · W A L A C H I A
Strehaia · Filiaşi · Craiova · Slatina · Piteşti
D O L J · Segarcea · Leu · Osica de Sus
Galicea Mare · Bîrca · Roşiori-de-Vede · T E L E O R M A N
Bechet · Corabia · Turnu Măgurele · Alexandria · Giurgiu

BACĂU · Moineşti · Crasna
Comăneşti · Dărmăneşti · Răcăciuni
Gheorghe · Gheorghiu-Dej
Adjud · Tecuci · Bîrlad
VRANCEA · Focşani · Galati
Rîmnicu Sărat · Brăila · Măcin · Tulcea
BRĂILA · Traian
Buzău · Ploieşti · BUCUREŞTI · Bucharest
I A L O M I T A · C Ă L Ă R A Ş I · Cernavodă · Medgidia · Constanţa
Giurgiu · Ruse · Ruschuk · Silistra · Dunărea (Dánube)

U.S.S.R.

UKRAINIAN S.S.R.
Komrat · Chadyr-Lunga · Kagul
Ozero Yalpukh · Ozero Kitai · Ozero Sasyk
Reni · Ismail · Kiliya · Vilkovo
Galati · Dunay (Danube) · Bratul Chilia
Ostrov Letea · Bratul Sulina
Tulcea · Sulina · Vîlcu Gheorghe
Babadag · Ostrov Dranov
Lacul Razelm · Gura Portiţei
Lacul Sinoe · Siutghiol · Constanţa
D O B R O G E A · Mangalia
Dobrich Bazargic · Shabla (Şabla)
Kavarna (Cavarna) · Nos Kaliakra

B U L G A R I A

Vidin · Lom · Kozloduy · Oryakhovo · Pleven
Mikhaylovgrad · Vratsa · Berkovitsa · Mezdra
Sofiya (Sofia) · Botevgrad · Etropole
S r e d n a   G o r a
Plovdiv (Philippopolis) · Pazardzhik · Stara Zagora
K H A S K O V O · Khaskovo · Kŭrdzhali
Iztochni Rodopi · Sredni Rodopi
Razlog · Bansko

V A R N A · Varna
R A Z G R A D · Razgrad · Tŭrgovishte
Shumen (Kolarovgrad) · Novi Pazar
Preslavska Planina · Provadiya
B U R G A S · Burgas · Burgaski Zaliv
Sliven · Yambol · Nova Zagora
Aytos · Nesebŭr · Pomorie (Ankhialo)
Sozopol · Michurin (Tsarevo)
Malko Tŭrnovo · Rezovo

B L A C K   S E A

T U R K E Y

K I R K L A R E L I · Edirne (Adrianople)
Istranca Dağları · 1018
Lüleburgaz · Babaeski · Kırklareli
Çorlu · Tekirdağ · Çatalca
İSTANBUL · Üsküdar · Beykoz
Karadeniz Boğazı (Bosporus)

G R E E C E

Drama · Xanthi · Komotini
Nestos · Serrai · Sidhirokastron

COPYRIGHT GEORGE PHILIP & SON LTD

8   9   10   11   12   13

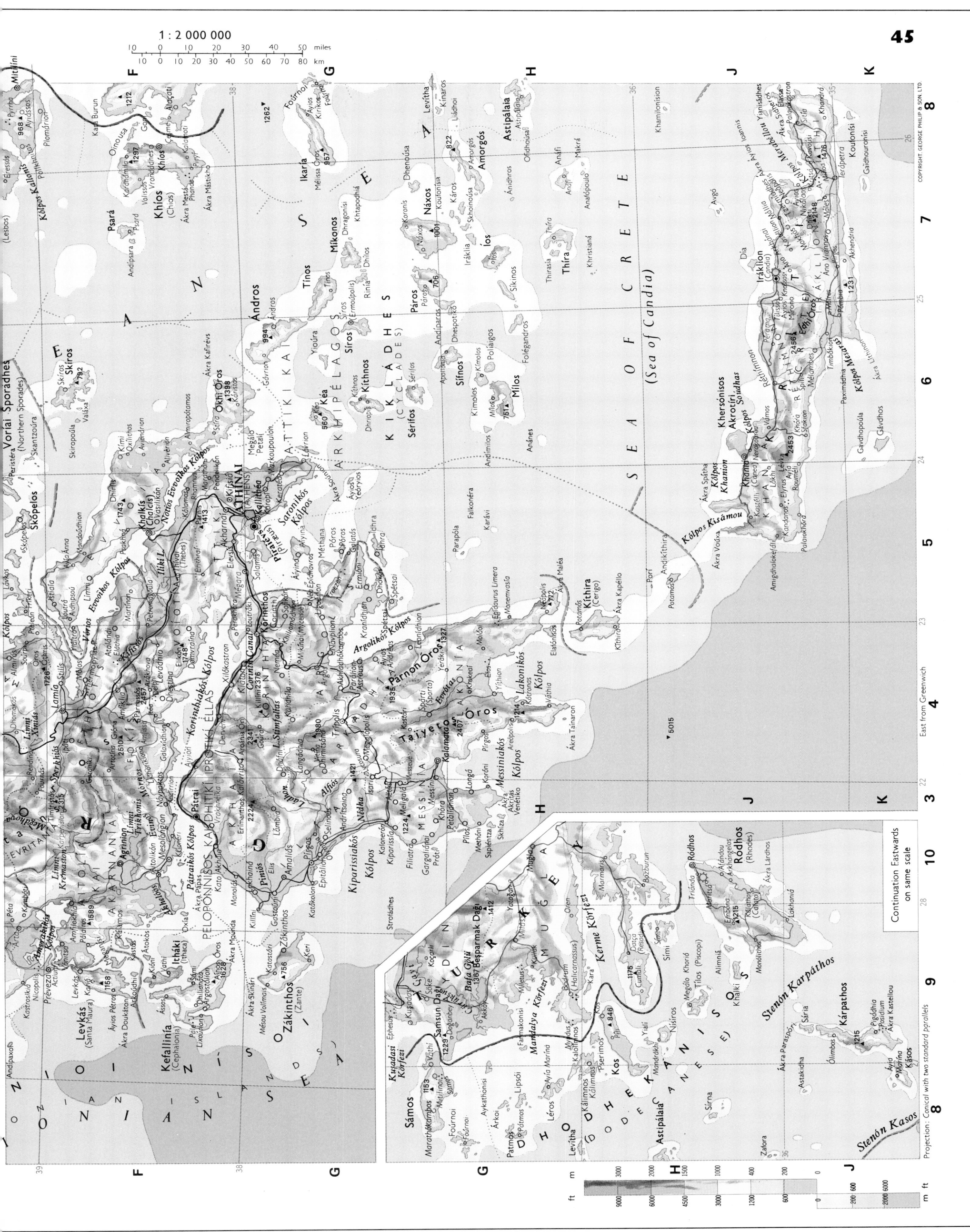

1 : 2 000 000

10   0   10   20   30   40   50 miles
10 0 10 20 30 40 50 60 70 80 km

F   G   H   J   K

8
7
6
5
4
3

East from Greenwich

Continuation Eastwards
on same scale

10
9
8

Projection: Conical with two standard parallels

Sea and island labels

(Lesbos)
Mittlíni
Eresós
Ayiássos
Plomárion
968 ▲
Kólpos Kallonís
Kará Burun
Oinoússa
1212 ▲
1297 ▲
Khíos (Chios)
Volissós
Kardhámila
Vrondádos
Khíos
Ákra Mésta
Ákra Mastikhó
Pirgí
Psará
Antípsara
1262 ▼
Foúrnoi
Áyios Kírikos
Ikaría
1041 ▲
957 ▲
Mélissa
822 ▲
Dhenoúsa
Khinaros
Lévirtha
Liádhoi
Astipálaia
Khamilonísion
Ofidhoúsa
Makrá
Anáfi
Amorgós
Amorgós
Koufonísi
Kéros
Khtapodhiá
Skhinoúsa
Iráklia
Dhonoússa
Koronís
Náxos
1001 ▲
Náxos
Ándhros
Avgó
Analípsou

Voríai Sporádhes (Northern Sporades)
Peristéra
Skántzoura
Skópelos
Skiropoúla
Skíros
Skíros
792 ▲
Ákra Kafiréus
Óthri Óros
1398 ▲
Mikonos
Dhragonísi
Dhílos
Rínia
Síros (Ermoúpolis)
Yioúra
Tínos
Tínos
560 ▲
Kéa
994 ▲
Ándros
Andros
Megálo Petáli
Markópoulon
Ándros

ARKHIPÉLAGOS
KIKLÁDHES
(CYCLADES)

Sérifos
Sérifos
Sífnos
Kímolos
Mílos
751 ▲
Mílos
Andímilos
Ananés
Políaigos
Sikínos
Íos
Íos
706 ▲
Páros
Páros
Antíparos
Dhespotikó
Dhrionísi
Apolloniá
Kíthnos
Kýthnos
Kíthnos

Thirasía
Thíra
Khristianá
Thíra

SEA OF CRETE
(Sea of Candia)

Falkonéra
Karáví
Parapóla
Falkonéra

Dia
Iráklion (Candia)
Knossós
Pezá
2148 ▲
KRÍTI (CRETE)
Timbákion
Kólpos Mesará
Paximádha

Ákra Líthinon
Gávdhos
Gavdhopoúla

Akhendriá

Ierápetra
Koutsounári
Gaidhouronísi

Áyios Nikólaos
Sitía
Ákra Sídheros
Palaiókastron
Knandí
1476 ▲
Khandrás
DHÍKTI
2148 ▲

Ákra Spátha
Kólpos Khaníon
Khaniá (Canea)
Soúdhas
Kólpos Soúdhas
Rodhopós
Khersónisos Akrotiri
Réthimnon
2456 ▲
ÍDHI ÓROS
2453 ▲
RÉTHIMNON
Vámos
Amaríou
Melámbes

Kólpos Kisámou
Andikíthira
Ákra Voúxa
Kándanos
Palaiokhóra
Ákra Krios
Elýros
Ayía Rouméli
LÉVKA
Loútro
Ayía Roúmeli
Timbákion

Southern region
Kíthira (Cerigo)
Ákra Kapéllo
Pótamos
Kíthira
Elafónisos
Néapolis
712 ▲
Monemvasía
Ákra Maléa
Pórt
Parnon Óros 1937 ▲
Léonidhion
Kranídhion
Ídhra
Spétsai
Spétsai
Ermióni
Galatás
Póros
Méthana
Aíyina
Aíyina
Salamís
Piraiévs (Piraeus)
ATHÍNAI (ATHENS)
Kifisiá
Kallithéa
Eleusís
Mégara
Saronikós Kólpos
Ákra Soúnion
Lávrion
Markópoulon
Kiáton

5015 ▼

ÁTTIKI (ATTICA)
Pendéli
Parnís 1413 ▲
Khalkís (Chalcis)
Óros
Dhrósia
Vasilikón
1743 ▲
Váthia
Néa Ártaki
Kími
Aliverion
Amárinthos
Ákra Kafiréus
Kárystos
Dhírfis
Amfíkleia

EVVOIA (EUBOEA)
Nótios Evvoïkós Kólpos
Khálkis
Kímí
Kárystos

Istiaía
Óreoi
Limni
Loutrá Aidhipsoú

Stilís
Lamía
1726 ▲
Néon Monastírion
Domokós

FTHIÓTIS
Stereá Ellás
2315 ▲
Karpenísion
Ayrínion
AITOLÍA KAÍ AKARNANÍA
ÁKARNANÍA
Mesolóngion
Astakós
Vónitsa
Amfilokhía
Árta
Amvrakikós Kólpos

VOIOTÍA (BOEOTIA)
Livádhia
Orkhomenós
Thívai (Thebes)
Erithraí
Elikón Óros 1748 ▲
Dhístomon
Leivadhiá

Peloponnese
Patrai
Aíyion
Kalávrita
2341 ▲
2357 ▲
Kiáton
Kiáto
KÓRINTHÍA
Kórinthos (Corinth)
Corinth Canal
Megára
Loutráki

ILÍA
Pírgos
Olympia
Krestena
Amaliás
Gastoúni
Pineiós
Vartholomió
Killíni
Ándravida
Lekhainá
Manolás

AKHAÍA
AKHAÍA
ARKADHÍA
Tripolis
L. Stimfalías
Levídhi
Vitína
Dhimitsána
Megalópolis
Ládhon
2224 ▲

PELOPÓNNISOS KAÍ DHITIKÍ IPÍROTIKÍ ELLÁS

Kiparissía
Kiparissiakós Kólpos
Filiatrá
Gargalíani
Khóra
Pílos (Navarino)
Methóni
Sapiéntza
Skhíza
Ákra Akrítas
Petalídhi
Koróni
Messíni
Kalamata
Taíyetos Óros 2407 ▲
MESSÍNIA
Meligalá
MessinIakós Kólpos
Longá
Pírgos
Khóra
Koróni
Lakonikós Kólpos
Ákra Tainaron
Areópolis
Yíthion
Skála
Spárti (Sparta)
LAKONÍA
Évrotas
Kastóri
1421 ▲
Molάoi

Argolikós Kólpos
Ástros
ARGOLÍS
Náfplion
Árgos
Návplion
Mikínai
Tolón

Ionian Islands
IÓNIOI NÍSOI
Levkás (Santa Maura)
Levkás
Kalamos
Meganísi
Árkoudi
Ákra Dhoukáton
Ithaki (Ithaca)
1158 ▲
Sámi
Fiskárdhon
Kefallinía (Cephalonia)
Argostólion
1628 ▲
Páli
Likoúrion
Lixoúrion
Póros
Zákinthos (Zante)
Zákinthos
756 ▲
Mésou Volímais
Ákra Skinári
Katástári
Strofádhes
Proti
IÓNIAN SEA
IONIAN SEA

Dodecanese inset
YDIN
BÜYÜK MÉNDERES
Aydın
Söke
Kuşadası
Kuşadası Körfezi
Ephesos
Vízhi
1229 ▲
Sámos
Sámos
Marathókambos
Mitilíni
1153 ▲
Fournoi
Foúrnoi

AKRA
Samsun Dağı
1237 ▲
Miletus
Söke
Didim
Akköy
Milas
Mylasa (Halicarnassus)
Bodrum (Halicarnassus)
Mandalya Körfezi
Güllük
Güllük
Farmakonísi
Léros
Lipsói
Aykathónisi
Arkoi
Pátmos
Léros
Kálimnos
Psérimos
1367 ▲
Beşparmak Dağı
1142 ▲
Babadağ
Yataǧan
Marmaris
Muǧla
MUǦLA
Kerme Körfezi
Datça (Reşadiye)
Knidos
Símí
Kara
Bozburun
Sími
Kástellórizon
Çine

DHODHEKÁNISOS (DODECANESE)
Kos
Kos (Cos)
Astipálaia
846 ▲
Yialí
Nísiros
1215 ▲
Kálimnos
Astakídha
Tílos (Piscopi)
Khálki
Mandráki
Megálo Khorió
Ólimbos
Ródhos (Rhodes)
Ródhos
Triánda
Ákra Láardhos
Ákra Prasonísi
Líndhos
Emboná
1215 ▲
Kattaviá
Khalkí

Kárpathos
Kárpathos
Ólimbos
Pigádhia
Ákra Kastéllou
Saría
Stenón Karpáthos
Ayía Marína
Kásos
Stenón Kásos

Depth/height legend

m   ft
    9000
3000
    6000
2000
    4500
1500
    3000
1000
    1200
400
    600
200
    0
0
200
600
    2000
6000
m   ft

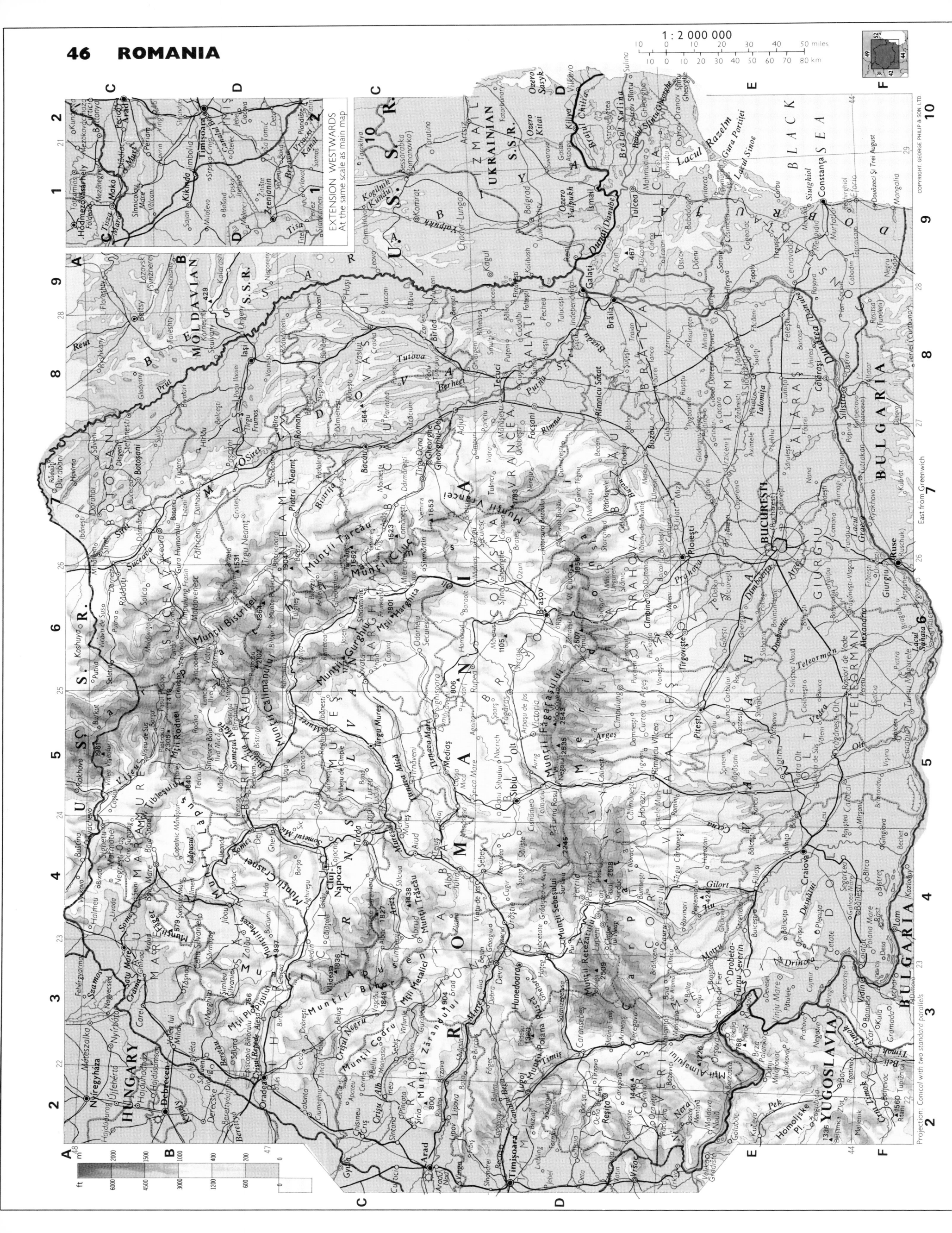

1 : 2 000 000

EXTENSION WESTWARDS
At the same scale as main map

BLACK SEA

MOLDAVIAN S.S.R.

U K R A I N I A N   S.S.R.

U . S . S . R .

U . S . S . R .

HUNGARY

YUGOSLAVIA

BULGARIA

BUCUREŞTI
(Bucharest)

T R A N S Y L V A N I A

C A R P A Ţ I I

M O L D O V A

Projection: Conical with two standard parallels

East from Greenwich

COPYRIGHT GEORGE PHILIP & SON LTD

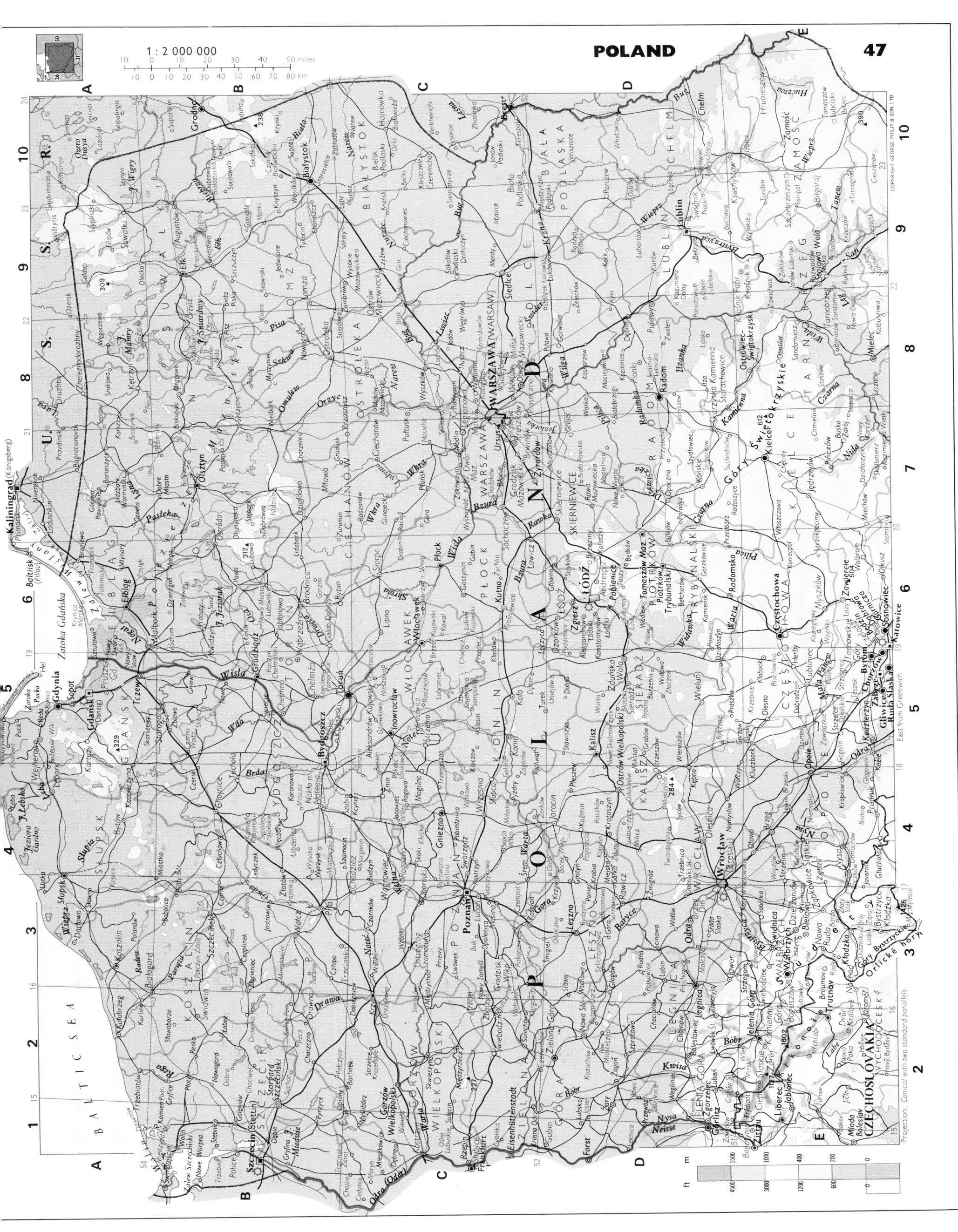

1 : 2 000 000

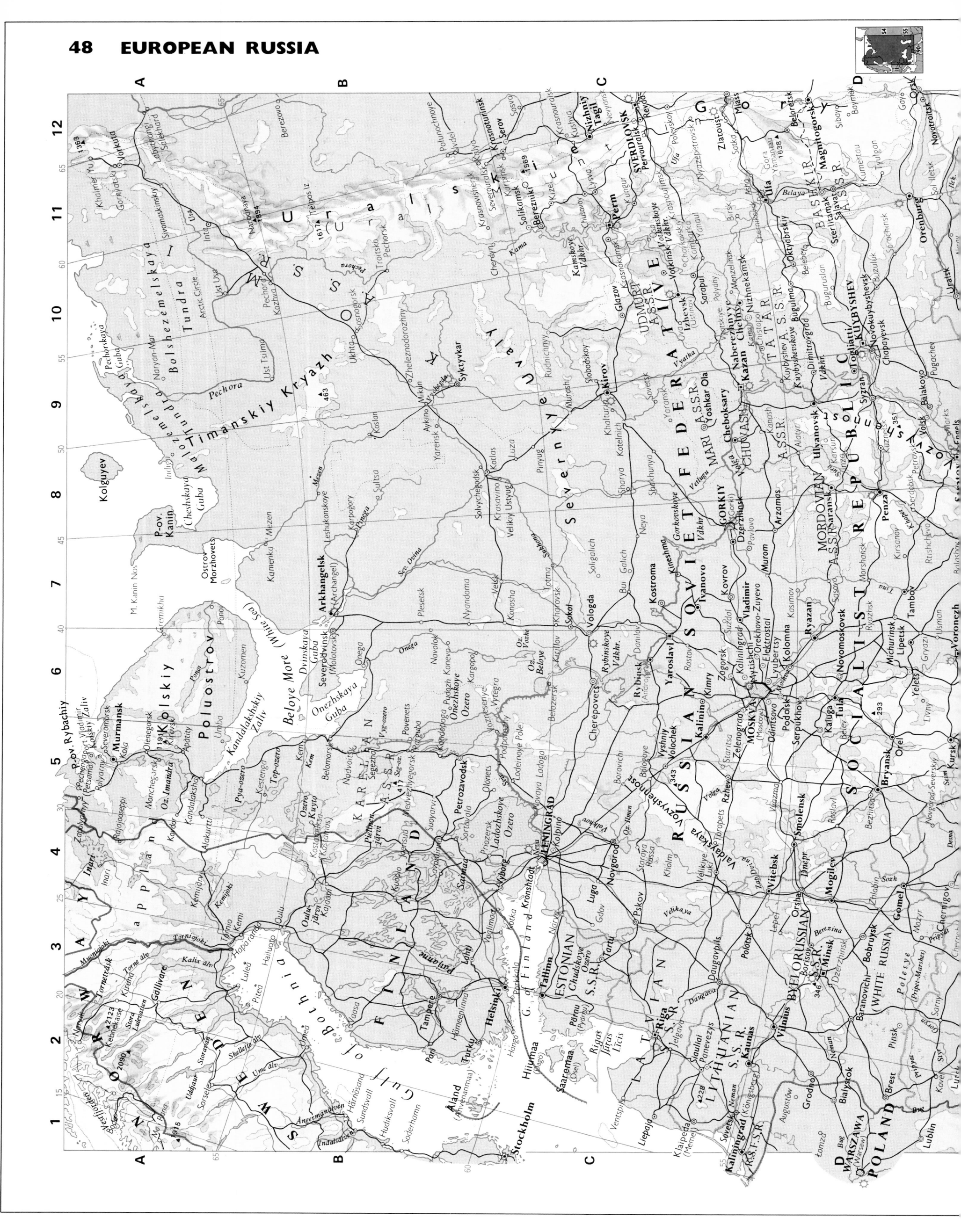

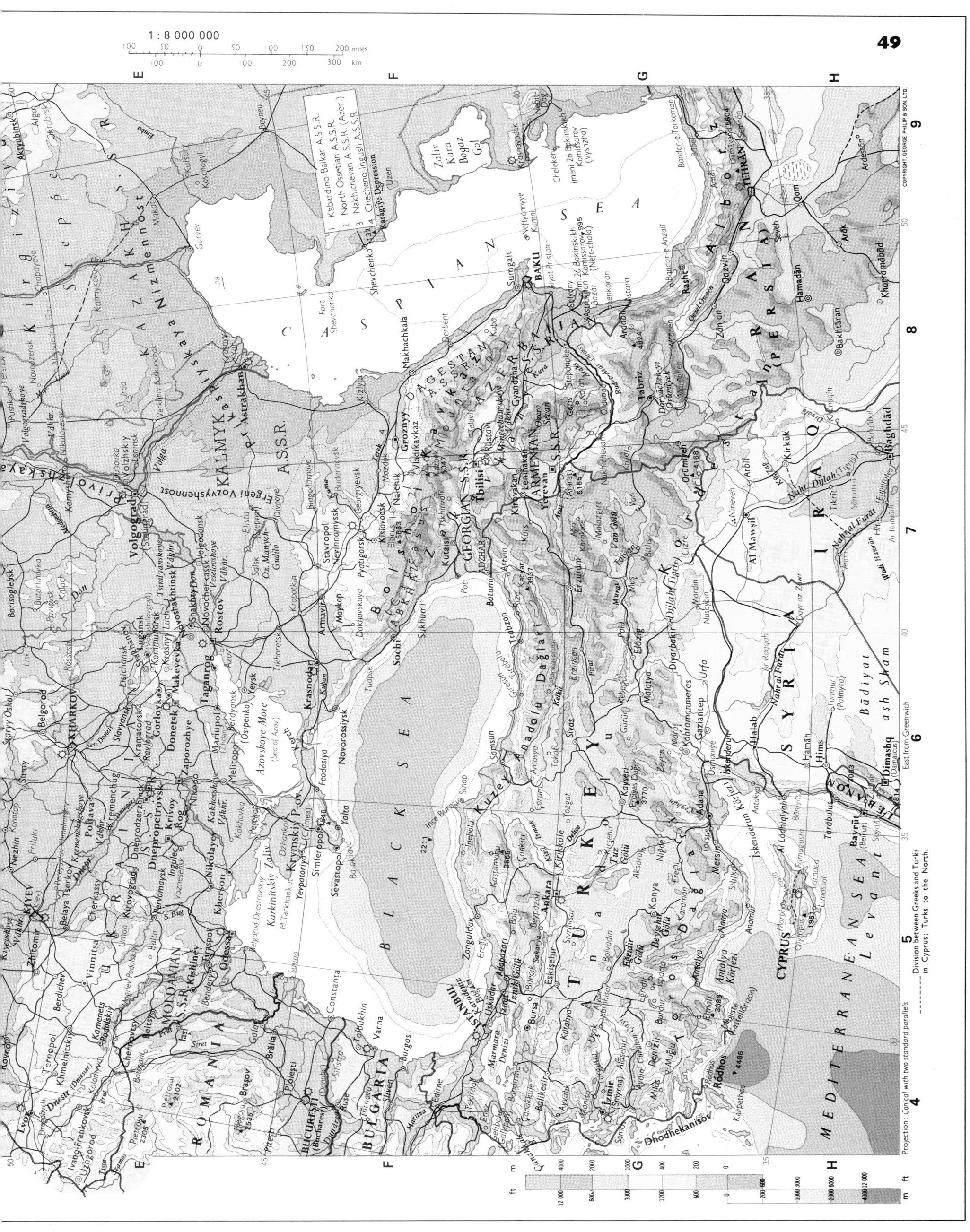

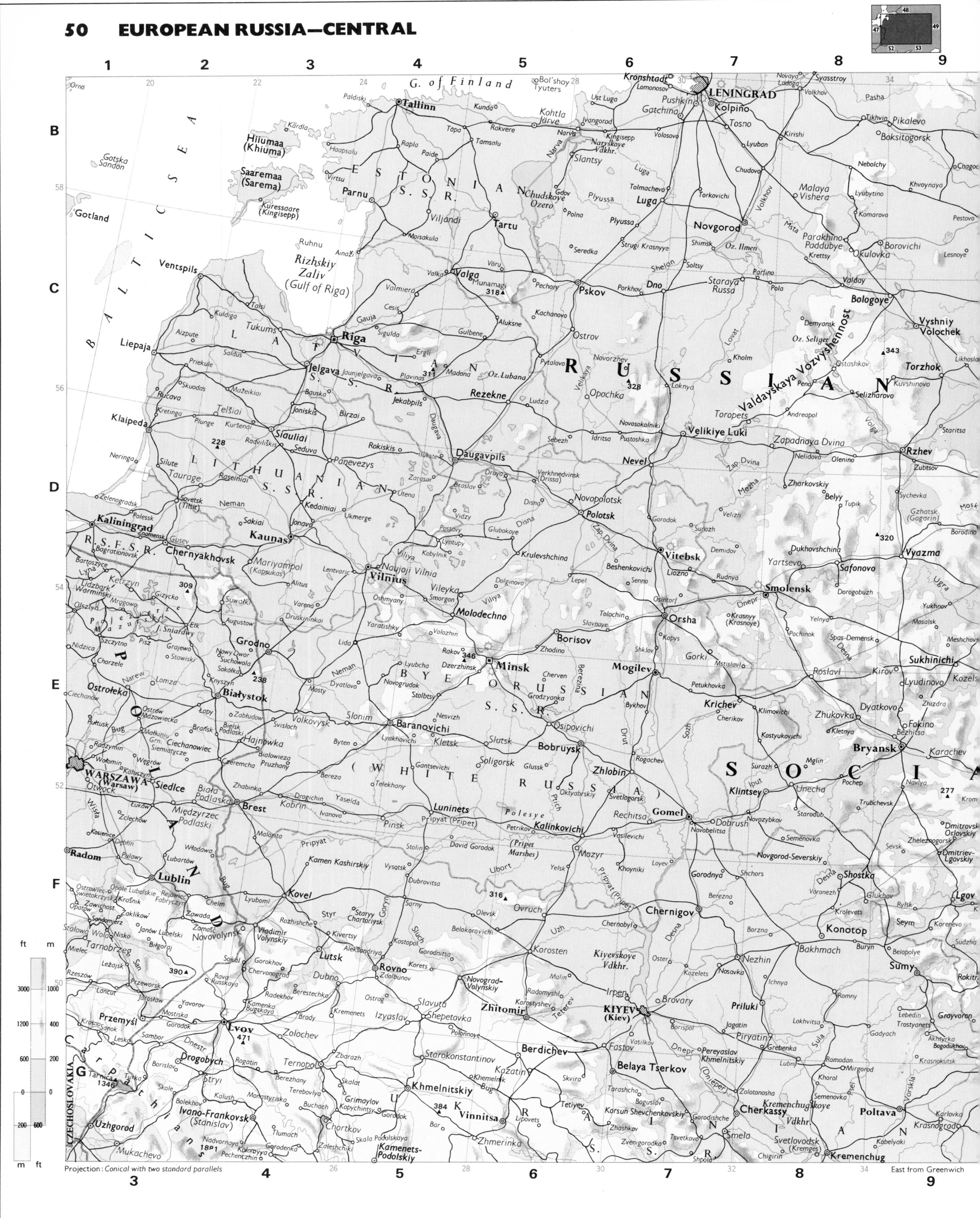

1 : 4 000 000

50   0   50   100 miles
50   0   50   100   150 km

S O V I E T   F E D E R A T I V E

S O C I A L I S T   R E P U B L I C

UDMURT A.S.S.R.

MARI A.S.S.R.

CHUVASH A.S.S.R.

TATAR A.S.S.R.

MORDOVIAN A.S.S.R.

KAZAKH S.S.R.

Cherepovets · Vologda · Sokol · Rybinsk (Andropov) · Yaroslavl · Kostroma · Ivanovo · Shuya · Kovrov · Vladimir · Dzerzhinsk · GORKIY · Cheboksary · Zelenodolsk · Kazan · Nizhnekamsk · Chistopol

Kalinin · Kalyazin · Dubna · Klin · Zelenograd · Mytishchi · Balashikha · MOSKVA (Moscow) · Lyubertsy · Podolsk · Serpukhov · Kaluga · Tula · Novomoskovsk · Orel · Yelets · Lipetsk · Voronezh · Belgorod · Kharkov · Kupyansk

Ryazan · Kolomna · Michurinsk · Tambov · Borisoglebsk · Balashov · Saratov · Engels

Arzamas · Saransk · Ruzayevka · Penza · Kuznetsk · Syzran · Ulyanovsk · Dimitrovgrad · Togliatti · KUYBYSHEV · Novokuybyshevsk · Chapayevsk

Kirov · Novovyatsk · Kotelnich · Glazov · Omutninsk

Volsk · Balakovo · Pugachev · Kamyshin · Volzhskiy · Volgograd (Stalingrad)

Kotlas areas: Totma · Nikolsk · Sharya · Murashi

COPYRIGHT. GEORGE PHILIP & SON. LTD.

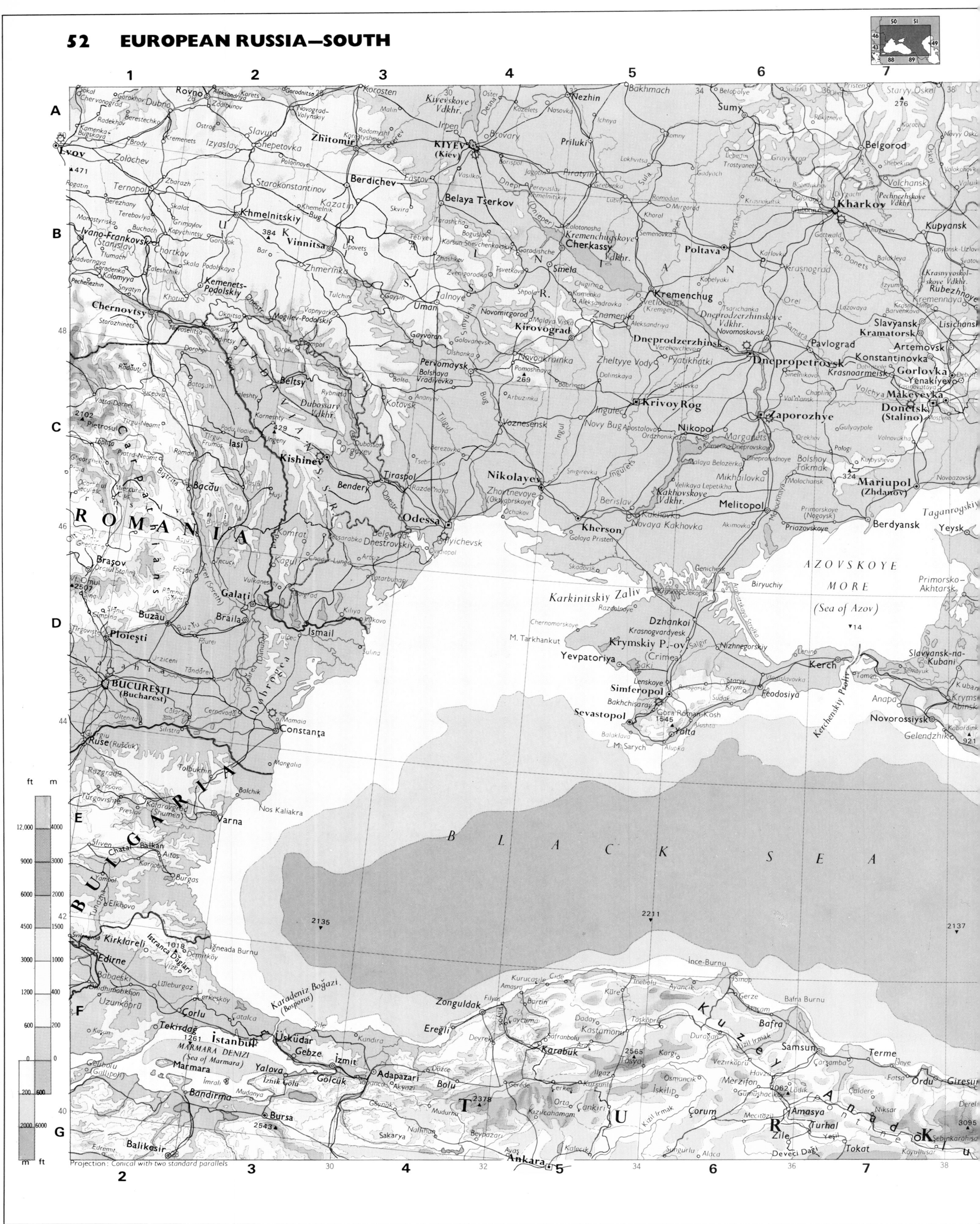

Projection : Conical with two standard parallels

1 : 4 000 000

50   0   50   100 miles

50   0   50   100   150 km

8   9   10   11   12   13   14   15

East from Greenwich   40

COPYRIGHT GEORGE PHILIP & SON LTD.

1 : 4 000 000

50   0   50   100 miles

50   0   50   150 km

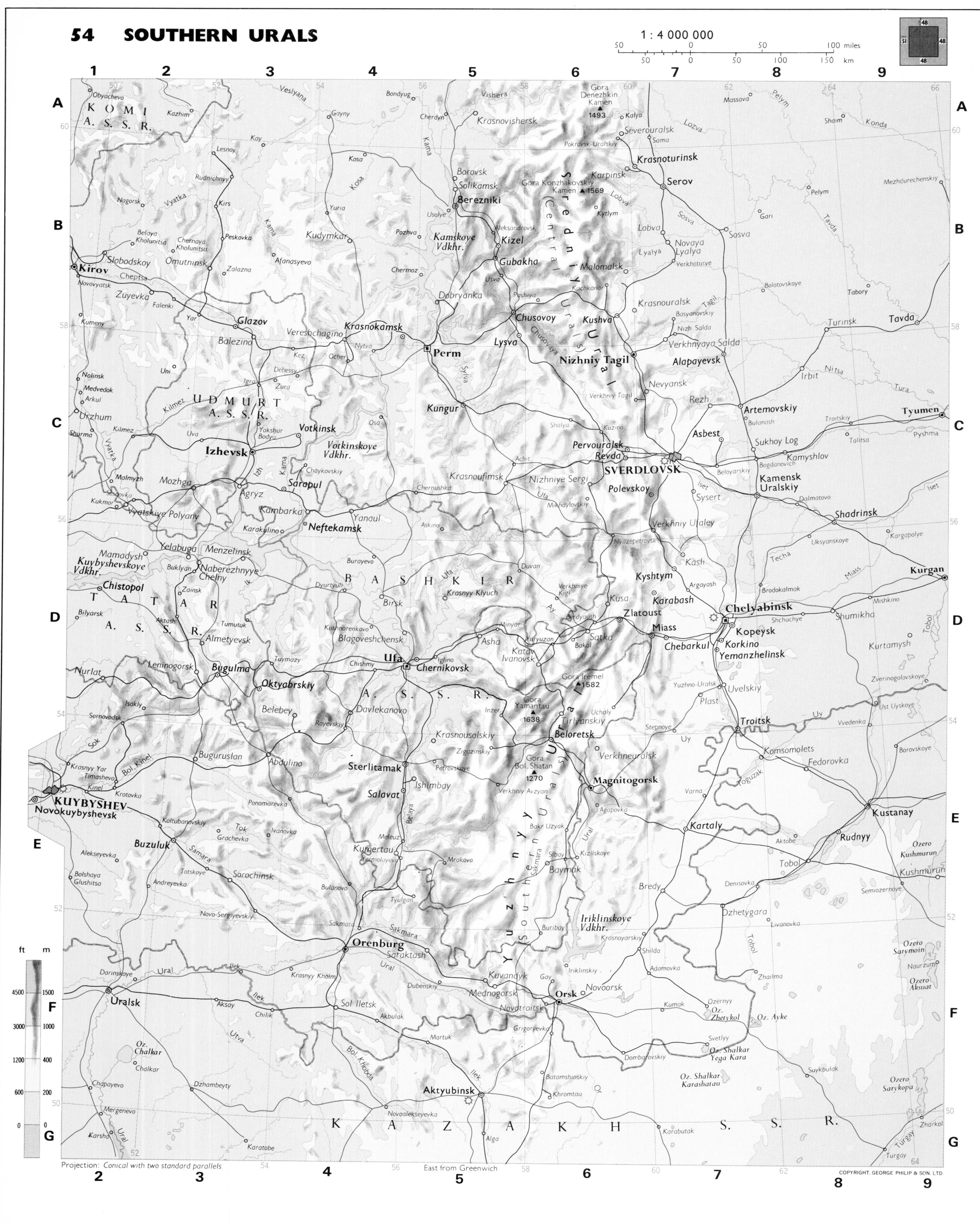

A
KOMI A.S.S.R.
Obyachevo   Kazhim   Gayny   Bondyug   Vishera   Gora Denezhkin Kamen ▲1493   Massava   Pelym   Shaim   Konda

Nogorsk   Vyatka   Kosa   Cherdyn   Krasnovishersk   Kalya   Lozva   Mezhdurechenskiy
Kirs   Kosa   Kama   Borovsk   Pokrovsk-Uralskiy   Severouralsk   Sama

B
Beloya Kholunitsa   Chernaya Kholunitsa   Peskovka   Kudymkar   Solikamsk   Gora Konzhakovskiy Kamen ▲1569   Karpinsk   Krasnoturinsk   Gari
Kirov   Slobodskoy   Omutninsk   Zalazna   Afanasyevo   Kamskoye Vdkhr.   Berezniki   Kizel   Kytlym   Lobva   Serov   Novaya Lyalya   Sosva   Botlovskoye   Tabory
Novovyatsk   Cheptsa   Kama   Usolye   Aleksandrovsk   Malomalsk   Lyalya   Verkhoturye   Turinsk   Tavda
Zuyevka   Zalazna   Pozhva   Gubakha   Kachkanar   Krasnouralsk   Tagil   Basyanovskiy

C
Kumeny   Glazov   Vereshchagino   Dobryanka   Pyshma   Chusovoy   Kushva   Nizh. Salda   Turinsk
Nolinsk   Balezino   Krasnokamsk   Nytva   Perm   Lysva   Nizhniy Tagil   Verkhnyaya Salda   Tavda
Medvedok   Uni   Kez   Ocher   Syva   Nevyansk   Irbit   Nitsa
Arkul   Igra   Zura   Debessy   Kungur   Verkhniy Tagil   Rezh   Artemovskiy   Tyumen
Urzhum   UDMURT A.S.S.R.   Osa   Shalya   Kuzino   Pervouralsk   Asbest   Troitskiy   Pyshma
Kilmez   Yakshur Bodya   Chaykovskiy   Krasnoufimsk   Nizhniye Sergi   Revda   Bulanash   Sukhoy Log   Talitsa
Izhevsk   Votkinsk   Votkinskoye Vdkhr.   Achit   SVERDLOVSK   Beloyarskiy   Kamensk Uralskiy   Kamyshlov   Pyshma
Malmyzh   Mozhga   Sarapul   Chernushka   Uta   Mikhaylovskiy   Polevskoy   Iset   Bogdanovich   Dalmatovo   Shadrinsk

D
Kukmor   Agryz   Kambarka   Yanaul   Askino   Duvan   Verkhniy Ufaley   Techa   Uksyanskoye   Kargapolye
Vyatskiye Polyany   Karakulino   Neftekamsk   Nyazepetrovsk   Kashi   Miass   Kurgan
Mamadysh   Menzelinsk   Burayevo   Uta   Verkhniye Kigi   Kyshtym   Argayash   Brodokalmak
Kuybyshevskoye Vdkhr.   Buklyan   Naberezhnyye Chelny   Dyurtyuli   Krasnyy Klyuch   Kusa   Kusa   Karabash   Chelyabinsk   Mishkino
Chistopol   Zainsk   Birsk   Kushnarenkovo   Asha   Minyar   Zlatoust   Miass   Kopeysk   Shumikha
Bilyarsk   Aktash   Tumutuk   Blagoveshchensk   Katav Ivanovsk   Satka   Bakal   Chebarkul   Korkino   Kurtamysh
TATAR A.S.S.R.   Almetyevsk   BASHKIR   Yuryuzan   Gora Iremel ▲1582   Yemanzhelinsk   Zverinogolovskoye
Nurlat   Leninogorsk   Bugulma   Tuymazy   Chishmy   Iglino   Ufa   Gora Yamantau 1638   Yuzhno-Uralsk   Uvelskiy   Ust Uyskoye
Sernovodsk   Isakly   Oktyabrskiy   Chernikovsk   Inzer   Uchaly   Plast   Troitsk   Vvedenka
Belebey   A. S. S. R.   Tirlyanskiy   Stepnoye   Uy
Krasnyy Yar   Davlekanovo   Krasnousolskiy   Beloretsk   Verkhneuralsk   Komsomolets   Borovskoye

E
Timashevo   Buguruslan   Abdulino   Rayevskiy   Zigazinskiy   Gora Bol. Shatan ▲1270   Magnitogorsk   Varna   Fedorovka
Krotovka   Sterlitamak   Petrovskoye   Verkhniy Avzyan   Agapovka   Kartaly   Kustanay
KUYBYSHEV   Kinel   Ponomarevka   Ishimbay   Bakr Uzyak   Rudnyy
Novokuybyshevsk   Koltubanovskiy   Tok   Ivanovka   Salavat   Sibay   Baymak   Aktobe   Ozero Kushmurun
Buzuluk   Alekseyevka   Grachevka   Kumertau   Yarmolovka   Mrakovo   Kiziliskoye   Tobol   Kushmurun
Bolshaya Glushitsa   Samara   Totskoye   Andreyevka   Bulanovo   Tyulgan   Buribay   Iriklinskoye Vdkhr.   Bredy   Denisovka   Semiozernaye

F
Sol   Novo-Sergiyevskiy   Sakmara   Sakmara   Orenburg   Saraktash   Krasnoyarskiy   Shilda   Dzhetygara   Livanovka   Ozero Sarymoin
Darinskoye   Ural   Ilek   Ural   Kuvandyk   Gay   Iriklinskiy   Adamovka   Zhaima   Naurzum   Ozero Aksuat
Uralsk   Aksay   Ilek   Krasnyy Kholm   Dubenskiy   Mednogorsk   Novoorsk   Kumak   Oz. Zhetykol   Oz. Ayke
Chilik   Sol Iletsk   Akbulak   Orsk   Novotroitsk   Svetlyy   Oz. Shalkar Yega Kara   Ozero Sarykopa
Chapayevo   Utva   Martuk   Bol. Khoba   Grigoryevka   Dombarovskiy   Oz. Shalkar Karashatau   Suykbulak

G
Mergenevo   Oz. Chalkar   Dzhambeyty   Ilek   Aktyubinsk   Batamshinskiy   Khromtau   Turgay
Karsha   Ural   Chalkar   Novoalekseyevka   KAZAKH S. S. R.   Karabutak   Zhaīkol
Karatobe   Alga   Turgay

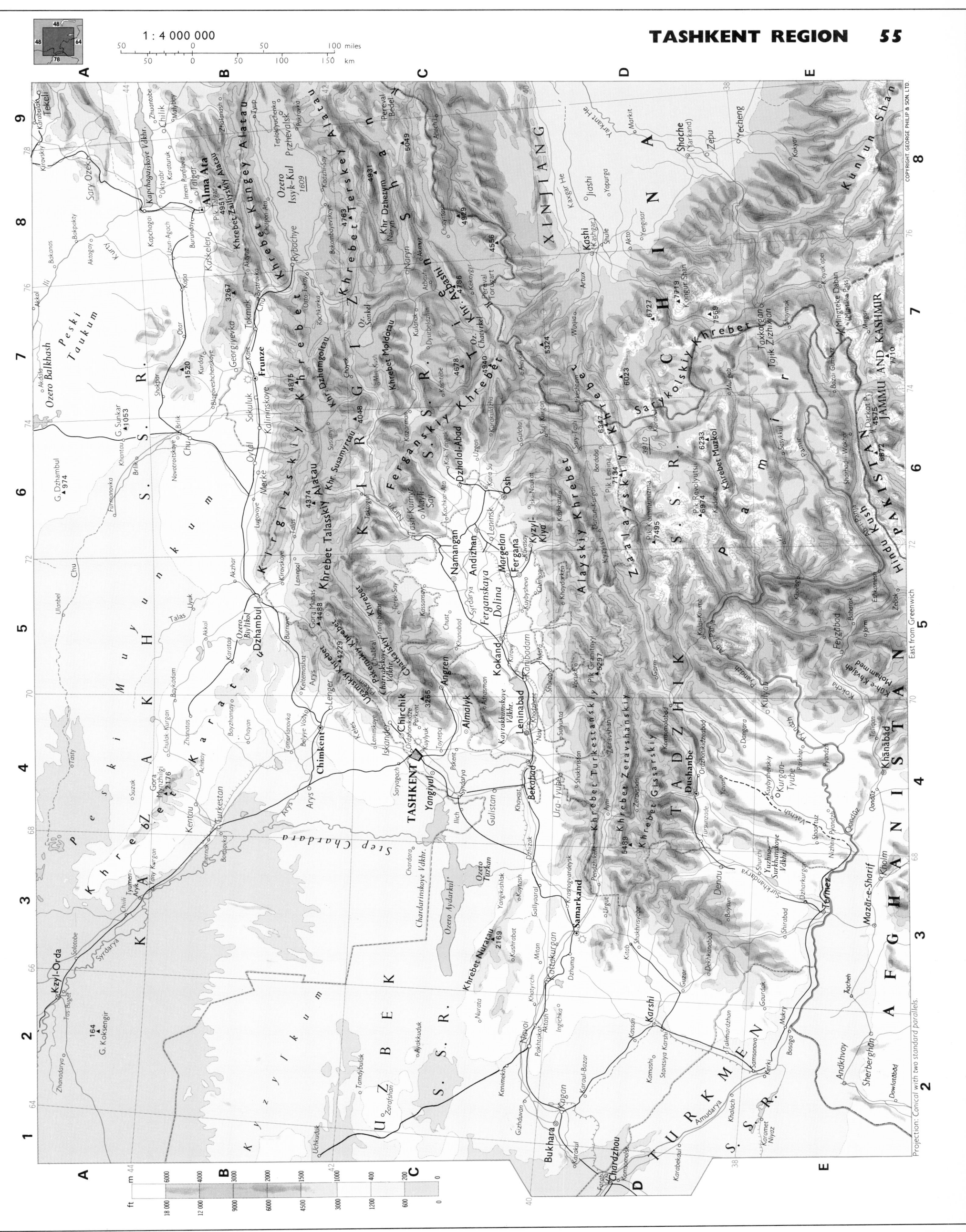

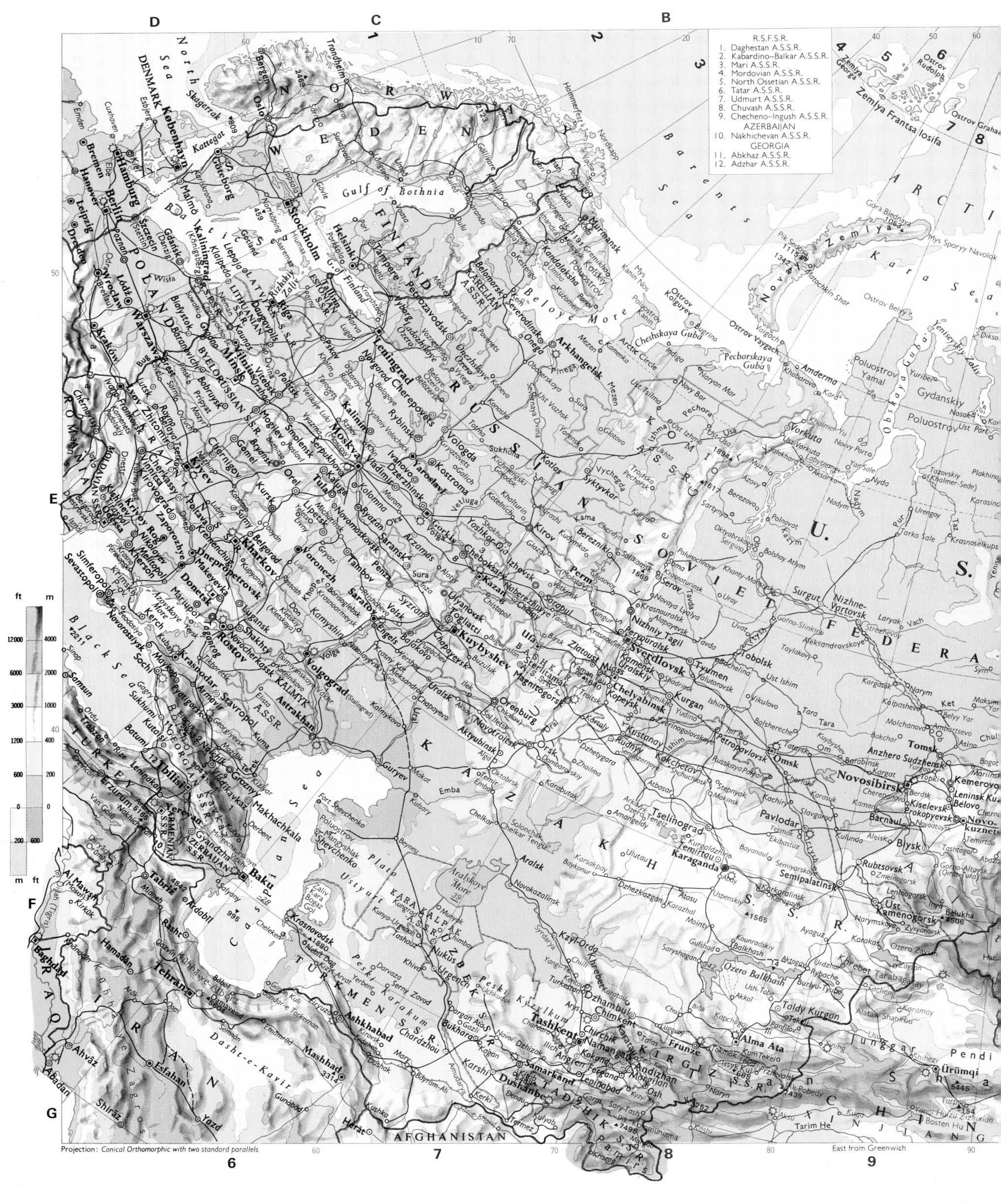

R.S.F.S.R.
1. Daghestan A.S.S.R.
2. Kabardino–Balkar A.S.S.R.
3. Mari A.S.S.R.
4. Mordovian A.S.S.R.
5. North Ossetian A.S.S.R.
6. Tatar A.S.S.R.
7. Udmurt A.S.S.R.
8. Chuvash A.S.S.R.
9. Checheno–Ingush A.S.S.R.
AZERBAIJAN
10. Nakhichevan A.S.S.R.
GEORGIA
11. Abkhaz A.S.S.R.
12. Adzhar A.S.S.R.

Projection: Conical Orthomorphic with two standard parallels

East from Greenwich

1 : 16 000 000

57

Boundaries of U.S.S.R.
Boundaries of S.S.R.
Boundaries of A.S.S.R.

COPYRIGHT. GEORGE PHILIP & SON. LTD.

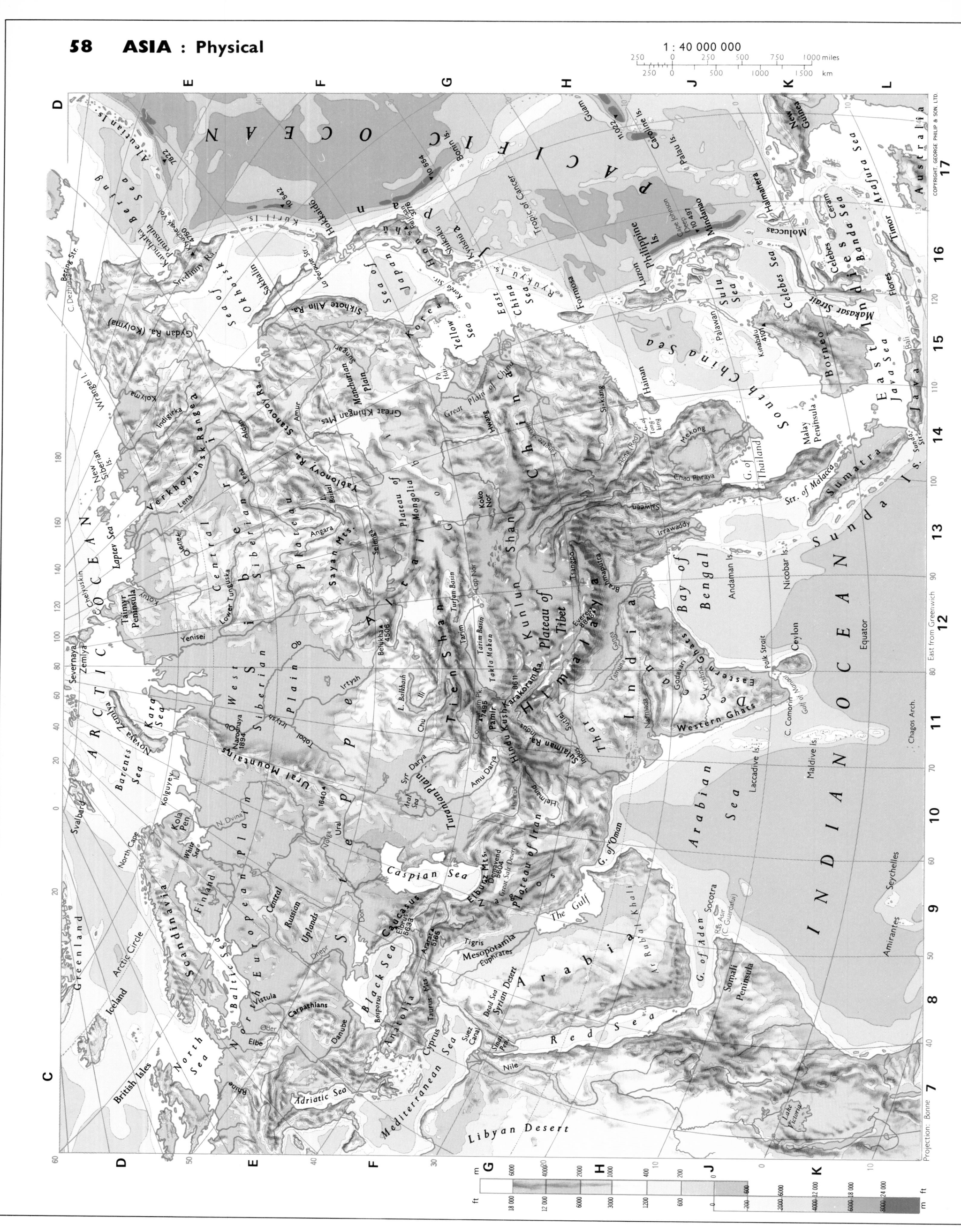

1 : 40 000 000

250   0   250   500   750   1000 miles
250   0   500   1000   1500 km

Projection: Bonne

COPYRIGHT. GEORGE PHILIP & SON LTD.

PACIFIC OCEAN

ARCTIC OCEAN

INDIAN OCEAN

China

Steppe

Plateau of Tibet

Himalaya

Arabia

Mediterranean Sea

Libyan Desert

Red Sea

Caspian Sea

Black Sea

Bay of Bengal

South China Sea

Arabian Sea

Sunda Is.

Australia

m ft
18 000 6000
12 000 4000
6000   2000
3000   1000
1200   400
600   200
0
-200   -600
-2000 -6000
-4000 -12 000
-6000 -18 000
-8000 -24 000

1 : 40 000 000

250 0 250 500 750 1000 miles
250 0 500 1000 1500 km

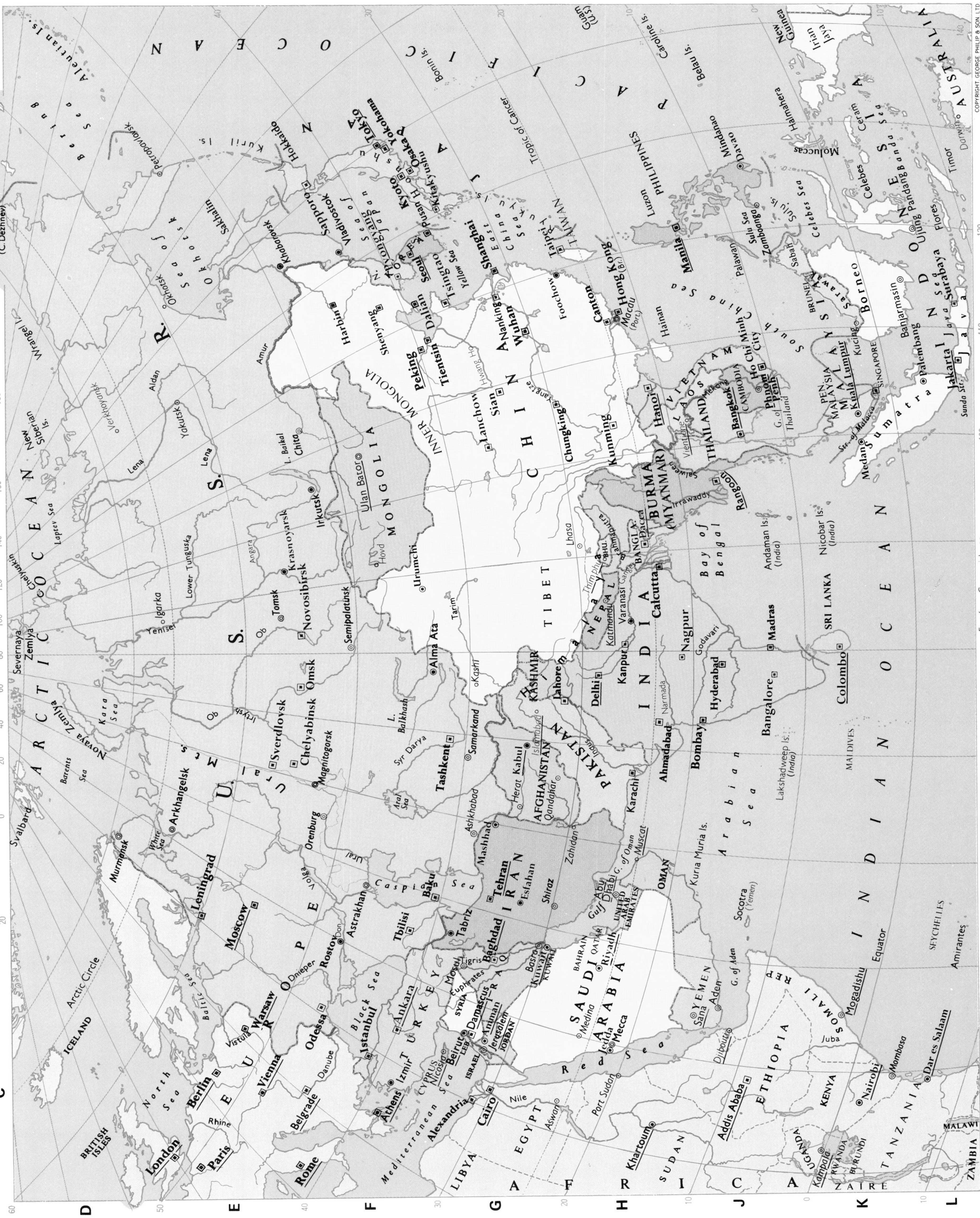

PACIFIC OCEAN

ARCTIC OCEAN

INDIAN OCEAN

U.S.S.R.

CHINA

MONGOLIA
INNER MONGOLIA

TIBET

INDIA

IRAN

IRAQ

SAUDI ARABIA

TURKEY

PAKISTAN

AFGHANISTAN

KASHMIR

NEPAL

BURMA MYANMAR

THAILAND

VIETNAM

LAOS

CAMBODIA

MALAYSIA

INDONESIA

PHILIPPINES

JAPAN

AUSTRALIA

ETHIOPIA

SOMALI REP.

EGYPT

LIBYA

SUDAN

KENYA

TANZANIA

ZAIRE

ZAMBIA

MALAWI

UGANDA

EUROPE

Capital cities: Peking

Moscow, Leningrad, Warsaw, Vienna, Berlin, London, Paris, Rome, Belgrade, Athens, Istanbul, Ankara, Baghdad, Tehran, Tbilisi, Baku, Kuwait, Riyadh, Mecca, Medina, Sana, Aden, Addis Ababa, Khartoum, Cairo, Jerusalem, Amman, Damascus, Beirut, Nicosia, Kabul, Islamabad, Delhi, Kathmandu, Dacca, Thimphu, Lhasa, Rangoon, Bangkok, Vientiane, Phnom Penh, Ho Chi Minh City, Hanoi, Kuala Lumpur, Singapore, Jakarta, Manila, Peking, Ulan Bator, Seoul, Tokyo, Colombo, Kuching, Nairobi, Kampala, Mogadishu, Dar es Salaam

Projection: Bonne

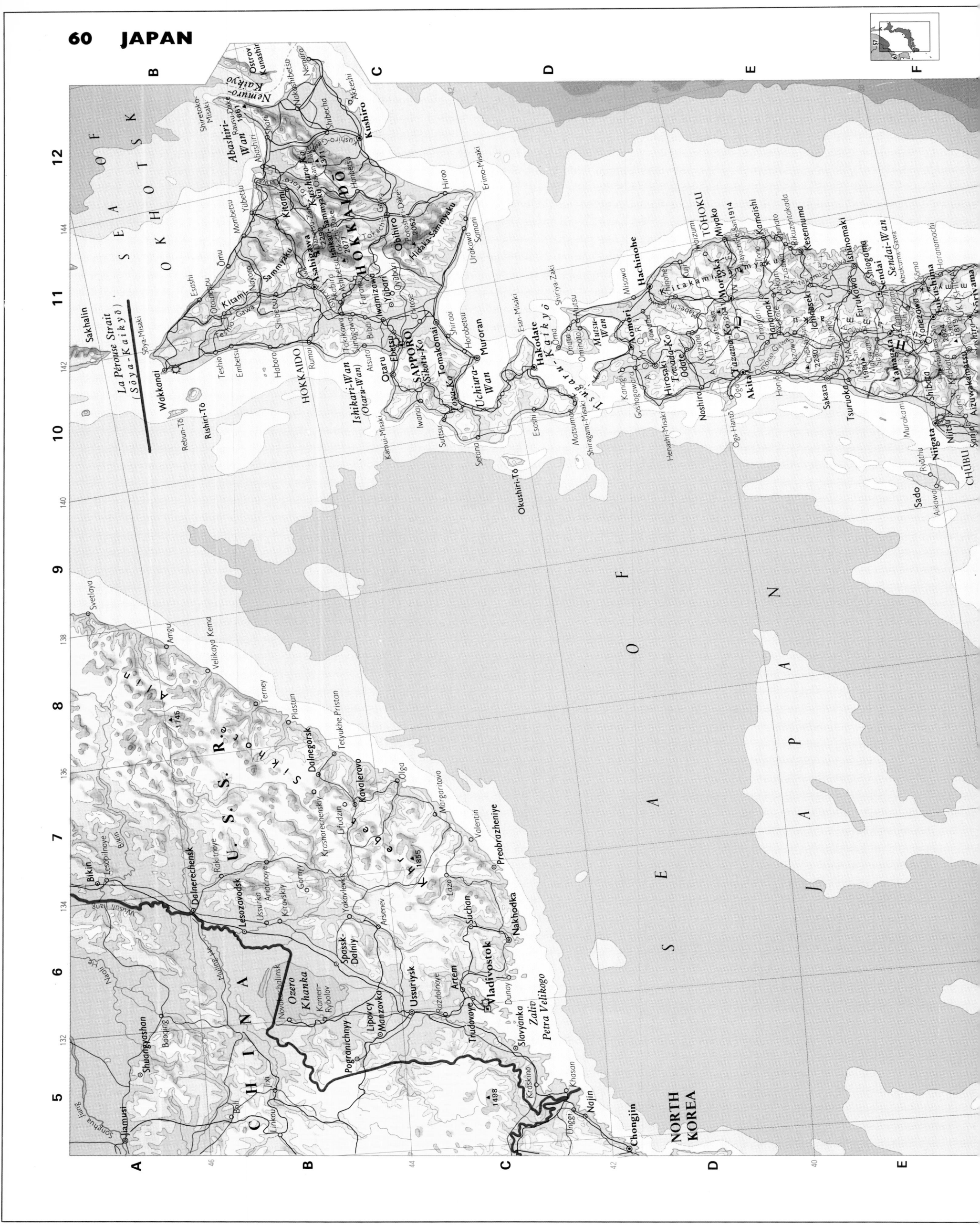

SEA OF OKHOTSK

Ostrov Kunashiri

Nemuro-Kaikyo

Shiretoko-Misaki

Rausu-Dake 1661

Abashiri-Wan

Kushiro-Ko

Kushiro

Enruma-Misaki

HOKKAIDO

Sammyaku

Kitami

Sammyaku

Asahizawa

Ashizawa 2290

Daisetsu-Zan 2077

Hidaka-Sammyaku 2052

Hiroo

Sapporo

SAPPORO

Shikotu-Ko

Toya-Ko

Tomakomai

Uchiura-Wan

Muroran

Hakodate

Tsugaru-Kaikyo

Esan-Misaki

Okushiri-To

La Pérouse Strait
(Sōya-Kaikyō)

Sakhalin

Wakkanai

Rebun-To

Rishiri-To

HOKKAIDO

Ishikari-Wan
(Otaru-Wan)

Otaru

Ebetsu

Iwamizawa

Yubari

Kamui-Misaki

Suttsu

TŌHOKU

Miyako

Kesennuma

Hachinohe

Aomori

AKITA

Towada-Ko
Odate

Noshiro

Akita

Sakata

Tsuruoka

YAMAGATA

Yamagata

Yonezawa

Shibata

Niigata

CHŪBU

Sado

Ryōtsu

SEA OF JAPAN

U.S.S.R.

Svetlaya

Amgu

Velikaya Kema

Terney

Plastun

Dalnegorsk

Sikhote Alin

Dalnerechensk

Bikin

Lesozavodsk

Ussurka

Kirovsky

Gornyy

Krasnorechensky

Arsenev

Lazo

Margaritovo

Valentin

Preobrazheniye

Olga

Kavalerovo

CHINA

Jiamusi

Shuangyashan

Baoqing

Linkou

Ozero Khanka

Spassk-Dalniy

Ussuriysk

Artem

Vladivostok

Nakhodka

Zaliv Petra Velikogo

Pogranichnyy

Slavyanka

Kraskino

Najin

Chongjin

NORTH KOREA

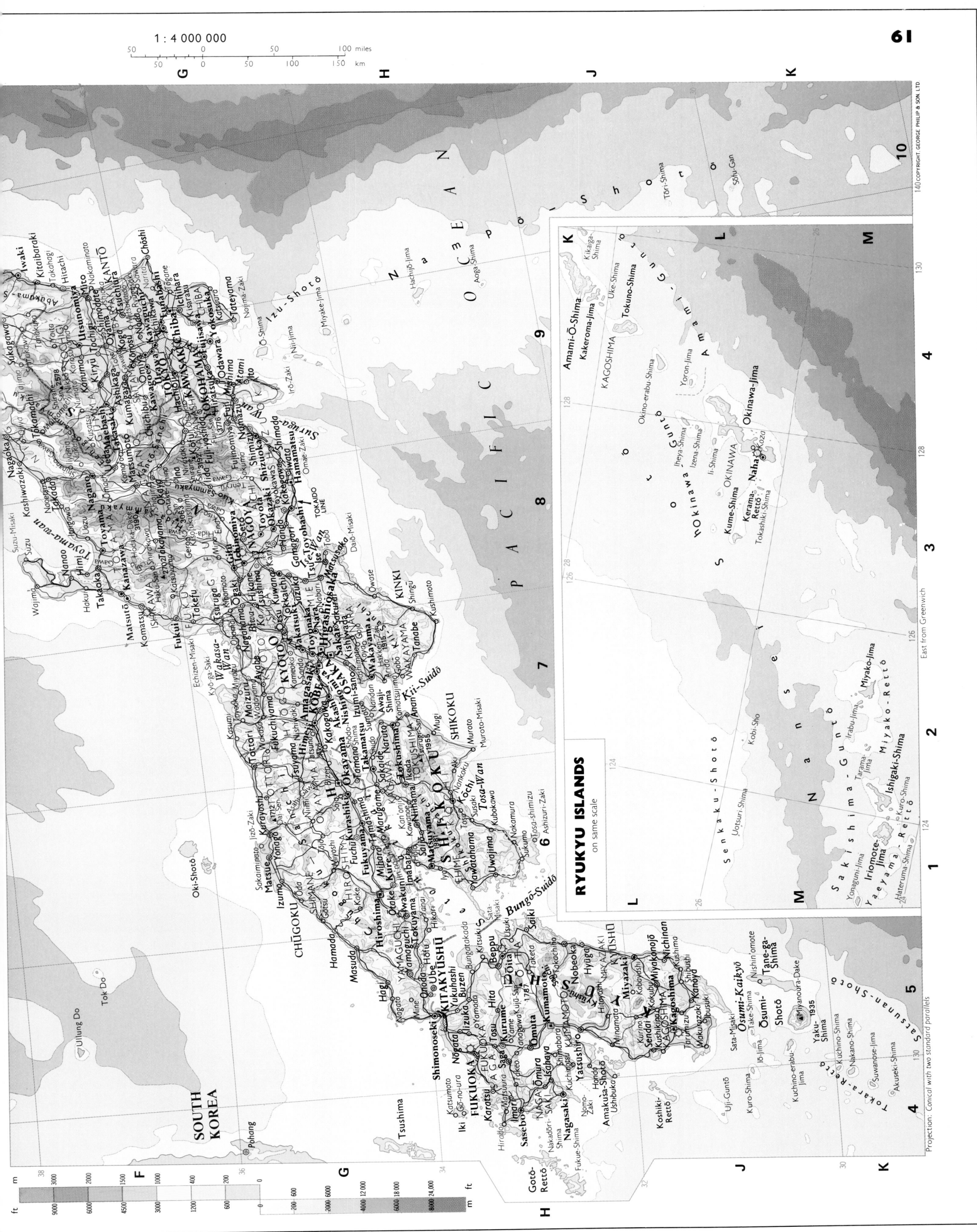

1 : 4 000 000

50   0   50   100 miles
50   0   50   100   150   km

G   H   J   K

RYUKYU ISLANDS
on same scale

PACIFIC OCEAN

SOUTH
KOREA

Tsushima

Ullung Do

Tok Do

Pohang

CHŪGOKU

SHIKOKU

KINKI

KYOTO
KOBE
OSAKA
NAGOYA

TOKYO
YOKOHAMA
CHIBA
KAWASAKI
KANTŌ

Hiroshima
YAMAGUCHI
KITAKYŪSHŪ
Shimonoseki
FUKUOKA
Kurume
Nagasaki
Sasebo
Kumamoto
Ōita
Beppu
Miyazaki
KAGOSHIMA
Sendai

Amami-Ō-Shima
Kakeroma-jima
Tokuno-Shima
Okino-erabu-Shima
Yoron-Jima
OKINAWA
Okinawa-jima
Naha
Kume-Shima
Kerama Rettō

Ishigaki-Shima
Miyako-jima
Iriomote-jima
Yonaguni-Jima

East from Greenwich

Projection: Conical with two standard parallels

COPYRIGHT. GEORGE PHILIP & SON LTD.

ft   m
38   3000
36   2000   9000 6000
34   1500   4500 3000
     1000   1200 600
     400   200
     0   0
     200   600
     2000   6000
     4000   12000
     8000   18000
            24000
m   ft

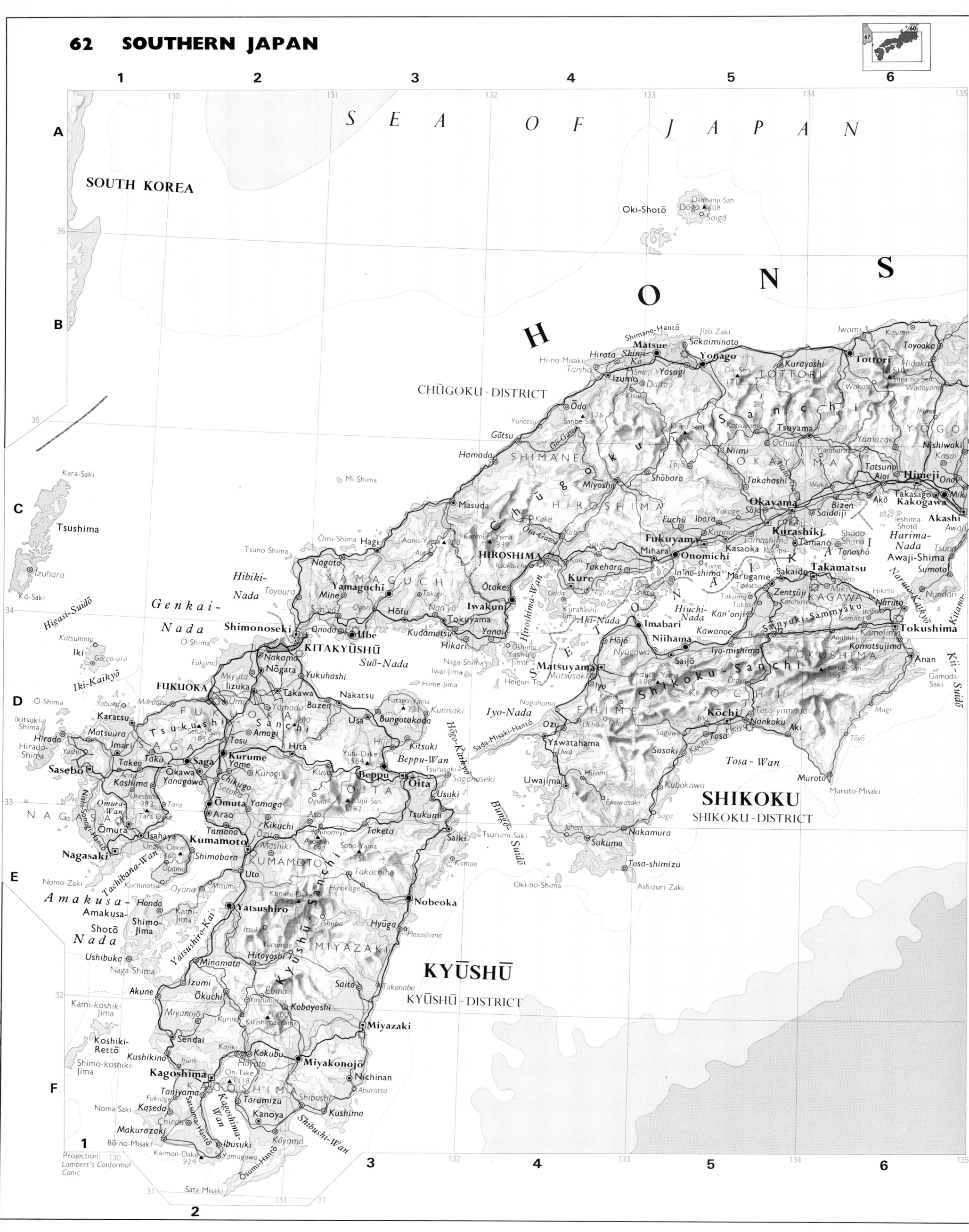

UNION OF SOVIET SOCIALIST

KAZAKH S.S.R.

MONGOLIA

Karaganda
Karsakpay
Dzhezkazgan
Semipalatinsk
Leninogorsk
Ust-Kamenogorsk
Belukha 4506
Zyryanovsk
Gorno-Altaysk
Rubtsovsk
Zapadnyy Sayan
Tannu Ola
Cheremkhovo
Angarsk
Irkutsk
Babushkin
Munku Sardyk 3491
Khubsugul
Hatgal
Hövsgöl Nuur

Mointy
Kounradski
Balkhash
Ozero Balkhash 342
Karkaralinsk
Ayaguz
Usharal
Zaysan
Ozero Zaysan
Khrebet Tarbagatay
Altay
Fuhai
Fuyun
Hyargas Nuur
Doröö Nuur
Hangayn Nuruu
Ulaangom
Ulan Bator
Dzuunmod

Frunze
Dzhambul
Issyk Kul
Alma Ata
1609
Yining
Ili
Bole
Ala Kul
Usheng
Dzhungarskiye Vorota
Karamay
Manas
Urumqi 5445
Gitai
Barkol Kazak Zizhixian
Hami
4925
Buyanhongor
Huld
Dalandzadgad

KIRGIZ S.S.R.
Namangan
Andizhan
Naryn
Pik Pobedy 7439
Wensu
Aksu
Kuqa
Korla
Bosten (Bagrax) Hu
Turpan
154
Aydingkol Hu
Kuruktag
Gaxun Nur

Artux
Kashi
Shule
Tarim He
Tarim Pendi
Lop Nor
Dunhuang
Anxi
Yumen
Alxa Zuoqi
Wuhai 2514

XINJIANG
Shache
Yecheng
Pishan
1635
Qiemo
Qarqan He
Ruoqiang
Altun Shan
Mengnai
Tsart
Har Hu
8346
Qilian Shan
Zhangye
Shandan
Yinchuan
NINGXIA HUIZU ZIZHIQU

Taxkorgan Tajik Zizhixian
Hotan (Khotan)
Yutian
Wuluk omushih Ling 7723
Huh Xil Shan
Da Qaidam
Qaidam Pendi
Golmud
Dulan
Qinghai Hu 3205
Gonghe
Xining
Wuwei
Pingluo
Guyuan
Qingyang

KARAKORAM
8611
Karakorum Shankou 5575
Togatax
Kun-Lun Shan
QINGHAI
Ngoring Hu
Gyaring Hu 4237
Maqen
Linxia
LANZHOU
Pingliang
Baoji

JAMMU & KASHMIR
8126
Srinagar
Leh
Aksai
Zhaxigang
Gar
Ngari
Bayan Har Shan
6994
Yushu
Yangtze
Tongren
Tianshui
Wudu

Nanda Devi 7817
Dehra Dun
Mapam Yumco
XIZANG
Tanggula (Dangla) Shan
Amdo
Nagqu
Siling Co 4495
Nam Co 4627
Qamdo
Garze
SICHUAN
Daxian
Mianyang

Meerut
Moradabad
DELHI
Aligarh
8221
Xainza
Namcha Barwa 7756
Bomi
Nyainqentanghla Shan
Lhasa
Daxue Shan
CHENGDU
Nanchong
Hechuan

Agra
KANPUR
Gwalior
Lucknow
Gorakhpur
Darbhanga
Naqmring
8848
Xigaze
Lhaze
Yarlung Zangbo Jiang
Yamdrok Yumco
Santai
Neijiang
Leshan
Zigong
Luzhou
Yibin
CHONGQING

Jhansi
Allahabad
NEPAL
Katmandu
Punakha
BHUTAN
Dibrugarh
Zunyi
Meitan

INDIA
Sagar
Varanasi
Patna
Gaya
Gauhati
Tezpur
Brahmaputra
GUIZHOU
Liuzhi
Guiyang

Jabalpur
Tropic of Cancer
Rajshahi
BANGLADESH
Khasi Hills
Imphal
382
Myitkyina
Dali
Xiaguan
Dongchuan
Anshun
Duyun

Ranchi
Asansol
Berhampore
Bhatpara
DHAKA
Narayanganj
Silchar
BURMA
Bhamo
KUNMING
Xingyi
Guilin

Raipur
Barddhaman
Khulna
Haora
CALCUTTA
Chittagong
Monywa
2650
Yuxi
Gejiu
Mengzi
Wenshan
Bose

Nagpur
Kharagpur
Baleshwar
Mandalay
3053
MYANMAR
NANNING

Chanda
Indravati
Cuttack
BAY OF
Akyab
Pegu Yoma
3143
Pingxiang
VIETNAM
Hanoi
Haiphong
Gulf of Tonkin

Warangal
Vizianagaram
Berhampur
BENGAL
Arakan Yoma
Victoria 3053
LAOS
THAILAND (SIAM)
Luang Prabang
2711
Mekong

Projection: Bonne
East from Greenwich

Scale: ft / m
18 000 / 6000
12 000 / 4000
9000 / 3000
6000 / 2000
4500 / 1500
3000 / 1000
1200 / 400
600 / 200
0 / 0
200 / 600
m / ft

1 : 12 000 000

| 100 | | 0 | 100 | 200 | 300 | 400 miles |
| 100 | 0 | 100 | 200 | 300 | 400 | 500 | 600 km |

REPUBLICS
Oz. Baykal
Ulan Ude
Chita
Bukachacha
Sretensk
Shimanovsk
Svobodny
Aleksandrovsk
C. Terpeniya
Sakhalin
Poronaysk
Komsomolsk
Nerchinsk
Yilehuli
Shan
Yablonovy Khrebet
Borzya
Oloyannaya
Blagoveshchensk
Aihui
Bureya
Troitskoye
L. Bolon
Khabarovsk
Dolinsk
Yuzhno-Sakhalinsk
Kholmsk
Tartarskiy Proliv
Manzhouli
Oroqen Zizhiqi
Obluchye
Birobidzhan
Amur
Kholmsk

Hulun Nur
Hailar
Nenjiang
Bei'an
Yichun
Hegang
Jiamusi
Shuangyashan
Bikin
La Perouse Str.
Wakkanai
Buir Nur
Butha Qi
Nan Jiang
Jixi
Mishan
Ozero Khanka
Ussuriysk
Asahigawa
HOKKAIDO
Kushiro
SAPPORO
Otaru
Muroran
C. Erimo
Horqin Youyi Qianqi (Ulan Hot)
Baicheng
HARBIN
Kuyu
Vladivostok
Nakhodka
Artem
Partizansk
Hakodate
Aomori
Hachinohe
Morioka
Akita
Sakata
Ishinomaki
Sado
Sendai
Niigata
Wajima
Koriyama
Utsunomiya
Kanazawa
Toyama
TOKYO
Kawasaki
NAGOYA
YOKOHAMA
KYOTO
Shizuoka
Yokosuka
KOBE OSAKA
Sakai
Hamamatsu
Wakayama
Okayama
Shikoku
Kochi
Matsuyama

SEA OF JAPAN

YELLOW SEA

EAST CHINA SEA

PACIFIC OCEAN

SOUTH CHINA SEA

COPYRIGHT GEORGE PHILIP & SON LTD

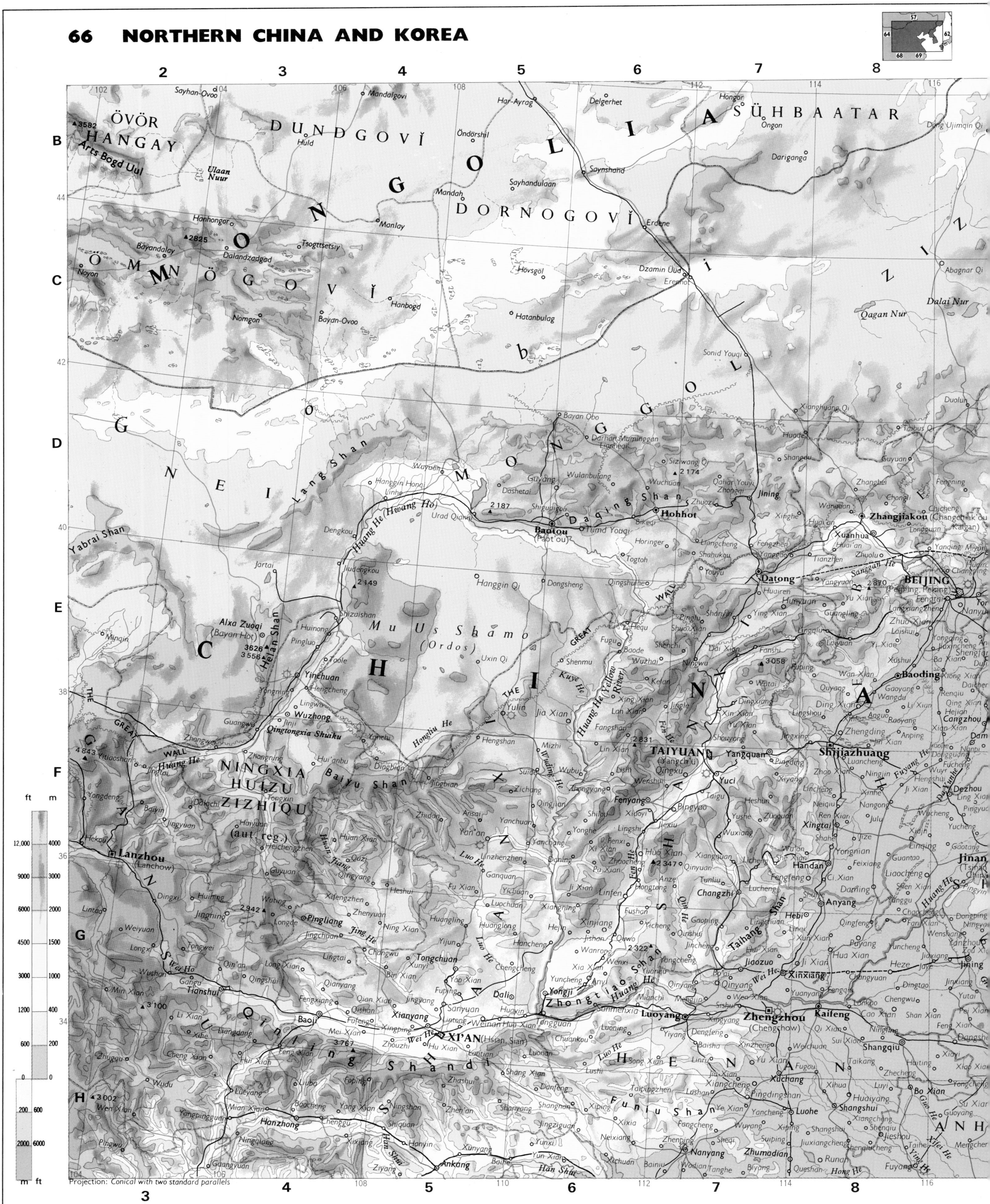

2   3   4   5   6   7   8

MONGOLIA

ÖVÖR HANGAY
Arts Bogd Uul
▲3582

DUNDGOVĬ

SÜHBAATAR

Sayhan-Ovoo
Mandalgovi
Har-Ayrag
Delgerhet
Hongor
Öndörshil
Ongon
Dar_ganga
Düng Ujimqin Qi

Huld
Saynshand
B

Hanhongor
Manlay
Sayhandulaan
Mandah
Erdene
Abnagar Qi

▲2825
Bayandalay
Dalandzadgad
Tsogttsetsiy
Hövsgöl
Dzamin Üüd
Erenhot
Qagan Nur
Dalai Nur

Noyon
MÖGOVĬ
Hanbogd
Hatanbulag
C

Nomgon
Bayan-Ovoo
b

Sonid Youqi
Xianghuang Qi
Duolun

GOBI
Bayan Obo
Darhan Muminggan Hanlieqi
Huade
Tabus

NEI
Wuyuan
MONGGOL
Guyang
Siziwang Qi
▲2174
Shandu
Guyuan
Zhangbei
Fengning

Langshan
Hanggin Hou
Linhe
Dashetai
Wulanbulang
Wuchuan
Qahar Youyi Zhongqi
Zhuozi
Jining
Wanquan
Chongli
Chicheng
D

Dengkou
2187
Shiguaigou
Daqing Shan
Hohhot
Xinghe
Hui'an
Zhuolu
Zhangjiakou (Changchiakow · Kalgan)
Longguan · Katgan
Yanqing
Miyun

Urad Qianqi
Baotou (Paot'ou)
Tumd Youqi
Horinger
Liangcheng
Fengzhen
Yanggao
Xuanhua
Huai'an
Tianzhen
Sanggan He
Yangyuan
Yu Xian
BEIJING (Peiping, Peking)
Fengtai

Huang He (Hwang Ho)
Togtoh
Qingshuihe
Huairen
Datong
▲2870
Guangling
Langfang Zhen
Zhuo Xian
Nanyu

Jartai
Jiudengkou
▲2149
Hanggin Qi
Dongsheng
Hequ
Shanyin
Ying Xian
Liaoyuan
Huaiyang Zheng
Shengfan
E

Shizuishan
Mu Us Shamo (Ordos)
Baode
Wuzhai
Dai Xian
Fanshi
Fuping
Wan Xian
Baoding

Alxa Zuoqi (Bayan Hot)
Huinong
Uxin Qi
Shenmu
Kelan
Xing Xian
Lan Xian
Ningwu
▲3058
Watai
Quyang
Gaoyang
Renqiu

Helan Shan
3626 3556
Pingluo
CHI
Yulin
Kuye He
Xing Xian
Jingle
Dingxiang
Ding Xian
Qing Xian

Yinchuan
Taole
Jia Xian
Huang He (Yellow River)
Fangshan
▲2831
Xin Xian
Lingshou
Anguo
Raoyang

Yongning
Hengcheng
Wuzhong
Mizhi
Lishi
TAIYUAN (Yangchu'u)
Yangquan
Zhengding
Anping

Qingtongxia Shuiku
Honglu He
Suide
Wuding He
Wubu
Fenyang
Yuci
SHIJIAZHUANG
Pingding
Zhao Xian
Dam

Zhongwei
Hengshan
Zichang
Qingjian
Shilou
Xiaoyi
Jiexiu
Xiangyuan
Wutai
Yongnian
Linqing
F

Huang He
WALL
Dingbian
Ansai
Yanchuan
Yonghe
Lingshi
Yushe
Zuoquan
Wuxiang
Xingtai
Jize
Guantao

▲4843 Yitiaoshan
GREAT
NINGXIA HUIZU ZIZHIQU (aut. reg.)
Baiyu Shan
Zhidan
Yan'an
Xi Xian
Renxi
Jiexiu
Xiangfen
Handan
Linxi
Gaotang

Hekou
Lanzhou (Lanchow)
Huan Xian
Luo He
Ganquan
Qingyang
Hua Shan
Daming
Nanle
Puyang

Dingxi
Huining
2942
Longde
Pingliang
Yijun
Xianglong
Linfen
Hongtong
Fushan
Qinshui
Changzhi
Hebi
Qingfeng
G

Weiyuan
Lintao
Tongwei
Jingning
Jingchuan
Ning Xian
Huangling
Hejin
Jishan
Qinyuan
Lucheng
Anyang
Heze

Longxi
Qin'an
Long Xian
Lingtai
Chongwu
Jing He
Tongchuan
Xunyi
Huangling
Hancheng
▲2322
Yangcheng
Jincheng
Xun Xian
Jining

Tianshui
Qinshui
Qianyang
Bin Xian
Yao Xian
Chengcheng
Xia Xian
Wenxi
Boai
Qinyang
Xinxiang
Changyuan
Dingtao

3'100
Li Xian
Liangdang
Fengxiang
Qian Xian
Yaozhou
Dali
Yongji
Yuncheng
Anyi
Huang He
Wei He
Xinxiang
Lankao

Zhugqu
Cheng Xian
Qianyang
Mei Xian
Sanyuan
Liquan
Weinan
Hua Xian
Sanmenxia
Luoyang
Zhengzhou (Chengchow)
Kaifeng
Shan Xian

Wudu
Hui Xian
Xianyang
Weinan
Tongguan
Lingbao
Miaodi
Xingyang
Qi Xian
Cao Xian

QINLING SHAN
Fengfxiang
3767
Wei He
XI'AN (Hsian, Sian)
Luonan
Luoning
Yiyang
Dengfeng
Baisha
Xinzheng
Weichuan
Shangqiu

Lüeyang
Baoji
Zhouzhi
Hu Xian
Lantian
Chuankou
Luo He
Song Xian
HENAN
Xuchang
Xihua

Pingwu
Ningqiang
Foping
Zhashui
Shang Xian
Danfeng
Lushi
Linru
Xiangcheng
Fugou
Luyi

H
▲3002
Wen Xian
Yang Xian
Ningshan
Shiquan
Shanyang
Xixia
Xichuan
Funiu Shan
Neixiang
Pingdingshan
Luohe
Shangshui
Bo Xian

Guangyuan
Qingchuan
Chenggu
Hanzhong
Han Shan
Xunyang
Xixiang
Zhenping
Sheqi
Wuyang
Suiping
ANH

Pingwu
Ningqiang
Ziyang
Ankang
Baihe
Han Shui
Yun Xian
Danjiang
Nanyang
Zhumadian
Biyang
Queshan

Projection: Conical with two standard parallels

Scale (ft / m)

ft	m
12,000	4000
9000	3000
6000	2000
4500	1500
3000	1000
1200	400
600	200
0	0
200	600
2000	6000
m	ft

3   4   5   6   7   8

1 : 4 800 000

50   0   50   100   150 miles
50   0   50   100   150   200   km

9   10   11   12   13   14   15   16

HINGAN

Horqin Youyi Qianqi   Zhenlai   HARBIN
(Haerhbin)   Jixi   Ozero
Khanka

Baicheng   Zhaoyuan   Acheng   Yanshou   Turiy Rog
Tao'an   Daan   Songhua Jiang   Shangzhi   Yimianpo   Linkou
Anguang   Fuyu   Changchunling   Huachae   Hengdaohezi   U.S.S.R.
Tuquan   Qian Gorlos   Shenjingzi   Shanhetun   Zhangguangcailing   Mudanjiang   Maqiaohe   Pogranichnyy
Tongyu   Nong'an   Dehui   Shulan   1 690   Hailin   Muling   Suiyang   Sifenhe   Golenki

Jarud Qi   Fulongquan   Gongzhuling   Yushu   Ning'an   Dongning   Ussuriysk
Changling   Jilin   Jiaohe   Emu   Wangqing   (Voroshilov)   Razdolnoye
Xinkai He   Huaidezhen   Kirin   Huangnidadian   Dunhua   Daxinggou   Tavrichanka   Artem

CHANGCHUN   Maolin   Panshi   Antu   Helong   Mingyuegue   Yanji   Krasnino   Vladivostok
Huaide   Shuangyang   1677   Tumen   Hunchun   Posyet   Slavyanka

HEILONGJIANG

NORTH KOREA

SOUTH KOREA

SEA   OF   JAPAN

Bo Hai
(Gulf of Chihli)

HUANG HAI
(Yellow Sea)

JAPAN

East from Greenwich   COPYRIGHT. GEORGE PHILIP & SON. LTD.

9   10   11   12   13   14   15

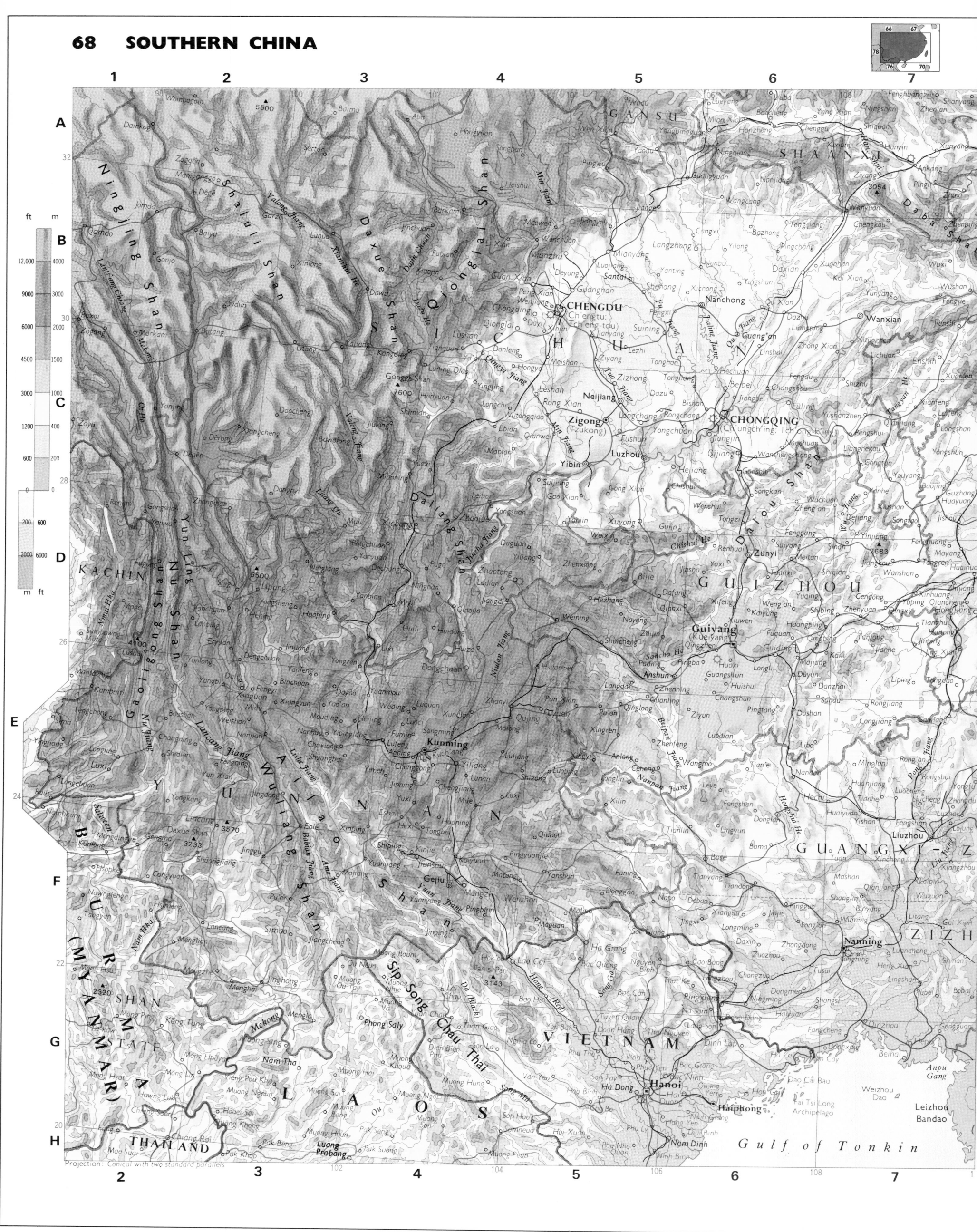

1 : 4 800 000

50   0   50   100   150 miles
50   0   50   100   150   200 km

8   9   10   11   12   13   14

A

JIANGSU

Shangqiu Xipng Xuchang Shengli Guo He Guzhen Hongze Dongtai
Yunxi Fangcheng Xiping Shangcai Jieshou Taihe Xifei He Mengcheng Hu Gaoyou Xinghua
Nelxiang Zhumadian Runan Hong He Fuyang Yingshang Madian Fengyang Huaiyin Gaoyou Gaoyou Hai'an
Nanyang Biyang Xincai Yinshang Fengtai Bengbu Tianchang Yangzhou Taizhou Tai Xing Rugao Rudong
Zhenping Tanghe Huai He Shou Xian Huainan Dingyuan Lai'an Yizheng Zhenjiang Jiangdu Jiangyin Nantong Qidong

HENAN Zhengyang Chengxi Hefei Chu Xian Puko (Chenchiang) Danyang Jingjiang
Xiangfan Zaoyang Xinyang Huangchuan Lu'an Zhegao **NANJING** Meishui Changzhou Changshu Jiading
Fangcheng Dongjinwan Sui Xian Yingshan Hong'an Chao Hu He Xian Nanjng Meishan Wuxi Kunshan Baoshan
Fang Xian Baokang Nanzhang Maping Macheng Chaohu Wuwei Nanyi Hu Langxi Suzhou Qingpu **SHANGHAI**
Shennongjia Jingshan Anlu Yunmeng Xiaogan Tongcheng Tongling Xuancheng Wuxing Jiaxing (Changhai)
Xuejiaping Zhongxiang Tianmen Hanchuan **WUHAN** Yuexi Datong Jing Xian Qingyang Ningguo Fengxian Songjiang

HUBEI Hankou Huanggang Anqing Taiping Chengde Haiyan **Hangzhou** (Hangchow: Hangchow)
Yichang Dongyang Jinkou Hanyang Huangshi Qichun Wangjiang Jingde Lin'an Hangzhou Wan Daqu Shan
(Kiang) Zhijiang Jiangling Qianjiang Daye Meichuan Susong Dongzhi 1810 Changhua **Shaoxing** Putuo Zhoushan Dao
Yidu Shashi Honghu Hanli Pengze Shita Yi Xian Tunxi Tonglu Fuyang Zhenhai
Songzi Gong'an Haoxue Xiannng Yangxin Jiujiang Shimenjie Qimen Xiuning She Xian Fuchun Jiang **Ningbo** (Ningpo)

ZHEJIANG

Wufeng Gong'an Haoxue Ruichang De'an Duchang Jingdezhen Kaihua Lanxi Jin Xian Dongyang Tiantai Linhai Niutou Shan
Shishou Linxiang Pugi Poyang Leping Dexing Yushan Longyou Qu Xian **Jinhua** Xianju Huangyan
Shimen Linli Nan Xian Pingjiang Xiushui Shan Yongxiu Anyi Wannian Hengfeng Jiangshan Wuyi Lishui Haimen
Sangzhi Dayong Hanshou Nanchang Yuganxian Yiyang Jin Jiang Shangrao Guixi Longquan Yunhe Wenzhou
Cili Changde Yueyang Ningxiang Tonggu Shanggao Jin Gao'an Dongxiang Yujiang Hexi Wencheng (Wenchow)
Zi Shui Yiyang Xiangyin **Nanchang** Fengcheng Yiyang Yanshan Pucheng Zherong Bei'an
Yuanling Anhua Ningxiang Xiangyin Fengxin Linchuan Jinxi Chong'an Zheng Songxi Fuding Nanji Shan
Chenxi Xupu Loudi **Changsha** Wanzai Xinyu Yichun Chongren Zixi Guangze Shuiji Zhenghe Dongyuan Wu'an

HUNAN Xiangtan Zhuzhou Linchuan Yihuang Nanfeng Jian'ou Pingnan Sansha Daqu Xiapu

JIANGXI Pingxiang Gaokeng Anfu Lishui Xinfeng Nancheng Taining Jianyang Nanping Gutian Ningde
Xiangtan Xinhua Lianyuan Chaling Ji'an Guangchang Taihe Jiangle Nanping Shunchang 1629 Luoyuan Fuying Dao
Shaoyang Hengyang Hengyang Anren Yongxin Yongfeng Ningdu Shaowu Jian'ou Min Jiang Fuzhou (Foochow: Fuchow)
Xue.feng Shan Qiyang Chaling Ling Xian Suichuan Wan'an Ninghua Qingliu Youxi Minqing Mazu Dao
Hengyang Huangyangsi Chongning Leiyang 2164 Ningdu Longquan Qingliu Sanming Yongtai Changle
Wugong Qidong Yongxing Shicheng Xingguo Qin Jiang Ninghua Qinglu Yongan Minhou Fuqing Huanghua Wan

FUJIAN Guidong Shadi Yudu Longgou Changting Datian Xiongyou Putian Nanri Dao
Qianyang Shaoyang Yongxing **Ganzhou** Ruijin Lianchng Maiyuan Dehua Xinghua Wan
Dong'an Zixing Chongyi Shangyou Huichang Zhangping Nan'an Quanzhou (Chuanchou)
Suiping Lianzhou Xintian Chen Xian Dayu Nankang Xinfeng Anyuan Zhangzhou Anxi Quanzhou
Ning'an Xing'an Guiyang Jiahe Dao Xian Renhua Quannan Waping Wuping Shanghang Hua'an Tong'an Xiamen (Hsiamen: Amoy)
Guilin Jianyang Lingchuan Linwu Yizhang Longnan Longnan Xunwu Tong'an Jinmen Dao
Yangshuo Guanyang Lanshan Lechang Pingshi Dingnan Huachuan Zhangzhou Longhai
Xingshan Lipu Zhaoping Liangtian Leichong Shixing Heping Lianping Nanjing Zhao'an

GUANGXI ZHU Gongcheng Pingle Ruyuan Wengyuan **Shaoguan** Mei Xian Han Jiang Pinghe Zhangpu
Xiuren Zhaoping Mengshan Zhongxin Lianping Longchuan Meixian Xingning Dabu Yunxiao Dongshan
Zhaoqing Wengcheng Heping Xingning Jiaoling Pingyuan Nan'ao
Pingnan Wuzhou Fengkai Zijin Heyuan Longmen Zengcheng Dapu Chao'an Jieyang Nan'ao Shantou (Swatow)
Xun Jiang Xi Jiang Foshan Zengcheng Boluo Huizhou Haifeng Jieyang Puning Xiamen
Suiping Teng Xian Zhaoqing Sanshui **Guangzhou** (Canton) Shilong Dongguan Lufeng Huilai

GUANGDONG Jiangmen Panyu Heping Shunde Huidong Honghai Wan Tainan

Yulin Beiliu Gaozhou Zhongshan Xiaolan **HONG KONG** (U.K.) Kowloon
Luchuan 1703 Gaolan Dao **Macao** (Macao) (Port.) Dangan Liedao

Tropic of Cancer

Huazhou Wuchuan Xuchang Gaolan Dao Shangchuan Dao Huang **TAIWAN (FORMOSA)**

Lianjiang Huilong Huizhou Danshui Jilong
Zhanjiang Donghai Dao Taoyuan **TAIBEI** (Taipei)
Leizhou Wan Naozhou Dao Xinzhu Daxi Yilan Luodong
Xuwen Hai'an Yuanli Xue Shan 3931 Luodong Hualian

Zhanghua Taichung (Taichung) Huadian
Erlin Yunlin Jiayi Yu Shan 3997 Toman
Dongjun Beigang Baihe Jiali
Tainan Jiali Taidong Huoshao Dao
Gaoxiong (Kaohsiung) Pingdong Fangliao
Eluanbi Lan Yu

Taiwan Shan

Taiwan Strait

Luzon Strait

Tungsha Tao

S O U T H   C H I N A   S E A

B

C

D

E

F

G

H

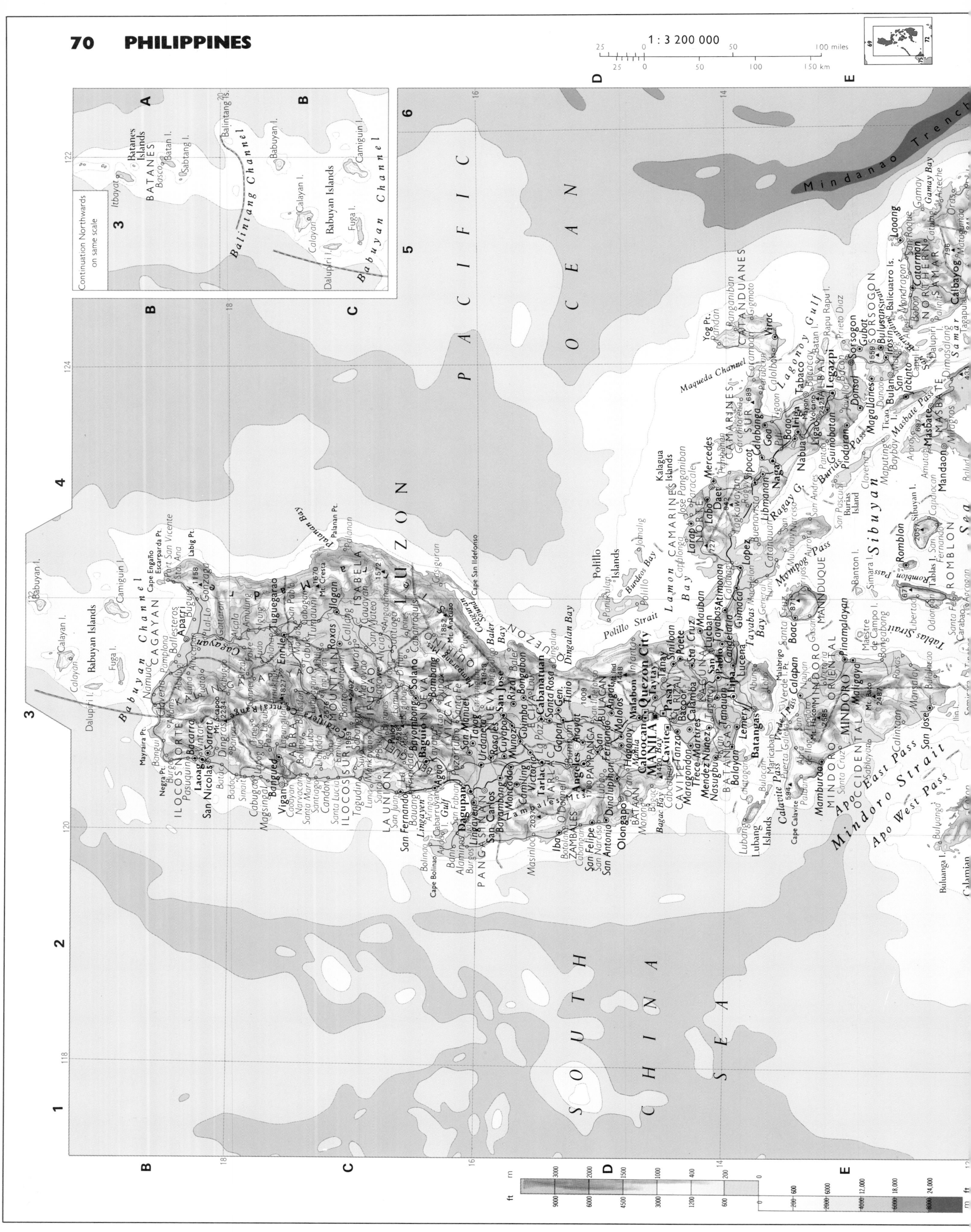

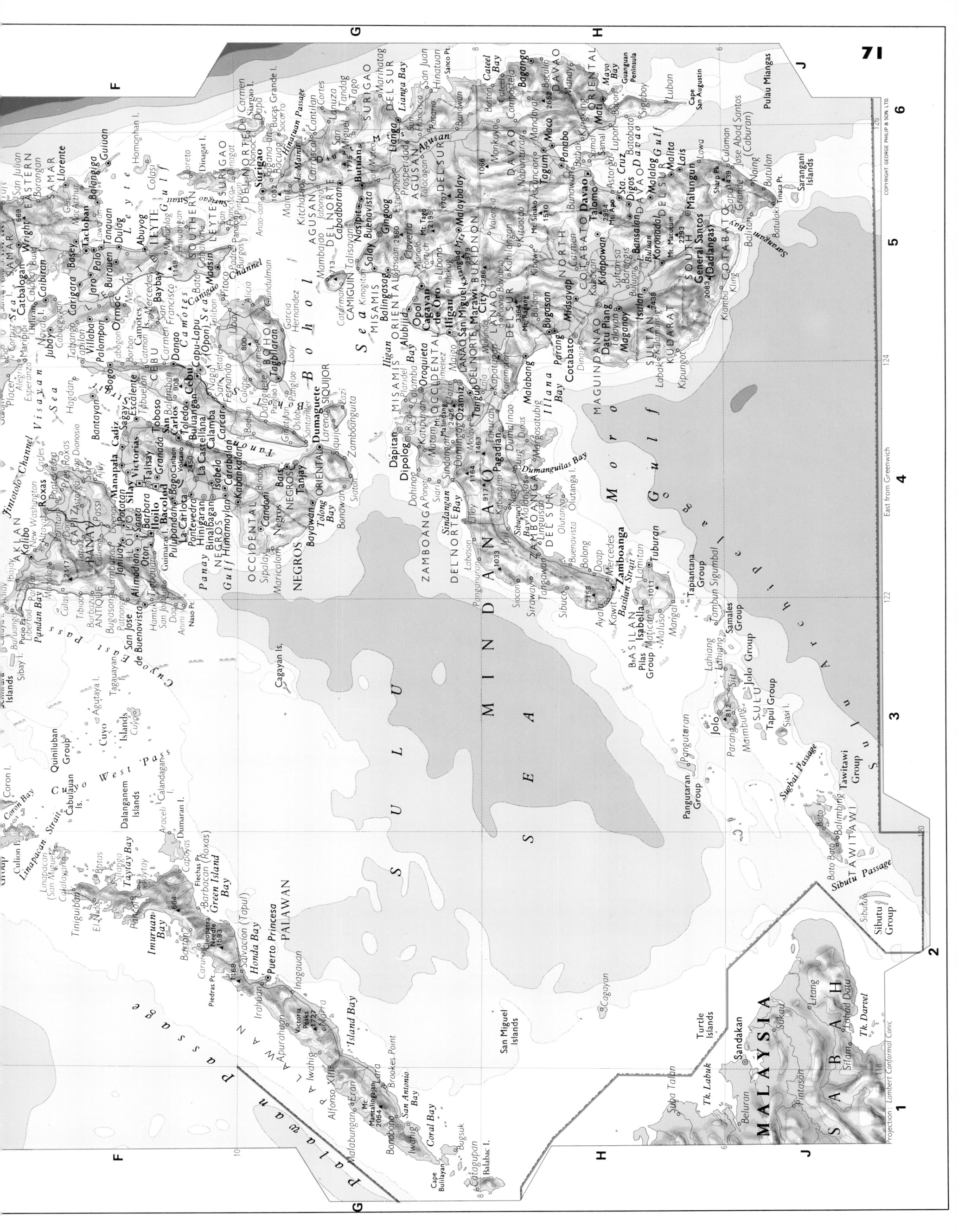

Projection: Lambert Conformal Conic.

East from Greenwich

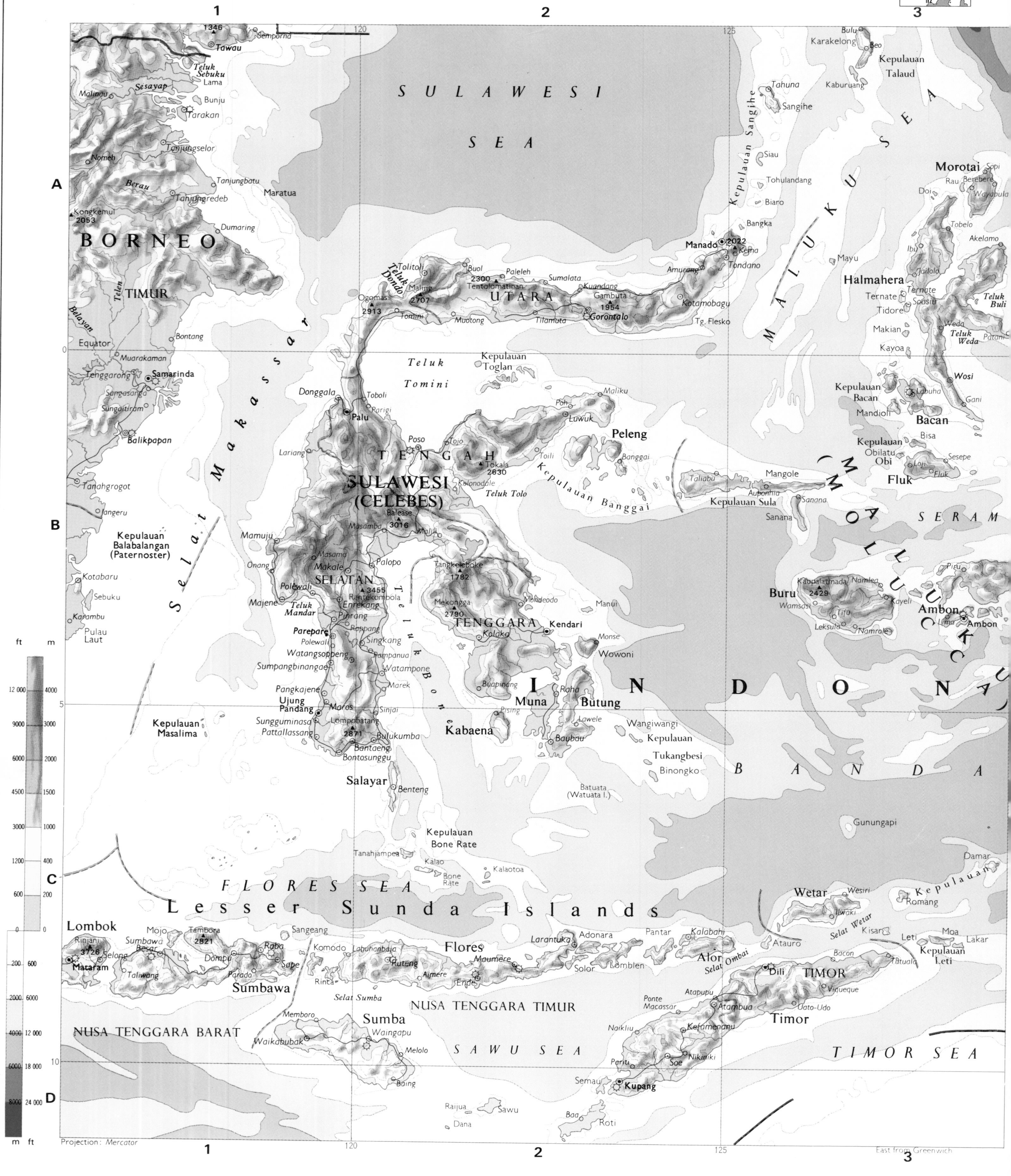

SULAWESI SEA

1346
Tawau
Semporna
Karakelong Beo
Kepulauan Talaud
Teluk Sebuku
Lama
Malinau
Sesayap
Bunju
Tarakan
Tahuna
Kaburuang
Bulu

Nomeh
Berau
Tanjungselor
Siau
Tohulandang
Biaro
Bangka
Bangka
Morotai Sopi
Rau Berebere
Wayabula

Kongkemul
2053
Tanjungbatu
Maratua
Kepulauan Sangihe
Doi
Ibu
Jailolo
Tobelo
Akelamo

A

BORNEO
Dumaring
Manado 2022 Kema
Amurang
Tondano
Ternate
Halmahera
Soasiu
TIMUR
Tolitoli
Teluk Dondo
Buol
Paleleh
Sumalata
Kuandang
Kotamobagu
Tg. Flesko
Tidore
Makian
Weda
Teluk Buli

Telen
Ogomas
Malimo
2300
Tentolomatinan
Gambuta
1954
Mayu
Kayoa
Teluk Weda
Patani

Equator
Muarakaman
2913
2707
Tomini
Muotong
Tilamuta
Gorontalo
UTARA
Kepulauan Bacan
Wosi

Samarinda
Donggala
Toboli
Parigi
Kepulauan Toglan
Teluk Tomini
Poh
Maliku
Luwuk
Peleng
Mandioli
Bacan
Bisa

Sungguminasa
Palu
Poso
Tojo
Toili
Banggai
Kepulauan Banggai
Mangole
Kepulauan Obilatu
Obi
Sesepe
Loji Fluk

Balikpapan
Lariang
TENGAH
2630
Kolonodale
Teluk Tolo
Taliabu
Auponhia
Sanana
Fluk

Tanahgrogot
SULAWESI (CELEBES)
Masamba
3016
Kepulauan Sula
Sanana

B

Jangeru
Balease
Kulu
Mamuju
Masama
Is Palopo
Kaupalamada Namlea
Pipu

Kepulauan Balabalangan (Paternoster)
Onang
Makale
Tangkeleboke
1782
Mendeodo
Manui
Buru 2429
Tifu Kayeli
Ambon

Kotabaru
Polewali
SELATAN
3455
Rantekombola
Mekongga
2790
Wamsasi
Leksula
Namlea
Ambon

Sebuku
Majene
Enrekang
Pinrang
Kolaka
Monse
TENGGARA
Kendari

Karambu
Teluk Mandar
Parepare
Pinrang
Raspang
Singkang
TELUK BONE
Wowoni

Pulau Laut
Polewali
Watansoppeng
Rappang
Pampanua
Watampone
Monse

Sumpangbinangae
Marek
INDONESIA

Pangkajene
Buapinang
Raha
Muna
Butung

Kepulauan Masalima
Ujung Pandang
Maros
Sinjai
Pising
Baybau
Lawele
Wangiwangi

Sunguminasa
Lompobatang
2871
Kabaena
Kepulauan Tukangbesi

Pattallassang
Bantaeng
Bulukumba
Binongko
BANDA

Bontosunggu
Salayar
Benteng
Batuata (Watuata I.)

Kepulauan Bone Rate
Gunungapi

Tanahjampea
Kalao
FLORES SEA
Kalaotoa
Damar

Lombok
Mojo
Tambora
2821
Sangeang
Bone Rate
Wetar
Wesiri
Ilwaki
Romang
Kepulauan

Rinjani
3726
Mataram
Sumbawa Besar
Raba
Komodo
Labuhanbaja
Ruteng
Larantuka
Adonara
Pantar
Kalabahi
Ataura
Bacan
Leti
Moa
Lakar

Selong
Taliwang
Dompu
Sape
Maumere
Solor
Lomblen
Alor
Selat Ombai
Dili
TIMOR
Btuala
Kepulauan Leti

Lesser Sunda Islands
Parado
Rinta
Aimere
Ende
Ponte
Macassar
Atapupu
Atambua
Timor
Qto-Udo
Viqueque

Sumbawa
Selat Sumba
Flores
NUSA TENGGARA TIMUR
Naikliu
Kefamenanu

NUSA TENGGARA BARAT
Memboro
Sumba
Waingapu
SAWU SEA
Periti
Soe
Nikiniki

Waikabubak
Melolo
Semau
Kupang
TIMOR SEA

Baing
Raijua
Sawu
Baa
Roti
Dana

ft m
12 000
9000
6000
4500
3000
1200
600
0

m
4000
3000
2000
1000
400
200
0

200 600
2000 6000
4000 12 000
6000 18 000
8000 24 000
m ft

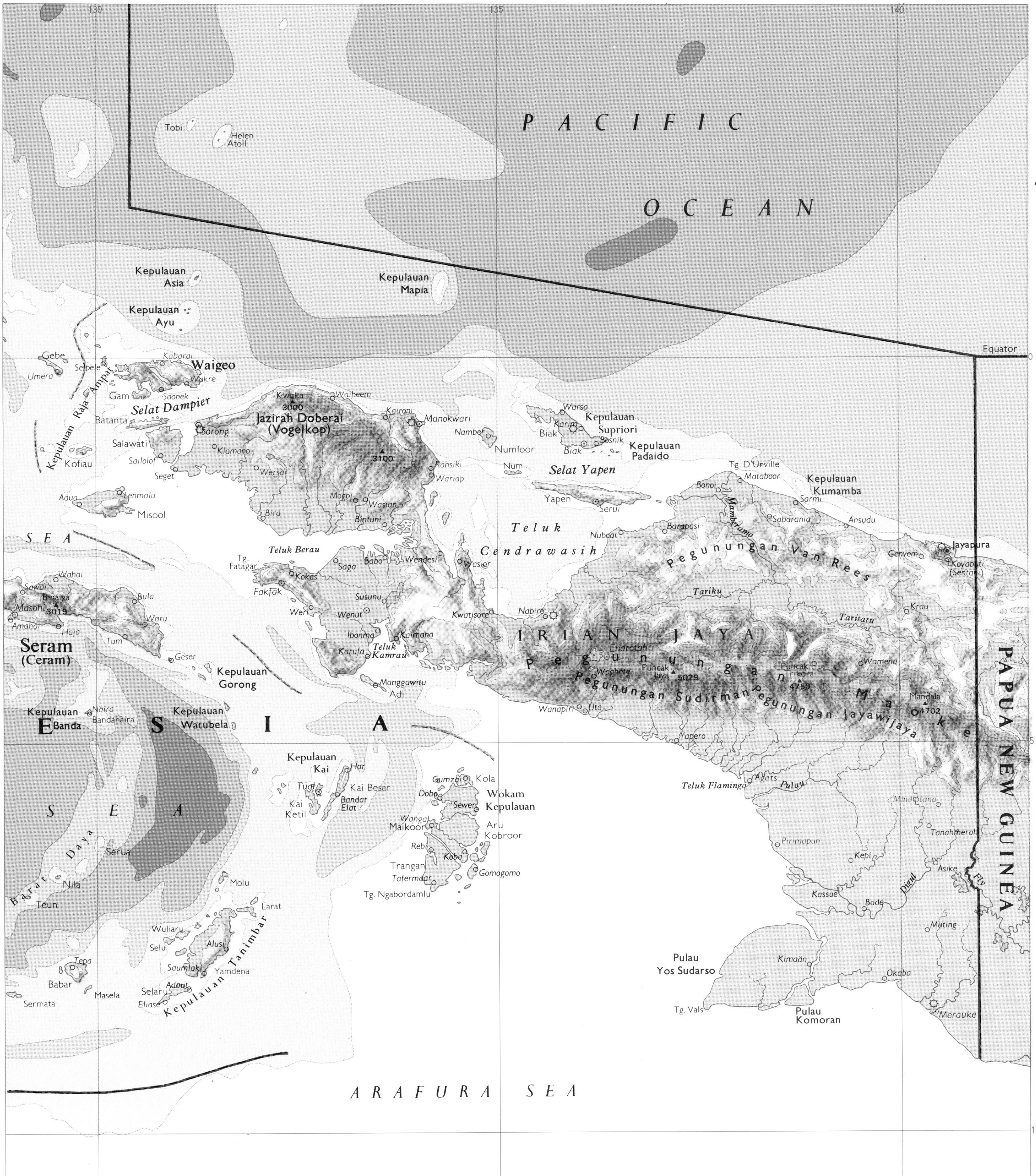

1 : 5 600 000

50 0 50 100 150 200 miles
50 0 50 100 150 200 250 300 km

4 5 6

130 135 140

P A C I F I C

O C E A N

A

Tobi

Helen
Atoll

Kepulauan
Asia

Kepulauan
Mapia

Kepulauan
Ayu

Equator

Gebe
Kabarai
Umera
Selpele
Waigeo
Wakre
Gam
Saonek
Selat Dampier
Batanta
Sorong
Klamono
Salawati
Sailolof
Kofiau
Seget
Adua
Lenmalu
Misool
Bira

Kepulauan Raja Ampat

Kwoka
3000
Waibeem
Kaironi
Jazirah Doberai
(Vogelkop)
Manokwari
Nambel
3100
Ransiki
Wariap
Mogol
Wasian
Bintuni

Warsa
Warsa
Kepulauan
Supriori
Biak
Bosnik
Biak
Num
Numfoor
Selat Yapen
Yapen
Serui
Kepulauan
Padaido

Bonoi
Mataboor
Tg. D'Urville
Kepulauan
Kumamba
Sarmi
Sabarania
Ansudu

Jayapura
Genyem
Koyabuti
(Sentani)

B

S E A

Wahai
Sowai
Binaiya
Masohi 3019
Amahai Haja
Seram
(Ceram)

Tg.
Fatagar
Kokas
Fakfak
Weri

Teluk Berau
Saga
Babo
Susunu
Wenut
Ibonma

Wendesi

Teluk
Cendrawasih
Wasior

Nuboai
Nabire
Kwatisore

Pegunungan Van Rees
Tariku
Taritatu
Krau

Bula
Waru
Tum
Geser
Kepulauan
Gorong

Kaimana
Teluk
Kamrau
Karufa
Manggawitu
Adi

I R I A N   J A Y A

Endarotali
Wopheng
Puncak
Jaya 5029
Uta
Wanapiri
Yapero

P e g u n u n g a n
Puncak
Trikora
4750
Pegunungan Sudirman Pegunungan Jayawijaya

Wamena

M a o k e
Mandala
4702

Kepulauan
Banda
Naira
Bandanaira
Kepulauan
Watubela

E   S   I   A

Kepulauan
Kai
Har
Tual
Kai Besar
Kai
Ketil
Bandar
Elat

Gumzai Kola
Dobo Sewer
Wokam
Kepulauan
Wangel
Maikoor
Rebi
Aru
Kobroor
Koba
Trangan
Tafermaar
Gomogomo
Tg. Ngabordamlu

Teluk Flaminga
Agats
Pulau

Mindiptana
Tanahmerah

S   E   A

Barat Daya
Serua
Nila
Molu
Teun
Larat

Pirimapun
Kepi
Kassue
Bade
Digul
Asike
Fly

Muting

Babar
Wuliaru
Selu
Alusi
Saumlaki
Yamdena
Sermata Masela
Selaru Adaut
Eliase
Kepulauan Tanimbar

Pulau
Yos Sudarso

Kimaän
Okaba

Tanahmerah

C

Tg. Vals
Pulau
Komoran
Merauke

A R A F U R A   S E A

D

P A P U A   N E W   G U I N E A

130 135 140 COPYRIGHT GEORGE PHILIP & SON LTD

4 5 6

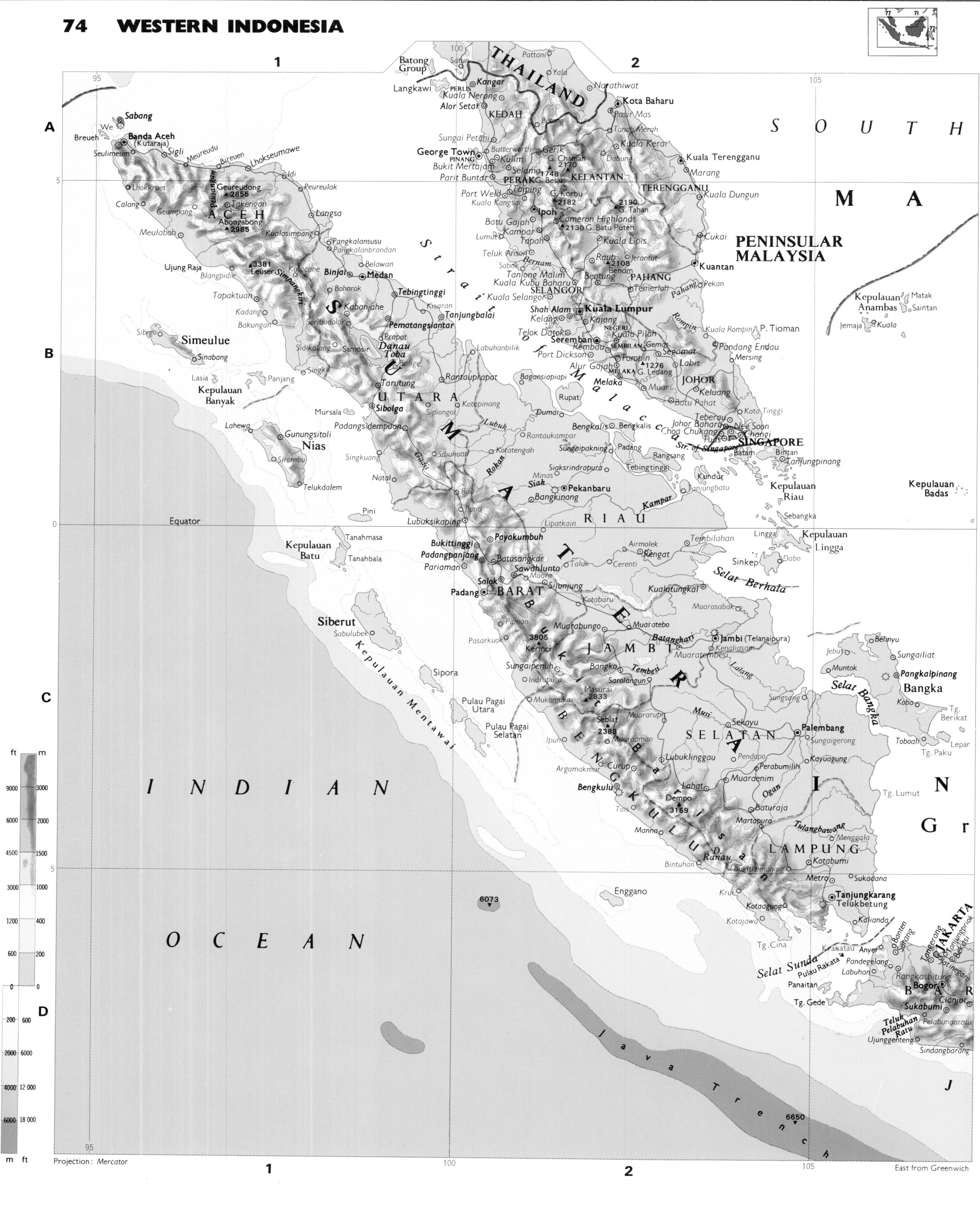

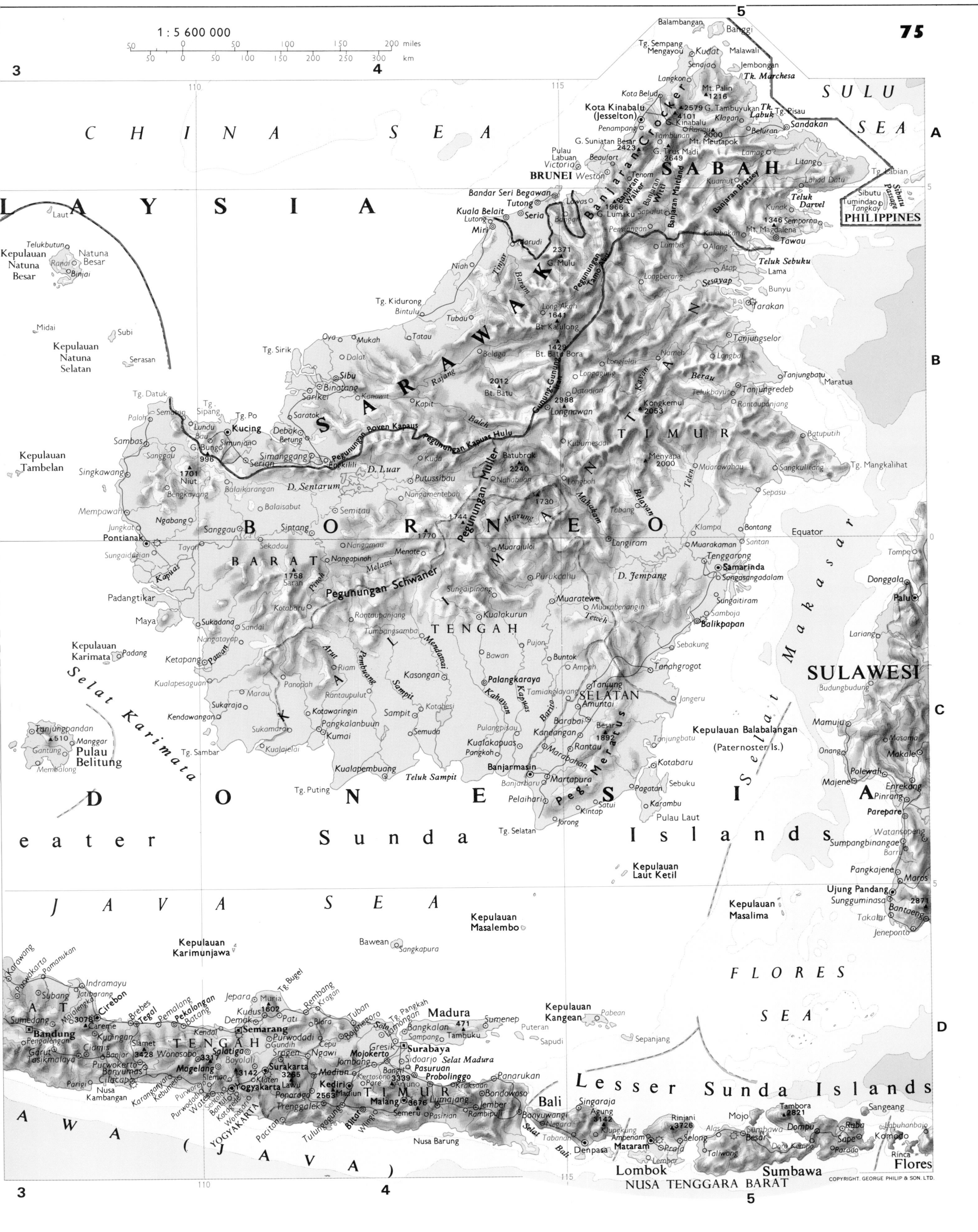

1 : 5 600 000

50   0   50   100   150   200 miles
50   0   50   100   150   200   250   300 km

3

C H I N A   S E A

4

115

5

Balambangan

Tg. Sampang
Mengayou · Kudat   Malawali
Sendjai   Jembongan
Langkon   Tk. Marchesa

A

Mt. Palin
▲1216

Kota Beludu   Banggi

S U L U
S E A

Kota Kinabalu
(Jesselton)   ▲2579 G. Tambuyukan Tk.
▲4101   Tg. Labuk   Pisau
G. Kinabalu   Klagan
Penampang   Rangin   Sandakan
Beluran
G. Suniatan Besar   Mt. Meutapok
2423   Timbunan   2000
Pulau
Labuan
Victoria   Beaufort   G. Trus Madi   Lamag
2649   Litang   Tg. Labian

BRUNEI   Weston   **SABAH**   Lahad Datu

Bandar Seri Begawan   Tenom   Walker   Maitland   Teluk
Tutong   Lowas   1966   Darvel   1346 Semporna
Kuala Belait   Seria   Lumaku   Pensiangan   Mt. Magdalena
Lutong   Alang   Teluk Sebuku
Miri   Lumbis   Atop   Lama

PHILIPPINES

Marudi   Bunyu

Niah   2371   Longberang   Sesayap   Tarakan
G. Mulu   Long Akah   Nameh
Tg. Kidurong   1641   Longpanang   Tanjungselor
Bintulu   Bt. Kalulong   Longgaung   Longbei
Tubau   1429   Tanjungbatu   Maratua
Oya · Mukah   Dalat   Bt. Batu Bora   Berau   Tanjungredeb
Tatau   2012   Telukbayur
Tg. Sirik   Beloga   Bt. Batu   Kongkemul   Batuputih
Sibu   Kapit   2988   ▲2053
Binatang   Rejang   Longnawan   Tg. Mangkalihat
Sarikei   Kanowit   Datadian   Sepaso

S A R A W A K   *K A L I M A N T A N   T I M U R*

Saratok   Balch   Kubumesaai
Debak   Betung   Pegunungan Boven Kapaus   Menyapa   Samboja
Lubau   Pegunungan Kapaus Hulu   2000
Kucing   Serian   Kuda   Batubrak   Muarawahau   Sangkulirang
G. Bungo   Engkilili   D. Luar   2240   Longboh   Telen   Santan
996   Putussibau   Nahabuan   Belayan   Makaham   Equator

B O R N E O

Sambas   1701   Balaikarangan   D. Sentarum   1730   Longiram
Niut   Bengkayang   Nangamentebah   1744   Murung   Muarakaman
Semitau   1770   Muarajuloi   Longnawan
Mempawah   Ngabang   Sanggau   Sintang   Nangamau   Santan

B A R A T   Tg. Mangkalihat

Padangtikar   Tayan   Sekadau   Melawi   Tenggarong
Maya   Nangapinoh   Menote   ● Samarinda
Kapuas   Sungaidjaran   1758   Purukcahu   Songosangadalam
Pontianak   Saran   Muaratewe   Sungaitiram

Kepulauan   Ngatayap   Sungaipinang   D. Jempang   ● Balikpapan
Karimata   Pawan   Kotabaru   Rantaupanjang   Samboja
Padang   Ketapang   Tumbangsamba   Muarabenangin   Sebakung
Kualapesaguan   Mendawai   Teweh   Tanahgrogot
Kendawangan   Panopah   Kasongan   Bawan   Pujon

K A L I M A N T A N   T E N G A H

Marau   Riam   Sampit   Buntok   Ampeh
Sukaraja   Pembuang   Kotabesi   Kualakurun   **Palangkaraya**
Sukadana   Kotawaringin   Sampit   Tamiangiayang
Sandai   Pangkalanbuun   Semuda   Pulangpisau   Tanjung

SULAWESI

Kumai   Pangkoh   Kahayan   **SELATAN**   Mamuju
Sukamara   Kualajelai   Barito   Amuntai   Masama
Kualakapuas   Barabai   Makale
Kualapembuang   1892   Marabahan   Rantau   Kotabaru
Teluk Sampit   Kandangan   Polewali
Tg. Puting   **Banjarmasin**   Majene   Enrekang

I N D O N E S I A

Tg. Selatan   Banjarbaru   Martapura   Sebuku   Pinrang
Pelaihari   Pagatan   **Parepare**
Jorong   Kintap   Pulau Laut   Kepulauan Balabalangan
Satui   Karambu   (Paternoster Is.)   Watansoping

G r e a t e r   *S u n d a*   *I s l a n d s*   Sumpangbinangae   Barri

Kepulauan   Pangkajene
Laut Ketil   Maros

Kepulauan   **Ujung Pandang**
Masalima   Sungguminasa   ▲2871

J A V A   S E A   Kepulauan   Bantaeng
Masalima   Takalar
Jeneponto

Kepulauan
Karimunjawa   Kepulauan   Masalembo
Bawean · Sangkapura

F L O R E S
S E A

Kepulauan
Kangean

Karawang · Pomanukan   Tg. Bugel   Madura
Subang   Jatibarang   Jepara   Muria   Rembang   Sumenep   Sepanjang
Indramayu   Brebes   Pemalang   471   Pati   Kragan   Tuban   Sampang
Pomanukan   ● **Cirebon**   Tegal   Pekalongan   Demak   Gundih   Lamongan   Bangkalan   Puteran
Sumedang   3078   Batang   1602   Kudus   Purwodadi   Ngawi   Gresik   Sampang   Tambuku   Sapudi
▲   Kuningan   Kendal   Slamet   Pati   Bidra   Bojonegoro   **Surabaya**
Bandung   Careme   ● **Semarang**   Sragen   Madiun   Sidoarjo   Pasuruan

Lesser   Sunda   Islands

Pengalengan   Ciamis   3428 Wonosobo   Boyolali   Jombang   **Mojokerto**   Probolinggo
Garut   3142   **Surakarta**   **Kediri**   Arjuno   Panarukan
Tasikmalaya   Banjar   3319   **Magelang**   Madiun   3339   **Pasuruan**   Bondowoso
Purwokerto   Banyumas   **Yogyakarta**   Lawu   2563   Pare   3676   Jember   Singaraja

T E N G A H   *T I M U R*   Rinjani
3726

Cilacap   Sleman   Kebumen   Ponorogo   Blitar   Lumajang   Rembipu   **Bali**   Tambora
Nusa   Karanganyar   Trenggalek   Tulungagung   Semeru   Pasirian   ▲2821
Kambangan   **YOGYAKARTA**   Wlingi   Agung   Mojo
3142   Dompu
Pacitan   Rinca
Klungkung   Raba
Mataram   Selong   Sumbawa   Sape   Parado
Nusa Barung   Denpasar   Negara   Ampenam   Alas   Sape
Praja   Taliwang   Dompo   **Flores**
Lombok   **Sumbawa**   Labuhanbaio
Selat   Komodo
Bali   Tabanan

A W A   *S u n d a*   Bali

3   110   **4**   115   **5**

J A V A   *NUSA TENGGARA BARAT*

COPYRIGHT GEORGE PHILIP & SON. LTD.

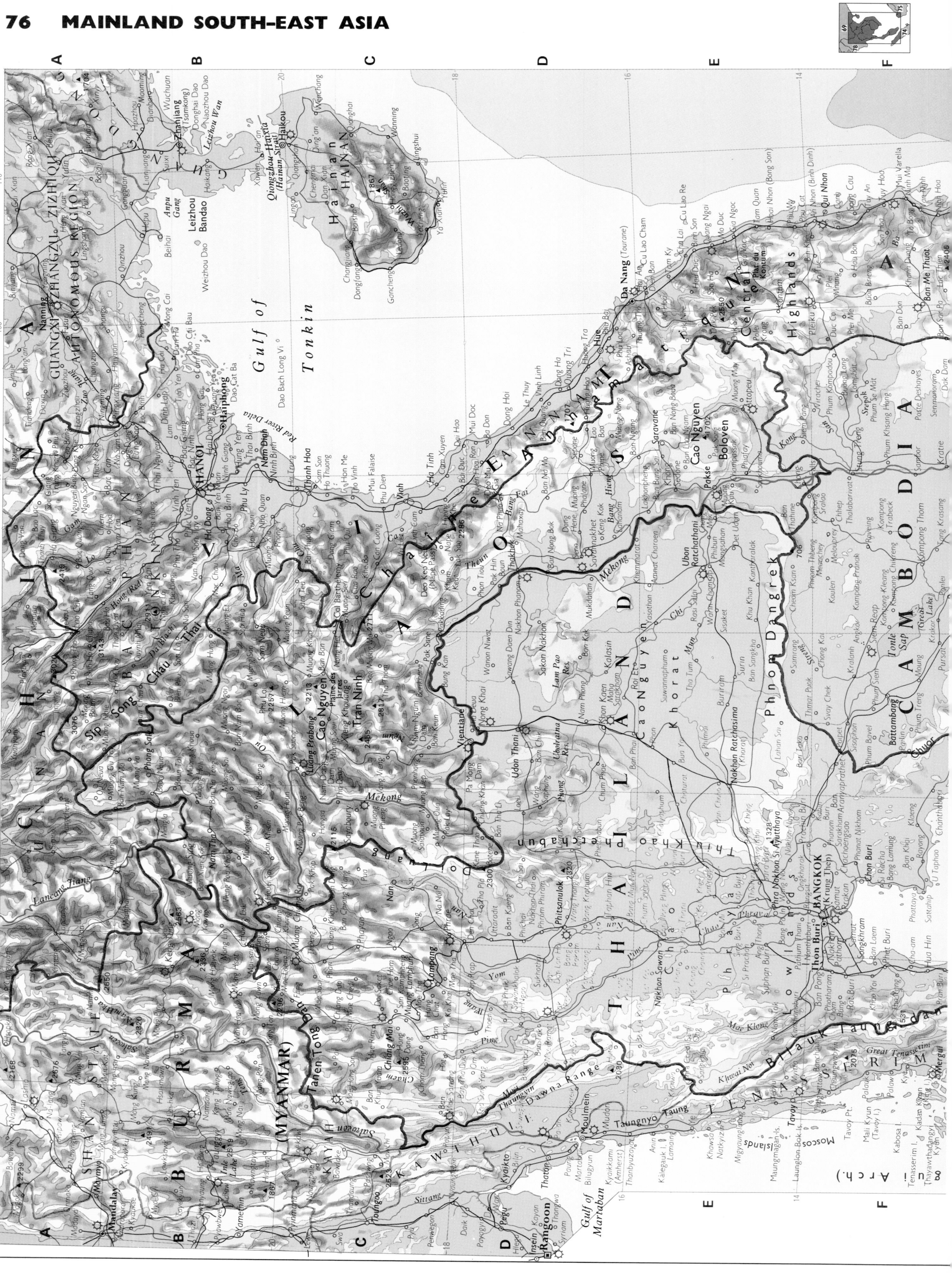

CHINA

GUANGXI ZHUANGZU ZIZHIQU (AUTONOMOUS REGION)

YUNNAN

HAINAN

Gulf of Tonkin

TONKIN

BAC PHAN

LAOS

VIETNAM

ANNAM

Annamitic Chain

Central Highlands

CAMBODIA

THAILAND

BURMA (MYANMAR)

SHAN STATE

KAYAH

Dawna Range

Tenasserim

TENASSERIM

Khorat

Phnom Dangrek

Central Lowlands

Thiu Khao Phetchabun

Menam Lowlands

HANOI

Haiphong

Red River Delta

Thanh Hoa

Vinh

Da Nang (Tourane)

Hue

Luang Prabang

Vientiane

Cao Nguyen

Boloven

Pakse

Ubon Ratchathani

Nakhon Ratchasima (Khorat)

BANGKOK (Krung Thep)

Thon Buri

Ayutthaya

Phitsanulok

Chiang Mai

Lampang

Battambang

Tonle Sap (Great Lake)

Phnom Penh

Mandalay

Rangoon

Pegu

Moulmein

Tavoy (Tavoy)

Mergui

Nanning

Zhanjiang

Leizhou Bandao

Haikou

Qiongzhou Haixia (Hainan Strait)

Gulf of Marthaban

Mekong

Lancang Jiang

Salween

Gulf of Tonkin

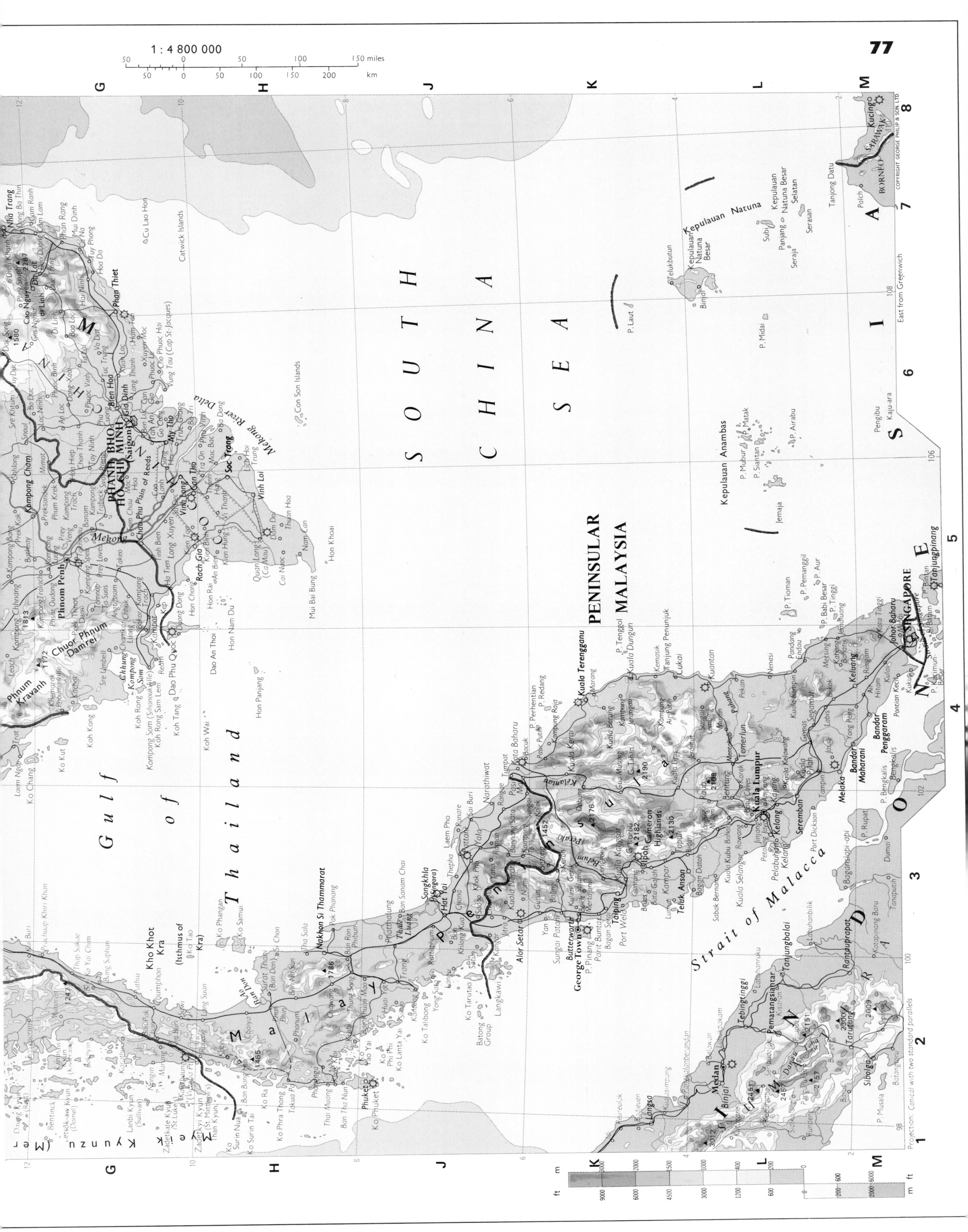

1 : 4 800 000

50   0   50   100   150 miles
50 0 50 100 150 200 km

SOUTH

CHINA

SEA

Gulf

of

Thailand

PENINSULAR
MALAYSIA

Kepulauan Natuna

Kepulauan
Natuna Besar

Tanjong Datu

BORNEO

Kepulauan Anambas

Strait of Malacca

SINGAPORE

Isthmus of
Kra (Isthmus of
Kra)

Kuala Lumpur

George Town
Butterworth

Alor Setar

Nakhon Si Thammarat

Songkhla
(Singora)

Hat Yai

Kuala Terengganu

Melaka

Phnom Penh

HO CHI MINH
(Saigon)
PHANH BHO

Mekong River Delta

Soc Trang

Medan

Pematangsiantar

Tebingtinggi

East from Greenwich

Projection: Conical with two standard parallels

COPYRIGHT GEORGE PHILIP & SON LTD

ft   m
9000
6000
4500
3000
1200
600
0

m   ft
6000
2000
1000
400
200
0

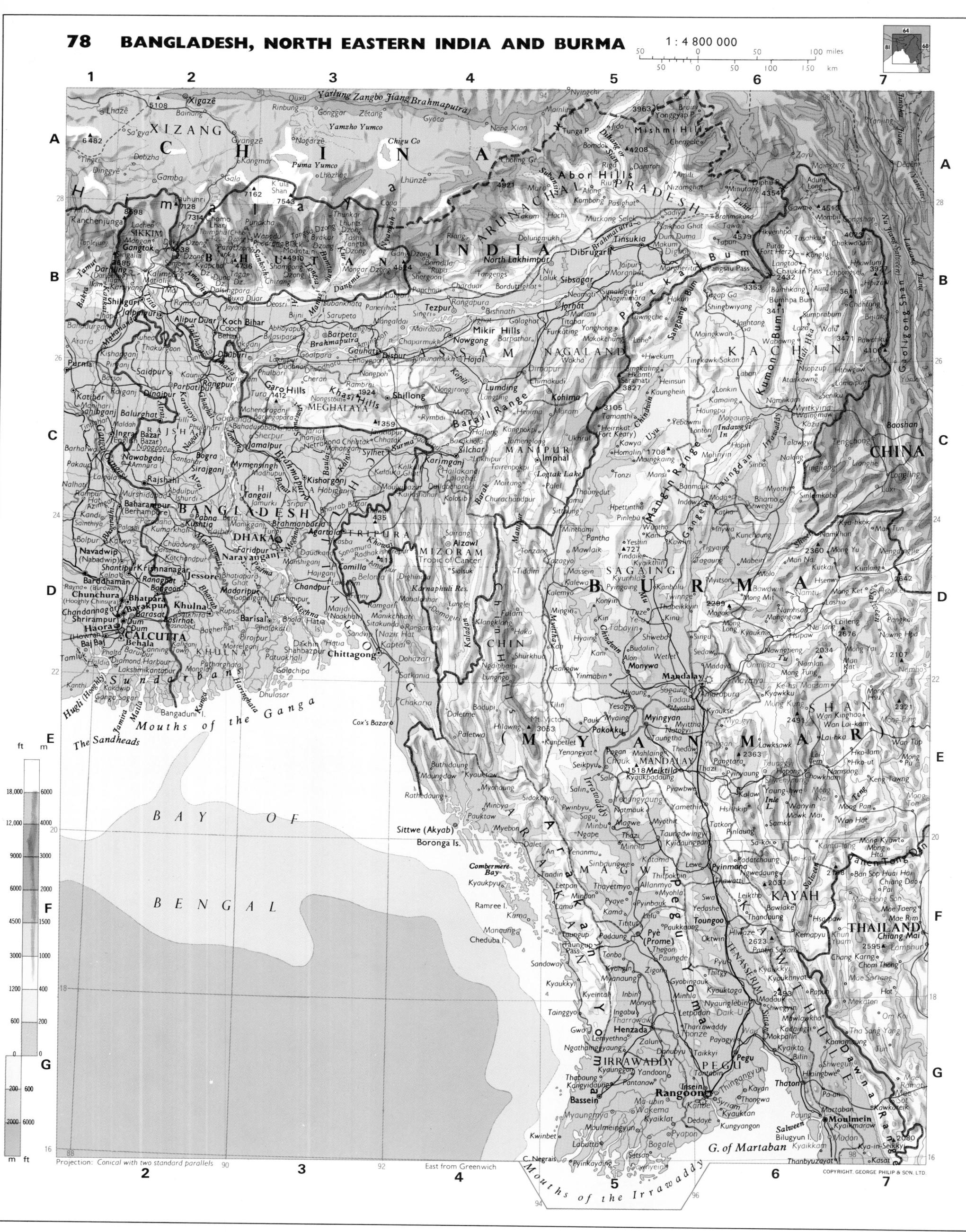

1 : 4 800 000

50   0   50   100 miles

50   0   50   100   150 km

| 1 | 2 | 3 | 4 | 5 | 6 | 7 |

XIZANG

Yarlung Zangbo Jiang Brahmaputra

C H I N A

ARUNACHAL PRADESH

Abor Hills

Mishmi Hills

SIKKIM

BHUTAN

I N D I A

NAGALAND

KACHIN

ASSAM

Mikir Hills

MEGHALAYA

Garo Hills

Khasi Hills

Barail Range

MANIPUR

Imphal

CHINA

BANGLADESH

DHAKA

TRIPURA

MIZORAM

Tropic of Cancer

SAGAING

BURMA

CALCUTTA

KHULNA

Chittagong

CHIN

MANDALAY

SHAN

Sundarbans

Mouths of the Ganga

The Sandheads

Cox's Bazar

Sittwe (Akyab)

Boronga Is.

B A Y   O F

B E N G A L

Combermere Bay

MAGWE

MYANMAR

KAYAH

THAILAND

Chiang Mai

Ramree I.

Cheduba I.

IRRAWADDY

PEGU

Bassein

Rangoon

Moulmein

G. of Martaban

Mouths of the Irrawaddy

C. Negrais

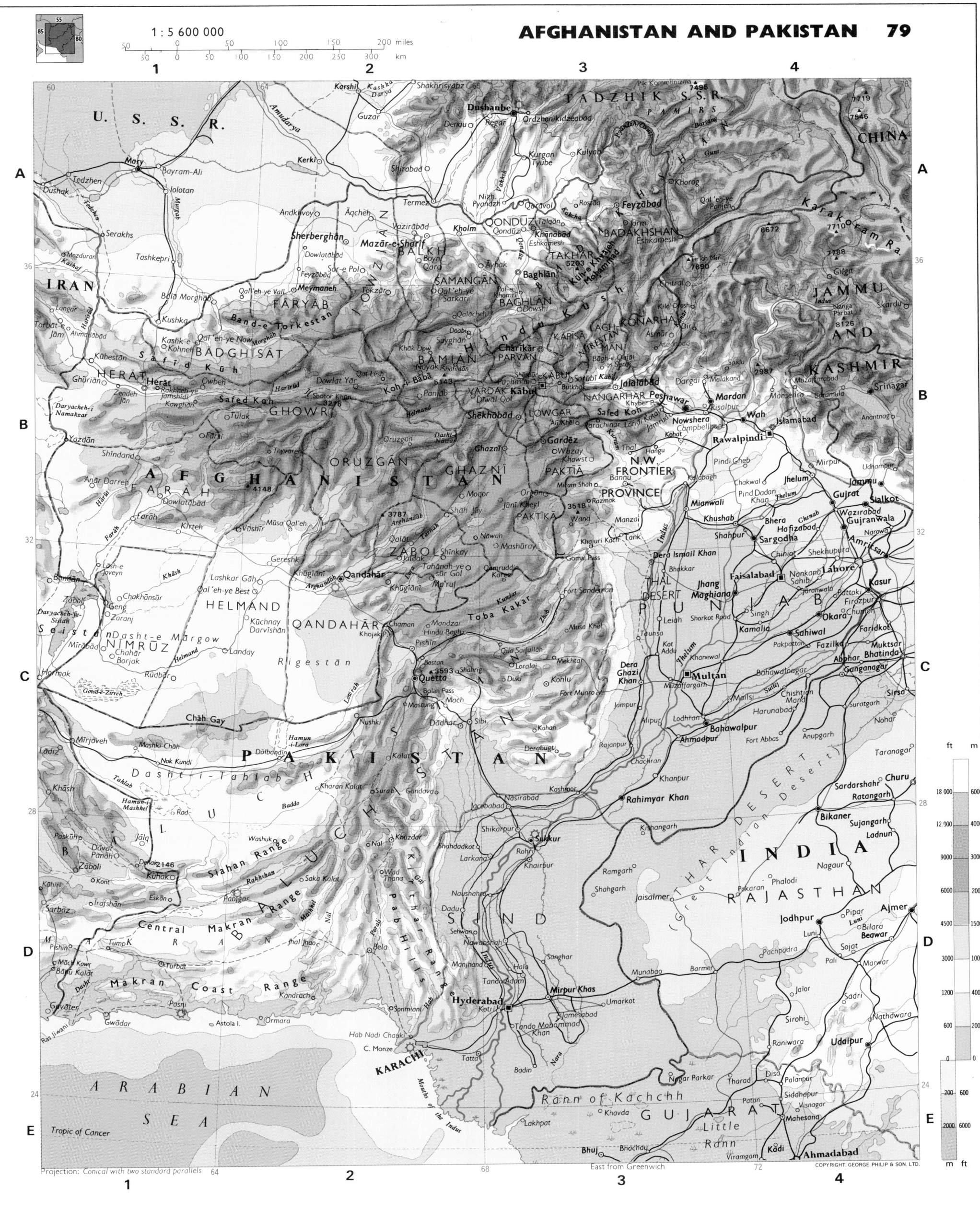

1 : 5 600 000

Projection: Conical with two standard parallels

East from Greenwich

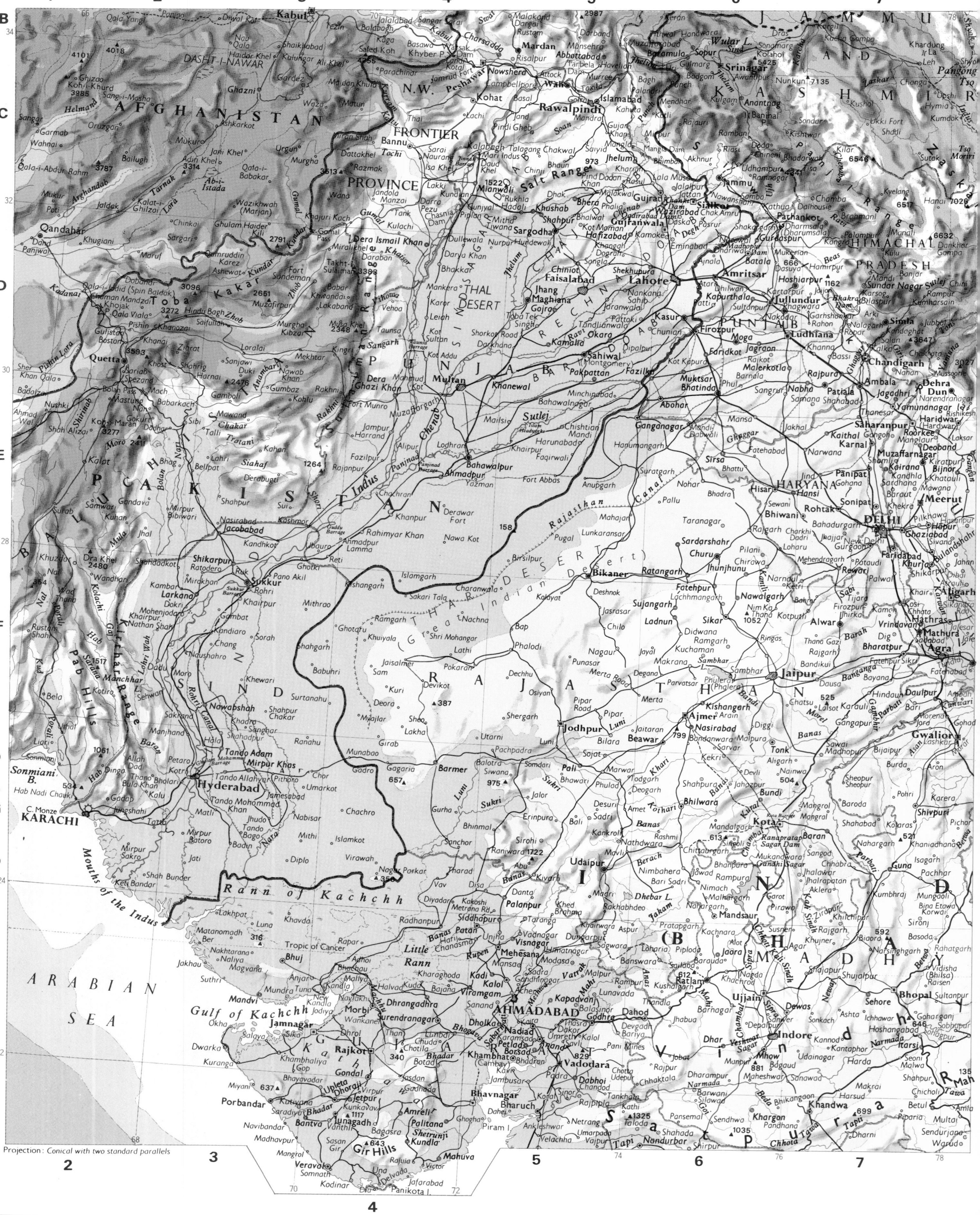

AFGHANISTAN

PAKISTAN

BALUCHISTAN

N.W. FRONTIER PROVINCE

PUNJAB

SIND

THAL DESERT

THAR DESERT (Great Indian Desert)

RAJASTHAN

HARYANA

HIMACHAL PRADESH

KASHMIR

JAMMU

GUJARAT

MADHYA PRADESH

ARABIAN SEA

Rann of Kachchh

Little Rann

Gulf of Kachchh

Mouths of the Indus

Salt Range

Kakar Range

Kirthar Range

Sulaiman Range

Pab Hills

Gir Hills

Tropic of Cancer

Kabul · Kandahar · Ghazni · Quetta · Peshawar · Rawalpindi · Islamabad · Mardan · Kohat · Bannu · Dera Ismail Khan · Dera Ghazi Khan · Multan · Lahore · Amritsar · Jullundur · Ludhiana · Chandigarh · Simla · Jammu · Srinagar · Sialkot · Gujranwala · Faisalabad · Jhang · Sargodha · Bahawalpur · Rahimyar Khan · Sukkur · Shikarpur · Jacobabad · Larkana · Hyderabad · KARACHI · Mirpur Khas · Jaisalmer · Jodhpur · Barmer · Bikaner · Ganganagar · Hisar · Rohtak · DELHI · New Delhi · Meerut · Saharanpur · Dehra Dun · Haridwar · Karnal · Panipat · Sonipat · Ghaziabad · Aligarh · Mathura · Agra · Gwalior · Bharatpur · Jaipur · Ajmer · Beawar · Udaipur · Bhilwara · Kota · Bundi · Ahmadabad · Vadodara · Rajkot · Jamnagar · Bhavnagar · Bhuj · Porbandar · Junagadh · Veraval · Indore · Ujjain · Dewas · Bhopal · Ratlam

Sutlej · Indus · Chenab · Jhelum · Ravi · Beas · Luni · Banas · Chambal · Narmada · Tapti · Mahi · Sabarmati

Projection: Conical with two standard parallels

ft m
18,000 6000
12,000 4000
9000   3000
6000   2000
4500   1500
3000   1000
1200   400
600   200
0   0
        200 600
        2000 6000
m ft

ARABIAN SEA

1 : 4 800 000
50 0 50 100 miles
50 0 50 100 150 km
8 9 10
JAMMU AND KASHMIR
On same scale as Main Map
5 6 7
A B C D E F G H J
C H I N A
Karakoram Range
Deosai Mountains
N.W. FRONTIER PROVINCE
PUNJAB
JAMMU AND KASHMIR
Zaskar Mountains
Ladakh Range
HIMACHAL PRADESH
Kunlun Shan
SODA PLAINS
Aksai Chin
Nganglong Kangri
Gangdisê Shan
XIZANG (TIBET)
NEPAL
Mahabharat Range
Siwalik Range
UTTAR PRADESH
BIHAR
MADHYA PRADESH
BANGLADESH
BHUTAN
SIKKIM
ASSAM
Rajmahal Hills
Kaimur Hills
Maikala Range
Garo Hills
Sundarbans
Mouths of the Ganga
The Sandheads
Mt. Everest 8848
Kanchenjunga
Katmandu
Lucknow
Kanpur
Allahabad
Varanasi
Patna
Calcutta
Srinagar
Rawalpindi
Islamabad
Jammu
Dhaka
Jabalpur
Ranchi
Jamshedpur
East from Greenwich
8 9 10 11 12 13

COPYRIGHT, GEORGE PHILIP & SON, LTD.

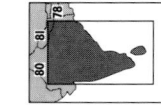

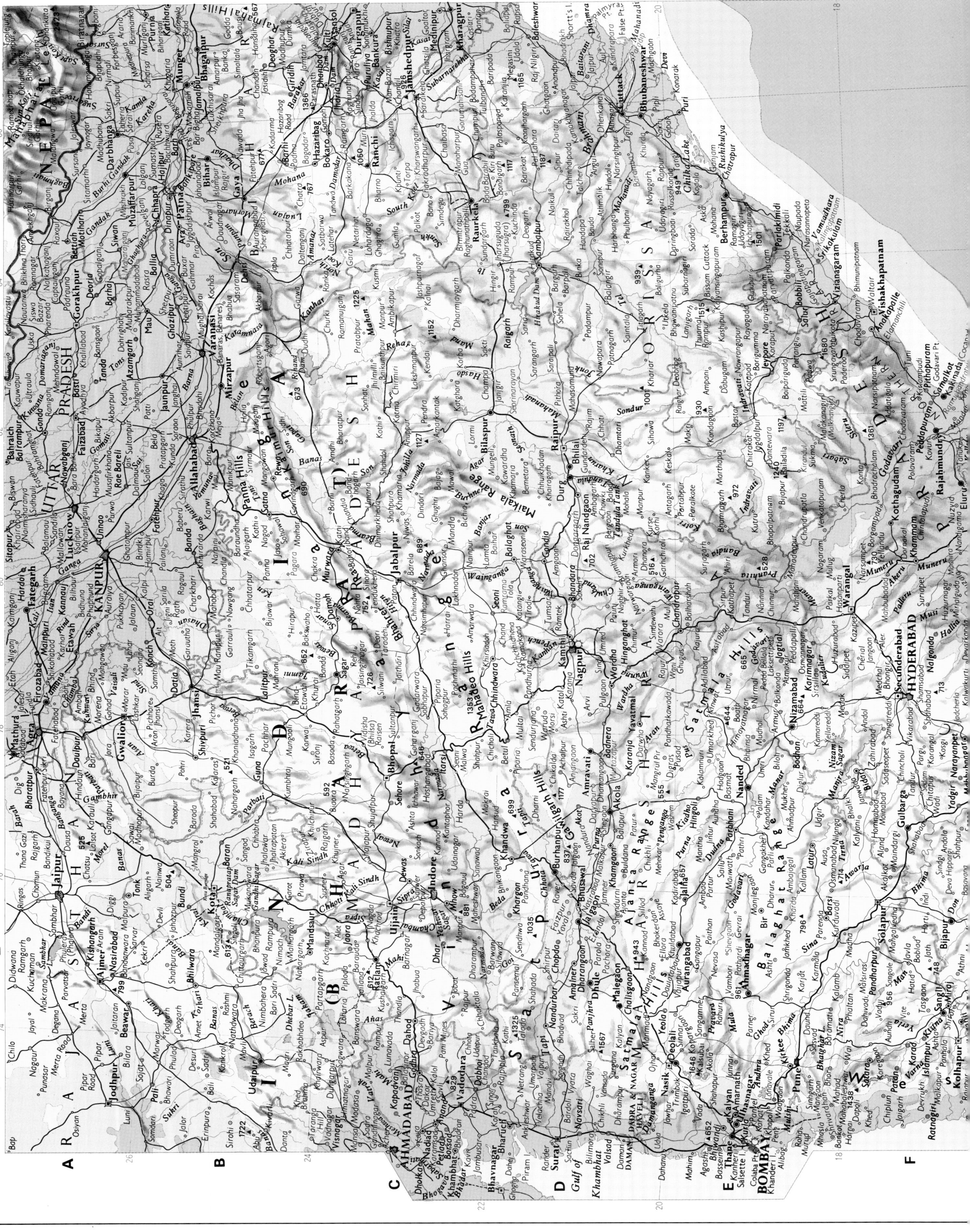

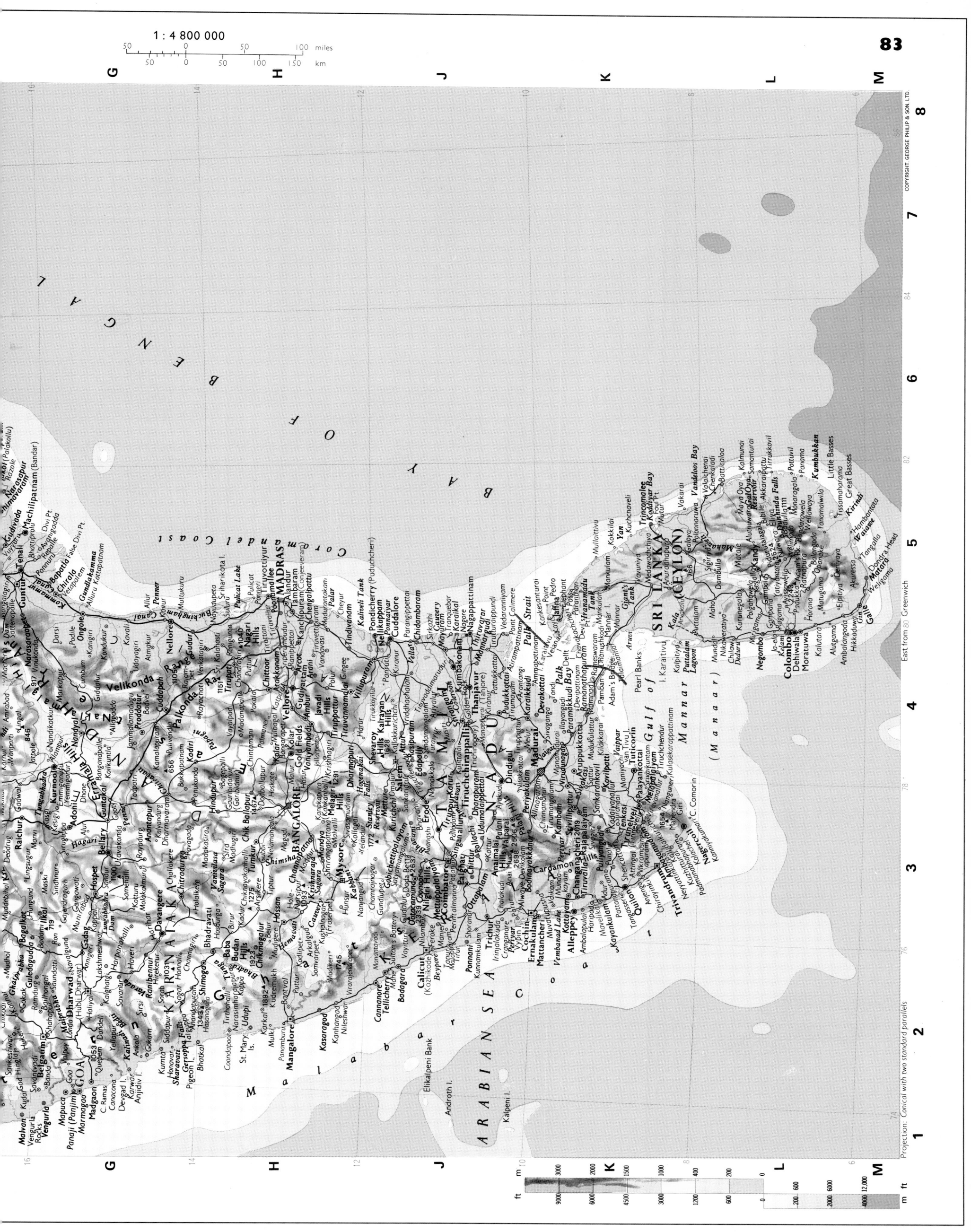

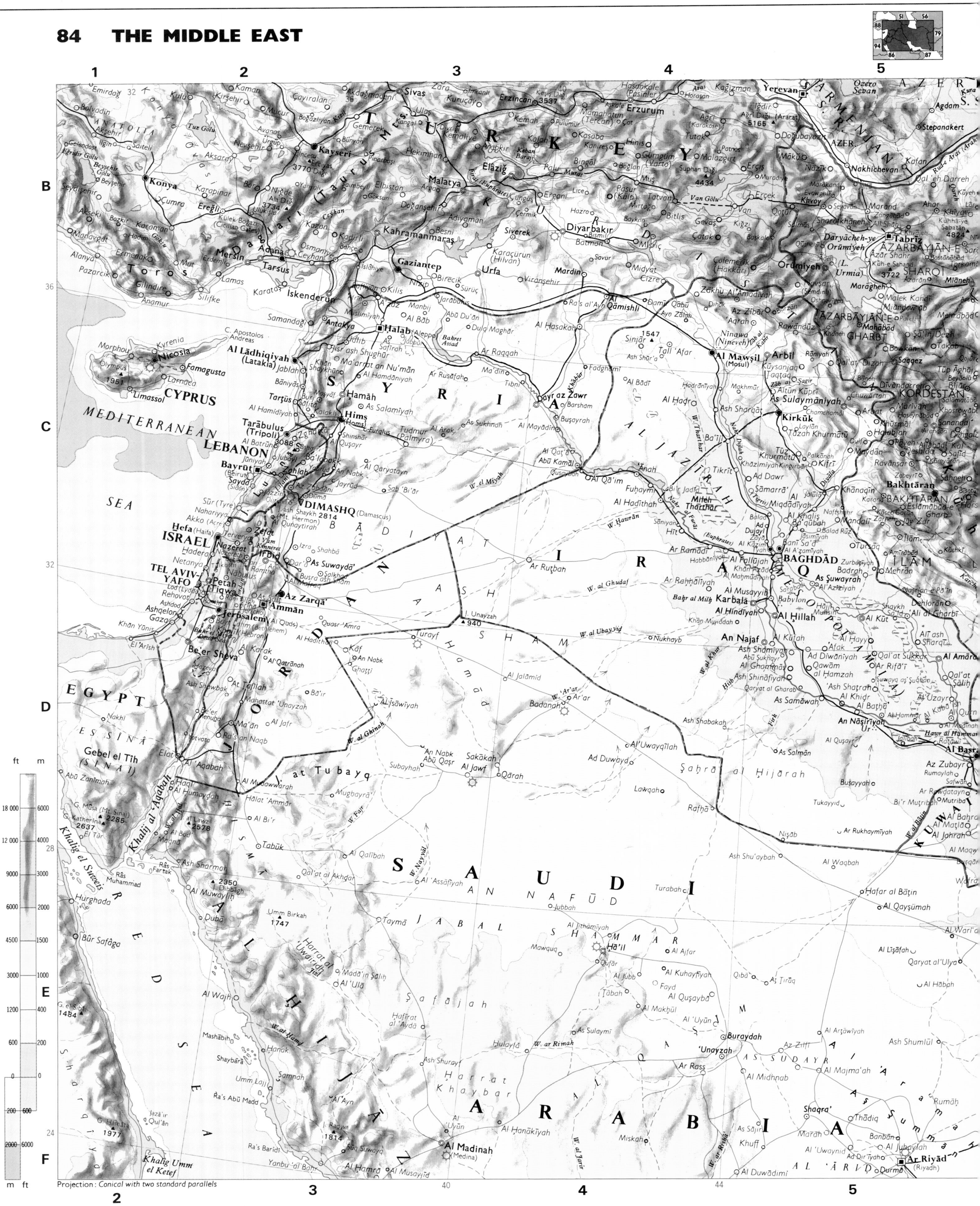

1   2   3   4   5

A

B

TURKEY

ANATOLIA

Konya

Kayseri

Malatya

Elâzığ

Diyarbakır

Erzurum

Yerevan

ARMENIAN S.S.R.

AZER.

Tabriz

ĀZARBĀYJĀN-E GHARBI

ĀZARBĀYJĀN-E SHARQĪ

Orūmīyeh

Mersin
Tarsus
Adana
Gaziantep
Urfa
Mardin
Al Qāmishlī
Al Mawşil (Mosul)
Arbīl
KORDESTĀN
Kirkūk

C

CYPRUS
Nicosia
Famagusta
Limassol

MEDITERRANEAN

SEA

Al Lādhiqīyah (Latakia)
Halab
Aleppo
SYRIA
Ḥamāh
Ar Raqqah
Dayr az Zawr
Tarṭūs
Ḥimṣ (Homs)
Tarābulus (Tripoli)
LEBANON
Bayrūt (Beirut)
Şaydā
AL JAZĪRAH

As Sulaymānīyah

Sāmarrā'

Tudmur (Palmyra)

Tikrīt

Bakhtārān

D

ISRAEL
Ḥefa (Haifa)
TEL AVIV-YAFO
DIMASHQ (Damascus)
Jerusalem (Al Quds)
'Ammān
Az Zarqā'
JORDAN
Be'er Sheva

Ar Ruṭbah

IRAQ
BAGHDĀD
Karbalā'
An Najaf
Al Hillah
Al Kūt
Al 'Amārah

Al Baṣrah
Az Zubayr

EGYPT
SINAI
Gebel el Tih (SINAI)
Al 'Aqabah
Khalīj al 'Aqabah

AN NAFŪD

SAUDI

Ḥā'il

E

RED SEA

HIJĀZ

Tabūk

Buraydah
'Unayzah
Ar Rass

AL 'ĀRID

F

ARABIA

Al Madīnah (Medina)

Ar Riyāḍ (Riyadh)

KUWAIT

Projection: Conical with two standard parallels

2   3   40   4   44   5

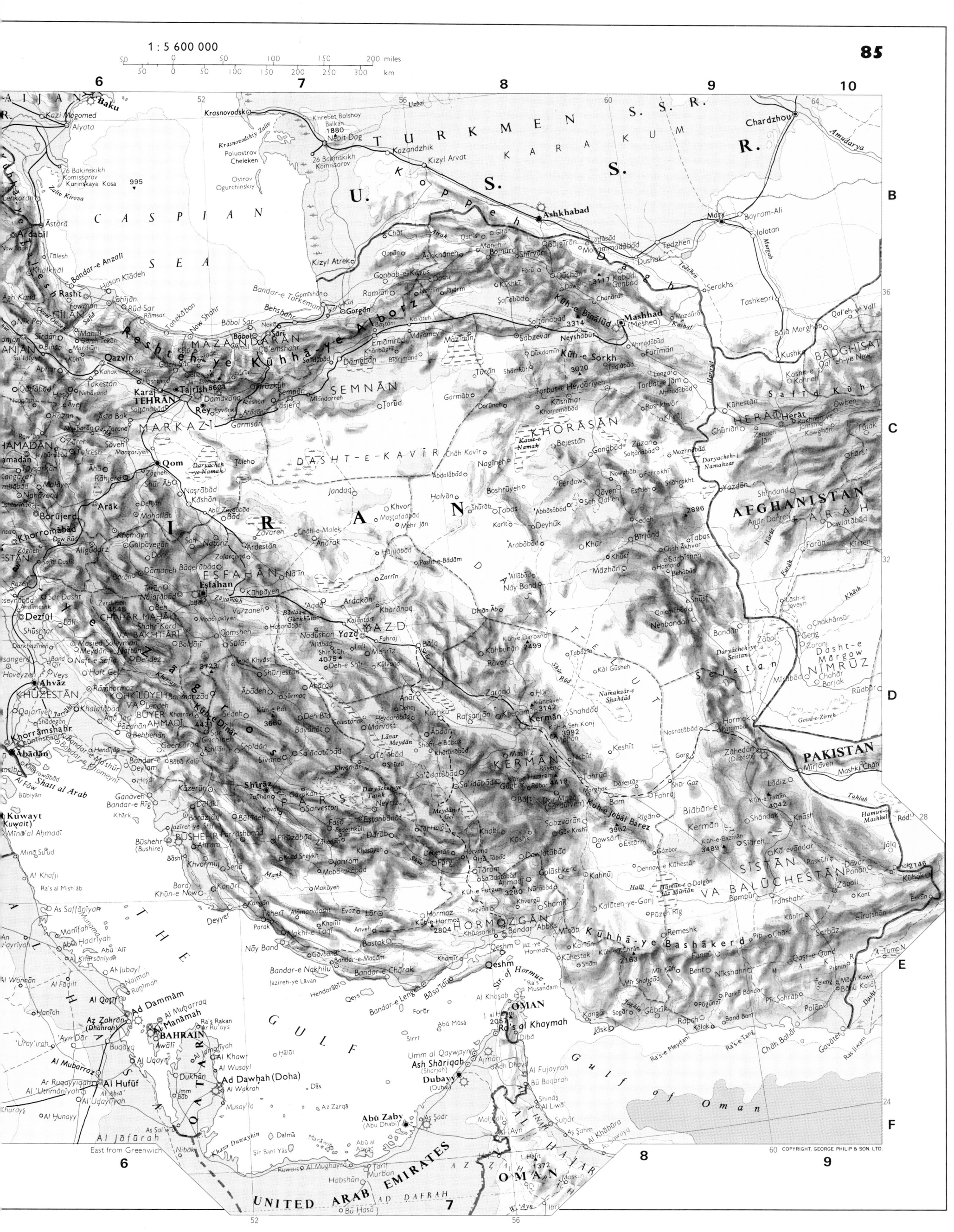

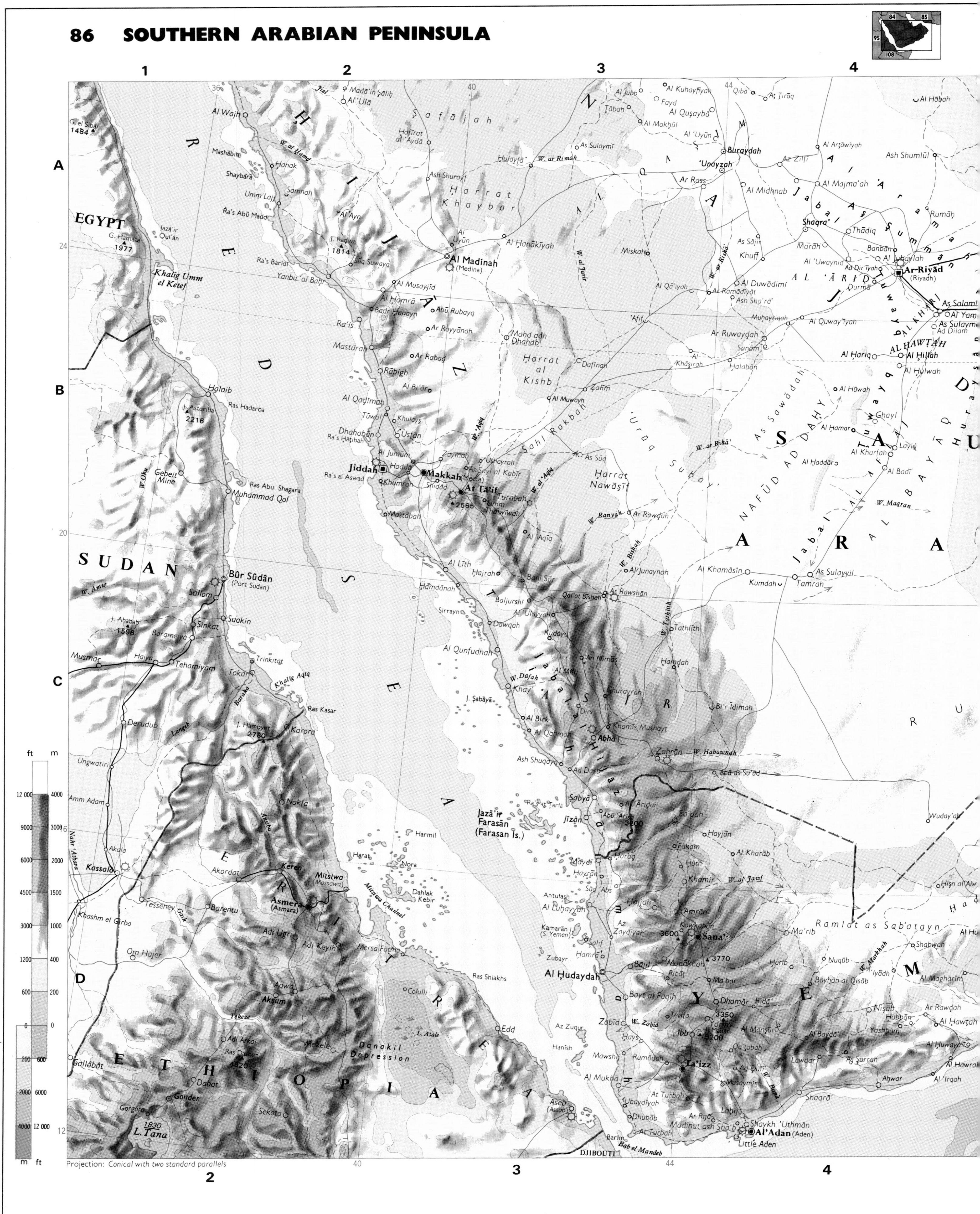

84 85
95
108

1 2 3 4

A

B

C

D

EGYPT

G. el Sibâ'i
1484

G. Hamâta
1977

Mashâbih
Hanak
Shaybârâ
Umm Lajj
Ra's Abū Madd

Al Wajh
Tjal
Madā'in Şālih
Al 'Ulā
Hafīrat al 'Aydā
Hulayfā'
W. ar Rimah

HIJAZ

Şafā'jah

N

Al Kuhayfiyah
Al Jubb
Fayd
Al Quşaybā
Al Makhūl
Al 'Uyūn

Qibā
Aş Tirāq
Al Hābah
Al Arţāwīyah
Ash Shumlūl

Bur0aydah
'Unayzah
Ar Rass
Al Majma'ah
Az Zilfī
Al Midhnab

Khalig Umm el Ketef

Ra's Bāridī
Yanbu' al Baḥr
Al Musayyid
Al Homrā
Badr Hunayn
Ra'īs

Al 'Ayn
J. Radwā
1814
Al 'Uyūn
Al Honākīyah
Miskah

Al Madinah (Medina)

Harrat Khaybar

Al Qā'iyah
'Afīf

Ar Ruwaydah

Shaqra'
Thādiq
Rumāḥ
Banbān
Marāh
Al 'Uwaynid
Ad Dir'īyah
Ar-Riyād (Riyadh)
Durma
As Salamī

SUDAN

Halaib
Ras Hadarba
Astarība
2216

Gebeit Mine
Ras Abu Shagara
Muhammad Qol

Mastūrah
Rābigh
Al Bī'ar

Ar Rabaq
Mahd adh Dhahab

Harrat al Kishb

Al Quway'īyah
Ad Dilam
Al Yam
As Sulaymī

AL HAWTAH
Al Hilah
Al Hulwah
Al Hariq
Al Khāşirah
Dāfinah

As SAWĀDAH
Al Hūwah
Al Hamar
Ghayl
Al Haddah
Al Hūwah
Laylā
Al Kharfah
Al Badī'

Bûr Sûdân (Port Sudan)
Sallom
Suakin
Sinkat
J. Abadah
1596
Barameiya
Tehamiyam
Musmar
Hai'ya
Trinkitat
Tokar
Derudub

Al Qadīmah
Tūwal
Dhahabān
Ra's Hâtibah
Al Jumūm

Jiddah
Hadda
Khumrah
Makkah (Mecca)
Shidād
At Tā'if
2566
Umm Thalwīwan
Turabah

Zaymah
Ushayrah
As Sayl al Kabīr
W. al 'Aqiq

Sahl Rakbah
Al Muwayh

'Urūq Subay'

Harrat Nawāşīt

Al Khişrah
Halabān

SA
NAFŪD AD DAHY

AL 'ĀRID

HU
Jabal Al Ţuwayq

Khulays
Usfān
Mastabah

Ranyah
Ar Rawdah

Al Junaynah

Kumdah
Tamrah
As Sulayyil

ARA

W. Maqran

Ra's al Aswad

Al Līth
Hajrah

Banī Sār
Baljurshi
Al Ulayyah
Dawqah

Qal'at bīshah
Ar Rawshan

W. Tabbah
Tathlīth

Hamdānah
Sirrayn

Al Qunfudhah

Kudays
An Nimāş
Al Miftā

Hamdah

R
U

Musmar
Haiya
Ungwatiri
Amm Adam
Kassala

Derudub
Langeb
J. Hamoyet
2780
Karora
Ras Kasar
Khalig Aqiq

J. Şabāyā
Al Birk
Al Qahmah

W. Dūfah
Khay...

Jabal 'Asīr

Dirs
Ghurayrah
Bi'r Idimah

Khamīs Mushayt
Abhā
3200
Zahrān
W. Habawnah
Abū as Su'ūd

Akala
Mitsiwa
(Massawa)

Ash Shuqayq
Ad Darb

Wuday'ah

Nakfa
Arebu

ERITREA

Akordat
Keren
Adi Ugri

Harat
Nora

Jazā'ir Farasān (Farasan Is.)

Ra's Tartā
Şabyā
Al 'Āriḍah
Jīzān
Hayjān
Al Kharāb

Fakam
Hayjān

Hişn al Abr
Khamir
W. al Jawf

Tessenei
Barentu
Asmera (Asmara)
Adi Keyih
Mersa Fatma
Dahlak Kebir
Antufash
Al Luhayyah

Harad
Khamir
Şa'dah
Hūth
W. al Jawf
Nuqūb
Shabwah

Om Hajer

Adwa
Aksum

Colulli
Kamarān (S. Yemen)
Salif
Zaydīyah
Az Zubayr
Hamrā'

Şa'fān
Sāq 'Abs
Hajjah
Amrān
Munakhah
3600
Kawkabān
Sana' (Şan'ā')

Ma'rib
Ribāt
Ramlat as Sab'atayn
Al Hu...

M

Khashm el Garba
Gallābāt

ETHIOPIA

Adi Arkoi
Ras Dashen
...
Dabat
Gondor
Gorgora
1830
L. Tana
Sekota
Mekele

Tekeze

Ras Shiakhs
Al Hudaydah

Danakil Depression

Colulli
L. Asale

Az Zuqur
Hanish

Edd

Mawshij

Bājil
Bayt al Faqīh
Zabīd
W. Zabīd
Hays
Rumādah
Al Mukhā
Ubaydīyah

Dhamār
Tefla
3350
Ibb
3200
Ma'bar

3770
Al Manşūr
La'izz
Al Bayḍ
Al Dhāli'
Musayyir
Laḥij

Yashbum
Nişāb
Hubbān
Al Hawtah
Al Rawḍah
Al Mogharīm

Lawdar
Aṣ Şurrah
Al Huwaymto
Aḥwar
Al Hawta
Al Irqah

YEME

Ar Rijā'
Shaykh 'Uthmān
Madīnat ash Sha'b
Al'Adan (Aden)
Little Aden

Dhubāb
At Turbah
Barim
Bab el Mandeb

DJIBOUTI

Aşeb (Assab)

40 3 44 4

Projection: Conical with two standard parallels

ft m
12 000 4000
9000   3000
6000   2000
4500   1500
3000   1000
1200   400
600   200
0   0
200   600
2000   6000
4000 12 000
m ft

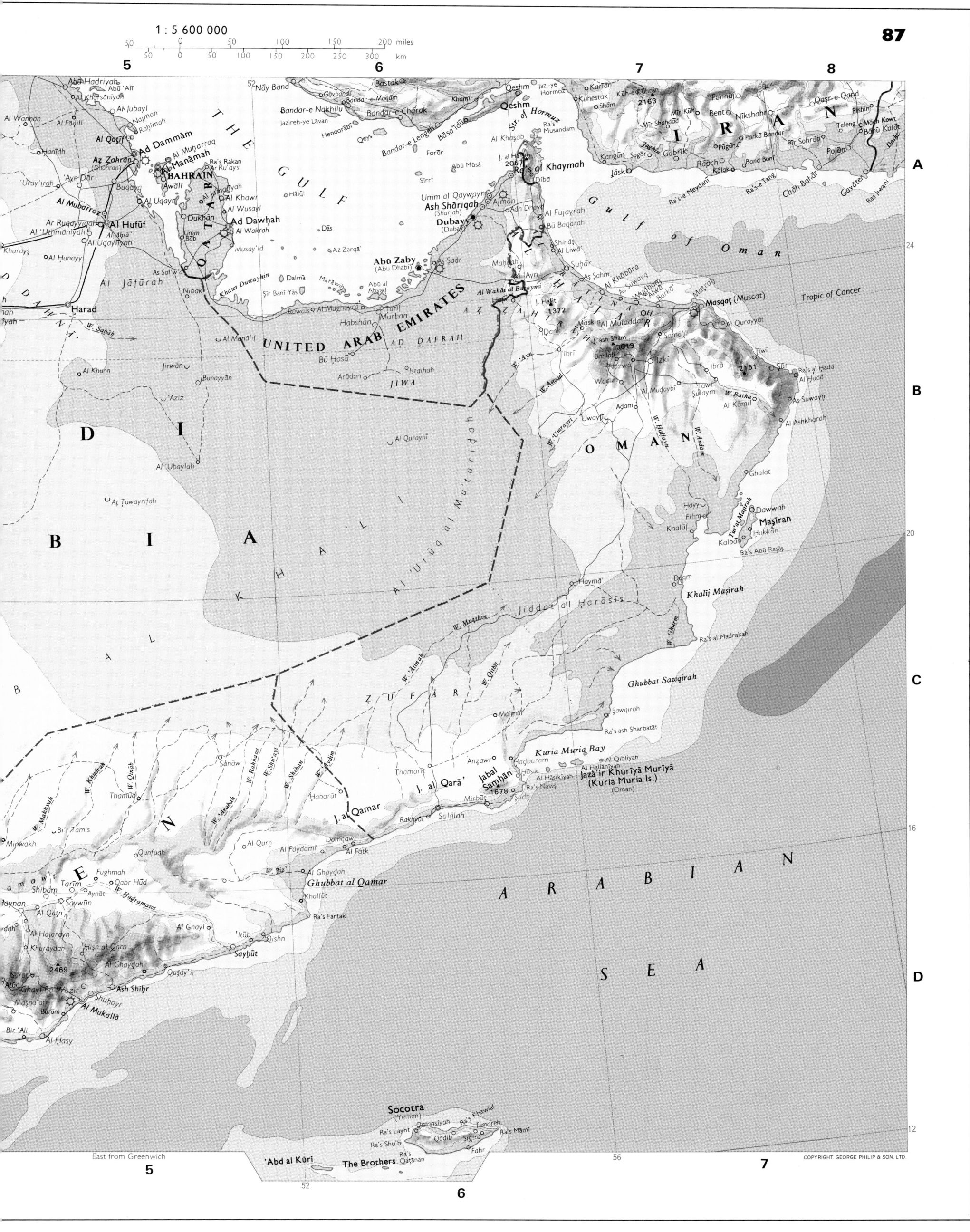

1 : 5 600 000

50   0   50   100   150   200 miles

50   0   50   100   150   200   250   300 km

5   **6**   **7**   **8**

Abū Hadriyah
Abū 'Alī
Al Kharsānīyah
Al Jubayl
Al Wannān
Al Faḍilī
Najmah
Raḥīmah
Al Qaṭīf
'Uray'irah
Ḥanīdh
Az Zahrān
(Dhahran)
Ad Dammām
Al Muḥarraq
Al Manāmah
Ra's Rakan
Ra's Ru'ays
BAHRAIN
Awālī
Ayn Dār
Buqayq
Al Mubarraz
Ar Ruqayyiqah
Al Ḥufūf
Al 'Uthmānīyah
Al Jishā
Al 'Uḍaylīyah
Ḥawr al 'Udayd
Dukhān
Umm Bāb
Ad Dawḥah
Al Wakrah
Khurayṣ
Al Hunayy

Nāy Band
52
Bastak
Gāvbandi
Bandar-e Magām
Bandar-e Nakhīlū
Bandar-e Chārak
Jazīreh-ye Lāvan
Hendorābī
Qeys
Forūr
Abū Mūsā
Sirrī
Bandar-e Lengeh
Bāsa Īdū
Khamīr
Qeshm
Jaz.-ye Hormoz
Qeshm
Ra's Musandam
Str. of Hormuz
J. al Ḥarīm
2057
Ra's al Khaymah

Qarān
Kūh-e Kūhrān
2163
Mīr Kūh
Fannūj
Bent
Nīkshahr
Qaṣr-e Qand
Pīshīn
Kūhestak
Shām
Mīr Shahdād
Parkā Bandar
Gavāter
Mīān Kowr
Bānū Kalāt
Kangūn
Sogar
Gābrīk
Rāpch
Kūlak
Band Bont
Rāsk
Jāsk
Ra's-e Meydānī
Ra's-e Tang
Chāh Bahār
Ra's Jiwan

I R A N

Al Wusayl
Al Khawr
Aḍ Ḍayyah
Al Bidāyah
Umm al Qaywayn
Ajmān
Adh Dhayd
Ash Shāriqah
(Sharjah)
Dibā
Ḍ
Dubayy
(Dubai)
Al Fujayrah
Bū Baqarah

Dās
Az Zarqā'
Shināṣ
Al Liwā'
Ṣuḥār
Khawr Dūwayhin
Marāwiḥ
Abū al Abyaḍ
Şīr Banī Yās
Dalmā
Maḥaḍah
Al 'Ayn
Al Khābūra
Aş Şaḥm
Aş Şadr
Abū Zaby
(Abu Dhabi)
Aş Şuwayq
As Sīb

G U L F   o f   O M A N

T H E   G U L F

Ḥārad
Jirwān
Al Khunn
Bunayyān
'Azīz
Al 'Ubaylah
Aḍ Ṭuwayrifah

Ruwais
Al Mughayrā'
Ṭarīf
Murban
Habshān
Bū Ḥasā
Arādah
Istaihah
Al Manā'if
Al Qurayni'

U N I T E D   A R A B   E M I R A T E S
AD   DAFRAH
JIWA

Al Wāḥāt al Buraymī
Ḥaīl
1372
J. Ḥafīt
Dank
Ibrī
Maskin
3019
Bahlā
Izkī
Nizwā
Manaḥ
Adam
Uwayfī
Wadām
Al Muḍaybī
Ibrā
2151
Sūr
Ra's al Ḥadd
Al Ḥadd
Ṭīwī
Samā'il
Bidbid
Jawr Sulaym
W. Baṭḥa
Al Kāmil
As Suwayḥ
Al Ashkharah

Masqaṭ (Muscat)
Al Muṭaddah
Al Quryyāt

Tropic of Cancer

O M A N

J   I   D   D   A   T
A   Z   Z   A   H   I   R   A
Al 'Urūq al Mu'tariḍah

Al Qarnī

R   U   B   '   A   L   K   H   A   L   I

Ghalat

Hayy
Filim
Khalūf
Kalhāt
Ra's Abū Raṣaṣ
Dawwah
Hukkān
Maṣīrah
Khalīj Maṣīrah

Haymā'

Jiddat al Ḥarāsīs

Dīqm
Ra's al Madrakah

W. Muqshin

Ghubbat Sawqirah

Z   U   F   A   R

Ma'mūl
Şawqirah
Ra's ash Sharbatāt

Anzawr
Ḥaqbaram
Al Hāsik
Al Ḥallānīyah
Al Qibliyah
Kuria Muria Bay
Jazā'ir Khurīyā Murīyā
(Kuria Muria Is.)
(Oman)

Sanāw
Thamarīt
J. al Qarā'
Jabal
Samḥān
1678
Mirbāṭ
Ra's Naws
Ḥabarūt
Rakhyūt
Salālah

Y E M E N

Thamūd
Minwakh
Bi'r Ḥamis
Al Khudrah
Shibām
Tarīm
Qabr Hūd
Aynāt
Saywūn
Al Qarn
Al Hajarayn
Khuraydah
2469
Ghayl Bā Wazīr
Ash Shiḥr
Shuḥayr
Būrūm
Al Mukallā
Bir 'Alī
Al Ḥasy

Qunfudh
Fughmah
Damqawt
Al Fūtk
Al Qurḥ
Al Faydamī
W. Jīz
Al Ghaydah
Ghubbat al Qamar
Khalfūt
Ra's Fartak

J. al Qamar

Ra's 'Itāb
Qishn
Sayḥūt
Quṣay'ir

A R A B I A N

S E A

Ra's Shu'b
Socotra
(Yemen)
Qaṭanslyah
Ra's Khawlaf
Ra's Layht
Qādīb
Ra's Timareh
Siqīra
Ra's Māmī
Fahr

'Abd al Kūri
Ra's Qaṭanan
The Brothers

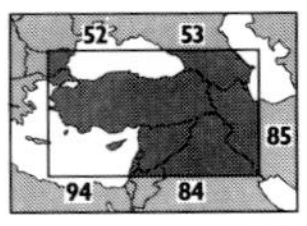

BULGARIA

GREECE

THRACE

MYSIA

LYDIA

CARIA

Dhodhekánisos
(Dodecanese)

LYCIA

BITHYNIA

PAPHLAGONIA

GALATIA

Anadolu (Anatolia)

PHRYGIA

PISIDIA

LYCAONIA

PAMPHYLIA

Toros Dağları (Taurus Mountains)

CILICIA

CATAONIA

CAPPADOCIA

TUR

Kuzey Ana

BLACK SEA

MEDITERRANEAN SEA

CYPRUS

LEBANON

ISTANBUL
Ankara
İzmir (Smyrna)
Bursa
Konya
Adana
Kayseri
Samsun
Zonguldak
Eskişehir
Kütahya
Balıkesir
Manisa
Aydın
Denizli
Isparta
Burdur
Antalya
Mersin (İçel)
Tarsus
Kahramanmaraş
Gaziantep
İskenderun
Antakya (Hatay)
Halab (Aleppo)
Nicosia
Famagusta
Larnaca
Limassol
Bayrut (Beirut)
Dimashq (Damascus)
Hims (Homs)
Hamāh
Tarābulus (Tripoli)

Tolbukhin
Kolarovgrad
Varna
Burgas
Edirne
Tekirdağ
Çanakkale

Projection: Conical with two standard parallels

Provinces in Turkey are named after the chief towns which are underlined.

Division between Greeks and Turks in Cyprus; Turks to the North.

- - - -

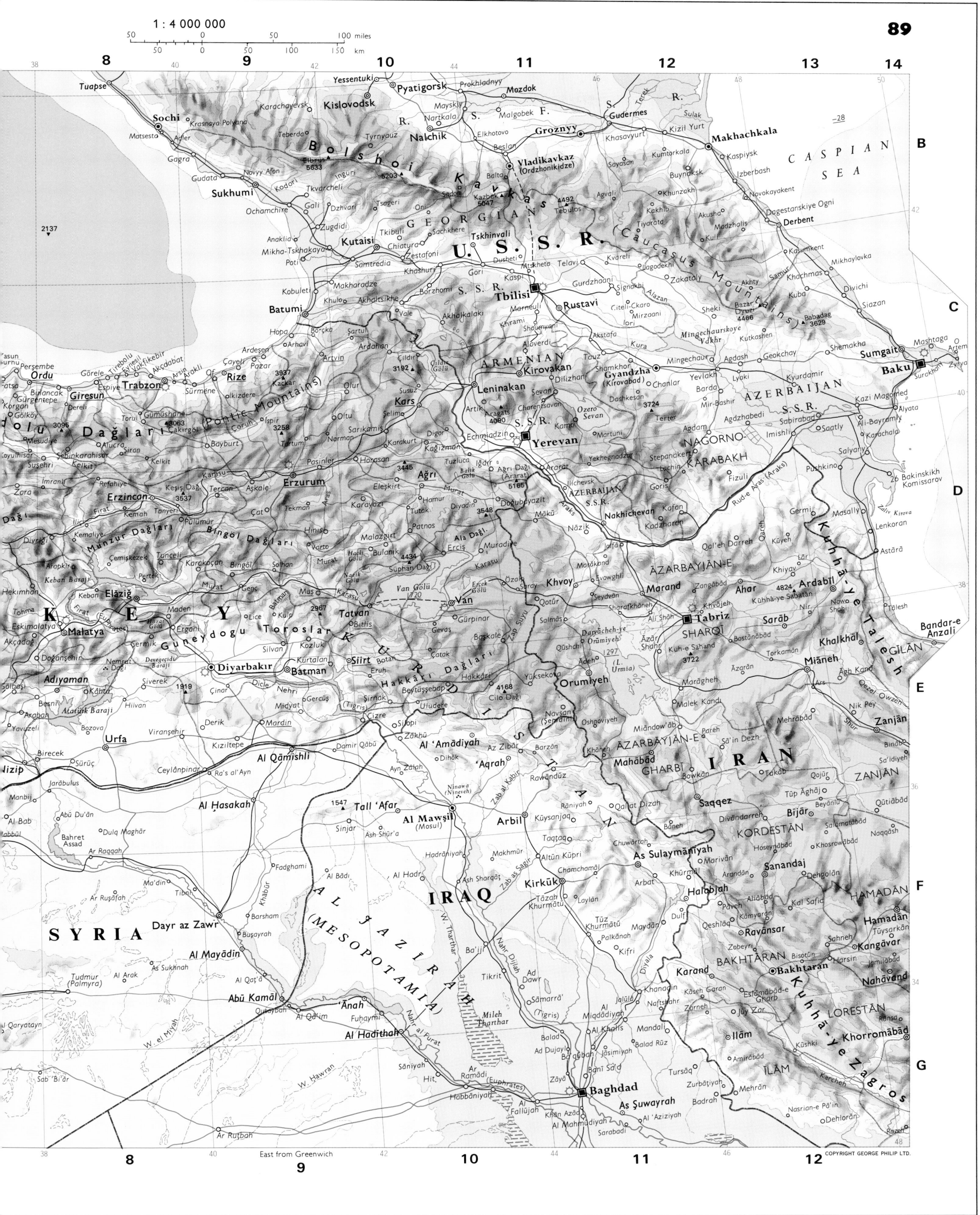

89

1 : 4 000 000

50   0   50   100 miles
50   0   50   100   150 km

East from Greenwich

COPYRIGHT GEORGE PHILIP LTD.

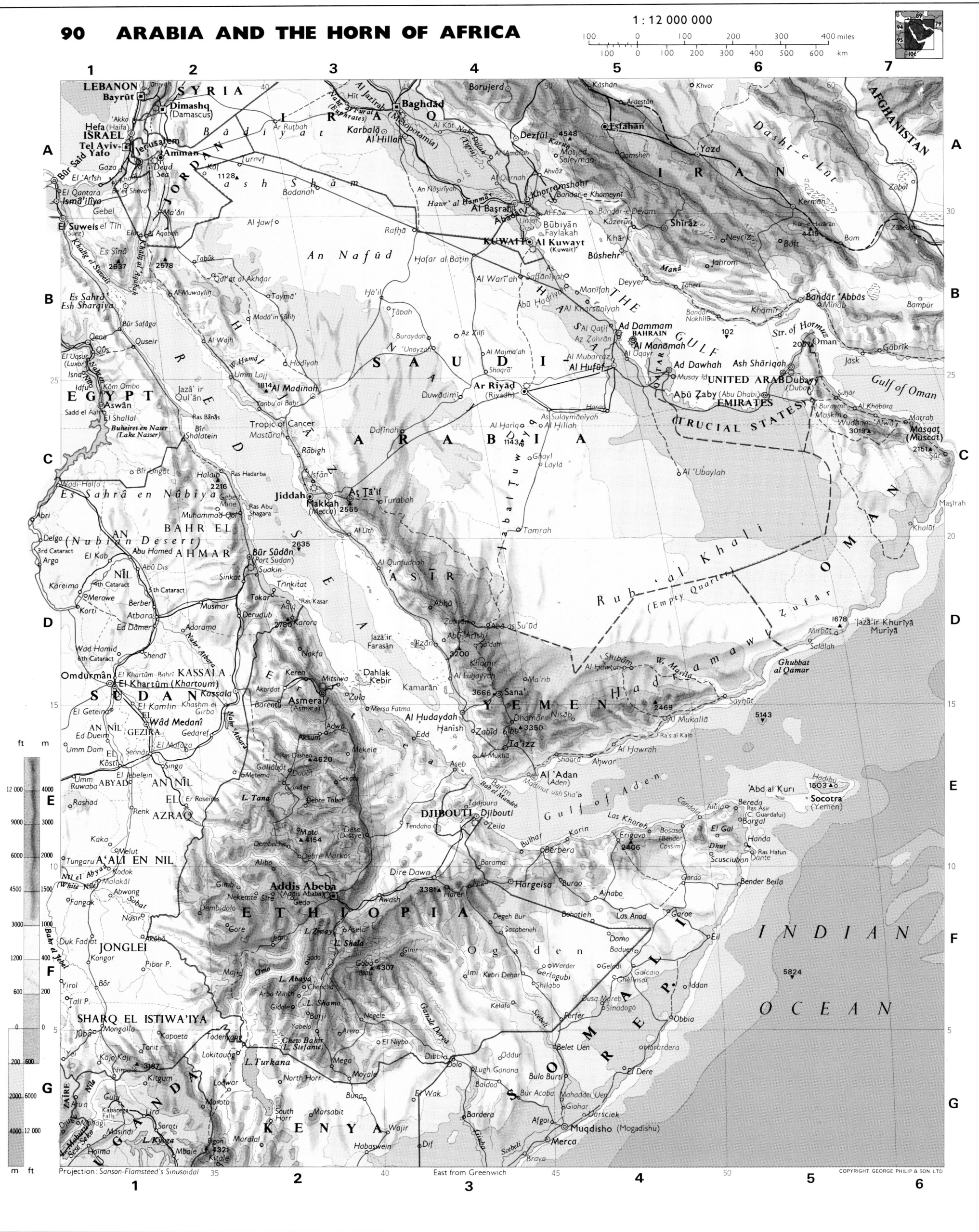

1 : 12 000 000

100   0   100   200   300   400 miles

100 0 100 200 300 400 500 600 km

1   **2**   **3**   **4**   **5**   **6**   **7**

LEBANON   SYRIA   Al Jazīrah   Boruǰerd   Kāshān   Khvor   AFGHANISTAN
Bayrūt   Dimashq (Damascus)   Baghdad   IRAQ   Ardestān   Yazd   Dashti-e Lūt
'Akka   Hefa (Haifa)   Karbalā   Al Hillah   Dezfūl   4548   Eṣfahān
ISRAEL   Amman   Mesopotamia   Karūn   Masjed Soleymān   Qomsheh   Zābol

A   Tel Aviv-Yafo   Jerusalem   Bādiyat   Karbalā   An Nāṣirīyah   Ahvāz   Khorramshahr   Shīrāz   Neyrīz   Kermān   Bam   Zāhedān   A
Bûr Saîd   Gaza   Dead Sea   1128   Badanah   Hawr al Hammār   Al 'Amārah   Al Qurnah   Al Baṣrah   Bandar-e Deyam   Būshehr   4419
El 'Arîsh   El Sheva   Juvī   ash Shām   An Nafūd   KUWAIT Al Kuwayt (Kuwait)   Khārk   Jahrom   Bampūr

B   El Suweis (Suez)   el Tih   Es Sînâ   2578   Al Jawf   Rafḥā   Hafar al Bāṭin   Manīfah   Az Zubayr   Deyyer   Ṭāherī   Bandar 'Abbās   B
Es Sahrâ' Esh Sharqîya   2637   Tabūk   Al Muwaylih   Taymā'   Hā'il   Abū Ḥadrīyah   THE GULF   Khamīr   Mināb
Bûr Safâga   Qal'at al Akhdar   Buraydah   Az Zilfī   Al Qaṭīf   Ad Dammam BAHRAIN   102   Oman   2057   Str. of Hormuz
Qena   Quseir   Al Wajh   Madā'in Sālih   'Unayzah   Al Majma'ah   Al Manāmah   QATAR   Jask   Gūbrik

C   Qûs   Jazā'ir Qul'ān   Hadīyah   SAUDI   Ar Riyād (Riyadh)   Al Mubarraz   Ad Dawhah   Ash Shāriqah   UNITED ARAB Dubay (Dubai)   Gulf of Oman   C
El Uqsur (Luxor)   Kôm Ombo   Aswân   1814 Al Madīnah   Yanbu' al Baḥr   Duwādimī   Al Ḥufūf   Musay'īd   Abū Ẓaby (Abu Dhabi) EMIRATES   Suḥar
Idfu   Isnâ   Sadd el 'Alî   Ras Bānās   Rābigh   Tropic of Cancer   Mastūrah   As Sulaymānīyah   Harad   TRUCIAL STATES   Al Buraymī   Al Khābūra
Buheiret en Naser (Lake Nasser)   Ras Shalatein   Dafīnah   ARABIA   Al Ḥariq   Al Hillah   Maskin   3019   Masqaṭ (Muscat)   2151   Ṣūr

Wadi Halfa   Halaib   Ras Hadarba   Jiddah   Makkah (Mecca)   At Ṭā'if   Turabah   Ghayl   Laylā   Al 'Ubaylah   OMAN   Maṣīrah
Es Sahrâ en Nûbiya   2216   Gebeit Mine   Usfān   2565   1143   Jabal Tuwayq
D   Abri   (Nubian Desert)   Muhammad Qol   Ras Abu Shagara   Al Lith   Al Qunfudhah   Tamrah   Rub' al Khali (Empty Quarter)   Zufār   1678 Jazā'ir Khurīyā Murīyā   D
Delgo   BAHR EL   AHMAR   2635   Khalūf
3rd Cataract   Abu Hamed   Bûr Sûdân (Port Sudan)   RED   Abha   Mirbat   Ghubbat al Qamar
Argo   El Kab   Suakin   'Asīr   Zahrān   Abū as Su'ūd   Hadramawt   Salālah
Kareima   Abū Dis   Sinkat   SEA   3200   Najrān   Sa'dah   Shibām   W. Masila   Sayhūt

NÎL   4th Cataract   Musmar   Trinkitat   Jazā'ir Farasān   Jīzān   Khamir   Al Euḥayyah   1678
Merowe   Berber   Tokar   Ras Kasar   2786   Karora   3666   Sana   Ma'rib   5143
Atbara   Derudub   Ras Kasar   Nakfa   YEMEN   2469   Al Mukallā   Hadibu   1503
E   Kortî   Ed Dâmer   Adarama   Keren   Mitsiwa   Dahlak Kebir   Kamarān   Dhamār   Nisāb   Sayhūt   Ra's al Kalb   E
Omdurmân   Wad Hamid   Kassala   Akordat   Zula   Al Ḥudaydah   Zabīd   Ibb   3350   Ahwar   'Abd al Kuri   Socotra (Yemen)
El Khartûm Bahri   KASSALA   Barentu   Asmera (Asmara)   Mersa Fatma   Hanish   Ta'izz   Al Hawrah   Bosaso (Bender Cassim)   El Gal   Ras Asir (C. Guardafui)
El Khartûm (Khartoum)   Kashm el Girba   Adwa   Mekele   Al Mukha   Bāb el Mandeb   Asab   Las Khareh   Candala   Bereda   Dhut
SUDAN   El Geteina   El Kamlin   Gedaref   Aksum   Gallabat   Al 'Adan (Aden)   Gulf of Aden   Bargal   Handa

INDIAN   OCEAN

F   AN NÎL   El Matena   Ras Dashen 4620   Adigrat   DJIBOUTI Djibouti   Zeila   Bulhar   Berbera   Erigavo   2406   Ras Hafun   F
Ed Dueim   Singa   Gonder   Sekota   Tendaho   Karin   Scusciuban   Dante
GEZIRA   Sennâr   Debre Tabor   Borama   Aibabo   Gardo   Bender Beila
Umm Ruwaba   El Jebelein   L. Tana   Hargeisa   Burao   Las Anod
ABYAD   Rashad   Er Roseires   Dese (Dessye)   Dire Dawa   3381   Harer   Degeh Bur   Garoe
AN NÎL   Kaka   Melut   4154   Debre Markos   Awash   Jijiga   Sasabeneh   Domo   Eil

Tungaru   A'ALI EN NIL   Dembecha   Addis Abeba (Addis Ababa) Geda   Ogaden   Werder   Gelgioi   5824
Nîl el Abyad   Kodok   Aliba   Nekemte   Sire   Imi   Kebri Dehar   Ghelinsor
G   White Nile   Malakal   Gimbio   ETHIOPIA   L. Ziway   Ginir   Shilabo   Obbia   G
Fangak   JONGLEI   Gore   Dembidolo   Asela   Gode 4307   Kelafo   Sinadogo
Bahr el Jebel   Abwong   Sobat   Nasir   Sodo   Shala   Bitata   Werder   Ferfer   Sebeli   Hararder
Duk Fadiat   Pibor P.   Maji   Omo   L. Abaya   Chencha   Negele   Ganale Dorya   Dusa Mreb   El Dere

Yirol   Bôr   Gidole   L. Shamo   Yabelo   SOMALI REP.   Belet Uen   Obbia
SHARQ EL ISTIWA'IYA   Kongor   Arba Minch   Burji   Arero   Dolo   Ugh Ganana   Oddur   Dibbo
Jûba   Mongalla   Chew Bahir (L. Stefanie)   El Niybo   Moyale   Baidoa   Bardera   Bur Acaba   Mahaddei Uen   Giohar
Yei   Kajo Kaji   Torit   Todenyang   Lokitaung   L. Turkana   Mega   Lugh Ganana   Afgoi   Warsciek
Nimule   3187   North Horr   Dolo   Bulo Burti   Muqdisho (Mogadishu)
Gulu   UGANDA   Moroto   Marsabit   Wajir   KENYA   Merca
Kabarega Falls   Lira   Soroti   South Horr   Moroto   Dif   Scebeli   Braya
Hoima   Masindi   Egon 4321   Mbale   Kitale   Marsabit   Habaswein   Dif

ft   m
12 000   4000
9000   3000
6000   2000
4500   1500
3000   1000
1200   400
600   200
0   0
200   600
2000   6000
4000   12 000
m   ft

Projection: Sanson-Flamsteed's Sinusoidal   **1**   35   **2**   40   East from Greenwich   45   **4**   50   **5**   **6**   COPYRIGHT. GEORGE PHILIP & SON. LTD.

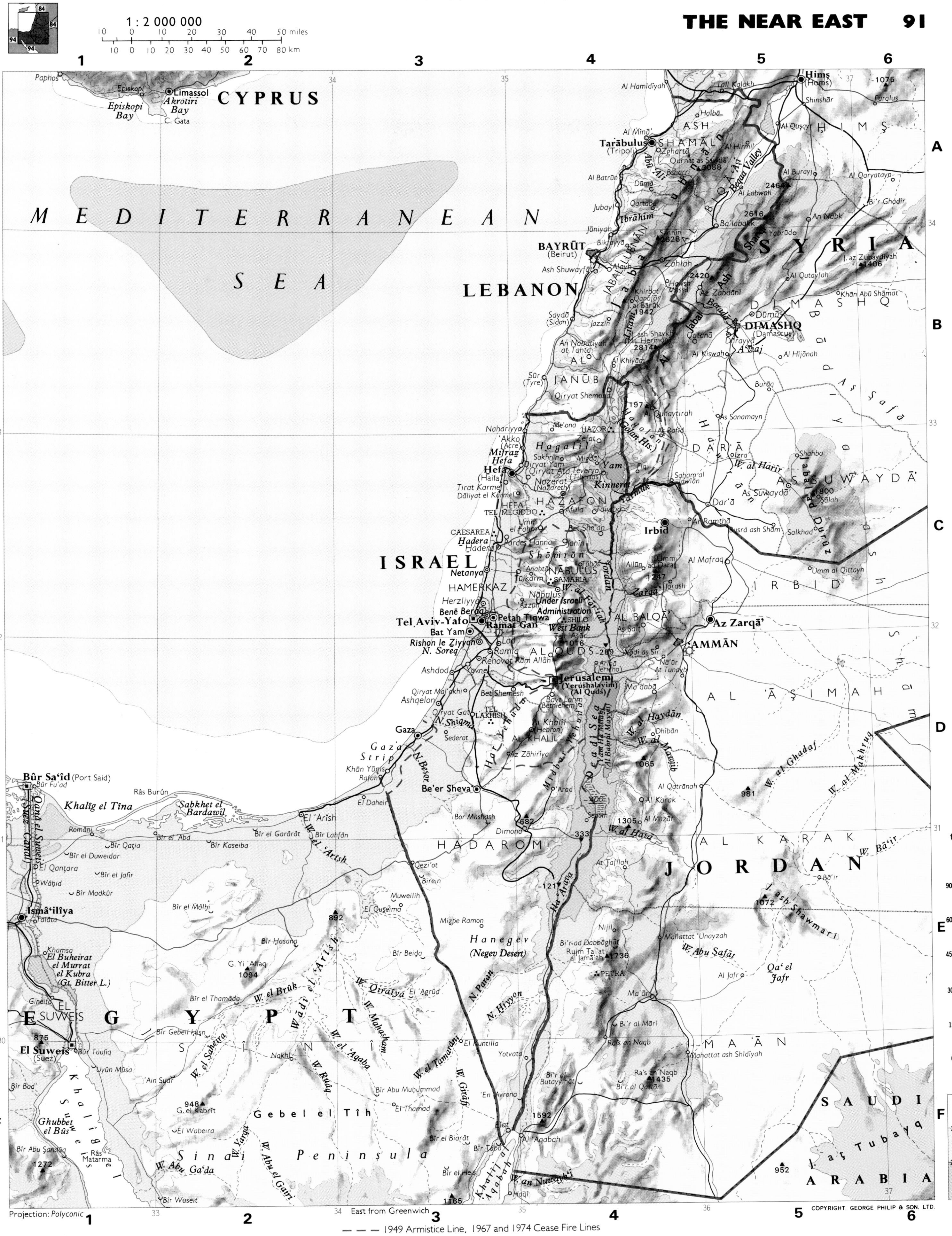

1 : 2 000 000

10   0   10   20   30   40   50 miles
10   0   10   20   30   40   50   70   80 km

CYPRUS

Paphos
Limassol
Episkopi
Akrotiri Bay
Episkopi Bay
C. Gata

M E D I T E R R A N E A N

S E A

LEBANON

BAYRŪT
(Beirut)

Al Hamidiyah
Tall Kalakh
Hịmş (Homs)
1076
Furqlus
Al Minā'
ASH SHAMĀL
Zgharta
Tarābulus (Tripoli)
Al Batrūn
Qartaba
Abu 'Alī
Dūmā
Qurnat as Sawdā'
3088
Bsharri
Jubayl
Ibrāhīm
Al Hirmil
Al Labwah
2468
Bekaa Valley
Halba
Al Quşayr
Al Burayj
Al Qaryatayn
Bi'r Ghādîr
HỊMŞ

Jūniyah
Biklîya
Zahlah
2616
Shanīn
Ba'labakk
An Nabk

SYRIA
J. az Zubaydīyah
4406

Alayh
Zahlah
2420
Az Zabdāni
Al Qutayfah
Khān Abū Shāmat
Ash Shuwayfāt
Khirbat Qanāfar
al Barūk 1942
Hawsh
DIMASHQ
Dūmā
DIMASHQ (Damascus)
A'zaj
Dārayyā
DIMASHQ

Saydā (Sidon)
Jazzīn
Ash Shaykh (Mt. Hermon) 2814
Al Khiyām
Al Kiswah
Al Hījānah

Şūr (Tyre)
AL JANŪB
Qiryat Shemona
1972
Al Qunaytirah
As Sanamayn
Burāq

Nahariyya
Me'ona
'Akko (Acre)
HAZOR
Zefat
Golan Hts.
Ad Rafīd
DAR'Ā
Izra
W. al Harīr
Shahba
AS SUWAYDĀ'
Mifraz Hefa
Hagalil
Sakhnīn
Miqdal
Yam
Sahwat al Qamh
As Sanamayn
Hefa (Haifa)
Qiryat Yam
Qiryat Ata Teverya (Tiberias)
Kinneret
Yarmūk
Dar'ā
As Suwaydā'
1800
Şālih
Tirat Karmel
Nazerat (Nazareth)
Dāliyat el Karmel
Yāmūn
Qadārīyān
Umm Qittayn

HEFA
TEL MEGIDDO
Afula
'Ayn Dīwān
Umm el Fahm
Bet She'an
An Ramthā
Jenin
Irbid
busrā ash Shām
Salkhad
IRBID

CAESAREA
Hadera
Pardes Hanna
Shōmrōn
Allūn
Umm ad Daraj
Umm al Qittayn

ISRAEL
Netanya
Tulkarm
NABULUS
SAMARIA
1247
Zarqā'
Jarash
Aṭ Ṭafīlah

HAMERKAZ
Herzliyya
Nablus
Under Israeli Administration
AL BALQĀ'
Az Zarqā'

Benē Beraq
Petah Tiqwa
SHILO
West Bank
As Salt
AMMĀN
Tel Aviv-Yafo
Ramat Gan
Tel Aṣūr
Na'ūr
Bat Yam
1016
Wādî as Sīr
An Sīr
Rishon le Ziyyon
Lod
AL QUDS -289
Rehovot
Ram Allāh
At Tunayb
N. Soreq
Ramla
Yavne
Arīha (Jericho)
Ashdod
Jerusalem (Yerushalayim) (Al Quds)
Ma'dabā

Qiryat Mal'akhi
Bet Shemesh
Bayt Laḥm (Bethlehem)
Ashqelon
Qiryat Gat
Al Khalīl (Hebron)
Gaza
LAKHISH
N. Shiqma
Sederot
Az Zāhirīya
W. al Haydān
Dhibān
AL KHALĪL
1065

Gaza Strip
Khān Yūnis
Rafāh
Be'er Sheva
'Arad
W. al Mawjib
981
Al Qatrānah
W. al Ghadaf

Bûr Sa'îd (Port Said)
Bûr Fu'ad
Rās Burūn
Sabkhet el Bardawîl
El 'Arîsh
Bor Mashash
Al Mazār
Seqom
Al Karak
W. al Makhrug

Khalîg el Tîna
Români
Bîr el 'Abd
W. el 'Arîsh
El Daheir
Dimona -682
1305
AL KARAK

Ismâ'îlîya
Bîr Qaţia
El Qanţara
Bîr el Garârât
Bîr el Lahfân
Qezi'ot
-333
W. al Ḥasa
HADAROM
W. al Ḥasa

Wāḥid
Bîr el Jafir
Bîr Kaseiba
Birein
At Tafilah
JORDAN

El Buheirat el Murra el Kubra (Gt. Bitter L.)
Bîr Madkūr
Bîr el Mālḥi
El Quşeima
Muweilih
Mizpe Ramon
-121
I. ash Shawmari
1072

G. Yi 'Allaq 1094
Bîr Hasana
Bîr Beiḍa
Hanegev (Negev Desert)
Nijīl
Maḥaṭṭat 'Unayzah
W. Abu Şafāt

El Agrûd
Bi'r ad Dabbōghāt
Ruim Tal'at al Jamā'a
Qa' el Jafr
SUWEIS
Khamsa
Bîr el Thamāda
W. el Brûk
W. Qiratya
El Agrûd
N. Paran
-736
PETRA
Ma'ān
El Jafr

EGYPT
W. Mahakhem
N. Hiyyon
Ra's an Naqb 1435
MA'ĀN

EL SUWEIS
875
W. el Saḥeira
Nakhl
W. el 'Aqaba
El Kuntilla
Rās an Naqb
Mahaṭṭat ash Shidīyah
El Suweis (Suez)
Bûr Taufiq
Yotvata
Bi'r al Qaṭar

Bîr Bad'
Uyūn Mûsa
W. el Tamarāni
Bîr Abu Muḥammad
'En Avrona
Bi'r al Mūrī

Ghubbet el Bûs
948 G. el Kabrît
El Wabeira
El Thamad
1592
SAUDI
Bîr Abu Şandûq
1272 Rās Matarma
Gebel el Tîh
Elat
Al 'Aqabah
952
I. at Tubayq
ARABIA

Sinai Peninsula
W. Yarqa
W. Abu Ga'da
W. Abu el Gairi
Bîr el Biarât
W. el Heisi
Khalîg el 'Aqaba
W. an Nuwaybi'
Haql
1165

Projection: Polyconic

East from Greenwich

ft   m
9000   3000
6000   2000
4500   1500
3000   1000
1200   400
600   200
0   0
600   200
2000   6000
m   ft

- - - 1949 Armistice Line, 1967 and 1974 Cease Fire Lines

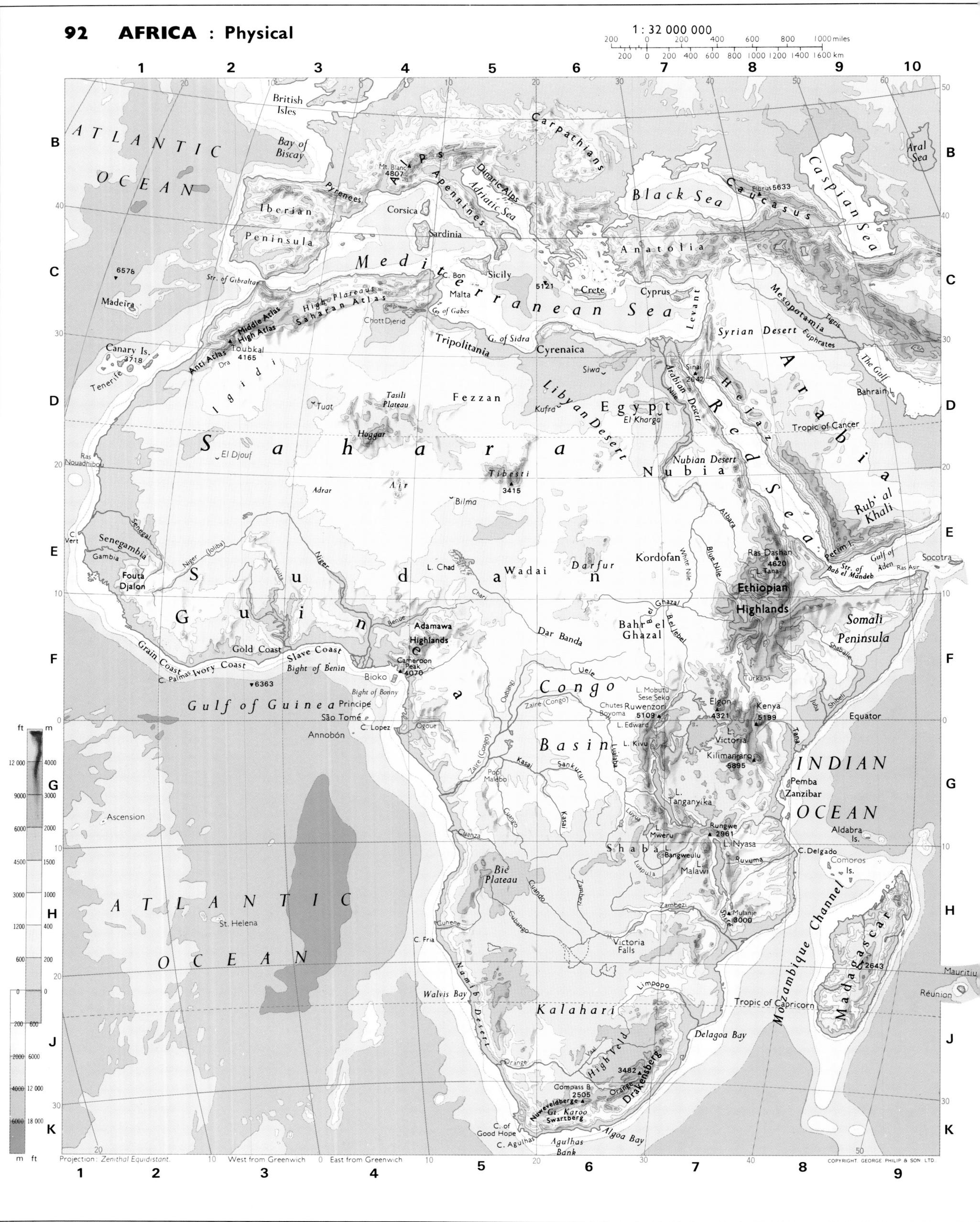

1 : 32 000 000

ATLANTIC OCEAN

British Isles

Bay of Biscay

Pyrenees

Iberian Peninsula

Corsica

Sardinia

Alps
Mt. Blanc 4807

Apennines

Dinaric Alps

Adriatic Sea

Carpathians

Black Sea

Caucasus
Elbrus 5633

Aral Sea

Caspian Sea

Mediterranean Sea

Anatolia

Crete

Cyprus

Levant

Mesopotamia

Syrian Desert

Tigris

Euphrates

The Gulf

Bahrain

Madeira

6578

Str. of Gibraltar

Canary Is. 3718

Tenerife

Middle Atlas
High Atlas
Anti Atlas
Toubkal
Dra 4165

High Plateaus
Saharan Atlas

Chott Djerid

C. Bon

Sicily

Malta

5121

G. of Gabes

Tripolitania

G. of Sidra

Cyrenaica

Igidi

Tuat

Tasili Plateau

Fezzan

Siwa

Libyan Desert

Egypt

El Kharga

Kufra

Sinai
2642

Arabian Desert

Nile

Hejaz

Red Sea

Tropic of Cancer

Arabia

Ras Nouadhibou

Sahara

El Djouf

Hoggar

Air

Bilma

Adrar

Tibesti
3415

Nubian Desert

Nubia

Rub' al Khali

C. Vert

Senegambia

Gambia

Senegal

Niger (Joliba)

Volta

Niger

L. Chad

Chari

Wadai

Darfur

Kordofan

White Nile

Blue Nile

Atbara

Ras Dashan
4620
L. Tana

Peri Im.

Str. of Bab el Mandeb

Gulf of Aden

Ras Asir

Socotra

Fouta Djalon

Sudan

Guinea

Benue

Adamawa Highlands

Cameroon Peak 4070

Bioko

Dar Banda

Bahr el Ghazal

Bahr el Ghazal

Bel Jebel

Ethiopian Highlands

Somali Peninsula

Shabeli

Grain Coast

Gold Coast

Ivory Coast

C. Palmas

Slave Coast

Bight of Benin

6363

Bight of Bonny

Principe

Uele

Oubangui

Zaire (Congo)

Congo Basin

L. Mobutu Sese Seko

Chutes Boyoma

Ruwenzori
5109

Elgon
4321

Kenya
5199

Juba

Gulf of Guinea

São Tomé

Annobón

C. Lopez

Ogoue

Zaire (Congo)

L. Edward

L. Kivu

Lualaba

ft.

Victoria

Kilimanjaro
5895

Equator

INDIAN OCEAN

Kasai

Pool Malebo

Kasai

Sankuru

L. Tanganyika

Pemba

Zanzibar

Ascension

Cuango

Cuanza

Luvua

Mweru

Rungwe
2961

L. Nyasa

Ruvuma

C. Delgado

Aldabra Is.

Comoros Is.

Shaba

Bangweulu

Malawi

Atlantic Ocean

St. Helena

Bié Plateau

Cuando

Luapula

Zambezi

Shire

Mulanje
3000

Mozambique Channel

Madagascar
2643

Cunene

C. Fria

Cubango

Victoria Falls

Namib Desert

Walvis Bay

Mauritiu

Réunion

Limpopo

Kalahari

Tropic of Capricorn

Delagoa Bay

Orange

Vaal

High Veld

3482
Drakensberg

Compass B.
2505

Nuweveldberge

Gt. Karoo

Swartberg

C. of Good Hope

C. Agulhas

Agulhas Bank

Orange

Algoa Bay

Projection: Zenithal Equidistant.

COPYRIGHT GEORGE PHILIP & SON LTD.

West from Greenwich

East from Greenwich

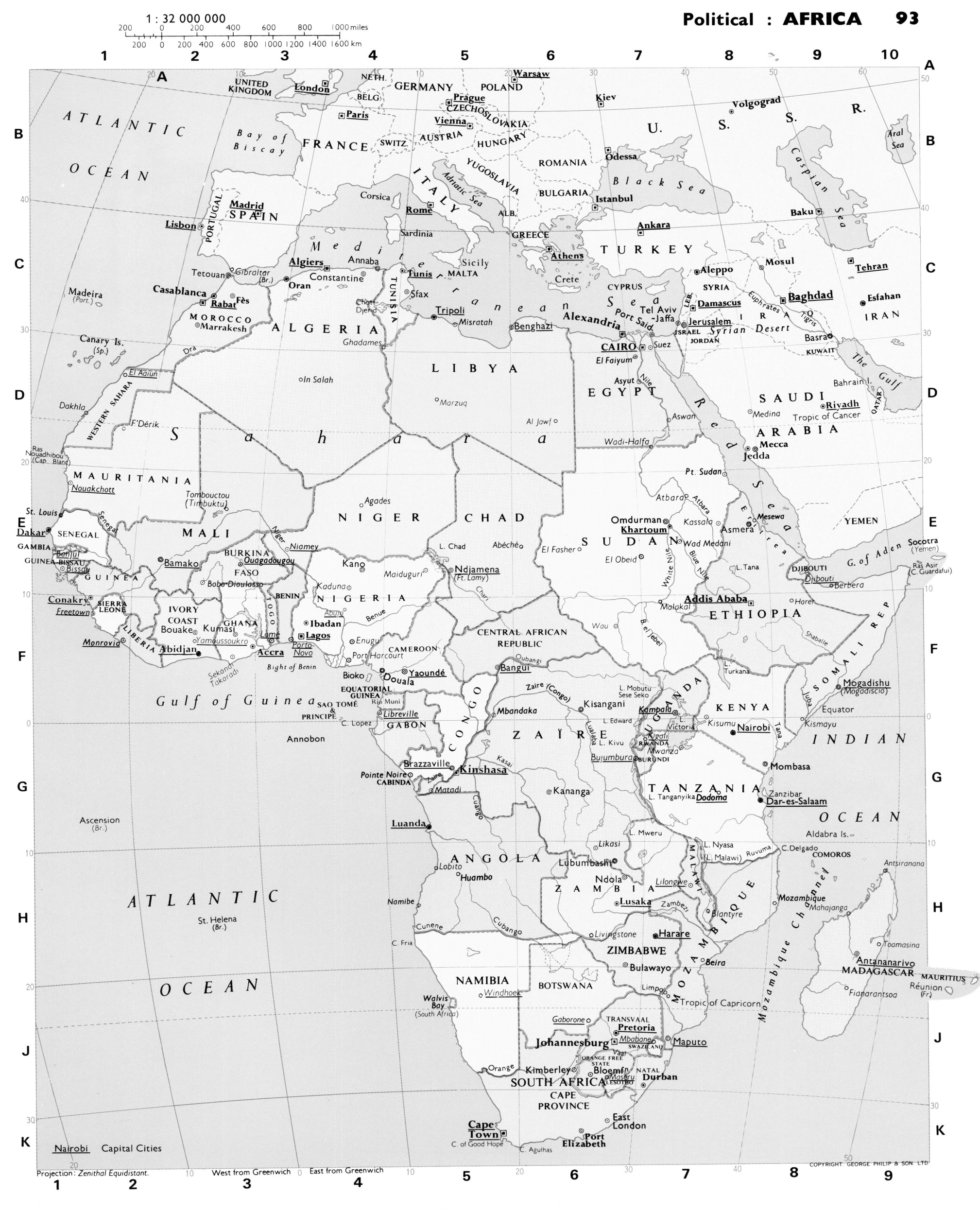

1 : 32 000 000

200 0 200 400 600 800 1000 miles
200 0 200 400 600 800 1000 1200 1400 1600 km

ATLANTIC

OCEAN

UNITED KINGDOM
London
NETH.
BELG.
GERMANY
POLAND
Warsaw
Kiev
Volgograd

Paris
Prague
CZECHOSLOVAKIA
Vienna
AUSTRIA
HUNGARY
ROMANIA
Odessa
U. S. S. R.
Baku
Aral Sea

Bay of Biscay
FRANCE
SWITZ.
YUGOSLAVIA
BULGARIA
Black Sea
Caspian Sea

Madrid
SPAIN
Lisbon
PORTUGAL
Corsica
ITALY
Rome
Sardinia
Adriatic Sea
Istanbul
Ankara
TURKEY
GREECE
Athens
Crete
Aleppo
Mosul
Tehran

Casablanca
Rabat
Fès
Algiers
Oran
Constantine
Annaba
TUNISIA
Tunis
Sfax
MALTA
Sicily
Mediterranean Sea
CYPRUS
SYRIA
Damascus
Baghdad
Esfahan

Tetouan
Gibraltar (Br.)
Tel Aviv-Jaffa
ISRAEL
Jerusalem
LEB.
I.Q.
IRAN

MOROCCO
Marrakesh
ALGERIA
Chott Djerid
Ghadames
Tripoli
Misratah
Benghazi
Alexandria
Port Said
Suez
CAIRO
JORDAN
Syrian Desert
Basra
KUWAIT
The Gulf
Bahrain I.
QATAR

Canary Is. (Sp.)
Dra
In Salah
LIBYA
Marzuq
Al Jawf
EGYPT
El Faiyum
Asyut
Aswan
Wadi-Halfa
Medina
Riyadh
Tropic of Cancer

Dakhla
WESTERN SAHARA
El Aaiun
F'Dérik
Sahara
SAUDI ARABIA
Mecca
Jedda

Ras Nouadhibou (Cap. Blanc)
MAURITANIA
Nouakchott
Tombouctou (Timbuktu)
Agades
NIGER
CHAD
SUDAN
Omdurman
Khartoum
Atbara
Kassala
Asmera
Mesewa
Pt. Sudan
YEMEN
Red Sea
Socotra (Yemen)

St. Louis
Dakar
SENEGAL
Senegal
MALI
Niger
Niamey
Kano
L. Chad
Abéché
El Fasher
Wad Medani
Blue Nile
DJIBOUTI
Djibouti
Berbera
G. of Aden
Ras Asir (C. Guardafui)

GAMBIA
Banjul
GUINEA-BISSAU
Bissau
BURKINA FASO
Ouagadougou
Bamako
Bobo-Dioulasso
Kaduna
Maiduguri
Ndjamena (Ft. Lamy)
Chari
El Obeid
White Nile
L. Tana
Addis Ababa
Harer

Conakry
Freetown
SIERRA LEONE
GUINEA
IVORY COAST
Bouake
GHANA
Kumasi
TOGO
BENIN
Abuja
NIGERIA
Ibadan
Lagos
Porto-Novo
Benue
CENTRAL AFRICAN REPUBLIC
Bangui
Oubangi
Wau
Bahr el Jebel
Malakal
ETHIOPIA
L. Turkana
SOMALI REP.

Monrovia
LIBERIA
Yamoussoukro
Abidjan
Accra
Lome
Sekondi Takoradi
Bight of Benin
Enugu
Port Harcourt
CAMEROON
Yaoundé
Douala
Bioko
Shabelle
Mogadishu (Mogadiscio)

Gulf of Guinea
SAO TOMÉ & PRINCIPE
EQUATORIAL GUINEA
Rio Muni
Libreville
GABON
C. Lopez
CONGO
Zaire (Congo)
ZAÏRE
Kisangani
Mbandaka
L. Mobutu Sese Seko
L. Edward
UGANDA
Kampala
L. Victoria
Kigali
RWANDA
Kisumu
KENYA
Nairobi
Tana
Kismayu
Equator
INDIAN

Annobon
Brazzaville
Kinshasa
Pointe Noire
CABINDA
Matadi
Kasai
Kwango
Kananga
L. Kivu
BURUNDI
Bujumbura
Mwanza
L. Tanganyika
TANZANIA
Dodoma
Mombasa
Zanzibar
Dar-es-Salaam
OCEAN

Ascension (Br.)
Luanda
ANGOLA
Likasi
L. Mweru
Aldabra Is.
COMOROS
Antsiranana

St. Helena (Br.)
Lobito
Huambo
Lubumbashi
Ndola
ZAMBIA
L. Nyasa (L. Malawi)
Ruvuma
C. Delgado
Mozambique
Mahajanga

Namibe
Lusaka
Zambezi
MALAWI
Lilongwe
Blantyre
MOZAMBIQUE
Mozambique Channel

ATLANTIC
Cunene
Cubango
Livingstone
Harare
ZIMBABWE
Bulawayo
Beira
Antananarivo
MADAGASCAR
MAURITIUS
Réunion (Fr.)
Toamasina

OCEAN
C. Fria
NAMIBIA
BOTSWANA
Limpopo
Tropic of Capricorn
Fianarantsoa

Walvis Bay (South Africa)
Windhoek
Gaborone
TRANSVAAL
Pretoria
Mbabane
SWAZILAND
Maputo

Johannesburg
ORANGE FREE STATE
Vaal
Bloemfontein
Maseru
LESOTHO
NATAL
Durban

Orange
Kimberley
SOUTH AFRICA
CAPE PROVINCE
East London

Cape Town
C. of Good Hope
C. Agulhas
Port Elizabeth

Nairobi Capital Cities

Projection : Zenithal Equidistant.
West from Greenwich   East from Greenwich

COPYRIGHT. GEORGE PHILIP & SON. LTD.

1 : 6 400 000

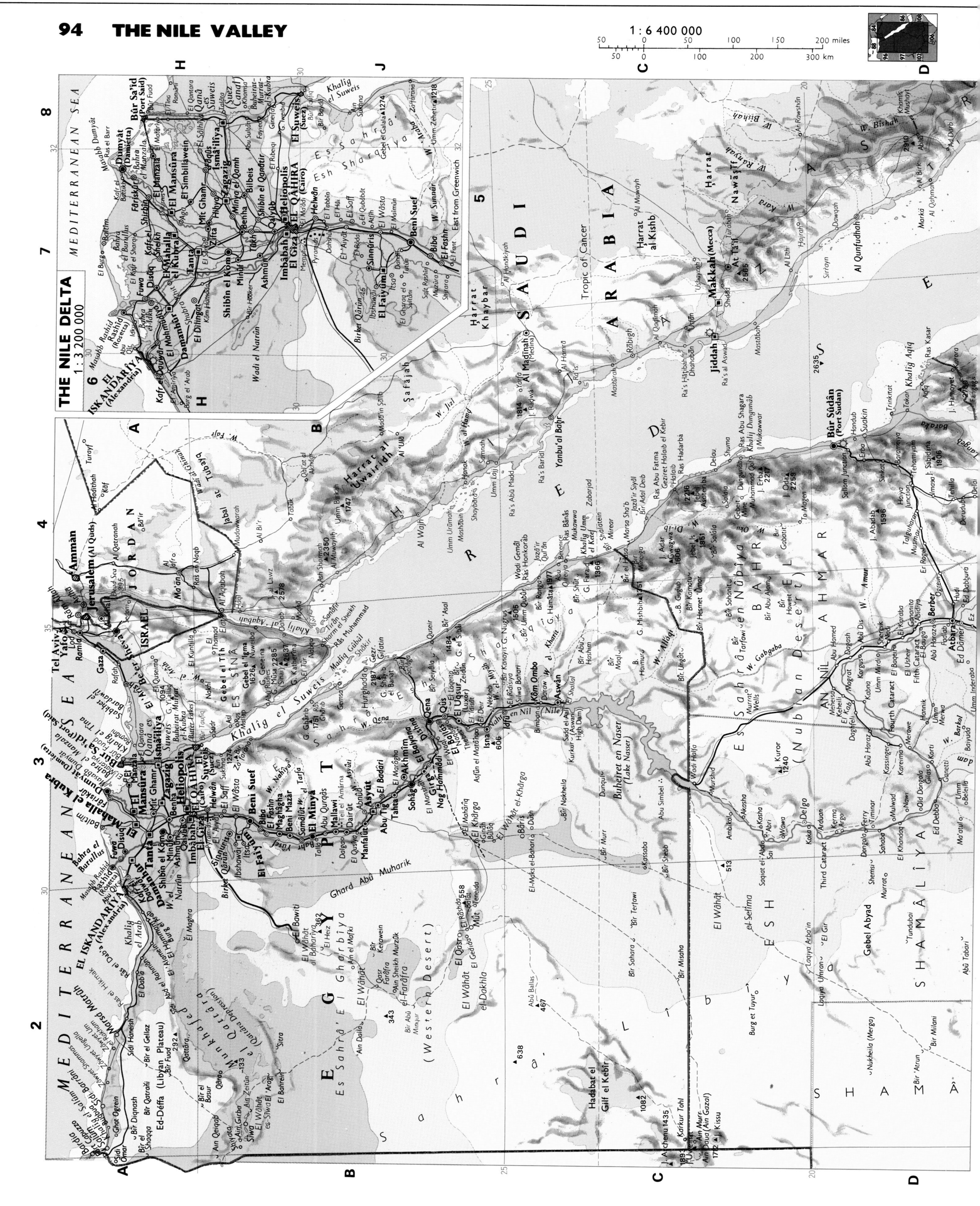

THE NILE DELTA
1 : 3 200 000

Projection : Lambert's Equivalent Azimuthal

East from Greenwich

YEMEN

Jazā'ir Farasān

Jabal at Ṭaʿiz

DJIBOUTI

ETHIOPIA

Asmera (Āsmara)

Mekelē

Aksum

Adwa

Gonder

L. Tana

Dese (Dessye)

Debre Markos

ADDIS ABEBA (Addis Ababa)

Debre Zeyit

Nazret

Dire Dawa

HARERGE

Jima

GAMO-GOFA

L. Turkana (L. Rudolf)

KENYA

SOMALI REP.

SUDAN

Khartoum

El Khartûm (Khartoum)

Omdurman

El Khartûm Bahri

Wad Medani

Kassala

Gedaref

Khashm el Girba

Shendi

Ed Dueim

El Obeid

DARFUR

El Fâsher

KORDOFAN

En Nahud

Kadugli

BAHR EL GHAZAL

Wau

Waw

UPPER NILE

Malakâl

Nasir

CENTRAL AFRICAN REPUBLIC

UGANDA

ZAIRE

Juba

ft
m
4000
3000
2000
1500
1000
400
200
0
12,000
9000
6000
4500
3000
1200
600
200
0
200-60
ft
m

EGYPT

ALGERIA

TUNISIA

Countries / Regions
- LIBYA
- EGYPT
- ALGERIA
- TUNISIA
- SICILIA
- MALTA

Seas and Waters
- MEDITERRANEAN SEA
- Khalij Surt (Gulf of Sidra)
- Dodecanese

Major Places
- Banghāzī (Benghazi)
- Tarābulus (Tripoli)
- TUNIS
- Bizerte
- Sousse
- Sfax
- Gabès
- Monastir
- Kairouan
- CONSTANTINE
- Annaba
- Skikda
- Catánia
- Siracusa
- Ragusa
- Valletta
- Iráklion
- Zāwiyat al Baydā
- Al Marj
- Al Jabal al Akhḍar
- Darnah
- Ajdābiyah
- Surt
- Miṣrātah
- Al Khums
- Zlīṭan
- Gharyān
- Nālūt
- Ghudāmis
- Sabhā (Sebha)
- Marzūq
- Ghāt
- Djanet
- Ad Diffah
- Sahrā
- BARQA (CYRENAICA)
- AL HAMMĀDAH AL ḤAMRĀ
- SAHARĀ
- Sarir Calanscio
- Sarir Nerastro
- Sarir Tibasti
- Plateau du Tinrhert
- Idehan Marzūq
- Idehan Ubari
- Téneré
- Tibesti
- Libyan Plateau
- Gilf el Kebir
- Hadabat el Gilf el Kebir
- Al Kufrah
- Al Jawf
- Jabal as Sawdā'
- Al Ḥarūj al Aswad
- Jabal Waddān
- Waddān
- Hūn
- Zillah
- Marādah
- Tropic of Cancer

Spot heights
- 2328
- 1338
- 1165
- 2264 Adrar
- 1428
- 840
- 1200
- 945
- 583
- 573
- 638
- 1082
- 716
- 133

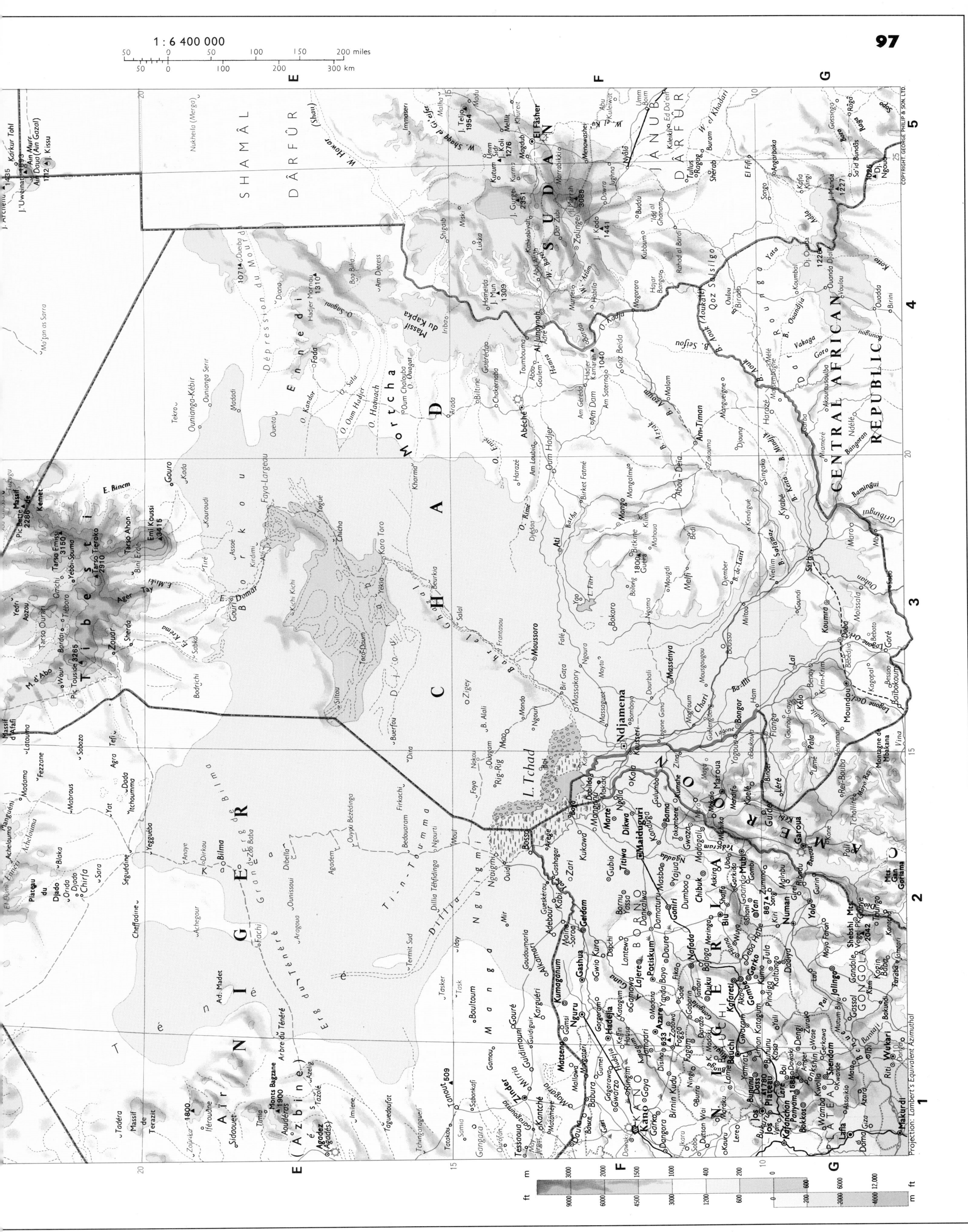

1 : 6 400 000

SHAMÂL DÂRFÛR (Shau)

DÂRFÛR

JANUB

El Fâsher

T   C   H   A   D

Ennedi

Tibesti

N   I   G   E   R

Ad. Madet

E(Aïzbine)

Aïr

Agadez

CENTRAL AFRICAN REPUBLIC

L. Tchad

Ndjamena

BORNO

K A N O

N I G E R I A

CAMEROON

Projection: Lambert's Equivalent Azimuthal

m   ft

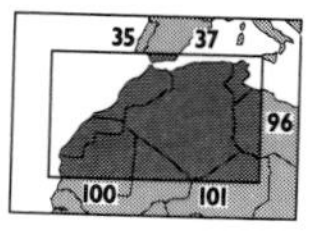

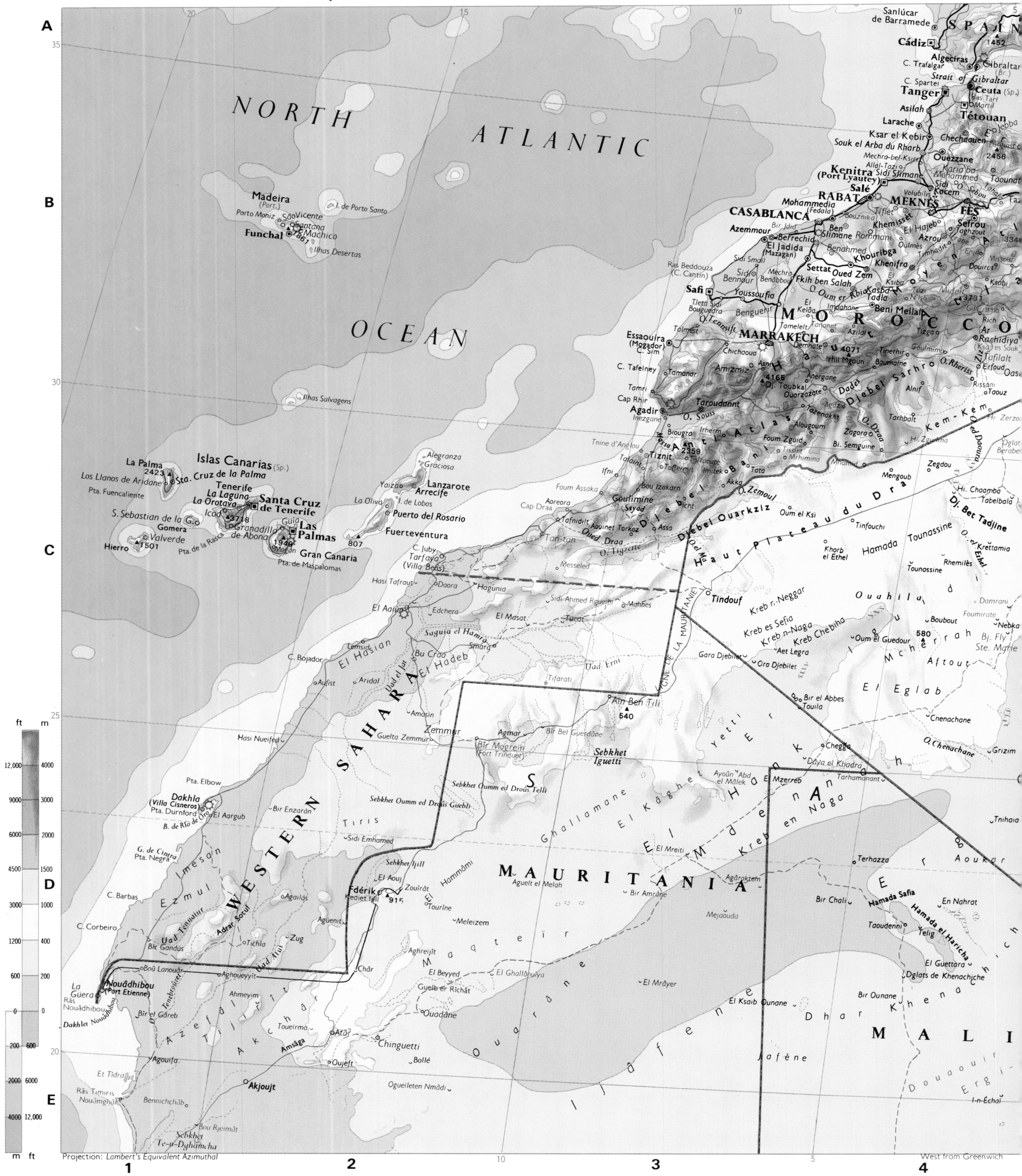

NORTH ATLANTIC OCEAN

SPAIN

Sanlúcar de Barrameda
Cádiz
Algeciras
Gibraltar (Br.)
C. Trafalgar
C. Spartel
Ceuta (Sp.)
Strait of Gibraltar
Tanger
Asilah
Larache
Ksar el Kebir
Souk el Arba du Rharb
Chechaouen
Ouezzane
Kenitra (Port Lyautey)
Sidi Slimane
Salé
RABAT
MEKNÈS
FES
Sefrou
Mohammedia (Fedala)
CASABLANCA
Azemmour
Berrechid
Ben Slimane
Settat
Oued Zem
Khouribga
El Jadida (Mazagan)
Khenifra
Ras Beddouza (C. Cantin)
Safi
Youssoufia
Fkih ben Salah
Beni Mellal
Essaouira (Mogador)
C. Sim
MARRAKECH
Chichaoua
MOROCCO
C. Tafelney
Tamanar
Agadir
Inezgane
Taroudannt
Dj. Toubkal 4165
Moyen Atlas
Haut Atlas
Tiznit
Ifni
Goulimine
Tan-tan
Tarfaya (Villa Bens)
C. Juby

Islas Canarias (Sp.)
La Palma
Sta. Cruz de la Palma
Los Llanos de Aridane
Pta. Fuencaliente
Tenerife
La Laguna
La Orotava
Santa Cruz de Tenerife
Icod
S. Sebastián de la Gomera
Gomera
Valverde
Hierro
Granadilla de Abona
Las Palmas
Gran Canaria
Pta. de Maspalomas
Lanzarote
Arrecife
Alegranza
Graciosa
La Oliva
I. de Lobos
Puerto del Rosario
Fuerteventura

WESTERN SAHARA
El Aaiún
Smara
El Hagounia
Daora
Edchera
El Masat
Bu Craa
El Hadeb
C. Bojador
El Hasian
Aridal
Guelta Zemmour
Zemmour
Bir Enzarán
Dakhla (Villa Cisneros)
Pta. Durnford
El Aargub
G. de Cintra
Pta. Negra
Tiris
Sidi Emhamed
Sebkhet Ijill
Fdérik
Kediet Ijill 915
Zouïrât
Tourine
Nouâdhibou (Port Etienne)
La Güera
Ras Nouâdhibou
Dakhlet Nouâdhibou
Akjoujt
Atar
Chinguetti
Ouadâne

MAURITANIA
Tindouf
Hamada Tounassine
El Eglab
El Mreiti
Terhazza
Taoudenni
Hamada Safi
En Nahrat

MALI

ft   m
12,000   4000
9000   3000
6000   2000
4500   1500
3000   1000
1200   400
600   200
0   0
200   600
2000   6000
4000   12,000
m   ft

1 : 6 400 000

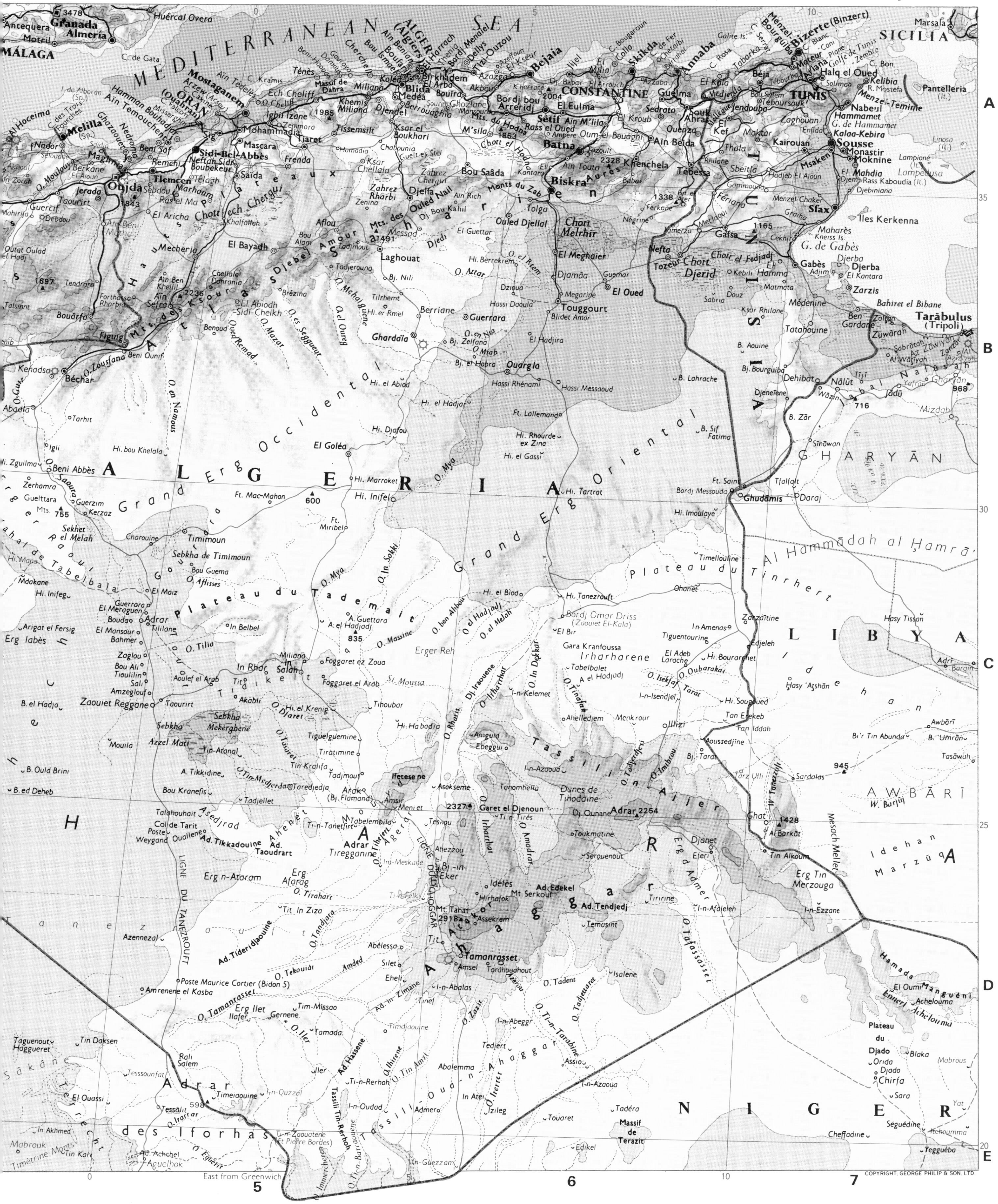

50 0 100 150 200 miles
50 0 100 200 300 km

MEDITERRANEAN SEA

MÁLAGA · Antequera · Granada · Almería · Motril · Huércal Overa

ORAN · Mostaganem · Arzew · Oujda · Tlemcen · Sidi-Bel-Abbès · Mascara · Saïda

ALGIERS (Alger) · Blida · Médéa · Bou Saâda · Djelfa · Laghouat · Ghardaïa · Ouargla

CONSTANTINE · Sétif · Batna · Biskra · Touggourt · El Oued · Tébessa

TUNIS · Bizerte (Binzert) · Sousse · Sfax · Gabès · Gafsa · Kairouan · SICILIA

ALGERIA

Grand Erg Occidental · Grand Erg Oriental · Plateau du Tademaït

In Salah · Timimoun · Adrar · Reggane · Tamanrasset · Djanet · Ghat

Ahaggar · Tassili n'Ajjer · Mt. Tahat 2918

LIBYA · Tarābulus (Tripoli) · Ghudāmis · Awbārī · Idehan Marzūq

NIGER · Adrar des Iforhas

COPYRIGHT. GEORGE PHILIP & SON. LTD.

East from Greenwich

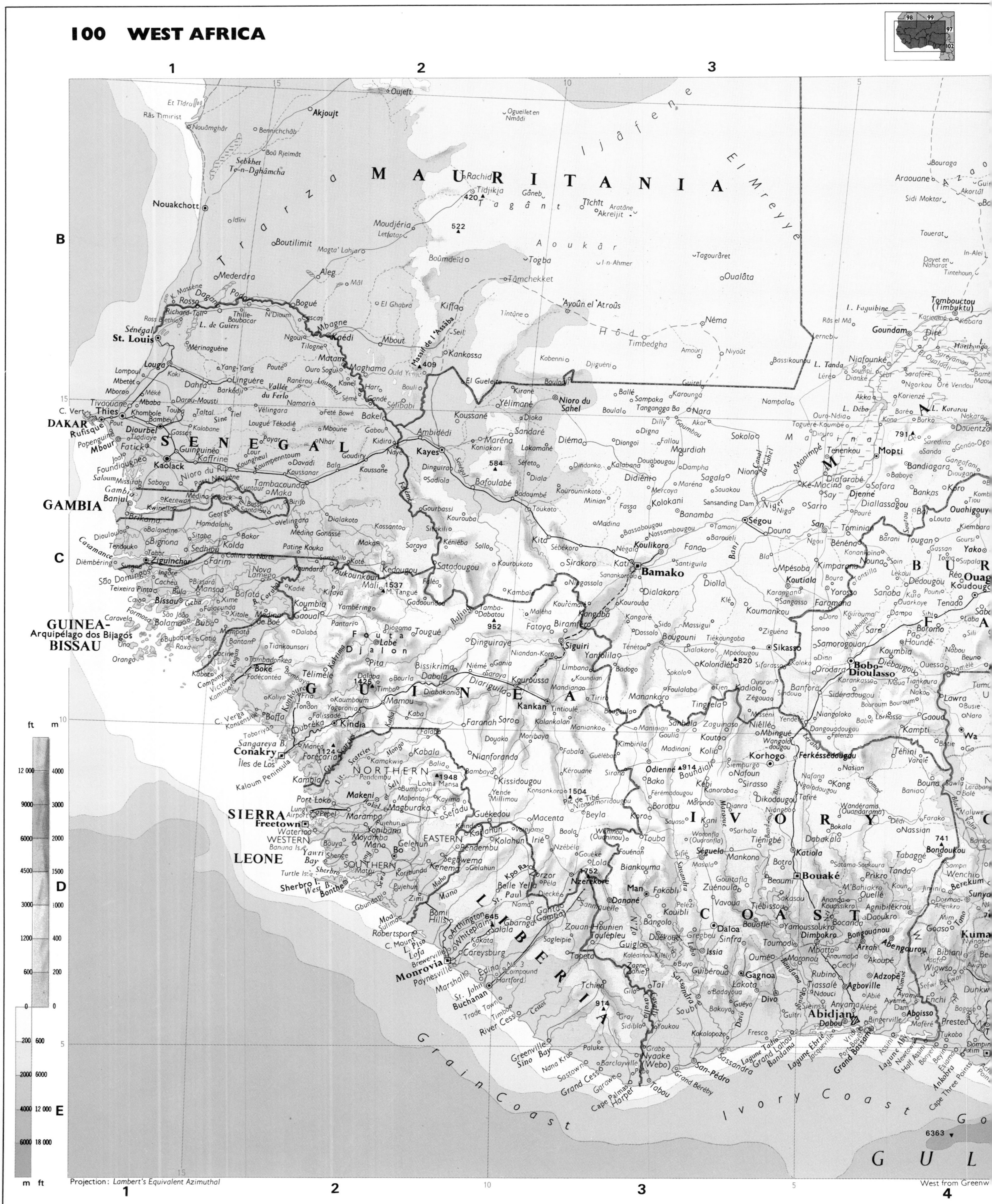

MAURITANIA

SENEGAL

GAMBIA

GUINEA-BISSAU
Arquipélago dos Bijagós

GUINEA

SIERRA LEONE

LIBERIA

IVORY COAST

MALI

BURKINA FASO

DAKAR

Nouakchott

St. Louis

Banjul

Conakry

Freetown

Monrovia

Abidjan

Bamako

Bobo-Dioulasso

Grain Coast

Ivory Coast

GULF

Projection: Lambert's Equivalent Azimuthal

West from Greenwich

ft	m
12 000	4000
9000	3000
6000	2000
4500	1500
3000	1000
1200	400
600	200
0	0
600	200
6000	2000
12 000	4000
18 000	6000

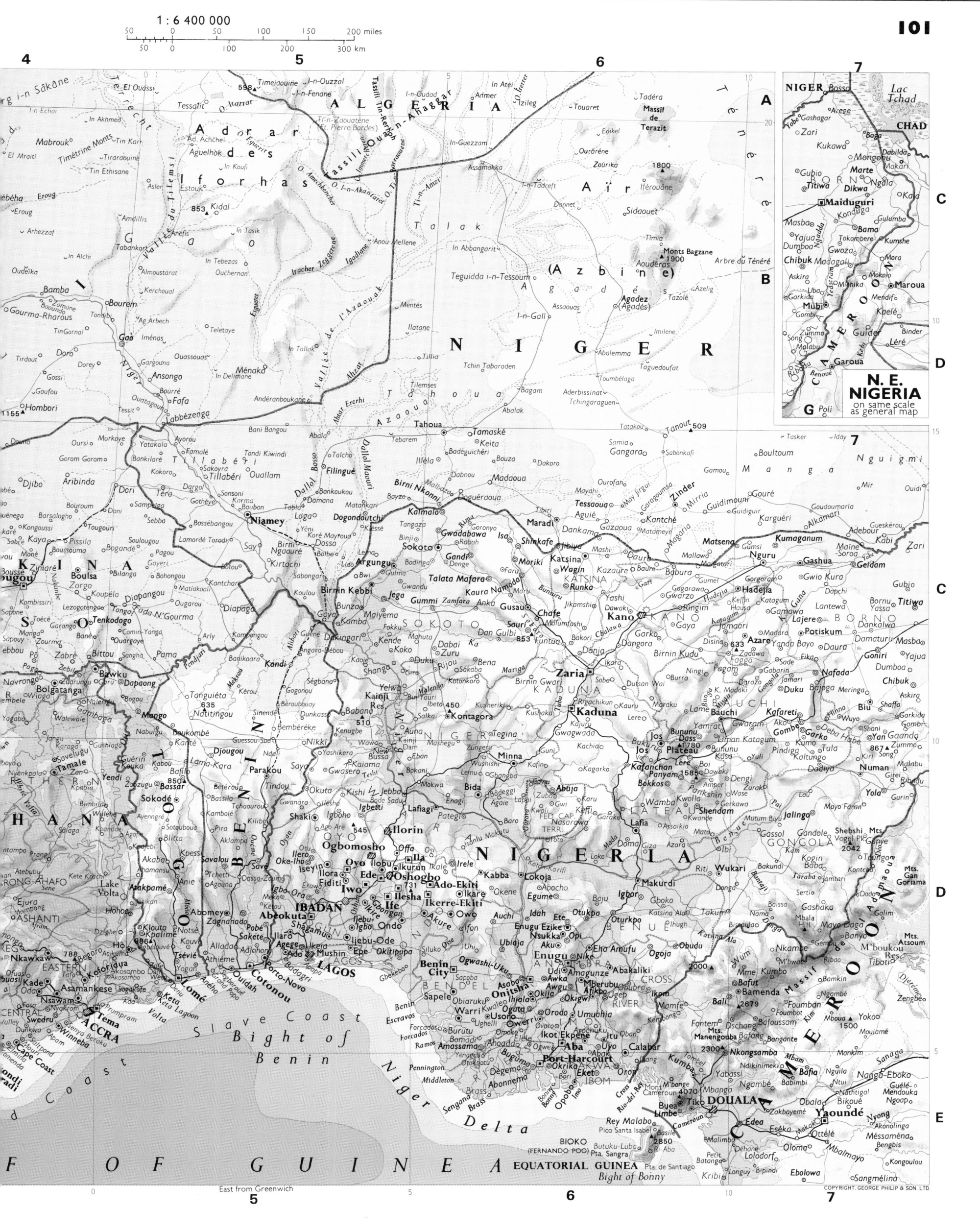

1 : 6 400 000

50   0   50   100   150   200 miles
50   0   50   100   200   300 km

4   5   6   7

ALGERIA

A d r a r   d e s   I f o r h a s

NIGER

A ï r (Azbine)

A g a d e s

N I G E R

NIGER   Bosso
CHAD

Maiduguri

CAMEROON
Maroua

**N. E.
NIGERIA**
on same scale
as general map

B U R K I N A   F A S O

Niamey

Sokoto

Katsina

Kano
KANO

BORNO

Zinder

Manga

Nguigmi

SOKOTO

KADUNA
Kaduna

BAUCHI

Zaria

Jos
Plateau

GONGOLA

Bauchi

Gombe

Yola

Kaffareti

Bolgatanga

T O G O

B E N I N

Parakou

NIGER

Abuja
FED. CAP.
TERR.

Minna

Bida

Lafia

PLATEAU

Makurdi

BENUE

CAMEROON

Mts.
Gan
Goriama

G H A N A

Tamale

OYO

Ogbomosho
IBADAN
Ilorin

Oshogbo

ONDO
Akure

ANAMBRA
Onitsha
Enugu

CROSS
RIVER

Bamenda

ACCRA
Tema

LAGOS
Cotonou
Porto-Novo

Abeokuta
OGUN
Ijebu-Ode

BENDEL
Benin
City

Warri

RIVERS
Port-Harcourt

IMO
Aba

AKWA
IBOM
Calabar

Buea
Limbe

DOUALA

Yaoundé

Slave Coast

*Bight of
Benin*

Niger
Delta

C A M E R O O N

G U L F   O F   G U I N E A

BIOKO
(FERNANDO POO)

Pico Santa Isabel

EQUATORIAL GUINEA

Bight of Bonny

East from Greenwich

5   6   7

COPYRIGHT. GEORGE PHILIP & SON, LTD.

A

B

C

D

E

F

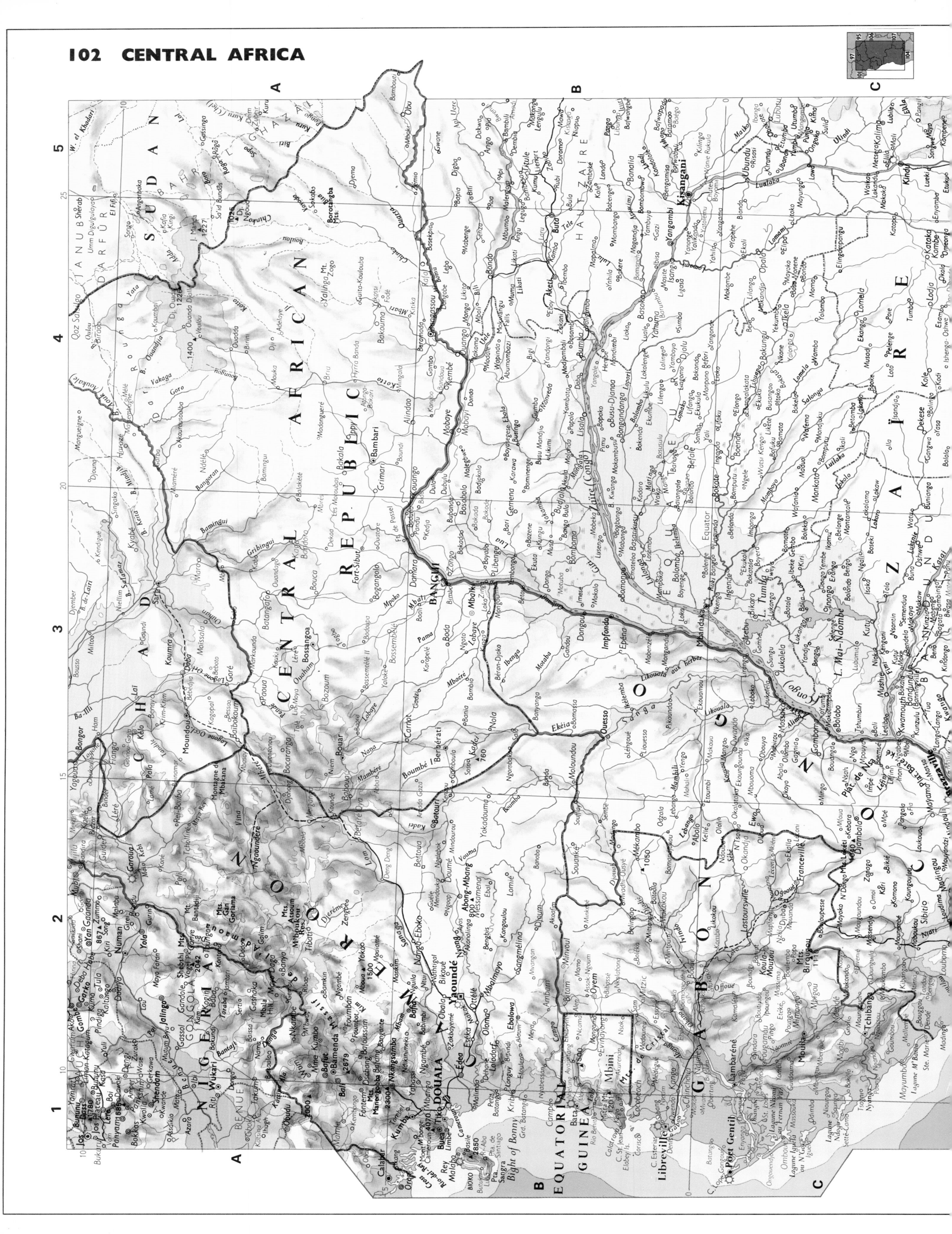

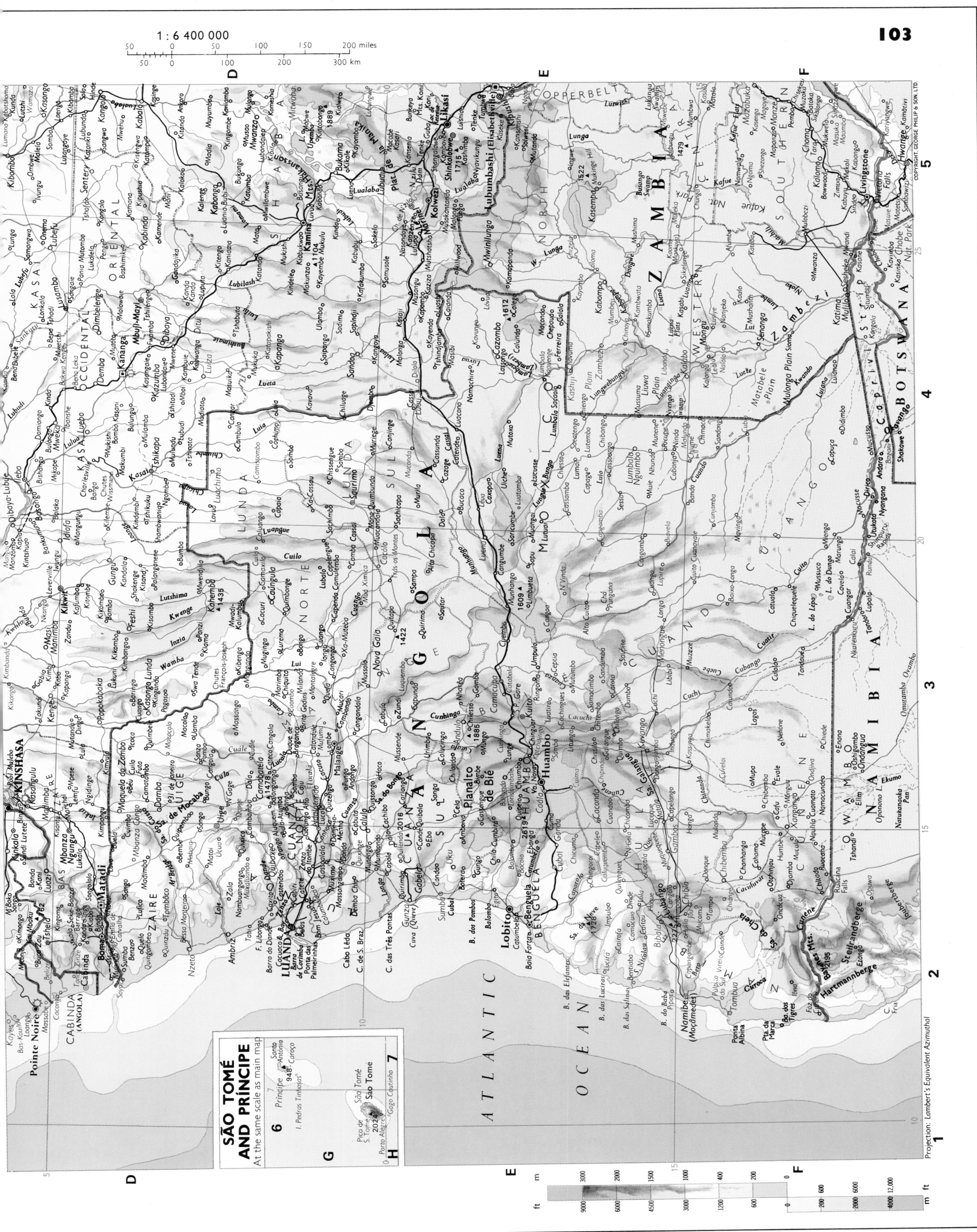

1 : 6 400 000

Projection: Lambert's Equivalent Azimuthal

COPYRIGHT. GEORGE PHILIP & SON LTD.

SÃO TOMÉ AND PRÍNCIPE
At the same scale as main map

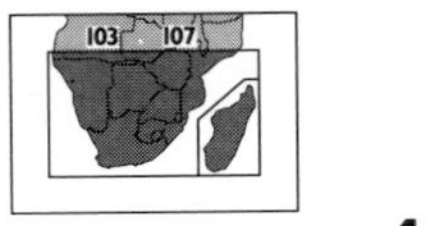

1   2   3   4

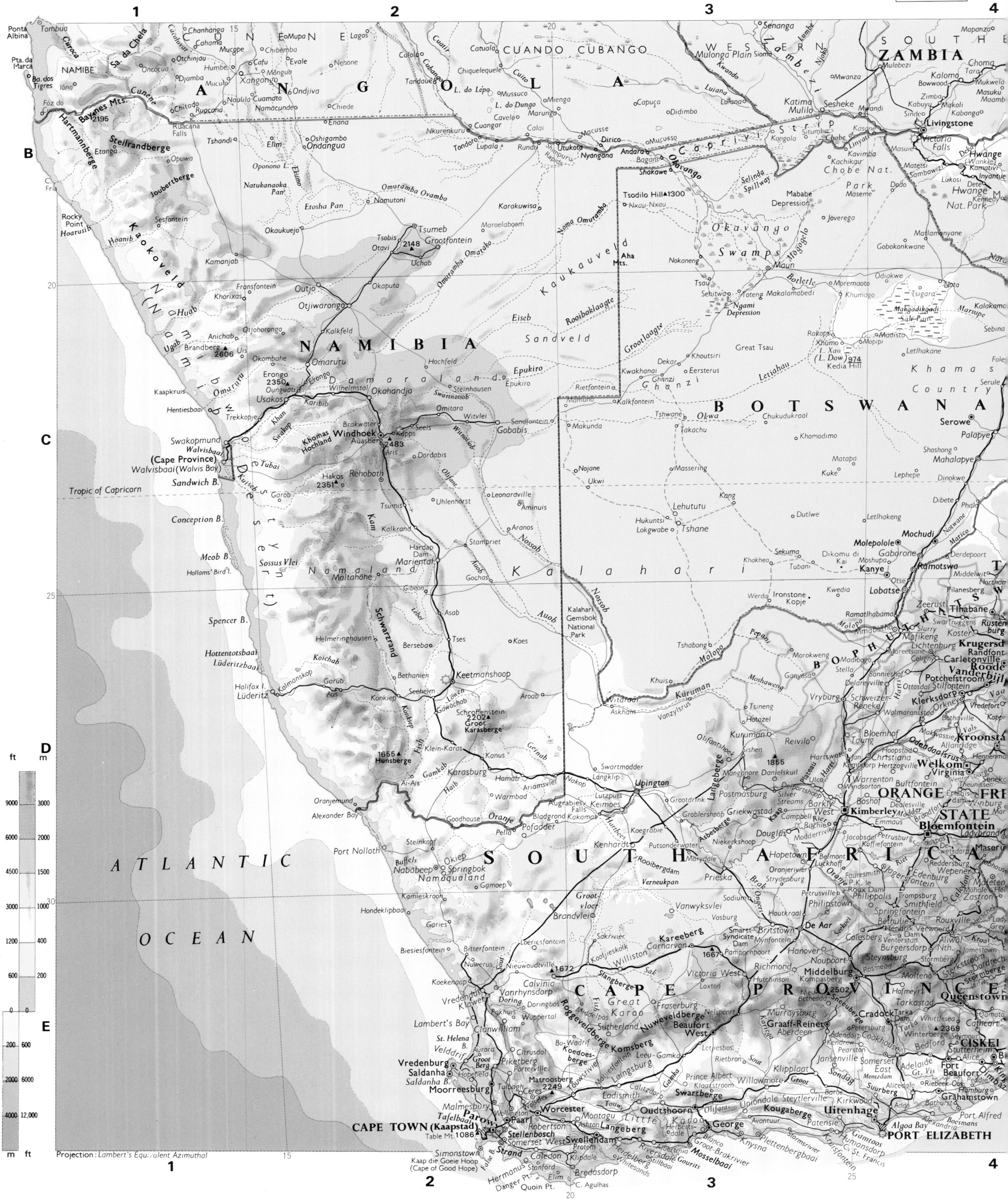

ZAMBIA

ANGOLA

CUANDO CUBANGO

WESTERN

Caprivi Strip

Livingstone

Victoria Falls

Hwange Nat. Park

Chobe Nat. Park

NAMIBIA

Etosha Pan

Tsumeb
Grootfontein

Kaokoveld

OKAVANGO Swamps

BOTSWANA

Serowe
Palapye
Mahalapye

Kalahari

Windhoek

Khomas Hochland

Swakopmund
Walvisbaai (Walvis Bay)
(Cape Province)

Tropic of Capricorn

Namib Desert

Rehoboth

Maltahohe

Kalahari Gemsbok National Park

Molepolole
Gaborone
Kanye
Lobatse
Ramotswa

Luderitz

Keetmanshoop

BOPHUTHATSWANA

Mafikeng
Lichtenburg
Krugersdorp
Potchefstroom
Klerksdorp

Kuruman

Vryburg

Bloemhof
Christiana

Welkom
Virginia

ORANGE FREE STATE

Kimberley
Bloemfontein

ATLANTIC OCEAN

Port Nolloth

SOUTH

AFRICA

Springbok
Namaqualand

Upington

De Aar

Carnarvon

Great Karoo

Beaufort West

CAPE PROVINCE

Queenstown

CISKEI

Fort Beaufort

Worcester

CAPE TOWN (Kaapstad)
Table Mt 1086

Stellenbosch

George

Oudtshoorn

Uitenhage

PORT ELIZABETH
Algoa Bay

Projection: Lambert's Equivalent Azimuthal

Kaap die Goeie Hoop
(Cape of Good Hope)

C. Agulhas

1 : 6 400 000

50   0   50   100   150   200 miles
50   0   100   200   300 km

MALAWI

ZAMBÉZIA

MOZAMBIQUE CHANNEL

ZIMBABWE

HARARE

Chitungwiza

Bulawayo

MASHONALAND
WEST

MASHONALAND
CENTRAL

MATEBELELAND
NORTH

Gweru

Masvingo

Zvishavane

VENDA

MATABELELAND
SOUTH

Beira

Nova Lusitânia

MOZAMBIQUE

Mahajanga

MADAGASCAR

ANTANANARIVO

Antsirabe

Fianarantsoa

FIANARANTSOA

Toliara

MOZAMBIQUE CHANNEL

Antsiranana

ANTSIRANANA

Toamasina

Ile de
Juan de Nova
(Réunion)

Iles Glorieuses
(Réunion)

PRETORIA

JOHANNESBURG

Benoni
Springs

Soweto
Germiston

Vereeniging

Sasolburg

Maputo
(Lourenço Marques)

SWAZILAND

Manzini

TRANSVAAL

NATAL

LESOTHO

Pietermaritzburg

Mpumalanga
KwaMashu
DURBAN
Umlazi

Umtata

East London

INDIAN

OCEAN

Tropic of Capricorn

Taolanaro

East from Greenwich

MADAGASCAR

On same scale as General Map

COPYRIGHT. GEORGE PHILIP & SON. LTD.

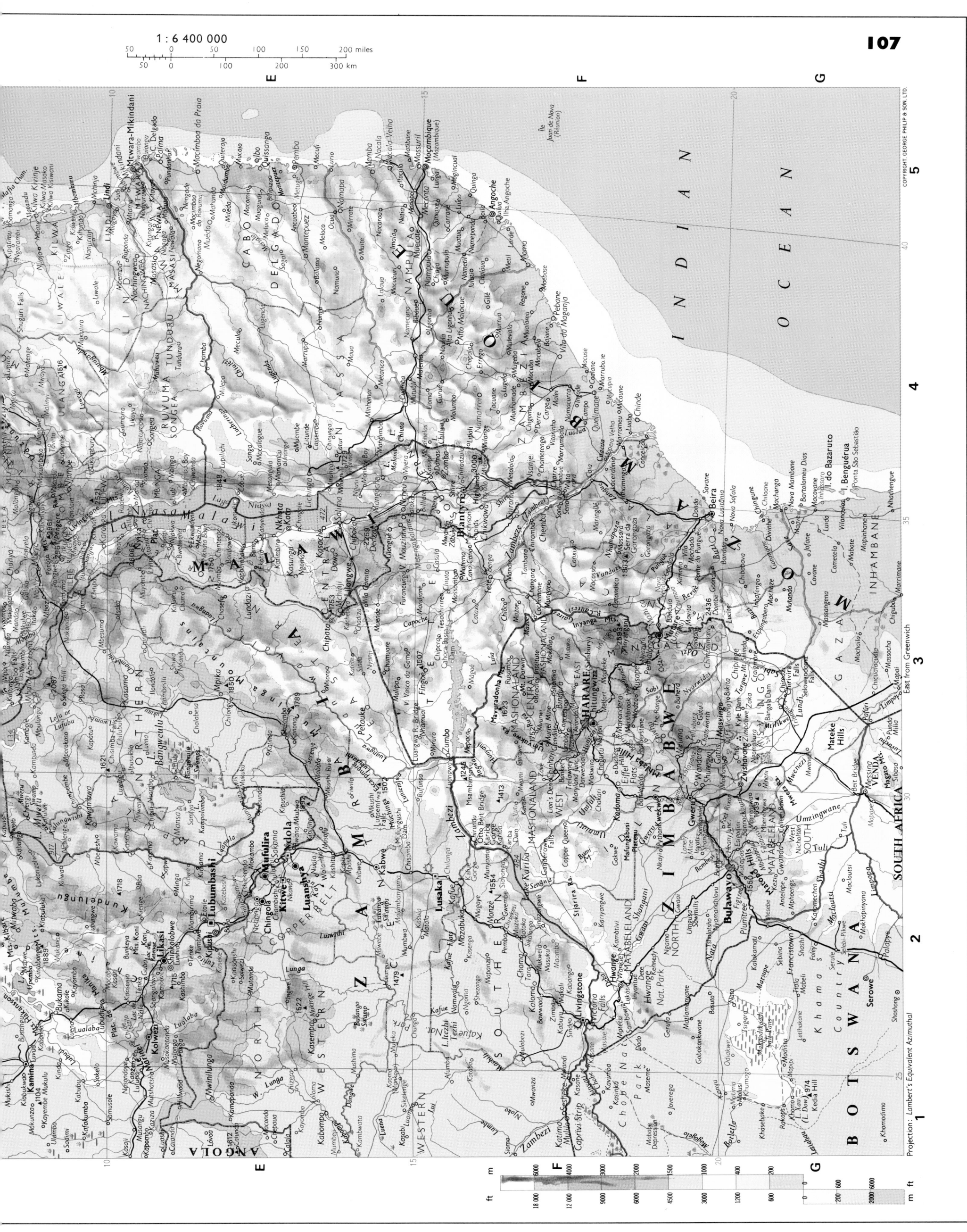

1 : 6 400 000

50   0   50   100   150   200 miles

50   0   100   200   300 km

INDIAN

OCEAN

COPYRIGHT GEORGE PHILIP & SON LTD.

Projection: Lambert's Equivalent Azimuthal

East from Greenwich

1 : 6 400 000

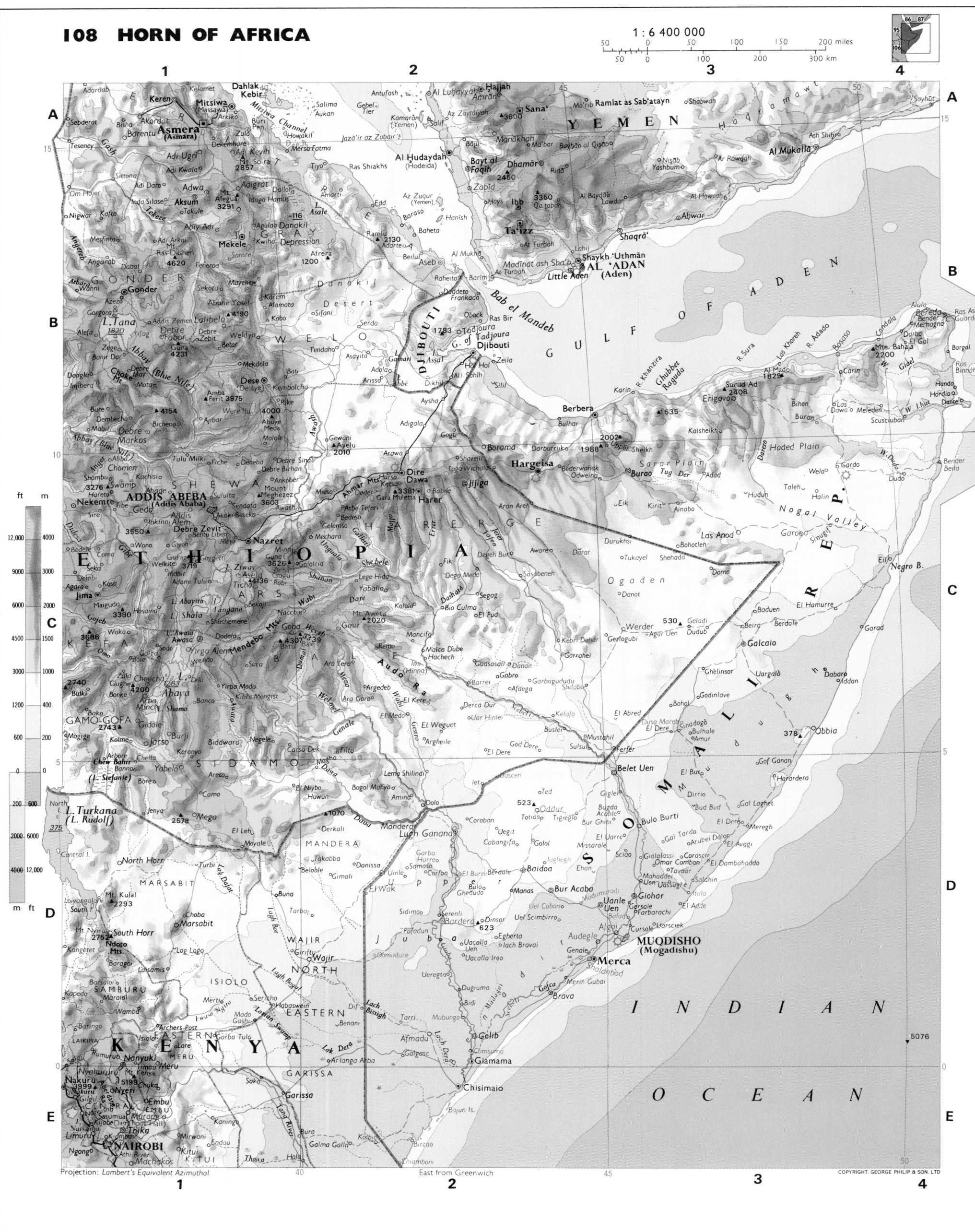

1 2 3 4 5 6 7 8 9 10

A
Mediterranean Sea Bayrūt SYRIA Baghdād IRAN AFGHANISTAN Rawalpindi XIZANG Xi'an CHINA
El Iskandariya Tel Aviv Yafo ISRAEL LEB. Dimashq Euphrates Esfahān Qandahār Lahore Mt. Yarlung Zangbo Chengdu Wuhan Nanjing Shanghai
Banghāzī Jerusalem IRAQ Karbalā Al Başrah Ābādān Quetta Everest 8848 Chongqing Hangzhou Nanchang
El Qāhira El Suweis JORDAN KUWAIT Zahedān PAKISTAN Indus Delhi Katmandu NEPAL Changsha Guiyang Wenzhou

B
LIBYA EGYPT Asyūt Nile SAUDI BAHRAIN QATAR UNITED G. of Oman Multan Agra Brahmaputra BHUTAN Kunming Fuzhou
Aswān L. Nasser Al Madīnah Ar Riyād ARAB Karachi Kanpur Ganga BANGLADESH Dhaka Guangzhou
CHAD Tropic of Cancer ARABIA EMIRATES INDIA Varanasi Chittagong Hong TAIWAN
Wadi Halfa Jiddah Makkah OMAN G. of Kutch Ahmadabad Calcutta Mandalay Hong Kong
Dongola Būr Sūdān Narmada Cuttack BURMA Hainan

C
Omdurmān El Khartūm Mitsiwa YEMEN Arabian Bombay Pune Hyderabad Bay of Rangoon THAILAND G. of Tonkin
SUDAN Asmera Al 'Adan Sea Krishna Bengal Bangkok Paracel Is.
L. Tana Ras Dashan Gulf of Aden Socotra (Yemen) Arabian Bangalore Madras Andaman Is. (India) CAMBODIA Phnom Penh South
CENTRAL DJIBOUTI Ras 'Asir (C. Guardafui) Basin Lakshadweep Is. (India) Mergui Arch. Ho Chi Minh Phanh Bho China

D
Addis Abeba Berbera Madurai SRI LANKA (CEYLON) Nicobar Is. (India) Isthmus of Kra Gulf of Sea
AFRICA ETHIOPIA 4620 4307 Batu 5824 5875 Pidurutalagala 2524 Thailand George Town
Wāw Mongalla Carlesberg MALDIVES Colombo Natuna BRUNEI SABAH BORNEO
L. Turkana SOMALI REP. Somali Kuala Lumpur MALAYSIA Kuching SARAWAK

E
ZAÏRE L. Mobutu Sese Seko UGANDA Muqdisho Ridge Chagos Archipelago (Br.) Diego Garcia Nias MALAYSIA Singapore
Kisangani Kampala Entebbe KENYA Mt. Kenya 5199 Basin Equator SEYCHELLES Mentawei Is. Borneo
L. Edward L. Victoria Nairobi 5895 Victoria Mahe Sumatera Bangka INDONESIA
RWANDA Mwanza Kilimanjaro Amirante Is. Des Roches Coetivy Is. Palembang Java Sea
BURUNDI Mombasa 'Alphonse' Jakarta Semarang Flores Sea

F
Bukama L. Kivu TANZANIA Pemba Zanzibar Aldabra Is. St. Pierre Sunda Strait Bandung Java Surabaya
L. Mweru Dar es Salaam Providence Bali Lombok Sumbawa
Lubumbashi ZAMBIA L. Bangweulu Farquhar Is. Agalega I. Cocos or Keeling Is. (Austral.) Christmas I. (Austral.) 7450
ANGOLA Lusaka L. Malawi COMOROS Tromelin I. 4819 6327
Lilongwe Moçambique Cargados Garajos

G
NAMIBIA ZIMBABWE Blantyre MADAGASCAR Rodriguez MAURITIUS N.W. Cape Onslow
BOTSWANA Harare Beira Toamasina Mascarene Tropic of Capricorn Shark Bay WESTERN
Gaborone Bulawayo Antananarivo 5322 Port St. Louis Mascarene Islands AUSTRALIA
Johannesburg Pretoria 2643 Denis Réunion (Fr.) Geraldton AUSTRALIA
Kimberley Maputo Bassas da India (Fr.) Mascarene Basin Kalgoorlie
SOUTH AFRICA Bloemfontein Ntlenyana I. Europa (Fr.) Toliara 6400 1491 1104 Perth Geographe Bay

H
Cape Town Durban Madagascar Equatorial Limit of Icebergs Fremantle
Port Elizabeth Basin Amsterdam I. (Fr.) Albany
East London St. Paul I. (Fr.)

J
Agulhas 5778 Crozet Southeast Indian Rise
Basin Pr. Edward Is. (S.A.) Basin Crozet Is. (Fr.) 2899
Marion I. Hog I. Possession I.

K
Atlantic Indian Ridge Kerguelen (Fr.) I. McDonald Is. Heard I. (Austral.) 5141 5202
Extreme Limit of Pack Ice
5848

L
4850 4691
Antarctic Circle Wilkes Land
Queen Maud Land Enderby Land Adélie Land

M

ft m
18 000 6000
12 000 4000
6000 2000
3000 1000
1200 400
600 200
0 0
200 600
2000 6000
4000 12 000
6000 18 000
m ft

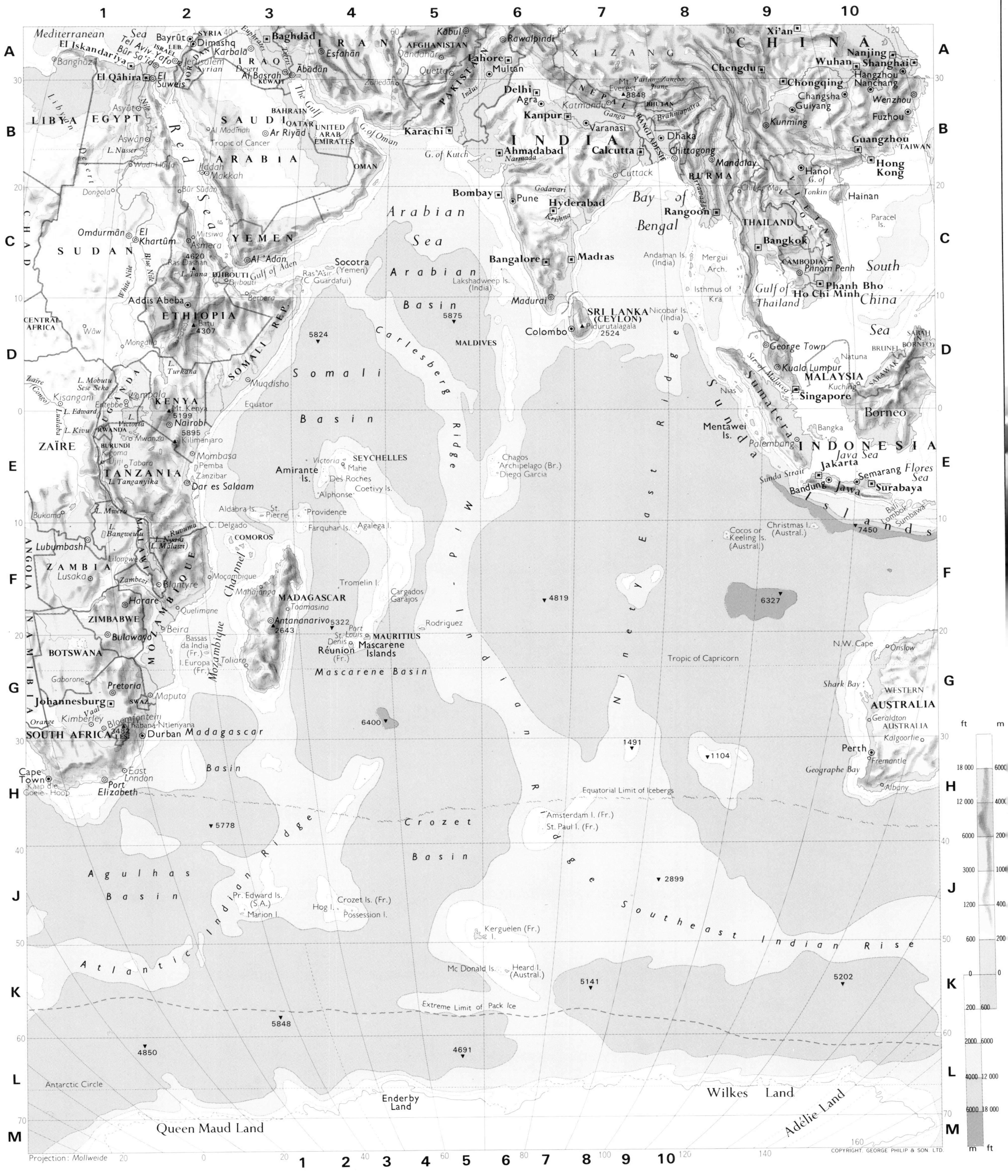

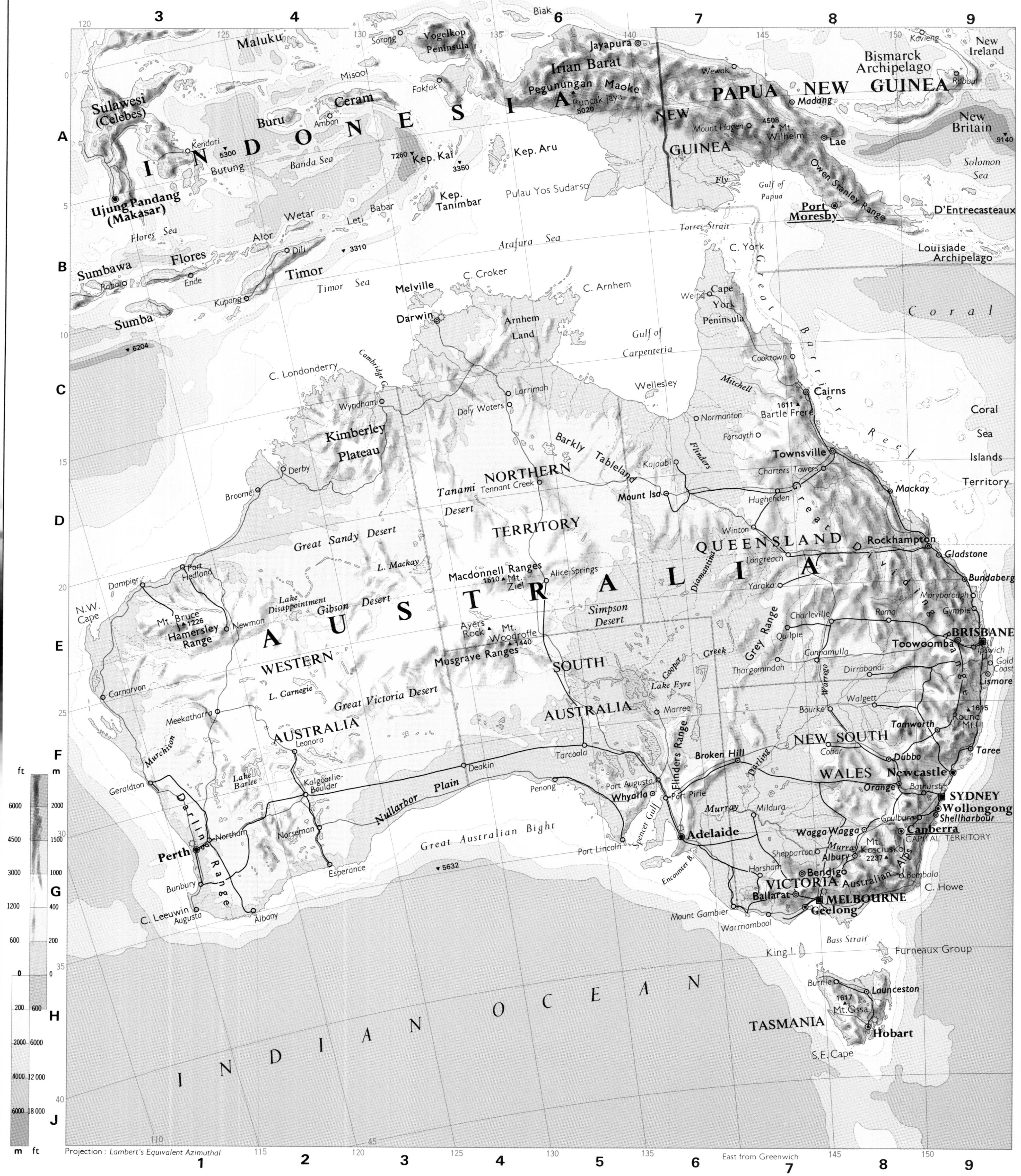

INDONESIA

Maluku
Sulawesi (Celebes)
Ceram
Buru
Ambon
Kendari
Butung
Banda Sea
Ujung Pandang (Makasar)
Flores Sea
Sumbawa
Flores
Sumba
Babao
Ende
Kupang
Timor
Timor Sea
Sorong
Vogelkop Peninsula
Misool
Fakfak
Kep. Kai
Kep. Aru
Kep. Tanimbar
Wetar
Leti
Babar
Alor
Dili
Biak
Jayapura
Irian Barat
Pegunungan Maoke
Puncak Jaya 5020
Pulau Yos Sudarso
Arafura Sea
Torres Strait

PAPUA NEW GUINEA

New Ireland
Bismarck Archipelago
Wewak
Madang
Mount Hagen
Mt. Wilhelm 4508
Lae
New Britain
9140
Solomon Sea
Fly
Gulf of Papua
Port Moresby
Owen Stanley Range
D'Entrecasteaux
Louisiade Archipelago

AUSTRALIA

C. York
Cape York Peninsula
Weipa
Gulf of Carpentaria
Melville
C. Croker
C. Arnhem
Darwin
Arnhem Land
Wellesley
Cooktown
Cairns
Coral Sea
Coral Sea Islands Territory
C. Londonderry
Cambridge G.
Wyndham
Larrimah
Daly Waters
Mitchell
Normanton
Forsayth
Bartle Frere 1611
Townsville
Charters Towers
Kimberley Plateau
Derby
Broome
NORTHERN TERRITORY
Tanami Desert
Tennant Creek
Barkly Tableland
Kajabbi
Mount Isa
Hughenden
Mackay
Winton
QUEENSLAND
Rockhampton
Gladstone
Longreach
Bundaberg
Maryborough
Gympie
Port Hedland
Dampier
N.W. Cape
Great Sandy Desert
L. Mackay
Macdonnell Ranges
Mt. Ziel 1510
Alice Springs
Simpson Desert
Yaraka
Diamantina
Mt. Bruce 1726
Hamersley Range
Newman
Lake Disappointment
Gibson Desert
Ayers Rock
Mt. Woodroffe 1440
Musgrave Ranges
SOUTH AUSTRALIA
Lake Eyre
Cooper Creek
Grey Range
Charleville
Roma
Quilpie
Toowoomba
BRISBANE
Ipswich
Gold Coast
Lismore
Carnarvon
L. Carnegie
Great Victoria Desert
Marree
Thargomindah
Cunnamulla
Bourke
Walgett
Tamworth
Round Mt. 1615
WESTERN AUSTRALIA
Leonora
Meekatharra
Broken Hill
Flinders Range
Warrego
Dirranbandi
NEW SOUTH WALES
Cobar
Dubbo
Taree
Murchison
Geraldton
Lake Barlee
Kalgoorlie-Boulder
Tarcoola
Deakin
Nullarbor Plain
Penong
Port Augusta
Port Pirie
Whyalla
Spencer Gulf
Darling
Mildura
Wagga Wagga
Orange
Bathurst
Newcastle
SYDNEY
Wollongong
Shellharbour
Northam
Norseman
Great Australian Bight
Port Lincoln
Adelaide
Murray
Goulburn
Canberra CAPITAL TERRITORY
Mt. Kosciusko 2237
PERTH
Darling Range
Bunbury
C. Leeuwin
Augusta
Albany
Esperance 5632
Shepparton
Horsham
Bendigo
VICTORIA
Ballarat
Australian Alps
Bombala
C. Howe
MELBOURNE
Geelong
Mount Gambier
Warrnambool
Encounter B.
King I.
Bass Strait
Furneaux Group
TASMANIA
Burnie
Launceston
Mt. Ossa 1617
Hobart
S.E. Cape

INDIAN OCEAN

ft / m scale:
6000 2000
4500 1500
3000 1000
1200 400
600 200
0 0
600 -200
6000 2000
12000 4000
18000 6000

Projection: Lambert's Equivalent Azimuthal
East from Greenwich

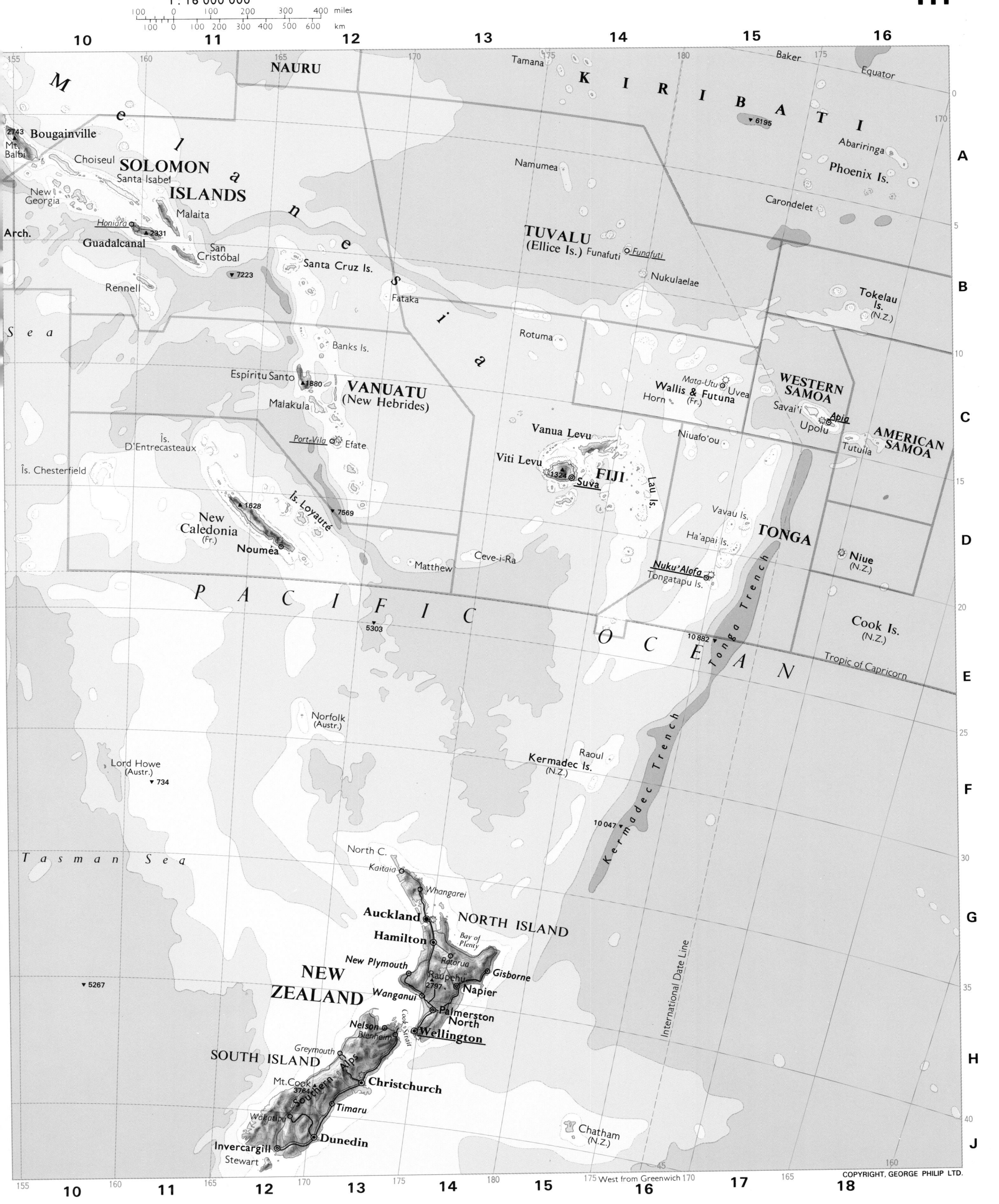

1 : 16 000 000

100 0 100 200 300 400 miles
100 0 100 200 300 400 500 600 km

10   11   12   13   14   15   16

155   160   165   170   175   180   175   170

NAURU

Tamana

K I R I B A T I

▼6195

Baker

Equator

M
e
l
a
n
e
s
i
a

▲2743 Bougainville
Mt.
Balbi

Choiseul

Santa Isabel

SOLOMON

ISLANDS

New
Georgia

Arch.

Honiara

▲2331

Guadalcanal

Malaita

San
Cristóbal

Rennell

▼7223

Sea

Fataka

Namumea

Abariringa

Phoenix Is.

Carondelet

Tokelau
Is.
(N.Z.)

TUVALU
(Ellice Is.) Funafuti ○Funafuti

Nukulaelae

Rotuma

Santa Cruz Is.

Banks Is.

Espíritu Santo ▲1880

VANUATU
(New Hebrides)

Malakula

Mata-Utu ○Uvea
Wallis & Futuna
Horn   (Fr.)

WESTERN
SAMOA

Savai'i
Upolu

Apia

AMERICAN
SAMOA

Tutuila

Îs.
D'Entrecasteaux

Port-Vila ○Efate

Vanua Levu

Viti Levu

▲1324 ○Suva FIJI

Niuafo'ou

Lau Is.

Î. Chesterfield

▼1628

Îs. Loyauté

▼7569

New
Caledonia
(Fr.)

Nouméa ○

Matthew

Ceve-i-Ra

Vavau Is.

Ha'apai Is.

TONGA

Niue
(N.Z.)

P A C I F I C

▼5303

Nuku'Alofa ○
Tongatapu Is.

Tonga Trench

▼10 882

Cook Is.
(N.Z.)

Tropic of Capricorn

O C E A N

Norfolk
(Austr.)

Raoul

Kermadec Is.
(N.Z.)

Kermadec Trench

▼10 047

Lord Howe
(Austr.)

▼734

Tasman Sea

North C.

Kaitaia ○

Whangarei

Auckland ○○

NORTH ISLAND

Hamilton ○

Bay of
Plenty

New Plymouth

Rotorua ○

Ruapehu
2797

Gisborne ○

NEW
ZEALAND

Wanganui ○

Napier ○

Palmerston
North ○

▼5267

Nelson ○
Blenheim ○
Cook Strait

Wellington ○

Greymouth ○

SOUTH ISLAND

Southern Alps

Mt.Cook
3764

Christchurch ○

Wakatipu

Timaru ○

Chatham
(N.Z.)

Invercargill ○
Stewart

Dunedin ○

International Date Line

A
B
C
D
E
F
G
H
J

0
170
5
10
15
20
25
30
35
40

155   160   165   170   175   180   175 West from Greenwich 170   165   160

10   11   12   13   14   15   16   17   18

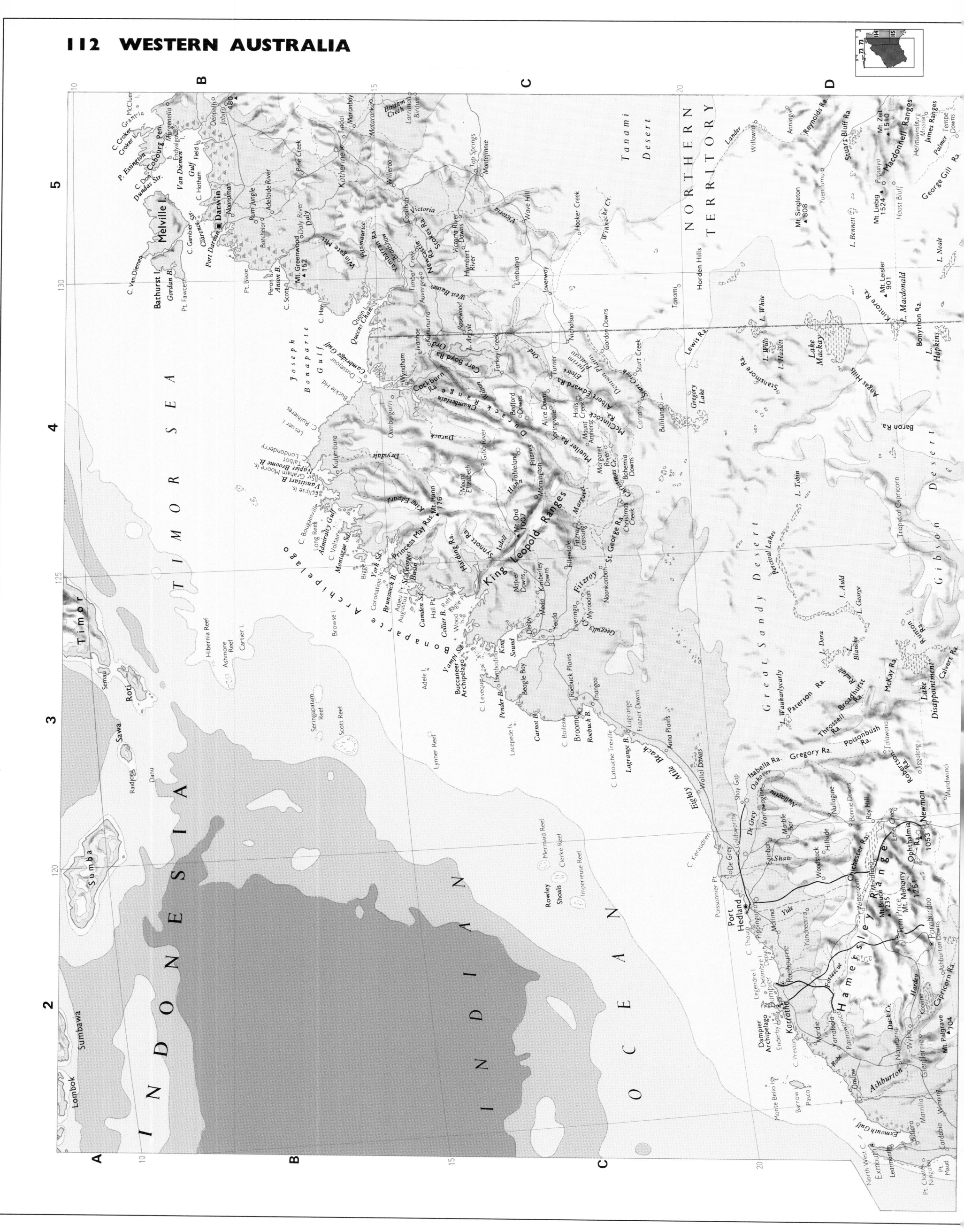

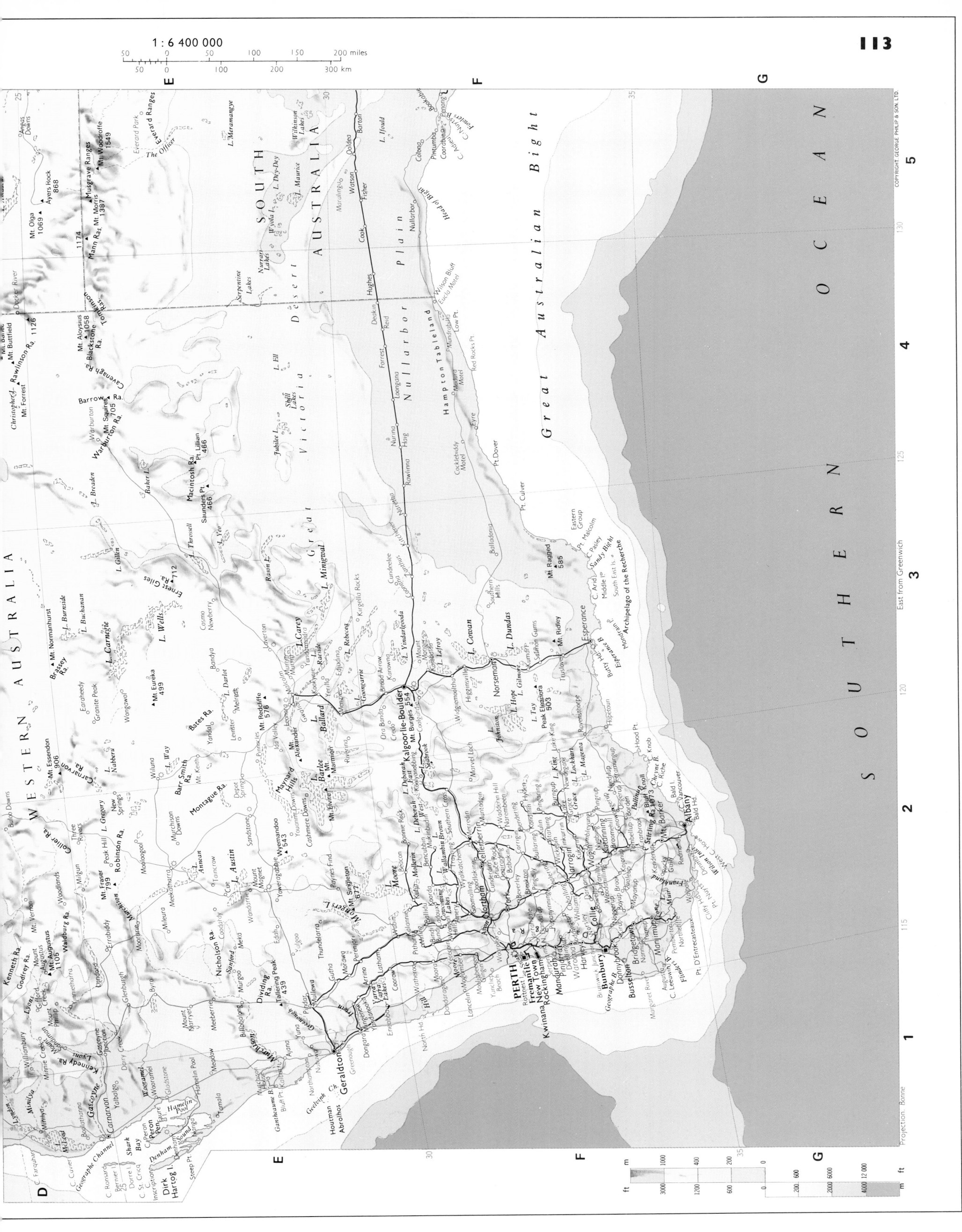

113

1 : 6 400 000

50   0   50   100   150   200 miles
50   0   100   200   300 km

E

Projection: Bonne

East from Greenwich

COPYRIGHT GEORGE PHILIP & SON LTD

WESTERN AUSTRALIA

SOUTH AUSTRALIA

Great Victoria Desert

Nullarbor Plain

Hampton Tableland

Great Australian Bight

SOUTHERN OCEAN

Everard Ranges
The Officer
Ayers Rock 868
Mt. Olga 1069
Mann Ras. Mt. Morris 1387
Musgrave Ranges
Mt Woodroffe 1549
L. Meramangye
Wilkinson Lakes
L. Dey-Dey
L. Maurice
1174
Serpentine Lakes
Nurrai Lakes

Mt. Barker
Christopher I.
Rawlinson Ra.
Mt Buttfield 1126
Mt Forrest
Cavenagh Ra.
Mt. Aloysius 1058
Mt. Blackstone Ra.
Barrow Ra.
Warburton
Mt. Squires Ra.
Warburton Ra. 105

Kennedy Ra.
Godfrey Ra.
Mount Augustus 1105
Waldburg Ra.
Lyons
Collier Ra.
Three Rivers
Peak Hill
L. Gregory
New Springs
Carnarvon Ra.
Brassey Ra.
L. Buchanan
L. Carnegie
Ernest Giles Ra. 712
L. Gillen
Throssell
L. Yeo
Macintosh Ra.
Saunders Pt. 466
Pt. Lilian 466

Geographe Channel
Shark Bay
Denham
Hamelin Pool
Gascoyne Jn.
Carnarvon
Minnie Creek
Gascoyne
Mt. Vernon
Mt. Essendon 906
Mt Normanhurst
Earaheedy
Granite Peak
Wongawol
L. Wells
Baker L.
L. Breaden
Montague Ra.
Bates Ra.
Mt. Eureka 499
L. Carey

Geraldton
Greenough
Dongara
Houtman Abrolhos
North Hd.
Greenough Ch.
Gullewa
Mullewa
Yalgoo
Morawa
Perenjori
Dalwallinu
Dividing Peak 439
Talbingering Peak
Cue
Mount Magnet
Sandstone
Meekatharra
Murchison Downs
Cosmo Newberry
Laverton
L. Minigwal
L. Rason E.

PERTH
Fremantle
Rottnest I.
New Town
Kwinana
Rockingham
Mandurah
Pinjarra
Harvey
Collie
Bunbury
Busselton
Margaret River
C. Leeuwin
Augusta
Albany
King George Sd.
Mt Barker
Stirling Ra. 1073
Esperance
Norseman
Kalgoorlie-Boulder 554
Mt Burges
Coolgardie
Kambalda
L. Lefroy
L. Cowan
L. Dundas
L. Johnston
Peak Eleanora 503
Mt Ridley
Archipelago of the Recherche

Great Australian Bight
Wilson Bluff
Eucla Motel
Mundrabilla
Nullarbor
Koonalda
Eyre
Cocklebiddy Motel
Madura Motel
Pt. Culver
Pt. Dover
Israelite B.
Cape Arid
Middle I.
South East Is.
Cape Pasley

Kalgoorlie
Coolgardie
Southern Cross
Merredin
Kellerberrin
York
Northam
Beverley
Brookton
Corrigin
Narrogin
Wagin
Katanning
Kojonup
Cranbrook
Mt. Barker

ft   m
3000 1000
1200 400
600   200
0   0
      m
200   600
2000 6000
4000 12000
ft

D

E

F

G

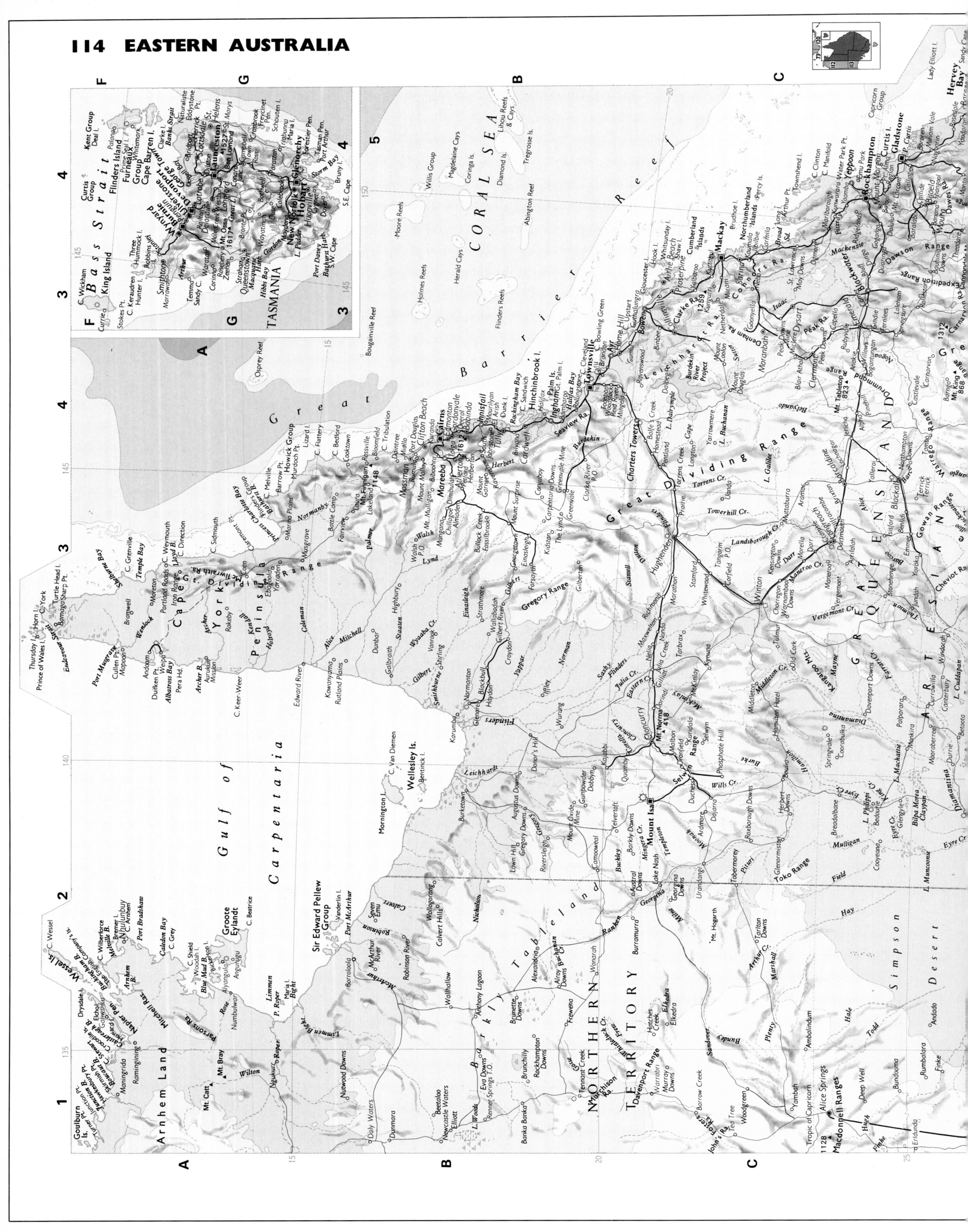

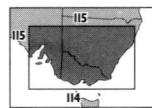

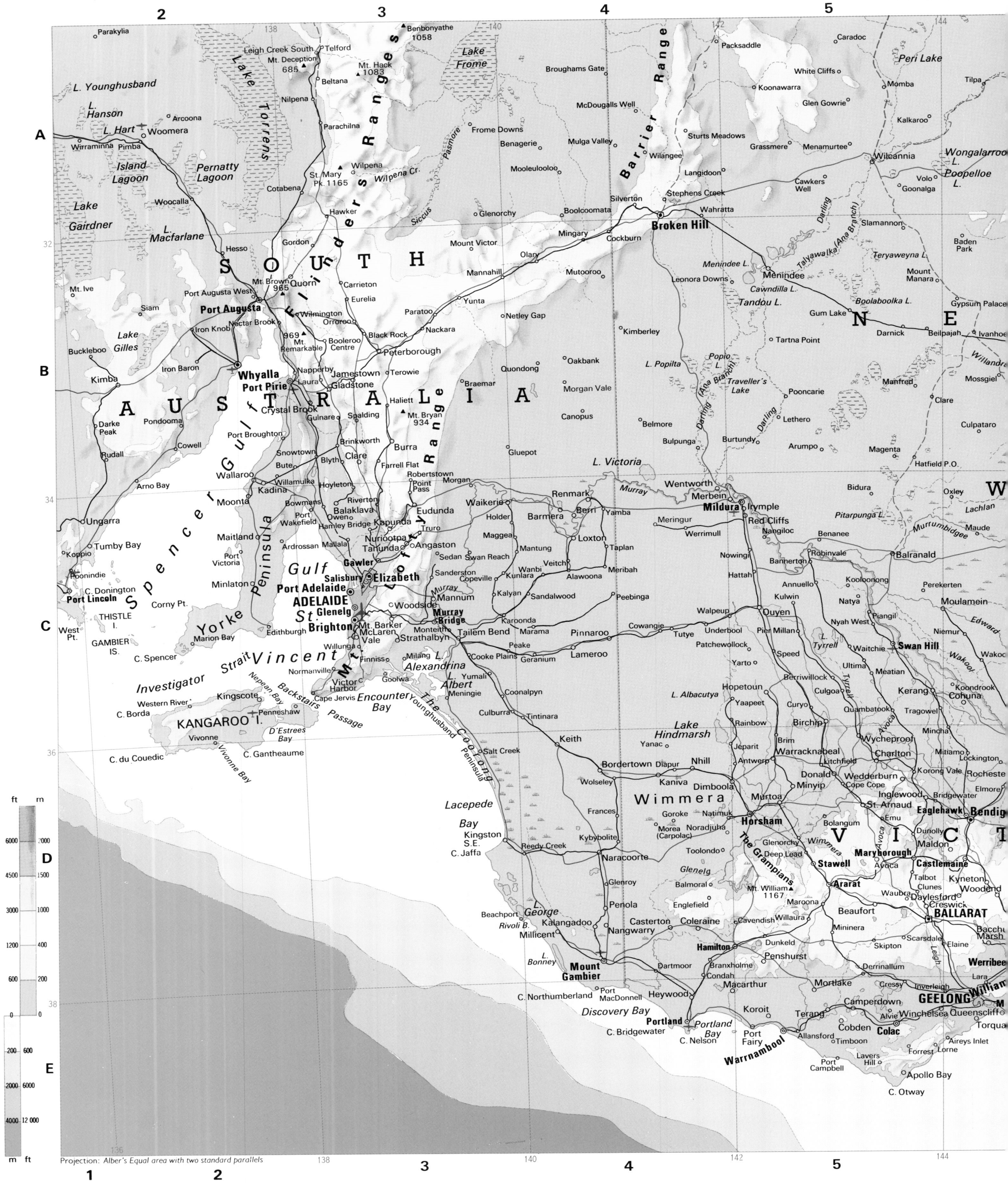

2　3　4　5

Parakylia　Benbonyathe 1058　Packsaddle　Caradoc　Peri Lake
Leigh Creek South　Telford　Broughams Gate　White Cliffs　Tilpa
Mt. Deception 685　Beltana　McDougalls Well　Koonawarra　Momba
L. Younghusband　Nilpena　Glen Gowrie　Kalkaroo
L. Hanson　Parachilna　Lake Frome　Benagerie　Mulga Valley　Sturts Meadows　Grassmere　Menamurtee
L. Hart　Arcoona　Frome Downs　Pasmore　Langidoon　Wilcannia
Wirraminna　Woomera　St. Mary Pk. 1165　Wilpena　Mooleulooloo　Wilangee　Wongalarroo L.
Pimba　Wilpena Cr.　Silverton　Poopelloe L.
Island Lagoon　Pernatty Lagoon　Cotabena　Stephens Creek　Cawkers Well　Baden Park
Mt. Ive　Hawker　Glenorchy　Boolcoomata　Wahratta
Lake Gairdner　Hesso　Gordon　Mount Victor　Cockburn　Broken Hill　Slamannon
L. Macfarlane　Mannahill　Olary　Menindee L.　Teryaweyna L.
Mt. Brown 965　Quorn　Carrieton　Yunta　Leonora Downs　Menindee　Mount Manara
Port Augusta West　Eurelia　Paratoo　Mutooroo　Tandou L.　Boolaboolka L.
Port Augusta　Wilmington　Black Rock　Netley Gap　Gum Lake　Gypsum Palace
Nectar Brook　Orroroo　Nackara　Kimberley　Tartna Point　Darnick　Ivanhoe
Iron Knob　969 Mt. Remarkable　Booleroo Centre　Peterborough　Oakbank　Popio L.　Poncarie
Iron Baron　Napperby　Terowie　Quondong　L. Popilta　Traveller's Lake　Manfred
Buckleboo　Laura　Jamestown　Braemar　Morgan Vale　Belmore　Lethero　Clare
Kimba　Whyalla　Gladstone　Burtundy　Culparoo
Port Pirie　Crystal Brook　Canopus　Bulpunga　Arumpo　Magenta
Darke Peak　Pondooma　Gulnare　Spalding　Mt. Bryan 934　Gluepot　L. Victoria　Hatfield P.O.
Iron Baron　Port Broughton　Snowtown　Blyth　Clare　Farrell Flat　Wentworth
Rudall　Cowell　Bute　Burra　Renmark　Murray　Bidura　Oxley
Wallaroo　Willamulka　Hoyleton　Robertstown　Berri　Mildura　Pitarpunga L.
Arno Bay　Kadina　Bowmans　Balaklava　Point Pass　Morgan　Waikerie　Yamba　Irymple　Maude
Moonta　Riverton　Eudunda　Holder　Barmera　Meringur　Red Cliffs　Benanee
Ungarra　Maitland　Port Wakefield　Hamley Bridge　Kapunda　Truro　Maggea　Loxton　Werrimull　Nangiloc　Balranald
Tumby Bay　Ardrossan　Mallala　Nuriootpa　Angaston　Sedan　Swan Reach　Wanbi　Veitch　Taplan　Nowingi　Robinvale
Koppio　Port Victoria　Owen　Tanunda　Sanderston　Copeville　Kunlara　Meribah　Hattah
Poonindie　Minlaton　Gawler　Salisbury　Elizabeth　Kalyan　Sandalwood　Walpeup　Ouyen
Port Lincoln　Corny Pt.　Port Adelaide　Mannum　Peebinga　Kulwin　Kooloonong　Natya
West Pt.　THISTLE I.　ADELAIDE　St. Woodside　Murray　Karoonda　Cowangie　Tutye　Pier Millan　Piangil
GAMBIER IS.　Marion Bay　Glenelg　Murray Bridge　Marama　Pinnaroo　Underbool　Patchewollock　Speed
C. Spencer　Brighton　Mt. Barker　Monteith　Peake　Yarto　Ultima　Swan Hill
Investigator Strait　Vincent　McLaren Vale　Strathalbyn　Tailem Bend　Geranium　Lameroo　Berriwillock　Waitchie
Edithburgh　Willunga　Cooke Plains　Tintinara　Rainbow　Meatian
Kangaroo I.　Normanville　Milang L. Alexandrina　Coonalpyn　Hopetoun　Yaapeet　Birchip　Kerang
Western River　Kingscote　Victor Harbor　Albert　Meningie　Culburra　L. Albacutya　Curyo　Quambatook
C. Borda　Vivonne　Goolwa　L. Yumali　L. Albert　Jeparit　Brim　Avoca　Tragowel
Penneshaw　D'Estrees Bay　Encounter Bay　Lake Hindmarsh　Warracknabeal　Wycheproof　Mincha
C. du Couedic　Vivonne Bay　Salt Creek　Keith　Yanac　Antwerp　Litchfield　Charlton
C. Gantheaume　The Coorong　Bordertown　Diapur　Nhill　Donald　Cope Cope　Korong Vale　Rochester
Lacepede Bay　Wolseley　Kaniva　Dimboola　Minyip　Wedderburn　Elmore
Kingston S.E.　Frances　Goroke　Natimuk　Murtoa　St. Arnaud　Inglewood　Bridgewater
C. Jaffa　Wimmera　Horsham　Emu　Dunolly　Maldon
Reedy Creek　Kybybolite　Morea Noradjuha (Carpolac)　Glenorchy　Wimmera　Maryborough　Castlemaine
Naracoorte　Toolondo　The Grampians　Deep Lead　Stawell　Avoca　Talbot　Kyneton
Glenelg　Balmoral　Mt. William 1167　Ararat　Clunes　Woodend
George　Glenroy　Englefield　Maroona　Waubra　Daylesford　Creswick
Beachport　Kalangadoo　Casterton　Coleraine　Cavendish Willaura　Beaufort　BALLARAT
Rivoli B.　Millicent　Nangwarry　Dunkeld　Mininera　Scarsdale　Elaine
L. Bonney　Penola　Hamilton　Penshurst　Skipton　Derrinallum　Werribee
Mount Gambier　Dartmoor　Branxholme Condah　Macarthur　Mortlake　Cressy　Inverleigh
Port MacDonnell　Heywood　Koroit　Camperdown　Terang　Winchelsea　GEELONG
C. Northumberland　Discovery Bay　Portland　Cobden　Colac　Torquay
C. Bridgewater　Portland Bay　Port Fairy　Allansford　Timboon　Aireys Inlet
Warrnambool　C. Nelson　Port Campbell　Lavers Hill　Forrest　Lorne
Apollo Bay
C. Otway

SOUTH AUSTRALIA

Flinders Ranges · **Mt. Lofty Range** · **Spencer Gulf** · **Yorke Peninsula** · **Gulf St. Vincent** · **The Younghusband Peninsula** · **Wimmera** · **VICTORIA** · **Barrier Range** · **Darling** · **Murrumbidgee** · **Lachlan** · **NEW SOUTH WALES**

ft m
6000 2000
4500 1500
3000 1000
1200 400
600 200
0 0
200 600
2000 6000
4000 12000
m ft

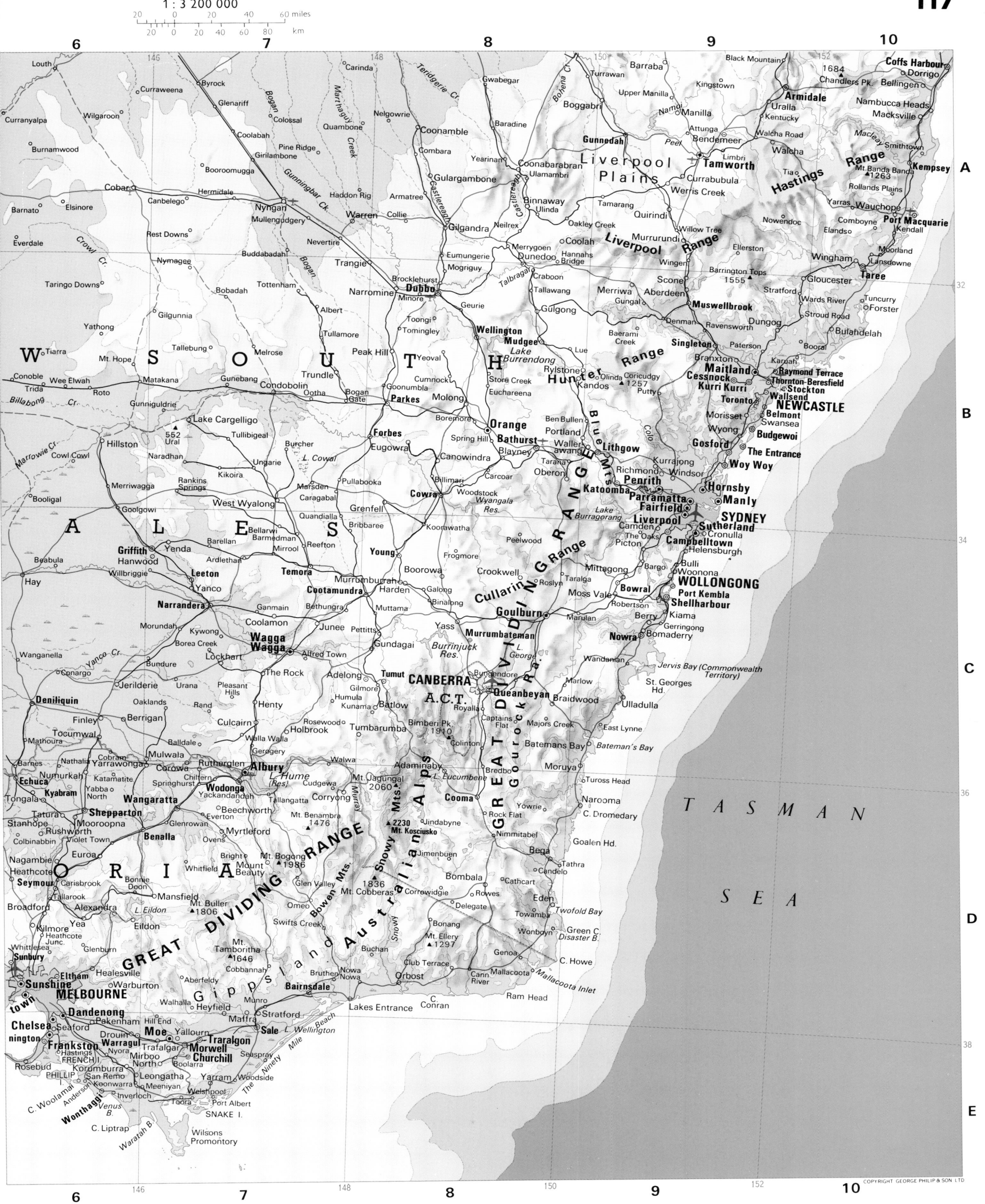

1 : 3 200 000

20   0   20   40   60 miles
20   0   20   40   60   80   km

6   7   8   9   10

Louth
Currawena
Curranyalpa
Wilgaroon
Burnamwood
Barnato
Elsinore
Everdale
Conoble
Trida
Wee Elwah
Yathong
Tiarra
Mt. Hope
Billabong
Booligal
Hay
Beabula
Hillston
Merriwagga
Goolgowi
Roto
Gunnigudrie
Naradhan
Rankins Springs
Barellan
Ardlethan
Griffith
Hanwood
Willbriggie
Yenda
Leeton
Yanco
Narrandera
Morundah
Kywong
Borea Creek
Wanganella
Conargo
Jerilderie
Urana
Rand
Deniliquin
Finley
Tocumwal
Mathoura
Barnes
Nathalia
Cobram
Mulwala
Numurkah
Yarrawonga
Corowa
Echuca
Kyabram
Katamatite
Springhurst
Chiltern
Wangaratta
Tongala
Taturra
Stanhope
Rushworth
Mooroopna
Shepparton
Colbinabbin
Violet Town
Benalla
Nagambie
Heathcote
Euroa
Seymour
Carisbrook
Tallarook
Kilmore
Heathcote Junc.
Broadford
Alexandra
Yea
Whittlesea
Glenburn
Sunbury
Healesville
Warburton
Eltham
Sunshine
town
MELBOURNE
Dandenong
Chelsea
nington
Seaford
Frankston
Rosebud
FRENCH I.
PHILLIP
C. Woolamai
Wonthaggi
C. Liptrap

Cobar
Canbelego
Hermidale
Nyngan
Mullengudgery
Nevertire
Buddabadah
Nymagee
Gilgunnia
Matakana
Condobolin
Gunebang
Tullibigeal
Lake Cargelligo
552 Ural
Kikoira
Ungarie
L. Cowal
Burcher
West Wyalong
Caragabal
Quandialla
Bribbaree
Reefton
Barmedman
Mirrool
Temora
Ganmain
Coolamon
Junee
Lockhart
Bundure
The Rock
Oaklands
Berrigan
Balldale
Culcairn
Walla Walla
Gerogery
Rutherglen
Albury
Wodonga
Yackandandah
Beechworth
Everton
Glenrowan
Myrtleford
Ovens
Bright
Whitfield
Mount Beauty
Mansfield
Mt. Buller
1806
L. Eildon
Eildon
Omeo
Glen Valley
GREAT
Mt. Tamboritha
1646
Aberfeldy
Cobbannah
Walhalla
Heyfield
Gippsland
Warragul
Nyora
Mirboo North
Korumburra
San Remo
Leongatha
Koonwarra
Meeniyan
Inverloch
Toora
Venus B.
SNAKE I.
Waratah B.
Wilsons Promontory

Carinda
Coolabah
Colossal
Booroomugga
Cabon
Pine Ridge
Girilambone
Haddon Rig
Warren
Collie
Gilgandra
Trangie
Brocklehurst
Narromine
Minore
DUBBO
Toongi
Tomingley
Peak Hill
Trundle
Tullamore
Melrose
Parkes
Bogan Gate
Forbes
Eugowra
Grenfell
Caragabal
Young
Murrumburrah
Cootamundra
Harden
Bethungra
Junee
Pettitts
Gundagai
Adelong
Tumut
Gilmore
Humula
Kunama
Batlow
Holbrook
Tumbarumba
Rosewood
Walla Walla
Adaminaby
Cudgewa
Tallangatta
Corryong
Mt. Jagungal
2060
L. Eucumbene
Snowy
Mt. Kosciusko
2230
Jindabyne
Jimenbuen
Cooma
DIVIDING
Mt. Bogong
1986
Mt. Benambra
1476
Bonang
Mt. Cobberas 1836
Swifts Creek
Bowen Mts.
Buchan
RANGE
Mt. Ellery
1297
Nowa Nowa
Bruthen
Bairnsdale
Stratford
Maffra
Sale
L. Wellington
Traralgon
Morwell
Churchill
Trafalgar
Moe
Yallourn
Yarram
Welshpool
Woodside
Port Albert
Seaspray
The Ninety Mile Beach

Gwabegar
Baradine
Coonamble
Combara
Yearinan
Ulamambri
Merrygoen
Mogriguy
Geurie
Wellington
Mudgee
Lake Burrendong
Store Creek
Molong
Orange
Spring Hill
Bathurst
Blayney
Canowindra
Billimari
Carcoar
Woodstock
Cowra
Wyangala Res.
Koorawatha
Boorowa
Frogmore
Crookwell
Galong
Muttama
Binalong
Yass
Murrumbateman
Gundagai
Burrinjuck Res.
Bimberi Pk.
1910
Colinton
CANBERRA
A.C.T.
Queanbeyan
Royalla
Captains Flat
Bredbo
Nimmitabel
Bombala
Delegate
Bonang
Orbost
Cann River
Conran

Turrawan
Boggabri
Coonabarabran
Tamarang
Binnaway
Ulinda
Coolah
Dunedoo
Hannahs Bridge
Talbragar
Craboon
Tallawang
Gulgong
Rylstone
Kandos
Ben Bullen
Portland
Wallerawang
Blaxland
Oberon
Taralga
Roslyn
Goulburn
Marulan
Murrumbateman
L. George
Byangendore
Braidwood
Major's Creek
Araluen
East Lynne
Batemans Bay
Moruya
Tuross Head
Narooma
Bega
Candelo
Wyndham
Towamba
Eden
Green C.
Disaster B.
Genoa
Mallacoota
Mallacoota Inlet
C. Howe
Ram Head

Barraba
Upper Manilla
Namoi
Gunnedah
Liverpool Plains
Currabubula
Werris Creek
Quirindi
Tamarang
Willow Tree
Murrurundi
Wingen
Scone
Aberdeen
Merriwa
Gungal
Denman
Muswellbrook
Baerami Creek
Putty
Coricudgy
1257
Olinda
Hunter Range
Singleton
Branxton
Maitland
Cessnock
Kurri Kurri
Paterson
Ravensworth
Dungog
Stroud Road
Bulahdelah
Booral
Stratford
Wards River
Gloucester
Wingham
Taree
Tuncurry
Forster

Black Mountain
Kingstown
Manilla
Attunga
Walcha Road
Walcha
Nowendoo
Ellerston
Barrington Tops
1555
Kandah
Raymond Terrace
Thornton-Beresfield
Stockton
Wallsend
NEWCASTLE
Belmont
Swansea
Morisset
Toronto
Wyong
Budgewoi
The Entrance
Woy Woy
Gosford
Hornsby
Manly
SYDNEY
Parramatta
Fairfield
Liverpool
Sutherland
Cronulla
Campbelltown
Helensburgh
Bulli
Woonona
WOLLONGONG
Port Kembla
Shellharbour
Kiama
Gerringong
Bomaderry
Nowra
Berry
Robertson
Moss Vale
Bowral
Mittagong
Bargo
Picton
The Oaks
Camden

1684
Chandlers Pk.
Armidale
Uralla
Kentucky
Tia
Mt Banda Banda
1263
Rollands Plains
Yarras
Wauchope
Kendall
Moorland
Lansdowne
Coffs Harbour
Dorrigo
Bellingen
Nambucca Heads
Macksville
Smithtown
Kempsey
Port Macquarie

W   S   O   U   T   H

A   L   E   S

V   I   C   T   O   R   I   A

Great Dividing Range
Cullarin Range
Gourock Ra.
Liverpool Range
Blue Mts.
Snowy Mts.
Australian Alps

T A S M A N

S E A

Jervis Bay (Commonwealth Territory)
St. Georges Hd.
C. Dromedary
Goalen Hd.
Bateman's Bay
Twofold Bay

32
34
36
38

A
B
C
D
E

146   148   150   152

6   7   8   9   10

COPYRIGHT GEORGE PHILIP & SON LTD

1 : 2 800 000

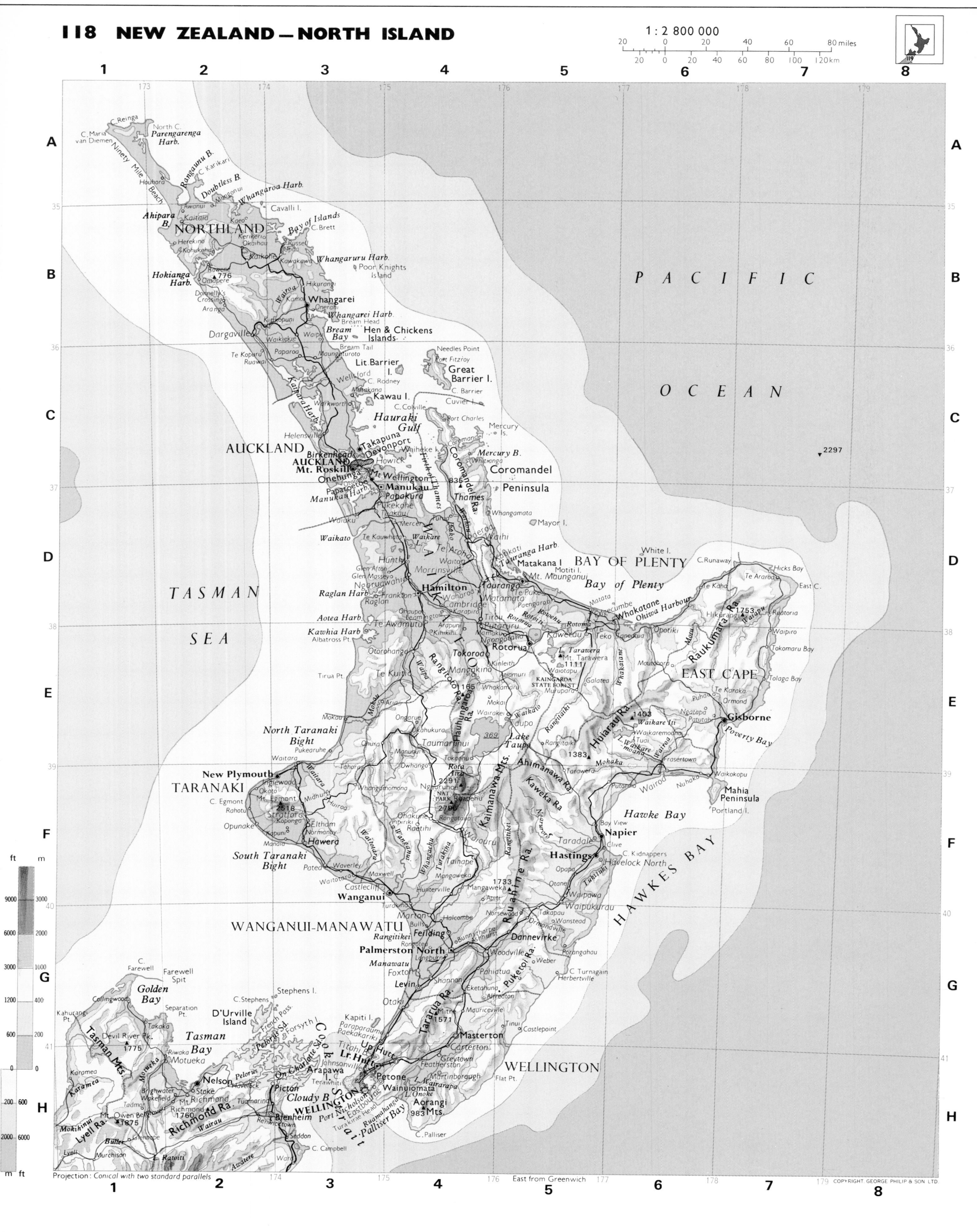

Projection: Conical with two standard parallels   East from Greenwich   COPYRIGHT. GEORGE PHILIP & SON LTD.

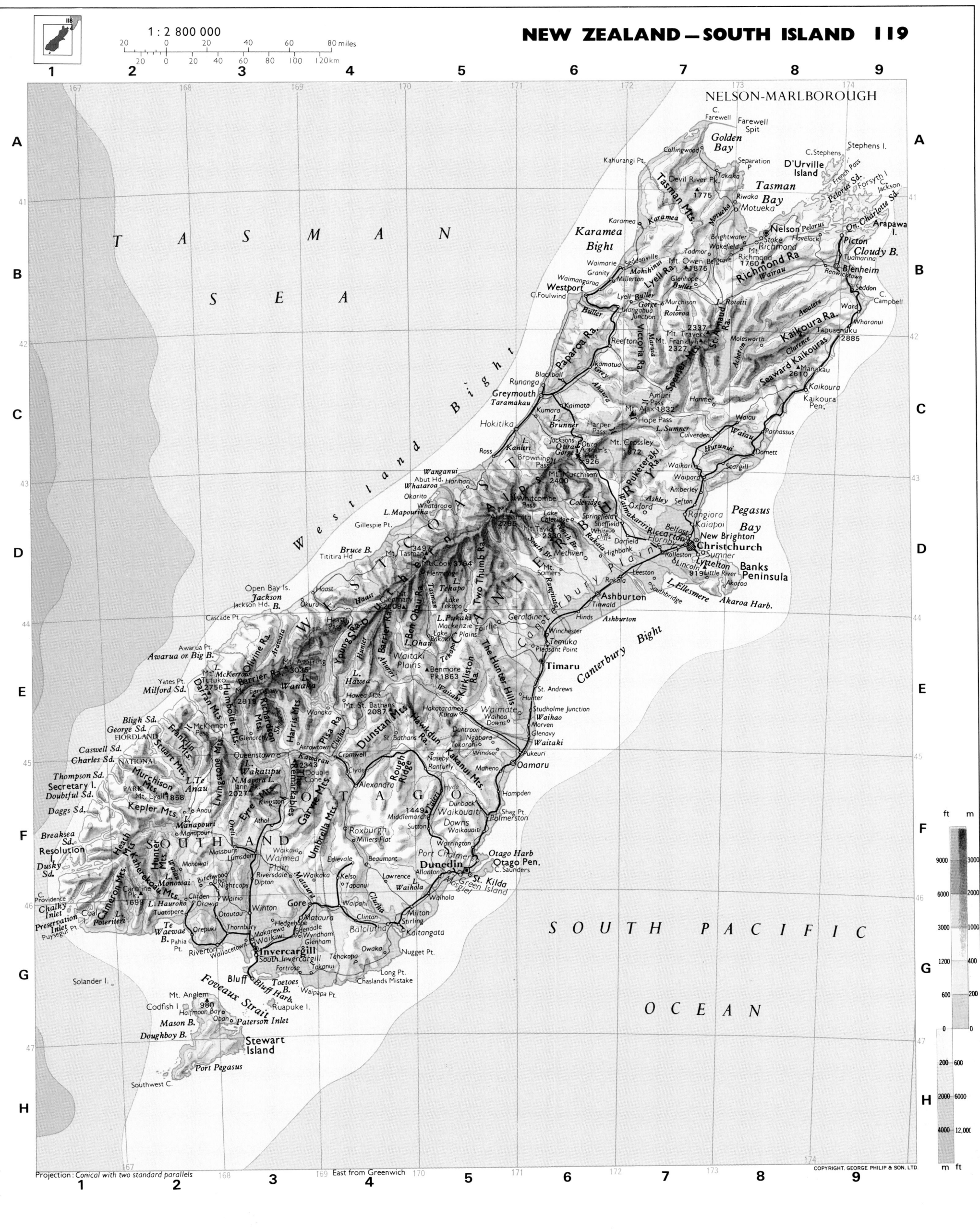

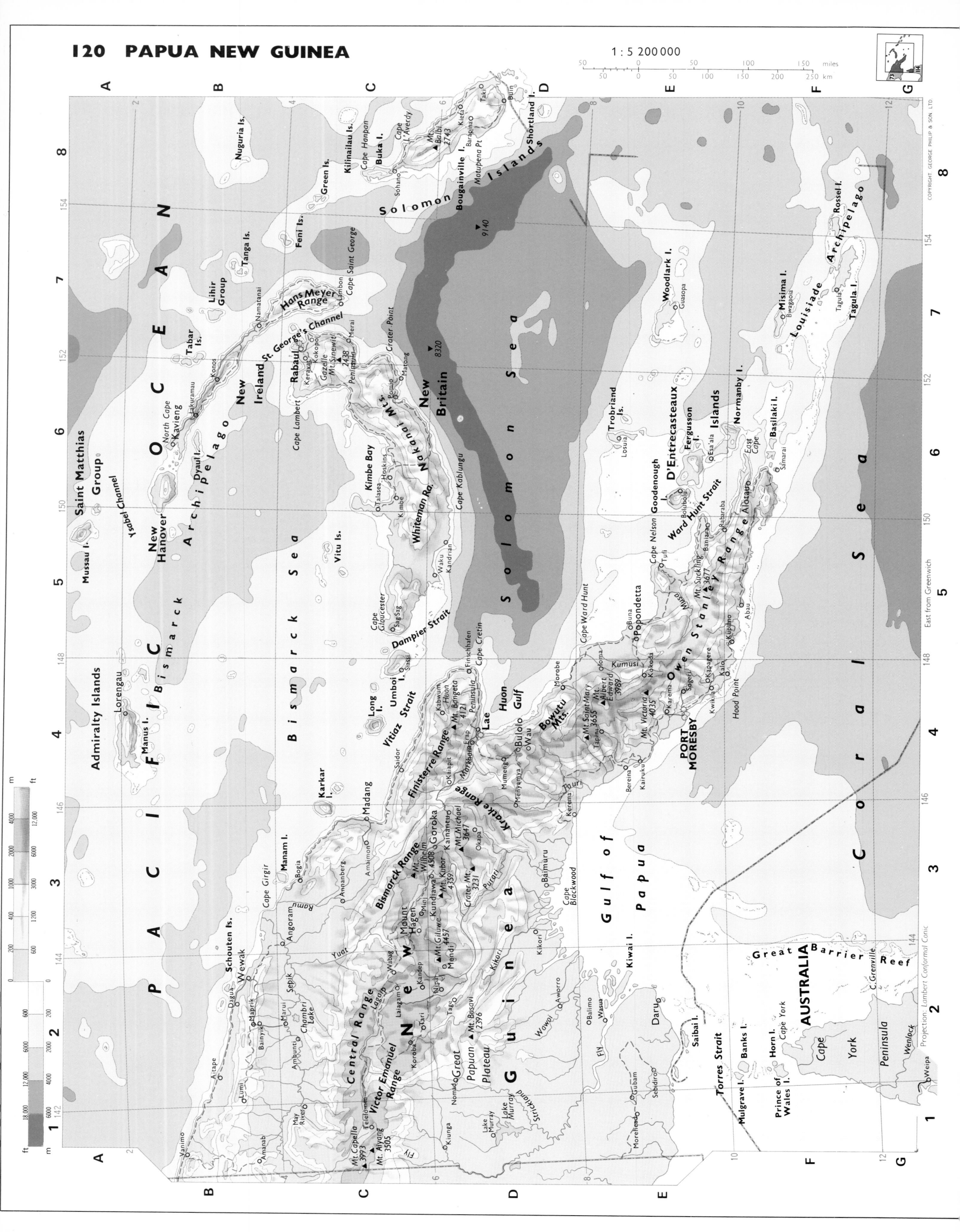

1 : 5 200 000

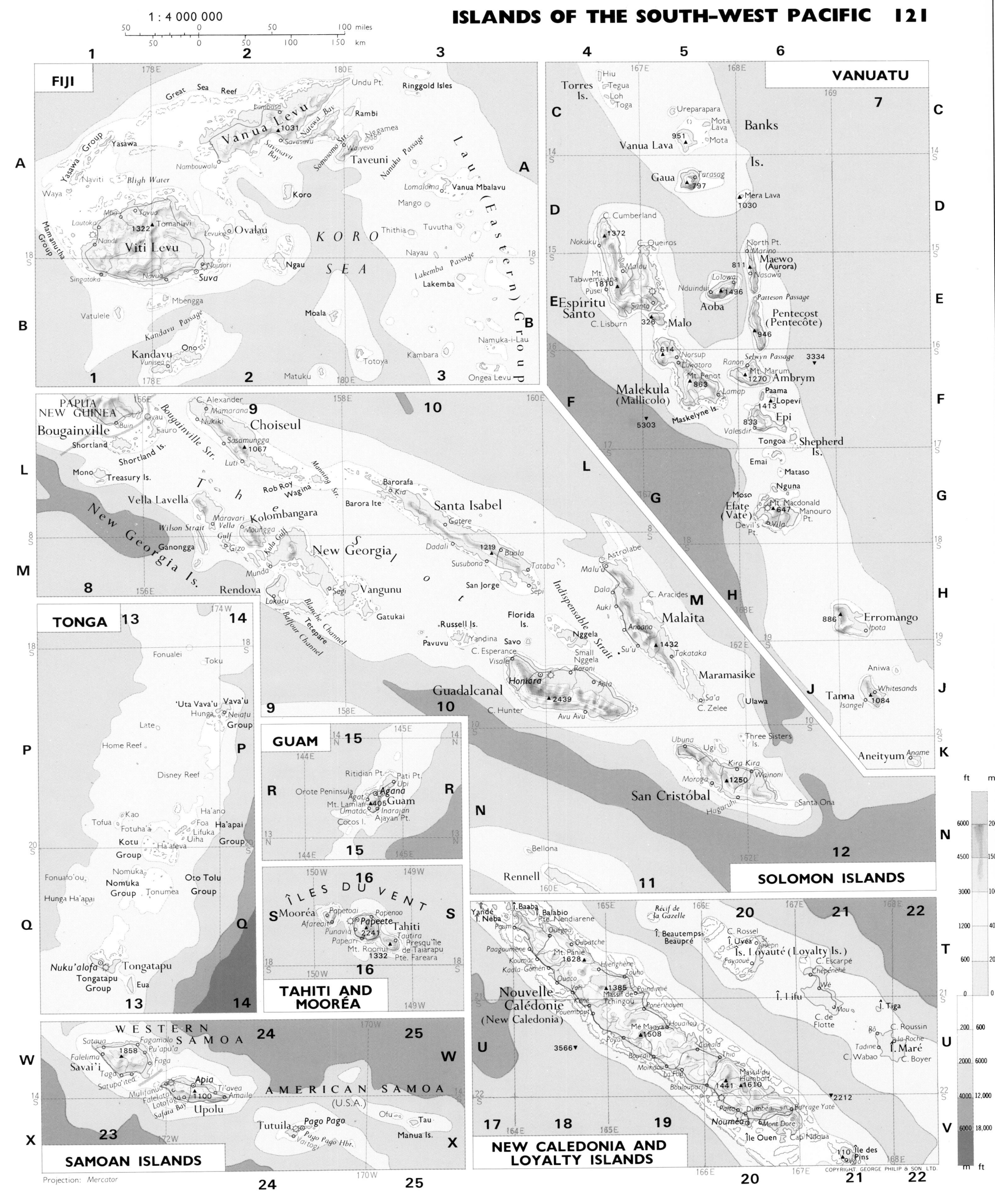

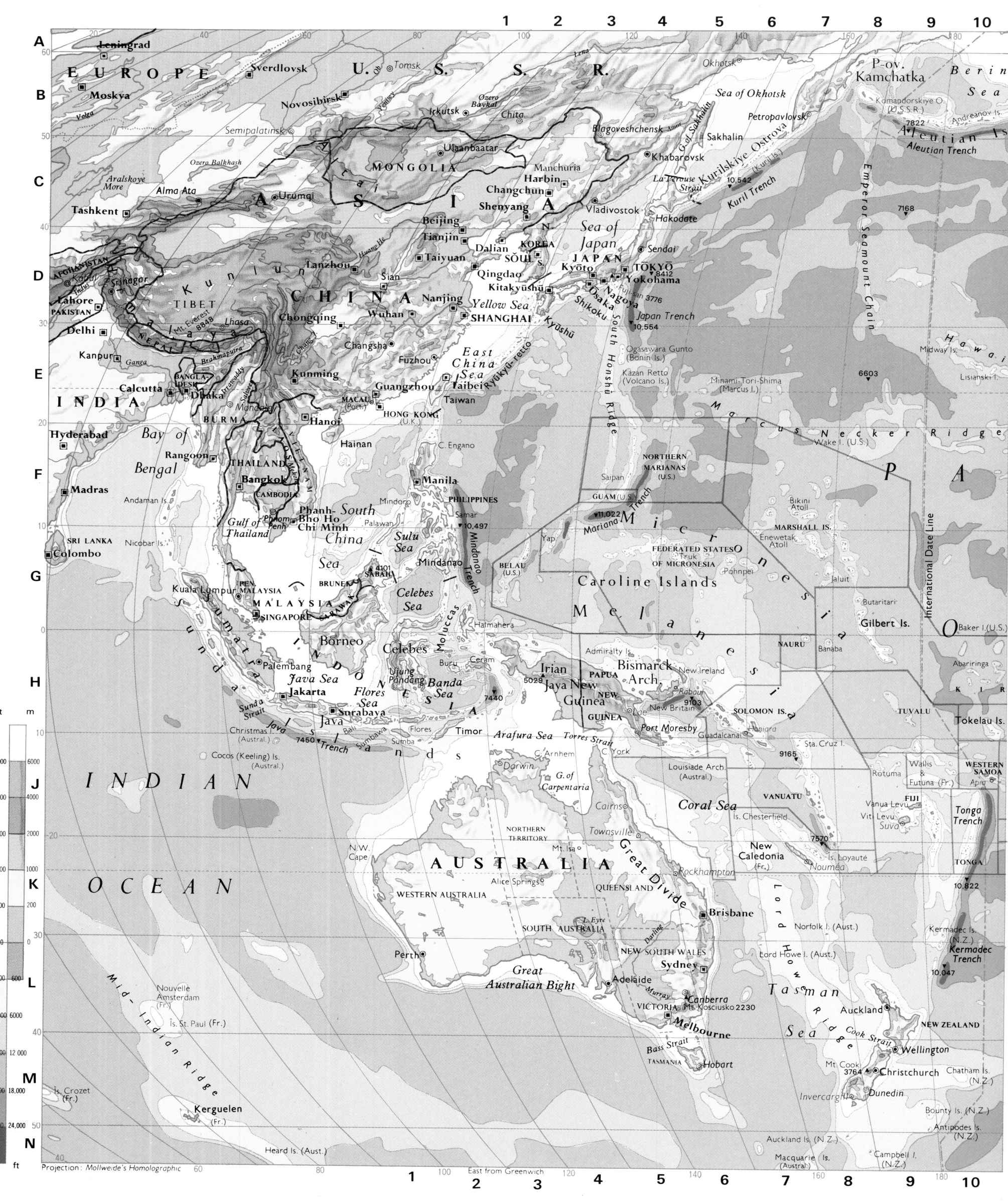

Projection: Mollweide's Homolographic

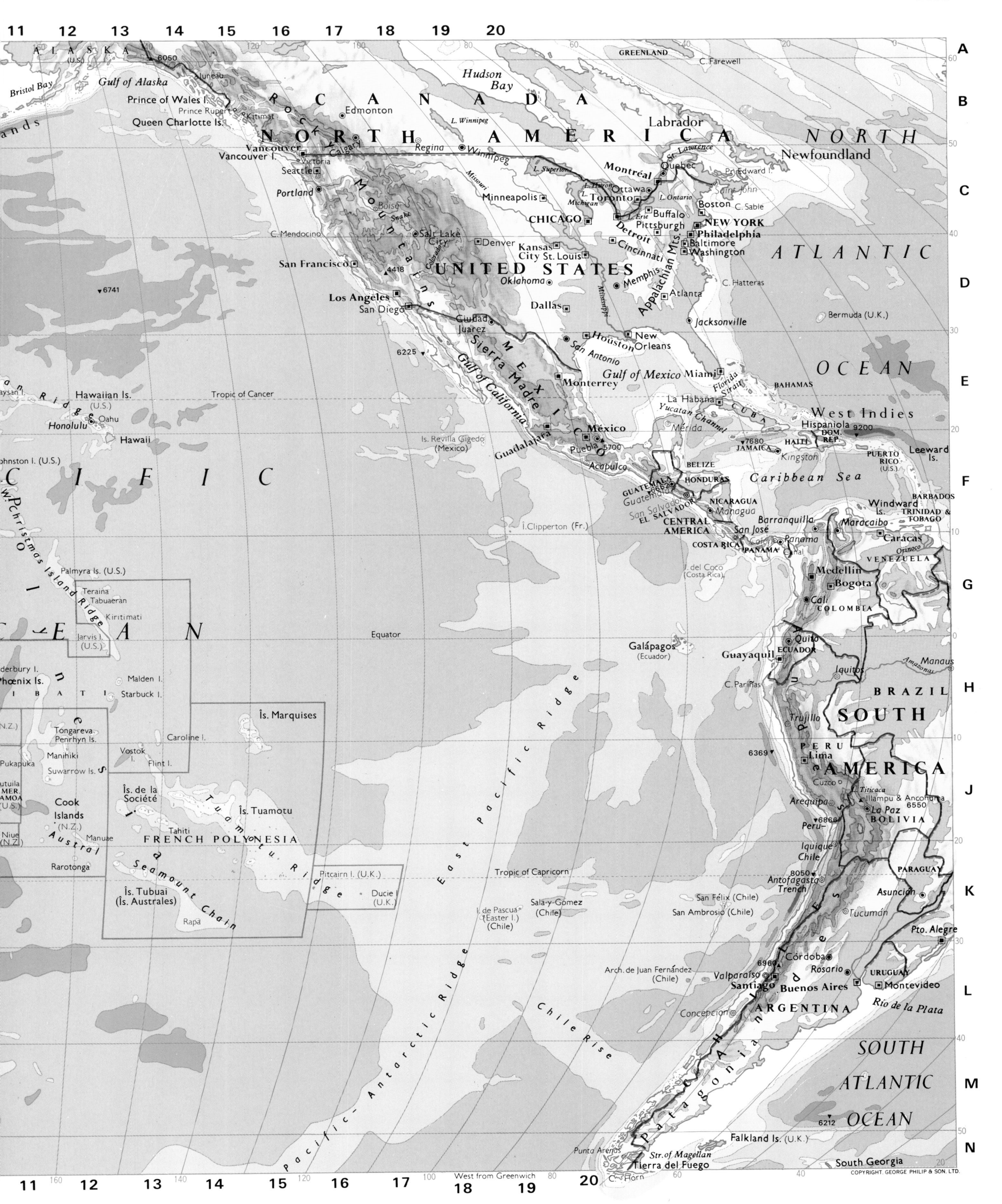

1 : 43 200 000

11 12 13 14 15 16 17 18 19 20

A
B
C
D
E
F
G
H
J
K
L
M
N

60
50
40
30
20
10
0
10
20
30
40
50

ALASKA
(U.S.)
6050
Bristol Bay
Gulf of Alaska
Prince of Wales I.
Queen Charlotte Is.
Prince Rupert
Kitimat
Juneau

C A N A D A
NORTH   AMERICA
Edmonton
L. Winnipeg
Hudson Bay
GREENLAND
C. Farewell
Labrador
NORTH
Newfoundland

Vancouver
Vancouver I.
Victoria
Seattle
Portland
Calgary
Regina
Winnipeg
Missouri
Montréal
St. Lawrence
Québec
Pr. Edward I.

Minneapolis
L. Superior
St. John
Ottawa
Toronto
L. Huron
Michigan
L. Ontario
L. Erie
Boston
C. Sable
Buffalo
Pittsburgh
Cincinnati
Detroit
NEW YORK
Philadelphia
Baltimore
Washington

C. Mendocino
Salt Lake City
Denver
Kansas City
St. Louis
CHICAGO
Appalachian Mts.
C. Hatteras

San Francisco
4418
UNITED STATES
Oklahoma
Memphis
Atlanta
Jacksonville
Bermuda (U.K.)

6741

Los Angeles
San Diego
Dallas
New Orleans
Houston
San Antonio
Monterrey
Gulf of Mexico
Miami
Florida Strait
ATLANTIC
OCEAN

Ciudad Juárez
6225
Sierra Madre
M E X I C O
Gulf of California
BAHAMAS
CUBA
La Habana
Yucatan Channel
Mérida
West Indies

Hawaiian Is.
(U.S.)
Tropic of Cancer

Honolulu
Oahu
Hawaii
Is. Revilla Gigedo
(Mexico)
México
5700
Guadalajara
Puebla
Acapulco
HAITI
7680
JAMAICA
Kingston
Hispaniola
DOM.
REP.
9200
PUERTO RICO
(U.S.)
Leeward
Is.

Johnston I. (U.S.)
BELIZE
HONDURAS
Caribbean Sea
BARBADOS
TRINIDAD & TOBAGO

P A C I F I C
GUATEMALA
3837
Guatemala
San Salvador
EL SALVADOR
NICARAGUA
Managua
CENTRAL AMERICA
Windward Is.

I. Clipperton (Fr.)
COSTA RICA
San José
Panama
PANAMA
Barranquilla
Maracaibo
Caracas
VENEZUELA

Palmyra Is. (U.S.)
Teraina
Tabuaerān
Kiritimati
I. del Coco
(Costa Rica)
Colón
Canal
Medellín
Bogota
Cali
COLOMBIA

Jarvis I.
(U.S.)
Orinoco

O C E A N
Equator
Quito
ECUADOR
Manaus

Christmas Island Ridge
Galápagos
(Ecuador)
Guayaquil
Iquitos
Amazonas

Phoenix Is.
derbury I.
Malden I.
Starbuck I.
C. Pariñas
B R A Z I L
SOUTH

KIRIBATI
Trujillo
A M E R I C A

Tongareva
Penrhyn Is.
Îs. Marquises
6369
PERU
Lima

Manihiki
Suwarrow Is.
Vostok I.
Caroline I.
Cuzco
Titicaca
Illampu & Ancohuma
6550

Pukapuka
AMER.
SAMOA
Flint I.
Îs. de la Société
Îs. Tuamotu
Arequipa
La Paz
BOLIVIA

Cook Islands
(N.Z.)
Tahiti
Manuae
6868
Peru
Iquique
Chile

Niue
(N.Z.)
Austral
Rarotonga
FRENCH POLYNESIA
Tuamotu Ridge
Tropic of Capricorn
8050
Antofagasta
Trench
PARAGUAY

Îs. Tubuai
(Îs. Australes)
Rapa
Seamount Chain
Pitcairn I. (U.K.)
Ducie I.
(U.K.)
East Pacific Ridge
I. de Pascua
(Easter I.)
(Chile)
Sala-y-Gomez
(Chile)
San Félix (Chile)
San Ambrosio (Chile)
Asunción
Tucumán
Pto. Alegre

6960
Córdoba
Rosario
URUGUAY
Montevideo

Arch. de Juan Fernández
(Chile)
Valparaíso
Santiago
Buenos Aires
Río de la Plata

Concepción
ARGENTINA

Pacific - Antarctic Ridge
Chile Rise
SOUTH
ATLANTIC
OCEAN
6212

Patagonia
Falkland Is. (U.K.)
Punta Arenas
Str. of Magellan
Tierra del Fuego
C. Horn
South Georgia

West from Greenwich

11 12 13 14 15 16 17 18 19 20
160 140 120 100 80 60 40

COPYRIGHT. GEORGE PHILIP & SON. LTD.

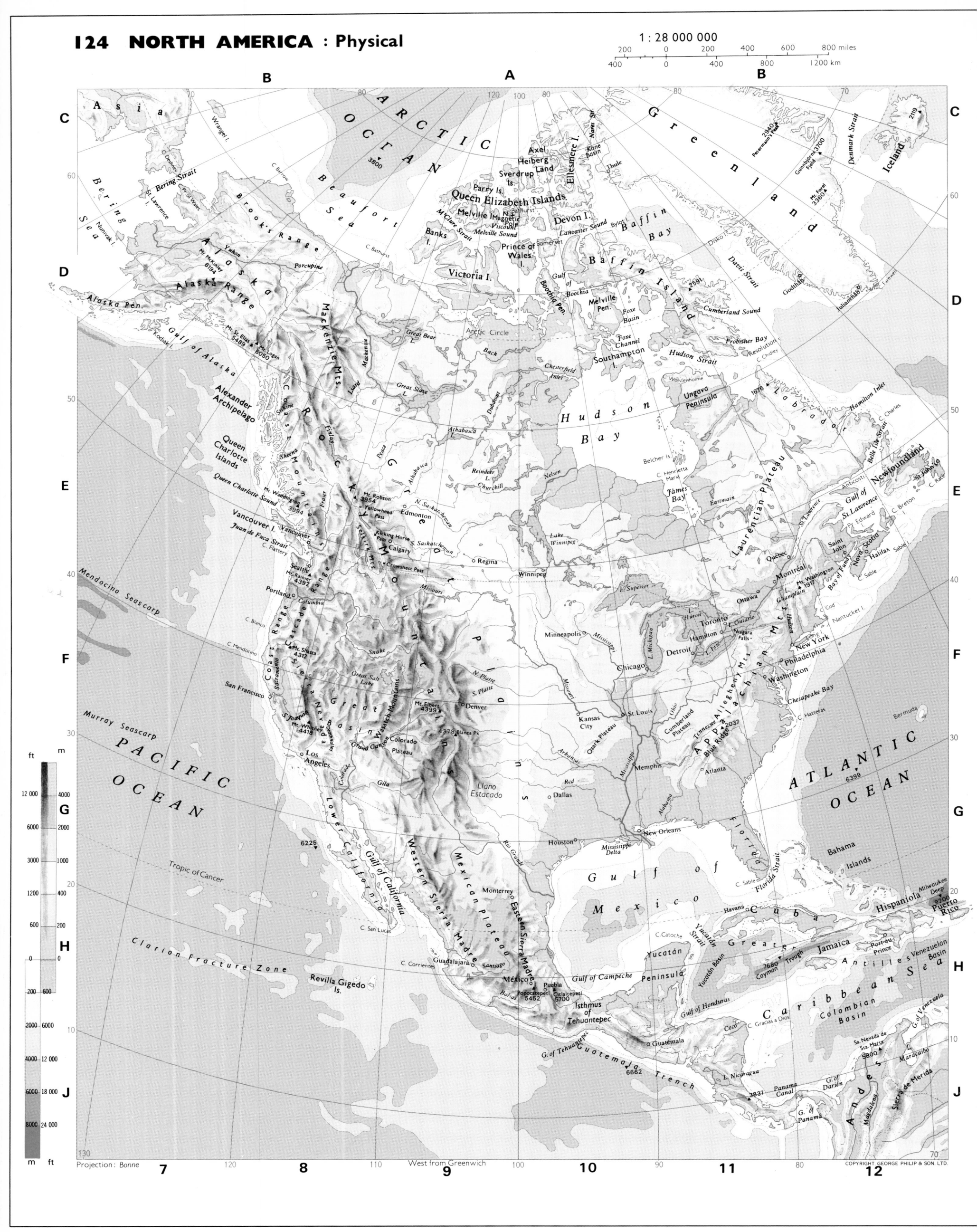

1 : 28 000 000

Projection: Bonne

West from Greenwich

COPYRIGHT GEORGE PHILIP & SON, LTD.

1 : 28 000 000

200   0   200   400   600   800 miles
400   0   400   800   1200 km

ARCTIC OCEAN

GREENLAND (Denmark)

ICELAND
Reykjavik
Denmark Strait

U.S.S.R.

Bering Strait
Bering Sea

Beaufort Sea

Queen Elizabeth Is.
Ellesmere I.

Baffin Bay
Baffin I.
BAFFIN

Davis Strait
C. Farvel
Godthaab

ALASKA
Yukon
Fairbanks
Arctic Circle
Anchorage
Gulf of Alaska
Juneau

Porcupine
Whitehorse

YUKON TERRITORY

INUVIK
Victoria I.
KITIKMEOT

NORTHWEST TERRITORIES

Mackenzie
Great Bear L.
Back
KEEWATIN
Dubawnt
Yellowknife
FORT SMITH
Great Slave L.
Liard
Finlay

Hudson Strait
NEWFOUNDLAND

Hudson Bay

CANADA

Peace
L. Athabasca
Churchill
Nelson
Labrador
Eastmain
St. Lawrence
St. John's
SPM

BRITISH COLUMBIA
Skeena
Fraser
ALBERTA
Edmonton
N. Saskatchewan
S. Saskatchewan
Calgary
SASKATCHEWAN
Regina
MANITOBA
L. Winnipeg
Winnipeg
ONTARIO
QUÉBEC
Québec
PR. EDWARD
Charlottetown
NEW BRUNS. WICK
NOVA SCOTIA
Halifax
Fredericton
MAINE

Victoria
Vancouver
WASHINGTON
Seattle
Olympia
Portland
Salem
Columbia
OREGON

Montréal
Ottawa
Montpelier
VER. N.H. Concord
Boston
MASS.
Albany
Providence
Hartford
NEW YORK
Toronto
Buffalo
NEW YORK
L. Ontario
Detroit
Cleveland
PENNSYLVANIA
N.J. Philadelphia
Harrisburg
Pittsburgh
Trenton
N. DEL. Dover
Baltimore
Annapolis
WEST VIRGINIA
Washington D.C.
M.
Richmond
VIRGINIA

MONTANA
Helena
Missouri
NORTH DAKOTA
Bismarck
MINNESOTA
L. Superior
L. Michigan
L. Huron
WISCONSIN
MICHIGAN
Lansing
Madison
Milwaukee
Chicago
IOWA
Des Moines
ILLINOIS
INDIANA
Indianapolis
OHIO
Columbus
Toledo
Frankfort
Cincinnati
KENTUCKY
L. Erie

IDAHO
Boise
Snake
WYOMING
Cheyenne
N. Platte
NEBRASKA
Lincoln
Springfield
Jefferson City
St. Louis
MISSOURI

SOUTH DAKOTA
Pierre
St. Paul
Minneapolis

NEVADA
Carson City
Salt Lake City
UTAH
COLORADO
Denver
Arkansas
KANSAS
Topeka
Kansas City

Sacramento
San Francisco
San Jose
CALIFORNIA
Las Vegas
Colorado
LOS ANGELES
San Diego
ARIZONA
Phoenix
Tucson
Gila
Santa Fe
NEW MEXICO
Albuquerque
OKLAHOMA
Oklahoma City
Red River
ARKANSAS
Little Rock
Memphis
TENNESSEE
Nashville
Tennessee
NORTH CAROLINA
Raleigh
Columbia
SOUTH CAROLINA
Charleston
Bermuda (Br.)

UNITED STATES

El Paso
Dallas
TEXAS
Austin
Rio Grande
Houston
LOUISIANA
Baton Rouge
New Orleans
Mississippi
MISSISSIPPI
Jackson
ALABAMA
Montgomery
GEORGIA
Atlanta
Alabama
Birmingham
Tallahassee
Jacksonville
FLORIDA
Tampa
Miami
St. of Florida
C. Sable
Nassau
BAHAMAS
Turks & Caicos (Br.)

PACIFIC OCEAN

ATLANTIC OCEAN

Tropic of Cancer

MEXICO
Monterrey
Guadalajara
MEXICO
Revilla Gigedo Is. (Mexico)

Gulf of Mexico

Havana
CUBA
Cayman Is. (Br.)
JAMAICA
Kingston
HAITI
Port-au-Prince
DOMINICAN REP.
Santo Domingo
San Juan
PUERTO RICO

Caribbean Sea

Belmopan
BELIZE
GUATEMALA
Guatemala
HONDURAS
Tegucigalpa
EL SALVADOR
San Salvador
NICARAGUA
Managua
L. Nicaragua
COSTA RICA
San José
PANAMA
Panamá

Maracaibo
Barranquilla
VENEZUELA
Medellín
COLOMBIA
Bogotá
SOUTH AMERICA

Washington Capital Cities
◉ U.S. State Capitals and Canadian Provincial Capitals

C	CONNECTICUT	N.H.	NEW HAMPSHIRE
D.	DELAWARE	N.J.	NEW JERSEY
D.C.	DISTRICT OF COLUMBIA	R.I.	RHODE ISLAND
M.	MARYLAND	VER.	VERMONT
MASS.	MASSACHUSETTS	SPM	ST. PIERRE ET MIQUELON

Projection: Bonne

West from Greenwich

COPYRIGHT GEORGE PHILIP & SON LTD.

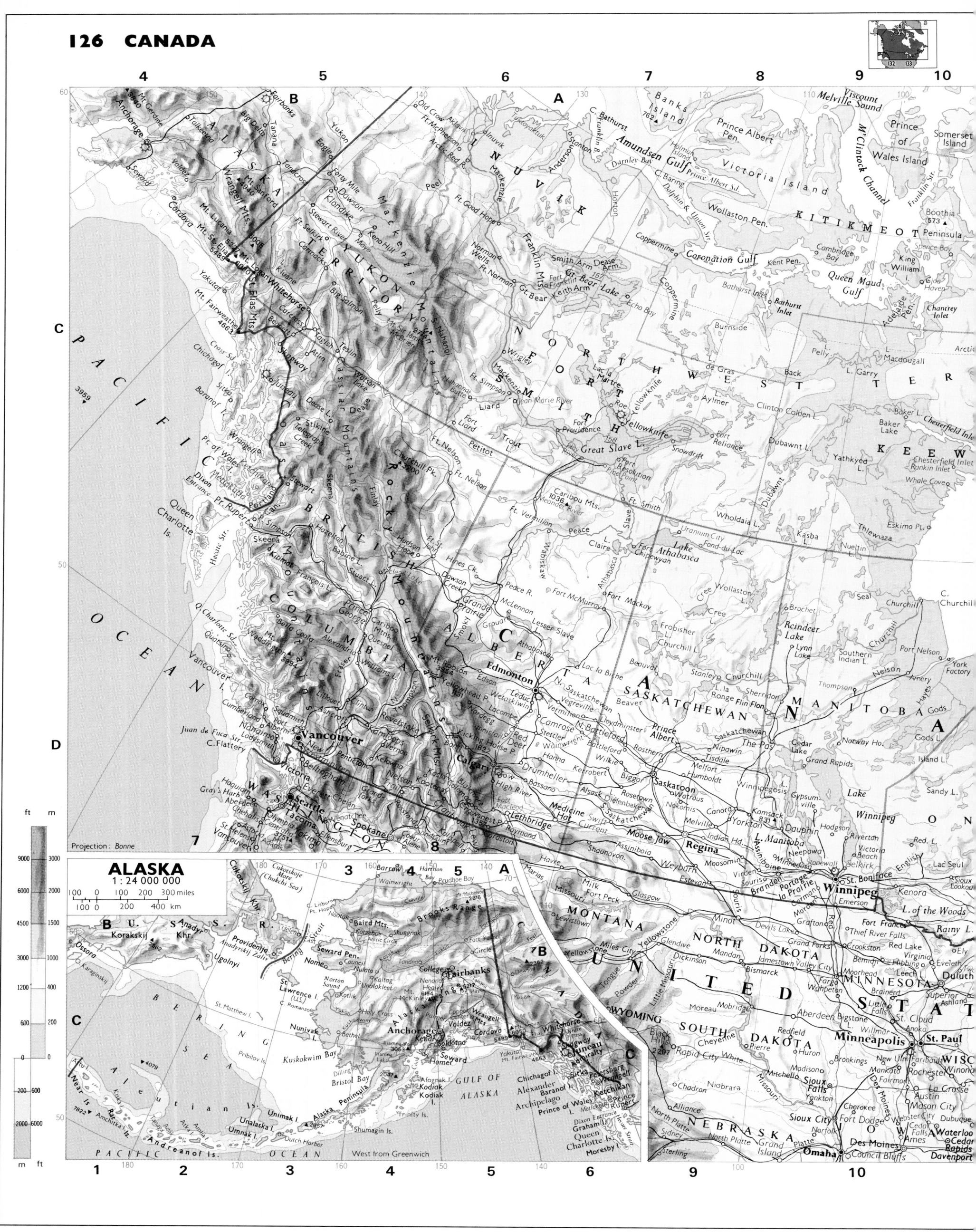

PACIFIC OCEAN

ALASKA

YUKON TERRITORY

BRITISH COLUMBIA

NORTH WEST TERRITOR

KITIKMEOT

KEEW

ALBERTA

SASKATCHEWAN

MANITOBA

Amundsen Gulf

Victoria Island

Banks Island

Coronation Gulf

Great Slave L.

Lake Athabasca

Vancouver

Edmonton

Calgary

Saskatoon

Regina

Winnipeg

WASHINGTON

Seattle

Spokane

MONTANA

NORTH DAKOTA

SOUTH DAKOTA

MINNESOTA

WISC

WYOMING

NEBRASKA

Minneapolis   St. Paul

Duluth

Omaha

UNITED STATES

Projection: Bonne

ALASKA
1 : 24 000 000
100 0   100 200 300 miles
100 0   200   400 km

BERING SEA

Anchorage

Fairbanks

Brooks Range

Seward Pen.

Aleutian Is.

GULF OF ALASKA

PACIFIC OCEAN

West from Greenwich

ft   m
9000 3000
6000 2000
4500 1500
3000 1000
1200 400
600   200
0   0
200   600
2000 6000
m   ft

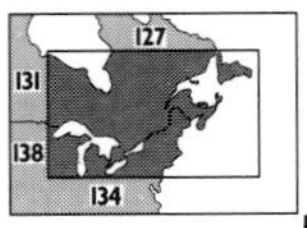

N. W. TERRITORIES

MANITOBA

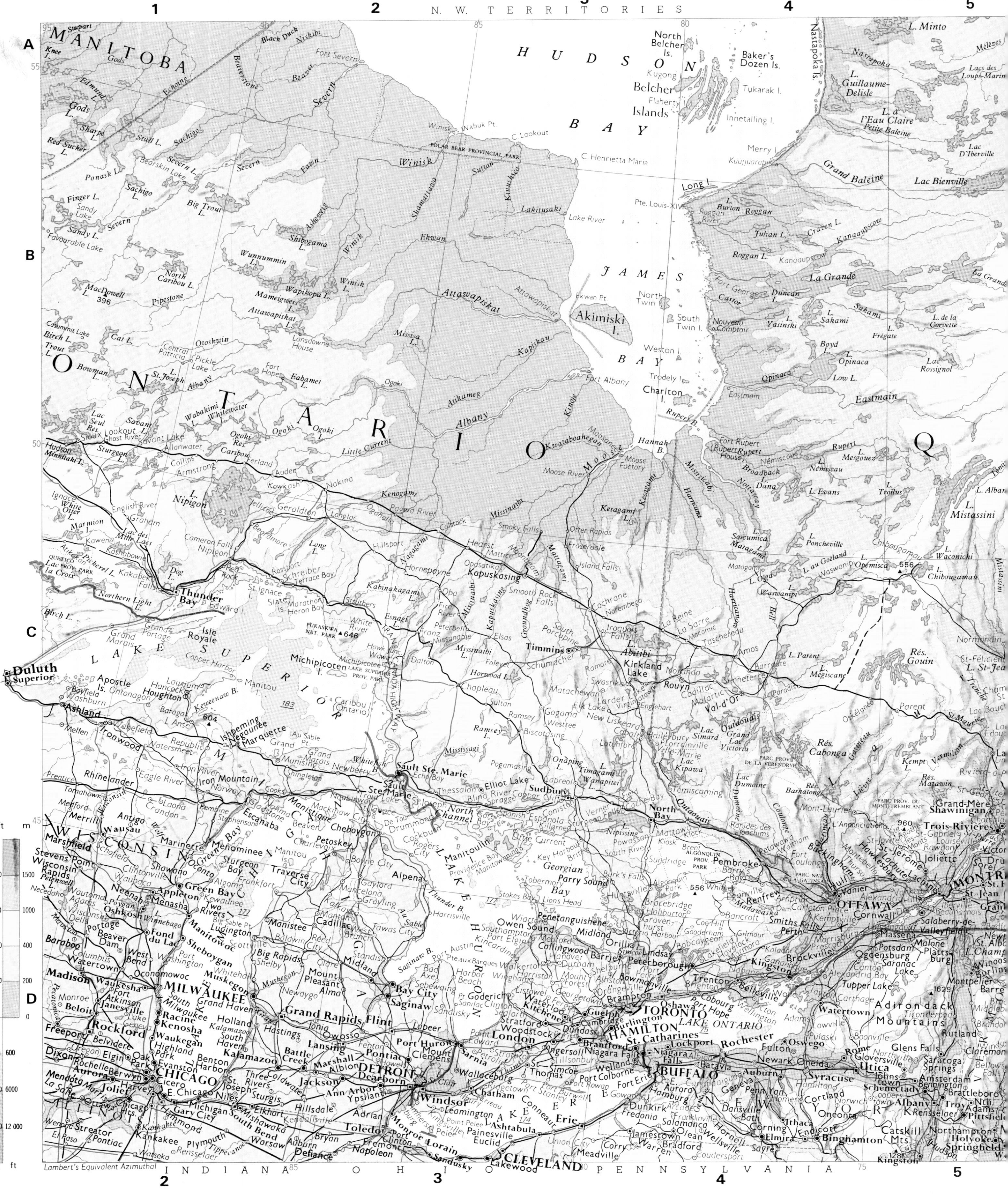

ONTARIO

HUDSON BAY

JAMES BAY

LAKE SUPERIOR

LAKE HURON

LAKE ONTARIO

LAKE ERIE

WISCONSIN

MICHIGAN

INDIANA   OHIO   PENNSYLVANIA

Belcher Islands
Flaherty I.
North Belcher Is.
Baker's Dozen Is.
Kugong
Tukarak I.
Innetalling I.
Akimiski I.
North Twin I.
South Twin I.
Weston I.
Trodely I.
Charlton

Polar Bear Provincial Park
Winisk
Sutton
C. Henrietta Maria
C. Lookout
Winisk Pt.   Wabuk Pt.
Lake River
Attawapiskat
Ekwan
Kapiskau
Albany
Fort Albany
Moose Factory
Moose River
Moosonee
Kwataboahegan
Hannah B.
Fort Rupert (Rupert House)
Rupert B.
Broadback
Nottoway
Eastmain
Fort George
La Grande
Duncan
Castor
Yasinski
Sakami
Boyd
Opinaca
Low L.
Opemisca
Chibougamau

Thunder Bay
Duluth
Superior
Ashland
Ironwood
Marquette
Negaunee
Ishpeming
Iron Mountain
Escanaba
Green Bay
Appleton
Oshkosh
Fond du Lac
Sheboygan
Milwaukee
Madison
Racine
Kenosha
Waukegan
Rockford
Freeport
Chicago
Joliet
Gary
Hammond

Sault Ste. Marie
Timmins
Kirkland Lake
Rouyn
Noranda
Val-d'Or
North Bay
Sudbury
Elliot Lake
Espanola
Parry Sound
Georgian Bay
Manitoulin I.
Owen Sound
Collingwood
Barrie
Orillia
Peterborough
Lindsay
Bowmanville
Oshawa
Toronto
Hamilton
St. Catharines
Niagara Falls
Buffalo
London
Sarnia
Windsor
Detroit
Dearborn
Ann Arbor
Toledo
Cleveland
Lakewood
Sandusky
Lorain
Erie

Ottawa
Cornwall
Brockville
Kingston
Belleville
Trenton
Pembroke
Renfrew
Smiths Falls
Perth
Rochester
Syracuse
Utica
Watertown
Oswego
Adirondack Mountains
Albany
Schenectady
Troy
Saratoga Springs
Glens Falls

Montréal
Trois-Rivières
Shawinigan
Grand-Mère
St-Jérôme
Joliette
Hull
Buckingham

Lambert's Equivalent Azimuthal

ft   m
4500   1500
3000   1000
1200   400
600   200
0   0
200   600
2000   6000
4000   12000
m   ft

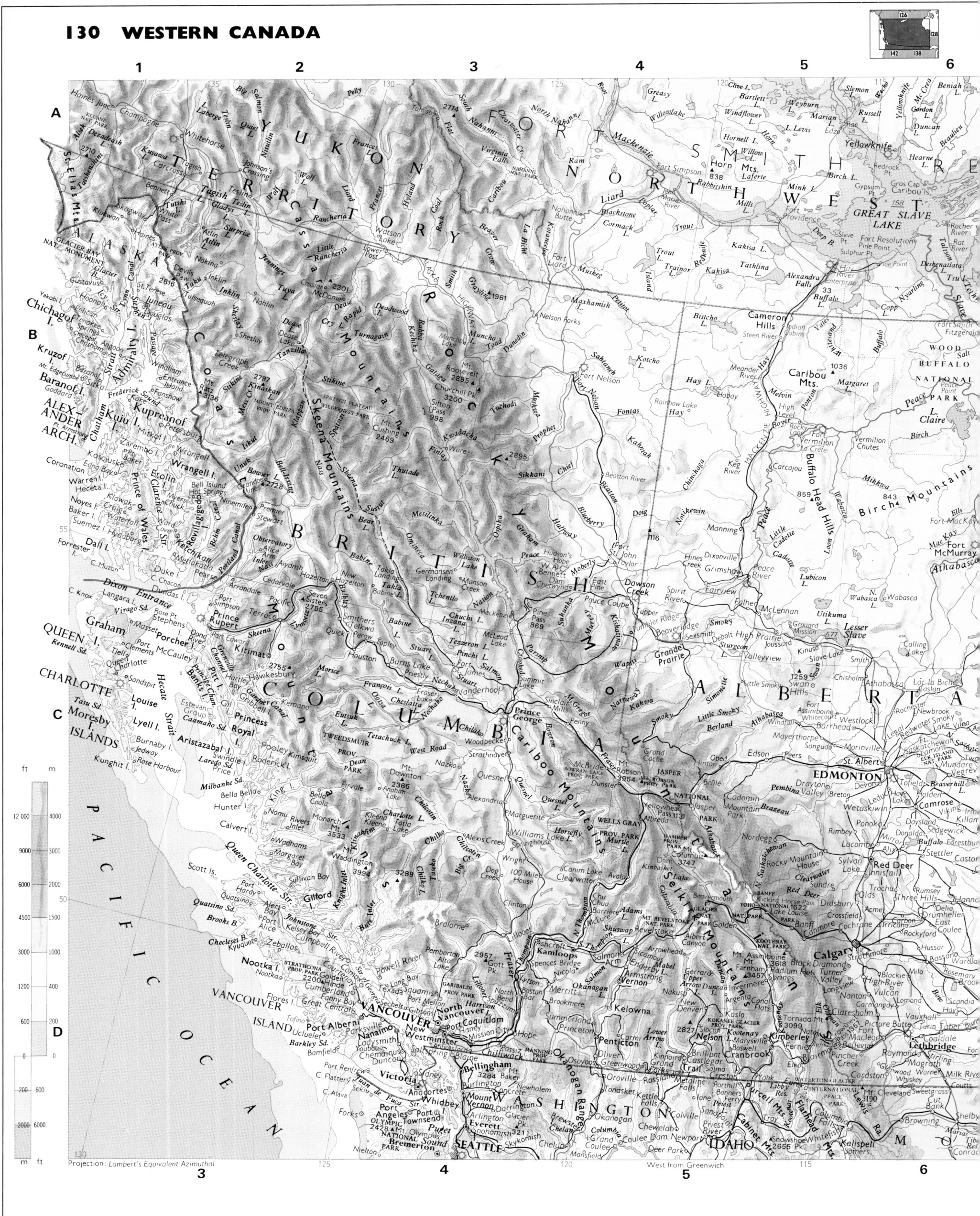

1 : 5 600 000

50 0 50 100 150 200 miles
50 0 50 100 150 200 250 300 km

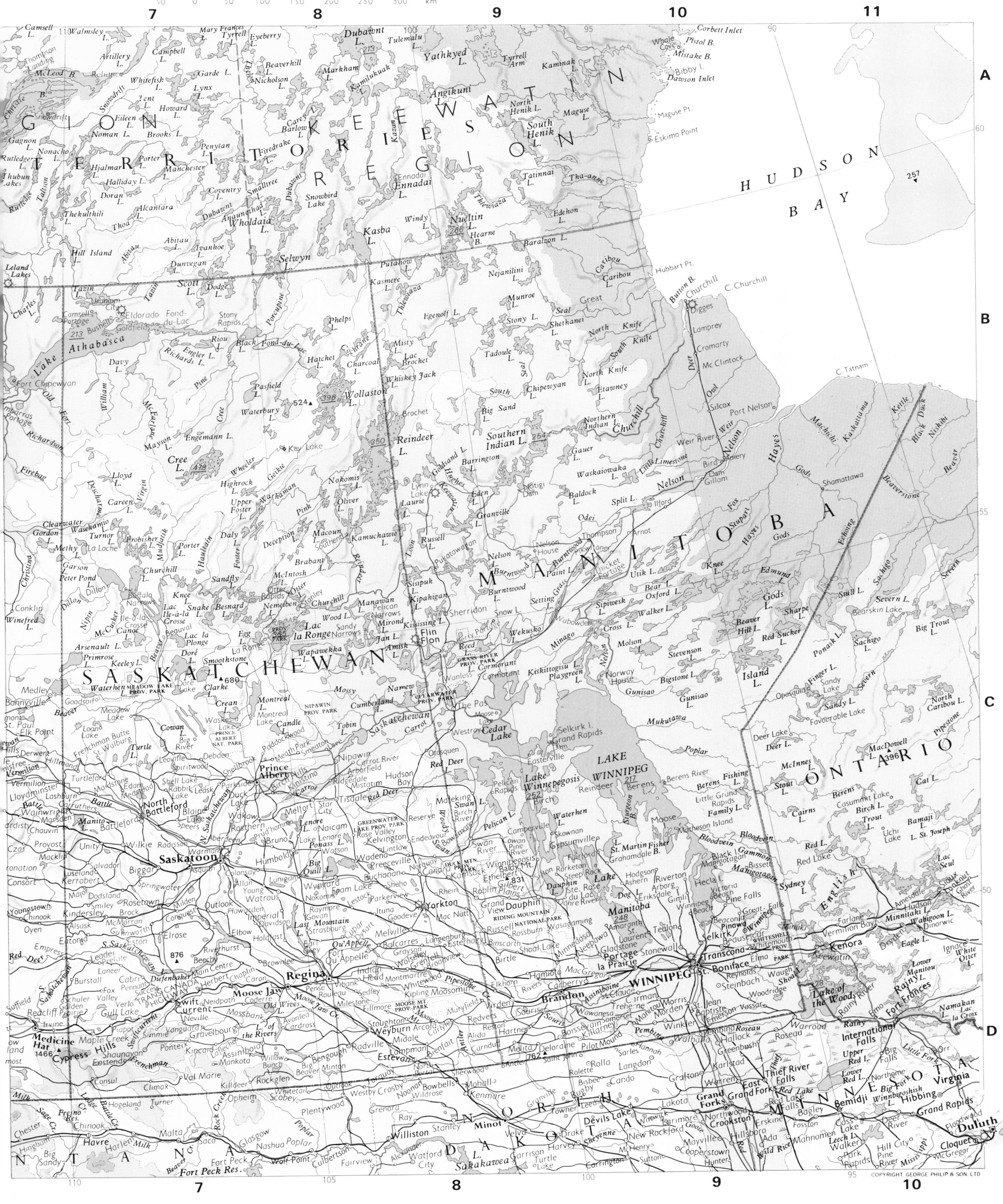

HUDSON BAY

KEEWATIN REGION

TERRITORIES

MANITOBA

SASKATCHEWAN

ONTARIO

NORTH DAKOTA

MINNESOTA

MONTANA

Lake Athabasca

Lake Winnipeg

Lake Winnipegosis

Cedar Lake

Reindeer L.

Wollaston

Cree L.

Southern Indian L.

Saskatoon

Prince Albert

North Battleford

Regina

Moose Jaw

Swift Current

Medicine Hat

Winnipeg

Brandon

Portage la Prairie

Selkirk

Dauphin

The Pas

Flin Flon

Yorkton

Kenora

Fort Frances

International Falls

Churchill

Thompson

Grand Forks

Bemidji

Duluth

Minot

Devils Lake

Williston

Havre

Fort Peck Res.

Lake of the Woods

TRANS CANADA HIGHWAY

COPYRIGHT GEORGE PHILIP & SON LTD

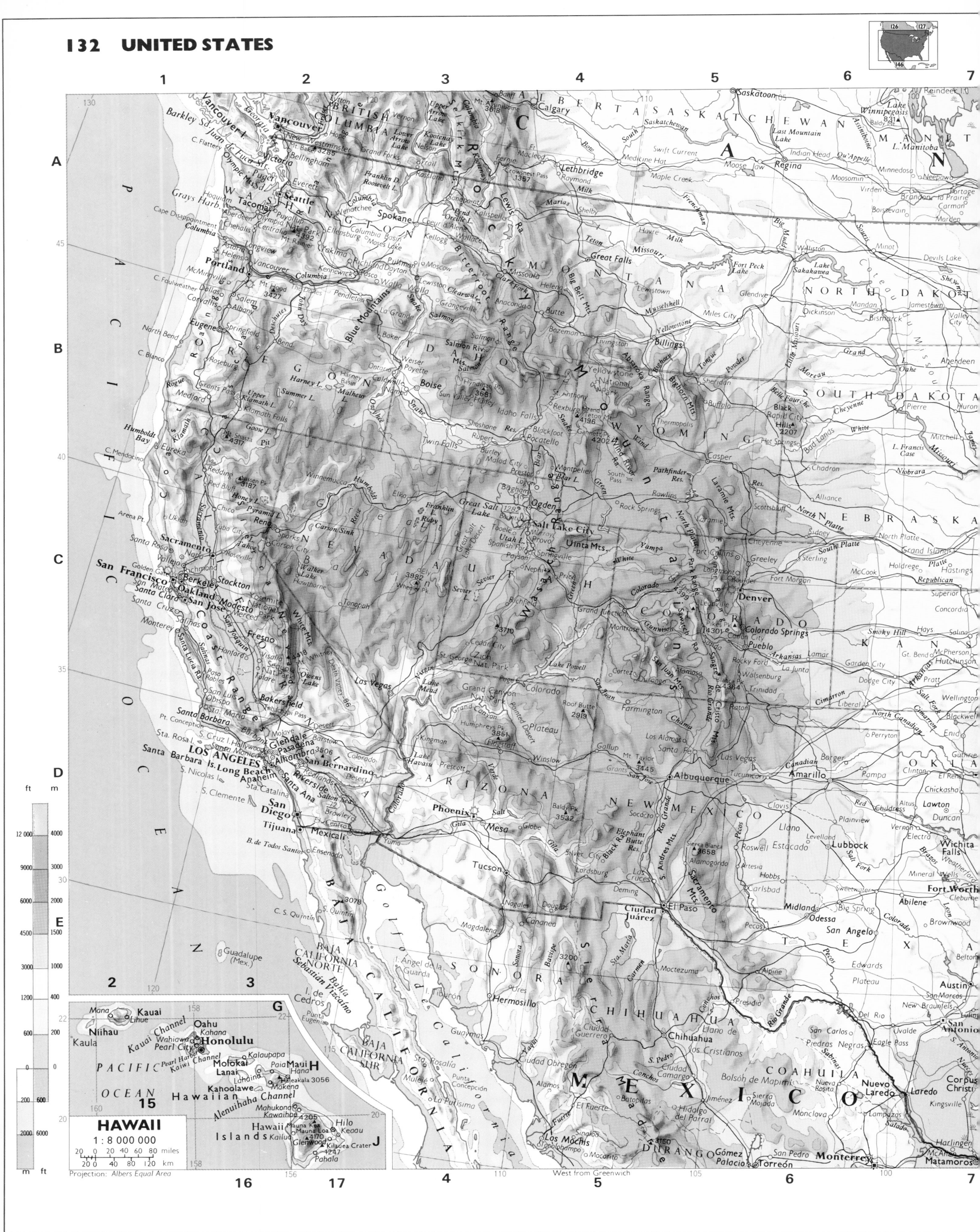

1 : 9 600 000

50   50   100 150 200 250 300 miles
50   0   50 100 150 200 250 300 350 400 450 km

8   9   10   11   12   13

Winnipeg Lake Winnipeg Lake of the Woods Trout Lake L. St. Joseph English L. Seul Lake Nipigon

MINNESOTA Duluth **Lake Superior** Sault Ste. Marie **Lake Huron** North Bay Ottawa **MONTRÉAL** Québec **MAINE** NEW BRUNSWICK

Minneapolis **St. Paul** **WISCONSIN** Green Bay **Lake Michigan** **TORONTO** **Lake Ontario** Rochester **Buffalo** Syracuse Albany **Boston**

Madison **Milwaukee** Grand Rapids Lansing **DETROIT** **Lake Erie** Cleveland **NEW YORK**

CHICAGO South Bend Ft. Wayne Toledo Akron Youngstown **PENNSYLVANIA** Newark **PHILADELPHIA**

Des Moines **IOWA** Peoria **ILLINOIS** **INDIANA** **Pittsburgh** **Baltimore**

Omaha Lincoln **Kansas City** **St. Louis** **MISSOURI** **Indianapolis** **Cincinnati** **WEST VIRGINIA** **Washington D.C.** **Richmond** **VIRGINIA** Norfolk

Wichita Springfield **KENTUCKY** **Louisville** Lexington Roanoke

Tulsa **Oklahoma City** Fort Smith **Memphis** **TENNESSEE** Nashville Knoxville Asheville **NORTH CAROLINA** Raleigh

Little Rock **ARKANSAS** Chattanooga Charlotte Greensboro Winston-Salem

Dallas Shreveport **MISSISSIPPI** **ALABAMA** **Birmingham** **Atlanta** **GEORGIA** **SOUTH CAROLINA** Columbia Charleston

Houston Beaumont Lake Charles Baton Rouge **LOUISIANA** **New Orleans** Mobile Montgomery Columbus Savannah Jacksonville

Galveston **GULF OF MEXICO** Tallahassee **FLORIDA** Orlando **Tampa** St. Petersburg

Brownsville Rio Grande Miami West Palm Beach **BAHAMAS** Grand Bahama I. Gt. Abaco Eleuthera I.

Key West Florida Bay Andros I.

ATLANTIC OCEAN

8   9   10   11   12

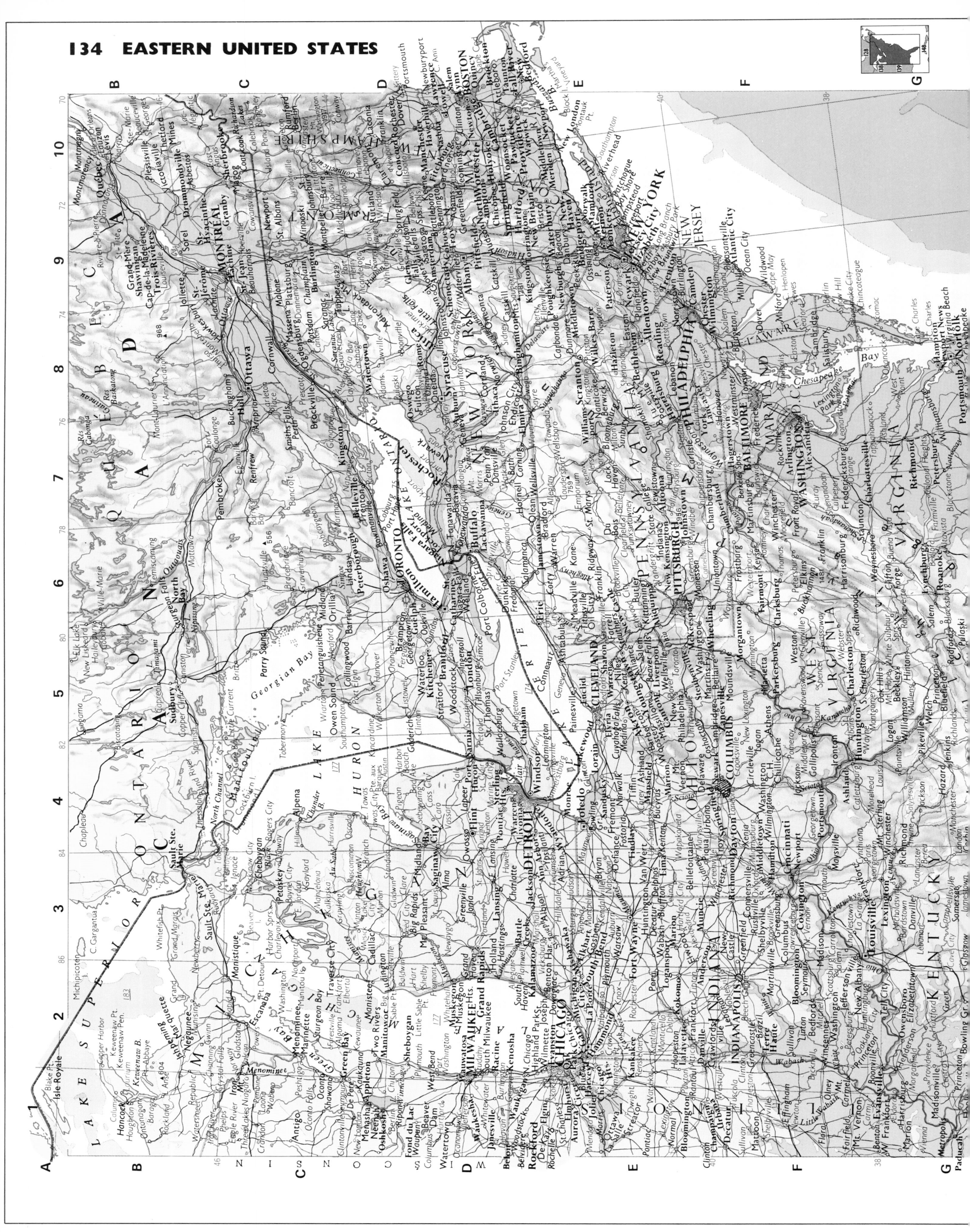

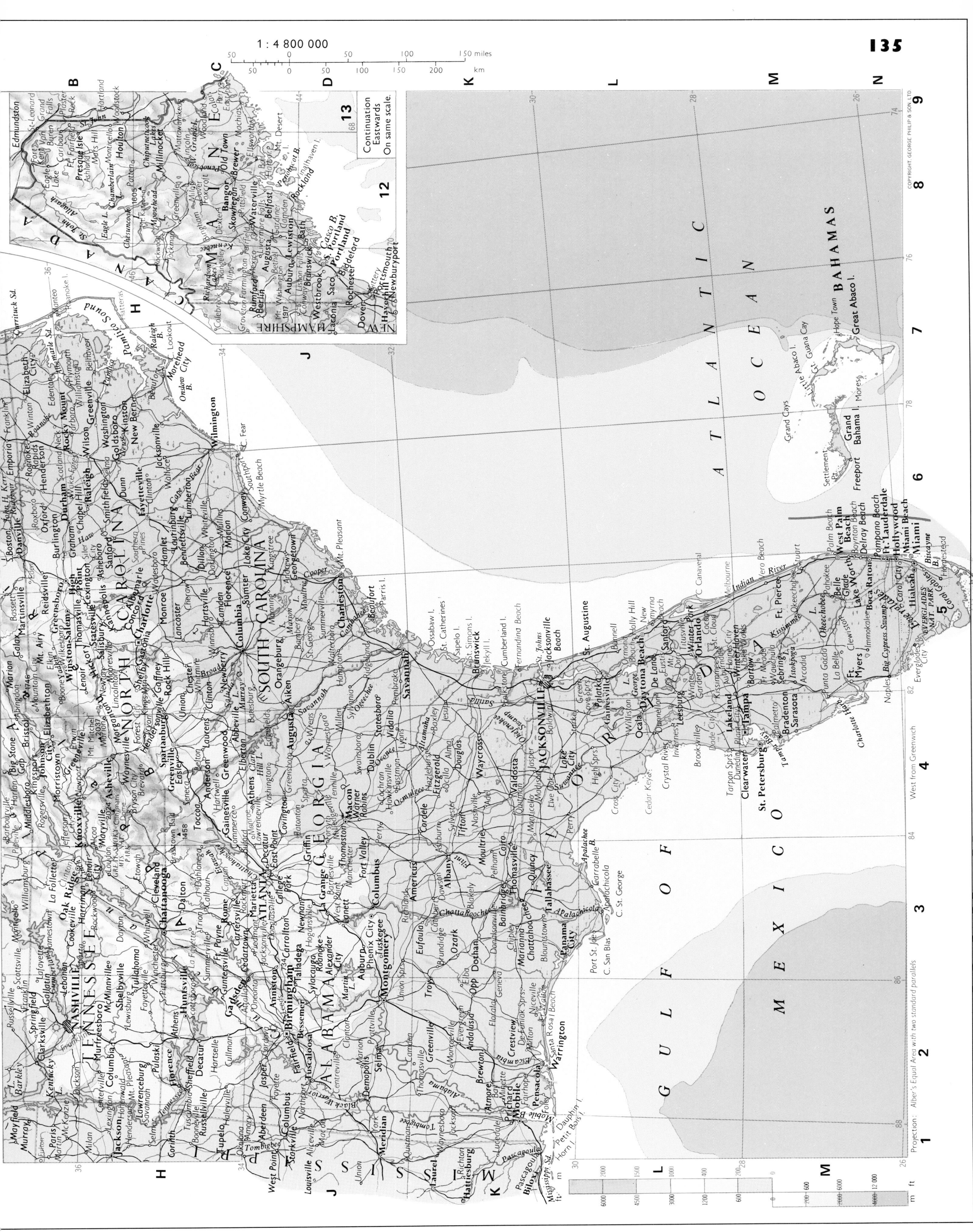

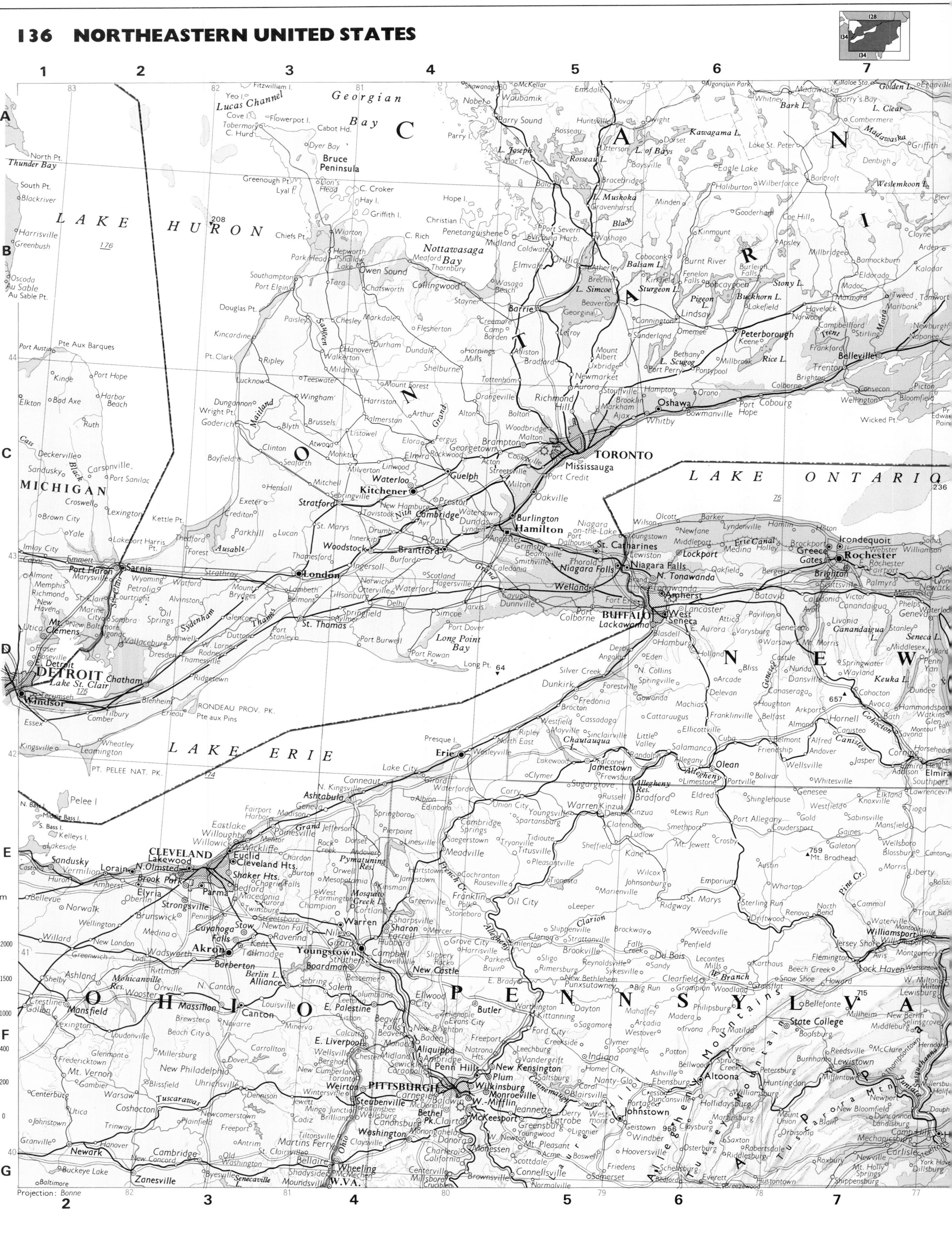

1   2   3   4   5   6   7

LAKE HURON

Georgian Bay

Lucas Channel
Cove I.
Tobermory
C. Hurd
Flowerpot I.
Dyer Bay
Bruce Peninsula
C. Croker
Lion's Head
Hay I.
Griffith I.

Fitzwilliam I.
Yeo I.
Cabot Hd.

Shawanaga I.
Nobel
Waubamik
McKellar
Ensdale
Novar
Algonquin Park
Whitney
Bark L.
Barry's Bay
Combermere
Golden L.
Eganville

Parry Sound
Rosseau
Huntsville
Dwight
Dorset
Kawagama L.
Wilberforce
Bancroft
Westemkoon I.

North Pt.
Thunder Bay
South Pt.
Blackriver
Harrisville
Greenbush
Oscoda
Au Sable
Au Sable Pt.
Port Austin
Pte Aux Barques

ONTARIO

L. Joseph
L. MacTier
L. of Bays
Rosseau L.
Baysville
Bracebridge
Gravenhurst
Black
Port Severn
Victoria Harb.
Midland
Coldwater
Washago
Orillia
Atherley

L. Muskoka
Minden
Gooderham
Coe Hill
Haliburton

Kinmount
Cobocconk
Fenelon Falls
Bobcaygeon
Stony L.
Apsley
Millbridge
Bannockburn
Eldorado
Madoc
Tweed
Marmora
Marlbank

LAKE ONTARIO

MICHIGAN

Detroit
Windsor
Sarnia
Port Huron

OHIO

Cleveland
Akron
Youngstown
Canton

PENNSYLVANIA

Pittsburgh
Erie
Williamsport
Altoona
Johnstown
State College

NEW YORK

Buffalo
Rochester
Niagara Falls
Jamestown
Olean

Toronto
Mississauga
Hamilton
Kitchener
Guelph
London
Brantford
St. Catharines

LAKE ERIE

W. VA.
Wheeling

Projection: Bonne

1:2 000 000

MONTREAL QUEBEC MAINE VERMONT NEW HAMPSHIRE

Ottawa Hull

Lake Champlain

Adirondack Mountains

Green Mountains White Mountains

NEW YORK MASSACHUSETTS

Albany Schenectady Troy Utica Syracuse

Springfield Worcester BOSTON Cambridge

Catskill Mts. CONNECTICUT RHODE ISLAND

Hartford Providence New Haven Bridgeport

Scranton Wilkes-Barre Allentown Bethlehem

NEW JERSEY NEW YORK Newark Jersey City Elizabeth

Long Island Long Beach

PENNSYLVANIA Reading PHILADELPHIA Camden Trenton

ATLANTIC OCEAN

West from Greenwich

COPYRIGHT. GEORGE PHILIP & SON. LTD.

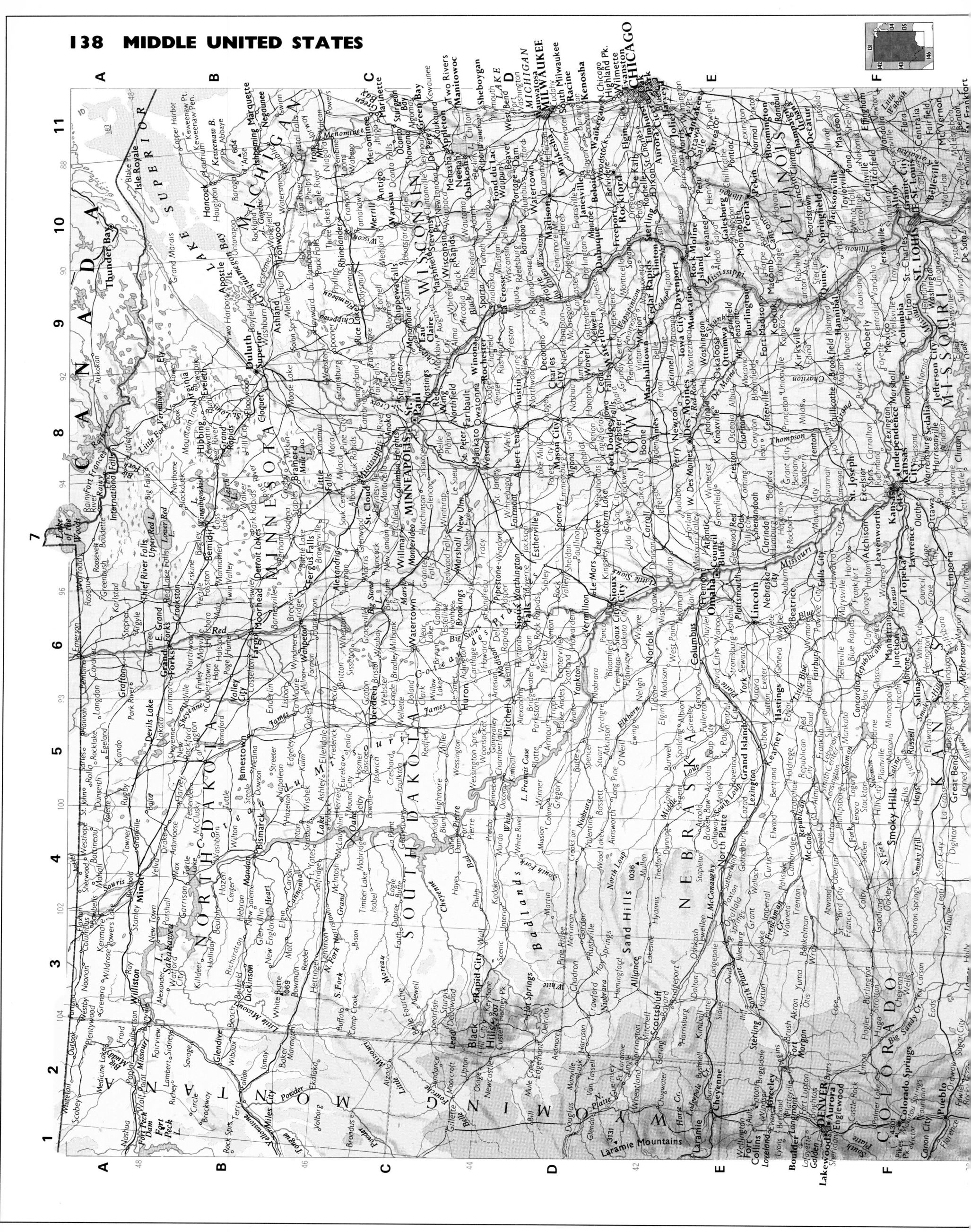

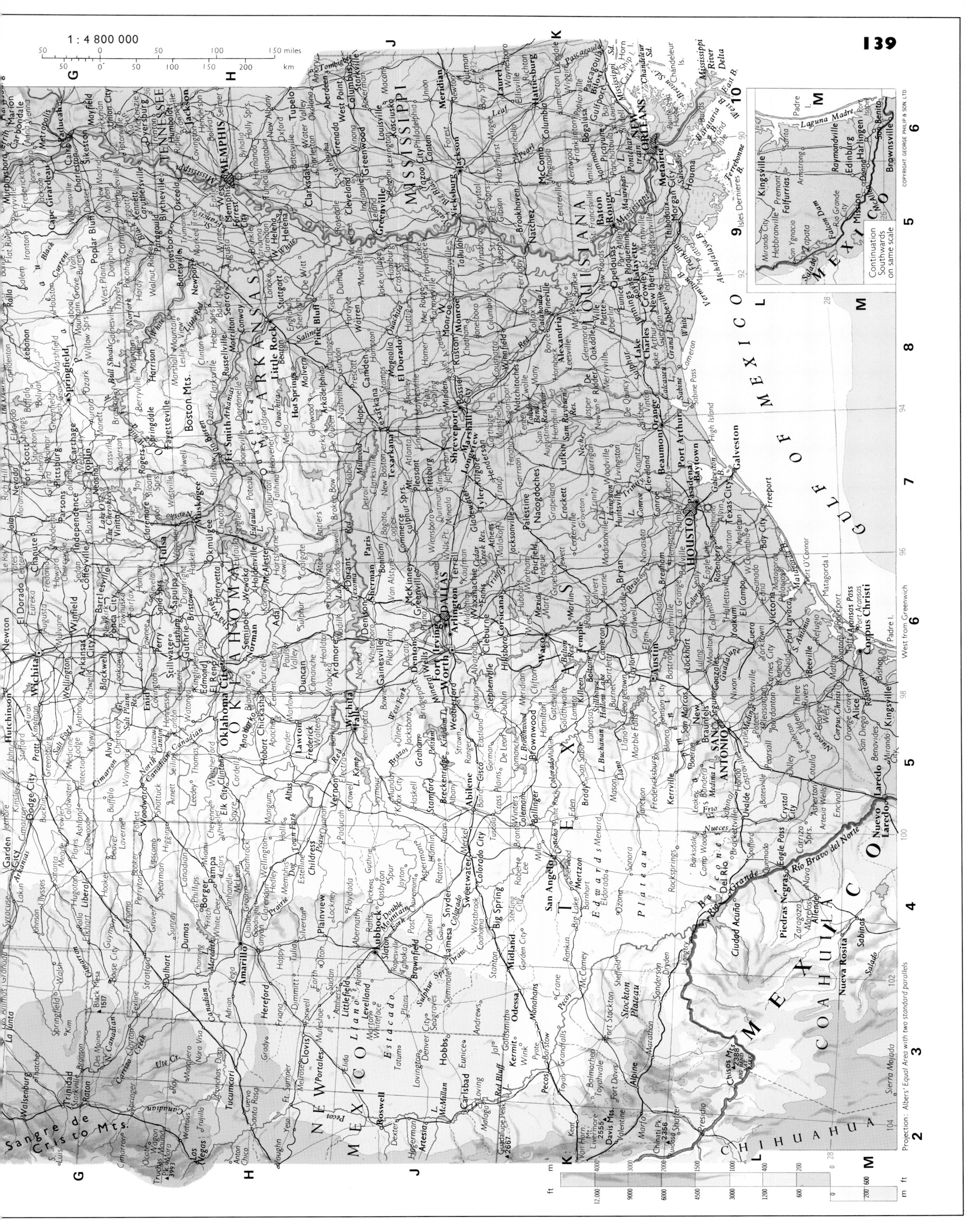

1 : 4 800 000

COPYRIGHT. GEORGE PHILIP & SON, LTD.

Projection: Alber's Equal Area with two standard parallels

Continuation Southwards on same scale

IOWA

WISCON(SIN)

MISSOURI

ILLIN(OIS)

KANSAS

Projection: Bonne

ft   m
1200   400
600   200
0   0

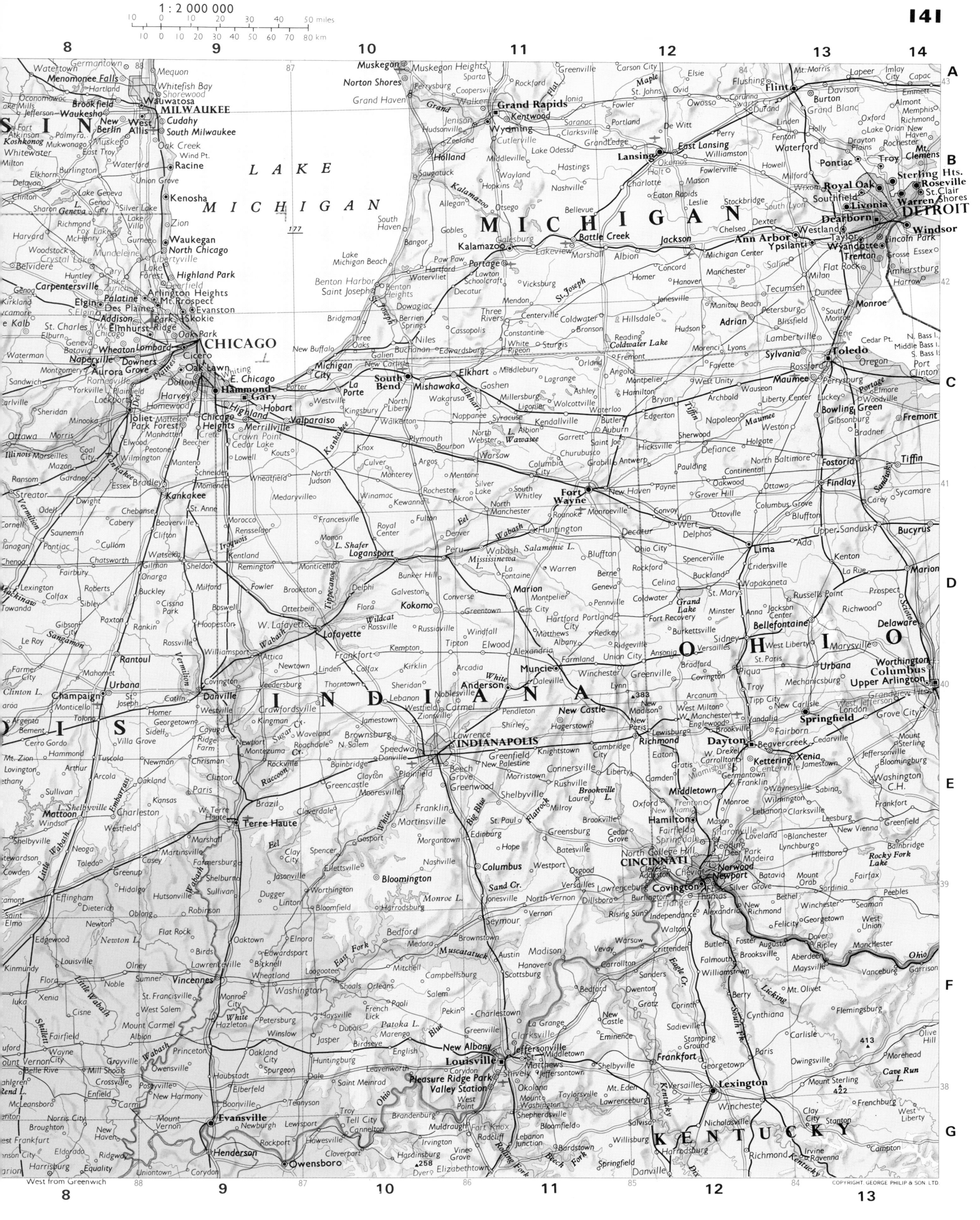

1 : 4 800 000

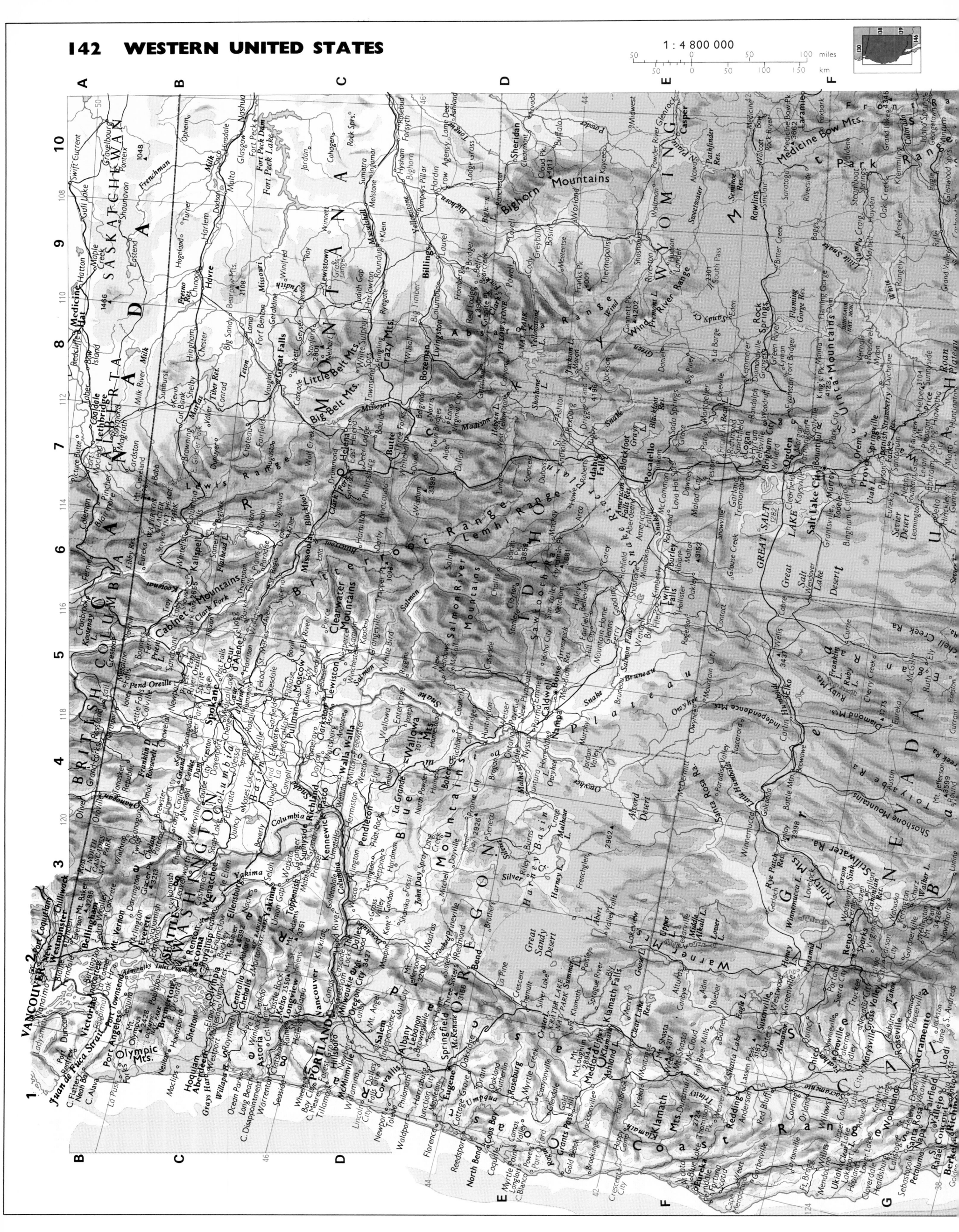

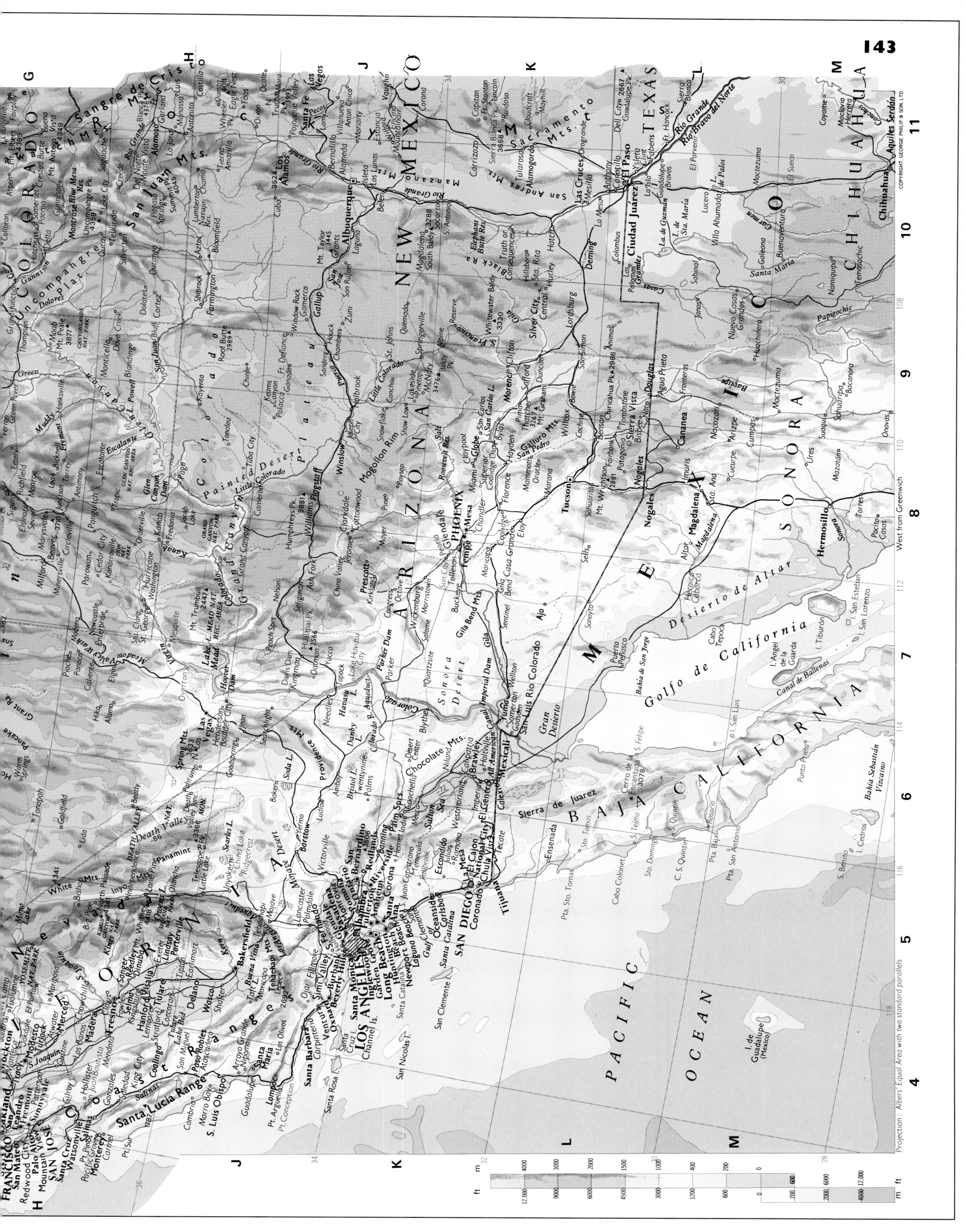

Projection: Albers' Equal Area with two standard parallels

West from Greenwich

SEATTLE-PORTLAND REGION
On same scale

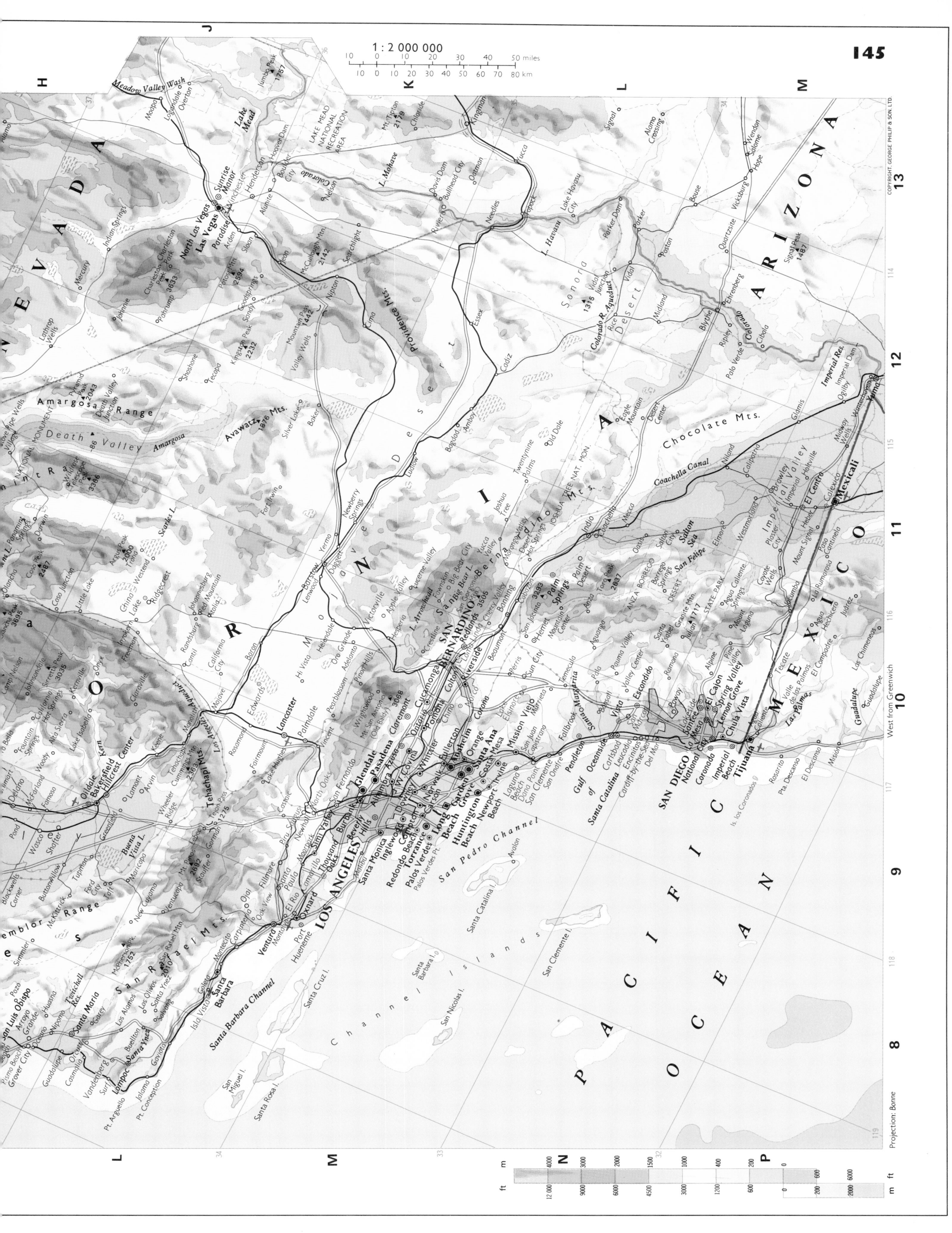

1 : 2 000 000

10   0   10   20   30   40   50 miles
10   0   10 20 30 40 50 60 70 80 km

COPYRIGHT GEORGE PHILIP & SON, LTD.

Projection: Bonne

West from Greenwich

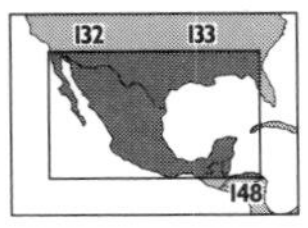

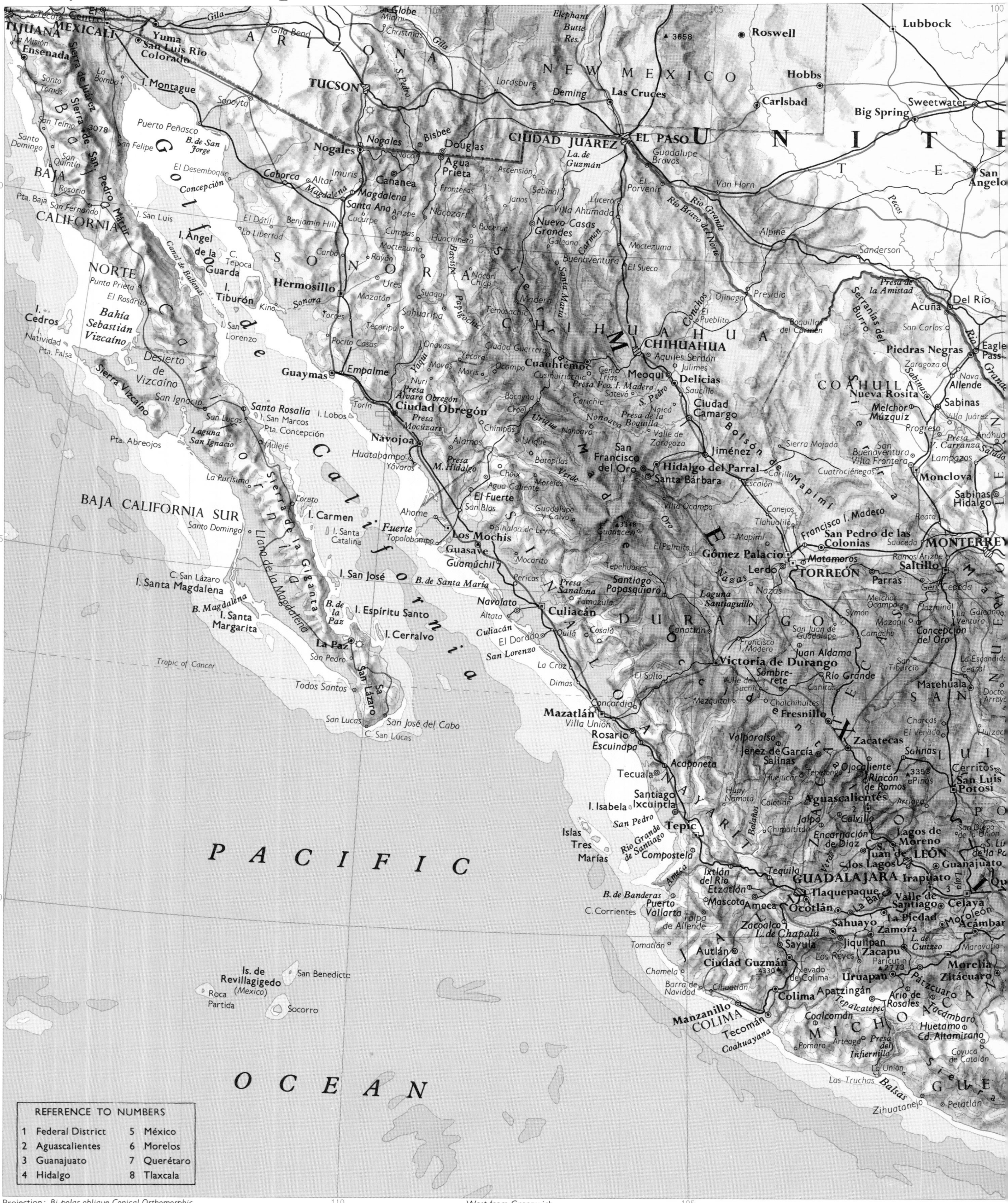

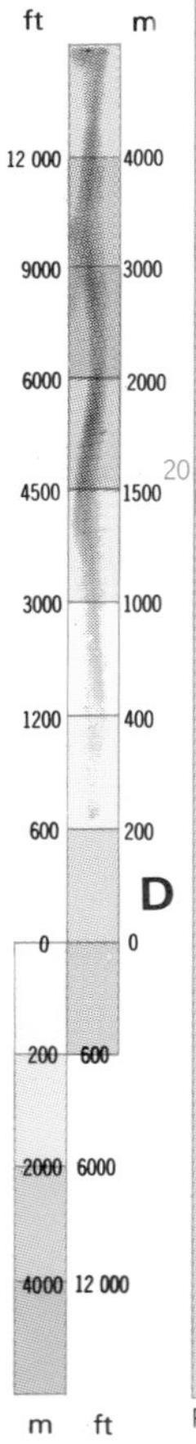

PACIFIC

OCEAN

Projection: Bi-polar oblique Conical Orthomorphic

West from Greenwich

REFERENCE TO NUMBERS
1 Federal District 5 México
2 Aguascalientes 6 Morelos
3 Guanajuato 7 Querétaro
4 Hidalgo 8 Tlaxcala

ft m
12 000 4000
9000 3000
6000 2000
4500 1500
3000 1000
1200 400
600 200
0 0
200 600
2000 6000
4000 12 000
m ft

Tijuana, MEXICALI, Tecate, El Centro, Yuma, San Luis Río Colorado, Ensenada, La Misión, Santo Tomás, San Telmo, San Quintín, Santo Domingo, Rosario, San Fernando, Pta. Baja, La Bomba, I. Montague, Puerto Peñasco, San Felipe, El Desemboque, Concepción, Caborca, Altar, Imuris, Magdalena, Santa Ana, Arizpe, Cucurpe, Nogales, Nogales, Cananea, Agua Prieta, Douglas, Bisbee, Naco, Fronteras, Nacozari, Cumpas, Moctezuma

ARIZONA, SONORA, CHIHUAHUA, COAHUILA, DURANGO, NUEVO LEÓN, SINALOA, NAYARIT, JALISCO, COLIMA, MICHOACÁN, GUERRERO, SAN LUIS POTOSÍ, ZACATECAS

NEW MEXICO, UNITED STATES

TUCSON, Globe, Miami, Christmas, Gila Bend, Lordsburg, Deming, Las Cruces, CIUDAD JUÁREZ, EL PASO, Roswell, Hobbs, Carlsbad, Big Spring, Sweetwater, Lubbock, San Angelo, Van Horn, Alpine, Sanderson, Del Río, Acuña, Eagle Pass, Piedras Negras, Nueva Rosita, Sabinas, Allende, Melchor Múzquiz, Monclova

Elephant Butte Res., 3658, 3078

BAJA CALIFORNIA NORTE, BAJA CALIFORNIA SUR, Golfo de California, Gulf of California

Hermosillo, Guaymas, Empalme, Ciudad Obregón, Navojoa, Huatabampo, Yávaros, Los Mochis, Topolobampo, Ahome, El Fuerte, San Blas, Guasave, Guamúchil, Navolato, Culiacán, Altata, Mazatlán, Rosario, Escuinapa, Tecuala, Acaponeta, Santiago Ixcuintla, Tepic, Compostela, Ixtlán del Río, Etzatlán, Mascota, Ameca, Puerto Vallarta, Tepa de Allende, GUADALAJARA, Tlaquepaque, Orotlán, Zacoalco, Sayula, Autlán, Ciudad Guzmán, Colima, MANZANILLO, Tecomán, Coahuayana, Apatzingán, Uruapan, Coalcomán

CHIHUAHUA, Cuauhtémoc, Aquiles Serdán, Meoqui, Delicias, Camargo, Jiménez, Hidalgo del Parral, Santa Bárbara, San Francisco del Oro, Escalón, Nuevo Casas Grandes, Villa Ahumada, Buenaventura, El Sueco, Ojinaga, Presidio

MONTERREY, SALTILLO, TORREÓN, Gómez Palacio, Lerdo, Parras, Matamoros, Victoria de Durango, Sombrerete, Río Grande, Fresnillo, ZACATECAS, Valparaíso, Jerez de García Salinas, San Luis Potosí, Matehuala, Aguascalientes, Lagos de Moreno, S. Juan de los Lagos, LEÓN, Guanajuato, Irapuato, Celaya, La Piedad, Zamora, Zacapu, Pátzcuaro, MORELIA, Zitácuaro, Tepalcatepec, Ario de Rosales, Tacámbaro, Huetamo, Cd. Altamirano, Coyuca de Catalán, Petatlán, Zihuatanejo, Las Truchas

Is. de Revillagigedo (Mexico), San Benedicto, Roca Partida, Socorro

I. Cedros, I. Natividad, Bahía Sebastián Vizcaíno, Desierto de Vizcaíno, Sierra Vizcaíno, San Ignacio, Laguna San Ignacio, Pta. Abreojos, La Purísima, Comondú, Loreto, I. Carmen, I. Santa Catalina, Santa Rosalía, Mulegé, I. San José, B. de Santa María, La Paz, San Pedro, San José del Cabo, C. San Lucas, Todos Santos, Tropic of Cancer, I. Santa Margarita, I. Santa Magdalena, C. San Lázaro, B. Magdalena, B. de la Paz, I. Espíritu Santo, I. Cerralvo

Sierra Madre Occidental, Sierra Madre Oriental

Río Bravo del Norte, Río Grande, Pecos, Río Conchos, Boquillas del Carmen, Presa de la Amistad

I. Tiburón, I. Ángel de la Guarda, Canal de Ballenas, I. San Lorenzo, Punta Prieta, El Rosarito

1 : 6 400 000

50   0   50   100   150   200 miles
50   0   100   200   300 km

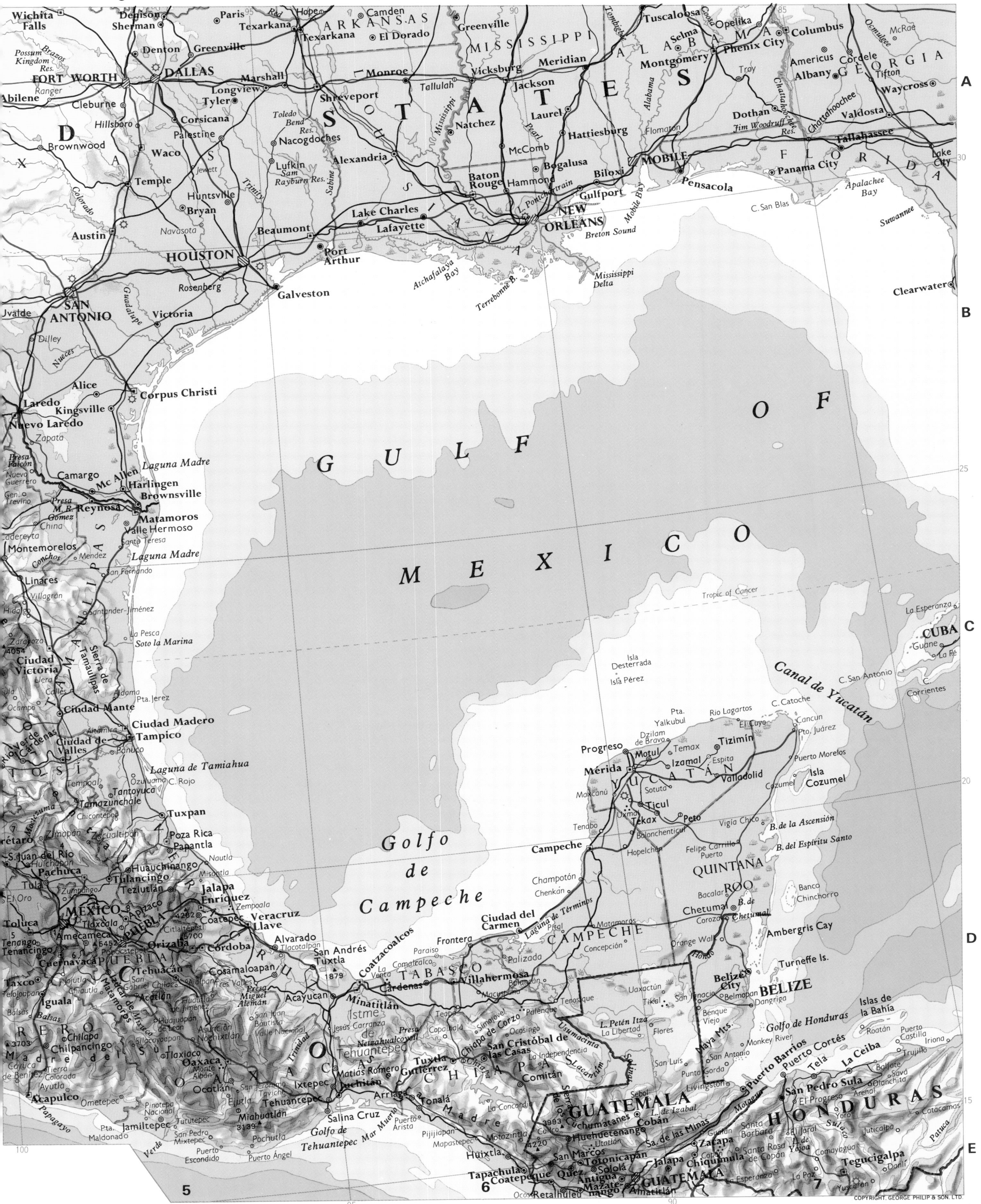

5   6   7   8

GULF OF MEXICO

Golfo de Campeche

UNITED STATES

TEXAS
ARKANSAS
MISSISSIPPI
ALABAMA
GEORGIA
FLORIDA
LOUISIANA

Wichita Falls, Denison, Sherman, Paris, Texarkana, Camden, Greenville, Tuscaloosa, Opelika, Columbus, McRae, Osmulgee
Denton, Greenville, El Dorado, Selma, Phenix City, Americus, Cordele
FORT WORTH, DALLAS, Marshall, Monroe, Vicksburg, Meridian, Montgomery, Troy, Albany, Tifton, Waycross
Abilene, Cleburne, Longview, Tyler, Shreveport, Jackson, Dothan, Valdosta
Brownwood, Corsicana, Palestine, Nacogdoches, Natchez, Laurel, Tallahassee
Waco, Alexandria, McComb, Hattiesburg, Flomaton, Lake City
Temple, Huntsville, Bryan, Baton Rouge, Bogalusa, Biloxi, MOBILE, Pensacola, Panama City, Apalachee Bay
Austin, Lake Charles, Hammond, Gulfport, Mobile Bay, Suwannee
SAN ANTONIO, HOUSTON, Beaumont, Lafayette, NEW ORLEANS, Breton Sound, Clearwater
Victoria, Port Arthur, Galveston
Uvalde, Rosenberg
Alice, Corpus Christi
Laredo, Kingsville
Nuevo Laredo, Matamoros

MEXICO
Tropic of Cancer

CUBA
Guane, La Fé
Canal de Yucatán, C. San Antonio, Corrientes, C. Catoche

YUCATÁN
Progreso, Mérida, Motul, Izamal, Tizimín, Cancun, Pto. Juárez
Valladolid, Cozumel, Isla Cozumel
Ticul, Peto
QUINTANA ROO
Campeche, Champotón, Chetumal
CAMPECHE
Ciudad del Carmen, Frontera, Villahermosa
TABASCO
Coatzacoalcos, Minatitlán

BELIZE
Belize City, Belmopan, Turneffe Is., Ambergris Cay

GUATEMALA
HONDURAS
San Pedro Sula, Puerto Barrios, Puerto Cortés, La Ceiba, Tegucigalpa, Islas de la Bahía

MEXICO
Ciudad Victoria, Ciudad Mante, Ciudad Madero, Tampico, Ciudad Valles
Tuxpan, Poza Rica, Papantla
Pachuca, Tulancingo, Teziutlán, Jalapa Enríquez, Veracruz
MÉXICO, PUEBLA, Orizaba, Córdoba, Veracruz Llave, Alvarado
Toluca, Cuernavaca, Tehuacán, San Andrés Tuxtla
Taxco, Iguala, Acayucan
Chilpancingo, Oaxaca, Tuxtla Gutiérrez, San Cristóbal de las Casas, Comitán
Acapulco, Tehuantepec, Salina Cruz, Golfo de Tehuantepec
CHIAPAS, GUATEMALA, Tapachula, Coatepeque, Quezaltenango

COPYRIGHT. GEORGE PHILIP & SON, LTD

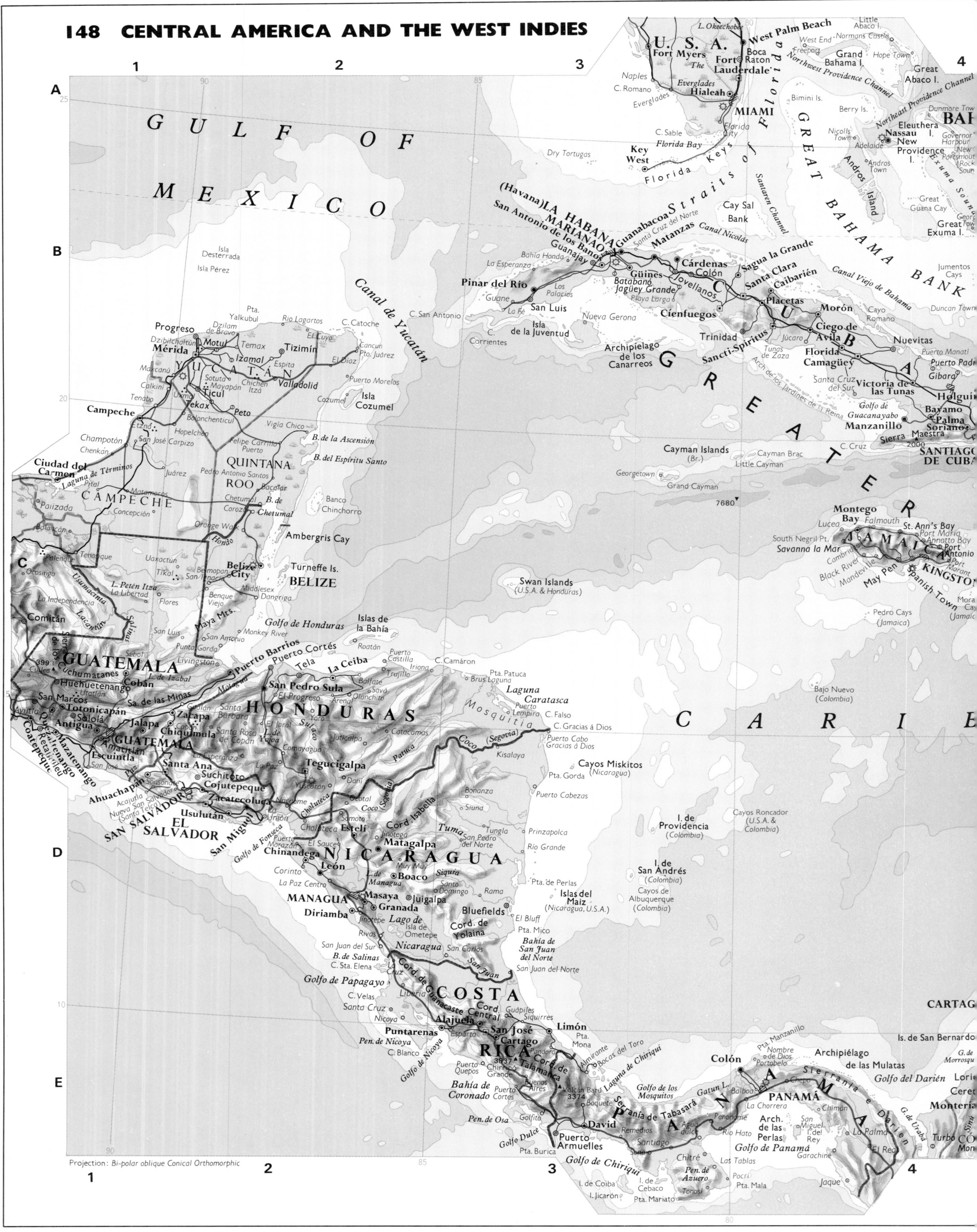

A

B

C

D

E

1   2   3   4

25

20

15

10

GULF OF MEXICO

U.S.A.
Fort Myers
Naples
C. Romano
Everglades
Hialeah
MIAMI
C. Sable
Florida Bay
Dry Tortugas
Key West
Florida Keys
Straits of Florida
West Palm Beach
Boca Raton
Fort Lauderdale
West End
Grand Bahama I.
Hope Town
Little Abaco I.
Normans Castle
Great Abaco I.
Northwest Providence Channel
Bimini Is.
Berry Is.
Eleuthera
Nassau
New Providence
Andros Town
Andros Island
BAH
Great Guana Cay
Great Exuma I.
Jumentos Cays
Duncan Town

(Havana) LA HABANA
MARIANAO
Guanabacoa
San Antonio de los Baños
Guanajay
Bahía Honda
La Esperanza
Pinar del Río
Guane
La Fé
Los Palacios
San Luis
C. San Antonio
C. Corrientes
Isla de la Juventud
Nueva Gerona
Archipiélago de los Canarreos
Santa Cruz del Norte
Matanzas
Canal Nicolás
Cárdenas
Colón
Jovellanos
Güines
Batabanó
Jagüey Grande
Playa Larga
Cienfuegos
Sagua la Grande
Santa Clara
Caibarién
Placetas
Trinidad
Sancti-Spíritus
Júcaro
Tunas de Zaza
Golfo de Guacanayabo
Morón
Cayo Romano
Ciego de Avila
Florida
Camagüey
Santa Cruz del Sur
Arch. de los Jardines de la Reina
Nuevitas
Puerto Manatí
Puerto Padre
Gibara
Holguín
Victoria de las Tunas
Bayamo
Palma Soriano
Manzanillo
Sierra Maestra
C. Cruz
SANTIAGO DE CUBA

Canal Viejo de Bahama

CUBA

GREATER

Cay Sal Bank

Cayman Islands (Br.)
Georgetown
Grand Cayman
Cayman Brac
Little Cayman

7680

Swan Islands (U.S.A. & Honduras)

Montego Bay
Lucea
Falmouth
St. Ann's Bay
Port Maria
Annotto Bay
Port Antonio
South Negril Pt.
Savanna la Mar
Black River
Mandeville
May Pen
Spanish Town
KINGSTON
JAMAI
Pedro Cays (Jamaica)

CARIB

Isla Desterrada
Isla Pérez

Progreso
Dzilam
Pta. Yalkubul
Río Lagartos
C. Catoche
Cancún
Pto. Juárez
Motul
Temax
El Cuyo
Dzibilchaltún
Mérida
Izamal
Tizimín
Espita
YUCATÁN
Maxcanú
Sotuta
Mayapán
Chichén Itzá
Valladolid
Puerto Morelos
Ticul
Tekax
Peto
Isla Cozumel
Calkiní
Uman
Oxkutzcab
Campeche
Champotón
Chenkán
Hecelchakán
Bolonchenticul
Hopelchén
Vigía Chico
B. de la Ascensión
B. del Espíritu Santo
Ciudad del Carmen
Laguna de Términos
Pital
Palizada
Atasta
Balancán
QUINTANA ROO
Pedro Antonio Santos
Juárez
Felipe Carrillo Puerto
Bacalar
B. de Chetumal
Chetumal
Corozal
Banco Chinchorro
Ambergris Cay
Palenque
Tenosique
CAMPECHE
Matamoros
Concepción
Uaxactún
Tikal
Flores
L. Petén Itza
La Libertad
San Luis
Benque Viejo
Belmopan
San Ignacio
Orange Walk
Hondo
Belize City
Turneffe Is.
Middlesex
Dangriga
BELIZE
Ocosingo
Sebol
Comitán
La Independencia
Lacantún
Usumacinta
Sa. de los Cuchumatanes
Huehuetenango
Cobán
Livingston
Puerto Barrios
Puerto Cortés
Golfo de Honduras
Islas de la Bahía
Roatán
Maya Mts.
Punta Gorda
Monkey River
San Antonio

GUATEMALA
899
Cobán
San Marcos
Totonicapán
Sololá
Jalapa
Zacapa
Chiquimula
Santa Rosa de Copán
HONDURAS
Antigua
GUATEMALA
Amatitlán
Chimaltenango
Escuintla
Santa Ana
Ahuachapán
Acajutla
Nuevo San Salvador (Santa Tecla)
SAN SALVADOR
Cojutepeque
Zacatecoluca
EL SALVADOR
Usulután
San Miguel
La Unión
Golfo de Fonseca
Chinandega
León
Corinto
La Paz Centro
MANAGUA
Diriamba
Masaya
Granada
Jinotepe
Rivas
San Juan del Sur
B. de Salinas
C. Sta. Elena
Golfo de Papagayo
C. Velas
Santa Cruz
Nicoya
Pen. de Nicoya
C. Blanco
Golfo de Nicoya
Puntarenas
Esparta
Puerto Quepos
Bahía de Coronado
Puerto Cortés
Pen. de Osa
Golfo Dulce
Golfito
Pta. Burica
Puerto Armuelles
Golfo de Chiriquí
I. de Coiba
I. de Cebaco
I. Jicarón
Pta. Mariato
David
Remedios
Pocrí
Jaqué

Tela
La Ceiba
Balfate
Savá
Olanchito
San Pedro Sula
El Progreso
Santa Bárbara
L. de Yojoa
Yoro
Sulaco
Arenal
L. de Izabal
Motagua
Gualán
Jalapa
El Jícaro
Comayagua
Juticalpa
Catacamas
Tegucigalpa
Danlí
Nacaome
Choluteca
El Sauce
Somoto
Estelí
Jinotega
Matagalpa
San Pedro del Norte
Chalatenango
Morazán
San Vicente
NICARAGUA
Muy Muy
Boaco
Juigalpa
Santo Domingo
Rama
Siquia
Cord. Isabella
Tuma
San Carlos
Lago de Nicaragua
Isla de Ometepe
Cord. de Guanacaste
Liberia
COSTA RICA
Alajuela
San José
Cartago
Cord. Central
Cord. de Talamanca
3637
Chirripó Grande
Buenos Aires
Volcán Barú
3377
Boquete
Limón
Pta. Mona
Siquirres
Guápiles
Almirante
Bocas del Toro
Laguna de Chiriquí
Golfo de los Mosquitos
Colón
Nombre de Dios
Portobelo
PANAMÁ
Chitré
Las Tablas
Pen. de Azuero
Tonosí

Río Lempira
Copán
La Esperanza
Catacamas
Coco (Segovia)
Kisalaya
Puerto Cabo Gracias á Dios
C. Gracias á Dios
Laguna Caratasca
Puerto Lempira
Mosquitia
Brus Laguna
Pta. Patuca
C. Camarón
Iriona
Trujillo
Pta. Castilla
Patuca
Coco
Bonanza
Siuna
Prinzapolca
Tungla
Bonanza
Río Grande
Puerto Cabezas
Cayos Miskitos (Nicaragua)
Pta. Gorda
Bluefields
El Bluff
Pta. Mico
Cord. de Yolaina
Bahía de San Juan del Norte
San Juan del Norte
San Juan
Islas del Maíz (Nicaragua, U.S.A.)
Pta. de Perlas

I. de Providencia (Colombia)
Cayos Roncador (U.S.A. & Colombia)
Bajo Nuevo (Colombia)
I. de San Andrés (Colombia)
Cayos de Albuquerque (Colombia)

CARTAG

CARTAGE

PANAMÁ
Balboa
La Chorrera
Penonomé
Río Hato
Santiago
Aguadulce
Chimán
San Miguel I. del Rey
Arch. de las Perlas
Golfo de Panamá
Sierranía de Tabasará
Serranía del Darién
Archipiélago de las Mulatas
Golfo del Darién
Is. de San Bernardo
Sierrania del Darién
G. de Morrosqu
G. de Urabá
Turbo
El Real
Montería
Loric
Cereté
La Palma

90   85   80

1   2   3   4

1 : 6 400 000

50   0   50   100   150   200 miles

50   0   100   200   300 km

5   6   7   8

A

A T L A N T I C

Tropic of Cancer

B

O C E A N

ft   m

12,000   4000

9000   3000

6000   2000

1200   400

600   200

0

200   600

2000   6000

4000   12,000

6000   18,000

8000   24,000

m   ft

MAS

Arthur's Town

The Bight   Cat I.

San Salvador
(Watling I., Guanahani)

Conception I.

andy   Rum Cay
Cay

Long I.

Clarence
Town

Crooked I.   Plana Cays

Richmond   Crooked I.
Albert   Snug
Town   Corner   Atwood or
Samana Cay

Cay Verde   Mira por vos Cay

Acklins I.

Mayaguana I.

Caicos Passage

Cay Santa
Domingo

Hogsty Reef   Caicos
Islands
(Br.)   Turks Islands
(Br.)

Turks I. Passage

Little Inagua I.

Lake Rose

Banes   Great
Inagua I.

Antilla   Moa
Mayarí

Matthew
Town

Baracoa

Guantánamo   Pta. de
Maisí   Î. de
la Tortue
Paso de los Vientos
(Windward/Jean-Rabel)   Port-de-Paix
Cap-à-Foux   Cap-Haïtien
Fort-Liberté   Monte Cristi
La Isabela
Puerto Plata
C. Frances Viejo

Milwaukee
Deep
9200   Puerto Rico Trench

Puerto Rico Trench

San Francisco de Macoris

Santiago de
los Cabelleros
La Vega   Nagua
Sánchez
Sabana de La Mar   Virgin Gorda
St. Thomas   Tortola   Anegada
Virgin Is.
(Br.)   Sombrero (Anguilla)

Gonaïves   Central   Bayamón   San Juan
Carolina   Virgin Is.
(U.S.A.)   Anguilla (Br.)
St.-Martin (Guad.)   St-Barthélemy (Fr.)

St.-Marc   Hinche   Aguadilla   Arecibo   Fajardo   Road Town
Charlotte Amalie
St. Thomas   Anegada Passage

Jérémie   Î. de la Gonâve   DOMINICAN
REP.   San Pedro   Higüey   C. Engaño   Caguas   St. Maarten (Neth.)   Saba (Neth.)   Barbuda
PORT-
AU-PRINCE   San Juan   de Macoris   La Romana   1338   Ponce   Carolina   Guayama   St. Eustatius
(Neth.)   CHRISTOPHER-   ANTIGUA
& BARBUDA
Massif de la Hotte   Petit Goâve   Azua de   B. de   Mayagüez   Basseterre   NEVIS   St. Johns
Les Cayes   2280   Barahona   Compostela   Yuma   Isla   Canal de la Mona   Nevis   Antigua
Jacmel   Bani   Mona   (U.S.A.)   PUERTO   Frederiksted   St. Croix   Redonda   Montserrat
Aquin   San Cristóbal   I. Saona   RICO   Christiansted   (U.S.A.)

Navassa I.   Dame
(U.S.A.)   Marie   SANTO DOMINGO   (U.S.A.)

C. Carcasse   Pointe-à-Gravois   Î.-à-Vache   Pedernales   I. Beata   C. Beata   Guadeloupe Passage

H I S P A N I O L A   Ste-Rose   Moule   Désirade

A N T I L L E S   E   S   S   GUADELOUPE   Pointe-à-Pitre
(Fr.)   Basse-Terre   Marie-Galante (Fr.)
Grand-Bourg
I. des Saintes
(Guad.)   Dominica Passage
I. de Aves (Bird I.)
(Venezuela)   Portsmouth   DOMINICA
Roseau

Martinique Passage
Mt. Pelée
1397   Ste-Marie
François
Rivière-Pilo
Fort-de-France   MARTINIQUE
St. Lucia Channel (Fr.)
Castries   ST. LUCIA
Soufrière

St. Vincent Passage
Soufrière 1234   ST. VINCENT
Kingstown   Speightstown
Bridgetown   BARBADOS
& THE

C

D

B E A N   S E A

W   I   N   D   W   A   R   D   I   S   L   A   N   D   S

L   E   S   S   E   R   A   N   T   I   L   L   E   S

L   E   E   W   A   R   D   I   S   L   A   N   D   S

L E S S E R   A N T I L L E S

Hillsborough   The Grenadines
St. George's   GRENADA

I. Blanquilla (Ven.)

Pta. Gallinas   Aruba
(Neth.)   Curaçao   Bonaire   I. Los Hermanos
(Ven.)   Tobago

C. San Román   NETH.
ANTILLES   Is. de Aves
(Ven.)   I. Orchila
(Ven.)   I. Los Testigos
(Ven.)   Scarborough
Galera
Pt.

Pen. de la
Guajira   Pta.
Espada   Pen. de
Paraguaná   Willemstad   Is. Los Roques
(Ven.)   I. Margarita
NUEVA   La Asunción
ESPARTA   Porlamar   Pen. de Paria   Port of
Spain   Arima   Galera
Pt.

Ríohacha   Uribia   GUAJIRA   Punto Fijo   Puerto
Cumarebo   I. La Tortuga
(Ven.)   Carúpano   Río
Caribe   Güiria   TRINIDAD   Río Claro

Santa
Marta   C. San Juan
de Guía   Punta
Cardón   Coro   La Vela de Coro   Maiquetía
La Guaira   CARACAS   C. Codera   Higuerote   Cumaná   SUCRE   Caripito   San Fernando   TRINIDAD
& TOBAGO

BARRAN-
QUILLA   Cienaga   Sierra Nevada de
Santa Marta
5800   San
Rafael   FALCÓN   Mene de Mauroa   Tocuyo   Puerto
Cabello   Maracay   DISTRITO
FEDERAL   Puerto
La Cruz   Barcelona   Caicara   Maturín   DELTA
Baranoa   Soledad   La
Concepción   Altagracia   Carora   San Felipe   YARACUY   Valencia   MIRANDA   Los Teques   Ocumare del Tuy   Anaco   MONAGAS   Tucupita   AMACUR
Sabanalarga   Santa Rita   CARABOBO   San Juan de   Aragua de
Fundación   Valledupar   Villa del
Rosario   Ciudad   Mene   BARQUISIMETO   Maritagua de   los Morros de Orituco   Barcelona   El Tigre
Calamar   Agustín   Cabimas   Ojeda   LARA   El Tocuyo   San Carlos   Villa   Cantaura
Arjona   Codazzi   Machiques   Lago de   COJEDES   El Sombrero   Valle de la   Pariaguán   ANZOÁTEGUI   Ciudad Guayana
Plato   Zambrano   CÉSAR   Maracaibo   TRUJILLO   Acarigua   Pascua   El Pao   Upata
El Carmen   ZULIA   La Ceiba   PORTUGUESA   El Baúl   GUÁRICO   Santa María   El Tigre   Sierra Imataca
de Bolívar   Magangué   Betijoque   Trujillo   Calabozo   de Ipire   Soledad   Tumeremo
Sincé-   Mompós   Catatumbo   Valera   Guanare   Ciudad   Guasipati
lejo   Encontrados   San Carlos   Barinas   Ciudad Guayana
Sahagún   del Zulia   MÉRIDA   BARINAS   Ciudad Bolívar   El Callao
San Marcos   NORTE   Cordillera de Mérida   Libertad   San   Mapire
Sincé   Majagual   SANTANDER   Ciudad   Fernando de   Emb. de Guri
Planeta   Ocaña   Bolivia   Apure   V E N E Z U E L A
Rica   Banco   TACHIRA   Santa   Río de Nutrias   Achaguas   Apure
DOBA   Ayapel   Bolívar   Simití   Cúcuta   Bárbara   Caicara

E

Santa
Marta   C. San Juan   Valencia

West from Greenwich   COPYRIGHT. GEORGE PHILIP & SON. LTD.

75   70   65   60

5   6   7

150 SOUTH AMERICA : Physical

1 : 24 000 000

100   0   100 200 300 400 500 miles
100   0   200   400   600   800 km

Labels (geographic features)

Sa. Nevada de Santa Marta
Barranquilla
Maracaibo ▲5800
G. of Darien
Panama Canal
Margarita
Tobago I.
Caracas
Trinidad
5994▾

Medellín
Cordillera Occidental
Cordillera Central
Cordillera Oriental
Magdalena
Cordá. de Mérida
L. Maracaibo
Orinoco
Georgetown
C. Orange

Cali
Bogotá
Llanos
Meta
Guaviare
Guiana Highlands
Serra de Tumucumaque
ATLANTIC OCEAN

Gulf of Panama
Caquetá
Sierra Pacaraima
▲2810 Roraima
Caroni
Caura
Essequibo

C. de San Francisco
Quito Cotopaxi ▲5897
Chimborazo ▲6267
Napo
Putumayo
Japurá
Negro
Manaus
Amazon
Marajó I.
Pará
Belém
Equator

Guayaquil
G. of Guayaquil
Pta. Pariñas
Pta. Aguja
Lobos Is.
Marañón
Ucayali
Juruá
Purus
Madeira
Amazon
Fortaleza
São Roque
C. Branco

Andes
Huascarán ▲6768
Selva
Juruá
Purus
Madeira
Roosevelt
Tapajós
Xingu
Araguaia
Tocantins
Plateau of Borborema
Recife

Chile
Lima
Chincha Is.
Madre de Dios
Guaporé
Mamoré
Araguaia
Tocantins
São Francisco
Salvador

PACIFIC
Peru Trench
L. Titicaca
Ancohuma & Illampu ▲6550
La Paz
Bolivian Plateau
Plateau of Mato Grosso
Brasília
Brazilian Highlands
Abrolhos Bank

L. Poopó
Pilcomayo
Paraguay
Parná
Belo Horizonte
Serra da Mantiqueira
▲2890 Pico da Bandeira

OCEAN
Tropic of Capricorn
8050
Atacama Desert
Gran Chaco
Asunción
São Paulo
Rio de Janeiro
C. Frio

S. Félix
S. Ambrosio
Ojos del Salado ▲6863
Tucumán
Salado
Paraná
Iguaçu Falls
Uruguay
Serra do Mar
Porto Alegre
Lagoa dos Patos

Salinas Grandes
Córdoba
L. Mar Chiquita
Sierra de Córdoba
Entre Rios
Pampas

Aconcagua ▲6960
Uspallata Pass
Santiago
Valparaíso
Arch. de Juan Fernández
Rosario
Buenos Aires
La Plata
Montevideo
Río de la Plata

Colorado
Negro
Bahía Blanca
Pta. Mogotes

SOUTH
Chile Rise
G. of San Matias
Valdés Peninsula
Argentine Basin

ATLANTIC
Chiloé I.
Chonos Archipelago
Patagonia
G. of San Jorge

Taitao Peninsula
▲4058 S. Valentín
G. of Peñas
6212▾

OCEAN
Wellington
Madre de Dios I.
West Falkland
Falkland Islands
East Falkland
Magellan's Strait
Santa Inés
Cockburn Chan.
Tierra del Fuego
Staten I.
Beagle Chan.
C. Horn

Projection: Lambert's Equivalent Azimuthal

West from Greenwich

COPYRIGHT GEORGE PHILIP & SON LTD

Elevation scale

ft / m

18 000 / 6000
12 000 / 4000
9000 / 3000
6000 / 2000
3000 / 1000
1200 / 400
600 / 200
0 / 0

m / ft
0 / 40
200 / 600
2000 / 6000
4000 / 12 000
6000 / 18 000
8000 / 24 000

1 : 24 000 000

100   0   100   200   300   500 miles
100   0   200   400   600   800 km

1   **2**   **3**   **4**   **5**   **6**

A

COSTA
RICA
San José
PANAMA
Panamá
Golfo de
Darién
Golfo de
Panamá

Barranquilla
Cartagena
Maracaibo
Barquisimeto
Valencia
Caracas

TRINIDAD
AND
TOBAGO
Port of Spain

B

Cúcuta
San
Cristóbal
Bucaramanga
Medellín

VENEZUELA

Orinoco
Ciudad Guayana

Georgetown

Paramaribo
GUYANA   SURINAM   FRENCH
GUIANA
Cayenne
C. Orange

NORTH
ATLANTIC
OCEAN

Cali
Bogotá
COLOMBIA
Meta
Magdalena
Orinoco

Esequibo
Corantijn

C. de San
Francisco
Caquetá

Quito
ECUADOR
Guayaquil
G. de Guayaquil
Napo
Putumayo

Japurá
Negro

Branco

Amazonas
(Amazon)
Ilha de
Marajó
Belém

Equator

São Luís
Fortaleza (Ceara)

C

Iquitos
Marañón
PERU
Chiclayo
Trujillo
Chimbote

Juruá
Purus
Madeira

Aripuanã
Tapajós
Xingu
Tocantins
Santarém
Manaus

Parnaíba
Teresina

C. de São Roque
Natal
João Pessoa
Recife
(Pernambuco)
Maceió

10

Callao
Lima
Cuzco
Madre de Dios
Pôrto Velho
Guaporé

B R A Z I L
Araguaia
São Francisco

Aracaju

D

Titicaca
Arequipa
La Paz
Cochabamba
BOLIVIA
Sucre
Santa Cruz
Mamoré

Cuiabá
Brasília
Goiânia

Salvador

Iquique
Campo Grande
Belo
Horizonte
Vitória
Ribeirão
Prêto
Juiz de Fora
Campos

20

Antofagasto
Tropic of Capricorn
PARAGUAY
Paraguay
Paraná
Londrina
Campinas   Niterói
SÃO
PAULO   Santos   RIO DE JANEIRO

Isla San Felix
(Chile)
Isla San Ambrosio
(Chile)

Salta
San Miguel
de Tucumán
Resistencia
Corrientes
Asunción
Uruguay
Curitiba

E

CHILE
ARGENTINA
Córdoba
San Juan
Santa Fe
Paraná
Rosario
URUGUAY
Pôrto
Alegre
Lagoa dos Patos
Pelotas

SOUTH

30

Viña del Mar
Valparaíso
Santiago
Mendoza
Santa Fe

BUENOS
AIRES
La
Plata
Río de la Plata
Montevideo
Mar del Plata

ATLANTIC

F

Talca
Concepción
Valdivia
Puerto Montt

Bahía Blanca
Colorado
Negro
Viedma

OCEAN

40

PACIFIC
OCEAN
Arch de Juan Fernández
(Chile)

Chubut
Golfo
Comodoro Rivadavia
San Jorge

G

G. de Penas

FALKLAND ISLANDS

Punta
Arenas
Strait of Magellan
West Falkland
(U.K.)
Stanley
East Falkland

H

Cape Horn
Tierra del Fuego
West from Greenwich

Projection : Lambert's Equivalent Azimuthal

COPYRIGHT. GEORGE PHILIP & SON, LTD.

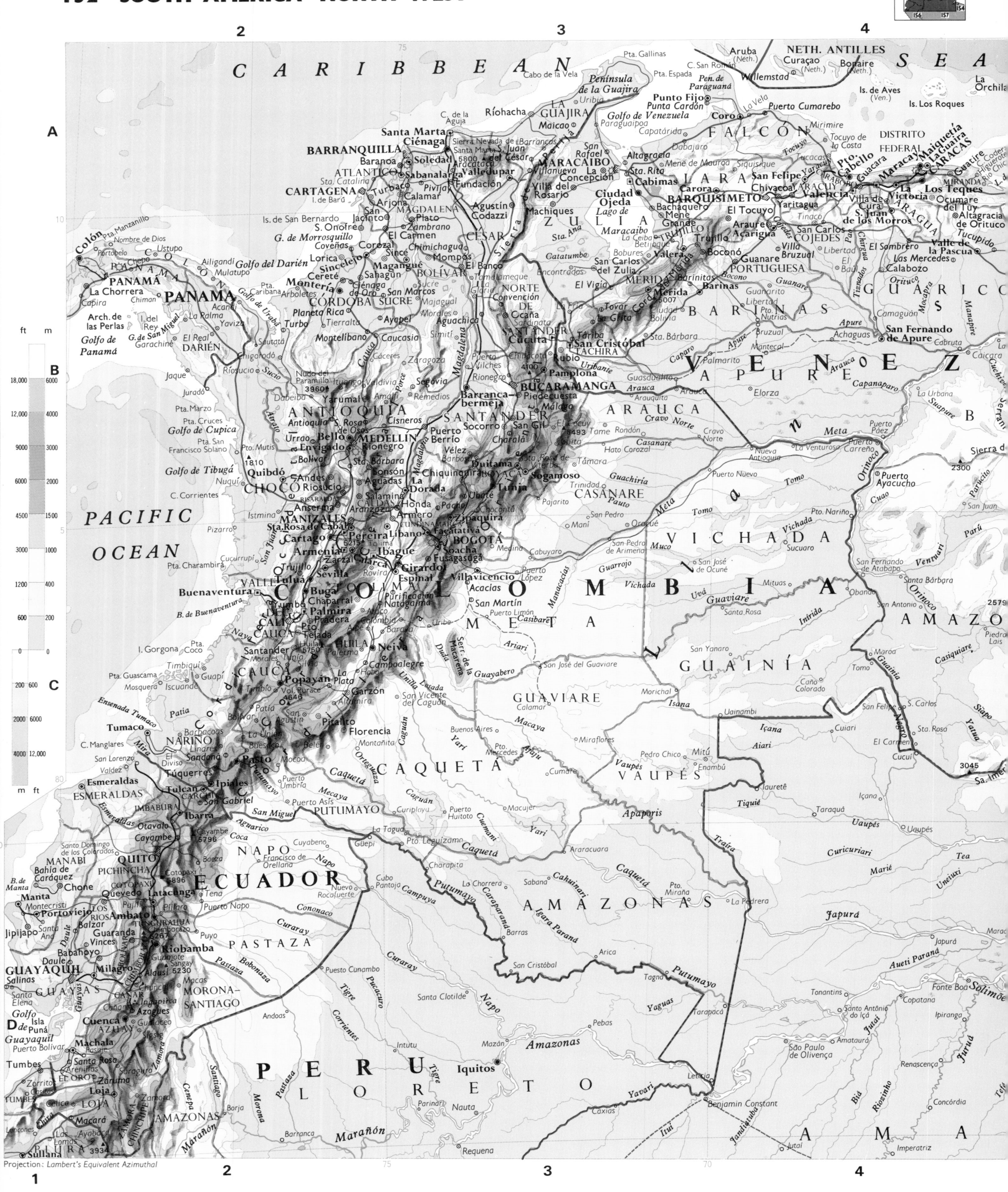

Projection: *Lambert's Equivalent Azimuthal*

1 : 6 400 000

50 0 50 100 150 200 miles
50 0 100 200 300 km

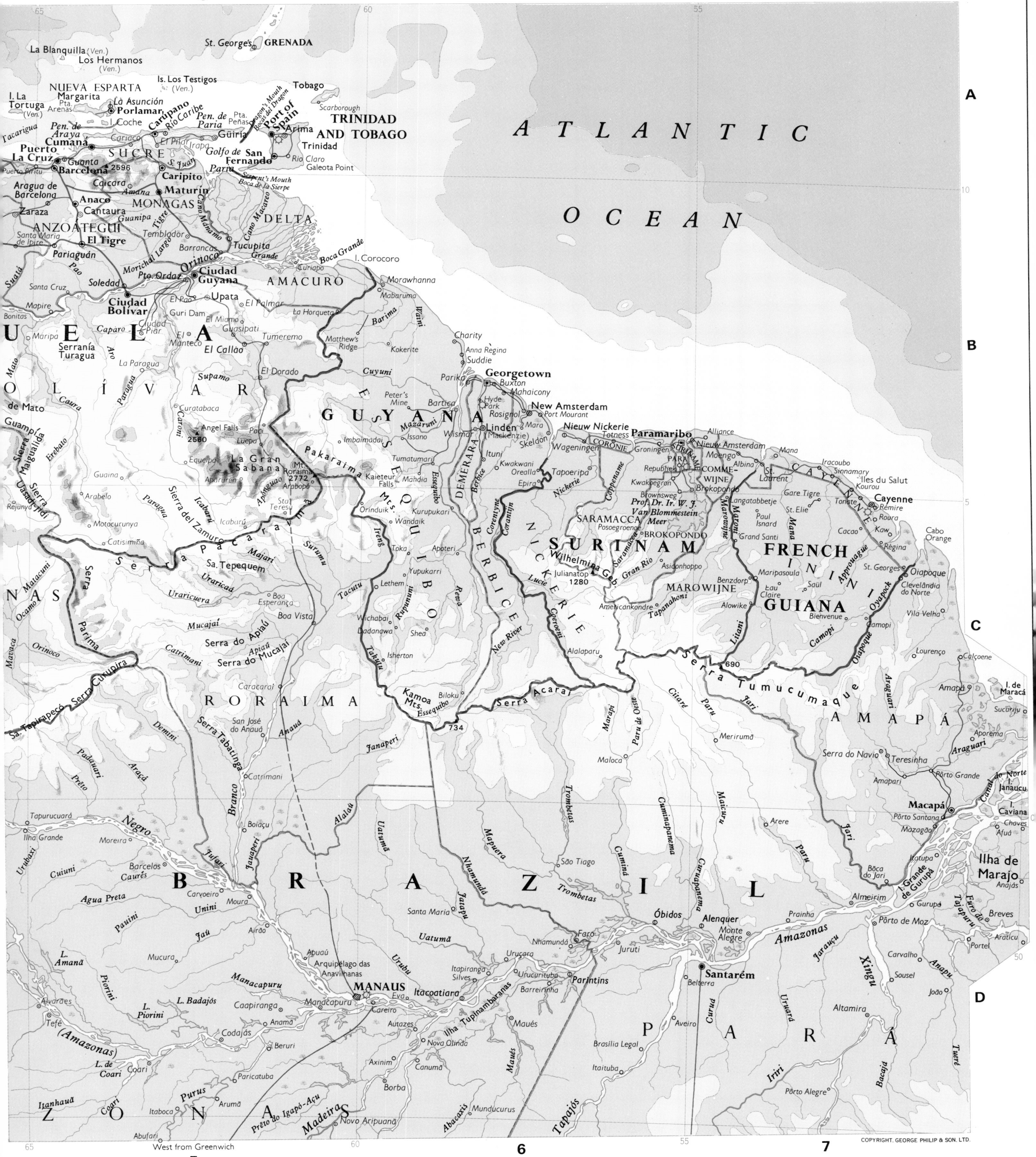

5 6 7

65 60 55

GRENADA
St. George's
La Blanquilla (Ven.)
Los Hermanos (Ven.)
Is. Los Testigos (Ven.)
NUEVA ESPARTA
Margarita
La Asunción
I. La Tortuga (Ven.)
Pta. Arenas
Porlamar
Coche
Carúpano
Pen. de Araya
Cumaná
SUCRE
Río Caribe
Pen. de Paria
Güiria
Irapa
Golfo de San
Tobago
Scarborough
TRINIDAD AND TOBAGO
Trinidad
Port of Spain
Arima
Boca del Dragon
Serpent's Mouth
Río Claro
Galeota Point

A

ATLANTIC

OCEAN

Puerto La Cruz
Guanta
Barcelona
2596
Caicara
Caripito
Maturín
Amana
MONAGAS
Anaco
Cantaura
Guanipa
Tigre
DELTA
Tucupita
Boca Grande
Zaraza
ANZOÁTEGUI
El Tigre
Temblador
Barrancas
Orinoco
Boca Grande
I. Corocoro
Santa María de Ipire
Pariaguán
Pao
Morichal Largo
Pto. Ordaz
Ciudad Guyana
Curiapo
Morawhanna
Mabaruma
AMACURO

B

UELA
Mapire
Santa Cruz
Soledad
El Pao
Upata
Bonitas
Ciudad Bolívar
Guri Dam
El Miamo
El Palmar
La Horqueta
Barima
Charity
Cáparo
Ciudad Piar
Caroní
Caura
Mática
El Callao
El Manteco
Tumeremo
Matthew's Ridge
Kokerite
Waini
Anna Regina
Suddie
Serranía Turagua
La Paragua
Aro
El Dorado
Cuyuni
Parika
Georgetown
Buxton
Mahaicony
New Amsterdam
OLÍVAR
de Mato
Supamo
Peter's Mine
Bartica
Hyde Park
Rosignol
Port Mourant
Guampía
Curataraca
GUYANA
Mazaruni
Issano
Wismar
Linden (Mackenzie)
Mara
Nieuw Nickerie
Paramaribo
Nieuw Amsterdam
Alliance
Mana
Iracoubo
Sinnamary
Errebato
Angel Falls
2580
Poti
Luepa
Imbaimadai
Tumatumari
Kaieteur Falls
Ituni
Kwakwani
Orealla
Tapoeripa
Nickerie
TOTNESS
CORONIE
Groningen
Wageningen
Republiek
PARA
Brownsweg
Moengo
Albina
St. Laurent
Kourou
CAYENNE
Cayenne
Rémire
Iles du Salut
Sierra Maigualida
La Gran Sabana
Mt. Roraima 2772
Arabopó
Orinduik
Kurupukari
Wandaik
Apoteri
Epira
Prof. Dr. Ir. W.J. Van Blommestein Meer
SURINAM
Saramacca
Posoegroene
Grand Santi
Paul Isnard
Gare Tigre
St. Elie
FRENCH GUIANA
Roura
Kaw
Cacao
Régina
Cabo Orange
Equador
Stat. Teresa
Irebu
Toka
Yupukarri
Reina
Wilhelmina Geb.
Julianatop 1280
Gran Rio
Asidonhoppo
MAROWIJNE
Benzdorp
Maripasoula
Saül
Eau Claire
Alowike
Bienvenue
Camopi
St. Georges
Oiapoque
Clevelândia do Norte
Paraguá
Motocurunya
Arabelo
Guaina
Apararú
Orinduik
Lethem
Rapununi
Wichabai
Dadanawa
Shea
Alalaparu
Taponahoni
Litani
GUIANA
690
Vila Velha
NAS
Motocurunya
Catisimiña
Sa. Tepequem
Uraricoera
Boa Esperança
Boa Vista
Serra do Apiaú
Apiaú
Serra do Mucajaí
Isherton
New River
Serra Acarai
Serra Tumucumaque
AMAPÁ
Lourenço
Calçoene
Orinoco
Parima
Mucajaí
Catrimani
Caracaraí
Kamoa Mts.
Biloku
Essequibo
734
Serra do Navio
Amapá
I. de Maracá
Sucuríju
Aporema
Araguari
Teresinha
Sa. Tapirapecó
Serra Curupira
Demini
San José do Anauá
RORAIMA
Anauá
Janaperi
Meirumã
Maloca
Paru de Oeste
Jari
Amapari
Pôrto Grande
Araguari
Serra Tabatinga
Catrimani
Boiaçu
Trombetas
Cuminá
Paru
Curuá
Canal do Norte
Janaucu
Macapá
Pôrto Santana
Mazagão
Caviana
Afuá
Chaves
Ilha de Marajó
Tapurucuará
Preto
Branco
Alalaú
Uatumã
Mapuera
Nhamundá
Trombetas
São Tiago
Caxipanema
Carrapanema
Almeirim
I. Grande de Gurupá
Gurupá
Breves
Anajás
Ilha Grande
Moreira
Carvoeiro
Unini
Moura
Airão
Apuaú
Santa Maria
Jatapu
Urucará
Faro
Óbidos
Alenquer
Monte Alegre
Prainha
Pôrto de Moz
Araticu
Portel
BRAZIL
Barcelos
Caurés
Agua Preta
Jaú
Jauaperi
Arquipélago das Anavilhanas
Uatumã
Urubu
Silves
Itapiranga
Urucurituba
Nhamundá
Juruti
Amazonas
Jarauçu
Breves
João
Pauini
Mucura
Apuaú
Manacapuru
Eva
Itacoatiara
Barreirinha
Parintins
Santarém
Belterra
Carvalho
Sousel
Anapu
L. Amaná
Piorini
MANAUS
Mandacapuru
Careiro
Ilha Tupinambaranas
Maués
Brasília Legal
PARÁ
Altamira
Xingu
Urará
Tefé
L. Badajós
L. Piorini
Caapiranga
Anamã
Autazes
Maués
Aveiro
Itaituba
Iriri
(Amazonas)
L. de Coari
Coari
Codajás
Beruri
Nova Olinda
Axinim
Canumã
Tapajós
Pôrto Alegre
Bacajá
ZONA
Itanhaũa
Coari
Purus
Itaboca
Arumã
Borba
Munducurus
Abacaxis
Novo Aripuanã
Madeiras
Prêto do Igapó-Açu
Abufari
Tiuré

C

D

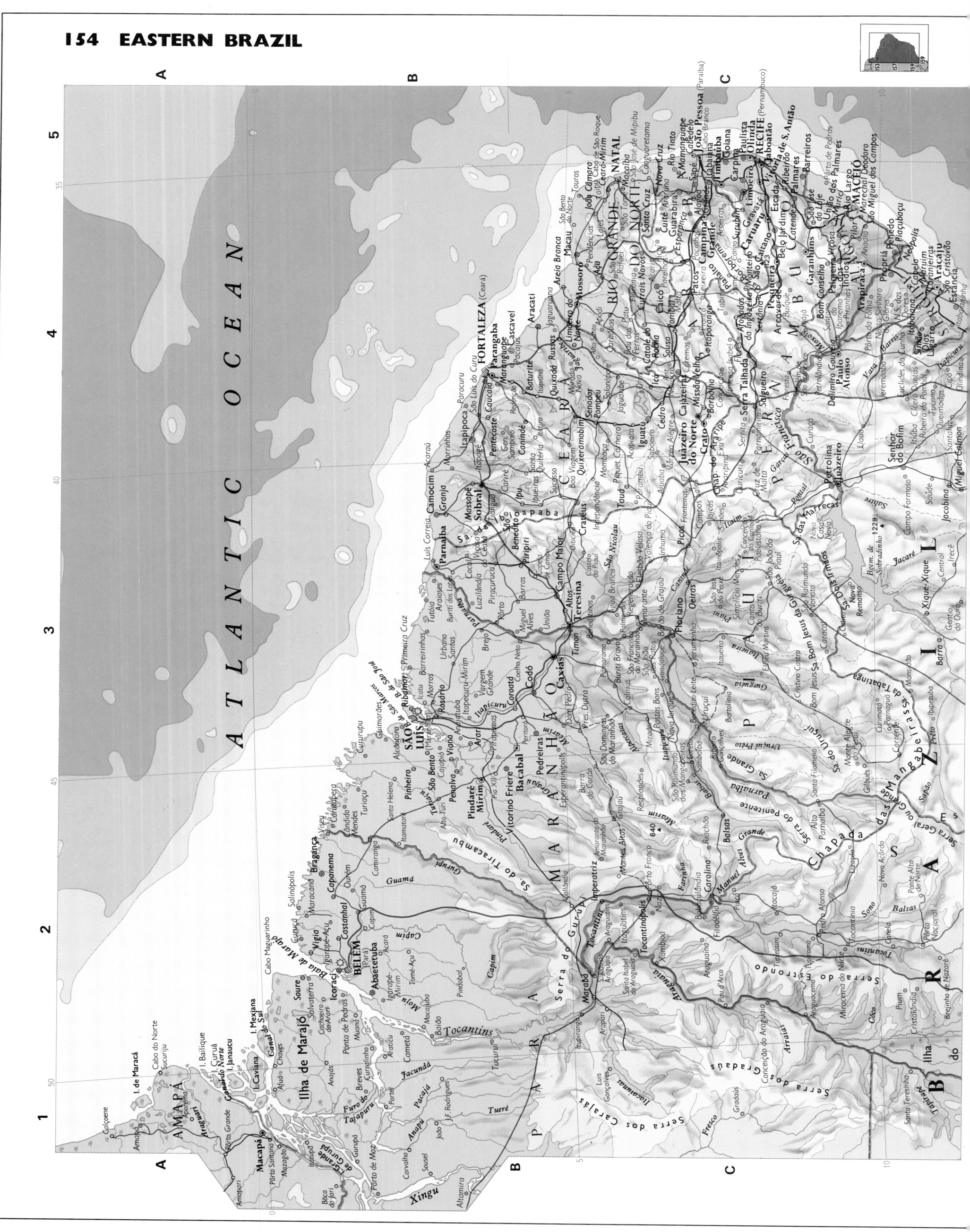

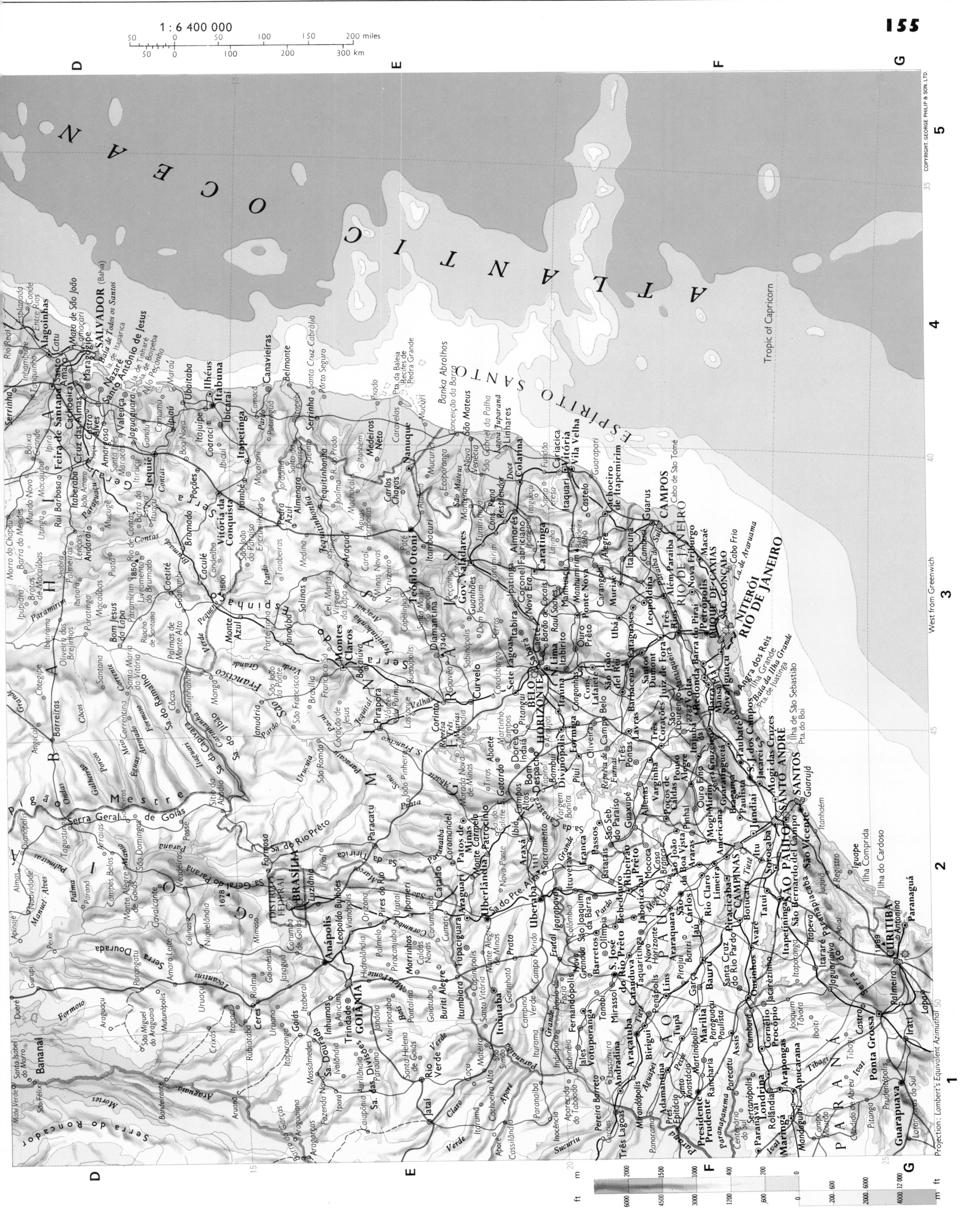

1 : 6 400 000

50   0   50   100   150   200 miles
50   0   100   200   300 km

D   15   E   20   F   25   G

ATLANTIC OCEAN

5

COPYRIGHT. GEORGE PHILIP & SON LTD.

35

4

Tropic of Capricorn

40

ESPIRITO SANTO

SALVADOR (Bahia)

3

West from Greenwich

45

RIO DE JANEIRO

2

NITERÓI
RIO DE JANEIRO

SÃO PAULO
SANTO ANDRE
SANTOS

BRASILIA
DISTRITO FEDERAL

GOIANIA

MINAS GERAIS

BELO HORIZONTE

PARANÁ

CURITIBA

1

Projection: Lambert's Equivalent Azimuthal 50

D   15   E   20   F   25   G

ft   m
6000 ─ 2000
4500 ─ 1500
3000 ─ 1000
1200 ─ 400
600 ─ 200
0 ─ 0
200 ─ 600
2000 ─ 6000
4000 ─ 12 000
m   ft

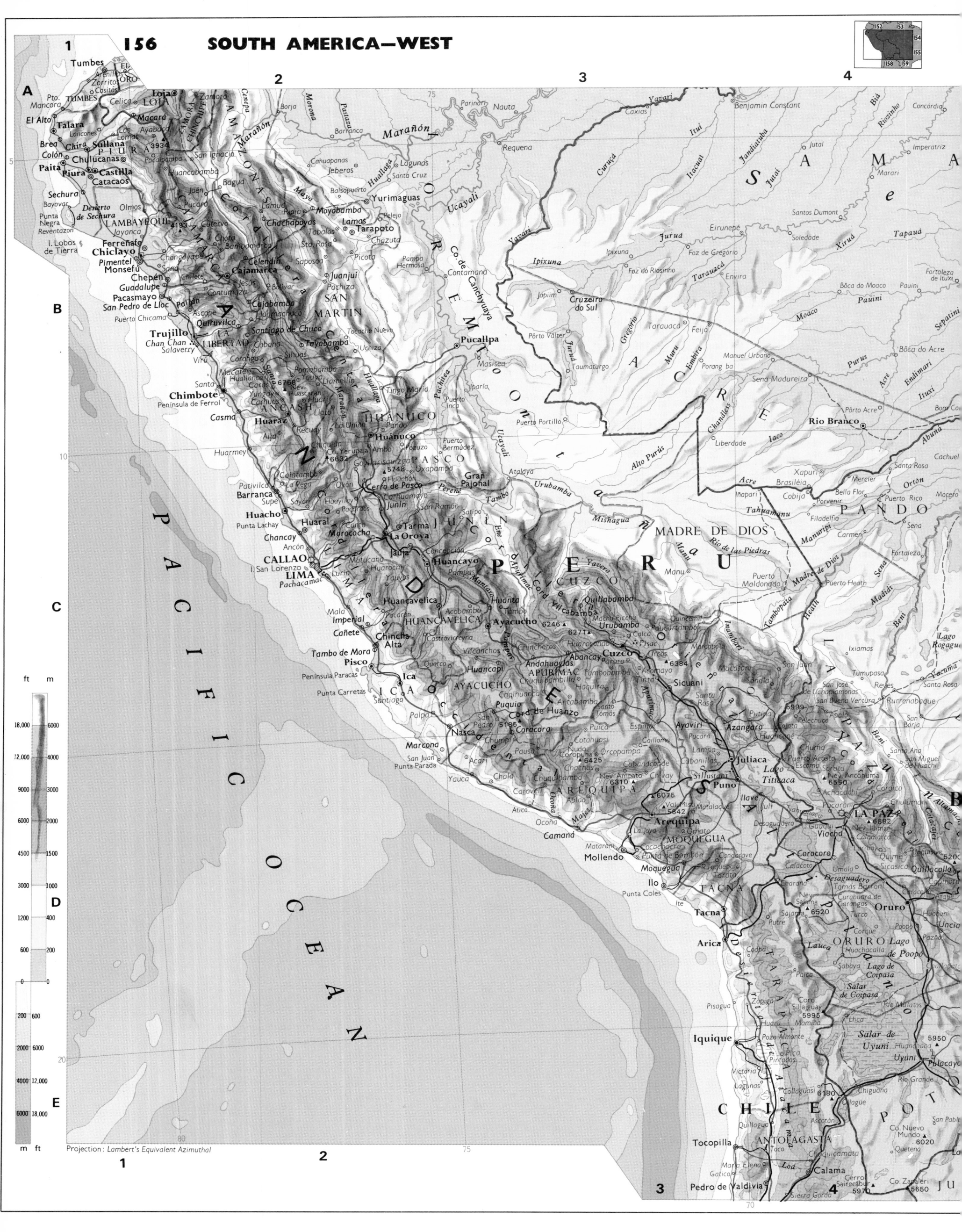

A

B

C

D

E

1   2   3   4

ft m
18,000   6000
12,000   4000
9000   3000
6000   2000
4500   1500
3000   1000
1200   400
600   200
0   0
200   600
2000   6000
4000   12,000
6000   18,000
m   ft

PACIFIC

OCEAN

PERU

Tumbes
Pto. TUMBES
El Alto
Talara
Brea
Colón
Paita
Piura Castilla
Catacaos
Sechura
Bayovar
Punta Negra
Reventazon
I. Lobos de Tierra
LAMBAYEQUE
Ferreñafe
Chiclayo
Pimentel
Monsefú
Chepén
Guadalupe
Pacasmayo
San Pedro de Lloc
Puerto Chicama
Trujillo
Chan Chan Salaverry
LA LIBERTAD
Chimbote
Península de Ferrol
Casma
Huaraz
ANCASH
Huarmey
Barranca
Supe
Huacho
Punta Lachay
Huaral
Chancay
Ancón
CALLAO
LIMA
Pachacamac
Mala
Imperial
Cañete
Tambo de Mora
Pisco
Península Paracas
Punta Carretas
Ica
ICA
Santiago
Palpa
Nasca
Marcona
San Juan
Punta Parada
Yauca
Chala
Caravelí
Atico
Ocoña
Camaná
Mollendo
Ilo
Punta Coles

Loja
LOJA
Macará
Zamora
Celica
Ayabaca
Sullana
Chira
Chulucanas
PIURA
Olmos
Huancabamba
Jaén
Cutervo
Chota
Celendín
Cajamarca
CAJAMARCA
Bolívar
Cajabamba
Huamachuco
Santiago de Chuco
Tayabamba
Cabana
Sihuas
Pomabamba
Carhuaz
Yungay
Recuay
La Unión
Huánuco
HUANUCO
Ambo
Oxapampa
Cerro de Pasco
PASCO
Junín
Tarma
La Oroya
Morococha
Jauja
Concepción
Huancayo
JUNIN
HUANCAVELICA
Huancavelica
Acobamba
Castrovirreyna
Pilpichaca
Huaytará
Huancapi
Ayacucho
AYACUCHO
Cangallo
Puquio
Coracora
Chumpi
Pausa
Chuquibamba
AREQUIPA
Arequipa
MOQUEGUA
Moquegua
TACNA
Tacna
Arica

SAN MARTIN
Moyobamba
Rioja
Chachapoyas
Lamas Tarapoto
Juanjuí
Tingo María
Pucallpa

Yurimaguas
Lagunas
Santa Cruz

CHILE
Iquique
Tocopilla
ANTOFAGASTA
Pedro de Valdivia
Calama

BOLIVIA
LA PAZ
Viacha
Corocoro
ORURO
Oruro
Uyuni
Salar de Uyuni
Lago de Poopó
Lago de Coipasa
Salar de Coipasa

MADRE DE DIOS
PANDO
Rio Branco

CUZCO
Cuzco
Sicuani
Ayaviri
Azángaro
Juliaca
Puno
PUNO
Lago Titicaca

Projection: Lambert's Equivalent Azimuthal

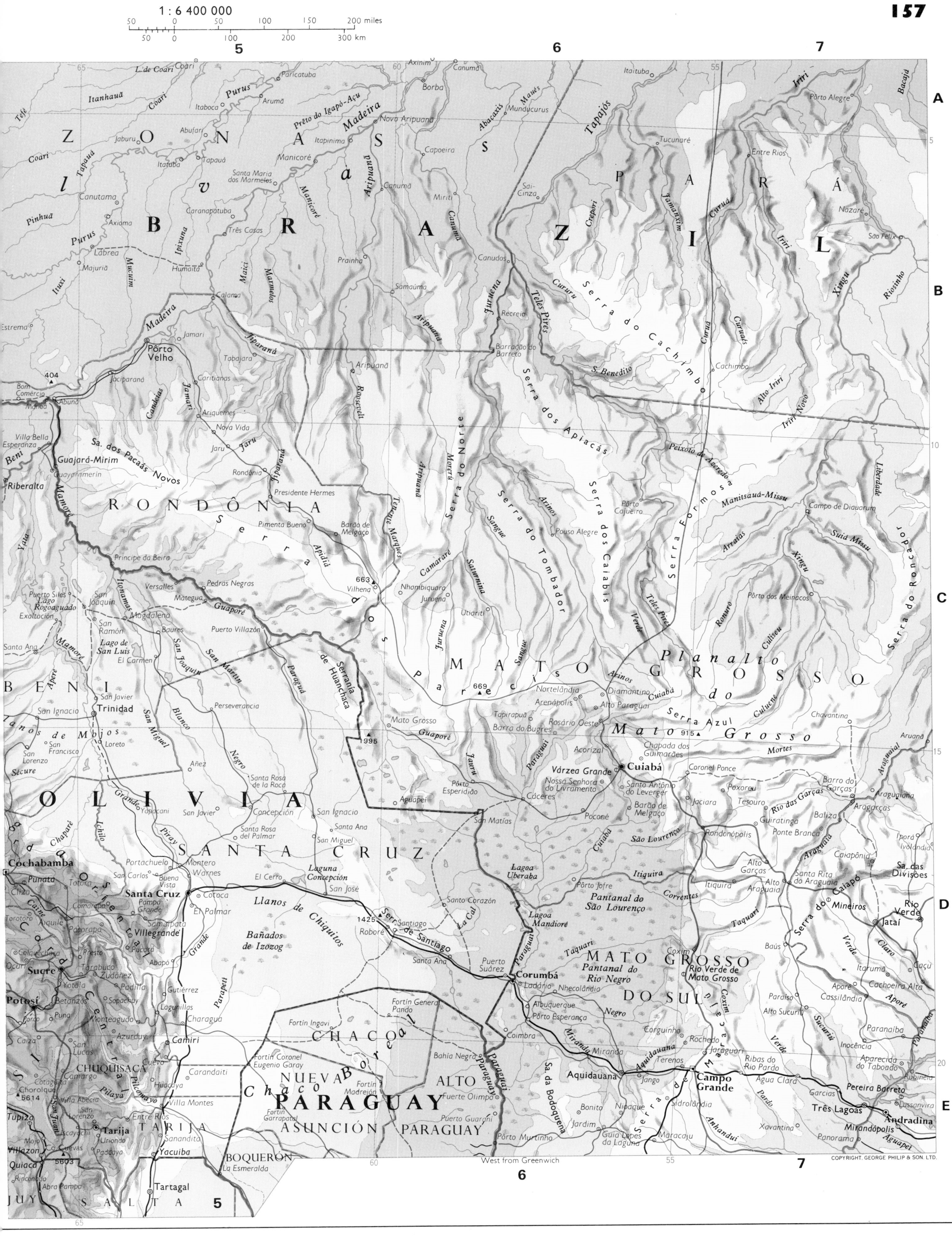

1 : 6 400 000

50   0   50   100   150   200 miles
50   0   100   200   300 km

5   **6**   **7**

A

B

C

D

E

L. de Coari   Coari
Itanhauá   Purus   Paricatuba
Tefé   Axinim   Canumã   Itaituba   Iriri   Pôrto Alegre   Bacaiá
Itaboca   Prêto do Igapó-Açu   Madeira   Borba   Maués   Mundurucus
Coari   Aruma   Abufari   Abacaxis   Tapajós   Tucunaré   Entre Rios
Canutama   Itatuba   Tapauá   Novo Aripuanã   Capoeira   São Félix
Pinhua   Purus   Santa Maria dos Marmelos   Itapinima   Miriti   Saí-Cinza   Nazaré
Iuiá   Axioma   Manicoré   Crepori   Riosinho
Estrema   Labrea   Ipixuna   Três Casas   Manicoré   Prainha   Canudos   Xingu
Majuria   Mucum   Samaúma   Recreio   Telles Pires   Cachimbo
Humaitá   Maici   Marmelos   Barracão do Barreto   S. Benedito   Curuá
Madeira   Calama   Aripuanã   Alto Iriri
Pôrto Velho   Jamari   Jiparaná   Aripuanã   Peixoto de Azeredo

Z O N A S   B R A Z I L   P A R Á
Z

404   Bom Comércio   Abuná   Jaciparaná   Tabajara   Aripuanã   Juruena   Serra dos Apiacás   Pôrto Cajueiro   Manitsauá-Missu   Campo de Diauarum   Libertade
Villa Bella   Guayaramerín   Sa. dos Pacaás Novos   Nova Vida   Jaru   Jaru   Rondônia   Presidente Hermes   Serra do Norte   Arinos   Pouso Alegre   Serra do Cachimb   Suiá Missu
Esperanza   Beni   Guajará-Mirim   Ariquemes   Moreru   Sangue   Serra dos Caiabis   Serra Formosa   Arraias   Xingu
Riberalta   R O N D Ô N I A   Pimenta Bueno   Barão de Melgaço   Nhambiquara   Juruena   Tombador   Telles Pires   Romoro   Pôrto dos Meinacos   Serra do Roncador
Ixiá   Puerto Siles   San Joaquín   Príncipe da Beira   Versalles   Pedras Negras   663 Vilhena   Camararé   Saturnina   Utiariti   Verde   Culiseu   Chavantina
Lago Rogoaguado   Exaltación   San Ramón   Magdalena   Baures   Puerto Villazón   Guaporé   M A T O   G R O S S O   Arinos   Nortelândia   Diamantino   Cuiabá   **P l a n a l t o**   Aruana
Santa Ana   San Carmen   Serranía de Huanchaca   669   Mato Grosso   Arenápolis   Alto Paraguai   Serra Azul   Chapada dos Guimarães   Mortes   Aragariana
B E N I   San Javier   Trinidad   San Martín   Paraguá   Guaporé   Barra do Bugres   Rosário Oeste   915   **M a t o   G r o s s o**   Barro do Garças   Aragarças
Apere   San Ignacio   Perseverancia   995   Acorizal   Várzea Grande   **Cuiabá**   Coronel Ponce   Rondonópolis   Baliza   Araguaiana
Llanos de Mojos   San Francisco   Loreto   San Miguel   Blanco   Negro   Santa Rosa de la Roca   Concepción   Pôsto Esperidião   Cáceres   Nossa Senhora do Livramento   Santo Antônio do Leverger   Poxoreu   Tesouro   Rio das Garças   Ponte Branca   Iporá   Ivolândia
Secure   San Lorenzo   Añez   San Javier   Santa Ana   San Ignacio   San Matías   Poconé   Barão de Melgaço   Jaciara   Guiratinga   Capônia   Sa. das Divisões
B O L I V I A   Grande   Yapacani   San Miguel   Cuiabá   São Lourenço   Alto Garças   Santa Rita do Araguaia   Jiapó   Rio Verde
Cochabamba   Portachuelo   Montero   **S A N T A   C R U Z**   Laguna Concepción   Lagoa Uberaba   Itiquira   Correntes   Itiquira   Alto Araguaia   Mineiros   Jataí
Punata   San Carlos   Buena Vista   Warnes   El Cerro   San José   Santo Corazón   La Cal   Pôrto Jofre   Pantanal do São Lourenço   Taquari   Baús   Verde   Claro   Caçu
Cliza   Totora   Comarapa   Pampa Grande   Cotoca   El Palmar   1425   Serra de Santiago   Lagoa Mandioré   **M A T O   G R O S S O**   Aporé   Itarumã   Cachoeira Alta   Aporé
Toropata   Aiquile   Samaipata   Roboré   Llanos de Chiquitos   Santa Ana   Puerto Suárez   Taquari   **D O   S U L**   Paraíso   Cassilândia
Sucre   Presto   Pucará   Abapó   Grande   Bañados de Izozog   Corumbá   Pantanal do Rio Negro   Rio Verde de Mato Grosso   Alto Sucuriú   Paranaíba
Yotala   Tarabuco   Padilla   Ladário   Nhecolândia   Negro   Coxim   Inocência   Aparecida do Taboado
Potosí   Zudáñez   Gutiérrez   Parapeti   Fortín General Pando   Albuquerque   Corguinho   Verde   Sucuriú
Betanzos   Sopachuy   Lagunillas   Charagua   Pôrto Esperança   Miranda   Rochedo   Paraguai   Ribas do Rio Pardo   Agua Clara   Panorama
Puna   Monteagudo   Fortín Ingavi   Coimbra   Miranda   Aquidauana   Jango   Taboado   Rubinea
CHUQUISACA   Camargo   Azurduy   Camiri   Fortín Coronel Eugenio Garay   Carandaiti   Bahía Negra   Sa. da Bodoquena   Terenos   **Campo Grande**   Garcias   Cussanvira   Pereira Barreto
5614   Choroloque   Cuevas   Fortín Madreión   **C H A C O**   Fuerte Olimpo   Bonita   Nioaque   Sidrolândia   **Três Lagoas**   **Andradina**
Chorolque   Villa Abecia   **N U E V A**   Fortín Garrapatal   Puerto Guaraní   Guia Lopes da Laguna   Jardim   Maracaju   Mirandópolis
Tupiza   Villa Montes   **P A R A G U A Y**   Fortín   **A L T O**   Pôrto Murtinho   Xavantina   Aguapei
Caiza   **TARIJA**   **ASUNCIÓN**   **PARAGUAY**
Tarija   Uriondo   Sanandita   Padcaya
Quiaca   5603   Yacuiba   **BOQUERÓN**   La Esmeralda
Villazón   Abra Pampa   **JUJUY   SALTA**   Tartagal   **5**

West from Greenwich

6   **7**

COPYRIGHT. GEORGE PHILIP & SON.LTD.

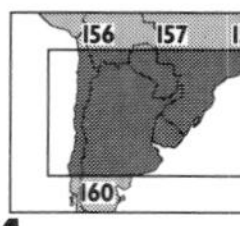

PACIFIC OCEAN

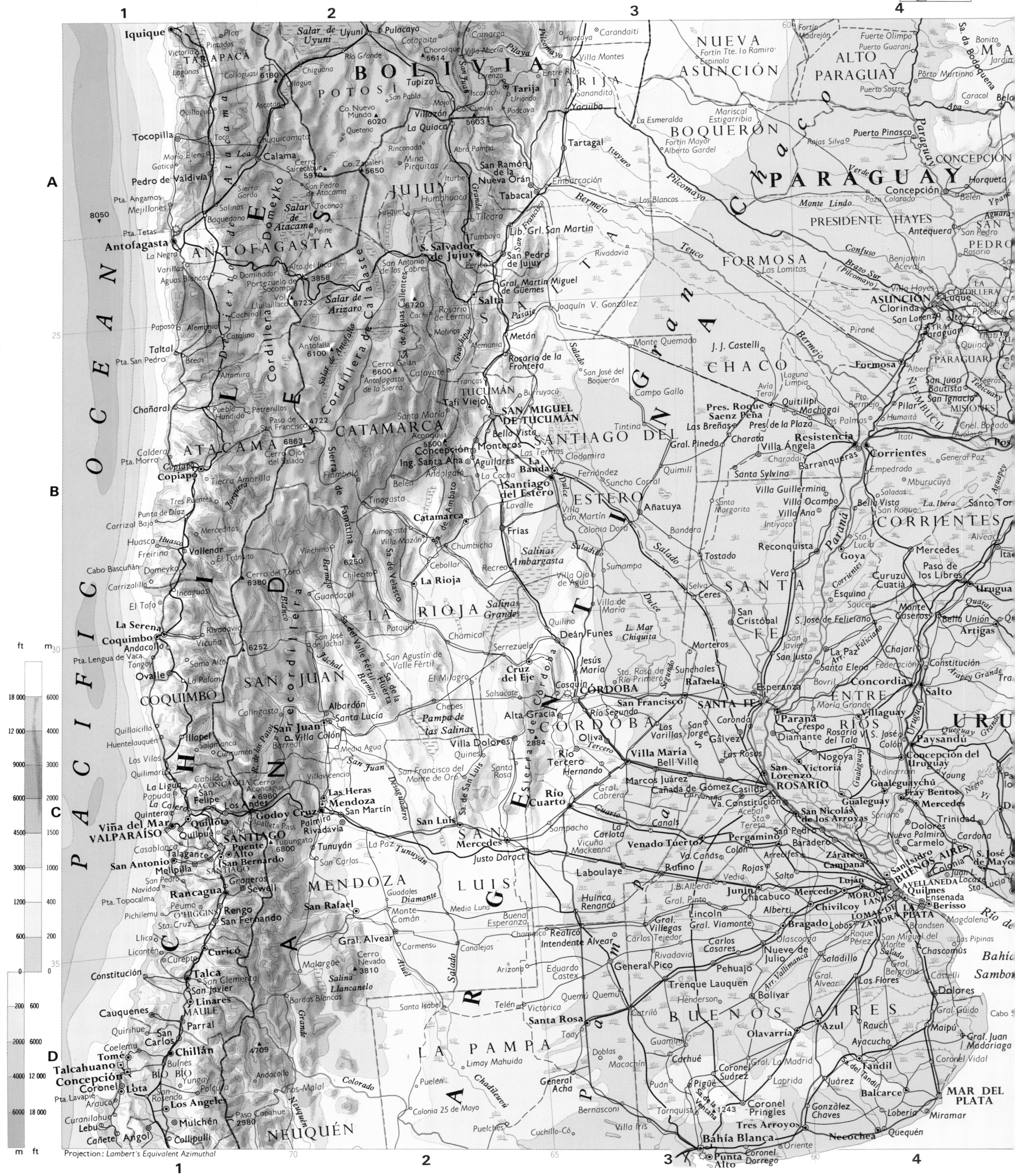

BOLIVIA

PARAGUAY

NUEVA ASUNCIÓN

ALTO PARAGUAY

BOQUERÓN

PRESIDENTE HAYES

FORMOSA

CHACO

POTOSÍ

TARAPACÁ

ANTOFAGASTA

JUJUY

SALTA

TARIJA

Iquique
Salar de Uyuni
Pulacayo
Tocopilla
Calama
Chuquicamata
Pedro de Valdivia
Antofagasta
Mejillones
Pta. Tetas
8050

La Quiaca
Villazón
San Ramón de la Nueva Orán
Tabacal
Embarcación
Humahuaca
Tilcara
S. Salvador de Jujuy
San Pedro de Jujuy
Perico
Gral. Martín Miguel de Güemes
Salta
Metán
Rosario de la Frontera

Concepción
Belén
Asunción
Clorinda
Formosa

TUCUMÁN

CATAMARCA

SANTIAGO DEL ESTERO

SANTA FE

CORRIENTES

ATACAMA

LA RIOJA

CÓRDOBA

SAN JUAN

SAN LUIS

MENDOZA

COQUIMBO

BUENOS AIRES

LA PAMPA

NEUQUÉN

URUGUAY

San Miguel de Tucumán
Tafí Viejo
Concepción
Monteros
Aguilares
La Banda
Santiago del Estero
Frías
Catamarca
Añatuya
Tostado
Reconquista
Goya
Corrientes
Resistencia
Formosa
Saenz Peña
Pres. Roque Saenz Peña
Quitilipi
Machagai
Charata

La Rioja
Chilecito
Chamical
Dean Funes
Cruz del Eje
Córdoba
San Francisco
Santa Fe
Paraná
Rafaela
Esperanza
Concordia
Salto
Paysandú

San Juan
Villa Dolores
Villa María
Bell Ville
Río Cuarto
Rosario
San Nicolás de los Arroyos
Pergamino
Venado Tuerto
Campana
Zárate
Buenos Aires
La Plata

Mendoza
Godoy Cruz
San Martín
San Rafael
Gral. Alvear
Santa Rosa
Bolívar
Olavarría
Tandil
Mar del Plata
Bahía Blanca
Tres Arroyos
Necochea

La Serena
Coquimbo
Ovalle
Valparaíso
Viña del Mar
Santiago
San Bernardo
Rancagua
San Fernando
Curicó
Talca
Linares
Chillán
Concepción
Talcahuano
Coronel
Lota
Los Angeles

Projection: Lambert's Equivalent Azimuthal

1 : 6 400 000

50   0   50   100   150   200 miles
50   0   100   200   300 km

MATO GROSSO
DO SUL

Nioaque
Guia Lopes
da Laguna
Maracaju
Dourados
Ponta Pora
Pedro Juan Caballero
Amambay
Cord. de
Amambay
Amambai

PARAGUAY
MISIONES
Encarnación
Obera
San Javier
Santa Rosa
Apóstoles

RIO GRANDE

DO SUL

Santana do
Livramento
Rivera

URUGUAY
Tacuarembó
Melo
San Gregorio
Treinta y Tres
Santa Vitória do Palmar
Aigua
Minas
Rocha
San Carlos
Maldonado
MONTEVIDEO
Rio de la Plata

Três Lagoas
Andradina
Xavantina
Mirandópolis
Panorama
Pres. Epitácio
Adamantina
Presidente Prudente
Martinópolis
Rancharia
Paranavaí
Nova Esperança
Rolândia
Maringá
Cianorte
Mandaguari
Apucarana
Umuarama
Cruzeiro do Oeste
Guaíra
Goio Erê
Cascavel
Foz do Iguaçu
Iguazú Dam
Itaipu Dam
Iguazú Falls

BRAZIL
PARANÁ
Guarapuava
Ponta Grossa
Palmeira
CURITIBA
Antonina
Paranaguá
Guaratuba
União da Vitória
Rio Negro
Mafra
São Francisco do Sul
Joinvile
Caçador
Blumenau
Itajaí
SANTA CATARINA
Brusque
Rio do Sul
Ilha de Santa Catarina
Florianópolis
Tubarão
Laguna
Criciúma
Ararangua
Cabo Santa Marta Grande
Vacaria
Bento Gonçalves
Caxias do Sul
Passo Fundo
Carazinho
Cruz Alta
Santa Maria
Santa Cruz do Sul
Montenegro
Nôvo Hamburgo
Taquara
São Leopoldo
Canoas
Viamão
PÔRTO ALEGRE
Osorio
Rio Pardo
Cachoeira do Sul
São Gabriel
Dom Pedrito
Bagé
Pelotas
Rio Grande
Jaguarão
Lagoa dos Patos
Lagoa Mangueira

ATLANTIC

OCEAN

São Sebastião
do Paraíso
Passos
Batatais
Mococa
Ribeirão Prêto
S. José do Rio Prêto
Olímpia
Mirassol
Araçatuba
Birigui
Catanduva
Jaboticabal
Bebedouro
Guaxupé
São Carlos
Araraquara
Bauru
Lins
Penápolis
Tupã
SÃO PAULO
Marília
Garça
Jaú
Bariri
Rio Claro
Limeira
Americana
Piracicaba
CAMPINAS
Botucatu
Tietê
Avaré
Tatuí
Sorocaba
Jundiaí
Itapetininga
SÃO PAULO
São Bernardo del Campo
SANTO ANDRÉ
Mogi das Cruzes
São Vicente
SANTOS
Guarujá
Ilha de São Sebastião
Itanhaém
Iguape
Ilha Comprida
Ilha do Cardoso
Registro
Paranapiacaba
Jaguariaíva
Castro

BELO HORIZONTE
Lima
Itabirito
Congonhas
Ouro Prêto
Ponte Nova
Pico da Bandeira 2890
Vitória
Itaquari
Vila Velha
Guarapari
Cachoeiro de Itapemirim
Castelo
Carangola
Muriaé
Itaperuna
Alegre
Guarus
CAMPOS
Cabo de São Tomé
Macaé
Nova Friburgo
RIO DE JANEIRO
NITERÓI
RIO DE JANEIRO
Cabo Frio
La. de Araruama
Tropic of Capricorn
DUQUE DE CAXIAS
SÃO GONÇALO
Nova Iguaçu
Angra dos Reis
Ilha Grande
Barra do Piraí
Volta Redonda
Barra Mansa
Resende
Petrópolis
Juiz de Fora
Leopoldina
Cataguases
Ubá
Além Paraíba
Barbacena
São João del Rei
Lavras
Três Corações
Varginha
Alfenas
Pouso Alegre
Poços de Caldas
Três Pontas
Campo Belo
Oliveira
Cons. Lafaiete
Represa de Furnas
Taubaté
J. dos Campos
Jacareí
Guaratinguetá
Cruzeiro
Aparecida
Lorena
Mogi-Mirim

COPYRIGHT. GEORGE PHILIP & SON. LTD

West from Greenwich

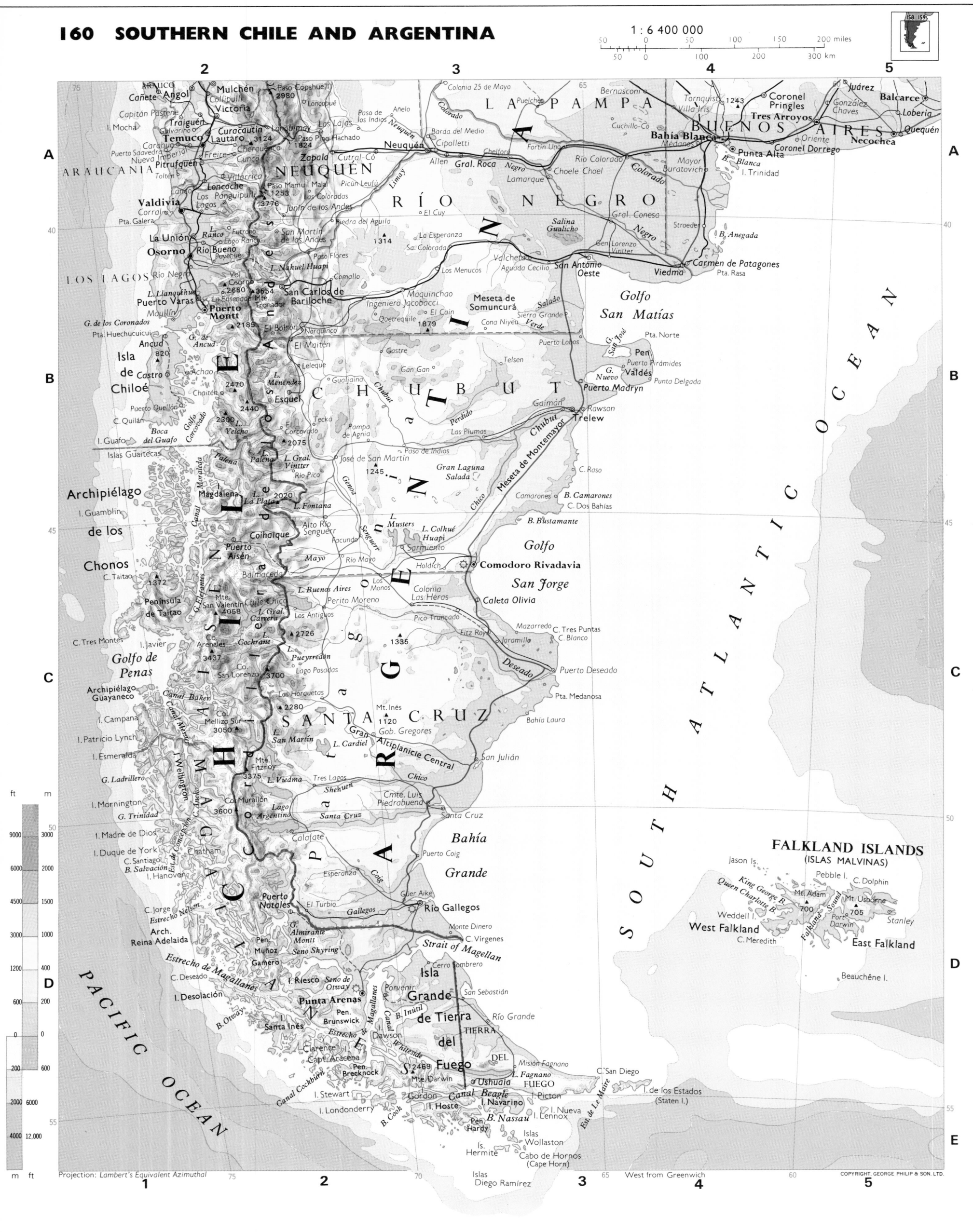

INDEX

The index contains the names of all the principal places and features shown on the World Maps. Each name is followed by an additional entry in italics giving the country or region within which it is located. The alphabetical order of names composed of two or more words is governed primarily by the first word and then by the second. This is an example of the rule:

Mīr Kūh, *Iran*	**85 E8**	26 22 N	58 55 E
Mīr Shahdād, *Iran*	**85 E8**	26 15 N	58 29 E
Miraj, *India*	**82 F2**	16 50 N	74 45 E
Miram Shah, *Pakistan*	**79 B3**	33 0 N	70 2 E
Miramar, *Mozam.*	**105 C6**	23 50 S	35 35 E

Physical features composed of a proper name (Erie) and a description (Lake) are positioned alphabetically by the proper name. The description is positioned after the proper name and is usually abbreviated:

Erie, L., *N. Amer.* . . . . **136 D4** 42 15 N 81 0 W

Where a description forms part of a settlement or administrative name however, it is always written in full and put in its true alphabetic position:

Mount Morris, *U.S.A.* . . . . . . **136 D7** 42 43 N 77 50 W

Names beginning with M' and Mc are indexed as if they were spelt Mac. Names beginning St. are alphabetised under Saint, but Sankt, Sint, Sant', Santa and San are all spelt in full and are alphabetised accordingly. If the same place name occurs two or more times in the index and all are in the same country, each is followed by the name of the administrative subdivision in which it is located. The names are placed in the alphabetical order of the subdivisions. For example:

Jackson, *Ky., U.S.A.*	**134 G4**	37 35 N	83 22 W
Jackson, *Mich., U.S.A.*	**141 B12**	42 18 N	84 25 W
Jackson, *Minn., U.S.A.*	**138 D7**	43 35 N	95 0 W

The number in bold type which follows each name in the index refers to the number of the map page where that feature or place will be found. This is usually the largest scale at which the place or feature appears.

The letter and figure which are in bold type immediately after the page number give the grid square on the map page, within which the feature is situated. The letter represents the latitude and the figure the longitude.

In some cases the feature itself may fall within the specified square, while the name is outside. This is usually the case only with features which are larger than a grid square.

For a more precise location the geographical coordinates which follow the letter/figure references give the latitude and the longitude of each place. The first set of figures represent the latitude which is the distance north or south of the Equator measured as an angle at the centre of the earth. The Equator is latitude 0°, the North Pole is 90°N, and the South Pole 90°S.

The second set of figures represent the longitude, which is the distance East or West of the prime meridian, which runs through Greenwich, England. Longitude is also measured as an angle at the centre of the earth and is given East or West of the prime meridian, from 0° to 180° in either direction.

The unit of measurement for latitude and longitude is the degree, which is subdivided into 60 minutes. Each index entry states the position of a place in degrees and minutes, a space being left between the degrees and the minutes.

The latitude is followed by N(orth) or S(outh) and the longitude by E(ast) or W(est).

Rivers are indexed to their mouths or confluences, and carry the symbol ➛ after their names. A solid square ■ follows the name of a country while, an open square ☐ refers to a first order administrative area.

ABBREVIATIONS USED IN THE INDEX

A.C.T. — Australian Capital Territory
A.S.S.R. — Autonomous Soviet Socialist Republic
Afghan. — Afghanistan
Ala. — Alabama
Alta. — Alberta
Amer. — America(n)
Arch. — Archipelago
Ariz. — Arizona
Ark. — Arkansas
Atl. Oc. — Atlantic Ocean
B. — Baie, Bahía, Bay, Bucht, Bugt
B.C. — British Columbia
Bangla. — Bangladesh
Barr. — Barrage
C. — Cabo, Cap, Cape, Coast
C.A.R. — Central African Republic
C. Prov. — Cape Province
Calif. — California
Cent. — Central
Chan. — Channel
Colo. — Colorado
Conn. — Connecticut
Cord. — Cordillera
Cr. — Creek
Czech. — Czechoslovakia
D.C. — District of Columbia
Del. — Delaware
Dep. — Dependency
Des. — Desert
Dist. — District
Dj. — Djebel
Domin. — Dominica
Dom. Rep. — Dominican Republic
E. — East
El Salv. — El Salvador

Eq. Guin. — Equatorial Guinea
Fla. — Florida
Falk. Is. — Falkland Is.
G. — Golfe, Golfo, Gulf, Guba, Gebel
Ga. — Georgia
Gt. — Great, Greater
Guinea-Biss. — Guinea-Bissau
H.K. — Hong Kong
H.P. — Himachal Pradesh
Hants. — Hampshire
Harb. — Harbor, Harbour
Hd. — Head
Hts. — Heights
I.(s). — Île, Ilha, Insel, Isla, Island, Isle
Ill. — Illinois
Ind. — Indiana
Ind. Oc. — Indian Ocean
Ivory C. — Ivory Coast
J. — Jabal, Jebel, Jazira
Junc. — Junction
K. — Kap, Kapp
Kans. — Kansas
Kep. — Kepulauan
Ky. — Kentucky
L. — Lac, Lacul, Lago, Lagoa, Lake, Limni, Loch, Lough
La. — Louisiana
Liech. — Liechtenstein
Lux. — Luxembourg
Mad. P. — Madhya Pradesh
Madag. — Madagascar
Man. — Manitoba
Mass. — Massachusetts
Md. — Maryland
Me. — Maine

Medit. S. — Mediterranean Sea
Mich. — Michigan
Minn. — Minnesota
Miss. — Mississippi
Mo. — Missouri
Mont. — Montana
Mozam. — Mozambique
Mt.(e). — Mont, Monte, Monti, Montaña, Mountain
N. — Nord, Norte, North, Northern, Nouveau
N.B. — New Brunswick
N.C. — North Carolina
N. Cal. — New Caledonia
N. Dak. — North Dakota
N.H. — New Hampshire
N.I. — North Island
N.J. — New Jersey
N. Mex. — New Mexico
N.S. — Nova Scotia
N.S.W. — New South Wales
N.W.T. — North West Territory
N.Y. — New York
N.Z. — New Zealand
Nebr. — Nebraska
Neths. — Netherlands
Nev. — Nevada
Nfld. — Newfoundland
Nic. — Nicaragua
O. — Oued, Ouadi
Occ. — Occidentale
Okla. — Oklahoma
Ont. — Ontario
Or. — Orientale
Oreg. — Oregon
Os. — Ostrov

Oz. — Ozero
P. — Pass, Passo, Pasul, Pulau
P.E.I. — Prince Edward Island
Pa. — Pennsylvania
Pac. Oc. — Pacific Ocean
Papua N.G. — Papua New Guinea
Pass. — Passage
Pen. — Peninsula, Péninsule
Phil. — Philippines
Pk. — Park, Peak
Plat. — Plateau
P-ov. — Poluostrov
Prov. — Province, Provincial
Pt. — Point
Pta. — Ponta, Punta
Pte. — Pointe
Qué. — Québec
Queens. — Queensland
R. — Rio, River
R.I. — Rhode Island
R.S.F.S.R. — Russian Soviet Federative Socialist Republic
Ra.(s). — Range(s)
Raj. — Rajasthan
Reg. — Region
Rep. — Republic
Res. — Reserve, Reservoir
S. — San, South, Sea
Si. Arabia — Saudi Arabia
S.C. — South Carolina
S. Dak. — South Dakota
S.I. — South Island
S.S.R. — Soviet Socialist Republic
Sa. — Serra, Sierra
Sask. — Saskatchewan
Scot. — Scotland

Sd. — Sound
Sev. — Severnaya
Sib. — Siberia
Sprs. — Springs
St. — Saint, Sankt, Sint
Sta. — Santa, Station
Ste. — Sainte
Sto. — Santo
Str. — Strait, Stretto
Switz. — Switzerland
Tas. — Tasmania
Tenn. — Tennessee
Tex. — Texas
Tg. — Tanjung
Trin. & Tob. — Trinidad & Tobago
U.A.E. — United Arab Emirates
U.K. — United Kingdom
U.S.A. — United States of America
U.S.S.R. — Union of Soviet Socialist Republics
Ut. P. — Uttar Pradesh
Va. — Virginia
Vdkhr. — Vodokhranilishche
Vf. — Vîrful
Vic. — Victoria
Vol. — Volcano
Vt. — Vermont
W. — Wadi, West
W. Va. — West Virginia
Wash. — Washington
Wis. — Wisconsin
Wlkp. — Wielkopolski
Wyo. — Wyoming
Yorks. — Yorkshire

162 Aachen

A

Aachen, *Germany* 26 E2 50 47N 6 4 E
Aadorf, *Switz.* 29 B7 47 30N 8 55 E
Aalborg = Ålborg, *Denmark* 15 G3 57 2N 9 54 E
Aalen, *Germany* 27 G6 48 49N 10 6 E
A'âli en Nîl □, *Sudan* 95 F3 9 30N 31 30 E
Aalsmeer, *Neths.* 20 D5 52 17N 4 43 E
Aalst, *Belgium* 21 G4 50 56N 4 2 E
Aalst, *Neths.* 21 F6 51 23N 5 29 E
Aalten, *Neths.* 20 E9 51 56N 6 35 E
Aalter, *Belgium* 21 F2 51 5N 3 28 E
Aarau, *Switz.* 28 B6 47 23N 8 4 E
Aarberg, *Switz.* 28 B4 47 2N 7 16 E
Aardenburg, *Belgium* 21 F2 51 16N 3 28 E
Aare →, *Switz.* 28 A6 47 33N 8 14 E
Aargau □, *Switz.* 28 B6 47 26N 8 10 E
Aarhus = Århus, *Denmark* 15 H4 56 8N 10 11 E
Aarle, *Neths.* 21 F7 51 30N 5 38 E
Aarschot, *Belgium* 21 G5 50 59N 4 49 E
Aarsele, *Belgium* 21 G2 51 0N 3 26 E
Aartrijke, *Belgium* 21 F2 51 7N 3 6 E
Aarwangen, *Switz.* 28 B5 47 15N 7 46 E
Aba, *China* 68 A3 32 59N 101 42 E
Aba, *Nigeria* 101 D6 5 10N 7 19 E
Aba, *Zaïre* 106 B3 3 58N 30 17 E
Âbâ, Jazîrat, *Sudan* 95 E3 13 30N 32 31 E
Abacaxis →, *Brazil* 153 D6 3 54 S 58 47W
Ābādān, *Iran* 85 D6 30 22N 48 20 E
Abade, *Ethiopia* 95 F4 9 22N 38 3 E
Ābādeh, *Iran* 85 D7 31 8N 52 40 E
Abadin, *Spain* 36 B3 43 21N 7 29W
Abadla, *Algeria* 99 B4 31 2N 2 45W
Abaeté, *Brazil* 155 E2 19 9 S 45 27W
Abaeté →, *Brazil* 155 E2 18 2 S 45 12W
Abaetetuba, *Brazil* 154 B2 1 40 S 48 50W
Abagnar Qi, *China* 66 C9 43 52N 116 2 E
Abai, *Paraguay* 159 B4 25 58 S 55 54W
Abak, *Nigeria* 101 E6 4 58N 7 50 E
Abakaliki, *Nigeria* 101 D6 6 22N 8 2 E
Abakan, *U.S.S.R.* 57 D10 53 40N 91 10 E
Abalemma, *Niger* 101 B6 16 12N 7 50 E
Abana, *Turkey* 88 C6 41 59N 34 1 E
Abancay, *Peru* 156 C3 13 35 S 72 55W
Abanilla, *Spain* 35 G3 38 12N 1 3W
Abano Terme, *Italy* 39 C8 45 22N 11 46 E
Abapó, *Bolivia* 157 D5 18 48 S 63 25W
Abarán, *Spain* 35 G3 38 12N 1 23W
Abariringa, *Kiribati* 122 H10 2 50 S 171 40W
Abarqū, *Iran* 85 D7 31 10N 53 20 E
Abashiri, *Japan* 60 C12 44 0N 144 15 E
Abashiri-Wan, *Japan* 60 C12 44 0N 144 30 E
Abau, *Papua N. G.* 120 F5 10 11 S 148 46 E
Abaújszántó, *Hungary* 31 C14 48 16N 21 12 E
Abay, *U.S.S.R.* 56 E8 49 38N 72 53 E
Abaya, L., *Ethiopia* 95 F4 6 30N 37 50 E
Abaza, *U.S.S.R.* 56 D10 52 39N 90 6 E
Abbadia San Salvatore, *Italy* 39 F8 42 53N 11 40 E
'Abbāsābād, *Iran* 85 C8 33 34N 58 23 E
Abbay = Nîl el Azraq →, *Sudan* 95 D3 15 38N 32 31 E
Abbaye, Pt., *U.S.A.* 134 B1 46 58N 88 4W
Abbé, L., *Ethiopia* 95 E5 11 8N 41 47 E
Abbeville, *France* 23 B8 50 6N 1 49 E
Abbeville, *La., U.S.A.* 139 L8 30 0N 92 7W
Abbeville, *S.C., U.S.A.* 135 H4 34 12N 82 21W
Abbiategrasso, *Italy* 38 C5 45 23N 8 55 E
Abbieglassie, *Australia* 115 D4 27 15 S 147 28 E
Abbot Ice Shelf, *Antarctica* 7 D16 73 0 S 92 0W
Abbotsford, *Canada* 130 D4 49 5N 122 20W
Abbotsford, *U.S.A.* 138 C9 44 55N 90 20W
Abbottabad, *Pakistan* 80 B5 34 10N 73 15 E
Abcoude, *Neths.* 20 D5 52 17N 4 59 E
Abd al Kūrī, *Ind. Oc.* 87 D6 12 5N 52 20 E
Ābdar, *Iran* 85 D7 30 16N 55 19 E
'Abdolābād, *Iran* 85 C8 34 12N 56 30 E
Abdulino, *U.S.S.R.* 54 E3 53 42N 53 40 E
Abéché, *Chad* 97 F4 13 50N 20 35 E
Abejar, *Spain* 34 D2 41 48N 2 47W
Abekr, *Sudan* 95 E2 12 45N 28 50 E
Abêlessa, *Algeria* 99 D5 22 58N 4 47 E
Abengourou, *Ivory C.* 100 D4 6 42N 3 27W
Åbenrå, *Denmark* 15 J3 55 3N 9 25 E
Abensberg, *Germany* 27 G7 48 49N 11 51 E
Abeokuta, *Nigeria* 101 D5 7 3N 3 19 E
Aber, *Uganda* 106 B3 2 12N 32 25 E
Aberaeron, *U.K.* 17 E3 52 15N 4 16W
Aberayron = Aberaeron, *U.K.* 17 E3 52 15N 4 16W
Abercorn = Mbala, *Zambia* 107 D3 8 46 S 31 24 E
Abercorn, *Australia* 115 D5 25 12 S 151 5 E
Aberdare, *U.K.* 17 F4 51 43N 3 27W
Aberdare Ra., *Kenya* 106 C4 0 15 S 36 50 E
Aberdeen, *Australia* 117 B9 32 9 S 150 56 E
Aberdeen, *Canada* 131 C7 52 20N 106 8W
Aberdeen, *S. Africa* 104 E3 32 28 S 24 2 E
Aberdeen, *U.K.* 18 D6 57 9N 2 6W
Aberdeen, *Ala., U.S.A.* 135 J1 33 49N 88 33W
Aberdeen, *Idaho, U.S.A.* 142 E7 42 57N 112 50W
Aberdeen, *Ohio, U.S.A.* 141 F13 38 39N 83 46W
Aberdeen, *S. Dak., U.S.A.* 138 C5 45 30N 98 30W
Aberdeen, *Wash., U.S.A.* 144 D3 47 0N 123 50W
Aberdovey = Aberdyfi, *U.K.* 17 E3 52 33N 4 3W
Aberdyfi, *U.K.* 17 E3 52 33N 4 3W
Aberfeldy, *Australia* 117 D7 37 42 S 146 22 E
Aberfeldy, *U.K.* 18 E5 56 37N 3 50W
Abergaria-a-Velha, *Portugal* 36 E2 40 41N 8 32W
Abergavenny, *U.K.* 17 F4 51 49N 3 1W
Abernathy, *U.S.A.* 139 J4 33 49N 101 49W
Abert, L., *U.S.A.* 142 E3 42 40N 120 8W
Aberystwyth, *U.K.* 17 E3 52 25N 4 6W
Abha, *Si. Arabia* 94 D5 18 0N 42 34 E
Abhar, *Iran* 85 B6 36 9N 49 13 E
Abhayapuri, *India* 78 B3 26 24N 90 38 E
Abidiya, *Sudan* 94 D3 18 18N 34 3 E
Abidjan, *Ivory C.* 100 D4 5 26N 3 58W
Abilene, *Kans., U.S.A.* 138 F6 39 0N 97 16W
Abilene, *Tex., U.S.A.* 139 J5 32 22N 99 40W
Abingdon, *U.K.* 17 F6 51 40N 1 17W
Abingdon, *Ill., U.S.A.* 140 D6 40 53N 90 23W
Abingdon, *Va., U.S.A.* 135 G5 36 46N 81 56W
Abington Reef, *Australia* 114 B4 18 0 S 149 35 E
Abitau →, *Canada* 131 B7 59 53N 109 3W
Abitau L., *Canada* 131 A7 60 27N 107 15W
Abitibi L., *Canada* 128 C4 48 40N 79 40W
Abiy Adi, *Ethiopia* 95 E4 13 39N 39 3 E
Abkhaz A.S.S.R. □, *U.S.S.R.* 53 E9 43 0N 41 0 E
Abkit, *U.S.S.R.* 57 C16 64 10N 157 10 E
Abminga, *Australia* 115 D1 26 8 S 134 51 E
Abnûb, *Egypt* 94 B3 27 18N 31 4 E
Abo, Massif d', *Chad* 97 D3 21 41N 16 8 E
Abocho, *Nigeria* 101 D6 7 35N 6 56 E
Abohar, *India* 80 D6 30 10N 74 10 E
Aboisso, *Ivory C.* 100 D4 5 30N 3 5W
Abolo, *Congo* 102 B2 0 8N 14 16 E
Abomey, *Benin* 101 D5 7 10N 2 5 E
Abondance, *France* 25 B10 46 18N 6 43 E
Abong-Mbang, *Cameroon* 102 B2 4 0N 13 8 E
Abongabong, *Indonesia* 74 B1 4 15N 96 48 E
Abonnema, *Nigeria* 101 E6 4 41N 6 49 E
Abony, *Hungary* 31 D13 47 12N 20 3 E
Aboso, *Ghana* 100 D4 5 23N 1 57W
Abou-Deïa, *Chad* 97 F3 11 20N 19 20 E
Abou Goulem, *Chad* 97 F4 13 37N 21 38 E
Aboyne, *U.K.* 18 D6 57 4N 2 48W
Abra Pampa, *Argentina* 158 A2 22 43 S 65 42W
Abrantes, *Portugal* 37 F2 39 24N 8 7W
Abraveses, *Portugal* 36 E3 40 41N 7 55W
Abreojos, Pta., *Mexico* 146 B2 26 50N 113 40W
Abreschviller, *France* 23 D14 48 39N 7 6 E
Abri, *Esh Shamâliya, Sudan* 94 C3 20 50N 30 27 E
Abri, *Janub Kordofân, Sudan* 95 E3 11 40N 30 21 E
Abrolhos, Banka, *Brazil* 155 E4 18 0 S 38 0W
Abrud, *Romania* 46 C4 46 19N 23 5 E
Abruzzi □, *Italy* 39 F11 42 15N 14 0 E
Absaroka Ra., *U.S.A.* 142 D9 44 40N 110 0W
Abū al Khaṣīb, *Iraq* 85 D6 30 25N 48 0 E
Abū 'Alī, *Si. Arabia* 85 E6 27 20N 49 27 E
Abū 'Alī →, *Lebanon* 91 A4 34 25N 35 50 E
Abu 'Arīsh, *Si. Arabia* 86 C3 16 53N 42 48 E
Abû Ballas, *Egypt* 94 C2 24 26N 27 36 E
Abu Deleiq, *Sudan* 95 D3 15 57N 33 48 E
Abu Dhabi = Abū Ẓāby, *U.A.E.* 85 E7 24 28N 54 22 E
Abû Dis, *Sudan* 94 D3 19 12N 33 38 E
Abû Dom, *Sudan* 95 D3 16 18N 32 25 E
Abū Du'ān, *Syria* 84 B3 36 25N 38 15 E
Abu el Gairi, W. →, *Egypt* 91 F2 29 35N 33 30 E
Abû Gabra, *Sudan* 95 E2 11 2N 26 50 E
Abu Ga'da, W. →, *Egypt* 91 F1 29 15N 32 53 E
Abû Gubeiha, *Sudan* 95 E3 11 30N 31 15 E
Abu Habl, Khawr →, *Sudan* 95 E3 12 37N 31 0 E
Abū Ḥadrīyah, *Si. Arabia* 85 E6 27 20N 48 58 E
Abu Hamed, *Sudan* 94 D3 19 32N 33 13 E
Abu Haraz, *An Nîl el Azraq, Sudan* 95 E3 14 35N 33 30 E
Abû Haraz, *Esh Shamâliya, Sudan* 94 D3 19 8N 32 18 E
Abû Higar, *Sudan* 95 E3 12 50N 33 59 E
Abū Kamāl, *Syria* 84 C4 34 30N 41 0 E
Abū Madd, Ra's, *Si. Arabia* 84 E3 24 50N 37 7 E
Abu Matariq, *Sudan* 95 E2 10 59N 26 9 E
Abu Qir, *Egypt* 94 H7 31 18N 30 0 E
Abu Qireiya, *Egypt* 94 C4 24 5N 35 28 E
Abu Qurqâs, *Egypt* 94 J7 28 1N 30 44 E
Abū Rașāș, Ra's, *Oman* 87 B7 20 10N 58 38 E
Abū Rubayq, *Si. Arabia* 86 B2 23 44N 39 42 E
Abu Ṣafāt, W. →, *Jordan* 91 E5 30 24N 36 7 E
Abū Simbel, *Egypt* 94 C3 22 18N 31 40 E
Abū Şukhayr, *Iraq* 84 D5 31 54N 44 30 E
Abu Tig, *Egypt* 94 B3 27 4N 31 15 E
Abu Tiga, *Sudan* 95 E3 12 47N 34 12 E
Abû Zabad, *Sudan* 95 E2 12 25N 29 10 E
Abū Ẓāby, *U.A.E.* 85 E7 24 28N 54 22 E
Abū Zeydābād, *Iran* 85 C6 33 54N 51 45 E
Abufari, *Brazil* 157 B5 5 25 S 62 59W
Abuja, *Nigeria* 101 D6 9 16N 7 2 E
Abukuma-Gawa →, *Japan* 60 E10 38 6N 140 52 E
Abukuma-Sammyaku, *Japan* 60 F10 37 30N 140 45 E
Abumombazi, *Zaïre* 102 B4 3 42N 22 10 E
Abunã, *Brazil* 157 B4 9 40 S 65 20W
Abunã →, *Brazil* 157 B4 9 41 S 65 20W
Aburatsu, *Japan* 62 F3 31 34N 131 24 E
Aburo, *Zaïre* 106 B3 2 4N 30 53 E
Abut Hd., *N.Z.* 119 D5 43 7 S 170 15 E
Abwong, *Sudan* 95 F3 9 2N 32 14 E
Åby, *Sweden* 15 F10 58 40N 16 10 E
Aby, Lagune, *Ivory C.* 100 D4 5 15N 3 14W
Acacías, *Colombia* 152 C3 3 59N 73 46W
Acajutla, *El Salv.* 148 D2 13 36N 89 50W
Açailândia, *Brazil* 154 C2 5 0 S 47 30W
Acámbaro, *Mexico* 146 D4 20 0N 100 40W
Acanthus, *Greece* 44 D5 40 27N 23 47 E
Acaponeta, *Mexico* 146 C3 22 30N 105 20W
Acapulco, *Mexico* 147 D5 16 51N 99 56W
Acarai, Serra, *Brazil* 153 C6 1 50N 57 50W
Acaraú, *Brazil* 154 B3 2 53 S 40 7W
Acari, *Brazil* 154 C4 6 31 S 36 38W
Acarí, *Peru* 156 D3 15 25 S 74 36W
Acarigua, *Venezuela* 152 B4 9 33N 69 12W
Acatlán, *Mexico* 147 D5 18 10N 98 3W
Acayucan, *Mexico* 147 D6 17 59N 94 58W
Accéglio, *Italy* 38 D3 44 28N 6 59 E
Accomac, *U.S.A.* 134 G8 37 43N 75 40W
Accous, *France* 24 F3 43 0N 0 36W
Accra, *Ghana* 101 D4 5 35N 0 6W
Accrington, *U.K.* 16 D5 53 46N 2 22W
Acebal, *Argentina* 158 C3 33 20 S 60 50W
Aceh □, *Indonesia* 70 D1 4 15N 97 30 E
Acerenza, *Italy* 41 B8 40 50N 15 58 E
Acerra, *Italy* 41 B7 40 57N 14 22 E
Aceuchal, *Spain* 37 G4 38 39N 6 30W
Achacachi, *Bolivia* 156 D4 16 3 S 68 43W
Achaguas, *Venezuela* 152 B4 7 46N 68 14W
Achalpur, *India* 82 D3 21 22N 77 32 E
Achao, *Chile* 160 B2 42 28 S 73 30W
Achel, *Belgium* 21 F6 51 15N 5 29 E
Acheng, *China* 67 B14 45 30N 126 58 E
Achenkirch, *Austria* 30 D4 47 32N 11 45 E
Achensee, *Austria* 30 D4 47 26N 11 45 E
Acher, *India* 80 H5 23 10N 72 32 E
Achern, *Germany* 27 G4 48 37N 8 5 E
Acheron →, *N.Z.* 119 C8 42 16 S 173 4 E
Achill, *Ireland* 19 C2 53 56N 9 55W
Achill Hd., *Ireland* 19 C1 53 59N 10 15W
Achill I., *Ireland* 19 C1 53 58N 10 5W
Achill Sd., *Ireland* 19 C2 53 53N 9 55W
Achim, *Germany* 26 B5 53 1N 9 2 E
Achinsk, *U.S.S.R.* 57 D10 56 20N 90 20 E
Achisay, *U.S.S.R.* 55 B4 43 35N 68 53 E
Achit, *U.S.S.R.* 54 C5 56 48N 57 54 E
Achol, *Sudan* 95 F3 6 35N 31 32 E
Acıgöl, *Turkey* 88 E3 37 50N 29 50 E
Acireale, *Italy* 41 E8 37 37N 15 9 E
Ackerman, *U.S.A.* 139 J10 33 20N 89 8W
Ackley, *U.S.A.* 140 B3 42 33N 93 3W
Acklins I., *Bahamas* 149 B5 22 30N 74 0W
Acme, *Canada* 130 C6 51 33N 113 30W
Acobamba, *Peru* 156 C3 12 52 S 74 35W
Acomayo, *Peru* 156 C3 13 55 S 71 38W
Aconcagua □, *Chile* 158 C1 32 15 S 70 30W
Aconcagua, Cerro, *Argentina* 158 C2 32 39 S 70 0W
Aconquija, Mt., *Argentina* 158 B2 27 0 S 66 0W
Acopiara, *Brazil* 154 C4 6 6 S 39 27W
Açores, Is. dos = Azores, *Atl. Oc.* 8 E6 38 44N 29 0W
Acorizal, *Brazil* 157 D6 15 12 S 56 22W
Acquapendente, *Italy* 39 F8 42 45N 11 50 E
Acquasanta, *Italy* 39 F10 42 46N 13 24 E
Acquaviva delle Fonti, *Italy* 41 B9 40 53N 16 50 E
Acqui, *Italy* 38 D5 44 40N 8 28 E
Acraman, L., *Australia* 115 E2 32 2 S 135 23 E
Acre = 'Akko, *Israel* 91 C4 32 55N 35 4 E
Acre □, *Brazil* 156 B3 9 1 S 71 0W
Acre →, *Brazil* 156 B4 8 45 S 67 22W
Acri, *Italy* 41 C9 39 29N 16 23 E
Acs, *Hungary* 31 D11 47 42N 18 2 E
Actium, *Greece* 45 F2 38 57N 20 45 E
Acton, *Canada* 136 C4 43 38N 80 3W
Açu, *Brazil* 154 C4 5 34 S 36 54W
Ad Dahnā, *Si. Arabia* 87 A5 24 30N 48 10 E
Aḍ Ḍāliʻ, *Yemen* 86 D4 13 42N 44 44 E
Ad Dammām, *Si. Arabia* 85 E6 26 20N 50 5 E
Ad Darb, *Si. Arabia* 86 C3 18 2N 43 7 E
Ad Dawhah, *Qatar* 85 E6 25 15N 51 35 E
Ad Dawr, *Iraq* 84 C4 34 27N 43 47 E
Aḍ Ḍiffah, *Libya* 96 B4 30 30N 24 30 E
Ad Dilam, *Si. Arabia* 86 B4 23 55N 47 10 E
Ad Dir'īyah, *Si. Arabia* 84 E5 24 44N 46 35 E
Ad Dīwānīyah, *Iraq* 84 D5 32 0N 45 0 E
Ad Dujayl, *Iraq* 84 C5 33 51N 44 14 E
Ad Durūz, J., *Jordan* 91 C5 32 35N 36 40 E
Ada, *Ghana* 101 D5 5 44N 0 40 E
Ada, *Minn., U.S.A.* 138 B6 47 20N 96 30W
Ada, *Ohio, U.S.A.* 141 D13 40 46N 83 49W
Ada, *Okla., U.S.A.* 139 H6 34 50N 96 45W
Ada, *Yugoslavia* 42 B5 45 49N 20 9 E
Adad, *Somali Rep.* 108 C3 9 27N 46 49 E
Adaja →, *Spain* 36 D6 41 32N 4 52W
Ådalslinden, *Sweden* 14 A10 63 27N 16 55 E
Adam, *Oman* 87 B7 22 15N 57 28 E
Adam, Mt., *Falk. Is.* 160 D4 51 34 S 60 4W
Adamantina, *Brazil* 155 F1 21 42 S 51 4W
Adamaoua, Massif de l', *Cameroon* 101 D7 7 20N 12 20 E
Adamawa Highlands = Adamaoua, Massif de l', *Cameroon* 101 D7 7 20N 12 20 E
Adamello, Mt., *Italy* 38 B7 46 10N 10 34 E
Adami Tulu, *Ethiopia* 95 F4 7 53N 38 41 E
Adaminaby, *Australia* 117 D8 36 0 S 148 45 E
Adamovka, *U.S.S.R.* 54 F6 51 32N 59 56 E
Adams, *Mass., U.S.A.* 137 D11 42 38N 73 8W
Adams, *N.Y., U.S.A.* 137 C8 43 50N 76 3W
Adams, *Wis., U.S.A.* 138 D10 43 59N 89 50W
Adams, Mt., *U.S.A.* 144 D5 46 10N 121 28W
Adam's Bridge, *Sri Lanka* 83 K4 9 15N 79 40 E
Adams L., *Canada* 130 C5 51 10N 119 40W
Adam's Peak, *Sri Lanka* 83 L5 6 48N 80 30 E
Adamuz, *Spain* 37 G6 38 2N 4 32W
Adana, *Turkey* 88 E6 37 0N 35 16 E
Adana □, *Turkey* 88 E6 37 0N 35 30 E
Adanero, *Spain* 36 E6 40 56N 4 36W
Adapazarı, *Turkey* 88 C4 40 48N 30 25 E
Adarama, *Sudan* 95 D3 17 10N 34 52 E
Adare, C., *Antarctica* 7 D11 71 0 S 171 0 E
Adaut, *Indonesia* 71 F8 8 8 S 131 7 E
Adavale, *Australia* 115 D3 25 52 S 144 32 E
Adda →, *Italy* 38 C6 45 8N 9 53 E
Addis Ababa = Addis Abeba, *Ethiopia* 95 F4 9 2N 38 42 E
Addis Abeba, *Ethiopia* 95 F4 9 2N 38 42 E
Addis Alem, *Ethiopia* 95 F4 9 0N 38 17 E
Addison, *Ill., U.S.A.* 141 C8 41 56N 88 2W
Addison, *N.Y., U.S.A.* 136 D7 42 9N 77 15W
Addo, *S. Africa* 104 E4 33 32 S 25 45 E
Addyston, *U.S.A.* 141 E12 39 8N 84 43W
Adebour, *Niger* 97 F2 13 17N 11 50 E
Ādeh, *Iran* 84 B5 37 42N 45 11 E
Adel, *Ga., U.S.A.* 135 K4 31 10N 83 28W
Adel, *Iowa, U.S.A.* 140 C2 41 37N 94 1W
Adelaide, *Australia* 116 C3 34 52 S 138 30 E
Adelaide, *Bahamas* 148 A4 25 4N 77 31W
Adelaide, *S. Africa* 104 E4 32 42 S 26 20 E
Adelaide I., *Antarctica* 7 C17 67 15 S 68 30W
Adelaide Pen., *Canada* 126 B10 68 15N 97 30W
Adelaide River, *Australia* 112 B5 13 15 S 131 7 E
Adelanto, *U.S.A.* 145 L9 34 35N 117 22W
Adelboden, *Switz.* 28 D5 46 29N 7 33 E
Adele I., *Australia* 112 C3 15 32 S 123 9 E
Adélie, Terre, *Antarctica* 7 C10 68 0 S 140 0 E
Ademuz, *Spain* 34 E3 40 5N 1 13W
Aden = Al 'Adan, *Yemen* 86 D4 12 45N 45 0 E
Aden, G. of, *Asia* 90 E4 12 30N 47 30 E
Adendorp, *S. Africa* 104 E3 32 15 S 24 30 E
Adh Dhayd, *U.A.E.* 85 E7 25 17N 55 53 E
Adhoi, *India* 80 H4 23 26N 70 32 E
Adi, *Indonesia* 71 E8 4 15 S 133 30 E
Adi Daro, *Ethiopia* 95 E4 14 20N 38 14 E
Adi Keyih, *Ethiopia* 95 E4 14 51N 39 22 E
Adi Kwala, *Ethiopia* 95 E4 14 38N 38 48 E
Adi Ugri, *Ethiopia* 95 E4 14 58N 38 48 E
Adieu, C., *Australia* 113 F5 32 0 S 132 10 E
Adieu Pt., *Australia* 112 C3 15 14 S 124 35 E
Adigala, *Ethiopia* 95 E5 10 24N 42 15 E
Adige →, *Italy* 39 C9 45 9N 12 20 E
Adigrat, *Ethiopia* 95 E4 14 20N 39 26 E
Adilabad, *India* 82 E4 19 33N 78 20 E
Adin, *U.S.A.* 142 F3 41 10N 121 0W
Adinkerke, *Belgium* 21 F1 51 5N 2 36 E
Adirondack Mts., *U.S.A.* 137 C10 44 0N 74 15W
Adıyaman, *Turkey* 89 E8 37 45N 38 16 E
Adiyaman □, *Turkey* 89 E8 37 30N 38 10 E
Adjim, *Tunisia* 96 B2 33 47N 10 50 E
Adjohon, *Benin* 101 D5 6 41N 2 32 E
Adjud, *Romania* 46 C8 46 7N 27 10 E
Adjumani, *Uganda* 106 B3 3 20N 31 50 E
Adlavik Is., *Canada* 129 A8 55 2N 57 45W
Adler, *U.S.S.R.* 53 E8 43 28N 39 52 E
Adliswil, *Switz.* 29 B7 47 19N 8 32 E
Admer, *Algeria* 99 D6 20 21N 5 27 E
Admer, Erg d', *Algeria* 99 D6 24 0N 9 5 E
Admiralty G., *Australia* 112 B4 14 20 S 125 55 E
Admiralty I., *U.S.A.* 126 C6 57 40N 134 35W
Admiralty Inlet, *U.S.A.* 142 C2 48 0N 122 40W
Admiralty Is., *Papua N. G.* 120 B4 2 0 S 147 0 E
Ado, *Nigeria* 101 D5 6 36N 2 56 E
Ado Ekiti, *Nigeria* 101 D6 7 38N 5 12 E
Adok, *Sudan* 95 F3 8 10N 30 20 E
Adola, *Ethiopia* 95 E5 11 14N 41 44 E
Adonara, *Indonesia* 71 F6 8 15 S 123 5 E
Adoni, *India* 83 G3 15 33N 77 18 E
Adony, *Hungary* 31 D11 47 6N 18 52 E
Adour →, *France* 24 E2 43 32N 1 32W
Adra, *India* 81 H12 23 30N 86 42 E
Adra, *Spain* 35 J1 36 43N 3 3W
Adrano, *Italy* 41 E7 37 40N 14 49 E
Adrar, *Algeria* 99 C4 27 51N 0 11W
Adrasman, *U.S.S.R.* 55 C4 40 38N 69 58 E
Adré, *Chad* 97 F4 13 40N 22 20 E
Adrī, *Libya* 96 C2 27 32N 13 2 E
Ádria, *Italy* 39 C9 45 4N 12 3 E
Adrian, *Mich., U.S.A.* 141 C12 41 55N 84 5W
Adrian, *Mo., U.S.A.* 140 F2 38 24N 94 21W
Adrian, *Tex., U.S.A.* 139 H3 35 19N 102 37W
Adriatic Sea, *Europe* 10 G8 43 0N 16 0 E
Adua, *Indonesia* 71 E7 1 45 S 129 50 E
Adula, *Switz.* 29 D8 46 30N 9 3 E
Adung Long, *Burma* 78 A6 28 7N 97 42 E
Adur, *India* 83 K3 9 8N 76 40 E
Adwa, *Ethiopia* 95 E4 14 15N 38 52 E
Adzhar A.S.S.R. □, *U.S.S.R.* 53 F10 41 30N 42 0 E
Adzopé, *Ivory C.* 100 D4 6 7N 3 49W
Æolian Is. = Eólie, Is., *Italy* 41 D7 38 30N 14 50 E
Aerhtai Shan, *Mongolia* 64 B4 46 40N 92 45 E
Ærø, *Denmark* 15 K4 54 52N 10 25 E
Ærøskøbing, *Denmark* 15 K4 54 53N 10 24 E
Aesch, *Switz.* 28 B5 47 28N 7 36 E
Aëtós, *Greece* 45 G3 37 15N 21 50 E
Afafi, Massif d', *Niger* 97 D3 22 11N 15 10 E
'Afak, *Iraq* 84 C5 32 4N 45 15 E
Afanasyevo, *U.S.S.R.* 54 B3 58 52N 53 15 E
Afándou, *Greece* 32 C10 36 18N 28 12 E
Afarag, Erg, *Algeria* 99 D5 23 50N 2 47 E
Afars & Issas, Terr. of = Djibouti ■, *Africa* 90 E3 12 0N 43 0 E
Afdega, *Ethiopia* 108 C2 6 4N 43 30 E
Affreville = Khemis Miliana, *Algeria* 99 A5 36 11N 2 14 E
Affton, *U.S.A.* 140 F6 38 33N 90 20W
Afghanistan ■, *Asia* 79 B2 33 0N 65 0 E
Afgoi, *Somali Rep.* 90 G3 2 7N 44 59 E
'Afīf, *Si. Arabia* 86 B3 23 53N 42 56 E
Afikpo, *Nigeria* 101 D6 5 53N 7 54 E
Aflou, *Algeria* 99 B5 34 7N 2 3 E
Afmadu, *Somali Rep.* 108 D2 0 31N 42 4 E
Afogados da Ingàzeira, *Brazil* 154 C4 7 45 S 37 39W
Afognak I., *U.S.A.* 126 C4 58 10N 152 50W
Afragola, *Italy* 41 B7 40 54N 14 15 E
Afrera, *Ethiopia* 95 E5 13 16N 41 5 E
'Afrīn, *Syria* 84 B3 36 32N 36 50 E
Afşin, *Turkey* 88 D7 38 14N 36 55 E
Afton, *U.S.A.* 137 D9 42 14N 75 31W
Aftout, *Algeria* 98 C4 26 50N 3 45W
Afuá, *Brazil* 153 D7 0 15 S 50 20W
Afula, *Israel* 91 C4 32 37N 35 17 E
Afyonkarahisar, *Turkey* 88 D4 38 45N 30 33 E
Afyonkarahisar □, *Turkey* 88 D4 38 45N 30 30 E
Aga, *Egypt* 94 H7 30 55N 31 10 E
Agadès = Agadez, *Niger* 97 E1 16 58N 7 59 E
Agadez, *Niger* 97 E1 16 58N 7 59 E
Agadir, *Morocco* 98 B3 30 28N 9 55W
Agaete, *Canary Is.* 33 F4 28 6N 15 43W
Agailás, *Mauritania* 98 D2 22 37N 14 22W
Agana, *Guam* 121 R15 13 28N 144 45 E
Agapa, *U.S.S.R.* 57 B9 71 27N 89 15 E
Agapovka, *U.S.S.R.* 54 E6 53 18N 59 8 E
Agar, *India* 80 H7 23 40N 76 2 E
Agaro, *Ethiopia* 95 F4 7 50N 36 38 E
Agartala, *India* 78 D3 23 50N 91 23 E
Agăş, *Romania* 46 C7 46 28N 26 15 E
Agassiz, *Canada* 130 D4 49 14N 121 46W
Agats, *Indonesia* 71 F9 5 33 S 138 0 E
Agbélouvé, *Togo* 101 D5 6 35N 1 14 E
Agboville, *Ivory C.* 100 D4 5 55N 4 15W
Agdam, *U.S.S.R.* 53 G12 40 0N 46 58 E
Agdash, *U.S.S.R.* 53 F12 40 44N 47 22 E
Agde, *France* 24 E7 43 19N 3 28 E
Agde, C. d', *France* 24 E7 43 16N 3 28 E
Agdz, *Morocco* 98 B3 30 47N 6 30W
Agdzhabedi, *U.S.S.R.* 53 F12 40 5N 47 27 E

Agen, France — 24 D4 44 12N 0 38 E
Ageo, Japan — 63 B11 35 58N 139 36 E
Ager Tay, Chad — 97 E3 20 0N 17 41 E
Agersø, Denmark — 15 J5 55 13N 11 12 E
Ageyevo, U.S.S.R. — 51 D10 54 10N 36 27 E
Agger, Denmark — 15 H2 56 47N 8 13 E
Aggius, Italy — 40 B2 40 56N 9 4 E
Āgh Kand, Iran — 85 B6 37 15N 48 4 E
Aghoueyyît, Mauritania — 98 D1 21 10N 15 6W
Aginskoye, U.S.S.R. — 57 D12 51 6N 114 32 E
Agira, Italy — 41 E7 37 40N 14 30 E
Ağlasun, Turkey — 88 E4 37 39N 30 31 E
Agly →, France — 24 F7 42 46N 3 3 E
Agnibilékrou, Ivory C. — 100 D4 7 10N 3 11W
Agnita, Romania — 46 D5 45 59N 24 40 E
Agnone, Italy — 41 A7 41 49N 14 20 E
Ago, Japan — 63 C8 34 20N 136 51 E
Agofie, Ghana — 101 D5 8 27N 0 15 E
Agogna →, Italy — 38 C5 45 4N 8 52 E
Agogo, Sudan — 95 F2 7 50N 28 45 E
Agon, France — 22 C5 49 2N 1 34W
Agön, Sweden — 14 C11 61 34N 17 23 E
Ågordo, Italy — 39 B9 46 18N 12 2 E
Agout →, France — 24 E5 43 47N 1 41 E
Agra, India — 80 F7 27 17N 77 58 E
Agramunt, Spain — 34 D6 41 48N 1 6 E
Ágreda, Spain — 34 D3 41 51N 1 55W
Ağri, Turkey — 89 D10 39 44N 43 4 E
Ağri □, Turkey — 89 D10 39 45N 43 5 E
Agri →, Italy — 41 B9 40 13N 16 44 E
Ağrı Daği, Turkey — 89 D11 39 50N 44 15 E
Ağrı Karakose, Turkey — 89 D10 39 44N 43 3 E
Agrigento, Italy — 40 E6 37 19N 13 33 E
Agrinion, Greece — 45 F3 38 37N 21 27 E
Agrópoli, Italy — 41 B7 40 23N 14 59 E
Agryz, U.S.S.R. — 54 C3 56 33N 53 2 E
Água Branca, Brazil — 154 C3 5 50 S 42 40W
Agua Caliente, Baja Calif. N., Mexico — 145 N10 32 29N 116 59W
Agua Caliente, Sinaloa, Mexico — 146 B3 26 30N 108 20W
Agua Caliente Springs, U.S.A. — 145 N10 32 56N 116 19W
Água Clara, Brazil — 157 E7 20 25 S 52 45W
Agua Hechicero, Mexico — 145 N10 32 26N 116 14W
Agua Preta →, Brazil — 153 D5 1 41 S 63 48W
Agua Prieta, Mexico — 146 A3 31 20N 109 32W
Aguachica, Colombia — 152 B3 8 19N 73 38W
Aguada Cecilio, Argentina — 160 B3 40 51 S 65 51W
Aguadas, Colombia — 152 B2 5 40N 75 38W
Aguadilla, Puerto Rico — 149 C6 18 27N 67 10W
Aguadulce, Panama — 148 E3 8 15N 80 32W
Aguanga, U.S.A. — 145 M10 33 27N 116 51W
Aguanish, Canada — 129 B7 50 14N 62 2W
Aguanus →, Canada — 129 B7 50 13N 62 5W
Aguapeí, Brazil — 157 D6 16 12 S 59 43W
Aguapeí →, Brazil — 155 F1 21 0 S 51 0W
Aguapey →, Argentina — 158 B4 29 7 S 56 36W
Aguaray Guazú →, Paraguay — 158 A4 24 47 S 57 19W
Aguarico →, Ecuador — 152 D2 0 59 S 75 11W
Aguas →, Spain — 34 D4 41 20N 0 30W
Aguas Blancas, Chile — 158 A2 24 15 S 69 55W
Aguas Calientes, Sierra de, Argentina — 158 B2 25 26 S 66 40W
Águas Formosas, Brazil — 155 E3 17 5 S 40 57W
Aguascalientes, Mexico — 146 C4 21 53N 102 12W
Aguascalientes □, Mexico — 146 C4 22 0N 102 20W
Agudo, Spain — 37 G6 38 59N 4 52W
Águeda, Portugal — 36 E2 40 34N 8 27W
Agueda →, Spain — 36 D4 41 2N 6 56W
Aguié, Niger — 101 C6 13 31N 7 46 E
Aguilafuente, Spain — 36 D6 41 13N 4 7W
Aguilar, Spain — 37 H6 37 31N 4 40W
Aguilar de Campóo, Spain — 36 C6 42 47N 4 15W
Aguilares, Argentina — 158 B2 27 26 S 65 35W
Aguilas, Spain — 35 H3 37 23N 1 35W
Agüimes, Canary Is. — 33 G4 27 58N 15 27W
Aguja, C. de la, Colombia — 152 A3 11 18N 74 12W
Agulaa, Ethiopia — 95 E4 13 40N 39 40 E
Agulhas, C., S. Africa — 104 E3 34 52 S 20 0 E
Agulo, Canary Is. — 33 F2 28 11N 17 12W
Agung, Indonesia — 70 F5 8 20 S 115 28 E
Agur, Uganda — 106 B3 2 28N 32 55 E
Agusan →, Phil. — 71 C7 9 0N 125 30 E
Agustín Codazzi, Colombia — 152 A3 10 2N 73 14W
Agvali, U.S.S.R. — 53 E12 42 36N 46 8 E
Aha Mts., Botswana — 104 B3 19 45 S 21 0 E
Ahaggar, Algeria — 99 D6 23 0N 6 30 E
Ahamansu, Ghana — 101 D5 7 38N 0 35 E
Ahar, Iran — 84 B5 38 35N 47 0 E
Ahaura, N.Z. — 119 C6 42 21 S 171 34 E
Ahaus, Germany — 26 C3 52 4N 7 1 E
Ahelledjem, Algeria — 99 C6 26 37N 6 58 E
Ahimanawa Ra., N.Z. — 118 F5 39 3 S 176 30 E
Ahipara B., N.Z. — 118 B2 35 5 S 173 5 E
Ahiri, India — 82 E5 19 30N 80 0 E
Ahlen, Germany — 26 D3 51 45N 7 52 E
Ahmad Wal, Pakistan — 80 E1 29 18N 65 58 E
Ahmadābād, India — 80 H5 23 0N 72 40 E
Aḥmadābād, Khorāsān, Iran — 85 C9 35 3N 60 50 E
Aḥmadābād, Khorāsān, Iran — 85 C8 35 49N 59 42 E
Aḥmadī, Iran — 85 E8 27 56N 56 42 E
Ahmadnagar, India — 82 E2 19 7N 74 46 E
Ahmadpur, Pakistan — 80 E4 29 12N 71 10 E
Ahmar, Ethiopia — 95 F5 9 20N 41 15 E
Ahmedabad = Ahmadabad, India — 80 H5 23 0N 72 40 E
Ahmednagar = Ahmadnagar, India — 82 E2 19 7N 74 46 E
Ahoada, Nigeria — 101 D6 5 8N 6 36 E
Ahome, Mexico — 146 B3 25 55N 109 11W
Ahr →, Germany — 26 E3 50 33N 7 17 E
Ahram, Iran — 85 D6 28 52N 51 16 E
Ahrax Pt., Malta — 32 D1 35 59N 14 22 E
Ahrensbök, Germany — 26 A6 54 2N 10 34 E
Ahrweiler, Germany — 26 E3 50 31N 7 3 E
Āhū, Iran — 85 C6 34 33N 50 2 E
Ahuachapán, El Salv. — 148 D2 13 54N 89 52W

Ahuriri →, N.Z. — 119 E5 44 31 S 170 12 E
Ahvāz, Iran — 85 D6 31 20N 48 40 E
Ahvenanmaa = Åland, Finland — 13 F16 60 15N 20 0 E
Ahwar, Yemen — 86 D4 13 30N 46 40 E
Ahzar, Mali — 101 B5 15 30N 3 20 E
Aiari →, Brazil — 152 C4 1 22N 68 36W
Aichach, Germany — 27 G7 48 28N 11 9 E
Aichi □, Japan — 63 C9 35 0N 137 15 E
Aidone, Italy — 41 E7 37 26N 14 26 E
Aiello Cálabro, Italy — 41 C9 39 6N 16 12 E
Aigle, Switz. — 28 D3 46 18N 6 58 E
Aignay-le-Duc, France — 23 E11 47 40N 4 43 E
Aigoual, Mt., France — 24 D7 44 8N 3 35 E
Aigre, France — 24 C4 45 54N 0 1 E
Aigua, Uruguay — 159 C5 34 13 S 54 46W
Aigueperse, France — 24 B7 46 3N 3 12 E
Aigues →, France — 25 D8 44 7N 4 43 E
Aigues-Mortes, France — 25 E8 43 35N 4 12 E
Aigues-Mortes, G. d', France — 25 E8 43 31N 4 3 E
Aiguilles, France — 25 D10 44 47N 6 51 E
Aiguillon, France — 24 D4 44 18N 0 21 E
Aigurande, France — 24 B5 46 27N 1 49 E
Aihui, China — 65 A7 50 10N 127 30 E
Aija, Peru — 156 B2 9 50 S 77 45W
Aikawa, Japan — 60 E9 38 2N 138 15 E
Aiken, U.S.A. — 135 J5 33 34N 81 50W
Ailao Shan, China — 68 F3 24 0N 101 20 E
Aillant-sur-Tholon, France — 23 E10 47 52N 3 20 E
Aillik, Canada — 129 A8 55 11N 59 18W
Ailly-sur-Noye, France — 23 C9 49 45N 2 20 E
Ailsa Craig, U.K. — 18 F3 55 15N 5 7W
'Ailūn, Jordan — 91 C4 32 18N 35 47 E
Aim, U.S.S.R. — 57 D14 59 0N 133 55 E
Aimere, Indonesia — 71 F6 8 45 S 121 3 E
Aimogasta, Argentina — 158 B2 28 33 S 66 50W
Aimorés, Brazil — 155 E3 19 30 S 41 4W
Ain □, France — 25 B9 46 5N 5 20 E
Ain →, France — 25 C9 45 45N 5 11 E
Ain Beïda, Algeria — 99 A6 35 50N 7 29 E
Aïn Ben Khellil, Algeria — 99 B4 33 15N 0 49W
Aïn Ben Tili, Mauritania — 98 C3 25 59N 9 27W
Aïn Beni Mathar, Morocco — 99 B4 34 1N 2 0W
Aïn Benian, Algeria — 99 A5 36 48N 2 55 E
Ain Dalla, Egypt — 94 B2 27 20N 27 23 E
Ain el Mafki, Egypt — 94 B2 27 30N 28 15 E
Aïn M'lila, Algeria — 99 A6 36 2N 6 35 E
Ain Girba, Egypt — 94 B2 29 20N 25 14 E
Aïn Qeiqab, Egypt — 94 B1 29 42N 24 55 E
Aïn-Sefra, Algeria — 99 B4 32 47N 0 37W
Aïn Sheikh Murzûk, Egypt — 94 B2 26 47N 27 45 E
'Ain Sudr, Egypt — 91 F2 29 50N 33 6 E
Ain Sukhna, Egypt — 94 J8 29 32N 32 20 E
Aïn-Témouchent, Algeria — 99 A4 35 16N 1 8W
Ain Touta, Algeria — 99 A6 35 26N 5 54 E
Ain Zeitûn, Egypt — 94 B2 29 10N 25 48 E
Aïn Zorah, Morocco — 99 B4 34 37N 3 32W
Ainabo, Somali Rep. — 90 F4 9 0N 46 25 E
Aïnaži, U.S.S.R. — 50 C4 57 50N 24 24 E
Aínos Óros, Greece — 45 F2 38 10N 20 35 E
Ainsworth, U.S.A. — 138 D5 42 33N 99 52W
Aioi, Japan — 62 C6 34 48N 134 28 E
Aipe, Colombia — 152 C2 3 13N 75 15W
Aiquile, Bolivia — 157 D4 18 10 S 65 10W
Air, Niger — 97 E1 18 30N 8 0 E
Air Hitam, Malaysia — 77 M4 1 55N 103 11 E
Airaines, France — 23 C8 49 58N 1 55 E
Airão, Brazil — 153 D5 1 56 S 61 22W
Airdrie, Canada — 130 C6 51 18N 114 2W
Airdrie, U.K. — 18 F5 55 53N 3 57W
Aire, I. del, Spain — 33 B11 39 48N 4 16 E
Aire →, France — 23 B9 50 37N 2 22 E
Aire →, U.K. — 16 D7 53 42N 0 55W
Aire-sur-la-Lys, France — 23 B9 50 37N 2 22 E
Aire-sur-l'Adour, France — 24 E3 43 42N 0 15W
Aireys Inlet, Australia — 116 E6 38 29 S 144 5 E
Airlie Beach, Australia — 114 C4 20 16 S 148 43 E
Airolo, Switz. — 29 C7 46 32N 8 37 E
Airvault, France — 22 F6 46 50N 0 8W
Aisch →, Germany — 27 F7 49 46N 11 1 E
Aisen □, Chile — 160 C2 46 30 S 73 0W
Aisne □, France — 23 C10 49 42N 3 40 E
Aisne →, France — 23 C9 49 26N 2 50 E
Aitana, Sierra de, Spain — 35 G4 38 35N 0 24W
Aitape, Papua N. G. — 120 B2 3 11 S 142 22 E
Aitkin, U.S.A. — 138 B8 46 32N 93 43W
Aitolía Kai Akarnanía □, Greece — 45 F3 38 45N 21 18 E
Aitolikón, Greece — 45 F3 38 26N 21 21 E
Aiuaba, Brazil — 154 C3 6 38 S 40 7W
Aiud, Romania — 46 C4 46 19N 23 44 E
Aix-en-Provence, France — 25 E9 43 32N 5 27 E
Aix-la-Chapelle = Aachen, Germany — 26 E2 50 47N 6 4 E
Aix-les-Bains, France — 25 C9 45 41N 5 53 E
Aixe-sur-Vienne, France — 24 C5 45 47N 1 9 E
Aiyang, Mt., Papua N. G. — 120 C1 5 10 S 141 20 E
Aiyansh, Canada — 130 B3 55 17N 129 2W
Aíyina, Greece — 45 G5 37 45N 23 26 E
Aiyínion, Greece — 44 D4 40 28N 22 28 E
Aíyion, Greece — 45 F4 38 15N 22 5 E
Aizawl, India — 78 D4 23 40N 92 44 E
Aizenay, France — 22 F5 46 44N 1 38W
Aizpute, U.S.S.R. — 50 C2 56 43N 21 40 E
Aizuwakamatsu, Japan — 60 F9 37 30N 139 56 E
Ajaccio, France — 25 G12 41 55N 8 40 E
Ajaccio, G. d', France — 25 G12 41 52N 8 40 E
Ajaju →, Colombia — 152 C3 0 59N 72 20W
Ajalpan, Mexico — 147 D5 18 22N 97 15W
Ajanta Ra., India — 82 D2 20 28N 75 50 E
Ajax, Canada — 136 C5 43 50N 79 1W
Ajax, Mt., N.Z. — 119 C7 42 35 S 172 5 E
Ajayan Pt., Guam — 121 R15 13 15N 144 43 E
Ajdâbiyah, Libya — 96 B4 30 54N 20 4 E
Ajdovščina, Yugoslavia — 39 C10 45 54N 13 54 E
Ajibar, Ethiopia — 95 E4 10 35N 38 36 E
Ajka, Hungary — 31 D10 47 4N 17 31 E
'Ajmān, U.A.E. — 87 A6 25 25N 55 30 E
Ajmer, India — 80 F6 26 28N 74 37 E
Ajo, U.S.A. — 143 K7 32 18N 112 54W

Ajoie, Switz. — 28 B4 47 22N 7 0 E
Ajok, Sudan — 95 F2 9 15N 28 28 E
Ak Dağ, Antalya, Turkey — 88 E3 36 30N 29 45 E
Ak Dağ, Sivas, Turkey — 88 D7 39 40N 36 25 E
Akaba, Togo — 101 D5 8 10N 1 2 E
Akabira, Japan — 60 C11 43 33N 142 5 E
Akabli, Algeria — 99 C5 26 49N 1 31 E
Akaishi-Dake, Japan — 63 B10 35 27N 138 9 E
Akaishi-Sammyaku, Japan — 63 B10 35 25N 138 10 E
Akaki Beseka, Ethiopia — 95 F4 8 55N 38 45 E
Akala, Sudan — 95 D4 15 39N 36 13 E
Akamas □, Cyprus — 32 D11 35 3N 32 18 E
Akanthou, Cyprus — 32 D12 35 22N 33 45 E
Akaroa, N.Z. — 119 D7 43 49 S 172 59 E
Akaroa Harbour, N.Z. — 119 D7 43 50 S 172 55 E
Akasha, Sudan — 94 C3 21 10N 30 32 E
Akashi, Japan — 62 C6 34 45N 134 58 E
Akbou, Algeria — 99 A5 36 31N 4 31 E
Akbulak, U.S.S.R. — 54 F4 51 1N 55 37 E
Akçaabat, Turkey — 89 C8 41 1N 39 34 E
Akçakoca, Turkey — 88 C4 41 5N 31 8 E
Akchâr, Mauritania — 98 D2 20 20N 14 28W
Akdağmadeni, Turkey — 88 D6 39 39N 35 53 E
Akdala, U.S.S.R. — 55 A7 45 2N 74 35 E
Akechi, Japan — 63 B9 35 18N 137 23 E
Akelamo, Indonesia — 71 D7 1 35N 129 40 E
Akershus fylke □, Norway — 14 E5 60 0N 11 10 E
Akeru →, India — 82 F5 17 25N 80 5 E
Aketi, Zaïre — 102 B4 2 38N 23 47 E
Akhaïa □, Greece — 45 F3 38 5N 21 45 E
Akhalkalaki, U.S.S.R. — 53 F10 41 27N 43 25 E
Akhaltsikhe, U.S.S.R. — 53 F10 41 40N 43 0 E
Akharnaí, Greece — 45 F5 38 5N 23 44 E
Akhelóös →, Greece — 45 F3 38 36N 21 14 E
Akhendria, Greece — 45 K5 34 58N 25 16 E
Akhéron →, Greece — 44 E2 39 20N 20 29 E
Akhladhókambos, Greece — 45 G4 37 31N 22 35 E
Akhmîm, Egypt — 94 B3 26 31N 31 47 E
Akhnur, India — 81 C6 32 52N 74 45 E
Akhtopol, Bulgaria — 43 E12 42 6N 27 56 E
Akhtubinsk, U.S.S.R. — 53 B12 48 13N 46 7 E
Akhty, U.S.S.R. — 53 F12 41 30N 47 45 E
Akhtyrka, U.S.S.R. — 50 F9 50 25N 35 0 E
Aki, Japan — 62 D5 33 30N 133 54 E
Aki-Nada, Japan — 62 C4 34 5N 132 40 E
Akiéni, Gabon — 102 C2 1 11 S 13 53 E
Akimiski I., Canada — 128 B3 52 50N 81 30W
Akimovka, U.S.S.R. — 52 C6 46 44N 35 0 E
Akita, Japan — 60 E10 39 45N 140 7 E
Akita □, Japan — 60 E10 39 40N 140 30 E
Akjoujt, Mauritania — 100 B2 19 45N 14 15W
Akka, Morocco — 98 C3 29 22N 8 9W
Akkeshi, Japan — 60 C12 43 2N 144 51 E
'Akko, Israel — 91 C4 32 55N 35 4 E
Akkol, Kazakh S.S.R., U.S.S.R. — 55 B5 43 36N 70 45 E
Akkol, Kazakh S.S.R., U.S.S.R. — 56 E8 45 0N 75 39 E
Akköy, Turkey — 45 G9 37 30N 27 18 E
Akkrum, Neths. — 20 B7 53 3N 5 50 E
Aklampa, Benin — 101 D5 8 15N 2 10 E
Aklavik, Canada — 126 B6 68 12N 135 0W
Akmonte, Spain — 37 H4 37 13N 6 38W
Akmuz, U.S.S.R. — 55 C8 41 15N 76 10 E
Aknoul, Morocco — 99 B4 34 40N 3 55W
Akō, Japan — 62 C6 34 45N 134 24 E
Ako, Nigeria — 101 C7 10 19N 10 48 E
Akobo →, Ethiopia — 95 F3 7 48N 33 3 E
Akola, India — 82 D3 20 42N 77 2 E
Akonolinga, Cameroon — 101 E7 3 50N 12 18 E
Akordat, Ethiopia — 95 D4 15 30N 37 40 E
Akosombo Dam, Ghana — 101 D5 6 20N 0 5 E
Akot, India — 82 D3 21 10N 77 10 E
Akot, Sudan — 95 F3 6 31N 30 9 E
Akpatok I., Canada — 127 B13 60 25N 68 8W
Akranes, Iceland — 12 D3 64 19N 21 58W
Akreïjit, Mauritania — 100 B3 18 19N 9 11W
Akrítas Venétiko, Ákra, Greece — 45 H3 36 43N 21 54 E
Akron, Colo., U.S.A. — 138 E3 40 13N 103 15W
Akron, Ind., U.S.A. — 141 C10 41 2N 86 1W
Akron, Ohio, U.S.A. — 136 E3 41 7N 81 31W
Akrotiri, Cyprus — 32 E11 34 36N 32 57 E
Akrotíri, Ákra, Greece — 44 D7 40 26N 25 27 E
Akrotiri Bay, Cyprus — 32 E12 34 35N 33 10 E
Aksai Chih, India — 81 B8 35 15N 79 55 E
Aksaray, Turkey — 88 D6 38 25N 34 2 E
Aksarka, U.S.S.R. — 56 C7 66 31N 67 50 E
Aksay, U.S.S.R. — 54 F3 51 11N 53 0 E
Akşehir, Turkey — 88 D4 38 18N 31 30 E
Akşehir Gölü, Turkey — 88 D4 38 30N 31 25 E
Aksenovo Zilovskoye, U.S.S.R. — 57 D12 53 20N 117 40 E
Aksha, U.S.S.R. — 57 D12 50 17N 117 40 E
Akstafa, U.S.S.R. — 53 F11 41 7N 45 27 E
Aksu, China — 64 B3 41 5N 80 10 E
Aksu →, Turkey — 88 E4 36 41N 30 54 E
Aksuat, Ozero, U.S.S.R. — 54 F9 51 30N 64 34 E
Aksum, Ethiopia — 95 E4 14 5N 38 40 E
Aktash, R.S.F.S.R., U.S.S.R. — 54 D3 55 2N 52 7 E
Aktash, Uzbek S.S.R., U.S.S.R. — 55 D2 39 55N 65 55 E
Aktogay, Kazakh S.S.R., U.S.S.R. — 55 A8 44 25N 76 44 E
Aktogay, Kazakh S.S.R., U.S.S.R. — 56 E8 46 57N 79 40 E
Aktyubinsk, U.S.S.R. — 49 D10 50 17N 57 10 E
Aktyuz, U.S.S.R. — 55 B8 42 54N 76 7 E
Aku, Nigeria — 101 D6 6 40N 7 18 E
Akula, Zaïre — 102 B4 2 22N 20 12 E
Akune, Japan — 62 E2 32 1N 130 12 E
Akure, Nigeria — 101 D6 7 15N 5 5 E
Akureyri, Iceland — 12 D4 65 40N 18 6W
Akuseki-Shima, Japan — 61 K4 29 27N 129 37 E
Akusha, U.S.S.R. — 53 E12 42 18N 47 30 E
Akwa-Ibom □, Nigeria — 101 E6 4 30N 7 30 E
Akyab = Sittwe, Burma — 78 E4 20 18N 92 45 E
Akyazı, Turkey — 88 C4 40 40N 30 38 E
Al Abyār, Libya — 96 B4 32 9N 20 29 E
Al 'Adan, Yemen — 86 D4 12 45N 45 0 E
Al Aḥsā, Si. Arabia — 85 E6 25 50N 49 0 E
Al Ajfar, Si. Arabia — 84 E4 27 26N 43 0 E

Al Amādīyah, Iraq — 84 B4 37 5N 43 30 E
Al Amārah, Iraq — 84 D5 31 55N 47 15 E
Al 'Aqabah, Jordan — 91 F4 29 31N 35 0 E
Al Aqīq, Si. Arabia — 86 B3 20 39N 41 25 E
Al Arak, Syria — 84 C3 34 38N 38 35 E
Al 'Aramah, Si. Arabia — 84 E5 25 30N 46 0 E
Al 'Arīḍah, Si. Arabia — 86 C3 17 3N 43 5 E
Al Arṭāwīyah, Si. Arabia — 84 E5 26 31N 45 20 E
Al Ashkhara, Oman — 87 C6 21 50N 59 30 E
Al 'Āṣimah □, Jordan — 91 D5 31 40N 36 30 E
Al 'Aṣṣāfīyah, Si. Arabia — 84 D3 28 17N 38 59 E
Al 'Ayn, Oman — 85 E7 24 15N 55 45 E
Al 'Ayn, Si. Arabia — 84 E3 25 4N 38 6 E
Al 'Azamīyah, Iraq — 84 C5 32 54N 45 4 E
Al 'Azīzīyah, Iraq — 84 C5 32 54N 45 4 E
Al 'Azīzīyah, Libya — 96 B2 32 30N 13 1 E
Al Bāb, Syria — 84 B3 36 23N 37 29 E
Al Bad', Si. Arabia — 84 D2 28 28N 35 1 E
Al Bādī, Iraq — 84 C4 35 56N 41 32 E
Al Badī', Si. Arabia — 86 B4 20 0N 46 35 E
Al Baḥrah, Kuwait — 84 D5 29 40N 47 52 E
Al Balqā' □, Jordan — 91 C4 32 5N 35 45 E
Al Barkāt, Libya — 96 D2 24 56N 10 14 E
Al Bārūk, J., Lebanon — 91 B4 33 39N 35 40 E
Al Baṣrah, Iraq — 84 D5 30 30N 47 50 E
Al Baṭḥā, Iraq — 84 D5 31 6N 45 53 E
Al Batrūn, Lebanon — 91 A4 34 15N 35 40 E
Al Bayāḍ, Si. Arabia — 86 B4 22 0N 47 0 E
Al Bayḍā', Yemen — 86 D4 14 5N 45 42 E
Al Bayḍā, Libya — 96 B4 32 0N 21 30 E
Al Bi'ār, Si. Arabia — 86 B2 22 39N 39 40 E
Al Bir, Si. Arabia — 84 D3 28 51N 36 16 E
Al Birk, Si. Arabia — 86 C3 18 13N 41 33 E
Al Bu'ayrāt, Libya — 96 B3 31 24N 15 44 E
Al Buraymī, Syria — 91 A5 34 15N 36 46 E
Al Fallūjah, Iraq — 84 C4 33 20N 43 55 E
Al Fatk, Yemen — 87 C6 16 31N 52 41 E
Al Fāw, Iraq — 85 D6 30 0N 48 30 E
Al Faydamī, Yemen — 87 C6 16 25N 52 26 E
Al Fujayrah, U.A.E. — 85 E8 25 7N 56 18 E
Al Ghadaf, W. →, Jordan — 91 D5 31 26N 36 43 E
Al Ghammās, Iraq — 84 D5 31 45N 44 37 E
Al Gharīb, Libya — 96 A2 32 35N 21 11 E
Al Ghaydah, Yemen — 87 C6 16 13N 52 11 E
Al Ghaydah, Yemen — 87 D5 14 55N 50 0 E
Al Ghayl, Yemen — 87 D5 15 30N 50 54 E
Al Hābah, Si. Arabia — 84 E5 27 10N 47 0 E
Al Ḥadd, Oman — 87 C6 22 32N 59 48 E
Al Ḥaddār, Si. Arabia — 86 B4 21 58N 45 57 E
Al Ḥadīthah, Iraq — 84 C4 34 0N 41 13 E
Al Ḥadīthah, Si. Arabia — 84 D3 31 28N 37 8 E
Al Ḥājānah, Syria — 91 B5 33 18N 36 6 E
Al Ḥajarayn, Yemen — 87 D5 15 29N 48 20 E
Al Ḥallānīyah, Oman — 87 C7 17 30N 56 1 E
Al Ḥāmad, Syria — 84 C3 31 30N 39 30 E
Al Ḥamar, Si. Arabia — 86 B4 22 26N 46 12 E
Al Ḥamdānīyah, Syria — 84 C3 35 25N 36 50 E
Al Ḥamidīyah, Syria — 91 A4 34 42N 35 57 E
Al Ḥammādah al Ḥamrā', Libya — 96 C2 29 30N 12 0 E
Al Ḥammar, Iraq — 84 D5 30 57N 46 51 E
Al Ḥamrā', Si. Arabia — 86 A2 24 2N 38 55 E
Al Ḥarīq, Si. Arabia — 86 B4 23 29N 46 27 E
Al Ḥarīr, W. →, Syria — 91 C4 32 44N 35 59 E
Al Ḥarūj al Aswad, Libya — 96 C3 27 0N 17 10 E
Al Ḥasā, Jordan — 91 D4 31 4N 35 29 E
Al Ḥasakah, Syria — 84 B4 36 35N 40 45 E
Al Ḥawrah, Yemen — 86 D4 13 50N 47 35 E
Al Ḥawṭah, Yemen — 87 D4 14 23N 47 24 E
Al Ḥawṭah □, Si. Arabia — 86 B4 23 30N 47 0 E
Al Ḥaydān, W. →, Jordan — 91 D4 31 29N 35 34 E
Al Ḥayy, Iraq — 84 C5 32 5N 46 5 E
Al Ḥijāz, Si. Arabia — 86 A2 26 0N 37 30 E
Al Ḥillah, Iraq — 84 C5 32 30N 44 25 E
Al Ḥillah, Si. Arabia — 86 B4 23 35N 46 50 E
Al Ḥirmil, Lebanon — 91 A5 34 26N 36 24 E
Al Hoceïma, Morocco — 98 A4 35 8N 3 58W
Al Ḥudaydah, Yemen — 86 D3 14 50N 43 0 E
Al Ḥufrah, Awbārī, Libya — 96 C2 25 32N 14 1 E
Al Ḥufrah, Misrātah, Libya — 96 C3 29 5N 18 3 E
Al Ḥufūf, Si. Arabia — 85 E6 25 25N 49 45 E
Al Ḥulwah, Si. Arabia — 86 B4 23 24N 46 48 E
Al Ḥumaydah, Si. Arabia — 84 D2 29 14N 34 56 E
Al Ḥunayy, Si. Arabia — 85 E6 25 58N 48 45 E
Al Ḥuraydah, Yemen — 87 D5 15 36N 48 12 E
Al Ḥusayyāt, Libya — 96 B4 30 24N 20 37 E
Al Ḥūwah, Si. Arabia — 86 B4 23 2N 45 48 E
Al Ḥuwaymī, Yemen — 86 D4 13 23N 44 28 E
Al Irq, Libya — 96 C4 29 5N 21 35 E
Al 'Irqah, Yemen — 86 D4 13 39N 47 22 E
Al Īsāwīyah, Si. Arabia — 84 D3 30 43N 37 59 E
Al Ittiḥad = Madīnat ash Sha'b, Yemen — 86 D4 12 50N 45 0 E
Al Jabal al Akhḍar, Libya — 96 B4 32 0N 21 30 E
Al Jafr, Jordan — 91 E5 30 18N 36 14 E
Al Jaghbūb, Libya — 96 C5 29 42N 24 38 E
Al Jahrah, Kuwait — 84 D5 29 25N 47 40 E
Al Jalāmīd, Si. Arabia — 84 D3 31 20N 39 45 E
Al Jamalīyah, Qatar — 85 E6 25 37N 51 5 E
Al Janūb □, Lebanon — 91 B4 33 20N 35 20 E
Al Jawf, Libya — 96 D4 24 10N 23 24 E
Al Jawf, Si. Arabia — 84 D3 29 55N 39 40 E
Al Jazirah, Iraq — 84 C5 33 30N 44 0 E
Al Jazirah, Libya — 96 C4 26 10N 21 20 E
Al Jithāmīyah, Si. Arabia — 84 E4 27 41N 41 43 E
Al Jubayl, Si. Arabia — 85 E6 27 0N 49 50 E
Al Jubaylah, Si. Arabia — 84 E5 24 55N 46 25 E
Al Jubb, Si. Arabia — 84 E4 27 11N 42 17 E
Al Jumūm, Si. Arabia — 86 B2 21 37N 39 42 E
Al Junaynah, Sudan — 97 F4 13 27N 22 45 E
Al Kabā'ish, Iraq — 84 D5 30 58N 47 0 E
Al Kāmil, Oman — 87 B7 22 13N 59 12 E
Al Karak, Jordan — 91 D4 31 11N 35 42 E
Al Karak □, Jordan — 91 E5 31 0N 36 0 E
Al Kāzim Tyah, Iraq — 84 C5 33 22N 44 12 E
Al Khābūra, Oman — 87 B7 23 57N 57 5 E
Al Khalīl, Jordan — 91 D4 31 32N 35 6 E
Al Khamāsīn, Si. Arabia — 86 B4 20 29N 44 46 E

Ampasindava, Helodranon' 165

Alimnía, Greece 32 C9 36 16N 27 43 E
Alindao, C.A.R. 102 A4 5 2N 21 13 E
Alingsås, Sweden 15 G6 57 56N 12 31 E
Alipur, Pakistan 80 E4 29 25N 70 55 E
Alipur Duar, India 78 B2 26 30N 89 35 E
Aliquippa, U.S.A. 136 F4 40 38N 80 18W
Aliste →, Spain 36 D5 41 34N 5 58W
Alitus, U.S.S.R. 50 D4 54 24N 24 3 E
Alivérion, Greece 45 F6 38 24N 24 2 E
Aliwal North, S. Africa 104 E4 30 45 S 26 45 E
Alix, Canada 130 C6 52 24N 113 11W
Aljezur, Portugal 37 H2 37 18N 8 49W
Aljustrel, Portugal 37 H2 37 55N 8 10W
Alkamari, Niger 97 F2 13 27N 11 10 E
Alken, Belgium 21 G6 50 53N 5 18 E
Alkmaar, Neths. 20 C5 52 37N 4 45 E
All American Canal, U.S.A. 143 K6 32 45N 115 0W
Allada, Benin 101 D5 6 41N 2 9 E
Allah Dad, Pakistan 80 G2 25 38N 67 34 E
Allahabad, India 81 G9 25 25N 81 58 E
Allakh-Yun, U.S.S.R. 57 C14 60 50N 137 5 E
Allal Tazi, Morocco 98 B3 34 30N 6 20W
Allan, Canada 131 C7 51 53N 106 4W
Allanche, France 24 C6 45 14N 2 57 E
Allanmyo, Burma 78 F5 19 30N 95 17 E
Allanridge, S. Africa 104 D4 27 45 S 26 40 E
Allansford, Australia 116 E5 38 26 S 142 39 E
Allanton, N.Z. 119 F5 45 55 S 170 15 E
Allanwater, Canada 128 B1 50 14N 90 10W
Allaqi, Wadi →, Egypt 94 C3 23 7N 32 47 E
Allariz, Spain 36 C3 42 11N 7 50W
Allassac, France 24 C5 45 15N 1 29 E
Alle, Belgium 21 J5 49 51N 4 58 E
Allegan, U.S.A. 141 B11 42 32N 85 52W
Allegany, U.S.A. 136 D6 42 6N 78 30W
Allegheny →, U.S.A. 136 F5 40 27N 80 0W
Allegheny Plateau, U.S.A. 134 G6 38 0N 80 0W
Allegheny Res., U.S.A. 136 E6 42 0N 78 55W
Allègre, France 24 C7 45 12N 3 41 E
Allen, Argentina 160 A3 38 58 S 67 50W
Allen, L., Ireland 19 B3 54 12N 8 5W
Allende, Mexico 146 B4 28 20N 100 50W
Allentown, U.S.A. 137 F9 40 36N 75 30W
Allentsteig, Austria 30 C8 48 41N 15 20 E
Alleppey, India 83 K3 9 30N 76 28 E
Aller →, Germany 26 C5 52 57N 9 10 E
Alleur, Belgium 21 G7 50 39N 5 31 E
Allevard, France 25 C10 45 24N 6 5 E
Alliance, Surinam 153 B7 5 50N 54 50W
Alliance, Nebr., U.S.A. 138 D3 42 10N 102 50W
Alliance, Ohio, U.S.A. 136 F3 40 53N 81 7W
Allier □, France 24 B6 46 25N 2 40 E
Allier →, France 23 F10 46 57N 3 4 E
Allingåbro, Denmark 15 H4 56 28N 10 20 E
Allison, U.S.A. 140 B4 42 45N 92 48W
Alliston, Canada 128 D4 44 9N 79 52W
Alloa, U.K. 18 E5 56 7N 3 49W
Allora, Australia 115 D5 28 2 S 152 0 E
Allos, France 25 D10 44 15N 6 38 E
Alluitsup Paa = Sydprøven, Greenland 6 C5 60 30N 45 35W
Alma, Canada 129 C5 48 35N 71 40W
Alma, Ga., U.S.A. 135 K4 31 33N 82 28W
Alma, Kans., U.S.A. 138 F6 39 1N 96 22W
Alma, Mich., U.S.A. 134 D3 43 25N 84 40W
Alma, Nebr., U.S.A. 138 E5 40 10N 99 25W
Alma, Wis., U.S.A. 138 C9 44 19N 91 54W
Alma Ata, U.S.S.R. 55 B8 43 15N 76 57 E
Almada, Portugal 37 G1 38 40N 9 9W
Almaden, Australia 114 B3 17 22 S 144 40 E
Almadén, Spain 37 G6 38 49N 4 52W
Almagro, Spain 37 G7 38 50N 3 45W
Almalyk, U.S.S.R. 55 C4 40 50N 69 35 E
Almanor, L., U.S.A. 142 F3 40 15N 121 11W
Almansa, Spain 35 G3 38 51N 1 5W
Almanza, Spain 36 C5 42 39N 5 3W
Almanzor, Pico de, Spain 36 E5 40 15N 5 18W
Almanzora →, Spain 35 H3 37 14N 1 46W
Almas, Brazil 155 D2 11 33 S 47 9W
Almaş, Mţii., Romania 46 E3 44 49N 22 12 E
Almazán, Spain 34 D2 41 30N 2 30W
Almazora, Spain 34 F4 39 57N 0 3W
Almeirim, Brazil 153 D7 1 30 S 52 34W
Almeirim, Portugal 37 F2 39 12N 8 37W
Almelo, Neths. 20 D9 52 22N 6 42 E
Almenar, Spain 34 D2 41 43N 2 12W
Almenara, Brazil 155 E3 16 11 S 40 42W
Almenara, Spain 34 F4 39 46N 0 14W
Almenara, Sierra de, Spain 35 H3 37 34N 1 32W
Almendralejo, Spain 37 G4 38 41N 6 26W
Almería, Spain 35 J2 36 52N 2 27W
Almería □, Spain 35 H2 37 20N 2 20W
Almería, G. de, Spain 35 J2 36 41N 2 28W
Almetyevsk, U.S.S.R. 54 D3 54 53N 52 20 E
Almirante, Panama 148 E3 9 10N 82 30W
Almirante Montt, G., Chile 160 D2 51 52 S 72 50W
Almiropótamos, Greece 45 F6 38 16N 24 11 E
Almirós, Greece 45 E4 39 11N 22 45 E
Almiroú, Kólpos, Greece 32 D6 35 23N 24 20 E
Almodôvar, Portugal 37 H2 37 31N 8 2W
Almodóvar del Campo, Spain 37 G6 38 43N 4 10W
Almogia, Spain 37 J6 36 50N 4 32W
Almonaster la Real, Spain 37 H4 37 52N 6 48W
Almont, U.S.A. 136 D1 42 53N 83 2W
Almonte, Canada 137 A8 45 14N 76 12W
Almonte →, Spain 37 F4 39 41N 6 28W
Almora, India 81 E8 29 38N 79 40 E
Almoradi, Spain 35 G4 38 7N 0 46W
Almorox, Spain 36 E6 40 14N 4 24W
Almoustarat, Mali 101 B5 17 35N 0 8 E
Almuñécar, Spain 37 J7 36 43N 3 41W
Alnif, Morocco 98 B3 31 10N 5 8W
Alnwick, U.K. 16 B6 55 25N 1 42W
Aloi, Uganda 106 B3 2 16N 33 10 E
Alon, Burma 78 D5 22 12N 95 5 E
Alor, Indonesia 71 F6 8 15 S 124 30 E
Alor Setar, Malaysia 77 J3 6 7N 100 22 E
Alora, Spain 37 J6 36 49N 4 46W
Alosno, Spain 37 H3 37 33N 7 7W
Alotau, Papua N. G. 120 F6 10 16 S 150 30 E
Alougoum, Morocco 98 B3 30 17N 6 56W
Aloysius, Mt., Australia 113 E4 26 0 S 128 38 E
Alpaugh, U.S.A. 144 K7 35 53N 119 29W
Alpedrinha, Portugal 36 E3 40 6N 7 27W
Alpena, U.S.A. 134 C4 45 6N 83 24W
Alpercatas →, Brazil 154 C3 6 2 S 44 19W
Alpes-de-Haute-Provence □, France 25 D10 44 8N 6 10 E
Alpes-Maritimes □, France 25 E11 43 55N 7 10 E
Alpha, Australia 114 C4 23 39 S 146 37 E
Alpha, U.S.A. 140 C6 41 11N 90 23W
Alphen, Neths. 21 F5 51 29N 4 58 E
Alphen aan den Rijn, Neths. 20 D5 52 7N 4 40 E
Alphonse, Seychelles 109 E4 7 0 S 52 45 E
Alpiarça, Portugal 37 F2 39 15N 8 35W
Alpine, Ariz., U.S.A. 143 K9 33 57N 109 4W
Alpine, Calif., U.S.A. 145 N10 32 50N 116 46W
Alpine, Tex., U.S.A. 139 K3 30 25N 103 35W
Alpnach, Switz. 29 C6 46 57N 8 17 E
Alps, Europe 10 F7 46 30N 9 30 E
Alpu, Turkey 88 D4 39 46N 30 58 E
Alrø, Denmark 15 J4 55 52N 10 5 E
Alroy Downs, Australia 114 B2 19 20 S 136 5 E
Alsace, France 23 D14 48 15N 7 25 E
Alsask, Canada 131 C7 51 21N 109 59W
Alsásua, Spain 34 C2 42 54N 2 10W
Alsen, Sweden 14 A7 63 23N 13 56 E
Alsfeld, Germany 26 E5 50 44N 9 19 E
Alsónémedi, Hungary 31 D12 47 20N 19 15 E
Alsten, Norway 12 D12 65 58N 12 40 E
Alta, Norway 12 B17 69 57N 23 10 E
Alta, Sierra, Spain 34 E3 40 31N 1 30W
Alta Gracia, Argentina 158 C3 31 40 S 64 30W
Alta Lake, Canada 130 C4 50 10N 123 0W
Alta Sierra, U.S.A. 145 K8 35 42N 118 33W
Altaelva →, Norway 12 B17 69 46N 23 45 E
Altafjorden, Norway 12 A17 70 5N 23 5 E
Altagracia, Venezuela 152 A3 10 45N 71 30W
Altagracia de Orituco, Venezuela 152 B4 9 52N 66 23W
Altai = Aerhtai Shan, Mongolia 64 B4 46 40N 92 45 E
Altamachi →, Bolivia 156 D4 16 8 S 66 50W
Altamaha →, U.S.A. 135 K5 31 19N 81 17W
Altamira, Brazil 153 D7 3 12 S 52 10W
Altamira, Chile 158 B2 25 47 S 69 51W
Altamira, Colombia 152 C2 2 3N 75 47W
Altamira, Mexico 147 C5 22 24N 97 55W
Altamira, Cuevas de, Spain 36 B6 43 20N 4 5W
Altamont, Ill., U.S.A. 141 E8 39 4N 88 45W
Altamont, N.Y., U.S.A. 137 D10 42 43N 74 3W
Altamura, Italy 41 B9 40 50N 16 33 E
Altanbulag, Mongolia 64 A5 50 16N 106 30 E
Altar, Mexico 146 A2 30 40N 111 50W
Altata, Mexico 146 C3 24 30N 108 0W
Altavista, U.S.A. 134 G6 37 9N 79 22W
Altay, China 64 B3 47 48N 88 10 E
Altdorf, Switz. 29 C7 46 52N 8 36 E
Alte Mellum, Germany 26 B4 53 45N 8 6 E
Altea, Spain 35 G4 38 38N 0 2W
Altenberg, Germany 26 E9 50 46N 13 47 E
Altenbruch, Germany 26 B4 53 48N 8 44 E
Altenburg, Germany 26 E8 50 59N 12 28 E
Altenkirchen, Mecklenburg-Vorpommern, Germany 26 A9 54 38N 13 20 E
Altenkirchen, Rhld-Pfz., Germany 26 E3 50 41N 7 38 E
Altenmarkt, Austria 30 D7 47 43N 14 39 E
Altenteptow, Germany 26 B9 53 42N 13 15 E
Alter do Chão, Portugal 37 F3 39 12N 7 40W
Altıntas, Turkey 88 D4 39 4N 30 10 E
Altiplano, Bolivia 156 D4 17 0 S 68 0W
Altkirch, France 23 E14 47 37N 7 15 E
Altmühl →, Germany 27 G7 48 54N 11 54 E
Alto Adige = Trentino-Alto Adige □, Italy 38 B8 46 30N 11 0 E
Alto Araguaia, Brazil 157 D7 17 15 S 53 20W
Alto Cuchumatanes = Cuchumatanes, Sierra de los, Guatemala 148 C1 15 35N 91 25W
Alto Cuito, Angola 103 E3 13 27 S 18 49 E
Alto del Inca, Chile 158 A2 24 10 S 68 10W
Alto Garças, Brazil 157 D7 16 56 S 53 32W
Alto Iriri →, Brazil 157 B7 8 50 S 53 25W
Alto Ligonha, Mozam. 107 F4 15 30 S 38 11 E
Alto Molocue, Mozam. 107 F4 15 50 S 37 35 E
Alto Paraguai, Brazil 157 C6 14 30 S 56 31W
Alto Paraguay □, Paraguay 158 A4 21 0 S 58 30W
Alto Paraná □, Paraguay 159 B5 25 30 S 54 50W
Alto Parnaíba, Brazil 154 C2 9 6 S 45 57W
Alto Purús →, Peru 156 B3 9 12 S 70 28W
Alto Río Senguerr, Argentina 160 C2 45 2 S 70 50W
Alto Santo, Brazil 154 C4 5 31 S 38 15W
Alto Sucuriú, Brazil 157 D7 19 19 S 52 47W
Alto Turi, Brazil 154 B2 2 54 S 45 38W
Alton, Canada 136 C4 43 54N 80 5W
Alton, U.S.A. 140 F6 38 55N 90 5W
Alton Downs, Australia 115 D2 26 7 S 138 57 E
Altoona, Iowa, U.S.A. 140 C3 41 39N 93 28W
Altoona, Pa., U.S.A. 136 F6 40 32N 78 24W
Altopáscio, Italy 38 E7 43 50N 10 40 E
Altos, Brazil 154 C3 5 3 S 42 28W
Altötting, Germany 27 G8 48 14N 12 41 E
Altstätten, Switz. 29 B9 47 22N 9 33 E
Altūn Kūprī, Iraq 84 C5 35 45N 44 9 E
Altun Shan, China 64 C3 38 30N 88 0 E
Alturas, U.S.A. 142 F3 41 36N 120 37W
Altus, U.S.A. 139 H5 34 30N 99 25W
Alucra, Turkey 53 F8 40 22N 38 47 E
Aluksne, U.S.S.R. 50 C5 57 24N 27 3 E
Alùla, Somali Rep. 90 E5 11 50N 50 45 E
Alunite, U.S.A. 145 K12 35 59N 114 55W
Alupka, U.S.S.R. 52 D6 44 23N 34 2 E
Alushta, U.S.S.R. 52 D6 44 40N 34 25 E
Alusi, Indonesia 71 F8 7 35 S 131 40 E
Alustante, Spain 34 E3 40 36N 1 40W
Al'Uzayr, Iraq 84 D5 31 19N 47 25 E
Alva, U.S.A. 139 G5 36 50N 98 50W
Alvaiázere, Portugal 36 F2 39 49N 8 23W
Älvängen, Sweden 15 G6 57 58N 12 8 E
Alvarado, Mexico 147 D5 18 40N 95 50W
Alvarado, U.S.A. 139 J6 32 25N 97 15W
Alvarães, Brazil 153 D5 3 12 S 64 50W
Alvaro Obregón, Presa, Mexico 146 B3 27 55N 109 52W
Alvdal, Norway 14 B4 62 6N 10 37 E
Alvear, Argentina 158 B4 29 5 S 56 30W
Alverca, Portugal 37 G1 38 56N 9 1W
Alveringen, Belgium 21 F1 51 1N 2 43 E
Alvesta, Sweden 13 H13 56 54N 14 35 E
Alvie, Australia 116 E5 38 14 S 143 30 E
Alvin, U.S.A. 139 L7 29 23N 95 12W
Alvinston, Canada 136 D3 42 49N 81 52W
Alvito, Portugal 37 G3 38 15N 8 0W
Älvkarleby, Sweden 13 F14 60 34N 17 26 E
Alvros, Sweden 14 B8 62 3N 14 38 E
Älvsborgs län □, Sweden 15 F6 58 30N 12 30 E
Älvsbyn, Sweden 12 D16 65 40N 21 0 E
Alvsered, Sweden 15 G6 57 14N 12 51 E
Alwar, India 80 F7 27 38N 76 34 E
Alwaye, India 83 J3 10 8N 76 24 E
Alxa Zuoqi, China 66 E3 38 50N 105 40 E
Alyaskitovyy, U.S.S.R. 57 C15 64 45N 141 30 E
Alyata, U.S.S.R. 53 G13 39 58N 49 25 E
Alyth, U.K. 18 E5 56 38N 3 15W
Alzada, U.S.A. 138 C2 45 3N 104 22W
Alzano Lombardo, Italy 38 C6 45 44N 9 43 E
Alzette →, Lux. 21 J8 49 45N 6 6 E
Alzey, Germany 27 F4 49 48N 8 4 E
Am Dam, Chad 97 F4 12 40N 20 35 E
Am Géréda, Chad 97 F4 12 53N 21 14 E
Am-Timan, Chad 97 F4 11 0N 20 10 E
Amacuro □, Venezuela 153 B5 8 50N 61 5W
Amadeus, L., Australia 113 D5 24 54 S 131 0 E
Amâdi, Sudan 95 F3 5 29N 30 25 E
Amadi, Zaïre 106 B2 3 40N 26 40 E
Amadjuak, Canada 127 B12 64 0N 72 39W
Amadjuak L., Canada 127 B12 65 0N 71 8W
Amadora, Portugal 37 G1 38 45N 9 13W
Amagasaki, Japan 63 C7 34 42N 135 20 E
Amager, Denmark 15 J6 55 37N 12 35 E
Amagi, Japan 62 D2 33 25N 130 39 E
Amahai, Indonesia 73 B3 3 20 S 128 55 E
Amaimon, Papua N. G. 120 C3 5 12 S 145 30 E
Amakusa-Nada, Japan 62 E2 32 35N 130 5 E
Amakusa-Shotō, Japan 62 E2 32 15N 130 10 E
Amalapuram, India 83 F5 16 35N 81 55 E
Amalfi, Colombia 152 B2 6 55N 75 4W
Amalfi, Italy 41 B7 40 39N 14 34 E
Amaliás, Greece 45 G3 37 47N 21 22 E
Amalner, India 82 D2 21 5N 75 5 E
Amambaí, Brazil 159 A4 23 5 S 55 13W
Amambaí →, Brazil 159 A5 23 22 S 53 56W
Amambay □, Paraguay 159 A4 23 0 S 56 0W
Amambay, Cordillera de, S. Amer. 159 A4 23 0 S 55 45W
Amami-Guntō, Japan 61 L4 27 16N 129 21 E
Amami-Ō-Shima, Japan 61 L4 28 0N 129 0 E
Amana →, Venezuela 153 B5 9 45N 62 39W
Amaná, L., Brazil 153 D5 2 35 S 64 40W
Amanab, Papua N. G. 120 B1 3 40 S 141 14 E
Amanda Park, U.S.A. 144 C3 47 28N 123 55W
Amándola, Italy 39 F10 42 59N 13 21 E
Amangeldy, U.S.S.R. 56 D7 50 10N 65 10 E
Amantea, Italy 41 C9 39 8N 16 3 E
Amapá, Brazil 153 C7 2 5N 50 50W
Amapá □, Brazil 153 C7 1 40N 52 0W
Amapari, Brazil 153 C7 0 37N 51 39W
Amara, Sudan 95 E3 10 25N 34 10 E
Amarante, Brazil 154 C3 6 14 S 42 50W
Amarante, Portugal 36 D2 41 16N 8 5W
Amarante do Maranhão, Brazil 154 C2 5 36 S 46 45W
Amaranth, Canada 131 C9 50 36N 98 43W
Amarapura, Burma 78 E6 21 54N 96 3 E
Amaravati →, India 83 J4 11 0N 78 15 E
Amareleja, Portugal 37 G3 38 12N 7 13W
Amargosa, Brazil 155 D4 13 2 S 39 36W
Amargosa →, U.S.A. 145 J10 36 14N 116 51W
Amargosa Ra., U.S.A. 145 J10 36 25N 116 40W
Amári, Greece 32 D6 35 13N 24 40 E
Amarillo, U.S.A. 139 H4 35 14N 101 46W
Amarnath, India 82 E1 19 12N 73 22 E
Amaro, Mt., Italy 39 F11 42 5N 14 6 E
Amaro Leite, Brazil 155 D2 13 58 S 49 9W
Amarpur, India 81 G12 25 5N 87 0 E
Amasra, Turkey 88 C5 41 45N 32 23 E
Amassama, Nigeria 101 D6 5 1N 6 2 E
Amasya, Turkey 88 C6 40 40N 35 50 E
Amasya □, Turkey 88 C6 40 40N 35 50 E
Amataurá, Brazil 152 D4 3 29 S 68 6W
Amatikulu, S. Africa 105 D5 29 3 S 31 33 E
Amatitlán, Guatemala 148 D1 14 29N 90 38W
Amatrice, Italy 39 F10 42 38N 13 16 E
Amay, Belgium 21 G6 50 33N 5 19 E
Amazon = Amazonas →, S. Amer. 153 D8 0 5 S 50 0W
Amazonas □, Brazil 157 B5 5 0 S 65 0W
Amazonas □, Peru 156 B2 5 0 S 78 0W
Amazonas □, Venezuela 152 C4 3 30N 66 0W
Amazonas →, S. Amer. 153 D8 0 5 S 50 0W
Ambad, India 82 E2 19 38N 75 50 E
Ambahakily, Madag. 105 C7 21 36 S 43 41 E
Ambala, India 80 D7 30 23N 76 56 E
Ambalangoda, Sri Lanka 83 L5 6 15N 80 5 E
Ambalapulai, India 83 K3 9 25N 76 25 E
Ambalavao, Madag. 105 C8 21 50 S 46 56 E
Ambalindum, Australia 114 C2 23 23 S 135 0 E
Ambam, Cameroon 102 B2 2 20N 11 15 E
Ambanja, Madag. 105 A8 13 40 S 48 27 E
Ambarchik, U.S.S.R. 57 C17 69 40N 162 20 E
Ambarijeby, Madag. 105 A8 14 56 S 47 41 E
Ambaro, Helodranon', Madag. 105 A8 13 23 S 48 38 E
Ambartsevo, U.S.S.R. 56 D9 57 30N 83 52 E
Ambasamudram, India 83 K3 8 43N 77 25 E
Ambato, Ecuador 152 D2 1 5 S 78 42W
Ambato, Sierra de, Argentina 158 B2 28 25 S 66 10W
Ambato Boeny, Madag. 105 B8 16 28 S 46 43 E
Ambatofinandrahana, Madag. 105 C8 20 33 S 46 48 E
Ambatolampy, Madag. 105 B8 19 20 S 47 35 E
Ambatondrazaka, Madag. 105 B8 17 55 S 48 28 E
Ambatosoratra, Madag. 105 B8 17 37 S 48 31 E
Ambenja, Madag. 105 B8 15 17 S 46 58 E
Amberg, Germany 27 F7 49 25N 11 52 E
Ambergris Cay, Belize 147 D7 18 0N 88 0W
Ambérieu-en-Bugey, France 25 C9 45 57N 5 20 E
Amberley, N.Z. 119 D7 43 9 S 172 44 E
Ambert, France 24 C7 45 33N 3 44 E
Ambidédi, Mali 100 C2 14 35N 11 47W
Ambikapur, India 81 H10 23 15N 83 15 E
Ambikol, Sudan 94 C3 21 20N 30 50 E
Ambilobé, Madag. 105 A8 13 10 S 49 3 E
Ambinanindrano, Madag. 105 C8 20 5 S 48 23 E
Ambjörnarp, Sweden 15 G7 57 25N 13 17 E
Ambleside, U.K. 16 C5 54 26N 2 58W
Amblève, Belgium 21 H8 50 21N 6 10 E
Amblève →, Belgium 21 H7 50 25N 5 45 E
Ambo, Ethiopia 95 E4 12 20N 37 30 E
Ambo, Peru 156 C2 10 5 S 76 10W
Ambodifototra, Madag. 105 B8 16 59 S 49 52 E
Ambodilazana, Madag. 105 B8 18 6 S 49 10 E
Ambohimahasoa, Madag. 105 C8 21 7 S 47 13 E
Ambohimanga, Madag. 105 C8 20 52 S 47 36 E
Ambohitra, Madag. 105 A8 12 30 S 49 10 E
Ambon, Indonesia 71 E7 3 35 S 128 20 E
Ambon, Indonesia 72 B3 3 43 S 128 12 E
Amboseli L., Kenya 106 C4 2 40 S 37 10 E
Ambositra, Madag. 105 C8 20 31 S 47 25 E
Ambovombé, Madag. 105 D8 25 11 S 46 5 E
Amboy, Calif., U.S.A. 145 L11 34 33N 115 51W
Amboy, Ill., U.S.A. 140 C7 41 44N 89 20W
Amboyna I., S. China Sea 70 C4 7 50N 112 50 E
Ambridge, U.S.A. 136 F4 40 36N 80 15W
Ambriz, Angola 103 D2 7 48 S 13 8 E
Ambunti, Papua N. G. 120 C2 4 13 S 142 52 E
Ambur, India 83 H4 12 48N 78 43 E
Amby, Australia 115 D4 26 30 S 148 11 E
Amchitka I., U.S.A. 126 C1 51 30N 179 0 E
Amderma, U.S.S.R. 56 C7 69 45N 61 30 E
Ameca, Mexico 146 C4 20 30N 104 0W
Ameca →, Mexico 146 C3 20 40N 105 15W
Amecameca, Mexico 147 D5 19 7N 98 46W
Ameland, Neths. 20 B7 53 27N 5 45 E
Amélia, Italy 39 F9 42 34N 12 25 E
Amélie-les-Bains-Palalda, France 24 F6 42 29N 2 41 E
Amen, U.S.S.R. 57 C19 68 45N 180 0 E
Amendolaro, Italy 41 C9 39 58N 16 34 E
America, Neths. 21 F7 51 27N 5 59 E
American Falls, U.S.A. 142 E7 42 46N 112 56W
American Falls Res., U.S.A. 142 E7 43 0N 112 50W
American Highland, Antarctica 7 D6 73 0 S 75 0 E
American Samoa ■, Pac. Oc. 121 X24 14 20 S 170 40W
Americana, Brazil 159 A6 22 45 S 47 20W
Americus, U.S.A. 135 K3 32 0N 84 10W
Amersfoort, Neths. 20 D6 52 9N 5 23 E
Amersfoort, S. Africa 105 D4 26 59 S 29 53 E
Amery, Australia 113 F2 31 9 S 117 5 E
Amery, Canada 131 B10 56 34N 94 3W
Amery Ice Shelf, Antarctica 7 C6 69 30 S 72 0 E
Ames, U.S.A. 140 C3 42 0N 93 40W
Amesbury, U.S.A. 137 D14 42 50N 70 52W
Amfíklia, Greece 45 F4 38 38N 22 35 E
Amfilokhía, Greece 45 F3 38 52N 21 9 E
Amfípolis, Greece 44 D5 40 48N 23 52 E
Ámfissa, Greece 45 F4 38 32N 22 22 E
Amga, U.S.S.R. 57 C14 60 50N 132 0 E
Amga →, U.S.S.R. 57 C14 62 38N 134 32 E
Amgu, U.S.S.R. 57 E14 45 45N 137 15 E
Amgun →, U.S.S.R. 57 D14 52 56N 139 38 E
Amherst, Canada 129 C7 45 48N 64 8W
Amherst, Mass., U.S.A. 137 D12 42 21N 72 30W
Amherst, N.Y., U.S.A. 136 D6 42 59N 78 48W
Amherst, Ohio, U.S.A. 136 E2 41 23N 82 15W
Amherst, Tex., U.S.A. 139 J3 34 0N 102 24W
Amherst I., Canada 137 B8 44 8N 76 43W
Amherstburg, Canada 128 D3 42 6N 83 6W
Amiata, Mte., Italy 39 F8 42 54N 11 40 E
Amiens, France 23 C9 49 54N 2 16 E
Amigdhalokefáli, Greece 45 J5 35 23N 23 30 E
Amili, India 78 A5 28 25N 95 52 E
Amindaion, Greece 44 D3 40 42N 21 42 E
Amīrābād, Iran 84 C5 33 20N 46 16 E
Amirante Is., Seychelles 109 E4 6 0 S 53 0 E
Amisk L., Canada 131 C8 54 35N 102 15W
Amistad, Presa de la, Mexico 146 B4 29 24N 101 0W
Amite, U.S.A. 139 K9 30 47N 90 31W
Amizmiz, Morocco 98 B3 31 12N 8 15W
Åmli, Norway 15 F2 58 45N 8 32 E
Amlwch, U.K. 16 D3 53 24N 4 21W
Amm Adam, Sudan 95 D4 16 20N 36 1 E
'Ammān, Jordan 91 D4 31 57N 35 52 E
Ammanford, U.K. 17 F3 51 48N 4 4W
Ammassalik = Angmagssalik, Greenland 6 C6 65 40N 37 20W
Ammerån, Sweden 14 A10 63 9N 16 13 E
Ammerån →, Sweden 14 A10 63 9N 16 13 E
Ammersee, Germany 27 H7 48 0N 11 7 E
Ammerzoden, Neths. 20 E6 51 45N 5 13 E
Amnat Charoen, Thailand 76 E5 15 51N 104 38 E
Amo Jiang →, China 68 F3 23 0N 101 50 E
Āmol, Iran 85 B7 36 23N 52 20 E
Amorebieta, Spain 34 B2 43 13N 2 44W
Amoret, U.S.A. 140 F2 38 15N 94 35W
Amorgós, Greece 45 H7 36 50N 25 57 E
Amory, U.S.A. 135 J1 33 59N 88 29W
Amos, Canada 128 C4 48 35N 78 5W
Åmot, Buskerud, Norway 14 E3 59 54N 9 54 E
Åmot, Telemark, Norway 14 E2 59 34N 8 0 E
Åmotsdal, Norway 14 E2 59 37N 8 26 E
Amour, Djebel, Algeria 99 B5 33 42N 1 37 E
Amoy = Xiamen, China 69 E12 24 25N 118 4 E
Ampang, Malaysia 77 L3 3 8N 101 45 E
Ampanihy, Madag. 105 C7 24 40 S 44 45 E
Ampasindava, Helodranon', Madag. 105 A8 13 40 S 48 15 E

166 Ampasindava, Saikanosy

Ampasindava, Saikanosy, *Madag.* **105 A8** 13 42 S 47 55 E
Ampato, Nevado, *Peru* **156 D3** 15 40 S 71 56W
Ampenan, *Indonesia* **70 F5** 8 35 S 116 13 E
Amper, *Nigeria* **101 D6** 9 25N 9 40 E
Amper →, *Germany* **27 G7** 48 30N 11 57 E
Ampère, *Algeria* **99 A6** 35 44N 5 27 E
Ampezzo, *Italy* **39 B9** 46 25N 12 48 E
Amposta, *Spain* **34 E5** 40 43N 0 34 E
Ampotaka, *Madag.* **105 D7** 25 3 S 44 41 E
Ampoza, *Madag.* **105 C7** 22 20 S 44 44 E
Amqui, *Canada* **129 C6** 48 28N 67 27W
'Amrān, *Yemen* **86 D3** 15 41N 43 55 E
Amravati, *India* **82 D3** 20 55N 77 45 E
Amreli, *India* **80 J4** 21 35N 71 17 E
Amrenene el Kasba, *Algeria* **99 D5** 22 10N 0 30 E
Amriswil, *Switz.* **29 A8** 47 33N 9 18 E
Amritsar, *India* **80 D6** 31 35N 74 57 E
Amroha, *India* **81 E8** 28 53N 78 30 E
Amrum, *Germany* **26 A4** 54 37N 8 21 E
Amsel, *Algeria* **99 D6** 22 47N 5 29 E
Amsterdam, *Neths.* **20 D5** 52 23N 4 54 E
Amsterdam, *U.S.A.* **137 D10** 42 58N 74 10W
Amsterdam, I., *Ind. Oc.* **109 H6** 38 30 S 77 30 E
Amstetten, *Austria* **30 C7** 48 7N 14 51 E
Amudarya →, *U.S.S.R.* **56 E6** 43 40N 59 0 E
Amundsen Gulf, *Canada* **126 A7** 71 0N 124 0W
Amundsen Sea, *Antarctica* **7 D15** 72 0 S 115 0W
Amuntai, *Indonesia* **70 E5** 2 28 S 115 25 E
Amur, *Somali Rep.* **108 C3** 5 16N 46 30 E
Amur →, *U.S.S.R.* **57 D15** 52 56N 141 10 E
Amurang, *Indonesia* **71 D6** 1 5N 124 40 E
Amuri Pass, *N.Z.* **119 C7** 42 31 S 172 11 E
Amurrio, *Spain* **34 B2** 43 3N 3 0W
Amursk, *U.S.S.R.* **57 D14** 50 14N 136 54 E
Amurzet, *U.S.S.R.* **57 E14** 47 50N 131 5 E
Amusco, *Spain* **36 C6** 42 10N 4 28W
Amvrakikós Kólpos, *Greece* **45 F2** 39 0N 20 55 E
Amvrosiyevka, *U.S.S.R.* **53 C8** 47 43N 38 30 E
Amzeglouf, *Algeria* **99 C5** 26 50N 0 1 E
An, *Burma* **78 F5** 19 48N 94 0 E
An Bien, *Vietnam* **77 H5** 9 45N 105 0 E
An Hoa, *Vietnam* **76 E7** 15 40N 108 5 E
An Khe, *Vietnam* **76 F7** 13 57N 108 39 E
An Nabatīyah at Tahta, *Lebanon* **91 B4** 33 23N 35 27 E
An Nabk, *Si. Arabia* **84 D3** 31 20N 37 20 E
An Nabk, *Syria* **91 A5** 34 2N 36 44 E
An Nabk Abū Qaṣr, *Si. Arabia* **84 D3** 30 21N 38 34 E
An Nafūd, *Si. Arabia* **84 D4** 28 15N 41 0 E
An Najaf, *Iraq* **84 C5** 32 3N 44 15 E
An Nāṣirīyah, *Iraq* **84 D5** 31 0N 46 15 E
An Nawfalīyah, *Libya* **96 B3** 30 54N 17 58 E
An Nhon, *Vietnam* **76 F7** 13 55N 109 7 E
An Nîl □, *Sudan* **94 D3** 19 30N 33 0 E
An Nîl el Abyad □, *Sudan* **95 E3** 14 0N 32 15 E
An Nîl el Azraq □, *Sudan* **95 E3** 12 30N 34 30 E
An Nimāṣ, *Si. Arabia* **86 C3** 19 7N 42 8 E
An Nu'ayrīyah, *Si. Arabia* **85 E6** 27 30N 48 30 E
An Nuwayb'ī, W. →, *Si. Arabia* **91 F3** 29 18N 34 57 E
An Thoi, Dao, *Vietnam* **77 H5** 9 58N 104 0 E
An Uaimh, *Ireland* **19 C5** 53 39N 6 40W
Anabar →, *U.S.S.R.* **57 B12** 73 8N 113 36 E
Anabuki, *Japan* **62 C6** 34 2N 134 11 E
Anaco, *Venezuela* **153 B5** 9 27N 64 28W
Anaconda, *U.S.A.* **142 C7** 46 7N 113 0W
Anacortes, *U.S.A.* **144 B4** 48 30N 122 40W
Anadarko, *U.S.A.* **139 H5** 35 4N 98 15W
Anadia, *Brazil* **154 C4** 9 42 S 36 18W
Anadia, *Portugal* **36 E2** 40 26N 8 27W
Anadolu, *Turkey* **88 D4** 39 0N 30 0 E
Anadyr, *U.S.S.R.* **57 C18** 64 35N 177 20 E
Anadyr →, *U.S.S.R.* **57 C18** 64 55N 176 5 E
Anadyrskiy Zaliv, *U.S.S.R.* **57 C19** 64 0N 180 0 E
Anáfi, *Greece* **45 H7** 36 22N 25 48 E
Anafópoulo, *Greece* **45 H7** 36 17N 25 50 E
Anaga, Pta. de, *Canary Is.* **33 F3** 28 34N 16 9W
Anagni, *Italy* **40 A6** 41 44N 13 8 E
'Ānah, *Iraq* **84 C4** 34 25N 42 0 E
Anaheim, *U.S.A.* **145 M9** 33 50N 118 0W
Anahim Lake, *Canada* **130 C3** 52 28N 125 18W
Anáhuac, *Mexico* **146 B4** 27 14N 100 9W
Anai Mudi, Mt., *India* **83 J3** 10 12N 77 4 E
Anaimalai Hills, *India* **83 J3** 10 20N 76 40 E
Anajás, *Brazil* **154 B2** 0 59 S 49 57W
Anajatuba, *Brazil* **154 B3** 3 16 S 44 37W
Anakapalle, *India* **82 F6** 17 42N 83 6 E
Anakie, *Australia* **114 C4** 23 32 S 147 45 E
Anaklia, *U.S.S.R.* **53 E9** 42 22N 41 35 E
Analalava, *Madag.* **105 A8** 14 35 S 48 0 E
Análipsis, *Greece* **32 A3** 39 36N 19 55 E
Anamã, *Brazil* **153 D5** 3 35 S 61 22W
Anambar →, *Pakistan* **80 D3** 30 15N 68 50 E
Anambas, Kepulauan, *Indonesia* **70 D3** 3 20N 106 30 E
Anambas Is. = Anambas, Kepulauan, *Indonesia* **70 D3** 3 20N 106 30 E
Aname, *Vanuatu* **121 K7** 20 8 S 169 47 E
Anamoose, *U.S.A.* **138 B4** 47 55N 100 20W
Anamosa, *U.S.A.* **140 B5** 42 7N 91 30W
Anamur, *Turkey* **88 E5** 36 8N 32 58 E
Anamur Burnu, *Turkey* **88 E5** 36 2N 32 47 E
Anan, *Japan* **62 D6** 33 54N 134 40 E
Anand, *India* **80 H5** 22 32N 72 59 E
Anandpur, *India* **82 D8** 21 16N 86 13 E
Anánes, *Greece* **45 H6** 36 33N 24 9 E
Anantapur, *India* **83 G3** 14 39N 77 42 E
Anantnag, *India* **81 C6** 33 45N 75 10 E
Ananyev, *U.S.S.R.* **52 C3** 47 44N 29 47 E
Anapa, *U.S.S.R.* **52 D7** 44 55N 37 25 E
Anapodháris →, *Greece* **32 E7** 34 59N 25 20 E
Anápolis, *Brazil* **155 E2** 16 15 S 48 50W
Anapu →, *Brazil* **153 D7** 1 53 S 50 53W
Anār, *Iran* **85 D7** 30 55N 55 13 E
Anār Darreh, *Afghan.* **79 B1** 32 46N 61 39 E
Anārak, *Iran* **85 C7** 33 25N 53 40 E
Anatolia = Anadolu, *Turkey* **88 D4** 39 0N 30 0 E
Anatone, *U.S.A.* **142 C5** 46 9N 117 4W
Anatsogno, *Madag.* **105 C7** 23 33 S 43 46 E
Añatuya, *Argentina* **158 B3** 28 20 S 62 50W
Anauá →, *Brazil* **153 C5** 0 58N 61 21W
Anaunethad L., *Canada* **131 A8** 60 55N 104 25W
Anavilhanas, Arquipélago das, *Brazil* **153 D5** 2 42 S 60 45W
Anaye, *Niger* **97 E2** 19 15N 12 50 E
Anbyŏn, *N. Korea* **67 E14** 39 1N 127 35 E
Ancash □, *Peru* **156 B2** 9 30 S 77 45W
Ancenis, *France* **22 E5** 47 21N 1 10W
Ancho, Canal, *Chile* **160 D2** 50 0 S 74 20W
Anchor Bay, *U.S.A.* **144 G3** 38 48N 123 34W
Anchorage, *U.S.A.* **126 B5** 61 10N 149 50W
Anci, *China* **66 E9** 39 20N 116 40 E
Ancohuma, Nevada, *Bolivia* **156 D4** 16 0 S 68 50W
Ancón, *Peru* **156 C2** 11 50 S 77 10W
Ancona, *Italy* **39 E10** 43 37N 13 30 E
Ancud, *Chile* **160 B2** 42 0 S 73 50W
Ancud, G. de, *Chile* **160 B2** 42 0 S 73 0W
Anda, *China* **65 B7** 46 24N 125 19 E
Andacollo, *Argentina* **158 D1** 37 10 S 70 42W
Andacollo, *Chile* **158 C1** 30 5 S 71 10W
Andado, *Australia* **114 D2** 25 25 S 135 15 E
Andahuaylas, *Peru* **156 C3** 13 40 S 73 25W
Andalgalá, *Argentina* **158 B2** 27 40 S 66 30W
Åndalsnes, *Norway* **14 B1** 62 35N 7 43 E
Andalucía □, *Spain* **37 H6** 37 35N 5 0W
Andalusia, *U.S.A.* **135 K2** 31 19N 86 30W
Andalusia □ = Andalucía □, *Spain* **37 H6** 37 35N 5 0W
Andaman Is., *Ind. Oc.* **58 H13** 12 30N 92 30 E
Andaman Sea, *Ind. Oc.* **70 B1** 13 0N 96 0 E
Andara, *Namibia* **104 B3** 18 2 S 21 9 E
Andaraí, *Brazil* **155 D3** 12 48 S 41 20W
Andeer, *Switz.* **29 C8** 46 36N 9 26 E
Andelfingen, *Switz.* **29 A7** 47 36N 8 41 E
Andelot, *France* **23 D12** 48 15N 5 18 E
Andenne, *Belgium* **21 H6** 50 28N 5 5 E
Andéranboukane, *Mali* **101 B5** 15 26N 3 2 E
Anderlecht, *Belgium* **21 G4** 50 50N 4 19 E
Anderlues, *Belgium* **21 H4** 50 25N 4 16 E
Andermatt, *Switz.* **29 C7** 46 38N 8 35 E
Andernach, *Germany* **26 E3** 50 24N 7 25 E
Andernos-les-Bains, *France* **24 D2** 44 44N 1 6W
Anderslöv, *Sweden* **15 J7** 55 26N 13 19 E
Anderson, *Calif., U.S.A.* **142 F2** 40 30N 122 19W
Anderson, *Ind., U.S.A.* **141 D11** 40 5N 85 40W
Anderson, *Mo., U.S.A.* **139 G7** 36 43N 94 29W
Anderson, *S.C., U.S.A.* **135 H4** 34 32N 82 40W
Anderson →, *Canada* **126 B7** 69 42N 129 0W
Anderson, Mt., *S. Africa* **105 D5** 25 5 S 30 42 E
Andes, *Colombia* **156 C2** 10 0 S 75 53W
Andes, Cord. de los, *S. Amer.* **156 E4** 20 0 S 68 0W
Andfjorden, *Norway* **12 B14** 69 10N 16 20 E
Andhra, L., *India* **82 E1** 18 54N 73 32 E
Andhra Pradesh □, *India* **83 F4** 18 0N 79 0 E
Andikíthira, *Greece* **45 J5** 35 52N 23 15 E
Andīmeshk, *Iran* **85 C6** 32 27N 48 21 E
Andímilos, *Greece* **45 H6** 36 47N 24 12 E
Andíparos, *Greece* **45 H7** 37 0N 25 3 E
Andípaxoi, *Greece* **45 E2** 39 9N 20 13 E
Andípsara, *Greece* **45 F7** 38 30N 25 29 E
Andírrion, *Greece* **45 F3** 38 24N 21 46 E
Andizhan, *U.S.S.R.* **55 C6** 41 10N 72 15 E
Andkhvoy, *Afghan.* **79 A2** 36 52N 65 8 E
Andoany, *Madag.* **105 A8** 13 25 S 48 16 E
Andoas, *Peru* **152 D2** 2 55 S 76 25W
Andol, *India* **82 F4** 17 51N 78 4 E
Andong, *S. Korea* **67 F15** 36 40N 128 43 E
Andongwei, *China* **67 G10** 35 6N 119 20 E
Andorra ■, *Europe* **34 C6** 42 30N 1 30 E
Andorra La Vella, *Andorra* **34 C6** 42 31N 1 32 E
Andover, *U.K.* **17 F6** 51 13N 1 29W
Andover, *Mass., U.S.A.* **137 D13** 42 40N 71 8W
Andover, *N.Y., U.S.A.* **136 D7** 42 11N 77 48W
Andover, *Ohio, U.S.A.* **136 E4** 41 35N 80 35W
Andradina, *Brazil* **155 F1** 20 54 S 51 23W
Andrahary, Mt., *Madag.* **105 A8** 13 37 S 49 17 E
Andraitx, *Spain* **33 B9** 39 39N 2 25 E
Andramasina, *Madag.* **105 B8** 19 11 S 47 35 E
Andranopasy, *Madag.* **105 C7** 21 17 S 43 44 E
Andreanof Is., *U.S.A.* **126 C2** 52 0N 178 0W
Andreapol, *U.S.S.R.* **50 C8** 56 40N 32 17 E
Andrespol, *Poland* **47 D6** 51 45N 19 34 E
Andrewilla, *Australia* **115 D2** 26 31 S 139 17 E
Andrews, *S.C., U.S.A.* **135 J6** 33 29N 79 30W
Andrews, *Tex., U.S.A.* **139 J3** 32 18N 102 33W
Andreyevka, *U.S.S.R.* **54 E2** 52 19N 51 55 E
Ándria, *Italy* **41 A9** 41 13N 16 17 E
Andriba, *Madag.* **105 B8** 17 30 S 46 58 E
Andrijevica, *Yugoslavia* **42 E4** 42 45N 19 48 E
Andrítsaina, *Greece* **45 G3** 37 29N 21 52 E
Androka, *Madag.* **105 C7** 24 58 S 44 2 E
Andropov = Rybinsk, *U.S.S.R.* **51 B11** 58 5N 38 50 E
Ándros, *Greece* **45 G6** 37 50N 24 57 E
Andros I., *Bahamas* **148 B4** 24 30N 78 0W
Andros Town, *Bahamas* **148 B4** 24 43N 77 47W
Andrychów, *Poland* **31 B12** 49 51N 19 18 E
Andújar, *Spain* **37 G6** 38 3N 4 5W
Andulo, *Angola* **103 E3** 11 25 S 16 45 E
Anegada, B., *Argentina* **160 B4** 40 20 S 62 20W
Anegada I., *Virgin Is.* **149 C7** 18 45N 64 20W
Anegada Passage, *W. Indies* **149 C7** 18 15N 63 45W
Anécho, *Togo* **101 D5** 6 12N 1 34 E
Aneityum, *Vanuatu* **121 K7** 20 12 S 169 45 E
Añelo, *Argentina* **160 A3** 38 20 S 68 45W
Anergane, *Morocco* **98 B3** 31 4N 7 14W
Aneto, Pico de, *Spain* **34 C5** 42 37N 0 40 E
Añez, *Bolivia* **157 D5** 15 40 S 63 10W
Anfu, *China* **69 D10** 27 21N 114 40 E
Ang Thong, *Thailand* **76 E3** 14 35N 100 31 E
Angamos, Punta, *Chile* **158 A1** 23 1 S 70 32W
Angara →, *U.S.S.R.* **57 D10** 58 30N 97 0 E
Angarab, *Ethiopia* **95 E4** 13 11N 37 7 E
Angarsk, *U.S.S.R.* **57 D11** 52 30N 104 0 E
Angas Downs, *Australia* **113 E5** 25 2 S 132 14 E
Angas Hills, *Australia* **112 D4** 23 0 S 127 50 E
Angaston, *Australia* **116 C3** 34 30 S 139 8 E
Ånge, *Sweden* **14 B9** 62 31N 15 35 E
Ángel de la Guarda, I., *Mexico* **146 B2** 29 30N 113 30W
Angel Falls, *Venezuela* **153 B5** 5 57N 62 30W
Angeles, *Phil.* **71 A6** 15 9N 120 33 E
Ängelholm, *Sweden* **15 H6** 56 15N 12 58 E
Angellala, *Australia* **115 D4** 26 24 S 146 54 E
Angels Camp, *U.S.A.* **144 G6** 38 8N 120 30W
Anger →, *Ethiopia* **95 F4** 9 37N 36 6 E
Angereb →, *Ethiopia* **95 E4** 13 45N 36 40 E
Ångermanälven →, *Sweden* **14 B12** 62 40N 18 0 E
Angermünde, *Germany* **26 B10** 53 1N 14 0 E
Angers, *Canada* **137 A9** 45 31N 75 29W
Angers, *France* **22 E6** 47 30N 0 35W
Angerville, *France* **23 D9** 48 19N 2 0 E
Ängesån →, *Sweden* **12 C17** 66 50N 22 15 E
Anghiari, *Italy* **39 E9** 43 32N 12 3 E
Angical, *Brazil* **155 D3** 12 0 S 44 42W
Angikuni L., *Canada* **131 A9** 62 0N 100 0W
Angkor, *Cambodia* **76 F4** 13 22N 103 50 E
Anglem Mt., *N.Z.* **119 G2** 46 45 S 167 53 E
Anglés, *Spain* **34 D7** 41 57N 2 38 E
Anglesey, *U.K.* **16 D3** 53 17N 4 20W
Anglet, *France* **24 E2** 43 29N 1 31W
Angleton, *U.S.A.* **139 L7** 29 12N 95 23W
Angleur, *Belgium* **21 G7** 50 36N 5 35 E
Anglin →, *France* **24 B4** 46 42N 0 52 E
Anglisidhes, *Cyprus* **32 E12** 34 51N 33 27 E
Anglure, *France* **23 D10** 48 35N 3 50 E
Angmagssalik, *Greenland* **6 C6** 65 40N 37 20W
Ango, *Zaïre* **106 B2** 4 10N 26 5 E
Angoche, *Mozam.* **107 F4** 16 8 S 39 55 E
Angoche, I., *Mozam.* **107 F4** 16 20 S 39 50 E
Angol, *Chile* **158 D1** 37 56 S 72 45W
Angola, *Ind., U.S.A.* **141 C12** 41 40N 85 0W
Angola, *N.Y., U.S.A.* **136 D5** 42 38N 79 2W
Angola ■, *Africa* **103 E3** 12 0 S 18 0 E
Angoon, *U.S.A.* **130 B2** 57 40N 134 40W
Angoram, *Papua N. G.* **120 C3** 4 4 S 144 4 E
Angoulême, *France* **24 C4** 45 39N 0 10 E
Angoumois, *France* **24 C4** 45 50N 0 25 E
Angra dos Reis, *Brazil* **159 A7** 23 0 S 44 10W
Angren, *U.S.S.R.* **55 C5** 41 1N 70 12 E
Angtassom, *Cambodia* **77 G5** 11 1N 104 41 E
Angu, *Zaïre* **106 B1** 3 25N 24 28 E
Anguang, *China* **67 B12** 45 15N 123 45 E
Anguilla, *W. Indies* **149 C7** 18 14N 63 5W
Anguo, *China* **66 E8** 38 28N 115 15 E
Angurugu, *Australia* **114 A2** 14 0 S 136 25 E
Angus, Braes of, *U.K.* **18 E5** 56 51N 3 10W
Anhanduí →, *Brazil* **159 A5** 21 46 S 52 9W
Anhée, *Belgium* **21 H5** 50 18N 4 53 E
Anholt, *Denmark* **15 H5** 56 42N 11 33 E
Anhua, *China* **69 C8** 28 23N 111 12 E
Anhui □, *China* **69 B11** 32 0N 117 0 E
Anhwei □ = Anhui □, *China* **69 B11** 32 0N 117 0 E
Anichab, *Namibia* **104 C1** 21 0 S 14 46 E
Anicuns, *Brazil* **155 E2** 16 28 S 49 58W
Ánidhros, *Greece* **45 H7** 36 38N 25 43 E
Anie, *Togo* **101 D5** 7 42N 1 8 E
Animas, *U.S.A.* **143 L9** 31 58N 108 58W
Änimskog, *Sweden* **15 F6** 58 53N 12 35 E
Anina, *Romania* **42 B6** 45 6N 21 51 E
Anita, *U.S.A.* **140 C2** 41 27N 94 46W
Anivorano, *Madag.* **105 B8** 18 44 S 48 58 E
Aniwa, *Vanuatu* **121 J7** 19 17 S 169 35 E
Anjangaon, *India* **82 D3** 21 10N 77 20 E
Anjar, *India* **80 H4** 23 6N 70 10 E
Anjidiv I., *India* **83 G2** 14 40N 74 10 E
Anjō, *Japan* **63 C9** 34 57N 137 5 E
Anjou, *France* **22 E6** 47 20N 0 15W
Anjozorobe, *Madag.* **105 B8** 18 22 S 47 52 E
Anju, *N. Korea* **67 E13** 39 36N 125 40 E
Anka, *Nigeria* **101 C6** 12 13N 5 58 E
Ankaboa, Tanjona, *Madag.* **105 C7** 21 58 S 43 20 E
Ankang, *China* **66 H5** 32 40N 109 1 E
Ankara, *Turkey* **88 D5** 39 57N 32 54 E
Ankara □, *Turkey* **88 D5** 39 55N 32 50 E
Ankaramena, *Madag.* **105 C8** 21 57 S 46 39 E
Ankazoabo, *Madag.* **105 C7** 22 18 S 44 31 E
Ankazobe, *Madag.* **105 B8** 18 20 S 47 10 E
Ankeny, *U.S.A.* **140 C3** 41 44N 93 36W
Ankisabe, *Madag.* **105 B8** 19 17 S 46 29 E
Anklam, *Germany* **26 B9** 53 48N 13 40 E
Ankleshwar, *India* **82 D1** 21 38N 73 3 E
Ankober, *Ethiopia* **95 F4** 9 35N 39 40 E
Ankoro, *Zaïre* **106 D2** 6 45 S 26 55 E
Anlong, *China* **68 E5** 25 2N 105 27 E
Anlu, *China* **69 B9** 31 15N 113 45 E
Anmyŏn-do, *S. Korea* **67 F14** 36 25N 126 25 E
Ånn, *Sweden* **14 A6** 63 19N 12 34 E
Ann, C., *U.S.A.* **137 D14** 42 39N 70 37W
Ann Arbor, *U.S.A.* **141 B13** 42 17N 83 45W
Anna, *Ill., U.S.A.* **139 G10** 37 28N 89 10W
Anna, *Ohio, U.S.A.* **141 D12** 40 24N 84 11W
Anna, *U.S.S.R.* **51 F12** 51 28N 40 23 E
Anna Plains, *Australia* **112 C3** 19 17 S 121 37 E
Anna Regina, *Guyana* **153 B6** 7 10N 58 30W
Annaba, *Algeria* **99 A6** 36 50N 7 46 E
Annaberg-Buchholz, *Germany* **26 E8** 50 34N 12 58 E
Annaka, *Japan* **63 A10** 36 19N 138 54 E
Annalee →, *Ireland* **19 B4** 54 3N 7 15W
Annam = Trung-Phan, *Vietnam* **76 E7** 16 0N 108 0 E
Annamitique, Chaîne, *Asia* **76 D6** 17 0N 106 0 E
Annan, *U.K.* **18 G5** 54 57N 3 17W
Annan →, *U.K.* **18 G5** 54 58N 3 18W
Annanberg, *Papua N. G.* **120 C3** 4 52 S 144 42 E
Annapolis, *U.S.A.* **134 F7** 39 0N 76 30W
Annapolis Royal, *Canada* **129 D6** 44 44N 65 32W
Annapurna, *Nepal* **81 E10** 28 34N 83 50 E
Annean, L., *Australia* **113 E2** 26 54 S 118 14 E
Anneberg, *Sweden* **15 G6** 57 32N 12 6 E
Annecy, *France* **25 C10** 45 55N 6 8 E
Annecy, L. d', *France* **25 C10** 45 52N 6 10 E
Annemasse, *France* **25 B10** 46 12N 6 16 E
Anning, *China* **68 E4** 24 55N 102 26 E
Anningie, *Australia* **112 D5** 21 50 S 133 7 E
Anniston, *U.S.A.* **135 J3** 33 45N 85 50W
Annobón, *Atl. Oc.* **93 G4** 1 25 S 5 36 E
Annonay, *France* **25 C8** 45 15N 4 40 E
Annot, *France* **25 E10** 43 58N 6 38 E
Annotto Bay, *Jamaica* **148 C4** 18 17N 76 45W
Annuello, *Australia* **116 C5** 34 53 S 142 55 E
Annville, *U.S.A.* **137 F8** 40 18N 76 32W
Annweiler, *Germany* **27 F3** 49 12N 7 58 E
Áno Arkhánai, *Greece* **45 J7** 35 16N 25 11 E
Áno Porróia, *Greece* **44 C5** 41 17N 23 2 E
Áno Viánnos, *Greece* **32 D7** 35 2N 25 21 E
Anoano, *Solomon Is.* **121 M11** 8 59 S 160 46 E
Anoka, *U.S.A.* **138 C8** 45 10N 93 26W
Anorotsangana, *Madag.* **105 A8** 13 56 S 47 55 E
Anóyia, *Greece* **32 D6** 35 16N 24 52 E
Anping, *Hebei, China* **66 E8** 38 15N 115 30 E
Anping, *Liaoning, China* **67 D12** 41 5N 123 30 E
Anpu Gang, *China* **68 G7** 21 25N 109 50 E
Anqing, *China* **69 B11** 30 30N 117 3 E
Anqiu, *China* **67 F10** 36 25N 119 10 E
Anren, *China* **69 D9** 26 43N 113 18 E
Ans, *Belgium* **21 G7** 50 39N 5 32 E
Ansai, *China* **66 F5** 36 50N 109 20 E
Ansbach, *Germany* **27 F6** 49 17N 10 34 E
Anseba →, *Ethiopia* **95 D4** 16 0N 38 30 E
Anserma, *Colombia* **152 B2** 5 13N 75 48W
Anseroeul, *Belgium* **21 G3** 50 43N 3 32 E
Anshan, *China* **65 B7** 41 3N 122 58 E
Anshan, *Liaoning, China* **67 D12** 41 5N 122 58 E
Anshun, *China* **68 D5** 26 18N 105 57 E
Ansião, *Portugal* **36 F2** 39 56N 8 27W
Ansirabe, *Madag.* **105 B8** 19 55 S 47 2 E
Ansley, *U.S.A.* **138 E5** 41 19N 99 24W
Ansó, *Spain* **34 C4** 42 51N 0 48W
Anson, *U.S.A.* **139 J5** 32 46N 99 54W
Anson B., *Australia* **112 B5** 13 20 S 130 6 E
Ansongo, *Mali* **101 B5** 15 25N 0 35 E
Ansonia, *Conn., U.S.A.* **137 E11** 41 21N 73 6W
Ansonia, *Ohio, U.S.A.* **141 D12** 40 13N 84 38W
Anstruther, *U.K.* **18 E6** 56 14N 2 40W
Ansudu, *Indonesia* **71 E9** 2 11 S 139 22 E
Antabamba, *Peru* **156 C3** 14 40 S 73 0W
Antakya, *Turkey* **88 E7** 36 14N 36 10 E
Antalaha, *Madag.* **105 A9** 14 57 S 50 20 E
Antalya, *Turkey* **88 E4** 36 52N 30 45 E
Antalya □, *Turkey* **88 E4** 36 55N 30 45 E
Antalya Körfezi, *Turkey* **88 E4** 36 15N 31 30 E
Antananarivo, *Madag.* **105 B8** 18 55 S 47 31 E
Antananarivo □, *Madag.* **105 B8** 19 0 S 47 0 E
Antanimbaribe, *Madag.* **105 C7** 21 30 S 44 48 E
Antarctic Pen., *Antarctica* **7 C18** 67 0 S 60 0W
Antarctica **7 E3** 90 0 S 0 0 E
Antelope, *Zimbabwe* **107 G2** 21 2 S 28 31 E
Antenor Navarro, *Brazil* **154 C4** 6 44 S 38 27W
Antequera, *Paraguay* **158 A4** 24 8 S 57 7W
Antequera, *Spain* **37 H6** 37 5N 4 33W
Antero, Mt., *U.S.A.* **143 G10** 38 45N 106 15W
Anthemoús, *Greece* **44 D5** 40 31N 23 15 E
Anthony, *Kans., U.S.A.* **139 G5** 37 8N 98 2W
Anthony, *N. Mex., U.S.A.* **143 K10** 32 1N 106 37W
Anthony Lagoon, *Australia* **114 B2** 18 0 S 135 30 E
Anti Atlas, *Morocco* **98 C3** 30 0N 8 30W
Anti-Lebanon = Ash Sharqi, Al Jabal, *Lebanon* **91 B5** 33 40N 36 10 E
Antibes, *France* **25 E11** 43 34N 7 6 E
Antibes, C. d', *France* **25 E11** 43 31N 7 7 E
Anticosti, I. d', *Canada* **129 C7** 49 30N 63 0W
Antifer, C. d', *France* **22 C7** 49 41N 0 10 E
Antigo, *U.S.A.* **138 C10** 45 8N 89 5W
Antigonish, *Canada* **129 C7** 45 38N 61 58W
Antigua, *Canary Is.* **33 F5** 28 24N 14 1W
Antigua, *Guatemala* **148 D1** 14 34N 90 41W
Antigua, *W. Indies* **149 C7** 17 0N 61 50W
Antigua & Barbuda ■, *W. Indies* **149 C7** 17 20N 61 48W
Antilla, *Cuba* **148 B4** 20 40N 75 50W
Antimony, *U.S.A.* **143 G8** 38 7N 112 0W
Antioch, *U.S.A.* **144 G5** 38 5N 121 45W
Antioche, Pertuis d', *France* **24 B2** 46 6N 1 20W
Antioquia, *Colombia* **152 B2** 6 40N 75 55W
Antioquia □, *Colombia* **152 B2** 7 0N 75 30W
Antipodes Is., *Pac. Oc.* **122 M9** 49 45 S 178 40 E
Antler, *U.S.A.* **138 A4** 48 58N 101 18W
Antler →, *Canada* **131 D8** 49 8N 101 0W
Antlers, *U.S.A.* **139 H7** 34 15N 95 35W
Antofagasta, *Chile* **158 A1** 23 50 S 70 30W
Antofagasta □, *Chile* **158 A2** 24 0 S 69 0W
Antofagasta de la Sierra, *Argentina* **158 B2** 26 5 S 67 20W
Antofalla, *Argentina* **158 B2** 25 30 S 68 5W
Antofalla, Salar de, *Argentina* **158 B2** 25 40 S 67 45W
Antoing, *Belgium* **21 G2** 50 34N 3 27 E
Anton, *U.S.A.* **139 J3** 33 49N 102 5W
Anton Chico, *U.S.A.* **143 J11** 35 12N 105 5W
Antongila, Helodrano, *Madag.* **105 B8** 15 30 S 49 50 E
Antonibé, *Madag.* **105 B8** 15 7 S 47 24 E
Antonibé, Presqu'île d', *Madag.* **105 A8** 14 55 S 47 20 E
Antonina, *Brazil* **159 B6** 25 26 S 48 42W
Antonito, *U.S.A.* **143 H10** 37 4N 106 1W
Antonovo, *U.S.S.R.* **53 B14** 49 25N 51 42 E
Antrain, *France* **22 D5** 48 28N 1 30W
Antrim, *U.K.* **19 B5** 54 43N 6 13W
Antrim □, *U.K.* **19 B5** 54 55N 6 20W
Antrim, Mts. of, *U.K.* **19 B5** 54 57N 6 8W
Antrim Plateau, *Australia* **112 C4** 18 8 S 128 20 E
Antrodoco, *Italy* **39 F10** 42 25N 13 4 E
Antropovo, *U.S.S.R.* **51 B13** 58 26N 42 51 E
Antsalova, *Madag.* **105 B7** 18 40 S 44 37 E
Antsiranana, *Madag.* **105 A8** 12 25 S 49 20 E
Antsohihy, *Madag.* **105 A8** 14 50 S 47 59 E
Antsohimbondrona Seranana, *Madag.* **105 A8** 13 7 S 48 48 E
Antu, *China* **67 C15** 42 30N 128 20 E
Antufash, *Yemen* **86 D3** 15 42N 42 25 E
Antwerp = Antwerpen, *Belgium* **21 F4** 51 13N 4 25 E
Antwerp, *Australia* **116 D5** 36 17 S 142 4 E
Antwerp, *N.Y., U.S.A.* **137 B9** 44 12N 75 36W

Ariquemes 167

Antwerp, *Ohio, U.S.A.* **141 C12** 41 11N 84 45W
Antwerpen, *Belgium* **21 F4** 51 13N 4 25 E
Antwerpen □, *Belgium* **21 F5** 51 15N 4 40 E
Anupgarh, *India* **80 E5** 29 10N 73 10 E
Anuradhapura, *Sri Lanka* **83 K5** 8 22N 80 28 E
Anveh, *Iran* **85 E7** 27 23N 54 11 E
Anvers = Antwerpen, *Belgium* **21 F4** 51 13N 4 25 E
Anvers I., *Antarctica* **7 C17** 64 30 S 63 40W
Anxi, *Fujian, China* **69 E12** 25 2N 118 12 E
Anxi, *Gansu, China* **64 B4** 40 30N 95 43 E
Anxiang, *China* **69 C9** 29 27N 112 11 E
Anxious B., *Australia* **115 E1** 33 24 S 134 45 E
Anyama, *Ivory C.* **100 D4** 5 30N 4 3W
Anyang, *China* **66 F8** 36 5N 114 21 E
Anyer, *Indonesia* **74 D3** 6 4 S 105 53 E
Anyi, *Jiangxi, China* **69 C10** 28 49N 115 25 E
Anyi, *Shanxi, China* **66 G6** 35 2N 111 2 E
Anyuan, *China* **69 E10** 25 9N 115 21 E
Anza, *U.S.A.* **145 M10** 33 35N 116 39W
Anzawr, *Oman* **87 C6** 17 28N 52 50 E
Anze, *China* **66 F7** 36 10N 112 12 E
Anzhero-Sudzhensk, *U.S.S.R.* **56 D9** 56 10N 86 0 E
Ánzio, *Italy* **40 A5** 41 28N 12 37 E
Anzoátegui □, *Venezuela* **153 B5** 9 0N 64 30W
Aoga-Shima, *Japan* **63 E11** 32 28N 139 46 E
Aoiz, *Spain* **34 C3** 42 46N 1 22W
Aomori, *Japan* **60 D10** 40 45N 140 45 E
Aomori □, *Japan* **60 D10** 40 45N 140 40 E
Aonla, *India* **81 E8** 28 16N 79 11 E
Aono-Yama, *Japan* **62 C3** 34 28N 131 48 E
Aorangi Mts., *N.Z.* **118 H4** 41 28 S 175 22 E
Aosta, *Italy* **38 C4** 45 43N 7 20 E
Aotea Harbour, *N.Z.* **118 E3** 38 0 S 174 50 E
Aoudéras, *Niger* **97 E1** 17 45N 8 20 E
Aouinet Torkoz, *Morocco* **98 C3** 28 31N 9 46W
Aoukar, *Mali* **98 D4** 23 50N 2 45W
Aouker, *Mauritania* **100 B3** 17 40N 10 0W
Aoulef el Arab, *Algeria* **99 C5** 26 55N 1 2 E
Apa →, *S. Amer.* **158 A4** 22 6 S 58 2W
Apache, *U.S.A.* **139 H5** 34 53N 98 22W
Apalachee B., *U.S.A.* **135 L4** 30 0N 84 0W
Apalachicola, *U.S.A.* **135 L3** 29 40N 85 0W
Apalachicola →, *U.S.A.* **135 L3** 29 40N 85 0W
Apapa, *Nigeria* **101 D5** 6 25N 3 25 E
Apaporis →, *Colombia* **152 D4** 1 23 S 69 25W
Aparecida do Taboado, *Brazil* **155 F1** 20 5 S 51 5W
Aparri, *Phil.* **71 A6** 18 22N 121 38 E
Aparurén, *Venezuela* **153 B5** 5 6N 62 8W
Apateu, *Romania* **46 C2** 46 36N 21 47 E
Apatin, *Yugoslavia* **42 B4** 45 40N 19 0 E
Apàtity, *U.S.S.R.* **48 A5** 67 34N 33 22 E
Apatzingán, *Mexico* **146 D4** 19 0N 102 20W
Apeldoorn, *Neths.* **20 D7** 52 13N 5 57 E
Apeldoornsch Kanal →, *Neths.* **20 D8** 52 29N 6 5 E
Apen, *Germany* **26 B3** 53 12N 7 47 E
Apennines = Appennini, *Italy* **38 E7** 44 0N 10 0 E
Apere →, *Bolivia* **157 C4** 13 44 S 65 18W
Apia, *W. Samoa* **121 W24** 13 50 S 171 50W
Apiacás, Serra dos, *Brazil* **157 B6** 9 50 S 57 0W
Apiaú →, *Brazil* **153 C5** 2 39N 61 12W
Apiaú, Serra do, *Brazil* **153 C5** 2 30N 62 0W
Apidiá →, *Brazil* **157 C5** 11 39 S 61 11W
Apinajé, *Brazil* **155 D2** 11 31 S 48 18W
Apiti, *N.Z.* **118 F4** 39 58 S 175 54 E
Apizaco, *Mexico* **147 D5** 19 26N 98 9W
Aplao, *Peru* **156 D3** 16 0 S 72 40W
Apo, Mt., *Phil.* **71 C7** 6 53N 125 14 E
Apodi, *Brazil* **154 C4** 5 39 S 37 48W
Apolakkiá, *Greece* **32 C9** 36 5N 27 48 E
Apolakkiá, Órmos, *Greece* **32 C9** 36 5N 27 45 E
Apolda, *Germany* **26 D7** 51 1N 11 30 E
Apollo Bay, *Australia* **116 E5** 38 45 S 143 40 E
Apollonia = Marsá Susah, *Libya* **96 B4** 32 52N 21 59 E
Apollonia, *Greece* **45 H6** 36 58N 24 43 E
Apolo, *Bolivia* **156 C4** 14 30 S 68 30W
Apónguao →, *Venezuela* **153 C5** 4 48N 61 36W
Aporé, *Brazil* **157 D7** 18 58 S 52 1W
Aporé →, *Brazil* **155 E1** 19 27 S 50 57W
Aporema, *Brazil* **154 A1** 1 14N 50 49W
Apostle Is., *U.S.A.* **138 B9** 47 0N 90 30W
Apóstoles, *Argentina* **159 B4** 28 0 S 56 0W
Apostolos Andreas, C., *Cyprus* **32 D13** 35 42N 34 35 E
Apostolovo, *U.S.S.R.* **52 C5** 47 39N 33 39 E
Apoteri, *Guyana* **153 C6** 4 2N 58 32W
Appalachian Mts., *U.S.A.* **124 F12** 38 0N 80 0W
Appelscha, *Neths.* **20 C8** 52 57N 6 21 E
Appennini, *Italy* **38 E7** 44 0N 10 0 E
Appennino Ligure, *Italy* **38 D6** 44 30N 9 0 E
Appenzell, *Switz.* **29 B8** 47 20N 9 25 E
Appenzell-Ausser Rhoden □, *Switz.* **29 B8** 47 23N 9 23 E
Appenzell-Inner Rhoden □, *Switz.* **29 B8** 47 20N 9 25 E
Appiano, *Italy* **39 B8** 46 27N 11 17 E
Appingedam, *Neths.* **20 B9** 53 19N 6 51 E
Apple Hill, *Canada* **137 A10** 45 13N 74 46W
Apple Valley, *U.S.A.* **145 L9** 34 30N 117 11W
Appleby, *U.K.* **16 C5** 54 35N 2 29W
Appleton, *U.S.A.* **134 C1** 44 17N 88 25W
Appleton City, *U.S.A.* **140 F2** 38 11N 94 2W
Approuague, *Fr. Guiana* **153 C7** 4 20N 52 0W
Approuague →, *Fr. Guiana* **153 C7** 4 30N 51 57W
Apricena, *Italy* **41 A8** 41 47N 15 25 E
Aprigliano, *Italy* **41 C9** 39 17N 16 19 E
Aprília, *Italy* **40 A5** 41 38N 12 38 E
Apsheronsk, *U.S.S.R.* **53 D8** 44 28N 39 42 E
Apt, *France* **25 E9** 43 53N 5 24 E
Apuane, Alpi, *Italy* **38 D7** 44 7N 10 14 E
Apuaú, *Brazil* **153 D5** 2 25 S 60 53W
Apucarana, *Brazil* **159 A5** 23 55 S 51 33W
Apulia = Púglia □, *Italy* **41 B9** 41 0N 16 30 E
Apure □, *Venezuela* **152 B4** 7 10N 68 50W
Apure →, *Venezuela* **152 B4** 7 37N 66 25W
Apurímac □, *Peru* **156 C3** 14 0 S 73 0W
Apurimac →, *Peru* **156 C3** 12 17 S 73 56W
Apuseni, Munţii, *Romania* **46 C3** 46 30N 22 45 E
Aqabah = Al 'Aqabah, *Jordan* **91 F4** 29 31N 35 0 E
'Aqabah, Khalīj al, *Red Sea* **84 D2** 28 15N 33 20 E
Āqcheh, *Afghan.* **79 A2** 36 56N 66 11 E
'Aqdā, *Iran* **85 C7** 32 26N 53 37 E
Aqīq, *Sudan* **94 D4** 18 14N 38 12 E
Aqīq, Khalīg, *Sudan* **94 D4** 18 20N 38 10 E
'Aqīq, W. al →, *Si. Arabia* **86 B3** 20 16N 41 40 E
Aqrah, *Iraq* **84 B4** 36 46N 43 45 E
Aquidauana, *Brazil* **157 E6** 20 30 S 55 50W
Aquidauana →, *Brazil* **157 D6** 19 44 S 56 50W
Aquiles Serdán, *Mexico* **146 B3** 28 37N 105 54W
Aquin, *Haiti* **149 C5** 18 16N 73 24W
Ar Rabaḍ, *Si. Arabia* **86 B2** 23 11N 39 52 E
Ar Rachidiya, *Morocco* **98 B4** 31 58N 4 20W
Ar Rafīd, *Syria* **91 C4** 32 57N 35 52 E
Ar Raḥḥālīyah, *Iraq* **84 C4** 32 44N 43 23 E
Ar Ramādī, *Iraq* **84 C4** 33 25N 43 20 E
Ar Ramādīyāt, *Si. Arabia* **86 A3** 24 18N 43 52 E
Ar Raml, *Libya* **96 C3** 26 45N 19 40 E
Ar Ramthā, *Jordan* **91 C5** 32 34N 36 0 E
Ar Raqqah, *Syria* **84 C3** 36 0N 38 55 E
Ar Rass, *Si. Arabia* **84 E4** 25 50N 43 40 E
Ar Rawḍah, *Si. Arabia* **86 B3** 21 16N 42 50 E
Ar Rawḍah, *Yemen* **86 D4** 14 28N 47 17 E
Ar Rawshān, *Si. Arabia* **86 B3** 20 2N 42 36 E
Ar Rayyānah, *Si. Arabia* **86 B2** 23 32N 39 45 E
Ar Rifa'i, *Si. Arabia* **84 D5** 31 50N 46 10 E
Ar Rijā', *Yemen* **86 D4** 13 1N 44 35 E
Ar Riyāḍ, *Si. Arabia* **84 E5** 24 41N 46 42 E
Ar Ru'ays, *Qatar* **85 E6** 26 8N 51 12 E
Ar Rukhaymīyah, *Iraq* **84 D5** 29 22N 45 38 E
Ar Ruqayyidah, *Si. Arabia* **85 E6** 25 21N 49 34 E
Ar Ruṣāfah, *Syria* **84 C3** 35 52N 36 53 E
Ar Ruṭbah, *Iraq* **84 C4** 33 0N 40 15 E
Ar Ruwayḍah, *Si. Arabia* **86 B4** 23 40N 44 40 E
Ara, *India* **81 G11** 25 35N 84 32 E
'Arab, Bahr el →, *Sudan* **95 F2** 9 0N 29 30 E
Arab, Khalîg el, *Egypt* **94 H6** 30 55N 29 0 E
'Arabābād, *Iran* **85 C8** 33 2N 57 41 E
'Arabah, W. →, *Yemen* **87 C5** 18 5N 51 26 E
Araban, *Turkey* **89 E7** 37 28N 37 3 E
Arabatskaya Strelka, *U.S.S.R.* **52 D6** 45 40N 35 0 E
Arabba, *Italy* **39 B8** 46 30N 11 51 E
Arabelo, *Venezuela* **153 C5** 4 55N 64 13W
Arabia, *Asia* **90 C4** 25 0N 45 0 E
Arabian Desert = Es Sahrâ' Esh Sharqîya, *Egypt* **94 B3** 27 30N 32 30 E
Arabian Gulf = Gulf, The, *Asia* **85 E6** 27 0N 50 0 E
Arabian Sea, *Ind. Oc.* **58 H10** 16 0N 65 0 E
Araç, *Turkey* **88 C5** 41 15N 33 21 E
Aracaju, *Brazil* **154 D4** 10 55 S 37 4W
Aracataca, *Colombia* **152 A3** 10 38N 74 9W
Aracati, *Brazil* **154 B4** 4 30 S 37 44W
Araçatuba, *Brazil* **159 A5** 21 10 S 50 30W
Aracena, *Spain* **37 H4** 37 53N 6 38W
Aracena, Sierra de, *Spain* **37 H4** 37 50N 6 50W
Aracides, C., *Solomon Is.* **121 M11** 8 21 S 161 0 E
Araçuaí, *Brazil* **155 E3** 16 52 S 42 4W
Araçuaí →, *Brazil* **155 E3** 16 46 S 42 2W
'Arad, *Israel* **91 D4** 31 15N 35 12 E
Arad, *Romania* **46 C2** 46 10N 21 20 E
Arad □, *Romania* **46 C3** 46 20N 22 0 E
Arada, *Chad* **97 F4** 15 0N 20 20 E
Aradhippou, *Cyprus* **32 E12** 34 57N 33 36 E
Aradu Nou, *Romania* **46 C2** 46 8N 21 20 E
Arafura Sea, *E. Indies* **71 F9** 9 0 S 135 0 E
Aragarças, *Brazil* **157 D7** 15 55 S 52 15W
Aragats, *U.S.S.R.* **53 F11** 40 30N 44 15 E
Aragón □, *Spain* **34 D4** 41 25N 0 40W
Aragón →, *Spain* **34 C3** 42 13N 1 44W
Aragona, *Italy* **40 E6** 37 24N 13 36 E
Aragua □, *Venezuela* **152 B4** 10 0N 67 10W
Aragua de Barcelona, *Venezuela* **153 B5** 9 28N 64 49W
Araguacema, *Brazil* **154 C2** 8 50 S 49 20W
Araguaçu, *Brazil* **155 D2** 12 49 S 49 51W
Araguaia →, *Brazil* **154 C2** 5 21 S 48 41W
Araguaiana, *Brazil* **157 D7** 15 43 S 51 51W
Araguaína, *Brazil* **154 C2** 7 12 S 48 12W
Araguari, *Brazil* **155 E2** 18 38 S 48 11W
Araguari →, *Brazil* **153 C8** 1 15N 49 55W
Araguatins, *Brazil* **154 C2** 5 38 S 48 7W
Araioses, *Brazil* **154 B3** 2 53 S 41 55W
Arak, *Algeria* **99 C5** 25 20N 3 45 E
Arāk, *Iran* **85 C6** 34 0N 49 40 E
Arakan □, *Burma* **78 F5** 19 0N 94 15 E
Arakan Yoma, *Burma* **78 F5** 20 0N 94 40 E
Arákhova, *Greece* **45 F4** 38 28N 22 35 E
Arakkonam, *India* **83 H4** 13 7N 79 43 E
Arakli, *Turkey* **89 C9** 41 6N 40 2 E
Araks = Aras, Rūd-e →, *Iran* **84 B5** 39 10N 47 10 E
Aral Sea = Aralskoye More, *U.S.S.R.* **56 E7** 44 30N 60 0 E
Aralsk, *U.S.S.R.* **56 E7** 46 50N 61 20 E
Aralskoye More, *U.S.S.R.* **56 E7** 44 30N 60 0 E
Aramac, *Australia* **114 C4** 22 58 S 145 14 E
Arambag, *India* **81 H12** 22 53N 87 48 E
Aran Areh, *Ethiopia* **108 C2** 9 2N 43 54 E
Aran I., *Ireland* **19 B3** 55 0N 8 30W
Aran Is., *Ireland* **19 C2** 53 5N 9 42W
Aranda de Duero, *Spain* **34 D1** 41 39N 3 42W
Arandān, *Iran* **84 C5** 35 23N 46 55 E
Arand-elovac, *Yugoslavia* **42 C5** 44 18N 20 27 E
Aranga, *N.Z.* **118 B2** 35 44 S 173 40 E
Arani, *India* **83 H4** 12 43N 79 19 E
Aranjuez, *Spain* **36 E7** 40 1N 3 40W
Aranos, *Namibia* **104 C2** 24 9 S 19 7 E
Aransas Pass, *U.S.A.* **139 M6** 27 55N 97 9W
Aranzazu, *Colombia* **152 B2** 5 16N 75 30W
Arao, *Japan* **62 E2** 32 59N 130 25 E
Araouane, *Mali* **100 B4** 18 55N 3 30W
Arapahoe, *U.S.A.* **138 E5** 40 22N 99 53W
Arapari, *Brazil* **154 C2** 5 34 S 49 15W
Arapawa I., *N.Z.* **119 B9** 41 11 S 174 17 E
Arapey Grande →, *Uruguay* **158 C4** 30 55 S 57 49W
Arapiraca, *Brazil* **154 C4** 9 45 S 36 39W
Arapkir, *Turkey* **89 D8** 39 5N 38 30 E
Arapongas, *Brazil* **159 A5** 23 29 S 51 28W
Arapuni, *N.Z.* **118 E4** 38 4 S 175 39 E
Ar'ar, *Si. Arabia* **84 D4** 30 59N 41 2 E
Araracuara, *Colombia* **152 D3** 0 24 S 72 17W
Araranguá, *Brazil* **159 B6** 29 0 S 49 30W
Araraquara, *Brazil* **155 F2** 21 50 S 48 0W
Ararás, Serra das, *Brazil* **159 B5** 25 0 S 53 10W
Ararat, *Australia* **116 D5** 37 16 S 143 0 E
Ararat, Mt. = Ağrı Dağı, *Turkey* **89 D11** 39 50N 44 15 E
Arari, *Brazil* **154 B3** 3 28 S 44 47W
Araria, *India* **81 F12** 26 9N 87 33 E
Araripe, Chapada do, *Brazil* **154 C4** 7 20 S 40 0W
Araripina, *Brazil* **154 C3** 7 33 S 40 34W
Araruama, L. de, *Brazil* **155 F3** 22 53 S 42 12W
Araruna, *Brazil* **154 C4** 6 52 S 35 44W
Aras, Rūd-e →, *Iran* **84 B5** 39 10N 47 10 E
Araticu, *Brazil* **154 B2** 1 58 S 49 51W
Arauca, *Colombia* **152 B3** 7 0N 70 40W
Arauca □, *Colombia* **152 B3** 6 40N 71 0W
Arauca →, *Venezuela* **152 B4** 7 24N 66 35W
Arauco, *Chile* **158 D1** 37 16 S 73 25W
Arauco □, *Chile* **158 D1** 37 40 S 73 25W
Araújos, *Brazil* **155 E2** 19 56 S 45 14W
Arauquita, *Colombia* **152 B3** 7 2N 71 25W
Araure, *Venezuela* **152 B4** 9 34N 69 13W
Arawa, *Ethiopia* **95 F5** 9 57N 41 58 E
Arawata →, *N.Z.* **119 E3** 44 0 S 168 40 E
Araxá, *Brazil* **155 E2** 19 35 S 46 55W
Araya, Pen. de, *Venezuela* **153 A5** 10 40N 64 0W
Arba Minch, *Ethiopia* **95 F4** 6 0N 37 30 E
Arbat, *Iraq* **84 C5** 35 25N 45 35 E
Arbatax, *Italy* **40 C2** 39 57N 9 42 E
Arbaza, *U.S.S.R.* **57 D10** 52 40N 92 30 E
Arbedo, *Switz.* **29 D8** 46 12N 9 3 E
Arbīl, *Iraq* **84 B5** 36 15N 44 5 E
Arbois, *France* **23 F12** 46 55N 5 46 E
Arboletes, *Colombia* **152 B2** 8 51N 76 26W
Arbon, *Switz.* **29 A8** 47 31N 9 26 E
Arbore, *Ethiopia* **95 F4** 5 3N 36 50 E
Arborea, *Italy* **40 C1** 39 46N 8 34 E
Arborfield, *Canada* **131 C8** 53 6N 103 39W
Arborg, *Canada* **131 C9** 50 54N 97 13W
Arbrå, *Sweden* **14 C10** 61 28N 16 22 E
Arbroath, *U.K.* **18 E6** 56 34N 2 35W
Arbuckle, *U.S.A.* **144 F4** 39 3N 122 2W
Arbus, *Italy* **40 C1** 39 30N 8 33 E
Arbuzinka, *U.S.S.R.* **52 C4** 47 0N 31 59 E
Arc, *France* **23 E12** 47 28N 5 34 E
Arc →, *France* **25 C10** 45 34N 6 12 E
Arcachon, *France* **24 D2** 44 40N 1 10W
Arcachon, Bassin d', *France* **24 D2** 44 42N 1 10W
Arcade, *U.S.A.* **136 D6** 42 34N 78 25W
Arcadia, *Fla., U.S.A.* **135 M5** 27 20N 81 50W
Arcadia, *Ind., U.S.A.* **141 D10** 40 10N 86 1W
Arcadia, *Iowa, U.S.A.* **140 B1** 42 5N 95 3W
Arcadia, *La., U.S.A.* **139 J8** 32 34N 92 53W
Arcadia, *Nebr., U.S.A.* **138 E5** 41 29N 99 4W
Arcadia, *Pa., U.S.A.* **136 F6** 40 46N 78 54W
Arcadia, *Wis., U.S.A.* **138 C9** 44 13N 91 29W
Arcanum, *U.S.A.* **141 E12** 39 59N 84 33W
Arcata, *U.S.A.* **142 F1** 40 55N 124 4W
Arcévia, *Italy* **39 E9** 43 29N 12 58 E
Archangel = Arkhangelsk, *U.S.S.R.* **48 B7** 64 40N 41 0 E
Archar, *Bulgaria* **42 D7** 43 50N 22 54 E
Archbald, *U.S.A.* **137 E9** 41 30N 75 31W
Archbold, *U.S.A.* **141 C12** 41 31N 84 18W
Archena, *Spain* **35 G3** 38 9N 1 16W
Archer →, *Australia* **114 A3** 13 28 S 141 41 E
Archer B., *Australia* **114 A3** 13 20 S 141 30 E
Archers Post, *Kenya* **106 B4** 0 35N 37 35 E
Archidona, *Spain* **37 H6** 37 6N 4 22W
Arci, Monte, *Italy* **40 C1** 39 47N 8 44 E
Arcidosso, *Italy* **39 F8** 42 51N 11 30 E
Arcila = Asilah, *Morocco* **98 A3** 35 29N 6 0W
Arcis-sur-Aube, *France* **23 D11** 48 32N 4 10 E
Arckaringa, *Australia* **115 D1** 27 56 S 134 45 E
Arckaringa Cr. →, *Australia* **115 D2** 28 10 S 135 22 E
Arco, *Italy* **38 C7** 45 55N 10 54 E
Arco, *U.S.A.* **142 E7** 43 45N 113 16W
Arcola, *Canada* **131 D8** 49 40N 102 30W
Arcola, *U.S.A.* **141 E8** 39 41N 88 19W
Arcoona, *Australia* **116 A2** 31 2 S 137 1 E
Arcos, *Spain* **34 D2** 41 12N 2 16W
Arcos de los Frontera, *Spain* **37 J5** 36 45N 5 49W
Arcos de Valdevez, *Portugal* **36 D2** 41 55N 8 22W
Arcot, *India* **83 H4** 12 53N 79 20 E
Arcoverde, *Brazil* **154 C4** 8 25 S 37 4W
Arctic Bay, *Canada* **127 A11** 73 1N 85 7W
Arctic Ocean, *Arctic* **6 B18** 78 0N 160 0W
Arctic Red River, *Canada* **126 B6** 67 15N 134 0W
Arda →, *Bulgaria* **43 F11** 41 40N 26 29 E
Arda →, *Italy* **38 C6** 44 53N 9 52 E
Ardabīl, *Iran* **85 B6** 38 15N 48 18 E
Ardahan, *Turkey* **89 C10** 41 7N 42 41 E
Ardakān = Sepīdān, *Iran* **85 D7** 30 20N 52 5 E
Ardales, *Spain* **37 J6** 36 53N 4 51W
Årdalstangen, *Norway* **14 C1** 61 14N 7 43 E
Ardatov, *U.S.S.R.* **51 D15** 54 51N 46 15 E
Ardea, *Greece* **44 D4** 40 58N 22 3 E
Ardèche □, *France* **25 D8** 44 42N 4 16 E
Ardèche →, *France* **25 D8** 44 16N 4 39 E
Ardee, *Ireland* **19 C5** 53 51N 6 32W
Arden, *Canada* **136 B8** 44 43N 76 56W
Arden, *Denmark* **15 H3** 56 46N 9 52 E
Arden, *Calif., U.S.A.* **144 G5** 38 36N 121 33W
Arden, *Nev., U.S.A.* **145 J11** 36 1N 115 14W
Ardenne, *Belgium* **23 C12** 49 50N 5 5 E
Ardennes □, *France* **23 C11** 49 35N 4 40 E
Ardentes, *France* **23 F8** 46 45N 1 50 E
Ardeşen, *Turkey* **89 C9** 41 12N 41 2 E
Ardestān, *Iran* **85 C7** 33 20N 52 25 E
Ardgour, *U.K.* **18 E3** 56 45N 5 25W
Árdhas →, *Greece* **44 C8** 41 36N 26 25 E
Ardila →, *Portugal* **37 G3** 38 12N 7 28W
Ardino, *Bulgaria* **43 F10** 41 34N 25 9 E
Ardlethan, *Australia* **117 C7** 34 22 S 146 53 E
Ardmore, *Australia* **114 C2** 21 39 S 139 11 E
Ardmore, *Okla., U.S.A.* **139 H6** 34 10N 97 5W
Ardmore, *Pa., U.S.A.* **137 G9** 39 58N 75 18W
Ardmore, *S. Dak., U.S.A.* **138 D3** 43 0N 103 40W
Ardnacrusha, *Ireland* **19 D3** 52 43N 8 38W
Ardnamurchan, Pt. of, *U.K.* **18 E2** 56 44N 6 14W
Ardooie, *Belgium* **21 G2** 50 59N 3 13 E
Ardore Marina, *Italy* **41 D9** 38 11N 16 10 E
Ardres, *France* **23 B8** 50 50N 1 59 E
Ardrossan, *Australia* **116 C2** 34 26 S 137 53 E
Ardrossan, *U.K.* **18 F4** 55 39N 4 50W
Ards □, *U.K.* **19 B6** 54 35N 5 30W
Ards Pen., *U.K.* **19 B6** 54 30N 5 25W
Ardud, *Romania* **46 B3** 47 37N 22 52 E
Ardunac, *Turkey* **53 F10** 41 8N 42 5 E
Åre, *Sweden* **14 A7** 63 22N 13 15 E
Arecibo, *Puerto Rico* **149 C6** 18 29N 66 42W
Areia Branca, *Brazil* **154 C4** 5 0 S 37 0W
Arena, Pt., *U.S.A.* **144 G3** 38 57N 123 44W
Arenales, Cerro, *Chile* **160 C2** 47 5 S 73 40W
Arenápolis, *Brazil* **157 C6** 14 26 S 56 49W
Arenas, *Spain* **36 B6** 43 17N 4 50W
Arenas de San Pedro, *Spain* **36 E5** 40 12N 5 5W
Arendal, *Norway* **15 F2** 58 28N 8 46 E
Arendonk, *Belgium* **21 F6** 51 19N 5 5 E
Arendsee, *Germany* **26 C7** 52 52N 11 27 E
Arenillas, *Ecuador* **152 D1** 3 33 S 80 10W
Arenys de Mar, *Spain* **34 D7** 41 35N 2 33 E
Arenzano, *Italy* **38 D5** 44 24N 8 40 E
Arenzville, *U.S.A.* **140 E6** 39 53N 90 22W
Areópolis, *Greece* **45 H4** 36 40N 22 22 E
Arequipa, *Peru* **156 D3** 16 20 S 71 30W
Arequipa □, *Peru* **156 D3** 16 0 S 72 50W
Arere, *Brazil* **153 D7** 0 16 S 53 52W
Arero, *Ethiopia* **95 G4** 4 41N 38 50 E
Arès, *France* **24 D2** 44 47N 1 8W
Arévalo, *Spain* **36 D6** 41 3N 4 43W
Arezzo, *Italy* **39 E8** 43 28N 11 50 E
Arga →, *Spain* **34 C3** 42 18N 1 47W
Argalastí, *Greece* **44 E5** 39 13N 23 13 E
Argamakmur, *Indonesia* **70 E2** 3 35 S 102 0 E
Argamasilla de Alba, *Spain* **35 F1** 39 8N 3 5W
Arganda, *Spain* **34 E1** 40 19N 3 26W
Arganil, *Portugal* **36 E2** 40 13N 8 3W
Argayash, *U.S.S.R.* **54 D7** 55 29N 60 52 E
Argelès-Gazost, *France* **24 F3** 43 0N 0 6W
Argelès-sur-Mer, *France* **24 F7** 42 34N 3 1 E
Argens →, *France* **25 E10** 43 24N 6 44 E
Argent-sur-Sauldre, *France* **23 E9** 47 33N 2 25 E
Argenta, *Italy* **39 D8** 44 37N 11 50 E
Argenta, *U.S.A.* **141 E8** 39 59N 88 49W
Argentan, *France* **22 D6** 48 45N 0 1W
Argentário, Mte., *Italy* **39 F8** 42 23N 11 11 E
Argentat, *France* **24 C5** 45 6N 1 56 E
Argentera, *Italy* **38 D3** 44 23N 6 58 E
Argentera, Monte del, *Italy* **38 D4** 44 12N 7 5 E
Argenteuil, *France* **23 D9** 48 57N 2 14 E
Argentia, *Canada* **129 C9** 47 18N 53 58W
Argentiera, C. dell', *Italy* **40 B1** 40 44N 8 8 E
Argentière, Aiguilles d', *Switz.* **28 E4** 45 58N 7 2 E
Argentina ■, *S. Amer.* **160 A3** 35 0 S 66 0W
Argentina Is., *Antarctica* **7 C17** 66 0 S 64 0W
Argentino, L., *Argentina* **160 D2** 50 10 S 73 0W
Argenton-Château, *France* **22 F6** 46 59N 0 27W
Argenton-sur-Creuse, *France* **24 B5** 46 36N 1 30 E
Argeş □, *Romania* **46 E5** 45 0N 24 45 E
Argeş →, *Romania* **46 E7** 44 12N 26 14 E
Arghandab →, *Afghan.* **79 C2** 31 30N 64 15 E
Argo, *Sudan* **94 D3** 19 28N 30 30 E
Argolikós Kólpos, *Greece* **45 G4** 37 20N 22 52 E
Argolís □, *Greece* **45 G4** 37 38N 22 50 E
Argonne, *France* **23 C12** 49 10N 5 0 E
Árgos, *Greece* **45 G4** 37 40N 22 43 E
Argos, *U.S.A.* **141 C10** 41 14N 86 15W
Árgos Orestikón, *Greece* **44 D3** 40 27N 21 26 E
Argostólion, *Greece* **45 F2** 38 12N 20 33 E
Arguedas, *Spain* **34 C3** 42 11N 1 36W
Arguello, Pt., *U.S.A.* **145 L6** 34 34N 120 40W
Arguineguín, *Canary Is.* **33 G4** 27 46N 15 41W
Argun →, *U.S.S.R.* **57 D13** 53 20N 121 28 E
Argungu, *Nigeria* **101 C5** 12 40N 4 31 E
Argus Pk., *U.S.A.* **145 K9** 35 52N 117 26W
Argyle, *U.S.A.* **138 A6** 48 23N 96 49W
Argyle, L., *Australia* **112 C4** 16 20 S 128 40 E
Arhavi, *Turkey* **89 C9** 41 21N 41 18 E
Århus, *Denmark* **15 H4** 56 8N 10 11 E
Århus Amtskommune □, *Denmark* **15 H4** 56 15N 10 15 E
Aria, *N.Z.* **118 E4** 38 33 S 175 0 E
Ariadnoye, *U.S.S.R.* **60 B7** 45 8N 134 25 E
Ariamsvlei, *Namibia* **104 D2** 28 9 S 19 51 E
Ariana, *Tunisia* **96 A2** 36 52N 10 12 E
Ariano Irpino, *Italy* **41 A8** 41 10N 15 4 E
Ariano nel Polèsine, *Italy* **39 D9** 44 56N 12 5 E
Ariari →, *Colombia* **152 C3** 2 35N 72 47W
Aribinda, *Burkina Faso* **101 C4** 14 17N 0 52W
Arica, *Chile* **156 D3** 18 32 S 70 20W
Arica, *Colombia* **152 D3** 2 0 S 71 50W
Arico, *Canary Is.* **33 F3** 28 9N 16 29W
Arid, C., *Australia* **113 F3** 34 1 S 123 10 E
Arida, *Japan* **63 C7** 34 5N 135 8 E
Ariège □, *France* **24 F5** 42 56N 1 30 E
Ariège →, *France* **24 E5** 43 30N 1 25 E
Arieş →, *Romania* **46 C4** 46 24N 23 20 E
Arīḥā, *Syria* **84 C3** 35 49N 36 35 E
Arilje, *Yugoslavia* **42 D5** 43 44N 20 7 E
Aríllá, Ákra, *Greece* **32 A3** 39 43N 19 39 E
Arima, *Trin. & Tob.* **149 D7** 10 38N 61 17W
Arinos →, *Brazil* **157 C6** 10 25 S 58 20W
Ario de Rosales, *Mexico* **146 D4** 19 12N 102 0W
Aripuanã, *Brazil* **157 B5** 9 25 S 60 30W
Aripuanã →, *Brazil* **157 B5** 5 7 S 60 25W
Ariquemes, *Brazil* **157 B5** 9 55 S 63 6W

168 Arisaig

Arisaig, *U.K.* **18 E3** 56 55N 5 50W
Arîsh, W. el →, *Egypt* **94 H8** 31 9N 33 49 E
Arismendi, *Venezuela* **152 B4** 8 29N 68 22W
Arissa, *Ethiopia* **95 E5** 11 10N 41 35 E
Aristazabal I., *Canada* **130 C3** 52 40N 129 10W
Arita, *Japan* **62 D1** 33 11N 129 54 E
Arivaca, *U.S.A.* **143 L8** 31 37N 111 25W
Arivonimamo, *Madag.* **105 B8** 19 1 S 47 11 E
Ariyalur, *India* **83 J4** 11 8N 79 8 E
Ariza, *Spain* **34 D2** 41 19N 2 3W
Arizaro, Salar de, *Argentina* **158 A2** 24 40 S 67 50W
Arizona, *Argentina* **158 D2** 35 45 S 65 25W
Arizona □, *U.S.A.* **143 J8** 34 20N 111 30W
Arizpe, *Mexico* **146 A2** 30 20N 110 11W
Arjeplog, *Sweden* **12 C15** 66 3N 18 2 E
Arjona, *Colombia* **152 A2** 10 14N 75 22W
Arjona, *Spain* **37 H6** 37 56N 4 4W
Arjuno, *Indonesia* **71 G15** 7 49 S 112 34 E
Arka, *U.S.S.R.* **57 C15** 60 15N 142 0 E
Arkadak, *U.S.S.R.* **51 F13** 51 58N 43 19 E
Arkadelphia, *U.S.A.* **139 H8** 34 5N 93 0W
Arkadhía □, *Greece* **45 G4** 37 30N 22 20 E
Arkaig, L., *U.K.* **18 E3** 56 58N 5 10W
Arkalyk, *U.S.S.R.* **56 D7** 50 13N 66 50 E
Arkansas □, *U.S.A.* **139 H8** 35 0N 92 30W
Arkansas →, *U.S.A.* **139 J9** 33 48N 91 4W
Arkansas City, *U.S.A.* **139 G6** 37 4N 97 3W
Árkathos →, *Greece* **44 E3** 39 20N 21 4 E
Arkhángelos, *Greece* **32 C10** 36 13N 28 7 E
Arkhangelsk, *U.S.S.R.* **48 B7** 64 40N 41 0 E
Arkhangelskoye, *U.S.S.R.* **51 F12** 51 32N 40 58 E
Arkiko, *Ethiopia* **95 D4** 15 33N 39 30 E
Árkoi, *Greece* **45 G8** 37 24N 26 44 E
Arkona, Kap, *Germany* **26 A9** 54 41N 13 26 E
Arkösund, *Sweden* **15 F10** 58 29N 16 56 E
Arkoúdhi, *Greece* **45 F2** 38 33N 20 43 E
Arkticheskiy, Mys, *U.S.S.R.* **57 A10** 81 10N 95 0 E
Arkul, *U.S.S.R.* **54 C2** 57 17N 50 3 E
Arlanc, *France* **24 C7** 45 25N 3 42 E
Arlanza →, *Spain* **36 C6** 42 6N 4 9W
Arlanzón →, *Spain* **36 C6** 42 3N 4 17W
Arlberg Pass, *Austria* **27 H6** 47 9N 10 12 E
Arlee, *U.S.A.* **142 C6** 47 10N 114 4W
Arles, *France* **25 E8** 43 41N 4 40 E
Arlesheim, *Switz.* **28 B5** 47 30N 7 37 E
Arlington, *S. Africa* **105 D4** 28 1 S 27 53 E
Arlington, *Oreg., U.S.A.* **142 D3** 45 48N 120 6W
Arlington, *S. Dak., U.S.A.* **138 C6** 44 25N 97 4W
Arlington, *Va., U.S.A.* **134 F7** 38 52N 77 5W
Arlington, *Wash., U.S.A.* **144 B4** 48 11N 122 4W
Arlington Heights, *U.S.A.* **141 B9** 42 5N 87 59W
Arlon, *Belgium* **21 J7** 49 42N 5 49 E
Arlöv, *Sweden* **15 J7** 55 38N 13 5 E
Arly, *Burkina Faso* **101 C5** 11 35N 1 28 E
Armagh, *U.K.* **19 B5** 54 22N 6 40W
Armagh □, *U.K.* **19 B5** 54 18N 6 37W
Armagnac, *France* **24 E4** 43 50N 0 10 E
Armançon →, *France* **23 E10** 47 59N 3 30 E
Armavir, *U.S.S.R.* **53 D9** 45 2N 41 7 E
Armenia, *Colombia* **152 C2** 4 35N 75 45W
Armenian S.S.R. □, *U.S.S.R.* **53 F11** 40 20N 44 0 E
Armeniş, *Romania* **46 D3** 45 13N 22 17 E
Armenistís, Ákra, *Greece* **32 C9** 36 8N 27 42 E
Armentières, *France* **23 B9** 50 40N 2 50 E
Armidale, *Australia* **117 A9** 30 30 S 151 40 E
Armour, *U.S.A.* **138 D5** 43 20N 98 25W
Armstrong, *B.C., Canada* **130 C5** 50 25N 119 10W
Armstrong, *Ont., Canada* **128 B2** 50 18N 89 4W
Armstrong, *U.S.A.* **139 M6** 26 59N 97 48W
Armstrong →, *Australia* **112 C5** 16 35 S 131 40 E
Armur, *India* **82 E4** 18 48N 78 16 E
Arnaía, *Greece* **44 D5** 40 30N 23 40 E
Arnarfjörður, *Iceland* **12 D2** 65 48N 23 40W
Arnaud →, *Canada* **127 C13** 60 0N 70 0W
Arnauti, C., *Cyprus* **32 D11** 35 6N 32 17 E
Arnay-le-Duc, *France* **23 E11** 47 10N 4 27 E
Arnedillo, *Spain* **34 C2** 42 13N 2 14W
Arnedo, *Spain* **34 C2** 42 12N 2 5W
Arnemuiden, *Neths.* **21 F3** 51 30N 3 40 E
Árnes, *Iceland* **12 C3** 66 1N 21 31W
Årnes, *Norway* **14 D5** 60 7N 11 28 E
Arnett, *U.S.A.* **139 G5** 36 9N 99 44W
Arnhem, *Neths.* **20 E7** 51 58N 5 55 E
Arnhem, C., *Australia* **114 A2** 12 20 S 137 30 E
Arnhem B., *Australia* **114 A2** 12 20 S 136 10 E
Arnhem Land, *Australia* **114 A1** 13 10 S 134 30 E
Árnissa, *Greece* **44 D3** 40 47N 21 49 E
Arno →, *Italy* **38 E7** 43 41N 10 17 E
Arno Bay, *Australia* **116 B2** 33 54 S 136 34 E
Arnold, *Calif., U.S.A.* **144 G6** 38 15N 120 20W
Arnold, *Nebr., U.S.A.* **138 E4** 41 29N 100 10W
Arnoldstein, *Austria* **30 E6** 46 33N 13 43 E
Arnon →, *France* **23 E9** 47 13N 2 1 E
Arnot, *Canada* **131 B9** 55 56N 96 41W
Arnøy, *Norway* **12 A16** 70 9N 20 40 E
Arnprior, *Canada* **128 C4** 45 26N 76 21W
Arnsberg, *Germany* **26 D4** 51 25N 8 2 E
Arnstadt, *Germany* **26 E6** 50 50N 10 56 E
Aro →, *Venezuela* **153 B5** 8 1N 64 11W
Aroab, *Namibia* **104 D2** 26 41 S 19 39 E
Aroánia Óri, *Greece* **45 G4** 37 56N 22 12 E
Aroche, *Spain* **37 H4** 37 56N 6 57W
Aroeiras, *Brazil* **154 C4** 7 31 S 35 41W
Arolla, *Switz.* **28 D4** 46 2N 7 29 E
Arolsen, *Germany* **26 D5** 51 23N 9 1 E
Aron →, *France* **24 B7** 46 50N 3 28 E
Arona, *Italy* **38 C5** 45 45N 8 32 E
Arosa, *Switz.* **29 C9** 46 47N 9 41 E
Arosa, Ria de, *Spain* **36 C2** 42 28N 8 57W
Arpajon, *France* **23 D9** 48 36N 2 15 E
Arpajon-sur-Cère, *France* **24 D6** 44 53N 2 28 E
Arpino, *Italy* **40 A6** 41 40N 13 35 E
Arque, *Bolivia* **156 D4** 17 48 S 66 23W
Arrabury, *Australia* **115 D3** 26 45 S 141 0 E
Arraias, *Brazil* **155 D2** 12 56 S 46 57W
Arraias →, *Mato Grosso, Brazil* **157 C7** 11 10 S 53 35W
Arraias →, *Pará, Brazil* **154 C2** 7 30 S 49 20W
Arraiolos, *Portugal* **37 G3** 38 44N 7 59W
Arran, *U.K.* **18 F3** 55 34N 5 12W
Arrandale, *Canada* **130 C3** 54 57N 130 0W
Arras, *France* **23 B9** 50 17N 2 46 E
Arrats →, *France* **24 D4** 44 6N 0 52 E
Arreau, *France* **24 F4** 42 54N 0 22 E
Arrecife, *Canary Is.* **33 F6** 28 57N 13 37W
Arrecifes, *Argentina* **158 C3** 34 6 S 60 9W
Arrée, Mts. d', *France* **22 D3** 48 26N 3 55W
Arriaga, *Chiapas, Mexico* **147 D6** 16 15N 93 52W
Arriaga, *San Luis Potosí, Mexico* **146 C4** 21 55N 101 23W
Arrilalah P.O., *Australia* **114 C3** 23 43 S 143 54 E
Arrino, *Australia* **113 E2** 29 30 S 115 40 E
Arrojado →, *Brazil* **155 D3** 13 24 S 44 20W
Arromanches-les-Bains, *France* **22 C6** 49 20N 0 38W
Arronches, *Portugal* **37 F3** 39 8N 7 16W
Arros →, *France* **24 E3** 43 40N 0 2W
Arrou, *France* **22 D8** 48 6N 1 8 E
Arrow, L., *Ireland* **19 B3** 54 3N 8 20W
Arrow Rock Res., *U.S.A.* **142 E6** 43 45N 115 50W
Arrowhead, *Canada* **130 C5** 50 40N 117 55W
Arrowhead, L., *U.S.A.* **145 L9** 34 16N 117 10W
Arrowsmith, Mt., *N.Z.* **119 D5** 43 20 S 170 55 E
Arrowtown, *N.Z.* **119 E3** 44 57 S 168 50 E
Arroyo de la Luz, *Spain* **37 F4** 39 30N 6 38W
Arroyo Grande, *U.S.A.* **145 K6** 35 9N 120 32W
Ars, *Denmark* **15 H3** 56 48N 9 30 E
Ars, *Iran* **84 B5** 37 9N 47 46 E
Ars-en-Ré, *France* **24 B2** 46 12N 1 31W
Ars-sur-Moselle, *France* **23 C13** 49 5N 6 4 E
Arsenault L., *Canada* **131 B7** 55 6N 108 32W
Arsenev, *U.S.S.R.* **60 B6** 44 10N 133 15 E
Arsi □, *Ethiopia* **95 F4** 7 45N 39 0 E
Arsiero, *Italy* **39 C8** 45 49N 11 22 E
Arsikere, *India* **83 H3** 13 15N 76 15 E
Arsin, *Turkey* **89 C8** 41 8N 39 55 E
Arsk, *U.S.S.R.* **51 C16** 56 10N 49 50 E
Árta, *Greece* **45 E3** 39 8N 21 2 E
Artá, *Spain* **33 B10** 39 41N 3 21 E
Árta □, *Greece* **44 E3** 39 15N 21 5 E
Arteaga, *Mexico* **146 D4** 18 50N 102 20W
Arteijo, *Spain* **36 B2** 43 19N 8 29W
Artem, *U.S.S.R.* **60 C6** 43 22N 132 13 E
Artem, Ostrov, *U.S.S.R.* **53 F14** 40 28N 50 20 E
Artemovsk, *R.S.F.S.R., U.S.S.R.* **57 D10** 54 45N 93 35 E
Artemovsk, *Ukraine S.S.R., U.S.S.R.* **52 B8** 48 35N 38 0 E
Artemovski, *U.S.S.R.* **53 C9** 47 45N 40 16 E
Artemovskiy, *U.S.S.R.* **54 C7** 57 21N 61 54 E
Artenay, *France* **23 D8** 48 5N 1 50 E
Artern, *Germany* **26 D7** 51 22N 11 18 E
Artesa de Segre, *Spain* **34 D6** 41 54N 1 3 E
Artesia = Mosomane, *Botswana* **104 C4** 24 2 S 26 19 E
Artesia, *U.S.A.* **139 J2** 32 55N 104 25W
Artesia Wells, *U.S.A.* **139 L5** 28 17N 99 18W
Artesian, *U.S.A.* **138 C6** 44 2N 97 54W
Arth, *Switz.* **29 B7** 47 4N 8 31 E
Arthez-de-Béarn, *France* **24 E3** 43 29N 0 38W
Arthington, *Liberia* **100 D2** 6 35N 10 45W
Arthur, *U.S.A.* **141 E8** 39 43N 88 28W
Arthur →, *Australia* **114 G3** 41 2 S 144 40 E
Arthur Cr. →, *Australia* **114 C2** 22 30 S 136 25 E
Arthur Pt., *Australia* **114 C5** 22 7 S 150 3 E
Arthur's Pass, *N.Z.* **119 C6** 42 54 S 171 35 E
Arthur's Town, *Bahamas* **149 B4** 24 38N 75 42W
Artigas, *Uruguay* **158 C4** 30 20 S 56 30W
Artik, *U.S.S.R.* **53 F10** 40 38N 43 58 E
Artillery L., *Canada* **131 A7** 63 9N 107 52W
Artois, *France* **23 B9** 50 20N 2 30 E
Artotína, *Greece* **45 F4** 38 42N 22 2 E
Artsiz, *U.S.S.R.* **52 C3** 46 4N 29 26 E
Artvin, *Turkey* **53 F9** 41 14N 41 44 E
Artvin □, *Turkey* **89 C9** 41 10N 41 50 E
Aru, Kepulauan, *Indonesia* **71 F8** 6 0 S 134 30 E
Aru Is. = Aru, Kepulauan, *Indonesia* **71 F8** 6 0 S 134 30 E
Aru Meru □, *Tanzania* **106 C4** 3 20 S 36 50 E
Arua, *Uganda* **106 B3** 3 1N 30 58 E
Aruanã, *Brazil* **155 D1** 14 54 S 51 10W
Aruba, *Neth. Ant.* **149 D6** 12 30N 70 0W
Arucas, *Canary Is.* **33 F4** 28 7N 15 32W
Arudy, *France* **24 E3** 43 7N 0 28W
Arumã, *Brazil* **153 D5** 4 44 S 62 8W
Arumpo, *Australia* **116 B5** 33 48 S 142 55 E
Arun →, *Nepal* **81 F12** 26 55N 87 10 E
Arunachal Pradesh □, *India* **78 B5** 28 0N 95 0 E
Aruppukkottai, *India* **83 K4** 9 31N 78 8 E
Arusha, *Tanzania* **106 C4** 3 20 S 36 40 E
Arusha □, *Tanzania* **106 C4** 4 0 S 36 30 E
Arusha Chini, *Tanzania* **106 C4** 3 32 S 37 20 E
Arut →, *Indonesia* **75 C4** 2 42 S 111 34 E
Aruvi →, *Sri Lanka* **83 K4** 8 48N 79 53 E
Aruwimi →, *Zaïre* **106 B1** 1 13N 23 36 E
Arvada, *U.S.A.* **142 D10** 44 43N 106 6W
Arvakalu, *Sri Lanka* **83 K4** 8 20N 79 58 E
Arve →, *France* **25 B10** 46 11N 6 8 E
Árvi, *Greece* **32 E7** 34 59N 25 28 E
Arvi, *India* **82 D4** 20 59N 78 16 E
Arvida, *Canada* **129 C5** 48 25N 71 14W
Arvidsjaur, *Sweden* **12 D15** 65 35N 19 10 E
Arvika, *Sweden* **13 G12** 59 40N 12 36 E
Arvin, *U.S.A.* **145 K8** 35 12N 118 50W
Arxan, *China* **65 B6** 47 11N 119 57 E
Aryirádhes, *Greece* **32 B3** 39 27N 19 58 E
Aryiroúpolis, *Greece* **32 D6** 35 17N 24 20 E
Arys, *U.S.S.R.* **55 B4** 42 26N 68 48 E
Arys →, *U.S.S.R.* **55 B4** 42 45N 68 15 E
Arzachena, *Italy* **40 A2** 41 5N 9 27 E
Arzamas, *U.S.S.R.* **51 D13** 55 27N 43 55 E
Arzew, *Algeria* **99 A4** 35 50N 0 23W
Arzgir, *U.S.S.R.* **53 D11** 45 18N 44 23 E
Arzignano, *Italy* **39 C8** 45 30N 11 20 E
As, *Belgium* **21 F7** 51 1N 5 35 E
Aš, *Czech.* **30 A5** 50 13N 12 12 E
Aş Şadr, *U.A.E.* **85 E7** 24 40N 54 41 E
Aş Şafā, *Syria* **91 B6** 33 10N 37 0 E
'As Saffānīyah, *Si. Arabia* **85 D6** 28 5N 48 50 E
As Safīrah, *Syria* **84 B3** 36 5N 37 21 E
Aş Şahm, *Oman* **85 E8** 24 10N 56 53 E
As Sājir, *Si. Arabia* **84 E5** 25 11N 44 36 E
As Salamīyah, *Si. Arabia* **86 A4** 24 12N 47 18 E
As Salamīyah, *Syria* **84 C3** 35 1N 37 2 E
As Salt, *Jordan* **91 C4** 32 2N 35 43 E
As Sal'w'a, *Qatar* **85 E6** 24 23N 50 50 E
As Samāwah, *Iraq* **84 D5** 31 15N 45 15 E
As Sanamayn, *Syria* **91 B5** 33 3N 36 10 E
As Sawādah, *Si. Arabia* **86 B4** 22 24N 44 28 E
As Sayl al Kabīr, *Si. Arabia* **86 B3** 21 38N 40 25 E
As Sukhnah, *Syria* **84 C3** 34 52N 38 52 E
As Sulaymānīyah, *Iraq* **84 C5** 35 35N 45 29 E
As Sulaymānīyah, *Si. Arabia* **86 A4** 24 9N 47 18 E
As Sulaymī, *Si. Arabia* **84 E4** 26 17N 41 21 E
As Sulayyil, *Si. Arabia* **86 B4** 20 27N 45 34 E
As Sulţan, *Libya* **96 B3** 31 4N 17 8 E
As Summān, *Si. Arabia* **84 E5** 25 0N 47 0 E
As Sūq, *Si. Arabia* **86 B3** 21 54N 42 3 E
Aş Şurrah, *Yemen* **86 D4** 13 57N 46 14 E
As Suwaydā', *Syria* **91 C5** 32 40N 36 30 E
As Suwaydā' □, *Syria* **91 C5** 32 45N 36 45 E
As Suwayh, *Oman* **87 B7** 22 10N 59 33 E
As Suwayq, *Oman* **87 B7** 23 51N 57 26 E
Aş Şuwayrah, *Iraq* **84 C5** 32 55N 45 0 E
Asab, *Namibia* **104 D2** 25 30 S 18 0 E
Asaba, *Nigeria* **101 D6** 6 12N 6 38 E
Asafo, *Ghana* **100 D4** 6 20N 2 40W
Asahi, *Japan* **63 B12** 35 43N 140 39 E
Asahi-Gawa →, *Japan* **62 C5** 34 36N 133 58 E
Asahigawa, *Japan* **60 C11** 43 46N 142 22 E
Asale, L., *Ethiopia* **95 E5** 14 0N 40 20 E
Asama-Yama, *Japan* **63 A10** 36 24N 138 31 E
Asamankese, *Ghana* **101 D4** 5 50N 0 40W
Asansol, *India* **81 H12** 23 40N 87 1 E
Åsarna, *Sweden* **14 B8** 62 39N 14 22 E
Asbe Teferi, *Ethiopia* **95 F5** 9 4N 40 49 E
Asbesberge, *S. Africa* **104 D3** 29 0 S 23 0 E
Asbest, *U.S.S.R.* **54 C7** 57 0N 61 30 E
Asbestos, *Canada* **129 C5** 45 47N 71 58W
Asbury Park, *U.S.A.* **137 F10** 40 15N 74 1W
Ascensión, *Mexico* **146 A3** 31 6N 107 59W
Ascensión, B. de la, *Mexico* **147 D7** 19 50N 87 20W
Ascension I., *Atl. Oc.* **9 J7** 8 0 S 14 15W
Aschach, *Austria* **30 C7** 48 22N 14 2 E
Aschaffenburg, *Germany* **27 F5** 49 58N 9 8 E
Aschendorf, *Germany* **26 B3** 53 2N 7 22 E
Aschersleben, *Germany* **26 D7** 51 45N 11 28 E
Asciano, *Italy* **39 E8** 43 14N 11 32 E
Áscoli Piceno, *Italy* **39 F10** 42 51N 13 34 E
Áscoli Satriano, *Italy* **41 A8** 41 11N 15 32 E
Ascona, *Switz.* **29 D7** 46 9N 8 46 E
Ascope, *Peru* **156 B2** 7 46 S 79 8W
Ascotán, *Chile* **158 A2** 21 45 S 68 17W
Aseb, *Ethiopia* **90 E3** 13 0N 42 40 E
Asedjrad, *Algeria* **99 D5** 24 51N 1 29 E
Asela, *Ethiopia* **95 F4** 8 0N 39 0 E
Asenovgrad, *Bulgaria* **43 E9** 42 1N 24 51 E
Asfeld, *France* **23 C11** 49 27N 4 5 E
Asfûn el Matâ'na, *Egypt* **94 B3** 25 26N 32 30 E
Åsgårdstrand, *Norway* **14 E4** 59 22N 10 27 E
Asgata, *Cyprus* **32 E12** 34 46N 33 15 E
Ash Fork, *U.S.A.* **143 J7** 35 14N 112 32W
Ash Grove, *U.S.A.* **139 G8** 37 21N 93 36W
Ash Shamāl □, *Lebanon* **91 A5** 34 25N 36 0 E
Ash Shāmīyah, *Iraq* **84 D5** 31 55N 44 35 E
Ash Sha'rā', *Si. Arabia* **86 A4** 24 16N 44 11 E
Ash Shāriqah, *U.A.E.* **85 E7** 25 23N 55 26 E
Ash Sharmah, *Si. Arabia* **84 D2** 28 1N 35 16 E
Ash Sharqāt, *Iraq* **84 C4** 35 27N 43 16 E
Ash Sharqi, Al Jabal, *Lebanon* **91 B5** 33 40N 36 10 E
Ash Shaţrah, *Iraq* **84 D5** 31 30N 46 10 E
Ash Shawbak, *Jordan* **84 D2** 30 32N 35 34 E
Ash Shawmari, J., *Jordan* **91 E5** 30 35N 36 35 E
Ash Shaykh, J., *Lebanon* **91 B4** 33 25N 35 50 E
Ash Shiḩr, *Yemen* **87 D5** 14 45N 49 36 E
Ash Shināfīyah, *Iraq* **84 D5** 31 35N 44 39 E
Ash Shu'aybah, *Si. Arabia* **84 E5** 27 53N 44 43 E
Ash Shumlūl, *Si. Arabia* **84 E5** 26 31N 47 20 E
Ash Shuqayq, *Si. Arabia* **86 C3** 17 44N 42 1 E
Ash Shūr'a, *Iraq* **84 C4** 35 58N 43 13 E
Ash Shurayf, *Si. Arabia* **84 E3** 25 43N 39 14 E
Ash Shuwayfāt, *Lebanon* **91 B4** 33 45N 35 30 E
Asha, *U.S.S.R.* **54 D5** 55 0N 57 16 E
Ashanti □, *Ghana* **101 D4** 7 30N 1 30W
Ashau, *Vietnam* **76 D6** 16 6N 107 22 E
Ashburn, *U.S.A.* **135 K4** 31 42N 83 40W
Ashburton, *N.Z.* **119 D6** 43 53 S 171 48 E
Ashburton →, *Australia* **112 D1** 21 40 S 114 56 E
Ashburton, North Branch →, *N.Z.* **119 D6** 43 54 S 171 44 E
Ashburton, South Branch →, *N.Z.* **119 D6** 43 54 S 171 44 E
Ashburton Downs, *Australia* **112 D2** 23 25 S 117 4 E
Ashby de la Zouch, *U.K.* **16 E6** 52 45N 1 29W
Ashcroft, *Canada* **130 C4** 50 40N 121 20W
Ashdod, *Israel* **91 D3** 31 49N 34 35 E
Asheboro, *U.S.A.* **135 H6** 35 43N 79 46W
Asherton, *U.S.A.* **139 L5** 28 25N 99 43W
Asheville, *U.S.A.* **135 H4** 35 39N 82 30W
Asheweig →, *Canada* **128 B2** 54 17N 87 12W
Ashford, *Australia* **115 D5** 29 15 S 151 3 E
Ashford, *U.K.* **17 F8** 51 8N 0 53 E
Ashford, *U.S.A.* **142 C2** 46 45N 122 2W
Ashibetsu, *Japan* **60 C11** 43 31N 142 11 E
Ashikaga, *Japan* **63 A11** 36 28N 139 29 E
Ashio, *Japan* **63 A11** 36 38N 139 27 E
Ashizuri-Zaki, *Japan* **62 E5** 32 44N 133 0 E
Ashkarkot, *Afghan.* **80 C2** 33 3N 67 58 E
Ashkhabad, *U.S.S.R.* **56 F6** 38 0N 57 50 E
Ashland, *Ill., U.S.A.* **140 E7** 39 53N 90 0W
Ashland, *Kans., U.S.A.* **139 G5** 37 13N 99 43W
Ashland, *Ky., U.S.A.* **134 F4** 38 25N 82 40W
Ashland, *Maine, U.S.A.* **129 C6** 46 34N 68 26W
Ashland, *Mont., U.S.A.* **142 D10** 45 41N 106 12W
Ashland, *Nebr., U.S.A.* **138 E6** 41 5N 96 27W
Ashland, *Ohio, U.S.A.* **136 F2** 40 52N 82 20W
Ashland, *Oreg., U.S.A.* **142 E2** 42 10N 122 38W
Ashland, *Pa., U.S.A.* **137 F8** 40 45N 76 22W
Ashland, *Va., U.S.A.* **134 G7** 37 46N 77 30W
Ashland, *Wis., U.S.A.* **138 B9** 46 40N 90 52W
Ashley, *Ill., U.S.A.* **140 F7** 38 20N 89 11W
Ashley, *Ind., U.S.A.* **141 C11** 41 32N 85 4W
Ashley, *N. Dak., U.S.A.* **138 B5** 46 3N 99 23W
Ashley, *Pa., U.S.A.* **137 E9** 41 12N 75 55W
Ashley →, *N.Z.* **119 D7** 43 17 S 172 44 E
Ashmont, *Canada* **130 C6** 54 7N 111 35W
Ashmore Reef, *Australia* **112 B3** 12 14 S 123 5 E
Ashmûn, *Egypt* **94 H7** 30 18N 30 55 E
Ashq'elon, *Israel* **91 D3** 31 42N 34 35 E
Ashtabula, *U.S.A.* **136 E4** 41 52N 80 50W
Ashti, *India* **82 E2** 18 50N 75 15 E
Ashton, *S. Africa* **104 E3** 33 50 S 20 5 E
Ashton, *U.S.A.* **142 D8** 44 6N 111 30W
Ashton under Lyne, *U.K.* **16 D5** 53 30N 2 8W
Ashuanipi, L., *Canada* **129 B6** 52 45N 66 15W
Ashurst, *N.Z.* **118 G4** 40 16 S 175 45 E
Asia **58 E11** 45 0N 75 0 E
Asia, Kepulauan, *Indonesia* **71 D8** 1 0N 131 13 E
Āsīā Bak, *Iran* **85 C6** 35 19N 50 30 E
Asiago, *Italy* **39 C8** 45 52N 11 30 E
Asidonhoppo, *Surinam* **153 C6** 3 50N 55 30W
Asifabad, *India* **82 E4** 19 20N 79 24 E
Asike, *Indonesia* **71 F10** 6 39 S 140 24 E
Asilah, *Morocco* **98 A3** 35 29N 6 0W
Asinara, *Italy* **40 A1** 41 5N 8 15 E
Asinara, G. dell', *Italy* **40 B1** 41 0N 8 30 E
Asino, *U.S.S.R.* **56 D9** 57 0N 86 0 E
'Asīr □, *Si. Arabia* **86 C3** 18 40N 42 30 E
Asir, Ras, *Somali Rep.* **90 E5** 11 55N 51 10 E
Aska, *India* **82 E7** 19 2N 84 42 E
Aşkale, *Turkey* **89 D9** 39 55N 40 41 E
Asker, *Norway* **14 E4** 59 50N 10 26 E
Askersund, *Sweden* **15 F8** 58 53N 14 55 E
Askham, *S. Africa* **104 D3** 26 59 S 20 47 E
Askim, *Norway* **14 E5** 59 35N 11 10 E
Askino, *U.S.S.R.* **54 C5** 56 5N 56 34 E
Askja, *Iceland* **12 D5** 65 3N 16 48W
Asl, *Egypt* **94 J8** 29 33N 32 44 E
Āsmār, *Afghan.* **79 B3** 35 10N 71 27 E
Asmara = Asmera, *Ethiopia* **95 D4** 15 19N 38 55 E
Asmera, *Ethiopia* **95 D4** 15 19N 38 55 E
Asnæs, *Denmark* **15 J5** 55 40N 11 0 E
Asni, *Morocco* **98 B3** 31 17N 7 58W
Aso, *Japan* **62 E3** 32 55N 131 5 E
Aso-Zan, *Japan* **62 E3** 32 53N 131 6 E
Ásola, *Italy* **38 C7** 45 12N 10 25 E
Asoteriba, Jebel, *Sudan* **94 C4** 21 51N 36 30 E
Asotin, *U.S.A.* **142 C5** 46 20N 117 3W
Aspe, *Spain* **35 G4** 38 20N 0 40W
Aspen, *U.S.A.* **143 G10** 39 12N 106 56W
Aspendos, *Turkey* **88 E4** 36 54N 31 7 E
Aspermont, *U.S.A.* **139 J4** 33 11N 100 15W
Aspiring, Mt., *N.Z.* **119 E3** 44 23 S 168 46 E
Aspres-sur-Buëch, *France* **25 D9** 44 32N 5 44 E
Asprókavos, Ákra, *Greece* **32 B4** 39 21N 20 6 E
Aspromonte, *Italy* **41 D8** 38 10N 15 55 E
Aspur, *India* **80 H6** 23 58N 74 7 E
Asquith, *Canada* **131 C7** 52 8N 107 13W
Assa, *Morocco* **98 C3** 28 35N 9 6W
Assâba, *Mauritania* **100 B2** 16 10N 11 45W
Assam □, *India* **78 C4** 26 0N 93 0 E
Assamakka, *Niger* **101 B6** 19 21N 5 38 E
Asse, *Belgium* **21 H4** 50 24N 4 10 E
Assebroek, *Belgium* **21 F2** 51 11N 3 17 E
Assekrem, *Algeria* **99 D6** 23 16N 5 49 E
Asséminí, *Italy* **40 C2** 39 18N 9 0 E
Assen, *Neths.* **20 C9** 53 0N 6 35 E
Assendelft, *Neths.* **20 D5** 52 29N 4 45 E
Assenede, *Belgium* **21 F3** 51 14N 3 46 E
Assens, *Århus, Denmark* **15 H4** 56 41N 10 3 E
Assens, *Fyn, Denmark* **15 J3** 55 16N 9 55 E
Assesse, *Belgium* **21 H6** 50 22N 5 2 E
Assini, *Ivory C.* **100 D4** 5 9N 3 17W
Assiniboia, *Canada* **131 D7** 49 40N 105 59W
Assiniboine →, *Canada* **131 D9** 49 53N 97 8W
Assis, *Brazil* **159 A5** 22 40 S 50 20W
Assisi, *Italy* **39 E9** 43 4N 12 36 E
Ássos, *Greece* **45 F2** 38 22N 20 33 E
Assumption, *U.S.A.* **140 E7** 39 31N 89 3W
Assus, *Turkey* **44 E8** 39 32N 26 22 E
Assynt, L., *U.K.* **18 C3** 58 25N 5 15W
Astaffort, *France* **24 D4** 44 4N 0 40 E
Astakidha, *Greece* **45 J8** 35 53N 26 50 E
Astara, *U.S.S.R.* **89 D13** 38 30N 48 50 E
Asten, *Neths.* **21 F7** 51 24N 5 45 E
Asteroúsia, *Greece* **32 E7** 34 59N 25 3 E
Asti, *Italy* **38 D5** 44 54N 8 11 E
Astipálaia, *Greece* **45 H8** 36 32N 26 22 E
Astorga, *Spain* **36 C4** 42 29N 6 8W
Astoria, *Ill., U.S.A.* **140 D6** 40 14N 90 21W
Astoria, *Oreg., U.S.A.* **144 D3** 46 16N 123 50W
Åstorp, *Sweden* **15 H6** 56 6N 12 55 E
Astrakhan, *U.S.S.R.* **53 C13** 46 25N 48 5 E
Astrakhan-Bazàr, *U.S.S.R.* **49 G8** 39 14N 48 30 E
Astudillo, *Spain* **36 C6** 42 12N 4 22W
Asturias, *Spain* **36 B5** 43 15N 6 0W
Asunción, *Paraguay* **158 B4** 25 10 S 57 30W
Asunción Nochixtlán, *Mexico* **147 D5** 17 28N 97 14W
Asutri, *Sudan* **95 D4** 15 25N 35 45 E
Aswa →, *Uganda* **106 B3** 3 43N 31 55 E
Aswad, Ras al, *Si. Arabia* **86 B2** 21 20N 39 0 E
Aswân, *Egypt* **94 C3** 24 4N 32 57 E
Aswân High Dam = Sadd el Aali, *Egypt* **94 C3** 23 54N 32 54 E
Asyût, *Egypt* **94 B3** 27 11N 31 4 E
Asyûti, Wadi →, *Egypt* **94 B3** 27 11N 31 16 E
Aszód, *Hungary* **31 D12** 47 39N 19 28 E
At Ţafīlah, *Jordan* **91 E4** 30 45N 35 30 E
At Tā'if, *Si. Arabia* **86 B3** 21 5N 40 27 E
At Tāj, *Libya* **96 D4** 24 13N 23 18 E
At Tamīmī, *Libya* **96 B4** 32 20N 23 4 E
Aţ Ţirāq, *Si. Arabia* **84 E5** 27 19N 44 33 E
At Turbah, *Yemen* **86 D4** 13 13N 44 7 E
At Turbah, *Yemen* **86 D3** 12 40N 43 30 E
Aţ Ţuwayrifah, *Si. Arabia* **87 B5** 21 30N 49 35 E
Atacama □, *Chile* **158 B2** 27 30 S 70 0W
Atacama, Desierto de, *Chile* **158 A2** 24 0 S 69 20W
Atacama, Salar de, *Chile* **158 A2** 23 30 S 68 20W
Ataco, *Colombia* **152 C2** 3 35N 75 23W

Azogues 169

Atakor, Algeria 99 D6 23 27N 5 31 E
Atakpamé, Togo 101 D5 7 31N 1 13 E
Atalándi, Greece 45 F4 38 39N 22 58 E
Atalaya, Peru 156 C3 10 45 S 73 50W
Atalaya de Femes, Canary Is. 33 F6 28 56N 13 47W
Ataléia, Brazil 155 E3 18 3 S 41 6W
Atambua, Indonesia 72 C2 9 7 S 124 54 E
Atami, Japan 63 B11 35 5N 139 4 E
Atankawng, Burma 78 C6 25 50N 97 47 E
Atapupu, Indonesia 71 F6 9 0 S 124 51 E
Atâr, Mauritania 98 D2 20 30N 13 5W
Atara, U.S.S.R. 57 C13 63 10N 129 10 E
Ataram, Erg n-, Algeria 99 D5 23 57N 2 0 E
Atarfe, Spain 37 H7 37 13N 3 40W
Atascadero, U.S.A. 143 J3 35 32N 120 44W
Atascadero, Calif., U.S.A. 144 K6 35 29N 120 40W
Atasu, U.S.S.R. 56 E8 48 30N 71 0 E
Atauro, Indonesia 71 F7 8 10 S 125 30 E
Atbara, Sudan 94 D3 17 42N 33 59 E
'Atbara →, Sudan 94 D3 17 40N 33 56 E
Atbasar, U.S.S.R. 56 D7 51 48N 68 20 E
Atbashi, U.S.S.R. 55 C7 41 10N 75 48 E
Atbashi, Khrebet, U.S.S.R. 55 C7 40 50N 75 30 E
Atchafalaya B., U.S.A. 139 L9 29 30N 91 20W
Atchison, U.S.A. 138 F7 39 40N 95 10W
Atebubu, Ghana 101 D4 7 47N 1 0W
Ateca, Spain 34 D3 41 20N 1 49W
Aterno →, Italy 39 F10 42 11N 13 51 E
Atesine, Alpi, Italy 38 B8 46 55N 11 30 E
Atessa, Italy 39 F11 42 5N 14 27 E
Ath, Belgium 21 G3 50 38N 3 47 E
Athabasca, Canada 130 C6 54 45N 113 20W
Athabasca →, Canada 131 B6 58 40N 110 50W
Athabasca, L., Canada 131 B7 59 15N 109 15W
Athboy, Ireland 19 C5 53 37N 6 55W
Athenry, Ireland 19 C3 53 18N 8 45W
Athens = Athínai, Greece 45 G5 37 58N 23 46 E
Athens, Ala., U.S.A. 135 H2 34 49N 86 58W
Athens, Ga., U.S.A. 135 J4 33 56N 83 24W
Athens, N.Y., U.S.A. 137 D11 42 15N 73 48W
Athens, Ohio, U.S.A. 134 F4 39 25N 82 6W
Athens, Pa., U.S.A. 137 E8 41 57N 76 36W
Athens, Tenn., U.S.A. 135 H3 35 45N 84 38W
Athens, Tex., U.S.A. 139 J7 32 11N 95 48W
Atherley, Canada 136 B5 44 37N 79 20W
Atherton, Australia 114 B4 17 17 S 145 30 E
Athiéme, Benin 101 D5 6 37N 1 40 E
Athienou, Cyprus 32 D12 35 3N 33 32 E
Athínai, Greece 45 G5 37 58N 23 46 E
Athlone, Ireland 19 C4 53 26N 7 57W
Athna, Cyprus 32 D12 35 3N 33 47 E
Athni, India 82 F2 16 44N 75 6 E
Athol, N.Z. 119 F3 45 30 S 168 35 E
Atholl, Forest of, U.K. 18 E5 56 51N 3 50W
Atholville, Canada 129 C6 47 59N 66 43W
Áthos, Greece 44 D6 40 9N 24 22 E
Athus, Belgium 21 J7 49 34N 5 50 E
Ati, Chad 97 F3 13 13N 18 20 E
Ati, Sudan 95 E2 13 5N 29 2 E
Atiak, Uganda 106 B3 3 12N 32 2 E
Atiamuri, N.Z. 118 E5 38 24 S 176 5 E
Atico, Peru 156 D3 16 14 S 73 40W
Atienza, Spain 34 D2 41 12N 2 52W
Atikokan, Canada 128 C1 48 45N 91 37W
Atikonak L., Canada 129 B7 52 40N 64 32W
'Ātinah, W. →, Oman 87 C6 18 23N 53 28 E
Atirampattinam, India 83 J4 10 28N 79 20 E
Atka, U.S.S.R. 57 C16 60 50N 151 48 E
Atkarsk, U.S.S.R. 51 F14 51 55N 45 2 E
Atkinson, Ill., U.S.A. 140 C6 41 25N 90 1W
Atkinson, Nebr., U.S.A. 138 D5 42 35N 98 59W
Atlanta, Ga., U.S.A. 135 J3 33 50N 84 24W
Atlanta, Ill., U.S.A. 140 D7 40 16N 89 14W
Atlanta, Mo., U.S.A. 140 E4 39 54N 92 29W
Atlanta, Tex., U.S.A. 139 J7 33 7N 94 8W
Atlantic, U.S.A. 138 E7 41 25N 95 0W
Atlantic City, U.S.A. 134 F8 39 25N 74 25W
Atlantic Ocean 8 H7 0 0 20 0W
Atlántico □, Colombia 152 A3 10 45N 75 0W
Atlas Mts. = Haut Atlas, Morocco 98 B4 32 30N 5 0W
Atlin, Canada 130 B2 59 31N 133 41W
Atlin, L., Canada 130 B2 59 26N 133 45W
Atmakur, India 83 G4 14 37N 79 40 E
Atmore, U.S.A. 135 K2 31 2N 87 30W
Atō, Japan 62 C3 34 25N 131 40 E
Atoka, U.S.A. 139 H6 34 22N 96 10W
Atokos, Greece 45 F2 38 28N 20 49 E
Atolia, U.S.A. 145 K9 35 19N 117 37W
Atouguia, Portugal 37 F1 39 20N 9 20W
Atoyac →, Mexico 147 D5 16 30N 97 31W
Atrak →, Iran 85 B8 37 50N 57 0 E
Ätran, Sweden 15 G6 57 7N 12 57 E
Atrato →, Colombia 152 B2 8 17N 76 58W
Atrauli, India 80 E8 28 2N 78 20 E
Atri, Italy 39 F11 42 35N 14 0 E
Atsbi, Ethiopia 95 E4 13 52N 39 50 E
Atsoum, Mts., Cameroon 101 D7 6 41N 12 57 E
Atsugi, Japan 63 B11 35 25N 139 21 E
Atsumi, Japan 63 C9 34 35N 137 4 E
Atsumi-Wan, Japan 63 C9 34 44N 137 13 E
Atsuta, Japan 60 C10 43 24N 141 26 E
Attalla, U.S.A. 135 H2 34 2N 86 5W
Attáviros, Greece 32 C9 36 12N 27 50 E
Attawapiskat, Canada 128 B3 52 56N 82 24W
Attawapiskat →, Canada 128 B3 52 57N 82 18W
Attawapiskat, L., Canada 128 B2 52 18N 87 54W
Attendorn, Germany 26 D3 51 8N 7 54 E
Attersee, Austria 30 D6 47 55N 13 32 E
Attert, Belgium 21 J7 49 45N 5 47 E
Attica, U.S.A. 141 D9 40 20N 87 15W
Attichy, France 23 C10 49 25N 3 3 E
Attigny, France 23 C11 49 28N 4 35 E
Attikamagen L., Canada 129 B6 55 0N 66 30W
Attikí □, Greece 45 F5 38 10N 23 40 E
Attleboro, U.S.A. 137 E13 41 56N 71 18W
Attock, Pakistan 80 C5 33 52N 72 20 E
Attopeu, Laos 76 E6 14 48N 106 50 E
Attunga, Australia 117 A9 30 55 S 150 50 E
Attur, India 83 J4 11 35N 78 30 E
'Atūd, Yemen 86 D4 13 53N 48 10 E
Atuel →, Argentina 158 D2 36 17 S 66 50W
Atvacik, Turkey 88 D2 39 36N 26 24 E
Åtvidaberg, Sweden 15 F10 58 12N 16 0 E
Atwater, U.S.A. 144 H6 37 21N 120 37W
Atwood, Canada 136 C3 43 40N 81 1W
Atwood, U.S.A. 138 F4 39 52N 101 3W
Au Sable →, U.S.A. 134 C4 44 25N 83 20W
Au Sable Pt., U.S.A. 128 C2 46 40N 86 10W
Aubagne, France 25 E9 43 17N 5 37 E
Aubange, Belgium 21 J7 49 34N 5 48 E
Aubarca, C., Spain 33 B7 39 4N 1 22 E
Aube □, France 23 D11 48 15N 4 10 E
Aube →, France 23 D10 48 34N 3 43 E
Aubel, Belgium 21 G7 50 42N 5 51 E
Aubenas, France 25 D8 44 37N 4 24 E
Aubenton, France 23 C11 49 50N 4 12 E
Auberry, U.S.A. 144 H7 37 7N 119 29W
Aubigny-sur-Nère, France 23 E9 47 30N 2 24 E
Aubin, France 24 D6 44 33N 2 15 E
Aubrac, Mts. d', France 24 D7 44 40N 3 2 E
Auburn, Ala., U.S.A. 135 J3 32 37N 85 30W
Auburn, Calif., U.S.A. 144 G5 38 53N 121 4W
Auburn, Ill., U.S.A. 140 E7 39 36N 89 45W
Auburn, Ind., U.S.A. 141 C11 41 20N 85 5W
Auburn, N.Y., U.S.A. 137 D8 42 57N 76 39W
Auburn, Nebr., U.S.A. 138 E7 40 25N 95 50W
Auburn, Wash., U.S.A. 144 C4 47 18N 122 13W
Auburn Ra., Australia 115 D5 25 15 S 150 30 E
Auburndale, U.S.A. 135 L5 28 5N 81 45W
Aubusson, France 24 C6 45 57N 2 11 E
Auch, France 24 E4 43 39N 0 36 E
Auchel, France 23 B9 50 30N 2 29 E
Auchi, Nigeria 101 D6 7 6N 6 13 E
Auckland, N.Z. 118 C3 36 52 S 174 46 E
Auckland □, N.Z. 118 E6 38 35 S 177 0 E
Auckland Is., Pac. Oc. 122 N8 50 40 S 166 5 E
Aude □, France 24 E6 43 8N 2 28 E
Aude →, France 24 E7 43 13N 3 14 E
Audegle, Somali Rep. 108 D2 1 59N 44 50 E
Auden, Canada 128 B2 50 14N 87 53W
Auderghem, Belgium 21 G4 50 49N 4 26 E
Auderville, France 22 C5 49 43N 1 57W
Audierne, France 22 D2 48 1N 4 34W
Audincourt, France 23 E13 47 30N 6 50 E
Audo, Ethiopia 95 F5 6 20N 41 50 E
Audubon, U.S.A. 140 C2 41 43N 94 56W
Aue, Germany 26 E8 50 34N 12 43 E
Auerbach, Germany 26 E8 50 30N 12 25 E
Aueti Paraná →, Brazil 152 D4 1 51 S 65 37W
Aufist, W. Sahara 98 C2 25 44N 14 39W
Augathella, Australia 115 D4 25 48 S 146 35 E
Augrabies Falls, S. Africa 104 D3 28 35 S 20 20 E
Augsburg, Germany 27 G6 48 22N 10 54 E
Augusta, Italy 41 E8 37 14N 15 12 E
Augusta, Ark., U.S.A. 139 H9 35 17N 91 25W
Augusta, Ga., U.S.A. 135 J5 33 29N 81 59W
Augusta, Ill., U.S.A. 140 D6 40 14N 90 57W
Augusta, Kans., U.S.A. 139 G6 37 40N 97 0W
Augusta, Ky., U.S.A. 141 F13 38 47N 84 0W
Augusta, Maine, U.S.A. 129 D6 44 20N 69 46W
Augusta, Mont., U.S.A. 142 C7 47 30N 112 29W
Augusta, Wis., U.S.A. 138 C9 44 41N 91 8W
Augustenborg, Denmark 15 K3 54 57N 9 53 E
Augustów, Poland 47 B10 53 51N 23 0 E
Augustus, Mt., Australia 112 D2 24 20 S 116 50 E
Augustus Downs, Australia 114 B2 18 35 S 139 55 E
Augustus I., Australia 112 C3 15 20 S 124 30 E
Aukan, Ethiopia 95 D5 15 29N 40 50 E
Auki, Solomon Is. 121 M11 8 45 S 160 42 E
Aukum, U.S.A. 144 G6 38 34N 120 43W
Auld, L., Australia 112 D3 22 25 S 123 50 E
Aulla, Italy 38 D7 44 12N 10 0 E
Aulnay, France 24 B3 46 2N 0 22W
Aulne →, France 22 D2 48 17N 4 16W
Aulnoye-Aymeries, France 23 B10 50 12N 3 50 E
Ault, France 22 B8 50 8N 1 26 E
Ault, U.S.A. 138 E2 40 40N 104 42W
Aulus-les-Bains, France 24 F5 42 49N 1 19 E
Aumale, France 23 C8 49 46N 1 46 E
Aumont-Aubrac, France 24 D7 44 43N 3 17 E
Auna, Nigeria 101 C5 10 9N 4 42 E
Aundh, India 82 F2 17 33N 74 23 E
Aunis, France 24 B3 46 5N 0 50W
Auponhia, Indonesia 71 E7 1 58 S 125 27 E
Aups, France 25 E10 43 37N 6 15 E
Aur, P., Malaysia 77 L5 2 35N 104 10 E
Aura, Burma 78 B6 26 59N 97 57 E
Auraiya, India 81 F8 26 28N 79 33 E
Aurangabad, Bihar, India 81 G11 24 45N 84 18 E
Aurangabad, Maharashtra, India 82 E2 19 50N 75 23 E
Auray, France 22 E4 47 40N 2 59W
Aurès, Algeria 99 A6 35 8N 6 30 E
Aurich, Germany 26 B3 53 28N 7 30 E
Aurilândia, Brazil 155 E1 16 44 S 50 28W
Aurillac, France 24 D6 44 55N 2 26 E
Auronza, Italy 39 B9 46 33N 12 27 E
Aurora = Maewo, Vanuatu 121 E6 15 10 S 168 10 E
Aurora, Canada 136 C5 44 0N 79 28W
Aurora, S. Africa 104 E2 32 40 S 18 29 E
Aurora, Colo., U.S.A. 138 F2 39 44N 104 55W
Aurora, Ill., U.S.A. 141 C8 41 42N 88 12W
Aurora, Mo., U.S.A. 139 G8 36 58N 93 42W
Aurora, Nebr., U.S.A. 138 E6 40 55N 98 0W
Aurora, Ohio, U.S.A. 136 E3 41 21N 81 20W
Aurskog, Norway 14 E5 59 55N 11 26 E
Aurukun Mission, Australia 114 A3 13 20 S 141 45 E
Aus, Namibia 104 D2 26 35 S 16 12 E
Auschwitz = Oświecim, Poland 31 A12 50 2N 19 11 E
Aust-Agder fylke □, Norway 13 G9 58 55N 7 40 E
Austerlitz = Slavkov, Czech. 31 B9 49 10N 16 52 E
Austin, Ind., U.S.A. 141 F11 38 45N 85 49W
Austin, Minn., U.S.A. 138 D8 43 37N 92 59W
Austin, Nev., U.S.A. 142 G5 39 30N 117 1W
Austin, Pa., U.S.A. 136 E6 41 40N 78 7W
Austin, Tex., U.S.A. 139 K6 30 20N 97 45W
Austin, L., Australia 113 E2 27 40 S 118 0 E
Austral Downs, Australia 114 C2 20 30 S 137 45 E
Austral Is. = Tubuai Is., Pac. Oc. 123 K13 25 0 S 150 0W
Austral Seamount Chain, Pac. Oc. 123 K13 24 0 S 150 0W
Australia ■, Oceania 110 E6 23 0 S 135 0 E
Australian Alps, Australia 117 D8 36 30 S 148 30 E
Australian Capital Territory □, Australia 115 F4 35 30 S 149 0 E
Austria ■, Europe 30 E7 47 0N 14 0 E
Austvågøy, Norway 12 B13 68 20N 14 40 E
Autazes, Brazil 153 D6 3 35 S 59 8W
Autelbas, Belgium 21 J7 49 39N 5 52 E
Auterive, France 24 E5 43 21N 1 29 E
Authie →, France 23 B8 50 22N 1 38 E
Authon-du-Perche, France 22 D7 48 12N 0 54 E
Autlán, Mexico 146 D4 19 40N 104 30W
Autun, France 23 F11 46 58N 4 17 E
Auvelais, Belgium 21 H5 50 27N 4 38 E
Auvergne, Australia 112 C5 15 39 S 130 1 E
Auvergne, France 24 C7 45 20N 3 15 E
Auvergne, Mts. d', France 24 C6 45 20N 2 55 E
Auvézère →, France 24 C4 45 12N 0 50 E
Auxerre, France 23 E10 47 48N 3 32 E
Auxi-le-Château, France 23 B9 50 15N 2 8 E
Auxonne, France 23 E12 47 10N 5 20 E
Auxvasse, U.S.A. 140 E5 39 1N 91 54W
Auzances, France 24 B6 46 2N 2 30 E
Auzat-sur-Allier, France 24 C7 45 27N 3 19 E
Ava, U.S.A. 140 G7 37 53N 89 30W
Avallon, France 23 E10 47 30N 3 53 E
Avalon, U.S.A. 145 M8 33 21N 118 20W
Avalon Pen., Canada 129 C9 47 30N 53 20W
Avanigadda, India 83 G5 16 0N 80 56 E
Avaré, Brazil 159 A6 23 4 S 48 58W
Ávas, Greece 44 D7 40 57N 25 56 E
Avawatz Mts., U.S.A. 145 K10 35 30N 116 20W
Aveiro, Brazil 153 D6 3 10 S 55 5W
Aveiro, Portugal 36 E2 40 37N 8 38W
Aveiro □, Portugal 36 E2 40 40N 8 35W
Āvej, Iran 85 C6 35 40N 49 15 E
Avelgem, Belgium 21 G2 50 47N 3 27 E
Avellaneda, Argentina 158 C4 34 50 S 58 10W
Avellino, Italy 41 B7 40 54N 14 46 E
Avenal, U.S.A. 144 K6 36 0N 120 8W
Avenches, Switz. 28 C4 46 53N 7 2 E
Averøya, Norway 14 A1 63 5N 7 35 E
Aversa, Italy 41 B7 40 58N 14 11 E
Avery, U.S.A. 142 C6 47 22N 115 56W
Aves, I. de, W. Indies 149 C7 15 45N 63 55W
Aves, Is. de, Venezuela 149 D6 12 0N 67 30W
Avesnes-sur-Helpe, France 23 B10 50 8N 3 55 E
Avesta, Sweden 13 F14 60 9N 16 10 E
Aveyron □, France 24 D6 44 22N 2 45 E
Aveyron →, France 24 D5 44 5N 1 16 E
Avezzano, Italy 39 F10 42 2N 13 24 E
Avgó, Greece 45 J7 35 33N 25 37 E
Aviá Terai, Argentina 158 B3 26 45 S 60 50W
Aviano, Italy 39 B9 46 3N 12 35 E
Avigliana, Italy 38 C4 45 7N 7 13 E
Avigliano, Italy 41 B8 40 44N 15 41 E
Avignon, France 25 E8 43 57N 4 50 E
Ávila, Spain 36 E6 40 39N 4 43W
Ávila □, Spain 36 E6 40 30N 5 0W
Ávila, Sierra de, Spain 36 E5 40 40N 5 15W
Avila Beach, U.S.A. 145 K6 35 11N 120 44W
Avilés, Spain 36 B5 43 35N 5 57W
Avionárion, Greece 45 F6 38 31N 24 8 E
Avisio →, Italy 39 B8 46 7N 11 5 E
Aviston, U.S.A. 140 F7 38 36N 89 36W
Aviz, Portugal 37 F3 39 4N 7 53W
Avize, France 23 D11 48 59N 4 1 E
Avoca, U.S.A. 136 D7 42 24N 77 25W
Avoca →, Australia 116 C5 35 40 S 143 43 E
Avola, Canada 130 C5 51 45N 119 19W
Avola, Italy 41 F8 36 56N 15 7 E
Avon, Ill., U.S.A. 140 D6 40 40N 90 26W
Avon, N.Y., U.S.A. 136 D7 42 55N 77 42W
Avon, S. Dak., U.S.A. 138 D5 43 0N 98 3W
Avon □, U.K. 17 F5 51 30N 2 40W
Avon →, Australia 113 F2 31 40 S 116 7 E
Avon →, Avon, U.K. 17 F5 51 30N 2 43W
Avon →, Hants., U.K. 17 G6 50 44N 1 45W
Avon →, Warks., U.K. 17 F5 51 57N 2 9W
Avondale, Zimbabwe 107 F3 17 43 S 30 58 E
Avonlea, Canada 131 D8 50 0N 105 0W
Avonmore, Canada 137 A10 45 10N 74 58W
Avonmouth, U.K. 17 F5 51 30N 2 42W
Avramov, Bulgaria 43 E11 42 45N 26 38 E
Avranches, France 22 D5 48 40N 1 20W
Avre →, France 22 D8 48 47N 1 22 E
Avrig, Romania 46 D5 45 43N 24 21 E
Avtovac, Yugoslavia 42 D3 43 9N 18 35 E
Avu Avu, Solomon Is. 121 M11 9 50 S 160 22 E
Awag el Baqar, Sudan 95 E3 10 10N 33 10 E
A'waj →, Syria 91 B5 33 23N 36 20 E
Awaji, Japan 63 C7 34 32N 135 1 E
Awaji-Shima, Japan 62 C6 34 30N 134 50 E
'Awālī, Bahrain 85 E6 26 0N 50 30 E
Awantipur, India 81 C6 33 55N 75 3 E
Awanui, N.Z. 118 B2 35 4 S 173 17 E
Awarja →, India 82 F3 17 5N 76 15 E
Awarua B., N.Z. 119 E3 44 28 S 168 4 E
Awarua Pt., N.Z. 119 E3 44 15 S 168 5 E
Awasa, L., Ethiopia 95 F4 7 0N 38 30 E
Awash, Ethiopia 90 F3 9 1N 40 10 E
Awash →, Ethiopia 95 E5 11 45N 41 5 E
Awaso, Ghana 100 D4 6 15N 2 22W
Awatere →, N.Z. 119 B9 41 37 S 174 10 E
Awbārī, Libya 96 C2 26 46N 12 57 E
Awbārī □, Libya 96 C2 26 35N 12 46 E
Awe, L., U.K. 18 E3 56 15N 5 15W
Aweil, Sudan 95 F2 8 42N 27 20 E
Awgu, Nigeria 101 D6 6 4N 7 24 E
Awjilah, Libya 96 C4 29 8N 21 7 E
Aworro, Papua N. G. 120 D2 7 43 S 143 11 E
Ax-les-Thermes, France 24 F5 42 44N 1 50 E
Axarfjördur, Iceland 12 C5 66 15N 16 45W
Axel, Neths. 21 F3 51 16N 3 55 E
Axel Heiberg I., Canada 6 B3 80 0N 90 0W
Axim, Ghana 100 E4 4 51N 2 15W
Aximim, Brazil 153 D6 4 2 S 59 22W
Axintele, Romania 46 E7 44 37N 26 47 E
Axioma, Brazil 157 B5 6 45 S 64 31W
Axiós →, Greece 44 D4 40 57N 22 35 E
Axminster, U.K. 17 G4 50 47N 3 1W
Axvall, Sweden 15 F7 58 23N 13 34 E
Aÿ, France 23 C11 49 3N 4 1 E
Ay →, U.S.S.R. 54 C5 56 8N 57 40 E
Ayaantang, Eq. Guin. 102 B2 1 58N 10 24 E
Ayabaca, Peru 156 A2 4 40 S 79 53W
Ayabe, Japan 63 B7 35 20N 135 20 E
Ayacucho, Argentina 158 D4 37 5 S 58 20W
Ayacucho, Peru 156 C3 13 0 S 74 0W
Ayaguz, U.S.S.R. 56 E9 48 10N 80 10 E
Ayakkuduk, U.S.S.R. 55 C2 41 12N 65 12 E
Ayakudi, India 83 J3 10 28N 77 56 E
Ayamonte, Spain 37 H3 37 12N 7 24W
Ayan, U.S.S.R. 57 D14 56 30N 138 16 E
Ayancık, Turkey 52 F6 41 57N 34 35 E
Ayapel, Colombia 152 B2 8 19N 75 9W
Ayas, Turkey 52 F5 40 2N 32 21 E
Ayaviri, Peru 156 C3 14 50 S 70 35W
Āybak, Afghan. 79 A3 36 15N 68 5 E
Aybastı, Turkey 88 C7 40 41N 37 23 E
Aydim, W. →, Oman 87 C6 18 8N 53 8 E
Aydın, Turkey 88 E2 37 51N 27 51 E
Aydin □, Turkey 88 E3 37 50N 28 0 E
Aye, Belgium 21 H6 50 14N 5 18 E
Ayenngré, Togo 101 D5 8 40N 1 1 E
Ayer's Cliff, Canada 137 A12 45 10N 72 3W
Ayers Rock, Australia 113 E5 25 23 S 131 5 E
Ayiá, Greece 44 E4 39 43N 22 45 E
Ayía Aikateríni, Ákra, Greece 32 A3 39 50N 19 50 E
Ayía Ánna, Greece 45 F5 38 52N 23 24 E
Ayía Dhéka, Greece 32 D6 35 3N 24 58 E
Ayía Gálini, Greece 32 D6 35 6N 24 41 E
Ayía Marína, Kásos, Greece 45 J8 35 27N 26 53 E
Ayía Marína, Leros, Greece 45 G8 37 11N 26 48 E
Ayia Napa, Cyprus 32 E13 34 59N 34 0 E
Ayía Paraskeví, Greece 44 E8 39 14N 26 16 E
Áyia Phyla, Cyprus 32 E12 34 43N 33 1 E
Ayía Rouméli, Greece 45 J5 35 14N 23 58 E
Ayia Varvára, Greece 32 D7 35 8N 25 1 E
Ayiássos, Greece 45 E8 39 5N 26 23 E
Áyion Óros, Greece 44 D6 40 25N 24 6 E
Áyios Amvrósios, Cyprus 32 D12 35 20N 33 35 E
Áyios Andréas, Greece 45 G4 37 21N 22 45 E
Áyios Evstrátios, Greece 44 E6 39 34N 24 58 E
Áyios Ioánnis, Ákra, Greece 32 D7 35 20N 25 40 E
Áyios Isidhoros, Greece 32 C9 36 9N 27 51 E
Áyios Kiríkos, Greece 45 G8 37 34N 26 17 E
Áyios Matthaíos, Greece 32 B3 39 30N 19 47 E
Áyios Mírono, Greece 45 J7 35 15N 25 1 E
Áyios Nikólaos, Greece 32 D7 35 11N 25 41 E
Áyios Pétros, Greece 45 F2 38 38N 20 33 E
Áyios Seryios, Cyprus 32 D12 35 12N 33 53 E
Ayios Theodhoros, Cyprus 32 D13 35 22N 34 1 E
Áyios Yeóryios, Greece 45 G5 37 28N 23 57 E
Aykathonisi, Greece 45 G9 37 28N 27 0 E
Ayke, Ozero, U.S.S.R. 54 F7 50 57N 61 36 E
Aykin, U.S.S.R. 48 B8 62 15N 49 56 E
Aylesbury, U.K. 17 F7 51 48N 0 49W
Aylmer, Canada 136 D4 42 46N 80 59W
Aylmer L., Canada 126 B8 64 0N 110 8W
'Ayn al Ghazālah, Libya 96 B4 32 10N 23 20 E
'Ayn Zaqqūt, Libya 96 C3 29 0N 19 30 E
Ayna, Spain 35 G2 38 34N 2 3W
Aynāt, Yemen 87 C5 16 4N 49 9 E
Ayni, U.S.S.R. 55 D4 39 23N 68 32 E
Ayolas, Paraguay 158 B4 27 10 S 56 59W
Ayom, Sudan 95 F2 7 49N 28 23 E
Ayon, Ostrov, U.S.S.R. 57 C17 69 50N 169 0 E
Ayora, Spain 35 F3 39 3N 1 3W
Ayr, Australia 114 B4 19 35 S 147 25 E
Ayr, U.K. 18 F4 55 28N 4 37W
Ayr →, U.K. 18 F4 55 29N 4 40W
Ayrancı, Turkey 88 E5 37 21N 33 41 E
Ayre, Pt. of, U.K. 16 C3 54 27N 4 21W
Aysha, Ethiopia 95 E5 10 50N 42 23 E
Aytos, Bulgaria 43 E12 42 42N 27 16 E
Aytoska Planina, Bulgaria 43 E12 42 45N 27 30 E
Ayu, Kepulauan, Indonesia 71 D8 0 35N 131 5 E
Ayutla, Guatemala 148 D1 14 40N 92 10W
Ayutla, Mexico 147 D5 16 58N 99 17W
Ayvacık, Turkey 88 C7 40 59N 36 38 E
Ayvalık, Turkey 88 D2 39 20N 26 46 E
Aywaille, Belgium 21 H7 50 28N 5 40 E
Az Zabdānī, Syria 91 B5 33 43N 36 5 E
Az Zāhirīyah, Jordan 91 D3 31 25N 34 58 E
Az Zahrān, Si. Arabia 85 E6 26 10N 50 7 E
Az Zarqā, Jordan 91 C5 32 5N 36 4 E
Az Zāwiyah, Libya 96 B2 32 52N 12 56 E
Az Zaydīyah, Yemen 86 D3 15 20N 43 1 E
Az Zībār, Iraq 84 B5 36 52N 44 4 E
Az-Zilfī, Si. Arabia 84 E5 26 12N 44 52 E
Az Zubayr, Iraq 84 D5 30 20N 47 50 E
Az Zuqur, Yemen 86 D3 14 0N 42 45 E
Azambuja, Portugal 37 F2 39 4N 8 51W
Azamgarh, India 81 F10 26 5N 83 13 E
Azangaro, Peru 156 C3 14 55 S 70 13W
Azaouak, Vallée de l', Mali 101 B5 15 50N 3 20 E
Āzār Shahr, Iran 84 B5 37 45N 45 59 E
Āzarbāyjān-e Gharbī □, Iran 84 B5 37 0N 44 30 E
Āzarbāyjān-e Sharqī □, Iran 84 B5 37 20N 47 0 E
Azare, Nigeria 101 C7 11 55N 10 10 E
Azay-le-Rideau, France 22 E7 47 16N 0 30 E
A'zāz, Syria 84 B3 36 36N 37 4 E
Azazga, Algeria 99 A5 36 48N 4 22 E
Azbine = Aïr, Niger 97 E1 18 30N 8 0 E
Azefal, Mauritania 98 D2 21 0N 14 45W
Azeffoun, Algeria 99 A5 36 51N 4 26 E
Azemmour, Morocco 98 B3 33 20N 9 20W
Azerbaijan S.S.R. □, U.S.S.R. 53 F13 40 20N 48 0 E
Azezo, Ethiopia 95 E4 12 28N 37 15 E
Azimganj, India 81 G13 24 14N 88 16 E
Aznalcóllar, Spain 37 H4 37 32N 6 17W
Azogues, Ecuador 152 D2 2 35 S 78 0W

170 Azores

Azores, Atl. Oc. 8 E6 38 44N 29 0W
Azov, U.S.S.R. 53 C8 47 3N 39 25 E
Azov Sea = Azovskoye More, U.S.S.R. 52 D7 46 0N 36 30 E
Azovskoye More, U.S.S.R. 52 D7 46 0N 36 30 E
Azovy, U.S.S.R. 56 C7 64 55N 64 35 E
Azpeitia, Spain 34 B2 43 12N 2 19W
Azrou, Morocco 98 B3 33 28N 5 19W
Aztec, U.S.A. 143 H10 36 54N 108 0W
Azúa, Dom. Rep. 149 C5 18 25N 70 44W
Azuaga, Spain 37 G5 38 16N 5 39W
Azuara, Spain 34 D4 41 15N 0 53W
Azuay □, Ecuador 152 D2 2 55 S 79 0W
Azuer →, Spain 37 F7 39 8N 3 36W
Azuero, Pen. de, Panama 148 E3 7 30N 80 30W
Azul, Argentina 158 D4 36 42 S 59 43W
Azul, Serra, Brazil 157 C7 14 50 S 54 50W
Azurduy, Bolivia 157 D5 19 59 S 64 29W
Azusa, U.S.A. 145 L9 34 8N 117 52W
Azzaba, Algeria 99 A6 36 48N 7 6 E
Azzano Décimo, Italy 39 C9 45 53N 12 46 E
'Azzūn, Jordan 91 C4 32 10N 35 2 E

B

Ba Don, Vietnam 76 D6 17 45N 106 26 E
Ba Dong, Vietnam 77 H6 9 40N 106 33 E
Ba Ngoi = Cam Lam, Vietnam 77 G7 11 54N 109 10 E
Ba Ria, Vietnam 77 G6 10 30N 107 10 E
Ba Tri, Vietnam 77 G6 10 2N 106 36 E
Ba Xian, China 66 E9 39 8N 116 22 E
Baa, Indonesia 71 F6 10 50 S 123 0 E
Baaba, I., N. Cal. 121 T18 20 3 S 164 59 E
Baamonde, Spain 36 B3 43 7N 7 44W
Baar, Switz. 29 B7 47 12N 8 32 E
Baarle Nassau, Belgium 21 F5 51 27N 4 56 E
Baarlo, Neths. 21 F8 51 20N 6 6 E
Baarn, Neths. 20 D6 52 12N 5 17 E
Bab el Mandeb, Red Sea 86 D3 12 35N 43 25 E
Baba, Bulgaria 43 E8 42 44N 23 59 E
Baba Burnu, Turkey 44 E8 39 29N 26 2 E
Baba dag, U.S.S.R. 53 F13 41 0N 48 19 E
Bābā Kalū, Iran 85 D6 30 7N 50 49 E
Babaçulândia, Brazil 154 C2 7 13 S 47 46W
Babadag, Romania 46 E9 44 53N 28 44 E
Babaeski, Turkey 43 F12 41 26N 27 6 E
Babahoyo, Ecuador 152 D2 1 40 S 79 30W
Babakin, Australia 113 F2 32 7 S 118 1 E
Babana, Nigeria 101 C5 10 31N 3 46 E
Babar, Algeria 99 A6 35 10N 7 6 E
Babar, Indonesia 71 F7 8 0 S 129 30 E
Babar, Pakistan 80 D3 31 7N 69 32 E
Babarkach, Pakistan 80 E3 29 45N 68 0 E
Babayevo, U.S.S.R. 51 B9 59 24N 35 55 E
Babb, U.S.A. 142 B7 48 56N 113 27W
Babenhausen, Germany 27 F4 49 57N 8 56 E
Babi Besar, P., Malaysia 77 L4 2 25N 103 59 E
Babia Gora, Europe 31 B12 49 38N 19 38 E
Babian Jiang →, China 68 F3 22 55N 101 47 E
Babile, Ethiopia 95 F5 9 16N 42 11 E
Babinda, Australia 114 B4 17 20 S 145 56 E
Babine, Canada 130 B3 55 22N 126 37W
Babine →, Canada 130 B3 55 45N 127 44W
Babine L., Canada 130 C3 54 48N 126 0W
Babo, Indonesia 71 E8 2 30 S 133 30 E
Babócsa, Hungary 31 E10 46 2N 17 21 E
Bābol, Iran 85 B7 36 40N 52 50 E
Bābol Sar, Iran 85 B7 36 45N 52 45 E
Baborów, Poland 31 A11 50 7N 18 1 E
Baboua, C.A.R. 102 A2 5 49N 14 58 E
Babuna, Yugoslavia 42 F6 41 30N 21 40 E
Babura, Nigeria 101 C6 12 51N 8 59 E
Babusar Pass, Pakistan 81 B5 35 12N 73 59 E
Babušnica, Yugoslavia 42 D7 43 7N 22 27 E
Babuyan Chan., Phil. 71 A6 18 40N 121 30 E
Babylon, Iraq 84 C5 32 40N 44 30 E
Bač, Yugoslavia 42 B4 45 29N 19 17 E
Bac Can, Vietnam 76 A5 22 8N 105 49 E
Bac Giang, Vietnam 76 B6 21 16N 106 11 E
Bac Ninh, Vietnam 76 B6 21 13N 106 4 E
Bac Phan, Vietnam 76 B5 22 0N 105 0 E
Bac Quang, Vietnam 76 A5 22 30N 104 48 E
Bacabal, Brazil 154 B3 4 15 S 44 45W
Bacajá →, Brazil 153 D7 3 25 S 51 50W
Bacalar, Mexico 147 D7 18 50N 87 27W
Bacan, Indonesia 71 F7 8 27 S 126 27 E
Bacan, Kepulauan, Indonesia 71 E7 0 35 S 127 30 E
Bacan, Pulau, Indonesia 71 E7 0 50 S 127 30 E
Bacarra, Phil. 71 A6 18 15N 120 37 E
Bacău, Romania 46 C7 46 35N 26 55 E
Bacău □, Romania 46 C7 46 30N 26 45 E
Baccarat, France 23 D13 48 28N 6 42 E
Bacchus Marsh, Australia 116 D6 37 43 S 144 27 E
Bacerac, Mexico 146 A3 30 18N 108 50W
Băceşti, Romania 46 C8 46 50N 27 11 E
Bach Long Vi, Dao, Vietnam 76 B6 20 10N 107 40 E
Bachaquero, Venezuela 152 B3 9 56N 71 8W
Bacharach, Germany 27 E3 50 3N 7 46 E
Bachelina, U.S.S.R. 56 D7 57 45N 67 20 E
Bachuma, Ethiopia 95 F4 6 48N 35 53 E
Bačina, Yugoslavia 42 D6 43 42N 21 23 E
Back →, Canada 126 B9 65 10N 104 0W
Bačka Palanka, Yugoslavia 42 B4 45 17N 19 27 E
Bačka Topola, Yugoslavia 42 B4 45 49N 19 39 E
Bäckefors, Sweden 15 F6 58 48N 12 9 E
Bački Petrovac, Yugoslavia 42 B4 45 29N 19 32 E
Backnang, Germany 27 G5 48 57N 9 26 E
Backstairs Passage, Australia 116 C3 35 40 S 138 5 E
Bacolod, Phil. 71 B6 10 40N 122 57 E
Bacqueville-en-Caux, France 22 C8 49 47N 1 0 E
Bacs-Kiskun □, Hungary 31 E12 46 43N 19 30 E
Bácsalmás, Hungary 31 E12 46 8N 19 17 E
Bacuk, Malaysia 77 J4 6 4N 102 25 E
Bād, Iran 85 C7 33 41N 52 1 E
Bad →, U.S.A. 138 C4 44 22N 100 22W
Bad Aussee, Austria 30 D6 47 43N 13 45 E
Bad Axe, U.S.A. 136 C2 43 48N 82 59W
Bad Bergzabern, Germany 27 F4 49 6N 8 0 E
Bad Berleburg, Germany 26 D4 51 3N 8 22 E
Bad Bevensen, Germany 26 B6 53 5N 10 34 E
Bad Bramstedt, Germany 26 B5 53 56N 9 53 E
Bad Brückenau, Germany 27 E5 50 17N 9 48 E
Bad Doberan, Germany 26 A7 54 6N 11 55 E
Bad Driburg, Germany 26 D5 51 44N 9 0 E
Bad Ems, Germany 27 E3 50 22N 7 44 E
Bad Frankenhausen, Germany 26 D7 51 21N 11 3 E
Bad Freienwalde, Germany 26 C10 52 47N 14 3 E
Bad Godesberg, Germany 26 E3 50 41N 7 4 E
Bad Hersfeld, Germany 26 E5 50 52N 9 42 E
Bad Hofgastein, Austria 30 D6 47 17N 13 6 E
Bad Homburg, Germany 27 E4 50 17N 8 33 E
Bad Honnef, Germany 26 E3 50 39N 7 13 E
Bad Ischl, Austria 30 D6 47 44N 13 38 E
Bad Kissingen, Germany 27 E6 50 11N 10 5 E
Bad Königshofen, Germany 27 E6 50 18N 10 29 E
Bad Kreuznach, Germany 27 F3 49 47N 7 47 E
Bad Laasphe, Germany 26 E4 50 56N 8 23 E
Bad Lands, U.S.A. 138 D3 43 40N 102 10W
Bad Langensalza, Germany 26 D6 51 6N 10 40 E
Bad Lauterberg, Germany 26 D6 51 38N 10 29 E
Bad Leonfelden, Austria 30 C7 48 31N 14 18 E
Bad Lippspringe, Germany 26 D4 51 47N 8 46 E
Bad Mergentheim, Germany 27 F5 49 29N 9 47 E
Bad Münstereifel, Germany 26 E2 50 33N 6 46 E
Bad Muskau, Germany 26 D10 51 33N 14 43 E
Bad Nauheim, Germany 27 E4 50 24N 8 45 E
Bad Oeynhausen, Germany 26 C4 52 16N 8 45 E
Bad Oldesloe, Germany 26 B6 53 48N 10 22 E
Bad Orb, Germany 27 E5 50 16N 9 21 E
Bad Pyrmont, Germany 26 D5 51 59N 9 15 E
Bad Ragaz, Switz. 29 C9 47 0N 9 30 E
Bad Reichenhall, Germany 27 H8 47 44N 12 53 E
Bad Säckingen, Germany 27 H3 47 34N 7 56 E
Bad Salzuflen, Germany 26 C4 52 8N 8 44 E
Bad Segeberg, Germany 26 B6 53 58N 10 16 E
Bad Tölz, Germany 27 H7 47 43N 11 34 E
Bad Urach, Germany 27 G5 48 29N 9 25 E
Bad Waldsee, Germany 27 H5 47 56N 9 46 E
Bad Wildungen, Germany 26 D5 51 7N 9 10 E
Bad Wimpfen, Germany 27 F5 49 12N 9 10 E
Bad Windsheim, Germany 27 F6 49 29N 10 25 E
Badagara, India 83 J2 11 35N 75 40 E
Badagri, Nigeria 101 D5 6 25N 2 55 E
Badajós, L., Brazil 153 D5 3 15 S 62 50W
Badajoz, Spain 37 G4 38 50N 6 59W
Badajoz □, Spain 37 G4 38 40N 6 30W
Badakhshān □, Afghan. 79 A3 36 30N 71 0 E
Badalona, Spain 34 D7 41 26N 2 15 E
Badalzai, Afghan. 80 E1 29 50N 65 35 E
Badampahar, India 82 C8 22 10N 86 10 E
Badanah, Si. Arabia 84 D4 30 58N 41 30 E
Badarinath, India 81 D8 30 45N 79 30 E
Badas, Brunei 70 D4 4 33N 114 25 E
Badas, Kepulauan, Indonesia 70 D3 0 45N 107 5 E
Baddo →, Pakistan 79 D2 28 0N 64 20 E
Bade, Indonesia 71 F9 7 10 S 139 35 E
Baden, Austria 31 C9 48 1N 16 13 E
Baden, Switz. 29 B6 47 28N 8 18 E
Baden-Baden, Germany 27 G4 48 45N 8 15 E
Baden Park, Australia 116 B6 32 8 S 144 12 E
Baden-Württemberg □, Germany 27 G5 48 40N 9 0 E
Badenoch, U.K. 18 E4 56 59N 4 15W
Badgastein, Austria 30 D6 47 7N 13 9 E
Badger, Canada 129 C8 49 0N 56 4W
Badger, U.S.A. 144 J7 36 38N 119 1W
Bādghīsāt □, Afghan. 79 B1 35 0N 63 0 E
Badgom, India 81 B6 34 1N 74 45 E
Badhoevedorp, Neths. 20 D5 52 20N 4 47 E
Badia Polèsine, Italy 39 C8 45 6N 11 30 E
Badin, Pakistan 79 D3 24 38N 68 54 E
Badnera, India 82 D3 20 48N 77 44 E
Badogo, Mali 100 C3 11 2N 8 13W
Badong, China 69 B8 31 1N 110 23 E
Badr Ḥunayn, Si. Arabia 86 B2 23 44N 38 46 E
Baduen, Somali Rep. 90 F4 7 15N 47 40 E
Badulla, Sri Lanka 83 L5 7 1N 81 7 E
Badupi, Burma 78 E4 21 36N 93 27 E
Baena, Spain 37 H6 37 37N 4 20W
Baerami Creek, Australia 117 B9 32 27 S 150 27 E
Baexem, Neths. 21 F7 51 13N 5 53 E
Baeza, Ecuador 152 D2 0 25 S 77 53W
Baeza, Spain 35 H1 37 57N 3 25W
Bafa Gölü, Turkey 45 G9 37 30N 27 29 E
Bafang, Cameroon 101 D7 5 9N 10 11 E
Bafatá, Guinea-Biss. 100 C2 12 8N 14 40W
Baffin B., Canada 124 B13 72 0N 64 0W
Baffin I., Canada 127 B12 68 0N 75 0W
Bafia, Cameroon 101 E7 4 40N 11 10 E
Bafilo, Togo 101 D5 9 22N 1 22 E
Bafing →, Mali 100 C2 13 49N 10 50W
Bafliyūn, Syria 84 B3 36 37N 36 59 E
Baflo, Neths. 20 B9 53 22N 6 31 E
Bafoulabé, Mali 100 C2 13 50N 10 55W
Bafoussam, Cameroon 101 D7 5 28N 10 25 E
Bāfq, Iran 85 D7 31 40N 55 25 E
Bafra, Turkey 52 F6 41 34N 35 54 E
Bafra Burnu, Turkey 52 F6 41 44N 35 58 E
Bāft, Iran 85 D8 29 15N 56 38 E
Bafut, Cameroon 101 D7 6 6N 10 2 E
Bafwasende, Zaïre 106 B2 1 3N 27 5 E
Bagalkot, India 83 F2 16 10N 75 40 E
Bagamoyo, Tanzania 106 D4 6 28 S 38 55 E
Bagamoyo □, Tanzania 106 D4 6 20 S 38 30 E
Bagan Datoh, Malaysia 77 L3 3 59N 100 47 E
Bagan Serai, Malaysia 77 K3 5 1N 100 32 E
Baganga, Phil. 71 C7 7 34N 126 33 E
Bagani, Namibia 104 B3 18 7 S 21 41 E
Bagansiapiapi, Indonesia 70 D2 2 12N 100 50 E
Bagasra, India 80 J4 21 30N 71 0 E
Bagata, Zaïre 102 C3 3 44 S 17 57 E
Bagawi, Sudan 95 E3 12 20N 34 18 E
Bagdad, U.S.A. 145 L11 34 35N 115 53W
Bagdarin, U.S.S.R. 57 D12 54 26N 113 36 E
Bagé, Brazil 159 C5 31 20 S 54 15W
Bagenalstown = Muine Bheag, Ireland 19 D5 52 42N 6 57W
Baggs, U.S.A. 142 F10 41 8N 107 46W
Bagh, Pakistan 81 C5 33 59N 73 45 E
Baghdād, Iraq 84 C5 33 20N 44 30 E
Bagherhat, Bangla. 78 D2 22 40N 89 47 E
Bagheria, Italy 40 D6 38 5N 13 30 E
Baghlān, Afghan. 79 A3 36 12N 69 0 E
Baghlān □, Afghan. 79 B3 36 0N 68 30 E
Bagley, U.S.A. 138 B7 47 30N 95 22W
Bagnacavallo, Italy 39 D8 44 25N 11 58 E
Bagnara Cálabra, Italy 41 D8 38 16N 15 49 E
Bagnell Dam, U.S.A. 140 F4 38 14N 92 36W
Bagnères-de-Bigorre, France 24 E4 43 5N 0 9 E
Bagnères-de-Luchon, France 24 F4 42 47N 0 38 E
Bagni di Lucca, Italy 38 D7 44 1N 10 37 E
Bagno di Romagna, Italy 39 E8 43 50N 11 59 E
Bagnoles-de-l'Orne, France 22 D6 48 32N 0 25W
Bagnoli di Sopra, Italy 39 C8 45 13N 11 55 E
Bagnolo Mella, Italy 38 C7 45 27N 10 14 E
Bagnols-sur-Cèze, France 25 D8 44 10N 4 36 E
Bagnorégio, Italy 39 F9 42 38N 12 7 E
Bagolino, Italy 38 C7 45 49N 10 28 E
Bagotville, Canada 129 C5 48 22N 70 54W
Bagrdan, Yugoslavia 42 C6 44 5N 21 11 E
Bagua, Peru 156 B2 5 35 S 78 22W
Baguio, Phil. 71 A6 16 26N 120 34 E
Bahabón de Esgueva, Spain 34 D1 41 52N 3 43W
Bahadurabad Ghat, Bangla. 78 C2 25 11N 89 44 E
Bahadurgarh, India 80 E7 28 40N 76 57 E
Bahama, Canal Viejo de, W. Indies 148 B4 22 10N 77 30W
Bahamas ■, N. Amer. 149 B5 24 0N 75 0W
Baharampur, India 81 G13 24 2N 88 27 E
Baharîya, El Wâhât al, Egypt 94 J6 28 0N 28 50 E
Bahau, Malaysia 77 L4 2 48N 102 26 E
Bahawalnagar, Pakistan 79 C4 30 0N 73 15 E
Bahawalpur, Pakistan 79 C3 29 24N 71 40 E
Bahçe, Turkey 88 E7 37 13N 36 34 E
Baheri, India 81 E8 28 45N 79 34 E
Bahi, Tanzania 106 D4 5 58 S 35 21 E
Bahi Swamp, Tanzania 106 D4 6 10 S 35 0 E
Bahía = Salvador, Brazil 155 D4 13 0 S 38 30W
Bahía □, Brazil 155 D3 12 0 S 42 0W
Bahía, Is. de la, Honduras 148 C2 16 45N 86 15W
Bahía Blanca, Argentina 158 D3 38 35 S 62 13W
Bahía de Caráquez, Ecuador 152 D1 0 40 S 80 27W
Bahía Honda, Cuba 148 B3 22 54N 83 10W
Bahía Laura, Argentina 160 C3 48 10 S 66 30W
Bahía Negra, Paraguay 157 E6 20 5 S 58 5W
Bahir Dar, Ethiopia 95 E4 11 37N 37 10 E
Bahlah, Oman 87 B7 22 58N 57 18 E
Bahmanzād, Iran 85 D6 31 15N 51 47 E
Bahmer, Algeria 99 C4 27 32N 0 10W
Bahönye, Hungary 31 E10 46 25N 17 28 E
Bahr Aouk →, C.A.R. 102 A3 8 40N 19 0 E
Bahr el Ahmar □, Sudan 94 D4 20 0N 35 0 E
Bahr el Ghazâl □, Sudan 95 F2 7 0N 28 0 E
Bahr Salamat →, Chad 97 G3 9 20N 18 0 E
Bahr Yûsef →, Egypt 94 J7 28 25N 30 35 E
Bahra el Burullus, Egypt 94 H7 31 28N 30 48 E
Bahraich, India 81 F9 27 38N 81 37 E
Bahrain ■, Asia 85 E6 26 0N 50 35 E
Bahret Assad, Syria 84 C3 36 0N 38 15 E
Bahror, India 80 F7 27 51N 76 20 E
Bāhū Kalāt, Iran 85 E9 25 43N 61 25 E
Bai, Mali 100 C4 13 35N 3 28W
Bai Bung, Mui, Vietnam 77 H5 8 38N 104 44 E
Bai Duc, Vietnam 76 C5 18 3N 105 49 E
Bai Thuong, Vietnam 76 C5 19 54N 105 23 E
Baia Farta, Angola 103 E2 12 40 S 13 11 E
Baia Mare, Romania 46 B4 47 40N 23 35 E
Baia-Sprie, Romania 46 B4 47 41N 23 43 E
Baião, Brazil 154 B2 2 40 S 49 40W
Baïbokoum, Chad 97 G3 7 46N 15 43 E
Baicheng, China 67 B12 45 38N 122 42 E
Băicoi, Romania 46 D6 45 3N 25 52 E
Baidoa, Somali Rep. 90 G3 3 8N 43 30 E
Baie Comeau, Canada 129 C6 49 12N 68 10W
Baie-St-Paul, Canada 129 C5 47 28N 70 32W
Baie Trinité, Canada 129 C6 49 25N 67 20W
Baie Verte, Canada 129 C8 49 55N 56 12W
Baignes-Ste.-Radegonde, France 24 C3 45 23N 0 25W
Baigneux-les-Juifs, France 23 E11 47 31N 4 39 E
Baihe, China 66 H6 32 50N 110 5 E
Baihe, Taiwan 69 F13 23 24N 120 24 E
Ba'ījī, Iraq 84 C4 35 0N 43 30 E
Baikal, L. = Baykal, Oz., U.S.S.R. 57 D11 53 0N 108 0 E
Bailadila, Mt., India 82 E5 18 43N 81 15 E
Baile Atha Cliath = Dublin, Ireland 19 C5 53 20N 6 18W
Bailei, Ethiopia 95 F5 6 44N 40 18 E
Bailén, Spain 37 G7 38 8N 3 48W
Băileşti, Romania 46 E4 44 1N 23 20 E
Baileux, Belgium 21 H4 50 2N 4 23 E
Bailhongal, India 83 G2 15 55N 74 53 E
Bailique, Ilha, Brazil 154 A2 1 2N 49 58W
Bailleul, France 23 B9 50 44N 2 41 E
Bailundo, Angola 103 E3 12 10 S 15 50 E
Baima, China 68 A3 33 0N 100 26 E
Baimuru, Papua N. G. 120 D3 7 35 S 144 51 E
Bain-de-Bretagne, France 22 E5 47 50N 1 40W
Bainbridge, Ga., U.S.A. 135 K3 30 53N 84 34W
Bainbridge, Ind., U.S.A. 141 E10 39 46N 86 49W
Bainbridge, N.Y., U.S.A. 137 D9 42 17N 75 29W
Bainbridge, Ohio, U.S.A. 141 E13 39 14N 83 16W
Baing, Indonesia 71 F6 10 14 S 120 34 E
Bainiu, China 66 H7 32 50N 112 15 E
Bainville, U.S.A. 138 A2 48 8N 104 10W
Bainyik, Papua N. G. 120 C2 3 40 S 143 4 E
Bā'ir, Jordan 91 E5 30 45N 36 55 E
Baird, U.S.A. 139 J5 32 25N 99 25W
Baird Mts., U.S.A. 126 B3 67 10N 160 15W
Bairin Youqi, China 67 C10 43 30N 118 35 E
Bairin Zuoqi, China 67 C10 43 58N 119 15 E
Bairnsdale, Australia 117 D7 37 48 S 147 36 E
Baisha, China 66 G7 34 20N 112 32 E
Baïsole →, France 24 E4 43 26N 0 25 E
Baissa, Nigeria 101 D7 7 14N 10 38 E
Baitadi, Nepal 81 E9 29 35N 80 25 E
Baixa Grande, Brazil 155 D3 11 57 S 40 11W
Baiyin, China 66 F3 36 45N 104 14 E
Baiyü, China 68 B2 31 16N 98 50 E
Baiyu Shan, China 66 F4 37 15N 107 30 E
Baiyuda, Sudan 94 D3 17 35N 32 7 E
Baj Baj, India 81 H13 22 30N 88 5 E
Baja, Hungary 31 E11 46 12N 18 59 E
Baja, Pta., Mexico 146 B1 29 50N 116 0W
Baja California, Mexico 146 A1 31 10N 115 12W
Bajamar, Canary Is. 33 F3 28 33N 16 20W
Bajana, India 80 H4 23 7N 71 49 E
Bājgīrān, Iran 85 B8 37 36N 58 24 E
Bājil, Yemen 86 D3 15 4N 43 17 E
Bajimba, Mt., Australia 115 D5 29 17 S 152 6 E
Bajina Bašta, Yugoslavia 42 D4 43 58N 19 35 E
Bajmok, Yugoslavia 42 B4 45 57N 19 24 E
Bajo Nuevo, Caribbean 148 C4 15 40N 78 50W
Bajoga, Nigeria 101 C7 10 57N 11 20 E
Bajool, Australia 114 C5 23 40 S 150 35 E
Bak, Hungary 31 E9 46 43N 16 51 E
Bakal, U.S.S.R. 54 D6 54 56N 58 48 E
Bakala, C.A.R. 102 A4 6 15N 20 20 E
Bakanas, U.S.S.R. 55 A8 44 50N 76 15 E
Bakar, Yugoslavia 39 C11 45 18N 14 32 E
Bakchar, U.S.S.R. 56 D9 57 1N 82 5 E
Bakel, Neths. 21 F7 51 30N 5 45 E
Bakel, Senegal 100 C2 14 56N 12 20W
Baker, Calif., U.S.A. 145 K10 35 16N 116 8W
Baker, Mont., U.S.A. 138 B2 46 22N 104 12W
Baker, Oreg., U.S.A. 142 D5 44 50N 117 55W
Baker, Canal, Chile 160 C2 47 45 S 74 45W
Baker, L., Canada 126 B10 64 0N 96 0W
Baker I., Pac. Oc. 122 G10 0 10N 176 35W
Baker L., Australia 113 E4 26 54 S 126 5 E
Baker Lake, Canada 126 B10 64 20N 96 3W
Baker Mt., U.S.A. 142 B3 48 50N 121 49W
Bakers Creek, Australia 114 C4 21 13 S 149 7 E
Baker's Dozen Is., Canada 128 A4 56 45N 78 45W
Bakersfield, Calif., U.S.A. 145 K8 35 25N 119 0W
Bakersfield, Vt., U.S.A. 137 B12 44 46N 72 48W
Bakhchisaray, U.S.S.R. 52 D5 44 40N 33 45 E
Bakhmach, U.S.S.R. 50 F8 51 10N 32 45 E
Bākhtarān, Iran 84 C5 34 23N 47 0 E
Bakhtarān □, Iran 84 C5 34 0N 46 30 E
Bakinskikh Komissarov, im. 26, U.S.S.R. 89 D13 39 20N 49 15 E
Bakırdaği, Turkey 88 D6 38 13N 35 46 E
Bakırköy, Turkey 43 F13 41 2N 28 53 E
Bakkafjörður, Iceland 12 C6 66 2N 14 48W
Bakkagerði, Iceland 12 D7 65 31N 13 49W
Bakony →, Hungary 31 D10 47 35N 17 54 E
Bakony Forest = Bakony Hegyseg, Hungary 31 D10 47 10N 17 30 E
Bakony Hegyseg, Hungary 31 D10 47 10N 17 30 E
Bakori, Nigeria 101 C6 11 34N 7 25 E
Bakouma, C.A.R. 102 A4 5 40N 22 56 E
Bakov, Czech. 30 A7 50 27N 14 55 E
Bakpakty, U.S.S.R. 55 A8 44 35N 76 40 E
Bakr Uzyak, U.S.S.R. 54 E6 52 59N 58 38 E
Baku, U.S.S.R. 53 F13 40 25N 49 45 E
Bakutis Coast, Antarctica 7 D15 74 0 S 120 0W
Bakwa-Kenge, Zaïre 103 C4 4 51 S 22 4 E
Bala, Canada 136 A5 45 1N 79 37W
Bâlâ, Turkey 88 D5 39 32N 33 6 E
Bala, L., U.K. 16 E4 52 53N 3 38W
Bālā Morghāb, Afghan. 79 B1 35 35N 63 20 E
Balabac I., Phil. 70 C5 8 0N 117 0 E
Balabac Str., E. Indies 70 C5 7 53N 117 5 E
Balabagh, Afghan. 80 B4 34 25N 70 12 E
Balabakk, Lebanon 91 B5 34 0N 36 10 E
Balabalangan, Kepulauan, Indonesia 70 E5 2 20 S 117 30 E
Balabio, I., N. Cal. 121 T18 20 7 S 164 11 E
Bălăciţa, Romania 46 E4 44 23N 23 8 E
Balad, Iraq 84 C5 34 1N 44 9 E
Balad Rūz, Iraq 84 C5 33 42N 45 5 E
Bālādeh, Fārs, Iran 85 D6 29 17N 51 56 E
Bālādeh, Māzandaran, Iran 85 B6 36 12N 51 48 E
Balaghat, India 82 D5 21 49N 80 12 E
Balaghat Ra., India 82 E3 18 50N 76 30 E
Balaguer, Spain 34 D5 41 50N 0 50 E
Balakété, C.A.R. 102 A3 6 6N 19 54 E
Balakhna, U.S.S.R. 51 C13 56 25N 43 32 E
Balaklava, Australia 116 C3 34 7 S 138 22 E
Balaklava, U.S.S.R. 52 D5 44 30N 33 30 E
Balakleya, U.S.S.R. 52 B7 49 28N 36 55 E
Balakovo, U.S.S.R. 51 E15 52 4N 47 55 E
Balancán, Mexico 147 D6 17 48N 91 32W
Balanda, U.S.S.R. 51 F14 51 30N 44 40 E
Balangir, India 82 D6 20 43N 83 35 E
Balapur, India 82 D3 20 40N 76 45 E
Balashikha, U.S.S.R. 51 D10 55 49N 37 59 E
Balashov, U.S.S.R. 51 F13 51 30N 43 10 E
Balasinor, India 80 H5 22 57N 73 23 E
Balasore = Baleshwar, India 82 D8 21 35N 87 3 E
Balassagyarmat, Hungary 31 C12 48 4N 19 15 E
Balât, Egypt 94 B2 25 36N 29 19 E
Balaton, Hungary 31 E10 46 50N 17 40 E
Balatonfüred, Hungary 31 E10 46 58N 17 54 E
Balatonszentgyörgy, Hungary 31 E10 46 41N 17 19 E
Balazote, Spain 35 G2 38 54N 2 9W
Balbi, Mt., Papua N. G. 120 C8 5 55 S 154 58 E
Balboa, Panama 148 E4 9 0N 79 30W
Balbriggan, Ireland 19 C5 53 35N 6 10W
Balcarce, Argentina 158 D4 38 0 S 58 10W
Balcarres, Canada 131 C8 50 50N 103 35W

Barcoo 171

Balchik, Bulgaria .... 43 D13 43 28N 28 11 E
Balclutha, N.Z. .... 119 G4 46 15 S 169 45 E
Bald Hd., Australia ..... 113 G2 35 6 S 118 1 E
Bald I., Australia .... 113 F2 34 57 S 118 27 E
Bald Knob, U.S.A. 139 H9 35 20N 91 35W
Baldock L., Canada 131 B9 56 33N 97 57W
Baldwin, Fla., U.S.A. .. 135 K4 30 15N 82 10W
Baldwin, Mich., U.S.A. . 134 D3 43 54N 85 53W
Baldwinsville, U.S.A. ... 137 C8 43 10N 76 19W
Bale, Yugoslavia .... 39 C10 45 4N 13 46 E
Bale □, Ethiopia .... 95 F5 6 20N 41 30 E
Baleares □, Spain ...... 34 F8 39 30N 3 0 E
Baleares, Is., Spain ..... 33 B10 39 30N 3 0 E
Balearic Is. = Baleares, Is., Spain .... 33 B10 39 30N 3 0 E
Baleia, Pta. da, Brazil .. 155 E4 17 40 S 39 7W
Balen, Belgium .... 21 F6 51 10N 5 10 E
Băleni, Romania .... 46 D8 45 48N 27 51 E
Baler, Phil. .... 71 A6 15 46N 121 34 E
Balerna, Switz. .... 29 E8 45 52N 9 0 E
Baleshwar, India .... 82 D8 21 35N 87 3 E
Balezino, U.S.S.R. ..... 54 B3 58 2N 53 6 E
Balfate, Honduras 148 C2 15 48N 86 25W
Balfe's Creek, Australia . 114 C4 20 12 S 145 55 E
Balfour, S. Africa ...... 105 D4 26 38 S 28 35 E
Balfour Channel, Solomon Is. .... 121 M9 8 43 S 157 27 E
Balharshah, India ...... 82 E4 19 50N 79 23 E
Bali, Cameroon .... 101 D7 5 54N 10 0 E
Balí, Greece .... 32 D6 35 25N 24 47 E
Bali, Indonesia .... 70 F5 8 20 S 115 0 E
Bali □, Indonesia ...... 70 F5 8 20 S 115 0 E
Bali, Selat, Indonesia ... 71 H16 8 18 S 114 25 E
Baligród, Poland .... 31 B15 49 20N 22 17 E
Balık Gölü, Turkey ..... 89 D10 39 46N 43 34 E
Balıkeşir, Turkey .... 88 D2 39 35N 27 58 E
Balıkeşir □, Turkey ..... 88 D3 39 45N 28 0 E
Balikpapan, Indonesia ... 70 E5 1 10 S 116 55 E
Balimbing, Phil. .... 71 C5 5 5N 119 58 E
Balimo, Papua N. G. .... 120 E2 8 6 S 142 57 E
Baling, Malaysia .... 77 K3 5 41N 100 55 E
Baliza, Brazil .... 157 D7 16 0 S 52 20W
Baljurshi, Si. Arabia .... 86 C3 19 51N 41 33 E
Balk, Neths. .... 20 C7 52 54N 5 35 E
Balkan Mts. = Stara Planina, Bulgaria ..... 43 D8 43 15N 23 0 E
Balkh □, Afghan. ...... 79 A2 36 50N 67 0 E
Balkhash, U.S.S.R. ..... 56 E8 46 50N 74 50 E
Balkhash, Ozero, U.S.S.R. .... 56 E8 46 0N 74 50 E
Ballachulish, U.K. 18 E3 56 40N 5 10W
Balladonia, Australia .... 113 F3 32 27 S 123 51 E
Ballara, Australia ...... 116 B4 32 19 S 140 45 E
Ballarat, Australia ...... 115 F3 37 33 S 143 50 E
Ballard, L., Australia ... 113 E3 29 20 S 120 40 E
Ballater, U.K. 18 D5 57 2N 3 2W
Balldale, Australia ...... 117 C7 35 50 S 146 33 E
Ballenas, Canal de, Mexico 146 B2 29 10N 113 45W
Balleny Is., Antarctica .. 7 C11 66 30 S 163 0 E
Ballia, India .... 81 G11 25 46N 84 12 E
Ballidu, Australia ...... 113 F2 30 35 S 116 45 E
Ballina, Australia ...... 115 D5 28 50 S 153 31 E
Ballina, Mayo, Ireland .. 19 B2 54 7N 9 10W
Ballina, Tipp., Ireland .. 19 D3 52 49N 8 27W
Ballinasloe, Ireland 19 C3 53 20N 8 12W
Ballinger, U.S.A. 139 K5 31 45N 99 58W
Ballinrobe, Ireland 19 C2 53 36N 9 13W
Ballinskelligs B., Ireland 19 E1 51 46N 10 11W
Ballon, France .... 22 D7 48 10N 0 14 E
Ballycastle, U.K. 19 A5 55 12N 6 15W
Ballymena, U.K. 19 B5 54 53N 6 18W
Ballymena □, U.K. 19 B5 54 53N 6 18W
Ballymoney, U.K. 19 A5 55 5N 6 30W
Ballymoney □, U.K. 19 A5 55 5N 6 23W
Ballyshannon, Ireland ... 19 B3 54 30N 8 10W
Balmaceda, Chile .... 160 C2 46 0 S 71 50W
Balmazújváros, Hungary 31 D14 47 37N 21 21 E
Balmhorn, Switz. .... 28 D5 46 26N 7 42 E
Balmoral, Australia ..... 116 D4 37 15 S 141 48 E
Balmoral, U.K. 18 D5 57 3N 3 13W
Balmorhea, U.S.A. 139 K3 31 2N 103 41W
Balombo, Angola .... 103 E2 12 21 S 14 46 E
Balonne →, Australia .. 115 D4 28 47 S 147 56 E
Balrampur, India .... 81 F10 27 30N 82 20 E
Balranald, Australia .... 116 C5 34 38 S 143 33 E
Balş, Romania .... 46 E5 44 22N 24 5 E
Balsapuerto, Peru ...... 156 B2 5 48 S 76 33W
Balsas, Mexico 147 D5 18 0N 99 40W
Balsas →, Goiás, Brazil 154 C2 9 58 S 47 52W
Balsas →, Maranhão, Brazil .... 154 C3 7 15 S 44 35W
Balsas →, Mexico 146 D4 17 55N 102 10W
Bålsta, Sweden .... 14 E11 59 35N 17 30 E
Balsthal, Switz. .... 28 B5 47 19N 7 41 E
Balston Spa, U.S.A. 137 D11 43 0N 73 52W
Balta, Romania .... 46 E3 44 54N 22 38 E
Balta, U.S.A. 138 A4 48 12N 100 7W
Balta, R.S.F.S.R., U.S.S.R. .... 53 E11 42 58N 44 32 E
Balta, Ukraine S.S.R., U.S.S.R. .... 52 B3 48 2N 29 45 E
Baltanás, Spain 36 D6 41 56N 4 15W
Baltic Sea, Europe ...... 13 H15 57 0N 19 0 E
Baltîm, Egypt .... 94 H7 31 35N 31 10 E
Baltimore, Ireland 19 E2 51 29N 9 22W
Baltimore, U.S.A. 134 F7 39 18N 76 37W
Baltit, Pakistan .... 81 A6 36 15N 74 40 E
Baltrum, Germany ...... 26 B3 53 43N 7 25 E
Baluchistan □, Pakistan . 79 D2 27 30N 65 0 E
Balurghat, India .... 81 G13 25 15N 88 44 E
Balya, Turkey .... 88 D2 39 44N 27 35 E
Balygychan, U.S.S.R. ... 57 C16 63 56N 154 12 E
Balzar, Ecuador .... 152 D2 2 2 S 79 54W
Bam, Iran .... 85 D8 29 7N 58 14 E
Bama, China .... 68 E6 24 8N 107 12 E
Bama, Nigeria .... 101 C7 11 33N 13 41 E
Bamako, Mali 100 C3 12 34N 7 55W
Bamba, Mali 101 B4 17 5N 1 24W
Bamba, Zaïre .... 103 D3 5 45 S 18 23 E
Bambamarca, Peru ...... 156 B2 6 36 S 78 32W
Bambari, C.A.R. .... 102 A4 5 40N 20 35 E
Bambaroo, Australia .... 114 B4 18 50 S 146 10 E
Bamberg, Germany ..... 27 F6 49 54N 10 53 E
Bamberg, U.S.A. 135 J5 33 19N 81 1W
Bambesi, Ethiopia ...... 95 F3 9 45N 34 40 E
Bambey, Senegal 100 C1 14 42N 16 28W
Bambili, Zaïre .... 106 B2 3 40N 26 0 E
Bambuí, Brazil .... 155 F2 20 1 S 45 58W
Bamenda, Cameroon ... 101 D7 5 57N 10 11 E
Bamfield, Canada 130 D3 48 45N 125 10W
Bāmīān □, Afghan. .... 79 B2 35 0N 67 0 E
Bamiancheng, China .... 67 C13 43 15N 124 2 E
Bamingui, C.A.R. ...... 102 A4 7 34N 20 11 E
Bamkin, Cameroon ..... 101 D7 6 3N 11 27 E
Bampūr, Iran .... 85 E9 27 15N 60 21 E
Ban Aranyaprathet, Thailand .... 76 F4 13 41N 102 30 E
Ban Ban, Laos .... 76 C4 19 31N 103 30 E
Ban Bang Hin, Thailand 77 H2 9 32N 98 35 E
Ban Chiang Klang, Thailand .... 76 C3 19 25N 100 55 E
Ban Chik, Laos .... 76 D4 17 15N 102 22 E
Ban Choho, Thailand ... 76 E4 15 2N 102 9 E
Ban Dan Lan Hoi, Thailand .... 76 D2 17 0N 99 35 E
Ban Don = Surat Thani, Thailand .... 77 H2 9 6N 99 20 E
Ban Don, Vietnam ..... 76 F6 12 53N 107 48 E
Ban Don, Ao, Thailand . 77 H2 9 20N 99 25 E
Ban Dong, Thailand .... 76 C3 19 30N 100 59 E
Ban Hong, Thailand .... 76 C2 18 18N 98 50 E
Ban Kaeng, Thailand ... 76 D3 17 29N 100 7 E
Ban Keun, Laos .... 76 C4 18 22N 102 35 E
Ban Khai, Thailand .... 76 F3 12 46N 101 18 E
Ban Kheun, Laos ...... 76 B3 20 13N 101 7 E
Ban Khlong Kua, Thailand .... 77 J3 6 57N 100 8 E
Ban Khuan Mao, Thailand .... 77 J2 7 50N 99 37 E
Ban Khun Yuam, Thailand .... 76 C1 18 49N 97 57 E
Ban Ko Yai Chim, Thailand .... 77 G2 11 17N 99 26 E
Ban Kok, Thailand ..... 76 D4 16 40N 103 40 E
Ban Laem, Thailand .... 76 F2 13 13N 99 59 E
Ban Lao Ngam, Laos .... 76 E6 15 28N 106 10 E
Ban Le Kathe, Thailand 76 E2 15 49N 98 53 E
Ban Mae Chedi, Thailand 76 C2 19 11N 99 31 E
Ban Mae Laeng, Thailand 76 B2 20 1N 99 17 E
Ban Mae Sariang, Thailand .... 76 C1 18 10N 97 56 E
Ban Mê Thuôt = Buon Me Thuot, Vietnam ... 76 F7 12 40N 108 3 E
Ban Mi, Thailand ...... 76 E3 15 3N 100 32 E
Ban Muong Mo, Laos ... 76 C4 19 4N 103 58 E
Ban Na Mo, Laos ...... 76 D5 17 7N 105 40 E
Ban Na San, Thailand .. 77 H2 8 53N 99 52 E
Ban Na Tong, Laos .... 76 B3 20 56N 101 47 E
Ban Nam Bac, Laos .... 76 B4 20 38N 102 20 E
Ban Nam Ma, Laos .... 76 A3 22 2N 101 37 E
Ban Ngang, Laos ...... 76 E6 15 59N 106 11 E
Ban Nong Bok, Laos ... 76 D5 17 5N 104 48 E
Ban Nong Boua, Laos .. 76 E6 15 40N 106 33 E
Ban Nong Pling, Thailand 76 E3 15 40N 100 10 E
Ban Pak Chan, Thailand 77 G2 10 32N 98 51 E
Ban Phai, Thailand ..... 76 D4 16 4N 102 44 E
Ban Pong, Thailand .... 76 F2 13 50N 99 55 E
Ban Ron Phibun, Thailand .... 77 H2 8 9N 99 51 E
Ban Sanam Chai, Thailand .... 77 J3 7 33N 100 25 E
Ban Sangkha, Thailand . 76 E4 14 37N 103 52 E
Ban Tak, Thailand ..... 76 D2 17 2N 99 4 E
Ban Tako, Thailand .... 76 E4 14 5N 102 40 E
Ban Tha Dua, Thailand . 76 D2 17 59N 98 39 E
Ban Tha Li, Thailand .. 76 D3 17 37N 101 25 E
Ban Tha Nun, Thailand 77 H2 8 12N 98 18 E
Ban Thahine, Laos ..... 76 E5 14 12N 105 33 E
Ban Xien Kok, Laos .... 76 B3 20 54N 100 39 E
Ban Yen Nhan, Vietnam 76 B6 20 57N 106 2 E
Banā, Punta de la, Spain 34 E5 40 33N 0 40 E
Banā, W. →, Yemen ... 86 D4 13 3N 45 24 E
Banaba, Kiribati ...... 122 H8 0 45 S 169 50 E
Bañalbufar, Spain ..... 33 B9 39 42N 2 31 E
Banalia, Zaïre .... 106 B2 1 32N 25 5 E
Banam, Cambodia ..... 77 G5 11 20N 105 17 E
Banamba, Mali 100 C3 13 29N 7 22W
Banana, Australia ...... 114 C5 24 28 S 150 8 E
Bananal, I. do, Brazil .. 155 D1 11 30 S 50 30W
Banaras = Varanasi, India .... 81 G10 25 22N 83 0 E
Banas →, Gujarat, India 80 H4 23 45N 71 25 E
Banas →, Mad. P., India 81 G9 24 15N 81 30 E
Bânâs, Ras, Egypt ...... 94 C4 23 57N 35 50 E
Banaz, Turkey .... 88 D3 38 44N 29 46 E
Banbān, Si. Arabia ..... 84 E5 25 1N 46 35 E
Banbridge, U.K. 19 B5 54 21N 6 17W
Banbridge □, U.K. 19 B5 54 21N 6 16W
Banbury, U.K. 17 E6 52 4N 1 21W
Banchory, U.K. 18 D6 57 3N 2 30W
Bancroft, Canada 128 C4 45 3N 77 51W
Band, Romania .... 46 C5 46 30N 24 25 E
Band Bonī, Iran .... 85 E8 25 30N 59 33 E
Band-e Torkestān, Afghan. .... 79 B2 35 30N 64 0 E
Band Qīr, Iran .... 85 D6 31 39N 48 53 E
Banda, Cameroon ...... 102 B2 3 58N 14 32 E
Banda, India .... 81 G9 25 30N 80 26 E
Banda, Kepulauan, Indonesia .... 71 E7 4 37 S 129 50 E
Banda Aceh, Indonesia . 70 C1 5 35N 95 20 E
Banda Banda, Mt., Australia .... 117 A10 31 10 S 152 28 E
Banda Elat, Indonesia .. 71 F8 5 40 S 133 5 E
Banda Is. = Banda, Kepulauan, Indonesia . 71 E7 4 37 S 129 50 E
Banda Sea, Indonesia ... 71 F8 6 0 S 130 0 E
Bandai-San, Japan ..... 60 F10 37 36N 140 4 E
Bandama →, Ivory C. .. 100 D3 6 32N 5 30W
Bandān, Iran .... 85 D9 31 23N 60 44 E
Bandanaira, Indonesia .. 71 E7 4 32 S 129 54 E
Bandanwara, India ..... 80 F6 26 9N 74 38 E
Bandar = Machilipatnam, India .... 83 F5 16 12N 81 8 E
Bandār 'Abbās, Iran .... 85 E8 27 15N 56 15 E
Bandar-e Anzalī, Iran ... 85 B6 37 30N 49 30 E
Bandar-e Chārak, Iran .. 85 E7 26 45N 54 20 E
Bandar-e Deylam, Iran . 85 D6 30 5N 50 10 E
Bandar-e Khomeyni, Iran 85 D6 30 30N 49 5 E
Bandar-e Lengeh, Iran .. 85 E7 26 35N 54 58 E
Bandar-e Maqām, Iran .. 85 E7 26 56N 53 29 E
Bandar-e Ma'shur, Iran . 85 D6 30 35N 49 10 E
Bandar-e Nakhīlū, Iran . 85 E7 26 58N 53 30 E
Bandar-e Rīg, Iran ..... 85 D6 29 29N 50 38 E
Bandar-e Torkeman, Iran 85 B7 37 0N 54 10 E
Bandar Maharani = Muar, Malaysia ...... 77 L4 2 3N 102 34 E
Bandar Penggaram = Batu Pahat, Malaysia . 77 M4 1 50N 102 56 E
Bandar Seri Begawan, Brunei .... 70 D5 4 52N 115 0 E
Bandawe, Malawi ...... 107 E3 11 58 S 34 5 E
Bande, Belgium .... 21 H6 50 10N 5 25 E
Bande, Spain 36 C3 42 3N 7 58W
Bandeira, Pico da, Brazil 155 F3 20 26 S 41 47W
Bandeirante, Brazil ..... 155 D1 13 41 S 50 48W
Bandera, Argentina ..... 158 B3 28 55 S 62 20W
Bandera, U.S.A. 139 L5 29 45N 99 3W
Banderas, B. de, Mexico 146 C3 20 40N 105 30W
Bandia →, India ...... 82 E5 19 2N 80 28 E
Bandiagara, Mali 100 C4 14 12N 3 29W
Bandırma, Turkey ..... 88 C3 40 20N 28 0 E
Bandon, Ireland 19 E3 51 44N 8 45W
Bandon →, Ireland 19 E3 51 40N 8 41W
Bandoua, C.A.R. ...... 102 B4 4 39N 21 42 E
Bandula, Mozam. ...... 107 F3 19 0 S 33 7 E
Bandundu, Zaïre .... 102 C3 3 15 S 17 22 E
Bandung, Indonesia .... 71 G12 6 54 S 107 36 E
Bandya, Australia ...... 113 E3 27 40 S 122 5 E
Băneasa, Romania ..... 46 D8 45 56N 27 55 E
Bāneh, Iran .... 84 C5 35 59N 45 53 E
Bañeres, Spain 35 G4 38 44N 0 38W
Banes, Cuba 149 B4 21 0N 75 42W
Banff, Canada 130 C5 51 10N 115 34W
Banff, U.K. 18 D6 57 40N 2 32W
Banff Nat. Park, Canada 130 C5 51 30N 116 15W
Banfora, Burkina Faso .. 100 C4 10 40N 4 40W
Bang Fai →, Laos ..... 76 D5 16 57N 104 45 E
Bang Hieng →, Laos .. 76 D5 16 10N 105 10 E
Bang Krathum, Thailand 76 D3 16 34N 100 18 E
Bang Lamung, Thailand 76 F3 13 3N 100 56 E
Bang Mun Nak, Thailand 76 D3 16 2N 100 23 E
Bang Pa In, Thailand ... 76 E3 14 14N 100 35 E
Bang Rakam, Thailand . 76 D3 16 45N 100 7 E
Bang Saphan, Thailand . 77 G2 11 14N 99 28 E
Bangala Dam, Zimbabwe 107 G3 21 7 S 31 25 E
Bangalore, India .... 83 H3 12 59N 77 40 E
Bangante, Cameroon ... 101 D7 5 8N 10 32 E
Bangaon, India .... 81 H13 23 0N 88 47 E
Bangassou, C.A.R. ..... 102 B4 4 55N 23 7 E
Bangeta, Mt., Papua N. G. .... 120 D4 6 21 S 147 3 E
Banggai, Kepulauan, Indonesia .... 71 E6 1 40 S 123 30 E
Banggai Arch., Indonesia 72 B2 2 0 S 123 15 E
Banggi, P., Malaysia .... 70 C5 7 17N 117 12 E
Banghāzī, Libya .... 96 B4 32 11N 20 3 E
Banghāzī □, Libya ..... 96 B4 32 7N 20 4 E
Bangil, Indonesia ...... 71 G15 7 36 S 112 50 E
Bangjang, Sudan .... 95 E3 11 23N 32 41 E
Bangka, P., Sulawesi, Indonesia .... 71 D7 1 50N 125 5 E
Bangka, P., Sumatera, Indonesia .... 70 E3 2 0 S 105 50 E
Bangka, Selat, Indonesia 70 E3 2 30 S 105 30 E
Bangkalan, Indonesia ... 71 G15 7 2 S 112 46 E
Bangkinang, Indonesia .. 70 D2 0 18N 101 5 E
Bangko, Indonesia ..... 70 E2 2 5 S 102 9 E
Bangkok, Thailand ..... 76 F3 13 45N 100 35 E
Bangladesh ■, Asia .... 78 D3 24 0N 90 0 E
Bangolo, Ivory C. 100 D3 7 1N 7 29W
Bangong Co, India ..... 81 B8 35 50N 79 20 E
Bangor, Down, U.K. ... 19 B6 54 40N 5 40W
Bangor, Gwynedd, U.K. 16 D3 53 13N 4 9W
Bangor, Maine, U.S.A. . 129 D6 44 48N 68 42W
Bangor, Mich., U.S.A. .. 141 B10 42 18N 86 7W
Bangor, Pa., U.S.A. 137 F9 40 51N 75 13W
Bangu, Zaïre .... 102 C3 0 3 S 19 12 E
Bangued, Phil. .... 71 A6 17 40N 120 37 E
Bangui, C.A.R. .... 102 B3 4 23N 18 35 E
Banguru, Zaïre .... 106 B2 0 30N 27 10 E
Bangweulu, L., Zambia . 107 E3 11 0 S 30 0 E
Bangweulu Swamp, Zambia .... 107 E3 11 20 S 30 15 E
Bani, Dom. Rep. 149 C5 18 16N 70 22W
Bani →, Mali 100 C4 14 30N 4 12W
Bani, Djebel, Morocco .. 98 C3 29 16N 8 0W
Bani Bangou, Niger .... 101 B5 15 3N 2 42 E
Banī Sa'd, Iraq .... 84 C5 33 34N 44 32 E
Banī Sār, Si. Arabia .... 86 B3 20 6N 41 27 E
Banī Walīd, Libya ...... 96 B2 31 36N 13 53 E
Bania, Ivory C. 100 D4 9 4N 3 6W
Baniara, Papua N. G. ... 120 E5 9 44 S 149 54 E
Banihal Pass, India .... 81 C6 33 30N 75 12 E
Banīnah, Libya .... 96 B4 32 0N 20 12 E
Bānīyās, Syria .... 84 C3 35 10N 36 0 E
Banja Luka, Yugoslavia . 42 C2 44 49N 17 11 E
Banjar, Indonesia ..... 71 G13 7 24 S 108 30 E
Banjarmasin, Indonesia . 70 E4 3 20 S 114 35 E
Banjarnegara, Indonesia 71 G13 7 24 S 109 42 E
Banjul, Gambia 100 C1 13 28N 16 40W
Banka Banka, Australia . 114 B1 18 50 S 134 0 E
Banket, Zimbabwe ..... 107 F3 17 27 S 30 19 E
Bankilaré, Niger .... 101 C5 14 35N 0 44 E
Bankipore, India ...... 81 G11 25 35N 85 10 E
Banks, Is., Vanuatu .... 121 C5 13 50 S 167 30 E
Banks I., B.C., Canada . 130 C3 53 20N 130 0W
Banks I., N.W.T., Canada 126 A7 73 15N 121 30W
Banks I., Papua N. G. ... 120 F2 10 10 S 142 15 E
Banks Pen., N.Z. .... 119 D8 43 45 S 173 15 E
Banks Str., Australia ... 114 G4 40 40 S 148 10 E
Bankura, India .... 81 H12 23 11N 87 18 E
Bankya, Bulgaria ...... 42 E8 42 43N 23 8 E
Bann →, Down, U.K. .. 19 B5 54 30N 6 31W
Bann →, L'derry., U.K. 19 A5 55 10N 6 34W
Bannalec, France 22 E3 47 57N 3 42W
Bannang Sata, Thailand . 77 J3 6 16N 101 16 E
Bannerton, Australia ... 116 C5 34 42 S 142 47 E
Banning, U.S.A. 145 M10 33 58N 116 52W
Banningville = Bandundu, Zaïre ..... 102 C3 3 15 S 17 22 E
Bannockburn, Canada .. 136 B7 44 39N 77 33W
Bannockburn, U.K. 18 E5 56 5N 3 55W
Bannockburn, Zimbabwe 107 G2 20 17 S 29 48 E
Bannu, Pakistan .... 79 B3 33 0N 70 18 E
Bañolas, Spain .... 34 C7 42 16N 2 44 E
Banon, France .... 25 D9 44 2N 5 38 E
Baños de la Encina, Spain 37 G7 38 10N 3 46W
Baños de Molgas, Spain . 36 C3 42 15N 7 40W
Bánovce, Czech. .... 31 C11 48 44N 18 16 E
Banská Bystrica, Czech. . 31 C12 48 46N 19 14 E
Banská Štiavnica, Czech. 31 C11 48 25N 18 55 E
Bansko, Bulgaria ...... 43 F8 41 52N 23 28 E
Banswara, India .... 80 H6 23 32N 74 24 E
Banten, Indonesia ...... 71 G12 6 5 S 106 8 E
Bantry, Ireland 19 E2 51 40N 9 28W
Bantry B., Ireland 19 E2 51 35N 9 50W
Bantul, Indonesia ...... 71 G14 7 55 S 110 19 E
Bantva, India .... 80 J4 21 29N 70 12 E
Bantval, India .... 83 H2 12 55N 75 0 E
Banya, Bulgaria .... 43 E9 42 33N 24 50 E
Banyak, Kepulauan, Indonesia .... 70 D1 2 10N 97 10 E
Banyo, Cameroon ...... 101 D7 6 52N 11 45 E
Banyuls-sur-Mer, France 24 F7 42 28N 3 8 E
Banyumas, Indonesia ... 71 G13 7 32 S 109 18 E
Banyuwangi, Indonesia . 71 H16 8 13 S 114 21 E
Banzare Coast, Antarctica 7 C9 68 0 S 125 0 E
Banzyville = Mobayi, Zaïre .... 102 B4 4 15N 21 8 E
Bao Ha, Vietnam .... 76 A5 22 11N 104 21 E
Bao Lac, Vietnam ...... 76 A5 22 57N 105 40 E
Bao Loc, Vietnam ...... 77 G6 11 32N 107 48 E
Bao'an, China .... 69 F10 22 27N 114 10 E
Baocheng, China .... 66 H4 33 12N 106 56 E
Baode, China .... 66 E6 39 1N 111 5 E
Baodi, China .... 67 E9 39 38N 117 20 E
Baoding, China .... 66 E8 38 50N 115 28 E
Baoji, China .... 66 G4 34 20N 107 5 E
Baojing, China .... 68 C7 28 45N 109 41 E
Baokang, China .... 69 B8 31 54N 111 12 E
Baoro, C.A.R. .... 102 A3 5 40N 15 58 E
Baoshan, Shanghai, China 69 B13 31 27N 121 26 E
Baoshan, Yunnan, China 68 E2 25 10N 99 5 E
Baotou, China .... 66 D6 40 32N 110 2 E
Baoying, China .... 67 H10 33 17N 119 20 E
Bap, India .... 80 F5 27 23N 72 18 E
Bapatla, India .... 83 G5 15 55N 80 30 E
Bapaume, France ...... 23 B9 50 7N 2 50 E
Bāqerābād, Iran .... 85 C6 33 2N 51 58 E
Ba'qūbah, Iraq .... 84 C5 33 45N 44 50 E
Baquedano, Chile ..... 158 A2 23 20 S 69 52W
Bar, U.S.S.R. .... 52 B2 49 4N 27 40 E
Bar, Yugoslavia .... 42 E4 42 8N 19 8 E
Bar Bigha, India ...... 81 G11 25 21N 85 47 E
Bar Harbor, U.S.A. 129 D6 44 15N 68 20W
Bar-le-Duc, France .... 23 D12 48 47N 5 10 E
Bar-sur-Aube, France ... 23 D11 48 14N 4 40 E
Bar-sur-Seine, France ... 23 D11 48 7N 4 20 E
Barabai, Indonesia ..... 70 E5 2 32 S 115 34 E
Barabinsk, U.S.S.R. .... 56 D8 55 20N 78 20 E
Baraboo, U.S.A. 138 D10 43 28N 89 46W
Baracaldo, Spain 34 B2 43 18N 2 59W
Baracoa, Cuba 149 B5 20 20N 74 30W
Baradero, Argentina .... 158 C4 33 52 S 59 29W
Baradine, Australia .... 117 A8 30 56 S 149 4 E
Baraga, U.S.A. 138 B10 46 49N 88 29W
Barahona, Dom. Rep. ... 149 C5 18 13N 71 7W
Barahona, Spain 34 D2 41 17N 2 39W
Baraka →, Sudan ...... 94 D4 18 13N 37 35 E
Barakot, India .... 81 J11 21 33N 84 59 E
Barakpur, India .... 81 H13 22 44N 88 30 E
Barakula, Australia .... 115 D5 26 30 S 150 33 E
Baralaba, Australia .... 114 C4 24 13 S 149 50 E
Baralzon L., Canada ... 131 B9 60 0N 98 3W
Baramati, India .... 82 E2 18 11N 74 33 E
Baramba, India .... 82 D7 20 25N 85 23 E
Barameiya, Sudan ...... 94 D4 18 32N 36 38 E
Baramula, India .... 81 B6 34 15N 74 20 E
Baran, India .... 80 G7 25 9N 76 40 E
Baranoa, Colombia 152 A3 10 48N 74 55W
Baranof I., U.S.A. 130 B1 57 0N 135 10W
Baranovichi, U.S.S.R. .. 50 E5 53 10N 26 0 E
Baranów Sandomierski, Poland .... 47 E8 50 29N 21 30 E
Baranya □, Hungary ... 31 F11 46 0N 18 15 E
Barão de Cocais, Brazil . 155 E3 19 56 S 43 28W
Barão de Grajaú, Brazil 154 C3 6 45 S 43 1W
Barão de Melgaço, Mato Grosso, Brazil .. 157 D6 16 14 S 55 52W
Barão de Melgaço, Rondônia, Brazil ..... 157 C5 11 50 S 60 45W
Baraolt, Romania ...... 46 C6 46 5N 25 34 E
Barapasi, Indonesia ..... 71 E9 2 15 S 137 5 E
Barapina, Papua N. G. .. 120 D8 6 21 S 155 25 E
Barasat, India .... 81 H13 22 46N 88 31 E
Barat Daya, Kepulauan, Indonesia .... 71 F7 7 30 S 128 0 E
Barataria B., U.S.A. ... 139 L10 29 15N 89 45W
Baraut, India .... 80 E7 29 13N 77 7 E
Baraya, Colombia 152 C2 3 10N 75 4W
Barbacena, Brazil ..... 155 F3 21 15 S 43 56W
Barbacoas, Colombia ... 152 C2 1 45N 78 0W
Barbacoas, Venezuela .. 152 B4 9 29N 66 58W
Barbados ■, W. Indies .. 149 D8 13 0N 59 30W
Barbalha, Brazil .... 154 C4 7 19 S 39 17W
Barban, Yugoslavia .... 39 C11 45 5N 14 4 E
Barbastro, Spain ...... 34 C5 42 2N 0 5 E
Barbate, Spain 37 J5 36 13N 5 56W
Barberino di Mugello, Italy .... 39 D8 44 1N 11 15 E
Barberton, S. Africa .... 105 D5 25 42 S 31 2 E
Barberton, U.S.A. 136 E3 41 0N 81 40W
Barbezieux, France 24 C3 45 28N 0 9W
Barbosa, Colombia 152 B3 5 57N 73 37W
Barbourville, U.S.A. ... 135 G4 36 57N 83 52W
Barbuda, W. Indies 149 C7 17 30N 61 40W
Barcaldine, Australia ... 114 C4 23 43 S 145 6 E
Barcarrota, Spain 37 G4 38 31N 6 51W
Barcellona Pozzo di Gotto, Italy .... 41 D8 38 8N 15 15 E
Barcelona, Spain ...... 34 D7 41 21N 2 10 E
Barcelona, Venezuela ... 153 A5 10 10N 64 40W
Barcelona □, Spain .... 34 D7 41 30N 2 0 E
Barcelonette, France .... 25 D10 44 23N 6 40 E
Barcelos, Brazil ...... 153 D5 1 0 S 63 0W
Barcin, Poland .... 47 C4 52 52N 17 55 E
Barcoo →, Australia ... 114 D3 25 30 S 142 50 E

172 Barcs

Barcs, Hungary 31 F10 45 58N 17 28 E
Barczewo, Poland 47 B7 53 50N 20 42 E
Barda, U.S.S.R. 53 F12 40 25N 47 10 E
Barda del Medio, Argentina 160 A3 38 45 S 68 11W
Bardai, Chad 97 D3 21 25N 17 0 E
Bardas Blancas, Argentina 158 D2 35 49 S 69 45W
Barddhaman, India 81 H12 23 14N 87 39 E
Bardejov, Czech. 31 B14 49 18N 21 15 E
Bardera, Somali Rep. 90 G3 2 20N 42 27 E
Bardi, Italy 38 D6 44 38N 9 43 E
Bardia, Libya 96 B5 31 45N 25 5 E
Bardo, Poland 47 E3 50 31N 16 42 E
Bardoli, India 82 D1 21 12N 73 5 E
Bardolino, Italy 38 C7 45 33N 10 43 E
Bardsey I., U.K. 16 E3 52 46N 4 47W
Bardstown, U.S.A. 141 G11 37 50N 85 29W
Bareilly, India 81 E8 28 22N 79 27 E
Barellan, Australia 117 C7 34 16 S 146 24 E
Barentin, France 22 C7 49 33N 0 58 E
Barenton, France 22 D6 48 38N 0 50W
Barents Sea, Arctic 6 B9 73 0N 39 0 E
Barentu, Ethiopia 95 D4 15 2N 37 35 E
Barfleur, France 22 C5 49 40N 1 17W
Barfleur, Pte. de, France 22 C5 49 42N 1 16W
Barga, Italy 38 D7 44 5N 10 30 E
Bargal, Somali Rep. 90 E5 11 25N 51 0 E
Bargara, Australia 114 C5 24 50 S 152 25 E
Barge, Italy 38 D4 44 43N 7 19 E
Bargnop, Sudan 95 F2 9 32N 28 25 E
Bargo, Australia 117 C9 34 18 S 150 35 E
Bargteheide, Germany 26 B6 53 42N 10 13 E
Barguzin, U.S.S.R. 57 D11 53 37N 109 37 E
Barh, India 81 G11 25 29N 85 46 E
Barhaj, India 81 F10 26 18N 83 44 E
Barhi, India 81 G11 24 15N 85 25 E
Bari, India 80 F7 26 39N 77 39 E
Bari, Italy 41 A9 41 6N 16 52 E
Bari Doab, Pakistan 80 D5 30 20N 73 0 E
Bariadi □, Tanzania 106 C3 2 45 S 34 40 E
Barīm, Yemen 86 D3 12 39N 43 25 E
Barima →, Guyana 153 B5 8 33N 60 25W
Barinas, Venezuela 152 B3 8 36N 70 15W
Barinas □, Venezuela 152 B4 8 10N 69 50W
Baring, U.S.A. 140 D4 40 15N 92 12W
Baring, C., Canada 126 B8 70 0N 117 30W
Baringa, Zaïre 102 B4 0 45N 20 52 E
Baringo, Kenya 106 B4 0 47N 36 16 E
Baringo □, Kenya 106 B4 0 55N 36 0 E
Baringo, L., Kenya 106 B4 0 47N 36 16 E
Barinitas, Venezuela 152 B3 8 45N 70 25W
Baripada, India 82 D8 21 57N 86 45 E
Bariri, Brazil 155 F2 22 4 S 48 44W
Bârîs, Egypt 94 C3 24 42N 30 31 E
Barisal, Bangla. 78 D3 22 45N 90 20 E
Barisan, Bukit, Indonesia 70 E2 3 30 S 102 15 E
Barito →, Indonesia 70 E4 4 0 S 114 50 E
Barjac, France 25 D8 44 20N 4 22 E
Barjols, France 25 E10 43 34N 6 2 E
Barjūj, Wadi →, Libya 96 C2 25 26N 12 12 E
Bark L., Canada 136 A7 45 27N 77 51W
Barka = Baraka →, Sudan 94 D4 18 13N 37 35 E
Barkam, China 68 B4 31 51N 102 28 E
Barker, U.S.A. 136 C6 43 20N 78 35W
Barkley Sound, Canada 130 D3 48 50N 125 10W
Barkly Downs, Australia 114 C2 20 30 S 138 30 E
Barkly East, S. Africa 104 E4 30 58 S 27 33 E
Barkly Tableland, Australia 114 B2 17 50 S 136 40 E
Barkly West, S. Africa 104 D3 28 5 S 24 31 E
Barkol, China 64 B4 43 37N 93 2 E
Barkol, Wadi →, Sudan 94 D3 17 40N 32 0 E
Barksdale, U.S.A. 139 L4 29 47N 100 2W
Barlee, L., Australia 113 E2 29 15 S 119 30 E
Barlee, Mt., Australia 113 D4 24 38 S 128 13 E
Barletta, Italy 41 A9 41 20N 16 17 E
Barlinek, Poland 47 C2 53 0N 15 15 E
Barlovento, Canary Is. 33 F2 28 48N 17 48W
Barlow L., Canada 131 A8 62 0N 103 0W
Barmedman, Australia 117 C7 34 9 S 147 21 E
Barmer, India 80 G4 25 45N 71 20 E
Barmera, Australia 116 C4 34 15 S 140 28 E
Barmouth, U.K. 16 E3 52 44N 4 3W
Barmstedt, Germany 26 B5 53 47N 9 46 E
Barnagar, India 80 H6 23 7N 75 19 E
Barnard Castle, U.K. 16 C6 54 33N 1 55W
Barnato, Australia 117 A6 31 38 S 145 0 E
Barnaul, U.S.S.R. 56 D9 53 20N 83 40 E
Barnesville, U.S.A. 135 J3 33 6N 84 9W
Barnet, U.K. 17 F7 51 37N 0 15W
Barneveld, Neths. 20 D7 52 7N 5 36 E
Barneveld, U.S.A. 137 C9 43 16N 75 14W
Barneville-Cartevert, France 22 C5 49 23N 1 46W
Barngo, Australia 114 D4 25 3 S 147 20 E
Barnhart, U.S.A. 139 K4 31 10N 101 8W
Barnsley, U.K. 16 D6 53 33N 1 29W
Barnstaple, U.K. 17 F3 51 5N 4 3W
Barnsville, U.S.A. 138 B6 46 43N 96 28W
Baro, Nigeria 101 D6 8 35N 6 18 E
Baro →, Ethiopia 95 F3 8 26N 33 13 E
Baroda = Vadodara, India 80 H5 22 20N 73 10 E
Baroda, India 80 G7 25 29N 76 35 E
Baroe, S. Africa 104 E3 33 13 S 24 33 E
Baron Ra., Australia 112 D4 23 30 S 127 45 E
Barora Ite, Solomon Is. 121 L10 7 36 S 158 24 E
Barorafa, Solomon Is. 121 L10 7 30 S 158 20 E
Barpali, India 82 D6 21 11N 83 35 E
Barpathar, India 78 B4 26 17N 93 53 E
Barpeta, India 78 B3 26 20N 91 10 E
Barqin, Libya 96 C2 27 33N 13 34 E
Barques, Pte. aux, U.S.A. 134 C4 44 5N 82 55W
Barquinha, Portugal 37 F2 39 28N 8 25W
Barquísimeto, Venezuela 152 A4 10 4N 69 19W
Barr, France 23 D14 48 25N 7 28 E
Barra, Brazil 154 D3 11 5 S 43 10W
Barra, U.K. 18 E1 57 0N 7 30W
Barra, Sd. of, U.K. 18 D1 57 4N 7 25W
Barra da Estiva, Brazil 155 D3 13 38 S 41 19W
Barra de Navidad, Mexico 146 D4 19 12N 104 41W
Barra do Corda, Brazil 154 C2 5 30 S 45 10W
Barra do Dande, Angola 103 D2 8 28 S 13 22 E
Barra do Mendes, Brazil 155 D3 11 43 S 42 4W
Barra do Piraí, Brazil 155 F3 22 30 S 43 50W
Barra Falsa, Pta. da, Mozam. 105 C6 22 58 S 35 37 E
Barra Hd., U.K. 18 E1 56 47N 7 40W
Barra Mansa, Brazil 155 F3 22 35 S 44 12W
Barraba, Australia 117 A9 30 21 S 150 35 E
Barracão do Barreto, Brazil 157 B6 8 48 S 58 24W
Barrackpur = Barakpur, India 81 H13 22 44N 88 30 E
Barrafranca, Italy 41 E7 37 22N 14 10 E
Barranca, Lima, Peru 156 C2 10 45 S 77 50W
Barranca, Loreto, Peru 152 D2 4 50 S 76 50W
Barrancabermeja, Colombia 152 B3 7 0N 73 50W
Barrancas, Colombia 152 A3 10 57N 72 50W
Barrancas, Venezuela 153 B5 8 55N 62 5W
Barrancos, Portugal 37 G4 38 10N 6 58W
Barranqueras, Argentina 158 B4 27 30 S 59 0W
Barranquilla, Colombia 152 A3 11 0N 74 50W
Barras, Brazil 154 B3 4 15 S 42 18W
Barras, Colombia 152 D3 1 45 S 73 13W
Barraute, Canada 128 C4 48 26N 77 38W
Barre, Mass., U.S.A. 133 B12 42 26N 72 6W
Barre, Vt., U.S.A. 137 B12 44 15N 72 30W
Barre do Bugres, Brazil 157 D6 15 0 S 57 11W
Barreal, Argentina 158 C2 31 33 S 69 28W
Barrei, Ethiopia 108 C2 6 10N 42 49 E
Barreiras, Brazil 155 D3 12 8 S 45 0W
Barreirinha, Brazil 153 D6 2 47 S 57 3W
Barreirinhas, Brazil 154 B3 2 30 S 42 50W
Barreiro, Portugal 37 G1 38 40N 9 6W
Barreiros, Brazil 154 C4 8 49 S 35 12W
Barrême, France 25 E10 43 57N 6 23 E
Barren, Nosy, Madag. 105 B7 18 25 S 43 40 E
Barretos, Brazil 155 F2 20 30 S 48 35W
Barrhead, Canada 130 C6 54 10N 114 24W
Barrie, Canada 128 D4 44 24N 79 40W
Barrier, C., N.Z. 118 C4 36 25 S 175 32 E
Barrier Ra., Australia 116 A4 31 0 S 141 30 E
Barrier Ra., N.Z. 119 E4 44 15 S 169 32 E
Barrier Ra., N.Z. 119 E3 44 30 S 168 30 E
Barrière, Canada 130 C4 51 12N 120 7W
Barrington, U.S.A. 137 E13 41 43N 71 20W
Barrington L., Canada 131 B8 56 55N 100 15W
Barrington Tops, Australia 117 B9 32 6 S 151 28 E
Barringun, Australia 115 D4 29 1 S 145 41 E
Barro do Garças, Brazil 157 D7 15 54 S 52 16W
Barrow, U.S.A. 126 A4 71 16N 156 50W
Barrow, C., U.S.A. 124 B4 71 10N 156 20W
Barrow Creek, Australia 114 C1 21 30 S 133 55 E
Barrow I., Australia 112 D2 20 45 S 115 20 E
Barrow-in-Furness, U.K. 16 C4 54 8N 3 15W
Barrow Pt., Australia 114 A3 14 20 S 144 40 E
Barrow Ra., Australia 113 E4 26 0 S 127 40 E
Barrow Str., Canada 6 B3 74 20N 95 0W
Barruecopardo, Spain 36 D4 41 4N 6 40W
Barruelo, Spain 36 C6 42 54N 4 17W
Barry, U.K. 17 F4 51 23N 3 19W
Barry, U.S.A. 140 E5 39 42N 91 2W
Barry's Bay, Canada 128 C4 45 29N 77 41W
Barsalogho, Burkina Faso 101 C4 13 25N 1 3W
Barsat, Pakistan 81 A5 36 10N 72 45 E
Barsham, Syria 84 C4 35 21N 40 33 E
Barsi, India 82 E2 18 10N 75 50 E
Barsø, Denmark 15 J3 55 7N 9 33 E
Barstow, Calif., U.S.A. 145 L9 34 58N 117 2W
Barstow, Tex., U.S.A. 139 K3 31 28N 103 24W
Barth, Germany 26 A8 54 20N 12 36 E
Barthélemy, Col, Vietnam 76 C5 19 26N 104 6 E
Bartica, Guyana 153 B6 6 25N 58 40W
Bartin, Turkey 88 C5 41 38N 32 21 E
Bartle Frere, Australia 110 D8 17 27 S 145 50 E
Bartlesville, U.S.A. 139 G7 36 50N 95 58W
Bartlett, Calif., U.S.A. 144 J8 36 29N 118 2W
Bartlett, Tex., U.S.A. 139 K6 30 46N 97 30W
Bartlett, L., Canada 130 A5 63 5N 118 20W
Bartolomeu Dias, Mozam. 107 G4 21 10 S 35 8 E
Barton, Australia 113 F5 30 31 S 132 39 E
Barton upon Humber, U.K. 16 D7 53 41N 0 27W
Bartonville, U.S.A. 140 D7 40 39N 89 39W
Bartoszyce, Poland 47 A7 54 15N 20 55 E
Bartow, U.S.A. 135 M5 27 53N 81 49W
Barú, I. de, Colombia 152 A2 10 15N 75 35W
Barú, Volcan, Panama 148 E3 8 55N 82 35W
Barumba, Zaïre 106 B1 1 3N 23 37 E
Baruth, Germany 26 C9 52 3N 13 31 E
Barvaux, Belgium 21 H6 50 21N 5 29 E
Barvenkovo, U.S.S.R. 52 B7 48 57N 37 0 E
Barwani, India 80 H6 22 2N 74 57 E
Barycz →, Poland 47 D3 51 42N 16 15 E
Barysh, U.S.S.R. 51 E15 53 39N 47 8 E
Barzān, Iraq 84 B5 36 55N 44 3 E
Bas-Rhin □, France 23 D14 48 40N 7 30 E
Bašaid, Yugoslavia 42 B5 45 38N 20 25 E
Bāsa'idū, Iran 85 E7 26 35N 55 20 E
Basal, Pakistan 80 C5 33 33N 72 13 E
Basankusa, Zaïre 102 B3 1 5N 19 50 E
Basawa, Afghan. 80 B4 34 15N 70 50 E
Bascharage, Lux. 21 J7 49 34N 5 55 E
Bascuñán, C., Chile 158 B1 28 52 S 71 35W
Basècles, Belgium 21 G3 50 32N 3 39 E
Basel, Switz. 28 A5 47 35N 7 35 E
Basel-Stadt □, Switz. 28 A5 47 35N 7 35 E
Baselland □, Switz. 28 B5 47 26N 7 45 E
Basento →, Italy 41 B9 40 21N 16 50 E
Bāshī, Iran 85 D6 28 41N 51 4 E
Bashkir A.S.S.R. □, U.S.S.R. 54 E5 54 0N 57 0 E
Basilaki I., Papua N. G. 120 F6 10 35 S 151 0 E
Basilan, Phil. 71 C6 6 35N 122 0 E
Basilan Str., Phil. 71 C6 6 50N 122 0 E
Basildon, U.K. 17 F8 51 34N 0 29 E
Basilicata □, Italy 41 B9 40 30N 16 0 E
Basim = Washim, India 82 D3 20 3N 77 0 E
Basin, U.S.A. 142 D9 44 22N 108 2W
Basingstoke, U.K. 17 F6 51 15N 1 5W
Basirhat, Bangla. 78 D2 22 40N 88 54 E
Baška, Yugoslavia 39 D11 44 58N 14 45 E
Başkale, Turkey 89 D10 38 2N 43 59 E
Baskatong, Rés., Canada 128 C4 46 46N 75 50W
Basle = Basel, Switz. 28 A5 47 35N 7 35 E
Basmat, India 82 E3 19 15N 77 12 E
Basoda, India 80 H7 23 52N 77 54 E
Basodino, Switz. 29 D6 46 25N 8 28 E
Basoka, Zaïre 106 B1 1 16N 23 40 E
Basongo, Zaïre 103 C4 4 15 S 20 20 E
Basque, Pays, France 24 E2 43 15N 1 20W
Basque Provinces = País Vasco □, Spain 34 C2 42 50N 2 45W
Basra = Al Başrah, Iraq 84 D5 30 30N 47 50 E
Bass Rock, U.K. 18 E6 56 5N 2 40W
Bass Str., Australia 114 F4 39 15 S 146 30 E
Bassano, Canada 130 C6 50 48N 112 20W
Bassano del Grappa, Italy 39 C8 45 45N 11 45 E
Bassar, Togo 101 D5 9 19N 0 57 E
Basse Santa-Su, Gambia 100 C2 13 13N 14 15W
Basse-Terre, Guadeloupe 149 C7 16 0N 61 44W
Bassecourt, Switz. 28 B4 47 20N 7 15 E
Bassein, Burma 78 G5 16 45N 94 30 E
Bassein, India 82 E1 19 26N 72 48 E
Basseterre, St. Christopher-Nevis 149 C7 17 17N 62 43W
Bassett, Nebr., U.S.A. 138 D5 42 37N 99 30W
Bassett, Va., U.S.A. 135 G6 36 48N 79 59W
Bassevelde, Belgium 21 F3 51 15N 3 41 E
Bassi, India 80 D7 30 44N 76 21 E
Bassigny, France 23 E12 48 0N 5 30 E
Bassikounou, Mauritania 100 B3 15 55N 6 1W
Bassilly, Belgium 21 G3 50 40N 3 56 E
Bassum, Germany 26 C4 52 50N 8 42 E
Båstad, Sweden 15 H6 56 25N 12 51 E
Bastak, Iran 85 E7 27 15N 54 25 E
Baştām, Iran 85 B7 36 29N 55 4 E
Bastar, India 82 E5 19 15N 81 40 E
Bastelica, France 25 F13 42 1N 9 3 E
Basti, India 81 F10 26 52N 82 55 E
Bastia, France 25 F13 42 40N 9 30 E
Bastia Umbra, Italy 39 E9 43 4N 12 34 E
Bastogne, Belgium 21 H7 50 1N 5 43 E
Bastrop, U.S.A. 139 K6 30 5N 97 22W
Basyanovskiy, U.S.S.R. 54 B7 58 19N 60 44 E
Bat Yam, Israel 91 C3 32 2N 34 44 E
Bata, Eq. Guin. 102 B1 1 57N 9 50 E
Bata, Romania 46 C3 46 1N 22 4 E
Bataan, Phil. 71 B6 14 40N 120 25 E
Batabanó, Cuba 148 B3 22 40N 82 20W
Batabanó, G. de, Cuba 148 B3 22 30N 82 30W
Batac, Phil. 71 A6 18 3N 120 34 E
Batagoy, U.S.S.R. 57 C14 67 38N 134 38 E
Batak, Bulgaria 43 F9 41 57N 24 12 E
Batalha, Portugal 37 F2 39 40N 8 50W
Batam, Indonesia 74 B2 1 5N 104 3 E
Batama, Zaïre 106 B2 0 58N 26 33 E
Batamay, U.S.S.R. 57 C13 63 30N 129 15 E
Batamshinskiy, U.S.S.R. 54 F6 50 36N 58 16 E
Batang, China 68 B2 30 1N 99 0 E
Batang, Indonesia 71 G13 6 55 S 109 45 E
Batangafo, C.A.R. 102 A3 7 25N 18 20 E
Batangas, Phil. 71 B6 13 35N 121 10 E
Batanghari, Indonesia 74 C2 1 36 S 103 37 E
Batanta, Indonesia 71 E8 0 55 S 130 40 E
Batatais, Brazil 159 A6 20 54 S 47 37W
Batavia, Ind., U.S.A. 141 C8 41 55N 88 17W
Batavia, N.Y., U.S.A. 136 D6 43 0N 78 10W
Batavia, Ohio, U.S.A. 141 E12 39 5N 84 11W
Bataysk, U.S.S.R. 53 C8 47 3N 39 45 E
Batchelor, Australia 112 B5 13 4 S 131 1 E
Batéké, Plateau, Congo 102 C3 3 30 S 15 45 E
Bateman's B., Australia 117 C9 35 40 S 150 12 E
Batemans Bay, Australia 117 C9 35 44 S 150 11 E
Bates Ra., Australia 113 E3 27 27 S 121 5 E
Batesburg, U.S.A. 135 J5 33 54N 81 32W
Batesville, Ark., U.S.A. 139 H9 35 48N 91 40W
Batesville, Ind., U.S.A. 141 E11 39 18N 85 13W
Batesville, Miss., U.S.A. 139 H10 34 17N 89 58W
Batesville, Tex., U.S.A. 139 L5 28 59N 99 38W
Bath, U.K. 17 F5 51 22N 2 22W
Bath, Maine, U.S.A. 129 D6 43 50N 69 49W
Bath, N.Y., U.S.A. 136 D7 42 20N 77 17W
Batheay, Cambodia 77 G5 11 59N 104 57 E
Bathgate, U.K. 18 F5 55 54N 3 38W
Bathmen, Neths. 20 D8 52 15N 6 29 E
Bathurst = Banjul, Gambia 100 C1 13 28N 16 40W
Bathurst, Australia 117 B8 33 25 S 149 31 E
Bathurst, Canada 129 C6 47 37N 65 43W
Bathurst, S. Africa 104 E4 33 30 S 26 50 E
Bathurst, C., Canada 126 A7 70 34N 128 0W
Bathurst B., Australia 114 A3 14 16 S 144 25 E
Bathurst Harb., Australia 114 G4 43 15 S 146 10 E
Bathurst I., Australia 112 B5 11 30 S 130 10 E
Bathurst I., Canada 6 B2 76 0N 100 30W
Bathurst Inlet, Canada 126 B9 66 50N 108 1W
Batie, Burkina Faso 100 D4 9 53N 2 53W
Batlow, Australia 117 C8 35 31 S 148 9 E
Batman, Turkey 89 E9 37 55N 41 5 E
Batna, Algeria 99 A6 35 34N 6 15 E
Batoala, Gabon 102 B2 0 48N 13 27 E
Batočina, Yugoslavia 42 C6 44 7N 21 5 E
Batoka, Zambia 107 F2 16 45 S 27 15 E
Baton Rouge, U.S.A. 139 K9 30 30N 91 5W
Batong, Ko, Thailand 77 J2 6 32N 99 12 E
Bátonyterenye, Hungary 31 C12 48 3N 19 50 E
Batopilas, Mexico 146 B3 27 0N 107 45W
Batouri, Cameroon 102 B2 4 30N 14 25 E
Battambang, Cambodia 76 F4 13 7N 103 12 E
Batticaloa, Sri Lanka 83 L5 7 43N 81 45 E
Battice, Belgium 21 G7 50 39N 5 50 E
Battipáglia, Italy 41 B8 40 38N 15 0 E
Battle, U.K. 17 G8 50 55N 0 30 E
Battle →, Canada 131 C7 52 43N 108 15W
Battle Camp, Australia 114 B3 15 20 S 144 40 E
Battle Creek, U.S.A. 141 B11 42 20N 85 6W
Battle Ground, U.S.A. 144 E4 45 47N 122 32W
Battle Harbour, Canada 129 B8 52 16N 55 35W
Battle Lake, U.S.A. 138 B7 46 20N 95 43W
Battle Mountain, U.S.A. 142 F5 40 45N 117 0W
Battlefields, Zimbabwe 107 F2 18 37 S 29 47 E
Battleford, Canada 131 C7 52 45N 108 15W
Battonya, Hungary 31 E14 46 16N 21 3 E
Batu, Ethiopia 90 F2 6 55N 39 45 E
Batu, Kepulauan, Indonesia 70 E1 0 30 S 98 25 E
Batu Caves, Malaysia 77 L3 3 15N 101 40 E
Batu Gajah, Malaysia 77 K3 4 28N 101 3 E
Batu Is. = Batu, Kepulauan, Indonesia 70 E1 0 30 S 98 25 E
Batu Pahat, Malaysia 77 M4 1 50N 102 56 E
Batuata, Indonesia 71 F6 6 12 S 122 42 E
Batumi, U.S.S.R. 53 F9 41 30N 41 30 E
Baturaja, Indonesia 70 E2 4 11 S 104 15 E
Baturité, Brazil 154 B4 4 28 S 38 45W
Batusangkar, Indonesia 74 C2 0 27 S 100 35 E
Bau, Malaysia 70 D4 1 25N 110 9 E
Baubau, Indonesia 71 F6 5 25 S 122 38 E
Bauchi, Nigeria 101 C6 10 22N 9 48 E
Bauchi □, Nigeria 101 C7 10 30N 10 0 E
Baud, France 22 E3 47 52N 3 1W
Baudette, U.S.A. 138 A7 48 46N 94 35W
Baudour, Belgium 21 H3 50 29N 3 50 E
Bauer, C., Australia 115 E1 32 44 S 134 4 E
Baugé, France 22 E6 47 31N 0 8W
Bauhinia Downs, Australia 114 C4 24 35 S 149 18 E
Bauma, Switz. 29 B7 47 23N 8 53 E
Baume-les-Dames, France 23 E13 47 22N 6 22 E
Baunatal, Germany 26 D5 51 13N 9 25 E
Baunei, Italy 40 B2 40 2N 9 41 E
Baures, Bolivia 157 C5 13 35 S 63 35W
Bauru, Brazil 159 A6 22 10 S 49 0W
Baús, Brazil 157 D7 18 22 S 52 47W
Bauska, U.S.S.R. 50 C4 56 24N 25 15 E
Bautzen, Germany 26 D10 51 11N 14 25 E
Bavānāt, Iran 85 D7 30 28N 53 27 E
Bavanište, Yugoslavia 42 C5 44 49N 20 53 E
Bavaria = Bayern □, Germany 27 F7 49 7N 11 30 E
Båven, Sweden 14 F10 59 0N 16 56 E
Bavi Sadri, India 80 G6 24 28N 74 30 E
Bavispe →, Mexico 146 B3 29 30N 109 11W
Bawdwin, Burma 78 D6 23 5N 97 20 E
Bawean, Indonesia 70 F4 5 46 S 112 35 E
Bawku, Ghana 101 C4 11 3N 0 19W
Bawlake, Burma 78 F6 19 11N 97 21 E
Bawolung, China 68 C3 28 50N 101 16 E
Baxley, U.S.A. 135 K4 31 43N 82 23W
Baxoi, China 68 B1 30 1N 96 50 E
Baxter, U.S.A. 140 C3 41 49N 93 9W
Baxter Springs, U.S.A. 139 G7 37 3N 94 45W
Bay, L. de, Phil. 71 B6 14 20N 121 11 E
Bay Bulls, Canada 129 C9 47 19N 52 50W
Bay City, Mich., U.S.A. 134 D4 43 35N 83 51W
Bay City, Oreg., U.S.A. 142 D2 45 45N 123 58W
Bay City, Tex., U.S.A. 139 L7 28 59N 95 55W
Bay de Verde, Canada 129 C9 48 5N 52 54W
Bay Minette, U.S.A. 135 K2 30 54N 87 43W
Bay St. Louis, U.S.A. 139 K10 30 18N 89 22W
Bay Springs, U.S.A. 139 K10 31 58N 89 18W
Bay View, N.Z. 118 F5 39 25 S 176 50 E
Baya, Zaïre 107 E2 11 53 S 27 25 E
Bayamo, Cuba 148 B4 20 20N 76 40W
Bayamón, Puerto Rico 149 C6 18 24N 66 10W
Bayan Har Shan, China 64 C4 34 0N 98 0 E
Bayan Hot = Alxa Zuoqi, China 66 E3 38 50N 105 40 E
Bayan Obo, China 66 D5 41 52N 109 59 E
Bayan-Ovoo, Mongolia 66 C4 42 55N 106 5 E
Bayana, India 80 F7 26 55N 77 18 E
Bayanaul, U.S.S.R. 56 D8 50 45N 75 45 E
Bayandalay, Mongolia 66 C2 43 30N 103 29 E
Bayanhongor, Mongolia 64 B5 46 8N 102 43 E
Bayard, U.S.A. 138 E3 41 48N 103 17W
Baybay, Phil. 71 B6 10 40N 124 55 E
Bayburt, Turkey 89 C9 40 15N 40 20 E
Bayerischer Wald, Germany 27 G8 49 0N 12 50 E
Bayern □, Germany 27 F7 49 7N 11 30 E
Bayeux, France 22 C6 49 17N 0 42W
Bayfield, Canada 136 C3 43 34N 81 42W
Bayfield, U.S.A. 138 B9 46 50N 90 48W
Bayḥān al Qisāb, Yemen 86 D4 15 48N 45 44 E
Bayındır, Turkey 88 D2 38 13N 27 39 E
Baykadam, U.S.S.R. 55 B4 43 48N 69 58 E
Baykal, Oz., U.S.S.R. 57 D11 53 0N 108 0 E
Baykit, U.S.S.R. 57 C10 61 50N 95 50 E
Baykonur, U.S.S.R. 56 E7 47 48N 65 50 E
Baymak, U.S.S.R. 54 E6 52 36N 58 19 E
Baynes Mts., Namibia 104 B1 17 15 S 13 0 E
Bayombong, Phil. 71 A6 16 30N 121 10 E
Bayon, France 23 D13 48 30N 6 20 E
Bayona, Spain 36 C2 42 6N 8 52W
Bayonne, France 24 E2 43 30N 1 28W
Bayonne, U.S.A. 137 F10 40 41N 74 7W
Bayovar, Peru 156 B1 5 50 S 81 0W
Bayram-Ali, U.S.S.R. 56 F7 37 37N 62 10 E
Bayramiç, Turkey 88 D2 39 48N 26 36 E
Bayreuth, Germany 27 F7 49 56N 11 35 E
Bayrischzell, Germany 27 H8 47 39N 12 1 E
Bayrūt, Lebanon 91 B4 33 53N 35 31 E
Baysun, U.S.S.R. 55 D3 38 12N 67 12 E
Bayt al Faqīh, Yemen 86 D3 14 31N 43 19 E
Bayt Lahm, Jordan 91 D4 31 43N 35 12 E
Baytown, U.S.A. 139 L7 29 42N 94 57W
Bayzhansay, U.S.S.R. 55 B4 43 14N 69 54 E
Bayzo, Niger 101 C5 13 52N 4 35 E
Baza, Spain 35 H2 37 30N 2 47W
Bazar Dyuzi, U.S.S.R. 53 F12 41 12N 47 50 E
Bazarny Karabulak, U.S.S.R. 51 E15 52 15N 46 20 E
Bazarnyy Syzgan, U.S.S.R. 51 E15 53 45N 46 40 E
Bazartobe, U.S.S.R. 53 B14 49 26N 51 45 E
Bazaruto, I. do, Mozam. 105 C6 21 40 S 35 28 E
Bazas, France 24 D3 44 27N 0 13W
Bazhong, China 68 B6 31 52N 106 46 E
Bazmān, Kūh-e, Iran 85 D9 28 4N 60 1 E
Beabula, Australia 117 C6 34 26 S 145 9 E
Beach, U.S.A. 138 B3 46 57N 103 58W
Beach City, U.S.A. 136 F3 40 38N 81 35W
Beachport, Australia 116 D4 37 29 S 140 0 E
Beachy Hd., U.K. 17 G8 50 44N 0 16 E
Beacon, Australia 113 F2 30 26 S 117 52 E
Beacon, U.S.A. 137 E11 41 32N 73 58W
Beaconia, Canada 131 C9 50 25N 96 31W
Beagle, Canal, S. Amer. 160 E3 55 0 S 68 30W
Beagle Bay, Australia 112 C3 16 58 S 122 40 E
Bealanana, Madag. 105 A8 14 33 S 48 44 E
Beamsville, Canada 136 C5 43 12N 79 28W
Bear →, U.S.A. 144 G5 38 56N 121 36W
Béar, C., France 24 F7 42 31N 3 8 E

Bendela 173

Bear I., Ireland 19 E2 51 38N 9 50W
Bear L., B.C., Canada 130 B3 56 10N 126 52W
Bear L., Man., Canada 131 B9 55 8N 96 0W
Bear L., U.S.A. 142 F8 42 0N 111 20W
Bearcreek, U.S.A. 142 D9 45 11N 109 6W
Beardmore, Canada 128 C2 49 36N 87 57W
Beardmore Glacier, Antarctica 7 E11 84 30 S 170 0 E
Beardstown, U.S.A. 140 E6 40 0N 90 25W
Béarn, France 24 E3 43 20N 0 30W
Bearpaw Mts., U.S.A. 142 B9 48 15N 109 30W
Bearskin Lake, Canada 128 B1 53 58N 91 2W
Beas de Segura, Spain 35 G2 38 15N 2 53W
Beasain, Spain 34 B2 43 3N 2 11W
Beata, C., Dom. Rep. 149 C5 17 40N 71 30W
Beata, I., Dom. Rep. 149 C5 17 34N 71 31W
Beatrice, U.S.A. 138 E6 40 20N 96 40W
Beatrice, Zimbabwe 107 F3 18 15 S 30 55 E
Beatrice, C., Australia 114 A2 14 20 S 136 55 E
Beatton →, Canada 130 B4 56 15N 120 45W
Beatton River, Canada 130 B4 57 26N 121 20W
Beatty, U.S.A. 144 J10 36 58N 116 46W
Beaucaire, France 25 E8 43 48N 4 39 E
Beauce, Plaine de la, France 23 D8 48 10N 1 45 E
Beauceville, Canada 129 C5 46 13N 70 46W
Beauchêne, I., Falk. Is. 160 D5 52 55 S 59 15W
Beaudesert, Australia 115 D5 27 59 S 153 0 E
Beaufort, Australia 116 D5 37 25 S 143 25 E
Beaufort, Malaysia 70 C5 5 30N 115 40 E
Beaufort, N.C., U.S.A. 135 H7 34 45N 76 40W
Beaufort, S.C., U.S.A. 135 J5 32 25N 80 40W
Beaufort Sea, Arctic 124 B6 72 0N 140 0W
Beaufort West, S. Africa 104 E3 32 18 S 22 36 E
Beaugency, France 23 E8 47 47N 1 38 E
Beauharnois, Canada 128 C5 45 20N 73 52W
Beaujeu, France 25 B8 46 10N 4 35 E
Beaulieu →, Canada 130 A6 62 3N 113 11W
Beaulieu-sur-Dordogne, France 24 D5 44 58N 1 50 E
Beaulieu-sur-Mer, France 25 E11 43 42N 7 20 E
Beauly, U.K. 18 D4 57 29N 4 27W
Beauly →, U.K. 18 D4 57 26N 4 28W
Beaumaris, U.K. 16 D3 53 16N 4 7W
Beaumetz-lès-Loges, France 23 B9 50 15N 2 38 E
Beaumont, Belgium 21 H4 50 15N 4 14 E
Beaumont, France 24 D4 44 45N 0 46 E
Beaumont, N.Z. 119 F4 45 50 S 169 33 E
Beaumont, Calif., U.S.A. 145 M10 33 56N 116 58W
Beaumont, Tex., U.S.A. 139 K7 30 5N 94 8W
Beaumont-de-Lomagne, France 24 E5 43 53N 1 0 E
Beaumont-le-Roger, France 22 C7 49 4N 0 47 E
Beaumont-sur-Oise, France 23 C9 49 9N 2 17 E
Beaumont-sur-Sarthe, France 22 D7 48 13N 0 8 E
Beaune, France 23 E11 47 2N 4 50 E
Beaune-la-Rolande, France 23 D9 48 4N 2 25 E
Beaupréau, France 22 E6 47 12N 0 59W
Beauraing, Belgium 21 H5 50 7N 4 57 E
Beauséjour, Canada 131 C9 50 5N 96 35W
Beautemps-Beaupré, I., N. Cal. 121 K4 20 24 S 166 9 E
Beauvais, France 23 C9 49 25N 2 8 E
Beauval, Canada 131 B7 55 9N 107 37W
Beauvoir-sur-Mer, France 22 F4 46 55N 2 2W
Beauvoir-sur-Niort, France 24 B3 46 12N 0 30W
Beaver, Alaska, U.S.A. 126 B5 66 20N 147 30W
Beaver, Okla., U.S.A. 139 G4 36 52N 100 31W
Beaver, Pa., U.S.A. 136 F4 40 40N 80 18W
Beaver, Utah, U.S.A. 143 G7 38 20N 112 45W
Beaver →, B.C., Canada 130 B4 59 52N 124 20W
Beaver →, Ont., Canada 128 A2 55 55N 87 48W
Beaver →, Sask., Canada 131 B7 55 26N 107 45W
Beaver City, U.S.A. 138 E5 40 13N 99 50W
Beaver Dam, U.S.A. 138 D10 43 28N 88 50W
Beaver Falls, U.S.A. 136 F4 40 44N 80 20W
Beaver Hill L., Canada 131 C10 54 5N 94 50W
Beaver I., U.S.A. 134 C3 45 40N 85 31W
Beavercreek, U.S.A. 141 E12 39 43N 84 11W
Beaverhill L., Alta., Canada 130 C6 53 27N 112 32W
Beaverhill L., N.W.T., Canada 131 A8 63 2N 104 22W
Beaverlodge, Canada 130 B5 55 11N 119 29W
Beavermouth, Canada 130 C5 51 32N 117 23W
Beaverstone →, Canada 128 B2 54 59N 89 25W
Beaverton, Canada 136 B5 44 26N 79 9W
Beaverton, U.S.A. 144 E4 45 29N 122 48W
Beaverville, U.S.A. 141 D9 40 57N 87 39W
Beawar, India 80 F6 26 3N 74 18 E
Bebedouro, Brazil 159 A6 21 0 S 48 25W
Beboa, Madag. 105 B7 17 22 S 44 33 E
Bebra, Germany 26 E5 50 59N 9 48 E
Beccles, U.K. 17 E9 52 27N 1 33 E
Bečej, Yugoslavia 42 B5 45 36N 20 3 E
Beceni, Romania 46 D7 45 23N 26 48 E
Becerreá, Spain 36 C3 42 51N 7 10W
Béchar, Algeria 99 B4 31 38N 2 18W
Bechyně, Czech. 30 B7 49 17N 14 29 E
Beckley, U.S.A. 134 G5 37 50N 81 8W
Beckum, Germany 26 D4 51 46N 8 3 E
Bečva →, Czech. 31 B10 49 31N 17 40 E
Bédar, Spain 35 H3 37 11N 1 59W
Bédarieux, France 24 E7 43 37N 3 10 E
Bédarrides, France 25 D8 44 2N 4 54 E
Beddouza, Ras, Morocco 98 B3 32 33N 9 9W
Bedel, Pereval, U.S.S.R. 55 C9 41 26N 78 26 E
Bedele, Ethiopia 95 F4 8 31N 36 23 E
Bederkesa, Germany 26 B4 53 37N 8 50 E
Bederwanak, Somali Rep. 108 C2 9 34N 44 23 E
Bedeso, Ethiopia 95 F5 9 58N 40 52 E
Bedford, Canada 128 C5 45 7N 72 59W
Bedford, S. Africa 104 E4 32 40 S 26 10 E
Bedford, U.K. 17 E7 52 8N 0 29W
Bedford, Ind., U.S.A. 141 F10 38 50N 86 30W
Bedford, Iowa, U.S.A. 140 D2 40 40N 94 41W
Bedford, Ky., U.S.A. 141 F11 38 36N 85 19W
Bedford, Ohio, U.S.A. 136 E3 41 23N 81 32W
Bedford, Pa., U.S.A. 136 F6 40 1N 78 30W
Bedford, Va., U.S.A. 134 G6 37 25N 79 30W
Bedford, C., Australia 114 B4 15 14 S 145 21 E
Bedford Downs, Australia 112 C4 17 19 S 127 20 E
Bedfordshire □, U.K. 17 E7 52 4N 0 28W
Bedi, Chad 97 F3 11 6N 18 33 E
Będków, Poland 47 D6 51 36N 19 44 E
Bednja →, Yugoslavia 39 B13 46 12N 16 25 E
Bednodemyanovsk, U.S.S.R. 51 E13 53 55N 43 15 E
Bedónia, Italy 38 D6 44 28N 9 36 E
Bedourie, Australia 114 C2 24 30 S 139 30 E
Bedretto, Switz. 29 C7 46 31N 8 31 E
Bedum, Neths. 20 B9 53 18N 6 36 E
Będzin, Poland 47 E6 50 19N 19 7 E
Beech Fork →, U.S.A. 141 G11 37 55N 85 50W
Beech Grove, U.S.A. 141 E10 39 40N 86 2W
Beecher, U.S.A. 141 C9 41 21N 87 38W
Beechworth, Australia 117 D7 36 22 S 146 43 E
Beechy, Canada 131 C7 50 53N 107 24W
Beek, Gelderland, Neths. 20 E8 51 55N 6 11 E
Beek, Limburg, Neths. 21 G7 50 57N 5 48 E
Beek, Noord-Brabant, Neths. 21 E7 51 32N 5 38 E
Beekbergen, Neths. 20 D7 52 10N 5 58 E
Beelitz, Germany 26 C8 52 14N 12 58 E
Beenleigh, Australia 115 D5 27 43 S 153 10 E
Be'er Menuha, Israel 84 D2 30 19N 35 8 E
Be'er Sheva', Israel 91 D3 31 15N 34 48 E
Beersheba = Be'er Sheva', Israel 91 D3 31 15N 34 48 E
Beerta, Neths. 20 B10 53 11N 7 6 E
Beerze →, Neths. 20 E6 51 39N 5 20 E
Beesd, Neths. 20 E6 51 53N 5 11 E
Beeskow, Germany 26 C10 52 9N 14 14 E
Beeston, U.K. 16 E6 52 55N 1 11W
Beetaloo, Australia 114 B1 17 15 S 133 50 E
Beetsterzwaag, Neths. 20 B8 53 4N 6 5 E
Beetzendorf, Germany 26 C7 52 42N 11 6 E
Beeville, U.S.A. 139 L6 28 27N 97 44W
Befale, Zaïre 102 B4 0 25N 20 45 E
Befandriana, Madag. 105 C7 21 55 S 44 0 E
Befotaka, Madag. 105 C8 23 49 S 47 0 E
Bega, Australia 117 D8 36 41 S 149 51 E
Bega, Canalul, Romania 42 B5 45 37N 20 46 E
Bégard, France 22 D3 48 38N 3 18W
Bègles, France 24 D3 44 45N 0 35W
Begna →, Norway 14 D4 60 35N 10 0 E
Begonte, Spain 36 B3 43 10N 7 40W
Begusarai, India 81 G12 25 24N 86 9 E
Behābād, Iran 85 C8 32 24N 59 47 E
Behara, Madag. 105 C8 24 55 S 46 20 E
Behbehān, Iran 85 D6 30 30N 50 15 E
Behshahr, Iran 85 B7 36 45N 53 35 E
Bei Jiang →, China 69 F9 23 2N 112 58 E
Bei'an, China 65 B7 48 10N 126 20 E
Beigang, Taiwan 69 F13 23 38N 120 16 E
Beihai, China 68 G7 21 28N 109 6 E
Beijing, China 66 E9 39 55N 116 20 E
Beijing □, China 66 E9 39 55N 116 20 E
Beilen, Neths. 20 C8 52 52N 6 27 E
Beiliu, China 69 F8 22 41N 110 21 E
Beilngries, Germany 27 F7 49 1N 11 27 E
Beilpajah, Australia 116 B5 32 54 S 143 52 E
Beilul, Ethiopia 95 E5 13 2N 42 20 E
Beipiao, China 67 D11 41 52N 120 32 E
Beira, Mozam. 107 F3 19 50 S 34 52 E
Beira, Somali Rep. 108 C3 6 57N 47 19 E
Beirut = Bayrūt, Lebanon 91 B4 33 53N 35 31 E
Beitaolaizhao, China 67 B13 44 58N 125 58 E
Beitbridge, Zimbabwe 107 G3 22 12 S 30 0 E
Beiuş, Romania 46 C3 46 40N 22 21 E
Beizhen, Liaoning, China 67 D11 41 38N 121 54 E
Beizhen, Shandong, China 67 F10 37 20N 118 2 E
Beizhengzhen, China 67 B12 44 31N 123 30 E
Beja, Portugal 37 G3 38 2N 7 53W
Béja, Tunisia 96 A1 36 43N 9 12 E
Beja □, Portugal 37 H3 37 55N 7 55W
Bejaia, Algeria 99 A6 36 42N 5 2 E
Béjar, Spain 36 E5 40 23N 5 46W
Bejestān, Iran 85 C8 34 30N 58 5 E
Bekabad, U.S.S.R. 55 C4 40 13N 69 14 E
Bekasi, Indonesia 71 G12 6 14 S 106 59 E
Békés, Hungary 31 E14 46 47N 21 9 E
Békés □, Hungary 31 E14 46 45N 21 0 E
Békéscsaba, Hungary 31 E14 46 40N 21 5 E
Bekily, Madag. 105 C8 24 13 S 45 19 E
Bekkevoort, Belgium 21 G5 50 57N 4 58 E
Bekoji, Ethiopia 95 F4 7 40N 39 17 E
Bekok, Malaysia 77 L4 2 20N 103 7 E
Bekwai, Ghana 101 D4 6 30N 1 34W
Bela, India 81 G10 25 50N 82 0 E
Bela, Pakistan 79 D2 26 12N 66 20 E
Bela Crkva, Yugoslavia 42 C6 44 55N 21 27 E
Bela Palanka, Yugoslavia 42 D7 43 13N 22 17 E
Bela Vista, Brazil 158 A4 22 12 S 56 20W
Bela Vista, Mozam. 105 D5 26 10 S 32 44 E
Bélâbre, France 24 B5 46 34N 1 8 E
Belalcázar, Spain 37 G5 38 35N 5 10W
Belanovica, Yugoslavia 42 C5 44 15N 20 23 E
Belas, Angola 103 D2 8 55 S 13 9 E
Belau I., Pac. Oc. 122 G5 7 30N 134 30 E
Belavenona, Madag. 105 C8 24 50 S 47 4 E
Belawan, Indonesia 70 D1 3 33N 98 32 E
Belaya, Ethiopia 95 E4 11 25N 36 8 E
Belaya →, U.S.S.R. 54 D4 56 0N 54 32 E
Belaya Glina, U.S.S.R. 53 C9 46 5N 40 48 E
Belaya Kalitva, U.S.S.R. 53 B9 48 13N 40 50 E
Belaya Kholunitsa, U.S.S.R. 54 B2 58 41N 50 13 E
Belaya Tserkov, U.S.S.R. 50 G7 49 45N 30 10 E
Belayan →, Indonesia 75 C5 0 14 S 116 36 E
Belceşti, Romania 46 B8 47 19N 27 7 E
Bełchatów, Poland 47 D6 51 21N 19 22 E
Belcher Is., Canada 127 C12 56 15N 78 45W
Belchite, Spain 34 D4 41 18N 0 43W
Belden, U.S.A. 144 E5 40 2N 121 17W
Belebey, U.S.S.R. 54 D4 54 7N 54 7 E
Belém, Brazil 154 B2 1 20 S 48 30W
Belém de São Francisco, Brazil 154 C4 8 46 S 38 58W
Belén, Argentina 158 B2 27 40 S 67 5W
Belén, Colombia 152 C2 1 26N 75 56W
Belén, Paraguay 158 A4 23 30 S 57 6W
Belen, U.S.A. 143 J10 34 40N 106 50W
Belene, Bulgaria 43 D10 43 39N 25 10 E
Bélesta, France 24 F5 42 55N 1 56 E
Belet Uen, Somali Rep. 90 G4 4 30N 45 5 E
Belev, U.S.S.R. 51 E10 53 50N 36 5 E
Belfair, U.S.A. 144 C4 47 27N 122 50W
Belfast, N.Z. 119 D7 43 27 S 172 39 E
Belfast, S. Africa 105 D5 25 42 S 30 2 E
Belfast, U.K. 19 B6 54 35N 5 56W
Belfast, Maine, U.S.A. 129 D6 44 30N 69 0W
Belfast, N.Y., U.S.A. 136 D6 42 21N 78 9W
Belfast □, U.K. 19 B6 54 35N 5 56W
Belfast L., U.K. 19 B6 54 40N 5 50W
Belfeld, Neths. 21 F8 51 18N 6 6 E
Belfield, U.S.A. 138 B3 46 54N 103 11W
Belfort, France 23 E13 47 38N 6 50 E
Belfort, Territoire de □, France 23 E13 47 40N 6 55 E
Belfry, U.S.A. 142 D9 45 10N 109 2W
Belgaum, India 83 G2 15 55N 74 35 E
Belgioioso, Italy 38 C6 45 9N 9 21 E
Belgium ■, Europe 21 H6 50 30N 5 0 E
Belgorod, U.S.S.R. 51 F10 50 35N 36 35 E
Belgorod-Dnestrovskiy, U.S.S.R. 52 C4 46 11N 30 23 E
Belgrade = Beograd, Yugoslavia 42 C5 44 50N 20 37 E
Belgrade, U.S.A. 142 D8 45 50N 111 10W
Belgrove, N.Z. 119 B7 41 27 S 172 59 E
Belhaven, U.S.A. 135 H7 35 34N 76 35W
Beli Drim →, Europe 42 E5 42 6N 20 25 E
Beli Manastir, Yugoslavia 42 B3 45 45N 18 36 E
Beli Timok →, Yugoslavia 42 D7 43 53N 22 14 E
Belice →, Italy 40 E5 37 35N 12 55 E
Belin-Béliet, France 24 D3 44 29N 0 47W
Belinga, Gabon 102 B2 1 10N 13 2 E
Belinskiy, U.S.S.R. 51 E13 53 0N 43 25 E
Belinţ, Romania 46 D2 45 48N 21 54 E
Belinyu, Indonesia 70 E3 1 35 S 105 50 E
Belitung, Indonesia 70 E3 3 10 S 107 50 E
Beliu, Romania 46 C3 46 30N 22 0 E
Belize ■, Cent. Amer. 147 D7 17 0N 88 30W
Belize City, Belize 147 D7 17 25N 88 0W
Beljanica, Yugoslavia 42 C6 44 8N 21 43 E
Belkovskiy, Ostrov, U.S.S.R. 57 B14 75 32N 135 44 E
Bell →, Canada 128 C4 49 48N 77 38W
Bell Bay, Australia 114 G4 41 6 S 146 53 E
Bell I., Canada 129 B8 50 46N 55 35W
Bell-Irving →, Canada 130 B3 56 12N 129 5W
Bell Peninsula, Canada 127 B11 63 50N 82 0W
Bell Ville, Argentina 158 C3 32 40 S 62 40W
Bella Bella, Canada 130 C3 52 10N 128 10W
Bella Coola, Canada 130 C3 52 25N 126 40W
Bella Flor, Bolivia 156 C4 11 9 S 67 49W
Bella Unión, Uruguay 158 C4 30 15 S 57 40W
Bella Vista, Corrientes, Argentina 158 B4 28 33 S 59 0W
Bella Vista, Tucuman, Argentina 158 B2 27 10 S 65 25W
Bellac, France 24 B5 46 7N 1 3 E
Bellágio, Italy 38 C6 45 59N 9 15 E
Bellaire, U.S.A. 136 F4 40 1N 80 46W
Bellary, India 83 G3 15 10N 76 56 E
Bellata, Australia 115 D4 29 53 S 149 46 E
Belle, U.S.A. 140 F5 38 17N 91 43W
Belle Fourche, U.S.A. 138 C3 44 43N 103 52W
Belle Fourche →, U.S.A. 138 C3 44 25N 102 19W
Belle Glade, U.S.A. 135 M5 26 43N 80 38W
Belle-Ile, France 22 E3 47 20N 3 10W
Belle Isle, Canada 129 B8 51 57N 55 25W
Belle Isle, Str. of, Canada 129 B8 51 30N 56 30W
Belle-Isle-en-Terre, France 22 D3 48 33N 3 23W
Belle Plaine, Iowa, U.S.A. 140 C4 41 51N 92 18W
Belle Plaine, Minn., U.S.A. 138 C8 44 35N 93 48W
Belle Rive, U.S.A. 141 F8 38 14N 88 45W
Belle Yella, Liberia 100 D3 7 24N 10 0W
Belledonne, Chaîne de, France 25 C10 45 20N 6 10 E
Belledune, Canada 129 C6 47 55N 65 50W
Bellefontaine, U.S.A. 141 D13 40 20N 83 45W
Bellefonte, U.S.A. 136 F7 40 56N 77 45W
Bellegarde, France 23 E9 47 59N 2 26 E
Bellegarde-en-Marche, France 24 C6 45 59N 2 18 E
Bellegarde-sur-Valserine, France 25 B9 46 4N 5 50 E
Bellême, France 22 D7 48 22N 0 34 E
Belleoram, Canada 129 C8 47 31N 55 25W
Belleville, Canada 128 D4 44 10N 77 23W
Belleville, France 25 B8 46 7N 4 45 E
Belleville, Ill., U.S.A. 140 F7 38 30N 90 0W
Belleville, Kans., U.S.A. 138 F6 39 51N 97 38W
Belleville, N.Y., U.S.A. 137 C8 43 46N 76 10W
Belleville-sur-Vie, France 22 F5 46 46N 1 25W
Bellevue, Canada 130 D6 49 35N 114 22W
Bellevue, Idaho, U.S.A. 142 E6 43 25N 114 23W
Bellevue, Iowa, U.S.A. 140 B6 42 16N 90 26W
Bellevue, Mich., U.S.A. 141 B11 42 27N 85 1W
Bellevue, Ohio, U.S.A. 136 E2 41 20N 82 48W
Bellevue, Wash., U.S.A. 144 C4 47 37N 122 12W
Belley, France 25 C9 45 46N 5 41 E
Bellflower, U.S.A. 140 F5 39 0N 91 21W
Bellin, Canada 127 C13 60 0N 70 0W
Bellingen, Australia 117 A10 30 25 S 152 50 E
Bellingham, U.S.A. 144 B4 48 45N 122 27W
Bellingshausen Sea, Antarctica 7 C17 66 0 S 80 0W
Bellinzona, Switz. 29 D8 46 11N 9 1 E
Bello, Colombia 152 B2 6 20N 75 33W
Bellona, Solomon Is. 121 N10 11 17 S 159 47 E
Bellows Falls, U.S.A. 137 C12 43 10N 72 30W
Bellpat, Pakistan 80 E3 29 0N 68 5 E
Bellpuig, Spain 34 D6 41 37N 1 1 E
Belluno, Italy 39 B9 46 8N 12 13 E
Bellville, U.S.A. 139 L6 29 58N 96 18W
Bellwood, U.S.A. 136 F6 40 36N 78 21W
Bélmez, Spain 37 G5 38 17N 5 17W
Belmond, U.S.A. 140 B3 42 51N 93 37W
Belmont, Australia 117 B9 33 4 S 151 42 E
Belmont, Canada 136 D3 42 53N 81 5W
Belmont, S. Africa 104 D3 29 28 S 24 22 E
Belmont, U.S.A. 136 D6 42 14N 78 3W
Belmonte, Brazil 155 E4 16 0 S 39 0W
Belmonte, Portugal 36 E3 40 21N 7 20W
Belmonte, Spain 34 F2 39 34N 2 43W
Belmopan, Belize 147 D7 17 18N 88 30W
Belmore, Australia 116 B4 33 34 S 141 13 E
Belmullet, Ireland 19 B2 54 13N 9 58W
Belo Horizonte, Brazil 155 E3 19 55 S 43 56W
Belo Jardim, Brazil 154 C4 8 20 S 36 26W
Belo-sur-Mer, Madag. 105 C7 20 42 S 44 0 E
Belo-Tsiribihina, Madag. 105 B7 19 40 S 44 30 E
Belogorsk, R.S.F.S.R., U.S.S.R. 57 D13 51 0N 128 20 E
Belogorsk, Ukraine S.S.R., U.S.S.R. 52 D6 45 3N 34 35 E
Belogradchik, Bulgaria 42 D7 43 53N 22 15 E
Belogradets, Bulgaria 43 D12 43 22N 27 18 E
Beloha, Madag. 105 D8 25 10 S 45 3 E
Beloit, Kans., U.S.A. 138 F5 39 32N 98 9W
Beloit, Wis., U.S.A. 140 B7 42 35N 89 3W
Belokorovichi, U.S.S.R. 50 F6 51 7N 28 2 E
Belomorsk, U.S.S.R. 48 B5 64 35N 34 30 E
Belonia, India 78 D3 23 15N 91 30 E
Belopolye, U.S.S.R. 50 F9 51 14N 34 20 E
Beloretsk, U.S.S.R. 54 E6 53 58N 58 24 E
Belovo, U.S.S.R. 56 D9 54 30N 86 0 E
Beloyarskiy, U.S.S.R. 54 C7 56 45N 61 24 E
Beloye, Oz., U.S.S.R. 48 B6 60 10N 37 35 E
Beloye More, U.S.S.R. 48 A6 66 30N 38 0 E
Beloye Ozero, U.S.S.R. 53 D12 45 15N 46 50 E
Belozem, Bulgaria 43 E10 42 12N 25 2 E
Belozersk, U.S.S.R. 51 A10 60 0N 37 30 E
Belpasso, Italy 41 E8 37 37N 15 0 E
Belsele, Belgium 21 F4 51 9N 4 6 E
Belsito, Italy 40 E6 37 50N 13 47 E
Beltana, Australia 116 A3 30 48 S 138 25 E
Belterra, Brazil 153 D7 2 45 S 55 0W
Beltinci, Yugoslavia 39 B13 46 37N 16 20 E
Belton, S.C., U.S.A. 135 H4 34 31N 82 39W
Belton, Tex., U.S.A. 139 K6 31 4N 97 30W
Belton Res., U.S.A. 139 K6 31 8N 97 32W
Beltsy, U.S.S.R. 52 C3 47 48N 28 0 E
Belturbet, Ireland 19 B4 54 6N 7 28W
Belukha, U.S.S.R. 56 E9 49 50N 86 50 E
Beluran, Malaysia 70 C5 5 48N 117 35 E
Beluša, Czech. 31 B11 49 5N 18 27 E
Belušić, Yugoslavia 42 D6 43 50N 21 10 E
Belvedere Maríttimo, Italy 41 C8 39 37N 15 52 E
Belvès, France 24 D5 44 46N 1 0 E
Belvidere, Ill., U.S.A. 138 D10 42 15N 88 55W
Belvidere, N.J., U.S.A. 137 F9 40 48N 75 5W
Belvis de la Jara, Spain 37 F6 39 45N 4 57W
Belyando →, Australia 114 C4 21 38 S 146 50 E
Belyy, U.S.S.R. 50 D8 55 48N 32 51 E
Belyy, Ostrov, U.S.S.R. 56 B8 73 30N 71 0 E
Belyy Yar, U.S.S.R. 56 D9 58 26N 84 39 E
Belyye Vody, U.S.S.R. 55 B4 42 25N 69 50 E
Belzig, Germany 26 C8 52 8N 12 36 E
Belzoni, U.S.A. 139 J9 33 12N 90 30W
Bełżyce, Poland 47 D9 51 11N 22 17 E
Bemaraha, Lembalemban' i, Madag. 105 B7 18 40 S 44 45 E
Bemarivo, Madag. 105 C7 21 45 S 44 45 E
Bemarivo →, Madag. 105 B8 15 27 S 47 40 E
Bemavo, Madag. 105 C8 21 33 S 45 25 E
Bembéréke, Benin 101 C5 10 11N 2 43 E
Bembesi, Zimbabwe 107 G2 20 0 S 28 58 E
Bembesi →, Zimbabwe 107 F2 18 57 S 27 47 E
Bembézar →, Spain 37 H5 37 45N 5 13W
Bement, U.S.A. 141 E8 39 55N 88 34W
Bemidji, U.S.A. 138 B7 47 30N 94 50W
Bemmel, Neths. 20 E7 51 54N 5 54 E
Ben, Iran 85 C6 32 32N 50 45 E
Ben Bullen, Australia 117 B9 33 12 S 150 2 E
Ben Cruachan, U.K. 18 E3 56 26N 5 8W
Ben Dearg, U.K. 18 D4 57 47N 4 58W
Ben Gardane, Tunisia 96 B2 33 11N 11 11 E
Ben Hope, U.K. 18 C4 58 24N 4 36W
Ben Lawers, U.K. 18 E4 56 33N 4 13W
Ben Lomond, N.S.W., Australia 115 E5 30 1 S 151 43 E
Ben Lomond, Tas., Australia 114 G4 41 38 S 147 42 E
Ben Lomond, U.K. 18 E4 56 12N 4 39W
Ben Luc, Vietnam 77 G6 10 39N 106 29 E
Ben Macdhui, U.K. 18 D5 57 4N 3 40W
Ben Mhor, U.K. 18 D1 57 16N 7 21W
Ben More, Central, U.K. 18 E4 56 23N 4 31W
Ben More, Strath., U.K. 18 E2 56 26N 6 2W
Ben More Assynt, U.K. 18 C4 58 7N 4 51W
Ben Nevis, U.K. 18 E4 56 48N 4 58W
Ben Ohau Ra., N.Z. 119 E5 44 1 S 170 4 E
Ben Quang, Vietnam 76 D6 17 3N 106 55 E
Ben Slimane, Morocco 98 B3 33 38N 7 7W
Ben Tre, Vietnam 77 G6 10 3N 106 36 E
Ben Vorlich, U.K. 18 E4 56 22N 4 15W
Ben Wyvis, U.K. 18 D4 57 40N 4 35W
Bena, Nigeria 101 C6 11 20N 5 50 E
Bena Dibele, Zaïre 103 C4 4 4 S 22 50 E
Bena-Leka, Zaïre 103 D4 5 8 S 22 10 E
Bena-Tshadi, Zaïre 103 C4 4 40 S 22 49 E
Benadir, Somali Rep. 108 D2 1 30N 44 30 E
Benagalbón, Spain 37 J6 36 45N 4 15W
Benagerie, Australia 116 A4 31 25 S 140 22 E
Benahmed, Morocco 98 B3 33 4N 7 9W
Benalla, Australia 117 D7 36 30 S 146 0 E
Benambra, Mt., Australia 117 D7 36 31 S 147 34 E
Benamejí, Spain 37 H6 37 16N 4 33W
Benares = Varanasi, India 81 G10 25 22N 83 0 E
Bénat, C., France 25 E10 43 5N 6 22 E
Benavente, Portugal 37 G2 38 59N 8 49W
Benavente, Spain 36 C5 42 2N 5 43W
Benavides, Spain 36 C5 42 30N 5 54W
Benavides, U.S.A. 139 M5 27 35N 98 28W
Benbecula, U.K. 18 D1 57 26N 7 21W
Benbonyathe, Australia 116 A3 30 25 S 139 11 E
Bencubbin, Australia 113 F2 30 48 S 117 52 E
Bend, U.S.A. 142 D3 44 2N 121 15W
Bendel □, Nigeria 101 D6 6 0N 6 0 E
Bendela, Zaïre 102 C3 3 18 S 17 36 E

Brakel 177

Bonneval, France 22 D8 48 11N 1 24 E
Bonneville, France 25 B10 46 4N 6 24 E
Bonney, L., Australia 116 D4 37 50 S 140 20 E
Bonnie Doon, Australia 117 D6 37 2 S 145 53 E
Bonnie Downs, Australia 114 C3 22 7 S 143 50 E
Bonnie Rock, Australia 113 F2 30 29 S 118 22 E
Bonny, Nigeria 101 E6 4 25N 7 13 E
Bonny →, Nigeria 101 E6 4 20N 7 10 E
Bonny, Bight of, Africa 101 E6 3 30N 9 20 E
Bonny-sur-Loire, France 23 E9 47 33N 2 50 E
Bonnyville, Canada 131 C6 54 20N 110 45W
Bonoi, Indonesia 71 E9 1 45 S 137 41 E
Bonorva, Italy 40 B1 40 25N 8 47 E
Bonsall, U.S.A. 145 M9 33 16N 117 14W
Bontang, Indonesia 70 D5 0 10N 117 30 E
Bonthain, Indonesia 71 F5 5 34 S 119 56 E
Bonthe, S. Leone 100 D2 7 30N 12 33W
Bontoc, Phil. 71 A6 17 7N 120 58 E
Bonyeri, Ghana 100 D4 5 1N 2 46W
Bonyhád, Hungary 31 E11 46 18N 18 32 E
Bonython Ra., Australia 112 D4 23 40 S 128 45 E
Bookabie, Australia 113 F5 31 50 S 132 41 E
Booker, U.S.A. 139 G4 36 29N 100 30W
Boolaboolka L., Australia 116 B5 32 38 S 143 10 E
Boolarra, Australia 117 E7 38 20 S 146 20 E
Boolcoomata, Australia 116 A4 31 57 S 140 33 E
Booleroo Centre, Australia 116 B3 32 53 S 138 21 E
Booligal, Australia 117 B6 33 58 S 144 53 E
Boom, Belgium 21 F4 51 6N 4 20 E
Boonah, Australia 115 D5 27 58 S 152 41 E
Boone, Iowa, U.S.A. 140 B3 42 5N 93 53W
Boone, N.C., U.S.A. 135 G5 36 14N 81 43W
Booneville, Ark., U.S.A. 139 H8 35 10N 93 54W
Booneville, Miss., U.S.A. 135 H1 34 39N 88 34W
Boonville, Calif., U.S.A. 144 F3 39 1N 123 22W
Boonville, Ind., U.S.A. 141 F9 38 3N 87 13W
Boonville, Mo., U.S.A. 140 F4 38 57N 92 45W
Boonville, N.Y., U.S.A. 137 C9 43 31N 75 20W
Booral, Australia 117 B9 32 30 S 151 56 E
Boorindal, Australia 115 E4 30 22 S 146 11 E
Booroomugga, Australia 117 A7 31 17 S 146 27 E
Boorowa, Australia 117 C8 34 28 S 148 44 E
Boothia, Gulf of, Canada 127 A11 71 0N 90 0W
Boothia Pen., Canada 126 A10 71 0N 94 0W
Bootle, Cumb., U.K. 16 C4 54 17N 3 24W
Bootle, Mersey., U.K. 16 D4 53 28N 3 1W
Booué, Gabon 102 C2 0 5 S 11 55 E
Bophuthatswana □, S. Africa 104 D4 25 49 S 25 30 E
Boppard, Germany 27 E3 50 13N 7 36 E
Boquerón □, Paraguay 157 E6 23 0 S 60 0W
Boquete, Panama 148 E3 8 46N 82 27W
Boquilla, Presa de la, Mexico 146 B3 27 40N 105 30W
Boquillas del Carmen, Mexico 146 B4 29 17N 102 53W
Bor, Czech. 30 B5 49 41N 12 45 E
Bôr, Sudan 95 F3 6 10N 31 40 E
Bor, Turkey 88 E6 37 54N 34 32 E
Bor, Yugoslavia 42 C7 44 8N 22 7 E
Bor Mashash, Israel 91 D3 31 7N 34 50 E
Boradā →, Syria 91 B5 33 33N 36 34 E
Borah Pk., U.S.A. 142 D7 44 19N 113 46W
Borama, Somali Rep. 90 F3 9 55N 43 7 E
Borang, Sudan 95 G3 4 50N 30 59 E
Borangapara, India 78 C3 25 14N 90 14 E
Borås, Sweden 15 G6 57 43N 12 56 E
Borāzjān, Iran 85 D6 29 22N 51 10 E
Borba, Brazil 153 D6 4 12 S 59 34W
Borba, Portugal 37 G3 38 50N 7 26W
Borborema, Planalto da, Brazil 154 C4 7 0 S 37 0W
Borçka, Turkey 53 F9 41 25N 41 41 E
Borculo, Neths. 20 D9 52 7N 6 31 E
Bord Khūn-e Now, Iran 85 D6 28 3N 51 28 E
Borda, C., Australia 116 C2 35 45 S 136 34 E
Bordeaux, France 24 D3 44 50N 0 36W
Borden, Australia 113 F2 34 3 S 118 12 E
Borden, Canada 129 C7 46 18N 63 47W
Borden I., Canada 6 B2 78 30N 111 30W
Borders □, U.K. 18 F6 55 35N 2 50W
Bordertown, Australia 116 D4 36 19 S 140 45 E
Borðeyri, Iceland 12 D3 65 12N 21 6W
Bordighera, Italy 38 E4 43 47N 7 40 E
Bordj bou Arreridj, Algeria 99 A5 36 4N 4 45 E
Bordj Bourguiba, Tunisia 96 B2 32 12N 10 2 E
Bordj el Hobra, Algeria 99 B5 32 9N 4 51 E
Bordj Fly Ste. Marie, Algeria 98 C4 27 19N 2 32W
Bordj-in-Eker, Algeria 99 D6 24 9N 5 3 E
Bordj Menaiel, Algeria 99 A5 36 46N 3 43 E
Bordj Messouda, Algeria 99 B6 30 12N 9 25 E
Bordj Nili, Algeria 99 B5 33 28N 3 2 E
Bordj Omar Driss, Algeria 99 C6 28 10N 6 40 E
Bordj-Tarat, Algeria 99 C6 25 55N 9 3 E
Bordj Zelfana, Algeria 99 B5 32 27N 4 15 E
Bordoba, U.S.S.R. 55 D6 39 31N 73 16 E
Borea Creek, Australia 117 C7 35 5 S 146 35 E
Borek Wielkopolski, Poland 47 D4 51 54N 17 11 E
Boremore, Australia 117 B8 33 15 S 149 0 E
Borensberg, Sweden 15 F9 58 34N 15 17 E
Borgarnes, Iceland 12 D3 64 32N 21 55W
Børgefjellet, Norway 12 D12 65 20N 13 45 E
Borger, Neths. 20 C9 52 54N 6 44 E
Borger, U.S.A. 139 H4 35 40N 101 20W
Borgerhout, Belgium 21 F4 51 12N 4 28 E
Borghamn, Sweden 15 F8 58 23N 14 41 E
Borgholm, Sweden 13 H14 56 52N 16 39 E
Bórgia, Italy 41 D9 38 50N 16 30 E
Borgloon, Belgium 21 G6 50 48N 5 21 E
Borgo San Dalmazzo, Italy 38 D4 44 19N 7 29 E
Borgo San Lorenzo, Italy 39 E8 43 57N 11 21 E
Borgo Valsugano, Italy 39 B8 46 3N 11 27 E
Borgomanero, Italy 38 C5 45 41N 8 28 E
Borgonovo Val Tidone, Italy 38 C6 45 1N 9 28 E
Borgorose, Italy 39 F10 42 12N 13 14 E
Borgosésia, Italy 38 C5 45 43N 8 17 E
Borgvattnet, Sweden 14 A9 63 26N 15 48 E
Borikhane, Laos 76 C4 18 33N 103 43 E
Borislav, U.S.S.R. 50 G3 49 18N 23 28 E
Borisoglebsk, U.S.S.R. 51 F13 51 27N 42 5 E
Borisoglebskiy, U.S.S.R. 51 C13 56 28N 43 59 E
Borisov, U.S.S.R. 50 D6 54 17N 28 28 E
Borisovka, U.S.S.R. 55 B4 43 15N 68 10 E
Borispol, U.S.S.R. 50 F7 50 21N 30 59 E
Borja, Peru 152 D2 4 20 S 77 40W
Borja, Spain 34 D3 41 48N 1 34W
Borjas Blancas, Spain 34 D5 41 31N 0 52 E
Borken, Germany 26 D2 51 51N 6 52 E
Borkou, Chad 97 E3 18 15N 18 50 E
Borkum, Germany 26 B2 53 36N 6 42 E
Borlänge, Sweden 13 F13 60 29N 15 26 E
Borley, C., Antarctica 7 C5 66 15 S 52 30 E
Bormida →, Italy 38 D5 44 23N 8 13 E
Bórmio, Italy 38 B7 46 28N 10 22 E
Born, Neths. 21 F7 51 2N 5 49 E
Borna, Germany 26 D8 51 8N 12 31 E
Borndiep, Neths. 20 B7 53 27N 5 35 E
Borne, Neths. 20 D9 52 18N 6 46 E
Bornem, Belgium 21 F4 51 6N 4 14 E
Borneo, E. Indies 70 D5 1 0N 115 0 E
Bornholm, Denmark 13 J13 55 10N 15 0 E
Borno □, Nigeria 101 C7 12 30N 12 30 E
Bornos, Spain 37 J5 36 48N 5 42W
Bornu Yassa, Nigeria 101 C7 12 14N 12 25 E
Borobudur, Indonesia 71 G14 7 36 S 110 13 E
Borodino, U.S.S.R. 50 D9 55 31N 35 40 E
Borogontsy, U.S.S.R. 57 C14 62 42N 131 8 E
Boromo, Burkina Faso 100 C4 11 45N 2 58W
Boron, U.S.A. 145 L9 35 0N 117 39W
Boronga Is., Burma 78 F4 19 58N 93 6 E
Borongan, Phil. 71 B7 11 37N 125 26 E
Bororen, Australia 114 C5 24 13 S 151 33 E
Borotangba Mts., C.A.R. 95 F2 6 30N 25 0 E
Borovan, Bulgaria 43 D8 43 27N 23 45 E
Borovichi, U.S.S.R. 50 B8 58 25N 33 55 E
Borovsk, Moskva, U.S.S.R. 51 D10 55 12N 36 24 E
Borovsk, Urals, U.S.S.R. 54 B5 59 43N 56 40 E
Borovskoye, U.S.S.R. 54 E9 53 48N 64 12 E
Borrego Springs, U.S.A. 145 M10 33 15N 116 23W
Borriol, Spain 34 E4 40 4N 0 4W
Borroloola, Australia 114 B2 16 4 S 136 17 E
Borşa, Romania 46 B5 47 41N 24 50 E
Borsod-Abaúj-Zemplén □, Hungary 31 C14 48 20N 21 0 E
Borssele, Neths. 21 F3 51 26N 3 45 E
Bort-les-Orgues, France 24 C6 45 24N 2 29 E
Borth, U.K. 17 E3 52 29N 4 3W
Borujerd, Iran 85 C6 33 55N 48 50 E
Borzhomi, U.S.S.R. 53 F10 41 48N 43 28 E
Borzna, U.S.S.R. 50 F8 51 18N 32 26 E
Borzya, U.S.S.R. 57 D12 50 24N 116 31 E
Bosa, Italy 40 B1 40 17N 8 32 E
Bosaga, U.S.S.R. 55 E2 37 33N 65 41 E
Bosanska Brod, Yugoslavia 42 B3 45 10N 18 0 E
Bosanska Dubica, Yugoslavia 39 C13 45 10N 16 50 E
Bosanska Gradiška, Yugoslavia 42 B2 45 10N 17 15 E
Bosanska Kostajnica, Yugoslavia 39 C13 45 11N 16 33 E
Bosanska Krupa, Yugoslavia 39 D13 44 53N 16 10 E
Bosanski Novi, Yugoslavia 39 C13 45 2N 16 22 E
Bosanski Šamac, Yugoslavia 42 B3 45 3N 18 29 E
Bosansko Grahovo, Yugoslavia 39 D13 44 12N 16 26 E
Bosansko Petrovac, Yugoslavia 39 D13 44 35N 16 21 E
Bosaso, Somali Rep. 90 E4 11 12N 49 18 E
Bosavi, Mt., Papua N. G. 120 D2 6 30 S 142 49 E
Boscastle, U.K. 17 G3 50 42N 4 42W
Boscobel, U.S.A. 140 A6 43 8N 90 42W
Boscotrecase, Italy 41 B7 40 46N 14 28 E
Bose, China 68 F6 23 53N 106 35 E
Boshan, China 67 F9 36 28N 117 49 E
Boshoek, S. Africa 104 D4 25 30 S 27 9 E
Boshof, S. Africa 104 D4 28 31 S 25 13 E
Boshrūyeh, Iran 85 C8 33 50N 57 30 E
Bosilegrad, Yugoslavia 42 E7 42 30N 22 27 E
Boskoop, Neths. 20 D5 52 4N 4 40 E
Boskovice, Czech. 31 B9 49 29N 16 40 E
Bosna →, Yugoslavia 42 B3 45 4N 18 29 E
Bosna i Hercegovina □, Yugoslavia 42 D2 44 0N 17 0 E
Bosnia = Bosna i Hercegovina □, Yugoslavia 42 D2 44 0N 17 0 E
Bosnik, Indonesia 71 E9 1 5 S 136 10 E
Bōsō-Hantō, Japan 63 B12 35 20N 140 20 E
Bosobolo, Zaïre 102 B3 4 15N 19 50 E
Bosporus = Karadeniz Boğazı, Turkey 88 C3 41 10N 29 10 E
Bossangoa, C.A.R. 102 A3 6 35N 17 30 E
Bossekop, Norway 12 B17 69 57N 23 15 E
Bossembélé, C.A.R. 102 A3 5 25N 17 40 E
Bossembélé II, C.A.R. 102 A3 5 41N 16 38 E
Bossier City, U.S.A. 139 J8 32 28N 93 48W
Bosso, Niger 97 F2 13 43N 13 19 E
Bostānābād, Iran 84 B5 37 50N 46 50 E
Bosten Hu, China 64 B3 41 55N 87 40 E
Boston, U.K. 16 E7 52 59N 0 2W
Boston, U.S.A. 137 D13 42 20N 71 5W
Boston Bar, Canada 130 D4 49 52N 121 30W
Bosusulu, Zaïre 102 B4 0 50N 20 45 E
Bosut →, Yugoslavia 42 B3 45 20N 18 45 E
Boswell, Canada 130 D5 49 28N 116 45W
Boswell, Ind., U.S.A. 141 D9 40 30N 87 23W
Boswell, Okla., U.S.A. 139 H7 34 1N 95 50W
Boswell, Pa., U.S.A. 136 F5 40 9N 79 2W
Bosworth, U.S.A. 140 E3 39 28N 93 20W
Botad, India 80 H4 22 15N 71 40 E
Botan →, Turkey 89 E9 37 44N 41 47 E
Botany B., Australia 115 E5 34 0 S 151 14 E
Botene, Laos 76 D3 17 35N 101 12 E
Botevgrad, Bulgaria 43 E8 42 55N 23 47 E
Bothaville, S. Africa 104 D4 27 23 S 26 34 E
Bothnia, G. of, Europe 12 E16 63 0N 20 15 E
Bothwell, Australia 114 G4 42 20 S 147 1 E
Bothwell, Canada 136 D3 42 38N 81 52W
Boticas, Portugal 36 D3 41 41N 7 40W
Botletle →, Botswana 104 C3 20 10 S 23 15 E
Botoroaga, Romania 46 E6 44 8N 25 32 E
Botoşani, Romania 46 B7 47 42N 26 41 E
Botoşani □, Romania 46 B7 47 50N 26 50 E
Botro, Ivory C. 100 D3 7 51N 5 19W
Botswana ■, Africa 104 C3 22 0 S 24 0 E
Bottineau, U.S.A. 138 A4 48 49N 100 25W
Bottrop, Germany 21 E9 51 34N 6 59 E
Botucatu, Brazil 159 A6 22 55 S 48 30W
Botwood, Canada 129 C8 49 6N 55 23W
Bou Alam, Algeria 99 B5 33 50N 1 26 E
Bou Ali, Algeria 99 C4 27 11N 0 4W
Bou Djébéha, Mali 100 B4 18 25N 2 45W
Bou Guema, Algeria 99 C5 28 49N 0 19 E
Bou Ismael, Algeria 99 A5 36 38N 2 42 E
Bou Izakarn, Morocco 98 C3 29 12N 9 46W
Boû Lanouâr, Mauritania 98 D1 21 12N 16 34W
Bou Saâda, Algeria 99 A5 35 11N 4 9 E
Bou Salem, Tunisia 96 A1 36 45N 9 2 E
Bouaké, Ivory C. 100 D3 7 40N 5 2W
Bouanga, Congo 102 C3 2 7 S 16 8 E
Bouar, C.A.R. 102 A3 6 0N 15 40 E
Bouârfa, Morocco 99 B4 32 32N 1 58W
Bouca, C.A.R. 102 A3 6 45N 18 25 E
Boucau, France 24 E2 43 32N 1 29W
Boucaut B., Australia 114 A1 12 0 S 134 25 E
Bouches-du-Rhône □, France 25 E9 43 37N 5 2 E
Bouda, Algeria 99 C4 27 50N 0 27W
Boudenib, Morocco 98 B4 31 59N 3 31W
Boudry, Switz. 28 C3 46 57N 6 50 E
Boufarik, Algeria 99 A5 36 34N 2 58 E
Bougainville, C., Australia 112 B4 13 57 S 126 4 E
Bougainville I., Solomon Is. 121 L8 6 0 S 155 0 E
Bougainville Reef, Australia 114 B4 15 30 S 147 5 E
Bougainville Str., Solomon Is. 121 L9 6 40 S 156 10 E
Bougaroun, C., Algeria 99 A6 37 6N 6 30 E
Bougie = Bejaia, Algeria 99 A6 36 42N 5 2 E
Bougouni, Mali 100 C3 11 30N 7 20W
Bouillon, Belgium 21 J6 49 44N 5 3 E
Bouïra, Algeria 99 A5 36 20N 3 59 E
Boulder, Colo., U.S.A. 138 E2 40 3N 105 10W
Boulder, Mont., U.S.A. 142 C7 46 14N 112 4W
Boulder City, U.S.A. 145 K12 35 58N 114 50W
Boulder Creek, U.S.A. 144 H4 37 7N 122 7W
Boulder Dam = Hoover Dam, U.S.A. 145 K12 36 0N 114 45W
Boulembo, Gabon 102 C2 1 26 S 12 0 E
Bouli, Mauritania 100 B2 15 17N 12 18W
Boulia, Australia 114 C2 22 52 S 139 51 E
Bouligny, France 23 C12 49 17N 5 45 E
Boulogne →, France 22 E5 47 12N 1 47W
Boulogne-sur-Gesse, France 24 E4 43 18N 0 38 E
Boulogne-sur-Mer, France 23 B8 50 42N 1 36 E
Bouloire, France 22 E7 47 59N 0 45 E
Bouloupari, N. Cal. 121 U20 21 52 S 166 4 E
Boulsa, Burkina Faso 101 C4 12 39N 0 34W
Boultoum, Niger 97 F2 14 45N 10 25 E
Boumalne, Morocco 98 B3 31 25N 6 0W
Boun Neua, Laos 76 B3 21 38N 101 54 E
Boun Tai, Laos 76 B3 21 23N 101 58 E
Bouna, Ivory C. 100 D4 9 10N 3 0W
Boundary Pk., U.S.A. 144 H8 37 51N 118 21W
Boundiali, Ivory C. 100 D3 9 30N 6 20W
Bountiful, U.S.A. 142 F8 40 57N 111 58W
Bounty Is., Pac. Oc. 122 M9 48 0 S 178 30 E
Bourail, N. Cal. 121 U19 21 34 S 165 30 E
Bourbeuse →, U.S.A. 140 F6 38 24N 90 54W
Bourbon, U.S.A. 141 C10 41 18N 86 7W
Bourbon-Lancy, France 24 B7 46 37N 3 45 E
Bourbon-l'Archambault, France 24 B7 46 36N 3 4 E
Bourbonnais, France 24 B7 46 28N 3 0 E
Bourbonne-les-Bains, France 23 E12 47 54N 5 45 E
Bourem, Mali 101 B4 17 0N 0 24W
Bourg, France 24 C3 45 3N 0 34W
Bourg-Argental, France 25 C8 45 18N 4 32 E
Bourg-de-Péage, France 25 C9 45 2N 5 3 E
Bourg-en-Bresse, France 25 B9 46 13N 5 12 E
Bourg-St.-Andéol, France 25 D8 44 23N 4 39 E
Bourg-St.-Maurice, France 25 C10 45 35N 6 46 E
Bourg-St.-Pierre, Switz. 28 E4 45 57N 7 12 E
Bourganeuf, France 24 C5 45 57N 1 45 E
Bourges, France 23 E9 47 9N 2 25 E
Bourget, Canada 137 A9 45 26N 75 9W
Bourget, L. du, France 25 C9 45 44N 5 52 E
Bourgneuf, B. de, France 22 E4 47 3N 2 10W
Bourgneuf-en-Retz, France 22 E5 47 2N 1 58W
Bourgogne, France 23 F11 47 0N 4 50 E
Bourgoin-Jallieu, France 25 C9 45 36N 5 17 E
Bourgueil, France 22 E7 47 17N 0 10 E
Bourke, Australia 115 E4 30 8 S 145 55 E
Bournemouth, U.K. 17 G6 50 43N 1 53W
Bourriot-Bergonce, France 24 D3 44 7N 0 14W
Bouse, U.S.A. 145 M13 33 55N 114 0W
Boussac, France 24 B6 46 22N 2 13 E
Boussens, France 24 E4 43 12N 0 58 E
Bousso, Chad 97 F3 10 34N 16 52 E
Boussu, Belgium 21 H3 50 26N 3 48 E
Boutilimit, Mauritania 100 B2 17 45N 14 40W
Bouvet I. = Bouvetøya, Antarctica 9 P9 54 26 S 3 24 E
Bouvetøya, Antarctica 9 P9 54 26 S 3 24 E
Bouznika, Morocco 98 B3 33 46N 7 6W
Bouzonville, France 23 C13 49 17N 6 32 E
Bova Marina, Italy 41 E8 37 59N 15 56 E
Bovalino Marina, Italy 41 D9 38 9N 16 10 E
Bovec, Yugoslavia 39 B10 46 20N 13 33 E
Bovenkarspel, Neths. 20 C6 52 41N 5 14 E
Bovigny, Belgium 21 H7 50 12N 5 55 E
Bovill, U.S.A. 142 C5 46 58N 116 27W
Bovino, Italy 41 A8 41 15N 15 20 E
Bow Island, Canada 130 D6 49 50N 111 23W
Bowbells, U.S.A. 138 A3 48 47N 102 19W
Bowdle, U.S.A. 138 C5 45 30N 99 40W
Bowelling, Australia 113 F2 33 25 S 116 30 E
Bowen, Australia 114 C4 20 0 S 148 16 E
Bowen Mts., Australia 117 D7 37 0 S 147 50 E
Bowie, Ariz., U.S.A. 143 K9 32 15N 109 30W
Bowie, Tex., U.S.A. 139 J6 33 33N 97 50W
Bowkān, Iran 84 B5 36 31N 46 12 E
Bowland, Forest of, U.K. 16 D5 54 0N 2 30W
Bowling Green, Ky., U.S.A. 134 G2 37 0N 86 25W
Bowling Green, Mo., U.S.A. 140 E5 39 21N 91 12W
Bowling Green, Ohio, U.S.A. 141 C13 41 22N 83 40W
Bowling Green, C., Australia 114 B4 19 19 S 147 25 E
Bowman, U.S.A. 138 B3 46 12N 103 21W
Bowman I., Antarctica 7 C8 65 0 S 104 0 E
Bowmans, Australia 116 C3 34 10 S 138 17 E
Bowmanville, Canada 128 D4 43 55N 78 41W
Bowmore, U.K. 18 F2 55 45N 6 18W
Bowral, Australia 117 C9 34 26 S 150 27 E
Bowraville, Australia 115 E5 30 37 S 152 52 E
Bowron →, Canada 130 C4 54 3N 121 50W
Bowser L., Canada 130 B3 56 30N 129 30W
Bowsman, Canada 131 C8 52 14N 101 12W
Bowutu Mts., Papua N. G. 120 D4 7 45 S 147 10 E
Bowwood, Zambia 107 F2 17 5 S 26 20 E
Boxholm, Sweden 15 F9 58 12N 15 3 E
Boxmeer, Neths. 21 E7 51 38N 5 56 E
Boxtel, Neths. 21 E6 51 36N 5 20 E
Boyabat, Turkey 52 F6 41 28N 34 42 E
Boyabo, Zaïre 102 B3 3 43N 18 46 E
Boyaca = Casanare □, Colombia 152 B3 6 0N 73 0W
Boyce, U.S.A. 139 K8 31 25N 92 39W
Boyer →, Canada 130 B5 58 27N 115 57W
Boyer, C., N. Cal. 121 U22 21 37 S 168 6 E
Boyle, Ireland 19 C3 53 58N 8 19W
Boyne →, Ireland 19 C5 53 43N 6 15W
Boyne City, U.S.A. 134 C3 45 13N 85 1W
Boyni Qara, Afghan. 79 A2 36 20N 67 0 E
Boynton Beach, U.S.A. 135 M5 26 31N 80 3W
Boyolali, Indonesia 75 D4 7 32 S 110 35 E
Boyoma, Chutes, Zaïre 102 B5 0 35N 25 23 E
Boyup Brook, Australia 113 F2 33 50 S 116 23 E
Boz Dağ, Turkey 88 E3 37 18N 29 11 E
Boz Dağları, Turkey 88 D3 38 20N 28 0 E
Bozburun, Turkey 45 H10 36 43N 28 8 E
Bozcaada, Turkey 44 E8 39 49N 26 3 E
Bozdoğan, Turkey 88 E3 37 40N 28 17 E
Bozeman, U.S.A. 142 D8 45 40N 111 0W
Bozen = Bolzano, Italy 39 B8 46 30N 11 20 E
Bozene, Zaïre 102 B3 2 56N 19 12 E
Bożepole Wielkopolski, Poland 47 A4 54 33N 17 56 E
Boževac, Yugoslavia 42 C6 44 32N 21 24 E
Bozkır, Turkey 88 E5 37 11N 32 14 E
Bozouls, France 24 D6 44 28N 2 43 E
Bozoum, C.A.R. 102 A3 6 25N 16 35 E
Bozova, Turkey 89 E8 37 21N 38 32 E
Bozovici, Romania 46 E3 44 56N 22 1 E
Bozüyük, Turkey 88 D4 39 54N 30 1 E
Bra, Italy 38 D4 44 41N 7 50 E
Brabant □, Belgium 21 G5 50 46N 4 30 E
Brabant L., Canada 131 B8 55 58N 103 43W
Brabrand, Denmark 15 H4 56 9N 10 7 E
Brač, Yugoslavia 39 E13 43 20N 16 40 E
Bracadale, L., U.K. 18 D2 57 20N 6 30W
Bracciano, Italy 39 F9 42 6N 12 10 E
Bracciano, L. di, Italy 39 F9 42 8N 12 11 E
Bracebridge, Canada 128 C4 45 2N 79 19W
Brach, Libya 96 C2 27 31N 14 20 E
Bracieux, France 23 E8 47 30N 1 30 E
Bräcke, Sweden 14 B9 62 45N 15 26 E
Brackettville, U.S.A. 139 L4 29 21N 100 20W
Bracki Kanal, Yugoslavia 39 E13 43 24N 16 40 E
Brad, Romania 46 C3 46 10N 22 50 E
Brádano →, Italy 41 B9 40 23N 16 51 E
Bradenton, U.S.A. 135 M4 27 25N 82 35W
Bradford, Canada 136 B5 44 7N 79 34W
Bradford, U.K. 16 D6 53 47N 1 45W
Bradford, Ill., U.S.A. 140 C7 41 11N 89 39W
Bradford, Ohio, U.S.A. 141 D12 40 8N 84 27W
Bradford, Pa., U.S.A. 136 E6 41 58N 78 41W
Bradford, Vt., U.S.A. 137 C12 43 59N 72 9W
Brădiceni, Romania 46 D4 45 3N 23 4 E
Bradley, Ark., U.S.A. 139 J8 33 7N 93 39W
Bradley, Calif., U.S.A. 144 K6 35 52N 120 48W
Bradley, Ill., U.S.A. 141 C9 41 9N 87 52W
Bradley, S. Dak., U.S.A. 138 C6 45 10N 97 40W
Bradley Institute, Zimbabwe 107 F3 17 7 S 31 25 E
Bradore Bay, Canada 129 B8 51 27N 57 18W
Bradshaw, Australia 112 C5 15 21 S 130 16 E
Brady, U.S.A. 139 K5 31 8N 99 25W
Brædstrup, Denmark 15 J3 55 58N 9 37 E
Braemar, Australia 116 B3 33 12 S 139 35 E
Braeside, Canada 137 A8 45 28N 76 24W
Braga, Portugal 36 D2 41 35N 8 25W
Braga □, Portugal 36 D2 41 30N 8 30W
Bragado, Argentina 158 D3 35 2 S 60 27W
Bragança, Brazil 154 B2 1 0 S 47 2W
Bragança, Portugal 36 D4 41 48N 6 50W
Bragança □, Portugal 36 D4 41 30N 6 45W
Bragança Paulista, Brazil 159 A6 22 55 S 46 32W
Brahmanbaria, Bangla. 78 D3 23 58N 91 15 E
Brahmani →, India 78 D2 20 39N 86 46 E
Brahmaputra →, India 78 D2 23 58N 89 50 E
Braich-y-pwll, U.K. 16 E3 52 47N 4 46W
Braidwood, Australia 117 C8 35 27 S 149 49 E
Brăila, Romania 46 D8 45 19N 27 59 E
Brăila □, Romania 46 D8 45 5N 27 30 E
Braine-l'Alleud, Belgium 21 G4 50 42N 4 23 E
Braine-le-Comte, Belgium 21 G4 50 37N 4 8 E
Brainerd, U.S.A. 138 B7 46 20N 94 10W
Braintree, U.K. 17 F8 51 53N 0 34 E
Braintree, U.S.A. 137 D14 42 11N 71 0W
Brak →, S. Africa 104 D3 29 35 S 22 55 E
Brake, Niedersachsen, Germany 26 B4 53 19N 8 30 E
Brake, Nordrhein-Westfalen, Germany 26 D5 51 43N 9 12 E
Brakel, Neths. 20 E6 51 49N 5 5 E

178 Brakwater

Brakwater, Namibia 104 C2 22 28 S 17 3 E
Brålanda, Sweden 15 F6 58 34N 12 21 E
Bralorne, Canada 130 C4 50 50N 122 50W
Bramberg, Germany 27 E6 50 6N 10 40 E
Bramminge, Denmark 15 J2 55 28N 8 42 E
Brämön, Sweden 14 B11 62 14N 17 40 E
Brampton, Canada 128 D4 43 45N 79 45W
Bramsche, Germany 26 C3 52 25N 7 58 E
Bramwell, Australia 114 A3 12 8 S 142 37 E
Branco →, Brazil 153 D5 1 20 S 61 50W
Branco, C., Brazil 154 C5 7 9 S 34 47W
Brande, Denmark 15 J3 55 57N 9 8 E
Brandenburg, Germany 26 C8 52 24N 12 33 E
Brandenburg, U.S.A. 141 G10 38 0N 86 10W
Brandenburg □, Germany 26 C9 52 15N 13 0 E
Brandfort, S. Africa 104 D4 28 40 S 26 30 E
Brandon, Canada 131 D9 49 50N 99 57W
Brandon, U.S.A. 137 C11 43 48N 73 4W
Brandon B., Ireland 19 D1 52 17N 10 8W
Brandon Mt., Ireland 19 D1 52 15N 10 15W
Brandsen, Argentina 158 D4 35 10 S 58 15W
Brandval, Norway 14 D6 60 19N 12 1 E
Brandvlei, S. Africa 104 E3 30 25 S 20 30 E
Brandýs, Czech. 30 A7 50 10N 14 40 E
Branford, U.S.A. 137 E12 41 15N 72 48W
Braniewo, Poland 47 A6 54 25N 19 50 E
Bransfield Str., Antarctica 7 C18 63 0 S 59 0W
Brańsk, Poland 47 C9 52 45N 22 50 E
Branson, Colo., U.S.A. 139 G3 37 4N 103 53W
Branson, Mo., U.S.A. 139 G8 36 40N 93 18W
Brantford, Canada 128 D3 43 10N 80 15W
Brantôme, France 24 C4 45 22N 0 39 E
Branxholme, Australia 116 D4 37 52 S 141 49 E
Branxton, Australia 117 B9 32 38 S 151 21 E
Branzi, Italy 38 C6 46 0N 9 46 E
Bras d'Or, L., Canada 129 C7 45 50N 60 50W
Brasiléia, Brazil 156 C4 11 0 S 68 45W
Brasília, Brazil 155 E2 15 47 S 47 55W
Brasília Legal, Brazil 153 D6 3 49 S 55 36W
Braslav, U.S.S.R. 50 D5 55 38N 27 0 E
Braslovce, Yugoslavia 39 B12 46 21N 15 3 E
Braşov, Romania 46 D6 45 38N 25 35 E
Braşov □, Romania 46 D6 45 45N 25 15 E
Brass, Nigeria 101 E6 4 35N 6 14 E
Brass →, Nigeria 101 E6 4 15N 6 13 E
Brassac-les-Mines, France 24 C7 45 24N 3 20 E
Brasschaat, Belgium 21 F4 51 19N 4 27 E
Brassey, Banjaran, Malaysia 70 D5 5 0N 117 15 E
Brassey Ra., Australia 113 E3 25 8 S 122 15 E
Brasstown Bald, U.S.A. 135 H4 34 54N 83 45W
Bratan = Morozov, Bulgaria 43 E10 42 30N 25 10 E
Bratislava, Czech. 31 C10 48 10N 17 7 E
Bratsigovo, Bulgaria 43 E9 42 1N 24 22 E
Bratsk, U.S.S.R. 57 D11 56 10N 101 30 E
Brattleboro, U.S.A. 137 D12 42 53N 72 37W
Bratunac, Yugoslavia 42 C4 44 13N 19 21 E
Braunau, Austria 30 C6 48 15N 13 3 E
Braunschweig, Germany 26 C6 52 17N 10 28 E
Braunton, U.K. 17 F3 51 6N 4 9W
Brava, Somali Rep. 90 G3 1 20N 44 8 E
Bråviken, Sweden 14 F10 58 38N 16 32 E
Bravo del Norte →, Mexico 146 B5 25 57N 97 9W
Brawley, U.S.A. 145 N11 32 58N 115 30W
Bray, Mt., Australia 114 A1 14 0 S 134 30 E
Bray, Pays de, France 23 C8 49 46N 1 26 E
Bray-sur-Seine, France 23 D10 48 25N 3 14 E
Braymer, U.S.A. 140 E3 39 35N 93 48W
Brazeau →, Canada 130 C5 52 55N 115 14W
Brazil, U.S.A. 141 E9 39 32N 87 8W
Brazil ■, S. Amer. 155 D2 12 0 S 50 0W
Brazo Sur →, S. Amer. 158 B4 25 21 S 57 42W
Brazos →, U.S.A. 139 L7 28 53N 95 23W
Brazzaville, Congo 103 C3 4 9 S 15 12 E
Brčko, Yugoslavia 42 C3 44 54N 18 46 E
Brda →, Poland 47 B5 53 8N 18 8 E
Brea, Peru 156 A1 4 40 S 81 7W
Breadalbane, Australia 114 C2 23 50 S 139 35 E
Breadalbane, U.K. 18 E4 56 30N 4 15W
Breaden, L., Australia 113 E4 25 51 S 125 28 E
Breaksea Sd., N.Z. 119 F1 45 35 S 166 35 E
Bream B., N.Z. 118 B3 35 56 S 174 28 E
Bream Hd., N.Z. 118 B3 35 51 S 174 36 E
Bream Tail, N.Z. 118 C3 36 3 S 174 36 E
Breas, Chile 158 B1 25 29 S 70 24W
Brebes, Indonesia 71 G13 6 52 S 109 3 E
Brechin, Canada 136 B5 44 32N 79 10W
Brechin, U.K. 18 E6 56 44N 2 40W
Brecht, Belgium 21 F5 51 21N 4 38 E
Breckenridge, Colo., U.S.A. 142 G10 39 30N 106 2W
Breckenridge, Minn., U.S.A. 138 B6 46 20N 96 36W
Breckenridge, Mo., U.S.A. 140 E3 39 46N 93 48W
Breckenridge, Tex., U.S.A. 139 J5 32 48N 98 55W
Brecknock, Pen., Chile 160 D2 54 35 S 71 30W
Břeclav, Czech. 31 C9 48 46N 16 53 E
Brecon, U.K. 17 F4 51 57N 3 23W
Brecon Beacons, U.K. 17 F4 51 53N 3 27W
Breda, Neths. 21 E5 51 35N 4 45 E
Bredasdorp, S. Africa 104 E3 34 33 S 20 2 E
Bredbo, Australia 117 C8 35 58 S 149 10 E
Bredene, Belgium 21 F1 51 14N 2 59 E
Bredstedt, Germany 26 A4 54 37N 8 59 E
Bredy, U.S.S.R. 54 E7 52 26N 60 21 E
Bree, Belgium 21 F7 51 8N 5 35 E
Breezand, Neths. 20 C5 52 53N 4 49 E
Bregalnica →, Yugoslavia 42 F7 41 43N 22 9 E
Bregenz, Austria 30 D2 47 30N 9 45 E
Bregovo, Bulgaria 42 C7 44 9N 22 39 E
Bréhal, France 22 D5 48 53N 1 30W
Bréhat, I. de, France 22 D4 48 51N 3 0W
Breiðafjörður, Iceland 12 D2 65 15N 23 15W
Breil-sur-Roya, France 25 E11 43 56N 7 31 E
Breisach, Germany 27 G3 48 2N 7 37 E
Brejinho de Nazaré, Brazil 154 D2 11 1 S 48 34W
Brejo, Brazil 154 B3 3 41 S 42 47W
Bremen, Germany 26 B4 53 4N 8 47 E
Bremen □, Germany 26 B4 53 6N 8 46 E
Bremer I., Australia 114 A2 12 5 S 136 45 E
Bremerhaven, Germany 26 B4 53 34N 8 35 E
Bremerton, U.S.A. 144 C4 47 30N 122 38W
Bremervörde, Germany 26 B5 53 28N 9 10 E
Bremsnes, Norway 14 A1 63 6N 7 40 E
Brenes, Spain 37 H5 37 32N 5 54W
Brenham, U.S.A. 139 K6 30 5N 96 27W
Brenner Pass, Austria 30 D4 47 2N 11 30 E
Breno, Italy 38 C7 45 57N 10 20 E
Brent, Canada 128 C4 46 2N 78 29W
Brent, U.K. 17 F7 51 33N 0 18W
Brenta →, Italy 39 C9 45 11N 12 18 E
Brentwood, U.K. 17 F8 51 37N 0 19 E
Brentwood, U.S.A. 137 F11 40 47N 73 15W
Bréscia, Italy 38 C7 45 33N 10 13 E
Breskens, Neths. 21 F3 51 23N 3 33 E
Breslau = Wrocław, Poland 47 D4 51 5N 17 5 E
Bresle →, France 22 B8 50 4N 1 22 E
Bresles, France 23 C9 49 25N 2 13 E
Bressanone, Italy 39 B8 46 43N 11 40 E
Bressay, U.K. 18 A7 60 10N 1 5W
Bresse, France 23 F12 46 50N 5 10 E
Bressuire, France 22 F6 46 51N 0 30W
Brest, France 22 D2 48 24N 4 31W
Brest, U.S.S.R. 50 E3 52 10N 23 40 E
Bretagne, France 22 D4 48 10N 3 0W
Bretçu, Romania 46 C7 46 7N 26 18 E
Breteuil, Eure, France 22 D7 48 50N 0 53 E
Breteuil, Oise, France 23 C9 49 38N 2 18 E
Breton, Canada 130 C6 53 7N 114 28W
Breton, Pertuis, France 24 B2 46 17N 1 25W
Breton Sd., U.S.A. 139 L10 29 40N 89 12W
Brett, C., N.Z. 118 B3 35 10 S 174 20 E
Bretten, Germany 27 F4 49 2N 8 43 E
Breukelen, Neths. 20 D6 52 10N 5 0 E
Brevard, U.S.A. 135 H4 35 19N 82 42W
Breves, Brazil 154 B1 1 40 S 50 29W
Brevik, Norway 14 E3 59 4N 9 42 E
Brewarrina, Australia 115 E4 30 0 S 146 51 E
Brewer, U.S.A. 129 D6 44 43N 68 50W
Brewer, Mt., U.S.A. 144 J8 36 44N 118 28W
Brewster, N.Y., U.S.A. 137 E11 41 23N 73 37W
Brewster, Wash., U.S.A. 142 B4 48 10N 119 51W
Brewster, Kap, Greenland 6 B6 70 7N 22 0W
Brewton, U.S.A. 135 K2 31 9N 87 2W
Breyten, S. Africa 105 D5 26 16 S 30 0 E
Breytovo, U.S.S.R. 51 B10 58 18N 37 50 E
Brezhnev = Naberezhnyye Chelny, U.S.S.R. 54 D3 55 42N 52 19 E
Brežice, Yugoslavia 39 C12 45 54N 15 35 E
Brézina, Algeria 99 B5 33 4N 1 14 E
Březnice, Czech. 30 B6 49 32N 13 57 E
Breznik, Bulgaria 42 E7 42 44N 22 50 E
Brezno, Czech. 31 C12 48 50N 19 40 E
Brezovo, Bulgaria 43 E10 42 21N 25 5 E
Bria, C.A.R. 102 A4 6 30N 21 58 E
Briançon, France 25 D10 44 54N 6 39 E
Briare, France 23 E9 47 38N 2 45 E
Bribbaree, Australia 117 C7 34 10 S 147 51 E
Bribie I., Australia 115 D5 27 0 S 153 10 E
Bricquebec, France 22 C5 49 28N 1 38W
Bridgehampton, U.S.A. 137 F12 40 56N 72 19W
Bridgend, U.K. 17 F4 51 30N 3 35W
Bridgeport, Calif., U.S.A. 144 G7 38 14N 119 15W
Bridgeport, Conn., U.S.A. 137 E11 41 12N 73 12W
Bridgeport, Nebr., U.S.A. 138 E3 41 42N 103 10W
Bridgeport, Tex., U.S.A. 139 J6 33 15N 97 45W
Bridger, U.S.A. 142 D9 45 20N 108 58W
Bridgeton, U.S.A. 134 F8 39 29N 75 10W
Bridgetown, Australia 113 F2 33 58 S 116 7 E
Bridgetown, Barbados 149 D8 13 5N 59 30W
Bridgetown, Canada 129 D6 44 55N 65 18W
Bridgewater, Australia 116 D5 36 36 S 143 59 E
Bridgewater, Canada 129 D7 44 25N 64 31W
Bridgewater, Mass., U.S.A. 137 E14 41 59N 70 56W
Bridgewater, S. Dak., U.S.A. 138 D6 43 34N 97 29W
Bridgewater, C., Australia 116 E4 38 23 S 141 23 E
Bridgman, U.S.A. 141 C10 41 57N 86 33W
Bridgnorth, U.K. 17 E5 52 33N 2 25W
Bridgton, U.S.A. 137 B14 44 5N 70 41W
Bridgwater, U.K. 17 F5 51 7N 3 0W
Bridlington, U.K. 16 C7 54 6N 0 11W
Bridport, Australia 114 G4 40 59 S 147 23 E
Bridport, U.K. 17 G5 50 43N 2 45W
Brie, Plaine de la, France 23 D10 48 35N 3 10 E
Brie-Comte-Robert, France 23 D9 48 40N 2 35 E
Briec, France 22 D3 48 6N 4 0W
Brielle, Neths. 20 E4 51 54N 4 10 E
Brienne-le-Château, France 23 D11 48 24N 4 30 E
Brienon-sur-Armançon, France 23 E10 47 59N 3 38 E
Brienz, Switz. 28 C6 46 46N 8 2 E
Brienzersee, Switz. 28 C5 46 44N 7 53 E
Brig, Switz. 28 D5 46 18N 7 59 E
Brigg, U.K. 16 D7 53 33N 0 30W
Briggsdale, U.S.A. 138 E2 40 40N 104 20W
Brigham City, U.S.A. 142 F7 41 30N 112 1W
Bright, Australia 117 D7 36 42 S 146 56 E
Brighton, Australia 116 C3 35 5 S 138 30 E
Brighton, Canada 128 D4 44 2N 77 44W
Brighton, U.K. 17 G7 50 50N 0 9W
Brighton, Colo., U.S.A. 138 F2 39 59N 104 50W
Brighton, Ill., U.S.A. 140 E6 39 2N 90 8W
Brighton, Iowa, U.S.A. 140 C5 41 10N 91 49W
Brightwater, N.Z. 119 B8 41 22 S 173 9 E
Brignogan-Plage, France 22 D2 48 40N 4 20W
Brignoles, France 25 E10 43 25N 6 5 E
Brihuega, Spain 34 E2 40 45N 2 52W
Brikama, Gambia 100 C1 13 15N 16 45W
Brilliant, Canada 130 D5 49 19N 117 38W
Brilliant, U.S.A. 136 F4 40 15N 80 39W
Brilon, Germany 26 D4 51 23N 8 32 E
Brim, Australia 116 D5 36 3 S 142 27 E
Brimfield, U.S.A. 140 D7 40 50N 89 53W
Bríndisi, Italy 41 B10 40 39N 17 55 E
Brinje, Yugoslavia 39 D12 45 0N 15 9 E
Brinkley, U.S.A. 139 H9 34 55N 91 15W
Brinkworth, Australia 116 B3 33 42 S 138 26 E
Brinnon, U.S.A. 144 C4 47 41N 122 54W
Brion, I., Canada 129 C7 47 46N 61 26W
Brionne, France 22 C7 49 11N 0 43 E
Brionski, Yugoslavia 39 D10 44 55N 13 45 E
Brioude, France 24 C7 45 18N 3 24 E
Briouze, France 22 D6 48 42N 0 23W
Brisbane, Australia 115 D5 27 25 S 153 2 E
Brisbane →, Australia 115 D5 27 24 S 153 9 E
Brisighella, Italy 39 D8 44 14N 11 46 E
Bristol, U.K. 17 F5 51 26N 2 35W
Bristol, Conn., U.S.A. 137 E12 41 44N 72 57W
Bristol, Pa., U.S.A. 137 F10 40 6N 74 52W
Bristol, R.I., U.S.A. 137 E13 41 40N 71 15W
Bristol, S. Dak., U.S.A. 138 C6 45 25N 97 45W
Bristol, Tenn., U.S.A. 135 G4 36 36N 82 11W
Bristol B., U.S.A. 126 C4 58 0N 160 0W
Bristol Channel, U.K. 17 F3 51 18N 4 30W
Bristol I., Antarctica 7 B1 58 45 S 28 0W
Bristol L., U.S.A. 143 J5 34 23N 116 50W
Bristow, U.S.A. 139 H6 35 55N 96 28W
British Columbia □, Canada 130 C3 55 0N 125 15W
British Guiana = Guyana ■, S. Amer. 153 C6 5 0N 59 0W
British Honduras = Belize ■, Cent. Amer. 147 D7 17 0N 88 30W
British Isles, Europe 10 E5 54 0N 4 0W
Brits, S. Africa 105 D4 25 37 S 27 48 E
Britstown, S. Africa 104 E3 30 37 S 23 30 E
Britt, Canada 128 C3 45 46N 80 34W
Britt, U.S.A. 140 A3 43 6N 93 48W
Brittany = Bretagne, France 22 D4 48 10N 3 0W
Britton, U.S.A. 138 C6 45 50N 97 47W
Brive-la-Gaillarde, France 24 C5 45 10N 1 32 E
Briviesca, Spain 34 C1 42 32N 3 19W
Brixton, Australia 114 C3 23 32 S 144 57 E
Brlik, Kazakh S.S.R., U.S.S.R. 55 B6 43 40N 73 49 E
Brlik, Kazakh S.S.R., U.S.S.R. 55 A6 44 5N 73 31 E
Brno, Czech. 31 B9 49 10N 16 35 E
Bro, Sweden 14 E11 59 31N 17 38 E
Broach = Bharuch, India 82 D1 21 47N 73 0 E
Broad →, U.S.A. 135 J5 33 59N 81 39W
Broad Arrow, Australia 113 F3 30 23 S 121 15 E
Broad B., U.K. 18 C2 58 14N 6 16W
Broad Haven, Ireland 19 B2 54 20N 9 55W
Broad Law, U.K. 18 F5 55 30N 3 22W
Broad Sd., Australia 114 C4 22 0 S 149 45 E
Broadford, Australia 117 D6 37 14 S 145 4 E
Broadhurst Ra., Australia 112 D3 22 30 S 122 30 E
Broads, The, U.K. 16 E9 52 45N 1 30 E
Broadus, U.S.A. 138 C2 45 28N 105 27W
Broadview, Canada 131 C8 50 22N 102 35W
Broager, Denmark 15 K3 54 53N 9 40 E
Broaryd, Sweden 15 G7 57 7N 13 15 E
Brochet, Canada 131 B8 57 53N 101 40W
Brochet, L., Canada 131 B8 58 36N 101 35W
Brock, Canada 131 C7 51 26N 108 43W
Brocken, Germany 26 D6 51 48N 10 40 E
Brocklehurst, Australia 117 B8 32 9 S 148 38 E
Brockport, U.S.A. 136 C7 43 12N 77 56W
Brockton, U.S.A. 137 D13 42 8N 71 2W
Brockville, Canada 128 D4 44 35N 75 41W
Brockway, Mont., U.S.A. 138 B2 47 18N 105 46W
Brockway, Pa., U.S.A. 136 E6 41 14N 78 48W
Brocton, U.S.A. 136 D5 42 25N 79 26W
Brod, Yugoslavia 42 F6 41 35N 21 17 E
Brodarevo, Yugoslavia 42 D4 43 14N 19 44 E
Brodeur Pen., Canada 127 A11 72 30N 88 10W
Brodhead, U.S.A. 140 B7 42 37N 89 22W
Brodick, U.K. 18 F3 55 34N 5 9W
Brodnica, Poland 47 B6 53 15N 19 25 E
Brodokalmak, U.S.S.R. 54 D8 55 35N 62 6 E
Brody, U.S.S.R. 50 F4 50 5N 25 10 E
Broechem, Belgium 21 F5 51 11N 4 38 E
Broek, Neths. 20 D6 52 26N 5 0 E
Broek op Langedijk, Neths. 20 C5 52 41N 4 49 E
Brogan, U.S.A. 142 D5 44 14N 117 32W
Broglie, France 22 C7 49 2N 0 30 E
Brok, Poland 47 C8 52 43N 21 52 E
Broken Bow, Nebr., U.S.A. 138 E5 41 25N 99 35W
Broken Bow, Okla., U.S.A. 139 H7 34 2N 94 43W
Broken Hill = Kabwe, Zambia 107 E2 14 30 S 28 29 E
Broken Hill, Australia 116 A4 31 58 S 141 29 E
Brokind, Sweden 15 F9 58 13N 15 42 E
Brokopondo, Surinam 153 B7 5 3N 54 59W
Brokopondo □, Surinam 153 C6 4 30N 55 30W
Bromfield, U.K. 17 E5 52 25N 2 45W
Bromley, U.K. 17 F8 51 20N 0 5 E
Bronaugh, U.S.A. 140 G2 37 41N 94 28W
Brønderslev, Denmark 15 G3 57 16N 9 57 E
Brong-Ahafo □, Ghana 100 D4 7 50N 2 0W
Bronkhorstspruit, S. Africa 105 D4 25 46 S 28 45 E
Bronnitsy, U.S.S.R. 51 D11 55 27N 38 10 E
Bronson, U.S.A. 141 C11 41 52N 85 12W
Bronte, Italy 41 E7 37 48N 14 49 E
Bronte, U.S.A. 139 K4 31 54N 100 18W
Bronte Park, Australia 114 G4 42 8 S 146 30 E
Brook Park, U.S.A. 136 E4 41 24N 80 51W
Brookfield, U.S.A. 140 E3 39 50N 93 4W
Brookhaven, U.S.A. 139 K9 31 40N 90 25W
Brookings, Oreg., U.S.A. 142 E1 42 4N 124 10W
Brookings, S. Dak., U.S.A. 138 C6 44 20N 96 45W
Brooklin, Canada 136 C6 43 55N 78 55W
Brooklyn, U.S.A. 140 C4 41 44N 92 27W
Brookmere, Canada 130 D4 49 52N 120 53W
Brooks, Canada 130 C6 50 35N 111 55W
Brooks B., Canada 130 C3 50 15N 127 55W
Brooks L., Canada 131 A7 61 55N 106 35W
Brooks Ra., U.S.A. 126 B5 68 40N 147 0W
Brookston, U.S.A. 141 D10 40 36N 86 52W
Brooksville, Fla., U.S.A. 135 L4 28 32N 82 21W
Brooksville, Ky., U.S.A. 141 F12 38 41N 84 4W
Brookville, U.S.A. 141 E12 39 25N 85 0W
Brooloo, Australia 115 D5 26 30 S 152 43 E
Broom, L., U.K. 18 D3 57 55N 5 15W
Broome, Australia 112 C3 18 0 S 122 15 E
Broomehill, Australia 113 F2 33 51 S 117 39 E
Broons, France 22 D4 48 20N 2 16W
Brora, U.K. 18 C5 58 3N 3 50W
Brora →, U.K. 18 C5 58 4N 3 52W
Brosna →, Ireland 19 C4 53 8N 8 0W
Broşteni, Romania 46 B6 47 14N 25 43 E
Brotas de Macaúbas, Brazil 155 D3 12 0 S 42 38W
Brothers, U.S.A. 142 E3 43 56N 120 39W
Brøttum, Norway 14 C4 61 2N 10 34 E
Brou, France 22 D8 48 13N 1 11 E
Broughams Gate, Australia 116 A4 30 51 S 140 59 E
Broughton, U.S.A. 141 G8 37 56N 88 27W
Broughton Island, Canada 127 B13 67 33N 63 0W
Broughty Ferry, U.K. 18 E6 56 29N 2 50W
Broumov, Czech. 31 A9 50 35N 16 20 E
Brouwershaven, Neths. 20 E3 51 45N 3 55 E
Brouwershavensche Gat, Neths. 20 E3 51 46N 3 50 E
Brovary, U.S.S.R. 50 F7 50 34N 30 48 E
Brovst, Denmark 15 G3 57 6N 9 31 E
Browerville, U.S.A. 138 B7 46 3N 94 50W
Brown, Mt., Australia 116 B3 32 30 S 138 0 E
Brown, Pt., Australia 115 E1 32 32 S 133 50 E
Brown Willy, U.K. 17 G3 50 35N 4 34W
Brownfield, U.S.A. 139 J3 33 10N 102 15W
Browning, Ill., U.S.A. 140 D6 40 7N 90 22W
Browning, Mo., U.S.A. 140 D3 40 3N 93 12W
Browning, Mont., U.S.A. 142 B7 48 35N 113 0W
Browning Pass, N.Z. 119 C6 42 55 S 171 22 E
Brownlee, Canada 131 C7 50 43N 106 1W
Brownsburg, U.S.A. 141 E10 39 50N 86 26W
Brownstown, U.S.A. 141 F10 38 53N 86 3W
Brownsville, Oreg., U.S.A. 142 D2 44 29N 123 0W
Brownsville, Tenn., U.S.A. 139 H10 35 35N 89 15W
Brownsville, Tex., U.S.A. 139 N6 25 56N 97 25W
Brownsweg, Surinam 153 B6 5 5N 55 15W
Brownwood, U.S.A. 139 K5 31 45N 99 0W
Brownwood, L., U.S.A. 139 K5 31 51N 98 35W
Browse I., Australia 112 B3 14 7 S 123 33 E
Broye →, Switz. 28 C3 46 52N 6 58 E
Brozas, Spain 37 F4 39 37N 6 47W
Bruas, Malaysia 77 K3 4 30N 100 47 E
Bruay-en-Artois, France 23 B9 50 29N 2 33 E
Bruce, Mt., Australia 112 D2 22 37 S 118 8 E
Bruce B., N.Z. 119 D4 43 35 S 169 42 E
Bruce Pen., Canada 136 B3 45 0N 81 30W
Bruce Rock, Australia 113 F2 31 52 S 118 8 E
Bruche →, France 23 D14 48 34N 7 43 E
Bruchsal, Germany 27 F4 49 9N 8 39 E
Bruck an der Leitha, Austria 31 C9 48 1N 16 47 E
Bruck an der Mur, Austria 30 D8 47 24N 15 16 E
Brue →, U.K. 17 F5 51 10N 2 59W
Brugelette, Belgium 21 G3 50 35N 3 52 E
Bruges = Brugge, Belgium 21 F2 51 13N 3 13 E
Brugg, Switz. 28 B6 47 29N 8 11 E
Brugge, Belgium 21 F2 51 13N 3 13 E
Brühl, Germany 26 E2 50 49N 6 51 E
Bruinisse, Neths. 21 E4 51 40N 4 5 E
Brûlé, Canada 130 C5 53 15N 117 58W
Brûlon, France 22 E6 47 58N 0 15W
Brûly, Belgium 21 J5 49 58N 4 32 E
Brumado, Brazil 155 D3 14 14 S 41 40W
Brumado →, Brazil 155 D3 14 13 S 41 40W
Brumath, France 23 D14 48 43N 7 40 E
Brummen, Neths. 20 D8 52 5N 6 10 E
Brumunddal, Norway 14 D4 60 53N 10 56 E
Brunchilly, Australia 114 B1 18 50 S 134 30 E
Brundidge, U.S.A. 135 K3 31 43N 85 45W
Bruneau, U.S.A. 142 E6 42 57N 115 55W
Bruneau →, U.S.A. 142 E6 42 57N 115 58W
Brunei = Bandar Seri Begawan, Brunei 70 D5 4 52N 115 0 E
Brunei ■, Asia 70 D5 4 50N 115 0 E
Brunette Downs, Australia 114 B2 18 40 S 135 55 E
Brunflo, Sweden 14 A8 63 5N 14 50 E
Brunico, Italy 39 B8 46 50N 11 55 E
Brünig, P., Switz. 28 C6 46 46N 8 8 E
Brunkeberg, Norway 14 E2 59 26N 8 28 E
Brunna, Sweden 14 E11 59 52N 17 25 E
Brunnen, Switz. 29 C7 46 59N 8 37 E
Brunner, L., N.Z. 119 C6 42 37 S 171 27 E
Bruno, Canada 131 C7 52 20N 105 30W
Brunsbüttel, Germany 26 B5 53 52N 9 13 E
Brunssum, Neths. 21 G7 50 57N 5 59 E
Brunswick = Braunschweig, Germany 26 C6 52 17N 10 28 E
Brunswick, Ga., U.S.A. 135 K5 31 10N 81 30W
Brunswick, Maine, U.S.A. 129 D6 43 53N 69 50W
Brunswick, Md., U.S.A. 134 F7 39 20N 77 38W
Brunswick, Mo., U.S.A. 140 E4 39 26N 93 10W
Brunswick, Ohio, U.S.A. 136 E3 41 15N 81 50W
Brunswick, Pen. de, Chile 160 D2 53 30 S 71 30W
Brunswick B., Australia 112 C3 15 15 S 124 50 E
Brunswick Junction, Australia 113 F2 33 15 S 115 50 E
Bruntál, Czech. 31 B10 50 0N 17 27 E
Bruny I., Australia 114 G4 43 20 S 147 15 E
Brus Laguna, Honduras 148 C3 15 47N 84 35W
Brusartsi, Bulgaria 42 D8 43 40N 23 5 E
Brush, U.S.A. 138 E3 40 17N 103 33W
Brushton, U.S.A. 137 B10 44 50N 74 32W
Brusio, Switz. 29 D10 46 14N 10 8 E
Brusque, Brazil 159 B6 27 5 S 49 0W
Brussel, Belgium 21 G4 50 51N 4 21 E
Brussels = Brussel, Belgium 21 G4 50 51N 4 21 E
Brussels, Canada 136 C3 43 44N 81 15W
Brustem, Belgium 21 G6 50 48N 5 14 E
Bruthen, Australia 117 D7 37 42 S 147 50 E
Bruxelles = Brussel, Belgium 21 G4 50 51N 4 21 E
Bruyères, France 23 D13 48 10N 6 40 E
Brwinów, Poland 47 C7 52 9N 20 40 E
Bryagovo, Bulgaria 43 F10 41 58N 25 8 E
Bryan, Ohio, U.S.A. 141 C12 41 30N 84 30W

Buthidaung 179

Bryan, Tex., U.S.A. 139 K6 30 40N 96 27W
Bryan, Mt., Australia 116 B3 33 30 S 139 0 E
Bryanka, U.S.S.R. 53 B8 48 32N 38 45 E
Bryansk, U.S.S.R. 50 E9 53 13N 34 25 E
Bryanskoye, U.S.S.R. 53 D12 44 20N 47 10 E
Bryant, U.S.A. 138 C6 44 35N 97 28W
Bryne, Norway 13 G8 58 44N 5 38 E
Bryson City, U.S.A. 135 H4 35 28N 83 25W
Brza Palanka, Yugoslavia 42 C7 44 28N 22 27 E
Brzava →, Yugoslavia 42 B5 45 21N 20 45 E
Brzeg, Poland 47 E4 50 52N 17 30 E
Brzeg Din, Poland 47 D3 51 16N 16 41 E
Brześć Kujawski, Poland 47 C5 52 36N 18 55 E
Brzesko, Poland 31 B13 49 59N 20 34 E
Brzeszcze, Poland 31 B12 49 59N 19 10 E
Brzeziny, Poland 47 D6 51 49N 19 42 E
Brzozów, Poland 31 B15 49 41N 22 3 E
Bsharri, Lebanon 91 A5 34 15N 36 0 E
Bū Athlah, Libya 96 B3 30 9N 15 39 E
Bū Baqarah, U.A.E. 85 E8 25 35N 56 25 E
Bu Craa, W. Sahara 98 C2 26 45N 12 50W
Bū Ḩasā, U.A.E. 85 F7 23 30N 53 20 E
Bua Yai, Thailand 76 E4 15 33N 102 26 E
Buala, Solomon Is. 121 M10 8 10 S 159 35 E
Buapinang, Indonesia 71 E6 4 40 S 121 30 E
Buayan, Phil. 71 C7 6 3N 125 6 E
Buba, Guinea-Biss. 100 C2 11 40N 14 59W
Bubanda, Zaïre 102 B3 4 14N 19 38 E
Bubanza, Burundi 106 C2 3 6 S 29 23 E
Būbiyān, Kuwait 85 D6 29 45N 48 15 E
Bucak, Turkey 88 E4 37 28N 30 36 E
Bucaramanga, Colombia 152 B3 7 0N 73 0W
Buccaneer Arch., Australia 112 C3 16 7 S 123 20 E
Bucchiánico, Italy 39 F11 42 20N 14 10 E
Bucecea, Romania 46 B7 47 47N 26 28 E
Buchach, U.S.S.R. 50 G4 49 5N 25 25 E
Buchan, Australia 117 D8 37 30 S 148 12 E
Buchan, U.K. 18 D6 57 32N 2 8W
Buchan Ness, U.K. 18 D7 57 29N 1 48W
Buchanan, Canada 131 C8 51 40N 102 45W
Buchanan, Liberia 100 D2 5 57N 10 2W
Buchanan, U.S.A. 141 C10 41 50N 86 22W
Buchanan, L., Queens., Australia 114 C4 21 35 S 145 52 E
Buchanan, L., W. Austral., Australia 113 E3 25 33 S 123 2 E
Buchanan, L., U.S.A. 139 K5 30 50N 98 25W
Buchanan Cr. →, Australia 114 B2 19 13 S 136 33 E
Buchans, Canada 129 C8 48 50N 56 52W
Bucharest = Bucureşti, Romania 46 E7 44 27N 26 10 E
Buchholz, Germany 26 B5 53 19N 9 51 E
Buchloe, Germany 27 G6 48 3N 10 45 E
Buchon, Pt., U.S.A. 144 K6 35 15N 120 54W
Buchs, Switz. 29 B8 47 10N 9 28 E
Bückeburg, Germany 26 C5 52 16N 9 2 E
Buckeye, U.S.A. 143 K7 33 28N 112 40W
Buckhannon, U.S.A. 134 F5 39 2N 80 10W
Buckhaven, U.K. 18 E5 56 10N 3 2W
Buckie, U.K. 18 D6 57 40N 2 58W
Buckingham, Canada 128 C4 45 37N 75 24W
Buckingham, U.K. 17 F7 52 0N 0 59W
Buckingham B., Australia 114 A2 12 10 S 135 40 E
Buckingham Canal, India 83 H5 14 0N 80 5 E
Buckinghamshire □, U.K. 17 F7 51 50N 0 55W
Buckland, U.S.A. 141 D12 40 37N 84 16W
Buckle Hd., Australia 112 B4 14 26 S 127 52 E
Buckleboo, Australia 116 B2 32 54 S 136 12 E
Buckley, Ill., U.S.A. 141 D8 40 35N 88 2W
Buckley, Wash., U.S.A. 142 C2 47 10N 122 2W
Buckley →, Australia 114 C2 20 10 S 138 49 E
Bucklin, Kans., U.S.A. 139 G5 37 37N 99 40W
Bucklin, Mo., U.S.A. 140 E4 39 47N 92 53W
Bucks L., U.S.A. 144 F5 39 54N 121 12W
Buco Zau, Angola 103 C2 4 46 S 12 33 E
Bucquoy, France 23 B9 50 9N 2 43 E
Buctouche, Canada 129 C7 46 30N 64 45W
Bucureşti, Romania 46 E7 44 27N 26 10 E
Bucyrus, U.S.A. 141 D14 40 48N 82 58W
Budafok, Hungary 31 D12 47 26N 19 2 E
Budalin, Burma 78 D5 22 20N 95 10 E
Budapest, Hungary 31 D12 47 29N 19 5 E
Budaun, India 81 E8 28 5N 79 10 E
Budd Coast, Antarctica 7 C8 68 0 S 112 0 E
Buddabadah, Australia 117 A7 31 56 S 147 14 E
Budduso, Italy 40 B2 40 35N 9 18 E
Bude, U.K. 17 G3 50 49N 4 33W
Budel, Neths. 21 F7 51 17N 5 34 E
Budennovsk, U.S.S.R. 53 D11 44 50N 44 10 E
Budeşti, Romania 46 E7 44 13N 26 30 E
Budge Budge = Baj Baj, India 81 H13 22 30N 88 5 E
Budgewoi, Australia 117 B9 33 13 S 151 34 E
Búðareyri, Iceland 12 D6 65 2N 14 13W
Búðir, Iceland 12 D2 64 49N 23 23W
Budia, Spain 34 E2 40 38N 2 46W
Budjala, Zaïre 102 B3 2 50N 19 40 E
Búdrio, Italy 39 D8 44 31N 11 31 E
Budva, Yugoslavia 42 E3 42 17N 18 50 E
Budzyń, Poland 47 C3 52 54N 16 59 E
Buea, Cameroon 101 E6 4 10N 9 9 E
Buellton, U.S.A. 145 L6 34 37N 120 12W
Buena Vista, Bolivia 157 D5 17 27 S 63 40W
Buena Vista, Colo., U.S.A. 143 G10 38 56N 106 6W
Buena Vista, Va., U.S.A. 134 G6 37 47N 79 23W
Buena Vista L., U.S.A. 145 K7 35 15N 119 21W
Buenaventura, Colombia 152 C2 3 53N 77 4W
Buenaventura, Mexico 146 B3 29 50N 107 30W
Buenaventura, B. de, Colombia 152 C2 3 48N 77 17W
Buendía, Pantano de, Spain 34 E2 40 25N 2 43W
Buenópolis, Brazil 155 E3 17 54 S 44 11W
Buenos Aires, Argentina 158 C4 34 30 S 58 20W
Buenos Aires, Colombia 152 C3 1 36N 73 18W
Buenos Aires, Costa Rica 148 E3 9 10N 83 20W
Buenos Aires □, Argentina 158 D4 36 30 S 60 0W
Buenos Aires, L., Chile 160 C2 46 35 S 72 30W
Buesaco, Colombia 152 C2 1 23N 77 9W
Buffalo, Mo., U.S.A. 139 G8 37 40N 93 5W
Buffalo, N.Y., U.S.A. 136 D6 42 55N 78 50W
Buffalo, Okla., U.S.A. 139 G5 36 55N 99 42W
Buffalo, S. Dak., U.S.A. 138 C3 45 39N 103 31W
Buffalo, Wyo., U.S.A. 142 D10 44 25N 106 50W
Buffalo →, Canada 130 A5 60 5N 115 5W
Buffalo Head Hills, Canada 130 B5 57 25N 115 55W
Buffalo L., Canada 130 C6 52 27N 112 54W
Buffalo Narrows, Canada 131 B7 55 51N 108 29W
Buffels →, S. Africa 104 D2 29 36 S 17 3 E
Buford, U.S.A. 135 H4 34 5N 84 0W
Bug →, Poland 47 C8 52 31N 21 5 E
Bug →, U.S.S.R. 52 C4 46 59N 31 58 E
Buga, Colombia 152 C2 4 0N 76 15W
Buganda, Uganda 106 C3 0 0 31 30 E
Buganga, Uganda 106 C3 0 3 S 32 0 E
Bugeat, France 24 C5 45 36N 1 55 E
Bugel, Tanjung, Indonesia 70 F4 6 26 S 111 3 E
Buggenhout, Belgium 21 F4 51 1N 4 12 E
Bugibba, Malta 32 D1 35 57N 14 25 E
Bugojno, Yugoslavia 42 C2 44 2N 17 25 E
Bugsuk, Phil. 70 C5 8 15N 117 15 E
Bugulma, U.S.S.R. 54 D3 54 33N 52 48 E
Buguma, Nigeria 101 E6 4 42N 6 55 E
Bugun Shara, Mongolia 64 B5 49 0N 104 0 E
Bugun Shara, Mongolia 64 B5 49 0N 104 0 E
Buguruslan, U.S.S.R. 54 E3 53 39N 52 26 E
Buhăeşti, Romania 46 C8 46 47N 27 32 E
Buheirat-Murrat-el-Kubra, Egypt 94 H8 30 15N 32 40 E
Buhl, Idaho, U.S.A. 142 E6 42 35N 114 54W
Buhl, Minn., U.S.A. 138 B8 47 30N 92 46W
Buhuşi, Romania 46 C7 46 41N 26 45 E
Buick, U.S.A. 139 G9 37 38N 91 2W
Builth Wells, U.K. 17 E4 52 10N 3 26W
Buin, Papua N. G. 121 L8 6 48 S 155 42 E
Buinsk, U.S.S.R. 51 D16 55 0N 48 18 E
Buíque, Brazil 154 C4 8 37 S 37 9W
Buir Nur, Mongolia 65 B6 47 50N 117 42 E
Buis-les-Baronnies, France 25 D9 44 17N 5 16 E
Buitenpost, Neths. 20 B8 53 15N 6 9 E
Buitrago, Spain 36 E7 40 58N 3 38W
Bujalance, Spain 37 H6 37 54N 4 23W
Buján, Spain 36 C2 42 59N 8 36W
Bujanovac, Yugoslavia 42 E6 42 28N 21 44 E
Bujaraloz, Spain 34 D4 41 29N 0 10W
Buje, Yugoslavia 39 C10 45 24N 13 39 E
Bujumbura, Burundi 106 C2 3 16 S 29 18 E
Bük, Hungary 31 D9 47 22N 16 45 E
Buk, Poland 47 C3 52 21N 16 30 E
Buka I., Papua N. G. 120 C8 5 10 S 154 35 E
Bukachacha, U.S.S.R. 57 D12 52 55N 116 50 E
Bukama, Zaïre 107 D2 9 10 S 25 50 E
Bukavu, Zaïre 106 C2 2 20 S 28 52 E
Bukene, Tanzania 106 C3 4 15 S 32 48 E
Bukhara, U.S.S.R. 55 D2 39 48N 64 25 E
Bukima, Tanzania 106 C3 1 50 S 33 25 E
Bukit Mertajam, Malaysia 77 K3 5 22N 100 28 E
Bukittinggi, Indonesia 70 E2 0 20 S 100 20 E
Bukkapatnam, India 83 G3 14 14N 77 46 E
Buklyan, U.S.S.R. 54 D3 55 42N 52 10 E
Bukoba, Tanzania 106 C3 1 20 S 31 49 E
Bukoba □, Tanzania 106 C3 1 30 S 32 0 E
Bukowno, Poland 31 A12 50 17N 19 35 E
Bukuru, Nigeria 101 D6 9 42N 8 48 E
Bukuya, Uganda 106 B3 0 40N 31 52 E
Bula, Guinea-Biss. 100 C1 12 7N 15 43W
Bula, Indonesia 71 E8 3 6 S 130 30 E
Bülach, Switz. 29 A7 47 31N 8 32 E
Bulahdelah, Australia 117 B10 32 23 S 152 13 E
Bulan, Phil. 71 B6 12 40N 123 52 E
Bulanash, U.S.S.R. 54 C8 57 16N 62 0 E
Bulancak, Turkey 89 C8 40 56N 38 14 E
Bulandshahr, India 80 E7 28 28N 77 51 E
Bulanık, Turkey 89 D10 39 4N 42 14 E
Bulanovo, U.S.S.R. 54 E4 52 27N 55 10 E
Bûlâq, Egypt 94 B3 25 10N 30 38 E
Bulawayo, Zimbabwe 107 G2 20 7 S 28 32 E
Buldan, Turkey 88 D3 38 2N 28 50 E
Buldana, India 82 D3 20 30N 76 18 E
Bulgaria ■, Europe 43 E10 42 35N 25 30 E
Bulgroo, Australia 115 D3 25 47 S 143 58 E
Bulgunnia, Australia 115 E1 30 10 S 134 53 E
Bulhale, Somali Rep. 108 C3 5 20N 46 29 E
Bulhar, Somali Rep. 90 E3 10 25N 44 30 E
Buli, Teluk, Indonesia 71 D7 1 5N 128 25 E
Buliluyan, C., Phil. 70 C5 8 20N 117 15 E
Bulki, Ethiopia 95 F4 6 11N 36 31 E
Bulkley →, Canada 130 B3 55 15N 127 40W
Bull Shoals L., U.S.A. 139 G8 36 40N 93 5W
Bullange, Belgium 21 H8 50 24N 6 15 E
Bullaque →, Spain 37 G6 38 59N 4 17W
Bullara, Australia 112 D1 22 40 S 114 3 E
Bullaring, Australia 113 F2 32 30 S 117 45 E
Bullas, Spain 35 G3 38 2N 1 40W
Bulle, Switz. 28 C4 46 37N 7 3 E
Buller →, N.Z. 119 B6 41 44 S 171 36 E
Buller, Mt., Australia 117 D7 37 10 S 146 28 E
Buller Gorge, N.Z. 119 B7 41 40 S 172 10 E
Bulli, Australia 117 C9 34 15 S 150 57 E
Bullock Creek, Australia 114 B3 17 43 S 144 31 E
Bulloo →, Australia 115 D3 28 43 S 142 30 E
Bulloo Downs, Queens., Australia 115 D3 28 31 S 142 57 E
Bulloo Downs, W. Austral., Australia 112 D2 24 0 S 119 32 E
Bulloo L., Australia 115 D3 28 43 S 142 25 E
Bulls, N.Z. 118 G4 40 10 S 175 24 E
Bully-les-Mines, France 23 B9 50 27N 2 44 E
Bulnes, Chile 158 D1 36 42 S 72 19W
Bulo Burti, Somali Rep. 90 G4 3 50N 45 33 E
Bulo Ghedudo, Somali Rep. 108 D2 2 52N 43 1 E
Bulolo, Papua N. G. 120 D4 7 10 S 146 40 E
Bulongo, Zaïre 103 C4 4 45 S 21 30 E
Bulpunga, Australia 116 B4 33 47 S 141 45 E
Bulqiza, Albania 44 C2 41 30N 20 21 E
Bulsar = Valsad, India 82 D1 20 40N 72 58 E
Bultfontein, S. Africa 104 D4 28 18 S 26 10 E
Bulu Karakelong, Indonesia 71 D7 4 35N 126 50 E
Bulukumba, Indonesia 71 F6 5 33 S 120 11 E
Bulun, U.S.S.R. 57 B13 70 37N 127 30 E
Bulungu, Zaïre 103 D4 6 4 S 21 54 E
Bumba, Zaïre 102 B4 2 13N 22 30 E
Bumbiri I., Tanzania 106 C3 1 40 S 31 55 E
Bumhkang, Burma 78 B6 26 51N 97 40 E
Bumhpa Bum, Burma 78 B6 26 51N 97 14 E
Bumi →, Zimbabwe 107 F2 17 0 S 28 20 E
Bumtang →, Bhutan 78 B3 26 56N 90 53 E
Buna, Kenya 106 B4 2 58N 39 30 E
Buna, Papua N. G. 120 E5 8 42 S 148 27 E
Bunazi, Tanzania 106 C3 1 3 S 31 23 E
Bunbah, Khalīj, Libya 96 B4 32 20N 23 15 E
Bunbury, Australia 113 F2 33 20 S 115 35 E
Buncrana, Ireland 19 A4 55 8N 7 28W
Bundaberg, Australia 115 C5 24 54 S 152 22 E
Bünde, Germany 26 C4 52 11N 8 33 E
Bundey →, Australia 114 C2 21 46 S 135 37 E
Bundi, India 80 G6 25 30N 75 35 E
Bundooma, Australia 114 C1 24 54 S 134 16 E
Bundoran, Ireland 19 B3 54 24N 8 17W
Bundukia, Sudan 95 F3 5 14N 30 55 E
Bundure, Australia 117 C7 35 10 S 146 1 E
Bung Kan, Thailand 76 C4 18 23N 103 37 E
Bungatakada, Japan 62 D3 33 35N 131 25 E
Bungendore, Australia 117 C8 35 14 S 149 30 E
Bungil Cr. →, Australia 114 D4 27 5 S 149 5 E
Bungo-Suidō, Japan 62 E4 33 0N 132 15 E
Bungoma, Kenya 106 B3 0 34N 34 34 E
Bungu, Tanzania 106 D4 7 35 S 39 0 E
Bunia, Zaïre 106 B3 1 35N 30 20 E
Bunji, Pakistan 81 B6 35 45N 74 40 E
Bunker Hill, Ill., U.S.A. 140 E7 39 3N 89 57W
Bunker Hill, Ind., U.S.A. 141 D10 40 40N 86 6W
Bunkie, U.S.A. 139 K8 31 1N 92 12W
Bunnell, U.S.A. 135 L5 29 28N 81 12W
Bunnik, Neths. 20 D6 52 4N 5 12 E
Bunnythorpe, N.Z. 118 G4 40 16 S 175 39 E
Buñol, Spain 35 F4 39 25N 0 47W
Bunsbeek, Belgium 21 G5 50 50N 4 56 E
Bunschoten, Neths. 20 D6 52 14N 5 22 E
Buntok, Indonesia 70 E4 1 40 S 114 58 E
Bununu, Nigeria 101 D6 9 51N 9 32 E
Bununu Dass, Nigeria 101 C6 10 5N 9 31 E
Bünyan, Turkey 88 D6 38 51N 35 51 E
Bunyu, Indonesia 70 D5 3 35N 117 50 E
Bunza, Nigeria 101 C5 12 8N 4 0 E
Buol, Indonesia 71 D6 1 15N 121 32 E
Buon Brieng, Vietnam 76 F7 13 9N 108 12 E
Buon Me Thuot, Vietnam 76 F7 12 40N 108 3 E
Buong Long, Cambodia 76 F6 13 44N 106 59 E
Buorkhaya, Mys, U.S.S.R. 57 B14 71 50N 132 40 E
Buqayq, Si. Arabia 85 E6 26 0N 49 45 E
Buqbua, Egypt 94 A2 31 29N 25 29 E
Bur Acaba, Somali Rep. 90 G3 3 12N 44 20 E
Bûr Fuad, Egypt 94 H8 31 15N 32 20 E
Bur Ghibi, Somali Rep. 108 D3 3 56N 45 7 E
Bûr Safâga, Egypt 94 B3 26 43N 33 57 E
Bûr Sa'îd, Egypt 94 H8 31 16N 32 18 E
Bûr Sûdân, Sudan 94 D4 19 32N 37 9 E
Bûr Taufiq, Egypt 94 J8 29 54N 32 32 E
Bura, Kenya 106 C4 1 4 S 39 58 E
Buran, Somali Rep. 108 B3 10 14N 48 44 E
Burao, Somali Rep. 90 F4 9 32N 45 32 E
Burāq, Syria 91 B5 33 11N 36 29 E
Buras, U.S.A. 139 L10 29 20N 89 33W
Buraydah, Si. Arabia 84 E5 26 20N 44 8 E
Burayevo, U.S.S.R. 54 D4 55 50N 55 24 E
Burbank, U.S.A. 145 L8 34 9N 118 23W
Burcher, Australia 117 B7 33 30 S 147 16 E
Burdekin →, Australia 114 B4 19 38 S 147 25 E
Burdett, Canada 130 D6 49 50N 111 32W
Burdur, Turkey 88 E4 37 45N 30 17 E
Burdur □, Turkey 88 E4 37 45N 30 15 E
Burdur Gölü, Turkey 88 E4 37 44N 30 10 E
Burdwan = Barddhaman, India 81 H12 23 14N 87 39 E
Bure, Ethiopia 95 E4 10 40N 37 4 E
Bure →, U.K. 16 E9 52 38N 1 45 E
Büren, Germany 26 D4 51 33N 8 34 E
Buren, Neths. 20 E6 51 55N 5 20 E
Bureya →, U.S.S.R. 57 E13 49 27N 129 30 E
Burford, Canada 136 C4 43 7N 80 27W
Burg, Sachsen-Anhalt, Germany 26 C7 52 16N 11 50 E
Burg, Schleswig-Holstein, Germany 26 A7 54 25N 11 10 E
Burg el Arab, Egypt 94 H6 30 54N 29 32 E
Burg et Tuyur, Sudan 94 C2 20 55N 27 56 E
Burg Stargard, Germany 26 B9 53 29N 13 19 E
Burgas, Bulgaria 43 E12 42 33N 27 29 E
Burgaski Zaliv, Bulgaria 43 E12 42 30N 27 39 E
Burgdorf, Germany 26 C6 52 27N 10 0 E
Burgdorf, Switz. 28 B5 47 3N 7 37 E
Burgenland □, Austria 31 D9 47 20N 16 20 E
Burgeo, Canada 129 C8 47 37N 57 38W
Burgersdorp, S. Africa 104 E4 31 0 S 26 20 E
Burges, Mt., Australia 113 F3 30 50 S 121 5 E
Burghausen, Germany 27 G8 48 10N 12 50 E
Búrgio, Italy 40 E6 37 35N 13 18 E
Bürglen, Switz. 29 C7 46 53N 8 40 E
Burglengenfeld, Germany 27 F8 49 11N 12 2 E
Burgo de Osma, Spain 34 D1 41 35N 3 4W
Burgohondo, Spain 36 E6 40 26N 4 47W
Burgos, Spain 34 C1 42 21N 3 41W
Burgos □, Spain 34 C1 42 21N 3 42W
Burgstädt, Germany 26 E8 50 55N 12 49 E
Burgsvik, Sweden 13 H15 57 3N 18 19 E
Burguillos del Cerro, Spain 37 G4 38 23N 6 35W
Burgundy = Bourgogne, France 23 F11 47 0N 4 50 E
Burhanpur, India 82 D3 21 18N 76 14 E
Burhou, U.K. 22 C4 49 45N 2 15W
Buri Pen., Ethiopia 95 D4 15 25N 39 55 E
Burias, Phil. 71 B6 12 55N 123 5 E
Buribay, U.S.S.R. 54 F6 51 57N 58 10 E
Burica, Pta., Costa Rica 148 E3 8 3N 82 51W
Burigi, L., Tanzania 106 C3 2 2 S 31 22 E
Burin, Canada 129 C8 47 1N 55 14W
Buriram, Thailand 76 E4 15 0N 103 0 E
Buriti Alegre, Brazil 155 E2 18 9 S 49 3W
Buriti Bravo, Brazil 154 C3 5 50 S 43 50W
Buriti dos Lopes, Brazil 154 B3 3 10 S 41 52W
Burj Sāfitā, Syria 84 C3 34 48N 36 7 E
Burji, Ethiopia 95 F4 5 29N 37 51 E
Burkburnett, U.S.A. 139 H5 34 7N 98 35W
Burke, U.S.A. 142 C6 47 31N 115 56W
Burke →, Australia 114 C2 23 12 S 139 33 E
Burketown, Australia 114 B2 17 45 S 139 33 E
Burkettsville, U.S.A. 141 D12 40 21N 84 39W
Burkina Faso ■, Africa 100 C4 12 0N 1 0W
Burk's Falls, Canada 128 C4 45 37N 79 24W
Burley, U.S.A. 142 E7 42 37N 113 55W
Burlingame, U.S.A. 144 H4 37 35N 122 21W
Burlington, Canada 136 C5 43 18N 79 45W
Burlington, Colo., U.S.A. 138 F3 39 21N 102 18W
Burlington, Ill., U.S.A. 141 B8 42 43N 88 33W
Burlington, Iowa, U.S.A. 140 D5 40 50N 91 5W
Burlington, Kans., U.S.A. 138 F7 38 15N 95 47W
Burlington, Ky., U.S.A. 141 E12 39 2N 84 43W
Burlington, N.C., U.S.A. 135 G6 36 7N 79 27W
Burlington, N.J., U.S.A. 137 F10 40 5N 74 50W
Burlington, Vt., U.S.A. 137 B11 44 27N 73 14W
Burlington, Wash., U.S.A. 144 B4 48 29N 122 19W
Burlington, Wis., U.S.A. 134 D1 42 41N 88 18W
Burlyu-Tyube, U.S.S.R. 56 E8 46 30N 79 10 E
Burma ■, Asia 78 E6 21 0N 96 30 E
Burnaby I., Canada 130 C2 52 25N 131 19W
Burnamwood, Australia 117 A6 31 7 S 144 53 E
Burnet, U.S.A. 139 K5 30 45N 98 11W
Burney, U.S.A. 142 F3 40 56N 121 41W
Burngup, Australia 113 F2 33 2 S 118 42 E
Burnham, U.S.A. 136 F7 40 37N 77 34W
Burnie, Australia 114 G4 41 4 S 145 56 E
Burnley, U.K. 16 D5 53 47N 2 15W
Burnoye, U.S.S.R. 55 B5 42 36N 70 47 E
Burns, Oreg., U.S.A. 142 E4 43 40N 119 4W
Burns, Wyo., U.S.A. 138 E2 41 13N 104 18W
Burns Lake, Canada 130 C3 54 20N 125 45W
Burnside →, Canada 126 B9 66 51N 108 4W
Burnside, L., Australia 113 E3 25 22 S 123 0 E
Burnt River, Canada 136 B6 44 41N 78 42W
Burntwood →, Canada 131 B9 56 8N 96 34W
Burntwood L., Canada 131 B8 55 22N 100 26W
Burqān, Kuwait 84 D5 29 0N 47 57 E
Burra, Australia 116 B3 33 40 S 138 55 E
Burragorang, L., Australia 117 B9 33 52 S 150 37 E
Burramurra, Australia 114 C2 20 25 S 137 15 E
Burreli, Albania 44 C2 41 36N 20 1 E
Burren Junction, Australia 115 E4 30 7 S 148 59 E
Burrendong, L., Australia 117 B8 32 45 S 149 10 E
Burrendong Dam, Australia 115 E4 32 39 S 149 6 E
Burriana, Spain 34 F4 39 50N 0 4W
Burrinjuck Res., Australia 117 C8 35 0 S 148 36 E
Burro, Serranías del, Mexico 146 B4 29 0N 102 0W
Burruyacú, Argentina 158 B3 26 30 S 64 40W
Burry Port, U.K. 17 F3 51 41N 4 17W
Bursa, Turkey 88 C3 40 15N 29 5 E
Bursa □, Turkey 88 C4 40 10N 30 0 E
Burseryd, Sweden 15 G7 57 12N 13 17 E
Burstall, Canada 131 C7 50 39N 109 54W
Burton, U.S.A. 141 B13 43 0N 83 40W
Burton L., Canada 128 B4 54 45N 78 20W
Burton upon Trent, U.K. 16 E6 52 48N 1 39W
Burtundy, Australia 116 B5 33 45 S 142 15 E
Buru, Indonesia 71 E7 3 30 S 126 30 E
Burullus, Bahra el, Egypt 94 H7 31 25N 31 0 E
Burûm, Yemen 87 D5 14 22N 48 59 E
Burûn, Râs, Egypt 91 D2 31 14N 33 7 E
Burunday, U.S.S.R. 55 B8 43 20N 76 51 E
Burundi ■, Africa 106 C3 3 15 S 30 0 E
Bururi, Burundi 106 C2 3 57 S 29 37 E
Burutu, Nigeria 101 D6 5 20N 5 29 E
Burwell, U.S.A. 138 E5 41 49N 99 8W
Bury, U.K. 16 D5 53 36N 2 19W
Bury St. Edmunds, U.K. 17 E8 52 15N 0 42 E
Buryat A.S.S.R. □, U.S.S.R. 57 D12 53 0N 110 0 E
Buryn, U.S.S.R. 50 F8 51 13N 33 50 E
Burzenin, Poland 47 D5 51 28N 18 47 E
Busalla, Italy 38 D5 44 34N 8 58 E
Busango Swamp, Zambia 107 E2 14 15 S 25 45 E
Buşayrah, Syria 84 C4 35 9N 40 26 E
Buşayyah, Iraq 84 D5 30 0N 46 10 E
Busca, Italy 38 D4 44 31N 7 29 E
Bushati, Albania 44 C1 41 58N 19 34 E
Būshehr, Iran 85 D6 28 55N 50 55 E
Būshehr □, Iran 85 D6 28 20N 51 45 E
Bushell, Canada 131 B7 59 31N 108 45W
Bushenyi, Uganda 106 C3 0 35 S 30 10 E
Bushire = Būshehr, Iran 85 D6 28 55N 50 55 E
Bushnell, Ill., U.S.A. 138 E9 40 32N 90 30W
Bushnell, Nebr., U.S.A. 138 E3 41 18N 103 50W
Busia □, Kenya 106 B3 0 25N 34 6 E
Busie, Ghana 100 C4 10 29N 2 22W
Businga, Zaïre 102 B4 3 16N 20 59 E
Buskerud fylke □, Norway 14 D3 60 13N 9 0 E
Busko Zdrój, Poland 47 E7 50 28N 20 42 E
Buslei, Ethiopia 108 C2 5 28N 44 25 E
Busoga □, Uganda 106 B3 0 5N 33 30 E
Busovača, Yugoslavia 42 C2 44 6N 17 53 E
Busra ash Shām, Syria 91 C5 32 30N 36 25 E
Bussang, France 23 E13 47 50N 6 50 E
Busselton, Australia 113 F2 33 42 S 115 15 E
Busseto, Italy 38 D7 44 59N 10 2 E
Bussigny, Switz. 28 C3 46 33N 6 33 E
Bussum, Neths. 20 D6 52 16N 5 10 E
Bustamante, B., Argentina 160 C3 45 5 S 66 18W
Busto, C., Spain 36 B4 43 34N 6 28W
Busto Arsizio, Italy 38 C5 45 40N 8 50 E
Busu-Djanoa, Zaïre 102 B4 1 43N 21 23 E
Busuanga, Phil. 71 B6 12 10N 120 0 E
Büsum, Germany 26 A4 54 7N 8 50 E
Buta, Zaïre 106 B1 2 50N 24 53 E
Butare, Rwanda 106 C2 2 31 S 29 52 E
Butaritari, Kiribati 122 G9 3 30N 174 0 E
Bute, Australia 116 B3 33 51 S 138 2 E
Bute, U.K. 18 F3 55 48N 5 2W
Bute Inlet, Canada 130 C4 50 40N 124 53W
Butemba, Uganda 106 B3 1 9N 31 37 E
Butembo, Zaïre 106 B2 0 9N 29 18 E
Butera, Italy 41 E7 37 10N 14 10 E
Bütgenbach, Belgium 21 H8 50 26N 6 12 E
Butha Qi, China 65 B7 48 0N 122 32 E
Buthidaung, Burma 78 E4 20 52N 92 32 E

180 Butiaba

Butiaba, Uganda 106 B3 1 50N 31 20 E
Butkhāk, Afghan. 79 B3 34 30N 69 22 E
Butler, Ind., U.S.A. 141 C12 41 26N 84 52W
Butler, Ky., U.S.A. 141 F12 38 47N 84 22W
Butler, Mo., U.S.A. 140 F2 38 17N 94 18W
Butler, Pa., U.S.A. 136 F5 40 52N 79 52W
Butom Odrzánski, Poland 47 D2 51 44N 15 48 E
Bütschwil, Switz. 29 B8 47 23N 9 5 E
Butte, Mont., U.S.A. 142 C7 46 2N 112 31W
Butte, Nebr., U.S.A. 138 D5 42 56N 98 54W
Butte Creek →, U.S.A. 144 F5 39 12N 121 56W
Butterworth = Gcuwa, S. Africa 105 E4 32 20 S 28 11 E
Butterworth, Malaysia 77 K3 5 24N 100 23 E
Buttfield, Mt., Australia 113 D4 24 45 S 128 9 E
Button B., Canada 131 B10 58 45N 94 23W
Buttonwillow, U.S.A. 145 K7 35 24N 119 28W
Butty Hd., Australia 113 F3 33 54 S 121 39 E
Butuan, Phil. 71 C7 8 57N 125 33 E
Butuku-Luba, Eq. Guin. 101 E6 3 29N 8 33 E
Butung, Indonesia 71 F6 5 0 S 122 45 E
Buturlinovka, U.S.S.R. 51 F12 50 50N 40 35 E
Butzbach, Germany 26 E4 50 24N 8 40 E
Bützow, Germany 26 B7 53 51N 11 59 E
Buxar, India 81 G10 25 34N 83 58 E
Buxton, Guyana 153 B6 6 48N 58 2W
Buxton, S. Africa 104 D3 27 38 S 24 42 E
Buxton, U.K. 16 D6 53 16N 1 54W
Buxy, France 23 F11 46 44N 4 40 E
Buy, U.S.S.R. 51 B12 58 28N 41 28 E
Buyaga, U.S.S.R. 57 D13 59 50N 127 0 E
Buynaksk, U.S.S.R. 53 E12 42 48N 47 7 E
Büyük Kemikli Burun, Turkey 44 D8 40 20N 26 15 E
Büyük Menderes →, Turkey 88 E2 37 28N 27 11 E
Büyükçekmece, Turkey 43 F13 41 2N 28 35 E
Buzançais, France 22 F8 46 54N 1 25 E
Buzău, Romania 46 D7 45 10N 26 50 E
Buzău □, Romania 46 D7 45 20N 26 30 E
Buzău →, Romania 46 D8 45 26N 27 44 E
Buzău, Pasul, Romania 46 D7 45 35N 26 12 E
Buzen, Japan 62 D3 33 35N 131 5 E
Buzet, Yugoslavia 39 C10 45 24N 13 58 E
Buzi →, Mozam. 107 F3 19 50 S 34 43 E
Buziaş, Romania 46 D2 45 38N 21 36 E
Buzuluk, U.S.S.R. 54 E3 52 48N 52 12 E
Buzuluk →, U.S.S.R. 51 F13 50 15N 42 7 E
Buzzards Bay, U.S.A. 137 E14 41 45N 70 38W
Bwagaoia, Papua N. G. 120 F7 10 40 S 152 52 E
Bwana Mkubwe, Zaïre 107 E2 13 8 S 28 38 E
Byala, Ruse, Bulgaria 43 D10 43 28N 25 44 E
Byala, Varna, Bulgaria 43 E12 42 53N 27 55 E
Byala Slatina, Bulgaria 43 D8 43 26N 23 55 E
Byandovan, Mys, U.S.S.R. 53 G13 39 45N 49 28 E
Bychawa, Poland 47 D9 51 1N 22 36 E
Byczyna, Poland 47 D5 51 7N 18 12 E
Bydgoszcz, Poland 47 B5 53 10N 18 0 E
Bydgoszcz □, Poland 47 B4 53 16N 17 33 E
Byelorussian S.S.R. □, U.S.S.R. 50 E5 53 30N 27 0 E
Byers, U.S.A. 138 F2 39 46N 104 13W
Byesville, U.S.A. 136 G3 39 56N 81 32W
Byhalia, U.S.A. 139 H10 34 53N 89 41W
Bykhov, U.S.S.R. 50 E7 53 31N 30 14 E
Bykovo, U.S.S.R. 53 B11 49 50N 45 25 E
Bylas, U.S.A. 143 K8 33 11N 110 9W
Bylderup, Denmark 15 K3 54 57N 9 6 E
Bylot I., Canada 127 A12 73 13N 78 34W
Byrd, C., Antarctica 7 C17 69 38 S 76 7W
Byro, Australia 113 E2 26 5 S 116 11 E
Byrock, Australia 117 A7 30 40 S 146 27 E
Byron, U.S.A. 140 B7 42 8N 89 15W
Byron Bay, Australia 115 D5 28 43 S 153 37 E
Byrranga, Gory, U.S.S.R. 57 B11 75 0N 100 0 E
Byrum, Denmark 15 G5 57 16N 11 0 E
Byske, Sweden 12 D16 64 57N 21 11 E
Byske älv →, Sweden 12 D16 64 57N 21 13 E
Bystrovka, U.S.S.R. 55 B7 42 47N 75 42 E
Bystrzyca →, Lublin, Poland 47 D9 51 21N 22 46 E
Bystrzyca →, Wrocław, Poland 47 D3 51 12N 16 55 E
Bystrzyca Kłodzka, Poland 47 E3 50 19N 16 39 E
Byten, U.S.S.R. 50 E4 52 50N 25 27 E
Bytom, Poland 47 E5 50 25N 18 54 E
Bytów, Poland 47 A4 54 10N 17 30 E
Byumba, Rwanda 106 C3 1 35 S 30 4 E
Bzenec, Czech. 31 C10 48 58N 17 18 E
Bzura →, Poland 47 C7 52 25N 20 15 E

C

Ca →, Vietnam 76 C5 18 45N 105 45 E
Ca Mau = Quan Long, Vietnam 77 H5 9 7N 105 8 E
Ca Mau, Mui = Bai Bung, Mui, Vietnam 77 H5 8 38N 104 44 E
Ca Na, Vietnam 77 G7 11 20N 108 54 E
Caacupé, Paraguay 158 B4 25 23 S 57 5W
Caála, Angola 103 E3 12 46 S 15 30 E
Caamano Sd., Canada 130 C3 52 55N 129 25W
Caapiranga, Brazil 153 D5 3 18 S 61 13W
Caazapá, Paraguay 158 B4 26 8 S 56 19W
Caazapá □, Paraguay 159 B4 26 10 S 56 0W
Caballeria, C. de, Spain 33 A11 40 5N 4 5 E
Cabana, Peru 156 B2 8 25 S 78 5W
Cabanaconde, Peru 156 D3 15 38 S 71 58W
Cabañaquinta, Spain 36 B5 43 10N 5 38W
Cabanatuan, Phil. 71 A6 15 30N 120 58 E
Cabanes, Spain 34 E5 40 9N 0 2 E
Cabanillas, Peru 156 D3 15 38 S 70 28W
Cabano, Canada 129 C6 47 40N 68 56W
Čabar, Yugoslavia 39 C11 45 36N 14 39 E
Cabazon, U.S.A. 145 M10 33 55N 116 47W
Cabedelo, Brazil 154 C5 7 0 S 34 50W
Cabery, U.S.A. 141 D8 40 59N 88 12W
Cabeza del Buey, Spain 37 G5 38 44N 5 13W
Cabildo, Chile 158 C1 32 30 S 71 5W
Cabimas, Venezuela 152 A3 10 23N 71 25W
Cabinda, Angola 103 D2 5 33 S 12 11 E
Cabinda □, Angola 103 D2 5 0 S 12 30 E
Cabinet Mts., U.S.A. 142 C6 48 0N 115 30W
Cabiri, Angola 103 D2 8 52 S 13 39 E
Cabo Blanco, Argentina 160 C3 47 15 S 65 47W
Cabo Frio, Brazil 155 F3 22 51 S 42 3W
Cabo Pantoja, Peru 152 D2 1 0 S 75 10W
Cabo Raso, Argentina 160 B3 44 20 S 65 15W
Cabonga, Réservoir, Canada 128 C4 47 20N 76 40W
Cabool, U.S.A. 139 G8 37 10N 92 8W
Caboolture, Australia 115 D5 27 5 S 152 58 E
Cabora Bassa Dam = Cahora Bassa Dam, Mozam. 107 F3 15 20 S 32 50 E
Caborca, Mexico 146 A2 30 40N 112 10W
Cabot, Mt., U.S.A. 137 B13 44 30N 71 25W
Cabot Str., Canada 129 C8 47 15N 59 40W
Cabra, Spain 37 H6 37 30N 4 28W
Cabra del Santo Cristo, Spain 35 H1 37 42N 3 16W
Cábras, Italy 40 C1 39 57N 8 30 E
Cabrera, I., Spain 33 B9 39 8N 2 57 E
Cabrera, Sierra, Spain 36 C4 42 12N 6 40W
Cabri, Canada 131 C7 50 35N 108 25W
Cabriel →, Spain 35 F3 39 14N 1 3W
Cabruta, Venezuela 152 B4 7 50N 66 10W
Cabuyaro, Colombia 152 C3 4 18N 72 49W
Cacabelos, Spain 36 C4 42 36N 6 44W
Čačak, Yugoslavia 42 D5 43 54N 20 20 E
Cacao, Fr. Guiana 153 C7 4 33N 52 26W
Cáceres, Brazil 157 D6 16 5 S 57 40W
Cáceres, Colombia 152 B2 7 35N 75 20W
Cáceres, Spain 37 F4 39 26N 6 23W
Cáceres □, Spain 37 F5 39 45N 6 0W
Cache Bay, Canada 128 C4 46 22N 80 0W
Cache Cr. →, U.S.A. 144 G5 38 45N 121 43W
Cachepo, Portugal 37 H3 37 20N 7 49W
Cachéu, Guinea-Biss. 100 C1 12 14N 16 8W
Cachi, Argentina 158 B2 25 5 S 66 10W
Cachimbo, Brazil 157 B7 8 57 S 54 54W
Cachimbo, Serra do, Brazil 157 B6 9 30 S 55 30W
Cachingues, Angola 103 E3 13 5 S 16 43 E
Cachoeira, Brazil 155 D4 12 30 S 39 0W
Cachoeira Alta, Brazil 155 E1 18 48 S 50 58W
Cachoeira de Itapemirim, Brazil 155 F3 20 51 S 41 7W
Cachoeira do Sul, Brazil 159 C5 30 3 S 52 53W
Cachoeiro do Arari, Brazil 154 B2 1 1 S 48 58W
Cachopo, Portugal 37 H3 37 20N 7 49W
Cachuela Esperanza, Bolivia 157 C4 10 32 S 65 38W
Cacólo, Angola 103 E3 10 9 S 19 21 E
Caconda, Angola 103 E3 13 48 S 15 8 E
Cacongo, Angola 103 D2 5 11 S 12 5 E
Caçu, Brazil 155 E1 18 37 S 51 4W
Cacula, Angola 103 E2 14 29 S 14 10 E
Caculé, Brazil 155 D3 14 30 S 42 13W
Cacuso, Angola 103 D3 9 25 S 15 45 E
Cadarache, France 25 E9 43 41N 5 43 E
Čadca, Czech. 31 B11 49 26N 18 45 E
Caddo, U.S.A. 139 H6 34 8N 96 18W
Cadell Cr. →, Australia 114 C3 22 35 S 141 51 E
Cadenazzo, Switz. 29 D7 46 9N 8 57 E
Cader Idris, U.K. 16 E4 52 43N 3 56W
Cadí, Sierra del, Spain 34 C6 42 17N 1 42 E
Cadibarrawirracanna, L., Australia 115 D2 28 52 S 135 27 E
Cadillac, Canada 128 C4 48 14N 78 23W
Cadillac, France 24 D3 44 38N 0 20W
Cadillac, U.S.A. 134 C3 44 16N 85 25W
Cadiz, Phil. 71 B6 10 57N 123 15 E
Cádiz, Spain 37 J4 36 30N 6 20W
Cadiz, U.S.A. 136 F4 40 13N 81 0W
Cádiz □, Spain 37 J5 36 36N 5 45W
Cádiz, G. de, Spain 37 J4 36 40N 7 0W
Cadney Park, Australia 115 D1 27 55 S 134 3 E
Cadomin, Canada 130 C5 53 2N 117 20W
Cadotte →, Canada 130 B5 56 43N 117 10W
Cadours, France 24 E5 43 44N 1 2 E
Cadoux, Australia 113 F2 30 46 S 117 7 E
Caen, France 22 C6 49 10N 0 22W
Caernarfon, U.K. 16 D3 53 8N 4 17W
Caernarfon B., U.K. 16 D3 53 4N 4 40W
Caernarvon = Caernarfon, U.K. 16 D3 53 8N 4 17W
Caerphilly, U.K. 17 F4 51 34N 3 13W
Caesarea, Israel 91 C3 32 30N 34 53 E
Caeté, Brazil 155 E3 19 55 S 43 40W
Caetité, Brazil 155 D3 13 50 S 42 32W
Cafayate, Argentina 158 B2 26 2 S 66 0W
Cafifi, Colombia 152 B3 5 13N 71 4W
Cafu, Angola 103 F3 16 30 S 15 8 E
Cagayan →, Phil. 71 A6 18 25N 121 42 E
Cagayan de Oro, Phil. 71 C6 8 30N 124 40 E
Cagli, Italy 39 E9 43 32N 12 38 E
Cágliari, Italy 40 C2 39 15N 9 6 E
Cágliari, G. di, Italy 40 C2 39 8N 9 10 E
Cagnano Varano, Italy 41 A8 41 49N 15 47 E
Cagnes-sur-Mer, France 25 E11 43 40N 7 9 E
Caguán →, Colombia 152 D3 0 8 S 74 18W
Caguas, Puerto Rico 149 C6 18 14N 66 4W
Caha Mts., Ireland 19 E2 51 45N 9 40W
Cahama, Angola 103 F2 16 17 S 14 19 E
Caher, Ireland 19 D4 52 23N 7 56W
Cahersiveen, Ireland 19 E1 51 57N 10 13W
Cahora Bassa Dam, Mozam. 107 F3 15 20 S 32 50 E
Cahors, France 24 D5 44 27N 1 27 E
Cahuapanas, Peru 156 B2 5 15 S 77 0W
Cahuinari →, Colombia 152 D3 1 21 S 70 44W
Cai Bau, Dao, Vietnam 76 B6 21 10N 107 27 E
Cai Nuoc, Vietnam 77 H5 8 56N 105 1 E
Caia, Mozam. 107 F4 17 51 S 35 24 E
Caiabis, Serra dos, Brazil 157 C6 11 30 S 56 30W
Caianda, Angola 103 E4 11 2 S 23 31 E
Caiapó, Serra do, Brazil 157 D7 17 0 S 52 0W
Caiapônia, Brazil 157 D7 16 57 S 51 49W
Caibarién, Cuba 148 B4 22 30N 79 30W
Caicara, Bolívar, Venezuela 152 B4 7 38N 66 10W
Caicara, Monagas, Venezuela 153 B5 9 52N 63 38W
Caicó, Brazil 154 C4 6 20 S 37 0W
Caicos I., W. Indies 149 B5 21 40N 71 40W
Caicos Passage, W. Indies 149 B5 22 45N 72 45W
Cailloma, Peru 156 D3 15 9 S 71 45W
Caine →, Bolivia 157 D4 18 23 S 65 21W
Caird Coast, Antarctica 7 D1 75 0 S 25 0W
Cairn Gorm, U.K. 18 D5 57 7N 3 40W
Cairn Toul, U.K. 18 D5 57 3N 3 44W
Cairngorm Mts., U.K. 18 D5 57 6N 3 42W
Cairns, Australia 114 B4 16 57 S 145 45 E
Cairo = El Qâhira, Egypt 94 H7 30 1N 31 14 E
Cairo, Ga., U.S.A. 135 K3 30 52N 84 12W
Cairo, Ill., U.S.A. 139 G10 37 0N 89 10W
Cairo Montenotte, Italy 38 D5 44 23N 8 16 E
Caithness, Ord of, U.K. 18 C5 58 9N 3 37W
Caiundo, Angola 103 F3 15 50 S 17 28 E
Caiza, Bolivia 157 E4 20 2 S 65 40W
Cajabamba, Peru 156 B2 7 38 S 78 4W
Cajamarca, Peru 156 B2 7 5 S 78 28W
Cajamarca □, Peru 156 B2 6 15 S 78 50W
Cajapió, Brazil 154 B3 2 58 S 44 48W
Cajarc, France 24 D5 44 29N 1 50 E
Cajatambo, Peru 156 C2 10 30 S 77 2W
Cajàzeiras, Brazil 154 C4 6 52 S 38 30W
Čajetina, Yugoslavia 42 D4 43 47N 19 42 E
Čajniče, Yugoslavia 42 D4 43 34N 19 5 E
Çakirgol, Turkey 53 F8 40 33N 39 40 E
Čakovec, Yugoslavia 39 B13 46 23N 16 26 E
Çal, Turkey 88 D3 38 4N 29 23 E
Cala, Spain 37 H4 37 59N 6 21W
Cala →, Spain 37 H4 37 38N 6 5W
Cala Cadolar, Punta de, Spain 35 G6 38 38N 1 35 E
Cala d'Or, Spain 33 B10 39 23N 3 14 E
Cala Figuera, C., Spain 33 B9 39 27N 2 31 E
Cala Forcat, Spain 33 B10 40 0N 3 47 E
Cala Mayor, Spain 33 B9 39 33N 2 37 E
Cala Mezquida, Spain 33 B11 39 55N 4 16 E
Cala Millor, Spain 33 B10 39 35N 3 22 E
Cala Ratjada, Spain 33 B10 39 43N 3 27 E
Calabar, Nigeria 101 E6 4 57N 8 20 E
Calabozo, Venezuela 152 B4 9 0N 67 28W
Calábria □, Italy 41 C9 39 24N 16 30 E
Calaburras, Pta. de, Spain 37 J6 36 30N 4 38W
Calaceite, Spain 34 D5 41 1N 0 11 E
Calacota, Bolivia 156 D4 17 16 S 68 38W
Calafat, Romania 46 F3 43 58N 22 59 E
Calafate, Argentina 160 D2 50 19 S 72 15W
Calahorra, Spain 34 C3 42 18N 1 59W
Calais, France 23 B8 50 57N 1 56 E
Calais, U.S.A. 129 C6 45 11N 67 20W
Calais, Pas de, France 23 B8 50 30N 1 20 E
Calalaste, Cord. de, Argentina 158 B2 25 0 S 67 0W
Calama, Brazil 157 B5 8 0 S 62 50W
Calama, Chile 158 A2 22 30 S 68 55W
Calamar, Bolívar, Colombia 152 A3 10 15N 74 55W
Calamar, Vaupés, Colombia 152 C3 1 58N 72 32W
Calamarca, Bolivia 156 D4 16 55 S 68 9W
Calamian Group, Phil. 71 B5 11 50N 119 55 E
Calamocha, Spain 34 E3 40 50N 1 17W
Calán Porter, Spain 33 B11 39 52N 4 8 E
Calañas, Spain 37 H4 37 40N 6 53W
Calanda, Spain 34 E4 40 56N 0 15W
Calandula, Angola 103 D3 9 6 S 15 57 E
Calang, Indonesia 70 D1 4 37N 95 37 E
Calangiánus, Italy 40 B2 40 56N 9 12 E
Calanscio, Sarīr, Libya 96 C4 27 0N 21 30 E
Calapan, Phil. 71 B6 13 25N 121 7 E
Călăraşi, Romania 46 E8 44 12N 27 20 E
Călăraşi □, Romania 46 E8 44 10N 27 0 E
Calasparra, Spain 35 G3 38 14N 1 41W
Calatafimi, Italy 40 E5 37 56N 12 50 E
Calatayud, Spain 34 D3 41 20N 1 40W
Calato = Kálathos, Greece 45 H10 36 9N 28 8 E
Calauag, Phil. 71 B6 13 55N 122 15 E
Calavà, C., Italy 41 D7 38 11N 14 55 E
Calavite, C., Phil. 71 B6 13 26N 120 20 E
Calbayog, Phil. 71 B6 12 4N 124 38 E
Calbe, Germany 26 D7 51 57N 11 47 E
Calca, Peru 156 C3 13 22 S 72 0W
Calcasieu L., U.S.A. 139 L8 30 0N 93 17W
Calci, Italy 38 E7 43 44N 10 31 E
Calcutta, India 81 H13 22 36N 88 24 E
Caldaro, Italy 39 B8 46 23N 11 15 E
Caldas □, Colombia 152 B2 5 15N 75 30W
Caldas da Rainha, Portugal 37 F1 39 24N 9 8W
Caldas de Reyes, Spain 36 C2 42 36N 8 39W
Caldas Novas, Brazil 155 E2 17 45 S 48 38W
Calder →, U.K. 16 D6 53 44N 1 21W
Caldera, Chile 158 B1 27 5 S 70 55W
Caldwell, Idaho, U.S.A. 142 E5 43 45N 116 42W
Caldwell, Kans., U.S.A. 139 G6 37 5N 97 37W
Caldwell, Tex., U.S.A. 139 K6 30 30N 96 42W
Caledon, S. Africa 104 E2 34 14 S 19 26 E
Caledon →, S. Africa 104 E4 30 31 S 26 5 E
Caledon B., Australia 114 A2 12 45 S 137 0 E
Caledonia, Canada 136 C5 43 7N 79 58W
Caledonia, Mo., U.S.A. 140 G6 37 45N 90 46W
Caledonia, N.Y., U.S.A. 136 D7 42 57N 77 54W
Calella, Spain 34 D7 41 37N 2 40 E
Calemba, Angola 104 B2 16 0 S 15 44 E
Calenzana, France 25 F12 42 31N 8 51 E
Caleta Olivia, Argentina 160 C3 46 25 S 67 25W
Calexico, U.S.A. 145 N11 32 40N 115 33W
Calf of Man, U.K. 16 C3 54 3N 4 49W
Calgary, Canada 130 C6 51 0N 114 10W
Calheta, Madeira 33 D2 32 44N 17 11W
Calhoun, U.S.A. 135 H3 34 30N 84 55W
Cali, Colombia 152 C2 3 25N 76 35W
Calicut, India 83 J2 11 15N 75 43 E
Caliente, U.S.A. 143 H6 37 36N 114 34W
California, Mo., U.S.A. 140 F4 38 37N 92 30W
California, Pa., U.S.A. 136 F5 40 5N 79 55W
California □, U.S.A. 143 H4 37 25N 120 0W
California, Baja, Mexico 146 A1 32 10N 115 12W
California, Baja, T.N. □, Mexico 146 B2 30 0N 115 0W
California, Baja, T.S. □, Mexico 146 B2 25 50N 111 50W
California, G. de, Mexico 146 B2 27 0N 111 0W
California City, U.S.A. 145 K9 35 7N 117 57W
California Hot Springs, U.S.A. 145 K8 35 51N 118 41W
Călimăneşti, Romania 46 D5 45 14N 24 20 E
Călimani, Munţii, Romania 46 B6 47 12N 25 0 E
Călineşti, Romania 46 D5 45 21N 24 18 E
Calingasta, Argentina 158 C2 31 15 S 69 30W
Calipatria, U.S.A. 145 M11 33 8N 115 30W
Calistoga, U.S.A. 144 G4 38 36N 122 32W
Calitri, Italy 41 B8 40 54N 15 25 E
Calitzdorp, S. Africa 104 E3 33 33 S 21 42 E
Callabonna, L., Australia 115 D3 29 40 S 140 5 E
Callac, France 22 D3 48 25N 3 27W
Callander, U.K. 18 E4 56 15N 4 14W
Callantsoog, Neths. 20 C5 52 50N 4 42 E
Callao, Peru 156 C2 12 0 S 77 0W
Callaway, U.S.A. 138 E5 41 20N 99 56W
Callender, U.S.A. 140 B2 42 22N 94 17W
Calles, Mexico 147 C5 23 2N 98 42W
Callide, Australia 114 C5 24 18 S 150 28 E
Calling Lake, Canada 130 B6 55 15N 113 12W
Calliope, Australia 114 C5 24 0 S 151 16 E
Callosa de Ensarriá, Spain 35 G4 38 40N 0 8W
Callosa de Segura, Spain 35 G4 38 7N 0 53W
Calmar, U.S.A. 140 A5 43 11N 91 52W
Calola, Angola 103 F3 16 25 S 17 48 E
Calore →, Italy 41 A7 41 11N 14 28 E
Caloundra, Australia 115 D5 26 45 S 153 10 E
Calpe, Spain 35 G5 38 39N 0 3 E
Calpella, U.S.A. 144 F3 39 14N 123 12W
Calpine, U.S.A. 144 F6 39 40N 120 27W
Calstock, Canada 128 C3 49 47N 84 9W
Caltabellotta, Italy 40 E6 37 36N 13 11 E
Caltagirone, Italy 41 E7 37 13N 14 30 E
Caltanissetta, Italy 41 E7 37 30N 14 3 E
Calucinga, Angola 103 E3 11 18 S 16 12 E
Calulo, Angola 103 E2 10 1 S 14 56 E
Calumet, U.S.A. 134 B1 47 14N 88 27W
Calunda, Angola 103 E4 12 7 S 23 36 E
Caluquembe, Angola 103 E2 13 47 S 14 44 E
Caluso, Italy 38 C4 45 18N 7 52 E
Calvados □, France 22 C6 49 5N 0 15W
Calvert, U.S.A. 139 K6 30 59N 96 40W
Calvert →, Australia 114 B2 16 17 S 137 44 E
Calvert Hills, Australia 114 B2 17 15 S 137 20 E
Calvert I., Canada 130 C3 51 30N 128 0W
Calvert Ra., Australia 112 D3 24 0 S 122 30 E
Calvi, France 25 F12 42 34N 8 45 E
Calvillo, Mexico 146 C4 21 51N 102 43W
Calvinia, S. Africa 104 E2 31 28 S 19 45 E
Calw, Germany 27 G4 48 43N 8 44 E
Calwa, U.S.A. 144 J7 36 42N 119 46W
Calzada Almuradiel, Spain 35 G1 38 32N 3 28W
Calzada de Calatrava, Spain 37 G7 38 42N 3 46W
Cam →, U.K. 17 E8 52 21N 0 16 E
Cam Lam, Vietnam 77 G7 11 54N 109 10 E
Cam Pha, Vietnam 76 B6 21 7N 107 18 E
Cam Ranh, Vietnam 77 G7 11 54N 109 12 E
Cam Xuyen, Vietnam 76 C6 18 15N 106 0 E
Camabatela, Angola 103 D3 8 20 S 15 26 E
Camacã, Brazil 155 E4 15 24 S 39 30W
Camaçari, Brazil 155 D4 12 41 S 38 18W
Camacha, Madeira 33 D3 32 41N 16 49W
Camacho, Mexico 146 C4 24 25N 102 18W
Camacupa, Angola 103 E3 11 58 S 17 22 E
Camaguán, Venezuela 152 B4 8 6N 67 36W
Camagüey, Cuba 148 B4 21 20N 78 0W
Camaiore, Italy 38 E7 43 57N 10 18 E
Camamu, Brazil 155 D4 13 57 S 39 7W
Camaná, Peru 156 D3 16 30 S 72 50W
Camanche, U.S.A. 140 C6 41 47N 90 15W
Camanche Res., U.S.A. 144 G6 38 16N 120 51W
Camanongue, Angola 103 E4 11 24 S 20 17 E
Camaquã →, Brazil 159 C5 31 17 S 51 47W
Câmara de Lobos, Madeira 33 D3 32 39N 16 59W
Camararé →, Brazil 157 C6 12 15 S 58 55W
Camarat, C., France 25 E10 43 12N 6 41 E
Camaret, France 22 D2 48 16N 4 37W
Camargo, Bolivia 157 E4 20 38 S 65 15W
Camargue, France 25 E8 43 34N 4 34 E
Camarillo, U.S.A. 145 L7 34 13N 119 2W
Camariñas, Spain 36 B1 43 8N 9 12W
Camarón, C., Honduras 148 C2 16 0N 85 5W
Camarones, Argentina 160 B3 44 50 S 65 40W
Camarones, B., Argentina 160 B3 44 45 S 65 35W
Camas, U.S.A. 144 E4 45 35N 122 24W
Camas Valley, U.S.A. 142 E2 43 0N 123 46W
Camaxilo, Angola 103 D3 8 21 S 18 56 E
Cambados, Spain 36 C2 42 31N 8 49W
Cambamba, Angola 103 D2 8 53 S 14 44 E
Cambará, Brazil 159 A5 23 2 S 50 5W
Cambay = Khambhat, India 80 H5 22 23N 72 33 E
Cambil, Spain 35 H1 37 40N 3 33W
Cambo-les-Bains, France 24 E2 43 22N 1 23W
Cambodia ■, Asia 76 F5 12 15N 105 0 E
Camborne, U.K. 17 G2 50 13N 5 18W
Cambrai, France 23 B10 50 11N 3 14 E
Cambria, U.S.A. 144 K5 35 39N 121 6W
Cambrian Mts., U.K. 17 E4 52 25N 3 52W
Cambridge, Canada 128 D3 43 23N 80 15W
Cambridge, Jamaica 148 C4 18 18N 77 54W
Cambridge, N.Z. 118 D4 37 54 S 175 29 E
Cambridge, U.K. 17 E8 52 13N 0 8 E
Cambridge, Idaho, U.S.A. 142 D5 44 36N 116 40W
Cambridge, Ill., U.S.A. 140 C6 41 18N 90 12W
Cambridge, Iowa, U.S.A. 140 C3 41 54N 93 32W
Cambridge, Mass., U.S.A. 137 D13 42 20N 71 8W
Cambridge, Md., U.S.A. 134 F7 38 33N 76 2W
Cambridge, Minn., U.S.A. 138 C8 45 34N 93 15W
Cambridge, N.Y., U.S.A. 137 C11 43 2N 73 22W
Cambridge, Nebr., U.S.A. 138 E4 40 20N 100 12W
Cambridge, Ohio, U.S.A. 136 F3 40 1N 81 35W
Cambridge Bay, Canada 126 B9 69 10N 105 0W
Cambridge City, U.S.A. 141 E11 39 49N 85 10W
Cambridge G., Australia 112 B4 14 55 S 128 15 E

Chapala, L. de 183

Cavan, Ireland 19 C4 54 0N 7 22W
Cavan □, Ireland 19 C4 53 58N 7 10W
Cavárzere, Italy 39 C9 45 8N 12 6 E
Cave City, U.S.A. 134 G3 37 13N 85 57W
Cavenagh Ra., Australia 113 E4 26 12 S 127 55 E
Cavendish, Australia 116 D5 37 31 S 142 2 E
Caviana, I., Brazil 153 C7 0 10N 50 10W
Cavite, Phil. 71 B6 14 29N 120 55 E
Cavour, Italy 38 D4 44 47N 7 22 E
Cavtat, Yugoslavia 42 E3 42 35N 18 13 E
Cavuşcu Gölü, Turkey 88 D4 38 22N 31 53 E
Cawkers Well, Australia 116 A5 31 41 S 142 57 E
Cawndilla L., Australia 116 B5 32 30 S 142 15 E
Cawnpore = Kanpur, India 81 F9 26 28N 80 20 E
Caxias, Brazil 154 B3 4 55 S 43 20W
Caxias do Sul, Brazil 159 B5 29 10 S 51 10W
Caxine, C., Algeria 99 A4 35 56N 0 27W
Caxito, Angola 103 D2 8 30 S 13 30 E
Caxopa, Angola 103 E4 11 52 S 20 52 E
Çay, Turkey 88 D4 38 35N 31 1 E
Cay Sal Bank, Bahamas 148 B4 23 45N 80 0W
Cayambe, Ecuador 152 C2 0 2N 77 59W
Cayambe, Ecuador 152 C2 0 3N 78 8W
Çaycuma, Turkey 88 C5 41 25N 32 4 E
Çayeli, Turkey 89 C9 41 5N 40 45 E
Cayenne, Fr. Guiana 153 B7 5 5N 52 18W
Cayenne □, Fr. Guiana 153 C7 5 0N 53 0W
Cayeux-sur-Mer, France 23 B8 50 10N 1 30 E
Cayiralan, Turkey 88 D6 39 17N 35 38 E
Caylus, France 24 D5 44 15N 1 47 E
Cayman Brac, Cayman Is. 148 C4 19 43N 79 49W
Cayman Is., W. Indies 148 C3 19 40N 80 30W
Cayo Romano, Cuba 149 B4 22 0N 78 0W
Cayuga, Canada 136 D5 42 59N 79 50W
Cayuga, Ind., U.S.A. 141 E9 39 57N 87 38W
Cayuga, N.Y., U.S.A. 137 D8 42 54N 76 44W
Cayuga L., U.S.A. 137 D8 42 45N 76 45W
Cazaje, Angola 103 E4 11 2 S 20 45 E
Cazalla de la Sierra, Spain 37 H5 37 56N 5 45W
Căzăneşti, Romania 46 E8 44 36N 27 3 E
Cazaux et de Sanguinet, Étang de, France 24 D2 44 29N 1 10W
Cazères, France 24 E5 43 13N 1 5 E
Cazin, Yugoslavia 39 D12 44 57N 15 57 E
Čazma, Yugoslavia 39 C13 45 45N 16 39 E
Čazma →, Yugoslavia 39 C13 45 35N 16 29 E
Cazombo, Angola 103 E4 11 54 S 22 56 E
Cazorla, Spain 35 H1 37 55N 3 2W
Cazorla, Venezuela 152 B4 8 1N 67 0W
Cazorla, Sierra de, Spain 35 G2 38 5N 2 55W
Cea →, Spain 36 D5 42 0N 5 36W
Ceamurlia de Jos, Romania 46 E9 44 43N 28 47 E
Ceanannus Mor, Ireland 19 C5 53 42N 6 53W
Ceará = Fortaleza, Brazil 154 B4 3 45 S 38 35W
Ceará □, Brazil 154 C4 5 0 S 40 0W
Ceará Mirim, Brazil 154 C4 5 38 S 35 25W
Ceauru, L., Romania 46 E4 44 58N 23 11 E
Cebaco, I. de, Panama 148 E3 7 33N 81 9W
Cebollar, Argentina 158 B2 29 10 S 66 35W
Cebollera, Sierra de, Spain 34 D2 42 0N 2 30W
Cebreros, Spain 36 E6 40 27N 4 28W
Cebu, Phil. 71 B6 10 18N 123 54 E
Ceccano, Italy 40 A6 41 34N 13 18 E
Cece, Hungary 31 E11 46 46N 18 39 E
Čechi, Ivory C. 100 D4 6 15N 4 25W
Čechy, Czech. 30 B6 49 58N 13 30 E
Cecil Plains, Australia 115 D5 27 30 S 151 11 E
Cécina, Italy 38 E7 43 19N 10 33 E
Cécina →, Italy 38 E7 43 19N 10 29 E
Ceclavin, Spain 36 F4 39 50N 6 45W
Cedar →, U.S.A. 140 C5 41 17N 91 21W
Cedar City, U.S.A. 143 H7 37 41N 113 3W
Cedar Creek Res., U.S.A. 139 J6 32 4N 96 5W
Cedar Falls, Iowa, U.S.A. 140 B4 42 39N 92 29W
Cedar Falls, Wash., U.S.A. 144 C5 47 25N 121 45W
Cedar Grove, U.S.A. 141 E12 39 22N 84 56W
Cedar Key, U.S.A. 135 L4 29 9N 83 5W
Cedar L., Canada 131 C9 53 10N 100 0W
Cedar Lake, U.S.A. 141 C9 41 20N 87 25W
Cedar Point, U.S.A. 141 C13 41 44N 83 21W
Cedar Rapids, U.S.A. 140 C5 41 55N 91 38W
Cedartown, U.S.A. 135 H3 34 1N 85 15W
Cedarvale, Canada 130 B3 55 1N 128 22W
Cedarville, S. Africa 105 E4 30 23 S 29 3 E
Cedarville, Calif., U.S.A. 142 F3 41 37N 120 13W
Cedarville, Ill., U.S.A. 140 B7 42 23N 89 38W
Cedarville, Ohio, U.S.A. 141 E13 39 44N 83 49W
Cedeira, Spain 36 B2 43 39N 8 2W
Cedral, Mexico 146 C4 23 50N 100 42W
Cedrino →, Italy 40 B2 40 23N 9 44 E
Cedro, Brazil 154 C4 6 34 S 39 3W
Cedros, I. de, Mexico 146 B1 28 10N 115 20W
Ceduna, Australia 115 E1 32 7 S 133 46 E
Cedynia, Poland 47 C1 52 53N 14 12 E
Cefalù, Italy 41 D7 38 3N 14 1 E
Cega →, Spain 36 D6 41 33N 4 46W
Cegléd, Hungary 31 D12 47 11N 19 47 E
Céglie Messápico, Italy 41 B10 40 39N 17 31 E
Cehegín, Spain 35 G3 38 6N 1 48W
Ceheng, China 68 E5 24 58N 105 48 E
Cehu-Silvaniei, Romania 46 B4 47 24N 23 9 E
Ceica, Romania 46 C3 46 53N 22 10 E
Ceira →, Portugal 36 E2 40 13N 8 16W
Cekhira, Tunisia 96 B2 34 20N 10 5 E
Cela, Angola 103 E3 11 25 S 15 7 E
Celano, Italy 39 F10 42 6N 13 30 E
Celanova, Spain 36 C3 42 9N 7 58W
Celaya, Mexico 146 C4 20 31N 100 37W
Celebes = Sulawesi □, Indonesia 71 E6 2 0 S 120 0 E
Celebes Sea, Indonesia 71 D6 3 0N 123 0 E
Celendín, Peru 156 B2 6 52 S 78 10W
Čelić, Yugoslavia 42 C3 44 43N 18 47 E
Celica, Ecuador 152 D2 4 7 S 79 59W
Celina, U.S.A. 141 D12 40 32N 84 31W
Celje, Yugoslavia 39 B12 46 16N 15 18 E
Celldömölk, Hungary 31 D10 47 16N 17 10 E
Celle, Germany 26 C6 52 37N 10 4 E
Celles, Belgium 21 G2 50 42N 3 28 E
Celorico da Beira, Portugal 36 E3 40 38N 7 24W
Cement, U.S.A. 139 H5 34 56N 98 8W
Çemişgezek, Turkey 89 D8 39 3N 38 56 E
Cenepa →, Peru 152 D2 4 40 S 78 10W
Cengong, China 68 D7 27 13N 108 44 E
Ceno →, Italy 38 D7 44 4N 10 5 E
Centallo, Italy 38 D4 44 30N 7 35 E
Centenário do Sul, Brazil 155 F1 22 48 S 51 36W
Center, N. Dak., U.S.A. 138 B4 47 9N 101 17W
Center, Tex., U.S.A. 139 K7 31 50N 94 10W
Center Point, U.S.A. 140 B5 42 12N 91 46W
Centerfield, U.S.A. 143 G8 39 9N 111 56W
Centerville, Calif., U.S.A. 144 J7 36 44N 119 30W
Centerville, Iowa, U.S.A. 140 D4 40 45N 92 57W
Centerville, Mich., U.S.A. 141 C11 41 55N 85 32W
Centerville, Pa., U.S.A. 136 F5 40 3N 79 59W
Centerville, S. Dak., U.S.A. 138 D6 43 10N 96 58W
Centerville, Tenn., U.S.A. 135 H2 35 46N 87 29W
Centerville, Tex., U.S.A. 139 K7 31 15N 95 56W
Cento, Italy 39 D8 44 43N 11 16 E
Central, Brazil 154 D3 11 8 S 42 8W
Central, U.S.A. 143 K9 32 46N 108 9W
Central □, Kenya 106 C4 0 30 S 37 30 E
Central □, Malawi 107 E3 13 30 S 33 30 E
Central □, U.K. 18 E4 56 10N 4 30W
Central □, Zambia 107 E2 14 25 S 28 50 E
Central, Cordillera, Bolivia 157 D5 18 30 S 64 55W
Central, Cordillera, Colombia 152 C3 5 0N 75 0W
Central, Cordillera, Costa Rica 148 D3 10 10N 84 5W
Central, Cordillera, Dom. Rep. 149 C5 19 15N 71 0W
Central, Cordillera, Peru 156 B2 7 0 S 77 30W
Central, Sistema, Spain 36 E5 40 40N 5 55W
Central African Republic ■, Africa 102 A4 7 0N 20 0 E
Central City, Ky., U.S.A. 134 G2 37 20N 87 7W
Central City, Nebr., U.S.A. 138 E6 41 8N 98 0W
Central I., Kenya 106 B4 3 30N 36 0 E
Central Makran Range, Pakistan 79 D2 26 30N 64 15 E
Central Patricia, Canada 128 B1 51 30N 90 9W
Central Ra., Papua N. G. 120 C2 5 0 S 143 0 E
Central Russian Uplands, Europe 10 E13 54 0N 36 0 E
Central Siberian Plateau, U.S.S.R. 58 C14 65 0N 105 0 E
Centralia, Ill., U.S.A. 140 F7 38 32N 89 5W
Centralia, Mo., U.S.A. 140 E4 39 12N 92 6W
Centralia, Wash., U.S.A. 144 D4 46 46N 122 59W
Centreville, Ala., U.S.A. 135 J2 32 55N 87 7W
Centreville, Miss., U.S.A. 139 K9 31 10N 91 3W
Centúripe, Italy 41 E7 37 37N 14 41 E
Cephalonia = Kefallinía, Greece 45 F2 38 20N 20 30 E
Čepin, Yugoslavia 42 B3 45 32N 18 34 E
Ceprano, Italy 40 A6 41 33N 13 30 E
Ceptura, Romania 46 D7 45 1N 26 21 E
Cepu, Indonesia 71 G14 7 9 S 111 35 E
Ceram = Seram, Indonesia 71 E7 3 10 S 129 0 E
Ceram Sea = Seram Sea, Indonesia 71 E7 2 30 S 128 30 E
Cerbère, France 24 F7 42 26N 3 10 E
Cerbicales, Is., France 25 G13 41 33N 9 22 E
Cerbu, Romania 46 E5 44 46N 24 46 E
Cercal, Portugal 37 H2 37 48N 8 40W
Cercemaggiore, Italy 41 A7 41 27N 14 43 E
Cerdaña, Spain 34 C6 42 22N 1 35 E
Cerdedo, Spain 36 C2 42 33N 8 23W
Cère →, France 24 D5 44 55N 1 49 E
Cerea, Italy 39 C8 45 12N 11 13 E
Ceres, Argentina 158 B3 29 55 S 61 55W
Ceres, Brazil 155 E2 15 17 S 49 35W
Ceres, Italy 38 C4 45 19N 7 22 E
Ceres, S. Africa 104 E2 33 21 S 19 18 E
Ceres, U.S.A. 144 H6 37 35N 120 57W
Céret, France 24 F6 42 30N 2 42 E
Cereté, Colombia 152 B2 8 53N 75 48W
Cerfontaine, Belgium 21 H4 50 11N 4 26 E
Cerignola, Italy 41 A8 41 17N 15 53 E
Cerigo = Kíthira, Greece 45 H6 36 9N 24 12 E
Cérilly, France 24 B6 46 37N 2 50 E
Cerisiers, France 23 D10 48 8N 3 30 E
Cerizay, France 22 F6 46 50N 0 40W
Çerkeş, Turkey 88 C5 40 49N 32 52 E
Çerkezköy, Turkey 88 C2 41 17N 27 59 E
Cerknica, Yugoslavia 39 C11 45 48N 14 21 E
Cermerno, Yugoslavia 42 D5 43 35N 20 25 E
Çermik, Turkey 89 D8 38 8N 39 26 E
Cerna, Romania 46 D9 45 4N 28 17 E
Cerna →, Romania 46 E5 44 15N 24 25 E
Cernavodă, Romania 46 E9 44 22N 28 3 E
Cernay, France 23 E14 47 44N 7 10 E
Cernik, Yugoslavia 42 B2 45 17N 17 22 E
Cerralvo, I., Mexico 146 C3 24 20N 109 45W
Cerreto Sannita, Italy 41 A7 41 17N 14 34 E
Cerritos, Mexico 146 C4 22 27N 100 20W
Cerro Gordo, U.S.A. 141 E8 39 53N 88 44W
Cerro Sombrero, Chile 160 D3 52 45 S 69 15W
Certaldo, Italy 38 E8 43 32N 11 2 E
Cervaro →, Italy 41 A8 41 30N 15 52 E
Cervera, Spain 34 D6 41 40N 1 16 E
Cervera de Pisuerga, Spain 36 C6 42 51N 4 30W
Cervera del Río Alhama, Spain 34 C3 42 2N 1 58W
Cérvia, Italy 39 D9 44 15N 12 20 E
Cervignano del Friuli, Italy 39 C10 45 49N 13 20 E
Cervinara, Italy 41 A7 41 2N 14 36 E
Cervione, France 25 F13 42 20N 9 29 E
Cervo, Spain 36 B3 43 40N 7 24W
César □, Colombia 152 B3 9 0N 73 30W
Cesaro, Italy 41 E7 37 50N 14 38 E
Cesena, Italy 39 D9 44 9N 12 14 E
Cesenático, Italy 39 D9 44 12N 12 22 E
Cēsis, U.S.S.R. 50 C4 57 17N 25 28 E
Česká Lípa, Czech. 30 A7 50 45N 14 30 E
Česka Republika □, Czech. 30 B7 49 30N 14 40 E
Česká Třebová, Czech. 31 B9 49 54N 16 27 E
České Budějovice, Czech. 30 C7 48 55N 14 25 E
České Velenice, Czech. 30 C8 48 45N 15 1 E
Ceskomoravská Vrchovina, Czech. 30 B8 49 30N 15 40 E
Český Brod, Czech. 30 A7 50 4N 14 52 E
Český Krumlov, Czech. 30 C7 48 43N 14 21 E
Český Těšin, Czech. 31 B11 49 45N 18 39 E
Çeşme, Turkey 45 F8 38 20N 26 23 E
Cessnock, Australia 117 B9 32 50 S 151 21 E
Cestos →, Liberia 100 D3 5 40N 9 10W
Cetate, Romania 46 E4 44 7N 23 2 E
Cétin Grad, Yugoslavia 39 C12 45 9N 15 45 E
Cetina →, Yugoslavia 39 E13 43 26N 16 42 E
Cetinje, Yugoslavia 42 E3 42 23N 18 59 E
Cetraro, Italy 41 C8 39 30N 15 56 E
Ceuta, Morocco 98 A3 35 52N 5 18W
Ceva, Italy 38 D5 44 23N 8 3 E
Cévennes, France 24 D7 44 10N 3 50 E
Ceyhan, Turkey 88 E6 37 4N 35 47 E
Ceyhan →, Turkey 88 E6 36 38N 35 40 E
Ceylânpınar, Turkey 89 E9 36 50N 40 2 E
Ceylon = Sri Lanka ■, Asia 83 L5 7 30N 80 50 E
Cèze →, France 25 D8 44 6N 4 43 E
Cha-am, Thailand 76 F2 12 48N 99 58 E
Chá Pungana, Angola 103 E3 13 44 S 18 39 E
Chaam, Neths. 21 F5 51 30N 4 52 E
Chabeuil, France 25 D9 44 54N 5 3 E
Chablais, France 25 B10 46 20N 6 36 E
Chablis, France 23 E10 47 47N 3 48 E
Chabounia, Algeria 99 A5 35 30N 2 38 E
Chacabuco, Argentina 158 C3 34 40 S 60 27W
Chachapoyas, Peru 156 B2 6 15 S 77 50W
Chachasp, Peru 156 D3 15 30 S 72 15W
Chachoengsao, Thailand 76 F3 13 42N 101 5 E
Chachro, Pakistan 80 G4 25 5N 70 15 E
Chaco □, Argentina 158 B3 26 30 S 61 0W
Chaco □, Paraguay 158 B4 26 0 S 60 0W
Chad ■, Africa 97 F3 15 0N 17 15 E
Chad, L. = Tchad, L., Chad 97 F2 13 30N 14 30 E
Chadan, U.S.S.R. 57 D10 51 17N 91 35 E
Chadarinskoye Vdkhr., U.S.S.R. 55 C4 41 0N 68 20 E
Chadileuvú →, Argentina 158 D2 37 46 S 66 0W
Chadiza, Zambia 107 E3 14 45 S 32 27 E
Chadron, U.S.A. 138 D3 42 50N 103 0W
Chadyr-Lunga, U.S.S.R. 52 C3 46 3N 28 51 E
Chae Hom, Thailand 76 C2 18 43N 99 35 E
Chaem →, Thailand 76 C2 18 11N 98 38 E
Chaeryŏng, N. Korea 67 E13 38 24N 125 36 E
Chagda, U.S.S.R. 57 D14 58 45N 130 38 E
Chagny, France 23 F11 46 57N 4 45 E
Chagoda, U.S.S.R. 50 B9 59 10N 35 15 E
Chagos Arch., Ind. Oc. 58 K11 6 0 S 72 0 E
Chāh Ākhvor, Iran 85 C8 32 41N 59 40 E
Chāh Bahār, Iran 85 E9 25 20N 60 40 E
Chāh-e-Malek, Iran 85 D8 28 35N 59 7 E
Chāh Gay Hills, Afghan. 79 C2 29 30N 64 0 E
Chāh Kavīr, Iran 85 D7 31 45N 54 52 E
Chahār Borjak, Afghan. 79 C1 30 17N 62 3 E
Chahtung, Burma 78 B7 26 41N 98 10 E
Chaillé-les-Marais, France 24 B2 46 25N 1 2W
Chainat, Thailand 76 E3 15 11N 100 8 E
Chaitén, Chile 160 B2 42 55 S 72 43W
Chaiya, Thailand 77 H2 9 23N 99 14 E
Chaj Doab, Pakistan 80 C5 32 15N 73 0 E
Chajari, Argentina 158 C4 30 42 S 58 0W
Chakaria, Bangla. 78 E4 21 45N 92 5 E
Chake Chake, Tanzania 106 D4 5 15 S 39 45 E
Chakhānsūr, Afghan. 79 C1 31 10N 62 0 E
Chakonipau, L., Canada 129 A6 56 18N 68 30W
Chakradharpur, India 81 H11 22 45N 85 40 E
Chakwadam, Burma 78 B7 27 29N 98 31 E
Chakwal, Pakistan 79 B4 32 56N 72 53 E
Chala, Peru 156 D3 15 48 S 74 20W
Chalais, France 24 C4 45 16N 0 3 E
Chalakudi, India 83 J3 10 18N 76 20 E
Chalchihuites, Mexico 146 C4 23 29N 103 53W
Chalcis = Khalkís, Greece 45 F5 38 27N 23 42 E
Chaleur B., Canada 129 C6 47 55N 65 30W
Chalfant, U.S.A. 144 H8 37 32N 118 21W
Chalhuanca, Peru 156 C3 14 15 S 73 15W
Chalindrey, France 23 E12 47 43N 5 26 E
Chaling, China 69 D9 26 58N 113 30 E
Chalisgaon, India 82 D2 20 30N 75 10 E
Chalkar, U.S.S.R. 53 A14 50 40N 51 53 E
Chalkar, Ozero, U.S.S.R. 53 A14 50 50N 51 50 E
Chalky Inlet, N.Z. 119 G1 46 3 S 166 31 E
Challans, France 22 F5 46 50N 1 52W
Challapata, Bolivia 156 D4 18 53 S 66 50W
Challis, U.S.A. 142 D6 44 32N 114 25W
Chalna, India 81 H13 22 36N 89 35 E
Chalon-sur-Saône, France 23 F11 46 48N 4 50 E
Chalonnes-sur-Loire, France 22 E6 47 20N 0 45W
Châlons-sur-Marne, France 23 D11 48 58N 4 20 E
Châlus, France 24 C4 45 39N 0 58 E
Chalyaphum, Thailand 76 E4 15 48N 102 2 E
Cham, Germany 27 F8 49 12N 12 40 E
Cham, Switz. 29 B6 47 11N 8 28 E
Cham, Cu Lao, Vietnam 76 E7 15 57N 108 30 E
Chama, U.S.A. 143 H10 36 54N 106 35W
Chaman, Pakistan 79 C2 30 58N 66 25 E
Chamba, India 80 C7 32 35N 76 10 E
Chamba, Tanzania 107 E4 11 37 S 37 0 E
Chambal →, India 81 F8 26 29N 79 15 E
Chamberlain, U.S.A. 138 D5 43 50N 99 21W
Chamberlain →, Australia 112 C4 15 30 S 127 54 E
Chambers, U.S.A. 143 J9 35 13N 109 30W
Chambersburg, U.S.A. 134 F7 39 53N 77 41W
Chambéry, France 25 C9 45 34N 5 55 E
Chambly, Canada 137 A11 45 27N 73 17W
Chambord, Canada 129 C5 48 25N 72 6W
Chambri L., Papua N. G. 120 C2 4 15 S 143 10 E
Chamchamal, Iraq 84 C5 35 32N 44 50 E
Chamela, Mexico 146 D3 19 32N 105 5W
Chamical, Argentina 158 C2 30 22 S 66 27W
Chamkar Luong, Cambodia 77 G4 11 0N 103 45 E
Chamois, U.S.A. 140 F5 38 41N 91 46W
Chamonix-Mont-Blanc, France 25 C10 45 55N 6 51 E
Champa, India 81 H10 22 2N 82 43 E
Champagne, Canada 130 A1 60 49N 136 30W
Champagne, France 23 D11 48 40N 4 20 E
Champagne, Plaine de, France 23 D11 49 0N 4 30 E
Champagnole, France 23 F12 46 45N 5 55 E
Champaign, U.S.A. 141 D8 40 8N 88 14W
Champassak, Laos 76 E5 14 53N 105 52 E
Champaubert, France 23 D10 48 50N 3 45 E
Champdeniers, France 24 B3 46 29N 0 25W
Champeix, France 24 C7 45 37N 3 8 E
Champlain, Canada 134 B9 46 27N 72 24W
Champlain, U.S.A. 137 B11 44 59N 73 27W
Champlain, L., U.S.A. 137 B11 44 30N 73 20W
Champotón, Mexico 147 D6 19 20N 90 50W
Chamrajnagar, India 83 J3 11 52N 76 52 E
Chamusca, Portugal 37 F2 39 21N 8 29W
Chan Chan, Peru 156 B2 8 7 S 79 0W
Chana, Thailand 77 J3 6 55N 100 44 E
Chañaral, Chile 158 B1 26 23 S 70 40W
Chanārān, Iran 85 B8 36 39N 59 6 E
Chanasma, India 80 H5 23 44N 72 5 E
Chancay, Peru 156 C2 11 32 S 77 25W
Chancy, Switz. 28 D1 46 8N 5 58 E
Chandannagar, India 81 H13 22 52N 88 24 E
Chandausi, India 81 E8 28 27N 78 49 E
Chandeleur Is., U.S.A. 139 L10 29 48N 88 51W
Chandeleur Sd., U.S.A. 139 L10 29 58N 88 40W
Chandigarh, India 80 D7 30 43N 76 47 E
Chandler, Australia 115 D1 27 0 S 133 19 E
Chandler, Canada 129 C7 48 18N 64 46W
Chandler, Ariz., U.S.A. 143 K8 33 20N 111 56W
Chandler, Okla., U.S.A. 139 H6 35 43N 96 53W
Chandlers Pk., Australia 117 A9 30 15 S 151 48 E
Chandless →, Brazil 156 B4 9 8 S 69 51W
Chandpur, Bangla. 78 D3 23 8N 90 45 E
Chandpur, India 80 E8 29 8N 78 19 E
Chandrapur, India 82 E4 19 57N 79 25 E
Chānf, Iran 85 E9 26 38N 60 29 E
Chang, Pakistan 80 F3 26 59N 68 30 E
Chang, Ko, Thailand 77 G4 12 0N 102 23 E
Chang Jiang →, China 69 B13 31 48N 121 10 E
Changa, India 81 C7 33 53N 77 35 E
Changanacheri, India 83 K3 9 25N 76 31 E
Changane →, Mozam. 105 C5 24 30 S 33 30 E
Changbai, China 67 D15 41 25N 128 5 E
Changbai Shan, China 67 C15 42 20N 129 0 E
Changchiak'ou = Zhangjiakou, China 66 D8 40 48N 114 55 E
Ch'angchou = Changzhou, China 69 B12 31 47N 119 58 E
Changchun, China 67 C13 43 57N 125 17 E
Changchunling, China 67 B13 45 18N 125 27 E
Changde, China 69 C8 29 4N 111 35 E
Changdo-ri, N. Korea 67 E14 38 30N 127 40 E
Changfeng, China 69 A11 32 28N 117 10 E
Changhai = Shanghai, China 69 B13 31 15N 121 26 E
Changhua, China 69 B12 30 12N 119 12 E
Changhŭng, S. Korea 67 G14 34 41N 126 52 E
Changhŭngni, N. Korea 67 D15 40 24N 128 19 E
Changjiang, China 76 C7 19 20N 108 55 E
Changjin, N. Korea 67 D14 40 23N 127 15 E
Changjin-chŏsuji, N. Korea 67 D14 40 30N 127 15 E
Changle, China 69 E12 25 59N 119 27 E
Changli, China 67 E10 39 40N 119 13 E
Changling, China 67 B12 44 20N 123 58 E
Changlun, Malaysia 77 J3 6 25N 100 26 E
Changning, Hunan, China 69 D9 26 28N 112 22 E
Changning, Yunnan, China 68 E2 24 45N 99 30 E
Changping, China 66 D9 40 14N 116 12 E
Changsha, China 69 C9 28 12N 113 0 E
Changshan, China 69 C12 28 55N 118 27 E
Changshou, China 68 C6 29 51N 107 8 E
Changshu, China 69 B13 31 38N 120 43 E
Changshun, China 68 D6 26 3N 106 25 E
Changtai, China 69 E11 24 35N 117 42 E
Changting, China 69 E11 25 50N 116 22 E
Changwu, China 66 G4 35 10N 107 45 E
Changxing, China 69 B12 31 0N 119 55 E
Changyang, China 69 B8 30 30N 111 10 E
Changyi, China 67 F10 36 40N 119 30 E
Changyŏn, N. Korea 67 E13 38 15N 125 6 E
Changyuan, China 66 G8 35 15N 114 42 E
Changzhi, China 66 F7 36 10N 113 6 E
Changzhou, China 69 B12 31 47N 119 58 E
Chanhanga, Angola 103 F2 16 0 S 14 8 E
Chanlar, U.S.S.R. 53 F12 40 25N 46 10 E
Channapatna, India 83 H3 12 40N 77 15 E
Channel Is., U.K. 17 H5 49 30N 2 40W
Channel Is., U.S.A. 145 M7 33 55N 119 26W
Channel-Port aux Basques, Canada 129 C8 47 30N 59 9W
Channing, Mich., U.S.A. 134 B1 46 9N 88 1W
Channing, Tex., U.S.A. 139 H3 35 45N 102 20W
Chantada, Spain 36 C3 42 36N 7 46W
Chanthaburi, Thailand 76 F4 12 38N 102 12 E
Chantilly, France 23 C9 49 12N 2 29 E
Chantonnay, France 22 F5 46 40N 1 3W
Chantrey Inlet, Canada 126 B10 67 48N 96 20W
Chanute, U.S.A. 139 G7 37 45N 95 25W
Chanza →, Spain 37 H3 37 32N 7 30W
Chao Hu, China 69 B11 31 30N 117 30 E
Chao Phraya →, Thailand 76 F3 13 32N 100 36 E
Chao Phraya Lowlands, Thailand 76 E3 15 30N 100 0 E
Chao Xian, China 69 B11 31 38N 117 50 E
Chao'an, China 69 F11 23 42N 116 32 E
Chaocheng, China 66 F8 36 4N 115 37 E
Chaoyang, Guangdong, China 69 F11 23 17N 116 30 E
Chaoyang, Liaoning, China 67 D11 41 35N 120 22 E
Chapada dos Guimarães, Brazil 157 D6 15 26 S 55 45W
Chapala, Mozam. 107 F4 15 50 S 37 35 E
Chapala, L. de, Mexico 146 C4 20 10N 103 20W

184 Chaparé

Chaparé →, *Bolivia* **157 D5** 15 58 S 64 42W
Chaparmukh, *India* **78 B4** 26 12N 92 31 E
Chaparral, *Colombia* **152 C2** 3 43N 75 28W
Chapayevo, *U.S.S.R.* **53 A14** 50 25N 51 10 E
Chapayevsk, *U.S.S.R.* **51 E16** 53 0N 49 40 E
Chapecó, *Brazil* **159 B5** 27 14 S 52 41W
Chapel Hill, *U.S.A.* **135 H6** 35 53N 79 3W
Chapeyevo, *U.S.S.R.* **54 F2** 50 12N 51 10 E
Chapin, *U.S.A.* **140 E6** 39 46N 90 24W
Chapleau, *Canada* **128 C3** 47 50N 83 24W
Chaplin, *Canada* **131 C7** 50 28N 106 40W
Chaplino, *U.S.S.R.* **52 B7** 48 8N 36 15 E
Chaplygin, *U.S.S.R.* **51 E12** 53 15N 40 0 E
Châr, *Mauritania* **98 D2** 21 32N 12 45W
Chara, *U.S.S.R.* **57 D12** 56 54N 118 20 E
Charadai, *Argentina* **158 B4** 27 35 S 59 55W
Charagua, *Bolivia* **157 D5** 19 45 S 63 10W
Charalá, *Colombia* **152 B3** 6 17N 73 10W
Charambirá, Punta, *Colombia* **152 C2** 4 16N 77 32W
Charaña, *Bolivia* **156 D4** 17 30 S 69 25W
Charapita, *Colombia* **152 D3** 0 37 S 74 21W
Charata, *Argentina* **158 B3** 27 13 S 61 14W
Charcas, *Mexico* **146 C4** 23 10N 101 20W
Charcoal L., *Canada* **131 B8** 58 49N 102 22W
Chard, *U.K.* **17 G5** 50 52N 2 59W
Chardara, *U.S.S.R.* **55 C3** 41 16N 67 59 E
Chardara, Step, *U.S.S.R.* **55 B4** 42 20N 68 0 E
Chardarinskoye Vdkhr., *U.S.S.R.* **55 C4** 41 10N 68 15 E
Chardon, *U.S.A.* **136 E3** 41 34N 81 17W
Charduar, *India* **78 B4** 26 51N 92 46 E
Chardzhou, *U.S.S.R.* **55 D1** 39 6N 63 34 E
Charente □, *France* **24 C4** 45 50N 0 16 E
Charente →, *France* **24 C2** 45 57N 1 5W
Charente-Maritime □, *France* **24 C3** 45 45N 0 45W
Charentsavan, *U.S.S.R.* **53 F11** 40 35N 44 41 E
Chari →, *Chad* **97 F2** 12 58N 14 31 E
Chārīkār, *Afghan.* **79 B3** 35 0N 69 10 E
Chariton, *U.S.A.* **140 C3** 41 1N 93 19W
Chariton →, *U.S.A.* **140 E4** 39 19N 92 58W
Charity, *Guyana* **153 B6** 7 24N 58 36W
Charkhari, *India* **81 G8** 25 24N 79 45 E
Charkhi Dadri, *India* **80 E7** 28 37N 76 17 E
Charleroi, *Belgium* **21 H4** 50 24N 4 27 E
Charleroi, *U.S.A.* **136 F5** 40 8N 79 54W
Charles, C., *U.S.A.* **134 G8** 37 10N 75 59W
Charles City, *U.S.A.* **140 A4** 43 2N 92 41W
Charles L., *Canada* **131 B6** 59 50N 110 33W
Charles Sound, *N.Z.* **119 F2** 45 2 S 167 4 E
Charles Town, *U.S.A.* **134 F7** 39 20N 77 50W
Charleston, *Ill., U.S.A.* **134 F1** 39 30N 88 10W
Charleston, *Ill., U.S.A.* **141 E8** 39 30N 88 10W
Charleston, *Miss., U.S.A.* **139 H9** 34 2N 90 3W
Charleston, *Mo., U.S.A.* **139 G10** 36 52N 89 20W
Charleston, *S.C., U.S.A.* **135 J6** 32 47N 79 56W
Charleston, *W. Va., U.S.A.* **134 F5** 38 24N 81 36W
Charleston Pk., *U.S.A.* **145 J11** 36 16N 115 42W
Charlestown, *S. Africa* **105 D4** 27 26 S 29 53 E
Charlestown, *U.S.A.* **141 F11** 38 29N 85 40W
Charlesville, *Zaïre* **103 D4** 5 27 S 20 59 E
Charleville = Rath Luirc, *Ireland* **19 D3** 52 21N 8 40W
Charleville, *Australia* **115 D4** 26 24 S 146 15 E
Charleville-Mézières, *France* **23 C11** 49 44N 4 40 E
Charlevoix, *U.S.A.* **134 C3** 45 19N 85 14W
Charlieu, *France* **25 B8** 46 10N 4 10 E
Charlotte, *Mich., U.S.A.* **141 B12** 42 36N 84 48W
Charlotte, *N.C., U.S.A.* **135 H5** 35 16N 80 46W
Charlotte Amalie, *Virgin Is.* **149 C7** 18 22N 64 56W
Charlotte Harbor, *U.S.A.* **135 M4** 26 58N 82 4W
Charlottesville, *U.S.A.* **134 F6** 38 1N 78 30W
Charlottetown, *Canada* **129 C7** 46 14N 63 8W
Charlton, *Australia* **116 D5** 36 16 S 143 24 E
Charlton, *U.S.A.* **138 E8** 40 59N 93 20W
Charlton I., *Canada* **128 B4** 52 0N 79 20W
Charmes, *France* **23 D13** 48 22N 6 17 E
Charny, *Canada* **129 C5** 46 43N 71 15W
Charolles, *France* **25 B8** 46 27N 4 16 E
Chârost, *France* **23 F9** 46 58N 2 7 E
Charouine, *Algeria* **99 C4** 29 0N 0 15W
Charre, *Mozam.* **107 F4** 17 13 S 35 10 E
Charroux, *France* **24 B4** 46 9N 0 25 E
Charsadda, *Pakistan* **80 B4** 34 7N 71 45 E
Charters Towers, *Australia* **114 C4** 20 5 S 146 13 E
Chartres, *France* **22 D8** 48 29N 1 30 E
Charvakskoye Vdkhr., *U.S.S.R.* **55 C5** 41 35N 70 0 E
Chascomús, *Argentina* **158 D4** 35 30 S 58 0W
Chasefu, *Zambia* **107 E3** 11 55 S 33 8 E
Chaslands Mistake, *N.Z.* **119 G4** 46 38 S 169 22 E
Chasovnya-Uchurskaya, *U.S.S.R.* **57 D14** 57 15N 132 50 E
Chasseneuil-sur-Bonnieure, *France* **24 C4** 45 52N 0 29 E
Chāt, *Iran* **85 B7** 37 59N 55 16 E
Chatal Balkan = Udvoy Balkan, *Bulgaria* **43 E11** 42 50N 26 50 E
Château-Arnoux, *France* **25 D10** 44 6N 6 0 E
Château-Chinon, *France* **23 E10** 47 4N 3 56 E
Château d'Oex, *Switz.* **28 D4** 46 28N 7 8 E
Château-du-Loir, *France* **22 E7** 47 40N 0 25 E
Château-Gontier, *France* **22 E6** 47 50N 0 48W
Château-la-Vallière, *France* **22 E7** 47 30N 0 20 E
Château-Landon, *France* **23 D9** 48 8N 2 40 E
Château-Porcien, *France* **23 C11** 49 31N 4 13 E
Château-Renault, *France* **22 E7** 47 36N 0 56 E
Château-Salins, *France* **23 D13** 48 50N 6 30 E
Château-Thierry, *France* **23 C10** 49 3N 3 20 E
Châteaubourg, *France* **22 D5** 48 7N 1 25W
Châteaubriant, *France* **22 E5** 47 43N 1 23W
Châteaudun, *France* **22 D8** 48 3N 1 20 E
Châteaugiron, *France* **22 D5** 48 3N 1 30W
Châteaulin, *France* **22 D2** 48 11N 4 8W
Châteaumeillant, *France* **24 B6** 46 35N 2 12 E
Châteauneuf-du-Faou, *France* **22 D3** 48 11N 3 50W
Châteauneuf-en-Thymerais, *France* **22 D8** 48 35N 1 13 E
Châteauneuf-sur-Charente, *France* **24 C3** 45 36N 0 3W
Châteauneuf-sur-Cher, *France* **23 F9** 46 52N 2 18 E
Châteauneuf-sur-Loire, *France* **23 E9** 47 52N 2 13 E
Châteaurenard, *Bouches-du-Rhône, France* **25 E8** 43 53N 4 51 E
Châteaurenard, *Loiret, France* **23 E9** 47 56N 2 55 E
Châteauroux, *France* **23 F8** 46 50N 1 40 E
Châtel-St.-Denis, *Switz.* **28 C3** 46 32N 6 54 E
Châtelaillon-Plage, *France* **24 B2** 46 5N 1 5W
Châtelaudren, *France* **22 D4** 48 33N 2 59W
Chatelet, *Belgium* **21 H5** 50 24N 4 32 E
Châtelguyon, *France* **24 C7** 45 55N 3 4 E
Châtellerault, *France* **22 F7** 46 50N 0 30 E
Châtelus-Malvaleix, *France* **24 B6** 46 18N 2 1 E
Chatfield, *U.S.A.* **138 D9** 43 15N 91 58W
Chatham, *N.B., Canada* **129 C6** 47 2N 65 28W
Chatham, *Ont., Canada* **128 D3** 42 24N 82 11W
Chatham, *U.K.* **17 F8** 51 22N 0 32 E
Chatham, *Ill., U.S.A.* **140 E7** 39 40N 89 42W
Chatham, *La., U.S.A.* **139 J8** 32 22N 92 26W
Chatham, *N.Y., U.S.A.* **137 D11** 42 21N 73 32W
Chatham, I., *Chile* **160 D2** 50 40 S 74 25W
Chatham Is., *Pac. Oc.* **122 M10** 44 0 S 176 40W
Chatham Str., *U.S.A.* **130 B2** 57 0N 134 40W
Chatillon, *Italy* **38 C4** 45 45N 7 40 E
Châtillon-Coligny, *France* **23 E9** 47 50N 2 51 E
Châtillon-en-Bazois, *France* **23 E10** 47 3N 3 39 E
Châtillon-en-Diois, *France* **25 D9** 44 41N 5 29 E
Châtillon-sur-Indre, *France* **22 F8** 46 59N 1 10 E
Châtillon-sur-Loire, *France* **23 E9** 47 35N 2 44 E
Châtillon-sur-Marne, *France* **23 C10** 49 6N 3 44 E
Châtillon-sur-Seine, *France* **23 E11** 47 50N 4 33 E
Chatkal →, *U.S.S.R.* **55 C5** 41 38N 70 1 E
Chatkalskiy Khrebet, *U.S.S.R.* **55 C5** 41 30N 70 45 E
Chatmohar, *Bangla.* **81 G13** 24 15N 89 15 E
Chatra, *India* **81 G11** 24 12N 84 56 E
Chatrapur, *India* **82 E7** 19 22N 85 2 E
Chats, L. des, *Canada* **137 A8** 45 30N 76 20W
Chatsworth, *Canada* **136 B4** 44 27N 80 54W
Chatsworth, *U.S.A.* **141 D8** 40 45N 88 18W
Chatsworth, *Zimbabwe* **107 F3** 19 38 S 31 13 E
Chatta-Hantō, *Japan* **63 C8** 34 45N 136 55 E
Chattahoochee →, *U.S.A.* **135 K3** 30 43N 84 51W
Chattanooga, *U.S.A.* **135 H3** 35 2N 85 17W
Chaturat, *Thailand* **76 E3** 15 40N 101 51 E
Chatyrkel, Ozero, *U.S.S.R.* **55 C7** 40 40N 75 18 E
Chatyrtash, *U.S.S.R.* **55 C8** 40 55N 76 25 E
Chau Doc, *Vietnam* **77 G5** 10 42N 105 7 E
Chaudanne, Barr. de, *France* **25 E10** 43 51N 6 32 E
Chaudes-Aigues, *France* **24 D7** 44 51N 3 1 E
Chauffailles, *France* **25 B8** 46 13N 4 20 E
Chauk, *Burma* **78 E5** 20 53N 94 49 E
Chaukan Pass, *Burma* **78 B6** 27 8N 97 10 E
Chaulnes, *France* **23 C9** 49 48N 2 47 E
Chaumont, *France* **23 D12** 48 7N 5 8 E
Chaumont, *U.S.A.* **137 B8** 44 4N 76 9W
Chaumont-en-Vexin, *France* **23 C8** 49 16N 1 53 E
Chaumont-sur-Loire, *France* **22 E8** 47 29N 1 11 E
Chaunay, *France* **24 B4** 46 13N 0 9 E
Chauny, *France* **23 C10** 49 37N 3 12 E
Chausey, Is., *France* **22 D5** 48 52N 1 49W
Chaussin, *France* **23 F12** 46 59N 5 22 E
Chautauqua L., *U.S.A.* **136 D5** 42 7N 79 30W
Chauvigny, *France* **22 F7** 46 34N 0 39 E
Chauvin, *Canada* **131 C6** 52 45N 110 10W
Chavantina, *Brazil* **157 C7** 14 40 S 52 21W
Chaves, *Brazil* **154 B2** 0 15 S 49 55W
Chaves, *Portugal* **36 D3** 41 45N 7 32W
Chavuma, *Zambia* **103 E4** 13 4 S 22 40 E
Chawang, *Thailand* **77 H2** 8 25N 99 30 E
Chayan, *U.S.S.R.* **55 B4** 43 5N 69 25 E
Chayek, *U.S.S.R.* **55 C7** 41 55N 74 30 E
Chaykovskiy, *U.S.S.R.* **54 C4** 56 47N 54 9 E
Chazelles-sur-Lyon, *France* **25 C8** 45 39N 4 22 E
Chazuta, *Peru* **156 B2** 6 30 S 76 0W
Chazy, *U.S.A.* **137 B11** 44 52N 73 28W
Cheb, *Czech.* **30 A5** 50 9N 12 28 E
Chebanse, *U.S.A.* **141 D9** 41 0N 87 54W
Chebarkul, *U.S.S.R.* **54 D7** 55 0N 60 25 E
Cheboksary, *U.S.S.R.* **51 C15** 56 8N 47 12 E
Cheboygan, *U.S.A.* **134 C3** 45 38N 84 29W
Chebsara, *U.S.S.R.* **51 B11** 59 10N 38 59 E
Chech, Erg, *Africa* **98 D4** 25 0N 2 15W
Chechaouen, *Morocco* **98 A3** 35 9N 5 15W
Chechen, Os., *U.S.S.R.* **53 E12** 43 59N 47 40 E
Checheno-Ingush A.S.S.R. □, *U.S.S.R.* **53 E11** 43 30N 45 29 E
Chechon, *S. Korea* **67 F15** 37 8N 128 12 E
Chęciny, *Poland* **47 E7** 50 46N 20 28 E
Checleset B., *Canada* **130 C3** 50 5N 127 35W
Checotah, *U.S.A.* **139 H7** 35 31N 95 30W
Chedabucto B., *Canada* **129 C7** 45 25N 61 8W
Cheduba I., *Burma* **78 F4** 18 45N 93 40 E
Cheepie, *Australia* **115 D4** 26 33 S 145 1 E
Chef-Boutonne, *France* **24 B3** 46 7N 0 4W
Chegdomyn, *U.S.S.R.* **57 D14** 51 7N 133 1 E
Chegga, *Mauritania* **98 C3** 25 27N 5 40W
Chegutu, *Zimbabwe* **107 F3** 18 10 S 30 14 E
Chehalis, *U.S.A.* **144 D4** 46 44N 122 59W
Cheiron, Mt., *France* **25 E10** 43 49N 6 58 E
Cheju Do, *S. Korea* **67 H14** 33 29N 126 34 E
Chekalin, *U.S.S.R.* **51 D10** 54 10N 36 10 E
Chekiang = Zhejiang □, *China* **69 C13** 29 0N 120 0 E
Chel = Kuru, Bahr el →, *Sudan* **95 F2** 8 10N 26 50 E
Chela, Sa. da, *Angola* **103 F2** 16 20 S 13 20 E
Chelan, *U.S.A.* **142 C4** 47 49N 120 0W
Chelan, L., *U.S.A.* **142 B3** 48 5N 120 30W
Cheleken, *U.S.S.R.* **49 G9** 39 26N 53 7 E
Chelforó, *Argentina* **160 A3** 39 0 S 66 33W
Chéliff, O. →, *Algeria* **99 A5** 36 0N 0 8 E
Chelkar, *U.S.S.R.* **56 E6** 47 48N 59 39 E
Chelkar Tengiz, Solonchak, *U.S.S.R.* **56 E7** 48 0N 62 30 E
Chellala Dahrania, *Algeria* **99 B5** 33 2N 0 1 E
Chelles, *France* **23 D9** 48 52N 2 33 E
Chełm, *Poland* **47 D10** 51 8N 23 30 E
Chełm □, *Poland* **47 D10** 51 15N 23 30 E
Chełmek, *Poland* **31 A12** 50 6N 19 16 E
Chełmno, *Poland* **47 B5** 53 20N 18 30 E
Chelmsford, *U.K.* **17 F8** 51 44N 0 29 E
Chelmsford Dam, *S. Africa* **105 D4** 27 55 S 29 59 E
Chełmża, *Poland* **47 B5** 53 10N 18 39 E
Chelsea, *Australia* **117 E6** 38 5 S 145 8 E
Chelsea, *Mich., U.S.A.* **141 B12** 42 19N 84 1W
Chelsea, *Okla., U.S.A.* **139 G7** 36 35N 95 35W
Chelsea, *Vt., U.S.A.* **137 C12** 43 59N 72 27W
Cheltenham, *U.K.* **17 F5** 51 55N 2 5W
Chelva, *Spain* **34 F4** 39 45N 1 0W
Chelyabinsk, *U.S.S.R.* **54 D7** 55 10N 61 24 E
Chelyuskin, C., *U.S.S.R.* **58 B14** 77 30N 103 0 E
Chemainus, *Canada* **130 D4** 48 55N 123 42W
Chembar = Belinskiy, *U.S.S.R.* **51 E13** 53 0N 43 25 E
Chemillé, *France* **22 E6** 47 14N 0 45W
Chemnitz, *Germany* **26 E8** 50 50N 12 55 E
Chemult, *U.S.A.* **142 E3** 43 14N 121 47W
Chen, Gora, *U.S.S.R.* **57 C15** 65 16N 141 50 E
Chen Xian, *China* **69 E9** 25 47N 113 1 E
Chenab →, *Pakistan* **79 C3** 30 23N 71 2 E
Chenachane, O. →, *Algeria* **98 C4** 25 20N 3 20W
Chenango Forks, *U.S.A.* **137 D9** 42 15N 75 51W
Chencha, *Ethiopia* **95 F4** 6 15N 37 32 E
Chenchiang = Zhenjiang, *China* **69 A12** 32 11N 119 26 E
Chênée, *Belgium* **21 G7** 50 37N 5 37 E
Cheney, *U.S.A.* **142 C5** 47 29N 117 34W
Cheng Xian, *China* **66 H3** 33 43N 105 42 E
Chengalpattu, *India* **83 H4** 12 42N 79 58 E
Chengbu, *China* **69 D8** 26 18N 110 16 E
Chengcheng, *China* **66 G5** 35 8N 109 56 E
Chengchou = Zhengzhou, *China* **66 G7** 34 45N 113 34 E
Chengde, *China* **67 D9** 40 59N 117 58 E
Chengdong Hu, *China* **69 A11** 32 15N 116 20 E
Chengdu, *China* **68 B5** 30 38N 104 2 E
Chengele, *India* **78 A6** 28 47N 96 16 E
Chenggong, *China* **68 E4** 24 52N 102 56 E
Chenggu, *China* **66 H4** 33 10N 107 21 E
Chengjiang, *China* **68 E4** 24 39N 103 0 E
Chengkou, *China* **68 B7** 31 54N 108 31 E
Ch'engtu = Chengdu, *China* **68 B5** 30 38N 104 2 E
Chengwu, *China* **66 G8** 34 58N 115 50 E
Chengxi Hu, *China* **69 A11** 32 15N 116 10 E
Chengyang, *China* **67 F11** 36 18N 120 21 E
Chenjiagang, *China* **67 G10** 34 23N 119 47 E
Chenkán, *Mexico* **147 D6** 19 8N 90 58W
Chenoa, *U.S.A.* **141 D8** 40 45N 88 42W
Chenxi, *China* **69 C8** 28 2N 110 12 E
Cheo Reo, *Vietnam* **76 F7** 13 25N 108 28 E
Cheom Ksan, *Cambodia* **76 E5** 14 13N 104 56 E
Chepelare, *Bulgaria* **43 F9** 41 44N 24 40 E
Chepén, *Peru* **156 B2** 7 15 S 79 23W
Chépénéhé, *Vanuatu* **121 K5** 20 47 S 167 9 E
Chepes, *Argentina* **158 C2** 31 20 S 66 35W
Chepo, *Panama* **148 E4** 9 10N 79 6W
Cheptsa →, *U.S.S.R.* **51 B17** 58 36N 50 4 E
Cheptulil, Mt., *Kenya* **106 B4** 1 25N 35 35 E
Chequamegon B., *U.S.A.* **138 B9** 46 40N 90 30W
Cher □, *France* **23 E9** 47 10N 2 30 E
Cher →, *France* **22 E7** 47 21N 0 29 E
Cheran, *India* **78 C3** 25 45N 90 44 E
Cherasco, *Italy* **38 D4** 44 39N 7 50 E
Cheratte, *Belgium* **21 G7** 50 40N 5 41 E
Cheraw, *U.S.A.* **135 H6** 34 42N 79 54W
Cherbourg, *France* **22 C5** 49 39N 1 40W
Cherchell, *Algeria* **99 A5** 36 35N 2 12 E
Cherdakly, *U.S.S.R.* **51 D16** 54 25N 48 50 E
Cherdyn, *U.S.S.R.* **54 A5** 60 24N 56 29 E
Cheremkhovo, *U.S.S.R.* **57 D11** 53 8N 103 1 E
Cherepanovo, *U.S.S.R.* **56 D9** 54 15N 83 30 E
Cherepovets, *U.S.S.R.* **51 B10** 59 5N 37 55 E
Chergui, Chott ech, *Algeria* **99 B5** 34 21N 0 25 E
Cherikov, *U.S.S.R.* **50 E7** 53 32N 31 20 E
Cherkassy, *U.S.S.R.* **52 B5** 49 27N 32 4 E
Cherkessk, *U.S.S.R.* **53 D10** 44 15N 42 5 E
Cherlak, *U.S.S.R.* **56 D8** 54 15N 74 55 E
Chermoz, *U.S.S.R.* **54 B5** 58 46N 56 10 E
Chernak, *U.S.S.R.* **55 B4** 43 24N 68 2 E
Chernaya Kholunitsa, *U.S.S.R.* **54 B2** 58 51N 51 52 E
Cherni, *Bulgaria* **43 E8** 42 35N 23 18 E
Chernigov, *U.S.S.R.* **50 F7** 51 28N 31 20 E
Chernikovsk, *U.S.S.R.* **54 D5** 54 48N 56 8 E
Chernobyl, *U.S.S.R.* **50 F7** 51 13N 30 15 E
Chernogorsk, *U.S.S.R.* **57 D10** 53 49N 91 18 E
Chernomorskoye, *U.S.S.R.* **52 D5** 45 31N 32 40 E
Chernovskoye, *U.S.S.R.* **51 B15** 58 48N 47 20 E
Chernovtsy, *U.S.S.R.* **52 B1** 48 15N 25 52 E
Chernoye, *U.S.S.R.* **57 B9** 70 30N 89 10 E
Chernushka, *U.S.S.R.* **54 C5** 56 29N 56 3 E
Chernyakhovsk, *U.S.S.R.* **50 D2** 54 36N 21 48 E
Chernyshkovskiy, *U.S.S.R.* **53 B10** 48 30N 42 13 E
Chernyshovskiy, *U.S.S.R.* **57 C12** 63 0N 112 30 E
Cherokee, *Iowa, U.S.A.* **138 D7** 42 40N 95 30W
Cherokee, *Okla., U.S.A.* **139 G5** 36 45N 98 25W
Cherokees, L. O'The, *U.S.A.* **139 G7** 36 50N 95 12W
Cherquenco, *Chile* **160 A2** 38 35 S 72 0W
Cherry Creek, *U.S.A.* **142 G6** 39 50N 114 58W
Cherry Valley, *U.S.A.* **145 M10** 33 59N 116 57W
Cherryvale, *U.S.A.* **139 G7** 37 20N 95 33W
Cherskiy, *U.S.S.R.* **57 C17** 68 45N 161 18 E
Cherskogo Khrebet, *U.S.S.R.* **57 C15** 65 0N 143 0 E
Chertkovo, *U.S.S.R.* **53 B9** 49 25N 40 19 E
Cherven, *U.S.S.R.* **50 E6** 53 45N 28 28 E
Cherven-Bryag, *Bulgaria* **43 D9** 43 17N 24 7 E
Chervonograd, *U.S.S.R.* **50 F4** 50 25N 24 10 E
Cherwell →, *U.K.* **17 F6** 51 46N 1 18W
Chesapeake, *U.S.A.* **134 G7** 36 43N 76 15W
Chesapeake B., *U.S.A.* **134 G7** 38 0N 76 12W
Cheshire □, *U.K.* **16 D5** 53 14N 2 30W
Cheshskaya Guba, *U.S.S.R.* **48 A8** 67 20N 47 0 E
Cheslatta L., *Canada* **130 C3** 53 49N 125 20W
Chesley, *Canada* **136 B3** 44 17N 81 5W
Cheste, *Spain* **35 F4** 39 30N 0 41W
Chester, *U.K.* **16 D5** 53 12N 2 53W
Chester, *Calif., U.S.A.* **142 F3** 40 22N 121 14W
Chester, *Ill., U.S.A.* **139 G10** 37 58N 89 50W
Chester, *Mont., U.S.A.* **142 B8** 48 31N 111 0W
Chester, *Pa., U.S.A.* **134 F8** 39 54N 75 20W
Chester, *S.C., U.S.A.* **135 H5** 34 44N 81 13W
Chesterfield, *U.K.* **16 D6** 53 14N 1 26W
Chesterfield, Is., *N. Cal.* **122 J7** 19 52 S 158 15 E
Chesterfield Inlet, *Canada* **126 B10** 63 30N 90 45W
Chesterton Ra., *Australia* **115 D4** 25 30 S 147 27 E
Chesterville, *Canada* **137 A9** 45 6N 75 14W
Chesuncook L., *U.S.A.* **129 C6** 46 0N 69 10W
Chetaibi, *Algeria* **99 A6** 37 1N 7 20 E
Chéticamp, *Canada* **129 C7** 46 37N 60 59W
Chetumal, B. de, *Mexico* **147 D7** 18 40N 88 10W
Chetwynd, *Canada* **130 B4** 55 45N 121 36W
Chevanceaux, *France* **24 C3** 45 18N 0 14W
Cheviot, *U.S.A.* **141 E12** 39 10N 84 37W
Cheviot, The, *U.K.* **16 B5** 55 29N 2 8W
Cheviot Hills, *U.K.* **16 B5** 55 20N 2 30W
Cheviot Ra., *Australia* **114 D3** 25 20 S 143 45 E
Chew Bahir, *Ethiopia* **95 G4** 4 40N 36 50 E
Chewelah, *U.S.A.* **142 B5** 48 17N 117 43W
Cheyenne, *Okla., U.S.A.* **139 H5** 35 35N 99 40W
Cheyenne, *Wyo., U.S.A.* **138 E2** 41 9N 104 49W
Cheyenne →, *U.S.A.* **138 C4** 44 40N 101 15W
Cheyenne Wells, *U.S.A.* **138 F3** 38 51N 102 10W
Cheyne B., *Australia* **113 F2** 34 35 S 118 50 E
Chhabra, *India* **80 G7** 24 40N 76 54 E
Chhapra, *India* **81 G11** 25 48N 84 44 E
Chhata, *India* **80 F7** 27 42N 77 30 E
Chhatak, *Bangla.* **78 C3** 25 5N 91 37 E
Chhatarpur, *India* **81 G8** 24 55N 79 35 E
Chhep, *Cambodia* **76 F5** 13 45N 105 24 E
Chhindwara, *India* **81 H8** 22 2N 78 59 E
Chhlong, *Cambodia* **77 F5** 12 15N 105 58 E
Chhuk, *Cambodia* **77 G5** 10 46N 104 28 E
Chi →, *Thailand* **76 E5** 15 11N 104 43 E
Chiamis, *Indonesia* **71 G13** 7 20 S 108 21 E
Chiamussu = Jiamusi, *China* **65 B8** 46 40N 130 26 E
Chiang Dao, *Thailand* **76 C2** 19 22N 98 58 E
Chiang Kham, *Thailand* **76 C3** 19 32N 100 18 E
Chiang Khan, *Thailand* **76 D3** 17 52N 101 36 E
Chiang Khong, *Thailand* **76 B3** 20 17N 100 24 E
Chiang Mai, *Thailand* **76 C2** 18 47N 98 59 E
Chiang Saen, *Thailand* **76 B3** 20 16N 100 5 E
Chiange, *Angola* **103 F2** 15 35 S 13 40 E
Chiapa →, *Mexico* **147 D6** 16 42N 93 0W
Chiapa de Corzo, *Mexico* **147 D6** 16 42N 93 0W
Chiapas □, *Mexico* **147 D6** 17 0N 92 45W
Chiaramonte Gulfi, *Italy* **41 E7** 37 1N 14 41 E
Chiaravalle, *Italy* **39 E10** 43 38N 13 17 E
Chiaravalle Centrale, *Italy* **41 D9** 38 41N 16 25 E
Chiari, *Italy* **38 C6** 45 31N 9 55 E
Chiasso, *Switz.* **29 E8** 45 50N 9 2 E
Chiatura, *U.S.S.R.* **53 E10** 42 15N 43 17 E
Chiautla, *Mexico* **147 D5** 18 18N 98 34W
Chiávari, *Italy* **38 D6** 44 20N 9 20 E
Chiavenna, *Italy* **38 B6** 46 18N 9 23 E
Chiba, *Japan* **63 B12** 35 30N 140 7 E
Chiba □, *Japan* **63 B12** 35 30N 140 20 E
Chibabava, *Mozam.* **105 C5** 20 17 S 33 35 E
Chibatu, *Indonesia* **71 G12** 7 6 S 107 59 E
Chibemba, *Cunene, Angola* **103 F2** 15 48 S 14 8 E
Chibemba, *Huila, Angola* **103 F3** 16 20 S 15 20 E
Chibia, *Angola* **103 F2** 15 10 S 13 42 E
Chibougamau, *Canada* **128 C5** 49 56N 74 24W
Chibougamau L., *Canada* **128 C5** 49 50N 74 20W
Chibuk, *Nigeria* **101 C7** 10 52N 12 50 E
Chic-Chocs, Mts., *Canada* **129 C6** 48 55N 66 0W
Chicacole = Srikakulam, *India* **82 E6** 18 14N 83 58 E
Chicago, *U.S.A.* **141 C9** 41 53N 87 40W
Chicago Heights, *U.S.A.* **141 C9** 41 29N 87 37W
Chichagof I., *U.S.A.* **130 B1** 58 0N 136 0W
Chichaoua, *Morocco* **98 B3** 31 32N 8 44W
Chicheng, *China* **66 D8** 40 55N 115 55 E
Chichester, *U.K.* **17 G7** 50 50N 0 47W
Chichibu, *Japan* **63 A11** 36 5N 139 10 E
Ch'ich'ihaerh = Qiqihar, *China* **65 B7** 47 26N 124 0 E
Chickasha, *U.S.A.* **139 H6** 35 0N 98 0W
Chiclana de la Frontera, *Spain* **37 J4** 36 26N 6 9W
Chiclayo, *Peru* **156 B2** 6 42 S 79 50W
Chico, *U.S.A.* **144 F5** 39 45N 121 54W
Chico →, *Chubut, Argentina* **160 B3** 44 0 S 67 0W
Chico →, *Santa Cruz, Argentina* **160 D3** 50 0 S 68 30W
Chicomo, *Mozam.* **105 C5** 24 31 S 34 6 E
Chicontepec, *Mexico* **147 C5** 20 58N 98 10W
Chicopee, *U.S.A.* **137 D12** 42 6N 72 37W
Chicoutimi, *Canada* **129 C5** 48 28N 71 5W
Chicualacuala, *Mozam.* **105 C5** 22 6 S 31 42 E
Chidambaram, *India* **83 J4** 11 20N 79 45 E
Chidenguele, *Mozam.* **105 C5** 24 55 S 34 11 E
Chidley, C., *Canada* **127 B13** 60 23N 64 26W
Chiede, *Angola* **103 F3** 17 15 S 16 22 E
Chiefs Pt., *Canada* **136 B3** 44 41N 81 18W
Chiem Hoa, *Vietnam* **76 A5** 22 12N 105 17 E
Chiemsee, *Germany* **27 H8** 47 53N 12 27 E
Chiengi, *Zambia* **107 D2** 8 45 S 29 10 E
Chiengmai = Chiang Mai, *Thailand* **76 C2** 18 47N 98 59 E
Chiengo, *Angola* **103 E4** 13 20 S 21 55 E
Chienti →, *Italy* **39 E10** 43 18N 13 45 E
Chieri, *Italy* **38 D4** 45 0N 7 50 E

Cirium 185

Chiers →, France 23 C11 49 39N 4 59 E
Chiese →, Italy 38 C7 45 8N 10 25 E
Chieti, Italy 39 F11 42 22N 14 10 E
Chièvres, Belgium 21 G3 50 35N 3 48 E
Chifeng, China 67 C10 42 18N 118 58 E
Chigasaki, Japan 63 B11 35 19N 139 24 E
Chigirin, U.S.S.R. 52 B5 49 4N 32 38 E
Chignecto B., Canada 129 C7 45 30N 64 40W
Chigorodó, Colombia 152 B2 7 41N 76 42W
Chiguana, Bolivia 158 A2 21 0 S 67 58W
Chiha-ri, N. Korea 67 E14 38 40N 126 30 E
Chihli, G. of = Bo Hai, China 67 E10 39 0N 119 0 E
Chihuahua, Mexico 146 B3 28 40N 106 3W
Chihuahua □, Mexico 146 B3 28 40N 106 3W
Chiili, U.S.S.R. 55 A3 44 20N 66 15 E
Chik Bollapur, India 83 H3 13 25N 77 45 E
Chikhli, India 82 D3 20 20N 76 18 E
Chikmagalur, India 83 H2 13 15N 75 45 E
Chikodi, India 83 F2 16 26N 74 38 E
Chikugo, Japan 62 D2 33 14N 130 28 E
Chikuma-Gawa →, Japan 63 A10 36 59N 138 35 E
Chikwawa, Malawi 107 F3 16 2 S 34 50 E
Chilac, Mexico 147 D5 18 20N 97 24W
Chilako →, Canada 130 C4 53 53N 122 57W
Chilam Chavki, Pakistan 81 B6 35 5N 75 5 E
Chilanga, Zambia 107 F2 15 33 S 28 16 E
Chilapa, Mexico 147 D5 17 40N 99 11W
Chilas, Pakistan 81 B6 35 25N 74 5 E
Chilcotin →, Canada 130 C4 51 44N 122 23W
Childers, Australia 115 D5 25 15 S 152 17 E
Childress, U.S.A. 139 H4 34 30N 100 15W
Chile ■, S. Amer. 160 A2 35 0 S 72 0W
Chile Chico, Chile 160 C2 46 33 S 71 44W
Chile Rise, Pac. Oc. 123 L18 38 0 S 92 0W
Chilecito, Argentina 158 B2 29 10 S 67 30W
Chilete, Peru 156 B2 7 10 S 78 50W
Chilhowee, U.S.A. 140 F3 38 36N 93 51W
Chilia, Braţul →, Romania 46 D10 45 25N 29 20 E
Chilik, Kazakh S.S.R., U.S.S.R. 54 F3 51 7N 53 55 E
Chilik, Kirgiz S.S.R., U.S.S.R. 55 B9 43 33N 78 17 E
Chililabombwe, Zambia 107 E2 12 18 S 27 43 E
Chilin = Jilin, China 67 C14 43 44N 126 30 E
Chilka L., India 82 E7 19 40N 85 25 E
Chilko →, Canada 130 C4 52 0N 123 40W
Chilko, L., Canada 130 C4 51 20N 124 10W
Chillagoe, Australia 114 B3 17 7 S 144 33 E
Chillán, Chile 158 D1 36 40 S 72 10W
Chillicothe, Ill., U.S.A. 140 D7 40 55N 89 32W
Chillicothe, Mo., U.S.A. 140 E3 39 45N 93 30W
Chillicothe, Ohio, U.S.A. 134 F4 39 20N 82 58W
Chilliwack, Canada 130 D4 49 10N 121 54W
Chilo, India 80 F5 27 25N 73 32 E
Chiloane, I., Mozam. 105 C5 20 40 S 34 55 E
Chiloé □, Chile 160 B2 43 0 S 73 0W
Chiloé, I. de, Chile 160 B2 42 30 S 73 50W
Chilonda, Angola 103 E3 11 19 S 16 12 E
Chilpancingo, Mexico 147 D5 17 30N 99 30W
Chiltern, Australia 117 D7 36 10 S 146 36 E
Chiltern Hills, U.K. 17 F7 51 44N 0 42W
Chilton, U.S.A. 134 C1 44 1N 88 12W
Chiluage, Angola 103 D4 9 30 S 21 50 E
Chilubi, Zambia 107 E2 11 5 S 29 58 E
Chilubula, Zambia 107 E3 10 14 S 30 51 E
Chilumba, Malawi 107 E3 10 28 S 34 12 E
Chilwa, L., Malawi 107 F4 15 15 S 35 40 E
Chimaltitán, Mexico 146 C4 21 46N 103 50W
Chimán, Panama 148 E4 8 45N 78 40W
Chimay, Belgium 21 H4 50 3N 4 20 E
Chimbay, U.S.S.R. 56 E6 42 57N 59 47 E
Chimborazo, Ecuador 152 D2 1 29 S 78 55W
Chimborazo □, Ecuador 152 D2 1 0 S 78 40W
Chimbote, Peru 156 B2 9 0 S 78 35W
Chimion, U.S.S.R. 55 C5 40 15N 71 32 E
Chimishliya, U.S.S.R. 46 C9 46 34N 28 44 E
Chimkent, U.S.S.R. 55 B4 42 18N 69 36 E
Chimoio, Mozam. 107 F3 19 4 S 33 30 E
Chimpembe, Zambia 107 D2 9 31 S 29 33 E
Chin □, Burma 78 E4 22 0N 93 0 E
Chin Hills, Burma 78 D4 22 30N 93 30 E
Chin Ling Shan = Qinling Shandi, China 66 H5 33 50N 108 10 E
China, Mexico 147 B5 25 40N 99 20W
China ■, Asia 65 D6 30 0N 110 0 E
China Lake, U.S.A. 145 K9 35 44N 117 37W
Chinacota, Colombia 152 B3 7 37N 72 36W
Chinan = Jinan, China 66 F9 36 38N 117 1 E
Chinandega, Nic. 148 D2 12 35N 87 12W
Chinati Pk., U.S.A. 139 L2 30 0N 104 25W
Chincha Alta, Peru 156 C2 13 25 S 76 7W
Chinchilla, Australia 115 D5 26 45 S 150 38 E
Chinchilla de Monte Aragón, Spain 35 G3 38 53N 1 40W
Chinchón, Spain 34 E1 40 9N 3 26W
Chinchorro, Banco, Mexico 147 D7 18 35N 87 20W
Chinchou = Jinzhou, China 67 D11 41 5N 121 3 E
Chinchoua, Gabon 102 B1 0 1N 9 48 E
Chincoteague, U.S.A. 134 G8 37 58N 75 21W
Chinde, Mozam. 107 F4 18 35 S 36 30 E
Chindo, S. Korea 67 G14 34 28N 126 15 E
Chindwin →, Burma 78 E5 21 26N 95 15 E
Chineni, India 81 C6 33 2N 75 15 E
Chinga, Mozam. 107 F4 15 13 S 38 35 E
Chingola, Zambia 107 E2 12 31 S 27 53 E
Chingole, Malawi 107 E3 13 4 S 34 17 E
Chingoroi, Angola 103 E2 13 37 S 14 1 E
Ch'ingtao = Qingdao, China 67 F11 36 5N 120 20 E
Chinguar, Angola 103 E3 12 25 S 16 45 E
Chinguetti, Mauritania 98 D2 20 25N 12 24W
Chingune, Mozam. 105 C5 20 33 S 34 58 E
Chinhae, S. Korea 67 G15 35 9N 128 47 E
Chinhanguanine, Mozam. 105 D5 25 21 S 32 30 E
Chinhoyi, Zimbabwe 107 F3 17 20 S 30 8 E
Chiniot, Pakistan 79 C4 31 45N 73 0 E
Chínipas, Mexico 146 B3 27 22N 108 32W
Chinju, S. Korea 67 G15 35 12N 128 2 E
Chinle, U.S.A. 143 H9 36 14N 109 38W
Chinnamanur, India 83 K3 9 50N 77 24 E
Chinnampo, N. Korea 67 E13 38 52N 125 10 E
Chinnur, India 82 E4 18 57N 79 49 E
Chino, Japan 63 B10 35 59N 138 9 E
Chino, U.S.A. 145 L9 34 1N 117 41W
Chino Valley, U.S.A. 143 J7 34 54N 112 28W
Chinon, France 22 E7 47 10N 0 15 E
Chinook, Canada 131 C6 51 28N 110 59W
Chinook, U.S.A. 142 B9 48 35N 109 19W
Chinsali, Zambia 107 E3 10 30 S 32 2 E
Chintamani, India 83 H4 13 26N 78 3 E
Chióggia, Italy 39 C9 45 13N 12 15 E
Chíos = Khíos, Greece 45 F8 38 27N 26 9 E
Chipata, Zambia 107 E3 13 38 S 32 28 E
Chipewyan L., Canada 131 B9 58 0N 98 27W
Chipinge, Zimbabwe 107 G3 20 13 S 32 28 E
Chipiona, Spain 37 J4 36 44N 6 26W
Chipley, U.S.A. 135 K3 30 45N 85 32W
Chiplun, India 82 F1 17 31N 73 34 E
Chipman, Canada 129 C6 46 6N 65 53W
Chipoka, Malawi 107 E3 13 57 S 34 28 E
Chippenham, U.K. 17 F5 51 27N 2 7W
Chippewa →, U.S.A. 138 C8 44 25N 92 10W
Chippewa Falls, U.S.A. 138 C9 44 55N 91 22W
Chiprovtsi, Bulgaria 42 D7 43 24N 22 52 E
Chiquián, Peru 156 C2 10 10 S 77 0W
Chiquimula, Guatemala 148 D2 14 51N 89 37W
Chiquinquira, Colombia 152 B3 5 37N 73 50W
Chiquitos, Llanos de, Bolivia 157 D5 18 0 S 61 30W
Chir →, U.S.S.R. 53 B10 48 30N 43 0 E
Chirala, India 83 G5 15 50N 80 26 E
Chiramba, Mozam. 107 F3 16 55 S 34 39 E
Chiran, Japan 62 F2 31 22N 130 27 E
Chirawa, India 80 E6 28 14N 75 42 E
Chirayinkil, India 83 K3 8 41N 76 49 E
Chirchik, U.S.S.R. 55 C4 41 29N 69 35 E
Chirfa, Niger 97 D2 20 55N 12 22 E
Chirgua →, Venezuela 152 B4 8 54N 67 58W
Chiricahua Pk., U.S.A. 143 L9 31 53N 109 14W
Chiriquí, G. de, Panama 148 E3 8 0N 82 10W
Chiriquí, L. de, Panama 148 E3 9 10N 82 0W
Chirivira Falls, Zimbabwe 107 G3 21 10 S 32 12 E
Chirnogi, Romania 46 E7 44 7N 26 32 E
Chirpan, Bulgaria 43 E10 42 10N 25 19 E
Chirripó Grande, Cerro, Costa Rica 148 E3 9 29N 83 29W
Chisamba, Zambia 107 E2 14 55 S 28 20 E
Chishmy, U.S.S.R. 54 D4 54 35N 55 23 E
Chisholm, Canada 130 C6 54 55N 114 10W
Chishtian Mandi, Pakistan 80 E5 29 50N 72 55 E
Chishui, China 68 C5 28 30N 105 42 E
Chishui He →, China 68 C5 28 49N 105 50 E
Chisimaio, Somali Rep. 108 E2 0 22 S 42 32 E
Chisimba Falls, Zambia 107 E3 10 12 S 30 56 E
Chisineu Criş, Romania 46 C2 46 32N 21 37 E
Chisone →, Italy 38 D4 44 49N 7 25 E
Chisos Mts., U.S.A. 139 L3 29 20N 103 15W
Chistopol, U.S.S.R. 51 D17 55 25N 50 38 E
Chita, Colombia 152 B3 6 11N 72 28W
Chita, U.S.S.R. 57 D12 52 0N 113 35 E
Chitado, Angola 103 F2 17 10 S 14 8 E
Chitapur, India 82 F3 17 10N 77 5 E
Chitembo, Angola 103 E3 13 30 S 16 50 E
Chitipa, Malawi 107 D3 9 41 S 33 19 E
Chitose, Japan 60 C10 42 49N 141 39 E
Chitrakot, India 82 E5 19 10N 81 40 E
Chitral, Pakistan 79 B3 35 50N 71 56 E
Chitravati →, India 83 G4 14 45N 78 15 E
Chitré, Panama 148 E3 7 59N 80 27W
Chittagong, Bangla. 78 D3 22 19N 91 48 E
Chittagong □, Bangla. 78 C3 24 5N 91 0 E
Chittaurgarh, India 80 G6 24 52N 74 38 E
Chittoor, India 83 H4 13 15N 79 5 E
Chittur, India 83 J3 10 40N 76 45 E
Chitungwiza, Zimbabwe 107 F3 18 0 S 31 6 E
Chiumba, Angola 103 E3 12 29 S 16 8 E
Chiume, Angola 103 F4 15 3 S 21 14 E
Chiusa, Italy 39 B8 46 38N 11 34 E
Chiusi, Italy 39 E8 43 1N 11 58 E
Chiva, Spain 35 F4 39 27N 0 41W
Chivacoa, Venezuela 152 A4 10 10N 68 54W
Chivasso, Italy 38 C4 45 10N 7 52 E
Chivay, Peru 156 D3 15 40 S 71 35W
Chivhu, Zimbabwe 107 F3 19 2 S 30 52 E
Chivilcoy, Argentina 158 C4 34 55 S 60 0W
Chiwanda, Tanzania 107 E3 11 23 S 34 55 E
Chixi, China 69 G9 22 0N 112 58 E
Chizera, Zambia 107 E2 13 10 S 25 0 E
Chkalov = Orenburg, U.S.S.R. 54 F4 51 45N 55 6 E
Chkolovsk, U.S.S.R. 51 C13 56 50N 43 10 E
Chloride, U.S.A. 145 K12 35 25N 114 12W
Chlumec, Czech. 30 A8 50 9N 15 29 E
Chmielnik, Poland 47 E7 50 37N 20 43 E
Cho Bo, Vietnam 76 B5 20 46N 105 10 E
Cho-do, N. Korea 67 E13 38 30N 124 40 E
Cho Phuoc Hai, Vietnam 77 G6 10 26N 107 18 E
Choba, Kenya 106 B4 2 30N 38 5 E
Chobe National Park, Botswana 104 B4 18 0 S 25 0 E
Chochiwŏn, S. Korea 67 F14 36 37N 127 18 E
Chocianów, Poland 47 D2 51 27N 15 55 E
Chociwel, Poland 47 B2 53 29N 15 21 E
Chocó □, Colombia 152 B2 6 0N 77 0W
Chocontá, Colombia 152 B3 5 9N 73 41W
Choctawhatchee B., U.S.A. 133 D9 30 15N 86 30W
Chodaków, Poland 47 C7 52 16N 20 18 E
Chodavaram, India 82 F6 17 50N 82 57 E
Chodecz, Poland 47 C6 52 24N 19 2 E
Chodziez, Poland 47 C3 52 58N 16 58 E
Choele Choel, Argentina 160 A3 39 11 S 65 40W
Chōfu, Japan 63 B11 35 39N 139 33 E
Choiseul, Solomon Is. 121 L9 7 0 S 156 40 E
Choisy-le-Roi, France 23 D9 48 45N 2 24 E
Choix, Mexico 146 B3 26 40N 108 23W
Chojna, Poland 47 C1 52 58N 14 25 E
Chojnice, Poland 47 B4 53 42N 17 32 E
Chojnów, Poland 47 D2 51 18N 15 58 E
Chōkai-San, Japan 60 E10 39 6N 140 3 E
Choke, Ethiopia 95 E4 11 18N 37 15 E
Chokurdakh, U.S.S.R. 57 B15 70 38N 147 55 E
Cholame, U.S.A. 144 K6 35 44N 120 18W
Cholet, France 22 E6 47 4N 0 52W
Cholpon-Ata, U.S.S.R. 55 B8 42 40N 77 6 E
Choluteca, Honduras 148 D2 13 20N 87 14W
Choluteca →, Honduras 148 D2 13 0N 87 20W
Chom Bung, Thailand 76 F2 13 37N 99 36 E
Chom Thong, Thailand 76 C2 18 25N 98 41 E
Choma, Zambia 107 F2 16 48 S 26 59 E
Chomen Swamp, Ethiopia 95 F4 9 20N 37 10 E
Chomun, India 80 F6 27 15N 75 40 E
Chomutov, Czech. 30 A6 50 28N 13 23 E
Chon Buri, Thailand 76 F3 13 21N 101 1 E
Chon Thanh, Vietnam 77 G6 11 24N 106 36 E
Chonan, S. Korea 67 F14 36 48N 127 9 E
Chone, Ecuador 152 D2 0 40 S 80 0W
Chong Kai, Cambodia 76 F4 13 57N 103 35 E
Chong Mek, Thailand 76 E5 15 10N 105 27 E
Chong'an, China 69 D12 27 45N 118 0 E
Chongde, China 69 B13 30 32N 120 26 E
Chŏngdo, S. Korea 67 G15 35 38N 128 42 E
Chŏngha, S. Korea 67 F15 36 12N 129 21 E
Chongjin, N. Korea 67 D15 41 47N 129 50 E
Chŏngju, N. Korea 67 E13 39 40N 125 5 E
Chŏngju, S. Korea 67 F14 36 39N 127 27 E
Chongli, China 66 D8 40 58N 115 15 E
Chongming, China 69 B13 31 38N 121 23 E
Chongming Dao, China 69 B13 31 40N 121 30 E
Chongoyape, Peru 156 B2 6 35 S 79 25W
Chongqing, Sichuan, China 68 C6 29 35N 106 25 E
Chongqing, Sichuan, China 68 B4 30 38N 103 40 E
Chongren, China 69 D11 27 46N 116 3 E
Chŏngŭp, S. Korea 67 G14 35 35N 126 50 E
Chongzuo, China 68 F6 22 23N 107 20 E
Chŏnju, S. Korea 67 G14 35 50N 127 4 E
Chonos, Arch. de los, Chile 160 C2 45 0 S 75 0W
Chopda, India 82 D2 21 20N 75 15 E
Chopim →, Brazil 159 B5 25 35 S 53 5W
Chorbat La, India 81 B7 34 42N 76 37 E
Chorley, U.K. 16 D5 53 39N 2 39W
Chorolque, Cerro, Bolivia 158 A2 20 59 S 66 5W
Choroszcz, Poland 47 B9 53 10N 22 59 E
Chorregon, Australia 114 C3 22 40 S 143 32 E
Chortkov, U.S.S.R. 50 G4 49 2N 25 46 E
Chŏrwŏn, S. Korea 67 E14 38 15N 127 10 E
Chorzele, Poland 47 B7 53 15N 20 55 E
Chorzów, Poland 47 E5 50 18N 18 57 E
Chos-Malal, Argentina 158 D1 37 20 S 70 15W
Chosan, N. Korea 67 D13 40 50N 125 47 E
Chōshi, Japan 63 B12 35 45N 140 51 E
Choszczno, Poland 47 B2 53 7N 15 25 E
Chota, Peru 156 B2 6 33 S 78 39W
Choteau, U.S.A. 142 C7 47 50N 112 10W
Chotila, India 80 H4 22 23N 71 15 E
Chowchilla, U.S.A. 144 H6 37 11N 120 12W
Chowkham, Burma 78 E6 20 52N 97 28 E
Choybalsan, Mongolia 65 B6 48 4N 114 30 E
Chrisman, U.S.A. 141 E9 39 48N 87 41W
Christchurch, N.Z. 119 D7 43 33 S 172 47 E
Christchurch, U.K. 17 G6 50 44N 1 45W
Christian I., Canada 136 B4 44 50N 80 12W
Christiana, S. Africa 104 D4 27 52 S 25 8 E
Christiansfeld, Denmark 15 J3 55 21N 9 29 E
Christiansted, Virgin Is. 149 C7 17 45N 64 42W
Christie B., Canada 131 A6 62 32N 111 10W
Christina →, Canada 131 B6 56 40N 111 3W
Christmas Cr. →, Australia 112 C4 18 29 S 125 23 E
Christmas Creek, Australia 112 C4 18 29 S 125 23 E
Christmas I. = Kiritimati, Kiribati 123 G12 1 58N 157 27W
Christmas I., Ind. Oc. 109 F9 10 30 S 105 40 E
Christopher L., Australia 113 D4 24 49 S 127 42 E
Chrudim, Czech. 30 B8 49 58N 15 43 E
Chrzanów, Poland 31 A12 50 10N 19 21 E
Chtimba, Malawi 107 E3 10 35 S 34 13 E
Chu, U.S.S.R. 55 B6 43 36N 73 42 E
Chu →, U.S.S.R. 55 A3 45 0N 67 44 E
Chu →, Vietnam 76 C5 19 53N 105 45 E
Chu Chua, Canada 130 C4 51 22N 120 10W
Chu Lai, Vietnam 76 E7 15 28N 108 45 E
Chu Xian, China 69 A12 32 19N 118 20 E
Chuadanga, Bangla. 78 D2 23 38N 88 51 E
Ch'uanchou = Quanzhou, China 69 E12 24 55N 118 34 E
Chuankou, China 66 G6 34 20N 110 59 E
Chūbu □, Japan 63 A9 36 45N 137 30 E
Chubut □, Argentina 160 B3 43 30 S 69 0W
Chubut →, Argentina 160 B3 43 20 S 65 5W
Chuchi L., Canada 130 B4 55 12N 124 30W
Chudovo, U.S.S.R. 50 B7 59 10N 31 41 E
Chudskoye, Oz., U.S.S.R. 50 B5 58 13N 27 30 E
Chūgoku □, Japan 62 C5 35 0N 133 0 E
Chūgoku-Sanchi, Japan 62 C5 35 0N 133 0 E
Chuguyev, U.S.S.R. 52 B7 49 55N 36 45 E
Chugwater, U.S.A. 138 E2 41 48N 104 47W
Chukhloma, U.S.S.R. 51 B13 58 45N 42 40 E
Chukotskiy Khrebet, U.S.S.R. 57 C18 68 0N 175 0 E
Chukotskoye More, U.S.S.R. 57 C19 68 0N 175 0W
Chula, U.S.A. 140 E3 39 55N 93 29W
Chula Vista, U.S.A. 145 N9 32 39N 117 8W
Chulak-Kurgan, U.S.S.R. 55 B4 43 46N 69 9 E
Chulman, U.S.S.R. 57 D13 56 52N 124 52 E
Chulucanas, Peru 156 B1 5 8 S 80 10W
Chulumani, Bolivia 156 D4 16 24 S 67 31W
Chulym →, U.S.S.R. 56 D9 57 43N 83 51 E
Chum Phae, Thailand 76 D4 16 40N 102 6 E
Chum Saeng, Thailand 76 E3 15 55N 100 15 E
Chuma, Bolivia 156 D4 15 24 S 68 56W
Chumar, India 81 C8 32 40N 78 35 E
Chumbicha, Argentina 158 B2 29 0 S 66 10W
Chumerna, Bulgaria 43 E10 42 45N 25 55 E
Chumikan, U.S.S.R. 57 D14 54 40N 135 10 E
Chumphon, Thailand 77 G2 10 35N 99 14 E
Chumpi, Peru 156 D3 15 4 S 73 46W
Chumuare, Mozam. 107 E3 14 31 S 31 50 E
Chumunjin, S. Korea 67 F15 37 55N 128 54 E
Chuna →, U.S.S.R. 57 D10 57 47N 94 37 E
Chun'an, China 69 C12 29 35N 119 3 E
Chunchŏn, S. Korea 67 F14 37 58N 127 44 E
Chunchura, India 81 H13 22 53N 88 27 E
Chunga, Zambia 107 F2 15 0 S 26 2 E
Chunggang-ŭp, N. Korea 67 D14 41 48N 126 48 E
Chunghwa, N. Korea 67 E13 38 52N 125 47 E
Chungju, S. Korea 67 F14 36 58N 127 58 E
Chungking = Chongqing, China 68 C6 29 35N 106 25 E
Chungmu, S. Korea 67 G15 34 50N 128 20 E
Chungt'iaoshan = Zhongtiao Shan, China 66 G6 35 0N 111 10 E
Chunian, Pakistan 80 D6 30 57N 74 0 E
Chunya, Tanzania 107 D3 8 30 S 33 27 E
Chunya □, Tanzania 106 D3 7 48 S 33 0 E
Chunyang, China 67 C15 43 38N 129 23 E
Chuquibamba, Peru 156 D3 15 47 S 72 44W
Chuquibambilla, Peru 156 C3 14 7 S 72 41W
Chuquicamata, Chile 158 A2 22 15 S 69 0W
Chuquisaca □, Bolivia 157 E5 20 30 S 63 30W
Chur, Switz. 29 C9 46 52N 9 32 E
Churachandpur, India 78 C4 24 20N 93 40 E
Churchill, Canada 131 B10 58 47N 94 11W
Churchill →, Man., Canada 131 B10 58 47N 94 12W
Churchill →, Nfld., Canada 129 B7 53 19N 60 10W
Churchill, C., Canada 131 B10 58 46N 93 12W
Churchill Falls, Canada 129 B7 53 36N 64 19W
Churchill L., Canada 131 B7 55 55N 108 20W
Churchill Pk., Canada 130 B3 58 10N 125 10W
Churdan, U.S.A. 140 B2 42 9N 94 29W
Churfirsten, Switz. 29 B8 47 8N 9 17 E
Churu, India 80 E6 28 20N 74 50 E
Churubusco, U.S.A. 141 C11 41 14N 85 19W
Churwalden, Switz. 29 C9 46 47N 9 33 E
Chushal, India 81 C8 33 40N 78 40 E
Chusovaya →, U.S.S.R. 54 B5 58 18N 56 22 E
Chusovoy, U.S.S.R. 54 B5 58 15N 57 40 E
Chust, U.S.S.R. 55 C5 41 0N 71 13 E
Chuuronjang, N. Korea 67 D15 41 35N 129 40 E
Chuvash A.S.S.R.□, U.S.S.R. 51 D15 55 30N 47 0 E
Chuwārtah, Iraq 84 C5 35 43N 45 34 E
Chuxiong, China 68 E3 25 2N 101 28 E
Ci Xian, China 66 F8 36 20N 114 25 E
Ciacova, Romania 46 D2 45 35N 21 10 E
Ciamis, Indonesia 75 D3 7 20 S 108 21 E
Cianjur, Indonesia 71 G12 6 49 S 107 8 E
Cibadok, Indonesia 71 G12 6 53 S 106 47 E
Cibatu, Indonesia 71 G12 7 8 S 107 59 E
Cibola, U.S.A. 145 M12 33 17N 114 42W
Cicero, U.S.A. 134 E2 41 48N 87 48W
Cicero, Ill., U.S.A. 141 C9 41 51N 87 45W
Cícero Dantas, Brazil 154 D4 10 36 S 38 23W
Cidacos →, Spain 34 C3 42 21N 1 38W
Cide, Turkey 52 F5 41 53N 33 1 E
Ciechanów, Poland 47 C7 52 52N 20 38 E
Ciechanów □, Poland 47 C7 53 0N 20 30 E
Ciechanowiec, Poland 47 C9 52 40N 22 31 E
Ciechocinek, Poland 47 C5 52 53N 18 45 E
Ciego de Avila, Cuba 148 B4 21 50N 78 50W
Ciénaga, Colombia 152 A3 11 1N 74 15W
Ciénaga de Oro, Colombia 152 B2 8 53N 75 37W
Cienfuegos, Cuba 148 B3 22 10N 80 30W
Cieplice Sląskie Zdrój, Poland 47 E2 50 50N 15 40 E
Cierp, France 24 F4 42 55N 0 40 E
Cíes, Is., Spain 36 C2 42 12N 8 55W
Cieszanów, Poland 47 E10 50 14N 23 8 E
Cieszyn, Poland 31 B11 49 45N 18 35 E
Cieza, Spain 35 G3 38 17N 1 23W
Çifteler, Turkey 88 D4 39 22N 31 2 E
Cifuentes, Spain 34 E2 40 47N 2 37W
Cihanbeyli, Turkey 88 D5 38 40N 32 55 E
Cihuatlán, Mexico 146 D4 19 14N 104 35W
Cijara, Pantano de, Spain 37 F6 39 18N 4 52W
Cijulang, Indonesia 71 G13 7 42 S 108 27 E
Cikajang, Indonesia 71 G12 7 25 S 107 48 E
Cikampek, Indonesia 71 G12 6 23 S 107 28 E
Cilacap, Indonesia 71 G13 7 43 S 109 0 E
Çıldır, Turkey 53 F10 41 7N 43 8 E
Çıldır Gölü, Turkey 89 C10 41 5N 43 15 E
Cili, China 69 C8 29 30N 111 8 E
Cilicia, Turkey 88 E5 36 30N 33 40 E
Cîlnicu, Romania 46 E4 44 54N 23 4 E
Cilo Dağı, Turkey 89 E10 37 28N 43 55 E
Cima, U.S.A. 145 K11 35 14N 115 30W
Cimahi, Indonesia 71 G12 6 53 S 107 33 E
Cimarron, Kans., U.S.A. 139 G4 37 50N 100 20W
Cimarron, N. Mex., U.S.A. 139 G2 36 30N 104 52W
Cimarron →, U.S.A. 139 G6 36 10N 96 17W
Cimone, Mte., Italy 38 D7 44 10N 10 40 E
Cîmpic Turzii, Romania 46 C4 46 34N 23 53 E
Cîmpina, Romania 46 D6 45 10N 25 45 E
Cîmpulung, Argeş, Romania 46 D6 45 17N 25 3 E
Cîmpulung, Suceava, Romania 46 B6 47 32N 25 30 E
Cîmpuri, Romania 46 D7 46 0N 26 50 E
Çinar, Turkey 89 E9 37 46N 40 19 E
Cinca →, Spain 34 D5 41 26N 0 21 E
Cincer, Yugoslavia 42 D2 43 55N 17 5 E
Cincinnati, Iowa, U.S.A. 140 D4 40 38N 92 56W
Cincinnati, Ohio, U.S.A. 141 E12 39 10N 84 26W
Cîndeşti, Romania 46 D7 45 15N 26 42 E
Çine, Turkey 88 E3 37 37N 28 2 E
Ciney, Belgium 21 H6 50 18N 5 5 E
Cíngoli, Italy 39 E10 43 23N 13 10 E
Cinigiano, Italy 39 F8 42 53N 11 23 E
Cinto, Mte., France 25 F12 42 24N 8 54 E
Ciorani, Romania 46 E7 44 45N 26 25 E
Čiovo, Yugoslavia 39 E13 43 30N 16 17 E
Cipó, Brazil 154 D4 11 6 S 38 31W
Circeo, Monte, Italy 40 A6 41 14N 13 3 E
Çirçir, Turkey 88 C7 40 5N 36 47 E
Circle, Alaska, U.S.A. 126 B5 65 50N 144 10W
Circle, Mont., U.S.A. 138 B2 47 26N 105 35W
Circleville, Ohio, U.S.A. 134 F4 39 35N 82 57W
Circleville, Utah, U.S.A. 143 G7 38 12N 112 24W
Cirebon, Indonesia 71 G13 6 45 S 108 32 E
Cirencester, U.K. 17 F6 51 43N 1 59W
Cireşu, Romania 46 E3 44 47N 22 31 E
Cirey-sur-Vezouze, France 23 D13 48 35N 6 57 E
Ciriè, Italy 38 C4 45 14N 7 35 E
Cirium, Cyprus 32 E11 34 40N 32 53 E

Coromandel Coast 187

Colne, *U.K.* 16 D5 53 51N 2 11W
Colo →, *Australia* 117 B9 33 25 S 150 52 E
Cologna Véneta, *Italy* 39 C8 45 19N 11 21 E
Cologne = Köln,
Germany 26 E2 50 56N 6 58 E
Colom, I., *Spain* 33 B11 39 58N 4 16 E
Coloma, *U.S.A.* 144 G6 38 49N 120 53W
Colomb-Béchar =
Béchar, *Algeria* 99 B4 31 38N 2 18W
Colombey-les-Belles,
France 23 D12 48 32N 5 54 E
Colombey-les-Deux-
Églises, *France* 23 D11 48 13N 4 50 E
Colômbia, *Brazil* 155 F2 20 10 S 48 40W
Colombia ■, *S. Amer.* 152 C3 3 45N 73 0W
Colombier, *Switz.* 28 C3 46 58N 6 53 E
Colombo, *Sri Lanka* 83 L4 6 56N 79 58 E
Colome, *U.S.A.* 138 D5 43 20N 99 44W
Colón, *Argentina* 158 C4 32 12 S 58 10W
Colón, *Cuba* 148 B3 22 42N 80 54W
Colón, *Panama* 148 E4 9 20N 79 54W
Colón, *Peru* 156 B1 5 0 S 81 0W
Colona, *Australia* 113 F5 31 38 S 132 4 E
Colonella, *Italy* 39 F10 42 52N 13 50 E
Colonia, *Uruguay* 158 C4 34 25 S 57 50W
Colonia de San Jordi,
Spain 33 B9 39 19N 2 59 E
Colonia Dora, *Argentina* 158 B3 28 34 S 62 59W
Colonial Heights, *U.S.A.* 134 G7 37 19N 77 25W
Colonne, C. delle, *Italy* 41 C10 39 2N 17 11 E
Colonsay, *Canada* 131 C7 51 59N 105 52W
Colonsay, *U.K.* 18 E2 56 4N 6 12W
Colorado □, *U.S.A.* 132 C5 37 40N 106 0W
Colorado →, *Argentina* 160 A4 39 50 S 62 8W
Colorado →, *N. Amer.* 143 L6 31 45N 114 40W
Colorado →, *U.S.A.* 139 L7 28 36N 95 58W
Colorado City, *U.S.A.* 139 J4 32 25N 100 50W
Colorado Desert, *U.S.A.* 132 D3 34 20N 116 0W
Colorado Plateau, *U.S.A.* 143 H8 36 40N 110 30W
Colorado River
Aqueduct, *U.S.A.* 145 L12 34 17N 114 10W
Colorado Springs, *U.S.A.* 138 F2 38 55N 104 50W
Colorno, *Italy* 38 D7 44 55N 10 21 E
Colotlán, *Mexico* 146 C4 22 6N 103 16W
Colquechaca, *Bolivia* 157 D4 18 40 S 66 1W
Colton, *Calif., U.S.A.* 145 L9 34 4N 117 20W
Colton, *N.Y., U.S.A.* 137 B10 44 34N 74 58W
Colton, *Wash., U.S.A.* 142 C5 46 41N 117 6W
Columbia, *Ill., U.S.A.* 140 F6 38 26N 90 12W
Columbia, *La., U.S.A.* 139 J8 32 7N 92 5W
Columbia, *Miss., U.S.A.* 139 K10 31 16N 89 50W
Columbia, *Mo., U.S.A.* 140 F4 38 58N 92 20W
Columbia, *Pa., U.S.A.* 137 F8 40 2N 76 30W
Columbia, *S.C., U.S.A.* 135 J5 34 0N 81 0W
Columbia, *Tenn., U.S.A.* 135 H2 35 40N 87 0W
Columbia →, *N. Amer.* 142 C1 46 15N 124 5W
Columbia, C., *Canada* 6 A4 83 0N 70 0W
Columbia, District of □,
U.S.A. 134 F7 38 55N 77 0W
Columbia, Mt., *Canada* 130 C5 52 8N 117 20W
Columbia Basin, *U.S.A.* 142 C4 47 30N 118 30W
Columbia Falls, *U.S.A.* 142 B6 48 25N 114 16W
Columbia Heights,
U.S.A. 138 C8 45 5N 93 10W
Columbiana, *U.S.A.* 136 F4 40 53N 80 40W
Columbretes, Is., *Spain* 34 F5 39 50N 0 50 E
Columbus, *Ga., U.S.A.* 135 J3 32 30N 84 58W
Columbus, *Ind., U.S.A.* 141 E11 39 14N 85 55W
Columbus, *Kans., U.S.A.* 139 G7 37 15N 94 30W
Columbus, *Miss., U.S.A.* 135 J1 33 30N 88 26W
Columbus, *Mont., U.S.A.* 142 D9 45 38N 109 14W
Columbus, *N. Dak.,*
U.S.A. 138 A3 48 52N 102 48W
Columbus, *N. Mex.,*
U.S.A. 143 L10 31 54N 107 43W
Columbus, *Nebr., U.S.A.* 138 E6 41 30N 97 25W
Columbus, *Ohio, U.S.A.* 141 E13 39 57N 83 1W
Columbus, *Tex., U.S.A.* 139 L6 29 42N 96 33W
Columbus, *Wis., U.S.A.* 138 D10 43 20N 89 2W
Columbus Grove, *U.S.A.* 141 D12 40 55N 84 4W
Columbus Junction,
U.S.A. 140 C5 41 17N 91 22W
Colunga, *Spain* 36 B5 43 29N 5 16W
Colusa, *U.S.A.* 144 F4 39 15N 122 1W
Colville, *U.S.A.* 142 B5 48 33N 117 54W
Colville →, *U.S.A.* 126 A4 70 25N 151 0W
Colville, C., *N.Z.* 118 C4 36 29 S 175 21 E
Colwyn Bay, *U.K.* 16 D4 53 17N 3 44W
Coma, *Ethiopia* 95 F4 8 29N 36 53 E
Comácchio, *Italy* 39 D9 44 41N 12 10 E
Comalcalco, *Mexico* 147 D6 18 16N 93 13W
Comallo, *Argentina* 160 B2 41 0 S 70 5W
Comana, *Romania* 46 E7 44 10N 26 10 E
Comanche, *Okla., U.S.A.* 139 H6 34 27N 97 58W
Comanche, *Tex., U.S.A.* 139 K5 31 55N 98 35W
Comandante Luis
Piedrabuena, *Argentina* 160 C3 49 59 S 68 54W
Comănești, *Romania* 46 C7 46 25N 26 26 E
Comarapa, *Bolivia* 157 D5 17 54 S 64 29W
Comayagua, *Honduras* 148 D2 14 25N 87 37W
Combahee →, *U.S.A.* 135 J5 32 30N 80 31W
Combara, *Australia* 117 A8 31 10 S 148 22 E
Combeaufontaine, *France* 23 E12 47 38N 5 54 E
Comber, *Canada* 136 D2 42 14N 82 33W
Combermere Bay, *Burma* 78 F4 19 37N 93 34 E
Comblain-au-Pont,
Belgium 21 H7 50 29N 5 35 E
Combles, *France* 23 B9 50 2N 2 50 E
Combourg, *France* 22 D5 48 25N 1 46W
Comboyne, *Australia* 117 A10 31 34 S 152 27 E
Combronde, *France* 24 C7 45 58N 3 5 E
Comet, *Australia* 114 C4 23 36 S 148 38 E
Comilla, *Bangla.* 78 D3 23 28N 91 10 E
Comines, *Belgium* 21 G2 50 46N 3 0 E
Comino, *Malta* 32 C1 36 2N 14 20 E
Comino, C., *Italy* 40 B2 40 28N 9 47 E
Cómiso, *Italy* 41 F7 36 57N 14 35 E
Comitán, *Mexico* 147 D6 16 18N 92 9W
Commentry, *France* 24 B6 46 20N 2 46 E
Commerce, *Ga., U.S.A.* 135 H4 34 10N 83 25W
Commerce, *Tex., U.S.A.* 139 J7 33 15N 95 50W
Commercy, *France* 23 D12 48 43N 5 34 E
Commewijne □, *Surinam* 153 B7 5 25N 54 45W
Committee B., *Canada* 127 B11 68 30N 86 30W
Commonwealth B.,
Antarctica 7 C10 67 0 S 144 0 E
Commoron Cr. →,
Australia 115 D5 28 22 S 150 8 E
Communism Pk. =
Kommunizma, Pik,
U.S.S.R. 55 D6 39 0N 72 2 E
Como, *Italy* 38 C6 45 48N 9 5 E
Como, L. di, *Italy* 38 B6 46 5N 9 17 E
Comodoro Rivadavia,
Argentina 160 C3 45 50 S 67 40W
Comorin, C., *India* 83 K3 8 3N 77 40 E
Comoriște, *Romania* 46 D2 45 10N 21 35 E
Comoro Is. ■, *Ind. Oc.* 93 H8 12 10 S 44 15 E
Comox, *Canada* 130 D4 49 42N 124 55W
Compiègne, *France* 23 C9 49 24N 2 50 E
Comporta, *Portugal* 37 G2 38 22N 8 46W
Compostela, *Mexico* 146 C4 21 15N 104 53W
Comprida, I., *Brazil* 159 A6 24 50 S 47 42W
Compton, *U.S.A.* 145 M8 33 54N 118 13W
Compton Downs,
Australia 115 E4 30 28 S 146 30 E
Con Cuong, *Vietnam* 76 C5 19 2N 104 54 E
Con Son, Is., *Vietnam* 77 H6 8 41N 106 37 E
Cona Niyeu, *Argentina* 160 B3 41 58 S 67 0W
Conakry, *Guinea* 100 D2 9 29N 13 49W
Conara Junction,
Australia 114 G4 41 50 S 147 26 E
Conargo, *Australia* 117 C6 35 16 S 145 10 E
Concarneau, *France* 22 E3 47 52N 3 56W
Conceição, *Brazil* 154 C4 7 33 S 38 31W
Conceição, *Mozam.* 107 F4 18 47 S 36 7 E
Conceição da Barra,
Brazil 155 E4 18 35 S 39 45W
Conceição do Araguaia,
Brazil 154 C2 8 0 S 49 2W
Conceição do Canindé,
Brazil 154 C3 7 54 S 41 34W
Concepción, *Argentina* 158 B2 27 20 S 65 35W
Concepción, *Bolivia* 157 D5 16 15 S 62 8W
Concepción, *Chile* 158 D1 36 50 S 73 0W
Concepción, *Mexico* 147 D6 18 15N 90 5W
Concepción, *Paraguay* 158 A4 23 22 S 57 26W
Concepción, *Peru* 156 C2 11 54 S 75 19W
Concepción □, *Chile* 158 D1 37 0 S 72 30W
Concepción →, *Mexico* 146 A2 30 32N 113 2W
Concepción, Est. de,
Chile 160 D2 50 30 S 74 55W
Concepción, L., *Bolivia* 157 D5 17 20 S 61 20W
Concepción, Punta,
Mexico 146 B2 26 55N 111 59W
Concepción del Oro,
Mexico 146 C4 24 40N 101 30W
Concepción del Uruguay,
Argentina 158 C4 32 35 S 58 20W
Conception, Pt., *U.S.A.* 145 L6 34 30N 120 34W
Conception B., *Namibia* 104 C1 23 55 S 14 22 E
Conception I., *Bahamas* 149 B4 23 52N 75 9W
Concession, *Zimbabwe* 107 F3 17 27 S 30 56 E
Conchas Dam, *U.S.A.* 139 H2 35 25N 104 10W
Conche, *Canada* 129 B8 50 55N 55 58W
Concho, *U.S.A.* 143 J9 34 32N 109 43W
Concho →, *U.S.A.* 139 K5 31 30N 99 45W
Conchos →, *Chihuahua,*
Mexico 146 B4 29 32N 105 0W
Conchos →, *Tamaulipas,*
Mexico 147 B5 25 9N 98 35W
Concord, *Calif., U.S.A.* 144 H4 37 59N 122 2W
Concord, *Mich., U.S.A.* 141 B12 42 11N 84 38W
Concord, *N.C., U.S.A.* 135 H5 35 28N 80 35W
Concord, *N.H., U.S.A.* 137 C13 43 12N 71 30W
Concordia, *Argentina* 158 C4 31 20 S 58 2W
Concórdia, *Brazil* 152 D4 4 36 S 66 36W
Concordia, *Mexico* 146 C3 23 18N 106 2W
Concordia, *Kans., U.S.A.* 138 F6 39 35N 97 40W
Concordia, *Mo., U.S.A.* 140 F3 38 59N 93 34W
Concots, *France* 24 D5 44 26N 1 40 E
Concrete, *U.S.A.* 142 B3 48 35N 121 49W
Condah, *Australia* 116 D4 37 57 S 141 44 E
Condamine, *Australia* 115 D5 26 56 S 150 9 E
Condat, *France* 24 C6 45 21N 2 46 E
Condé, *Angola* 103 E2 10 50 S 14 37 E
Conde, *Brazil* 155 D4 11 49 S 37 37W
Conde, *U.S.A.* 138 C5 45 13N 98 5W
Condé-sur-l'Escaut,
France 23 B10 50 26N 3 34 E
Condé-sur-Noireau,
France 22 D6 48 51N 0 33W
Condeúba, *Brazil* 155 D3 14 52 S 42 0W
Condobolin, *Australia* 115 E4 33 4 S 147 6 E
Condom, *France* 24 E4 43 57N 0 22 E
Condon, *U.S.A.* 142 D3 45 15N 120 8W
Condove, *Italy* 38 C4 45 8N 7 19 E
Conegliano, *Italy* 39 C9 45 53N 12 18 E
Conejera, I., *Spain* 33 B9 39 11N 2 58 E
Conejos, *Mexico* 146 B4 26 14N 103 53W
Conflans-en-Jarnisy,
France 23 C12 49 10N 5 52 E
Confolens, *France* 24 B4 46 2N 0 40 E
Confuso →, *Paraguay* 158 B4 25 9 S 57 34W
Congjiang, *China* 68 E7 25 43N 108 52 E
Congleton, *U.K.* 16 D5 53 10N 2 12W
Congo = Zaïre →,
Africa 103 D2 6 4 S 12 24 E
Congo, *Brazil* 154 C4 7 48 S 36 40W
Congo (Kinshasa) =
Zaïre ■, *Africa* 103 C4 3 0 S 23 0 E
Congo ■, *Africa* 102 C3 1 0 S 16 0 E
Congo Basin, *Africa* 92 G6 0 10 S 24 30 E
Congonhas, *Brazil* 155 F3 20 30 S 43 52W
Congress, *U.S.A.* 143 J7 34 11N 112 56W
Conil, *Spain* 37 J4 36 17N 6 10W
Coniston, *Canada* 128 C3 46 29N 80 51W
Conjeeveram =
Kanchipuram, *India* 83 H4 12 52N 79 45 E
Conjuboy, *Australia* 114 B3 18 35 S 144 35 E
Conklin, *Canada* 131 B6 55 38N 111 5W
Conlea, *Australia* 115 E3 30 7 S 144 35 E
Conn, L., *Ireland* 19 B2 54 3N 9 15W
Connacht, *Ireland* 19 C3 53 23N 8 40W
Conneaut, *U.S.A.* 136 E4 41 55N 80 32W
Connecticut □, *U.S.A.* 137 E12 41 40N 72 40W
Connecticut →, *U.S.A.* 137 E12 41 17N 72 21W
Connell, *U.S.A.* 142 C4 46 36N 118 51W
Connellsville, *U.S.A.* 136 F5 40 3N 79 32W
Connemara, *Ireland* 19 C2 53 29N 9 45W
Connemaugh →, *U.S.A.* 136 F5 40 38N 79 42W
Connerré, *France* 22 D7 48 3N 0 30 E
Connersville, *U.S.A.* 141 E11 39 40N 85 10W
Connors Ra., *Australia* 114 C4 21 40 S 149 10 E
Conoble, *Australia* 117 B6 32 55 S 144 33 E
Cononaco →, *Ecuador* 152 D2 1 32 S 75 35W
Cononbridge, *U.K.* 18 D4 57 32N 4 30W
Conquest, *Canada* 131 C7 51 32N 107 14W
Conrad, *Iowa, U.S.A.* 140 B4 42 14N 92 52W
Conrad, *Mont., U.S.A.* 142 B8 48 11N 111 58W
Conran, C., *Australia* 117 D8 37 49 S 148 44 E
Conroe, *U.S.A.* 139 K7 30 15N 95 28W
Conselheiro Lafaiete,
Brazil 155 F3 20 40 S 43 48W
Conselheiro Pena, *Brazil* 155 E3 19 10 S 41 30W
Consort, *Canada* 131 C6 52 1N 110 46W
Constance = Konstanz,
Germany 27 H5 47 39N 9 10 E
Constance, L. =
Bodensee, *Europe* 29 A8 47 35N 9 25 E
Constanța, *Romania* 46 E9 44 14N 28 38 E
Constanța □, *Romania* 46 E9 44 15N 28 15 E
Constantina, *Spain* 37 H5 37 51N 5 40W
Constantine, *Algeria* 99 A6 36 25N 6 42 E
Constantine, *U.S.A.* 141 C11 41 50N 85 40W
Constitución, *Chile* 158 D1 35 20 S 72 30W
Constitución, *Uruguay* 158 C4 31 0 S 57 50W
Consuegra, *Spain* 37 F7 39 28N 3 36W
Consul, *Canada* 131 D7 49 20N 109 30W
Contact, *U.S.A.* 142 F6 41 50N 114 56W
Contai, *India* 81 J12 21 54N 87 46 E
Contamana, *Peru* 156 B3 7 19 S 74 55W
Contarina, *Italy* 39 C9 45 2N 12 13 E
Contas →, *Brazil* 155 D4 14 17 S 39 1W
Contes, *France* 25 E11 43 49N 7 19 E
Conthey, *Switz.* 28 D4 46 14N 7 18 E
Continental, *U.S.A.* 141 C12 41 6N 84 16W
Contoocook, *U.S.A.* 137 C13 43 13N 71 45W
Contra Costa, *Mozam.* 105 D5 25 9 S 33 30 E
Contres, *France* 22 E8 47 24N 1 26 E
Contrexéville, *France* 23 D12 48 10N 5 53 E
Contumaza, *Peru* 156 B2 7 23 S 78 57W
Convención, *Colombia* 152 B3 8 28N 73 21W
Conversano, *Italy* 41 B10 40 57N 17 8 E
Converse, *U.S.A.* 141 D11 40 34N 85 52W
Convoy, *U.S.A.* 141 D12 40 55N 84 43W
Conway = Conwy, *U.K.* 16 D4 53 17N 3 50W
Conway = Conwy →,
U.K. 16 D4 53 18N 3 50W
Conway, *Ark., U.S.A.* 139 H8 35 5N 92 30W
Conway, *N.H., U.S.A.* 137 C13 43 58N 71 8W
Conway, *S.C., U.S.A.* 135 J6 33 49N 79 2W
Conway, L., *Australia* 115 D2 28 17 S 135 35 E
Conwy, *U.K.* 16 D4 53 17N 3 50W
Conwy →, *U.K.* 16 D4 53 18N 3 50W
Coober Pedy, *Australia* 115 D1 29 1 S 134 43 E
Cooch Behar = Koch
Bihar, *India* 78 B2 26 22N 89 29 E
Coodardy, *Australia* 113 E2 27 15 S 117 39 E
Cook, *Australia* 113 F5 30 37 S 130 25 E
Cook, *U.S.A.* 138 B8 47 49N 92 39W
Cook, B., *Chile* 160 E3 55 10 S 70 0W
Cook, Mt., *N.Z.* 119 D5 43 36 S 170 9 E
Cook Inlet, *U.S.A.* 126 C4 59 0N 151 0W
Cook Is., *Pac. Oc.* 123 J12 17 0 S 160 0W
Cook Strait, *N.Z.* 118 H3 41 15 S 174 29 E
Cooke Plains, *Australia* 116 C3 35 23 S 139 34 E
Cookeville, *U.S.A.* 135 G3 36 12N 85 30W
Cookhouse, *S. Africa* 104 E4 32 44 S 25 47 E
Cookshire, *Canada* 137 A13 45 25N 71 38W
Cookstown, *U.K.* 19 B5 54 40N 6 43W
Cookstown □, *U.K.* 19 B5 54 40N 6 43W
Cooksville, *Canada* 136 C5 43 36N 79 35W
Cooktown, *Australia* 114 B4 15 30 S 145 16 E
Coolabah, *Australia* 117 A7 31 1 S 146 43 E
Cooladdi, *Australia* 115 D4 26 37 S 145 23 E
Coolah, *Australia* 117 A8 31 48 S 149 41 E
Coolamon, *Australia* 115 E4 34 46 S 147 8 E
Coolangatta, *Australia* 115 D5 28 11 S 153 29 E
Coolgardie, *Australia* 113 F3 30 55 S 121 8 E
Coolibah, *Australia* 112 C5 15 33 S 130 56 E
Coolidge, *U.S.A.* 143 K8 33 1N 111 35W
Coolidge Dam, *U.S.A.* 143 K8 33 10N 110 30W
Cooma, *Australia* 117 D8 36 12 S 149 8 E
Coon Rapids, *U.S.A.* 140 C2 41 53N 94 41W
Coonabarabran, *Australia* 117 A8 31 14 S 149 18 E
Coonalpyn, *Australia* 116 C3 35 43 S 139 52 E
Coonamble, *Australia* 117 A8 30 56 S 148 27 E
Coonana, *Australia* 113 F3 31 0 S 123 0 E
Coondapoor, *India* 83 H2 13 42N 74 40 E
Coongie, *Australia* 115 D3 27 9 S 140 8 E
Coongoola, *Australia* 115 D4 27 43 S 145 51 E
Cooninie, L., *Australia* 115 D2 26 4 S 139 59 E
Coonoor, *India* 83 J3 11 21N 76 45 E
Cooper, *U.S.A.* 139 J7 33 20N 95 40W
Cooper →, *U.S.A.* 135 J6 33 0N 79 55W
Cooper Cr. →, *N. Terr.,*
Australia 110 C5 12 7 S 132 41 E
Cooper Cr. →,
S. Austral., Australia 115 D2 28 29 S 137 46 E
Cooperstown, *N. Dak.,*
U.S.A. 138 B5 47 30N 98 6W
Cooperstown, *N.Y.,*
U.S.A. 137 D10 42 42N 74 57W
Coopersville, *U.S.A.* 141 A11 43 4N 85 57W
Coorabie, *Australia* 113 F5 31 54 S 132 18 E
Coorabulka, *Australia* 114 C3 23 41 S 140 20 E
Coorow, *Australia* 113 E2 29 53 S 116 2 E
Cooroy, *Australia* 115 D5 26 22 S 152 54 E
Coos Bay, *U.S.A.* 142 E1 43 26N 124 7W
Cootamundra, *Australia* 117 C8 34 36 S 148 1 E
Cootehill, *Ireland* 19 B4 54 5N 7 5W
Cooyar, *Australia* 115 D5 26 59 S 151 51 E
Cooyeana, *Australia* 114 C2 24 29 S 138 45 E
Copahue Paso, *Argentina* 158 D1 37 49 S 71 8W
Copainalá, *Mexico* 147 D6 17 8N 93 11W
Copán, *Honduras* 148 D2 14 50N 89 9W
Copatana, *Brazil* 152 D4 2 48 S 67 4W
Cope, *U.S.A.* 138 F3 39 44N 102 50W
Cope, C., *Spain* 35 H3 37 26N 1 28W
Cope Cope, *Australia* 116 D5 36 27 S 143 5 E
Copenhagen =
København, *Denmark* 15 J6 55 41N 12 34 E
Copertino, *Italy* 41 B11 40 17N 18 2 E
Copeville, *Australia* 116 C3 34 47 S 139 51 E
Copiapó, *Chile* 158 B1 27 30 S 70 20W
Copiapó →, *Chile* 158 B1 27 19 S 70 56W
Copley, *Australia* 116 A3 30 36 S 138 26 E
Copp L., *Canada* 130 A6 60 14N 114 40W
Copparo, *Italy* 39 D8 44 52N 11 49 E
Coppename →, *Surinam* 153 B6 5 48N 55 55W
Copper Center, *U.S.A.* 126 B5 62 10N 145 25W
Copper Cliff, *Canada* 128 C3 46 28N 81 4W
Copper Harbor, *U.S.A.* 134 B2 47 31N 87 55W
Copper Queen,
Zimbabwe 107 F2 17 29 S 29 18 E
Copperbelt □, *Zambia* 107 E2 13 15 S 27 30 E
Coppermine, *Canada* 126 B8 67 50N 115 5W
Coppermine →, *Canada* 126 B8 67 49N 116 4W
Copperopolis, *U.S.A.* 144 H6 37 58N 120 38W
Coquet →, *U.K.* 16 B6 55 18N 1 45W
Coquilhatville =
Mbandaka, *Zaïre* 102 B3 0 1N 18 18 E
Coquille, *U.S.A.* 142 E1 43 15N 124 12W
Coquimbo, *Chile* 158 C1 30 0 S 71 20W
Coquimbo □, *Chile* 158 C1 31 0 S 71 0W
Corabia, *Romania* 46 F5 43 48N 24 30 E
Coração de Jesus, *Brazil* 155 E3 16 43 S 44 22W
Coracora, *Peru* 156 D3 15 5 S 73 45W
Coradi, Is., *Italy* 41 B10 40 27N 17 10 E
Coral Gables, *U.S.A.* 135 N5 25 45N 80 16W
Coral Harbour, *Canada* 127 B11 64 8N 83 10W
Coral Sea, *Pac. Oc.* 122 J7 15 0 S 150 0 E
Coralville, *U.S.A.* 140 C5 41 42N 91 34W
Coralville Res., *U.S.A.* 140 C5 41 50N 91 40W
Corantijn →, *Surinam* 153 B6 5 50N 57 8W
Coraopolis, *U.S.A.* 136 F4 40 30N 80 10W
Corato, *Italy* 41 A9 41 12N 16 22 E
Corbeil-Essonnes, *France* 23 D9 48 36N 2 26 E
Corbie, *France* 23 C9 49 54N 2 30 E
Corbières, *France* 24 F6 42 55N 2 35 E
Corbigny, *France* 23 E10 47 16N 3 40 E
Corbin, *U.S.A.* 134 G3 37 0N 84 3W
Corbion, *Belgium* 21 J6 49 48N 5 0 E
Corbones →, *Spain* 37 H5 37 36N 5 39W
Corby Glen, *U.K.* 17 E7 52 49N 0 31W
Corcoles →, *Spain* 35 F1 39 40N 3 18W
Corcoran, *U.S.A.* 144 J7 36 6N 119 35W
Corcubión, *Spain* 36 C1 42 56N 9 12W
Cordele, *U.S.A.* 135 K4 31 55N 83 49W
Cordell, *U.S.A.* 139 H5 35 18N 99 0W
Cordenons, *Italy* 39 C9 45 59N 12 42 E
Cordes, *France* 24 D5 44 5N 1 57 E
Cordisburgo, *Brazil* 155 E3 19 7 S 44 21W
Córdoba, *Argentina* 158 C3 31 20 S 64 10W
Córdoba, *Mexico* 147 D5 18 50N 97 0W
Córdoba, *Spain* 37 H6 37 50N 4 50W
Córdoba □, *Argentina* 158 C3 31 22 S 64 15W
Córdoba □, *Colombia* 152 B2 8 20N 75 40W
Córdoba □, *Spain* 37 G6 38 5N 5 0W
Córdoba, Sierra de,
Argentina 158 C3 31 10 S 64 25W
Cordon, *Phil.* 71 A6 16 42N 121 32 E
Cordova, *Ala., U.S.A.* 135 J2 33 45N 87 12W
Cordova, *Alaska, U.S.A.* 126 B5 60 36N 145 45W
Cordova, *Ill., U.S.A.* 140 C6 41 41N 90 19W
Corella, *Spain* 34 C3 42 7N 1 48W
Corella →, *Australia* 114 B3 19 34 S 140 47 E
Coremas, *Brazil* 154 C4 7 1 S 37 58W
Corentyne →, *Guyana* 153 B6 5 50N 57 8W
Corfield, *Australia* 114 C3 21 40 S 143 21 E
Corfu = Kérkira, *Greece* 32 A3 39 38N 19 50 E
Corfu, Str of, *Greece* 32 A4 39 34N 20 0 E
Corgo, *Spain* 36 C3 42 56N 7 25W
Corguinho, *Brazil* 157 D7 19 53 S 54 52W
Cori, *Italy* 40 A5 41 39N 12 53 E
Coria, *Spain* 36 F4 39 58N 6 33W
Coricudgy, *Australia* 117 B9 32 51 S 150 24 E
Corigliano Cálabro, *Italy* 41 C9 39 36N 16 31 E
Coringa Is., *Australia* 114 B4 16 58 S 149 58 E
Corinna, *Australia* 114 G4 41 35 S 145 10 E
Corinth = Kórinthos,
Greece 45 G4 37 56N 22 55 E
Corinth, *Ky., U.S.A.* 141 F12 38 30N 84 34W
Corinth, *Miss., U.S.A.* 135 H1 34 54N 88 30W
Corinth, *N.Y., U.S.A.* 137 C11 43 15N 73 50W
Corinth, G. of =
Korinthiakós Kólpos,
Greece 45 F4 38 16N 22 30 E
Corinth Canal, *Greece* 45 G5 37 58N 23 0 E
Corinto, *Brazil* 155 E3 18 20 S 44 30W
Corinto, *Nic.* 148 D2 12 30N 87 10W
Corj □, *Romania* 46 D4 45 5N 23 25 E
Cork, *Ireland* 19 E3 51 54N 8 30W
Cork □, *Ireland* 19 E3 51 50N 8 50W
Cork Harbour, *Ireland* 19 E3 51 46N 8 16W
Corlay, *France* 22 D3 48 20N 3 5W
Corleone, *Italy* 40 E6 37 48N 13 16 E
Corleto Perticara, *Italy* 41 B9 40 23N 16 2 E
Çorlu, *Turkey* 43 F12 41 11N 27 49 E
Cormack L., *Canada* 130 A4 60 56N 121 37W
Cormóns, *Italy* 39 C10 45 58N 13 29 E
Cormorant, *Canada* 131 C8 54 14N 100 35W
Cormorant L., *Canada* 131 C8 54 15N 100 50W
Corn Is. = Maiz, Is. del,
Nic. 148 D3 12 15N 83 4W
Cornélio Procópio, *Brazil* 159 A5 23 7 S 50 40W
Cornell, *Ill., U.S.A.* 141 D8 40 58N 88 43W
Cornell, *Wis., U.S.A.* 138 C9 45 10N 91 8W
Corner Brook, *Canada* 129 C8 48 57N 57 58W
Corníglio, *Italy* 38 D7 44 29N 10 5 E
Corning, *Ark., U.S.A.* 139 G9 36 27N 90 34W
Corning, *Calif., U.S.A.* 142 G2 39 56N 122 9W
Corning, *Iowa, U.S.A.* 140 D2 40 57N 94 40W
Corning, *N.Y., U.S.A.* 136 D7 42 10N 77 3W
Corno, Monte, *Italy* 39 F10 42 28N 13 34 E
Cornwall, *Canada* 128 C5 45 2N 74 44W
Cornwall □, *U.K.* 17 G3 50 26N 4 40W
Corny Pt., *Australia* 116 C2 34 55 S 137 0 E
Coro, *Venezuela* 152 A4 11 25N 69 41W
Coroaci, *Brazil* 155 E3 18 35 S 42 17W
Coroatá, *Brazil* 154 B3 4 8 S 44 0W
Coroban, *Somali Rep.* 108 D2 3 58N 42 44 E
Corocoro, *Bolivia* 156 D4 17 15 S 68 28W
Corocoro, I., *Venezuela* 153 B5 8 30N 60 10W
Coroico, *Bolivia* 156 D4 16 0 S 67 50W
Coromandel, *Brazil* 155 E2 18 28 S 47 13W
Coromandel, *N.Z.* 118 C4 36 45 S 175 31 E
Coromandel Coast, *India* 83 H5 12 30N 81 0 E

190 Dangla

Dangla, *Ethiopia* **95 E4** 11 18N 36 56 E
Dangora, *Nigeria* **101 C6** 11 30N 8 7 E
Dangrek, Phnom, *Thailand* **76 E5** 14 15N 105 0 E
Dangriga, *Belize* **147 D7** 17 0N 88 13W
Dangshan, *China* **66 G9** 34 27N 116 22 E
Dangtu, *China* **69 B12** 31 32N 118 25 E
Dangyang, *China* **69 B8** 30 52N 111 44 E
Daniel, *U.S.A.* **142 E8** 42 56N 110 2W
Daniel's Harbour, *Canada* **129 B8** 50 13N 57 35W
Danielskuil, *S. Africa* **104 D3** 28 11 S 23 33 E
Danielson, *U.S.A.* **137 E13** 41 50N 71 52W
Danilov, *U.S.S.R.* **51 B12** 58 16N 40 13 E
Danilovgrad, *Yugoslavia* **42 E4** 42 38N 19 9 E
Danilovka, *U.S.S.R.* **51 F14** 50 25N 44 12 E
Daning, *China* **66 F6** 36 28N 110 45 E
Danissa, *Kenya* **106 B5** 3 15N 40 58 E
Danja, *Nigeria* **101 C6** 11 21N 7 30 E
Danje-ia-Menha, *Angola* **103 D2** 9 32 S 14 39 E
Ḍank, *Oman* **87 B7** 23 33N 56 16 E
Dankalwa, *Nigeria* **101 C7** 11 52N 12 12 E
Dankama, *Nigeria* **101 C6** 13 20N 7 44 E
Dankov, *U.S.S.R.* **51 E11** 53 20N 39 5 E
Danleng, *China* **68 B4** 30 1N 103 31 E
Danlí, *Honduras* **148 D2** 14 4N 86 35W
Dannemora, *Sweden* **13 F14** 60 12N 17 51 E
Dannemora, *U.S.A.* **137 B11** 44 41N 73 44W
Dannenberg, *Germany* **26 B7** 53 7N 11 4 E
Dannevirke, *N.Z.* **118 G5** 40 12 S 176 8 E
Dannhauser, *S. Africa* **105 D5** 28 0 S 30 3 E
Danot, *Ethiopia* **108 C3** 7 33N 45 17 E
Danshui, *Taiwan* **69 E13** 25 12N 121 25 E
Dansville, *U.S.A.* **136 D7** 42 32N 77 41W
Dantan, *India* **81 J12** 21 57N 87 20 E
Dante, *Somali Rep.* **108 B4** 10 25N 51 16 E
Danube →, *Europe* **46 D10** 45 20N 29 40 E
Danubyu, *Burma* **78 G5** 17 15N 95 35 E
Danukandi, *Bangla.* **78 D3** 23 32N 90 43 E
Danvers, *U.S.A.* **137 D14** 42 34N 70 55W
Danville, *Ill., U.S.A.* **141 D9** 40 10N 87 40W
Danville, *Ind., U.S.A.* **141 E10** 39 46N 86 32W
Danville, *Ky., U.S.A.* **141 G12** 37 40N 84 45W
Danville, *Va., U.S.A.* **135 G6** 36 40N 79 20W
Danyang, *China* **69 B12** 32 0N 119 31 E
Danzhai, *China* **68 D6** 26 11N 107 48 E
Danzig = Gdańsk, *Poland* **47 A5** 54 22N 18 40 E
Dao, *Phil.* **71 B6** 10 30N 121 57 E
Dão →, *Portugal* **36 E2** 40 20N 8 11W
Dao Xian, *China* **69 E8** 25 36N 111 31 E
Daocheng, *China* **68 C3** 29 0N 100 10 E
Daora, *W. Sahara* **98 C2** 27 5N 12 59W
Daoud = Aïn Beïda, *Algeria* **99 A6** 35 50N 7 29 E
Daoulas, *France* **22 D2** 48 22N 4 17W
Dapong, *Togo* **101 C5** 10 55N 0 16 E
Daqing Shan, *China* **66 D6** 40 40N 111 0 E
Daqu Shan, *China* **69 B14** 30 25N 122 20 E
Dar es Salaam, *Tanzania* **106 D4** 6 50 S 39 12 E
Dar Mazār, *Iran* **85 D8** 29 14N 57 20 E
Dar'ā, *Syria* **91 C5** 32 36N 36 7 E
Dar'ā □, *Syria* **91 C5** 32 55N 36 10 E
Dārāb, *Iran* **85 D7** 28 50N 54 30 E
Darabani, *Romania* **46 A7** 48 10N 26 39 E
Daraj, *Libya* **96 B2** 30 10N 10 28 E
Dārān, *Iran* **85 C6** 32 59N 50 24 E
Daraut Kurgan, *U.S.S.R.* **55 D6** 39 33N 72 11 E
Daravica, *Yugoslavia* **42 E5** 42 32N 20 8 E
Daraw, *Egypt* **94 C3** 24 22N 32 51 E
Dārayyā, *Syria* **91 B5** 33 28N 36 15 E
Darazo, *Nigeria* **101 C7** 11 1N 10 24 E
Darband, *Pakistan* **80 B5** 34 20N 72 50 E
Darband, Kūh-e, *Iran* **85 D8** 31 34N 57 8 E
Darbhanga, *India* **81 F11** 26 15N 85 55 E
Darburruk, *Somali Rep.* **108 C2** 9 44N 44 31 E
Darby, *U.S.A.* **142 C6** 46 2N 114 7W
Darda, *Yugoslavia* **42 B3** 45 40N 18 41 E
Dardanelle, *Ark., U.S.A.* **139 H8** 35 12N 93 9W
Dardanelle, *Calif., U.S.A.* **144 G7** 38 15N 119 50W
Dardanelles = Çanakkale Boğazı, *Turkey* **44 D8** 40 17N 26 32 E
Darende, *Turkey* **88 D7** 38 31N 37 30 E
Dārestān, *Iran* **85 D8** 29 9N 58 42 E
Darfield, *N.Z.* **119 D7** 43 29 S 172 7 E
Darfo, *Italy* **38 C7** 45 52N 10 11 E
Dargai, *Pakistan* **79 B3** 34 25N 71 55 E
Dargan Ata, *U.S.S.R.* **56 E7** 40 29N 62 10 E
Dargaville, *N.Z.* **118 B2** 35 57 S 173 52 E
Darhan Muminggan Lianheqi, *China* **66 D6** 41 40N 110 28 E
Dari, *Sudan* **95 F3** 5 48N 30 26 E
Darién, G. del, *Colombia* **152 B2** 9 0N 77 0W
Darién, Serranía del, *Colombia* **152 B2** 8 30N 77 30W
Dariganga, *Mongolia* **66 B7** 45 21N 113 45 E
Darinskoye, *U.S.S.R.* **54 F2** 51 20N 51 44 E
Darjeeling = Darjiling, *India* **81 F13** 27 3N 88 18 E
Darjiling, *India* **81 F13** 27 3N 88 18 E
Dark Cove, *Canada* **129 C9** 48 47N 54 13W
Darkan, *Australia* **113 F2** 33 20 S 116 43 E
Darke Peak, *Australia* **116 B2** 33 27 S 136 12 E
Darkhazīneh, *Iran* **85 D6** 31 54N 48 39 E
Darkot Pass, *Pakistan* **81 A5** 36 45N 73 26 E
Darling →, *Australia* **116 C4** 34 4 S 141 54 E
Darling Downs, *Australia* **115 D5** 27 30 S 150 30 E
Darling Ra., *Australia* **113 F2** 32 30 S 116 0 E
Darlington, *U.K.* **16 C6** 54 33N 1 33W
Darlington, *S.C., U.S.A.* **135 H6** 34 18N 79 50W
Darlington, *Wis., U.S.A.* **140 B6** 42 43N 90 7W
Darlot, L., *Australia* **113 E3** 27 48 S 121 35 E
Darłowo, *Poland* **47 A3** 54 25N 16 25 E
Dărmăneşti, *Romania* **46 C7** 46 21N 26 33 E
Darmstadt, *Germany* **27 F4** 49 51N 8 40 E
Darnah, *Libya* **96 B4** 32 40N 22 35 E
Darnah □, *Libya* **96 B4** 31 0N 23 40 E
Darnall, *S. Africa* **105 D5** 29 23 S 31 18 E
Darnétal, *France* **22 C8** 49 25N 1 10 E
Darney, *France* **23 D13** 48 5N 6 2 E
Darnick, *Australia* **116 B5** 32 48 S 143 38 E
Darnley, C., *Antarctica* **7 C6** 68 0 S 69 0 E
Darnley B., *Canada* **126 B7** 69 30N 123 30W
Daroca, *Spain* **34 D3** 41 9N 1 25W
Darr, *Australia* **114 C3** 23 13 S 144 7 E
Darr →, *Australia* **114 C3** 23 39 S 143 50 E
Darran Mts., *N.Z.* **119 E2** 44 37 S 167 59 E
Darrington, *U.S.A.* **142 B3** 48 14N 121 37W
Darsana, *Bangla.* **78 D2** 23 35N 88 48 E
Darsi, *India* **83 G4** 15 46N 79 44 E
Darsser Ort, *Germany* **26 A8** 54 29N 12 31 E
Dart →, *U.K.* **17 G4** 50 24N 3 36W
Dart, C., *Antarctica* **7 D14** 73 6 S 126 20W
Dartmoor, *Australia* **116 D4** 37 56 S 141 19 E
Dartmoor, *U.K.* **17 G4** 50 36N 4 0W
Dartmouth, *Australia* **114 C3** 23 31 S 144 44 E
Dartmouth, *Canada* **129 D7** 44 40N 63 30W
Dartmouth, *U.K.* **17 G4** 50 21N 3 35W
Dartmouth, L., *Australia* **115 D4** 26 4 S 145 18 E
Dartuch, C., *Spain* **33 B10** 39 55N 3 49 E
Daru, *Papua N. G.* **120 E2** 9 3 S 143 13 E
Daruvar, *Yugoslavia* **42 B2** 45 35N 17 14 E
Darvaza, *U.S.S.R.* **56 E6** 40 11N 58 24 E
Darvel, Teluk, *Malaysia* **71 D5** 4 50N 118 20 E
Darwha, *India* **82 D3** 20 15N 77 45 E
Darwin, *Australia* **112 B5** 12 25 S 130 51 E
Darwin, *U.S.A.* **145 J9** 36 15N 117 35W
Darwin, Mt., *Chile* **160 D3** 54 47 S 69 55W
Darwin River, *Australia* **112 B5** 12 50 S 130 58 E
Daryapur, *India* **82 D3** 20 55N 77 20 E
Dās, *U.A.E.* **85 E7** 25 20N 53 30 E
Dashetai, *China* **66 D5** 41 0N 109 5 E
Dashkesan, *U.S.S.R.* **53 F12** 40 2N 46 0 E
Dasht, *Iran* **85 B8** 37 17N 56 7 E
Dasht →, *Pakistan* **79 D1** 25 10N 61 40 E
Dasht-i-Nawar, *Afghan.* **80 C3** 33 52N 68 0 E
Daska, *Pakistan* **80 C6** 32 20N 74 20 E
Dassa-Zoume, *Benin* **101 D5** 7 46N 2 14 E
Dasseneiland, *S. Africa* **104 E2** 33 25 S 18 3 E
Datça, *Turkey* **45 H9** 36 46N 27 40 E
Datia, *India* **81 G8** 25 39N 78 27 E
Datian, *China* **69 E11** 25 40N 117 50 E
Datong, *Anhui, China* **69 B11** 30 48N 117 44 E
Datong, *Shanxi, China* **66 D7** 40 6N 113 18 E
Dattapur = Dhamangaon, *India* **82 D4** 20 45N 78 15 E
Datu, Tanjung, *Indonesia* **70 D3** 2 5N 109 39 E
Datu Piang, *Phil.* **71 C6** 7 2N 124 30 E
Daugava →, *U.S.S.R.* **50 C4** 57 4N 24 3 E
Daugavpils, *U.S.S.R.* **50 D5** 55 53N 26 32 E
Daulatabad, *India* **82 E2** 19 57N 75 15 E
Daule, *Ecuador* **152 D2** 1 56 S 79 56W
Daule →, *Ecuador* **152 D2** 2 10 S 79 52W
Daulpur, *India* **80 F7** 26 45N 77 59 E
Daun, *Germany* **27 E2** 50 10N 6 53 E
Daund, *India* **82 E2** 18 26N 74 40 E
Dauphin, *Canada* **131 C8** 51 9N 100 5W
Dauphin I., *U.S.A.* **135 K1** 30 16N 88 10W
Dauphin L., *Canada* **131 C9** 51 20N 99 45W
Dauphiné, *France* **25 C9** 45 15N 5 25 E
Daura, *Borno, Nigeria* **101 C7** 11 31N 11 24 E
Daura, *Kaduna, Nigeria* **101 C6** 13 2N 8 21 E
Dausa, *India* **80 F7** 26 52N 76 20 E
Davangere, *India* **83 G2** 14 25N 75 55 E
Davao, *Phil.* **71 C7** 7 0N 125 40 E
Davao, G. of, *Phil.* **71 C7** 6 30N 125 48 E
Dāvar Panāh, *Iran* **85 E9** 27 25N 62 15 E
Davenport, *Calif., U.S.A.* **144 H4** 37 1N 122 12W
Davenport, *Iowa, U.S.A.* **140 C6** 41 30N 90 40W
Davenport, *Wash., U.S.A.* **142 C4** 47 40N 118 5W
Davenport Downs, *Australia* **114 C3** 24 8 S 141 7 E
Davenport Ra., *Australia* **114 C1** 20 28 S 134 0 E
David, *Panama* **148 E3** 8 30N 82 30W
David City, *U.S.A.* **138 E6** 41 18N 97 10W
David Gorodok, *U.S.S.R.* **50 E5** 52 4N 27 8 E
Davidson, *Canada* **131 C7** 51 16N 105 59W
Davis, *U.S.A.* **144 G5** 38 33N 121 44W
Davis Dam, *U.S.A.* **145 K12** 35 11N 114 35W
Davis Inlet, *Canada* **129 A7** 55 50N 60 59W
Davis Mts., *U.S.A.* **139 K2** 30 42N 104 15W
Davis Sea, *Antarctica* **7 C7** 66 0 S 92 0 E
Davis Str., *N. Amer.* **127 B14** 65 0N 58 0W
Davlekanovo, *U.S.S.R.* **54 D4** 54 13N 55 3 E
Davos, *Switz.* **29 C9** 46 48N 9 49 E
Davy L., *Canada* **131 B7** 58 53N 108 18W
Dawa →, *Ethiopia* **95 G5** 4 11N 42 6 E
Dawaki, *Bauchi, Nigeria* **101 D6** 9 25N 9 33 E
Dawaki, *Kano, Nigeria* **101 C6** 12 5N 8 23 E
Dawes Ra., *Australia* **114 C5** 24 40 S 150 40 E
Dawna Range, *Burma* **78 G7** 16 30N 98 30 E
Dawnyein, *Burma* **78 G5** 15 54N 95 36 E
Dawqah, *Si. Arabia* **86 C3** 19 36N 40 54 E
Dawson, *Canada* **126 B6** 64 10N 139 30W
Dawson, *Ga., U.S.A.* **135 K3** 31 45N 84 28W
Dawson, *N. Dak., U.S.A.* **138 B5** 46 56N 99 45W
Dawson, I., *Chile* **160 D2** 53 50 S 70 50W
Dawson Creek, *Canada* **130 B4** 55 45N 120 15W
Dawson Inlet, *Canada* **131 A10** 61 50N 93 25W
Dawson Ra., *Australia* **114 C4** 24 30 S 149 48 E
Dawu, *China* **68 B3** 30 55N 101 10 E
Dawwah, *Oman* **87 B7** 20 33N 58 48 E
Dax, *France* **24 E2** 43 44N 1 3W
Daxi, *Taiwan* **69 E13** 24 52N 121 20 E
Daxian, *China* **68 B6** 31 15N 107 23 E
Daxin, *China* **68 F6** 22 50N 107 11 E
Daxindian, *China* **67 F11** 37 30N 120 50 E
Daxinggou, *China* **67 C15** 43 25N 129 40 E
Daxue Shan, *Sichuan, China* **68 B3** 30 30N 101 30 E
Daxue Shan, *Yunnan, China* **68 F2** 23 42N 99 48 E
Dayao, *China* **68 E3** 25 43N 101 20 E
Daye, *China* **69 B10** 30 6N 114 58 E
Dayi, *China* **68 B4** 30 41N 103 29 E
Daylesford, *Australia* **116 D6** 37 21 S 144 9 E
Dayong, *China* **69 C8** 29 11N 110 30 E
Dayr az Zawr, *Syria* **84 C4** 35 20N 40 5 E
Daysland, *Canada* **130 C6** 52 50N 112 20W
Dayton, *Iowa, U.S.A.* **140 B2** 42 14N 94 6W
Dayton, *Ky., U.S.A.* **141 E12** 39 47N 84 28W
Dayton, *Nev., U.S.A.* **144 F7** 39 15N 119 34W
Dayton, *Ohio, U.S.A.* **134 F3** 39 45N 84 10W
Dayton, *Pa., U.S.A.* **136 F5** 40 54N 79 18W
Dayton, *Tenn., U.S.A.* **135 H3** 35 30N 85 1W
Dayton, *Wash., U.S.A.* **142 C4** 46 20N 118 10W
Daytona Beach, *U.S.A.* **135 L5** 29 14N 81 0W
Dayu, *China* **69 E10** 25 24N 114 22 E
Dayville, *U.S.A.* **142 D4** 44 33N 119 37W
Dazhu, *China* **68 B6** 30 41N 107 15 E
Dazu, *China* **68 C5** 29 40N 105 42 E
De Aar, *S. Africa* **104 E3** 30 39 S 24 0 E
De Bilt, *Neths.* **20 D6** 52 6N 5 11 E
De Forest, *U.S.A.* **140 A7** 43 15N 89 20W
De Funiak Springs, *U.S.A.* **135 K2** 30 42N 86 10W
De Grey, *Australia* **112 D2** 20 12 S 119 12 E
De Grey →, *Australia* **112 D2** 20 12 S 119 13 E
De Kalb, *U.S.A.* **138 E10** 41 55N 88 45W
De Koog, *Neths.* **20 B5** 53 6N 4 46 E
De Land, *U.S.A.* **135 L5** 29 1N 81 19W
De Leon, *U.S.A.* **139 J5** 32 9N 98 35W
De Panne, *Belgium* **21 F1** 51 6N 2 34 E
De Pere, *U.S.A.* **134 C1** 44 28N 88 1W
De Queen, *U.S.A.* **139 H7** 34 3N 94 24W
De Quincy, *U.S.A.* **139 K8** 30 30N 93 27W
De Ridder, *U.S.A.* **139 K8** 30 48N 93 15W
De Rijp, *Neths.* **20 C5** 52 33N 4 51 E
De Smet, *U.S.A.* **138 C6** 44 25N 97 35W
De Soto, *U.S.A.* **140 F6** 38 7N 90 33W
De Tour, *U.S.A.* **134 C4** 45 59N 83 56W
De Witt, *Ark., U.S.A.* **139 H9** 34 19N 91 20W
De Witt, *Iowa, U.S.A.* **140 C6** 41 49N 90 33W
De Witt, *Mich., U.S.A.* **141 B12** 42 50N 84 33W
Dead Sea, *Asia* **86 A1** 31 30N 35 30 E
Deadwood, *U.S.A.* **138 C3** 44 23N 103 44W
Deadwood L., *Canada* **130 B3** 59 10N 128 30W
Deakin, *Australia* **113 F4** 30 46 S 128 58 E
Deal, *U.K.* **17 F9** 51 13N 1 25 E
Deal I., *Australia* **114 F4** 39 30 S 147 20 E
Dealesville, *S. Africa* **104 D4** 28 41 S 25 44 E
De'an, *China* **69 C10** 29 21N 115 46 E
Dean, Forest of, *U.K.* **17 F5** 51 50N 2 35W
Deán Funes, *Argentina* **158 C3** 30 20 S 64 20W
Dearborn, *Mich., U.S.A.* **128 D3** 42 18N 83 15W
Dearborn, *Mo., U.S.A.* **140 E2** 39 32N 94 46W
Dease →, *Canada* **130 B3** 59 56N 128 32W
Dease L., *Canada* **130 B2** 58 40N 130 5W
Dease Lake, *Canada* **130 B2** 58 25N 130 6W
Death Valley, *U.S.A.* **145 J10** 36 19N 116 52W
Death Valley Junction, *U.S.A.* **145 J10** 36 21N 116 30W
Death Valley Nat. Monument, *U.S.A.* **145 J10** 36 30N 117 0W
Deauville, *France* **22 C7** 49 23N 0 2 E
Deba Habe, *Nigeria* **101 C7** 10 14N 11 20 E
Debaltsevo, *U.S.S.R.* **52 B8** 48 22N 38 26 E
Debao, *China* **68 F6** 23 21N 106 46 E
Debar, *Yugoslavia* **42 F5** 41 31N 20 30 E
Debden, *Canada* **131 C7** 53 30N 106 50W
Debdou, *Morocco* **99 B4** 33 59N 3 0W
Debessy, *U.S.S.R.* **54 C3** 57 39N 53 49 E
Dębica, *Poland* **31 A14** 50 2N 21 25 E
Dęblin, *Poland* **47 D8** 51 34N 21 50 E
Debno, *Poland* **47 C1** 52 44N 14 41 E
Débo, L., *Mali* **100 B4** 15 14N 4 15W
Debolt, *Canada* **130 B5** 55 12N 118 1W
Deborah East, L., *Australia* **113 F2** 30 45 S 119 0 E
Deborah West, L., *Australia* **113 F2** 30 45 S 118 50 E
Debrc, *Yugoslavia* **42 C4** 44 38N 19 53 E
Debre Birhan, *Ethiopia* **95 F4** 9 41N 39 31 E
Debre Markos, *Ethiopia* **95 E4** 10 20N 37 40 E
Debre May, *Ethiopia* **95 E4** 11 20N 37 25 E
Debre Sina, *Ethiopia* **95 F4** 9 51N 39 50 E
Debre Tabor, *Ethiopia* **95 E4** 11 50N 38 26 E
Debre Zebit, *Ethiopia* **95 E4** 11 48N 38 30 E
Debrecen, *Hungary* **31 D14** 47 33N 21 42 E
Dečani, *Yugoslavia* **42 E5** 42 30N 20 10 E
Decatur, *Ala., U.S.A.* **135 H2** 34 35N 87 0W
Decatur, *Ga., U.S.A.* **135 J3** 33 47N 84 17W
Decatur, *Ill., U.S.A.* **140 E8** 39 50N 88 55W
Decatur, *Ind., U.S.A.* **141 D12** 40 50N 84 56W
Decatur, *Mich., U.S.A.* **141 B11** 42 7N 85 58W
Decatur, *Tex., U.S.A.* **139 J6** 33 15N 97 35W
Decazeville, *France* **24 D6** 44 34N 2 15 E
Deccan, *India* **82 F4** 18 0N 79 0 E
Deception, Mt., *Australia* **116 A3** 30 42 S 138 16 E
Deception L., *Canada* **131 B8** 56 33N 104 13W
Dechang, *China* **68 D4** 27 25N 102 11 E
Děčin, *Czech.* **30 A7** 50 47N 14 12 E
Decize, *France* **23 F10** 46 50N 3 28 E
Deckerville, *U.S.A.* **136 C2** 43 33N 82 46W
Decollatura, *Italy* **41 C9** 39 2N 16 21 E
Decorah, *U.S.A.* **138 D9** 43 20N 91 50W
Deda, *Romania* **46 C5** 46 56N 24 50 E
Dedaye, *Burma* **78 G5** 16 24N 95 53 E
Dedéagach = Alexandroúpolis, *Greece* **44 D7** 40 50N 25 54 E
Dedegöl Dağları, *Turkey* **88 E4** 37 15N 31 18 E
Dedemsvaart, *Neths.* **20 C8** 52 36N 6 28 E
Dedham, *U.S.A.* **137 D13** 42 14N 71 10W
Dedilovo, *U.S.S.R.* **51 E10** 53 59N 37 50 E
Dédougou, *Burkina Faso* **100 C4** 12 30N 3 25W
Deduru Oya, *Sri Lanka* **83 L4** 7 32N 79 50 E
Dedza, *Malawi* **107 E3** 14 20 S 34 20 E
Dee →, *Clwyd, U.K.* **16 D4** 53 15N 3 7W
Dee →, *Gramp., U.K.* **18 D6** 57 4N 2 7W
Deep B., *Canada* **130 A5** 61 15N 116 35W
Deep Lead, *Australia* **116 D5** 37 0 S 142 43 E
Deep River, *U.S.A.* **140 C4** 41 35N 92 22W
Deep Well, *Australia* **114 C1** 24 20 S 134 0 E
Deepwater, *Australia* **115 D5** 29 25 S 151 51 E
Deepwater, *U.S.A.* **140 F3** 38 18N 93 46W
Deer →, *Canada* **131 B10** 58 23N 94 13W
Deer Lake, *Nfld., Canada* **129 C8** 49 11N 57 27W
Deer Lake, *Ont., Canada* **131 C10** 52 36N 94 20W
Deer Lodge, *U.S.A.* **142 C7** 46 25N 112 40W
Deer Park, *Ohio, U.S.A.* **141 E12** 39 13N 84 23W
Deer Park, *Wash., U.S.A.* **142 C5** 47 55N 117 21W
Deer River, *U.S.A.* **138 B8** 47 21N 93 44W
Deeral, *Australia* **114 B4** 17 14 S 145 55 E
Deerdepoort, *S. Africa* **104 C4** 24 37 S 26 27 E
Deerlijk, *Belgium* **21 G2** 50 51N 3 22 E
Deferiet, *U.S.A.* **137 B9** 44 2N 75 41W
Defiance, *U.S.A.* **141 C12** 41 20N 84 20W
Dêgê, *China* **68 B2** 31 44N 98 39 E
Degebe →, *Portugal* **37 G3** 38 13N 7 29W
Degeh Bur, *Ethiopia* **90 F3** 8 11N 43 31 E
Degema, *Nigeria* **101 E6** 4 50N 6 48 E
Degersheim, *Switz.* **29 B8** 47 23N 9 12 E
Deggendorf, *Germany* **27 G8** 48 49N 12 59 E
Deh Bīd, *Iran* **85 D7** 30 39N 53 11 E
Deh-e Shīr, *Iran* **85 D7** 31 29N 53 45 E
Dehaj, *Iran* **85 D7** 30 42N 54 53 E
Dehak, *Iran* **79 D1** 27 11N 62 37 E
Dehdez, *Iran* **85 D6** 31 43N 50 17 E
Dehestān, *Iran* **85 D7** 28 30N 55 35 E
Dehgolān, *Iran* **84 C5** 35 17N 47 25 E
Dehibat, *Tunisia* **96 B2** 32 0N 10 47 E
Dehiwala, *Sri Lanka* **83 L4** 6 50N 79 51 E
Dehlorān, *Iran* **84 C5** 32 41N 47 16 E
Dehnow-e Kūhestān, *Iran* **85 E8** 27 58N 58 32 E
Dehra Dun, *India* **80 D8** 30 20N 78 4 E
Dehri, *India* **81 G11** 24 50N 84 15 E
Dehua, *China* **69 E12** 25 26N 118 14 E
Dehui, *China* **67 B13** 44 30N 125 40 E
Deinze, *Belgium* **21 G3** 50 59N 3 32 E
Dej, *Romania* **46 B4** 47 10N 23 52 E
Dejiang, *China* **68 C7** 28 18N 108 7 E
Dekemhare, *Ethiopia* **95 D4** 15 6N 39 0 E
Dekese, *Zaïre* **102 C4** 3 24 S 21 24 E
Dekhkanabad, *U.S.S.R.* **55 D3** 38 21N 66 30 E
Dekoa, *C.A.R.* **102 A3** 6 19N 19 4 E
Del Mar, *U.S.A.* **145 N9** 32 58N 117 16W
Del Norte, *U.S.A.* **143 H10** 37 40N 106 27W
Del Rio, *U.S.A.* **139 L4** 29 23N 100 50W
Delai, *Sudan* **94 D4** 17 21N 36 6 E
Delano, *U.S.A.* **145 K7** 35 48N 119 13W
Delareyville, *S. Africa* **104 D4** 26 41 S 25 26 E
Delavan, *Ill., U.S.A.* **140 D7** 40 22N 89 33W
Delavan, *Wis., U.S.A.* **138 D10** 42 40N 88 39W
Delaware, *U.S.A.* **141 D13** 40 20N 83 5W
Delaware □, *U.S.A.* **134 F8** 39 0N 75 40W
Delaware →, *U.S.A.* **134 F8** 39 20N 75 25W
Delaware B., *U.S.A.* **133 C12** 38 50N 75 0W
Delčevo, *Yugoslavia* **42 F7** 41 58N 22 46 E
Delegate, *Australia* **117 D8** 37 4 S 148 56 E
Delémont, *Switz.* **28 B4** 47 22N 7 20 E
Delft, *Neths.* **20 D4** 52 1N 4 22 E
Delft I., *Sri Lanka* **83 K4** 9 30N 79 40 E
Delfzijl, *Neths.* **20 B9** 53 20N 6 55 E
Delgado, C., *Mozam.* **107 E5** 10 45 S 40 40 E
Delgerhet, *Mongolia* **66 B6** 45 50N 110 30 E
Delgo, *Sudan* **94 C3** 20 6N 30 40 E
Delhi, *Canada* **136 D4** 42 51N 80 30W
Delhi, *India* **80 E7** 28 38N 77 17 E
Delhi, *U.S.A.* **137 D10** 42 17N 74 56W
Deli Jovan, *Yugoslavia* **42 C7** 44 13N 22 9 E
Delia, *Canada* **130 C6** 51 38N 112 23W
Delice, *Turkey* **88 D6** 39 54N 34 2 E
Delice →, *Turkey* **88 D6** 39 45N 34 15 E
Delicias, *Mexico* **146 B3** 28 10N 105 30W
Delījān, *Iran* **85 C6** 33 59N 50 40 E
Delitzsch, *Germany* **26 D8** 51 32N 12 22 E
Dell City, *U.S.A.* **143 L11** 31 58N 105 19W
Dell Rapids, *U.S.A.* **138 D6** 43 53N 96 44W
Delle, *France* **23 E14** 47 30N 7 2 E
Dellys, *Algeria* **99 A5** 36 57N 3 57 E
Delmar, *Iowa, U.S.A.* **140 C6** 42 0N 90 37W
Delmar, *N.Y., U.S.A.* **137 D11** 42 37N 73 47W
Delmenhorst, *Germany* **26 B4** 53 3N 8 37 E
Delmiro Gouveia, *Brazil* **154 C4** 9 24 S 38 6W
Delnice, *Yugoslavia* **39 C11** 45 23N 14 50 E
Delong, Ostrova, *U.S.S.R.* **57 B15** 76 40N 149 20 E
Deloraine, *Australia* **114 G4** 41 30 S 146 40 E
Deloraine, *Canada* **131 D8** 49 15N 100 29W
Delphi, *Greece* **45 F4** 38 28N 22 30 E
Delphi, *U.S.A.* **141 D10** 40 37N 86 40W
Delphos, *U.S.A.* **141 D12** 40 51N 84 17W
Delportshoop, *S. Africa* **104 D3** 28 22 S 24 20 E
Delray Beach, *U.S.A.* **135 M5** 26 27N 80 4W
Delsbo, *Sweden* **14 C10** 61 48N 16 32 E
Delta, *Colo., U.S.A.* **143 G9** 38 44N 108 5W
Delta, *Utah, U.S.A.* **142 G7** 39 21N 112 29W
Delta Amacuro □, *Venezuela* **153 B5** 8 30N 61 30W
Delungra, *Australia* **115 D5** 29 39 S 150 51 E
Delvina, *Albania* **44 E2** 39 59N 20 4 E
Delvinákion, *Greece* **44 E2** 39 57N 20 32 E
Demak, *Indonesia* **75 D4** 6 53 S 110 38 E
Demanda, Sierra de la, *Spain* **34 C2** 42 15N 3 0W
Demba, *Zaïre* **103 D4** 5 28 S 22 15 E
Demba Chio, *Angola* **103 D2** 9 41 S 13 41 E
Dembecha, *Ethiopia* **95 E4** 10 32N 37 30 E
Dembi, *Ethiopia* **95 F4** 8 5N 36 25 E
Dembia, *Zaïre* **106 B2** 3 33N 25 48 E
Dembidolo, *Ethiopia* **95 F3** 8 34N 34 50 E
Demer →, *Belgium* **21 G5** 50 57N 4 42 E
Demerara □, *Guyana* **153 B6** 6 0N 58 30W
Demetrias, *Greece* **44 E5** 39 22N 23 1 E
Demidov, *U.S.S.R.* **50 D7** 55 16N 31 30 E
Deming, *N. Mex., U.S.A.* **143 K10** 32 10N 107 50W
Deming, *Wash., U.S.A.* **144 B4** 48 49N 122 13W
Demini →, *Brazil* **153 D5** 0 46 S 62 56W
Demirci, *Turkey* **88 D3** 39 2N 28 38 E
Demirköy, *Turkey* **88 C2** 41 49N 27 45 E
Demmin, *Germany* **26 B9** 53 54N 13 2 E
Demnate, *Morocco* **98 B3** 31 44N 6 59W
Demonte, *Italy* **38 D4** 44 18N 7 18 E
Demopolis, *U.S.A.* **135 J2** 32 30N 87 48W
Dempo, *Indonesia* **70 E2** 4 2 S 103 15 E
Demyansk, *U.S.S.R.* **50 C8** 57 40N 32 27 E
Den Burg, *Neths.* **20 B5** 53 3N 4 47 E
Den Chai, *Thailand* **76 D3** 17 59N 100 4 E
Den Dungen, *Neths.* **21 E6** 51 41N 5 22 E
Den Haag = 's-Gravenhage, *Neths.* **20 D4** 52 7N 4 17 E
Den Ham, *Neths.* **20 D9** 52 28N 6 30 E
Den Helder, *Neths.* **20 C5** 52 57N 4 45 E
Den Hulst, *Neths.* **20 C8** 52 36N 6 16 E
Den Oever, *Neths.* **20 C6** 52 56N 5 2 E
Denain, *France* **23 B10** 50 20N 3 22 E
Denair, *U.S.A.* **144 H6** 37 32N 120 48W
Denau, *U.S.S.R.* **55 D3** 38 16N 67 54 E
Denbigh, *U.K.* **16 D4** 53 12N 3 26W
Dendang, *Indonesia* **70 E3** 3 7 S 107 56 E
Dender →, *Belgium* **21 F4** 51 2N 4 6 E
Denderhoutem, *Belgium* **21 G4** 50 53N 4 2 E
Denderleeuw, *Belgium* **21 G4** 50 54N 4 5 E
Dendermonde, *Belgium* **21 F4** 51 2N 4 5 E
Deneba, *Ethiopia* **95 F4** 9 47N 39 10 E
Denekamp, *Neths.* **20 D10** 52 22N 7 1 E

Dixon 191

Denezhkin Kamen, Gora,
U.S.S.R. . . . . **54 A6** 60 25N 59 32 E
Deng Deng, *Cameroon* . **102 A2** 5 12N 13 31 E
Deng Xian, *China* . . . . . . **69 A9** 32 34N 112 4 E
Dengchuan, *China* . . . . . **68 E3** 25 59N 100 3 E
Denge, *Nigeria* . . . . **101 C6** 12 52N 5 21 E
Dengfeng, *China* . . . . **66 G7** 34 25N 113 2 E
Dengi, *Nigeria* . . . . **101 D6** 9 25N 9 55 E
Dengkou, *China* . . . . **66 D4** 40 18N 106 55 E
Denham, *Australia* . . . . . **113 E1** 25 56 S 113 31 E
Denham Ra., *Australia* . **114 C4** 21 55 S 147 46 E
Denham Sd., *Australia* . . **113 E1** 25 45 S 113 15 E
Denia, *Spain* . . . . **35 G5** 38 49N 0 8 E
Denial B., *Australia* . . . . **115 E1** 32 14 S 133 32 E
Deniliquin, *Australia* . . . **117 C6** 35 30 S 144 58 E
Denison, *Iowa, U.S.A.* . . **138 E7** 42 0N 95 18W
Denison, *Tex., U.S.A.* . . **139 J6** 33 50N 96 40W
Denison Plains, *Australia* **112 C4** 18 35 S 128 0 E
Denisovka, *U.S.S.R.* . . . **54 E7** 52 28N 61 46 E
Denizli, *Turkey* . . . . **88 E3** 37 42N 29 2 E
Denizli □, *Turkey* . . . . . . **88 E3** 37 45N 29 5 E
Denman, *Australia* . . . . . **117 B9** 32 24 S 150 42 E
Denman Glacier,
Antarctica . . . . **7 C7** 66 45 S 99 25 E
Denmark, *Australia* . . . . **113 F2** 34 59 S 117 25 E
Denmark ■, *Europe* . . . . **15 J3** 55 30N 9 0 E
Denmark Str., *Atl. Oc.* . . **124 C17** 66 0N 30 0W
Dennison, *U.S.A.* **136 F3** 40 21N 81 21W
Denpasar, *Indonesia* . . . . **70 F5** 8 45 S 115 14 E
Denton, *Mont., U.S.A.* . **142 C9** 47 25N 109 56W
Denton, *Tex., U.S.A.* . . . **139 J6** 33 12N 97 10W
D'Entrecasteaux, Pt.,
Australia . . . . **113 F2** 34 50 S 115 57 E
D'Entrecasteaux Is.,
Papua N. G. . . . . **120 E6** 9 0 S 151 0 E
Dents du Midi, *Switz.* . . **28 D3** 46 10N 6 56 E
Denu, *Ghana* . . . . **101 D5** 6 4N 1 8 E
Denver, *Colo., U.S.A.* . . **138 F2** 39 45N 105 0W
Denver, *Ind., U.S.A.* . . **141 D10** 40 52N 86 5W
Denver, *Iowa, U.S.A.* . . **140 B4** 42 40N 92 20W
Denver City, *U.S.A.* . . . **139 J3** 32 58N 102 48W
Deoband, *India* . . . . **80 E7** 29 42N 77 43 E
Deobhog, *India* . . . . **82 E6** 19 53N 82 44 E
Deogarh, *India* . . . . **82 D7** 21 32N 84 45 E
Deoghar, *India* . . . . **81 G12** 24 30N 86 42 E
Deolali, *India* . . . . **82 E1** 19 58N 73 50 E
Deoli = Devli, *India* . . . **80 G6** 25 50N 75 20 E
Deoria, *India* . . . . **81 F10** 26 31N 83 48 E
Deosai Mts., *Pakistan* . . **81 B6** 35 40N 75 0 E
Deping, *China* . . . . **67 F9** 37 25N 116 58 E
Deposit, *U.S.A.* **137 D9** 42 5N 75 23W
Depot Springs, *Australia* **113 E3** 27 55 S 120 3 E
Deputatskiy, *U.S.S.R.* . . **57 C14** 69 18N 139 54 E
Dêqên, *China* . . . . **68 C2** 28 34N 98 51 E
Deqing, *China* . . . . **69 F8** 23 8N 111 42 E
Dera Ghazi Khan,
Pakistan . . . . **79 C3** 30 5N 70 43 E
Dera Ismail Khan,
Pakistan . . . . **79 C3** 31 50N 70 50 E
Derbent, *U.S.S.R.* . . . . . **53 E13** 42 5N 48 15 E
Derby, *Australia* . . . . **112 C3** 17 18 S 123 38 E
Derby, *U.K.* **16 E6** 52 55N 1 28W
Derby, *Conn., U.S.A.* . . **137 E11** 41 20N 73 5W
Derby, *N.Y., U.S.A.* . . . **136 D6** 42 40N 78 59W
Derbyshire □, *U.K.* **16 E6** 52 55N 1 28W
Derecske, *Hungary* . . . . . **31 D14** 47 20N 21 33 E
Dereli, *Turkey* . . . . **89 C8** 40 44N 38 26 E
Derg →, *U.K.* **19 B4** 54 42N 7 26W
Derg, L., *Ireland* **19 D3** 53 0N 8 20W
Dergachi, *U.S.S.R.* . . . . . **51 F10** 50 9N 36 11 E
Derik, *Turkey* . . . . **89 E9** 37 21N 40 18 E
Derinkuyu, *Turkey* . . . . . **88 D6** 38 22N 34 45 E
Dermantsi, *Bulgaria* . . . . **43 D9** 43 8N 24 17 E
Dernieres Isles, *U.S.A.* . **139 L9** 29 0N 90 45W
Dêrong, *China* . . . . **68 C2** 28 44N 99 9 E
Derrinallum, *Australia* . **116 D5** 37 57 S 143 15 E
Derry = Londonderry,
U.K. **19 B4** 55 0N 7 23W
Derryveagh Mts., *Ireland* **19 B3** 55 0N 8 4W
Derudub, *Sudan* . . . . **94 D4** 17 31N 36 7 E
Derval, *France* **22 E5** 47 40N 1 41W
Dervéni, *Greece* . . . . **45 F4** 38 8N 22 25 E
Derventa, *Yugoslavia* . . . **42 C2** 44 59N 17 55 E
Derwent, *Canada* **131 C6** 53 41N 110 58W
Derwent →, *Derby,*
U.K. **16 E6** 52 53N 1 17W
Derwent →, *N. Yorks.,*
U.K. **16 D7** 53 45N 0 57W
Derwent Water, *U.K.* . . **16 C4** 54 35N 3 9W
Des Moines, *Iowa,*
U.S.A. **140 C3** 41 35N 93 37W
Des Moines, *N. Mex.,*
U.S.A. **139 G3** 36 50N 103 51W
Des Moines →, *U.S.A.* . **138 E9** 40 23N 91 25W
Des Plaines, *U.S.A.* **141 B9** 42 3N 87 52W
Des Plaines →, *U.S.A.* . **141 C8** 41 23N 88 15W
Desaguadero →,
Argentina . . . . **158 C2** 34 30 S 66 46W
Desaguadero →, *Bolivia* **156 D4** 16 35 S 69 5W
Descanso, Pta., *Mexico* . **145 N9** 32 21N 117 3W
Descartes, *France* . . . . . . **24 B4** 46 59N 0 42 E
Deschaillons, *Canada* . . . **129 C5** 46 32N 72 7W
Descharme →, *Canada* . **131 B7** 56 51N 109 13W
Deschutes →, *U.S.A.* . . **142 D3** 45 30N 121 0W
Dese, *Ethiopia* . . . . **90 E2** 11 5N 39 40 E
Deseado, C., *Chile* . . . . . **160 D2** 52 45 S 74 42W
Desenzano del Gardo,
Italy . . . . **38 C7** 45 28N 10 32 E
Desert Center, *U.S.A.* . . **145 M11** 33 45N 115 27W
Desert Hot Springs,
U.S.A. **145 M10** 33 58N 116 30W
Désirade, I., *Guadeloupe* **149 C7** 16 18N 61 3W
Deskenatlata L., *Canada* **130 A6** 60 55N 112 3W
Desna →, *U.S.S.R.* . . . . **50 F7** 50 33N 30 32 E
Desnătui →, *Romania* . **46 E4** 44 15N 23 27 E
Desolación, I., *Chile* . . . **160 D2** 53 0 S 74 0W
Despeñaperros, Paso,
Spain **35 G1** 38 24N 3 30W
Despotovac, *Yugoslavia* . **42 C6** 44 6N 21 30 E
Dessau, *Germany* . . . . . . **26 D8** 51 49N 12 15 E
Dessel, *Belgium* . . . . **21 F6** 51 15N 5 7 E
Dessye = Dese, *Ethiopia* **90 E2** 11 5N 39 40 E
D'Estrees B., *Australia* . **116 C2** 35 55 S 137 45 E
Desuri, *India* . . . . **80 G5** 25 18N 73 35 E
Desvres, *France* . . . . **23 B8** 50 40N 1 48 E
Det Udom, *Thailand* . . . **76 E5** 14 54N 105 5 E
Deta, *Romania* . . . . **42 B6** 45 24N 21 13 E
Dete, *Zimbabwe* . . . . **107 F2** 18 38 S 26 50 E
Detinja →, *Yugoslavia* . **42 D4** 43 51N 19 45 E
Detmold, *Germany* . . . . . **26 D4** 51 55N 8 50 E
Detour Pt., *U.S.A.* **134 C2** 45 37N 86 35W
Detroit, *Mich., U.S.A.* . . **128 D3** 42 23N 83 5W
Detroit, *Tex., U.S.A.* . . . **139 J7** 33 40N 95 10W
Detroit Lakes, *U.S.A.* . . **138 B7** 46 50N 95 50W
Deurne, *Belgium* . . . . **21 F4** 51 12N 4 24 E
Deurne, *Neths.* . . . . **21 F7** 51 27N 5 49 E
Deutsche Bucht,
Germany . . . . **26 A4** 54 15N 8 0 E
Deutschlandsberg, *Austria* **30 E8** 46 49N 15 14 E
Deux-Sèvres □, *France* . **22 F6** 46 35N 0 20W
Deva, *Romania* . . . . **46 D3** 45 53N 22 55 E
Devakottai, *India* . . . . . . **83 K4** 9 55N 78 45 E
Devaprayag, *India* . . . . . . **81 D8** 30 13N 78 35 E
Dévaványa, *Hungary* . . . **31 D13** 47 2N 20 59 E
Deveci Dağı, *Turkey* . . . **52 F7** 40 10N 36 0 E
Deveci Dağları, *Turkey* . . **88 C6** 40 10N 35 50 E
Devecser, *Hungary* . . . . . **31 D10** 47 6N 17 26 E
Develi, *Turkey* . . . . **88 D6** 38 23N 35 29 E
Deventer, *Neths.* . . . . . . **20 D8** 52 15N 6 10 E
Deveron →, *U.K.* **18 D6** 57 40N 2 31W
Devesel, *Romania* . . . . . . **46 E3** 44 28N 22 41 E
Devgad I., *India* . . . . **83 G2** 14 48N 74 5 E
Devgadh Bariya, *India* . . **80 H5** 22 40N 73 55 E
Devil River Pk., *N.Z.* . . **119 A7** 40 56 S 172 37 E
Devils Den, *U.S.A.* **144 K7** 35 46N 119 58W
Devils Lake, *U.S.A.* **138 A5** 48 5N 98 50W
Devils Paw, *Canada* **130 B2** 58 47N 134 0W
Devil's Pt., *Sri Lanka* . . . **83 K5** 9 26N 80 6 E
Devil's Pt., *Vanuatu* . . . **121 G6** 17 44 S 168 11 E
Devin, *Bulgaria* . . . . **43 F9** 41 44N 24 24 E
Devizes, *U.K.* **17 F6** 51 21N 2 0W
Devli, *India* . . . . **80 G6** 25 50N 75 20 E
Devnya, *Bulgaria* . . . . . . **43 D12** 43 13N 27 33 E
Devolii →, *Albania* . . . . **44 D2** 40 57N 20 15 E
Devon, *Canada* **130 C6** 53 24N 113 44W
Devon □, *U.K.* **17 G4** 50 50N 3 40W
Devon I., *Canada* **6 B3** 75 10N 85 0W
Devonport, *Australia* . . . **114 G4** 41 10 S 146 22 E
Devonport, *N.Z.* . . . . **118 C3** 36 49 S 174 49 E
Devonport, *U.K.* **17 G3** 50 23N 4 11W
Devrek, *Turkey* . . . . **88 C4** 41 13N 31 57 E
Devrekâni, *Turkey* . . . . . **88 C5** 41 36N 33 50 E
Devrez →, *Turkey* . . . . . **88 C6** 41 6N 34 25 E
Dewas, *India* . . . . **80 H7** 22 59N 76 3 E
Dewetsdorp, *S. Africa* . . **104 D4** 29 33 S 26 39 E
Dewsbury, *U.K.* **16 D6** 53 42N 1 38W
Dexing, *China* . . . . **69 C11** 28 46N 117 30 E
Dexter, *Mich., U.S.A.* . . **141 B13** 42 20N 83 53W
Dexter, *Mo., U.S.A.* . . . **139 G10** 36 50N 90 0W
Dexter, *N. Mex., U.S.A.* **139 J2** 33 15N 104 25W
Dey-Dey, L., *Australia* . **113 E5** 29 12 S 131 4 E
Deyang, *China* . . . . **68 B5** 31 3N 104 27 E
Deyhūk, *Iran* . . . . **85 C8** 33 15N 57 30 E
Deyyer, *Iran* . . . . **85 E6** 27 55N 51 55 E
Dezadeash L., *Canada* . . **130 A1** 60 28N 136 58W
Dezfūl, *Iran* . . . . **85 C6** 32 20N 48 30 E
Dezhneva, Mys, *U.S.S.R.* **57 C19** 66 5N 169 40W
Dezhou, *China* . . . . **66 F9** 37 26N 116 18 E
Dháfni, *Greece* . . . . **45 G4** 37 48N 22 1 E
Dháfni, *Kríti, Greece* . . . **32 D7** 35 13N 25 3 E
Dhahaban, *Si. Arabia* . . . **86 B2** 21 58N 39 3 E
Dhahiriya = Az
Ẓāhirīyah, *Jordan* . . . . **91 D3** 31 25N 34 58 E
Dhahran = Aẓ Ẓahrān,
Si. Arabia . . . . **85 E6** 26 10N 50 7 E
Dhaka, *Bangla.* . . . . **78 D3** 23 43N 90 26 E
Dhaka □, *Bangla.* . . . . . **78 C3** 24 25N 90 25 E
Dhali, *Cyprus* . . . . **32 D12** 35 1N 33 25 E
Dhamangaon, *India* . . . . **82 D4** 20 45N 78 15 E
Dhamar, *Yemen* . . . . **86 D4** 14 30N 44 20 E
Dhamási, *Greece* . . . . **44 E4** 39 43N 22 11 E
Dhampur, *India* . . . . **81 E8** 29 19N 78 33 E
Dhamtari, *India* . . . . **82 D5** 20 42N 81 35 E
Dhanbad, *India* . . . . **81 H12** 23 50N 86 30 E
Dhankuta, *Nepal* . . . . . . **81 F12** 26 55N 87 40 E
Dhanora, *India* . . . . **82 D5** 20 20N 80 22 E
Dhar, *India* . . . . **80 H6** 22 35N 75 26 E
Dharampur, *Gujarat,*
India . . . . **82 D1** 20 32N 73 17 E
Dharampur, *Mad. P.,*
India . . . . **80 H6** 22 13N 75 18 E
Dharamsala =
Dharmsala, *India* . . . . . **80 C7** 32 16N 76 23 E
Dharapuram, *India* . . . . . **83 J3** 10 45N 77 34 E
Dharmapuri, *India* . . . . . **83 H4** 12 10N 78 10 E
Dharmavaram, *India* . . . **83 G3** 14 29N 77 44 E
Dharmsala, *India* . . . . . . **80 C7** 32 16N 76 23 E
Dharwad, *India* . . . . **83 G2** 15 22N 75 15 E
Dhaulagiri, *Nepal* . . . . . **81 E10** 28 39N 83 28 E
Dhebar, L., *India* . . . . . . **80 G6** 24 10N 74 0 E
Dheftera, *Cyprus* . . . . . . **32 D12** 35 5N 33 16 E
Dhenkanal, *India* . . . . . . **82 D7** 20 45N 85 35 E
Dhenoúsa, *Greece* . . . . . . **45 G7** 37 8N 25 48 E
Dherinia, *Cyprus* . . . . . . **32 D12** 35 3N 33 57 E
Dheskáti, *Greece* . . . . **44 E3** 39 55N 21 49 E
Dhespotikó, *Greece* . . . . **45 H6** 36 57N 24 58 E
Dhestina, *Greece* . . . . **45 F4** 38 25N 22 31 E
Dhiarrizos →, *Cyprus* . . **32 E11** 34 41N 32 34 E
Dhībān, *Jordan* . . . . **91 D4** 31 30N 35 46 E
Dhidhimótikhon, *Greece* **44 C8** 41 22N 26 29 E
Dhíkti Óros, *Greece* . . . . **32 D7** 35 8N 25 22 E
Dhilianáta, *Greece* . . . . . **45 F2** 38 15N 20 34 E
Dhílos, *Greece* . . . . **45 G7** 37 23N 25 15 E
Dhimitsána, *Greece* . . . . **45 G4** 37 36N 22 3 E
Dhírfis, *Greece* . . . . **45 F5** 38 40N 23 54 E
Dhodhekánisos, *Greece* . **45 H9** 36 35N 27 0 E
Dhokós, *Greece* . . . . **45 G5** 37 20N 23 20 E
Dholiana, *Greece* . . . . **44 E2** 39 54N 20 32 E
Dholka, *India* . . . . **80 H5** 22 44N 72 29 E
Dhomokós, *Greece* . . . . . **45 E4** 39 10N 22 18 E
Dhoraji, *India* . . . . **80 J4** 21 45N 70 37 E
Dhoxáton, *Greece* . . . . . . **44 C6** 41 9N 24 16 E
Dhragonísi, *Greece* . . . . **45 G7** 37 27N 25 29 E
Dhráhstis, Ákra, *Greece* **32 A3** 39 48N 19 40 E
Dhrangadhra, *India* . . . . **80 H4** 22 59N 71 31 E
Dhrápanon, Ákra, *Greece* **32 D6** 35 28N 24 14 E
Dhriopís, *Greece* . . . . . . **45 G6** 37 25N 24 35 E
Dhrol, *India* . . . . **80 H4** 22 33N 70 25 E
Dhubāb, *Yemen* . . . . **86 D3** 12 56N 43 25 E
Dhuburi, *India* . . . . **78 B2** 26 2N 89 59 E
Dhulasar, *Bangla.* . . . . . . **78 E3** 21 52N 90 14 E
Dhule, *India* . . . . **82 D2** 20 58N 74 50 E
Dhupdhara, *India* . . . . . . **78 B3** 26 10N 91 4 E
Dhut →, *Somali Rep.* . . **90 E5** 10 30N 50 0 E
Di Linh, *Vietnam* . . . . . . **77 G7** 11 35N 108 4 E
Di Linh, Cao Nguyen,
Vietnam . . . . **77 G7** 11 30N 108 0 E
Día, *Greece* . . . . **32 D7** 35 28N 25 14 E
Diablo, Mt., *U.S.A.* **144 H5** 37 53N 121 56W
Diablo Range, *U.S.A.* . . . **144 J5** 37 0N 121 5W
Diafarabé, *Mali* **100 C4** 14 9N 4 57W
Diagonal, *U.S.A.* **140 D2** 40 49N 94 20W
Diala, *Mali* **100 C3** 14 10N 9 58W
Dialakoro, *Mali* **100 C3** 12 18N 7 54W
Diallassagou, *Mali* **100 C4** 13 47N 3 41W
Diamante, *Argentina* . . . **158 C3** 32 5 S 60 40W
Diamante →, *Argentina* . **158 C2** 34 30 S 66 46W
Diamantina, *Brazil* . . . . . **155 E3** 18 17 S 43 40W
Diamantina →, *Australia* **115 D2** 26 45 S 139 10 E
Diamantino, *Brazil* . . . . . **157 C6** 14 30 S 56 30W
Diamond Harbour, *India* **81 H13** 22 11N 88 14 E
Diamond Is., *Australia* . . **114 B5** 17 25 S 151 5 E
Diamond Mts., *U.S.A.* . . **142 G6** 40 0N 115 58W
Diamond Springs, *U.S.A.* **144 G6** 38 42N 120 49W
Diamondville, *U.S.A.* . . . **142 F8** 41 51N 110 30W
Dianbai, *China* . . . . **69 G8** 21 33N 111 0 E
Diancheng, *China* . . . . . . **69 G8** 21 30N 111 4 E
Diano Marina, *Italy* . . . . **38 E5** 43 55N 8 3 E
Dianópolis, *Brazil* . . . . . . **155 D2** 11 38 S 46 50W
Dianra, *Ivory C.* **100 D3** 8 45N 6 14W
Diapaga, *Burkina Faso* . **101 C5** 12 5N 1 46 E
Diapangou, *Burkina Faso* **101 C5** 12 5N 0 10 E
Diapur, *Australia* . . . . . . **116 D4** 36 19 S 141 29 E
Diariguila, *Guinea* **100 C2** 10 35N 10 2W
Dībā, *Oman* . . . . **85 E8** 25 45N 56 16 E
Dibaya, *Zaïre* . . . . **103 D4** 6 30 S 22 57 E
Dibaya-Lubue, *Zaïre* . . . **103 C3** 4 12 S 19 54 E
Dibbi, *Ethiopia* . . . . **90 G3** 4 10N 41 52 E
Dibete, *Botswana* . . . . . . **104 C4** 23 45 S 26 32 E
Dibrugarh, *India* . . . . **78 B5** 27 29N 94 55 E
Dickeyville, *U.S.A.* **140 B6** 42 38N 90 36W
Dickinson, *U.S.A.* **138 B3** 46 50N 102 48W
Dickson, *U.S.A.* **135 G2** 36 5N 87 22W
Dickson City, *U.S.A.* **137 E9** 41 29N 75 40W
Dicomano, *Italy* . . . . **39 E8** 43 53N 11 30 E
Didam, *Neths.* . . . . **20 E8** 51 57N 6 8 E
Didesa, W. →, *Ethiopia* **95 E4** 10 2N 35 32 E
Didiéni, *Mali* **100 C3** 13 53N 8 6W
Didsbury, *Canada* **130 C6** 51 35N 114 10W
Didwana, *India* . . . . **80 F6** 27 23N 74 36 E
Die, *France* . . . . **25 D9** 44 47N 5 22 E
Diébougou, *Burkina Faso* **100 C4** 11 0N 3 15W
Diefenbaker L., *Canada* . **131 C7** 51 0N 106 55W
Diego Garcia, *Ind. Oc.* . . **109 E6** 7 50 S 72 50 E
Diekirch, *Lux.* . . . . **21 J8** 49 52N 6 10 E
Diélette, *France* **22 C5** 49 33N 1 52W
Diéma, *Mali* **100 C3** 14 32N 9 12W
Diémbéring, *Senegal* **100 C1** 12 29N 16 47W
Diemen, *Neths.* . . . . **20 D5** 52 21N 4 58 E
Dien Ban, *Vietnam* . . . . . **76 E7** 15 53N 108 16 E
Dien Bien, *Vietnam* . . . . **76 B4** 21 20N 103 0 E
Dien Khanh, *Vietnam* . . . **77 F7** 12 15N 109 6 E
Diepenbeek, *Belgium* . . . **21 G6** 50 54N 5 25 E
Diepenheim, *Neths.* . . . . . **20 D9** 52 12N 6 33 E
Diepenveen, *Neths.* . . . . . **20 D8** 52 18N 6 9 E
Diepholz, *Germany* . . . . . **26 C4** 52 37N 8 22 E
Diepoldsau, *Switz.* . . . . . **29 B9** 47 23N 9 40 E
Dieppe, *France* . . . . **22 C8** 49 54N 1 4 E
Dieren, *Neths.* . . . . **20 D8** 52 3N 6 6 E
Dierks, *U.S.A.* **139 H8** 34 9N 94 0W
Diessen, *Neths.* . . . . **21 F6** 51 29N 5 10 E
Diessenhofen, *Switz.* . . . . **29 A7** 47 42N 8 46 E
Diest, *Belgium* . . . . **21 G6** 50 58N 5 4 E
Dieterich, *U.S.A.* **141 E8** 39 4N 88 23W
Dietikon, *Switz.* . . . . **29 B6** 47 24N 8 24 E
Dieulefit, *France* . . . . **25 D9** 44 32N 5 4 E
Dieuze, *France* . . . . **23 D13** 48 49N 6 43 E
Diever, *Neths.* . . . . **20 C8** 52 51N 6 19 E
Differdange, *Lux.* . . . . . . **21 J7** 49 31N 5 54 E
Dig, *India* . . . . **80 F7** 27 28N 77 20 E
Digba, *Zaïre* . . . . **106 B2** 4 25N 25 48 E
Digboi, *India* . . . . **78 B5** 27 23N 95 38 E
Digby, *Canada* **129 D6** 44 38N 65 50W
Digges, *Canada* **131 B10** 58 40N 94 0W
Digges Is., *Canada* **127 B12** 62 40N 77 50W
Dighinala, *Bangla.* . . . . . **78 D4** 23 15N 92 5 E
Dighton, *U.S.A.* **138 F4** 38 30N 100 26W
Diglur, *India* . . . . **82 E3** 18 34N 77 33 E
Digne, *France* . . . . **25 D10** 44 5N 6 12 E
Digoin, *France* . . . . **24 B7** 46 29N 3 58 E
Digor, *Turkey* . . . . **89 C10** 40 22N 43 25 E
Digos, *Phil.* . . . . **71 C7** 6 45N 125 20 E
Digranes, *Iceland* **12 C6** 66 4N 14 44W
Digras, *India* . . . . **82 D3** 20 6N 77 45 E
Digul →, *Indonesia* . . . . **71 F9** 7 7 S 138 42 E
Dīhōk, *Iraq* . . . . **84 B3** 36 55N 38 57 E
Dijlah, Nahr →, *Asia* . . **84 D5** 31 0N 47 25 E
Dijle →, *Belgium* . . . . . . **21 G5** 50 58N 4 41 E
Dijon, *France* . . . . **23 E12** 47 20N 5 3 E
Dikala, *Sudan* . . . . **95 G3** 4 45N 31 28 E
Dikkil, *Djibouti* . . . . **95 E5** 11 8N 42 20 E
Dikomu di Kai, *Botswana* **104 C3** 24 58 S 24 36 E
Diksmuide, *Belgium* . . . . **21 F1** 51 2N 2 52 E
Dikson, *U.S.S.R.* . . . . **56 B9** 73 40N 80 5 E
Dikwa, *Nigeria* . . . . **101 C7** 12 4N 13 30 E
Dila, *Ethiopia* . . . . **95 F4** 6 21N 38 22 E
Dilbeek, *Belgium* . . . . **21 G4** 50 51N 4 17 E
Dili, *Indonesia* . . . . **71 F7** 8 39 S 125 34 E
Dilizhan, *U.S.S.R.* . . . . . . **53 F11** 40 46N 44 57 E
Dilj, *Yugoslavia* . . . . **42 B3** 45 29N 18 1 E
Dillard, *U.S.A.* **140 G5** 37 44N 91 13W
Dillenburg, *Germany* . . . . **26 E4** 50 44N 8 17 E
Dilley, *U.S.A.* **139 L5** 28 40N 99 12W
Dilling, *Sudan* . . . . **95 E2** 12 3N 29 35 E
Dillingen, *Germany* . . . . **27 G6** 48 32N 10 29 E
Dillingham, *U.S.A.* **126 C4** 59 5N 158 30W
Dillon, *Canada* **131 B7** 55 56N 108 35W
Dillon, *Mont., U.S.A.* . . . **142 D7** 45 9N 112 36W
Dillon, *S.C., U.S.A.* **135 H6** 34 26N 79 20W
Dillon →, *Canada* **131 B7** 55 56N 108 56W
Dillsboro, *U.S.A.* **141 E11** 39 1N 85 4W
Dilolo, *Zaïre* . . . . **103 E4** 10 28 S 22 18 E
Dilsen, *Belgium* . . . . **21 F7** 51 2N 5 44 E
Dilston, *Australia* . . . . . . **114 G4** 41 22 S 147 10 E
Dimapur, *India* . . . . **78 C4** 25 54N 93 45 E
Dimas, *Mexico* **146 C3** 23 43N 106 47W
Dimashq, *Syria* . . . . **91 B5** 33 30N 36 18 E
Dimashq □, *Syria* . . . . . . **91 B5** 33 30N 36 30 E
Dimbaza, *S. Africa* . . . . . **105 E4** 32 50 S 27 14 E
Dimbelenge, *Zaïre* . . . . . **103 D4** 5 33 S 23 7 E
Dimbokro, *Ivory C.* **100 D4** 6 45N 4 46W
Dimboola, *Australia* . . . . **116 D5** 36 28 S 142 7 E
Dîmboviţa □, *Romania* . **46 E6** 45 0N 25 30 E
Dîmboviţa →, *Romania* . **46 E7** 44 5N 26 35 E
Dîmbovnic →, *Romania* **46 E6** 44 28N 25 18 E
Dimbulah, *Australia* . . . . **114 B4** 17 8 S 145 4 E
Dimitrovgrad, *Bulgaria* . **43 E10** 42 5N 25 35 E
Dimitrovgrad, *U.S.S.R.* . **51 D16** 54 14N 49 39 E
Dimitrovgrad, *Yugoslavia* **42 D7** 43 2N 22 48 E
Dimitrovo = Pernik,
Bulgaria . . . . **42 E8** 42 35N 23 2 E
Dimmitt, *U.S.A.* **139 H3** 34 36N 102 16W
Dimo, *Sudan* . . . . **95 F2** 5 19N 29 10 E
Dimona, *Israel* . . . . **91 D4** 31 2N 35 1 E
Dimovo, *Bulgaria* . . . . . . **42 D7** 43 43N 22 50 E
Dinagat, *Phil.* . . . . **71 B7** 10 10N 125 40 E
Dinajpur, *Bangla.* . . . . . . **78 C2** 25 33N 88 43 E
Dinan, *France* **22 D4** 48 28N 2 2W
Dīnān Āb, *Iran* . . . . **85 C8** 32 4N 56 49 E
Dinant, *Belgium* . . . . **21 H5** 50 16N 4 55 E
Dinapur, *India* . . . . **81 G11** 25 38N 85 5 E
Dinar, *Turkey* . . . . **88 D4** 38 5N 30 10 E
Dinara Planina,
Yugoslavia . . . . **39 E13** 44 0N 16 30 E
Dinard, *France* **22 D4** 48 38N 2 6W
Dinaric Alps = Dinara
Planina, *Yugoslavia* . . . **39 E13** 44 0N 16 30 E
Dinder, Nahr ed →,
Sudan . . . . **95 E3** 14 6N 33 40 E
Dindi →, *India* . . . . **83 F4** 16 24N 78 15 E
Dindigul, *India* . . . . **83 J4** 10 25N 78 0 E
Ding Xian, *China* . . . . **66 E8** 38 30N 114 59 E
Dingbian, *China* . . . . **66 F4** 37 35N 107 32 E
Dingelstädt, *Germany* . . **26 D6** 51 19N 10 19 E
Dinghai, *China* . . . . **69 B14** 30 1N 122 6 E
Dingle, *Ireland* **19 D1** 52 9N 10 17W
Dingle B., *Ireland* **19 D1** 52 3N 10 20W
Dingmans Ferry, *U.S.A.* **137 E10** 41 13N 74 55W
Dingnan, *China* . . . . **69 E10** 24 45N 115 0 E
Dingo, *Australia* . . . . **114 C4** 23 38 S 149 19 E
Dingolfing, *Germany* . . . **27 G8** 48 38N 12 30 E
Dingtao, *China* . . . . **66 G8** 35 5N 115 35 E
Dinguiraye, *Guinea* **100 C2** 11 18N 10 49W
Dingwall, *U.K.* **18 D4** 57 36N 4 26W
Dingxi, *China* . . . . **66 G3** 35 30N 104 33 E
Dingxiang, *China* . . . . . . **66 E7** 38 30N 112 58 E
Dingyuan, *China* . . . . **69 A11** 32 32N 117 41 E
Dinh, Mui, *Vietnam* . . . . **77 G7** 11 22N 109 1 E
Dinh Lap, *Vietnam* . . . . . **76 B6** 21 33N 107 6 E
Dinhata, *India* . . . . **78 B2** 26 8N 89 27 E
Dinkel →, *Neths.* . . . . . . **20 D9** 52 30N 6 58 E
Dinokwe, *Botswana* . . . . **104 C4** 23 29 S 26 37 E
Dinosaur National
Monument, *U.S.A.* **142 F9** 40 30N 108 58W
Dinslaken, *Germany* . . . . **21 E9** 51 34N 6 41 E
Dinsor, *Somali Rep.* . . . . **108 D2** 2 24N 42 59 E
Dintel →, *Neths.* . . . . . . **21 E4** 51 39N 4 22 E
Dinteloord, *Neths.* . . . . . **21 E4** 51 38N 4 22 E
Dinuba, *U.S.A.* **144 J7** 36 31N 119 22W
Dinxperlo, *Neths.* . . . . . . **20 E9** 51 52N 6 30 E
Diósgyör, *Hungary* . . . . . **31 C13** 48 7N 20 43 E
Diosig, *Romania* . . . . **46 B3** 47 18N 22 2 E
Diourbel, *Senegal* **100 C1** 14 39N 16 12W
Diphu Pass, *India* . . . . . . **78 A6** 28 9N 97 20 E
Diplo, *Pakistan* . . . . **80 G3** 24 35N 69 35 E
Dipolog, *Phil.* . . . . **71 C6** 8 36N 123 20 E
Dipşa, *Romania* . . . . **46 C5** 46 58N 24 27 E
Dipton, *N.Z.* . . . . **119 F3** 45 54 S 168 22 E
Dir, *Pakistan* . . . . **79 B3** 35 8N 71 59 E
Diré, *Mali* **100 B4** 16 20N 3 25W
Dire Dawa, *Ethiopia* . . . . **90 F3** 9 35N 41 45 E
Diriamba, *Nic.* **148 D2** 11 51N 86 19W
Dirico, *Angola* . . . . **103 F4** 17 50 S 20 42 E
Dirk Hartog I., *Australia* **113 E1** 25 50 S 113 5 E
Dirkou, *Niger* . . . . **97 E2** 19 1N 12 53 E
Dirranbandi, *Australia* . . **115 D4** 28 33 S 148 17 E
Dirs, *Si. Arabia* . . . . **86 C3** 18 32N 42 5 E
Disa, *India* . . . . **80 G5** 24 18N 72 10 E
Disa, *Sudan* . . . . **95 E3** 12 5N 34 15 E
Disappointment, C.,
U.S.A. **142 C2** 46 20N 124 0W
Disappointment, L.,
Australia . . . . **112 D3** 23 20 S 122 40 E
Disaster B., *Australia* . . . **117 D8** 37 15 S 149 58 E
Discovery B., *Australia* . **116 E4** 38 10 S 140 40 E
Disentis, *Switz.* . . . . **29 C7** 46 42N 8 50 E
Dishna, *Egypt* . . . . **94 B3** 26 9N 32 32 E
Disina, *Nigeria* . . . . **101 C6** 11 35N 9 50 E
Disko, *Greenland* **6 C5** 69 45N 53 30W
Disko Bugt, *Greenland* . . **6 C5** 69 10N 52 0W
Disna, *U.S.S.R.* . . . . **50 D6** 55 32N 28 11 E
Disna →, *U.S.S.R.* . . . . . **50 D6** 55 34N 28 12 E
Disney Reef, *Tonga* . . . . **121 P13** 19 17 S 174 7W
Dison, *Belgium* . . . . **21 G7** 50 37N 5 51 E
Disteghil Sar, *Pakistan* . . **81 A6** 36 20N 75 12 E
Distrito Federal □, *Brazil* **155 E2** 15 45 S 47 45W
Distrito Federal □,
Venezuela **152 A4** 10 30N 66 55W
Disūq, *Egypt* . . . . **94 H7** 31 8N 30 35 E
Ditu, *Zaïre* . . . . **103 D4** 5 23 S 21 27 E
Diu, *India* . . . . **80 J4** 20 45N 70 58 E
Dīvāndarreh, *Iran* . . . . . . **84 C5** 35 55N 47 2 E
Dives →, *France* **22 C6** 49 18N 0 7W
Dives-sur-Mer, *France* . . **22 C6** 49 18N 0 8W
Divi Pt., *India* . . . . **83 G5** 15 59N 81 9 E
Divichi, *U.S.S.R.* . . . . **53 F13** 41 15N 48 57 E
Divide, *U.S.A.* **142 D7** 45 48N 112 47W
Dividing Ra., *Australia* . **113 E2** 27 45 S 116 0 E
Divinópolis, *Brazil* . . . . . **155 F3** 20 10 S 44 54W
Divisões, Serra dos,
Brazil . . . . **155 E1** 17 0 S 51 0W
Divnoye, *U.S.S.R.* . . . . . . **53 D10** 45 55N 43 21 E
Divo, *Ivory C.* **100 D3** 5 48N 5 15W
Divriği, *Turkey* . . . . **89 D8** 39 22N 38 7 E
Dīwāl Kol, *Afghan.* . . . . . **79 B2** 34 23N 67 52 E
Dix →, *U.S.A.* **141 G12** 37 49N 84 44W
Dixie Mt., *U.S.A.* **144 F6** 39 55N 120 16W
Dixon, *Calif., U.S.A.* . . . **144 G5** 38 27N 121 49W
Dixon, *Ill., U.S.A.* **140 C7** 41 50N 89 30W
Dixon, *Iowa, U.S.A.* . . . **140 C6** 41 45N 90 47W

192 Dixon

Dixon, Mo., U.S.A. 140 G4 37 59N 92 6W
Dixon, Mont., U.S.A. 142 C6 47 19N 114 25W
Dixon, N. Mex., U.S.A. 143 H11 36 15N 105 57W
Dixon Entrance, U.S.A. 130 C2 54 30N 132 0W
Dixonville, Canada 130 B5 56 32N 117 40W
Diyadin, Turkey 89 D10 39 33N 43 40 E
Diyarbakır, Turkey 89 E9 37 55N 40 18 E
Diyarbakir □, Turkey 89 E9 38 0N 40 10 E
Djado, Niger 97 D2 21 4N 12 14 E
Djado, Plateau du, Niger 97 D2 21 29N 12 21 E
Djakarta = Jakarta, Indonesia 71 G12 6 9 S 106 49 E
Djamâa, Algeria 99 B6 33 32N 5 59 E
Djamba, Angola 103 F2 16 45 S 13 58 E
Djambala, Congo 102 C2 2 32 S 14 30 E
Djanet, Algeria 99 D6 24 35N 9 32 E
Djaul I., Papua N. G. 120 B6 2 58 S 150 57 E
Djawa = Jawa, Indonesia 71 G14 7 0 S 110 0 E
Djebiniana, Tunisia 96 A2 35 1N 11 0 E
Djédaa, Chad 97 F3 13 31N 18 34 E
Djelfa, Algeria 99 B5 34 40N 3 15 E
Djema, C.A.R. 102 A5 6 3N 25 15 E
Djember, Chad 97 F3 10 25N 17 50 E
Djendel, Algeria 99 A5 36 15N 2 25 E
Djeneïene, Tunisia 96 B2 31 45N 10 9 E
Djenné, Mali 100 C4 14 0N 4 30W
Djenoun, Garet el, Algeria 99 C6 25 4N 5 31 E
Djerba, Tunisia 96 B2 33 52N 10 51 E
Djerid, Chott, Tunisia 96 B1 33 42N 8 30 E
Djiba, Gabon 102 C2 1 20 S 13 9 E
Djibo, Burkina Faso 101 C4 14 9N 1 35W
Djibouti, Djibouti 90 E3 11 30N 43 5 E
Djibouti ■, Africa 90 E3 12 0N 43 0 E
Djolu, Zaïre 102 B4 0 35N 22 5 E
Djougou, Benin 101 D5 9 40N 1 45 E
Djoum, Cameroon 102 B2 2 41N 12 35 E
Djourab, Chad 97 E3 16 40N 18 50 E
Djugu, Zaïre 106 B3 1 55N 30 35 E
Djúpivogur, Iceland 12 D6 64 39N 14 17W
Djursholm, Sweden 14 E12 59 25N 18 6 E
Djursland, Denmark 15 H4 56 27N 10 45 E
Dmitriev-Lgovskiy, U.S.S.R. 50 E9 52 10N 35 0 E
Dmitriya Lapteva, Proliv, U.S.S.R. 57 B15 73 0N 140 0 E
Dmitrov, U.S.S.R. 51 C10 56 25N 37 32 E
Dmitrovsk-Orlovskiy, U.S.S.R. 50 E9 52 29N 35 10 E
Dnepr →, U.S.S.R. 52 C5 46 30N 32 18 E
Dneprodzerzhinsk, U.S.S.R. 52 B6 48 32N 34 37 E
Dneprodzerzhinskoye Vdkhr., U.S.S.R. 52 B6 49 0N 34 0 E
Dnepropetrovsk, U.S.S.R. 52 B6 48 30N 35 0 E
Dneprorudnoye, U.S.S.R. 52 C6 47 21N 34 58 E
Dnestr →, U.S.S.R. 52 C4 46 18N 30 17 E
Dnestrovski = Belgorod, U.S.S.R. 51 F10 50 35N 36 35 E
Dnieper = Dnepr →, U.S.S.R. 52 C5 46 30N 32 18 E
Dniester = Dnestr →, U.S.S.R. 52 C4 46 18N 30 17 E
Dno, U.S.S.R. 50 C6 57 50N 29 58 E
Doabi, Afghan. 79 A3 36 1N 69 32 E
Doan Hung, Vietnam 76 B5 21 30N 105 10 E
Doba, Chad 97 G3 8 40N 16 50 E
Dobbiaco, Italy 39 B9 46 44N 12 13 E
Dobbyn, Australia 114 B3 19 44 S 140 2 E
Dobczyce, Poland 31 B13 49 52N 20 25 E
Döbeln, Germany 26 D9 51 7N 13 10 E
Doberai, Jazirah, Indonesia 71 E8 1 25 S 133 0 E
Dobiegniew, Poland 47 C2 52 59N 15 45 E
Doblas, Argentina 158 D3 37 5 S 64 0W
Dobo, Indonesia 71 F8 5 45 S 134 15 E
Doboj, Yugoslavia 42 C3 44 46N 18 6 E
Dobra, Konin, Poland 47 D5 51 55N 18 37 E
Dobra, Szczecin, Poland 47 B2 53 34N 15 20 E
Dobra, Dîmbovita, Romania 46 E6 44 52N 25 40 E
Dobra, Hunedoara, Romania 46 D3 45 54N 22 36 E
Dobre Miasto, Poland 47 B7 53 58N 20 26 E
Dobreta-Turnu-Severin, Romania 46 E3 44 39N 22 41 E
Dobrinishta, Bulgaria 43 F8 41 49N 23 34 E
Dobříš, Czech. 30 B7 49 46N 14 10 E
Dobrodzień, Poland 47 E5 50 45N 18 25 E
Dobropole, U.S.S.R. 52 B7 48 25N 37 2 E
Dobruja, Romania 46 E9 44 30N 28 15 E
Dobrush, U.S.S.R. 50 E7 52 28N 30 19 E
Dobryanka, U.S.S.R. 54 B5 58 27N 56 25 E
Dobrzyń nad Wisłą, Poland 47 C6 52 39N 19 22 E
Dobtong, Sudan 95 F3 6 25N 31 40 E
Doc, Mui, Vietnam 76 D6 17 58N 106 30 E
Doce →, Brazil 155 E4 19 37 S 39 49W
Doda, India 81 C6 33 10N 75 34 E
Dodecanese = Dhodhekánisos, Greece 45 H9 36 35N 27 0 E
Dodewaard, Neths. 20 E7 51 55N 5 39 E
Dodge Center, U.S.A. 138 C8 44 1N 92 50W
Dodge City, U.S.A. 139 G5 37 42N 100 0W
Dodge L., Canada 131 B7 59 50N 105 36W
Dodgeville, U.S.A. 140 B6 42 55N 90 8W
Dodo, Sudan 95 F2 5 10N 29 57 E
Dodola, Ethiopia 95 F4 6 59N 39 11 E
Dodoma, Tanzania 106 D4 6 8 S 35 45 E
Dodoma □, Tanzania 106 D4 6 0 S 36 0 E
Dodona, Greece 44 E2 39 40N 20 46 E
Dodsland, Canada 131 C7 51 50N 108 45W
Dodson, U.S.A. 142 B9 48 23N 108 16W
Doesburg, Neths. 20 D8 52 1N 6 9 E
Doetinchem, Neths. 20 E8 51 59N 6 18 E
Doftana, Romania 46 D6 45 11N 25 45 E
Dog Creek, Canada 130 C4 51 35N 122 14W
Dog L., Man., Canada 131 C9 51 2N 98 31W
Dog L., Ont., Canada 128 C2 48 48N 89 30W
Doğanbey, Turkey 45 G9 37 40N 27 10 E
Doğanşehir, Turkey 89 D7 38 5N 37 53 E
Dogger Bank, N. Sea 10 E6 54 50N 2 0 E
Dogliani, Italy 38 D4 44 35N 7 55 E
Dōgo, Japan 62 A5 36 15N 133 16 E
Dōgo-San, Japan 62 B5 35 2N 133 13 E
Dogondoutchi, Niger 101 C5 13 38N 4 2 E
Dogran, Pakistan 80 D5 31 48N 73 35 E
Doğubayazıt, Turkey 89 D11 39 31N 44 5 E
Doguéraoua, Niger 101 C6 14 0N 5 31 E
Doi, Indonesia 71 D7 2 14N 127 49 E
Doi Luang, Thailand 76 C3 18 30N 101 0 E
Doi Saket, Thailand 76 C2 18 52N 99 9 E
Doig →, Canada 130 B4 56 25N 120 40W
Dois Irmãos, Sa., Brazil 154 C3 9 0 S 42 30W
Dojransko Jezero, Yugoslavia 42 F7 41 13N 22 44 E
Dokka, Norway 13 F11 60 49N 10 7 E
Dokka →, Norway 14 D4 60 50N 10 6 E
Dokkum, Neths. 20 B7 53 20N 5 59 E
Dokkumer Ee →, Neths. 20 B7 53 18N 5 52 E
Dokri, Pakistan 80 F3 27 25N 68 7 E
Dol-de-Bretagne, France 22 D5 48 34N 1 47W
Doland, U.S.A. 138 C5 44 55N 98 5W
Dolbeau, Canada 129 C5 48 53N 72 18W
Dole, France 23 E12 47 7N 5 31 E
Doleib, Wadi →, Sudan 95 E3 12 10N 33 15 E
Dolgellau, U.K. 16 E4 52 44N 3 53W
Dolgelley = Dolgellau, U.K. 16 E4 52 44N 3 53W
Dolginovo, U.S.S.R. 50 D5 54 39N 27 29 E
Dolianova, Italy 40 C2 39 23N 9 11 E
Dolinskaya, U.S.S.R. 52 B5 48 6N 32 46 E
Dolj □, Romania 46 E4 44 10N 23 30 E
Dollart, Neths. 20 B10 53 20N 7 10 E
Dolna Banya, Bulgaria 43 E8 42 18N 23 44 E
Dolni Dŭbnik, Bulgaria 43 D9 43 24N 24 26 E
Dolo, Ethiopia 95 G5 4 11N 42 3 E
Dolo, Italy 39 C9 45 25N 12 4 E
Dolomites = Dolomiti, Italy 39 B8 46 30N 11 40 E
Dolomiti, Italy 39 B8 46 30N 11 40 E
Dolores, Argentina 158 D4 36 20 S 57 40W
Dolores, Uruguay 158 C4 33 34 S 58 15W
Dolores, U.S.A. 143 H9 37 30N 108 30W
Dolores →, U.S.A. 143 G9 38 49N 108 17W
Đolovo, Yugoslavia 42 C5 44 55N 20 52 E
Dolphin, C., Falk. Is. 160 D5 51 10 S 59 0W
Dolphin and Union Str., Canada 126 B8 69 5N 114 45W
Dolsk, Poland 47 D4 51 59N 17 3 E
Dolton, U.S.A. 141 C9 41 38N 87 36W
Dom, Switz. 28 D5 46 6N 7 50 E
Dom Joaquim, Brazil 155 E3 18 57 S 43 16W
Dom Pedrito, Brazil 159 C5 31 0 S 54 40W
Dom Pedro, Brazil 154 B3 4 59 S 44 27W
Doma, Nigeria 101 D6 8 25N 8 18 E
Domaniç, Turkey 88 D3 39 48N 29 36 E
Domasi, Malawi 107 F4 15 15 S 35 22 E
Domat Ems, Switz. 29 C8 46 50N 9 27 E
Domazlice, Czech. 30 B5 49 28N 12 58 E
Dombarovskiy, U.S.S.R. 54 F6 50 46N 59 32 E
Dombås, Norway 13 E10 62 4N 9 8 E
Dombasle-sur-Meurthe, France 23 D13 48 38N 6 21 E
Dombes, France 25 C9 45 58N 5 0 E
Dombóvár, Hungary 31 E11 46 21N 18 9 E
Dombrád, Hungary 31 C14 48 13N 21 54 E
Domburg, Neths. 21 E3 51 34N 3 30 E
Domérat, France 24 B6 46 21N 2 32 E
Domett, N.Z. 119 C8 42 53 S 173 12 E
Domeyko, Chile 158 B1 29 0 S 71 0W
Domeyko, Cordillera, Chile 158 A2 24 30 S 69 0W
Domfront, France 22 D6 48 37N 0 40W
Dominador, Chile 158 A2 24 21 S 69 20W
Dominica ■, W. Indies 149 C7 15 20N 61 20W
Dominica Passage, W. Indies 149 C7 15 10N 61 20W
Dominican Rep. ■, W. Indies 149 C5 19 0N 70 30W
Domiongo, Zaïre 103 C4 4 37 S 21 15 E
Dömitz, Germany 26 B7 53 9N 11 13 E
Domme, France 24 D5 44 48N 1 12 E
Dommel →, Neths. 21 E6 51 38N 5 20 E
Domo, Ethiopia 90 F4 7 50N 47 10 E
Domodóssola, Italy 38 B5 46 6N 8 19 E
Dompaire, France 23 D13 48 14N 6 14 E
Dompierre-sur-Besbre, France 24 B7 46 31N 3 41 E
Dompim, Ghana 100 D4 5 10N 2 5W
Dompu, Indonesia 72 C1 8 32 S 118 28 E
Domrémy-la-Pucelle, France 23 D12 48 26N 5 40 E
Domsjö, Sweden 14 A12 63 16N 18 41 E
Domville, Mt., Australia 115 D5 28 1 S 151 15 E
Domvraína, Greece 45 F4 38 15N 22 59 E
Domžale, Yugoslavia 39 B11 46 9N 14 35 E
Don →, India 83 F3 16 20N 76 15 E
Don →, Gramp., U.K. 18 D6 57 14N 2 5W
Don →, S. Yorks., U.K. 16 D7 53 41N 0 51W
Don →, U.S.S.R. 53 C8 47 4N 39 18 E
Don, C., Australia 112 B5 11 18 S 131 46 E
Don Benito, Spain 37 G5 38 53N 5 51W
Don Duong, Vietnam 77 G7 11 51N 108 35 E
Don Martín, Presa de, Mexico 146 B4 27 30N 100 50W
Dona Ana = Nhamaabué, Mozam. 107 F4 17 25 S 35 5 E
Donaghadee, U.K. 19 B6 54 38N 5 32W
Donald, Australia 116 D5 36 23 S 143 0 E
Donalda, Canada 130 C6 52 35N 112 34W
Donaldsonville, U.S.A. 139 K9 30 2N 91 0W
Donalsonville, U.S.A. 135 K3 31 3N 84 52W
Donau →, Austria 31 C10 48 10N 17 0 E
Donaueschingen, Germany 27 H4 47 57N 8 30 E
Donauwörth, Germany 27 G6 48 42N 10 47 E
Donawitz, Austria 30 D8 47 22N 15 4 E
Doncaster, U.K. 16 D6 53 31N 1 9W
Dondo, Angola 103 D2 9 45 S 14 25 E
Dondo, Mozam. 107 F3 19 33 S 34 46 E
Dondo, Zaïre 102 B4 4 11N 23 35 E
Dondo, Teluk, Indonesia 71 D6 0 29N 120 30 E
Dondra Head, Sri Lanka 83 M5 5 55N 80 40 E
Donegal, Ireland 19 B3 54 39N 8 8W
Donegal □, Ireland 19 B4 54 53N 8 0W
Donegal B., Ireland 19 B3 54 30N 8 35W
Donets →, U.S.S.R. 53 C9 47 33N 40 55 E
Donetsk, U.S.S.R. 52 C7 48 0N 37 45 E
Dong Ba Thin, Vietnam 77 F7 12 8N 109 13 E
Dong Dang, Vietnam 76 B6 21 54N 106 42 E
Dong Giam, Vietnam 76 C5 19 25N 105 31 E
Dong Ha, Vietnam 76 D6 16 55N 107 8 E
Dong Hene, Laos 76 D5 16 40N 105 18 E
Dong Hoi, Vietnam 76 D6 17 29N 106 36 E
Dong Jiang →, China 69 F10 23 6N 114 0 E
Dong Khe, Vietnam 76 A6 22 26N 106 27 E
Dong Ujimqin Qi, China 66 B9 45 32N 116 55 E
Dong Van, Vietnam 76 A5 23 16N 105 22 E
Dong Xoai, Vietnam 77 G6 11 32N 106 55 E
Donga, Nigeria 101 D7 7 45N 10 2 E
Dong'an, China 69 D8 26 23N 111 12 E
Dongara, Australia 113 E1 29 14 S 114 57 E
Dongargarh, India 82 D5 21 10N 80 40 E
Dongbei, China 67 D13 42 0N 125 0 E
Dongchuan, China 68 D4 26 8N 103 1 E
Dongen, Neths. 21 E5 51 38N 4 56 E
Donges, France 22 E4 47 18N 2 4W
Dongfang, China 76 C7 18 50N 108 33 E
Dongfeng, China 67 C13 42 40N 125 34 E
Donggala, Indonesia 71 E5 0 30 S 119 40 E
Donggan, China 68 F5 23 22N 105 9 E
Donggou, China 67 E13 39 52N 124 10 E
Dongguan, China 69 F9 22 58N 113 44 E
Dongguang, China 66 F9 37 50N 116 30 E
Donghai Dao, China 69 G8 21 0N 110 15 E
Dongjingcheng, China 67 B15 44 5N 129 10 E
Donglan, China 68 E6 24 30N 107 21 E
Dongliu, China 69 B11 30 13N 116 55 E
Dongmen, China 68 F6 22 20N 107 48 E
Dongning, China 67 B16 44 2N 131 5 E
Dongnyi, China 68 C3 28 3N 100 15 E
Dongo, Angola 103 E3 14 36 S 15 48 E
Dongola, Sudan 94 D3 19 9N 30 22 E
Dongou, Congo 102 B3 2 0N 18 5 E
Dongping, China 66 G9 35 55N 116 20 E
Dongshan, China 69 F11 23 43N 117 30 E
Dongsheng, China 66 E6 39 50N 110 0 E
Dongshi, Taiwan 69 E13 24 18N 120 49 E
Dongtai, China 67 H11 32 51N 120 21 E
Dongting Hu, China 69 C9 29 18N 112 45 E
Dongxiang, China 69 C11 28 11N 116 34 E
Dongxing, China 68 G7 21 34N 108 0 E
Dongyang, China 69 C13 29 13N 120 15 E
Dongzhi, China 69 B11 30 9N 117 0 E
Donington, C., Australia 116 C2 34 45 S 136 0 E
Doniphan, U.S.A. 139 G9 36 40N 90 50W
Donja Stubica, Yugoslavia 39 C13 45 59N 16 0 E
Donji Dušnik, Yugoslavia 42 D7 43 12N 22 5 E
Donji Miholjac, Yugoslavia 42 B3 45 45N 18 10 E
Donji Milanovac, Yugoslavia 42 C7 44 28N 22 6 E
Donji Vakuf, Yugoslavia 42 C2 44 8N 17 24 E
Dønna, Norway 12 C12 66 6N 12 30 E
Donna, U.S.A. 139 M5 26 12N 98 2W
Donnaconna, Canada 129 C5 46 41N 71 41W
Donnelly's Crossing, N.Z. 118 B2 35 42 S 173 38 E
Donnybrook, Australia 113 F2 33 34 S 115 48 E
Donnybrook, S. Africa 105 D4 29 59 S 29 48 E
Donora, U.S.A. 136 F5 40 11N 79 50W
Donor's Hill, Australia 114 B3 18 42 S 140 33 E
Donostia = San Sebastián, Spain 34 B3 43 17N 1 58W
Donque, Angola 103 F2 15 28 S 14 6 E
Donskoy, U.S.S.R. 51 E11 53 55N 38 15 E
Donya Lendava, Yugoslavia 39 B13 46 35N 16 25 E
Donzère, France 25 D8 44 28N 4 43 E
Donzère-Mondragon, Barr. de, France 25 D8 44 13N 4 42 E
Donzy, France 23 E10 47 20N 3 6 E
Doon →, U.K. 18 F4 55 26N 4 41W
Doorn, Neths. 20 D6 52 2N 5 20 E
Dora, L., Australia 112 D3 22 0 S 123 0 E
Dora Báltea →, Italy 38 C5 45 11N 8 5 E
Dora Riparia →, Italy 38 C4 45 5N 7 44 E
Doran L., Canada 131 A7 61 13N 108 6W
Dorchester, U.K. 17 G5 50 42N 2 28W
Dorchester, C., Canada 127 B12 65 27N 77 27W
Dordogne □, France 24 C4 45 5N 0 40 E
Dordogne →, France 24 C3 45 2N 0 36W
Dordrecht, Neths. 20 E5 51 48N 4 39 E
Dordrecht, S. Africa 104 E4 31 20 S 27 3 E
Dore →, France 24 C7 45 50N 3 35 E
Dore, Mts., France 24 C6 45 32N 2 50 E
Doré L., Canada 131 C7 54 46N 107 17W
Doré Lake, Canada 131 C7 54 38N 107 36W
Dores do Indaiá, Brazil 155 E2 19 27 S 45 36W
Dorfen, Germany 27 G8 48 16N 12 10 E
Dorgali, Italy 40 B2 40 18N 9 35 E
Dori, Burkina Faso 101 C4 14 3N 0 2W
Doring →, S. Africa 104 E2 31 54 S 18 39 E
Doringbos, S. Africa 104 E2 31 59 S 19 16 E
Dorion, Canada 128 C5 45 23N 74 3W
Dormaa-Ahenkro, Ghana 100 D4 7 15N 2 52W
Dormo, Ras, Ethiopia 95 E5 13 14N 42 35 E
Dornach, Switz. 28 B5 47 29N 7 37 E
Dornberg, Yugoslavia 39 C10 45 45N 13 50 E
Dornbirn, Austria 30 D2 47 25N 9 45 E
Dornes, France 23 F10 46 48N 3 18 E
Dornoch, U.K. 18 D4 57 52N 4 5W
Dornoch Firth, U.K. 18 D5 57 52N 4 0W
Dornogovĭ □, Mongolia 66 C6 44 0N 110 0 E
Doro, Mali 101 B4 16 9N 0 51W
Dorog, Hungary 31 D11 47 42N 18 45 E
Dorogobuzh, U.S.S.R. 50 D8 54 50N 33 18 E
Dorohoi, Romania 46 B7 47 56N 26 30 E
Döröö Nuur, Mongolia 64 B4 48 0N 93 0 E
Dorr, Iran 85 C6 33 17N 50 38 E
Dorre I., Australia 113 E1 25 13 S 113 12 E
Dorrigo, Australia 117 A10 30 20 S 152 44 E
Dorris, U.S.A. 142 F3 41 59N 121 58W
Dorset, Canada 136 A6 45 14N 78 54W
Dorset, U.S.A. 136 E4 41 4N 80 40W
Dorset □, U.K. 17 G5 50 48N 2 25W
Dorsten, Germany 26 D2 51 40N 6 55 E
Dortmund, Germany 26 D3 51 32N 7 28 E
Dörtyol, Turkey 88 E7 36 50N 36 13 E
Dorum, Germany 26 B4 53 40N 8 33 E
Doruma, Zaïre 106 B2 4 42N 27 33 E
Dorūneh, Iran 85 C8 35 10N 57 18 E
Dos Bahías, C., Argentina 160 B3 44 58 S 65 32W
Dos Hermanas, Spain 37 H5 37 16N 5 55W
Dos Palos, U.S.A. 144 J6 36 59N 120 37W
Dosso, Niger 101 C5 13 0N 3 13 E
Dothan, U.S.A. 135 K3 31 10N 85 25W
Dottignies, Belgium 21 G2 50 44N 3 19 E
Doty, U.S.A. 144 D3 46 38N 123 17W
Douai, France 23 B10 50 21N 3 4 E
Douala, Cameroon 101 E6 4 0N 9 45 E
Douarnenez, France 22 D2 48 6N 4 21W
Douăzeci Şi Trei August, Romania 46 F9 43 55N 28 40 E
Double Island Pt., Australia 115 D5 25 56 S 153 11 E
Doubrava →, Czech. 30 B8 49 40N 15 30 E
Doubs □, France 23 E13 47 10N 6 20 E
Doubs →, France 23 F12 46 53N 5 1 E
Doubtful Sd., N.Z. 119 F1 45 20 S 166 49 E
Doubtless B., N.Z. 118 A2 34 55 S 173 26 E
Doudeville, France 22 C7 49 43N 0 47 E
Doué-la-Fontaine, France 22 E6 47 11N 0 16W
Douentza, Mali 100 C4 14 58N 2 48W
Doughboy B., N.Z. 119 H2 47 2 S 167 40 E
Douglas, S. Africa 104 D3 29 4 S 23 46 E
Douglas, U.K. 16 C3 54 9N 4 29W
Douglas, Alaska, U.S.A. 130 B2 58 23N 134 24W
Douglas, Ariz., U.S.A. 143 L9 31 21N 109 30W
Douglas, Ga., U.S.A. 135 K4 31 32N 82 52W
Douglas, Wyo., U.S.A. 138 D2 42 45N 105 20W
Douglastown, Canada 129 C7 48 46N 64 24W
Douglasville, U.S.A. 135 J3 33 46N 84 43W
Douirat, Morocco 98 B4 33 2N 4 11W
Doukáton, Ákra, Greece 45 F2 38 34N 20 30 E
Doulevant-le-Château, France 23 D11 48 23N 4 55 E
Doullens, France 23 B9 50 10N 2 20 E
Doumé, Cameroon 102 B2 4 15N 13 25 E
Douna, Mali 100 C3 13 13N 6 0W
Dounan, Taiwan 69 F13 23 41N 120 26 E
Dounguila, Congo 102 C2 2 53 S 11 58 E
Dounreay, U.K. 18 C5 58 34N 3 44W
Dour, Belgium 21 H3 50 24N 3 46 E
Dourada, Serra, Brazil 155 D2 13 10 S 48 45W
Dourados, Brazil 159 A5 22 9 S 54 50W
Dourados →, Brazil 159 A5 21 58 S 54 18W
Dourdan, France 23 D9 48 30N 2 1 E
Douro →, Europe 36 D2 41 8N 8 40W
Douvaine, France 25 B10 46 19N 6 16 E
Douz, Tunisia 96 B1 33 25N 9 0 E
Douze →, France 24 E3 43 54N 0 30W
Dove →, U.K. 16 E6 52 51N 1 36W
Dove Creek, U.S.A. 143 H9 37 46N 108 59W
Dover, Australia 114 G4 43 18 S 147 2 E
Dover, U.K. 17 F9 51 7N 1 19 E
Dover, Del., U.S.A. 134 F8 39 10N 75 31W
Dover, Ky., U.S.A. 141 F13 38 43N 83 52W
Dover, N.H., U.S.A. 137 C14 43 12N 70 51W
Dover, N.J., U.S.A. 137 F10 40 53N 74 34W
Dover, Ohio, U.S.A. 136 F3 40 32N 81 30W
Dover, Pt., Australia 113 F4 32 32 S 125 32 E
Dover, Str. of, Europe 22 B8 51 0N 1 30 E
Dover-Foxcroft, U.S.A. 129 C6 45 14N 69 14W
Dover Plains, U.S.A. 137 E11 41 43N 73 35W
Dovey = Dyfi →, U.K. 17 E4 52 32N 4 0W
Dovrefjell, Norway 14 B3 62 15N 9 33 E
Dow Rūd, Iran 85 C6 33 28N 49 4 E
Dowa, Malawi 107 E3 13 38 S 33 58 E
Dowagiac, U.S.A. 141 C10 41 58N 86 8W
Dowgha'i, Iran 85 B8 36 54N 58 32 E
Dowlat Yār, Afghan. 79 B2 34 30N 65 45 E
Dowlatābād, Farāh, Afghan. 79 B1 32 47N 62 40 E
Dowlatābād, Fāryāb, Afghan. 79 A2 36 26N 64 55 E
Dowlatābād, Iran 85 D8 28 20N 56 40 E
Down □, U.K. 19 B6 54 20N 5 47W
Downers Grove, U.S.A. 141 C8 41 49N 88 1W
Downey, Calif., U.S.A. 145 M8 33 56N 118 7W
Downey, Utah, U.S.A. 142 E7 42 29N 112 3W
Downham Market, U.K. 17 E8 52 36N 0 22 E
Downieville, U.S.A. 144 F6 39 34N 120 50W
Downing, U.S.A. 140 D4 40 29N 92 22W
Downpatrick, U.K. 19 B6 54 20N 5 43W
Downpatrick Hd., Ireland 19 B2 54 20N 9 21W
Dowsārī, Iran 85 D8 28 25N 57 59 E
Dowshī, Afghan. 79 B3 35 35N 68 43 E
Doyle, U.S.A. 144 E6 40 2N 120 6W
Doylestown, U.S.A. 137 F9 40 21N 75 10W
Draa, C., Morocco 98 C2 28 47N 11 0W
Draa, Oued →, Morocco 98 C2 28 40N 11 10W
Drac →, France 25 C9 45 12N 5 42 E
Drachten, Neths. 20 B8 53 7N 6 5 E
Drăgăneşti, Romania 46 E5 44 9N 24 32 E
Drăgăneşti-Viaşca, Romania 46 E6 44 5N 25 33 E
Dragaš, Yugoslavia 42 E5 42 5N 20 35 E
Drăgăsani, Romania 46 E5 44 39N 24 17 E
Dragina, Yugoslavia 42 C4 44 30N 19 25 E
Dragocvet, Yugoslavia 42 D6 43 58N 21 15 E
Dragoman, Prokhod, Bulgaria 42 E7 42 58N 22 53 E
Dragonera, I., Spain 33 B9 39 35N 2 19 E
Dragovishtitsa, Bulgaria 42 E7 42 22N 22 39 E
Draguignan, France 25 E10 43 32N 6 27 E
Drain, U.S.A. 142 E2 43 45N 123 17W
Drake, Australia 115 D5 28 55 S 152 25 E
Drake, U.S.A. 138 B4 47 56N 100 21W
Drake Passage, S. Ocean 7 B17 58 0 S 68 0W
Drakensberg, S. Africa 105 E4 31 0 S 28 0 E
Dráma, Greece 44 C6 41 9N 24 10 E
Dráma □, Greece 44 C6 41 20N 24 0 E
Drammen, Norway 14 E4 59 42N 10 12 E
Drangajökull, Iceland 12 C2 66 9N 22 15W
Drangedal, Norway 14 E3 59 6N 9 3 E
Dranov, Ostrov, Romania 46 E10 44 55N 29 30 E
Dras, India 81 B6 34 25N 75 48 E
Drau = Drava →, Yugoslavia 31 F11 45 33N 18 55 E
Drava →, Yugoslavia 31 F11 45 33N 18 55 E
Draveil, France 23 D9 48 41N 2 25 E
Dravograd, Yugoslavia 39 B12 46 36N 15 5 E
Drawa →, Poland 47 C2 52 52N 15 59 E
Drawno, Poland 47 B2 53 13N 15 46 E
Drawsko Pomorskie, Poland 47 B2 53 35N 15 50 E
Drayton Plains, U.S.A. 141 B13 42 42N 83 23W
Drayton Valley, Canada 130 C6 53 12N 114 58W

East Point 193

Dreibergen, Neths. 20 D6 52 3N 5 17 E
Dren, Yugoslavia 42 D5 43 8N 20 44 E
Drenthe □, Neths. 20 C9 52 52N 6 40 E
Drentsche Hoofdvaart, Neths. 20 C8 52 39N 6 4 E
Drepanum, C., Cyprus 32 E11 34 54N 32 19 E
Dresden, Canada 136 D2 42 35N 82 11W
Dresden, Germany 26 D9 51 2N 13 45 E
Dreux, France 22 D8 48 44N 1 23 E
Drexel, U.S.A. 141 E12 39 45N 84 18W
Drezdenko, Poland 47 C2 52 50N 15 49 E
Driel, Neths. 20 E7 51 57N 5 49 E
Driffield = Great Driffield, U.K. 16 D7 54 0N 0 25W
Driftwood, U.S.A. 136 E6 41 22N 78 9W
Driggs, U.S.A. 142 E8 43 50N 111 8W
Drin i zi →, Albania 44 C2 41 37N 20 28 E
Drina →, Yugoslavia 42 C4 44 53N 19 21 E
Drincea →, Romania 46 E3 44 20N 22 55 E
Drînceni, Romania 46 C9 46 49N 28 10 E
Drini →, Albania 44 B2 42 20N 20 0 E
Drinjača →, Yugoslavia 42 C4 44 15N 19 8 E
Drivstua, Norway 14 B3 62 26N 9 47 E
Drniš, Yugoslavia 39 E13 43 51N 16 10 E
Drøbak, Norway 14 E4 59 39N 10 39 E
Drobin, Poland 47 C6 52 42N 19 58 E
Drogheda, Ireland 19 C5 53 45N 6 20W
Drogichin, U.S.S.R. 50 E4 52 15N 25 8 E
Drogobych, U.S.S.R. 50 G3 49 20N 23 30 E
Drohiczyn, Poland 47 C9 52 24N 22 39 E
Droitwich, U.K. 17 E5 52 16N 2 10W
Drôme □, France 25 D9 44 38N 5 15 E
Drôme →, France 25 D8 44 46N 4 46 E
Dromedary, C., Australia 117 D9 36 17 S 150 10 E
Dronero, Italy 38 D4 44 29N 7 22 E
Dronfield, Australia 114 C3 21 12 S 140 3 E
Dronne →, France 24 C3 45 2N 0 9W
Dronninglund, Denmark 15 G4 57 10N 10 19 E
Dronrijp, Neths. 20 B7 53 11N 5 39 E
Dropt →, France 24 D3 44 35N 0 6W
Drosendorf, Austria 30 C8 48 52N 15 37 E
Drouin, Australia 117 E6 38 10 S 145 53 E
Drouzhba, Bulgaria 43 D13 43 15N 28 0 E
Drumbo, Canada 136 C4 43 16N 80 35W
Drumheller, Canada 130 C6 51 25N 112 40W
Drummond, U.S.A. 142 C7 46 40N 113 4W
Drummond I., U.S.A. 128 C3 46 0N 83 40W
Drummond Pt., Australia 115 E2 34 9 S 135 16 E
Drummond Ra., Australia 114 C4 23 45 S 147 10 E
Drummondville, Canada 128 C5 45 55N 72 25W
Drumright, U.S.A. 139 H6 35 59N 96 38W
Drunen, Neths. 21 E6 51 41N 5 8 E
Druskininkai, U.S.S.R. 50 D3 54 3N 23 58 E
Drut →, U.S.S.R. 50 E7 53 3N 30 42 E
Druten, Neths. 20 E7 51 53N 5 36 E
Druya, U.S.S.R. 50 D5 55 45N 27 28 E
Druzhina, U.S.S.R. 57 C15 68 14N 145 18 E
Drvar, Yugoslavia 39 D13 44 21N 16 23 E
Drvenik, Yugoslavia 39 E13 43 27N 16 3 E
Drwęca →, Poland 47 C5 53 0N 18 42 E
Dry Tortugas, U.S.A. 148 B3 24 38N 82 55W
Dryanovo, Bulgaria 43 E10 42 59N 25 28 E
Dryden, Canada 131 D10 49 47N 92 50W
Dryden, U.S.A. 139 K3 30 3N 102 3W
Drygalski I., Antarctica 7 C7 66 0 S 92 0 E
Drysdale →, Australia 112 B4 13 59 S 126 51 E
Drysdale I., Australia 114 A2 11 41 S 136 0 E
Drzewiczka →, Poland 47 D7 51 36N 20 36 E
Dschang, Cameroon 101 D7 5 32N 10 3 E
Du Bois, U.S.A. 136 E6 41 8N 78 46W
Du Quoin, U.S.A. 140 G7 38 0N 89 10W
Duanesburg, U.S.A. 137 D10 42 45N 74 11W
Duaringa, Australia 114 C4 23 42 S 149 42 E
Ḍubā, Si. Arabia 84 E2 27 10N 35 40 E
Dubai = Dubayy, U.A.E. 85 E7 25 18N 55 20 E
Dubawnt →, Canada 131 A8 64 33N 100 6W
Dubawnt, L., Canada 131 A8 63 4N 101 42W
Dubayy, U.A.E. 85 E7 25 18N 55 20 E
Dubbeldam, Neths. 20 E5 51 47N 4 43 E
Dubbo, Australia 117 B8 32 11 S 148 35 E
Dubele, Zaïre 106 B2 2 56N 29 35 E
Dübendorf, Switz. 29 B7 47 24N 8 37 E
Dubenskiy, U.S.S.R. 54 F5 51 27N 56 38 E
Dubica, Yugoslavia 39 C13 45 11N 16 48 E
Dublin, Ireland 19 C5 53 20N 6 18W
Dublin, Ga., U.S.A. 135 J4 32 30N 82 34W
Dublin, Tex., U.S.A. 139 J5 32 5N 98 20W
Dublin □, Ireland 19 C5 53 24N 6 20W
Dubna, R.S.F.S.R., U.S.S.R. 51 C10 56 44N 37 10 E
Dubna, R.S.F.S.R., U.S.S.R. 51 D10 54 8N 36 59 E
Dubno, U.S.S.R. 50 F4 50 25N 25 45 E
Dubois, Idaho, U.S.A. 142 D7 44 7N 112 9W
Dubois, Ind., U.S.A. 141 F10 38 26N 86 48W
Dubossary, U.S.S.R. 52 C3 47 15N 29 10 E
Dubossary Vdkhr., U.S.S.R. 52 C3 47 30N 29 0 E
Dubovka, U.S.S.R. 53 B11 49 5N 44 50 E
Dubovskoye, U.S.S.R. 53 C10 47 28N 42 46 E
Dubrajpur, India 81 H12 23 48N 87 25 E
Dubréka, Guinea 100 D2 9 46N 13 31W
Dubrovitsa, U.S.S.R. 50 F5 51 31N 26 35 E
Dubrovnik, Yugoslavia 42 E3 42 39N 18 6 E
Dubrovskoye, U.S.S.R. 57 D12 58 55N 111 10 E
Dubulu, Zaïre 102 B4 4 18N 20 16 E
Dubuque, U.S.A. 140 B6 42 30N 90 41W
Duchang, China 69 C11 29 18N 116 12 E
Duchesne, U.S.A. 142 F8 40 14N 110 22W
Duchess, Australia 114 C2 21 20 S 139 50 E
Ducie I., Pac. Oc. 123 K15 24 40 S 124 48W
Duck Cr. →, Australia 112 D2 22 37 S 116 53 E
Duck Lake, Canada 131 C7 52 50N 106 16W
Duck Mountain Prov. Park, Canada 131 C8 51 45N 101 0W
Duckwall, Mt., U.S.A. 144 H6 37 58N 120 7W
Düdelange, Lux. 21 K8 49 29N 6 5 E
Duderstadt, Germany 26 D6 51 30N 10 15 E
Dudhnai, India 78 C3 25 59N 90 47 E
Düdingen, Switz. 28 C4 46 52N 7 12 E
Dudinka, U.S.S.R. 57 C9 69 30N 86 13 E
Dudley, U.K. 17 E5 52 30N 2 5W
Dudna →, India 82 E3 19 17N 76 54 E
Dudo, Somali Rep. 108 C4 9 20N 50 12 E
Dudub, Ethiopia 108 C3 6 55N 46 43 E
Dueñas, Spain 36 D6 41 52N 4 33W
Dueré, Brazil 155 D2 11 20 S 49 17W
Duero = Douro →, Europe 36 D2 41 8N 8 40W
Dūfah, W. →, Si. Arabia 86 C3 18 45N 41 49 E
Duffel, Belgium 21 F5 51 6N 4 30 E
Dufftown, U.K. 18 D5 57 26N 3 9W
Dufourspitz, Switz. 28 E5 45 56N 7 52 E
Dugger, U.S.A. 141 E9 39 4N 87 16W
Dugi Otok, Yugoslavia 39 E12 44 0N 15 3 E
Dugiuma, Somali Rep. 108 D2 1 15N 42 34 E
Dugo Selo, Yugoslavia 39 C13 45 51N 16 18 E
Duifken Pt., Australia 114 A3 12 33 S 141 38 E
Duisburg, Germany 26 D2 51 27N 6 42 E
Duitama, Colombia 152 B3 5 50N 73 2W
Duiveland, Neths. 21 E4 51 38N 4 0 E
Duiwelskloof, S. Africa 105 C5 23 42 S 30 10 E
Dukati, Albania 44 D1 40 16N 19 32 E
Dūkdamīn, Iran 85 C8 35 59N 57 43 E
Duke I., U.S.A. 130 C2 54 50N 131 20W
Dukelskýprůsmyk, Czech. 31 B14 49 25N 21 42 E
Dukhān, Qatar 85 E6 25 25N 50 50 E
Dukhovshchina, U.S.S.R. 50 D8 55 15N 32 27 E
Duki, Pakistan 79 C3 30 14N 68 25 E
Dukla, Poland 31 B14 49 30N 21 35 E
Duku, Bauchi, Nigeria 101 C7 10 43N 10 43 E
Duku, Sokoto, Nigeria 101 C5 11 11N 4 55 E
Dulce →, Argentina 158 C3 30 32 S 62 33W
Dulce, G., Costa Rica 148 E3 8 40N 83 20W
Dulf, Iraq 84 C5 35 7N 45 51 E
Dŭlgopol, Bulgaria 43 D12 43 3N 27 22 E
Dulit, Banjaran, Malaysia 70 D4 3 15N 114 30 E
Duliu, China 66 E9 39 2N 116 55 E
Dullewala, Pakistan 80 D4 31 50N 71 25 E
Dülmen, Germany 26 D3 51 49N 7 18 E
Dulovo, Bulgaria 43 D12 43 48N 27 9 E
Dulq Maghār, Syria 84 B3 36 22N 38 39 E
Dululu, Australia 114 C5 23 48 S 150 15 E
Duluth, U.S.A. 138 B8 46 48N 92 10W
Dum Dum, India 81 H13 22 39N 88 33 E
Dum Hadjer, Chad 97 F3 13 18N 19 41 E
Dūmā, Lebanon 91 A4 34 12N 35 50 E
Dūmā, Syria 91 B5 33 34N 36 24 E
Dumaguete, Phil. 71 C6 9 17N 123 15 E
Dumai, Indonesia 70 D2 1 35N 101 28 E
Dumaran, Phil. 71 B5 10 33N 119 50 E
Dumas, Ark., U.S.A. 139 J9 33 52N 91 30W
Dumas, Tex., U.S.A. 139 H4 35 50N 101 58W
Dumbarton, U.K. 18 F4 55 58N 4 35W
Dumbea, N. Cal. 121 V20 22 10 S 166 27 E
Dumbleyung, Australia 113 F2 33 17 S 117 42 E
Dumbo, Angola 103 E3 14 6 S 17 24 E
Dumbrăveni, Romania 46 C5 46 14N 24 34 E
Dumfries, U.K. 18 F5 55 4N 3 37W
Dumfries & Galloway □, U.K. 18 F5 55 5N 4 0W
Dumka, India 81 G12 24 12N 87 15 E
Dümmersee, Germany 26 C4 52 30N 8 21 E
Dumoine →, Canada 128 C4 46 13N 77 51W
Dumoine L., Canada 128 C4 46 55N 77 55W
Dumraon, India 81 G11 25 33N 84 8 E
Dumyât, Egypt 94 H7 31 24N 31 48 E
Dumyât, Masabb, Egypt 94 H7 31 28N 31 51 E
Dun-le-Palestel, France 24 B5 46 18N 1 39 E
Dun-sur-Auron, France 23 F9 46 53N 2 33 E
Duna →, Hungary 31 F11 45 51N 18 48 E
Dunaföldvár, Hungary 31 E11 46 50N 18 57 E
Dunaj →, Czech. 31 D11 47 50N 18 50 E
Dunajec →, Poland 31 A13 50 15N 20 44 E
Dunajska Streda, Czech. 31 D10 48 0N 17 37 E
Dunapatai, Hungary 31 E12 46 39N 19 4 E
Dunărea →, Romania 46 D10 45 20N 29 40 E
Dunaszekcsö, Hungary 31 E11 46 6N 18 45 E
Dunaújváros, Hungary 31 E11 47 0N 18 57 E
Dunav →, Yugoslavia 42 C6 44 47N 21 20 E
Dunavtsi, Bulgaria 42 D7 43 57N 22 53 E
Dunay, U.S.S.R. 60 C6 42 52N 132 22 E
Dunback, N.Z. 119 F5 45 23 S 170 36 E
Dunbar, Australia 114 B3 16 0 S 142 22 E
Dunbar, U.K. 18 F6 56 0N 2 32W
Dunblane, U.K. 18 E5 56 10N 3 58W
Duncan, Canada 130 D4 48 45N 123 40W
Duncan, Ariz., U.S.A. 143 K9 32 46N 109 6W
Duncan, Okla., U.S.A. 139 H6 34 25N 98 0W
Duncan, L., Canada 128 B4 53 29N 77 58W
Duncan L., Canada 130 A6 62 51N 113 58W
Duncan Town, Bahamas 148 B4 22 15N 75 45W
Duncannon, U.S.A. 136 F7 40 23N 77 2W
Dundalk, Canada 136 B4 44 10N 80 24W
Dundalk, Ireland 19 B5 54 1N 6 25W
Dundalk Bay, Ireland 19 C5 53 55N 6 15W
Dundas, Canada 128 D4 43 17N 79 59W
Dundas, L., Australia 113 F3 32 35 S 121 50 E
Dundas I., Canada 130 C2 54 30N 130 50W
Dundas Str., Australia 112 B5 11 15 S 131 35 E
Dundee, S. Africa 105 D5 28 11 S 30 15 E
Dundee, U.K. 18 E6 56 29N 3 0W
Dundee, U.S.A. 141 C13 41 57N 83 40W
Dundgovĭ □, Mongolia 66 B4 45 10N 106 0 E
Dundoo, Australia 115 D3 27 40 S 144 37 E
Dundrum, U.K. 19 B6 54 17N 5 50W
Dundrum B., U.K. 19 B6 54 12N 5 40W
Dundwara, India 81 F8 27 48N 79 9 E
Dunedin, N.Z. 119 F5 45 50 S 170 33 E
Dunedin, U.S.A. 135 L4 28 1N 82 45W
Dunedin →, Canada 130 B4 59 30N 124 5W
Dunfermline, U.K. 18 E5 56 5N 3 28W
Dungannon, Canada 136 C3 43 51N 81 36W
Dungannon, U.K. 19 B5 54 30N 6 47W
Dungannon □, U.K. 19 B5 54 30N 6 55W
Dungarpur, India 80 H5 23 52N 73 45 E
Dungeness, U.K. 17 G8 50 54N 0 59 E
Dungo, L. do, Angola 103 F3 17 15 S 19 0 E
Dungog, Australia 117 B9 32 22 S 151 46 E
Dungu, Zaïre 106 B2 3 40N 28 32 E
Dungunâb, Sudan 94 C4 21 10N 37 9 E
Dungunâb, Khalij, Sudan 94 C4 21 5N 37 12 E
Dunhinda Falls, Sri Lanka 83 L5 7 5N 81 6 E
Dunhua, China 67 C15 43 20N 128 14 E
Dunhuang, China 64 B4 40 8N 94 36 E
Dunières, France 25 C8 45 13N 4 20 E
Dunk I., Australia 114 B4 17 59 S 146 29 E
Dunkeld, Australia 116 D5 37 40 S 142 22 E
Dunkeld, U.K. 18 E5 56 34N 3 36W
Dunkerque, France 23 A9 51 2N 2 20 E
Dunkery Beacon, U.K. 17 F4 51 15N 3 37W
Dunkirk = Dunkerque, France 23 A9 51 2N 2 20 E
Dunkirk, U.S.A. 136 D5 42 30N 79 18W
Dunkuj, Sudan 95 E3 12 50N 32 49 E
Dunkwa, Central, Ghana 100 D4 6 0N 1 47W
Dunkwa, Central, Ghana 101 D4 5 30N 1 0W
Dunlap, U.S.A. 138 E7 41 50N 95 36W
Dunmanus B., Ireland 19 E2 51 31N 9 50W
Dunmara, Australia 114 B1 16 42 S 133 25 E
Dunmore, U.S.A. 137 E9 41 27N 75 38W
Dunmore Hd., Ireland 19 D1 52 10N 10 35W
Dunmore Town, Bahamas 148 A4 25 30N 76 39W
Dunn, U.S.A. 135 H6 35 18N 78 36W
Dunnellon, U.S.A. 135 L4 29 4N 82 28W
Dunnet Hd., U.K. 18 C5 58 38N 3 22W
Dunning, U.S.A. 138 E4 41 52N 100 4W
Dunnville, Canada 136 D5 42 54N 79 36W
Dunolly, Australia 116 D5 36 51 S 143 44 E
Dunoon, U.K. 18 F4 55 57N 4 56W
Dunqul, Egypt 94 C3 23 26N 31 37 E
Duns, U.K. 18 F6 55 47N 2 20W
Dunseith, U.S.A. 138 A4 48 49N 100 2W
Dunsmuir, U.S.A. 142 F2 41 10N 122 18W
Dunstable, U.K. 17 F7 51 53N 0 31W
Dunstan Mts., N.Z. 119 E4 44 53 S 169 35 E
Dunster, Canada 130 C5 53 8N 119 50W
Duntroon, N.Z. 119 E5 44 51 S 170 40 E
Dunvegan L., Canada 131 A7 60 8N 107 10W
Duolun, China 66 C9 42 12N 116 28 E
Duong Dong, Vietnam 77 G4 10 13N 103 58 E
Dupree, U.S.A. 138 C4 45 4N 101 35W
Dupuyer, U.S.A. 142 B7 48 11N 112 31W
Duqm, Oman 87 C7 19 39N 57 42 E
Duque de Caxias, Brazil 155 F3 22 45 S 43 19W
Duque de York, I., Chile 160 D1 50 37 S 75 25W
Durack →, Australia 112 C4 15 33 S 127 52 E
Durack Ra., Australia 112 C4 16 50 S 127 40 E
Durağan, Turkey 88 C6 41 25N 35 3 E
Durance →, France 25 E8 43 55N 4 45 E
Durand, Ill., U.S.A. 140 B7 42 26N 89 20W
Durand, Mich., U.S.A. 141 B13 42 54N 83 58W
Durango = Victoria de Durango, Mexico 146 C4 24 3N 104 39W
Durango, Spain 34 B2 43 13N 2 40W
Durango, U.S.A. 143 H10 37 16N 107 50W
Durango □, Mexico 146 C4 25 0N 105 0W
Duranillin, Australia 113 F2 33 30 S 116 45 E
Durant, Iowa, U.S.A. 140 C6 41 36N 90 54W
Durant, Okla., U.S.A. 139 J6 34 0N 96 25W
Duratón →, Spain 36 D6 41 37N 4 7W
Durazno, Uruguay 158 C4 33 25 S 56 31W
Durazzo = Durrësi, Albania 44 C1 41 19N 19 28 E
Durban, France 24 F6 42 59N 2 49 E
Durban, S. Africa 105 D5 29 49 S 31 1 E
Durbo, Somali Rep. 108 B4 11 37N 50 20 E
Dúrcal, Spain 37 J7 37 0N 3 34W
Đurd-evac, Yugoslavia 42 A2 46 2N 17 3 E
Düren, Germany 26 E2 50 48N 6 30 E
Durg, India 82 D5 21 15N 81 22 E
Durgapur, India 81 H12 23 30N 87 20 E
Durham, Canada 128 D3 44 10N 80 49W
Durham, U.K. 16 C6 54 47N 1 34W
Durham, Calif., U.S.A. 144 F5 39 39N 121 48W
Durham, N.C., U.S.A. 135 H6 36 0N 78 55W
Durham □, U.K. 16 C6 54 42N 1 45W
Durham Downs, Australia 115 D4 26 6 S 149 5 E
Ḍurmā, Si. Arabia 86 A4 24 37N 46 8 E
Durness, U.K. 18 C4 58 34N 4 45W
Durrësi, Albania 44 C1 41 19N 19 28 E
Durrie, Australia 114 D3 25 40 S 140 15 E
Dursunbey, Turkey 88 D3 39 35N 28 37 E
Durtal, France 22 E6 47 40N 0 18W
Duru, Zaïre 106 B2 4 14N 28 50 E
D'Urville, Tanjung, Indonesia 71 E9 1 28 S 137 54 E
D'Urville I., N.Z. 119 A8 40 50 S 173 55 E
Duryea, U.S.A. 137 E9 41 20N 75 45W
Dusa Mareb, Somali Rep. 90 F4 5 30N 46 15 E
Dûsh, Egypt 94 C3 24 35N 30 41 E
Dushak, U.S.S.R. 56 F7 37 13N 60 1 E
Dushan, China 68 E6 25 48N 107 30 E
Dushanbe, U.S.S.R. 55 D4 38 33N 68 48 E
Dusheti, U.S.S.R. 53 E11 42 10N 44 42 E
Dusky Sd., N.Z. 119 F1 45 47 S 166 30 E
Dussejour, C., Australia 112 B4 14 45 S 128 13 E
Düsseldorf, Germany 26 D2 51 15N 6 46 E
Dussen, Neths. 20 E5 51 44N 4 59 E
Duszniki-Zdrój, Poland 47 E3 50 24N 16 24 E
Dutch Harbor, U.S.A. 126 C3 53 54N 166 35W
Dutlwe, Botswana 104 C3 23 58 S 23 46 E
Dutsan Wai, Nigeria 101 C6 10 50N 8 10 E
Dutton, Canada 136 D3 42 39N 81 30W
Dutton →, Australia 114 C3 20 44 S 143 10 E
Duvan, U.S.S.R. 54 D5 55 42N 57 54 E
Duved, Sweden 14 A6 63 24N 12 55 E
Duvno, Yugoslavia 42 D2 43 42N 17 13 E
Duyun, China 68 D6 26 18N 107 29 E
Düzce, Turkey 88 C4 40 50N 31 10 E
Duzdab = Zāhedān, Iran 85 D9 29 30N 60 50 E
Dve Mogili, Bulgaria 43 D10 43 35N 25 55 E
Dvina, Sev. →, U.S.S.R. 48 B7 64 32N 40 30 E
Dvinsk = Daugavpils, U.S.S.R. 50 D5 55 53N 26 32 E
Dvinskaya Guba, U.S.S.R. 48 B6 65 0N 39 0 E
Dvor, Yugoslavia 39 C13 45 4N 16 22 E
Dvorce, Czech. 31 B10 49 50N 17 34 E
Dvur Králové, Czech. 30 A8 50 27N 15 50 E
Dwarka, India 80 H3 22 18N 69 8 E
Dwellingup, Australia 113 F2 32 43 S 116 4 E
Dwight, Canada 136 A5 45 20N 79 1W
Dwight, U.S.A. 141 C8 41 5N 88 25W
Dyakovskoya, U.S.S.R. 51 A12 60 5N 41 12 E
Dyatkovo, U.S.S.R. 50 E9 53 40N 34 27 E
Dyatlovo, U.S.S.R. 50 E4 53 28N 25 28 E
Dyer, U.S.A. 141 G10 37 24N 86 13W
Dyer, C., Canada 127 B13 66 40N 61 0W
Dyer Plateau, Antarctica 7 D17 70 45 S 65 30W
Dyerbeldzhin, U.S.S.R. 55 C7 41 13N 74 54 E
Dyersburg, U.S.A. 139 G10 36 2N 89 20W
Dyersville, U.S.A. 140 B5 42 29N 91 8W
Dyfed □, U.K. 17 F3 52 0N 4 30W
Dyfi →, U.K. 17 E4 52 32N 4 0W
Dyje →, Czech. 31 C9 48 37N 16 56 E
Dyle →, Belgium 21 G5 50 58N 4 41 E
Dynevor Downs, Australia 115 D3 28 10 S 144 20 E
Dynów, Poland 31 B15 49 50N 22 11 E
Dysart, Canada 131 C8 50 57N 104 2W
Dyurtyuli, U.S.S.R. 54 D4 55 9N 54 4 E
Dzamin Üüd, Mongolia 66 C6 43 50N 111 58 E
Dzerzhinsk, Byelorussian S.S.R., U.S.S.R. 50 E5 53 40N 27 1 E
Dzerzhinsk, R.S.F.S.R., U.S.S.R. 51 C13 56 14N 43 30 E
Dzhalal-Abad, U.S.S.R. 55 C6 40 56N 73 0 E
Dzhalinda, U.S.S.R. 57 D13 53 26N 124 0 E
Dzhambeyty, U.S.S.R. 53 A15 50 16N 52 35 E
Dzhambul, U.S.S.R. 55 B5 42 54N 71 22 E
Dzhambul, Gora, U.S.S.R. 55 A6 44 54N 73 0 E
Dzhankoi, U.S.S.R. 52 D6 45 40N 34 20 E
Dzhanybek, U.S.S.R. 53 B12 49 25N 46 50 E
Dzhardzhan, U.S.S.R. 57 C13 68 10N 124 10 E
Dzharkurgan, U.S.S.R. 55 E3 37 31N 67 25 E
Dzhelinde, U.S.S.R. 57 C12 70 0N 114 20 E
Dzhetygara, U.S.S.R. 54 E7 52 11N 61 12 E
Dzhetym, Khrebet, U.S.S.R. 55 C8 41 30N 77 0 E
Dzhezkazgan, U.S.S.R. 56 E7 47 44N 67 40 E
Dzhikimde, U.S.S.R. 57 D13 59 1N 121 47 E
Dzhizak, U.S.S.R. 55 C3 40 6N 67 50 E
Dzhugdzur, Khrebet, U.S.S.R. 57 D14 57 30N 138 0 E
Dzhuma, U.S.S.R. 55 D3 39 42N 66 40 E
Dzhumgoltau, Khrebet, U.S.S.R. 55 B7 42 15N 74 30 E
Dzhungarskiye Vorota, U.S.S.R. 64 B3 45 0N 82 0 E
Dzhvari, U.S.S.R. 53 E10 42 42N 42 4 E
Działdowo, Poland 47 B7 53 15N 20 15 E
Działoszyce, Poland 47 E7 50 22N 20 20 E
Działoszyn, Poland 47 D5 51 6N 18 50 E
Dzierzgoń, Poland 47 B6 53 58N 19 20 E
Dzierzoniów, Poland 47 E3 50 45N 16 39 E
Dzilam de Bravo, Mexico 147 C7 21 24N 88 53W
Dzioua, Algeria 99 B6 33 14N 5 14 E
Dziwnów, Poland 47 A1 54 2N 14 45 E
Dzungaria = Junggar Pendi, China 64 B3 44 30N 86 0 E
Dzungarian Gates = Dzhungarskiye Vorota, U.S.S.R. 64 B3 45 0N 82 0 E
Dzuumod, Mongolia 64 B5 47 45N 106 58 E

E

Eabamet, L., Canada 128 B2 51 30N 87 46W
Eads, U.S.A. 138 F3 38 30N 102 46W
Eagle, U.S.A. 142 G10 39 39N 106 55W
Eagle →, Canada 129 B8 53 36N 57 26W
Eagle Butt, U.S.A. 138 C4 45 1N 101 12W
Eagle Cr. →, U.S.A. 141 F11 38 36N 85 4W
Eagle Grove, U.S.A. 140 B3 42 37N 93 53W
Eagle L., Calif., U.S.A. 142 F3 40 35N 120 50W
Eagle L., Maine, U.S.A. 129 C6 46 23N 69 22W
Eagle Lake, U.S.A. 139 L6 29 35N 96 21W
Eagle Mountain, U.S.A. 145 M11 33 52N 115 26W
Eagle Nest, U.S.A. 143 H11 36 33N 105 13W
Eagle Pass, U.S.A. 139 L4 28 45N 100 35W
Eagle Pk., U.S.A. 144 G7 38 10N 119 25W
Eagle Pt., Australia 112 C3 16 11 S 124 23 E
Eagle River, U.S.A. 138 C10 45 55N 89 17W
Eagleville, U.S.A. 140 D3 40 28N 93 59W
Ealing, U.K. 17 F7 51 30N 0 19W
Earaheedy, Australia 113 E3 25 34 S 121 29 E
Earl Grey, Canada 131 C8 50 57N 104 43W
Earle, U.S.A. 139 H9 35 18N 90 26W
Earlimart, U.S.A. 145 K7 35 53N 119 16W
Earlville, U.S.A. 141 C8 41 35N 88 55W
Earn →, U.K. 18 E5 56 20N 3 19W
Earn, L., U.K. 18 E4 56 23N 4 14W
Earnslaw, Mt., N.Z. 119 E3 44 32 S 168 27 E
Earth, U.S.A. 139 H3 34 18N 102 30W
Easley, U.S.A. 135 H4 34 52N 82 35W
East Angus, Canada 129 C5 45 30N 71 40W
East Aurora, U.S.A. 136 D6 42 46N 78 38W
East B., U.S.A. 139 L10 29 2N 89 16W
East Beskids = Vychodné Beskydy, Europe 31 B15 49 20N 22 0 E
East Brady, U.S.A. 136 F5 40 59N 79 36W
East C., N.Z. 118 D7 37 42 S 178 35 E
East C., Papua N. G. 120 F6 10 13 S 150 53 E
East Chicago, U.S.A. 141 C9 41 40N 87 30W
East China Sea, Asia 65 C7 30 5N 126 0 E
East Coast □, N.Z. 118 E7 38 0 S 178 0 E
East Coast Bays, N.Z. 118 C3 36 46 S 174 46 E
East Coulee, Canada 130 C6 51 23N 112 27W
East Dubuque, U.S.A. 140 B6 42 29N 90 39W
East Falkland, Falk. Is. 160 D5 51 30 S 58 30W
East Grand Forks, U.S.A. 138 B6 47 55N 97 5W
East Greenwich, U.S.A. 137 E13 41 39N 71 27W
East Hartford, U.S.A. 137 E12 41 45N 72 39W
East Helena, U.S.A. 142 C8 46 37N 111 58W
East Indies, Asia 71 E6 0 0 120 0 E
East Jordan, U.S.A. 134 C3 45 10N 85 7W
East Lansing, U.S.A. 141 B12 42 44N 84 29W
East Liverpool, U.S.A. 136 F4 40 39N 80 35W
East London, S. Africa 105 E4 33 0 S 27 55 E
East Lynne, Australia 117 C9 35 35 S 150 16 E
East Main = Eastmain, Canada 128 B4 52 10N 78 30W
East Moline, U.S.A. 140 C6 41 31N 90 25W
East Orange, U.S.A. 137 F10 40 46N 74 13W
East Pacific Ridge, Pac. Oc. 123 J17 15 0 S 110 0W
East Pakistan = Bangladesh ■, Asia 78 D3 24 0N 90 0 E
East Palestine, U.S.A. 136 F4 40 50N 80 32W
East Peoria, U.S.A. 140 D7 40 40N 89 34W
East Pine, Canada 130 B4 55 48N 120 12W
East Pt., Canada 129 C7 46 27N 61 58W
East Point, U.S.A. 135 J3 33 40N 84 28W

194 East Providence

East Providence, *U.S.A.* **137 E13** 41 48N 71 22W
East Retford, *U.K.* **16 D7** 53 19N 0 55W
East St. Louis, *U.S.A.* **140 F6** 38 37N 90 4W
East Schelde → = Oosterschelde, *Neths.* **21 E4** 51 33N 4 0 E
East Siberian Sea, *U.S.S.R.* **57 B17** 73 0N 160 0 E
East Stroudsburg, *U.S.A.* **137 E9** 41 1N 75 11W
East Sussex □, *U.K.* **17 G8** 51 0N 0 20 E
East Tawas, *U.S.A.* **134 C4** 44 17N 83 31W
East Toorale, *Australia* **115 E4** 30 27 S 145 28 E
East Troy, *U.S.A.* **141 B8** 42 47N 88 24W
East Walker →, *U.S.A.* **144 G7** 38 52N 119 10W
Eastbourne, *N.Z.* **118 H3** 41 19 S 174 55 E
Eastbourne, *U.K.* **17 G8** 50 46N 0 18 E
Eastend, *Canada* **131 D7** 49 32N 108 50W
Easter Islands = Pascua, I. de, *Pac. Oc.* **123 K17** 27 0 S 109 0W
Eastern □, *Kenya* **106 C4** 0 0 38 30 E
Eastern □, *Uganda* **106 B3** 1 50N 33 45 E
Eastern Cr. →, *Australia* **114 C3** 20 40 S 141 35 E
Eastern Ghats, *India* **83 H4** 14 0N 78 50 E
Eastern Group = Lau Group, *Fiji* **121 A3** 17 0 S 178 30W
Eastern Group, *Australia* **113 F3** 33 30 S 124 30 E
Eastern Province □, *S. Leone* **100 D2** 8 15N 11 0W
Easterville, *Canada* **131 C9** 53 8N 99 49W
Easthampton, *U.S.A.* **137 D12** 42 15N 72 41W
Eastland, *U.S.A.* **139 J5** 32 26N 98 45W
Eastleigh, *U.K.* **17 G6** 50 58N 1 21W
Eastmain, *Canada* **128 B4** 52 10N 78 30W
Eastmain →, *Canada* **128 B4** 52 27N 78 26W
Eastman, *Canada* **137 A12** 45 18N 72 19W
Eastman, *Ga., U.S.A.* **135 J4** 32 13N 83 20W
Eastman, *Wis., U.S.A.* **140 A5** 43 10N 91 1W
Easton, *Md., U.S.A.* **134 F7** 38 47N 76 7W
Easton, *Pa., U.S.A.* **137 F9** 40 41N 75 15W
Easton, *Wash., U.S.A.* **144 C5** 47 14N 121 8W
Eastport, *U.S.A.* **129 D6** 44 57N 67 0W
Eastsound, *U.S.A.* **144 B4** 48 42N 122 55W
Eaton, *Colo., U.S.A.* **138 E2** 40 35N 104 42W
Eaton, *Ohio, U.S.A.* **141 E12** 39 45N 84 38W
Eaton Rapids, *U.S.A.* **141 B12** 42 31N 84 39W
Eatonia, *Canada* **131 C7** 51 13N 109 25W
Eatonton, *U.S.A.* **135 J4** 33 22N 83 24W
Eatontown, *U.S.A.* **137 F10** 40 18N 74 7W
Eatonville, *U.S.A.* **144 D4** 46 52N 122 16W
Eau Claire, *Fr. Guiana* **153 C7** 3 30N 53 40W
Eau Claire, *U.S.A.* **138 C9** 44 46N 91 30W
Eauze, *France* **24 E4** 43 53N 0 7 E
Ebagoola, *Australia* **114 A3** 14 15 S 143 12 E
Eban, *Nigeria* **101 D5** 9 40N 4 50 E
Ebangalakata, *Zaïre* **102 C4** 0 29 S 21 29 E
Ebbw Vale, *U.K.* **17 F4** 51 47N 3 12W
Ebebiyín, *Eq. Guin.* **102 B2** 2 9N 11 20 E
Ebeggui, *Algeria* **99 C6** 26 2N 6 0 E
Ebel, *Gabon* **102 B2** 0 7N 11 5 E
Ebeltoft, *Denmark* **13 H11** 56 12N 10 41 E
Ebensburg, *U.S.A.* **136 F6** 40 29N 78 43W
Ebensee, *Austria* **30 D6** 47 48N 13 46 E
Eber Gölü, *Turkey* **88 D4** 38 38N 31 11 E
Eberbach, *Germany* **27 F4** 49 27N 8 59 E
Eberswalde, *Germany* **26 C9** 52 49N 13 50 E
Ebetsu, *Japan* **60 C10** 43 7N 141 34 E
Ebian, *China* **68 C4** 29 11N 103 13 E
Ebikon, *Switz.* **29 B6** 47 5N 8 21 E
Ebingen, *Germany* **27 G5** 48 13N 9 1 E
Ebino, *Japan* **62 E2** 32 2N 130 48 E
Ebnat-Kappel, *Switz.* **29 B8** 47 16N 9 7 E
Eboli, *Italy* **41 B8** 40 39N 15 2 E
Ebolowa, *Cameroon* **101 E7** 2 55N 11 10 E
Ebrach, *Germany* **27 F6** 49 50N 10 30 E
Ébrié, Lagune, *Ivory C.* **100 D4** 5 12N 4 26W
Ebro →, *Spain* **34 E5** 40 43N 0 54 E
Ebro, Pantano del, *Spain* **36 C7** 43 0N 3 58W
Ebstorf, *Germany* **26 B6** 53 2N 10 23 E
Ecaussines-d' Enghien, *Belgium* **21 G4** 50 35N 4 11 E
Eceabat, *Turkey* **44 D8** 40 11N 26 21 E
Ech Cheliff, *Algeria* **99 A5** 36 10N 1 20 E
Echallens, *Switz.* **28 C3** 46 38N 6 38 E
Echeng, *China* **69 B10** 30 23N 114 50 E
Echigo-Sammyaku, *Japan* **61 F9** 36 50N 139 50 E
Echizen-Misaki, *Japan* **63 B7** 35 59N 135 57 E
Echmiadzin, *U.S.S.R.* **53 F11** 40 12N 44 19 E
Echo Bay, *N.W.T., Canada* **126 B8** 66 5N 117 55W
Echo Bay, *Ont., Canada* **128 C3** 46 29N 84 4W
Echoing →, *Canada* **131 B10** 55 51N 92 5W
Echt, *Neths.* **21 F7** 51 7N 5 52 E
Echternach, *Lux.* **21 J8** 49 49N 6 25 E
Echuca, *Australia* **117 D6** 36 10 S 144 20 E
Ecija, *Spain* **37 H5** 37 30N 5 10W
Eckernförde, *Germany* **26 A5** 54 26N 9 50 E
Eclipse Is., *Australia* **112 B4** 13 54 S 126 19 E
Écommoy, *France* **22 E7** 47 50N 0 17 E
Ecoporanga, *Brazil* **155 E3** 18 23 S 40 50W
Écos, *France* **23 C8** 49 9N 1 35 E
Écouché, *France* **22 D6** 48 42N 0 10W
Ecuador ■, *S. Amer.* **152 D2** 2 0 S 78 0W
Écueillé, *France* **22 E8** 47 5N 1 21 E
Ed, *Sweden* **15 F5** 58 55N 11 55 E
Ed Dabbura, *Sudan* **94 D3** 17 40N 34 15 E
Ed Dâmer, *Sudan* **94 D3** 17 27N 34 0 E
Ed Debba, *Sudan* **94 D3** 18 0N 30 51 E
Ed-Déffa, *Egypt* **94 A2** 30 40N 26 30 E
Ed Deim, *Sudan* **95 E2** 10 10N 28 20 E
Ed Dueim, *Sudan* **95 E3** 14 0N 32 10 E
Edah, *Australia* **113 E2** 28 16 S 117 10 E
Edam, *Canada* **131 C7** 53 11N 108 46W
Edam, *Neths.* **20 C6** 52 31N 5 3 E
Edapally, *India* **83 J4** 11 19N 78 3 E
Eday, *U.K.* **18 B6** 59 11N 2 47W
Edd, *Ethiopia* **90 E3** 14 0N 41 38 E
Eddrachillis B., *U.K.* **18 C3** 58 16N 5 10W
Eddystone, *U.K.* **17 G3** 50 11N 4 16W
Eddystone Pt., *Australia* **114 G4** 40 59 S 148 20 E
Eddyville, *U.S.A.* **140 C4** 41 9N 92 38W
Ede, *Neths.* **20 D7** 52 4N 5 40 E
Ede, *Nigeria* **101 D5** 7 45N 4 29 E
Édea, *Cameroon* **101 E7** 3 51N 10 9 E
Edegem, *Belgium* **21 F4** 51 10N 4 27 E
Edehon L., *Canada* **131 A9** 60 25N 97 15W
Edekel, Adrar, *Algeria* **99 D6** 23 56N 6 47 E
Eden, *Australia* **117 D8** 37 3 S 149 55 E
Eden, *N.C., U.S.A.* **135 G6** 36 29N 79 53W
Eden, *N.Y., U.S.A.* **136 D6** 42 39N 78 55W
Eden, *Tex., U.S.A.* **139 K5** 31 16N 99 50W
Eden, *Wyo., U.S.A.* **142 E9** 42 2N 109 27W
Eden →, *U.K.* **16 C4** 54 57N 3 2W
Eden L., *Canada* **131 B8** 56 38N 100 15W
Edenburg, *S. Africa* **104 D4** 29 43 S 25 58 E
Edendale, *N.Z.* **119 G3** 46 19 S 168 48 E
Edendale, *S. Africa* **105 D5** 29 39 S 30 18 E
Edenton, *U.S.A.* **135 G7** 36 5N 76 36W
Edenville, *S. Africa* **105 D4** 27 37 S 27 34 E
Eder →, *Germany* **26 D5** 51 15N 9 25 E
Ederstausee, *Germany* **26 D5** 51 11N 9 0 E
Edgar, *U.S.A.* **138 E6** 40 25N 98 0W
Edgartown, *U.S.A.* **137 E14** 41 22N 70 28W
Edge Hill, *U.K.* **17 E6** 52 7N 1 28W
Edgecumbe, *N.Z.* **118 D5** 37 59 S 176 47 E
Edgefield, *U.S.A.* **135 J5** 33 50N 81 59W
Edgeley, *U.S.A.* **138 B5** 46 27N 98 41W
Edgemont, *U.S.A.* **138 D3** 43 15N 103 53W
Edgeøya, *Svalbard* **6 B9** 77 45N 22 30 E
Edgerton, *Ohio, U.S.A.* **141 C12** 41 27N 84 45W
Edgerton, *Wis., U.S.A.* **140 B7** 42 50N 89 4W
Edgewood, *U.S.A.* **141 F8** 38 55N 88 40W
Edhessa, *Greece* **44 D4** 40 48N 22 5 E
Edievale, *N.Z.* **119 F4** 45 49 S 169 22 E
Edina, *Liberia* **100 D2** 6 0N 10 10W
Edina, *U.S.A.* **140 D4** 40 6N 92 10W
Edinburg, *Ill., U.S.A.* **140 E7** 39 39N 89 23W
Edinburg, *Ind., U.S.A.* **141 E11** 39 21N 85 58W
Edinburg, *Tex., U.S.A.* **139 M5** 26 22N 98 10W
Edinburgh, *U.K.* **18 F5** 55 57N 3 12W
Edirne, *Turkey* **43 F11** 41 40N 26 34 E
Edirne □, *Turkey* **88 C2** 41 40N 26 30 E
Edison, *U.S.A.* **144 B4** 48 33N 122 27W
Edithburgh, *Australia* **116 C2** 35 5 S 137 43 E
Edjeleh, *Algeria* **99 C6** 28 38N 9 50 E
Edjudina, *Australia* **113 E3** 29 48 S 122 23 E
Edmeston, *U.S.A.* **137 D9** 42 42N 75 15W
Edmond, *U.S.A.* **139 H6** 35 37N 97 30W
Edmonds, *U.S.A.* **144 C4** 47 47N 122 22W
Edmonton, *Australia* **114 B4** 17 2 S 145 46 E
Edmonton, *Canada* **130 C6** 53 30N 113 30W
Edmund L., *Canada* **131 C10** 54 45N 93 17W
Edmundston, *Canada* **129 C6** 47 23N 68 20W
Edna, *U.S.A.* **139 L6** 29 0N 96 40W
Edna Bay, *U.S.A.* **130 B2** 55 55N 133 40W
Edolo, *Italy* **38 B7** 46 10N 10 21 E
Edremit, *Turkey* **88 D2** 39 34N 27 0 E
Edremit Körfezi, *Turkey* **88 D2** 39 30N 26 45 E
Edsbyn, *Sweden* **14 C9** 61 23N 15 49 E
Edsele, *Sweden* **14 A10** 63 25N 16 32 E
Edson, *Canada* **130 C5** 53 35N 116 28W
Eduardo Castex, *Argentina* **158 D3** 35 50 S 64 18W
Edward →, *Australia* **116 C5** 35 5 S 143 30 E
Edward, L., *Africa* **106 C2** 0 25 S 29 40 E
Edward I., *Canada* **128 C2** 48 22N 88 37W
Edward River, *Australia* **114 A3** 14 59 S 141 26 E
Edward VII Land, *Antarctica* **7 E13** 80 0 S 150 0W
Edwards, *U.S.A.* **145 L9** 34 55N 117 51W
Edwards →, *U.S.A.* **140 C6** 41 10N 90 59W
Edwards Plateau, *U.S.A.* **139 K4** 30 30N 101 5W
Edwardsburg, *U.S.A.* **141 C10** 41 48N 86 6W
Edwardsport, *U.S.A.* **141 F9** 38 49N 87 15W
Edwardsville, *Ill., U.S.A.* **140 F7** 38 49N 89 57W
Edwardsville, *Pa., U.S.A.* **137 E9** 41 15N 75 56W
Edzo, *Canada* **130 A5** 62 49N 116 4W
Eefde, *Neths.* **20 D8** 52 10N 6 13 E
Eekloo, *Belgium* **21 F3** 51 11N 3 33 E
Eel →, *Ind., U.S.A.* **141 E10** 39 7N 86 58W
Eel →, *Ind., U.S.A.* **141 D10** 40 45N 86 22W
Eelde, *Neths.* **20 B9** 53 8N 6 34 E
Eem →, *Neths.* **20 D6** 52 16N 5 20 E
Eems →, *Neths.* **20 B9** 53 26N 6 57 E
Eems Kanaal, *Neths.* **20 B9** 53 18N 6 46 E
Eenrum, *Neths.* **20 B8** 53 22N 6 28 E
Eernegem, *Belgium* **21 F2** 51 8N 3 2 E
Eerste Valthermond, *Neths.* **20 C9** 52 53N 6 58 E
Efate, I., *Vanuatu* **121 G6** 17 40 S 168 25 E
Eferding, *Austria* **30 C7** 48 18N 14 1 E
Eferi, *Algeria* **99 D6** 24 30N 9 28 E
Effingham, *U.S.A.* **141 E8** 39 8N 88 30W
Effretikon, *Switz.* **29 B7** 47 25N 8 42 E
Eforie Sud, *Romania* **46 E9** 44 1N 28 37 E
Ega →, *Spain* **34 C3** 42 19N 1 55W
Égadi, Ísole, *Italy* **40 E5** 37 55N 12 16 E
Eganville, *Canada* **128 C4** 45 32N 77 5W
Egeland, *U.S.A.* **138 A5** 48 42N 99 6W
Egenolf L., *Canada* **131 B9** 59 3N 100 0W
Eger = Cheb, *Czech.* **30 A5** 50 9N 12 28 E
Eger, *Hungary* **31 D13** 47 53N 20 27 E
Eger →, *Hungary* **31 D13** 47 38N 20 50 E
Egersund, *Norway* **13 G9** 58 26N 6 1 E
Egg L., *Canada* **131 B7** 55 5N 105 30W
Eggenburg, *Austria* **30 C8** 48 38N 15 50 E
Eggenfelden, *Germany* **27 G8** 48 24N 12 46 E
Eggiwil, *Switz.* **28 C5** 46 52N 7 47 E
Egherta, *Somali Rep.* **108 D2** 2 4N 43 11 E
Éghezée, *Belgium* **21 G5** 50 35N 4 55 E
Eginbah, *Australia* **112 D2** 20 53 S 119 47 E
Egito, *Angola* **103 E2** 12 4 S 13 58 E
Égletons, *France* **24 C6** 45 24N 2 3 E
Eglisau, *Switz.* **29 A7** 47 35N 8 31 E
Egmond-aan-Zee, *Neths.* **20 C5** 52 37N 4 38 E
Egmont, C., *N.Z.* **118 F2** 39 16 S 173 45 E
Egmont, Mt., *N.Z.* **118 F3** 39 17 S 174 5 E
Eğridir, *Turkey* **88 E4** 37 52N 30 51 E
Eğridir Gölü, *Turkey* **88 E4** 37 53N 30 50 E
Egtved, *Denmark* **15 J3** 55 38N 9 18 E
Éguas →, *Brazil* **155 D3** 13 26 S 44 14W
Egume, *Nigeria* **101 D6** 7 30N 7 14 E
Éguzon, *France* **24 B5** 46 27N 1 33 E
Egvekinot, *U.S.S.R.* **57 C19** 66 19N 179 50W
Egyek, *Hungary* **31 D13** 47 39N 20 52 E
Egypt ■, *Africa* **94 J7** 28 0N 31 0 E
Eha Amufu, *Nigeria* **101 D6** 6 30N 7 46 E
Ehime □, *Japan* **62 D4** 33 30N 132 40 E
Ehingen, *Germany* **27 G5** 48 16N 9 43 E
Ehrenberg, *U.S.A.* **145 M12** 33 36N 114 31W
Ehrwald, *Austria* **30 D3** 47 24N 10 56 E
Eibar, *Spain* **34 B2** 43 11N 2 28W
Eibergen, *Neths.* **20 D9** 52 6N 6 39 E
Eichstatt, *Germany* **27 G7** 48 53N 11 12 E
Eider →, *Germany* **26 A4** 54 19N 8 58 E
Eidsvold, *Australia* **115 D5** 25 25 S 151 12 E
Eidsvoll, *Norway* **13 F11** 60 19N 11 14 E
Eifel, *Germany* **27 E2** 50 10N 6 45 E
Eiffel Flats, *Zimbabwe* **107 F3** 18 20 S 30 0 E
Eigg, *U.K.* **18 E2** 56 54N 6 10W
Eighty Mile Beach, *Australia* **112 C3** 19 30 S 120 40 E
Eil, *Somali Rep.* **90 F4** 8 0N 49 50 E
Eil, L., *U.K.* **18 E3** 56 50N 5 15W
Eildon, *Australia* **117 D6** 37 14 S 145 55 E
Eildon, L., *Australia* **115 F4** 37 10 S 146 0 E
Eileen L., *Canada* **131 A7** 62 16N 107 37W
Eilenburg, *Germany* **26 D8** 51 28N 12 38 E
Ein el Luweiqa, *Sudan* **95 E3** 14 5N 33 50 E
Einasleigh, *Australia* **114 B3** 18 32 S 144 5 E
Einasleigh →, *Australia* **114 B3** 17 30 S 142 17 E
Einbeck, *Germany* **26 D5** 51 48N 9 50 E
Eindhoven, *Neths.* **21 F6** 51 26N 5 28 E
Einsiedeln, *Switz.* **29 B7** 47 7N 8 46 E
Eire ■, *Europe* **19 D4** 53 0N 8 0W
Eiríksjökull, *Iceland* **12 D3** 64 46N 20 24W
Eirlandsche Gat, *Neths.* **20 B5** 53 12N 4 54 E
Eirunepé, *Brazil* **156 B4** 6 35 S 69 53W
Eisden, *Belgium* **21 G7** 50 59N 5 42 E
Eisenach, *Germany* **26 E6** 50 58N 10 18 E
Eisenberg, *Germany* **26 E7** 50 59N 11 50 E
Eisenerz, *Austria* **30 D7** 47 32N 14 54 E
Eisenhüttenstadt, *Germany* **26 C10** 52 9N 14 41 E
Eisenkappel, *Austria* **30 E7** 46 29N 14 36 E
Eisenstadt, *Austria* **31 D9** 47 51N 16 31 E
Eiserfeld, *Germany* **26 E3** 50 50N 7 59 E
Eisfeld, *Germany* **26 E6** 50 25N 10 54 E
Eisleben, *Germany* **26 D7** 51 31N 11 31 E
Ejby, *Denmark* **15 J3** 55 25N 9 56 E
Eje, Sierra del, *Spain* **36 C4** 42 24N 6 54W
Ejea de los Caballeros, *Spain* **34 C3** 42 7N 1 9W
Ejutla, *Mexico* **147 D5** 16 34N 96 44W
Ekalaka, *U.S.A.* **138 C2** 45 55N 104 30W
Ekalla, *Gabon* **102 C2** 1 27 S 14 0 E
Ekanga, *Zaïre* **102 C4** 2 23 S 23 14 E
Ekawasaki, *Japan* **62 D4** 33 13N 132 46 E
Ekeren, *Belgium* **21 F4** 51 17N 4 25 E
Eket, *Nigeria* **101 E6** 4 38N 7 56 E
Eketahuna, *N.Z.* **118 G4** 40 38 S 175 43 E
Ekhínos, *Greece* **44 C7** 41 16N 25 1 E
Ekibastuz, *U.S.S.R.* **56 D8** 51 50N 75 10 E
Ekimchan, *U.S.S.R.* **57 D14** 53 0N 133 0 E
Ekoli, *Zaïre* **102 C4** 0 23 S 24 13 E
Eksel, *Belgium* **21 F6** 51 9N 5 24 E
Ekwan →, *Canada* **128 B3** 53 12N 82 15W
Ekwan Pt., *Canada* **128 B3** 53 16N 82 7W
El Aaiún, *W. Sahara* **98 C2** 27 9N 13 12W
El Aargub, *Mauritania* **98 D1** 23 37N 15 52W
El Abiodh-Sidi-Cheikh, *Algeria* **99 B5** 32 53N 0 31 E
El Adde, *Somali Rep.* **108 D3** 2 35N 46 9 E
El 'Agrûd, *Egypt* **91 E3** 30 14N 34 24 E
El Aïoun, *Morocco* **99 B4** 34 33N 2 30W
El 'Aiyat, *Egypt* **94 J7** 29 36N 31 15 E
El Alamein, *Egypt* **94 H6** 30 48N 28 58 E
El Alto, *Peru* **156 A1** 4 15 S 81 14W
El 'Aqaba, W. →, *Egypt* **91 E2** 30 7N 33 54 E
El 'Arag, *Egypt* **94 B2** 28 40N 26 20 E
El Arahal, *Spain* **37 H5** 37 15N 5 33W
El Arenal, *Spain* **33 B9** 39 30N 2 45 E
El Aricha, *Algeria* **99 B4** 34 13N 1 10W
El Arïhā, *Jordan* **91 D4** 31 52N 35 27 E
El Arish, *Australia* **114 B4** 17 35 S 146 1 E
El 'Arîsh, *Egypt* **91 D2** 31 8N 33 50 E
El 'Arîsh, W. →, *Egypt* **91 D2** 31 8N 33 47 E
El Arrouch, *Algeria* **99 A6** 36 37N 6 53 E
El Asnam = Ech Cheliff, *Algeria* **99 A5** 36 10N 1 20 E
El Astillero, *Spain* **36 B7** 43 24N 3 49W
El Badâri, *Egypt* **94 B3** 27 4N 31 25 E
El Bahrein, *Egypt* **94 B2** 28 30N 26 25 E
El Ballâs, *Egypt* **94 B3** 26 2N 32 43 E
El Balyana, *Egypt* **94 B3** 26 10N 32 3 E
El Banco, *Colombia* **152 B3** 9 0N 73 58W
El Baqeir, *Sudan* **94 D3** 18 40N 33 40 E
El Barco de Ávila, *Spain* **36 E5** 40 21N 5 31W
El Barco de Valdeorras, *Spain* **36 C4** 42 23N 6 58W
El Bauga, *Sudan* **94 D3** 18 18N 33 52 E
El Baúl, *Venezuela* **152 B4** 8 57N 68 17W
El Bawiti, *Egypt* **94 J6** 28 25N 28 45 E
El Bayadh, *Algeria* **99 B5** 33 40N 1 1 E
El Bierzo, *Spain* **36 C4** 42 45N 6 30W
El Bluff, *Nic.* **148 D3** 11 59N 83 40W
El Bolsón, *Argentina* **160 B2** 41 55 S 71 30W
El Bonillo, *Spain* **35 G2** 38 57N 2 35W
El Brûk, W. →, *Egypt* **91 E2** 30 15N 33 50 E
El Buheirat □, *Sudan* **95 F3** 7 0N 30 0 E
El Bur, *Somali Rep.* **108 D3** 4 40N 46 37 E
El Caín, *Argentina* **160 B3** 41 38 S 68 19W
El Cajon, *U.S.A.* **145 N10** 32 49N 117 0W
El Callao, *Venezuela* **153 B5** 7 18N 61 50W
El Camp, *Spain* **34 D6** 41 5N 1 10 E
El Campo, *U.S.A.* **139 L6** 29 10N 96 20W
El Carmen, *Bolivia* **157 C5** 13 40 S 63 55W
El Carmen, *Venezuela* **152 C4** 1 16N 66 52W
El Castillo, *Spain* **37 H4** 37 41N 6 19W
El Centro, *U.S.A.* **145 N11** 32 50N 115 40W
El Cerro, *Bolivia* **157 D5** 17 30 S 61 40W
El Cerro, *Spain* **37 H4** 37 45N 6 57W
El Cocuy, *Colombia* **152 B3** 6 25N 72 27W
El Compadre, *Mexico* **145 N10** 32 20N 116 14W
El Corcovado, *Argentina* **160 B2** 43 25 S 71 35W
El Coronil, *Spain* **37 H5** 37 5N 5 38W
El Cuy, *Argentina* **160 A3** 39 55 S 68 25W
El Cuyo, *Mexico* **147 C7** 21 30N 87 40W
El Dab'a, *Egypt* **94 H6** 31 0N 28 27 E
El Daheir, *Egypt* **91 D3** 31 13N 34 10 E
El Dambahaddo, *Somali Rep.* **108 D3** 3 17N 46 40 E
El Deir, *Egypt* **94 B3** 25 25N 32 20 E
El Dere, *Ethiopia* **108 C2** 5 6N 43 5 E
El Dere, *Somali Rep.* **108 C3** 5 22N 46 11 E
El Dere, *Somali Rep.* **90 G4** 3 50N 47 8 E
El Descanso, *Mexico* **145 N10** 32 12N 116 58W
El Desemboque, *Mexico* **146 A2** 30 30N 112 57W
El Dilingat, *Egypt* **94 H7** 30 50N 30 31 E
El Diviso, *Colombia* **152 C2** 1 22N 78 14W
El Djem, *Tunisia* **96 A2** 35 18N 10 42 E
El Djouf, *Mauritania* **92 D3** 20 0N 9 0W
El Dorado, *Ark., U.S.A.* **139 J8** 33 10N 92 40W
El Dorado, *Kans., U.S.A.* **139 G6** 37 55N 96 56W
El Dorado, *Venezuela* **153 B5** 6 55N 61 37W
El Eglab, *Algeria* **98 C4** 26 20N 4 30W
El Escorial, *Spain* **36 E6** 40 35N 4 7W
El Eulma, *Algeria* **99 A6** 36 9N 5 42 E
El Faiyûm, *Egypt* **94 J7** 29 19N 30 50 E
El Fâsher, *Sudan* **95 E2** 13 33N 25 26 E
El Fashn, *Egypt* **94 J7** 28 50N 30 54 E
El Ferrol, *Spain* **36 B2** 43 29N 8 15W
El Fifi, *Sudan* **95 E2** 10 4N 25 0 E
El Fud, *Ethiopia* **108 C2** 7 15N 42 52 E
El Fuerte, *Mexico* **146 B3** 26 30N 108 40W
El Gal, *Somali Rep.* **90 E5** 10 58N 50 20 E
El Gebir, *Sudan* **95 E2** 13 40N 29 40 E
El Gedida, *Egypt* **94 B2** 25 40N 28 30 E
El Geteina, *Sudan* **95 E3** 14 50N 32 27 E
El Gezira □, *Sudan* **95 E3** 15 0N 33 0 E
El Gîza, *Egypt* **94 J7** 30 0N 31 10 E
El Goléa, *Algeria* **99 B5** 30 30N 2 50 E
El Guettar, *Algeria* **99 B5** 34 5N 4 38 E
El Hadeb, *W. Sahara* **98 C2** 25 51N 13 0W
El Hadjira, *Algeria* **99 B6** 32 36N 5 30 E
El Hagiz, *Sudan* **95 D4** 15 15N 35 50 E
El Hajeb, *Morocco* **98 B3** 33 43N 5 13W
El Hammam, *Egypt* **94 H6** 30 52N 29 25 E
El Hammâmi, *Mauritania* **98 D2** 23 3N 11 30W
El Hamurre, *Somali Rep.* **108 C3** 7 13N 48 54 E
El Hank, *Mauritania* **98 D3** 24 30N 7 0W
El Harrach, *Algeria* **99 A5** 36 45N 3 5 E
El Hasian, *W. Sahara* **98 C2** 26 20N 14 0W
El Hawata, *Sudan* **95 E3** 13 25N 34 42 E
El Heiz, *Egypt* **94 B2** 27 50N 28 40 E
El 'Idisât, *Egypt* **94 B3** 25 30N 32 35 E
El Iskandarîya, *Egypt* **94 H7** 31 0N 30 0 E
El Jadida, *Morocco* **98 B3** 33 11N 8 17W
El Jebelein, *Sudan* **95 E3** 12 40N 32 55 E
El Kab, *Sudan* **94 D3** 19 27N 32 46 E
El Kabrît, G., *Egypt* **91 F2** 29 42N 33 16 E
El Kala, *Algeria* **99 A6** 36 50N 8 30 E
El Kalâa, *Morocco* **98 B3** 32 4N 7 27W
El Kamlin, *Sudan* **95 D3** 15 3N 33 11 E
El Kantara, *Algeria* **99 A6** 35 14N 5 45 E
El Kantara, *Tunisia* **96 B2** 33 45N 10 58 E
El Karaba, *Sudan* **94 D3** 18 32N 33 41 E
El Kef, *Tunisia* **96 A1** 36 12N 8 47 E
El Khandaq, *Sudan* **94 D3** 18 30N 30 30 E
El Khârga, *Egypt* **94 B3** 25 30N 30 33 E
El Khartûm, *Sudan* **95 D3** 15 31N 32 35 E
El Khartûm □, *Sudan* **95 D3** 16 0N 33 0 E
El Khartûm Bahrî, *Sudan* **95 D3** 15 40N 32 31 E
El Khroub, *Algeria* **99 A6** 36 10N 6 55 E
El Kseur, *Algeria* **99 A5** 36 46N 4 49 E
El Ksiba, *Morocco* **98 B3** 32 45N 6 1W
El Kuntilla, *Egypt* **91 E3** 30 1N 34 45 E
El Laqâwa, *Sudan* **95 E2** 11 25N 29 1 E
El Laqeita, *Egypt* **94 B3** 25 50N 33 15 E
El Leiya, *Sudan* **95 D4** 16 15N 35 28 E
El Mafâza, *Sudan* **95 E3** 13 38N 34 30 E
El Mahalla el Kubra, *Egypt* **94 H7** 31 0N 31 0 E
El Mahârîq, *Egypt* **94 B3** 25 35N 30 35 E
El Mahmûdîya, *Egypt* **94 H7** 31 10N 30 32 E
El Maitén, *Argentina* **160 B2** 42 3 S 71 10W
El Maiz, *Algeria* **99 C4** 28 19N 0 9W
El-Maks el-Bahari, *Egypt* **94 C3** 24 30N 30 40 E
El Manshâh, *Egypt* **94 B3** 26 26N 31 50 E
El Mansour, *Algeria* **99 C4** 27 47N 0 14W
El Mansûra, *Egypt* **94 H7** 31 0N 31 19 E
El Mantico, *Venezuela* **153 B5** 7 38N 62 45W
El Manzala, *Egypt* **94 H7** 31 10N 31 50 E
El Marâgha, *Egypt* **94 B3** 26 35N 31 10 E
El Masid, *Sudan* **95 D3** 15 15N 33 0 E
El Matariya, *Egypt* **94 H8** 31 15N 32 0 E
El Medano, *Canary Is.* **33 F3** 28 3N 16 32W
El Meghaier, *Algeria* **99 B6** 33 55N 5 58 E
El Meraguen, *Algeria* **99 C4** 28 0N 0 7W
El Metemma, *Sudan* **95 D3** 16 50N 33 10 E
El Miamo, *Venezuela* **153 B5** 7 39N 61 46W
El Milagro, *Argentina* **158 C2** 30 59 S 65 59W
El Milia, *Algeria* **99 A6** 36 51N 6 13 E
El Minyâ, *Egypt* **94 J7** 28 7N 30 33 E
El Molar, *Spain* **34 E1** 40 42N 3 45W
El Mreyye, *Mauritania* **100 B3** 18 0N 6 0W
El Obeid, *Sudan* **95 E3** 13 8N 30 10 E
El Odaiya, *Sudan* **95 E2** 12 8N 28 12 E
El Oro, *Mexico* **147 D4** 19 48N 100 8W
El Oro □, *Ecuador* **152 D2** 3 30 S 79 50W
El Oued, *Algeria* **99 B6** 33 20N 6 58 E
El Palmar, *Bolivia* **157 D5** 17 50 S 63 9W
El Palmar, *Venezuela* **153 B5** 7 58N 61 53W
El Palmito, Presa, *Mexico* **146 B3** 25 40N 105 30W
El Panadés, *Spain* **34 D6** 41 10N 1 30 E
El Pardo, *Spain* **36 E7** 40 31N 3 47W
El Paso, *Ill., U.S.A.* **140 D7** 40 44N 89 1W
El Paso, *Tex., U.S.A.* **143 L10** 31 50N 106 30W
El Paso Robles, *U.S.A.* **144 K6** 35 38N 120 41W
El Pedernoso, *Spain* **35 F2** 39 29N 2 45W
El Pedroso, *Spain* **37 H5** 37 51N 5 45W
El Pobo de Dueñas, *Spain* **34 E3** 40 46N 1 39W
El Portal, *U.S.A.* **144 H7** 37 44N 119 49W
El Porvenir, *Mexico* **146 A3** 31 15N 105 51W
El Prat de Llobregat, *Spain* **34 D7** 41 18N 2 3 E
El Progreso, *Honduras* **148 C2** 15 26N 87 51W
El Provencío, *Spain* **35 F2** 39 23N 2 35W
El Pueblito, *Mexico* **146 B3** 29 3N 105 4W
El Pueblo, *Canary Is.* **33 F2** 28 36N 17 47W
El Qâhira, *Egypt* **94 H7** 30 1N 31 14 E
El Qantara, *Egypt* **91 E1** 30 51N 32 20 E
El Qasr, *Egypt* **94 B2** 25 44N 28 42 E
El Quseima, *Egypt* **91 E3** 30 40N 34 15 E
El Qusîya, *Egypt* **94 B3** 27 29N 30 44 E
El Râshda, *Egypt* **94 B2** 25 36N 28 57 E
El Reno, *U.S.A.* **139 H6** 35 30N 98 0W
El Ribero, *Spain* **36 C2** 42 30N 8 30W
El Rîdisiya, *Egypt* **94 C3** 24 56N 32 51 E
El Rio, *U.S.A.* **145 L7** 34 14N 119 10W
El Ronquillo, *Spain* **37 H4** 37 44N 6 10W

Ereğli 195

El Roque, Pta., Canary Is. 33 F4 28 10N 15 25W
El Rosarito, Mexico 146 B2 28 38N 114 4W
El Rubio, Spain 37 H6 37 22N 5 0W
El Saff, Egypt 94 J7 29 34N 31 16 E
El Saheira, W. →, Egypt 91 E2 30 5N 33 25 E
El Salto, Mexico 146 C3 23 47N 105 22W
El Salvador ■, Cent. Amer. 148 D2 13 50N 89 0W
El Sancejo, Spain 37 H5 37 4N 5 6W
El Sauce, Nic. 148 D2 13 0N 86 40W
El Shallal, Egypt 94 C3 24 0N 32 53 E
El Simbillawein, Egypt 94 H7 30 48N 31 13 E
El Sombrero, Venezuela 152 B4 9 23N 67 3W
El Suweis, Egypt 94 J8 29 58N 32 31 E
El Tamarâni, W. →, Egypt 91 E3 30 7N 34 43 E
El Thamad, Egypt 91 F3 29 40N 34 28 E
El Tigre, Venezuela 153 B5 8 44N 64 15W
El Tîh, G., Egypt 91 F2 29 40N 33 50 E
El Tîna, Khalîg, Egypt 91 D1 31 10N 32 40 E
El Tocuyo, Venezuela 152 B4 9 47N 69 48W
El Tofo, Chile 158 B1 29 22 S 71 18W
El Tránsito, Chile 158 B1 28 52 S 70 17W
El Tûr, Egypt 94 J8 28 14N 33 36 E
El Turbio, Argentina 160 D2 51 45 S 72 5W
El Uinle, Somali Rep. 108 D2 3 4N 41 42 E
El Uqsur, Egypt 94 B3 25 41N 32 38 E
El Vado, Spain 34 D1 41 2N 3 18W
El Vallés, Spain 34 D7 41 35N 2 20 E
El Venado, Mexico 146 C4 22 56N 101 10W
El Vigía, Venezuela 152 B3 8 38N 71 39W
El Wabeira, Egypt 91 F2 29 34N 33 6 E
El Wak, Kenya 106 B5 2 49N 40 56 E
El Wak, Somali Rep. 108 D2 2 44N 41 1 E
El Waqf, Egypt 94 B3 25 45N 32 15 E
El Wâsta, Egypt 94 J7 29 19N 31 12 E
El Weguet, Ethiopia 95 F5 5 28N 42 17 E
El Wuz, Sudan 95 D3 15 5N 30 7 E
Elafónisos, Greece 45 H4 36 29N 22 56 E
Elaine, Australia 116 D6 37 44 S 144 2 E
Elamanchili, India 82 F6 17 33N 82 50 E
Elands, Australia 117 A10 31 37 S 152 20 E
Elandsvlei, S. Africa 104 E2 32 19 S 19 31 E
Élassa, Greece 45 J8 35 18N 26 21 E
Elassón, Greece 44 E4 39 53N 22 12 E
Elat, Israel 91 F3 29 30N 34 56 E
Eláthia, Greece 45 F4 38 37N 22 46 E
Elâzığ, Turkey 89 D8 38 37N 39 14 E
Elâzığ □, Turkey 89 D8 38 40N 39 15 E
Elba, Italy 38 F7 42 48N 10 15 E
Elba, U.S.A. 135 K2 31 27N 86 4W
Elbasani, Albania 44 C2 41 9N 20 9 E
Elbasani-Berati □, Albania 44 D2 40 58N 20 0 E
Elbe, U.S.A. 144 D4 46 45N 122 10W
Elbe →, Europe 26 B5 53 50N 9 0 E
Elbe-Seiten Kanal, Germany 26 C6 52 45N 10 32 E
Elberfeld, U.S.A. 141 F9 38 10N 87 27W
Elbert, Mt., U.S.A. 143 G10 39 5N 106 27W
Elberta, U.S.A. 134 C2 44 35N 86 14W
Elberton, U.S.A. 135 H4 34 7N 82 51W
Elbeuf, France 22 C8 49 17N 1 2 E
Elbing = Elbląg, Poland 47 A6 54 10N 19 25 E
Elbistan, Turkey 88 D7 38 12N 36 11 E
Elbląg, Poland 47 A6 54 10N 19 25 E
Elbląg □, Poland 47 A6 54 15N 19 30 E
Elbow, Canada 131 C7 51 7N 106 35W
Elbrus, U.S.S.R. 53 E10 43 21N 42 30 E
Elburg, Neths. 20 D7 52 26N 5 50 E
Elburn, U.S.A. 141 C8 41 54N 88 28W
Elburz Mts. = Alborz, Reshteh-ye Kūhhā-ye, Iran 85 C7 36 0N 52 0 E
Elche, Spain 35 G4 38 15N 0 42W
Elche de la Sierra, Spain 35 G2 38 27N 2 3W
Elcho I., Australia 114 A2 11 55 S 135 45 E
Elda, Spain 35 G4 38 29N 0 47W
Eldon, Mo., U.S.A. 140 F4 38 20N 92 38W
Eldon, Wash., U.S.A. 144 C3 47 32N 123 4W
Eldora, U.S.A. 140 B3 42 20N 93 5W
Eldorado, Argentina 159 B5 26 28 S 54 43W
Eldorado, Canada 131 B7 59 35N 108 30W
Eldorado, Mexico 146 C3 24 20N 107 22W
Eldorado, Ill., U.S.A. 141 G8 37 50N 88 25W
Eldorado, Tex., U.S.A. 139 K4 30 52N 100 35W
Eldorado Springs, U.S.A. 139 G8 37 54N 93 59W
Eldoret, Kenya 106 B4 0 30N 35 17 E
Eldred, U.S.A. 136 E6 41 57N 78 24W
Eldridge, U.S.A. 140 C6 41 39N 90 35W
Elea, C., Cyprus 32 D13 35 19N 34 4 E
Electra, U.S.A. 139 H5 34 5N 99 0W
Elefantes →, Mozam. 105 C5 24 10 S 32 40 E
Elefantes, G., Chile 160 C2 46 28 S 73 49W
Elektrogorsk, U.S.S.R. 51 D11 55 56N 38 50 E
Elektrostal, U.S.S.R. 51 D11 55 41N 38 32 E
Elele, Nigeria 101 D6 5 5N 6 50 E
Elena, Bulgaria 43 E10 42 55N 25 53 E
Elephant Butte Res., U.S.A. 143 K10 33 45N 107 30W
Elephant I., Antarctica 7 C18 61 0 S 55 0W
Elephant Pass, Sri Lanka 83 K5 9 35N 80 25 E
Elesbão Veloso, Brazil 154 C3 6 13 S 42 8W
Eleshnitsa, Bulgaria 43 F8 41 52N 23 36 E
Eleşkirt, Turkey 89 D10 39 50N 42 50 E
Eleuthera, Bahamas 148 B4 25 0N 76 20W
Elevsís, Greece 45 F5 38 4N 23 26 E
Elevtheroúpolis, Greece 44 D6 40 52N 24 20 E
Elgepiggen, Norway 14 B5 62 10N 11 21 E
Elgeyo-Marakwet □, Kenya 106 B4 0 45N 35 30 E
Elgg, Switz. 29 B7 47 29N 8 52 E
Elgin, N.B., Canada 129 C6 45 48N 65 10W
Elgin, Ont., Canada 137 B8 44 36N 76 13W
Elgin, U.K. 18 D5 57 39N 3 20W
Elgin, Ill., U.S.A. 141 B8 42 5N 88 20W
Elgin, N. Dak., U.S.A. 138 B4 46 24N 101 46W
Elgin, Nebr., U.S.A. 138 E5 41 58N 98 3W
Elgin, Nev., U.S.A. 143 H6 37 21N 114 20W
Elgin, Oreg., U.S.A. 142 D5 45 37N 118 0W
Elgin, Tex., U.S.A. 139 K6 30 21N 97 22W
Elgon, Mt., Africa 106 B3 1 10N 34 30 E
Eliase, Indonesia 71 F8 8 21 S 130 48 E
Elida, U.S.A. 139 J3 33 56N 103 41W
Elikón, Greece 45 F4 38 18N 22 45 E
Elim, S. Africa 104 E2 34 35 S 19 45 E
Elin Pelin, Bulgaria 43 E8 42 40N 23 36 E
Elisabethville = Lubumbashi, Zaïre 107 E2 11 40 S 27 28 E
Eliseu Martins, Brazil 154 C3 8 13 S 43 42W
Elista, U.S.S.R. 53 C11 46 16N 44 14 E
Elizabeth, Australia 116 C3 34 42 S 138 41 E
Elizabeth, Ill., U.S.A. 140 B6 42 19N 90 13W
Elizabeth, N.J., U.S.A. 137 F10 40 37N 74 12W
Elizabeth City, U.S.A. 135 G7 36 18N 76 16W
Elizabethton, U.S.A. 135 G4 36 20N 82 13W
Elizabethtown, Ky., U.S.A. 134 G3 37 40N 85 54W
Elizabethtown, N.Y., U.S.A. 137 B11 44 13N 73 36W
Elizabethtown, Pa., U.S.A. 137 F8 40 8N 76 36W
Elizondo, Spain 34 B3 43 12N 1 30W
Ełk, Poland 47 B9 53 50N 22 21 E
Ełk →, Poland 47 B9 53 41N 22 28 E
Elk City, U.S.A. 139 H5 35 25N 99 25W
Elk Creek, U.S.A. 144 F4 39 36N 122 32W
Elk Grove, U.S.A. 144 G5 38 25N 121 22W
Elk Island Nat. Park, Canada 130 C6 53 35N 112 59W
Elk Lake, Canada 128 C3 47 40N 80 25W
Elk Point, Canada 131 C6 53 54N 110 55W
Elk River, Idaho, U.S.A. 142 C5 46 50N 116 8W
Elk River, Minn., U.S.A. 138 C8 45 17N 93 34W
Elkader, U.S.A. 140 B5 42 51N 91 24W
Elkedra, Australia 114 C2 21 9 S 135 33 E
Elkedra →, Australia 114 C2 21 8 S 136 22 E
Elkhart, Ind., U.S.A. 141 C11 41 42N 85 55W
Elkhart, Kans., U.S.A. 139 G4 37 3N 101 54W
Elkhart →, U.S.A. 141 C11 41 41N 85 58W
Elkhorn, Canada 131 D8 49 59N 101 14W
Elkhorn, U.S.A. 141 B8 42 40N 88 33W
Elkhorn →, U.S.A. 138 E6 41 7N 96 15W
Elkhotovo, U.S.S.R. 53 E11 43 19N 44 15 E
Elkhovo, Bulgaria 43 E11 42 10N 26 40 E
Elkin, U.S.A. 135 G5 36 17N 80 50W
Elkins, U.S.A. 134 F6 38 53N 79 53W
Elko, Canada 130 D5 49 20N 115 10W
Elko, U.S.A. 142 F6 40 50N 115 50W
Ell, L., Australia 113 E4 29 13 S 127 46 E
Ellecom, Neths. 20 D8 52 2N 6 6 E
Ellef Ringnes I., Canada 6 B2 78 30N 102 2W
Ellendale, Australia 112 C3 17 56 S 124 48 E
Ellendale, U.S.A. 138 B5 46 3N 98 30W
Ellensburg, U.S.A. 142 C3 47 0N 120 30W
Ellenville, U.S.A. 137 E10 41 42N 74 23W
Ellerston, Australia 117 A9 31 49 S 151 20 E
Ellery, Mt., Australia 117 D8 37 28 S 148 47 E
Ellesmere, L., N.Z. 119 H7 47 47 S 172 28 E
Ellesmere I., Canada 6 B4 79 30N 80 0W
Ellettsville, U.S.A. 141 E10 39 14N 86 38W
Ellezelles, Belgium 21 G3 50 44N 3 42 E
Ellice Is. = Tuvalu ■, Pac. Oc. 111 B14 8 0 S 178 0 E
Ellinwood, U.S.A. 138 F5 38 27N 98 37W
Elliot, Australia 114 B1 17 33 S 133 32 E
Elliot, S. Africa 105 E4 31 22 S 27 48 E
Elliot Lake, Canada 128 C3 46 25N 82 35W
Elliotdale = Xhora, S. Africa 105 E4 31 55 S 28 38 E
Ellis, U.S.A. 138 F5 39 0N 99 39W
Elliston, Australia 115 E1 33 39 S 134 53 E
Ellisville, U.S.A. 139 K10 31 38N 89 12W
Ellon, U.K. 18 D6 57 21N 2 5W
Ellore = Eluru, India 82 F5 16 48N 81 8 E
Ells →, Canada 130 B6 57 18N 111 40W
Ellsworth, U.S.A. 138 F5 38 47N 98 15W
Ellsworth Land, Antarctica 7 D16 76 0 S 89 0W
Ellsworth Mts., Antarctica 7 D16 78 30 S 85 0W
Ellwangen, Germany 27 G6 48 57N 10 9 E
Ellwood City, U.S.A. 136 F4 40 52N 80 19W
Elm, Switz. 29 C8 46 54N 9 10 E
Elma, Canada 131 D9 49 52N 95 55W
Elma, U.S.A. 144 D3 47 0N 123 30W
Elmadağ, Turkey 88 D5 39 55N 33 14 E
Elmalı, Turkey 88 E3 36 44N 29 56 E
Elmer, U.S.A. 140 E4 39 57N 92 39W
Elmhurst, U.S.A. 141 C9 41 52N 87 58W
Elmina, Ghana 101 D4 5 5N 1 21W
Elmira, Canada 136 C4 43 36N 80 33W
Elmira, U.S.A. 136 D8 42 8N 76 49W
Elmore, Australia 116 D6 36 30 S 144 37 E
Elmore, Calif., U.S.A. 145 M11 33 7N 115 49W
Elmore, Minn., U.S.A. 141 C13 41 29N 83 18W
Elmshorn, Germany 26 B5 53 44N 9 40 E
Elmvale, Canada 136 B5 44 35N 79 52W
Elmwood, U.S.A. 140 D7 40 47N 90 0W
Elne, France 24 F6 42 36N 2 58 E
Elnora, U.S.A. 141 F9 38 53N 87 5W
Elora, Canada 136 C4 43 41N 80 26W
Elorza, Venezuela 152 B4 7 3N 69 31W
Elos, Greece 45 H4 36 46N 22 43 E
Eloúnda, Greece 32 D7 35 16N 25 42 E
Eloy, U.S.A. 143 K8 32 46N 111 33W
Éloyes, France 23 D13 48 6N 6 36 E
Elrose, Canada 131 C7 51 12N 108 0W
Elsas, Canada 128 C3 48 32N 82 55W
Elsie, U.S.A. 144 E3 45 52N 123 35W
Elsinore = Helsingør, Denmark 15 H6 56 2N 12 35 E
Elsinore, Australia 117 A6 31 35 S 145 11 E
Elsinore, U.S.A. 143 G7 38 40N 112 2W
Elspe, Germany 26 D4 51 10N 8 1 E
Elspeet, Neths. 20 D7 52 17N 5 48 E
Elst, Neths. 20 E7 51 55N 5 51 E
Elster →, Germany 26 D7 51 25N 11 57 E
Elsterwerda, Germany 26 D9 51 27N 13 32 E
Elten, Neths. 20 E8 51 52N 6 9 E
Eltham, Australia 117 D6 37 43 S 145 12 E
Eltham, N.Z. 118 F3 39 26 S 174 19 E
Elton, U.S.S.R. 53 B12 49 5N 46 52 E
Eluanbi, Taiwan 69 G13 21 51N 120 50 E
Eluru, India 82 F5 16 48N 81 8 E
Elvas, Portugal 37 G3 38 50N 7 10W
Elven, France 22 E4 47 44N 2 36W
Elverum, Norway 14 D5 60 53N 11 34 E
Elvire →, Australia 112 C4 17 51 S 128 11 E
Elvo →, Italy 38 C5 45 23N 8 21 E
Elvran, Norway 14 A5 63 24N 11 3 E
Elwood, Ill., U.S.A. 141 C8 41 24N 88 7W
Elwood, Ind., U.S.A. 141 D11 40 20N 85 50W
Elwood, Nebr., U.S.A. 138 E5 40 38N 99 51W
Ely, U.K. 17 E8 52 24N 0 16 E
Ely, Minn., U.S.A. 138 B9 47 54N 91 52W
Ely, Nev., U.S.A. 142 G6 39 10N 114 50W
Elyria, U.S.A. 136 E2 41 22N 82 8W
Elyrus, Greece 45 J5 35 15N 23 45 E
Elz →, Germany 27 G3 48 21N 7 45 E
Emai, Vanuatu 121 G6 17 4 S 168 24 E
Emāmrūd, Iran 85 B7 36 30N 55 0 E
Emba, U.S.S.R. 56 E6 48 50N 58 8 E
Emba →, U.S.S.R. 49 E9 46 38N 53 14 E
Embarcación, Argentina 158 A3 23 10 S 64 0W
Embarras Portage, Canada 131 B6 58 27N 111 28W
Embarrass →, U.S.A. 141 F9 38 39N 87 37W
Embetsu, Japan 60 B10 44 44N 141 47 E
Embira →, Brazil 156 B3 7 19 S 70 15W
Embóna, Greece 32 C9 36 13N 27 51 E
Embrach, Switz. 29 B7 47 30N 8 36 E
Embrun, France 25 D10 44 34N 6 30 E
Embu, Kenya 106 C4 0 32 S 37 38 E
Embu □, Kenya 106 C4 0 30 S 37 35 E
Emden, Germany 26 B3 53 22N 7 12 E
Emerald, Australia 114 C4 23 32 S 148 10 E
Emerson, Canada 131 D9 49 0N 97 10W
Emery, U.S.A. 143 G8 38 59N 111 17W
Emet, Turkey 88 D3 39 20N 29 15 E
Emi Koussi, Chad 97 E3 19 45N 18 55 E
Emilia-Romagna □, Italy 38 D7 44 33N 10 40 E
Emilius, Mte., Italy 38 C4 45 41N 7 23 E
Eminabad, Pakistan 80 C6 32 2N 74 8 E
Emine, Nos, Bulgaria 43 E12 42 40N 27 56 E
Eminence, U.S.A. 141 F11 38 22N 85 11W
Emirdağ, Turkey 88 D4 39 2N 31 8 E
Emlenton, U.S.A. 136 E5 41 11N 79 41W
Emlichheim, Germany 26 C2 52 37N 6 51 E
Emme →, Switz. 28 B5 47 14N 7 32 E
Emmeloord, Neths. 20 C7 52 44N 5 46 E
Emmen, Neths. 20 C9 52 48N 6 57 E
Emmendingen, Germany 27 G3 48 7N 7 51 E
Emmental, Switz. 28 C4 46 55N 7 20 E
Emmer-Compascuum, Neths. 20 C10 52 49N 7 2 E
Emmerich, Germany 26 D2 51 50N 6 12 E
Emmet, Australia 114 C3 24 45 S 144 30 E
Emmetsburg, U.S.A. 140 A2 43 3N 94 40W
Emmett, U.S.A. 142 E5 43 51N 116 33W
Emöd, Hungary 31 D13 47 57N 20 47 E
Emona, Bulgaria 43 E12 42 43N 27 53 E
Empalme, Mexico 146 B2 28 1N 110 49W
Empangeni, S. Africa 105 D5 28 50 S 31 52 E
Empedrado, Argentina 158 B4 28 0 S 58 46W
Emperor Seamount Chain, Pac. Oc. 122 D9 40 0N 170 0 E
Empoli, Italy 38 E7 43 43N 10 57 E
Emporia, Kans., U.S.A. 138 F6 38 25N 96 10W
Emporia, Va., U.S.A. 135 G7 36 41N 77 32W
Emporium, U.S.A. 136 E6 41 30N 78 17W
Empress, Canada 131 C7 50 57N 110 0W
Emptinne, Belgium 21 H6 50 19N 5 8 E
Empty Quarter = Rub' al Khali, Si. Arabia 87 C5 18 0N 48 0 E
Ems →, Germany 26 B3 53 22N 7 15 E
Emsdale, Canada 136 A5 45 32N 79 19W
Emsdetten, Germany 26 C3 52 11N 7 31 E
Emu, Australia 116 D5 36 44 S 143 26 E
Emu, China 67 C15 43 40N 128 6 E
Emu Park, Australia 114 C5 23 13 S 150 50 E
'En 'Avrona, Israel 91 F4 29 43N 35 0 E
En Nahud, Sudan 95 E2 12 45N 28 25 E
Ena, Japan 63 B9 35 25N 137 25 E
Ena-San, Japan 63 B9 35 26N 137 36 E
Enafors, Sweden 14 A6 63 17N 12 20 E
Enambú, Colombia 152 C3 1 1N 70 17W
Enana, Namibia 104 B2 17 30 S 16 23 E
Enånger, Sweden 14 C11 61 30N 17 9 E
Enaratoli, Indonesia 71 E9 3 55 S 136 21 E
Enard B., U.K. 18 C3 58 5N 5 20W
Enare = Inarijärvi, Finland 12 B20 69 0N 28 0 E
Encantadas, Serra, Brazil 159 C5 30 40 S 53 0W
Encanto, C., Phil. 71 A6 15 45N 121 38 E
Encarnación, Paraguay 159 B4 27 15 S 55 50W
Encarnación de Diaz, Mexico 146 C4 21 30N 102 13W
Enchi, Ghana 100 D4 5 53N 2 48W
Encinal, U.S.A. 139 L5 28 3N 99 25W
Encinitas, U.S.A. 145 M9 33 3N 117 17W
Encino, U.S.A. 143 J11 34 38N 105 40W
Encontrados, Venezuela 152 B3 9 3N 72 14W
Encounter B., Australia 116 C3 35 45 S 138 45 E
Encruzilhada, Brazil 155 E3 15 31 S 40 54W
Ende, Indonesia 71 F6 8 45 S 121 40 E
Endeavour, Canada 131 C8 52 10N 102 39W
Endeavour Str., Australia 114 A3 10 45 S 142 0 E
Endelave, Denmark 15 J4 55 46N 10 18 E
Enderbury I., Kiribati 122 H10 3 8 S 171 5W
Enderby, Canada 130 C5 50 35N 119 10W
Enderby I., Australia 112 D2 20 35 S 116 30 E
Enderby Land, Antarctica 7 C5 66 0 S 53 0 E
Enderlin, U.S.A. 138 B6 46 37N 97 41W
Endicott, N.Y., U.S.A. 137 D8 42 6N 76 2W
Endicott, Wash., U.S.A. 142 C5 47 0N 117 45W
Endimari →, Brazil 156 B4 8 46 S 66 7W
Endröd, Hungary 31 E13 46 55N 20 47 E
Endyalgout I., Australia 112 B5 11 40 S 132 35 E
Ene →, Peru 156 C3 11 10 S 74 18W
Enewetak Atoll, Pac. Oc. 122 F8 11 30N 162 15 E
Enez, Turkey 44 D8 40 45N 26 5 E
Enfida, Tunisia 96 A2 36 6N 10 28 E
Enfield, U.K. 17 F7 51 39N 0 4W
Enfield, U.S.A. 141 F8 38 6N 88 20W
Engadin, Switz. 27 J6 46 45N 10 10 E
Engaño, C., Dom. Rep. 149 C6 18 30N 68 20W
Engaño, C., Phil. 71 A6 18 35N 122 23 E
Engcobo, S. Africa 105 E4 31 37 S 28 0 E
Engelberg, Switz. 29 C6 46 48N 8 26 E
Engels, U.S.S.R. 51 F15 51 28N 46 6 E
Engemann L., Canada 131 B7 58 0N 106 55W
Enger, Norway 14 D4 60 35N 10 20 E
Enggano, Indonesia 70 F2 5 20 S 102 40 E
Enghien, Belgium 21 G4 50 37N 4 2 E
Engil, Morocco 98 B4 33 12N 4 32W
Engkilili, Malaysia 70 D4 1 3N 111 42 E
England, U.S.A. 139 H9 34 30N 91 58W
England □, U.K. 11 E5 53 0N 2 0W
Englee, Canada 129 B8 50 45N 56 5W
Englefield, Australia 116 D4 37 21 S 141 48 E
Englehart, Canada 128 C4 47 49N 79 52W
Engler L., Canada 131 B7 59 8N 106 52W
Englewood, Colo., U.S.A. 138 F2 39 40N 105 0W
Englewood, Kans., U.S.A. 139 G5 37 7N 99 59W
Englewood, Ohio, U.S.A. 141 E12 39 53N 84 18W
English, U.S.A. 141 F10 38 20N 86 28W
English →, Canada 131 C10 50 35N 93 30W
English →, U.S.A. 140 C5 41 29N 91 32W
English Bazar = Ingraj Bazar, India 81 G13 24 58N 88 10 E
English Channel, Europe 17 H6 50 0N 2 0W
English River, Canada 128 C1 49 14N 91 0W
Enid, U.S.A. 139 G6 36 26N 97 52W
Enipévs →, Greece 44 E4 39 22N 22 17 E
Enkhuizen, Neths. 20 C6 52 42N 5 17 E
Enköping, Sweden 14 E11 59 37N 17 4 E
Enle, China 68 F3 24 0N 101 9 E
Enna, Italy 41 E7 37 34N 14 15 E
Ennadai, Canada 131 A8 61 8N 100 53W
Ennadai L., Canada 131 A8 61 0N 101 0W
Ennedi, Chad 97 E4 17 15N 22 0 E
Enngonia, Australia 115 D4 29 21 S 145 50 E
Ennis, Ireland 19 D3 52 51N 8 59W
Ennis, Mont., U.S.A. 142 D8 45 20N 111 42W
Ennis, Tex., U.S.A. 139 J6 32 15N 96 40W
Enniskillen, U.K. 19 B4 54 20N 7 40W
Ennistimon, Ireland 19 D2 52 56N 9 18W
Enns, Austria 30 C7 48 12N 14 28 E
Enns →, Austria 30 C7 48 14N 14 32 E
Enontekiö, Finland 12 B17 68 23N 23 37 E
Enping, China 69 F9 22 16N 112 21 E
Enrekang, Indonesia 72 B1 3 34 S 119 47 E
Enriquillo, L., Dom. Rep. 149 C5 18 20N 72 5W
Ens, Neths. 20 C7 52 38N 5 50 E
Enschede, Neths. 20 D9 52 13N 6 53 E
Ensenada, Argentina 158 C4 34 55 S 57 55W
Ensenada, Mexico 146 A1 31 50N 116 50W
Enshi, China 68 B7 30 18N 109 29 E
Enshū-Nada, Japan 63 C9 34 27N 137 38 E
Ensiola, Pta., Spain 33 B9 39 7N 2 55 E
Ensisheim, France 23 E14 47 50N 7 20 E
Entebbe, Uganda 106 B3 0 4N 32 28 E
Enter, Neths. 20 D9 52 17N 6 35 E
Enterprise, Canada 130 A5 60 47N 115 45W
Enterprise, Oreg., U.S.A. 142 D5 45 30N 117 18W
Enterprise, Utah, U.S.A. 143 H7 37 37N 113 36W
Entlebuch, Switz. 28 C6 46 59N 8 4 E
Entre Ríos, Bolivia 158 A3 21 30 S 64 25W
Entre Rios, Bahia, Brazil 155 D4 11 56 S 38 5W
Entre Rios, Pará, Brazil 157 B7 5 24 S 54 21W
Entre Ríos □, Argentina 158 C4 30 30 S 58 30W
Entrepeñas, Pantano de, Spain 34 E2 40 34N 2 42W
Enugu, Nigeria 101 D6 6 20N 7 30 E
Enugu Ezike, Nigeria 101 D6 7 0N 7 29 E
Enumclaw, U.S.A. 144 C5 47 12N 122 0W
Envermeu, France 22 C8 49 53N 1 15 E
Envigado, Colombia 152 B2 6 10N 75 35W
Envira, Brazil 156 B3 7 18 S 70 13W
Enz →, Germany 27 F5 49 1N 9 6 E
Enza →, Italy 38 D7 44 54N 10 31 E
Enzan, Japan 63 B10 35 42N 138 44 E
Eólie, Is., Italy 41 D7 38 30N 14 50 E
Epanomí, Greece 44 D4 40 25N 22 59 E
Epe, Neths. 20 D7 52 21N 5 59 E
Epe, Nigeria 101 D5 6 36N 3 59 E
Epéna, Congo 102 B3 1 22N 17 29 E
Épernay, France 23 C10 49 3N 3 56 E
Épernon, France 23 D8 48 35N 1 40 E
Ephesus, Turkey 45 G9 37 50N 27 33 E
Ephraim, U.S.A. 142 G8 39 21N 111 37W
Ephrata, U.S.A. 142 C4 47 20N 119 32W
Epi, Vanuatu 121 F6 16 43 S 168 15 E
Epidaurus Limera, Greece 45 H5 36 46N 23 0 E
Epila, Spain 34 D3 41 36N 1 17W
Épinac-les-Mines, France 23 F11 46 59N 4 31 E
Épinal, France 23 D13 48 10N 6 27 E
Epira, Guyana 153 B6 5 5N 57 20W
Episcopia Bihorului, Romania 46 B2 47 12N 21 55 E
Episkopi, Cyprus 32 E11 34 40N 32 54 E
Episkopí, Greece 32 D6 35 20N 24 20 E
Episkopi Bay, Cyprus 32 E11 34 35N 32 50 E
Epitálion, Greece 45 G3 37 37N 21 30 E
Epping, U.K. 17 F8 51 42N 0 8 E
Epukiro, Namibia 104 C2 21 40 S 19 9 E
Equality, U.S.A. 141 G8 37 44N 88 20W
Equatorial Guinea ■, Africa 102 B1 2 0N 8 0 E
Equeipa, Venezuela 153 B5 5 22N 62 43W
Er Rahad, Sudan 95 E3 12 45N 30 32 E
Er Rif, Morocco 99 A4 35 1N 4 1W
Er Roseires, Sudan 95 E3 11 55N 34 30 E
Er Yébigué, Chad 97 D3 22 30N 17 30 E
Erandol, India 82 D2 20 56N 75 20 E
Erap, Papua N. G. 120 D4 6 37 S 146 51 E
Erāwadī Myit = Irrawaddy →, Burma 78 G5 15 50N 95 6 E
Erba, Italy 38 C6 45 49N 9 12 E
Erba, Sudan 94 D4 19 5N 36 51 E
Erbaa, Turkey 88 C7 40 42N 36 36 E
Erçek Gölü, Turkey 89 D10 38 39N 43 35 E
Ercha, U.S.S.R. 57 C15 69 45N 147 20 E
Erçiş, Turkey 89 D10 39 2N 43 21 E
Erciyaş Dağı, Turkey 88 D6 38 30N 35 30 E
Erdao Jiang →, China 67 C14 43 0N 127 0 E
Erdek, Turkey 88 C2 40 23N 27 47 E
Erdemli, Turkey 88 E6 36 36N 34 19 E
Erdene, Mongolia 66 B6 44 13N 111 10 E
Erding, Germany 27 G7 48 18N 11 55 E
Erdre →, France 22 E5 47 13N 1 32W
Erebato →, Venezuela 153 B5 5 54N 64 16W
Erebus, Mt., Antarctica 7 D11 77 35 S 167 0 E
Erechim, Brazil 159 B5 27 35 S 52 15W
Ereğli, Konya, Turkey 88 E6 37 31N 34 4 E
Ereğli, Zonguldak, Turkey 88 C4 41 15N 31 24 E

196 Erei, Monti

Erei, Monti, Italy 41 E7 37 20N 14 20 E
Erembodegem, Belgium 21 G4 50 56N 4 4 E
Erenhot, China 66 C7 43 48N 112 2 E
Eresma →, Spain 36 D6 41 26N 4 45W
Eressós, Greece 45 E7 39 11N 25 57 E
Erfenisdam, S. Africa 104 D4 28 30 S 26 50 E
Erfoud, Morocco 98 B4 31 30N 4 15W
Erft →, Germany 26 D2 51 11N 6 44 E
Erfurt, Germany 26 E7 50 58N 11 2 E
Ergani, Turkey 89 D8 38 17N 39 49 E
Ergene →, Turkey 43 F11 41 1N 26 22 E
Ergeni Vozvyshennost, U.S.S.R. 53 C11 47 0N 44 0 E
Ergli, U.S.S.R. 50 C4 56 54N 25 38 E
Eria →, Spain 36 C5 42 3N 5 44W
Eriba, Sudan 95 D4 16 40N 36 10 E
Eriboll, L., U.K. 18 C4 58 28N 4 41W
Erica, Neths. 20 C9 52 43N 6 56 E
Érice, Italy 40 D5 38 4N 12 34 E
Erie, Mich., U.S.A. 141 C13 41 47N 83 31W
Erie, Pa., U.S.A. 136 D4 42 10N 80 7W
Erie, L., N. Amer. 136 D4 42 15N 81 0W
Erie Canal, U.S.A. 136 C7 43 15N 78 0W
Erieau, Canada 136 D3 42 16N 81 57W
Erigavo, Somali Rep. 90 E4 10 35N 47 20 E
Erikoúsa, Greece 44 E1 39 55N 19 14 E
Erikoúsa, Kérkira, Greece 32 G18 39 53N 19 34 E
Eriksdale, Canada 131 C9 50 52N 98 7W
Erikslund, Sweden 14 B9 62 31N 15 54 E
Erímanthos, Greece 45 G3 37 57N 21 50 E
Erimo-misaki, Japan 60 D11 41 50N 143 15 E
Eriswil, Switz. 28 B5 47 5N 7 46 E
Erithraí, Greece 45 F5 38 13N 23 20 E
Eritrea □, Ethiopia 95 E4 14 0N 38 30 E
Erjas →, Portugal 37 F3 39 40N 7 1W
Erlangen, Germany 27 F7 49 35N 11 2 E
Erldunda, Australia 114 D1 25 14 S 133 12 E
Erlin, Taiwan 69 F13 23 55N 120 21 E
Ermelo, Neths. 20 D7 52 18N 5 35 E
Ermelo, S. Africa 105 D4 26 31 S 29 59 E
Ermenak, Turkey 88 E5 36 38N 33 0 E
Ermióni, Greece 45 G5 37 23N 23 15 E
Ermones, Greece 32 A3 39 37N 19 46 E
Ermoúpolis = Síros, Greece 45 G6 37 28N 24 57 E
Ernakulam = Cochin, India 83 K3 9 59N 76 22 E
Erne →, Ireland 19 B3 54 30N 8 16W
Erne, Lower L., U.K. 19 B4 54 26N 7 46W
Erne, Upper L., U.K. 19 B4 54 14N 7 22W
Ernée, France 22 D6 48 18N 0 56W
Ernest Giles Ra., Australia 113 E3 27 0 S 123 45 E
Ernstberg, Germany 27 E2 50 14N 6 46 E
Erode, India 83 J3 11 24N 77 45 E
Eromanga, Australia 115 D3 26 40 S 143 11 E
Erongo, Namibia 104 C2 21 39 S 15 58 E
Erp, Neths. 21 E7 51 36N 5 37 E
Erquelinnes, Belgium 21 H4 50 19N 4 8 E
Erquy, France 22 D4 48 38N 2 29W
Erquy, C. d', France 22 D4 48 39N 2 29W
Err, Piz d', Switz. 29 C9 46 34N 9 43 E
Errabiddy, Australia 113 E2 25 25 S 117 5 E
Erramala Hills, India 83 G4 15 30N 78 15 E
Errer →, Ethiopia 95 F5 7 32N 42 35 E
Errigal, Ireland 19 A3 55 2N 8 8W
Erris Hd., Ireland 19 B2 54 19N 10 0W
Erromango, Vanuatu 121 H7 18 45 S 169 5 E
Erseka, Albania 44 D2 40 22N 20 40 E
Erskine, U.S.A. 138 B7 47 37N 96 0W
Erstein, France 23 D14 48 25N 7 38 E
Erstfeld, Switz. 29 C7 46 50N 8 38 E
Ertil, U.S.S.R. 51 F12 51 55N 40 50 E
Ertvelde, Belgium 21 F3 51 11N 3 45 E
Eruh, Turkey 89 E10 37 46N 42 13 E
Eruwa, Nigeria 101 D5 7 33N 3 26 E
Ervy-le-Châtel, France 23 D10 48 2N 3 55 E
Erwin, U.S.A. 135 G4 36 10N 82 28W
Eryuan, China 68 D2 26 7N 99 57 E
Erzgebirge, Germany 26 E9 50 25N 13 0 E
Erzin, U.S.S.R. 57 D10 50 15N 95 10 E
Erzincan, Turkey 89 D8 39 46N 39 30 E
Erzincan □, Turkey 89 D8 39 45N 39 30 E
Erzurum, Turkey 89 D9 39 57N 41 15 E
Erzurum □, Turkey 89 D9 39 55N 41 15 E
Es Caló, Spain 33 C8 38 40N 1 30 E
Es Caná, Spain 33 B8 39 2N 1 36 E
Es Sahrâ' Esh Sharqîya, Egypt 94 B3 27 30N 32 30 E
Es Sînâ', Egypt 94 J8 29 0N 34 0 E
Es Sûkî, Sudan 95 E3 13 20N 33 58 E
Esa'ala, Papua N. G. 120 E6 9 45 S 150 49 E
Esambo, Zaïre 102 C4 3 48 S 23 30 E
Esan-Misaki, Japan 60 D10 41 40N 141 10 E
Esashi, Hokkaidō, Japan 60 B11 44 56N 142 35 E
Esashi, Hokkaidō, Japan 60 D10 41 52N 140 7 E
Esbjerg, Denmark 15 J2 55 29N 8 29 E
Escada, Brazil 154 C4 8 22 S 35 8W
Escalante, U.S.A. 143 H8 37 47N 111 37W
Escalante →, U.S.A. 143 H8 37 17N 110 53W
Escalón, Mexico 146 B4 26 46N 104 20W
Escalona, Spain 36 E6 40 9N 4 29W
Escambia →, U.S.A. 135 K2 30 32N 87 15W
Escanaba, U.S.A. 134 C2 45 44N 87 5W
Escarpé, C., Vanuatu 121 K5 20 41 S 167 13 E
Escaut →, Belgium 21 F3 51 2N 3 45 E
Esch-sur-Alzette, Lux. 21 J8 49 32N 6 0 E
Eschede, Germany 26 C6 52 44N 10 13 E
Escholzmatt, Switz. 28 C5 46 55N 7 56 E
Eschwege, Germany 26 D6 51 10N 10 3 E
Eschweiler, Germany 26 E2 50 49N 6 14 E
Escoma, Bolivia 156 D4 15 40 S 69 8W
Escondido, U.S.A. 145 M9 33 9N 117 4W
Escuinapa, Mexico 146 C3 22 50N 105 50W
Escuintla, Guatemala 148 D1 14 20N 90 48W
Eséka, Cameroon 101 E7 3 41N 10 44 E
Esens, Germany 26 B3 53 40N 7 35 E
Esera →, Spain 34 C5 42 6N 0 15 E
Eşfahān, Iran 85 C6 33 0N 51 30 E
Esfideh, Iran 85 C8 33 39N 59 46 E
Esgueva →, Spain 36 D6 41 40N 4 43W
Esh Sham = Dimashq, Syria 91 B5 33 30N 36 18 E
Esh Shamâlîya □, Sudan 94 D2 19 0N 29 0 E
Eshan, China 68 E4 24 11N 102 24 E
Eshkamesh, Afghan. 79 A3 36 23N 69 19 E
Eshowe, S. Africa 105 D5 28 50 S 31 30 E
Esiama, Ghana 100 E4 4 56N 2 25W
Esino →, Italy 39 E10 43 39N 13 22 E
Esk →, Dumf. & Gall., U.K. 18 G5 54 58N 3 4W
Esk →, N. Yorks., U.K. 16 C7 54 27N 0 36W
Eskān, Iran 79 D1 26 48N 63 9 E
Eskifjörður, Iceland 12 D7 65 3N 13 55W
Eskilstuna, Sweden 14 E10 59 22N 16 32 E
Eskimalatya, Turkey 89 D8 38 24N 38 22 E
Eskimo Pt., Canada 131 A10 61 10N 94 15W
Eskişehir, Turkey 88 D4 39 50N 30 35 E
Eskişehir □, Turkey 88 D4 39 40N 31 0 E
Esla →, Spain 36 D4 41 29N 6 3W
Esla, Pantano del, Spain 36 D4 41 29N 6 3W
Eslāmābād-e Gharb, Iran 84 C5 34 10N 46 30 E
Eslöv, Sweden 15 J7 55 50N 13 20 E
Eşme, Turkey 88 D3 38 23N 28 58 E
Esmeralda, I., Chile 160 C1 48 55 S 75 25W
Esmeraldas, Ecuador 152 C2 1 0N 79 40W
Esmeraldas □, Ecuador 152 C2 0 40N 79 30W
Esmeraldas →, Ecuador 152 C2 0 58N 79 38W
Esneux, Belgium 21 G7 50 32N 5 33 E
Espada, Pta., Colombia 152 A3 12 5N 71 7W
Espalion, France 24 D6 44 32N 2 47 E
Espalmador, I., Spain 33 C7 38 47N 1 26 E
Espanola, Canada 128 C3 46 15N 81 46W
Espardell, I. del, Spain 33 C7 38 48N 1 29 E
Esparraguera, Spain 34 D6 41 33N 1 52 E
Esparta, Costa Rica 148 E3 9 59N 84 40W
Espejo, Spain 37 H6 37 40N 4 34W
Esperança, Brazil 154 C4 7 1 S 35 51W
Esperance, Australia 113 F3 33 45 S 121 55 E
Esperance B., Australia 113 F3 33 48 S 121 55 E
Esperantinópolis, Brazil 154 B3 4 53 S 44 53W
Esperanza, Santa Cruz, Argentina 160 D2 51 1 S 70 49W
Esperanza, Santa Fe, Argentina 158 C3 31 29 S 61 3W
Espéraza, France 24 F6 42 56N 2 14 E
Espichel, C., Portugal 37 G1 38 22N 9 16W
Espiel, Spain 37 G5 38 11N 5 1W
Espigão, Serra do, Brazil 159 B5 26 35 S 50 30W
Espinal, Colombia 152 C3 4 9N 74 53W
Espinar, Peru 156 C3 14 51 S 71 24W
Espinazo, Sierra del = Espinhaço, Serra do, Brazil 155 E3 17 30 S 43 30W
Espinhaço, Serra do, Brazil 155 E3 17 30 S 43 30W
Espinho, Portugal 36 D2 41 1N 8 38W
Espinilho, Serra do, Brazil 159 B5 28 30 S 55 0W
Espino, Venezuela 152 B4 8 34N 66 1W
Espinosa de los Monteros, Spain 36 B7 43 5N 3 34W
Espírito Santo □, Brazil 155 F3 20 0 S 40 45W
Espíritu Santo, Vanuatu 121 E4 15 15 S 166 50 E
Espíritu Santo, B. del, Mexico 147 D7 19 15N 87 0W
Espíritu Santo, I., Mexico 146 C2 24 30N 110 23W
Espita, Mexico 147 C7 21 1N 88 19W
Espiye, Turkey 89 C8 40 56N 38 43 E
Esplanada, Brazil 155 D4 11 47 S 37 57W
Espluga de Francolí, Spain 34 D6 41 24N 1 7 E
Espuña, Sierra, Spain 35 H3 37 51N 1 35W
Espungabera, Mozam. 105 C5 20 29 S 32 45 E
Esquel, Argentina 160 B2 42 55 S 71 20W
Esquina, Argentina 158 C4 30 0 S 59 30W
Essaouira, Morocco 98 B3 31 32N 9 42W
Essebie, Zaïre 106 B3 2 58N 30 40 E
Essen, Belgium 21 F4 51 28N 4 28 E
Essen, Germany 26 D2 51 28N 6 59 E
Essendon, Mt., Australia 113 E3 25 0 S 120 29 E
Essequibo □, Guyana 153 B6 7 0N 59 0W
Essequibo →, Guyana 153 B6 6 50N 58 30W
Essex, Canada 136 D2 42 10N 82 49W
Essex, Calif., U.S.A. 145 L11 34 44N 115 15W
Essex, Ill., U.S.A. 141 C8 41 11N 88 11W
Essex, N.Y., U.S.A. 137 B11 44 17N 73 21W
Essex □, U.K. 17 F8 51 48N 0 30 E
Esslingen, Germany 27 G5 48 43N 9 19 E
Essonne □, France 23 D9 48 30N 2 20 E
Essvik, Sweden 14 B11 62 18N 17 24 E
Estaca, Pta. del, Spain 36 B3 43 46N 7 42W
Estadilla, Spain 34 C5 42 4N 0 16 E
Estados, I. de Los, Argentina 160 D4 54 40 S 64 30W
Estagel, France 24 F6 42 47N 2 40 E
Eşţahbānāt, Iran 85 D7 29 8N 54 4 E
Estallenchs, Spain 33 B9 39 39N 2 29 E
Estância, Brazil 154 D4 11 16 S 37 26W
Estancia, U.S.A. 143 J10 34 50N 106 1W
Estārm, Iran 85 D8 28 21N 58 21 E
Estarreja, Portugal 36 E2 40 45N 8 35W
Estats, Pic d', Spain 34 C6 42 40N 1 24 E
Estavayer-le-Lac, Switz. 28 C3 46 51N 6 51 E
Estcourt, S. Africa 105 D4 29 0 S 29 53 E
Este, Italy 39 C8 45 12N 11 40 E
Esteban, Spain 36 B4 43 33N 6 5W
Estelí, Nic. 148 D2 13 9N 86 22W
Estella, Spain 34 C2 42 40N 2 2W
Estelline, S. Dak., U.S.A. 138 C6 44 39N 96 52W
Estelline, Tex., U.S.A. 139 H4 34 35N 100 27W
Estena →, Spain 37 F6 39 23N 4 44W
Estepa, Spain 37 H6 37 17N 4 52W
Estepona, Spain 37 J5 36 24N 5 7W
Esterhazy, Canada 131 C8 50 37N 102 5W
Esternay, France 23 D10 48 44N 3 33 E
Esterri de Aneu, Spain 34 C6 42 38N 1 5 E
Estevan, Canada 131 D8 49 10N 102 59W
Estevan Group, Canada 130 C3 53 3N 129 38W
Estherville, U.S.A. 138 D7 43 25N 94 50W
Estissac, France 23 D10 48 16N 3 48 E
Eston, Canada 131 C7 51 8N 108 40W
Estonian S.S.R. □, U.S.S.R. 50 B4 58 30N 25 30 E
Estoril, Portugal 37 G1 38 42N 9 23W
Estouk, Mali 101 B5 18 14N 1 2 E
Estrêla, Serra da, Portugal 36 E3 40 10N 7 45W
Estrella, Spain 35 G1 38 25N 3 35W
Estremoz, Portugal 37 G3 38 51N 7 39W
Estrondo, Serra do, Brazil 154 C2 7 20 S 48 0W
Esztergom, Hungary 31 D11 47 47N 18 44 E
Et Tîdra, Mauritania 100 B1 19 45N 16 20W
Étables-sur-Mer, France 22 D4 48 38N 2 51W
Etadunna, Australia 115 D2 28 43 S 138 38 E
Etah, India 81 F8 27 35N 78 40 E
Étain, France 23 C12 49 13N 5 38 E
Etalle, Belgium 21 J7 49 40N 5 36 E
Etamamu, Canada 129 B8 50 18N 59 59W
Étampes, France 23 D9 48 26N 2 10 E
Étang-sur-Arroux, France 25 B8 46 51N 4 11 E
Etanga, Namibia 104 B1 17 55 S 13 0 E
Étaples, France 23 B8 50 30N 1 39 E
Etawah, India 81 F8 26 48N 79 6 E
Etawah →, U.S.A. 135 H3 34 20N 84 15W
Etawney L., Canada 131 B9 57 50N 96 50W
Ete, Nigeria 101 D6 7 2N 7 28 E
Éthe, Belgium 21 J7 49 35N 5 35 E
Ethel, U.S.A. 144 D4 46 32N 122 46W
Ethel, Oued el →, Algeria 98 C4 28 31N 3 37W
Ethel Creek, Australia 112 D3 22 55 S 120 11 E
Ethelbert, Canada 131 C8 51 32N 100 25W
Ethiopia ■, Africa 90 F3 8 0N 40 0 E
Ethiopian Highlands, Ethiopia 92 E7 10 0N 37 0 E
Etive, L., U.K. 18 E3 56 30N 5 12W
Etna, Italy 41 E8 37 45N 15 0 E
Etoile, Zaïre 107 E2 11 33 S 27 30 E
Etolin I., U.S.A. 130 B2 56 5N 132 20W
Etosha Pan, Namibia 104 B2 18 40 S 16 30 E
Etoumbi, Congo 102 C2 0 1 S 14 57 E
Etowah, U.S.A. 135 H3 35 20N 84 30W
Étrépagny, France 23 C8 49 18N 1 36 E
Étretat, France 22 C7 49 42N 0 12 E
Etropole, Bulgaria 43 E9 42 50N 24 0 E
Ettelbruck, Lux. 21 J8 49 51N 6 5 E
Etten, Neths. 21 E5 51 34N 4 38 E
Ettlingen, Germany 27 G4 48 58N 8 25 E
Ettrick Water →, U.K. 18 F6 55 31N 2 55W
Etuku, Zaïre 102 C5 3 42 S 25 45 E
Etzatlán, Mexico 146 C4 20 48N 104 5W
Eu, France 22 B8 50 3N 1 26 E
Eua, Tonga 121 Q13 21 22 S 174 56W
Euboea = Évvoia, Greece 45 F6 38 30N 24 0 E
Euchareena, Australia 117 B8 32 57 S 149 6 E
Eucla Motel, Australia 113 F4 31 41 S 128 52 E
Euclid, U.S.A. 136 E3 41 32N 81 31W
Euclides da Cunha, Brazil 154 D4 10 31 S 39 1W
Eucumbene, L., Australia 117 D8 36 2 S 148 40 E
Eudora, U.S.A. 139 J9 33 5N 91 17W
Eudunda, Australia 116 C3 34 12 S 139 7 E
Eufaula, Ala., U.S.A. 135 K3 31 55N 85 11W
Eufaula, Okla., U.S.A. 139 H7 35 20N 95 33W
Eufaula, L., U.S.A. 139 H7 35 15N 95 28W
Eugene, U.S.A. 142 E2 44 0N 123 8W
Eugowra, Australia 117 B8 33 22 S 148 24 E
Eulo, Australia 115 D4 28 10 S 145 3 E
Eumungerie, Australia 117 A8 31 56 S 148 36 E
Eunice, La., U.S.A. 139 K8 30 35N 92 28W
Eunice, N. Mex., U.S.A. 139 J3 32 30N 103 10W
Eupen, Belgium 21 G8 50 37N 6 3 E
Euphrates = Furāt, Nahr al →, Asia 84 D5 31 0N 47 25 E
Eure □, France 22 C8 49 10N 1 0 E
Eure →, France 22 C8 49 18N 1 12 E
Eure-et-Loir □, France 22 D8 48 22N 1 30 E
Eureka, Canada 6 B3 80 0N 85 56W
Eureka, Calif., U.S.A. 142 F1 40 50N 124 8W
Eureka, Ill., U.S.A. 140 D7 40 43N 89 16W
Eureka, Kans., U.S.A. 139 G6 37 50N 96 20W
Eureka, Mo., U.S.A. 140 F6 38 30N 90 38W
Eureka, Mont., U.S.A. 142 B6 48 53N 115 6W
Eureka, Nev., U.S.A. 142 G5 39 32N 116 2W
Eureka, S. Dak., U.S.A. 138 C5 45 49N 99 38W
Eureka, Utah, U.S.A. 142 G7 39 58N 112 9W
Eureka, Mt., Australia 113 E3 26 35 S 121 35 E
Eurelia, Australia 116 B3 32 33 S 138 35 E
Euroa, Australia 117 D6 36 44 S 145 35 E
Europa, Picos de, Spain 36 B6 43 10N 4 49W
Europa, Pta. de, Gib. 37 J5 36 3N 5 21W
Europa Pt. = Europa, Pta. de, Gib. 37 J5 36 3N 5 21W
Europe 10 F10 50 0N 20 0 E
Europoort, Neths. 20 E4 51 57N 4 10 E
Euskirchen, Germany 26 E2 50 40N 6 45 E
Eustis, U.S.A. 135 L5 28 54N 81 36W
Eutin, Germany 26 A6 54 7N 10 38 E
Eutsuk L., Canada 130 C3 53 20N 126 45W
Eva, Brazil 153 D6 3 9 S 59 56W
Eva Downs, Australia 114 B1 18 1 S 134 52 E
Evale, Angola 103 F3 16 33 S 15 44 E
Evans, U.S.A. 138 E2 40 25N 104 43W
Evans Head, Australia 115 D5 29 7 S 153 27 E
Evans L., Canada 128 B4 50 50N 77 0W
Evans Mills, U.S.A. 137 B9 44 6N 75 48W
Evansdale, U.S.A. 140 B4 42 30N 92 17W
Evanston, Ill., U.S.A. 141 C9 42 0N 87 40W
Evanston, Wyo., U.S.A. 142 F8 41 10N 111 0W
Evansville, Ill., U.S.A. 140 F7 38 5N 89 56W
Evansville, Ind., U.S.A. 141 G9 37 55N 87 35W
Evansville, Wis., U.S.A. 140 B7 42 47N 89 18W
Évaux-les-Bains, France 24 B6 46 12N 2 29 E
Evaz, Iran 85 E7 27 46N 53 59 E
Eveleth, U.S.A. 138 B8 47 29N 92 46W
Evensk, U.S.S.R. 57 C16 62 12N 159 30 E
Evenstad, Norway 14 C5 61 25N 11 7 E
Everard, L., Australia 115 E2 31 30 S 135 0 E
Everard Park, Australia 113 E5 27 1 S 132 43 E
Everard Ras., Australia 113 E5 27 5 S 132 28 E
Everdale, Australia 117 A6 31 52 S 144 46 E
Evere, Belgium 21 G4 50 52N 4 25 E
Everest, Mt., Nepal 81 E12 28 5N 86 58 E
Everett, Pa., U.S.A. 136 F6 40 2N 78 24W
Everett, Wash., U.S.A. 144 C4 48 0N 122 10W
Evergem, Belgium 21 F3 51 7N 3 43 E
Everglades, U.S.A. 135 N5 26 0N 80 30W
Everglades City, U.S.A. 135 N5 25 52N 81 23W
Everglades Nat. Park., U.S.A. 135 N5 25 27N 80 53W
Evergreen, U.S.A. 135 K2 31 28N 86 55W
Everson, U.S.A. 142 B2 48 57N 122 22W
Everton, Australia 117 D7 36 25 S 146 33 E
Evesham, U.K. 17 E6 52 6N 1 57W
Évian-les-Bains, France 25 B10 46 24N 6 35 E
Evinayong, Eq. Guin. 102 B2 1 26N 10 35 E
Évinos →, Greece 45 F3 38 27N 21 40 E
Évisa, France 25 F12 42 15N 8 48 E
Évora, Portugal 37 G3 38 33N 7 57W
Évora □, Portugal 37 G3 38 33N 7 50W
Evowghlī, Iran 84 B5 38 43N 45 13 E
Évreux, France 22 C8 49 3N 1 8 E
Evritania □, Greece 45 E3 39 5N 21 30 E
Évron, France 22 D6 48 10N 0 24W
Évros □, Greece 44 C8 41 10N 26 0 E
Evrótas →, Greece 45 H4 36 50N 22 40 E
Évvoia, Greece 45 F6 38 30N 24 0 E
Évvoia □, Greece 45 F5 38 40N 23 40 E
Ewe, L., U.K. 18 D3 57 49N 5 38W
Ewing, Mo., U.S.A. 140 E5 40 0N 91 43W
Ewing, Nebr., U.S.A. 138 D5 42 18N 98 22W
Ewo, Congo 102 C2 0 48 S 14 45 E
Exaltación, Bolivia 157 C4 13 10 S 65 20W
Excelsior Springs, U.S.A. 140 E2 39 20N 94 10W
Excideuil, France 24 C5 45 20N 1 4 E
Exe →, U.K. 17 G4 50 38N 3 27W
Exeter, Canada 136 C3 43 21N 81 29W
Exeter, U.K. 17 G4 50 43N 3 31W
Exeter, Calif., U.S.A. 144 J7 36 17N 119 9W
Exeter, N.H., U.S.A. 137 D14 43 0N 70 58W
Exeter, Nebr., U.S.A. 138 E6 40 43N 97 30W
Exira, U.S.A. 140 C2 41 35N 94 52W
Exloo, Neths. 20 C9 52 53N 6 52 E
Exmes, France 22 D7 48 45N 0 10 E
Exmoor, U.K. 17 F4 51 10N 3 59W
Exmouth, Australia 112 D1 21 54 S 114 10 E
Exmouth, U.K. 17 G4 50 37N 3 26W
Exmouth G., Australia 112 D1 22 15 S 114 15 E
Expedition Ra., Australia 114 C4 24 30 S 149 12 E
Extremadura □, Spain 37 F4 39 30N 6 5W
Exuma Sound, Bahamas 148 B4 24 30N 76 20W
Eyasi, L., Tanzania 106 C4 3 30 S 35 0 E
Eyeberry L., Canada 131 A8 63 8N 104 43W
Eyemouth, U.K. 18 F6 55 53N 2 5W
Eygurande, France 24 C6 45 40N 2 26 E
Eyjafjörður, Iceland 12 C4 66 15N 18 30W
Eymet, France 24 D4 44 40N 0 25 E
Eymoutiers, France 24 C5 45 40N 1 45 E
Eynesil, Turkey 89 C8 41 3N 39 9 E
Eyrarbakki, Iceland 12 E3 63 52N 21 9W
Eyre, Australia 113 F4 32 15 S 126 18 E
Eyre (North), L., Australia 115 D2 28 30 S 137 20 E
Eyre (South), L., Australia 115 D2 29 18 S 137 25 E
Eyre, L., Australia 110 F6 29 30 S 137 26 E
Eyre Cr. →, Australia 115 D2 26 40 S 139 0 E
Eyre Mts., N.Z. 119 F3 45 25 S 168 25 E
Eyre Pen., Australia 115 E2 33 30 S 136 17 E
Eyvānkī, Iran 85 C6 35 24N 51 56 E
Ez Zeidab, Sudan 94 D3 17 25N 33 55 E
Ezcaray, Spain 34 C2 42 19N 3 0W
Ezine, Turkey 44 E8 39 48N 26 20 E
Ezmul, Mauritania 98 D1 22 15N 15 40W
Ezouza →, Cyprus 32 E11 34 44N 32 27 E

F

Fabens, U.S.A. 143 L10 31 30N 106 8W
Fåborg, Denmark 15 J4 55 6N 10 15 E
Fabriano, Italy 39 E9 43 20N 12 52 E
Făcăeni, Romania 46 E8 44 32N 27 53 E
Facatativá, Colombia 152 C3 4 49N 74 22W
Fachi, Niger 97 E2 18 6N 11 34 E
Facture, France 24 D3 44 39N 0 58W
Fada, Chad 97 E4 17 13N 21 34 E
Fada-n-Gourma, Burkina Faso 101 C5 12 10N 0 30 E
Fadd, Hungary 31 E11 46 28N 18 49 E
Faddeyevskiy, Ostrov, U.S.S.R. 57 B15 76 0N 144 0 E
Fadghāmī, Syria 84 C4 35 53N 40 52 E
Fadlab, Sudan 94 D3 17 42N 34 2 E
Faenza, Italy 39 D8 44 17N 11 53 E
Fafa, Mali 101 B5 15 22N 0 48 E
Fafe, Portugal 36 D2 41 27N 8 11W
Faga, W. Samoa 121 W23 13 39 S 172 8W
Fagam, Nigeria 101 C7 11 1N 10 1 E
Fagamalo, W. Samoa 121 W23 13 25 S 172 21W
Făgăras, Romania 46 D5 45 48N 24 58 E
Făgăras, Munţii, Romania 46 D5 45 40N 24 40 E
Fågelsjö, Sweden 14 C8 61 50N 14 35 E
Fagernes, Norway 13 F10 60 59N 9 14 E
Fagersta, Sweden 13 F13 60 1N 15 46 E
Făget, Romania 46 D3 45 52N 22 10 E
Făget, Munţii, Romania 46 B4 47 40N 23 10 E
Fagnano, L., Argentina 160 D3 54 30 S 68 0W
Fagnano Castello, Italy 41 C9 39 31N 16 4 E
Fagnières, France 23 D11 48 58N 4 20 E
Fahlīān, Iran 85 D6 30 11N 51 28 E
Fahr, Yemen 87 D6 12 26N 54 8 E
Fahraj, Kermān, Iran 85 D8 29 0N 59 0 E
Fahraj, Yazd, Iran 85 D7 31 46N 54 36 E
Faial, Madeira 33 D3 32 47N 16 53W
Faido, Switz. 29 D7 46 29N 8 48 E
Fair Hd., U.K. 19 A5 55 14N 6 10W
Fair Oaks, U.S.A. 144 G5 38 39N 121 16W
Fairbank, U.S.A. 143 L8 31 44N 110 12W
Fairbanks, U.S.A. 126 B5 64 50N 147 50W
Fairborn, U.S.A. 141 E12 39 52N 84 2W
Fairbury, Ill., U.S.A. 141 D8 40 45N 88 31W
Fairbury, Nebr., U.S.A. 138 E6 40 5N 97 5W
Fairfax, Ohio, U.S.A. 141 E13 39 5N 83 37W
Fairfax, Okla., U.S.A. 139 G6 36 37N 96 45W
Fairfield, Australia 117 B9 33 53 S 150 57 E
Fairfield, Ala., U.S.A. 135 J2 33 30N 87 0W
Fairfield, Calif., U.S.A. 144 G4 38 14N 122 1W
Fairfield, Conn., U.S.A. 137 E11 41 8N 73 16W
Fairfield, Idaho, U.S.A. 142 E6 43 21N 114 46W
Fairfield, Ill., U.S.A. 141 F8 38 20N 88 20W
Fairfield, Iowa, U.S.A. 140 D5 41 0N 91 58W
Fairfield, Mont., U.S.A. 142 C8 47 40N 112 0W
Fairfield, Ohio, U.S.A. 141 E12 39 21N 84 34W
Fairfield, Tex., U.S.A. 139 K7 31 40N 96 0W
Fairford, Canada 131 C9 51 37N 98 45W
Fairhope, U.S.A. 135 K2 30 35N 87 50W

Finike 197

Fairlie, *N.Z.* **119 E5** 44 5 S 170 49 E
Fairmead, *U.S.A.* **144 H6** 37 5N 120 10W
Fairmont, *Minn., U.S.A.* **138 D7** 43 37N 94 30W
Fairmont, *W. Va., U.S.A.* **134 F5** 39 29N 80 10W
Fairmount, *U.S.A.* **145 L8** 34 45N 118 26W
Fairplay, *U.S.A.* **143 G11** 39 9N 105 40W
Fairport, *N.Y., U.S.A.* **136 C7** 43 8N 77 29W
Fairport, *Ohio, U.S.A.* **136 E3** 41 45N 81 17W
Fairview, *Australia* **114 B3** 15 31 S 144 17 E
Fairview, *Canada* **130 B5** 56 5N 118 25W
Fairview, *N. Dak., U.S.A.* **138 B2** 47 49N 104 7W
Fairview, *Okla., U.S.A.* **139 G5** 36 19N 98 30W
Fairview, *Utah, U.S.A.* **142 G8** 39 50N 111 0W
Fairweather, Mt., *U.S.A.* **126 C6** 58 55N 137 45W
Faisalabad, *Pakistan* **79 C4** 31 30N 73 5 E
Faith, *U.S.A.* **138 C3** 45 2N 102 4W
Faizabad, *India* **81 F10** 26 45N 82 10 E
Faizpur, *India* **82 D2** 21 14N 75 49 E
Fajardo, *Puerto Rico* **149 C6** 18 20N 65 39W
Fakam, *Yemen* **86 C3** 16 38N 43 49 E
Fakfak, *Indonesia* **71 E8** 3 0S 132 15 E
Fakiya, *Bulgaria* **43 E12** 42 10N 27 6 E
Fakobli, *Ivory C.* **100 D3** 7 23N 7 23W
Fakse, *Denmark* **15 J6** 55 15N 12 8 E
Fakse B., *Denmark* **15 J6** 55 11N 12 15 E
Fakse Ladeplads, *Denmark* **15 J6** 55 11N 12 9 E
Faku, *China* **67 C12** 42 32N 123 21 E
Falaise, *France* **22 D6** 48 54N 0 12W
Falaise, Mui, *Vietnam* **76 C5** 19 6N 105 45 E
Falakrón Óros, *Greece* **44 C5** 41 15N 23 58 E
Falam, *Burma* **78 D4** 23 0N 93 45 E
Falces, *Spain* **34 C3** 42 24N 1 48W
Fălciu, *Romania* **46 C9** 46 17N 28 7 E
Falcón □, *Venezuela* **152 A4** 11 0N 69 50W
Falcón, C., *Spain* **33 C7** 38 50N 1 23 E
Falcon, C., *Algeria* **99 A4** 35 50N 0 50W
Falcon Dam, *U.S.A.* **139 M5** 26 50N 99 20W
Falconara Marittima, *Italy* **39 E10** 43 37N 13 23 E
Falconer, *U.S.A.* **136 D5** 42 7N 79 13W
Faléa, *Mali* **100 C2** 12 16N 11 17W
Falelatai, *W. Samoa* **121 W24** 13 55 S 171 59W
Falelima, *W. Samoa* **121 W23** 13 32 S 172 41W
Falenki, *U.S.S.R.* **54 B2** 58 22N 51 35 E
Faleshty, *U.S.S.R.* **52 C2** 47 32N 27 44 E
Falfurrias, *U.S.A.* **139 M5** 27 14N 98 8W
Falher, *Canada* **130 B5** 55 44N 117 15W
Faliraki, *Greece* **32 C10** 36 22N 28 12 E
Falkenberg, *Germany* **26 D9** 51 34N 13 13 E
Falkenberg, *Sweden* **15 H6** 56 54N 12 30 E
Falkensee, *Germany* **26 C9** 52 35N 13 6 E
Falkenstein, *Germany* **26 E8** 50 27N 12 24 E
Falkirk, *U.K.* **18 F5** 56 0N 3 47W
Falkland, East, I., *Falk. Is.* **160 D5** 51 40 S 58 30W
Falkland, West, I., *Falk. Is.* **160 D5** 51 40 S 60 0W
Falkland Is., *Atl. Oc.* **160 D5** 51 30 S 59 0W
Falkland Is. Dependency □, *Atl. Oc.* **7 B1** 57 0 S 40 0W
Falkland Sd., *Falk. Is.* **160 D5** 52 0 S 60 0W
Falkonéra, *Greece* **45 H5** 36 50N 23 52 E
Falköping, *Sweden* **15 F7** 58 12N 13 33 E
Fall River, *U.S.A.* **137 E13** 41 45N 71 5W
Fall River Mills, *U.S.A.* **142 F3** 41 1N 121 30W
Fallbrook, *U.S.A.* **143 K5** 33 25N 117 12W
Fallbrook, *U.S.A.* **145 M9** 33 23N 117 15W
Fallon, *Mont., U.S.A.* **138 B2** 46 52N 105 8W
Fallon, *Nev., U.S.A.* **142 G4** 39 31N 118 51W
Falls City, *Nebr., U.S.A.* **138 E7** 40 5N 95 40W
Falls City, *Oreg., U.S.A.* **142 D2** 44 54N 123 29W
Falls Creek, *U.S.A.* **136 E6** 41 8N 78 49W
Falmouth, *Jamaica* **148 C4** 18 30N 77 40W
Falmouth, *U.K.* **17 G2** 50 9N 5 5W
Falmouth, *U.S.A.* **141 F12** 38 40N 84 20W
False B., *S. Africa* **104 E2** 34 15 S 18 40 E
False Divi Pt., *India* **83 G5** 15 43N 80 50 E
Falset, *Spain* **34 D5** 41 7N 0 50 E
Falso, C., *Honduras* **148 C3** 15 12N 83 21W
Falster, *Denmark* **15 K5** 54 45N 11 55 E
Falsterbo, *Sweden* **15 J6** 55 23N 12 50 E
Fălticeni, *Romania* **46 B7** 47 21N 26 20 E
Falun, *Sweden* **13 F13** 60 37N 15 37 E
Famagusta, *Cyprus* **32 D12** 35 8N 33 55 E
Famagusta Bay, *Cyprus* **32 D13** 35 15N 34 0 E
Famatina, Sierra de, *Argentina* **158 B2** 27 30 S 68 0W
Family L., *Canada* **131 C9** 51 54N 95 27W
Famoso, *U.S.A.* **145 K7** 35 37N 119 12W
Fan Xian, *China* **66 G8** 35 55N 115 38 E
Fana, *Mali* **100 C3** 13 0N 6 56W
Fanárion, *Greece* **44 E3** 39 24N 21 47 E
Fandriana, *Madag.* **105 C8** 20 14 S 47 21 E
Fang, *Thailand* **76 C2** 19 55N 99 13 E
Fang Xian, *China* **69 A8** 32 3N 110 40 E
Fangchang, *China* **69 B12** 31 5N 118 4 E
Fangcheng, *Guangxi Zhuangzu, China* **68 G7** 21 42N 108 21 E
Fangcheng, *Henan, China* **66 H7** 33 18N 112 59 E
Fangliao, *Taiwan* **69 F13** 22 22N 120 38 E
Fangshan, *China* **66 E6** 38 3N 111 25 E
Fangzi, *China* **67 F10** 36 33N 119 10 E
Fani i Madh →, *Albania* **44 C2** 41 56N 20 16 E
Fanjiatun, *China* **67 C13** 43 40N 125 15 E
Fannich, L., *U.K.* **18 D4** 57 40N 5 0W
Fannūj, *Iran* **85 E8** 26 35N 59 38 E
Fanny Bay, *Canada* **130 D4** 49 37N 124 48W
Fanø, *Denmark* **15 J2** 55 25N 8 25 E
Fano, *Italy* **39 E10** 43 50N 13 0 E
Fanshaw, *U.S.A.* **130 B2** 57 11N 133 30W
Fanshi, *China* **66 E7** 39 12N 113 20 E
Fao = Al Fāw, *Iraq* **85 D6** 30 0N 48 30 E
Faqirwali, *Pakistan* **80 E5** 29 27N 73 0 E
Fara in Sabina, *Italy* **39 F9** 42 13N 12 44 E
Farab, *U.S.S.R.* **55 D1** 39 9N 63 36 E
Faradje, *Zaïre* **106 B2** 3 50N 29 45 E
Farafangana, *Madag.* **105 C8** 22 49 S 47 50 E
Farâfra, El Wâhât el-, *Egypt* **94 B2** 27 15N 28 20 E
Farāh, *Afghan.* **79 B1** 32 20N 62 7 E
Farāh □, *Afghan.* **79 B1** 32 25N 62 10 E
Farahalana, *Madag.* **105 A9** 14 26 S 50 10 E
Faraid, Gebel, *Egypt* **94 C4** 23 33N 35 19 E
Faramana, *Burkina Faso* **100 C4** 11 56N 4 45W
Faranah, *Guinea* **100 C2** 10 3N 10 45W
Farasān, Jazā'ir, *Si. Arabia* **86 C3** 16 45N 41 55 E
Farasan Is. = Farasān, Jazā'ir, *Si. Arabia* **86 C3** 16 45N 41 55 E
Faratsiho, *Madag.* **105 B8** 19 24 S 46 57 E
Farbarachi, *Somali Rep.* **108 D3** 2 30N 45 30 E
Fardes →, *Spain* **35 H2** 37 35N 3 0W
Fareham, *U.K.* **17 G6** 50 52N 1 11W
Farewell, C., *N.Z.* **119 A7** 40 29 S 172 43 E
Farewell C. = Farvel, Kap, *Greenland* **124 D15** 59 48N 43 55W
Farewell Spit, *N.Z.* **119 A8** 40 35 S 173 0 E
Fargo, *U.S.A.* **138 B6** 46 52N 96 40W
Fari'a →, *Jordan* **91 C4** 32 12N 35 27 E
Faribault, *U.S.A.* **138 C8** 44 15N 93 19W
Faridkot, *India* **80 D6** 30 44N 74 45 E
Faridpur, *Bangla.* **78 D2** 23 15N 89 55 E
Färila, *Sweden* **14 C9** 61 48N 15 50 E
Farim, *Guinea-Biss.* **100 C1** 12 27N 15 9W
Farīmān, *Iran* **85 C8** 35 40N 59 49 E
Farina, *Australia* **115 E2** 30 3 S 138 15 E
Farinha →, *Brazil* **154 C2** 6 51 S 47 30W
Fariones, Pta., *Canary Is.* **33 E6** 29 13N 13 28W
Fâriskûr, *Egypt* **94 H7** 31 20N 31 43 E
Farmakonisi, *Greece* **45 G9** 37 17N 27 8 E
Farmer City, *U.S.A.* **141 D8** 40 15N 88 39W
Farmersburg, *U.S.A.* **141 E9** 39 15N 87 23W
Farmerville, *U.S.A.* **139 J8** 32 48N 92 23W
Farmington, *Calif., U.S.A.* **144 H6** 37 56N 121 0W
Farmington, *Ill., U.S.A.* **140 D7** 40 42N 90 0W
Farmington, *Iowa, U.S.A.* **140 D5** 40 38N 91 44W
Farmington, *Mo., U.S.A.* **140 G6** 37 47N 90 25W
Farmington, *N.H., U.S.A.* **137 C13** 43 25N 71 7W
Farmington, *N. Mex., U.S.A.* **143 H9** 36 45N 108 28W
Farmington, *Utah, U.S.A.* **142 F8** 41 0N 111 12W
Farmington →, *U.S.A.* **137 E12** 41 51N 72 38W
Farmland, *U.S.A.* **141 D11** 40 15N 85 5W
Farmville, *U.S.A.* **134 G6** 37 19N 78 22W
Farnborough, *U.K.* **17 F7** 51 17N 0 46W
Farne Is., *U.K.* **16 B6** 55 38N 1 37W
Farnham, *Canada* **137 A12** 45 17N 72 59W
Faro, *Brazil* **153 D6** 2 10 S 56 39W
Faro, *Portugal* **37 H3** 37 2N 7 55W
Fårö, *Sweden* **13 H15** 57 55N 19 5 E
Faro □, *Portugal* **37 H2** 37 12N 8 10W
Faroe Is. = Føroyar, *Atl. Oc.* **8 B8** 62 0N 7 0W
Farquhar, C., *Australia* **113 D1** 23 50 S 113 36 E
Farquhar Is., *Seychelles* **109 F4** 11 0 S 52 0 E
Farrars Cr. →, *Australia* **114 D3** 25 35 S 140 43 E
Farrāshband, *Iran* **85 D7** 28 57N 52 5 E
Farrell, *U.S.A.* **136 E4** 41 13N 80 29W
Farrell Flat, *Australia* **116 B3** 33 48 S 138 48 E
Farrokhī, *Iran* **85 C8** 33 50N 59 31 E
Farruch, C., *Spain* **33 B10** 39 47N 3 21 E
Farrukhabad-cum-Fatehgarh, *India* **81 F8** 27 30N 79 32 E
Fārs □, *Iran* **85 D7** 29 30N 55 0 E
Fársala, *Greece* **44 E4** 39 17N 22 23 E
Fārsī, *Afghan.* **79 B1** 33 47N 63 15 E
Farsø, *Denmark* **15 H3** 56 46N 9 19 E
Farsund, *Norway* **13 G9** 58 5N 6 55 E
Fartak, Râs, *Si. Arabia* **84 D2** 28 5N 34 34 E
Fartak, Ra's, *Yemen* **87 D6** 15 38N 52 15 E
Fartura, Serra da, *Brazil* **159 B5** 26 21 S 52 52W
Faru, *Nigeria* **101 C6** 12 48N 6 12 E
Fārūj, *Iran* **85 B8** 37 14N 58 14 E
Farum, *Denmark* **15 J6** 55 49N 12 21 E
Farvel, Kap, *Greenland* **124 D15** 59 48N 43 55W
Farwell, *U.S.A.* **139 H3** 34 25N 103 0W
Fāryāb □, *Afghan.* **79 B2** 36 0N 65 0 E
Fasā, *Iran* **85 D7** 29 0N 53 39 E
Fasano, *Italy* **41 B10** 40 50N 17 20 E
Fashoda, *Sudan* **95 F3** 9 50N 32 2 E
Fastnet Rock, *Ireland* **19 E2** 51 22N 9 37W
Fastov, *U.S.S.R.* **50 F6** 50 7N 29 57 E
Fatagar, Tanjung, *Indonesia* **71 E8** 2 46 S 131 57 E
Fatehgarh, *India* **81 F8** 27 25N 79 35 E
Fatehpur, *Raj., India* **80 F6** 28 0N 74 40 E
Fatehpur, *Ut. P., India* **81 G9** 25 56N 81 13 E
Fatesh, *U.S.S.R.* **51 E9** 52 8N 35 57 E
Fatick, *Senegal* **100 C1** 14 19N 16 27W
Fatima, *Canada* **129 C7** 47 24N 61 53W
Fátima, *Portugal* **37 F2** 39 37N 8 39W
Fatoya, *Guinea* **100 C3** 11 37N 9 10W
Faucille, Col de la, *France* **25 B10** 46 22N 6 2 E
Faulkton, *U.S.A.* **138 C5** 45 4N 99 8W
Faulquemont, *France* **23 C13** 49 3N 6 36 E
Fauquembergues, *France* **23 B9** 50 36N 2 5 E
Faure I., *Australia* **113 E1** 25 52 S 113 50 E
Făurei, *Romania* **46 D8** 45 6N 27 19 E
Fauresmith, *S. Africa* **104 D4** 29 44 S 25 17 E
Fauro, *Solomon Is.* **121 L9** 6 55 S 156 7 E
Fauske, *Norway* **12 C13** 67 17N 15 25 E
Fauvillers, *Belgium* **21 J7** 49 51N 5 40 E
Favara, *Italy* **40 E6** 37 19N 13 39 E
Favaritx, C., *Spain* **33 B11** 40 0N 4 15 E
Favignana, *Italy* **40 E5** 37 56N 12 18 E
Favignana, I., *Italy* **40 E5** 37 56N 12 18 E
Favourable Lake, *Canada* **128 B1** 52 50N 93 39W
Fawn →, *Canada* **128 A2** 55 20N 87 35W
Fawnskin, *U.S.A.* **145 L10** 34 16N 116 56W
Faxaflói, *Iceland* **12 D2** 64 29N 23 0W
Faya-Largeau, *Chad* **97 E3** 17 58N 19 6 E
Fayaoué, *Vanuatu* **121 K4** 20 38 S 166 33 E
Fayd, *Si. Arabia* **84 E4** 27 1N 42 52 E
Fayence, *France* **25 E10** 43 38N 6 42 E
Fayette, *Ala., U.S.A.* **135 J2** 33 40N 87 50W
Fayette, *Iowa, U.S.A.* **140 B5** 42 51N 91 48W
Fayette, *Mo., U.S.A.* **140 E4** 39 10N 92 40W
Fayette, *Ohio, U.S.A.* **141 C12** 41 40N 84 20W
Fayetteville, *Ark., U.S.A.* **139 G7** 36 5N 94 5W
Fayetteville, *N.C., U.S.A.* **135 H6** 35 0N 78 58W
Fayetteville, *Tenn., U.S.A.* **135 H2** 35 8N 86 30W
Fayón, *Spain* **34 D5** 41 15N 0 20 E
Fazenda Libongo, *Angola* **103 D2** 8 24 S 13 24 E
Fazenda Nova, *Brazil* **155 E1** 16 11 S 50 48W
Fazilka, *India* **80 D6** 30 27N 74 2 E
Fazilpur, *Pakistan* **80 E4** 29 18N 70 29 E
Fdérik, *Mauritania* **98 D2** 22 40N 12 45W
Feale →, *Ireland* **19 D2** 52 26N 9 40W
Fear, C., *U.S.A.* **135 J7** 33 51N 78 0W
Feather →, *U.S.A.* **142 G3** 38 47N 121 36W
Feather Falls, *U.S.A.* **144 F5** 39 36N 121 16W
Featherston, *N.Z.* **118 H4** 41 6 S 175 20 E
Featherstone, *Zimbabwe* **107 F3** 18 42 S 30 55 E
Fécamp, *France* **22 C7** 49 45N 0 22 E
Fedala = Mohammedia, *Morocco* **98 B3** 33 44N 7 21W
Federación, *Argentina* **158 C4** 31 0 S 57 55W
Fedeshkūh, *Iran* **85 D7** 28 49N 53 50 E
Fedjadj, Chott el, *Tunisia* **96 B1** 33 52N 9 14 E
Fedorovka, *U.S.S.R.* **54 E8** 53 38N 62 42 E
Fehérgyarmat, *Hungary* **31 D15** 48 0N 22 30 E
Fehmarn, *Germany* **26 A7** 54 26N 11 10 E
Fei Xian, *China* **67 G9** 35 18N 117 59 E
Feijó, *Brazil* **156 B3** 8 9 S 70 21W
Feilding, *N.Z.* **118 G4** 40 13 S 175 35 E
Feira de Santana, *Brazil* **155 D4** 12 15 S 38 57W
Feixiang, *China* **66 F8** 36 30N 114 45 E
Fejér □, *Hungary* **31 D11** 47 9N 18 30 E
Fejø, *Denmark* **15 K5** 54 55N 11 30 E
Feke, *Turkey* **88 E6** 37 48N 35 56 E
Fekete →, *Hungary* **31 F11** 45 47N 18 15 E
Felanitx, *Spain* **33 B10** 39 28N 3 9 E
Feldbach, *Austria* **30 E8** 46 57N 15 52 E
Feldberg, *Baden-W., Germany* **27 H3** 47 51N 7 58 E
Feldberg, *Mecklenburg-Vorpommern, Germany* **26 B9** 53 20N 13 26 E
Feldkirch, *Austria* **30 D2** 47 15N 9 37 E
Feldkirchen, *Austria* **30 E7** 46 44N 14 6 E
Felicity, *U.S.A.* **141 F12** 38 51N 84 6W
Felipe Carrillo Puerto, *Mexico* **147 D7** 19 38N 88 3W
Felixlândia, *Brazil* **155 E3** 18 47 S 44 55W
Felixstowe, *U.K.* **17 F9** 51 58N 1 22 E
Felletin, *France* **24 C6** 45 53N 2 11 E
Felton, *U.K.* **16 B6** 55 18N 1 42W
Felton, *U.S.A.* **144 H4** 37 3N 122 4W
Feltre, *Italy* **39 B8** 46 1N 11 55 E
Femø, *Denmark* **15 K5** 54 58N 11 53 E
Femunden, *Norway* **14 B5** 62 10N 11 53 E
Fen He →, *China* **66 G6** 35 36N 110 42 E
Fenelon Falls, *Canada* **136 B6** 44 32N 78 45W
Feneroa, *Ethiopia* **95 E4** 13 5N 39 3 E
Feng Xian, *Jiangsu, China* **66 G9** 34 43N 116 35 E
Feng Xian, *Shaanxi, China* **66 H4** 33 54N 106 40 E
Fengári, *Greece* **44 D7** 40 25N 25 32 E
Fengcheng, *Jiangxi, China* **69 C10** 28 12N 115 48 E
Fengcheng, *Liaoning, China* **67 D13** 40 28N 124 5 E
Fengdu, *China* **68 C6** 29 55N 107 41 E
Fengfeng, *China* **66 F8** 36 28N 114 8 E
Fenggang, *China* **68 D6** 27 57N 107 47 E
Fenghua, *China* **69 C13** 29 40N 121 25 E
Fenghuang, *China* **68 D7** 27 57N 109 29 E
Fenghuangzui, *China* **68 A7** 33 30N 109 23 E
Fengjie, *China* **68 B7** 31 5N 109 36 E
Fengkai, *China* **69 F8** 23 24N 111 30 E
Fengle, *China* **69 B9** 31 29N 112 29 E
Fengning, *China* **66 D9** 41 10N 116 33 E
Fengqing, *China* **68 E2** 24 38N 99 55 E
Fengqiu, *China* **66 G8** 35 2N 114 25 E
Fengrun, *China* **67 E10** 39 48N 118 8 E
Fengshan, *Guangxi Zhuangzu, China* **68 E7** 24 39N 109 15 E
Fengshan, *Guangxi Zhuangzu, China* **68 E6** 24 31N 107 3 E
Fengtai, *Anhui, China* **69 A11** 32 50N 116 40 E
Fengtai, *Beijing, China* **66 E9** 39 50N 116 18 E
Fengxian, *China* **69 B13** 30 55N 121 26 E
Fengxiang, *China* **66 G4** 34 29N 107 25 E
Fengxin, *China* **69 C10** 28 41N 115 18 E
Fengyang, *China* **67 H9** 32 51N 117 29 E
Fengyi, *China* **68 E3** 25 37N 100 20 E
Fengzhen, *China* **66 D7** 40 25N 113 2 E
Feni Is., *Papua N. G.* **120 C7** 4 0 S 153 40 E
Fenit, *Ireland* **19 D2** 52 17N 9 51W
Fennimore, *U.S.A.* **140 B6** 42 58N 90 41W
Fenny, *Bangla.* **78 D3** 22 55N 91 32 E
Feno, C. de, *France* **25 G12** 41 58N 8 33 E
Fenoarivo Afovoany, *Madag.* **105 B8** 18 26 S 46 34 E
Fenoarivo Atsinanana, *Madag.* **105 B8** 17 22 S 49 25 E
Fens, The, *U.K.* **16 E8** 52 45N 0 2 E
Fenton, *U.S.A.* **141 B13** 42 47N 83 44W
Fenxi, *China* **66 F6** 36 40N 111 31 E
Fenyang, *China* **65 C6** 37 19N 111 46 E
Fenyang, *Shanxi, China* **66 F6** 37 18N 111 48 E
Fenyi, *China* **69 D10** 27 45N 114 47 E
Feodosiya, *U.S.S.R.* **52 D6** 45 2N 35 28 E
Fer, C. de, *Algeria* **99 A6** 37 3N 7 10 E
Ferdows, *Iran* **85 C8** 33 58N 58 2 E
Fère-Champenoise, *France* **23 D10** 48 45N 3 59 E
Fère-en-Tardenois, *France* **23 C10** 49 10N 3 30 E
Ferentino, *Italy* **40 A6** 41 42N 13 14 E
Ferfer, *Somali Rep.* **90 F4** 5 4N 45 9 E
Fergana, *U.S.S.R.* **55 C5** 40 23N 71 19 E
Ferganskaya Dolina, *U.S.S.R.* **55 C5** 40 50N 71 30 E
Ferganskiy Khrebet, *U.S.S.R.* **55 C6** 41 0N 73 50 E
Fergus, *Canada* **128 D3** 43 43N 80 24W
Fergus Falls, *U.S.A.* **138 B6** 46 18N 96 7W
Ferguson, *U.S.A.* **140 F6** 38 45N 90 18W
Fergusson I., *Papua N. G.* **120 E6** 9 30 S 150 45 E
Fériana, *Tunisia* **96 B1** 34 59N 8 33 E
Feričanci, *Yugoslavia* **42 B3** 45 32N 18 0 E
Ferkane, *Algeria* **99 B6** 34 37N 7 26 E
Ferkéssédougou, *Ivory C.* **100 D3** 9 35N 5 6W
Ferlach, *Austria* **30 E7** 46 32N 14 18 E
Ferland, *Canada* **128 B2** 50 19N 88 27W
Ferlo, Vallée du, *Senegal* **100 B2** 15 15N 14 15W
Fermanagh □, *U.K.* **19 B4** 54 21N 7 40W
Fermo, *Italy* **39 E10** 43 10N 13 42 E
Fermoselle, *Spain* **36 D4** 41 19N 6 27W
Fermoy, *Ireland* **19 D3** 52 4N 8 18W
Fernán Nuñéz, *Spain* **37 H6** 37 40N 4 44W
Fernández, *Argentina* **158 B3** 27 55 S 63 50W
Fernandina Beach, *U.S.A.* **135 K5** 30 40N 81 30W
Fernando de Noronha, *Brazil* **154 B5** 4 0 S 33 10W
Fernando Póo = Bioko, *Eq. Guin.* **101 E6** 3 30N 8 40 E
Fernandópolis, *Brazil* **155 F1** 20 16 S 50 14W
Ferndale, *Calif., U.S.A.* **142 F1** 40 37N 124 12W
Ferndale, *Wash., U.S.A.* **144 B4** 48 51N 122 41W
Fernie, *Canada* **130 D5** 49 30N 115 5W
Fernlees, *Australia* **114 C4** 23 51 S 148 7 E
Fernley, *U.S.A.* **142 G4** 39 36N 119 14W
Feroke, *India* **83 J2** 11 9N 75 46 E
Ferozepore = Firozpur, *India* **80 D6** 30 55N 74 40 E
Férai, *Greece* **44 D8** 40 53N 26 10 E
Ferrandina, *Italy* **41 B9** 40 30N 16 28 E
Ferrara, *Italy* **39 D8** 44 50N 11 36 E
Ferrato, C., *Italy* **40 C2** 39 18N 9 39 E
Ferreira do Alentejo, *Portugal* **37 G2** 38 4N 8 6W
Ferreñafe, *Peru* **156 B2** 6 42 S 79 50W
Ferrerías, *Spain* **33 B11** 39 59N 4 1 E
Ferret, C., *France* **24 D2** 44 38N 1 15W
Ferrette, *France* **23 E14** 47 30N 7 20 E
Ferriday, *U.S.A.* **139 K9** 31 35N 91 33W
Ferrières, *France* **23 D9** 48 5N 2 48 E
Ferriete, *Italy* **38 D6** 44 40N 9 30 E
Ferrol, Pen. de, *Peru* **156 B2** 9 10 S 78 35W
Ferron, *U.S.A.* **143 G8** 39 3N 111 3W
Ferros, *Brazil* **155 E3** 19 14 S 43 2W
Ferryland, *Canada* **129 C9** 47 2N 52 53W
Ferrysburg, *U.S.A.* **141 A10** 43 5N 86 13W
Fertile, *U.S.A.* **138 B6** 47 31N 96 18W
Fertília, *Italy* **40 B1** 40 37N 8 13 E
Fertöszentmiklós, *Hungary* **31 D9** 47 35N 16 53 E
Fès, *Morocco* **98 B4** 34 0N 5 0W
Feschaux, *Belgium* **21 H5** 50 9N 4 54 E
Feshi, *Zaïre* **103 D3** 6 8 S 18 10 E
Fessenden, *U.S.A.* **138 B5** 47 42N 99 38W
Festus, *U.S.A.* **140 F6** 38 13N 90 24W
Feteşti, *Romania* **46 E8** 44 22N 27 51 E
Fethiye, *Turkey* **88 E3** 36 36N 29 10 E
Fetlar, *U.K.* **18 A8** 60 36N 0 52W
Feuerthalen, *Switz.* **29 A7** 47 37N 8 38 E
Feuilles →, *Canada* **127 C12** 58 47N 70 4W
Feurs, *France* **25 C8** 45 45N 4 13 E
Feyzābād, *Badākhshān, Afghan.* **79 A3** 37 7N 70 33 E
Feyzābād, *Fāryāb, Afghan.* **79 A2** 36 17N 64 52 E
Fezzan, *Libya* **92 D5** 27 0N 15 0 E
Ffestiniog, *U.K.* **16 E4** 52 58N 3 56W
Fiambalá, *Argentina* **158 B2** 27 45 S 67 37W
Fianarantsoa, *Madag.* **105 C8** 21 26 S 47 5 E
Fianarantsoa □, *Madag.* **105 B8** 19 30 S 47 0 E
Fianga, *Cameroon* **97 G3** 9 55N 15 9 E
Fibiş, *Romania* **46 D2** 45 57N 21 26 E
Fichtelgebirge, *Germany* **27 E8** 50 10N 12 0 E
Ficksburg, *S. Africa* **105 D4** 28 51 S 27 53 E
Fidenza, *Italy* **38 D7** 44 51N 10 3 E
Fiditi, *Nigeria* **101 D5** 7 45N 3 53 E
Field, *Canada* **128 C3** 46 31N 80 1W
Field →, *Australia* **114 C2** 23 48 S 138 0 E
Field I., *Australia* **112 B5** 12 5 S 132 23 E
Fieri, *Albania* **44 D1** 40 43N 19 33 E
Fiesch, *Switz.* **28 D6** 46 25N 8 12 E
Fife □, *U.K.* **18 E5** 56 13N 3 2W
Fife Ness, *U.K.* **18 E6** 56 17N 2 35W
Fifth Cataract, *Sudan* **94 D3** 18 22N 33 50 E
Figeac, *France* **24 D6** 44 37N 2 2 E
Figline Valdarno, *Italy* **39 E8** 43 37N 11 28 E
Figtree, *Zimbabwe* **107 G2** 20 22 S 28 20 E
Figueira Castelo Rodrigo, *Portugal* **36 E4** 40 57N 6 58W
Figueira da Foz, *Portugal* **36 E2** 40 7N 8 54W
Figueiró dos Vinhos, *Portugal* **36 F2** 39 55N 8 16W
Figueras, *Spain* **34 C7** 42 18N 2 58 E
Figuig, *Morocco* **99 B4** 32 5N 1 11W
Fihaonana, *Madag.* **105 B8** 18 36 S 47 12 E
Fiherenana, *Madag.* **105 B8** 18 29 S 48 24 E
Fiherenana →, *Madag.* **105 C7** 23 19 S 43 37 E
Fiji ■, *Pac. Oc.* **121 A2** 17 20 S 179 0 E
Fika, *Nigeria* **101 C7** 11 15N 11 13 E
Filabres, Sierra de los, *Spain* **35 H2** 37 13N 2 20W
Filadelfia, *Bolivia* **156 C4** 11 20 S 68 46W
Filadélfia, *Brazil* **154 C2** 7 21 S 47 30W
Filadelfia, *Italy* **41 D9** 38 47N 16 17 E
Fil'akovo, *Czech.* **31 C12** 48 17N 19 50 E
Filer, *U.S.A.* **142 E6** 42 30N 114 35W
Filey, *U.K.* **16 C7** 54 13N 0 18W
Filfla, *Malta* **32 D1** 35 47N 14 24 E
Filiaşi, *Romania* **46 E4** 44 32N 23 31 E
Filiátes, *Greece* **44 E2** 39 38N 20 16 E
Filiatrá, *Greece* **45 G3** 37 9N 21 35 E
Filicudi, *Italy* **41 D7** 38 35N 14 33 E
Filim, *Oman* **87 B7** 20 37N 58 12 E
Filiouri →, *Greece* **44 C7** 41 15N 25 40 E
Filipów, *Poland* **47 A9** 54 11N 22 37 E
Filipstad, *Sweden* **13 G13** 59 43N 14 9 E
Filisur, *Switz.* **29 C9** 46 41N 9 40 E
Fillmore, *Canada* **131 D8** 49 50N 103 25W
Fillmore, *Calif., U.S.A.* **145 L8** 34 23N 118 58W
Fillmore, *Utah, U.S.A.* **143 G7** 38 58N 112 20W
Filottrano, *Italy* **39 E10** 43 28N 13 20 E
Filyos, *Turkey* **52 F5** 41 34N 32 4 E
Finale Ligure, *Italy* **38 D5** 44 10N 8 21 E
Finale nell' Emília, *Italy* **39 D8** 44 50N 11 18 E
Fiñana, *Spain* **35 H2** 37 10N 2 50W
Finch, *Canada* **137 A9** 45 11N 75 7W
Findhorn →, *U.K.* **18 D5** 57 38N 3 38W
Findlay, *U.S.A.* **141 C13** 41 5N 83 41W
Finger L., *Canada* **131 C10** 53 33N 93 30W
Fingõe, *Mozam.* **107 E3** 14 55 S 31 50 E
Finike, *Turkey* **88 E4** 36 21N 30 10 E

Gadap 199

Fouriesburg, *S. Africa* **104 D4** 28 38 S 28 14 E
Fourmies, *France* **23 B11** 50 1N 4 2 E
Fournás, *Greece* **45 E3** 39 3N 21 52 E
Foúrnoi, *Greece* **45 G8** 37 36N 26 32 E
Fours, *France* **23 F10** 46 50N 3 42 E
Fouta Djalon, *Guinea* **100 C2** 11 20N 12 10W
Foux, Cap-à-, *Haiti* **149 C5** 19 43N 73 27W
Foveaux Str., *N.Z.* **119 G3** 46 42 S 168 10 E
Fowey, *U.K.* **17 G3** 50 20N 4 39W
Fowler, *Calif., U.S.A.* **144 J7** 36 41N 119 41W
Fowler, *Colo., U.S.A.* **138 F3** 38 10N 104 0W
Fowler, *Ind., U.S.A.* **141 D9** 40 37N 87 19W
Fowler, *Kans., U.S.A.* **139 G4** 37 28N 100 7W
Fowler, *Mich., U.S.A.* **141 B12** 43 0N 84 45W
Fowlers B., *Australia* **113 F5** 31 59 S 132 34 E
Fowlerton, *U.S.A.* **139 L5** 28 26N 98 50W
Fowlerville, *U.S.A.* **141 B12** 42 40N 84 4W
Fox →, *Canada* **131 B10** 56 3N 93 18W
Fox Valley, *Canada* **131 C7** 50 30N 109 25W
Foxe Basin, *Canada* **127 B12** 66 0N 77 0W
Foxe Chan., *Canada* **127 B12** 65 0N 80 0W
Foxe Pen., *Canada* **127 B12** 65 0N 76 0W
Foxhol, *Neths.* **20 B9** 53 10N 6 43 E
Foxpark, *U.S.A.* **142 F10** 41 4N 106 6W
Foxton, *N.Z.* **118 G4** 40 29 S 175 18 E
Foyle, Lough, *U.K.* **19 A4** 55 6N 7 8W
Foynes, *Ireland* **19 D2** 52 37N 9 5W
Foz, *Spain* **36 B3** 43 33N 7 20W
Fóz do Cunene, *Angola* **103 F2** 17 15 S 11 48 E
Foz do Gregório, *Brazil* **156 B3** 6 47 S 70 44W
Foz do Iguaçu, *Brazil* **159 B5** 25 30 S 54 30W
Foz do Riosinho, *Brazil* **156 B3** 7 11 S 71 50W
Frackville, *U.S.A.* **137 F8** 40 46N 76 15W
Fraga, *Spain* **34 D5** 41 32N 0 21 E
Fraire, *Belgium* **21 H5** 50 16N 4 31 E
Frameries, *Belgium* **21 H3** 50 24N 3 54 E
Framingham, *U.S.A.* **137 D13** 42 18N 71 26W
Frampol, *Poland* **47 E9** 50 41N 22 40 E
Franca, *Brazil* **155 F2** 20 33 S 47 30W
Francavilla al Mare, *Italy* **39 F11** 42 25N 14 16 E
Francavilla Fontana, *Italy* **41 B10** 40 32N 17 35 E
France ■, *Europe* **11 F6** 47 0N 3 0 E
Frances, *Australia* **116 D4** 36 41 S 140 55 E
Frances →, *Canada* **130 A3** 60 16N 129 10W
Frances L., *Canada* **130 A3** 61 23N 129 30W
Francés Viejo, C., *Dom. Rep.* **149 C6** 19 40N 69 55W
Francesville, *U.S.A.* **141 D10** 40 59N 86 53W
Franceville, *Gabon* **102 C2** 1 40 S 13 32 E
Franche-Comté, *France* **23 F12** 46 50N 5 55 E
Franches Montagnes, *Switz.* **28 B4** 47 10N 7 0 E
Francisco de Orellana, *Ecuador* **152 D2** 0 28 S 76 58W
Francisco I. Madero, *Coahuila, Mexico* **146 B4** 25 48N 103 18W
Francisco I. Madero, *Durango, Mexico* **146 C4** 24 32N 104 22W
Francisco Sá, *Brazil* **155 E3** 16 28 S 43 30W
Francistown, *Botswana* **105 C4** 21 7 S 27 33 E
Francofonte, *Italy* **41 E7** 37 13N 14 50 E
François, *Canada* **129 C8** 47 35N 56 45W
François L., *Canada* **130 C3** 54 0N 125 30W
Francorchamps, *Belgium* **21 H7** 50 27N 5 57 E
Franeker, *Neths.* **20 B7** 53 12N 5 33 E
Frankado, *Djibouti* **95 E5** 12 30N 43 12 E
Frankenberg, *Germany* **26 D4** 51 3N 8 47 E
Frankenthal, *Germany* **27 F4** 49 32N 8 21 E
Frankenwald, *Germany* **27 E7** 50 18N 11 36 E
Frankford, *U.S.A.* **140 E5** 39 29N 91 19W
Frankfort, *S. Africa* **105 D4** 27 17 S 28 30 E
Frankfort, *Ind., U.S.A.* **141 D10** 40 20N 86 33W
Frankfort, *Kans., U.S.A.* **138 F6** 39 42N 96 26W
Frankfort, *Ky., U.S.A.* **141 F12** 38 12N 84 52W
Frankfort, *Mich., U.S.A.* **134 C2** 44 38N 86 14W
Frankfort, *Ohio, U.S.A.* **141 E13** 39 24N 83 11W
Frankfurt am Main, *Germany* **27 E4** 50 7N 8 40 E
Frankfurt an der Oder, *Germany* **26 C10** 52 20N 14 31 E
Fränkische Alb, *Germany* **27 F7** 49 20N 11 30 E
Fränkische Rezal →, *Germany* **27 F7** 49 11N 11 1 E
Fränkische Saale →, *Germany* **27 E5** 50 30N 9 42 E
Fränkische Schweiz, *Germany* **27 F7** 49 45N 11 10 E
Frankland →, *Australia* **113 G2** 35 0 S 116 48 E
Franklin, *Ill., U.S.A.* **140 E6** 39 37N 90 3W
Franklin, *Ind., U.S.A.* **141 E10** 39 29N 86 3W
Franklin, *Ky., U.S.A.* **135 G2** 36 40N 86 30W
Franklin, *La., U.S.A.* **139 L9** 29 45N 91 30W
Franklin, *Mass., U.S.A.* **137 D13** 42 4N 71 23W
Franklin, *N.H., U.S.A.* **137 C13** 43 28N 71 39W
Franklin, *Nebr., U.S.A.* **138 E5** 40 9N 98 55W
Franklin, *Ohio, U.S.A.* **141 E12** 39 34N 84 18W
Franklin, *Pa., U.S.A.* **136 E5** 41 22N 79 45W
Franklin, *Tenn., U.S.A.* **135 H2** 35 54N 86 53W
Franklin, *Va., U.S.A.* **135 G7** 36 40N 76 58W
Franklin, *W. Va., U.S.A.* **134 F6** 38 38N 79 21W
Franklin, L., *U.S.A.* **142 F6** 40 20N 115 26W
Franklin B., *Canada* **126 B7** 69 45N 126 0W
Franklin D. Roosevelt L., *U.S.A.* **142 B4** 48 30N 118 16W
Franklin I., *Antarctica* **7 D11** 76 10 S 168 30 E
Franklin Mts., *Canada* **126 B7** 65 0N 125 0W
Franklin Mts., *N.Z.* **119 E2** 44 55 S 167 45 E
Franklin Str., *Canada* **126 A10** 72 0N 96 0W
Franklinton, *U.S.A.* **139 K9** 30 53N 90 10W
Franklinville, *U.S.A.* **136 D6** 42 21N 78 28W
Franklyn Mt., *N.Z.* **119 C7** 42 4 S 172 42 E
Franks Peak, *U.S.A.* **142 E9** 43 50N 109 5W
Frankston, *Australia* **117 E6** 38 8 S 145 8 E
Frankton Junc., *N.Z.* **118 D4** 37 47 S 175 16 E
Fränsta, *Sweden* **14 B10** 62 30N 16 11 E
Frantsa Iosifa, Zemlya, *U.S.S.R.* **56 A6** 82 0N 55 0 E
Franz, *Canada* **128 C3** 48 25N 84 30W
Franz Josef Land = Frantsa Iosifa, Zemlya, *U.S.S.R.* **56 A6** 82 0N 55 0 E
Franzburg, *Germany* **26 A8** 54 9N 12 52 E
Frascati, *Italy* **40 A5** 41 48N 12 41 E
Fraser →, *B.C., Canada* **130 D4** 49 7N 123 11W
Fraser →, *Nfld., Canada* **129 A7** 56 39N 62 10W
Fraser, Mt., *Australia* **113 E2** 25 35 S 118 20 E
Fraser I., *Australia* **115 D5** 25 15 S 153 10 E
Fraser Lake, *Canada* **130 C4** 54 0N 124 50W
Fraserburg, *S. Africa* **104 E3** 31 55 S 21 30 E
Fraserburgh, *U.K.* **18 D6** 57 41N 2 3W
Fraserdale, *Canada* **128 C3** 49 55N 81 37W
Frasertown, *N.Z.* **118 E6** 38 58 S 177 28 E
Frashëri, *Albania* **44 D2** 40 23N 20 26 E
Frasne, *France* **23 F13** 46 50N 6 10 E
Frauenfeld, *Switz.* **29 A7** 47 34N 8 54 E
Fray Bentos, *Uruguay* **158 C4** 33 10 S 58 15W
Frazier Downs, *Australia* **112 C3** 18 48 S 121 42 E
Frechilla, *Spain* **36 C6** 42 8N 4 50W
Fredericia, *Denmark* **15 J3** 55 34N 9 45 E
Frederick, *Md., U.S.A.* **134 F7** 39 25N 77 23W
Frederick, *Okla., U.S.A.* **139 H5** 34 22N 99 0W
Frederick, *S. Dak., U.S.A.* **138 C5** 45 55N 98 29W
Frederick Sd., *U.S.A.* **130 B2** 57 10N 134 0W
Fredericksburg, *Tex., U.S.A.* **139 K5** 30 17N 98 55W
Fredericksburg, *Va., U.S.A.* **134 F7** 38 16N 77 29W
Frederickstown, *U.S.A.* **139 G9** 37 35N 90 15W
Frederico I. Madero, Presa, *Mexico* **146 B3** 28 7N 105 40W
Fredericton, *Canada* **129 C6** 45 57N 66 40W
Fredericton Junc., *Canada* **129 C6** 45 41N 66 40W
Frederikshåb, *Greenland* **6 C5** 62 0N 49 43W
Frederikshavn, *Denmark* **15 G4** 57 28N 10 31 E
Frederikssund, *Denmark* **15 J6** 55 50N 12 3 E
Frederiksted, *Virgin Is.* **149 C7** 17 43N 64 53W
Fredonia, *Ariz., U.S.A.* **143 H7** 36 59N 112 36W
Fredonia, *Kans., U.S.A.* **139 G7** 37 34N 95 50W
Fredonia, *N.Y., U.S.A.* **136 D5** 42 26N 79 20W
Fredrikstad, *Norway* **14 E4** 59 13N 10 57 E
Freeburg, *U.S.A.* **140 F5** 38 19N 91 56W
Freehold, *U.S.A.* **137 F10** 40 15N 74 18W
Freel Pk., *U.S.A.* **144 G7** 38 52N 119 53W
Freeland, *U.S.A.* **137 E9** 41 3N 75 48W
Freels, C., *Canada* **129 C9** 49 15N 53 30W
Freeman, *Calif., U.S.A.* **145 K9** 35 35N 117 53W
Freeman, *Mo., U.S.A.* **140 F2** 38 37N 94 30W
Freeman, *S. Dak., U.S.A.* **138 D6** 43 25N 97 20W
Freeport, *Bahamas* **148 A4** 26 30N 78 47W
Freeport, *Canada* **129 D6** 44 15N 66 20W
Freeport, *Ill., U.S.A.* **140 B7** 42 18N 89 40W
Freeport, *N.Y., U.S.A.* **137 F11** 40 39N 73 35W
Freeport, *Tex., U.S.A.* **139 L7** 28 55N 95 22W
Freetown, *S. Leone* **100 D2** 8 30N 13 17W
Frégate, L., *Canada* **128 B5** 53 15N 74 45W
Fregenal de la Sierra, *Spain* **37 G4** 38 10N 6 39W
Fregene, *Italy* **40 A5** 41 50N 12 12 E
Fréhel, C., *France* **22 D4** 48 40N 2 20W
Freiberg, *Germany* **26 E9** 50 55N 13 20 E
Freiburg = Fribourg, *Switz.* **28 C4** 46 49N 7 9 E
Freiburg, *Baden-W., Germany* **27 H3** 48 0N 7 52 E
Freiburg, *Niedersachsen, Germany* **26 B5** 53 49N 9 17 E
Freiburger Alpen, *Switz.* **28 C4** 46 37N 7 10 E
Freire, *Chile* **160 A2** 38 54 S 72 38W
Freirina, *Chile* **158 B1** 28 30 S 71 10W
Freising, *Germany* **27 G7** 48 24N 11 47 E
Freistadt, *Austria* **30 C7** 48 30N 14 30 E
Freital, *Germany* **26 E9** 51 0N 13 40 E
Fréjus, *France* **25 E10** 43 25N 6 44 E
Fremantle, *Australia* **113 F2** 32 7 S 115 47 E
Fremont, *Calif., U.S.A.* **144 H4** 37 32N 122 1W
Fremont, *Ind., U.S.A.* **141 C12** 41 44N 84 56W
Fremont, *Mich., U.S.A.* **134 D3** 43 29N 85 59W
Fremont, *Nebr., U.S.A.* **138 E6** 41 30N 96 30W
Fremont, *Ohio, U.S.A.* **141 C13** 41 20N 83 5W
Fremont →, *U.S.A.* **143 G8** 38 15N 110 20W
Fremont, L., *U.S.A.* **142 E9** 43 0N 109 50W
French Camp, *U.S.A.* **144 H5** 37 53N 121 16W
French Cr. →, *U.S.A.* **136 E5** 41 22N 79 50W
French Guiana ■, *S. Amer.* **153 C7** 4 0N 53 0W
French I., *Australia* **117 E6** 38 20 S 145 22 E
French Lick, *U.S.A.* **141 F10** 38 33N 86 37W
French Pass, *N.Z.* **119 A8** 40 55 S 173 55 E
French Polynesia □, *Pac. Oc.* **123 K13** 20 0 S 145 0W
French Terr. of Afars & Issas = Djibouti ■, *Africa* **90 E3** 12 0N 43 0 E
Frenchburg, *U.S.A.* **141 G13** 37 57N 83 38W
Frenchglen, *U.S.A.* **142 E4** 42 48N 119 0W
Frenchman →, *N. Amer.* **142 B10** 48 24N 107 5W
Frenchman Butte, *Canada* **131 C7** 53 35N 109 38W
Frenchman Creek →, *U.S.A.* **138 E4** 40 13N 100 50W
Frenda, *Algeria* **99 A5** 35 2N 1 1 E
Fresco →, *Brazil* **157 B7** 7 15 S 51 30W
Freshfield, C., *Antarctica* **7 C10** 68 25 S 151 10 E
Fresnay-sur-Sarthe, *France* **22 D7** 48 17N 0 1 E
Fresnillo, *Mexico* **146 C4** 23 10N 103 0W
Fresno, *U.S.A.* **144 J7** 36 47N 119 50W
Fresno Alhandiga, *Spain* **36 E5** 40 42N 5 37W
Fresno Res., *U.S.A.* **142 B9** 48 40N 110 0W
Freudenstadt, *Germany* **27 G4** 48 27N 8 25 E
Freux, *Belgium* **21 J6** 49 59N 5 27 E
Frévent, *France* **23 B9** 50 15N 2 17 E
Frew →, *Australia* **114 C2** 20 0 S 135 38 E
Frewena, *Australia* **114 B2** 19 25 S 135 25 E
Freycinet Pen., *Australia* **114 G4** 42 10 S 148 25 E
Freyming-Merlebach, *France* **23 C13** 49 8N 6 48 E
Freyung, *Germany* **27 G9** 48 48N 13 33 E
Fria, *Guinea* **100 C2** 10 27N 13 38W
Fria, C., *Namibia* **104 B1** 18 0 S 12 0 E
Friant, *U.S.A.* **144 J7** 36 59N 119 43W
Frías, *Argentina* **158 B2** 28 40 S 65 5W
Fribourg, *Switz.* **28 C4** 46 49N 7 9 E
Fribourg □, *Switz.* **28 C4** 46 40N 7 0 E
Frick, *Switz.* **28 A6** 47 31N 8 1 E
Friday Harbor, *U.S.A.* **144 B3** 48 32N 123 1W
Friedberg, *Bayern, Germany* **27 G6** 48 21N 10 59 E
Friedberg, *Hessen, Germany* **27 E4** 50 21N 8 46 E
Friedland, *Germany* **26 B9** 53 40N 13 33 E
Friedrichshafen, *Germany* **27 H5** 47 39N 9 29 E
Friedrichskoog, *Germany* **26 A4** 54 1N 8 52 E
Friedrichstadt, *Germany* **26 A5** 54 23N 9 6 E
Friendly Is. = Tonga ■, *Pac. Oc.* **121 P13** 19 50 S 174 30W
Friesach, *Austria* **30 E7** 46 57N 14 24 E
Friesack, *Germany* **26 C8** 52 43N 12 35 E
Friesche Wad, *Neths.* **20 B7** 53 22N 5 44 E
Friesland □, *Neths.* **20 B7** 53 5N 5 50 E
Friesoythe, *Germany* **26 B3** 53 1N 7 51 E
Frillesås, *Sweden* **15 G6** 57 20N 12 12 E
Frio →, *U.S.A.* **139 L5** 28 30N 98 10W
Friona, *U.S.A.* **139 H3** 34 40N 102 42W
Frisian Is., *Europe* **26 B2** 53 30N 6 0 E
Fristad, *Sweden* **15 G7** 57 50N 13 0 E
Fritch, *U.S.A.* **139 H4** 35 40N 101 35W
Fritsla, *Sweden* **15 G6** 57 33N 12 47 E
Fritzlar, *Germany* **26 D5** 51 8N 9 19 E
Friuli-Venezia Giulia □, *Italy* **39 C10** 46 0N 13 0 E
Frobisher B., *Canada* **127 B13** 62 30N 66 0W
Frobisher Bay = Iqaluit, *Canada* **127 B13** 63 44N 68 31W
Frobisher L., *Canada* **131 B7** 56 20N 108 15W
Frogmore, *Australia* **117 C8** 34 15 S 148 52 E
Frohavet, *Norway* **12 E10** 63 50N 9 35 E
Froid, *U.S.A.* **138 A2** 48 20N 104 29W
Froid-Chapelle, *Belgium* **21 H4** 50 9N 4 19 E
Frolovo, *U.S.S.R.* **53 B10** 49 45N 43 40 E
Fromberg, *U.S.A.* **142 D9** 45 25N 108 58W
Frombork, *Poland* **47 A6** 54 21N 19 41 E
Frome, *U.K.* **17 F5** 51 16N 2 17W
Frome, L., *Australia* **116 A3** 30 45 S 139 45 E
Frome Downs, *Australia* **116 A3** 31 13 S 139 45 E
Frómista, *Spain* **36 C6** 42 16N 4 25W
Front Range, *U.S.A.* **142 G11** 40 0N 105 40W
Front Royal, *U.S.A.* **134 F6** 38 55N 78 10W
Fronteira, *Portugal* **37 F3** 39 3N 7 39W
Fronteiras, *Brazil* **154 C3** 7 5 S 40 37W
Frontera, *Canary Is.* **33 G2** 27 47N 17 59W
Frontera, *Mexico* **147 D6** 18 30N 92 40W
Frontignan, *France* **24 E7** 43 27N 3 45 E
Frosinone, *Italy* **40 A6** 41 38N 13 20 E
Frosolone, *Italy* **41 A7** 41 34N 14 27 E
Frostburg, *U.S.A.* **134 F6** 39 43N 78 57W
Frostisen, *Norway* **12 B14** 68 14N 17 10 E
Frouard, *France* **23 D13** 48 47N 6 8 E
Frøya, *Norway* **12 E10** 63 43N 8 40 E
Fruges, *France* **23 B9** 50 30N 2 8 E
Frumoasa, *Romania* **46 C6** 46 28N 25 48 E
Frunze, *U.S.S.R.* **55 B7** 42 54N 74 46 E
Fruška Gora, *Yugoslavia* **42 B4** 45 7N 19 30 E
Frutal, *Brazil* **155 F2** 20 0 S 49 0W
Frutigen, *Switz.* **28 C5** 46 35N 7 38 E
Frýdek-Místek, *Czech.* **31 B11** 49 40N 18 20 E
Frýdlant, *Severočeský, Czech.* **30 A8** 50 56N 15 9 E
Frýdlant, *Severomoravsky, Czech.* **31 B11** 49 35N 18 20 E
Fryvaldov = Jeseník, *Czech.* **31 B10** 50 0N 17 8 E
Fthiótis □, *Greece* **45 F4** 38 50N 22 25 E
Fu Jiang →, *China* **68 C6** 30 0N 106 16 E
Fu Xian, *Liaoning, China* **67 E11** 39 38N 121 58 E
Fu Xian, *Shaanxi, China* **66 G5** 36 0N 109 20 E
Fu'an, *China* **69 D12** 27 11N 119 36 E
Fubian, *China* **68 B4** 31 17N 102 22 E
Fucécchio, *Italy* **38 E7** 43 44N 10 51 E
Fucheng, *China* **66 F9** 37 50N 116 10 E
Fuchou = Fuzhou, *China* **69 D12** 26 5N 119 16 E
Fuchū, *Hiroshima, Japan* **62 C5** 34 34N 133 14 E
Fūchū, *Tōkyō, Japan* **63 B11** 35 40N 139 29 E
Fuchuan, *China* **69 E8** 24 50N 111 5 E
Fuchun Jiang →, *China* **69 B13** 30 5N 120 5 E
Fúcino, Conca del, *Italy* **39 F10** 42 1N 13 31 E
Fuding, *China* **69 D13** 27 20N 120 12 E
Fuencaliente, *Canary Is.* **33 F2** 28 28N 17 50W
Fuencaliente, *Spain* **37 G6** 38 25N 4 18W
Fuencaliente, Pta., *Canary Is.* **33 F2** 28 27N 17 51W
Fuengirola, *Spain* **37 J6** 36 32N 4 41W
Fuente Alamo, *Albacete, Spain* **35 G3** 38 44N 1 24W
Fuente Álamo, *Murcia, Spain* **35 H3** 37 42N 1 6W
Fuente de Cantos, *Spain* **37 G4** 38 15N 6 18W
Fuente del Maestre, *Spain* **37 G4** 38 31N 6 28W
Fuente el Fresno, *Spain* **37 F7** 39 14N 3 46W
Fuente Ovejuna, *Spain* **37 G5** 38 15N 5 25W
Fuentes de Andalucía, *Spain* **37 H5** 37 28N 5 20W
Fuentes de Ebro, *Spain* **34 D4** 41 31N 0 38W
Fuentes de León, *Spain* **37 G4** 38 5N 6 32W
Fuentes de Oñoro, *Spain* **36 E4** 40 33N 6 52W
Fuentesaúco, *Spain* **36 D5** 41 15N 5 30W
Fuerte →, *Mexico* **146 B3** 25 50N 109 25W
Fuerte Olimpo, *Paraguay* **158 A4** 21 0 S 57 51W
Fuerteventura, *Canary Is.* **33 F6** 28 30N 14 0W
Fufeng, *China* **66 G5** 34 22N 108 0 E
Fughmah, *Yemen* **87 C5** 16 9N 49 26 E
Fugløysund, *Norway* **12 A16** 70 15N 20 20 E
Fugong, *China* **68 D2** 27 5N 98 47 E
Fugou, *China* **66 G8** 34 3N 114 25 E
Fugu, *China* **66 E6** 39 2N 111 3 E
Fuhai, *China* **64 B3** 47 2N 87 25 E
Fuḩaymī, *Iraq* **84 C4** 34 16N 42 10 E
Fuji, *Japan* **63 B10** 35 9N 138 39 E
Fuji-no-miya, *Japan* **63 B10** 35 10N 138 40 E
Fuji-San, *Japan* **63 B10** 35 22N 138 44 E
Fuji-yoshida, *Japan* **63 B10** 35 30N 138 46 E
Fujian □, *China* **69 E12** 26 0N 118 0 E
Fujieda, *Japan* **63 C10** 34 52N 138 16 E
Fujioka, *Japan* **63 A11** 36 15N 139 5 E
Fujisawa, *Japan* **63 B11** 35 22N 139 29 E
Fukaya, *Japan* **63 A11** 36 12N 139 12 E
Fukien = Fujian □, *China* **69 E12** 26 0N 118 0 E
Fukuchiyama, *Japan* **63 B7** 35 19N 135 9 E
Fukue-Shima, *Japan* **61 H4** 32 40N 128 45 E
Fukui, *Japan* **63 A8** 36 5N 136 10 E
Fukui □, *Japan* **63 B8** 36 0N 136 12 E
Fukuma, *Japan* **62 D2** 33 46N 130 28 E
Fukuoka, *Japan* **62 D2** 33 39N 130 21 E
Fukuoka □, *Japan* **62 D3** 33 30N 131 0 E
Fukuroi, *Japan* **63 C9** 34 45N 137 55 E
Fukushima, *Japan* **60 F10** 37 44N 140 28 E
Fukushima □, *Japan* **60 F10** 37 30N 140 15 E
Fukuyama, *Japan* **62 C5** 34 35N 133 20 E
Fulda, *Germany* **26 E5** 50 32N 9 41 E
Fulda →, *Germany* **26 D5** 51 27N 9 40 E
Fuling, *China* **68 C6** 29 40N 107 20 E
Fullerton, *Calif., U.S.A.* **145 M9** 33 52N 117 58W
Fullerton, *Nebr., U.S.A.* **138 E6** 41 25N 98 0W
Fulongquan, *China* **67 B13** 44 20N 124 42 E
Fulton, *Ill., U.S.A.* **140 C6** 41 52N 90 11W
Fulton, *Ind., U.S.A.* **141 D10** 40 57N 86 16W
Fulton, *Mo., U.S.A.* **140 F5** 38 50N 91 55W
Fulton, *N.Y., U.S.A.* **137 C8** 43 20N 76 22W
Fulton, *Tenn., U.S.A.* **135 G1** 36 31N 88 53W
Fuluälven, *Sweden* **14 C7** 61 18N 13 4 E
Fulufjället, *Sweden* **14 C6** 61 32N 12 41 E
Fumay, *France* **23 C11** 49 58N 4 40 E
Fumel, *France* **24 D4** 44 30N 0 58 E
Fumin, *China* **68 E4** 25 10N 102 20 E
Funabashi, *Japan* **63 B12** 35 45N 140 0 E
Funafuti, *Pac. Oc.* **111 B14** 8 30 S 179 0 E
Funchal, *Madeira* **33 D3** 32 38N 16 54W
Fundación, *Colombia* **152 A3** 10 31N 74 11W
Fundão, *Brazil* **155 E3** 19 55 S 40 24W
Fundão, *Portugal* **36 E3** 40 8N 7 30W
Fundy, B. of, *Canada* **129 D6** 45 0N 66 0W
Funing, *Hebei, China* **67 E10** 39 53N 119 12 E
Funing, *Jiangsu, China* **67 H10** 33 45N 119 50 E
Funing, *Yunnan, China* **68 F5** 23 35N 105 45 E
Funiu Shan, *China* **66 H7** 33 30N 112 20 E
Funsi, *Ghana* **100 C4** 10 21N 1 54W
Funtua, *Nigeria* **101 C6** 11 30N 7 18 E
Fuping, *Hebei, China* **66 E8** 38 48N 114 12 E
Fuping, *Shaanxi, China* **66 G5** 34 42N 109 10 E
Fuqing, *China* **69 E12** 25 41N 119 21 E
Fuquan, *China* **68 D6** 26 40N 107 27 E
Fur, *Denmark* **15 H3** 56 50N 9 0 E
Furano, *Japan* **60 C11** 43 21N 142 23 E
Furāt, Nahr al →, *Asia* **84 D5** 31 0N 47 25 E
Fürg, *Iran* **85 D7** 28 18N 55 13 E
Furkapass, *Switz.* **29 C7** 46 34N 8 35 E
Furmanov, *U.S.S.R.* **51 C12** 57 10N 41 9 E
Furmanovka, *U.S.S.R.* **55 A6** 44 17N 72 57 E
Furmanovo, *U.S.S.R.* **53 B13** 49 42N 49 25 E
Furnás, *Spain* **33 B8** 39 3N 1 32 E
Furnas, Reprêsa de, *Brazil* **155 F2** 20 50 S 45 30W
Furneaux Group, *Australia* **114 G4** 40 10 S 147 50 E
Furness, *U.K.* **16 C4** 54 14N 3 8W
Furqlus, *Syria* **91 A6** 34 36N 37 8 E
Fürstenau, *Germany* **26 C3** 52 32N 7 40 E
Fürstenberg, *Germany* **26 B9** 53 11N 13 9 E
Fürstenfeld, *Austria* **30 D9** 47 3N 16 3 E
Fürstenfeldbruck, *Germany* **27 G7** 48 10N 11 15 E
Fürstenwalde, *Germany* **26 C10** 52 20N 14 3 E
Fürth, *Germany* **27 F7** 49 29N 11 0 E
Furth im Wald, *Germany* **27 F8** 49 19N 12 51 E
Furtwangen, *Germany* **27 G4** 48 3N 8 14 E
Furukawa, *Japan* **60 E10** 38 34N 140 58 E
Furusund, *Sweden* **14 E12** 59 40N 18 55 E
Fury and Hecla Str., *Canada* **127 B11** 69 56N 84 0W
Fusagasuga, *Colombia* **152 C3** 4 21N 74 22W
Fuscaldo, *Italy* **41 C9** 39 25N 16 1 E
Fushan, *Shandong, China* **67 F11** 37 30N 121 15 E
Fushan, *Shanxi, China* **66 G6** 35 58N 111 51 E
Fushë Arrëzi, *Albania* **44 B2** 42 4N 20 2 E
Fushun, *Liaoning, China* **67 D12** 41 50N 123 56 E
Fushun, *Sichuan, China* **68 C5** 29 13N 104 52 E
Fusio, *Switz.* **29 D7** 46 27N 8 40 E
Fusong, *China* **67 C14** 42 20N 127 15 E
Füssen, *Germany* **27 H6** 47 35N 10 43 E
Fusui, *China* **68 F6** 22 40N 107 56 E
Futago-Yama, *Japan* **62 D3** 33 35N 131 36 E
Futrono, *Chile* **160 B2** 40 8 S 72 24W
Futuna, *Wall. & F. Is.* **122 J9** 14 25 S 178 20 E
Fuwa, *Egypt* **94 H7** 31 12N 30 33 E
Fuxin, *China* **67 C11** 42 5N 121 48 E
Fuyang, *Anhui, China* **66 H8** 33 0N 115 48 E
Fuyang, *Zhejiang, China* **69 B12** 30 5N 119 57 E
Fuyang He →, *China* **66 E9** 38 12N 117 0 E
Fuying Dao, *China* **69 D13** 26 34N 120 9 E
Fuyu, *China* **67 B13** 45 12N 124 43 E
Fuyuan, *China* **68 E5** 25 40N 104 16 E
Füzesgyarmat, *Hungary* **31 D14** 47 6N 21 14 E
Fuzhou, *China* **69 D12** 26 5N 119 16 E
Fylde, *U.K.* **16 D5** 53 50N 2 58W
Fyn, *Denmark* **15 J4** 55 20N 10 30 E
Fyne, L., *U.K.* **18 F3** 56 0N 5 20W
Fyns Amtskommune □, *Denmark* **15 J4** 55 15N 10 30 E
Fyresvatn, *Norway* **14 E2** 59 6N 8 10 E

G

Gaanda, *Nigeria* **101 C7** 10 10N 12 27 E
Gabarin, *Nigeria* **101 C7** 11 8N 10 27 E
Gabas →, *France* **24 E3** 43 46N 0 42W
Gabela, *Angola* **103 E2** 11 0 S 14 24 E
Gabès, *Tunisia* **96 B2** 33 53N 10 2 E
Gabès, G. de, *Tunisia* **96 B2** 34 0N 10 30 E
Gabgaba, W. →, *Egypt* **94 C3** 22 10N 33 5 E
Gabin, *Poland* **47 C6** 52 23N 19 41 E
Gabon ■, *Africa* **102 C2** 0 10 S 10 0 E
Gaborone, *Botswana* **104 C4** 24 45 S 25 57 E
Gabriels, *U.S.A.* **137 B10** 44 26N 74 12W
Gābrīk, *Iran* **85 E8** 25 44N 58 28 E
Gabro, *Ethiopia* **108 C2** 6 18N 43 16 E
Gabrovo, *Bulgaria* **43 E10** 42 52N 25 19 E
Gacé, *France* **22 D7** 48 49N 0 20 E
Gāch Sār, *Iran* **85 B6** 36 7N 51 19 E
Gachsārān, *Iran* **85 D6** 30 15N 50 45 E
Gacko, *Yugoslavia* **42 D3** 43 10N 18 33 E
Gadag, *India* **83 G2** 15 30N 75 45 E
Gadamai, *Sudan* **95 D4** 17 11N 36 10 E
Gadap, *Pakistan* **80 G2** 25 5N 67 28 E

200 Gadarwara

Gadarwara, India 81 H8 22 50N 78 50 E
Gadebusch, Germany 26 B7 53 41N 11 6 E
Gadein, Sudan 95 F2 8 10N 28 45 E
Gadhada, India 80 J4 22 0N 71 35 E
Gadmen, Switz. 29 C6 46 45N 8 16 E
Gádor, Sierra de, Spain 35 J2 36 57N 2 45W
Gadsden, Ala., U.S.A. 135 H3 34 1N 86 0W
Gadsden, Ariz., U.S.A. 143 K6 32 35N 114 47W
Gadwal, India 83 F3 16 10N 77 50 E
Gadyach, U.S.S.R. 50 F9 50 21N 34 0 E
Gadzi, C.A.R. 102 B3 4 47N 16 42 E
Găeşti, Romania 46 E6 44 48N 25 19 E
Gaeta, Italy 40 A6 41 12N 13 35 E
Gaeta, G. di, Italy 40 B6 41 0N 13 25 E
Gaffney, U.S.A. 135 H5 35 3N 81 40W
Gafsa, Tunisia 96 B1 34 24N 8 43 E
Gagarin, U.S.S.R. 50 D9 55 38N 35 0 E
Gagetown, Canada 129 C6 45 46N 66 10W
Gagino, U.S.S.R. 51 D14 55 15N 45 1 E
Gagliano del Capo, Italy 41 C11 39 50N 18 23 E
Gagnoa, Ivory C. 100 D3 6 56N 5 16W
Gagnon, Canada 129 B6 51 50N 68 5W
Gagnon, L., Canada 131 A6 62 3N 110 27W
Gagra, U.S.S.R. 53 E9 43 20N 40 10 E
Gahini, Rwanda 106 C3 1 50 S 30 30 E
Gahmar, India 81 G10 25 27N 83 49 E
Gai Xian, China 67 D12 40 22N 122 20 E
Gaibanda, Bangla. 78 C2 25 20N 89 36 E
Gaïdhouronísi, Greece 32 E7 34 53N 25 41 E
Gail, U.S.A. 139 J4 32 48N 101 25W
Gail →, Austria 30 E6 46 36N 13 53 E
Gaillac, France 24 E5 43 54N 1 54 E
Gaillon, France 22 C8 49 10N 1 20 E
Gaimán, Argentina 160 B3 43 10 S 65 25W
Gaines, U.S.A. 136 E7 41 46N 77 35W
Gainesville, Fla., U.S.A. 135 L4 29 38N 82 20W
Gainesville, Ga., U.S.A. 135 H4 34 17N 83 47W
Gainesville, Mo., U.S.A. 139 G8 36 35N 92 26W
Gainesville, Tex., U.S.A. 139 J6 33 40N 97 10W
Gainsborough, U.K. 16 D7 53 23N 0 46W
Gairdner, L., Australia 116 A2 31 30 S 136 0 E
Gairloch, L., U.K. 18 D3 57 43N 5 45W
Gais, Switz. 29 B8 47 22N 9 27 E
Gaj, Yugoslavia 42 B2 45 28N 17 3 E
Gakuch, Pakistan 81 A5 36 7N 73 45 E
Gal Laghet, Somali Rep. 108 D3 4 9N 47 10 E
Gal Oya Res., Sri Lanka 83 L5 7 5N 81 30 E
Gal Tardo, Somali Rep. 108 D3 3 34N 45 58 E
Galachipa, Bangla. 78 D3 22 8N 90 26 E
Galán, Cerro, Argentina 158 B2 25 55 S 66 52W
Galana →, Kenya 106 C5 3 9 S 40 8 E
Galangue, Angola 103 E3 13 42 S 16 9 E
Galangue, Serra, Angola 103 E3 14 18 S 15 52 E
Galanta, Czech. 31 C10 48 11N 17 45 E
Galápagos, Pac. Oc. 123 H18 0 0 91 0W
Galashiels, U.K. 18 F6 55 37N 2 50W
Galatás, Greece 45 G5 37 30N 23 26 E
Galatea, N.Z. 118 E5 38 24 S 176 45 E
Galaţi, Romania 46 D9 45 27N 28 2 E
Galaţi □, Romania 46 D8 45 45N 27 30 E
Galatia, Turkey 88 D5 39 30N 33 0 E
Galatina, Italy 41 B11 40 10N 18 10 E
Galátone, Italy 41 B11 40 8N 18 3 E
Galax, U.S.A. 135 G5 36 42N 80 57W
Galaxídhion, Greece 45 F4 38 22N 22 23 E
Galbraith, Australia 114 B3 16 25 S 141 30 E
Galcaio, Somali Rep. 90 F4 6 30N 47 30 E
Galdhøpiggen, Norway 14 C2 61 38N 8 18 E
Galeana, Mexico 146 C4 24 50N 100 4W
Galela, Indonesia 71 D7 1 50N 127 49 E
Galena, U.S.A. 140 B6 42 25N 90 26W
Galera, Spain 35 H2 37 45N 2 33W
Galera, Pta., Chile 160 A2 39 59 S 73 43W
Galera Point, Trin. & Tob. 149 D7 10 8N 61 0W
Galesburg, Ill., U.S.A. 140 D6 40 57N 90 23W
Galesburg, Mich., U.S.A. 141 B11 42 17N 85 26W
Galeton, U.S.A. 136 E7 41 43N 77 40W
Galgasc, Somali Rep. 108 D2 0 11N 41 38 E
Galheirão →, Brazil 155 D2 12 23 S 45 5W
Galheiros, Brazil 155 D2 13 18 S 46 25W
Gali, U.S.S.R. 53 E9 42 37N 41 46 E
Galicea Mare, Romania 46 E4 44 4N 23 19 E
Galich, U.S.S.R. 51 B13 58 23N 42 12 E
Galiche, Bulgaria 43 D8 43 34N 23 50 E
Galicia □, Spain 36 C3 42 43N 7 45W
Galien, U.S.A. 141 C10 41 48N 86 30W
Galilee = Hagalil, Israel 91 C4 32 53N 35 18 E
Galilee, L., Australia 114 C4 22 20 S 145 50 E
Galilee, Sea of = Yam Kinneret, Israel 91 C4 32 45N 35 35 E
Galinoporni, Cyprus 32 D13 35 31N 34 18 E
Galion, U.S.A. 136 F2 40 43N 82 48W
Galite, Is. de la, Tunisia 99 A6 37 30N 8 59 E
Galiuro Mts., U.S.A. 143 K8 32 40N 110 30W
Gallabat, Sudan 95 E4 12 58N 36 11 E
Gallardon, France 23 D8 48 32N 1 42 E
Gallarte, Italy 38 C5 45 40N 8 48 E
Gallatin, Mo., U.S.A. 140 E3 39 55N 93 58W
Gallatin, Tenn., U.S.A. 135 G2 36 24N 86 27W
Galle, Sri Lanka 83 L5 6 5N 80 10 E
Gállego →, Spain 34 D4 41 39N 0 51W
Gallegos →, Argentina 160 D3 51 35 S 69 0W
Galley Hd., Ireland 19 E3 51 32N 8 56W
Galliate, Italy 38 C5 45 27N 8 44 E
Gallinas, Pta., Colombia 152 A3 12 28N 71 40W
Gallipoli = Gelibolu, Turkey 44 D8 40 28N 26 43 E
Gallípoli, Italy 41 B11 40 8N 18 0 E
Gallipolis, U.S.A. 134 F4 38 50N 82 10W
Gällivare, Sweden 12 C16 67 9N 20 40 E
Gallo, C., Italy 40 D6 38 13N 13 19 E
Gallocanta, L. de, Spain 34 E3 40 58N 1 30W
Galloway, U.K. 18 G4 55 0N 4 25W
Galloway, Mull of, U.K. 18 G4 54 38N 4 50W
Gallup, U.S.A. 143 J9 35 30N 108 45W
Gallur, Spain 34 D3 41 52N 1 19W
Gallyaaral, U.S.S.R. 55 C3 40 2N 67 35 E
Galong, Australia 117 C8 34 37 S 148 34 E
Galt, Calif., U.S.A. 144 G5 38 15N 121 18W
Galt, Mo., U.S.A. 140 D3 40 8N 93 23W
Galtström, Sweden 14 B11 62 10N 17 30 E
Galtür, Austria 30 E3 46 58N 10 11 E
Galty Mts., Ireland 19 D3 52 22N 8 10W
Galtymore, Ireland 19 D3 52 22N 8 12W
Galva, U.S.A. 140 C6 41 10N 90 3W
Galvarino, Chile 160 A2 38 24 S 72 47W
Galve de Sorbe, Spain 34 D1 41 13N 3 10W
Galveston, Ind., U.S.A. 141 D10 40 35N 86 11W
Galveston, Tex., U.S.A. 139 L7 29 15N 94 48W
Galveston B., U.S.A. 139 L7 29 30N 94 50W
Gálvez, Argentina 158 C3 32 0 S 61 14W
Gálvez, Spain 37 F6 39 42N 4 16W
Galway, Ireland 19 C2 53 16N 9 4W
Galway □, Ireland 19 C2 53 16N 9 3W
Galway B., Ireland 19 C2 53 10N 9 20W
Gam, Indonesia 73 B4 0 27 S 130 36 E
Gam →, Vietnam 76 B5 21 55N 105 12 E
Gamagori, Japan 63 C9 34 50N 137 14 E
Gamari, L., Ethiopia 95 E5 11 32N 41 40 E
Gamawa, Nigeria 101 C7 12 10N 10 31 E
Gamba, Angola 103 E3 11 42 S 17 14 E
Gambaga, Ghana 101 C4 10 30N 0 28W
Gambat, Pakistan 80 F3 27 17N 68 26 E
Gambela, Ethiopia 95 F3 8 14N 34 38 E
Gambia ■, W. Afr. 100 C1 13 25N 16 0W
Gambia →, W. Afr. 100 C1 13 28N 16 34W
Gambier, C., Australia 112 B5 11 56 S 130 57 E
Gambier Is., Australia 116 C2 35 3 S 136 30 E
Gambo, C.A.R. 102 B4 4 39N 22 16 E
Gamboli, Pakistan 80 E3 29 53N 68 24 E
Gamboma, Congo 102 C3 1 55 S 15 52 E
Gamboula, C.A.R. 102 B3 4 8N 15 9 E
Gambuta, Indonesia 72 A2 0 30N 123 20 E
Gamerco, U.S.A. 143 J9 35 33N 108 56W
Gamlakarleby = Kokkola, Finland 12 E17 63 50N 23 8 E
Gammon →, Canada 131 C9 51 24N 95 44W
Gammouda, Tunisia 96 A1 35 3N 9 39 E
Gamoda-Saki, Japan 62 D6 33 50N 134 45 E
Gamu-Gofa □, Ethiopia 95 F4 5 40N 36 40 E
Gan, France 24 E3 43 12N 0 27W
Gan Gan, Argentina 160 B3 42 30 S 68 10W
Gan Goriama, Mts., Cameroon 101 D7 7 44N 12 45 E
Gan Jiang →, China 69 C11 29 15N 116 0 E
Ganado, Ariz., U.S.A. 143 J9 35 46N 109 41W
Ganado, Tex., U.S.A. 139 L6 29 4N 96 31W
Gananoque, Canada 128 D4 44 20N 76 10W
Ganaveh, Iran 85 D6 29 35N 50 35 E
Gand = Gent, Belgium 21 F3 51 2N 3 42 E
Ganda, Angola 103 E2 13 3 S 14 35 E
Gandak →, India 81 G11 25 39N 85 13 E
Gandava, Pakistan 79 C2 28 32N 67 32 E
Gander, Canada 129 C9 48 58N 54 35W
Gander L., Canada 129 C9 48 58N 54 35W
Ganderowe Falls, Zimbabwe 107 F2 17 20 S 29 10 E
Gandesa, Spain 34 D5 41 3N 0 26 E
Gandhi Sagar, India 80 G6 24 40N 75 40 E
Gandi, Nigeria 101 C6 12 55N 5 49 E
Gandía, Spain 35 G4 38 58N 0 9W
Gandino, Italy 38 C6 45 50N 9 52 E
Gando, Pta., Canary Is. 33 G4 27 55N 15 22W
Gandole, Nigeria 101 D7 8 28N 11 35 E
Gandu, Brazil 155 D4 13 45 S 39 30W
Ganedidalem = Gani, Indonesia 71 E7 0 48 S 128 14 E
Ganetti, Sudan 94 D3 18 0N 31 10 E
Ganga →, India 81 H14 23 20N 90 30 E
Ganga, Mouths of the, India 81 J14 21 30N 90 0 E
Ganganagar, India 80 E5 29 56N 73 56 E
Gangapur, India 80 F7 26 32N 76 49 E
Gangara, Niger 97 F1 14 35N 8 29 E
Gangaw, Burma 78 D5 22 5N 94 5 E
Gangawati, India 83 G3 15 30N 76 36 E
Ganges = Ganga →, India 81 H14 23 20N 90 30 E
Ganges, France 24 E7 43 56N 3 42 E
Gangoh, India 80 E7 29 46N 77 18 E
Gangtok, India 78 B2 27 20N 88 37 E
Gangu, China 66 G3 34 40N 105 15 E
Gangyao, China 67 B14 44 12N 126 37 E
Gani, Indonesia 71 E7 0 48 S 128 14 E
Ganj, India 81 F8 27 45N 78 57 E
Gannat, France 24 B7 46 7N 3 11 E
Gannett Pk., U.S.A. 142 E9 43 15N 109 38W
Gannvalley, U.S.A. 138 C5 44 3N 98 57W
Ganongga, Solomon Is. 121 M9 8 5 S 156 35 E
Ganquan, China 66 F5 36 20N 109 20 E
Gänserdorf, Austria 31 C9 48 20N 16 43 E
Ganshui, China 68 C6 28 40N 106 40 E
Gansu □, China 66 G3 36 0N 104 0 E
Ganta, Liberia 100 D3 7 15N 8 59W
Gantheaume, C., Australia 116 D2 36 4 S 137 32 E
Gantheaume B., Australia 113 E1 27 40 S 114 10 E
Gantsevichi, U.S.S.R. 50 E5 52 49N 26 30 E
Ganyem, Indonesia 71 E10 2 46 S 140 12 E
Ganyu, China 67 G10 34 50N 119 8 E
Ganyushkino, U.S.S.R. 53 C13 46 35N 49 20 E
Ganzhou, China 69 E10 25 51N 114 56 E
Gao, Mali 101 B5 18 0N 1 0 E
Gao Xian, China 68 C5 28 21N 104 32 E
Gao'an, China 69 C10 28 26N 115 17 E
Gaohe, China 69 F9 22 46N 112 57 E
Gaohebu, China 69 B11 30 43N 116 49 E
Gaokeng, China 69 D9 27 40N 113 58 E
Gaolan Dao, China 69 G9 21 55N 113 10 E
Gaoligong Shan, China 68 E2 24 45N 98 45 E
Gaomi, China 67 F10 36 20N 119 42 E
Gaoping, China 66 G7 35 45N 112 55 E
Gaotang, China 66 F9 36 50N 116 15 E
Gaoua, Burkina Faso 100 C4 10 20N 3 8W
Gaoual, Guinea 100 C2 11 45N 13 25W
Gaoxiong, Taiwan 69 F13 22 38N 120 18 E
Gaoyang, China 66 E8 38 40N 115 45 E
Gaoyou, China 69 A12 32 47N 119 26 E
Gaoyou Hu, China 67 H10 32 45N 119 20 E
Gaoyuan, China 67 F9 37 8N 117 58 E
Gaozhou, China 69 G8 21 58N 110 50 E
Gap, France 25 D10 44 33N 6 5 E
Gar, China 64 C2 32 10N 79 58 E
Garachico, Canary Is. 33 F3 28 22N 16 46W
Garachiné, Panama 148 E4 8 0N 78 12W
Garad, Somali Rep. 108 C3 6 57N 49 24 E
Garafia, Canary Is. 33 F2 28 48N 17 57W
Garajonay, Canary Is. 33 F2 28 7N 17 14W
Garanhuns, Brazil 154 C4 8 50 S 36 30W
Garawe, Liberia 100 E3 4 35N 8 0W
Garba Harre, Somali Rep. 108 D2 3 19N 42 13 E
Garba Tula, Kenya 106 B4 0 30N 38 32 E
Garbagududu, Ethiopia 108 C2 6 12N 43 50 E
Garber, U.S.A. 139 G6 36 30N 97 36W
Garberville, U.S.A. 142 F2 40 11N 123 50W
Garça, Brazil 155 F2 22 14 S 49 37W
Garças →, Mato Grosso, Brazil 157 D7 15 54 S 52 16W
Garças →, Pernambuco, Brazil 154 C4 8 43 S 39 41W
Garcias, Brazil 157 E7 20 34 S 52 13W
Gard, Somali Rep. 90 F4 9 30N 49 6 E
Gard □, France 25 D8 44 2N 4 10 E
Gard →, France 25 E8 43 51N 4 37 E
Garda, L. di, Italy 38 C7 45 40N 10 40 E
Gardanne, France 25 E9 43 27N 5 27 E
Garde L., Canada 131 A7 62 50N 106 13W
Gardelegen, Germany 26 C7 52 32N 11 21 E
Garden City, Kans., U.S.A. 139 G4 38 0N 100 45W
Garden City, Mo., U.S.A. 140 F2 38 34N 94 12W
Garden City, Tex., U.S.A. 139 K4 31 52N 101 28W
Garden Grove, U.S.A. 145 M9 33 47N 117 55W
Gardēz, Afghan. 79 B3 33 37N 69 9 E
Gardhíki, Greece 45 F3 38 50N 21 55 E
Gardiner, U.S.A. 142 D8 45 3N 110 42W
Gardiners I., U.S.A. 137 E12 41 4N 72 5W
Gardner, Ill., U.S.A. 141 C8 41 12N 88 17W
Gardner, Mass., U.S.A. 137 D13 42 35N 71 58W
Gardner Canal, Canada 130 C3 53 27N 128 8W
Gardnerville, U.S.A. 144 G7 38 59N 119 47W
Gardno, Jezioro, Poland 47 A4 54 40N 17 7 E
Gare Tigre, Fr. Guiana 153 C7 4 58N 53 9W
Garešnica, Yugoslavia 42 B1 45 36N 16 56 E
Garéssio, Italy 38 D5 44 12N 8 1 E
Garey, U.S.A. 145 L6 34 53N 120 19W
Garfield, U.S.A. 142 C5 47 3N 117 8W
Gargaliánoi, Greece 45 G3 37 4N 21 38 E
Gargan, Mt., France 24 C5 45 37N 1 39 E
Gargano, Mte., Italy 41 A8 41 43N 15 43 E
Gargouna, Mali 101 B5 15 56N 0 13 E
Garhshankar, India 80 D7 31 13N 76 11 E
Gari, U.S.S.R. 54 B8 59 26N 62 21 E
Garibaldi Prov. Park, Canada 130 D4 49 50N 122 40W
Garies, S. Africa 104 E2 30 32 S 17 59 E
Garigliano →, Italy 40 A6 41 13N 13 44 E
Garissa, Kenya 106 C4 0 25 S 39 40 E
Garissa □, Kenya 106 C5 0 20 S 40 0 E
Garkida, Nigeria 101 C7 10 27N 12 36 E
Garko, Nigeria 101 C6 11 45N 8 53 E
Garland, U.S.A. 142 F7 41 47N 112 10W
Garlasco, Italy 38 C5 45 11N 8 55 E
Garm, U.S.S.R. 55 D5 39 0N 70 20 E
Garmāb, Iran 85 C8 35 25N 56 45 E
Garmisch-Partenkirchen, Germany 27 H7 47 30N 11 5 E
Garmsār, Iran 85 C7 35 20N 52 25 E
Garner, U.S.A. 140 A3 43 4N 93 37W
Garnett, U.S.A. 138 F7 38 18N 95 12W
Garo Hills, India 81 G14 25 30N 90 30 E
Garoe, Somali Rep. 90 F4 8 25N 48 33 E
Garonne →, France 24 C3 45 2N 0 36W
Garonne, Canal Latéral à la →, France 24 D4 44 15N 0 18 E
Garoua, Cameroon 101 D7 9 19N 13 21 E
Garrel, Germany 26 C3 52 58N 7 59 E
Garrett, U.S.A. 141 C11 41 21N 85 8W
Garrigue, France 24 E7 43 40N 4 5 E
Garrison, Ky., U.S.A. 141 F13 38 36N 83 10W
Garrison, Mont., U.S.A. 142 C7 46 30N 112 56W
Garrison, N. Dak., U.S.A. 138 B4 47 39N 101 27W
Garrison, Tex., U.S.A. 139 K7 31 50N 94 28W
Garrison Res. = Sakakawea, L., U.S.A. 138 B4 47 30N 102 0W
Garrovillas, Spain 37 F4 39 40N 6 33W
Garrucha, Spain 35 H3 37 11N 1 49W
Garry →, U.K. 18 E5 56 47N 3 47W
Garry L., Canada 126 B9 65 58N 100 18W
Garsen, Kenya 106 C5 2 20 S 40 5 E
Garson L., Canada 131 B6 56 19N 110 2W
Gartempe →, France 24 B4 46 47N 0 49 E
Gartz, Germany 26 B10 53 12N 14 23 E
Garu, Ghana 101 C4 10 55N 0 11W
Garub, Namibia 104 D2 26 37 S 16 0 E
Garut, Indonesia 71 G12 7 14 S 107 53 E
Garvão, Portugal 37 H2 37 42N 8 21W
Garvie Mts., N.Z. 119 F3 45 30 S 168 50 E
Garwa = Garoua, Cameroon 101 D7 9 19N 13 21 E
Garwa, India 81 G10 24 11N 83 47 E
Garwolin, Poland 47 D8 51 55N 21 38 E
Gary, U.S.A. 141 C9 41 35N 87 20W
Garz, Germany 26 A9 54 17N 13 21 E
Garzê, China 68 B3 31 38N 100 1 E
Garzón, Colombia 152 C2 2 10N 75 40W
Gas City, U.S.A. 141 D11 40 29N 85 36W
Gas-San, Japan 60 E10 38 32N 140 1 E
Gasan Kuli, U.S.S.R. 56 F6 37 40N 54 20 E
Gascogne, France 24 E4 43 45N 0 20 E
Gascogne, G. de, Europe 34 B3 44 0N 2 0W
Gasconade, U.S.A. 140 F5 38 40N 91 33W
Gasconade →, U.S.A. 140 F5 38 41N 91 33W
Gascony = Gascogne, France 24 E4 43 45N 0 20 E
Gascoyne →, Australia 113 D1 24 52 S 113 37 E
Gascoyne Junc. T.O., Australia 113 E2 25 2 S 115 17 E
Gascueña, Spain 34 E2 40 18N 2 31W
Gash, Wadi →, Ethiopia 95 D4 16 48N 35 51 E
Gashaka, Nigeria 101 D7 7 20N 11 29 E
Gasherbrum, Pakistan 81 B7 35 40N 76 40 E
Gashua, Nigeria 101 C7 12 54N 11 0 E
Gaspé, Canada 129 C7 48 52N 64 30W
Gaspé, C. de, Canada 129 C7 48 48N 64 7W
Gaspé, Pén. de, Canada 129 C6 48 45N 65 40W
Gaspésie, Parc Prov. de la, Canada 129 C6 48 55N 65 50W
Gassaway, U.S.A. 134 F5 38 42N 80 43W
Gasselte, Neths. 20 C9 52 58N 6 48 E
Gasselternijveen, Neths. 20 C9 52 59N 6 51 E
Gássino Torinese, Italy 38 C4 45 8N 7 50 E
Gassol, Nigeria 101 D7 8 34N 10 25 E
Gastonia, U.S.A. 135 H5 35 17N 81 10W
Gastoúni, Greece 45 G3 37 51N 21 15 E
Gastoúri, Greece 44 E1 39 34N 19 54 E
Gastre, Argentina 160 B3 42 20 S 69 15W
Gata, C., Cyprus 32 E12 34 34N 33 2 E
Gata, C. de, Spain 35 J2 36 41N 2 13W
Gata, Sierra de, Spain 36 E4 40 20N 6 45W
Gataga →, Canada 130 B3 58 35N 126 59W
Gătaia, Romania 46 D2 45 26N 21 30 E
Gatchina, U.S.S.R. 50 B7 59 35N 30 9 E
Gates, U.S.A. 136 C7 43 9N 77 42W
Gateshead, U.K. 16 C6 54 57N 1 37W
Gatesville, U.S.A. 139 K6 31 29N 97 45W
Gaths, Zimbabwe 107 G3 20 2 S 30 32 E
Gatico, Chile 158 A1 22 29 S 70 20W
Gâtinais, France 23 D9 48 5N 2 40 E
Gâtine, Hauteurs de, France 24 B3 46 35N 0 45W
Gatineau →, Canada 128 C4 45 27N 75 42W
Gatineau, Parc de la, Canada 128 C4 45 40N 76 0W
Gattinara, Italy 38 C5 45 37N 8 22 E
Gatukai, Solomon Is. 121 M10 8 45 S 158 15 E
Gatun, L., Panama 148 E4 9 7N 79 56W
Gatyana, S. Africa 105 E4 32 16 S 28 31 E
Gau, Fiji 121 B2 18 2 S 179 18 E
Gaucín, Spain 37 J5 36 31N 5 19W
Gauer L., Canada 131 B9 57 0N 97 50W
Gauhati, India 81 F14 26 10N 91 45 E
Gauja →, U.S.S.R. 50 C4 57 10N 24 16 E
Gaula →, Norway 12 E11 63 21N 10 14 E
Gaurain-Ramecroix, Belgium 21 G3 50 36N 3 30 E
Gaurdak, U.S.S.R. 55 E3 37 50N 66 4 E
Gausta, Norway 14 E2 59 50N 8 37 E
Gausta, Mt., Norway 13 G10 59 48N 8 40 E
Gāv Koshī, Iran 85 D8 28 38N 57 12 E
Gavá, Spain 34 D7 41 18N 2 0 E
Gāvakān, Iran 85 D7 29 37N 53 10 E
Gavarnie, France 24 F3 42 44N 0 1W
Gavāter, Iran 85 E9 25 10N 61 31 E
Gāvbandī, Iran 85 E7 27 12N 53 4 E
Gavdhopoúla, Greece 32 E6 34 56N 24 0 E
Gávdhos, Greece 32 E6 34 50N 24 5 E
Gavere, Belgium 21 G3 50 55N 3 40 E
Gavião, Portugal 37 F3 39 28N 7 56W
Gaviota, U.S.A. 145 L6 34 29N 120 13W
Gävleborgs län □, Sweden 14 C10 61 30N 16 15 E
Gavorrano, Italy 38 F7 42 55N 10 49 E
Gavray, France 22 D5 48 55N 1 20W
Gavrilov Yam, U.S.S.R. 51 C11 57 18N 39 49 E
Gávrion, Greece 45 G6 37 54N 24 44 E
Gawachab, Namibia 104 D2 27 4 S 17 55 E
Gawai, Burma 78 B6 27 56N 97 30 E
Gawilgarh Hills, India 82 D3 21 15N 76 45 E
Gawler, Australia 116 C3 34 30 S 138 42 E
Gaxun Nur, China 64 B5 42 22N 100 30 E
Gay, U.S.S.R. 54 F6 51 27N 58 27 E
Gaya, India 81 G11 24 47N 85 4 E
Gaya, Niger 101 C5 11 52N 3 28 E
Gaya, Nigeria 101 C6 11 57N 9 0 E
Gaylord, U.S.A. 134 C3 45 1N 84 41W
Gayndah, Australia 115 D5 25 35 S 151 32 E
Gayny, U.S.S.R. 54 A4 60 18N 54 19 E
Gaysin, U.S.S.R. 52 B3 48 57N 28 25 E
Gayvoron, U.S.S.R. 52 B3 48 22N 29 52 E
Gaza, Egypt 91 D3 31 30N 34 28 E
Gaza □, Mozam. 105 C5 23 10 S 32 45 E
Gaza Strip, Egypt 91 D3 31 29N 34 25 E
Gazaoua, Niger 97 F1 13 32N 7 55 E
Gāzbor, Iran 85 D8 28 5N 58 51 E
Gazelle Pen., Papua N. G. 120 C7 4 40 S 152 0 E
Gazi, Zaïre 106 B1 1 3N 24 30 E
Gaziantep, Turkey 88 E7 37 6N 37 23 E
Gaziantep □, Turkey 88 E7 37 0N 37 0 E
Gazipaşa, Turkey 88 E5 36 16N 32 18 E
Gazli, U.S.S.R. 56 E7 40 14N 63 24 E
Gbarnga, Liberia 100 D3 7 19N 9 13W
Gbekebo, Nigeria 101 D5 6 20N 4 56 E
Gboko, Nigeria 101 D6 7 17N 9 4 E
Gbongan, Nigeria 101 D5 7 28N 4 20 E
Gcuwa, S. Africa 105 E4 32 20 S 28 11 E
Gdańsk, Poland 47 A5 54 22N 18 40 E
Gdańsk □, Poland 47 A5 54 10N 18 30 E
Gdańska, Zatoka, Poland 47 A6 54 30N 19 20 E
Gdov, U.S.S.R. 50 B5 58 48N 27 55 E
Gdynia, Poland 47 A5 54 35N 18 33 E
Gebe, Indonesia 71 D7 0 5N 129 25 E
Gebeit Mine, Sudan 94 C4 21 3N 36 29 E
Gebel Mûsa, Egypt 94 J8 28 32N 33 59 E
Gebze, Turkey 88 C3 40 47N 29 25 E
Gecha, Ethiopia 95 F4 7 30N 35 18 E
Gedaref, Sudan 95 E4 14 2N 35 28 E
Gede, Tanjung, Indonesia 70 F3 6 46 S 105 12 E
Gedinne, Belgium 21 J5 49 59N 4 56 E
Gediz, Turkey 88 D3 39 1N 29 24 E
Gediz →, Turkey 88 D2 38 35N 26 48 E
Gedo, Ethiopia 95 F4 9 2N 37 25 E
Gèdre, France 24 F4 42 47N 0 2 E
Gedser, Denmark 15 K5 54 35N 11 55 E
Gedser Odde, Denmark 15 K5 54 30N 11 58 E
Geegully Cr. →, Australia 112 C3 18 32 S 123 41 E
Geel, Belgium 21 F5 51 10N 4 59 E
Geelong, Australia 116 E6 38 10 S 144 22 E
Geelvink Chan., Australia 113 E1 28 30 S 114 0 E
Geer →, Belgium 21 G7 50 51N 5 42 E
Geesthacht, Germany 26 B6 53 25N 10 20 E
Geffen, Neths. 20 E6 51 44N 5 28 E
Geidam, Nigeria 101 C7 12 57N 11 57 E
Geikie →, Canada 131 B8 57 45N 103 52W
Geili, Sudan 95 D3 16 1N 32 37 E
Geilo, Norway 14 D2 60 32N 8 14 E
Geinica, Czech. 31 C13 48 51N 20 55 E
Geisingen, Germany 27 H4 47 55N 8 37 E
Geislingen, Germany 27 G5 48 37N 9 51 E
Geita, Tanzania 106 C3 2 48 S 32 12 E
Geita □, Tanzania 106 C3 2 50 S 32 10 E
Gejiu, China 68 F4 23 20N 103 10 E
Gel →, Sudan 95 F2 7 5N 29 10 E

Givors 201

Gel River, Sudan 95 F2 7 5N 29 10 E
Gela, Italy 41 E7 37 6N 14 18 E
Gela, G. di, Italy 41 F7 37 0N 14 8 E
Geladi, Ethiopia 90 F4 6 59N 46 30 E
Gelderland □, Neths. 20 D8 52 5N 6 10 E
Geldermalsen, Neths. 20 E6 51 53N 5 17 E
Geldern, Germany 26 D2 51 32N 6 18 E
Geldrop, Neths. 21 F7 51 25N 5 32 E
Geleen, Neths. 21 G7 50 57N 5 49 E
Gelehun, S. Leone 100 D2 8 20N 11 40W
Gelendost, Turkey 88 D4 38 7N 31 1 E
Gelendzhik, U.S.S.R. 52 D8 44 33N 38 10 E
Gelib, Somali Rep. 108 D2 0 29N 42 46 E
Gelibolu, Turkey 44 D8 40 28N 26 43 E
Gelidonya Burnu, Turkey 88 E4 36 12N 30 24 E
Gelnhausen, Germany 27 E5 50 12N 9 12 E
Gelsenkirchen, Germany 26 D3 51 30N 7 5 E
Gelting, Germany 26 A5 54 43N 9 53 E
Gemas, Malaysia 77 L4 2 37N 102 36 E
Gembloux, Belgium 21 G5 50 34N 4 43 E
Gemena, Zaïre 102 B3 3 13N 19 48 E
Gemerek, Turkey 88 D7 39 15N 36 10 E
Gemert, Neths. 21 E7 51 33N 5 41 E
Gemlik, Turkey 88 C3 40 26N 29 9 E
Gemona del Friuli, Italy 39 B10 46 16N 13 7 E
Gemsa, Egypt 94 B3 27 39N 33 35 E
Gemünden, Germany 27 E5 50 3N 9 43 E
Genale, Ethiopia 95 F4 6 0N 39 30 E
Genale, Somali Rep. 108 D2 1 48N 44 42 E
Genappe, Belgium 21 G5 50 37N 4 30 E
Genç, Turkey 89 D9 38 44N 40 34 E
Gençay, France 24 B4 46 23N 0 23 E
Gendringen, Neths. 20 E8 51 52N 6 21 E
Gendt, Neths. 20 E7 51 53N 5 59 E
Geneina, Gebel, Egypt 94 J8 29 2N 33 55 E
Genemuiden, Neths. 20 C8 52 38N 6 2 E
General Acha, Argentina 158 D3 37 20 S 64 38W
General Alvear, Buenos Aires, Argentina 158 D4 36 0 S 60 0W
General Alvear, Mendoza, Argentina 158 D2 35 0 S 67 40W
General Artigas, Paraguay 158 B4 26 52 S 56 16W
General Belgrano, Argentina 158 D4 36 35 S 58 47W
General Cabrera, Argentina 158 C3 32 53 S 63 52W
General Carrera, L., Chile 160 C2 46 35 S 72 0W
General Cepeda, Mexico 146 B4 25 23N 101 27W
General Conesa, Argentina 160 B4 40 6 S 64 25W
General Guido, Argentina 158 D4 36 40 S 57 50W
General Juan Madariaga, Argentina 158 D4 37 0 S 57 0W
General La Madrid, Argentina 158 D3 37 17 S 61 20W
General Lorenzo Vintter, Argentina 160 B4 40 45 S 64 26W
General MacArthur, Phil. 71 B7 11 18N 125 28 E
General Martin Miguel de Güemes, Argentina 158 A3 24 50 S 65 0W
General Paz, Argentina 158 B4 27 45 S 57 36W
General Pico, Argentina 158 D3 35 45 S 63 50W
General Pinedo, Argentina 158 B3 27 15 S 61 20W
General Pinto, Argentina 158 C3 34 45 S 61 50W
General Sampaio, Brazil 154 B4 4 2 S 39 29W
General Santos, Phil. 71 C7 6 5N 125 14 E
General Toshevo, Bulgaria 43 D13 43 42N 28 6 E
General Trevino, Mexico 147 B5 26 14N 99 29W
General Trías, Mexico 146 B3 28 21N 106 22W
General Viamonte, Argentina 158 D3 35 1 S 61 3W
General Villegas, Argentina 158 D3 35 5 S 63 0W
General Vintter, L., Argentina 160 B2 43 55 S 71 40W
Generoso, Mte., Switz. 29 E8 45 56N 9 2 E
Genesee, Idaho, U.S.A. 142 C5 46 31N 116 59W
Genesee, Pa., U.S.A. 136 E7 41 59N 77 54W
Genesee →, U.S.A. 136 C7 43 16N 77 36W
Geneseo, Ill., U.S.A. 140 C6 41 25N 90 10W
Geneseo, Kans., U.S.A. 138 F5 38 32N 98 8W
Geneseo, N.Y., U.S.A. 136 D7 42 49N 77 49W
Geneva = Genève, Switz. 28 D2 46 12N 6 9 E
Geneva, Ala., U.S.A. 135 K3 31 2N 85 52W
Geneva, Ill., U.S.A. 141 C8 41 53N 88 18W
Geneva, Ind., U.S.A. 141 D12 40 36N 84 57W
Geneva, N.Y., U.S.A. 136 D8 42 53N 77 0W
Geneva, Nebr., U.S.A. 138 E6 40 35N 97 35W
Geneva, Ohio, U.S.A. 136 E4 41 49N 80 58W
Geneva, L. = Léman, Lac, Switz. 28 D3 46 26N 6 30 E
Geneva, L., U.S.A. 141 B8 42 38N 88 30W
Genève, Switz. 28 D2 46 12N 6 9 E
Genève □, Switz. 28 D2 46 10N 6 10 E
Geng, Afghan. 79 C1 31 22N 61 28 E
Gengenbach, Germany 27 G4 48 25N 8 2 E
Gengma, China 68 F2 23 32N 99 20 E
Genichesk, U.S.S.R. 52 C6 46 12N 34 50 E
Genil →, Spain 37 H5 37 42N 5 19W
Génissiat, Barr. de, France 25 B9 46 1N 5 48 E
Genk, Belgium 21 G7 50 58N 5 32 E
Genkai-Nada, Japan 62 D2 34 0N 130 0 E
Genlis, France 23 E12 47 11N 5 12 E
Gennargentu, Mti. del, Italy 40 C2 40 0N 9 10 E
Gennep, Neths. 21 E7 51 41N 5 59 E
Gennes, France 22 E6 47 20N 0 17W
Genoa = Génova, Italy 38 D5 44 24N 8 56 E
Genoa, Australia 117 D8 37 29 S 149 35 E
Genoa, Ill., U.S.A. 141 B8 42 6N 88 42W
Genoa, N.Y., U.S.A. 137 D8 42 40N 76 32W
Genoa, Nebr., U.S.A. 138 E6 41 31N 97 44W
Genoa, Nev., U.S.A. 144 F7 39 2N 119 50W
Genoa →, Argentina 160 B2 44 55 S 70 5W
Genoa City, U.S.A. 141 B8 42 30N 88 20W
Génova, Italy 38 D5 44 24N 8 56 E
Génova, G. di, Italy 38 E6 44 0N 9 0 E
Gent, Belgium 21 F3 51 2N 3 42 E
Gentbrugge, Belgium 21 F3 51 3N 3 47 E
Genthin, Germany 26 C8 52 24N 12 10 E
Gentio do Ouro, Brazil 154 D3 11 25 S 42 30W
Geographe B., Australia 113 F2 33 30 S 115 15 E
Geographe Chan., Australia 113 D1 24 30 S 113 0 E
Geokchay, U.S.S.R. 53 F12 40 42N 47 43 E
Georga, Zemlya, U.S.S.R. 56 A5 80 30N 49 0 E
George, S. Africa 104 E3 33 58 S 22 29 E
George →, Canada 129 A6 58 49N 66 10W
George, L., N.S.W., Australia 117 C8 35 10 S 149 25 E
George, L., S. Austral., Australia 116 D4 37 25 S 140 0 E
George, L., W. Austral., Australia 112 D3 22 45 S 123 40 E
George, L., Uganda 106 B3 0 5N 30 10 E
George, L., Fla., U.S.A. 135 L5 29 15N 81 35W
George, L., N.Y., U.S.A. 137 C11 43 30N 73 30W
George Gill Ra., Australia 112 D5 24 22 S 131 45 E
George River = Port Nouveau-Québec, Canada 127 C13 58 30N 65 59W
George Sound, N.Z. 119 E2 44 52 S 167 25 E
George Town, Bahamas 148 B4 23 33N 75 47W
George Town, Malaysia 77 K3 5 25N 100 15 E
George V Land, Antarctica 7 C10 69 0 S 148 0 E
George VI Sound, Antarctica 7 D17 71 0 S 68 0W
George West, U.S.A. 139 L5 28 18N 98 5W
Georgetown, Australia 114 B3 18 17 S 143 33 E
Georgetown, Ont., Canada 128 D4 43 40N 79 56W
Georgetown, P.E.I., Canada 129 C7 46 13N 62 24W
Georgetown, Cayman Is. 148 C3 19 20N 81 24W
Georgetown, Gambia 100 C2 13 30N 14 47W
Georgetown, Guyana 153 B6 6 50N 58 12W
Georgetown, Calif., U.S.A. 144 G6 38 54N 120 50W
Georgetown, Colo., U.S.A. 142 G11 39 46N 105 49W
Georgetown, Ill., U.S.A. 141 E9 39 59N 87 38W
Georgetown, Ky., U.S.A. 134 F3 38 13N 84 33W
Georgetown, Ohio, U.S.A. 141 F13 38 50N 83 50W
Georgetown, S.C., U.S.A. 135 J6 33 22N 79 15W
Georgetown, Tex., U.S.A. 139 K6 30 40N 97 45W
Georgi Dimitrov, Bulgaria 43 E8 42 15N 23 54 E
Georgi Dimitrov, Yazovir, Bulgaria 43 E10 42 37N 25 18 E
Georgia □, U.S.A. 135 K5 32 0N 82 0W
Georgia, Str. of, Canada 130 D4 49 25N 124 0W
Georgian B., Canada 128 C3 45 15N 81 0W
Georgian S.S.R. □, U.S.S.R. 53 F10 42 0N 43 0 E
Georgievsk, U.S.S.R. 53 D10 44 12N 43 28 E
Georgina →, Australia 114 C2 23 30 S 139 47 E
Georgina Downs, Australia 114 C2 21 10 S 137 40 E
Georgiu-Dezh, U.S.S.R. 51 F11 51 3N 39 30 E
Georgiyevka, U.S.S.R. 55 B7 43 3N 74 43 E
Gera, Germany 26 E8 50 53N 12 11 E
Geraardsbergen, Belgium 21 G3 50 45N 3 53 E
Geral, Serra, Bahia, Brazil 155 D3 14 0 S 41 0W
Geral, Serra, Goiás, Brazil 154 D2 11 15 S 46 30W
Geral, Serra, Sta. Catarina, Brazil 159 B6 26 25 S 50 0W
Geral de Goiás, Serra, Brazil 155 D2 12 0 S 46 0W
Geral do Paranã Serra, Brazil 155 E2 15 0 S 47 30W
Gerald, U.S.A. 140 F5 38 24N 91 21W
Geraldine, N.Z. 119 E6 44 5 S 171 15 E
Geraldine, U.S.A. 142 C8 47 36N 110 18W
Geraldton, Australia 113 E1 28 48 S 114 32 E
Geraldton, Canada 128 C2 49 44N 86 59W
Geranium, Australia 116 C4 35 23 S 140 11 E
Gérardmer, France 23 D13 48 3N 6 50 E
Gercüş, Turkey 89 E9 37 34N 41 23 E
Gerede, Turkey 52 F5 40 45N 32 10 E
Gereshk, Afghan. 79 C2 31 47N 64 35 E
Gérgal, Spain 35 H2 37 7N 2 31W
Gerik, Malaysia 77 K3 5 50N 101 15 E
Gering, U.S.A. 138 E3 41 51N 103 30W
Gerlach, U.S.A. 142 F4 40 43N 119 27W
Gerlachovka, Czech. 31 B13 49 11N 20 7 E
Gerlogubi, Ethiopia 90 F4 6 53N 45 3 E
German Planina, Yugoslavia 42 E7 42 20N 22 0 E
Germansen Landing, Canada 130 B4 55 43N 124 40W
Germantown, U.S.A. 141 E12 39 38N 84 22W
Germany ■, Europe 26 E6 51 0N 10 0 E
Germersheim, Germany 27 F4 49 13N 8 20 E
Germiston, S. Africa 105 D4 26 15 S 28 10 E
Gernsheim, Germany 27 F4 49 44N 8 29 E
Gero, Japan 63 B9 35 48N 137 14 E
Gerolstein, Germany 27 E2 50 12N 6 40 E
Gerolzhofen, Germany 27 F6 49 54N 10 21 E
Gerona, Spain 34 D7 41 58N 2 46 E
Gerona □, Spain 34 C7 42 11N 2 30 E
Gérouville, Belgium 21 J6 49 37N 5 26 E
Gerrard, Canada 130 C5 50 30N 117 17W
Gerringong, Australia 117 C9 34 46 S 150 47 E
Gers □, France 24 E4 43 35N 0 30 E
Gers →, France 24 D4 44 9N 0 39 E
Gersfeld, Germany 26 E5 50 27N 9 57 E
Gersoppa Falls, India 83 G2 14 12N 74 46 E
Gerze, Turkey 88 C6 41 48N 35 12 E
Geseke, Germany 26 D4 51 38N 8 29 E
Geser, Indonesia 71 E8 3 50 S 130 54 E
Gesso →, Italy 38 D4 44 24N 7 33 E
Gestro, Wabi →, Ethiopia 95 G5 4 12N 42 2 E
Gesves, Belgium 21 H6 50 24N 5 4 E
Getafe, Spain 36 E7 40 18N 3 44W
Gethsémani, Canada 129 B7 50 13N 60 40W
Gettysburg, Pa., U.S.A. 134 F7 39 47N 77 18W
Gettysburg, S. Dak., U.S.A. 138 C5 45 3N 99 56W
Getz Ice Shelf, Antarctica 7 D14 75 0 S 130 0W
Geul →, Neths. 21 G7 50 53N 5 43 E
Geureudong, Mt., Indonesia 74 B1 4 13N 96 42 E
Geurie, Australia 117 B8 32 22 S 148 50 E
Gevaş, Turkey 89 D10 38 15N 43 6 E
Gévaudan, France 24 D7 44 40N 3 40 E
Gevgelija, Yugoslavia 42 F7 41 9N 22 30 E
Gévora →, Spain 37 G4 38 53N 6 57W
Gex, France 25 B10 46 21N 6 3 E
Geyikli, Turkey 44 E8 39 50N 26 12 E
Geyser, U.S.A. 142 C8 47 17N 110 30W
Geyserville, U.S.A. 144 G4 38 42N 122 54W
Geysir, Iceland 12 D3 64 19N 20 18W
Geyve, Turkey 88 C4 40 30N 30 18 E
Ghâbat el Arab = Wang Kai, Sudan 95 F2 9 3N 29 23 E
Ghaghara →, India 81 G11 25 45N 84 40 E
Ghalat, Oman 87 B7 21 6N 58 53 E
Ghalla, Wadi el →, Sudan 95 E2 10 25N 27 32 E
Ghallamane, Mauritania 98 D3 23 15N 10 0W
Ghana ■, W. Afr. 101 D4 8 0N 1 0W
Ghansor, India 81 H9 22 39N 80 1 E
Ghanzi, Botswana 104 C3 21 50 S 21 34 E
Ghanzi □, Botswana 104 C3 21 50 S 21 45 E
Gharb el Istiwa'iya □, Sudan 95 G3 5 0N 30 0 E
Gharbîya, Es Sahrâ el, Egypt 94 B2 27 40N 26 30 E
Ghard Abû Muharik, Egypt 94 B3 26 50N 30 0 E
Ghardaïa, Algeria 99 B5 32 20N 3 37 E
Ghârib, G., Egypt 94 J8 28 6N 32 54 E
Ghârib, Râs, Egypt 94 J8 28 6N 33 18 E
Gharm, W. →, Oman 87 C7 19 57N 57 38 E
Gharyān, Libya 96 B2 32 10N 13 0 E
Gharyān □, Libya 96 B2 30 35N 12 0 E
Ghat, Libya 96 D2 24 59N 10 11 E
Ghatal, India 81 H12 22 40N 87 46 E
Ghatampur, India 81 F9 26 8N 80 13 E
Ghatere, Solomon Is. 121 L10 7 55 S 159 0 E
Ghatprabha →, India 83 F2 16 15N 75 20 E
Ghaţţī, Si. Arabia 84 D3 31 16N 37 31 E
Ghawdex = Gozo, Malta 32 C1 36 3N 14 13 E
Ghayl, Si. Arabia 86 B4 21 40N 46 20 E
Ghayl Bā Wazīr, Yemen 87 D5 14 47N 49 22 E
Ghazal, Bahr el →, Chad 97 F3 13 0N 15 47 E
Ghazâl, Bahr el →, Sudan 95 F3 9 31N 30 25 E
Ghazaouet, Algeria 99 A4 35 8N 1 50W
Ghaziabad, India 80 E7 28 42N 77 26 E
Ghazipur, India 81 G10 25 38N 83 35 E
Ghaznī, Afghan. 79 B3 33 30N 68 28 E
Ghaznī □, Afghan. 79 B3 32 10N 68 20 E
Ghedi, Italy 38 C7 45 24N 10 16 E
Ghelari, Romania 46 D3 45 38N 22 45 E
Ghèlinsor, Somali Rep. 90 F4 6 28N 46 39 E
Ghent = Gent, Belgium 21 F3 51 2N 3 42 E
Gheorghe Gheorghiu-Dej, Romania 46 C7 46 17N 26 47 E
Gheorgheni, Romania 46 C6 46 43N 25 41 E
Ghergani, Romania 46 E6 44 37N 25 37 E
Gherla, Romania 46 B4 47 2N 23 57 E
Ghilarza, Italy 40 B1 40 8N 8 50 E
Ghisonaccia, France 25 F13 42 1N 9 26 E
Ghisoni, France 25 F13 42 7N 9 12 E
Ghizao, Afghan. 80 C1 33 20N 65 44 E
Ghizar →, Pakistan 81 A5 36 15N 73 43 E
Ghod →, India 82 E2 18 30N 74 35 E
Ghogha, India 80 J5 21 40N 72 20 E
Ghot Ogrein, Egypt 94 A2 31 10N 25 20 E
Ghotaru, India 80 F4 27 20N 70 1 E
Ghotki, Pakistan 80 E3 28 5N 69 21 E
Ghowr □, Afghan. 79 B2 34 0N 64 20 E
Ghudaf, W. al →, Iraq 84 C4 32 56N 43 30 E
Ghudāmis, Libya 96 B1 30 11N 9 29 E
Ghughri, India 81 H9 22 39N 80 41 E
Ghugus, India 82 E4 19 58N 79 12 E
Ghulam Mohammad Barrage, Pakistan 80 G3 25 30N 68 20 E
Ghurayrah, Si. Arabia 86 C3 18 37N 42 41 E
Ghūriān, Afghan. 79 B1 34 17N 61 25 E
Gia Dinh, Vietnam 77 G6 10 49N 106 42 E
Gia Lai = Pleiku, Vietnam 76 F7 13 57N 108 0 E
Gia Nghia, Vietnam 77 G6 11 58N 107 42 E
Gia Ngoc, Vietnam 76 E7 14 50N 108 58 E
Gia Vuc, Vietnam 76 E7 14 42N 108 34 E
Giamama, Somali Rep. 108 D2 0 4N 42 44 E
Gian, Phil. 71 C7 5 45N 125 20 E
Giannutri, Italy 38 F8 42 16N 11 5 E
Giant Forest, U.S.A. 144 J8 36 36N 118 43W
Giant Mts. = Krkonoše, Czech. 30 A8 50 50N 15 35 E
Giants Causeway, U.K. 19 A5 55 15N 6 30W
Giarabub = Al Jaghbūb, Libya 96 C4 29 42N 24 38 E
Giarre, Italy 41 E8 37 44N 15 10 E
Giaveno, Italy 38 C4 45 3N 7 20 E
Gibara, Cuba 148 B4 21 9N 76 11W
Gibb River, Australia 112 C4 16 26 S 126 26 E
Gibbon, U.S.A. 138 E5 40 49N 98 45W
Gibe →, Ethiopia 95 F4 7 20N 37 36 E
Gibellina, Italy 40 E6 37 48N 13 0 E
Gibraléon, Spain 37 H4 37 23N 6 58W
Gibraltar, Europe 37 J5 36 7N 5 22W
Gibraltar, Str. of, Medit. S. 37 K5 35 55N 5 40W
Gibson City, U.S.A. 141 D8 40 28N 88 22W
Gibson Desert, Australia 112 D4 24 0 S 126 0 E
Gibsonburg, U.S.A. 141 C13 41 23N 83 19W
Gibsons, Canada 130 D4 49 24N 123 32W
Gibsonville, U.S.A. 144 F6 39 46N 120 54W
Giddalur, India 83 G4 15 20N 78 57 E
Giddings, U.S.A. 139 K6 30 11N 96 58W
Gidole, Ethiopia 95 F4 5 40N 37 25 E
Gien, France 23 E9 47 40N 2 36 E
Giessen, Germany 26 E4 50 34N 8 40 E
Gieten, Neths. 20 B9 53 1N 6 46 E
Gīfān, Iran 85 B8 37 54N 57 28 E
Gifatin, Geziret, Egypt 94 B3 27 10N 33 50 E
Gifford Creek, Australia 112 D2 24 3 S 116 16 E
Gifhorn, Germany 26 C6 52 29N 10 32 E
Gifu, Japan 63 B8 35 30N 136 45 E
Gifu □, Japan 63 B9 35 40N 137 0 E
Gigant, U.S.S.R. 53 C9 46 28N 41 20 E
Giganta, Sa. de la, Mexico 146 B2 25 30N 111 30W
Gigen, Bulgaria 43 D9 43 40N 24 28 E
Gigha, U.K. 18 F3 55 42N 5 45W
Giglei, Somali Rep. 108 C3 5 25N 45 20 E
Giglio, Italy 38 F7 42 20N 10 52 E
Gignac, France 24 E7 43 39N 3 32 E
Gigüela →, Spain 35 F1 39 8N 3 44W
Gijón, Spain 36 B5 43 32N 5 42W
Gil I., Canada 130 C3 53 12N 129 15W
Gila →, U.S.A. 143 K6 32 43N 114 33W
Gila Bend, U.S.A. 143 K7 33 0N 112 46W
Gila Bend Mts., U.S.A. 143 K7 33 15N 113 0W
Gīlān □, Iran 85 B6 37 0N 50 0 E
Gilău, Romania 46 C4 46 45N 23 23 E
Gilbert →, Australia 114 B3 16 35 S 141 15 E
Gilbert Is., Kiribati 122 G9 1 0N 176 0 E
Gilbert Plains, Canada 131 C8 51 9N 100 28W
Gilbert River, Australia 114 B3 18 9 S 142 52 E
Gilberton, Australia 114 B3 19 16 S 143 35 E
Gilbués, Brazil 154 C2 9 50 S 45 21W
Gilf el Kebîr, Hadabat el, Egypt 94 C2 23 50N 25 50 E
Gilford I., Canada 130 C3 50 40N 126 30W
Gilgandra, Australia 117 A8 31 43 S 148 39 E
Gilgil, Kenya 106 C4 0 30 S 36 20 E
Gilgit, India 81 B6 35 50N 74 15 E
Gilgit →, Pakistan 81 B6 35 44N 74 37 E
Gilgunnia, Australia 117 B7 32 26 S 146 2 E
Giljeva Planina, Yugoslavia 42 D5 43 9N 20 0 E
Gillam, Canada 131 B10 56 20N 94 40W
Gilleleje, Denmark 15 H6 56 8N 12 19 E
Gillen, L., Australia 113 E3 26 11 S 124 38 E
Gilles, L., Australia 116 B2 32 50 S 136 45 E
Gillespie, U.S.A. 140 E7 39 7N 89 49W
Gillespies Pt., N.Z. 119 D4 43 24 S 169 49 E
Gillette, U.S.A. 138 C2 44 20N 105 30W
Gilliat, Australia 114 C3 20 40 S 141 28 E
Gillingham, U.K. 17 F8 51 23N 0 34 E
Gilly, Belgium 21 H4 50 25N 4 29 E
Gilman, U.S.A. 141 D9 40 46N 88 0W
Gilman City, U.S.A. 140 D3 40 8N 93 53W
Gilmer, U.S.A. 139 J7 32 44N 94 55W
Gilmore, Australia 117 C8 35 20 S 148 12 E
Gilmore, L., Australia 113 F3 32 29 S 121 37 E
Gilmour, Canada 128 D4 44 48N 77 37W
Gilo →, Ethiopia 95 F3 8 10N 33 15 E
Gilort →, Romania 46 E4 44 38N 23 32 E
Gilroy, U.S.A. 144 H5 37 1N 121 37W
Giluwe, Mt., Papua N. G. 120 D2 6 8 S 143 52 E
Gilze, Neths. 21 E5 51 32N 4 57 E
Gimbi, Ethiopia 95 F4 9 3N 35 42 E
Gimigliano, Italy 41 D9 38 58N 16 32 E
Gimli, Canada 131 C9 50 40N 97 0W
Gimone →, France 24 E5 44 0N 1 6 E
Gimont, France 24 E4 43 38N 0 52 E
Gin →, Sri Lanka 83 L5 6 5N 80 7 E
Gin Gin, Australia 115 D5 25 0 S 151 58 E
Ginâh, Egypt 94 B3 25 21N 30 30 E
Gindie, Australia 114 C4 23 44 S 148 8 E
Gingin, Australia 113 F2 31 22 S 115 54 E
Gîngiova, Romania 46 F4 43 54N 23 50 E
Ginir, Ethiopia 90 F3 7 6N 40 40 E
Ginosa, Italy 41 B9 40 35N 16 45 E
Ginzo de Limia, Spain 36 C3 42 3N 7 47W
Giohar, Somali Rep. 90 G4 2 48N 45 30 E
Gióia, G. di, Italy 41 D8 38 30N 15 50 E
Gióia del Colle, Italy 41 B9 40 49N 16 55 E
Gióia Tauro, Italy 41 D8 38 26N 15 53 E
Gioiosa Iónica, Italy 41 D9 38 20N 16 19 E
Gióna, Óros, Greece 45 F4 38 38N 22 14 E
Giovi, Passo dei, Italy 38 D5 44 33N 8 57 E
Giovinazzo, Italy 41 A9 41 10N 16 40 E
Gir Hills, India 80 J4 21 0N 71 0 E
Girab, India 80 F4 26 2N 70 38 E
Girâfi, W. →, Egypt 91 F3 29 58N 34 39 E
Giraltovce, Czech. 31 B14 49 7N 21 32 E
Girard, Ill., U.S.A. 140 E7 39 27N 89 48W
Girard, Kans., U.S.A. 139 G7 37 30N 94 50W
Girard, Ohio, U.S.A. 136 E4 41 10N 80 42W
Girard, Pa., U.S.A. 136 D4 42 1N 80 21W
Girardot, Colombia 152 C3 4 18N 74 48W
Girdle Ness, U.K. 18 D6 57 9N 2 2W
Giresun, Turkey 89 C8 40 55N 38 30 E
Giresun □, Turkey 89 C8 40 30N 38 30 E
Girga, Egypt 94 B3 26 17N 31 55 E
Girgir, C., Papua N. G. 120 B3 3 50 S 144 35 E
Giridih, India 81 G12 24 10N 86 21 E
Girifalco, Italy 41 D9 38 49N 16 25 E
Girilambone, Australia 117 A7 31 16 S 146 57 E
Giro, Nigeria 101 C5 11 7N 4 42 E
Giromagny, France 23 E13 47 45N 6 50 E
Gironde □, France 24 D3 44 45N 0 30W
Gironde →, France 24 C2 45 32N 1 7W
Gironella, Spain 34 C6 42 2N 1 53 E
Giru, Australia 114 B4 19 30 S 147 5 E
Girvan, U.K. 18 F4 55 15N 4 50W
Gisborne, N.Z. 118 E7 38 39 S 178 5 E
Gisenyi, Rwanda 106 C2 1 41 S 29 15 E
Gisors, France 23 C8 49 15N 1 47 E
Gissarskiy, Khrebet, U.S.S.R. 55 D4 39 0N 69 0 E
Gistel, Belgium 21 F1 51 9N 2 59 E
Giswil, Switz. 28 C6 46 50N 8 11 E
Gitega, Burundi 106 C2 3 26 S 29 56 E
Gits, Belgium 21 G2 51 0N 3 6 E
Giuba →, Somali Rep. 90 G3 1 30N 42 35 E
Giubiasco, Switz. 29 D8 46 11N 9 1 E
Giugliano in Campania, Italy 41 B7 40 55N 14 12 E
Giulianova, Italy 39 F10 42 45N 13 58 E
Giurgeni, Romania 46 E8 44 45N 27 48 E
Giurgiu, Romania 46 F6 43 52N 25 57 E
Giurgiu □, Romania 46 E7 44 20N 26 0 E
Give, Denmark 15 J3 55 51N 9 13 E
Givet, France 23 B11 50 8N 4 49 E
Givors, France 25 C8 45 35N 4 45 E

202 Givry

Givry, Belgium 21 H4 50 23N 4 2 E
Givry, France 23 F11 46 41N 4 46 E
Giyon, Ethiopia 95 F4 8 33N 38 1 E
Giza = El Gîza, Egypt 94 J7 30 0N 31 10 E
Gizhduvan, U.S.S.R. 55 C2 40 6N 64 41 E
Gizhiga, U.S.S.R. 57 C17 62 3N 160 30 E
Gizhiginskaya Guba, U.S.S.R. 57 C16 61 0N 158 0 E
Gizo, Solomon Is. 121 M9 8 7 S 156 50 E
Giżycko, Poland 47 A8 54 2N 21 48 E
Gizzeria, Italy 41 D9 38 57N 16 10 E
Gjegjan, Albania 44 C2 41 58N 20 3 E
Gjerstad, Norway 14 F3 58 54N 9 0 E
Gjirokastra, Albania 44 D2 40 7N 20 10 E
Gjoa Haven, Canada 126 B10 68 20N 96 8W
Gjøl, Denmark 15 G3 57 4N 9 42 E
Gjøvik, Norway 14 D4 60 47N 10 43 E
Gjuhës, Kep-i-, Albania 44 D1 40 28N 19 15 E
Glace Bay, Canada 129 C8 46 11N 59 58W
Glacier B., U.S.A. 130 B1 58 30N 136 10W
Glacier Nat. Park, Canada 130 C5 51 15N 117 30W
Glacier Park, U.S.A. 142 B7 48 30N 113 18W
Glacier Peak, U.S.A. 142 B3 48 7N 121 7W
Gladewater, U.S.A. 139 J7 32 30N 94 58W
Gladstone, Queens., Australia 114 C5 23 52 S 151 16 E
Gladstone, S. Austral., Australia 116 B3 33 15 S 138 22 E
Gladstone, W. Austral., Australia 113 E1 25 57 S 114 17 E
Gladstone, Canada 131 C9 50 13N 98 57W
Gladstone, Mich., U.S.A. 134 C2 45 52N 87 1W
Gladstone, Mo., U.S.A. 140 E2 39 13N 94 35W
Gladwin, U.S.A. 134 D3 43 59N 84 29W
Gladys L., Canada 130 B2 59 50N 133 0W
Głagów Małapolski, Poland 31 A14 50 10N 21 56 E
Gláma, Iceland 12 D2 65 48N 23 0W
Glåma →, Norway 14 E4 59 12N 10 57 E
Glamis, U.S.A. 145 N11 33 0N 115 4W
Glamoč, Yugoslavia 39 D13 44 3N 16 51 E
Glan, Sweden 15 F10 58 37N 16 0 E
Glanerbrug, Neths. 20 D9 52 13N 6 58 E
Glarner Alpen, Switz. 29 C8 46 50N 9 0 E
Glärnisch, Switz. 29 C8 47 0N 9 0 E
Glarus, Switz. 29 B8 47 3N 9 4 E
Glarus □, Switz. 29 C8 47 0N 9 5 E
Glasco, Kans., U.S.A. 138 F6 39 25N 97 50W
Glasco, N.Y., U.S.A. 137 D11 42 3N 73 57W
Glasgow, U.K. 18 F4 55 52N 4 14W
Glasgow, Ky., U.S.A. 134 G3 37 2N 85 55W
Glasgow, Mo., U.S.A. 140 E4 39 14N 92 51W
Glasgow, Mont., U.S.A. 142 B10 48 12N 106 35W
Glastonbury, U.K. 17 F5 51 9N 2 42W
Glastonbury, U.S.A. 137 E12 41 42N 72 27W
Glatt →, Switz. 29 B7 47 28N 8 32 E
Glattfelden, Switz. 29 A7 47 33N 8 30 E
Glauchau, Germany 26 E8 50 50N 12 33 E
Glazov, U.S.S.R. 51 B18 58 9N 52 40 E
Gleisdorf, Austria 30 D8 47 6N 15 44 E
Gleiwitz = Gliwice, Poland 47 E5 50 22N 18 41 E
Glen, U.S.A. 137 B13 44 7N 71 10W
Glen Affric, U.K. 18 D4 57 15N 5 0W
Glen Afton, N.Z. 118 D4 37 37 S 175 4 E
Glen Canyon Dam, U.S.A. 143 H8 37 0N 111 25W
Glen Canyon Nat. Recreation Area, U.S.A. 143 H8 37 30N 111 0W
Glen Coe, U.K. 18 E4 56 40N 5 0W
Glen Cove, U.S.A. 137 F11 40 51N 73 37W
Glen Garry, U.K. 18 D3 57 3N 5 7W
Glen Gowrie, Australia 116 A5 31 4 S 143 10 E
Glen Innes, Australia 115 D5 29 44 S 151 44 E
Glen Lyon, U.S.A. 137 E8 41 10N 76 7W
Glen Massey, N.Z. 118 D4 37 38 S 175 2 E
Glen Mor, U.K. 18 D4 57 12N 4 37W
Glen Moriston, U.K. 18 D4 57 10N 4 58W
Glen Orchy, U.K. 18 E4 56 27N 4 52W
Glen Spean, U.K. 18 E4 56 53N 4 40W
Glen Ullin, U.S.A. 138 B4 46 48N 101 46W
Glen Valley, Australia 117 D7 36 54 S 147 28 E
Glénan, Is. de, France 22 E3 47 42N 4 0W
Glenariff, Australia 117 A7 30 50 S 146 33 E
Glenavy, N.Z. 119 E6 44 54 S 171 7 E
Glenburgh, Australia 113 E2 25 26 S 116 6 E
Glenburn, Australia 117 D6 37 27 S 145 26 E
Glencoe, Canada 136 D3 42 45N 81 43W
Glencoe, S. Africa 105 D5 28 11 S 30 11 E
Glencoe, U.S.A. 138 C7 44 45N 94 10W
Glendale, Ariz., U.S.A. 143 K7 33 40N 112 8W
Glendale, Calif., U.S.A. 145 L8 34 7N 118 18W
Glendale, Oreg., U.S.A. 142 E2 42 44N 123 29W
Glendale, Zimbabwe 107 F3 17 22 S 31 5 E
Glendive, U.S.A. 138 B2 47 7N 104 40W
Glendo, U.S.A. 138 D2 42 30N 105 0W
Glenelg, Australia 116 C3 34 58 S 138 31 E
Glenelg →, Australia 116 E4 38 4 S 140 59 E
Glenflorrie, Australia 112 D2 22 55 S 115 59 E
Glengarriff, Ireland 19 E2 51 45N 9 33W
Glengyle, Australia 114 C2 24 48 S 139 37 E
Glenham, N.Z. 119 G3 46 26 S 168 52 E
Glenhope, N.Z. 119 B7 41 40 S 172 39 E
Glenmary, Mt., N.Z. 119 D4 43 55 S 169 55 E
Glenmora, U.S.A. 139 K8 31 1N 92 34W
Glenmorgan, Australia 115 D4 27 14 S 149 42 E
Glenn, U.S.A. 144 F4 39 31N 122 1W
Glenns Ferry, U.S.A. 142 E6 43 0N 115 15W
Glenorchy, S. Austral., Australia 116 A3 31 55 S 139 46 E
Glenorchy, Tas., Australia 114 G4 42 49 S 147 18 E
Glenorchy, Vic., Australia 116 D5 36 55 S 142 41 E
Glenorchy, N.Z. 119 E3 44 51 S 168 24 E
Glenore, Australia 114 B3 17 50 S 141 12 E
Glenormiston, Australia 114 C2 22 55 S 138 50 E
Glenreagh, Australia 115 E5 30 2 S 153 1 E
Glenrock, U.S.A. 142 E11 42 53N 105 55W
Glenrothes, U.K. 18 E5 56 12N 3 11W
Glenrowan, Australia 117 D7 36 29 S 146 13 E
Glenroy, Australia 116 D4 37 13 S 140 48 E
Glens Falls, U.S.A. 137 C11 43 20N 73 40W
Glenties, Ireland 19 B3 54 48N 8 18W
Glenville, U.S.A. 134 F5 38 56N 80 50W
Glenwood, Alta., Canada 130 D6 49 21N 113 31W
Glenwood, Nfld., Canada 129 C9 49 0N 54 58W
Glenwood, Ark., U.S.A. 139 H8 34 20N 93 30W
Glenwood, Hawaii, U.S.A. 132 J17 19 29N 155 10W
Glenwood, Iowa, U.S.A. 138 E7 41 7N 95 41W
Glenwood, Minn., U.S.A. 138 C7 45 38N 95 21W
Glenwood, Wash., U.S.A. 144 D5 46 1N 121 17W
Glenwood Springs, U.S.A. 142 G10 39 39N 107 21W
Gletsch, Switz. 29 C6 46 34N 8 22 E
Glina, Yugoslavia 39 C13 45 20N 16 6 E
Glinojeck, Poland 47 C7 52 49N 20 21 E
Glittertind, Norway 14 C2 61 40N 8 32 E
Gliwice, Poland 47 E5 50 22N 18 41 E
Globe, U.S.A. 143 K8 33 25N 110 53W
Glodeanu Siliştea, Romania 46 E7 44 50N 26 48 E
Glödnitz, Austria 30 E7 46 53N 14 7 E
Glodyany, U.S.S.R. 46 B8 47 45N 27 31 E
Gloggnitz, Austria 30 D8 47 41N 15 56 E
Głogów, Poland 47 D3 51 37N 16 5 E
Głogowek, Poland 47 E4 50 21N 17 53 E
Glorieuses, Is., Ind. Oc. 105 A8 11 30 S 47 20 E
Glossop, U.K. 16 D6 53 27N 1 56W
Gloucester, Australia 117 B9 32 0 S 151 59 E
Gloucester, U.K. 17 F5 51 52N 2 15W
Gloucester, U.S.A. 137 D14 42 38N 70 39W
Gloucester, C., Papua N. G. 120 C5 5 26 S 148 21 E
Gloucester I., Australia 114 C4 20 0 S 148 30 E
Gloucestershire □, U.K. 17 F5 51 44N 2 10W
Gloversville, U.S.A. 137 C10 43 5N 74 18W
Glovertown, Canada 129 C9 48 40N 54 3W
Główno, Poland 47 D6 51 59N 19 42 E
Głubczyce, Poland 31 A10 50 13N 17 52 E
Glubokiy, U.S.S.R. 53 B9 48 35N 40 25 E
Glubokoye, U.S.S.R. 50 D5 55 10N 27 45 E
Glŭbovo, Bulgaria 43 E10 42 8N 25 55 E
Głuchołazy, Poland 47 E4 50 19N 17 24 E
Glücksburg, Germany 26 A5 54 48N 9 34 E
Glückstadt, Germany 26 B5 53 46N 9 28 E
Gluepot, Australia 116 B4 33 45 S 140 0 E
Glukhov, U.S.S.R. 50 F8 51 40N 33 58 E
Glussk, U.S.S.R. 50 E6 52 53N 28 41 E
Glyngøre, Denmark 15 H2 56 46N 8 52 E
Gmünd, Kärnten, Austria 30 E6 46 54N 13 31 E
Gmünd, Niederösterreich, Austria 30 C8 48 45N 15 0 E
Gmunden, Austria 30 D6 47 55N 13 48 E
Gnali, Gabon 102 C2 2 34 S 11 18 E
Gnarp, Sweden 14 B11 62 3N 17 16 E
Gnesta, Sweden 14 E11 59 3N 17 17 E
Gniew, Poland 47 B5 53 50N 18 50 E
Gniewkowo, Poland 47 C5 52 54N 18 25 E
Gniezno, Poland 47 C4 52 30N 17 35 E
Gnjilane, Yugoslavia 42 E6 42 28N 21 29 E
Gnoien, Germany 26 B8 53 58N 12 41 E
Gnowangerup, Australia 113 F2 33 58 S 117 59 E
Go Cong, Vietnam 77 G6 10 22N 106 40 E
Gō-no-ura, Japan 62 D1 33 44N 129 40 E
Go Quao, Vietnam 77 H5 9 43N 105 17 E
Goa, India 83 G1 15 33N 73 59 E
Goa □, India 83 G1 15 33N 73 59 E
Goalen Hd., Australia 117 D9 36 33 S 150 4 E
Goalpara, India 78 B3 26 10N 90 40 E
Goalundo Ghat, Bangla. 81 H13 23 50N 89 47 E
Goaso, Ghana 100 D4 6 48N 2 30W
Goat Fell, U.K. 18 F3 55 37N 5 11W
Goba, Ethiopia 90 F2 7 1N 39 59 E
Goba, Mozam. 105 D5 26 15 S 32 13 E
Gobabis, Namibia 104 C2 22 30 S 19 0 E
Gobernador Gregores, Argentina 160 C2 48 46 S 70 15W
Gobi, Asia 66 C6 44 0N 111 0 E
Gobichettipalayam, India 83 J3 11 31N 77 21 E
Gobles, U.S.A. 141 B11 42 22N 85 53W
Gobō, Japan 63 D7 33 53N 135 10 E
Gobo, Sudan 95 F3 5 40N 31 10 E
Goch, Germany 26 D2 51 40N 6 9 E
Gochas, Namibia 104 C2 24 59 S 18 55 E
Godavari →, India 82 F6 16 25N 82 18 E
Godavari Point, India 82 F6 17 0N 82 20 E
Godbout, Canada 129 C6 49 20N 67 38W
Godda, India 81 G12 24 50N 87 13 E
Goddua, Libya 96 C2 26 26N 14 19 E
Godech, Bulgaria 42 D8 43 1N 23 4 E
Godegård, Sweden 15 F9 58 43N 15 8 E
Goderich, Canada 128 D3 43 45N 81 41W
Goderville, France 22 C7 49 38N 0 22 E
Godfrey, U.S.A. 140 F6 38 57N 90 11W
Godhavn, Greenland 6 C5 69 15N 53 38W
Godhra, India 80 H5 22 49N 73 40 E
Godinlave, Somali Rep. 108 C3 5 54N 46 38 E
Gödöllö, Hungary 31 D12 47 38N 19 25 E
Godoy Cruz, Argentina 158 C2 32 56 S 68 52W
Gods →, Canada 131 B10 56 22N 92 51W
Gods L., Canada 131 C10 54 40N 94 15W
Godthåb, Greenland 127 B14 64 10N 51 35W
Godwin Austen = K2, Mt., Pakistan 81 B7 35 58N 76 32 E
Goeie Hoop, Kaap die = Good Hope, C. of, S. Africa 104 E2 34 24 S 18 30 E
Goéland, L. au, Canada 128 C4 49 50N 76 48W
Goeree, Neths. 20 E4 51 50N 4 0 E
Goes, Neths. 21 F3 51 30N 3 55 E
Gogama, Canada 128 C3 47 35N 81 43W
Gogango, Australia 114 C5 23 40 S 150 2 E
Gogebic, L., U.S.A. 138 B10 46 20N 89 34W
Gogolin, Poland 47 E5 50 30N 18 0 E
Gogra = Ghaghara →, India 81 G11 25 45N 84 40 E
Gogriâl, Sudan 95 F2 8 30N 28 8 E
Goiana, Brazil 154 C5 7 33 S 34 59W
Goianésia, Brazil 155 E2 15 18 S 49 7W
Goiânia, Brazil 155 E2 16 43 S 49 20W
Goiás, Brazil 155 E1 15 55 S 50 10W
Goiás □, Brazil 154 D2 12 10 S 48 0W
Goiatuba, Brazil 155 E2 18 1 S 49 23W
Goio-Ere, Brazil 159 A5 24 12 S 53 1W
Goirle, Neths. 21 E6 51 31N 5 4 E
Góis, Portugal 36 E2 40 10N 8 6W
Goisern, Austria 30 D6 47 38N 13 38 E
Gojam □, Ethiopia 95 E4 10 55N 36 30 E
Gojeb, Wabi →, Ethiopia 95 F4 7 12N 36 40 E
Gojō, Japan 63 C7 34 21N 135 42 E
Gojra, Pakistan 80 D5 31 10N 72 40 E
Gokak, India 83 F2 16 11N 74 52 E
Gokarannath, India 81 F9 27 57N 80 39 E
Gokarn, India 83 G2 14 33N 74 17 E
Gökçeada, Turkey 44 D7 40 10N 25 50 E
Gökırmak →, Turkey 88 C6 41 25N 35 8 E
Göksu →, Turkey 88 E6 36 19N 34 5 E
Göksun, Turkey 88 D7 38 2N 36 30 E
Gokurt, Pakistan 80 E2 29 40N 67 26 E
Gola, India 81 E9 28 3N 80 32 E
Golaghat, India 78 B5 26 30N 94 0 E
Golakganj, India 81 F13 26 8N 89 52 E
Golan Heights = Hagolan, Syria 91 C4 33 0N 35 45 E
Golāshkerd, Iran 85 E8 27 59N 57 16 E
Golaya Pristen, U.S.S.R. 52 C5 46 29N 32 32 E
Gölbaşı, Adiyaman, Turkey 89 E7 37 43N 37 25 E
Gölbaşı, Ankara, Turkey 88 D5 39 47N 32 49 E
Golchikha, U.S.S.R. 6 B12 71 45N 83 30 E
Golconda, U.S.A. 142 F5 40 58N 117 32W
Gölcük, Kocaeli, Turkey 88 C3 40 42N 29 48 E
Gölcük, Niğde, Turkey 88 D6 38 14N 34 47 E
Gold Beach, U.S.A. 142 E1 42 25N 124 25W
Gold Coast, Australia 115 D5 28 0 S 153 25 E
Gold Coast, W. Afr. 101 E4 4 0N 1 40W
Gold Hill, U.S.A. 142 E2 42 28N 123 2W
Goldach, Switz. 29 B8 47 28N 9 28 E
Gołdap, Poland 47 A9 54 19N 22 18 E
Goldau, Switz. 29 B7 47 3N 8 33 E
Goldberg, Germany 26 B8 53 34N 12 6 E
Golden, Canada 130 C5 51 20N 116 59W
Golden, Colo., U.S.A. 138 F2 39 42N 105 15W
Golden, Ill., U.S.A. 140 D5 40 7N 91 1W
Golden B., N.Z. 119 A7 40 40 S 172 50 E
Golden Gate, U.S.A. 142 H2 37 54N 122 30W
Golden Hinde, Canada 130 D3 49 40N 125 44W
Golden Lake, Canada 136 A7 45 34N 77 21W
Golden Prairie, Canada 131 C7 50 13N 109 37W
Golden Rock, India 83 J4 10 45N 78 48 E
Golden Vale, Ireland 19 D3 52 33N 8 17W
Goldendale, U.S.A. 142 D3 45 53N 120 48W
Goldfield, U.S.A. 143 H5 37 45N 117 13W
Goldfields, Canada 131 B7 59 28N 108 29W
Goldsand L., Canada 131 B8 57 2N 101 8W
Goldsboro, U.S.A. 135 H7 35 24N 77 59W
Goldsmith, U.S.A. 139 K3 32 0N 102 40W
Goldsworthy, Australia 112 D2 20 21 S 119 30 E
Goldthwaite, U.S.A. 139 K5 31 25N 98 32W
Golegã, Portugal 37 F2 39 24N 8 29W
Goleniów, Poland 47 B1 53 35N 14 50 E
Golestānak, Iran 85 D7 30 36N 54 14 E
Goleta, U.S.A. 145 L7 34 27N 119 50W
Golfito, Costa Rica 148 E3 8 41N 83 5W
Golfo Aranci, Italy 40 B2 41 0N 9 35 E
Gölgeli Dağları, Turkey 88 E3 37 10N 28 55 E
Goliad, U.S.A. 139 L6 28 40N 97 22W
Golija, Crna Gora, Yugoslavia 42 D3 43 5N 18 45 E
Golija, Srbija, Yugoslavia 42 D5 43 22N 20 15 E
Golina, Poland 47 C5 52 15N 18 4 E
Gölköy, Turkey 89 C7 40 41N 37 37 E
Göllersdorf, Austria 31 C9 48 29N 16 7 E
Golo →, France 25 F13 42 31N 9 32 E
Golol, Somali Rep. 108 D2 3 38N 43 49 E
Golovanevsk, U.S.S.R. 52 B4 48 25N 30 30 E
Golpāyegān, Iran 85 C6 33 27N 50 18 E
Gölpazarı, Turkey 88 C4 40 16N 30 18 E
Golra, Pakistan 80 C5 33 37N 72 56 E
Golspie, U.K. 18 D5 57 58N 3 58W
Golub Dobrzyń, Poland 47 B6 53 7N 19 2 E
Golubac, Yugoslavia 42 C6 44 38N 21 38 E
Golungo Alto, Angola 103 D2 9 8 S 14 46 E
Golyam Perelik, Bulgaria 43 F9 41 36N 24 33 E
Golyama Kamchiya →, Bulgaria 43 D12 43 10N 27 55 E
Goma, Rwanda 106 C2 2 11 S 29 18 E
Goma, Zaïre 106 C2 1 37 S 29 10 E
Gomati →, India 81 G10 25 32N 83 11 E
Gombari, Zaïre 106 B2 2 45N 29 3 E
Gombe, Nigeria 101 C7 10 19N 11 2 E
Gombe →, Tanzania 106 C3 4 38 S 31 40 E
Gombi, Nigeria 101 C7 10 12N 12 30 E
Gomel, U.S.S.R. 50 E7 52 28N 31 0 E
Gomera, Canary Is. 33 F2 28 7N 17 14W
Gómez Palacio, Mexico 146 B4 25 40N 104 0W
Gomīshān, Iran 85 B7 37 4N 54 6 E
Gommern, Germany 26 C7 52 54N 11 47 E
Gomogomo, Indonesia 71 F8 6 39 S 134 43 E
Gomotartsi, Bulgaria 42 C7 44 6N 22 57 E
Gompa = Ganta, Liberia 100 D3 7 15N 8 59W
Gomphoi, Greece 44 E3 39 31N 21 27 E
Goms, Switz. 28 D6 46 27N 8 15 E
Gonābād, Iran 85 C8 34 15N 58 45 E
Gonaïves, Haiti 149 C5 19 20N 72 42W
Gonâve, G. de la, Haiti 149 C5 19 29N 72 42W
Gonâve, I. de la, Haiti 149 C5 18 45N 73 0W
Gonbab-e Kāvūs, Iran 85 B7 37 20N 55 25 E
Gönc, Hungary 31 C14 48 28N 21 14 E
Gonda, India 81 F9 27 9N 81 58 E
Gondal, India 80 J4 21 58N 70 52 E
Gonder, Ethiopia 95 E4 12 39N 37 30 E
Gonder □, Ethiopia 95 E4 12 55N 37 30 E
Gondia, India 82 D5 21 23N 80 10 E
Gondola, Mozam. 107 F3 19 10 S 33 37 E
Gondomar, Portugal 36 D2 41 10N 8 35W
Gondomar, Spain 36 C2 42 7N 8 45W
Gondrecourt-le-Château, France 23 D12 48 31N 5 30 E
Gönen, Turkey 88 C2 40 6N 27 39 E
Gong Xian, China 68 C5 28 23N 104 47 E
Gong'an, China 69 B9 30 7N 112 12 E
Gongcheng, China 69 E8 24 50N 110 49 E
Gongga Shan, China 68 C3 29 40N 101 55 E
Gongguan, China 68 G7 21 48N 109 36 E
Gonghe, China 64 C5 36 18N 100 32 E
Gongola □, Nigeria 101 D7 8 0N 12 0 E
Gongola →, Nigeria 101 D7 9 30N 12 4 E
Gongolgon, Australia 115 E4 30 21 S 146 54 E
Gongshan, China 68 D2 27 43N 98 29 E
Gongtan, China 68 C7 28 55N 108 20 E
Goniadz, Poland 47 B9 53 30N 22 44 E
Goniri, Nigeria 101 C7 11 30N 12 15 E
Gonjo, China 68 B2 30 52N 98 17 E
Gonnesa, Italy 40 C1 39 17N 8 27 E
Gónnos, Greece 44 E4 39 52N 22 29 E
Gonnosfanadiga, Italy 40 C1 39 30N 8 39 E
Gonzales, Calif., U.S.A. 144 J5 36 35N 121 30W
Gonzales, Tex., U.S.A. 139 L6 29 30N 97 30W
González Chaves, Argentina 158 D3 38 2 S 60 5W
Good Hope, C. of, S. Africa 104 E2 34 24 S 18 30 E
Goodenough I., Papua N. G. 120 E6 9 20 S 150 15 E
Gooderham, Canada 128 D4 44 54N 78 21W
Goodeve, Canada 131 C8 51 4N 103 10W
Gooding, U.S.A. 142 E6 43 0N 114 44W
Goodland, U.S.A. 138 F4 39 22N 101 44W
Goodnight, U.S.A. 139 H4 35 4N 101 13W
Goodooga, Australia 115 D4 29 3 S 147 28 E
Goodsoil, Canada 131 C7 54 24N 109 13W
Goodsprings, U.S.A. 143 J6 35 51N 115 30W
Goole, U.K. 16 D7 53 42N 0 52W
Goolgowi, Australia 117 B6 33 58 S 145 41 E
Goolwa, Australia 116 C3 35 30 S 138 47 E
Goomalling, Australia 113 F2 31 15 S 116 49 E
Goombalie, Australia 115 D4 29 59 S 145 26 E
Goonalga, Australia 116 A5 31 45 S 143 37 E
Goonda, Mozam. 107 F3 19 48 S 33 57 E
Goondiwindi, Australia 115 D5 28 30 S 150 21 E
Goongarrie, L., Australia 113 F3 30 3 S 121 9 E
Goonumbla, Australia 117 B8 32 59 S 148 11 E
Goonyella, Australia 114 C4 21 47 S 147 58 E
Goor, Neths. 20 D9 52 13N 6 33 E
Gooray, Australia 115 D5 28 25 S 150 2 E
Goose →, Canada 129 B7 53 20N 60 35W
Goose L., U.S.A. 142 F3 42 0N 120 30W
Gooty, India 83 G3 15 7N 77 41 E
Gopalganj, Bangla. 78 D2 23 1N 89 50 E
Gopalganj, India 81 F11 26 28N 84 30 E
Goppenstein, Switz. 28 D5 46 23N 7 46 E
Göppingen, Germany 27 G5 48 42N 9 40 E
Gor, Spain 35 H2 37 23N 2 58W
Góra, Leszno, Poland 47 D3 51 40N 16 31 E
Góra, Płock, Poland 47 C7 52 39N 20 6 E
Góra Kalwaria, Poland 47 D8 51 59N 21 14 E
Gorakhpur, India 81 F10 26 47N 83 23 E
Goražde, Yugoslavia 42 D3 43 38N 18 58 E
Gorbatov, U.S.S.R. 51 C13 56 12N 43 2 E
Gorbea, Peña, Spain 34 B2 43 1N 2 50W
Gorda, U.S.A. 144 K5 35 53N 121 26W
Gorda, Pta., Nic. 148 D3 14 20N 83 10W
Gorda, Pta., Canary Is. 33 F2 28 45N 18 0W
Gordan B., Australia 112 B5 11 35 S 130 10 E
Gordon, U.S.A. 138 D3 42 49N 102 12W
Gordon →, Australia 114 G4 42 27 S 145 30 E
Gordon, I., Chile 160 D3 54 55 S 69 30W
Gordon Downs, Australia 112 C4 18 48 S 128 33 E
Gordon L., Alta., Canada 131 B6 56 30N 110 25W
Gordon L., N.W.T., Canada 130 A6 63 5N 113 11W
Gordonia, S. Africa 104 D3 28 13 S 21 10 E
Gordonvale, Australia 114 B4 17 5 S 145 50 E
Gore, Australia 115 D5 28 17 S 151 30 E
Goré, Chad 97 G3 7 59N 16 31 E
Gore, Ethiopia 95 F4 8 12N 35 32 E
Gore, N.Z. 119 G3 46 5 S 168 58 E
Gore Bay, Canada 128 C3 45 57N 82 28W
Görele, Turkey 89 C8 41 2N 39 0 E
Gorg, Iran 85 D8 29 29N 59 43 E
Gorgān, Iran 85 B7 36 50N 54 29 E
Gorgona, Italy 38 E6 43 27N 9 52 E
Gorgona, I., Colombia 156 A2 3 0N 78 10W
Gorgora, Ethiopia 95 E4 12 15N 37 17 E
Gorham, U.S.A. 137 B13 44 23N 71 10W
Gori, U.S.S.R. 53 F11 42 0N 44 7 E
Gorin, U.S.A. 140 D4 40 22N 92 1W
Gorinchem, Neths. 20 E5 51 50N 4 59 E
Gorinhatã, Brazil 155 E2 19 15 S 49 45W
Goritsy, U.S.S.R. 51 C10 57 4N 36 43 E
Gorízia, Italy 39 C10 45 56N 13 37 E
Górka, Poland 47 D3 51 39N 16 58 E
Gorki = Gorkiy, U.S.S.R. 51 C14 56 20N 44 0 E
Gorki, U.S.S.R. 50 D7 54 17N 30 59 E
Gorkiy, U.S.S.R. 51 C14 56 20N 44 0 E
Gorkovskoye Vdkhr., U.S.S.R. 51 C13 57 2N 43 4 E
Gørlev, Denmark 15 J5 55 30N 11 15 E
Gorlice, Poland 31 B14 49 35N 21 11 E
Görlitz, Germany 26 D10 51 10N 14 59 E
Gorlovka, U.S.S.R. 52 B8 48 19N 38 5 E
Gorman, Calif., U.S.A. 145 L8 34 47N 118 51W
Gorman, Tex., U.S.A. 139 J5 32 15N 98 43W
Gorna Dzhumayo = Blagoevgrad, Bulgaria 42 E8 42 2N 23 5 E
Gorna Oryakhovitsa, Bulgaria 43 D10 43 7N 25 40 E
Gornja Radgona, Yugoslavia 39 B13 46 40N 16 2 E
Gornja Tuzla, Yugoslavia 42 C3 44 35N 18 46 E
Gornji Grad, Yugoslavia 39 B11 46 20N 14 52 E
Gornji Milanovac, Yugoslavia 42 D5 44 0N 20 29 E
Gornji Vakuf, Yugoslavia 42 D2 43 57N 17 34 E
Gorno Ablanovo, Bulgaria 43 D10 43 37N 25 43 E
Gorno-Altaysk, U.S.S.R. 56 D9 51 50N 86 5 E
Gorno Slinkino, U.S.S.R. 56 C8 60 5N 70 0 E
Gornyatski, U.S.S.R. 48 A11 67 32N 64 3 E
Gornyi, U.S.S.R. 60 B6 44 57N 133 59 E
Gornyy, U.S.S.R. 51 F16 51 50N 48 30 E
Gorodenka, U.S.S.R. 52 B1 48 41N 25 29 E
Gorodets, U.S.S.R. 51 C13 56 38N 43 28 E
Gorodishche, R.S.F.S.R., U.S.S.R. 51 E14 53 13N 45 40 E
Gorodishche, Ukraine S.S.R., U.S.S.R. 52 B4 49 17N 31 27 E
Gorodnitsa, U.S.S.R. 50 F5 50 46N 27 19 E
Gorodnya, U.S.S.R. 50 F7 51 55N 31 33 E
Gorodok, Byelorussian S.S.R., U.S.S.R. 50 D7 55 30N 30 3 E

Greenock 203

Gorodok, *Ukraine S.S.R., U.S.S.R.* **50 G3** 49 46N 23 32 E
Goroka, *Papua N. G.* **120 D3** 6 7 S 145 25 E
Goroke, *Australia* **116 D4** 36 43 S 141 29 E
Gorokhov, *U.S.S.R.* **50 F4** 50 30N 24 45 E
Gorokhovets, *U.S.S.R.* **51 C13** 56 13N 42 39 E
Gorom Gorom, *Burkina Faso* **101 C4** 14 26N 0 14W
Goromonzi, *Zimbabwe* **107 F3** 17 52 S 31 22 E
Gorongose →, *Mozam.* **105 C5** 20 30 S 34 40 E
Gorongoza, *Mozam.* **107 F3** 18 44 S 34 2 E
Gorongoza, Sa. da, *Mozam.* **107 F3** 18 27 S 34 2 E
Gorontalo, *Indonesia* **71 D6** 0 35N 123 5 E
Goronyo, *Nigeria* **101 C6** 13 29N 5 39 E
Górowo Iławeckie, *Poland* **47 A7** 54 17N 20 30 E
Gorredijk, *Neths.* **20 C8** 53 0N 6 3 E
Gorron, *France* **22 D6** 48 25N 0 50W
Gorssel, *Neths.* **20 D8** 52 12N 6 12 E
Gort, *Ireland* **19 C3** 53 4N 8 50W
Gortis, *Greece* **32 D6** 35 4N 24 58 E
Gorumahisani, *India* **82 C8** 22 20N 86 24 E
Gorzkowice, *Poland* **47 D6** 51 13N 19 36 E
Gorzno, *Poland* **47 B6** 53 12N 19 38 E
Gorzów Śląski, *Poland* **47 D5** 51 3N 18 22 E
Gorzów Wielkopolski, *Poland* **47 C2** 52 43N 15 15 E
Gorzów Wielkopolski □, *Poland* **47 C2** 52 45N 15 30 E
Göschenen, *Switz.* **29 C7** 46 40N 8 36 E
Gose, *Japan* **63 C7** 34 27N 135 44 E
Gosford, *Australia* **117 B9** 33 23 S 151 18 E
Goshen, *Calif., U.S.A.* **144 J7** 36 21N 119 25W
Goshen, *Ind., U.S.A.* **141 C11** 41 36N 85 46W
Goshen, *N.Y., U.S.A.* **137 E10** 41 23N 74 21W
Goshogawara, *Japan* **60 D10** 40 48N 140 27 E
Goslar, *Germany* **26 D6** 51 55N 10 23 E
Gospič, *Yugoslavia* **39 D12** 44 35N 15 23 E
Gosport, *U.K.* **17 G6** 50 48N 1 8W
Gosport, *U.S.A.* **141 E10** 39 21N 86 40W
Gossau, *Switz.* **29 B8** 47 25N 9 15 E
Gosse →, *Australia* **114 B1** 19 32 S 134 37 E
Gostivar, *Yugoslavia* **42 F5** 41 48N 20 57 E
Gostyń, *Poland* **47 D4** 51 50N 17 3 E
Gostynin, *Poland* **47 C6** 52 26N 19 29 E
Göta älv →, *Sweden* **15 G5** 57 42N 11 54 E
Göta kanal, *Sweden* **13 G12** 58 50N 13 58 E
Göteborg, *Sweden* **15 G5** 57 43N 11 59 E
Göteborgs och Bohus län □, *Sweden* **13 G11** 58 30N 11 30 E
Gotemba, *Japan* **63 B10** 35 18N 138 56 E
Götene, *Sweden* **15 F7** 58 32N 13 30 E
Gotha, *Germany* **26 E6** 50 56N 10 42 E
Gothenburg, *U.S.A.* **138 E4** 40 58N 100 8W
Gotland, *Sweden* **13 H15** 57 30N 18 33 E
Gotse Delchev, *Bulgaria* **43 F8** 41 43N 23 46 E
Gotska Sandön, *Sweden* **13 G15** 58 24N 19 15 E
Gōtsu, *Japan* **62 C4** 35 0N 132 14 E
Göttingen, *Germany* **26 D5** 51 31N 9 55 E
Gottwald, *U.S.S.R.* **52 B7** 49 39N 36 27 E
Gottwaldov, *Czech.* **31 B10** 49 14N 17 40 E
Goubangzi, *China* **67 D11** 41 20N 121 52 E
Gouda, *Neths.* **20 D5** 52 1N 4 42 E
Goúdhoura, Ákra, *Greece* **32 E8** 34 59N 26 6 E
Goudiry, *Senegal* **100 C2** 14 15N 12 45W
Gough I., *Atl. Oc.* **9 N8** 40 10 S 9 45W
Gouin, Rés., *Canada* **128 C5** 48 35N 74 40W
Gouitafla, *Ivory C.* **100 D3** 7 30N 5 53W
Goulburn, *Australia* **117 C8** 34 44 S 149 44 E
Goulburn Is., *Australia* **114 A1** 11 40 S 133 20 E
Goulia, *Ivory C.* **100 C3** 10 1N 7 11W
Goulimine, *Morocco* **98 C3** 28 56N 10 0W
Goulmina, *Morocco* **98 B4** 31 41N 4 57W
Gouménissa, *Greece* **44 D4** 40 56N 22 37 E
Gounou-Gaya, *Chad* **97 G3** 9 38N 15 31 E
Goúra, *Greece* **45 G4** 37 56N 22 20 E
Gouraya, *Algeria* **99 A5** 36 31N 1 56 E
Gourdon, *France* **24 D5** 44 44N 1 23 E
Gouré, *Niger* **97 F2** 14 0N 10 10 E
Gouri, *Chad* **97 E3** 19 36N 19 36 E
Gourits →, *S. Africa* **104 E3** 34 21 S 21 52 E
Gourma Rharous, *Mali* **101 B4** 16 55N 1 50W
Goúrnais, *Greece* **32 D7** 35 19N 25 16 E
Gournay-en-Bray, *France* **23 C8** 49 29N 1 44 E
Gourock Ra., *Australia* **117 D8** 36 0 S 149 25 E
Goursi, *Burkina Faso* **100 C4** 12 42N 2 37W
Gouvêa, *Brazil* **155 E3** 18 27 S 43 44W
Gouverneur, *U.S.A.* **137 B9** 44 18N 75 30W
Gouviá, *Greece* **32 A3** 39 39N 19 50 E
Gouzon, *France* **24 B6** 46 12N 2 14 E
Govan, *Canada* **131 C8** 51 20N 105 0W
Governador Valadares, *Brazil* **155 E3** 18 15 S 41 57W
Governor's Harbour, *Bahamas* **148 A4** 25 10N 76 14W
Gowan Ra., *Australia* **114 D4** 25 0 S 145 0 E
Gowanda, *U.S.A.* **136 D6** 42 29N 78 58W
Gower, *U.K.* **17 F3** 51 35N 4 10W
Gowna, L., *Ireland* **19 C4** 53 52N 7 35W
Gowrie, *U.S.A.* **140 B2** 42 17N 94 17W
Goya, *Argentina* **158 B4** 29 10 S 59 10W
Goyder Lagoon, *Australia* **115 D2** 27 3 S 138 58 E
Goyllarisquisga, *Peru* **156 C2** 10 31 S 76 24W
Göynük, *Turkey* **88 C4** 40 24N 30 48 E
Goz Beïda, *Chad* **97 F4** 12 10N 21 20 E
Goz Regeb, *Sudan* **95 D4** 16 3N 35 33 E
Gozdnica, *Poland* **47 D2** 51 28N 15 4 E
Gozo, *Malta* **32 C1** 36 3N 14 13 E
Graaff-Reinet, *S. Africa* **104 E3** 32 13 S 24 32 E
Grabill, *U.S.A.* **141 C12** 41 13N 84 57W
Grabow, *Germany* **26 B7** 53 17N 11 31 E
Grabów, *Poland* **47 D5** 51 31N 18 7 E
Grabs, *Switz.* **29 B8** 47 11N 9 27 E
Gračac, *Yugoslavia* **39 D12** 44 18N 15 57 E
Gračanica, *Yugoslavia* **42 C3** 44 43N 18 18 E
Graçay, *France* **23 E8** 47 10N 1 50 E
Grace, *U.S.A.* **142 E8** 42 38N 111 46W
Graceville, *U.S.A.* **138 C6** 45 36N 96 23W
Grachevka, *U.S.S.R.* **54 E3** 52 55N 52 52 E
Gracias a Dios, C., *Honduras* **148 D3** 15 0N 83 10W
Graciosa, I., *Canary Is.* **33 E6** 29 15N 13 32W
Gradačac, *Yugoslavia* **42 C3** 44 52N 18 26 E
Gradaús, *Brazil* **154 C1** 7 43 S 51 11W
Gradaús, Serra dos, *Brazil* **154 C1** 8 0 S 50 45W
Gradeška Planina, *Yugoslavia* **42 F7** 41 30N 22 15 E
Gradets, *Bulgaria* **43 E11** 42 46N 26 30 E
Grado, *Italy* **39 C10** 45 40N 13 20 E
Grado, *Spain* **36 B4** 43 23N 6 4W
Gradule, *Australia* **115 D4** 28 32 S 149 15 E
Grady, *U.S.A.* **139 H3** 34 52N 103 15W
Graeca, Lacul, *Romania* **46 E7** 44 5N 26 10 E
Graénalon, L., *Iceland* **12 D5** 64 10N 17 20W
Grafenau, *Germany* **27 G9** 48 51N 13 24 E
Gräfenberg, *Germany* **27 F7** 49 39N 11 15 E
Grafton, *Australia* **115 D5** 29 38 S 152 58 E
Grafton, *Ill., U.S.A.* **140 F6** 38 58N 90 26W
Grafton, *N. Dak., U.S.A.* **138 A6** 48 30N 97 25W
Gragnano, *Italy* **41 B7** 40 42N 14 30 E
Graham, *Canada* **128 C1** 49 20N 90 30W
Graham, *N.C., U.S.A.* **135 G6** 36 5N 79 22W
Graham, *Tex., U.S.A.* **139 J5** 33 7N 98 38W
Graham →, *Canada* **130 B4** 56 31N 122 17W
Graham Bell, Os., *U.S.S.R.* **56 A7** 81 0N 62 0 E
Graham I., *Canada* **130 C2** 53 40N 132 30W
Graham Land, *Antarctica* **7 C17** 65 0 S 64 0W
Graham Mt., *U.S.A.* **143 K9** 32 46N 109 58W
Grahamdale, *Canada* **131 C9** 51 23N 98 30W
Grahamstown, *S. Africa* **104 E4** 33 19 S 26 31 E
Grahovo, *Yugoslavia* **42 E3** 42 40N 18 40 E
Graïba, *Tunisia* **96 B2** 34 30N 10 13 E
Graide, *Belgium* **21 J6** 49 58N 5 4 E
Graie, Alpi, *Europe* **38 C4** 45 30N 7 10 E
Grain Coast, *W. Afr.* **100 E3** 4 20N 10 0W
Grajaú, *Brazil* **154 C2** 5 50 S 46 4W
Grajaú →, *Brazil* **154 B3** 3 41 S 44 48W
Grajewo, *Poland* **47 B9** 53 39N 22 30 E
Gramada, *Bulgaria* **42 D7** 43 49N 22 39 E
Gramat, *France* **24 D5** 44 48N 1 43 E
Grammichele, *Italy* **41 E7** 37 12N 14 37 E
Grámmos, Óros, *Greece* **44 D2** 40 18N 20 47 E
Grampian □, *U.K.* **18 D6** 57 20N 3 0W
Grampian Highlands = Grampian Mts., *U.K.* **18 E5** 56 50N 4 0W
Grampian Mts., *U.K.* **18 E5** 56 50N 4 0W
Gran →, *Surinam* **153 C6** 4 1N 55 30W
Gran Altiplanicie Central, *Argentina* **160 C3** 49 0 S 69 30W
Gran Canaria, *Canary Is.* **33 G4** 27 55N 15 35W
Gran Chaco, *S. Amer.* **158 B3** 25 0 S 61 0W
Gran Paradiso, *Italy* **38 C4** 45 33N 7 17 E
Gran Sasso d'Italia, *Italy* **39 F10** 42 25N 13 30 E
Granada, *Nic.* **148 D2** 11 58N 86 0W
Granada, *Spain* **35 H1** 37 10N 3 35W
Granada, *U.S.A.* **139 F3** 38 5N 102 20W
Granada □, *Spain* **37 H8** 37 18N 3 0W
Granadilla de Abona, *Canary Is.* **33 F3** 28 7N 16 33W
Granard, *Ireland* **19 C4** 53 47N 7 30W
Granbury, *U.S.A.* **139 J6** 32 28N 97 48W
Granby, *Canada* **128 C5** 45 25N 72 45W
Grand →, *Mich., U.S.A.* **141 A10** 43 4N 86 15W
Grand →, *Mo., U.S.A.* **140 E3** 39 23N 93 6W
Grand →, *S. Dak., U.S.A.* **138 C4** 45 40N 100 32W
Grand Bahama, *Bahamas* **148 A4** 26 40N 78 30W
Grand Bank, *Canada* **129 C8** 47 6N 55 48W
Grand Bassam, *Ivory C.* **100 D4** 5 10N 3 49W
Grand Béréby, *Ivory C.* **100 E3** 4 38N 6 55W
Grand Blanc, *U.S.A.* **141 B13** 42 56N 83 38W
Grand-Bourg, *Guadeloupe* **149 C7** 15 53N 61 19W
Grand Canal = Yun Ho →, *China* **67 E9** 39 10N 117 10 E
Grand Canyon, *U.S.A.* **143 H7** 36 3N 112 9W
Grand Canyon National Park, *U.S.A.* **143 H7** 36 15N 112 20W
Grand Cayman, *Cayman Is.* **148 C3** 19 20N 81 20W
Grand Cess, *Liberia* **100 E3** 4 40N 8 12W
Grand Coulee, *U.S.A.* **142 C4** 47 48N 119 1W
Grand Coulee Dam, *U.S.A.* **142 C4** 48 0N 118 50W
Grand Erg de Bilma, *Niger* **97 E2** 18 30N 14 0 E
Grand Erg Occidental, *Algeria* **99 B5** 30 20N 1 0 E
Grand Erg Oriental, *Algeria* **99 C6** 30 0N 6 30 E
Grand Falls, *Canada* **129 C8** 48 56N 55 40W
Grand Forks, *Canada* **130 D5** 49 0N 118 30W
Grand Forks, *U.S.A.* **138 B6** 47 55N 97 3W
Grand-Fougeray, *France* **22 E5** 47 44N 1 43W
Grand Haven, *U.S.A.* **141 A10** 43 3N 86 13W
Grand I., *U.S.A.* **134 B2** 46 30N 86 40W
Grand Island, *U.S.A.* **138 E5** 40 59N 98 25W
Grand Isle, *U.S.A.* **139 L10** 29 15N 89 58W
Grand Junction, *Colo., U.S.A.* **143 G9** 39 0N 108 30W
Grand Junction, *Iowa, U.S.A.* **140 B2** 42 2N 94 14W
Grand Lac Victoria, *Canada* **128 C4** 47 35N 77 35W
Grand Lahou, *Ivory C.* **100 D3** 5 10N 5 5W
Grand L., *N.B., Canada* **129 C6** 45 57N 66 7W
Grand L., *Nfld., Canada* **129 C8** 49 0N 57 30W
Grand L., *Nfld., Canada* **129 B7** 53 40N 60 30W
Grand Lake, *U.S.A.* **142 F11** 40 20N 105 54W
Grand L., *La., U.S.A.* **139 L8** 29 55N 92 45W
Grand L., *Ohio, U.S.A.* **141 D12** 40 32N 84 25W
Grand Ledge, *U.S.A.* **141 B12** 42 45N 84 45W
Grand-Leez, *Belgium* **21 G5** 50 35N 4 45 E
Grand-Lieu, L. de, *France* **22 E5** 47 6N 1 40W
Grand Manan I., *Canada* **129 D6** 44 45N 66 52W
Grand Marais, *Canada* **138 B9** 47 45N 90 25W
Grand Marais, *U.S.A.* **134 B3** 46 39N 85 59W
Grand-Mère, *Canada* **128 C5** 46 36N 72 40W
Grand Popo, *Benin* **101 D5** 6 15N 1 57 E
Grand Portage, *U.S.A.* **128 C2** 47 58N 89 41W
Grand Rapids, *Canada* **131 C9** 53 12N 99 19W
Grand Rapids, *Mich., U.S.A.* **141 B10** 42 57N 86 40W
Grand Rapids, *Minn., U.S.A.* **138 B8** 47 15N 93 29W
Grand River, *U.S.A.* **140 D3** 40 49N 93 58W
Grand St-Bernard, Col du, *Switz.* **28 E4** 45 50N 7 10 E
Grand Santi, *Fr. Guiana* **153 C7** 4 20N 54 24W
Grand Teton, *U.S.A.* **142 E8** 43 54N 111 50W
Grand Valley, *U.S.A.* **142 G9** 39 30N 108 2W
Grand View, *Canada* **131 C8** 51 10N 100 42W
Grandas de Salime, *Spain* **36 B4** 43 13N 6 53W
Grande →, *Jujuy, Argentina* **158 A2** 24 20 S 65 2W
Grande →, *Mendoza, Argentina* **158 D2** 36 52 S 69 45W
Grande →, *Bolivia* **157 D5** 15 51 S 64 39W
Grande →, *Bahia, Brazil* **154 D3** 11 30 S 44 30W
Grande →, *Minas Gerais, Brazil* **155 F1** 20 6 S 51 4W
Grande →, *Spain* **35 F4** 39 6N 0 48W
Grande →, *U.S.A.* **139 N6** 25 57N 97 9W
Grande →, *Venezuela* **153 B5** 8 36N 61 39W
Grande, B., *Argentina* **160 D3** 50 30 S 68 20W
Grande, I., *Brazil* **155 F3** 23 9 S 44 14W
Grande, Serra, *Goiás, Brazil* **154 D2** 11 15 S 46 30W
Grande, Serra, *Piauí, Brazil* **154 C2** 8 0 S 45 10W
Grande Baie, *Canada* **129 C5** 48 19N 70 52W
Grande Baleine, R. de la →, *Canada* **128 A4** 55 16N 77 47W
Grande Cache, *Canada* **130 C5** 53 53N 119 8W
Grande de Santiago →, *Mexico* **146 C3** 21 20N 105 50W
Grande Dixence, Barr. de la, *Switz.* **28 D4** 46 5N 7 23 E
Grande-Entrée, *Canada* **129 C7** 47 30N 61 40W
Grande Prairie, *Canada* **130 B5** 55 10N 118 50W
Grande-Rivière, *Canada* **129 C7** 48 26N 64 30W
Grande Sauldre →, *France* **23 E9** 47 27N 2 5 E
Grande-Vallée, *Canada* **129 C6** 49 14N 65 8W
Grandes-Bergeronnes, *Canada* **129 C6** 48 16N 69 35W
Grandfalls, *U.S.A.* **139 K3** 31 21N 102 51W
Grandoe Mines, *Canada* **130 B3** 56 29N 129 54W
Grândola, *Portugal* **37 G2** 38 12N 8 35W
Grandpré, *France* **23 C11** 49 20N 4 50 E
Grandson, *Switz.* **28 C3** 46 49N 6 39 E
Grandview, *Mo., U.S.A.* **140 F2** 38 53N 94 32W
Grandview, *Wash., U.S.A.* **142 C4** 46 13N 119 58W
Grandview Heights, *U.S.A.* **141 E13** 39 58N 83 2W
Grandvilliers, *France* **23 C8** 49 40N 1 57 E
Graneros, *Chile* **158 C1** 34 5 S 70 45W
Grangemouth, *U.K.* **18 E5** 56 1N 3 43W
Granger, *Wash., U.S.A.* **142 C3** 46 25N 120 5W
Granger, *Wyo., U.S.A.* **142 F9** 41 35N 109 58W
Grangeville, *U.S.A.* **142 D5** 45 57N 116 4W
Granite City, *U.S.A.* **140 F6** 38 45N 90 3W
Granite Falls, *U.S.A.* **138 C7** 44 45N 95 35W
Granite Mt., *U.S.A.* **145 M10** 33 5N 116 28W
Granite Peak, *Australia* **113 E3** 25 40 S 121 20 E
Granite Pk., *U.S.A.* **142 D9** 45 8N 109 52W
Granitnyy, Pik, *U.S.S.R.* **55 D5** 39 32N 70 20 E
Granity, *N.Z.* **119 B6** 41 39 S 171 51 E
Granja, *Brazil* **154 B3** 3 7 S 40 50W
Granja de Moreruela, *Spain* **36 D5** 41 48N 5 44W
Granja de Torrehermosa, *Spain* **37 G5** 38 19N 5 35W
Granollers, *Spain* **34 D7** 41 39N 2 18 E
Gransee, *Germany* **26 C9** 53 0N 13 10 E
Grant, *U.S.A.* **138 E4** 40 53N 101 42W
Grant, Mt., *U.S.A.* **142 G4** 38 34N 118 48W
Grant City, *U.S.A.* **140 D2** 40 30N 94 25W
Grant I., *Australia* **112 B5** 11 10 S 132 52 E
Grant Range Mts., *U.S.A.* **143 G6** 38 30N 115 30W
Grantham, *U.K.* **16 E7** 52 55N 0 39W
Grantown-on-Spey, *U.K.* **18 D5** 57 19N 3 36W
Grants, *U.S.A.* **143 J10** 35 14N 107 51W
Grants Pass, *U.S.A.* **142 E2** 42 30N 123 22W
Grantsburg, *U.S.A.* **138 C8** 45 46N 92 44W
Grantsville, *U.S.A.* **142 F7** 40 35N 112 32W
Granville, *France* **22 D5** 48 50N 1 35W
Granville, *U.S.A.* **140 C7** 41 17N 89 15W
Granville, *N. Dak., U.S.A.* **138 A4** 48 18N 100 48W
Granville, *N.Y., U.S.A.* **134 D9** 43 24N 73 16W
Granville L., *Canada* **131 B8** 56 18N 100 30W
Grao de Gandía, *Spain* **35 G4** 39 0N 0 7W
Grapeland, *U.S.A.* **139 K7** 31 30N 95 31W
Gras, L. de, *Canada* **126 B8** 64 30N 110 30W
Graskop, *S. Africa* **105 C5** 24 56 S 30 49 E
Grass →, *Canada* **131 B9** 56 3N 96 33W
Grass Range, *U.S.A.* **142 C9** 47 0N 109 0W
Grass River Prov. Park, *Canada* **131 C8** 54 40N 100 50W
Grass Valley, *Calif., U.S.A.* **144 F6** 39 18N 121 0W
Grass Valley, *Oreg., U.S.A.* **142 D3** 45 22N 120 48W
Grassano, *Italy* **41 B9** 40 38N 16 17 E
Grasse, *France* **25 E10** 43 38N 6 56 E
Grassmere, *Australia* **116 A5** 31 24 S 142 38 E
Gratis, *U.S.A.* **141 E12** 39 38N 84 32W
Gratz, *U.S.A.* **141 F12** 38 28N 84 57W
Graubünden □, *Switz.* **29 C9** 46 45N 9 30 E
Graulhet, *France* **24 E5** 43 45N 1 59 E
Graus, *Spain* **34 C5** 42 11N 0 20 E
Gravatá, *Brazil* **154 C4** 8 10 S 35 29W
Grave, *Neths.* **20 E7** 51 46N 5 44 E
Grave, Pte. de, *France* **24 C2** 45 34N 1 4W
's-Graveland, *Neths.* **20 D6** 52 15N 5 7 E
Gravelbourg, *Canada* **131 D7** 49 50N 106 35W
Gravelines, *France* **23 B9** 50 59N 2 10 E
's-Gravendeel, *Neths.* **20 E5** 51 47N 4 37 E
's-Gravenhage, *Neths.* **20 D4** 52 7N 4 17 E
Gravenhurst, *Canada* **136 B5** 44 52N 79 20W
's-Gravenpolder, *Neths.* **21 F3** 51 28N 3 54 E
's-Gravenzande, *Neths.* **20 E4** 52 0N 4 9 E
Gravesend, *Australia* **115 D5** 29 35 S 150 20 E
Gravesend, *U.K.* **17 F8** 51 25N 0 22 E
Gravina di Púglia, *Italy* **41 B9** 40 48N 16 25 E
Gravois, Pointe-à-, *Haiti* **149 C5** 18 15N 73 56W
Gravone →, *France* **25 G12** 41 58N 8 45 E
Gray, *France* **23 E12** 47 22N 5 35 E
Grayling, *U.S.A.* **134 C3** 44 40N 84 42W
Grayling →, *Canada* **130 B3** 59 21N 125 0W
Grays Harbor, *U.S.A.* **142 C1** 46 55N 124 8W
Grays L., *U.S.A.* **142 E8** 43 8N 111 30W
Grays River, *U.S.A.* **144 D3** 46 21N 123 37W
Grayson, *Canada* **131 C8** 50 45N 102 40W
Grayville, *U.S.A.* **141 F9** 38 16N 88 0W
Graz, *Austria* **30 D8** 47 4N 15 27 E
Grazalema, *Spain* **37 J5** 36 46N 5 23W
Grdelica, *Yugoslavia* **42 E7** 42 55N 22 3 E
Greasy L., *Canada* **130 A4** 62 55N 122 12W
Great Abaco I., *Bahamas* **148 A4** 26 25N 77 10W
Great Artesian Basin, *Australia* **114 C3** 23 0 S 144 0 E
Great Australian Bight, *Australia* **113 F5** 33 30 S 130 0 E
Great Bahama Bank, *Bahamas* **148 B4** 23 15N 78 0W
Great Barrier I., *N.Z.* **118 C4** 36 11 S 175 25 E
Great Barrier Reef, *Australia* **114 B4** 18 0 S 146 50 E
Great Barrington, *U.S.A.* **137 D11** 42 11N 73 22W
Great Basin, *U.S.A.* **124 F8** 40 0N 116 30W
Great Bear →, *Canada* **126 B7** 65 0N 124 0W
Great Bear L., *Canada* **126 B8** 65 30N 120 0W
Great Bena, *U.S.A.* **137 E9** 41 57N 75 45W
Great Bend, *U.S.A.* **138 F5** 38 25N 98 55W
Great Blasket I., *Ireland* **19 D1** 52 5N 10 30W
Great Britain, *Europe* **10 E5** 54 0N 2 15W
Great Central, *Canada* **130 D3** 49 20N 125 10W
Great Dividing Ra., *Australia* **114 C4** 23 0 S 146 0 E
Great Driffield, *U.K.* **16 D7** 54 0N 0 25W
Great Exuma I., *Bahamas* **148 B4** 23 30N 75 50W
Great Falls, *Canada* **131 C9** 50 27N 96 1W
Great Falls, *U.S.A.* **142 C8** 47 27N 111 12W
Great Fish = Groot Vis →, *S. Africa* **104 E4** 33 28 S 27 5 E
Great Guana Cay, *Bahamas* **148 B4** 24 0N 76 20W
Great Harbour Deep, *Canada* **129 B8** 50 25N 56 32W
Great Inagua I., *Bahamas* **149 B5** 21 0N 73 20W
Great Indian Desert = Thar Desert, *India* **80 F5** 28 0N 72 0 E
Great I., *Canada* **131 B9** 58 53N 96 35W
Great Karoo, *S. Africa* **104 E3** 31 55 S 21 0 E
Great Lake, *Australia* **114 G4** 41 50 S 146 40 E
Great Ormes Head, *U.K.* **16 D4** 53 20N 3 52W
Great Ouse →, *U.K.* **16 E8** 52 47N 0 22 E
Great Palm I., *Australia* **114 B4** 18 45 S 146 40 E
Great Papuan Plateau, *Papua N. G.* **120 D2** 6 30 S 142 25 E
Great Plains, *N. Amer.* **124 E9** 47 0N 105 0W
Great Ruaha →, *Tanzania* **106 D4** 7 56 S 37 52 E
Great Saint Bernard P. = Grand St-Bernard, Col du, *Switz.* **28 E4** 45 50N 7 10 E
Great Salt Lake, *U.S.A.* **124 E8** 41 0N 112 30W
Great Salt Lake Desert, *U.S.A.* **142 F7** 40 20N 113 50W
Great Salt Plains Res., *U.S.A.* **139 G5** 36 40N 98 15W
Great Sandy Desert, *Australia* **112 D3** 21 0 S 124 0 E
Great Scarcies →, *S. Leone* **100 D2** 9 0N 13 0W
Great Sea Reef, *Fiji* **121 A2** 16 15 S 179 0 E
Great Slave L., *Canada* **130 A5** 61 23N 115 38W
Great Smoky Mts. Nat. Park, *U.S.A.* **135 H4** 35 39N 83 30W
Great Stour = Stour →, *U.K.* **17 F9** 51 15N 1 20 E
Great Victoria Desert, *Australia* **113 E4** 29 30 S 126 30 E
Great Wall, *China* **66 E5** 38 30N 109 30 E
Great Whernside, *U.K.* **16 C6** 54 9N 1 59W
Great Yarmouth, *U.K.* **16 E9** 52 40N 1 45 E
Greater Antilles, *W. Indies* **149 C5** 17 40N 74 0W
Greater London □, *U.K.* **17 F7** 51 31N 0 6W
Greater Manchester □, *U.K.* **16 D5** 53 30N 2 15W
Greater Sunda Is., *Indonesia* **70 F4** 7 0 S 112 0 E
Grebbestad, *Sweden* **15 F5** 58 42N 11 15 E
Grebenka, *U.S.S.R.* **50 F8** 50 9N 32 22 E
Greco, C., *Cyprus* **32 E13** 34 57N 34 5 E
Greco, Mte., *Italy* **40 A6** 41 48N 14 0 E
Gredos, Sierra de, *Spain* **36 E6** 40 20N 5 0W
Greece, *U.S.A.* **136 C7** 43 13N 77 41W
Greece ■, *Europe* **44 E5** 40 0N 23 0 E
Greeley, *Colo., U.S.A.* **138 E2** 40 30N 104 40W
Greeley, *Nebr., U.S.A.* **138 E5** 41 36N 98 32W
Green →, *Ky., U.S.A.* **134 G2** 37 54N 87 30W
Green →, *Utah, U.S.A.* **143 G9** 38 11N 109 53W
Green B., *U.S.A.* **134 C2** 45 0N 87 30W
Green Bay, *U.S.A.* **134 C2** 44 30N 88 0W
Green C., *Australia* **117 D9** 37 13 S 150 1 E
Green City, *U.S.A.* **140 D4** 40 16N 92 57W
Green Cove Springs, *U.S.A.* **135 L5** 29 59N 81 40W
Green Is., *Papua N. G.* **120 C8** 4 35 S 154 10 E
Green River, *U.S.A.* **143 G8** 38 59N 110 10W
Greenbank, *U.S.A.* **144 B4** 48 6N 122 34W
Greenbush, *Mich., U.S.A.* **136 B1** 44 35N 83 19W
Greenbush, *Minn., U.S.A.* **138 A6** 48 46N 96 10W
Greencastle, *U.S.A.* **141 E10** 39 40N 86 48W
Greene, *Iowa, U.S.A.* **140 B4** 42 54N 92 48W
Greene, *N.Y., U.S.A.* **137 D9** 42 20N 75 45W
Greenfield, *Calif., U.S.A.* **144 J5** 36 19N 121 15W
Greenfield, *Calif., U.S.A.* **145 K8** 35 15N 119 0W
Greenfield, *Ill., U.S.A.* **140 E6** 39 21N 90 12W
Greenfield, *Ind., U.S.A.* **141 E11** 39 47N 85 51W
Greenfield, *Iowa, U.S.A.* **140 C2** 41 18N 94 28W
Greenfield, *Mass., U.S.A.* **137 D12** 42 38N 72 38W
Greenfield, *Miss., U.S.A.* **139 G8** 37 28N 93 50W
Greenfield, *Ohio, U.S.A.* **141 E13** 39 21N 83 23W
Greenfield Park, *Canada* **137 A11** 45 29N 73 29W
Greenland ■, *N. Amer.* **127 B15** 66 0N 45 0W
Greenland Sea, *Arctic* **6 B7** 73 0N 10 0W
Greenock, *U.K.* **18 F4** 55 57N 4 46W

204 Greenore

Greenore, *Ireland* **19 B5** 54 2N 6 8W
Greenough →, *Australia* **113 E1** 28 51 S 114 38 E
Greenport, *U.S.A.* **137 E12** 41 5N 72 23W
Greensboro, *Ga., U.S.A.* **135 J4** 33 34N 83 12W
Greensboro, *N.C., U.S.A.* **135 G6** 36 7N 79 46W
Greensburg, *Ind., U.S.A.* **141 E11** 39 20N 85 30W
Greensburg, *Kans., U.S.A.* **139 G5** 37 38N 99 20W
Greensburg, *Pa., U.S.A.* **136 F5** 40 18N 79 31W
Greentown, *U.S.A.* **141 D11** 40 29N 85 58W
Greenup, *U.S.A.* **141 E8** 39 15N 88 10W
Greenville, *Liberia* **100 D3** 5 1N 9 6W
Greenville, *Ala., U.S.A.* **135 K2** 31 50N 86 37W
Greenville, *Calif., U.S.A.* **144 E6** 40 8N 120 57W
Greenville, *Ill., U.S.A.* **140 F7** 38 53N 89 22W
Greenville, *Ind., U.S.A.* **141 F11** 38 22N 85 59W
Greenville, *Maine, U.S.A.* **129 C6** 45 30N 69 32W
Greenville, *Mich., U.S.A.* **141 A11** 43 12N 85 14W
Greenville, *Miss., U.S.A.* **139 J9** 33 25N 91 0W
Greenville, *N.C., U.S.A.* **135 H7** 35 37N 77 26W
Greenville, *Ohio, U.S.A.* **141 D12** 40 5N 84 38W
Greenville, *Pa., U.S.A.* **136 E4** 41 23N 80 22W
Greenville, *S.C., U.S.A.* **135 H4** 34 54N 82 24W
Greenville, *Tenn., U.S.A.* **135 G4** 36 13N 82 51W
Greenville, *Tex., U.S.A.* **139 J6** 33 5N 96 5W
Greenwater Lake Prov. Park, *Canada* **131 C8** 52 32N 103 30W
Greenwich, *U.K.* **17 F8** 51 28N 0 0 E
Greenwich, *Conn., U.S.A.* **137 E11** 41 1N 73 38W
Greenwich, *N.Y., U.S.A.* **137 C11** 43 2N 73 36W
Greenwich, *Ohio, U.S.A.* **136 E2** 41 1N 82 32W
Greenwood, *Canada* **130 D5** 49 10N 118 40W
Greenwood, *Ind., U.S.A.* **141 E10** 39 37N 86 7W
Greenwood, *Miss., U.S.A.* **139 J9** 33 30N 90 4W
Greenwood, *S.C., U.S.A.* **135 H4** 34 13N 82 13W
Greenwood, Mt., *Australia* **112 B5** 13 48 S 130 4 E
Gregório →, *Brazil* **156 B3** 6 50 S 70 46W
Gregory, *U.S.A.* **138 D5** 43 14N 99 20W
Gregory →, *Australia* **114 B2** 17 53 S 139 17 E
Gregory, L., *S. Austral., Australia* **115 D2** 28 55 S 139 0 E
Gregory, L., *W. Austral., Australia* **113 E2** 25 38 S 119 58 E
Gregory Downs, *Australia* **114 B2** 18 35 S 138 45 E
Gregory L., *Australia* **112 D4** 20 0 S 127 40 E
Gregory Ra., *Queens., Australia* **114 B3** 19 30 S 143 40 E
Gregory Ra., *W. Austral., Australia* **112 D3** 21 20 S 121 12 E
Greiffenberg, *Germany* **26 B9** 53 6N 13 57 E
Greifswald, *Germany* **26 A9** 54 6N 13 23 E
Greifswalder Bodden, *Germany* **26 A9** 54 12N 13 35 E
Grein, *Austria* **30 C7** 48 14N 14 51 E
Greiner Wald, *Austria* **30 C8** 48 30N 15 0 E
Greiz, *Germany* **26 E8** 50 39N 12 12 E
Gremikha, *U.S.S.R.* **48 A6** 67 50N 39 40 E
Grenå, *Denmark* **15 H4** 56 25N 10 53 E
Grenada, *U.S.A.* **139 J10** 33 45N 89 50W
Grenada ■, *W. Indies* **149 D7** 12 10N 61 40W
Grenade, *France* **24 E5** 43 47N 1 17 E
Grenadines, *W. Indies* **149 D7** 12 40N 61 20W
Grenchen, *Switz.* **28 B4** 47 12N 7 24 E
Grenen, *Denmark* **15 G4** 57 44N 10 40 E
Grenfell, *Australia* **117 B8** 33 52 S 148 8 E
Grenfell, *Canada* **131 C8** 50 30N 102 56W
Grenoble, *France* **25 C9** 45 12N 5 42 E
Grenora, *U.S.A.* **138 A3** 48 38N 103 54W
Grenville, C., *Australia* **114 A3** 12 0 S 143 13 E
Grenville Chan., *Canada* **130 C3** 53 40N 129 46W
Gréoux-les-Bains, *France* **25 E9** 43 45N 5 52 E
Gresham, *U.S.A.* **144 E4** 45 30N 122 25W
Gresik, *Indonesia* **71 G15** 7 13 S 112 38 E
Grëssoney St. Jean, *Italy* **38 C4** 45 49N 7 47 E
Gretna Green, *U.K.* **18 G5** 55 0N 3 3W
Grevelingen Krammer, *Neths.* **20 E4** 51 44N 4 0 E
Greven, *Germany* **26 C3** 52 7N 7 36 E
Grevená, *Greece* **44 D3** 40 4N 21 25 E
Grevená □, *Greece* **44 D3** 40 2N 21 25 E
Grevenbroich, *Germany* **26 D2** 51 6N 6 32 E
Grevenmacher, *Lux.* **21 J8** 49 41N 6 26 E
Grevesmühlen, *Germany* **26 B7** 53 51N 11 10 E
Grevie, *Sweden* **15 H6** 56 22N 12 46 E
Grey →, *N.Z.* **119 C6** 42 27 S 171 12 E
Grey, C., *Australia* **114 A2** 13 0 S 136 35 E
Grey Ra., *Australia* **115 D3** 27 0 S 143 30 E
Grey Res., *Canada* **129 C8** 48 20N 56 30W
Greybull, *U.S.A.* **142 D9** 44 30N 108 3W
Greymouth, *N.Z.* **119 C6** 42 29 S 171 13 E
Greytown, *N.Z.* **118 H4** 41 5 S 175 29 E
Greytown, *S. Africa* **105 D5** 29 1 S 30 36 E
Gribanovskiy, *U.S.S.R.* **51 F12** 51 28N 41 50 E
Gribbell I., *Canada* **130 C3** 53 23N 129 0W
Gridley, *U.S.A.* **144 F5** 39 27N 121 47W
Griekwastad, *S. Africa* **104 D3** 28 49 S 23 15 E
Griffin, *U.S.A.* **135 J3** 33 17N 84 14W
Griffith, *Australia* **117 C7** 34 18 S 146 2 E
Grigoryevka, *U.S.S.R.* **54 F6** 50 48N 58 18 E
Grijpskerk, *Neths.* **20 B8** 53 16N 6 18 E
Grillby, *Sweden* **14 E11** 59 38N 17 15 E
Grimari, *C.A.R.* **102 A4** 5 43N 20 6 E
Grimaylov, *U.S.S.R.* **50 G5** 49 20N 26 5 E
Grimbergen, *Belgium* **21 G4** 50 56N 4 22 E
Grimes, *U.S.A.* **144 F5** 39 4N 121 54W
Grimma, *Germany* **26 D8** 51 14N 12 44 E
Grimmen, *Germany* **26 A9** 54 6N 13 2 E
Grimsby, *Canada* **136 C5** 43 12N 79 34W
Grimsby, *U.K.* **16 D7** 53 35N 0 5W
Grimselpass, *Switz.* **29 C6** 46 34N 8 23 E
Grímsey, *Iceland* **12 C5** 66 33N 17 58W
Grimshaw, *Canada* **130 B5** 56 10N 117 40W
Grimstad, *Norway* **15 F2** 58 22N 8 35 E
Grindelwald, *Switz.* **28 C6** 46 38N 8 2 E
Grindsted, *Denmark* **15 J2** 55 46N 8 55 E
Grindu, *Romania* **46 E7** 44 44N 26 50 E
Grinnell, *U.S.A.* **140 C4** 41 45N 92 43W
Griñón, *Spain* **36 E7** 40 13N 3 51W
Grintavec, *Yugoslavia* **39 B11** 46 22N 14 32 E
Grip, *Norway* **14 A1** 63 16N 7 37 E
Gris-Nez, C., *France* **23 B8** 50 52N 1 35 E
Grisolles, *France* **24 E5** 43 49N 1 19 E
Grisons = Graubünden □, *Switz.* **29 C9** 46 45N 9 30 E
Grivegnée, *Belgium* **21 G7** 50 37N 5 36 E
Grmeč Planina, *Yugoslavia* **39 D13** 44 43N 16 16 E
Groais I., *Canada* **129 B8** 50 55N 55 35W
Groblersdal, *S. Africa* **105 D4** 25 15 S 29 25 E
Grobming, *Austria* **30 D6** 47 27N 13 54 E
Grocka, *Yugoslavia* **42 C5** 44 40N 20 42 E
Gródek, *Poland* **47 B10** 53 6N 23 40 E
Grodkow, *Poland* **47 E4** 50 43N 17 21 E
Grodno, *U.S.S.R.* **50 E3** 53 42N 23 52 E
Grodzisk Mázowiecki, *Poland* **47 C7** 52 7N 20 37 E
Grodzisk Wielkopolski, *Poland* **47 C3** 52 15N 16 22 E
Grodzyanka, *U.S.S.R.* **50 E6** 53 31N 28 42 E
Groenlo, *Neths.* **20 D9** 52 2N 6 37 E
Groesbeck, *U.S.A.* **139 K6** 31 32N 96 34W
Groesbeek, *Neths.* **20 E7** 51 47N 5 58 E
Groix, *France* **22 E3** 47 38N 3 29W
Groix, I. de, *France* **22 E3** 47 38N 3 28W
Grójec, *Poland* **47 D7** 51 50N 20 58 E
Grolloo, *Neths.* **20 C9** 52 56N 6 41 E
Gronau, *Niedersachsen, Germany* **26 C5** 52 5N 9 47 E
Gronau, *Nordrhein-Westfalen, Germany* **26 C3** 52 13N 7 2 E
Grong, *Norway* **12 D12** 64 25N 12 8 E
Groningen, *Neths.* **20 B9** 53 15N 6 35 E
Groningen, *Surinam* **153 B6** 5 48N 55 28W
Groningen □, *Neths.* **20 B9** 53 16N 6 40 E
Groninger Wad, *Neths.* **20 B9** 53 27N 6 30 E
Gronsveld, *Neths.* **21 G7** 50 49N 5 44 E
Groom, *U.S.A.* **139 H4** 35 12N 100 59W
Groot →, *S. Africa* **104 E3** 33 45 S 24 36 E
Groot Berg →, *S. Africa* **104 E2** 32 47 S 18 8 E
Groot-Brakrivier, *S. Africa* **104 E3** 34 2 S 22 18 E
Groot-Kei →, *S. Africa* **105 E4** 32 41 S 28 22 E
Groot Vis →, *S. Africa* **104 E4** 33 28 S 27 5 E
Groote Eylandt, *Australia* **114 A2** 14 0 S 136 40 E
Grootebroek, *Neths.* **20 C6** 52 41N 5 13 E
Grootfontein, *Namibia* **104 B2** 19 31 S 18 6 E
Grootlaagte →, *Africa* **104 C3** 20 55 S 21 27 E
Grootvloer, *S. Africa* **104 E3** 30 0 S 20 40 E
Gros C., *Canada* **130 A6** 61 59N 113 32W
Grosa, Pta., *Spain* **33 B8** 39 6N 1 36 E
Grósio, *Italy* **38 B7** 46 18N 10 17 E
Grosne →, *France* **25 B8** 46 42N 4 56 E
Gross Glockner, *Austria* **30 D5** 47 5N 12 40 E
Grossenbrode, *Germany* **26 A7** 54 21N 11 4 E
Grossenhain, *Germany* **26 D9** 51 17N 13 32 E
Grosseto, *Italy* **38 F8** 42 45N 11 7 E
Grossgerungs, *Austria* **30 C7** 48 34N 14 57 E
Groswater B., *Canada* **129 B8** 54 20N 57 40W
Grote Gette →, *Neths.* **21 G6** 50 51N 5 6 E
Grote Nete →, *Belgium* **21 F5** 51 8N 4 34 E
Groton, *Conn., U.S.A.* **137 E12** 41 22N 72 12W
Groton, *S. Dak., U.S.A.* **138 C5** 45 27N 98 6W
Grottáglie, *Italy* **41 B10** 40 32N 17 25 E
Grottaminarda, *Italy* **41 A8** 41 5N 15 4 E
Grottammare, *Italy* **39 F10** 42 59N 13 52 E
Grouard Mission, *Canada* **130 B5** 55 33N 116 9W
Grouin, Pte. du, *France* **22 D5** 48 43N 1 51W
Groundhog →, *Canada* **128 C3** 48 45N 82 58W
Grouse Creek, *U.S.A.* **142 F7** 41 44N 113 57W
Grouw, *Neths.* **20 B7** 53 5N 5 51 E
Grove City, *Ohio, U.S.A.* **141 E13** 39 53N 83 6W
Grove City, *Pa., U.S.A.* **136 E4** 41 10N 80 5W
Groveland, *U.S.A.* **144 H6** 37 50N 120 14W
Grover City, *U.S.A.* **145 K6** 35 7N 120 37W
Grover Hill, *U.S.A.* **141 C12** 41 1N 84 29W
Groveton, *N.H., U.S.A.* **137 B13** 44 34N 71 30W
Groveton, *Tex., U.S.A.* **139 K7** 31 5N 95 4W
Grožnjan, *Yugoslavia* **39 C10** 45 22N 13 43 E
Groznyy, *U.S.S.R.* **53 E11** 43 20N 45 45 E
Grubbenvorst, *Neths.* **21 F8** 51 25N 6 9 E
Grubišno Polje, *Yugoslavia* **42 B2** 45 44N 17 12 E
Grudovo, *Bulgaria* **43 E12** 42 21N 27 10 E
Grudusk, *Poland* **47 B7** 53 3N 20 38 E
Grudziądz, *Poland* **47 B5** 53 30N 18 47 E
Gruissan, *France* **24 E7** 43 8N 3 7 E
Grumo Áppula, *Italy* **41 A9** 41 2N 16 43 E
Grünberg, *Germany* **26 E4** 50 37N 8 55 E
Grundy Center, *U.S.A.* **140 B4** 42 22N 92 45W
Gruver, *U.S.A.* **139 G4** 36 19N 101 20W
Gruyères, *Switz.* **28 C4** 46 35N 7 4 E
Gruža, *Yugoslavia* **42 D5** 43 54N 20 46 E
Gryazi, *U.S.S.R.* **51 E11** 52 30N 39 58 E
Gryazovets, *U.S.S.R.* **51 B12** 58 50N 40 10 E
Grybów, *Poland* **31 B13** 49 36N 20 55 E
Gryfice, *Poland* **47 B2** 53 55N 15 13 E
Gryfino, *Poland* **47 B1** 53 16N 14 29 E
Gryfow Sl., *Poland* **47 D2** 51 2N 15 24 E
Gstaad, *Switz.* **28 D4** 46 28N 7 18 E
Gua Musang, *Malaysia* **77 K3** 4 53N 101 58 E
Guacanayabo, G. de, *Cuba* **148 B4** 20 40N 77 20W
Guacara, *Venezuela* **152 A4** 10 14N 67 53W
Guachípas →, *Argentina* **158 B2** 25 40 S 65 30W
Guachiría →, *Colombia* **152 B3** 5 27N 70 36W
Guadajoz →, *Spain* **37 H6** 37 50N 4 51W
Guadalajara, *Mexico* **146 C4** 20 40N 103 20W
Guadalajara, *Spain* **34 E1** 40 37N 3 12W
Guadalajara □, *Spain* **34 E2** 40 47N 2 30W
Guadalcanal, *Solomon Is.* **121 M11** 9 32 S 160 12 E
Guadalcanal, *Spain* **37 G5** 38 5N 5 52W
Guadalén →, *Spain* **37 G7** 38 5N 3 32W
Guadales, *Argentina* **158 C2** 34 30 S 67 55W
Guadalete →, *Spain* **37 J4** 36 35N 6 13W
Guadalhorce →, *Spain* **37 J6** 36 41N 4 27W
Guadalimar →, *Spain* **35 G1** 38 5N 3 28W
Guadalmena →, *Spain* **35 G2** 38 19N 2 56W
Guadalmez →, *Spain* **37 G5** 38 46N 5 4W
Guadalope →, *Spain* **34 D4** 41 15N 0 3W
Guadalquivir →, *Spain* **37 J4** 36 47N 6 22W
Guadalupe = Guadeloupe ■, *W. Indies* **149 C7** 16 20N 61 40W
Guadalupe, *Brazil* **154 C3** 6 44 S 43 47W
Guadalupe, *Mexico* **145 N10** 32 4N 116 32W
Guadalupe, *Spain* **37 F5** 39 27N 5 17W
Guadalupe, *U.S.A.* **145 L6** 34 59N 120 33W
Guadalupe →, *Mexico* **145 N10** 32 6N 116 51W
Guadalupe →, *U.S.A.* **139 L6** 28 30N 96 53W
Guadalupe, Sierra de, *Spain* **37 F5** 39 28N 5 30W
Guadalupe Bravos, *Mexico* **146 A3** 31 20N 106 10W
Guadalupe Pk., *U.S.A.* **143 L11** 31 50N 105 30W
Guadalupe y Calvo, *Mexico* **146 B3** 26 6N 106 58W
Guadarrama, Sierra de, *Spain* **36 E7** 41 0N 4 0W
Guadeloupe ■, *W. Indies* **149 C7** 16 20N 61 40W
Guadeloupe Passage, *W. Indies* **149 C7** 16 50N 62 15W
Guadiamar →, *Spain* **37 J4** 36 55N 6 24W
Guadiana →, *Portugal* **37 H3** 37 14N 7 22W
Guadiana Menor →, *Spain* **35 H1** 37 56N 3 15W
Guadiaro →, *Spain* **37 J5** 36 17N 5 17W
Guadiato →, *Spain* **37 H5** 37 48N 5 5W
Guadiela →, *Spain* **34 E2** 40 22N 2 49W
Guadix, *Spain* **35 H1** 37 18N 3 11W
Guafo, Boca del, *Chile* **160 B2** 43 35 S 74 0W
Guafo, I., *Chile* **160 B2** 43 35 S 74 50W
Guainía □, *Colombia* **152 C4** 2 30N 69 0W
Guainía →, *Colombia* **152 C4** 2 1N 67 7W
Guaíra, *Brazil* **159 A5** 24 5 S 54 10W
Guaitecas, Is., *Chile* **160 B2** 44 0 S 74 30W
Guajará-Mirim, *Brazil* **157 C4** 10 50 S 65 20W
Guajira □, *Colombia* **152 A3** 11 30N 72 30W
Guajira, Pen. de la, *Colombia* **152 A3** 12 0N 72 0W
Gualaceo, *Ecuador* **152 D2** 2 54 S 78 47W
Gualán, *Guatemala* **148 C2** 15 8N 89 22W
Gualdo Tadino, *Italy* **39 E9** 43 14N 12 46 E
Gualeguay, *Argentina* **158 C4** 33 10 S 59 14W
Gualeguaychú, *Argentina* **158 C4** 33 3 S 59 31W
Gualicho, Salina, *Argentina* **160 B3** 40 25 S 65 20W
Gualjaina, *Argentina* **160 B2** 42 45 S 70 30W
Guam, *Pac. Oc.* **121 R15** 13 27N 144 45 E
Guamá, *Brazil* **154 B2** 1 37 S 47 29W
Guamá →, *Brazil* **154 B2** 1 29 S 48 30W
Guamblin, I., *Chile* **160 B2** 44 50 S 75 0W
Guaminí, *Argentina* **158 D3** 37 1 S 62 28W
Guamote, *Ecuador* **152 D2** 1 56 S 78 43W
Guampí, Sierra de, *Venezuela* **153 B4** 6 0N 65 35W
Guamúchil, *Mexico* **146 B3** 25 25N 108 3W
Guan Xian, *China* **68 B4** 31 2N 103 38 E
Guanabacoa, *Cuba* **148 B3** 23 8N 82 18W
Guanacaste, Cordillera del, *Costa Rica* **148 D2** 10 40N 85 4W
Guanaceví, *Mexico* **146 B3** 25 40N 106 0W
Guanahani = San Salvador, *Bahamas* **149 B5** 24 0N 74 40W
Guanajay, *Cuba* **148 B3** 22 56N 82 42W
Guanajuato, *Mexico* **146 C4** 21 0N 101 20W
Guanajuato □, *Mexico* **146 C4** 20 40N 101 20W
Guanambi, *Brazil* **155 D3** 14 13 S 42 47W
Guanare, *Venezuela* **152 B4** 8 42N 69 12W
Guanare →, *Venezuela* **152 B4** 8 13N 67 46W
Guandacol, *Argentina* **158 B2** 29 30 S 68 40W
Guane, *Cuba* **148 B3** 22 10N 84 7W
Guang'an, *China* **68 B6** 30 28N 106 35 E
Guangchang, *China* **69 D11** 26 50N 116 21 E
Guangde, *China* **69 B12** 30 54N 119 25 E
Guangdong □, *China* **69 F9** 23 0N 113 0 E
Guangfeng, *China* **69 C12** 28 20N 118 15 E
Guanghan, *China* **68 B5** 30 58N 104 17 E
Guanghua, *China* **69 A8** 32 22N 111 38 E
Guangji, *China* **69 C10** 29 52N 115 30 E
Guangling, *China* **66 E8** 39 47N 114 22 E
Guangning, *China* **69 F9** 23 40N 112 22 E
Guangrao, *China* **67 F10** 37 5N 118 25 E
Guangshun, *China* **68 D6** 26 8N 106 21 E
Guangwu, *China* **66 F3** 37 48N 105 57 E
Guangxi Zhuangzu Zizhiqu □, *China* **68 F7** 24 0N 109 0 E
Guangyuan, *China* **68 A5** 32 26N 105 51 E
Guangze, *China* **69 D11** 27 30N 117 12 E
Guangzhou, *China* **69 F9** 23 5N 113 10 E
Guanhães, *Brazil* **155 E3** 18 47 S 42 57W
Guanipa →, *Venezuela* **153 B5** 9 56N 62 26W
Guanling, *China* **68 E5** 25 56N 105 35 E
Guannan, *China* **67 G10** 34 8N 119 21 E
Guanta, *Venezuela* **153 A5** 10 14N 64 36W
Guantánamo, *Cuba* **149 B4** 20 10N 75 14W
Guantao, *China* **66 F8** 36 42N 115 25 E
Guanyang, *China* **69 E8** 25 30N 111 8 E
Guanyun, *China* **67 G10** 34 20N 119 18 E
Guapí, *Colombia* **152 C2** 2 36N 77 54W
Guápiles, *Costa Rica* **148 D3** 10 10N 83 46W
Guaporé →, *Brazil* **157 C4** 11 55 S 65 4W
Guaqui, *Bolivia* **156 D4** 16 41 S 68 54W
Guara, Sierra de, *Spain* **34 C4** 42 19N 0 15W
Guarabira, *Brazil* **154 C4** 6 51 S 35 29W
Guaranda, *Ecuador* **152 D2** 1 36 S 79 0W
Guarapari, *Brazil* **155 F3** 20 40 S 40 30W
Guarapuava, *Brazil* **155 G1** 25 20 S 51 30W
Guaratinguetá, *Brazil* **159 A6** 22 49 S 45 9W
Guaratuba, *Brazil* **159 B6** 25 53 S 48 38W
Guarda, *Portugal* **36 E3** 40 32N 7 20W
Guarda □, *Portugal* **36 E3** 40 40N 7 20W
Guardafui, C. = Asir, Ras, *Somali Rep.* **90 E5** 11 55N 51 10 E
Guardamar del Segura, *Spain* **35 G4** 38 5N 0 39W
Guardavalle, *Italy* **41 D9** 38 31N 16 30 E
Guardiagrele, *Italy* **39 F11** 42 11N 14 11 E
Guardo, *Spain* **36 C6** 42 47N 4 50W
Guareña, *Spain* **37 G4** 38 51N 6 6W
Guareña →, *Spain* **36 D5** 41 29N 5 23W
Guaria □, *Paraguay* **158 B4** 25 45 S 56 30W
Guárico □, *Venezuela* **152 B4** 8 40N 66 35W
Guarrojo →, *Colombia* **152 C3** 4 6N 70 42W
Guarujá, *Brazil* **159 A6** 24 2 S 46 25W
Guarus, *Brazil* **155 F3** 21 44 S 41 20W
Guasave, *Mexico* **146 B3** 25 34N 108 27W
Guascama, Pta., *Colombia* **152 C2** 2 32N 78 24W
Guasdualito, *Venezuela* **152 B3** 7 15N 70 44W
Guasipati, *Venezuela* **153 B5** 7 28N 61 54W
Guasopa, *Papua N. G.* **120 E7** 9 12 S 152 56 E
Guastalla, *Italy* **38 D7** 44 55N 10 40 E
Guatemala, *Guatemala* **148 D1** 14 40N 90 22W
Guatemala ■, *Cent. Amer.* **148 C1** 15 40N 90 30W
Guatire, *Venezuela* **152 A4** 10 28N 66 32W
Guaviare □, *Colombia* **152 C3** 2 0N 72 30W
Guaviare →, *Colombia* **152 C4** 4 3N 67 44W
Guaxupé, *Brazil* **159 A6** 21 10 S 47 5W
Guayabero →, *Colombia* **152 C3** 2 36N 72 47W
Guayama, *Puerto Rico* **149 C6** 17 59N 66 7W
Guayaneco, Arch., *Chile* **160 C1** 47 45 S 75 10W
Guayaquil, *Ecuador* **152 D2** 2 15 S 79 52W
Guayaquil, G. de, *Ecuador* **152 D1** 3 10 S 81 0W
Guayaramerín, *Bolivia* **157 C4** 10 48 S 65 23W
Guayas →, *Ecuador* **152 D2** 2 36 S 79 52W
Guaymas, *Mexico* **146 B2** 27 59N 110 54W
Guazhou, *China* **69 A12** 32 17N 119 21 E
Guba, *Zaïre* **107 E2** 10 38 S 26 27 E
Gubakha, *U.S.S.R.* **54 B5** 58 52N 57 36 E
Gûbâl, Madîq, *Egypt* **94 B3** 27 30N 34 0 E
Gubam, *Papua N. G.* **120 E1** 8 39 S 141 53 E
Gúbbio, *Italy* **39 E9** 43 20N 12 34 E
Gubin, *Poland* **47 D1** 51 57N 14 43 E
Gubio, *Nigeria* **101 C7** 12 30N 12 42 E
Gubkin, *U.S.S.R.* **51 F10** 51 17N 37 32 E
Guča, *Yugoslavia* **42 D5** 43 46N 20 15 E
Gudalur, *India* **83 J3** 11 30N 76 29 E
Gudata, *U.S.S.R.* **53 E9** 43 7N 40 10 E
Gudbrandsdalen, *Norway* **13 F10** 61 33N 9 55 E
Gudenå, *Denmark* **15 H3** 56 27N 9 40 E
Gudermes, *U.S.S.R.* **53 E12** 43 24N 46 5 E
Gudivada, *India* **83 F5** 16 30N 81 3 E
Gudiyattam, *India* **83 H4** 12 57N 78 55 E
Gudur, *India* **83 G4** 14 12N 79 55 E
Guebwiller, *France* **23 E14** 47 55N 7 12 E
Guecho, *Spain* **34 B2** 43 21N 2 59W
Guékédou, *Guinea* **100 D2** 8 40N 10 5W
Guelma, *Algeria* **99 A6** 36 25N 7 29 E
Guelph, *Canada* **128 D3** 43 35N 80 20W
Guelt es Stel, *Algeria* **99 A5** 35 12N 3 1 E
Guelttara, *Algeria* **99 C4** 29 23N 2 10W
Guemar, *Algeria* **99 B6** 33 30N 6 49 E
Guéméné-Penfao, *France* **22 E5** 47 38N 1 50W
Guéméné-sur-Scorff, *France* **22 D3** 48 4N 3 13W
Guéné, *Benin* **101 C5** 11 44N 3 16 E
Güepí, *Peru* **152 D2** 0 9 S 75 10W
Guer, *France* **22 E4** 47 54N 2 8W
Güer Aike, *Argentina* **160 D3** 51 39 S 69 35W
Guera Pk., *Chad* **97 F3** 11 55N 18 12 E
Guérande, *France* **22 E4** 47 20N 2 26W
Guercif, *Morocco* **99 B4** 34 14N 3 21W
Guéréda, *Chad* **97 F4** 14 31N 22 5 E
Guéret, *France* **24 B5** 46 11N 1 51 E
Guérigny, *France* **23 E10** 47 6N 3 10 E
Guerneville, *U.S.A.* **144 G4** 38 30N 123 0W
Guernica, *Spain* **34 B2** 43 19N 2 40W
Guernsey, *U.K.* **17 H5** 49 30N 2 35W
Guernsey, *U.S.A.* **138 D2** 42 19N 104 45W
Guerrara, *Oasis, Algeria* **99 B5** 32 51N 4 22 E
Guerrara, *Saoura, Algeria* **99 C4** 28 5N 0 8W
Guerrero □, *Mexico* **147 D5** 17 30N 100 0W
Guerzim, *Algeria* **99 C4** 29 39N 1 40W
Gueugnon, *France* **25 B8** 46 36N 4 4 E
Gueydan, *U.S.A.* **139 K8** 30 3N 92 30W
Gügher, *Iran* **85 D8** 29 28N 56 27 E
Guglionesi, *Italy* **41 A7** 41 55N 14 54 E
Gui Jiang →, *China* **69 F8** 23 30N 111 15 E
Gui Xian, *China* **68 F7** 23 8N 109 35 E
Guia, *Canary Is.* **33 F4** 28 8N 15 38W
Guia de Isora, *Canary Is.* **33 F3** 28 12N 16 46W
Guia Lopes da Laguna, *Brazil* **159 A4** 21 26 S 56 7W
Guichi, *China* **69 B11** 30 39N 117 27 E
Guider, *Cameroon* **101 D7** 9 56N 13 57 E
Guidimouni, *Niger* **97 F1** 13 42N 9 31 E
Guiding, *China* **68 D6** 26 34N 107 11 E
Guidong, *China* **69 D9** 26 7N 113 57 E
Guiglo, *Ivory C.* **100 D3** 6 45N 7 30W
Guijá, *Mozam.* **105 C5** 24 27 S 33 0 E
Guijo de Coria, *Spain* **36 E4** 40 6N 6 28W
Guildford, *U.K.* **17 F7** 51 14N 0 34W
Guilford, *U.S.A.* **129 C6** 45 12N 69 25W
Guilin, *China* **69 E8** 25 18N 110 15 E
Guillaumes, *France* **25 D10** 44 5N 6 52 E
Guillestre, *France* **25 D10** 44 39N 6 40 E
Guilvinec, *France* **22 E2** 47 48N 4 17W
Güímar, *Canary Is.* **33 F3** 28 18N 16 24W
Guimarães, *Brazil* **154 B3** 2 9 S 44 42W
Guimarães, *Portugal* **36 D2** 41 28N 8 24W
Guimaras, *Phil.* **71 B6** 10 35N 122 37 E
Guinda, *U.S.A.* **144 G4** 38 50N 122 12W
Guinea ■, *W. Afr.* **100 C2** 10 20N 11 30W
Guinea, Gulf of, *Atl. Oc.* **101 E5** 3 0N 2 30 E
Guinea-Bissau ■, *Africa* **100 C2** 12 0N 15 0W
Güines, *Cuba* **148 B3** 22 50N 82 0W
Guingamp, *France* **22 D3** 48 34N 3 10W
Guipavas, *France* **22 D2** 48 26N 4 29W
Guiping, *China* **69 F8** 23 21N 110 2 E
Guipúzcoa □, *Spain* **34 B2** 43 12N 2 15W
Guir, O. →, *Algeria* **99 B4** 31 29N 2 17W
Guiratinga, *Brazil* **157 D7** 16 21 S 53 45W
Güiria, *Venezuela* **153 A5** 10 32N 62 18W
Guiscard, *France* **23 C10** 49 40N 3 1 E
Guise, *France* **23 C10** 49 52N 3 35 E
Guitiriz, *Spain* **36 B3** 43 11N 7 50W
Guiuan, *Phil.* **71 B7** 11 5N 125 55 E
Guixi, *China* **69 C11** 28 16N 117 15 E
Guiyang, *Guizhou, China* **68 D6** 26 32N 106 40 E
Guiyang, *Hunan, China* **69 E9** 25 46N 112 42 E
Guizhou □, *China* **68 D6** 27 0N 107 0 E
Gujan-Mestras, *France* **24 D2** 44 38N 1 4W
Gujarat □, *India* **80 H4** 23 20N 71 0 E
Gujiang, *China* **69 D10** 27 11N 114 47 E
Gujranwala, *Pakistan* **79 B4** 32 10N 74 12 E
Gujrat, *Pakistan* **79 B4** 32 40N 74 2 E
Gukovo, *U.S.S.R.* **53 B8** 48 1N 39 58 E
Gulargambone, *Australia* **117 A8** 31 20 S 148 30 E
Gulbarga, *India* **82 F3** 17 20N 76 50 E
Gulbene, *U.S.S.R.* **50 C5** 57 8N 26 52 E
Gulcha, *U.S.S.R.* **55 C6** 40 19N 73 26 E
Guledagudda, *India* **83 F2** 16 3N 75 48 E

Hamilton Inlet 205

Gulf, The, Asia 85 E6 27 0N 50 0 E
Gulfport, U.S.A. 139 K10 30 21N 89 3W
Gulgong, Australia 117 B8 32 20 S 149 49 E
Gulin, China 68 C5 28 1N 105 50 E
Gulistan, Pakistan 80 D2 30 30N 66 35 E
Gulistan, U.S.S.R. 55 C4 40 29N 68 46 E
Gull Lake, Canada 131 C7 50 10N 108 29W
Gullegem, Belgium 21 G2 50 51N 3 13 E
Güllük, Turkey 88 E2 37 14N 27 35 E
Gulma, Nigeria 101 C5 12 40N 4 23 E
Gulmarg, India 81 B6 34 3N 74 25 E
Gülnar, Turkey 88 E5 36 19N 33 24 E
Gulnare, Australia 116 B3 33 27 S 138 27 E
Gulpen, Neths. 21 G7 50 49N 5 53 E
Gülpinar, Turkey 44 E8 39 32N 26 10 E
Gülşehir, Turkey 88 D6 38 44N 34 37 E
Gulshad, U.S.S.R. 56 E8 46 45N 74 25 E
Gulsvik, Norway 14 D3 60 24N 9 38 E
Gulu, Uganda 106 B3 2 48N 32 17 E
Gulwe, Tanzania 106 D4 6 30 S 36 25 E
Gulyaypole, U.S.S.R. 52 C7 47 45N 36 21 E
Gum Lake, Australia 116 B5 32 42 S 143 9 E
Gumal →, Pakistan 80 D4 31 40N 71 50 E
Gumbaz, Pakistan 80 D3 30 2N 69 0 E
Gumel, Nigeria 101 C6 12 39N 9 22 E
Gumiel de Hizán, Spain 34 D1 41 46N 3 41W
Gumlu, Australia 114 B4 19 53 S 147 41 E
Gumma □, Japan 63 A10 36 30N 138 20 E
Gummersbach, Germany 26 D3 51 2N 7 32 E
Gummi, Nigeria 101 C6 12 4N 5 9 E
Gümüşhaciköy, Turkey 52 F6 40 50N 35 18 E
Gümüşhane, Turkey 89 C8 40 30N 39 30 E
Gümüşhane □, Turkey 89 C8 40 35N 39 25 E
Gumzai, Indonesia 71 F8 5 28 S 134 42 E
Guna, Ethiopia 95 E4 11 50N 37 40 E
Guna, India 80 G7 24 40N 77 19 E
Gundagai, Australia 117 C8 35 3 S 148 6 E
Gundelfingen, Germany 27 G6 48 33N 10 22 E
Gundih, Indonesia 71 G14 7 10 S 110 56 E
Gundlakamma →, India 83 G5 15 30N 80 15 E
Gunebang, Australia 117 B7 33 1 S 146 38 E
Guneydogu Toroslar, Turkey 89 D9 38 40N 40 30 E
Gungal, Australia 117 B9 32 17 S 150 32 E
Gungu, Zaïre 103 D3 5 43 S 19 20 E
Gunisao →, Canada 131 C9 53 56N 97 53W
Gunisao L., Canada 131 C9 53 33N 96 15W
Gunnbjørn Fjeld, Greenland 6 C6 68 55N 29 47W
Gunnedah, Australia 117 A9 30 59 S 150 15 E
Gunniguldrie, Australia 117 B7 33 12 S 146 8 E
Gunningbar Cr. →, Australia 117 A7 31 14 S 147 6 E
Gunnison, Colo., U.S.A. 143 G10 38 32N 106 56W
Gunnison, Utah, U.S.A. 142 G8 39 11N 111 48W
Gunnison →, U.S.A. 143 G9 39 3N 108 30W
Gunpowder, Australia 114 B2 19 42 S 139 22 E
Guntakal, India 83 G3 15 11N 77 27 E
Guntersville, U.S.A. 135 H2 34 18N 86 16W
Guntong, Malaysia 77 K3 4 36N 101 3 E
Guntur, India 83 F5 16 23N 80 30 E
Gunungapi, Indonesia 71 F7 6 45 S 126 30 E
Gunungsitoli, Indonesia 70 D1 1 15N 97 30 E
Gunupur, India 82 E6 19 5N 83 50 E
Günz →, Germany 27 G6 48 27N 10 16 E
Gunza, Angola 103 E2 10 50 S 13 50 E
Günzburg, Germany 27 G6 48 27N 10 16 E
Gunzenhausen, Germany 27 F6 49 6N 10 45 E
Guo He →, China 67 H9 32 59N 117 10 E
Guoyang, China 66 H9 33 32N 116 12 E
Gupis, Pakistan 81 A5 36 15N 73 20 E
Gura Humorului, Romania 46 B6 47 35N 25 53 E
Gura-Teghii, Romania 46 D7 45 30N 26 25 E
Gurag, Ethiopia 95 F4 8 20N 38 20 E
Gurdaspur, India 80 C6 32 5N 75 31 E
Gurdon, U.S.A. 139 J8 33 55N 93 10W
Gurdzhaani, U.S.S.R. 53 F11 41 43N 45 52 E
Gurgaon, India 80 E7 28 27N 77 1 E
Gürgentepe, Turkey 89 C8 40 45N 38 18 E
Gurghiu, Munţii, Romania 46 C6 46 41N 25 15 E
Gurguéia →, Brazil 154 C3 6 50 S 43 24W
Gurha, India 80 G4 25 12N 71 39 E
Guri, Embalse de, Venezuela 153 B5 7 50N 62 52W
Gurk →, Austria 30 E7 46 35N 14 31 E
Gurkha, Nepal 81 E11 28 5N 84 40 E
Gurley, Australia 115 D4 29 45 S 149 48 E
Gurnee, U.S.A. 141 B9 42 22N 87 55W
Gurué, Mozam. 107 F4 15 25 S 36 58 E
Gurun, Malaysia 77 K3 5 49N 100 27 E
Gürün, Turkey 88 D7 38 43N 37 15 E
Gurupá, Brazil 153 D7 1 25 S 51 35W
Gurupá, I. Grande de, Brazil 153 D7 1 25 S 51 45W
Gurupi, Brazil 155 D2 11 43 S 49 4W
Gurupi →, Brazil 154 B2 1 13 S 46 6W
Gurupi, Serra do, Brazil 154 C2 5 0 S 47 50W
Guryev, U.S.S.R. 53 C15 47 5N 52 0 E
Gus-Khrustalnyy, U.S.S.R. 51 D12 55 42N 40 44 E
Gusau, Nigeria 101 C6 12 12N 6 40 E
Gusev, U.S.S.R. 50 D3 54 35N 22 10 E
Gushan, China 67 E12 39 50N 123 35 E
Gushi, China 69 A10 32 11N 115 41 E
Gushiago, Ghana 101 D4 9 55N 0 15W
Gusinje, Yugoslavia 42 E4 42 35N 19 50 E
Gusinoozersk, U.S.S.R. 57 D11 51 16N 106 27 E
Gúspini, Italy 40 C1 39 32N 8 38 E
Güssing, Austria 31 D9 47 3N 16 20 E
Gustanj, Yugoslavia 39 B11 46 36N 14 49 E
Gustine, U.S.A. 144 H6 37 14N 121 0W
Güstrow, Germany 26 B8 53 47N 12 12 E
Gusum, Sweden 15 F10 58 16N 16 30 E
Guta = Kalárovo, Czech. 31 D11 47 54N 18 0 E
Gütersloh, Germany 26 D4 51 54N 8 25 E
Gutha, Australia 113 E2 28 58 S 115 55 E
Guthalongra, Australia 114 B4 19 52 S 147 50 E
Guthrie, U.S.A. 139 H6 35 55N 97 30W
Guthrie Center, U.S.A. 140 C2 41 41N 94 30W
Gutian, China 69 D12 26 32N 118 43 E
Gutiérrez, Bolivia 157 D5 19 25 S 63 34W
Guttannen, Switz. 29 C6 46 38N 8 18 E
Guttenberg, U.S.A. 140 B5 42 46N 91 10W
Guyana ■, S. Amer. 153 C6 5 0N 59 0W
Guyang, China 66 D6 41 0N 110 5 E
Guyenne, France 24 D4 44 30N 0 40 E
Guymon, U.S.A. 139 G4 36 45N 101 30W
Guyra, Australia 115 E5 30 15 S 151 40 E
Guyuan, Hebei, China 66 D8 41 37N 115 40 E
Guyuan, Ningxia Huizu, China 66 G4 36 0N 106 20 E
Guzar, U.S.S.R. 55 D3 38 36N 66 15 E
Guzhang, China 68 C7 28 42N 109 58 E
Guzhen, China 67 H9 33 22N 117 18 E
Guzinozersk, U.S.S.R. 57 D11 51 20N 106 35 E
Guzmán, L. de, Mexico 146 A3 31 25N 107 25W
Gwa, Burma 78 G5 17 36N 94 34 E
Gwaai, Zimbabwe 107 F2 19 15 S 27 45 E
Gwabegar, Australia 117 A8 30 31 S 149 0 E
Gwadabawa, Nigeria 101 C6 13 28N 5 15 E
Gwādar, Pakistan 79 D1 25 10N 62 18 E
Gwagwada, Nigeria 101 C6 10 15N 7 15 E
Gwalia, Australia 113 E3 28 54 S 121 20 E
Gwalior, India 80 F8 26 12N 78 10 E
Gwanda, Zimbabwe 107 G2 20 55 S 29 0 E
Gwandu, Nigeria 101 C5 12 30N 4 41 E
Gwane, Zaïre 106 B2 4 45N 25 48 E
Gwaram, Nigeria 101 C7 10 15N 10 25 E
Gwarzo, Nigeria 101 C6 12 20N 8 55 E
Gwda →, Poland 47 B3 53 3N 16 44 E
Gweebarra B., Ireland 19 B3 54 52N 8 21W
Gweedore, Ireland 19 A3 55 4N 8 15W
Gwent □, U.K. 17 F5 51 45N 2 55W
Gweru, Zimbabwe 107 F2 19 28 S 29 45 E
Gwi, Nigeria 101 D6 9 0N 7 10 E
Gwinn, U.S.A. 134 B2 46 15N 87 29W
Gwio Kura, Nigeria 101 C7 12 40N 11 2 E
Gwol, Ghana 100 C4 10 58N 1 59W
Gwoza, Nigeria 101 C7 11 5N 13 40 E
Gwydir →, Australia 115 D4 29 27 S 149 48 E
Gwynedd □, U.K. 16 E4 53 0N 4 0W
Gyandzha, U.S.S.R. 53 F12 40 45N 46 20 E
Gyaring Hu, China 64 C4 34 50N 97 40 E
Gydanskiy P-ov., U.S.S.R. 56 C8 70 0N 78 0 E
Gympie, Australia 115 D5 26 11 S 152 38 E
Gyobingauk, Burma 78 F5 18 13N 95 39 E
Gyoda, Japan 63 A11 36 10N 139 30 E
Gyoma, Hungary 31 E13 46 56N 20 50 E
Gyöngyös, Hungary 31 D12 47 48N 19 56 E
Györ, Hungary 31 D10 47 41N 17 40 E
Györ-Sopron □, Hungary 31 D10 47 40N 17 20 E
Gypsum Palace, Australia 116 B6 32 37 S 144 9 E
Gypsum Pt., Canada 130 A6 61 53N 114 35W
Gypsumville, Canada 131 C9 51 45N 98 40W
Gyula, Hungary 31 E14 46 38N 21 17 E
Gzhatsk = Gagarin, U.S.S.R. 50 D9 55 38N 35 0 E

H

Ha 'Arava →, Israel 91 E4 30 50N 35 20 E
Ha Coi, Vietnam 76 B6 21 26N 107 46 E
Ha Dong, Vietnam 76 B5 20 58N 105 46 E
Ha Giang, Vietnam 76 A5 22 50N 104 59 E
Ha Tien, Vietnam 77 G5 10 23N 104 29 E
Ha Tinh, Vietnam 76 C5 18 20N 105 54 E
Ha Trung, Vietnam 76 C5 19 58N 105 50 E
Haacht, Belgium 21 G5 50 59N 4 37 E
Ha'afeva, Tonga 121 P13 19 57 S 174 43W
Haag, Germany 27 G8 48 11N 12 12 E
Haaksbergen, Neths. 20 D9 52 9N 6 45 E
Haaltert, Belgium 21 G4 50 55N 4 1 E
Haamstede, Neths. 21 E3 51 42N 3 45 E
Ha'ano, Tonga 121 P13 19 41 S 174 18W
Ha'apai Group, Tonga 121 P13 19 47 S 174 27W
Haapamäki, Finland 12 E18 62 18N 24 28 E
Haapsalu, U.S.S.R. 50 B3 58 56N 23 30 E
Haarlem, Neths. 20 D5 52 23N 4 39 E
Haast, N.Z. 119 D4 43 51 S 169 1 E
Haast →, N.Z. 119 D4 43 50 S 169 2 E
Haast Bluff, Australia 112 D5 23 22 S 132 0 E
Haast Pass, N.Z. 119 E4 44 6 S 169 21 E
Haastrecht, Neths. 20 E5 52 0N 4 47 E
Hab Nadi Chauki, Pakistan 80 G2 25 0N 66 50 E
Ḩabarūt, Yemen 87 C6 17 18N 52 44 E
Habaswein, Kenya 106 B4 1 2N 39 30 E
Ḩabawnah, W. →, Si. Arabia 86 C4 17 57N 44 58 E
Habay, Canada 130 B5 58 50N 118 44W
Habay-la-Neuve, Belgium 21 J7 49 44N 5 38 E
Ḩabbān, Yemen 86 D4 14 21N 47 5 E
Ḩabbānīyah, Iraq 84 C4 33 17N 43 29 E
Habiganj, Bangla. 78 C3 24 24N 91 30 E
Haboro, Japan 60 B10 44 22N 141 42 E
Haccourt, Belgium 21 G7 50 44N 5 40 E
Hachenburg, Germany 26 E3 50 40N 7 49 E
Hachijō-Jima, Japan 63 D11 33 5N 139 45 E
Hachinohe, Japan 60 D10 40 30N 141 29 E
Hachiōji, Japan 63 B11 35 40N 139 20 E
Hachŏn, N. Korea 67 D15 41 29N 129 2 E
Hachy, Belgium 21 J7 49 42N 5 41 E
Hacıbektaş, Turkey 88 D6 38 56N 34 33 E
Hacılar, Turkey 88 D6 38 38N 35 26 E
Hackensack, U.S.A. 137 F10 40 53N 74 3W
Haçli Gölü, Turkey 89 D10 39 0N 42 17 E
Hadali, Pakistan 80 C5 32 16N 72 11 E
Hadarba, Ras, Sudan 94 C4 22 4N 36 51 E
Hadarom □, Israel 91 E4 31 0N 35 0 E
Ḩadbaram, Oman 87 C6 17 27N 55 15 E
Hadd, Ras al, Oman 87 B7 22 35N 59 50 E
Ḩaddā, Si. Arabia 86 B2 21 27N 39 34 E
Haddington, U.K. 18 F6 55 57N 2 48W
Haddon Rig, Australia 117 A7 31 27 S 147 52 E
Haded Plain, Somali Rep. 108 C3 9 46N 48 2 E
Hadejia, Nigeria 101 C7 12 30N 10 5 E
Hadejia →, Nigeria 101 C7 12 50N 10 51 E
Haden, Australia 115 D5 27 13 S 151 54 E
Ḩadera, Israel 91 C3 32 27N 34 55 E
Ḩadera, N. →, Israel 91 C3 32 28N 34 52 E
Haderslev, Denmark 15 J3 55 15N 9 30 E
Hadházteglás, Hungary 31 D14 47 40N 21 40 E
Hadhramaut = Ḩaḑramawt, Yemen 87 D5 15 30N 49 30 E
Hadım, Turkey 88 E5 36 58N 32 26 E
Hadjeb El Aïoun, Tunisia 96 A1 35 21N 9 32 E
Hadong, S. Korea 67 G14 35 5N 127 44 E
Ḩaḑramawt, Yemen 87 D5 15 30N 49 30 E
Ḩaḑramawt, W. →, Yemen 87 D5 16 0N 48 53 E
Ḩadrānīyah, Iraq 84 C4 35 38N 43 14 E
Hadrian's Wall, U.K. 16 C5 55 0N 2 30W
Hadsten, Denmark 15 H4 56 19N 10 3 E
Hadsund, Denmark 15 H4 56 44N 10 8 E
Haeju, N. Korea 67 E13 38 3N 125 45 E
Haenam, S. Korea 67 G14 34 34N 126 35 E
Haerhpin = Harbin, China 67 B14 45 48N 126 40 E
Hafar al Bāţin, Si. Arabia 84 D5 28 25N 46 0 E
Hafik, Turkey 88 D7 39 51N 37 23 E
Ḩafīrat al 'Aydā, Si. Arabia 84 E3 26 26N 39 12 E
Ḩafit, Oman 87 B6 23 59N 55 49 E
Hafizabad, Pakistan 80 C5 32 5N 73 40 E
Haflong, India 78 C4 25 10N 93 5 E
Hafnarfjörður, Iceland 12 D3 64 4N 21 57W
Hafun, Ras, Somali Rep. 90 E5 10 29N 51 30 E
Hagalil, Israel 91 C4 32 53N 35 18 E
Hagari →, India 83 G3 15 40N 77 0 E
Hagen, Germany 26 D3 51 21N 7 29 E
Hagenow, Germany 26 B7 53 25N 11 10 E
Hagerman, U.S.A. 139 J2 33 5N 104 22W
Hagerstown, Ind., U.S.A. 141 E11 39 55N 85 10W
Hagerstown, Md., U.S.A. 134 F7 39 39N 77 46W
Hagetmau, France 24 E3 43 39N 0 37W
Hagfors, Sweden 13 F12 60 3N 13 45 E
Häggenås, Sweden 14 A8 63 24N 14 55 E
Hagi, Iceland 12 D2 65 28N 23 25W
Hagi, Japan 62 C3 34 30N 131 22 E
Hagolan, Syria 91 C4 33 0N 35 45 E
Hagondange-Briey, France 23 C13 49 16N 6 11 E
Hags Hd., Ireland 19 D2 52 57N 9 30W
Hague, C. de la, France 22 C5 49 44N 1 56W
Hague, The = 's-Gravenhage, Neths. 20 D4 52 7N 4 17 E
Haguenau, France 23 D14 48 49N 7 47 E
Hai □, Tanzania 106 C4 3 10 S 37 10 E
Hai Duong, Vietnam 76 B6 20 56N 106 19 E
Hai'an, Guangdong, China 69 G8 20 18N 110 11 E
Hai'an, Jiangsu, China 69 A13 32 37N 120 27 E
Haicheng, Fujian, China 69 E11 24 23N 117 48 E
Haicheng, Liaoning, China 67 D12 40 50N 122 45 E
Haidar Khel, Afghan. 80 C3 33 58N 68 38 E
Haifa = Ḩefa, Israel 91 C4 32 46N 35 0 E
Haifeng, China 69 F10 22 58N 115 10 E
Haig, Australia 113 F4 30 55 S 126 10 E
Haiger, Germany 26 E4 50 44N 8 12 E
Haikang, China 69 G8 20 52N 110 8 E
Haikou, China 65 D6 20 1N 110 16 E
Ḩā'il, Si. Arabia 84 E4 27 28N 41 45 E
Hailakandi, India 78 C4 24 42N 92 34 E
Hailar, China 65 B6 49 10N 119 38 E
Hailey, U.S.A. 142 E6 43 30N 114 15W
Haileybury, Canada 128 C4 47 30N 79 38W
Hailin, China 67 B15 44 37N 129 30 E
Hailing Dao, China 69 G8 21 35N 111 47 E
Hailong, China 67 C13 42 32N 125 40 E
Hailuoto, Finland 12 D18 65 3N 24 45 E
Haimen, Guangdong, China 69 F11 23 15N 116 38 E
Haimen, Jiangsu, China 69 B13 31 52N 121 10 E
Haimen, Zhejiang, China 69 C13 28 40N 121 24 E
Hainan □, China 65 E5 19 0N 109 30 E
Hainaut □, Belgium 21 H4 50 30N 4 0 E
Hainburg, Austria 31 C9 48 9N 16 56 E
Haines, U.S.A. 142 D5 44 51N 117 59W
Haines City, U.S.A. 135 L5 28 6N 81 35W
Haines Junction, Canada 130 A1 60 45N 137 30W
Hainfeld, Austria 30 C8 48 3N 15 48 E
Haining, China 69 B13 30 28N 120 40 E
Haiphong, Vietnam 64 D5 20 47N 106 41 E
Haiti ■, W. Indies 149 C5 19 0N 72 30W
Haiya Junction, Sudan 94 D4 18 20N 36 21 E
Haiyan, China 69 B13 30 28N 120 58 E
Haiyang, China 67 F11 36 47N 121 9 E
Haiyuan, Guangxi Zhuangzu, China 68 F6 22 8N 107 35 E
Haiyuan, Ningxia Huizu, China 66 F3 36 35N 105 52 E
Haizhou, China 67 G10 34 37N 119 7 E
Haizhou Wan, China 67 G10 34 50N 119 20 E
Haja, Indonesia 71 E7 3 19 S 129 37 E
Hajar Bangar, Sudan 97 F4 10 40N 22 45 E
Hajdú-Bihar □, Hungary 31 D14 47 30N 21 30 E
Hajdúböszörmény, Hungary 31 D14 47 40N 21 30 E
Hajdúdurog, Hungary 31 D14 47 48N 21 30 E
Hajdúnánás, Hungary 31 D14 47 50N 21 26 E
Hajdúsámson, Hungary 31 D14 47 37N 21 42 E
Hajdúszoboszló, Hungary 31 D14 47 27N 21 22 E
Hajiganj, Bangla. 78 D3 23 15N 90 50 E
Hajipur, India 81 G11 25 45N 85 13 E
Ḩajjah, Yemen 86 D3 15 42N 43 36 E
Ḩājjī Muḩsin, Iraq 84 C5 32 35N 45 29 E
Ḩājjīābād, Eşfahan, Iran 85 C7 33 41N 54 50 E
Ḩājjīābād, Hormozgān, Iran 85 D7 28 19N 55 55 E
Hajnówka, Poland 47 C10 52 47N 23 35 E
Ḩajrah, Si. Arabia 86 B3 20 14N 41 3 E
Haka, Burma 78 D4 22 39N 93 37 E
Hakansson, Mts., Zaïre 103 D5 8 40 S 25 45 E
Håkantorp, Sweden 15 F6 58 18N 12 55 E
Hakataramea, N.Z. 119 E5 44 43 S 170 30 E
Ḩakkan, Oman 87 B7 20 22N 56 58 E
Hakkâri, Turkey 89 E10 37 34N 43 44 E
Hakkâri □, Turkey 89 E11 37 30N 44 0 E
Hakkâri Dağları, Turkey 89 E10 37 45N 42 35 E
Hakken-Zan, Japan 63 C7 34 10N 135 54 E
Hakodate, Japan 60 D10 41 45N 140 44 E
Hakota, Japan 63 A12 36 5N 140 30 E
Haku-San, Japan 63 A8 36 9N 136 46 E
Hakui, Japan 61 F8 36 53N 136 47 E
Hakun, Burma 78 B5 26 46N 95 42 E
Hala, Pakistan 79 D3 25 43N 68 20 E
Ḩalab, Syria 84 B3 36 10N 37 15 E
Ḩalaban, Si. Arabia 86 B4 23 29N 44 23 E
Ḩalabjah, Iraq 84 C5 35 10N 45 58 E
Halaib, Sudan 94 C4 22 12N 36 30 E
Halanzy, Belgium 21 J7 49 33N 5 44 E
Hālāt' Ammār, Si. Arabia 84 D3 29 10N 36 4 E
Halbā, Lebanon 91 A5 34 34N 36 6 E
Halberstadt, Germany 26 D7 51 53N 11 2 E
Halcombe, N.Z. 118 G4 40 8 S 175 30 E
Halcon, Mt., Phil. 71 B6 13 0N 121 30 E
Halden, Norway 14 E5 59 9N 11 23 E
Haldensleben, Germany 26 C7 52 17N 11 30 E
Haldwani, India 81 E8 29 31N 79 30 E
Hale, U.S.A. 140 E3 39 36N 93 20W
Hale →, Australia 114 C2 24 56 S 135 53 E
Haleakala Crater, U.S.A. 132 H16 20 43N 156 12W
Halen, Belgium 21 G6 50 57N 5 6 E
Haleyville, U.S.A. 135 H2 34 15N 87 40W
Half Assini, Ghana 100 D4 5 1N 2 50W
Halfmoon Bay, N.Z. 119 G3 46 50 S 168 5 E
Halfway →, Canada 130 B4 56 12N 121 32W
Haliburton, Canada 128 C4 45 3N 78 30W
Halicarnassus, Turkey 45 G9 37 3N 27 30 E
Halifax, Australia 114 B4 18 32 S 146 22 E
Halifax, Canada 129 D7 44 38N 63 35W
Halifax, U.K. 16 D6 53 43N 1 51W
Halifax B., Australia 114 B4 18 50 S 147 0 E
Halifax I., Namibia 104 D2 26 38 S 15 4 E
Halīl →, Iran 85 E8 27 40N 58 30 E
Halin, Somali Rep. 108 C3 9 6N 48 37 E
Hall, Austria 30 D4 47 17N 11 30 E
Hall Beach, Canada 127 B11 68 46N 81 12W
Hall Pt., Australia 112 C3 15 40 S 124 23 E
Hallands län □, Sweden 15 H6 56 50N 12 50 E
Hallands Väderö, Sweden 15 H6 56 27N 12 34 E
Hallandsås, Sweden 15 H7 56 22N 13 0 E
Halle, Belgium 21 G4 50 44N 4 13 E
Halle, Nordrhein-Westfalen, Germany 26 C4 52 4N 8 20 E
Halle, Sachsen-Anhalt, Germany 26 D8 51 29N 12 0 E
Hällefors, Sweden 13 G13 59 47N 14 31 E
Hallein, Austria 30 D6 47 40N 13 5 E
Hällekis, Sweden 15 F7 58 38N 13 27 E
Hallett, Australia 116 B3 33 25 S 138 55 E
Hallettsville, U.S.A. 139 L6 29 28N 96 57W
Hällevadsholm, Sweden 15 F5 58 35N 11 33 E
Hallia →, India 82 F4 16 55N 79 20 E
Halliday, U.S.A. 138 B3 47 20N 102 25W
Halliday L., Canada 131 A7 61 21N 108 56W
Hallim, S. Korea 67 H14 33 24N 126 15 E
Hallingdal →, Norway 13 F10 60 34N 9 12 E
Hällnäs, Sweden 12 D15 64 19N 19 36 E
Hallock, U.S.A. 131 D9 48 47N 97 0W
Halls Creek, Australia 112 C4 18 16 S 127 38 E
Hallstahammar, Sweden 14 E10 59 38N 16 15 E
Hallstatt, Austria 30 D6 47 33N 13 38 E
Hallstead, U.S.A. 137 E9 41 56N 75 45W
Halmahera, Indonesia 71 D7 0 40N 128 0 E
Halmeu, Romania 46 B4 47 57N 23 2 E
Halmstad, Sweden 15 H6 56 41N 12 52 E
Halq el Oued, Tunisia 96 A2 36 53N 10 18 E
Hals, Denmark 15 H4 56 59N 10 18 E
Halsafjorden, Norway 14 A2 63 5N 8 10 E
Hälsingborg = Helsingborg, Sweden 15 H6 56 3N 12 42 E
Halstad, U.S.A. 138 B6 47 21N 96 50W
Haltdalen, Norway 14 B5 62 56N 11 8 E
Haltern, Germany 26 D3 51 44N 7 10 E
Halul, Qatar 85 E7 25 40N 52 40 E
Ḩalvān, Iran 85 C8 33 57N 56 15 E
Ham, France 23 C10 49 45N 3 4 E
Ham Tan, Vietnam 77 G6 10 40N 107 45 E
Ham Yen, Vietnam 76 A5 22 4N 105 3 E
Hamab, Namibia 104 D2 28 7 S 19 16 E
Hamad, Sudan 95 D3 15 20N 33 32 E
Hamada, Japan 62 C4 34 56N 132 4 E
Hamadān, Iran 85 C6 34 52N 48 32 E
Hamadān □, Iran 85 C6 35 0N 49 0 E
Hamadia, Algeria 99 A5 35 28N 1 57 E
Hamāh, Syria 84 C3 35 5N 36 40 E
Hamakita, Japan 63 C9 34 45N 137 47 E
Hamamatsu, Japan 63 C9 34 45N 137 45 E
Hamar, Norway 14 D5 60 48N 11 7 E
Hamarøy, Norway 12 B13 68 5N 15 38 E
Hamâta, Gebel, Egypt 94 C4 24 17N 35 0 E
Hamber Prov. Park, Canada 130 C5 52 20N 118 0W
Hamburg, Germany 26 B5 53 32N 9 59 E
Hamburg, Ark., U.S.A. 139 J9 33 15N 91 47W
Hamburg, Iowa, U.S.A. 138 E7 40 37N 95 38W
Hamburg, N.Y., U.S.A. 136 D6 42 44N 78 50W
Hamburg, Pa., U.S.A. 137 F9 40 33N 76 0W
Hamburg □, Germany 26 B6 53 30N 10 0 E
Ḩamḑ, W. al →, Si. Arabia 84 E3 24 55N 36 20 E
Ḩamḑah, Si. Arabia 86 C3 19 2N 43 36 E
Ḩamdānah, Si. Arabia 86 C3 19 59N 40 34 E
Hamden, U.S.A. 137 E12 41 21N 72 56W
Hame □, Finland 13 F18 61 30N 24 0 E
Hämeenlinna, Finland 13 F18 61 0N 24 28 E
Hamélé, Ghana 100 C4 10 56N 2 45W
Hamelin Pool, Australia 113 E1 26 22 S 114 20 E
Hameln, Germany 26 C5 52 7N 9 24 E
Hamer Koke, Ethiopia 95 F4 5 15N 36 45 E
Hamerkaz □, Israel 91 C3 32 15N 34 55 E
Hamersley Ra., Australia 112 D2 22 0 S 117 45 E
Hamhung, N. Korea 67 E14 39 54N 127 30 E
Hami, China 64 B4 42 55N 93 25 E
Hamilton, Australia 116 D5 37 45 S 142 2 E
Hamilton, Canada 128 D4 43 15N 79 50W
Hamilton, N.Z. 118 D4 37 47 S 175 19 E
Hamilton, U.K. 18 F4 55 47N 4 2W
Hamilton, Ill., U.S.A. 140 D5 40 24N 91 21W
Hamilton, Ind., U.S.A. 141 C12 41 33N 84 56W
Hamilton, Mo., U.S.A. 138 F8 39 45N 93 59W
Hamilton, Mo., U.S.A. 140 E3 39 45N 93 59W
Hamilton, Mont., U.S.A. 142 C6 46 20N 114 6W
Hamilton, N.Y., U.S.A. 137 D9 42 49N 75 31W
Hamilton, Ohio, U.S.A. 141 E12 39 20N 84 35W
Hamilton, Tex., U.S.A. 139 K5 31 40N 98 5W
Hamilton →, Australia 114 C2 23 30 S 139 47 E
Hamilton City, U.S.A. 144 F4 39 45N 122 1W
Hamilton Hotel, Australia 114 C3 22 45 S 140 40 E
Hamilton Inlet, Canada 129 B8 54 0N 57 30W

Hinchinbrook I. 207

Hazlehurst, Miss., U.S.A. 139 K9 31 52N 90 24W
Hazleton, Ind., U.S.A. 141 F9 38 29N 87 34W
Hazleton, Pa., U.S.A. 137 F9 40 58N 76 0W
Hazlett, L., Australia 112 D4 21 30 S 128 48 E
Hazor, Israel 91 B4 33 2N 35 32 E
He Xian, Anhui, China 69 B12 31 45N 118 20 E
He Xian, Guangxi Zhuangzu, China 69 E8 24 27N 111 30 E
Head of Bight, Australia 113 F5 31 30 S 131 25 E
Headlands, Zimbabwe 107 F3 18 15 S 32 2 E
Healdsburg, U.S.A. 144 G4 38 33N 122 51W
Healdton, U.S.A. 139 H6 34 16N 97 31W
Healesville, Australia 117 D6 37 35 S 145 30 E
Heanor, U.K. 16 D6 53 1N 1 20W
Heard I., Ind. Oc. 109 K6 53 0 S 74 0 E
Hearne, U.S.A. 139 K6 30 54N 96 35W
Hearne B., Canada 131 A9 60 10N 99 10W
Hearne L., Canada 130 A6 62 20N 113 10W
Hearst, Canada 128 C3 49 40N 83 41W
Heart →, U.S.A. 138 B4 46 40N 100 51W
Heart's Content, Canada 129 C9 47 54N 53 27W
Heath →, Bolivia 156 C4 12 31 S 68 38W
Heath Mts., N.Z. 119 F2 45 39 S 167 9 E
Heath Pt., Canada 129 C7 49 8N 61 40W
Heath Steele, Canada 129 C6 47 17N 66 5W
Heathcote, Australia 117 D6 36 56 S 144 45 E
Heavener, U.S.A. 139 H7 34 54N 94 36W
Hebbronville, U.S.A. 139 M5 27 20N 98 40W
Hebei □, China 66 E9 39 0N 116 0 E
Hebel, Australia 115 D4 28 58 S 147 47 E
Heber, U.S.A. 145 N11 32 44N 115 32W
Heber Springs, U.S.A. 139 H9 35 29N 91 59W
Hebert, Canada 131 C7 50 30N 107 10W
Hebgen, L., U.S.A. 142 D8 44 50N 111 15W
Hebi, China 66 G8 35 57N 114 7 E
Hebrides, U.K. 18 D2 57 30N 7 0W
Hebron = Al Khalīl, Jordan 91 D4 31 32N 35 6 E
Hebron, Canada 127 C13 58 5N 62 30W
Hebron, N. Dak., U.S.A. 138 B3 46 56N 102 2W
Hebron, Nebr., U.S.A. 138 E6 40 15N 97 33W
Hecate Str., Canada 130 C2 53 10N 130 30W
Hechi, China 68 E7 24 40N 108 2 E
Hechingen, Germany 27 G4 48 20N 8 58 E
Hechtel, Belgium 21 F6 51 8N 5 22 E
Hechuan, China 68 B6 30 2N 106 12 E
Hecla, U.S.A. 138 C5 45 56N 98 8W
Hecla I., Canada 131 C9 51 10N 96 43W
Heddal, Norway 14 E3 59 36N 9 9 E
Hédé, France 22 D5 48 18N 1 49W
Hede, Sweden 14 B7 62 23N 13 30 E
Hedemora, Sweden 13 F13 60 18N 15 58 E
Hedgehope, N.Z. 119 G3 46 12 S 168 34 E
Hedley, U.S.A. 139 H4 34 53N 100 39W
Hedmark fylke □, Norway 14 C5 61 17N 11 40 E
Hedrick, U.S.A. 140 C4 41 11N 92 19W
Hedrum, Norway 14 E4 59 7N 10 5 E
Heeg, Neths. 20 C7 52 58N 5 37 E
Heegermeer, Neths. 20 C7 52 56N 5 32 E
Heemskerk, Neths. 20 C5 52 31N 4 40 E
Heemstede, Neths. 20 D5 52 22N 4 37 E
Heer, Neths. 21 G7 50 50N 5 43 E
Heerde, Neths. 20 D8 52 24N 6 2 E
's Heerenburg, Neths. 20 E8 51 53N 6 16 E
Heerenveen, Neths. 20 C7 52 57N 5 55 E
Heerhugowaard, Neths. 20 C5 52 40N 4 51 E
Heerlen, Neths. 21 G7 50 55N 5 58 E
Heers, Belgium 21 G6 50 45N 5 18 E
Heesch, Neths. 20 E7 51 44N 5 32 E
Heestert, Belgium 21 G2 50 47N 3 25 E
Heeze, Neths. 21 F7 51 23N 5 35 E
Hefa, Israel 91 C4 32 46N 35 0 E
Hefa □, Israel 91 C4 32 40N 35 0 E
Hefei, China 69 B11 31 52N 117 18 E
Hegang, China 65 B8 47 20N 130 19 E
Hegyalja, Hungary 31 C14 48 25N 21 25 E
Heichengzhen, China 66 F4 36 24N 106 3 E
Heide, Germany 26 A5 54 10N 9 7 E
Heidelberg, Germany 27 F4 49 23N 8 41 E
Heidelberg, C. Prov., S. Africa 104 E3 34 6 S 20 59 E
Heidelberg, Trans., S. Africa 105 D4 26 30 S 28 23 E
Heidenheim, Germany 27 G6 48 40N 10 10 E
Heigun-To, Japan 62 D4 33 47N 132 14 E
Heijing, China 68 E3 25 22N 101 44 E
Heilbron, S. Africa 105 D4 27 16 S 27 59 E
Heilbronn, Germany 27 F5 49 8N 9 13 E
Heiligenblut, Austria 30 D5 47 2N 12 51 E
Heiligenhafen, Germany 26 A6 54 21N 10 58 E
Heiligenstadt, Germany 26 D6 51 22N 10 9 E
Heilongjiang □, China 67 A14 48 0N 126 0 E
Heilunkiang = Heilongjiang □, China 67 A14 48 0N 126 0 E
Heino, Neths. 20 D8 52 26N 6 14 E
Heinola, Finland 13 F19 61 13N 26 2 E
Heinsch, Belgium 21 J7 49 42N 5 44 E
Heinsun, Burma 78 C5 25 52N 95 35 E
Heirnkut, Burma 78 C5 25 14N 94 44 E
Heishan, China 67 D12 41 40N 122 5 E
Heishui, Liaoning, China 67 C10 42 8N 119 30 E
Heishui, Sichuan, China 68 A4 32 4N 103 2 E
Heist, Belgium 21 F2 51 20N 3 15 E
Heist-op-den-Berg, Belgium 21 F5 51 5N 4 44 E
Hejaz = Al Ḥijāz, Si. Arabia 86 A2 26 0N 37 30 E
Hejian, China 66 E9 38 25N 116 5 E
Hejiang, China 68 C5 28 43N 105 46 E
Hejin, China 66 G6 35 35N 110 42 E
Hekelgem, Belgium 21 G4 50 55N 4 7 E
Hekımhan, Turkey 89 D7 38 50N 37 55 E
Hekinan, Japan 63 C9 34 52N 137 0 E
Hekla, Iceland 12 E4 63 56N 19 35W
Hekou, Gansu, China 66 F2 36 10N 103 28 E
Hekou, Guangdong, China 69 F9 23 13N 112 45 E
Hekou, Yunnan, China 64 D5 22 30N 103 59 E
Hel, Poland 47 A5 54 37N 18 47 E
Helagsfjället, Sweden 14 B6 62 54N 12 25 E
Helan Shan, China 66 E3 38 30N 105 55 E
Helchteren, Belgium 21 F6 51 4N 5 22 E
Helden, Neths. 21 F8 51 19N 6 0 E
Helechosa, Spain 37 F6 39 22N 4 53W
Helena, Ark., U.S.A. 139 H9 34 30N 90 35W
Helena, Mont., U.S.A. 142 C7 46 40N 112 5W
Helendale, U.S.A. 145 L9 34 44N 117 19W
Helensburgh, Australia 117 C9 34 11 S 151 1 E
Helensburgh, U.K. 18 F4 56 0N 4 44W
Helensville, N.Z. 118 C3 36 41 S 174 29 E
Helgeroa, Norway 14 F3 59 0N 9 45 E
Helgoland, Germany 26 A3 54 10N 7 51 E
Heligoland = Helgoland, Germany 26 A3 54 10N 7 51 E
Heliopolis, Egypt 94 H7 30 6N 31 17 E
Hellebæk, Denmark 15 H6 56 4N 12 32 E
Hellendoorn, Neths. 20 D8 52 24N 6 27 E
Hellevoetsluis, Neths. 20 E4 51 50N 4 8 E
Hellín, Spain 35 G3 38 31N 1 40W
Helmand □, Afghan. 79 C2 31 20N 64 0 E
Helmand →, Afghan. 79 C1 31 12N 61 34 E
Helme →, Germany 26 D7 51 40N 11 20 E
Helmond, Neths. 21 F7 51 29N 5 41 E
Helmsdale, U.K. 18 C5 58 7N 3 40W
Helmstedt, Germany 26 C7 52 16N 11 0 E
Helnæs, Denmark 15 J4 55 9N 10 0 E
Helong, China 67 C15 42 40N 129 0 E
Helper, U.S.A. 142 G8 39 44N 110 56W
Helsingborg, Sweden 15 H6 56 3N 12 42 E
Helsinge, Denmark 15 H6 56 2N 12 12 E
Helsingfors, Finland 13 F18 60 15N 25 3 E
Helsingør, Denmark 15 H6 56 2N 12 35 E
Helsinki, Finland 13 F18 60 15N 25 3 E
Helska, Mierzeja, Poland 47 A5 54 45N 18 40 E
Helston, U.K. 17 G2 50 7N 5 17W
Helvellyn, U.K. 16 C4 54 31N 3 1W
Helvoirt, Neths. 21 E6 51 38N 5 14 E
Helwân, Egypt 94 J7 29 50N 31 20 E
Hemavati →, India 83 H3 12 30N 76 20 E
Hemet, U.S.A. 145 M10 33 45N 116 59W
Hemingford, U.S.A. 138 D3 42 21N 103 4W
Hemphill, U.S.A. 139 K8 31 21N 93 49W
Hempstead, U.S.A. 139 K6 30 5N 96 5W
Hemse, Sweden 13 H15 57 15N 18 22 E
Hemsö, Sweden 14 B12 62 43N 18 5 E
Hen & Chickens Is., N.Z. 118 B3 35 58 S 174 45 E
Henan □, China 66 H8 34 0N 114 0 E
Henares →, Spain 34 E1 40 24N 3 30W
Henashi-Misaki, Japan 60 D9 40 37N 139 51 E
Hendaye, France 24 E2 43 23N 1 47W
Hendek, Turkey 88 C4 40 48N 30 44 E
Henderson, Argentina 158 D3 36 18 S 61 43W
Henderson, Ky., U.S.A. 141 G9 37 50N 87 38W
Henderson, N.C., U.S.A. 135 G6 36 20N 78 25W
Henderson, Nev., U.S.A. 145 J12 36 2N 115 0W
Henderson, Pa., U.S.A. 135 H1 35 25N 88 40W
Henderson, Tex., U.S.A. 139 J7 32 5N 94 49W
Hendersonville, U.S.A. 135 H4 35 21N 82 28W
Hendījān, Iran 85 D6 30 14N 49 43 E
Hendon, Australia 115 D5 28 5 S 151 50 E
Hendorf, Romania 46 C5 46 4N 24 55 E
Heng Xian, China 68 F7 22 40N 109 17 E
Hengcheng, China 66 E4 38 18N 106 28 E
Hengdaohezi, China 67 B15 44 52N 129 0 E
Hengelo, Gelderland, Neths. 20 D8 52 3N 6 19 E
Hengelo, Overijssel, Neths. 20 D9 52 16N 6 48 E
Hengfeng, China 69 C10 28 12N 115 48 E
Hengshan, Hunan, China 69 D9 27 16N 112 45 E
Hengshan, Shaanxi, China 66 F5 37 58N 109 5 E
Hengshui, China 66 F8 37 41N 115 40 E
Hengyang, Hunan, China 69 D9 26 52N 112 33 E
Hengyang, Hunan, China 69 D9 26 59N 112 22 E
Hénin-Beaumont, France 23 B9 50 25N 2 58 E
Henlopen, C., U.S.A. 134 F8 38 48N 75 5W
Hennan, Sweden 14 B9 62 3N 15 46 E
Hennebont, France 22 E3 47 49N 3 19W
Hennenman, S. Africa 104 D4 27 59 S 27 1 E
Hennepin, U.S.A. 140 C7 41 15N 89 21W
Hennessey, U.S.A. 139 G6 36 8N 97 53W
Hennigsdorf, Germany 26 C9 52 38N 13 13 E
Henrichemont, France 23 E9 47 20N 2 30 E
Henrietta, U.S.A. 139 J5 33 50N 98 15W
Henrietta, Ostrov, U.S.S.R. 57 B16 77 6N 156 30 E
Henrietta Maria C., Canada 128 A3 55 9N 82 20W
Henry, U.S.A. 140 C7 41 5N 89 20W
Henryetta, U.S.A. 139 H7 35 30N 96 0W
Hensall, Canada 136 C3 43 26N 81 30W
Hentiyn Nuruu, Mongolia 65 B5 48 30N 108 30 E
Henty, Australia 115 F4 35 30 S 147 0 E
Henzada, Burma 78 G5 17 38N 95 26 E
Hephaestia, Greece 44 E7 39 55N 25 14 E
Heping, China 69 E10 24 29N 115 0 E
Heppner, U.S.A. 142 D4 45 21N 119 34W
Hepu, China 68 G7 21 40N 109 12 E
Hepworth, Canada 136 B3 44 37N 81 9W
Heqing, China 68 D3 26 37N 100 11 E
Hequ, China 66 E6 39 20N 111 15 E
Héraðsflói, Iceland 12 D6 65 42N 14 12W
Héraðsvötn →, Iceland 12 D4 65 45N 19 25W
Herald Cays, Australia 114 B4 16 58 S 149 9 E
Herāt, Afghan. 79 B1 34 20N 62 7 E
Herāt □, Afghan. 79 B1 35 0N 62 0 E
Hérault □, France 24 E7 43 34N 3 15 E
Hérault →, France 24 E7 43 17N 3 26 E
Herbault, France 22 E8 47 36N 1 8 E
Herbert →, Australia 114 B4 18 31 S 146 17 E
Herbert Downs, Australia 114 C2 23 7 S 139 9 E
Herberton, Australia 114 B4 17 20 S 145 25 E
Herbertville, N.Z. 118 G5 40 30 S 176 33 E
Herbignac, France 22 E4 47 27N 2 18W
Herborn, Germany 26 E4 50 40N 8 19 E
Herby, Poland 47 E5 50 45N 18 50 E
Hercegnovi, Yugoslavia 42 E3 42 30N 18 33 E
Hercegovina = Bosna i Hercegovina □, Yugoslavia 42 D2 44 0N 17 0 E
Herculaneum, U.S.A. 140 F6 38 16N 90 23W
Herðubreið, Iceland 12 D5 65 11N 16 21W
Hereford, U.K. 17 E5 52 4N 2 42W
Hereford, U.S.A. 139 H3 34 50N 102 28W
Hereford and Worcester □, U.K. 17 E5 52 10N 2 30W
Herefoss, Norway 15 F2 58 32N 8 23 E
Herekino, N.Z. 118 B2 35 18 S 173 11 E
Herent, Belgium 21 G5 50 54N 4 40 E
Herentals, Belgium 21 F5 51 12N 4 51 E
Herenthout, Belgium 21 F5 51 8N 4 45 E
Herfølge, Denmark 15 J6 55 26N 12 9 E
Herford, Germany 26 C4 52 7N 8 40 E
Héricourt, France 23 E13 47 32N 6 45 E
Herington, U.S.A. 138 F6 38 43N 97 0W
Herisau, Switz. 29 B8 47 22N 9 17 E
Hérisson, France 24 B6 46 32N 2 42 E
Herjehogna, Norway 13 F12 61 43N 12 7 E
Herk →, Belgium 21 G6 50 56N 5 12 E
Herkenbosch, Neths. 21 F8 51 9N 6 4 E
Herkimer, U.S.A. 137 D10 43 0N 74 59W
Herlong, U.S.A. 144 E6 40 8N 120 8W
Herm, Chan. Is. 22 C4 49 30N 2 28W
Hermagor-Pressegger See, Austria 30 E6 46 38N 13 23 E
Herman, U.S.A. 138 C6 45 51N 96 8W
Hermann, U.S.A. 138 F9 38 40N 91 25W
Hermannsburg, Germany 26 C6 52 49N 10 6 E
Hermannsburg Mission, Australia 112 D5 23 57 S 132 45 E
Hermanus, S. Africa 104 E2 34 27 S 19 12 E
Herment, France 24 C6 45 45N 2 24 E
Hermidale, Australia 117 A7 31 30 S 146 42 E
Hermiston, U.S.A. 142 D4 45 50N 119 16W
Hermitage, N.Z. 119 D5 43 44 S 170 5 E
Hermitage, U.S.A. 140 G3 37 56N 93 19W
Hermite, I., Chile 160 E3 55 50 S 68 0W
Hermon, Mt. = Ash Shaykh, J., Lebanon 91 B4 33 25N 35 50 E
Hermosillo, Mexico 146 B2 29 10N 111 0W
Hernád →, Hungary 31 D14 47 56N 21 8 E
Hernandarias, Paraguay 159 B5 25 20 S 54 40W
Hernandez, U.S.A. 144 J6 36 24N 120 46W
Hernando, Argentina 158 C3 32 28 S 63 40W
Hernando, U.S.A. 139 H10 34 50N 89 59W
Herne, Belgium 21 G4 50 44N 4 2 E
Herne, Germany 21 E10 51 33N 7 12 E
Herne Bay, U.K. 17 F9 51 22N 1 8 E
Herning, Denmark 15 H2 56 8N 8 58 E
Heroica = Caborca, Mexico 146 A2 30 40N 112 10W
Heroica Nogales = Nogales, Mexico 146 A2 31 20N 110 56W
Heron Bay, Canada 128 C2 48 40N 86 25W
Herradura, Pta. de la, Canary Is. 33 F5 28 26N 14 8W
Herreid, U.S.A. 138 C4 45 53N 100 5W
Herrera, Spain 37 H6 37 26N 4 55W
Herrera de Alcántar, Spain 37 F3 39 39N 7 25W
Herrera de Pisuerga, Spain 36 C6 42 35N 4 20W
Herrera del Duque, Spain 37 F5 39 10N 5 3W
Herrick, Australia 114 G4 41 5 S 147 55 E
Herrin, U.S.A. 139 G10 37 50N 89 0W
Herrljunga, Sweden 15 F7 58 5N 13 1 E
Hersbruck, Germany 27 F7 49 30N 11 25 E
Herseaux, Belgium 21 G2 50 43N 3 15 E
Herselt, Belgium 21 F5 51 3N 4 53 E
Hersonissos, Greece 32 D7 35 18N 25 22 E
Herstal, Belgium 21 G7 50 40N 5 38 E
Hertford, U.K. 17 F7 51 47N 0 4W
Hertfordshire □, U.K. 17 F7 51 51N 0 5W
's-Hertogenbosch, Neths. 21 E6 51 42N 5 17 E
Hertzogville, S. Africa 104 D4 28 9 S 25 30 E
Hervás, Spain 36 E5 40 16N 5 52W
Herve, Belgium 21 G7 50 38N 5 48 E
Herwijnen, Neths. 20 E6 51 50N 5 7 E
Herzberg, Brandenburg, Germany 26 D9 51 40N 13 13 E
Herzberg, Niedersachsen, Germany 26 D6 51 38N 10 20 E
Herzele, Belgium 21 G3 50 53N 3 53 E
Herzliyya, Israel 91 C3 32 10N 34 50 E
Herzogenbuchsee, Switz. 28 B5 47 11N 7 42 E
Herzogenburg, Austria 30 C8 48 17N 15 41 E
Ḥeṣār, Fārs, Iran 85 D6 29 52N 50 16 E
Ḥeṣār, Markazī, Iran 85 C6 35 49N 49 24 E
Hesdin, France 23 B9 50 21N 2 2 E
Hesel, Germany 26 B3 53 18N 7 36 E
Heshui, China 66 G5 36 0N 108 0 E
Heshun, China 66 F7 37 22N 113 32 E
Hesperange, Lux. 21 J8 49 35N 6 10 E
Hesperia, U.S.A. 145 L9 34 25N 117 18W
Hesse = Hessen □, Germany 26 E5 50 40N 9 20 E
Hessen □, Germany 26 E5 50 40N 9 20 E
Hetch Hetchy Aqueduct, U.S.A. 144 H5 37 36N 121 25W
Hettinger, U.S.A. 138 C3 46 0N 102 38W
Hettstedt, Germany 26 D7 51 39N 11 30 E
Heugem, Neths. 21 G7 50 49N 5 42 E
Heule, Belgium 21 G2 50 51N 3 15 E
Heusden, Belgium 21 F6 51 2N 5 17 E
Heusden, Neths. 20 E6 51 44N 5 8 E
Hève, C. de la, France 22 C7 49 30N 0 5 E
Heverlee, Belgium 21 G5 50 52N 4 42 E
Heves □, Hungary 31 D13 47 50N 20 0 E
Hewett, C., Canada 127 A13 70 16N 67 45W
Hexham, U.K. 16 C5 54 58N 2 7W
Hexi, Yunnan, China 68 E4 24 9N 102 38 E
Hexi, Zhejiang, China 69 D12 27 58N 119 38 E
Hexigten Qi, China 67 C9 43 18N 117 30 E
Hexrivier, S. Africa 104 E2 33 30 S 19 35 E
Ḥeydarābād, Iran 85 D7 30 33N 55 38 E
Heyfield, Australia 117 D7 37 59 S 146 47 E
Heysham, U.K. 16 C5 54 5N 2 53W
Heythuysen, Neths. 21 F7 51 15N 5 55 E
Heyuan, China 69 F10 23 39N 114 40 E
Heywood, Australia 116 E4 38 8 S 141 37 E
Heze, China 66 G8 35 14N 115 20 E
Hezhang, China 68 D5 27 8N 104 41 E
Hi-no-Misaki, Japan 62 B4 35 26N 132 38 E
Hi Vista, U.S.A. 145 L9 34 45N 117 46W
Hialeah, U.S.A. 135 N5 25 49N 80 17W
Hiawatha, Kans., U.S.A. 138 F7 39 55N 95 33W
Hiawatha, Utah, U.S.A. 142 G8 39 29N 111 1W
Hibbing, U.S.A. 138 B8 47 30N 93 0W
Hibbs B., Australia 114 G4 42 35 S 145 15 E
Hibernia Reef, Australia 112 B3 12 0 S 123 23 E
Hibiki-Nada, Japan 62 D2 34 0N 130 0 E
Hickory, U.S.A. 135 H5 35 46N 81 17W
Hicks, Pt., Australia 117 D8 37 49 S 149 17 E
Hicks Bay, N.Z. 118 D7 37 34 S 178 21 E
Hicksville, N.Y., U.S.A. 137 F11 40 46N 73 30W
Hicksville, Ohio, U.S.A. 141 C12 41 18N 84 46W
Hida, Romania 46 B4 47 10N 23 19 E
Hida-Gawa →, Japan 63 B9 35 26N 137 3 E
Hida-Sammyaku, Japan 63 A9 36 30N 137 40 E
Hida-Sanchi, Japan 63 A9 36 10N 137 0 E
Hidaka, Japan 62 B6 35 30N 134 44 E
Hidaka-Sammyaku, Japan 60 C11 42 35N 142 45 E
Hidalgo, Mexico 147 C5 24 15N 99 26W
Hidalgo, U.S.A. 141 E8 39 9N 88 9W
Hidalgo □, Mexico 147 C5 20 30N 99 10W
Hidalgo, Presa M., Mexico 146 B3 26 30N 108 35W
Hidalgo, Pta. del, Canary Is. 33 F3 28 33N 16 19W
Hidalgo del Parral, Mexico 146 B3 26 58N 105 40W
Hiddensee, Germany 26 A9 54 30N 13 6 E
Hidrolândia, Brazil 155 E2 17 0 S 49 15W
Hieflau, Austria 30 D7 47 36N 14 46 E
Hiendelaencina, Spain 34 D2 41 5N 3 0W
Hienghène, N. Cal. 121 T18 20 41 S 164 56 E
Hierapolis, Turkey 88 E3 37 57N 28 50 E
Hierro, Canary Is. 33 G1 27 44N 18 0 E
Higashi-matsuyama, Japan 63 A11 36 2N 139 25 E
Higashiajima-San, Japan 60 F10 37 40N 140 10 E
Higashiōsaka, Japan 63 C7 34 40N 135 37 E
Higasi-Suidō, Japan 62 D1 34 0N 129 30 E
Higbee, U.S.A. 140 E4 39 19N 92 31W
Higgins, U.S.A. 139 G4 36 9N 100 1W
Higgins Corner, U.S.A. 144 F5 39 2N 121 5W
Higginsville, Australia 113 F3 31 42 S 121 38 E
Higginsville, U.S.A. 140 E3 39 4N 93 43W
High Atlas = Haut Atlas, Morocco 98 B4 32 30N 5 0W
High I., Canada 129 A7 56 40N 61 10W
High Island, U.S.A. 139 L7 29 32N 94 22W
High Level, Canada 130 B5 58 31N 117 8W
High Point, U.S.A. 135 H6 35 57N 79 58W
High Prairie, Canada 130 B5 55 30N 116 30W
High River, Canada 130 C6 50 30N 113 50W
High Springs, U.S.A. 135 L4 29 50N 82 40W
High Wycombe, U.K. 17 F7 51 37N 0 45W
Highbank, N.Z. 119 D6 43 37 S 171 45 E
Highbury, Australia 114 B3 16 25 S 143 9 E
Highland, Ill., U.S.A. 140 F7 38 44N 89 41W
Highland, Ind., U.S.A. 141 C9 41 33N 87 28W
Highland, Wis., U.S.A. 140 A6 43 6N 90 21W
Highland □, U.K. 18 D4 57 30N 5 0W
Highland Park, U.S.A. 141 B9 42 10N 87 50W
Highmore, U.S.A. 138 C5 44 35N 99 26W
Highrock L., Canada 131 B7 57 5N 105 32W
Higüay, Dom. Rep. 149 C6 18 37N 68 42W
Hihya, Egypt 94 H7 30 40N 31 36 E
Hiiumaa, U.S.S.R. 50 B3 58 50N 22 45 E
Híjar, Spain 34 D4 41 10N 0 27W
Ḥijāz □, Si. Arabia 86 B3 24 0N 40 0 E
Hijāz, Jabal al, Si. Arabia 86 C3 19 45N 41 55 E
Hiji, Japan 62 D3 33 22N 131 32 E
Hijken, Neths. 20 C9 52 54N 6 30 E
Hijo = Tagum, Phil. 71 C7 7 33N 125 53 E
Hikari, Japan 62 D3 33 58N 131 58 E
Hiketa, Japan 62 C6 34 13N 134 24 E
Hiko, U.S.A. 144 H11 37 30N 115 13W
Hikone, Japan 63 B8 35 15N 136 10 E
Hikurangi, N.Z. 118 B3 35 36 S 174 17 E
Hikurangi, Mt., N.Z. 118 E5 38 21 S 176 52 E
Hilawng, Burma 78 E4 21 23N 93 48 E
Hildburghhausen, Germany 27 E6 50 24N 10 43 E
Hildesheim, Germany 26 C5 52 9N 9 55 E
Hill →, Australia 113 F2 30 23 S 115 3 E
Hill City, Idaho, U.S.A. 142 E6 43 20N 115 2W
Hill City, Kans., U.S.A. 138 F5 39 25N 99 51W
Hill City, Minn., U.S.A. 138 B8 46 57N 93 35W
Hill City, S. Dak., U.S.A. 138 D3 43 58N 103 35W
Hill End, Australia 117 E7 38 1 S 146 9 E
Hill Island L., Canada 131 A7 60 30N 109 50W
Hillared, Sweden 15 G7 57 37N 13 10 E
Hillcrest Center, U.S.A. 145 K8 35 23N 118 57W
Hillegom, Neths. 20 D5 52 18N 4 35 E
Hillerød, Denmark 15 J6 55 56N 12 19 E
Hilli, Bangla. 78 C2 25 17N 89 1 E
Hillingdon, U.K. 17 F7 51 33N 0 29W
Hillman, U.S.A. 134 C4 45 5N 83 52W
Hillmond, Canada 131 C7 53 26N 109 41W
Hillsboro, Ill., U.S.A. 140 E7 39 9N 89 29W
Hillsboro, Iowa, U.S.A. 140 D5 40 50N 91 42W
Hillsboro, Kans., U.S.A. 138 F6 38 22N 97 10W
Hillsboro, Mo., U.S.A. 140 F6 38 14N 90 34W
Hillsboro, N. Dak., U.S.A. 138 B6 47 23N 97 9W
Hillsboro, N.H., U.S.A. 137 C13 43 8N 71 56W
Hillsboro, N. Mex., U.S.A. 143 K10 33 0N 107 35W
Hillsboro, Ohio, U.S.A. 141 E13 39 12N 83 37W
Hillsboro, Oreg., U.S.A. 144 E4 45 31N 123 0W
Hillsboro, Tex., U.S.A. 139 J6 32 5N 97 10W
Hillsborough, Grenada 149 D7 12 28N 61 28W
Hillsdale, Mich., U.S.A. 141 C12 41 55N 84 40W
Hillsdale, N.Y., U.S.A. 137 D11 42 11N 73 30W
Hillside, Australia 112 D2 21 45 S 119 23 E
Hillsport, Canada 128 C2 49 27N 85 34W
Hillston, Australia 117 B6 33 30 S 145 31 E
Hilo, U.S.A. 132 J17 19 44N 155 5W
Hilton, U.S.A. 136 C7 43 16N 77 48W
Hilvan, Turkey 89 E8 37 34N 38 58 E
Hilvarenbeek, Neths. 21 F6 51 29N 5 8 E
Hilversum, Neths. 20 D6 52 14N 5 10 E
Himachal Pradesh □, India 80 D7 31 30N 77 0 E
Himalaya, Asia 81 E11 29 0N 84 0 E
Himara, Albania 44 D1 40 8N 19 43 E
Hime-Jima, Japan 62 D3 33 43N 131 40 E
Himeji, Japan 62 C6 34 50N 134 40 E
Himi, Japan 63 A8 36 50N 136 55 E
Himmerland, Denmark 15 H3 56 45N 9 30 E
Ḥimṣ, Syria 91 A5 34 40N 36 45 E
Ḥims □, Syria 91 A6 34 30N 37 0 E
Hinche, Haiti 149 C5 19 9N 72 1W
Hinchinbrook I., Australia 114 B4 18 20 S 146 15 E

210 Icabarú

Icabarú →, *Venezuela* **153 C5** 4 45N 62 15W
Içana, *Brazil* **152 C4** 0 21N 67 19W
Içana →, *Brazil* **152 C4** 0 26N 67 19W
Icatu, *Brazil* **154 B3** 2 46 S 44 4W
Içel = Mersin, *Turkey* **88 E6** 36 51N 34 36 E
Içel □, *Turkey* **88 E6** 36 45N 34 0 E
Iceland ■, *Atl. Oc.* **12 D4** 64 45N 19 0W
Icha, *U.S.S.R.* **57 D16** 55 30N 156 0 E
Ich'ang = Yichang, *China* **69 B8** 30 40N 111 20 E
Ichchapuram, *India* **82 E7** 19 10N 84 40 E
Ichihara, *Japan* **63 B12** 35 28N 140 5 E
Ichikawa, *Japan* **63 B11** 35 44N 139 55 E
Ichilo →, *Bolivia* **157 D5** 15 57 S 64 50W
Ichinohe, *Japan* **60 D10** 40 13N 141 17 E
Ichinomiya, *Gifu, Japan* **63 B8** 35 18N 136 48 E
Ichinomiya, *Kumamoto, Japan* **62 E3** 32 58N 131 5 E
Ichinoseki, *Japan* **60 E10** 38 55N 141 8 E
Ichnya, *U.S.S.R.* **50 F8** 50 52N 32 24 E
Ichŏn, *S. Korea* **67 F14** 37 17N 127 27 E
Icht, *Morocco* **98 C3** 29 6N 8 54W
Ichtegem, *Belgium* **21 F2** 51 5N 3 1 E
Icó, *Brazil* **154 C4** 6 24 S 38 51W
Icod, *Canary Is.* **33 F3** 28 22N 16 43W
Icoraci, *Brazil* **154 B2** 1 18 S 48 28W
Icy Str., *U.S.A.* **130 B1** 58 20N 135 30W
Ida Grove, *U.S.A.* **138 D7** 42 20N 95 25W
Ida Valley, *Australia* **113 E3** 28 42 S 120 29 E
Idabel, *U.S.A.* **139 J7** 33 53N 94 50W
Idaga Hamus, *Ethiopia* **95 E4** 14 13N 39 48 E
Idah, *Nigeria* **101 D6** 7 5N 6 40 E
Idaho □, *U.S.A.* **142 D7** 44 10N 114 0W
Idaho City, *U.S.A.* **142 E6** 43 50N 115 52W
Idaho Falls, *U.S.A.* **142 E7** 43 30N 112 1W
Idaho Springs, *U.S.A.* **142 G11** 39 49N 105 30W
Idanha-a-Nova, *Portugal* **36 F3** 39 50N 7 15W
Idar-Oberstein, *Germany* **27 F3** 49 43N 7 19 E
Idd el Ghanam, *Sudan* **97 F4** 11 30N 24 19 E
Iddan, *Somali Rep.* **90 F4** 6 10N 48 55 E
Idehan, *Libya* **96 C2** 27 10N 11 30 E
Idehan Marzūq, *Libya* **96 D2** 24 50N 13 51 E
Idelès, *Algeria* **99 D6** 23 50N 5 53 E
Idfû, *Egypt* **94 C3** 24 55N 32 49 E
Ídhi Óros, *Greece* **32 D6** 35 15N 24 45 E
Ídhra, *Greece* **45 G5** 37 20N 23 28 E
Idi, *Indonesia* **70 C1** 5 2N 97 37 E
Idiofa, *Zaïre* **103 C3** 4 55 S 19 42 E
Idku, Bahra el, *Egypt* **94 H7** 31 18N 30 18 E
Idlib, *Syria* **84 C3** 35 55N 36 36 E
Idria, *U.S.A.* **144 J6** 36 25N 120 41W
Idrija, *Yugoslavia* **39 C11** 46 0N 14 5 E
Idritsa, *U.S.S.R.* **50 C6** 56 25N 28 30 E
Idstein, *Germany* **27 E4** 50 13N 8 17 E
Idutywa, *S. Africa* **105 E4** 32 8 S 28 18 E
Ieper, *Belgium* **21 G1** 50 51N 2 53 E
Ierápetra, *Greece* **32 E7** 35 0N 25 44 E
Ierissós, *Greece* **44 D5** 40 22N 23 52 E
Ierissóu Kólpos, *Greece* **44 D5** 40 27N 23 57 E
Ierzu, *Italy* **40 C2** 39 48N 9 32 E
Ieshima-Shotō, *Japan* **62 C6** 34 40N 134 32 E
Iesi, *Italy* **39 E10** 43 32N 13 12 E
Ifach, Punta, *Spain* **35 G5** 38 38N 0 5 E
'Ifâl, W. al →, *Si. Arabia* **84 D2** 28 7N 35 3 E
Ifanadiana, *Madag.* **105 C8** 21 19 S 47 39 E
Ife, *Nigeria* **101 D5** 7 30N 4 31 E
Iférouâne, *Niger* **97 E1** 19 5N 8 24 E
Iffley, *Australia* **114 B3** 18 53 S 141 12 E
Ifni, *Morocco* **98 C2** 29 29N 10 12W
Ifon, *Nigeria* **101 D6** 6 58N 5 40 E
Iforas, Adrar des, *Mali* **101 B5** 19 40N 1 40 E
Ifould, L., *Australia* **113 F5** 30 52 S 132 6 E
Ifrane, *Morocco* **98 B3** 33 33N 5 7W
Iga, *Japan* **63 C8** 34 45N 136 10 E
Iganga, *Uganda* **106 B3** 0 37N 33 28 E
Igara Paraná →, *Colombia* **152 D3** 2 9 S 71 47W
Igarapava, *Brazil* **155 F2** 20 3 S 47 47W
Igarapé Açu, *Brazil* **154 B2** 1 4 S 47 33W
Igarapé-Mirim, *Brazil* **154 B2** 1 59 S 48 58W
Igarka, *U.S.S.R.* **57 C9** 67 30N 86 33 E
Igatimi, *Paraguay* **159 A4** 24 5 S 55 40W
Igatpuri, *India* **82 E1** 19 40N 73 35 E
Igbetti, *Nigeria* **101 D5** 8 44N 4 8 E
Igbo-Ora, *Nigeria* **101 D5** 7 29N 3 15 E
Igboho, *Nigeria* **101 D5** 8 53N 3 50 E
Iğdır, *Turkey* **89 D11** 39 55N 44 2 E
Iggesund, *Sweden* **14 C11** 61 39N 17 10 E
Ighil Izane, *Algeria* **99 A5** 35 44N 0 31 E
Iglésias, *Italy* **40 C1** 39 19N 8 27 E
Igli, *Algeria* **99 B4** 30 25N 2 19W
Iglino, *U.S.S.R.* **54 D5** 54 50N 56 26 E
Igloolik, *Canada* **127 B11** 69 20N 81 49W
Igma, Gebel el, *Egypt* **94 J8** 28 55N 34 0 E
Ignace, *Canada* **128 C1** 49 30N 91 40W
İğneada Burnu, *Turkey* **88 C3** 41 53N 28 2 E
Igoshevo, *U.S.S.R.* **51 B13** 59 25N 42 35 E
Igoumenítsa, *Greece* **44 E2** 39 32N 20 18 E
Igra, *U.S.S.R.* **54 C3** 57 33N 53 7 E
Iguaçu →, *Brazil* **159 B5** 25 36 S 54 36W
Iguaçu, Cat. del, *Brazil* **159 B5** 25 41 S 54 26W
Iguaçu Falls = Iguaçu, Cat. del, *Brazil* **159 B5** 25 41 S 54 26W
Iguala, *Mexico* **147 D5** 18 20N 99 40W
Igualada, *Spain* **34 D6** 41 37N 1 37 E
Iguape, *Brazil* **155 F2** 24 43 S 47 33W
Iguassu = Iguaçu →, *Brazil* **159 B5** 25 36 S 54 36W
Iguatu, *Brazil* **154 C4** 6 20 S 39 18W
Iguéla, *Gabon* **102 C1** 2 0 S 9 16 E
Igunga □, *Tanzania* **106 C3** 4 20 S 33 45 E
Iheya-Shima, *Japan* **61 L3** 27 4N 127 58 E
Ihiala, *Nigeria* **101 D6** 5 51N 6 55 E
Ihosy, *Madag.* **105 C8** 22 24 S 46 8 E
Ihotry, L., *Madag.* **105 C7** 21 56 S 43 41 E
Ii, *Finland* **12 D18** 65 19N 25 22 E
Ii-Shima, *Japan* **61 L3** 26 43N 127 47 E
Iida, *Japan* **63 B9** 35 35N 137 50 E
Iijoki →, *Finland* **12 D18** 65 20N 25 20 E
Iisalmi, *Finland* **12 E19** 63 32N 27 10 E
Iiyama, *Japan* **61 F9** 36 51N 138 22 E
Iizuka, *Japan* **62 D2** 33 38N 130 42 E
Ijâfene, *Mauritania* **98 D3** 20 40N 8 0W
Ijebu-Igbo, *Nigeria* **101 D5** 6 56N 4 1 E
Ijebu-Ode, *Nigeria* **101 D5** 6 47N 3 58 E
IJmuiden, *Neths.* **20 D5** 52 28N 4 35 E
IJssel →, *Neths.* **20 C7** 52 35N 5 50 E
IJsselmeer, *Neths.* **20 C6** 52 45N 5 20 E
IJsselmuiden, *Neths.* **20 C7** 52 34N 5 57 E
IJsselstein, *Neths.* **20 D6** 52 1N 5 2 E
Ijuí →, *Brazil* **159 B4** 27 58 S 55 20W
Ijūin, *Japan* **62 F2** 31 37N 130 24 E
IJzendijke, *Neths.* **21 F3** 51 19N 3 37 E
IJzer →, *Belgium* **21 F1** 51 9N 2 44 E
Ik →, *U.S.S.R.* **54 D3** 55 55N 52 36 E
Ikale, *Nigeria* **101 D6** 7 40N 5 37 E
Ikare, *Nigeria* **101 D6** 7 32N 5 40 E
Ikaría, *Greece* **45 G8** 37 35N 26 10 E
Ikast, *Denmark* **15 H3** 56 8N 9 10 E
Ikawa, *Japan* **63 B10** 35 13N 138 15 E
Ikeda, *Japan* **62 C5** 34 1N 133 48 E
Ikeja, *Nigeria* **101 D5** 6 36N 3 23 E
Ikela, *Zaïre* **102 C4** 1 6 S 23 6 E
Ikenge, *Zaïre* **102 C3** 0 8 S 18 8 E
Ikerre-Ekiti, *Nigeria* **101 D6** 7 25N 5 19 E
Ikhtiman, *Bulgaria* **43 E8** 42 27N 23 48 E
Iki, *Japan* **62 D1** 33 45N 129 42 E
Iki-Kaikyō, *Japan* **62 D1** 33 40N 129 45 E
Ikimba L., *Tanzania* **106 C3** 1 30 S 31 20 E
Ikire, *Nigeria* **101 D5** 7 23N 4 15 E
Ikitsuki-Shima, *Japan* **62 D1** 33 23N 129 26 E
İkizdere, *Turkey* **89 C9** 40 46N 40 32 E
Ikom, *Nigeria* **101 D6** 6 0N 8 42 E
Ikopa →, *Madag.* **105 B8** 16 45 S 46 40 E
Ikot Ekpene, *Nigeria* **101 D6** 5 12N 7 40 E
'Ikrimah, *Libya* **96 B4** 32 2N 23 41 E
Ikungu, *Tanzania* **106 C3** 1 33 S 33 42 E
Ikuno, *Japan* **62 B6** 35 10N 134 48 E
Ikurun, *Nigeria* **101 D5** 7 54N 4 40 E
Ila, *Nigeria* **101 D5** 8 0N 4 39 E
Ilagan, *Phil.* **71 A6** 17 7N 121 53 E
Īlām, *Iran* **84 C5** 33 0N 46 0 E
Ilam, *Nepal* **81 F12** 26 58N 87 58 E
Ilanskiy, *U.S.S.R.* **57 D10** 56 14N 96 3 E
Ilanz, *Switz.* **29 C8** 46 46N 9 12 E
Ilaro, *Nigeria* **101 D5** 6 53N 3 3 E
Iława, *Poland* **47 B6** 53 36N 19 34 E
Ilayangudi, *India* **83 K4** 9 34N 78 37 E
Ilbilbie, *Australia* **114 C4** 21 45 S 149 20 E
Ile-à-la-Crosse, *Canada* **131 B7** 55 27N 107 53W
Ile-à-la-Crosse, Lac, *Canada* **131 B7** 55 40N 107 45W
Île-de-France, *France* **23 D9** 49 0N 2 20 E
Ilebo, *Zaïre* **103 C4** 4 17 S 20 55 E
Ileje □, *Tanzania* **107 D3** 9 30 S 33 25 E
Ilek, *U.S.S.R.* **54 F3** 51 32N 53 21 E
Ilek →, *U.S.S.R.* **54 F3** 51 30N 53 22 E
Ilero, *Nigeria* **101 D5** 8 0N 3 20 E
Ilesha, *Kwara, Nigeria* **101 D5** 8 57N 3 28 E
Ilesha, *Oyo, Nigeria* **101 D5** 7 37N 4 40 E
Ilford, *Canada* **131 B9** 56 4N 95 35W
Ilfracombe, *Australia* **114 C3** 23 30 S 144 30 E
Ilfracombe, *U.K.* **17 F3** 51 13N 4 8W
Ilgaz, *Turkey* **88 C5** 40 55N 33 37 E
Ilgaz Dağları, *Turkey* **88 C5** 41 10N 33 50 E
Ilgın, *Turkey* **88 D4** 38 16N 31 55 E
Ilha Grande, *Brazil* **153 D4** 0 27 S 65 2W
Ilha Grande, B. da, *Brazil* **155 F3** 23 9 S 44 30W
Ílhavo, *Portugal* **36 E2** 40 33N 8 43W
Ilhéus, *Brazil* **155 D4** 14 49 S 39 2W
Ili →, *U.S.S.R.* **55 A8** 45 53N 77 10 E
Ilia, *Romania* **46 D3** 45 57N 22 40 E
Ilia □, *Greece* **45 G3** 37 45N 21 35 E
Iliç, *Turkey* **89 D8** 39 27N 38 33 E
Ilich, *U.S.S.R.* **55 C4** 40 50N 68 27 E
Iliff, *U.S.A.* **138 E3** 40 50N 103 3W
Iligan, *Phil.* **71 C6** 8 12N 124 13 E
Ilíki, L., *Greece* **45 F5** 38 24N 23 15 E
Iliodhrómia, *Greece* **44 E5** 39 12N 23 50 E
Ilion, *U.S.A.* **137 D9** 43 0N 75 3W
Ilirska-Bistrica, *Yugoslavia* **39 C11** 45 34N 14 14 E
Ilkal, *India* **83 G3** 15 57N 76 8 E
Ilkeston, *U.K.* **16 E6** 52 59N 1 19W
Illampu = Ancohuma, Nevada, *Bolivia* **156 D4** 16 0 S 68 50W
Illana B., *Phil.* **71 C6** 7 35N 123 45 E
Illapel, *Chile* **158 C1** 32 0 S 71 10W
Ille-et-Vilaine □, *France* **22 D5** 48 10N 1 30W
Ille-sur-Têt, *France* **24 F6** 42 40N 2 38 E
Iller →, *Germany* **27 G5** 48 23N 9 58 E
Illescas, *Spain* **36 E7** 40 8N 3 51W
Illetas, *Spain* **33 B9** 39 32N 2 35 E
Illiers-Combray, *France* **22 D8** 48 18N 1 15 E
Illimani, *Bolivia* **156 D4** 16 30 S 67 50W
Illinois □, *U.S.A.* **140 D7** 40 15N 89 30W
Illinois →, *U.S.A.* **140 F6** 38 55N 90 28W
Illiopolis, *U.S.A.* **140 E7** 39 51N 89 15W
Illium = Troy, *Turkey* **44 E8** 39 57N 26 12 E
Illizi, *Algeria* **99 C6** 26 31N 8 32 E
Illora, *Spain* **37 H7** 37 17N 3 53W
Ilm →, *Germany* **26 D7** 51 7N 11 45 E
Ilmen, Oz., *U.S.S.R.* **50 B7** 58 15N 31 10 E
Ilmenau, *Germany* **26 E6** 50 41N 10 55 E
Ilo, *Peru* **156 D3** 17 40 S 71 20W
Ilobu, *Nigeria* **101 D5** 7 45N 4 25 E
Iloilo, *Phil.* **71 B6** 10 45N 122 33 E
Ilok, *Yugoslavia* **42 B4** 45 15N 19 20 E
Ilora, *Nigeria* **101 D5** 7 45N 3 50 E
Ilorin, *Nigeria* **101 D5** 8 30N 4 35 E
Iloulya, *U.S.S.R.* **53 B11** 49 15N 44 2 E
Ilovatka, *U.S.S.R.* **51 F14** 50 30N 45 50 E
Ilovlya →, *U.S.S.R.* **53 B10** 49 14N 43 54 E
Iłowa, *Poland* **47 D2** 51 30N 15 10 E
Ilubabor □, *Ethiopia* **95 F4** 7 25N 35 0 E
Ilukste, *U.S.S.R.* **50 D5** 55 55N 26 20 E
Ilva Mică, *Romania* **46 B5** 47 17N 24 40 E
Ilwaco, *U.S.A.* **144 D2** 46 19N 124 3W
Ilwaki, *Indonesia* **71 F7** 7 55 S 126 30 E
Ilyichevsk, *U.S.S.R.* **52 C4** 46 10N 30 35 E
Iłża, *Poland* **47 D8** 51 10N 21 15 E
Iłżanka →, *Poland* **47 D8** 51 14N 21 48 E
Imabari, *Japan* **62 C5** 34 4N 133 0 E
Imaichi, *Japan* **63 A11** 36 43N 139 46 E
Imaloto →, *Madag.* **105 C8** 23 27 S 45 13 E
İmamoğlu, *Turkey* **88 E6** 37 15N 35 38 E
Imandra, Oz., *U.S.S.R.* **48 A5** 67 30N 33 0 E
Imari, *Japan* **62 D1** 33 15N 129 52 E
Imasa, *Sudan* **94 D4** 18 0N 36 12 E
Imathía □, *Greece* **44 D4** 40 30N 22 15 E
Imbâbah, *Egypt* **94 H7** 30 5N 31 12 E
Imbabura □, *Ecuador* **152 C2** 0 30N 78 45W
Imbaimadai, *Guyana* **153 B5** 5 44N 60 17W
Imbler, *U.S.A.* **142 D5** 45 31N 118 0W
Imdahane, *Morocco* **98 B3** 32 8N 7 0W
imeni 26 Bakinskikh Komissarov, *Azerbaijan, U.S.S.R.* **49 G8** 39 19N 49 12 E
imeni 26 Bakinskikh Komissarov, *Turkmen S.S.R., U.S.S.R.* **49 G9** 39 22N 54 10 E
Imeni Panfilova, *U.S.S.R.* **55 B8** 43 23N 77 7 E
Imeni Poliny Osipenko, *U.S.S.R.* **57 D14** 52 30N 136 29 E
Imeri, Serra, *Brazil* **152 C4** 0 50N 65 25W
Imerimandroso, *Madag.* **105 B8** 17 26 S 48 35 E
Imesan, *Mauritania* **98 D1** 22 54N 15 30W
Imi, *Ethiopia* **90 F3** 6 28N 42 10 E
Imishly, *U.S.S.R.* **53 G13** 39 49N 48 4 E
Imitek, *Morocco* **98 C3** 29 43N 8 10W
Imlay, *U.S.A.* **142 F4** 40 45N 118 9W
Imlay City, *U.S.A.* **136 D1** 43 0N 83 2W
Immenstadt, *Germany* **27 H6** 47 34N 10 13 E
Immingham, *U.K.* **16 D7** 53 37N 0 12W
Immokalee, *U.S.A.* **135 M5** 26 25N 81 26W
Imo □, *Nigeria* **101 D6** 5 15N 7 20 E
Imola, *Italy* **39 D8** 44 20N 11 42 E
Imotski, *Yugoslavia* **42 D2** 43 27N 17 12 E
Imperatriz, *Amazonas, Brazil* **156 B4** 5 18 S 67 11W
Imperatriz, *Maranhão, Brazil* **154 C2** 5 30 S 47 29W
Impéria, *Italy* **38 E5** 43 52N 8 3 E
Imperial, *Canada* **131 C7** 51 21N 105 28W
Imperial, *Peru* **156 C2** 13 4 S 76 21W
Imperial, *Calif., U.S.A.* **145 N11** 32 52N 115 34W
Imperial, *Nebr., U.S.A.* **138 E4** 40 38N 101 39W
Imperial Beach, *U.S.A.* **145 N9** 32 35N 117 8W
Imperial Dam, *U.S.A.* **145 N12** 32 50N 114 30W
Imperial Res., *U.S.A.* **145 N12** 32 53N 114 28W
Imperial Valley, *U.S.A.* **145 N11** 32 55N 115 30W
Imperieuse Reef, *Australia* **112 C2** 17 36 S 118 50 E
Impfondo, *Congo* **102 B3** 1 40N 18 0 E
Imphal, *India* **78 C4** 24 48N 93 56 E
Imphy, *France* **24 B7** 46 55N 3 16 E
İmralı, *Turkey* **88 C3** 40 32N 28 31 E
Imranlı, *Turkey* **89 D8** 39 54N 38 7 E
İmroz = Gökçeada, *Turkey* **44 D7** 40 10N 25 50 E
Imst, *Austria* **30 D3** 47 15N 10 44 E
Imuruan B., *Phil.* **71 B5** 10 40N 119 10 E
In Belbel, *Algeria* **99 C5** 27 55N 1 12 E
In Delimane, *Mali* **101 B5** 15 52N 1 31 E
In Rhar, *Algeria* **99 C5** 27 10N 1 59 E
In Salah, *Algeria* **99 C5** 27 10N 2 32 E
In Tallak, *Mali* **101 B5** 16 19N 3 15 E
Ina, *Japan* **63 B9** 35 50N 137 55 E
Ina-Bonchi, *Japan* **63 B9** 35 45N 137 58 E
Inajá, *Brazil* **154 C4** 8 54 S 37 49W
Inangahua Junction, *N.Z.* **119 B6** 41 52 S 171 59 E
Inanwatan, *Indonesia* **71 E8** 2 10 S 132 14 E
Iñapari, *Peru* **156 C4** 11 0 S 69 40W
Inarajan, *Guam* **121 R15** 13 16N 144 45 E
Inari, *Finland* **12 B19** 68 54N 27 5 E
Inarijärvi, *Finland* **12 B20** 69 0N 28 0 E
Inawashiro-Ko, *Japan* **60 F10** 37 29N 140 6 E
Inazawa, *Japan* **63 B8** 35 15N 136 47 E
Inca, *Spain* **33 B9** 39 43N 2 54 E
Incaguasi, *Chile* **158 B1** 29 12 S 71 5W
İnce-Burnu, *Turkey* **52 E6** 42 7N 34 56 E
İncekum Burnu, *Turkey* **88 E5** 36 13N 33 57 E
Inchon, *S. Korea* **67 F14** 37 27N 126 40 E
Incio, *Spain* **36 C3** 42 39N 7 21W
İncirliova, *Turkey* **88 E2** 37 50N 27 41 E
Incomáti →, *Mozam.* **105 D5** 25 46 S 32 43 E
Inda Silase, *Ethiopia* **95 E4** 14 10N 38 15 E
Indalsälven →, *Sweden* **14 B11** 62 36N 17 30 E
Indaw, *Burma* **78 C6** 24 15N 96 5 E
Indbir, *Ethiopia* **95 F4** 8 7N 37 52 E
Independence, *Calif., U.S.A.* **144 J8** 36 51N 118 14W
Independence, *Iowa, U.S.A.* **140 B5** 42 27N 91 52W
Independence, *Kans., U.S.A.* **139 G7** 37 10N 95 43W
Independence, *Ky., U.S.A.* **141 F12** 38 57N 84 33W
Independence, *Mo., U.S.A.* **140 E2** 39 3N 94 25W
Independence, *Oreg., U.S.A.* **142 D2** 44 53N 123 12W
Independence Fjord, *Greenland* **6 A6** 82 10N 29 0W
Independence Mts., *U.S.A.* **142 F5** 41 30N 116 2W
Independência, *Brazil* **154 C3** 5 23 S 40 19W
Independenţa, *Romania* **46 D8** 45 25N 27 42 E
Inderborskiy, *U.S.S.R.* **53 B14** 48 30N 51 42 E
Index, *U.S.A.* **144 C5** 47 50N 121 33W
India ■, *Asia* **59 H11** 20 0N 78 0 E
Indian →, *U.S.A.* **135 M5** 27 59N 80 34W
Indian Cabins, *Canada* **130 B5** 59 52N 117 40W
Indian Harbour, *Canada* **129 B8** 54 27N 57 13W
Indian Head, *Canada* **131 C8** 50 30N 103 41W
Indian Ocean **58 K11** 5 0 S 75 0 E
Indian Springs, *U.S.A.* **145 J11** 36 35N 115 40W
Indiana, *U.S.A.* **136 F5** 40 38N 79 9W
Indiana □, *U.S.A.* **141 E11** 40 0N 86 0W
Indianapolis, *U.S.A.* **141 E10** 39 42N 86 10W
Indianola, *Iowa, U.S.A.* **140 C3** 41 20N 93 32W
Indianola, *Miss., U.S.A.* **139 J9** 33 27N 90 40W
Indiapora, *Brazil* **155 E1** 19 57 S 50 17W
Indiga, *U.S.S.R.* **48 A8** 67 50N 48 50 E
Indigirka →, *U.S.S.R.* **57 B15** 70 48N 148 54 E
Inđija, *Yugoslavia* **42 B5** 45 6N 20 7 E
Indio, *U.S.A.* **145 M10** 33 46N 116 15W
Indispensable Strait, *Solomon Is.* **121 M11** 9 0 S 160 30 E
Indonesia ■, *Asia* **70 F5** 5 0 S 115 0 E
Indore, *India* **80 H6** 22 42N 75 53 E
Indramayu, *Indonesia* **71 G13** 6 20 S 108 19 E
Indravati →, *India* **82 E5** 19 20N 80 20 E
Indre □, *France* **23 F8** 46 50N 1 39 E
Indre →, *France* **22 E7** 47 16N 0 11 E
Indre-et-Loire □, *France* **22 E7** 47 20N 0 40 E
Indungo, *Angola* **103 E3** 14 48 S 16 17 E
Indus →, *Pakistan* **79 D2** 24 20N 67 47 E
Indus, Mouth of the, *Pakistan* **79 E3** 24 0N 68 0 E
Industry, *U.S.A.* **140 D6** 40 20N 90 36W
İnebolu, *Turkey* **88 C5** 41 55N 33 40 E
İnegöl, *Turkey* **88 C3** 40 5N 29 31 E
Inés, Mt., *Argentina* **160 C3** 48 30 S 69 40W
Ineu, *Romania* **46 C2** 46 26N 21 51 E
Inezgane, *Morocco* **98 B3** 30 25N 9 29W
Infantes, *Spain* **35 G1** 38 43N 3 1W
Infiernillo, Presa del, *Mexico* **146 D4** 18 9N 102 0W
Infiesto, *Spain* **36 B5** 43 21N 5 21W
Inganda, *Zaïre* **102 C4** 0 5 S 20 57 E
Ingapirca, *Ecuador* **152 D2** 2 38 S 78 56W
Ingelmunster, *Belgium* **21 G2** 50 56N 3 16 E
Ingende, *Zaïre* **102 C3** 0 12 S 18 57 E
Ingeniero Jacobacci, *Argentina* **160 B3** 41 20 S 69 36W
Ingenio, *Canary Is.* **33 G4** 27 55N 15 26W
Ingenio Santa Ana, *Argentina* **158 B2** 27 25 S 65 40W
Ingersoll, *Canada* **136 C4** 43 4N 80 55W
Ingham, *Australia* **114 B4** 18 43 S 146 10 E
Ingichka, *U.S.S.R.* **55 D2** 39 47N 65 58 E
Ingleborough, *U.K.* **16 C5** 54 11N 2 23W
Inglewood, *Queens., Australia* **115 D5** 28 25 S 151 2 E
Inglewood, *Vic., Australia* **116 D5** 36 29 S 143 53 E
Inglewood, *N.Z.* **118 F3** 39 9 S 174 14 E
Inglewood, *U.S.A.* **145 M8** 33 58N 118 21W
Ingólfshöfði, *Iceland* **12 E5** 63 48N 16 39W
Ingolstadt, *Germany* **27 G7** 48 45N 11 26 E
Ingomar, *U.S.A.* **142 C10** 46 35N 107 21W
Ingonish, *Canada* **129 C7** 46 42N 60 18W
Ingore, *Guinea-Biss.* **100 C1** 12 24N 15 48W
Ingraj Bazar, *India* **81 G13** 24 58N 88 10 E
Ingrid Christensen Coast, *Antarctica* **7 C6** 69 30 S 76 0 E
Ingul →, *U.S.S.R.* **52 C5** 46 50N 32 15 E
Ingulec, *U.S.S.R.* **52 C5** 47 42N 33 14 E
Ingulets →, *U.S.S.R.* **52 C5** 46 41N 32 48 E
Inguri →, *U.S.S.R.* **53 E9** 42 38N 41 35 E
Ingwavuma, *S. Africa* **105 D5** 27 9 S 31 59 E
Inhaca, I., *Mozam.* **105 D5** 26 1 S 32 57 E
Inhafenga, *Mozam.* **105 C5** 20 36 S 33 53 E
Inhambane, *Mozam.* **105 C6** 23 54 S 35 30 E
Inhambane □, *Mozam.* **105 C5** 22 30 S 34 20 E
Inhambupe, *Brazil* **155 D4** 11 47 S 38 21W
Inhaminga, *Mozam.* **107 F4** 18 26 S 35 0 E
Inharrime, *Mozam.* **105 C6** 24 30 S 35 0 E
Inharrime →, *Mozam.* **105 C6** 24 30 S 35 0 E
Inhuma, *Brazil* **154 C3** 6 40 S 41 42W
Inhumas, *Brazil* **155 E2** 16 22 S 49 30W
Iniesta, *Spain* **35 F3** 39 27N 1 45W
Ining = Yining, *China* **64 B3** 43 58N 81 10 E
Inini □, *Fr. Guiana* **153 C7** 4 0N 53 0W
Inírida →, *Colombia* **152 C4** 3 55N 67 52W
Inishbofin, *Ireland* **19 C1** 53 35N 10 12W
Inishmore, *Ireland* **19 C2** 53 8N 9 45W
Inishowen, *Ireland* **19 A4** 55 14N 7 15W
Injune, *Australia* **115 D4** 25 53 S 148 32 E
Inklin, *Canada* **130 B2** 58 56N 133 5W
Inklin →, *Canada* **130 B2** 58 50N 133 10W
Inkom, *U.S.A.* **142 E7** 42 51N 112 15W
Inle L., *Burma* **78 E6** 20 30N 96 58 E
Inn →, *Austria* **27 G9** 48 35N 13 28 E
Innamincka, *Australia* **115 D3** 27 44 S 140 46 E
Inner Hebrides, *U.K.* **18 E2** 57 0N 6 30W
Inner Mongolia = Nei Monggol Zizhiqu □, *China* **66 D7** 42 0N 112 0 E
Inner Sound, *U.K.* **18 D3** 57 30N 5 55W
Innerkip, *Canada* **136 C4** 43 13N 80 42W
Innerkirchen, *Switz.* **28 C6** 46 43N 8 14 E
Innerste →, *Germany* **26 C5** 52 45N 9 40 E
Innetalling I., *Canada* **128 A4** 56 0N 79 0W
Innisfail, *Australia* **114 B4** 17 33 S 146 5 E
Innisfail, *Canada* **130 C6** 52 0N 113 57W
In'no-shima, *Japan* **62 C5** 34 19N 133 10 E
Innsbruck, *Austria* **30 D4** 47 16N 11 23 E
Inny →, *Ireland* **19 C4** 53 30N 7 50W
Ino, *Japan* **62 D5** 33 33N 133 26 E
Inocência, *Brazil* **155 E1** 19 47 S 51 48W
Inongo, *Zaïre* **102 C3** 1 55 S 18 30 E
Inoni, *Congo* **102 C3** 3 4 S 15 39 E
Inoucdjouac, *Canada* **127 C12** 58 25N 78 15W
Inowrocław, *Poland* **47 C5** 52 50N 18 12 E
Inpundong, *N. Korea* **67 D14** 41 25N 126 34 E
Inquisivi, *Bolivia* **156 D4** 16 50 S 67 10W
Ins, *Switz.* **28 B4** 47 1N 7 7 E
Inscription, C., *Australia* **113 E1** 25 29 S 112 59 E
Insein, *Burma* **78 G6** 16 50N 96 5 E
Însurăţei, *Romania* **46 E8** 44 50N 27 40 E
Inta, *U.S.S.R.* **48 A11** 66 5N 60 8 E
Intendente Alvear, *Argentina* **158 D3** 35 12 S 63 32W
Interior, *U.S.A.* **138 D4** 43 46N 101 59W
Interlaken, *Switz.* **23 F14** 46 41N 7 50 E
International Falls, *U.S.A.* **138 A8** 48 36N 93 25W
Intiyaco, *Argentina* **158 B3** 28 43 S 60 5W
Intragna, *Switz.* **29 D7** 46 11N 8 42 E
Intutu, *Peru* **152 D3** 3 32 S 74 48W
Inubō-Zaki, *Japan* **63 B12** 35 42N 140 52 E
Inútil, B., *Chile* **160 D2** 53 30 S 70 15W
Inuvik, *Canada* **126 B6** 68 16N 133 40W
Inuyama, *Japan* **63 B8** 35 23N 136 56 E
Inveraray, *U.K.* **18 E3** 56 13N 5 5W
Inverbervie, *U.K.* **18 E6** 56 50N 2 17W
Invercargill, *N.Z.* **119 G3** 46 24 S 168 24 E
Inverell, *Australia* **115 D5** 29 45 S 151 8 E
Invergordon, *U.K.* **18 D4** 57 41N 4 10W
Inverleigh, *Australia* **116 E6** 38 38 S 144 3 E
Invermere, *Canada* **130 C5** 50 30N 116 2W
Inverness, *Canada* **129 C7** 46 15N 61 19W
Inverness, *U.K.* **18 D4** 57 29N 4 12W
Inverness, *U.S.A.* **135 L4** 28 50N 82 20W
Inverurie, *U.K.* **18 D6** 57 15N 2 21W
Inverway, *Australia* **112 C4** 17 50 S 129 38 E

Izyum 211

Investigator Group, Australia 115 E1 34 45 S 134 20 E
Investigator Str., Australia 116 C2 35 30 S 137 0 E
Inya, U.S.S.R. 56 D9 50 28N 86 37 E
Inyanga, Zimbabwe 107 F3 18 12 S 32 40 E
Inyangani, Zimbabwe 107 F3 18 5 S 32 50 E
Inyantue, Zimbabwe 107 F2 18 30 S 26 40 E
Inyo Mts., U.S.A. 143 H5 37 0N 118 0W
Inyokern, U.S.A. 145 K9 35 38N 117 48W
Inywa, Burma 78 D6 23 56N 96 17 E
Inza, U.S.S.R. 51 E15 53 55N 46 25 E
Inzer, U.S.S.R. 54 D5 54 14N 57 34 E
Inzhavino, U.S.S.R. 51 E13 52 22N 42 30 E
Iō-Jima, Japan 61 J5 30 48N 130 18 E
Ioánnina, Greece 44 E2 39 42N 20 47 E
Ioánnina □, Greece 44 E2 39 39N 20 57 E
Iola, U.S.A. 139 G7 38 0N 95 20W
Ioma, Papua N. G. 120 E4 8 19 S 147 52 E
Ion Corvin, Romania 46 E8 44 7N 27 50 E
Iona, U.K. 18 E2 56 20N 6 25W
Ione, Calif., U.S.A. 144 G6 38 20N 120 56W
Ione, Wash., U.S.A. 142 B5 48 44N 117 29W
Ionia, U.S.A. 141 B11 42 59N 85 7W
Ionian Is. = Iónioi Nísoi, Greece 45 F2 38 40N 20 0 E
Ionian Sea, Europe 10 H9 37 30N 17 30 E
Iónioi Nísoi, Greece 45 F2 38 40N 20 0 E
Iori →, U.S.S.R. 53 F12 41 3N 46 17 E
Íos, Greece 45 H7 36 41N 25 20 E
Iowa □, U.S.A. 138 D8 42 18N 93 30W
Iowa →, U.S.A. 140 C5 41 10N 91 1W
Iowa City, U.S.A. 140 C5 41 40N 91 35W
Iowa Falls, U.S.A. 140 B3 42 30N 93 15W
Ipala, Tanzania 106 C3 4 30 S 32 52 E
Ipameri, Brazil 155 E2 17 44 S 48 9W
Iparía, Peru 156 B3 9 17 S 74 29W
Ipáti, Greece 45 F4 38 52N 22 14 E
Ipatinga, Brazil 155 E3 19 32 S 42 30W
Ipatovo, U.S.S.R. 53 D10 45 45N 42 50 E
Ipel →, Europe 31 C12 48 10N 19 35 E
Ipiales, Colombia 152 C2 0 50N 77 37W
Ipiaú, Brazil 155 D4 14 8 S 39 44W
Ipin = Yibin, China 68 C5 28 45N 104 32 E
Ipirá, Brazil 155 D4 12 10 S 39 44W
Ipiranga, Brazil 152 D4 3 13 S 65 57W
Ípiros □, Greece 44 E2 39 30N 20 30 E
Ipixuna, Brazil 156 B3 7 0 S 71 40W
Ipixuna →, Amazonas, Brazil 156 B3 7 11 S 71 51W
Ipixuna →, Amazonas, Brazil 157 B5 5 45 S 63 2W
Ipoh, Malaysia 77 K3 4 35N 101 5 E
Iporá, Brazil 155 D1 11 23 S 50 40W
Ippy, C.A.R. 102 A4 6 5N 21 7 E
Ipsala, Turkey 44 D8 40 55N 26 23 E
Ipsárion Óros, Greece 44 D6 40 40N 24 40 E
Ipswich, Australia 115 D5 27 35 S 152 40 E
Ipswich, U.K. 17 E9 52 4N 1 9 E
Ipswich, Mass., U.S.A. 137 D14 42 40N 70 50W
Ipswich, S. Dak., U.S.A. 138 C5 45 28N 99 1W
Ipu, Brazil 154 B3 4 23 S 40 44W
Ipueiras, Brazil 154 B3 4 33 S 40 43W
Ipupiara, Brazil 155 D3 11 49 S 42 37W
Iput →, U.S.S.R. 50 E7 52 26N 31 2 E
Iqaluit, Canada 127 B13 63 44N 68 31W
Iquique, Chile 156 E3 20 19 S 70 5W
Iquitos, Peru 152 D3 3 45 S 73 10W
Irabu-Jima, Japan 61 M2 24 50N 125 10 E
Iracoubo, Fr. Guiana 153 B7 5 30N 53 10W
Īrafshān, Iran 85 E9 26 42N 61 56 E
Iráklia, Greece 45 H7 36 50N 25 28 E
Iráklion, Greece 32 D7 35 20N 25 12 E
Iráklion □, Greece 32 D7 35 10N 25 10 E
Irako-Zaki, Japan 63 C9 34 35N 137 1 E
Irala, Paraguay 159 B5 25 55 S 54 35W
Iramba □, Tanzania 106 C3 4 30 S 34 30 E
Iran ■, Asia 85 C7 33 0N 53 0 E
Iran, Gunung-Gunung, Malaysia 70 D4 2 20N 114 50 E
Iran Ra. = Iran, Gunung-Gunung, Malaysia 70 D4 2 20N 114 50 E
Iranamadu Tank, Sri Lanka 83 K5 9 23N 80 29 E
Īrānshahr, Iran 85 E9 27 15N 60 40 E
Irapa, Venezuela 153 A5 10 34N 62 35W
Irapuato, Mexico 146 C4 20 40N 101 30W
Iraq ■, Asia 84 C5 33 0N 44 0 E
Irarrar, O. →, Mali 99 E5 20 0N 1 30 E
Irati, Brazil 159 B5 25 25 S 50 38W
Irbid, Jordan 91 C4 32 35N 35 48 E
Irbid □, Jordan 91 C5 32 15N 36 35 E
Irbit, U.S.S.R. 54 C8 57 41N 63 3 E
Irebu, Zaïre 102 C3 0 40 S 17 46 E
Irecê, Brazil 154 D3 11 18 S 41 52W
Iregua →, Spain 34 C7 42 27N 2 24 E
Ireland ■, Europe 19 D4 53 0N 8 0W
Ireland's Eye, Ireland 19 C5 53 25N 6 4W
Irele, Nigeria 101 D6 7 40N 5 40 E
Iremel, Gora, U.S.S.R. 54 D6 54 33N 58 50 E
Ireng →, Brazil 153 C6 3 33N 59 51W
Iret, U.S.S.R. 57 C16 60 3N 154 20 E
Irgiz, Bolshaya →, U.S.S.R. 51 E16 52 10N 49 10 E
Irhârharene, Algeria 99 C6 27 37N 7 30 E
Irharrhar, O. →, Algeria 99 C6 28 3N 6 15 E
Irherm, Morocco 98 B3 30 7N 8 18W
Irhil Mgoun, Morocco 98 B3 31 30N 6 28W
Irhyangdong, N. Korea 67 D15 41 15N 129 30 E
Iri, S. Korea 67 G14 35 59N 127 0 E
Irian Jaya □, Indonesia 71 E9 4 0 S 137 0 E
Iriba, Chad 97 E4 15 7N 22 15 E
Irié, Guinea 100 D3 8 15N 9 10W
Iriklinskiy, U.S.S.R. 54 F6 51 39N 58 38 E
Iriklinskoye Vdkhr., U.S.S.R. 54 F6 52 0N 59 0 E
Iringa, Tanzania 106 D4 7 48 S 35 43 E
Iringa □, Tanzania 106 D4 7 48 S 35 43 E
Irinjalakuda, India 83 J3 10 21N 76 14 E
Iriomote-Jima, Japan 61 M1 24 19N 123 48 E
Iriona, Honduras 148 C2 15 57N 85 11W
Iriri →, Brazil 153 D7 3 52 S 52 37W
Iriri Novo →, Brazil 157 B7 8 46 S 53 22W
Irish Republic ■, Europe 19 D4 53 0N 8 0W
Irish Sea, Europe 16 D3 54 0N 5 0W
Irkeshtam, U.S.S.R. 55 D6 39 41N 73 55 E
Irkineyeva, U.S.S.R. 57 D10 58 30N 96 49 E
Irkutsk, U.S.S.R. 57 D11 52 18N 104 20 E
Irma, Canada 131 C6 52 55N 111 14W
Irō-Zaki, Japan 63 C10 34 36N 138 51 E
Iroise, Mer d', France 22 D2 48 15N 4 45W
Iron Baron, Australia 116 B2 32 58 S 137 11 E
Iron Gate = Portile de Fier, Europe 46 E3 44 42N 22 30 E
Iron Knob, Australia 116 B2 32 46 S 137 8 E
Iron Mountain, U.S.A. 134 C1 45 49N 88 4W
Iron Ra., Australia 114 A3 12 46 S 143 16 E
Iron River, U.S.A. 138 B10 46 6N 88 40W
Ironbridge, U.K. 17 E5 52 38N 2 29W
Irondequoit, U.S.A. 136 C7 43 13N 77 35W
Ironstone Kopje, Botswana 104 D3 25 17 S 24 5 E
Ironton, Mo., U.S.A. 139 G9 37 40N 90 40W
Ironton, Ohio, U.S.A. 134 F4 38 35N 82 40W
Ironwood, U.S.A. 138 B9 46 30N 90 10W
Iroquois →, U.S.A. 141 C9 41 5N 87 49W
Iroquois Falls, Canada 128 C3 48 46N 80 41W
Irpen, U.S.S.R. 50 F7 50 30N 30 15 E
Irrara Cr. →, Australia 115 D4 29 35 S 145 31 E
Irrawaddy □, Burma 78 G5 17 0N 95 0 E
Irrawaddy →, Burma 78 G5 15 50N 95 6 E
Irsina, Italy 41 B9 40 45N 16 15 E
Irtysh →, U.S.S.R. 56 C7 61 4N 68 52 E
Irumu, Zaïre 106 B2 1 32N 29 53 E
Irún, Spain 34 B3 43 20N 1 52W
Irurzun, Spain 34 C3 42 55N 1 50W
Irvine, Canada 131 D6 49 57N 110 16W
Irvine, U.K. 18 F4 55 37N 4 40W
Irvine, U.S.A. 141 G13 37 42N 83 58W
Irvine, Calif., U.S.A. 145 M9 33 41N 117 46W
Irvinestown, U.K. 19 B4 54 28N 7 38W
Irvington, U.S.A. 141 G10 37 53N 86 17W
Irvona, U.S.A. 136 F6 40 46N 78 35W
Irwin →, Australia 113 E1 29 15 S 114 54 E
Irymple, Australia 116 C5 34 14 S 142 8 E
Is-sur-Tille, France 23 E12 47 30N 5 8 E
Isa, Nigeria 101 C6 13 14N 6 24 E
Isaac →, Australia 114 C4 22 55 S 149 20 E
Isabel, U.S.A. 138 C4 45 27N 101 22W
Isabela, I., Mexico 146 C3 21 51N 105 55W
Isabella, Phil. 71 C6 6 40N 122 10 E
Isabella, Cord., Nic. 148 D2 13 30N 85 25W
Isabella Ra., Australia 112 D3 21 0 S 121 4 E
Ísafjarðardjúp, Iceland 12 C2 66 10N 23 0W
Ísafjörður, Iceland 12 C2 66 5N 23 9W
Isagarh, India 80 G7 24 48N 77 51 E
Isahaya, Japan 62 E2 32 52N 130 2 E
Isaka, Tanzania 106 C3 3 56 S 32 59 E
Isakly, U.S.S.R. 54 D2 54 8N 51 32 E
Isana = Içana →, Brazil 152 C4 0 26N 67 19W
Isangi, Zaïre 102 B4 0 52N 24 10 E
Isar →, Germany 27 G8 48 49N 12 58 E
Isarco →, Italy 39 B8 46 57N 11 18 E
Ísari, Greece 45 G4 37 22N 22 0 E
Isbergues, France 23 B9 50 36N 2 28 E
Isbiceni, Romania 46 F5 43 45N 24 40 E
Iscayachi, Bolivia 157 E4 21 31 S 65 3W
Íschia, Italy 40 B6 40 45N 13 51 E
Iscuandé, Colombia 152 C2 2 28N 77 59W
Isdell →, Australia 112 C3 16 27 S 124 51 E
Ise, Japan 63 C8 34 25N 136 45 E
Ise-Heiya, Japan 63 C8 34 40N 136 30 E
Ise-Wan, Japan 63 C8 34 43N 136 43 E
Isefjord, Denmark 15 J5 55 53N 11 50 E
Iseltwald, Switz. 28 C5 46 43N 7 58 E
Isenthal, Switz. 29 C7 46 55N 8 34 E
Iseo, Italy 38 C7 45 40N 10 3 E
Iseo, L. d', Italy 38 C7 45 45N 10 3 E
Iseramagazi, Tanzania 106 C3 4 37 S 32 10 E
Isère □, France 25 C9 45 15N 5 40 E
Isère →, France 25 D8 44 59N 4 51 E
Iserlohn, Germany 26 D3 51 22N 7 40 E
Isérnia, Italy 41 A7 41 35N 14 12 E
Isesaki, Japan 63 A11 36 19N 139 12 E
Iseyin, Nigeria 101 D5 8 0N 3 36 E
Isfara, U.S.S.R. 55 C5 40 7N 70 38 E
Isherton, Guyana 153 C6 2 20N 59 25W
Ishigaki-Shima, Japan 61 M2 24 20N 124 10 E
Ishikari-Gawa →, Japan 60 C10 43 15N 141 23 E
Ishikari-Sammyaku, Japan 60 C11 43 30N 143 0 E
Ishikari-Wan, Japan 60 C10 43 25N 141 1 E
Ishikawa □, Japan 63 A8 36 30N 136 30 E
Ishim, U.S.S.R. 56 D7 56 10N 69 30 E
Ishim →, U.S.S.R. 56 D8 57 45N 71 10 E
Ishimbay, U.S.S.R. 54 E5 53 28N 56 2 E
Ishinomaki, Japan 60 E10 38 32N 141 20 E
Ishioka, Japan 63 A12 36 11N 140 16 E
Ishizuchi-Yama, Japan 62 D5 33 45N 133 6 E
Ishkashim, U.S.S.R. 55 E5 36 44N 71 37 E
Ishkuman, Pakistan 81 A5 36 30N 73 50 E
Ishmi, Albania 44 C1 41 33N 19 34 E
Ishpeming, U.S.A. 134 B2 46 30N 87 40W
Ishurdi, Bangla. 78 C2 24 9N 89 3 E
Isigny-sur-Mer, France 22 C5 49 19N 1 6W
Isil Kul, U.S.S.R. 56 D8 54 55N 71 16 E
Isiolo, Kenya 106 B4 0 24N 37 33 E
Isiolo □, Kenya 106 B4 2 30N 37 30 E
Isipingo Beach, S. Africa 105 E5 30 0 S 30 57 E
Isiro, Zaïre 106 B2 2 53N 27 40 E
Isisford, Australia 114 C3 24 15 S 144 21 E
Iskander, U.S.S.R. 55 C4 41 36N 69 41 E
İskederun, Turkey 88 E7 36 9N 36 35 E
İskenderun, Turkey 88 E7 36 32N 36 10 E
İskenderun Körfezi, Turkey 88 E6 36 40N 35 50 E
Iski-Naukat, U.S.S.R. 55 C6 40 16N 72 36 E
İskilip, Turkey 52 F6 40 45N 34 29 E
Iskŭr →, Bulgaria 43 D9 43 45N 24 25 E
Iskŭr, Yazovir, Bulgaria 43 E8 42 23N 23 30 E
Iskut →, Canada 130 B2 56 45N 131 49W
Isla →, U.K. 18 E5 56 32N 3 20W
Isla Cristina, Spain 37 H3 37 13N 7 17W
Isla Vista, U.S.A. 145 L7 34 27N 119 52W
İslâhiye, Turkey 88 E7 37 0N 36 35 E
Islamabad, Pakistan 79 B4 33 40N 73 10 E
Islamkot, Pakistan 80 G4 24 42N 70 13 E
Islampur, India 82 F2 17 2N 74 20 E
Island →, Canada 130 A4 60 25N 121 12W
Island Falls, Canada 128 C3 49 35N 81 20W
Island Falls, U.S.A. 129 C6 46 0N 68 16W
Island L., Canada 131 C10 53 47N 94 25W
Island Lagoon, Australia 116 A2 31 30 S 136 40 E
Island Pond, U.S.A. 137 B13 44 50N 71 50W
Islands, B. of, Canada 129 C8 49 11N 58 15W
Islands, B. of, N.Z. 118 B3 35 15 S 174 6 E
Islay, U.K. 18 F2 55 46N 6 10W
Isle →, France 24 D3 44 55N 0 15W
Isle aux Morts, Canada 129 C8 47 35N 59 0W
Isle of Wight □, U.K. 17 G6 50 40N 1 20W
Isle Royale, U.S.A. 138 B10 48 0N 88 50W
Isleta, U.S.A. 143 J10 34 58N 106 46W
Isleton, U.S.A. 144 G5 38 10N 121 37W
Ismail, U.S.S.R. 52 D3 45 22N 28 46 E
Ismâ'ilîya, Egypt 94 H8 30 37N 32 18 E
Ismaning, Germany 27 G7 48 14N 11 41 E
Ismay, U.S.A. 138 B2 46 33N 104 44W
Isna, Egypt 94 B3 25 17N 32 30 E
Isogstalo, India 81 B8 34 15N 78 46 E
Isola del Gran Sasso d'Italia, Italy 39 F10 42 30N 13 40 E
Ísola del Liri, Italy 40 A6 41 39N 13 32 E
Ísola della Scala, Italy 38 C8 45 16N 11 0 E
Ísola di Capo Rizzuto, Italy 41 D10 38 56N 17 5 E
Isparta, Turkey 88 E4 37 47N 30 30 E
Isparta □, Turkey 88 E4 38 0N 31 0 E
Isperikh, Bulgaria 43 D11 43 43N 26 50 E
Íspica, Italy 41 F7 36 47N 14 53 E
Ispir, Turkey 53 F9 40 28N 41 1 E
Israel ■, Asia 91 D3 32 0N 34 50 E
Issano, Guyana 153 B6 5 49N 59 26W
Issia, Ivory C. 100 D3 6 33N 6 33W
Issoire, France 24 C7 45 32N 3 15 E
Issoudun, France 23 F9 46 57N 2 0 E
Issyk-Kul, Ozero, U.S.S.R. 55 B8 42 25N 77 15 E
Ist, Yugoslavia 39 D11 44 17N 14 47 E
Istaihah, U.A.E. 85 F7 23 19N 54 4 E
İstanbul, Turkey 88 C3 41 0N 29 0 E
İstanbul □, Turkey 88 C3 41 0N 29 0 E
Istiaía, Greece 45 F5 38 57N 23 9 E
Istmina, Colombia 152 B2 5 10N 76 39W
Istok, Yugoslavia 42 E5 42 45N 20 24 E
Istokpoga, L., U.S.A. 135 M5 27 22N 81 14W
Istra, U.S.S.R. 51 D10 55 55N 36 50 E
Istra, Yugoslavia 39 C11 45 10N 14 0 E
İstranca Dağları, Turkey 43 F12 41 48N 27 36 E
Istres, France 25 E8 43 31N 4 59 E
Istria = Istra, Yugoslavia 39 C11 45 10N 14 0 E
Itá, Paraguay 158 B4 25 29 S 57 21W
'Itāb, Yemen 87 D5 15 20N 51 29 E
Itabaiana, Paraíba, Brazil 154 C4 7 18 S 35 19W
Itabaiana, Sergipe, Brazil 154 D4 10 41 S 37 37W
Itabaianinha, Brazil 154 D4 11 16 S 37 47W
Itaberaba, Brazil 155 D3 12 32 S 40 18W
Itaberaí, Brazil 155 E2 16 2 S 49 48W
Itabira, Brazil 155 E3 19 37 S 43 13W
Itabirito, Brazil 155 F3 20 15 S 43 48W
Itaboca, Brazil 153 D5 4 50 S 62 40W
Itabuna, Brazil 155 D4 14 48 S 39 16W
Itacajá, Brazil 154 C2 8 19 S 47 46W
Itacaunas →, Brazil 154 C2 5 21 S 49 8W
Itacoatiara, Brazil 153 D6 3 8 S 58 25W
Itacuaí →, Brazil 156 A3 4 20 S 70 12W
Itaguaçu, Brazil 155 E3 19 48 S 40 51W
Itaguari →, Brazil 155 D3 14 11 S 44 40W
Itaguatins, Brazil 154 C2 5 47 S 47 29W
Itaim →, Brazil 154 C3 7 2 S 42 2W
Itainópolis, Brazil 154 C3 7 24 S 41 31W
Itaipu Dam, Brazil 159 B5 25 30 S 54 30W
Itaituba, Brazil 153 D6 4 10 S 55 50W
Itajaí, Brazil 159 B6 27 50 S 48 39W
Itajubá, Brazil 155 F2 22 24 S 45 30W
Itajuípe, Brazil 155 D4 14 41 S 39 22W
Itaka, Tanzania 107 D3 8 50 S 32 49 E
Itako, Japan 63 B12 35 56N 140 33 E
Italy ■, Europe 11 G8 42 0N 13 0 E
Itamataré, Brazil 154 B2 2 16 S 46 24W
Itambacuri, Brazil 155 E3 18 1 S 41 42W
Itambé, Brazil 155 E3 15 15 S 40 37W
Itampolo, Madag. 105 C7 24 41 S 43 57 E
Itanhauã →, Brazil 153 D5 4 45 S 63 48W
Itanhém, Brazil 155 E3 17 9 S 40 20W
Itano, Japan 62 C6 34 7N 134 28 E
Itapaci, Brazil 155 D2 14 57 S 49 34W
Itapagé, Brazil 154 B4 3 41 S 39 34W
Itaparica, I. de, Brazil 155 D4 12 54 S 38 42W
Itapebi, Brazil 155 E4 15 56 S 39 32W
Itapecuru-Mirim, Brazil 154 B3 3 24 S 44 20W
Itaperuna, Brazil 155 F3 21 10 S 41 54W
Itapetinga, Brazil 155 E3 15 15 S 40 15W
Itapetininga, Brazil 159 A6 23 36 S 48 7W
Itapeva, Brazil 159 A6 23 59 S 48 59W
Itapicuru →, Bahia, Brazil 154 D4 11 47 S 37 32W
Itapicuru →, Maranhão, Brazil 154 B3 2 52 S 44 12W
Itapinima, Brazil 157 B5 5 25 S 60 44W
Itapipoca, Brazil 154 B4 3 30 S 39 35W
Itapiranga, Brazil 153 D6 2 45 S 58 1W
Itapiúna, Brazil 154 B4 4 33 S 38 57W
Itaporanga, Brazil 154 C4 7 18 S 38 0W
Itapuá □, Paraguay 159 B4 26 40 S 55 40W
Itapuranga, Brazil 155 E2 15 40 S 49 59W
Itaquari, Brazil 155 F3 20 20 S 40 25W
Itaquatiara, Brazil 153 D6 2 58 S 58 30W
Itaquí, Brazil 158 B4 29 8 S 56 30W
Itararé, Brazil 159 A6 24 6 S 49 23W
Itarsi, India 80 H7 22 36N 77 51 E
Itarumã, Brazil 155 E1 18 42 S 51 25W
Itatí, Argentina 158 B4 27 16 S 58 15W
Itatira, Brazil 154 B4 4 30 S 39 37W
Itatuba, Brazil 157 B5 5 46 S 63 20W
Itatupa, Brazil 153 D7 0 37 S 51 12W
Itaueira, Brazil 154 C3 7 36 S 43 2W
Itaueira →, Brazil 154 C3 6 41 S 42 55W
Itaúna, Brazil 155 F3 20 4 S 44 34W
Itchen →, U.K. 17 G6 50 57N 1 20W
Ite, Peru 156 D3 17 55 S 70 57W
Itéa, Greece 45 F4 38 25N 22 25 E
Itezhi Tezhi, L., Zambia 107 F2 15 30 S 25 30 E
Ithaca = Itháki, Greece 45 F2 38 25N 20 40 E
Ithaca, U.S.A. 137 D8 42 25N 76 30W
Itháki, Greece 45 F2 38 25N 20 40 E
Itinga, Brazil 155 E3 16 36 S 41 47W
Itiquira, Brazil 157 D7 17 12 S 54 7W
Itiquira →, Brazil 157 D6 17 18 S 56 44W
Itiruçu, Brazil 155 D3 13 31 S 40 9W
Itiúba, Brazil 154 D4 10 43 S 39 51W
Ito, Japan 63 C11 34 58N 139 5 E
Itoigawa, Japan 61 F8 37 2N 137 51 E
Iton →, France 22 C8 49 9N 1 12 E
Itonamas →, Bolivia 157 C5 12 28 S 64 24W
Itsa, Egypt 94 J7 29 15N 30 47 E
Itsukaichi, Japan 62 C4 34 22N 132 22 E
Itsuki, Japan 62 E2 32 24N 130 50 E
Íttiri, Italy 40 B1 40 38N 8 32 E
Ittoqqortoormiit = Scoresbysund, Greenland 6 B6 70 20N 23 0W
Itu, Brazil 159 A6 23 17 S 47 15W
Itu, Nigeria 101 D6 5 10N 7 58 E
Ituaçu, Brazil 155 D3 13 50 S 41 18W
Ituango, Colombia 152 B2 7 4N 75 45W
Ituiutaba, Brazil 155 E2 19 0 S 49 25W
Itumbiara, Brazil 155 E2 18 20 S 49 10W
Ituna, Canada 131 C8 51 10N 103 24W
Itunge Port, Tanzania 107 D3 9 40 S 33 55 E
Ituni, Guyana 153 B6 5 28N 58 15W
Itupiranga, Brazil 154 C2 5 9 S 49 20W
Iturama, Brazil 155 E1 19 44 S 50 11W
Iturbe, Argentina 158 A2 23 0 S 65 25W
Ituri →, Zaïre 106 B2 1 40N 27 1 E
Iturup, Ostrov, U.S.S.R. 57 E15 45 0N 148 0 E
Ituverava, Brazil 155 F2 20 20 S 47 47W
Ituxi →, Brazil 157 B5 7 18 S 64 51W
Ituyuro →, Argentina 158 A3 22 40 S 63 50W
Itzehoe, Germany 26 B5 53 56N 9 31 E
Iuka, U.S.A. 141 F8 38 37N 88 47W
Ivaí →, Brazil 159 A5 23 18 S 53 42W
Ivalo, Finland 12 B19 68 38N 27 35 E
Ivalojoki →, Finland 12 B19 68 40N 27 40 E
Ivangorod, U.S.S.R. 50 B6 59 37N 28 40 E
Ivangrad, Yugoslavia 42 E4 42 51N 19 52 E
Ivanhoe, N.S.W., Australia 116 B6 32 56 S 144 20 E
Ivanhoe, W. Austral., Australia 112 C4 15 41 S 128 41 E
Ivanhoe, U.S.A. 144 J7 36 23N 119 13W
Ivanhoe L., Canada 131 A7 60 25N 106 30W
Ivanić Grad, Yugoslavia 39 C13 45 41N 16 25 E
Ivanjica, Yugoslavia 42 D5 43 35N 20 12 E
Ivanjšcice, Yugoslavia 39 B13 46 12N 16 13 E
Ivankoyskoye Vdkhr., U.S.S.R. 51 C10 56 37N 36 32 E
Ivano-Frankovsk, U.S.S.R. 50 G4 48 40N 24 40 E
Ivanovka, U.S.S.R. 54 E3 52 34N 53 23 E
Ivanovo, Byelorussian S.S.R., U.S.S.R. 50 E4 52 7N 25 29 E
Ivanovo, R.S.F.S.R., U.S.S.R. 51 C12 57 5N 41 0 E
Ivato, Madag. 105 C8 20 37 S 47 10 E
Ivaylovgrad, Bulgaria 43 F11 41 32N 26 8 E
Ivdel, U.S.S.R. 48 B11 60 42N 60 24 E
Ive, Mt., Australia 116 B2 32 25 S 136 5 E
Ivindo →, Gabon 102 C2 0 9 S 12 9 E
Ivinheima →, Brazil 159 A5 23 14 S 53 42W
Iviza = Ibiza, Spain 33 C7 38 54N 1 26 E
Ivohibe, Madag. 105 C8 22 31 S 46 57 E
Ivolândia, Brazil 155 E1 16 34 S 50 51W
Ivory Coast ■, Africa 100 D4 7 30N 5 0W
Ivrea, Italy 38 C4 45 30N 7 52 E
Ivugivik, Canada 127 B12 62 24N 77 55W
Iwahig, Phil. 70 C5 8 36N 117 32 E
Iwai-Jima, Japan 62 D3 33 47N 131 58 E
Iwaizumi, Japan 60 E10 39 50N 141 45 E
Iwaki, Japan 61 F10 37 3N 140 55 E
Iwakuni, Japan 62 C4 34 15N 132 8 E
Iwami, Japan 62 B6 35 32N 134 15 E
Iwamizawa, Japan 60 C10 43 12N 141 46 E
Iwanai, Japan 60 C10 42 58N 140 30 E
Iwase, Japan 63 A12 36 21N 140 6 E
Iwata, Japan 63 C9 34 42N 137 51 E
Iwate □, Japan 60 E10 39 30N 141 30 E
Iwate-San, Japan 60 E10 39 51N 141 0 E
Iwo, Nigeria 101 D5 7 39N 4 9 E
Iwonicz-Zdrój, Poland 31 B14 49 37N 21 47 E
Iwungu, Zaïre 103 D3 5 16 S 19 17 E
Ixiamas, Bolivia 156 C4 13 50 S 68 5W
Ixopo, S. Africa 105 E5 30 11 S 30 5 E
Ixtepec, Mexico 147 D5 16 32N 95 10W
Ixtlán del Río, Mexico 146 C4 21 5N 104 21W
'Iyādh, Yemen 86 D4 14 59N 46 51 E
Iyo, Japan 62 D4 33 45N 132 45 E
Iyo-mishima, Japan 62 D5 33 58N 133 30 E
Iyo-Nada, Japan 62 D4 33 40N 132 20 E
Izabal, L. de, Guatemala 148 C2 15 30N 89 10W
Izamal, Mexico 147 C7 20 56N 89 1W
Izberbash, U.S.S.R. 53 E12 42 35N 47 52 E
Izbica, Poland 47 E10 50 53N 23 10 E
Izbica Kujawska, Poland 47 C5 52 25N 18 30 E
Izegem, Belgium 21 G2 50 55N 3 12 E
Izena-Shima, Japan 61 L3 26 56N 127 56 E
Izgrev, Bulgaria 43 D11 43 36N 26 58 E
Izh →, U.S.S.R. 54 D3 55 58N 52 38 E
Izhevsk, U.S.S.R. 54 C3 56 51N 53 14 E
Izkī, Oman 87 B7 22 56N 57 46 E
İzmir, Turkey 88 D2 38 25N 27 8 E
İzmir □, Turkey 88 D2 38 25N 27 10 E
İzmit, Turkey 88 C3 40 45N 29 50 E
Iznajar, Spain 37 H6 37 15N 4 19W
Iznalloz, Spain 35 H1 37 24N 3 30W
İznik Gölü, Turkey 88 C3 40 27N 29 30 E
Izobil'nyy, U.S.S.R. 53 D9 45 25N 41 44 E
Izola, Yugoslavia 39 C10 45 32N 13 39 E
Izozog, Bañados de, Bolivia 157 D5 18 48 S 62 10W
Izra, Syria 91 C5 32 51N 36 15 E
Iztochni Rodopi, Bulgaria 43 F10 41 45N 25 30 E
Izu-Hantō, Japan 63 C11 34 45N 139 0 E
Izu-Shotō, Japan 61 G10 34 30N 140 0 E
Izuhara, Japan 62 C1 34 12N 129 17 E
Izumi, Japan 62 E2 32 5N 130 22 E
Izumi-sano, Japan 63 C7 34 23N 135 18 E
Izumiotsu, Japan 63 C7 34 30N 135 24 E
Izumo, Japan 62 B4 35 20N 132 46 E
Izyaslav, U.S.S.R. 50 F5 50 5N 26 50 E
Izyum, U.S.S.R. 52 B7 49 12N 37 19 E

212 J.F. Rodrigues

J

J.F. Rodrigues, Brazil .. 154 B1 2 55 S 50 20W
Jaba, Ethiopia .... 95 F4 6 20N 35 7 E
Jabal el Awlîya, Sudan .. 95 D3 15 10N 32 31 E
Jabal Lubnān, Lebanon . 91 B4 33 45N 35 40 E
Jabalón →, Spain 37 G6 38 53N 4 5W
Jabalpur, India .... 81 H8 23 9N 79 58 E
Jabbūl, Syria .... 84 B3 36 4N 37 30 E
Jablah, Syria .... 84 C3 35 20N 36 0 E
Jablanac, Yugoslavia .... 39 D11 44 42N 14 56 E
Jablonec, Czech. .... 30 A8 50 43N 15 10 E
Jablonica, Czech. ...... 31 C10 48 37N 17 26 E
Jabłonowo, Poland ..... 47 B6 53 23N 19 10 E
Jaboatão, Brazil .... 154 C4 8 7 S 35 1W
Jaboticabal, Brazil ..... 159 A6 21 15 S 48 17W
Jabukovac, Yugoslavia .. 42 C7 44 22N 22 21 E
Jaburu, Brazil .... 157 B5 5 30 S 64 0W
Jaca, Spain 34 C4 42 35N 0 33W
Jacaré →, Brazil ...... 154 D3 10 3 S 42 13W
Jacareí, Brazil .... 159 A6 23 20 S 46 0W
Jacarèzinho, Brazil .... 159 A6 23 5 S 49 58W
Jáchymov, Czech. ...... 30 A5 50 22N 12 55 E
Jaciara, Brazil .... 157 D7 15 59 S 54 57W
Jacinto, Brazil .... 155 E3 16 10 S 40 17W
Jaciparaná, Brazil ..... 157 B5 9 15 S 64 23W
Jackman, U.S.A. 129 C5 45 35N 70 17W
Jacksboro, U.S.A. 139 J5 33 14N 98 15W
Jackson, Australia ...... 115 D4 26 39 S 149 39 E
Jackson, Ala., U.S.A. .. 135 K2 31 32N 87 53W
Jackson, Calif., U.S.A. . 144 G6 38 19N 120 47W
Jackson, Ky., U.S.A. ... 134 G4 37 35N 83 22W
Jackson, Mich., U.S.A. . 141 B12 42 18N 84 25W
Jackson, Minn., U.S.A. . 138 D7 43 35N 95 0W
Jackson, Miss., U.S.A. .. 139 J9 32 20N 90 10W
Jackson, Mo., U.S.A. ... 139 G10 37 25N 89 42W
Jackson, Ohio, U.S.A. .. 134 F4 39 0N 82 40W
Jackson, Tenn., U.S.A. . 135 H1 35 40N 88 50W
Jackson, Wyo., U.S.A. .. 142 E8 43 30N 110 49W
Jackson, C., N.Z. ...... 119 A9 40 59 S 174 20 E
Jackson, L., U.S.A. 142 E8 43 55N 110 40W
Jackson B., N.Z. .... 119 D3 43 58 S 168 42 E
Jackson Center, U.S.A. . 141 D12 40 27N 84 4W
Jackson Hd., N.Z. ..... 119 D3 43 58 S 168 37 E
Jacksons, N.Z. .... 119 C6 42 46 S 171 32 E
Jacksonville, Ala., U.S.A. 135 J3 33 49N 85 45W
Jacksonville, Calif., U.S.A. 144 H6 37 52N 120 24W
Jacksonville, Fla., U.S.A. 135 K5 30 15N 81 38W
Jacksonville, Ill., U.S.A. 140 E6 39 42N 90 15W
Jacksonville, N.C., U.S.A. 135 H7 34 50N 77 29W
Jacksonville, Oreg., U.S.A. 142 E2 42 19N 122 56W
Jacksonville, Tex., U.S.A. 139 K7 31 58N 95 19W
Jacksonville Beach, U.S.A. 135 K5 30 19N 81 26W
Jacmel, Haiti 149 C5 18 14N 72 32W
Jacob Lake, U.S.A. 143 H7 36 45N 112 12W
Jacobabad, Pakistan ... 79 C3 28 20N 68 29 E
Jacobina, Brazil .... 154 D3 11 11 S 40 30W
Jacques-Cartier, Mt., Canada 129 C6 48 57N 66 0W
Jacqueville, Ivory C. 100 D4 5 12N 4 25W
Jacuí →, Brazil .... 159 C5 30 2 S 51 15W
Jacumba, U.S.A. 145 N10 32 37N 116 11W
Jacundá →, Brazil .... 154 B1 1 57 S 50 26W
Jade, Germany .... 26 B4 53 22N 8 14 E
Jadebusen, Germany ... 26 B4 53 30N 8 15 E
Jadoigne, Belgium ..... 21 G5 50 43N 4 52 E
Jadotville = Likasi, Zaïre 107 E2 10 55 S 26 48 E
Jadovnik, Yugoslavia ... 42 D4 43 20N 19 45 E
Jadów, Poland .... 47 C8 52 28N 21 38 E
Jadraque, Spain 34 E2 40 55N 2 55W
Jādū, Libya .... 96 B2 32 0N 12 0 E
Jaén, Peru .... 156 B2 5 25 S 78 40W
Jaén, Spain 37 H7 37 44N 3 43W
Jaén □, Spain 37 H7 37 50N 3 30W
Jafène, Africa 98 D3 20 35N 5 30W
Jaffa = Tel Aviv-Yafo, Israel .... 91 C3 32 4N 34 48 E
Jaffa, C., Australia ..... 116 D3 36 58 S 139 40 E
Jaffna, Sri Lanka ...... 83 K5 9 45N 80 2 E
Jagadhri, India .... 80 D7 30 10N 77 20 E
Jagadishpur, India ..... 81 G11 25 30N 84 21 E
Jagdalpur, India .... 82 E6 19 3N 82 0 E
Jagersfontein, S. Africa . 104 D4 29 44 S 25 27 E
Jagst →, Germany ..... 27 F5 49 14N 9 11 E
Jagtial, India .... 82 E4 18 50N 79 0 E
Jaguaquara, Brazil ..... 155 D4 13 32 S 39 58W
Jaguariaíva, Brazil .... 159 A6 24 10 S 49 50W
Jaguaribe, Brazil ...... 154 C4 5 53 S 38 37W
Jaguaribe →, Brazil ... 154 B4 4 25 S 37 45W
Jaguaruana, Brazil .... 154 B4 4 50 S 37 47W
Jagüey Grande, Cuba ... 148 B3 22 35N 81 7W
Jagungal, Mt., Australia . 117 D8 36 8 S 148 22 E
Jahangirabad, India .... 80 E8 28 19N 78 4 E
Jahrom, Iran .... 85 D7 28 30N 53 31 E
Jaicós, Brazil .... 154 C3 7 21 S 41 8W
Jailolo, Indonesia ..... 71 D7 1 5N 127 30 E
Jailolo, Selat, Indonesia . 71 D7 0 5N 129 5 E
Jaintiapur, Bangla. .... 78 C4 25 8N 92 7 E
Jaipur, India .... 80 F6 27 0N 75 50 E
Jājarm, Iran .... 85 B8 36 58N 56 27 E
Jajce, Yugoslavia ...... 42 C2 44 19N 17 17 E
Jajpur, India .... 82 D8 20 53N 86 22 E
Jakarta, Indonesia ..... 71 G12 6 9 S 106 49 E
Jakobstad, Finland .... 12 E17 63 40N 22 43 E
Jakupica, Yugoslavia ... 42 F6 41 45N 21 22 E
Jal, U.S.A. 139 J3 32 8N 103 8W
Jalalabad, Afghan. ..... 79 B3 34 30N 70 29 E
Jalalabad, India .... 81 F8 27 41N 79 42 E
Jalalpur Jattan, Pakistan 80 C6 32 38N 74 11 E
Jalama, U.S.A. 145 L6 34 29N 120 29W
Jalapa, Guatemala 148 D2 14 39N 89 59W
Jalapa Enríquez, Mexico 147 D5 19 32N 96 55W
Jalaun, India .... 81 F8 26 8N 79 25 E
Jaldak, Afghan. .... 79 C2 31 58N 66 43 E
Jales, Brazil .... 155 F1 20 10 S 50 33W
Jaleswar, Nepal .... 81 F11 26 38N 85 48 E
Jalgaon, Maharashtra, India .... 82 D3 21 2N 76 31 E
Jalgaon, Maharashtra, India .... 82 D2 21 0N 75 42 E
Jalhay, Belgium .... 21 G7 50 33N 5 58 E
Jalībah, Iraq .... 84 D5 30 35N 46 32 E
Jalingo, Nigeria .... 101 D7 8 55N 11 25 E
Jalisco □, Mexico 146 D4 20 0N 104 0W
Jalkot, Pakistan .... 81 B5 35 14N 73 24 E
Jallas →, Spain 36 C1 42 54N 9 8W
Jalna, India .... 82 E2 19 48N 75 38 E
Jalón →, Spain 34 D3 41 47N 1 4W
Jalpa, Mexico 146 C4 21 38N 102 58W
Jalpaiguri, India .... 78 B2 26 32N 88 46 E
Jalq, Iran .... 79 D1 27 35N 62 46 E
Jaluit I., Pac. Oc. ..... 122 G8 6 0N 169 30 E
Jalūlā, Iraq .... 84 C5 34 16N 45 10 E
Jamaari, Nigeria ...... 101 C6 11 44N 9 53 E
Jamaica, U.S.A. 140 C2 41 51N 94 18W
Jamaica ■, W. Indies ... 148 C4 18 10N 77 30W
Jamalpur, Bangla. ..... 78 C2 24 52N 89 56 E
Jamalpur, India .... 81 G12 25 18N 86 28 E
Jamalpurganj, India ... 81 H13 23 2N 88 1 E
Jamanxim →, Brazil ... 157 A6 4 43 S 56 18W
Jamari, Brazil .... 157 B5 8 45 S 63 27W
Jamari →, Brazil ..... 157 B5 8 27 S 63 30W
Jambe, Indonesia ...... 71 E8 1 15 S 132 10 E
Jambes, Belgium ...... 21 H5 50 27N 4 52 E
Jambi, Indonesia ...... 70 E2 1 38 S 103 30 E
Jambi □, Indonesia .... 70 E2 1 30 S 102 30 E
Jambusar, India .... 80 H5 22 3N 72 51 E
James →, U.S.A. 138 D6 42 52N 97 18W
James B., Canada 127 C12 51 30N 80 0W
James Ras., Australia ... 112 D5 24 10 S 132 30 E
James Ross I., Antarctica 7 C18 63 58 S 57 50W
Jamesport, U.S.A. 140 E3 39 58N 93 48W
Jamestown, Australia ... 116 B3 33 10 S 138 32 E
Jamestown, S. Africa ... 104 E4 31 6 S 26 45 E
Jamestown, Ind., U.S.A. 141 E10 39 56N 86 38W
Jamestown, Ky., U.S.A. 134 G3 37 0N 85 5W
Jamestown, Mo., U.S.A. 140 F4 38 48N 92 30W
Jamestown, N. Dak., U.S.A. 138 B5 46 54N 98 42W
Jamestown, N.Y., U.S.A. 136 D5 42 5N 79 18W
Jamestown, Ohio, U.S.A. 141 E13 39 39N 83 44W
Jamestown, Pa., U.S.A. 136 E4 41 32N 80 27W
Jamestown, Tenn., U.S.A. 135 G3 36 25N 85 0W
Jamīlābād, Iran .... 85 C6 34 24N 48 28 E
Jamiltepec, Mexico 147 D5 16 17N 97 49W
Jamkhandi, India ...... 82 F2 16 30N 75 15 E
Jammalamadugu, India . 83 G4 14 51N 78 25 E
Jammerbugt, Denmark .. 15 G3 57 15N 9 20 E
Jammu, India .... 80 C6 32 43N 74 54 E
Jammu & Kashmir □, India .... 81 B7 34 25N 77 0 E
Jamnagar, India .... 80 H4 22 30N 70 6 E
Jamner, India .... 82 D2 20 45N 75 52 E
Jamoigne, Belgium ..... 21 J6 49 41N 5 24 E
Jampur, Pakistan ..... 79 C3 29 39N 70 40 E
Jamrud, Pakistan ..... 79 B3 33 59N 71 24 E
Jamshedpur, India ..... 81 H12 22 44N 86 12 E
Jamtara, India .... 81 H12 23 59N 86 49 E
Jämtlands län □, Sweden 14 B7 62 40N 13 50 E
Jamuna →, Bangla. .... 78 D2 23 51N 89 45 E
Jamurki, Bangla. ..... 78 C3 24 9N 90 2 E
Jan Kempdorp, S. Africa 104 D3 27 55 S 24 51 E
Jan L., Canada 131 C8 54 56N 102 55W
Jan Mayen, Arctic 6 B7 71 0N 9 0W
Janaúba, Brazil .... 155 E3 15 48 S 43 19W
Janaucu, I., Brazil 154 A1 0 30N 50 10W
Jand, Pakistan .... 80 C5 33 30N 72 6 E
Janda, L. de la, Spain ... 37 J5 36 15N 5 45W
Jandaia, Brazil .... 155 E1 17 6 S 50 7W
Jandaq, Iran .... 85 C7 34 3N 54 22 E
Jandia, Canary Is. 33 F5 28 6N 14 21W
Jandia, Pta. de, Canary Is. 33 F5 28 3N 14 31W
Jandiatuba →, Brazil .. 152 D4 3 28 S 68 42W
Jandola, Pakistan ..... 80 C4 32 20N 70 9 E
Jandowae, Australia ... 115 D5 26 45 S 151 7 E
Jandrain-Jandrenouilles, Belgium .... 21 G5 50 40N 4 58 E
Jándula →, Spain 37 G6 38 3N 4 6W
Jane Pk., N.Z. .... 119 F3 45 15 S 168 20 E
Janesville, U.S.A. 140 B7 42 39N 89 1W
Jango, Ghana 101 C4 10 5N 1 0W
Jangoo, Brazil .... 157 E6 20 27 S 55 29W
Jangoon, India .... 82 F4 17 44N 79 5 E
Janhtang Ga, Burma ... 78 B6 26 32N 96 38 E
Jānī Kheyl, Afghan. ... 79 B3 32 46N 68 24 E
Janikowo, Poland ..... 47 C5 52 45N 18 7 E
Janīn, Jordan .... 91 C4 32 28N 35 18 E
Janinà = Ioánnina □, Greece .... 44 E2 39 39N 20 57 E
Janja, Yugoslavia ..... 42 C4 44 40N 19 17 E
Janjevo, Yugoslavia ... 42 E6 42 35N 21 19 E
Janjina, Yugoslavia ... 42 E2 42 58N 17 25 E
Janos, Mexico 146 A3 30 45N 108 10W
Jánoshalma, Hungary ... 31 E12 46 18N 19 21 E
Jánosháza, Hungary ... 31 D10 47 8N 17 12 E
Jánossomorja, Hungary . 31 D10 47 47N 17 11 E
Janów, Poland .... 47 E6 50 44N 19 27 E
Janów Lubelski, Poland . 47 E9 50 48N 22 23 E
Janów Podlaski, Poland . 47 C10 52 11N 23 11 E
Janowiec Wielkopolski, Poland .... 47 C4 52 45N 17 30 E
Januária, Brazil ...... 155 E3 15 25 S 44 25W
Janub Dârfûr □, Sudan . 95 E2 11 0N 25 0 E
Janub Kordofân □, Sudan 95 E3 12 0N 30 0 E
Janubio, Canary Is. ... 33 F6 28 56N 13 50W
Janville, France ...... 23 D8 48 10N 1 50 E
Janzé, France 22 E5 47 55N 1 28W
Jaora, India .... 80 H6 23 40N 75 10 E
Japan ■, Asia .... 61 G8 36 0N 136 0 E
Japan, Sea of, Asia ... 60 E7 40 0N 135 0 E
Japan Trench, Pac. Oc. . 122 D6 32 0N 142 0 E
Japen = Yapen, Indonesia .... 71 E9 1 50 S 136 0 E
Japurá →, Brazil ..... 152 D4 3 8 S 65 46W
Jaque, Panama 152 B2 7 27N 78 8W
Jarābulus, Syria ...... 84 B3 36 49N 38 1 E
Jaraguá, Brazil .... 155 E2 15 45 S 49 20W
Jaraguari, Brazil ..... 157 E7 20 9 S 54 35W
Jaraicejo, Spain 37 F5 39 40N 5 49W
Jaraiz, Spain 36 E5 40 4N 5 45W
Jarama →, Spain 34 E1 40 2N 3 39W
Jaramillo, Argentina .... 160 C3 47 10 S 67 7W
Jarandilla, Spain 36 E5 40 8N 5 39W
Jaranwala, Pakistan .... 79 C4 31 15N 73 26 E
Jarash, Jordan .... 91 C4 32 17N 35 54 E
Jarauçu →, Brazil .... 153 D7 1 48 S 52 22W
Jardas al 'Abīd, Libya .. 96 B4 32 18N 20 59 E
Jardim, Brazil .... 158 A4 21 28 S 56 2W
Jardín →, Spain 35 G2 38 50N 2 10W
Jardines de la Reina, Is., Cuba 148 B4 20 50N 78 50W
Jargalang, China ..... 67 C12 43 5N 122 55 E
Jargalant = Hovd, Mongolia .... 64 B4 48 2N 91 37 E
Jargeau, France ...... 23 E9 47 50N 2 1 E
Jari →, Brazil .... 153 D7 1 9 S 51 54W
Jarīr, W. al →, Si. Arabia .... 84 E4 25 38N 42 30 E
Jarmen, Germany ..... 26 B9 53 56N 13 20 E
Jarnac, France 24 C3 45 40N 0 11W
Jarny, France .... 23 C12 49 9N 5 53 E
Jarocin, Poland ...... 47 D4 51 59N 17 29 E
Jaroměr, Czech. ..... 30 A8 50 22N 15 52 E
Jarosław, Poland ..... 31 A15 50 2N 22 42 E
Järpås, Sweden ...... 15 F6 58 23N 12 57 E
Järpen, Sweden ...... 14 A7 63 21N 13 26 E
Jarrahdale, Australia .... 113 F2 32 24 S 116 5 E
Jarres, Plaine des, Laos . 76 C4 19 27N 103 10 E
Jarso, Ethiopia ...... 95 F4 5 15N 37 30 E
Jartai, China .... 66 E3 39 45N 105 48 E
Jaru, Brazil .... 157 C5 10 26 S 62 27W
Jaru →, Brazil ...... 157 C5 10 5 S 61 59W
Jarud Qi, China ..... 67 B11 44 28N 120 50 E
Jarvis, Canada 136 D4 42 53N 80 6W
Jarvis I., Pac. Oc. .... 123 H12 0 15 S 159 55W
Jarvornik, Czech. .... 31 A10 50 23N 17 2 E
Jarwa, India .... 81 F10 27 38N 82 30 E
Jaša Tomić, Yugoslavia . 42 B5 45 26N 20 50 E
Jasien, Poland ...... 47 D2 51 46N 15 0 E
Jāsimīyah, Iraq ...... 84 C5 33 45N 44 41 E
Jasin, Malaysia ..... 77 L4 2 20N 102 26 E
Jāsk, Iran .... 85 E8 25 38N 57 45 E
Jasło, Poland .... 31 B14 49 45N 21 30 E
Jason, Is., Falk. Is. .... 160 D4 51 0 S 61 0W
Jasonville, U.S.A. 141 E9 39 10N 87 13W
Jasper, Alta., Canada ... 130 C5 52 55N 118 5W
Jasper, Ont., Canada ... 137 B9 44 52N 75 57W
Jasper, Ala., U.S.A. 135 J2 33 48N 87 16W
Jasper, Fla., U.S.A. 135 K4 30 31N 82 58W
Jasper, Ind., U.S.A. 141 F10 38 24N 86 56W
Jasper, Minn., U.S.A. .. 138 D6 43 52N 96 22W
Jasper, Tex., U.S.A. 139 K8 30 59N 93 58W
Jasper Nat. Park, Canada 130 C5 52 50N 118 8W
Jassy = Iaşi, Romania .. 46 B8 47 10N 27 40 E
Jastrebarsko, Yugoslavia 39 C12 45 41N 15 39 E
Jastrowie, Poland .... 47 B3 53 26N 16 49 E
Jastrzębie Zdrój, Poland 31 B11 49 57N 18 35 E
Jászapáti, Hungary .... 31 D13 47 32N 20 10 E
Jászárokszállás, Hungary 31 D13 47 39N 20 1 E
Jászberény, Hungary ... 31 D12 47 30N 19 55 E
Jászkiser, Hungary .... 31 D13 47 27N 20 20 E
Jászladány, Hungary ... 31 D13 47 23N 20 10 E
Jataí, Brazil .... 155 E1 17 58 S 51 48W
Jatapu →, Brazil .... 153 D6 2 13 S 58 17W
Jati, Pakistan .... 80 G3 24 20N 68 19 E
Jatibarang, Indonesia ... 71 G13 6 28 S 108 18 E
Jatinegara, Indonesia ... 71 G12 6 13 S 106 52 E
Játiva, Spain 35 G4 39 0N 0 32W
Jatobal, Brazil ...... 154 B2 4 35 S 49 33W
Jáu, Angola .... 103 F2 15 12 S 13 31 E
Jaú, Brazil .... 159 A6 22 10 S 48 30W
Jaú →, Brazil ...... 153 D5 1 54 S 61 26W
Jauaperí →, Brazil ... 153 D5 1 26 S 61 35W
Jauche, Belgium ..... 21 G5 50 41N 4 57 E
Jauja, Peru .... 156 C2 11 45 S 75 15W
Jaunjelgava, U.S.S.R. ... 50 C4 56 35N 25 0 E
Jaunpur, India ...... 81 G10 25 46N 82 44 E
Jauru →, Brazil ..... 157 D6 16 22 S 57 46W
Java = Jawa, Indonesia . 71 G14 7 0 S 110 0 E
Java Sea, Indonesia .... 70 E3 4 35 S 107 15 E
Java Trench, Ind. Oc. ... 74 D3 9 0 S 105 0 E
Javadi Hills, India .... 83 H4 12 40N 78 40 E
Jávea, Spain .... 35 G5 38 48N 0 10 E
Javhlant = Ulyasutay, Mongolia .... 64 B4 47 56N 97 28 E
Javier, I., Chile ..... 160 C2 47 5 S 74 25W
Javla, India .... 82 F2 17 18N 75 9 E
Javron, France 22 D6 48 25N 0 25W
Jawa, Indonesia ..... 71 G14 7 0 S 110 0 E
Jawf, W. al →, Yemen .. 86 D4 15 50N 45 30 E
Jawor, Poland ...... 47 D3 51 4N 16 11 E
Jaworzno, Poland .... 31 A12 50 13N 19 11 E
Jay, U.S.A. 139 G7 36 25N 94 46W
Jaya, Puncak, Indonesia . 71 E9 3 57 S 137 17 E
Jayanca, Peru ...... 156 B2 6 24 S 79 50W
Jayanti, India ...... 78 B2 26 45N 89 40 E
Jayapura, Indonesia ... 71 E10 2 28 S 140 38 E
Jayawijaya, Pegunungan, Indonesia .... 71 F9 5 0 S 139 0 E
Jayrūd, Syria .... 84 C3 33 49N 36 44 E
Jayton, U.S.A. 139 J4 33 17N 100 35W
Jazīreh-ye Shīf, Iran .... 85 D6 29 4N 50 54 E
Jazminal, Mexico 146 C4 24 56N 101 25W
Jazzīn, Lebanon ..... 91 B4 33 31N 35 35 E
Jean, U.S.A. 145 K11 35 47N 115 20W
Jean Marie River, Canada 130 A4 61 32N 120 38W
Jean Rabel, Haiti 149 C5 19 50N 73 5W
Jeanerette, U.S.A. 139 L9 29 52N 91 38W
Jeanette, Ostrov, U.S.S.R. .... 57 B16 76 43N 158 0 E
Jeannette, U.S.A. 136 F5 40 20N 79 36W
Jebba, Morocco 98 A4 35 11N 4 43W
Jebba, Nigeria ...... 101 D5 9 9N 4 48 E
Jebel, Bahr el →, Sudan 95 F3 9 30N 30 25 E
Jebel Qerri, Sudan .... 95 D3 16 16N 32 50 E
Jeberos, Peru ...... 156 B2 5 15 S 76 10W
Jedburgh, U.K. 18 F6 55 28N 2 33W
Jedda = Jiddah, Si. Arabia .... 86 B2 21 29N 39 10 E
Jedlicze, Poland ..... 31 B14 49 43N 21 40 E
Jedlnia-Letnisko, Poland 47 D8 51 25N 21 19 E
Jędrzejów, Poland .... 47 E7 50 35N 20 15 E
Jedwabne, Poland .... 47 B9 53 17N 22 18 E
Jedway, Canada 130 C2 52 17N 131 14W
Jeetzel →, Germany ... 26 B7 53 9N 11 6 E
Jefferson, Iowa, U.S.A. . 140 B2 42 3N 94 25W
Jefferson, Ohio, U.S.A. . 136 E4 41 40N 80 46W
Jefferson, Tex., U.S.A. . 139 J7 32 45N 94 23W
Jefferson, Wis., U.S.A. . 138 D10 43 0N 88 49W
Jefferson, Mt., Nev., U.S.A. 142 G5 38 51N 117 0W
Jefferson, Mt., Oreg., U.S.A. 142 D3 44 45N 121 50W
Jefferson City, Mo., U.S.A. 140 F4 38 34N 92 10W
Jefferson City, Tenn., U.S.A. 135 G4 36 8N 83 30W
Jeffersontown, U.S.A. .. 141 F11 38 17N 85 44W
Jeffersonville, Ind., U.S.A. 141 F11 38 20N 85 42W
Jeffersonville, Ohio, U.S.A. 141 E13 39 38N 83 34W
Jega, Nigeria .... 101 C5 12 15N 4 23 E
Jekabpils, U.S.S.R. .... 50 C4 56 29N 25 57 E
Jelenia Góra, Poland ... 47 E2 50 50N 15 45 E
Jelenia Góra □, Poland . 47 E2 51 0N 15 30 E
Jelgava, U.S.S.R. ..... 13 H17 56 41N 23 49 E
Jelica, Yugoslavia .... 42 D5 43 50N 20 17 E
Jelli, Sudan .... 95 F3 5 25N 31 45 E
Jellicoe, Canada 128 C2 49 40N 87 30W
Jelšava, Czech. ..... 31 C13 48 37N 20 15 E
Jemaja, Indonesia .... 70 D3 3 5N 105 45 E
Jemaluang, Malaysia ... 77 L4 2 16N 103 52 E
Jemappes, Belgium ... 21 H3 50 27N 3 54 E
Jember, Indonesia .... 71 H15 8 11 S 113 41 E
Jembongan, Malaysia ... 70 C5 6 45N 117 20 E
Jemeppe, Belgium .... 21 G7 50 37N 5 30 E
Jemnice, Czech. ..... 30 B8 49 1N 15 34 E
Jena, Germany ...... 26 E7 50 56N 11 33 E
Jena, U.S.A. 139 K8 31 41N 92 7W
Jenbach, Austria .... 30 D4 47 24N 11 47 E
Jendouba, Tunisia .... 96 A1 36 29N 8 47 E
Jeneponto, Indonesia ... 72 C1 5 41 S 119 42 E
Jenkins, U.S.A. 134 G4 37 13N 82 41W
Jenner, U.S.A. 144 G3 38 27N 123 7W
Jennings, La., U.S.A. .. 139 K8 30 10N 92 45W
Jennings, Mo., U.S.A. .. 140 F6 38 43N 90 16W
Jennings →, Canada .. 130 B2 59 38N 132 5W
Jepara, Indonesia .... 75 D3 7 40 S 109 14 E
Jeparit, Australia .... 116 D5 36 8 S 142 1 E
Jequié, Brazil ...... 155 D3 13 51 S 40 5W
Jequitaí →, Brazil ... 155 E3 17 4 S 44 50W
Jequitinhonha, Brazil ... 155 E3 16 30 S 41 0W
Jequitinhonha →, Brazil 155 E4 15 51 S 38 53W
Jerada, Morocco 99 B4 34 17N 2 10W
Jerantut, Malaysia .... 77 L4 3 56N 102 22 E
Jérémie, Haiti 149 C5 18 40N 74 10W
Jeremoabo, Brazil .... 154 D4 10 4 S 38 21W
Jerez, Punta, Mexico ... 147 C5 22 58N 97 40W
Jerez de García Salinas, Mexico 146 C4 22 39N 103 0W
Jerez de la Frontera, Spain 37 J4 36 41N 6 7W
Jerez de los Caballeros, Spain 37 G4 38 20N 6 45W
Jericho = Arīḩā, Syria .. 84 C3 35 49N 36 35 E
Jericho = El Arīḩā, Jordan .... 91 D4 31 52N 35 27 E
Jericho, Australia .... 114 C4 23 38 S 146 6 E
Jerichow, Germany ... 26 C8 52 30N 12 2 E
Jerico Springs, U.S.A. .. 140 G2 37 37N 94 1W
Jerilderie, Australia ... 117 C6 35 20 S 145 41 E
Jermyn, U.S.A. 137 E9 41 31N 75 31W
Jerome, U.S.A. 143 J8 34 50N 112 0W
Jersey, Chan. Is. 17 H5 49 13N 2 7W
Jersey City, U.S.A. ... 137 F10 40 41N 74 8W
Jersey Shore, U.S.A. ... 136 E7 41 17N 77 18W
Jerseyville, U.S.A. ... 140 E6 39 5N 90 20W
Jerusalem, Israel .... 91 D4 31 47N 35 10 E
Jervis B., Australia ... 117 C9 35 8 S 150 46 E
Jesenice, Yugoslavia ... 39 B11 46 28N 14 3 E
Jeseník, Czech. ..... 31 B10 50 0N 17 8 E
Jesenké, Czech. ..... 31 C13 48 20N 20 10 E
Jesselton = Kota Kinabalu, Malaysia ... 70 C5 6 0N 116 4 E
Jessnitz, Germany .... 26 D8 51 42N 12 19 E
Jessore, Bangla. ..... 78 D2 23 10N 89 10 E
Jesup, U.S.A. 135 K5 31 36N 81 54W
Jesup, U.S.A. 140 B4 42 29N 92 4W
Jesús, Peru .... 156 B2 7 15 S 78 25W
Jesús Carranza, Mexico . 147 D5 17 28N 95 1W
Jesús María, Argentina .. 158 C3 30 59 S 64 5W
Jetmore, U.S.A. 139 F5 38 10N 99 57W
Jetpur, India .... 80 J4 21 45N 70 10 E
Jette, Belgium ...... 21 G4 50 53N 4 20 E
Jevnaker, Norway .... 14 D4 60 15N 10 26 E
Jewell, U.S.A. 140 B3 42 20N 93 39W
Jewett, Ohio, U.S.A. .. 136 F3 40 22N 81 2W
Jewett, Tex., U.S.A. .. 139 K6 31 20N 96 8W
Jewett City, U.S.A. ... 137 E13 41 36N 71 58W
Jeyḩūnābād, Iran .... 85 C6 34 58N 48 59 E
Jeypore, India ...... 82 E6 18 50N 82 38 E
Jeziorak, Jezioro, Poland 47 B6 53 40N 19 35 E
Jeziorany, Poland .... 47 B7 53 58N 20 46 E
Jeziorka →, Poland ... 47 D7 51 59N 20 57 E
Jhajjar, India ...... 80 E7 28 37N 76 42 E
Jhal Jhao, Pakistan ... 79 D2 26 20N 65 35 E
Jhalakati, Bangla. ... 78 D3 22 39N 90 12 E
Jhalawar, India ..... 80 G7 24 40N 76 10 E
Jhang Maghiana, Pakistan 79 C4 31 15N 72 22 E
Jhansi, India ...... 81 G8 25 30N 78 36 E
Jharia, India ...... 81 H12 23 45N 86 26 E
Jharsuguda, India .... 82 D7 21 56N 84 5 E
Jhelum, Pakistan .... 79 B4 33 0N 73 45 E
Jhelum →, Pakistan ... 80 D5 31 20N 72 10 E
Jhunjhunu, India .... 80 E6 28 10N 75 30 E
Ji Xian, Hebei, China ... 66 F8 37 35N 115 30 E
Ji Xian, Henan, China ... 66 G8 35 22N 114 5 E
Ji Xian, Shanxi, China .. 66 F6 36 7N 110 40 E
Jia Xian, Henan, China . 66 H7 33 59N 113 12 E
Jia Xian, Shaanxi, China 66 E6 38 12N 110 28 E
Jiading, China ..... 69 B13 31 22N 121 15 E
Jiahe, China .... 69 E9 25 38N 112 19 E
Jiali, Taiwan .... 69 F13 23 12N 120 10 E
Jialing Jiang →, China . 68 C6 29 30N 106 20 E
Jiamusi, China ..... 65 B8 46 40N 130 26 E
Ji'an, Jiangxi, China ... 69 D10 27 6N 114 59 E
Ji'an, Jilin, China .... 67 D14 41 5N 126 10 E
Jianchang, China .... 67 D11 40 55N 120 35 E
Jianchangying, China ... 67 D10 40 10N 118 50 E
Jianchuan, China .... 68 D2 26 38N 99 55 E
Jiande, China ...... 69 C12 29 23N 119 15 E
Jiangbei, China ..... 68 C6 29 40N 106 34 E

K

214 Kadiri

Kadiri, *India* 83 G4 14 12N 78 13 E
Kadirli, *Turkey* 88 E7 37 23N 36 5 E
Kadiyevka = Stakhanov, *U.S.S.R.* 53 B8 48 35N 38 40 E
Kadoka, *U.S.A.* 138 D4 43 50N 101 31W
Kadom, *U.S.S.R.* 51 D13 54 37N 42 30 E
Kadoma, *Zimbabwe* 107 F2 18 20 S 29 52 E
Kâdugli, *Sudan* 95 E2 11 0N 29 45 E
Kaduna, *Nigeria* 101 C6 10 30N 7 21 E
Kaduna □, *Nigeria* 101 C6 11 0N 7 30 E
Kadzhi-Say, *U.S.S.R.* 55 B8 42 8N 77 10 E
Kaédi, *Mauritania* 100 B2 16 9N 13 28W
Kaelé, *Cameroon* 101 C7 10 7N 14 27 E
Kaeng Khoï, *Thailand* 76 E3 14 35N 101 0 E
Kaeo, *N.Z.* 118 B2 35 6 S 173 49 E
Kaesŏng, *N. Korea* 67 F14 37 58N 126 35 E
Kāf, *Si. Arabia* 84 D3 31 25N 37 29 E
Kafakumba, *Zaïre* 103 D4 9 38 S 23 46 E
Kafan, *U.S.S.R.* 89 D12 39 18N 46 15 E
Kafanchan, *Nigeria* 101 D6 9 40N 8 20 E
Kafareti, *Nigeria* 101 C7 10 25N 11 12 E
Kaffrine, *Senegal* 100 C1 14 8N 15 36W
Kafia Kingi, *Sudan* 102 A4 9 20N 24 25 E
Kafinda, *Zambia* 107 E3 12 32 S 30 20 E
Kafirévs, Ákra, *Greece* 45 F6 38 9N 24 38 E
Kafr el Dauwâr, *Egypt* 94 H7 31 8N 30 8 E
Kafr el Sheikh, *Egypt* 94 H7 31 15N 30 50 E
Kafue, *Zambia* 107 F2 15 46 S 28 9 E
Kafue Flats, *Zambia* 107 F2 15 40 S 27 25 E
Kafue Nat. Park, *Zambia* 107 F2 15 0 S 25 30 E
Kafulwe, *Zambia* 107 D2 9 0 S 29 1 E
Kaga, *Afghan.* 80 B4 34 14N 70 10 E
Kaga, *Japan* 63 A8 36 16N 136 15 E
Kaga Bandoro, *C.A.R.* 102 A3 7 0N 19 10 E
Kagan, *U.S.S.R.* 55 D2 39 43N 64 33 E
Kagawa □, *Japan* 62 C6 34 15N 134 0 E
Kagera □, *Tanzania* 106 C3 2 0 S 31 30 E
Kagera →, *Uganda* 106 C3 0 57 S 31 47 E
Kağizman, *Turkey* 89 C10 40 5N 43 10 E
Kagoshima, *Japan* 62 F2 31 35N 130 33 E
Kagoshima □, *Japan* 62 F2 31 30N 130 30 E
Kagoshima-Wan, *Japan* 62 F2 31 25N 130 40 E
Kagul, *U.S.S.R.* 52 D3 45 50N 28 15 E
Kahak, *Iran* 85 B6 36 6N 49 46 E
Kahama, *Tanzania* 106 C3 4 8 S 32 30 E
Kahama □, *Tanzania* 106 C3 3 50 S 32 0 E
Kahang, *Malaysia* 77 L4 2 12N 103 32 E
Kahayan →, *Indonesia* 70 E4 3 40 S 114 0 E
Kahe, *Tanzania* 106 C4 3 30 S 37 25 E
Kahemba, *Zaïre* 103 D3 7 18 S 18 55 E
Kaherekoau Mts., *N.Z.* 119 F2 45 45 S 167 15 E
Kahil, Djebel bou, *Algeria* 99 B5 34 26N 4 0 E
Kahniah →, *Canada* 130 B4 58 15N 120 55W
Kahnūj, *Iran* 85 E8 27 55N 57 40 E
Kahoka, *U.S.A.* 140 D5 40 25N 91 42W
Kahoolawe, *U.S.A.* 132 H16 20 33N 156 35W
Kahramanmaraş, *Turkey* 88 E7 37 37N 36 53 E
Kahramanmaraş □, *Turkey* 88 E7 37 35N 36 33 E
Kâhta, *Turkey* 89 E8 37 46N 38 36 E
Kahurangi, Pt., *N.Z.* 119 A7 40 50 S 172 10 E
Kahuta, *Pakistan* 80 C5 33 35N 73 24 E
Kai, Kepulauan, *Indonesia* 71 F8 5 55 S 132 45 E
Kai Besar, *Indonesia* 71 F8 5 35 S 133 0 E
Kai Is. = Kai, Kepulauan, *Indonesia* 71 F8 5 55 S 132 45 E
Kai-Ketil, *Indonesia* 71 F8 5 45 S 132 40 E
Kai Xian, *China* 68 B7 31 11N 108 21 E
Kaiama, *Nigeria* 101 D5 9 36N 4 1 E
Kaiapit, *Papua N. G.* 120 D4 6 18 S 146 18 E
Kaiapoi, *N.Z.* 119 D7 43 24 S 172 40 E
Kaibara, *Japan* 63 B7 35 8N 135 5 E
Kaieteur Falls, *Guyana* 153 B6 5 1N 59 10W
Kaifeng, *China* 65 C6 34 49N 114 30 E
Kaifeng, *Henan, China* 66 G8 34 48N 114 21 E
Kaihua, *China* 69 C12 29 12N 118 20 E
Kaikohe, *N.Z.* 118 B2 35 25 S 173 49 E
Kaikoura, *N.Z.* 119 C8 42 25 S 173 43 E
Kaikoura Pen., *N.Z.* 119 C8 42 25 S 173 43 E
Kaikoura Ra., *N.Z.* 119 B8 41 59 S 173 41 E
Kailahun, *S. Leone* 100 D2 8 18N 10 39W
Kailashahar, *India* 78 C4 24 19N 92 0 E
Kaili, *China* 68 D6 26 33N 107 59 E
Kailu, *China* 67 C11 43 38N 121 18 E
Kailua, *U.S.A.* 132 J17 19 39N 156 0W
Kaimana, *Indonesia* 71 E8 3 39 S 133 45 E
Kaimanawa Mts., *N.Z.* 118 F4 39 15 S 175 56 E
Kaimata, *N.Z.* 119 C6 42 34 S 171 28 E
Kaimganj, *India* 81 F8 27 33N 79 24 E
Kaimon-Dake, *Japan* 62 F2 31 11N 130 32 E
Kaimur Hills, *India* 81 G10 24 30N 82 0 E
Kainan, *Japan* 63 C7 34 9N 135 12 E
Kainantu, *Papua N. G.* 120 D3 6 18 S 145 52 E
Kaingaroa Forest, *N.Z.* 118 E5 38 24 S 176 30 E
Kainji Res., *Nigeria* 101 C5 10 1N 4 40 E
Kaipara Harbour, *N.Z.* 118 C3 36 25 S 174 14 E
Kaiping, *China* 69 F9 22 23N 112 42 E
Kaipokok B., *Canada* 129 B8 54 54N 59 47W
Kairana, *India* 80 E7 29 24N 77 15 E
Kaironi, *Indonesia* 71 E8 0 47 S 133 40 E
Kairouan, *Tunisia* 96 A2 35 45N 10 5 E
Kairuku, *Papua N. G.* 120 E4 8 51 S 146 35 E
Kaiserslautern, *Germany* 27 F3 49 30N 7 43 E
Kaitaia, *N.Z.* 118 B2 35 8 S 173 17 E
Kaitangata, *N.Z.* 119 G4 46 17 S 169 51 E
Kaithal, *India* 80 E7 29 48N 76 26 E
Kaitu →, *Pakistan* 80 C4 33 10N 70 30 E
Kaiwi Channel, *U.S.A.* 132 H16 21 13N 157 30W
Kaiyang, *China* 68 D6 27 4N 106 59 E
Kaiyuan, *Liaoning, China* 67 C13 42 28N 124 1 E
Kaiyuan, *Yunnan, China* 68 F4 23 40N 103 12 E
Kajaani, *Finland* 12 D19 64 17N 27 46 E
Kajabbi, *Australia* 114 C3 20 0 S 140 1 E
Kajana = Kajaani, *Finland* 12 D19 64 17N 27 46 E
Kajang, *Malaysia* 77 L3 2 59N 101 48 E
Kajiado, *Kenya* 106 C4 1 53 S 36 48 E
Kajiado □, *Kenya* 106 C4 2 0 S 36 30 E
Kajiki, *Japan* 62 F2 31 44N 130 40 E
Kajo Kaji, *Sudan* 95 G3 3 58N 31 40 E
Kaka, *Sudan* 95 E3 10 38N 32 10 E
Kakabeka Falls, *Canada* 128 C2 48 24N 89 37W
Kakamas, *S. Africa* 104 D3 28 45 S 20 33 E
Kakamega, *Kenya* 106 B3 0 20N 34 46 E
Kakamega □, *Kenya* 106 B3 0 20N 34 46 E
Kakamigahara, *Japan* 63 B8 35 28N 136 48 E
Kakanj, *Yugoslavia* 42 C3 44 9N 18 7 E
Kakanui Mts., *N.Z.* 119 F5 45 10 S 170 30 E
Kake, *Japan* 62 C4 34 36N 132 19 E
Kakegawa, *Japan* 63 C10 34 45N 138 1 E
Kakeroma-Jima, *Japan* 61 K4 28 8N 129 14 E
Kakhib, *U.S.S.R.* 53 E12 42 28N 46 34 E
Kakhovka, *U.S.S.R.* 52 C5 46 40N 33 15 E
Kakhovskoye Vdkhr., *U.S.S.R.* 52 C6 47 5N 34 16 E
Kakinada, *India* 82 F6 16 57N 82 11 E
Kakisa →, *Canada* 130 A5 61 3N 118 10W
Kakisa L., *Canada* 130 A5 60 56N 117 43W
Kakogawa, *Japan* 62 C6 34 46N 134 51 E
Kakwa →, *Canada* 130 C5 54 37N 118 28W
Kāl Gūsheh, *Iran* 85 D8 30 59N 58 12 E
Kal Safīd, *Iran* 84 C5 34 52N 47 23 E
Kala, *Nigeria* 101 C7 12 2N 14 40 E
Kala Oya →, *Sri Lanka* 83 K4 8 20N 79 45 E
Kalaa-Kebira, *Tunisia* 96 A2 35 59N 10 32 E
Kalabagh, *Pakistan* 79 B3 33 0N 71 28 E
Kalabahi, *Indonesia* 71 F6 8 13 S 124 31 E
Kalabáka, *Greece* 44 E3 39 42N 21 39 E
Kalabo, *Zambia* 103 E4 14 58 S 22 40 E
Kalach, *U.S.S.R.* 51 F12 50 22N 41 0 E
Kalach na Donu, *U.S.S.R.* 53 B10 48 43N 43 32 E
Kaladar, *Canada* 136 B7 44 37N 77 5W
Kalahari, *Africa* 104 C3 24 0 S 21 30 E
Kalahari Gemsbok Nat. Park, *S. Africa* 104 D3 25 30 S 20 30 E
Kalai-Khumb, *U.S.S.R.* 55 D5 38 28N 70 46 E
Kālak, *Iran* 85 E8 25 29N 59 22 E
Kalakamati, *Botswana* 105 C4 20 40 S 27 25 E
Kalakan, *U.S.S.R.* 57 D12 55 15N 116 45 E
Kalakh, *Syria* 84 C3 34 55N 36 10 E
K'alak'unlun Shank'ou, *Pakistan* 81 B7 35 33N 77 46 E
Kalam, *Pakistan* 81 B5 35 34N 72 30 E
Kalama, *U.S.A.* 144 E4 46 0N 122 55W
Kalama, *Zaïre* 106 C2 2 52 S 28 35 E
Kalamariá, *Greece* 44 D4 40 33N 22 55 E
Kalamata, *Greece* 45 G4 37 3N 22 10 E
Kalamazoo, *U.S.A.* 141 B11 42 20N 85 35W
Kalamazoo →, *U.S.A.* 141 B10 42 40N 86 12W
Kalamb, *India* 82 E2 18 3N 74 48 E
Kalambo Falls, *Tanzania* 107 D3 8 37 S 31 35 E
Kálamos, *Attikí, Greece* 45 F5 38 17N 23 52 E
Kálamos, *Pelopónnisos, Greece* 45 F2 38 37N 20 55 E
Kalamoti, *Greece* 45 F8 38 15N 26 4 E
Kalangadoo, *Australia* 116 D4 37 34 S 140 41 E
Kalannie, *Australia* 113 F2 30 22 S 117 5 E
Kalāntarī, *Iran* 85 C7 32 10N 54 8 E
Kalao, *Indonesia* 71 F6 7 21 S 121 0 E
Kalaotoa, *Indonesia* 71 F6 7 20 S 121 50 E
Kalärne, *Sweden* 14 B10 62 59N 16 8 E
Kalárovo, *Czech.* 31 D11 47 54N 18 0 E
Kalasin, *Thailand* 76 D4 16 26N 103 30 E
Kalat, *Pakistan* 79 C2 29 8N 66 31 E
Kalāteh, *Iran* 85 B7 36 33N 55 41 E
Kalāteh-ye-Ganj, *Iran* 85 E8 27 31N 57 55 E
Kálathos, *Greece* 45 H10 36 9N 28 8 E
Kalaus →, *U.S.S.R.* 53 D11 45 40N 44 7 E
Kalávrita, *Greece* 45 F4 38 3N 22 8 E
Kalaw, *Burma* 78 E6 20 38N 96 34 E
Kalbān, *Oman* 87 B7 20 18N 58 38 E
Kalbarri, *Australia* 113 E1 27 40 S 114 10 E
Kale, *Turkey* 88 E3 37 27N 28 49 E
Kalecik, *Turkey* 88 C5 40 4N 33 26 E
Kalehe, *Zaïre* 106 C2 2 6 S 28 50 E
Kalema, *Tanzania* 106 C3 1 12 S 31 55 E
Kalemie, *Zaïre* 106 D2 5 55 S 29 9 E
Kalemyo, *Burma* 78 D5 23 11N 94 4 E
Kalety, *Poland* 47 E5 50 35N 18 52 E
Kalewa, *Burma* 78 D5 23 10N 94 15 E
Kálfafellsstaður, *Iceland* 12 D6 64 11N 15 53W
Kalgan = Zhangjiakou, *China* 66 D8 40 48N 114 55 E
Kalgoorlie-Boulder, *Australia* 113 F3 30 40 S 121 22 E
Kaliakra, Nos, *Bulgaria* 43 D13 43 21N 28 30 E
Kalianda, *Indonesia* 70 F3 5 50 S 105 45 E
Kalibo, *Phil.* 71 B6 11 43N 122 22 E
Kaliganj, *Bangla.* 81 H13 22 25N 89 8 E
Kalima, *Zaïre* 106 C2 2 33 S 26 32 E
Kalimantan, *Indonesia* 70 E4 0 0 114 0 E
Kalimantan Barat □, *Indonesia* 70 E4 0 0 110 30 E
Kalimantan Selatan □, *Indonesia* 70 E5 2 30 S 115 30 E
Kalimantan Tengah □, *Indonesia* 70 E4 2 0 S 113 30 E
Kalimantan Timur □, *Indonesia* 70 D5 1 30N 116 30 E
Kálimnos, *Greece* 45 H9 37 0N 27 0 E
Kalimpong, *India* 81 F13 27 4N 88 35 E
Kalinadi →, *India* 83 G2 14 50N 74 7 E
Kalinin, *U.S.S.R.* 51 C9 56 55N 35 55 E
Kaliningrad, *R.S.F.S.R., U.S.S.R.* 50 D2 54 42N 20 32 E
Kaliningrad, *R.S.F.S.R., U.S.S.R.* 51 D10 55 58N 37 54 E
Kalininskoye, *U.S.S.R.* 55 B6 42 50N 73 49 E
Kalinkovichi, *U.S.S.R.* 50 E6 52 12N 29 20 E
Kalinovik, *Yugoslavia* 42 D3 43 31N 18 29 E
Kalipetrovo, *Bulgaria* 43 C12 44 5N 27 14 E
Kaliro, *Uganda* 106 B3 0 56N 33 30 E
Kalirrákhi, *Greece* 44 D6 40 40N 24 35 E
Kalispell, *U.S.A.* 142 B6 48 10N 114 22W
Kalisz, *Poland* 47 D5 51 45N 18 8 E
Kalisz □, *Poland* 47 D5 51 30N 18 0 E
Kalisz Pomorski, *Poland* 47 B2 53 17N 15 55 E
Kaliua, *Tanzania* 106 D3 5 5 S 31 48 E
Kaliveli Tank, *India* 83 H4 12 5N 79 50 E
Kalix →, *Sweden* 12 D17 65 50N 23 11 E
Kalka, *India* 80 D7 30 46N 76 57 E
Kalkan, *Turkey* 88 E3 36 15N 29 23 E
Kalkaroo, *Australia* 116 A5 31 12 S 143 54 E
Kalkaska, *U.S.A.* 134 C3 44 44N 85 11W
Kalkfeld, *Namibia* 104 C2 20 57 S 16 14 E
Kalkfontein, *Botswana* 104 C3 22 4 S 20 57 E
Kalkrand, *Namibia* 104 C2 24 1 S 17 35 E
Kallakkurichchi, *India* 83 J4 11 44N 79 1 E
Kållandsö, *Sweden* 15 F7 58 40N 13 5 E
Kallidaikurichi, *India* 83 K3 8 38N 77 31 E
Kallithéa, *Greece* 45 G5 37 55N 23 41 E
Kallmeti, *Albania* 44 C1 41 51N 19 41 E
Kallonís, Kólpos, *Greece* 45 E8 39 10N 26 10 E
Kallsjön, *Sweden* 12 E12 63 38N 13 0 E
Kalmalo, *Nigeria* 101 C6 13 40N 5 20 E
Kalmar, *Sweden* 13 H14 56 40N 16 20 E
Kalmthout, *Belgium* 21 F4 51 23N 4 29 E
Kalmyk A.S.S.R. □, *U.S.S.R.* 53 C12 46 5N 46 1 E
Kalmykovo, *U.S.S.R.* 53 B14 49 0N 51 47 E
Kalna, *India* 81 H13 23 13N 88 25 E
Kalo, *Papua N. G.* 120 F4 10 1 S 147 48 E
Kalocsa, *Hungary* 31 E12 46 32N 19 0 E
Kalofer, *Bulgaria* 43 E9 42 37N 24 59 E
Kalokhorio, *Cyprus* 32 E12 34 51N 33 2 E
Kaloko, *Zaïre* 103 D5 6 47 S 25 48 E
Kalol, *Gujarat, India* 80 H5 22 37N 73 31 E
Kalol, *Gujarat, India* 80 H5 23 15N 72 33 E
Kalolímnos, *Greece* 45 G9 37 4N 27 8 E
Kalomo, *Zambia* 107 F2 17 0 S 26 30 E
Kalona, *U.S.A.* 140 C5 41 29N 91 43W
Kaloneróin, *Greece* 45 G3 37 20N 21 38 E
Kalpi, *India* 81 F8 26 8N 79 47 E
Kalrayan Hills, *India* 83 J4 11 45N 78 40 E
Kalsubai, *India* 82 E1 19 35N 73 45 E
Kaltbrunn, *Switz.* 29 B8 47 13N 9 2 E
Kaltungo, *Nigeria* 101 D7 9 48N 11 19 E
Kalu, *Pakistan* 80 G2 25 5N 67 39 E
Kaluga, *U.S.S.R.* 51 D10 54 35N 36 10 E
Kalulushi, *Zambia* 107 E2 12 50 S 28 3 E
Kalundborg, *Denmark* 15 J5 55 41N 11 5 E
Kalush, *U.S.S.R.* 50 G4 49 3N 24 23 E
Kałuszyn, *Poland* 47 C8 52 13N 21 52 E
Kalutara, *Sri Lanka* 83 L5 6 35N 80 0 E
Kalwaria, *Poland* 31 B12 49 53N 19 41 E
Kalya, *U.S.S.R.* 54 A6 60 15N 59 59 E
Kalyan, *Australia* 116 C3 34 55 S 139 49 E
Kalyan, *India* 82 D2 20 30N 74 3 E
Kalyazin, *U.S.S.R.* 51 C10 57 15N 37 55 E
Kama, *Burma* 78 F5 19 1N 95 4 E
Kama, *Zaïre* 106 C2 3 30 S 27 5 E
Kama →, *U.S.S.R.* 54 D3 55 45N 52 0 E
Kamachumu, *Tanzania* 106 C3 1 37 S 31 37 E
Kamae, *Japan* 62 E3 32 48N 131 56 E
Kamaing, *Burma* 78 C6 25 26N 96 35 E
Kamaishi, *Japan* 60 E10 39 16N 141 53 E
Kamakura, *Japan* 63 B11 35 19N 139 33 E
Kamalia, *Pakistan* 80 D5 30 44N 72 42 E
Kamamaung, *Burma* 78 G6 17 21N 97 40 E
Kamandorskiye Ostrava, *U.S.S.R.* 57 D17 55 0N 167 0 E
Kamapanda, *Zambia* 107 E1 12 5 S 24 0 E
Kamaran, *Yemen* 86 D3 15 21N 42 35 E
Kamashi, *U.S.S.R.* 55 D2 38 51N 65 23 E
Kamativi, *Zimbabwe* 107 F2 18 15 S 27 27 E
Kamba, *Nigeria* 101 C5 11 50N 3 45 E
Kambalda, *Australia* 113 F3 31 10 S 121 37 E
Kambam, *India* 83 K3 9 45N 77 16 E
Kambar, *Pakistan* 80 F3 27 37N 68 1 E
Kambarka, *U.S.S.R.* 54 C4 56 15N 54 11 E
Kambia, *S. Leone* 100 D2 9 3N 12 53W
Kambolé, *Zambia* 107 D3 8 47 S 30 48 E
Kambos, *Cyprus* 32 D11 35 2N 32 44 E
Kambove, *Zaïre* 107 E2 10 51 S 26 33 E
Kambuie, *Zaïre* 103 D4 6 59 S 22 19 E
Kamchatka, P-ov., *U.S.S.R.* 57 D17 57 0N 160 0 E
Kamen, *U.S.S.R.* 56 D9 53 50N 81 30 E
Kamen Kashirskiy, *U.S.S.R.* 50 F4 51 39N 24 56 E
Kamen-Rybolov, *U.S.S.R.* 60 B6 44 46N 132 2 E
Kamenets-Podolskiy, *U.S.S.R.* 52 B2 48 45N 26 10 E
Kamenica, *Srbija, Yugoslavia* 42 D7 43 27N 22 27 E
Kamenica, *Srbija, Yugoslavia* 42 C4 44 25N 19 40 E
Kamenice, *Czech.* 30 B8 49 18N 15 2 E
Kamenjak, Rt., *Yugoslavia* 39 D10 44 47N 13 55 E
Kamenka, *R.S.F.S.R., U.S.S.R.* 48 A7 65 58N 44 0 E
Kamenka, *R.S.F.S.R., U.S.S.R.* 51 E14 53 10N 44 5 E
Kamenka, *R.S.F.S.R., U.S.S.R.* 51 F11 50 47N 39 20 E
Kamenka, *Ukraine S.S.R., U.S.S.R.* 52 B5 49 3N 32 6 E
Kamenka Bugskaya, *U.S.S.R.* 50 F4 50 8N 24 16 E
Kamenka Dneprovskaya, *U.S.S.R.* 52 C6 47 29N 34 14 E
Kameno, *Bulgaria* 43 E12 42 34N 27 18 E
Kamenolomini, *U.S.S.R.* 53 C9 47 40N 40 14 E
Kamensk-Shakhtinskiy, *U.S.S.R.* 53 B9 48 23N 40 20 E
Kamensk Uralskiy, *U.S.S.R.* 54 C8 56 25N 62 2 E
Kamenskiy, *R.S.F.S.R., U.S.S.R.* 51 F14 50 48N 45 25 E
Kamenskiy, *R.S.F.S.R., U.S.S.R.* 53 B9 49 20N 41 15 E
Kamenskoye, *U.S.S.R.* 57 C17 62 45N 165 30 E
Kamenyak, *Bulgaria* 43 D11 43 24N 26 57 E
Kamenz, *Germany* 26 D10 51 17N 14 7 E
Kameoka, *Japan* 63 C7 35 0N 135 35 E
Kameyama, *Japan* 63 C8 34 51N 136 27 E
Kami, *Albania* 44 B2 42 17N 20 18 E
Kami-Jima, *Japan* 62 E2 32 27N 130 20 E
Kami-koshiki-Jima, *Japan* 62 F1 31 50N 129 52 E
Kamiah, *U.S.A.* 142 C5 46 12N 116 2W
Kamień Krajeński, *Poland* 47 B4 53 32N 17 32 E
Kamień Pomorski, *Poland* 47 B1 53 57N 14 43 E
Kamienna →, *Poland* 47 D8 51 6N 21 47 E
Kamienna Góra, *Poland* 47 E3 50 47N 16 2 E
Kamieńsk, *Poland* 47 D6 51 12N 19 29 E
Kamieskroon, *S. Africa* 104 E2 30 9 S 17 56 E
Kamiita, *Japan* 62 C6 34 6N 134 22 E
Kamilukuak, L., *Canada* 131 A8 62 22N 101 40W
Kamina, *Zaïre* 103 D5 8 45 S 25 0 E
Kaminak L., *Canada* 131 A10 62 10N 95 0W
Kaminoyama, *Japan* 60 E10 38 9N 140 17 E
Kamioka, *Japan* 63 A9 36 25N 137 15 E
Kamiros, *Greece* 32 C9 36 20N 27 56 E
Kamituga, *Zaïre* 106 C2 3 2 S 28 10 E
Kamloops, *Canada* 130 C4 50 40N 120 20W
Kamnik, *Yugoslavia* 39 B11 46 14N 14 37 E
Kamo, *Japan* 60 F9 37 39N 139 3 E
Kamo, *N.Z.* 118 B3 35 42 S 174 20 E
Kamo, *U.S.S.R.* 53 F11 40 21N 45 7 E
Kamoa Mts., *Guyana* 153 C6 1 30N 59 0W
Kamogawa, *Japan* 63 B12 35 5N 140 5 E
Kamoke, *Pakistan* 80 C6 32 4N 74 4 E
Kamp →, *Austria* 30 C8 48 23N 15 42 E
Kampala, *Uganda* 106 B3 0 20N 32 30 E
Kampar, *Malaysia* 77 K3 4 18N 101 9 E
Kampar →, *Indonesia* 70 D2 0 30N 103 8 E
Kampen, *Neths.* 20 C7 52 33N 5 53 E
Kamperland, *Neths.* 21 E3 51 34N 3 43 E
Kamphaeng Phet, *Thailand* 76 D2 16 28N 99 30 E
Kampolombo, L., *Zambia* 107 E2 11 37 S 29 42 E
Kampong To, *Thailand* 77 J3 6 3N 101 13 E
Kampot, *Cambodia* 77 G5 10 36N 104 10 E
Kampsville, *U.S.A.* 140 E6 39 18N 90 37W
Kamptee, *India* 82 D4 21 9N 79 19 E
Kampti, *Burkina Faso* 100 C4 10 7N 3 25W
Kampuchea = Cambodia ■, *Asia* 76 F5 12 15N 105 0 E
Kampung →, *Indonesia* 71 F9 5 44 S 138 24 E
Kampung Air Putih, *Malaysia* 77 K4 4 15N 103 10 E
Kampung Jerangau, *Malaysia* 77 K4 4 50N 103 10 E
Kampung Raja, *Malaysia* 77 K4 5 45N 102 35 E
Kampungbaru = Tolitoli, *Indonesia* 71 D6 1 5N 120 50 E
Kamrau, Teluk, *Indonesia* 71 E8 3 30 S 133 36 E
Kamsack, *Canada* 131 C8 51 34N 101 54W
Kamskoye Ustye, *U.S.S.R.* 51 D16 55 10N 49 20 E
Kamskoye Vdkhr., *U.S.S.R.* 48 C10 58 0N 56 0 E
Kamuchawie L., *Canada* 131 B8 56 18N 101 59W
Kamui-Misaki, *Japan* 60 C10 43 20N 140 21 E
Kāmyārān, *Iran* 84 C5 34 47N 46 56 E
Kamyshin, *U.S.S.R.* 51 F14 50 10N 45 24 E
Kamyshlov, *U.S.S.R.* 54 C8 56 50N 62 43 E
Kamyzyak, *U.S.S.R.* 53 C13 46 4N 48 10 E
Kan, *Burma* 78 D5 22 25N 94 5 E
Kanaaupscow, *Canada* 128 B4 54 2N 76 30W
Kanab, *U.S.A.* 143 H7 37 3N 112 29W
Kanab Creek, *U.S.A.* 143 H7 37 0N 112 40W
Kanagawa □, *Japan* 63 B11 35 20N 139 20 E
Kanagi, *Japan* 60 D10 40 54N 140 27 E
Kanairiktok →, *Canada* 129 A7 55 2N 60 18W
Kanakapura, *India* 83 H3 12 33N 77 28 E
Kanália, *Greece* 44 E4 39 30N 22 53 E
Kananga, *Zaïre* 103 D4 5 55 S 22 18 E
Kanarraville, *U.S.A.* 143 H7 37 34N 113 12W
Kanash, *U.S.S.R.* 51 D15 55 30N 47 32 E
Kanaskat, *U.S.A.* 144 C5 47 19N 121 54W
Kanastraíon, Ákra, *Greece* 44 E5 39 57N 23 45 E
Kanawha →, *U.S.A.* 134 F4 38 50N 82 8W
Kanazawa, *Japan* 63 A8 36 30N 136 38 E
Kanbalu, *Burma* 78 D5 23 12N 95 31 E
Kanchanaburi, *Thailand* 76 E2 14 2N 99 31 E
Kanchenjunga, *Nepal* 81 F13 27 50N 88 10 E
Kanchipuram, *India* 83 H4 12 52N 79 45 E
Kańczuga, *Poland* 31 B15 49 59N 22 25 E
Kanda Kanda, *Zaïre* 103 D4 6 52 S 23 48 E
Kandahar = Qandahār, *Afghan.* 79 C2 31 32N 65 30 E
Kandalaksha, *U.S.S.R.* 48 A5 67 9N 32 30 E
Kandalakshkiy Zaliv, *U.S.S.R.* 48 A6 66 0N 35 0 E
Kandangan, *Indonesia* 70 E5 2 50 S 115 20 E
Kandanos, *Greece* 45 J5 35 19N 23 44 E
Kandanos, *Kriti, Greece* 32 D5 35 20N 23 45 E
Kandavu, *Fiji* 121 B2 19 0 S 178 15 E
Kandavu Passage, *Fiji* 121 B2 18 45 S 178 0 E
Kandep, *Papua N. G.* 120 C2 5 54 S 143 32 E
Kander →, *Switz.* 28 C5 46 33N 7 38 E
Kandersteg, *Switz.* 28 D5 46 28N 7 40 E
Kandhíla, *Greece* 45 G4 37 46N 22 22 E
Kandhkot, *Pakistan* 80 E3 28 16N 69 8 E
Kandhla, *India* 80 E7 29 18N 77 19 E
Kandi, *Benin* 101 C5 11 7N 2 55 E
Kandi, *India* 81 H13 23 58N 88 5 E
Kandıra, *Turkey* 88 C4 41 4N 30 9 E
Kandla, *India* 80 H4 23 0N 70 10 E
Kandos, *Australia* 117 B8 32 45 S 149 58 E
Kandrian, *Papua N. G.* 120 D5 6 14 S 149 37 E
Kandy, *Sri Lanka* 83 L5 7 18N 80 43 E
Kane, *U.S.A.* 136 E6 41 39N 78 53W
Kane Basin, *Canada* 6 B4 79 1N 70 0W
Kanevskaya, *U.S.S.R.* 53 C8 46 3N 39 3 E
Kanfanar, *Yugoslavia* 39 C10 45 7N 13 50 E
Kangaba, *Mali* 100 C3 11 56N 8 25W
Kangal, *Turkey* 88 D7 39 14N 37 23 E
Kangān, *Fārs, Iran* 85 E7 27 50N 52 3 E
Kangān, *Hormozgān, Iran* 85 E8 25 48N 57 28 E
Kangar, *Malaysia* 77 J3 6 27N 100 12 E
Kangaroo I., *Australia* 116 C2 35 45 S 137 0 E
Kangavar, *Iran* 85 C6 34 40N 48 0 E
Kangding, *China* 68 B3 30 2N 101 57 E
Kăngdong, *N. Korea* 67 E14 39 9N 126 5 E
Kangean, Kepulauan, *Indonesia* 70 F5 6 55 S 115 23 E
Kangean Is. = Kangean, Kepulauan, *Indonesia* 70 F5 6 55 S 115 23 E
Kanggye, *N. Korea* 67 D14 41 0N 126 35 E
Kanggyŏng, *S. Korea* 67 F14 36 10N 127 0 E
Kanghwa, *S. Korea* 67 F14 37 45N 126 30 E
Kangnŭng, *S. Korea* 67 F15 37 45N 128 54 E
Kango, *Gabon* 102 B2 0 11N 10 5 E
Kangoya, *Zaïre* 103 D4 9 55 S 22 48 E
Kangping, *China* 67 C12 42 43N 123 18 E
Kangpokpi, *India* 78 C4 25 8N 93 58 E
Kangyidaung, *Burma* 78 G5 16 56N 94 54 E
Kanhangad, *India* 83 H2 12 21N 74 58 E
Kanheri, *India* 82 E1 19 13N 72 50 E

Kaunas 215

Kani, *Ivory C.* **100 D3** 8 29N 6 36W
Kaniama, *Zaïre* **103 D4** 7 30 S 24 12 E
Kaniapiskau ⟶, *Canada* **129 A6** 56 40N 69 30W
Kaniapiskau L., *Canada* **129 B6** 54 10N 69 55W
Kanibadam, *U.S.S.R.* **55 C5** 40 17N 70 25 E
Kanieri, L., *N.Z.* **119 C6** 42 50 S 171 10 E
Kanin, P-ov., *U.S.S.R.* **48 A8** 68 0N 45 0 E
Kanin Nos, Mys,
U.S.S.R. **48 A7** 68 45N 43 20 E
Kanina, *Albania* **44 D1** 40 23N 19 30 E
Kaniva, *Australia* **116 D4** 36 22 S 141 18 E
Kanjiža, *Yugoslavia* **42 A5** 46 3N 20 4 E
Kanjut Sar, *Pakistan* **81 A6** 36 7N 75 25 E
Kankakee, *U.S.A.* **141 C9** 41 6N 87 50W
Kankakee ⟶, *U.S.A.* **141 C8** 41 23N 88 16W
Kankan, *Guinea* **100 C3** 10 23N 9 15W
Kanker, *India* **82 D5** 20 10N 81 40 E
Kankunskiy, *U.S.S.R.* **57 D13** 57 37N 126 8 E
Kanmuri-Yama, *Japan* **62 C4** 34 30N 132 4 E
Kannabe, *Japan* **62 C5** 34 32N 133 23 E
Kannapolis, *U.S.A.* **135 H5** 35 32N 80 37W
Kannauj, *India* **81 F8** 27 3N 79 56 E
Kano, *Nigeria* **101 C6** 12 2N 8 30 E
Kano □, *Nigeria* **101 C6** 11 45N 9 0 E
Kan'onji, *Japan* **62 C5** 34 7N 133 39 E
Kanoroba, *Ivory C.* **100 D3** 9 7N 6 8W
Kanowha, *U.S.A.* **140 B3** 42 57N 93 47W
Kanowit, *Malaysia* **70 D4** 2 14N 112 20 E
Kanowna, *Australia* **113 F3** 30 32 S 121 31 E
Kanoya, *Japan* **62 F2** 31 25N 130 50 E
Kanpetlet, *Burma* **78 E4** 21 10N 93 59 E
Kanpur, *India* **81 F9** 26 28N 80 20 E
Kansas, *U.S.A.* **141 E9** 39 33N 87 56W
Kansas □, *U.S.A.* **138 F6** 38 40N 98 0W
Kansas ⟶, *U.S.A.* **138 F7** 39 7N 94 36W
Kansas City, *Kans.,*
U.S.A. **140 E2** 39 5N 94 40W
Kansas City, *Mo., U.S.A.* **140 E2** 39 3N 94 30W
Kansenia, *Zaïre* **107 E2** 10 20 S 26 0 E
Kansk, *U.S.S.R.* **57 D10** 56 20N 95 37 E
Kansŏng, *S. Korea* **67 E15** 38 24N 128 30 E
Kansu = Gansu □, *China* **66 G3** 36 0N 104 0 E
Kant, *U.S.S.R.* **55 B7** 42 53N 74 51 E
Kantang, *Thailand* **77 J2** 7 25N 99 31 E
Kantché, *Niger* **97 F1** 13 31N 8 30 E
Kanté, *Togo* **101 D5** 9 57N 1 3 E
Kantemirovka, *U.S.S.R.* **53 B8** 49 43N 39 55 E
Kantharalak, *Thailand* **76 E5** 14 39N 104 39 E
Kantō □, *Japan* **63 A11** 36 15N 139 30 E
Kantō-Heiya, *Japan* **63 B11** 36 0N 139 30 E
Kantō-Sanchi, *Japan* **63 B10** 35 59N 138 50 E
Kantu-long, *Burma* **78 F6** 19 57N 97 36 E
Kanturk, *Ireland* **19 D3** 52 10N 8 55W
Kanuma, *Japan* **63 A11** 36 34N 139 42 E
Kanus, *Namibia* **104 D2** 27 50 S 18 39 E
Kanye, *Botswana* **104 C4** 24 55 S 25 28 E
Kanzenze, *Zaïre* **103 E5** 10 30 S 25 12 E
Kanzi, Ras, *Tanzania* **106 D4** 7 1 S 39 33 E
Kao, *Fiji* **121 P13** 19 40 S 175 1W
Kaohsiung = Gaoxiong,
Taiwan **69 F13** 22 38N 120 18 E
Kaokoveld, *Namibia* **104 B1** 19 15 S 14 30 E
Kaolack, *Senegal* **100 C1** 14 5N 16 8W
Kaoshan, *China* **67 B13** 44 38N 124 50 E
Kaouar, *Niger* **97 E2** 19 5N 12 52 E
Kapadvanj, *India* **80 H5** 23 5N 73 0 E
Kapagere, *Papua N. G.* **120 E4** 9 46 S 147 42 E
Kapanga, *Zaïre* **103 D4** 8 30 S 22 40 E
Kapchagai, *U.S.S.R.* **55 B8** 43 51N 77 14 E
Kapchagaiskoye Vdkhr.,
U.S.S.R. **55 B8** 43 45N 77 50 E
Kapellen, *Belgium* **21 F4** 51 19N 4 25 E
Kapéllo, Ákra, *Greece* **45 H5** 36 9N 23 3 E
Kapema, *Zaïre* **107 E2** 10 45 S 28 22 E
Kapfenberg, *Austria* **30 D8** 47 26N 15 18 E
Kapia, *Zaïre* **103 C3** 4 17 S 19 46 E
Kapiri Mposhi, *Zambia* **107 E2** 13 59 S 28 43 E
Kāpīsā □, *Afghan.* **79 B3** 35 0N 69 20 E
Kapiskau ⟶, *Canada* **128 B3** 52 47N 81 55W
Kapit, *Malaysia* **70 D4** 2 0N 112 55 E
Kapiti I., *N.Z.* **118 G3** 40 50 S 174 56 E
Kapka, Massif du, *Chad* **97 E4** 15 7N 21 45 E
Kaplice, *Czech.* **30 C7** 48 42N 14 30 E
Kapoe, *Thailand* **77 H2** 9 34N 98 32 E
Kapoeta, *Sudan* **95 G3** 4 50N 33 35 E
Kápolnásnyék, *Hungary* **31 D11** 47 16N 18 41 E
Kaponga, *N.Z.* **118 F3** 39 29 S 174 9 E
Kapos ⟶, *Hungary* **31 E11** 46 44N 18 30 E
Kaposvár, *Hungary* **31 E10** 46 25N 17 47 E
Kapowsin, *U.S.A.* **144 D4** 46 59N 122 13W
Kappeln, *Germany* **26 A5** 54 37N 9 56 E
Kapps, *Namibia* **104 C2** 22 32 S 17 18 E
Kaprije, *Yugoslavia* **39 E12** 43 42N 15 43 E
Kaprijke, *Belgium* **21 F3** 51 13N 3 38 E
Kapsan, *N. Korea* **67 D15** 41 4N 128 19 E
Kapsukas =
Mariyampole, *U.S.S.R.* **50 D3** 54 33N 23 19 E
Kapuas, *Indonesia* **75 C4** 3 10 S 114 5 E
Kapuas ⟶, *Indonesia* **70 E3** 0 25 S 109 20 E
Kapuas Hulu,
Pegunungan, *Malaysia* **70 D4** 1 30N 113 30 E
Kapuas Hulu Ra. =
Kapuas Hulu,
Pegunungan, *Malaysia* **70 D4** 1 30N 113 30 E
Kapulo, *Zaïre* **107 D2** 8 18 S 29 15 E
Kapunda, *Australia* **116 C3** 34 20 S 138 56 E
Kapuni, *N.Z.* **118 F3** 39 29 S 174 8 E
Kapurthala, *India* **80 D6** 31 23N 75 25 E
Kapuskasing, *Canada* **128 C3** 49 25N 82 30W
Kapuskasing ⟶, *Canada* **128 C3** 49 49N 82 0W
Kapustin Yar, *U.S.S.R.* **53 B11** 48 37N 45 40 E
Kaputar, *Australia* **115 E5** 30 15 S 150 10 E
Kaputir, *Kenya* **106 B4** 2 5N 35 28 E
Kapuvár, *Hungary* **31 D10** 47 36N 17 1 E
Kara, *Turkey* **45 H9** 36 58N 27 30 E
Kara, *U.S.S.R.* **56 C7** 69 10N 65 0 E
Kara Bogaz Gol, Zaliv,
U.S.S.R. **49 F9** 41 0N 53 30 E
Kara Kalpak A.S.S.R. □,
U.S.S.R. **56 E6** 43 0N 58 0 E
Kara Kum = Karakum,
Peski, *U.S.S.R.* **56 F7** 39 30N 60 0 E
Kara-Saki, *Japan* **62 C1** 34 41N 129 30 E
Kara Sea, *U.S.S.R.* **56 B8** 75 0N 70 0 E
Kara Su, *U.S.S.R.* **55 C6** 40 44N 72 53 E
Karabash, *U.S.S.R.* **54 D7** 55 29N 60 14 E
Karabekaul, *U.S.S.R.* **55 D2** 38 30N 64 8 E
Karabük, *Turkey* **52 F5** 41 12N 32 37 E
Karabulak, *U.S.S.R.* **55 A9** 44 54N 78 30 E
Karaburun, *Turkey* **45 F8** 38 41N 26 28 E
Karaburuni, *Albania* **44 D1** 40 25N 19 20 E
Karabutak, *U.S.S.R.* **54 G7** 49 59N 60 14 E
Karacabey, *Turkey* **88 C3** 40 12N 28 21 E
Karacasu, *Turkey* **88 E3** 37 43N 28 35 E
Karachala, *U.S.S.R.* **53 G13** 39 45N 48 53 E
Karachayevsk, *U.S.S.R.* **53 E9** 43 50N 41 55 E
Karachev, *U.S.S.R.* **50 E9** 53 10N 35 5 E
Karachi, *Pakistan* **79 D2** 24 53N 67 0 E
Karád, *Hungary* **31 E10** 46 41N 17 51 E
Karad, *India* **82 F2** 17 15N 74 10 E
Karadeniz Boğazı, *Turkey* **88 C3** 41 10N 29 10 E
Karaga, *Ghana* **101 D4** 9 58N 0 28W
Karaganda, *U.S.S.R.* **56 E8** 49 50N 73 10 E
Karagayly, *U.S.S.R.* **56 E8** 49 26N 76 0 E
Karaginskiy, Ostrov,
U.S.S.R. **57 D17** 58 45N 164 0 E
Karagiye Depression,
U.S.S.R. **49 F9** 43 27N 51 45 E
Karagüney Dağları,
Turkey **88 C6** 40 30N 34 40 E
Karagwe □, *Tanzania* **106 C3** 2 0 S 31 0 E
Karaikal, *India* **83 J4** 10 59N 79 50 E
Karaikkudi, *India* **83 J4** 10 5N 78 45 E
Karaisali, *Turkey* **88 E6** 37 16N 35 2 E
Karaitivu I., *Sri Lanka* **83 K4** 9 45N 79 52 E
Karaj, *Iran* **85 C6** 35 48N 51 0 E
Karak, *Malaysia* **77 L4** 3 25N 102 2 E
Karakas, *U.S.S.R.* **56 E9** 48 20N 83 30 E
Karakitang, *Indonesia* **71 D7** 3 14N 125 28 E
Karakoçan, *Turkey* **89 D9** 38 57N 40 2 E
Karakoram Pass, *Pakistan* **81 B7** 35 33N 77 50 E
Karakoram Ra., *Pakistan* **81 B7** 35 30N 77 0 E
Karakul, *Tadzhik S.S.R.,*
U.S.S.R. **55 D6** 39 2N 73 33 E
Karakul, *Uzbek S.S.R.,*
U.S.S.R. **55 D1** 39 22N 63 50 E
Karakuldzha, *U.S.S.R.* **55 C6** 40 39N 73 26 E
Karakulino, *U.S.S.R.* **54 C3** 56 1N 53 43 E
Karakum, Peski, *U.S.S.R.* **56 F7** 39 30N 60 0 E
Karakurt, *Turkey* **89 C10** 40 10N 42 37 E
Karal, *Chad* **97 F2** 12 50N 14 46 E
Karalon, *U.S.S.R.* **57 D12** 57 5N 115 50 E
Karaman, *Turkey* **88 E5** 37 14N 33 13 E
Karamay, *China* **64 B3** 45 30N 84 58 E
Karambu, *Indonesia* **70 E5** 3 53 S 116 6 E
Karamea, *N.Z.* **119 B7** 41 14 S 172 6 E
Karamea ⟶, *N.Z.* **119 B7** 41 13 S 172 26 E
Karamea Bight, *N.Z.* **119 B6** 41 22 S 171 40 E
Karamet Niyaz, *U.S.S.R.* **55 E2** 37 45N 64 34 E
Karamoja □, *Uganda* **106 B3** 3 0N 34 15 E
Karamsad, *India* **80 H5** 22 35N 72 50 E
Karand, *Iran* **84 C5** 34 16N 46 15 E
Karanganyar, *Indonesia* **71 G13** 7 38 S 109 37 E
Karanja, *India* **82 D3** 20 29N 77 31 E
Karapınar, *Turkey* **88 E5** 37 43N 33 32 E
Karapiro, *N.Z.* **118 D4** 37 53 S 175 32 E
Karasburg, *Namibia* **104 D2** 28 0 S 18 44 E
Karasino, *U.S.S.R.* **56 C9** 66 50N 86 50 E
Karasjok, *Norway* **12 B18** 69 27N 25 30 E
Karasu, *Turkey* **88 C4** 41 4N 30 46 E
Karasu ⟶, *Turkey* **89 D8** 39 42N 39 25 E
Karasuk, *U.S.S.R.* **56 D8** 53 44N 78 2 E
Karasuyama, *Japan* **63 A12** 36 39N 140 9 E
Karataş Burnu, *Turkey* **88 E6** 36 32N 35 1 E
Karatau, *U.S.S.R.* **55 B5** 43 10N 70 28 E
Karatau, Khrebet,
U.S.S.R. **55 B4** 43 30N 69 30 E
Karatepe, *Turkey* **88 E7** 37 22N 36 16 E
Karativu, *Sri Lanka* **83 K4** 8 22N 79 47 E
Karatobe, *U.S.S.R.* **54 G3** 49 44N 53 30 E
Karatoya ⟶, *India* **78 C2** 24 7N 89 36 E
Karaturuk, *U.S.S.R.* **55 B8** 43 35N 77 50 E
Karaul-Bazar, *U.S.S.R.* **55 D2** 39 30N 64 48 E
Karauli, *India* **80 F7** 26 30N 77 4 E
Karávi, *Greece* **45 H5** 36 49N 23 37 E
Karavostasi, *Cyprus* **32 D11** 35 8N 32 50 E
Karawa, *Zaïre* **102 B4** 3 18N 20 17 E
Karawang, *Indonesia* **71 G12** 6 30 S 107 15 E
Karawanken, *Europe* **30 E7** 46 30N 14 40 E
Karayazı, *Turkey* **89 D10** 39 41N 42 9 E
Karazhal, *U.S.S.R.* **56 E8** 48 2N 70 49 E
Karbalā, *Iraq* **84 C5** 32 36N 44 3 E
Kårböle, *Sweden* **14 C9** 61 59N 15 22 E
Karcag, *Hungary* **31 D13** 47 19N 20 57 E
Karcha ⟶, *Pakistan* **81 B7** 34 45N 76 10 E
Karda, *U.S.S.R.* **57 D11** 55 0N 103 16 E
Kardhámila, *Greece* **45 F8** 38 35N 26 5 E
Kardhítsa, *Greece* **44 E3** 39 23N 21 54 E
Kardhítsa □, *Greece* **44 E3** 39 15N 21 50 E
Kärdla, *U.S.S.R.* **50 B3** 58 50N 22 40 E
Kareeberge, *S. Africa* **104 E3** 30 59 S 21 50 E
Kareima, *Sudan* **94 D3** 18 30N 31 49 E
Karelian A.S.S.R. □,
U.S.S.R. **48 A5** 65 30N 32 30 E
Karema, *Papua N. G.* **120 E4** 9 12 S 147 18 E
Kārevāndar, *Iran* **85 E9** 27 53N 60 44 E
Kargapolye, *U.S.S.R.* **54 D9** 55 57N 64 24 E
Kargasok, *U.S.S.R.* **56 D9** 59 3N 80 53 E
Kargat, *U.S.S.R.* **56 D9** 55 10N 80 15 E
Kargı, *Turkey* **52 F6** 41 11N 34 30 E
Kargil, *India* **81 B7** 34 32N 76 12 E
Kargopol, *U.S.S.R.* **48 B6** 61 30N 38 58 E
Kargowa, *Poland* **47 C2** 52 5N 15 51 E
Karguéri, *Niger* **97 F2** 13 27N 10 30 E
Karia ba Mohammed,
Morocco **98 B3** 34 22N 5 12W
Kariaí, *Greece* **44 D6** 40 14N 24 19 E
Karīān, *Iran* **85 E8** 26 57N 57 14 E
Kariba, *Zimbabwe* **107 F2** 16 28 S 28 50 E
Kariba, L., *Zimbabwe* **107 F2** 16 40 S 28 25 E
Kariba Dam, *Zimbabwe* **107 F2** 16 30 S 28 35 E
Kariba Gorge, *Zambia* **107 F2** 16 30 S 28 50 E
Karibib, *Namibia* **104 C2** 22 0 S 15 56 E
Karikari, C., *N.Z.* **118 A2** 34 46 S 173 24 E
Karimata, Kepulauan,
Indonesia **70 E3** 1 25 S 109 0 E
Karimata, Selat,
Indonesia **70 E3** 2 0 S 108 40 E
Karimata I. = Karimata,
Kepulauan, *Indonesia* **70 E3** 1 25 S 109 0 E
Karimnagar, *India* **82 E4** 18 26N 79 10 E
Karimunjawa, Kepulauan,
Indonesia **70 F4** 5 50 S 110 30 E
Karin, *Somali Rep.* **90 E4** 10 50N 45 52 E
Káristos, *Greece* **45 F6** 38 1N 24 29 E
Karīt, *Iran* **85 C8** 33 29N 56 55 E
Kariya, *Japan* **63 C9** 34 58N 137 1 E
Karkal, *India* **83 H2** 13 15N 74 56 E
Karkar I., *Papua N. G.* **120 C4** 4 40 S 146 0 E
Karkaralinsk, *U.S.S.R.* **56 E8** 49 26N 75 30 E
Karkinitskiy Zaliv,
U.S.S.R. **52 D5** 45 56N 33 0 E
Karkur Tohl, *Egypt* **94 C2** 22 5N 25 5 E
Karl Libknekht, *U.S.S.R.* **50 F9** 51 40N 35 35 E
Karl-Marx-Stadt =
Chemnitz, *Germany* **26 E8** 50 50N 12 55 E
Karla, L. = Voiviïs
Límni, *Greece* **44 E4** 39 30N 22 45 E
Karlino, *Poland* **47 A2** 54 3N 15 53 E
Karlobag, *Yugoslavia* **39 D12** 44 32N 15 5 E
Karlovac, *Yugoslavia* **39 C12** 45 31N 15 36 E
Karlovka, *U.S.S.R.* **52 B6** 49 29N 35 8 E
Karlovy Vary, *Czech.* **30 A5** 50 13N 12 51 E
Karlsbad = Karlovy
Vary, *Czech.* **30 A5** 50 13N 12 51 E
Karlsborg, *Sweden* **15 F8** 58 33N 14 33 E
Karlshamn, *Sweden* **13 H13** 56 10N 14 51 E
Karlskoga, *Sweden* **13 G13** 59 22N 14 33 E
Karlskrona, *Sweden* **13 H13** 56 10N 15 35 E
Karlsruhe, *Germany* **27 F4** 49 3N 8 23 E
Karlstad, *Sweden* **13 G12** 59 23N 13 30 E
Karlstad, *U.S.A.* **138 A6** 48 38N 96 30W
Karlstadt, *Germany* **27 F5** 49 57N 9 46 E
Karnal, *India* **80 E7** 29 42N 77 2 E
Karnali ⟶, *Nepal* **81 E9** 28 45N 81 16 E
Karnaphuli Res., *Bangla.* **78 D4** 22 40N 92 20 E
Karnataka □, *India* **83 H3** 13 15N 77 0 E
Karnes City, *U.S.A.* **139 L6** 28 53N 97 53W
Karnische Alpen, *Europe* **30 E6** 46 36N 13 0 E
Kärnten □, *Austria* **30 E6** 46 52N 13 30 E
Karo, *Mali* **100 C4** 12 16N 3 18W
Karoi, *Zimbabwe* **107 F2** 16 48 S 29 45 E
Karonga, *Malawi* **107 D3** 9 57 S 33 55 E
Karoonda, *Australia* **116 C3** 35 1 S 139 59 E
Karora, *Sudan* **94 D4** 17 44N 38 15 E
Káros, *Greece* **45 H7** 36 54N 25 40 E
Karousádhes, *Greece* **44 E1** 39 47N 19 45 E
Karpasia □, *Cyprus* **32 D13** 35 32N 34 15 E
Kárpathos, *Greece* **45 J9** 35 37N 27 10 E
Kárpathos, Stenón,
Greece **45 J9** 36 0N 27 30 E
Karpinsk, *U.S.S.R.* **54 B7** 59 45N 60 1 E
Karpogory, *U.S.S.R.* **48 B7** 63 59N 44 27 E
Karrebæk, *Denmark* **15 J5** 55 12N 11 39 E
Kars, *Turkey* **53 F10** 40 40N 43 5 E
Kars □, *Turkey* **89 C10** 40 40N 43 0 E
Karsakpay, *U.S.S.R.* **56 E7** 47 55N 66 40 E
Karsha, *U.S.S.R.* **53 B14** 49 45N 51 35 E
Karshi, *U.S.S.R.* **55 D2** 38 53N 65 48 E
Karsiyang, *India* **81 F13** 26 56N 88 18 E
Karst, *Yugoslavia* **39 C11** 45 35N 14 0 E
Karsun, *U.S.S.R.* **51 D15** 54 14N 46 57 E
Kartál Óros, *Greece* **44 C7** 41 15N 25 13 E
Kartaly, *U.S.S.R.* **54 E7** 53 3N 60 40 E
Kartapur, *India* **80 D6** 31 27N 75 32 E
Karthaus, *U.S.A.* **136 E6** 41 8N 78 9W
Kartuzy, *Poland* **47 A5** 54 22N 18 10 E
Karuah, *Australia* **117 B9** 32 37 S 151 56 E
Karufa, *Indonesia* **71 E8** 3 50 S 133 20 E
Karumba, *Australia* **114 B3** 17 31 S 140 50 E
Karumo, *Tanzania* **106 C3** 2 25 S 32 50 E
Karumwa, *Tanzania* **106 C3** 3 12 S 32 38 E
Karungu, *Kenya* **106 C3** 0 50 S 34 10 E
Karup, *Denmark* **15 H3** 56 19N 9 10 E
Karur, *India* **83 J4** 10 59N 78 2 E
Karviná, *Czech.* **31 B11** 49 53N 18 25 E
Karwi, *India* **81 G9** 25 12N 80 57 E
Kaş, *Turkey* **88 E3** 36 11N 29 37 E
Kasache, *Malawi* **107 E3** 13 25 S 34 20 E
Kasai, *Japan* **62 C6** 34 55N 134 52 E
Kasai ⟶, *Zaïre* **103 C3** 3 30 S 16 10 E
Kasai Occidental □, *Zaïre* **103 D4** 6 0 S 22 0 E
Kasai Oriental □, *Zaïre* **103 D4** 5 0 S 24 30 E
Kasaji, *Zaïre* **103 E4** 10 25 S 23 27 E
Kasama, *Japan* **63 A12** 36 23N 140 16 E
Kasama, *Zambia* **107 E3** 10 16 S 31 9 E
Kasan-dong, *N. Korea* **67 D14** 41 18N 126 55 E
Kasane, *Namibia* **104 B3** 17 34 S 24 50 E
Kasanga, *Tanzania* **107 D3** 8 30 S 31 10 E
Kasangulu, *Zaïre* **103 C3** 4 33 S 15 15 E
Kasaoka, *Japan* **62 C5** 34 30N 133 30 E
Kasaragod, *India* **83 H2** 12 30N 74 58 E
Kasat, *Burma* **78 G7** 15 56N 98 13 E
Kasba, *Bangla.* **78 D3** 23 45N 91 2 E
Kasba L., *Canada* **131 A8** 60 20N 102 10W
Kasba Tadla, *Morocco* **98 B3** 32 36N 6 17W
Kaseda, *Japan* **62 F2** 31 25N 130 19 E
Kāseh Garān, *Iran* **84 C5** 34 5N 46 2 E
Kasempa, *Zambia* **107 E2** 13 30 S 25 44 E
Kasenga, *Zaïre* **107 E2** 10 20 S 28 45 E
Kasese, *Uganda* **106 B3** 0 13N 30 3 E
Kasewa, *Zambia* **107 E2** 14 28 S 28 53 E
Kasganj, *India* **81 F8** 27 48N 78 42 E
Kashabowie, *Canada* **128 C1** 48 40N 90 26W
Kāshān, *Iran* **85 C6** 34 5N 51 30 E
Kashi, *China* **64 C2** 39 30N 76 2 E
Kashihara, *Japan* **63 C7** 34 27N 135 46 E
Kashima, *Ibaraki, Japan* **63 B12** 35 58N 140 38 E
Kashima, *Saga, Japan* **62 D2** 33 7N 130 6 E
Kashima-Nada, *Japan* **63 B12** 36 0N 140 45 E
Kashimbo, *Zaïre* **107 E2** 11 12 S 26 19 E
Kashin, *U.S.S.R.* **51 C10** 57 20N 37 36 E
Kashipur, *Orissa, India* **82 E6** 19 16N 83 3 E
Kashipur, *Ut. P., India* **81 E8** 29 15N 79 0 E
Kashira, *U.S.S.R.* **51 D11** 54 45N 38 10 E
Kashiwa, *Japan* **63 B11** 35 52N 139 59 E
Kashiwazaki, *Japan* **61 F9** 37 22N 138 33 E
Kashk-e Kohneh, *Afghan.* **79 B1** 34 55N 62 30 E
Kashkasu, *U.S.S.R.* **55 D6** 39 54N 72 44 E
Kāshmar, *Iran* **85 C8** 35 16N 58 26 E
Kashmir, *Asia* **81 C7** 34 0N 76 0 E
Kashmor, *Pakistan* **79 C3** 28 28N 69 32 E
Kashpirovka, *U.S.S.R.* **51 E16** 53 0N 48 30 E
Kashun Noerh = Gaxun
Nur, *China* **64 B5** 42 22N 100 30 E
Kasimov, *U.S.S.R.* **51 D12** 54 55N 41 20 E
Kasinge, *Zaïre* **106 D2** 6 15 S 26 58 E
Kasiruta, *Indonesia* **71 E7** 0 25 S 127 12 E
Kaskaskia ⟶, *U.S.A.* **140 G7** 37 58N 89 57W
Kaskattama ⟶, *Canada* **131 B10** 57 3N 90 4W
Kaskelan, *U.S.S.R.* **55 B8** 43 20N 76 35 E
Kaskinen, *Finland* **12 E16** 62 22N 21 15 E
Kaskö, *Finland* **12 E16** 62 22N 21 15 E
Kasli, *U.S.S.R.* **54 D7** 55 53N 60 46 E
Kaslo, *Canada* **130 D5** 49 55N 116 55W
Kasmere L., *Canada* **131 B8** 59 34N 101 10W
Kasongan, *Indonesia* **75 C4** 2 0 S 113 23 E
Kasongo, *Zaïre* **106 C2** 4 30 S 26 33 E
Kasongo Lunda, *Zaïre* **103 D3** 6 35 S 16 49 E
Kásos, *Greece* **45 J8** 35 20N 26 55 E
Kásos, Stenón, *Greece* **45 J8** 35 30N 26 30 E
Kaspi, *U.S.S.R.* **53 F11** 41 54N 44 17 E
Kaspichan, *Bulgaria* **43 D12** 43 18N 27 11 E
Kaspiysk, *U.S.S.R.* **53 E12** 42 52N 47 40 E
Kaspiyskiy, *U.S.S.R.* **53 D12** 45 22N 47 23 E
Kassab ed Doleib, *Sudan* **95 E3** 13 30N 33 35 E
Kassaba, *Egypt* **94 C2** 22 40N 29 55 E
Kassala, *Sudan* **95 D4** 15 30N 36 0 E
Kassalâ □, *Sudan* **95 D4** 15 20N 36 26 E
Kassan, *U.S.S.R.* **55 D2** 39 2N 65 35 E
Kassándra, *Greece* **44 E5** 40 0N 23 30 E
Kassansay, *U.S.S.R.* **55 C5** 41 15N 71 31 E
Kassel, *Germany* **26 D5** 51 19N 9 32 E
Kassinger, *Sudan* **94 D3** 18 46N 31 51 E
Kassiópi, *Greece* **32 A3** 39 48N 19 53 E
Kassue, *Indonesia* **71 F9** 6 58 S 139 21 E
Kastamonu, *Turkey* **88 C5** 41 25N 33 43 E
Kastamonu □, *Turkey* **88 C6** 41 20N 34 0 E
Kastav, *Yugoslavia* **39 C11** 45 22N 14 20 E
Kastélli, *Greece* **32 D5** 35 29N 23 38 E
Kastéllion, *Greece* **32 D7** 35 12N 25 20 E
Kastellou, Ákra, *Greece* **45 J9** 35 30N 27 15 E
Kasterlee, *Belgium* **21 F5** 51 15N 4 59 E
Kastóri, *Greece* **45 G4** 37 10N 22 17 E
Kastoría, *Greece* **44 D3** 40 30N 21 19 E
Kastoría □, *Greece* **44 D3** 40 30N 21 15 E
Kastorías, L., *Greece* **44 D3** 40 30N 21 20 E
Kastornoye, *U.S.S.R.* **51 F11** 51 55N 38 2 E
Kastós, *Greece* **45 F2** 38 35N 20 55 E
Kástron, *Greece* **44 E7** 39 50N 25 2 E
Kastrosikiá, *Greece* **45 E2** 39 6N 20 36 E
Kasugai, *Japan* **63 B8** 35 12N 136 59 E
Kasukabe, *Japan* **63 B11** 35 58N 139 49 E
Kasulu, *Tanzania* **106 C3** 4 37 S 30 5 E
Kasulu □, *Tanzania* **106 C3** 4 37 S 30 5 E
Kasumi, *Japan* **62 B6** 35 38N 134 38 E
Kasumiga-Ura, *Japan* **63 B12** 36 0N 140 25 E
Kasumkent, *U.S.S.R.* **53 F13** 41 47N 48 15 E
Kasungu, *Malawi* **107 E3** 13 0 S 33 29 E
Kasur, *Pakistan* **79 C4** 31 5N 74 25 E
Kata, *U.S.S.R.* **57 D11** 58 46N 102 40 E
Kataba, *Zambia* **107 F2** 16 5 S 25 10 E
Katako Kombe, *Zaïre* **102 C4** 3 25 S 24 20 E
Katákolon, *Greece* **45 G3** 37 38N 21 19 E
Katale, *Tanzania* **106 C3** 4 52 S 31 7 E
Katamatite, *Australia* **117 D6** 36 6 S 145 41 E
Katanda, *Kivu, Zaïre* **106 C2** 0 55 S 29 21 E
Katanda, *Shaba, Zaïre* **103 D4** 7 52 S 24 13 E
Katangi, *India* **82 D4** 21 56N 79 50 E
Katangli, *U.S.S.R.* **57 D15** 51 42N 143 14 E
Katapakishi, *Zaïre* **103 D4** 8 15 S 22 49 E
Katastári, *Greece* **45 G2** 37 50N 20 45 E
Katav Ivanovsk, *U.S.S.R.* **54 D6** 54 45N 58 12 E
Katavi Swamp, *Tanzania* **106 D3** 6 50 S 31 10 E
Katchiungo, *Angola* **103 E3** 12 35 S 16 13 E
Kateríni, *Greece* **44 D4** 40 18N 22 37 E
Katherîna, Gebel, *Egypt* **94 J8** 28 30N 33 57 E
Katherine, *Australia* **112 B5** 14 27 S 132 20 E
Kathiawar, *India* **80 H4** 22 20N 71 0 E
Kathikas, *Cyprus* **32 E11** 34 55N 32 25 E
Kati, *Mali* **100 C3** 12 41N 8 4W
Katihar, *India* **81 G12** 25 34N 87 36 E
Katikati, *N.Z.* **118 D4** 37 32 S 175 57 E
Katima Mulilo, *Zambia* **104 B3** 17 28 S 24 13 E
Katimbira, *Malawi* **107 E3** 12 40 S 34 0 E
Katingan =
Mendawai ⟶,
Indonesia **70 E4** 3 30 S 113 0 E
Katiola, *Ivory C.* **100 D3** 8 10N 5 10W
Katlanovo, *Yugoslavia* **42 F6** 41 52N 21 40 E
Katmandu, *Nepal* **81 F11** 27 45N 85 20 E
Kato Akhaïa, *Greece* **45 F3** 38 8N 21 33 E
Káto Arkhánai, *Greece* **32 D7** 35 15N 25 10 E
Káto Khorió, *Greece* **32 D7** 35 3N 25 47 E
Kato Pyrgos, *Cyprus* **32 D11** 35 11N 32 41 E
Káto Stavros, *Greece* **44 D5** 40 39N 23 43 E
Katol, *India* **82 D4** 21 17N 78 38 E
Katompe, *Zaïre* **103 D5** 6 2 S 26 23 E
Katonga ⟶, *Uganda* **106 B3** 0 34N 31 50 E
Katoomba, *Australia* **117 B9** 33 41 S 150 19 E
Katowice, *Poland* **47 E6** 50 17N 19 5 E
Katowice □, *Poland* **47 E6** 50 10N 19 0 E
Katrine, L., *U.K.* **18 E4** 56 15N 4 30W
Katrineholm, *Sweden* **14 E10** 59 9N 16 12 E
Katsepe, *Madag.* **105 B8** 15 45 S 46 15 E
Katsina, *Nigeria* **101 C6** 13 0N 7 32 E
Katsina □, *Nigeria* **101 C6** 12 30N 7 30 E
Katsina Ala ⟶, *Nigeria* **101 D6** 7 10N 9 30 E
Katsumoto, *Japan* **62 D1** 33 51N 129 42 E
Katsuta, *Japan* **63 A12** 36 25N 140 31 E
Katsuura, *Japan* **63 B12** 35 10N 140 20 E
Katsuyama, *Japan* **63 A8** 36 3N 136 30 E
Kattakurgan, *U.S.S.R.* **55 D3** 39 55N 66 15 E
Kattavía, *Greece* **32 D9** 35 57N 27 46 E
Kattegatt, *Denmark* **15 H5** 57 0N 11 20 E
Katumba, *Zaïre* **103 D5** 7 40 S 25 17 E
Katungu, *Kenya* **106 C5** 2 55 S 40 3 E
Katwa, *India* **81 H13** 23 30N 88 5 E
Katwijk-aan-Zee, *Neths.* **20 D4** 52 12N 4 24 E
Katy, *Poland* **47 D3** 51 2N 16 45 E
Kauai, *U.S.A.* **132 H15** 22 0N 159 30W
Kauai Chan., *U.S.A.* **132 H15** 21 45N 158 50W
Kaub, *Germany* **27 E3** 50 5N 7 46 E
Kaufbeuren, *Germany* **27 H6** 47 50N 10 37 E
Kaufman, *U.S.A.* **139 J6** 32 35N 96 20W
Kaukauna, *U.S.A.* **134 C1** 44 20N 88 13W
Kaukauveld, *Namibia* **104 C3** 20 0 S 20 15 E
Kaukonen, *Finland* **12 C18** 67 31N 24 53 E
Kauliranta, *Finland* **12 C17** 66 27N 23 41 E
Kaunas, *U.S.S.R.* **50 D3** 54 54N 23 54 E

216 Kaunghein

Kaunghein, *Burma* 78 C5 25 41N 95 26 E
Kaupalatmada, Mt., *Indonesia* 72 B3 3 30 S 126 10 E
Kaura Namoda, *Nigeria* 101 C6 12 37N 6 33 E
Kautokeino, *Norway* 12 B17 69 0N 23 4 E
Kavacha, *U.S.S.R.* 57 C17 60 16N 169 51 E
Kavadarci, *Yugoslavia* 42 F7 41 26N 22 3 E
Kavaja, *Albania* 44 C1 41 11N 19 33 E
Kavak, *Turkey* 88 C7 41 4N 36 3 E
Kavalerovo, *U.S.S.R.* 60 B7 44 15N 135 4 E
Kavali, *India* 83 G5 14 55N 80 1 E
Kavälla, *Greece* 44 D6 40 57N 24 28 E
Kavälla □, *Greece* 44 C6 41 5N 24 30 E
Kavälla Kólpos, *Greece* 44 D6 40 50N 24 25 E
Kavār, *Iran* 85 D7 29 11N 52 44 E
Kavarna, *Bulgaria* 43 D13 43 26N 28 22 E
Kavieng, *Papua N. G.* 120 B6 2 36 S 150 51 E
Kavos, *Greece* 32 B4 39 23N 20 3 E
Kavoúsi, *Greece* 45 J7 35 7N 25 51 E
Kaw, *Fr. Guiana* 153 C7 4 30N 52 15W
Kawa, *Sudan* 95 E3 13 42N 32 34 E
Kawachi-Nagano, *Japan* 63 C7 34 28N 135 31 E
Kawagama L., *Canada* 136 A6 45 18N 78 45W
Kawagoe, *Japan* 63 B11 35 55N 139 29 E
Kawaguchi, *Japan* 63 B11 35 52N 139 45 E
Kawaihae, *U.S.A.* 132 H17 20 3N 155 50W
Kawakawa, *N.Z.* 118 B3 35 23 S 174 6 E
Kawambwa, *Zambia* 107 D2 9 48 S 29 3 E
Kawanoe, *Japan* 62 C5 34 1N 133 34 E
Kawarau, *N.Z.* 119 F3 45 3 S 168 45 E
Kawardha, *India* 81 J9 22 0N 81 17 E
Kawasaki, *Japan* 63 B11 35 35N 139 42 E
Kawau I., *N.Z.* 118 C3 36 25 S 174 52 E
Kaweka Ra., *N.Z.* 118 F5 39 17 S 176 19 E
Kawene, *Canada* 128 C1 48 45N 91 15W
Kawerau, *N.Z.* 118 E5 38 7 S 176 42 E
Kawhia Harbour, *N.Z.* 118 E3 38 5 S 174 51 E
Kawio, Kepulauan, *Indonesia* 71 D7 4 30N 125 30 E
Kawkabān, *Yemen* 86 D3 15 30N 43 54 E
Kawkareik, *Burma* 78 G7 16 33N 98 14 E
Kawlin, *Burma* 78 D5 23 47N 95 41 E
Kawthoolei = Kawthule □, *Burma* 78 G6 18 0N 97 30 E
Kawthule □, *Burma* 78 G6 18 0N 97 30 E
Kawya, *Burma* 78 C5 24 50N 94 58 E
Kay, *U.S.S.R.* 54 B3 59 57N 52 59 E
Kaya, *Burkina Faso* 101 C4 13 4N 1 10W
Kayah □, *Burma* 78 F6 19 15N 97 15 E
Kayan, *Burma* 78 G6 16 54N 96 34 E
Kayan →, *Indonesia* 70 D5 2 55N 117 35 E
Kayankulam, *India* 83 K3 9 10N 76 33 E
Kaycee, *U.S.A.* 142 E10 43 45N 106 46W
Kayeli, *Indonesia* 71 E7 3 20 S 127 10 E
Kayenta, *U.S.A.* 143 H8 36 46N 110 15W
Kayes, *Congo* 102 C2 4 25 S 11 41 E
Kayes, *Mali* 100 C2 14 25N 11 30W
Kayima, *S. Leone* 100 D2 8 54N 11 15W
Kayl, *Lux.* 21 K8 49 29N 6 2 E
Kayoa, *Indonesia* 71 D7 0 1N 127 28 E
Kayomba, *Zambia* 107 E1 13 11 S 24 2 E
Kayoro, *Ghana* 101 C4 11 0N 1 28W
Kayrakkumskoye Vdkhr., *U.S.S.R.* 55 C5 40 20N 70 0 E
Kayrunnera, *Australia* 115 E3 30 40 S 142 30 E
Kaysatskoye, *U.S.S.R.* 53 B12 49 47N 46 49 E
Kayseri, *Turkey* 88 D6 38 45N 35 30 E
Kayseri □, *Turkey* 88 D7 38 40N 36 0 E
Kaysville, *U.S.A.* 142 F8 41 2N 111 58W
Kayuagung, *Indonesia* 70 E2 3 24 S 104 50 E
Kazachinskoye, *U.S.S.R.* 57 D11 56 16N 107 36 E
Kazachye, *U.S.S.R.* 57 B14 70 52N 135 58 E
Kazakh S.S.R. □, *U.S.S.R.* 56 E8 50 0N 70 0 E
Kazan, *U.S.S.R.* 51 D16 55 48N 49 3 E
Kazan-Rettō, *Pac. Oc.* 122 E6 25 0N 141 0 E
Kazanlúk, *Bulgaria* 43 E10 42 38N 25 20 E
Kazanskaya, *U.S.S.R.* 53 B9 49 50N 41 10 E
Kazarman, *U.S.S.R.* 55 C6 41 24N 73 59 E
Kazatin, *U.S.S.R.* 52 B3 49 45N 28 50 E
Kazbek, *U.S.S.R.* 53 E11 42 42N 44 30 E
Kāzerūn, *Iran* 85 D6 29 38N 51 40 E
Kazhim, *U.S.S.R.* 54 A2 60 21N 51 33 E
Kazi Magomed, *U.S.S.R.* 53 F13 40 3N 49 0 E
Kazimierz Dolny, *Poland* 47 D8 51 19N 21 57 E
Kazimierza Wielka, *Poland* 47 E7 50 15N 20 30 E
Kazincbarcika, *Hungary* 31 C13 48 17N 20 36 E
Kazo, *Japan* 63 A11 36 7N 139 36 E
Kaztalovka, *U.S.S.R.* 53 B13 49 47N 48 43 E
Kazu, *Burma* 78 C6 25 27N 97 46 E
Kazumba, *Zaïre* 103 D4 6 25 S 22 5 E
Kazuno, *Japan* 60 D10 40 10N 140 45 E
Kazym →, *U.S.S.R.* 56 C7 63 54N 65 50 E
Kcynia, *Poland* 47 C4 53 0N 17 30 E
Ke-hsi Mansam, *Burma* 78 E6 21 56N 97 50 E
Ké-Macina, *Mali* 100 C3 13 58N 5 22W
Kéa, *Greece* 45 G6 37 35N 24 22 E
Keams Canyon, *U.S.A.* 143 J8 35 53N 110 9W
Kearney, *Mo., U.S.A.* 140 E2 39 22N 94 22W
Kearney, *Nebr., U.S.A.* 138 E5 40 45N 99 3W
Keban, *Turkey* 89 D8 38 50N 38 50 E
Keban Baraji, *Turkey* 89 D8 38 34N 38 21 E
Kébi, *Ivory C.* 100 D3 9 18N 6 37W
Kebili, *Tunisia* 96 B1 33 47N 9 0 E
Kebnekaise, *Sweden* 12 C15 67 53N 18 33 E
Kebri Dehar, *Ethiopia* 90 F3 6 45N 44 17 E
Kebumen, *Indonesia* 71 G13 7 42 S 109 40 E
Kecel, *Hungary* 31 E12 46 31N 19 16 E
Kechika →, *Canada* 130 B3 59 41N 127 12W
Kecskemét, *Hungary* 31 E12 46 57N 19 42 E
Kedada, *Ethiopia* 95 F4 5 25N 35 58 E
Kedainiai, *U.S.S.R.* 50 D4 55 15N 24 2 E
Kedgwick, *Canada* 129 C6 47 40N 67 20W
Kédhros Óros, *Greece* 32 D6 35 11N 24 37 E
Kedia Hill, *Botswana* 104 C3 21 28 S 24 37 E
Kediri, *Indonesia* 71 G15 7 51 S 112 1 E
Kédougou, *Senegal* 100 C2 12 35N 12 10W
Kedzierzyn, *Poland* 47 E5 50 20N 18 12 E
Keeler, *U.S.A.* 144 J9 36 29N 117 52W
Keeley L., *Canada* 131 C7 54 54N 108 8W
Keeling Is. = Cocos Is., *Ind. Oc.* 109 F8 12 10 S 96 55 E
Keene, *Calif., U.S.A.* 145 K8 35 13N 118 33W
Keene, *N.H., U.S.A.* 137 D12 42 57N 72 17W
Keeper Hill, *Ireland* 19 D3 52 46N 8 17W
Keer-Weer, C., *Australia* 114 A3 14 0 S 141 32 E
Keerbergen, *Belgium* 21 F5 51 1N 4 38 E
Keeseville, *U.S.A.* 137 B11 44 29N 73 30W
Keeten Mastgat, *Neths.* 21 E4 51 36N 4 0 E
Keetmanshoop, *Namibia* 104 D2 26 35 S 18 8 E
Keewatin, *U.S.A.* 138 B8 47 23N 93 0W
Keewatin □, *Canada* 131 A10 63 20N 95 0W
Keewatin →, *Canada* 131 B8 56 29N 100 46W
Kefa □, *Ethiopia* 95 F4 6 55N 36 30 E
Kefallinía, *Greece* 45 F2 38 20N 20 30 E
Kefamenanu, *Indonesia* 71 F6 9 28 S 124 29 E
Keffi, *Nigeria* 101 D6 8 55N 7 43 E
Kefken, *Turkey* 88 C4 41 11N 30 14 E
Keflavík, *Iceland* 12 D2 64 2N 22 35W
Keg River, *Canada* 130 B5 57 54N 117 55W
Kegalla, *Sri Lanka* 83 L5 7 15N 80 21 E
Kegaska, *Canada* 129 B7 50 9N 61 18W
Kehl, *Germany* 27 G3 48 34N 7 50 E
Keighley, *U.K.* 16 D6 53 52N 1 54W
Keimoes, *S. Africa* 104 D3 28 41 S 20 59 E
Keita, *Niger* 101 C6 14 46N 5 56 E
Keith, *Australia* 116 D4 36 6 S 140 20 E
Keith, *U.K.* 18 D6 57 33N 2 58W
Keith Arm, *Canada* 126 B7 64 20N 122 15W
Keithsburg, *U.S.A.* 140 C6 41 6N 90 56W
Kekaygyr, *U.S.S.R.* 55 C7 40 42N 75 32 E
Kekri, *India* 80 G6 26 0N 75 10 E
Kël, *U.S.S.R.* 57 C13 69 30N 124 10 E
Kelamet, *Ethiopia* 95 D4 16 0N 38 30 E
Kelan, *China* 66 E6 38 43N 111 31 E
Kelang, *Malaysia* 77 L3 3 2N 101 26 E
Kelani Ganga →, *Sri Lanka* 83 L4 6 58N 79 50 E
Kelantan →, *Malaysia* 77 J4 6 13N 102 14 E
Kelcyra, *Albania* 44 D2 40 22N 20 12 E
Keles →, *U.S.S.R.* 55 C4 41 1N 68 37 E
Kelheim, *Germany* 27 G7 48 58N 11 57 E
Kelibia, *Tunisia* 96 A2 36 50N 11 3 E
Kelkit, *Turkey* 89 C8 40 7N 39 16 E
Kelkit →, *Turkey* 88 C7 40 45N 36 32 E
Kellé, *Congo* 102 C2 0 8 S 14 38 E
Keller, *U.S.A.* 142 B4 48 2N 118 44W
Kellerberrin, *Australia* 113 F2 31 36 S 117 38 E
Kellett, C., *Canada* 6 B1 72 0N 126 0W
Kelleys I., *U.S.A.* 136 E2 41 35N 82 42W
Kellogg, *U.S.A.* 142 C5 47 30N 116 5W
Kelloselkä, *Finland* 12 C20 66 56N 28 53 E
Kells = Ceanannus Mor, *Ireland* 19 C5 53 42N 6 53W
Kélo, *Chad* 97 G3 9 10N 15 45 E
Kelokedhara, *Cyprus* 32 E11 34 48N 32 39 E
Kelowna, *Canada* 130 D5 49 50N 119 25W
Kelsey Bay, *Canada* 130 C3 50 25N 126 0W
Kelseyville, *U.S.A.* 144 G4 38 59N 122 50W
Kelso, *N.Z.* 119 F4 45 54 S 169 15 E
Kelso, *U.K.* 18 F6 55 36N 2 27W
Kelso, *U.S.A.* 144 D4 46 10N 122 57W
Keltemashat, *U.S.S.R.* 55 B5 42 25N 70 8 E
Keluang, *Malaysia* 77 L4 2 3N 103 18 E
Kelvington, *Canada* 131 C8 52 10N 103 30W
Kem, *U.S.S.R.* 48 B5 65 0N 34 38 E
Kem →, *U.S.S.R.* 48 B5 64 57N 34 41 E
Kem-Kem, *Morocco* 98 B4 30 40N 4 30W
Kema, *Indonesia* 71 D7 1 22N 125 8 E
Kemah, *Turkey* 89 D8 39 32N 39 5 E
Kemaliye, *Turkey* 89 D8 39 16N 38 29 E
Kemano, *Canada* 130 C3 53 35N 128 0W
Kemapyu, *Burma* 78 F6 18 49N 97 19 E
Kemasik, *Malaysia* 77 K4 4 25N 103 27 E
Kembé, *C.A.R.* 102 B4 4 36N 21 54 E
Kembolcha, *Ethiopia* 95 E4 11 2N 39 42 E
Kemer, *Turkey* 88 E4 36 35N 30 33 E
Kemerovo, *U.S.S.R.* 56 D9 55 20N 86 5 E
Kemi, *Finland* 12 D18 65 44N 24 34 E
Kemi älv = Kemijoki →, *Finland* 12 D18 65 47N 24 32 E
Kemijärvi, *Finland* 12 C19 66 43N 27 22 E
Kemijoki →, *Finland* 12 D18 65 47N 24 32 E
Kemmel, *Belgium* 21 G1 50 47N 2 50 E
Kemmerer, *U.S.A.* 142 F8 41 52N 110 30W
Kemmuna = Comino, *Malta* 32 C1 36 2N 14 20 E
Kemp L., *U.S.A.* 139 J5 33 45N 99 15W
Kemp Land, *Antarctica* 7 C5 69 0 S 55 0 E
Kempsey, *Australia* 117 A10 31 1 S 152 50 E
Kempt, L., *Canada* 128 C5 47 25N 74 22W
Kempten, *Germany* 27 H6 47 42N 10 18 E
Kempton, *U.S.A.* 141 D10 40 16N 86 14W
Kemptville, *Canada* 128 D4 45 0N 75 38W
Kenadsa, *Algeria* 99 B4 31 48N 2 26W
Kendal, *Indonesia* 70 F4 6 56 S 110 14 E
Kendal, *U.K.* 16 C5 54 19N 2 44W
Kendall, *Australia* 117 A10 31 35 S 152 44 E
Kendall →, *Australia* 114 A3 14 4 S 141 35 E
Kendallville, *U.S.A.* 141 C11 41 25N 85 15W
Kendari, *Indonesia* 71 E6 3 50 S 122 30 E
Kendawangan, *Indonesia* 70 E4 2 32 S 110 17 E
Kende, *Nigeria* 101 C5 11 30N 4 12 E
Kendenup, *Australia* 113 F2 34 30 S 117 38 E
Kendervicës, Mal e., *Albania* 44 D1 40 15N 19 52 E
Kendrapara, *India* 82 D8 20 35N 86 30 E
Kendrew, *S. Africa* 104 E3 32 32 S 24 30 E
Kendrick, *U.S.A.* 142 C5 46 43N 116 41W
Kene Thao, *Laos* 76 D3 17 44N 101 10 E
Kenedy, *U.S.A.* 139 L6 28 49N 97 51W
Kenema, *S. Leone* 100 D2 7 50N 11 14W
Keng Kok, *Laos* 76 D5 16 26N 105 12 E
Keng Tawng, *Burma* 78 E7 20 45N 98 18 E
Kengeni, *Zaïre* 102 C3 2 59 S 17 36 E
Kenge, *Zaïre* 103 C3 4 50 S 17 4 E
Kengeja, *Tanzania* 106 D4 5 26 S 39 45 E
Kenhardt, *S. Africa* 104 D3 29 19 S 21 12 E
Kenimekh, *U.S.S.R.* 55 C2 40 16N 65 7 E
Kenitra, *Morocco* 98 B3 34 15N 6 40W
Kenli, *China* 67 F10 37 30N 118 20 E
Kenmare, *Ireland* 19 E2 51 52N 9 35W
Kenmare, *U.S.A.* 138 A3 48 40N 102 4W
Kenmare →, *Ireland* 19 E2 51 40N 10 0W
Kennebec, *U.S.A.* 138 D5 43 56N 99 54W
Kennedy, *Zimbabwe* 107 F2 18 52 S 27 10 E
Kennedy Ra., *Australia* 113 D2 24 45 S 115 10 E
Kennet →, *U.K.* 17 F7 51 24N 0 58W
Kenneth Ra., *Australia* 112 D2 23 50 S 117 8 E
Kennett, *U.S.A.* 139 G9 36 7N 90 5W
Kennewick, *U.S.A.* 142 C4 46 11N 119 2W
Kénogami, *Canada* 129 C5 48 25N 71 15W
Kenogami →, *Canada* 128 B3 51 6N 84 28W
Kenora, *Canada* 131 D10 49 47N 94 29W
Kenosha, *U.S.A.* 141 B9 42 33N 87 48W
Kensington, *Canada* 129 C7 46 28N 63 34W
Kensington, *U.S.A.* 138 F5 39 48N 99 2W
Kensington Downs, *Australia* 114 C3 22 31 S 144 19 E
Kent, *Ohio, U.S.A.* 136 E3 41 8N 81 20W
Kent, *Oreg., U.S.A.* 142 D3 45 11N 120 45W
Kent, *Tex., U.S.A.* 139 K2 31 5N 104 12W
Kent, *Wash., U.S.A.* 144 C4 47 23N 122 14W
Kent □, *U.K.* 17 F8 51 12N 0 40 E
Kent Group, *Australia* 114 F4 39 30 S 147 20 E
Kent Pen., *Canada* 126 B9 68 30N 107 0W
Kentau, *U.S.S.R.* 55 B4 43 32N 68 36 E
Kentland, *U.S.A.* 141 D9 40 45N 87 25W
Kenton, *U.S.A.* 141 D13 40 40N 83 35W
Kentucky, *Australia* 117 A9 30 45 S 151 28 E
Kentucky □, *U.S.A.* 134 G3 37 20N 85 0W
Kentucky →, *U.S.A.* 141 F11 38 41N 85 11W
Kentucky L., *U.S.A.* 135 G2 36 25N 88 0W
Kentville, *Canada* 129 C7 45 6N 64 29W
Kentwood, *U.S.A.* 139 K9 31 0N 90 30W
Kentwood, *La., U.S.A.* 139 K9 30 56N 90 31W
Kenya ■, *Africa* 106 B4 1 0N 38 0 E
Kenya, Mt., *Kenya* 106 C4 0 10 S 37 18 E
Kenzou, *Cameroon* 102 B3 4 10N 15 2 E
Keo Neua, Deo, *Vietnam* 76 C5 18 23N 105 10 E
Keokuk, *U.S.A.* 140 D5 40 25N 91 24W
Keosauqua, *U.S.A.* 140 D5 40 44N 91 58W
Keota, *U.S.A.* 140 C5 41 22N 91 57W
Kep, *Cambodia* 77 G5 10 29N 104 19 E
Kep, *Vietnam* 76 B6 21 24N 106 16 E
Kepi, *Indonesia* 71 F9 6 32 S 139 19 E
Kepice, *Poland* 47 A3 54 16N 16 51 E
Kepler Mts., *N.Z.* 119 F2 45 25 S 167 20 E
Kępno, *Poland* 47 D4 51 18N 17 58 E
Kepsut, *Turkey* 88 D3 39 40N 28 9 E
Kerala □, *India* 83 J3 11 0N 76 15 E
Kerama-Rettō, *Japan* 61 L3 26 5N 127 15 E
Keran, *Pakistan* 81 B5 34 35N 73 59 E
Kerang, *Australia* 116 C5 35 40 S 143 55 E
Keratéa, *Greece* 45 G5 37 48N 23 58 E
Keraudren, C., *Australia* 112 C2 19 58 S 119 45 E
Keravat, *Papua N. G.* 120 C7 4 17 S 152 2 E
Kerch, *U.S.S.R.* 52 D7 45 20N 36 20 E
Kerchenskiy Proliv, *U.S.S.R.* 52 D7 45 10N 36 30 E
Kerchoual, *Mali* 101 B5 17 12N 0 20 E
Kerema, *Papua N. G.* 120 D3 7 58 S 145 50 E
Kerempe Burnu, *Turkey* 88 B5 42 2N 33 20 E
Keren, *Ethiopia* 95 D4 15 45N 38 28 E
Kerewan, *Gambia* 100 C1 13 29N 16 10W
Kerguelen, *Ind. Oc.* 109 J5 49 15 S 69 10 E
Keri, *Greece* 45 G2 37 40N 20 49 E
Keri Kera, *Sudan* 95 E3 12 21N 32 42 E
Kericho, *Kenya* 106 C4 0 22 S 35 15 E
Kericho □, *Kenya* 106 C4 0 30 S 35 15 E
Kerikeri, *N.Z.* 118 B2 35 12 S 173 59 E
Kerinci, *Indonesia* 70 E2 1 40 S 101 15 E
Kerkdriel, *Neths.* 20 E6 51 47N 5 20 E
Kerkenna, Is., *Tunisia* 96 B2 34 48N 11 11 E
Kerki, *U.S.S.R.* 55 E2 37 50N 65 12 E
Kerkinítis, Límni, *Greece* 44 C5 41 12N 23 10 E
Kérkira, *Greece* 32 A3 39 38N 19 50 E
Kerkrade, *Neths.* 21 G8 50 53N 6 4 E
Kerma, *Sudan* 94 D3 19 33N 30 32 E
Kermadec Is., *Pac. Oc.* 122 L10 30 0 S 178 15W
Kermadec Trench, *Pac. Oc.* 122 L10 30 30 S 176 0W
Kermān, *Iran* 85 D8 30 15N 57 1 E
Kerman, *U.S.A.* 144 J6 36 43N 120 4W
Kermān □, *Iran* 85 D8 30 0N 57 0 E
Kermānshāh = Bākhtarān, *Iran* 84 C5 34 23N 47 0 E
Kerme Körfezi, *Turkey* 45 H9 36 55N 27 50 E
Kermen, *Bulgaria* 43 E11 42 30N 26 16 E
Kermit, *U.S.A.* 139 K3 31 56N 103 3W
Kern →, *U.S.A.* 145 K7 35 16N 119 18W
Kerns, *Switz.* 29 C6 46 54N 8 17 E
Kernville, *U.S.A.* 145 K8 35 45N 118 26W
Keroh, *Malaysia* 77 K3 5 43N 101 1 E
Kerrobert, *Canada* 131 C7 51 56N 109 8W
Kerrville, *U.S.A.* 139 K5 30 1N 99 8W
Kerry □, *Ireland* 19 D2 52 7N 9 35W
Kerry Hd., *Ireland* 19 D2 52 26N 9 56W
Kersa, *Ethiopia* 95 F5 9 28N 41 48 E
Kerteminde, *Denmark* 15 J4 55 28N 10 39 E
Kertosono, *Indonesia* 71 G15 7 38 S 112 9 E
Kerulen →, *Asia* 65 B6 48 48N 117 0 E
Kerzaz, *Algeria* 99 C4 29 29N 1 37W
Kerzers, *Switz.* 28 C4 46 59N 7 12 E
Kesagami →, *Canada* 128 B4 51 40N 79 45W
Kesagami L., *Canada* 128 B3 50 23N 80 15W
Keşan, *Turkey* 44 D8 40 49N 26 38 E
Kesch, Piz, *Switz.* 29 C9 46 38N 9 53 E
Kesennuma, *Japan* 60 E10 38 54N 141 35 E
Keshit, *Iran* 85 D8 29 43N 58 17 E
Keşiş Dağ, *Turkey* 89 D8 39 47N 39 46 E
Keski-Suomen lääni □, *Finland* 12 E18 63 0N 25 30 E
Keskin, *Turkey* 88 D5 39 40N 33 36 E
Kessel, *Belgium* 21 F5 51 8N 4 38 E
Kessel, *Neths.* 21 F8 51 17N 6 3 E
Kessel-Lo, *Belgium* 21 G5 50 53N 4 43 E
Kestell, *S. Africa* 105 D4 28 17 S 28 42 E
Kestenga, *U.S.S.R.* 48 A5 66 0N 31 50 E
Kesteren, *Neths.* 20 E7 51 56N 5 34 E
Keswick, *U.K.* 16 C4 54 35N 3 9W
Keszthely, *Hungary* 31 E10 46 50N 17 15 E
Ket →, *U.S.S.R.* 56 D9 58 55N 81 32 E
Keta, *Ghana* 101 D5 5 49N 1 0 E
Ketapang, *Indonesia* 70 E4 1 55 S 110 0 E
Ketchikan, *U.S.A.* 126 C6 55 25N 131 40W
Ketchum, *U.S.A.* 142 E6 43 41N 114 27W
Kete Krachi, *Ghana* 101 D4 7 46N 0 1W
Ketef, Khalîg Umm el, *Egypt* 94 C4 23 40N 35 35 E
Ketelmeer, *Neths.* 20 C7 52 36N 5 46 E
Keti Bandar, *Pakistan* 80 G2 24 8N 67 27 E
Ketri, *India* 80 E6 28 1N 75 50 E
Kętrzyn, *Poland* 47 A8 54 7N 21 22 E
Kettering, *U.K.* 17 E7 52 24N 0 44W
Kettering, *U.S.A.* 141 E12 39 41N 84 10W
Kettle →, *Canada* 131 B11 56 40N 89 34W
Kettle Falls, *U.S.A.* 142 B4 48 41N 118 2W
Kettleman City, *U.S.A.* 144 J7 36 1N 119 58W
Kety, *Poland* 31 B12 49 51N 19 16 E
Kevin, *U.S.A.* 142 B8 48 45N 111 58W
Kewanee, *U.S.A.* 140 C7 41 18N 89 55W
Kewanna, *U.S.A.* 141 C10 41 1N 86 25W
Kewaunee, *U.S.A.* 134 C2 44 27N 87 30W
Keweenaw B., *U.S.A.* 134 B1 46 56N 88 23W
Keweenaw Pen., *U.S.A.* 134 B2 47 30N 88 0W
Keweenaw Pt., *U.S.A.* 134 B2 47 26N 87 40W
Key Harbour, *Canada* 128 C3 45 50N 80 45W
Key West, *U.S.A.* 133 F10 24 33N 82 0W
Keyesport, *U.S.A.* 140 F7 38 45N 89 17W
Keyser, *U.S.A.* 134 F6 39 26N 79 0W
Keystone, *U.S.A.* 138 D3 43 54N 103 27W
Keytesville, *U.S.A.* 140 E4 39 26N 92 56W
Kez, *U.S.S.R.* 54 C3 57 55N 53 46 E
Kezhma, *U.S.S.R.* 57 D11 58 59N 101 9 E
Kežmarok, *Czech.* 31 B13 49 10N 20 28 E
Khabarovo, *U.S.S.R.* 56 C7 69 30N 60 30 E
Khabarovsk, *U.S.S.R.* 57 E14 48 30N 135 5 E
Khabr, *Iran* 85 D8 28 51N 56 22 E
Khābūr →, *Syria* 84 C4 35 0N 40 30 E
Khachmas, *U.S.S.R.* 53 F13 41 31N 48 42 E
Khachrod, *India* 80 H6 23 25N 75 20 E
Khadari, W. el →, *Sudan* 95 E2 10 29N 27 15 E
Khadro, *Pakistan* 80 F3 26 11N 68 50 E
Khadyzhensk, *U.S.S.R.* 53 D8 44 26N 39 32 E
Khadzhilyangar, *India* 81 B8 35 45N 79 20 E
Khagaria, *India* 81 G12 25 30N 86 32 E
Khaipur, *Bahawalpur, Pakistan* 80 E5 29 34N 72 17 E
Khaipur, *Hyderabad, Pakistan* 80 F3 27 32N 68 49 E
Khair, *India* 80 F7 27 57N 77 46 E
Khairabad, *India* 81 F9 27 33N 80 47 E
Khairagarh, *India* 81 J9 21 27N 81 2 E
Khairpur, *Pakistan* 79 D3 27 32N 68 49 E
Khāk Dow, *Afghan.* 79 B2 34 57N 67 16 E
Khakhea, *Botswana* 104 C3 24 48 S 23 22 E
Khalach, *U.S.S.R.* 55 D2 38 4N 64 52 E
Khalafābād, *Iran* 85 D6 30 54N 49 24 E
Khalfallah, *Algeria* 99 B5 34 20N 0 16 E
Khalfūt, *Yemen* 87 D6 15 52N 52 10 E
Khalilabad, *India* 81 F10 26 48N 83 5 E
Khalīlī, *Iran* 85 E7 27 38N 53 17 E
Khalkhāl, *Iran* 85 B6 37 37N 48 32 E
Khálki, *Greece* 44 E4 39 36N 22 30 E
Khalkidhikí □, *Greece* 44 D5 40 25N 23 20 E
Khalkís, *Greece* 45 F5 38 27N 23 42 E
Khalmer-Sede = Tazovskiy, *U.S.S.R.* 56 C8 67 30N 78 44 E
Khalmer Yu, *U.S.S.R.* 48 A12 67 58N 65 1 E
Khalturin, *U.S.S.R.* 51 B16 58 40N 48 50 E
Khalūf, *Oman* 90 C6 20 30N 58 13 E
Kham Keut, *Laos* 76 C5 18 15N 104 43 E
Khamaria, *India* 82 C5 23 10N 80 52 E
Khamas Country, *Botswana* 104 C4 21 45 S 26 30 E
Khambat, G. of, *India* 80 J5 20 45N 72 30 E
Khambhaliya, *India* 80 H3 22 14N 69 41 E
Khambhat, *India* 80 H5 22 23N 72 33 E
Khamgaon, *India* 82 D3 20 42N 76 37 E
Khamilonísion, *Greece* 45 J8 35 50N 26 15 E
Khamīr, *Iran* 85 E7 26 57N 55 36 E
Khamir, *Yemen* 86 C4 16 2N 44 0 E
Khamīs Mushayṭ, *Si. Arabia* 86 C3 18 18N 42 44 E
Khammam, *India* 82 F5 17 11N 80 6 E
Khamsa, *Egypt* 91 E1 30 27N 32 23 E
Khān Abū Shāmat, *Syria* 91 B5 33 39N 36 53 E
Khān Azād, *Iraq* 84 C5 33 7N 44 22 E
Khān Mujiddah, *Iraq* 84 C4 32 21N 43 48 E
Khān Shaykhūn, *Syria* 84 C3 35 26N 36 38 E
Khān Yūnis, *Egypt* 91 D3 31 21N 34 18 E
Khānābād, *Afghan.* 79 A3 36 45N 69 5 E
Khanabad, *U.S.S.R.* 55 C5 40 59N 70 38 E
Khānaqīn, *Iraq* 84 C5 34 23N 45 25 E
Khānbāghī, *Iran* 85 B7 36 10N 55 25 E
Khandrá, *Greece* 45 J8 35 3N 26 8 E
Khandwa, *India* 82 D3 21 49N 76 22 E
Khandyga, *U.S.S.R.* 57 C14 62 42N 135 35 E
Khāneh, *Iran* 84 B5 36 41N 45 8 E
Khanewal, *Pakistan* 79 C3 30 20N 71 55 E
Khanh Duong, *Vietnam* 76 F7 12 44N 108 44 E
Khaniá, *Greece* 32 D6 35 30N 24 4 E
Khaniá □, *Greece* 32 D6 35 30N 24 0 E
Khaníon, Kólpos, *Greece* 32 D5 35 33N 23 55 E
Khanka, Ozero, *Asia* 57 E14 45 0N 132 24 E
Khanna, *India* 80 D7 30 42N 76 16 E
Khanpur, *Pakistan* 79 C3 28 42N 70 35 E
Khantau, *U.S.S.R.* 55 A6 44 13N 73 48 E
Khanty-Mansiysk, *U.S.S.R.* 56 C7 61 0N 69 0 E
Khapalu, *Pakistan* 81 B7 35 10N 76 20 E
Khapcheranga, *U.S.S.R.* 57 E12 49 42N 112 24 E
Kharagpur, *India* 81 H12 22 20N 87 25 E
Khárakas, *Greece* 32 D7 35 1N 25 7 E
Kharan Kalat, *Pakistan* 79 C2 28 34N 65 21 E
Kharānaq, *Iran* 85 C7 32 20N 54 45 E
Kharda, *India* 82 E2 18 40N 75 34 E
Khardung La, *India* 81 B7 34 20N 77 43 E
Khârga, El Wâhât el, *Egypt* 94 B3 25 10N 30 35 E
Khargon, *India* 82 D2 21 45N 75 40 E
Kharit, Wadi el →, *Egypt* 94 C3 24 26N 33 3 E
Khārk, Jazireh, *Iran* 85 D6 29 15N 50 28 E
Kharkov, *U.S.S.R.* 52 B7 49 58N 36 20 E
Kharmanli, *Bulgaria* 43 F10 41 55N 25 55 E
Kharovsk, *U.S.S.R.* 51 B12 59 56N 40 13 E
Khartoum = El Khartûm, *Sudan* 95 D3 15 31N 32 35 E
Khasan, *U.S.S.R.* 60 C5 42 25N 130 40 E
Khasavyurt, *U.S.S.R.* 53 E12 43 16N 46 40 E
Khāsh, *Iran* 85 D9 28 15N 61 15 E
Khashm el Girba, *Sudan* 95 E4 14 59N 35 58 E
Khashuri, *U.S.S.R.* 53 F10 41 58N 43 35 E
Khasi Hills, *India* 78 C3 25 30N 91 30 E
Khaskovo, *Bulgaria* 43 F10 41 56N 25 30 E
Khatanga, *U.S.S.R.* 57 B11 72 0N 102 20 E

Kirovskiy 217

Khatanga →, U.S.S.R. 57 B11 72 55N 106 0 E
Khatangskiy Zaliv, U.S.S.R. 6 B13 73 45N 112 0 E
Khatauli, India 80 E7 29 17N 77 43 E
Khātūnābād, Iran 85 C6 35 30N 51 40 E
Khatyrchi, U.S.S.R. 55 C2 40 2N 65 58 E
Khatyrka, U.S.S.R. 57 C18 62 3N 175 15 E
Khavast, U.S.S.R. 55 C4 40 10N 68 49 E
Khawlaf, Ra's, Yemen 87 D6 12 40N 54 7 E
Khay', Si. Arabia 86 C3 18 45N 41 24 E
Khaybar, Harrat, Si. Arabia 84 E4 25 45N 40 0 E
Khaydarken, U.S.S.R. 55 D5 39 57N 71 20 E
Khāzimiyah, Iraq 84 C4 34 46N 43 37 E
Khazzān Jabal el Awliyâ, Sudan 95 D3 15 24N 32 20 E
Khe Bo, Vietnam 76 C5 19 8N 104 41 E
Khe Long, Vietnam 76 B5 21 29N 104 46 E
Khed, Maharashtra, India 82 F1 17 43N 73 27 E
Khed, Maharashtra, India 82 E1 18 51N 73 56 E
Khekra, India 80 E7 28 52N 77 20 E
Khemarak Phouminville, Cambodia 77 G4 11 37N 102 59 E
Khemelnik, U.S.S.R. 52 B2 49 33N 27 58 E
Khemis Miliana, Algeria 99 A5 36 11N 2 14 E
Khemissèt, Morocco 98 B3 33 50N 6 1W
Khemmarat, Thailand 76 D5 16 10N 105 15 E
Khenāmān, Iran 85 D8 30 27N 56 29 E
Khenchela, Algeria 99 A6 35 28N 7 11 E
Khenifra, Morocco 98 B3 32 58N 5 46W
Kherrata, Algeria 99 A6 36 27N 5 13 E
Khérson, Greece 44 C4 41 5N 22 47 E
Kherson, U.S.S.R. 52 C5 46 35N 32 35 E
Khersónisos Akrotíri, Greece 32 D6 35 30N 24 10 E
Kheta →, U.S.S.R. 57 B11 71 54N 102 6 E
Khiliomódhion, Greece 45 G4 37 48N 22 51 E
Khilok, U.S.S.R. 57 D12 51 30N 110 45 E
Khimki, U.S.S.R. 51 D10 55 50N 37 20 E
Khíos, Greece 45 F8 38 27N 26 9 E
Khirbat Qanāfār, Lebanon 91 B4 33 39N 35 43 E
Khisar-Momina Banya, Bulgaria 43 E9 42 30N 24 44 E
Khiuma = Hiiumaa, U.S.S.R. 50 B3 58 50N 22 45 E
Khiva, U.S.S.R. 56 E7 41 30N 60 18 E
Khīyāv, Iran 84 B5 38 30N 47 45 E
Khlebarovo, Bulgaria 43 D11 43 37N 26 15 E
Khlong Khlung, Thailand 76 D2 16 12N 99 43 E
Khmelnitskiy, U.S.S.R. 50 G5 49 23N 27 0 E
Khmer Rep. = Cambodia ■, Asia 76 F5 12 15N 105 0 E
Khoai, Hon, Vietnam 77 H5 8 26N 104 50 E
Khodzhent, U.S.S.R. 55 C4 40 14N 69 37 E
Khojak P., Afghan. 79 C2 30 55N 66 30 E
Khok Kloi, Thailand 77 H2 8 17N 98 19 E
Khok Pho, Thailand 77 J3 6 43N 101 6 E
Khokholskiy, U.S.S.R. 51 F11 51 35N 38 40 E
Kholm, Afghan. 79 A2 36 45N 67 40 E
Kholm, U.S.S.R. 50 C7 57 10N 31 15 E
Kholmsk, U.S.S.R. 57 E15 47 40N 142 5 E
Khomas Hochland, Namibia 104 C2 22 40 S 16 0 E
Khomayn, Iran 85 C6 33 40N 50 7 E
Khon Kaen, Thailand 76 D4 16 30N 102 47 E
Khong, Laos 76 E5 14 7N 105 51 E
Khong Sedone, Laos 76 E5 15 34N 105 49 E
Khonu, U.S.S.R. 57 C15 66 30N 143 12 E
Khoper →, U.S.S.R. 51 G13 49 30N 42 20 E
Khor el 'Atash, Sudan 95 E3 13 20N 34 15 E
Khóra, Greece 45 G3 37 3N 21 42 E
Khóra Sfakíon, Greece 32 D6 35 15N 24 9 E
Khorāsān □, Iran 85 C8 34 0N 58 0 E
Khorat = Nakhon Ratchasima, Thailand 76 E4 14 59N 102 12 E
Khorat, Cao Nguyen, Thailand 76 E4 15 30N 102 50 E
Khorb el Ethel, Algeria 98 C3 28 30N 6 17W
Khorixas, Namibia 104 C1 20 16 S 14 59 E
Khorog, U.S.S.R. 55 E5 37 30N 71 36 E
Khorol, U.S.S.R. 52 B5 49 48N 33 15 E
Khorramābād, Khorāsān, Iran 85 C8 35 6N 57 57 E
Khorramābād, Lorestān, Iran 85 C6 33 30N 48 25 E
Khorrāmshahr, Iran 85 D6 30 29N 48 15 E
Khosravī, Iran 85 D6 30 48N 51 28 E
Khosrowābād, Khuzestān, Iran 85 D6 30 10N 48 25 E
Khosrowābād, Kordestān, Iran 84 C5 35 31N 47 38 E
Khosūyeh, Iran 85 D7 28 32N 54 26 E
Khotin, U.S.S.R. 52 B2 48 31N 26 27 E
Khouribga, Morocco 98 B3 32 58N 6 57W
Khowai, Bangla. 78 C3 24 5N 91 40 E
Khoyniki, U.S.S.R. 50 F6 51 54N 29 55 E
Khrami →, U.S.S.R. 53 F11 41 30N 45 0 E
Khrenovoye, U.S.S.R. 51 F12 51 4N 40 16 E
Khristianá, Greece 45 H7 36 14N 25 13 E
Khromtau, U.S.S.R. 54 F6 50 17N 58 27 E
Khrysokhou B., Cyprus 32 D11 35 6N 32 25 E
Khtapodhiá, Greece 45 G7 37 24N 25 34 E
Khu Khan, Thailand 76 E5 14 42N 104 12 E
Khudrah, W. →, Yemen 87 C5 18 10N 50 20 E
Khuff, Si. Arabia 84 E5 24 55N 44 53 E
Khūgīānī, Qandahar, Afghan. 79 C2 31 34N 66 32 E
Khūgīānī, Qandahar, Afghan. 79 C2 31 28N 65 14 E
Khulayş, Si. Arabia 86 B2 22 9N 39 19 E
Khulna, Bangla. 78 D2 22 45N 89 34 E
Khulna □, Bangla. 78 D2 22 25N 89 35 E
Khulo, U.S.S.R. 53 F10 41 33N 42 19 E
Khumago, Botswana 104 C3 20 26 S 24 32 E
Khumrah, Si. Arabia 86 B2 21 22N 39 13 E
Khūnsorkh, Iran 85 E8 27 9N 56 7 E
Khunzakh, U.S.S.R. 53 E12 42 35N 46 42 E
Khūr, Iran 85 C8 32 55N 58 18 E
Khurai, India 80 G8 24 3N 78 23 E
Khuraydah, Yemen 87 D5 15 33N 48 18 E
Khurayş, Si. Arabia 85 E6 25 6N 48 2 E
Khūrīyā Mūrīyā, Jazā 'ir, Oman 87 C6 17 30N 55 58 E
Khurja, India 80 E7 28 15N 77 58 E
Khūsf, Iran 85 C8 32 46N 58 53 E
Khushab, Pakistan 79 B4 32 20N 72 20 E
Khuzdar, Pakistan 79 D2 27 52N 66 30 E
Khūzestān □, Iran 85 D6 31 0N 49 0 E
Khvājeh, Iran 84 B5 38 9N 46 35 E
Khvājeh Moḥammad, Kūh-e, Afghan. 79 A3 36 22N 70 17 E
Khvalynsk, U.S.S.R. 51 E16 52 30N 48 2 E
Khvānsār, Iran 85 D7 29 56N 54 8 E
Khvatovka, U.S.S.R. 51 E15 52 24N 46 32 E
Khvor, Iran 85 C7 33 45N 55 0 E
Khvorgū, Iran 85 E8 27 34N 56 27 E
Khvormūj, Iran 85 D6 28 40N 51 30 E
Khvoy, Iran 84 B5 38 35N 45 0 E
Khvoynaya, U.S.S.R. 50 B9 58 58N 34 28 E
Khyber Pass, Afghan. 79 B3 34 10N 71 8 E
Kia, Solomon Is. 121 L10 7 32 S 158 26 E
Kiabukwa, Zaïre 103 D4 8 40 S 24 48 E
Kiadho →, India 82 E3 19 37N 77 40 E
Kiama, Australia 117 C9 34 40 S 150 50 E
Kiamba, Phil. 71 C6 6 2N 124 46 E
Kiambi, Zaïre 106 D2 7 15 S 28 0 E
Kiambu, Kenya 106 C4 1 8 S 36 50 E
Kiangsi = Jiangxi □, China 69 D11 27 30N 116 0 E
Kiangsu = Jiangsu □, China 67 H11 33 0N 120 0 E
Kiáton, Greece 45 F4 38 2N 22 43 E
Kibæk, Denmark 15 H2 56 2N 8 51 E
Kibanga Port, Uganda 106 B3 0 10N 32 58 E
Kibangou, Congo 102 C2 3 26 S 12 22 E
Kibara, Tanzania 106 C3 2 8 S 33 30 E
Kibare, Mts., Zaïre 106 D2 8 25 S 27 10 E
Kibombo, Zaïre 103 C5 3 57 S 25 53 E
Kibondo, Tanzania 106 C3 3 35 S 30 45 E
Kibondo □, Tanzania 106 C3 4 0 S 30 55 E
Kibumbu, Burundi 106 C2 3 32 S 29 45 E
Kibungu, Rwanda 106 C3 2 10 S 30 32 E
Kibuye, Burundi 106 C2 3 39 S 29 59 E
Kibuye, Rwanda 106 C2 2 3 S 29 21 E
Kibwesa, Tanzania 106 D2 6 30 S 29 58 E
Kibwezi, Kenya 106 C4 2 27 S 37 57 E
Kičevo, Yugoslavia 42 F5 41 34N 20 59 E
Kichiga, U.S.S.R. 57 D17 59 50N 163 5 E
Kicking Horse Pass, Canada 130 C5 51 28N 116 16W
Kidal, Mali 101 B5 18 26N 1 22 E
Kidderminster, U.K. 17 E5 52 24N 2 13W
Kidete, Tanzania 106 D4 6 25 S 37 17 E
Kidira, Senegal 100 C2 14 28N 12 13W
Kidnappers, C., N.Z. 118 F6 39 38 S 177 5 E
Kidston, Australia 114 B3 18 52 S 144 8 E
Kidugallo, Tanzania 106 D4 6 49 S 38 15 E
Kiel, Germany 26 A6 54 16N 10 8 E
Kiel Kanal = Nord-Ostsee Kanal, Germany 26 A5 54 15N 9 40 E
Kielce, Poland 47 E7 50 52N 20 42 E
Kielce □, Poland 47 E7 50 40N 20 40 E
Kieldrecht, Belgium 21 F4 51 17N 4 11 E
Kieler Bucht, Germany 26 A6 54 30N 10 30 E
Kien Binh, Vietnam 77 H5 9 55N 105 19 E
Kien Tan, Vietnam 77 G5 10 7N 105 17 E
Kienge, Zaïre 107 E2 10 30 S 27 30 E
Kiessé, Niger 101 C5 13 29N 4 1 E
Kieta, Papua N. G. 120 D8 6 12 S 155 36 E
Kiev = Kiyev, U.S.S.R. 50 F7 50 30N 30 28 E
Kiffa, Mauritania 100 B2 16 37N 11 24W
Kifisiá, Greece 45 F5 38 4N 23 49 E
Kifissós →, Greece 45 F5 38 35N 23 20 E
Kifrī, Iraq 84 C5 34 45N 45 0 E
Kigali, Rwanda 106 C3 1 59 S 30 4 E
Kigarama, Tanzania 106 C3 1 1 S 31 50 E
Kigoma □, Tanzania 106 D3 5 0 S 30 0 E
Kigoma-Ujiji, Tanzania 106 C2 4 55 S 29 36 E
Kigomasha, Ras, Tanzania 106 C4 4 58 S 38 58 E
Kihee, Australia 115 D3 27 23 S 142 37 E
Kihikihi, N.Z. 118 E4 38 2 S 175 22 E
Kii-Hantō, Japan 63 D7 34 0N 135 45 E
Kii-Sanchi, Japan 63 C8 34 20N 136 0 E
Kii-Suidō, Japan 62 D6 33 40N 134 45 E
Kikaiga-Shima, Japan 61 K4 28 19N 129 59 E
Kikinda, Yugoslavia 42 B5 45 50N 20 30 E
Kikládhes, Greece 45 G6 37 20N 24 30 E
Kikládhes □, Greece 45 H7 37 0N 25 0 E
Kikoira, Australia 117 B7 33 39 S 146 40 E
Kikori, Papua N. G. 120 D3 7 25 S 144 15 E
Kikori →, Papua N. G. 120 D3 7 38 S 144 20 E
Kikuchi, Japan 62 E2 32 59N 130 47 E
Kikwit, Zaïre 103 D3 5 0 S 18 45 E
Kila' Drosh, Pakistan 79 B3 35 33N 71 52 E
Kilakkarai, India 83 K4 9 12N 78 47 E
Kílalki, Greece 45 H9 36 15N 27 35 E
Kilauea Crater, U.S.A. 132 J17 19 24N 155 17W
Kilchberg, Switz. 29 B7 47 18N 8 33 E
Kilcoy, Australia 115 D5 26 59 S 152 30 E
Kilembe, Zaïre 103 D3 5 42 S 19 55 E
Kilgore, U.S.A. 139 J7 32 22N 94 55W
Kilifi, Kenya 106 C4 3 40 S 39 48 E
Kilifi □, Kenya 106 C4 3 30 S 39 40 E
Kilimanjaro, Tanzania 106 C4 3 7 S 37 20 E
Kilimanjaro □, Tanzania 106 C4 4 0 S 38 0 E
Kilinailau Is., Papua N. G. 120 C8 4 45 S 155 20 E
Kilindini, Kenya 106 C4 4 4 S 39 40 E
Kilis, Turkey 88 E7 36 42N 37 6 E
Kiliya, U.S.S.R. 52 D3 45 28N 29 16 E
Kilju, N. Korea 67 D15 40 57N 129 25 E
Kilkee, Ireland 19 D2 52 41N 9 40W
Kilkieran B., Ireland 19 C2 53 18N 9 45W
Kilkís, Greece 44 D4 40 58N 22 57 E
Kilkís □, Greece 44 C4 41 5N 22 50 E
Killala, Ireland 19 B2 54 13N 9 12W
Killala B., Ireland 19 B2 54 20N 9 12W
Killaloe, Ireland 19 D3 52 48N 8 28W
Killaloe Sta., Canada 136 A7 45 33N 77 25W
Killam, Canada 130 C6 52 47N 111 51W
Killarney, Australia 115 D5 28 20 S 152 18 E
Killarney, Canada 128 C3 45 55N 81 30W
Killarney, Ireland 19 D2 52 2N 9 30W
Killarney, Lakes of, Ireland 19 E2 52 0N 9 30W
Killary Harbour, Ireland 19 C2 53 38N 9 52W
Killdeer, Canada 131 D7 49 6N 106 22W
Killdeer, U.S.A. 138 B3 47 26N 102 48W
Killeen, U.S.A. 139 K6 31 7N 97 45W
Killiecrankie, Pass of, U.K. 18 E5 56 44N 3 46W
Killin, U.K. 18 E4 56 28N 4 20W
Killíni, Ilía, Greece 45 G3 37 55N 21 8 E
Killíni, Korinthía, Greece 45 G4 37 54N 22 25 E
Killybegs, Ireland 19 B3 54 38N 8 26W
Kilmarnock, U.K. 18 F4 55 36N 4 30W
Kilmez, U.S.S.R. 54 C2 56 58N 50 55 E
Kilmez →, U.S.S.R. 54 C2 56 58N 50 28 E
Kilmore, Australia 117 D6 37 25 S 144 53 E
Kilondo, Tanzania 107 D3 9 45 S 34 20 E
Kilosa, Tanzania 106 D4 6 48 S 37 0 E
Kilosa □, Tanzania 106 D4 6 48 S 37 0 E
Kilrush, Ireland 19 D2 52 39N 9 30W
Kilwa □, Tanzania 107 D4 9 0 S 39 0 E
Kilwa Kisiwani, Tanzania 107 D4 8 58 S 39 32 E
Kilwa Kivinje, Tanzania 107 D4 8 45 S 39 25 E
Kilwa Masoko, Tanzania 107 D4 8 55 S 39 30 E
Kim, U.S.A. 139 G3 37 18N 103 20W
Kimaam, Indonesia 71 F9 7 58 S 138 53 E
Kimamba, Tanzania 106 D4 6 45 S 37 10 E
Kimba, Australia 116 B2 33 8 S 136 23 E
Kimball, Nebr., U.S.A. 138 E3 41 17N 103 40W
Kimball, S. Dak., U.S.A. 138 D5 43 47N 98 57W
Kimbe, Papua N. G. 120 C6 5 33 S 150 11 E
Kimbe B., Papua N. G. 120 C6 5 15 S 150 30 E
Kimberley, Australia 116 B4 32 50 S 141 4 E
Kimberley, Canada 130 D5 49 40N 115 59W
Kimberley, S. Africa 104 D3 28 43 S 24 46 E
Kimberley Downs, Australia 112 C3 17 24 S 124 22 E
Kimberley Plateau, Australia 110 D4 16 20 S 127 0 E
Kimberly, U.S.A. 142 E6 42 33N 114 25W
Kimchaek, N. Korea 67 D15 40 40N 129 10 E
Kimchŏn, S. Korea 67 F15 36 11N 128 4 E
Kími, Greece 45 F6 38 38N 24 6 E
Kimje, S. Korea 67 G14 35 48N 126 45 E
Kímolos, Greece 45 H6 36 48N 24 37 E
Kimovsk, U.S.S.R. 51 E11 54 0N 38 29 E
Kimparana, Mali 100 C4 12 48N 5 0W
Kimry, U.S.S.R. 51 C10 56 55N 37 15 E
Kimsquit, Canada 130 C3 52 45N 126 57W
Kimstad, Sweden 15 F9 58 35N 15 58 E
Kimvula, Zaïre 103 D3 5 44 S 15 58 E
Kinabalu, Malaysia 70 C5 6 3N 116 14 E
Kínaros, Greece 45 H8 36 59N 26 15 E
Kinaskan L., Canada 130 B2 57 38N 130 8W
Kinbasket L., Canada 130 C5 52 0N 118 10W
Kincaid, Canada 131 D7 49 40N 107 0W
Kincaid, U.S.A. 140 E7 39 35N 89 25W
Kincardine, Canada 128 D3 44 10N 81 40W
Kinda, Kasai Or., Zaïre 103 D5 9 18 S 25 4 E
Kinda, Shaba, Zaïre 103 C4 4 47 S 21 48 E
Kinder Scout, U.K. 16 D6 53 24N 1 53W
Kindersley, Canada 131 C7 51 30N 109 10W
Kindia, Guinea 100 D2 10 0N 12 52W
Kindu, Zaïre 102 C5 2 55 S 25 50 E
Kinel, U.S.S.R. 54 E2 53 15N 50 40 E
Kineshma, U.S.S.R. 51 C13 57 30N 42 5 E
Kinesi, Tanzania 106 C3 1 25 S 33 50 E
King, L., Australia 113 F2 33 10 S 119 35 E
King, Mt., Australia 114 D4 25 10 S 147 30 E
King City, Calif., U.S.A. 144 J5 36 11N 121 8W
King City, Mo., U.S.A. 140 D2 40 3N 94 31W
King Cr. →, Australia 114 C2 24 35 S 139 30 E
King Edward →, Australia 112 B4 14 14 S 126 35 E
King Frederick VI Land = Kong Frederik VI.s Kyst, Greenland 6 C5 63 0N 43 0W
King George B., Falk. Is. 160 D4 51 30 S 60 30W
King George I., Antarctica 7 C18 60 0 S 60 0W
King George Is., Canada 127 C11 57 20N 80 30W
King I. = Kadan Kyun, Burma 70 B1 12 30N 98 20 E
King I., Australia 114 F3 39 50 S 144 0 E
King I., Canada 130 C3 52 10N 127 40W
King Leopold Ras., Australia 112 C4 17 30 S 125 45 E
King Sd., Australia 112 C3 16 50 S 123 20 E
King William I., Canada 126 B10 69 10N 97 25W
King William's Town, S. Africa 104 E4 32 51 S 27 22 E
Kingaroy, Australia 115 D5 26 32 S 151 51 E
Kingfisher, U.S.A. 139 H6 35 50N 97 55W
Kingirbān, Iraq 84 C5 34 40N 44 54 E
Kingisepp = Kuressaare, U.S.S.R. 50 B3 58 15N 22 30 E
Kingisepp, U.S.S.R. 50 B6 59 25N 28 40 E
Kingman, Ariz., U.S.A. 145 K12 35 12N 114 2W
Kingman, Ind., U.S.A. 141 E9 39 58N 87 18W
Kingman, Kans., U.S.A. 139 G5 37 41N 98 9W
Kingoonya, Australia 115 E2 30 55 S 135 19 E
Kings →, U.S.A. 144 J7 36 10N 119 50W
Kings Canyon National Park, U.S.A. 144 J8 37 0N 118 35W
King's Lynn, U.K. 16 E8 52 45N 0 25 E
Kings Mountain, U.S.A. 135 H5 35 13N 81 20W
King's Peak, U.S.A. 142 F8 40 46N 110 27W
Kingsbridge, U.K. 17 G4 50 17N 3 46W
Kingsburg, U.S.A. 144 J7 36 35N 119 36W
Kingsbury, U.S.A. 141 C10 41 31N 86 42W
Kingscote, Australia 116 C2 35 40 S 137 38 E
Kingscourt, Ireland 19 C5 53 55N 6 48W
Kingsley, U.S.A. 138 D7 42 37N 95 58W
Kingsport, U.S.A. 135 G4 36 33N 82 36W
Kingston, Canada 128 D4 44 14N 76 30W
Kingston, Jamaica 148 C4 18 0N 76 50W
Kingston, N.Z. 119 F3 45 20 S 168 43 E
Kingston, Mo., U.S.A. 140 E2 39 38N 94 2W
Kingston, N.Y., U.S.A. 137 E11 41 55N 74 0W
Kingston, Pa., U.S.A. 137 E9 41 19N 75 58W
Kingston, R.I., U.S.A. 137 E13 41 29N 71 30W
Kingston Pk., U.S.A. 145 K11 35 45N 115 54W
Kingston South East, Australia 116 D3 36 51 S 139 55 E
Kingston upon Hull, U.K. 16 D7 53 45N 0 20W
Kingston-upon-Thames, U.K. 17 F7 51 23N 0 20W
Kingstown, Australia 117 A9 30 29 S 151 6 E
Kingstown, St. Vincent 149 D7 13 10N 61 10W
Kingstree, U.S.A. 135 J6 33 40N 79 48W
Kingsville, Canada 128 D3 42 2N 82 45W
Kingsville, U.S.A. 139 M6 27 30N 97 53W
Kingussie, U.K. 18 D4 57 5N 4 2W
Kinistino, Canada 131 C7 52 57N 105 2W
Kinkala, Congo 103 C2 4 18 S 14 49 E
Kinki □, Japan 63 D8 33 45N 136 0 E
Kinleith, N.Z. 118 E4 38 20 S 175 56 E
Kinmount, Canada 136 B6 44 48N 78 45W
Kinmundy, U.S.A. 141 F8 38 46N 88 51W
Kinna, Sweden 15 G6 57 32N 12 42 E
Kinnaird, Canada 130 D5 49 17N 117 39W
Kinnairds Hd., U.K. 18 D7 57 40N 2 0W
Kinnared, Sweden 15 G7 57 2N 13 7 E
Kino, Mexico 146 B2 28 45N 111 59W
Kinoje →, Canada 128 B3 52 8N 81 25W
Kinomoto, Japan 63 B8 35 30N 136 13 E
Kinoni, Uganda 106 C3 0 41 S 30 28 E
Kinrooi, Belgium 21 F7 51 9N 5 45 E
Kinross, U.K. 18 E5 56 13N 3 25W
Kinsale, Ireland 19 E3 51 42N 8 31W
Kinsale, Old Hd. of, Ireland 19 E3 51 37N 8 32W
Kinshasa, Zaïre 103 C3 4 20 S 15 15 E
Kinsley, U.S.A. 139 G5 37 55N 99 30W
Kinston, U.S.A. 135 H7 35 18N 77 35W
Kintampo, Ghana 101 D4 8 5N 1 41W
Kintap, Indonesia 70 E5 3 51 S 115 13 E
Kintore Ra., Australia 112 D4 23 15 S 128 47 E
Kintyre, U.K. 18 F3 55 30N 5 35W
Kintyre, Mull of, U.K. 18 F3 55 17N 5 55W
Kinu, Burma 78 D5 22 46N 95 37 E
Kinu-Gawa →, Japan 63 B11 35 36N 139 57 E
Kinushseo →, Canada 128 A3 55 15N 83 45W
Kinuso, Canada 130 B5 55 20N 115 25W
Kinyangiri, Tanzania 106 C3 4 25 S 34 37 E
Kinzig →, Germany 27 G3 48 37N 7 49 E
Kinzua, U.S.A. 136 E6 41 52N 78 58W
Kinzua Dam, U.S.A. 136 E6 41 53N 79 0W
Kióni, Greece 45 F2 38 27N 20 41 E
Kiosk, Canada 128 C4 46 6N 78 53W
Kiowa, Kans., U.S.A. 139 G5 37 3N 98 30W
Kiowa, Okla., U.S.A. 139 H7 34 45N 95 50W
Kipahigan L., Canada 131 B8 55 20N 101 55W
Kipanga, Tanzania 106 D4 6 15 S 35 20 E
Kiparissía, Greece 45 G3 37 15N 21 40 E
Kiparissiakós Kólpos, Greece 45 G3 37 25N 21 25 E
Kipembawe, Tanzania 106 D3 7 38 S 33 27 E
Kipengere Ra., Tanzania 107 D3 9 12 S 34 15 E
Kipili, Tanzania 106 D3 7 28 S 30 32 E
Kipini, Kenya 106 C5 2 30 S 40 32 E
Kipling, Canada 131 C8 50 6N 102 38W
Kipushi, Zaïre 107 E2 11 48 S 27 12 E
Kira Kira, Solomon Is. 121 N11 10 27 S 161 56 E
Kirandul, India 82 E5 18 33N 81 10 E
Kiratpur, India 80 E8 29 32N 78 12 E
Kirchberg, Switz. 28 B5 47 5N 7 35 E
Kirchhain, Germany 26 E4 50 49N 8 54 E
Kirchheim, Germany 27 G5 48 38N 9 20 E
Kirchheim-Bolanden, Germany 27 F4 49 40N 8 0 E
Kirchschlag, Austria 31 D9 47 30N 16 19 E
Kirensk, U.S.S.R. 57 D11 57 50N 107 55 E
Kirgella Rocks, Australia 113 F3 30 5 S 122 50 E
Kirgiz S.S.R. □, U.S.S.R. 55 C7 42 0N 75 0 E
Kirgiziya Steppe, U.S.S.R. 49 E10 50 0N 55 0 E
Kiri, Zaïre 102 C3 1 29 S 19 0 E
Kiri Buru, India 82 D7 22 0N 85 0 E
Kiribati ■, Pac. Oc. 122 H9 5 0 S 176 0 E
Kırıkhan, Turkey 88 E7 36 31N 36 21 E
Kırıkkale, Turkey 88 D5 39 51N 33 32 E
Kirikopuni, N.Z. 118 B3 35 50 S 174 1 E
Kirillov, U.S.S.R. 51 B11 59 51N 38 14 E
Kirin = Jilin, China 67 C14 43 44N 126 30 E
Kirin = Jilin □, China 67 C14 44 0N 127 0 E
Kirindi →, Sri Lanka 83 L5 6 15N 81 20 E
Kirishi, U.S.S.R. 50 B7 59 28N 31 59 E
Kirishima-Yama, Japan 62 F2 31 58N 130 55 E
Kiritimati, Kiribati 123 G12 1 58N 157 27W
Kırka, Turkey 88 D4 39 16N 30 31 E
Kirkcaldy, U.K. 18 E5 56 7N 3 10W
Kirkcudbright, U.K. 18 G4 54 50N 4 3W
Kirkee, India 82 E1 18 34N 73 56 E
Kirkenær, Norway 14 D6 60 27N 12 3 E
Kirkenes, Norway 12 B21 69 40N 30 5 E
Kirkintilloch, U.K. 18 F4 55 57N 4 10W
Kirkjubæjarklaustur, Iceland 12 E4 63 47N 18 4W
Kirkland, Ariz., U.S.A. 143 J7 34 29N 112 46W
Kirkland, Ill., U.S.A. 141 B8 42 5N 88 51W
Kirkland Lake, Canada 128 C3 48 9N 80 2W
Kırklareli, Turkey 43 F12 41 44N 27 15 E
Kırklareli □, Turkey 43 F12 41 45N 27 15 E
Kirklin, U.S.A. 141 D10 40 12N 86 22W
Kirkliston Ra., N.Z. 119 E5 44 25 S 170 34 E
Kirksville, U.S.A. 140 D4 40 8N 92 35W
Kirkūk, Iraq 84 C5 35 30N 44 21 E
Kirkwall, U.K. 18 C6 58 59N 2 59W
Kirkwood, S. Africa 104 E4 33 22 S 25 15 E
Kirkwood, U.S.A. 140 F6 38 35N 90 24W
Kirlampudi, India 82 F6 17 12N 82 12 E
Kirn, Germany 27 F3 49 46N 7 29 E
Kirov, R.S.F.S.R., U.S.S.R. 50 D9 54 3N 34 20 E
Kirov, R.S.F.S.R., U.S.S.R. 54 B1 58 35N 49 40 E
Kirovabad = Gyandzha, U.S.S.R. 53 F12 40 45N 46 20 E
Kirovakan, U.S.S.R. 53 F11 40 48N 44 30 E
Kirovo, U.S.S.R. 55 C5 40 26N 70 36 E
Kirovo-Chepetsk, U.S.S.R. 51 B17 58 28N 50 0 E
Kirovograd, U.S.S.R. 52 B5 48 35N 32 20 E
Kirovsk, R.S.F.S.R., U.S.S.R. 48 A5 67 48N 33 50 E
Kirovsk, Turkmen S.S.R., U.S.S.R. 56 F7 37 42N 60 23 E
Kirovsk, Ukraine S.S.R., U.S.S.R. 53 B8 48 35N 38 30 E
Kirovski, U.S.S.R. 53 D13 45 51N 48 11 E
Kirovskiy, Kamchatka, U.S.S.R. 57 D16 54 27N 155 42 E

218 Kirovskiy

Kirovskiy, Kazakh S.S.R., U.S.S.R. **55 A9** 44 52N 78 12 E
Kirovskiy, R.S.F.S.R., U.S.S.R. **60 B6** 45 7N 133 30 E
Kirovskoye, U.S.S.R. **55 B5** 42 39N 71 35 E
Kirriemuir, U.K. **18 E6** 56 41N 2 58W
Kirs, U.S.S.R. **54 B3** 59 21N 52 14 E
Kirsanov, U.S.S.R. **51 E13** 52 35N 42 40 E
Kırşehir, Turkey **88 D6** 39 14N 34 5 E
Kırşehir □, Turkey **88 D6** 39 10N 34 10 E
Kirstonia, S. Africa **104 D3** 25 30 S 23 45 E
Kirtachi, Niger **101 C5** 12 52N 2 30 E
Kīrteh, Afghan. **79 B1** 32 15N 63 0 E
Kirthar Range, Pakistan **79 D2** 27 0N 67 0 E
Kiruna, Sweden **12 C16** 67 52N 20 15 E
Kirundu, Zaïre **102 C5** 0 50 S 25 35 E
Kirup, Australia **113 F2** 33 40 S 115 50 E
Kirya, U.S.S.R. **51 D15** 55 5N 46 45 E
Kiryū, Japan **63 A11** 36 24N 139 20 E
Kisaga, Tanzania **106 C3** 4 30 S 34 23 E
Kisalaya, Nic. **148 D3** 14 40N 84 3W
Kisambo, Zaïre **103 D3** 6 25 S 18 14 E
Kisámou, Kólpos, Greece **32 D5** 35 30N 23 38 E
Kisanga, Zaïre **106 B2** 2 30N 26 35 E
Kisangani, Zaïre **106 B2** 0 35N 25 15 E
Kisantu, Zaïre **103 D3** 5 7 S 15 5 E
Kisar, Indonesia **71 F7** 8 5 S 127 10 E
Kisaran, Indonesia **70 D1** 3 0N 99 37 E
Kisarawe, Tanzania **106 D4** 6 53 S 39 0 E
Kisarawe □, Tanzania **106 D4** 7 3 S 39 0 E
Kisarazu, Japan **63 B11** 35 23N 139 55 E
Kisbér, Hungary **31 D11** 47 30N 18 2 E
Kiselevsk, U.S.S.R. **56 D9** 54 5N 86 39 E
Kishanganga →, Pakistan **81 B5** 34 18N 73 28 E
Kishanganj, India **81 F13** 26 3N 88 14 E
Kishangarh, India **80 F4** 27 50N 70 30 E
Kishi, Nigeria **101 D5** 9 1N 3 52 E
Kishinev, U.S.S.R. **52 C3** 47 0N 28 50 E
Kishiwada, Japan **63 C7** 34 28N 135 22 E
Kishorganj, Bangla. **78 C3** 24 26N 90 40 E
Kishtwar, India **81 C6** 33 20N 75 48 E
Kishwaukee →, U.S.A. **140 B7** 42 12N 89 8W
Kisii, Kenya **106 C3** 0 40 S 34 45 E
Kisii □, Kenya **106 C3** 0 40 S 34 45 E
Kisiju, Tanzania **106 D4** 7 23 S 39 19 E
Kısır Dağ, Turkey **53 F10** 41 0N 43 5 E
Kisizi, Uganda **106 C2** 1 0 S 29 58 E
Kiska I., U.S.A. **126 C1** 52 0N 177 30 E
Kiskatinaw →, Canada **130 B4** 56 8N 120 10W
Kiskittogisu L., Canada **131 C9** 54 13N 98 20W
Kiskomárom = Zalakomár, Hungary **31 E10** 46 33N 17 10 E
Kiskörös, Hungary **31 E12** 46 37N 19 20 E
Kiskundorozsma, Hungary **31 E13** 46 16N 20 5 E
Kiskunfélegyháza, Hungary **31 E12** 46 42N 19 53 E
Kiskunhalas, Hungary **31 E12** 46 28N 19 37 E
Kiskunmajsa, Hungary **31 E12** 46 30N 19 48 E
Kislovodsk, U.S.S.R. **53 E10** 43 50N 42 45 E
Kismayu = Chisimaio, Somali Rep. **108 E2** 0 22 S 42 32 E
Kiso-Gawa →, Japan **63 B8** 35 20N 136 45 E
Kiso-Sammyaku, Japan **63 B9** 35 45N 137 45 E
Kisofukushima, Japan **63 B9** 35 52N 137 43 E
Kisoro, Uganda **106 C2** 1 17 S 29 48 E
Kispest, Hungary **31 D12** 47 27N 19 9 E
Kissidougou, Guinea **100 D2** 9 5N 10 5W
Kissimmee, U.S.A. **135 L5** 28 18N 81 22W
Kissimmee →, U.S.A. **135 M5** 27 20N 80 55W
Kississing L., Canada **131 B8** 55 10N 101 20W
Kissónerga, Cyprus **32 E11** 34 49N 32 24 E
Kistanje, Yugoslavia **39 E12** 43 58N 15 55 E
Kisújszállás, Hungary **31 D13** 47 12N 20 50 E
Kisuki, Japan **62 B4** 35 17N 132 54 E
Kisumu, Kenya **106 C3** 0 3 S 34 45 E
Kisvárda, Hungary **31 C15** 48 14N 22 4 E
Kiswani, Tanzania **106 C4** 4 5 S 37 57 E
Kiswere, Tanzania **107 D4** 9 27 S 39 30 E
Kit Carson, U.S.A. **138 F3** 38 48N 102 45W
Kita, Mali **100 C3** 13 5N 9 25W
Kita-Ura, Japan **63 B12** 36 0N 140 34 E
Kitab, U.S.S.R. **55 D3** 39 7N 66 52 E
Kitaibaraki, Japan **61 F10** 36 50N 140 45 E
Kitakami, Japan **60 E10** 39 20N 141 10 E
Kitakami-Gawa →, Japan **60 E10** 38 25N 141 19 E
Kitakami-Sammyaku, Japan **60 E10** 39 30N 141 30 E
Kitakata, Japan **60 F9** 37 39N 139 52 E
Kitakyūshū, Japan **62 D2** 33 50N 130 50 E
Kitale, Kenya **106 B4** 1 0N 35 0 E
Kitami, Japan **60 C11** 43 48N 143 54 E
Kitami-Sammyaku, Japan **60 B11** 44 22N 142 43 E
Kitangiri, L., Tanzania **106 C3** 4 5 S 34 20 E
Kitano-Kaikyō, Japan **62 C6** 34 17N 134 58 E
Kitaya, Tanzania **107 E5** 10 38 S 40 8 E
Kitchener, Australia **113 F3** 30 55 S 124 8 E
Kitchener, Canada **128 D3** 43 27N 80 29W
Kitega = Gitega, Burundi **106 C2** 3 26 S 29 56 E
Kitengo, Zaïre **103 D4** 7 26 S 24 8 E
Kiteto □, Tanzania **106 D4** 5 0 S 37 0 E
Kitgum, Uganda **106 B3** 3 17N 32 52 E
Kíthira, Greece **45 H6** 36 9N 24 12 E
Kíthnos, Greece **45 G6** 37 26N 24 27 E
Kiti, Cyprus **32 E12** 34 50N 33 34 E
Kiti, C., Cyprus **32 E12** 34 48N 33 36 E
Kitikmeot □, Canada **126 B9** 70 0N 110 0W
Kitimat, Canada **130 C3** 54 3N 128 38W
Kitinen →, Finland **12 C19** 67 34N 26 40 E
Kitiyab, Sudan **95 D3** 17 13N 33 35 E
Kítros, Greece **44 D4** 40 22N 22 34 E
Kitsuki, Japan **62 D3** 33 35N 131 37 E
Kittakittaooloo, L., Australia **115 D2** 28 3 S 138 14 E
Kittanning, U.S.A. **136 F5** 40 49N 79 30W
Kittatinny Mts., U.S.A. **137 F10** 41 0N 75 0W
Kittery, U.S.A. **135 D10** 43 7N 70 42W
Kitui, Kenya **106 C4** 1 17 S 38 0 E
Kitui □, Kenya **106 C4** 1 30 S 38 25 E
Kitwe, Zambia **107 E2** 12 54 S 28 13 E
Kitzbühel, Austria **30 D5** 47 27N 12 24 E
Kitzingen, Germany **27 F6** 49 44N 10 9 E
Kivalo, Finland **12 C19** 66 18N 26 0 E
Kivarli, India **80 G5** 24 33N 72 46 E
Kividhes, Cyprus **32 E11** 34 46N 32 51 E
Kivotós, Greece **44 D3** 40 13N 21 26 E
Kivu □, Zaïre **106 C2** 3 10 S 27 0 E
Kivu, L., Zaïre **106 C2** 1 48 S 29 0 E
Kiwai I., Papua N. G. **120 E2** 8 35 S 143 30 E
Kiyev, U.S.S.R. **50 F7** 50 30N 30 28 E
Kiyevskoye Vdkhr., U.S.S.R. **50 F7** 51 0N 30 25 E
Kizel, U.S.S.R. **54 B5** 59 3N 57 40 E
Kiziguru, Rwanda **106 C3** 1 46 S 30 23 E
Kızıl Irmak →, Turkey **52 F6** 41 44N 35 58 E
Kizil Jilga, India **81 B8** 35 26N 78 50 E
Kizil Yurt, U.S.S.R. **53 E12** 43 13N 46 54 E
Kızılcahamam, Turkey **52 F5** 40 30N 32 30 E
Kızılhisar, Turkey **88 E3** 37 32N 29 17 E
Kızılırmak, Turkey **88 C5** 40 21N 33 59 E
Kizilskoye, U.S.S.R. **54 E6** 52 44N 58 54 E
Kızıltepe, Turkey **89 E9** 37 12N 40 35 E
Kizimkazi, Tanzania **106 D4** 6 28 S 39 30 E
Kizlyar, U.S.S.R. **53 E12** 43 51N 46 40 E
Kizyl-Arvat, U.S.S.R. **56 F6** 38 58N 56 15 E
Kjellerup, Denmark **15 H3** 56 17N 9 25 E
Kladanj, Yugoslavia **42 C3** 44 14N 18 42 E
Kladnica, Yugoslavia **42 D5** 43 23N 20 2 E
Kladno, Czech. **30 A7** 50 10N 14 7 E
Kladovo, Yugoslavia **42 C7** 44 36N 22 33 E
Klaeng, Thailand **76 F3** 12 47N 101 39 E
Klagenfurt, Austria **30 E7** 46 38N 14 20 E
Klagshamn, Sweden **15 J6** 55 32N 12 53 E
Klagstorp, Sweden **15 J7** 55 22N 13 23 E
Klaipeda, U.S.S.R. **50 D2** 55 43N 21 10 E
Klamath →, U.S.A. **142 F1** 41 40N 124 4W
Klamath Falls, U.S.A. **142 E3** 42 20N 121 50W
Klamath Mts., U.S.A. **142 F2** 41 20N 123 0W
Klangklang, Burma **78 D4** 22 41N 93 26 E
Klanjec, Yugoslavia **39 B12** 46 3N 15 45 E
Klappan →, Canada **130 B3** 58 0N 129 43W
Klarälven →, Sweden **13 G12** 59 23N 13 32 E
Klaten, Indonesia **71 G14** 7 43 S 110 36 E
Klatovy, Czech. **30 B6** 49 23N 13 18 E
Klawak, U.S.A. **130 B2** 55 35N 133 0W
Klawer, S. Africa **104 E2** 31 44 S 18 36 E
Klazienaveen, Neths. **20 C10** 52 44N 7 0 E
Kłecko, Poland **47 C4** 52 38N 17 25 E
Kleczew, Poland **47 C5** 52 22N 18 9 E
Kleena Kleene, Canada **130 C4** 52 0N 124 59W
Klein, U.S.A. **142 C9** 46 26N 108 31W
Klein-Karas, Namibia **104 D2** 27 33 S 18 7 E
Kleine Gette →, Belgium **21 G6** 50 51N 5 6 E
Kleine Nete →, Belgium **21 F5** 51 12N 4 46 E
Klekovača, Yugoslavia **39 D13** 44 25N 16 32 E
Klenovec, Czech. **31 C12** 48 36N 19 54 E
Klenovec, Yugoslavia **42 F5** 41 32N 20 49 E
Klerksdorp, S. Africa **104 D4** 26 53 S 26 38 E
Kleszczele, Poland **47 C10** 52 35N 23 19 E
Kletnya, U.S.S.R. **50 E8** 53 23N 33 12 E
Kletsk, U.S.S.R. **50 E5** 53 5N 26 45 E
Kletskaïa Kletskiy, U.S.S.R. **56 E5** 49 20N 43 0 E
Kletskiy, U.S.S.R. **53 B10** 49 20N 43 0 E
Kleve, Germany **26 D2** 51 46N 6 10 E
Klickitat, U.S.A. **142 D3** 45 50N 121 10W
Klickitat →, U.S.A. **144 E5** 45 42N 121 17W
Klidhes, Cyprus **32 D13** 35 42N 34 36 E
Klimovichi, U.S.S.R. **50 E8** 53 36N 32 0 E
Klin, U.S.S.R. **51 C10** 56 20N 36 48 E
Klinaklini →, Canada **130 C3** 51 21N 125 40W
Klintsey, U.S.S.R. **50 E8** 52 50N 32 10 E
Klipdale, S. Africa **104 E2** 34 19 S 19 57 E
Klipplaat, S. Africa **104 E3** 33 1 S 24 22 E
Klisura, Bulgaria **43 E9** 42 40N 24 28 E
Klitmøller, Denmark **15 G2** 57 3N 8 30 E
Kljajićevo, Yugoslavia **42 B4** 45 45N 19 17 E
Ključ, Yugoslavia **39 D13** 44 32N 16 48 E
Kłobuck, Poland **47 E5** 50 55N 18 55 E
Kłodawa, Poland **47 C5** 52 15N 18 55 E
Kłodzko, Poland **47 E3** 50 28N 16 38 E
Kloetinge, Neths. **21 F3** 51 30N 3 56 E
Klondike, Canada **126 B6** 64 0N 139 26W
Kloosterzande, Neths. **21 F4** 51 22N 4 1 E
Klosi, Albania **44 C2** 41 28N 20 10 E
Klosterneuburg, Austria **31 C9** 48 18N 16 19 E
Klosters, Switz. **29 C9** 46 52N 9 52 E
Kloten, Switz. **29 B7** 47 27N 8 35 E
Klötze, Germany **26 C7** 52 38N 11 9 E
Klouto, Togo **101 D5** 6 57N 0 44 E
Kluane L., Canada **126 B6** 61 15N 138 40W
Kluczbork, Poland **47 E5** 50 58N 18 12 E
Klundert, Neths. **21 E5** 51 40N 4 32 E
Klyuchevskaya, Guba, U.S.S.R. **57 D17** 55 50N 160 30 E
Knaresborough, U.K. **16 C6** 54 1N 1 29W
Knee L., Man., Canada **131 B10** 55 3N 94 45W
Knee L., Sask., Canada **131 B7** 55 51N 107 0W
Kneïss, Is., Tunisia **96 B2** 34 22N 10 18 E
Knesselare, Belgium **21 F2** 51 9N 3 26 E
Knezha, Bulgaria **43 D9** 43 30N 24 5 E
Knić, Yugoslavia **42 D5** 43 53N 20 45 E
Knight Inlet, Canada **130 C3** 50 45N 125 40W
Knighton, U.K. **17 E4** 52 21N 3 2W
Knights Ferry, U.S.A. **144 H6** 37 50N 120 40W
Knights Landing, U.S.A. **144 G5** 38 50N 121 43W
Knightstown, U.S.A. **141 E11** 39 49N 85 32W
Knin, Yugoslavia **39 D13** 44 1N 16 17 E
Knittelfeld, Austria **30 D7** 47 13N 14 51 E
Knjaževac, Yugoslavia **42 D7** 43 35N 22 18 E
Knob, C., Australia **113 F2** 34 32 S 119 16 E
Knockmealdown Mts., Ireland **19 D4** 52 16N 8 0W
Knokke, Belgium **21 F2** 51 20N 3 17 E
Knossós, Greece **32 D7** 35 16N 25 10 E
Knox, U.S.A. **141 C10** 41 18N 86 36W
Knox, C., Canada **130 C2** 54 11N 133 5W
Knox City, U.S.A. **139 J5** 33 26N 99 49W
Knox Coast, Antarctica **7 C8** 66 30 S 108 0 E
Knoxville, Iowa, U.S.A. **140 C4** 41 20N 92 55W
Knoxville, Tenn., U.S.A. **135 H4** 35 58N 83 57W
Knurów, Poland **31 A11** 50 13N 18 38 E
Knutshø, Norway **14 B3** 62 18N 9 41 E
Knysna, S. Africa **104 E3** 34 2 S 23 2 E
Knyszyn, Poland **47 B9** 53 20N 22 56 E
Ko Kha, Thailand **76 C2** 18 11N 99 24 E
Kō-Saki, Japan **62 C1** 34 5N 129 13 E
Ko Tao, Thailand **77 G2** 10 6N 99 48 E
Koartac, Canada **127 B13** 60 55N 69 40W
Koba, Aru, Indonesia **71 F8** 6 37 S 134 37 E
Koba, Bangka, Indonesia **70 E3** 2 26 S 106 14 E
Kobarid, Yugoslavia **39 B10** 46 15N 13 30 E
Kobayashi, Japan **62 F2** 31 56N 130 59 E
Kobdo = Hovd, Mongolia **64 B4** 48 2N 91 37 E
Kōbe, Japan **63 C7** 34 45N 135 10 E
Kobelyaki, U.S.S.R. **52 B6** 49 11N 34 9 E
København, Denmark **15 J6** 55 41N 12 34 E
Kōbi-Sho, Japan **61 M1** 25 56N 123 41 E
Koblenz, Germany **27 E3** 50 21N 7 36 E
Koblenz, Switz. **28 A6** 47 37N 8 14 E
Kobo, Ethiopia **95 E4** 12 2N 39 56 E
Kobo, Zaïre **103 C3** 4 54 S 17 9 E
Kobrin, U.S.S.R. **50 E4** 52 15N 24 22 E
Kobroor, Kepulauan, Indonesia **71 F8** 6 10 S 134 30 E
Kobuchizawa, Japan **63 B10** 35 52N 138 19 E
Kobuleti, U.S.S.R. **53 F9** 41 55N 41 45 E
Kobylin, Poland **47 D4** 51 43N 17 12 E
Kobyłka, Poland **47 C8** 52 21N 21 10 E
Kobylkino, U.S.S.R. **51 D13** 54 8N 43 56 E
Kobylnik, U.S.S.R. **50 D5** 54 58N 26 39 E
Kocaeli = İzmit, Turkey **88 C3** 40 45N 29 50 E
Kocaeli □, Turkey **88 C3** 40 45N 29 55 E
Kočane, Yugoslavia **42 D6** 43 12N 21 52 E
Koćani, Yugoslavia **42 F7** 41 55N 22 25 E
Koçarlı, Turkey **45 G9** 37 45N 27 43 E
Koceljevo, Yugoslavia **42 C4** 44 28N 19 50 E
Kočevje, Yugoslavia **39 C11** 45 39N 14 50 E
Koch Bihar, India **78 B2** 26 22N 89 29 E
Kochang, S. Korea **67 G14** 35 41N 127 55 E
Kochas, India **81 G10** 25 15N 83 56 E
Kocher →, Germany **27 F5** 49 14N 9 12 E
Kocheya, U.S.S.R. **57 D13** 52 32N 120 42 E
Kōchi, Japan **62 D5** 33 30N 133 35 E
Kōchi □, Japan **62 D5** 33 40N 133 30 E
Kōchi-Heiya, Japan **62 D5** 33 28N 133 30 E
Kochiu = Gejiu, China **68 F4** 23 20N 103 10 E
Kochkor-Ata, U.S.S.R. **55 C6** 41 1N 72 29 E
Kochkorka, U.S.S.R. **55 B7** 42 13N 75 46 E
Kock, Poland **47 D9** 51 38N 22 27 E
Kodaira, Japan **63 B11** 35 44N 139 29 E
Koddiyar B., Sri Lanka **83 K5** 8 33N 81 15 E
Kodiak, U.S.A. **126 C4** 57 30N 152 45W
Kodiak I., U.S.A. **126 C4** 57 30N 152 45W
Kodinar, India **80 J4** 20 46N 70 46 E
Kodori →, U.S.S.R. **53 E9** 42 47N 41 10 E
Koekelare, Belgium **21 F1** 51 5N 2 59 E
Koersel, Belgium **21 F6** 51 3N 5 17 E
Koes, Namibia **104 D2** 26 0 S 19 15 E
Koffiefontein, S. Africa **104 D4** 29 30 S 25 0 E
Kofiau, Indonesia **71 E7** 1 11 S 129 50 E
Köflach, Austria **30 D8** 47 4N 15 5 E
Koforidua, Ghana **101 D4** 6 3N 0 17W
Kōfu, Japan **63 B10** 35 40N 138 30 E
Koga, Japan **63 A11** 36 11N 139 43 E
Kogaluk →, Canada **129 A7** 56 12N 61 44W
Kogan, Australia **115 D5** 27 2 S 150 40 E
Kogin Baba, Nigeria **101 D7** 7 55N 11 35 E
Koh-i-Bābā, Afghan. **79 B2** 34 30N 67 0 E
Koh-i-Khurd, Afghan. **80 C1** 33 30N 65 59 E
Kohat, Pakistan **79 B3** 33 40N 71 29 E
Kohima, India **78 C5** 25 35N 94 10 E
Kohkīlūyeh va Būyer Aḥmadi □, Iran **85 D6** 31 30N 50 30 E
Kohler Ra., Antarctica **7 D15** 77 0 S 110 0W
Kohtla Järve, U.S.S.R. **50 B5** 59 20N 27 20 E
Kohukohu, N.Z. **118 B2** 35 22 S 173 38 E
Koin-dong, N. Korea **67 D14** 40 28N 126 18 E
Kojetín, Czech. **31 B10** 49 21N 17 20 E
Kojima, Japan **62 C5** 34 30N 133 50 E
Kōjo, Japan **62 C5** 34 33N 133 55 E
Kojŏ, N. Korea **67 E14** 38 58N 127 58 E
Kojonup, Australia **113 F2** 33 48 S 117 10 E
Kojūr, Iran **85 B6** 36 23N 51 43 E
Kok Yangak, U.S.S.R. **55 C6** 41 2N 73 12 E
Koka, Sudan **94 C3** 20 5N 30 35 E
Kokand, U.S.S.R. **55 C5** 40 30N 70 57 E
Kokanee Glacier Prov. Park, Canada **130 D5** 49 47N 117 10W
Kokas, Indonesia **71 E8** 2 42 S 132 26 E
Kokava, Czech. **31 C12** 48 35N 19 50 E
Kokchetav, U.S.S.R. **56 D7** 53 20N 69 25 E
Kokemäenjoki, Finland **13 F16** 61 32N 21 44 E
Kokerite, Guyana **153 B6** 7 12N 59 35W
Kokhma, U.S.S.R. **51 C12** 56 55N 41 18 E
Kokiri, N.Z. **119 C6** 42 29 S 171 25 E
Kokkola, Finland **12 E17** 63 50N 23 8 E
Koko, Nigeria **101 C5** 11 28N 4 29 E
Kokoda, Papua N. G. **120 E4** 8 54 S 147 47 E
Kokolopozo, Ivory C. **100 D3** 5 8N 6 5W
Kokomo, U.S.A. **141 D10** 40 30N 86 6W
Kokonau, Indonesia **71 E9** 4 43 S 136 26 E
Kokopo, Papua N. G. **120 C7** 4 22 S 152 19 E
Kokoro, Niger **101 C5** 14 12N 0 55 E
Koksan, N. Korea **67 E14** 38 46N 126 40 E
Koksengir, Gora, U.S.S.R. **55 A2** 44 21N 65 6 E
Koksoak →, Canada **127 C13** 58 30N 68 10W
Kokstad, S. Africa **105 E4** 30 32 S 29 29 E
Kokubu, Japan **62 F2** 31 44N 130 46 E
Kokuora, U.S.S.R. **57 B15** 71 35N 144 50 E
Kola, Indonesia **71 F8** 5 35 S 134 30 E
Kola, U.S.S.R. **48 A5** 68 45N 33 8 E
Kola Pen. = Kolskiy Poluostrov, U.S.S.R. **48 A6** 67 30N 38 0 E
Kolachel, India **83 K3** 8 10N 77 15 E
Kolahoi, India **81 B6** 34 12N 75 22 E
Kolahun, Liberia **100 D2** 8 15N 10 4W
Kolaka, Indonesia **71 E6** 4 3 S 121 46 E
Kolar, India **83 H4** 13 12N 78 15 E
Kolar Gold Fields, India **83 H4** 12 58N 78 16 E
Kolari, Finland **12 C17** 67 20N 23 48 E
Kolašin, Yugoslavia **42 E4** 42 50N 19 31 E
Kolby Kås, Denmark **15 J4** 55 48N 10 32 E
Kolchugino, U.S.S.R. **51 C11** 56 17N 39 22 E
Kolda, Senegal **100 C2** 12 55N 14 57W
Kolding, Denmark **15 J3** 55 30N 9 29 E
Kole, Zaïre **102 C4** 3 16 S 22 42 E
Koléa, Algeria **99 A5** 36 38N 2 46 E
Kolepom = Yos Sudarso, Pulau, Indonesia **71 F9** 8 0 S 138 30 E
Kolguyev, Ostrov, U.S.S.R. **48 A8** 69 20N 48 30 E
Kolham, Neths. **20 B9** 53 11N 6 44 E
Kolhapur, India **82 F2** 16 43N 74 15 E
Kolia, Ivory C. **100 D3** 9 46N 6 28W
Kolín, Czech. **30 A8** 50 2N 15 9 E
Kolind, Denmark **15 H4** 56 21N 10 34 E
Kölleda, Germany **26 D7** 51 11N 11 14 E
Kollegal, India **83 H3** 12 9N 77 9 E
Kolleru L., India **82 F5** 16 40N 81 10 E
Kollum, Neths. **20 B8** 53 17N 6 10 E
Kolmanskop, Namibia **104 D2** 26 45 S 15 14 E
Köln, Germany **26 E2** 50 56N 6 58 E
Kolno, Poland **47 B8** 53 25N 21 56 E
Koło, Poland **47 C5** 52 14N 18 40 E
Kołobrzeg, Poland **47 A2** 54 10N 15 35 E
Kologriv, U.S.S.R. **51 B14** 58 48N 44 25 E
Kolokani, Mali **100 C3** 13 35N 7 45W
Kolombangara, Solomon Is. **121 M9** 8 0 S 157 5 E
Kolomna, U.S.S.R. **51 D11** 55 8N 38 45 E
Kolomyya, U.S.S.R. **52 B1** 48 31N 25 2 E
Kolondiéba, Mali **100 C3** 11 5N 6 54W
Kolonodale, Indonesia **71 E6** 2 3 S 121 25 E
Kolosib, India **78 C4** 24 15N 92 45 E
Kolpashevo, U.S.S.R. **56 D9** 58 20N 83 5 E
Kolpino, U.S.S.R. **50 B7** 59 44N 30 39 E
Kolpny, U.S.S.R. **51 E10** 52 12N 37 10 E
Kolskiy Poluostrov, U.S.S.R. **48 A6** 67 30N 38 0 E
Kolskiy Zaliv, U.S.S.R. **48 A5** 69 23N 34 0 E
Koltubanovskiy, U.S.S.R. **54 E3** 52 57N 52 2 E
Kolubara →, Yugoslavia **42 C5** 44 35N 20 15 E
Kolumna, Poland **47 D6** 51 36N 19 14 E
Koluszki, Poland **47 D6** 51 45N 19 46 E
Kolwezi, Zaïre **107 E2** 10 40 S 25 25 E
Kolyberovo, U.S.S.R. **51 D11** 55 15N 38 40 E
Kolyma →, U.S.S.R. **57 C17** 69 30N 161 0 E
Kolymskoye, Okhotsko, U.S.S.R. **57 C16** 63 0N 157 0 E
Kôm Ombo, Egypt **94 C3** 24 25N 32 52 E
Komagene, Japan **63 B9** 35 44N 137 58 E
Komaki, Japan **63 B8** 35 17N 136 55 E
Komandorskie Is. = Komandorskiye, Ostrov, U.S.S.R. **57 D17** 55 0N 167 0 E
Komandorskiye, Ostrov, U.S.S.R. **57 D17** 55 0N 167 0 E
Komárno, Czech. **31 D11** 47 49N 18 5 E
Komárom, Hungary **31 D11** 47 43N 18 7 E
Komárom □, Hungary **31 D11** 47 35N 18 20 E
Komarovo, U.S.S.R. **50 B8** 58 38N 33 40 E
Komatipoort, S. Africa **105 D5** 25 25 S 31 55 E
Komatou Yialou, Cyprus **32 D13** 35 25N 34 8 E
Komatsu, Japan **63 A8** 36 25N 136 30 E
Komatsujima, Japan **62 D6** 34 0N 134 35 E
Kombissiri, Burkina Faso **101 C4** 12 4N 1 20W
Kombo, Gabon **102 C2** 0 20 S 12 22 E
Kombori, Burkina Faso **100 C4** 13 26N 3 56W
Kombóti, Greece **45 E3** 39 6N 21 5 E
Komen, Yugoslavia **39 C10** 45 49N 13 45 E
Komenda, Ghana **101 D4** 5 4N 1 28W
Komi A.S.S.R. □, U.S.S.R. **48 B10** 64 0N 55 0 E
Komiža, Yugoslavia **39 E13** 43 3N 16 11 E
Komló, Hungary **31 E11** 46 15N 18 16 E
Kommamur Canal, India **83 G5** 16 0N 80 25 E
Kommunarsk, U.S.S.R. **53 B8** 48 30N 38 45 E
Kommunizma, Pik, U.S.S.R. **55 D6** 39 0N 72 2 E
Komodo, Indonesia **71 F5** 8 37 S 119 20 E
Komoé, Ivory C. **100 D4** 5 12N 3 44W
Komono, Congo **102 C2** 3 10 S 13 20 E
Komoran, Pulau, Indonesia **71 F9** 8 18 S 138 45 E
Komoro, Japan **63 A10** 36 19N 138 26 E
Komotini, Greece **44 C7** 41 9N 25 26 E
Komovi, Yugoslavia **42 E4** 42 41N 19 39 E
Kompasberg, S. Africa **104 E3** 31 45 S 24 32 E
Kompong Bang, Cambodia **77 F5** 12 24N 104 40 E
Kompong Cham, Cambodia **77 G5** 12 0N 105 30 E
Kompong Chhnang, Cambodia **77 F5** 12 20N 104 35 E
Kompong Chikreng, Cambodia **76 F5** 13 5N 104 18 E
Kompong Kleang, Cambodia **76 F5** 13 6N 104 8 E
Kompong Luong, Cambodia **77 G5** 11 49N 104 48 E
Kompong Pranak, Cambodia **76 F5** 13 35N 104 55 E
Kompong Som, Cambodia **77 G4** 10 38N 103 30 E
Kompong Som, Chhung, Cambodia **77 G4** 10 50N 103 32 E
Kompong Speu, Cambodia **77 G5** 11 26N 104 32 E
Kompong Sralao, Cambodia **76 E5** 14 5N 105 46 E
Kompong Thom, Cambodia **76 F5** 12 35N 104 51 E
Kompong Trabeck, Cambodia **76 F5** 13 6N 105 14 E
Kompong Trabeck, Cambodia **77 G5** 11 9N 105 28 E
Kompong Trach, Cambodia **77 G5** 11 25N 105 48 E
Kompong Tralach, Cambodia **77 G5** 11 54N 104 47 E
Komrat, U.S.S.R. **52 C3** 46 18N 28 40 E
Komsberg, S. Africa **104 E3** 32 40 S 20 45 E
Komsomolabad, U.S.S.R. **55 D4** 38 50N 69 55 E
Komsomolets, U.S.S.R. **54 E8** 53 45N 62 2 E
Komsomolets, Ostrov, U.S.S.R. **57 A10** 80 30N 95 0 E
Komsomolsk, R.S.F.S.R., U.S.S.R. **51 C12** 57 2N 40 20 E
Komsomolsk, R.S.F.S.R., U.S.S.R. **57 D14** 50 30N 137 0 E
Komsomolsk, Turkmen S.S.R., U.S.S.R. **55 D1** 39 2N 63 36 E
Komsomolskiy, U.S.S.R. **51 E16** 53 30N 49 30 E

Krasnoye 219

Konakovo, U.S.S.R. 51 C10 56 52N 36 45 E
Konarhá □, Afghan. 79 B3 35 30N 71 3 E
Konārī, Iran 85 D6 28 13N 51 36 E
Konawa, U.S.A. 139 H6 34 59N 96 46W
Konch, India 81 G8 26 0N 79 10 E
Kondagaon, India 82 E5 19 35N 81 35 E
Kondakovo, U.S.S.R. 57 C16 69 36N 152 0 E
Konde, Tanzania 106 C4 4 57 S 39 45 E
Kondiá, Greece 44 E7 39 49N 25 10 E
Kondinin, Australia 113 F2 32 34 S 118 8 E
Kondo, Zaïre 103 D2 5 35 S 13 0 E
Kondoa, Tanzania 106 C4 4 55 S 35 50 E
Kondoa □, Tanzania 106 D4 5 0 S 36 0 E
Kondókali, Greece 32 A3 39 38N 19 51 E
Kondopaga, U.S.S.R. 48 B5 62 12N 34 17 E
Kondratyevo, U.S.S.R. 57 D10 57 22N 98 15 E
Konduga, Nigeria 101 C7 11 35N 13 26 E
Kondukur, India 83 G4 15 12N 79 57 E
Koné, N. Cal. 121 U18 21 4 S 164 52 E
Konevo, U.S.S.R. 48 B6 62 8N 39 20 E
Kong, Ivory C. 100 D4 8 54N 4 36W
Kong →, Cambodia 76 F5 13 32N 105 58 E
Kong, Koh, Cambodia 77 G4 11 20N 103 0 E
Kong Christian IX.s Land, Greenland 6 C6 68 0N 36 0W
Kong Christian X.s Land, Greenland 6 B6 74 0N 29 0W
Kong Franz Joseph Fd., Greenland 6 B6 73 20N 24 30W
Kong Frederik IX.s Land, Greenland 6 C5 67 0N 52 0W
Kong Frederik VI.s Kyst, Greenland 6 C5 63 0N 43 0W
Kong Frederik VIII.s Land, Greenland 6 B6 78 30N 26 0W
Kong Oscar Fjord, Greenland 6 B6 72 20N 24 0W
Kongbo, C.A.R. 102 B4 4 44N 21 23 E
Kongeå, Denmark 15 J3 55 24N 9 39 E
Kongju, S. Korea 67 F14 36 30N 127 0 E
Kongkemul, Indonesia 75 B4 1 52N 112 11 E
Konglu, Burma 78 B6 27 13N 97 57 E
Kongolo, Kasai Or., Zaïre 103 D4 5 26 S 24 49 E
Kongolo, Shaba, Zaïre 106 D2 5 22 S 27 0 E
Kongor, Sudan 95 F3 7 1N 31 27 E
Kongoussi, Burkina Faso 101 C4 13 19N 1 32W
Kongsberg, Norway 14 E3 59 39N 9 39 E
Kongsvinger, Norway 14 D6 60 12N 12 2 E
Kongwa, Tanzania 106 D4 6 11 S 36 26 E
Koni, Zaïre 107 E2 10 40 S 27 11 E
Koni, Mts., Zaïre 107 E2 10 36 S 27 10 E
Koniecpol, Poland 47 E6 50 46N 19 40 E
Königsberg = Kaliningrad, U.S.S.R. 50 D2 54 42N 20 32 E
Königslutter, Germany 26 C6 52 14N 10 50 E
Königswusterhausen, Germany 26 C9 52 19N 13 38 E
Konin, Poland 47 C5 52 12N 18 15 E
Konin □, Poland 47 C5 52 15N 18 30 E
Konispoli, Albania 44 E2 39 42N 20 10 E
Kónitsa, Greece 44 D2 40 5N 20 48 E
Köniz, Switz. 28 C4 46 56N 7 25 E
Konjic, Yugoslavia 42 D2 43 42N 17 58 E
Konjice, Yugoslavia 39 B12 46 20N 15 28 E
Konkiep, Namibia 104 D2 26 49 S 17 15 E
Konkouré →, Guinea 100 D2 9 50N 13 42W
Könnern, Germany 26 D7 51 40N 11 45 E
Konnur, India 83 F2 16 14N 74 49 E
Kono, S. Leone 100 D2 8 30N 11 5W
Konolfingen, Switz. 28 C5 46 54N 7 38 E
Konongo, Ghana 101 D4 6 40N 1 15W
Konos, Papua N. G. 120 B6 3 10 S 151 44 E
Konosha, U.S.S.R. 48 B7 61 0N 40 5 E
Kōnosu, Japan 63 A11 36 3N 139 31 E
Konotop, U.S.S.R. 50 F8 51 12N 33 7 E
Końskie, Poland 47 D7 51 15N 20 23 E
Konstantinovka, U.S.S.R. 52 B7 48 32N 37 39 E
Konstantinovski, U.S.S.R. 53 C9 47 33N 41 10 E
Konstantynów Łódźki, Poland 47 D6 51 45N 19 20 E
Konstanz, Germany 27 H5 47 39N 9 10 E
Kont, Iran 85 E9 26 55N 61 50 E
Kontagora, Nigeria 101 C6 10 23N 5 27 E
Kontich, Belgium 21 F4 51 8N 4 26 E
Kontum, Vietnam 76 E7 14 24N 108 0 E
Kontum, Plateau du, Vietnam 76 E7 14 30N 108 30 E
Konya, Turkey 88 E5 37 52N 32 35 E
Konya □, Turkey 88 E5 37 46N 32 20 E
Konya Ovasi, Turkey 88 D5 38 30N 33 0 E
Konyin, Burma 78 D5 22 58N 94 42 E
Konz, Germany 27 F2 49 41N 6 36 E
Konza, Kenya 106 C4 1 45 S 37 7 E
Konzhakovskiy Kamen, Gora, U.S.S.R. 54 B6 59 38N 59 8 E
Kookynie, Australia 113 E3 29 17 S 121 22 E
Kooline, Australia 112 D2 22 57 S 116 20 E
Kooloonong, Australia 116 C5 34 48 S 143 10 E
Koolyanobbing, Australia 113 F2 30 48 S 119 36 E
Koondrook, Australia 116 C6 35 33 S 144 8 E
Koonibba, Australia 115 E1 31 54 S 133 25 E
Koorawatha, Australia 117 C8 34 2 S 148 33 E
Koorda, Australia 113 F2 30 48 S 117 35 E
Kooskia, U.S.A. 142 C6 46 9N 115 59W
Kootenai →, Canada 142 B5 49 15N 117 39W
Kootenay L., Canada 130 D5 49 45N 116 50W
Kootenay Nat. Park, Canada 130 C5 51 0N 116 0W
Kootjieskolk, S. Africa 104 E3 31 15 S 20 21 E
Kopa, U.S.S.R. 55 B7 43 31N 75 50 E
Kopanovka, U.S.S.R. 53 C12 47 28N 46 50 E
Kopaonik Planina, Yugoslavia 42 D6 43 10N 21 50 E
Kopargaon, India 82 E2 19 51N 74 28 E
Kópavogur, Iceland 12 D3 64 6N 21 55W
Koper, Yugoslavia 39 C10 45 31N 13 44 E
Kopervik, Norway 13 G8 59 17N 5 17 E
Kopeysk, U.S.S.R. 54 D7 55 7N 61 37 E
Kopi, Australia 115 E2 33 24 S 135 40 E
Köping, Sweden 14 E10 59 31N 16 3 E
Kopiste, Yugoslavia 39 F13 42 48N 16 42 E
Kopliku, Albania 44 B1 42 15N 19 25 E
Köpmanholmen, Sweden 14 A12 63 10N 18 35 E
Koppal, India 83 G3 15 23N 76 5 E
Koppang, Norway 14 C5 61 34N 11 3 E
Kopparberg, Sweden 13 G13 59 52N 15 0 E
Kopparbergs län □, Sweden 13 F13 61 20N 14 15 E
Kopperå, Norway 14 A5 63 24N 11 50 E
Koppies, S. Africa 105 D4 27 20 S 27 30 E
Koppio, Australia 116 C1 34 26 S 135 51 E
Koprivlen, Bulgaria 43 F8 41 36N 23 53 E
Koprivnica, Yugoslavia 39 B13 46 12N 16 45 E
Koprivshtitsa, Bulgaria 43 E9 42 40N 24 19 E
Kopychintsy, U.S.S.R. 50 G4 49 7N 25 58 E
Kopys, U.S.S.R. 50 D7 54 20N 30 17 E
Korab, Yugoslavia 42 F5 41 44N 20 40 E
Korakiána, Greece 32 A3 39 42N 19 45 E
Koraput, India 82 E6 18 50N 82 40 E
Korba, India 81 H10 22 20N 82 45 E
Korbach, Germany 26 D4 51 17N 8 50 E
Korbu, G., Malaysia 77 K3 4 41N 101 18 E
Korça, Albania 44 D2 40 37N 20 50 E
Korça □, Albania 44 D2 40 40N 20 50 E
Korce = Korça, Albania 44 D2 40 37N 20 50 E
Korčula, Yugoslavia 39 F14 42 57N 17 8 E
Korčulanski Kanal, Yugoslavia 39 E13 43 3N 16 40 E
Kord Kūy, Iran 85 B7 36 48N 54 7 E
Kord Sheykh, Iran 85 D7 28 31N 52 53 E
Kordestān □, Iran 84 C5 36 0N 47 0 E
Korea, North ■, Asia 67 E14 40 0N 127 0 E
Korea, South ■, Asia 67 G15 36 0N 128 0 E
Korea Bay, Korea 67 E13 39 0N 124 0 E
Korea Strait, Asia 67 H15 34 0N 129 30 E
Koregaon, India 82 F2 17 40N 74 10 E
Korenevo, U.S.S.R. 50 F9 51 27N 34 55 E
Korenovsk, U.S.S.R. 53 D8 45 30N 39 22 E
Korets, U.S.S.R. 50 F5 50 40N 27 5 E
Korgan, Turkey 89 C7 40 44N 37 13 E
Korgus, Sudan 94 D3 19 16N 33 29 E
Korhogo, Ivory C. 100 D3 9 29N 5 28W
Koribundu, S. Leone 100 D2 7 41N 11 46W
Korim, Indonesia 71 E9 0 58 S 136 10 E
Korinthía □, Greece 45 G4 37 50N 22 35 E
Korinthiakós Kólpos, Greece 45 F4 38 16N 22 30 E
Kórinthos, Greece 45 G4 37 56N 22 55 E
Korioumé, Mali 100 B4 16 35N 3 0W
Korissa, Limni, Greece 32 B3 39 27N 19 53 E
Kōriyama, Japan 60 F10 37 24N 140 23 E
Korkino, U.S.S.R. 54 D7 54 54N 61 23 E
Korkuteli, Turkey 88 E4 37 2N 30 11 E
Korla, China 64 B3 41 45N 86 4 E
Kormakiti, C., Cyprus 32 D11 35 23N 32 56 E
Körmend, Hungary 31 D9 47 5N 16 35 E
Kornat, Yugoslavia 39 E12 43 50N 15 20 E
Korneshty, U.S.S.R. 52 C3 47 21N 28 1 E
Korneuburg, Austria 31 C9 48 20N 16 20 E
Kornsjø, Norway 14 F5 58 57N 11 39 E
Kornstad, Norway 14 B1 62 58N 7 27 E
Koro, Fiji 121 A2 17 19 S 179 23 E
Koro, Ivory C. 100 D3 8 32N 7 30W
Koro, Mali 100 C4 14 1N 2 58W
Koro Sea, Fiji 121 A3 17 30 S 179 45W
Koro Toro, Chad 97 E3 16 5N 18 30 E
Koroba, Papua N. G. 120 C2 5 44 S 142 47 E
Korocha, U.S.S.R. 51 F10 50 55N 37 30 E
Köroğlu Dağları, Turkey 88 C4 40 30N 31 50 E
Korogwe, Tanzania 106 D4 5 5 S 38 25 E
Korogwe □, Tanzania 106 D4 5 0 S 38 20 E
Koroit, Australia 116 E5 38 18 S 142 24 E
Korong Vale, Australia 116 D5 36 22 S 143 45 E
Koróni, Greece 45 H3 36 48N 21 57 E
Korónia, Limni, Greece 44 D5 40 47N 23 37 E
Koronís, Greece 45 G7 37 12N 25 35 E
Koronowo, Poland 47 B4 53 19N 17 55 E
Koror, Pac. Oc. 71 C8 7 20N 134 28 E
Körös →, Hungary 31 E13 46 43N 20 12 E
Köröstarcsa, Hungary 31 E14 46 53N 21 3 E
Korosten, U.S.S.R. 50 F6 50 57N 28 25 E
Korotoyak, U.S.S.R. 51 F11 51 1N 39 2 E
Korraraika, Helodranon' i, Madag. 105 B7 17 45 S 43 57 E
Korsakov, U.S.S.R. 57 E15 46 36N 142 42 E
Korshunovo, U.S.S.R. 57 D12 58 37N 110 10 E
Korsör, Denmark 13 J11 55 20N 11 9 E
Korsun Shevchenkovskiy, U.S.S.R. 52 B4 49 26N 31 16 E
Korsze, Poland 47 A8 54 11N 21 9 E
Kortemark, Belgium 21 F2 51 2N 3 3 E
Kortessem, Belgium 21 G6 50 52N 5 23 E
Korti, Sudan 94 D3 18 6N 31 33 E
Kortrijk, Belgium 21 G2 50 50N 3 17 E
Korumburra, Australia 117 E6 38 26 S 145 50 E
Korwai, India 80 G8 24 7N 78 5 E
Koryakskiy Khrebet, U.S.S.R. 57 C18 61 0N 171 0 E
Koryŏng, S. Korea 67 G15 35 44N 128 15 E
Kos, Greece 45 H9 36 50N 27 15 E
Kosa, Ethiopia 95 F4 7 50N 36 50 E
Kosa, U.S.S.R. 54 B4 59 56N 55 0 E
Kosa →, U.S.S.R. 54 A4 60 11N 55 10 E
Kosaya Gora, U.S.S.R. 51 D10 54 10N 37 30 E
Koschagyl, U.S.S.R. 49 E9 46 40N 54 0 E
Kościan, Poland 47 C3 52 5N 16 40 E
Kościerzyna, Poland 47 A4 54 8N 17 59 E
Kosciusko, U.S.A. 139 J10 33 3N 89 34W
Kosciusko, Mt., Australia 117 D8 36 27 S 148 16 E
Kosciusko I., U.S.A. 130 B2 56 0N 133 40W
Kösély →, Hungary 31 D14 47 25N 21 5 E
Kosgi, India 83 F3 16 58N 77 43 E
Kosha, Sudan 94 C3 20 50N 30 30 E
Koshigaya, Japan 63 B11 35 54N 139 48 E
K'oshih = Kashi, China 64 C2 39 30N 76 2 E
Koshiki-Rettō, Japan 62 F1 31 45N 129 49 E
Koshkonong, L., U.S.A. 141 B8 42 55N 88 58W
Kōshoku, Japan 63 A10 36 38N 138 6 E
Koshtëbë, U.S.S.R. 55 C7 41 5N 74 15 E
Kosi, India 80 F7 27 48N 77 29 E
Kosi-meer, S. Africa 105 D5 27 0 S 32 50 E
Košice, Czech. 31 C14 48 42N 21 15 E
Kosjerić, Yugoslavia 42 D4 44 0N 19 55 E
Koskhinoú, Greece 32 C10 36 23N 28 13 E
Koslan, U.S.S.R. 48 B8 63 28N 48 52 E
Kosŏng, N. Korea 67 E15 38 40N 128 22 E
Kosovo, Soc. Aut. Pokrajina □, Yugoslavia 42 E6 42 30N 21 0 E
Kosovska-Mitrovica, Yugoslavia 42 E5 42 54N 20 52 E
Kostajnica, Yugoslavia 39 C13 45 17N 16 30 E
Kostamuksa, U.S.S.R. 48 B5 62 34N 32 44 E
Kostanjevica, Yugoslavia 39 C12 45 51N 15 27 E
Kostelec, Czech. 31 A9 50 14N 16 35 E
Kostenets, Bulgaria 43 E8 42 15N 23 52 E
Koster, S. Africa 104 D4 25 52 S 26 54 E
Kôstî, Sudan 95 E3 13 8N 32 43 E
Kostolac, Yugoslavia 42 C6 44 37N 21 15 E
Kostopol, U.S.S.R. 50 F5 50 51N 26 22 E
Kostroma, U.S.S.R. 51 C12 57 50N 40 58 E
Kostromskoye Vdkhr., U.S.S.R. 51 C12 57 52N 40 49 E
Kostrzyn, Gorzow Wlkp., Poland 47 C1 52 35N 14 39 E
Kostrzyn, Poznań, Poland 47 C4 52 24N 17 14 E
Kostyukovichi, U.S.S.R. 50 E8 53 20N 32 4 E
Koszalin, Poland 47 A3 54 11N 16 8 E
Koszalin □, Poland 47 B3 53 40N 16 10 E
Köszeg, Hungary 31 D9 47 23N 16 33 E
Kot Addu, Pakistan 79 C3 30 30N 71 0 E
Kot Moman, Pakistan 80 C5 32 13N 73 0 E
Kota, India 80 G6 25 14N 75 49 E
Kota Baharu, Malaysia 77 J4 6 7N 102 14 E
Kota Belud, Malaysia 70 C5 6 21N 116 26 E
Kota Kinabalu, Malaysia 70 C5 6 0N 116 4 E
Kota Tinggi, Malaysia 77 M4 1 44N 103 53 E
Kotaagung, Indonesia 70 F2 5 38 S 104 29 E
Kotabaru, Indonesia 70 E5 3 20 S 116 20 E
Kotabumi, Indonesia 70 E2 4 49 S 104 54 E
Kotagede, Indonesia 71 G14 7 54 S 110 26 E
Kotamobagu, Indonesia 71 D6 0 57N 124 31 E
Kotaneelee →, Canada 130 A4 60 11N 123 42W
Kotawaringin, Indonesia 70 E4 2 28 S 111 27 E
Kotchandpur, Bangla. 78 D2 23 24N 89 1 E
Kotcho L., Canada 130 B4 59 7N 121 12W
Kotel, Bulgaria 43 E11 42 52N 26 26 E
Kotelnich, U.S.S.R. 51 B16 58 20N 48 10 E
Kotelnikovo, U.S.S.R. 53 C10 47 38N 43 8 E
Kotelnyy, Ostrov, U.S.S.R. 57 B14 75 10N 139 0 E
Kothagudam, India 82 F5 17 30N 80 40 E
Kothapet, India 82 E4 19 21N 79 28 E
Köthen, Germany 26 D7 51 44N 11 59 E
Kothi, India 81 G9 24 45N 80 40 E
Kotiro, Pakistan 80 F2 26 17N 67 13 E
Kotka, Finland 13 F19 60 28N 26 58 E
Kotlas, U.S.S.R. 48 B8 61 15N 47 0 E
Kotlenska Planina, Bulgaria 43 E11 42 56N 26 30 E
Kotli, Pakistan 80 C5 33 30N 73 55 E
Kotmul, Pakistan 81 B6 35 32N 75 10 E
Kotohira, Japan 62 C5 34 11N 133 49 E
Kotonkoro, Nigeria 101 C6 11 3N 5 58 E
Kotor, Yugoslavia 42 E3 42 25N 18 47 E
Kotor Varoš, Yugoslavia 42 C2 44 38N 17 22 E
Kotoriba, Yugoslavia 39 B13 46 23N 16 48 E
Kotovo, U.S.S.R. 51 F14 50 22N 44 45 E
Kotovsk, U.S.S.R. 52 C3 47 45N 29 35 E
Kotputli, India 80 F7 27 43N 76 12 E
Kotri, Pakistan 79 D3 25 22N 68 22 E
Kotri →, India 82 E5 19 15N 80 35 E
Kótronas, Greece 45 H4 36 38N 22 29 E
Kötschach-Mauthen, Austria 30 E6 46 41N 13 1 E
Kottayam, India 83 K3 9 35N 76 33 E
Kottur, India 83 J3 10 34N 76 56 E
Kotuy →, U.S.S.R. 57 B11 71 54N 102 6 E
Kotzebue, U.S.A. 126 B3 66 50N 162 40W
Kouango, C.A.R. 102 B4 5 0N 20 10 E
Koudekerke, Neths. 21 F3 51 29N 3 33 E
Koudougou, Burkina Faso 100 C4 12 10N 2 20W
Koufonisi, Greece 32 E8 34 56N 26 8 E
Koufonísia, Greece 45 H7 36 57N 25 35 E
Kougaberge, S. Africa 104 E3 33 48 S 23 50 E
Kouibli, Ivory C. 100 D3 7 15N 7 14W
Kouilou →, Congo 103 C2 4 10 S 12 5 E
Kouki, C.A.R. 102 A3 7 22N 17 3 E
Koula Moutou, Gabon 102 C2 1 15 S 12 25 E
Koulen, Cambodia 76 F5 13 50N 104 40 E
Koulikoro, Mali 100 C3 12 40N 7 50W
Kouloúra, Greece 32 A3 39 42N 19 54 E
Koúm-bournoú, Ákra, Greece 32 C10 36 15N 28 11 E
Koumac, N. Cal. 121 T18 20 33 S 164 17 E
Koumala, Australia 114 C4 21 38 S 149 15 E
Koumankou, Mali 100 C3 11 58N 6 6W
Koumbia, Burkina Faso 100 C4 11 10N 3 50W
Koumbia, Guinea 100 C2 11 48N 13 29W
Koumboum, Guinea 100 C2 10 25N 13 0W
Koumpenntoum, Senegal 100 C2 13 59N 14 34W
Koumra, Chad 97 G3 8 50N 17 35 E
Koundara, Guinea 100 C2 12 29N 13 18W
Koundé, C.A.R. 102 A2 6 7N 14 38 E
Kounradskiy, U.S.S.R. 56 E8 46 59N 75 0 E
Kountze, U.S.A. 139 K7 30 20N 94 22W
Koupéla, Burkina Faso 101 C4 12 11N 0 21W
Kouris →, Cyprus 32 E11 34 38N 32 54 E
Kourizo, Passe de, Chad 96 D3 22 28N 15 27 E
Kourou, Fr. Guiana 153 B7 5 9N 52 39W
Kouroussa, Guinea 100 C3 10 45N 9 45W
Koussané, Mali 100 C2 14 53N 11 14W
Kousseri, Cameroon 97 F2 12 0N 14 55 E
Koutiala, Mali 100 C3 12 25N 5 23W
Kouto, Ivory C. 100 D3 9 53N 6 25W
Kouts, U.S.A. 141 C9 41 18N 87 2W
Kouvé, Togo 101 D5 6 25N 1 25 E
Kovačica, Yugoslavia 42 B5 45 5N 20 38 E
Kovdor, U.S.S.R. 48 A5 67 34N 30 24 E
Kovel, U.S.S.R. 50 F4 51 10N 24 20 E
Kovilpatti, India 83 K3 9 10N 77 50 E
Kovin, Yugoslavia 42 C5 44 44N 20 59 E
Kovrov, U.S.S.R. 51 C12 56 25N 41 25 E
Kovur, Andhra Pradesh, India 82 F5 17 3N 81 39 E
Kovur, Andhra Pradesh, India 83 G5 14 30N 80 1 E
Kowal, Poland 47 C6 52 32N 19 7 E
Kowalewo Pomorskie, Poland 47 B5 53 10N 18 52 E
Kowanyama, Australia 114 B3 15 29 S 141 44 E
Kowghān, Afghan. 79 B1 34 12N 63 2 E
Kowkash, Canada 128 B2 50 20N 87 12W
Kowloon, H.K. 69 F10 22 20N 114 15 E
Kowŏn, N. Korea 67 E14 39 26N 127 14 E
Koyabuti, Indonesia 71 E10 2 36 S 140 37 E
Kōyama, Japan 62 F2 31 20N 130 56 E
Köyceğiz, Turkey 88 E3 36 57N 28 40 E
Koytash, U.S.S.R. 55 C3 40 11N 67 19 E
Koyuk, U.S.A. 126 B3 64 55N 161 20W
Koyukuk →, U.S.A. 126 B4 64 56N 157 30W
Koyulhisar, Turkey 52 F7 40 20N 37 52 E
Koza, Japan 61 L3 26 19N 127 46 E
Kozan, Turkey 88 E6 37 26N 35 50 E
Kozáni, Greece 44 D3 40 19N 21 47 E
Kozáni □, Greece 44 D3 40 18N 21 45 E
Kozara, Yugoslavia 39 D14 45 0N 17 0 E
Kozarac, Yugoslavia 39 D13 44 58N 16 48 E
Kozelsk, U.S.S.R. 50 D9 54 2N 35 48 E
Kozhikode = Calicut, India 83 J2 11 15N 75 43 E
Kozhva, U.S.S.R. 48 A10 65 10N 57 0 E
Koziegłowy, Poland 47 E6 50 37N 19 8 E
Kozienice, Poland 47 D8 51 35N 21 34 E
Kozje, Yugoslavia 39 B12 46 5N 15 35 E
Kozle, Poland 47 E5 50 20N 18 8 E
Kozloduy, Bulgaria 43 D8 43 45N 23 42 E
Kozlovets, Bulgaria 43 D10 43 30N 25 20 E
Kozlu, Turkey 88 C4 41 26N 31 45 E
Kozluk, Turkey 89 D9 38 11N 41 31 E
Koźmin, Poland 47 D4 51 48N 17 27 E
Kozmodemyansk, U.S.S.R. 51 C15 56 20N 46 36 E
Kōzu-Shima, Japan 63 C11 34 13N 139 10 E
Kozuchów, Poland 47 D2 51 45N 15 31 E
Kpabia, Ghana 101 D4 9 10N 0 20W
Kpalimé, Togo 101 D5 6 57N 0 44 E
Kpandae, Ghana 101 D4 8 30N 0 2W
Kpessi, Togo 101 D5 8 4N 1 16 E
Kra, Isthmus of = Kra, Kho Khot, Thailand 77 G2 10 15N 99 30 E
Kra, Kho Khot, Thailand 77 G2 10 15N 99 30 E
Kra Buri, Thailand 77 G2 10 22N 98 46 E
Krabbendijke, Neths. 21 F4 51 26N 4 7 E
Krabi, Thailand 77 H2 8 4N 98 55 E
Kragan, Indonesia 71 G14 6 43 S 111 38 E
Kragerø, Norway 14 F3 58 52N 9 25 E
Kragujevac, Yugoslavia 42 C5 44 2N 20 56 E
Krajenka, Poland 47 B3 53 18N 16 59 E
Krakatau = Rakata, Pulau, Indonesia 70 F3 6 10 S 105 20 E
Krakor, Cambodia 76 F5 12 32N 104 12 E
Kraków, Poland 31 A12 50 4N 19 57 E
Kraków □, Poland 31 B13 50 0N 20 0 E
Kraksaan, Indonesia 71 G15 7 43 S 113 23 E
Kråkstad, Norway 14 E4 59 39N 10 55 E
Kralanh, Cambodia 76 F4 13 35N 103 25 E
Králíky, Czech. 31 A9 50 6N 16 45 E
Kraljevo, Yugoslavia 42 D5 43 44N 20 41 E
Kralovice, Czech. 30 B6 49 59N 13 29 E
Královský Chlmec, Czech. 31 C15 48 27N 22 0 E
Kralupy, Czech. 30 A7 50 13N 14 20 E
Kramatorsk, U.S.S.R. 52 B7 48 50N 37 30 E
Kramfors, Sweden 14 B11 62 55N 17 48 E
Kramis, C., Algeria 99 A5 36 26N 0 45 E
Krångede, Sweden 14 A10 63 9N 16 10 E
Kraniá, Greece 44 E3 39 53N 21 18 E
Kranidhion, Greece 45 G5 37 20N 23 10 E
Kranj, Yugoslavia 39 B11 46 16N 14 22 E
Kranjska Gora, Yugoslavia 39 B10 46 29N 13 48 E
Krankskop, S. Africa 105 D5 28 0 S 30 47 E
Krapina, Yugoslavia 39 B12 46 10N 15 52 E
Krapina →, Yugoslavia 39 C12 45 50N 15 50 E
Krapivna, U.S.S.R. 51 E10 53 58N 37 10 E
Krapkowice, Poland 47 E4 50 29N 17 56 E
Krasavino, U.S.S.R. 48 B8 60 58N 46 29 E
Krashyy Klyuch, U.S.S.R. 54 D5 55 23N 56 39 E
Kraskino, U.S.S.R. 57 E14 42 44N 130 48 E
Kraslice, Czech. 30 A5 50 19N 12 31 E
Krasnaya Gorbatka, U.S.S.R. 51 D12 55 52N 41 45 E
Krasnaya Polyana, U.S.S.R. 53 E9 43 40N 40 13 E
Kraśnik, Poland 47 E9 50 55N 22 5 E
Kraśnik Fabryczny, Poland 47 E9 50 58N 22 11 E
Krasnoarmeisk, U.S.S.R. 52 B7 48 18N 37 11 E
Krasnoarmeysk, R.S.F.S.R., U.S.S.R. 51 F14 51 0N 45 42 E
Krasnoarmeysk, R.S.F.S.R., U.S.S.R. 53 B11 48 30N 44 25 E
Krasnodar, U.S.S.R. 53 D8 45 5N 39 0 E
Krasnodon, U.S.S.R. 53 B8 48 17N 39 44 E
Krasnodonetskaya, U.S.S.R. 53 B9 48 5N 40 50 E
Krasnogorskiy, U.S.S.R. 51 C16 56 10N 48 28 E
Krasnograd, U.S.S.R. 52 B6 49 27N 35 27 E
Krasnogvardeysk, U.S.S.R. 55 D3 39 46N 67 16 E
Krasnogvardeyskoye, U.S.S.R. 53 D9 45 52N 41 33 E
Krasnogvardyesk, U.S.S.R. 52 D6 45 32N 34 16 E
Krasnokamsk, U.S.S.R. 54 B4 58 4N 55 48 E
Krasnokutsk, U.S.S.R. 50 F9 50 10N 34 50 E
Krasnoperekopsk, U.S.S.R. 52 D5 46 0N 33 54 E
Krasnorechenskiy, U.S.S.R. 60 B7 44 41N 135 14 E
Krasnoselkupsk, U.S.S.R. 56 C9 65 20N 82 10 E
Krasnoslobodsk, R.S.F.S.R., U.S.S.R. 51 D13 54 25N 43 45 E
Krasnoslobodsk, R.S.F.S.R., U.S.S.R. 53 B11 48 42N 44 33 E
Krasnoturinsk, U.S.S.R. 54 B7 59 46N 60 12 E
Krasnoufimsk, U.S.S.R. 54 C5 56 57N 57 46 E
Krasnouralsk, U.S.S.R. 54 B7 58 21N 60 3 E
Krasnousolskiy, U.S.S.R. 54 E5 53 54N 56 27 E
Krasnovishersk, U.S.S.R. 54 A5 60 23N 57 3 E
Krasnovodsk, U.S.S.R. 49 G9 40 0N 52 52 E
Krasnoyarsk, U.S.S.R. 57 D10 56 8N 93 0 E
Krasnoyarskiy, U.S.S.R. 54 F6 51 58N 59 55 E
Krasnoye = Krasnyy, U.S.S.R. 50 D7 54 25N 31 30 E

220 Krasnoye

Krasnoye, Kalmyk A.S.S.R., U.S.S.R. 53 C11 46 16N 45 0 E
Krasnoye, R.S.F.S.R., U.S.S.R. 51 B15 59 15N 47 40 E
Krasnozavodsk, U.S.S.R. 51 C11 56 27N 38 25 E
Krasny Liman, U.S.S.R. 52 B7 48 58N 37 50 E
Krasny Sulin, U.S.S.R. 53 C9 47 52N 40 8 E
Krasnystaw, Poland 47 E10 50 57N 23 5 E
Krasnyy, U.S.S.R. 50 D7 54 25N 31 30 E
Krasnyy Kholm, R.S.F.S.R., U.S.S.R. 51 B10 58 10N 37 10 E
Krasnyy Kholm, R.S.F.S.R., U.S.S.R. 54 F4 51 35N 54 9 E
Krasnyy Kut, U.S.S.R. 51 F15 50 50N 47 0 E
Krasnyy Luch, U.S.S.R. 53 B8 48 13N 39 0 E
Krasnyy Profintern, U.S.S.R. 51 C12 57 45N 40 27 E
Krasnyy Yar, Kalmyk A.S.S.R., U.S.S.R. 53 C13 46 43N 48 23 E
Krasnyy Yar, R.S.F.S.R., U.S.S.R. 51 F14 50 42N 44 45 E
Krasnyy Yar, R.S.F.S.R., U.S.S.R. 54 E2 53 30N 50 22 E
Krasnyye Baki, U.S.S.R. 51 C14 57 8N 45 10 E
Krasnyyoskolskoye Vdkhr., U.S.S.R. 52 B7 49 30N 37 30 E
Kraszna →, Hungary 31 C15 48 4N 22 20 E
Kratie, Cambodia 76 F6 12 32N 106 10 E
Kratke Ra., Papua N. G. 120 D4 6 45 S 146 0 E
Kratovo, Yugoslavia 42 E7 42 6N 22 10 E
Krau, Indonesia 71 E10 3 19 S 140 5 E
Kravanh, Chuor Phnum, Cambodia 77 G4 12 0N 103 32 E
Krefeld, Germany 26 D2 51 20N 6 32 E
Krémaston, Límni, Greece 45 F3 38 52N 21 30 E
Kremenchug, U.S.S.R. 52 B5 49 5N 33 25 E
Kremenchugskoye Vdkhr., U.S.S.R. 52 B5 49 20N 32 30 E
Kremenets, U.S.S.R. 52 A1 50 8N 25 43 E
Kremenica, Yugoslavia 44 D3 40 55N 21 25 E
Kremennaya, U.S.S.R. 52 B8 49 1N 38 10 E
Kremges = Svetlovodsk, U.S.S.R. 50 G8 49 2N 33 13 E
Kremikovtsi, Bulgaria 43 E8 42 46N 23 28 E
Kremmen, Germany 26 C9 52 45N 13 1 E
Kremmling, U.S.A. 142 F10 40 10N 106 30W
Kremnica, Czech. 31 C11 48 45N 18 50 E
Krems, Austria 30 C8 48 25N 15 36 E
Kremsmünster, Austria 30 C7 48 3N 14 8 E
Kretinga, U.S.S.R. 50 D2 55 53N 21 15 E
Krettamia, Algeria 98 C4 28 47N 3 27W
Krettsy, U.S.S.R. 50 B8 58 15N 32 30 E
Kreuzberg, Germany 27 E5 50 22N 9 58 E
Kreuzlingen, Switz. 29 A8 47 38N 9 10 E
Kribi, Cameroon 101 E6 2 57N 9 56 E
Krichem, Bulgaria 43 E9 42 8N 24 28 E
Krichev, U.S.S.R. 50 E7 53 45N 31 50 E
Krim, Yugoslavia 39 C11 45 53N 14 30 E
Krimpen, Neths. 20 E5 51 55N 4 34 E
Krionéri, Greece 45 F3 38 20N 21 35 E
Kriós, Ákra, Greece 32 D5 35 13N 23 34 E
Krishna →, India 83 G5 15 57N 80 59 E
Krishnagiri, India 83 H4 12 32N 78 16 E
Krishnanagar, India 81 H13 23 24N 88 33 E
Krishnaraja Sagara, India 83 H3 12 20N 76 30 E
Kristiansand, Norway 13 G10 58 9N 8 1 E
Kristianstad, Sweden 13 H13 56 2N 14 9 E
Kristianstads län □, Sweden 13 H13 56 15N 14 0 E
Kristiansund, Norway 14 A1 63 7N 7 45 E
Kristiinankaupunki, Finland 12 E16 62 16N 21 21 E
Kristinehamn, Sweden 13 G13 59 18N 14 13 E
Kristinestad, Finland 12 E16 62 16N 21 21 E
Kríti, Greece 32 D7 35 15N 25 0 E
Kritsá, Greece 32 D7 35 10N 25 41 E
Kriva →, Yugoslavia 42 E6 42 5N 21 47 E
Kriva Palanka, Yugoslavia 42 E7 42 11N 22 19 E
Krivaja →, Yugoslavia 42 C3 44 27N 18 9 E
Krivelj, Yugoslavia 42 C7 44 8N 22 5 E
Krivoy Rog, U.S.S.R. 52 C5 47 51N 33 20 E
Križevci, Yugoslavia 39 B13 46 3N 16 32 E
Krk, Yugoslavia 39 C11 45 8N 14 40 E
Krka →, Yugoslavia 39 C12 45 50N 15 30 E
Krkonoše, Czech. 30 A8 50 50N 15 35 E
Krnov, Czech. 31 A10 50 5N 17 40 E
Krobia, Poland 47 D3 51 47N 16 59 E
Kročehlavy, Czech. 30 A7 50 8N 14 9 E
Krokeaí, Greece 45 H4 36 53N 22 32 E
Krokodil →, Mozam. 105 D5 25 14 S 32 18 E
Krokom, Sweden 14 A8 63 20N 14 30 E
Krokowa, Poland 47 A5 54 47N 18 9 E
Krolevets, U.S.S.R. 50 F8 51 35N 33 20 E
Kroměříz, Czech. 31 B10 49 18N 17 21 E
Krommenie, Neths. 20 D5 52 30N 4 46 E
Krompachy, Czech. 31 C13 48 54N 20 52 E
Kromy, U.S.S.R. 50 E9 52 40N 35 48 E
Kronach, Germany 27 E7 50 14N 11 19 E
Kronobergs län □, Sweden 13 H13 56 45N 14 30 E
Kronprins Olav Kyst, Antarctica 7 C5 69 0 S 42 0 E
Kronshtadt, U.S.S.R. 50 A6 60 5N 29 45 E
Kroonstad, S. Africa 104 D4 27 43 S 27 19 E
Kröpelin, Germany 26 A7 54 4N 11 48 E
Kropotkin, R.S.F.S.R., U.S.S.R. 53 D9 45 28N 40 28 E
Kropotkin, R.S.F.S.R., U.S.S.R. 57 D12 59 0N 115 30 E
Kropp, Germany 26 A5 54 24N 9 32 E
Krościenko, Poland 31 B13 49 29N 20 25 E
Krośniewice, Poland 47 C6 52 15N 19 11 E
Krosno, Poland 31 B14 49 42N 21 46 E
Krosno □, Poland 31 B15 49 35N 22 0 E
Krosno Odrzańskie, Poland 47 C2 52 3N 15 7 E
Krotoszyn, Poland 47 D4 51 42N 17 23 E
Krotovka, U.S.S.R. 54 E2 53 18N 51 10 E
Kroussón, Greece 32 D6 35 13N 24 59 E
Krraba, Albania 44 C2 41 13N 20 0 E
Krško, Yugoslavia 39 C12 45 57N 15 30 E
Krstača, Yugoslavia 42 E5 42 57N 20 8 E
Kruger Nat. Park, S. Africa 105 C5 23 30 S 31 40 E
Krugersdorp, S. Africa 105 D4 26 5 S 27 46 E
Kruiningen, Neths. 21 F4 51 27N 4 2 E
Kruisfontein, S. Africa 104 E3 33 59 S 24 43 E
Kruishoutem, Belgium 21 G3 50 54N 3 32 E
Kruisland, Neths. 21 E4 51 34N 4 25 E
Kruja, Albania 44 C1 41 32N 19 46 E
Krulevshchina, U.S.S.R. 50 D5 55 5N 27 45 E
Kruma, Albania 44 B2 42 14N 20 28 E
Krumbach, Germany 27 G6 48 15N 10 22 E
Krumovgrad, Bulgaria 43 F10 41 29N 25 38 E
Krung Thep = Bangkok, Thailand 76 F3 13 45N 100 35 E
Krupanj, Yugoslavia 42 C4 44 25N 19 22 E
Krupina, Czech. 31 C12 48 22N 19 5 E
Krupinica →, Czech. 31 C11 48 15N 18 52 E
Kruševac, Yugoslavia 42 D6 43 35N 21 28 E
Kruševo, Yugoslavia 42 F6 41 23N 21 19 E
Kruszwica, Poland 47 C5 52 40N 18 20 E
Kruzof I., U.S.A. 130 B1 57 10N 135 40W
Krymsk Abinsk, U.S.S.R. 52 D8 44 50N 38 0 E
Krymskiy Poluostrov, U.S.S.R. 52 D6 45 0N 34 0 E
Krynica, Poland 31 B13 49 25N 20 57 E
Krynica Morska, Poland 47 A6 54 23N 19 28 E
Krynki, Poland 47 B10 53 17N 23 43 E
Krzepice, Poland 47 E5 50 58N 18 50 E
Krzeszów, Poland 47 E9 50 24N 22 21 E
Krzeszowice, Poland 31 A12 50 8N 19 37 E
Krzna →, Poland 47 D9 51 59N 22 47 E
Krzywiń, Poland 47 D3 51 58N 16 50 E
Krzyż, Poland 47 C3 52 52N 16 0 E
Ksabi, Morocco 98 B4 32 51N 4 13W
Ksar Chellala, Algeria 99 A5 35 13N 2 19 E
Ksar el Boukhari, Algeria 99 A5 35 51N 2 52 E
Ksar el Kebir, Morocco 98 B3 35 0N 6 0W
Ksar es Souk = Ar Rachidiya, Morocco 98 B4 31 58N 4 20W
Ksar Rhilane, Tunisia 96 B1 33 0N 9 39 E
Ksour, Mts. des, Algeria 99 B4 32 45N 0 30W
Kstovo, U.S.S.R. 51 C14 56 12N 44 13 E
Kuala, Indonesia 70 D3 2 55N 105 47 E
Kuala Berang, Malaysia 77 K4 5 5N 103 1 E
Kuala Dungun, Malaysia 77 K4 4 45N 103 25 E
Kuala Kangsar, Malaysia 77 K3 4 46N 100 56 E
Kuala Kelawang, Malaysia 77 L4 2 56N 102 5 E
Kuala Kerai, Malaysia 77 K4 5 30N 102 12 E
Kuala Kubu Baharu, Malaysia 77 L3 3 34N 101 39 E
Kuala Lipis, Malaysia 77 K4 4 10N 102 3 E
Kuala Lumpur, Malaysia 77 L3 3 9N 101 41 E
Kuala Nerang, Malaysia 77 J3 6 16N 100 37 E
Kuala Pilah, Malaysia 77 L4 2 45N 102 15 E
Kuala Rompin, Malaysia 77 L4 2 49N 103 29 E
Kuala Selangor, Malaysia 77 L3 3 20N 101 15 E
Kuala Terengganu, Malaysia 77 K4 5 20N 103 8 E
Kualajelai, Indonesia 70 E4 2 58 S 110 46 E
Kualakapuas, Indonesia 70 E4 2 55 S 114 20 E
Kualakurun, Indonesia 70 E4 1 10 S 113 50 E
Kualapembuang, Indonesia 70 E4 3 14 S 112 38 E
Kualasimpang, Indonesia 70 D1 4 17N 98 3 E
Kuancheng, China 67 D10 40 37N 118 30 E
Kuandang, Indonesia 71 D6 0 56N 123 1 E
Kuandian, China 67 D13 40 45N 124 45 E
Kuangchou = Guangzhou, China 69 F9 23 5N 113 10 E
Kuantan, Malaysia 77 L4 3 49N 103 20 E
Kuba, U.S.S.R. 53 F13 41 21N 48 32 E
Kuban →, U.S.S.R. 52 D7 45 20N 37 30 E
Kubenskoye, Oz., U.S.S.R. 51 B11 59 40N 39 25 E
Kuberle, U.S.S.R. 53 C10 47 0N 42 20 E
Kubokawa, Japan 62 D5 33 12N 133 8 E
Kubor, Mt., Papua N. G. 120 D3 6 10 S 144 44 E
Kubrat, Bulgaria 43 D11 43 49N 26 31 E
Kučevo, Yugoslavia 42 C6 44 30N 21 40 E
Kucha Gompa, India 81 B7 34 25N 76 56 E
Kuchaman, India 80 F6 27 13N 74 47 E
Kuchenspitze, Austria 30 D3 47 7N 10 12 E
Kuchino-eruba-Jima, Japan 61 J5 30 28N 130 12 E
Kuchino-Shima, Japan 61 K4 29 57N 129 55 E
Kuchinotsu, Japan 62 E2 32 36N 130 11 E
Kucing, Malaysia 70 D4 1 33N 110 25 E
Kuçove = Qytet Stalin, Albania 44 D1 40 47N 19 57 E
Kücük Kuyu, Turkey 44 E8 39 35N 26 27 E
Kud →, Pakistan 80 F2 26 5N 66 20 E
Kudalier →, India 82 E4 18 35N 79 48 E
Kudamatsu, Japan 62 D3 34 0N 131 52 E
Kudara, U.S.S.R. 55 D6 38 25N 72 39 E
Kudat, Malaysia 70 C5 6 55N 116 55 E
Kudayd, Si. Arabia 86 C3 19 21N 41 48 E
Kudremukh, India 83 H2 13 15N 75 20 E
Kudus, Indonesia 71 G14 6 48 S 110 51 E
Kudymkar, U.S.S.R. 54 B4 59 1N 54 39 E
Kueiyang = Guiyang, China 68 D6 26 32N 106 40 E
Kufstein, Austria 30 D5 47 35N 12 11 E
Kugong I., Canada 128 A4 56 18N 79 50W
Kūh-e Dīnār, Iran 85 D6 30 40N 51 0 E
Kūh-e-Hazārām, Iran 85 D8 29 35N 57 20 E
Kūhak, Iran 79 D1 27 12N 63 10 E
Kūhbonān, Iran 85 D8 31 23N 56 19 E
Kūhestak, Iran 85 E8 26 47N 57 2 E
Kūhestān, Afghan. 79 B1 34 39N 61 12 E
Kūhīn, Iran 85 C6 35 13N 48 25 E
Kūhīrī, Iran 85 E9 26 55N 61 2 E
Kuhnsdorf, Austria 30 E7 46 37N 14 38 E
Kūhpāyeh, Eşfahan, Iran 85 C7 32 44N 52 20 E
Kūhpāyeh, Kermān, Iran 85 D8 30 35N 57 15 E
Kui Buri, Thailand 77 F2 12 3N 99 52 E
Kuinre, Neths. 20 C7 52 47N 5 51 E
Kuito, Angola 103 E3 12 22 S 16 55 E
Kujang, N. Korea 67 E14 39 57N 126 1 E
Kuji, Japan 60 D10 40 11N 141 46 E
Kujū-San, Japan 62 D3 33 5N 131 15 E
Kujukuri-Heiya, Japan 63 B12 35 45N 140 30 E
Kukavica, Yugoslavia 42 E6 42 48N 21 57 E
Kukawa, Nigeria 101 C7 12 58N 13 27 E
Kukerin, Australia 113 F2 33 13 S 118 0 E
Kukësi, Albania 44 B2 42 5N 20 20 E
Kukësi □, Albania 44 B2 42 25N 20 15 E
Kukmor, U.S.S.R. 54 C2 56 11N 50 54 E
Kukup, Malaysia 77 M4 1 20N 103 27 E
Kukvidze, U.S.S.R. 51 F13 50 40N 43 15 E
Kula, Bulgaria 42 D7 43 52N 22 36 E
Kula, Yugoslavia 42 B4 45 37N 19 32 E
Kula Gulf, Solomon Is. 121 M9 8 5 S 157 18 E
Kulai, Malaysia 77 M4 1 44N 103 35 E
Kulal, Mt., Kenya 106 B4 2 42N 36 57 E
Kulaly, Os., U.S.S.R. 53 D14 45 0N 50 0 E
Kulanak, U.S.S.R. 55 C7 41 22N 75 30 E
Kulasekarappattinam, India 83 K4 8 20N 78 5 E
Kuldiga, U.S.S.R. 50 C2 56 58N 21 59 E
Kuldja = Yining, China 64 B3 43 58N 81 10 E
Kuldu, Sudan 95 E2 12 50N 28 30 E
Kulebaki, U.S.S.R. 51 D13 55 22N 42 25 E
Kulen Vakuf, Yugoslavia 39 D13 44 35N 16 2 E
Kulgam, India 81 C6 33 36N 75 2 E
Kuli, U.S.S.R. 53 E12 42 2N 47 12 E
Kulim, Malaysia 77 K3 5 22N 100 34 E
Kulin, Australia 113 F2 32 40 S 118 2 E
Kulja, Australia 113 F2 30 28 S 117 18 E
Küllük, Turkey 45 G9 37 12N 27 36 E
Kulm, U.S.A. 138 B5 46 22N 98 58W
Kulmbach, Germany 27 E7 50 6N 11 27 E
Kulp, Turkey 89 D9 38 29N 41 2 E
Kulsary, U.S.S.R. 49 E9 46 59N 54 1 E
Kultay, U.S.S.R. 53 D14 45 5N 51 40 E
Kulti, India 81 H12 23 43N 86 50 E
Kulu, Turkey 88 D5 39 5N 33 4 E
Kulumbura, Australia 112 B4 13 55 S 126 35 E
Kulunda, U.S.S.R. 56 D8 52 35N 78 57 E
Kulungar, Afghan. 80 C3 34 0N 69 2 E
Kūlvand, Iran 85 D7 31 21N 54 35 E
Kulwin, Australia 116 C5 35 0 S 142 42 E
Kulyab, U.S.S.R. 55 E4 37 55N 69 50 E
Kum Tekei, U.S.S.R. 56 E8 43 10N 79 30 E
Kuma, Japan 62 D4 33 39N 132 54 E
Kuma →, U.S.S.R. 53 D12 44 55N 47 0 E
Kumaganum, Nigeria 101 C7 13 8N 10 38 E
Kumagaya, Japan 63 A11 36 9N 139 22 E
Kumai, Indonesia 70 E4 2 44 S 111 43 E
Kumak, U.S.S.R. 54 F7 51 10N 60 8 E
Kumamba, Kepulauan, Indonesia 71 E9 1 36 S 138 45 E
Kumamoto, Japan 62 E2 32 45N 130 45 E
Kumamoto □, Japan 62 E2 32 55N 130 55 E
Kumano, Japan 63 D8 33 54N 136 5 E
Kumano-Nada, Japan 63 D8 33 47N 136 20 E
Kumanovo, Yugoslavia 42 E6 42 9N 21 42 E
Kumara, N.Z. 119 C6 42 37 S 171 12 E
Kumarkhali, Bangla. 78 D2 23 51N 89 15 E
Kumarl, Australia 113 F3 32 47 S 121 33 E
Kumasi, Ghana 100 D4 6 41N 1 38W
Kumba, Cameroon 101 E6 4 36N 9 24 E
Kumbakonam, India 83 J4 10 58N 79 25 E
Kumbarilla, Australia 115 D5 27 15 S 150 55 E
Kumbo, Cameroon 101 D7 6 15N 10 36 E
Kumbukkan Oya →, Sri Lanka 83 L5 6 35N 81 40 E
Kŭmchŏn, N. Korea 67 E14 38 10N 126 29 E
Kumdah, Si. Arabia 86 B4 20 23N 45 5 E
Kumdok, India 81 C8 33 32N 78 10 E
Kume-Shima, Japan 61 L3 26 20N 126 47 E
Kumeny, U.S.S.R. 54 B1 58 10N 49 47 E
Kumertau, U.S.S.R. 54 E4 52 46N 55 47 E
Kŭmhwa, S. Korea 67 E14 38 17N 127 28 E
Kumi, Uganda 106 B3 1 30N 33 58 E
Kumkale, Turkey 44 E8 40 0N 26 13 E
Kumla, Sweden 13 G13 59 8N 15 10 E
Kumluca, Turkey 88 E4 36 11N 30 17 E
Kummerower See, Germany 26 B8 53 47N 12 52 E
Kumo, Nigeria 101 C7 10 1N 11 12 E
Kumon Bum, Burma 78 B6 26 30N 97 15 E
Kumotori-Yama, Japan 63 B10 35 51N 138 57 E
Kumta, India 83 G2 14 29N 74 25 E
Kumtorkala, U.S.S.R. 53 E12 43 2N 46 50 E
Kumusi →, Papua N. G. 120 E5 8 16 S 148 13 E
Kumylzhenskaya, U.S.S.R. 53 B10 49 51N 42 38 E
Kunágota, Hungary 31 E14 46 26N 21 3 E
Kunama, Australia 117 C8 35 35 S 148 4 E
Kunashir, Ostrov, U.S.S.R. 57 E15 44 0N 146 0 E
Kunda, U.S.S.R. 50 B5 59 30N 26 34 E
Kundiawa, Papua N. G. 120 D3 6 2 S 145 1 E
Kundla, India 80 J4 21 21N 71 25 E
Kundur, Indonesia 74 C3 3 8 S 107 48 E
Kungala, Australia 115 D5 29 58 S 153 7 E
Kungälv, Sweden 15 G5 57 53N 11 59 E
Kungey Alatau, Khrebet, U.S.S.R. 55 B8 42 50N 77 0 E
Kunghit I., Canada 130 C2 52 6N 131 3W
Kungrad, U.S.S.R. 56 E6 43 6N 58 54 E
Kungsbacka, Sweden 15 G6 57 30N 12 5 E
Kungu, Zaïre 102 B3 2 47N 19 12 E
Kungur, U.S.S.R. 54 C5 57 25N 56 57 E
Kungurri, Australia 114 C4 21 3 S 148 46 E
Kungyangon, Burma 78 G6 16 27N 96 20 E
Kunhar →, Pakistan 81 B5 34 20N 73 30 E
Kunhegyes, Hungary 31 D13 47 22N 20 36 E
Kunimi-Dake, Japan 62 E3 32 33N 131 1 E
Kuningan, Indonesia 71 G13 6 59 S 108 29 E
Kunisaki, Japan 62 D3 33 33N 131 45 E
Kunlara, Australia 116 C3 34 54 S 139 55 E
Kunlong, Burma 78 D7 23 20N 98 50 E
Kunlun Shan, Asia 64 C3 36 0N 86 30 E
Kunmadaras, Hungary 31 D13 47 28N 20 45 E
Kunming, China 68 E4 25 1N 102 41 E
Kunnamkulam, India 83 J3 10 38N 76 7 E
Kunrade, Neths. 21 G7 50 53N 5 57 E
Kunsan, S. Korea 67 G14 35 59N 126 45 E
Kunshan, China 69 B13 31 22N 120 58 E
Kunszentmárton, Hungary 31 E13 46 50N 20 20 E
Kununurra, Australia 112 C4 15 40 S 128 50 E
Kunwarara, Australia 114 C5 22 55 S 150 9 E
Kunya-Urgench, U.S.S.R. 56 E6 42 19N 59 10 E
Künzelsau, Germany 27 F5 49 17N 9 41 E
Kuopio, Finland 12 E19 62 53N 27 35 E
Kuopion lääni □, Finland 12 E19 63 25N 27 10 E
Kupa →, Yugoslavia 39 C13 45 28N 16 24 E
Kupang, Indonesia 71 F6 10 19 S 123 39 E
Kupiano, Papua N. G. 120 F4 10 4 S 148 14 E
Kupres, Yugoslavia 42 C2 44 1N 17 15 E
Kupyansk, U.S.S.R. 52 B7 49 52N 37 35 E
Kupyansk-Uzlovoi, U.S.S.R. 52 B7 49 45N 37 34 E
Kuqa, China 64 B3 41 35N 82 30 E
Kur →, Bhutan 78 B3 26 50N 91 0 E
Kura →, U.S.S.R. 53 G13 39 50N 49 20 E
Kurahashi-Jima, Japan 62 C4 34 8N 132 31 E
Kuranda, Australia 114 B4 16 48 S 145 35 E
Kurashiki, Japan 62 C5 34 40N 133 50 E
Kurayoshi, Japan 62 B5 35 26N 133 50 E
Kurday, U.S.S.R. 55 B7 43 21N 74 59 E
Kurdistan, Asia 89 E10 37 20N 43 30 E
Kurduvadi, India 82 E2 18 8N 75 29 E
Kŭrdzhali, Bulgaria 43 F10 41 38N 25 21 E
Kure, Japan 62 C4 34 14N 132 32 E
Küre, Turkey 88 C5 41 48N 33 43 E
Küre Dağları, Turkey 88 C6 41 50N 34 10 E
Kuressaare, U.S.S.R. 50 B3 58 15N 22 30 E
Kurgaldzhino, U.S.S.R. 56 D8 50 35N 70 20 E
Kurgan, U.S.S.R. 54 D9 55 26N 65 18 E
Kurgan-Tyube, U.S.S.R. 55 E4 37 50N 68 47 E
Kurganinsk, U.S.S.R. 53 D9 44 54N 40 34 E
Kurgannaya = Kurganinsk, U.S.S.R. 53 D9 44 54N 40 34 E
Kuria Maria Is. = Khūrīyā Mūrīyā, Jazā 'ir, Oman 87 C6 17 30N 55 58 E
Kuria Muria B., Oman 87 C6 17 40N 55 45 E
Kurichchi, India 83 J3 11 36N 77 35 E
Kuridala, Australia 114 C3 21 16 S 140 29 E
Kurigram, Bangla. 78 C2 25 49N 89 39 E
Kurihashi, Japan 63 A11 36 8N 139 42 E
Kuril Is. = Kurilskiye Ostrova, U.S.S.R. 57 E16 45 0N 150 0 E
Kuril Trench, Pac. Oc. 122 C7 44 0N 153 0 E
Kurilsk, U.S.S.R. 57 E15 45 14N 147 53 E
Kurilskiye Ostrova, U.S.S.R. 57 E16 45 0N 150 0 E
Kuringen, Belgium 21 G6 50 56N 5 18 E
Kurino, Japan 62 F2 31 57N 130 43 E
Kurkur, Egypt 94 C3 23 50N 32 0 E
Kurkūrah, Libya 96 B4 31 30N 20 1 E
Kurla, India 82 E1 19 5N 72 52 E
Kurlovskiy, U.S.S.R. 51 D12 55 25N 40 40 E
Kurmuk, Sudan 95 E3 10 33N 34 21 E
Kurnool, India 83 G4 15 45N 78 0 E
Kuro-Shima, Kagoshima, Japan 61 J4 30 50N 129 57 E
Kuro-Shima, Okinawa, Japan 61 M2 24 14N 124 1 E
Kurobe-Gawe →, Japan 63 A9 36 55N 137 25 E
Kurogi, Japan 62 D2 33 12N 130 40 E
Kurovskoye, U.S.S.R. 51 D11 55 35N 38 55 E
Kurow, N.Z. 119 E5 44 44 S 170 29 E
Kurów, Poland 47 D9 51 23N 22 12 E
Kurrajong, Australia 117 B9 33 33 S 150 42 E
Kurram →, Pakistan 79 B3 32 36N 71 20 E
Kurri Kurri, Australia 117 B9 32 50 S 151 28 E
Kursavka, U.S.S.R. 53 D10 44 29N 42 32 E
Kuršenai, U.S.S.R. 50 C3 56 1N 23 3 E
Kursk, U.S.S.R. 51 F10 51 42N 36 11 E
Kuršumlija, Yugoslavia 42 D6 43 9N 21 19 E
Kuršumlijska Banja, Yugoslavia 42 D6 43 3N 21 11 E
Kurşunlu, Turkey 88 C5 40 51N 33 15 E
Kurtalan, Turkey 89 E9 37 56N 41 44 E
Kurtamysh, U.S.S.R. 54 D9 54 55N 64 27 E
Kurty →, U.S.S.R. 55 A8 44 16N 76 42 E
Kuru, Bahr el →, Sudan 95 F2 8 10N 26 50 E
Kurucaşile, Turkey 88 C5 41 49N 32 42 E
Kuruktag, China 64 B3 41 0N 89 0 E
Kuruman, S. Africa 104 D3 27 28 S 23 28 E
Kuruman →, S. Africa 104 D3 26 56 S 20 39 E
Kurume, Japan 62 D2 33 15N 130 30 E
Kurunegala, Sri Lanka 83 L5 7 30N 80 23 E
Kurupukari, Guyana 153 C6 4 43N 58 37W
Kurya, U.S.S.R. 57 C11 61 15N 108 10 E
Kus Gölü, Turkey 88 C2 40 10N 27 55 E
Kusa, U.S.S.R. 54 D6 55 20N 59 29 E
Kuşada Körfezi, Turkey 45 G9 37 56N 27 0 E
Kuşadası, Turkey 45 G9 37 52N 27 15 E
Kusatsu, Gumma, Japan 63 A10 36 37N 138 36 E
Kusatsu, Shiga, Japan 63 C7 34 58N 135 57 E
Kusawa L., Canada 130 A1 60 20N 136 13W
Kusel, Germany 27 F3 49 31N 7 25 E
Kushchevskaya, U.S.S.R. 53 C8 46 33N 39 35 E
Kushikino, Japan 62 F2 31 44N 130 16 E
Kushima, Japan 62 F3 31 29N 131 14 E
Kushimoto, Japan 63 D7 33 28N 135 47 E
Kushiro, Japan 60 C12 43 0N 144 25 E
Kushiro →, Japan 60 C12 42 59N 144 23 E
Kūshk, Iran 85 D8 28 46N 56 51 E
Kushka, U.S.S.R. 56 F7 35 20N 62 18 E
Kūshkī, Īlām, Iran 84 C5 33 31N 47 13 E
Kūshkī, Khorāsān, Iran 85 B8 37 2N 57 26 E
Kūshkū, Iran 85 E7 27 19N 53 28 E
Kushmurun, U.S.S.R. 54 E9 52 27N 64 36 E
Kushmurun, Ozero, U.S.S.R. 54 E9 52 40N 64 48 E
Kushnarenkovo, U.S.S.R. 54 D4 55 6N 55 22 E
Kushol, India 81 C7 33 40N 76 36 E
Kushrabat, U.S.S.R. 55 C3 40 18N 66 32 E
Kushtia, Bangla. 78 D2 23 55N 89 5 E
Kushum →, U.S.S.R. 53 B14 49 0N 50 20 E
Kushva, U.S.S.R. 54 B6 58 18N 59 45 E
Kuskokwim →, U.S.A. 126 B3 60 17N 162 27W
Kuskokwim Bay, U.S.A. 126 C3 59 50N 162 56W
Küsnacht, Switz. 29 B7 47 19N 8 35 E
Kussharo-Ko, Japan 60 C12 43 38N 144 21 E
Küssnacht, Switz. 29 B6 47 5N 8 26 E
Kustanay, U.S.S.R. 54 E8 53 10N 63 35 E
Kusu, Japan 62 D3 33 16N 131 9 E
Kut, Ko, Thailand 77 G4 11 40N 102 35 E
Kutacane, Indonesia 74 B1 3 50N 97 50 E
Kütahya, Turkey 88 D4 39 30N 30 2 E
Kütahya □, Turkey 88 D3 39 10N 29 30 E
Kutaisi, U.S.S.R. 53 E10 42 19N 42 40 E
Kutaraja = Banda Aceh, Indonesia 70 C1 5 35N 95 20 E
Kutch, Gulf of = Kachchh, Gulf of, India 80 H3 22 50N 69 15 E

Lachen 221

Kutch, Rann of = Kachchh, Rann of, *India* **80 H4** 24 0N 70 0 E
Kutina, *Yugoslavia* **39 C13** 45 29N 16 48 E
Kutiyana, *India* **80 J4** 21 36N 70 2 E
Kutjevo, *Yugoslavia* **42 B2** 45 23N 17 55 E
Kutkai, *Burma* **78 D6** 23 27N 97 56 E
Kutkashen, *U.S.S.R.* **53 F12** 40 58N 47 47 E
Kutná Hora, *Czech.* **30 B8** 49 57N 15 16 E
Kutno, *Poland* **47 C6** 52 15N 19 23 E
Kuttabul, *Australia* **114 C4** 21 5 S 148 48 E
Kutu, *Zaïre* **102 C3** 2 40 S 18 11 E
Kutum, *Sudan* **95 E1** 14 10N 24 40 E
Kúty, *Czech.* **31 C10** 48 40N 17 3 E
Kuujjuaq, *Canada* **127 C13** 58 6N 68 15W
Kuŭp-tong, *N. Korea* **67 D14** 40 45N 126 1 E
Kuurne, *Belgium* **21 G2** 50 51N 3 18 E
Kuvandyk, *U.S.S.R.* **54 F5** 51 28N 57 21 E
Kuvango, *Angola* **103 E3** 14 28 S 16 20 E
Kuvasay, *U.S.S.R.* **55 C5** 40 18N 71 59 E
Kuvshinovo, *U.S.S.R.* **50 C9** 57 2N 34 11 E
Kuwait = Al Kuwayt, *Kuwait* **84 D5** 29 30N 48 0 E
Kuwait ■, *Asia* **84 D5** 29 30N 47 30 E
Kuwana, *Japan* **63 B8** 35 5N 136 43 E
Kuybyshev, *R.S.F.S.R., U.S.S.R.* **51 E17** 53 8N 50 6 E
Kuybyshev, *R.S.F.S.R., U.S.S.R.* **56 D8** 55 27N 78 19 E
Kuybyshevo, *Ukraine S.S.R., U.S.S.R.* **52 C7** 47 25N 36 40 E
Kuybyshevo, *Uzbek S.S.R., U.S.S.R.* **55 C5** 40 20N 71 15 E
Kuybyshevskiy, *U.S.S.R.* **55 E4** 37 52N 68 44 E
Kuybyshevskoye Vdkhr., *U.S.S.R.* **51 D16** 55 2N 49 30 E
Kuye He →, *China* **66 E6** 38 23N 110 46 E
Kūyeh, *Iran* **84 B5** 38 45N 47 57 E
Kuylyuk, *U.S.S.R.* **55 C4** 41 14N 69 17 E
Kūysanjaq, *Iraq* **84 B5** 36 5N 44 38 E
Kuyto, Oz., *U.S.S.R.* **48 B5** 64 40N 31 0 E
Kuyumba, *U.S.S.R.* **57 C10** 60 58N 96 59 E
Kuzey Anadolu Dağları, *Turkey* **88 C6** 41 30N 35 0 E
Kuzhithurai, *India* **83 K3** 8 18N 77 11 E
Kuzino, *U.S.S.R.* **54 C6** 57 1N 59 27 E
Kuzmin, *Yugoslavia* **42 B4** 45 2N 19 25 E
Kuznetsk, *U.S.S.R.* **51 E15** 53 12N 46 40 E
Kuzomen, *U.S.S.R.* **48 A6** 66 22N 36 50 E
Kvænangen, *Norway* **12 A16** 70 5N 21 15 E
Kvam, *Norway* **14 C3** 61 40N 9 42 E
Kvareli, *U.S.S.R.* **53 F11** 41 27N 45 47 E
Kvarner, *Yugoslavia* **39 D11** 44 50N 14 10 E
Kvarnerič, *Yugoslavia* **39 D11** 44 43N 14 37 E
Kviteseid, *Norway* **14 E2** 59 24N 8 29 E
Kwabhaca, *S. Africa* **105 E4** 30 51 S 29 0 E
Kwadacha →, *Canada* **130 B3** 57 28N 125 38W
Kwakhanai, *Botswana* **104 C3** 21 39 S 21 16 E
Kwakoegron, *Surinam* **153 B6** 5 12N 55 25W
Kwale, *Kenya* **106 C4** 4 15 S 39 31 E
Kwale, *Nigeria* **101 D6** 5 46N 6 26 E
Kwale □, *Kenya* **106 C4** 4 15 S 39 10 E
KwaMashu, *S. Africa* **105 D5** 29 45 S 30 58 E
Kwamouth, *Zaïre* **102 C3** 3 9 S 16 12 E
Kwando →, *Africa* **103 F4** 18 27 S 23 32 E
Kwangdaeri, *N. Korea* **67 D14** 40 31N 127 32 E
Kwangju, *S. Korea* **67 G14** 35 9N 126 54 E
Kwango →, *Zaïre* **102 C3** 3 14 S 17 22 E
Kwangsi-Chuang = Guangxi Zhuangzu Zizhiqu □, *China* **68 F7** 24 0N 109 0 E
Kwangtung = Guangdong □, *China* **69 F9** 23 0N 113 0 E
Kwara □, *Nigeria* **101 D6** 8 0N 5 0 E
Kwataboahegan →, *Canada* **128 B3** 51 9N 80 50W
Kwatisore, *Indonesia* **71 E8** 3 18 S 134 50 E
Kweichow = Guizhou □, *China* **68 D6** 27 0N 107 0 E
Kwekwe, *Zimbabwe* **107 F2** 18 58 S 29 48 E
Kwidzyn, *Poland* **47 B5** 53 44N 18 55 E
Kwikila, *Papua N. G.* **120 E4** 9 49 S 147 38 E
Kwimba □, *Tanzania* **106 C3** 3 0 S 33 0 E
Kwinana New Town, *Australia* **113 F2** 32 15 S 115 47 E
Kwisa →, *Poland* **47 D2** 51 34N 15 24 E
Kwoka, *Indonesia* **71 E8** 0 31 S 132 27 E
Kya-in-Seikkyi, *Burma* **78 G7** 16 2N 98 8 E
Kyabé, *Chad* **97 G3** 9 30N 19 0 E
Kyabra Cr. →, *Australia* **115 D3** 25 36 S 142 55 E
Kyabram, *Australia* **115 F4** 36 19 S 145 4 E
Kyaiklat, *Burma* **78 G5** 16 25N 95 40 E
Kyaikmaraw, *Burma* **78 G6** 16 23N 97 44 E
Kyaikthin, *Burma* **78 D5** 23 32N 95 40 E
Kyaikto, *Burma* **76 D1** 17 20N 97 3 E
Kyakhta, *U.S.S.R.* **57 D11** 50 30N 106 25 E
Kyancutta, *Australia* **115 E2** 33 8 S 135 33 E
Kyangin, *Burma* **78 F5** 18 20N 95 20 E
Kyaukhnyat, *Burma* **78 F6** 18 15N 97 31 E
Kyaukse, *Burma* **78 E6** 21 36N 96 10 E
Kyauktaw, *Burma* **78 E4** 20 51N 92 59 E
Kyawkku, *Burma* **78 E6** 21 48N 96 56 E
Kyburz, *U.S.A.* **144 G6** 38 47N 120 18W
Kybybolite, *Australia* **116 D4** 36 53 S 140 55 E
Kyeintali, *Burma* **78 G5** 18 0N 94 29 E
Kyenjojo, *Uganda* **106 B3** 0 40N 30 37 E
Kyidaunggan, *Burma* **78 F6** 19 53N 96 12 E
Kyle Dam, *Zimbabwe* **107 G3** 20 15 S 31 0 E
Kyle of Lochalsh, *U.K.* **18 D3** 57 17N 5 43W
Kyll →, *Germany* **27 F2** 49 48N 6 42 E
Kyllburg, *Germany* **27 E2** 50 2N 6 35 E
Kyneton, *Australia* **116 D6** 37 10 S 144 29 E
Kynuna, *Australia* **114 C3** 21 37 S 141 55 E
Kyō-ga-Saki, *Japan* **63 B7** 35 45N 135 15 E
Kyoga, L., *Uganda* **106 B3** 1 35N 33 0 E
Kyogle, *Australia* **115 D5** 28 40 S 153 0 E
Kyongju, *S. Korea* **67 G15** 35 51N 129 14 E
Kyŏngsŏng, *N. Korea* **67 D15** 41 35N 129 36 E
Kyōto, *Japan* **63 C7** 35 0N 135 45 E
Kyōto □, *Japan* **63 B7** 35 15N 135 45 E
Kyparissovouno, *Cyprus* **32 D12** 35 19N 33 10 E
Kyperounda, *Cyprus* **32 E11** 34 56N 32 58 E
Kyren, *U.S.S.R.* **57 D11** 51 45N 101 45 E
Kyrenia, *Cyprus* **32 D12** 35 20N 33 20 E
Kyritz, *Germany* **26 C8** 52 57N 12 25 E
Kyshtym, *U.S.S.R.* **54 D7** 55 42N 60 34 E
Kystatyam, *U.S.S.R.* **57 C13** 67 20N 123 10 E
Kytal Ktakh, *U.S.S.R.* **57 C13** 65 30N 123 40 E
Kythréa, *Cyprus* **32 D12** 35 15N 33 29 E
Kytlym, *U.S.S.R.* **54 B6** 59 30N 59 12 E
Kyu-hkok, *Burma* **78 C7** 24 4N 98 4 E
Kyulyunken, *U.S.S.R.* **57 C14** 64 10N 137 5 E
Kyunhla, *Burma* **78 D5** 23 25N 95 15 E
Kyuquot, *Canada* **130 C3** 50 3N 127 25W
Kyurdamir, *U.S.S.R.* **53 F13** 40 25N 48 3 E
Kyūshū, *Japan* **62 E3** 33 0N 131 0 E
Kyūshū □, *Japan* **62 E3** 33 0N 131 0 E
Kyūshū-Sanchi, *Japan* **62 E3** 32 35N 131 17 E
Kyustendil, *Bulgaria* **42 E7** 42 16N 22 41 E
Kyusyur, *U.S.S.R.* **57 B13** 70 39N 127 15 E
Kywong, *Australia* **117 C7** 34 58 S 146 44 E
Kyzyl, *U.S.S.R.* **57 D10** 51 50N 94 30 E
Kyzyl-Kiya, *U.S.S.R.* **55 C6** 40 16N 72 8 E
Kyzylkum, Peski, *U.S.S.R.* **55 B2** 42 30N 65 0 E
Kyzylsu →, *U.S.S.R.* **55 D6** 39 11N 72 2 E
Kzyl-Orda, *U.S.S.R.* **55 A2** 44 48N 65 28 E

L

La Albuera, *Spain* **37 G4** 38 45N 6 49W
La Alcarria, *Spain* **34 E2** 40 31N 2 45W
La Algaba, *Spain* **37 H4** 37 27N 6 1W
La Almarcha, *Spain* **34 F2** 39 41N 2 24W
La Almunia de Doña Godina, *Spain* **34 D3** 41 29N 1 23W
La Asunción, *Venezuela* **153 A5** 11 2N 63 53W
La Banda, *Argentina* **158 B3** 27 45 S 64 10W
La Bañeza, *Spain* **36 C5** 42 17N 5 54W
La Barca, *Mexico* **146 C4** 20 20N 102 40W
La Barge, *U.S.A.* **142 E8** 42 12N 110 4W
La Bassée, *France* **23 B9** 50 31N 2 49 E
La Bastide-Puylaurent, *France* **24 D7** 44 35N 3 55 E
La Baule, *France* **22 E4** 47 17N 2 24W
La Belle, *Fla., U.S.A.* **135 M5** 26 45N 81 22W
La Belle, *Mo., U.S.A.* **140 D5** 40 7N 91 55W
La Biche →, *Canada* **130 B4** 59 57N 123 50W
La Bisbal, *Spain* **34 D8** 41 58N 3 2 E
La Blanquilla, *Venezuela* **153 A5** 11 51N 64 37W
La Bomba, *Mexico* **146 A1** 31 53N 115 2W
La Bresse, *France* **23 D13** 48 2N 6 53 E
La Bureba, *Spain* **34 C1** 42 36N 3 24W
La Cal →, *Bolivia* **157 D6** 17 27 S 58 15W
La Calera, *Chile* **158 C1** 32 50 S 71 10W
La Campiña, *Spain* **37 H6** 37 45N 4 45W
La Canal, *Spain* **33 C7** 38 51N 1 23 E
La Cañiza, *Spain* **36 C2** 42 13N 8 16W
La Capelle, *France* **23 C10** 49 59N 3 50 E
La Carlota, *Argentina* **158 C3** 33 30 S 63 20W
La Carolina, *Spain* **37 G7** 38 17N 3 38W
La Cavalerie, *France* **24 D7** 44 1N 3 10 E
La Ceiba, *Honduras* **148 C2** 15 40N 86 50W
La Chaise-Dieu, *France* **24 C7** 45 18N 3 42 E
La Chaize-le-Vicomte, *France* **22 F5** 46 40N 1 18W
La Chapelle d'Angillon, *France* **23 E9** 47 21N 2 25 E
La Chapelle-Glain, *France* **22 E5** 47 38N 1 11W
La Charité-sur-Loire, *France* **23 E10** 47 10N 3 1 E
La Chartre-sur-le-Loir, *France* **22 E7** 47 44N 0 34 E
La Châtaigneraie, *France* **24 B3** 46 39N 0 44W
La Châtre, *France* **24 B6** 46 35N 2 0 E
La Chaux de Fonds, *Switz.* **28 B3** 47 7N 6 50 E
La Chorrera, *Colombia* **152 D3** 0 44 S 73 1W
La Ciotat, *France* **25 E9** 43 10N 5 37 E
La Clayette, *France* **25 B8** 46 17N 4 19 E
La Cocha, *Argentina* **158 B2** 27 50 S 65 40W
La Concepción = Ri-Aba, *Eq. Guin.* **101 E6** 3 28N 8 40 E
La Concepción, *Venezuela* **152 A3** 10 30N 71 50W
La Concordia, *Mexico* **147 D6** 16 8N 92 38W
La Conner, *U.S.A.* **142 B2** 48 22N 122 27W
La Coruña, *Spain* **36 B2** 43 20N 8 25W
La Coruña □, *Spain* **36 B2** 43 10N 8 30W
La Côte, *Switz.* **28 D2** 46 25N 6 15 E
La Côte-St.-André, *France* **25 C9** 45 24N 5 15 E
La Courtine-le-Trucq, *France* **24 C6** 45 41N 2 15 E
La Crau, *France* **25 E8** 43 32N 4 40 E
La Crete, *Canada* **130 B5** 58 11N 116 24W
La Crosse, *Kans., U.S.A.* **138 F5** 38 33N 99 20W
La Crosse, *Wis., U.S.A.* **138 D9** 43 48N 91 13W
La Cruz, *Costa Rica* **148 D2** 11 4N 85 39W
La Cruz, *Mexico* **146 C3** 23 55N 106 54W
La Dorada, *Colombia* **152 B3** 5 30N 74 40W
La Ensenada, *Chile* **160 B2** 41 12 S 72 33W
La Escondida, *Mexico* **146 C5** 24 6N 99 55W
La Esmeralda, *Paraguay* **158 A3** 22 16 S 62 33W
La Esperanza, *Argentina* **160 B3** 40 26 S 68 32W
La Esperanza, *Cuba* **148 B3** 22 46N 83 44W
La Esperanza, *Honduras* **148 D2** 14 15N 88 10W
La Estrada, *Spain* **36 C2** 42 43N 8 27W
La Fayette, *U.S.A.* **135 H3** 34 44N 85 15W
La Fé, *Cuba* **148 B3** 22 2N 84 15W
La Fère, *France* **23 C10** 49 39N 3 21 E
La Ferté-Bernard, *France* **22 D7** 48 10N 0 40 E
La Ferté-Macé, *France* **22 D6** 48 35N 0 22W
La Ferté-St.-Aubin, *France* **23 E8** 47 42N 1 57 E
La Ferté-sous-Jouarre, *France* **23 D10** 48 56N 3 8 E
La Ferté-Vidame, *France* **22 D7** 48 37N 0 53 E
La Flèche, *France* **22 E6** 47 42N 0 4W
La Foa, *N. Cal.* **121 U19** 21 43 S 165 50 E
La Follette, *U.S.A.* **135 G3** 36 23N 84 9W
La Fontaine, *U.S.A.* **141 D11** 40 40N 85 43W
La Fregeneda, *Spain* **36 E4** 40 58N 6 54W
La Fría, *Venezuela* **152 B3** 8 13N 72 15W
La Fuente de San Esteban, *Spain* **36 E4** 40 49N 6 15W
La Gineta, *Spain* **35 F2** 39 8N 2 1W
La Gloria, *Colombia* **152 B3** 8 37N 73 48W
La Gran Sabana, *Venezuela* **153 B5** 5 30N 61 30W
La Grand-Combe, *France* **25 D8** 44 13N 4 2 E
La Grande, *U.S.A.* **142 D4** 45 15N 118 10W
La Grande-Motte, *France* **25 E8** 43 23N 4 5 E
La Grange, *U.S.A.* **144 H6** 37 42N 120 27W
La Grange, *Ga., U.S.A.* **135 J3** 33 4N 85 0W
La Grange, *Ky., U.S.A.* **134 F3** 38 20N 85 20W
La Grange, *Mo., U.S.A.* **140 D5** 40 3N 91 35W
La Grange, *Tex., U.S.A.* **139 L6** 29 54N 96 52W
La Grita, *Venezuela* **152 B3** 8 8N 71 59W
La Guaira, *Venezuela* **152 A4** 10 36N 66 56W
La Guardia, *Spain* **36 D2** 41 56N 8 52W
La Gudiña, *Spain* **36 C3** 42 4N 7 8W
La Güera, *Mauritania* **98 D1** 20 51N 17 0W
La Guerche-de-Bretagne, *France* **22 E5** 47 57N 1 16W
La Guerche-sur-l'Aubois, *France* **23 F9** 46 58N 2 56 E
La Habana, *Cuba* **148 B3** 23 8N 82 22W
La Harpe, *U.S.A.* **140 D6** 40 30N 91 0W
La Haye-du-Puits, *France* **22 C5** 49 17N 1 33W
La Horqueta, *Venezuela* **153 B5** 7 55N 60 20W
La Horra, *Spain* **36 D7** 41 44N 3 53W
La Independencia, *Mexico* **147 D6** 16 31N 91 47W
La Isabela, *Dom. Rep.* **149 C5** 19 58N 71 2W
La Jara, *U.S.A.* **143 H11** 37 16N 106 0W
La Joya, *Peru* **156 D3** 16 43 S 71 52W
La Junquera, *Spain* **34 C7** 42 25N 2 53 E
La Junta, *U.S.A.* **139 F3** 38 5N 103 30W
La Laguna, *Canary Is.* **33 F3** 28 28N 16 18W
La Libertad, *Guatemala* **148 C1** 16 47N 90 7W
La Libertad, *Mexico* **146 B2** 29 55N 112 41W
La Libertad □, *Peru* **156 B2** 8 0 S 78 30W
La Ligua, *Chile* **158 C1** 32 30 S 71 16W
La Línea de la Concepción, *Spain* **37 J5** 36 15N 5 23W
La Loche, *Canada* **131 B7** 56 29N 109 26W
La Londe-les-Maures, *France* **25 E10** 43 8N 6 14 E
La Lora, *Spain* **36 C7** 42 45N 4 0W
La Loupe, *France* **22 D8** 48 29N 1 1 E
La Louvière, *Belgium* **21 H4** 50 27N 4 10 E
La Machine, *France* **23 F10** 46 54N 3 27 E
La Maddalena, *Italy* **40 A2** 41 13N 9 25 E
La Malbaie, *Canada* **129 C5** 47 40N 70 10W
La Mancha, *Spain* **35 F2** 39 10N 2 54W
La Mariña, *Spain* **36 B3** 43 30N 7 40W
La Mesa, *Calif., U.S.A.* **145 N9** 32 48N 117 5W
La Mesa, *N. Mex., U.S.A.* **143 K10** 32 6N 106 48W
La Misión, *Mexico* **146 A1** 32 5N 116 50W
La Moille, *U.S.A.* **140 C7** 41 32N 89 17W
La Moine →, *U.S.A.* **140 E6** 39 58N 90 32W
La Monte, *U.S.A.* **140 F3** 38 47N 93 27W
La Mothe-Achard, *France* **22 F5** 46 37N 1 40W
La Motte, *France* **25 D10** 44 20N 6 3 E
La Motte-Chalançon, *France* **25 D9** 44 30N 5 21 E
La Moure, *U.S.A.* **138 B5** 46 27N 98 17W
La Muela, *Spain* **34 D3** 41 36N 1 7W
La Mure, *France* **25 D9** 44 55N 5 48 E
La Negra, *Chile* **158 A1** 23 46 S 70 18W
La Neuveville, *Switz.* **28 B4** 47 4N 7 6 E
La Oliva, *Canary Is.* **33 F6** 28 36N 13 57W
La Oraya, *Peru* **156 C2** 11 32 S 75 54W
La Orotava, *Canary Is.* **33 F3** 28 22N 16 31W
La Pacaudière, *France* **24 B7** 46 11N 3 52 E
La Palma, *Canary Is.* **33 F2** 28 40N 17 50W
La Palma, *Panama* **148 E4** 8 15N 78 0W
La Palma, *Spain* **37 H4** 37 21N 6 38W
La Paloma, *Chile* **158 C1** 30 35 S 71 0W
La Pampa □, *Argentina* **158 D2** 36 50 S 66 0W
La Paragua, *Venezuela* **153 B5** 6 50N 63 20W
La Paz, *Entre Ríos, Argentina* **158 C4** 30 50 S 59 45W
La Paz, *San Luis, Argentina* **158 C2** 33 30 S 67 20W
La Paz, *Bolivia* **156 D4** 16 20 S 68 10W
La Paz, *Honduras* **148 D2** 14 20N 87 47W
La Paz, *Mexico* **146 C2** 24 10N 110 20W
La Paz □, *Bolivia* **156 D4** 15 30 S 68 0W
La Paz Centro, *Nic.* **148 D2** 12 20N 86 41W
La Pedrera, *Colombia* **152 D4** 1 18 S 69 43W
La Perouse Str., *Asia* **60 B11** 45 40N 142 0 E
La Pesca, *Mexico* **147 C5** 23 46N 97 47W
La Piedad, *Mexico* **146 C4** 20 20N 102 1W
La Pine, *U.S.A.* **142 E3** 43 40N 121 30W
La Plant, *U.S.A.* **138 C4** 45 11N 100 40W
La Plata, *Argentina* **158 D4** 35 0 S 57 55W
La Plata, *Colombia* **152 C2** 2 23N 75 53W
La Plata, *U.S.A.* **140 D4** 40 2N 92 29W
La Plata, L., *Argentina* **160 B2** 44 55 S 71 50W
La Pobla de Lillet, *Spain* **34 C6** 42 16N 1 59 E
La Pola de Gordón, *Spain* **36 C5** 42 51N 5 41W
La Porte, *U.S.A.* **141 C10** 41 36N 86 43W
La Porte City, *U.S.A.* **140 B4** 42 19N 92 12W
La Puebla, *Spain* **34 F8** 39 46N 3 1 E
La Puebla de Cazalla, *Spain* **37 H5** 37 10N 5 20W
La Puebla de los Infantes, *Spain* **37 H5** 37 47N 5 24W
La Puebla de Montalbán, *Spain* **36 F6** 39 52N 4 22W
La Puerta, *Spain* **35 G2** 38 22N 2 45W
La Punt, *Switz.* **29 C9** 46 35N 9 56 E
La Purísima, *Mexico* **146 B2** 26 10N 112 4W
La Push, *U.S.A.* **144 C2** 47 55N 124 38W
La Quiaca, *Argentina* **158 A2** 22 5 S 65 35W
La Rambla, *Spain* **37 H6** 37 37N 4 45W
La Reine, *Canada* **128 C4** 48 50N 79 30W
La Réole, *France* **24 D3** 44 35N 0 1W
La Restinga, *Canary Is.* **33 G2** 27 38N 17 59W
La Rioja, *Argentina* **158 B2** 29 20 S 67 0W
La Rioja □, *Argentina* **158 B2** 29 30 S 67 0W
La Rioja □, *Spain* **34 C2** 42 20N 2 20W
La Robla, *Spain* **36 C5** 42 50N 5 41W
La Roche, *Switz.* **28 C4** 46 42N 7 7 E
La Roche-Bernard, *France* **22 E4** 47 31N 2 19W
La Roche-Canillac, *France* **24 C5** 45 12N 1 57 E
La Roche-en-Ardenne, *Belgium* **21 H7** 50 11N 5 35 E
La Roche-sur-Yon, *France* **22 F5** 46 40N 1 25W
La Rochefoucauld, *France* **24 C4** 45 44N 0 24 E
La Rochelle, *France* **24 B2** 46 10N 1 9W
La Roda, *Albacete, Spain* **35 F2** 39 13N 2 15W
La Roda, *Sevilla, Spain* **37 H6** 37 12N 4 46W
La Romana, *Dom. Rep.* **149 C6** 18 27N 68 57W
La Ronge, *Canada* **131 B7** 55 5N 105 20W
La Rue, *U.S.A.* **141 D13** 40 35N 83 23W
La Rumorosa, *Mexico* **145 N10** 32 33N 116 4W
La Sabina, *Spain* **33 C7** 38 44N 1 25 E
La Sagra, *Spain* **35 H2** 37 57N 2 35W
La Salle, *U.S.A.* **140 C7** 41 20N 89 6W
La Sanabria, *Spain* **36 D4** 42 0N 6 30W
La Santa, *Canary Is.* **33 E6** 29 5N 13 40W
La Sarraz, *Switz.* **28 C3** 46 38N 6 32 E
La Sarre, *Canada* **128 C4** 48 45N 79 15W
La Scie, *Canada* **129 C8** 49 57N 55 36W
La Selva, *Spain* **34 D7** 42 0N 2 45 E
La Selva Beach, *U.S.A.* **144 J5** 36 56N 121 51W
La Serena, *Chile* **158 B1** 29 55 S 71 10W
La Serena, *Spain* **37 G5** 38 45N 5 40W
La Seyne, *France* **25 E9** 43 7N 5 52 E
La Sila, *Italy* **41 C9** 39 15N 16 35 E
La Solana, *Spain* **35 G1** 38 59N 3 14W
La Souterraine, *France* **24 B5** 46 15N 1 30 E
La Spézia, *Italy* **38 D6** 44 8N 9 50 E
La Suze-sur-Sarthe, *France* **22 E7** 47 53N 0 2 E
La Tagua, *Colombia* **152 C3** 0 3N 74 40W
La Teste, *France* **24 D2** 44 37N 1 8W
La Tortuga, *Venezuela* **149 D6** 11 0N 65 22W
La Tour-du-Pin, *France* **25 C9** 45 33N 5 27 E
La Tranche-sur-Mer, *France* **22 F5** 46 20N 1 27W
La Tremblade, *France* **24 C2** 45 46N 1 8W
La Tuque, *Canada* **128 C5** 47 30N 72 50W
La Unión, *Chile* **160 B2** 40 10 S 73 0W
La Unión, *Colombia* **152 C2** 1 35N 77 5W
La Unión, *El Salv.* **148 D2** 13 20N 87 50W
La Unión, *Mexico* **146 D4** 17 58N 101 49W
La Unión, *Peru* **156 B2** 9 43 S 76 45W
La Unión, *Spain* **35 H4** 37 38N 0 53W
La Urbana, *Venezuela* **152 B4** 7 8N 66 56W
La Vecilla, *Spain* **36 C5** 42 51N 5 27W
La Vega, *Dom. Rep.* **149 C5** 19 20N 70 30W
La Vega, *Peru* **156 C2** 10 41 S 77 44W
La Vela, *Venezuela* **152 A4** 11 27N 69 34W
La Veleta, *Spain* **37 H7** 37 1N 3 22W
La Venta, *Mexico* **147 D6** 18 8N 94 3W
La Ventura, *Mexico* **146 C4** 24 38N 100 54W
La Venturosa, *Colombia* **152 B4** 6 8N 68 48W
La Victoria, *Venezuela* **152 A4** 10 14N 67 20W
La Voulte-sur-Rhône, *France* **25 D8** 44 48N 4 46 E
La Zarza, *Spain* **37 H4** 37 42N 6 51W
Laa, *Austria* **31 C9** 48 43N 16 23 E
Laaber →, *Germany* **27 G8** 48 55N 12 30 E
Laage, *Germany* **26 B8** 53 55N 12 21 E
Laba →, *U.S.S.R.* **53 D8** 45 11N 39 42 E
Laban, *Burma* **78 C6** 25 52N 96 40 E
Labastide-Murat, *France* **24 D5** 44 39N 1 33 E
Labastide-Rouairoux, *France* **24 E6** 43 28N 2 39 E
Labbézenga, *Mali* **101 B5** 15 2N 0 48 E
Labdah = Leptis Magna, *Libya* **96 B2** 32 40N 14 12 E
Labe = Elbe →, *Europe* **26 B5** 53 50N 9 0 E
Labé, *Guinea* **100 C2** 11 24N 12 16W
Laberec →, *Czech.* **31 C14** 48 37N 21 58 E
Laberge, L., *Canada* **130 A1** 61 11N 135 12W
Labin, *Yugoslavia* **39 C11** 45 5N 14 8 E
Labinsk, *U.S.S.R.* **53 D9** 44 40N 40 48 E
Labis, *Malaysia* **77 L4** 2 22N 103 2 E
Labiszyn, *Poland* **47 C4** 52 57N 17 54 E
Laboe, *Germany* **26 A6** 54 25N 10 13 E
Laboka, *Gabon* **102 B2** 0 19N 11 32 E
Labouheyre, *France* **24 D3** 44 13N 0 55W
Laboulaye, *Argentina* **158 C3** 34 10 S 63 30W
Labra, Peña, *Spain* **36 B6** 43 3N 4 26W
Labrador, Coast of □, *Canada* **129 B7** 53 20N 61 0W
Labrador City, *Canada* **129 B6** 52 57N 66 55W
Lábrea, *Brazil* **157 B5** 7 15 S 64 51W
Labrède, *France* **24 D3** 44 41N 0 32W
Labuan, Pulau, *Malaysia* **75 C5** 5 21N 115 13 E
Labuha, *Indonesia* **71 E7** 0 30 S 127 30 E
Labuhan, *Indonesia* **71 G11** 6 22 S 105 50 E
Labuhanbajo, *Indonesia* **71 F6** 8 28 S 120 1 E
Labuissière, *Belgium* **21 H4** 50 19N 4 11 E
Labuk, Telok, *Malaysia* **70 C5** 6 10N 117 50 E
Labutta, *Burma* **78 G5** 16 9N 94 46 E
Labyrinth, L., *Australia* **115 E2** 30 40 S 135 11 E
Labytnangi, *U.S.S.R.* **48 A12** 66 39N 66 21 E
Łabżenica, *Poland* **47 B4** 53 18N 17 15 E
Lac Allard, *Canada* **129 B7** 50 33N 63 24W
Lac Bouchette, *Canada* **129 C5** 48 16N 72 11W
Lac du Flambeau, *U.S.A.* **138 B10** 46 1N 89 51W
Lac Édouard, *Canada* **128 C5** 47 40N 72 16W
Lac La Biche, *Canada* **130 C6** 54 45N 111 58W
Lac la Martre, *Canada* **126 B8** 63 8N 117 16W
Lac-Mégantic, *Canada* **129 C5** 45 35N 70 53W
Lac Seul, Res., *Canada* **128 B1** 50 25N 92 30W
Lac Thien, *Vietnam* **76 F7** 12 25N 108 11 E
Lacanau, *France* **24 D2** 44 58N 1 5W
Lacanau, Étang de, *France* **24 D2** 44 58N 1 7W
Lacantúm →, *Mexico* **147 D6** 16 36N 90 40W
Lacara →, *Spain* **37 G4** 38 55N 6 25W
Lacaune, *France* **24 E6** 43 43N 2 40 E
Lacaune, Mts. de, *France* **24 E6** 43 43N 2 50 E
Laccadive Is. = Lakshadweep Is., *Ind. Oc.* **109 C6** 10 0N 72 30 E
Lacepede B., *Australia* **116 D3** 36 40 S 139 40 E
Lacepede Is., *Australia* **112 C3** 16 55 S 122 0 E
Lacerdónia, *Mozam.* **107 F4** 18 3 S 35 35 E
Lacey, *U.S.A.* **144 C4** 47 7N 122 49W
Lachay, Pta., *Peru* **156 C2** 11 17 S 77 44W
Lachen, *India* **78 B2** 27 46N 88 36 E
Lachen, *Switz.* **29 B7** 47 12N 8 51 E

222 Lachhmangarh

Lachhmangarh, India ... 80 F6 27 50N 75 4 E
Lachi, Pakistan ... 80 C4 33 25N 71 20 E
Lachine, Canada ... 128 C5 45 30N 73 40W
Lachlan →, Australia .. 116 C5 34 22 S 143 55 E
Lachute, Canada ... 128 C5 45 39N 74 21W
Lackawanna, U.S.A. ... 136 D6 42 49N 78 50W
Lacolle, Canada ... 137 A11 45 5N 73 22W
Lacombe, Canada ... 130 C6 52 30N 113 44W
Lacon, U.S.A. ... 140 C7 41 2N 89 24W
Lacona, Iowa, U.S.A. .. 140 C3 41 11N 93 23W
Lacona, N.Y., U.S.A. .. 137 C8 43 37N 76 5W
Láconi, Italy ... 40 C2 39 54N 9 4 E
Laconia, U.S.A. ... 137 C13 43 32N 71 30W
Lacq, France ... 24 E3 43 25N 0 35W
Lacrosse, U.S.A. ... 142 C5 46 51N 117 58W
Ladakh Ra., India ... 81 C8 34 0N 78 0 E
Ladário, Brazil ... 157 D6 19 1 S 57 35W
Ladd, U.S.A. ... 140 C7 41 23N 89 13W
Laddonia, U.S.A. ... 140 E5 39 15N 91 39W
Lądekzdrój, Poland ... 47 E3 50 21N 16 53 E
Ládhon →, Greece ... 45 G3 37 40N 21 50 E
Lâdik, Turkey ... 52 F6 40 57N 35 58 E
Ladismith, S. Africa ... 104 E3 33 28 S 21 15 E
Lādīz, Iran ... 85 D9 28 55N 61 15 E
Ladnun, India ... 80 F6 27 38N 74 25 E
Ladoga, L. = Ladozhskoye Ozero, U.S.S.R. ... 48 B5 61 15N 30 30 E
Ladon, France ... 23 E9 48 0N 2 30 E
Ladozhskoye Ozero, U.S.S.R. ... 48 B5 61 15N 30 30 E
Ladrillero, G., Chile ... 160 C1 49 20 S 75 35W
Lady Grey, S. Africa ... 104 E4 30 43 S 27 13 E
Ladybrand, S. Africa ... 104 D4 29 9 S 27 29 E
Ladysmith, Canada ... 130 D4 49 0N 123 49W
Ladysmith, S. Africa ... 105 D4 28 32 S 29 46 E
Ladysmith, U.S.A. ... 138 C9 45 27N 91 4W
Lae, Papua N. G. ... 120 D4 6 40 S 147 2 E
Laem Ngop, Thailand ... 77 F4 12 10N 102 26 E
Laem Pho, Thailand ... 77 J3 6 55N 101 19 E
Læsø, Denmark ... 15 G4 57 15N 10 53 E
Læsø Rende, Denmark . 15 G4 57 20N 10 45 E
Lafayette, Colo., U.S.A. 138 F2 40 0N 105 2W
Lafayette, Ind., U.S.A. . 141 D10 40 25N 86 54W
Lafayette, La., U.S.A. . 139 K9 30 18N 92 0W
Lafayette, Tenn., U.S.A. 135 G3 36 35N 86 0W
Laferte →, Canada ... 130 A5 61 53N 117 44W
Lafia, Nigeria ... 101 D6 8 30N 8 34 E
Lafiagi, Nigeria ... 101 D6 8 52N 5 20 E
Lafleche, Canada ... 131 D7 49 45N 106 40W
Lafon, Sudan ... 95 F3 5 5N 32 29 E
Laforsen, Sweden ... 14 C9 61 56N 15 3 E
Lagaip →, Papua N. G. 120 C2 5 4 S 142 52 E
Lagan →, Sweden ... 15 H7 56 56N 13 58 E
Lagan →, U.K. ... 19 B6 54 35N 5 55W
Lagarfljót →, Iceland .. 12 D6 65 40N 14 18W
Lagarto, Brazil ... 154 D4 10 54 S 37 41W
Lage, Germany ... 26 D4 51 58N 8 47 E
Lage, Spain ... 36 B2 43 13N 9 0W
Lage-Mierde, Neths. ... 21 F6 51 25N 5 9 E
Lågen →, Norway ... 13 F11 61 8N 10 25 E
Lägerdorf, Germany ... 26 B5 53 53N 9 35 E
Laghmān □, Afghan. ... 79 B3 34 20N 70 0 E
Laghouat, Algeria ... 99 B5 33 50N 2 59 E
Lagnieu, France ... 25 C9 45 55N 5 20 E
Lagny, France ... 23 D9 48 52N 2 44 E
Lago, Italy ... 41 C9 39 9N 16 8 E
Lago Posadas, Argentina 160 C2 47 30 S 71 40W
Lago Ranco, Chile ... 160 B2 40 19 S 72 30W
Lagôa, Portugal ... 37 H2 37 8N 8 27W
Lagoaça, Portugal ... 36 D4 41 11N 6 44W
Lagodekhi, U.S.S.R. ... 53 F12 41 50N 46 22 E
Lagónegro, Italy ... 41 B8 40 8N 15 45 E
Lagonoy Gulf, Phil. ... 71 B6 13 50N 123 50 E
Lagos, Nigeria ... 101 D5 6 25N 3 27 E
Lagos, Portugal ... 37 H2 37 5N 8 41W
Lagos de Moreno, Mexico 146 C4 21 21N 101 55W
Lagrange, Australia ... 112 C3 18 45 S 121 43 E
Lagrange, U.S.A. ... 141 C11 41 39N 85 25W
Lagrange B., Australia .. 112 C3 18 38 S 121 42 E
Laguardia, Spain ... 34 C2 42 33N 2 35W
Laguépie, France ... 24 D5 44 8N 1 57 E
Laguna, Brazil ... 159 B6 28 30 S 48 50W
Laguna, U.S.A. ... 143 J10 35 3N 107 28W
Laguna Beach, U.S.A. .. 145 M9 33 31N 117 52W
Laguna de la Janda, Spain ... 37 J5 36 15N 5 45W
Laguna Limpia, Argentina 158 B4 26 32 S 59 45W
Laguna Madre, U.S.A. .. 147 B5 27 0N 97 20W
Lagunas, Chile ... 158 A2 21 0 S 69 45W
Lagunas, Peru ... 156 B2 5 10 S 75 35W
Lagunillas, Bolivia ... 157 D5 19 38 S 63 43W
Lahad Datu, Malaysia .. 71 D5 5 0N 118 20 E
Lahan Sai, Thailand ... 76 E4 14 25N 102 52 E
Lahanam, Laos ... 76 D5 16 16N 105 16 E
Laharpur, India ... 81 F9 27 43N 80 56 E
Lahat, Indonesia ... 70 E2 3 45 S 103 30 E
Lahe, Burma ... 78 B5 26 20N 95 26 E
Lahewa, Indonesia ... 70 D1 1 22N 97 12 E
Laḥij, Yemen ... 86 D4 13 4N 44 53 E
Lāhījān, Iran ... 85 B6 37 10N 50 6 E
Lahn →, Germany ... 27 E3 50 17N 7 38 E
Laholm, Sweden ... 15 H7 56 30N 13 2 E
Laholmsbukten, Sweden 15 H6 56 30N 12 45 E
Lahontan Res., U.S.A. . 142 G4 39 28N 118 58W
Lahore, Pakistan ... 79 C4 31 32N 74 22 E
Lahpongsel, Burma ... 78 B7 27 7N 98 25 E
Lahr, Germany ... 27 G3 48 20N 7 52 E
Lahti, Finland ... 13 F18 60 58N 25 40 E
Lahtis = Lahti, Finland . 13 F18 60 58N 25 40 E
Laï, Chad ... 97 G3 9 25N 16 18 E
Lai Chau, Vietnam ... 76 A4 22 5N 103 3 E
Lai-hka, Burma ... 78 E6 21 16N 97 40 E
Laiagam, Papua N. G. .. 120 C2 5 33 S 143 30 E
Lai'an, China ... 69 A12 32 28N 118 30 E
Laibin, China ... 68 F7 23 42N 109 14 E
Laidley, Australia ... 115 D5 27 39 S 152 20 E
Laifeng, China ... 68 C7 29 27N 109 20 E
L'Aigle, France ... 22 D7 48 46N 0 38 E
Laignes, France ... 23 E11 47 50N 4 20 E
L'Aiguillon-sur-Mer, France ... 24 B2 46 20N 1 18W
Laikipia □, Kenya ... 106 B4 0 30N 36 30 E
Laingsburg, S. Africa ... 104 E3 33 9 S 20 52 E
Lairg, U.K. ... 18 C4 58 1N 4 24W
Laishui, China ... 66 E8 39 23N 115 45 E
Laiwu, China ... 67 F9 36 15N 117 40 E
Laixi, China ... 67 F11 36 50N 120 31 E
Laiyang, China ... 67 F11 36 59N 120 45 E
Laiyuan, China ... 66 E8 39 20N 114 40 E
Laizhou Wan, China ... 67 F10 37 30N 119 30 E
Laja →, Mexico ... 146 C4 20 55N 100 46W
Lajere, Nigeria ... 101 C7 12 10N 11 25 E
Lajes, Rio Grande do N., Brazil ... 154 C4 5 41 S 36 14W
Lajes, Sta. Catarina, Brazil ... 159 B5 27 48 S 50 20W
Lajinha, Brazil ... 155 F3 20 9 S 41 37W
Lajkovac, Yugoslavia ... 42 C5 44 27N 20 14 E
Lajosmizse, Hungary ... 31 D12 47 3N 19 32 E
Lak Sao, Laos ... 76 C5 18 11N 104 59 E
Lakaband, Pakistan ... 80 D3 31 2N 69 15 E
Lakar, Indonesia ... 71 F7 8 15 S 128 17 E
Lakatoro, Vanuatu ... 121 F5 16 0 S 167 0 E
Lake Alpine, U.S.A. ... 144 G7 38 29N 120 0W
Lake Andes, U.S.A. ... 138 D5 43 10N 98 32W
Lake Anse, U.S.A. ... 134 B1 46 42N 88 25W
Lake Arthur, U.S.A. ... 139 K8 30 8N 92 40W
Lake Cargelligo, Australia 117 B7 33 15 S 146 22 E
Lake Charles, U.S.A. ... 139 K8 30 15N 93 10W
Lake City, Colo., U.S.A. 143 G10 38 3N 107 27W
Lake City, Fla., U.S.A. . 135 K4 30 10N 82 40W
Lake City, Iowa, U.S.A. 140 B2 42 12N 94 42W
Lake City, Mich., U.S.A. 134 C3 44 20N 85 10W
Lake City, Minn., U.S.A. 138 C8 44 28N 92 21W
Lake City, Pa., U.S.A. . 136 D4 42 2N 80 20W
Lake City, S.C., U.S.A. 135 J6 33 51N 79 44W
Lake Coleridge, N.Z. ... 119 D6 43 17 S 171 30 E
Lake Forest, U.S.A. ... 141 B9 42 15N 87 50W
Lake Geneva, U.S.A. ... 141 B8 42 36N 88 26W
Lake George, U.S.A. ... 137 C11 43 25N 73 43W
Lake Grace, Australia .. 113 F2 33 7 S 118 28 E
Lake Harbour, Canada . 127 B13 62 50N 69 50W
Lake Havasu City, U.S.A. ... 145 L12 34 25N 114 29W
Lake Hughes, U.S.A. ... 145 L8 34 41N 118 26W
Lake Isabella, U.S.A. ... 145 K8 35 38N 118 28W
Lake King, Australia ... 113 F2 33 5 S 119 45 E
Lake Lenore, Canada ... 131 C8 52 24N 104 59W
Lake Louise, Canada ... 130 C5 51 30N 116 10W
Lake Mead Nat. Rec. Area, U.S.A. ... 145 K12 36 0N 114 30W
Lake Michigan Beach, U.S.A. ... 141 B10 42 13N 86 25W
Lake Mills, Iowa, U.S.A. 138 D8 43 23N 93 33W
Lake Mills, Wis., U.S.A. 141 A8 43 5N 88 55W
Lake Murray, Papua N. G. ... 120 D1 6 48 S 141 29 E
Lake Nash, Australia ... 114 C2 20 57 S 138 0 E
Lake Odessa, U.S.A. ... 141 B11 42 47N 85 8W
Lake Orion, U.S.A. ... 141 B13 42 47N 83 14W
Lake Providence, U.S.A. 139 J9 32 49N 91 12W
Lake Pukaki, N.Z. ... 119 E5 44 11 S 170 8 E
Lake River, Canada ... 128 B3 54 30N 82 31W
Lake Superior Prov. Park, Canada ... 128 C3 47 45N 84 45W
Lake Tekapo, N.Z. ... 119 E5 44 0 S 170 30 E
Lake Villa, U.S.A. ... 141 B8 42 25N 88 5W
Lake Village, U.S.A. ... 139 J9 33 20N 91 19W
Lake Wales, U.S.A. ... 135 M5 27 55N 81 32W
Lake Worth, U.S.A. ... 135 M5 26 36N 80 3W
Lakefield, Canada ... 136 B6 44 25N 78 16W
Lakeland, Australia ... 114 B3 15 49 S 144 57 E
Lakeland, U.S.A. ... 135 M5 28 0N 82 0W
Lakemba, Fiji ... 121 B3 18 13 S 178 47W
Lakeport, U.S.A. ... 144 F4 39 1N 122 56W
Lakes Entrance, Australia 117 D8 37 50 S 148 0 E
Lakeside, Ariz., U.S.A. . 143 J9 34 12N 109 59W
Lakeside, Calif., U.S.A. 145 N10 32 52N 116 55W
Lakeside, Nebr., U.S.A. 138 D3 42 5N 102 24W
Lakeview, U.S.A. ... 142 E3 42 15N 120 22W
Lakewood, Colo., U.S.A. 138 F2 39 44N 105 3W
Lakewood, N.J., U.S.A. 137 F10 40 5N 74 13W
Lakewood, Ohio, U.S.A. 136 E3 41 28N 81 50W
Lakewood Center, U.S.A. 144 C4 47 11N 122 32W
Lakhaniá, Greece ... 32 D9 35 58N 27 54 E
Lakhipur, Assam, India . 78 C4 24 48N 93 0 E
Lakhipur, Assam, India . 78 B3 26 2N 90 18 E
Lakhonpheng, Laos ... 76 E5 15 54N 105 34 E
Lakhpat, India ... 80 H3 23 48N 68 47 E
Laki, Iceland ... 12 D4 64 4N 18 14W
Lakin, U.S.A. ... 139 G4 37 58N 101 18W
Lakitusaki →, Canada . 128 B3 54 21N 82 25W
Lákkoi, Greece ... 32 D5 35 24N 23 57 E
Lakonía □, Greece ... 45 H4 36 55N 22 30 E
Lakonikós Kólpos, Greece 45 H4 36 40N 22 40 E
Lakota, Ivory C. ... 100 D3 5 50N 5 30W
Lakota, U.S.A. ... 138 A5 48 5N 98 22W
Laksefjorden, Norway .. 12 A19 70 45N 26 50 E
Lakselv, Norway ... 12 A18 70 2N 24 56 E
Lakshadweep Is., Ind. Oc. ... 109 C6 10 0N 72 30 E
Laksham, Bangla. ... 78 D3 23 14N 91 8 E
Lakshmeshwar, India ... 83 G2 15 9N 75 28 E
Lakshmikantapur, India . 81 H13 22 5N 88 20 E
Lakshmipur, Bangla. ... 78 D3 22 58N 90 50 E
Lakuramau, Papua N. G. 120 B6 2 54 S 151 15 E
Lala Musa, Pakistan ... 80 C5 32 40N 73 57 E
Lalago, Tanzania ... 106 C3 3 28 S 33 58 E
Lalapanzi, Zimbabwe ... 107 F3 19 20 S 30 15 E
Lalganj, India ... 81 G11 25 52N 85 13 E
Lalibela, Ethiopia ... 95 E4 12 2N 39 2 E
Lalin, China ... 67 B14 45 12N 127 0 E
Lalín, Spain ... 36 C2 42 40N 8 5W
Lalinde, France ... 24 D4 44 50N 0 44 E
Lalitapur, India ... 81 G8 24 42N 78 28 E
Lam, Vietnam ... 76 B6 21 21N 106 31 E
Lam Pao Res., Thailand 76 D4 16 50N 103 15 E
Lama Kara, Togo ... 101 D5 9 30N 1 15 E
Lamaipum, Burma ... 78 C6 25 40N 97 57 E
Lamap, Vanuatu ... 121 F5 16 26 S 167 43 E
Lamar, Colo., U.S.A. ... 138 F3 38 9N 102 35W
Lamar, Mo., U.S.A. ... 139 G7 37 30N 94 20W
Lamarque, Argentina ... 160 A3 39 24 S 65 40W
Lamas, Peru ... 156 B2 6 28 S 76 31W
Lamastre, France ... 25 D8 44 59N 4 35 E
Lambach, Austria ... 30 C6 48 6N 13 51 E
Lamballe, France ... 22 D4 48 29N 2 31W
Lambaréné, Gabon ... 102 C2 0 41 S 10 12 E
Lambasa, Fiji ... 121 A2 16 30 S 179 10 E
Lambay I., Ireland ... 19 C6 53 30N 6 0W
Lambayeque □, Peru ... 156 B2 6 45 S 80 0W
Lambert, U.S.A. ... 138 B2 47 44N 104 39W
Lambert, C., Papua N. G. ... 120 C6 4 11 S 151 31 E
Lambert Glacier, Antarctica ... 7 D6 71 0 S 70 0 E
Lamberts Bay, S. Africa 104 E2 32 5 S 18 17 E
Lambesc, France ... 25 E9 43 39N 5 16 E
Lámbia, Greece ... 45 G3 37 52N 21 53 E
Lambon, Papua N. G. .. 120 C7 4 45 S 152 48 E
Lambro →, Italy ... 38 C6 45 8N 9 32 E
Lame, Nigeria ... 101 C6 10 30N 9 20 E
Lame Deer, U.S.A. ... 142 D10 45 45N 106 40W
Lamego, Portugal ... 36 D3 41 5N 7 52W
Lamèque, Canada ... 129 C7 47 45N 64 38W
Lameroo, Australia ... 116 C4 35 19 S 140 33 E
Lamesa, U.S.A. ... 139 J4 32 45N 101 57W
Lamía, Greece ... 45 F4 38 55N 22 26 E
Lammermuir Hills, U.K. 18 F6 55 50N 2 40W
Lamon Bay, Phil. ... 71 B6 14 30N 122 20 E
Lamongan, Indonesia ... 75 D4 7 7 S 112 25 E
Lamoni, U.S.A. ... 140 D3 40 37N 93 56W
Lamont, Canada ... 130 C6 53 46N 112 50W
Lamont, Calif., U.S.A. . 145 K8 35 15N 118 55W
Lamont, Iowa, U.S.A. .. 140 B5 42 36N 91 40W
Lampa, Peru ... 156 D3 15 22 S 70 22W
Lampang, Thailand ... 76 C2 18 16N 99 32 E
Lampasas, U.S.A. ... 139 K5 31 5N 98 10W
Lampaul, France ... 22 D1 48 28N 5 7W
Lampazos de Naranjo, Mexico ... 146 B4 27 2N 100 32W
Lampeter, U.K. ... 17 E3 52 6N 4 6W
Lampione, Medit. S. ... 96 A2 35 33N 12 20 E
Lampman, Canada ... 131 D8 49 25N 102 50W
Lamprechtshausen, Austria ... 30 D5 48 0N 12 58 E
Lamprey, Canada ... 131 B10 58 33N 94 8W
Lampung □, Indonesia .. 70 F2 5 30 S 104 30 E
Lamu, Burma ... 78 F5 19 14N 94 10 E
Lamu, Kenya ... 106 C5 2 16 S 40 55 E
Lamu □, Kenya ... 106 C5 2 0 S 40 45 E
Lamud, Peru ... 156 B2 6 10 S 77 57W
Lamy, U.S.A. ... 143 J11 35 30N 105 58W
Lan Xian, China ... 66 E6 38 15N 111 35 E
Lan Yu, Taiwan ... 69 F13 22 5N 121 35 E
Lanai I., U.S.A. ... 132 H16 20 50N 156 55W
Lanak La, India ... 81 B8 34 27N 79 32 E
Lanaken, Belgium ... 21 G7 50 53N 5 39 E
Lanak'o Shank'ou = Lanak La, India ... 81 B8 34 27N 79 32 E
Lanao, L., Phil. ... 71 C6 7 52N 124 15 E
Lanark, Canada ... 137 A8 45 1N 76 22W
Lanark, U.K. ... 18 F5 55 40N 3 48W
Lancang, China ... 68 F2 22 36N 99 58 E
Lancang Jiang →, China 68 G3 21 40N 101 10 E
Lancashire □, U.K. ... 16 D5 53 40N 2 30W
Lancaster, Canada ... 137 A10 45 10N 74 30W
Lancaster, U.K. ... 16 C5 54 3N 2 48W
Lancaster, Calif., U.S.A. 145 L8 34 47N 118 8W
Lancaster, Ky., U.S.A. . 134 G3 37 40N 84 40W
Lancaster, Mo., U.S.A. . 140 D4 40 31N 92 32W
Lancaster, N.H., U.S.A. 137 B13 44 27N 71 33W
Lancaster, N.Y., U.S.A. 136 D6 42 53N 78 43W
Lancaster, Pa., U.S.A. . 137 F8 40 4N 76 19W
Lancaster, S.C., U.S.A. . 135 H5 34 45N 80 47W
Lancaster, Wis., U.S.A. . 140 B6 42 48N 90 43W
Lancaster Sd., Canada . 127 A11 74 13N 84 0W
Lancer, Canada ... 131 C7 50 48N 108 53W
Lanchow = Lanzhou, China ... 66 F2 36 1N 103 52 E
Lanciano, Italy ... 39 F11 42 15N 14 22 E
Lanco, Chile ... 160 A2 39 24 S 72 46W
Lancones, Peru ... 156 A1 4 30 S 80 30W
Lancun, China ... 67 F11 36 25N 120 10 E
Łańcut, Poland ... 31 A15 50 10N 22 13 E
Lancy, Switz. ... 28 D2 46 12N 6 8 E
Landau, Bayern, Germany ... 27 G8 48 41N 12 41 E
Landau, Rhld-Pfz., Germany ... 27 F4 49 12N 8 7 E
Landay, Afghan. ... 79 C1 30 31N 63 47 E
Landeck, Austria ... 30 D3 47 9N 10 34 E
Landen, Belgium ... 21 G6 50 45N 5 3 E
Lander, U.S.A. ... 142 E9 42 50N 108 49W
Lander →, Australia ... 112 D5 22 0 S 132 0 E
Landerneau, France ... 22 D2 48 28N 4 17W
Landeryd, Sweden ... 15 G7 57 7N 13 15 E
Landes, France ... 24 E3 44 0N 1 0W
Landes □, France ... 24 E3 43 57N 0 48W
Landete, Spain ... 34 F3 39 56N 1 25W
Landi Kotal, Pakistan ... 79 B3 34 7N 71 6 E
Landivisiau, France ... 22 D2 48 31N 4 6W
Landor, Australia ... 113 E2 25 10 S 116 54 E
Landquart, Switz. ... 29 C9 46 58N 9 32 E
Landquart →, Switz. ... 29 C9 46 50N 9 47 E
Landrecies, France ... 23 B10 50 7N 3 40 E
Land's End, U.K. ... 17 G2 50 4N 5 43W
Landsberg, Germany ... 27 G6 48 3N 10 52 E
Landsborough Cr. →, Australia ... 114 C3 22 28 S 144 35 E
Landshut, Germany ... 27 G8 48 31N 12 10 E
Landskrona, Sweden ... 15 J6 55 53N 12 50 E
Landstuhl, Germany ... 27 F3 49 25N 7 34 E
Landvetter, Sweden ... 15 G6 57 41N 12 17 E
Laneffe, Belgium ... 21 H5 50 17N 4 30 E
Lanesboro, U.S.A. ... 137 E9 41 57N 75 34W
Lanett, U.S.A. ... 135 J3 33 0N 85 15W
Lang Bay, Canada ... 130 D4 49 45N 124 21W
Lang Qua, Vietnam ... 76 A5 22 16N 104 27 E
Lang Shan, China ... 66 D4 41 0N 106 30 E
Lang Son, Vietnam ... 76 B6 21 52N 106 42 E
Lang Suan, Thailand ... 77 H2 9 57N 99 4 E
Langádhas, Greece ... 44 D5 40 46N 23 2 E
Langádhia, Greece ... 45 G4 37 43N 22 1 E
Långan →, Sweden ... 14 A8 63 19N 14 44 E
Langar, Iran ... 85 C9 35 23N 60 25 E
Langara I., Canada ... 130 C2 54 14N 133 1W
Langatabbetje, Surinam . 153 C7 4 59N 54 28W
Langdai, China ... 68 D5 26 6N 105 21 E
Langdon, U.S.A. ... 138 A5 48 47N 98 24W
Langdorp, Belgium ... 21 G5 50 59N 4 52 E
Langeac, France ... 24 C7 45 7N 3 29 E
Langeais, France ... 22 E7 47 20N 0 24 E
Langeb Baraka →, Sudan ... 94 D4 17 28N 36 50 E
Langeberg, S. Africa ... 104 E3 33 55 S 21 0 E
Langeberge, S. Africa .. 104 D3 28 15 S 22 33 E
Langeland, Denmark ... 15 K4 54 56N 10 48 E
Langemark, Belgium ... 21 G1 50 55N 2 55 E
Langen, Germany ... 27 F4 49 59N 8 40 E
Langenburg, Canada ... 131 C8 50 51N 101 43W
Langeness, Germany ... 26 A4 54 34N 8 35 E
Langenlois, Austria ... 30 C8 48 29N 15 40 E
Langenthal, Switz. ... 28 B5 47 13N 7 47 E
Langeoog, Germany ... 26 B3 53 44N 7 33 E
Langeskov, Denmark ... 15 J4 55 22N 10 35 E
Langesund, Norway ... 14 F3 59 0N 9 45 E
Länghem, Sweden ... 15 G7 57 36N 13 14 E
Langhirano, Italy ... 38 D7 44 39N 10 16 E
Langholm, U.K. ... 18 F6 55 9N 2 59W
Langidoon, Australia ... 116 A5 31 36 S 142 2 E
Langjökull, Iceland ... 12 D3 64 39N 20 12W
Langkawi, P., Malaysia . 77 J2 6 25N 99 45 E
Langklip, S. Africa ... 104 D3 28 12 S 20 20 E
Langkon, Malaysia ... 70 C5 6 30N 116 40 E
Langlade, St- P. & M. .. 129 C8 46 50N 56 20W
Langlois, U.S.A. ... 142 E1 42 54N 124 26W
Langnau, Switz. ... 28 C5 46 56N 7 47 E
Langogne, France ... 24 D7 44 43N 3 50 E
Langon, France ... 24 D3 44 33N 0 16W
Langøya, Norway ... 12 B13 68 45N 14 50 E
Langres, France ... 23 E12 47 52N 5 20 E
Langres, Plateau de, France ... 23 E12 47 45N 5 3 E
Langsa, Indonesia ... 70 D1 4 30N 97 57 E
Långsele, Sweden ... 14 A11 63 12N 17 4 E
Langtao, Burma ... 78 B6 27 15N 97 34 E
Langting, India ... 78 C4 25 31N 93 7 E
Langtry, U.S.A. ... 139 L4 29 50N 101 33W
Langu, Thailand ... 77 J2 6 53N 99 47 E
Languedoc, France ... 24 E7 43 58N 4 5 E
Langwies, Switz. ... 29 C9 46 50N 9 44 E
Langxi, China ... 69 B12 31 10N 119 12 E
Langxiangzhen, China ... 66 E9 39 43N 116 8 E
Langzhong, China ... 68 B5 31 38N 105 58 E
Lanigan, Canada ... 131 C7 51 51N 105 2W
Lankao, China ... 66 G8 34 48N 114 50 E
Lannemezan, France ... 24 E4 43 8N 0 23 E
Lannilis, France ... 22 D2 48 35N 4 32W
Lannion, France ... 22 D3 48 46N 3 29W
L'Annonciation, Canada 128 C5 46 25N 74 55W
Lanouaille, France ... 24 C5 45 24N 1 9 E
Lanping, China ... 68 D2 26 28N 99 15 E
Lansdale, U.S.A. ... 137 F9 40 14N 75 18W
Lansdowne, Australia ... 117 A10 31 48 S 152 30 E
Lansdowne, Canada ... 137 B8 44 24N 76 1W
Lansdowne House, Canada ... 128 B2 52 14N 87 53W
L'Anse, U.S.A. ... 128 C2 46 47N 88 28W
L'Anse au Loup, Canada 129 B8 51 32N 56 50W
Lansford, U.S.A. ... 137 F9 40 48N 75 55W
Lanshan, China ... 69 E9 25 24N 112 10 E
Lansing, U.S.A. ... 141 B12 42 47N 84 40W
Lanslebourg-Mont-Cenis, France ... 25 C10 45 17N 6 52 E
Lanta Yai, Ko, Thailand 77 J2 7 35N 99 3 E
Lantian, China ... 66 G5 34 11N 109 20 E
Lanus, Argentina ... 158 C4 34 44 S 58 27W
Lanusei, Italy ... 40 C2 39 53N 9 31 E
Lanxi, China ... 69 C12 29 13N 119 28 E
Lanzarote, Canary Is. ... 33 F6 29 0N 13 40W
Lanzhou, China ... 66 F2 36 1N 103 52 E
Lanzo Torinese, Italy ... 38 C4 45 16N 7 29 E
Lao →, Italy ... 41 C8 39 45N 15 45 E
Lao Bao, Laos ... 76 D6 16 35N 106 30 E
Lao Cai, Vietnam ... 76 A4 22 30N 103 57 E
Laoag, Phil. ... 71 A6 18 7N 120 34 E
Laoang, Phil. ... 71 B7 12 32N 125 8 E
Laoha He →, China ... 67 C11 43 25N 120 35 E
Laon, France ... 23 C10 49 33N 3 35 E
Laona, U.S.A. ... 134 C1 45 32N 88 41W
Laos ■, Asia ... 76 D5 17 45N 105 0 E
Lapa, Brazil ... 159 B6 25 46 S 49 44W
Lapalisse, France ... 24 B7 46 15N 3 38 E
Laparan, Phil. ... 71 C6 6 0N 120 0 E
Lapeer, U.S.A. ... 141 A13 43 3N 83 20W
Lapi □, Finland ... 12 C19 67 0N 27 0 E
Lapithos, Cyprus ... 32 D12 35 21N 33 11 E
Lapland = Lappland, Europe ... 12 B18 68 7N 24 0 E
Laporte, U.S.A. ... 137 E8 41 27N 76 30W
Lapovo, Yugoslavia ... 42 C6 44 10N 21 2 E
Lappland, Europe ... 12 B18 68 7N 24 0 E
Laprida, Argentina ... 158 D3 37 34 S 60 45W
Laptev Sea, U.S.S.R. ... 57 B13 76 0N 125 0 E
Lapuş, Munţii, Romania 46 B4 47 20N 23 50 E
Lăpuşul →, Romania ... 46 B4 47 25N 23 40 E
Łapy, Poland ... 47 C9 52 59N 22 52 E
L'Áquila, Italy ... 39 F10 42 21N 13 24 E
Lār, Āzarbājān-e Sharqī, Iran ... 84 B5 38 30N 47 52 E
Lār, Fārs, Iran ... 85 E7 27 40N 54 14 E
Lara, Australia ... 116 E6 38 2 S 144 26 E
Lara □, Venezuela ... 152 A4 10 10N 69 50W
Larabanga, Ghana ... 100 D4 9 16N 1 56W
Laracha, Spain ... 36 B2 43 15N 8 35W
Larache, Morocco ... 98 A3 35 10N 6 5W
Laragne-Montéglin, France ... 25 D9 44 18N 5 49 E
Laramie, U.S.A. ... 138 E2 41 20N 105 38W
Laramie Mts., U.S.A. ... 138 E2 42 0N 105 30W
Laranjeiras, Brazil ... 154 D4 10 48 S 37 10W
Laranjeiras do Sul, Brazil 159 B5 25 23 S 52 23W
Larantuka, Indonesia ... 71 F6 8 21 S 122 55 E
Larap, Phil. ... 71 B6 14 18N 122 39 E
Larat, Indonesia ... 71 F8 7 0 S 132 0 E
L'Arbresle, France ... 25 C8 45 50N 4 36 E
Larde, Mozam. ... 107 F4 16 28 S 39 43 E
Larder Lake, Canada ... 128 C4 48 5N 79 40W
Lardhos, Ákra, Greece ... 32 C10 36 4N 28 10 E
Lardhos, Órmos, Greece 32 C10 36 4N 28 2 E
Laredo, Spain ... 34 B1 43 26N 3 28W
Laredo, U.S.A. ... 139 M5 27 34N 99 29W
Laredo Sd., Canada ... 130 C3 52 30N 128 53W
Laren, Neths. ... 20 D6 52 16N 5 14 E
Largentière, France ... 25 D8 44 34N 4 18 E
L'Argentière-la-Bessée, France ... 25 D10 44 47N 6 33 E

224 Leninsk-Kuznetskiy

Leninsk-Kuznetskiy, U.S.S.R. 56 D9 54 44N 86 10 E
Leninskaya Sloboda, U.S.S.R. 51 C14 56 7N 44 29 E
Leninskoye, R.S.F.S.R., U.S.S.R. 51 B15 58 23N 47 3 E
Leninskoye, R.S.F.S.R., U.S.S.R. 57 E14 47 56N 132 38 E
Leninskoye, Uzbek S.S.R., U.S.S.R. 55 C4 41 45N 69 23 E
Lenk, Switz. 28 D4 46 27N 7 28 E
Lenkoran, U.S.S.R. 89 D13 39 45N 48 50 E
Lenmalu, Indonesia 71 E8 1 45 S 130 15 E
Lenne →, Germany 26 D3 51 25N 7 30 E
Lennox, I., Chile 160 E3 55 18 S 66 50W
Lennoxville, Canada 137 A13 45 22N 71 51W
Leno, Italy 38 C7 45 24N 10 14 E
Lenoir, U.S.A. 135 H5 35 55N 81 36W
Lenoir City, U.S.A. 135 H3 35 40N 84 20W
Lenora, U.S.A. 138 F4 39 39N 100 1W
Lenore L., Canada 131 C8 52 30N 104 59W
Lenox, Iowa, U.S.A. 140 D2 40 53N 94 34W
Lenox, Mass., U.S.A. 137 D11 42 20N 73 18W
Lens, Belgium 21 G3 50 33N 3 54 E
Lens, France 23 B9 50 26N 2 50 E
Lens St. Remy, Belgium 21 G6 50 39N 5 7 E
Lensk, U.S.S.R. 57 C12 60 48N 114 55 E
Lenskoye, U.S.S.R. 52 D6 45 3N 34 1 E
Lent, Neths. 20 E7 51 52N 5 52 E
Lenti, Hungary 31 E9 46 37N 16 33 E
Lentini, Italy 41 E8 37 18N 15 0 E
Lentvaric, U.S.S.R. 50 D4 54 39N 25 3 E
Lenwood, U.S.A. 145 L9 34 53N 117 7W
Lenzburg, Switz. 28 B6 47 23N 8 11 E
Lenzen, Germany 26 B7 53 6N 11 26 E
Lenzerheide, Switz. 29 C9 46 44N 9 34 E
Léo, Burkina Faso 100 C4 11 3N 2 2W
Leoben, Austria 30 D8 47 22N 15 5 E
Leola, U.S.A. 138 C5 45 47N 98 58W
Leominster, U.K. 17 E5 52 15N 2 43W
Leominster, U.S.A. 137 D13 42 32N 71 45W
Léon, France 24 E2 43 53N 1 18W
León, Mexico 146 C4 21 7N 101 30W
León, Nic. 148 D2 12 20N 86 51W
León, Spain 36 C5 42 38N 5 34W
Leon, U.S.A. 140 D3 40 40N 93 40W
León □, Spain 36 C5 42 40N 5 55W
León, Montañas de, Spain 36 C4 42 30N 6 18W
Leonardtown, U.S.A. 134 F7 38 19N 76 39W
Leone, Mte., Switz. 28 D6 46 15N 8 5 E
Leonforte, Italy 41 E7 37 39N 14 22 E
Leongatha, Australia 117 E6 38 30 S 145 58 E
Leonídhion, Greece 45 G4 37 9N 22 52 E
Leonora, Australia 113 E3 28 49 S 121 19 E
Leonora Downs, Australia 116 B5 32 29 S 142 5 E
Léopold II, Lac = Mai-Ndombe, L., Zaïre 102 C3 2 0 S 18 20 E
Leopoldina, Brazil 155 F3 21 28 S 42 40W
Leopoldo Bulhões, Brazil 155 E2 16 37 S 48 46W
Leopoldsburg, Belgium 21 F6 51 7N 5 13 E
Léopoldville = Kinshasa, Zaïre 103 C3 4 20 S 15 15 E
Leoti, U.S.A. 138 F4 38 31N 101 19W
Leoville, Canada 131 C7 53 39N 107 33W
Lépa, L. do, Angola 103 F3 17 0 S 19 0 E
Lepe, Spain 37 H3 37 15N 7 12W
Lepel, U.S.S.R. 50 D6 54 50N 28 40 E
Lepikha, U.S.S.R. 57 C13 64 45N 125 55 E
Leping, China 69 C11 28 47N 117 7 E
Lepontine, Alpi, Italy 29 D6 46 22N 8 27 E
Lepsény, Hungary 31 E11 47 0N 18 15 E
Leptis Magna, Libya 96 B2 32 40N 14 12 E
Lequeitio, Spain 34 B2 43 20N 2 32W
Lercara Friddi, Italy 40 E6 37 42N 13 36 E
Lerdo, Mexico 146 B4 25 32N 103 32W
Léré, C.A.R. 102 A3 6 46N 17 25 E
Léré, Chad 97 G2 9 39N 14 13 E
Lere, Nigeria 101 D6 9 43N 9 18 E
Leribe, Lesotho 105 D4 28 51 S 28 3 E
Lérici, Italy 38 D6 44 4N 9 58 E
Lérida, Spain 34 D5 41 37N 0 39 E
Lérida □, Spain 34 C6 42 6N 1 0 E
Lérins, Is. de, France 25 E11 43 31N 7 3 E
Lerma, Spain 36 D7 42 0N 3 47W
Léros, Greece 45 G8 37 10N 26 50 E
Lérouville, France 23 D12 48 44N 5 30 E
Lerwick, U.K. 18 A7 60 10N 1 10W
Les, Romania 46 C2 46 58N 21 50 E
Les Abrets, France 25 C9 45 32N 5 35 E
Les Andelys, France 22 C8 49 15N 1 25 E
Les Arcs, France 25 E10 43 27N 6 29 E
Les Baux-de-Provence, France 25 E8 43 45N 4 51 E
Les Bois, Switz. 28 B3 47 11N 6 50 E
Les Cayes, Haiti 149 C5 18 15N 73 46W
Les Diablerets, Switz. 28 D4 46 22N 7 10 E
Les Échelles, France 25 C9 45 26N 5 46 E
Les Essarts, France 22 F5 46 47N 1 12W
Les Étroits, Canada 129 C6 47 24N 68 54W
Les Eyzies-de-Tayac-Sireuil, France 24 D5 44 56N 1 1 E
Les Herbiers, France 22 F5 46 52N 1 1W
Les Minquiers, Chan. Is. 22 D4 48 58N 2 8W
Les Ponts-de-Cé, France 22 E6 47 25N 0 30W
Les Riceys, France 23 E11 47 59N 4 22 E
Les Sables-d'Olonne, France 24 B2 46 30N 1 45W
Les Vans, France 25 D8 44 25N 4 7 E
Les Verrières, Switz. 28 C2 46 55N 6 28 E
Lesbos = Lésvos, Greece 45 E8 39 10N 26 20 E
Leshan, China 68 C4 29 33N 103 41 E
Leshukonskoye, U.S.S.R. 48 B8 64 54N 45 46 E
Lésina, L. di, Italy 39 G12 41 53N 15 25 E
Lesja, Norway 14 B2 62 7N 8 51 E
Lesjaverk, Norway 14 B2 62 12N 8 34 E
Lesko, Poland 31 B15 49 30N 22 23 E
Leskov I., Antarctica 7 B1 56 0 S 28 0W
Leskovac, Yugoslavia 42 E6 43 0N 21 58 E
Leskoviku, Albania 44 D2 40 10N 20 34 E
Leslie, Ark., U.S.A. 139 H8 35 50N 92 35W
Leslie, Mich., U.S.A. 141 B12 42 27N 84 26W
Lesna, Poland 47 E2 51 0N 15 15 E
Lesneven, France 22 D2 48 35N 4 20W
Lešnica, Yugoslavia 42 C4 44 39N 19 20 E
Lesnoy, U.S.S.R. 54 B3 59 47N 52 9 E
Lesnoye, U.S.S.R. 50 B9 58 15N 35 18 E
Lesopilnoye, U.S.S.R. 60 A7 46 44N 134 20 E
Lesotho ■, Africa 105 D4 29 40 S 28 0 E
Lesozavodsk, U.S.S.R. 57 E14 45 30N 133 29 E
Lesparre-Médoc, France 24 C3 45 18N 0 57W
Lessay, France 22 C5 49 14N 1 30W
Lesse →, Belgium 21 H5 50 15N 4 54 E
Lesser Antilles, W. Indies 149 D7 15 0N 61 0W
Lesser Slave L., Canada 130 B5 55 30N 115 25W
Lesser Sunda Is., Indonesia 71 F6 7 0 S 120 0 E
Lessines, Belgium 21 G3 50 42N 3 50 E
Lester, U.S.A. 144 C5 47 12N 121 29W
Lestock, Canada 131 C8 51 19N 103 59W
Lesuer I., Australia 112 B4 13 50 S 127 17 E
Lésvos, Greece 45 E8 39 10N 26 20 E
Leszno, Poland 47 D3 51 50N 16 30 E
Leszno □, Poland 47 D3 51 45N 16 30 E
Letchworth, U.K. 17 F7 51 58N 0 13W
Letea, Ostrov, Romania 46 D10 45 18N 29 20 E
Lethbridge, Canada 130 D6 49 45N 112 45W
Lethem, Guyana 153 C6 3 20N 59 50W
Lethero, Australia 116 B5 33 33 S 142 30 E
Leti, Kepulauan, Indonesia 71 F7 8 10 S 128 0 E
Leti Is. = Leti, Kepulauan, Indonesia 71 F7 8 10 S 128 0 E
Letiahau →, Botswana 104 C3 21 16 S 24 0 E
Leticia, Colombia 152 D4 4 9 S 70 0W
Leting, China 67 E10 39 23N 118 55 E
Letjiesbos, S. Africa 104 E3 32 34 S 22 16 E
Letlhakeng, Botswana 104 C3 24 0 S 24 59 E
Letpadan, Burma 78 G5 17 45N 95 45 E
Letpan, Burma 78 F5 19 28N 94 10 E
Letterkenny, Ireland 19 B4 54 57N 7 42W
Leu, Romania 46 E5 44 10N 24 0 E
Léua, Angola 103 E4 11 34 S 20 32 E
Leucadia, U.S.A. 145 M9 33 4N 117 18W
Leucate, France 24 F7 42 56N 3 3 E
Leucate, Étang de, France 24 F7 42 50N 3 0 E
Leuk, Switz. 28 D5 46 19N 7 37 E
Leukerbad, Switz. 28 D5 46 24N 7 36 E
Leupegem, Belgium 21 G3 50 50N 3 36 E
Leuser, G., Indonesia 70 D1 3 46N 97 12 E
Leutkirch, Germany 27 H6 47 49N 10 1 E
Leuven, Belgium 21 G5 50 52N 4 42 E
Leuze, Hainaut, Belgium 21 G3 50 36N 3 37 E
Leuze, Namur, Belgium 21 G5 50 33N 4 54 E
Lev Tolstoy, U.S.S.R. 51 E11 53 13N 39 29 E
Levádhia, Greece 45 F4 38 27N 22 54 E
Levan, U.S.A. 142 G8 39 37N 111 52W
Levanger, Norway 12 E11 63 45N 11 19 E
Levani, Albania 44 D1 40 40N 19 28 E
Levant, I. du, France 25 E10 43 3N 6 28 E
Lévanto, Italy 38 D6 44 10N 9 37 E
Levanzo, Italy 40 E5 38 0N 12 19 E
Levelland, U.S.A. 139 J3 33 38N 102 23W
Leven, U.K. 18 E6 56 12N 3 0W
Leven, L., U.K. 18 E5 56 12N 3 22W
Leven, Toraka, Madag. 105 A8 12 30 S 47 45 E
Levens, France 25 E11 43 50N 7 12 E
Leveque C., Australia 112 C3 16 20 S 123 0 E
Leverano, Italy 41 B11 40 16N 18 0 E
Leverkusen, Germany 26 D2 51 2N 6 59 E
Leverville, Zaïre 103 C3 4 50 S 18 44 E
Levet, France 23 F9 46 56N 2 22 E
Levice, Czech. 31 C11 48 13N 18 35 E
Levico, Italy 39 C8 46 0N 11 18 E
Levie, France 25 G13 41 40N 9 7 E
Levier, France 23 F13 46 58N 6 8 E
Levin, N.Z. 118 G4 40 37 S 175 18 E
Lévis, Canada 129 C5 46 48N 71 9W
Levis, L., Canada 130 A5 62 37N 117 58W
Levítha, Greece 45 H8 37 0N 26 28 E
Levittown, N.Y., U.S.A. 137 F11 40 41N 73 31W
Levittown, Pa., U.S.A. 137 F10 40 10N 74 51W
Levka, Bulgaria 43 F11 41 52N 26 15 E
Lévka Óri, Greece 32 D6 35 18N 24 3 E
Levkás, Greece 45 F2 38 40N 20 43 E
Levkímmi, Greece 32 B4 39 25N 20 3 E
Levkímmi, Ákra, Greece 32 B4 39 29N 20 4 E
Levkôsia = Nicosia, Cyprus 32 D12 35 10N 33 25 E
Levoča, Czech. 31 B13 49 2N 20 35 E
Levroux, France 23 F8 46 59N 1 38 E
Levski, Bulgaria 43 D10 43 21N 25 10 E
Levskigrad, Bulgaria 43 E9 42 38N 24 47 E
Levuka, Fiji 121 A2 17 34 S 179 0 E
Lewe, Burma 78 F6 19 38N 96 7 E
Lewellen, U.S.A. 138 E3 41 22N 102 5W
Lewes, U.K. 17 G8 50 53N 0 2 E
Lewes, U.S.A. 134 F8 38 45N 75 8W
Lewin Brzeski, Poland 47 E4 50 45N 17 37 E
Lewis, U.K. 18 C2 58 10N 6 40W
Lewis →, U.S.A. 144 E4 45 51N 122 48W
Lewis, Butt of, U.K. 18 C2 58 30N 6 12W
Lewis Ra., Australia 112 D4 20 3 S 128 50 E
Lewis Ra., U.S.A. 142 C7 48 0N 113 15W
Lewisburg, Ohio, U.S.A. 141 E12 39 51N 84 33W
Lewisburg, Pa., U.S.A. 136 F8 40 57N 76 57W
Lewisburg, Tenn., U.S.A. 135 H2 35 29N 86 46W
Lewisport, U.S.A. 141 G10 37 56N 86 54W
Lewisporte, Canada 129 C8 49 15N 55 3W
Lewiston, U.S.A. 142 C5 46 25N 117 0W
Lewistown, Ill., U.S.A. 140 D6 40 24N 90 9W
Lewistown, Mont., U.S.A. 142 C9 47 0N 109 25W
Lewistown, Pa., U.S.A. 136 F7 40 37N 77 33W
Lexington, Ill., U.S.A. 138 E10 40 37N 88 47W
Lexington, Ky., U.S.A. 141 F12 38 6N 84 30W
Lexington, Miss., U.S.A. 139 J9 33 8N 90 2W
Lexington, Mo., U.S.A. 140 E3 39 7N 93 55W
Lexington, N.C., U.S.A. 135 H5 35 50N 80 13W
Lexington, Nebr., U.S.A. 138 E5 40 48N 99 45W
Lexington, Ohio, U.S.A. 136 F2 40 41N 82 35W
Lexington, Oreg., U.S.A. 142 D4 45 29N 119 46W
Lexington, Tenn., U.S.A. 135 H1 35 38N 88 25W
Lexington Park, U.S.A. 134 F7 38 16N 76 27W
Leye, China 68 E6 24 48N 106 29 E
Leyre →, France 24 D2 44 39N 1 1W
Leysin, Switz. 28 D4 46 21N 7 0 E
Leyte, Phil. 71 B7 11 0N 125 0 E
Lezajsk, Poland 47 E9 50 16N 22 25 E
Lezay, France 24 B4 46 15N 0 1 E
Lezha, Albania 44 C1 41 47N 19 42 E
Lezhi, China 68 B5 30 19N 104 58 E
Lézignan-Corbières, France 24 E6 43 13N 2 43 E
Lezoux, France 24 C7 45 49N 3 21 E
Lgov, U.S.S.R. 50 F9 51 42N 35 16 E
Lhasa, China 64 D4 29 25N 90 58 E
Lhazê, China 64 D3 29 5N 87 38 E
Lhokkruet, Indonesia 70 D1 4 55N 95 24 E
Lhokseumawe, Indonesia 70 C1 5 10N 97 10 E
Lhuntsi Dzong, India 78 B3 27 39N 91 10 E
Li, Thailand 76 D2 17 48N 98 57 E
Li Shui →, China 69 C9 29 24N 112 1 E
Li Xian, Gansu, China 66 G3 34 10N 105 5 E
Li Xian, Hebei, China 66 E8 38 30N 115 35 E
Li Xian, Hunan, China 69 C8 29 36N 111 42 E
Li Xian, Sichuan, China 68 B4 31 23N 103 13 E
Lia-Moya, C.A.R. 102 A3 6 54N 16 17 E
Liádhoi, Greece 45 H8 36 50N 26 11 E
Lian Xian, China 69 E9 24 51N 112 22 E
Liancheng, China 69 E11 25 42N 116 40 E
Lianga, Phil. 71 C7 8 38N 126 6 E
Liangcheng, Nei Mongol Zizhiqu, China 66 D7 40 28N 112 25 E
Liangcheng, Shandong, China 67 G10 35 32N 119 37 E
Liangdang, China 66 H4 33 56N 106 18 E
Lianghekou, China 68 C7 29 11N 108 44 E
Liangping, China 68 B6 30 38N 107 47 E
Lianhua, China 69 D9 27 3N 113 54 E
Lianjiang, Fujian, China 69 D12 26 12N 119 27 E
Lianjiang, Guangdong, China 69 G8 21 40N 110 20 E
Lianping, China 69 E10 24 26N 114 30 E
Lianshan, China 69 E9 24 38N 112 8 E
Lianshanguan, China 67 D12 40 53N 123 43 E
Lianshui, China 67 H10 33 42N 119 20 E
Lianyuan, China 69 D8 27 40N 111 38 E
Lianyungang, China 67 G10 34 40N 119 11 E
Liao He →, China 67 D11 41 0N 121 50 E
Liaocheng, China 66 F8 36 28N 115 58 E
Liaodong Bandao, China 67 E12 40 0N 122 30 E
Liaodong Wan, China 67 D11 40 20N 121 10 E
Liaoning □, China 65 B7 41 40N 122 30 E
Liaoning □, Liaoning, China 67 D12 42 0N 122 0 E
Liaoyang, China 67 D12 41 15N 122 58 E
Liaoyuan, China 67 C13 42 58N 125 2 E
Liaozhong, China 67 D12 41 23N 122 50 E
Liapádhes, Greece 44 E1 39 42N 19 40 E
Liard →, Canada 130 A4 61 51N 121 18W
Liari, Pakistan 80 G2 25 37N 66 30 E
Líbano, Colombia 152 C2 4 55N 75 4W
Libau = Liepaja, U.S.S.R. 50 C2 56 30N 21 0 E
Libby, U.S.A. 142 B6 48 20N 115 33W
Libenge, Zaïre 102 B3 3 40N 18 55 E
Liberal, Kans., U.S.A. 139 G4 37 4N 101 0W
Liberal, Mo., U.S.A. 139 G7 37 35N 94 30W
Liberdade, Brazil 156 C3 10 5 S 70 20W
Liberdade →, Brazil 157 B7 9 40 S 52 17W
Liberec, Czech. 30 A8 50 47N 15 7 E
Liberia, Costa Rica 148 D2 10 40N 85 30W
Liberia ■, W. Afr. 100 D3 6 30N 9 30W
Libertad, Venezuela 152 B4 8 20N 69 37W
Liberty, Ind., U.S.A. 141 E12 39 38N 84 56W
Liberty, Mo., U.S.A. 140 E2 39 15N 94 24W
Liberty, Tex., U.S.A. 139 K7 30 5N 94 50W
Liberty Center, U.S.A. 141 C12 41 27N 84 1W
Libertyville, U.S.A. 141 B9 42 18N 87 57W
Libiaz, Poland 31 A12 50 7N 19 21 E
Libibi, Angola 103 E3 14 42 S 17 44 E
Libin, Belgium 21 J6 49 59N 5 15 E
Lîbîya, Sahrâ', Africa 96 C4 25 0N 25 0 E
Libo, China 68 E6 25 22N 107 53 E
Libobo, Tanjung, Indonesia 71 E7 0 54 S 128 28 E
Libode, S. Africa 105 E4 31 33 S 29 2 E
Libohava, Albania 44 D2 40 3N 20 10 E
Libonda, Zambia 103 E4 14 28 S 23 12 E
Libourne, France 24 D3 44 55N 0 14W
Libramont, Belgium 21 J6 49 55N 5 23 E
Librazhdi, Albania 44 C2 41 12N 20 22 E
Libreville, Gabon 102 B1 0 25N 9 26 E
Libya ■, N. Afr. 96 C3 27 0N 17 0 E
Libyan Desert = Lîbîya, Sahrâ', Africa 96 C4 25 0N 25 0 E
Libyan Plateau = Ed-Déffa, Egypt 94 A2 30 40N 26 30 E
Licantén, Chile 158 D1 35 55 S 72 0W
Licata, Italy 40 E6 37 6N 13 55 E
Lice, Turkey 89 D9 38 27N 40 39 E
Licheng, China 66 F7 36 28N 113 20 E
Lichfield, U.K. 16 E6 52 40N 1 50W
Lichinga, Mozam. 107 E4 13 13 S 35 11 E
Lichtaart, Belgium 21 F5 51 13N 4 55 E
Lichtenburg, S. Africa 104 D4 26 8 S 26 8 E
Lichtenfels, Germany 27 E7 50 7N 11 4 E
Lichtenvoorde, Neths. 20 E9 51 59N 6 34 E
Lichtervelde, Belgium 21 F2 51 2N 3 9 E
Lichuan, Hubei, China 68 B7 30 18N 108 57 E
Lichuan, Jiangxi, China 69 D11 27 18N 116 55 E
Licking, South Fork →, U.S.A. 141 F12 38 40N 84 19W
Licosa, Punta, Italy 41 B7 40 15N 14 53 E
Lida, U.S.A. 143 H5 37 30N 117 30W
Lida, U.S.S.R. 50 E4 53 53N 25 15 E
Lidingö, Sweden 14 E12 59 22N 18 8 E
Lidköping, Sweden 15 F7 58 31N 13 14 E
Lido, Italy 39 C9 45 25N 12 23 E
Lido, Niger 101 C5 12 54N 3 44 E
Lido di Roma = Óstia, Lido di, Italy 40 A5 41 43N 12 17 E
Lidzbark, Poland 47 B6 53 15N 19 49 E
Lidzbark Warminski, Poland 47 A7 54 7N 20 34 E
Liebenwalde, Germany 26 C9 52 51N 13 23 E
Lieberose, Germany 26 D10 51 59N 14 18 E
Liebig, Mt., Australia 112 D5 23 18 S 131 22 E
Liebling, Romania 46 D2 45 36N 21 20 E
Liechtenstein ■, Europe 29 B9 47 8N 9 35 E
Liederkerke, Belgium 21 G4 50 52N 4 5 E
Liège, Belgium 21 G7 50 38N 5 35 E
Liège □, Belgium 21 G7 50 32N 5 35 E
Liegnitz = Legnica, Poland 47 D3 51 12N 16 10 E
Liempde, Neths. 21 E6 51 35N 5 23 E
Lienart, Zaïre 106 B2 3 3N 25 31 E
Lienyünchiangshih = Lianyungang, China 67 G10 34 40N 119 11 E
Lienz, Austria 30 E5 46 50N 12 46 E
Liepaja, U.S.S.R. 50 C2 56 30N 21 0 E
Lier, Belgium 21 F5 51 7N 4 34 E
Lierneux, Belgium 21 H7 50 17N 5 47 E
Lieshout, Neths. 21 E7 51 31N 5 36 E
Liești, Romania 46 D8 45 38N 27 34 E
Liestal, Switz. 28 B5 47 29N 7 44 E
Liévin, France 23 B9 50 24N 2 47 E
Lièvre →, Canada 128 C4 45 31N 75 26W
Liezen, Austria 30 D7 47 34N 14 15 E
Lifford, Ireland 19 B4 54 50N 7 30W
Liffré, France 22 D5 48 12N 1 30W
Lifjell, Norway 14 E2 59 27N 8 45 E
Lifudzin, U.S.S.R. 60 B7 44 21N 134 58 E
Lifuka, Tonga 121 P13 19 48 S 174 21W
Lightning Ridge, Australia 115 D4 29 22 S 148 0 E
Lignano, Italy 39 C10 45 42N 13 8 E
Ligny-en-Barrois, France 23 D12 48 36N 5 20 E
Ligny-le-Châtel, France 23 E10 47 54N 3 45 E
Ligoúrion, Greece 45 G5 37 37N 23 2 E
Ligueil, France 22 E7 47 2N 0 49 E
Liguria □, Italy 38 D6 44 30N 9 0 E
Ligurian Sea, Italy 38 E6 43 20N 9 0 E
Lihir Group, Papua N. G. 120 B7 3 0 S 152 35 E
Lihou Reefs and Cays, Australia 114 B5 17 25 S 151 40 E
Lihue, U.S.A. 132 H15 21 59N 159 24W
Lijiang, China 68 D3 26 55N 100 20 E
Likasi, Zaïre 107 E2 10 55 S 26 48 E
Likati, Zaïre 102 B4 3 20N 24 0 E
Likhoslavl, U.S.S.R. 50 C9 57 12N 35 30 E
Likhovski, U.S.S.R. 53 B9 48 10N 40 10 E
Likokou, Gabon 102 C2 0 12 S 12 48 E
Likoma I., Malawi 107 E3 12 3 S 34 45 E
Likumburu, Tanzania 107 D4 9 43 S 35 8 E
L'Île-Bouchard, France 22 E7 47 7N 0 26 E
L'Ile-Rousse, France 25 F12 42 38N 8 57 E
Liling, China 69 D9 27 42N 113 29 E
Lille, Belgium 21 F5 51 15N 4 50 E
Lille, France 23 B10 50 38N 3 3 E
Lille Bælt, Denmark 15 J3 55 20N 9 45 E
Lillebonne, France 22 C7 49 30N 0 32 E
Lillehammer, Norway 14 C4 61 8N 10 30 E
Lillers, France 23 B9 50 35N 2 28 E
Lillesand, Norway 15 F2 58 15N 8 23 E
Lilleshall, U.K. 17 E5 52 45N 2 22W
Lillestrøm, Norway 14 E5 59 58N 11 5 E
Lillian Point, Mt., Australia 113 E4 27 40 S 126 6 E
Lillo, Spain 34 F1 39 45N 3 20W
Lillooet →, Canada 130 D4 49 15N 121 57W
Lilongwe, Malawi 107 E3 14 0 S 33 48 E
Liloy, Phil. 71 C6 8 4N 122 39 E
Lim →, Yugoslavia 42 D4 43 45N 19 15 E
Lima, Indonesia 71 E7 3 37 S 128 4 E
Lima, Peru 156 C2 12 0 S 77 0W
Lima, Mont., U.S.A. 142 D7 44 41N 112 38W
Lima, Ohio, U.S.A. 141 D12 40 42N 84 5W
Lima □, Peru 156 C2 12 3 S 77 3W
Lima →, Portugal 36 D2 41 41N 8 50W
Limages, Canada 137 A9 45 20N 75 16W
Liman, U.S.S.R. 53 D12 45 45N 47 12 E
Limanowa, Poland 31 B13 49 42N 20 22 E
Limassol, Cyprus 32 E12 34 42N 33 1 E
Limavady, U.K. 19 A5 55 3N 6 58W
Limavady □, U.K. 19 B5 55 0N 6 55W
Limay →, Argentina 160 A3 39 0 S 68 0W
Limay Mahuida, Argentina 158 D2 37 10 S 66 45W
Limbang, Brunei 70 D5 4 42N 115 6 E
Limbara, Monti, Italy 40 B2 40 50N 9 10 E
Limbdi, India 80 H4 22 34N 71 51 E
Limbe, Cameroon 101 E6 4 1N 9 10 E
Limbourg, Belgium 21 G7 50 37N 5 56 E
Limbri, Australia 117 A9 31 3 S 151 5 E
Limbueta, Angola 103 E3 12 30 S 18 42 E
Limbunya, Australia 112 C4 17 14 S 129 50 E
Limburg, Germany 27 E4 50 22N 8 4 E
Limburg □, Belgium 21 F6 51 2N 5 25 E
Limburg □, Neths. 21 F7 51 20N 5 55 E
Limeira, Brazil 159 A6 22 35 S 47 28W
Limenária, Greece 44 D6 40 38N 24 32 E
Limerick, Ireland 19 D3 52 40N 8 38W
Limerick □, Ireland 19 D3 52 30N 8 50W
Limestone, U.S.A. 136 D6 42 2N 78 39W
Limestone →, Canada 131 B10 56 31N 94 7W
Limfjorden, Denmark 15 H3 56 55N 9 0 E
Limia = Lima →, Portugal 36 D2 41 41N 8 50W
Limmared, Sweden 15 G7 57 34N 13 20 E
Limmat →, Switz. 29 B6 47 26N 8 20 E
Limmen, Neths. 20 C5 52 34N 4 42 E
Limmen Bight, Australia 114 A2 14 40 S 135 35 E
Limmen Bight →, Australia 114 B2 15 7 S 135 44 E
Límni, Greece 45 F5 38 43N 23 18 E
Límnos, Greece 44 E7 39 50N 25 5 E
Limoeiro, Brazil 154 C4 7 52 S 35 27W
Limoeiro do Norte, Brazil 154 C4 5 5 S 38 0W
Limoges, France 24 C5 45 50N 1 15 E
Limón, Costa Rica 148 E3 10 0N 83 2W
Limon, U.S.A. 138 F3 39 18N 103 38W
Limone Piemonte, Italy 38 D4 44 12N 7 32 E
Limousin, France 24 C5 45 30N 1 30 E
Limousin, Plateaux du, France 24 C5 45 45N 1 15 E
Limoux, France 24 E6 43 4N 2 12 E
Limpopo →, Africa 105 D5 25 5 S 33 30 E
Limuru, Kenya 106 C4 1 2 S 36 35 E
Lin Xian, China 66 F6 37 57N 110 58 E
Lin'an, China 69 B12 30 15N 119 42 E
Linares, Chile 158 D1 35 50 S 71 40W
Linares, Colombia 152 C2 1 23N 77 31W
Linares, Mexico 147 C5 24 50N 99 40W
Linares, Spain 35 G1 38 10N 3 40W
Linares □, Chile 158 D1 36 0 S 71 0W

Línas Mte., *Italy* **40 C1** 39 25N 8 38 E
Lincang, *China* **68 F3** 23 58N 100 1 E
Lincheng, *China* **66 F8** 37 25N 114 30 E
Linchuan, *China* **69 D11** 27 57N 116 15 E
Lincoln, *Argentina* **158 C3** 34 55 S 61 30W
Lincoln, *N.Z.* **119 D7** 43 38 S 172 30 E
Lincoln, *U.K.* **16 D7** 53 14N 0 32W
Lincoln, *Calif., U.S.A.* **144 G5** 38 54N 121 17W
Lincoln, *Ill., U.S.A.* **140 D7** 40 10N 89 20W
Lincoln, *Kans., U.S.A.* **138 F5** 39 6N 98 9W
Lincoln, *Maine, U.S.A.* **129 C6** 45 27N 68 29W
Lincoln, *N.H., U.S.A.* **137 B13** 44 3N 71 40W
Lincoln, *N. Mex., U.S.A.* **143 K11** 33 30N 105 26W
Lincoln, *Nebr., U.S.A.* **138 E6** 40 50N 96 42W
Lincoln Park, *U.S.A.* **141 B13** 42 15N 83 11W
Lincoln Sea, *Arctic* **6 A5** 84 0N 55 0W
Lincoln Wolds, *U.K.* **16 D7** 53 20N 0 5W
Lincolnshire □, *U.K.* **16 D7** 53 14N 0 32W
Lincolnton, *U.S.A.* **135 H5** 35 30N 81 15W
L'Incudine, *France* **25 G13** 41 50N 9 12 E
Lind, *U.S.A.* **142 C4** 47 0N 118 33W
Linda, *U.S.A.* **144 F5** 39 6N 121 34W
Lindau, *Germany* **27 H5** 47 33N 9 41 E
Linde →, *Neths.* **20 C7** 52 50N 5 57 E
Linden, *Calif., U.S.A.* **144 G5** 38 1N 121 5W
Linden, *Ind., U.S.A.* **141 D10** 40 11N 86 54W
Linden, *Mich., U.S.A.* **141 B13** 42 49N 83 47W
Linden, *Tex., U.S.A.* **139 J7** 33 0N 94 20W
Lindenheuvel, *Neths.* **21 G7** 50 59N 5 48 E
Lindenhurst, *U.S.A.* **137 F11** 40 41N 73 23W
Linderöd, *Sweden* **15 J7** 55 56N 13 47 E
Linderödsåsen, *Sweden* **15 J7** 55 53N 13 53 E
Lindesnes, *Norway* **10 D7** 57 58N 7 3 E
Líndhos, *Greece* **32 C10** 36 6N 28 4 E
Lindi, *Tanzania* **107 D4** 9 58 S 39 38 E
Lindi □, *Tanzania* **107 D4** 9 40 S 38 30 E
Lindi →, *Zaïre* **106 B2** 0 33N 25 5 E
Lindoso, *Portugal* **36 D2** 41 52N 8 11W
Lindow, *Germany* **26 C8** 52 58N 12 58 E
Lindsay, *Canada* **128 D4** 44 22N 78 43W
Lindsay, *Calif., U.S.A.* **144 J7** 36 14N 119 6W
Lindsay, *Okla., U.S.A.* **139 H6** 34 51N 97 37W
Lindsborg, *U.S.A.* **138 F6** 38 35N 97 40W
Lineville, *U.S.A.* **140 D3** 40 35N 93 31W
Linfen, *China* **66 F6** 36 3N 111 30 E
Ling Xian, *Hunan, China* **69 D9** 26 29N 113 48 E
Ling Xian, *Shandong, China* **66 F9** 37 22N 116 30 E
Lingao, *China* **76 C7** 19 56N 109 42 E
Lingayen, *Phil.* **71 A6** 16 1N 120 14 E
Lingayen G., *Phil.* **71 A6** 16 10N 120 15 E
Lingbi, *China* **67 H9** 33 33N 117 33 E
Lingchuan, *Guangxi Zhuangzu, China* **69 E8** 25 26N 110 21 E
Lingchuan, *Shanxi, China* **66 G7** 35 45N 113 12 E
Lingen, *Germany* **26 C3** 52 32N 7 21 E
Lingga, *Indonesia* **70 E2** 0 12 S 104 37 E
Lingga, Kepulauan, *Indonesia* **70 E2** 0 10 S 104 30 E
Lingga Arch. = Lingga, Kepulauan, *Indonesia* **70 E2** 0 10 S 104 30 E
Lingle, *U.S.A.* **138 D2** 42 10N 104 18W
Lingling, *China* **69 D8** 26 17N 111 37 E
Lingqiu, *China* **66 E8** 39 28N 114 22 E
Lingshan, *China* **68 F7** 22 25N 109 18 E
Lingshi, *China* **66 F6** 36 48N 111 48 E
Lingshou, *China* **66 E8** 38 20N 114 20 E
Lingshui, *China* **76 C8** 18 27N 110 0 E
Lingtai, *China* **66 G4** 35 0N 107 40 E
Linguère, *Senegal* **100 B1** 15 25N 15 5W
Lingwu, *China* **66 E4** 38 6N 106 20 E
Lingyuan, *China* **67 D10** 41 10N 119 15 E
Lingyun, *China* **68 E6** 25 2N 106 35 E
Linh Cam, *Vietnam* **76 C5** 18 31N 105 31 E
Linhai, *China* **69 C13** 28 50N 121 8 E
Linhares, *Brazil* **155 E3** 19 25 S 40 4W
Linhe, *China* **66 D4** 40 48N 107 20 E
Linjiang, *China* **67 D14** 41 50N 127 0 E
Linköping, *Sweden* **15 F9** 58 28N 15 36 E
Linkou, *China* **67 B16** 45 15N 130 18 E
Linli, *China* **69 C8** 29 27N 111 30 E
Linlithgow, *U.K.* **18 F5** 55 58N 3 38W
Linn, *U.S.A.* **140 F5** 38 29N 91 51W
Linneus, *U.S.A.* **140 E3** 39 53N 93 11W
Linnhe, L., *U.K.* **18 E3** 56 36N 5 25W
Linosa, I., *Medit. S.* **96 A2** 35 51N 12 50 E
Linqi, *China* **66 G7** 35 45N 113 52 E
Linqing, *China* **66 F8** 36 50N 115 42 E
Linqu, *China* **67 F10** 36 25N 118 30 E
Linru, *China* **66 G7** 34 11N 112 52 E
Lins, *Brazil* **159 A6** 21 40 S 49 44W
Linshui, *China* **68 B6** 30 21N 106 57 E
Lintao, *China* **66 G2** 35 18N 103 52 E
Linth →, *Switz.* **27 H5** 47 7N 9 7 E
Linthal, *Switz.* **29 C8** 46 54N 9 0 E
Lintlaw, *Canada* **131 C8** 52 4N 103 14W
Linton, *Canada* **129 C5** 47 15N 72 16W
Linton, *Ind., U.S.A.* **141 F9** 39 0N 87 10W
Linton, *N. Dak., U.S.A.* **138 B4** 46 21N 100 12W
Lintong, *China* **66 G5** 34 20N 109 10 E
Linville, *Australia* **115 D5** 26 50 S 152 11 E
Linwood, *Canada* **136 C4** 43 35N 80 43W
Linwu, *China* **69 E9** 25 19N 112 31 E
Linxi, *China* **67 C10** 43 36N 118 2 E
Linxia, *China* **64 C5** 35 36N 103 10 E
Linxiang, *China* **69 C9** 29 28N 113 23 E
Linyanti →, *Africa* **104 B4** 17 50 S 25 5 E
Linyi, *China* **67 G10** 35 5N 118 21 E
Linz, *Austria* **30 C7** 48 18N 14 18 E
Linz, *Germany* **26 E3** 50 33N 7 18 E
Linzhenzhen, *China* **66 F5** 36 30N 109 59 E
Linzi, *China* **67 F10** 36 50N 118 20 E
Lion, G. du, *France* **25 E8** 43 10N 4 0 E
Lionárisso, *Cyprus* **32 D13** 35 28N 34 8 E
Lioni, *Italy* **41 B8** 40 52N 15 10 E
Lion's Den, *Zimbabwe* **107 F3** 17 15 S 30 5 E
Lion's Head, *Canada* **128 D3** 44 58N 81 15W
Liouesso, *Congo* **102 B3** 1 2N 15 43 E
Liozno, *U.S.S.R.* **50 D7** 55 0N 30 50 E
Lipa, *Phil.* **71 B6** 13 57N 121 10 E
Lipali, *Mozam.* **107 F4** 15 50 S 35 50 E
Lípari, *Italy* **41 D7** 38 26N 14 58 E
Lípari, Is., *Italy* **41 D7** 38 30N 14 50 E
Lipetsk, *U.S.S.R.* **51 E11** 52 37N 39 35 E
Lipiany, *Poland* **47 B1** 53 2N 14 58 E
Liping, *China* **68 D7** 26 15N 109 7 E
Lipkany, *U.S.S.R.* **52 B2** 48 14N 26 48 E
Lipljan, *Yugoslavia* **42 E6** 42 31N 21 7 E
Lipnik, *Czech.* **31 B10** 49 32N 17 36 E
Lipno, *Poland* **47 C6** 52 49N 19 15 E
Lipova, *Romania* **42 A6** 46 8N 21 42 E
Lipovcy Manzovka, *U.S.S.R.* **60 B6** 44 12N 132 26 E
Lipovets, *U.S.S.R.* **52 B3** 49 12N 29 1 E
Lippe →, *Germany* **26 D2** 51 39N 6 38 E
Lippstadt, *Germany* **26 D4** 51 40N 8 19 E
Lipscomb, *U.S.A.* **139 G4** 36 16N 100 16W
Lipsko, *Poland* **47 D8** 51 9N 21 40 E
Lipsói, *Greece* **45 G8** 37 19N 26 50 E
Liptovsky Svaty Milkulaš, *Czech.* **31 B12** 49 6N 19 35 E
Liptrap C., *Australia* **117 E6** 38 50 S 145 55 E
Lipu, *China* **69 E8** 24 30N 110 22 E
Lira, *Uganda* **106 B3** 2 17N 32 57 E
Liri →, *Italy* **40 A6** 41 25N 13 52 E
Liria, *Spain* **34 F4** 39 37N 0 35W
Lisala, *Zaïre* **102 B4** 2 12N 21 38 E
Lisboa, *Portugal* **37 G1** 38 42N 9 10W
Lisboa □, *Portugal* **37 G1** 39 0N 9 12W
Lisbon = Lisboa, *Portugal* **37 G1** 38 42N 9 10W
Lisbon, *N. Dak., U.S.A.* **138 B6** 46 30N 97 46W
Lisbon, *N.H., U.S.A.* **137 B13** 44 13N 71 52W
Lisbon, *Ohio, U.S.A.* **136 F4** 40 45N 80 42W
Lisburn, *U.K.* **19 B5** 54 30N 6 9W
Lisburne, C., *U.S.A.* **126 B3** 68 50N 166 0W
Liscannor, B., *Ireland* **19 D2** 52 57N 9 24W
Liscia →, *Italy* **40 A2** 41 11N 9 9 E
Lishe Jiang →, *China* **68 E3** 24 15N 101 35 E
Lishi, *China* **66 F6** 37 31N 111 8 E
Lishu, *China* **67 C13** 43 20N 124 18 E
Lishui, *Jiangsu, China* **69 B12** 31 38N 119 2 E
Lishui, *Zhejiang, China* **69 C12** 28 28N 119 54 E
Lisianski I., *Pac. Oc.* **122 E10** 26 2N 174 0W
Lisichansk, *U.S.S.R.* **52 B8** 48 55N 38 30 E
Lisieux, *France* **22 C7** 49 10N 0 12 E
L'Isle-Adam, *France* **23 C9** 49 6N 2 14 E
L'Isle-Jourdain, *Gers, France* **24 E5** 43 36N 1 5 E
L'Isle-Jourdain, *Vienne, France* **24 B4** 46 13N 0 31 E
L'Isle-sur-le-Doubs, *France* **23 E13** 47 26N 6 34 E
Lisle-sur-Tarn, *France* **24 E5** 43 52N 1 49 E
Lismore, *Australia* **115 D5** 28 44 S 153 21 E
Lismore, *Ireland* **19 D4** 52 8N 7 58W
Lisse, *Neths.* **20 D5** 52 16N 4 33 E
List, *Germany* **26 A4** 55 1N 8 26 E
Lista, *Norway* **13 G9** 58 7N 6 39 E
Lista, *Sweden* **13 G14** 59 19N 16 16 E
Lister, Mt., *Antarctica* **7 D11** 78 0 S 162 0 E
Liston, *Australia* **115 D5** 28 39 S 152 6 E
Listowel, *Canada* **128 D3** 43 44N 80 58W
Listowel, *Ireland* **19 D2** 52 27N 9 30W
Lit-et-Mixe, *France* **24 D2** 44 2N 1 15W
Litang, *Guangxi Zhuangzu, China* **68 F7** 23 12N 109 8 E
Litang, *Sichuan, China* **68 B3** 30 1N 100 17 E
Litang, *Malaysia* **71 C5** 5 27N 118 31 E
Litang Qu →, *China* **68 C3** 28 4N 101 32 E
Litani →, *Lebanon* **91 B4** 33 20N 35 15 E
Litchfield, *Australia* **116 D5** 36 18 S 142 52 E
Litchfield, *Calif., U.S.A.* **144 E6** 40 24N 120 23W
Litchfield, *Conn., U.S.A.* **137 E11** 41 44N 73 12W
Litchfield, *Ill., U.S.A.* **140 E7** 39 10N 89 40W
Litchfield, *Minn., U.S.A.* **138 C7** 45 5N 94 31W
Liteni, *Romania* **46 B7** 47 32N 26 32 E
Lithgow, *Australia* **117 B9** 33 25 S 150 8 E
Líthinon, Ákra, *Greece* **32 E6** 34 55N 24 44 E
Lithuanian S.S.R. □, *U.S.S.R.* **50 D4** 55 30N 24 0 E
Litija, *Yugoslavia* **39 B11** 46 3N 14 50 E
Litókhoron, *Greece* **44 D4** 40 8N 22 34 E
Litoměřice, *Czech.* **30 A7** 50 33N 14 10 E
Litomysl, *Czech.* **31 B9** 49 52N 16 20 E
Litschau, *Austria* **30 C8** 48 58N 15 4 E
Little Abaco I., *Bahamas* **148 A4** 26 50N 77 30W
Little Aden, *Yemen* **86 D4** 12 45N 44 52 E
Little Barrier I., *N.Z.* **118 C4** 36 12 S 175 8 E
Little Belt Mts., *U.S.A.* **142 C8** 46 50N 111 0W
Little Blue →, *U.S.A.* **138 F6** 39 41N 96 40W
Little Bushman Land, *S. Africa* **104 D2** 29 10 S 18 10 E
Little Cadotte →, *Canada* **130 B5** 56 41N 117 6W
Little Cayman, I., *Cayman Is.* **148 C3** 19 41N 80 3W
Little Churchill →, *Canada* **131 B9** 57 30N 95 22W
Little Colorado →, *U.S.A.* **143 H8** 36 11N 111 48W
Little Current, *Canada* **128 C3** 45 55N 82 0W
Little Current →, *Canada* **128 B3** 50 57N 84 36W
Little Falls, *Minn., U.S.A.* **138 C7** 45 58N 94 19W
Little Falls, *N.Y., U.S.A.* **137 C10** 43 3N 74 50W
Little Fork →, *U.S.A.* **138 A8** 48 31N 93 35W
Little Grand Rapids, *Canada* **131 C9** 52 0N 95 29W
Little Humboldt →, *U.S.A.* **142 F5** 41 0N 117 43W
Little Inagua I., *Bahamas* **149 B5** 21 40N 73 50W
Little Karoo, *S. Africa* **104 E3** 33 45 S 21 0 E
Little Lake, *U.S.A.* **145 K9** 35 58N 117 58W
Little Laut Is. = Laut Ketil, Kepulauan, *Indonesia* **70 E5** 4 45 S 115 40 E
Little Minch, *U.K.* **18 D2** 57 35N 6 45W
Little Missouri →, *U.S.A.* **138 B3** 47 30N 102 25W
Little Namaqualand, *S. Africa* **104 D2** 29 0 S 17 9 E
Little Ouse →, *U.K.* **17 E8** 52 25N 0 50 E
Little Rann, *India* **80 H4** 23 25N 71 25 E
Little Red →, *U.S.A.* **139 H9** 35 11N 91 27W
Little River, *N.Z.* **119 D7** 43 45 S 172 49 E
Little Rock, *U.S.A.* **139 H8** 34 41N 92 10W
Little Ruaha →, *Tanzania* **106 D4** 7 57 S 37 53 E
Little Sable Pt., *U.S.A.* **134 D2** 43 40N 86 32W
Little Sioux →, *U.S.A.* **138 E6** 41 49N 96 4W
Little Smoky →, *Canada* **130 C5** 54 44N 117 11W
Little Snake →, *U.S.A.* **142 F9** 40 27N 108 26W
Little Valley, *U.S.A.* **136 D6** 42 15N 78 48W
Little Wabash →, *U.S.A.* **141 G8** 37 54N 88 5W
Little York, *U.S.A.* **140 C6** 41 1N 90 45W
Littlefield, *U.S.A.* **139 J3** 33 57N 102 17W
Littlefork, *U.S.A.* **138 A8** 48 24N 93 35W
Littlehampton, *U.K.* **17 G7** 50 48N 0 32W
Littleton, *U.S.A.* **137 B13** 44 19N 71 47W
Liu He →, *China* **67 D11** 40 55N 121 35 E
Liu Jiang →, *China* **68 F7** 23 55N 109 30 E
Liuba, *China* **66 H4** 33 38N 106 55 E
Liucheng, *China* **68 E7** 24 38N 109 14 E
Liugou, *China* **67 D10** 40 57N 118 15 E
Liuhe, *China* **67 C13** 42 17N 125 43 E
Liuheng Dao, *China* **69 C14** 29 40N 122 5 E
Liukang Tenggaja, *Indonesia* **71 F5** 6 45 S 118 50 E
Liuli, *Tanzania* **107 E3** 11 3 S 34 38 E
Liuwa Plain, *Zambia* **103 E4** 14 20 S 22 30 E
Liuyang, *China* **69 C9** 28 10N 113 37 E
Liuzhou, *China* **68 E7** 24 22N 109 22 E
Liuzhuang, *China* **67 H11** 33 12N 120 18 E
Livada, *Romania* **46 B4** 47 52N 23 5 E
Livadherón, *Greece* **44 D3** 40 2N 21 57 E
Livadhia, *Cyprus* **32 E12** 34 57N 33 38 E
Livanovka, *U.S.S.R.* **54 E7** 52 6N 61 59 E
Livarot, *France* **22 D7** 48 58N 0 9 E
Live Oak, *Calif., U.S.A.* **144 F5** 39 17N 121 40W
Live Oak, *Fla., U.S.A.* **135 K4** 30 17N 83 0W
Liveras, *Cyprus* **32 D11** 35 23N 32 57 E
Liveringa, *Australia* **112 C3** 18 3 S 124 10 E
Livermore, *U.S.A.* **144 H5** 37 41N 121 47W
Livermore, Mt., *U.S.A.* **139 K2** 30 45N 104 8W
Liverpool, *Australia* **117 B9** 33 54 S 150 58 E
Liverpool, *Canada* **129 D7** 44 5N 64 41W
Liverpool, *U.K.* **16 D5** 53 25N 3 0W
Liverpool Plains, *Australia* **117 A9** 31 15 S 150 15 E
Liverpool Ra., *Australia* **117 A9** 31 50 S 150 30 E
Livingston, *Guatemala* **148 C2** 15 50N 88 50W
Livingston, *Calif., U.S.A.* **144 H6** 37 23N 120 43W
Livingston, *Mont., U.S.A.* **142 D8** 45 40N 110 40W
Livingston, *Tex., U.S.A.* **139 K7** 30 44N 94 54W
Livingston, *Wis., U.S.A.* **140 B6** 42 54N 90 26W
Livingstone, *Zambia* **107 F2** 17 46 S 25 52 E
Livingstone Mts., *N.Z.* **119 F3** 45 15 S 168 9 E
Livingstone Mts., *Tanzania* **107 D3** 9 40 S 34 20 E
Livingstonia, *Malawi* **107 E3** 10 38 S 34 5 E
Livno, *Yugoslavia* **42 D2** 43 50N 17 0 E
Livny, *U.S.S.R.* **51 E10** 52 30N 37 30 E
Livonia, *U.S.A.* **141 B13** 42 25N 83 23W
Livorno, *Italy* **38 E7** 43 32N 10 18 E
Livramento, *Brazil* **159 C4** 30 55 S 55 30W
Livramento do Brumado, *Brazil* **155 D3** 13 39 S 41 50W
Livron-sur-Drôme, *France* **25 D8** 44 46N 4 51 E
Liwale, *Tanzania* **107 D4** 9 48 S 37 58 E
Liwale □, *Tanzania* **107 D4** 9 0 S 38 0 E
Liwiec →, *Poland* **47 C8** 52 36N 21 34 E
Lixi, *China* **68 D3** 26 23N 101 59 E
Lixoúrion, *Greece* **45 F2** 38 14N 20 24 E
Liyang, *China* **69 B12** 31 26N 119 28 E
Lizard I., *Australia* **114 A4** 14 42 S 145 30 E
Lizard Pt., *U.K.* **17 H2** 49 57N 5 11W
Lizarda, *Brazil* **154 C2** 9 36 S 46 41W
Lizzano, *Italy* **41 B10** 40 23N 17 25 E
Ljig, *Yugoslavia* **42 C5** 44 13N 20 18 E
Ljubija, *Yugoslavia* **39 D13** 44 55N 16 35 E
Ljubinje, *Yugoslavia* **42 E3** 42 58N 18 5 E
Ljubljana, *Yugoslavia* **39 B11** 46 4N 14 33 E
Ljubno, *Yugoslavia* **39 B11** 46 25N 14 46 E
Ljubovija, *Yugoslavia* **42 C4** 44 11N 19 22 E
Ljubuški, *Yugoslavia* **42 D2** 43 12N 17 34 E
Ljung, *Sweden* **15 F7** 58 1N 13 3 E
Ljungan →, *Sweden* **14 B11** 62 18N 17 23 E
Ljungaverk, *Sweden* **14 B10** 62 30N 16 5 E
Ljungby, *Sweden* **13 H12** 56 49N 13 55 E
Ljusdal, *Sweden* **14 C10** 61 46N 16 3 E
Ljusnan →, *Sweden* **13 F14** 61 12N 17 8 E
Ljusne, *Sweden* **13 F14** 61 13N 17 7 E
Ljutomer, *Yugoslavia* **39 B13** 46 31N 16 11 E
Llagostera, *Spain* **34 D7** 41 50N 2 54 E
Llamellín, *Peru* **156 B2** 9 0 S 76 54W
Llancanelo, Salina, *Argentina* **158 D2** 35 40 S 69 8W
Llandeilo, *U.K.* **17 F3** 51 53N 4 3W
Llandovery, *U.K.* **17 F4** 51 59N 3 49W
Llandrindod Wells, *U.K.* **17 E4** 52 15N 3 23W
Llandudno, *U.K.* **16 D4** 53 19N 3 51W
Llanelli, *U.K.* **17 F3** 51 41N 4 11W
Llanes, *Spain* **36 B6** 43 25N 4 50W
Llangollen, *U.K.* **16 E4** 52 58N 3 10W
Llanidloes, *U.K.* **17 E4** 52 28N 3 31W
Llano, *U.S.A.* **139 K5** 30 45N 98 41W
Llano →, *U.S.A.* **139 K5** 30 50N 98 25W
Llano Estacado, *U.S.A.* **139 J3** 34 0N 103 0W
Llanos, *S. Amer.* **150 B2** 5 0N 71 35W
Llanquihue □, *Chile* **160 B2** 41 30 S 73 0W
Llanquihue, L., *Chile* **160 B1** 41 10 S 75 50W
Llebetx, C., *Spain* **33 B9** 39 33N 2 18 E
Llentrisca, C., *Spain* **33 C7** 38 52N 1 15 E
Llera, *Mexico* **147 C5** 23 19N 99 1W
Llerena, *Spain* **37 G5** 38 17N 6 0W
Llica, *Bolivia* **156 D4** 19 52 S 68 16W
Llico, *Chile* **158 C1** 34 46 S 72 5W
Llobregat →, *Spain* **34 D7** 41 19N 2 9 E
Lloret de Mar, *Spain* **34 D7** 41 41N 2 53 E
Lloyd B., *Australia* **114 A3** 12 45 S 143 27 E
Lloyd L., *Canada* **131 B7** 57 22N 108 57W
Lloydminster, *Canada* **131 C7** 53 17N 110 0W
Lluchmayor, *Spain* **33 B9** 39 29N 2 53 E
Llullaillaco, Volcán, *S. Amer.* **158 A2** 24 43 S 68 30W
Lo, *Belgium* **21 G1** 50 59N 2 45 E
Lo →, *Vietnam* **76 B5** 21 18N 105 25 E
Loa, *U.S.A.* **143 G8** 38 18N 111 40W
Loa →, *Chile* **158 A1** 21 26 S 70 41W
Loano, *Italy* **38 D5** 44 8N 8 14 E
Lobatse, *Botswana* **104 D4** 25 12 S 25 40 E
Löbau, *Germany* **26 D10** 51 5N 14 42 E
Lobaye →, *C.A.R.* **102 B3** 3 41N 18 35 E
Lobbes, *Belgium* **21 H4** 50 21N 4 16 E
Lobenstein, *Germany* **26 E7** 50 25N 11 39 E
Lobería, *Argentina* **158 D4** 38 10 S 58 40W
Łobez, *Poland* **47 B2** 53 38N 15 39 E
Lobito, *Angola* **103 E2** 12 18 S 13 35 E
Lobón, Canal de, *Spain* **37 G4** 38 50N 6 55W
Lobos, *Argentina* **158 D4** 35 10 S 59 0W
Lobos, I., *Mexico* **146 B2** 27 15N 110 30W
Lobos, Is., *Peru* **150 C1** 6 57 S 80 45W
Lobos, I. de, *Canary Is.* **33 F6** 28 45N 13 50W
Lobos de Tierra, I., *Peru* **156 B1** 6 27 S 80 52W
Lobva, *U.S.S.R.* **54 B7** 59 10N 60 30 E
Lobva →, *U.S.S.R.* **54 B7** 59 8N 60 48 E
Loc Binh, *Vietnam* **76 B6** 21 46N 106 54 E
Loc Ninh, *Vietnam* **77 G6** 11 50N 106 34 E
Locarno, *Switz.* **29 D7** 46 10N 8 47 E
Lochaber, *U.K.* **18 E4** 56 55N 5 0W
Lochcarron, *U.K.* **18 D3** 57 25N 5 30W
Lochem, *Neths.* **20 D8** 52 9N 6 26 E
Loches, *France* **22 E8** 47 7N 1 0 E
Lochgelly, *U.K.* **18 E5** 56 7N 3 18W
Lochgilphead, *U.K.* **18 E3** 56 2N 5 37W
Lochinver, *U.K.* **18 C3** 58 9N 5 15W
Lochnagar, *Australia* **114 C4** 23 33 S 145 38 E
Lochnagar, *U.K.* **18 E5** 56 57N 3 14W
Łochów, *Poland* **47 C8** 52 33N 21 42 E
Lochy →, *U.K.* **18 E3** 56 52N 5 3W
Lock, *Australia* **115 E2** 33 34 S 135 46 E
Lock Haven, *U.S.A.* **136 E7** 41 7N 77 31W
Lockeford, *U.S.A.* **144 G5** 38 10N 121 9W
Lockeport, *Canada* **129 D6** 43 47N 65 4W
Lockerbie, *U.K.* **18 F5** 55 7N 3 21W
Lockhart, *Australia* **117 C7** 35 14 S 146 40 E
Lockhart, *U.S.A.* **139 L6** 29 55N 97 40W
Lockhart, L., *Australia* **113 F2** 33 15 S 119 3 E
Lockington, *Australia* **116 D6** 36 16 S 144 34 E
Lockney, *U.S.A.* **139 H4** 34 7N 101 27W
Lockport, *Ill., U.S.A.* **141 C8** 41 35N 88 3W
Lockport, *N.Y., U.S.A.* **136 C6** 43 12N 78 42W
Locminé, *France* **22 E4** 47 54N 2 51W
Locri, *Italy* **41 D9** 38 14N 16 14 E
Locronan, *France* **22 D2** 48 7N 4 15W
Loctudy, *France* **22 E2** 47 50N 4 12W
Locust Cr. →, *U.S.A.* **140 E3** 39 40N 93 17W
Lod, *Israel* **91 D3** 31 57N 34 54 E
Lodeinoye Pole, *U.S.S.R.* **48 B5** 60 44N 33 33 E
Lodève, *France* **24 E7** 43 44N 3 19 E
Lodge Grass, *U.S.A.* **142 D10** 45 21N 107 20W
Lodgepole, *U.S.A.* **138 E3** 41 12N 102 40W
Lodgepole Cr. →, *U.S.A.* **138 E2** 41 20N 104 30W
Lodhran, *Pakistan* **80 E4** 29 32N 71 30 E
Lodi, *Italy* **38 C6** 45 19N 9 30 E
Lodi, *U.S.A.* **144 G5** 38 12N 121 16W
Lodja, *Zaïre* **102 C4** 3 30 S 23 23 E
Lodosa, *Spain* **34 C2** 42 25N 2 4W
Lödöse, *Sweden* **15 F6** 58 2N 12 9 E
Lodwar, *Kenya* **106 B4** 3 10N 35 40 E
Łódź, *Poland* **47 D6** 51 45N 19 27 E
Łódź □, *Poland* **47 D6** 51 45N 19 27 E
Loei, *Thailand* **76 D3** 17 29N 101 35 E
Loenen, *Neths.* **20 D8** 52 7N 6 1 E
Loengo, *Zaïre* **103 C5** 4 48 S 26 30 E
Loeriesfontein, *S. Africa* **104 E2** 31 0 S 19 26 E
Lofer, *Austria* **30 D5** 47 35N 12 41 E
Lofoten, *Norway* **12 B13** 68 30N 15 0 E
Lofsdalen, *Sweden* **14 B7** 62 10N 13 20 E
Lofsen →, *Sweden* **14 B7** 62 7N 13 57 E
Logan, *Kans., U.S.A.* **138 F5** 39 40N 99 35W
Logan, *Ohio, U.S.A.* **134 F4** 39 25N 82 22W
Logan, *Utah, U.S.A.* **142 F8** 41 45N 111 50W
Logan, *W. Va., U.S.A.* **134 G5** 37 51N 81 59W
Logan, Mt., *Canada* **126 B5** 60 31N 140 22W
Logan Pass, *U.S.A.* **130 D6** 48 41N 113 44W
Logandale, *U.S.A.* **145 J12** 36 36N 114 29W
Logansport, *Ind., U.S.A.* **141 D10** 40 45N 86 21W
Logansport, *La., U.S.A.* **139 K8** 31 58N 93 58W
Logo, *Sudan* **95 F3** 5 20N 30 18 E
Logone →, *Chad* **97 F3** 12 6N 15 2 E
Logroño, *Spain* **34 C2** 42 28N 2 27W
Logrosán, *Spain* **37 F5** 39 20N 5 32W
Løgstør, *Denmark* **15 H3** 56 58N 9 14 E
Loh, *Vanuatu* **121 C4** 13 21 S 166 38 E
Lohardaga, *India* **81 H11** 23 27N 84 45 E
Lohr, *Germany* **27 F5** 50 0N 9 35 E
Lohrville, *U.S.A.* **140 B2** 42 17N 94 33W
Loi-kaw, *Burma* **78 F6** 19 40N 97 17 E
Loimaa, *Finland* **13 F17** 60 50N 23 5 E
Loir →, *France* **22 E6** 47 33N 0 32W
Loir-et-Cher □, *France* **22 E8** 47 40N 1 20 E
Loire □, *France* **25 C8** 45 40N 4 5 E
Loire →, *France* **22 E4** 47 16N 2 10W
Loire-Atlantique □, *France* **22 E5** 47 25N 1 40W
Loiret □, *France* **23 E9** 47 55N 2 30 E
Loitz, *Germany* **26 B9** 53 58N 13 8 E
Loja, *Ecuador* **156 A2** 3 59 S 79 16W
Loja, *Spain* **37 H6** 37 10N 4 10W
Loja □, *Ecuador* **152 D2** 4 0 S 79 13W
Loji, *Indonesia* **71 E7** 1 38 S 127 28 E
Loka, *Sudan* **95 G3** 4 13N 31 0 E
Lokandu, *Zaïre* **102 C5** 2 30 S 25 45 E
Løken, *Norway* **14 E5** 59 48N 11 29 E
Lokeren, *Belgium* **21 F3** 51 6N 3 59 E
Lokhvitsa, *U.S.S.R.* **50 F8** 50 25N 33 18 E
Lokichokio, *Kenya* **106 B3** 4 19N 34 13 E
Lokitaung, *Kenya* **106 B4** 4 12N 35 48 E
Lokka, *Finland* **12 C19** 67 55N 27 35 E
Løkken, *Denmark* **15 G3** 57 22N 9 41 E
Løkken Verk, *Norway* **14 A3** 63 7N 9 43 E
Loknya, *U.S.S.R.* **50 C7** 56 49N 30 4 E
Lokoja, *Nigeria* **101 D6** 7 47N 6 45 E
Lokolama, *Zaïre* **102 C3** 2 35 S 19 50 E
Lokuru, *Solomon Is.* **121 M9** 8 20 S 157 0 E
Lol →, *Sudan* **95 F2** 9 13N 26 30 E
Lola, *Guinea* **100 D3** 7 52N 8 29W
Lola, Mt., *U.S.A.* **144 F6** 39 26N 120 22W
Lolibai, Gebel, *Sudan* **95 G3** 3 50N 33 0 E
Lolimi, *Sudan* **95 G3** 4 35N 34 0 E
Loliondo, *Tanzania* **106 C4** 2 2 S 35 39 E
Lolland, *Denmark* **15 K5** 54 45N 11 30 E
Lollar, *Germany* **26 E4** 50 39N 8 43 E
Lolo, *U.S.A.* **142 C6** 46 50N 114 8W

226 Lolodorf

Lolodorf, *Cameroon* .... **101 E7** 3 16N 10 49 E
Lolowai, *Vanuatu* ...... **121 E6** 15 18 S 168 0 E
Lom, *Bulgaria* .... **43 D8** 43 48N 23 12 E
Lom →, *Bulgaria* ...... **42 D8** 43 45N 23 15 E
Lom Kao, *Thailand* .... **76 D3** 16 53N 101 14 E
Lom Sak, *Thailand* ..... **76 D3** 16 47N 101 15 E
Loma, *U.S.A.* **142 C8** 47 59N 110 29W
Loma Linda, *U.S.A.* **145 L9** 34 3N 117 16W
Lomaloma, *Fiji* .... **121 A3** 17 17 S 178 59W
Lomami →, *Zaïre* ..... **102 B4** 0 46N 24 16 E
Lomas de Zamóra, *Argentina* .... **158 C4** 34 45 S 58 25W
Lombadina, *Australia* .. **112 C3** 16 31 S 122 54 E
Lombard, *U.S.A.* **141 C8** 41 53N 88 1W
Lombardia □, *Italy* ..... **38 C6** 45 35N 9 45 E
Lombardy = Lombardia □, *Italy* ... **38 C6** 45 35N 9 45 E
Lombe, *Angola* .... **103 D3** 9 27 S 16 13 E
Lombez, *France* .... **24 E4** 43 29N 0 55 E
Lomblen, *Indonesia* .... **71 F6** 8 30 S 123 32 E
Lombok, *Indonesia* ..... **70 F5** 8 45 S 116 30 E
Lomé, *Togo* .... **101 D5** 6 9N 1 20 E
Lomela, *Zaïre* .... **102 C4** 2 19 S 23 15 E
Lomela →, *Zaïre* ...... **102 C4** 0 15 S 20 40 E
Lomello, *Italy* .... **38 C5** 45 5N 8 46 E
Lometa, *U.S.A.* **139 K5** 31 15N 98 25W
Lomié, *Cameroon* .... **102 B2** 3 13N 13 38 E
Lomma, *Sweden* .... **15 J7** 55 43N 13 6 E
Lomme →, *Belgium* ..... **21 H6** 50 8N 5 10 E
Lommel, *Belgium* .... **21 F6** 51 14N 5 19 E
Lomond, *Canada* **130 C6** 50 24N 112 36W
Lomond, L., *U.K.* **18 E4** 56 8N 4 38W
Lomonosov, *U.S.S.R.* .. **50 B6** 59 57N 29 53 E
Lomphat, *Cambodia* .... **76 F6** 13 30N 106 59 E
Lompobatang, *Indonesia* **71 F5** 5 24 S 119 56 E
Lompoc, *U.S.A.* **145 L6** 34 41N 120 32W
Lomsegga, *Norway* ...... **14 C2** 61 49N 8 21 E
Łomza, *Poland* .... **47 B9** 53 10N 22 2 E
Łomza □, *Poland* ...... **47 C9** 53 0N 22 30 E
Lonavale, *India* .... **82 E1** 18 46N 73 29 E
Loncoche, *Chile* .... **160 A2** 39 20 S 72 50W
Loncopuè, *Argentina* ... **160 A2** 38 4 S 70 37W
Londa, *India* .... **83 G2** 15 30N 74 30 E
Londerzeel, *Belgium* .... **21 G4** 51 0N 4 19 E
Londiani, *Kenya* .... **106 C4** 0 10 S 35 33 E
Londinières, *France* .... **22 C8** 49 50N 1 25 E
London, *Canada* **128 D3** 42 59N 81 15W
London, *U.K.* **17 F7** 51 30N 0 5W
London, *Ky., U.S.A.* ... **134 G3** 37 11N 84 5W
London, *Ohio, U.S.A.* .. **141 E13** 39 54N 83 28W
London, Greater □, *U.K.* **17 F7** 51 30N 0 5W
London Mills, *U.S.A.* ... **140 D6** 40 43N 90 11W
Londonderry, *U.K.* **19 B4** 55 0N 7 23W
Londonderry □, *U.K.* .. **19 B4** 55 0N 7 20W
Londonderry, C., *Australia* .... **112 B4** 13 45 S 126 55 E
Londonderry, I., *Chile* .. **160 E2** 55 0 S 71 0W
Londrina, *Brazil* .... **159 A5** 23 18 S 51 10W
Londuimbale, *Angola* ... **103 E3** 12 15 S 15 19 E
Lone Pine, *U.S.A.* **144 J8** 36 35N 118 2W
Long Beach, *Calif., U.S.A.* **145 M8** 33 46N 118 12W
Long Beach, *N.Y., U.S.A.* **137 F11** 40 35N 73 40W
Long Beach, *Wash., U.S.A.* **144 D2** 46 20N 124 1W
Long Branch, *U.S.A.* ... **137 F11** 40 19N 74 0W
Long Creek, *U.S.A.* **142 D4** 44 43N 119 6W
Long Eaton, *U.K.* **16 E6** 52 54N 1 16W
Long I., *Australia* ...... **114 C4** 22 8 S 149 53 E
Long I., *Bahamas* **149 B4** 23 20N 75 10W
Long I., *Papua N. G.* ... **120 C4** 5 20 S 147 5 E
Long I., *U.S.A.* **137 F11** 40 50N 73 20W
Long Island Sd., *U.S.A.* **137 E12** 41 10N 73 0W
Long L., *Canada* **128 C2** 49 30N 86 50W
Long Lake, *U.S.A.* **137 C10** 43 57N 74 25W
Long Pine, *U.S.A.* **138 D5** 42 33N 99 41W
Long Pt., *Nfld., Canada* **129 C8** 48 47N 58 46W
Long Pt., *Ont., Canada* . **136 D4** 42 35N 80 2W
Long Pt., *N.Z.* .... **119 G4** 46 34 S 169 36 E
Long Point B., *Canada* . **136 D4** 42 40N 80 10W
Long Range Mts., *Canada* **129 C8** 49 30N 57 30W
Long Reef, *Australia* ... **112 B4** 14 1 S 125 48 E
Long Str. = Longa, Proliv, *U.S.S.R.* ...... **6 C16** 70 0N 175 0 E
Long Thanh, *Vietnam* ... **77 G6** 10 47N 106 57 E
Long Xian, *China* ...... **66 G4** 34 55N 106 55 E
Long Xuyen, *Vietnam* .. **77 G5** 10 19N 105 28 E
Longa, *Angola* .... **103 E3** 14 42 S 18 32 E
Longá, *Greece* .... **45 H3** 36 53N 21 55 E
Longa, Proliv, *U.S.S.R.* . **6 C16** 70 0N 175 0 E
Long'an, *China* .... **68 F6** 23 10N 107 40 E
Longarone, *Italy* .... **39 B9** 46 15N 12 18 E
Longburn, *N.Z.* .... **118 G4** 40 23 S 175 35 E
Longchang, *China* ...... **68 C5** 29 18N 105 15 E
Longchi, *China* .... **68 C4** 29 25N 103 24 E
Longchuan, *Guangdong, China* .... **69 E10** 24 5N 115 17 E
Longchuan, *Yunnan, China* .... **68 E1** 24 23N 97 58 E
Longde, *China* .... **66 G4** 35 30N 106 20 E
Longeau, *France* .... **23 E12** 47 47N 5 20 E
Longford, *Australia* ..... **114 G4** 41 32 S 147 3 E
Longford, *Ireland* **19 C4** 53 43N 7 50W
Longford □, *Ireland* **19 C4** 53 42N 7 45W
Longguan, *China* .... **66 D8** 40 45N 115 30 E
Longhua, *China* .... **67 D9** 41 18N 117 45 E
Longhui, *China* .... **69 D8** 27 7N 111 2 E
Longido, *Tanzania* ..... **106 C4** 2 43 S 36 42 E
Longiram, *Indonesia* .... **70 E5** 0 5 S 115 45 E
Longkou, *Jiangxi, China* **69 D10** 26 8N 115 10 E
Longkou, *Shandong, China* .... **67 F11** 37 40N 120 18 E
Longlac, *Canada* **128 C2** 49 45N 86 25W
Longli, *China* .... **68 D6** 26 25N 106 58 E
Longlier, *Belgium* ...... **21 J6** 49 52N 5 27 E
Longlin, *China* .... **68 E5** 24 47N 105 20 E
Longling, *China* .... **68 E2** 24 37N 98 39 E
Longmen, *China* .... **69 F10** 23 40N 114 18 E
Longming, *China* .... **68 F6** 22 59N 107 7 E
Longmont, *U.S.A.* **138 E2** 40 10N 105 4W
Longnan, *China* .... **69 E10** 24 55N 114 47 E
Longnawan, *Indonesia* .. **70 D4** 1 51N 114 55 E
Longobucco, *Italy* ...... **41 C9** 39 27N 16 37 E
Longquan, *China* .... **69 C12** 28 7N 119 10 E
Longreach, *Australia* ... **114 C3** 23 28 S 144 14 E
Longshan, *China* .... **68 C7** 29 29N 109 25 E
Longsheng, *China* ...... **69 E8** 25 48N 110 0 E
Longton, *Australia* ..... **114 C4** 20 58 S 145 55 E
Longtown, *U.K.* **17 F5** 51 58N 2 59W
Longué-Jumelles, *France* **22 E6** 47 22N 0 8W
Longueau, *France* ...... **23 C9** 49 52N 2 21 E
Longueuil, *Canada* **137 A11** 45 32N 73 28W
Longuyon, *France* ...... **23 C12** 49 27N 5 35 E
Longview, *Canada* **130 C6** 50 32N 114 10W
Longview, *Tex., U.S.A.* . **139 J7** 32 30N 94 45W
Longview, *Wash., U.S.A.* **144 D4** 46 9N 122 58W
Longvilly, *Belgium* ..... **21 H7** 50 2N 5 50 E
Longwy, *France* .... **23 C12** 49 30N 5 46 E
Longxi, *China* .... **66 G3** 34 53N 104 40 E
Longyou, *China* .... **69 C12** 29 1N 119 8 E
Longzhou, *China* .... **68 F6** 22 22N 106 50 E
Lonigo, *Italy* .... **39 C8** 45 23N 11 22 E
Löningen, *Germany* .... **26 C3** 52 43N 7 44 E
Lonja →, *Yugoslavia* ... **39 C13** 45 30N 16 40 E
Lonkin, *Burma* .... **78 C6** 25 39N 96 22 E
Lonoke, *U.S.A.* **139 H9** 34 48N 91 57W
Lonquimay, *Chile* ...... **160 A2** 38 26 S 71 14W
Lons-le-Saunier, *France* . **23 F12** 46 40N 5 31 E
Lønstrup, *Denmark* .... **15 G3** 57 29N 9 47 E
Loogootee, *U.S.A.* **141 F10** 38 41N 86 55W
Lookout, C., *Canada* ... **128 A3** 55 18N 83 56W
Lookout, C., *U.S.A.* ... **135 H7** 34 30N 76 30W
Loolmalasin, *Tanzania* .. **106 C4** 3 0 S 35 53 E
Loon →, *Alta., Canada* **130 B5** 57 8N 115 3W
Loon →, *Man., Canada* **131 B8** 55 53N 101 59W
Loon Lake, *Canada* **131 C7** 54 2N 109 10W
Loon-op-Zand, *Neths.* .. **21 E6** 51 38N 5 5 E
Loongana, *Australia* .... **113 F4** 30 52 S 127 5 E
Loop Hd., *Ireland* **19 D2** 52 34N 9 55W
Loosduinen, *Neths.* ..... **20 D4** 52 3N 4 14 E
Lop Buri, *Thailand* ..... **76 E3** 14 48N 100 37 E
Lop Nor = Lop Nur, *China* .... **64 B4** 40 20N 90 10 E
Lop Nur, *China* .... **64 B4** 40 20N 90 10 E
Lopare, *Yugoslavia* ..... **42 C3** 44 39N 18 46 E
Lopatin, *U.S.S.R.* ...... **53 E12** 43 50N 47 35 E
Lopatina, G., *U.S.S.R.* . **57 D15** 50 47N 143 10 E
Lopaye, *Sudan* .... **95 F3** 6 37N 33 40 E
Lopera, *Spain* **37 H6** 37 56N 4 14W
Lopevi, *Vanuatu* .... **121 F6** 16 30 S 168 21 E
Lopez, C., *Gabon* ...... **102 C1** 0 47 S 8 40 E
Lopez I., *Gabon* .... **102 C1** 0 50 S 8 47 E
Loppersum, *Neths.* ..... **20 B9** 53 20N 6 44 E
Lopphavet, *Norway* ..... **12 A16** 70 27N 21 15 E
Lora →, *Afghan.* ...... **79 C2** 31 35N 65 50 E
Lora, Hamun-i-, *Pakistan* **79 C2** 29 38N 64 58 E
Lora Cr. →, *Australia* .. **115 D2** 28 10 S 135 22 E
Lora del Río, *Spain* **37 H5** 37 39N 5 33W
Lorain, *U.S.A.* **136 E2** 41 28N 82 55W
Loraine, *U.S.A.* **140 D5** 40 9N 91 13W
Loralai, *Pakistan* .... **79 C3** 30 20N 68 41 E
Lorca, *Spain* **35 H3** 37 41N 1 42W
Lord Howe I., *Pac. Oc.* . **122 L7** 31 33 S 159 6 E
Lord Howe Ridge, *Pac. Oc.* .... **122 L8** 30 0 S 162 30 E
Lordsburg, *U.S.A.* **143 K9** 32 22N 108 45W
Lorengau, *Papua N. G.* . **120 B4** 2 1 S 147 15 E
Loreto, *Bolivia* .... **157 D5** 15 13 S 64 40W
Loreto, *Brazil* .... **154 C2** 7 5 S 45 10W
Loreto, *Italy* .... **39 E10** 43 26N 13 36 E
Loreto, *Mexico* **146 B2** 26 1N 111 21W
Loreto □, *Peru* .... **152 E3** 5 0 S 75 0W
Loreto Aprutina, *Italy* .. **39 F10** 42 24N 13 59 E
Lorgues, *France* .... **25 E10** 43 28N 6 22 E
Lorica, *Colombia* **152 B2** 9 14N 75 49W
Lorient, *France* **22 E3** 47 45N 3 23W
Lorimor, *U.S.A.* **140 C2** 41 7N 94 3W
Lorn, *U.K.* **18 E3** 56 26N 5 10W
Lorn, Firth of, *U.K.* **18 E3** 56 20N 5 40W
Lorne, *Australia* .... **116 E5** 38 33 S 143 59 E
Lorovouno, *Cyprus* ..... **32 D11** 35 8N 32 36 E
Lörrach, *Germany* ..... **27 H3** 47 36N 7 38 E
Lorraine, *France* .... **23 D13** 48 53N 6 0 E
Lorrainville, *Canada* **128 C4** 47 21N 79 23W
Los, Îles de, *Guinea* **100 D2** 9 30N 13 50W
Los Alamos, *Calif., U.S.A.* **145 L6** 34 44N 120 17W
Los Alamos, *N. Mex., U.S.A.* **143 J10** 35 57N 106 17W
Los Altos, *U.S.A.* **144 H4** 37 23N 122 7W
Los Andes, *Chile* ...... **158 C1** 32 50 S 70 40W
Los Angeles, *Chile* ..... **158 D1** 37 28 S 72 23W
Los Angeles, *U.S.A.* **145 M8** 34 0N 118 10W
Los Angeles Aqueduct, *U.S.A.* **145 K9** 35 25N 118 0W
Los Antiguos, *Argentina* **160 C2** 46 35 S 71 40W
Los Banos, *U.S.A.* **144 H6** 37 8N 120 56W
Los Barrios, *Spain* **37 J5** 36 11N 5 30W
Los Blancos, *Argentina* . **158 A3** 23 40 S 62 30W
Los Cristianos, *Canary Is.* **33 F3** 28 3N 16 42W
Los Gatos, *U.S.A.* **144 H5** 37 14N 121 59W
Los Hermanos, *Venezuela* **149 D7** 11 45N 64 25W
Los Islotes, *Canary Is.* .. **33 E6** 29 4N 13 44W
Los Lagos, *Chile* .... **160 A2** 39 51 S 72 50W
Los Llanos de Aridane, *Canary Is.* **33 F2** 28 38N 17 54W
Los Lomas, *Peru* .... **156 A1** 4 40 S 80 10W
Los Lunas, *U.S.A.* **143 J10** 34 48N 106 47W
Los Menucos, *Argentina* **160 B3** 40 50 S 68 10W
Los Mochis, *Mexico* **146 B3** 25 45N 109 5W
Los Monegros, *Spain* ... **34 D4** 41 29N 0 13W
Los Monos, *Argentina* .. **160 C3** 46 1 S 69 36W
Los Olivos, *U.S.A.* **145 L6** 34 40N 120 7W
Los Palacios, *Cuba* **148 B3** 22 35N 83 15W
Los Palacios y Villafranca, *Spain* **37 H5** 37 10N 5 55W
Los Reyes, *Mexico* **146 D4** 19 34N 102 30W
Los Ríos □, *Ecuador* ... **152 D2** 1 30 S 79 25W
Los Roques, *Venezuela* . **152 A4** 11 50N 66 45W
Los Santos de Maimona, *Spain* **37 G4** 38 27N 6 22W
Los Teques, *Venezuela* .. **152 A4** 10 21N 67 2W
Los Testigos, *Venezuela* . **153 A5** 11 23N 63 6W
Los Vilos, *Chile* .... **158 C1** 32 10 S 71 30W
Los Yébenes, *Spain* **37 F7** 39 36N 3 55W
Losada →, *Colombia* .. **152 C3** 2 12N 73 55W
Loshkalakh, *U.S.S.R.* ... **57 C15** 62 45N 147 20 E
Łosice, *Poland* .... **47 C9** 52 13N 22 43 E
Lošinj, *Yugoslavia* ...... **39 D11** 44 30N 14 30 E
Losser, *Neths.* .... **20 D10** 52 16N 7 1 E
Lossiemouth, *U.K.* **18 D5** 57 43N 3 17W
Losuia, *Papua N. G.* ... **120 E6** 8 30 S 151 4 E
Lot □, *France* .... **24 D5** 44 39N 1 40 E
Lot →, *France* .... **24 D4** 44 18N 0 20 E
Lot-et-Garonne □, *France* **24 D4** 44 22N 0 30 E
Lota, *Chile* .... **158 D1** 37 5 S 73 10W
Løten, *Norway* .... **14 D5** 60 51N 11 21 E
Loțfābād, *Iran* .... **85 B8** 37 32N 59 20 E
Lothair, *S. Africa* ...... **105 D5** 26 22 S 30 27 E
Lothian □, *U.K.* **18 F6** 55 50N 3 0W
Lothiers, *France* .... **23 F8** 46 42N 1 33 E
Lotofaga, *W. Samoa* .... **121 X24** 14 1 S 171 30W
Lötschbergtunnel, *Switz.* **28 D5** 46 26N 7 43 E
Lottefors, *Sweden* ...... **14 C10** 61 25N 16 24 E
Lotzwil, *Switz.* .... **28 B5** 47 12N 7 48 E
Loubomo, *Congo* ...... **102 C2** 4 9 S 12 47 E
Loudéac, *France* **22 D4** 48 11N 2 47W
Loudi, *China* .... **69 D8** 27 42N 111 59 E
Loudima, *Congo* .... **102 C2** 4 6 S 13 5 E
Loudon, *U.S.A.* **135 H3** 35 35N 84 22W
Loudonville, *U.S.A.* **136 F2** 40 40N 82 15W
Loudun, *France* .... **22 E7** 47 3N 0 5 E
Loué, *France* **22 E6** 47 59N 0 9W
Loue →, *France* .... **23 E12** 47 1N 5 28 E
Louga, *Senegal* **100 B1** 15 45N 16 5W
Loughborough, *U.K.* **16 E6** 52 46N 1 11W
Loughrea, *Ireland* **19 C3** 53 11N 8 33W
Loughros More B., *Ireland* **19 B3** 54 48N 8 30W
Louhans, *France* .... **25 B9** 46 38N 5 12 E
Louis Trichardt, *S. Africa* **105 C4** 23 1 S 29 43 E
Louis XIV, Pte., *Canada* **128 B4** 54 37N 79 45W
Louisa, *U.S.A.* **134 F4** 38 5N 82 40W
Louisbourg, *Canada* **129 C8** 45 55N 60 0W
Louisburg, *U.S.A.* **140 F2** 38 37N 94 41W
Louise I., *Canada* **130 C2** 52 55N 131 50W
Louiseville, *Canada* **128 C5** 46 20N 72 56W
Louisiade Arch., *Papua N. G.* .... **120 F7** 11 10 S 153 0 E
Louisiana, *U.S.A.* **140 E6** 39 25N 91 0W
Louisiana □, *U.S.A.* **139 K9** 30 50N 92 0W
Louisville, *Ky., U.S.A.* . **141 F11** 38 15N 85 45W
Louisville, *Miss., U.S.A.* **139 J10** 33 7N 89 3W
Loukouo, *Congo* .... **102 C2** 3 38 S 14 39 E
Loulay, *France* **24 B3** 46 3N 0 30W
Loulé, *Portugal* **37 H3** 37 9N 8 0W
Louny, *Czech.* .... **30 A6** 50 20N 13 48 E
Loup City, *U.S.A.* **138 E5** 41 19N 98 57W
Lourdes, *France* **24 E3** 43 6N 0 3W
Lourdes-du-Blanc-Sablon, *Canada* **129 B8** 51 24N 57 12W
Lourenço, *Brazil* **153 C7** 2 30N 51 40W
Lourenço-Marques = Maputo, *Mozam.* .... **105 D5** 25 58 S 32 32 E
Loures, *Portugal* **37 G1** 38 50N 9 9W
Lourinhã, *Portugal* **37 F1** 39 14N 9 17W
Lousã, *Portugal* **36 E2** 40 7N 8 14W
Louth, *Australia* .... **117 A6** 30 30 S 145 8 E
Louth, *Ireland* **19 C5** 53 47N 6 33W
Louth, *U.K.* .... **16 D8** 53 23N 0 0 E
Louth □, *Ireland* **19 C5** 53 55N 6 30W
Loutrá Aidhipsoú, *Greece* **45 F5** 38 54N 23 2 E
Loutráki, *Greece* .... **45 G4** 37 58N 22 57 E
Louvain = Leuven, *Belgium* .... **21 G5** 50 52N 4 42 E
Louveigné, *Belgium* .... **21 G7** 50 32N 5 42 E
Louviers, *France* .... **22 C8** 49 12N 1 10 E
Louwsburg, *S. Africa* ... **105 D5** 27 37 S 31 7 E
Lovat →, *U.S.S.R.* ..... **50 B7** 58 14N 30 28 E
Lovćen, *Yugoslavia* ..... **42 E3** 42 23N 18 51 E
Love, *Canada* **131 C8** 53 29N 104 10W
Lovech, *Bulgaria* .... **43 D9** 43 8N 24 42 E
Loveland, *Colo., U.S.A.* **138 E2** 40 27N 105 4W
Loveland, *Ohio, U.S.A.* **141 E12** 39 16N 84 16W
Lovell, *U.S.A.* **142 D9** 44 51N 108 20W
Lovelock, *U.S.A.* **142 F4** 40 17N 118 25W
Lóvere, *Italy* .... **38 C7** 45 50N 10 4 E
Loves Park, *U.S.A.* **140 B7** 42 19N 89 3W
Loviisa = Lovisa, *Finland* **13 F19** 60 28N 26 12 E
Lovilia, *U.S.A.* **140 C4** 41 8N 92 55W
Loving, *U.S.A.* **139 J2** 32 17N 104 4W
Lovington, *Ill., U.S.A.* .. **141 E8** 39 43N 88 38W
Lovington, *N. Mex., U.S.A.* **139 J3** 33 0N 103 20W
Lovios, *Spain* **36 D2** 41 55N 8 4W
Lovisa, *Finland* .... **13 F19** 60 28N 26 12 E
Lovosice, *Czech.* .... **30 A7** 50 30N 14 2 E
Lovran, *Yugoslavia* ..... **39 C11** 45 18N 14 15 E
Lovrin, *Romania* .... **46 D1** 45 58N 20 48 E
Low Pt., *Australia* ..... **113 F4** 32 25 S 127 25 E
Lowa, *Zaïre* .... **106 C2** 1 25 S 25 47 E
Lowa →, *Zaïre* .... **106 C2** 1 24 S 25 51 E
Lowden, *U.S.A.* **140 C6** 41 52N 90 56W
Lowell, *Ind., U.S.A.* **141 C9** 41 18N 87 25W
Lowell, *Mass., U.S.A.* .. **137 D13** 42 38N 71 19W
Lower Arrow L., *Canada* **130 D5** 49 40N 118 5W
Lower Austria = Niederösterreich □, *Austria* .... **30 C8** 48 25N 15 40 E
Lower California = Baja California, *Mexico* **146 A1** 31 10N 115 12W
Lower California = California, Baja, *Mexico* **146 A1** 32 10N 115 12W
Lower Hutt, *N.Z.* ...... **118 H3** 41 10 S 174 55 E
Lower L., *U.S.A.* **142 F3** 41 17N 120 3W
Lower Lake, *U.S.A.* **144 G4** 38 56N 122 36W
Lower Post, *Canada* **130 B3** 59 58N 128 30W
Lower Red L., *U.S.A.* .. **138 B7** 48 0N 94 50W
Lower Saxony = Niedersachsen □, *Germany* .... **26 C5** 52 45N 9 0 E
Lower Tunguska = Tunguska, Nizhnyaya →, *U.S.S.R.* .... **57 C9** 65 48N 88 4 E
Lowestoft, *U.K.* .... **17 E9** 52 29N 1 44 E
Łowicz, *Poland* .... **47 C6** 52 6N 19 55 E
Lowry City, *U.S.A.* **140 F3** 38 8N 93 44W
Lowville, *U.S.A.* **137 C9** 43 48N 75 30W
Loxton, *Australia* ...... **116 C4** 34 28 S 140 31 E
Loxton, *S. Africa* ...... **104 E3** 31 30 S 22 22 E
Loyalton, *U.S.A.* **144 F6** 39 41N 120 14W
Loyalty Is. = Loyauté, Is., *N. Cal.* .... **121 K4** 20 50 S 166 30 E
Loyang = Luoyang, *China* .... **66 G7** 34 40N 112 26 E
Loyauté, Is., *N. Cal.* .... **121 K4** 20 50 S 166 30 E
Loyev, *U.S.S.R.* .... **50 F7** 51 56N 30 46 E
Loyoro, *Uganda* .... **106 B3** 3 22N 34 14 E
Lož, *Yugoslavia* .... **39 C11** 45 43N 14 30 E
Lozère □, *France* ...... **24 D7** 44 35N 3 30 E
Loznica, *Yugoslavia* .... **42 C4** 44 32N 19 14 E
Lozovaya, *U.S.S.R.* .... **52 B7** 49 0N 36 20 E
Lozva →, *U.S.S.R.* .... **54 B8** 59 36N 62 20 E
Luachimo, *Angola* ...... **103 D4** 7 23 S 20 48 E
Luacono, *Angola* .... **103 E4** 11 15 S 21 37 E
Lualaba →, *Zaïre* ..... **102 B5** 0 26N 25 20 E
Luampa, *Zambia* .... **107 F1** 15 4 S 24 20 E
Lu'an, *China* .... **69 B11** 31 45N 116 29 E
Luan Chau, *Vietnam* .... **76 B4** 21 38N 103 24 E
Luan He →, *China* .... **67 E10** 39 20N 119 5 E
Luan Xian, *China* ...... **67 E10** 39 40N 118 40 E
Luancheng, *Guangxi Zhuangzu, China* .... **68 F7** 22 48N 108 55 E
Luancheng, *Hebei, China* **66 F8** 37 53N 114 40 E
Luanda, *Angola* .... **103 D2** 8 50 S 13 15 E
Luanda □, *Angola* ..... **103 D2** 9 0 S 13 10 E
Luang Prabang, *Laos* ... **76 C4** 19 52N 102 10 E
Luang Thale, *Thailand* .. **77 J3** 7 30N 100 15 E
Luangwa, *Zambia* ...... **107 F3** 15 35 S 30 16 E
Luangwa →, *Zambia* .. **107 E3** 14 25 S 30 25 E
Luangwa Valley, *Zambia* **107 E3** 13 30 S 31 30 E
Luanne, *China* .... **67 D9** 40 55N 117 40 E
Luanping, *China* .... **67 D9** 40 53N 117 23 E
Luanshya, *Zambia* ..... **107 E2** 13 3 S 28 28 E
Luapula □, *Zambia* .... **107 E2** 11 0 S 29 0 E
Luapula →, *Africa* .... **107 D2** 9 26 S 28 33 E
Luarca, *Spain* **36 B4** 43 32N 6 32W
Luashi, *Zaïre* .... **103 E4** 10 50 S 23 36 E
Luau, *Angola* .... **103 E4** 10 40 S 22 10 E
Lubaczów, *Poland* ..... **47 E10** 50 10N 23 8 E
Lubalo, *Angola* .... **103 D3** 9 10 S 19 15 E
Lubań, *Poland* .... **47 D2** 51 5N 15 15 E
Lubana, Ozero, *U.S.S.R.* **50 C5** 56 45N 27 0 E
Lubang Is., *Phil.* ...... **71 B6** 13 50N 120 12 E
Lubango, *Angola* ...... **103 E2** 14 55 S 13 30 E
Lubartów, *Poland* ..... **47 D9** 51 28N 22 42 E
Lubawa, *Poland* .... **47 B6** 53 30N 19 48 E
Lubbeek, *Belgium* ..... **21 G5** 50 54N 4 50 E
Lübben, *Germany* ..... **26 D9** 51 56N 13 54 E
Lübbenau, *Germany* ... **26 D9** 51 49N 13 59 E
Lubbock, *U.S.A.* **139 J4** 33 40N 101 53W
Lübeck, *Germany* ..... **26 B6** 53 52N 10 41 E
Lübecker Bucht, *Germany* .... **26 A7** 54 3N 11 0 E
Lubefu, *Zaïre* .... **103 C4** 4 47 S 24 27 E
Lubefu →, *Zaïre* ..... **103 C4** 4 10 S 23 0 E
Lubero = Luofu, *Zaïre* . **106 C2** 0 10 S 29 15 E
Lubicon L., *Canada* **130 B5** 56 23N 115 56W
Lubień Kujawski, *Poland* **47 C6** 52 23N 19 9 E
Lubin, *Poland* .... **47 D3** 51 24N 16 11 E
Lublin, *Poland* .... **47 D9** 51 12N 22 38 E
Lublin □, *Poland* ...... **47 D9** 51 5N 22 30 E
Lubliniec, *Poland* ...... **47 E5** 50 43N 18 45 E
Lubnān, J., *Lebanon* ... **91 B4** 33 50N 35 45 E
Lubny, *U.S.S.R.* .... **50 F8** 50 3N 32 58 E
Lubon, *Poland* .... **47 C3** 52 21N 16 51 E
Lubongola, *Zaïre* ...... **106 C2** 2 35 S 27 50 E
Lubotin, *Czech.* .... **31 B13** 49 17N 20 53 E
Lubraniec, *Poland* ..... **47 C5** 52 33N 18 50 E
Lubsko, *Poland* .... **47 D1** 51 45N 14 57 E
Lübtheen, *Germany* .... **26 B7** 53 18N 11 4 E
Lubuagan, *Phil.* .... **71 A6** 17 21N 121 10 E
Lubudi →, *Zaïre* ..... **103 D5** 9 0 S 25 35 E
Lubuk Antu, *Malaysia* .. **70 D4** 1 3N 111 50 E
Lubukklinggau, *Indonesia* **70 E2** 3 15 S 102 55 E
Lubuksikaping, *Indonesia* **70 D2** 0 10N 100 15 E
Lubumbashi, *Zaïre* ..... **107 E2** 11 40 S 27 28 E
Lubunda, *Zaïre* .... **103 D5** 5 12 S 26 41 E
Lubungu, *Zambia* ...... **107 E2** 14 35 S 26 24 E
Lubutu, *Zaïre* .... **106 C2** 0 45 S 26 30 E
Luc An Chau, *Vietnam* . **76 A5** 22 6N 104 43 E
Luc-en-Diois, *France* ... **25 D9** 44 36N 5 28 E
Lucala, *Angola* .... **103 D3** 9 7 S 15 58 E
Lucan, *Canada* **136 C3** 43 11N 81 24W
Lucca, *Italy* .... **38 E7** 43 50N 10 30 E
Luce Bay, *U.K.* **18 G4** 54 45N 4 48W
Lucea, *Jamaica* **148 C4** 18 25N 78 10W
Lucedale, *U.S.A.* **135 K1** 30 55N 88 34W
Lucena, *Phil.* .... **71 B6** 13 56N 121 37 E
Lucena, *Spain* **37 H6** 37 27N 4 31W
Lucena del Cid, *Spain* .. **34 E4** 40 9N 0 17W
Lučenec, *Czech.* .... **31 C12** 48 18N 19 42 E
Lucens, *Switz.* .... **28 C3** 46 43N 6 51 E
Lucera, *Italy* .... **41 A8** 41 30N 15 20 E
Lucerne = Luzern, *Switz.* **29 B6** 47 3N 8 18 E
Lucerne, *U.S.A.* **144 F4** 39 6N 122 48W
Lucerne Valley, *U.S.A.* . **145 L10** 34 27N 116 57W
Lucero, *Mexico* **146 A3** 30 49N 106 30W
Luchena →, *Spain* **35 H3** 37 44N 1 50W
Lucheng, *China* .... **66 F7** 36 20N 113 11 E
Lucheringo →, *Mozam.* **107 E4** 11 43 S 36 17 E
Lüchow, *Germany* ...... **26 C7** 52 58N 11 8 E
Luchuan, *China* .... **69 F8** 22 21N 110 12 E
Lucie →, *Surinam* **153 C6** 3 35N 57 38W
Lucira, *Angola* .... **103 E2** 14 0 S 12 35 E
Luckau, *Germany* ...... **26 D9** 51 50N 13 43 E
Luckenwalde, *Germany* . **26 C9** 52 5N 13 11 E
Luckey, *U.S.A.* **141 C13** 41 27N 83 29W
Lucknow, *India* .... **81 F9** 26 50N 81 0 E
Luçon, *France* **24 B2** 46 28N 1 10W
Lucusse, *Angola* .... **103 E4** 12 32 S 20 48 E
Lüda = Dalian, *China* .. **67 E11** 38 50N 121 40 E
Luda Kamchiya →, *Bulgaria* .... **43 D12** 43 3N 27 29 E
Ludbreg, *Yugoslavia* .... **39 B13** 46 15N 16 38 E
Lüdenscheid, *Germany* .. **26 D3** 51 13N 7 37 E
Lüderitz, *Namibia* ..... **104 D2** 26 41 S 15 8 E
Ludewe □, *Tanzania* ... **107 E3** 10 0 S 34 50 E
Ludhiana, *India* .... **80 D6** 30 57N 75 56 E
Ludian, *China* .... **68 D4** 27 10N 103 33 E
Luding Qiao, *China* .... **68 C4** 29 53N 102 12 E
Lüdinghausen, *Germany* **26 D3** 51 46N 7 28 E
Ludington, *U.S.A.* **134 D2** 43 58N 86 27W
Ludlow, *U.K.* **17 E5** 52 23N 2 42W
Ludlow, *Calif., U.S.A.* .. **145 L10** 34 43N 116 10W

MacLeod, B. 227

Ludlow, *Vt., U.S.A.* 137 C12 43 25N 72 40W
Ludus, *Romania* 46 C5 46 29N 24 5 E
Ludvika, *Sweden* 13 F13 60 8N 15 14 E
Ludwigsburg, *Germany* 27 G5 48 53N 9 11 E
Ludwigshafen, *Germany* 27 F4 49 27N 8 27 E
Ludwigslust, *Germany* 26 B7 53 19N 11 28 E
Ludza, *U.S.S.R.* 50 C5 56 32N 27 43 E
Lue, *Australia* 117 B8 32 38 S 149 50 E
Luebo, *Zaïre* 103 D4 5 21 S 21 23 E
Lueki, *Zaïre* 102 C5 3 20 S 25 48 E
Luena, *Angola* 103 E3 12 13 S 19 51 E
Luena, *Zaïre* 107 D2 9 28 S 25 43 E
Luena, *Zambia* 107 E3 10 40 S 30 25 E
Luepa, *Venezuela* 153 B5 5 43N 61 31W
Lüeyang, *China* 66 H4 33 22N 106 10 E
Lufeng, *Guangdong, China* 69 F10 22 57N 115 38 E
Lufeng, *Yunnan, China* 68 E4 25 0N 102 5 E
Lufico, *Angola* 103 D2 6 24 S 13 23 E
Lufira →, *Zaïre* 107 D2 9 30 S 27 0 E
Lufkin, *U.S.A.* 139 K7 31 25N 94 40W
Lufupa, *Zaïre* 103 E4 10 37 S 24 56 E
Luga, *U.S.S.R.* 50 B6 58 40N 29 55 E
Luga →, *U.S.S.R.* 50 B6 59 40N 28 18 E
Lugang, *Taiwan* 69 E13 24 4N 120 23 E
Lugano, *Switz.* 29 E7 46 0N 8 57 E
Lugano, L. di, *Switz.* 29 E8 46 0N 9 0 E
Lugansk, *U.S.S.R.* 53 B8 48 38N 39 15 E
Lugard's Falls, *Kenya* 106 C4 3 6 S 38 41 E
Lugela, *Mozam.* 107 F4 16 25 S 36 43 E
Lugenda →, *Mozam.* 107 E4 11 25 S 38 33 E
Lugh Ganana, *Somali Rep.* 90 G3 3 48N 42 34 E
Lugnvik, *Sweden* 14 B11 62 56N 17 55 E
Lugo, *Italy* 39 D8 44 25N 11 53 E
Lugo, *Spain* 36 B3 43 2N 7 35W
Lugo □, *Spain* 36 C3 43 0N 7 30W
Lugoj, *Romania* 42 B6 45 42N 21 57 E
Lugones, *Spain* 36 B5 43 26N 5 50W
Lugovoye, *U.S.S.R.* 55 B6 42 55N 72 43 E
Luhe, *China* 69 A12 32 19N 118 50 E
Luhe →, *Germany* 26 B6 53 18N 10 11 E
Luhuo, *China* 68 B3 31 21N 100 48 E
Luiana, *Angola* 103 F4 17 25 S 22 59 E
Luino, *Italy* 38 C5 45 58N 8 42 E
Luís Correia, *Brazil* 154 B3 3 0 S 41 35W
Luís Gonçalves, *Brazil* 154 C1 3 37 S 50 25W
Luitpold Coast, *Antarctica* 7 D1 78 30 S 32 0W
Luiza, *Zaïre* 103 D4 7 40 S 22 30 E
Luizi, *Zaïre* 106 D2 6 0 S 27 25 E
Luján, *Argentina* 158 C4 34 45 S 59 5W
Lujiang, *China* 69 B11 31 20N 117 15 E
Lukala, *Zaïre* 103 D2 5 31 S 14 32 E
Lukanga Swamp, *Zambia* 107 E2 14 30 S 27 40 E
Lukenie →, *Zaïre* 102 C3 3 0 S 18 50 E
Lukhisaral, *India* 81 G12 25 11N 86 5 E
Lŭki, *Bulgaria* 43 F9 41 50N 24 43 E
Lukk, *Libya* 96 B4 32 1N 24 46 E
Lukolela, *Equateur, Zaïre* 102 C3 1 10 S 17 12 E
Lukolela, *Kasai Or., Zaïre* 103 D4 5 23 S 24 32 E
Lukosi, *Zimbabwe* 107 F2 18 30 S 26 30 E
Lukovit, *Bulgaria* 43 D9 43 13N 24 11 E
Łuków, *Poland* 47 D9 51 55N 22 23 E
Lukoyanov, *U.S.S.R.* 51 D14 55 2N 44 29 E
Lule älv →, *Sweden* 12 D17 65 35N 22 10 E
Luleå, *Sweden* 12 D17 65 35N 22 10 E
Lüleburgaz, *Turkey* 43 F12 41 23N 27 22 E
Luliang, *China* 68 E4 25 0N 103 40 E
Luling, *U.S.A.* 139 L6 29 45N 97 40W
Lulong, *China* 67 E10 39 53N 118 51 E
Lulonga →, *Zaïre* 102 B3 1 0N 18 10 E
Lulua →, *Zaïre* 103 C4 4 30 S 20 30 E
Luluabourg = Kananga, *Zaïre* 103 D4 5 55 S 22 18 E
Lumai, *Angola* 103 E4 13 13 S 21 25 E
Lumajang, *Indonesia* 71 H15 8 8 S 113 13 E
Lumbala Kaquengue, *Angola* 103 E4 12 39 S 22 34 E
Lumbala N'guimbo, *Angola* 103 E4 14 18 S 21 18 E
Lumberton, *Miss., U.S.A.* 139 K10 31 4N 89 28W
Lumberton, *N.C., U.S.A.* 135 H6 34 37N 78 59W
Lumberton, *N. Mex., U.S.A.* 143 H10 36 58N 106 57W
Lumbres, *France* 23 B9 50 40N 2 5 E
Lumbwa, *Kenya* 106 C4 0 12 S 35 28 E
Lumding, *India* 78 C4 25 46N 93 10 E
Lumi, *Papua N. G.* 120 B2 3 30 S 142 2 E
Lummen, *Belgium* 21 G6 50 59N 5 12 E
Lumsden, *N.Z.* 119 F3 45 44 S 168 27 E
Lumut, *Malaysia* 77 K3 4 13N 100 37 E
Lumut, Tg., *Indonesia* 70 E3 3 50 S 105 58 E
Lunan, *China* 68 E4 24 40N 103 18 E
Lunavada, *India* 80 H5 23 8N 73 37 E
Lunca, *Romania* 46 B6 47 22N 25 1 E
Lund, *Sweden* 15 J7 55 44N 13 12 E
Lund, *U.S.A.* 142 G6 38 53N 115 0W
Lunda Norte □, *Angola* 103 D4 8 0 S 20 0 E
Lunda Sul □, *Angola* 103 E4 10 0 S 20 0 E
Lundazi, *Zambia* 107 E3 12 20 S 33 7 E
Lunde, *Norway* 14 E3 59 17N 9 5 E
Lunderskov, *Denmark* 15 J3 55 29N 9 19 E
Lundi →, *Zimbabwe* 107 G3 21 43 S 32 34 E
Lundu, *Malaysia* 70 D3 1 40N 109 50 E
Lundy, *U.K.* 17 F3 51 10N 4 41W
Lune →, *U.K.* 16 D5 54 0N 2 51W
Lüneburg, *Germany* 26 B6 53 15N 10 23 E
Lüneburg Heath = Lüneburger Heide, *Germany* 26 C6 53 0N 10 0 E
Lüneburger Heide, *Germany* 26 C6 53 0N 10 0 E
Lunel, *France* 25 E8 43 39N 4 9 E
Lünen, *Germany* 26 D3 51 36N 7 31 E
Lunenburg, *Canada* 129 D7 44 22N 64 18W
Lunéville, *France* 23 D13 48 36N 6 30 E
Lunga →, *Zambia* 107 E2 14 34 S 26 25 E
Lungern, *Switz.* 28 C6 46 48N 8 10 E
Lungi Airport, *S. Leone* 100 D2 8 40N 13 17W
Lunglei, *India* 78 D4 22 55N 92 45 E
Lungngo, *Burma* 78 E4 21 57N 93 36 E
Luni, *India* 80 G5 26 0N 73 6 E
Luni →, *India* 80 G4 24 41N 71 14 E
Luninets, *U.S.S.R.* 50 E5 52 15N 26 50 E
Luning, *U.S.A.* 142 G4 38 30N 118 10W
Lunino, *U.S.S.R.* 51 E14 53 35N 45 6 E
Lunner, *Norway* 14 D4 60 19N 10 35 E
Lunsemfwa →, *Zambia* 107 E3 14 54 S 30 12 E
Lunsemfwa Falls, *Zambia* 107 E2 14 30 S 29 6 E
Lunteren, *Neths.* 20 D7 52 5N 5 38 E
Luo He →, *China* 66 G6 34 35N 110 20 E
Luocheng, *China* 68 E7 24 48N 108 53 E
Luochuan, *China* 66 G5 35 45N 109 26 E
Luoci, *China* 68 E4 25 19N 102 18 E
Luodian, *China* 68 E6 25 24N 106 43 E
Luoding, *China* 69 F8 22 45N 111 40 E
Luodong, *Taiwan* 69 E13 24 41N 121 46 E
Luofu, *Zaïre* 106 C2 0 10 S 29 15 E
Luohe, *China* 66 H8 33 32N 114 2 E
Luojiang, *China* 68 B5 31 18N 104 33 E
Luonan, *China* 66 G6 34 5N 110 10 E
Luoning, *China* 66 G6 34 35N 111 40 E
Luoshan, *China* 69 A10 32 13N 114 30 E
Luotian, *China* 69 B10 30 46N 115 22 E
Luoyang, *China* 66 G7 34 40N 112 26 E
Luoyuan, *China* 69 D12 26 28N 119 30 E
Luozi, *Zaïre* 103 C2 4 54 S 14 0 E
Luozigou, *China* 67 C16 43 42N 130 18 E
Lupeni, *Romania* 46 D4 45 21N 23 13 E
Lupilichi, *Mozam.* 107 E4 11 47 S 35 13 E
Lupire, *Angola* 103 E3 14 36 S 19 29 E
Łupków, *Poland* 31 B15 49 15N 22 4 E
Lupoing, *China* 68 E5 24 53N 104 21 E
Luquan, *China* 68 E4 25 35N 102 25 E
Luque, *Paraguay* 158 B4 25 19 S 57 25W
Luque, *Spain* 37 H6 37 35N 4 16W
Luray, *U.S.A.* 134 F6 38 39N 78 26W
Lure, *France* 23 E13 47 40N 6 30 E
Luremo, *Angola* 103 D3 8 30 S 17 50 E
Lurgan, *U.K.* 19 B5 54 28N 6 20W
Luribay, *Bolivia* 156 D4 17 6 S 67 39W
Lurin, *Peru* 156 C2 12 17 S 76 52W
Lusaka, *Zambia* 107 F2 15 28 S 28 16 E
Lusambo, *Zaïre* 103 C4 4 58 S 23 28 E
Lusangaye, *Zaïre* 103 C5 4 54 S 26 0 E
Luseland, *Canada* 131 C7 52 5N 109 24W
Lushan, *Henan, China* 66 H7 33 45N 112 55 E
Lushan, *Sichuan, China* 68 B4 30 12N 102 52 E
Lushi, *China* 66 G6 34 3N 111 3 E
Lushnja, *Albania* 44 D1 40 55N 19 41 E
Lushoto, *Tanzania* 106 C4 4 47 S 38 20 E
Lushoto □, *Tanzania* 106 C4 4 45 S 38 20 E
Lushui, *China* 68 E2 25 58N 98 44 E
Lüshun, *China* 67 E11 38 45N 121 15 E
Lusignan, *France* 24 B4 46 26N 0 8 E
Lusigny-sur-Barse, *France* 23 D11 48 16N 4 15 E
Lusk, *U.S.A.* 138 D2 42 47N 104 27W
Lussac-les-Châteaux, *France* 24 B4 46 24N 0 43 E
Lussanvira, *Brazil* 155 F1 20 42 S 51 7W
Luta = Dalian, *China* 67 E11 38 50N 121 40 E
Lutembo, *Angola* 103 E4 13 26 S 21 16 E
Luti, *Solomon Is.* 121 L9 7 14 S 157 0 E
Luton, *U.K.* 17 F7 51 53N 0 24W
Lutong, *Malaysia* 70 D4 4 28N 114 0 E
Lutry, *Switz.* 28 C3 46 31N 6 42 E
Lutsk, *U.S.S.R.* 50 F4 50 50N 25 15 E
Lutuai, *Angola* 103 E4 12 41 S 20 7 E
Lützow Holmbukta, *Antarctica* 7 C4 69 10 S 37 30 E
Lutzputs, *S. Africa* 104 D3 28 3 S 20 40 E
Luverne, *U.S.A.* 138 D6 43 35N 96 12W
Luvo, *Angola* 103 D2 5 51 S 14 5 E
Luvua, *Zaïre* 103 D5 8 48 S 25 17 E
Luvua →, *Zaïre* 106 D2 6 50 S 27 30 E
Luwegu →, *Tanzania* 107 D4 8 31 S 37 23 E
Luwuk, *Indonesia* 71 E6 0 56 S 122 47 E
Luxembourg, *Lux.* 21 J8 49 37N 6 9 E
Luxembourg □, *Belgium* 21 J7 49 58N 5 30 E
Luxembourg ■, *Europe* 21 J8 49 45N 6 0 E
Luxeuil-les-Bains, *France* 23 E13 47 49N 6 24 E
Luxi, *Hunan, China* 69 C8 28 20N 110 7 E
Luxi, *Yunnan, China* 68 E4 24 40N 103 55 E
Luxi, *Yunnan, China* 68 E2 24 27N 98 36 E
Luxor = El Uqsur, *Egypt* 94 B3 25 41N 32 38 E
Luy →, *France* 24 E2 43 39N 1 9W
Luy-de-Béarn →, *France* 24 E3 43 39N 0 48W
Luy-de-France →, *France* 24 E3 43 39N 0 48W
Luyi, *China* 66 H8 33 50N 115 35 E
Luyksgestel, *Neths.* 21 F6 51 17N 5 20 E
Luz-St.-Sauveur, *France* 24 F4 42 53N 0 0 E
Luza, *U.S.S.R.* 48 B8 60 39N 47 10 E
Luzern, *Switz.* 29 B6 47 3N 8 18 E
Luzern □, *Switz.* 28 B5 47 2N 7 55 E
Luzhai, *China* 68 E7 24 29N 109 42 E
Luzhou, *China* 68 C5 28 52N 105 20 E
Luziânia, *Brazil* 155 E2 16 20 S 48 0W
Luzilândia, *Brazil* 154 B3 3 28 S 42 22W
Luzon, *Phil.* 71 A6 16 0N 121 0 E
Luzy, *France* 23 F10 46 47N 3 58 E
Luzzi, *Italy* 41 C9 39 28N 16 17 E
Lvov, *U.S.S.R.* 50 G4 49 50N 24 0 E
Lwówek, *Poland* 47 C3 52 28N 16 10 E
Lwówek Śląski, *Poland* 47 D2 51 7N 15 38 E
Lyakhovichi, *U.S.S.R.* 50 E5 53 2N 26 32 E
Lyakhovskiye, Ostrova, *U.S.S.R.* 57 B15 73 40N 141 0 E
Lyaki, *U.S.S.R.* 53 F12 40 34N 47 22 E
Lyall Mt., *N.Z.* 119 F2 45 16 S 167 32 E
Lyallpur = Faisalabad, *Pakistan* 79 C4 31 30N 73 5 E
Lyalya →, *U.S.S.R.* 54 B7 59 9N 61 29 E
Lyaskovets, *Bulgaria* 43 D10 43 6N 25 44 E
Lycaonia, *Turkey* 88 E5 38 0N 33 0 E
Lychen, *Germany* 26 B9 53 13N 13 20 E
Lycia, *Turkey* 88 E3 36 30N 29 30 E
Lycksele, *Sweden* 12 D15 64 38N 18 40 E
Lycosura, *Greece* 45 G4 37 20N 22 3 E
Lydda = Lod, *Israel* 91 D3 31 57N 34 54 E
Lydenburg, *S. Africa* 105 D5 25 10 S 30 29 E
Lydia, *Turkey* 88 D3 39 0N 28 0 E
Lyell, *N.Z.* 119 B7 41 48 S 172 4 E
Lyell I., *Canada* 130 C2 52 40N 131 35W
Lyell Ra., *N.Z.* 119 B7 41 38 S 172 20 E
Lygnern, *Sweden* 15 G6 57 30N 12 15 E
Lyman, *U.S.A.* 142 F8 41 24N 110 15W
Lyme Regis, *U.K.* 17 G5 50 44N 2 57W
Lymington, *U.K.* 17 G6 50 46N 1 32W
Łyńa →, *Poland* 47 A8 54 37N 21 14 E
Lynchburg, *Ohio, U.S.A.* 141 E13 39 15N 83 48W
Lynchburg, *Va., U.S.A.* 134 G6 37 23N 79 10W
Lynd →, *Australia* 114 B3 16 28 S 143 18 E
Lynd Ra., *Australia* 115 D4 25 30 S 149 20 E
Lynden, *Canada* 136 C4 43 14N 80 9W
Lynden, *U.S.A.* 144 B4 48 56N 122 32W
Lyndhurst, *Queens., Australia* 114 B3 19 12 S 144 20 E
Lyndhurst, *S. Austral., Australia* 115 E2 30 15 S 138 18 E
Lyndon →, *Australia* 113 D1 23 29 S 114 6 E
Lyndonville, *N.Y., U.S.A.* 136 C6 43 19N 78 25W
Lyndonville, *Vt., U.S.A.* 137 B12 44 32N 72 1W
Lyngdal, *Norway* 14 E3 59 54N 9 32 E
Lynher Reef, *Australia* 112 C3 15 27 S 121 55 E
Lynn, *Ind., U.S.A.* 141 D12 40 3N 84 56W
Lynn, *Mass., U.S.A.* 137 D14 42 28N 70 57W
Lynn Canal, *U.S.A.* 130 B1 58 50N 135 20W
Lynn Lake, *Canada* 131 B8 56 51N 101 3W
Lynnwood, *U.S.A.* 144 C4 47 49N 122 19W
Lynton, *U.K.* 17 F4 51 14N 3 50W
Lyntupy, *U.S.S.R.* 50 D5 55 4N 26 23 E
Lynx L., *Canada* 131 A7 62 25N 106 15W
Lyø, *Denmark* 15 J4 55 3N 10 9 E
Lyon, *France* 25 C8 45 46N 4 50 E
Lyonnais, *France* 25 C8 45 45N 4 15 E
Lyons = Lyon, *France* 25 C8 45 46N 4 50 E
Lyons, *Colo., U.S.A.* 138 E2 40 17N 105 15W
Lyons, *Ga., U.S.A.* 135 J4 32 10N 82 15W
Lyons, *Kans., U.S.A.* 138 F5 38 24N 98 13W
Lyons, *N.Y., U.S.A.* 136 C8 43 3N 77 0W
Lyrestad, *Sweden* 15 F8 58 48N 14 4 E
Lys = Leie →, *Belgium* 23 A10 51 2N 3 45 E
Lysá, *Czech.* 30 A7 50 11N 14 51 E
Lysekil, *Sweden* 15 F5 58 17N 11 26 E
Lyskovo, *U.S.S.R.* 51 D14 56 0N 45 3 E
Lyss, *Switz.* 28 B4 47 4N 7 19 E
Lysva, *U.S.S.R.* 54 B5 58 7N 57 49 E
Lytle, *U.S.A.* 139 L5 29 14N 98 46W
Lyttelton, *N.Z.* 119 D7 43 35 S 172 44 E
Lytton, *Canada* 130 C4 50 13N 121 31W
Lyuban, *U.S.S.R.* 50 B7 59 16N 31 18 E
Lyubcha, *U.S.S.R.* 50 E5 53 46N 26 1 E
Lyubertsy, *U.S.S.R.* 51 D10 55 39N 37 50 E
Lyubim, *U.S.S.R.* 51 B12 58 20N 40 39 E
Lyubimets, *Bulgaria* 43 F11 41 50N 26 5 E
Lyuboml, *U.S.S.R.* 50 F4 51 11N 24 4 E
Lyubotin, *U.S.S.R.* 52 B7 50 0N 36 0 E
Lyubytino, *U.S.S.R.* 50 B8 58 50N 33 16 E
Lyudinovo, *U.S.S.R.* 50 E9 53 52N 34 28 E

M

Ma →, *Vietnam* 76 C5 19 47N 105 56 E
Ma'adaba, *Jordan* 91 E4 30 43N 35 47 E
Maamba, *Zambia* 104 B4 17 17 S 26 28 E
Ma'ān, *Jordan* 91 E4 30 12N 35 44 E
Ma'ān □, *Jordan* 91 F5 30 0N 36 0 E
Ma'anshan, *China* 69 B12 31 44N 118 29 E
Maarheeze, *Neths.* 21 F7 51 19N 5 36 E
Maarianhamina, *Finland* 13 F15 60 5N 19 55 E
Maarn, *Neths.* 20 D6 52 3N 5 22 E
Ma'arrat an Nu'mān, *Syria* 84 C3 35 43N 36 43 E
Maarssen, *Neths.* 20 D6 52 9N 5 2 E
Maartensdijk, *Neths.* 20 D6 52 9N 5 10 E
Maas →, *Neths.* 20 E5 51 45N 4 32 E
Maasbracht, *Belgium* 21 F7 51 9N 5 54 E
Maasbree, *Neths.* 21 F8 51 22N 6 3 E
Maasdam, *Neths.* 20 E5 51 48N 4 34 E
Maasdijk, *Neths.* 20 E4 51 58N 4 13 E
Maaseik, *Belgium* 21 F7 51 6N 5 45 E
Maasland, *Neths.* 20 E4 51 57N 4 16 E
Maasniel, *Neths.* 21 F8 51 12N 6 1 E
Maassluis, *Neths.* 20 E4 51 56N 4 16 E
Maastricht, *Neths.* 21 G7 50 50N 5 40 E
Maave, *Mozam.* 105 C5 21 4 S 34 47 E
Ma'bar, *Yemen* 86 D4 14 48N 44 17 E
Mabaruma, *Guyana* 153 B6 8 10N 59 50W
Mabein, *Burma* 78 D6 23 29N 96 37 E
Mabel L., *Canada* 130 C5 50 35N 118 43W
Mabenge, *Zaïre* 106 B1 4 15N 24 12 E
Mabian, *China* 68 C4 28 47N 103 37 E
Mablethorpe, *U.K.* 16 D8 53 21N 0 14 E
Maboma, *Zaïre* 106 B2 2 30N 28 10 E
Maboukou, *Congo* 102 C2 3 39 S 12 31 E
Mabrouk, *Mali* 101 B4 19 29N 1 15W
Mabton, *U.S.A.* 142 C3 46 15N 120 12W
Mabungo, *Somali Rep.* 108 D2 0 49N 42 35 E
Mac Bac, *Vietnam* 77 H6 9 46N 106 7 E
Macachín, *Argentina* 158 D3 37 10 S 63 43W
Macaé, *Brazil* 155 F3 22 20 S 41 43W
Macaíba, *Brazil* 154 C4 5 51 S 35 21W
Macajuba, *Brazil* 155 D3 12 9 S 40 22W
McAlester, *U.S.A.* 139 H7 34 57N 95 46W
McAllen, *U.S.A.* 139 M5 26 12N 98 15W
Macamic, *Canada* 128 C4 48 45N 79 0W
Macao = Macau ■, *China* 65 D6 22 16N 113 35 E
Macão, *Portugal* 37 F3 39 35N 7 59W
Macapá, *Brazil* 153 C7 0 5N 51 4W
Macará, *Ecuador* 152 D2 4 23 S 79 57W
Macarani, *Brazil* 155 E3 15 33 S 40 24W
Macarena, Serranía de la, *Colombia* 152 C3 2 45N 73 55W
Macarthur, *Australia* 116 E5 38 5 S 142 0 E
McArthur →, *Australia* 114 B2 15 54 S 136 40 E
McArthur, Port, *Australia* 114 B2 16 4 S 136 23 E
McArthur River, *Australia* 114 B2 16 27 S 136 7 E
Macas, *Ecuador* 152 D2 2 19 S 78 7W
Macate, *Peru* 156 B2 8 48 S 78 7W
Macau, *Brazil* 154 C4 5 15 S 36 40W
Macau ■, *China* 65 D6 22 16N 113 35 E
Macaúbas, *Brazil* 155 D3 13 2 S 42 42W
Macaya →, *Colombia* 152 C3 0 59N 72 20W
McBride, *Canada* 130 C4 53 20N 120 19W
McCall, *U.S.A.* 142 D5 44 55N 116 6W
McCamey, *U.S.A.* 139 K3 31 8N 102 15W
McCammon, *U.S.A.* 142 E7 42 41N 112 11W
McCauley I., *Canada* 130 C2 53 40N 130 15W
McCleary, *U.S.A.* 144 C3 47 3N 123 16W
Macclesfield, *U.K.* 16 D5 53 16N 2 9W
McClintock, *Canada* 131 B10 57 50N 94 10W
McClintock Ra., *Australia* 112 C4 18 44 S 127 38 E
McCloud, *U.S.A.* 142 F2 41 14N 122 5W
McCluer I., *Australia* 112 B5 11 5 S 133 0 E
McClure, *U.S.A.* 136 F7 40 42N 77 20W
McClure, L., *U.S.A.* 144 H6 37 35N 120 16W
M'Clure Str., *Canada* 124 B8 75 0N 119 0W
McClusky, *U.S.A.* 138 B4 47 30N 100 31W
McComb, *U.S.A.* 139 K9 31 13N 90 30W
McConaughy, L., *U.S.A.* 138 E4 41 20N 101 40W
McCook, *U.S.A.* 138 E4 40 15N 100 35W
McCullough Mt., *U.S.A.* 145 K11 35 35N 115 13W
McCusker →, *Canada* 131 B7 55 32N 108 39W
McDame, *Canada* 130 B3 59 44N 128 59W
McDermitt, *U.S.A.* 142 F5 42 0N 117 45W
Macdonald, L., *Australia* 112 D4 23 30 S 129 0 E
Macdonald, Mt., *Vanuatu* 121 G6 17 36 S 168 23 E
McDonald Is., *Ind. Oc.* 109 K6 53 0 S 73 0 E
Macdonnell Ras., *Australia* 112 D5 23 40 S 133 0 E
McDouall Peak, *Australia* 115 D1 29 51 S 134 55 E
Macdougall L., *Canada* 126 B10 66 0N 98 27W
McDougalls Well, *Australia* 116 A4 31 8 S 141 15 E
MacDowell L., *Canada* 128 B1 52 15N 92 45W
Macduff, *U.K.* 18 D6 57 40N 2 30W
Maceda, *Spain* 36 C3 42 16N 7 39W
Macedonia = Makedhonía □, *Greece* 44 D4 40 39N 22 0 E
Macedonia = Makedonija □, *Yugoslavia* 42 F6 41 53N 21 40 E
Maceió, *Brazil* 154 C4 9 40 S 35 41W
Maceira, *Portugal* 37 F2 39 41N 8 55W
Macenta, *Guinea* 100 D3 8 35N 9 32W
Macerata, *Italy* 39 E10 43 19N 13 28 E
McFarland, *U.S.A.* 145 K7 35 41N 119 14W
McFarlane →, *Canada* 131 B7 59 12N 107 58W
Macfarlane, L., *Australia* 116 B2 32 0 S 136 40 E
McGehee, *U.S.A.* 139 J9 33 40N 91 25W
McGill, *U.S.A.* 142 G6 39 27N 114 50W
Macgillycuddy's Reeks, *Ireland* 19 D2 52 2N 9 45W
MacGregor, *Canada* 131 D9 49 57N 98 48W
McGregor, *U.S.A.* 140 A5 43 5N 91 15W
McGregor →, *Canada* 130 B4 55 10N 122 0W
McGregor Ra., *Australia* 115 D3 27 0 S 142 45 E
Mach Kowr, *Iran* 85 E9 25 48N 61 28 E
Machacalis, *Brazil* 155 E3 17 5 S 40 45W
Machado = Jiparaná →, *Brazil* 157 B5 8 3 S 62 52W
Machagai, *Argentina* 158 B3 26 56 S 60 2W
Machakos, *Kenya* 106 C4 1 30 S 37 15 E
Machakos □, *Kenya* 106 C4 1 30 S 37 15 E
Machala, *Ecuador* 152 D2 3 20 S 79 57W
Machanga, *Mozam.* 105 C6 20 59 S 35 0 E
Machattie, L., *Australia* 114 C2 24 50 S 139 48 E
Machava, *Mozam.* 105 D5 25 54 S 32 28 E
Machece, *Mozam.* 107 F4 19 15 S 35 32 E
Machecoul, *France* 22 F5 47 0N 1 49W
Machelen, *Belgium* 21 G4 50 55N 4 26 E
Macheng, *China* 69 B10 31 12N 115 2 E
McHenry, *U.S.A.* 141 B8 42 21N 88 16W
Machevna, *U.S.S.R.* 57 C18 61 20N 172 20 E
Machezo, *Spain* 37 F6 39 21N 4 20W
Machias, *U.S.A.* 129 D6 44 40N 67 28W
Machichaco, C., *Spain* 34 B2 43 28N 2 47W
Machichi →, *Canada* 131 B10 57 3N 92 6W
Machico, *Madeira* 33 D3 32 43N 16 44W
Machida, *Japan* 63 B11 35 28N 139 23 E
Machilipatnam, *India* 83 F5 16 12N 81 8 E
Machiques, *Venezuela* 152 A3 10 4N 72 34W
Machupicchu, *Peru* 156 C3 13 8 S 72 30W
Machynlleth, *U.K.* 17 E4 52 36N 3 51W
Maciejowice, *Poland* 47 D8 51 36N 21 26 E
McIlwraith Ra., *Australia* 114 A3 13 50 S 143 20 E
Măcin, *Romania* 46 D9 45 16N 28 8 E
Macina, *Mali* 100 C4 14 50N 5 0W
McIntosh, *U.S.A.* 138 C4 45 57N 101 20W
McIntosh L., *Canada* 131 B8 55 45N 105 0W
Macintosh Ra., *Australia* 113 E4 27 39 S 125 32 E
Macintyre →, *Australia* 115 D5 28 37 S 150 47 E
Macizo Galaico, *Spain* 36 C3 42 30N 7 30W
Mackay, *Australia* 114 C4 21 8 S 149 11 E
Mackay, *U.S.A.* 142 E7 43 58N 113 37W
MacKay →, *Canada* 130 B6 57 10N 111 38W
Mackay, L., *Australia* 112 D4 22 30 S 129 0 E
McKay Ra., *Australia* 112 D3 23 0 S 122 30 E
McKeesport, *U.S.A.* 136 F5 40 21N 79 50W
McKenna, *U.S.A.* 144 D4 46 56N 122 33W
Mackenzie, *Canada* 130 B4 55 20N 123 5W
Mackenzie, *Guyana* 153 B6 6 0N 58 17W
McKenzie, *U.S.A.* 135 G1 36 10N 88 31W
Mackenzie →, *Australia* 114 C4 23 38 S 149 46 E
Mackenzie →, *Canada* 126 B6 69 10N 134 20W
McKenzie →, *U.S.A.* 142 D2 44 2N 123 6W
Mackenzie Highway, *Canada* 130 B5 58 0N 117 15W
Mackenzie Mts., *Canada* 126 B7 64 0N 130 0W
Mackenzie Plains, *N.Z.* 119 E5 44 10 S 170 25 E
McKerrow L., *N.Z.* 119 E3 44 25 S 168 5 E
Mackinaw, *U.S.A.* 140 D7 40 32N 89 21W
Mackinaw →, *U.S.A.* 140 D7 40 33N 89 44W
Mackinaw City, *U.S.A.* 134 C3 45 47N 84 44W
McKinlay, *Australia* 114 C3 21 16 S 141 18 E
McKinlay →, *Australia* 114 C3 20 50 S 141 28 E
McKinley, Mt., *U.S.A.* 126 B4 63 2N 151 0W
McKinley Sea, *Arctic* 6 A7 84 0N 10 0W
McKinney, *U.S.A.* 139 J6 33 10N 96 40W
McKinnon Pass, *N.Z.* 119 E3 44 52 S 168 12 E
Mackinnon Road, *Kenya* 106 C4 3 40 S 39 1 E
Macksville, *Australia* 117 A10 30 40 S 152 56 E
McLaren Vale, *Australia* 116 C3 35 13 S 138 31 E
McLaughlin, *U.S.A.* 138 C4 45 50N 100 50W
Maclean, *Australia* 115 D5 29 26 S 153 16 E
McLean, *Ill., U.S.A.* 140 D7 40 19N 89 10W
McLean, *Tex., U.S.A.* 139 H4 35 15N 100 35W
McLeansboro, *U.S.A.* 138 F10 38 5N 88 30W
Maclear, *S. Africa* 105 E4 31 2 S 28 23 E
Macleay →, *Australia* 117 A10 30 56 S 153 0 E
McLennan, *Canada* 130 B5 55 42N 116 50W
MacLeod, B., *Canada* 131 A7 62 53N 110 0W

Manti 229

Malargüe, *Argentina* 158 D2 35 32 S 69 30W
Malartic, *Canada* 128 C4 48 9N 78 9W
Malatya, *Turkey* 89 D8 38 25N 38 20 E
Malatya □, *Turkey* 89 D8 38 15N 38 0 E
Malawi ■, *Africa* 107 E3 11 55 S 34 0 E
Malawi, L., *Africa* 107 E3 12 30 S 34 30 E
Malay Pen., *Asia* 77 J3 7 25N 100 0 E
Malaya Belozërka, *U.S.S.R.* 52 C6 47 12N 34 56 E
Malaya Vishera, *U.S.S.R.* 50 B8 58 55N 32 25 E
Malaya Viska, *U.S.S.R.* 52 B4 48 39N 31 36 E
Malaybalay, *Phil.* 71 C7 8 5N 125 7 E
Malāyer, *Iran* 85 C6 34 19N 48 51 E
Malaysia ■, *Asia* 70 D4 5 0N 110 0 E
Malazgirt, *Turkey* 89 D10 39 10N 42 33 E
Malbon, *Australia* 114 C3 21 5 S 140 17 E
Malbooma, *Australia* 115 E1 30 41 S 134 11 E
Malbork, *Poland* 47 A6 54 3N 19 1 E
Malca Dube, *Ethiopia* 108 C2 6 47N 42 4 E
Malcésine, *Italy* 38 C7 45 46N 10 48 E
Malchin, *Germany* 26 B8 53 43N 12 44 E
Malchow, *Germany* 26 B8 53 29N 12 25 E
Malcolm, *Australia* 113 E3 28 51 S 121 25 E
Malcolm, Pt., *Australia* 113 F3 33 48 S 123 45 E
Malczyce, *Poland* 47 D3 51 14N 16 29 E
Maldegem, *Belgium* 21 F2 51 14N 3 26 E
Malden, *Mass., U.S.A.* 137 D13 42 26N 71 5W
Malden, *Mo., U.S.A.* 139 G10 36 35N 90 0W
Malden I., *Kiribati* 123 H12 4 3 S 155 1W
Maldives ■, *Ind. Oc.* 109 D6 5 0N 73 0 E
Maldon, *Australia* 116 D6 37 0 S 144 6 E
Maldonado, *Uruguay* 159 C5 34 59 S 55 0W
Maldonado, Punta, *Mexico* 147 D5 16 19N 98 35W
Malé, *Italy* 38 B7 46 20N 10 55 E
Malé Karpaty, *Czech.* 31 C10 48 30N 17 20 E
Maléa, Ákra, *Greece* 45 H5 36 28N 23 7 E
Malebo, Pool, *Africa* 103 C3 4 17 S 15 20 E
Malegaon, *India* 82 D2 20 30N 74 38 E
Malei, *Mozam.* 107 F4 17 12 S 36 58 E
Malek Kandī, *Iran* 84 B5 37 9N 46 6 E
Malela, *Bas Zaïre, Zaïre* 103 D2 5 59 S 12 37 E
Malela, *Kivu, Zaïre* 103 C5 4 22 S 26 8 E
Malema, *Mozam.* 107 E4 14 57 S 37 20 E
Máleme, *Greece* 32 D5 35 31N 23 49 E
Malerkotla, *India* 80 D6 30 32N 75 58 E
Máles, *Greece* 32 D7 35 6N 25 35 E
Malesherbes, *France* 23 D9 48 15N 2 24 E
Maleshevska Planina, *Europe* 42 F8 41 38N 23 7 E
Malestroit, *France* 22 E4 47 49N 2 25W
Malfa, *Italy* 41 D7 38 35N 14 50 E
Malgobek, *U.S.S.R.* 53 E11 43 30N 44 34 E
Malgomaj, *Sweden* 12 D14 64 40N 16 30 E
Malgrat, *Spain* 34 D7 41 39N 2 46 E
Malha, *Sudan* 95 D2 15 8N 25 10 E
Malheur →, *U.S.A.* 142 D5 44 3N 116 59W
Malheur L., *U.S.A.* 142 E4 43 19N 118 42W
Mali, *Guinea* 100 C2 12 10N 12 20W
Mali ■, *Africa* 100 B4 17 0N 3 0W
Mali Hka →, *Burma* 78 C6 25 42N 97 30 E
Mali Kanal, *Yugoslavia* 42 B4 45 36N 19 24 E
Malibu, *U.S.A.* 145 L8 34 2N 118 41W
Malik, *Indonesia* 71 E6 0 39 S 123 16 E
Malili, *Indonesia* 71 E6 2 42 S 121 6 E
Malimba, Mts., *Zaïre* 106 D2 7 30 S 29 30 E
Malin, *U.S.S.R.* 50 F6 50 46N 29 3 E
Malindi, *Kenya* 106 C5 3 12 S 40 5 E
Malines = Mechelen, *Belgium* 21 F4 51 2N 4 29 E
Maling, *Indonesia* 71 D6 1 0N 121 0 E
Malinyi, *Tanzania* 107 D4 8 56 S 36 0 E
Malipo, *China* 68 F5 23 7N 104 42 E
Maliqi, *Albania* 44 D2 40 45N 20 48 E
Malita, *Phil.* 71 C7 6 19N 125 39 E
Maljenik, *Yugoslavia* 42 D6 43 59N 21 55 E
Malkapur, *Maharashtra, India* 82 F3 16 57N 76 17 E
Malkapur, *Maharashtra, India* 82 D1 20 53N 73 58 E
Malkara, *Turkey* 88 C2 40 53N 26 53 E
Małkinia Górna, *Poland* 47 C9 52 42N 22 5 E
Malko Tŭrnovo, *Bulgaria* 43 F12 41 59N 27 31 E
Mallacoota, *Australia* 117 D8 37 40 S 149 40 E
Mallacoota Inlet, *Australia* 117 D8 37 34 S 149 40 E
Mallaig, *U.K.* 18 E3 57 0N 5 50W
Mallala, *Australia* 116 C3 34 26 S 138 30 E
Mallard, *U.S.A.* 140 B2 42 56N 94 41W
Mallawan, *India* 81 F9 27 4N 80 12 E
Mallawi, *Egypt* 94 B3 27 44N 30 44 E
Malleco □, *Chile* 160 A2 38 10 S 72 20W
Mallemort, *France* 25 E9 43 43N 5 11 E
Málles Venosta, *Italy* 38 B7 46 42N 10 32 E
Mállia, *Greece* 32 D7 35 17N 25 27 E
Mallión, Kólpos, *Greece* 32 D7 35 19N 25 27 E
Mallorca, *Spain* 33 B10 39 30N 3 0 E
Mallorytown, *Canada* 137 B9 44 29N 75 53W
Mallow, *Ireland* 19 D3 52 8N 8 40W
Malmberget, *Sweden* 12 C16 67 11N 20 40 E
Malmédy, *Belgium* 21 H8 50 25N 6 2 E
Malmesbury, *S. Africa* 104 E2 33 28 S 18 41 E
Malmö, *Sweden* 15 J6 55 36N 12 59 E
Malmöhus län □, *Sweden* 15 J7 55 45N 13 30 E
Malmslätt, *Sweden* 15 F9 58 27N 15 33 E
Malmyzh, *U.S.S.R.* 54 C2 56 31N 50 41 E
Malnaş, *Romania* 46 C6 46 2N 25 49 E
Malo, *Vanuatu* 121 E5 15 40 S 167 11 E
Malo Konare, *Bulgaria* 43 E9 42 12N 24 24 E
Maloarkhangelsk, *U.S.S.R.* 51 E10 52 28N 36 30 E
Maloca, *Brazil* 153 C6 0 43N 55 57W
Maloja, *Switz.* 29 D9 46 25N 9 35 E
Maloja, P., *Switz.* 29 D9 46 23N 9 42 E
Malolos, *Phil.* 71 B6 14 50N 120 49 E
Malomalsk, *U.S.S.R.* 54 B6 58 45N 59 53 E
Malombe L., *Malawi* 107 E4 14 40 S 35 15 E
Malomir, *Bulgaria* 43 E11 42 16N 26 30 E
Malone, *U.S.A.* 137 B10 44 50N 74 19W
Malong, *China* 68 E4 25 24N 103 34 E
Malonga, *Zaïre* 103 E4 10 24 S 23 10 E
Malorad, *Bulgaria* 43 D8 43 28N 23 41 E
Malorita, *U.S.S.R.* 50 F4 51 50N 24 3 E
Maloyaroslovets, *U.S.S.R.* 51 D10 55 2N 36 20 E
Malozemelskaya Tundra, *U.S.S.R.* 48 A9 67 0N 50 0 E
Malpartida, *Spain* 37 F4 39 26N 6 30W
Malpaso, *Canary Is.* 33 G1 27 43N 18 3W
Malpelo, *Colombia* 156 A1 4 3N 81 35W
Malpica, *Spain* 36 B2 43 19N 8 50W
Malprabha →, *India* 83 F3 16 20N 76 5 E
Malta, *Brazil* 154 C4 6 54 S 37 31W
Malta, *Idaho, U.S.A.* 142 E7 42 15N 113 30W
Malta, *Mont., U.S.A.* 142 B10 48 20N 107 55W
Malta ■, *Europe* 32 D2 35 50N 14 30 E
Malta Channel, *Medit. S.* 40 F6 36 40N 14 0 E
Maltahöhe, *Namibia* 104 C2 24 55 S 17 0 E
Malters, *Switz.* 28 B6 47 3N 8 11 E
Malton, *Canada* 136 C5 43 42N 79 38W
Malton, *U.K.* 16 C7 54 9N 0 48W
Malu'a, *Solomon Is.* 121 M11 8 0 S 160 0 E
Maluku, *Indonesia* 71 E7 1 0 S 127 0 E
Maluku □, *Indonesia* 71 E7 3 0 S 128 0 E
Maluku Sea, *Indonesia* 71 E6 4 0 S 124 0 E
Malumfashi, *Nigeria* 101 C6 11 48N 7 39 E
Malvalli, *India* 83 H3 12 28N 77 8 E
Malvan, *India* 83 F1 16 2N 73 30 E
Malvern, *U.S.A.* 139 H8 34 22N 92 50W
Malvik, *Norway* 14 A4 63 25N 10 40 E
Malvinas, Is. = Falkland Is., *Atl. Oc.* 160 D5 51 30 S 59 0W
Malya, *Tanzania* 106 C3 3 5 S 33 38 E
Malybay, *U.S.S.R.* 55 B9 43 30N 78 25 E
Malyy Lyakhovskiy, Ostrov, *U.S.S.R.* 57 B15 74 7N 140 36 E
Mama, *U.S.S.R.* 57 D12 58 18N 112 54 E
Mamadysh, *U.S.S.R.* 54 D2 55 44N 51 23 E
Mamaia, *Romania* 46 E9 44 18N 28 37 E
Mamaku, *N.Z.* 118 E5 38 5 S 176 8 E
Mamanguape, *Brazil* 154 C4 6 50 S 35 4W
Mamasa, *Indonesia* 71 E5 2 55 S 119 20 E
Mambasa, *Zaïre* 106 B2 1 22N 29 3 E
Mamberamo →, *Indonesia* 71 E9 2 0 S 137 50 E
Mambilima Falls, *Zambia* 107 E2 10 31 S 28 45 E
Mambirima, *Zaïre* 107 E2 11 25 S 27 33 E
Mambo, *Tanzania* 106 C4 4 52 S 38 22 E
Mambrui, *Kenya* 106 C5 3 5 S 40 5 E
Mamburao, *Phil.* 71 B6 13 13N 120 39 E
Mameigwess L., *Canada* 128 B2 52 35N 87 50W
Mamer, *Lux.* 21 J8 49 38N 6 2 E
Mamers, *France* 22 D7 48 21N 0 22 E
Mamfe, *Cameroon* 101 D6 5 50N 9 15 E
Māmī, Ra's, *Yemen* 87 D6 12 32N 54 30 E
Mamiña, *Chile* 156 E4 20 5 S 69 14W
Mámmola, *Italy* 41 D9 38 23N 16 13 E
Mammoth, *U.S.A.* 143 K8 32 46N 110 43W
Mammoth, *U.S.A.* 57 C13 63 0N 110 0 E
Mamoré →, *Bolivia* 157 C4 10 23 S 65 53W
Mamou, *Guinea* 100 C2 10 15N 12 0W
Mampatá, *Guinea-Biss.* 100 C2 11 54N 14 53W
Mampong, *Ghana* 101 D4 7 6N 1 26W
Mamry, Jezioro, *Poland* 47 A8 54 5N 21 50 E
Mamuil Malal, Paso, *S. Amer.* 160 A2 39 35 S 71 28W
Mamuju, *Indonesia* 71 E5 2 41 S 118 50 E
Ma'mūl, *Oman* 87 C6 18 8N 55 16 E
Man, *Ivory C.* 100 D3 7 30N 7 40W
Man →, *India* 82 F2 17 31N 75 32 E
Man, I. of, *U.K.* 16 C3 54 15N 4 30W
Man Na, *Burma* 78 D6 23 27N 97 19 E
Man Tun, *Burma* 78 D7 23 52N 98 38 E
Mana, *Fr. Guiana* 153 B7 5 45N 53 55W
Mana →, *Fr. Guiana* 153 B7 5 45N 53 55W
Måna →, *Norway* 14 E2 59 55N 8 50 E
Manaar, G. of = Mannar, G. of, *Asia* 83 K4 8 30N 79 0 E
Manabí □, *Ecuador* 152 D1 0 40 S 80 5W
Manacacías →, *Colombia* 152 C3 4 23N 72 4W
Manacapuru, *Brazil* 153 D5 3 16 S 60 37W
Manacapuru →, *Brazil* 153 D5 3 18 S 60 37W
Manacor, *Spain* 33 B10 39 34N 3 13 E
Manado, *Indonesia* 71 D6 1 29N 124 51 E
Manage, *Belgium* 21 G4 50 31N 4 15 E
Managua, *Nic.* 148 D2 12 6N 86 20W
Managua, L., *Nic.* 148 D2 12 20N 86 30W
Manaia, *N.Z.* 118 F3 39 33 S 174 8 E
Manakara, *Madag.* 105 C8 22 8 S 48 1 E
Manakau Mt., *N.Z.* 119 C8 42 15 S 173 42 E
Manākhah, *Yemen* 86 D3 15 5N 43 44 E
Manakino, *N.Z.* 118 E4 38 22 S 175 47 E
Manam I., *Papua N. G.* 120 C3 4 5 S 145 0 E
Manambao →, *Madag.* 105 B7 17 35 S 44 0 E
Manambato, *Madag.* 105 A8 13 43 S 49 7 E
Manambolo →, *Madag.* 105 B7 19 18 S 44 22 E
Manambolosy, *Madag.* 105 B8 16 2 S 49 40 E
Mananara, *Madag.* 105 B8 16 10 S 49 46 E
Mananara →, *Madag.* 105 C8 23 21 S 47 42 E
Mananjary, *Madag.* 105 C8 21 13 S 48 20 E
Manantenina, *Madag.* 105 C8 24 17 S 47 19 E
Manaos = Manaus, *Brazil* 153 D6 3 0 S 60 0W
Manapire →, *Venezuela* 152 B4 7 42N 66 7W
Manapouri, *N.Z.* 119 F2 45 34 S 167 39 E
Manapouri, L., *N.Z.* 119 F2 45 32 S 167 32 E
Manar →, *India* 82 E3 18 50N 77 20 E
Manār, Jabal, *Yemen* 86 D4 14 2N 44 17 E
Manas, *China* 64 B3 44 17N 85 56 E
Manas, *Somali Rep.* 108 D2 2 57N 43 28 E
Manas, Gora, *U.S.S.R.* 55 B5 42 22N 71 2 E
Manaslu, *Nepal* 81 E11 28 33N 84 33 E
Manasquan, *U.S.A.* 137 F10 40 7N 74 3W
Manassa, *U.S.A.* 143 H11 37 12N 105 58W
Manaung, *Burma* 78 F4 18 45N 93 40 E
Manaus, *Brazil* 153 D6 3 0 S 60 0W
Manavgat, *Turkey* 88 E4 36 47N 31 26 E
Manawan L., *Canada* 131 B8 55 24N 103 14W
Manawatu →, *N.Z.* 118 G4 40 28 S 175 12 E
Manay, *Phil.* 71 C7 7 17N 126 33 E
Manbij, *Syria* 84 B3 36 31N 37 57 E
Mancelona, *U.S.A.* 134 C3 44 54N 85 5W
Mancha Real, *Spain* 37 H7 37 48N 3 39W
Manche □, *France* 22 C5 49 10N 1 20W
Manchegorsk, *U.S.S.R.* 48 A5 67 40N 32 40 E
Manchester, *U.K.* 16 D5 53 30N 2 15W
Manchester, *Calif., U.S.A.* 144 G3 38 58N 123 41W
Manchester, *Conn., U.S.A.* 137 E12 41 47N 72 30W
Manchester, *Ga., U.S.A.* 135 J3 32 53N 84 32W
Manchester, *Iowa, U.S.A.* 140 B5 42 28N 91 27W
Manchester, *Ky., U.S.A.* 134 G4 37 9N 83 45W
Manchester, *Mich., U.S.A.* 141 B12 42 9N 84 2W
Manchester, *N.H., U.S.A.* 137 D13 42 58N 71 29W
Manchester, *N.Y., U.S.A.* 136 D7 42 56N 77 16W
Manchester, *Vt., U.S.A.* 137 C11 43 10N 73 5W
Manchester L., *Canada* 131 A7 61 28N 107 29W
Manchouli, *China* 10 H10 49 46N 117 24 E
Manchuria = Dongbei, *China* 67 D13 42 0N 125 0 E
Manciano, *Italy* 39 F8 42 35N 11 30 E
Mancifa, *Ethiopia* 95 F5 6 53N 41 50 E
Mancora, Pta., *Peru* 156 A1 4 9 S 81 1W
Mand →, *Iran* 85 D7 28 20N 52 30 E
Manda, *Chunya, Tanzania* 106 D3 6 51 S 32 29 E
Manda, *Ludewe, Tanzania* 107 E3 10 30 S 34 40 E
Mandabé, *Madag.* 105 C7 21 0 S 44 55 E
Mandaguari, *Brazil* 159 A5 23 32 S 51 42W
Mandah, *Mongolia* 66 B5 44 27N 108 2 E
Mandal, *Norway* 13 G9 58 2N 7 25 E
Mandalay, *Burma* 78 E6 22 0N 96 4 E
Mandale = Mandalay, *Burma* 78 E6 22 0N 96 4 E
Mandalgovi, *Mongolia* 66 B4 45 45N 106 10 E
Mandalī, *Iraq* 84 C5 33 43N 45 28 E
Mandalya Körfezi, *Turkey* 45 G9 37 15N 27 20 E
Mandan, *U.S.A.* 138 B4 46 50N 101 0W
Mandapeta, *India* 82 F5 16 47N 81 56 E
Mandar, Teluk, *Indonesia* 71 E5 3 35 S 119 15 E
Mandas, *Italy* 40 C2 39 40N 9 8 E
Mandasor = Mandsaur, *India* 80 G6 24 3N 75 8 E
Mandaue, *Phil.* 71 B6 10 20N 123 56 E
Mandelieu-la-Napoule, *France* 25 E10 43 34N 6 57 E
Mandera, *Kenya* 106 B5 3 55N 41 53 E
Mandera □, *Kenya* 106 B5 3 30N 41 0 E
Manderfeld, *Belgium* 21 H8 50 20N 6 20 E
Mandi, *India* 80 D7 31 39N 76 58 E
Mandimba, *Mozam.* 107 E4 14 20 S 35 40 E
Mandioli, *Indonesia* 71 E7 0 40 S 127 20 E
Mandioré, L., *S. Amer.* 157 D6 18 8 S 57 33W
Mandji I. = Lopez I., *Gabon* 102 C1 0 50 S 8 47 E
Mandla, *India* 81 H9 22 39N 80 30 E
Mandø, *Denmark* 15 J2 55 18N 8 33 E
Mandoto, *Madag.* 105 B8 19 34 S 46 17 E
Mandoúdhion, *Greece* 45 F5 38 48N 23 29 E
Mandra, *Pakistan* 80 C5 33 23N 73 12 E
Mandráki, *Greece* 45 H9 36 36N 27 11 E
Mandrare →, *Madag.* 105 D8 25 10 S 46 30 E
Mandritsara, *Madag.* 105 B8 15 50 S 48 49 E
Mandsaur, *India* 80 G6 24 3N 75 8 E
Mandurah, *Australia* 113 F2 32 36 S 115 48 E
Mandúria, *Italy* 41 B10 40 25N 17 38 E
Mandvi, *India* 80 H3 22 51N 69 22 E
Mandya, *India* 83 H3 12 30N 77 0 E
Mandzai, *Pakistan* 80 D2 30 55N 67 6 E
Mané, *Burkina Faso* 101 C4 12 59N 1 21W
Maneh, *Iran* 85 B8 37 39N 57 7 E
Manengouba, Mts., *Cameroon* 101 E6 5 0N 9 50 E
Maner →, *India* 82 E4 18 30N 79 40 E
Maneroo, *Australia* 114 C3 23 22 S 143 53 E
Maneroo Cr. →, *Australia* 114 C3 23 21 S 143 53 E
Manfalût, *Egypt* 94 B3 27 20N 30 52 E
Manfred, *Australia* 116 B5 33 19 S 143 45 E
Manfredónia, *Italy* 41 A8 41 40N 15 55 E
Manfredónia, G. di, *Italy* 41 A9 41 30N 16 10 E
Manga, *Brazil* 155 D3 14 46 S 43 56W
Manga, *Burkina Faso* 101 C4 11 40N 1 4W
Manga, *Niger* 97 F2 15 0N 14 0 E
Mangabeiras, Chapada das, *Brazil* 154 D2 10 0 S 46 30W
Mangalagiri, *India* 83 F5 16 26N 80 36 E
Mangaldai, *India* 78 B4 26 26N 92 2 E
Mangalia, *Romania* 46 F9 43 50N 28 35 E
Mangalore, *Australia* 117 D6 36 56 S 145 10 E
Mangalore, *India* 83 H2 12 55N 74 47 E
Manganeses, *Spain* 36 D5 41 45N 5 43W
Mangaon, *India* 82 E1 18 15N 73 20 E
Mangaweka, *N.Z.* 118 F4 39 48 S 175 47 E
Mangaweka, Mt., *N.Z.* 118 F5 39 49 S 176 5 E
Mange, *Zaïre* 102 B4 0 54N 20 30 E
Manggar, *Indonesia* 70 E3 2 50 S 108 10 E
Manggawitu, *Indonesia* 71 E8 4 8 S 133 32 E
Mangin Range, *Burma* 78 C5 24 15N 95 45 E
Mangkalihat, Tanjung, *Indonesia* 71 D5 1 2N 118 59 E
Mangla Dam, *Pakistan* 81 C5 33 9N 73 44 E
Manglares, C., *Colombia* 152 C2 1 36N 79 2W
Manglaur, *India* 80 E7 29 44N 77 49 E
Mangnai, *China* 64 C4 37 52N 91 43 E
Mango, *Togo* 101 C5 10 20N 0 30 E
Mangoche, *Malawi* 107 E4 14 25 S 35 16 E
Mangoky →, *Madag.* 105 C7 21 29 S 43 41 E
Mangole, *Indonesia* 71 E7 1 50 S 125 55 E
Mangombe, *Zaïre* 106 C2 1 20 S 26 48 E
Mangonui, *N.Z.* 118 B2 35 1 S 173 32 E
Mangualde, *Portugal* 36 E3 40 38N 7 48W
Mangueigne, *Chad* 97 F4 10 30N 21 15 E
Mangueira, L. da, *Brazil* 159 C5 33 0 S 52 50W
Manguéni, Hamada, *Niger* 96 D2 22 35N 12 40 E
Mangum, *U.S.A.* 139 H5 34 50N 99 30W
Mangyshlak Poluostrov, *U.S.S.R.* 53 D15 44 30N 52 30 E
Mangyshlakskiy Zaliv, *U.S.S.R.* 53 D14 44 40N 50 50 E
Manhattan, *U.S.A.* 138 F6 39 10N 96 40W
Manhatten, *U.S.A.* 141 C9 41 26N 87 59W
Manhiça, *Mozam.* 105 D5 25 23 S 32 49 E
Manhuaçu, *Brazil* 155 F3 20 15 S 42 2W
Manhumirim, *Brazil* 155 F3 20 22 S 41 57W
Maní, *Colombia* 152 C3 4 49N 72 17W
Mania →, *Madag.* 105 B8 19 42 S 45 22 E
Maniago, *Italy* 39 B9 46 11N 12 40 E
Manica, *Mozam.* 105 B5 18 58 S 32 59 E
Manica e Sofala □, *Mozam.* 105 B5 19 10 S 33 45 E
Manicaland □, *Zimbabwe* 107 F3 19 0 S 32 30 E
Manicoré, *Brazil* 157 B5 5 48 S 61 16W
Manicoré →, *Brazil* 157 B5 5 51 S 61 19W
Manicouagan →, *Canada* 129 C6 49 30N 68 30W
Manīfah, *Si. Arabia* 85 E6 27 44N 49 0 E
Manifold, *Australia* 114 C5 22 41 S 150 40 E
Manifold, C., *Australia* 114 C5 22 41 S 150 50 E
Maniganggo, *China* 68 B2 31 56N 99 10 E
Manigotagan, *Canada* 131 C9 51 6N 96 18W
Manihiki, *Cook Is.* 123 J11 10 24 S 161 1W
Manika, Plateau de la, *Zaïre* 107 E2 10 0 S 25 5 E
Manikganj, *Bangla.* 78 D3 23 52N 90 0 E
Manila, *Phil.* 71 B6 14 40N 121 3 E
Manila, *U.S.A.* 142 F9 41 0N 109 44W
Manila B., *Phil.* 71 B6 14 40N 120 35 E
Manilla, *Australia* 117 A9 30 45 S 150 43 E
Manimpé, *Mali* 100 C3 14 11N 5 28W
Maningrida, *Australia* 114 A1 12 3 S 134 13 E
Manipur □, *India* 78 C5 25 0N 94 0 E
Manipur →, *Burma* 78 D5 23 45N 94 20 E
Manisa, *Turkey* 88 D2 38 38N 27 30 E
Manisa □, *Turkey* 88 D3 38 40N 28 0 E
Manistee, *U.S.A.* 134 C2 44 15N 86 20W
Manistee →, *U.S.A.* 134 C2 44 15N 86 21W
Manistique, *U.S.A.* 134 C2 45 59N 86 18W
Manito, *U.S.A.* 140 D7 40 25N 89 47W
Manito L., *Canada* 131 C7 52 43N 109 43W
Manitoba □, *Canada* 131 B9 55 30N 97 0W
Manitoba, L., *Canada* 131 C9 51 0N 98 45W
Manitou, *Canada* 131 D9 49 15N 98 32W
Manitou Beach, *U.S.A.* 141 C12 41 58N 84 19W
Manitou I., *U.S.A.* 128 C2 47 22N 87 30W
Manitou Is., *U.S.A.* 134 C3 45 8N 86 0W
Manitou L., *Canada* 129 B6 50 55N 65 17W
Manitou Springs, *U.S.A.* 138 F2 38 52N 104 55W
Manitoulin I., *Canada* 128 C3 45 40N 82 30W
Manitowaning, *Canada* 128 C3 45 46N 81 49W
Manitowoc, *U.S.A.* 134 C2 44 8N 87 40W
Manitsauá-Missu →, *Brazil* 157 C7 10 58 S 53 20W
Manizales, *Colombia* 152 B2 5 5N 75 32W
Manja, *Madag.* 105 C7 21 26 S 44 20 E
Manjacaze, *Mozam.* 105 C5 24 45 S 34 0 E
Manjakandriana, *Madag.* 105 B8 18 55 S 47 47 E
Manjeri, *India* 83 J3 11 7N 76 11 E
Manjhand, *Pakistan* 79 D3 25 50N 68 10 E
Manjil, *Iran* 85 B6 36 46N 49 30 E
Manjimup, *Australia* 113 F2 34 15 S 116 6 E
Manjra →, *India* 82 E3 18 49N 77 52 E
Mankato, *Kans., U.S.A.* 138 F5 39 49N 98 11W
Mankato, *Minn., U.S.A.* 138 C8 44 8N 93 59W
Mankayane, *Swaziland* 105 D5 26 40 S 31 4 E
Mankono, *Ivory C.* 100 D3 8 1N 6 10W
Mankota, *Canada* 131 D7 49 25N 107 5W
Manlay, *Mongolia* 66 B4 44 9N 107 0 E
Manlleu, *Spain* 34 C7 42 2N 2 17 E
Manly, *Australia* 117 B9 33 48 S 151 17 E
Manmad, *India* 82 D2 20 18N 74 28 E
Mann Ras., *Australia* 113 E5 26 6 S 130 5 E
Manna, *Indonesia* 70 E2 4 25 S 102 55 E
Mannahill, *Australia* 116 B4 32 25 S 140 0 E
Mannar, *Sri Lanka* 83 K4 9 1N 79 54 E
Mannar, G. of, *Asia* 83 K4 8 30N 79 0 E
Mannar I., *Sri Lanka* 83 K4 9 5N 79 45 E
Mannargudi, *India* 83 J4 10 45N 79 51 E
Männedorf, *Switz.* 29 B7 47 15N 8 43 E
Mannheim, *Germany* 27 F4 49 28N 8 29 E
Manning, *Canada* 130 B5 56 53N 117 39W
Manning, *Oreg., U.S.A.* 144 E3 45 45N 123 13W
Manning, *S.C., U.S.A.* 135 J5 33 40N 80 9W
Manning Prov. Park, *Canada* 130 D4 49 5N 120 45W
Manning Str., *Solomon Is.* 121 L10 7 30 S 158 0 E
Mannington, *U.S.A.* 134 F5 39 35N 80 25W
Mannu →, *Italy* 40 C2 39 15N 9 32 E
Mannu, C., *Italy* 40 B1 40 2N 8 24 E
Mannum, *Australia* 116 C3 34 50 S 139 20 E
Mano, *S. Leone* 100 D2 8 3N 12 2W
Manoa, *Bolivia* 157 B4 9 40 S 65 27W
Manokwari, *Indonesia* 71 E8 0 54 S 134 0 E
Manolás, *Greece* 45 F3 38 4N 21 21 E
Manombo, *Madag.* 105 C7 22 57 S 43 28 E
Manono, *Zaïre* 106 D2 7 15 S 27 25 E
Manosque, *France* 25 E9 43 49N 5 47 E
Manouane, L., *Canada* 129 B5 50 45N 70 45W
Manouro, Pt., *Vanuatu* 121 G6 17 41 S 168 36 E
Manpojin, *N. Korea* 67 D14 41 6N 126 24 E
Manresa, *Spain* 34 D6 41 48N 1 50 E
Mansa, *Gujarat, India* 80 H5 23 27N 72 45 E
Mansa, *Punjab, India* 80 E6 30 0N 75 27 E
Mansa, *Zambia* 107 E2 11 13 S 28 55 E
Mansehra, *Pakistan* 80 B5 34 20N 73 15 E
Mansel I., *Canada* 127 B12 62 0N 80 0W
Mansfield, *Australia* 117 D7 37 4 S 146 6 E
Mansfield, *U.K.* 16 D6 53 8N 1 12W
Mansfield, *La., U.S.A.* 139 J8 32 2N 93 40W
Mansfield, *Mass., U.S.A.* 137 D13 42 2N 71 12W
Mansfield, *Ohio, U.S.A.* 136 F2 40 45N 82 30W
Mansfield, *Pa., U.S.A.* 136 E7 41 48N 77 4W
Mansfield, *Wash., U.S.A.* 142 C4 47 51N 119 44W
Mansi, *Burma* 78 C5 24 48N 95 52 E
Mansidão, *Brazil* 154 D3 10 43 S 44 2W
Mansilla de las Mulas, *Spain* 36 C5 42 30N 5 25W
Mansle, *France* 24 C4 45 52N 0 12 E
Manso →, *Brazil* 155 D2 13 50 S 47 0W
Mansoa, *Guinea-Biss.* 100 C1 12 0N 15 20W
Manson, *U.S.A.* 140 B2 42 32N 94 32W
Manson Creek, *Canada* 130 B4 55 37N 124 32W
Mansoura, *Algeria* 99 A5 36 1N 4 31 E
Manta, *Ecuador* 152 D1 1 0S 80 40W
Manta, B. de, *Ecuador* 152 D1 0 54 S 80 44W
Mantalingajan, Mt., *Phil.* 70 C5 8 55N 117 45 E
Mantare, *Tanzania* 106 C3 2 42 S 33 13 E
Manteca, *U.S.A.* 144 H5 37 50N 121 12W
Mantecal, *Venezuela* 152 B4 7 34N 69 17W
Mantena, *Brazil* 155 E3 18 47 S 40 59W
Manteno, *U.S.A.* 141 C9 41 15N 87 50W
Manteo, *U.S.A.* 135 H8 35 55N 75 41W
Mantes-la-Jolie, *France* 23 D8 48 58N 1 41 E
Manthani, *India* 82 E4 18 40N 79 35 E
Manthelan, *France* 22 E7 47 9N 0 47 E
Manti, *U.S.A.* 142 G8 39 23N 111 32W

230 Mantiqueira, Serra da

Mantiqueira, Serra da, Brazil 155 F3 22 0 S 44 0W
Manton, U.S.A. 134 C3 44 23N 85 25W
Mantorp, Sweden 15 F9 58 21N 15 20 E
Mántova, Italy 38 C7 45 20N 10 42 E
Mänttä, Finland 12 E18 62 0N 24 40 E
Mantua = Mántova, Italy 38 C7 45 20N 10 42 E
Mantung, Australia 116 C4 34 35 S 140 3 E
Manturovo, U.S.S.R. 51 B14 58 30N 44 30 E
Manu, Peru 156 C3 12 10 S 70 51W
Manu →, Peru 156 C3 12 16 S 70 55W
Manua Is., Amer. Samoa 121 X25 14 13 S 169 35W
Manuae, Cook Is. 123 J12 19 30 S 159 0W
Manuel Alves →, Brazil 155 D2 11 19 S 48 28W
Manuel Alves Grande →, Brazil 154 C2 7 27 S 47 35W
Manuel Urbano, Brazil 156 B4 8 53 S 69 18W
Manui, Indonesia 71 E6 3 35 S 123 5 E
Manukau, N.Z. 118 D3 37 1 S 174 55 E
Manukau Harbour, N.Z. 118 D3 37 3 S 174 45 E
Manunui, N.Z. 118 E4 38 54 S 175 21 E
Manuripi →, Bolivia 156 C4 11 6 S 67 36W
Manus I., Papua N. G. 120 B4 2 0 S 147 0 E
Manvi, India 83 G3 15 57N 76 59 E
Manville, U.S.A. 138 D2 42 48N 104 36W
Manwath, India 82 E3 19 19N 76 32 E
Many, U.S.A. 139 K8 31 36N 93 28W
Manyara, L., Tanzania 106 C4 3 40 S 35 50 E
Manych →, U.S.S.R. 53 C8 47 15N 39 25 E
Manych-Gudilo, Oz., U.S.S.R. 53 C10 46 24N 42 38 E
Manyonga →, Tanzania 106 C3 4 10 S 34 15 E
Manyoni, Tanzania 106 D3 5 45 S 34 55 E
Manyoni □, Tanzania 106 D3 6 30 S 34 30 E
Manzai, Pakistan 79 B3 32 12N 70 15 E
Manzala, Bahra el, Egypt 94 H7 31 10N 31 56 E
Manzanares, Spain 35 F1 39 2N 3 22W
Manzaneda, Cabeza de, Spain 36 C3 42 12N 7 15W
Manzanillo, Cuba 148 B4 20 20N 77 31W
Manzanillo, Mexico 146 D4 19 0N 104 20W
Manzanillo, Pta., Panama 148 E4 9 30N 79 40W
Manzano Mts., U.S.A. 143 J10 34 30N 106 45W
Manzarīyeh, Iran 85 C6 34 53N 50 50 E
Manzhouli, China 65 B6 49 35N 117 25 E
Manzini, Swaziland 105 D5 26 30 S 31 25 E
Mao, Chad 97 F3 14 4N 15 19 E
Maoke, Pegunungan, Indonesia 71 E9 3 40 S 137 30 E
Maolin, China 67 C12 43 58N 123 30 E
Maoming, China 69 G8 21 50N 110 54 E
Maowen, China 68 B4 31 41N 103 49 E
Maoxing, China 67 B13 45 28N 124 40 E
Mapam Yumco, China 64 C3 30 45N 81 28 E
Mapastepec, Mexico 147 D6 15 26N 92 54W
Mapia, Kepulauan, Indonesia 71 D8 0 50N 134 20 E
Mapimí, Mexico 146 B4 25 50N 103 50W
Mapimí, Bolsón de, Mexico 146 B4 27 30N 104 15W
Maping, China 69 B9 31 34N 113 32 E
Mapinga, Tanzania 106 D4 6 40 S 39 12 E
Mapinhane, Mozam. 105 C6 22 20 S 35 0 E
Mapire, Venezuela 153 B5 7 45N 64 42W
Maple →, U.S.A. 141 B12 42 58N 84 56W
Maple Creek, Canada 131 D7 49 55N 109 29W
Maple Valley, U.S.A. 144 C4 47 25N 122 3W
Mapleton, U.S.A. 142 D2 44 4N 123 58W
Mapourika, L., N.Z. 119 D5 43 16 S 170 12 E
Maprik, Papua N. G. 120 B2 3 44 S 143 3 E
Mapuca, India 83 G1 15 36N 73 46 E
Mapuera →, Brazil 153 D6 1 5 S 57 2W
Maputo, Mozam. 105 D5 25 58 S 32 32 E
Maputo, B. de, Mozam. 105 D5 25 50 S 32 45 E
Maqiaohe, China 67 B16 44 40N 130 30 E
Maqnā, Si. Arabia 84 D2 28 25N 34 50 E
Maqran, W. →, Si. Arabia 86 B4 20 55N 47 12 E
Maqteïr, Mauritania 98 D2 21 50N 11 40W
Maquela do Zombo, Angola 103 D3 6 0 S 15 15 E
Maquinchao, Argentina 160 B3 41 15 S 68 50W
Maquoketa, U.S.A. 140 B6 42 4N 90 40W
Mar, Serra do, Brazil 159 B6 25 30 S 49 0W
Mar Chiquita, L., Argentina 158 C3 30 40 S 62 50W
Mar del Plata, Argentina 158 D4 38 0 S 57 30W
Mar Menor, L., Spain 35 H4 37 40N 0 45W
Mara, Guyana 153 B6 6 0N 57 36W
Mara, India 78 A5 28 11N 94 14 E
Mara, Tanzania 106 C3 1 30 S 34 32 E
Mara □, Tanzania 106 C3 1 45 S 34 20 E
Maraã, Brazil 152 D4 1 52 S 65 25W
Marabá, Brazil 154 C2 5 20 S 49 5W
Maracá, I. de, Brazil 153 C7 2 10N 50 30W
Maracaibo, Venezuela 152 A3 10 40N 71 37W
Maracaibo, L. de, Venezuela 152 B3 9 40N 71 30W
Maracaju, Brazil 159 A4 21 38 S 55 9W
Maracajú, Serra de, Brazil 157 E6 23 57 S 55 1W
Maracanã, Brazil 154 B2 0 46 S 47 27W
Maracás, Brazil 155 D3 13 26 S 40 18W
Maracay, Venezuela 152 A4 10 15N 67 28W
Marādah, Libya 96 C3 29 15N 19 15 E
Maradi, Niger 101 C6 13 29N 7 20 E
Maradun, Nigeria 101 C6 12 35N 6 18 E
Marāgheh, Iran 84 B5 37 30N 46 12 E
Maragogipe, Brazil 155 D4 12 46 S 38 55W
Marāh, Si. Arabia 84 E5 25 0N 45 35 E
Marajó, B. de, Brazil 154 B2 1 0 S 48 30W
Marajó, I. de, Brazil 154 B2 1 0 S 49 30W
Marākand, Iran 84 B5 38 51N 45 16 E
Maralal, Kenya 106 B4 1 0N 36 38 E
Maralinga, Australia 113 F5 30 13 S 131 32 E
Marama, Australia 116 C4 35 10 S 140 10 E
Maramasike, Solomon Is. 121 M11 9 30 S 161 25 E
Marampa, S. Leone 100 D2 8 45N 12 28W
Maramureş □, Romania 46 B5 47 45N 24 0 E
Maran, Malaysia 77 L4 3 35N 102 45 E
Marana, U.S.A. 143 K8 32 30N 111 9W
Maranboy, Australia 112 B5 14 40 S 132 39 E
Maranchón, Spain 34 D2 41 6N 2 15W
Marand, Iran 84 B5 38 30N 45 45 E
Marang, Malaysia 77 K4 5 12N 103 13 E
Maranguape, Brazil 154 B4 3 55 S 38 50W
Maranhão = São Luís, Brazil 154 B3 2 39 S 44 15W
Maranhão □, Brazil 154 C2 5 0 S 46 0W
Marano, L. di, Italy 39 C10 45 42N 13 13 E
Maranoa →, Australia 115 D4 27 50 S 148 37 E
Marañón →, Peru 156 A3 4 30 S 73 35W
Marão, Mozam. 105 C5 24 18 S 34 2 E
Marapi →, Brazil 153 C6 0 37N 55 58W
Marari, Brazil 156 B4 5 43 S 67 47W
Maraş = Kahramanmaraş, Turkey 88 E7 37 37N 36 53 E
Mărăşeşti, Romania 46 D8 45 52N 27 14 E
Maratea, Italy 41 C8 39 59N 15 43 E
Marateca, Portugal 37 G2 38 34N 8 40W
Marathasa □, Cyprus 32 E11 34 59N 32 51 E
Marathókambos, Greece 45 G8 37 43N 26 42 E
Marathon, Australia 114 C3 20 51 S 143 32 E
Marathon, Canada 128 C2 48 44N 86 23W
Marathón, Greece 45 F5 38 11N 23 58 E
Marathon, Iowa, U.S.A. 140 B2 42 52N 94 59W
Marathon, N.Y., U.S.A. 137 D8 42 25N 76 3W
Marathon, Tex., U.S.A. 139 K3 30 15N 103 15W
Marathóvouno, Cyprus 32 D12 35 13N 33 37 E
Maratua, Indonesia 71 D5 2 10N 118 35 E
Maraú, Brazil 155 D4 14 6 S 39 0W
Maravatío, Mexico 146 D4 19 51N 100 25W
Marāwih, U.A.E. 85 E7 24 18N 53 18 E
Marbella, Spain 37 J6 36 30N 4 57W
Marble Bar, Australia 112 D2 21 9 S 119 44 E
Marble Falls, U.S.A. 139 K5 30 30N 98 15W
Marblehead, U.S.A. 137 D14 42 29N 70 51W
Marburg, Germany 26 E4 50 49N 8 36 E
Marby, Sweden 14 A8 63 7N 14 18 E
Marcal →, Hungary 31 D10 47 41N 17 32 E
Marcali, Hungary 31 E10 46 35N 17 25 E
Marcapata, Peru 156 C3 13 31 S 70 52W
Marcaria, Italy 38 C7 45 7N 10 34 E
Marceline, U.S.A. 140 E4 39 43N 92 57W
March, U.K. 17 E8 52 33N 0 5 E
Marchal, Zaïre 103 D2 5 16 S 14 58 E
Marchand = Rommani, Morocco 98 B3 33 31N 6 40W
Marche, France 24 B5 46 5N 1 20 E
Marche □, Italy 39 E10 43 22N 13 10 E
Marche-en-Famenne, Belgium 21 H6 50 14N 5 19 E
Marchena, Spain 37 H5 37 18N 5 23W
Marches = Marche □, Italy 39 E10 43 22N 13 10 E
Marciana Marina, Italy 38 F7 42 44N 10 12 E
Marcianise, Italy 41 A7 41 3N 14 16 E
Marcigny, France 25 B8 46 17N 4 2 E
Marcillat-en-Combraille, France 24 B6 46 12N 2 38 E
Marcinelle, Belgium 21 H4 50 24N 4 26 E
Marck, France 23 B8 50 57N 1 57 E
Marckolsheim, France 23 D14 48 10N 7 30 E
Marcona, Peru 156 D3 15 10 S 75 0W
Marcos Juárez, Argentina 158 C3 32 42 S 62 5W
Marcus I. = Minami-Tori-Shima, Pac. Oc. 122 E7 24 0N 153 45 E
Marcus Necker Ridge, Pac. Oc. 122 F9 20 0N 175 0 E
Marcy Mt., U.S.A. 137 B11 44 7N 73 55W
Mardan, Pakistan 79 B4 34 20N 72 0 E
Mardie, Australia 112 D2 21 12 S 115 59 E
Mardin, Turkey 89 E9 37 20N 40 43 E
Maré, I., N. Cal. 121 U22 21 30 S 168 0 E
Marechal Deodoro, Brazil 154 C4 9 43 S 35 54W
Maree L., U.K. 18 D3 57 40N 5 30W
Mareeba, Australia 114 B4 16 59 S 145 28 E
Marek = Stanke Dimitrov, Bulgaria 42 E8 42 17N 23 9 E
Marek, Indonesia 71 E6 4 41 S 120 24 E
Maremma, Italy 38 F8 42 45N 11 15 E
Maréna, Mali 100 C3 14 0N 7 20W
Marenberg, Yugoslavia 39 B12 46 38N 15 13 E
Marengo, U.S.A. 140 C4 41 42N 92 5W
Marennes, France 24 C2 45 49N 1 7W
Marenyi, Kenya 106 C4 4 22 S 39 8 E
Marerano, Madag. 105 C7 21 23 S 44 52 E
Maréttimo, Italy 40 E5 37 58N 12 5 E
Mareuil-sur-Lay, France 24 B2 46 32N 1 14W
Marfa, U.S.A. 139 K2 30 15N 104 5W
Marfa Pt., Malta 32 D1 35 59N 14 19 E
Marganets, U.S.S.R. 52 C6 47 40N 34 40 E
Margaret →, Australia 112 C4 18 9 S 125 41 E
Margaret Bay, Canada 130 C3 51 20N 127 35W
Margaret L., Canada 130 B5 58 56N 115 25W
Margaret River, Australia 112 C4 18 38 S 126 52 E
Margarita, I. de, Venezuela 153 A5 11 0N 64 0W
Margarítion, Greece 44 E2 39 22N 20 26 E
Margaritovo, U.S.S.R. 60 C7 43 25N 134 45 E
Margate, S. Africa 105 E5 30 50 S 30 20 E
Margate, U.K. 17 F9 51 23N 1 24 E
Margelan, U.S.S.R. 55 C5 40 27N 71 42 E
Margeride, Mts. de la, France 24 D7 44 43N 3 38 E
Margherita, India 78 B5 27 16N 95 40 E
Margherita di Savoia, Italy 41 A9 41 25N 16 5 E
Marghita, Romania 46 B3 47 22N 22 22 E
Margonin, Poland 47 C4 52 58N 17 5 E
Marguerite, Canada 130 C4 52 30N 122 25W
Marhoum, Algeria 99 B4 34 27N 0 11W
Mari A.S.S.R. □, U.S.S.R. 51 C16 56 30N 48 0 E
María Elena, Chile 158 A2 22 18 S 69 40W
María Grande, Argentina 158 C4 31 45 S 59 55W
Maria I., N. Terr., Australia 114 A2 14 52 S 135 45 E
Maria I., Tas., Australia 114 G4 42 35 S 148 0 E
Maria van Diemen, C., N.Z. 118 A1 34 29 S 172 40 E
Mariager, Denmark 15 H4 56 40N 10 0 E
Mariager Fjord, Denmark 15 H4 56 42N 10 19 E
Mariakani, Kenya 106 C4 3 50 S 39 27 E
Marian L., Canada 130 A5 63 0N 116 15W
Mariana Trench, Pac. Oc. 122 F6 13 0N 145 0 E
Marianao, Cuba 148 B3 23 8N 82 24W
Mariani, India 78 B5 26 39N 94 19 E
Marianna, Ark., U.S.A. 139 H9 34 48N 90 48W
Marianna, Fla., U.S.A. 135 K3 30 45N 85 15W
Mariánské Lázně, Czech. 30 B5 49 48N 12 41 E
Marias →, U.S.A. 142 C8 47 56N 110 30W
Mariato, Punta, Panama 148 E3 7 12N 80 52W
Mariazell, Austria 30 D8 47 47N 15 19 E
Ma'rib, Yemen 86 D4 15 25N 45 21 E
Maribo, Denmark 15 K5 54 48N 11 30 E
Maribor, Yugoslavia 39 B12 46 36N 15 40 E
Marico →, Africa 104 C4 23 35 S 26 57 E
Maricopa, Ariz., U.S.A. 143 K7 33 5N 112 2W
Maricopa, Calif., U.S.A. 145 K7 35 7N 119 27W
Marîdî, Sudan 95 G2 4 55N 29 25 E
Marîdi, Wadi →, Sudan 95 F2 6 15N 29 21 E
Marié →, Brazil 152 D4 0 27 S 66 26W
Marie Byrd Land, Antarctica 7 D14 79 30 S 125 0W
Marie-Galante, Guadeloupe 149 C7 15 56N 61 16W
Mariecourt, Canada 127 B12 61 30N 72 0W
Mariefred, Sweden 14 E11 59 15N 17 12 E
Mariehamn, Finland 13 F15 60 5N 19 55 E
Marienbad = Mariánské Lázně, Czech. 30 B5 49 48N 12 41 E
Marienberg, Germany 26 E9 50 40N 13 10 E
Marienberg, Neths. 20 D9 52 2N 6 35 E
Marienbourg, Belgium 21 H5 50 6N 4 31 E
Mariental, Namibia 104 C2 24 36 S 18 0 E
Marienville, U.S.A. 136 E5 41 27N 79 8W
Mariestad, Sweden 15 F7 58 43N 13 50 E
Marietta, Ga., U.S.A. 135 J3 33 55N 84 30W
Marietta, Ohio, U.S.A. 134 F5 39 27N 81 27W
Marieville, Canada 137 A11 45 26N 73 10W
Marignane, France 25 E9 43 25N 5 13 E
Mariinsk, U.S.S.R. 56 D9 56 10N 87 20 E
Mariinskiy Posad, U.S.S.R. 51 C15 56 10N 47 45 E
Marília, Brazil 159 A6 22 13 S 50 0W
Marillana, Australia 112 D2 22 37 S 119 16 E
Marimba, Angola 103 D3 8 28 S 17 8 E
Marín, Spain 36 C2 42 23N 8 42W
Marina, U.S.A. 144 J5 36 41N 121 48W
Marina di Cirò, Italy 41 C10 39 22N 17 8 E
Marina Plains, Australia 114 A3 14 37 S 143 57 E
Marinduque, Phil. 71 B6 13 25N 122 0 E
Marine City, U.S.A. 134 D4 42 45N 82 29W
Marineo, Italy 40 E6 37 57N 13 23 E
Marinette, U.S.A. 134 C2 45 4N 87 40W
Maringá, Brazil 159 A5 23 26 S 52 2W
Marinha Grande, Portugal 37 F2 39 45N 8 56W
Marion, Ala., U.S.A. 135 J2 32 33N 87 20W
Marion, Ill., U.S.A. 139 G10 37 45N 88 55W
Marion, Ind., U.S.A. 141 D11 40 35N 85 40W
Marion, Iowa, U.S.A. 140 B5 42 2N 91 36W
Marion, Kans., U.S.A. 138 F6 38 25N 97 2W
Marion, Mich., U.S.A. 134 C3 44 7N 85 8W
Marion, N.C., U.S.A. 135 H5 35 42N 82 0W
Marion, Ohio, U.S.A. 141 D13 40 38N 83 8W
Marion, S.C., U.S.A. 135 H6 34 11N 79 22W
Marion, Va., U.S.A. 135 G5 36 51N 81 29W
Marion, L., U.S.A. 135 J5 33 30N 80 15W
Marion Bay, Australia 116 C2 35 12 S 136 59 E
Marion I., Ind. Oc. 109 J2 47 0 S 38 0 E
Maripa, Venezuela 153 B4 7 26N 65 9W
Maripasoula, Fr. Guiana 153 C7 3 40N 54 4W
Mariposa, U.S.A. 144 H7 37 31N 119 59W
Mariscal Estigarribia, Paraguay 158 A3 22 3 S 60 40W
Maritime Alps = Maritimes, Alpes, Europe 25 D11 44 10N 7 10 E
Maritimes, Alpes, Europe 25 D11 44 10N 7 10 E
Maritsa, Bulgaria 43 E10 42 1N 25 50 E
Maritsa, Greece 32 C10 36 22N 28 10 E
Maritsa →, Bulgaria 43 F11 41 40N 26 34 E
Mariupol, U.S.S.R. 52 C7 47 5N 37 31 E
Marīvān, Iran 84 C5 35 30N 46 25 E
Mariyampole, U.S.S.R. 50 D3 54 33N 23 19 E
Markah, W. →, Yemen 86 D4 14 59N 46 36 E
Markam, China 68 C2 29 42N 98 38 E
Markapur, India 83 G4 15 44N 79 19 E
Markazī □, Iran 85 C6 35 0N 49 30 E
Markdale, Canada 136 B4 44 19N 80 39W
Marke, Belgium 21 G2 50 48N 3 14 E
Marked Tree, U.S.A. 139 H9 35 35N 90 24W
Markelsdorfer Huk, Germany 26 A7 54 33N 11 0 E
Marken, Neths. 20 D6 52 26N 5 12 E
Markermeer, Neths. 20 C6 52 33N 5 15 E
Market Drayton, U.K. 16 E5 52 55N 2 30W
Market Harborough, U.K. 17 E7 52 29N 0 55W
Markham, Canada 136 C5 43 52N 79 16W
Markham →, Papua N. G. 120 D4 6 41 S 147 2 E
Markham, Mt., Antarctica 7 E11 83 0 S 164 0 E
Markham L., Canada 131 A8 62 30N 102 35W
Marki, Poland 47 C8 52 20N 21 2 E
Markleeville, U.S.A. 144 G7 38 44N 119 47W
Markoupoulon, Greece 45 G5 37 53N 23 57 E
Markovac, Yugoslavia 42 C6 44 14N 21 7 E
Markovo, U.S.S.R. 57 C17 64 40N 169 40 E
Markoye, Burkina Faso 101 C5 14 39N 0 2 E
Marks, U.S.S.R. 51 F15 51 45N 46 50 E
Marksville, U.S.A. 139 K8 31 10N 92 2W
Markt Schwaben, Germany 27 G7 48 14N 11 49 E
Marktredwitz, Germany 27 E8 50 1N 12 2 E
Marla, Australia 115 D1 27 19 S 133 33 E
Marlboro, U.S.A. 137 D13 42 19N 71 33W
Marlborough, Australia 114 C4 22 46 S 149 52 E
Marlborough □, N.Z. 119 B8 41 45 S 173 33 E
Marlborough Downs, U.K. 17 F6 51 25N 1 55W
Marle, France 23 C10 49 43N 3 47 E
Marlin, U.S.A. 139 K6 31 25N 96 50W
Marlow, Germany 26 A8 54 8N 12 34 E
Marlow, U.S.A. 139 H6 34 40N 97 58W
Marly-le-Grand, Switz. 28 C4 46 47N 7 10 E
Marmagao, India 83 G1 15 25N 73 56 E
Marmande, France 24 D4 44 30N 0 10 E
Marmara, Turkey 52 F2 40 35N 27 38 E
Marmara, Sea of = Marmara Denizi, Turkey 88 C3 40 45N 28 15 E
Marmara Denizi, Turkey 88 C3 40 45N 28 15 E
Marmara Gölü, Turkey 88 D3 38 37N 28 0 E
Marmaris, Turkey 88 E3 36 50N 28 14 E
Marmarth, U.S.A. 138 B3 46 21N 103 52W
Marmelos →, Brazil 157 B5 6 6 S 61 46W
Marmion, Mt., Australia 113 E2 29 16 S 119 50 E
Marmion L., Canada 128 C1 48 55N 91 20W
Marmolada, Mte., Italy 39 B8 46 25N 11 55 E
Marmolejo, Spain 37 G6 38 3N 4 13W
Marmora, Canada 128 D4 44 28N 77 41W
Marnay, France 23 E12 47 16N 5 48 E
Marne, Germany 26 B5 53 57N 9 1 E
Marne □, France 23 D11 48 50N 4 10 E
Marne →, France 23 D9 48 48N 2 24 E
Marneuli, U.S.S.R. 53 F11 41 30N 44 48 E
Maro, Chad 97 G3 8 30N 19 0 E
Maroa, Venezuela 152 C4 2 43N 67 33W
Maroala, Madag. 105 B8 15 23 S 47 59 E
Maroantsetra, Madag. 105 B8 15 26 S 49 44 E
Maromandia, Madag. 105 A8 14 13 S 48 5 E
Marondera, Zimbabwe 107 F3 18 5 S 31 42 E
Maroni →, Fr. Guiana 153 B7 5 30N 54 0W
Marónia, Greece 44 D7 40 53N 25 24 E
Maronne →, France 24 C5 45 5N 1 56 E
Maroochydore, Australia 115 D5 26 29 S 153 5 E
Maroona, Australia 116 D5 37 27 S 142 54 E
Maros, Indonesia 72 C1 5 0 S 119 34 E
Maros →, Hungary 31 E13 46 15N 20 13 E
Marosakoa, Madag. 105 B8 15 26 S 46 38 E
Marostica, Italy 39 C8 45 44N 11 40 E
Maroua, Cameroon 101 C7 10 40N 14 20 E
Marovoay, Madag. 105 B8 16 6 S 46 39 E
Marowijne □, Surinam 153 C7 4 0N 55 0W
Marowijne →, Surinam 153 B7 5 45N 53 58W
Marquard, S. Africa 104 D4 28 40 S 27 28 E
Marqueira, Portugal 37 G1 38 41N 9 9W
Marquesas Is. = Marquises, Is., Pac. Oc. 123 H14 9 30 S 140 0W
Marquette, U.S.A. 134 B2 46 30N 87 21W
Marquise, France 23 B8 50 50N 1 40 E
Marquises, Is., Pac. Oc. 123 H14 9 30 S 140 0W
Marra, Gebel, Sudan 95 F2 7 20N 27 35 E
Marracuene, Mozam. 105 D5 25 45 S 32 35 E
Marradi, Italy 39 D8 44 5N 11 37 E
Marrakech, Morocco 98 B3 31 9N 8 0W
Marrawah, Australia 114 G3 40 55 S 144 42 E
Marrecas, Serra das, Brazil 154 C3 9 0 S 41 0W
Marree, Australia 115 D2 29 39 S 138 1 E
Marrilla, Australia 112 D1 22 31 S 114 25 E
Marrimane, Mozam. 105 C5 22 58 S 33 34 E
Marromeu, Mozam. 105 B6 18 15 S 36 25 E
Marroquí, Punta, Spain 37 K5 36 0N 5 37W
Marrowie Cr. →, Australia 117 B6 33 23 S 145 40 E
Marrubane, Mozam. 107 F4 18 0 S 37 0 E
Marrum, Neths. 20 B7 53 19N 5 48 E
Marrupa, Mozam. 107 E4 13 8 S 37 30 E
Marsa Brega, Libya 96 B3 30 24N 19 37 E
Marsá Matrûh, Egypt 94 A2 31 19N 27 9 E
Marsá Susah, Libya 96 B4 32 52N 21 59 E
Marsabit, Kenya 106 B4 2 18N 38 0 E
Marsabit □, Kenya 106 B4 2 45N 37 45 E
Marsala, Italy 40 E5 37 48N 12 25 E
Marsalforn, Malta 32 C1 36 4N 14 15 E
Marsberg, Germany 26 D4 51 28N 8 52 E
Marsciano, Italy 39 F9 42 54N 12 20 E
Marsden, Australia 117 B7 33 47 S 147 32 E
Marsdiep, Neths. 20 C5 52 58N 4 46 E
Marseillan, France 24 E7 43 23N 3 31 E
Marseille, France 25 E9 43 18N 5 23 E
Marseilles = Marseille, France 25 E9 43 18N 5 23 E
Marseilles, U.S.A. 141 C8 41 20N 88 43W
Marsh I., U.S.A. 139 L9 29 35N 91 50W
Marsh L., U.S.A. 138 C7 45 5N 96 0W
Marshall, Liberia 100 D2 6 8N 10 22W
Marshall, Ark., U.S.A. 139 H8 35 58N 92 40W
Marshall, Ill., U.S.A. 141 E9 39 23N 87 42W
Marshall, Mich., U.S.A. 141 B12 42 17N 84 59W
Marshall, Minn., U.S.A. 138 C7 44 25N 95 45W
Marshall, Mo., U.S.A. 140 E3 39 8N 93 15W
Marshall, Tex., U.S.A. 139 J7 32 29N 94 20W
Marshall →, Australia 114 C2 22 59 S 136 59 E
Marshall Is., Pac. Oc. 122 G9 9 0N 171 0 E
Marshalltown, U.S.A. 140 B4 42 5N 92 56W
Marshfield, Mo., U.S.A. 139 G8 37 20N 92 58W
Marshfield, Wis., U.S.A. 138 C9 44 42N 90 10W
Marshūn, Iran 85 B6 36 19N 49 23 E
Mársico Nuovo, Italy 41 B8 40 26N 15 43 E
Märsta, Sweden 14 E11 59 37N 17 52 E
Marstal, Denmark 15 K4 54 51N 10 30 E
Marstrand, Sweden 15 G5 57 53N 11 35 E
Mart, U.S.A. 139 K6 31 34N 96 51W
Marta →, Italy 39 F8 42 14N 11 42 E
Martaban, Burma 78 G6 16 30N 97 35 E
Martaban, G. of, Burma 78 G6 16 5N 96 30 E
Martano, Italy 41 B11 40 14N 18 18 E
Martapura, Kalimantan, Indonesia 70 E4 3 22 S 114 47 E
Martapura, Sumatera, Indonesia 70 E2 4 19 S 104 22 E
Marte, Nigeria 101 C7 12 23N 13 46 E
Martel, France 24 D5 44 57N 1 37 E
Martelange, Belgium 21 J7 49 49N 5 43 E
Martensdale, U.S.A. 140 C3 41 23N 93 45W
Martés, Sierra, Spain 35 F4 39 20N 1 0W
Martha's Vineyard, U.S.A. 137 E14 41 25N 70 35W
Martigné-Ferchaud, France 22 E5 47 50N 1 20W
Martigny, Switz. 28 D4 46 6N 7 3 E
Martigues, France 25 E9 43 24N 5 4 E
Martil, Morocco 98 A3 35 36N 5 15W
Martin, Czech. 31 B11 49 6N 18 48 E
Martin, S. Dak., U.S.A. 138 D4 43 11N 101 45W
Martin, Tenn., U.S.A. 139 G10 36 23N 88 51W
Martín →, Spain 34 D4 41 18N 0 19W
Martin, L., U.S.A. 135 J3 32 45N 85 50W
Martina, Switz. 29 C10 46 53N 10 28 E
Martina Franca, Italy 41 B10 40 42N 17 20 E
Martinborough, N.Z. 118 H4 41 14 S 175 29 E
Martinez, U.S.A. 144 G4 38 1N 122 8W
Martinho Campos, Brazil 155 E2 19 20 S 45 13W

Mbozi 231

Martinique ■, *W. Indies* **149 D7** 14 40N 61 0W
Martinique Passage, *W. Indies* **149 C7** 15 15N 61 0W
Martínon, *Greece* **45 F5** 38 35N 23 15 E
Martinópolis, *Brazil* **159 A5** 22 11 S 51 12W
Martins Ferry, *U.S.A.* **136 F4** 40 5N 80 46W
Martinsberg, *Austria* **30 C8** 48 22N 15 9 E
Martinsburg, *Pa., U.S.A.* **136 F6** 40 18N 78 21W
Martinsburg, *W. Va., U.S.A.* **134 F7** 39 30N 77 57W
Martinsville, *Ill., U.S.A.* **141 E9** 39 20N 87 53W
Martinsville, *Ind., U.S.A.* **141 E10** 39 29N 86 23W
Martinsville, *Va., U.S.A.* **135 G6** 36 41N 79 52W
Marton, *N.Z.* **118 G4** 40 4 S 175 23 E
Martorell, *Spain* **34 D6** 41 28N 1 56 E
Martos, *Spain* **37 H7** 37 44N 3 58W
Martūbah, *Libya* **96 B4** 32 35N 22 46 E
Martuk, *U.S.S.R.* **54 F5** 50 46N 56 31 E
Martuni, *U.S.S.R.* **53 F11** 40 9N 45 10 E
Maru, *Nigeria* **101 C6** 12 22N 6 22 E
Marudi, *Malaysia* **70 D4** 4 11N 114 19 E
Ma'ruf, *Afghan.* **79 C2** 31 30N 67 6 E
Marugame, *Japan* **62 C5** 34 15N 133 40 E
Marúggio, *Italy* **41 B10** 40 20N 17 33 E
Marui, *Papua N. G.* **120 C2** 4 4 S 143 2 E
Maruia →, *N.Z.* **119 B7** 41 47 S 172 13 E
Maruim, *Brazil* **154 D4** 10 45 S 37 5W
Marulan, *Australia* **117 C9** 34 43 S 150 3 E
Marum, *Neths.* **20 B8** 53 9N 6 16 E
Marum, Mt., *Vanuatu* **121 F6** 16 15 S 168 7 E
Marunga, *Angola* **103 F4** 17 28 S 20 2 E
Marungu, Mts., *Zaïre* **106 D3** 7 30 S 30 0 E
Maruoka, *Japan* **63 A8** 36 9N 136 16 E
Marvast, *Iran* **85 D7** 30 30N 54 15 E
Marvejols, *France* **24 D7** 44 33N 3 19 E
Marwar, *India* **80 G5** 25 43N 73 45 E
Mary, *U.S.S.R.* **56 F7** 37 40N 61 50 E
Mary Frances L., *Canada* **131 A7** 63 19N 106 13W
Mary Kathleen, *Australia* **114 C2** 20 44 S 139 48 E
Maryborough, *Queens., Australia* **115 D5** 25 31 S 152 37 E
Maryborough, *Vic., Australia* **116 D5** 37 0 S 143 44 E
Maryfield, *Canada* **131 D8** 49 50N 101 35W
Maryland □, *U.S.A.* **134 F7** 39 10N 76 40W
Maryland Junction, *Zimbabwe* **107 F3** 17 45 S 30 31 E
Maryport, *U.K.* **16 C4** 54 43N 3 30W
Mary's Harbour, *Canada* **129 B8** 52 18N 55 51W
Marystown, *Canada* **129 C8** 47 10N 55 10W
Marysvale, *U.S.A.* **143 G7** 38 25N 112 17W
Marysville, *Canada* **130 D5** 49 35N 116 0W
Marysville, *Calif., U.S.A.* **144 F5** 39 14N 121 40W
Marysville, *Kans., U.S.A.* **138 F6** 39 50N 96 49W
Marysville, *Mich., U.S.A.* **136 D2** 42 55N 82 29W
Marysville, *Ohio, U.S.A.* **141 D13** 40 15N 83 20W
Marysville, *Wash., U.S.A.* **144 B4** 48 3N 122 11W
Maryvale, *Australia* **115 D5** 28 4 S 152 12 E
Maryville, *Mo., U.S.A.* **140 D2** 40 21N 94 52W
Maryville, *Tenn., U.S.A.* **135 H4** 35 50N 84 0W
Marzo, Punta, *Colombia* **152 B2** 6 50N 77 42W
Marzūq, *Libya* **96 C2** 25 53N 13 57 E
Masahunga, *Tanzania* **106 C3** 2 6 S 33 18 E
Masai, *Malaysia* **77 M4** 1 29N 103 55 E
Masai Steppe, *Tanzania* **106 C4** 4 30 S 36 30 E
Masaka, *Uganda* **106 C3** 0 21 S 31 45 E
Masalembo, Kepulauan, *Indonesia* **70 F4** 5 35 S 114 30 E
Masalima, Kepulauan, *Indonesia* **70 F5** 5 4 S 117 5 E
Masamba, *Indonesia* **71 E6** 2 30 S 120 15 E
Masan, *S. Korea* **67 G15** 35 11N 128 32 E
Masanasa, *Spain* **35 F4** 39 25N 0 25W
Masasi, *Tanzania* **107 E4** 10 45 S 38 52 E
Masasi □, *Tanzania* **107 E4** 10 45 S 38 50 E
Masaya, *Nic.* **148 D2** 12 0N 86 7W
Masba, *Nigeria* **101 C7** 10 35N 13 1 E
Masbate, *Phil.* **71 B6** 12 21N 123 36 E
Mascara, *Algeria* **99 A5** 35 26N 0 6 E
Mascarene Is., *Ind. Oc.* **109 G4** 22 0 S 55 0 E
Mascota, *Mexico* **146 C4** 20 30N 104 50W
Mascoutah, *U.S.A.* **140 F7** 38 29N 89 48W
Masela, *Indonesia* **71 F7** 8 9 S 129 51 E
Maseru, *Lesotho* **104 D4** 29 18 S 27 30 E
Mashaba, *Zimbabwe* **107 G3** 20 2 S 30 29 E
Mashābih, *Si. Arabia* **84 E3** 25 35N 36 30 E
Mashan, *China* **68 F7** 23 40N 108 11 E
Masherbrum, *Pakistan* **81 B7** 35 38N 76 18 E
Mashhad, *Iran* **85 B8** 36 20N 59 35 E
Mashi, *Nigeria* **101 C6** 13 0N 7 54 E
Mashiki, *Japan* **62 E2** 32 51N 130 53 E
Mashīz, *Iran* **85 D8** 29 56N 56 37 E
Mashkel, Hamun-i-, *Pakistan* **79 C1** 28 30N 63 0 E
Mashki Chāh, *Pakistan* **79 C1** 29 5N 62 30 E
Mashonaland Central □, *Zimbabwe* **105 B5** 17 30 S 31 0 E
Mashonaland East □, *Zimbabwe* **105 B5** 18 0 S 32 0 E
Mashonaland West □, *Zimbabwe* **105 B4** 17 30 S 29 30 E
Mashtaga, *U.S.S.R.* **53 F13** 40 35N 49 57 E
Masi, *Norway* **12 B17** 69 26N 23 40 E
Masi Manimba, *Zaïre* **103 C3** 4 40 S 17 54 E
Masindi, *Uganda* **106 B3** 1 40N 31 43 E
Masindi Port, *Uganda* **106 B3** 1 43N 32 2 E
Maşīrah, Khalīj, *Oman* **87 B7** 20 10N 58 10 E
Maşīrah, Tur'at, *Oman* **87 B7** 20 30N 58 40 E
Masisea, *Peru* **156 B3** 8 35 S 74 22W
Masisi, *Zaïre* **106 C2** 1 23 S 28 49 E
Masjed Soleyman, *Iran* **85 D6** 31 55N 49 18 E
Mask, L., *Ireland* **19 C2** 53 36N 9 24W
Maskelyne Is., *Vanuatu* **121 F5** 16 32 S 167 49 E
Maski, *India* **83 G3** 15 56N 76 46 E
Maslen Nos, *Bulgaria* **43 E12** 42 18N 27 48 E
Maslinica, *Yugoslavia* **39 E13** 43 24N 16 13 E
Maşna'ah, *Yemen* **87 D5** 14 27N 48 17 E
Masnou, *Spain* **34 D7** 41 28N 2 20 E
Masoala, Tanjon' i, *Madag.* **105 B9** 15 59 S 50 13 E
Masoarivo, *Madag.* **105 B7** 19 3 S 44 19 E
Masohi, *Indonesia* **71 E7** 3 20 S 128 55 E
Masomeloka, *Madag.* **105 C8** 20 17 S 48 37 E
Mason, *Mich., U.S.A.* **141 B12** 42 35N 84 27W
Mason, *Nev., U.S.A.* **144 G7** 38 56N 119 8W
Mason, *Ohio, U.S.A.* **141 E12** 39 22N 84 19W
Mason, *Tex., U.S.A.* **139 K5** 30 45N 99 15W
Mason B., *N.Z.* **119 G2** 46 55 S 167 45 E
Mason City, *Ill., U.S.A.* **140 D7** 40 12N 89 42W
Mason City, *Iowa, U.S.A.* **140 A3** 43 9N 93 12W
Maspalomas, *Canary Is.* **33 G4** 27 46N 15 35W
Maspalomas, Pta., *Canary Is.* **33 G4** 27 43N 15 36W
Masqat, *Oman* **87 B7** 23 37N 58 36 E
Massa, *Congo* **102 C3** 3 45 S 15 29 E
Massa, *Italy* **38 D7** 44 2N 10 7 E
Massa, O. →, *Morocco* **98 B3** 30 2N 9 40W
Massa Maríttima, *Italy* **38 E7** 43 3N 10 52 E
Massachusetts □, *U.S.A.* **137 D13** 42 25N 72 0W
Massachusetts B., *U.S.A.* **137 D14** 42 30N 70 45W
Massafra, *Italy* **41 B10** 40 35N 17 8 E
Massaguet, *Chad* **97 F3** 12 28N 15 26 E
Massakory, *Chad* **97 F3** 13 0N 15 49 E
Massanella, *Spain* **33 B9** 39 48N 2 51 E
Massangena, *Mozam.* **105 C5** 21 34 S 33 0 E
Massapê, *Brazil* **154 B3** 3 31 S 40 19W
Massarosa, *Italy* **38 E7** 43 53N 10 17 E
Massat, *France* **24 F5** 42 53N 1 21 E
Massava, *U.S.S.R.* **54 A8** 60 40N 62 6 E
Massawa = Mitsiwa, *Ethiopia* **95 D4** 15 35N 39 25 E
Massena, *U.S.A.* **137 B10** 44 52N 74 55W
Massénya, *Chad* **97 F3** 11 21N 16 9 E
Masset, *Canada* **130 C2** 54 2N 132 10W
Massiac, *France* **24 C7** 45 15N 3 11 E
Massif Central, *France* **24 D7** 44 55N 3 0 E
Massillon, *U.S.A.* **136 F3** 40 47N 81 30W
Massinga, *Mozam.* **105 C6** 23 15 S 35 22 E
Masson, *Canada* **137 A9** 45 32N 75 25W
Masson I., *Antarctica* **7 C7** 66 10 S 93 20 E
Mastābah, *Si. Arabia* **86 B2** 20 49N 39 26 E
Mastanli = Momchilgrad, *Bulgaria* **43 F10** 41 33N 25 23 E
Masterton, *N.Z.* **118 G4** 40 56 S 175 39 E
Mástikho, Ákra, *Greece* **45 F8** 38 10N 26 2 E
Mastuj, *Pakistan* **81 A5** 36 20N 72 36 E
Mastung, *Pakistan* **79 C2** 29 50N 66 56 E
Mastūrah, *Si. Arabia* **86 B2** 23 7N 38 52 E
Masuda, *Japan* **62 C3** 34 40N 131 51 E
Masuika, *Zaïre* **103 D4** 7 37 S 22 32 E
Masvingo, *Zimbabwe* **107 G3** 20 8 S 30 49 E
Masvingo □, *Zimbabwe* **107 G3** 21 0 S 31 30 E
Maswa □, *Tanzania* **106 C3** 3 30 S 34 0 E
Maşyāf, *Syria* **84 C3** 35 4N 36 20 E
Mata de São João, *Brazil* **155 D4** 12 31 S 38 17W
Mata Utu, *Wall. & F. Is.* **111 C15** 13 17 S 176 8W
Matabeleland North □, *Zimbabwe* **107 F2** 19 0 S 28 0 E
Matabeleland South □, *Zimbabwe* **107 G2** 21 0 S 29 0 E
Mataboor, *Indonesia* **71 E9** 1 41 S 138 3 E
Matachel →, *Spain* **37 G4** 38 50N 6 17W
Matachewan, *Canada* **128 C3** 47 56N 80 39W
Matacuni →, *Venezuela* **153 C4** 3 2N 65 16W
Matadi, *Zaïre* **103 D2** 5 52 S 13 31 E
Matagalpa, *Nic.* **148 D2** 13 0N 85 58W
Matagami, *Canada* **128 C4** 49 45N 77 34W
Matagami, L., *Canada* **128 C4** 49 50N 77 40W
Matagorda, *U.S.A.* **139 L7** 28 43N 95 55W
Matagorda B., *U.S.A.* **139 L6** 28 30N 96 15W
Matagorda I., *U.S.A.* **139 L6** 28 10N 96 40W
Matak, P., *Indonesia* **77 L6** 3 18N 106 16 E
Matakana, *Australia* **117 B6** 32 59 S 145 54 E
Matakana, *N.Z.* **118 C3** 36 21 S 174 43 E
Matakana I., *N.Z.* **118 D5** 36 21 S 174 43 E
Matala, *Angola* **103 E3** 14 46 S 15 4 E
Mátala, *Greece* **32 E6** 34 59N 24 45 E
Matalaque, *Peru* **156 D3** 16 26 S 70 49W
Matale, *Sri Lanka* **83 L5** 7 30N 80 37 E
Matam, *Senegal* **100 B2** 15 34N 13 17W
Matamata, *N.Z.* **118 D4** 37 48 S 175 47 E
Matameye, *Niger* **97 F1** 13 26N 8 28 E
Matamoros, *Campeche, Mexico* **147 D6** 18 50N 90 50W
Matamoros, *Coahuila, Mexico* **146 B4** 25 33N 103 15W
Matamoros, *Puebla, Mexico* **147 D5** 18 2N 98 17W
Matamoros, *Tamaulipas, Mexico* **147 B5** 25 50N 97 30W
Ma'ṭan as Sarra, *Libya* **97 D4** 21 45N 22 0 E
Matandu →, *Tanzania* **107 D3** 8 45 S 34 19 E
Matane, *Canada* **129 C6** 48 50N 67 33W
Matang, *China* **68 F5** 23 30N 104 7 E
Matankari, *Niger* **101 C5** 13 46N 4 1 E
Matanzas, *Cuba* **148 B3** 23 0N 81 40W
Matapan, C. = Taínaron, Ákra, *Greece* **45 H4** 36 22N 22 27 E
Matapédia, *Canada* **129 C6** 48 0N 66 59W
Matara, *Sri Lanka* **83 M5** 5 58N 80 30 E
Mataram, *Indonesia* **70 F5** 8 41 S 116 10 E
Matarani, *Peru* **156 D3** 17 0 S 72 10W
Mataranka, *Australia* **112 B5** 14 55 S 133 4 E
Matarma, Râs, *Egypt* **91 E1** 30 27N 32 44 E
Mataró, *Spain* **34 D7** 41 32N 2 29 E
Matarraña →, *Spain* **34 D5** 41 14N 0 22 E
Mataruška Banja, *Yugoslavia* **42 D5** 43 40N 20 45 E
Mataso, *Vanuatu* **121 G6** 17 14 S 168 26 E
Matata, *N.Z.* **118 D5** 37 54 S 176 48 E
Matatiele, *S. Africa* **105 E4** 30 20 S 28 49 E
Mataura, *N.Z.* **119 G3** 46 11 S 168 51 E
Mataura →, *N.Z.* **119 G3** 46 34 S 168 44 E
Mategua, *Bolivia* **157 C5** 13 1 S 62 48W
Matehuala, *Mexico* **146 C4** 23 40N 100 40W
Mateira, *Brazil* **155 E1** 18 54 S 50 30W
Mateke Hills, *Zimbabwe* **107 G3** 21 48 S 31 0 E
Matélica, *Italy* **39 E10** 43 15N 13 0 E
Matera, *Italy* **41 B9** 40 40N 16 37 E
Mátészalka, *Hungary* **31 D15** 47 58N 22 20 E
Matetsi, *Zimbabwe* **107 F2** 18 12 S 26 0 E
Mateur, *Tunisia* **96 A1** 37 0N 9 40 E
Matfors, *Sweden* **14 B11** 62 21N 17 2 E
Matha, *France* **24 C3** 45 52N 0 20W
Matheson Island, *Canada* **131 C9** 51 45N 96 56W
Mathis, *U.S.A.* **139 L6** 28 4N 97 48W
Mathoura, *Australia* **117 C6** 35 50 S 144 55 E
Mathura, *India* **80 F7** 27 30N 77 40 E
Mati, *Phil.* **71 C7** 6 55N 126 15 E
Mati →, *Albania* **44 C1** 41 40N 19 35 E
Matías Romero, *Mexico* **147 D5** 16 53N 95 2W
Matibane, *Mozam.* **107 E5** 14 49 S 40 45 E
Matima, *Botswana* **104 C3** 20 15 S 24 26 E
Matlock, *U.K.* **16 D6** 53 8N 1 32W
Matmata, *Tunisia* **96 B1** 33 37N 9 59 E
Matna, *Sudan* **95 E4** 13 49N 35 10 E
Mato →, *Venezuela* **153 B4** 7 9N 65 7W
Mato, Serrania de, *Venezuela* **152 B4** 6 25N 65 25W
Mato Grosso □, *Brazil* **157 C7** 14 0 S 55 0W
Mato Grosso, Planalto do, *Brazil* **157 D7** 15 0 S 55 0W
Mato Grosso do Sul □, *Brazil* **157 D7** 18 0 S 55 0W
Matochkin Shar, *U.S.S.R.* **56 B6** 73 10N 56 40 E
Matong, *Papua N. G.* **120 C6** 5 36 S 151 50 E
Matopo Hills, *Zimbabwe* **107 G2** 20 36 S 28 20 E
Matopos, *Zimbabwe* **107 G2** 20 20 S 28 29 E
Matosinhos, *Portugal* **36 D2** 41 11N 8 42W
Matour, *France* **25 B8** 46 19N 4 29 E
Matrah, *Oman* **87 B7** 23 37N 58 30 E
Matsena, *Nigeria* **101 C7** 13 5N 10 5 E
Matsesta, *U.S.S.R.* **53 E8** 43 34N 39 51 E
Matsubara, *Japan* **63 C7** 34 33N 135 34 E
Matsudo, *Japan* **63 B11** 35 47N 139 54 E
Matsue, *Japan* **62 B5** 35 25N 133 10 E
Matsumae, *Japan* **60 D10** 41 26N 140 7 E
Matsumoto, *Japan* **63 A10** 36 15N 138 0 E
Matsusaka, *Japan* **63 C8** 34 34N 136 32 E
Matsutō, *Japan* **63 A8** 36 31N 136 34 E
Matsuura, *Japan* **62 D1** 33 20N 129 49 E
Matsuyama, *Japan* **62 D4** 33 45N 132 45 E
Matsuzaki, *Japan* **63 C10** 34 43N 138 50 E
Mattagami →, *Canada* **128 B3** 50 43N 81 29W
Mattancheri, *India* **83 K3** 9 50N 76 15 E
Mattawa, *Canada* **128 C4** 46 20N 78 45W
Mattawamkeag, *U.S.A.* **129 C6** 45 30N 68 21W
Matterhorn, *Switz.* **28 E5** 45 58N 7 39 E
Mattersburg, *Austria* **31 D9** 47 44N 16 24 E
Matteson, *U.S.A.* **141 C9** 41 30N 87 42W
Matthew Town, *Bahamas* **149 B5** 20 57N 73 40W
Matthews, *U.S.A.* **141 D11** 40 23N 85 31W
Matthew's Ridge, *Guyana* **153 B5** 7 37N 60 10W
Mattice, *Canada* **128 C3** 49 40N 83 20W
Mattituck, *U.S.A.* **137 F12** 40 58N 72 32W
Mattmar, *Sweden* **14 A7** 63 18N 13 45 E
Matuba, *Mozam.* **105 C5** 24 28 S 32 49 E
Matucana, *Peru* **156 C2** 11 55 S 76 25W
Matuku, *Fiji* **121 B2** 19 10 S 179 44 E
Matun, *Afghan.* **80 C3** 33 22N 69 58 E
Maturín, *Venezuela* **153 B5** 9 45N 63 11W
Matveyev Kurgan, *U.S.S.R.* **53 C8** 47 35N 38 47 E
Mau, *India* **81 G10** 25 56N 83 33 E
Mau Escarpment, *Kenya* **106 C4** 0 40 S 36 0 E
Mau Ranipur, *India* **81 G8** 25 16N 79 8 E
Maubeuge, *France* **23 B10** 50 17N 3 57 E
Maubourguet, *France* **24 E4** 43 29N 0 1 E
Maud, Pt., *Australia* **112 D1** 23 6 S 113 45 E
Maude, *Australia* **116 C6** 34 29 S 144 18 E
Maués, *Brazil* **153 D6** 3 20 S 57 45W
Maui, *U.S.A.* **132 H16** 20 45N 156 20W
Maulamyaing = Moulmein, *Burma* **78 G6** 16 30N 97 40 E
Maule □, *Chile* **158 D1** 36 5 S 72 30W
Mauléon-Licharre, *France* **24 E3** 43 14N 0 54W
Maullín, *Chile* **160 B2** 41 38 S 73 37W
Maulvibazar, *Bangla.* **78 C3** 24 29N 91 42 E
Maumee, *U.S.A.* **141 C13** 41 35N 83 40W
Maumee →, *U.S.A.* **141 C13** 41 42N 83 28W
Maumere, *Indonesia* **71 F6** 8 38 S 122 13 E
Maun, *Botswana* **104 C3** 20 0 S 23 26 E
Mauna Kea, *U.S.A.* **132 J17** 19 50N 155 28W
Mauna Loa, *U.S.A.* **132 H16** 21 8N 157 10W
Maungaturoto, *N.Z.* **118 C3** 36 6 S 174 23 E
Maungdow, *Burma* **78 E4** 20 50N 92 21 E
Maupin, *U.S.A.* **142 D3** 45 12N 121 9W
Maure-de-Bretagne, *France* **22 E5** 47 53N 1 58W
Maurepas L., *U.S.A.* **139 K9** 30 18N 90 35W
Maures, *France* **25 E10** 43 15N 6 15 E
Mauriac, *France* **24 C6** 45 13N 2 19 E
Maurice, L., *Australia* **113 E5** 29 30 S 131 0 E
Mauriceville, *N.Z.* **118 G4** 40 45 S 175 42 E
Mauritania ■, *Africa* **98 D3** 20 50N 10 0W
Mauritius ■, *Ind. Oc.* **109 G4** 20 0 S 57 0 E
Mauron, *France* **22 D4** 48 9N 2 18W
Maurs, *France* **24 D6** 44 43N 2 12 E
Mauston, *U.S.A.* **138 D9** 43 48N 90 5W
Mauterndorf, *Austria* **30 D6** 47 9N 13 40 E
Mauvezin, *France* **24 E4** 43 44N 0 53 E
Mauzé-sur-le-Mignon, *France* **24 B3** 46 12N 0 41W
Mavaca →, *Venezuela* **153 C4** 2 31N 65 11W
Mavelikara, *India* **83 K3** 9 14N 76 32 E
Mavinga, *Angola* **103 F4** 15 50 S 20 21 E
Mavli, *India* **80 G5** 24 45N 73 55 E
Mavrova, *Albania* **44 D1** 40 26N 19 32 E
Mavuradonha Mts., *Zimbabwe* **107 F3** 16 30 S 31 30 E
Mawa, *Zaïre* **106 B2** 2 45N 26 40 E
Mawana, *India* **80 E7** 29 6N 77 58 E
Mawand, *Pakistan* **80 E3** 29 33N 68 38 E
Mawk Mai, *Burma* **78 E6** 20 14N 97 37 E
Mawlaik, *Burma* **78 D5** 23 40N 94 26 E
Mawlawkho, *Burma* **78 G6** 17 50N 97 38 E
Mawquq, *Si. Arabia* **84 E4** 27 25N 41 8 E
Mawshij, *Yemen* **86 D3** 13 43N 43 17 E
Mawson Coast, *Antarctica* **7 C6** 68 30 S 63 0 E
Max, *U.S.A.* **138 B4** 47 50N 101 20W
Maxcanú, *Mexico* **147 C6** 20 40N 92 0W
Maxesibeni, *S. Africa* **105 E4** 30 49 S 29 23 E
Maxhamish L., *Canada* **130 B4** 59 50N 123 17W
Maxixe, *Mozam.* **105 C6** 23 54 S 35 17 E
Maxville, *Canada* **137 A10** 45 17N 74 51W
Maxwell, *N.Z.* **118 F3** 39 51 S 174 49 E
Maxwell, *U.S.A.* **144 F4** 39 17N 122 11W
Maxwelton, *Australia* **114 C3** 20 43 S 142 41 E
May Downs, *Australia* **114 C4** 22 38 S 148 55 E
May Pen, *Jamaica* **148 C4** 17 58N 77 15W
May River, *Papua N. G.* **120 C1** 4 19 S 141 58 E
Maya, *Indonesia* **75 C3** 1 10 S 109 35 E
Maya, *Spain* **34 B3** 43 12N 1 29W
Maya →, *U.S.S.R.* **57 D14** 54 31N 134 41 E
Maya Mts., *Belize* **147 D7** 16 30N 89 0W
Mayaguana, *Bahamas* **149 B5** 22 30N 72 44W
Mayagüez, *Puerto Rico* **149 C6** 18 12N 67 9W
Mayahi, *Niger* **101 C6** 13 58N 7 40 E
Mayals, *Spain* **34 D5** 41 22N 0 30 E
Mayama, *Congo* **102 C2** 3 51 S 14 54 E
Mayāmey, *Iran* **85 B7** 36 24N 55 42 E
Mayang, *China* **68 D7** 27 53N 109 49 E
Mayarí, *Cuba* **149 B4** 20 40N 75 41W
Mayavaram = Mayuram, *India* **83 J4** 11 3N 79 42 E
Maybell, *U.S.A.* **142 F9** 40 30N 108 4W
Maychew, *Ethiopia* **95 E4** 12 50N 39 31 E
Maydān, *Iraq* **84 C5** 34 55N 45 37 E
Maydena, *Australia* **114 G4** 42 45 S 146 30 E
Maydī, *Yemen* **86 C3** 16 19N 42 48 E
Maydos, *Turkey* **44 D8** 40 13N 26 20 E
Mayen, *Germany* **27 E3** 50 18N 7 10 E
Mayenne, *France* **22 D6** 48 20N 0 38W
Mayenne □, *France* **22 D6** 48 10N 0 40W
Mayenne →, *France* **22 E6** 47 30N 0 32W
Mayer, *U.S.A.* **143 J7** 34 28N 112 17W
Mayerthorpe, *Canada* **130 C5** 53 57N 115 8W
Mayfield, *U.S.A.* **135 G1** 36 45N 88 40W
Mayhill, *U.S.A.* **143 K11** 32 58N 105 30W
Maykop, *U.S.S.R.* **53 D9** 44 35N 40 25 E
Mayli-Say, *U.S.S.R.* **55 C6** 41 17N 72 24 E
Maymyo, *Burma* **76 A1** 22 2N 96 28 E
Maynard, *U.S.A.* **144 C4** 47 59N 122 55W
Maynard Hills, *Australia* **113 E2** 28 28 S 119 49 E
Mayne →, *Australia* **114 C3** 23 40 S 141 55 E
Maynooth, *Ireland* **19 C5** 53 22N 6 38W
Mayo, *Canada* **126 B6** 63 38N 135 57W
Mayo □, *Ireland* **19 C2** 53 47N 9 7W
Mayo →, *Argentina* **160 C3** 45 45 S 69 45W
Mayo →, *Peru* **156 B2** 6 38 S 76 15W
Mayo L., *Canada* **126 B6** 63 45N 135 0W
Mayoko, *Zaïre* **102 C2** 2 18 S 12 49 E
Mayon Volcano, *Phil.* **71 B6** 13 15N 123 41 E
Mayor I., *N.Z.* **118 D5** 37 16 S 176 17 E
Mayorga, *Spain* **36 C5** 42 10N 5 16W
Mayskiy, *U.S.S.R.* **53 E11** 43 47N 44 2 E
Mayson L., *Canada* **131 B7** 57 55N 107 10W
Maysville, *Ky., U.S.A.* **141 F13** 38 39N 83 46W
Maysville, *Mo., U.S.A.* **140 E2** 39 53N 94 21W
Mayu, *Indonesia* **71 D7** 1 30N 126 30 E
Mayumba, *Gabon* **102 C2** 3 25 S 10 39 E
Mayuram, *India* **83 J4** 11 3N 79 42 E
Mayville, *N. Dak., U.S.A.* **138 B6** 47 30N 97 23W
Mayville, *N.Y., U.S.A.* **136 D5** 42 14N 79 31W
Mayya, *U.S.S.R.* **57 C14** 61 44N 130 18 E
Mazabuka, *Zambia* **107 F2** 15 52 S 27 44 E
Mazagán = El Jadida, *Morocco* **98 B3** 33 11N 8 17W
Mazagão, *Brazil* **153 D7** 0 7 S 51 16W
Mazamet, *France* **24 E6** 43 30N 2 20 E
Mazán, *Peru* **152 D3** 3 30 S 73 0W
Māzandarān □, *Iran* **85 B7** 36 30N 52 0 E
Mazapil, *Mexico* **146 C4** 24 38N 101 34W
Mazar, O. →, *Algeria* **99 B5** 31 50N 1 36 E
Mazar-e Sharīf, *Afghan.* **79 A2** 36 41N 67 0 E
Mazara del Vallo, *Italy* **40 E5** 37 40N 12 34 E
Mazarredo, *Argentina* **160 C3** 47 10 S 66 50W
Mazarrón, *Spain* **35 H3** 37 38N 1 19W
Mazarrón, G. de, *Spain* **35 H3** 37 27N 1 19W
Mazaruni →, *Guyana* **153 B6** 6 25N 58 35W
Mazatán, *Mexico* **146 B2** 29 0N 110 8W
Mazatenango, *Guatemala* **148 D1** 14 35N 91 30W
Mazatlán, *Mexico* **146 C3** 23 10N 106 30W
Mažeikiai, *U.S.S.R.* **50 C3** 56 20N 22 20 E
Māzhān, *Iran* **85 C8** 32 30N 59 0 E
Mazīnān, *Iran* **85 B8** 36 19N 56 56 E
Mazoe, *Mozam.* **107 F3** 16 42 S 33 7 E
Mazoe →, *Mozam.* **107 F3** 16 20 S 33 30 E
Mazomanie, *U.S.A.* **140 A7** 43 11N 89 48W
Mazon, *U.S.A.* **141 C8** 41 14N 88 25W
Mazowe, *Zimbabwe* **107 F3** 17 28 S 30 58 E
Mazrûb, *Sudan* **95 E2** 14 0N 29 20 E
Mazu Dao, *China* **69 D12** 26 10N 119 55 E
Mazurian Lakes = Mazurski, Pojezierze, *Poland* **47 B8** 53 50N 21 0 E
Mazurski, Pojezierze, *Poland* **47 B8** 53 50N 21 0 E
Mazzarino, *Italy* **41 E7** 37 19N 14 12 E
Mba, *Fiji* **121 A1** 17 33 S 177 41 E
Mbaba, *Senegal* **100 C1** 14 59N 16 44W
Mbabane, *Swaziland* **105 D5** 26 18 S 31 6 E
Mbagne, *Mauritania* **100 B2** 16 6N 14 47W
M'bahiakro, *Ivory C.* **100 D4** 7 33N 4 19W
Mbaïki, *C.A.R.* **102 B3** 3 53N 18 1 E
Mbakana, Mt. de, *Cameroon* **102 A3** 7 57N 15 6 E
Mbala, *Zambia* **107 D3** 8 46 S 31 24 E
Mbale, *Uganda* **106 B3** 1 8N 34 12 E
Mbalmayo, *Cameroon* **101 E7** 3 33N 11 33 E
Mbamba Bay, *Tanzania* **107 E3** 11 13 S 34 49 E
Mbandaka, *Zaïre* **102 B3** 0 1N 18 18 E
Mbanga, *Cameroon* **101 E6** 4 30N 9 33 E
Mbanza Congo, *Angola* **103 D2** 6 18 S 14 16 E
Mbanza Ngungu, *Zaïre* **103 D2** 5 12 S 14 53 E
Mbarara, *Uganda* **106 C3** 0 35 S 30 40 E
Mbashe →, *S. Africa* **105 E4** 32 15 S 28 54 E
Mbatto, *Ivory C.* **100 D4** 6 28N 4 22W
Mbengga, *Fiji* **121 B2** 18 23 S 178 8 E
Mbenkuru →, *Tanzania* **107 D4** 9 25 S 39 50 E
Mberengwa, *Zimbabwe* **107 G2** 20 29 S 29 57 E
Mberengwa, Mt., *Zimbabwe* **107 G2** 20 37 S 29 55 E
Mberubu, *Nigeria* **101 D6** 6 10N 7 38 E
Mbesuma, *Zambia* **107 E3** 10 0 S 32 2 E
Mbeya, *Tanzania* **107 D3** 8 54 S 33 29 E
Mbeya □, *Tanzania* **106 D3** 8 15 S 33 30 E
Mbigou, *Gabon* **102 C2** 1 53 S 11 56 E
Mbinga, *Tanzania* **107 E4** 10 50 S 35 0 E
Mbinga □, *Tanzania* **107 E4** 10 50 S 35 0 E
Mbini □, *Eq. Guin.* **102 B2** 1 30N 10 0 E
Mboki, *C.A.R.* **95 F2** 5 19N 25 58 E
Mboli, *Zaïre* **102 B4** 4 8N 23 9 E
Mboro, *Senegal* **100 B1** 15 9N 16 54W
Mboune, *Senegal* **100 C2** 14 42N 13 34W
Mbouoma, *Congo* **102 C3** 0 52 S 15 4 E
Mbour, *Senegal* **100 C1** 14 22N 16 54W
Mbout, *Mauritania* **100 B2** 16 1N 12 38W
Mbozi □, *Tanzania* **107 D3** 9 0 S 32 50 E

232 Mbrés

Mbrés, *C.A.R.* **102 A3** 6 40N 19 48 E
Mbuji-Mayi, *Zaïre* **103 D4** 6 9 S 23 40 E
Mbulu, *Tanzania* **106 C4** 3 45 S 35 30 E
Mbulu □, *Tanzania* **106 C4** 3 52 S 35 33 E
Mburucuyá, *Argentina* **158 B4** 28 1 S 58 14W
Mcherrah, *Algeria* **98 C4** 27 0N 4 30W
Mchinja, *Tanzania* **107 D4** 9 44 S 39 45 E
Mchinji, *Malawi* **107 E3** 13 47 S 32 58 E
Mdennah, *Mauritania* **98 D3** 24 37N 6 0W
Mead, L., *U.S.A.* **145 J12** 36 1N 114 44W
Meade, *U.S.A.* **139 G4** 37 18N 100 25W
Meadow, *Australia* **113 E1** 26 35 S 114 40 E
Meadow Lake, *Canada* **131 C7** 54 10N 108 26W
Meadow Lake Prov. Park, *Canada* **131 C7** 54 27N 109 0W
Meadow Valley Wash →, *U.S.A.* **145 J12** 36 39N 114 35W
Meadville, *Mo., U.S.A.* **140 E3** 39 47N 93 18W
Meadville, *Pa., U.S.A.* **136 E4** 41 39N 80 9W
Meaford, *Canada* **128 D3** 44 36N 80 35W
Mealhada, *Portugal* **36 E2** 40 22N 8 27W
Mealy Mts., *Canada* **129 B8** 53 10N 58 0W
Meander River, *Canada* **130 B5** 59 2N 117 42W
Meares, C., *U.S.A.* **142 D2** 45 37N 124 0W
Mearim →, *Brazil* **154 B3** 3 4 S 44 35W
Meath □, *Ireland* **19 C5** 53 32N 6 40W
Meath Park, *Canada* **131 C7** 53 27N 105 22W
Meatian, *Australia* **116 C5** 35 34 S 143 21 E
Meaulne, *France* **24 B6** 46 36N 2 36 E
Meaux, *France* **23 D9** 48 58N 2 50 E
Mebechi-Gawa →, *Japan* **60 D10** 40 31N 141 31 E
Mecanhelas, *Mozam.* **107 F4** 15 12 S 35 54 E
Mecaya →, *Colombia* **152 C2** 0 29N 75 11W
Mecca = Makkah, *Si. Arabia* **86 B2** 21 30N 39 54 E
Mecca, *U.S.A.* **145 M10** 33 37N 116 3W
Mechanicsburg, *U.S.A.* **136 F8** 40 12N 77 0W
Mechanicsville, *U.S.A.* **140 C5** 41 54N 91 16W
Mechanicville, *U.S.A.* **137 D11** 42 54N 73 41W
Mechara, *Ethiopia* **95 F5** 8 36N 40 20 E
Mechelen, *Antwerpen, Belgium* **21 F4** 51 2N 4 29 E
Mechelen, *Limburg, Belgium* **21 G7** 50 58N 5 41 E
Mecheria, *Algeria* **99 B4** 33 35N 0 18W
Mechernich, *Germany* **26 E2** 50 35N 6 39 E
Mechetinskaya, *U.S.S.R.* **53 C9** 46 45N 40 32 E
Mechra Benâbbou, *Morocco* **98 B3** 32 39N 7 48W
Mecidiye, *Turkey* **44 D8** 40 38N 26 32 E
Mecitözü, *Turkey* **52 F6** 40 32N 35 17 E
Mecklenburg-Vorpommern □, *Germany* **26 B8** 53 50N 12 0 E
Mecklenburger Bucht, *Germany* **26 A7** 54 20N 11 40 E
Meconta, *Mozam.* **107 E4** 14 59 S 39 50 E
Meda, *Australia* **112 C3** 17 22 S 123 59 E
Meda, *Portugal* **36 E3** 40 57N 7 18W
Medak, *India* **82 E4** 18 1N 78 15 E
Medan, *Indonesia* **70 D1** 3 40N 98 38 E
Médanos, *Argentina* **160 A4** 38 50 S 62 42W
Medanosa, Pta., *Argentina* **160 C3** 48 8 S 66 0W
Medaryville, *U.S.A.* **141 C10** 41 4N 86 55W
Medawachchiya, *Sri Lanka* **83 K5** 8 30N 80 30 E
Medéa, *Algeria* **99 A5** 36 12N 2 50 E
Mededa, *Yugoslavia* **42 D4** 43 44N 19 15 E
Médégué, *Gabon* **102 B2** 0 37N 10 8 E
Medeiros Neto, *Brazil* **155 E3** 17 20 S 40 14W
Medel, Pic, *Switz.* **29 C7** 46 34N 8 55 E
Medellín, *Colombia* **152 B2** 6 15N 75 35W
Medemblik, *Neths.* **20 C6** 52 46N 5 8 E
Médenine, *Tunisia* **96 B2** 33 21N 10 30 E
Mederdra, *Mauritania* **100 B1** 17 0N 15 38W
Medford, *Mass., U.S.A.* **137 D13** 42 25N 71 7W
Medford, *Oreg., U.S.A.* **142 E2** 42 20N 122 52W
Medford, *Wis., U.S.A.* **138 C9** 45 9N 90 21W
Medgidia, *Romania* **46 E9** 44 15N 28 19 E
Medi, *Sudan* **95 F3** 5 4N 30 42 E
Media Agua, *Argentina* **158 C2** 31 58 S 68 25W
Media Luna, *Argentina* **158 C2** 34 45 S 66 44W
Mediapolis, *U.S.A.* **140 D5** 41 0N 91 10W
Mediaş, *Romania* **46 C5** 46 9N 24 22 E
Medical Lake, *U.S.A.* **142 C5** 47 35N 117 42W
Medicina, *Italy* **39 D8** 44 29N 11 38 E
Medicine Bow, *U.S.A.* **142 F10** 41 56N 106 11W
Medicine Bow Pk., *U.S.A.* **142 F10** 41 21N 106 19W
Medicine Bow Ra., *U.S.A.* **142 F10** 41 10N 106 25W
Medicine Hat, *Canada* **131 D6** 50 0N 110 45W
Medicine Lake, *U.S.A.* **138 A2** 48 30N 104 30W
Medicine Lodge, *U.S.A.* **139 G5** 37 20N 98 37W
Medina = Al Madīnah, *Si. Arabia* **84 E3** 24 35N 39 52 E
Medina, *Brazil* **155 E3** 16 15 S 41 29W
Medina, *Colombia* **152 C3** 4 30N 73 21W
Medina, *N. Dak., U.S.A.* **138 B5** 46 57N 99 20W
Medina, *N.Y., U.S.A.* **136 C6** 43 15N 78 27W
Medina, *Ohio, U.S.A.* **136 E3** 41 9N 81 50W
Medina →, *U.S.A.* **139 L5** 29 10N 98 20W
Medina de Ríoseco, *Spain* **36 D5** 41 53N 5 3W
Medina del Campo, *Spain* **36 D6** 41 18N 4 55W
Medina L., *U.S.A.* **139 L5** 29 35N 98 58W
Medina-Sidonia, *Spain* **37 J5** 36 28N 5 57W
Medinaceli, *Spain* **34 D2** 41 12N 2 30W
Medinipur, *India* **81 H12** 22 25N 87 21 E
Mediterranean Sea, *Europe* **92 C5** 35 0N 15 0 E
Medjerda, O. →, *Tunisia* **96 A2** 37 7N 10 13 E
Medley, *Canada* **131 C6** 54 25N 110 16W
Mednogorsk, *U.S.S.R.* **54 F5** 51 24N 57 37 E
Médoc, *France* **24 C3** 45 10N 0 50W
Medora, *U.S.A.* **141 F10** 38 49N 86 10W
Médouneu, *Gabon* **102 B2** 0 57N 10 47 E
Medstead, *Canada* **131 C7** 53 19N 108 5W
Medulin, *Yugoslavia* **39 D10** 44 49N 13 55 E
Medveda, *Yugoslavia* **42 E6** 42 50N 21 32 E
Medveditsa →, *R.S.F.S.R., U.S.S.R.* **51 G13** 49 35N 42 41 E
Medveditsa →, *R.S.F.S.R., U.S.S.R.* **51 C10** 57 5N 37 30 E
Medvedok, *U.S.S.R.* **54 C2** 57 20N 50 1 E
Medvezhi, Ostrava, *U.S.S.R.* **57 B17** 71 0N 161 0 E
Medvezhyegorsk, *U.S.S.R.* **48 B5** 63 0N 34 25 E
Medway →, *U.K.* **17 F8** 51 28N 0 45 E
Medyn, *U.S.S.R.* **51 D9** 54 58N 35 52 E
Medzev, *Czech.* **31 C13** 48 43N 20 55 E
Medzilaborce, *Czech.* **31 B14** 49 17N 21 52 E
Meeberrie, *Australia* **113 E2** 26 57 S 115 51 E
Meekatharra, *Australia* **113 E2** 26 32 S 118 29 E
Meeker, *U.S.A.* **142 F10** 40 1N 107 58W
Meeniyan, *Australia* **117 E7** 38 35 S 146 0 E
Meer, *Belgium* **21 F5** 51 27N 4 45 E
Meerane, *Germany* **26 E8** 50 51N 12 30 E
Meerbeke, *Belgium* **21 G4** 50 50N 4 3 E
Meerhout, *Belgium* **21 F6** 51 7N 5 4 E
Meerle, *Belgium* **21 F5** 51 29N 4 48 E
Meersburg, *Germany* **27 H5** 47 42N 9 16 E
Meerssen, *Neths.* **21 G7** 50 53N 5 50 E
Meerut, *India* **80 E7** 29 1N 77 42 E
Meeteetse, *U.S.A.* **142 D9** 44 10N 108 56W
Meeuwen, *Belgium* **21 F7** 51 6N 5 31 E
Mega, *Ethiopia* **95 G4** 3 57N 38 19 E
Megálo Khorío, *Greece* **45 H9** 36 27N 27 24 E
Megálo Petalí, *Greece* **45 G6** 38 0N 24 15 E
Megalópolis, *Greece* **45 G4** 37 25N 22 7 E
Meganísi, *Greece* **45 F2** 38 39N 20 48 E
Mégara, *Greece* **45 G5** 37 58N 23 22 E
Megarine, *Algeria* **99 B6** 33 14N 6 2 E
Megdhova →, *Greece* **45 E3** 39 10N 21 45 E
Megève, *France* **25 C10** 45 51N 6 37 E
Meghalaya □, *India* **78 C3** 25 50N 91 0 E
Meghezez, *Ethiopia* **95 F4** 9 18N 39 26 E
Meghna →, *Bangla.* **78 D3** 22 50N 90 50 E
Mégiscane, L., *Canada* **128 C4** 48 35N 75 55W
Mehadia, *Romania* **46 E3** 44 56N 22 23 E
Mehaigne →, *Belgium* **21 G6** 50 32N 5 13 E
Mehaïguene, O. →, *Algeria* **99 B5** 32 15N 2 59 E
Mehedinţi □, *Romania* **46 E3** 44 40N 22 45 E
Meheisa, *Sudan* **94 D3** 19 38N 32 57 E
Mehndawal, *India* **81 F10** 26 58N 83 5 E
Mehr Jān, *Iran* **85 C7** 33 50N 55 6 E
Mehrābād, *Iran* **84 B5** 36 53N 47 55 E
Mehrān, *Iran* **84 C5** 33 7N 46 10 E
Mehrīz, *Iran* **85 D7** 31 35N 54 28 E
Mehun-sur-Yèvre, *France* **23 E9** 47 10N 2 13 E
Mei Jiang →, *China* **69 E11** 24 25N 116 35 E
Mei Xian, *Guangdong, China* **69 E11** 24 16N 116 6 E
Mei Xian, *Shaanxi, China* **66 G4** 34 18N 107 55 E
Meia Ponte →, *Brazil* **155 E2** 18 32 S 49 36W
Meicheng, *China* **69 C12** 29 29N 119 16 E
Meichengzhen, *China* **69 C8** 28 9N 111 40 E
Meichuan, *China* **69 B10** 30 8N 115 31 E
Meiganga, *Cameroon* **102 A2** 6 30N 14 25 E
Meijel, *Neths.* **21 F7** 51 21N 5 53 E
Meiktila, *Burma* **78 E5** 20 53N 95 54 E
Meilen, *Switz.* **29 B7** 47 16N 8 39 E
Meiningen, *Germany* **26 E6** 50 32N 10 25 E
Meio →, *Brazil* **155 D3** 13 36 S 44 7W
Meira, Sierra de, *Spain* **36 B3** 43 15N 7 15W
Meiringen, *Switz.* **28 C6** 46 43N 8 12 E
Meishan, *China* **68 B4** 30 3N 103 23 E
Meissen, *Germany* **26 D9** 51 10N 13 29 E
Meissner, *Germany* **26 D5** 51 13N 9 51 E
Meitan, *China* **68 D6** 27 45N 107 29 E
Mejillones, *Chile* **158 A1** 23 10 S 70 30W
Meka, *Australia* **113 E2** 27 25 S 116 48 E
Mékambo, *Gabon* **102 B2** 1 2N 13 50 E
Mekdela, *Ethiopia* **95 E4** 11 24N 39 10 E
Mekele, *Ethiopia* **95 E4** 13 33N 39 30 E
Mekhtar, *Pakistan* **79 C3** 30 30N 69 15 E
Meknès, *Morocco* **98 B3** 33 57N 5 33W
Meko, *Nigeria* **101 D5** 7 27N 2 52 E
Mekong →, *Asia* **77 H6** 9 30N 106 15 E
Mekongga, *Indonesia* **71 E6** 3 39 S 121 15 E
Melagiri Hills, *India* **83 H3** 12 20N 77 30 E
Melah, Sebkhet el, *Algeria* **99 C4** 29 20N 1 30W
Melaka, *Malaysia* **77 L4** 2 15N 102 15 E
Melalap, *Malaysia* **70 C5** 5 10N 116 5 E
Mélambes, *Greece* **32 D6** 35 8N 24 40 E
Melanesia, *Pac. Oc.* **122 H7** 4 0 S 155 0 E
Melapalaiyam, *India* **83 K3** 8 39N 77 44 E
Melawi →, *Indonesia* **75 B4** 0 5N 111 29 E
Melbourne, *Australia* **117 D6** 37 50 S 145 0 E
Melbourne, *Fla., U.S.A.* **135 L5** 28 4N 80 35W
Melbourne, *Iowa, U.S.A.* **140 C3** 41 57N 93 6W
Melcher, *U.S.A.* **140 C3** 41 13N 93 15W
Melchor Múzquiz, *Mexico* **146 B4** 27 50N 101 30W
Melchor Ocampo, *Mexico* **146 C4** 24 52N 101 40W
Méldola, *Italy* **39 D9** 44 7N 12 3 E
Meldorf, *Germany* **26 A5** 54 5N 9 5 E
Meleden, *Somali Rep.* **108 B3** 10 25N 49 51 E
Melegnano, *Italy* **38 C6** 45 21N 9 20 E
Melenci, *Yugoslavia* **42 B5** 45 32N 20 20 E
Melenki, *U.S.S.R.* **51 D12** 55 20N 41 37 E
Meleuz, *U.S.S.R.* **54 E4** 52 58N 55 55 E
Mélèzes →, *Canada* **127 C12** 57 30N 71 0W
Melfi, *Chad* **97 F3** 11 0N 17 59 E
Melfi, *Italy* **41 B8** 41 0N 15 33 E
Melfort, *Canada* **131 C8** 52 50N 104 37W
Melfort, *Zimbabwe* **107 F3** 18 0 S 31 25 E
Melgaço, *Madeira* **36 C2** 42 7N 8 15W
Melgar de Fernamental, *Spain* **36 C6** 42 27N 4 17W
Melhus, *Norway* **14 A4** 63 17N 10 18 E
Melick, *Neths.* **21 F8** 51 10N 6 1 E
Melide, *Switz.* **29 E7** 45 57N 8 57 E
Meligalá, *Greece* **45 G3** 37 15N 21 59 E
Melilla, *Morocco* **99 A4** 35 21N 2 57W
Melipilla, *Chile* **158 C1** 33 42 S 71 15W
Mélissa, Ákra, *Greece* **32 D6** 35 6N 24 33 E
Mélissa Óros, *Greece* **45 G8** 37 32N 26 4 E
Melita, *Canada* **131 D8** 49 15N 101 0W
Mélito di Porto Salvo, *Italy* **41 E8** 37 55N 15 47 E
Melitopol, *U.S.S.R.* **52 C6** 46 50N 35 22 E
Melk, *Austria* **30 C8** 48 13N 15 20 E
Mellansel, *Sweden* **12 E15** 63 25N 18 17 E
Melle, *Belgium* **21 G3** 51 0N 3 49 E
Melle, *France* **24 B3** 46 14N 0 10W
Melle, *Germany* **26 C4** 52 12N 8 20 E
Mellégue, O. →, *Tunisia* **96 A1** 36 32N 8 51 E
Mellen, *U.S.A.* **138 B9** 46 19N 90 36W
Mellerud, *Sweden* **15 F6** 58 41N 12 28 E
Mellette, *U.S.A.* **138 C5** 45 11N 98 29W
Mellid, *Spain* **36 C2** 42 55N 8 1W
Mellieha, *Malta* **32 D1** 35 57N 14 21 E
Mellit, *Sudan* **95 E2** 14 7N 25 34 E
Mellizo Sur, Cerro, *Chile* **160 C2** 48 33 S 73 10W
Mellrichstadt, *Germany* **27 E6** 50 26N 10 19 E
Melnik, *Bulgaria* **43 F8** 41 30N 23 25 E
Mělník, *Czech.* **30 A7** 50 22N 14 23 E
Melo, *Uruguay* **159 C5** 32 20 S 54 10W
Melolo, *Indonesia* **71 F6** 9 53 S 120 40 E
Melouprey, *Cambodia* **76 F5** 13 48N 105 16 E
Melovoye, *U.S.S.R.* **53 B9** 49 25N 40 5 E
Melrhir, Chott, *Algeria* **99 B6** 34 25N 6 24 E
Melrose, *N.S.W., Australia* **117 B7** 32 42 S 146 57 E
Melrose, *W. Austral., Australia* **113 E3** 27 50 S 121 15 E
Melrose, *U.K.* **18 F6** 55 35N 2 44W
Melrose, *Iowa, U.S.A.* **140 D3** 40 59N 93 3W
Melrose, *N. Mex., U.S.A.* **139 H3** 34 27N 103 33W
Mels, *Switz.* **29 B8** 47 3N 9 25 E
Melsele, *Belgium* **21 F4** 51 13N 4 17 E
Melstone, *U.S.A.* **142 C10** 46 36N 107 50W
Melsungen, *Germany* **26 D5** 51 8N 9 34 E
Melton Mowbray, *U.K.* **16 E7** 52 46N 0 52W
Melun, *France* **23 D9** 48 32N 2 39 E
Melur, *India* **83 J4** 10 2N 78 23 E
Melut, *Sudan* **95 E3** 10 30N 32 13 E
Melville, *Canada* **131 C8** 50 55N 102 50W
Melville, C., *Australia* **114 A3** 14 11 S 144 30 E
Melville, L., *Canada* **129 B8** 53 30N 60 0W
Melville B., *Australia* **114 A2** 12 0 S 136 45 E
Melville I., *Australia* **112 B5** 11 30 S 131 0 E
Melville I., *Canada* **124 B8** 75 30N 112 0W
Melville Pen., *Canada* **127 B11** 68 0N 84 0W
Melvin →, *Canada* **130 B5** 59 11N 117 31W
Mélykút, *Hungary* **31 E12** 46 11N 19 25 E
Memaliaj, *Albania* **44 D1** 40 25N 19 58 E
Memba, *Mozam.* **107 E5** 14 11 S 40 30 E
Memboro, *Indonesia* **71 F5** 9 30 S 119 30 E
Membrilla, *Spain* **35 G1** 38 59N 3 21W
Memel = Klaipeda, *U.S.S.R.* **50 D2** 55 43N 21 10 E
Memel, *S. Africa* **105 D4** 27 38 S 29 36 E
Memmingen, *Germany* **27 H6** 47 59N 10 12 E
Mempawah, *Indonesia* **70 D3** 0 30N 109 5 E
Memphis, *Mo., U.S.A.* **140 D4** 40 28N 92 10W
Memphis, *Tenn., U.S.A.* **139 H10** 35 7N 90 0W
Memphis, *Tex., U.S.A.* **139 H4** 34 45N 100 30W
Mena, *U.S.A.* **139 H7** 34 40N 94 15W
Mena →, *Ethiopia* **95 F5** 5 40N 40 50 E
Menai Strait, *U.K.* **16 D3** 53 14N 4 10W
Ménaka, *Mali* **101 B5** 15 59N 2 18 E
Menaldum, *Neths.* **20 B7** 53 13N 5 40 E
Menamurtee, *Australia* **116 A5** 31 25 S 143 11 E
Menan = Chao Phraya →, *Thailand* **76 F3** 13 32N 100 36 E
Menarandra →, *Madag.* **105 D7** 25 17 S 44 30 E
Menard, *U.S.A.* **139 K5** 30 57N 99 48W
Menasha, *U.S.A.* **134 C1** 44 13N 88 27W
Menate, *Indonesia* **70 E4** 0 12 S 113 3 E
Mendawai →, *Indonesia* **70 E4** 3 30 S 113 0 E
Mende, *France* **24 D7** 44 31N 3 30 E
Mendebo, *Ethiopia* **95 F4** 7 0N 39 22 E
Mendez, *Mexico* **147 B5** 25 7N 98 34W
Mendhar, *India* **81 C6** 33 35N 74 10 E
Mendi, *Ethiopia* **95 F4** 9 47N 35 4 E
Mendi, *Papua N. G.* **120 D2** 6 11 S 143 39 E
Mendip Hills, *U.K.* **17 F5** 51 17N 2 40W
Mendocino, *U.S.A.* **142 G2** 39 26N 123 50W
Mendocino, C., *U.S.A.* **142 F1** 40 26N 124 25W
Mendon, *U.S.A.* **141 C11** 42 0N 85 27W
Mendota, *Calif., U.S.A.* **144 J6** 36 46N 120 24W
Mendota, *Ill., U.S.A.* **140 C7** 41 35N 89 5W
Mendoza, *Argentina* **158 C2** 32 50 S 68 52W
Mendoza □, *Argentina* **158 C2** 33 0 S 69 0W
Mendrisio, *Switz.* **29 E7** 45 52N 8 59 E
Mene Grande, *Venezuela* **152 B3** 9 49N 70 56W
Menemen, *Turkey* **88 D2** 38 34N 27 3 E
Menen, *Belgium* **21 G2** 50 47N 3 7 E
Menéndez, L., *Argentina* **160 B2** 42 40 S 71 51W
Menfi, *Italy* **40 E5** 37 36N 12 57 E
Mengcheng, *China* **69 A11** 33 18N 116 31 E
Mengdingjie, *China* **68 F2** 23 31N 98 58 E
Mengeš, *Yugoslavia* **39 B11** 46 24N 14 35 E
Menggala, *Indonesia* **70 E3** 4 30 S 105 15 E
Menghai, *China* **68 G3** 21 49N 100 55 E
Mengibar, *Spain* **37 H7** 37 58N 3 48W
Mengjin, *China* **66 G7** 34 55N 112 45 E
Mengla, *China* **68 G3** 21 20N 101 25 E
Menglian, *China* **68 F2** 22 21N 99 27 E
Mengoub, *Algeria* **98 C3** 29 49N 5 26W
Mengshan, *China* **69 E8** 24 14N 110 55 E
Mengyin, *China* **67 G9** 35 40N 117 58 E
Mengzhe, *China* **68 F3** 22 2N 100 15 E
Mengzi, *China* **68 F4** 23 20N 103 22 E
Menihek L., *Canada* **129 B6** 54 0N 67 0W
Menin = Menen, *Belgium* **21 G2** 50 47N 3 7 E
Menindee, *Australia* **116 B5** 32 20 S 142 25 E
Menindee L., *Australia* **116 B5** 32 20 S 142 25 E
Meningie, *Australia* **116 C3** 35 50 S 139 18 E
Menlo Park, *U.S.A.* **144 H4** 37 27N 122 12W
Menominee, *U.S.A.* **134 C2** 45 9N 87 39W
Menominee →, *U.S.A.* **134 C2** 45 5N 87 36W
Menomonee Falls, *U.S.A.* **141 A8** 43 11N 88 7W
Menomonie, *U.S.A.* **138 C9** 44 50N 91 54W
Menongue, *Angola* **103 E3** 14 48 S 17 52 E
Menorca, *Spain* **33 B11** 40 0N 4 0 E
Mentakab, *Malaysia* **77 L4** 3 29N 102 21 E
Mentawai, Kepulauan, *Indonesia* **70 E1** 2 0 S 99 0 E
Menton, *France* **25 E11** 43 50N 7 29 E
Mentone, *U.S.A.* **141 C10** 41 10N 86 2W
Mentor, *U.S.A.* **136 E3** 41 40N 81 21W
Mentz Dam, *S. Africa* **104 E4** 33 10 S 25 9 E
Menyamya, *Papua N. G.* **120 D3** 7 10 S 145 59 E
Menzel-Bourguiba, *Tunisia* **96 A1** 37 9N 9 49 E
Menzel Chaker, *Tunisia* **96 B2** 35 0N 10 26 E
Menzel-Temime, *Tunisia* **96 A2** 36 46N 11 0 E
Menzelinsk, *U.S.S.R.* **54 D3** 55 53N 53 1 E
Menzies, *Australia* **113 E3** 29 40 S 121 2 E
Me'ona, *Israel* **91 B4** 33 1N 35 15 E
Meoqui, *Mexico* **146 B3** 28 17N 105 29W
Mepaco, *Mozam.* **107 F3** 15 57 S 30 48 E
Meppel, *Neths.* **20 C8** 52 42N 6 12 E
Meppen, *Germany* **26 C3** 52 41N 7 20 E
Mequinenza, *Spain* **34 D5** 41 22N 0 17 E
Mequon, *U.S.A.* **141 A9** 43 14N 87 59W
Mer Rouge, *U.S.A.* **139 J9** 32 47N 91 48W
Mera Lava, *Vanuatu* **121 D6** 14 25 S 168 3 E
Merabéllou, Kólpos, *Greece* **32 D7** 35 10N 25 50 E
Merai, *Papua N. G.* **120 C7** 4 52 S 152 19 E
Meramangye, L., *Australia* **113 E5** 28 25 S 132 13 E
Meramec →, *U.S.A.* **140 F6** 38 23N 90 54W
Meran = Merano, *Italy* **39 B8** 46 40N 11 10 E
Merano, *Italy* **39 B8** 46 40N 11 10 E
Merate, *Italy* **38 C6** 45 42N 9 23 E
Merauke, *Indonesia* **71 F10** 8 29 S 140 24 E
Merbabu, *Indonesia* **71 G14** 7 30 S 110 40 E
Merbein, *Australia* **116 C5** 34 10 S 142 2 E
Merca, *Somali Rep.* **90 G3** 1 48N 44 50 E
Mercadal, *Spain* **33 B11** 39 59N 4 5 E
Mercato Saraceno, *Italy* **39 E9** 43 57N 12 11 E
Merced, *U.S.A.* **144 H6** 37 18N 120 30W
Merced Pk., *U.S.A.* **144 H7** 37 36N 119 24W
Mercedes, *Buenos Aires, Argentina* **158 C4** 34 40 S 59 30W
Mercedes, *Corrientes, Argentina* **158 B4** 29 10 S 58 5W
Mercedes, *San Luis, Argentina* **158 C2** 33 40 S 65 21W
Mercedes, *Uruguay* **158 C4** 33 12 S 58 0W
Merceditas, *Chile* **158 B1** 28 20 S 70 35W
Mercer, *N.Z.* **118 D4** 37 16 S 175 5 E
Mercer, *Mo., U.S.A.* **140 D3** 40 31N 93 32W
Mercer, *Pa., U.S.A.* **136 E4** 41 14N 80 13W
Merchtem, *Belgium* **21 G4** 50 58N 4 14 E
Mercier, *Bolivia* **156 C4** 10 42 S 68 5W
Mercury, *U.S.A.* **145 J11** 36 40N 115 58W
Mercury B., *N.Z.* **118 C4** 36 48 S 175 45 E
Mercury Is., *N.Z.* **118 C4** 36 37 S 175 52 E
Mercy C., *Canada* **127 B13** 65 0N 63 30W
Merdrignac, *France* **22 D4** 48 11N 2 27W
Mere, *Belgium* **21 G3** 50 55N 3 58 E
Meredith, C., *Falk. Is.* **160 D4** 52 15 S 60 40W
Meredith, L., *U.S.A.* **139 H4** 35 30N 101 35W
Meredosia, *U.S.A.* **140 E6** 39 50N 90 34W
Meregh, *Somali Rep.* **108 D3** 3 46N 47 18 E
Merei, *Romania* **46 D7** 45 7N 26 43 E
Merelbeke, *Belgium* **21 G3** 51 0N 3 45 E
Méréville, *France* **23 D9** 48 20N 2 5 E
Merga = Nukheila, *Sudan* **94 D2** 19 1N 26 21 E
Mergenevo, *U.S.S.R.* **54 G2** 49 56N 51 18 E
Mergenevsky, *U.S.S.R.* **53 B14** 49 59N 51 15 E
Mergui Arch. = Myeik Kyunzu, *Burma* **77 G1** 11 30N 97 30 E
Meribah, *Australia* **116 C4** 34 43 S 140 51 E
Mérida, *Mexico* **147 C7** 20 9N 89 40W
Mérida, *Spain* **37 G4** 38 55N 6 25W
Mérida, *Venezuela* **152 B3** 8 24N 71 8W
Mérida □, *Venezuela* **152 B3** 8 30N 71 10W
Mérida, Cord. de, *Venezuela* **152 B3** 9 0N 71 0W
Meriden, *U.S.A.* **137 E12** 41 33N 72 47W
Meridian, *Calif., U.S.A.* **144 F5** 39 9N 121 55W
Meridian, *Idaho, U.S.A.* **142 E5** 43 41N 116 25W
Meridian, *Miss., U.S.A.* **135 J1** 32 20N 88 42W
Meridian, *Tex., U.S.A.* **139 K6** 31 55N 97 37W
Mering, *Germany* **27 G7** 48 15N 11 0 E
Meriruma, *Brazil* **153 C7** 1 15N 54 50W
Merke, *U.S.S.R.* **55 B6** 42 52N 73 11 E
Merkel, *U.S.A.* **139 J5** 32 30N 100 0W
Merksem, *Belgium* **21 F4** 51 16N 4 25 E
Merksplas, *Belgium* **21 F5** 51 22N 4 52 E
Mermaid Reef, *Australia* **112 C2** 17 6 S 119 36 E
Mern, *Denmark* **15 J6** 55 3N 12 3 E
Merowe, *Sudan* **94 D3** 18 29N 31 46 E
Merredin, *Australia* **113 F2** 31 28 S 118 18 E
Merrick, *U.K.* **18 F4** 55 8N 4 30W
Merrickville, *Canada* **137 B9** 44 55N 75 50W
Merrill, *Oreg., U.S.A.* **142 E3** 42 2N 121 37W
Merrill, *Wis., U.S.A.* **138 C10** 45 11N 89 41W
Merrillville, *U.S.A.* **141 C9** 41 29N 87 20W
Merriman, *U.S.A.* **138 D4** 42 55N 101 42W
Merritt, *Canada* **130 C4** 50 10N 120 45W
Merriwa, *Australia* **117 B9** 32 6 S 150 22 E
Merriwagga, *Australia* **117 B6** 33 47 S 145 43 E
Merry I., *Canada* **128 A4** 55 29N 77 31W
Merrygoen, *Australia* **117 A8** 31 51 S 149 12 E
Merryville, *U.S.A.* **139 K8** 30 47N 93 31W
Mersa Fatma, *Ethiopia* **90 E3** 14 57N 40 17 E
Mersch, *Lux.* **21 J8** 49 44N 6 7 E
Merseburg, *Germany* **26 D8** 51 20N 12 0 E
Mersey →, *U.K.* **16 D5** 53 20N 2 56W
Merseyside □, *U.K.* **16 D5** 53 25N 2 55W
Mersin, *Turkey* **88 E6** 36 51N 34 36 E
Mersing, *Malaysia* **77 L4** 2 25N 103 50 E
Merta, *India* **80 F6** 26 39N 74 4 E
Mertert, *Lux.* **21 J8** 49 43N 6 29 E
Merthyr Tydfil, *U.K.* **17 F4** 51 45N 3 23W
Mértola, *Portugal* **37 H3** 37 40N 7 40W
Mertzig, *Lux.* **21 J8** 49 51N 6 1 E
Mertzon, *U.S.A.* **139 K4** 31 17N 100 48W
Méru, *France* **23 C9** 49 13N 2 8 E
Meru, *Kenya* **106 B4** 0 3N 37 40 E
Meru, *Tanzania* **106 C4** 3 15 S 36 46 E
Meru □, *Kenya* **106 B4** 0 3N 37 46 E
Merville, *France* **23 B9** 50 38N 2 38 E
Méry-sur-Seine, *France* **23 D10** 48 31N 3 54 E
Merzifon, *Turkey* **52 F6** 41 53N 35 32 E
Merzig, *Germany* **27 F2** 49 26N 6 37 E
Merzouga, Erg Tin, *Algeria* **99 D7** 24 0N 11 4 E
Mesa, *U.S.A.* **143 K8** 33 20N 111 56W
Mesach Mellet, *Libya* **96 D2** 24 30N 11 30 E
Mesagne, *Italy* **41 B10** 40 34N 17 48 E
Mesanagrós, *Greece* **32 C9** 36 1N 27 49 E
Mesaoría □, *Cyprus* **32 D12** 35 12N 33 14 E
Mesarás, Kólpos, *Greece* **32 D6** 35 6N 24 47 E
Meschede, *Germany* **26 D4** 51 20N 8 17 E
Mesfinto, *Ethiopia* **95 E4** 13 20N 37 22 E
Mesgouez, L., *Canada* **128 B5** 51 20N 75 0W
Meshchovsk, *U.S.S.R.* **50 D9** 54 22N 35 17 E
Meshed = Mashhad, *Iran* **85 B8** 36 20N 59 35 E
Meshoppen, *U.S.A.* **137 E8** 41 36N 76 3W

Mingera Cr. 233

Meshra er Req, *Sudan* **95 F2** 8 25N 29 18 E
Mesick, *U.S.A.* **134 C3** 44 24N 85 42W
Mesilinka →, *Canada* **130 B4** 56 6N 124 30W
Mesilla, *U.S.A.* **143 K10** 32 20N 106 50W
Meslay-du-Maine, *France* **22 E6** 47 58N 0 33W
Mesocco, *Switz.* **29 D8** 46 23N 9 12 E
Mesolóngion, *Greece* **45 F3** 38 21N 21 28 E
Mesopotamia = Al Jazirah, *Iraq* **84 C5** 33 30N 44 0 E
Mesoraca, *Italy* **41 C9** 39 5N 16 47 E
Mésou Volímais, *Greece* **45 G2** 37 53N 20 35 E
Mesquite, *U.S.A.* **143 H6** 36 47N 114 6W
Mess Cr. →, *Canada* **130 B2** 57 55N 131 14W
Messac, *France* **22 E5** 47 49N 1 50W
Messad, *Algeria* **99 B5** 34 8N 3 30 E
Messalo →, *Mozam.* **107 E4** 12 25 S 39 15 E
Méssaména, *Cameroon* **101 E7** 3 48N 12 49 E
Messancy, *Belgium* **21 J7** 49 36N 5 49 E
Messeue, *Greece* **45 G3** 37 12N 21 58 E
Messier, Canal, *Chile* **160 C2** 48 20 S 74 33W
Messina, *Italy* **41 D8** 38 10N 15 32 E
Messina, *S. Africa* **105 C5** 22 20 S 30 5 E
Messina, Str. di, *Italy* **41 D8** 38 5N 15 35 E
Messíni, *Greece* **45 G4** 37 4N 22 1 E
Messínia □, *Greece* **45 G4** 37 10N 22 0 E
Messiniakós, Kólpos, *Greece* **45 H4** 36 45N 22 5 E
Messkirch, *Germany* **27 H5** 47 59N 9 7 E
Messonghi, *Greece* **32 B3** 39 29N 19 56 E
Mesta →, *Bulgaria* **43 F9** 41 30N 24 12 E
Mestà, Ákra, *Greece* **45 F7** 38 16N 25 53 E
Mestanza, *Spain* **37 G6** 38 35N 4 4W
Město Teplá, *Czech.* **30 B5** 49 59N 12 52 E
Mestre, *Italy* **39 C9** 45 30N 12 13 E
Mestre, Espigão, *Brazil* **155 D2** 12 30 S 46 10W
Městys Zelezná Ruda, *Czech.* **30 B6** 49 8N 13 15 E
Meta, *U.S.A.* **140 F4** 38 19N 92 10W
Meta □, *Colombia* **152 C3** 3 30N 73 0W
Meta →, *S. Amer.* **152 B4** 6 12N 67 28W
Metairie, *U.S.A.* **139 L9** 29 59N 90 9W
Metalici, Munţii, *Romania* **46 C3** 46 15N 22 50 E
Metaline Falls, *U.S.A.* **142 B5** 48 52N 117 22W
Metamora, *U.S.A.* **140 D7** 40 47N 89 22W
Metán, *Argentina* **158 B3** 25 30 S 65 0W
Metangula, *Mozam.* **107 E3** 12 40 S 34 50 E
Metauro →, *Italy* **39 E10** 43 50N 13 3 E
Metema, *Ethiopia* **95 E4** 12 56N 36 13 E
Metengobalame, *Mozam.* **107 E3** 14 49 S 34 30 E
Méthana, *Greece* **45 G5** 37 35N 23 23 E
Methóni, *Greece* **45 H3** 36 49N 21 42 E
Methven, *N.Z.* **119 D6** 43 38 S 171 40 E
Methy L., *Canada* **131 B7** 56 28N 109 30W
Metil, *Mozam.* **107 F4** 16 24 S 39 0 E
Metkovets, *Bulgaria* **43 D8** 43 37N 23 10 E
Metković, *Yugoslavia* **42 D2** 43 6N 17 39 E
Metlakatla, *U.S.A.* **130 B2** 55 10N 131 33W
Metlaoui, *Tunisia* **96 B1** 34 24N 8 24 E
Metlika, *Yugoslavia* **39 C12** 45 40N 15 20 E
Metro, *Indonesia* **74 D3** 5 5 S 105 20 E
Metropolis, *U.S.A.* **139 G10** 37 10N 88 47W
Métsovon, *Greece* **44 E3** 39 48N 21 12 E
Mettet, *Belgium* **21 H5** 50 19N 4 41 E
Mettuppalaiyam, *India* **83 J3** 11 18N 76 59 E
Mettur, *India* **83 J3** 11 48N 77 47 E
Metz, *France* **23 C13** 49 8N 6 10 E
Meulaboh, *Indonesia* **70 D1** 4 11N 96 3 E
Meulan, *France* **23 C8** 49 3N 1 55 E
Meung-sur-Loire, *France* **23 E8** 47 50N 1 40 E
Meureudu, *Indonesia* **70 C1** 5 19N 96 10 E
Meurthe →, *France* **23 D13** 48 47N 6 9 E
Meurthe-et-Moselle □, *France* **23 D13** 48 52N 6 0 E
Meuse □, *France* **23 C12** 49 8N 5 25 E
Meuse →, *Europe* **21 G7** 50 45N 5 41 E
Meuselwitz, *Germany* **26 D8** 51 3N 12 18 E
Mexborough, *U.K.* **16 D6** 53 29N 1 18W
Mexia, *U.S.A.* **139 K6** 31 38N 96 32W
Mexiana, I., *Brazil* **154 B2** 0 0 49 30W
Mexicali, *Mexico* **146 A1** 32 40N 115 30W
México, *Mexico* **147 D5** 19 20N 99 10W
Mexico, *Maine, U.S.A.* **137 B14** 44 35N 70 30W
Mexico, *Mo., U.S.A.* **140 E5** 39 10N 91 55W
México □, *Mexico* **146 D5** 19 20N 99 10W
Mexico ■, *Cent. Amer.* **146 C4** 25 0N 105 0W
Mexico, G. of, *Cent. Amer.* **147 C7** 25 0N 90 0W
Meyenburg, *Germany* **26 B8** 53 19N 12 15 E
Meymac, *France* **24 C6** 45 32N 2 10 E
Meymaneh, *Afghan.* **79 B2** 35 53N 64 38 E
Meyrargues, *France* **25 E9** 43 38N 5 32 E
Meyrueis, *France* **24 D7** 44 12N 3 27 E
Meyssac, *France* **24 C5** 45 3N 1 40 E
Mezdra, *Bulgaria* **43 D8** 43 12N 23 42 E
Mèze, *France* **24 E7** 43 27N 3 36 E
Mezen, *U.S.S.R.* **48 A7** 65 50N 44 20 E
Mezen →, *U.S.S.R.* **48 A7** 66 11N 43 59 E
Mézenc, Mt., *France* **25 D8** 44 54N 4 11 E
Mezeş, Munţii, *Romania* **46 B4** 47 5N 23 5 E
Mezha →, *U.S.S.R.* **50 D7** 55 50N 31 45 E
Mezhdurechenskiy, *U.S.S.R.* **54 B9** 59 36N 65 56 E
Mézidon, *France* **22 C6** 49 5N 0 1W
Mézilhac, *France* **25 D8** 44 49N 4 21 E
Mézin, *France* **24 D4** 44 4N 0 16 E
Mezőberény, *Hungary* **31 E14** 46 49N 21 3 E
Mezőfalva, *Hungary* **31 E11** 46 55N 18 49 E
Mezőhegyes, *Hungary* **31 E13** 46 19N 20 49 E
Mezőkövácsháza, *Hungary* **31 E13** 46 25N 20 57 E
Mezőkövesd, *Hungary* **31 D13** 47 49N 20 35 E
Mézos, *France* **24 D2** 44 5N 1 10W
Mezőtúr, *Hungary* **31 E13** 46 58N 20 41 E
Mezquital, *Mexico* **146 C4** 23 29N 104 23W
Mezzolombardo, *Italy* **38 B8** 46 13N 11 5 E
Mgeta, *Tanzania* **107 D4** 8 22 S 36 6 E
Mglin, *U.S.S.R.* **50 E8** 53 2N 32 50 E
Mhlaba Hills, *Zimbabwe* **107 F3** 18 30 S 30 30 E
Mhow, *India* **80 H6** 22 33N 75 50 E
Mi-Shima, *Japan* **62 C3** 34 46N 131 9 E
Miahuatlán, *Mexico* **147 D5** 16 21N 96 36W
Miajadas, *Spain* **37 F5** 39 9N 5 54W
Miallo, *Australia* **114 B4** 16 28 S 145 22 E
Miami, *Ariz., U.S.A.* **143 K8** 33 25N 110 54W
Miami, *Fla., U.S.A.* **135 N5** 25 45N 80 15W
Miami, *Tex., U.S.A.* **139 H4** 35 44N 100 38W
Miami →, *U.S.A.* **134 F3** 39 20N 84 40W
Miami Beach, *U.S.A.* **135 N5** 25 49N 80 6W
Miamisburg, *U.S.A.* **141 E12** 39 40N 84 11W
Mian Xian, *China* **66 H4** 33 10N 106 32 E
Mianchi, *China* **66 G6** 34 48N 111 48 E
Mīāndowāb, *Iran* **84 B5** 37 0N 46 5 E
Miandrivazo, *Madag.* **105 B8** 19 31 S 45 29 E
Mīāneh, *Iran* **84 B5** 37 30N 47 40 E
Mianning, *China* **68 C4** 28 32N 102 9 E
Mianwali, *Pakistan* **79 B3** 32 38N 71 28 E
Mianyang, *Hubei, China* **69 B9** 30 25N 113 25 E
Mianyang, *Sichuan, China* **68 B5** 31 22N 104 47 E
Mianzhu, *China* **68 B5** 31 22N 104 7 E
Miaoli, *Taiwan* **69 E13** 24 37N 120 49 E
Miarinarivo, *Madag.* **105 B8** 18 57 S 46 55 E
Miass, *U.S.S.R.* **54 D7** 54 59N 60 6 E
Miass →, *U.S.S.R.* **54 C9** 56 6N 64 30 E
Miasteczko Kraj, *Poland* **47 B4** 53 7N 17 1 E
Miastko, *Poland* **47 B3** 54 0N 16 58 E
Micăsasa, *Romania* **46 C5** 46 7N 24 7 E
Michael, Mt., *Papua N. G.* **120 D3** 6 27 S 145 22 E
Michalovce, *Czech.* **31 C14** 48 47N 21 58 E
Michelstadt, *Germany* **27 F5** 49 40N 9 0 E
Michigan □, *U.S.A.* **133 B9** 44 40N 85 40W
Michigan, L., *U.S.A.* **134 D2** 44 0N 87 0W
Michigan Center, *U.S.A.* **141 B12** 42 14N 84 20W
Michigan City, *U.S.A.* **141 C10** 41 42N 86 56W
Michikamau L., *Canada* **129 B7** 54 20N 63 10W
Michipicoten, *Canada* **128 C3** 47 55N 84 55W
Michipicoten I., *Canada* **128 C2** 47 40N 85 40W
Michoacan □, *Mexico* **146 D4** 19 0N 102 0W
Michurin, *Bulgaria* **43 E12** 42 9N 27 51 E
Michurinsk, *U.S.S.R.* **51 E12** 52 58N 40 27 E
Miclere, *Australia* **114 C4** 22 34 S 147 32 E
Mico, Pta., *Nic.* **148 D3** 12 0N 83 30W
Micronesia, Federated States of ■, *Pac. Oc.* **122 G7** 9 0N 150 0 E
Mid Glamorgan □, *U.K.* **17 F4** 51 40N 3 25W
Mid-Indian Ridge, *Ind. Oc.* **109 H6** 30 0 S 75 0 E
Midai, P., *Indonesia* **75 B3** 3 0N 107 47 E
Midale, *Canada* **131 D8** 49 25N 103 20W
Middagsfjället, *Sweden* **14 A6** 63 27N 12 19 E
Middelbeers, *Neths.* **21 F6** 51 28N 5 15 E
Middelburg, *Neths.* **21 F3** 51 30N 3 36 E
Middelburg, *C. Prov., S. Africa* **104 E4** 31 30 S 25 0 E
Middelburg, *Trans., S. Africa* **105 D4** 25 49 S 29 28 E
Middelfart, *Denmark* **15 J3** 55 30N 9 43 E
Middelharnis, *Neths.* **20 E4** 51 46N 4 10 E
Middelkerke, *Belgium* **21 F1** 51 11N 2 49 E
Middelrode, *Neths.* **21 E6** 51 41N 5 26 E
Middelwit, *S. Africa* **104 C4** 24 51 S 27 3 E
Middle →, *U.S.A.* **140 C3** 41 26N 93 30W
Middle Alkali L., *U.S.A.* **142 F3** 41 30N 120 3W
Middle Fork Feather →, *U.S.A.* **144 F5** 39 35N 121 25W
Middle I., *Australia* **113 F3** 34 6 S 123 11 E
Middle Loup →, *U.S.A.* **138 E5** 41 17N 98 23W
Middle Raccoon →, *U.S.A.* **140 C3** 41 35N 93 35W
Middleboro, *U.S.A.* **137 E14** 41 56N 70 52W
Middleburg, *N.Y., U.S.A.* **137 D10** 42 36N 74 19W
Middleburg, *Pa., U.S.A.* **136 F7** 40 46N 77 5W
Middlebury, *Ind., U.S.A.* **141 C11** 41 41N 85 42W
Middlebury, *Vt., U.S.A.* **137 B11** 44 2N 73 9W
Middlemarch, *N.Z.* **119 F5** 45 30 S 170 9 E
Middleport, *U.S.A.* **134 F4** 39 0N 82 5W
Middlesboro, *U.S.A.* **133 C10** 36 40N 83 40W
Middlesboro, *U.S.A.* **135 G4** 36 36N 83 43W
Middlesbrough, *U.K.* **16 C6** 54 35N 1 14W
Middlesex, *Belize* **148 C2** 17 2N 88 31W
Middlesex, *U.S.A.* **137 F10** 40 36N 74 30W
Middleton, *Australia* **114 C3** 22 22 S 141 32 E
Middleton, *Canada* **129 D6** 44 57N 65 4W
Middleton, *U.S.A.* **140 A7** 43 6N 89 30W
Middletown, *Calif., U.S.A.* **144 G4** 38 45N 122 37W
Middletown, *Conn., U.S.A.* **137 E12** 41 37N 72 40W
Middletown, *N.Y., U.S.A.* **137 E10** 41 28N 74 28W
Middletown, *Ohio, U.S.A.* **141 E12** 39 29N 84 25W
Middletown, *Pa., U.S.A.* **137 F8** 40 12N 76 44W
Middleville, *U.S.A.* **141 B11** 42 43N 85 28W
Midelt, *Morocco* **98 B4** 32 46N 4 44W
Midhirst, *N.Z.* **118 F3** 39 17 S 174 18 E
Midi, Canal du →, *France* **24 E5** 43 45N 1 21 E
Midi d'Ossau, Pic du, *France* **24 F3** 42 50N 0 26W
Midland, *Canada* **128 D4** 44 45N 79 50W
Midland, *Calif., U.S.A.* **145 M12** 33 52N 114 48W
Midland, *Mich., U.S.A.* **134 D3** 43 37N 84 17W
Midland, *Pa., U.S.A.* **136 F4** 40 39N 80 27W
Midland, *Tex., U.S.A.* **139 K3** 32 0N 102 3W
Midlands □, *Zimbabwe* **107 F2** 19 40 S 29 0 E
Midleton, *Ireland* **19 E3** 51 52N 8 12W
Midlothian, *U.S.A.* **139 J6** 32 30N 97 0W
Midongy, Tangorombohitr' i, *Madag.* **105 C8** 23 30 S 47 0 E
Midongy Atsimo, *Madag.* **105 C8** 23 35 S 47 1 E
Midou →, *France* **24 E3** 43 54N 0 30W
Midouze →, *France* **24 E3** 43 48N 0 51W
Midu, *China* **68 E3** 25 18N 100 30 E
Midway Is., *Pac. Oc.* **122 E10** 28 13N 177 22W
Midway Wells, *U.S.A.* **145 N11** 32 41N 115 7W
Midwest, *U.S.A.* **142 E10** 43 27N 106 19W
Midwolda, *Neths.* **20 B9** 53 12N 6 52 E
Midyat, *Turkey* **89 E9** 37 25N 41 23 E
Midzur, *Bulgaria* **42 D7** 43 24N 22 40 E
Mie □, *Japan* **63 C8** 34 30N 136 10 E
Miechów, *Poland* **47 E7** 50 21N 20 5 E
Miedwie, Jezioro, *Poland* **47 B1** 53 17N 14 54 E
Międzybód, *Poland* **47 D4** 51 25N 17 34 E
Międzychód, *Poland* **47 C2** 52 35N 15 53 E
Międzylesie, *Poland* **47 E3** 50 8N 16 40 E
Międzyrzec Podlaski, *Poland* **47 D9** 51 58N 22 45 E
Międzyrzecz, *Poland* **47 C2** 52 26N 15 35 E
Międzyzdroje, *Poland* **47 B1** 53 56N 14 26 E
Miejska, *Poland* **47 D3** 51 39N 16 58 E
Miélan, *France* **24 E4** 43 27N 0 19 E
Mielec, *Poland* **47 E8** 50 15N 21 25 E
Mienga, *Angola* **103 F3** 17 12 S 19 48 E
Miercurea Ciuc, *Romania* **46 C6** 46 21N 25 48 E
Mieres, *Spain* **36 B5** 43 18N 5 48W
Mierlo, *Neths.* **21 F7** 51 27N 5 37 E
Mieroszów, *Poland* **47 E3** 50 40N 16 11 E
Mieso, *Ethiopia* **95 F5** 9 15N 40 43 E
Mieszkowice, *Poland* **47 C1** 52 47N 14 30 E
Mifflintown, *U.S.A.* **136 F7** 40 34N 77 24W
Mifraz Hefa, *Israel* **91 C4** 32 52N 35 0 E
Migdāl, *Israel* **91 C4** 32 51N 35 30 E
Migennes, *France* **23 E10** 47 58N 3 31 E
Migliarino, *Italy* **39 D8** 44 45N 11 56 E
Miguel Alemán, Presa, *Mexico* **147 D5** 18 15N 96 40W
Miguel Alves, *Brazil* **154 B3** 4 11 S 42 55W
Miguel Calmon, *Brazil* **154 D3** 11 26 S 40 36W
Mihaliççık, *Turkey* **88 D4** 39 53N 31 30 E
Mihara, *Japan* **62 C5** 34 24N 133 5 E
Mihara-Yama, *Japan* **63 C11** 34 43N 139 23 E
Mijares →, *Spain* **34 F4** 39 55N 0 1W
Mijas, *Spain* **37 J6** 36 36N 4 40W
Mikese, *Tanzania* **106 D4** 6 48 S 37 55 E
Mikha-Tskhakaya, *U.S.S.R.* **53 E10** 42 15N 42 7 E
Mikhailovka, *U.S.S.R.* **52 C6** 47 36N 35 16 E
Mikhaylov, *U.S.S.R.* **51 D11** 54 14N 39 0 E
Mikhaylovgrad, *Bulgaria* **43 D8** 43 27N 23 16 E
Mikhaylovka, *Azerbaijan, U.S.S.R.* **53 F13** 41 31N 48 52 E
Mikhaylovka, *R.S.F.S.R., U.S.S.R.* **51 F13** 50 3N 43 5 E
Mikhaylovski, *U.S.S.R.* **54 C6** 56 27N 59 7 E
Mikhnevo, *U.S.S.R.* **51 D10** 55 4N 37 59 E
Miki, *Hyōgo, Japan* **62 C6** 34 48N 134 59 E
Miki, *Kagawa, Japan* **62 C6** 34 12N 134 7 E
Mikínai, *Greece* **45 G4** 37 43N 22 46 E
Mikkeli, *Finland* **13 F19** 61 43N 27 15 E
Mikkeli □, *Finland* **12 E19** 62 0N 27 0 E
Mikkwa →, *Canada* **130 B6** 58 25N 114 46W
Mikniya, *Sudan* **95 D3** 17 0N 33 45 E
Mikołajki, *Poland* **47 B8** 53 49N 21 37 E
Mikołów, *Poland* **31 A11** 50 10N 18 50 E
Míkonos, *Greece* **45 G7** 37 30N 25 25 E
Mikrí Préspa, Límni, *Greece* **44 D3** 40 47N 21 3 E
Mikrón Dhérion, *Greece* **44 C8** 41 19N 26 6 E
Mikstat, *Poland* **47 D4** 51 32N 17 59 E
Mikulov, *Czech.* **31 C9** 48 48N 16 39 E
Mikumi, *Tanzania* **106 D4** 7 26 S 37 0 E
Mikun, *U.S.S.R.* **48 B9** 62 20N 50 0 E
Mikuni, *Japan* **63 A8** 36 13N 136 9 E
Mikuni-Tōge, *Japan* **63 A10** 36 50N 138 50 E
Mikura-Jima, *Japan* **63 D11** 33 52N 139 36 E
Milaca, *U.S.A.* **138 C8** 45 45N 93 40W
Milagro, *Ecuador* **152 D2** 2 11 S 79 36W
Milan = Milano, *Italy* **38 C6** 45 28N 9 10 E
Milan, *Ill., U.S.A.* **140 C6** 41 27N 90 34W
Milan, *Mich., U.S.A.* **141 B13** 42 5N 83 40W
Milan, *Mo., U.S.A.* **140 D3** 40 10N 93 5W
Milan, *Tenn., U.S.A.* **135 H1** 35 55N 88 45W
Milang, *S. Austral., Australia* **115 E2** 32 2 S 139 10 E
Milang, *S. Austral., Australia* **116 C3** 35 24 S 138 58 E
Milange, *Mozam.* **107 F4** 16 3 S 35 45 E
Milano, *Italy* **38 C6** 45 28N 9 10 E
Milâs, *Turkey* **88 E2** 37 20N 27 50 E
Milatos, *Greece* **32 D7** 35 18N 25 34 E
Milazzo, *Italy* **41 D8** 38 13N 15 13 E
Milbank, *U.S.A.* **138 C6** 45 17N 96 38W
Milden, *Canada* **131 C7** 51 29N 107 32W
Mildmay, *Canada* **136 B3** 44 3N 81 7W
Mildura, *Australia* **116 C5** 34 13 S 142 9 E
Mile, *China* **68 E4** 24 28N 103 20 E
Miléai, *Greece* **44 E5** 39 20N 23 9 E
Mileh Tharthār, *Iraq* **84 C4** 34 0N 43 15 E
Miles, *Australia* **115 D5** 26 40 S 150 9 E
Miles, *U.S.A.* **139 K4** 31 39N 100 11W
Miles City, *U.S.A.* **138 B2** 46 24N 105 50W
Milestone, *Canada* **131 D8** 49 59N 104 31W
Mileto, *Italy* **41 D9** 38 37N 16 3 E
Miletto, Mte., *Italy* **41 A7** 41 26N 14 23 E
Miletus, *Turkey* **45 G9** 37 30N 27 18 E
Mileura, *Australia* **113 E2** 26 22 S 117 20 E
Milevsko, *Czech.* **30 B7** 49 27N 14 21 E
Milford, *Calif., U.S.A.* **144 E6** 40 10N 120 22W
Milford, *Conn., U.S.A.* **137 E11** 41 13N 73 4W
Milford, *Del., U.S.A.* **134 F8** 38 52N 75 27W
Milford, *Ill., U.S.A.* **141 D9** 40 40N 87 43W
Milford, *Mass., U.S.A.* **137 D13** 42 8N 71 30W
Milford, *Mich., U.S.A.* **141 B13** 42 35N 83 36W
Milford, *Pa., U.S.A.* **137 E10** 41 20N 74 47W
Milford, *Utah, U.S.A.* **143 G7** 38 20N 113 0W
Milford Haven, *U.K.* **17 F2** 51 43N 5 2W
Milford Sd., *N.Z.* **119 E2** 44 41 S 167 47 E
Milgun, *Australia* **113 D2** 24 56 S 118 18 E
Milh, Bahr al, *Iraq* **84 C4** 32 40N 43 35 E
Miliana, Aïn Salah, *Algeria* **99 C5** 27 20N 2 32 E
Miliana, *Médéa, Algeria* **99 A5** 36 20N 2 15 E
Milicz, *Poland* **47 D4** 51 31N 17 19 E
Miling, *Australia* **113 F2** 30 30 S 116 17 E
Militello in Val di Catánia, *Italy* **41 E7** 37 16N 14 46 E
Milk →, *N. Amer.* **142 B10** 48 5N 106 15W
Milk, Wadi el →, *Sudan* **94 D3** 17 55N 30 20 E
Milk River, *Canada* **130 D6** 49 10N 112 5W
Mill, *Neths.* **21 E7** 51 41N 5 48 E
Mill City, *U.S.A.* **142 D2** 44 45N 122 28W
Mill I., *Antarctica* **7 C8** 66 0 S 101 30 E
Mill Shoals, *U.S.A.* **141 F8** 38 15N 88 21W
Mill Valley, *U.S.A.* **144 H4** 37 54N 122 32W
Millau, *France* **24 D7** 44 8N 3 4 E
Millbridge, *Canada* **136 B7** 44 41N 77 36W
Millbrook, *Canada* **136 B6** 44 10N 78 29W
Mille Lacs, L., *U.S.A.* **138 B8** 46 15N 93 30W
Mille Lacs, L. des, *Canada* **128 C1** 48 45N 90 35W
Milledgeville, *Ga., U.S.A.* **135 J4** 33 7N 83 15W
Milledgeville, *Ill., U.S.A.* **140 C7** 41 58N 89 46W
Millen, *U.S.A.* **135 J5** 32 50N 81 57W
Miller, *U.S.A.* **138 C5** 44 35N 98 59W
Millerovo, *U.S.S.R.* **53 B9** 48 57N 40 28 E
Miller's Flat, *N.Z.* **119 F4** 45 39 S 169 23 E
Millersburg, *Ind., U.S.A.* **141 C11** 41 32N 85 42W
Millersburg, *Ohio, U.S.A.* **136 F3** 40 32N 81 52W
Millersburg, *Pa., U.S.A.* **136 F8** 40 32N 76 58W
Millerton, *N.Z.* **119 B6** 41 39 S 171 54 E
Millerton, *U.S.A.* **137 E11** 41 57N 73 32W
Millerton L., *U.S.A.* **144 J7** 37 0N 119 42W
Millevaches, Plateau de, *France* **24 C6** 45 45N 2 0 E
Millicent, *Australia* **116 D4** 37 34 S 140 21 E
Millingen, *Neths.* **20 E8** 51 52N 6 2 E
Millinocket, *U.S.A.* **129 C6** 45 45N 68 45W
Millmerran, *Australia* **115 D5** 27 53 S 151 16 E
Mills L., *Canada* **130 A5** 61 30N 118 20W
Millsboro, *U.S.A.* **136 G5** 40 0N 80 0W
Milltown Malbay, *Ireland* **19 D2** 52 51N 9 25W
Millville, *U.S.A.* **134 F8** 39 22N 75 0W
Millwood Res., *U.S.A.* **139 J8** 33 45N 94 0W
Milly-la-Forêt, *France* **23 D9** 48 24N 2 28 E
Milna, *Yugoslavia* **39 E13** 43 20N 16 28 E
Milne →, *Australia* **114 C2** 21 10 S 137 33 E
Milne Inlet, *Canada* **127 A12** 72 30N 80 0W
Milnor, *U.S.A.* **138 B6** 46 19N 97 29W
Milo, *Canada* **130 C6** 50 34N 112 53W
Mílos, *Greece* **45 H6** 36 44N 24 25 E
Miloševo, *Yugoslavia* **42 B5** 45 42N 20 20 E
Miłosław, *Poland* **47 C4** 52 12N 17 32 E
Milparinka P.O., *Australia* **115 D3** 29 46 S 141 57 E
Milroy, *U.S.A.* **141 E11** 39 30N 85 28W
Miltenberg, *Germany* **27 F5** 49 41N 9 13 E
Milton, *Canada* **136 C5** 43 31N 79 53W
Milton, *N.Z.* **119 G4** 46 7 S 169 59 E
Milton, *U.K.* **18 D4** 57 18N 4 32W
Milton, *Calif., U.S.A.* **144 G6** 38 3N 120 51W
Milton, *Fla., U.S.A.* **135 K2** 30 38N 87 0W
Milton, *Iowa, U.S.A.* **140 D4** 40 41N 92 10W
Milton, *Pa., U.S.A.* **136 F8** 41 0N 76 53W
Milton, *Wis., U.S.A.* **141 B8** 42 47N 88 56W
Milton-Freewater, *U.S.A.* **142 D4** 45 57N 118 24W
Milton Keynes, *U.K.* **17 E7** 52 3N 0 42W
Miltou, *Chad* **97 F3** 10 14N 17 26 E
Milverton, *Canada* **136 C4** 43 34N 80 55W
Milwaukee, *U.S.A.* **141 A9** 43 9N 87 58W
Milwaukee Deep, *Atl. Oc.* **8 G2** 19 50N 68 0W
Milwaukie, *U.S.A.* **144 E4** 45 27N 122 39W
Mim, *Ghana* **100 D4** 6 57N 2 33W
Mimizan, *France* **24 D2** 44 12N 1 13W
Mimon, *Czech.* **30 A7** 50 38N 14 43 E
Mimongo, *Gabon* **102 C2** 1 11 S 11 36 E
Mimoso, *Brazil* **155 E2** 15 10 S 48 5W
Min Chiang →, *China* **69 E12** 26 0N 119 35 E
Min Jiang →, *China* **68 C5** 28 45N 104 40 E
Min-Kush, *U.S.S.R.* **55 C7** 41 4N 74 28 E
Min Xian, *China* **66 G3** 34 25N 104 5 E
Mina, *U.S.A.* **143 G4** 38 21N 118 9W
Mina Pirquitas, *Argentina* **158 A2** 22 40 S 66 30W
Mīnā Su'ud, *Si. Arabia* **85 D6** 28 45N 48 28 E
Mīnā'al Aḥmadī, *Kuwait* **85 D6** 29 5N 48 10 E
Mīnāb, *Iran* **85 E8** 27 10N 57 1 E
Minago →, *Canada* **131 C9** 54 33N 98 59W
Minakami, *Japan* **63 A10** 36 49N 138 59 E
Minaki, *Canada* **131 D10** 49 59N 94 40W
Minakuchi, *Japan* **63 C8** 34 58N 136 10 E
Minamata, *Japan* **62 E2** 32 10N 130 30 E
Minami-Tori-Shima, *Pac. Oc.* **122 E7** 24 0N 153 45 E
Minas, *Uruguay* **159 C4** 34 20 S 55 10W
Minas, Sierra de las, *Guatemala* **148 C2** 15 9N 89 31W
Minas Basin, *Canada* **129 C7** 45 20N 64 12W
Minas de Rio Tinto, *Spain* **37 H4** 37 42N 6 35W
Minas de San Quintín, *Spain* **37 G6** 38 49N 4 23W
Minas Gerais □, *Brazil* **155 E2** 18 50 S 46 0W
Minas Novas, *Brazil* **155 E3** 17 15 S 42 36W
Minatitlán, *Mexico* **147 D6** 17 58N 94 35W
Minbu, *Burma* **78 E5** 20 10N 94 52 E
Minbya, *Burma* **78 E4** 20 22N 93 16 E
Mincio →, *Italy* **38 C7** 45 4N 10 59 E
Mindanao, *Phil.* **71 C7** 8 0N 125 0 E
Mindanao Sea = Bohol Sea, *Phil.* **71 C6** 9 0N 124 0 E
Mindanao Trench, *Pac. Oc.* **71 B7** 12 0N 126 6 E
Mindel →, *Germany* **27 G6** 48 31N 10 23 E
Mindelheim, *Germany* **27 G6** 48 4N 10 30 E
Minden, *Canada* **136 B6** 44 55N 78 43W
Minden, *Germany* **26 C4** 52 18N 8 45 E
Minden, *La., U.S.A.* **139 J8** 32 40N 93 20W
Minden, *Nev., U.S.A.* **144 G7** 38 57N 119 48W
Mindiptana, *Indonesia* **71 F10** 5 55 S 140 22 E
Mindon, *Burma* **78 F5** 19 21N 94 44 E
Mindoro, *Phil.* **71 B6** 13 0N 121 0 E
Mindoro Str., *Phil.* **71 B6** 12 30N 120 30 E
Mindouli, *Congo* **103 C2** 4 12 S 14 28 E
Mine, *Japan* **62 C3** 34 12N 131 7 E
Minehead, *U.K.* **17 F4** 51 12N 3 29W
Mineiros, *Brazil* **157 D7** 17 34 S 52 34W
Mineola, *U.S.A.* **139 J7** 32 40N 95 30W
Mineral King, *U.S.A.* **144 J8** 36 27N 118 36W
Mineral Point, *U.S.A.* **140 B6** 42 52N 90 11W
Mineral Wells, *U.S.A.* **139 J5** 32 50N 98 5W
Mineralnyye Vody, *U.S.S.R.* **53 D10** 44 2N 43 8 E
Minersville, *Pa., U.S.A.* **137 F8** 40 11N 76 17W
Minersville, *Utah, U.S.A.* **143 G7** 38 14N 112 58W
Minerva, *U.S.A.* **136 F3** 40 43N 81 8W
Minervino Murge, *Italy* **41 A9** 41 6N 16 4 E
Minetto, *U.S.A.* **137 C8** 43 24N 76 28W
Mingan, *Canada* **129 B7** 50 20N 64 0W
Mingary, *Australia* **116 B4** 32 8 S 140 45 E
Mingechaur, *U.S.S.R.* **53 F12** 40 45N 47 0 E
Mingechaurskoye Vdkhr., *U.S.S.R.* **53 F12** 40 56N 47 20 E
Mingela, *Australia* **114 B4** 19 52 S 146 38 E
Mingenew, *Australia* **113 E2** 29 12 S 115 21 E
Mingera Cr. →, *Australia* **114 C2** 20 38 S 137 45 E

234 Minggang

Minggang, China 69 A10 32 24N 114 3 E
Mingin, Burma 78 D5 22 50N 94 30 E
Minglanilla, Spain 34 F3 39 34N 1 38W
Minglun, China 68 E7 25 10N 108 21 E
Mingorria, Spain 36 E6 40 45N 4 40W
Mingt'iehkaitafan = Mintaka Pass, Pakistan 81 A6 37 0N 74 58 E
Mingxi, China 69 D11 26 18N 117 12 E
Mingyuegue, China 67 C15 43 2N 128 50 E
Minhou, China 69 E12 26 0N 119 15 E
Minićevo, Yugoslavia 42 D7 43 42N 22 18 E
Minidoka, U.S.A. 142 E7 42 47N 113 34W
Minier, U.S.A. 140 D7 40 26N 89 19W
Minigwal, L., Australia 113 E3 29 31 S 123 14 E
Minilya, Australia 113 D1 23 55 S 114 0 E
Minilya ~▸, Australia 113 D1 23 45 S 114 0 E
Mininera, Australia 116 D5 37 37 S 142 58 E
Minipi, L., Canada 129 B7 52 25N 60 45W
Minj, Papua N. G. 120 C3 5 54 S 144 37 E
Mink L., Canada 130 A5 61 54N 117 40W
Minlaton, Australia 116 C2 34 45 S 137 35 E
Minna, Nigeria 101 D6 9 37N 6 30 E
Minneapolis, Kans., U.S.A. 138 F6 39 11N 97 40W
Minneapolis, Minn., U.S.A. 138 C8 44 58N 93 20W
Minnedosa, Canada 131 C9 50 14N 99 50W
Minnesota □, U.S.A. 138 B8 46 40N 94 0W
Minnesund, Norway 14 D5 60 23N 11 14 E
Minnie Creek, Australia 113 D2 24 3 S 115 42 E
Minnipa, Australia 115 E2 32 51 S 135 9 E
Minnitaki L., Canada 128 C1 49 57N 92 10W
Mino, Japan 63 B8 35 32N 136 55 E
Miño ~▸, Spain 36 D2 41 52N 8 40W
Mino-Kamo, Japan 63 B9 35 23N 137 2 E
Mino-Mikawa-Kōgen, Japan 63 B9 35 10N 137 23 E
Minoa, Greece 45 J7 35 6N 25 45 E
Minobu, Japan 63 B10 35 22N 138 26 E
Minobu-Sanchi, Japan 63 B10 35 14N 138 20 E
Minonk, U.S.A. 140 D7 40 54N 89 2W
Minooka, U.S.A. 141 C8 41 27N 88 16W
Minorca = Menorca, Spain 33 B11 40 0N 4 0 E
Minore, Australia 117 B8 32 14 S 148 27 E
Minot, U.S.A. 138 A4 48 10N 101 15W
Minqin, China 66 E2 38 38N 103 20 E
Minqing, China 69 D12 26 15N 118 50 E
Minsen, Germany 26 B3 53 43N 7 58 E
Minsk, U.S.S.R. 50 E5 53 52N 27 30 E
Mińsk Mazowiecki, Poland 47 C8 52 10N 21 33 E
Minster, U.S.A. 141 D12 40 24N 84 23W
Mintaka Pass, Pakistan 81 A6 37 0N 74 58 E
Minthami, Burma 78 D5 23 55N 94 16 E
Minto, U.S.A. 126 B5 64 55N 149 20W
Minton, Canada 131 D8 49 10N 104 35W
Mintoum, Gabon 102 B2 0 27N 12 16 E
Minturn, U.S.A. 142 G10 39 35N 106 25W
Minturno, Italy 40 A6 41 15N 13 43 E
Minûf, Egypt 94 H7 30 26N 30 52 E
Minusinsk, U.S.S.R. 57 D10 53 50N 91 20 E
Minutang, India 78 A6 28 15N 96 30 E
Minvoul, Gabon 102 B2 2 9N 12 8 E
Minwakh, Yemen 87 C5 16 48N 48 6 E
Minya el Qamh, Egypt 94 H7 30 31N 31 21 E
Minyar, U.S.S.R. 54 D5 55 4N 57 33 E
Minyip, Australia 116 D5 36 29 S 142 36 E
Mionica, Yugoslavia 42 C5 44 14N 20 6 E
Mir, Niger 97 F2 14 5N 11 59 E
Mir-Bashir, U.S.S.R. 53 F12 40 20N 46 58 E
Mīr Kūh, Iran 85 E8 26 22N 58 55 E
Mīr Shahdād, Iran 85 E8 26 15N 58 29 E
Mira, Italy 39 C9 45 26N 12 9 E
Mira, Portugal 36 E2 40 26N 8 44W
Mira ~▸, Colombia 152 C2 1 36N 79 1W
Mira ~▸, Portugal 37 H2 37 43N 8 47W
Mira por vos Cay, Bahamas 149 B5 22 9N 74 30W
Mīrābād, Afghan. 79 C1 30 25N 61 50 E
Mirabella Eclano, Italy 41 A7 41 3N 14 59 E
Miracema do Norte, Brazil 154 C2 9 33 S 48 24W
Mirador, Brazil 154 C3 6 22 S 44 22W
Miraflores, Colombia 152 C3 1 25N 72 13W
Miraj, India 82 F2 16 50N 74 45 E
Miram Shah, Pakistan 79 B3 33 0N 70 2 E
Miramar, Argentina 158 D4 38 15 S 57 50W
Miramar, Mozam. 105 C6 23 50 S 35 35 E
Miramas, France 25 E8 43 33N 4 59 E
Mirambeau, France 24 C3 45 23N 0 35W
Miramichi B., Canada 129 C7 47 15N 65 0W
Miramont-de-Guyenne, France 24 D4 44 37N 0 21 E
Miranda, Brazil 157 E6 20 10 S 56 15W
Miranda □, Venezuela 152 A4 10 15N 66 25W
Miranda ~▸, Brazil 157 D6 19 25 S 57 20W
Miranda de Ebro, Spain 34 C2 42 41N 2 57W
Miranda do Corvo, Spain 36 E2 40 6N 8 20W
Miranda do Douro, Portugal 36 D4 41 30N 6 16W
Mirande, France 24 E4 43 31N 0 25 E
Mirandela, Portugal 36 D3 41 32N 7 10W
Mirando City, U.S.A. 139 M5 27 28N 98 59W
Mirandola, Italy 38 D8 44 53N 11 2 E
Mirandópolis, Brazil 159 A5 21 9 S 51 6W
Mirango, Malawi 107 E3 13 32 S 34 58 E
Mirani, Australia 114 C4 21 9 S 148 53 E
Mirano, Italy 39 C9 45 29N 12 6 E
Mirassol, Brazil 159 A6 20 46 S 49 28W
Mirbāţ, Oman 87 C6 17 0N 54 45 E
Mirboo North, Australia 117 E7 38 24 S 146 10 E
Mirear, Egypt 94 C4 23 15N 35 41 E
Mirebeau, Côte-d'Or, France 23 E12 47 25N 5 20 E
Mirebeau, Vienne, France 22 F7 46 49N 0 10 E
Mirecourt, France 23 D13 48 20N 6 10 E
Mirgorod, U.S.S.R. 50 G8 49 58N 33 37 E
Miri, Malaysia 70 D4 4 23N 113 59 E
Miriam Vale, Australia 114 C5 24 20 S 151 33 E
Mirim, L., S. Amer. 159 C5 32 45 S 52 50W
Mirimire, Venezuela 152 A4 11 10N 68 43W
Miriti, Brazil 157 B6 6 15 S 59 0W
Mirnyy, U.S.S.R. 57 C12 62 33N 113 53 E
Miroč, Yugoslavia 42 C7 44 32N 22 16 E
Mirond L., Canada 131 B8 55 6N 102 47W
Mirosławiec, Poland 47 B3 53 20N 16 5 E
Mirpur, Pakistan 79 B4 33 32N 73 56 E
Mirpur Bibiwari, Pakistan 80 E2 28 33N 67 44 E
Mirpur Khas, Pakistan 79 D3 25 30N 69 0 E
Mirpur Sakro, Pakistan 80 G2 24 33N 67 41 E
Mirria, Niger 97 F1 13 43N 9 7 E
Mirror, Canada 130 C6 52 30N 113 7W
Mîrşani, Romania 46 E4 44 1N 23 59 E
Mirsk, Poland 47 E2 50 58N 15 23 E
Miryang, S. Korea 67 G15 35 31N 128 44 E
Mirzaani, U.S.S.R. 53 F12 41 24N 46 5 E
Mirzapur, India 81 G10 25 10N 82 34 E
Mirzapur-cum-Vindhyachal = Mirzapur, India 81 G10 25 10N 82 34 E
Misantla, Mexico 147 D5 19 56N 96 50W
Misawa, Japan 60 D10 40 41N 141 24 E
Miscou I., Canada 129 C7 47 57N 64 31W
Mish'āb, Ra'as al, Si. Arabia 85 D6 28 15N 48 43 E
Mishagua ~▸, Peru 156 C3 11 12 S 72 58W
Mishan, China 65 B8 45 37N 131 48 E
Mishawaka, U.S.A. 141 C10 41 40N 86 8W
Mishbih, Gebel, Egypt 94 C3 22 38N 34 44 E
Mishima, Japan 63 B10 35 10N 138 52 E
Mishkino, U.S.S.R. 54 D8 55 20N 63 55 E
Mishmi Hills, India 78 A6 29 0N 96 0 E
Misilmeri, Italy 40 D6 38 2N 13 25 E
Misima I., Papua N. G. 120 F7 10 40 S 152 45 E
Misión, Mexico 145 N10 32 6N 116 53W
Misión Fagnano, Argentina 160 D3 54 32 S 67 17W
Misiones □, Argentina 159 B5 27 0 S 55 0W
Misiones □, Paraguay 158 B4 27 0 S 56 0W
Miskah, Si. Arabia 84 E4 24 49N 42 56 E
Miskitos, Cayos, Nic. 148 D3 14 26N 82 50W
Miskolc, Hungary 31 C13 48 7N 20 50 E
Misoke, Zaïre 106 C2 0 42 S 28 2 E
Misool, Indonesia 71 E8 1 52 S 130 10 E
Misrātah, Libya 96 B3 32 24N 15 3 E
Misrātah □, Libya 96 C3 29 0N 16 0 E
Missanabie, Canada 128 C3 48 20N 84 6W
Missão Velha, Brazil 154 C4 7 15 S 39 10W
Missinaibi ~▸, Canada 128 B3 50 43N 81 29W
Missinaibi L., Canada 128 C3 48 23N 83 40W
Mission, S. Dak., U.S.A. 138 D4 43 21N 100 36W
Mission, Tex., U.S.A. 139 M5 26 15N 98 20W
Mission City, Canada 130 D4 49 10N 122 15W
Mission Viejo, U.S.A. 145 M9 33 41N 117 46W
Missisa L., Canada 128 B2 52 20N 85 7W
Mississagi ~▸, Canada 128 C3 46 15N 83 9W
Mississinewa Res., U.S.A. 141 D10 40 46N 86 3W
Mississippi □, U.S.A. 133 D9 33 0N 90 0W
Mississippi ~▸, U.S.A. 139 L10 29 0N 89 15W
Mississippi, Delta of the, U.S.A. 139 L9 29 15N 90 30W
Mississippi L., Canada 137 A8 45 5N 76 10W
Mississippi Sd., U.S.A. 139 K10 30 25N 89 0W
Missoula, U.S.A. 142 C7 46 52N 114 0W
Missour, Morocco 98 B4 33 3N 4 0W
Missouri □, U.S.A. 138 F8 38 25N 92 30W
Missouri ~▸, U.S.A. 138 F9 38 50N 90 8W
Missouri Valley, U.S.A. 138 E7 41 33N 95 53W
Mist, U.S.A. 144 E3 45 59N 123 15W
Mistake B., Canada 131 A10 62 8N 93 0W
Mistassini ~▸, Canada 129 C5 48 42N 72 20W
Mistassini L., Canada 128 B5 51 0N 73 30W
Mistastin L., Canada 129 A7 55 57N 63 20W
Mistatim, Canada 131 C8 52 52N 103 22W
Mistelbach, Austria 31 C9 48 34N 16 34 E
Misterbianco, Italy 41 E8 37 32N 15 2 E
Mistretta, Italy 41 E7 37 56N 14 20 E
Misty L., Canada 131 B8 58 53N 101 40W
Misugi, Japan 63 C8 34 31N 136 16 E
Misumi, Japan 62 E2 32 37N 130 27 E
Mît Ghamr, Egypt 94 H7 30 42N 31 12 E
Mitaka, Japan 63 B11 35 40N 139 33 E
Mitan, U.S.S.R. 55 C3 40 5N 66 35 E
Mitatib, Sudan 95 D4 15 59N 36 12 E
Mitchell, Australia 115 D4 26 29 S 147 58 E
Mitchell, Canada 136 C3 43 28N 81 12W
Mitchell, Ind., U.S.A. 141 F10 38 42N 86 25W
Mitchell, Nebr., U.S.A. 138 E3 41 58N 103 45W
Mitchell, Oreg., U.S.A. 142 D3 44 31N 120 8W
Mitchell, S. Dak., U.S.A. 138 D6 43 40N 98 0W
Mitchell ~▸, Australia 114 B3 15 12 S 141 35 E
Mitchell, Mt., U.S.A. 135 H4 35 40N 82 20W
Mitchell Ras., Australia 114 A2 12 49 S 135 36 E
Mitchelstown, Ireland 19 D3 52 16N 8 18W
Mitha Tiwana, Pakistan 80 C5 32 13N 72 6 E
Míthimna, Greece 44 E8 39 20N 26 12 E
Mitiamo, Australia 116 D6 36 12 S 144 15 E
Mitilíni, Greece 45 E8 39 6N 26 35 E
Mitilinoí, Greece 45 G8 37 42N 26 56 E
Mito, Japan 63 A12 36 20N 140 30 E
Mitre, Mt., N.Z. 118 G4 40 50 S 175 30 E
Mitsinjo, Madag. 105 B8 16 1 S 45 52 E
Mitsiwa, Ethiopia 95 D4 15 35N 39 25 E
Mitsiwa Channel, Ethiopia 95 D5 15 30N 40 0 E
Mitsukaidō, Japan 63 A11 36 1N 139 59 E
Mittagong, Australia 117 C9 34 28 S 150 29 E
Mittelland, Switz. 28 C4 46 50N 7 23 E
Mittelland Kanal, Germany 26 C3 52 23N 7 45 E
Mittenwalde, Germany 26 C9 52 16N 13 33 E
Mitterteich, Germany 27 F8 49 57N 12 15 E
Mittweida, Germany 26 E9 50 59N 13 0 E
Mitú, Colombia 152 C3 1 8N 70 3W
Mituas, Colombia 152 C4 3 52N 68 49W
Mitumba, Tanzania 106 D3 7 8 S 31 2 E
Mitumba, Chaîne des, Zaïre 106 D2 7 0 S 27 30 E
Mitwaba, Zaïre 107 D2 8 2 S 27 17 E
Mityana, Uganda 106 B3 0 23N 32 2 E
Mitzic, Gabon 102 B2 0 45N 11 40 E
Miura, Japan 63 B11 35 12N 139 40 E
Mixteco ~▸, Mexico 147 D5 18 11N 98 30W
Miyagi □, Japan 60 E10 38 15N 140 45 E
Miyâh, W. el ~▸, Egypt 94 C3 25 0N 33 23 E
Miyah, W. el ~▸, Syria 84 C3 34 44N 39 57 E
Miyake-Jima, Japan 63 C11 34 5N 139 30 E
Miyako, Japan 60 E10 39 40N 141 59 E
Miyako-Jima, Japan 61 M2 24 45N 125 20 E
Miyako-Rettō, Japan 61 M2 24 24N 125 0 E
Miyakonojō, Japan 62 F3 31 40N 131 5 E
Miyanojō, Japan 62 F2 31 54N 130 27 E
Miyanoura-Dake, Japan 61 J5 30 20N 130 31 E
Miyata, Japan 62 D2 33 49N 130 42 E
Miyazaki, Japan 62 F3 31 56N 131 30 E
Miyazaki □, Japan 62 E3 32 30N 131 30 E
Miyazu, Japan 63 B7 35 35N 135 10 E
Miyet, Bahr el = Dead Sea, Asia 86 A1 31 30N 35 30 E
Miyi, China 68 D4 26 47N 102 9 E
Miyoshi, Japan 62 C4 34 48N 132 51 E
Miyun, China 66 D9 40 28N 116 50 E
Miyun Shuiku, China 67 D9 40 30N 117 0 E
Mizamis = Ozamis, Phil. 71 C6 8 15N 123 50 E
Mizdah, Libya 96 B2 31 30N 13 0 E
Mizen Hd., Ireland 19 E2 51 27N 9 50W
Mizhi, China 66 F6 37 47N 110 12 E
Mizil, Romania 46 E7 44 59N 26 29 E
Mizoram □, India 78 D4 23 30N 92 40 E
Mizpe Ramon, Israel 91 E3 30 34N 34 49 E
Mizuho, Japan 63 B7 35 6N 135 17 E
Mizunami, Japan 63 B9 35 22N 137 15 E
Mizusawa, Japan 60 E10 39 8N 141 8 E
Mjöbäck, Sweden 15 G6 57 28N 12 53 E
Mjölby, Sweden 15 F9 58 20N 15 10 E
Mjörn, Sweden 15 G6 57 55N 12 25 E
Mjøsa, Norway 14 D5 60 48N 11 0 E
Mkata, Tanzania 106 D4 5 45 S 38 20 E
Mkokotoni, Tanzania 106 D4 5 55 S 39 15 E
Mkomazi, Tanzania 106 C4 4 40 S 38 7 E
Mkomazi ~▸, S. Africa 105 E5 30 12 S 30 50 E
Mkulwe, Tanzania 107 D3 8 37 S 32 20 E
Mkumbi, Ras, Tanzania 106 D4 7 38 S 39 55 E
Mkushi, Zambia 107 E2 14 25 S 29 15 E
Mkushi River, Zambia 107 E2 13 32 S 29 45 E
Mkuze, S. Africa 105 D5 27 10 S 32 0 E
Mkuze ~▸, S. Africa 105 D5 27 45 S 32 30 E
Mladá Boleslav, Czech. 30 A7 50 27N 14 53 E
Mladenovac, Yugoslavia 42 C5 44 28N 20 44 E
Mlala Hills, Tanzania 106 D3 6 50 S 31 40 E
Mlange, Malawi 107 F4 16 2 S 35 33 E
Mlava ~▸, Yugoslavia 42 C6 44 45N 21 13 E
Mława, Poland 47 B7 53 9N 20 25 E
Mlinište, Yugoslavia 39 D13 44 15N 16 50 E
Mljet, Yugoslavia 42 E2 42 43N 17 30 E
Mljetski Kanal, Yugoslavia 42 E2 42 48N 17 35 E
Młynary, Poland 47 A6 54 12N 19 46 E
Mmabatho, S. Africa 104 D4 25 49 S 25 30 E
Mme, Cameroon 101 D7 6 18N 10 14 E
Mo i Rana, Norway 12 C13 66 15N 14 7 E
Moa, Indonesia 71 F7 8 0 S 128 0 E
Moa ~▸, S. Leone 100 D2 6 59N 11 36W
Moab, U.S.A. 143 G9 38 40N 109 35W
Moabi, Gabon 102 C2 2 24 S 10 59 E
Moaco ~▸, Brazil 156 B4 7 41 S 68 18W
Moala, Fiji 121 B2 18 36 S 179 53 E
Moalie Park, Australia 115 D3 29 42 S 143 3 E
Moaña, Spain 36 C2 42 18N 8 43W
Moba, Zaïre 106 D2 7 0 S 29 48 E
Mobara, Japan 63 B12 35 25N 140 18 E
Mobārakābād, Iran 85 D7 28 24N 53 20 E
Mobārakīyeh, Iran 85 C6 35 5N 51 47 E
Mobaye, C.A.R. 102 B4 4 25N 21 5 E
Mobayi, Zaïre 102 B4 4 15N 21 8 E
Moberly, U.S.A. 140 E4 39 25N 92 25W
Moberly ~▸, Canada 130 B4 56 12N 120 55W
Mobile, U.S.A. 135 K1 30 41N 88 3W
Mobile B., U.S.A. 135 K2 30 30N 88 0W
Mobridge, U.S.A. 138 C4 45 31N 100 28W
Mobutu Sese Seko, L., Africa 106 B3 1 30N 31 0 E
Moc Chau, Vietnam 76 B5 20 50N 104 38 E
Moc Hoa, Vietnam 77 G5 10 46N 105 56 E
Mocabe Kasari, Zaïre 103 D3 7 12 S 15 0 E
Mocabe Kasari, Zaïre 107 D2 9 58 S 26 12 E
Mocajuba, Brazil 154 B2 2 35 S 49 30W
Moçambique, Mozam. 107 F5 15 3 S 40 42 E
Moçâmedes = Namibe, Angola 103 F2 15 7 S 12 11 E
Mocapra ~▸, Venezuela 152 B4 7 56N 66 46W
Mocha, I., Chile 160 A2 38 22 S 73 56W
Mochudi, Botswana 104 C4 24 27 S 26 7 E
Mocimboa da Praia, Mozam. 107 E5 11 25 S 40 20 E
Mociu, Romania 46 C5 46 46N 24 3 E
Moclips, U.S.A. 144 C2 47 14N 124 10W
Mocoa, Colombia 152 C2 1 7N 76 35W
Mococa, Brazil 159 A6 21 28 S 47 0W
Mocorito, Mexico 146 B3 25 30N 107 53W
Moctezuma, Mexico 146 B3 29 50N 109 0W
Moctezuma ~▸, Mexico 147 C5 21 59N 98 34W
Mocuba, Mozam. 107 F4 16 54 S 36 57 E
Mocúzari, Presa, Mexico 146 B3 27 10N 109 10W
Moda, Burma 78 C6 24 22N 96 29 E
Modane, France 25 C10 45 12N 6 40 E
Modasa, India 80 H5 23 30N 73 21 E
Modave, Belgium 21 H6 50 27N 5 18 E
Modder ~▸, S. Africa 104 D3 29 2 S 24 37 E
Modderrivier, S. Africa 104 D3 29 2 S 24 38 E
Módena, Italy 38 D7 44 39N 10 55 E
Modena, U.S.A. 143 H7 37 55N 113 56W
Modesto, U.S.A. 144 H6 37 43N 121 0W
Módica, Italy 41 F7 36 52N 14 45 E
Modigliana, Italy 39 D8 44 9N 11 48 E
Modjamboli, Zaïre 102 B4 2 28N 22 6 E
Modlin, Poland 47 C7 52 24N 20 41 E
Mödling, Austria 31 C9 48 5N 16 17 E
Modo, Sudan 95 F3 5 31N 30 33 E
Modra, Czech. 31 C10 48 19N 17 20 E
Modriča, Yugoslavia 42 C3 44 57N 18 17 E
Moe, Australia 117 E7 38 12 S 146 19 E
Moebase, Mozam. 107 F4 17 3 S 38 41 E
Moëlan-sur-Mer, France 22 E3 47 49N 3 38W
Moengo, Surinam 153 B7 5 45N 54 20W
Moergestel, Neths. 21 E6 51 33N 5 11 E
Moers, Germany 21 F9 51 27N 6 38 E
Moësa ~▸, Switz. 29 D8 46 12N 9 10 E
Moffat, U.K. 18 F5 55 20N 3 27W
Moga, India 80 D6 30 48N 75 8 E
Mogadishu = Muqdisho, Somali Rep. 90 G4 2 2N 45 25 E
Mogador = Essaouira, Morocco 98 B3 31 32N 9 42W
Mogadouro, Portugal 36 D4 41 22N 6 47W
Mogalakwena ~▸, S. Africa 105 C4 22 38 S 28 40 E
Mogami ~▸, Japan 60 E10 38 45N 140 0 E
Mogán, Canary Is. 33 G4 27 53N 15 43W
Mogaung, Burma 78 C6 25 20N 97 0 E
Møgeltønder, Denmark 15 K2 54 57N 8 48 E
Mogente, Spain 35 G4 38 52N 0 45W
Mogho, Ethiopia 95 G5 4 54N 40 16 E
Mogi das Cruzes, Brazil 159 A6 23 31 S 46 11W
Mogi-Guaçu ~▸, Brazil 159 A6 20 53 S 48 10W
Mogi-Mirim, Brazil 159 A6 22 29 S 47 0W
Mogielnica, Poland 47 D7 51 42N 20 41 E
Mogilev, U.S.S.R. 50 E7 53 55N 30 18 E
Mogilev-Podolskiy, U.S.S.R. 52 B2 48 20N 27 40 E
Mogilno, Poland 47 C4 52 39N 17 55 E
Mogincual, Mozam. 107 F5 15 35 S 40 25 E
Mogliano Véneto, Italy 39 C9 45 33N 12 15 E
Mogocha, U.S.S.R. 57 D12 53 40N 119 50 E
Mogoi, Indonesia 71 E8 1 55 S 133 10 E
Mogok, Burma 78 D6 23 0N 96 40 E
Mogriguy, Australia 117 B8 32 3 S 148 40 E
Moguer, Spain 37 H4 37 15N 6 52W
Mogumber, Australia 113 F2 31 2 S 116 3 E
Mohács, Hungary 31 F11 45 58N 18 41 E
Mohaka ~▸, N.Z. 118 F6 39 7 S 177 12 E
Mohales Hoek, Lesotho 104 E4 30 7 S 27 26 E
Mohall, U.S.A. 138 A4 48 46N 101 30W
Moḩammadābād, Iran 85 B8 37 52N 59 5 E
Mohammadia, Algeria 99 A5 35 33N 0 3 E
Mohammedia, Morocco 98 B3 33 44N 7 21W
Mohave, L., U.S.A. 145 K12 35 25N 114 36W
Mohawk ~▸, U.S.A. 137 D11 42 47N 73 42W
Möhne ~▸, Germany 26 D3 51 29N 7 57 E
Mohnyin, Burma 78 C6 24 47N 96 22 E
Moholm, Sweden 15 F8 58 37N 14 5 E
Mohoro, Tanzania 106 D4 8 6 S 39 8 E
Moia, Sudan 95 F2 5 3N 28 2 E
Moidart, L., U.K. 18 E3 56 47N 5 40W
Moinabad, India 82 F3 17 44N 77 16 E
Moindou, N. Cal. 121 U19 21 42 S 165 41 E
Moineşti, Romania 46 C7 46 28N 26 31 E
Mointy, U.S.S.R. 56 E8 47 10N 73 18 E
Moirans, France 25 C9 45 20N 5 33 E
Moirans-en-Montagne, France 25 B9 46 26N 5 43 E
Moíres, Greece 32 D6 35 4N 24 56 E
Moisakula, U.S.S.R. 50 B4 58 3N 25 12 E
Moisie, Canada 129 B6 50 12N 66 1W
Moisie ~▸, Canada 129 B6 50 14N 66 5W
Moissac, France 24 D5 44 7N 1 5 E
Moïssala, Chad 97 G3 8 21N 17 46 E
Moita, Portugal 37 G2 38 38N 8 58W
Mojácar, Spain 35 H3 37 6N 1 55W
Mojados, Spain 36 D6 41 26N 4 40W
Mojave, U.S.A. 145 K8 35 8N 118 8W
Mojave Desert, U.S.A. 145 L10 35 0N 116 30W
Mojiang, China 68 F3 23 37N 101 35 E
Mojo, Bolivia 158 A2 21 48 S 65 33W
Mojo, Ethiopia 95 F4 8 35N 39 5 E
Mojokerto, Indonesia 71 G15 7 28 S 112 26 E
Mojos, Llanos de, Bolivia 157 D5 15 10 S 65 0W
Moju ~▸, Brazil 154 B2 1 40 S 48 25W
Mokai, N.Z. 118 E4 38 32 S 175 56 E
Mokambo, Zaïre 107 E2 12 25 S 28 20 E
Mokameh, India 81 G11 25 24N 85 55 E
Mokane, U.S.A. 140 F5 38 41N 91 53W
Mokau, N.Z. 118 E3 38 42 S 174 39 E
Mokau ~▸, N.Z. 118 E3 38 35 S 174 35 E
Mokelumne ~▸, U.S.A. 144 G5 38 23N 121 25W
Mokelumne Hill, U.S.A. 144 G6 38 18N 120 43W
Mokhós, Greece 32 D7 35 16N 25 27 E
Mokhotlong, Lesotho 105 D4 29 22 S 29 2 E
Mokihinui ~▸, N.Z. 119 B6 41 33 S 171 58 E
Moknine, Tunisia 96 A2 35 35N 10 58 E
Mokpalin, Burma 78 G6 17 26N 96 53 E
Mokra Gora, Yugoslavia 42 E5 42 50N 20 30 E
Mokronog, Yugoslavia 39 C12 45 57N 15 9 E
Moksha ~▸, U.S.S.R. 51 D12 54 45N 41 53 E
Mokshan, U.S.S.R. 51 E14 53 25N 44 35 E
Mol, Belgium 21 F6 51 11N 5 5 E
Mola, C. de la, Spain 34 F9 39 40N 4 20 E
Mola di Bari, Italy 41 A10 41 3N 17 5 E
Moláoi, Greece 45 H4 36 49N 22 56 E
Molat, Yugoslavia 39 D11 44 15N 14 50 E
Molchanovo, U.S.S.R. 56 D9 57 40N 83 50 E
Mold, U.K. 16 D4 53 10N 3 10W
Moldava nad Bodvou, Czech. 31 C14 48 38N 21 0 E
Moldavia = Moldova, Romania 46 C8 46 30N 27 0 E
Moldavian S.S.R. □, U.S.S.R. 52 C3 47 0N 28 0 E
Molde, Norway 12 E9 62 45N 7 9 E
Moldotau, Khrebet, U.S.S.R. 55 C7 41 35N 75 0 E
Moldova, Romania 46 C8 46 30N 27 0 E
Moldova Nouă, Romania 46 E2 44 45N 21 41 E
Moldoveanu, Romania 46 D5 45 36N 24 45 E
Molepolole, Botswana 104 C4 24 28 S 25 28 E
Moléson, Switz. 28 C4 46 33N 7 1 E
Molesworth, N.Z. 119 C8 42 5 S 173 16 E
Molfetta, Italy 41 A9 41 12N 16 35 E
Molina de Aragón, Spain 34 E3 40 46N 1 52W
Moline, U.S.A. 140 C6 41 30N 90 30W
Molinella, Italy 39 D8 44 38N 11 40 E
Molinos, Argentina 158 B2 25 28 S 66 15W
Moliro, Zaïre 106 D3 8 12 S 30 30 E
Molise □, Italy 39 G11 41 45N 14 30 E
Moliterno, Italy 41 B8 40 14N 15 50 E
Mollahat, Bangla. 81 H13 22 56N 89 48 E
Mölle, Sweden 15 H6 56 17N 12 31 E
Molledo, Spain 36 B6 43 8N 4 6W
Mollendo, Peru 156 D3 17 0 S 72 0W
Mollerin, L., Australia 113 F2 30 30 S 117 35 E
Mollerusa, Spain 34 D5 41 37N 0 54 E
Mollina, Spain 37 H6 37 8N 4 38W
Mölln, Germany 26 B6 53 37N 10 41 E
Mölltorp, Sweden 15 F8 58 30N 14 26 E
Mölndal, Sweden 15 G6 57 40N 12 3 E
Molo, Burma 78 D6 23 22N 96 53 E
Molochansk, U.S.S.R. 52 C6 47 15N 35 35 E
Molochnaya ~▸, U.S.S.R. 52 C6 47 0N 35 30 E
Molodechno, U.S.S.R. 50 D5 54 20N 26 50 E

Moral de Calatrava 235

Molokai, *U.S.A.* 132 H16 21 8N 157 0W
Moloma →, *U.S.S.R.* 51 B16 58 20N 48 15 E
Molong, *Australia* 117 B8 33 5 S 148 54 E
Molopo →, *Africa* 104 D3 27 30 S 20 13 E
Mólos, *Greece* 45 F4 38 47N 22 37 E
Molotov = Perm, *U.S.S.R.* 54 C5 58 0N 56 10 E
Moloundou, *Cameroon* 102 B3 2 8N 15 15 E
Molsheim, *France* 23 D14 48 33N 7 29 E
Molson L., *Canada* 131 C9 54 22N 96 40W
Molteno, *S. Africa* 104 E4 31 22 S 26 22 E
Molu, *Indonesia* 71 F8 6 45 S 131 40 E
Molucca Sea = Maluku Sea, *Indonesia* 71 E6 4 0 S 124 0 E
Moluccas = Maluku, *Indonesia* 71 E7 1 0 S 127 0 E
Moma, *Mozam.* 107 F4 16 47 S 39 4 E
Moma, *Zaïre* 102 C4 1 35 S 23 52 E
Momba, *Australia* 116 A5 30 58 S 143 30 E
Mombaça, *Brazil* 154 C4 5 43 S 39 45W
Mombasa, *Kenya* 106 C4 4 2 S 39 43 E
Mombetsu, *Japan* 60 B11 44 21N 143 22 E
Mombil, *Burma* 78 B7 27 46N 98 6 E
Mombuey, *Spain* 36 C4 42 3N 6 20W
Momchilgrad, *Bulgaria* 43 F10 41 33N 25 23 E
Momence, *U.S.A.* 141 C9 41 10N 87 40W
Momi, *Zaïre* 106 C2 1 42 S 27 0 E
Momignies, *Belgium* 21 H4 50 2N 4 10 E
Mompós, *Colombia* 152 B3 9 14N 74 26W
Møn, *Denmark* 15 K6 54 57N 12 15 E
Mona, Canal de la, *W. Indies* 149 C6 18 30N 67 45W
Mona, I., *Puerto Rico* 149 C6 18 5N 67 54W
Mona, Pta., *Costa Rica* 148 E3 9 37N 82 36W
Mona, Pta., *Spain* 37 J7 36 43N 3 45W
Mona Quimbundo, *Angola* 103 D3 9 55 S 19 58 E
Monach Is., *U.K.* 18 D1 57 32N 7 40W
Monaco ■, *Europe* 25 E11 43 46N 7 23 E
Monadhliath Mts., *U.K.* 18 D4 57 10N 4 4W
Monagas □, *Venezuela* 153 B5 9 20N 63 0W
Monaghan, *Ireland* 19 B5 54 15N 6 58W
Monaghan □, *Ireland* 19 B5 54 15N 7 0W
Monahans, *U.S.A.* 139 K3 31 35N 102 50W
Monapo, *Mozam.* 107 E5 14 56 S 40 19 E
Monarch Mt., *Canada* 130 C3 51 55N 125 57W
Monastir = Bitola, *Yugoslavia* 42 F6 41 5N 21 10 E
Monastir, *Tunisia* 96 A2 35 50N 10 49 E
Monastyriska, *U.S.S.R.* 50 G4 49 8N 25 14 E
Moncada, *Spain* 34 F4 39 30N 0 24W
Moncalieri, *Italy* 38 D4 45 0N 7 40 E
Moncalvo, *Italy* 38 C5 45 3N 8 15 E
Moncão, *Portugal* 36 C2 42 4N 8 27W
Moncarapacho, *Portugal* 37 H3 37 5N 7 46W
Moncayo, Sierra del, *Spain* 34 D3 41 48N 1 50W
Mönchengladbach, *Germany* 26 D2 51 12N 6 23 E
Monchique, *Portugal* 37 H2 37 19N 8 38W
Monclova, *Mexico* 146 B4 26 50N 101 30W
Moncontour, *France* 22 D4 48 22N 2 38W
Moncoutant, *France* 24 B3 46 43N 0 35W
Moncton, *Canada* 129 C7 46 7N 64 51W
Mondego →, *Portugal* 36 E2 40 9N 8 52W
Mondego, C., *Portugal* 36 E2 40 11N 8 54W
Mondeodo, *Indonesia* 71 E6 3 34 S 122 9 E
Mondo, *Chad* 97 F3 13 47N 15 32 E
Mondolfo, *Italy* 39 E10 43 45N 13 8 E
Mondoñedo, *Spain* 36 B3 43 25N 7 23W
Mondoví, *Italy* 38 D4 44 23N 7 49 E
Mondovi, *U.S.A.* 138 C9 44 37N 91 40W
Mondragon, *France* 25 D8 44 13N 4 44 E
Mondragone, *Italy* 40 A6 41 8N 13 52 E
Mondrain I., *Australia* 113 F3 34 9 S 122 14 E
Monduli □, *Tanzania* 106 C4 3 0 S 36 0 E
Monemvasía, *Greece* 45 H5 36 41N 23 3 E
Monessen, *U.S.A.* 136 F5 40 9N 79 50W
Monesterio, *Spain* 37 G4 38 6N 6 15W
Monestier-de-Clermont, *France* 25 D9 44 55N 5 38 E
Monett, *U.S.A.* 139 G8 36 55N 93 56W
Monfalcone, *Italy* 39 C10 45 49N 13 32 E
Monflanquin, *France* 24 D4 44 32N 0 47 E
Monforte, *Portugal* 37 F3 39 6N 7 25W
Monforte de Lemos, *Spain* 36 C3 42 31N 7 33W
Mong Hta, *Burma* 78 F7 19 50N 98 35 E
Mong Ket, *Burma* 78 D7 23 8N 98 22 E
Mong Kung, *Burma* 78 E6 21 35N 97 35 E
Mong Kyawt, *Burma* 78 F7 19 56N 98 45 E
Mong Nai, *Burma* 78 E6 20 32N 97 46 E
Mong Ping, *Burma* 78 E7 21 22N 99 2 E
Mong Pu, *Burma* 78 E7 20 55N 98 44 E
Mong Ton, *Burma* 78 E7 20 17N 98 45 E
Mong Tung, *Burma* 78 D6 22 2N 97 41 E
Mong Yai, *Burma* 78 D7 22 21N 98 3 E
Monga, *Zaïre* 102 B4 4 12N 22 49 E
Mongalla, *Sudan* 95 F3 5 8N 31 42 E
Mongers, L., *Australia* 113 E2 29 25 S 117 5 E
Monghyr = Munger, *India* 81 G12 25 23N 86 30 E
Mongla, *Bangla.* 78 D2 22 8N 89 35 E
Mongngaw, *Burma* 78 D6 22 47N 96 59 E
Mongo, *Chad* 97 F3 12 14N 18 43 E
Mongó, *Eq. Guin.* 102 B2 1 52N 10 10 E
Mongolia ■, *Asia* 64 B5 47 0N 103 0 E
Mongomo, *Eq. Guin.* 102 B2 1 38N 11 19 E
Mongonu, *Nigeria* 101 C7 12 40N 13 32 E
Mongororo, *Chad* 97 F4 12 3N 22 26 E
Mongu, *Zambia* 103 F4 15 16 S 23 12 E
Mõngua, *Angola* 103 F3 16 43 S 15 20 E
Monistrol-d'Allier, *France* 24 D7 44 58N 3 38 E
Monistrol-sur-Loire, *France* 25 C8 45 17N 4 11 E
Monkey Bay, *Malawi* 107 E4 14 7 S 35 1 E
Monkey River, *Belize* 147 D7 16 22N 88 29W
Mońki, *Poland* 47 B9 53 23N 22 48 E
Monkira, *Australia* 114 C3 24 46 S 140 30 E
Monkoto, *Zaïre* 102 C4 1 38 S 20 35 E
Monmouth, *U.K.* 17 F5 51 48N 2 43W
Monmouth, *U.S.A.* 140 D6 40 50N 90 40W
Mono, *Solomon Is.* 121 L8 7 20 S 155 35 E
Mono, L., *U.S.A.* 144 H7 38 0N 119 9W
Monolith, *U.S.A.* 145 K8 35 7N 118 22W
Monólithos, *Greece* 32 C9 36 7N 27 45 E
Monon, *U.S.A.* 141 D10 40 52N 86 53W
Monona, *Iowa, U.S.A.* 140 A5 43 3N 91 24W
Monona, *Wis., U.S.A.* 140 A7 43 4N 89 20W
Monongahela, *U.S.A.* 136 F5 40 12N 79 56W
Monópoli, *Italy* 41 B10 40 57N 17 18 E
Monor, *Hungary* 31 D12 47 21N 19 27 E
Monóvar, *Spain* 35 G4 38 28N 0 53W
Monowai, *N.Z.* 119 F2 45 53 S 167 31 E
Monowai, L., *N.Z.* 119 F2 45 53 S 167 25 E
Monqoumba, *C.A.R.* 102 B3 3 33N 18 40 E
Monreal del Campo, *Spain* 34 E3 40 47N 1 20W
Monreale, *Italy* 40 D6 38 6N 13 16 E
Monroe, *Ga., U.S.A.* 135 J4 33 47N 83 43W
Monroe, *Iowa, U.S.A.* 140 C3 41 31N 93 6W
Monroe, *La., U.S.A.* 139 J8 32 32N 92 4W
Monroe, *Mich., U.S.A.* 141 C13 41 55N 83 26W
Monroe, *N.C., U.S.A.* 135 H5 35 2N 80 37W
Monroe, *N.Y., U.S.A.* 137 E10 41 19N 74 11W
Monroe, *Ohio, U.S.A.* 141 E12 39 27N 84 22W
Monroe, *Utah, U.S.A.* 143 G7 38 45N 112 5W
Monroe, *Wash., U.S.A.* 144 C5 47 51N 121 58W
Monroe, *Wis., U.S.A.* 140 B7 42 38N 89 40W
Monroe City, *U.S.A.* 140 E5 39 40N 91 40W
Monroe Res., *U.S.A.* 141 E10 39 1N 86 31W
Monroeville, *Ala., U.S.A.* 135 K2 31 33N 87 15W
Monroeville, *Ind., U.S.A.* 141 D12 40 59N 84 52W
Monroeville, *Pa., U.S.A.* 136 F5 40 26N 79 45W
Monrovia, *Liberia* 100 D2 6 18N 10 47W
Monrovia, *U.S.A.* 143 J4 34 7N 118 1W
Mons, *Belgium* 21 H3 50 27N 3 58 E
Monsaraz, *Portugal* 37 G3 38 28N 7 22W
Monse, *Indonesia* 71 E6 4 0 S 123 10 E
Monsefú, *Peru* 156 B2 6 52 S 79 52W
Monségur, *France* 24 D4 44 38N 0 4 E
Monsélice, *Italy* 39 C8 45 16N 11 46 E
Monster, *Neths.* 20 D4 52 1N 4 10 E
Mont Cenis, Col du, *France* 25 C10 45 15N 6 55 E
Mont-de-Marsan, *France* 24 E3 43 54N 0 31W
Mont-Joli, *Canada* 129 C6 48 37N 68 10W
Mont-Laurier, *Canada* 128 C4 46 35N 75 30W
Mont-St.-Michel, Le = Le Mont-St.-Michel, *France* 22 D5 48 40N 1 30W
Mont-sous-Vaudrey, *France* 23 F12 46 58N 5 36 E
Mont-sur-Marchienne, *Belgium* 21 H4 50 23N 4 24 E
Mont Tremblant Prov. Park, *Canada* 128 C5 46 30N 74 30W
Montabaur, *Germany* 26 E3 50 26N 7 49 E
Montagnac, *France* 24 E7 43 29N 3 28 E
Montagnana, *Italy* 39 C8 45 13N 11 29 E
Montagu, *S. Africa* 104 E3 33 45 S 20 8 E
Montagu I., *Antarctica* 7 B1 58 25 S 26 20W
Montague, *Canada* 129 C7 46 10N 62 39W
Montague, *U.S.A.* 142 F2 41 47N 122 30W
Montague, I., *Mexico* 146 A2 31 40N 114 56W
Montague Ra., *Australia* 113 E2 27 15 S 119 30 E
Montague Sd., *Australia* 112 B4 14 28 S 125 20 E
Montaigu, *France* 22 F5 46 59N 1 18W
Montalbán, *Spain* 34 E4 40 50N 0 45W
Montalbano di Elicona, *Italy* 41 D8 38 1N 15 0 E
Montalbano Iónico, *Italy* 41 B9 40 17N 16 33 E
Montalbo, *Spain* 34 F2 39 53N 2 42W
Montalcino, *Italy* 39 E8 43 4N 11 30 E
Montalegre, *Portugal* 36 D3 41 49N 7 47W
Montalto di Castro, *Italy* 39 F8 42 20N 11 36 E
Montalto Uffugo, *Italy* 41 C9 39 25N 16 9 E
Montalvo, *U.S.A.* 145 L7 34 15N 119 12W
Montamarta, *Spain* 36 D5 41 39N 5 49W
Montaña, *Peru* 156 B3 6 0 S 73 0W
Montana, *Switz.* 28 D4 46 19N 7 29 E
Montana □, *U.S.A.* 132 A5 47 0N 110 0W
Montaña Clara, I., *Canary Is.* 33 E6 29 17N 13 33W
Montánchez, *Spain* 37 F4 39 15N 6 8W
Montañita, *Colombia* 152 C2 1 22N 75 28W
Montargis, *France* 23 E9 47 59N 2 43 E
Montauban, *France* 24 D5 44 2N 1 21 E
Montauk, *U.S.A.* 137 E13 41 3N 71 57W
Montauk Pt., *U.S.A.* 137 E13 41 4N 71 52W
Montbard, *France* 23 E11 47 38N 4 20 E
Montbéliard, *France* 23 E13 47 31N 6 48 E
Montblanch, *Spain* 34 D6 41 23N 1 4 E
Montbrison, *France* 25 C8 45 36N 4 3 E
Montcalm, Pic de, *France* 24 F5 42 40N 1 25 E
Montceau-les-Mines, *France* 23 F11 46 40N 4 23 E
Montchanin, *France* 25 B8 46 47N 4 30 E
Montclair, *U.S.A.* 137 F10 40 53N 74 13W
Montcornet, *France* 23 C11 49 40N 4 1 E
Montcuq, *France* 24 D5 44 21N 1 13 E
Montdidier, *France* 23 C9 49 38N 2 35 E
Monte Albán, *Mexico* 147 D5 17 2N 96 45W
Monte Alegre, *Brazil* 153 D7 2 0 S 54 0W
Monte Alegre de Goiás, *Brazil* 155 D2 13 14 S 47 10W
Monte Alegre de Minas, *Brazil* 155 E2 18 52 S 48 52W
Monte Azul, *Brazil* 155 E3 15 9 S 42 53W
Monte Bello Is., *Australia* 112 D2 20 30 S 115 45 E
Monte-Carlo, *Monaco* 25 E11 43 46N 7 23 E
Monte Carmelo, *Brazil* 155 E2 18 43 S 47 29W
Monte Caseros, *Argentina* 158 C4 30 10 S 57 50W
Monte Comán, *Argentina* 158 C2 34 40 S 67 53W
Monte Cristi, *Dom. Rep.* 149 C5 19 52N 71 39W
Monte Dinero, *Argentina* 160 D3 52 18 S 68 33W
Monte Lindo →, *Paraguay* 158 A4 23 56 S 57 12W
Monte Quemado, *Argentina* 158 B3 25 53 S 62 41W
Monte Redondo, *Portugal* 36 F2 39 53N 8 50W
Monte Rio, *U.S.A.* 144 G4 38 28N 123 0W
Monte San Giovanni, *Italy* 40 A6 41 39N 13 33 E
Monte San Savino, *Italy* 39 E8 43 20N 11 42 E
Monte Sant' Ángelo, *Italy* 41 A8 41 42N 15 59 E
Monte Santu, C. di, *Italy* 40 B2 40 5N 9 42 E
Monte Vista, *U.S.A.* 143 H10 37 40N 106 8W
Monteagudo, *Argentina* 159 B5 27 14 S 54 8W
Monteagudo, *Bolivia* 157 D5 19 49 S 63 59W
Montealegre, *Spain* 35 G3 38 48N 1 17W
Montebello, *Canada* 128 C5 45 40N 74 55W
Montebelluna, *Italy* 39 C9 45 47N 12 3 E
Montebourg, *France* 22 C5 49 30N 1 20W
Montecastrilli, *Italy* 39 F9 42 40N 12 30 E
Montecatini Terme, *Italy* 38 E7 43 55N 10 48 E
Montecito, *U.S.A.* 145 L7 34 26N 119 40W
Montecristi, *Ecuador* 152 D1 1 0 S 80 40W
Montecristo, *Italy* 38 F7 42 20N 10 20 E
Montefalco, *Italy* 39 F9 42 53N 12 38 E
Montefiascone, *Italy* 39 F9 42 31N 12 2 E
Montefrío, *Spain* 37 H7 37 20N 4 0W
Montegnée, *Belgium* 21 G7 50 38N 5 31 E
Montego Bay, *Jamaica* 148 C4 18 30N 78 0W
Montegranaro, *Italy* 39 E10 43 13N 13 38 E
Monteiro, *Brazil* 154 C4 7 48 S 37 2W
Monteith, *Australia* 116 C3 35 11 S 139 23 E
Montejicar, *Spain* 35 H1 37 33N 3 30W
Montejinnie, *Australia* 112 C5 16 40 S 131 38 E
Montelíbano, *Colombia* 152 B2 8 5N 75 29W
Montélimar, *France* 25 D8 44 33N 4 45 E
Montella, *Italy* 41 B8 40 50N 15 2 E
Montellano, *Spain* 37 J5 36 59N 5 36W
Montello, *U.S.A.* 138 D10 43 49N 89 21W
Montelupo Fiorentino, *Italy* 38 E8 43 44N 11 2 E
Montemor-o-Novo, *Portugal* 37 G2 38 40N 8 12W
Montemor-o-Velho, *Portugal* 36 E2 40 11N 8 40W
Montemorelos, *Mexico* 147 B5 25 11N 99 42W
Montendre, *France* 24 C3 45 16N 0 26W
Montenegro = Crna Gora □, *Yugoslavia* 42 E4 42 40N 19 20 E
Montenegro, *Brazil* 159 B5 29 39 S 51 29W
Montenero di Bisaccia, *Italy* 39 G11 41 58N 14 47 E
Montepuez, *Mozam.* 107 E4 13 8 S 38 59 E
Montepuez →, *Mozam.* 107 E5 12 32 S 40 27 E
Montepulciano, *Italy* 39 E8 43 5N 11 46 E
Montereale, *Italy* 39 F10 42 31N 13 13 E
Montereau-Fault-Yonne, *France* 23 D9 48 22N 2 57 E
Monterey, *Calif., U.S.A.* 144 J5 36 35N 121 57W
Monterey, *Ind., U.S.A.* 141 C10 41 11N 86 30W
Monterey B., *U.S.A.* 144 J5 36 50N 121 55W
Montería, *Colombia* 152 B2 8 46N 75 53W
Montero, *Bolivia* 157 D5 17 20 S 63 15W
Monteros, *Argentina* 158 B2 27 11 S 65 30W
Monterotondo, *Italy* 39 F9 42 3N 12 36 E
Monterrey, *Mexico* 146 B4 25 40N 100 30W
Montes Altos, *Brazil* 154 C2 5 50 S 47 4W
Montes Claros, *Brazil* 155 E3 16 30 S 43 50W
Montesano, *U.S.A.* 144 D3 46 58N 123 39W
Montesárchio, *Italy* 41 A7 41 5N 14 37 E
Montescaglioso, *Italy* 41 B9 40 34N 16 40 E
Montesilvano, *Italy* 39 F11 42 30N 14 8 E
Montevarchi, *Italy* 39 E8 43 30N 11 32 E
Montevideo, *Uruguay* 159 C4 34 50 S 56 11W
Montevideo, *U.S.A.* 138 C7 44 55N 95 40W
Montezuma, *Ind., U.S.A.* 141 E9 39 47N 87 22W
Montezuma, *Iowa, U.S.A.* 140 C4 41 32N 92 35W
Montfaucon, *France* 23 C12 49 16N 5 8 E
Montfaucon-en-Velay, *France* 25 C8 45 11N 4 20 E
Montfort, *France* 22 D5 48 9N 1 58W
Montfort, *Neths.* 21 F7 51 7N 5 58 E
Montfort-l'Amaury, *France* 23 D8 48 47N 1 49 E
Montgenèvre, *France* 25 D10 44 56N 6 43 E
Montgomery = Sahiwal, *Pakistan* 79 C4 30 45N 73 8 E
Montgomery, *U.K.* 17 E4 52 34N 3 9W
Montgomery, *Ala., U.S.A.* 135 J2 32 20N 86 20W
Montgomery, *Ill., U.S.A.* 141 C8 41 44N 88 21W
Montgomery, *W. Va., U.S.A.* 134 F5 38 9N 81 21W
Montgomery City, *U.S.A.* 140 F5 38 59N 91 30W
Montguyon, *France* 24 C3 45 12N 0 12W
Monthey, *Switz.* 28 D3 46 15N 6 56 E
Monticelli d'Ongina, *Italy* 38 C6 45 3N 9 56 E
Monticello, *Ark., U.S.A.* 139 J9 33 40N 91 48W
Monticello, *Fla., U.S.A.* 135 K4 30 35N 83 50W
Monticello, *Ill., U.S.A.* 141 D8 40 1N 88 34W
Monticello, *Ind., U.S.A.* 141 D10 40 40N 86 45W
Monticello, *Iowa, U.S.A.* 140 B5 42 18N 91 12W
Monticello, *Ky., U.S.A.* 135 G3 36 52N 84 50W
Monticello, *Minn., U.S.A.* 138 C8 45 17N 93 52W
Monticello, *Miss., U.S.A.* 139 K9 31 35N 90 8W
Monticello, *Mo., U.S.A.* 140 D5 40 7N 91 43W
Monticello, *N.Y., U.S.A.* 137 E10 41 37N 74 42W
Monticello, *Utah, U.S.A.* 143 H9 37 55N 109 27W
Montichiari, *Italy* 38 C7 45 28N 10 29 E
Montier-en-Der, *France* 23 D11 48 30N 4 45 E
Montignac, *France* 24 C5 45 4N 1 10 E
Montignies-sur-Sambre, *Belgium* 21 H4 50 24N 4 29 E
Montigny, *France* 23 C13 49 7N 6 10 E
Montigny-sur-Aube, *France* 23 E11 47 57N 4 45 E
Montijo, *Spain* 37 G4 38 52N 6 39W
Montijo, Presa de, *Spain* 37 G4 38 55N 6 26W
Montilla, *Spain* 37 H6 37 36N 4 40W
Montlhéry, *France* 23 D9 48 39N 2 15 E
Montluçon, *France* 24 B6 46 22N 2 36 E
Montmagny, *Canada* 129 C5 46 58N 70 34W
Montmarault, *France* 24 B6 46 19N 2 57 E
Montmartre, *Canada* 131 C8 50 14N 103 27W
Montmédy, *France* 23 C12 49 30N 5 20 E
Montmélian, *France* 25 C10 45 30N 6 4 E
Montmirail, *France* 23 D10 48 51N 3 30 E
Montmoreau-St.-Cybard, *France* 24 C4 45 23N 0 8 E
Montmorency, *Canada* 129 C5 46 53N 71 11W
Montmorillon, *France* 24 B4 46 26N 0 50 E
Montmort, *France* 23 D10 48 55N 3 49 E
Monto, *Australia* 114 C5 24 52 S 151 6 E
Montoir-sur-le-Loir, *France* 22 E7 47 45N 0 52 E
Montório al Vomano, *Italy* 39 F10 42 35N 13 38 E
Montoro, *Spain* 37 G6 38 1N 4 27W
Montour Falls, *U.S.A.* 136 D8 42 20N 76 51W
Montpelier, *Idaho, U.S.A.* 142 E8 42 15N 111 20W
Montpelier, *Ind., U.S.A.* 141 D11 40 33N 85 17W
Montpelier, *Ohio, U.S.A.* 141 C12 41 34N 84 40W
Montpelier, *Vt., U.S.A.* 137 B12 44 15N 72 38W
Montpellier, *France* 24 E7 43 37N 3 52 E
Montpezat-de-Quercy, *France* 24 D5 44 15N 1 30 E
Montpon-Ménestérol, *France* 24 D4 45 0N 0 11 E
Montréal, *Canada* 128 C5 45 31N 73 34W
Montréal, *France* 24 E6 43 13N 2 8 E
Montreal L., *Canada* 131 C7 54 20N 105 45W
Montreal Lake, *Canada* 131 C7 54 3N 105 46W
Montredon-Labessonnié, *France* 24 E6 43 45N 2 18 E
Montréjeau, *France* 24 E4 43 6N 0 35 E
Montrésor, *France* 22 E8 47 10N 1 10 E
Montreuil, *France* 23 B8 50 27N 1 45 E
Montreuil-Bellay, *France* 22 E6 47 8N 0 9W
Montreux, *Switz.* 28 D3 46 26N 6 55 E
Montrevault, *France* 22 E5 47 17N 1 2W
Montrevel-en-Bresse, *France* 25 B9 46 21N 5 8 E
Montrichard, *France* 22 E8 47 20N 1 10 E
Montrose, *U.K.* 18 E6 56 43N 2 28W
Montrose, *Colo., U.S.A.* 143 G10 38 30N 107 52W
Montrose, *Pa., U.S.A.* 137 E9 41 50N 75 55W
Montrose, L., *U.S.A.* 140 F3 38 18N 93 50W
Monts, Pte. des, *Canada* 129 C6 49 20N 67 12W
Monts-sur-Guesnes, *France* 22 F7 46 55N 0 13 E
Montsalvy, *France* 24 D6 44 41N 2 30 E
Montsant, Sierra de, *Spain* 34 D6 41 17N 1 0 E
Montsauche, *France* 23 E11 47 13N 4 2 E
Montsech, Sierra del, *Spain* 34 D5 42 0N 0 45 E
Montseny, *Spain* 34 D2 41 55N 2 25W
Montserrat, *Spain* 34 D6 41 36N 1 49 E
Montserrat, *W. Indies* 149 C7 16 40N 62 10W
Montuenga, *Spain* 36 D6 41 3N 4 38W
Montuiri, *Spain* 33 B9 39 34N 2 59 E
Monveda, *Zaïre* 102 B4 2 52N 21 30 E
Monyo, *Burma* 78 G5 17 59N 95 30 E
Monywa, *Burma* 78 D5 22 7N 95 11 E
Monza, *Italy* 38 C6 45 35N 9 15 E
Monze, *Zambia* 107 F2 16 17 S 27 29 E
Monze, C., *Pakistan* 79 D2 24 47N 66 37 E
Monzón, *Spain* 34 D5 41 52N 0 10 E
Mooi River, *S. Africa* 105 D4 29 13 S 29 50 E
Mook, *Neths.* 20 E7 51 46N 5 54 E
Mo'oka, *Japan* 63 A12 36 26N 140 1 E
Moolawatana, *Australia* 115 D2 29 55 S 139 45 E
Mooleulooloo, *Australia* 116 A4 31 36 S 140 32 E
Mooliabeenee, *Australia* 113 F2 31 20 S 116 2 E
Mooloogool, *Australia* 113 E2 26 2 S 119 5 E
Moomin Cr. →, *Australia* 115 D4 29 44 S 149 20 E
Moonah →, *Australia* 114 C2 22 3 S 138 33 E
Moonbeam, *Canada* 128 C3 49 20N 82 10W
Moonda, L., *Australia* 114 D3 25 52 S 140 25 E
Moonie, *Australia* 115 D5 27 46 S 150 20 E
Moonie →, *Australia* 115 D4 29 19 S 148 43 E
Moonta, *Australia* 116 C2 34 6 S 137 32 E
Moora, *Australia* 113 F2 30 37 S 115 58 E
Mooraberree, *Australia* 114 D3 25 13 S 140 54 E
Moorarie, *Australia* 113 E2 25 56 S 117 35 E
Moorcroft, *U.S.A.* 138 C2 44 17N 104 58W
Moore →, *Australia* 113 F2 31 22 S 115 30 E
Moore, L., *Australia* 113 E2 29 50 S 117 35 E
Moore Reefs, *Australia* 114 B4 16 0 S 149 5 E
Moorefield, *U.S.A.* 134 F6 39 5N 78 59W
Moores Res., *U.S.A.* 137 B13 44 45N 71 50W
Mooresville, *Ind., U.S.A.* 141 E10 39 37N 86 22W
Mooresville, *N.C., U.S.A.* 135 H5 35 36N 80 45W
Moorfoot Hills, *U.K.* 18 F5 55 44N 3 8W
Moorhead, *U.S.A.* 138 B6 46 51N 96 44W
Moorland, *Australia* 117 A10 31 46 S 152 38 E
Mooroopna, *Australia* 117 D6 36 25 S 145 22 E
Moorpark, *U.S.A.* 145 L8 34 17N 118 53W
Moorreesburg, *S. Africa* 104 E2 33 6S 18 38 E
Moorslede, *Belgium* 21 G2 50 54N 3 4 E
Moosburg, *Germany* 27 G7 48 28N 11 57 E
Moose →, *Canada* 128 B3 51 20N 80 25W
Moose Factory, *Canada* 128 B3 51 16N 80 32W
Moose I., *Canada* 131 C9 51 42N 97 10W
Moose Jaw, *Canada* 131 C7 50 24N 105 30W
Moose Jaw →, *Canada* 131 C7 50 34N 105 18W
Moose Lake, *Canada* 131 C8 53 43N 100 20W
Moose Lake, *U.S.A.* 138 B8 46 27N 92 48W
Moose Mountain Cr. →, *Canada* 131 D8 49 13N 102 12W
Moose Mountain Prov. Park, *Canada* 131 D8 49 48N 102 25W
Moose River, *Canada* 128 B3 50 48N 81 17W
Moosehead L., *U.S.A.* 129 C6 45 34N 69 40W
Moosomin, *Canada* 131 C8 50 9N 101 40W
Moosonee, *Canada* 128 B3 51 17N 80 39W
Moosup, *U.S.A.* 137 E13 41 44N 71 52W
Mopeia Velha, *Mozam.* 107 F4 17 30 S 35 40 E
Mopipi, *Botswana* 104 C3 21 6 S 24 55 E
Mopoi, *C.A.R.* 102 A5 5 6N 26 54 E
Mopti, *Mali* 100 C4 14 30N 4 0W
Moqatta, *Sudan* 95 E4 14 38N 35 50 E
Moquegua, *Peru* 156 D3 17 15 S 70 46W
Moquegua □, *Peru* 156 D3 16 50 S 70 55W
Mór, *Hungary* 31 D11 47 25N 18 12 E
Móra, *Portugal* 37 G2 38 55N 8 10W
Mora, *Sweden* 13 F13 61 2N 14 38 E
Mora, *Minn., U.S.A.* 138 C8 45 52N 93 19W
Mora, *N. Mex., U.S.A.* 143 J11 35 58N 105 21W
Mora de Ebro, *Spain* 34 D5 41 6N 0 38 E
Mora de Rubielos, *Spain* 34 E4 40 15N 0 45W
Mora la Nueva, *Spain* 34 D5 41 7N 0 39 E
Morača →, *Yugoslavia* 42 E4 42 20N 19 9 E
Morada Nova, *Brazil* 154 C4 5 7 S 38 23W
Morada Nova de Minas, *Brazil* 155 E2 18 37 S 45 22W
Moradabad, *India* 81 E8 28 50N 78 50 E
Morafenobe, *Madag.* 105 B7 17 50 S 44 53 E
Morąg, *Poland* 47 B6 53 55N 19 56 E
Moral de Calatrava, *Spain* 35 G1 38 51N 3 33W

236 Moraleja

Moraleja, *Spain* 36 E4 40 6N 6 43W
Morales, *Colombia* 152 C2 2 45N 76 38W
Moramanga, *Madag.* 105 B8 18 56 S 48 12 E
Moran, *Kans., U.S.A.* 139 G7 37 53N 94 35W
Moran, *Wyo., U.S.A.* 142 E8 43 53N 110 37W
Moranbah, *Australia* 114 C4 22 1 S 148 6 E
Morano Cálabro, *Italy* 41 C9 39 51N 16 8 E
Morant Cays, *Jamaica* 148 C4 17 22N 76 0W
Morant Pt., *Jamaica* 148 C4 17 55N 76 12W
Morar, L., *U.K.* 18 E3 56 57N 5 40W
Moratalla, *Spain* 35 G3 38 14N 1 49W
Moratuwa, *Sri Lanka* 83 L4 6 45N 79 55 E
Morava →, *Czech.* 31 C9 48 10N 16 59 E
Moravia, *U.S.A.* 140 D4 40 50N 92 50W
Moravian Hts. = Ceskomoravská Vrchovina, *Czech.* 30 B8 49 30N 15 40 E
Moravica →, *Yugoslavia* 42 D5 43 52N 20 8 E
Moravice →, *Czech.* 31 B10 49 50N 17 43 E
Moravița, *Romania* 42 B6 45 17N 21 14 E
Moravská Třebová, *Czech.* 31 B9 49 45N 16 40 E
Moravské Budějovice, *Czech.* 30 B8 49 4N 15 49 E
Morawa, *Australia* 113 E2 29 13 S 116 0 E
Morawhanna, *Guyana* 153 B6 8 30N 59 40W
Moray Firth, *U.K.* 18 D5 57 50N 3 30W
Morbach, *Germany* 27 F3 49 48N 7 7 E
Morbegno, *Italy* 38 B6 46 8N 9 34 E
Morbi, *India* 80 H4 22 50N 70 42 E
Morbihan □, *France* 22 E4 47 55N 2 50W
Morcenx, *France* 24 D3 44 3N 0 55W
Mordelles, *France* 22 D5 48 5N 1 52W
Morden, *Canada* 131 D9 49 15N 98 10W
Mordovian A.S.S.R. □, *U.S.S.R.* 51 D14 54 20N 44 30 E
Mordovo, *U.S.S.R.* 51 E12 52 6N 40 50 E
Mordy, *Poland* 47 C9 52 13N 22 31 E
Møre og Romsdal fylke □, *Norway* 14 B2 62 30N 8 0 E
Morea, *Australia* 116 D4 36 45 S 141 18 E
Morea, *Greece* 10 H10 37 45N 22 10 E
Moreau →, *U.S.A.* 138 C4 45 15N 100 43W
Morecambe, *U.K.* 16 C5 54 5N 2 52W
Morecambe B., *U.K.* 16 C5 54 7N 3 0W
Moree, *Australia* 115 D4 29 28 S 149 54 E
Morehead, *Papua N. G.* 120 E1 8 41 S 141 41 E
Morehead, *U.S.A.* 141 F13 38 12N 83 22W
Morehead City, *U.S.A.* 135 H7 34 46N 76 44W
Morelia, *Mexico* 146 D4 19 40N 101 11W
Morella, *Australia* 114 C3 23 0 S 143 52 E
Morella, *Spain* 34 E4 40 35N 0 5W
Morelos, *Mexico* 146 B3 26 42N 107 40W
Morelos □, *Mexico* 147 D5 18 40N 99 10W
Morena, Sierra, *Spain* 37 G7 38 20N 4 0W
Morenci, *Ariz., U.S.A.* 143 K9 33 7N 109 20W
Morenci, *Mich., U.S.A.* 141 C12 41 43N 84 13W
Moreni, *Romania* 46 E6 44 59N 25 36 E
Morero, *Bolivia* 157 C4 11 9 S 66 15W
Moreru →, *Brazil* 157 C6 10 10 S 59 15W
Moresby I., *Canada* 130 C2 52 30N 131 40W
Morestel, *France* 25 C9 45 40N 5 28 E
Moret-sur-Loing, *France* 23 D9 48 22N 2 58 E
Moreton, *Australia* 114 A3 12 22 S 142 40 E
Moreton I., *Australia* 115 D5 27 10 S 153 25 E
Moreuil, *France* 23 C9 49 46N 2 30 E
Morey, *Spain* 33 B10 39 44N 3 20 E
Morez, *France* 25 B10 46 31N 6 2 E
Morgan, *Australia* 116 C3 34 2 S 139 35 E
Morgan, *U.S.A.* 142 F8 41 3N 111 44W
Morgan City, *U.S.A.* 139 L9 29 40N 91 15W
Morgan Hill, *U.S.A.* 144 H5 37 8N 121 39W
Morgan Vale, *Australia* 116 B4 33 10 S 140 32 E
Morganfield, *U.S.A.* 134 G2 37 40N 87 55W
Morganton, *U.S.A.* 135 H5 35 46N 81 48W
Morgantown, *Ind., U.S.A.* 141 E10 39 22N 86 16W
Morgantown, *W. Va., U.S.A.* 134 F6 39 39N 79 58W
Morgat, *France* 22 D2 48 15N 4 32W
Morgenzon, *S. Africa* 105 D4 26 45 S 29 36 E
Morges, *Switz.* 28 C2 46 31N 6 29 E
Morghak, *Iran* 85 D8 29 7N 57 54 E
Morhange, *France* 23 D13 48 55N 6 38 E
Mori, *Italy* 38 C7 45 51N 10 59 E
Morialmée, *Belgium* 21 H5 50 17N 4 35 E
Morice L., *Canada* 130 C3 53 50N 127 40W
Morichal, *Colombia* 152 C3 2 10N 70 34W
Morichal Largo →, *Venezuela* 153 B5 9 27N 62 25W
Moriguchi, *Japan* 63 C7 34 44N 135 34 E
Moriki, *Nigeria* 101 C6 12 52N 6 30 E
Morinville, *Canada* 130 C6 53 49N 113 41W
Morioka, *Japan* 60 E10 39 45N 141 8 E
Moris, *Mexico* 146 B3 28 8N 108 32W
Morisset, *Australia* 117 B9 33 6 S 151 30 E
Morlaàs, *France* 24 E3 43 21N 0 18W
Morlaix, *France* 22 D3 48 36N 3 52W
Morlanwelz, *Belgium* 21 H4 50 28N 4 15 E
Mormanno, *Italy* 41 C8 39 53N 15 59 E
Mormant, *France* 23 D9 48 37N 2 52 E
Mornington, *Vic., Australia* 117 E6 38 15 S 145 5 E
Mornington, *W. Austral., Australia* 112 C4 17 31 S 126 6 E
Mornington, I., *Chile* 160 C1 49 50 S 75 30W
Mornington I., *Australia* 114 B2 16 30 S 139 30 E
Mórnos →, *Greece* 45 F3 38 25N 21 50 E
Moro, *Sudan* 95 E3 10 50N 30 9 E
Moro G., *Phil.* 71 C6 6 30N 123 0 E
Morobe, *Papua N. G.* 120 D4 7 49 S 147 38 E
Morocco, *U.S.A.* 141 D9 40 57N 87 27W
Morocco ■, *N. Afr.* 98 B3 32 0N 5 50W
Morococha, *Peru* 156 C2 11 40 S 76 5W
Morogoro, *Tanzania* 106 D4 6 50 S 37 40 E
Morogoro □, *Tanzania* 106 D4 8 0 S 37 0 E
Moroleón, *Mexico* 146 C4 20 8N 101 32W
Morombe, *Madag.* 105 C7 21 45 S 43 22 E
Moron, *Argentina* 158 C4 34 39 S 58 37W
Morón, *Cuba* 148 B4 22 8N 78 39W
Morón de Almazán, *Spain* 34 D2 41 29N 2 27W
Morón de la Frontera, *Spain* 37 H5 37 6N 5 28W
Morona →, *Peru* 152 D2 4 40 S 77 10W
Morona-Santiago □, *Ecuador* 152 D2 2 30 S 78 0W
Morondava, *Madag.* 105 C7 20 17 S 44 17 E
Morondo, *Ivory C.* 100 D3 8 57N 6 47W
Morongo Valley, *U.S.A.* 145 L10 34 3N 116 37W
Moronou, *Ivory C.* 100 D4 6 16N 4 59W
Morotai, *Indonesia* 71 D7 2 10N 128 30 E
Moroto, *Uganda* 106 B3 2 28N 34 42 E
Moroto Summit, *Kenya* 106 B3 2 30N 34 43 E
Morozov, *Bulgaria* 43 E10 42 30N 25 10 E
Morozovsk, *U.S.S.R.* 53 B9 48 25N 41 50 E
Morpeth, *U.K.* 16 B6 55 11N 1 41W
Morphou, *Cyprus* 32 D11 35 12N 32 59 E
Morphou Bay, *Cyprus* 32 D11 35 15N 32 50 E
Morrelganj, *Bangla.* 78 D2 22 28N 89 51 E
Morrilton, *U.S.A.* 139 H8 35 10N 92 45W
Morrinhos, *Ceara, Brazil* 154 B3 3 14 S 40 7W
Morrinhos, *Minas Gerais, Brazil* 155 E2 17 45 S 49 10W
Morrinsville, *N.Z.* 118 D4 37 40 S 175 32 E
Morris, *Canada* 131 D9 49 25N 97 22W
Morris, *Ill., U.S.A.* 141 C8 41 20N 88 20W
Morris, *Minn., U.S.A.* 138 C7 45 33N 95 56W
Morris, Mt., *Australia* 113 E5 26 9 S 131 4 E
Morrisburg, *Canada* 128 D4 44 55N 75 7W
Morrison, *U.S.A.* 140 C7 41 47N 89 58W
Morrisonville, *U.S.A.* 140 E7 39 25N 89 27W
Morristown, *Ariz., U.S.A.* 143 K7 33 54N 112 35W
Morristown, *Ind., U.S.A.* 141 E11 39 40N 85 42W
Morristown, *N.J., U.S.A.* 137 F10 40 48N 74 30W
Morristown, *S. Dak., U.S.A.* 138 C4 45 57N 101 44W
Morristown, *Tenn., U.S.A.* 135 G4 36 18N 83 20W
Morro, Pta., *Chile* 158 B1 27 6 S 71 0W
Morro Bay, *U.S.A.* 144 K6 35 27N 120 54W
Morro del Jable, *Canary Is.* 33 F5 28 3N 14 23W
Morro do Chapéu, *Brazil* 155 D3 11 33 S 41 9W
Morro Jable, Pta. de, *Canary Is.* 33 F5 28 2N 14 20W
Morros, *Brazil* 154 B3 2 52 S 44 3W
Morrosquillo, G. de, *Colombia* 148 E4 9 35N 75 40W
Morrumbene, *Mozam.* 105 C6 23 31 S 35 16 E
Mors, *Denmark* 15 H2 56 50N 8 45 E
Morshansk, *U.S.S.R.* 51 E12 53 28N 41 50 E
Mörsil, *Sweden* 14 A7 63 19N 13 40 E
Mortagne →, *France* 23 D13 48 33N 6 27 E
Mortagne-au-Perche, *France* 22 D7 48 31N 0 33 E
Mortagne-sur-Gironde, *France* 24 C3 45 28N 0 47W
Mortagne-sur-Sèvre, *France* 22 F6 46 59N 0 57W
Mortain, *France* 22 D6 48 40N 0 57W
Mortara, *Italy* 38 C5 45 15N 8 43 E
Mortcha, *Chad* 97 E4 16 0N 21 10 E
Morteau, *France* 23 E13 47 3N 6 35 E
Morteros, *Argentina* 158 C3 30 50 S 62 0W
Mortes, R. das →, *Brazil* 155 D1 11 45 S 50 44W
Mortlake, *Australia* 116 E5 38 5 S 142 50 E
Morton, *Ill., U.S.A.* 140 D7 40 37N 89 28W
Morton, *Tex., U.S.A.* 139 J3 33 39N 102 49W
Morton, *Wash., U.S.A.* 144 D4 46 33N 122 17W
Mortsel, *Belgium* 21 F4 51 11N 4 27 E
Morundah, *Australia* 117 C7 34 57 S 146 19 E
Moruya, *Australia* 117 C9 35 58 S 150 3 E
Morvan, *France* 23 E11 47 5N 4 3 E
Morven, *Australia* 115 D4 26 22 S 147 5 E
Morven, *N.Z.* 119 E6 44 50 S 171 6 E
Morvern, *U.K.* 18 E3 56 38N 5 44W
Morwell, *Australia* 117 E7 38 10 S 146 22 E
Moryń, *Poland* 47 C1 52 51N 14 22 E
Morzhovets, Ostrov, *U.S.S.R.* 48 A7 66 44N 42 35 E
Mosalsk, *U.S.S.R.* 50 D9 54 30N 34 55 E
Mosbach, *Germany* 27 F5 49 21N 9 9 E
Mošćenice, *Yugoslavia* 39 C11 45 17N 14 16 E
Mosciano Sant' Ángelo, *Italy* 39 F10 42 42N 13 52 E
Moscos Is., *Burma* 76 F1 14 0N 97 30 E
Moscow = Moskva, *U.S.S.R.* 51 D10 55 45N 37 35 E
Moscow, *U.S.A.* 142 C5 46 45N 116 59W
Moselle □, *France* 23 D13 48 59N 6 33 E
Moses Lake, *U.S.A.* 142 C4 47 9N 119 17W
Mosgiel, *N.Z.* 119 F5 45 53 S 170 21 E
Moshi, *Tanzania* 106 C4 3 22 S 37 18 E
Moshi □, *Tanzania* 106 C4 3 22 S 37 18 E
Moshupa, *Botswana* 104 C4 24 46 S 25 29 E
Mošina, *Poland* 47 C3 52 15N 16 50 E
Mosjøen, *Norway* 12 D12 65 51N 13 12 E
Moskenesøya, *Norway* 12 C12 67 58N 13 0 E
Moskenstraumen, *Norway* 12 C12 67 47N 12 45 E
Moskva, *U.S.S.R.* 51 D10 55 45N 37 35 E
Moskva →, *U.S.S.R.* 51 D11 55 5N 38 51 E
Moslavačka Gora, *Yugoslavia* 39 C13 45 40N 16 37 E
Moso, *Vanuatu* 121 G6 17 30 S 168 15 E
Mosomane, *Botswana* 104 C4 24 2 S 26 19 E
Mosonmagyaróvár, *Hungary* 31 D10 47 52N 17 18 E
Mošorin, *Yugoslavia* 42 B5 45 19N 20 4 E
Mospino, *U.S.S.R.* 52 C8 47 52N 38 0 E
Mosquera, *Colombia* 152 C2 2 35N 78 24W
Mosquero, *U.S.A.* 139 H3 35 48N 103 57W
Mosqueruela, *Spain* 34 E4 40 21N 0 27W
Mosquitia, *Honduras* 148 C3 15 20N 84 10W
Mosquitos, G. de los, *Panama* 148 E3 9 15N 81 10W
Moss, *Norway* 14 E4 59 27N 10 40 E
Moss Vale, *Australia* 117 C9 34 32 S 150 25 E
Mossaka, *Congo* 102 C3 1 15 S 16 45 E
Mossâmedes, *Brazil* 155 E1 16 7 S 50 11W
Mossbank, *Canada* 131 D7 49 56N 105 56W
Mossburn, *N.Z.* 119 F3 45 41 S 168 15 E
Mosselbaai, *S. Africa* 104 E3 34 11 S 22 8 E
Mossendjo, *Congo* 102 C2 2 55 S 12 42 E
Mosses, Col des, *Switz.* 28 D4 46 25N 7 7 E
Mossgiel, *Australia* 116 B6 33 15 S 144 5 E
Mossman, *Australia* 114 B4 16 21 S 145 15 E
Mossoró, *Brazil* 154 C4 5 10 S 37 15W
Mossuril, *Mozam.* 107 E5 14 58 S 40 42 E
Mossy →, *Canada* 131 C8 54 5N 102 58W
Most, *Czech.* 30 A6 50 31N 13 38 E
Mosta, *Malta* 32 D1 35 54N 14 24 E
Moşţafáābād, *Iran* 85 C7 33 39N 54 53 E
Mostaganem, *Algeria* 99 A5 35 54N 0 5 E
Mostar, *Yugoslavia* 42 D2 43 22N 17 50 E
Mostardas, *Brazil* 159 C5 31 2 S 50 51W
Mostefa, Rass, *Tunisia* 96 A2 36 55N 11 3 E
Mostiska, *U.S.S.R.* 50 G3 49 48N 23 4 E
Móstoles, *Spain* 36 E7 40 19N 3 53W
Mosty, *U.S.S.R.* 50 E4 53 27N 24 38 E
Mosul = Al Mawşil, *Iraq* 84 B4 36 15N 43 5 E
Mosulpo, *S. Korea* 67 H14 33 20N 126 17 E
Mota, *Vanuatu* 121 C5 13 49 S 167 42 E
Mota del Cuervo, *Spain* 34 F2 39 30N 2 52W
Mota del Marqués, *Spain* 36 D5 41 38N 5 11W
Mota Lava, *Vanuatu* 121 C5 13 40 S 167 40 E
Motagua →, *Guatemala* 148 C2 15 44N 88 14W
Motala, *Sweden* 15 F9 58 32N 15 1 E
Motegi, *Japan* 63 A12 36 32N 140 11 E
Motherwell, *U.K.* 18 F5 55 48N 4 0W
Motihari, *India* 81 F11 26 30N 84 55 E
Motilla del Palancar, *Spain* 34 F3 39 34N 1 55W
Motiti I., *N.Z.* 118 D5 37 38 S 176 25 E
Motnik, *Yugoslavia* 39 B11 46 14N 14 54 E
Motocurunya, *Venezuela* 153 C5 4 24N 64 5W
Motovun, *Yugoslavia* 39 C10 45 20N 13 50 E
Motozintla de Mendoza, *Mexico* 147 D6 15 21N 92 14W
Motril, *Spain* 35 J1 36 31N 3 37W
Motru →, *Romania* 46 E4 44 32N 23 31 E
Mott, *U.S.A.* 138 B3 46 25N 102 29W
Móttola, *Italy* 41 B10 40 38N 17 2 E
Motu, *N.Z.* 118 E6 38 18 S 177 40 E
Motu →, *N.Z.* 118 D6 37 51 S 177 35 E
Motueka, *N.Z.* 119 B8 41 7 S 173 1 E
Motueka →, *N.Z.* 119 B8 41 5 S 173 1 E
Motul, *Mexico* 147 C7 21 0N 89 20W
Motupena Pt., *Papua N. G.* 120 D8 6 30 S 155 10 E
Mouanda, *Gabon* 102 C2 1 28 S 13 7 E
Mouchalagane →, *Canada* 129 B6 50 56N 68 41W
Moúdhros, *Greece* 44 E7 39 50N 25 18 E
Mouding, *China* 68 E3 25 20N 101 28 E
Moudjeria, *Mauritania* 100 B2 17 50N 12 28W
Moudon, *Switz.* 28 C3 46 40N 6 49 E
Mougoundou, *Congo* 102 C2 2 40 S 12 41 E
Mouila, *Gabon* 102 C2 1 50 S 11 0 E
Mouka, *C.A.R.* 102 A4 7 16N 21 52 E
Moulamein, *Australia* 116 C6 35 3 S 144 1 E
Mouliana, *Greece* 32 D7 35 10N 25 59 E
Moulins, *France* 24 B7 46 35N 3 19 E
Moulmein, *Burma* 78 G6 16 30N 97 40 E
Moulmeingyun, *Burma* 78 G5 16 23N 95 16 E
Moulouya, O. →, *Morocco* 99 A4 35 5N 2 25W
Moulton, *Iowa, U.S.A.* 140 D4 40 41N 92 41W
Moulton, *Tex., U.S.A.* 139 L6 29 35N 97 8W
Moultrie, *U.S.A.* 135 K4 31 11N 83 47W
Moultrie, L., *U.S.A.* 135 J5 33 25N 80 10W
Mound City, *Mo., U.S.A.* 138 E7 40 2N 95 25W
Mound City, *S. Dak., U.S.A.* 138 C4 45 46N 100 3W
Moúnda, Ákra, *Greece* 45 F2 38 5N 20 45 E
Moundou, *Chad* 97 G3 8 40N 16 10 E
Moundsville, *U.S.A.* 136 G4 39 53N 80 43W
Mounembé, *Congo* 102 C2 3 20 S 12 32 E
Moung, *Cambodia* 76 F4 12 46N 103 27 E
Moungoudi, *Congo* 102 C2 2 45 S 11 46 E
Mount Airy, *U.S.A.* 135 G5 36 31N 80 37W
Mount Albert, *Canada* 136 B5 44 8N 79 19W
Mount Amherst, *Australia* 112 C4 18 24 S 126 58 E
Mount Angel, *U.S.A.* 142 D2 45 4N 122 46W
Mount Augustus, *Australia* 112 D2 24 20 S 116 56 E
Mount Ayr, *U.S.A.* 140 D2 40 43N 94 14W
Mount Barker, *S. Austral., Australia* 116 C3 35 5 S 138 52 E
Mount Barker, *W. Austral., Australia* 113 F2 34 38 S 117 40 E
Mount Beauty, *Australia* 117 D7 36 47 S 147 10 E
Mount Carmel, *U.S.A.* 141 F9 38 20N 87 48W
Mount Carroll, *U.S.A.* 140 B7 42 6N 89 59W
Mount Clemens, *U.S.A.* 128 D3 42 35N 82 50W
Mount Coolon, *Australia* 114 C4 21 25 S 147 25 E
Mount Darwin, *Zimbabwe* 107 F3 16 47 S 31 38 E
Mount Desert I., *U.S.A.* 129 D6 44 15N 68 25W
Mount Dora, *U.S.A.* 135 L5 28 49N 81 32W
Mount Douglas, *Australia* 114 C4 21 35 S 146 50 E
Mount Eba, *Australia* 115 E2 30 11 S 135 40 E
Mount Eden, *U.S.A.* 141 F11 38 3N 85 9W
Mount Edgecumbe, *U.S.A.* 130 B1 57 8N 135 22W
Mount Elizabeth, *Australia* 112 C4 16 0 S 125 50 E
Mount Fletcher, *S. Africa* 105 E4 30 40 S 28 30 E
Mount Forest, *Canada* 128 D3 43 59N 80 43W
Mount Gambier, *Australia* 116 D4 37 50 S 140 46 E
Mount Garnet, *Australia* 114 B4 17 37 S 145 6 E
Mount Hagen, *Papua N. G.* 120 C3 5 52 S 144 16 E
Mount Hope, *N.S.W., Australia* 117 B6 32 51 S 145 51 E
Mount Hope, *S. Austral., Australia* 115 E2 34 7 S 135 23 E
Mount Hope, *U.S.A.* 134 G5 37 52N 81 9W
Mount Horeb, *U.S.A.* 140 B7 43 0N 89 42W
Mount Howitt, *Australia* 115 D3 26 31 S 142 16 E
Mount Isa, *Australia* 114 C2 20 42 S 139 26 E
Mount Keith, *Australia* 113 E3 27 15 S 120 30 E
Mount Laguna, *U.S.A.* 145 N10 32 52N 116 25W
Mount Larcom, *Australia* 114 C5 23 48 S 150 59 E
Mount Lofty Ra., *Australia* 116 C3 34 35 S 139 5 E
Mount McKinley Nat. Park, *U.S.A.* 126 B5 64 0N 150 0W
Mount Magnet, *Australia* 113 E2 28 2 S 117 47 E
Mount Manara, *Australia* 116 B5 32 29 S 143 58 E
Mount Margaret, *Australia* 115 D3 26 54 S 143 21 E
Mount Maunganui, *N.Z.* 118 D5 37 40 S 176 14 E
Mount Molloy, *Australia* 114 B4 16 42 S 145 20 E
Mount Monger, *Australia* 113 F3 31 0 S 122 0 E
Mount Morgan, *Australia* 114 C5 23 40 S 150 25 E
Mount Morris, *U.S.A.* 136 D7 42 43N 77 50W
Mount Mulligan, *Australia* 114 B3 16 45 S 144 47 E
Mount Narryer, *Australia* 113 E2 26 30 S 115 55 E
Mount Olive, *U.S.A.* 140 E7 39 4N 89 44W
Mount Olivet, *U.S.A.* 141 F12 38 32N 84 2W
Mount Olympus = Uludağ, *Turkey* 88 C3 40 4N 29 13 E
Mount Orab, *U.S.A.* 141 E13 39 5N 83 56W
Mount Oxide Mine, *Australia* 114 B2 19 30 S 139 29 E
Mount Pearl, *Canada* 129 C9 47 31N 52 47W
Mount Perry, *Australia* 115 D5 25 13 S 151 42 E
Mount Phillips, *Australia* 112 D2 24 25 S 116 15 E
Mount Pleasant, *Iowa, U.S.A.* 140 D5 40 58N 91 35W
Mount Pleasant, *Mich., U.S.A.* 134 D3 43 35N 84 47W
Mount Pleasant, *Pa., U.S.A.* 136 F5 40 9N 79 31W
Mount Pleasant, *S.C., U.S.A.* 135 J6 32 45N 79 48W
Mount Pleasant, *Tenn., U.S.A.* 135 H2 35 31N 87 11W
Mount Pleasant, *Tex., U.S.A.* 139 J7 33 5N 95 0W
Mount Pleasant, *Utah, U.S.A.* 142 G8 39 40N 111 29W
Mount Pocono, *U.S.A.* 137 E9 41 8N 75 21W
Mount Pulaski, *U.S.A.* 140 D7 40 1N 89 17W
Mount Rainier Nat. Park, *U.S.A.* 144 D5 46 50N 121 43W
Mount Revelstoke Nat. Park, *Canada* 130 C5 51 5N 118 30W
Mount Robson Prov. Park, *Canada* 130 C5 53 0N 119 0W
Mount Roskill, *N.Z.* 118 C3 36 55 S 174 45 E
Mount Sandiman, *Australia* 113 D2 24 25 S 115 30 E
Mount Shasta, *U.S.A.* 142 F2 41 20N 122 18W
Mount Signal, *U.S.A.* 145 N11 32 39N 115 37W
Mount Somers, *N.Z.* 119 D6 43 45 S 171 27 E
Mount Sterling, *Ill., U.S.A.* 140 E6 39 59N 90 40W
Mount Sterling, *Ky., U.S.A.* 141 F13 38 3N 83 57W
Mount Sterling, *Ohio, U.S.A.* 141 E13 39 43N 83 16W
Mount Surprise, *Australia* 114 B3 18 10 S 144 17 E
Mount Union, *U.S.A.* 136 F7 40 22N 77 51W
Mount Vernon, *Australia* 112 D2 24 9 S 118 2 E
Mount Vernon, *Ill., U.S.A.* 141 F8 38 19N 88 55W
Mount Vernon, *Ind., U.S.A.* 138 F10 38 17N 88 57W
Mount Vernon, *Iowa, U.S.A.* 140 C5 41 55N 91 23W
Mount Vernon, *N.Y., U.S.A.* 137 F11 40 57N 73 49W
Mount Vernon, *Ohio, U.S.A.* 136 F2 40 20N 82 30W
Mount Vernon, *Wash., U.S.A.* 144 B4 48 25N 122 20W
Mount Victor, *Australia* 116 B3 32 11 S 139 44 E
Mount Washington, *U.S.A.* 141 F11 38 3N 85 33W
Mount Wellington, *N.Z.* 118 C3 36 55 S 174 52 E
Mount Zion, *U.S.A.* 141 E8 39 46N 88 53W
Mountain Center, *U.S.A.* 145 M10 33 42N 116 44W
Mountain City, *Nev., U.S.A.* 142 F6 41 54N 116 0W
Mountain City, *Tenn., U.S.A.* 135 G5 36 30N 81 50W
Mountain Grove, *U.S.A.* 139 G8 37 5N 92 20W
Mountain Home, *Ark., U.S.A.* 139 G8 36 20N 92 25W
Mountain Home, *Idaho, U.S.A.* 142 E6 43 11N 115 45W
Mountain Iron, *U.S.A.* 138 B8 47 30N 92 37W
Mountain Park, *Canada* 130 C5 52 50N 117 15W
Mountain Pass, *U.S.A.* 145 K11 35 29N 115 35W
Mountain View, *Ark., U.S.A.* 139 H8 35 52N 92 10W
Mountain View, *Calif., U.S.A.* 144 H4 37 26N 122 5W
Mountainair, *U.S.A.* 143 J10 34 35N 106 15W
Moura, *Australia* 114 C4 24 35 S 149 58 E
Moura, *Brazil* 153 D5 1 32 S 61 38W
Moura, *Portugal* 37 G3 38 7N 7 30W
Mourão, *Portugal* 37 G3 38 22N 7 22W
Mourdi, Dépression du, *Chad* 97 E4 18 10N 23 0 E
Mourdiah, *Mali* 100 C3 14 35N 7 25W
Mourenx-Ville-Nouvelle, *France* 24 E3 43 22N 0 38W
Mouri, *Ghana* 101 D4 5 6N 1 14W
Mourilyan, *Australia* 114 B4 17 35 S 146 3 E
Mourmelon-le-Grand, *France* 23 C11 49 8N 4 22 E
Mourne →, *U.K.* 19 B4 54 45N 7 39W
Mourne Mts., *U.K.* 19 B5 54 10N 6 0W
Mournies, *Greece* 32 D6 35 29N 24 1 E
Mouscron, *Belgium* 21 G2 50 45N 3 12 E
Moussoro, *Chad* 97 F3 13 41N 16 35 E
Mouthe, *France* 23 F13 46 44N 6 12 E
Moutier, *Switz.* 28 B4 47 16N 7 21 E
Moûtiers, *France* 25 C10 45 29N 6 32 E
Moutohara, *N.Z.* 118 E6 38 27 S 177 32 E
Moutong, *Indonesia* 71 D6 0 28N 121 13 E
Mouy, *France* 23 C9 49 18N 2 20 E
Mouzáki, *Greece* 44 E3 39 25N 21 37 E
Movas, *Mexico* 146 B3 28 10N 109 25W
Moville, *Ireland* 19 A4 55 11N 7 3W
Moweaqua, *U.S.A.* 140 E7 39 37N 89 1W
Moxhe, *Belgium* 21 G6 50 38N 5 5 E
Moxico □, *Angola* 103 E4 12 0 S 20 30 E
Moxotó →, *Brazil* 154 C4 9 19 S 38 14W
Moy →, *Ireland* 19 B3 54 5N 8 50W
Moyale, *Kenya* 90 G2 3 30N 39 0 E
Moyamba, *S. Leone* 100 D2 8 4N 12 30W
Moyen Atlas, *Morocco* 98 B4 33 0N 5 0W
Moyle □, *U.K.* 19 A5 55 10N 6 15W

Mu'tariḑah, Al 'Urūq al 237

Moyo, *Indonesia* .... **70 F5** 8 10 S 117 40 E
Moyobamba, *Peru* ...... **156 B2** 6 0 S 77 0W
Moyyero →, *U.S.S.R.* . **57 C11** 68 44N 103 42 E
Mozambique = Moçambique, *Mozam.* **107 F5** 15 3 S 40 42 E
Mozambique ■, *Africa* . **107 F4** 19 0 S 35 0 E
Mozambique Chan., *Africa* .... **105 F7** 17 30 S 42 30 E
Mozdok, *U.S.S.R.* .... **53 E11** 43 45N 44 48 E
Mozdūrān, *Iran* .... **85 B9** 36 9N 60 35 E
Mozhaysk, *U.S.S.R.* ..... **51 D10** 55 30N 36 2 E
Mozhga, *U.S.S.R.* .... **54 C3** 56 26N 52 15 E
Mozhnābād, *Iran* .... **85 C9** 34 7N 60 6 E
Mozirje, *Yugoslavia* .... **39 B11** 46 22N 14 58 E
Mozyr, *U.S.S.R.* .... **50 E6** 52 5N 29 15 E
Mpanda, *Tanzania* ..... **106 D3** 6 23 S 31 1 E
Mpanda □, *Tanzania* ... **106 D3** 6 23 S 31 40 E
Mpésoba, *Mali* **100 C3** 12 31N 5 39W
Mpika, *Zambia* .... **107 E3** 11 51 S 31 25 E
Mpulungu, *Zambia* ..... **107 D3** 8 51 S 31 5 E
Mpumalanga, *S. Africa* . **105 D5** 29 50 S 30 33 E
Mpwapwa, *Tanzania* .... **106 D4** 6 23 S 36 30 E
Mpwapwa □, *Tanzania* . **106 D4** 6 30 S 36 20 E
Mrągowo, *Poland* ...... **47 B8** 53 52N 21 18 E
Mrakovo, *U.S.S.R.* ...... **54 E5** 52 43N 56 38 E
Mramor, *Yugoslavia* .... **42 D6** 43 20N 21 45 E
Mrimina, *Morocco* **98 C3** 29 50N 7 9W
Mrkonjić Grad, *Yugoslavia* .... **42 C2** 44 26N 17 4 E
Mrkopalj, *Yugoslavia* ... **39 C11** 45 21N 14 52 E
Mrocza, *Poland* .... **47 B4** 53 16N 17 35 E
Msab, Oued en →, *Algeria* .... **99 B6** 32 25N 5 20 E
Msaken, *Tunisia* .... **96 A2** 35 49N 10 33 E
Msambansovu, *Zimbabwe* **107 F3** 15 50 S 30 3 E
M'sila, *Algeria* .... **99 A5** 35 46N 4 30 E
Msoro, *Zambia* .... **107 E3** 13 35 S 31 50 E
Msta →, *U.S.S.R.* ...... **50 B7** 58 25N 31 20 E
Mstislavl, *U.S.S.R.* ..... **50 E7** 54 0N 31 50 E
Mszana Dolna, *Poland* .. **31 B13** 49 41N 20 5 E
Mszczonów, *Poland* .... **47 D7** 51 58N 20 33 E
Mtama, *Tanzania* ...... **107 E4** 10 17 S 39 21 E
Mtilikwe →, *Zimbabwe* **107 G3** 21 9 S 31 30 E
Mtsensk, *U.S.S.R.* ..... **51 E10** 53 25N 36 30 E
Mtskheta, *U.S.S.R.* ..... **53 F11** 41 52N 44 45 E
Mtubatuba, *S. Africa* ... **105 D5** 28 30 S 32 8 E
Mtwara-Mikindani, *Tanzania* .... **107 E5** 10 20 S 40 20 E
Mu →, *Burma* .... **78 E5** 21 56N 95 38 E
Mu Gia, Deo, *Vietnam* . **76 D5** 17 40N 105 47 E
Mu Us Shamo, *China* ... **66 E5** 39 0N 109 0 E
Muacandalo, *Angola* .... **103 E3** 10 2 S 19 40 E
Muaná, *Brazil* .... **154 B2** 1 25 S 49 15W
Muanda, *Zaïre* .... **103 D2** 6 0 S 12 20 E
Muang Chiang Rai, *Thailand* .... **76 C2** 19 52N 99 50 E
Muang Lamphun, *Thailand* .... **76 C2** 18 40N 99 2 E
Muang Pak Beng, *Laos* . **76 C3** 19 54N 101 8 E
Muar, *Malaysia* .... **77 L4** 2 3N 102 34 E
Muarabungo, *Indonesia* . **70 E2** 1 28 S 102 52 E
Muaraenim, *Indonesia* .. **70 E2** 3 40 S 103 50 E
Muarajuloi, *Indonesia* .. **70 E4** 0 12 S 114 3 E
Muarakaman, *Indonesia* . **70 E5** 0 2 S 116 45 E
Muaratebo, *Indonesia* ... **70 E2** 1 30 S 102 26 E
Muaratembesi, *Indonesia* **70 E2** 1 42 S 103 8 E
Muaratewe, *Indonesia* .. **70 E4** 0 58 S 114 52 E
Mubarakpur, *India* ..... **81 F10** 26 6N 83 18 E
Mubarraz = Al Mubarraz, *Si. Arabia* . **85 E6** 25 30N 49 40 E
Mubende, *Uganda* ...... **106 B3** 0 33N 31 22 E
Mubi, *Nigeria* .... **101 C7** 10 18N 13 16 E
Mubur, P., *Indonesia* ... **77 L6** 3 20N 106 12 E
Mucajaí →, *Brazil* **153 C5** 2 25N 60 52W
Mucajaí, Serra do, *Brazil* **153 C5** 2 23N 61 10W
Mucari, *Angola* .... **103 D3** 9 30 S 16 54 E
Muchachos, Roque de los, *Canary Is.* **33 F2** 28 44N 17 52W
Mücheln, *Germany* ..... **26 D7** 51 18N 11 49 E
Muchinga Mts., *Zambia* . **107 E3** 11 30 S 31 30 E
Muchkapskiy, *U.S.S.R.* . **51 F13** 51 52N 42 28 E
Muck, *U.K.* **18 E2** 56 50N 6 15W
Muckadilla, *Australia* .. **115 D4** 26 35 S 148 23 E
Muco →, *Colombia* **152 C3** 4 15N 70 21W
Mucoma, *Angola* ...... **103 F2** 15 18 S 13 39 E
Muconda, *Angola* ...... **103 E4** 10 31 S 21 15 E
Mucuim →, *Brazil* ..... **157 B5** 6 33 S 64 18W
Mucur, *Turkey* .... **88 D6** 39 3N 34 22 E
Mucura, *Brazil* .... **153 D5** 2 31 S 62 43W
Mucuri, *Brazil* .... **155 E4** 18 0 S 39 36W
Mucurici, *Brazil* .... **155 E3** 18 6 S 40 31W
Mucusso, *Angola* .... **103 F4** 18 1 S 21 25 E
Muda, *Canary Is.* **33 F6** 28 34N 13 57W
Mudan Jiang →, *China* . **67 A15** 46 20N 129 30 E
Mudanjiang, *China* ..... **67 B15** 44 38N 129 30 E
Mudanya, *Turkey* ...... **52 F3** 40 25N 28 50 E
Muddy →, *U.S.A.* **143 H8** 38 0N 110 22W
Mudgee, *Australia* ..... **117 B8** 32 32 S 149 31 E
Mudjatik →, *Canada* ... **131 B7** 56 1N 107 36W
Mudon, *Burma* .... **78 G6** 16 15N 97 44 E
Mudugh, *Somali Rep.* ... **108 C3** 7 0N 47 30 E
Mudurnu, *Turkey* ...... **88 C4** 40 27N 31 12 E
Muecate, *Mozam.* ...... **107 E4** 14 55 S 39 40 E
Muêda, *Mozam.* .... **107 E4** 11 36 S 39 28 E
Mueller Ra., *Australia* .. **112 C4** 18 18 S 126 46 E
Muende, *Mozam.* .... **107 E3** 14 28 S 33 0 E
Muerto, Mar, *Mexico* ... **147 D6** 16 10N 94 10W
Muertos, Punta de los, *Spain* **35 J3** 36 57N 1 54W
Mufindi □, *Tanzania* ... **107 D4** 8 30 S 35 20 E
Mufu Shan, *China* ...... **69 C10** 29 20N 114 30 E
Mufulira, *Zambia* ...... **107 E2** 12 32 S 28 15 E
Mufumbiro Range, *Africa* **106 C2** 1 25 S 29 30 E
Mugardos, *Spain* **36 B2** 43 27N 8 15W
Muge, *Portugal* **37 F2** 39 3N 8 40W
Muge →, *Portugal* **37 F2** 39 8N 8 44W
Múggia, *Italy* .... **39 C10** 45 36N 13 47 E
Mughayrā', *Si. Arabia* .. **84 D3** 29 17N 37 41 E
Mugi, *Japan* .... **62 D6** 33 40N 134 25 E
Mugia, *Spain* **36 B1** 43 3N 9 10W
Mugila, Mts., *Zaïre* ..... **106 D2** 7 0 S 28 50 E
Muğla, *Turkey* .... **88 E3** 37 15N 28 22 E
Muğla □, *Turkey* .... **88 E3** 37 0N 28 0 E
Müglizh, *Bulgaria* ...... **43 E10** 42 37N 25 32 E
Mugu, *Nepal* .... **81 E10** 29 45N 82 30 E
Muhammad, Râs, *Egypt* **94 B3** 27 44N 34 16 E
Muhammad Qol, *Sudan* . **94 C4** 20 53N 37 9 E
Muhammadabad, *India* . **81 F10** 26 4N 83 25 E
Muḩayriqah, *Si. Arabia* . **86 B4** 23 59N 45 4 E
Muhesi →, *Tanzania* ... **106 D4** 7 0 S 35 20 E
Muheza □, *Tanzania* ... **106 D4** 5 0 S 39 0 E
Mühldorf, *Germany* .... **27 G8** 48 14N 12 33 E
Mühlhausen, *Germany* .. **26 D6** 51 12N 10 29 E
Mühlig Hofmann fjella, *Antarctica* .... **7 D3** 72 30 S 5 0 E
Muhutwe, *Tanzania* .... **106 C3** 1 35 S 31 45 E
Muiden, *Neths.* .... **20 D6** 52 20N 5 4 E
Muikamachi, *Japan* ..... **61 F9** 37 15N 138 50 E
Muine Bheag, *Ireland* ... **19 D5** 52 42N 6 57W
Muiños, *Spain* **36 D3** 41 58N 7 59W
Muir, L., *Australia* ..... **113 F2** 34 30 S 116 40 E
Mukachevo, *U.S.S.R.* ... **50 G3** 48 27N 22 45 E
Mukah, *Malaysia* .... **70 D4** 2 55N 112 5 E
Mukawwa, Geziret, *Egypt* **94 C4** 23 55N 35 53 E
Mukdahan, *Thailand* ... **76 D5** 16 32N 104 43 E
Mukden = Shenyang, *China* .... **67 D12** 41 48N 123 27 E
Mukhtolovo, *U.S.S.R.* .. **51 D13** 55 29N 43 15 E
Mukhtuya = Lensk, *U.S.S.R.* .... **57 C12** 60 48N 114 55 E
Mukinbudin, *Australia* .. **113 F2** 30 55 S 118 5 E
Mukishi, *Zaïre* .... **103 D4** 8 30 S 24 44 E
Mukomuko, *Indonesia* .. **70 E2** 2 30 S 101 10 E
Mukomwenze, *Zaïre* .... **106 D2** 6 49 S 27 15 E
Mukry, *U.S.S.R.* .... **55 E2** 37 54N 65 12 E
Muktsar, *India* .... **80 D6** 30 30N 74 30 E
Mukur, *Afghan.* .... **80 C2** 32 50N 67 42 E
Mukutawa →, *Canada* . **131 C9** 53 10N 97 24W
Mukwela, *Zambia* ...... **107 F2** 17 0 S 26 40 E
Mukwonago, *U.S.A.* **141 B8** 42 52N 88 20W
Mula, *Spain* **35 G3** 38 3N 1 33W
Mula →, *India* .... **82 E2** 18 34N 74 21 E
Mulange, *Zaïre* .... **106 C2** 3 40 S 27 10 E
Mulberry Grove, *U.S.A.* **140 F7** 38 55N 89 16W
Mulchén, *Chile* .... **158 D1** 37 45 S 72 20W
Mulde →, *Germany* .... **26 D8** 51 50N 12 15 E
Muldraugh, *U.S.A.* **141 G11** 37 56N 85 59W
Mule Creek, *U.S.A.* **138 D2** 43 19N 104 8W
Muleba, *Tanzania* ...... **106 C3** 1 50 S 31 37 E
Muleba □, *Tanzania* ... **106 C3** 2 0 S 31 30 E
Mulegns, *Switz.* .... **29 C9** 46 32N 9 38 E
Muleshoe, *U.S.A.* **139 H3** 34 17N 102 42W
Mulga Valley, *Australia* . **116 A4** 31 8 S 141 3 E
Mulgathing, *Australia* ... **115 E1** 30 15 S 134 8 E
Mulgrave, *Canada* **129 C7** 45 38N 61 31W
Mulgrave I., *Papua N. G.* **120 F2** 10 5 S 142 10 E
Mulhacén, *Spain* **35 H1** 37 4N 3 20W
Mülheim, *Germany* ..... **26 D2** 51 26N 6 53 E
Mulhouse, *France* ...... **23 E14** 47 40N 7 20 E
Muli, *China* .... **68 D3** 27 52N 101 8 E
Mulifanua, *W. Samoa* ... **121 W24** 13 50 S 171 59W
Muling, *China* .... **67 B16** 44 35N 130 10 E
Mull, *U.K.* **18 E3** 56 27N 6 0W
Mullaittvu, *Sri Lanka* ... **83 K5** 9 15N 80 49 E
Mullen, *U.S.A.* **138 D4** 42 5N 101 0W
Mullengudgery, *Australia* **117 A7** 31 43 S 147 23 E
Mullens, *U.S.A.* **134 G5** 37 34N 81 22W
Muller, Pegunungan, *Indonesia* .... **70 D4** 0 30N 113 30 E
Mullet Pen., *Ireland* **19 B1** 54 10N 10 2W
Mullewa, *Australia* ..... **113 E2** 28 29 S 115 30 E
Müllheim, *Germany* .... **27 H3** 47 48N 7 37 E
Mulligan →, *Australia* .. **114 D2** 25 0 S 139 0 E
Mullin, *U.S.A.* **139 K5** 31 33N 98 38W
Mullingar, *Ireland* **19 C4** 53 31N 7 20W
Mullins, *U.S.A.* **135 H6** 34 12N 79 15W
Mullumbimby, *Australia* **115 D5** 28 30 S 153 30 E
Mulobezi, *Zambia* ...... **107 F2** 16 45 S 25 7 E
Mulshi L., *India* .... **82 E1** 18 30N 73 48 E
Multai, *India* .... **82 D4** 21 50N 78 21 E
Multan, *Pakistan* .... **79 C3** 30 15N 71 36 E
Multrå, *Sweden* .... **14 A11** 63 10N 17 24 E
Mulumbe, Mts., *Zaïre* .. **107 D2** 8 40 S 27 30 E
Mulungushi Dam, *Zambia* **107 E2** 14 48 S 28 48 E
Mulvane, *U.S.A.* **139 G6** 37 30N 97 15W
Mulwad, *Sudan* .... **94 D3** 18 45N 30 39 E
Mulwala, *Australia* ..... **117 C7** 35 59 S 146 0 E
Mumbondo, *Angola* ..... **103 E2** 10 9 S 14 15 E
Mumbwa, *Zambia* ...... **107 F2** 15 0 S 27 0 E
Mumeng, *Papua N. G.* . **120 D4** 7 1 S 146 37 E
Mumra, *U.S.S.R.* ...... **53 D12** 45 45N 47 41 E
Mun →, *Thailand* ..... **76 E5** 15 19N 105 30 E
Muna, *Indonesia* .... **71 F6** 5 0 S 122 30 E
Munamagi, *U.S.S.R.* .... **50 C5** 57 43N 27 4 E
Münchberg, *Germany* ... **27 E7** 50 11N 11 48 E
Müncheberg, *Germany* .. **26 C10** 52 30N 14 9 E
München, *Germany* ..... **27 G7** 48 8N 11 33 E
Munchen-Gladbach = Mönchengladbach, *Germany* .... **26 D2** 51 12N 6 23 E
Muncho Lake, *Canada* .. **130 B3** 59 0N 125 50W
Munchŏn, *N. Korea* .... **67 E14** 39 14N 127 19 E
Münchwilen, *Switz.* ..... **29 B7** 47 28N 8 59 E
Muncie, *U.S.A.* **141 D11** 40 10N 85 20W
Muncoonie, L., *Australia* **114 D2** 25 12 S 138 40 E
Munda, *Solomon Is.* .... **121 M9** 8 20 S 157 16 E
Mundakayam, *India* .... **83 K3** 9 30N 76 50 E
Mundala, *Indonesia* .... **71 E10** 4 30 S 141 0 E
Mundare, *Canada* **130 C6** 53 35N 112 20W
Munday, *U.S.A.* **139 J5** 33 26N 99 39W
Münden, *Germany* ..... **26 D5** 51 25N 9 42 E
Mundiwindi, *Australia* .. **112 D3** 23 47 S 120 9 E
Mundo →, *Spain* **35 G2** 38 30N 2 15W
Mundo Novo, *Brazil* .... **155 D3** 11 50 S 40 29W
Mundra, *India* .... **80 H3** 22 54N 69 48 E
Mundrabilla, *Australia* .. **113 F4** 31 52 S 127 51 E
Munducurus, *Brazil* .... **153 D6** 4 47 S 58 16W
Munenga, *Angola* ...... **103 E2** 10 2 S 14 41 E
Munera, *Spain* **35 F2** 39 2N 2 29W
Muneru →, *India* ...... **83 F5** 16 45N 80 3 E
Mungallala, *Australia* ... **115 D4** 26 28 S 147 34 E
Mungallala Cr. →, *Australia* .... **115 D4** 28 53 S 147 5 E
Mungana, *Australia* .... **114 B3** 17 8 S 144 27 E
Mungaoli, *India* .... **80 G8** 24 24N 78 7 E
Mungari, *Mozam.* ...... **107 F3** 17 12 S 33 30 E
Mungbere, *Zaïre* .... **106 B2** 2 36N 28 28 E
Munger, *India* .... **81 G12** 25 23N 86 30 E
Mungindi, *Australia* .... **115 D4** 28 58 S 149 1 E
Munhango, *Angola* ..... **103 E3** 12 10 S 18 38 E
Munich = München, *Germany* .... **27 G7** 48 8N 11 33 E
Munising, *U.S.A.* **134 B2** 46 25N 86 39W
Munka-Ljungby, *Sweden* **15 H6** 56 16N 12 58 E
Munkedal, *Sweden* ..... **15 F5** 58 28N 11 40 E
Munku-Sardyk, *U.S.S.R.* **57 D11** 51 45N 100 20 E
Münnerstadt, *Germany* . **27 E6** 50 15N 10 11 E
Muñoz Gamero, Pen., *Chile* .... **160 D2** 52 30 S 73 5W
Munro, *Australia* .... **117 D7** 37 56 S 147 11 E
Munroe L., *Canada* **131 B9** 59 13N 98 35W
Munsan, *S. Korea* ...... **67 F14** 37 51N 126 48 E
Munshiganj, *Bangla.* .... **78 D3** 23 33N 90 32 E
Münsingen, *Switz.* ...... **28 C5** 46 52N 7 32 E
Munster, *France* .... **23 D14** 48 2N 7 8 E
Munster, *Niedersachsen, Germany* .... **26 C6** 52 59N 10 5 E
Münster, *Nordrhein-Westfalen, Germany* .... **26 D3** 51 58N 7 37 E
Münster, *Switz.* .... **29 D6** 46 29N 8 17 E
Munster □, *Ireland* **19 D3** 52 20N 8 40W
Muntadgin, *Australia* ... **113 F2** 31 45 S 118 33 E
Muntele Mare, *Romania* **46 C4** 46 30N 23 12 E
Muntok, *Indonesia* ..... **70 E3** 2 5 S 105 10 E
Munyak, *U.S.S.R.* ...... **56 E6** 43 30N 59 15 E
Munyama, *Zambia* ..... **107 F2** 16 5 S 28 31 E
Muong Beng, *Laos* ..... **76 B3** 20 23N 101 46 E
Muong Boum, *Vietnam* . **76 A4** 22 24N 102 49 E
Muong Et, *Laos* .... **76 B5** 20 49N 104 1 E
Muong Hai, *Laos* ...... **76 B3** 21 3N 101 49 E
Muong Hiem, *Laos* ..... **76 B4** 20 5N 103 22 E
Muong Houn, *Laos* ..... **76 B3** 20 8N 101 23 E
Muong Hung, *Vietnam* .. **76 B4** 20 56N 103 53 E
Muong Kau, *Laos* ...... **76 E5** 15 6N 105 47 E
Muong Khao, *Laos* ..... **76 C4** 19 38N 103 32 E
Muong Khoua, *Laos* .... **76 B4** 21 5N 102 31 E
Muong Liep, *Laos* ..... **76 C3** 18 29N 101 40 E
Muong May, *Laos* ..... **76 E6** 14 49N 106 56 E
Muong Ngeun, *Laos* .... **76 B3** 20 36N 101 3 E
Muong Ngoi, *Laos* ..... **76 B4** 20 43N 102 41 E
Muong Nhie, *Vietnam* .. **76 A4** 22 12N 102 28 E
Muong Nong, *Laos* ..... **76 D6** 16 22N 106 30 E
Muong Ou Tay, *Laos* ... **76 A3** 22 7N 101 48 E
Muong Oua, *Laos* ...... **76 C3** 18 18N 101 20 E
Muong Peun, *Laos* ..... **76 B4** 20 13N 103 52 E
Muong Phalane, *Laos* .. **76 D5** 16 39N 105 34 E
Muong Phieng, *Laos* ... **76 C3** 19 6N 101 32 E
Muong Phine, *Laos* .... **76 D6** 16 32N 106 2 E
Muong Sai, *Laos* ...... **76 B3** 20 42N 101 59 E
Muong Saiapoun, *Laos* . **76 C3** 18 24N 101 31 E
Muong Sen, *Vietnam* ... **76 C5** 19 24N 104 8 E
Muong Sing, *Laos* ..... **76 B3** 21 11N 101 9 E
Muong Son, *Laos* ...... **76 B4** 20 27N 103 19 E
Muong Soui, *Laos* ..... **76 C4** 19 33N 102 52 E
Muong Va, *Laos* ...... **76 B4** 21 53N 102 19 E
Muong Xia, *Vietnam* ... **76 B5** 20 19N 104 50 E
Muonio, *Finland* .... **12 C17** 67 57N 23 40 E
Muotathal, *Switz.* ...... **29 C7** 46 58N 8 46 E
Mupa, *Angola* .... **103 F3** 16 5 S 15 50 E
Muping, *China* .... **67 F11** 37 22N 121 36 E
Muqaddam, Wadi →, *Sudan* .... **94 D3** 18 4N 31 30 E
Muqdisho, *Somali Rep.* . **90 G4** 2 2N 45 25 E
Muqshin, W. →, *Oman* **87 C6** 19 44N 55 14 E
Muquequete, *Angola* ... **103 E2** 14 50 S 14 16 E
Mur →, *Austria* .... **30 E9** 46 35N 16 3 E
Mur-de-Bretagne, *France* **22 D4** 48 12N 3 0W
Mura →, *Yugoslavia* ... **39 B13** 46 18N 16 53 E
Muradiye, *Turkey* ...... **89 D10** 39 0N 43 44 E
Murakami, *Japan* ...... **60 E9** 38 14N 139 29 E
Murallón, Cuerro, *Chile* **160 C2** 49 48 S 73 30W
Muralto, *Switz.* .... **29 D7** 46 11N 8 49 E
Muranda, *Rwanda* ...... **106 C2** 1 52 S 29 20 E
Murang'a, *Kenya* .... **106 C4** 0 45 S 37 9 E
Murashi, *U.S.S.R.* ..... **51 B16** 59 30N 49 0 E
Murat, *France* .... **24 C6** 45 7N 2 53 E
Murat →, *Turkey* ...... **89 D8** 38 39N 39 50 E
Muratlı, *Turkey* .... **88 C2** 41 10N 27 29 E
Murau, *Austria* .... **30 D7** 47 6N 14 10 E
Muravera, *Italy* .... **40 C2** 39 25N 9 35 E
Murayama, *Japan* ...... **60 E10** 38 30N 140 25 E
Murban, *U.A.E.* .... **85 F7** 23 50N 53 45 E
Murça, *Portugal* **36 D3** 41 24N 7 28W
Murchison, *N.Z.* .... **119 B7** 41 49 S 172 21 E
Murchison →, *Australia* **113 E1** 27 45 S 114 0 E
Murchison, Mt., *Antarctica* .... **7 D11** 73 0 S 168 0 E
Murchison Falls = Kabarega Falls, *Uganda* **106 B3** 2 15N 31 30 E
Murchison House, *Australia* .... **113 E1** 27 39 S 114 14 E
Murchison Mt., *N.Z.* ... **119 D6** 43 0 S 171 22 E
Murchison Mts., *N.Z.* .. **119 F2** 45 13 S 167 23 E
Murchison Ra., *Australia* **114 C1** 20 0 S 134 10 E
Murchison Rapids, *Malawi* .... **107 F3** 15 55 S 34 35 E
Murcia, *Spain* **35 G3** 38 20N 1 10W
Murcia □, *Spain* **35 H3** 37 50N 1 30W
Murdo, *U.S.A.* **138 D4** 43 56N 100 43W
Murdoch Pt., *Australia* .. **114 A3** 14 37 S 144 55 E
Mureş □, *Romania* .... **46 C5** 46 45N 24 40 E
Mureş →, *Romania* .... **46 C1** 46 15N 20 13 E
Mureşul = Mureş →, *Romania* .... **46 C1** 46 15N 20 13 E
Muret, *France* .... **24 E5** 43 30N 1 20 E
Murfatlar, *Romania* .... **46 E9** 44 10N 28 26 E
Murfreesboro, *U.S.A.* .. **135 H2** 35 50N 86 21W
Murg, *Switz.* .... **29 B8** 47 6N 9 13 E
Murg →, *Germany* .... **27 G4** 48 55N 8 10 E
Murgab, *U.S.S.R.* ..... **55 D7** 38 10N 74 2 E
Murgeni, *Romania* ..... **46 C9** 46 12N 28 1 E
Murgenthal, *Switz.* ..... **28 B5** 47 16N 7 50 E
Murgon, *Australia* ..... **115 D5** 26 15 S 151 54 E
Murgoo, *Australia* ..... **113 E2** 27 24 S 116 28 E
Muri, *Switz.* .... **29 B6** 47 17N 8 21 E
Muria, *Indonesia* ...... **71 G14** 6 36 S 110 53 E
Muriaé, *Brazil* .... **155 F3** 21 8 S 42 23W
Murias de Paredes, *Spain* **36 C4** 42 52N 6 11W
Murici, *Brazil* .... **154 C4** 9 19 S 35 56W
Muriége, *Angola* .... **103 D4** 9 58 S 21 11 E
Muriel Mine, *Zimbabwe* **107 F3** 17 14 S 30 40 E
Murila, *Angola* .... **103 E4** 10 44 S 20 20 E
Müritz See, *Germany* ... **26 B8** 53 25N 12 40 E
Murka, *Kenya* .... **106 C4** 3 27 S 38 0 E
Murmansk, *U.S.S.R.* ... **48 A5** 68 57N 33 10 E
Murmerwoude, *Neths.* .. **20 B8** 53 18N 6 0 E
Murnau, *Germany* ..... **27 H7** 47 40N 11 11 E
Muro, *France* .... **25 F12** 42 34N 8 54 E
Muro, *Spain* .... **33 B10** 39 44N 3 3 E
Muro, C. de, *France* .... **25 G12** 41 44N 8 37 E
Muro Lucano, *Italy* ..... **41 B8** 40 45N 15 30 E
Murom, *U.S.S.R.* ...... **51 D13** 55 35N 42 3 E
Muroran, *Japan* .... **60 C10** 42 25N 141 0 E
Muros, *Spain* **36 C1** 42 45N 9 5W
Muros y de Noya, Ría de, *Spain* **36 C2** 42 45N 9 0W
Muroto, *Japan* .... **62 D6** 33 18N 134 9 E
Muroto-Misaki, *Japan* .. **62 D6** 33 15N 134 10 E
Murowana Goślina, *Poland* .... **47 C4** 52 35N 17 0 E
Murphy, *U.S.A.* **142 E5** 43 11N 116 33W
Murphys, *U.S.A.* **144 G6** 38 8N 120 28W
Murphysboro, *U.S.A.* ... **139 G10** 37 50N 89 20W
Murrat, *Sudan* .... **94 D2** 18 51N 29 33 E
Murray, *Iowa, U.S.A.* .. **140 C3** 41 3N 93 57W
Murray, *Ky., U.S.A.* ... **135 G1** 36 40N 88 20W
Murray, *Utah, U.S.A.* .. **142 F8** 40 41N 111 58W
Murray →, *Australia* .. **116 C3** 35 20 S 139 22 E
Murray →, *Canada* **130 B4** 56 11N 120 45W
Murray, L., *Papua N. G.* **120 D1** 7 0 S 141 35 E
Murray, L., *U.S.A.* **135 H5** 34 8N 81 30W
Murray Bridge, *Australia* **116 C3** 35 6 S 139 14 E
Murray Downs, *Australia* **114 C1** 21 4 S 134 40 E
Murray Harbour, *Canada* **129 C7** 46 0N 62 28W
Murraysburg, *S. Africa* . **104 E3** 31 58 S 23 47 E
Murrayville, *U.S.A.* **140 E6** 39 35N 90 15W
Murree, *Pakistan* ...... **80 C5** 33 56N 73 28 E
Murrieta, *U.S.A.* **145 M9** 33 33N 117 13W
Murrin Murrin, *Australia* **113 E3** 28 58 S 121 33 E
Murrumbidgee →, *Australia* .... **116 C5** 34 43 S 143 12 E
Murrumburrah, *Australia* **117 C8** 34 32 S 148 22 E
Murrurundi, *Australia* .. **117 A9** 31 42 S 150 51 E
Mursala, *Indonesia* ..... **70 D1** 1 41N 98 28 E
Murshid, *Sudan* .... **94 C3** 21 40N 31 10 E
Murshidabad, *India* ..... **81 G13** 24 11N 88 19 E
Murska Sobota, *Yugoslavia* .... **39 B13** 46 39N 16 12 E
Murtazapur, *India* ...... **82 D3** 20 40N 77 25 E
Murten, *Switz.* .... **28 C4** 46 56N 7 4 E
Murtensee, *Switz.* ...... **28 C4** 46 56N 7 7 E
Murtle L., *Canada* **130 C5** 52 8N 119 38W
Murtoa, *Australia* ...... **116 D5** 36 35 S 142 28 E
Murtosa, *Portugal* **36 E2** 40 44N 8 40W
Muru →, *Brazil* .... **156 B3** 8 9 S 70 45W
Murungu, *Tanzania* .... **106 C3** 4 12 S 31 10 E
Murupara, *N.Z.* .... **118 E5** 38 28 S 176 42 E
Murwara, *India* .... **81 H9** 23 46N 80 28 E
Murwillumbah, *Australia* **115 D5** 28 18 S 153 27 E
Mürz →, *Austria* ...... **30 D8** 47 30N 15 25 E
Mürzzuschlag, *Austria* .. **30 D8** 47 36N 15 41 E
Muş, *Turkey* .... **89 D9** 38 45N 41 30 E
Muş □, *Turkey* .... **89 D9** 38 45N 41 30 E
Musa, *Zaïre* .... **102 B3** 2 40N 19 18 E
Musa →, *Papua N. G.* . **120 E5** 9 3 S 148 55 E
Mûsa, G., *Egypt* .... **94 J8** 28 33N 33 59 E
Musa Khel, *Pakistan* .... **79 C3** 30 59N 69 52 E
Mūsá Qal'eh, *Afghan.* .. **79 B2** 32 20N 64 50 E
Musala, *Bulgaria* .... **43 E8** 42 13N 23 37 E
Musan, *N. Korea* ...... **67 C15** 42 12N 129 12 E
Musangu, *Zaïre* .... **103 E4** 10 28 S 23 55 E
Musasa, *Tanzania* ..... **106 C3** 3 25 S 31 30 E
Musashino, *Japan* ..... **63 B11** 35 42N 139 34 E
Musay'īd, *Qatar* .... **85 E6** 25 0N 51 33 E
Musaymīr, *Yemen* ...... **86 D4** 13 27N 44 37 E
Muscat = Masqat, *Oman* **87 B7** 23 37N 58 36 E
Muscat & Oman = Oman ■, *Asia* .... **87 B7** 23 0N 58 0 E
Muscatine, *U.S.A.* **140 C5** 41 25N 91 5W
Muscoda, *U.S.A.* **140 A6** 43 11N 90 27W
Musel, *Spain* **36 B5** 43 34N 5 42W
Musgrave, *Australia* .... **114 A3** 14 47 S 143 30 E
Musgrave Ras., *Australia* **113 E5** 26 0 S 132 0 E
Mushie, *Zaïre* .... **102 C3** 2 56 S 16 55 E
Mushin, *Nigeria* .... **101 D5** 6 32N 3 21 E
Musi →, *India* .... **82 F4** 16 41N 79 40 E
Musi →, *Indonesia* .... **70 E2** 2 20 S 104 56 E
Muskeg →, *Canada* **130 A4** 60 20N 123 20W
Muskegon, *U.S.A.* **141 A10** 43 15N 86 17W
Muskegon →, *U.S.A.* .. **134 D2** 43 25N 86 25W
Muskegon Heights, *U.S.A.* **141 A10** 43 12N 86 17W
Muskogee, *U.S.A.* **139 H7** 35 50N 95 25W
Muskwa →, *Canada* ... **130 B4** 58 47N 122 48W
Muslīmiyah, *Syria* ...... **84 B3** 36 19N 37 12 E
Musmar, *Sudan* .... **94 D4** 18 13N 35 40 E
Musofu, *Zambia* .... **107 E2** 13 30 S 29 0 E
Musoma, *Tanzania* ..... **106 C3** 1 30 S 33 48 E
Musoma □, *Tanzania* ... **106 C3** 1 50 S 34 30 E
Musquaro, L., *Canada* .. **129 B7** 50 38N 61 5W
Musquodoboit Harbour, *Canada* **129 D7** 44 50N 63 9W
Mussau I., *Papua N. G.* **120 A5** 1 30 S 149 40 E
Musselburgh, *U.K.* **18 F5** 55 57N 3 3W
Musselkanaal, *Neths.* ... **20 C10** 52 57N 7 0 E
Musselshell →, *U.S.A.* . **142 C10** 47 21N 107 58W
Mussende, *Angola* ..... **103 E3** 10 32 S 16 5 E
Mussidan, *France* ...... **24 C4** 45 2N 0 22 E
Mussolo, *Angola* .... **103 D3** 9 59 S 17 19 E
Mussomeli, *Italy* .... **40 E6** 37 35N 13 43 E
Musson, *Belgium* ...... **21 J7** 49 33N 5 42 E
Mussoorie, *India* .... **80 D8** 30 27N 78 6 E
Mussuco, *Angola* ...... **103 F3** 17 2 S 19 3 E
Mustafakemalpaşa, *Turkey* .... **88 C3** 40 2N 28 24 E
Mustahil, *Ethiopia* ...... **108 C2** 5 16N 44 45 E
Mustang, *Nepal* .... **81 E10** 29 10N 83 55 E
Musters, L., *Argentina* . **160 C3** 45 20 S 69 25W
Musudan, *N. Korea* ... **67 D15** 40 50N 129 43 E
Muswellbrook, *Australia* **117 B9** 32 16 S 150 56 E
Muszyna, *Poland* ...... **31 B13** 49 22N 20 55 E
Mût, *Egypt* .... **94 B2** 25 28N 28 58 E
Mut, *Turkey* .... **88 E5** 36 40N 33 28 E
Mutanda, *Mozam.* ..... **105 C5** 21 0 S 33 34 E
Mutanda, *Zambia* ..... **107 E2** 12 24 S 26 13 E
Mutaray, *U.S.S.R.* ..... **57 C11** 60 56N 101 0 E
Mutare, *Zimbabwe* .... **107 F3** 18 58 S 32 38 E
Mu'tariḑah, Al 'Urūq al, *Si. Arabia* .... **87 B6** 21 15N 54 0 E

238 Muting

Muting, Indonesia 71 F10 7 23 S 140 20 E
Mutooroo, Australia 116 B4 32 26 S 140 55 E
Mutoto, Zaïre 103 D4 5 42 S 22 42 E
Mutshatsha, Zaïre 103 E4 10 35 S 24 20 E
Mutsu, Japan 60 D10 41 5N 140 55 E
Mutsu-Wan, Japan 60 D10 41 5N 140 55 E
Muttaburra, Australia 114 C3 22 38 S 144 29 E
Muttama, Australia 117 C8 34 46 S 148 8 E
Mutuáli, Mozam. 107 E4 14 55 S 37 0 E
Mutunópolis, Brazil 155 D2 13 40 S 49 15W
Muvatupusha, India 83 K3 9 53N 76 35 E
Muweilih, Egypt 91 E3 30 42N 34 19 E
Muxima, Angola 103 D2 9 33 S 13 58 E
Muy Muy, Nic. 148 D2 12 39N 85 36W
Muya, U.S.S.R. 57 D12 56 27N 115 50 E
Muyinga, Burundi 106 C3 3 14 S 30 33 E
Muyunkum, Peski, U.S.S.R. 55 A5 44 12N 71 0 E
Muzaffarabad, Pakistan 81 B5 34 25N 73 30 E
Muzaffargarh, Pakistan 79 C3 30 5N 71 14 E
Muzaffarnagar, India 80 E7 29 26N 77 40 E
Muzaffarpur, India 81 F11 26 7N 85 23 E
Muzeze, Angola 103 F3 15 3 S 17 43 E
Muzhi, U.S.S.R. 56 C7 65 25N 64 40 E
Muzillac, France 22 E4 47 35N 2 30W
Muzkol, Khrebet, U.S.S.R. 55 D6 38 22N 73 20 E
Muzon C., U.S.A. 130 C2 54 40N 132 40W
Mvadhi-Ousyé, Gabon 102 B2 1 13N 13 12 E
Mvam, Gabon 102 C1 0 13 S 9 39 E
Mvôlô, Sudan 95 F2 6 2N 29 53 E
Mvuma, Zimbabwe 107 F3 19 16 S 30 30 E
Mvurwi, Zimbabwe 107 F3 17 0 S 30 57 E
Mwadui, Tanzania 106 C3 3 26 S 33 32 E
Mwambo, Tanzania 107 E5 10 30 S 40 22 E
Mwandi, Zambia 107 F1 17 30 S 24 51 E
Mwanza, Tanzania 106 C3 2 30 S 32 58 E
Mwanza, Zaïre 103 D5 7 55 S 26 43 E
Mwanza, Zambia 107 F1 16 58 S 24 28 E
Mwanza □, Tanzania 106 C3 2 0 S 33 0 E
Mwaya, Tanzania 107 D3 9 32 S 33 55 E
Mweelrea, Ireland 19 C2 53 37N 9 48W
Mweka, Zaïre 103 C4 4 50 S 21 34 E
Mwendjila, Zaïre 103 D3 7 12 S 18 51 E
Mwene, Zaïre 103 D4 6 35 S 22 27 E
Mwenezi, Zimbabwe 107 G3 21 15 S 30 48 E
Mwenezi →, Mozam. 107 G3 22 40 S 31 50 E
Mwenga, Zaïre 106 C2 3 1 S 28 28 E
Mweru, L., Zambia 107 D2 9 0 S 28 40 E
Mweza Range, Zimbabwe 107 G3 21 0 S 30 0 E
Mwilambwe, Zaïre 103 D5 8 7 S 25 5 E
Mwimbi, Tanzania 107 D3 8 38 S 31 39 E
Mwinilunga, Zambia 107 E1 11 43 S 24 25 E
My Tho, Vietnam 77 G6 10 29N 106 23 E
Mya, O. →, Algeria 99 B5 30 46N 4 54 E
Myajlar, India 80 F4 26 15N 70 20 E
Myanaung, Burma 78 F5 18 18N 95 22 E
Myanmar = Burma ■, Asia 78 E6 21 0N 96 30 E
Myaungmya, Burma 78 G5 16 30N 94 40 E
Mycenae = Mikínai, Greece 45 G4 37 43N 22 46 E
Myeik Kyunzu, Burma 77 G1 11 30N 97 30 E
Myerstown, U.S.A. 137 F8 40 22N 76 18W
Myingyan, Burma 78 E5 21 30N 95 20 E
Myitkyina, Burma 78 C6 25 24N 97 26 E
Myittha →, Burma 78 D5 23 12N 94 17 E
Myjava, Czech. 31 C10 48 41N 17 37 E
Mymensingh, Bangla. 78 C3 24 45N 90 24 E
Myndus, Turkey 45 G9 37 3N 27 14 E
Mynydd Du, U.K. 17 F4 51 45N 3 45W
Mynzhilgi, Gora, U.S.S.R. 55 B4 43 48N 68 51 E
Mýrdalsjökull, Iceland 12 E4 63 40N 19 6W
Myroodah, Australia 112 C3 18 7 S 124 16 E
Myrtle Beach, U.S.A. 135 J6 33 43N 78 50W
Myrtle Creek, U.S.A. 142 E2 43 0N 123 9W
Myrtle Point, U.S.A. 142 E1 43 0N 124 4W
Myrtleford, Australia 117 D7 36 34 S 146 44 E
Myrtou, Cyprus 32 D12 35 18N 33 4 E
Mysen, Norway 14 E5 59 33N 11 20 E
Mysia, Turkey 88 D2 39 50N 27 0 E
Myslenice, Poland 31 B12 49 51N 19 57 E
Myślibórz, Poland 47 C1 52 55N 14 50 E
Mysłowice, Poland 31 A12 50 15N 19 12 E
Mysore = Karnataka □, India 83 H3 13 15N 77 0 E
Mysore, India 83 H3 12 17N 76 41 E
Mystic, Conn., U.S.A. 137 E13 41 21N 71 58W
Mystic, Iowa, U.S.A. 140 D4 40 47N 92 57W
Myszków, Poland 47 E6 50 45N 19 22 E
Myszyniec, Poland 47 B8 53 23N 21 21 E
Mythen, Switz. 29 B7 47 2N 8 42 E
Mytishchi, U.S.S.R. 51 D10 55 50N 37 50 E
Myton, U.S.A. 142 F8 40 10N 110 2W
Mývatn, Iceland 12 D5 65 36N 17 0W
Mže →, Czech. 30 B6 49 46N 13 24 E
Mzimba, Malawi 107 E3 11 55 S 33 39 E
Mzimkulu →, S. Africa 105 E5 30 44 S 30 28 E
Mzimvubu →, S. Africa 105 E4 31 38 S 29 33 E
Mzuzu, Malawi 107 E3 11 30 S 33 55 E

N

N' Dioum, Senegal 100 B2 16 31N 14 39W
Na-lang, Burma 78 D6 22 42N 97 33 E
Na Noi, Thailand 76 C3 18 19N 100 43 E
Na Phao, Laos 76 D5 17 35N 105 44 E
Na Sam, Vietnam 76 A6 22 3N 106 37 E
Na San, Vietnam 76 B5 21 12N 104 2 E
Naab →, Germany 27 F8 49 1N 12 2 E
Naaldwijk, Neths. 20 E4 51 59N 4 13 E
Na'am, Sudan 95 F2 9 42N 28 27 E
Naantali, Finland 13 F17 60 29N 22 2 E
Naarden, Neths. 20 D6 52 18N 5 9 E
Nababiep, S. Africa 104 D2 29 36 S 17 46 E
Nabadwip = Navadwip, India 81 H13 23 34N 88 20 E
Nabari, Japan 63 C8 34 37N 136 5 E
Nabawa, Australia 113 E1 28 30 S 114 48 E
Nabberu, L., Australia 113 E3 25 50 S 120 30 E
Nabburg, Germany 27 F8 49 27N 12 11 E
Naberezhnyye Chelny, U.S.S.R. 54 D3 55 42N 52 19 E
Nabeul, Tunisia 96 A2 36 30N 10 44 E
Nabha, India 80 D7 30 26N 76 14 E
Nabīd, Iran 85 D8 29 40N 57 38 E
Nabire, Indonesia 71 E9 3 15 S 135 26 E
Nabisar, Pakistan 80 G3 25 8N 69 40 E
Nabisipi →, Canada 129 B7 50 14N 62 13W
Nabiswera, Uganda 106 B3 1 27N 32 15 E
Nablus = Nābulus, Jordan 91 C4 32 14N 35 15 E
Naboomspruit, S. Africa 105 C4 24 32 S 28 40 E
Nābulus, Jordan 91 C4 32 14N 35 15 E
Nābulus □, Jordan 91 C4 32 20N 35 20 E
Nacala, Mozam. 107 E5 14 31 S 40 34 E
Nacala-Velha, Mozam. 107 E5 14 32 S 40 34 E
Nacaome, Honduras 148 D2 13 31N 87 30W
Nacaroa, Mozam. 107 E4 14 22 S 39 56 E
Naches, U.S.A. 142 C3 46 48N 120 42W
Naches →, U.S.A. 144 D6 46 38N 120 31W
Nachikatsuura, Japan 63 D7 33 33N 135 58 E
Nachingwea, Tanzania 107 E4 10 23 S 38 49 E
Nachingwea □, Tanzania 107 E4 10 30 S 38 30 E
Nachna, India 80 F4 27 34N 71 41 E
Náchod, Czech. 31 A9 50 25N 16 8 E
Nacimiento Res., U.S.A. 144 K6 35 46N 121 0W
Nacka, Sweden 14 E12 59 17N 18 12 E
Nackara, Australia 116 B3 32 48 S 139 12 E
Naco, Mexico 146 A3 31 20N 109 56W
Naco, U.S.A. 143 L9 31 24N 109 58W
Nacogdoches, U.S.A. 139 K7 31 33N 94 39W
Nácori Chico, Mexico 146 B3 29 39N 109 1W
Nacozari, Mexico 146 A3 30 24N 109 39W
Nadi, Sudan 94 D3 18 40N 33 41 E
Nadiad, India 80 H5 22 41N 72 56 E
Nădlac, Romania 46 C1 46 10N 20 50 E
Nador, Morocco 99 A4 35 14N 2 58W
Nadur, Malta 32 C1 36 2N 14 17 E
Nadūshan, Iran 85 C7 32 2N 53 35 E
Nadvoitsy, U.S.S.R. 48 B5 63 52N 34 14 E
Nadvornaya, U.S.S.R. 52 B1 48 37N 24 30 E
Nadym, U.S.S.R. 56 C8 65 35N 72 42 E
Nadym →, U.S.S.R. 56 C8 66 12N 72 0 E
Næstved, Denmark 15 J5 55 13N 11 44 E
Nafada, Nigeria 101 C7 11 8N 11 20 E
Näfels, Switz. 29 B8 47 6N 9 4 E
Naftshahr, Iran 84 C5 34 0N 45 30 E
Nafūsah, Jabal, Libya 96 B2 32 12N 12 30 E
Nag Hammâdi, Egypt 94 B3 26 2N 32 18 E
Naga, Phil. 71 B6 13 38N 123 15 E
Naga, Kreb en, Africa 98 D3 24 12N 6 0W
Naga-Shima, Kagoshima, Japan 62 E2 32 10N 130 9 E
Naga-Shima, Yamaguchi, Japan 62 D4 33 49N 132 5 E
Nagagami →, Canada 128 C3 49 40N 84 40W
Nagahama, Ehime, Japan 62 D4 33 36N 132 29 E
Nagahama, Shiga, Japan 63 B8 35 23N 136 16 E
Nagai, Japan 60 E10 38 6N 140 2 E
Nagaland □, India 78 C5 26 0N 94 30 E
Nagambie, Australia 117 D6 36 47 S 145 10 E
Nagano, Japan 63 A10 36 40N 138 10 E
Nagano □, Japan 63 A10 36 15N 138 0 E
Nagaoka, Japan 61 F9 37 27N 138 51 E
Nagappattinam, India 83 J4 10 46N 79 51 E
Nagar Parkar, Pakistan 80 G4 24 28N 70 46 E
Nagara →, Japan 63 B8 35 40N 136 43 E
Nagari Hills, India 83 H4 13 3N 79 45 E
Nagarjuna Sagar, India 83 F4 16 35N 79 17 E
Nagasaki, Japan 62 E1 32 47N 129 50 E
Nagasaki □, Japan 62 E1 32 50N 129 40 E
Nagato, Japan 62 C3 34 19N 131 5 E
Nagaur, India 80 F5 27 15N 73 45 E
Nagbhir, India 82 D4 20 34N 79 55 E
Nagercoil, India 83 K3 8 12N 77 26 E
Nagina, India 81 E8 29 30N 78 30 E
Nagīneh, Iran 85 C8 34 20N 57 15 E
Nagir, Pakistan 81 A6 36 12N 74 42 E
Nagold, Germany 27 G4 48 33N 8 43 E
Nagold →, Germany 27 G4 48 52N 8 42 E
Nagoorin, Australia 114 C5 24 17 S 151 15 E
Nagornyy, U.S.S.R. 57 D13 55 58N 124 57 E
Nagorsk, U.S.S.R. 54 B2 59 18N 50 48 E
Nagoya, Japan 63 B8 35 10N 136 50 E
Nagpur, India 82 D4 21 8N 79 10 E
Nagua, Dom. Rep. 149 C6 19 23N 69 50W
Nagyatád, Hungary 31 E10 46 14N 17 22 E
Nagyecsed, Hungary 31 D15 47 53N 22 24 E
Nagykanizsa, Hungary 31 E10 46 28N 17 0 E
Nagykörös, Hungary 31 D12 47 5N 19 48 E
Nagyléta, Hungary 31 D14 47 23N 21 55 E
Naha, Japan 61 L3 26 13N 127 42 E
Nahanni Butte, Canada 130 A4 61 2N 123 31W
Nahanni Nat. Park, Canada 130 A4 61 15N 125 0W
Nahariyya, Israel 84 C2 33 1N 35 5 E
Nahāvand, Iran 85 C6 34 10N 48 22 E
Nahe →, Germany 27 F3 49 58N 7 57 E
Nahīya, Wadi →, Egypt 94 J7 28 55N 31 0 E
Nahlin, Canada 130 B2 58 55N 131 38W
Nahuel Huapi, L., Argentina 160 B2 41 0 S 71 32W
Naicá, Mexico 146 B3 27 53N 105 31W
Naicam, Canada 131 C8 52 30N 104 30W
Nā'ifah, Si. Arabia 90 D5 19 59N 50 46 E
Naila, Germany 27 E7 50 19N 11 43 E
Nain, Canada 129 A7 56 34N 61 40W
Nā'īn, Iran 85 C7 32 54N 53 0 E
Naini Tal, India 81 E8 29 30N 79 30 E
Naintré, France 22 F7 46 46N 0 29 E
Naipu, Romania 46 E6 44 12N 25 47 E
Naira, Indonesia 71 E8 4 28 S 130 0 E
Nairn, U.K. 18 D5 57 35N 3 54W
Nairobi, Kenya 106 C4 1 17 S 36 48 E
Naivasha, Kenya 106 C4 0 40 S 36 30 E
Naivasha, L., Kenya 106 C4 0 48 S 36 20 E
Najac, France 24 D5 44 14N 1 58 E
Najafābād, Iran 85 C6 32 40N 51 15 E
Nájera, Spain 34 C2 42 26N 2 48W
Najerilla →, Spain 34 C2 42 32N 2 48W
Najibabad, India 80 E8 29 40N 78 20 E
Najin, N. Korea 67 C16 42 12N 130 15 E
Najmah, Si. Arabia 85 E6 26 42N 50 6 E
Naju, S. Korea 67 G14 35 3N 126 43 E
Naka →, Japan 63 A12 36 20N 140 36 E
Nakadōri-Shima, Japan 61 H4 32 57N 129 4 E
Nakalagba, Zaïre 106 B2 2 50N 27 58 E
Nakama, Japan 62 D2 33 56N 130 43 E
Nakaminato, Japan 63 A12 36 21N 140 36 E
Nakamura, Japan 62 E4 32 59N 132 56 E
Nakanai Mts., Papua N. G. 120 C6 5 40 S 151 0 E
Nakano, Japan 63 A10 36 45N 138 22 E
Nakano-Shima, Japan 61 K4 29 51N 129 52 E
Nakanojō, Japan 63 A10 36 35N 138 51 E
Nakashibetsu, Japan 60 C12 43 33N 144 59 E
Nakatsu, Japan 62 D3 33 34N 131 15 E
Nakatsugawa, Japan 63 B9 35 29N 137 30 E
Nakfa, Ethiopia 95 D4 16 40N 38 32 E
Nakhichevan, U.S.S.R. 89 D11 39 12N 45 15 E
Nakhichevan A.S.S.R. □, U.S.S.R. 49 G8 39 14N 45 30 E
Nakhl, Egypt 91 F2 29 55N 33 43 E
Nakhl-e Taqī, Iran 85 E7 27 28N 52 36 E
Nakhodka, U.S.S.R. 57 E14 42 53N 132 54 E
Nakhon Nayok, Thailand 76 E3 14 12N 101 13 E
Nakhon Pathom, Thailand 76 F3 13 49N 100 3 E
Nakhon Phanom, Thailand 76 D5 17 23N 104 43 E
Nakhon Ratchasima, Thailand 76 E4 14 59N 102 12 E
Nakhon Sawan, Thailand 76 E3 15 35N 100 10 E
Nakhon Si Thammarat, Thailand 77 H3 8 29N 100 0 E
Nakhon Thai, Thailand 76 D3 17 5N 100 44 E
Nakina, B.C., Canada 130 B2 59 12N 132 52W
Nakina, Ont., Canada 128 B2 50 10N 86 40W
Nakło nad Notecią, Poland 47 B4 53 9N 17 38 E
Nakodar, India 80 D6 31 8N 75 31 E
Nakskov, Denmark 15 K5 54 50N 11 8 E
Näkten, Sweden 14 B8 62 48N 14 38 E
Naktong →, S. Korea 67 G15 35 7N 128 57 E
Nakuru, Kenya 106 C4 0 15 S 36 4 E
Nakuru □, Kenya 106 C4 0 15 S 35 5 E
Nakuru, L., Kenya 106 C4 0 23 S 36 5 E
Nakusp, Canada 130 C5 50 20N 117 45W
Nal →, Pakistan 79 D2 25 20N 65 30 E
Nalchik, U.S.S.R. 53 E10 43 30N 43 33 E
Nälden, Sweden 14 A8 63 21N 14 14 E
Näldsjön, Sweden 14 A8 63 25N 14 15 E
Nalerigu, Ghana 101 C4 10 35N 0 25W
Nalgonda, India 82 F4 17 6N 79 15 E
Nalhati, India 81 G12 24 17N 87 52 E
Nalinnes, Belgium 21 H4 50 19N 4 27 E
Nallamalai Hills, India 83 G4 15 30N 78 50 E
Nallıhan, Turkey 88 C4 40 11N 31 20 E
Nalón →, Spain 36 B4 43 32N 6 4W
Nālūt, Libya 96 B2 31 54N 11 0 E
Nam Can, Vietnam 77 H5 8 46N 104 59 E
Nam Co, China 64 C4 30 30N 90 45 E
Nam Dinh, Vietnam 76 B6 20 25N 106 5 E
Nam Du, Hon, Vietnam 77 H5 9 41N 104 21 E
Nam Ngum Dam, Laos 76 C4 18 35N 102 34 E
Nam-Phan, Vietnam 77 G6 10 30N 106 0 E
Nam Phong, Thailand 76 D4 16 42N 102 52 E
Nam Tha, Laos 76 B3 20 58N 101 30 E
Nam Tok, Thailand 76 E2 14 21N 99 4 E
Namachire, Angola 103 E4 11 26 S 22 43 E
Namacunde, Angola 103 F3 17 18 S 15 50 E
Namacurra, Mozam. 105 B6 17 30 S 36 50 E
Namak, Daryācheh-ye, Iran 85 C7 34 30N 52 0 E
Namak, Kavir-e, Iran 85 C8 34 30N 57 30 E
Namakkal, India 83 J4 11 13N 78 13 E
Namaland, Namibia 104 C2 24 30 S 17 0 E
Namangan, U.S.S.R. 55 C5 41 0N 71 40 E
Namapa, Mozam. 107 E4 13 43 S 39 50 E
Namaqualand, S. Africa 104 E2 30 0 S 17 25 E
Namasagali, Uganda 106 B3 1 2N 33 0 E
Namatanai, Papua N. G. 120 B7 3 40 S 152 29 E
Namber, Indonesia 71 E8 1 2 S 134 49 E
Nambour, Australia 115 D5 26 32 S 152 58 E
Nambouwalu, Fiji 121 A2 17 0 S 178 45 E
Nambucca Heads, Australia 117 A10 30 37 S 153 0 E
Namcha Barwa, China 64 D4 29 40N 95 10 E
Namche Bazar, Nepal 81 F12 27 51N 86 47 E
Namchonjŏm, N. Korea 67 E14 38 15N 126 26 E
Namêche, Belgium 21 H6 50 28N 5 0 E
Namecunda, Mozam. 107 E4 14 54 S 37 37 E
Nameh, Indonesia 70 D5 2 34N 116 21 E
Nameponda, Mozam. 107 F4 15 50 S 39 50 E
Namerikawa, Japan 63 A9 36 46N 137 20 E
Náměšt' nad Oslavou, Czech. 31 B9 49 12N 16 10 E
Námestovo, Czech. 31 B12 49 24N 19 25 E
Nametil, Mozam. 107 F4 15 40 S 39 21 E
Namew L., Canada 131 C8 54 14N 101 56W
Namhsan, Burma 78 D6 22 48N 97 2 E
Namib Desert = Namibwoestyn, Namibia 104 C2 22 30 S 15 0 E
Namibe, Angola 103 F2 15 7 S 12 11 E
Namibe □, Angola 103 F2 16 35 S 12 30 E
Namibia ■, Africa 104 C2 22 0 S 18 9 E
Namibwoestyn, Namibia 104 C2 22 30 S 15 0 E
Namkhan, Burma 78 D6 23 50N 97 41 E
Namlea, Indonesia 71 E7 3 18 S 127 5 E
Namoi →, Australia 117 A8 30 12 S 149 30 E
Namous, O. en →, Algeria 99 B4 31 0N 0 15W
Nampa, U.S.A. 142 E5 43 34N 116 34W
Nampō-Shotō, Japan 61 J10 32 0N 140 0 E
Nampula, Mozam. 107 F4 15 6 S 39 15 E
Namrole, Indonesia 71 E7 3 46 S 126 46 E
Namsen →, Norway 12 D11 64 27N 11 42 E
Namsos, Norway 12 D11 64 29N 11 30 E
Namtay, U.S.S.R. 57 C13 62 43N 129 37 E
Namtu, Burma 78 D6 23 5N 97 28 E
Namtumbo, Tanzania 107 E4 10 30 S 36 4 E
Namu, Canada 130 C3 51 52N 127 50W
Namur, Belgium 21 H5 50 27N 4 52 E
Namur □, Belgium 21 H6 50 17N 5 0 E
Namutoni, Namibia 104 B2 18 49 S 16 55 E
Namwala, Zambia 107 F2 15 44 S 26 30 E
Namwŏn, S. Korea 67 G14 35 23N 127 23 E
Namysłów, Poland 47 D4 51 6N 17 42 E
Nan, Thailand 76 C3 18 48N 100 46 E
Nan →, Thailand 76 E3 15 42N 100 9 E
Nan Xian, China 69 C9 29 20N 112 22 E
Nana, Romania 46 E7 44 17N 26 34 E
Nanaimo, Canada 130 D4 49 10N 124 0W
Nanam, N. Korea 67 D15 41 44N 129 40 E
Nanan, China 69 E12 24 59N 118 21 E
Nanango, Australia 115 D5 26 40 S 152 0 E
Nan'ao, China 69 F11 23 28N 117 5 E
Nanao, Japan 61 F8 37 0N 137 0 E
Nanbu, China 68 B6 31 18N 106 3 E
Nanchang, China 69 C10 28 42N 115 55 E
Nancheng, China 69 D11 27 33N 116 35 E
Nanching = Nanjing, China 65 C6 32 2N 118 47 E
Nanchong, China 68 B6 30 43N 106 2 E
Nanchuan, China 68 C6 29 9N 107 6 E
Nancy, France 23 D13 48 42N 6 12 E
Nanda Devi, India 81 D8 30 23N 79 59 E
Nandan, China 68 E6 24 58N 107 29 E
Nandan, Japan 62 C6 34 10N 134 42 E
Nanded, India 82 E3 19 10N 77 20 E
Nandewar Ra., Australia 115 E5 30 15 S 150 35 E
Nandi □, Kenya 106 B4 0 15N 35 0 E
Nandikotkur, India 83 G4 15 52N 78 18 E
Nandura, India 82 D3 20 52N 76 25 E
Nandurbar, India 82 D2 21 20N 74 15 E
Nandyal, India 83 G4 15 30N 78 30 E
Nanfeng, Guangdong, China 69 F8 23 45N 111 47 E
Nanfeng, Jiangxi, China 69 D11 27 12N 116 28 E
Nanga, Australia 113 E1 26 7 S 113 45 E
Nanga-Eboko, Cameroon 101 E7 4 41N 12 22 E
Nanga Parbat, Pakistan 81 B6 35 10N 74 35 E
Nangade, Mozam. 107 E4 11 5 S 39 36 E
Nangapinoh, Indonesia 70 E4 0 20 S 111 44 E
Nangarhár □, Afghan. 79 B3 34 20N 70 0 E
Nangatayap, Indonesia 70 E4 1 32 S 110 34 E
Nangeya Mts., Uganda 106 B3 3 30N 33 30 E
Nangis, France 23 D10 48 33N 3 1 E
Nangong, China 66 F8 37 23N 115 22 E
Nangwarry, Australia 116 D4 37 33 S 140 48 E
Nanhua, China 68 E3 25 13N 101 21 E
Nanhuang, China 67 F11 36 58N 121 48 E
Nanhui, China 69 B13 31 5N 121 44 E
Nanjangud, India 83 H3 12 6N 76 43 E
Nanjeko, Zambia 107 F1 15 31 S 23 30 E
Nanji Shan, China 69 D13 27 27N 121 4 E
Nanjian, China 68 E3 25 2N 100 25 E
Nanjiang, China 68 A6 32 28N 106 51 E
Nanjing, Fujian, China 69 E11 24 25N 117 20 E
Nanjing, Jiangsu, China 65 C6 32 2N 118 47 E
Nanjirinji, Tanzania 107 D4 9 41 S 39 5 E
Nankana Sahib, Pakistan 80 D5 31 27N 73 38 E
Nankang, China 69 E10 25 40N 114 45 E
Nanking = Nanjing, China 65 C6 32 2N 118 47 E
Nankoku, Japan 62 D5 33 39N 133 44 E
Nanling, China 69 B12 30 55N 118 20 E
Nanning, China 68 F7 22 48N 108 20 E
Nannup, Australia 113 F2 33 59 S 115 48 E
Nanpan Jiang →, China 68 E6 25 10N 106 5 E
Nanpara, India 81 F9 27 52N 81 33 E
Nanpi, China 66 E9 38 2N 116 45 E
Nanping, Fujian, China 69 D12 26 38N 118 10 E
Nanping, Henan, China 69 C9 29 55N 112 3 E
Nanri Dao, China 69 E12 25 15N 119 25 E
Nanripe, Mozam. 107 E4 13 52 S 38 52 E
Nansei-Shotō = Ryūkyū-rettō, Japan 61 M3 26 0N 126 0 E
Nansen Sd., Canada 6 A3 81 0N 91 0W
Nansio, Tanzania 106 C3 2 3 S 33 4 E
Nant, France 24 D7 44 1N 3 18 E
Nantes, France 22 E5 47 12N 1 33W
Nanteuil-le-Haudouin, France 23 C9 49 9N 2 48 E
Nantiat, France 24 B5 46 1N 1 11 E
Nanticoke, U.S.A. 137 E8 41 12N 76 1W
Nanton, Canada 130 C6 50 21N 113 46W
Nantong, China 69 A13 32 1N 120 52 E
Nantua, France 25 B9 46 10N 5 35 E
Nantucket I., U.S.A. 124 E12 41 16N 70 3W
Nanuku Passage, Fiji 121 A3 16 45 S 179 15W
Nanuque, Brazil 155 E3 17 50 S 40 21W
Nanutarra, Australia 112 D2 22 32 S 115 30 E
Nanxiong, China 69 E10 25 6N 114 15 E
Nanyang, China 66 H7 33 11N 112 30 E
Nanyi Hu, China 69 B12 31 5N 119 0 E
Nan'yō, Japan 62 C3 34 3N 131 49 E
Nanyuan, China 66 E9 39 44N 116 22 E
Nanyuki, Kenya 106 B4 0 2N 37 4 E
Nanzhang, China 69 B8 31 45N 111 50 E
Náo, C. de la, Spain 35 G5 38 44N 0 14 E
Naococane L., Canada 129 B5 52 50N 70 45W
Naoetsu, Japan 61 F9 37 12N 138 10 E
Naogaon, Bangla. 78 C2 24 52N 88 52 E
Náousa, Greece 44 D4 40 42N 22 9 E
Naozhou Dao, China 69 G8 20 55N 110 20 E
Napa, U.S.A. 144 G4 38 18N 122 17W
Napa →, U.S.A. 144 G4 38 10N 122 19W
Napanee, Canada 128 D4 44 15N 77 0W
Napanoch, U.S.A. 137 E10 41 44N 74 22W
Nape, Laos 76 C5 18 18N 105 6 E
Nape Pass = Keo Neua, Deo, Vietnam 76 C5 18 23N 105 10 E
Naperville, U.S.A. 141 C8 41 46N 88 9W
Napf, Switz. 28 B5 47 1N 7 56 E
Napier, N.Z. 118 F5 39 30 S 176 56 E
Napier Broome B., Australia 112 B4 14 2 S 126 37 E
Napier Downs, Australia 112 C3 17 11 S 124 36 E
Napier Pen., Australia 114 A2 12 4 S 135 43 E
Naples = Nápoli, Italy 41 B7 40 50N 14 17 E
Naples, U.S.A. 135 M5 26 10N 81 45W
Napo, China 68 F5 23 22N 105 50 E
Napo □, Ecuador 152 D2 0 30 S 77 0W
Napo →, Peru 152 D3 3 20 S 72 40W
Napoleon, N. Dak., U.S.A. 138 B5 46 32N 99 49W
Napoleon, Ohio, U.S.A. 141 C12 41 24N 84 7W
Nápoli, Italy 41 B7 40 50N 14 17 E
Nápoli, G. di, Italy 41 B7 40 40N 14 10 E
Napopo, Zaïre 106 B2 4 15N 28 0 E
Nappa Merrie, Australia 115 D3 27 36 S 141 7 E
Nappanee, U.S.A. 141 C11 41 27N 86 0W
Naqâda, Egypt 94 B3 25 53N 32 42 E

Neusiedler See 239

Naqqāsh, *Iran* **85 C6** 35 40N 49 6 E
Nara, *Japan* **63 C7** 34 40N 135 49 E
Nara, *Mali* **100 B3** 15 10N 7 20W
Nara □, *Japan* **63 C8** 34 30N 136 0 E
Nara Canal, *Pakistan* **80 G3** 24 30N 69 20 E
Nara Visa, *U.S.A.* **139 H3** 35 39N 103 10W
Naracoorte, *Australia* **116 D4** 36 58 S 140 45 E
Naradhan, *Australia* **117 B7** 33 34 S 146 17 E
Narasapur, *India* **83 F5** 16 26N 81 40 E
Narasaropet, *India* **83 F5** 16 14N 80 4 E
Narathiwat, *Thailand* **77 J3** 6 30N 101 48 E
Narayanganj, *Bangla.* **78 D3** 23 40N 90 33 E
Narayanpet, *India* **82 F3** 16 45N 77 30 E
Narbonne, *France* **24 E7** 43 11N 3 0 E
Narcea →, *Spain* **36 B4** 43 33N 6 44W
Nardīn, *Iran* **85 B7** 37 3N 55 59 E
Nardò, *Italy* **41 B11** 40 10N 18 0 E
Narembeen, *Australia* **113 F2** 32 7 S 118 24 E
Nares Str., *Arctic* **124 B13** 80 0N 70 0W
Naretha, *Australia* **113 F3** 31 0 S 124 45 E
Narew, *Poland* **47 C10** 52 55N 23 31 E
Narew →, *Poland* **47 C7** 52 26N 20 41 E
Nari →, *Pakistan* **80 F2** 28 0N 67 40 E
Narindra, Helodranon' i, *Madag.* **105 A8** 14 55 S 47 30 E
Narino □, *Colombia* **152 C2** 1 30N 78 0W
Narita, *Japan* **63 B12** 35 47N 140 19 E
Narmada →, *India* **80 J5** 21 38N 72 36 E
Narman, *Turkey* **89 C9** 40 26N 41 57 E
Narnaul, *India* **80 E7** 28 5N 76 11 E
Narni, *Italy* **39 F9** 42 30N 12 30 E
Naro, *Ghana* **100 C4** 10 22N 2 27W
Naro, *Italy* **40 E6** 37 18N 13 48 E
Naro Fominsk, *U.S.S.R.* **51 D10** 55 23N 36 43 E
Narodnaya, *U.S.S.R.* **48 A10** 65 5N 59 58 E
Narok, *Kenya* **106 C4** 1 55 S 35 52 E
Narok □, *Kenya* **106 C4** 1 20 S 36 30 E
Narón, *Spain* **36 B2** 43 32N 8 9W
Narooma, *Australia* **117 D9** 36 14 S 150 4 E
Narowal, *Pakistan* **79 B4** 32 6N 74 52 E
Narrabri, *Australia* **115 E4** 30 19 S 149 46 E
Narran →, *Australia* **115 D4** 28 37 S 148 12 E
Narrandera, *Australia* **117 C7** 34 42 S 146 31 E
Narraway →, *Canada* **130 B5** 55 44N 119 55W
Narrogin, *Australia* **113 F2** 32 58 S 117 14 E
Narromine, *Australia* **117 B8** 32 12 S 148 12 E
Narsampet, *India* **82 F4** 17 57N 79 58 E
Narsimhapur, *India* **81 H8** 22 54N 79 14 E
Nartkala, *U.S.S.R.* **53 E10** 43 33N 43 51 E
Naruto, *Kantō, Japan* **62 C6** 34 11N 134 37 E
Narutō, *Shikoku, Japan* **63 B12** 35 36N 140 25 E
Naruto-Kaikyō, *Japan* **62 C6** 34 14N 134 39 E
Narva, *U.S.S.R.* **50 B6** 59 23N 28 12 E
Narva →, *U.S.S.R.* **50 B6** 59 27N 28 2 E
Narvik, *Norway* **12 B14** 68 28N 17 26 E
Narvskoye Vdkhr., *U.S.S.R.* **50 B6** 59 18N 28 14 E
Narwana, *India* **80 E7** 29 39N 76 6 E
Naryan-Mar, *U.S.S.R.* **48 A9** 68 0N 53 0 E
Naryilco, *Australia* **115 D3** 28 37 S 141 53 E
Narym, *U.S.S.R.* **56 D9** 59 0N 81 30 E
Narymskoye, *U.S.S.R.* **56 E9** 49 10N 84 15 E
Naryn, *U.S.S.R.* **55 C7** 41 26N 75 58 E
Naryn →, *U.S.S.R.* **55 C5** 40 52N 71 36 E
Nasa, *Norway* **12 C13** 66 29N 15 23 E
Nasarawa, *Nigeria* **101 D6** 8 32N 7 41 E
Năsăud, *Romania* **46 B5** 47 19N 24 29 E
Nasawa, *Vanuatu* **121 E6** 15 0 S 168 0 E
Naseby, *N.Z.* **119 F5** 45 1 S 170 10 E
Naselle, *U.S.A.* **144 D3** 46 22N 123 49W
Naser, Buheirat en, *Egypt* **94 C3** 23 0N 32 30 E
Nashua, *Iowa, U.S.A.* **140 B4** 42 55N 92 34W
Nashua, *Mont., U.S.A.* **142 B10** 48 10N 106 25W
Nashua, *N.H., U.S.A.* **137 D13** 42 50N 71 25W
Nashville, *Ark., U.S.A.* **139 J8** 33 56N 93 50W
Nashville, *Ga., U.S.A.* **135 K4** 31 3N 83 15W
Nashville, *Ill., U.S.A.* **140 F7** 38 21N 89 23W
Nashville, *Ind., U.S.A.* **141 E10** 39 12N 86 14W
Nashville, *Mich., U.S.A.* **141 B11** 42 36N 85 5W
Nashville, *Tenn., U.S.A.* **135 G2** 36 12N 86 46W
Našice, *Yugoslavia* **42 B3** 45 32N 18 4 E
Nasielsk, *Poland* **47 C7** 52 35N 20 50 E
Nasik, *India* **82 E1** 19 58N 73 50 E
Nasirabad, *India* **80 F6** 26 15N 74 45 E
Naskaupi →, *Canada* **129 B7** 53 47N 60 51W
Naso, *Italy* **41 D7** 38 8N 14 46 E
Naşriān-e Pā'īn, *Iran* **84 C5** 32 52N 46 52 E
Nass →, *Canada* **130 C3** 55 0N 129 40W
Nassau, *Bahamas* **148 A4** 25 5N 77 20W
Nassau, *U.S.A.* **137 D11** 42 30N 73 34W
Nassau, B., *Chile* **160 E3** 55 20 S 68 0W
Nasser, L. = Naser, Buheirat en, *Egypt* **94 C3** 23 0N 32 30 E
Nasser City = Kôm Ombo, *Egypt* **94 C3** 24 25N 32 52 E
Nassian, *Ivory C.* **100 D4** 8 28N 3 28W
Nässjö, *Sweden* **13 H13** 57 39N 14 42 E
Näsviken, *Sweden* **14 C10** 61 46N 16 52 E
Nata, *Botswana* **104 C4** 20 12 S 26 12 E
Natagaima, *Colombia* **152 C2** 3 37N 75 6W
Natal, *Brazil* **154 C4** 5 47 S 35 13W
Natal, *Canada* **130 D6** 49 43N 114 51W
Natal, *Indonesia* **70 D1** 0 35N 99 7 E
Natal □, *S. Africa* **105 D5** 28 30 S 30 30 E
Natalinci, *Yugoslavia* **42 C5** 44 15N 20 49 E
Naţanz, *Iran* **85 C6** 33 30N 51 55 E
Natashquan, *Canada* **129 B7** 50 14N 61 46W
Natashquan →, *Canada* **129 B7** 50 7N 61 50W
Natchez, *U.S.A.* **139 K9** 31 35N 91 25W
Natchitoches, *U.S.A.* **139 K8** 31 47N 93 4W
Naters, *Switz.* **28 D5** 46 19N 7 58 E
Natewa B., *Fiji* **121 A2** 16 35 S 179 40 E
Nathalia, *Australia* **117 D6** 36 1 S 145 13 E
Nathdwara, *India* **80 G5** 24 55N 73 50 E
Nati, Pta., *Spain* **33 A10** 40 3N 3 50 E
Natimuk, *Australia* **116 D5** 36 42 S 142 0 E
Nation →, *Canada* **130 B4** 55 30N 123 32W
National City, *U.S.A.* **145 N9** 32 39N 117 7W
Natitingou, *Benin* **101 C5** 10 20N 1 26 E
Natividad, I., *Mexico* **146 B1** 27 50N 115 10W
Natogyi, *Burma* **78 E5** 21 25N 95 39 E
Natoma, *U.S.A.* **138 F5** 39 14N 99 0W
Natron, L., *Tanzania* **106 C4** 2 20 S 36 0 E
Natrona Heights, *U.S.A.* **136 F5** 40 39N 79 43W
Natrûn, W. el →, *Egypt* **94 H7** 30 25N 30 13 E
Natuna Besar, Kepulauan, *Indonesia* **77 L7** 4 0N 108 15 E
Natuna Is. = Natuna Besar, Kepulauan, *Indonesia* **77 L7** 4 0N 108 15 E
Natuna Selatan, Kepulauan, *Indonesia* **75 B3** 2 45N 109 0 E
Natural Bridge, *U.S.A.* **137 B9** 44 5N 75 30W
Naturaliste, C., *Australia* **114 G4** 40 50 S 148 15 E
Natya, *Australia* **116 C5** 34 57 S 143 13 E
Nau, *U.S.S.R.* **55 C4** 40 9N 69 22 E
Nau Qala, *Afghan.* **80 B3** 34 5N 68 5 E
Naubinway, *U.S.A.* **128 C2** 46 7N 85 27W
Naucelle, *France* **24 D6** 44 13N 2 20 E
Nauders, *Austria* **30 E3** 46 54N 10 30 E
Nauen, *Germany* **26 C8** 52 36N 12 52 E
Naugatuck, *U.S.A.* **137 E11** 41 28N 73 4W
Naujoji Vilnia, *U.S.S.R.* **50 D4** 54 48N 25 27 E
Naumburg, *Germany* **26 D7** 51 10N 11 48 E
Nā'ūr at Tunayb, *Jordan* **91 D4** 31 48N 35 57 E
Nauru ■, *Pac. Oc.* **122 H8** 1 0 S 166 0 E
Naurzum, *U.S.S.R.* **54 F9** 51 32N 64 34 E
Naushahra = Nowshera, *Pakistan* **79 B4** 34 0N 72 0 E
Nausori, *Fiji* **121 B2** 18 2 S 178 32 E
Nauta, *Peru* **152 D3** 4 31 S 73 35W
Nautla, *Mexico* **147 C5** 20 20N 96 50W
Nauvoo, *U.S.A.* **140 D5** 40 33N 91 23W
Nava, *Mexico* **146 B4** 28 25N 100 46W
Nava del Rey, *Spain* **36 D5** 41 22N 5 6W
Navacerrada, Puerto de, *Spain* **36 E7** 40 47N 4 0W
Navadwip, *India* **81 H13** 23 34N 88 20 E
Navahermosa, *Spain* **37 F6** 39 41N 4 28W
Navajo Res., *U.S.A.* **143 H10** 36 55N 107 30W
Navalcarnero, *Spain* **36 E6** 40 17N 4 5W
Navalmoral de la Mata, *Spain* **36 F5** 39 52N 5 33W
Navalvillar de Pela, *Spain* **37 F5** 39 9N 5 24W
Navan = An Uaimh, *Ireland* **19 C5** 53 39N 6 40W
Navarino, I., *Chile* **160 E3** 55 0 S 67 40W
Navarra □, *Spain* **34 C3** 42 40N 1 40W
Navarre, *U.S.A.* **136 F3** 40 43N 81 31W
Navarrenx, *France* **24 E3** 43 20N 0 45W
Navarro, *U.S.A.* **144 F3** 39 10N 123 32W
Navasota, *U.S.A.* **139 K6** 30 20N 96 5W
Navassa, *W. Indies* **149 C5** 18 30N 75 0W
Nave, *Italy* **38 C7** 45 35N 10 17 E
Naver →, *U.K.* **18 C4** 58 34N 4 15W
Navia, *Spain* **36 B4** 43 35N 6 42W
Navia →, *Spain* **36 B4** 43 15N 6 50W
Navia de Suarna, *Spain* **36 C4** 42 58N 6 59W
Navidad, *Chile* **158 C1** 33 57 S 71 50W
Navlya, *U.S.S.R.* **50 E9** 52 53N 34 30 E
Navoi, *U.S.S.R.* **55 C2** 40 9N 65 22 E
Navojoa, *Mexico* **146 B3** 27 0N 109 30W
Navolato, *Mexico* **146 C3** 24 47N 107 42W
Navolok, *U.S.S.R.* **48 B6** 62 33N 39 57 E
Návpaktos, *Greece* **45 F3** 38 23N 21 50 E
Návplion, *Greece* **45 G4** 37 33N 22 50 E
Navrongo, *Ghana* **101 C4** 10 51N 1 3W
Navsari, *India* **82 D1** 20 57N 72 59 E
Nawa Kot, *Pakistan* **80 E4** 28 21N 71 24 E
Nawabganj, *Bangla.* **78 C2** 24 35N 88 14 E
Nawabganj, *Ut. P., India* **81 F9** 26 56N 81 14 E
Nawabganj, *Ut. P., India* **81 E8** 28 32N 79 40 E
Nawabshah, *Pakistan* **79 D3** 26 15N 68 25 E
Nawada, *India* **81 G11** 24 50N 85 33 E
Nāwah, *Afghan.* **79 B2** 32 19N 67 53 E
Nawakot, *Nepal* **81 F11** 27 55N 85 10 E
Nawalgarh, *India* **80 F6** 27 50N 75 15 E
Nawanshahr, *India* **81 C6** 32 33N 74 48 E
Nawapara, *India* **82 D6** 20 46N 82 33 E
Nawāsīf, Harrat, *Si. Arabia* **86 B3** 21 20N 42 10 E
Nawi, *Sudan* **94 D3** 18 32N 30 50 E
Nawng Hpa, *Burma* **78 D7** 22 30N 98 30 E
Nawş, Ra's, *Oman* **87 C6** 17 15N 55 16 E
Náxos, *Greece* **45 G7** 37 8N 25 25 E
Nay, *France* **24 E3** 43 10N 0 18W
Nāy Band, *Iran* **85 E7** 27 20N 52 40 E
Naya →, *Colombia* **152 C2** 3 13N 77 22W
Nayakhan, *U.S.S.R.* **57 C16** 61 56N 159 0 E
Nayarit □, *Mexico* **146 C4** 22 0N 105 0W
Nayé, *Senegal* **100 C2** 14 28N 12 12W
Nayong, *China* **68 D5** 26 50N 105 20 E
Nayoro, *Japan* **60 B11** 44 21N 142 28 E
Nayyāl, W. →, *Si. Arabia* **84 D3** 28 35N 39 4 E
Nazaré, *Bahia, Brazil* **155 D4** 13 2 S 39 0W
Nazaré, *Goiás, Brazil* **154 C2** 6 23 S 47 40W
Nazaré, *Pará, Brazil* **157 B7** 6 25 S 52 29W
Nazaré, *Portugal* **37 F1** 39 36N 9 4W
Nazareth = Nazerat, *Israel* **91 C4** 32 42N 35 17 E
Nazas, *Mexico* **146 B4** 25 10N 104 6W
Nazas →, *Mexico* **146 B4** 25 35N 103 25W
Naze, The, *U.K.* **17 F9** 51 53N 1 19 E
Nazerat, *Israel* **91 C4** 32 42N 35 17 E
Nāzīk, *Iran* **84 B5** 39 1N 45 4 E
Nazik Gölü, *Turkey* **89 D10** 38 50N 42 16 E
Nazilli, *Turkey* **88 E3** 37 55N 28 15 E
Nazir Hat, *Bangla.* **78 D3** 22 35N 91 49 E
Nazko, *Canada* **130 C4** 53 1N 123 37W
Nazko →, *Canada* **130 C4** 53 7N 123 34W
Nazret, *Ethiopia* **95 F4** 8 32N 39 22 E
Nazwá, *Oman* **87 B7** 22 56N 57 32 E
Nchanga, *Zambia* **107 E2** 12 30 S 27 49 E
Ncheu, *Malawi* **107 E3** 14 50 S 34 47 E
Ndala, *Tanzania* **106 C3** 4 45 S 33 15 E
Ndalatando, *Angola* **103 D2** 9 12 S 14 48 E
Ndali, *Benin* **101 D5** 9 50N 2 46 E
Ndareda, *Tanzania* **106 C4** 4 12 S 35 30 E
Ndélé, *C.A.R.* **102 A4** 8 25N 20 36 E
Ndendé, *Gabon* **102 C2** 2 22 S 11 23 E
Ndjamena, *Chad* **97 F2** 12 10N 14 59 E
Ndjolé, *Gabon* **102 C2** 0 10 S 10 45 E
Ndola, *Zambia* **107 E2** 13 0 S 28 34 E
Ndoto Mts., *Kenya* **106 B4** 2 0N 37 0 E
Ndoua, C., *N. Cal.* **121 V20** 22 24 S 166 56 E
Nduguti, *Tanzania* **106 C3** 4 18 S 34 41 E
Nduindui, *Vanuatu* **121 E5** 15 24 S 167 46 E
Nea →, *Norway* **14 A5** 63 15N 11 0 E
Néa Epídhavros, *Greece* **45 G5** 37 40N 23 7 E
Néa Flippiás, *Greece* **44 E2** 39 12N 20 53 E
Néa Kallikrátia, *Greece* **44 D5** 40 21N 23 1 E
Néa Víssi, *Greece* **44 C8** 41 34N 26 33 E
Neagari, *Japan* **63 A8** 36 26N 136 25 E
Neagh, Lough, *U.K.* **19 B5** 54 35N 6 25W
Neah Bay, *U.S.A.* **144 B2** 48 25N 124 40W
Neale, L., *Australia* **112 D5** 24 15 S 130 0 E
Neamţ □, *Romania* **46 C7** 47 0N 26 20 E
Neápolis, *Kozan, Greece* **44 D3** 40 20N 21 24 E
Neápolis, *Kríti, Greece* **32 D7** 35 15N 25 37 E
Neápolis, *Lakonia, Greece* **45 H5** 36 27N 23 8 E
Near Is., *U.S.A.* **126 C1** 53 0N 172 0 E
Neath, *U.K.* **17 F4** 51 39N 3 49W
Nebbou, *Burkina Faso* **101 C4** 11 9N 1 51W
Nebine Cr. →, *Australia* **115 D4** 29 27 S 146 56 E
Nebit Dag, *U.S.S.R.* **49 G9** 39 30N 54 22 E
Nebolchy, *U.S.S.R.* **50 B8** 59 8N 33 18 E
Nebraska □, *U.S.A.* **138 E5** 41 30N 100 0W
Nebraska City, *U.S.A.* **138 E7** 40 40N 95 52W
Nébrodi, Monti, *Italy* **41 E7** 37 55N 14 50 E
Necedah, *U.S.A.* **138 C9** 44 2N 90 7W
Nechako →, *Canada* **130 C4** 53 30N 122 44W
Neches →, *U.S.A.* **139 L8** 29 55N 93 52W
Neckar →, *Germany* **27 F4** 49 31N 8 26 E
Necochea, *Argentina* **158 D4** 38 30 S 58 50W
Nectar Brook, *Australia* **116 B2** 32 43 S 137 57 E
Nedelišće, *Yugoslavia* **39 B13** 46 23N 16 22 E
Neder Rijn →, *Neths.* **20 E8** 51 57N 6 2 E
Nederbrakel, *Belgium* **21 G3** 50 48N 3 46 E
Nederweert, *Neths.* **21 F7** 51 17N 5 45 E
Nédha →, *Greece* **45 G3** 37 25N 21 45 E
Nedroma, *Algeria* **99 A4** 35 1N 1 45W
Neede, *Neths.* **20 D9** 52 8N 6 37 E
Needles, *U.S.A.* **145 L12** 34 50N 114 35W
Needles, The, *U.K.* **17 G6** 50 39N 1 35W
Needles Pt., *N.Z.* **118 C4** 36 3 S 175 25 E
Ñeembucú □, *Paraguay* **158 B4** 27 0 S 58 0W
Neemuch = Nimach, *India* **80 G6** 24 30N 74 56 E
Neenah, *U.S.A.* **134 C1** 44 10N 88 30W
Neepawa, *Canada* **131 C9** 50 15N 99 30W
Neer, *Neths.* **21 F7** 51 16N 5 59 E
Neerpelt, *Belgium* **21 F6** 51 13N 5 26 E
Neft-chala = imeni 26 Bakinskikh Komissarov, *U.S.S.R.* **49 G8** 39 19N 49 12 E
Nefta, *Tunisia* **96 B1** 33 53N 7 50 E
Neftah Sidi Boubekeur, *Algeria* **99 A5** 35 1N 0 4 E
Neftegorsk, *U.S.S.R.* **53 D8** 44 25N 39 45 E
Neftekumsk, *U.S.S.R.* **53 D11** 44 46N 44 50 E
Neftenbach, *Switz.* **29 A7** 47 32N 8 41 E
Neftyannyye Kamni, *U.S.S.R.* **49 F9** 40 20N 50 55 E
Negapatam = Nagappattinam, *India* **83 J4** 10 46N 79 51 E
Negaunee, *U.S.A.* **134 B2** 46 30N 87 36W
Negele, *Ethiopia* **90 F2** 5 20N 39 36 E
Negev Desert = Hanegev, *Israel* **91 E4** 30 50N 35 0 E
Negoiul, Vf., *Romania* **46 D5** 45 38N 24 35 E
Negombo, *Sri Lanka* **83 L4** 7 12N 79 50 E
Negotin, *Yugoslavia* **42 C7** 44 16N 22 37 E
Negotino, *Yugoslavia* **42 F7** 41 29N 22 9 E
Negra, Peña, *Spain* **36 C4** 42 11N 6 30W
Negra, Pta., *Mauritania* **98 D1** 22 54N 16 18W
Negra, Pta., *Peru* **156 B1** 6 6 S 81 10W
Negra Pt., *Phil.* **71 A6** 18 40N 120 50 E
Negrais C., *Burma* **78 G5** 16 0N 94 12 E
Negreira, *Spain* **36 C2** 42 54N 8 45W
Negreşti, *Romania* **46 C8** 46 50N 27 30 E
Négrine, *Algeria* **99 B6** 34 30N 7 30 E
Negro →, *Argentina* **160 B4** 41 2 S 62 47W
Negro →, *Bolivia* **157 C5** 14 11 S 63 7W
Negro →, *Brazil* **153 D6** 3 0 S 60 0W
Negro →, *Uruguay* **159 C4** 33 24 S 58 22W
Negros, *Phil.* **71 C6** 9 30N 122 40 E
Negru Vodă, *Romania* **46 F9** 43 47N 28 21 E
Nehalem →, *U.S.A.* **144 E3** 45 40N 123 56W
Nehāvand, *Iran* **85 C6** 35 56N 49 31 E
Nehbandān, *Iran* **85 D9** 31 35N 60 5 E
Neheim, *Germany* **26 D3** 51 27N 7 58 E
Nehoiaşu, *Romania* **46 D7** 45 24N 26 20 E
Nei Monggol Zizhiqu □, *China* **66 D7** 42 0N 112 0 E
Neiafu, *Tonga* **121 P14** 18 39 S 173 59W
Neichiang, *China* **10 D12** 29 35N 105 0 E
Neidpath, *Canada* **131 C7** 50 12N 107 20W
Neihart, *U.S.A.* **142 C8** 47 0N 110 44W
Neijiang, *China* **68 C5** 29 35N 104 55 E
Neilrex, *Australia* **117 A8** 31 44 S 149 20 E
Neilton, *U.S.A.* **142 C2** 47 24N 123 52W
Neiqiu, *China* **66 F8** 37 15N 114 30 E
Neira de Jusá, *Spain* **36 C3** 42 53N 7 14W
Neisse →, *Europe* **26 C10** 52 4N 14 46 E
Neiva, *Colombia* **152 C2** 2 56N 75 18W
Neixiang, *China* **66 H6** 33 10N 111 52 E
Nejanilini L., *Canada* **131 B9** 59 33N 97 48W
Nejo, *Ethiopia* **95 F4** 9 30N 35 28 E
Nekā, *Iran* **85 B7** 36 39N 53 19 E
Nekemte, *Ethiopia* **95 F4** 9 4N 36 30 E
Nêkheb, *Egypt* **94 B3** 25 10N 32 48 E
Neksø, *Denmark* **13 J13** 55 4N 15 8 E
Nelas, *Portugal* **36 E3** 40 32N 7 52W
Nelia, *Australia* **114 C3** 20 39 S 142 12 E
Nelidovo, *U.S.S.R.* **50 C8** 56 13N 32 49 E
Neligh, *U.S.A.* **138 D5** 42 11N 98 2W
Nelkan, *U.S.S.R.* **57 D14** 57 40N 136 4 E
Nellikuppam, *India* **83 J4** 11 46N 79 43 E
Nellore, *India* **83 G4** 14 27N 79 59 E
Nelma, *U.S.S.R.* **57 E14** 47 39N 139 0 E
Nelson, *Canada* **130 D5** 49 30N 117 20W
Nelson, *N.Z.* **119 B8** 41 18 S 173 16 E
Nelson, *U.K.* **16 D5** 53 50N 2 14W
Nelson, *U.S.A.* **143 J7** 35 35N 113 16W
Nelson □, *N.Z.* **119 C7** 42 11 S 172 15 E
Nelson →, *Canada* **131 C9** 54 33N 98 2W
Nelson, C., *Australia* **116 E4** 38 26 S 141 32 E
Nelson, C., *Papua N. G.* **120 E5** 9 0 S 149 20 E
Nelson, Estrecho, *Chile* **160 D2** 51 30 S 75 0W
Nelson Forks, *Canada* **130 B4** 59 30N 124 0W
Nelson House, *Canada* **131 B9** 55 47N 98 51W
Nelson L., *Canada* **131 B8** 55 48N 100 7W
Nelspoort, *S. Africa* **104 E3** 32 7 S 23 0 E
Nelspruit, *S. Africa* **105 D5** 25 29 S 30 59 E
Néma, *Mauritania* **100 B3** 16 40N 7 15W
Neman →, *U.S.S.R.* **50 D2** 55 25N 21 10 E
Ņeméa, *Greece* **45 G4** 37 49N 22 40 E
Nemeiben L., *Canada* **131 B7** 55 20N 105 20W
Nemira, *Romania* **46 C7** 46 17N 26 19 E
Nemours, *France* **23 D9** 48 16N 2 40 E
Nemunas = Neman →, *U.S.S.R.* **50 D2** 55 25N 21 10 E
Nemuro, *Japan* **60 C12** 43 20N 145 35 E
Nemuro-Kaikyō, *Japan* **60 C12** 43 30N 145 30 E
Nemuy, *U.S.S.R.* **57 D14** 55 40N 136 9 E
Nen Jiang →, *China* **67 B13** 45 28N 124 30 E
Nenagh, *Ireland* **19 D3** 52 52N 8 11W
Nenana, *U.S.A.* **126 B5** 64 30N 149 20W
Nenasi, *Malaysia* **77 L4** 3 9N 103 23 E
Nendiarene, Pte., *N. Cal.* **121 T18** 20 14 S 164 19 E
Nene →, *U.K.* **16 E8** 52 38N 0 13 E
Nenjiang, *China* **65 B7** 49 10N 125 10 E
Neno, *Malawi* **107 F3** 15 25 S 34 40 E
Nenusa, Kepulauan, *Indonesia* **71 D7** 4 45N 127 1 E
Neodesha, *U.S.A.* **139 G7** 37 30N 95 37W
Neoga, *U.S.A.* **141 E8** 39 19N 88 27W
Néon Petrítsi, *Greece* **44 C5** 41 16N 23 15 E
Neópolis, *Brazil* **154 D4** 10 18 S 36 35W
Neosho, *U.S.A.* **139 G7** 36 56N 94 28W
Neosho →, *U.S.A.* **139 H7** 35 59N 95 10W
Nepal ■, *Asia* **81 F11** 28 0N 84 30 E
Nepalganj, *Nepal* **81 E9** 28 5N 81 40 E
Nephi, *U.S.A.* **142 G8** 39 43N 111 52W
Nephin, *Ireland* **19 B2** 54 1N 9 21W
Nepomuk, *Czech.* **30 B6** 49 29N 13 35 E
Neptune City, *U.S.A.* **137 F10** 40 13N 74 4W
Néra →, *Romania* **42 C6** 44 48N 21 25 E
Nérac, *France* **24 D4** 44 8N 0 21 E
Nerastro, Sarīr, *Libya* **96 D4** 24 20N 20 37 E
Nerchinsk, *U.S.S.R.* **57 D12** 52 0N 116 39 E
Nerchinskiy Zavod, *U.S.S.R.* **57 D12** 51 20N 119 40 E
Nereju, *Romania* **46 D7** 45 43N 26 43 E
Nerekhta, *U.S.S.R.* **51 C12** 57 26N 40 38 E
Néret L., *Canada* **129 B5** 54 45N 70 44W
Neretva →, *Yugoslavia* **42 D2** 43 1N 17 27 E
Neretvanski Kanal, *Yugoslavia* **42 D2** 43 7N 17 10 E
Neringa, *U.S.S.R.* **50 D2** 55 30N 21 5 E
Nerja, *Spain* **37 J7** 36 43N 3 55W
Nerl →, *U.S.S.R.* **51 C12** 56 11N 40 34 E
Nerokoúrou, *Greece* **45 J6** 35 29N 24 3 E
Nerpio, *Spain* **35 G2** 38 11N 2 16W
Nerva, *Spain* **37 H4** 37 42N 6 30W
Nes, *Iceland* **12 D5** 65 53N 17 24W
Nes, *Neths.* **20 B7** 53 26N 5 47 E
Nesbyen, *Norway* **14 D3** 60 34N 9 35 E
Nesebŭr, *Bulgaria* **43 E12** 42 41N 27 46 E
Neskaupstaður, *Iceland* **12 D7** 65 9N 13 42W
Nesland, *Norway* **14 E1** 59 31N 7 59 E
Neslandsvatn, *Norway* **14 F3** 58 57N 9 10 E
Nesle, *France* **23 C9** 49 45N 2 53 E
Nesodden, *Norway* **14 E4** 59 48N 10 40 E
Nesque →, *France* **25 E8** 43 59N 4 59 E
Ness, L., *U.K.* **18 D4** 57 15N 4 30W
Nesslau, *Switz.* **29 B8** 47 14N 9 13 E
Nestórion, *Greece* **44 D3** 40 24N 21 5 E
Néstos →, *Greece* **44 C6** 41 20N 24 35 E
Nesttun, *Norway* **13 F8** 60 19N 5 21 E
Nesvizh, *U.S.S.R.* **50 E5** 53 14N 26 38 E
Netanya, *Israel* **91 C3** 32 20N 34 51 E
Nète →, *Belgium* **21 F4** 51 7N 4 14 E
Netherdale, *Australia* **114 C4** 21 10 S 148 33 E
Netherlands ■, *Europe* **20 E7** 52 0N 5 30 E
Netherlands Antilles ■, *S. Amer.* **152 A4** 12 15N 69 0W
Netherlands Guiana = Surinam ■, *S. Amer.* **153 C6** 4 0N 56 0W
Netley Gap, *Australia* **116 B3** 32 43 S 139 59 E
Neto →, *Italy* **41 C10** 39 13N 17 8 E
Netrakona, *Bangla.* **78 C3** 24 53N 90 47 E
Nettancourt, *France* **23 D11** 48 51N 4 57 E
Nettilling L., *Canada* **127 B12** 66 30N 71 0W
Nettuno, *Italy* **40 A5** 41 29N 12 40 E
Netzahualcoyotl, Presa, *Mexico* **147 D6** 17 10N 93 30W
Neu-Isenburg, *Germany* **27 E4** 50 3N 8 42 E
Neu-Ulm, *Germany* **27 G6** 48 23N 10 2 E
Neubrandenburg, *Germany* **26 B9** 53 33N 13 17 E
Neubukow, *Germany* **26 A7** 54 1N 11 40 E
Neuburg, *Germany* **27 G7** 48 43N 11 11 E
Neuchâtel, *Switz.* **28 C3** 47 0N 6 55 E
Neuchâtel □, *Switz.* **28 C3** 47 0N 6 55 E
Neuchâtel, Lac de, *Switz.* **28 C3** 46 53N 6 50 E
Neudau, *Austria* **30 D9** 47 11N 16 6 E
Neuenegg, *Switz.* **28 C4** 46 54N 7 18 E
Neuenhaus, *Germany* **26 C2** 52 30N 6 55 E
Neuf-Brisach, *France* **23 D14** 48 1N 7 30 E
Neufahrn, *Germany* **27 G8** 48 44N 12 11 E
Neufchâteau, *Belgium* **21 J6** 49 50N 5 25 E
Neufchâteau, *France* **23 D12** 48 21N 5 40 E
Neufchâtel-en-Bray, *France* **22 C8** 49 44N 1 26 E
Neufchâtel-sur-Aisne, *France* **23 C11** 49 26N 4 1 E
Neuhaus, *Germany* **26 B6** 53 16N 10 54 E
Neuhausen, *Switz.* **29 A7** 47 41N 8 37 E
Neuillé-Pont-Pierre, *France* **22 E7** 47 33N 0 33 E
Neuilly-St.-Front, *France* **23 C10** 49 10N 3 15 E
Neukalen, *Germany* **26 B8** 53 49N 12 48 E
Neumarkt, *Germany* **27 F7** 49 16N 11 28 E
Neumarkt-Sankt Veit, *Germany* **27 G8** 48 22N 12 30 E
Neumünster, *Germany* **26 A5** 54 4N 9 58 E
Neung-sur-Beuvron, *France* **23 E8** 47 30N 1 50 E
Neunkirchen, *Austria* **30 D9** 47 43N 16 4 E
Neunkirchen, *Germany* **27 F3** 49 23N 7 12 E
Neuquén, *Argentina* **160 A3** 38 55 S 68 0W
Neuquén □, *Argentina* **158 D2** 38 0 S 69 50W
Neuquén →, *Argentina* **160 A3** 38 59 S 68 0W
Neuruppin, *Germany* **26 C8** 52 56N 12 48 E
Neuse →, *U.S.A.* **135 H7** 35 5N 76 30W
Neusiedl, *Austria* **31 D9** 47 57N 16 50 E
Neusiedler See, *Austria* **31 D9** 47 50N 16 47 E

240 Neuss

Neuss, Germany 21 F9 51 12N 6 39 E
Neussargues-Moissac, France 24 C7 45 9N 3 0 E
Neustadt, Baden-W., Germany 27 H4 47 54N 8 13 E
Neustadt, Bayern, Germany 27 F8 49 42N 12 10 E
Neustadt, Bayern, Germany 27 G7 48 48N 11 47 E
Neustadt, Bayern, Germany 27 F6 49 34N 10 37 E
Neustadt, Bayern, Germany 27 E7 50 23N 11 7 E
Neustadt, Brandenburg, Germany 26 C8 52 50N 12 27 E
Neustadt, Hessen, Germany 26 E5 50 51N 9 9 E
Neustadt, Niedersachsen, Germany 26 C5 52 30N 9 30 E
Neustadt, Rhld-Pfz., Germany 27 F4 49 21N 8 10 E
Neustadt, Schleswig-Holstein, Germany 26 A6 54 6N 10 49 E
Neustadt, Thüringen, Germany 26 E7 50 45N 11 43 E
Neustrelitz, Germany 26 B9 53 22N 13 4 E
Neuvic, France 24 C6 45 23N 2 16 E
Neuville, Belgium 21 H5 50 11N 4 32 E
Neuville-aux-Bois, France 23 D9 48 4N 2 3 E
Neuville-de-Poitou, France 24 B4 46 41N 0 15 E
Neuville-sur-Saône, France 25 C8 45 52N 4 51 E
Neuvy-le-Roi, France 22 E7 47 36N 0 36 E
Neuvy-St.-Sépulchre, France 24 B5 46 35N 1 48 E
Neuvy-sur-Barangeon, France 23 E9 47 20N 2 15 E
Neuwerk, Germany 26 B4 53 55N 8 30 E
Neuwied, Germany 26 E3 50 26N 7 29 E
Neva →, U.S.S.R. 48 C5 59 50N 30 30 E
Nevada, Iowa, U.S.A. 140 B3 42 1N 93 27W
Nevada, Mo., U.S.A. 139 G7 37 51N 94 22W
Nevada □, U.S.A. 142 G5 39 20N 117 0W
Nevada, Sierra, Spain 35 H1 37 3N 3 15W
Nevada, Sierra, U.S.A. 142 G3 39 0N 120 30W
Nevada City, U.S.A. 144 F6 39 20N 121 0W
Nevado, Cerro, Argentina 158 D2 35 30 S 68 32W
Nevanka, U.S.S.R. 57 D10 56 31N 98 55 E
Nevasa, India 82 E2 19 34N 75 0 E
Nevel, U.S.S.R. 50 D6 56 0N 29 55 E
Nevele, Belgium 21 F3 51 3N 3 33 E
Nevers, France 23 F10 47 0N 3 9 E
Nevertire, Australia 117 A7 31 50 S 147 44 E
Nevesinje, Yugoslavia 42 D3 43 14N 18 6 E
Neville, Canada 131 D7 49 58N 107 39W
Nevinnomyssk, U.S.S.R. 53 D10 44 40N 42 0 E
Nevis, W. Indies 149 C7 17 0N 62 30W
Nevrokop = Gotse Delchev, Bulgaria 43 F8 41 43N 23 46 E
Nevşehir, Turkey 88 D6 38 33N 34 40 E
Nevşehir □, Turkey 88 D6 38 50N 34 40 E
Nevyansk, U.S.S.R. 54 C7 57 30N 60 13 E
New →, Guyana 153 C6 3 20N 57 37W
New Albany, Ind., U.S.A. 141 F11 38 20N 85 50W
New Albany, Miss., U.S.A. 139 H10 34 30N 89 0W
New Albany, Pa., U.S.A. 137 E8 41 35N 76 28W
New Amsterdam, Guyana 153 B6 6 15N 57 36W
New Angledool, Australia 115 D4 29 5 S 147 55 E
New Athens, U.S.A. 140 F7 38 19N 89 53W
New Bedford, U.S.A. 137 E14 41 40N 70 52W
New Berlin, Ill., U.S.A. 140 E7 39 44N 89 55W
New Berlin, Wis., U.S.A. 141 B8 42 59N 88 6W
New Bern, U.S.A. 135 H7 35 8N 77 3W
New Bethlehem, U.S.A. 136 F5 41 0N 79 22W
New Bloomfield, U.S.A. 136 F7 40 24N 77 12W
New Boston, U.S.A. 139 J7 33 27N 94 21W
New Braunfels, U.S.A. 139 L5 29 43N 98 9W
New Brighton, N.Z. 119 D7 43 29 S 172 43 E
New Brighton, U.S.A. 136 F4 40 42N 80 19W
New Britain, Papua N. G. 120 C6 5 50 S 150 20 E
New Britain, U.S.A. 137 E12 41 41N 72 47W
New Brunswick, U.S.A. 137 F10 40 30N 74 28W
New Brunswick □, Canada 129 C6 46 50N 66 30W
New Buffalo, U.S.A. 141 C10 41 47N 86 45W
New Bussa, Nigeria 101 D5 9 53N 4 31 E
New Caledonia, Pac. Oc. 121 U19 21 0 S 165 0 E
New Canton, U.S.A. 140 E5 39 37N 91 8W
New Carlisle, Ind., U.S.A. 141 C10 41 45N 86 32W
New Carlisle, Ohio, U.S.A. 141 E12 39 56N 84 2W
New Castile = Castilla La Mancha □, Spain 37 F7 39 30N 3 30W
New Castle, Ind., U.S.A. 141 E11 39 55N 85 23W
New Castle, Ky., U.S.A. 141 F11 38 26N 85 10W
New Castle, Pa., U.S.A. 136 F4 41 0N 80 20W
New City, U.S.A. 137 E11 41 8N 74 0W
New Cumberland, U.S.A. 136 F4 40 30N 80 36W
New Cuyama, U.S.A. 145 L7 34 57N 119 38W
New Delhi, India 80 E7 28 37N 77 13 E
New Denver, Canada 130 D5 50 0N 117 25W
New Don Pedro Res., U.S.A. 144 H6 37 43N 120 24W
New England, U.S.A. 138 B3 46 36N 102 47W
New England Ra., Australia 115 E5 30 20 S 151 45 E
New Forest, U.K. 17 G6 50 53N 1 40W
New Franklin, U.S.A. 140 E4 39 1N 92 44W
New Georgia Is., Solomon Is. 121 M9 8 15 S 157 30 E
New Glarus, U.S.A. 140 B7 42 49N 89 38W
New Glasgow, Canada 129 C7 45 35N 62 36W
New Guinea, Oceania 122 H5 4 0 S 136 0 E
New Hamburg, Canada 136 C4 43 23N 80 42W
New Hampshire □, U.S.A. 137 C13 43 40N 71 40W
New Hampton, U.S.A. 140 A4 43 2N 92 20W
New Hanover, Papua N. G. 120 B6 2 30 S 150 10 E
New Hanover, S. Africa 105 D5 29 22 S 30 31 E
New Harmony, U.S.A. 141 F9 38 7N 87 56W
New Haven, Conn., U.S.A. 137 E12 41 20N 72 54W
New Haven, Ill., U.S.A. 141 G8 37 55N 88 8W
New Haven, Ind., U.S.A. 141 C11 41 4N 85 1W
New Haven, Mich., U.S.A. 136 D2 42 44N 82 46W
New Haven, Mo., U.S.A. 140 F5 38 37N 91 13W
New Hazelton, Canada 130 B3 55 20N 127 30W
New Hebrides = Vanuatu ■, Pac. Oc. 121 E6 15 0 S 168 0 E
New Iberia, U.S.A. 139 K9 30 2N 91 54W
New Ireland, Papua N. G. 120 B6 3 20 S 151 50 E
New Jersey □, U.S.A. 137 F10 40 30N 74 10W
New Kensington, U.S.A. 136 F5 40 36N 79 43W
New Lexington, U.S.A. 134 F4 39 40N 82 15W
New Liskeard, Canada 128 C4 47 31N 79 41W
New London, Conn., U.S.A. 137 E12 41 23N 72 8W
New London, Iowa, U.S.A. 140 D5 40 55N 91 24W
New London, Minn., U.S.A. 138 C7 45 17N 94 55W
New London, Mo., U.S.A. 140 E5 39 35N 91 24W
New London, Ohio, U.S.A. 136 E2 41 4N 82 25W
New London, Wis., U.S.A. 138 C10 44 23N 88 43W
New Madison, U.S.A. 141 E12 39 58N 84 43W
New Madrid, U.S.A. 139 G10 36 40N 89 30W
New Meadows, U.S.A. 142 D5 45 0N 116 32W
New Melones L., U.S.A. 144 H6 37 57N 120 31W
New Mexico □, U.S.A. 132 D5 34 30N 106 0W
New Miami, U.S.A. 141 E12 39 26N 84 32W
New Milford, Conn., U.S.A. 137 E11 41 35N 73 25W
New Milford, Pa., U.S.A. 137 E9 41 50N 75 45W
New Norcia, Australia 113 F2 30 57 S 116 13 E
New Norfolk, Australia 114 G4 42 46 S 147 2 E
New Orleans, U.S.A. 139 L9 30 0N 90 5W
New Palestine, U.S.A. 141 E11 39 45N 85 52W
New Paris, U.S.A. 141 E12 39 55N 84 48W
New Pekin, U.S.A. 141 F10 38 31N 86 2W
New Philadelphia, U.S.A. 136 F3 40 29N 81 25W
New Plymouth, N.Z. 118 F3 39 4 S 174 5 E
New Plymouth, U.S.A. 142 E5 43 58N 116 49W
New Providence, Bahamas 148 A4 25 25N 78 35W
New Radnor, U.K. 17 E4 52 15N 3 10W
New Richmond, Ohio, U.S.A. 141 F12 38 57N 84 17W
New Richmond, Wis., U.S.A. 138 C8 45 6N 92 34W
New Roads, U.S.A. 139 K9 30 43N 91 30W
New Rochelle, U.S.A. 137 F11 40 55N 73 46W
New Rockford, U.S.A. 138 B5 47 44N 99 7W
New Salem, U.S.A. 138 B4 46 51N 101 25W
New Scone, U.K. 18 E5 56 25N 3 26W
New Sharon, U.S.A. 140 C4 41 28N 92 39W
New Siberian Is. = Novosibirskiye Ostrava, U.S.S.R. 57 B15 75 0N 142 0 E
New Smyrna Beach, U.S.A. 135 L5 29 0N 80 50W
New South Wales □, Australia 115 E4 33 0 S 146 0 E
New Springs, Australia 113 E3 25 49 S 120 1 E
New Town, U.S.A. 138 B3 48 0N 102 30W
New Ulm, U.S.A. 138 C7 44 15N 94 30W
New Vienna, U.S.A. 141 E13 39 19N 83 42W
New Virginia, U.S.A. 140 C3 41 11N 93 44W
New Waterford, Canada 129 C7 46 13N 60 4W
New Westminster, Canada 130 D4 49 13N 122 55W
New York □, U.S.A. 137 D9 42 40N 76 0W
New York City, U.S.A. 137 F11 40 45N 74 0W
New Zealand ■, Oceania 118 G5 40 0 S 176 0 E
Newala, Tanzania 107 E4 10 58 S 39 18 E
Newala □, Tanzania 107 E4 10 46 S 39 20 E
Newark, Del., U.S.A. 134 F8 39 42N 75 45W
Newark, N.J., U.S.A. 137 F10 40 41N 74 12W
Newark, N.Y., U.S.A. 136 C7 43 2N 77 10W
Newark, Ohio, U.S.A. 136 F2 40 5N 82 24W
Newark-on-Trent, U.K. 16 D7 53 6N 0 48W
Newaygo, U.S.A. 134 D3 43 25N 85 48W
Newberg, Mo., U.S.A. 140 G5 37 55N 91 54W
Newberg, Oreg., U.S.A. 142 D2 45 22N 123 0W
Newberry, Mich., U.S.A. 134 B3 46 20N 85 32W
Newberry, S.C., U.S.A. 135 H5 34 17N 81 37W
Newberry Springs, U.S.A. 145 L10 34 50N 116 41W
Newbrook, Canada 130 C6 54 24N 112 57W
Newburgh, Ind., U.S.A. 141 G9 37 57N 87 24W
Newburgh, N.Y., U.S.A. 137 E10 41 30N 74 1W
Newbury, U.K. 17 F6 51 24N 1 19W
Newbury, U.S.A. 137 B12 44 7N 72 6W
Newburyport, U.S.A. 137 D14 42 48N 70 50W
Newcastle, Australia 117 B9 33 0 S 151 46 E
Newcastle, Canada 129 C6 47 1N 65 38W
Newcastle, S. Africa 105 D4 27 45 S 29 58 E
Newcastle, U.K. 19 B6 54 13N 5 54W
Newcastle, Calif., U.S.A. 144 G5 38 50N 121 8W
Newcastle, Wyo., U.S.A. 138 D2 43 50N 104 12W
Newcastle Emlyn, U.K. 17 E3 52 2N 4 29W
Newcastle Ra., Australia 112 C5 15 45 S 130 15 E
Newcastle-under-Lyme, U.K. 16 D5 53 2N 2 15W
Newcastle-upon-Tyne, U.K. 16 C6 54 59N 1 37W
Newcastle Waters, Australia 114 B1 17 30 S 133 28 E
Newdegate, Australia 113 F2 33 6 S 119 0 E
Newell, U.S.A. 138 C3 44 48N 103 25W
Newfoundland □, Canada 129 B8 53 0N 58 0W
Newhalem, U.S.A. 130 D4 48 41N 121 16W
Newhall, U.S.A. 145 L8 34 23N 118 32W
Newham, U.K. 17 F8 51 31N 0 2 E
Newhaven, U.K. 17 G8 50 47N 0 4 E
Newkirk, U.S.A. 139 G6 36 52N 97 3W
Newman, Australia 112 D2 23 18 S 119 45 E
Newman, Calif., U.S.A. 144 H5 37 19N 121 1W
Newman, Ill., U.S.A. 141 E9 39 48N 87 59W
Newmarket, Canada 136 B5 44 3N 79 28W
Newmarket, Ireland 19 D3 52 13N 9 0W
Newmarket, U.K. 17 E8 52 15N 0 23 E
Newmarket, U.S.A. 137 C14 43 4N 70 57W
Newnan, U.S.A. 135 J3 33 22N 84 48W
Newport, Gwent, U.K. 17 F5 51 35N 3 0W
Newport, I. of W., U.K. 17 G6 50 42N 1 18W
Newport, Shrops., U.K. 17 E5 52 47N 2 22W
Newport, Ark., U.S.A. 139 H9 35 38N 91 15W
Newport, Ind., U.S.A. 141 E9 39 53N 87 26W
Newport, Ky., U.S.A. 141 E12 39 5N 84 23W
Newport, N.H., U.S.A. 137 C12 43 23N 72 8W
Newport, Oreg., U.S.A. 142 D1 44 41N 124 2W
Newport, Pa., U.S.A. 136 F7 40 28N 77 8W
Newport, R.I., U.S.A. 137 E13 41 13N 71 19W
Newport, Tenn., U.S.A. 135 H4 35 59N 83 12W
Newport, Vt., U.S.A. 137 B12 44 57N 72 17W
Newport, Wash., U.S.A. 142 B5 48 11N 117 2W
Newport Beach, U.S.A. 145 M9 33 40N 117 58W
Newport News, U.S.A. 134 G7 37 2N 76 30W
Newquay, U.K. 17 G2 50 24N 5 6W
Newry, U.K. 19 B5 54 10N 6 20W
Newry & Mourne □, U.K. 19 B5 54 10N 6 15W
Newton, Ill., U.S.A. 141 F8 38 59N 88 10W
Newton, Iowa, U.S.A. 140 C3 41 40N 93 3W
Newton, Mass., U.S.A. 137 D13 42 21N 71 12W
Newton, Miss., U.S.A. 139 J10 32 19N 89 10W
Newton, N.C., U.S.A. 135 H5 35 42N 81 10W
Newton, N.J., U.S.A. 137 E10 41 3N 74 46W
Newton, Tex., U.S.A. 139 K8 30 54N 93 42W
Newton Abbot, U.K. 17 G4 50 32N 3 37W
Newton Boyd, Australia 115 D5 29 45 S 152 16 E
Newton Stewart, U.K. 18 G4 54 57N 4 30W
Newtonmore, U.K. 18 D4 57 4N 4 7W
Newtown, U.K. 17 E4 52 31N 3 19W
Newtown, U.S.A. 140 D3 40 22N 93 20W
Newtownabbey □, U.K. 19 B6 54 45N 6 0W
Newtownards, U.K. 19 B6 54 37N 5 40W
Newville, U.S.A. 136 F7 40 10N 77 24W
Nexon, France 24 C5 45 41N 1 11 E
Neya, U.S.S.R. 51 B13 58 21N 43 49 E
Neyrīz, Iran 85 D7 29 15N 54 19 E
Neyshābūr, Iran 85 B8 36 10N 58 50 E
Neyyattinkara, India 83 K3 8 26N 77 5 E
Nezhin, U.S.S.R. 50 F7 51 5N 31 55 E
Nezperce, U.S.A. 142 C5 46 13N 116 15W
Ngabang, Indonesia 70 D3 0 23N 109 55 E
Ngabordamlu, Tanjung, Indonesia 71 F8 6 56 S 134 11 E
N'Gage, Angola 103 D3 7 46 S 15 15 E
Ngaiphaipi, Burma 78 D4 22 14N 93 15 E
Ngambé, Cameroon 101 D7 5 48N 11 29 E
Ngami Depression, Botswana 104 C3 20 30 S 22 46 E
Ngamo, Zimbabwe 107 F2 19 3 S 27 32 E
Nganjuk, Indonesia 71 G14 7 32 S 111 55 E
Ngao, Thailand 76 C2 18 46N 99 59 E
Ngaoundéré, Cameroon 102 A2 7 15N 13 35 E
Ngapara, N.Z. 119 E5 44 57 S 170 46 E
Ngara, Tanzania 106 C3 2 29 S 30 40 E
Ngara □, Tanzania 106 C3 2 29 S 30 40 E
Ngaruawahia, N.Z. 118 D4 37 42 S 175 11 E
Ngaruroro →, N.Z. 118 F5 39 34 S 176 55 E
Ngatapa, N.Z. 118 E6 38 32 S 177 45 E
Ngathainggyaung, Burma 78 G5 17 24N 95 5 E
Ngauruhoe, Mt., N.Z. 118 F4 39 13 S 175 45 E
Ngawi, Indonesia 71 G14 7 24 S 111 26 E
Nggela, Solomon Is. 121 M11 9 5 S 160 15 E
Nghia Lo, Vietnam 76 B5 21 33N 104 28 E
Ngidinga, Zaïre 103 D3 5 37 S 15 17 E
Ngo, Congo 102 C3 2 29 S 15 45 E
N'Gola, Angola 103 E2 14 10 S 14 30 E
Ngoma, Malawi 107 E3 13 8 S 33 45 E
Ngomahura, Zimbabwe 107 G3 20 26 S 30 43 E
Ngomba, Tanzania 107 D3 8 20 S 32 53 E
Ngongotaha, N.Z. 118 E5 38 5 S 176 12 E
Ngop, Sudan 95 F3 6 17N 30 9 E
Ngoring Hu, China 64 C4 34 55N 97 5 E
Ngorkou, Mali 100 B4 15 40N 3 41W
Ngorongoro, Tanzania 106 C4 3 11 S 35 32 E
Ngouri, Chad 97 F3 13 38N 15 22 E
Ngourti, Niger 97 E2 15 19N 13 12 E
Ngozi, Burundi 106 C2 2 54 S 29 50 E
Ngudu, Tanzania 106 C3 2 58 S 33 25 E
Nguigmi, Niger 97 F2 14 20N 13 20 E
Ngukurr, Australia 114 A1 14 44 S 134 44 E
Ngunga, Tanzania 106 C3 3 37 S 33 37 E
Nguru, Nigeria 101 C7 12 56N 10 29 E
Nguru Mts., Tanzania 106 D4 6 0 S 37 30 E
Nguyen Binh, Vietnam 76 A5 22 39N 105 56 E
Nha Trang, Vietnam 77 F7 12 16N 109 10 E
Nhacoongo, Mozam. 105 C6 24 18 S 35 14 E
Nhamaabué, Mozam. 107 F4 17 25 S 35 5 E
Nhambiquara, Brazil 157 C6 12 50 S 59 49W
Nhamundá, Brazil 153 D6 2 14 S 56 43W
Nhamundá →, Brazil 153 D6 2 12 S 56 41W
Nhangutazi, L., Mozam. 105 C5 24 0 S 34 30 E
Nhecolândia, Brazil 157 D6 19 17 S 56 58W
Nhill, Australia 116 D4 36 18 S 141 40 E
Nho Quan, Vietnam 76 B5 20 18N 105 45 E
Nhulunbuy, Australia 114 A2 12 10 S 137 20 E
Nhundo, Angola 103 E4 14 25 S 21 23 E
Nia-nia, Zaïre 106 B2 1 30N 27 40 E
Niafounké, Mali 100 B4 16 0N 4 5W
Niagara, U.S.A. 134 C2 45 45N 88 0W
Niagara Falls, Canada 128 D4 43 7N 79 5W
Niagara Falls, U.S.A. 124 E12 43 5N 79 0W
Niagara-on-the-Lake, Canada 136 C5 43 15N 79 4W
Niah, Malaysia 70 D4 3 58N 113 46 E
Niamey, Niger 101 C5 13 27N 2 6 E
Nianforando, Guinea 100 D2 9 37N 10 36W
Nianfors, Sweden 14 C10 61 36N 16 46 E
Niangara, Zaïre 106 B2 3 42N 27 50 E
Niangua →, U.S.A. 140 G4 38 0N 92 48W
Nias, Indonesia 70 D1 1 0N 97 30 E
Niassa □, Mozam. 107 E4 13 30 S 36 0 E
Nibāk, Si. Arabia 87 A5 24 25N 50 50 E
Nibbiano, Italy 38 D6 44 54N 9 20 E
Nibe, Denmark 15 H3 56 59N 9 38 E
Nicaragua ■, Cent. Amer. 148 D2 11 40N 85 30W
Nicaragua, L. de, Nic. 148 D2 12 0N 85 30W
Nicastro, Italy 41 D9 38 58N 16 18 E
Nice, France 25 E11 43 42N 7 14 E
Niceville, U.S.A. 135 K2 30 30N 86 30W
Nichinan, Japan 62 F3 31 38N 131 23 E
Nicholás, Canal, W. Indies 148 B3 23 30N 80 5W
Nicholasville, U.S.A. 141 G12 37 54N 84 31W
Nichols, U.S.A. 137 D8 42 1N 76 22W
Nicholson, Australia 112 C4 18 2 S 128 54 E
Nicholson, U.S.A. 137 E9 41 37N 75 47W
Nicholson →, Australia 114 B2 17 31 S 139 36 E
Nicholson Ra., Australia 113 E2 27 15 S 116 45 E
Nickerie □, Surinam 153 C6 4 0N 57 0W
Nickerie →, Surinam 153 B6 5 58N 57 0W
Nicobar Is., Ind. Oc. 58 J13 9 0N 93 0 E
Nicoclí, Colombia 152 B2 8 26N 76 48W
Nicola, Canada 130 C4 50 12N 120 40W
Nicolet, Canada 128 C5 46 17N 72 35W
Nicolls Town, Bahamas 148 A4 25 8N 78 0W
Nicopolis, Greece 45 E2 39 2N 20 37 E
Nicosia, Cyprus 32 D12 35 10N 33 25 E
Nicosia, Italy 41 E7 37 45N 14 22 E
Nicótera, Italy 41 D8 38 33N 15 57 E
Nicoya, Costa Rica 148 D2 10 9N 85 27W
Nicoya, G. de, Costa Rica 148 E3 10 0N 85 0W
Nicoya, Pen. de, Costa Rica 148 E2 9 45N 85 40W
Nidau, Switz. 28 B4 47 7N 7 15 E
Nidd →, U.K. 16 C6 54 1N 1 32W
Nidda, Germany 26 E5 50 24N 9 2 E
Nidda →, Germany 27 E4 50 6N 8 34 E
Nidwalden □, Switz. 29 C6 46 50N 8 25 E
Nidzica, Poland 47 B7 53 25N 20 28 E
Niebüll, Germany 26 A4 54 47N 8 49 E
Nied →, Germany 23 C13 49 23N 6 40 E
Niederaula, Germany 26 E5 50 48N 9 37 E
Niederbipp, Switz. 28 B5 47 16N 7 42 E
Niederbronn-les-Bains, France 23 D14 48 57N 7 39 E
Niedere Tauern, Austria 30 D7 47 20N 14 0 E
Niederösterreich □, Austria 30 C8 48 25N 15 40 E
Niedersachsen □, Germany 26 C5 52 45N 9 0 E
Niefang, Eq. Guin. 102 B2 1 50N 10 14 E
Niekerkshoop, S. Africa 104 D3 29 19 S 22 51 E
Niel, Belgium 21 F4 51 7N 4 20 E
Niellé, Ivory C. 100 C3 10 5N 5 38W
Niem, C.A.R. 102 A3 6 12N 15 14 E
Niemba, Zaïre 106 D2 5 58 S 28 24 E
Niemcza, Poland 47 E3 50 42N 16 47 E
Niemodlin, Poland 47 E4 50 38N 17 38 E
Niemur, Australia 116 C6 35 17 S 144 9 E
Nienburg, Germany 26 C5 52 38N 9 15 E
Niepołomice, Poland 31 A13 50 3N 20 13 E
Niers →, Germany 26 D2 51 35N 6 13 E
Niesen, Switz. 28 C5 46 38N 7 39 E
Niesky, Germany 26 D10 51 18N 14 48 E
Nieszawa, Poland 47 C5 52 52N 18 50 E
Nieu Bethesda, S. Africa 104 E3 31 51 S 24 34 E
Nieuw-Amsterdam, Neths. 20 C9 52 43N 6 52 E
Nieuw Amsterdam, Surinam 153 B6 5 53N 55 5W
Nieuw Beijerland, Neths. 20 E4 51 49N 4 20 E
Nieuw-Dordrecht, Neths. 20 C9 52 45N 6 59 E
Nieuw Loosdrecht, Neths. 20 D6 52 12N 5 8 E
Nieuw Nickerie, Surinam 153 B6 6 0N 56 59W
Nieuw-Schoonebeek, Neths. 20 C10 52 39N 7 0 E
Nieuw-Vennep, Neths. 20 D5 52 16N 4 38 E
Nieuw-Vossemeer, Neths. 21 E4 51 34N 4 12 E
Nieuwe-Niedorp, Neths. 20 C5 52 44N 4 54 E
Nieuwe-Pekela, Neths. 20 B9 53 5N 6 58 E
Nieuwe-Schans, Neths. 20 B10 53 11N 7 12 E
Nieuwendijk, Neths. 20 E5 51 46N 4 55 E
Nieuwerkerken, Belgium 21 G6 50 52N 5 12 E
Nieuwkoop, Neths. 20 D5 52 9N 4 48 E
Nieuwleusen, Neths. 20 C8 52 34N 6 17 E
Nieuwnamen, Neths. 21 F4 51 18N 4 9 E
Nieuwolda, Neths. 20 B9 53 15N 6 58 E
Nieuwoudtville, S. Africa 104 E2 31 23 S 19 7 E
Nieuwpoort, Belgium 21 F1 51 8N 2 45 E
Nieuwveen, Neths. 20 D5 52 12N 4 46 E
Nieves, Spain 36 C2 42 7N 8 26W
Nieves, Pico de las, Canary Is. 33 G4 27 57N 15 35W
Nièvre □, France 23 E10 47 10N 3 40 E
Nigata, Japan 62 C4 34 13N 132 39 E
Niğde, Turkey 88 E6 37 58N 34 40 E
Niğde □, Turkey 88 E6 38 0N 34 30 E
Nigel, S. Africa 105 D4 26 27 S 28 25 E
Niger □, Nigeria 101 D6 10 0N 5 0 E
Niger ■, W. Afr. 97 E2 17 30N 10 0 E
Niger →, W. Afr. 101 D6 5 33N 6 33 E
Nigeria ■, W. Afr. 101 D6 8 30N 8 0 E
Nightcaps, N.Z. 119 F3 45 57 S 168 2 E
Nigrita, Greece 44 D5 40 56N 23 29 E
Nihtaur, India 81 E8 29 20N 78 23 E
Nii-Jima, Japan 63 C11 34 20N 139 15 E
Niigata, Japan 60 F9 37 58N 139 0 E
Niigata □, Japan 61 F9 37 15N 138 45 E
Niihama, Japan 62 D5 33 55N 133 16 E
Niihau, U.S.A. 132 H14 21 55N 160 10W
Niimi, Japan 62 C5 34 59N 133 28 E
Niitsu, Japan 60 F9 37 48N 139 7 E
Nījar, Spain 35 J2 36 53N 2 15W
Nijil, Jordan 91 E4 30 32N 35 33 E
Nijkerk, Neths. 20 D7 52 13N 5 30 E
Nijlen, Belgium 21 F5 51 10N 4 40 E
Nijmegen, Neths. 20 E7 51 50N 5 52 E
Nijverdal, Neths. 20 D8 52 22N 6 28 E
Nīk Pey, Iran 85 B6 36 50N 48 10 E
Nike, Nigeria 101 D6 6 26N 7 29 E
Nikel, U.S.S.R. 12 B21 69 24N 30 12 E
Nikiniki, Indonesia 71 F6 9 49 S 124 30 E
Nikítas, Greece 44 D5 40 13N 23 34 E
Nikki, Benin 101 D5 9 58N 3 12 E
Nikkō, Japan 63 A11 36 45N 139 35 E
Nikolayev, U.S.S.R. 52 C5 46 58N 32 0 E
Nikolayevsk, U.S.S.R. 51 G14 50 0N 45 35 E
Nikolayevsk-na-Amur, U.S.S.R. 57 D15 53 8N 140 44 E
Nikolsk, U.S.S.R. 51 B14 59 30N 45 28 E
Nikolskoye, U.S.S.R. 57 D17 55 12N 166 0 E
Nikopol, Bulgaria 43 D9 43 43N 24 54 E
Nikopol, U.S.S.R. 52 C6 47 35N 34 25 E

North Walsham 241

Niksar, *Turkey* **52 F7** 40 31N 37 2 E
Nīkshahr, *Iran* **85 E9** 26 15N 60 10 E
Nikšić, *Yugoslavia* **42 E3** 42 50N 18 57 E
Nîl, Nahr en →, *Africa* **94 H7** 30 10N 31 6 E
Nîl el Abyad →, *Sudan* **95 D3** 15 38N 32 31 E
Nîl el Azraq →, *Sudan* **95 D3** 15 38N 32 31 E
Niland, *U.S.A.* **145 M11** 33 16N 115 30W
Nile = Nîl, Nahr en →,
Africa **94 H7** 30 10N 31 6 E
Nile □, *Uganda* **106 B3** 2 0N 31 30 E
Nile Delta, *Egypt* **94 H7** 31 40N 31 0 E
Niles, *U.S.A.* **136 E4** 41 8N 80 40W
Nilgiri Hills, *India* **83 J3** 11 30N 76 30 E
Nilo Peçanha, *Brazil* **155 D4** 13 37 S 39 6W
Nilpena, *Australia* **116 A3** 30 58 S 138 20 E
Nimach, *India* **80 G6** 24 30N 74 56 E
Nimbahera, *India* **80 G6** 24 37N 74 45 E
Nîmes, *France* **25 E8** 43 50N 4 23 E
Nimfaíon, Ákra-, *Greece* **44 D6** 40 5N 24 20 E
Nimmitabel, *Australia* **117 D8** 36 29 S 149 15 E
Nimneryskiy, *U.S.S.R.* **57 D13** 57 50N 125 10 E
Nimule, *Sudan* **95 G3** 3 32N 32 3 E
Nin, *Yugoslavia* **39 D12** 44 16N 15 12 E
Nīnawá, *Iraq* **84 B4** 36 25N 43 10 E
Ninda, *Angola* **103 E4** 14 47 S 21 24 E
Nindigully, *Australia* **115 D4** 28 21 S 148 50 E
Ninemile, *U.S.A.* **130 B2** 56 0N 130 7W
Ninety Mile Beach, *N.Z.* **118 A2** 34 48 S 173 0 E
Ninety Mile Beach, The,
Australia **117 E7** 38 15 S 147 24 E
Nineveh = Nīnawá, *Iraq* **84 B4** 36 25N 43 10 E
Ning Xian, *China* **66 G4** 35 30N 107 58 E
Ningaloo, *Australia* **112 D1** 22 41 S 113 41 E
Ning'an, *China* **67 B15** 44 22N 129 20 E
Ningbo, *China* **69 C13** 29 51N 121 28 E
Ningcheng, *China* **67 D10** 41 32N 119 53 E
Ningde, *China* **69 D12** 26 38N 119 23 E
Ningdu, *China* **69 D10** 26 25N 115 59 E
Ninggang, *China* **69 D9** 26 42N 113 55 E
Ningguo, *China* **69 B12** 30 35N 119 0 E
Ninghai, *China* **69 C13** 29 15N 121 27 E
Ninghua, *China* **69 D11** 26 14N 116 45 E
Ningjin, *China* **66 F8** 37 35N 114 57 E
Ningjing Shan, *China* **68 C2** 30 0N 98 20 E
Ninglang, *China* **68 D3** 27 20N 100 55 E
Ningling, *China* **66 G8** 34 25N 115 22 E
Ningming, *China* **68 F6** 22 8N 107 4 E
Ningnan, *China* **68 D4** 27 5N 102 36 E
Ningpo = Ningbo, *China* **69 C13** 29 51N 121 28 E
Ningpo, *China* **10 A11** 29 53N 121 33 E
Ningqiang, *China* **66 H4** 32 47N 106 15 E
Ningshan, *China* **66 H5** 33 21N 108 21 E
Ningsia Hui A.R. =
Ningxia Huizu
Zizhiqu □, *China* **66 F4** 38 0N 106 0 E
Ningwu, *China* **66 E7** 39 0N 112 18 E
Ningxia Huizu Zizhiqu □,
China **66 F4** 38 0N 106 0 E
Ningxiang, *China* **69 C9** 28 15N 112 30 E
Ningyang, *China* **66 G9** 35 47N 116 45 E
Ningyuan, *China* **69 E8** 25 37N 111 57 E
Ninh Binh, *Vietnam* **76 B5** 20 15N 105 55 E
Ninh Giang, *Vietnam* **76 B6** 20 44N 106 24 E
Ninh Hoa, *Vietnam* **76 F7** 12 30N 109 7 E
Ninh Ma, *Vietnam* **76 F7** 12 48N 109 21 E
Ninove, *Belgium* **21 G4** 50 51N 4 2 E
Nioaque, *Brazil* **159 A4** 21 5 S 55 50W
Niobrara, *U.S.A.* **138 D6** 42 48N 97 59W
Niobrara →, *U.S.A.* **138 D6** 42 45N 98 0W
Nioki, *Zaïre* **102 C3** 2 47 S 17 40 E
Niono, *Mali* **100 C3** 14 15N 6 0W
Nioro du Rip, *Senegal* **100 C1** 13 40N 15 50W
Nioro du Sahel, *Mali* **100 B3** 15 15N 9 30W
Niort, *France* **24 B3** 46 19N 0 29W
Nipa, *Papua N. G.* **120 D2** 6 9 S 143 29 E
Nipani, *India* **83 F2** 16 20N 74 25 E
Nipawin, *Canada* **131 C8** 53 20N 104 0W
Nipawin Prov. Park,
Canada **131 C8** 54 0N 104 37W
Nipigon, *Canada* **128 C2** 49 0N 88 17W
Nipigon, L., *Canada* **128 C2** 49 50N 88 30W
Nipin →, *Canada* **131 B7** 55 46N 108 35W
Nipishish L., *Canada* **129 B7** 54 12N 60 45W
Nipissing L., *Canada* **128 C4** 46 20N 80 0W
Nipomo, *U.S.A.* **145 K6** 35 4N 120 29W
Nipton, *U.S.A.* **145 K11** 35 28N 115 16W
Niquelândia, *Brazil* **155 D2** 14 33 S 48 23W
Nīr, *Iran* **84 B5** 38 2N 47 59 E
Nira →, *India* **82 F2** 17 58N 75 8 E
Nirasaki, *Japan* **63 B10** 35 42N 138 27 E
Nirmal, *India* **82 E4** 19 3N 78 20 E
Nirmali, *India* **81 F12** 26 20N 86 35 E
Niš, *Yugoslavia* **42 D6** 43 19N 21 58 E
Nisa, *Portugal* **37 F3** 39 30N 7 41W
Nişāb, *Yemen* **86 D4** 14 25N 46 29 E
Nišava →, *Yugoslavia* **42 D6** 43 20N 21 46 E
Niscemi, *Italy* **41 E7** 37 8N 14 21 E
Nishi-Sonogi-Hantō,
Japan **62 E1** 32 55N 129 45 E
Nishinomiya, *Japan* **63 C7** 34 45N 135 20 E
Nishin'omote, *Japan* **61 J5** 30 43N 130 59 E
Nishio, *Japan* **63 C9** 34 52N 137 3 E
Nishiwaki, *Japan* **62 C6** 34 59N 134 58 E
Nísíros, *Greece* **45 H9** 36 35N 27 12 E
Niskibi →, *Canada* **128 A2** 56 29N 88 9W
Nisko, *Poland* **47 E9** 50 35N 22 7 E
Nispen, *Neths.* **21 F4** 51 29N 4 28 E
Nisporeny, *U.S.S.R.* **46 B9** 47 4N 28 10 E
Nisqually →, *U.S.A.* **144 C4** 47 6N 122 42W
Nissáki, *Greece* **32 A3** 39 43N 19 52 E
Nissan →, *Sweden* **15 H6** 56 40N 12 51 E
Nissedal, *Norway* **14 E2** 59 10N 8 30 E
Nisser, *Norway* **14 E2** 59 7N 8 28 E
Nissum Fjord, *Denmark* **15 H2** 56 20N 8 11 E
Nistelrode, *Neths.* **21 E7** 51 42N 5 34 E
Nisutlin →, *Canada* **130 A2** 60 14N 132 34W
Nitchequon, *Canada* **129 B5** 53 10N 70 58W
Niterói, *Brazil* **155 F3** 22 52 S 43 0W
Nith →, *U.K.* **18 F5** 55 20N 3 5W
Nitra, *Czech.* **31 C11** 48 19N 18 4 E
Nitra →, *Czech.* **31 D11** 47 46N 18 10 E
Nitsa →, *U.S.S.R.* **54 C9** 57 29N 64 33 E
Nittedal, *Norway* **14 D4** 60 1N 10 57 E
Nittendau, *Germany* **27 F8** 49 12N 12 16 E
Niuafo'ou, *Tonga* **111 D15** 15 30 S 175 58W
Niue, *Cook Is.* **111 D17** 19 2 S 169 54W
Niulan Jiang →, *China* **68 D4** 27 30N 103 5 E
Niut, *Indonesia* **70 D4** 0 55N 110 6 E
Niutou Shan, *China* **69 C13** 29 5N 121 59 E
Niuzhuang, *China* **67 D12** 40 58N 122 28 E
Nivelles, *Belgium* **21 G4** 50 35N 4 20 E
Nivernais, *France* **23 E10** 47 15N 3 30 E
Nixon, *U.S.A.* **139 L6** 29 17N 97 45W
Nizam Sagar, *India* **82 E3** 18 10N 77 58 E
Nizamabad, *India* **82 E4** 18 45N 78 7 E
Nizamghat, *India* **78 A5** 28 20N 95 45 E
Nizhiye Sergi, *U.S.S.R.* **54 C6** 56 40N 59 18 E
Nizhne Kolymsk,
U.S.S.R. **57 C17** 68 34N 160 55 E
Nizhneangarsk, *U.S.S.R.* **57 D11** 55 47N 109 30 E
Nizhnegorskiy, *U.S.S.R.* **52 D6** 45 27N 34 38 E
Nizhnekamsk, *U.S.S.R.* **54 D2** 55 38N 51 49 E
Nizhneudinsk, *U.S.S.R.* **57 D10** 54 54N 99 3 E
Nizhnevartovsk, *U.S.S.R.* **56 C8** 60 56N 76 38 E
Nizhneyansk, *U.S.S.R.* **57 B14** 71 26N 136 4 E
Nizhniy Lomov, *U.S.S.R.* **51 E13** 53 34N 43 38 E
Nizhniy Novgorod =
Gorkiy, *U.S.S.R.* **51 C14** 56 20N 44 0 E
Nizhniy Pyandzh,
U.S.S.R. **55 E4** 37 12N 68 35 E
Nizhniy Tagil, *U.S.S.R.* **54 C6** 57 55N 59 57 E
Nizhny Salda, *U.S.S.R.* **54 B7** 58 8N 60 42 E
Nizhnyaya Tunguska →,
U.S.S.R. **57 C10** 64 20N 93 0 E
Nizip, *Turkey* **89 E7** 37 5N 37 50 E
Nizké Tatry, *Czech.* **31 C12** 48 55N 19 30 E
Nizza Monferrato, *Italy* **38 D5** 44 46N 8 22 E
Njakwa, *Malawi* **107 E3** 11 1 S 33 56 E
Njanji, *Zambia* **107 E3** 14 25 S 31 46 E
Njinjo, *Tanzania* **107 D4** 8 48 S 38 54 E
Njombe, *Tanzania* **107 D3** 9 20 S 34 50 E
Njombe □, *Tanzania* **107 D3** 9 20 S 34 49 E
Njombe →, *Tanzania* **106 D4** 6 56 S 35 6 E
Nkambe, *Cameroon* **101 D7** 6 35N 10 40 E
Nkana, *Zambia* **107 E2** 12 50 S 28 8 E
Nkawkaw, *Ghana* **101 D4** 6 36N 0 49W
Nkayi, *Zimbabwe* **107 F2** 19 41 S 29 20 E
Nkhota Kota, *Malawi* **107 E3** 12 56 S 34 15 E
Nkolabona, *Gabon* **102 B2** 1 14N 11 43 E
Nkone, *Zaïre* **102 C4** 1 2 S 22 20 E
Nkongsamba, *Cameroon* **101 E6** 4 55N 9 55 E
Nkunga, *Zaïre* **103 C3** 4 41 S 18 34 E
Nkurenkuru, *Namibia* **104 B2** 17 42 S 18 32 E
Nkwanta, *Ghana* **100 D4** 6 10N 2 10W
Noakhali = Maijdi,
Bangla. **78 D3** 22 48N 91 10 E
Noatak, *U.S.A.* **126 B3** 67 32N 162 59W
Nobel, *Canada* **136 A4** 45 25N 80 6W
Nobeoka, *Japan* **62 E3** 32 36N 131 41 E
Nōbi-Heiya, *Japan* **63 B8** 35 15N 136 45 E
Noble, *U.S.A.* **141 F8** 38 42N 88 14W
Noblejas, *Spain* **34 F1** 39 58N 3 26W
Noblesville, *U.S.A.* **141 D11** 40 1N 85 59W
Noce →, *Italy* **38 B8** 46 9N 11 4 E
Nocera Inferiore, *Italy* **41 B7** 40 45N 14 37 E
Nocera Terinese, *Italy* **41 C9** 39 2N 16 9 E
Nocera Umbra, *Italy* **39 E9** 43 8N 12 47 E
Noci, *Italy* **41 B10** 40 47N 17 7 E
Nockatunga, *Australia* **115 D3** 27 42 S 142 42 E
Nocona, *U.S.A.* **139 J6** 33 48N 97 45W
Nocrich, *Romania* **46 D5** 45 55N 24 26 E
Noda, *Japan* **63 B11** 35 56N 139 52 E
Noel, *U.S.A.* **139 G7** 36 36N 94 29W
Nogal Valley,
Somali Rep. **108 C3** 8 35N 48 35 E
Nogales, *Mexico* **146 A2** 31 20N 110 56W
Nogales, *U.S.A.* **143 L8** 31 33N 110 56W
Nogat →, *Poland* **47 A6** 54 17N 19 17 E
Nōgata, *Japan* **62 D2** 33 48N 130 44 E
Nogent-en-Bassigny,
France **23 D12** 48 1N 5 20 E
Nogent-le-Rotrou, *France* **22 D7** 48 20N 0 50 E
Nogent-sur-Seine, *France* **23 D10** 48 30N 3 30 E
Noggerup, *Australia* **113 F2** 33 32 S 116 5 E
Noginsk, *Moskva,*
U.S.S.R. **51 D11** 55 50N 38 25 E
Noginsk, *Sib., U.S.S.R.* **57 C10** 64 30N 90 50 E
Nogoa →, *Australia* **114 C4** 23 40 S 147 55 E
Nogoyá, *Argentina* **158 C4** 32 24 S 59 48W
Nógrád □, *Hungary* **31 D12** 48 0N 19 30 E
Nogueira de Ramuin,
Spain **36 C3** 42 21N 7 43W
Noguera Pallaresa →,
Spain **34 D5** 41 55N 0 55 E
Noguera Ribagorzana →,
Spain **34 D5** 41 40N 0 43 E
Nohar, *India* **80 E6** 29 11N 74 49 E
Noire, Mt., *France* **22 D3** 48 11N 3 40W
Noirétable, *France* **24 C7** 45 48N 3 46 E
Noirmoutier, I. de,
France **22 F4** 46 58N 2 10W
Noirmoutier-en-l'Ile,
France **22 F4** 47 0N 2 14W
Nojane, *Botswana* **104 C3** 23 15 S 20 14 E
Nojima-Zaki, *Japan* **63 C11** 34 54N 139 53 E
Nok Kundi, *Pakistan* **79 C1** 28 50N 62 45 E
Nokaneng, *Botswana* **104 B3** 19 40 S 22 17 E
Nokhtuysk, *U.S.S.R.* **57 D12** 60 0N 117 45 E
Nokomis, *Canada* **131 C8** 51 35N 105 0W
Nokomis, *U.S.A.* **140 E7** 39 18N 89 18W
Nokomis L., *Canada* **131 B8** 57 0N 103 0W
Nokou, *Chad* **97 F2** 14 35N 14 47 E
Nol, *Sweden* **15 G6** 57 56N 12 5 E
Nola, *C.A.R.* **102 B3** 3 35N 16 4 E
Nola, *Italy* **41 B7** 40 54N 14 29 E
Nolay, *France* **23 F11** 46 58N 4 35 E
Noli, C. di, *Italy* **38 D5** 44 12N 8 26 E
Nolinsk, *U.S.S.R.* **54 C1** 57 28N 49 57 E
Noma Omuramba →,
Namibia **104 B3** 18 52 S 20 53 E
Noma-Saki, *Japan* **62 F2** 31 25N 130 7 E
Nomad, *Papua N. G.* **120 D2** 6 19 S 142 13 E
Noman L., *Canada* **131 A7** 62 15N 108 55W
Nombre de Dios, *Panama* **148 E4** 9 34N 79 28W
Nome, *U.S.A.* **126 B3** 64 30N 165 24W
Nomo-Zaki, *Japan* **62 E1** 32 35N 129 44 E
Nomuka, *Tonga* **121 Q13** 20 17 S 174 48W
Nomuka Group, *Tonga* **121 Q13** 20 20 S 174 48W
Nonacho L., *Canada* **131 A7** 61 42N 109 40W
Nonancourt, *France* **22 D8** 48 47N 1 11 E
Nonant-le-Pin, *France* **22 D7** 48 42N 0 12 E
Nonda, *Australia* **114 C3** 20 40 S 142 28 E
Nong Chang, *Thailand* **76 E2** 15 23N 99 51 E
Nong Het, *Laos* **76 C4** 19 29N 103 59 E
Nong Khai, *Thailand* **76 D4** 17 50N 102 46 E
Nong'an, *China* **67 B13** 44 25N 125 5 E
Nongoma, *S. Africa* **105 D5** 27 58 S 31 35 E
Nonoava, *Mexico* **146 B3** 27 28N 106 44W
Nonthaburi, *Thailand* **76 F3** 13 51N 100 34 E
Nontron, *France* **24 C4** 45 31N 0 40 E
Nonza, *France* **25 F13** 42 47N 9 21 E
Noonamah, *Australia* **112 B5** 12 40 S 131 4 E
Noonan, *U.S.A.* **138 A3** 48 51N 102 59W
Noondoo, *Australia* **115 D4** 28 35 S 148 30 E
Noonkanbah, *Australia* **112 C3** 18 30 S 124 50 E
Noord-Bergum, *Neths.* **20 B8** 53 14N 6 1 E
Noord Brabant □, *Neths.* **21 E6** 51 40N 5 0 E
Noord Holland □, *Neths.* **20 D5** 52 30N 4 45 E
Noordbeveland, *Neths.* **21 E3** 51 35N 3 50 E
Noordeloos, *Neths.* **20 E5** 51 55N 4 56 E
Noordhollandsch Kanaal,
Neths. **20 C5** 52 55N 4 48 E
Noordhorn, *Neths.* **20 B8** 53 16N 6 24 E
Noordoostpolder, *Neths.* **20 C7** 52 45N 5 45 E
Noordwijk aan Zee,
Neths. **20 D4** 52 14N 4 26 E
Noordwijk-Binnen, *Neths.* **20 D4** 52 14N 4 27 E
Noordwijkerhout, *Neths.* **20 D5** 52 16N 4 30 E
Noordzee Kanaal, *Neths.* **20 D5** 52 28N 4 35 E
Noorwolde, *Neths.* **20 C8** 52 54N 6 8 E
Nootka, *Canada* **130 D3** 49 38N 126 38W
Nootka I., *Canada* **130 D3** 49 32N 126 42W
Nóqui, *Angola* **103 D2** 5 55 S 13 30 E
Nora, *Ethiopia* **95 D5** 16 6N 40 4 E
Nora Springs, *U.S.A.* **140 A4** 43 9N 93 0W
Noranda, *Canada* **128 C4** 48 20N 79 0W
Norborne, *U.S.A.* **140 E3** 39 18N 93 40W
Nórcia, *Italy* **39 F10** 42 50N 13 5 E
Norco, *U.S.A.* **145 M9** 33 56N 117 33W
Nord □, *France* **23 B10** 50 15N 3 30 E
Nord-Ostsee Kanal,
Germany **26 A5** 54 15N 9 40 E
Nord-Trøndelag fylke □,
Norway **12 D12** 64 20N 12 10 E
Nordagutu, *Norway* **14 E3** 59 25N 9 20 E
Nordaustlandet, *Svalbard* **6 B9** 79 14N 23 0 E
Nordborg, *Denmark* **15 J3** 55 5N 9 50 E
Nordby, *Århus, Denmark* **15 J4** 55 58N 10 32 E
Nordby, *Ribe, Denmark* **15 J2** 55 27N 8 24 E
Norddeich, *Germany* **26 B3** 53 37N 7 10 E
Nordegg, *Canada* **130 C5** 52 29N 116 5W
Norden, *Germany* **26 B3** 53 35N 7 12 E
Nordenham, *Germany* **26 B4** 53 29N 8 28 E
Norderhov, *Norway* **14 D4** 60 7N 10 17 E
Norderney, *Germany* **26 B3** 53 42N 7 15 E
Nordfriesische Inseln,
Germany **26 A4** 54 40N 8 20 E
Nordhausen, *Germany* **26 D6** 51 29N 10 47 E
Nordhorn, *Germany* **26 C3** 52 27N 7 4 E
Nordjyllands
Amtskommune □,
Denmark **15 H4** 57 0N 10 0 E
Nordkapp, *Norway* **12 A18** 71 10N 25 44 E
Nordkapp, *Svalbard* **6 A9** 80 31N 20 0 E
Nordkinn, *Norway* **10 A11** 71 8N 27 40 E
Nordland fylke □,
Norway **12 D12** 65 40N 13 0 E
Nördlingen, *Germany* **27 G6** 48 50N 10 30 E
Nordrhein-Westfalen □,
Germany **26 D3** 51 45N 7 30 E
Nordstrand, *Germany* **26 A4** 54 27N 8 50 E
Nordvik, *U.S.S.R.* **57 B12** 74 2N 111 32 E
Nore, *Norway* **14 D3** 60 10N 9 0 E
Norefjell, *Norway* **14 D3** 60 16N 9 29 E
Norembega, *Canada* **128 C3** 48 59N 80 43W
Noresund, *Norway* **14 D3** 60 11N 9 37 E
Norfolk, *Nebr., U.S.A.* **138 D6** 42 3N 97 25W
Norfolk, *Va., U.S.A.* **134 G7** 36 40N 76 15W
Norfolk □, *U.K.* **16 E9** 52 39N 1 0 E
Norfolk Broads, *U.K.* **16 E9** 52 30N 1 15 E
Norfolk I., *Pac. Oc.* **111 F12** 28 58 S 168 3 E
Norfork Res., *U.S.A.* **139 G8** 36 13N 92 15W
Norg, *Neths.* **20 B8** 53 4N 6 28 E
Norilsk, *U.S.S.R.* **57 C9** 69 20N 88 6 E
Norley, *Australia* **115 D3** 27 45 S 143 48 E
Norma, Mt., *Australia* **114 C3** 20 55 S 140 42 E
Normal, *U.S.A.* **140 D8** 40 30N 88 55W
Norman, *U.S.A.* **139 H6** 35 12N 97 30W
Norman →, *Australia* **114 B3** 19 18 S 141 51 E
Norman Wells, *Canada* **126 B7** 65 17N 126 51W
Normanby, *N.Z.* **118 F3** 39 32 S 174 18 E
Normanby →, *Australia* **114 A3** 14 23 S 144 10 E
Normanby I.,
Papua N. G. **120 F6** 10 5 S 151 5 E
Normandie, *France* **22 D7** 48 45N 0 10 E
Normandie, Collines de,
France **22 D6** 48 45N 0 45W
Normandin, *Canada* **128 C5** 48 49N 72 31W
Normandy = Normandie,
France **22 D7** 48 45N 0 10 E
Normanhurst, Mt.,
Australia **113 E3** 25 4 S 122 30 E
Normanton, *Australia* **114 B3** 17 40 S 141 10 E
Normanville, *Australia* **116 C3** 35 27 S 138 18 E
Norquay, *Canada* **131 C8** 51 53N 102 5W
Norquinco, *Argentina* **160 B2** 41 51 S 70 55W
Norrbotten □, *Sweden* **12 C17** 66 30N 22 30 E
Norrby, *Sweden* **12 D15** 64 55N 18 15 E
Nørre Åby, *Denmark* **15 J3** 55 27N 9 52 E
Nørre Nebel, *Denmark* **15 J2** 55 47N 8 17 E
Nørresundby, *Denmark* **15 G3** 57 5N 9 52 E
Norris, *U.S.A.* **142 D8** 45 40N 111 40W
Norris City, *U.S.A.* **141 G8** 37 59N 88 20W
Norristown, *U.S.A.* **137 F9** 40 9N 75 21W
Norrköping, *Sweden* **15 F10** 58 37N 16 11 E
Norrland, *Sweden* **12 E13** 62 15N 15 45 E
Norrtälje, *Sweden* **14 E12** 59 46N 18 42 E
Norseman, *Australia* **113 F3** 32 8 S 121 43 E
Norsewood, *N.Z.* **118 G5** 40 3 S 176 13 E
Norsholm, *Sweden* **15 F9** 58 31N 15 59 E
Norsk, *U.S.S.R.* **57 D14** 52 30N 130 5 E
Norsup, *Vanuatu* **121 F5** 16 3 S 167 24 E
Norte, Pta., *Argentina* **160 B4** 42 5 S 63 46W
Norte, Pta. del,
Canary Is. **33 G2** 27 51N 17 57W
Norte de Santander □,
Colombia **152 B3** 8 0N 73 0W
Nortelândia, *Brazil* **157 C6** 14 25 S 56 48W
North Adams, *U.S.A.* **137 D11** 42 42N 73 6W
North America **124 F10** 40 0N 100 0W
North Atlantic Ocean,
Atl. Oc. **8 F4** 30 0N 50 0W
North Baltimore, *U.S.A.* **141 C13** 41 11N 83 41W
North Battleford, *Canada* **131 C7** 52 50N 108 17W
North Bay, *Canada* **128 C4** 46 20N 79 30W
North Belcher Is.,
Canada **128 A4** 56 50N 79 50W
North Bend, *Canada* **130 D4** 49 50N 121 27W
North Bend, *Oreg.,*
U.S.A. **142 E1** 43 28N 124 14W
North Bend, *Pa., U.S.A.* **136 E7** 41 20N 77 42W
North Bend, *Wash.,*
U.S.A. **144 C5** 47 30N 121 47W
North Berwick, *U.K.* **18 E6** 56 4N 2 44W
North Berwick, *U.S.A.* **137 C14** 43 18N 70 43W
North Buganda □,
Uganda **106 B3** 1 0N 32 0 E
North Canadian →,
U.S.A. **139 H7** 35 17N 95 31W
North C., *Canada* **129 C7** 47 2N 60 20W
North C., *N.Z.* **118 A2** 34 23 S 173 4 E
North C., *Papua N. G.* **120 B6** 2 32 S 150 50 E
North Caribou L.,
Canada **128 B1** 52 50N 90 40W
North Carolina □, *U.S.A.* **135 H6** 35 30N 80 0W
North Channel, *Canada* **128 C3** 46 0N 83 0W
North Channel, *U.K.* **18 G3** 55 0N 5 30W
North Chicago, *U.S.A.* **141 B9** 42 19N 87 50W
North College Hill,
U.S.A. **141 E12** 39 13N 84 33W
North Dakota □, *U.S.A.* **138 B5** 47 30N 100 0W
North Dandalup,
Australia **113 F2** 32 30 S 115 57 E
North Down □, *U.K.* **19 B6** 54 40N 5 45W
North Downs, *U.K.* **17 F8** 51 17N 0 30 E
North East, *U.S.A.* **136 D5** 42 17N 79 50W
North East Frontier
Agency = Arunachal
Pradesh □, *India* **78 B5** 28 0N 95 0 E
North East Providence
Chan., *W. Indies* **148 A4** 26 0N 76 0W
North Eastern □, *Kenya* **106 B5** 1 30N 40 0 E
North English, *U.S.A.* **140 C4** 41 31N 92 5W
North Esk →, *U.K.* **18 E6** 56 44N 2 25W
North European Plain,
Europe **10 E11** 55 0N 25 0 E
North Fabius →, *U.S.A.* **140 E5** 39 54N 91 28W
North Foreland, *U.K.* **17 F9** 51 22N 1 28 E
North Fork, *U.S.A.* **144 H7** 37 14N 119 21W
North Fork, Salt →,
U.S.A. **140 E5** 39 26N 91 53W
North Fork
American →, *U.S.A.* **144 G5** 38 45N 121 8W
North Fork Feather →,
U.S.A. **144 F5** 39 17N 121 38W
North Frisian Is. =
Nordfriesische Inseln,
Germany **26 A4** 54 40N 8 20 E
North Henik L., *Canada* **131 A9** 61 45N 97 40W
North Highlands, *U.S.A.* **144 G5** 38 40N 121 25W
North Horr, *Kenya* **106 B4** 3 20N 37 8 E
North I., *Kenya* **106 B4** 4 5N 36 5 E
North I., *N.Z.* **118 E4** 38 0 S 175 0 E
North Judson, *U.S.A.* **141 C10** 41 13N 86 46W
North Kingsville, *U.S.A.* **136 E4** 41 53N 80 42W
North Knife →, *Canada* **131 B10** 58 53N 94 45W
North Koel →, *India* **81 G10** 24 45N 83 50 E
North Korea ■, *Asia* **67 E14** 40 0N 127 0 E
North Lakhimpur, *India* **78 B5** 27 14N 94 7 E
North Las Vegas, *U.S.A.* **145 J11** 36 15N 115 6W
North Liberty, *U.S.A.* **141 C10** 41 32N 86 26W
North Loup →, *U.S.A.* **138 E5** 41 17N 98 23W
North Magnetic Pole,
Canada **6 B2** 77 58N 102 8 E
North Manchester,
U.S.A. **141 D11** 41 0N 85 46W
North Minch, *U.K.* **18 C3** 58 5N 5 55W
North Nahanni →,
Canada **130 A4** 62 15N 123 20W
North Olmsted, *U.S.A.* **136 E3** 41 25N 81 56W
North Ossetian
A.S.S.R. □, *U.S.S.R.* **53 E11** 43 30N 44 30 E
North Pagai, I. = Pagai
Utara, *Indonesia* **70 E2** 2 35 S 100 0 E
North Palisade, *U.S.A.* **144 H8** 37 6N 118 32W
North Platte, *U.S.A.* **138 E4** 41 10N 100 50W
North Platte →, *U.S.A.* **138 E4** 41 15N 100 45W
North Pt., *Canada* **129 C7** 47 5N 64 0W
North Pt., *Vanuatu* **121 D6** 14 56 S 168 6 E
North Pole, *Arctic* **6 A** 90 0N 0 0 E
North Portal, *Canada* **131 D8** 49 0N 102 33W
North Powder, *U.S.A.* **142 D5** 45 2N 117 59W
North Ronaldsay, *U.K.* **18 B6** 59 20N 2 30W
North Saskatchewan →,
Canada **131 C7** 53 15N 105 5W
North Sea, *Europe* **10 D6** 56 0N 4 0 E
North Sporades = Voríai
Sporádhes, *Greece* **45 E5** 39 15N 23 30 E
North Sydney, *Canada* **129 C7** 46 12N 60 15W
North Taranaki Bight,
N.Z. **118 E3** 38 50 S 174 15 E
North Thompson →,
Canada **130 C4** 50 40N 120 20W
North Tonawanda,
U.S.A. **136 C6** 43 5N 78 50W
North Troy, *U.S.A.* **137 B12** 44 59N 72 24W
North Truchas Pk.,
U.S.A. **143 J11** 36 0N 105 30W
North Twin I., *Canada* **128 B4** 53 20N 80 0W
North Tyne →, *U.K.* **16 C5** 54 59N 2 7W
North Uist, *U.K.* **18 D1** 57 40N 7 15W
North Vancouver, *Canada* **130 D4** 49 25N 123 3W
North Vernon, *U.S.A.* **141 F11** 39 0N 85 35W
North Wabasca L.,
Canada **130 B6** 56 0N 113 55W
North Walsham, *U.K.* **16 E9** 52 49N 1 22 E

Olivine Ra. 243

Nyurba, *U.S.S.R.* **57 C12** 63 17N 118 28 E
Nzega, *Tanzania* **106 C3** 4 10 S 33 12 E
Nzega □, *Tanzania* **106 C3** 4 10 S 33 10 E
N'Zérékoré, *Guinea* **100 D3** 7 49N 8 48W
Nzeto, *Angola* **103 D2** 7 10 S 12 52 E
Nzilo, Chutes de, *Zaïre* **103 E5** 10 18 S 25 27 E
Nzubuka, *Tanzania* **106 C3** 4 45 S 32 50 E

O

Ō-Shima, *Fukuoka, Japan* **62 D2** 33 54N 130 25 E
Ō-Shima, *Nagasaki, Japan* **62 C1** 34 29N 129 33 E
Ō-Shima, *Shizuoka, Japan* **63 C11** 34 44N 139 24 E
Oacoma, *U.S.A.* **138 D5** 43 50N 99 26W
Oahe Dam, *U.S.A.* **138 C4** 44 28N 100 25W
Oahe L., *U.S.A.* **138 C4** 45 30N 100 25W
Oahu, *U.S.A.* **132 H16** 21 30N 158 0W
Oak Creek, *Colo., U.S.A.* **142 F10** 40 15N 106 59W
Oak Creek, *Wis., U.S.A.* **141 B9** 42 52N 87 55W
Oak Harbour, *U.S.A.* **144 B4** 48 20N 122 38W
Oak Hill, *U.S.A.* **134 G5** 38 0N 81 7W
Oak Lawn, *U.S.A.* **141 C9** 41 43N 87 44W
Oak Park, *U.S.A.* **141 C9** 41 53N 87 47W
Oak Ridge, *U.S.A.* **135 G3** 36 1N 84 12W
Oak View, *U.S.A.* **145 L7** 34 24N 119 18W
Oakan-Dake, *Japan* **60 C12** 43 27N 144 10 E
Oakbank, *Australia* **116 B4** 33 4 S 140 33 E
Oakdale, *Calif., U.S.A.* **144 H6** 37 45N 120 55W
Oakdale, *La., U.S.A.* **139 K8** 30 50N 92 38W
Oakengates, *U.K.* **16 E5** 52 42N 2 29W
Oakes, *U.S.A.* **138 B5** 46 14N 98 4W
Oakesdale, *U.S.A.* **142 C5** 47 11N 117 15W
Oakey, *Australia* **115 D5** 27 25 S 151 43 E
Oakford, *U.S.A.* **140 D7** 40 6N 89 58W
Oakham, *U.K.* **16 E7** 52 40N 0 43W
Oakhurst, *U.S.A.* **144 H7** 37 19N 119 40W
Oakland, *Calif., U.S.A.* **144 H4** 37 50N 122 18W
Oakland, *Ill., U.S.A.* **141 E8** 39 39N 88 2W
Oakland, *Oreg., U.S.A.* **142 E2** 43 23N 123 18W
Oakland City, *U.S.A.* **141 F9** 38 20N 87 20W
Oaklands, *Australia* **117 C7** 35 34 S 146 10 E
Oakley, *Idaho, U.S.A.* **142 E7** 42 14N 113 55W
Oakley, *Kans., U.S.A.* **138 F4** 39 8N 100 51W
Oakley Creek, *Australia* **117 A8** 31 37 S 149 46 E
Oakover →, *Australia* **112 D3** 21 0 S 120 40 E
Oakridge, *U.S.A.* **142 E2** 43 47N 122 31W
Oaktown, *U.S.A.* **141 F9** 38 52N 87 27W
Oakville, *U.S.A.* **144 D3** 46 50N 123 14W
Oakwood, *U.S.A.* **141 C12** 41 6N 84 23W
Oamaru, *N.Z.* **119 F5** 45 5 S 170 59 E
Ōamishirasato, *Japan* **63 B12** 35 31N 140 18 E
Oarai, *Japan* **63 A12** 36 21N 140 34 E
Oasis, *Calif., U.S.A.* **145 M10** 33 28N 116 6W
Oasis, *Nev., U.S.A.* **144 H9** 37 29N 117 55W
Oates Land, *Antarctica* **7 C11** 69 0 S 160 0 E
Oatman, *U.S.A.* **145 K12** 35 1N 114 19W
Oaxaca, *Mexico* **147 D5** 17 2N 96 40W
Oaxaca □, *Mexico* **147 D5** 17 0N 97 0W
Ob →, *U.S.S.R.* **56 C7** 66 45N 69 30 E
Oba, *Canada* **128 C3** 49 4N 84 7W
Obala, *Cameroon* **101 E7** 4 9N 11 32 E
Obama, *Fukui, Japan* **63 B7** 35 30N 135 45 E
Obama, *Nagasaki, Japan* **62 E2** 32 43N 130 13 E
Oban, *U.K.* **18 E3** 56 25N 5 30W
Obbia, *Somali Rep.* **90 F4** 5 25N 48 30 E
Obdam, *Neths.* **20 C5** 52 41N 4 55 E
Obed, *Canada* **130 C5** 53 30N 117 10W
Ober-Aagau, *Switz.* **28 B5** 47 10N 7 45 E
Obera, *Argentina* **159 B4** 27 21 S 55 2W
Oberalppass, *Switz.* **29 C7** 46 39N 8 35 E
Oberalpstock, *Switz.* **29 C7** 46 45N 8 47 E
Oberammergau, *Germany* **27 H7** 47 35N 11 3 E
Oberdrauburg, *Austria* **30 E5** 46 44N 12 58 E
Oberengadin, *Switz.* **29 C9** 46 35N 9 55 E
Oberentfelden, *Switz.* **28 B6** 47 21N 8 2 E
Oberhausen, *Germany* **26 D2** 51 28N 6 50 E
Oberkirch, *Germany* **27 G4** 48 31N 8 5 E
Oberland, *Switz.* **28 C5** 46 35N 7 38 E
Oberlin, *Kans., U.S.A.* **138 F4** 39 52N 100 31W
Oberlin, *La., U.S.A.* **139 K8** 30 42N 92 42W
Oberlin, *Ohio, U.S.A.* **136 E2** 41 15N 82 10W
Obernai, *France* **23 D14** 48 28N 7 30 E
Oberndorf, *Germany* **27 G4** 48 17N 8 35 E
Oberon, *Australia* **117 B8** 33 45 S 149 52 E
Oberösterreich □, *Austria* **30 C7** 48 10N 14 0 E
Oberpfälzer Wald, *Germany* **27 F8** 49 30N 12 25 E
Obersiggenthal, *Switz.* **29 B6** 47 29N 8 18 E
Oberstdorf, *Germany* **27 H6** 47 25N 10 16 E
Oberting, *Gabon* **102 C1** 0 22 S 9 46 E
Oberwil, *Switz.* **28 A5** 47 32N 7 33 E
Obi, Kepulauan, *Indonesia* **71 E7** 1 23 S 127 45 E
Obi Is. = Obi, Kepulauan, *Indonesia* **71 E7** 1 23 S 127 45 E
Obiaruku, *Nigeria* **101 D6** 5 51N 6 9 E
Óbidos, *Brazil* **153 D6** 1 50 S 55 30W
Óbidos, *Portugal* **37 F1** 39 19N 9 10W
Obihiro, *Japan* **60 C11** 42 56N 143 12 E
Obilatu, *Indonesia* **71 E7** 1 25 S 127 20 E
Obilnoye, *U.S.S.R.* **53 C11** 47 32N 44 30 E
Obing, *Germany* **27 H8** 48 0N 12 25 E
Obisfelde, *Germany* **26 C6** 52 27N 10 57 E
Objat, *France* **24 C5** 45 16N 1 24 E
Oblong, *U.S.A.* **141 F9** 39 0N 87 55W
Obluchye, *U.S.S.R.* **57 E14** 49 1N 131 4 E
Obninsk, *U.S.S.R.* **51 D10** 55 8N 36 37 E
Obo, *C.A.R.* **102 A5** 5 20N 26 32 E
Obo, *Ethiopia* **95 G4** 3 46N 38 52 E
Oboa, Mt., *Uganda* **106 B3** 1 45N 34 45 E
Obock, *Djibouti* **95 E5** 12 0N 43 20 E
Oborniki, *Poland* **47 C3** 52 39N 16 50 E
Oborniki Śląskie, *Poland* **47 D3** 51 17N 16 53 E
Obouya, *Congo* **102 C3** 0 56 S 15 43 E
Oboyan, *U.S.S.R.* **51 F10** 51 13N 36 37 E
Obozerskaya, *U.S.S.R.* **56 C5** 63 20N 40 15 E
Obrenovac, *Yugoslavia* **42 C5** 44 40N 20 11 E
Obrovac, *Yugoslavia* **39 D12** 44 11N 15 41 E
Obruk, *Turkey* **88 D5** 38 18N 33 12 E
Observatory Inlet, *Canada* **130 B3** 55 10N 129 54W
Obshchi Syrt, *U.S.S.R.* **10 E16** 52 0N 53 0 E
Obskaya Guba, *U.S.S.R.* **56 C8** 69 0N 73 0 E
Obuasi, *Ghana* **101 D4** 6 17N 1 40W
Obubra, *Nigeria* **101 D6** 6 8N 8 20 E
Obwalden □, *Switz.* **28 C6** 46 55N 8 15 E
Obyachevo, *U.S.S.R.* **54 A1** 60 20N 49 37 E
Obzor, *Bulgaria* **43 E12** 42 50N 27 52 E
Ocala, *U.S.A.* **135 L4** 29 11N 82 5W
Ocamo →, *Venezuela* **153 C4** 2 48N 65 14W
Ocampo, *Mexico* **146 B3** 28 9N 108 24W
Ocaña, *Colombia* **152 B3** 8 15N 73 20W
Ocaña, *Spain* **34 F1** 39 55N 3 30W
Ocanomowoc, *U.S.A.* **138 D10** 43 7N 88 30W
Ocate, *U.S.A.* **139 G2** 36 12N 104 59W
Occidental, Cordillera, *Colombia* **152 C2** 5 0N 76 0W
Occidental, Cordillera, *Peru* **156 C3** 14 0 S 74 0W
Ocean City, *N.J., U.S.A.* **134 F8** 39 18N 74 34W
Ocean City, *Wash., U.S.A.* **144 C2** 47 4N 124 10W
Ocean I. = Banaba, *Kiribati* **122 H8** 0 45 S 169 50 E
Ocean Park, *U.S.A.* **144 D2** 46 30N 124 2W
Oceano, *U.S.A.* **145 K6** 35 6N 120 37W
Oceanport, *U.S.A.* **137 F10** 40 20N 74 3W
Oceanside, *U.S.A.* **145 M9** 33 13N 117 26W
Ochagavia, *Spain* **34 C3** 42 55N 1 5W
Ochamchire, *U.S.S.R.* **53 E9** 42 46N 41 32 E
Ochamps, *Belgium* **21 J6** 49 56N 5 16 E
Ocher, *U.S.S.R.* **54 C4** 57 53N 54 42 E
Ochiai, *Japan* **62 B5** 35 1N 133 45 E
Ochil Hills, *U.K.* **18 E5** 56 14N 3 40W
Ochre River, *Canada* **131 C9** 51 4N 99 47W
Ochsenfurt, *Germany* **27 F6** 49 38N 10 3 E
Ochsenhausen, *Germany* **27 G5** 48 4N 9 57 E
Ocilla, *U.S.A.* **135 K4** 31 35N 83 12W
Ocmulgee →, *U.S.A.* **135 K4** 31 58N 82 32W
Ocna Mureş, *Romania* **46 C4** 46 23N 23 55 E
Ocna Sibiului, *Romania* **46 D5** 45 52N 24 2 E
Ocnele Mari, *Romania* **46 D5** 45 8N 24 18 E
Ocoña, *Peru* **156 D3** 16 26 S 73 8W
Ocoña →, *Peru* **156 D3** 16 28 S 73 8W
Oconee →, *U.S.A.* **135 K4** 31 58N 82 32W
Oconomowoc, *U.S.A.* **141 A8** 43 6N 88 30W
Oconto, *U.S.A.* **134 C2** 44 52N 87 53W
Oconto Falls, *U.S.A.* **134 C1** 44 52N 88 10W
Ocosingo, *Mexico* **147 D6** 17 10N 92 15W
Ocotal, *Nic.* **148 D2** 13 41N 86 31W
Ocotlán, *Mexico* **146 C4** 20 21N 102 42W
Ocquier, *Belgium* **21 H6** 50 24N 5 24 E
Ocreza →, *Portugal* **37 F3** 39 32N 7 50W
Ócsa, *Hungary* **31 D12** 47 17N 19 15 E
Octave, *U.S.A.* **143 J7** 34 10N 112 43W
Octeville, *France* **22 C5** 49 38N 1 40W
Ocumare del Tuy, *Venezuela* **152 A4** 10 7N 66 46W
Ocuri, *Bolivia* **157 D4** 18 45 S 65 50W
Oda, *Ghana* **101 D4** 5 50N 0 51W
Oda, *Ehime, Japan* **62 D4** 33 36N 132 53 E
Ōda, *Shimane, Japan* **62 B4** 35 11N 132 30 E
Oda, J., *Sudan* **94 C4** 20 21N 36 39 E
Ódáðahraun, *Iceland* **12 D5** 65 5N 17 0W
Ödåkra, *Sweden* **15 H6** 56 7N 12 45 E
Odate, *Japan* **60 D10** 40 16N 140 34 E
Odawara, *Japan* **63 B11** 35 20N 139 6 E
Odda, *Norway* **13 F9** 60 3N 6 35 E
Odder, *Denmark* **15 J4** 55 58N 10 10 E
Oddur, *Somali Rep.* **90 G3** 4 11N 43 52 E
Ödeborg, *Sweden* **15 F5** 58 32N 11 58 E
Odei →, *Canada* **131 B9** 56 6N 96 54W
Odell, *U.S.A.* **141 D8** 41 0N 88 31W
Odemira, *Portugal* **37 H2** 37 35N 8 40W
Ödemiş, *Turkey* **88 D3** 38 15N 28 0 E
Odendaalsrus, *S. Africa* **104 D4** 27 48 S 26 45 E
Odense, *Denmark* **15 J4** 55 22N 10 23 E
Odenwald, *Germany* **27 F5** 49 30N 9 0 E
Oder →, *Germany* **26 B10** 53 33N 14 38 E
Oderzo, *Italy* **39 C9** 45 47N 12 29 E
Odessa, *Canada* **137 B8** 44 17N 76 43W
Odessa, *Mo., U.S.A.* **140 F3** 39 0N 93 57W
Odessa, *Tex., U.S.A.* **139 K3** 31 51N 102 23W
Odessa, *Wash., U.S.A.* **142 C4** 47 19N 118 35W
Odessa, *U.S.S.R.* **52 C4** 46 30N 30 45 E
Odiakwe, *Botswana* **104 C4** 20 12 S 25 17 E
Odiel →, *Spain* **37 H4** 37 10N 6 55W
Odienné, *Ivory C.* **100 D3** 9 30N 7 34W
Odintsovo, *U.S.S.R.* **51 D10** 55 39N 37 15 E
Odobeşti, *Romania* **46 D8** 45 43N 27 4 E
Odolanów, *Poland* **47 D4** 51 34N 17 40 E
O'Donnell, *U.S.A.* **139 J4** 33 0N 101 48W
Odoorn, *Neths.* **20 C9** 52 51N 6 51 E
Odorheiu Secuiesc, *Romania* **46 C6** 46 21N 25 21 E
Odoyevo, *U.S.S.R.* **51 E10** 53 56N 36 42 E
Odra →, *Poland* **47 B1** 53 33N 14 38 E
Odra →, *Spain* **36 C6** 42 14N 4 17W
Odweina, *Somali Rep.* **108 C3** 9 25N 45 4 E
Odžaci, *Yugoslavia* **42 B4** 45 30N 19 17 E
Odžak, *Yugoslavia* **42 B3** 45 3N 18 18 E
Odzi, *Zimbabwe* **105 B5** 19 0 S 32 20 E
Oedelem, *Belgium* **21 F2** 51 10N 3 21 E
Oegstgeest, *Neths.* **20 D4** 52 11N 4 29 E
Oeiras, *Brazil* **154 C3** 7 0 S 42 8W
Oeiras, *Portugal* **37 G1** 38 41N 9 18W
Oelrichs, *U.S.A.* **138 D3** 43 11N 103 14W
Oelsnitz, *Germany* **26 E8** 50 24N 12 11 E
Oelwein, *U.S.A.* **138 D9** 42 41N 91 55W
Oenpelli, *Australia* **112 B5** 12 20 S 133 4 E
Of, *Turkey* **89 C9** 40 59N 40 23 E
O'Fallon, *U.S.A.* **140 F6** 38 50N 90 43W
Ofanto →, *Italy* **41 A9** 41 22N 16 13 E
Offa, *Nigeria* **101 D5** 8 13N 4 42 E
Offenbach, *Germany* **27 E4** 50 6N 8 46 E
Offenburg, *Germany* **27 G3** 48 29N 7 56 E
Offerdal, *Sweden* **14 A8** 63 28N 14 0 E
Offida, *Italy* **39 F10** 42 56N 13 40 E
Offranville, *France* **22 C8** 49 52N 1 1 E
Ofidhousa, *Greece* **45 H8** 36 33N 26 8 E
Ofotfjorden, *Norway* **12 B14** 68 27N 16 40 E
Ofu, *Amer. Samoa* **121 X25** 14 11 S 169 41W
Ōfunato, *Japan* **60 E10** 39 4N 141 43 E
Oga, *Japan* **60 E9** 39 55N 139 50 E
Oga-Hantō, *Japan* **60 E9** 39 58N 139 47 E
Ogaden, *Ethiopia* **108 C3** 7 30N 45 30 E
Ogahalla, *Canada* **128 B2** 50 6N 85 51W
Ōgaki, *Japan* **63 B8** 35 21N 136 37 E
Ogallala, *U.S.A.* **138 E4** 41 12N 101 40W
Ogan →, *Indonesia* **74 C2** 3 1 S 104 44 E
Ogasawara Gunto, *Pac. Oc.* **122 E6** 27 0N 142 0 E
Ogbomosho, *Nigeria* **101 D5** 8 1N 4 11 E
Ogden, *Iowa, U.S.A.* **140 B3** 42 3N 94 0W
Ogden, *Utah, U.S.A.* **142 F7** 41 13N 112 1W
Ogdensburg, *U.S.A.* **137 B9** 44 40N 75 27W
Ogeechee →, *U.S.A.* **135 K5** 31 51N 81 6W
Ogilby, *U.S.A.* **145 N12** 32 49N 114 50W
Oglesby, *U.S.A.* **140 C7** 41 21N 89 3W
Oglio →, *Italy* **38 C7** 45 2N 10 39 E
Ogmore, *Australia* **114 C4** 22 37 S 149 35 E
Ognon →, *France* **23 E12** 47 16N 5 28 E
Ogo Mas, *Indonesia* **72 A2** 0 50N 120 5 E
Ogoja, *Nigeria* **101 D6** 6 38N 8 39 E
Ogoki →, *Canada* **128 B2** 51 38N 85 57W
Ogoki L., *Canada* **128 B2** 50 50N 87 10W
Ogoki Res., *Canada* **128 B2** 50 45N 88 15W
Ogooué →, *Gabon* **102 C1** 1 0 S 9 0 E
Ōgori, *Japan* **62 C3** 34 6N 131 24 E
Ogosta →, *Bulgaria* **43 D8** 43 48N 23 55 E
Ogowe = Ogooué →, *Gabon* **102 C1** 1 0 S 9 0 E
Ogr = Sharafa, *Sudan* **95 E2** 11 59N 27 7 E
Ograżden, *Yugoslavia* **42 F7** 41 30N 22 50 E
Ogrein, *Sudan* **94 D3** 17 55N 34 50 E
Ogulin, *Yugoslavia* **39 C12** 45 16N 15 16 E
Ogun □, *Nigeria* **101 D5** 7 0N 3 0 E
Oguni, *Japan* **62 D3** 33 11N 131 8 E
Oguta, *Nigeria* **101 D6** 5 44N 6 44 E
Ogwashi-Uku, *Nigeria* **101 D6** 6 15N 6 30 E
Ogwe, *Nigeria* **101 E6** 5 0N 7 14 E
Ohai, *N.Z.* **119 F3** 45 55 S 168 0 E
Ohakune, *N.Z.* **118 F4** 39 24 S 175 24 E
Ohanet, *Algeria* **99 C6** 28 44N 8 46 E
Ōhara, *Japan* **63 B12** 35 15N 140 23 E
Ohata, *Japan* **60 D10** 41 24N 141 10 E
Ohau, L., *N.Z.* **119 E4** 44 15 S 169 53 E
Ohaupo, *N.Z.* **118 D4** 37 56 S 175 20 E
Ohey, *Belgium* **21 H6** 50 26N 5 8 E
Ohio □, *U.S.A.* **134 E3** 40 20N 84 10W
Ohio →, *U.S.A.* **134 G1** 36 59N 89 8W
Ohio City, *U.S.A.* **141 D12** 40 46N 84 37W
Ohiwa Harbour, *N.Z.* **118 D6** 37 59 S 177 10 E
Ohre →, *Czech.* **30 A7** 50 30N 14 10 E
Ohre →, *Germany* **26 C7** 52 18N 11 47 E
Ohrid, *Yugoslavia* **42 F5** 41 8N 20 52 E
Ohridsko, Jezero, *Yugoslavia* **42 F5** 41 8N 20 52 E
Ohrigstad, *S. Africa* **105 C5** 24 39 S 30 36 E
Öhringen, *Germany* **27 F5** 49 11N 9 31 E
Ohura, *N.Z.* **118 E3** 38 51 S 174 59 E
Oiapoque →, *Brazil* **153 C7** 4 8N 51 40W
Oikou, *China* **67 E9** 38 35N 117 42 E
Oil City, *U.S.A.* **136 E5** 41 26N 79 40W
Oildale, *U.S.A.* **145 K7** 35 25N 119 1W
Oinousa, *Greece* **45 F8** 38 33N 26 14 E
Oirschot, *Neths.* **21 F6** 51 30N 5 18 E
Oise □, *France* **23 C9** 49 28N 2 30 E
Oise →, *France* **23 D9** 49 0N 2 4 E
Oisterwijk, *Neths.* **21 E6** 51 35N 5 12 E
Ōita, *Japan* **62 D3** 33 14N 131 36 E
Ōita □, *Japan* **62 D3** 33 15N 131 30 E
Oiticica, *Brazil* **154 C3** 5 3 S 41 5W
Ojai, *U.S.A.* **145 L7** 34 28N 119 16W
Ojinaga, *Mexico* **146 B4** 29 34N 104 25W
Ojiya, *Japan* **61 F9** 37 18N 138 48 E
Ojos del Salado, Cerro, *Argentina* **158 B2** 27 0 S 68 40W
Oka →, *U.S.S.R.* **51 C13** 56 20N 43 59 E
Okaba, *Indonesia* **71 F9** 8 6 S 139 42 E
Okahandja, *Namibia* **104 C2** 22 0 S 16 59 E
Okahukura, *N.Z.* **118 E4** 38 48 S 175 14 E
Okaihau, *N.Z.* **118 B2** 35 19 S 173 47 E
Okanagan L., *Canada* **130 D5** 50 0N 119 30W
Okandja, *Gabon* **102 C2** 0 35 S 13 45 E
Okanogan, *U.S.A.* **142 B4** 48 6N 119 43W
Okanogan →, *U.S.A.* **142 B4** 48 6N 119 43W
Okány, *Hungary* **31 E14** 46 52N 21 21 E
Okapa, *Papua N. G.* **120 D3** 6 38 S 145 39 E
Okaputa, *Namibia* **104 C2** 20 5 S 17 0 E
Okara, *Pakistan* **79 C4** 30 50N 73 31 E
Okarito, *N.Z.* **119 D5** 43 15 S 170 9 E
Okato, *N.Z.* **118 F2** 39 12 S 173 53 E
Okaukuejo, *Namibia* **104 B2** 19 10 S 16 0 E
Okavango Swamps, *Botswana* **104 B3** 18 45 S 22 45 E
Okawa, *Japan* **62 D2** 33 9N 130 21 E
Okawville, *U.S.A.* **140 F7** 38 26N 89 33W
Okaya, *Japan* **63 A10** 36 5N 138 10 E
Okayama, *Japan* **62 C5** 34 40N 133 54 E
Okayama □, *Japan* **62 C5** 35 0N 133 50 E
Okazaki, *Japan* **63 C9** 34 57N 137 10 E
Oke-Iho, *Nigeria* **101 D5** 8 1N 3 18 E
Okeechobee, *U.S.A.* **135 M5** 27 16N 80 46W
Okeechobee, L., *U.S.A.* **135 M5** 27 0N 80 50W
Okefenokee Swamp, *U.S.A.* **135 K4** 30 50N 82 15W
Okehampton, *U.K.* **17 G3** 50 44N 4 1W
Okene, *Nigeria* **101 D6** 7 32N 6 11 E
Oker →, *Germany* **26 C6** 52 30N 10 22 E
Okha, *U.S.S.R.* **57 D15** 53 40N 143 0 E
Ókhi Óros, *Greece* **45 F6** 38 5N 24 25 E
Okhotsk, *U.S.S.R.* **57 D15** 59 20N 143 10 E
Okhotsk, Sea of, *Asia* **57 D15** 55 0N 145 0 E
Okhotskiy Perevoz, *U.S.S.R.* **57 C14** 61 52N 135 35 E
Okhotsko Kolymskoye, *U.S.S.R.* **57 C16** 63 0N 157 0 E
Oki-no-Shima, *Japan* **62 E4** 32 44N 132 33 E
Oki-Shotō, *Japan* **62 A5** 36 5N 133 15 E
Okiep, *S. Africa* **104 D2** 29 39 S 17 53 E
Okigwi, *Nigeria* **101 D6** 5 52N 7 20 E
Okija, *Nigeria* **101 D6** 5 54N 6 55 E
Okinawa □, *Japan* **61 L4** 26 40N 128 0 E
Okinawa-Guntō, *Japan* **61 L4** 26 40N 128 0 E
Okinawa-Jima, *Japan* **61 L4** 26 32N 128 0 E
Okino-erabu-Shima, *Japan* **61 L4** 27 21N 128 33 E
Okitipupa, *Nigeria* **101 D5** 6 31N 4 50 E
Oklahoma □, *U.S.A.* **139 H6** 35 20N 97 30W
Oklahoma City, *U.S.A.* **139 H6** 35 25N 97 30W
Okmulgee, *U.S.A.* **139 H7** 35 38N 96 0W
Oknitsa, *U.S.S.R.* **52 B2** 48 25N 27 30 E
Okolo, *Uganda* **106 B3** 2 37N 31 8 E
Okolona, *Ky., U.S.A.* **141 F11** 38 8N 85 41W
Okolona, *Miss., U.S.A.* **139 J10** 34 0N 88 45W
Okonek, *Poland* **47 B3** 53 32N 16 51 E
Okrika, *Nigeria* **101 E6** 4 40N 7 10 E
Oktabrsk, *U.S.S.R.* **49 E10** 49 28N 57 25 E
Oktyabr, *U.S.S.R.* **55 B8** 43 41N 77 12 E
Oktyabrsk, *U.S.S.R.* **51 E16** 53 11N 48 40 E
Oktyabrskiy, *Byelorussian S.S.R., U.S.S.R.* **50 E6** 52 38N 28 53 E
Oktyabrskiy, *R.S.F.S.R., U.S.S.R.* **54 D3** 54 28N 53 28 E
Oktyabrskoy Revolyutsii, Os., *U.S.S.R.* **57 B10** 79 30N 97 0 E
Oktyabrskoye = Zhovtnevoye, *U.S.S.R.* **52 C5** 46 54N 32 3 E
Oktyabrskoye, *U.S.S.R.* **56 C7** 62 28N 66 3 E
Ōkuchi, *Japan* **62 E2** 32 4N 130 37 E
Okulovka, *U.S.S.R.* **50 B8** 58 25N 33 19 E
Okuru, *N.Z.* **119 D3** 43 55 S 168 55 E
Okushiri-Tō, *Japan* **60 C9** 42 15N 139 30 E
Okuta, *Nigeria* **101 D5** 9 14N 3 12 E
Okwa →, *Botswana* **104 C3** 22 30 S 23 0 E
Ola, *U.S.A.* **139 H8** 35 2N 93 10W
Ólafsfjörður, *Iceland* **12 C4** 66 4N 18 39W
Ólafsvík, *Iceland* **12 D2** 64 53N 23 43W
Olancha, *U.S.A.* **145 J8** 36 15N 118 1W
Olancha Pk., *U.S.A.* **145 J8** 36 15N 118 7W
Olanchito, *Honduras* **148 C2** 15 30N 86 30W
Öland, *Sweden* **13 H14** 56 45N 16 38 E
Olargues, *France* **24 E6** 43 34N 2 53 E
Olary, *Australia* **116 B4** 32 18 S 140 19 E
Olascoaga, *Argentina* **158 D3** 35 15 S 60 39W
Olathe, *U.S.A.* **138 F7** 38 50N 94 50W
Olavarría, *Argentina* **158 D3** 36 55 S 60 20W
Oława, *Poland* **47 E4** 50 57N 17 20 E
Ólbia, *Italy* **40 B2** 40 55N 9 30 E
Ólbia, G. di, *Italy* **40 B2** 40 55N 9 35 E
Old Bahama Chan. = Bahama, Canal Viejo de, *W. Indies* **148 B4** 22 10N 77 30W
Old Baldy Pk. = San Antonio, Mt., *U.S.A.* **145 L9** 34 17N 117 38W
Old Castile = Castilla y Leon □, *Spain* **36 D6** 42 0N 5 0W
Old Castle, *Ireland* **19 C4** 53 46N 7 10W
Old Cork, *Australia* **114 C3** 22 57 S 141 52 E
Old Crow, *Canada* **126 B6** 67 30N 139 55W
Old Dale, *U.S.A.* **145 L11** 34 8N 115 47W
Old Dongola, *Sudan* **94 D3** 18 11N 30 44 E
Old Fletton, *U.K.* **17 E7** 52 34N 0 13W
Old Forge, *N.Y., U.S.A.* **137 C10** 43 43N 74 58W
Old Forge, *Pa., U.S.A.* **137 E9** 41 20N 75 46W
Old Fort →, *Canada* **131 B6** 58 36N 110 24W
Old Shinyanga, *Tanzania* **106 C3** 3 33 S 33 27 E
Old Speck, Mt., *U.S.A.* **137 B14** 44 35N 70 57W
Old Town, *U.S.A.* **129 D6** 45 0N 68 41W
Old Wives L., *Canada* **131 C7** 50 5N 106 0W
Oldbury, *U.K.* **17 F5** 51 38N 2 30W
Oldeani, *Tanzania* **106 C4** 3 22 S 35 35 E
Oldenburg, *Niedersachsen, Germany* **26 B4** 53 10N 8 10 E
Oldenburg, *Schleswig-Holstein, Germany* **26 A6** 54 16N 10 53 E
Oldenzaal, *Neths.* **20 D9** 52 19N 6 53 E
Oldham, *U.K.* **16 D5** 53 33N 2 8W
Oldman →, *Canada* **130 D6** 49 57N 111 42W
Olds, *Canada* **130 C6** 51 50N 114 10W
Olean, *U.S.A.* **136 D6** 42 8N 78 25W
Olecko, *Poland* **47 A9** 54 2N 22 31 E
Oléggio, *Italy* **38 C5** 45 36N 8 38 E
Oleiros, *Portugal* **36 F3** 39 56N 7 56W
Olekma →, *U.S.S.R.* **57 C13** 60 22N 120 42 E
Olekminsk, *U.S.S.R.* **57 C13** 60 25N 120 30 E
Olema, *U.S.A.* **144 G4** 38 3N 122 47W
Olen, *Belgium* **21 F5** 51 9N 4 52 E
Olenegorsk, *U.S.S.R.* **48 A5** 68 9N 33 18 E
Olenek, *U.S.S.R.* **57 C12** 68 28N 112 18 E
Olenek →, *U.S.S.R.* **57 B13** 73 0N 120 10 E
Olenino, *U.S.S.R.* **50 C8** 56 15N 33 30 E
Oléron, I. d', *France* **24 C2** 45 55N 1 15W
Oleśnica, *Poland* **47 D4** 51 13N 17 22 E
Olesno, *Poland* **47 E5** 50 51N 18 26 E
Olevsk, *U.S.S.R.* **50 F5** 51 12N 27 39 E
Olga, *U.S.S.R.* **57 E14** 43 50N 135 14 E
Olga, L., *Canada* **128 C4** 49 47N 77 15W
Olga, Mt., *Australia* **113 E5** 25 20 S 130 50 E
Ølgod, *Denmark* **15 J2** 55 49N 8 36 E
Olhão, *Portugal* **37 H3** 37 3N 7 48W
Olib, *Yugoslavia* **39 D11** 44 23N 14 44 E
Oliena, *Italy* **40 B2** 40 18N 9 22 E
Oliete, *Spain* **34 D4** 41 1N 0 41W
Olifants →, *Africa* **105 C5** 23 57 S 31 58 E
Olifantshoek, *S. Africa* **104 D3** 27 57 S 22 42 E
Ólimbos, *Greece* **45 J9** 35 44N 27 11 E
Ólimbos, Óros, *Greece* **44 D4** 40 6N 22 23 E
Olímpia, *Brazil* **159 A6** 20 44 S 48 54W
Olin, *U.S.A.* **140 C5** 42 0N 91 9W
Olinda, *Brazil* **154 C5** 8 1 S 34 51W
Olindiná, *Brazil* **154 D4** 11 22 S 38 21W
Olite, *Spain* **34 C3** 42 29N 1 40W
Oliva, *Argentina* **158 C3** 32 0 S 63 38W
Oliva, *Spain* **35 G4** 38 58N 0 9W
Oliva, Punta del, *Spain* **36 B5** 43 37N 5 28W
Oliva de la Frontera, *Spain* **37 G4** 38 17N 6 54W
Olivares, *Spain* **34 F2** 39 46N 2 20W
Olive Hill, *U.S.A.* **141 F13** 38 18N 83 13W
Olivehurst, *U.S.A.* **144 F5** 39 6N 121 34W
Oliveira, *Brazil* **155 F3** 20 39 S 44 50W
Oliveira de Azemeis, *Portugal* **36 E2** 40 49N 8 29W
Oliveira dos Brejinhos, *Brazil* **155 D3** 12 19 S 42 54W
Olivenza, *Spain* **37 G3** 38 41N 7 9W
Oliver, *Canada* **130 D5** 49 13N 119 37W
Oliver L., *Canada* **131 B8** 56 56N 103 22W
Olivine Ra., *N.Z.* **119 E3** 44 15 S 168 30 E

244 Olivone

Olivone, *Switz.* 29 C7 46 32N 8 57 E
Olkhovka, *U.S.S.R.* 53 B11 49 48N 44 32 E
Olkusz, *Poland* 47 E6 50 18N 19 33 E
Ollagüe, *Chile* 158 A2 21 15 S 68 10W
Olloy, *Belgium* 21 H5 50 5N 4 36 E
Olmedo, *Spain* 36 D6 41 20N 4 43W
Olmos, *Peru* 156 B2 5 59 S 79 46W
Olney, *Ill., U.S.A.* 141 F8 38 40N 88 5W
Olney, *Tex., U.S.A.* 139 J5 33 25N 98 45W
Oloma, *Cameroon* 101 E7 3 29N 11 19 E
Olomane →, *Canada* 129 B7 50 14N 60 37W
Olombo, *Congo* 102 C3 1 18 S 15 53 E
Olomouc, *Czech.* 31 B10 49 38N 17 12 E
Olonets, *U.S.S.R.* 48 B5 61 10N 33 0 E
Olongapo, *Phil.* 71 B6 14 50N 120 18 E
Oloron, Gave d' →, *France* 24 E2 43 33N 1 5W
Oloron-Ste.-Marie, *France* 24 E3 43 11N 0 38W
Olot, *Spain* 34 C7 42 11N 2 30 E
Olovo, *Yugoslavia* 42 C3 44 3N 19 0 E
Olovo, *Yugoslavia* 42 C3 44 8N 18 35 E
Olovyannaya, *U.S.S.R.* 57 D12 50 58N 115 35 E
Oloy →, *U.S.S.R.* 57 C16 66 29N 159 29 E
Olpe, *Germany* 26 D3 51 2N 7 50 E
Olshanka, *U.S.S.R.* 52 B4 48 16N 30 58 E
Olshany, *U.S.S.R.* 52 A6 50 3N 35 53 E
Olst, *Neths.* 20 D8 52 20N 6 7 E
Olsztyn, *Poland* 47 B7 53 48N 20 29 E
Olsztyn □, *Poland* 47 B8 54 0N 21 0 E
Olsztynek, *Poland* 47 B7 53 34N 20 19 E
Olt □, *Romania* 46 E5 44 20N 24 30 E
Olt →, *Romania* 46 F5 43 43N 24 51 E
Olten, *Switz.* 28 B5 47 21N 7 53 E
Olteniţa, *Romania* 46 E7 44 7N 26 42 E
Olton, *U.S.A.* 139 H3 34 16N 102 7W
Oltu, *Turkey* 89 C9 40 35N 41 58 E
Olur, *Turkey* 89 C10 40 49N 42 8 E
Olvega, *Spain* 34 D3 41 47N 2 0W
Olvera, *Spain* 37 J5 36 55N 5 18W
Olymbos, *Cyprus* 32 D12 35 21N 33 45 E
Olympia, *Greece* 45 G3 37 39N 21 39 E
Olympia, *U.S.A.* 144 D4 47 0N 122 58W
Olympic Mts., *U.S.A.* 144 C3 47 50N 123 45W
Olympic Nat. Park, *U.S.A.* 144 C3 47 48N 123 30W
Olympus, *Cyprus* 32 E11 34 56N 32 52 E
Olympus, Mt. = Ólimbos, Óros, *Greece* 44 D4 40 6N 22 23 E
Olympus, Mt., *U.S.A.* 144 C3 47 52N 123 40W
Olyphant, *U.S.A.* 137 E9 41 27N 75 36W
Om →, *U.S.S.R.* 56 D8 54 59N 73 22 E
Om Hajer, *Ethiopia* 95 E4 14 20N 36 41 E
Om Koi, *Thailand* 76 D2 17 48N 98 22 E
Ōma, *Japan* 60 D10 41 45N 141 5 E
Ōmachi, *Japan* 63 A9 36 30N 137 50 E
Omae-Zaki, *Japan* 63 C10 34 36N 138 14 E
Ōmagari, *Japan* 60 E10 39 27N 140 29 E
Omagh, *U.K.* 19 B4 54 36N 7 20W
Omagh □, *U.K.* 19 B4 54 35N 7 15W
Omaha, *U.S.A.* 138 E7 41 15N 95 55W
Omak, *U.S.A.* 142 B4 48 24N 119 31W
Omalos, *Greece* 32 D5 35 19N 23 55 E
Oman ■, *Asia* 87 B7 23 0N 58 0 E
Oman, G. of, *Asia* 85 E8 24 30N 58 30 E
Omapere, *N.Z.* 118 B2 35 37 S 173 25 E
Omar Combon, *Somali Rep.* 108 D3 3 10N 45 47 E
Omaruru, *Namibia* 104 C2 21 26 S 16 0 E
Omaruru →, *Namibia* 104 C1 22 7 S 14 15 E
Omate, *Peru* 156 D3 16 45 S 71 0W
Ombai, Selat, *Indonesia* 71 F6 8 30 S 124 50 E
Omboué, *Gabon* 102 C1 1 35 S 9 15 E
Ombrone →, *Italy* 38 F8 42 39N 11 0 E
Omchi, *Chad* 97 D3 21 22N 17 53 E
Omdurmân, *Sudan* 95 D3 15 40N 32 28 E
Ōme, *Japan* 63 B11 35 47N 139 15 E
Omegna, *Italy* 38 C5 45 52N 8 23 E
Omeonga, *Zaïre* 102 C4 3 40 S 24 22 E
Ometepe, I. de, *Nic.* 148 D2 11 32N 85 35W
Ometepec, *Mexico* 147 D5 16 39N 98 23W
Ōmi-Shima, *Ehime, Japan* 62 C5 34 15N 133 0 E
Ōmi-Shima, *Yamaguchi, Japan* 62 C3 34 25N 131 9 E
Omihachiman, *Japan* 63 B8 35 7N 136 3 E
Ominato, *Japan* 60 D10 41 17N 141 10 E
Omineca →, *Canada* 130 B4 56 3N 124 16W
Omiš, *Yugoslavia* 39 E13 43 28N 16 40 E
Omišalj, *Yugoslavia* 39 C11 45 13N 14 32 E
Omitara, *Namibia* 104 C2 22 16 S 18 2 E
Ōmiya, *Japan* 63 B11 35 54N 139 38 E
Omme Å →, *Denmark* 15 J2 55 56N 8 32 E
Ommen, *Neths.* 20 C8 52 31N 6 26 E
Ömnögovĭ □, *Mongolia* 66 C3 43 15N 104 0 E
Omo →, *Ethiopia* 95 F4 6 25N 36 10 E
Omodhos, *Cyprus* 32 E11 34 51N 32 48 E
Omolon →, *U.S.S.R.* 57 C16 68 42N 158 36 E
Omono-Gawa →, *Japan* 60 E10 39 46N 140 3 E
Omsk, *U.S.S.R.* 56 D8 55 0N 73 12 E
Omsukchan, *U.S.S.R.* 57 C16 62 32N 155 48 E
Ōmu, *Japan* 60 B11 44 34N 142 58 E
Omul, Vf., *Romania* 46 D6 45 27N 25 29 E
Omulew →, *Poland* 47 B8 53 5N 21 33 E
Ōmura, *Japan* 62 E1 32 56N 129 57 E
Omura-Wan, *Japan* 62 E1 32 57N 129 52 E
Omurtag, *Bulgaria* 43 D11 43 8N 26 26 E
Ōmuta, *Japan* 62 D2 33 5N 130 26 E
Omutninsk, *U.S.S.R.* 54 B3 58 45N 52 4 E
On, *Belgium* 21 H6 50 11N 5 18 E
On-Take, *Japan* 62 F2 31 35N 130 39 E
Oña, *Spain* 34 C1 42 43N 3 25W
Onaga, *U.S.A.* 138 F6 39 32N 96 12W
Onalaska, *U.S.A.* 138 D9 43 53N 91 14W
Onamia, *U.S.A.* 138 B8 46 4N 93 38W
Onancock, *U.S.A.* 134 G8 37 42N 75 49W
Onang, *Indonesia* 71 E5 3 2 S 118 49 E
Onaping L., *Canada* 128 C3 47 3N 81 30W
Onarga, *U.S.A.* 141 D8 40 43N 88 1W
Onarhā, *Afghan.* 79 B3 35 30N 71 0 E
Oñate, *Spain* 34 B2 43 3N 2 25W
Onavas, *Mexico* 146 B3 28 28N 109 30W
Onawa, *U.S.A.* 138 D6 42 2N 96 2W
Onaway, *U.S.A.* 134 C3 45 21N 84 11W
Oncesti, *Romania* 46 F6 43 56N 25 52 E
Oncócua, *Angola* 103 F2 16 30 S 13 25 E
Onda, *Spain* 34 F4 39 55N 0 17W
Ondaejin, *N. Korea* 67 D15 41 34N 129 40 E
Ondangua, *Namibia* 104 B2 17 57 S 16 4 E
Ondárroa, *Spain* 34 B2 43 19N 2 25W
Ondas →, *Brazil* 155 D3 12 8 S 44 55W
Ondava →, *Czech.* 31 C14 48 27N 21 48 E
Onderdijk, *Neths.* 20 C6 52 45N 5 8 E
Ondjiva, *Angola* 103 F3 16 48 S 15 50 E
Ondo, *Japan* 62 C4 34 11N 132 32 E
Ondo, *Nigeria* 101 D5 7 4N 4 47 E
Ondo □, *Nigeria* 101 D6 7 0N 5 0 E
Öndörshil, *Mongolia* 66 B5 45 13N 108 5 E
Öndverðarnes, *Iceland* 12 D2 64 52N 24 0W
Onega, *U.S.S.R.* 48 B6 64 0N 38 10 E
Onega →, *U.S.S.R.* 48 B6 63 58N 37 55 E
Onega, G. of = Onezhskaya Guba, *U.S.S.R.* 48 B6 64 30N 37 0 E
Onega, L. = Onezhskoye Ozero, *U.S.S.R.* 48 B6 62 0N 35 30 E
Onehunga, *N.Z.* 118 C3 36 55 S 174 48 E
Oneida, *Ill., U.S.A.* 140 C6 41 4N 90 13W
Oneida, *N.Y., U.S.A.* 137 C9 43 5N 75 40W
Oneida L., *U.S.A.* 137 C9 43 12N 76 0W
O'Neill, *U.S.A.* 138 D5 42 30N 98 38W
Onekotan, Ostrov, *U.S.S.R.* 57 E16 49 25N 154 45 E
Onema, *Zaïre* 103 C4 4 35 S 24 30 E
Oneonta, *Ala., U.S.A.* 135 J2 33 58N 86 29W
Oneonta, *N.Y., U.S.A.* 137 D9 42 26N 75 5W
Onerahi, *N.Z.* 118 B3 35 45 S 174 22 E
Onezhskaya Guba, *U.S.S.R.* 48 B6 64 30N 37 0 E
Onezhskoye Ozero, *U.S.S.R.* 48 B6 62 0N 35 30 E
Ongarue, *N.Z.* 118 E4 38 42 S 175 19 E
Ongea Levu, *Fiji* 121 B3 19 8 S 178 24W
Ongerup, *Australia* 113 F2 33 58 S 118 28 E
Ongjin, *N. Korea* 67 F13 37 56N 125 21 E
Ongkharak, *Thailand* 76 E3 14 8N 101 1 E
Ongniud Qi, *China* 67 C10 43 0N 118 38 E
Ongoka, *Zaïre* 106 C2 1 20 S 26 0 E
Ongole, *India* 83 G5 15 33N 80 2 E
Ongon, *Mongolia* 66 B7 45 41N 113 5 E
Onguren, *U.S.S.R.* 57 D11 53 38N 107 36 E
Onhaye, *Belgium* 21 H5 50 15N 4 50 E
Oni, *U.S.S.R.* 53 E10 42 33N 43 26 E
Onida, *U.S.A.* 138 C4 44 42N 100 5W
Onilahy →, *Madag.* 105 C7 23 34 S 43 45 E
Onitsha, *Nigeria* 101 D6 6 6N 6 42 E
Onmaka, *Burma* 78 D6 22 17N 96 41 E
Ono, *Fiji* 121 B2 18 55 S 178 29 E
Ono, *Fukui, Japan* 63 B8 35 59N 136 29 E
Ono, *Hyōgo, Japan* 62 C6 34 51N 134 56 E
Onoda, *Japan* 62 C3 34 2N 131 25 E
Onoke, L., *N.Z.* 118 H4 41 22 S 175 8 E
Onomichi, *Japan* 62 C5 34 25N 133 12 E
Onpyŏng-ni, *S. Korea* 67 H14 33 25N 126 55 E
Ons, Is. d', *Spain* 36 C2 42 23N 8 55W
Onsala, *Sweden* 15 G6 57 26N 12 0 E
Onslow, *Australia* 112 D2 21 40 S 115 12 E
Onslow B., *U.S.A.* 135 H7 34 20N 77 20W
Onstwedde, *Neths.* 20 B10 53 2N 7 4 E
Ontake-San, *Japan* 63 B9 35 53N 137 29 E
Ontaneda, *Spain* 36 B7 43 12N 3 57W
Ontario, *Calif., U.S.A.* 145 L9 34 2N 117 40W
Ontario, *Oreg., U.S.A.* 142 D5 44 1N 117 1W
Ontario □, *Canada* 128 B2 52 0N 88 10W
Ontario, L., *N. Amer.* 128 D4 43 40N 78 0W
Onteniente, *Spain* 35 G4 38 50N 0 35W
Ontonagon, *U.S.A.* 138 B10 46 52N 89 19W
Ontur, *Spain* 35 G3 38 38N 1 29W
Onyx, *U.S.A.* 145 K8 35 41N 118 14W
Oodnadatta, *Australia* 115 D2 27 33 S 135 30 E
Ooldea, *Australia* 113 F5 30 27 S 131 50 E
Ooltgensplaat, *Neths.* 21 E4 51 41N 4 21 E
Oombulgurri, *Australia* 112 C4 15 15 S 127 45 E
Oona River, *Canada* 130 C2 53 57N 130 16W
Oordegem, *Belgium* 21 G3 50 58N 3 54 E
Oorindi, *Australia* 114 C3 20 40 S 141 1 E
Oost-Vlaanderen □, *Belgium* 21 F3 51 5N 3 50 E
Oost-Vlieland, *Neths.* 20 B6 53 18N 5 4 E
Oostakker, *Belgium* 21 F3 51 6N 3 46 E
Oostburg, *Neths.* 21 F3 51 19N 3 30 E
Oostduinkerke, *Belgium* 21 F1 51 7N 2 41 E
Oostelijk-Flevoland, *Neths.* 20 C7 52 31N 5 38 E
Oostende, *Belgium* 21 F1 51 15N 2 54 E
Oosterbeek, *Neths.* 20 E7 51 59N 5 51 E
Oosterdijk, *Neths.* 20 C6 52 44N 5 14 E
Oosterend, *Friesland, Neths.* 20 B6 53 24N 5 23 E
Oosterend, *Noord-Holland, Neths.* 20 B5 53 5N 4 52 E
Oosterhout, *Noord-Brabant, Neths.* 21 E7 51 53N 5 50 E
Oosterhout, *Noord-Brabant, Neths.* 21 E5 51 39N 4 47 E
Oosterschelde, *Neths.* 21 E4 51 33N 4 0 E
Oosterwolde, *Neths.* 20 C8 53 0N 6 17 E
Oosterzele, *Belgium* 21 G3 50 57N 3 48 E
Oostkamp, *Belgium* 21 F2 51 9N 3 14 E
Oostmalle, *Belgium* 21 F5 51 18N 4 44 E
Oostrozebekke, *Belgium* 21 G2 50 55N 3 21 E
Oostvleteven, *Belgium* 21 G1 50 56N 2 45 E
Oostvoorne, *Neths.* 20 E4 51 55N 4 5 E
Oostzaan, *Neths.* 20 D5 52 26N 4 52 E
Ootacamund, *India* 83 J3 11 30N 76 44 E
Ootha, *Australia* 117 B7 33 6 S 147 29 E
Ootmarsum, *Neths.* 20 D9 52 24N 6 54 E
Ootsa L., *Canada* 130 C3 53 50N 126 2W
Opaka, *Bulgaria* 43 D11 43 28N 26 10 E
Opala, *U.S.S.R.* 57 D16 51 58N 156 30 E
Opala, *Zaïre* 102 C4 0 40 S 24 20 E
Opalenica, *Poland* 47 C3 52 18N 16 24 E
Opan, *Bulgaria* 43 E10 42 13N 25 41 E
Opanake, *Sri Lanka* 83 L5 6 35N 80 40 E
Opapa, *N.Z.* 118 F5 39 47 S 176 42 E
Opasatika, *Canada* 128 C3 49 30N 82 50W
Opasquia, *Canada* 131 C10 53 16N 93 34W
Opatija, *Yugoslavia* 39 C11 45 21N 14 17 E
Opatów, *Poland* 47 E8 50 50N 21 27 E
Opava, *Czech.* 31 B10 49 57N 17 58 E
Opeinde, *Neths.* 20 B8 53 8N 6 4 E
Opelousas, *U.S.A.* 139 K8 30 35N 92 7W
Opémisca, L., *Canada* 128 C5 49 56N 74 52W
Open Bay Is., *N.Z.* 119 D3 43 51 S 168 51 E
Opglabbeek, *Belgium* 21 F7 51 3N 5 35 E
Opheim, *U.S.A.* 142 B10 48 52N 106 30W
Ophthalmia Ra., *Australia* 112 D2 23 15 S 119 30 E
Opi, *Nigeria* 101 D6 6 36N 7 28 E
Opinaca →, *Canada* 128 B4 52 15N 78 2W
Opinaca L., *Canada* 128 B4 52 39N 76 20W
Opiskotish, L., *Canada* 129 B6 53 10N 67 50W
Oploo, *Neths.* 21 E7 51 37N 5 52 E
Opmeer, *Neths.* 20 C5 52 42N 4 57 E
Opobo, *Nigeria* 101 E6 4 35N 7 34 E
Opochka, *U.S.S.R.* 50 C6 56 42N 28 45 E
Opoczno, *Poland* 47 D7 51 22N 20 18 E
Opole, *Poland* 47 E4 50 42N 17 58 E
Opole □, *Poland* 47 E4 50 40N 17 56 E
Oporto = Porto, *Portugal* 36 D2 41 8N 8 40W
Opotiki, *N.Z.* 118 E6 38 1 S 177 19 E
Opp, *U.S.A.* 135 K2 31 19N 86 13W
Oppegård, *Norway* 14 E4 59 48N 10 48 E
Oppenheim, *Germany* 27 F4 49 50N 8 22 E
Opperdoes, *Neths.* 20 C6 52 45N 5 4 E
Oppido Mamertina, *Italy* 41 D8 38 16N 15 59 E
Oppland fylke □, *Norway* 14 C3 61 15N 9 40 E
Oppstad, *Norway* 14 D5 60 17N 11 40 E
Oprtalj, *Yugoslavia* 39 C10 45 23N 13 50 E
Opua, *N.Z.* 118 B3 35 19 S 174 9 E
Opunake, *N.Z.* 118 F2 39 26 S 173 52 E
Opuzen, *Yugoslavia* 42 D2 43 1N 17 34 E
Oquawka, *U.S.A.* 140 D6 40 56N 90 57W
Ora, *Cyprus* 32 E12 34 51N 33 12 E
Ora, *Italy* 39 B8 46 20N 11 19 E
Ora Banda, *Australia* 113 F3 30 20 S 121 0 E
Oracle, *U.S.A.* 143 K8 32 36N 110 46W
Oradea, *Romania* 46 B2 47 2N 21 58 E
Öræfajökull, *Iceland* 12 D5 64 2N 16 39W
Orahovac, *Yugoslavia* 42 E5 42 24N 20 40 E
Orahovica, *Yugoslavia* 42 B2 45 35N 17 52 E
Orai, *India* 81 G8 25 58N 79 30 E
Oraison, *France* 25 E9 43 55N 5 55 E
Oran, *Algeria* 99 A4 35 45N 0 39W
Oran, *Argentina* 158 A3 23 10 S 64 20W
Orange = Oranje →, *S. Africa* 104 D2 28 41 S 16 28 E
Orange, *Australia* 117 B8 33 15 S 149 7 E
Orange, *France* 25 D8 44 8N 4 47 E
Orange, *Calif., U.S.A.* 145 M9 33 47N 117 51W
Orange, *Mass., U.S.A.* 137 D12 42 35N 72 15W
Orange, *Tex., U.S.A.* 139 K8 30 10N 93 50W
Orange, *Va., U.S.A.* 134 F6 38 17N 78 5W
Orange, C., *Brazil* 153 C7 4 20N 51 30W
Orange Cove, *U.S.A.* 144 J7 36 38N 119 19W
Orange Free State □, *S. Africa* 104 D4 28 30 S 27 0 E
Orange Grove, *U.S.A.* 139 M6 27 57N 97 57W
Orange Walk, *Belize* 147 D7 18 6N 88 33W
Orangeburg, *U.S.A.* 135 J5 33 35N 80 53W
Orangeville, *Canada* 136 D3 43 55N 80 5W
Orangeville, *U.S.A.* 140 B7 42 28N 89 39W
Oranienburg, *Germany* 26 C9 52 45N 13 15 E
Oranje →, *S. Africa* 104 D2 28 41 S 16 28 E
Oranje Vrystaat = Orange Free State □, *S. Africa* 104 D4 28 30 S 27 0 E
Oranjemund, *Namibia* 104 D2 28 38 S 16 29 E
Oranjerivier, *S. Africa* 104 D3 29 40 S 24 12 E
Oras, *Phil.* 71 B7 12 9N 125 28 E
Orašje, *Yugoslavia* 42 B3 45 1N 18 42 E
Orăştie, *Romania* 46 D4 45 50N 23 10 E
Oraşul Stalin = Braşov, *Romania* 46 D6 45 38N 25 35 E
Orava →, *Czech.* 31 B12 49 24N 19 20 E
Oravita, *Romania* 42 B6 45 2N 21 43 E
Orawia, *N.Z.* 119 G2 46 1 S 167 50 E
Orb →, *France* 24 E7 43 15N 3 18 E
Orba →, *Italy* 38 D5 44 53N 8 37 E
Ørbæk, *Denmark* 15 J4 55 17N 10 39 E
Orbe, *Switz.* 28 C3 46 43N 6 32 E
Orbec, *France* 22 C7 49 1N 0 23 E
Orbetello, *Italy* 39 F8 42 26N 11 11 E
Órbigo →, *Spain* 36 C5 42 5N 5 42W
Orbost, *Australia* 117 D8 37 40 S 148 29 E
Orce, *Spain* 35 H2 37 44N 2 28W
Orce →, *Spain* 35 H2 37 44N 2 28W
Orchies, *France* 23 B10 50 28N 3 14 E
Orchila, I., *Venezuela* 152 A4 11 48N 66 10W
Orco →, *Italy* 38 C4 45 10N 7 52 E
Orcopampa, *Peru* 156 D3 15 20 S 72 23W
Orcutt, *U.S.A.* 145 L6 34 52N 120 27W
Ord →, *Australia* 112 C4 15 33 S 128 15 E
Ord, Mt., *Australia* 112 C4 17 20 S 125 34 E
Ordenes, *Spain* 36 B2 43 5N 8 29W
Orderville, *U.S.A.* 143 H7 37 18N 112 43W
Ording, *Germany* 26 A4 54 23N 8 32 E
Ordos = Mu Us Shamo, *China* 66 E5 39 0N 109 0 E
Ordu, *Turkey* 89 C7 40 55N 37 53 E
Ordu □, *Turkey* 89 C7 41 0N 37 50 E
Orduña, *Álava, Spain* 34 C7 42 58N 2 58 E
Orduña, *Granada, Spain* 35 H1 37 20N 3 30W
Ordway, *U.S.A.* 138 F3 38 15N 103 42W
Ordzhonikidze = Vladikavkaz, *U.S.S.R.* 53 E11 43 0N 44 35 E
Ordzhonikidze, *Ukraine S.S.R., U.S.S.R.* 52 C6 47 39N 34 3 E
Ordzhonikidze, *Uzbek S.S.R., U.S.S.R.* 55 C4 41 21N 69 22 E
Ordzhonikidzeabad, *U.S.S.R.* 55 D4 38 34N 69 1 E
Ore, *Zaïre* 106 B2 3 17N 29 30 E
Ore Mts. = Erzgebirge, *Germany* 26 E9 50 25N 13 0 E
Orealla, *Guyana* 153 B6 5 15N 57 23W
Orebić, *Yugoslavia* 42 E2 43 0N 17 11 E
Örebro, *Sweden* 13 G13 59 20N 15 18 E
Örebro län □, *Sweden* 13 G13 59 27N 15 0 E
Oregon, *Ill., U.S.A.* 140 B7 42 1N 89 20W
Oregon, *Ohio, U.S.A.* 141 C13 41 38N 83 25W
Oregon, *Wis., U.S.A.* 140 B7 42 56N 89 23W
Oregon □, *U.S.A.* 142 E3 44 0N 121 0W
Oregon City, *U.S.A.* 144 E4 45 21N 122 35W
Orekhov, *U.S.S.R.* 52 C6 47 30N 35 48 E
Orekhovo-Zuyevo, *U.S.S.R.* 51 D11 55 50N 38 55 E
Orel, *U.S.S.R.* 51 E10 52 57N 36 3 E
Orel →, *U.S.S.R.* 52 B6 48 30N 34 54 E
Orellana, Canal de, *Spain* 37 F5 39 2N 6 0W
Orellana, Pantano de, *Spain* 37 F5 39 5N 5 10W
Orellana la Vieja, *Spain* 37 F5 39 1N 5 32W
Orem, *U.S.A.* 142 F8 40 20N 111 45W
Ören, *Turkey* 45 G9 37 3N 27 57 E
Orenburg, *U.S.S.R.* 54 F4 51 45N 55 6 E
Orense, *Spain* 36 C3 42 19N 7 55W
Orense □, *Spain* 36 C3 42 15N 7 51W
Orepuki, *N.Z.* 119 G2 46 19 S 167 46 E
Orestiás, *Greece* 44 C8 41 30N 26 33 E
Øresund, *Europe* 15 J6 55 45N 12 45 E
Oreti →, *N.Z.* 119 G3 46 28 S 168 14 E
Orford Ness, *U.K.* 17 E9 52 6N 1 31 E
Orgaña, *Spain* 34 C6 42 13N 1 20 E
Organos, Pta. de los, *Canary Is.* 33 F2 28 12N 17 17W
Orgaz, *Spain* 37 F7 39 39N 3 53W
Orgeyev, *U.S.S.R.* 52 C3 47 24N 28 50 E
Orgon, *France* 25 E9 43 47N 5 3 E
Orgūn, *Afghan.* 79 B3 32 55N 69 12 E
Orhaneli, *Turkey* 88 D3 39 54N 28 59 E
Orhangazi, *Turkey* 88 C3 40 29N 29 18 E
Orhon Gol →, *Mongolia* 64 A5 50 21N 106 0 E
Ória, *Italy* 41 B10 40 30N 17 38 E
Orient, *Australia* 115 D3 28 7 S 142 50 E
Orient, *U.S.A.* 140 C2 41 12N 94 25W
Oriental, Cordillera, *Bolivia* 157 D4 17 0 S 66 0W
Oriental, Cordillera, *Colombia* 152 B3 6 0N 73 0W
Oriente, *Argentina* 158 D3 38 44 S 60 37W
Origny-Ste.-Benoîte, *France* 23 C10 49 50N 3 30 E
Orihuela, *Spain* 35 G4 38 7N 0 55W
Orihuela del Tremedal, *Spain* 34 E3 40 33N 1 39W
Oriku, *Albania* 44 D1 40 20N 19 30 E
Orinduik, *Guyana* 153 C5 4 40N 60 3W
Orinoco →, *Venezuela* 153 B5 9 15N 61 30W
Orion, *U.S.A.* 140 C6 41 21N 90 23W
Orissa □, *India* 82 E7 20 0N 84 0 E
Oristano, *Italy* 40 C1 39 54N 8 35 E
Oristano, G. di, *Italy* 40 C1 39 50N 8 22 E
Orituco →, *Venezuela* 152 B4 8 45N 67 27W
Orizaba, *Mexico* 147 D5 18 50N 97 10W
Orizare, *Bulgaria* 43 E12 42 44N 27 39 E
Orizona, *Brazil* 155 E2 17 3 S 48 18W
Orjen, *Yugoslavia* 42 E3 42 35N 18 34 E
Orjiva, *Spain* 35 J1 36 53N 3 24W
Orkanger, *Norway* 14 A3 63 18N 9 52 E
Örkelljunga, *Sweden* 15 H7 56 17N 13 17 E
Örkény, *Hungary* 31 D12 47 9N 19 26 E
Orkla →, *Norway* 14 A3 63 18N 9 51 E
Orkney, *S. Africa* 104 D4 26 58 S 26 40 E
Orkney □, *U.K.* 18 C6 59 0N 3 0W
Orkney Is., *U.K.* 18 C6 59 0N 3 0W
Orla, *Poland* 47 C10 52 42N 23 20 E
Orland, *Calif., U.S.A.* 144 F4 39 46N 122 12W
Orland, *Ind., U.S.A.* 141 C11 41 47N 85 12W
Orlando, *U.S.A.* 135 L5 28 30N 81 25W
Orlando, C. d', *Italy* 41 D7 38 10N 14 43 E
Orléanais, *France* 23 E9 48 0N 2 0 E
Orléans, *France* 23 E8 47 54N 1 52 E
Orleans, *U.S.A.* 137 B12 44 49N 72 10W
Orléans, I. d', *Canada* 129 C5 46 54N 70 58W
Orlice →, *Czech.* 30 A9 50 5N 16 10 E
Orlické Hory, *Czech.* 31 A9 50 15N 16 30 E
Orlik, *U.S.S.R.* 57 D10 52 30N 99 55 E
Orlov, *Czech.* 31 B13 49 17N 20 51 E
Orlov Gay, *U.S.S.R.* 51 F16 50 56N 48 19 E
Orlovat, *Yugoslavia* 42 B5 45 14N 20 33 E
Ormara, *Pakistan* 79 D2 25 16N 64 33 E
Ormea, *Italy* 38 D4 44 9N 7 54 E
Ormília, *Greece* 44 D5 40 16N 23 39 E
Ormoc, *Phil.* 71 B6 11 0N 124 37 E
Ormond, *N.Z.* 118 E6 38 33 S 177 56 E
Ormond Beach, *U.S.A.* 135 L5 29 13N 81 5W
Ormondville, *N.Z.* 118 G5 40 5 S 176 19 E
Ormož, *Yugoslavia* 39 B13 46 25N 16 10 E
Ormstown, *Canada* 137 A11 45 8N 74 0W
Ornans, *France* 23 E13 47 7N 6 10 E
Orne □, *France* 22 D7 48 40N 0 5 E
Orne →, *France* 22 C6 49 18N 0 15W
Orneta, *Poland* 47 A7 54 8N 20 9 E
Ørnhøj, *Denmark* 15 H2 56 13N 8 34 E
Ornö, *Sweden* 14 E12 59 4N 18 24 E
Örnsköldsvik, *Sweden* 14 A12 63 17N 18 40 E
Oro, *N. Korea* 67 D14 40 1N 127 27 E
Oro →, *Mexico* 146 B3 25 35N 105 2W
Oro Grande, *U.S.A.* 145 L9 34 36N 117 20W
Orobie, Alpi, *Italy* 38 B7 46 7N 10 0 E
Orocué, *Colombia* 152 C3 4 48N 71 20W
Orodo, *Nigeria* 101 D6 5 34N 7 4 E
Orogrande, *U.S.A.* 143 K10 32 20N 106 4W
Orol, *Spain* 36 B3 43 34N 7 39W
Oromocto, *Canada* 129 C6 45 54N 66 29W
Oron, *Nigeria* 101 E6 4 48N 8 14 E
Oron, *Switz.* 28 C3 46 34N 6 50 E
Orono, *Canada* 136 C6 43 59N 78 37W
Oropesa, *Spain* 36 F5 39 57N 5 10W
Oroqen Zizhiqi, *China* 65 A7 50 34N 123 43 E
Oroquieta, *Phil.* 71 C6 8 32N 123 44 E
Orós, *Brazil* 154 C4 6 15 S 38 55W
Orosei, G. di, *Italy* 40 B2 40 15N 9 40 E
Orosháza, *Hungary* 31 E13 46 32N 20 42 E
Orote Pen., *Guam* 121 R15 13 26N 144 38 E
Orotukan, *U.S.S.R.* 57 C16 62 16N 151 42 E
Oroville, *Calif., U.S.A.* 144 F5 39 31N 121 30W
Oroville, *Wash., U.S.A.* 142 B4 48 58N 119 30W
Oroville Res., *U.S.A.* 144 F5 39 33N 121 29W
Orrick, *U.S.A.* 140 E2 39 13N 94 7W
Orroroo, *Australia* 116 B3 32 43 S 138 38 E
Orrville, *U.S.A.* 136 F3 40 50N 81 46W
Orsara di Púglia, *Italy* 41 A8 41 17N 15 16 E
Orsha, *U.S.S.R.* 50 D7 54 30N 30 25 E
Orsières, *Switz.* 28 D4 46 2N 7 9 E
Orsk, *U.S.S.R.* 54 F6 51 12N 58 34 E
Ørslev, *Denmark* 15 J5 55 3N 11 56 E
Orsogna, *Italy* 39 F11 42 13N 14 17 E
Orşova, *Romania* 46 E3 44 41N 22 25 E

Paatsi 245

Ørsted, Denmark 15 H4 56 30N 10 20 E
Orta, L. d', Italy 38 C5 45 48N 8 21 E
Orta Nova, Italy 41 A8 41 20N 15 40 E
Ortaca, Turkey 88 E3 36 49N 28 45 E
Ortaköy, Çorum, Turkey 88 C6 40 16N 35 15 E
Ortaköy, Niğde, Turkey 88 D6 38 44N 34 3 E
Orte, Italy 39 F9 42 28N 12 23 E
Ortegal, C., Spain 36 B3 43 43N 7 52W
Orteguaza →, Colombia 152 C2 0 43N 75 16W
Orthez, France 24 E3 43 29N 0 48W
Ortho, Belgium 21 H7 50 8N 5 37 E
Ortigueira, Spain 36 B3 43 40N 7 50W
Orting, U.S.A. 144 C4 47 6N 122 12W
Ortles, Italy 38 B7 46 31N 10 33 E
Orto, Tokay, U.S.S.R. 55 B8 42 20N 76 1 E
Ortón →, Bolivia 156 C4 10 50 S 67 0W
Ortona, Italy 39 F11 42 21N 14 24 E
Orūmīyeh, Iran 84 B5 37 40N 45 0 E
Orūmīyeh, Daryācheh-ye, Iran 84 B5 37 50N 45 30 E
Orune, Italy 40 B2 40 25N 9 20 E
Oruro, Bolivia 156 D4 18 0 S 67 9W
Oruro □, Bolivia 156 D4 18 40 S 67 30W
Orust, Sweden 15 F5 58 10N 11 40 E
Oruzgān □, Afghan. 79 B2 33 30N 66 0 E
Orvault, France 22 E5 47 17N 1 38W
Orvieto, Italy 39 F9 42 43N 12 8 E
Orwell, U.S.A. 136 E4 41 32N 80 52W
Orwell →, U.K. 17 E9 52 2N 1 12 E
Oryakhovo, Bulgaria 43 D8 43 40N 23 57 E
Orzinuovi, Italy 38 C6 45 24N 9 55 E
Orzyc →, Poland 47 C8 52 46N 21 14 E
Orzysz, Poland 47 B8 53 50N 21 58 E
Osa, U.S.S.R. 54 C4 57 17N 55 26 E
Osa →, Poland 47 B5 53 33N 18 46 E
Osa, Pen. de, Costa Rica 148 E3 8 0N 84 0W
Osage, Iowa, U.S.A. 138 D8 43 15N 92 50W
Osage, Wyo., U.S.A. 138 D2 43 59N 104 25W
Osage →, U.S.A. 140 F5 38 35N 91 57W
Osage City, U.S.A. 138 F7 38 43N 95 51W
Ōsaka, Japan 63 C7 34 40N 135 30 E
Ōsaka □, Japan 63 C7 34 30N 135 30 E
Ōsaka-Wan, Japan 63 C7 34 30N 135 18 E
Osan, S. Korea 67 F14 37 11N 127 4 E
Osawatomie, U.S.A. 138 F7 38 30N 94 55W
Osborne, U.S.A. 138 F5 39 30N 98 45W
Osceola, Ark., U.S.A. 139 H10 35 40N 90 0W
Osceola, Iowa, U.S.A. 140 C3 41 3N 93 20W
Osceola, Mo., U.S.A. 140 F3 38 3N 93 42W
Oschatz, Germany 26 D9 51 17N 13 8 E
Oschersleben, Germany 26 C7 52 2N 11 13 E
Óschiri, Italy 40 B2 40 43N 9 7 E
Oscoda, U.S.A. 136 B1 44 26N 83 20W
Osečina, Yugoslavia 42 C4 44 23N 19 34 E
Ösel = Saaremaa, U.S.S.R. 50 B3 58 30N 22 30 E
Osëry, U.S.S.R. 51 D11 54 52N 38 28 E
Osgood, U.S.A. 141 E11 39 8N 85 18W
Osh, U.S.S.R. 55 C6 40 37N 72 49 E
Oshawa, Canada 128 D4 43 50N 78 50W
Oshima, Japan 62 D4 33 55N 132 14 E
Oshkosh, Nebr., U.S.A. 138 E3 41 27N 102 20W
Oshkosh, Wis., U.S.A. 138 C10 44 3N 88 35W
Oshmyany, U.S.S.R. 50 D4 54 26N 25 52 E
Oshnovīyeh, Iran 84 B5 37 2N 45 6 E
Oshogbo, Nigeria 101 D5 7 48N 4 37 E
Oshtorīnān, Iran 85 C6 34 1N 48 38 E
Oshwe, Zaïre 102 C3 3 25 S 19 28 E
Osica de Jos, Romania 46 E5 44 14N 24 20 E
Osieczna, Poland 47 D3 51 55N 16 40 E
Osijek, Yugoslavia 42 B3 45 34N 18 41 E
Ósilo, Italy 40 B1 40 45N 8 41 E
Ósimo, Italy 39 E10 43 28N 13 30 E
Osintorf, U.S.S.R. 50 D7 54 40N 30 39 E
Osipenko = Berdyansk, U.S.S.R. 52 C7 46 45N 36 50 E
Osipovichi, U.S.S.R. 50 E6 53 19N 28 33 E
Osizweni, S. Africa 105 D5 27 49 S 30 7 E
Oskaloosa, U.S.A. 140 C4 41 18N 92 40W
Oskarshamn, Sweden 13 H14 57 15N 16 27 E
Oskélanéo, Canada 128 C4 48 5N 75 15W
Oskol →, U.S.S.R. 51 G10 49 6N 37 25 E
Oslo, Norway 14 E4 59 55N 10 45 E
Oslob, Phil. 71 C6 9 31N 123 26 E
Oslofjorden, Norway 14 E4 59 20N 10 35 E
Osmanabad, India 82 E3 18 5N 76 10 E
Osmancık, Turkey 52 F6 40 58N 34 47 E
Osmaniye, Turkey 88 E7 37 5N 36 10 E
Ösmo, Sweden 14 F11 58 58N 17 55 E
Osnabrück, Germany 26 C4 52 16N 8 2 E
Ośno Lubuskie, Poland 47 C1 52 28N 14 51 E
Osoblaha, Czech. 31 A10 50 17N 17 44 E
Osogovska Planina, Yugoslavia 42 E7 42 10N 22 30 E
Osor, Italy 39 D11 44 42N 14 24 E
Osorio, Brazil 159 B5 29 53 S 50 17W
Osorno, Chile 160 B2 40 25 S 73 0W
Osorno, Spain 36 C6 42 24N 4 22W
Osorno □, Chile 160 B2 40 34 S 73 9W
Osorno, Vol., Chile 160 B2 41 0 S 72 30W
Osoyoos, Canada 130 D5 49 0N 119 30W
Ospika →, Canada 130 B4 56 20N 124 0W
Osprey Reef, Australia 114 A4 13 52 S 146 36 E
Oss, Neths. 20 E7 51 46N 5 32 E
Ossa, Mt., Australia 114 G4 41 52 S 146 3 E
Óssa, Oros, Greece 44 E4 39 47N 22 42 E
Ossa de Montiel, Spain 35 G2 38 58N 2 45W
Ossabaw I., U.S.A. 135 K5 31 45N 81 8W
Osse →, France 24 D4 44 7N 0 17 E
Ossendrecht, Neths. 21 F4 51 24N 4 20 E
Ossining, U.S.A. 137 E11 41 9N 73 50W
Ossipee, U.S.A. 137 C13 43 41N 71 9W
Ossokmanuan L., Canada 129 B7 53 25N 65 0W
Ossora, U.S.S.R. 57 D17 59 20N 163 13 E
Ostashkov, U.S.S.R. 50 C8 57 4N 33 2 E
Oste →, Germany 26 B5 53 30N 9 12 E
Ostend = Oostende, Belgium 21 F1 51 15N 2 54 E
Oster, U.S.S.R. 50 F7 50 57N 30 53 E
Osterburg, Germany 26 C7 52 47N 11 44 E
Osterburken, Germany 27 F5 49 26N 9 25 E
Österdalälven →, Sweden 13 F12 61 30N 13 45 E
Östergötlands län □, Sweden 15 F9 58 35N 15 45 E
Osterholz-Scharmbeck, Germany 26 B4 53 14N 8 48 E
Østerild, Denmark 15 G2 57 2N 8 51 E
Ostermundigen, Switz. 28 C4 46 58N 7 27 E
Östersund, Sweden 14 A8 63 10N 14 38 E
Østfold fylke □, Norway 14 E5 59 25N 11 25 E
Ostfriesische Inseln, Germany 26 B3 53 45N 7 15 E
Ostfriesland, Germany 26 B3 53 20N 7 30 E
Óstia, Lido di, Italy 40 A5 41 43N 12 17 E
Ostiglía, Italy 39 C8 45 4N 11 9 E
Ostra, Italy 39 E10 43 40N 13 5 E
Ostrava, Czech. 31 B11 49 51N 18 18 E
Ostróda, Poland 47 B6 53 42N 19 58 E
Ostrog, U.S.S.R. 50 F5 50 20N 26 30 E
Ostrogozhsk, U.S.S.R. 51 F11 50 55N 39 7 E
Ostrogróg Sźamotuły, Poland 47 C3 52 37N 16 33 E
Ostrołęka, Poland 47 B8 53 4N 21 32 E
Ostrołeka □, Poland 47 C8 53 0N 21 30 E
Ostrov, Bulgaria 43 D9 43 40N 24 9 E
Ostrov, Romania 46 E9 44 6N 27 24 E
Ostrov, U.S.S.R. 50 C6 57 25N 28 20 E
Ostrów Lubelski, Poland 47 D9 51 29N 22 51 E
Ostrów Mazowiecka, Poland 47 C8 52 50N 21 51 E
Ostrów Wielkopolski, Poland 47 D4 51 36N 17 44 E
Ostrowiec-Świętokrzyski, Poland 47 E8 50 55N 21 22 E
Ostrozac, Yugoslavia 42 D2 43 43N 17 49 E
Ostrzeszów, Poland 47 D4 51 25N 17 52 E
Ostseebad-Külungsborn, Germany 26 A7 54 10N 11 40 E
Osttirol □, Austria 27 J8 46 50N 12 30 E
Ostuni, Italy 41 B10 40 44N 17 34 E
Osum →, Bulgaria 43 D9 43 40N 24 50 E
Osumi →, Albania 44 D2 40 40N 20 10 E
Ōsumi-Hantō, Japan 62 F2 31 20N 130 55 E
Ōsumi-Kaikyō, Japan 61 J5 30 55N 131 0 E
Ōsumi-Shotō, Japan 61 J5 30 30N 130 0 E
Osuna, Spain 37 H5 37 14N 5 8W
Oswego, U.S.A. 137 C8 43 29N 76 30W
Oswestry, U.K. 16 E4 52 52N 3 3W
Oświecim, Poland 31 A12 50 2N 19 11 E
Ōta, Japan 63 A11 36 18N 139 22 E
Ota-Gawa →, Japan 62 C4 34 21N 132 18 E
Otago □, N.Z. 119 E4 44 44 S 169 10 E
Otago Harbour, N.Z. 119 F5 45 47 S 170 42 E
Otago Pen., N.Z. 119 F5 45 48 S 170 39 E
Otahuhu, N.Z. 118 C3 36 56 S 174 51 E
Ōtake, Japan 62 C4 34 12N 132 13 E
Ōtaki, Japan 63 B12 35 17N 140 15 E
Otaki, N.Z. 118 G4 40 45 S 175 10 E
Otane, N.Z. 118 F5 39 54 S 176 39 E
Otar, U.S.S.R. 55 B7 43 32N 75 12 E
Otaru, Japan 60 C10 43 10N 141 0 E
Otaru-Wan = Ishikari-Wan, Japan 60 C10 43 25N 141 1 E
Otautau, N.Z. 119 G3 46 9 S 168 1 E
Otava →, Czech. 30 B7 49 26N 14 12 E
Otavalo, Ecuador 152 C2 0 13N 78 20W
Otavi, Namibia 104 B2 19 40 S 17 24 E
Otchinjau, Angola 103 F2 16 30 S 13 56 E
Otelec, Romania 46 D1 45 36N 20 50 E
Otero de Rey, Spain 36 B3 43 6N 7 36W
Othello, U.S.A. 142 C4 46 53N 119 8W
Othonoí, Greece 44 E1 39 52N 19 22 E
Óthris, Óros, Greece 45 E4 39 4N 22 42 E
Otira, N.Z. 119 C6 42 49 S 171 35 E
Otira Gorge, N.Z. 119 C6 42 53 S 171 33 E
Otis, U.S.A. 138 E3 40 12N 102 58W
Otjiwarongo, Namibia 104 C2 20 30 S 16 33 E
Otmuchów, Poland 47 E4 50 28N 17 10 E
Oto Tolu Group, Tonga 121 Q13 20 21 S 174 32W
Otočac, Yugoslavia 39 D12 44 53N 15 12 E
Otoineppu, Japan 60 B11 44 44N 142 16 E
Otorohanga, N.Z. 118 E4 38 12 S 175 14 E
Otoskwin →, Canada 128 B2 52 13N 88 6W
Otosquen, Canada 131 C8 53 17N 102 1W
Ōtoyo, Japan 62 D5 33 43N 133 45 E
Otranto, Italy 41 B11 40 9N 18 28 E
Otranto, C. d', Italy 41 B11 40 7N 18 30 E
Otranto, Str. of, Italy 41 B11 40 15N 18 40 E
Otse, S. Africa 104 D4 25 2 S 25 45 E
Otsego, U.S.A. 141 B11 42 27N 85 42W
Ōtsu, Japan 63 C7 35 0N 135 50 E
Ōtsuki, Japan 63 B10 35 36N 138 57 E
Otta, Norway 14 C3 61 46N 9 32 E
Ottapalam, India 83 J3 10 46N 76 23 E
Ottawa = Outaouais →, Canada 128 C5 45 27N 74 8W
Ottawa, Canada 128 C4 45 27N 75 42W
Ottawa, Ill., U.S.A. 138 E10 41 20N 88 55W
Ottawa, Kans., U.S.A. 138 F7 38 40N 95 6W
Ottawa, Ohio, U.S.A. 141 C12 41 1N 84 3W
Ottawa Is., Canada 127 C11 59 35N 80 10W
Ottélé, Cameroon 101 E7 3 38N 11 19 E
Ottensheim, Austria 30 C7 48 21N 14 12 E
Otter L., Canada 131 B8 55 35N 104 39W
Otter Rapids, Ont., Canada 128 B3 50 11N 81 39W
Otter Rapids, Sask., Canada 131 B8 55 38N 104 44W
Otterbein, U.S.A. 141 D9 40 29N 87 6W
Otterndorf, Germany 26 B4 53 47N 8 52 E
Otterup, Denmark 15 J4 55 30N 10 22 E
Otterville, Canada 136 D4 42 55N 80 36W
Otterville, U.S.A. 140 F4 38 42N 93 0W
Ottignies, Belgium 21 G5 50 40N 4 33 E
Otto Beit Bridge, Zimbabwe 107 F2 15 59 S 28 56 E
Ottosdal, S. Africa 104 D4 26 46 S 25 59 E
Ottoshoop, S. Africa 104 D4 25 45 S 25 58 E
Ottoville, U.S.A. 141 D12 40 57N 84 22W
Ottsjö, Sweden 14 A7 63 13N 13 2 E
Ottumwa, U.S.A. 140 D4 41 0N 92 25W
Otu, Nigeria 101 D5 8 14N 3 22 E
Otukpa, Nigeria 101 D6 7 9N 7 41 E
Oturkpo, Nigeria 101 D6 7 16N 8 8 E
Otway, B., Chile 160 D2 53 30 S 74 0W
Otway, C., Australia 116 E5 38 52 S 143 30 E
Otwock, Poland 47 C8 52 5N 21 20 E
Ötz, Austria 30 D3 47 13N 10 53 E
Ötz →, Austria 30 D3 47 14N 10 50 E
Ötztaler Alpen, Austria 30 E4 46 56N 11 0 E
Ou →, Laos 76 B4 20 4N 102 13 E
Ou Neua, Laos 76 A3 22 18N 101 48 E
Ou-Sammyaku, Japan 60 E10 39 20N 140 35 E
Ouachita →, U.S.A. 139 K9 31 38N 91 49W
Ouachita, L., U.S.A. 139 H8 34 40N 93 25W
Ouachita Mts., U.S.A. 139 H7 34 50N 94 30W
Ouaco, N. Cal. 121 T18 20 50 S 164 29 E
Ouadâne, Mauritania 98 D2 20 50N 11 40W
Ouadda, C.A.R. 102 A4 8 15N 22 20 E
Ouagadougou, Burkina Faso 101 C4 12 25N 1 30W
Ouagam, Chad 97 F2 14 22N 14 42 E
Ouahigouya, Burkina Faso 100 C4 13 31N 2 25W
Ouahila, Algeria 98 C4 27 50N 5 0W
Ouahran = Oran, Algeria 99 A4 35 45N 0 39W
Oualâta, Mauritania 100 B3 17 20N 6 55W
Ouallene, Algeria 99 D5 24 41N 1 11 E
Ouanda Djallé, C.A.R. 102 A4 8 55N 22 53 E
Ouandago, C.A.R. 102 A3 7 13N 18 50 E
Ouango, C.A.R. 102 B4 4 19N 22 30 E
Ouarâne, Mauritania 98 D2 21 0N 10 30W
Ouargla, Algeria 99 B6 31 59N 5 16 E
Ouarkziz, Djebel, Algeria 98 C3 28 50N 8 0W
Ouarzazate, Morocco 98 B3 30 55N 6 50W
Ouatagouna, Mali 101 B5 15 11N 0 43 E
Ouatere, C.A.R. 102 A3 5 30N 19 8 E
Oubangi →, Zaïre 102 C3 0 30 S 17 50 E
Oubarakai, O. →, Algeria 99 C6 27 20N 9 0 E
Oubatche, N. Cal. 121 T18 20 26 S 164 39 E
Ouche →, France 23 E12 47 6N 5 16 E
Oud-Beijerland, Neths. 20 E4 51 50N 4 25 E
Oud-Gastel, Neths. 21 E4 51 35N 4 28 E
Oud Turnhout, Belgium 21 F6 51 19N 5 0 E
Ouddorp, Neths. 20 E3 51 50N 3 57 E
Oude-Pekela, Neths. 20 B10 53 6N 7 0 E
Oude Rijn →, Neths. 20 D4 52 12N 4 24 E
Oudega, Neths. 20 B8 53 8N 6 0 E
Oudenaarde, Belgium 21 G3 50 50N 3 37 E
Oudenbosch, Neths. 21 E5 51 35N 4 32 E
Oudenburg, Belgium 21 F2 51 11N 3 1 E
Ouderkerk, Utrecht, Neths. 20 D5 52 18N 4 55 E
Ouderkerk, Zuid-Holland, Neths. 20 E5 51 56N 4 38 E
Oudeschild, Neths. 20 B5 53 2N 4 50 E
Oudewater, Neths. 20 D5 52 2N 4 52 E
Oudkarspel, Neths. 20 C5 52 43N 4 49 E
Oudon, France 22 E5 47 22N 1 19W
Oudtshoorn, S. Africa 104 E3 33 35 S 22 14 E
Oued Zem, Morocco 98 B3 32 52N 6 34W
Ouégoa, N. Cal. 121 T18 20 20 S 164 26 E
Ouellé, Ivory C. 100 D4 7 26N 4 1W
Ouen, I., N. Cal. 121 V20 22 26 S 166 49 E
Ouenza, Algeria 99 A6 35 57N 8 4 E
Ouessa, Burkina Faso 100 C4 11 4N 2 47W
Ouessant, I. d', France 22 D1 48 28N 5 6W
Ouesso, Congo 102 B3 1 37N 16 5 E
Ouest, Pte., Canada 129 C7 49 52N 64 40W
Ouezzane, Morocco 98 B3 34 51N 5 35W
Ouffet, Belgium 21 H6 50 26N 5 28 E
Ouidah, Benin 101 D5 6 25N 2 0 E
Ouistreham, France 22 C6 49 17N 0 18W
Oujda, Morocco 99 B4 34 41N 1 55W
Oujeft, Mauritania 98 D2 20 2N 13 0W
Ould Yenjé, Mauritania 100 B2 15 38N 12 16W
Ouled Djellal, Algeria 99 B6 34 28N 5 2 E
Ouled Naïl, Mts. des, Algeria 99 B5 34 30N 3 30 E
Oulmès, Morocco 98 B3 33 17N 6 0W
Oulu, Finland 12 D18 65 1N 25 29 E
Oulu □, Finland 12 D19 65 10N 27 20 E
Oulujärvi, Finland 12 D19 64 25N 27 15 E
Oulujoki →, Finland 12 D18 65 1N 25 30 E
Oulx, Italy 38 C3 45 2N 6 49 E
Oum Chalouba, Chad 97 E4 15 48N 20 46 E
Oum-el-Bouaghi, Algeria 99 A6 35 55N 7 6 E
Oum el Ksi, Algeria 98 C3 29 4N 6 59W
Oum-er-Rbia, O. →, Morocco 98 B3 33 19N 8 21W
Oumè, Ivory C. 100 D3 6 21N 5 27W
Ounane, Dj., Algeria 99 C6 25 4N 7 19 E
Ounguati, Namibia 104 C2 22 0 S 15 46 E
Ounianga-Kébir, Chad 97 E4 19 4N 20 29 E
Ounianga Sérir, Chad 97 E4 18 54N 20 51 E
Our →, Lux. 21 J8 49 55N 6 5 E
Ouray, U.S.A. 143 G10 38 3N 107 40W
Ourcq →, France 23 C10 49 1N 3 1 E
Oureg, Oued el →, Algeria 99 B5 32 34N 2 10 E
Ourém, Brazil 154 B2 1 33 S 47 6W
Ouricuri, Brazil 154 C3 7 53 S 40 5W
Ourinhos, Brazil 159 A6 23 0 S 49 54W
Ourique, Portugal 37 H2 37 38N 8 16W
Ouro Fino, Brazil 159 A6 22 16 S 46 25W
Ouro Prêto, Brazil 155 F3 20 20 S 43 30W
Ouro Sogui, Senegal 100 B2 15 36N 13 19W
Oursi, Burkina Faso 101 C4 14 41N 0 27W
Ourthe →, Belgium 21 H7 50 29N 5 35 E
Ouse, Australia 114 G4 42 38 S 146 42 E
Ouse →, E. Susx., U.K. 17 G8 50 43N 0 3 E
Ouse →, N. Yorks., U.K. 16 C8 54 3N 0 7 E
Oust, France 24 F5 42 52N 1 13 E
Oust →, France 22 E4 47 35N 2 6W
Outaouais →, Canada 128 C5 45 27N 74 8W
Outardes →, Canada 129 C6 49 24N 69 30W
Outat Oulad el Haj, Morocco 99 B4 33 22N 3 42W
Outer Hebrides, U.K. 18 D1 57 30N 7 40W
Outer I., Canada 129 B8 51 10N 58 35W
Outes, Spain 36 C2 42 52N 8 55W
Outjo, Namibia 104 C2 20 5 S 16 7 E
Outlook, Canada 131 C7 51 30N 107 0W
Outlook, U.S.A. 138 A2 48 53N 104 46W
Outreau, France 23 B8 50 40N 1 36 E
Ouvèze →, France 25 E8 43 59N 4 51 E
Ouyen, Australia 116 C5 35 1 S 142 22 E
Ouzouer-le-Marché, France 23 E8 47 54N 1 32 E
Ovada, Italy 38 D5 44 39N 8 40 E
Ovalau, Fiji 121 A2 17 40 S 178 48 E
Ovalle, Chile 158 C1 30 33 S 71 18W
Ovar, Portugal 36 E2 40 51N 8 40W
Ovejas, Colombia 152 B2 9 32N 75 14W
Ovens, Australia 117 D7 36 35 S 146 46 E
Overdinkel, Neths. 20 D10 52 14N 7 2 E
Overflakkee, Neths. 20 E4 51 44N 4 10 E
Overijse, Belgium 21 G5 50 47N 4 32 E
Overijssel □, Neths. 20 D9 52 25N 6 35 E
Overijsselsch Kanaal →, Neths. 20 C8 52 31N 6 6 E
Overland, U.S.A. 140 F6 38 41N 90 23W
Overpelt, Belgium 21 F6 51 12N 5 20 E
Overton, U.S.A. 145 J12 36 32N 114 31W
Övertorneå, Sweden 12 C17 66 23N 23 38 E
Ovid, Colo., U.S.A. 138 E3 41 0N 102 17W
Ovid, Mich., U.S.A. 141 A12 43 1N 84 22W
Ovidiopol, U.S.S.R. 52 C4 46 15N 30 30 E
Oviedo, Spain 36 B5 43 25N 5 50W
Oviedo □, Spain 36 B5 43 20N 6 0W
Oviken, Sweden 14 B8 63 0N 14 23 E
Oviksfjällen, Sweden 14 B7 63 0N 13 49 E
Övör Hangay □, Mongolia 66 B2 45 0N 102 30 E
Ovoro, Nigeria 101 D6 5 26N 7 16 E
Ovruch, U.S.S.R. 50 F6 51 25N 28 45 E
Owaka, N.Z. 119 G4 46 27 S 169 40 E
Owando, Congo 102 C3 0 29 S 15 55 E
Owase, Japan 63 C8 34 7N 136 12 E
Owatonna, U.S.A. 138 C8 44 3N 93 10W
Owbeh, Afghan. 79 B1 34 28N 63 10 E
Owego, U.S.A. 137 D8 42 6N 76 17W
Owen, Australia 116 C3 34 15 S 138 32 E
Owen Falls, Uganda 106 B3 0 30N 33 5 E
Owen Mt., N.Z. 119 B7 41 35 S 172 33 E
Owen Sound, Canada 128 D3 44 35N 80 55W
Owen Stanley Ra., Papua N. G. 120 E4 8 30 S 147 0 E
Owendo, Gabon 102 B1 0 17N 9 30 E
Owens →, U.S.A. 144 J9 36 32N 117 59W
Owens L., U.S.A. 145 J9 36 20N 118 0W
Owensboro, U.S.A. 141 G9 37 40N 87 5W
Owensville, Ind., U.S.A. 141 F9 38 16N 87 41W
Owensville, Mo., U.S.A. 140 F5 38 20N 91 30W
Owenton, U.S.A. 141 F12 38 32N 84 50W
Owerri, Nigeria 101 D6 5 29N 7 0 E
Owhango, N.Z. 118 F4 39 0 S 175 23 E
Owingsville, U.S.A. 141 F13 38 9N 83 46W
Owl →, Canada 131 B10 57 51N 92 44W
Owo, Nigeria 101 D6 7 10N 5 39 E
Owosso, U.S.A. 141 B12 43 0N 84 10W
Owyhee, U.S.A. 142 F5 42 0N 116 3W
Owyhee →, U.S.A. 142 E5 43 46N 117 2W
Owyhee, L., U.S.A. 142 E5 43 40N 117 16W
Ox Mts., Ireland 19 B3 54 6N 9 0W
Oxapampa, Peru 156 C2 10 33 S 75 26W
Oxelösund, Sweden 15 F11 58 43N 17 15 E
Oxford, N.Z. 119 D7 43 18 S 172 11 E
Oxford, U.K. 17 F6 51 45N 1 15W
Oxford, Iowa, U.S.A. 140 C5 41 43N 91 47W
Oxford, Mich., U.S.A. 141 B13 42 49N 83 16W
Oxford, Miss., U.S.A. 139 H10 34 22N 89 30W
Oxford, N.C., U.S.A. 135 G6 36 19N 78 36W
Oxford, Ohio, U.S.A. 141 E12 39 30N 84 40W
Oxford L., Canada 131 C9 54 51N 95 37W
Oxfordshire □, U.K. 17 F6 51 45N 1 15W
Oxía, Greece 45 F3 38 16N 21 5 E
Oxílithos, Greece 45 F6 38 35N 24 7 E
Oxley, Australia 116 C6 34 11 S 144 6 E
Oxnard, U.S.A. 145 L7 34 10N 119 14W
Oxus = Amudarya →, U.S.S.R. 56 E6 43 40N 59 0 E
Oya, Malaysia 70 D4 2 55N 111 55 E
Oyabe, Japan 63 A8 36 47N 136 56 E
Oyama, Japan 63 A11 36 18N 139 48 E
Oyana, Japan 62 E2 32 32N 130 30 E
Oyapock →, Fr. Guiana 153 C7 4 8N 51 40W
Oyem, Gabon 102 B2 1 34N 11 31 E
Oyen, Canada 131 C6 51 22N 110 28W
Øyeren, Norway 14 E5 59 50N 11 15 E
Oykel →, U.K. 18 D4 57 55N 4 26W
Oymyakon, U.S.S.R. 57 C15 63 25N 142 44 E
Oyo, Nigeria 101 D5 7 46N 3 56 E
Oyo □, Nigeria 101 D5 8 0N 3 30 E
Oyón, Peru 156 C2 10 37 S 76 47W
Oyonnax, France 25 B9 46 16N 5 40 E
Oyster Bay, U.S.A. 137 F11 40 52N 73 32W
Oytal, U.S.S.R. 55 B6 42 54N 73 17 E
Ōyūbari, Japan 60 C11 43 1N 142 5 E
Özalp, Turkey 89 D10 38 39N 43 59 E
Ozamis, Phil. 71 C6 8 15N 123 50 E
Ozark, Ala., U.S.A. 135 K3 31 29N 85 39W
Ozark, Ark., U.S.A. 139 H8 35 30N 93 50W
Ozark, Mo., U.S.A. 139 G8 37 0N 93 15W
Ozark Plateau, U.S.A. 139 G9 37 20N 91 40W
Ozarks, L. of the, U.S.A. 140 F4 38 10N 92 40W
Ózd, Hungary 31 C13 48 14N 20 15 E
Ozërnyy, U.S.S.R. 54 F7 51 8N 60 50 E
Ozette, L., U.S.A. 144 B2 48 6N 124 38W
Ozieri, Italy 40 B2 40 35N 9 0 E
Ozimek, Poland 47 E5 50 41N 18 11 E
Ozona, U.S.A. 139 K4 30 43N 101 11W
Ozorków, Poland 47 D6 51 57N 19 16 E
Ozren, Yugoslavia 42 D3 43 55N 18 29 E
Ozu, Ehime, Japan 62 D4 33 30N 132 33 E
Ozu, Kumamoto, Japan 62 E2 32 52N 130 52 E
Ozuluama, Mexico 147 C5 21 40N 97 50W
Ozun, Romania 46 D6 45 47N 25 50 E

P

P.K. le Roux Dam, S. Africa 104 E3 30 4 S 24 40 E
Pa, Burkina Faso 100 C4 11 33N 3 19W
Pa-an, Burma 78 G6 16 51N 97 40 E
Pa Mong Dam, Thailand 76 D4 18 0N 102 22 E
Paagoumène, N. Cal. 121 T18 20 29 S 164 11 E
Paal, Belgium 21 F6 51 2N 5 10 E
Paama, Vanuatu 121 F6 16 28 S 168 14 E
Paamiut = Frederikshåb, Greenland 6 C5 62 0N 49 43W
Paar →, Germany 27 G6 48 13N 10 59 E
Paarl, S. Africa 104 E2 33 45 S 18 56 E
Paatsi →, U.S.S.R. 12 B20 68 55N 29 0 E

246 Paauilo

Paauilo, U.S.A. 132 H17 20 3N 155 22W
Pab Hills, Pakistan 79 D2 26 30N 66 45 E
Pabianice, Poland 47 D6 51 40N 19 20 E
Pabna, Bangla. 78 C2 24 1N 89 18 E
Pabo, Uganda 106 B3 3 1N 32 10 E
Pacaás Novos, Serra dos, Brazil 157 C5 10 45 S 64 15W
Pacaipampa, Peru 156 B2 5 35 S 79 39W
Pacaja →, Brazil 154 B1 1 56 S 50 50W
Pacajus, Brazil 154 B4 4 10 S 38 31W
Pacaraima, Sierra, Venezuela 153 C5 4 0N 62 30W
Pacarán, Peru 156 C2 12 50 S 76 3W
Pacaraos, Peru 156 C2 11 12 S 76 42W
Pacasmayo, Peru 156 B2 7 20 S 79 35W
Paceco, Italy 40 E5 37 59N 12 32 E
Pachacamac, Peru 156 C2 12 14 S 77 53W
Pachhar, India 80 G7 24 40N 77 42 E
Pachino, Italy 41 F8 36 43N 15 4 E
Pachitea →, Peru 156 B3 8 46 S 74 33W
Pachiza, Peru 156 B2 7 16 S 76 46W
Pacho, Colombia 152 B3 5 8N 74 10W
Pachora, India 82 D2 20 38N 75 29 E
Pachuca, Mexico 147 C5 20 10N 98 40W
Pacific, Canada 130 C3 54 48N 128 28W
Pacific, U.S.A. 140 F6 38 29N 90 45W
Pacific-Antarctic Ridge, Pac. Oc. 123 M16 43 0 S 115 0W
Pacific Grove, U.S.A. 144 J5 36 38N 121 58W
Pacific Ocean, Pac. Oc. 123 G14 10 0N 140 0W
Pacifica, U.S.A. 144 H4 37 36N 122 30W
Pacitan, Indonesia 71 H14 8 12 S 111 7 E
Packsaddle, Australia 116 A4 30 36 S 141 58 E
Packwood, U.S.A. 144 D5 46 36N 121 40W
Pacov, Czech. 30 B8 49 27N 15 0 E
Pacsa, Hungary 31 E10 46 44N 17 2 E
Pacuí →, Brazil 155 E2 16 46 S 45 1W
Paczków, Poland 47 E4 50 28N 17 0 E
Padaido, Kepulauan, Indonesia 71 E9 1 5 S 138 0 E
Padang, Indonesia 70 E2 1 0 S 100 20 E
Padangpanjang, Indonesia 70 E2 0 40 S 100 20 E
Padangsidempuan, Indonesia 70 D1 1 30N 99 15 E
Padangtikar, Indonesia 75 C3 0 44 S 109 15 E
Padatchuang, Burma 78 F5 19 46N 94 48 E
Padauari →, Brazil 153 D5 0 15 S 64 5W
Padborg, Denmark 15 K3 54 49N 9 21 E
Padcaya, Bolivia 157 E5 21 52 S 64 48W
Paddockwood, Canada 131 C7 53 30N 105 30W
Paderborn, Germany 26 D4 51 42N 8 44 E
Padeşul, Romania 46 D3 45 40N 22 22 E
Padilla, Bolivia 157 D5 19 19 S 64 20W
Padina, Romania 46 E8 44 50N 27 8 E
Padloping Island, Canada 127 B13 67 0N 62 50W
Padma →, Bangla. 78 D3 23 22N 90 32 E
Padmanabhapuram, India 83 K3 8 16N 77 17 E
Pádova, Italy 39 C8 45 24N 11 52 E
Padra, India 80 H5 22 15N 73 7 E
Padrauna, India 81 F10 26 54N 83 59 E
Padre I., U.S.A. 139 M6 27 0N 97 20W
Padro, Mte., France 25 F12 42 28N 8 59 E
Padrón, Spain 36 C2 42 41N 8 39W
Padstow, U.K. 17 G3 50 33N 4 57W
Padua = Pádova, Italy 39 C8 45 24N 11 52 E
Paducah, Ky., U.S.A. 134 G1 37 0N 88 40W
Paducah, Tex., U.S.A. 139 H4 34 3N 100 16W
Padul, Spain 37 H7 37 1N 3 38W
Padula, Italy 41 B8 40 20N 15 40 E
Padwa, India 82 E6 18 27N 82 47 E
Paekakariki, N.Z. 118 G3 40 59 S 174 58 E
Paengaroa, N.Z. 118 D5 37 49 S 176 29 E
Paengnyong-do, S. Korea 67 F13 37 57N 124 40 E
Paeroa, N.Z. 118 D4 37 23 S 175 41 E
Paesana, Italy 38 D4 44 40N 7 18 E
Pafúri, Mozam. 105 C5 22 28 S 31 17 E
Pag, Yugoslavia 39 D11 44 30N 14 50 E
Paga, Ghana 101 C4 11 1N 1 8W
Pagadian, Phil. 71 C6 7 55N 123 30 E
Pagai Selatan, P., Indonesia 70 E2 3 0 S 100 15 E
Pagai Utara, Indonesia 70 E2 2 35 S 100 0 E
Pagalu = Annobón, Atl. Oc. 93 G4 1 25 S 5 36 E
Pagastikós Kólpos, Greece 44 E5 39 15N 23 0 E
Pagatan, Indonesia 70 E5 3 33 S 115 59 E
Page, Ariz., U.S.A. 143 H8 36 57N 111 27W
Page, N. Dak., U.S.A. 138 B6 47 11N 97 37W
Paglieta, Italy 39 F11 42 10N 14 30 E
Pagny-sur-Moselle, France 23 D13 48 59N 6 2 E
Pago Pago, Amer. Samoa 121 X24 14 16 S 170 43W
Pagosa Springs, U.S.A. 143 H10 37 16N 107 4W
Pagwa River, Canada 128 B2 50 2N 85 14W
Pahala, U.S.A. 132 J17 19 12N 155 25W
Pahang →, Malaysia 77 L4 3 30N 103 9 E
Pahia Pt., N.Z. 119 G2 46 20 S 167 41 E
Pahiatua, N.Z. 118 G4 40 27 S 175 50 E
Pahokee, U.S.A. 135 M5 26 50N 80 40W
Pahrump, U.S.A. 145 J11 36 15N 116 0W
Pahute Mesa, U.S.A. 144 H10 37 25N 116 50W
Pai, Thailand 76 C2 19 19N 98 27 E
Paia, U.S.A. 132 H16 20 54N 156 22W
Paicines, U.S.A. 144 J5 36 44N 121 17W
Paide, U.S.S.R. 50 B4 58 57N 25 31 E
Paignton, U.K. 17 G4 50 26N 3 33W
Paiján, Peru 156 B2 7 42 S 79 20W
Päijänne, Finland 13 F18 61 30N 25 30 E
Paimbœuf, France 22 E4 47 17N 2 3W
Paimpol, France 22 D3 48 48N 3 4W
Painan, Indonesia 70 E2 1 21 S 100 34 E
Painesville, U.S.A. 136 E3 41 42N 81 18W
Paint Hills = Nouveau Comptoir, Canada 128 B4 53 0N 78 49W
Paint L., Canada 131 B9 55 28N 97 57W
Paint Rock, U.S.A. 139 K5 31 30N 99 56W
Painted Desert, U.S.A. 143 J8 36 0N 111 30W
Paintsville, U.S.A. 134 G4 37 50N 82 50W
País Vasco □, Spain 34 C2 42 50N 2 45W
Paisley, Canada 136 B3 44 18N 81 16W
Paisley, U.K. 18 F4 55 51N 4 27W
Paisley, U.S.A. 142 E3 42 43N 120 40W
Paita, N. Cal. 121 V20 22 8 S 166 22 E
Paita, Peru 156 B1 5 11 S 81 9W
Paiva →, Portugal 36 D2 41 4N 8 16W
Paizhou, China 69 B9 30 12N 113 55 E
Pajares, Spain 36 B5 43 1N 5 46W
Pajares, Puerto de, Spain 36 C5 42 58N 5 46W
Pajeczno, Poland 47 D6 51 10N 19 0 E
Pak Lay, Laos 76 C3 18 15N 101 27 E
Pak Phanang, Thailand 77 H3 8 21N 100 12 E
Pak Sane, Laos 76 C4 18 22N 103 39 E
Pak Song, Laos 76 E6 15 11N 106 14 E
Pak Suong, Laos 76 C4 19 58N 102 15 E
Pakala, India 83 H4 13 29N 79 8 E
Pakaraima Mts., Guyana 153 B6 6 0N 60 0W
Pakenham, Australia 117 E6 38 6 S 145 30 E
Pákhnes, Greece 32 D6 35 16N 24 4 E
Pakhtakor, U.S.S.R. 55 C2 40 2N 65 46 E
Pakistan ■, Asia 79 C3 30 0N 70 0 E
Pakistan, East = Bangladesh ■, Asia 78 D3 24 0N 90 0 E
Pakkading, Laos 76 C4 18 19N 103 59 E
Pakokku, Burma 78 E5 21 20N 95 0 E
Pakosc, Poland 47 C5 52 48N 18 6 E
Pakpattan, Pakistan 79 C4 30 25N 73 27 E
Pakrac, Yugoslavia 42 B2 45 27N 17 12 E
Paks, Hungary 31 E11 46 38N 18 55 E
Pakse, Laos 76 E5 15 5N 105 52 E
Paktīā □, Afghan. 79 B3 33 0N 69 15 E
Paktīkā □, Afghan. 79 B3 32 30N 69 0 E
Pakwach, Uganda 106 B3 2 28N 31 27 E
Pala, Chad 97 G3 9 25N 15 5 E
Pala, U.S.A. 145 M9 33 22N 117 5W
Pala, Zaïre 106 D2 6 45 S 29 30 E
Palabek, Uganda 106 B3 3 22N 32 33 E
Palacios, U.S.A. 139 L6 28 44N 96 12W
Palafrugell, Spain 34 D8 41 55N 3 10 E
Palagiano, Italy 41 B10 40 35N 17 2 E
Palagonía, Italy 41 E7 37 20N 14 43 E
Palagruža, Yugoslavia 39 F13 42 24N 16 15 E
Palaiokastron, Greece 45 J8 35 12N 26 18 E
Palaiókastron, Kriti, Greece 32 D8 35 12N 26 15 E
Palaiokhóra, Greece 32 D5 35 16N 23 39 E
Pálairos, Greece 45 F2 38 45N 20 51 E
Palakol, India 83 F5 16 31N 81 46 E
Palam, India 82 E3 19 0N 77 0 E
Palamás, Greece 44 E4 39 26N 22 4 E
Palamós, Spain 34 D8 41 50N 3 10 E
Palampur, India 80 C7 32 10N 76 30 E
Palana, Australia 114 F4 39 45 S 147 55 E
Palana, U.S.S.R. 57 D16 59 10N 159 59 E
Palanan, Phil. 71 A6 17 8N 122 29 E
Palanan Pt., Phil. 71 A6 17 17N 122 30 E
Palandri, Pakistan 81 C5 33 42N 73 40 E
Palangkaraya, Indonesia 70 E4 2 16 S 113 56 E
Palani, India 83 J3 10 30N 77 30 E
Palani Hills, India 83 J3 10 14N 77 33 E
Palanpur, India 80 G5 24 10N 72 25 E
Palapye, Botswana 104 C4 22 30 S 27 7 E
Palar →, India 83 H5 12 27N 80 13 E
Palas, Pakistan 81 B5 35 4N 73 14 E
Palatine, U.S.A. 141 B8 42 7N 88 3W
Palatka, U.S.A. 135 L5 29 40N 81 40W
Palatka, U.S.S.R. 57 C16 60 6N 150 54 E
Palawan, Phil. 70 C5 9 30N 118 30 E
Palayankottai, India 83 K3 8 45N 77 45 E
Palazzo, Pte., France 25 F12 42 28N 8 30 E
Palazzo San Gervásio, Italy 41 B8 40 53N 15 58 E
Palazzolo Acreide, Italy 41 E7 37 4N 14 54 E
Palca, Chile 156 D4 19 7 S 69 9W
Paldiski, U.S.S.R. 50 B4 59 23N 24 9 E
Pale, Yugoslavia 42 D3 43 50N 18 38 E
Palel, India 78 C5 24 27N 94 2 E
Paleleh, Indonesia 71 D6 1 10N 121 50 E
Palembang, Indonesia 70 E2 3 0 S 104 50 E
Palena →, Chile 160 B2 43 50 S 73 50W
Palena, L., Chile 160 B2 43 55 S 71 40W
Palencia, Spain 36 C6 42 1N 4 34W
Palencia □, Spain 36 C6 42 31N 4 33W
Paleokastrítsa, Greece 32 A3 39 40N 19 41 E
Paleometokho, Cyprus 32 D12 35 7N 33 11 E
Palermo, Colombia 152 C2 2 54N 75 26W
Palermo, Italy 40 D6 38 8N 13 20 E
Palermo, U.S.A. 142 G3 39 30N 121 37W
Palestine, Asia 91 D4 32 0N 35 0 E
Palestine, U.S.A. 139 K7 31 42N 95 35W
Palestrina, Italy 40 A5 41 50N 12 52 E
Paletwa, Burma 78 E4 21 10N 92 50 E
Palghat, India 83 J3 10 46N 76 42 E
Palgrave, Mt., Australia 112 D2 23 22 S 115 58 E
Pali, India 80 G5 25 50N 73 20 E
Palinuro, C., Italy 41 B8 40 1N 15 14 E
Palisade, U.S.A. 138 E4 40 21N 101 10W
Paliseul, Belgium 21 J6 49 54N 5 8 E
Palitana, India 80 J4 21 32N 71 49 E
Palizada, Mexico 147 D6 18 18N 92 8W
Palizzi, Italy 41 E8 37 58N 15 59 E
Palk Bay, Asia 83 K4 9 30N 79 15 E
Palk Strait, Asia 83 K4 10 0N 79 45 E
Palkānah, Iraq 84 C5 35 49N 44 26 E
Palkonda, India 82 E6 18 36N 83 48 E
Palkonda Ra., India 83 H4 13 50N 79 20 E
Palla Road = Dinokwe, Botswana 104 C4 23 29 S 26 37 E
Pallanza = Verbánia, Italy 38 C5 45 56N 8 43 E
Pallasovka, U.S.S.R. 51 F15 50 4N 47 0 E
Pallerú →, India 83 F5 16 45N 80 2 E
Pallisa, Uganda 106 B3 1 12N 33 43 E
Palliser, C., N.Z. 118 H4 41 37 S 175 14 E
Palliser B., N.Z. 118 H4 41 26 S 175 5 E
Pallu, India 80 E6 28 59N 74 14 E
Palm Beach, U.S.A. 135 M6 26 46N 80 0W
Palm Desert, U.S.A. 145 M10 33 43N 116 22W
Palm Is., Australia 114 B4 18 40 S 146 35 E
Palm Springs, U.S.A. 145 M10 33 51N 116 35W
Palma, Mozam. 107 E5 10 46 S 40 29 E
Palma →, Brazil 155 D2 12 33 S 47 52W
Palma, B. de, Spain 33 B9 39 30N 2 39 E
Palma de Mallorca, Spain 33 B9 39 35N 2 39 E
Palma del Río, Spain 37 H5 37 43N 5 17W
Palma di Montechiaro, Italy 40 E6 37 12N 13 46 E
Palma Soriano, Cuba 148 B4 20 15N 76 0W
Palmanova, Italy 39 C10 45 54N 13 18 E
Palmares, Brazil 154 C4 8 41 S 35 28W
Palmarito, Venezuela 152 B3 7 37N 70 10W
Palmarola, Italy 40 B5 40 57N 12 50 E
Palmas, Brazil 159 B5 26 29 S 52 0W
Palmas, C., Liberia 100 E3 4 27N 7 46W
Pálmas, G. di, Italy 40 D1 39 0N 8 30 E
Palmas de Monte Alto, Brazil 155 D3 14 16 S 43 10W
Palmdale, U.S.A. 145 L8 34 36N 118 7W
Palmeira, Brazil 155 G2 25 25 S 50 0W
Palmeira dos Índios, Brazil 154 C4 9 25 S 36 37W
Palmeirais, Brazil 154 C3 6 0 S 43 0W
Palmeiras →, Brazil 155 D2 12 22 S 47 8W
Palmeirinhas, Pta. das, Angola 103 D2 9 2 S 12 57 E
Palmela, Portugal 37 G2 38 32N 8 57W
Palmelo, Brazil 155 E2 17 20 S 48 27W
Palmer, U.S.A. 126 B5 61 35N 149 10W
Palmer →, Australia 114 B3 16 0 S 142 26 E
Palmer Arch., Antarctica 7 C17 64 15 S 65 0W
Palmer Lake, U.S.A. 138 F2 39 10N 104 52W
Palmer Land, Antarctica 7 D18 73 0 S 60 0W
Palmerston, Canada 136 C4 43 50N 80 51W
Palmerston, N.Z. 119 F5 45 29 S 170 43 E
Palmerston North, N.Z. 118 G4 40 21 S 175 39 E
Palmerton, U.S.A. 137 F9 40 47N 75 36W
Palmetto, U.S.A. 135 M4 27 33N 82 33W
Palmi, Italy 41 D8 38 21N 15 51 E
Palmira, Argentina 158 C2 32 59 S 68 34W
Palmira, Colombia 152 C2 3 32N 76 16W
Palmyra = Tudmur, Syria 84 C3 34 36N 38 15 E
Palmyra, Ill., U.S.A. 140 E7 39 26N 90 0W
Palmyra, Mo., U.S.A. 140 E5 39 45N 91 30W
Palmyra, N.Y., U.S.A. 136 C7 43 5N 77 18W
Palmyra, Wis., U.S.A. 141 B8 42 52N 88 36W
Palmyra Is., Pac. Oc. 123 G11 5 52N 162 5W
Palo Alto, U.S.A. 144 H4 37 25N 122 8W
Palo del Colle, Italy 41 A9 41 4N 16 43 E
Palo Verde, U.S.A. 145 M12 33 26N 114 45W
Palombara Sabina, Italy 39 F9 42 4N 12 45 E
Palopo, Indonesia 71 E6 3 0 S 120 16 E
Palos, C. de, Spain 35 H4 37 38N 0 40W
Palos Verdes, U.S.A. 145 M8 33 48N 118 23W
Palos Verdes, Pt., U.S.A. 145 M8 33 43N 118 26W
Palouse, U.S.A. 142 C5 46 59N 117 5W
Palpa, Peru 156 C2 14 30 S 75 15W
Palparara, Australia 114 C3 24 47 S 141 28 E
Pålsboda, Sweden 14 E9 59 3N 15 22 E
Palu, Indonesia 71 E5 1 0 S 119 52 E
Palu, Turkey 49 G7 38 45N 40 0 E
Paluan, Phil. 71 B6 13 26N 120 29 E
Palwal, India 80 E7 28 8N 77 19 E
Pama, Burkina Faso 101 C5 11 19N 0 44 E
Pamanukan, Indonesia 71 G12 6 16 S 107 49 E
Pamban I., India 83 K4 9 15N 79 20 E
Pamekasan, Indonesia 71 G15 7 10 S 113 28 E
Pamiers, France 24 E5 43 7N 1 39 E
Pamir →, U.S.S.R. 55 E6 37 1N 72 41 E
Pamirs, U.S.S.R. 55 E6 37 40N 73 0 E
Pamlico →, U.S.A. 135 H7 35 25N 76 30W
Pamlico Sd., U.S.A. 135 H8 35 20N 76 0W
Pampa, U.S.A. 139 H4 35 35N 100 58W
Pampa de Agma, Argentina 160 B3 43 45 S 69 40W
Pampa de las Salinas, Argentina 158 C2 32 1 S 66 58W
Pampa Grande, Bolivia 157 D5 18 5 S 64 6W
Pampa Hermosa, Peru 156 B2 7 7 S 75 4W
Pampanua, Indonesia 71 E6 4 16 S 120 8 E
Pamparato, Italy 38 D4 44 16N 7 54 E
Pampas, Argentina 158 D3 35 0 S 63 0W
Pampas, Peru 156 C3 12 20 S 74 50W
Pampas →, Peru 156 C3 13 24 S 73 12W
Pamphylia, Turkey 88 E4 37 0N 31 20 E
Pamplona, Colombia 152 B3 7 23N 72 39W
Pamplona, Spain 34 C3 42 48N 1 38W
Pampoenpoort, S. Africa 104 E3 31 3 S 22 40 E
Pamukkale, Turkey 88 E3 37 57N 28 50 E
Pan Xian, China 68 E5 25 46N 104 38 E
Pana, U.S.A. 140 E7 39 25N 89 10W
Panaca, U.S.A. 143 H6 37 51N 114 23W
Panagyurishte, Bulgaria 43 E9 42 30N 24 15 E
Panaitan, Indonesia 71 G11 6 36 S 105 12 E
Panaji, India 83 G1 15 25N 73 50 E
Panamá, Panama 148 E4 9 0N 79 25W
Panama ■, Cent. Amer. 148 E4 8 48N 79 55W
Panamá, G. de, Panama 148 E4 8 4N 79 20W
Panama Canal, Panama 148 E4 9 10N 79 37W
Panama City, U.S.A. 135 K3 30 10N 85 41W
Panamint Ra., U.S.A. 145 J9 36 20N 117 20W
Panamint Springs, U.S.A. 145 J9 36 20N 117 28W
Panão, Peru 156 B2 9 55 S 75 55W
Panare, Thailand 77 J3 6 51N 101 30 E
Panarea, Italy 41 D8 38 38N 15 3 E
Panaro →, Italy 38 D8 44 55N 11 25 E
Panarukan, Indonesia 71 G15 7 42 S 113 56 E
Panay, Phil. 71 B6 11 10N 122 30 E
Panay, G., Phil. 71 B6 11 0N 122 30 E
Pancake Ra., U.S.A. 143 G6 38 30N 116 0W
Pančevo, Yugoslavia 42 C5 44 52N 20 41 E
Panciu, Romania 46 D8 45 54N 27 8 E
Pancorbo, Paso, Spain 34 C1 42 32N 3 5W
Pandan, Phil. 71 B6 11 45N 122 10 E
Pandegelang, Indonesia 71 G12 6 25 S 106 5 E
Pandharpur, India 82 F2 17 41N 75 20 E
Pandhurna, India 82 D4 21 36N 78 35 E
Pandilla, Spain 34 D1 41 32N 3 43W
Pando, Uruguay 159 C4 34 44 S 56 0W
Pando □, Bolivia 156 C4 11 20 S 67 40W
Pando, L. = Hope, L., Australia 115 D2 28 24 S 139 18 E
Pandokrátor, Greece 32 A3 39 45N 19 50 E
Pandora, Costa Rica 148 E3 9 43N 83 3W
Pandu, Zaïre 102 B3 4 59N 19 16 E
Panevezys, U.S.S.R. 50 D4 55 42N 24 25 E
Panfilov, U.S.S.R. 56 E9 44 10N 80 0 E
Panfilovo, U.S.S.R. 51 F13 50 25N 42 46 E
Panga, Zaïre 106 B2 1 52N 26 18 E
Pangaíon Óros, Greece 44 D6 40 50N 24 0 E
Pangala, Congo 102 C2 4 1 S 13 52 E
Pangalanes, Canal des, Madag. 105 C8 22 48 S 47 50 E
Pangani, Tanzania 106 D4 5 25 S 38 58 E
Pangani □, Tanzania 106 D4 5 25 S 39 0 E
Pangani →, Tanzania 106 D4 5 26 S 38 58 E
Pangfou = Bengbu, China 67 H9 32 58N 117 20 E
Pangil, Zaïre 106 C2 3 10 S 26 35 E
Pangkah, Tanjung, Indonesia 71 G15 6 51 S 112 33 E
Pangkai, Burma 78 D7 22 40N 98 40 E
Pangkajene, Indonesia 71 E5 4 46 S 119 34 E
Pangkalanbrandan, Indonesia 70 D1 4 1N 98 20 E
Pangkalanbuun, Indonesia 70 E4 2 41 S 111 37 E
Pangkalansusu, Indonesia 70 D1 4 2N 98 13 E
Pangkalpinang, Indonesia 70 E3 2 0 S 106 0 E
Pangkoh, Indonesia 70 E4 3 5 S 114 8 E
Pangnirtung, Canada 127 B13 66 8N 65 54W
Pangrango, Indonesia 71 G12 6 46 S 107 1 E
Pangsau Pass, Burma 78 B6 27 15N 96 10 E
Pangtara, Burma 78 E6 20 57N 96 40 E
Panguipulli, Chile 160 A2 39 38 S 72 20W
Panguitch, U.S.A. 143 H7 37 52N 112 30W
Pangutaran Group, Phil. 71 C6 6 18N 120 34 E
Panhandle, U.S.A. 139 H4 35 23N 101 23W
Pani Mines, India 80 H5 22 29N 73 50 E
Pania-Mutombo, Zaïre 103 D4 5 11 S 23 51 E
Panié, Mt., N. Cal. 121 T18 20 36 S 164 46 E
Panipat, India 80 E7 29 25N 77 2 E
Panjal Range, India 80 C7 32 30N 76 50 E
Panjgur, Pakistan 79 D2 27 0N 64 5 E
Panjim = Panaji, India 83 G1 15 25N 73 50 E
Panjwai, Afghan. 80 D1 31 26N 65 27 E
Pankshin, Nigeria 101 D6 9 16N 9 25 E
Panmunjŏm, N. Korea 67 F14 37 59N 126 38 E
Panna, India 81 G9 24 40N 80 15 E
Panna Hills, India 81 G9 24 40N 81 15 E
Pano Lefkara, Cyprus 32 E12 34 53N 33 20 E
Pano Panayia, Cyprus 32 E11 34 55N 32 38 E
Panora, U.S.A. 140 C2 41 41N 94 22W
Panorama, Brazil 159 A5 21 21 S 51 51W
Pánormon, Greece 32 D6 35 25N 24 41 E
Panruti, India 83 J4 11 46N 79 35 E
Panshan, China 67 D12 41 3N 122 2 E
Panshi, China 67 C14 42 58N 126 5 E
Pantar, Indonesia 71 F6 8 28 S 124 10 E
Pantelleria, Italy 40 F5 36 52N 12 0 E
Pantha, Burma 78 D5 23 55N 94 35 E
Pantin Sakan, Burma 78 F6 18 38N 97 33 E
Pantón, Spain 36 C3 42 31N 7 37W
Pánuco, Mexico 147 C5 22 0N 98 15W
Panyam, Nigeria 101 D6 9 27N 9 8 E
Panyu, China 69 F9 22 51N 113 20 E
Pao →, Anzoátegui, Venezuela 153 B5 8 6N 64 17W
Pao →, Apure, Venezuela 152 B4 8 33N 68 1W
Páola, Italy 41 C9 39 21N 16 2 E
Paola, Malta 32 D2 35 52N 14 30 E
Paola, U.S.A. 138 F7 38 36N 94 50W
Paoli, U.S.A. 141 F10 38 33N 86 28W
Paonia, U.S.A. 143 G10 38 56N 107 37W
Paoting = Baoding, China 66 E8 38 50N 115 28 E
Paot'ou = Baotou, China 66 D6 40 32N 110 2 E
Paoua, C.A.R. 102 A3 7 9N 16 20 E
Pápa, Hungary 31 D10 47 22N 17 30 E
Papagayo →, Mexico 147 D5 16 36N 99 43W
Papagayo, G. de, Costa Rica 148 D2 10 30N 85 50W
Papagni →, India 83 G3 15 35N 77 45 E
Papakura, N.Z. 118 D3 37 4 S 174 59 E
Papantla, Mexico 147 C5 20 30N 97 30W
Papar, Malaysia 70 C5 5 45N 116 0 E
Paparoa, N.Z. 118 C3 36 6 S 174 16 E
Paparoa Ra., N.Z. 119 C6 42 5 S 171 35 E
Pápas, Ákra, Greece 45 F3 38 13N 21 20 E
Papatoetoe, N.Z. 118 C3 36 59 S 174 51 E
Papenburg, Germany 26 B3 53 7N 7 25 E
Paphlagonia, Turkey 88 C5 41 30N 33 0 E
Paphos, Cyprus 32 E11 34 46N 32 25 E
Papien Chiang = Da →, Vietnam 76 B5 21 15N 105 20 E
Papigochic →, Mexico 146 B3 29 9N 109 40W
Paposo, Chile 158 B1 25 0 S 70 30W
Papoutsa, Cyprus 32 E12 34 54N 33 4 E
Papua, G. of, Papua N. G. 120 E3 9 0 S 144 50 E
Papua New Guinea ■, Oceania 120 E3 8 0 S 145 0 E
Papuča, Yugoslavia 39 D12 44 22N 15 30 E
Papudo, Chile 158 C1 32 29 S 71 27W
Papuk, Yugoslavia 42 B2 45 30N 17 30 E
Papun, Burma 78 F6 18 2N 97 30 E
Papunya, Australia 112 D5 23 15 S 131 54 E
Pará = Belém, Brazil 154 B2 1 20 S 48 30W
Pará □, Brazil 157 A7 3 20 S 52 0W
Pará □, Surinam 153 B6 5 20N 55 5W
Parábita, Italy 41 B11 40 3N 18 8 E
Paraburdoo, Australia 112 D2 23 14 S 117 32 E
Paracas, Pen., Peru 156 C2 13 53 S 76 20W
Paracatu, Brazil 155 E2 17 10 S 46 50W
Paracatu →, Brazil 155 E2 16 30 S 45 4W
Paracel Is. = Hsisha Chuntao, Pac. Oc. 70 A4 15 50N 112 0 E
Parachilna, Australia 116 A3 31 10 S 138 21 E
Parachinar, Pakistan 79 B3 33 55N 70 5 E
Paraćin, Yugoslavia 42 D6 43 54N 21 27 E
Paracuru, Brazil 154 B4 3 24 S 39 4W
Parada, Punta, Peru 156 D2 15 22 S 75 11W
Paradas, Spain 37 H5 37 18N 5 29W
Paradela, Spain 36 C3 42 44N 7 37W
Paradhísi, Greece 32 C10 36 18N 28 7 E
Paradip, India 82 D8 20 15N 86 35 E
Paradise, Calif., U.S.A. 144 F5 39 46N 121 37W
Paradise, Mont., U.S.A. 142 C6 47 27N 114 17W
Paradise, Nev., U.S.A. 145 J11 36 4N 115 7W
Paradise →, Canada 129 B8 53 27N 57 19W
Paradise Valley, U.S.A. 142 F5 41 30N 117 28W
Parado, Indonesia 71 F5 8 42 S 118 30 E
Paradyz, Poland 47 D7 51 19N 20 2 E
Paragould, U.S.A. 139 G9 36 5N 90 30W
Paraguá →, Bolivia 157 C5 13 34 S 61 53W
Paragua →, Venezuela 153 B5 6 55N 62 55W
Paraguaçu →, Brazil 155 D4 12 45 S 38 54W
Paraguaçu Paulista, Brazil 159 A5 22 22 S 50 35W
Paraguaipoa, Venezuela 152 A3 11 21N 71 57W
Paraguaná, Pen. de, Venezuela 152 A4 12 0N 70 0W
Paraguarí, Paraguay 158 B4 25 36 S 57 0W
Paraguarí □, Paraguay 158 B4 26 0 S 57 10W

248 Pekin

Pekin, U.S.A. **140 D7** 40 35N 89 40W
Peking = Beijing, China **66 E9** 39 55N 116 20 E
Pelabuhan Kelang, Malaysia **77 L3** 3 0N 101 23 E
Pelabuhan Ratu, Teluk, Indonesia **71 G12** 7 5 S 106 30 E
Pelabuhanratu, Indonesia **71 G12** 7 0 S 106 32 E
Pélagos, Greece **44 E6** 39 17N 24 4 E
Pelaihari, Indonesia **70 E4** 3 55 S 114 45 E
Pelat, Mt., France **25 D10** 44 16N 6 42 E
Pełczyce, Poland **47 B2** 53 3N 15 16 E
Peleaga, Romania **46 D3** 45 22N 22 55 E
Pelechuco, Bolivia **156 C4** 14 48 S 69 4W
Pelée, Mt., Martinique **149 D7** 14 48N 61 10W
Pelee, Pt., Canada **128 D3** 41 54N 82 31W
Pelee I., Canada **128 D3** 41 47N 82 40W
Pelejo, Peru **156 B2** 6 10 S 75 49W
Pelekech, Kenya **106 B4** 3 52N 35 8 E
Peleng, Indonesia **71 E6** 1 20 S 123 30 E
Pelham, U.S.A. **135 K3** 31 5N 84 6W
Pelhřimov, Czech. **30 B8** 49 24N 15 12 E
Pelican L., Canada **131 C8** 52 28N 100 20W
Pelican Narrows, Canada **131 B8** 55 10N 102 56W
Pelican Rapids, Canada **131 C8** 52 45N 100 42W
Peljesac, Yugoslavia **42 E2** 42 55N 17 25 E
Pelkosenniemi, Finland **12 C19** 67 6N 27 28 E
Pella, Greece **44 D4** 40 46N 22 23 E
Pella, S. Africa **104 D2** 29 1 S 19 6 E
Pella, U.S.A. **140 C4** 41 30N 92 54W
Pélla □, Greece **44 D4** 40 52N 22 0 E
Péllaro, Italy **41 D8** 38 1N 15 40 E
Pellworm, Germany **26 A4** 54 30N 8 40 E
Pelly →, Canada **126 B6** 62 47N 137 19W
Pelly Bay, Canada **127 B11** 68 38N 89 50W
Pelly L., Canada **126 B9** 66 0N 102 0W
Peloponnese = Pelopónnisos □, Greece **45 G4** 37 10N 22 0 E
Pelopónnisos □, Greece **45 G4** 37 10N 22 0 E
Peloritani, Monti, Italy **41 D8** 38 2N 15 25 E
Peloro, C., Italy **41 D8** 38 15N 15 40 E
Pelorus →, N.Z. **119 B8** 41 16 S 173 45 E
Pelorus Sd., N.Z. **119 A8** 40 59 S 173 59 E
Pelotas, Brazil **159 C5** 31 42 S 52 23W
Pelòvo, Bulgaria **43 D9** 43 26N 24 17 E
Pelvoux, Massif de, France **25 D10** 44 52N 6 20 E
Pelym →, U.S.S.R. **54 B8** 59 39N 63 26 E
Pemalang, Indonesia **71 G13** 6 53 S 109 23 E
Pematangsiantar, Indonesia **70 D1** 2 57N 99 5 E
Pemba, Mozam. **107 E5** 12 58 S 40 30 E
Pemba, Zambia **107 F2** 16 30 S 27 28 E
Pemba Channel, Tanzania **106 D4** 5 0 S 39 37 E
Pemba I., Tanzania **106 D4** 5 0 S 39 45 E
Pemberton, Australia **113 F2** 34 30 S 116 0 E
Pemberton, Canada **130 C4** 50 25N 122 50W
Pembina, U.S.A. **131 D9** 48 58N 97 15W
Pembina →, U.S.A. **131 D9** 49 0N 98 12W
Pembine, U.S.A. **134 C2** 45 38N 87 59W
Pembino, U.S.A. **138 A6** 48 58N 97 15W
Pembroke, Canada **128 C4** 45 50N 77 7W
Pembroke, U.K. **17 F3** 51 41N 4 57W
Pembroke, U.S.A. **135 J5** 32 5N 81 32W
Pembuang →, Indonesia **75 C4** 3 24 S 112 33 E
Pen-y-Ghent, U.K. **16 C5** 54 10N 2 15W
Peña, Sierra de la, Spain **34 C4** 42 32N 0 45W
Peña de Francia, Sierra de, Spain **36 E4** 40 32N 6 10W
Penafiel, Portugal **36 D2** 41 12N 8 17W
Peñafiel, Spain **36 D6** 41 35N 4 7W
Peñaflor, Spain **37 H5** 37 43N 5 21W
Peñalara, Pico, Spain **36 E7** 40 51N 3 57W
Penalva, Brazil **154 B2** 3 18 S 45 10W
Penamacôr, Portugal **36 E3** 40 10N 7 10W
Penang = Pinang, Malaysia **77 K3** 5 25N 100 15 E
Penápolis, Brazil **159 A6** 21 30 S 50 0W
Peñaranda de Bracamonte, Spain **36 E5** 40 53N 5 13W
Peñarroya-Pueblonuevo, Spain **37 G5** 38 19N 5 16W
Peñas, C. de, Spain **36 B5** 43 42N 5 52W
Penas, G. de, Chile **160 C2** 47 0 S 75 0W
Peñas, Pta., Venezuela **153 A5** 11 17N 62 0W
Peñas de San Pedro, Spain **35 G3** 38 44N 2 0W
Peñas del Chache, Canary Is. **33 E6** 29 6N 13 33W
Peñausende, Spain **36 D5** 41 17N 5 52W
Pench'i = Benxi, China **67 D12** 41 20N 123 48 E
Pend Oreille →, U.S.A. **142 B5** 49 4N 117 37W
Pend Oreille, L., U.S.A. **142 C5** 48 0N 116 30W
Pendálofon, Greece **44 D3** 40 14N 21 12 E
Pendelikón, Greece **45 F5** 38 10N 23 53 E
Pendembu, S. Leone **100 D2** 9 7N 12 14W
Pendências, Brazil **154 C4** 5 15 S 36 43W
Pender B., Australia **112 C3** 16 45 S 122 42 E
Pendleton, Calif., U.S.A. **145 M9** 33 16N 117 23W
Pendleton, Ind., U.S.A. **141 E11** 40 0N 85 45W
Pendleton, Oreg., U.S.A. **142 D4** 45 35N 118 50W
Pendzhikent, U.S.S.R. **55 D3** 39 29N 67 37 E
Penedo, Brazil **154 D4** 10 15 S 36 36W
Penetanguishene, Canada **128 D4** 44 50N 79 55W
Peng Xian, China **68 B4** 31 4N 103 32 E
Pengalengan, Indonesia **71 G12** 7 9 S 107 30 E
Penge, Kasai Or., Zaïre **103 D4** 5 30 S 24 33 E
Penge, Kivu, Zaïre **106 C2** 4 27 S 28 25 E
Penglai, China **67 F11** 37 48N 120 42 E
Pengshui, China **68 C7** 29 17N 108 12 E
Penguin, Australia **114 G4** 41 8 S 146 6 E
Pengxi, China **68 B5** 30 44N 105 45 E
Pengze, China **69 C11** 29 52N 116 32 E
Penhalonga, Zimbabwe **107 F3** 18 52 S 32 40 E
Peniche, Portugal **37 F1** 39 19N 9 22W
Penicuik, U.K. **18 F5** 55 50N 3 14W
Penida, Indonesia **70 F5** 8 45 S 115 30 E
Peninsular Malaysia □, Malaysia **77 L4** 4 0N 102 0 E
Peñíscola, Spain **34 E5** 40 22N 0 24 E
Penitente, Serra dos, Brazil **154 C2** 8 45 S 46 20W
Penmarch, France **22 E2** 47 49N 4 21W
Penmarch, Pte. de, France **22 E2** 47 48N 4 22W
Penn Hills, U.S.A. **136 F5** 40 28N 79 52W
Penn Yan, U.S.A. **136 D7** 42 39N 77 7W
Pennabilli, Italy **39 E9** 43 50N 12 17 E
Pennant, Canada **131 C7** 50 32N 108 14W
Penne, Italy **39 F10** 42 28N 13 56 E
Penner →, India **83 G5** 14 35N 80 10 E
Penneshaw, Australia **116 C2** 35 44 S 137 56 E
Pennine, Alpi, Alps **38 B4** 46 4N 7 30 E
Pennines, U.K. **16 C5** 54 50N 2 20W
Pennington, U.S.A. **144 F5** 39 15N 121 47W
Pennino, Mte., Italy **39 E9** 43 6N 12 54 E
Pennsylvania □, U.S.A. **134 E7** 40 50N 78 0W
Pennville, U.S.A. **141 D11** 40 30N 85 9W
Penny, Canada **130 C4** 53 51N 121 20W
Peno, U.S.S.R. **50 C8** 57 2N 32 49 E
Penola, Australia **116 D4** 37 25 S 140 48 E
Penong, Australia **110 G5** 31 59 S 133 5 E
Penong, S. Austral., Australia **113 F5** 31 56 S 133 1 E
Penonomé, Panama **148 E3** 8 31N 80 21W
Penot, Mt., Vanuatu **121 F5** 16 20 S 167 31 E
Penrith, Australia **117 B9** 33 43 S 150 38 E
Penrith, U.K. **16 C5** 54 40N 2 45W
Pensacola, U.S.A. **135 K2** 30 30N 87 10W
Pensacola Mts., Antarctica **7 E1** 84 0 S 40 0W
Pense, Canada **131 C8** 50 25N 104 59W
Penshurst, Australia **116 D5** 37 49 S 142 20 E
Pentecost = Pentecôte, Vanuatu **121 E6** 15 42 S 168 10 E
Pentecoste, Brazil **154 B4** 3 48 S 39 17W
Pentecôte, Vanuatu **121 E6** 15 42 S 168 10 E
Penticton, Canada **130 D5** 49 30N 119 38W
Pentland, Australia **114 C4** 20 32 S 145 25 E
Pentland Firth, U.K. **18 C5** 58 43N 3 10W
Pentland Hills, U.K. **18 F5** 55 48N 3 25W
Penukonda, India **83 G3** 14 5N 77 38 E
Penylan L., Canada **131 A7** 61 50N 106 20W
Penza, U.S.S.R. **51 E14** 53 15N 45 5 E
Penzance, U.K. **17 G2** 50 7N 5 32W
Penzberg, Germany **27 H7** 47 46N 11 23 E
Penzhino, U.S.S.R. **57 C17** 63 30N 167 55 E
Penzhinskaya Guba, U.S.S.R. **57 C17** 61 30N 163 0 E
Penzlin, Germany **26 B9** 53 32N 13 6 E
Peoria, Ariz., U.S.A. **143 K7** 33 40N 112 15W
Peoria, Ill., U.S.A. **140 D7** 40 40N 89 40W
Peoria Heights, U.S.A. **140 D7** 40 45N 89 35W
Peotone, U.S.A. **141 C9** 41 20N 87 48W
Pepingen, Belgium **21 G4** 50 46N 4 10 E
Pepinster, Belgium **21 G7** 50 34N 5 47 E
Peqini, Albania **44 C1** 41 4N 19 44 E
Pera Hd., Australia **114 A3** 12 55 S 141 37 E
Perabumilih, Indonesia **70 E2** 3 27 S 104 15 E
Perakhóra, Greece **45 F4** 38 2N 22 56 E
Perales de Alfambra, Spain **34 E4** 40 38N 1 0W
Perales del Puerto, Spain **36 E4** 40 10N 6 40W
Peralta, Spain **34 C3** 42 21N 1 49W
Pérama, Kérkira, Greece **32 A3** 39 34N 19 54 E
Pérama, Kriti, Greece **32 D6** 35 20N 24 40 E
Perast, Yugoslavia **42 E3** 42 31N 18 47 E
Percé, Canada **129 C7** 48 31N 64 13W
Perche, France **22 D8** 48 31N 1 1 E
Perche, Collines du, France **22 D7** 48 30N 0 40 E
Percival Lakes, Australia **112 D4** 21 25 S 125 0 E
Percy, France **22 D5** 48 55N 1 11W
Percy, U.S.A. **140 F7** 38 5N 89 41W
Percy Is., Australia **114 C5** 21 39 S 150 16 E
Perdido →, Argentina **160 B3** 42 55 S 67 0W
Perdido, Mte., Spain **24 F4** 42 40N 0 5 E
Perdu, Mt. = Perdido, Mte., Spain **24 F4** 42 40N 0 5 E
Pereira, Colombia **152 C2** 4 49N 75 43W
Pereira Barreto, Brazil **155 F1** 20 38 S 51 7W
Perekerten, Australia **116 C5** 34 55 S 143 40 E
Perekop, U.S.S.R. **52 C5** 46 10N 33 42 E
Perené →, Peru **156 C3** 11 9 S 74 14W
Perenjori, Australia **113 E2** 29 26 S 116 16 E
Pereslavi-Zalesskiy, U.S.S.R. **51 C11** 56 45N 38 50 E
Pereyaslav Khmelnitskiy, U.S.S.R. **50 F7** 50 3N 31 28 E
Pérez, I., Mexico **147 C7** 22 24N 89 42W
Perg, Austria **30 C7** 48 15N 14 38 E
Pergamino, Argentina **158 C3** 33 52 S 60 30W
Pérgine Valsugano, Italy **39 B8** 46 4N 11 15 E
Pérgola, Italy **39 E9** 43 35N 12 50 E
Perham, U.S.A. **138 B7** 46 36N 95 36W
Perhentian, Kepulauan, Malaysia **77 K4** 5 54N 102 42 E
Peri L., Australia **116 A5** 30 45 S 143 35 E
Periam, Romania **46 C1** 46 2N 20 59 E
Péribonca →, Canada **129 C5** 48 45N 72 5W
Péribonca, L., Canada **129 B5** 50 1N 71 10W
Perico, Argentina **158 A2** 24 20 S 65 5W
Pericos, Mexico **146 B3** 25 3N 107 42W
Périers, France **22 C5** 49 11N 1 25W
Périgord, France **24 D4** 45 0N 0 40 E
Périgueux, France **24 C4** 45 10N 0 42 E
Perijá, Sierra de, Colombia **152 B3** 9 30N 73 3W
Peristéra, Greece **45 E5** 39 15N 23 58 E
Peristerona →, Cyprus **32 D12** 35 8N 33 5 E
Perito Moreno, Argentina **160 C2** 46 36 S 70 56W
Peritoró, Brazil **154 B3** 4 20 S 44 18W
Perivol = Dragovishtitsa, Bulgaria **42 E7** 42 22N 22 39 E
Periyakulam, India **83 J3** 10 5N 77 30 E
Periyar →, India **83 J3** 10 15N 76 10 E
Periyar, L., India **83 K3** 9 25N 77 10 E
Perković, Yugoslavia **39 E13** 43 41N 16 10 E
Perlas, Arch. de las, Panama **148 E4** 8 41N 79 7W
Perlas, Punta de, Nic. **148 D3** 12 30N 83 30W
Perleberg, Germany **26 B7** 53 5N 11 50 E
Perlevka, U.S.S.R. **51 F11** 51 48N 38 57 E
Perlez, Yugoslavia **42 B5** 45 11N 20 22 E
Perm, U.S.S.R. **54 C5** 58 0N 56 10 E
Përmeti, Albania **44 D2** 40 15N 20 21 E
Pernambuco = Recife, Brazil **154 C5** 8 0 S 35 0W
Pernambuco □, Brazil **154 C4** 8 0 S 37 0W
Pernatty Lagoon, Australia **116 A2** 31 30 S 137 12 E
Pernik, Bulgaria **42 E8** 42 35N 23 2 E
Peron, C., Australia **113 E1** 25 30 S 113 30 E
Peron Is., Australia **112 B5** 13 9 S 130 4 E
Peron Pen., Australia **113 E1** 26 0 S 113 10 E
Péronne, France **23 C9** 49 55N 2 57 E
Péronnes, Belgium **21 H4** 50 27N 4 9 E
Perosa Argentina, Italy **38 D4** 44 57N 7 11 E
Perow, Canada **130 C3** 54 35N 126 10W
Perpendicular Pt., Australia **115 E5** 31 37 S 152 52 E
Perpignan, France **24 F6** 42 42N 2 53 E
Perris, U.S.A. **145 M9** 33 47N 117 14W
Perros-Guirec, France **22 D3** 48 49N 3 28W
Perry, Fla., U.S.A. **135 K4** 30 9N 83 40W
Perry, Ga., U.S.A. **135 J4** 32 25N 83 41W
Perry, Iowa, U.S.A. **140 C2** 41 48N 94 5W
Perry, Maine, U.S.A. **135 C12** 44 59N 67 20W
Perry, Mich., U.S.A. **141 B12** 42 50N 84 13W
Perry, Mo., U.S.A. **140 E5** 39 26N 91 40W
Perry, Okla., U.S.A. **139 G6** 36 20N 97 20W
Perrysburg, U.S.A. **141 C13** 41 34N 83 38W
Perryton, U.S.A. **139 G4** 36 28N 100 48W
Perryville, U.S.A. **139 G10** 37 42N 89 50W
Perşembe, Turkey **89 C7** 41 5N 37 46 E
Perseverancia, Bolivia **157 C5** 14 44 S 62 48W
Persia = Iran ■, Asia **85 C7** 33 0N 53 0 E
Persian Gulf = Gulf, The, Asia **85 E6** 27 0N 50 0 E
Perstorp, Sweden **15 H7** 56 10N 13 25 E
Pertek, Turkey **89 D8** 38 51N 39 19 E
Perth, Australia **113 F2** 31 57 S 115 52 E
Perth, Canada **128 D4** 44 55N 76 15W
Perth, U.K. **18 E5** 56 24N 3 27W
Perth Amboy, U.S.A. **137 F10** 40 31N 74 16W
Pertuis, France **25 E9** 43 42N 5 30 E
Peru, Ill., U.S.A. **140 C7** 41 18N 89 12W
Peru, Ind., U.S.A. **141 D10** 40 42N 86 5W
Peru ■, S. Amer. **152 D3** 4 0 S 75 0W
Peru-Chile Trench, Pac. Oc. **123 K20** 20 0 S 72 0W
Perúgia, Italy **39 E9** 43 6N 12 24 E
Perušić, Yugoslavia **39 D12** 44 40N 15 22 E
Péruwelz, Belgium **21 G3** 50 31N 3 36 E
Pervomaysk, R.S.F.S.R., U.S.S.R. **51 D13** 54 56N 43 58 E
Pervomaysk, Ukraine S.S.R., U.S.S.R. **52 B4** 48 10N 30 46 E
Pervouralsk, U.S.S.R. **54 C6** 56 55N 59 45 E
Perwez, Belgium **21 G5** 50 38N 4 48 E
Pes, Pta. del, Spain **33 C7** 38 46N 1 26 E
Pésaro, Italy **39 E9** 43 55N 12 53 E
Pescara, Italy **39 F11** 42 28N 14 13 E
Pescara →, Italy **39 F11** 42 28N 14 13 E
Peschanokopskoye, U.S.S.R. **53 C9** 46 14N 41 4 E
Péscia, Italy **38 E7** 43 54N 10 40 E
Pescina, Italy **39 G10** 42 0N 13 39 E
Peseux, Switz. **28 C3** 46 59N 6 53 E
Peshawar, Pakistan **79 B3** 34 2N 71 37 E
Peshkopia, Albania **44 C2** 41 41N 20 25 E
Peshovka, U.S.S.R. **54 B3** 59 4N 52 22 E
Peshtera, Bulgaria **43 E9** 42 2N 24 18 E
Peshtigo, U.S.A. **134 C2** 45 4N 87 46W
Peski, U.S.S.R. **51 F13** 51 14N 42 29 E
Peskovka, U.S.S.R. **51 B18** 59 23N 52 20 E
Pêso da Régua, Portugal **36 D3** 41 10N 7 47W
Pesqueira, Brazil **154 C4** 8 20 S 36 42W
Pessac, France **24 D3** 44 48N 0 37W
Pessoux, Belgium **21 H6** 50 17N 5 11 E
Pest □, Hungary **31 D12** 47 29N 19 5 E
Pestovo, U.S.S.R. **50 B9** 58 33N 35 42 E
Pestravka, U.S.S.R. **51 E16** 52 28N 49 57 E
Péta, Greece **45 E3** 39 10N 21 2 E
Petah Tiqwa, Israel **91 C3** 32 6N 34 53 E
Petalídhion, Greece **45 H3** 36 57N 21 55 E
Petaling Jaya, Malaysia **77 L3** 3 4N 101 42 E
Petaloudhes, Greece **32 C10** 36 18N 28 5 E
Petaluma, U.S.A. **144 G4** 38 13N 122 39W
Petange, Lux. **21 J7** 49 33N 5 55 E
Petatlán, Mexico **146 D4** 17 31N 101 16W
Petauke, Zambia **107 E3** 14 14 S 31 20 E
Petawawa, Canada **128 C4** 45 54N 77 17W
Petegem, Belgium **21 G3** 50 59N 3 32 E
Petén Itzá, L., Guatemala **148 C2** 16 58N 89 50W
Peter I.s Øy, Antarctica **7 C16** 69 0 S 91 0W
Peter Pond L., Canada **131 B7** 55 55N 108 44W
Peterbell, Canada **128 C3** 48 36N 83 21W
Peterborough, Australia **116 B3** 32 58 S 138 51 E
Peterborough, Canada **136 B6** 44 20N 78 20W
Peterborough, U.K. **17 E7** 52 35N 0 14W
Peterborough, U.S.A. **137 D13** 42 55N 71 59W
Peterhead, U.K. **18 D7** 57 30N 1 49W
Petermann Bjerg, Greenland **124 B17** 73 7N 28 25W
Peter's Mine, Guyana **153 B6** 6 14N 59 20W
Petersburg, Alaska, U.S.A. **130 B2** 56 50N 133 0W
Petersburg, Ill., U.S.A. **140 D7** 40 1N 89 51W
Petersburg, Ind., U.S.A. **141 F9** 38 30N 87 15W
Petersburg, Va., U.S.A. **134 G7** 37 17N 77 26W
Petersburg, W. Va., U.S.A. **134 F6** 38 59N 79 10W
Petford, Australia **114 B3** 17 20 S 144 58 E
Petília Policastro, Italy **41 C9** 39 7N 16 48 E
Petit Bois I., U.S.A. **135 K1** 30 16N 88 25W
Petit-Cap, Canada **129 C7** 49 3N 64 30W
Petit Goâve, Haiti **149 C5** 18 27N 72 51W
Petit Lac Manicouagan, Canada **129 B6** 51 25N 67 40W
Petit Saint Bernard, Col du, Italy **38 C3** 45 40N 6 52 E
Petitcodiac, Canada **129 C6** 45 57N 65 11W
Petite Baleine →, Canada **128 A4** 56 0N 76 45W
Petite Saguenay, Canada **129 C5** 48 15N 70 4W
Petitsikapau, L., Canada **129 B6** 54 37N 66 25W
Petlad, India **80 H5** 22 30N 72 45 E
Peto, Mexico **147 C7** 20 10N 88 53W
Petone, N.Z. **118 H3** 41 13 S 174 53 E
Petoskey, U.S.A. **134 C3** 45 22N 84 57W
Petra, Jordan **91 E4** 30 20N 35 22 E
Petra, Spain **33 B10** 39 37N 3 6 E
Petra, Ostrova, U.S.S.R. **6 B13** 76 15N 118 30 E
Petra Velikogo, Zaliv, U.S.S.R. **60 C6** 42 40N 132 0 E
Petralia, Italy **41 E7** 37 49N 14 4 E
Petrel, Spain **35 G4** 38 30N 0 46W
Petreto-Bicchisano, France **25 G12** 41 47N 8 58 E
Petrich, Bulgaria **43 F8** 41 24N 23 13 E
Petrijanec, Yugoslavia **39 B13** 46 23N 16 17 E
Petrikov, U.S.S.R. **50 E6** 52 11N 28 29 E
Petrila, Romania **46 D4** 45 29N 23 29 E
Petrinja, Yugoslavia **39 C13** 45 28N 16 18 E
Petrograd = Leningrad, U.S.S.R. **50 B7** 59 55N 30 20 E
Petrolândia, Brazil **154 C4** 9 5 S 38 20W
Petrolia, Canada **128 D3** 42 54N 82 9W
Petrolina, Brazil **154 C3** 9 24 S 40 30W
Petromagoúla, Greece **45 F5** 38 31N 23 0 E
Petropavlovsk, U.S.S.R. **56 D7** 54 53N 69 13 E
Petropavlovsk-Kamchatskiy, U.S.S.R. **57 D16** 53 3N 158 43 E
Petropavlovskiy = Akhtubinsk, U.S.S.R. **53 B12** 48 13N 46 7 E
Petrópolis, Brazil **155 F3** 22 33 S 43 9W
Petroşeni, Romania **46 D4** 45 28N 23 20 E
Petrova Gora, Yugoslavia **39 C12** 45 15N 15 45 E
Petrovac, Crna Gora, Yugoslavia **42 E3** 42 13N 18 57 E
Petrovac, Srbija, Yugoslavia **42 C6** 44 22N 21 26 E
Petrovaradin, Yugoslavia **42 B4** 45 16N 19 55 E
Petrovsk, U.S.S.R. **51 E14** 52 22N 45 19 E
Petrovsk-Zabaykalskiy, U.S.S.R. **57 D11** 51 20N 108 55 E
Petrovskoye = Svetlograd, U.S.S.R. **53 D10** 45 25N 42 58 E
Petrovskoye, U.S.S.R. **54 E5** 53 37N 56 23 E
Petrozavodsk, U.S.S.R. **48 B5** 61 41N 34 20 E
Petrus Steyn, S. Africa **105 D4** 27 38 S 28 8 E
Petrusburg, S. Africa **104 D4** 29 4 S 25 26 E
Pettitts, Australia **117 C8** 34 56 S 148 10 E
Petukhovka, U.S.S.R. **50 E7** 53 42N 30 54 E
Peumo, Chile **158 C1** 34 21 S 71 12W
Peureulak, Indonesia **70 D1** 4 48N 97 45 E
Peusangan →, Indonesia **74 A1** 5 16N 96 51 E
Pevek, U.S.S.R. **57 C18** 69 41N 171 19 E
Peveragno, Italy **38 D4** 44 20N 7 37 E
Peyrehorade, France **24 E2** 43 34N 1 7W
Peyruis, France **25 D9** 44 1N 5 56 E
Pézenas, France **24 E7** 43 28N 3 24 E
Pezinok, Czech. **31 C10** 48 17N 17 17 E
Pfaffenhofen, Germany **27 G7** 48 31N 11 31 E
Pfäffikon, Switz. **29 B7** 47 13N 8 46 E
Pfarrkirchen, Germany **27 G8** 48 25N 12 57 E
Pfeffenhausen, Germany **27 G7** 48 40N 11 58 E
Pforzheim, Germany **27 G4** 48 53N 8 43 E
Pfullendorf, Germany **27 H5** 47 55N 9 15 E
Pfungstadt, Germany **27 F4** 49 47N 8 36 E
Phaistós, Greece **32 D6** 35 2N 24 50 E
Phala, Botswana **104 C4** 23 45 S 26 50 E
Phalera = Phulera, India **80 F6** 26 52N 75 16 E
Phalodi, India **80 F5** 27 12N 72 24 E
Phalsbourg, France **23 D14** 48 46N 7 15 E
Phan, Thailand **76 C2** 19 28N 99 43 E
Phan Rang, Vietnam **77 G7** 11 34N 109 0 E
Phan Ri = Hoa Da, Vietnam **77 G7** 11 16N 108 40 E
Phan Thiet, Vietnam **77 G7** 11 1N 108 9 E
Phanae, Greece **45 F7** 38 8N 25 57 E
Phanat Nikhom, Thailand **76 F3** 13 27N 101 11 E
Phangan, Ko, Thailand **77 H3** 9 45N 100 0 E
Phangnga, Thailand **77 H2** 8 28N 98 30 E
Phanh Bho Ho Chi Minh, Vietnam **77 G6** 10 58N 106 40 E
Phanom Sarakham, Thailand **76 F3** 13 45N 101 21 E
Pharenda, India **81 F10** 27 5N 83 17 E
Phatthalung, Thailand **77 J3** 7 39N 100 6 E
Phayao, Thailand **76 C2** 19 11N 99 55 E
Phelps, N.Y., U.S.A. **136 D7** 42 57N 77 5W
Phelps, Wis., U.S.A. **138 B10** 46 2N 89 2W
Phelps L., Canada **131 B8** 59 15N 103 15W
Phenix City, U.S.A. **135 J3** 32 30N 84 55W
Phet Buri, Thailand **76 F2** 13 1N 99 55 E
Phetchabun, Thailand **76 D3** 16 25N 101 8 E
Phetchabun, Thiu Khao, Thailand **76 E3** 16 0N 101 20 E
Phetchaburi = Phet Buri, Thailand **76 F2** 13 1N 99 55 E
Phi Phi, Ko, Thailand **77 J2** 7 45N 98 46 E
Phiafay, Laos **76 E6** 14 48N 106 0 E
Phibun Mangsahan, Thailand **76 E5** 15 14N 105 14 E
Phichai, Thailand **76 D3** 17 22N 100 10 E
Phichit, Thailand **76 D3** 16 26N 100 22 E
Philadelphia, Miss., U.S.A. **139 J10** 32 47N 89 5W
Philadelphia, N.Y., U.S.A. **137 B9** 44 9N 75 40W
Philadelphia, Pa., U.S.A. **137 G9** 40 0N 75 10W
Philip, U.S.A. **138 C4** 44 4N 101 42W
Philippeville, Belgium **21 H5** 50 12N 4 33 E
Philippi, Greece **44 C6** 41 1N 24 16 E
Philippi L., Australia **114 C2** 24 20 S 138 55 E
Philippines ■, Asia **71 B6** 12 0N 123 0 E
Philippolis, S. Africa **104 E4** 30 15 S 25 16 E
Philippopolis = Plovdiv, Bulgaria **43 E9** 42 8N 24 44 E
Philipsburg, Mont., U.S.A. **142 C7** 46 20N 113 21W
Philipsburg, Pa., U.S.A. **136 F6** 40 53N 78 10W
Philipstown, S. Africa **104 E3** 30 28 S 24 30 E
Phillip I., Australia **117 E6** 38 30 S 145 12 E
Phillips, Tex., U.S.A. **139 H4** 35 48N 101 17W
Phillips, Wis., U.S.A. **138 C9** 45 41N 90 22W
Phillipsburg, Kans., U.S.A. **138 F5** 39 48N 99 20W
Phillipsburg, Pa., U.S.A. **137 F9** 40 43N 75 12W
Phillott, Australia **115 D4** 27 53 S 145 50 E
Philmont, U.S.A. **137 D11** 42 14N 73 37W
Philomath, U.S.A. **142 D2** 44 28N 123 21W
Phimai, Thailand **76 E4** 15 13N 102 30 E
Phitsanulok, Thailand **76 D3** 16 50N 100 12 E
Phnom Dangrek, Thailand **76 E5** 14 20N 104 0 E
Phnom Penh, Cambodia **77 G5** 11 33N 104 55 E

Playa Blanca 249

Phoenix, *Ariz., U.S.A.* **143 K7** 33 30N 112 10W
Phoenix, *N.Y., U.S.A.* **137 C8** 43 13N 76 18W
Phoenix Is., *Kiribati* **122 H10** 3 30 S 172 0W
Phoenixville, *U.S.A.* **137 F9** 40 12N 75 29W
Phon, *Thailand* **76 E4** 15 49N 102 36 E
Phon Tiou, *Laos* **76 D5** 17 53N 104 37 E
Phong →, *Thailand* **76 D4** 16 23N 102 56 E
Phong Saly, *Laos* **76 B4** 21 42N 102 9 E
Phong Tho, *Vietnam* **76 A4** 22 32N 103 21 E
Phonhong, *Laos* **76 C4** 18 30N 102 25 E
Phonum, *Thailand* **77 H2** 8 49N 98 48 E
Phosphate Hill, *Australia* **114 C2** 21 53 S 139 58 E
Photharam, *Thailand* **76 F2** 13 41N 99 51 E
Phra Chedi Sam Ong, *Thailand* **76 E2** 15 16N 98 23 E
Phra Nakhon Si Ayutthaya, *Thailand* **76 E3** 14 25N 100 30 E
Phra Thong, Ko, *Thailand* **77 H2** 9 5N 98 17 E
Phrae, *Thailand* **76 C3** 18 7N 100 9 E
Phrom Phiram, *Thailand* **76 D3** 17 2N 100 12 E
Phrygia, *Turkey* **88 D4** 38 40N 30 0 E
Phu Dien, *Vietnam* **76 C5** 18 58N 105 31 E
Phu Loi, *Laos* **76 B4** 20 14N 103 14 E
Phu Ly, *Vietnam* **76 B5** 20 35N 105 50 E
Phu Tho, *Vietnam* **76 B5** 21 24N 105 13 E
Phuc Yen, *Vietnam* **76 B5** 21 16N 105 45 E
Phuket, *Thailand* **77 J2** 7 52N 98 22 E
Phuket, Ko, *Thailand* **77 J2** 8 0N 98 22 E
Phulbari, *India* **78 C3** 25 55N 90 2 E
Phulera, *India* **80 F6** 26 52N 75 16 E
Phumiphon, Khuan, *Thailand* **76 D2** 17 15N 98 58 E
Phun Phin, *Thailand* **77 H2** 9 7N 99 12 E
Piacá, *Brazil* **154 C2** 7 42 S 47 18W
Piacenza, *Italy* **38 C6** 45 2N 9 42 E
Piaçubaçu, *Brazil* **154 D4** 10 24 S 36 25W
Piádena, *Italy* **38 C7** 45 8N 10 22 E
Piako →, *N.Z.* **118 D4** 37 12 S 175 30 E
Pialba, *Australia* **115 D5** 25 20 S 152 45 E
Pian Cr. →, *Australia* **115 E4** 30 2 S 148 12 E
Piana, *France* **25 F12** 42 15N 8 34 E
Pianella, *Italy* **39 F11** 42 24N 14 5 E
Piangil, *Australia* **116 C5** 35 5 S 143 20 E
Pianoro, *Italy* **39 D8** 44 20N 11 20 E
Pianosa, *Puglia, Italy* **39 F12** 42 12N 15 44 E
Pianosa, *Toscana, Italy* **38 F7** 42 36N 10 4 E
Piapot, *Canada* **131 D7** 49 59N 109 8W
Piare →, *Italy* **39 C9** 45 32N 12 44 E
Pias, *Portugal* **37 G3** 38 1N 7 29W
Piaseczno, *Poland* **47 C8** 52 5N 21 2 E
Piaski, *Poland* **47 D9** 51 8N 22 52 E
Piastów, *Poland* **47 C7** 52 12N 20 48 E
Piatã, *Brazil* **155 D3** 13 9 S 41 48W
Piatra, *Romania* **46 F6** 43 51N 25 9 E
Piatra Neamţ, *Romania* **46 C7** 46 56N 26 21 E
Piatra Olt, *Romania* **46 E5** 44 22N 24 16 E
Piauí □, *Brazil* **154 C3** 7 0 S 43 0W
Piaui →, *Brazil* **154 C3** 6 38 S 42 42W
Piave →, *Italy* **39 C9** 45 32N 12 44 E
Piazza Ármerina, *Italy* **41 E7** 37 21N 14 20 E
Pibor →, *Sudan* **95 F3** 7 35N 33 0 E
Pibor Post, *Sudan* **95 F3** 6 47N 33 3 E
Pica, *Chile* **156 E4** 20 35 S 69 25W
Picardie, *France* **23 C10** 49 50N 3 0 E
Picardie, Plaine de, *France* **23 C9** 50 0N 2 0 E
Picardy = Picardie, *France* **23 C10** 49 50N 3 0 E
Picayune, *U.S.A.* **139 K10** 30 31N 89 40W
Picerno, *Italy* **41 B8** 40 40N 15 37 E
Pichilemu, *Chile* **158 C1** 34 22 S 72 0W
Pichincha, □, *Ecuador* **152 D2** 0 10 S 78 40W
Pickerel L., *Canada* **128 C1** 48 40N 91 25W
Pickle Lake, *Canada* **128 B1** 51 30N 90 12W
Pico Truncado, *Argentina* **160 C3** 46 40 S 68 0W
Picos, *Brazil* **154 C3** 7 5 S 41 28W
Picos Ancares, Sierra de, *Spain* **36 C4** 42 51N 6 52W
Picota, *Peru* **156 B2** 6 54 S 76 24W
Picquigny, *France* **23 C9** 49 56N 2 10 E
Picton, *Australia* **117 C9** 34 12 S 150 34 E
Picton, *Canada* **128 D4** 44 1N 77 9W
Picton, *N.Z.* **119 B9** 41 18 S 174 3 E
Picton, I., *Chile* **160 E3** 55 2 S 66 57W
Pictou, *Canada* **129 C7** 45 41N 62 42W
Picture Butte, *Canada* **130 D6** 49 55N 112 45W
Picuí, *Brazil* **154 C4** 6 31 S 36 21W
Picún Leufú, *Argentina* **160 A3** 39 30 S 69 5W
Pidurutalagala, *Sri Lanka* **83 L5** 7 10N 80 50 E
Piedecuesta, *Colombia* **152 B3** 6 59N 73 3W
Piedicavallo, *Italy* **38 C4** 45 41N 7 57 E
Piedmont = Piemonte □, *Italy* **38 D4** 45 0N 7 30 E
Piedmont, *U.S.A.* **135 J3** 33 55N 85 39W
Piedmont Plateau, *U.S.A.* **135 J5** 34 0N 81 30W
Piedmonte d'Alife, *Italy* **41 A7** 41 22N 14 22 E
Piedra →, *Spain* **34 D3** 41 18N 1 47W
Piedra del Anguila, *Argentina* **160 B2** 40 2 S 70 4W
Piedra Lais, *Venezuela* **152 C4** 3 10N 65 50W
Piedrabuena, *Spain* **37 G6** 39 0N 4 10W
Piedrahita, *Spain* **36 E5** 40 28N 5 23W
Piedras, R. de las →, *Peru* **156 C4** 12 30 S 69 15W
Piedras Negras, *Mexico* **146 B4** 28 35N 100 35W
Piemonte □, *Italy* **38 D4** 45 0N 7 30 E
Piensk, *Poland* **47 D2** 51 16N 15 2 E
Pier Millan, *Australia* **116 C5** 35 14 S 142 40 E
Pierce, *U.S.A.* **142 C6** 46 29N 115 53W
Piercefield, *U.S.A.* **137 B10** 44 13N 74 35W
Piería □, *Greece* **44 D4** 40 13N 22 25 E
Pierre, *U.S.A.* **138 C4** 44 23N 100 20W
Pierre Bénite, Barrage de la, *France* **25 C8** 45 42N 4 49 E
Pierre-de-Bresse, *France* **25 B9** 46 54N 5 13 E
Pierrefeu-du-Var, *France* **25 E10** 43 13N 6 9 E
Pierrefonds, *France* **23 C9** 49 20N 2 58 E
Pierrefontaine-les-Varans, *France* **23 E13** 47 14N 6 32 E
Pierrefort, *France* **24 D6** 44 55N 2 50 E
Pierrelatte, *France* **25 D8** 44 23N 4 43 E
Pieštany, *Czech.* **31 C10** 48 38N 17 55 E
Piesting →, *Austria* **31 C9** 48 6N 16 40 E
Pieszyce, *Poland* **47 E3** 50 43N 16 33 E
Piet Retief, *S. Africa* **105 D5** 27 1 S 30 50 E
Pietarsaari = Jakobstad, *Finland* **12 E17** 63 40N 22 43 E
Pietermaritzburg, *S. Africa* **105 D5** 29 35 S 30 25 E
Pietersburg, *S. Africa* **105 C4** 23 54 S 29 25 E
Pietraperzia, *Italy* **41 E7** 37 26N 14 8 E
Pietrasanta, *Italy* **38 E7** 43 57N 10 12 E
Pietrosu, *Romania* **46 B6** 47 12N 25 8 E
Pietrosul, *Romania* **46 B5** 47 35N 24 43 E
Pieve di Cadore, *Italy* **39 B9** 46 25N 12 22 E
Pieve di Teco, *Italy* **38 D4** 44 3N 7 54 E
Pievepélago, *Italy* **38 D7** 44 12N 10 35 E
Pigádhia, *Greece* **45 J9** 35 30N 27 12 E
Pigadhítsa, *Greece* **44 E3** 39 59N 21 23 E
Pigeon, *U.S.A.* **134 D4** 43 50N 83 17W
Pigeon I., *India* **83 G2** 14 2N 74 20 E
Piggott, *U.S.A.* **139 G9** 36 20N 90 10W
Pigna, *Italy* **38 E4** 43 57N 7 40 E
Pigüe, *Argentina* **158 D3** 37 36 S 62 25W
Pihani, *India* **81 F9** 27 36N 80 15 E
Pijnacker, *Neths.* **20 D4** 52 1N 4 26 E
Pikalevo, *U.S.S.R.* **50 B9** 59 37N 34 0 E
Pikes Peak, *U.S.A.* **138 F2** 38 50N 105 10W
Piketberg, *S. Africa* **104 E2** 32 55 S 18 40 E
Pikeville, *U.S.A.* **134 G4** 37 30N 82 30W
Pikou, *China* **67 E12** 39 18N 122 22 E
Pikwitonei, *Canada* **131 B9** 55 35N 97 9W
Piła, *Poland* **47 B3** 53 10N 16 48 E
Pila, *Spain* **35 G3** 38 16N 1 11W
Piła □, *Poland* **47 C4** 53 0N 17 0 E
Pilaía, *Greece* **44 D4** 40 32N 22 59 E
Pilani, *India* **80 E6** 28 22N 75 33 E
Pilar, *Brazil* **154 C4** 9 36 S 35 56W
Pilar, *Paraguay* **158 B4** 26 50 S 58 20W
Pilas Group, *Phil.* **71 C6** 6 45N 121 35 E
Pilawa, *Poland* **47 D8** 51 57N 21 32 E
Pilaya →, *Bolivia* **157 E5** 20 55 S 64 4W
Pilcomayo →, *Paraguay* **158 B4** 25 21 S 57 42W
Píli, *Greece* **45 H9** 36 50N 27 15 E
Pilibhit, *India* **81 E8** 28 40N 79 50 E
Pilica →, *Poland* **47 D8** 51 52N 21 17 E
Pilion, *Greece* **44 E5** 39 27N 23 7 E
Pilis, *Hungary* **31 D12** 47 17N 19 35 E
Pilisvörösvár, *Hungary* **31 D11** 47 38N 18 56 E
Pilkhawa, *India* **80 E7** 28 43N 77 42 E
Pillaro, *Ecuador* **152 D2** 1 10 S 78 32W
Pílos, *Greece* **45 H3** 36 55N 21 42 E
Pilot Grove, *U.S.A.* **140 F4** 38 53N 92 55W
Pilot Mound, *Canada* **131 D9** 49 15N 98 54W
Pilot Point, *U.S.A.* **139 J6** 33 26N 97 0W
Pilot Rock, *U.S.A.* **142 D4** 45 30N 118 50W
Pilsen = Plzeň, *Czech.* **30 B6** 49 45N 13 22 E
Pilštanj, *Yugoslavia* **39 B12** 46 8N 15 39 E
Pilzno, *Poland* **31 B14** 49 58N 21 16 E
Pima, *U.S.A.* **143 K9** 32 54N 109 50W
Pimba, *Australia* **116 A2** 31 18 S 136 46 E
Pimenta Bueno, *Brazil* **157 C5** 11 35 S 61 10W
Pimentel, *Peru* **156 B2** 6 45 S 79 55W
Pina, *Spain* **34 D4** 41 29N 0 33W
Pinang, *Malaysia* **77 K3** 5 25N 100 15 E
Pinar, C. del, *Spain* **33 B10** 39 53N 3 12 E
Pinar del Río, *Cuba* **148 B3** 22 26N 83 40W
Pinarbaşi, *Turkey* **88 D7** 38 43N 36 23 E
Pincehely, *Hungary* **31 E11** 46 41N 18 27 E
Pinchang, *China* **68 B6** 31 36N 107 3 E
Pincher Creek, *Canada* **130 D6** 49 30N 113 57W
Pinchi L., *Canada* **130 C4** 54 38N 124 30W
Pinckneyville, *U.S.A.* **140 F7** 38 5N 89 20W
Pîncota, *Romania* **42 A6** 46 20N 21 45 E
Pińczów, *Poland* **47 E7** 50 32N 20 32 E
Pind Dadan Khan, *Pakistan* **80 C5** 32 36N 73 7 E
Pindar, *Australia* **113 E2** 28 30 S 115 47 E
Pindaré →, *Brazil* **154 B3** 3 17 S 44 47W
Pindaré Mirim, *Brazil* **154 B3** 3 37 S 45 21W
Pindi Gheb, *Pakistan* **80 C5** 33 14N 72 21 E
Pindiga, *Nigeria* **101 D7** 9 58N 10 53 E
Pindobal, *Brazil* **154 B2** 3 16 S 48 25W
Pindos Óros, *Greece* **44 E3** 40 0N 21 0 E
Pindus Mts. = Pindos Óros, *Greece* **44 E3** 40 0N 21 0 E
Pine, *U.S.A.* **143 J8** 34 27N 111 30W
Pine →, *Canada* **131 B7** 58 50N 105 38W
Pine, C., *Canada* **129 C9** 46 37N 53 32W
Pine Bluff, *U.S.A.* **139 H9** 34 10N 92 0W
Pine City, *U.S.A.* **138 C8** 45 46N 93 0W
Pine Falls, *Canada* **131 C9** 50 34N 96 11W
Pine Flat Res., *U.S.A.* **144 J7** 36 50N 119 20W
Pine Pass, *Canada* **130 B4** 55 25N 122 42W
Pine Point, *Canada* **130 A6** 60 50N 114 28W
Pine Ridge, *Australia* **117 A9** 31 30 S 150 28 E
Pine Ridge, *U.S.A.* **138 D3** 43 0N 102 35W
Pine River, *Canada* **131 C8** 51 45N 100 30W
Pine River, *U.S.A.* **138 B7** 46 43N 94 24W
Pine Valley, *U.S.A.* **145 N10** 32 50N 116 32W
Pinecrest, *U.S.A.* **144 G6** 38 12N 120 1W
Pinedale, *U.S.A.* **144 J7** 36 50N 119 48W
Pinega →, *U.S.S.R.* **48 B8** 64 8N 46 54 E
Pinehill, *Australia* **114 C4** 23 38 S 146 57 E
Pinerolo, *Italy* **38 D4** 44 47N 7 21 E
Pineto, *Italy* **39 F11** 42 36N 14 4 E
Pinetop, *U.S.A.* **143 J9** 34 10N 109 57W
Pinetown, *S. Africa* **105 D5** 29 48 S 30 54 E
Pinetree, *U.S.A.* **142 E11** 43 42N 105 52W
Pineville, *Ky., U.S.A.* **135 G4** 36 42N 83 42W
Pineville, *La., U.S.A.* **139 K8** 31 22N 92 30W
Piney, *France* **23 D11** 48 22N 4 21 E
Ping →, *Thailand* **76 E3** 15 42N 100 9 E
Pingaring, *Australia* **113 F2** 32 40 S 118 32 E
Pingba, *China* **68 D6** 26 23N 106 12 E
Pingchuan, *China* **68 D3** 27 35N 101 55 E
Pingding, *China* **66 F7** 37 47N 113 38 E
Pingdingshan, *China* **66 H7** 33 43N 113 27 E
Pingdong, *Taiwan* **69 F13** 22 39N 120 30 E
Pingdu, *China* **67 F10** 36 42N 119 59 E
Pingelly, *Australia* **113 F2** 32 32 S 117 5 E
Pingguo, *China* **68 F6** 23 19N 107 36 E
Pinghe, *China* **69 E11** 24 17N 117 21 E
Pinghu, *China* **69 B13** 30 40N 121 2 E
Pingjiang, *China* **69 C9** 28 45N 113 36 E
Pingle, *China* **69 E8** 24 40N 110 40 E
Pingli, *China* **68 A7** 32 27N 109 22 E
Pingliang, *China* **66 G4** 35 35N 106 31 E
Pinglu, *China* **66 E7** 39 31N 112 30 E
Pingluo, *China* **66 E4** 38 52N 106 30 E
Pingnan, *Fujian, China* **69 D12** 26 55N 119 0 E
Pingnan, *Guangxi Zhuangzu, China* **69 F8** 23 33N 110 22 E
Pingquan, *China* **67 D10** 41 1N 118 37 E
Pingrup, *Australia* **113 F2** 33 32 S 118 29 E
Pingtan, *China* **69 E12** 25 31N 119 47 E
Pingtang, *China* **68 E6** 25 49N 107 17 E
Pingwu, *China* **66 H3** 32 25N 104 30 E
Pingxiang, *Guangxi Zhuangzu, China* **68 F6** 22 6N 106 46 E
Pingxiang, *Jiangxi, China* **69 D9** 27 43N 113 48 E
Pingyao, *China* **66 F7** 37 12N 112 10 E
Pingyi, *China* **67 G9** 35 30N 117 35 E
Pingyin, *China* **66 F9** 36 20N 116 25 E
Pingyuan, *Guangdong, China* **69 E10** 24 37N 115 57 E
Pingyuan, *Shandong, China* **66 F9** 37 10N 116 22 E
Pingyuanjie, *China* **68 F4** 23 45N 103 48 E
Pinhal, *Brazil* **159 A6** 22 10 S 46 46W
Pinheiro, *Brazil* **154 B2** 2 31 S 45 5W
Pinhel, *Portugal* **36 E3** 40 50N 7 1W
Pinhuá →, *Brazil* **157 B5** 6 21 S 65 0W
Pini, *Indonesia* **70 D1** 0 10N 98 40 E
Piniós →, *Ilía, Greece* **45 G3** 37 48N 21 20 E
Piniós →, *Trikkala, Greece* **44 E4** 39 55N 22 10 E
Pinjarra, *Australia* **113 F2** 32 37 S 115 52 E
Pink →, *Canada* **131 B8** 56 50N 103 50W
Pinkafeld, *Austria* **31 D9** 47 22N 16 9 E
Pinlebu, *Burma* **78 C5** 24 5N 95 22 E
Pinnacles, *Australia* **113 E3** 28 12 S 120 26 E
Pinnacles, *U.S.A.* **144 J5** 36 33N 121 19W
Pinnaroo, *Australia* **116 C4** 35 17 S 140 53 E
Pinneberg, *Germany* **26 B5** 53 39N 9 48 E
Pino Hachado, Paso, *S. Amer.* **160 A2** 38 39 S 70 54W
Pinon Hills, *U.S.A.* **145 L9** 34 26N 117 39W
Pinos, *Mexico* **146 C4** 22 20N 101 40W
Pinos, Mt., *U.S.A.* **145 L7** 34 49N 119 8W
Pinos Pt., *U.S.A.* **143 H3** 36 38N 121 57W
Pinos Puente, *Spain* **37 H7** 37 15N 3 45W
Pinotepa Nacional, *Mexico* **147 D5** 16 19N 98 3W
Pinrang, *Indonesia* **71 E5** 3 46 S 119 41 E
Pins, I. des, *N. Cal.* **121 V21** 22 37 S 167 30 E
Pinsk, *U.S.S.R.* **50 E5** 52 10N 26 1 E
Pintados, *Chile* **156 E4** 20 35 S 69 40W
Pintumba, *Australia* **113 F5** 31 30 S 132 12 E
Pinyang, *China* **69 D13** 27 42N 120 31 E
Pinyug, *U.S.S.R.* **48 B8** 60 5N 48 0 E
Pinzolo, *Italy* **38 B7** 46 9N 10 45 E
Pio XII, *Brazil* **154 B2** 3 53 S 45 17W
Pioche, *U.S.A.* **143 H6** 38 0N 114 35W
Piombino, *Italy* **38 F7** 42 54N 10 30 E
Piombino, Canale di, *Italy* **38 F7** 42 50N 10 25 E
Pioner, Os., *U.S.S.R.* **57 B10** 79 50N 92 0 E
Pionki, *Poland* **47 D8** 51 29N 21 28 E
Piorini →, *Brazil* **153 D5** 3 23 S 63 30W
Piorini, L., *Brazil* **153 D5** 3 15 S 62 35W
Piotrków Trybunalski, *Poland* **47 D6** 51 23N 19 43 E
Piotrków Trybunalski □, *Poland* **47 D6** 51 30N 19 45 E
Piove di Sacco, *Italy* **39 C9** 45 18N 12 1 E
Pīp, *Iran* **85 E9** 26 45N 60 10 E
Pipar, *India* **80 F5** 26 25N 73 31 E
Piparia, *India* **80 H8** 22 45N 78 23 E
Pipéri, *Greece* **44 E6** 39 20N 24 19 E
Pipestone, *U.S.A.* **138 D6** 44 0N 96 20W
Pipestone →, *Canada* **128 B2** 52 53N 89 23W
Pipestone Cr. →, *Canada* **131 D8** 49 38N 100 15W
Pipiriki, *N.Z.* **118 F4** 39 28 S 175 5 E
Pipmuacan, Rés., *Canada* **129 C5** 49 45N 70 30W
Pippingarra, *Australia* **112 D2** 20 27 S 118 42 E
Pipriac, *France* **22 E5** 47 49N 1 58W
Piqua, *U.S.A.* **141 D12** 40 10N 84 10W
Piquet Carneiro, *Brazil* **154 C4** 5 48 S 39 25W
Piquiri →, *Brazil* **159 A5** 24 3 S 54 14W
Pīr Sohrāb, *Iran* **85 E9** 25 44N 60 54 E
Piracanjuba, *Brazil* **155 E2** 17 18 S 49 1W
Piracicaba, *Brazil* **159 A6** 22 45 S 47 40W
Piracuruca, *Brazil* **154 B3** 3 50 S 41 50W
Piræus = Piraiévs, *Greece* **45 G5** 37 57N 23 42 E
Piraiévs, *Greece* **45 G5** 37 57N 23 42 E
Piraiévs □, *Greece* **45 H5** 37 0N 23 30 E
Piráino, *Italy* **41 D7** 38 10N 14 52 E
Pirajuí, *Brazil* **159 A6** 21 59 S 49 29W
Piran, *Yugoslavia* **39 C10** 45 31N 13 33 E
Pirané, *Argentina* **158 B4** 25 42 S 59 6W
Piranhas, *Brazil* **154 C4** 9 27 S 37 46W
Pirano = Piran, *Yugoslavia* **39 C10** 45 31N 13 33 E
Pirapemas, *Brazil* **154 B3** 3 43 S 44 14W
Pirapora, *Brazil* **155 E3** 17 20 S 44 56W
Piray →, *Bolivia* **157 D5** 16 32 S 63 45W
Pirdop, *Bulgaria* **43 E9** 42 40N 24 10 E
Pires do Rio, *Brazil* **155 E2** 17 18 S 48 17W
Pirganj, *Bangla.* **78 C2** 25 51N 88 24 E
Pírgos, *Ilía, Greece* **45 G3** 37 40N 21 27 E
Pírgos, *Messinia, Greece* **45 H4** 36 50N 22 16 E
Pirgovo, *Bulgaria* **43 D10** 43 44N 25 43 E
Piriac-sur-Mer, *France* **22 E4** 47 22N 2 33W
Piribebuy, *Paraguay* **158 B4** 25 26 S 57 2W
Pirin Planina, *Bulgaria* **43 F8** 41 40N 23 30 E
Pirineos, *Spain* **34 C6** 42 40N 1 0 E
Piripiri, *Brazil* **154 B3** 4 15 S 41 46W
Piritu, *Venezuela* **152 B4** 9 23N 69 12W
Pirmasens, *Germany* **27 F3** 49 12N 7 30 E
Pirna, *Germany* **26 E9** 50 57N 13 57 E
Pirojpur, *Bangla.* **78 D3** 22 35N 90 1 E
Pirot, *Yugoslavia* **42 D7** 43 9N 22 39 E
Piru, *Indonesia* **71 E7** 3 4 S 128 12 E
Piru, *U.S.A.* **145 L8** 34 25N 118 48W
Piryatin, *U.S.S.R.* **50 F8** 50 15N 32 25 E
Piryí, *Greece* **45 F7** 38 13N 25 59 E
Pisa, *Italy* **38 E7** 43 43N 10 23 E
Pisa →, *Poland* **47 B8** 53 14N 21 52 E
Pisa Ra., *N.Z.* **119 E4** 44 52 S 169 12 E
Pisac, *Peru* **156 C3** 13 25 S 71 50W
Pisagua, *Chile* **156 D3** 19 40 S 70 15W
Pisarovina, *Yugoslavia* **39 C12** 45 35N 15 50 E
Pisciotta, *Italy* **41 B8** 40 7N 15 12 E
Pisco, *Peru* **156 C2** 13 50 S 76 12W
Piscu, *Romania* **46 D8** 45 30N 27 43 E
Písek, *Czech.* **30 B7** 49 19N 14 10 E
Pishan, *China* **64 C2** 37 30N 78 33 E
Pishin Lora →, *Pakistan* **80 E1** 29 9N 64 5 E
Pisidia, *Turkey* **88 E4** 37 30N 31 40 E
Pising, *Indonesia* **71 F6** 5 8 S 121 53 E
Pismo Beach, *U.S.A.* **145 K6** 35 9N 120 38W
Pissos, *France* **24 D3** 44 19N 0 49W
Pissouri, *Cyprus* **32 E11** 34 40N 32 42 E
Pisticci, *Italy* **41 B9** 40 24N 16 33 E
Pistóia, *Italy* **38 E7** 43 57N 10 53 E
Pistol B., *Canada* **131 A10** 62 25N 92 37W
Pisuerga →, *Spain* **36 D6** 41 33N 4 52W
Pisz, *Poland* **47 B8** 53 38N 21 49 E
Pitalito, *Colombia* **152 C2** 1 51N 76 2W
Pitanga, *Brazil* **155 F1** 24 46 S 51 44W
Pitangui, *Brazil* **155 E3** 19 40 S 44 54W
Pitarpunga, L., *Australia* **116 C5** 34 24 S 143 30 E
Pitcairn I., *Pac. Oc.* **123 K14** 25 5 S 130 5W
Pite älv →, *Sweden* **12 D16** 65 20N 21 25 E
Piteå, *Sweden* **12 D16** 65 20N 21 25 E
Piterka, *U.S.S.R.* **51 F15** 50 41N 47 29 E
Piteşti, *Romania* **46 E5** 44 52N 24 54 E
Pithapuram, *India* **82 F6** 17 10N 82 15 E
Pithara, *Australia* **113 F2** 30 20 S 116 35 E
Píthion, *Greece* **44 C8** 41 24N 26 40 E
Pithiviers, *France* **23 D9** 48 10N 2 13 E
Pitigliano, *Italy* **39 F8** 42 38N 11 40 E
Pitlochry, *U.K.* **18 E5** 56 43N 3 43W
Pitrufquén, *Chile* **160 A2** 38 59 S 72 39W
Pitsilia □, *Cyprus* **32 E12** 34 55N 33 0 E
Pitt I., *Canada* **130 C3** 53 30N 129 50W
Pittem, *Belgium* **21 F2** 51 1N 3 13 E
Pittsburg, *Kans., U.S.A.* **139 G7** 37 21N 94 43W
Pittsburg, *Tex., U.S.A.* **139 J7** 32 59N 94 58W
Pittsburgh, *U.S.A.* **136 F5** 40 25N 79 55W
Pittsfield, *Ill., U.S.A.* **140 E6** 39 35N 90 46W
Pittsfield, *Mass., U.S.A.* **137 D11** 42 28N 73 17W
Pittsfield, *N.H., U.S.A.* **137 C13** 43 17N 71 18W
Pittston, *U.S.A.* **137 E9** 41 19N 75 50W
Pittsworth, *Australia* **115 D5** 27 41 S 151 37 E
Pituri →, *Australia* **114 C2** 22 35 S 138 30 E
Piuí, *Brazil* **155 F2** 20 28 S 45 58W
Pium, *Brazil* **154 D2** 10 27 S 49 11W
Piura, *Peru* **156 B1** 5 15 S 80 38W
Piura □, *Peru* **156 B2** 5 10 S 80 0W
Piva →, *Yugoslavia* **42 D3** 43 20N 18 50 E
Pivijay, *Colombia* **152 A3** 10 28N 74 37W
Piwniczna, *Poland* **31 B13** 49 27N 20 42 E
Pixley, *U.S.A.* **144 K7** 35 58N 119 18W
Piyai, *Greece* **44 E3** 39 17N 21 25 E
Pizarro, *Colombia* **152 C2** 4 58N 77 22W
Pizol, *Switz.* **29 C8** 46 57N 9 23 E
Pizzo, *Italy* **41 D9** 38 44N 16 10 E
Placentia, *Canada* **129 C9** 47 20N 54 0W
Placentia B., *Canada* **129 C9** 47 0N 54 40W
Placerville, *U.S.A.* **144 G6** 38 47N 120 51W
Placetas, *Cuba* **148 B4** 22 15N 79 44W
Plačkovica, *Yugoslavia* **42 F7** 41 45N 22 30 E
Plaffeien, *Switz.* **28 C4** 46 45N 7 17 E
Plain Dealing, *U.S.A.* **139 J8** 32 56N 93 41W
Plainfield, *Ill., U.S.A.* **141 C8** 41 37N 88 12W
Plainfield, *N.J., U.S.A.* **137 F10** 40 37N 74 28W
Plains, *Kans., U.S.A.* **139 G4** 37 20N 100 35W
Plains, *Mont., U.S.A.* **142 C6** 47 27N 114 57W
Plains, *Tex., U.S.A.* **139 J3** 33 11N 102 50W
Plainview, *Nebr., U.S.A.* **138 D6** 42 25N 97 48W
Plainview, *Tex., U.S.A.* **139 H4** 34 10N 101 40W
Plainville, *U.S.A.* **138 F5** 39 18N 99 19W
Plainwell, *U.S.A.* **134 D3** 42 28N 85 40W
Plaisance, *France* **24 E4** 43 36N 0 3 E
Pláka, *Greece* **44 E7** 40 0N 25 24 E
Pláka, Ákra, *Greece* **32 D8** 35 11N 26 19 E
Plakenska Planina, *Yugoslavia* **42 F6** 41 14N 21 2 E
Plakhino, *U.S.S.R.* **56 C9** 67 45N 86 5 E
Planá, *Czech.* **30 B5** 49 50N 12 44 E
Plana Cays, *Bahamas* **149 B5** 22 38N 73 30W
Planada, *U.S.A.* **144 H6** 37 18N 120 19W
Plancoët, *France* **22 D4** 48 32N 2 13W
Plandište, *Yugoslavia* **42 B6** 45 16N 21 10 E
Planeta Rica, *Colombia* **152 B2** 8 25N 75 36W
Planina, *Slovenija, Yugoslavia* **39 B12** 46 10N 15 20 E
Planina, *Slovenija, Yugoslavia* **39 C11** 45 47N 14 19 E
Plankinton, *U.S.A.* **138 D5** 43 45N 98 27W
Plano, *U.S.A.* **139 J6** 33 0N 96 45W
Plant City, *U.S.A.* **135 M4** 28 0N 82 8W
Plaquemine, *U.S.A.* **139 K9** 30 20N 91 15W
Plasencia, *Spain* **36 E4** 40 3N 6 8W
Plaški, *Yugoslavia* **39 C12** 45 4N 15 22 E
Plast, *U.S.S.R.* **54 D7** 54 22N 60 50 E
Plaster City, *U.S.A.* **145 N11** 32 47N 115 51W
Plaster Rock, *Canada* **129 C6** 46 53N 67 22W
Plastun, *U.S.S.R.* **60 B8** 44 45N 136 19 E
Plata, Río de la, *S. Amer.* **158 C4** 34 45 S 57 30W
Platani →, *Italy* **40 E6** 37 23N 13 16 E
Plátanos, *Greece* **32 D5** 35 28N 23 33 E
Plateau □, *Nigeria* **101 D6** 8 0N 8 30 E
Plateau du Coteau du Missouri, *U.S.A.* **138 B4** 47 9N 101 5W
Platí, Ákra, *Greece* **44 D6** 40 27N 24 0 E
Plato, *Colombia* **152 B3** 9 47N 74 47W
Platta, Piz, *Switz.* **29 D9** 46 28N 9 35 E
Platte, *U.S.A.* **138 D5** 43 28N 98 50W
Platte →, *U.S.A.* **140 E2** 39 16N 94 50W
Platte City, *U.S.A.* **140 E2** 39 22N 94 47W
Platteville, *Colo., U.S.A.* **138 E2** 40 18N 104 47W
Platteville, *Wis., U.S.A.* **140 B6** 42 44N 90 29W
Plattling, *Germany* **27 G8** 48 46N 12 53 E
Plattsburg, *Miss., U.S.A.* **140 E2** 39 34N 94 27W
Plattsburg, *N.Y., U.S.A.* **137 B11** 44 41N 73 30W
Plattsmouth, *U.S.A.* **138 E7** 41 0N 95 50W
Plau, *Germany* **26 B8** 53 27N 12 16 E
Plauen, *Germany* **26 E8** 50 29N 12 9 E
Plav, *Yugoslavia* **42 E4** 42 38N 19 57 E
Plavinas, *U.S.S.R.* **50 C4** 56 35N 25 46 E
Plavnica, *Yugoslavia* **42 E4** 42 20N 19 13 E
Plavsk, *U.S.S.R.* **51 E10** 53 40N 37 18 E
Playa Blanca, *Canary Is.* **33 F6** 28 55N 13 37W

Radnevo 253

Puyehue, Chile 160 B2 40 40 S 72 37W
Puylaurens, France 24 E6 43 35N 2 0 E
Puyo, Ecuador 152 D2 1 28 S 77 59W
Puysegur Pt., N.Z. 119 G1 46 9 S 166 37 E
Pūzeh Rīg, Iran 85 E8 27 20N 58 40 E
Pwani □, Tanzania 106 D4 7 0 S 39 0 E
Pweto, Zaïre 107 D2 8 25 S 28 51 E
Pwinbyu, Burma 78 E5 20 23N 94 40 E
Pwllheli, U.K. 16 E3 52 54N 4 26W
Pya-ozero, U.S.S.R. 48 A5 66 5N 30 58 E
Pyana →, U.S.S.R. 51 D15 55 30N 46 0 E
Pyandzh, U.S.S.R. 55 E4 37 14N 69 6 E
Pyandzh →, Afghan. 79 A2 37 15N 67 15 E
Pyandzh →, U.S.S.R. 55 E4 37 6N 68 20 E
Pyapon, Burma 78 G5 16 20N 95 40 E
Pyasina →, U.S.S.R. 57 B9 73 30N 87 0 E
Pyatigorsk, U.S.S.R. 53 D10 44 2N 43 6 E
Pyatikhatki, U.S.S.R. 52 B5 48 28N 33 38 E
Pyaye, Burma 78 F5 19 12N 95 10 E
Pydna, Greece 44 D4 40 20N 22 34 E
Pyè, Burma 78 F5 18 49N 95 13 E
Pyinbauk, Burma 78 F5 19 10N 95 12 E
Pyinmana, Burma 78 F6 19 45N 96 12 E
Pyla, C., Cyprus 32 E12 34 56N 33 51 E
Pyŏktong, N. Korea 67 D13 40 50N 125 50 E
Pyŏnggang, N. Korea 67 E14 38 24N 127 17 E
Pyŏngtaek, S. Korea 67 F14 37 1N 127 4 E
P'yŏngyang, N. Korea 67 E13 39 0N 125 30 E
Pyote, U.S.A. 139 K3 31 34N 103 5W
Pyramid L., U.S.A. 142 G4 40 0N 119 30W
Pyramid Pk., U.S.A. 145 J10 36 25N 116 37W
Pyramids, Egypt 94 J7 29 58N 31 9 E
Pyrénées, Europe 24 F4 42 45N 0 18 E
Pyrénées-Atlantiques □, France 24 E3 43 10N 0 50W
Pyrénées-Orientales □, France 24 F6 42 35N 2 26 E
Pyrzyce, Poland 47 B1 53 10N 14 55 E
Pyshchug, U.S.S.R. 51 B14 58 57N 45 47 E
Pytalovo, U.S.S.R. 50 C5 57 5N 27 55 E
Pyttegga, Norway 14 B1 62 13N 7 42 E
Pyu, Burma 78 F6 18 30N 96 28 E
Pyzdry, Poland 47 C4 52 11N 17 42 E

Q

Qaanaaq = Thule, Greenland 6 B4 77 40N 69 0W
Qabr Hūd, Yemen 87 C5 16 9N 49 34 E
Qachasnek, S. Africa 105 E4 30 6 S 28 42 E
Qādib, Yemen 87 D6 12 37N 53 57 E
Qa'el Jafr, Jordan 91 E5 30 20N 36 25 E
Qa'emābād, Iran 85 D9 31 44N 60 2 E
Qā'emshahr, Iran 85 B7 36 30N 52 53 E
Qagan Nur, China 66 C8 43 30N 114 55 E
Qahar Youyi Zhongqi, China 66 D7 41 12N 112 40 E
Qahremānshahr = Bākhtarān, Iran 84 C5 34 23N 47 0 E
Qaidam Pendi, China 64 C4 37 0N 95 0 E
Qajarīyeh, Iran 85 D6 31 1N 48 22 E
Qala, Ras il, Malta 32 C1 36 1N 14 20 E
Qala-i-Jadid, Afghan. 80 D2 31 1N 66 25 E
Qala Yangi, Afghan. 80 B2 34 20N 66 30 E
Qalācheh, Afghan. 79 B2 35 30N 67 43 E
Qalansīyah, Yemen 87 D6 12 41N 53 29 E
Qalāt, Afghan. 79 B2 32 15N 66 58 E
Qal'at al Akhḍar, Si. Arabia 84 E3 28 0N 37 10 E
Qal'at Bīshah, Si. Arabia 86 C3 20 0N 42 36 E
Qal'at Sukkar, Iraq 84 D5 31 51N 46 5 E
Qal'eh Darreh, Iran 84 B5 38 47N 47 2 E
Qal'eh-ye Best, Afghan. 79 C2 31 30N 64 21 E
Qal'eh-ye Now, Afghan. 79 B1 35 0N 63 5 E
Qal'eh-ye Panjeh, Afghan. 79 A4 37 0N 72 35 E
Qal'eh-ye Sarkari, Afghan. 79 B2 35 54N 67 17 E
Qal'eh-ye Valī, Afghan. 79 B1 35 46N 63 45 E
Qalyûb, Egypt 94 H7 30 12N 31 11 E
Qamar, Ghubbat al, Yemen 87 C6 16 20N 52 30 E
Qamar, Jabal al, Oman 87 C6 16 48N 53 15 E
Qamdo, China 68 B1 31 15N 97 6 E
Qamruddin Karez, Pakistan 79 C3 31 45N 68 20 E
Qandahār, Afghan. 79 C2 31 32N 65 30 E
Qandahār □, Afghan. 79 C2 31 0N 65 0 E
Qapān, Iran 85 B7 37 40N 55 47 E
Qaqortoq = Julianehåb, Greenland 6 C5 60 43N 46 0W
Qâra, Egypt 94 B2 29 38N 26 30 E
Qarā', Jabal al, Oman 87 C6 17 15N 54 15 E
Qara Qash →, India 81 B8 35 0N 78 30 E
Qārah, Si. Arabia 84 D4 29 55N 40 3 E
Qarāvol, Afghan. 79 A3 37 14N 68 46 E
Qardud, Sudan 95 E2 10 20N 29 56 E
Qareh →, Iran 84 B5 39 25N 47 22 E
Qareh Tekān, Iran 85 B6 36 38N 49 29 E
Qarqan He →, China 64 C3 39 30N 88 30 E
Qarrasa, Sudan 95 E3 14 38N 32 5 E
Qartabā, Lebanon 91 A4 34 4N 35 50 E
Qaryat al Gharab, Iraq 84 D5 31 27N 44 48 E
Qaryat al 'Ulyā, Si. Arabia 84 E5 27 33N 47 42 E
Qasr 'Amra, Jordan 84 D3 31 48N 36 35 E
Qaṣr Bū Hadi, Libya 96 B3 31 1N 16 45 E
Qaṣr-e Qand, Iran 85 E9 26 15N 60 45 E
Qasr Farâfra, Egypt 94 B2 27 0N 28 1 E
Qat Lesh, Afghan. 79 B2 34 40N 66 18 E
Qa'ṭabah, Yemen 86 D4 13 51N 44 42 E
Qatanā, Syria 91 B5 33 26N 36 4 E
Qaṭānan, Ra's, Yemen 87 D6 12 21N 53 33 E
Qatar ■, Asia 85 E6 25 30N 51 15 E
Qatlīsh, Iran 85 B8 37 50N 57 19 E
Qattâra, Egypt 94 A2 30 12N 27 3 E
Qattâra, Munkhafed el, Egypt 94 B2 29 30N 27 30 E
Qattâra Depression = Qattâra, Munkhafed el, Egypt 94 B2 29 30N 27 30 E
Qawām al Ḥamzah, Iraq 84 D5 31 43N 44 58 E
Qāyen, Iran 85 C8 33 40N 59 10 E
Qazvin, Iran 85 B6 36 15N 50 0 E
Qena, Egypt 94 B3 26 10N 32 43 E
Qena, Wadi →, Egypt 94 B3 26 12N 32 44 E
Qeqertarsuag = Disko, Greenland 6 C5 69 45N 53 30W
Qeqertarsuaq = Godhavn, Greenland 6 C5 69 15N 53 38W
Qeshlāq, Iran 84 C5 34 55N 46 28 E
Qeshm, Iran 85 E8 26 55N 56 10 E
Qezi'ot, Israel 91 E3 30 52N 34 26 E
Qi Xian, China 66 G8 34 40N 114 48 E
Qian Gorlos, China 67 B13 45 5N 124 42 E
Qian Xian, China 66 G5 34 31N 108 15 E
Qiancheng, China 68 D7 27 12N 109 50 E
Qianjiang, Guangxi Zhuangzu, China 68 F7 23 38N 108 58 E
Qianjiang, Hubei, China 69 B9 30 24N 112 55 E
Qianjiang, Sichuan, China 68 C7 29 33N 108 47 E
Qianshan, China 69 B11 30 37N 116 35 E
Qianwei, China 68 C4 29 13N 103 56 E
Qianxi, China 68 D6 27 3N 106 3 E
Qianyang, Hunan, China 69 D8 27 18N 110 10 E
Qianyang, Shaanxi, China 66 G4 34 40N 107 8 E
Qianyang, Zhejiang, China 69 B12 30 11N 119 25 E
Qiaojia, China 68 D4 26 56N 102 58 E
Qibā', Si. Arabia 84 E5 27 24N 44 20 E
Qichun, China 69 B10 30 18N 115 25 E
Qidong, Hunan, China 69 D9 26 49N 112 7 E
Qidong, Jiangsu, China 69 B13 31 48N 121 38 E
Qijiang, China 68 C6 28 57N 106 35 E
Qila Saifullāh, Pakistan 79 C3 30 45N 68 17 E
Qilian Shan, China 64 C4 38 30N 96 0 E
Qimen, China 69 C11 29 50N 117 42 E
Qin He →, China 66 G7 35 1N 113 22 E
Qin Jiang →, China 69 D10 26 15N 115 55 E
Qin Ling = Qinling Shandi, China 66 H5 33 50N 108 10 E
Qināb, W. →, Yemen 87 C5 17 55N 49 59 E
Qin'an, China 66 G3 34 48N 105 40 E
Qing Xian, China 66 E9 38 35N 116 45 E
Qingcheng, China 67 F9 37 15N 117 40 E
Qingdao, China 67 F11 36 5N 120 20 E
Qingfeng, China 66 G8 35 52N 115 8 E
Qinghai □, China 64 C4 36 0N 98 0 E
Qinghai Hu, China 64 C5 36 40N 100 10 E
Qinghecheng, China 67 D13 41 15N 124 30 E
Qinghemen, China 67 D11 41 48N 121 25 E
Qingjian, China 66 F6 37 8N 110 8 E
Qingjiang, Jiangsu, China 67 H10 33 30N 119 2 E
Qingjiang, Jiangxi, China 69 C10 28 4N 115 29 E
Qingliu, China 69 D11 26 11N 116 48 E
Qinglong, China 68 E5 25 49N 105 12 E
Qingping, China 68 D6 26 39N 107 47 E
Qingpu, China 69 B13 31 10N 121 6 E
Qingshui, China 66 G4 34 48N 106 8 E
Qingshuihe, China 66 E6 39 55N 111 35 E
Qingtian, China 69 C13 28 12N 120 15 E
Qingtongxia Shuiku, China 66 F3 37 50N 105 58 E
Qingxi, China 68 D7 27 8N 108 43 E
Qingxu, China 66 F7 37 34N 112 22 E
Qingyang, Anhui, China 69 B11 30 38N 117 50 E
Qingyang, Gansu, China 66 F4 36 2N 107 55 E
Qingyi Jiang →, China 68 C4 29 32N 103 44 E
Qingyuan, Guangdong, China 69 F9 23 40N 112 59 E
Qingyuan, Liaoning, China 67 C13 42 10N 124 55 E
Qingyuan, Zhejiang, China 69 D12 27 36N 119 3 E
Qingyun, China 67 F9 37 45N 117 20 E
Qingzhen, China 68 D6 26 31N 106 25 E
Qinhuangdao, China 67 E10 39 56N 119 30 E
Qinling Shandi, China 66 H5 33 50N 108 10 E
Qinshui, China 66 G7 35 40N 112 8 E
Qinyang, China 66 G7 35 7N 112 57 E
Qinyuan, China 66 F7 36 29N 112 20 E
Qinzhou, China 68 G7 21 58N 108 38 E
Qionghai, China 76 C8 19 15N 110 26 E
Qionglai, China 68 B4 30 25N 103 31 E
Qionglai Shan, China 68 B4 31 0N 102 30 E
Qiongshan, China 76 C8 19 51N 110 26 E
Qiongzhou Haixia, China 76 B8 20 10N 110 15 E
Qiqihar, China 65 B7 47 26N 124 0 E
Qiraîya, W. →, Egypt 91 E3 30 27N 34 0 E
Qiryat Ata, Israel 91 C4 32 47N 35 6 E
Qiryat Gat, Israel 91 D3 31 32N 34 46 E
Qiryat Mal'akhi, Israel 91 D3 31 44N 34 44 E
Qiryat Shemona, Israel 91 B4 33 13N 35 35 E
Qiryat Yam, Israel 91 C4 32 51N 35 4 E
Qishan, China 66 G4 34 25N 107 38 E
Qishan, Taiwan 69 F13 22 52N 120 25 E
Qishn, Yemen 87 D5 15 26N 51 40 E
Qitai, China 64 B3 44 2N 89 35 E
Qitbīt, W. →, Oman 87 C6 19 15N 54 23 E
Qiubei, China 68 E5 24 2N 104 12 E
Qixia, China 67 F11 37 17N 120 52 E
Qiyang, China 69 D8 26 35N 111 50 E
Qojūr, Iran 84 B5 36 12N 47 55 E
Qom, Iran 85 C6 34 40N 51 0 E
Qomsheh, Iran 85 D6 32 0N 51 55 E
Qondūz, Afghan. 79 A3 36 50N 68 50 E
Qondūz □, Afghan. 79 A3 36 50N 68 50 E
Qu Jiang →, China 68 B6 30 1N 106 24 E
Qu Xian, Sichuan, China 68 B6 30 48N 106 58 E
Qu Xian, Zhejiang, China 69 C12 28 57N 118 54 E
Quackenbrück, Germany 26 C3 52 40N 7 59 E
Quairading, Australia 113 F2 32 0 S 117 21 E
Quakertown, U.S.A. 137 F9 40 27N 75 20W
Qualeup, Australia 113 F2 33 48 S 116 48 E
Quambatook, Australia 116 C5 35 49 S 143 34 E
Quambone, Australia 117 A7 30 57 S 147 53 E
Quamby, Australia 114 C3 20 22 S 140 17 E
Quan Long, Vietnam 77 H5 9 7N 105 8 E
Quanah, U.S.A. 139 H5 34 20N 99 45W
Quandialla, Australia 117 C7 34 1 S 147 47 E
Quang Ngai, Vietnam 76 E7 15 13N 108 58 E
Quang Yen, Vietnam 76 B6 20 56N 106 52 E
Quannan, China 69 E10 24 45N 114 33 E
Quantock Hills, U.K. 17 F4 51 8N 3 10W
Quanzhou, Fujian, China 69 E12 24 55N 118 34 E
Quanzhou, Guangxi Zhuangzu, China 69 E8 25 57N 111 5 E
Quaraí, Brazil 158 C4 30 15 S 56 20W
Quarré-les-Tombes, France 23 E11 47 21N 4 0 E
Quartu Sant' Elena, Italy 40 C2 39 15N 9 10 E
Quartzsite, U.S.A. 145 M12 33 44N 114 16W
Quatsino, Canada 130 C3 50 30N 127 40W
Quatsino Sd., Canada 130 C3 50 25N 127 58W
Qūchān, Iran 85 B8 37 10N 58 27 E
Queanbeyan, Australia 117 C8 35 17 S 149 14 E
Québec, Canada 129 C5 46 52N 71 13W
Québec □, Canada 129 C6 50 0N 70 0W
Quedlinburg, Germany 26 D7 51 47N 11 9 E
Queen Alexandra Ra., Antarctica 7 E11 85 0 S 170 0 E
Queen Charlotte, Canada 130 C2 53 15N 132 2W
Queen Charlotte Bay, Falk. Is. 160 D4 51 50 S 60 40W
Queen Charlotte Is., Canada 130 C2 53 20N 132 10W
Queen Charlotte Sd., N.Z. 119 B9 41 10 S 174 15 E
Queen Charlotte Str., Canada 130 C3 51 0N 128 0W
Queen City, U.S.A. 140 D4 40 25N 92 34W
Queen Elizabeth Is., Canada 124 B10 76 0N 95 0W
Queen Elizabeth Nat. Park, Uganda 106 C3 0 0 30 0 E
Queen Mary Land, Antarctica 7 D7 70 0 S 95 0 E
Queen Maud G., Canada 126 B9 68 15N 102 30W
Queen Maud Land, Antarctica 7 D3 72 30 S 12 0 E
Queen Maud Mts., Antarctica 7 E13 86 0 S 160 0W
Queens Chan., Australia 112 C4 15 0 S 129 30 E
Queenscliff, Australia 115 F3 38 16 S 144 39 E
Queensland □, Australia 114 C3 22 0 S 142 0 E
Queenstown, Australia 114 G4 42 4 S 145 35 E
Queenstown, N.Z. 119 F3 45 1 S 168 40 E
Queenstown, S. Africa 104 E4 31 52 S 26 52 E
Queets, U.S.A. 144 C2 47 32N 124 20W
Queguay Grande →, Uruguay 158 C4 32 9 S 58 9W
Queimadas, Brazil 154 D4 11 0 S 39 38W
Queiros, C., Vanuatu 121 D5 14 55 S 167 1 E
Quela, Angola 103 D3 9 10 S 16 56 E
Quelimane, Mozam. 107 F4 17 53 S 36 58 E
Quelpart = Cheju Do, S. Korea 67 H14 33 29N 126 34 E
Quemado, N. Mex., U.S.A. 143 J9 34 17N 108 28W
Quemado, Tex., U.S.A. 139 L4 28 58N 100 35W
Quemú-Quemú, Argentina 158 D3 36 3 S 63 36W
Quequén, Argentina 158 D4 38 30 S 58 30W
Querco, Peru 156 C3 13 50 S 74 52W
Querétaro, Mexico 146 C4 20 40N 100 23W
Querétaro □, Mexico 146 C5 20 30N 100 0W
Querfurt, Germany 26 D7 51 22N 11 33 E
Quesada, Spain 35 H1 37 51N 3 4W
Queshan, China 66 H8 32 55N 114 2 E
Quesnel, Canada 130 C4 53 0N 122 30W
Quesnel →, Canada 130 C4 52 58N 122 29W
Quesnel L., Canada 130 C4 52 30N 121 20W
Questa, U.S.A. 143 H11 36 45N 105 35W
Questembert, France 22 E4 47 40N 2 28W
Quetena, Bolivia 156 E4 22 10 S 67 25W
Quetico Prov. Park, Canada 128 C1 48 30N 91 45W
Quetrequile, Argentina 160 B3 41 33 S 69 22W
Quetta, Pakistan 79 C2 30 15N 66 55 E
Quevedo, Ecuador 152 D2 1 2 S 79 29W
Quezaltenango, Guatemala 148 D1 14 50N 91 30W
Quezon City, Phil. 71 B6 14 38N 121 0 E
Qufār, Si. Arabia 84 E4 27 26N 41 37 E
Qui Nhon, Vietnam 76 F7 13 40N 109 13 E
Quibala, Angola 103 E2 10 46 S 14 59 E
Quibaxe, Angola 103 D2 8 24 S 14 27 E
Quibdo, Colombia 152 B2 5 42N 76 40W
Quiberon, France 22 E3 47 29N 3 9W
Quíbor, Venezuela 152 B4 9 56N 69 37W
Quick, Canada 130 C3 54 36N 126 54W
Quickborn, Germany 26 B5 53 42N 9 52 E
Quiet L., Canada 130 A2 61 5N 133 5W
Quiévrain, Belgium 21 H3 50 24N 3 41 E
Quiindy, Paraguay 158 B4 25 58 S 57 14W
Quila, Mexico 146 C3 24 23N 107 13W
Quilán, C., Chile 160 B2 43 15 S 74 30W
Quilcene, U.S.A. 144 C4 47 49N 122 53W
Quilengues, Angola 103 E2 14 12 S 14 12 E
Quilimarí, Chile 158 C1 32 5 S 71 30W
Quilino, Argentina 158 C3 30 14 S 64 29W
Quillabamba, Peru 156 C3 12 50 S 72 50W
Quillacollo, Bolivia 156 D4 17 26 S 66 17W
Quillagua, Chile 158 A2 21 40 S 69 40W
Quillaicillo, Chile 158 C1 31 17 S 71 40W
Quillan, France 24 F6 42 53N 2 10 E
Quillebeuf-sur-Seine, France 22 C7 49 28N 0 30 E
Quillota, Chile 158 C1 32 54 S 71 16W
Quilmes, Argentina 158 C4 34 43 S 58 15W
Quilon, India 83 K3 8 50N 76 38 E
Quilpie, Australia 115 D3 26 35 S 144 11 E
Quilpué, Chile 158 C1 33 5 S 71 33W
Quilua, Mozam. 107 F4 16 17 S 39 54 E
Quimbele, Angola 103 D3 6 17 S 16 41 E
Quimbonge, Angola 103 D3 8 36 S 18 30 E
Quime, Bolivia 156 D4 17 2 S 67 15W
Quimilí, Argentina 158 B3 27 40 S 62 30W
Quimper, France 22 E2 48 0N 4 9W
Quimperlé, France 22 E3 47 53N 3 33W
Quinault →, U.S.A. 144 C2 47 23N 124 18W
Quincemil, Peru 156 C3 13 15 S 70 40W
Quincy, Calif., U.S.A. 144 F6 39 56N 120 56W
Quincy, Fla., U.S.A. 135 K3 30 34N 84 34W
Quincy, Ill., U.S.A. 138 F9 39 55N 91 20W
Quincy, Mass., U.S.A. 137 D14 42 14N 71 0W
Quincy, Wash., U.S.A. 142 C4 47 22N 119 56W
Quines, Argentina 158 C2 32 13 S 65 48W
Quinga, Mozam. 107 F5 15 49 S 40 15 E
Quingey, France 23 E12 47 7N 5 52 E
Quintana de la Serena, Spain 37 G5 38 45N 5 40W
Quintana Roo □, Mexico 147 D7 19 0N 88 0W
Quintanar de la Orden, Spain 34 F1 39 36N 3 5W
Quintanar de la Sierra, Spain 34 D2 41 57N 2 55W
Quintanar del Rey, Spain 35 F3 39 21N 1 56W
Quintero, Chile 158 C1 32 45 S 71 30W
Quintin, France 22 D4 48 26N 2 56W
Quinto, Spain 34 D4 41 25N 0 32W
Quinyambie, Australia 115 E3 30 15 S 141 0 E
Quípar →, Spain 35 G3 38 15N 1 40W
Quipungo, Angola 103 E2 14 37 S 14 40 E
Quirihue, Chile 158 D1 36 15 S 72 35W
Quirimbo, Angola 103 E2 10 36 S 14 12 E
Quirindi, Australia 117 A9 31 28 S 150 40 E
Quiroga, Spain 36 C3 42 28N 7 18W
Quiruvilca, Peru 156 B2 8 1 S 78 19W
Quissac, France 25 E8 43 55N 4 0 E
Quissanga, Mozam. 107 E5 12 24 S 40 28 E
Quitapa, Angola 103 E3 10 20 S 18 19 E
Quitilipi, Argentina 158 B3 26 50 S 60 13W
Quitman, Ga., U.S.A. 135 K4 30 49N 83 35W
Quitman, Miss., U.S.A. 135 J1 32 2N 88 42W
Quitman, Tex., U.S.A. 139 J7 32 48N 95 25W
Quito, Ecuador 152 D2 0 15 S 78 35W
Quixadá, Brazil 154 B4 4 55 S 39 0W
Quixaxe, Mozam. 107 F5 15 17 S 40 4 E
Quixeramobim, Brazil 154 C4 5 12 S 39 17W
Quixinge, Angola 103 D2 9 52 S 14 23 E
Quizenga, Angola 103 D3 9 21 S 15 28 E
Qujing, China 68 E4 25 32N 103 41 E
Qul'ân, Jazâ'ir, Egypt 94 C4 24 22N 35 31 E
Qumbu, S. Africa 105 E4 31 10 S 28 48 E
Quneitra, Syria 91 B4 33 7N 35 48 E
Qunfudh, Yemen 87 C5 16 39N 49 33 E
Quoin I., Australia 112 B4 14 54 S 129 32 E
Quoin Pt., S. Africa 104 E2 34 46 S 19 37 E
Quondong, Australia 116 B4 33 6 S 140 18 E
Quorn, Australia 116 B3 32 25 S 138 5 E
Qurein, Sudan 95 E3 13 30N 34 50 E
Qurnat as Sawdā', Lebanon 91 A5 34 18N 36 6 E
Qûs, Egypt 94 B3 25 55N 32 50 E
Qusaybah, Iraq 84 C4 34 24N 40 59 E
Quṣay'ir, Yemen 87 D5 14 55N 50 20 E
Quseir, Egypt 94 B3 26 7N 34 16 E
Qūshchī, Iran 84 B5 37 59N 45 3 E
Quthing, Lesotho 105 E4 30 25 S 27 36 E
Qūṭīābād, Iran 85 C6 35 47N 48 30 E
Quwo, China 66 G6 35 38N 111 25 E
Quyang, China 66 E8 38 35N 114 40 E
Quynh Nhai, Vietnam 76 B4 21 49N 103 33 E
Quzi, China 66 F4 36 20N 107 20 E
Qytet Stalin, Albania 44 D1 40 47N 19 57 E

R

Ra, Ko, Thailand 77 H2 9 13N 98 16 E
Råå, Sweden 15 J6 56 0N 12 45 E
Raab, Austria 30 C6 48 21N 13 39 E
Raahe, Finland 12 D18 64 40N 24 28 E
Raalte, Neths. 20 D8 52 23N 6 16 E
Raamsdonksveer, Neths. 21 E5 51 43N 4 52 E
Raasay, U.K. 18 D2 57 25N 6 4W
Raasay, Sd. of, U.K. 18 D2 57 30N 6 8W
Rab, Yugoslavia 39 D11 44 45N 14 45 E
Raba, Indonesia 71 F5 8 36 S 118 55 E
Rába →, Hungary 31 D10 47 38N 17 38 E
Raba →, Poland 31 A13 50 8N 20 30 E
Rabaçal →, Portugal 36 D3 41 30N 7 12W
Rabah, Nigeria 101 C6 13 5N 5 30 E
Rabai, Kenya 106 C4 3 50 S 39 31 E
Rabaraba, Papua N. G. 120 E5 9 58 S 149 49 E
Rabastens, France 24 E5 43 50N 1 43 E
Rabastens-de-Bigorre, France 24 E4 43 23N 0 9 E
Rabat, Malta 32 D1 35 53N 14 25 E
Rabat, Morocco 98 B3 34 2N 6 48W
Rabaul, Papua N. G. 120 C7 4 24 S 152 18 E
Rabbit →, Canada 130 B3 59 41N 127 12W
Rabbit Lake, Canada 131 C7 53 8N 107 46W
Rabbitskin →, Canada 130 A4 61 47N 120 42W
Rābigh, Si. Arabia 86 B2 22 50N 39 5 E
Rabka, Poland 31 B12 49 37N 19 59 E
Rābor, Iran 85 D8 29 17N 56 55 E
Rača, Yugoslavia 42 C6 44 14N 21 0 E
Răcale, Italy 41 C11 39 57N 18 6 E
Racalmuto, Italy 40 E6 37 25N 13 41 E
Răcăşdia, Romania 42 C6 44 59N 21 36 E
Racconigi, Italy 38 D4 44 47N 7 41 E
Raccoon →, U.S.A. 140 C3 41 35N 93 37W
Raccoon Cr. →, U.S.A. 141 E9 39 47N 87 23W
Race, C., Canada 129 C9 46 40N 53 5W
Rach Gia, Vietnam 77 G5 10 5N 105 5 E
Raciąż, Poland 47 C7 52 46N 20 10 E
Racibórz, Poland 31 A11 50 7N 18 18 E
Racine, U.S.A. 141 B9 42 41N 87 51W
Rackerby, U.S.A. 144 F5 39 26N 121 22W
Radama, Nosy, Madag. 105 A8 14 0 S 47 47 E
Radama, Saikanosy, Madag. 105 A8 14 16 S 47 53 E
Radan, Yugoslavia 42 E6 42 59N 21 29 E
Rădăuţi, Romania 46 B6 47 50N 25 59 E
Radbuza →, Czech. 30 B6 49 35N 13 5 E
Radcliff, U.S.A. 141 G11 37 51N 85 57W
Radeburg, Germany 26 D9 51 6N 13 55 E
Radeče, Yugoslavia 39 B12 46 5N 15 14 E
Radekhov, U.S.S.R. 50 F4 50 25N 24 32 E
Radew →, Poland 47 A2 54 2N 15 52 E
Radford, U.S.A. 134 G5 37 8N 80 32W
Radhanpur, India 80 H4 23 50N 71 38 E
Radiska →, Yugoslavia 42 F5 41 38N 20 37 E
Radisson, Canada 131 C7 52 30N 107 20W
Radium Hot Springs, Canada 130 C5 50 35N 116 2W
Radków, Poland 47 E3 50 30N 16 24 E
Radlin, Poland 31 A11 50 3N 18 29 E
Radna, Romania 42 A6 46 7N 21 41 E
Radnevo, Bulgaria 43 E10 42 17N 25 58 E

254 Radnice

Radnice, Czech. 30 B6 49 51N 13 35 E
Radnor Forest, U.K. 17 E4 52 17N 3 10W
Radolfzell, Germany 27 H4 47 44N 8 58 E
Radom, Poland 47 D8 51 23N 21 12 E
Radom □, Poland 47 D8 51 30N 21 0 E
Radomir, Bulgaria 42 E8 42 37N 23 4 E
Radomka →, Poland 47 D8 51 31N 21 11 E
Radomsko, Poland 47 D6 51 5N 19 28 E
Radomyshl, U.S.S.R. 50 F6 50 30N 29 12 E
Radomysl Wielki, Poland 31 A14 50 14N 21 15 E
Radoszyce, Poland 47 D7 51 4N 20 15 E
Radoviš, Yugoslavia 42 F7 41 38N 22 28 E
Radovljica, Yugoslavia 39 B11 46 22N 14 12 E
Radstadt, Austria 30 D6 47 24N 13 28 E
Radstock, U.K. 17 F5 51 17N 2 25W
Radstock, C., Australia 115 E1 33 12 S 134 20 E
Răducăneni, Romania 46 C8 46 58N 27 54 E
Raduša, Yugoslavia 42 E6 42 7N 21 15 E
Radviliškis, U.S.S.R. 50 D3 55 49N 23 33 E
Radville, Canada 131 D8 49 30N 104 15W
Radymno, Poland 31 B15 49 59N 22 52 E
Radzanów, Poland 47 C7 52 56N 20 8 E
Radziejów, Poland 47 C5 52 40N 18 30 E
Radzymin, Poland 47 C8 52 25N 21 11 E
Radzyń Chełmiński, Poland 47 B5 53 23N 18 55 E
Radzyń Podlaski, Poland 47 D9 51 47N 22 37 E
Rae, Canada 130 A5 62 50N 116 3W
Rae Bareli, India 81 F9 26 18N 81 20 E
Rae Isthmus, Canada 127 B11 66 40N 87 30W
Raeren, Belgium 21 G8 50 41N 6 7 E
Raeside, L., Australia 113 E3 29 20 S 122 0 E
Raetihi, N.Z. 118 F4 39 25 S 175 17 E
Rafaela, Argentina 158 C3 31 10 S 61 30W
Rafah, Egypt 91 D3 31 18N 34 14 E
Rafai, C.A.R. 102 B4 4 59N 23 58 E
Raffadali, Italy 40 E6 37 23N 13 29 E
Rafḩā, Si. Arabia 84 D4 29 35N 43 35 E
Rafsanjān, Iran 85 D8 30 30N 56 5 E
Raft Pt., Australia 112 C3 16 4 S 124 26 E
Ragag, Sudan 95 E1 10 59N 24 40 E
Ragged, Mt., Australia 113 F3 33 27 S 123 25 E
Raglan, Australia 114 C5 23 42 S 150 49 E
Raglan, N.Z. 118 D3 37 55 S 174 55 E
Raglan Harbour, N.Z. 118 D3 37 47 S 174 50 E
Ragunda, Sweden 14 A10 63 6N 16 23 E
Ragusa, Italy 41 F7 36 56N 14 42 E
Raha, Indonesia 71 E6 4 55 S 123 0 E
Rahad, Nahr ed →, Sudan 95 E3 14 28N 33 31 E
Rahad al Bardī, Sudan 97 F4 11 20N 23 40 E
Rahaeng = Tak, Thailand 76 D2 16 52N 99 8 E
Rahden, Germany 26 C4 52 26N 8 36 E
Raheita, Ethiopia 95 E5 12 46N 43 4 E
Raḩīmah, Si. Arabia 85 E6 26 42N 50 4 E
Rahimyar Khan, Pakistan 79 C3 28 30N 70 25 E
Rāhjerd, Iran 85 C6 34 22N 50 22 E
Rahotu, N.Z. 118 F2 39 20 S 173 49 E
Raichur, India 83 F3 16 10N 77 20 E
Raiganj, India 81 G13 25 37N 88 10 E
Raigarh, India 82 D6 21 56N 83 25 E
Raighar, India 82 E6 19 51N 82 6 E
Raijua, Indonesia 71 F6 10 37 S 121 36 E
Railton, Australia 114 G4 41 25 S 146 28 E
Rainbow, Australia 116 C5 35 55 S 142 0 E
Rainbow Lake, Canada 130 B5 58 30N 119 23W
Rainier, U.S.A. 144 D4 46 4N 122 58W
Rainier, Mt., U.S.A. 144 D5 46 50N 121 50W
Rainy L., Canada 131 D10 48 42N 93 10W
Rainy River, Canada 131 D10 48 43N 94 29W
Raipur, India 82 D5 21 17N 81 45 E
Raj Nandgaon, India 82 D5 21 5N 81 5 E
Raja, Ujung, Indonesia 70 D1 3 40N 96 25 E
Raja Ampat, Kepulauan, Indonesia 71 E8 0 30 S 130 0 E
Rajahmundry, India 82 F5 17 1N 81 48 E
Rajajooseppi, Finland 12 B20 68 28N 28 29 E
Rajang →, Malaysia 70 D4 2 30N 112 0 E
Rajapalaiyam, India 83 K3 9 25N 77 35 E
Rajasthan □, India 80 F5 26 45N 73 30 E
Rajasthan Canal, India 80 F5 28 0N 72 0 E
Rajauri, India 81 C6 33 25N 74 21 E
Rajbari, Bangla. 78 D2 23 47N 89 41 E
Rajgarh, Mad. P., India 80 G7 24 2N 76 45 E
Rajgarh, Raj., India 80 E6 28 40N 75 25 E
Rajgród, Poland 47 B9 53 42N 22 42 E
Rajhenburg, Yugoslavia 39 B12 46 1N 15 29 E
Rajkot, India 80 H4 22 15N 70 56 E
Rajmahal Hills, India 81 G12 24 30N 87 30 E
Rajpipla, India 82 D1 21 50N 73 30 E
Rajpura, India 80 D7 30 25N 76 32 E
Rajshahi, Bangla. 78 C2 24 22N 88 39 E
Rajshahi □, Bangla. 81 G13 25 0N 89 0 E
Rakaia, N.Z. 119 D7 43 45 S 172 1 E
Rakaia →, N.Z. 119 D7 43 36 S 172 15 E
Rakan, Ra's, Qatar 85 E6 26 10N 51 20 E
Rakaposhi, Pakistan 81 A6 36 10N 74 25 E
Rakata, Pulau, Indonesia 70 F3 6 10 S 105 20 E
Rakhawt, W. →, Yemen 87 C5 18 16N 51 50 E
Rakhneh-ye Jamshīdī, Afghan. 79 B1 34 22N 62 19 E
Rakhni, Pakistan 80 D3 30 4N 69 56 E
Rakhyūt, Oman 87 C6 16 44N 53 20 E
Rakitnoye, U.S.S.R. 60 B7 45 36N 134 17 E
Rakitovo, Bulgaria 43 F9 41 59N 24 5 E
Rakkestad, Norway 14 E5 59 25N 11 21 E
Rakoniewice, Poland 47 C3 52 10N 16 16 E
Rakops, Botswana 104 C3 21 1 S 24 28 E
Rákospalota, Hungary 31 D12 47 30N 19 5 E
Rakov, U.S.S.R. 50 E5 53 58N 26 59 E
Rakovica, Yugoslavia 39 D12 44 59N 15 38 E
Rakovník, Czech. 30 A6 50 6N 13 42 E
Rakovski, Bulgaria 43 E9 42 21N 24 57 E
Rakvere, U.S.S.R. 50 B5 59 30N 26 25 E
Raleigh, U.S.A. 135 H6 35 47N 78 39W
Raleigh B., U.S.A. 135 H7 34 50N 76 15W
Ralja, Yugoslavia 42 C5 44 33N 20 34 E
Ralls, U.S.A. 139 J4 33 40N 101 20W
Ram →, Canada 130 A4 62 1N 123 41W
Ram Allāh, Jordan 91 D4 31 55N 35 10 E
Ram Hd., Australia 117 D8 37 47 S 149 30 E
Rama, Nic. 148 D3 12 9N 84 15W
Ramacca, Italy 41 E7 37 24N 14 40 E
Ramachandrapuram, India 82 F6 16 50N 82 4 E
Ramales de la Victoria, Spain 34 B1 43 15N 3 28W
Ramalho, Serra do, Brazil 155 D3 13 45 S 44 0W
Raman, Thailand 77 J3 6 29N 101 18 E
Ramanathapuram, India 83 K4 9 25N 78 55 E
Ramanetaka, B. de, Madag. 105 A8 14 13 S 47 52 E
Ramas C., India 83 G1 15 5N 73 55 E
Ramat Gan, Israel 91 C3 32 4N 34 48 E
Ramatlhabama, S. Africa 104 D4 25 37 S 25 33 E
Ramban, India 81 C6 33 14N 75 12 E
Rambervillers, France 23 D13 48 20N 6 38 E
Rambi, Fiji 121 A3 16 30 S 179 59W
Rambipuji, Indonesia 71 H15 8 12 S 113 37 E
Rambouillet, France 23 D8 48 39N 1 50 E
Ramdurg, India 83 G2 15 58N 75 22 E
Ramea, Canada 129 C8 47 31N 57 23W
Ramechhap, Nepal 81 F12 27 25N 86 10 E
Ramelau, Indonesia 71 F7 8 55 S 126 22 E
Ramenskoye, U.S.S.R. 51 D11 55 32N 38 15 E
Ramgarh, Bihar, India 81 H11 23 40N 85 35 E
Ramgarh, Raj., India 80 F6 27 16N 75 14 E
Ramgarh, Raj., India 80 F4 27 30N 70 36 E
Rāmhormoz, Iran 85 D6 31 15N 49 35 E
Ramīān, Iran 85 B7 37 3N 55 16 E
Ramingining, Australia 114 A2 12 19 S 135 3 E
Ramla, Israel 91 D3 31 55N 34 52 E
Ramlat Zalṭan, Libya 96 C3 28 30N 19 30 E
Ramlu, Ethiopia 95 E5 13 32N 41 40 E
Ramme, Denmark 15 H2 56 30N 8 11 E
Ramnad = Ramanathapuram, India 83 K4 9 25N 78 55 E
Ramnagar, India 81 C6 32 47N 75 18 E
Ramnäs, Sweden 14 E10 59 46N 16 12 E
Ramon, U.S.S.R. 51 F11 51 55N 39 21 E
Ramona, U.S.A. 145 M10 33 1N 116 56W
Ramore, Canada 128 C3 48 30N 80 25W
Ramotswa, Botswana 104 C4 24 50 S 25 52 E
Rampur, H.P., India 80 D7 31 26N 77 43 E
Rampur, Mad. P., India 80 H5 23 25N 73 53 E
Rampur, Orissa, India 82 D6 21 48N 83 58 E
Rampur, Ut. P., India 81 E8 28 50N 79 5 E
Rampur Hat, India 81 G12 24 10N 87 50 E
Rampura, India 80 G6 24 30N 75 27 E
Rāmsar, Iran 85 B6 36 53N 50 41 E
Ramsel, Belgium 21 F5 51 2N 4 50 E
Ramsey, Canada 128 C3 47 25N 82 20W
Ramsey, U.K. 16 C3 54 20N 4 21W
Ramsey, U.S.A. 140 E7 39 8N 89 7W
Ramsgate, U.K. 17 F9 51 20N 1 25 E
Ramshai, India 78 B2 26 44N 88 51 E
Ramsjö, Sweden 14 B9 62 11N 15 37 E
Ramtek, India 82 D4 21 20N 79 15 E
Ramu →, Papua N. G. 120 C3 4 0 S 144 41 E
Ramvik, Sweden 14 B11 62 49N 17 51 E
Ranaghat, India 81 H13 23 15N 88 35 E
Ranahu, Pakistan 80 G3 25 55N 69 45 E
Ranau, Malaysia 70 C5 6 2N 116 40 E
Rancagua, Chile 158 C1 34 10 S 70 50W
Rance, Belgium 21 H4 50 9N 4 16 E
Rance →, France 22 D5 48 34N 1 59W
Rance, Barrage de la, France 22 D4 48 30N 2 3W
Rancharia, Brazil 155 F1 22 15 S 50 55W
Rancheria →, Canada 130 A3 60 13N 129 7W
Ranchester, U.S.A. 142 D10 44 57N 107 12W
Ranchi, India 81 H11 23 19N 85 27 E
Ranco, L., Chile 160 B2 40 15 S 72 25W
Rancu, Romania 46 E5 44 32N 24 15 E
Rand, Australia 117 C7 35 33 S 146 32 E
Randan, France 24 B7 46 2N 3 21 E
Randazzo, Italy 41 E7 37 53N 14 56 E
Randers, Denmark 15 H4 56 29N 10 1 E
Randers Fjord, Denmark 15 H4 56 37N 10 20 E
Randfontein, S. Africa 105 D4 26 8 S 27 45 E
Randle, U.S.A. 144 D5 46 32N 121 57W
Randolph, Mass., U.S.A. 137 D13 42 10N 71 3W
Randolph, N.Y., U.S.A. 136 D6 42 10N 78 59W
Randolph, Utah, U.S.A. 142 F8 41 43N 111 10W
Randolph, Vt., U.S.A. 137 C12 43 55N 72 39W
Randsfjord, Norway 14 D4 60 15N 10 25 E
Råne älv →, Sweden 12 D17 65 50N 22 20 E
Ranfurly, N.Z. 119 F5 45 7 S 170 6 E
Rangae, Thailand 77 J3 6 19N 101 44 E
Rangamati, Bangla. 78 D4 22 38N 92 12 E
Rangataua, N.Z. 118 F4 39 26 S 175 28 E
Rangaunu B., N.Z. 118 A2 34 51 S 173 15 E
Rångedala, Sweden 15 G7 57 47N 13 9 E
Rangeley, U.S.A. 137 B14 44 58N 70 33W
Rangely, U.S.A. 142 F9 40 3N 108 53W
Ranger, U.S.A. 139 J5 32 30N 98 42W
Rangia, India 78 B3 26 28N 91 38 E
Rangiora, N.Z. 119 D7 43 19 S 172 36 E
Rangitaiki, N.Z. 118 E5 38 52 S 176 24 E
Rangitaiki →, N.Z. 118 D5 37 54 S 176 49 E
Rangitata →, N.Z. 119 D6 43 45 S 171 15 E
Rangitikei →, N.Z. 118 G4 40 17 S 175 15 E
Rangitoto Ra., N.Z. 118 E4 38 25 S 175 35 E
Rangkasbitung, Indonesia 71 G12 6 21 S 106 15 E
Rangoon, Burma 78 G6 16 45N 96 20 E
Rangpur, Bangla. 78 C2 25 42N 89 22 E
Rangsang, Indonesia 74 B2 1 20N 103 30 E
Rangsit, Thailand 76 F3 13 59N 100 37 E
Ranibennur, India 83 G2 14 35N 75 30 E
Raniganj, India 81 H12 23 40N 87 5 E
Ranippettai, India 83 H4 12 56N 79 23 E
Rāniyah, Iraq 84 B5 36 15N 44 53 E
Ranken →, Australia 114 C2 20 31 S 137 36 E
Rankin, Ill., U.S.A. 141 D9 40 28N 87 54W
Rankin, Tex., U.S.A. 139 K4 31 16N 101 56W
Rankin Inlet, Canada 126 B10 62 30N 93 0W
Rankins Springs, Australia 117 B7 33 49 S 146 14 E
Rannoch, L., U.K. 18 E4 56 41N 4 20W
Rannoch Moor, U.K. 18 E4 56 38N 4 48W
Ranobe, Helodranon' i, Madag. 105 C7 23 3 S 43 33 E
Ranohira, Madag. 105 C8 22 29 S 45 24 E
Ranomafana, Toamasina, Madag. 105 B8 18 57 S 48 50 E
Ranomafana, Toliara, Madag. 105 C8 24 34 S 47 0 E
Ranong, Thailand 77 H2 9 56N 98 40 E
Rānsa, Iran 85 C6 33 39N 48 18 E
Ransiki, Indonesia 71 E8 1 30 S 134 10 E
Ransom, U.S.A. 141 C8 41 9N 88 39W
Rantau, Indonesia 70 E5 2 56 S 115 9 E
Rantauprapat, Indonesia 70 D1 2 15N 99 50 E
Rantekombola, Indonesia 71 E5 3 15 S 119 57 E
Rantoul, U.S.A. 141 D8 40 18N 88 10W
Ranum, Denmark 15 H3 56 54N 9 14 E
Ranyah, W. →, Si. Arabia 86 B3 21 18N 43 20 E
Raon l'Étape, France 23 D13 48 24N 6 50 E
Raoui, Erg er, Algeria 99 C4 29 0N 2 0W
Raoyang, China 66 E8 38 15N 115 45 E
Rapa, Pac. Oc. 123 K13 27 35 S 144 20W
Rapallo, Italy 38 D6 44 21N 9 12 E
Rāpch, Iran 85 E8 25 40N 59 15 E
Rapid →, Canada 130 B3 59 15N 129 5W
Rapid City, U.S.A. 138 D3 44 0N 103 0W
Rapid River, U.S.A. 134 C2 45 55N 87 0W
Rapides des Joachims, Canada 128 C4 46 13N 77 43W
Rapla, U.S.S.R. 50 B4 59 1N 24 52 E
Rapperswil, Switz. 29 B7 47 14N 8 45 E
Rarotonga, Cook Is. 123 K12 21 30 S 160 0W
Ra's al' Ayn, Syria 84 B4 36 51N 40 4 E
Ra's al Khaymah, U.A.E. 85 E8 25 50N 56 5 E
Ra's al-Unuf, Libya 96 B3 30 25N 18 15 E
Ra's an Naqb, Jordan 91 F4 30 0N 35 29 E
Ras Bânâs, Egypt 94 C4 23 57N 35 59 E
Ras Dashen, Ethiopia 95 E4 13 8N 38 26 E
Ras el Ma, Algeria 99 B4 34 26N 0 50W
Ras Mallap, Egypt 94 J8 29 18N 32 50 E
Râs Timirist, Mauritania 100 B1 19 21N 16 30W
Rasa, Punta, Argentina 160 B4 40 50 S 62 15W
Rasca, Pta. de la, Canary Is. 33 G3 27 59N 16 41W
Raseiniai, U.S.S.R. 50 D3 55 25N 23 5 E
Rashad, Sudan 95 E3 11 55N 31 0 E
Rashîd, Egypt 94 H7 31 21N 30 22 E
Rashîd, Masabb, Egypt 94 H7 31 22N 30 17 E
Rasht, Iran 85 B6 37 20N 49 40 E
Rasi Salai, Thailand 76 E5 15 20N 104 9 E
Rasipuram, India 83 J4 11 30N 78 15 E
Raška, Yugoslavia 42 D5 43 19N 20 39 E
Rason L., Australia 113 E3 28 45 S 124 25 E
Raşova, Romania 46 E8 44 15N 27 55 E
Rasovo, Bulgaria 43 D8 43 42N 23 17 E
Rasra, India 81 G10 25 50N 83 50 E
Rass el Oued, Algeria 99 A6 35 57N 5 2 E
Rasskazovo, U.S.S.R. 51 E12 52 35N 41 50 E
Rastatt, Germany 27 G4 48 50N 8 12 E
Rastu, Romania 46 F4 43 53N 23 16 E
Raszków, Poland 47 D4 51 43N 17 40 E
Rat Buri, Thailand 76 F2 13 30N 99 54 E
Rat Is., U.S.A. 126 C1 51 50N 178 15 E
Rat River, Canada 130 A6 61 7N 112 36W
Ratangarh, India 80 E6 28 5N 74 35 E
Raţāwī, Iraq 84 D5 30 38N 47 13 E
Rath, India 81 G8 25 36N 79 37 E
Rath Luirc, Ireland 19 D3 52 21N 8 40W
Rathbun Res., U.S.A. 140 D4 40 49N 92 53W
Rathedaung, Burma 78 E4 20 29N 92 45 E
Rathenow, Germany 26 C8 52 38N 12 23 E
Rathkeale, Ireland 19 D3 52 32N 8 57W
Rathlin, U.K. 19 A5 55 18N 6 14W
Rathlin O'Birne I., Ireland 19 B3 54 40N 8 50W
Ratibor = Racibórz, Poland 31 A11 50 7N 18 18 E
Rätikon, Austria 30 E2 47 0N 9 55 E
Ratlam, India 80 H6 23 20N 75 0 E
Ratnagiri, India 82 F1 16 57N 73 18 E
Ratnapura, Sri Lanka 83 L5 6 40N 80 20 E
Raton, U.S.A. 139 G2 37 0N 104 30W
Rattaphum, Thailand 77 J3 7 8N 100 16 E
Ratten, Austria 30 D8 47 28N 15 44 E
Rattray Hd., U.K. 18 D7 57 38N 1 50W
Ratz, Mt., Canada 130 B2 57 23N 132 12W
Ratzeburg, Germany 26 B6 53 41N 10 46 E
Raub, Malaysia 77 L3 3 47N 101 52 E
Rauch, Argentina 158 D4 36 45 S 59 5W
Raufarhöfn, Iceland 12 C6 66 27N 15 57W
Raufoss, Norway 14 D4 60 44N 10 37 E
Raukumara Ra., N.Z. 118 E6 38 5 S 177 55 E
Raul Soares, Brazil 155 F3 20 5 S 42 22W
Rauland, Norway 14 E2 59 43N 8 0 E
Rauma, Finland 13 F16 61 10N 21 30 E
Rauma →, Norway 14 B1 62 34N 7 43 E
Raurkela, India 81 H11 22 14N 84 50 E
Rausu-Dake, Japan 60 B12 44 4N 145 7 E
Rava Russkaya, U.S.S.R. 50 F3 50 15N 23 42 E
Ravānsar, Iran 84 C5 34 43N 46 40 E
Ravanusa, Italy 40 E6 37 16N 13 58 E
Rāvar, Iran 85 D8 31 20N 56 51 E
Ravels, Belgium 21 F6 51 22N 5 0 E
Ravena, U.S.A. 137 D11 42 28N 73 49W
Ravenna, Italy 39 D9 44 28N 12 15 E
Ravenna, Ky., U.S.A. 141 G13 37 42N 83 55W
Ravenna, Nebr., U.S.A. 138 E5 41 3N 98 58W
Ravenna, Ohio, U.S.A. 136 E3 41 11N 81 15W
Ravensburg, Germany 27 H5 47 48N 9 38 E
Ravenshoe, Australia 114 B4 17 37 S 145 29 E
Ravenstein, Neths. 20 E7 51 47N 5 39 E
Ravensthorpe, Australia 113 F3 33 35 S 120 2 E
Ravenswood, Australia 114 C4 20 6 S 146 54 E
Ravenswood, U.S.A. 134 F5 38 58N 81 47W
Ravensworth, Australia 117 B9 32 26 S 151 4 E
Ravenwood, U.S.A. 140 D2 40 23N 94 41W
Ravi →, Pakistan 80 D4 30 35N 71 49 E
Ravna Gora, Yugoslavia 39 C11 45 24N 14 50 E
Ravna Reka, Yugoslavia 42 D6 43 59N 21 35 E
Rawa Mazowiecka, Poland 47 D7 51 46N 20 12 E
Rawalpindi, Pakistan 79 B4 33 38N 73 8 E
Rawāndūz, Iraq 84 B5 36 40N 44 30 E
Rawang, Malaysia 77 L3 3 20N 101 35 E
Rawdon, Canada 128 C5 46 3N 73 40W
Rawene, N.Z. 118 B2 35 25 S 173 32 E
Rawicz, Poland 47 D3 51 36N 16 52 E
Rawka →, Poland 47 C7 52 9N 20 8 E
Rawlinna, Australia 113 F4 30 58 S 125 28 E
Rawlins, U.S.A. 142 F10 41 50N 107 20W
Rawlinson Ra., Australia 113 D4 24 40 S 128 30 E
Rawson, Argentina 160 B3 43 15 S 65 5W
Ray, U.S.A. 138 A3 48 21N 103 6W
Ray, C., Canada 129 C8 47 33N 59 15W
Rayachoti, India 83 G4 14 4N 78 50 E
Rayadurg, India 83 G3 14 40N 76 50 E
Rayagada, India 82 E6 19 15N 83 20 E
Raychikhinsk, U.S.S.R. 57 E13 49 46N 129 25 E
Rāyen, Iran 85 D8 29 34N 57 26 E
Rayevskiy, U.S.S.R. 54 D4 54 4N 54 56 E
Raymond, Canada 130 D6 49 30N 112 35W
Raymond, Calif., U.S.A. 144 H7 37 13N 119 54W
Raymond, Ill., U.S.A. 140 E7 39 19N 89 34W
Raymond, Wash., U.S.A. 144 D3 46 45N 123 48W
Raymond Terrace, Australia 117 B9 32 45 S 151 44 E
Raymondville, U.S.A. 139 M6 26 30N 97 50W
Raymore, Canada 131 C8 51 25N 104 31W
Rayne, U.S.A. 139 K8 30 16N 92 16W
Rayón, Mexico 146 B2 29 43N 110 35W
Rayong, Thailand 76 F3 12 40N 101 20 E
Raytown, U.S.A. 140 E2 39 1N 94 28W
Rayville, U.S.A. 139 J9 32 30N 91 45W
Raz, Pte. du, France 22 D2 48 2N 4 47W
Razan, Iran 85 C6 35 23N 49 2 E
Ražana, Yugoslavia 42 C4 44 6N 19 55 E
Ražanj, Yugoslavia 42 D6 43 40N 21 31 E
Razdelna, Bulgaria 43 D12 43 13N 27 41 E
Razdel'naya, U.S.S.R. 52 C4 46 50N 30 2 E
Razdolnoye, R.S.F.S.R., U.S.S.R. 60 C5 43 30N 131 52 E
Razdolnoye, Ukraine S.S.R., U.S.S.R. 52 D5 45 46N 33 29 E
Razeh, Iran 85 C6 32 47N 48 9 E
Razelm, Lacul, Romania 46 E10 44 50N 29 0 E
Razgrad, Bulgaria 43 D11 43 33N 26 34 E
Razlog, Bulgaria 43 F8 41 53N 23 28 E
Razmak, Pakistan 79 B3 32 45N 69 50 E
Razole, India 83 F5 16 36N 81 48 E
Ré, I. de, France 24 B2 46 12N 1 30W
Reading, U.K. 17 F7 51 27N 0 57W
Reading, Mich., U.S.A. 141 C12 41 50N 84 45W
Reading, Ohio, U.S.A. 141 E12 39 13N 84 26W
Reading, Pa., U.S.A. 137 F9 40 20N 75 53W
Real, Cordillera, Bolivia 156 D4 17 0 S 67 10W
Realicó, Argentina 158 D3 35 0 S 64 15W
Réalmont, France 24 E6 43 48N 2 10 E
Reata, Mexico 146 B4 26 8N 101 5W
Rebais, France 23 D10 48 50N 3 10 E
Rebecca, L., Australia 113 F3 30 0 S 122 15 E
Rebi, Indonesia 71 F8 6 23 S 134 7 E
Rebiana, Libya 96 D4 24 12N 22 10 E
Rebun-Tō, Japan 60 B10 45 23N 141 2 E
Recanati, Italy 39 E10 43 24N 13 32 E
Recaş, Romania 46 D2 45 46N 21 30 E
Recherche, Arch. of the, Australia 113 F3 34 15 S 122 50 E
Rechitsa, U.S.S.R. 50 E7 52 13N 30 15 E
Recht, Belgium 21 H8 50 20N 6 3 E
Recife, Brazil 154 C5 8 0 S 35 0W
Recklinghausen, Germany 21 E10 51 36N 7 10 E
Reconquista, Argentina 158 B4 29 10 S 59 45W
Recreio, Brazil 157 B6 8 0 S 58 25W
Recreo, Argentina 158 B2 29 25 S 65 10W
Recuay, Peru 156 B2 9 43 S 77 28W
Recz, Poland 47 B2 53 16N 15 31 E
Red →, N. Amer. 138 A6 50 24N 96 48W
Red →, U.S.A. 139 K9 31 0N 91 40W
Red Bank, U.S.A. 137 F10 40 21N 74 4W
Red Bay, Canada 129 B8 51 44N 56 25W
Red Bluff, U.S.A. 142 F2 40 11N 122 11W
Red Bluff L., U.S.A. 139 K3 31 59N 103 58W
Red Bud, U.S.A. 140 F7 38 13N 90 0W
Red Cliffs, Australia 116 C5 34 19 S 142 11 E
Red Cloud, U.S.A. 138 E5 40 8N 98 33W
Red Deer, Canada 130 C6 52 20N 113 50W
Red Deer →, Alta., Canada 131 C7 50 58N 110 0W
Red Deer →, Man., Canada 131 C8 52 53N 101 1W
Red Deer L., Canada 131 C8 52 55N 101 20W
Red Indian L., Canada 129 C8 48 35N 57 0W
Red Lake, Canada 131 C10 51 3N 93 49W
Red Lake Falls, U.S.A. 138 B6 47 54N 96 15W
Red Lodge, U.S.A. 142 D9 45 10N 109 10W
Red Mountain, U.S.A. 145 K9 35 22N 117 38W
Red Oak, U.S.A. 138 E7 41 0N 95 10W
Red Rock, Canada 128 C2 48 55N 88 15W
Red Rock, L., U.S.A. 140 C3 41 30N 93 15W
Red Rocks Pt., Australia 113 F4 32 13 S 127 32 E
Red Sea, Asia 90 C2 25 0N 36 0 E
Red Slate Mt., U.S.A. 144 H8 37 31N 118 52W
Red Sucker L., Canada 131 C10 54 9N 93 40W
Red Tower Pass = Turnu Rosu Pasul, Romania 46 D5 45 33N 24 17 E
Red Wing, U.S.A. 138 C8 44 32N 92 35W
Reda, Poland 47 A5 54 40N 18 19 E
Rédange, Lux. 21 J7 49 46N 5 52 E
Redbridge, U.K. 17 F8 51 35N 0 7 E
Redcar, U.K. 16 C6 54 37N 1 4W
Redcliff, Canada 131 C6 50 10N 110 50W
Redcliffe, Australia 115 D5 27 12 S 153 0 E
Redcliffe, Mt., Australia 113 E3 28 30 S 121 30 E
Reddersburg, S. Africa 104 D4 29 41 S 26 10 E
Redding, U.S.A. 142 F2 40 30N 122 25W
Redditch, U.K. 17 E6 52 18N 1 57W
Redenção, Brazil 154 B4 4 13 S 38 43W
Redfield, U.S.A. 138 C5 45 0N 98 30W
Redkey, U.S.A. 141 D11 40 21N 85 9W
Redknife →, Canada 130 A5 61 14N 119 22W
Redlands, U.S.A. 145 M9 34 0N 117 11W
Redmond, Australia 113 F2 34 55 S 117 40 E
Redmond, Oreg., U.S.A. 142 D3 44 19N 121 11W
Redmond, Wash., U.S.A. 144 C4 47 40N 122 7W
Redon, France 22 E4 47 40N 2 6W
Redonda, Antigua 149 C7 16 58N 62 19W
Redondela, Spain 36 C2 42 15N 8 38W
Redondo, Portugal 37 G3 38 39N 7 37W
Redondo Beach, U.S.A. 145 M8 33 52N 118 23W
Redrock Pt., Canada 130 A5 62 11N 115 2W
Redruth, U.K. 17 G2 50 14N 5 14W
Redvers, Canada 131 D8 49 35N 101 40W
Redwater, Canada 130 C6 53 55N 113 6W
Redwood, U.S.A. 137 B9 44 18N 75 48W
Redwood City, U.S.A. 144 H4 37 30N 122 15W
Redwood Falls, U.S.A. 138 C7 44 30N 95 2W
Ree, L., Ireland 19 C4 53 35N 8 0W

Ríohacha 255

Reed, L., Canada 131 C8 54 38N 100 30W
Reed City, U.S.A. 134 D3 43 52N 85 30W
Reeder, U.S.A. 138 B3 46 7N 102 52W
Reedley, U.S.A. 144 J7 36 36N 119 27W
Reedsburg, U.S.A. 138 D9 43 34N 90 5W
Reedsport, U.S.A. 142 E1 43 45N 124 4W
Reedy Creek, Australia 116 D4 36 58 S 140 2 E
Reefton, Australia 117 C7 34 15 S 147 27 E
Reefton, N.Z. 119 C6 42 6 S 171 51 E
Refahiye, Turkey 89 D8 39 54N 38 47 E
Refugio, U.S.A. 139 L6 28 18N 97 17W
Rega →, Poland 47 A2 54 10N 15 18 E
Regalbuto, Italy 41 E7 37 40N 14 38 E
Regar, U.S.S.R. 55 D4 38 30N 68 14 E
Regen, Germany 27 G9 48 58N 13 9 E
Regen →, Germany 27 F8 49 2N 12 6 E
Regeneração, Brazil 154 C3 6 15 S 42 41W
Regensburg, Germany 27 F8 49 1N 12 7 E
Regensdorf, Switz. 29 B6 47 26N 8 28 E
Réggio di Calábria, Italy 41 D8 38 7N 15 38 E
Réggio nell' Emilia, Italy 38 D7 44 42N 10 38 E
Regina, Canada 131 C8 50 27N 104 35W
Régina, Fr. Guiana 153 C7 4 19N 52 8W
Registro, Brazil 159 A6 24 29 S 47 49W
Reguengos de Monsaraz, Portugal 37 G3 38 25N 7 32W
Rehar →, India 81 H10 23 55N 82 40 E
Rehoboth, Namibia 104 C2 23 15 S 17 4 E
Rehovot, Israel 91 D3 31 54N 34 48 E
Rei-Bouba, Cameroon 102 A2 8 40N 14 15 E
Reichenbach, Germany 26 E8 50 36N 12 19 E
Reichenbach, Switz. 28 C5 46 38N 7 42 E
Reid, Australia 113 F4 30 49 S 128 26 E
Reid River, Australia 114 B4 19 40 S 146 48 E
Reiden, Switz. 28 B5 47 14N 7 59 E
Reidsville, U.S.A. 135 G6 36 21N 79 40W
Reigate, U.K. 17 F7 51 14N 0 11W
Reillo, Spain 34 F3 39 54N 1 53W
Reims, France 23 C11 49 15N 4 1 E
Reina Adelaida, Arch., Chile 160 D2 52 20 S 74 0W
Reinach, Aargau, Switz. 28 B6 47 14N 8 11 E
Reinach, Basel, Switz. 28 B5 47 29N 7 35 E
Reinbeck, U.S.A. 140 B4 42 18N 92 40W
Reindeer →, Canada 131 B8 55 36N 103 11W
Reindeer I., Canada 131 C9 52 30N 98 0W
Reindeer L., Canada 131 B8 57 15N 102 15W
Reinga, C., N.Z. 118 A1 34 25 S 172 43 E
Reinosa, Spain 36 B6 43 2N 4 15W
Reinosa, Paso, Spain 36 C6 42 56N 4 10W
Reitdiep, Neths. 20 B8 53 20N 6 20 E
Reitz, S. Africa 105 D4 27 48 S 28 29 E
Reivilo, S. Africa 104 D3 27 36 S 24 8 E
Rejmyre, Sweden 15 F9 58 50N 15 55 E
Rejowiec Fabryczny, Poland 47 D10 51 5N 23 17 E
Reka →, Yugoslavia 39 C11 45 40N 14 0 E
Rekinniki, U.S.S.R. 57 C17 60 51N 163 40 E
Rekovac, Yugoslavia 42 D6 43 51N 21 3 E
Reliance, Canada 131 A7 63 0N 109 20W
Remad, Oued →, Algeria 99 B4 33 28N 1 20W
Rémalard, France 22 D7 48 26N 0 47 E
Remarkable, Mt., Australia 116 B3 32 48 S 138 10 E
Rembang, Indonesia 71 G14 6 42 S 111 21 E
Remchi, Algeria 99 A4 35 2N 1 26W
Remedios, Colombia 152 B3 7 2N 74 41W
Remedios, Panama 148 E3 8 15N 81 50W
Remeshk, Iran 85 E8 26 55N 58 50 E
Remetea, Romania 46 C6 46 45N 25 29 E
Remich, Lux. 21 J8 49 32N 6 22 E
Remington, U.S.A. 141 D9 40 45N 87 8W
Rémire, Fr. Guiana 153 C7 4 53N 52 17W
Remiremont, France 23 D13 48 2N 6 36 E
Remo, Ethiopia 95 F5 6 48N 41 20 E
Remontnoye, U.S.S.R. 53 C10 46 34N 43 37 E
Remoulins, France 25 E8 43 55N 4 35 E
Remscheid, Germany 26 D3 51 11N 7 12 E
Ren Xian, China 66 F8 37 8N 114 40 E
Renascença, Brazil 152 D4 3 50 S 66 21W
Rend L., U.S.A. 140 F8 38 2N 88 58W
Rende, Italy 41 C9 39 19N 16 11 E
Rendeux, Belgium 21 H7 50 14N 5 30 E
Rendína, Greece 45 E3 39 4N 21 58 E
Rendova, Solomon Is. 121 M9 8 33 S 157 17 E
Rendsburg, Germany 26 A5 54 18N 9 41 E
Rene, U.S.S.R. 57 C19 66 2N 179 25W
Renfrew, Canada 128 C4 45 30N 76 40W
Renfrew, U.K. 18 F4 55 52N 4 24W
Rengat, Indonesia 70 E2 0 30 S 102 45 E
Rengo, Chile 158 C1 34 24 S 70 50W
Renhua, China 69 E9 25 5N 113 40 E
Renhuai, China 68 D6 27 48N 106 24 E
Reni, U.S.S.R. 52 D3 45 28N 28 15 E
Renigunta, India 83 H4 13 38N 79 30 E
Renk, Sudan 95 E3 11 50N 32 50 E
Renkum, Neths. 20 E7 51 58N 5 43 E
Renmark, Australia 116 C4 34 11 S 140 43 E
Rennell, Solomon Is. 121 N11 11 40 S 160 10 E
Rennell Sd., Canada 130 C2 53 23N 132 35W
Renner Springs T.O., Australia 114 B1 18 20 S 133 47 E
Rennes, France 22 D5 48 7N 1 41W
Rennes, Bassin de, France 22 E5 48 0N 1 30W
Reno, U.S.A. 144 F7 39 30N 119 50W
Reno →, Italy 39 D9 44 37N 12 17 E
Renovo, U.S.A. 136 E7 41 20N 77 47W
Renqiu, China 66 E9 38 43N 116 5 E
Rensselaer, Ind., U.S.A. 141 D9 40 57N 87 10W
Rensselaer, N.Y., U.S.A. 137 D11 42 38N 73 41W
Rentería, Spain 34 B3 43 19N 1 54W
Renton, U.S.A. 144 C4 47 30N 122 9W
Renwick, N.Z. 119 B8 41 30 S 173 51 E
Réo, Burkina Faso 100 C4 12 28N 2 35W
Reotipur, India 81 G10 25 33N 83 45 E
Repalle, India 83 F5 16 2N 80 45 E
Répcelak, Hungary 31 D10 47 24N 17 1 E
Republic, Mich., U.S.A. 134 B2 46 25N 87 59W
Republic, Wash., U.S.A. 142 B4 48 38N 118 42W
Republican →, U.S.A. 138 F6 39 3N 96 48W
Republican City, U.S.A. 138 E5 40 9N 99 20W
Republiek, Surinam 153 B6 5 30N 55 13W
Repulse Bay, Canada 127 B11 66 30N 86 30W
Requena, Peru 156 B3 5 5 S 73 52W
Requena, Spain 35 F3 39 30N 1 4W
Resadiye = Datça, Turkey 45 H9 36 46N 27 40 E
Reşadiye, Turkey 88 C7 40 23N 37 20 E
Resele, Sweden 14 A11 63 20N 17 5 E
Resen, Yugoslavia 42 F6 41 5N 21 0 E
Reserve, Canada 131 C8 52 28N 102 39W
Reserve, U.S.A. 143 K9 33 50N 108 54W
Resht = Rasht, Iran 85 B6 37 20N 49 40 E
Resistencia, Argentina 158 B4 27 30 S 59 0W
Reşiţa, Romania 42 B6 45 18N 21 53 E
Resko, Poland 47 B2 53 47N 15 25 E
Resolution I., Canada 127 B13 61 30N 65 0W
Resolution I., N.Z. 119 F1 45 40 S 166 40 E
Resplandes, Brazil 154 C2 6 17 S 45 13W
Resplendor, Brazil 155 E3 19 20 S 41 15W
Ressano Garcia, Mozam. 105 D5 25 25 S 32 0 E
Reston, Canada 131 D8 49 33N 101 6W
Reszel, Poland 47 A8 54 4N 21 10 E
Retalhuleu, Guatemala 148 D1 14 33N 91 46W
Reteag, Romania 46 B5 47 10N 24 0 E
Retenue, L. de, Zaïre 107 E2 11 0 S 27 0 E
Rethel, France 23 C11 49 30N 4 20 E
Rethem, Germany 26 C5 52 47N 9 25 E
Réthímnon, Greece 32 D6 35 18N 24 30 E
Réthímnon □, Greece 32 D6 35 23N 24 28 E
Retiche, Alpi, Switz. 29 D10 46 30N 10 0 E
Retie, Belgium 21 F6 51 16N 5 5 E
Retiers, France 22 E5 47 55N 1 23W
Retortillo, Spain 36 E4 40 48N 6 21W
Rétság, Hungary 31 D12 47 58N 19 10 E
Reuland, Belgium 21 H8 50 12N 6 8 E
Réunion ■, Ind. Oc. 109 G4 21 0 S 56 0 E
Reus, Spain 34 D6 41 10N 1 5 E
Reusel, Neths. 21 F6 51 21N 5 9 E
Reuss →, Switz. 29 B6 47 16N 8 24 E
Reutlingen, Germany 27 G5 48 28N 9 13 E
Reutte, Austria 30 D3 47 29N 10 42 E
Reuver, Neths. 21 F8 51 17N 6 5 E
Reval = Tallinn, U.S.S.R. 50 B4 59 22N 24 48 E
Revda, U.S.S.R. 54 C6 56 48N 59 57 E
Revel, France 24 E6 43 28N 2 0 E
Revelganj, India 81 G11 25 50N 84 40 E
Revelstoke, Canada 130 C5 51 0N 118 10W
Reventazón, Peru 156 B1 6 10 S 80 58W
Revigny-sur-Ornain, France 23 D11 48 49N 4 59 E
Revilla Gigedo, Is., Pac. Oc. 123 F16 18 40N 112 0W
Revillagigedo I., U.S.A. 130 B2 55 50N 131 20W
Revin, France 23 C11 49 55N 4 39 E
Revolyutsii, Pix, U.S.S.R. 55 D6 38 31N 72 21 E
Revuè →, Mozam. 107 F3 19 50 S 34 0 E
Rewa, India 81 G9 24 33N 81 25 E
Rewa →, Guyana 153 C6 3 19N 58 42W
Rewari, India 80 E7 28 15N 76 40 E
Rexburg, U.S.A. 142 E8 43 55N 111 50W
Rey, Iran 85 C6 35 35N 51 25 E
Rey, Rio del →, Nigeria 101 E6 4 30N 8 48 E
Rey Malabo, Eq. Guin. 101 E6 3 45N 8 50 E
Reyes, Bolivia 156 C4 14 19 S 67 23W
Reyes, Pt., U.S.A. 144 H3 37 59N 123 2W
Reykjahlið, Iceland 12 D5 65 40N 16 55W
Reykjanes, Iceland 12 E2 63 48N 22 40W
Reykjavík, Iceland 12 D3 64 10N 21 57W
Reynolds, Canada 131 D9 49 40N 95 55W
Reynolds, U.S.A. 140 C6 41 20N 90 40W
Reynolds Ra., Australia 112 D5 22 30 S 133 0 E
Reynoldsville, U.S.A. 136 E6 41 5N 78 58W
Reynosa, Mexico 147 B5 26 5N 98 18W
Rezekne, U.S.S.R. 50 C5 56 30N 27 17 E
Rezh, U.S.S.R. 54 C7 57 23N 61 24 E
Rezovo, Bulgaria 43 F13 42 0N 28 0 E
Rezvān, Iran 85 E8 27 34N 56 6 E
Rgotina, Yugoslavia 42 C7 44 1N 22 17 E
Rhamnus, Greece 45 F6 38 12N 24 3 E
Rharis, O. →, Algeria 99 C6 26 0N 5 4 E
Rhayader, U.K. 17 E4 52 19N 3 30W
Rheden, Neths. 20 D8 52 3N 6 3 E
Rhein, Canada 131 C8 51 25N 102 15W
Rhein →, Europe 20 E8 51 52N 6 2 E
Rhein-Main-Donau-Kanal, Germany 27 F7 49 1N 11 27 E
Rheinbach, Germany 26 E2 50 38N 6 54 E
Rheine, Germany 26 C3 52 17N 7 25 E
Rheineck, Switz. 29 B9 47 28N 9 31 E
Rheinfelden, Switz. 28 A5 47 32N 7 47 E
Rheinland-Pfalz □, Germany 27 F3 50 0N 7 0 E
Rheinsberg, Germany 26 B8 53 6N 12 52 E
Rheinwaldhorn, Switz. 29 D8 46 30N 9 3 E
Rhenen, Neths. 20 E7 51 58N 5 33 E
Rheriss, Oued →, Morocco 98 B4 30 50N 4 34W
Rheydt, Germany 26 D2 51 10N 6 24 E
Rhin = Rhein →, Europe 20 E8 51 52N 6 2 E
Rhinau, France 23 D14 48 19N 7 43 E
Rhine = Rhein →, Europe 20 E8 51 52N 6 2 E
Rhineland-Palatinate □ = Rheinland-Pfalz □, Germany 27 F3 50 0N 7 0 E
Rhinelander, U.S.A. 138 C10 45 38N 89 29W
Rhino Camp, Uganda 106 B3 3 0N 31 22 E
Rhir, Cap, Morocco 98 B3 30 38N 9 54W
Rhisnes, Belgium 21 G5 50 31N 4 48 E
Rho, Italy 38 C6 45 31N 9 2 E
Rhode Island □, U.S.A. 137 E13 41 38N 71 37W
Rhodes = Ródhos, Greece 32 C10 36 15N 28 10 E
Rhodesia = Zimbabwe ■, Africa 107 F3 19 0 S 30 0 E
Rhodope Mts. = Rhodopi Planina, Bulgaria 43 F9 41 40N 24 20 E
Rhodopi Planina, Bulgaria 43 F9 41 40N 24 20 E
Rhondda, U.K. 17 F4 51 39N 3 30W
Rhône □, France 25 C8 45 54N 4 35 E
Rhône →, France 25 E8 43 28N 4 42 E
Rhum, U.K. 18 E2 57 0N 6 20W
Rhyl, U.K. 16 D4 53 19N 3 29W
Rhymney, U.K. 17 F4 51 45N 3 17W
Ri-Aba, Eq. Guin. 101 E6 3 28N 8 40 E
Riachão, Brazil 154 C2 7 20 S 46 37W
Riacho de Santana, Brazil 155 D3 13 37 S 42 57W
Rialma, Brazil 155 E2 15 18 S 49 34W
Riang, India 78 B4 27 31N 92 56 E
Riaño, Spain 36 C6 42 59N 5 0W
Rians, France 25 E9 43 37N 5 44 E
Riansares →, Spain 34 F1 39 32N 3 18W
Riasi, India 81 C6 33 10N 74 50 E
Riau □, Indonesia 70 E2 0 0 102 35 E
Riau, Kepulauan, Indonesia 70 D2 0 30N 104 20 E
Riau Arch. = Riau, Kepulauan, Indonesia 70 D2 0 30N 104 20 E
Riaza, Spain 34 D1 41 18N 3 30W
Riaza →, Spain 34 D1 41 42N 3 55W
Riba de Saelices, Spain 34 E2 40 55N 2 17W
Ribadavia, Spain 36 C2 42 17N 8 8W
Ribadeo, Spain 36 B3 43 35N 7 5W
Ribadesella, Spain 36 B5 43 30N 5 7W
Ribamar, Brazil 154 B3 2 33 S 44 3W
Ribas, Spain 34 C7 42 19N 2 15 E
Ribas do Rio Pardo, Brazil 157 E7 20 27 S 53 46W
Ribāţ, Yemen 86 D4 14 18N 44 15 E
Ribble →, U.K. 16 C5 54 13N 2 20W
Ribe, Denmark 15 J2 55 19N 8 44 E
Ribeauvillé, France 23 D14 48 10N 7 20 E
Ribécourt, France 23 C9 49 30N 2 55 E
Ribeira, Spain 36 C2 42 36N 8 58W
Ribeira Brava, Madeira 33 D2 32 41N 17 4W
Ribeira do Pombal, Brazil 154 D4 10 50 S 38 32W
Ribeirão Prêto, Brazil 159 A6 21 10 S 47 50W
Ribeiro Gonçalves, Brazil 154 C2 7 32 S 45 14W
Ribemont, France 23 C10 49 47N 3 27 E
Ribera, Italy 40 E6 37 30N 13 13 E
Ribérac, France 24 C4 45 15N 0 20 E
Riberalta, Bolivia 157 C4 11 0 S 66 0W
Ribnica, Yugoslavia 39 C11 45 45N 14 45 E
Ribnitz-Damgarten, Germany 26 A8 54 14N 12 24 E
Ričany, Czech. 30 B7 50 0N 14 40 E
Riccarton, N.Z. 119 D7 43 32 S 172 37 E
Riccia, Italy 41 A7 41 30N 14 50 E
Riccione, Italy 39 E9 44 0N 12 39 E
Rice, U.S.A. 145 L12 34 5N 114 51W
Rice L., Canada 136 B6 44 12N 78 10W
Rice Lake, U.S.A. 138 C9 45 30N 91 42W
Rich, Morocco 98 B4 32 16N 4 30W
Rich Hill, U.S.A. 139 F7 38 5N 94 22W
Richards Bay, S. Africa 105 D5 28 48 S 32 6 E
Richards L., Canada 131 B7 59 10N 107 10W
Richardson →, Canada 131 B6 58 25N 111 14W
Richardson Mts., N.Z. 119 E3 44 49 S 168 34 E
Richardson Springs, U.S.A. 144 F5 39 51N 121 46W
Richardton, U.S.A. 138 B3 46 56N 102 22W
Riche, C., Australia 113 F2 34 36 S 118 47 E
Richelieu, France 22 F7 47 0N 0 20 E
Richey, U.S.A. 138 B2 47 42N 105 5W
Richfield, Idaho, U.S.A. 142 E6 43 2N 114 5W
Richfield, Utah, U.S.A. 143 G8 38 50N 112 0W
Richford, U.S.A. 137 B12 45 0N 72 40W
Richibucto, Canada 129 C7 46 42N 64 54W
Richland, Ga., U.S.A. 135 J3 32 7N 84 40W
Richland, Iowa, U.S.A. 140 C5 41 13N 92 0W
Richland, Mo., U.S.A. 140 G4 37 51N 92 26W
Richland, Oreg., U.S.A. 142 D5 44 49N 117 9W
Richland, Wash., U.S.A. 142 C4 46 15N 119 15W
Richland Center, U.S.A. 138 D9 43 21N 90 22W
Richlands, U.S.A. 134 G5 37 7N 81 49W
Richmond, N.S.W., Australia 117 B9 33 35 S 150 42 E
Richmond, Queens., Australia 114 C3 20 43 S 143 8 E
Richmond, N.Z. 119 B8 41 20 S 173 12 E
Richmond, S. Africa 105 D5 29 51 S 30 18 E
Richmond, U.K. 16 C6 54 24N 1 43W
Richmond, Calif., U.S.A. 144 H4 37 58N 122 21W
Richmond, Ind., U.S.A. 141 E12 39 50N 84 50W
Richmond, Ky., U.S.A. 141 G12 37 40N 84 20W
Richmond, Mich., U.S.A. 136 D2 42 47N 82 45W
Richmond, Mo., U.S.A. 138 F8 39 15N 93 58W
Richmond, Tex., U.S.A. 139 L7 29 32N 95 42W
Richmond, Utah, U.S.A. 142 F8 41 55N 111 48W
Richmond, Va., U.S.A. 134 G7 37 33N 77 27W
Richmond, Mt., N.Z. 119 B8 41 32 S 173 22 E
Richmond Ra., Australia 115 D5 29 0 S 152 45 E
Richmond Ra., N.Z. 119 B8 41 32 S 173 22 E
Richmond-upon-Thames, U.K. 17 F7 51 28N 0 18W
Richterswil, Switz. 29 B7 47 13N 8 43 E
Richton, U.S.A. 135 K1 31 23N 88 58W
Richwood, Ohio, U.S.A. 141 D13 40 26N 83 18W
Richwood, W. Va., U.S.A. 134 F5 38 17N 80 32W
Ricla, Spain 34 D3 41 31N 1 24W
Ricupe, Angola 103 E4 14 37 S 21 25 E
Ridā', Yemen 86 D4 14 25N 44 50 E
Ridderkerk, Neths. 20 E5 51 52N 4 35 E
Riddes, Switz. 28 D4 46 11N 7 14 E
Ridge Farm, U.S.A. 141 E9 39 54N 87 39W
Ridgecrest, U.S.A. 145 K9 35 37N 117 40W
Ridgedale, Canada 131 C8 53 0N 104 10W
Ridgefield, U.S.A. 144 E4 45 49N 122 45W
Ridgeland, U.S.A. 135 J5 32 30N 80 58W
Ridgelands, Australia 114 C5 23 16 S 150 17 E
Ridgetown, Canada 128 D3 42 26N 81 52W
Ridgeville, U.S.A. 141 D11 40 18N 85 2W
Ridgewood, U.S.A. 137 F10 40 59N 74 7W
Ridgway, Ill., U.S.A. 141 G8 37 48N 88 16W
Ridgway, Pa., U.S.A. 136 E6 41 25N 78 43W
Riding Mountain Nat. Park, Canada 131 C9 50 50N 100 0W
Ridley, Mt., Australia 113 F3 33 12 S 122 7 E
Ried, Austria 30 C6 48 14N 13 30 E
Riedlingen, Germany 27 G5 48 9N 9 28 E
Riel, Neths. 21 E6 51 31N 5 1 E
Rienza →, Italy 39 B8 46 49N 11 47 E
Riesa, Germany 26 D9 51 19N 13 19 E
Riesco, I., Chile 160 D2 52 55 S 72 40W
Riesi, Italy 41 E7 37 16N 14 4 E
Riet →, S. Africa 104 D3 29 0 S 23 54 E
Rieti, Italy 39 F9 42 23N 12 50 E
Rieupeyroux, France 24 D6 44 19N 2 12 E
Riez, France 25 E10 43 49N 6 6 E
Riffe, L., U.S.A. 144 D4 46 30N 122 20W
Rifle, U.S.A. 142 G10 39 40N 107 50W
Rifstangi, Iceland 12 C5 66 32N 16 12W
Rift Valley □, Kenya 106 B4 0 20N 36 0 E
Rig Rig, Chad 97 F2 14 13N 14 25 E
Riga, U.S.S.R. 50 C4 56 53N 24 8 E
Riga, G. of = Rīgas Jūras Līcis, U.S.S.R. 50 C3 57 40N 23 45 E
Rīgān, Iran 85 D8 28 37N 58 58 E
Rīgas Jūras Līcis, U.S.S.R. 50 C3 57 40N 23 45 E
Rigaud, Canada 137 A10 45 29N 74 18W
Rigby, U.S.A. 142 E8 43 41N 111 58W
Rīgestān □, Afghan. 79 C2 30 15N 65 0 E
Riggins, U.S.A. 142 D5 45 29N 116 26W
Rignac, France 24 D6 44 25N 2 16 E
Rigolet, Canada 129 B8 54 10N 58 23W
Riihimäki, Finland 13 F18 60 45N 24 48 E
Riiser-Larsen-halvøya, Antarctica 7 C4 68 0 S 35 0 E
Rijau, Nigeria 101 C6 11 8N 5 17 E
Rijeka, Yugoslavia 39 C11 45 20N 14 21 E
Rijeka Crnojevica, Yugoslavia 42 E4 42 24N 19 1 E
Rijen, Neths. 21 E5 51 35N 4 55 E
Rijkevorsel, Belgium 21 F5 51 21N 4 46 E
Rijn →, Neths. 20 D4 52 12N 4 21 E
Rijnsberg, Neths. 20 D4 52 11N 4 27 E
Rijsbergen, Neths. 21 E5 51 31N 4 41 E
Rijssen, Neths. 20 D9 52 19N 6 31 E
Rijswijk, Neths. 20 D4 52 4N 4 22 E
Rikā', W. ar →, Si. Arabia 86 B4 22 25N 44 50 E
Rike, Ethiopia 95 E4 10 50N 39 53 E
Rikuzentakada, Japan 60 E10 39 0N 141 40 E
Rila, Bulgaria 43 E8 42 7N 23 7 E
Rila Planina, Bulgaria 42 E8 42 10N 23 0 E
Riley, U.S.A. 142 E4 43 35N 119 33W
Rima →, Nigeria 101 C6 13 4N 5 10 E
Rimah, Wadi ar →, Si. Arabia 84 E4 26 5N 41 30 E
Rimavská Sobota, Czech. 31 C13 48 22N 20 2 E
Rimbey, Canada 130 C6 52 35N 114 15W
Rimbo, Sweden 14 E12 59 44N 18 21 E
Rimi, Nigeria 101 C6 12 58N 7 43 E
Rímini, Italy 39 D9 44 3N 12 33 E
Rîmna →, Romania 46 D8 45 36N 27 3 E
Rîmnicu Sărat, Romania 46 D8 45 26N 27 3 E
Rîmnicu Vîlcea, Romania 46 D5 45 9N 24 21 E
Rimouski, Canada 129 C6 48 27N 68 30W
Rimrock, U.S.A. 144 D5 46 38N 121 10W
Rinca, Indonesia 71 F5 8 45 S 119 35 E
Rincón de Romos, Mexico 146 C4 22 14N 102 18W
Rinconada, Argentina 158 A2 22 26 S 66 10W
Ringarum, Sweden 15 F10 58 21N 16 26 E
Ringe, Denmark 15 J4 55 13N 10 28 E
Ringgold Is., Fiji 121 A3 16 15 S 179 25W
Ringim, Nigeria 101 C6 12 13N 9 10 E
Ringkøbing, Denmark 15 H2 56 5N 8 15 E
Ringling, U.S.A. 142 C8 46 16N 110 56W
Ringsaker, Norway 14 D4 60 54N 10 45 E
Ringsted, Denmark 15 J5 55 25N 11 46 E
Ringvassøy, Norway 12 B15 69 56N 19 15 E
Rinía, Greece 45 G7 37 23N 25 13 E
Rinjani, Indonesia 70 F5 8 24 S 116 28 E
Rinteln, Germany 26 C5 52 11N 9 3 E
Río, Punta del, Spain 35 J2 36 49N 2 24W
Rio Branco, Brazil 156 B4 9 58 S 67 49W
Río Branco, Uruguay 159 C5 32 40 S 53 40W
Rio Brilhante, Brazil 159 A5 21 48 S 54 33W
Río Bueno, Chile 160 B2 40 19 S 72 58W
Río Chico, Venezuela 152 A4 10 19N 65 59W
Rio Claro, Brazil 159 A6 22 19 S 47 35W
Rio Claro, Trin. & Tob. 149 D7 10 20N 61 25W
Río Colorado, Argentina 160 A4 39 0 S 64 0W
Río Cuarto, Argentina 158 C3 33 10 S 64 25W
Rio das Pedras, Mozam. 105 C6 23 8 S 35 28 E
Rio de Contas, Brazil 155 D3 13 36 S 41 48W
Rio de Janeiro, Brazil 155 F3 23 0 S 43 12W
Rio de Janeiro □, Brazil 155 F3 22 50 S 43 0W
Rio do Prado, Brazil 155 E3 16 35 S 40 34W
Rio do Sul, Brazil 159 B6 27 13 S 49 37W
Río Gallegos, Argentina 160 D3 51 35 S 69 15W
Río Grande, Argentina 160 D3 53 50 S 67 45W
Río Grande, Bolivia 156 E4 20 51 S 67 17W
Rio Grande, Brazil 159 C5 32 0 S 52 20W
Río Grande, Mexico 146 C4 23 50N 103 2W
Río Grande, Nic. 148 D3 12 54N 83 33W
Rio Grande →, U.S.A. 139 N6 25 57N 97 9W
Rio Grande City, U.S.A. 139 M5 26 23N 98 49W
Río Grande del Norte →, N. Amer. 133 E7 26 0N 97 0W
Rio Grande do Norte □, Brazil 154 C4 5 40 S 36 0W
Rio Grande do Sul □, Brazil 159 C5 30 0 S 53 0W
Río Hato, Panama 148 E3 8 22N 80 10W
Río Lagartos, Mexico 147 C7 21 36N 88 10W
Rio Largo, Brazil 154 C4 9 28 S 35 50W
Rio Maior, Portugal 37 F2 39 19N 8 57W
Rio Marina, Italy 38 F7 42 48N 10 25 E
Río Mayo, Argentina 160 C2 45 40 S 70 15W
Río Mulatos, Bolivia 156 D4 19 40 S 66 50W
Río Muni = Mbini □, Eq. Guin. 102 B2 1 30N 10 0 E
Rio Negro, Brazil 159 B6 26 0 S 49 55W
Río Negro, Chile 160 B2 40 47 S 73 14W
Rio Negro, Pantanal do, Brazil 157 D6 19 0 S 56 0W
Rio Pardo, Brazil 159 C5 30 0 S 52 30W
Río Pico, Argentina 160 B2 44 0 S 70 22W
Rio Real, Brazil 155 D4 11 28 S 37 56W
Río Segundo, Argentina 158 C3 31 40 S 63 59W
Río Tercero, Argentina 158 C3 32 15 S 64 8W
Rio Tinto, Brazil 154 C4 6 48 S 35 5W
Rio Tinto, Portugal 36 D2 41 11N 8 34W
Rio Verde, Brazil 155 E1 17 50 S 51 0W
Río Verde, Mexico 147 C5 21 56N 99 59W
Rio Verde de Mato Grosso, Brazil 157 D7 18 56 S 54 52W
Rio Vista, U.S.A. 144 G5 38 11N 121 44W
Ríobamba, Ecuador 152 D2 1 50 S 78 45W
Ríohacha, Colombia 152 A3 11 33N 72 55W

S

San Angelo 259

St. Paul I., *Canada* **129 C7** 47 12N 60 9W
St.-Paul-lès-Dax, *France* **24 E2** 43 44N 1 3W
St.-Péray, *France* **25 D8** 44 57N 4 50 E
St.-Père-en-Retz, *France* **22 E4** 47 11N 2 2W
St. Peter, *U.S.A.* **138 C8** 44 21N 93 57W
St. Peter Port, *Chan. Is.* **17 H5** 49 27N 2 31W
St. Peters, *N.S., Canada* **129 C7** 45 40N 60 53W
St. Peters, *P.E.I., Canada* **129 C7** 46 25N 62 35W
St. Petersburg = Leningrad, *U.S.S.R.* **50 B7** 59 55N 30 20 E
St. Petersburg, *U.S.A.* **135 M4** 27 45N 82 40W
St.-Philbert-de-Grand-Lieu, *France* **22 E5** 47 2N 1 39W
St.-Pierre, *St- P. & M.* **129 C8** 46 46N 56 12W
St. Pierre, *Seychelles* **109 E3** 9 20 S 46 0 E
St-Pierre, L., *Canada* **128 C5** 46 12N 72 52W
St.-Pierre-d'Oléron, *France* **24 C2** 45 57N 1 19W
St.-Pierre-Église, *France* **22 C5** 49 40N 1 24W
St.-Pierre-en-Port, *France* **22 C7** 49 48N 0 30 E
St.-Pierre et Miquelon □, *St- P. & M.* **129 C8** 46 55N 56 10W
St.-Pierre-le-Moûtier, *France* **23 F10** 46 47N 3 7 E
St.-Pierre-sur-Dives, *France* **22 C6** 49 2N 0 1W
St.-Pieters Leew, *Belgium* **21 G4** 50 47N 4 16 E
St.-Pol-de-Léon, *France* **22 D3** 48 41N 4 0W
St.-Pol-sur-Mer, *France* **23 A9** 51 1N 2 20 E
St.-Pol-sur-Ternoise, *France* **23 B9** 50 23N 2 20 E
St.-Pons, *France* **24 E6** 43 30N 2 45 E
St.-Pourçain-sur-Sioule, *France* **24 B7** 46 18N 3 18 E
St.-Quay-Portrieux, *France* **22 D4** 48 39N 2 51W
St.-Quentin, *France* **23 C10** 49 50N 3 16 E
St.-Rambert-d'Albon, *France* **25 C8** 45 17N 4 49 E
St.-Raphaël, *France* **25 E10** 43 25N 6 46 E
St. Regis, *U.S.A.* **142 C6** 47 20N 115 3W
St.-Rémy-de-Provence, *France* **25 E8** 43 48N 4 50 E
St.-Renan, *France* **22 D2** 48 26N 4 37W
St.-Saëns, *France* **22 C8** 49 41N 1 16 E
St.-Sauveur-en-Puisaye, *France* **23 E10** 47 37N 3 12 E
St.-Sauveur-le-Vicomte, *France* **22 C5** 49 23N 1 32W
St.-Savin, *France* **24 B4** 46 34N 0 53 E
St.-Savinien, *France* **24 C3** 45 53N 0 42W
St. Sebastien, Tanjon' i, *Madag.* **105 A8** 12 26 S 48 44 E
St.-Seine-l'Abbaye, *France* **23 E11** 47 26N 4 47 E
St.-Sernin-sur-Rance, *France* **24 E6** 43 54N 2 35 E
St.-Servan-sur-Mer, *France* **22 D4** 48 38N 2 2W
St.-Sever, *France* **24 E3** 43 45N 0 35W
St.-Sever-Calvados, *France* **22 D5** 48 50N 1 3W
St-Siméon, *Canada* **129 C6** 47 51N 69 54W
St. Stephen, *Canada* **129 C6** 45 16N 67 17W
St.-Sulpice, *France* **24 E5** 43 46N 1 41 E
St.-Sulpice-Laurière, *France* **24 B5** 46 3N 1 29 E
St.-Syprien, *France* **24 F7** 42 37N 3 2 E
St.-Thégonnec, *France* **22 D3** 48 31N 3 57W
St. Thomas, *Canada* **128 D3** 42 45N 81 10W
St. Thomas, *Virgin Is.* **149 C7** 18 21N 64 55W
St-Tite, *Canada* **128 C5** 46 45N 72 34W
St.-Tropez, *France* **25 E10** 43 17N 6 38 E
St. Troud = Sint Truiden, *Belgium* **21 G6** 50 48N 5 10 E
St.-Vaast-la-Hougue, *France* **22 C5** 49 35N 1 17W
St.-Valéry-en-Caux, *France* **22 C7** 49 52N 0 43 E
St.-Valéry-sur-Somme, *France* **23 B8** 50 11N 1 38 E
St.-Vallier, *France* **25 C8** 45 11N 4 50 E
St.-Vallier-de-Thiey, *France* **25 E10** 43 42N 6 51 E
St.-Varent, *France* **22 F6** 46 53N 0 13W
St. Vincent, *C. Verde Is.* **8 G6** 18 0N 26 1W
St. Vincent, *W. Indies* **149 D7** 13 10N 61 10W
St. Vincent, G., *Australia* **116 C3** 35 0 S 138 0 E
St. Vincent and the Grenadines ■, *W. Indies* **149 D7** 13 0N 61 10W
St.-Vincent-de-Tyrosse, *France* **24 E2** 43 39N 1 19W
St. Vincent Passage, *W. Indies* **149 D7** 13 30N 61 0W
St-Vith, *Belgium* **21 H8** 50 17N 6 9 E
St.-Yrieix-la-Perche, *France* **24 C5** 45 31N 1 12 E
Ste.-Adresse, *France* **22 C7** 49 31N 0 5 E
Ste-Agathe-des-Monts, *Canada* **128 C5** 46 3N 74 17W
Ste-Anne de Beaupré, *Canada* **129 C5** 47 2N 70 58W
Ste-Anne-des-Monts, *Canada* **129 C6** 49 8N 66 30W
Ste-Croix, *Switz.* **28 C3** 46 49N 6 34 E
Ste.-Enimie, *France* **24 D7** 44 22N 3 26 E
Ste.-Foy-la-Grande, *France* **24 D4** 44 50N 0 13 E
Ste. Genevieve, *U.S.A.* **140 G6** 37 59N 90 2W
Ste.-Hermine, *France* **24 B2** 46 32N 1 4W
Ste.-Livrade-sur-Lot, *France* **24 D4** 44 24N 0 36 E
Ste-Marguerite →, *Canada* **129 B6** 50 9N 66 36W
Ste.-Marie, *Martinique* **149 D7** 14 48N 61 1W
Ste.-Marie-aux-Mines, *France* **23 D14** 48 15N 7 12 E
Ste-Marie de la Madeleine, *Canada* **129 C5** 46 26N 71 0W
Ste.-Maure-de-Touraine, *France* **22 E7** 47 7N 0 37 E
Ste.-Maxime, *France* **25 E10** 43 19N 6 39 E
Ste.-Menehould, *France* **23 C11** 49 5N 4 54 E
Ste.-Mère-Église, *France* **22 C5** 49 24N 1 19W
Ste.-Rose, *Guadeloupe* **149 C7** 16 20N 61 45W
Ste. Rose du Lac, *Canada* **131 C9** 51 4N 99 30W
Saintes, *France* **24 C3** 45 45N 0 37W
Saintes, I. des, *Guadeloupe* **149 C7** 15 50N 61 35W
Stes.-Maries-de-la-Mer, *France* **25 E8** 43 26N 4 26 E
Saintonge, *France* **24 C3** 45 40N 0 50W
Saipan, *Pac. Oc.* **122 F6** 15 12N 145 45 E
Sairecábur, Cerro, *Bolivia* **158 A2** 22 43 S 67 54W
Saitama □, *Japan* **63 A11** 36 25N 139 30 E
Saito, *Japan* **62 E3** 32 3N 131 24 E
Sajama, *Bolivia* **156 D4** 18 7 S 69 0W
Sajan, *Yugoslavia* **42 B5** 45 50N 20 20 E
Sajószentpéter, *Hungary* **31 C13** 48 12N 20 44 E
Sajum, *India* **81 C8** 33 20N 79 0 E
Sak →, *S. Africa* **104 E3** 30 52 S 20 25 E
Sakai, *Japan* **63 C7** 34 30N 135 30 E
Sakaide, *Japan* **62 C5** 34 15N 133 50 E
Sakaiminato, *Japan* **62 B5** 35 38N 133 11 E
Sakākah, *Si. Arabia* **84 D4** 30 0N 40 8 E
Sakakawea, L., *U.S.A.* **138 B4** 47 30N 102 0W
Sakami, L., *Canada* **128 B4** 53 15N 77 0W
Sâkâne, 'Erg i-n, *Mali* **98 D4** 20 30N 1 30W
Sakania, *Zaïre* **107 E2** 12 43 S 28 30 E
Sakarya = Adapazarı, *Turkey* **88 C4** 40 48N 30 25 E
Sakarya □, *Turkey* **88 C4** 40 45N 30 25 E
Sakarya →, *Turkey* **88 F4** 41 7N 30 39 E
Sakashima-Guntō, *Japan* **61 M2** 24 46N 124 0 E
Sakata, *Japan* **60 E9** 38 55N 139 50 E
Sakchu, *N. Korea* **67 D13** 40 23N 125 2 E
Sakeny →, *Madag.* **105 C8** 20 0 S 45 25 E
Sakété, *Benin* **101 D5** 6 40N 2 45 E
Sakhalin, *U.S.S.R.* **57 D15** 51 0N 143 0 E
Sakhalinskiy Zaliv, *U.S.S.R.* **57 D15** 54 0N 141 0 E
Sakhi Gopal, *India* **82 E7** 19 58N 85 50 E
Saki, *U.S.S.R.* **52 D5** 45 9N 33 34 E
Sakiai, *U.S.S.R.* **50 D3** 54 59N 23 0 E
Sakmara, *U.S.S.R.* **54 F4** 52 0N 55 20 E
Sakmara →, *U.S.S.R.* **54 F4** 51 46N 55 1 E
Sakon Nakhon, *Thailand* **76 D5** 17 10N 104 9 E
Sakrand, *Pakistan* **80 F3** 26 10N 68 15 E
Sakri, *India* **82 D2** 21 2N 74 20 E
Sakrivier, *S. Africa* **104 E3** 30 54 S 20 28 E
Sakskøbing, *Denmark* **15 K5** 54 49N 11 39 E
Saku, *Japan* **63 A10** 36 17N 138 31 E
Sakuma, *Japan* **63 B9** 35 3N 137 49 E
Sakura, *Japan* **63 B12** 35 43N 140 14 E
Sakurai, *Japan* **63 C7** 34 30N 135 51 E
Sal →, *U.S.S.R.* **53 C9** 47 31N 40 45 E
Šal'a, *Czech.* **31 C10** 48 10N 17 50 E
Sala, *Sweden* **13 G14** 59 58N 16 35 E
Sala Consilina, *Italy* **41 B8** 40 23N 15 35 E
Sala-y-Gómez, *Pac. Oc.* **123 K17** 26 28 S 105 28W
Salaberry-de-Valleyfield, *Canada* **128 C5** 45 15N 74 8W
Saladas, *Argentina* **158 B4** 28 15 S 58 40W
Saladillo, *Argentina* **158 D4** 35 40 S 59 55W
Salado →, *Buenos Aires, Argentina* **158 D4** 35 44 S 57 22W
Salado →, *La Pampa, Argentina* **160 A3** 37 30 S 67 0W
Salado →, *Río Negro, Argentina* **160 B3** 41 34 S 65 3W
Salado →, *Santa Fe, Argentina* **158 C3** 31 40 S 60 41W
Salado →, *Mexico* **146 B5** 26 52N 99 19W
Salaga, *Ghana* **101 D4** 8 31N 0 31W
Şalāh, *Syria* **91 C5** 32 40N 36 45 E
Sălaj □, *Romania* **46 B4** 47 15N 23 0 E
Sálakhos, *Greece* **32 C9** 36 17N 27 57 E
Salala, *Liberia* **100 D2** 6 42N 10 7W
Salala, *Sudan* **94 C4** 21 17N 36 16 E
Salālah, *Oman* **87 C6** 16 56N 53 59 E
Salamanca, *Chile* **158 C1** 31 46 S 70 59W
Salamanca, *Spain* **36 E5** 40 58N 5 39W
Salamanca, *U.S.A.* **136 D6** 42 10N 78 42W
Salamanca □, *Spain* **36 E5** 40 57N 5 40W
Salāmatābād, *Iran* **84 C5** 35 39N 47 50 E
Salamina, *Colombia* **152 B2** 5 25N 75 29W
Salamis, *Cyprus* **32 D12** 35 11N 33 54 E
Salamis, *Greece* **45 G5** 37 56N 23 30 E
Salamonie, Res., *U.S.A.* **141 D11** 40 45N 85 35W
Salar de Atacama, *Chile* **158 A2** 23 30 S 68 25W
Salar de Uyuni, *Bolivia* **156 E4** 20 30 S 67 45W
Sălard, *Romania* **46 B3** 47 12N 22 3 E
Salas, *Spain* **36 B4** 43 25N 6 15W
Salas de los Infantes, *Spain* **34 C1** 42 2N 3 17W
Salatiga, *Indonesia* **71 G14** 7 19 S 110 30 E
Salavat, *U.S.S.R.* **54 E4** 53 21N 55 55 E
Salaverry, *Peru* **156 B2** 8 15 S 79 0W
Salawati, *Indonesia* **71 E8** 1 7 S 130 52 E
Salayar, *Indonesia* **71 F6** 6 7 S 120 30 E
Salazar →, *Spain* **34 C3** 42 40N 1 20W
Salbris, *France* **23 E9** 47 25N 2 3 E
Salcia, *Romania* **46 F5** 43 56N 24 55 E
Salcombe, *U.K.* **17 G4** 50 14N 3 47W
Salda Gölü, *Turkey* **88 E3** 37 22N 29 41 E
Saldaña, *Spain* **36 C6** 42 32N 4 48W
Saldanha, *S. Africa* **104 E2** 33 0 S 17 58 E
Saldanha B., *S. Africa* **104 E2** 33 6 S 18 0 E
Saldus, *U.S.S.R.* **50 C3** 56 38N 22 30 E
Sale, *Australia* **117 E7** 38 6 S 147 6 E
Salé, *Morocco* **98 B3** 34 3N 6 48W
Sale, *U.K.* **16 D5** 53 26N 2 19W
Salekhard, *U.S.S.R.* **48 A12** 66 30N 66 35 E
Salem, *India* **83 J4** 11 40N 78 11 E
Salem, *Ill., U.S.A.* **140 F8** 38 38N 88 57W
Salem, *Ind., U.S.A.* **141 F10** 38 38N 86 6W
Salem, *Mass., U.S.A.* **137 D14** 42 29N 70 53W
Salem, *Mo., U.S.A.* **139 G9** 37 40N 91 30W
Salem, *N.J., U.S.A.* **134 F8** 39 34N 75 29W
Salem, *Ohio, U.S.A.* **136 F4** 40 52N 80 50W
Salem, *Oreg., U.S.A.* **142 D2** 45 0N 123 0W
Salem, *S. Dak., U.S.A.* **138 D6** 43 44N 97 23W
Salem, *Va., U.S.A.* **134 G5** 37 19N 80 8W
Salemi, *Italy* **40 E5** 37 49N 12 47 E
Salernes, *France* **25 E10** 43 34N 6 15 E
Salerno, *Italy* **41 B7** 40 40N 14 44 E
Salerno, G. di, *Italy* **41 B7** 40 35N 14 45 E
Salford, *U.K.* **16 D5** 53 30N 2 17W
Salgir →, *U.S.S.R.* **52 D6** 45 38N 35 1 E
Salgótarján, *Hungary* **31 C12** 48 5N 19 47 E
Salgueiro, *Brazil* **154 C4** 8 4 S 39 6W
Salies-de-Béarn, *France* **24 E3** 43 28N 0 56W
Şalif, *Yemen* **86 D3** 15 18N 42 41 E
Salihli, *Turkey* **88 D3** 38 28N 28 8 E
Salin, *Burma* **78 E5** 20 35N 94 40 E
Salina, *Italy* **41 D7** 38 35N 14 50 E
Salina, *U.S.A.* **138 F6** 38 50N 97 40W
Salina Cruz, *Mexico* **147 D5** 16 10N 95 10W
Salinas, *Brazil* **155 E3** 16 10 S 42 10W
Salinas, *Chile* **158 A2** 23 31 S 69 29W
Salinas, *Ecuador* **152 D1** 2 10 S 80 58W
Salinas, *U.S.A.* **144 J5** 36 40N 121 41W
Salinas →, *Guatemala* **147 D6** 16 28N 90 31W
Salinas →, *U.S.A.* **144 J5** 36 45N 121 48W
Salinas, B. de, *Nic.* **148 D2** 11 4N 85 45W
Salinas, C. de, *Spain* **33 B10** 39 16N 3 4 E
Salinas, Pampa de las, *Argentina* **158 C2** 31 58 S 66 42W
Salinas Ambargasta, *Argentina* **158 B3** 29 0 S 65 0W
Salinas de Hidalgo, *Mexico* **146 C4** 22 30N 101 40W
Salinas Grandes, *Argentina* **158 C3** 30 0 S 65 0W
Saline →, *Ark., U.S.A.* **139 J8** 33 10N 92 8W
Saline →, *Kans., U.S.A.* **138 F6** 38 51N 97 30W
Salines, *Spain* **33 B10** 39 21N 3 3 E
Salinópolis, *Brazil* **154 B2** 0 40 S 47 20W
Salins-les-Bains, *France* **23 F12** 46 58N 5 52 E
Salir, *Portugal* **37 H2** 37 14N 8 2W
Salisbury = Harare, *Zimbabwe* **107 F3** 17 43 S 31 2 E
Salisbury, *Australia* **116 C3** 34 46 S 138 40 E
Salisbury, *U.K.* **17 F6** 51 4N 1 48W
Salisbury, *Md., U.S.A.* **134 F8** 38 20N 75 38W
Salisbury, *Mo., U.S.A.* **140 E4** 39 25N 92 48W
Salisbury, *N.C., U.S.A.* **135 H5** 35 20N 80 29W
Salisbury Plain, *U.K.* **17 F6** 51 13N 1 50W
Săliște, *Romania* **46 D4** 45 45N 23 56 E
Salitre →, *Brazil* **154 C3** 9 29 S 40 39W
Salka, *Nigeria* **101 C5** 10 20N 4 58 E
Salkhad, *Jordan* **91 C5** 32 30N 36 43 E
Sallent, *Spain* **34 D6** 41 49N 1 54 E
Salles-Curan, *France* **24 D6** 44 11N 2 48 E
Salling, *Denmark* **15 H2** 56 40N 8 55 E
Sallisaw, *U.S.A.* **139 H7** 35 26N 94 45W
Sallom Junction, *Sudan* **94 D4** 19 17N 37 6 E
Salmās, *Iran* **84 B5** 38 11N 44 47 E
Salmerón, *Spain* **34 E2** 40 33N 2 29W
Salmo, *Canada* **130 D5** 49 10N 117 20W
Salmon, *U.S.A.* **142 D7** 45 12N 113 56W
Salmon →, *Canada* **130 C4** 54 3N 122 40W
Salmon →, *U.S.A.* **142 D5** 45 51N 116 46W
Salmon Arm, *Canada* **130 C5** 50 40N 119 15W
Salmon Falls, *U.S.A.* **142 E6** 42 48N 114 59W
Salmon Gums, *Australia* **113 F3** 32 59 S 121 38 E
Salmon Res., *Canada* **129 C8** 48 5N 56 0W
Salmon River Mts., *U.S.A.* **142 D6** 45 0N 114 30W
Salo, *Finland* **13 F17** 60 22N 23 10 E
Salò, *Italy* **38 C7** 45 37N 10 32 E
Salobreña, *Spain* **37 J7** 36 44N 3 35W
Salome, *U.S.A.* **145 M13** 33 51N 113 37W
Salon-de-Provence, *France* **25 E9** 43 39N 5 6 E
Salonica = Thessaloníki, *Greece* **44 D4** 40 38N 22 58 E
Salonta, *Romania* **46 C2** 46 49N 21 42 E
Salor →, *Spain* **37 F3** 39 39N 7 3W
Salou, C., *Spain* **34 D6** 41 3N 1 10 E
Salsacate, *Argentina* **158 C2** 31 20 S 65 5W
Salses, *France* **24 F6** 42 50N 2 55 E
Salsette I., *India* **82 E1** 19 5N 72 50 E
Salsk, *U.S.S.R.* **53 C9** 46 28N 41 30 E
Salso →, *Italy* **40 E6** 37 6N 13 55 E
Salsomaggiore, *Italy* **38 D6** 44 48N 9 59 E
Salt →, *Canada* **130 B6** 60 0N 112 25W
Salt →, *Ariz., U.S.A.* **143 K7** 33 23N 112 18W
Salt →, *Mo., U.S.A.* **140 E5** 39 29N 91 5W
Salt Creek, *Australia* **116 D3** 36 8 S 139 38 E
Salt Fork →, *U.S.A.* **139 G6** 36 37N 97 7W
Salt Lake City, *U.S.A.* **142 F8** 40 45N 111 58W
Salt Range, *Pakistan* **80 C5** 32 30N 72 25 E
Salta, *Argentina* **158 A2** 24 57 S 65 25W
Salta □, *Argentina* **158 A2** 24 48 S 65 30W
Saltcoats, *U.K.* **18 F4** 55 38N 4 47W
Saltfjorden, *Norway* **12 C13** 67 15N 14 10 E
Saltholm, *Denmark* **15 J6** 55 38N 12 43 E
Salthólmavík, *Iceland* **12 D3** 65 24N 21 57W
Saltillo, *Mexico* **146 B4** 25 30N 100 57W
Salto, *Argentina* **158 C3** 34 20 S 60 15W
Salto, *Uruguay* **158 C4** 31 27 S 57 50W
Salto da Divisa, *Brazil* **155 E4** 16 0 S 39 57W
Salton City, *U.S.A.* **145 M11** 33 29N 115 51W
Salton Sea, *U.S.A.* **145 M11** 33 20N 115 50W
Saltpond, *Ghana* **101 D4** 5 15N 1 3W
Saltsjöbaden, *Sweden* **14 E12** 59 15N 18 20 E
Saltville, *U.S.A.* **134 G5** 36 53N 81 46W
Saluda →, *U.S.A.* **135 J5** 34 0N 81 4W
Salûm, *Egypt* **94 A2** 31 31N 25 7 E
Salûm, Khâlig el, *Egypt* **94 A2** 31 30N 25 9 E
Salur, *India* **82 E6** 18 27N 83 18 E
Salut, Is. du, *Fr. Guiana* **153 B7** 5 15N 52 35W
Saluzzo, *Italy* **38 D4** 44 39N 7 29 E
Salvación, B., *Chile* **160 D1** 50 50 S 75 10W
Salvador, *Brazil* **155 D4** 13 0 S 38 30W
Salvador, *Canada* **131 C7** 52 10N 109 32W
Salvador, L., *U.S.A.* **139 L9** 29 46N 90 16W
Salvaterra, *Brazil* **154 B2** 0 46 S 48 31W
Salvaterra de Magos, *Portugal* **37 F2** 39 1N 8 47W
Salvisa, *U.S.A.* **141 G12** 37 54N 84 51W
Sálvora, I., *Spain* **36 C2** 42 30N 8 58W
Salween →, *Burma* **78 G6** 16 31N 97 37 E
Salyany, *U.S.S.R.* **89 D13** 39 10N 48 50 E
Salyersville, *U.S.A.* **134 G4** 37 45N 83 4W
Salza →, *Austria* **30 D7** 47 40N 14 43 E
Salzach →, *Austria* **30 C5** 48 12N 12 56 E
Salzburg, *Austria* **30 D6** 47 48N 13 2 E
Salzburg □, *Austria* **30 D6** 47 15N 13 0 E
Salzgitter, *Germany* **26 C6** 52 13N 10 22 E
Salzwedel, *Germany* **26 C7** 52 50N 11 11 E
Sam, *Gabon* **102 B2** 0 58N 11 16 E
Sam Neua, *Laos* **76 B5** 20 29N 104 5 E
Sam Ngao, *Thailand* **76 D2** 17 18N 99 0 E
Sam Rayburn Res., *U.S.A.* **139 K7** 31 15N 94 20W
Sam Son, *Vietnam* **76 C5** 19 44N 105 54 E
Sam Teu, *Laos* **76 C5** 19 59N 104 38 E
Sama, *U.S.S.R.* **54 A7** 60 12N 60 22 E
Sama de Langreo, *Spain* **36 B5** 43 18N 5 40W
Samacimbo, *Angola* **103 E3** 13 33 S 16 59 E
Samagaltai, *U.S.S.R.* **57 D10** 50 36N 95 3 E
Samā'il, *Oman* **87 B7** 23 40N 57 50 E
Samaipata, *Bolivia* **157 D5** 18 9 S 63 52W
Samales Group, *Phil.* **71 C6** 6 0N 122 0 E
Samalkot, *India* **82 F6** 17 3N 82 13 E
Samâlût, *Egypt* **94 J7** 28 20N 30 42 E
Samana, *India* **80 D7** 30 10N 76 13 E
Samana Cay, *Bahamas* **149 B5** 23 3N 73 45W
Samandağı, *Turkey* **88 E6** 36 5N 35 59 E
Samanga, *Tanzania* **107 D4** 8 20 S 39 13 E
Samangán □, *Afghan.* **79 A3** 36 15N 68 3 E
Samangwa, *Zaïre* **103 C4** 4 23 S 24 10 E
Samani, *Japan* **60 C11** 42 7N 142 56 E
Samar, *Phil.* **71 B7** 12 0N 125 0 E
Samara →, *U.S.S.R.* **54 E2** 53 10N 50 4 E
Samarai, *Papua N. G.* **120 F6** 10 39 S 150 41 E
Samaria = Shōmrōn, *Jordan* **91 C4** 32 15N 35 13 E
Samariá, *Greece* **32 D5** 35 17N 23 58 E
Samarinda, *Indonesia* **70 E5** 0 30 S 117 9 E
Samarkand, *U.S.S.R.* **55 D3** 39 40N 66 55 E
Sāmarrā, *Iraq* **84 C4** 34 12N 43 52 E
Samastipur, *India* **81 G11** 25 50N 85 50 E
Samatan, *France* **24 E4** 43 29N 0 55 E
Samaúma, *Brazil* **157 B5** 7 50 S 60 2W
Samba, *India* **81 C6** 32 32N 75 10 E
Samba, *Zaïre* **103 C5** 4 38 S 26 22 E
Samba Caju, *Angola* **103 D3** 8 46 S 15 24 E
Sambaíba, *Brazil* **154 C2** 7 8 S 45 21W
Sambalpur, *India* **82 D7** 21 28N 84 4 E
Sambar, Tanjung, *Indonesia* **70 E4** 2 59 S 110 19 E
Sambas, *Indonesia* **70 D3** 1 20N 109 20 E
Sambava, *Madag.* **105 A9** 14 16 S 50 10 E
Sambawizi, *Zimbabwe* **107 F2** 18 24 S 26 13 E
Sambhal, *India* **81 E8** 28 35N 78 37 E
Sambhar, *India* **80 F6** 26 52N 75 6 E
Sambiase, *Italy* **41 D9** 38 58N 16 16 E
Sambonifacio, *Italy* **38 C8** 45 24N 11 16 E
Sambor, *Cambodia* **76 F6** 12 46N 106 0 E
Sambor, *U.S.S.R.* **50 G3** 49 30N 23 10 E
Sambre →, *Europe* **21 H5** 50 27N 4 52 E
Sambuca di Sicilia, *Italy* **40 E6** 37 39N 13 6 E
Samburu □, *Kenya* **106 B4** 1 10N 37 0 E
Samchŏk, *S. Korea* **67 F15** 37 30N 129 10 E
Samchonpo, *S. Korea* **67 G15** 35 0N 128 6 E
Same, *Tanzania* **106 C4** 4 2 S 37 38 E
Samedan, *Switz.* **29 C9** 46 32N 9 52 E
Samer, *France* **23 B8** 50 38N 1 44 E
Samfya, *Zambia* **107 E2** 11 22 S 29 31 E
Samḩān, Jabal, *Oman* **87 C6** 17 12N 54 55 E
Sámi, *Greece* **45 F2** 38 15N 20 39 E
Samnah, *Si. Arabia* **84 E3** 25 10N 37 15 E
Samnaun, *Switz.* **29 C10** 46 57N 10 22 E
Samnū, *Libya* **96 C2** 27 15N 14 55 E
Samo Alto, *Chile* **158 C1** 30 22 S 71 0W
Samoan Is., *Pac. Oc.* **121 X24** 14 0 S 171 0W
Samobor, *Yugoslavia* **39 C12** 45 47N 15 44 E
Samoëns, *France* **25 B10** 46 5N 6 45 E
Samokov, *Bulgaria* **43 E8** 42 18N 23 35 E
Samoorombón, B., *Argentina* **158 D4** 36 5 S 57 20W
Samorogouan, *Burkina Faso* **100 C4** 11 21N 4 57W
Sámos, *Greece* **45 G8** 37 45N 26 50 E
Samos, *Spain* **36 C3** 42 44N 7 20W
Samoš, *Yugoslavia* **42 B5** 45 13N 20 49 E
Samosir, *Indonesia* **74 B1** 2 55N 98 50 E
Samothráki, *Évros, Greece* **44 D7** 40 28N 25 28 E
Samothráki, *Ípiros, Greece* **44 E1** 39 48N 19 31 E
Samothráki, *Kérkira, Greece* **32 A3** 39 48N 19 31 E
Samoylovka, *U.S.S.R.* **51 F13** 51 12N 43 43 E
Sampa, *Ghana* **100 D4** 8 0N 2 36W
Sampacho, *Argentina* **158 C3** 33 20 S 64 50W
Sampang, *Indonesia* **71 G15** 7 11 S 113 13 E
Samper de Calanda, *Spain* **34 D4** 41 11N 0 28W
Sampit, *Indonesia* **70 E4** 2 34 S 113 0 E
Sampit →, *Indonesia* **75 C4** 2 44 S 112 54 E
Sampit, Teluk, *Indonesia* **70 E4** 3 5 S 113 3 E
Samrée, *Belgium* **21 H7** 50 13N 5 39 E
Samrong, *Cambodia* **76 E4** 14 15N 103 30 E
Samrong, *Thailand* **76 E3** 15 10N 100 40 E
Samsø, *Denmark* **15 J4** 55 50N 10 35 E
Samsø Bælt, *Denmark* **15 J4** 55 45N 10 45 E
Samsonovo, *U.S.S.R.* **55 E2** 37 53N 65 15 E
Samsun, *Turkey* **88 C7** 41 15N 36 22 E
Samsun Dağı, *Turkey* **45 G9** 37 45N 27 10 E
Samtredia, *U.S.S.R.* **53 E10** 42 7N 42 24 E
Samui, Ko, *Thailand* **77 H3** 9 30N 100 0 E
Samun □, *Turkey* **88 C7** 41 10N 36 10 E
Samur →, *U.S.S.R.* **53 F13** 41 53N 48 32 E
Samusole, *Zaïre* **103 E4** 10 2 S 24 0 E
Samut Prakan, *Thailand* **76 F3** 13 32N 100 40 E
Samut Sakhon, *Thailand* **76 F3** 13 31N 100 13 E
Samut Songkhram →, *Thailand* **76 F3** 13 24N 100 1 E
Samwari, *Pakistan* **80 E2** 28 30N 66 46 E
San, *Mali* **100 C4** 13 15N 4 57W
San →, *Cambodia* **76 F5** 13 32N 105 57 E
San →, *Poland* **31 A14** 50 45N 21 51 E
San Adrián, C. de, *Spain* **36 B2** 43 21N 8 50W
San Agustín, *Colombia* **152 C2** 1 53N 76 16W
San Agustin, C., *Phil.* **71 C7** 6 20N 126 13 E
San Agustín de Valle Fértil, *Argentina* **158 C2** 30 35 S 67 30W
San Ambrosio, *Pac. Oc.* **123 K20** 26 28 S 79 53W
San Andreas, *U.S.A.* **144 G6** 38 15N 120 39W
San Andrés, I. de, *Caribbean* **148 D3** 12 42N 81 46W
San Andres Mts., *U.S.A.* **143 K10** 33 0N 106 45W
San Andrés Tuxtla, *Mexico* **147 D5** 18 30N 95 20W
San Angelo, *U.S.A.* **139 K4** 31 30N 100 30W

260 San Anselmo

San Anselmo, U.S.A. 144 H4 37 59N 122 34W
San Antonio, Belize 147 D7 16 15N 89 2W
San Antonio, Chile 158 C1 33 40 S 71 40W
San Antonio, N. Mex., U.S.A. 143 K10 33 58N 106 57W
San Antonio, Tex., U.S.A. 139 L5 29 30N 98 30W
San Antonio, Venezuela 152 C4 3 30N 66 44W
San Antonio →, U.S.A. 139 L6 28 30N 96 50W
San Antonio, C., Argentina 158 D4 36 15 S 56 40W
San Antonio, C., Cuba 148 B3 21 50N 84 57W
San Antonio, C. de, Spain 35 G5 38 48N 0 12 E
San Antonio, Mt., U.S.A. 145 L9 34 17N 117 38W
San Antonio Abad, Spain 33 C7 38 59N 1 19 E
San Antonio de los Baños, Cuba 148 B3 22 54N 82 31W
San Antonio de los Cobres, Argentina 158 A2 24 10 S 66 17W
San Antonio Oeste, Argentina 160 B4 40 40 S 65 0W
San Arcángelo, Italy 41 B9 40 14N 16 14 E
San Ardo, U.S.A. 144 J6 36 1N 120 54W
San Augustín, Canary Is. 33 G4 27 47N 15 32W
San Augustine, U.S.A. 139 K7 31 30N 94 7W
San Bartolomé, Canary Is. 33 F6 28 59N 13 37W
San Bartolomé de Tirajana, Canary Is. 33 G4 27 54N 15 34W
San Bartolomeo in Galdo, Italy 41 A8 41 23N 15 2 E
San Benedetto, Italy 38 C7 45 2N 10 57 E
San Benedetto del Tronto, Italy 39 F10 42 57N 13 52 E
San Benedicto, I., Mexico 146 D2 19 18N 110 49W
San Benito, U.S.A. 139 M6 26 5N 97 39W
San Benito →, U.S.A. 144 J5 36 53N 121 50W
San Benito Mt., U.S.A. 144 J6 36 22N 120 37W
San Bernardino, U.S.A. 145 L9 34 7N 117 18W
San Bernardino, Paso del, Switz. 29 D8 46 28N 9 11 E
San Bernardino Mts., U.S.A. 145 L10 34 10N 116 45W
San Bernardino Str., Phil. 71 B7 13 0N 125 0 E
San Bernardo, Chile 158 C1 33 40 S 70 50W
San Bernardo, I. de, Colombia 152 B2 9 45N 75 50W
San Blas, Mexico 146 B3 26 4N 108 46W
San Blas, Arch. de, Panama 148 E4 9 50N 78 31W
San Blas, C., U.S.A. 135 L3 29 40N 85 12W
San Borja, Bolivia 156 C4 14 50 S 66 52W
San Buenaventura, Bolivia 156 C4 14 28 S 67 35W
San Buenaventura, Mexico 146 B4 27 5N 101 32W
San Carlos = Butuku-Luba, Eq. Guin. 101 E6 3 29N 8 33 E
San Carlos, Argentina 158 C2 33 50 S 69 0W
San Carlos, Bolivia 157 D5 17 24 S 63 45W
San Carlos, Chile 158 D1 36 10 S 72 0W
San Carlos, Mexico 146 B4 29 0N 100 54W
San Carlos, Nic. 148 D3 11 12N 84 50W
San Carlos, Phil. 71 B6 10 29N 123 25 E
San Carlos, Spain 33 B8 39 3N 1 34 E
San Carlos, Uruguay 159 C5 34 46 S 54 58W
San Carlos, U.S.A. 143 K8 33 24N 110 27W
San Carlos, Amazonas, Venezuela 152 C4 1 55N 67 4W
San Carlos, Cojedes, Venezuela 152 B4 9 40N 68 36W
San Carlos de Bariloche, Argentina 160 B2 41 10 S 71 25W
San Carlos de la Rápita, Spain 34 E5 40 37N 0 35 E
San Carlos del Zulia, Venezuela 152 B3 9 1N 71 55W
San Carlos L., U.S.A. 143 K8 33 15N 110 25W
San Cataldo, Italy 40 E6 37 30N 13 58 E
San Celoni, Spain 34 D7 41 42N 2 30 E
San Clemente, Chile 158 D1 35 30 S 71 29W
San Clemente, Spain 35 F2 39 24N 2 25W
San Clemente, U.S.A. 145 M9 33 29N 117 36W
San Clemente I., U.S.A. 145 N8 32 53N 118 30W
San Constanzo, Italy 39 E10 43 46N 13 5 E
San Cristóbal, Argentina 158 C3 30 20 S 61 10W
San Cristóbal, Colombia 152 D3 2 18 S 73 2W
San Cristóbal, Dom. Rep. 149 C5 18 25N 70 6W
San Cristóbal, Mexico 147 D6 16 50N 92 33W
San Cristóbal, Solomon Is. 121 N11 10 30 S 161 0 E
San Cristóbal, Spain 33 B11 39 57N 4 3 E
San Cristóbal, Venezuela 152 B3 7 46N 72 14W
San Damiano d'Asti, Italy 38 D5 44 51N 8 4 E
San Daniele del Friuli, Italy 39 B10 46 10N 13 0 E
San Demétrio Corone, Italy 41 C9 39 34N 16 22 E
San Diego, Calif., U.S.A. 145 N9 32 43N 117 10W
San Diego, Tex., U.S.A. 139 M5 27 47N 98 15W
San Diego, C., Argentina 160 D3 54 40 S 65 10W
San Diego de la Unión, Mexico 146 C4 21 28N 100 52W
San Dimitri, Ras, Malta 32 C1 36 4N 14 11 E
San Donà di Piave, Italy 39 C9 45 38N 12 34 E
San Elpídio a Mare, Italy 39 E10 43 16N 13 41 E
San Estanislao, Paraguay 158 A4 24 39 S 56 26W
San Esteban de Gormaz, Spain 34 D1 41 34N 3 13W
San Felice sul Panaro, Italy 38 D8 44 51N 11 9 E
San Felipe, Chile 158 C1 32 43 S 70 42W
San Felipe, Colombia 152 C4 1 55N 67 6W
San Felipe, Mexico 146 A2 31 0N 114 52W
San Felipe, Venezuela 152 A4 10 20N 68 44W
San Felipe →, U.S.A. 145 M11 33 12N 115 49W
San Felíu de Guíxols, Spain 34 D8 41 45N 3 1 E
San Felíu de Llobregat, Spain 34 D7 41 23N 2 2 E
San Félix, Pac. Oc. 123 K20 26 23 S 80 0W
San Fernando, Chile 158 C1 34 30 S 71 0W
San Fernando, Mexico 146 B1 29 55N 115 10W
San Fernando, La Union, Phil. 71 A6 16 40N 120 23 E
San Fernando, Pampanga, Phil. 71 A6 15 5N 120 37 E
San Fernando, Baleares, Spain 33 C7 38 42N 1 28 E
San Fernando, Cádiz, Spain 37 J4 36 28N 6 17W
San Fernando, Trin. & Tob. 149 D7 10 20N 61 30W
San Fernando, U.S.A. 145 L8 34 15N 118 29W
San Fernando →, Mexico 146 C5 24 55N 98 10W
San Fernando de Apure, Venezuela 152 B4 7 54N 67 15W
San Fernando de Atabapo, Venezuela 152 C4 4 3N 67 42W
San Fernando di Púglia, Italy 41 A9 41 18N 16 5 E
San Francisco, Argentina 158 C3 31 30 S 62 5W
San Francisco, Bolivia 157 D4 15 16 S 65 31W
San Francisco, U.S.A. 144 H4 37 47N 122 30W
San Francisco →, U.S.A. 143 K9 32 59N 109 22W
San Francisco, Paso de, S. Amer. 158 B2 27 0 S 68 0W
San Francisco de Macorís, Dom. Rep. 149 C5 19 19N 70 15W
San Francisco del Monte de Oro, Argentina 158 C2 32 36 S 66 8W
San Francisco del Oro, Mexico 146 B3 26 52N 105 50W
San Francisco Javier, Spain 33 C7 38 42N 1 26 E
San Francisco Solano, Pta., Colombia 152 B2 6 18N 77 29W
San Fratello, Italy 41 D7 38 1N 14 33 E
San Gabriel, Ecuador 152 C2 0 36N 77 49W
San Gavino Monreale, Italy 40 C1 39 33N 8 47 E
San Gil, Colombia 152 B3 6 33N 73 8W
San Gimignano, Italy 38 E8 43 28N 11 3 E
San Giórgio di Nogaro, Italy 39 C10 45 50N 13 13 E
San Giórgio Iónico, Italy 41 B10 40 27N 17 23 E
San Giovanni Bianco, Italy 38 C6 45 52N 9 40 E
San Giovanni in Fiore, Italy 41 C9 39 16N 16 42 E
San Giovanni in Persiceto, Italy 39 D8 44 39N 11 12 E
San Giovanni Rotondo, Italy 41 A8 41 41N 15 42 E
San Giovanni Valdarno, Italy 39 E8 43 32N 11 30 E
San Giuliano Terme, Italy 38 E7 43 45N 10 26 E
San Gorgonio Mt., U.S.A. 145 L10 34 7N 116 51W
San Gottardo, Paso del, Switz. 29 C7 46 33N 8 33 E
San Gregorio, Uruguay 159 C4 32 37 S 55 40W
San Gregorio, U.S.A. 144 H4 37 20N 122 23W
San Guiseppe Iato, Italy 40 E6 37 57N 13 11 E
San Ignacio, Belize 147 D7 17 10N 89 0W
San Ignacio, Bolivia 157 D5 16 20 S 60 55W
San Ignacio, Mexico 146 B2 27 27N 113 0W
San Ignacio, Paraguay 158 B4 26 52 S 57 3W
San Ignacio, L., Mexico 146 B2 26 50N 113 11W
San Ildefonso, C., Phil. 71 A6 16 0N 122 1 E
San Isidro, Argentina 158 C4 34 29 S 58 31W
San Jacinto, Colombia 152 B2 9 50N 75 8W
San Jacinto, U.S.A. 145 M10 33 47N 116 57W
San Jaime, Spain 33 B11 39 54N 4 4 E
San Javier, Misiones, Argentina 159 B4 27 55 S 55 5W
San Javier, Santa Fe, Argentina 158 C4 30 40 S 59 55W
San Javier, Beni, Bolivia 157 C5 14 34 S 64 42W
San Javier, Santa Cruz, Bolivia 157 D5 16 18 S 62 30W
San Javier, Chile 158 D1 35 40 S 71 45W
San Javier, Spain 35 H4 37 49N 0 50W
San Jerónimo, Sa. de, Colombia 152 B2 8 0N 75 50W
San Jeronimo Taviche, Mexico 147 D5 16 38N 96 32W
San Joaquín, Bolivia 157 C5 13 4 S 64 49W
San Joaquin, U.S.A. 144 J6 36 36N 120 11W
San Joaquín, Venezuela 152 A4 10 16N 67 47W
San Joaquín →, Bolivia 157 C5 13 8 S 63 41W
San Joaquin →, U.S.A. 144 G5 38 4N 121 51W
San Joaquin Valley, U.S.A. 144 J6 37 0N 120 30W
San Jordi, Spain 33 B9 39 33N 2 46 E
San Jorge, Argentina 158 C3 31 54 S 61 50W
San Jorge, Spain 33 C7 38 54N 1 24 E
San Jorge, B. de, Mexico 146 A2 31 20N 113 20W
San Jorge, G., Argentina 160 C3 46 0 S 66 0W
San Jorge, G. de, Spain 34 E4 40 50N 0 55W
San José, Bolivia 157 D5 17 53 S 60 50W
San José, Costa Rica 148 E3 9 55N 84 2W
San José, Guatemala 148 D1 14 0N 90 50W
San José, Mexico 146 C2 25 0N 110 50W
San Jose, Phil. 71 A6 15 45N 120 55 E
San José, Spain 33 C7 38 55N 1 18 E
San Jose, Calif., U.S.A. 144 H5 37 20N 121 53W
San Jose, Ill., U.S.A. 140 D7 40 18N 89 36W
San Jose →, U.S.A. 143 J10 34 58N 106 7W
San Jose de Buenovista, Phil. 71 B6 12 27N 121 4 E
San José de Feliciano, Argentina 158 C4 30 26 S 58 46W
San José de Jáchal, Argentina 158 C2 30 15 S 68 46W
San José de Mayo, Uruguay 158 C4 34 27 S 56 40W
San José de Ocune, Colombia 152 C3 4 15N 70 20W
San José de Uchapiamonas, Bolivia 156 C4 14 13 S 68 5W
San José del Cabo, Mexico 146 C3 23 0N 109 40W
San José del Guaviare, Colombia 152 C3 2 35N 72 38W
San José do Anauá, Brazil 153 C5 0 58N 61 22W
San Juan, Argentina 158 C2 31 30 S 68 30W
San Juan, Colombia 152 B2 8 46N 76 32W
San Juan, Mexico 146 C4 21 20N 102 50W
San Juan, Ica, Peru 156 D2 15 22 S 75 7W
San Juan, Puno, Peru 156 C4 14 2 S 69 19W
San Juan, Phil. 71 C7 8 25N 126 20 E
San Juan, Puerto Rico 149 C6 18 28N 66 8W
San Juan □, Argentina 158 C2 31 9 S 69 0W
San Juan →, Argentina 158 C2 32 20 S 67 25W
San Juan →, Bolivia 157 E4 21 2 S 65 19W
San Juan →, Colombia 152 C2 4 3N 77 27W
San Juan →, Nic. 148 D3 10 56N 83 42W
San Juan →, Calif., U.S.A. 144 J5 36 14N 121 9W
San Juan →, Utah, U.S.A. 143 H8 37 20N 110 20W
San Juan →, Venezuela 153 A5 10 14N 62 38W
San Juan, C., Eq. Guin. 102 B1 1 5N 9 20 E
San Juan Bautista, Paraguay 158 B4 26 37 S 57 6W
San Juan Bautista, Spain 33 B8 39 5N 1 31 E
San Juan Bautista, U.S.A. 144 J5 36 51N 121 32W
San Juan Bautista Valle Nacional, Mexico 147 D5 17 47N 96 19W
San Juan Capistrano, U.S.A. 145 M9 33 29N 117 40W
San Juan de Guadalupe, Mexico 146 C4 24 38N 102 44W
San Juan de los Morros, Venezuela 152 B4 9 55N 67 21W
San Juan del César, Colombia 152 A3 10 46N 73 1W
San Juan del Norte, Nic. 148 D3 10 58N 83 40W
San Juan del Norte, B. de, Nic. 148 D3 11 0N 83 40W
San Juan del Puerto, Spain 37 H4 37 20N 6 50W
San Juan del Río, Mexico 147 C5 20 25N 100 0W
San Juan del Sur, Nic. 148 D2 11 20N 85 51W
San Juan I., U.S.A. 144 B3 48 32N 123 5W
San Juan Mts., U.S.A. 143 H10 37 30N 106 50W
San Julián, Argentina 160 C3 49 15 S 67 45W
San Just, Sierra de, Spain 34 E4 40 45N 0 49W
San Justo, Argentina 158 C3 30 47 S 60 30W
San Kamphaeng, Thailand 76 C2 18 45N 99 8 E
San Lázaro, C., Mexico 146 C2 24 50N 112 18W
San Lázaro, Sa., Mexico 146 C3 23 25N 110 0W
San Leandro, U.S.A. 144 H4 37 40N 122 6W
San Leonardo, Spain 34 D1 41 51N 3 5W
San Lorenzo, Argentina 158 C3 32 45 S 60 45W
San Lorenzo, Beni, Bolivia 157 D4 15 22 S 65 48W
San Lorenzo, Tarija, Bolivia 157 E5 21 26 S 64 47W
San Lorenzo, Ecuador 152 C2 1 15N 78 50W
San Lorenzo, Paraguay 158 B4 25 20 S 57 32W
San Lorenzo, Spain 33 B10 39 37N 3 17 E
San Lorenzo, Venezuela 152 B3 9 47N 71 4W
San Lorenzo →, Mexico 146 C3 24 15N 107 24W
San Lorenzo, I., Mexico 146 B2 28 35N 112 50W
San Lorenzo, I., Peru 156 C2 12 7 S 77 15W
San Lorenzo, Mt., Argentina 160 C2 47 40 S 72 20W
San Lorenzo de la Parrilla, Spain 34 F2 39 51N 2 22W
San Lorenzo de Morunys, Spain 34 C6 42 8N 1 35 E
San Lucas, Bolivia 157 E4 20 5 S 65 7W
San Lucas, Baja Calif. S., Mexico 146 C3 22 53N 109 54W
San Lucas, Baja Calif. S., Mexico 146 B2 27 10N 112 14W
San Lucas, U.S.A. 144 J5 36 8N 121 1W
San Lucas, C., Mexico 146 C3 22 50N 110 0W
San Lúcido, Italy 41 C9 39 18N 16 3 E
San Luis, Argentina 158 C2 33 20 S 66 20W
San Luis, Cuba 148 B3 22 17N 83 46W
San Luis, Guatemala 148 C2 16 14N 89 27W
San Luis, U.S.A. 143 H11 37 3N 105 26W
San Luis □, Argentina 158 C2 34 0 S 66 0W
San Luis, I., Mexico 146 B2 29 58N 114 26W
San Luis, L. de, Bolivia 157 C5 13 45 S 64 0W
San Luis, Sierra de, Argentina 158 C2 32 30 S 66 10W
San Luis de la Paz, Mexico 146 C4 21 19N 100 32W
San Luis Obispo, U.S.A. 145 K6 35 21N 120 38W
San Luis Potosí, Mexico 146 C4 22 9N 100 59W
San Luis Potosí □, Mexico 146 C4 22 10N 101 0W
San Luis Res., U.S.A. 144 H5 37 4N 121 5W
San Luis Río Colorado, Mexico 146 A2 32 29N 114 58W
San Marco Argentano, Italy 41 C9 39 34N 16 8 E
San Marco dei Cavoti, Italy 41 A7 41 20N 14 50 E
San Marco in Lámis, Italy 41 A8 41 43N 15 38 E
San Marcos, Colombia 152 B2 8 39N 75 8W
San Marcos, Guatemala 148 D1 14 59N 91 52W
San Marcos, Mexico 146 B2 27 13N 112 6W
San Marcos, U.S.A. 139 L6 29 53N 97 55W
San Marino ■, Europe 39 E9 43 56N 12 25 E
San Martín, Argentina 158 C2 33 5 S 68 28W
San Martín, Colombia 152 C3 3 42N 73 42W
San Martín →, Bolivia 157 C5 13 8 S 63 43W
San Martín, L., Argentina 160 C2 48 50 S 72 50W
San Martin de los Andes, Argentina 160 B2 40 10 S 71 20W
San Martín de Valdeiglesias, Spain 36 E6 40 21N 4 24W
San Martino de Calvi, Italy 38 C6 45 57N 9 41 E
San Mateo, Baleares, Spain 33 B7 39 3N 1 23 E
San Mateo, Valencia, Spain 34 E5 40 28N 0 10 E
San Mateo, U.S.A. 144 H4 37 32N 122 19W
San Matías, Bolivia 157 D6 16 25 S 58 20W
San Matías, G., Argentina 160 B4 41 30 S 64 0W
San Miguel, El Salv. 148 D2 13 30N 88 12W
San Miguel, Panama 148 E4 8 27N 78 55W
San Miguel, Spain 33 B7 39 3N 1 26 E
San Miguel, U.S.A. 144 K6 35 45N 120 42W
San Miguel, Venezuela 152 B4 9 40N 65 11W
San Miguel →, Bolivia 157 C5 13 52 S 63 56W
San Miguel →, S. Amer. 152 C2 0 25N 76 30W
San Miguel de Huachi, Bolivia 156 D4 15 40 S 67 15W
San Miguel de Salinas, Spain 35 H4 37 59N 0 47W
San Miguel de Tucumán, Argentina 158 B2 26 50 S 65 20W
San Miguel del Monte, Argentina 158 D4 35 23 S 58 50W
San Miguel I., U.S.A. 145 L6 34 2N 120 23W
San Miniato, Italy 38 E7 43 40N 10 50 E
San Narciso, Phil. 71 A6 15 2N 120 3 E
San Nicolás, Canary Is. 33 G4 27 58N 15 47W
San Nicolás de los Arroyas, Argentina 158 C3 33 25 S 60 10W
San Nicolas I., U.S.A. 145 M7 33 16N 119 30W
San Onofre, Colombia 152 B2 9 44N 75 32W
San Onofre, U.S.A. 145 M9 33 22N 117 34W
San Pablo, Bolivia 158 A2 21 43 S 66 38W
San Paolo di Civitate, Italy 41 A8 41 44N 15 16 E
San Pedro, Buenos Aires, Argentina 159 B5 26 30 S 54 10W
San Pedro, Jujuy, Argentina 158 A3 24 12 S 64 55W
San Pedro, Colombia 152 C3 4 56N 71 53W
San-Pédro, Ivory C. 100 E3 4 50N 6 33W
San Pedro, Mexico 146 C2 23 55N 110 17W
San Pedro, Peru 156 C3 14 49 S 74 5W
San Pedro □, Paraguay 158 A4 24 0 S 57 0W
San Pedro →, Chihuahua, Mexico 146 B3 28 20N 106 10W
San Pedro →, Michoacan, Mexico 146 D4 19 23N 103 51W
San Pedro →, Nayarit, Mexico 146 C3 21 45N 105 30W
San Pedro →, U.S.A. 143 K8 33 0N 110 50W
San Pedro, Pta., Chile 158 B1 25 30 S 70 38W
San Pedro, Sierra de, Spain 37 F4 39 18N 6 40W
San Pedro Channel, U.S.A. 145 M8 33 35N 118 25W
San Pedro de Arimena, Colombia 152 C3 4 37N 71 42W
San Pedro de Atacama, Chile 158 A2 22 55 S 68 15W
San Pedro de Jujuy, Argentina 158 A3 24 12 S 64 55W
San Pedro de las Colonias, Mexico 146 B4 25 50N 102 59W
San Pedro de Lloc, Peru 156 B2 7 15 S 79 28W
San Pedro de Macorís, Dom. Rep. 149 C6 18 30N 69 18W
San Pedro del Norte, Nic. 148 D3 13 4N 84 33W
San Pedro del Paraná, Paraguay 158 B4 26 43 S 56 13W
San Pedro del Pinatar, Spain 35 H4 37 50N 0 50W
San Pedro Mártir, Sierra, Mexico 146 A1 31 0N 115 30W
San Pedro Mixtepec, Mexico 147 D5 16 2N 97 7W
San Pedro Ocampo = Melchor Ocampo, Mexico 146 C4 24 52N 101 40W
San Pedro Sula, Honduras 148 C2 15 30N 88 0W
San Pietro, I., Italy 40 C1 39 9N 8 17 E
San Pietro Vernótico, Italy 41 B11 40 28N 18 0 E
San Quintín, Mexico 146 A1 30 29N 115 57W
San Rafael, Argentina 158 C2 34 40 S 68 21W
San Rafael, Calif., U.S.A. 144 H4 37 59N 122 32W
San Rafael, N. Mex., U.S.A. 143 J10 35 6N 107 58W
San Rafael, Venezuela 152 A3 10 58N 71 46W
San Rafael Mt., U.S.A. 145 L7 34 41N 119 52W
San Rafael Mts., U.S.A. 145 L7 34 40N 119 50W
San Ramón, Bolivia 157 C5 13 17 S 64 43W
San Ramón, Peru 156 C2 11 8 S 75 20W
San Ramón de la Nueva Orán, Argentina 158 A3 23 10 S 64 20W
San Remo, Italy 38 E4 43 48N 7 47 E
San Román, C., Venezuela 152 A4 12 12N 70 0W
San Roque, Argentina 158 B4 28 25 S 58 45W
San Roque, Spain 37 J5 36 17N 5 21W
San Rosendo, Chile 158 D1 37 16 S 72 43W
San Saba, U.S.A. 139 K5 31 12N 98 45W
San Salvador, Bahamas 149 B5 24 0N 74 40W
San Salvador, El Salv. 148 D2 13 40N 89 10W
San Salvador, Spain 33 B10 39 27N 3 11 E
San Salvador de Jujuy, Argentina 158 A3 24 10 S 64 48W
San Salvador I., Bahamas 149 B5 24 0N 74 32W
San Sebastián, Argentina 160 D3 53 10 S 68 30W
San Sebastián, Spain 34 B3 43 17N 1 58W
San Sebastián, Venezuela 152 B4 9 57N 67 11W
San Sebastian de la Gomera, Canary Is. 33 F2 28 5N 17 7W
San Serra, Spain 33 B10 39 43N 3 13 E
San Serverino Marche, Italy 39 E10 43 13N 13 10 E
San Simeon, U.S.A. 144 K5 35 44N 121 11W
San Simon, U.S.A. 143 K9 32 14N 109 16W
San Stéfano di Cadore, Italy 39 B9 46 34N 12 33 E
San Telmo, Mexico 146 A1 30 58N 116 6W
San Telmo, Spain 33 B9 39 35N 2 21 E
San Tiburcio, Mexico 146 C4 24 8N 101 32W
San Valentin, Mte., Chile 160 C2 46 30 S 73 30W
San Vicente de Alcántara, Spain 37 F3 39 22N 7 8W
San Vicente de la Barquera, Spain 36 B6 43 23N 4 29W
San Vicente del Caguán, Colombia 152 C3 2 7N 74 46W
San Vincenzo, Italy 38 E7 43 6N 10 29 E
San Vito, Italy 40 C2 39 26N 9 32 E
San Vito, C., Italy 40 D5 38 11N 12 41 E
San Vito al Tagliamento, Italy 39 C9 45 55N 12 50 E
San Vito Chietino, Italy 39 F11 42 19N 14 27 E

Senožeče 263

Scandinavia, *Europe* .... **12 E12** 64 0N 12 0 E
Scansano, *Italy* .... **39 F8** 42 40N 11 20 E
Scapa Flow, *U.K.* **18 C5** 58 52N 3 6W
Scappoose, *U.S.A.* **144 E4** 45 45N 122 53W
Scarborough, *Trin. & Tob.* **149 D7** 11 11N 60 42W
Scarborough, *U.K.* **16 C7** 54 17N 0 24W
Scargill, *N.Z.* .... **119 C7** 42 56 S 172 58 E
Scarsdale, *Australia* ..... **116 D5** 37 41 S 143 39 E
Scebeli, Wabi →, *Somali Rep.* .... **90 G3** 2 0N 44 0 E
Šćedro, *Yugoslavia* ..... **39 E13** 43 6N 16 43 E
Scenic, *U.S.A.* **138 D3** 43 49N 102 32W
Schaal See, *Germany* ... **26 B6** 53 40N 10 57 E
Schaan, *Liech.* .... **29 B9** 47 10N 9 31 E
Schaesberg, *Neths.* ..... **21 G8** 50 54N 6 0 E
Schaffen, *Belgium* ...... **21 G6** 51 0N 5 5 E
Schaffhausen, *Switz.* .... **29 A7** 47 42N 8 39 E
Schaffhausen □, *Switz.* . **29 A7** 47 42N 8 36 E
Schagen, *Neths.* .... **20 C5** 52 49N 4 48 E
Schaijk, *Neths.* .... **20 E7** 51 44N 5 38 E
Schalkhaar, *Neths.* ..... **20 D8** 52 17N 6 12 E
Schalkwijk, *Neths.* ...... **20 E6** 52 0N 5 11 E
Schangnau, *Switz.* ...... **28 C5** 46 50N 7 47 E
Schänis, *Switz.* .... **29 B8** 47 10N 9 3 E
Schärding, *Austria* ...... **30 C6** 48 27N 13 27 E
Scharhörn, *Germany* .... **26 B4** 53 58N 8 24 E
Scharnitz, *Austria* ...... **30 D4** 47 23N 11 15 E
Scheessel, *Germany* .... **26 B5** 53 10N 9 33 E
Schefferville, *Canada* ... **129 B6** 54 48N 66 50W
Scheibbs, *Austria* .... **30 C8** 48 1N 15 9 E
Schelde →, *Belgium* .... **21 F4** 51 15N 4 16 E
Schell City, *U.S.A.* **140 F2** 38 1N 94 7W
Schell Creek Ra., *U.S.A.* **142 G6** 39 15N 114 30W
Schenectady, *U.S.A.* **137 D11** 42 50N 73 58W
Scherfede, *Germany* .... **26 D5** 51 32N 9 2 E
Scherpenheuvel, *Belgium* **21 G5** 50 58N 4 58 E
Scherpenisse, *Neths.* .... **21 E4** 51 33N 4 6 E
Scherpenzeel, *Neths.* .... **20 D7** 52 5N 5 30 E
Schesaplana, *Switz.* ..... **29 B9** 47 5N 9 43 E
Schesslitz, *Germany* .... **27 F7** 49 59N 11 2 E
Scheveningen, *Neths.* ... **20 D4** 52 6N 4 16 E
Schiedam, *Neths.* .... **20 E4** 51 55N 4 25 E
Schiermonnikoog, *Neths.* **20 B8** 53 30N 6 15 E
Schiers, *Switz.* .... **29 C9** 46 58N 9 41 E
Schifferstadt, *Germany* .. **27 F4** 49 22N 8 23 E
Schifflange, *Lux.* .... **21 K8** 49 30N 6 1 E
Schijndel, *Neths.* .... **21 E6** 51 37N 5 27 E
Schiltigheim, *France* .... **23 D14** 48 35N 7 45 E
Schio, *Italy* .... **39 C8** 45 42N 11 21 E
Schipbeek, *Neths.* ...... **20 D8** 52 14N 6 10 E
Schipluiden, *Neths.* ..... **20 E4** 51 59N 4 19 E
Schirmeck, *France* ...... **23 D14** 48 29N 7 12 E
Schladming, *Austria* .... **30 D6** 47 23N 13 41 E
Schlei →, *Germany* ..... **26 A5** 54 45N 9 52 E
Schleiden, *Germany* .... **26 E2** 50 32N 6 26 E
Schleiz, *Germany* .... **26 E7** 50 35N 11 49 E
Schleswig, *Germany* .... **26 A5** 54 32N 9 34 E
Schleswig-Holstein □, *Germany* .... **26 A5** 54 10N 9 40 E
Schlieren, *Switz.* .... **29 B6** 47 26N 8 27 E
Schlüchtern, *Germany* .. **27 E5** 50 20N 9 32 E
Schmalkalden, *Germany* **26 E6** 50 43N 10 28 E
Schmölln, *Brandenburg, Germany* .... **26 B10** 53 15N 14 6 E
Schmölln, *Thüringen, Germany* .... **26 E8** 50 54N 12 22 E
Schneeberg, *Austria* .... **30 D8** 47 47N 15 48 E
Schneeberg, *Germany* .. **26 E8** 50 35N 12 39 E
Schneider, *U.S.A.* **141 C9** 41 13N 87 28W
Schoenberg, *Belgium* .... **21 H8** 50 17N 6 16 E
Schofield, *U.S.A.* **138 C10** 44 54N 89 39W
Scholls, *U.S.A.* **144 E4** 45 24N 122 56W
Schönberg, *Mecklenburg-Vorpommern, Germany* .... **26 B6** 53 50N 10 55 E
Schönberg, *Schleswig-Holstein, Germany* .... **26 A6** 54 23N 10 20 E
Schönebeck, *Germany* .. **26 C7** 52 2N 11 42 E
Schönenwerd, *Switz.* .... **28 B6** 47 23N 8 0 E
Schongau, *Germany* .... **27 H6** 47 49N 10 54 E
Schöningen, *Germany* .. **26 C6** 52 8N 10 57 E
Schoolcraft, *U.S.A.* **141 B11** 42 7N 85 38W
Schoondijke, *Neths.* .... **21 F3** 51 21N 3 33 E
Schoonebeek, *Neths.* ... **20 C9** 52 39N 6 52 E
Schoonhoven, *Neths.* ... **20 E5** 51 57N 4 51 E
Schoorl, *Neths.* .... **20 C5** 52 42N 4 42 E
Schortens, *Germany* .... **26 B3** 53 37N 7 51 E
Schoten, *Belgium* .... **21 F5** 51 16N 4 30 E
Schouten I., *Australia* .. **114 G4** 42 20 S 148 20 E
Schouten Is. = Supriori, Kepulauan, *Indonesia* . **71 E9** 1 0 S 136 0 E
Schouwen, *Neths.* .... **21 E3** 51 43N 3 45 E
Schramberg, *Germany* .. **27 G4** 48 12N 8 24 E
Schrankogl, *Austria* ..... **30 D4** 47 3N 11 7 E
Schreckhorn, *Switz.* .... **28 C6** 46 36N 8 7 E
Schreiber, *Canada* **128 C2** 48 45N 87 20W
Schrobenhausen, *Germany* .... **27 G7** 48 33N 11 16 E
Schruns, *Austria* .... **30 D2** 47 5N 9 56 E
Schuler, *Canada* **131 C6** 50 20N 110 6W
Schuls, *Switz.* .... **29 C10** 46 48N 10 18 E
Schumacher, *Canada* ... **128 C3** 48 30N 81 16W
Schüpfen, *Switz.* .... **28 B4** 47 2N 7 24 E
Schüpfheim, *Switz.* ..... **28 C6** 46 57N 8 2 E
Schurz, *U.S.A.* **142 G4** 38 57N 118 48W
Schuyler, *U.S.A.* **138 E6** 41 30N 97 3W
Schuylkill Haven, *U.S.A.* **137 F8** 40 37N 76 11W
Schwabach, *Germany* ... **27 F7** 49 19N 11 3 E
Schwäbisch Gmünd, *Germany* .... **27 G5** 48 49N 9 48 E
Schwäbisch Hall, *Germany* .... **27 F5** 49 7N 9 45 E
Schwäbische Alb, *Germany* .... **27 G5** 48 30N 9 30 E
Schwabmünchen, *Germany* .... **27 G6** 48 11N 10 45 E
Schwanden, *Switz.* ...... **29 C8** 46 58N 9 5 E
Schwandorf, *Germany* .. **27 F8** 49 20N 12 7 E
Schwaner, Pegunungan, *Indonesia* .... **70 E4** 1 0 S 112 30 E
Schwarmstedt, *Germany* **26 C5** 52 41N 9 37 E
Schwarzach →, *Austria* . **30 E5** 46 56N 12 35 E
Schwärze, *Germany* .... **26 C9** 52 50N 13 49 E
Schwarze Elster →, *Germany* .... **26 D8** 51 49N 12 51 E
Schwarzenberg, *Germany* **26 E8** 50 31N 12 49 E
Schwarzenburg, *Switz.* .. **28 C4** 46 49N 7 20 E
Schwarzwald, *Germany* . **27 H4** 48 0N 8 0 E
Schwaz, *Austria* .... **30 D4** 47 20N 11 44 E
Schwedt, *Germany* ..... **26 B10** 53 4N 14 18 E
Schweinfurt, *Germany* .. **27 E6** 50 3N 10 12 E
Schweizer Mittelland, *Switz.* .... **28 C4** 47 0N 7 15 E
Schweizer-Reneke, *S. Africa* .... **104 D4** 27 11 S 25 18 E
Schwenningen, *Germany* **27 G4** 48 3N 8 29 E
Schwerin, *Germany* ..... **26 B7** 53 37N 11 22 E
Schweriner See, *Germany* **26 B7** 53 45N 11 26 E
Schwetzingen, *Germany* . **27 F4** 49 22N 8 35 E
Schwyz, *Switz.* .... **29 B7** 47 2N 8 39 E
Schwyz □, *Switz.* .... **29 B7** 47 2N 8 39 E
Sciacca, *Italy* .... **40 E6** 37 30N 13 3 E
Sciao, *Somali Rep.* ..... **108 D3** 3 26N 45 21 E
Scicli, *Italy* .... **41 F7** 36 48N 14 41 E
Scilla, *Italy* .... **41 D8** 38 18N 15 44 E
Scilly, Isles of, *U.K.* **17 H1** 49 55N 6 15W
Ścinawa, *Poland* .... **47 D3** 51 25N 16 26 E
Scione, *Greece* .... **44 E5** 39 57N 23 36 E
Scioto →, *U.S.A.* **134 F4** 38 44N 83 0W
Scobey, *U.S.A.* **138 A2** 48 47N 105 30W
Scone, *Australia* .... **117 B9** 32 5 S 150 52 E
Scordia, *Italy* .... **41 E7** 37 19N 14 50 E
Scoresbysund, *Greenland* **6 B6** 70 20N 23 0W
Scorno, Punta dello, *Italy* **40 A1** 41 7N 8 23 E
Scotia, *Calif., U.S.A.* **142 F1** 40 36N 124 4W
Scotia, *N.Y., U.S.A.* **137 D11** 42 50N 73 58W
Scotia Sea, *Antarctica* ... **7 B18** 56 5 S 56 0W
Scotland, *U.S.A.* **138 D6** 43 10N 97 45W
Scotland □, *U.K.* **18 E5** 57 0N 4 0W
Scotland Neck, *U.S.A.* .. **135 G7** 36 6N 77 32W
Scott, C., *Australia* ..... **112 B4** 13 30 S 129 49 E
Scott City, *U.S.A.* **138 F4** 38 30N 100 52W
Scott Glacier, *Antarctica* **7 C8** 66 15 S 100 5 E
Scott I., *Antarctica* ..... **7 C11** 67 0 S 179 0 E
Scott Inlet, *Canada* **127 A12** 71 0N 71 0W
Scott Is., *Canada* **130 C3** 50 48N 128 40W
Scott L., *Canada* **131 B7** 59 55N 106 18W
Scott Reef, *Australia* ... **112 B3** 14 0 S 121 50 E
Scottburgh, *S. Africa* ... **105 E5** 30 15 S 30 47 E
Scottdale, *U.S.A.* **136 F5** 40 8N 79 35W
Scottsbluff, *U.S.A.* **138 E3** 41 55N 103 35W
Scottsboro, *U.S.A.* **135 H3** 34 40N 86 0W
Scottsburg, *U.S.A.* **141 F11** 38 40N 85 46W
Scottsdale, *Australia* .... **114 G4** 41 9 S 147 31 E
Scottsville, *Ky., U.S.A.* . **135 G2** 36 48N 86 10W
Scottsville, *N.Y., U.S.A.* **136 C7** 43 2N 77 47W
Scottville, *U.S.A.* **134 D2** 43 57N 86 18W
Scranton, *Iowa, U.S.A.* . **140 B2** 42 1N 94 33W
Scranton, *Pa., U.S.A.* .. **137 E9** 41 22N 75 41W
Scugog, L., *Canada* **136 B6** 44 10N 78 55W
Scunthorpe, *U.K.* **16 D7** 53 35N 0 38W
Scuol, *Switz.* .... **29 C10** 46 48N 10 17 E
Scusciuban, *Somali Rep.* **90 E5** 10 18N 50 12 E
Scutari = Üsküdar, *Turkey* .... **49 F4** 41 0N 29 5 E
Seabra, *Brazil* .... **155 D3** 12 25 S 41 46W
Seabrook, L., *Australia* . **113 F2** 30 55 S 119 40 E
Seaford, *U.S.A.* **134 F8** 38 37N 75 36W
Seaforth, *Canada* **128 D3** 43 35N 81 25W
Seagraves, *U.S.A.* **139 J3** 32 56N 102 30W
Seal →, *Canada* **131 B10** 59 4N 94 48W
Seal Cove, *Canada* **129 C8** 49 57N 56 22W
Seal L., *Canada* **129 B7** 54 20N 61 30W
Sealy, *U.S.A.* **139 L6** 29 46N 96 9W
Seaman, *U.S.A.* **141 F13** 38 57N 83 34W
Searchlight, *U.S.A.* **145 K12** 35 31N 114 55W
Searcy, *U.S.A.* **139 H9** 35 15N 91 45W
Searles L., *U.S.A.* **145 K9** 35 47N 117 17W
Seaside, *Calif., U.S.A.* .. **144 J5** 36 37N 121 50W
Seaside, *Oreg., U.S.A.* .. **144 E3** 45 59N 123 55W
Seaspray, *Australia* ..... **117 E7** 38 25 S 147 15 E
Seattle, *U.S.A.* **144 C4** 47 41N 122 15W
Seaview Ra., *Australia* .. **114 B4** 18 40 S 145 45 E
Seaward Kaikouras, Mts., *N.Z.* .... **119 C8** 42 10 S 173 44 E
Sebangka, *Indonesia* .... **74 B2** 0 7N 104 36 E
Sebastián Vizcaíno, B., *Mexico* **146 B2** 28 0N 114 30W
Sebastopol = Sevastopol, *U.S.S.R.* .... **52 D5** 44 35N 33 30 E
Sebastopol, *U.S.A.* **144 G4** 38 24N 122 49W
Sebderat, *Ethiopia* ...... **95 D4** 15 26N 36 42 E
Sebdou, *Algeria* **99 B4** 34 38N 1 19W
Seben, *Turkey* .... **88 C4** 40 24N 31 34 E
Sebeş, *Romania* .... **46 D4** 45 58N 23 34 E
Sebeşului, Munţii, *Romania* .... **46 D4** 45 36N 23 40 E
Sebewaing, *U.S.A.* **134 D4** 43 45N 83 27W
Sebezh, *U.S.S.R.* .... **50 C6** 56 14N 28 22 E
Sébi, *Mali* **100 B4** 15 50N 4 12W
Şebinkarahisar, *Turkey* . **52 F8** 40 22N 38 28 E
Sebiş, *Romania* .... **46 C3** 46 23N 22 13 E
Sebkhet Te-n-Dghâmcha, *Mauritania* **100 B1** 18 30N 15 55W
Sebkra Azzel Mati, *Algeria* .... **99 C5** 26 10N 0 43 E
Sebkra Mekerghene, *Algeria* .... **99 C5** 26 21N 1 30 E
Seblat, *Indonesia* ...... **74 C2** 3 14 S 101 38 E
Sebnitz, *Germany* ...... **26 E10** 50 58N 14 17 E
Sebou, Oued →, *Morocco* **98 B3** 34 16N 6 40W
Sebring, *Fla., U.S.A.* ... **135 M5** 27 30N 81 26W
Sebring, *Ohio, U.S.A.* .. **136 F3** 40 55N 81 2W
Sebringville, *Canada* **136 C3** 43 24N 81 4W
Sebta = Ceuta, *Morocco* **98 A3** 35 52N 5 18W
Sebuku, *Indonesia* ...... **70 E5** 3 30 S 116 25 E
Sebuku, Teluk, *Malaysia* **70 D5** 4 0N 118 10 E
Sečanj, *Yugoslavia* ..... **42 B5** 45 25N 20 47 E
Secchia →, *Italy* .... **38 C8** 45 4N 11 0 E
Sechelt, *Canada* **130 D4** 49 25N 123 42W
Sechura, *Peru* .... **156 B1** 5 39 S 80 50W
Sechura, Desierto de, *Peru* .... **156 B1** 6 0 S 80 30W
Seclin, *France* .... **23 B10** 50 33N 3 2 E
Secondigny, *France* **22 F6** 46 37N 0 26W
Sečovce, *Czech.* .... **31 C14** 48 42N 21 40 E
Secretary I., *N.Z.* .... **119 F1** 45 15 S 166 56 E
Secunderabad, *India* .... **82 F4** 17 28N 78 30 E
Sécure →, *Bolivia* ..... **157 D5** 15 10 S 64 52W
Sedalia, *U.S.A.* **140 F3** 38 40N 93 18W
Sedan, *Australia* .... **116 C3** 34 34 S 139 19 E
Sedan, *France* .... **23 C11** 49 43N 4 57 E
Sedan, *U.S.A.* **139 G6** 37 10N 96 11W
Sedano, *Spain* **34 C1** 42 43N 3 49W
Seddon, *N.Z.* .... **119 B9** 41 40 S 174 7 E
Seddonville, *N.Z.* .... **119 B7** 41 33 S 172 1 E
Sedeh, *Fārs, Iran* ...... **85 D7** 30 45N 52 11 E
Sedeh, *Khorāsān, Iran* .. **85 C8** 33 20N 59 14 E
Sederot, *Israel* .... **91 D3** 31 32N 34 37 E
Sedgewick, *Canada* **130 C6** 52 48N 111 41W
Sedhiou, *Senegal* **100 C1** 12 44N 15 30W
Sedičany, *Czech.* .... **30 B7** 49 40N 14 25 E
Sedico, *Italy* .... **39 B9** 46 8N 12 6 E
Sedienie, *Bulgaria* ...... **43 E9** 42 16N 24 33 E
Sedley, *Canada* **131 C8** 50 10N 104 0W
Sedova, Pik, *U.S.S.R.* .. **56 B6** 73 29N 54 58 E
Sedrata, *Algeria* .... **99 A6** 36 7N 7 31 E
Sedro Woolley, *U.S.A.* . **144 B4** 48 30N 122 15W
Sedrun, *Switz.* .... **29 C7** 46 36N 8 47 E
Seduva, *U.S.S.R.* .... **50 D3** 55 45N 23 45 E
Sedziszów Małapolski, *Poland* .... **31 A14** 50 5N 21 45 E
Seebad Ahlbeck, *Germany* .... **26 B10** 53 56N 14 10 E
Seefeld, *Austria* .... **30 D4** 47 19N 11 13 E
Seehausen, *Germany* .. **26 C7** 52 52N 11 43 E
Seeheim, *Namibia* ...... **104 D2** 26 50 S 17 45 E
Seekoei →, *S. Africa* .. **104 E4** 30 18 S 25 1 E
Seelaw, *Germany* ...... **26 C10** 52 32N 14 22 E
Sées, *France* .... **22 D7** 48 38N 0 10 E
Seesen, *Germany* .... **26 D6** 51 53N 10 10 E
Sefadu, *S. Leone* **100 D2** 8 35N 10 58W
Seferihisar, *Turkey* ..... **88 D2** 38 10N 26 50 E
Séfeto, *Mali* **100 C3** 14 8N 9 49W
Sefrou, *Morocco* **98 B4** 33 52N 4 52W
Sefton, *N.Z.* .... **119 D7** 43 15 S 172 41 E
Sefuri-San, *Japan* ...... **62 D2** 33 28N 130 18 E
Sefwi Bekwai, *Ghana* ... **100 D4** 6 10N 2 25W
Seg-ozero, *U.S.S.R.* .... **50 A8** 63 0N 33 10 E
Segag, *Ethiopia* .... **108 C2** 7 39N 42 50 E
Segamat, *Malaysia* ...... **77 L4** 2 30N 102 50 E
Segarcea, *Romania* ..... **46 E4** 44 6N 23 43 E
Segbwema, *S. Leone* **100 D2** 8 0N 11 0W
Seget, *Indonesia* .... **71 E8** 1 24 S 130 58 E
Segezha, *U.S.S.R.* ...... **48 B5** 63 44N 34 19 E
Seggueur, O. →, *Algeria* **99 B5** 32 4N 2 4 E
Segonzac, *France* **24 C3** 45 36N 0 14W
Segorbe, *Spain* **34 F4** 39 50N 0 30W
Ségou, *Mali* **100 C3** 13 30N 6 16W
Segovia = Coco →, *Cent. Amer.* **148 D3** 15 0N 83 8W
Segovia, *Colombia* **152 B3** 7 7N 74 42W
Segovia, *Spain* **36 E6** 40 57N 4 10W
Segovia □, *Spain* **36 E6** 40 55N 4 10W
Segré, *France* **22 E6** 47 40N 0 52W
Segre →, *Spain* .... **34 D5** 41 40N 0 43 E
Séguéla, *Ivory C.* **100 D3** 7 55N 6 40W
Seguin, *U.S.A.* **139 L6** 29 34N 97 58W
Segundo →, *Argentina* . **158 C3** 30 53 S 62 44W
Segura →, *Spain* **35 G4** 38 6N 0 54W
Segura, Sierra de, *Spain* **35 G2** 38 5N 2 45W
Seh Qal'eh, *Iran* .... **85 C8** 33 40N 58 24 E
Sehitwa, *Botswana* ..... **104 C3** 20 30 S 22 30 E
Sehore, *India* .... **80 H7** 23 10N 77 5 E
Sehwan, *Pakistan* ...... **79 D2** 26 28N 67 53 E
Şeica Mare, *Romania* ... **46 C5** 46 1N 24 7 E
Seikpyu, *Burma* .... **78 E5** 20 54N 94 48 E
Seiland, *Norway* .... **12 A17** 70 25N 23 15 E
Seiling, *U.S.A.* **139 G5** 36 10N 98 56W
Seille →, *France* .... **25 B8** 46 31N 4 57 E
Seilles, *Belgium* .... **21 H6** 50 30N 5 6 E
Sein, I. de, *France* **22 D2** 48 2N 4 52W
Seinäjoki →, *Finland* ... **12 E17** 62 40N 22 45 E
Seine →, *France* .... **22 C7** 49 26N 0 26 E
Seine, B. de la, *France* .. **22 C6** 49 40N 0 40W
Seine-et-Marne □, *France* **23 D10** 48 45N 3 0 E
Seine-Maritime □, *France* **22 C8** 49 40N 1 0 E
Seine-St.-Denis □, *France* **23 D9** 48 58N 2 24 E
Seini, *Romania* .... **46 B4** 47 44N 23 21 E
Seistan, *Iran* .... **85 D9** 30 50N 61 0 E
Sejerø, *Denmark* .... **15 J5** 55 54N 11 9 E
Sejerø Bugt, *Denmark* .. **15 J5** 55 53N 11 15 E
Sejny, *Poland* .... **47 A10** 54 6N 23 21 E
Seka, *Ethiopia* .... **95 F4** 8 10N 36 52 E
Sekayu, *Indonesia* ...... **70 E2** 2 51 S 103 51 E
Seke, *Tanzania* .... **106 C3** 3 20 S 33 31 E
Seke-Banza, *Zaïre* ..... **103 D2** 5 20 S 13 16 E
Sekenke, *Tanzania* ..... **106 C3** 4 18 S 34 11 E
Seki, *Japan* .... **63 B8** 35 29N 136 55 E
Sekigahara, *Japan* ...... **63 B8** 35 22N 136 28 E
Sekken Veøy, *Norway* ... **14 B1** 62 45N 7 30 E
Sekondi-Takoradi, *Ghana* **100 E4** 4 58N 1 45W
Sekuma, *Botswana* ..... **104 C3** 24 36 S 23 50 E
Selah, *U.S.A.* **142 C3** 46 44N 120 30W
Selama, *Malaysia* ...... **77 K3** 5 12N 100 42 E
Selárgius, *Italy* .... **40 C2** 39 14N 9 14 E
Selaru, *Indonesia* ...... **71 F8** 8 9 S 131 0 E
Selb, *Germany* .... **27 E8** 50 9N 12 9 E
Selby, *U.K.* **16 D6** 53 47N 1 5W
Selby, *U.S.A.* **138 C4** 45 34N 100 2W
Selca, *Yugoslavia* ...... **39 E13** 43 20N 16 50 E
Selçuk, *Turkey* .... **88 E2** 37 56N 27 22 E
Selden, *U.S.A.* **138 F4** 39 33N 100 39W
Sele →, *Italy* .... **41 B7** 40 27N 14 58 E
Selemdzha →, *U.S.S.R.* **57 D13** 51 42N 128 53 E
Selenga = Selenge Mörön →, *Asia* ...... **64 A5** 52 16N 106 16 E
Selenge, *Zaïre* .... **102 C3** 1 58 S 18 11 E
Selenge Mörön →, *Asia* **64 A5** 52 16N 106 16 E
Selenica, *Albania* ...... **44 D1** 40 33N 19 39 E
Selenter See, *Germany* . **26 A6** 54 19N 10 26 E
Sélestat, *France* .... **23 D14** 48 16N 7 26 E
Seletan, Tg., *Indonesia* . **70 E4** 4 10 S 114 40 E
Seletin, *Romania* .... **46 B6** 47 50N 25 12 E
Selevac, *Yugoslavia* .... **42 C5** 44 28N 20 52 E
Selfridge, *U.S.A.* **138 B4** 46 3N 100 57W
Sélibabi, *Mauritania* **100 B2** 15 10N 12 15W
Seliger, Oz., *U.S.S.R.* .. **50 C8** 57 15N 33 0 E
Seligman, *U.S.A.* **143 J7** 35 17N 112 56W
Şelim, *Turkey* .... **53 F10** 40 30N 42 46 E
Selîma, El Wâhât el, *Sudan* .... **94 C2** 21 22N 29 19 E
Selinda Spillway, *Botswana* .... **104 B3** 18 35 S 23 10 E
Selinoús, *Greece* .... **45 G3** 37 35N 21 37 E
Selizharovo, *U.S.S.R.* ... **50 C8** 56 51N 33 27 E
Seljord, *Norway* .... **14 E2** 59 30N 8 40 E
Selkirk, *Canada* **131 C9** 50 10N 96 55W
Selkirk, *U.K.* **18 F6** 55 33N 2 50W
Selkirk I., *Canada* **131 C9** 53 20N 99 6W
Selkirk Mts., *Canada* ... **130 C5** 51 15N 117 40W
Selles-sur-Cher, *France* . **23 E8** 47 16N 1 33 E
Selliá, *Greece* .... **32 D6** 35 12N 24 23 E
Sellières, *France* .... **23 F12** 46 50N 5 32 E
Sells, *U.S.A.* **143 L8** 31 57N 111 57W
Sellye, *Hungary* .... **31 F10** 45 52N 17 51 E
Selma, *Ala., U.S.A.* **135 J2** 32 30N 87 0W
Selma, *Calif., U.S.A.* **144 J7** 36 39N 119 39W
Selma, *N.C., U.S.A.* **135 H6** 35 32N 78 15W
Selmer, *U.S.A.* **135 H1** 35 9N 88 36W
Selo, *Greece* .... **44 C7** 41 10N 25 53 E
Selong, *Indonesia* ...... **75 D5** 8 39 S 116 32 E
Selongey, *France* .... **23 E12** 47 36N 5 11 E
Selowandoma Falls, *Zimbabwe* .... **107 G3** 21 15 S 31 50 E
Selpele, *Indonesia* ...... **71 E8** 0 1 S 130 5 E
Selsey Bill, *U.K.* **17 G7** 50 44N 0 47W
Seltz, *France* .... **23 D15** 48 54N 8 4 E
Selu, *Indonesia* .... **71 F8** 7 32 S 130 55 E
Sélune →, *France* **22 D5** 48 38N 1 22W
Selva, *Argentina* .... **158 B3** 29 50 S 62 0W
Selva, *Italy* .... **39 B8** 46 33N 11 46 E
Selva, *Spain* .... **34 D6** 41 13N 1 8 E
Selvas, *Brazil* .... **156 B4** 6 30 S 67 0W
Selwyn, *Australia* ...... **114 C3** 21 32 S 140 30 E
Selwyn L., *Canada* **131 B8** 60 0N 104 30W
Selwyn Passage, *Vanuatu* **121 F6** 16 3 S 168 12 E
Selwyn Ra., *Australia* ... **114 C3** 21 10 S 140 0 E
Seman →, *Albania* ..... **44 D1** 40 45N 19 50 E
Semara, *W. Sahara* **98 C2** 26 48N 11 41W
Semarang, *Indonesia* ... **71 G14** 7 0 S 110 26 E
Semau, *Indonesia* ...... **71 F6** 10 13 S 123 22 E
Sembabule, *Uganda* .... **106 C3** 0 4 S 31 25 E
Sembé, *Congo* .... **102 B2** 1 39N 14 36 E
Sémé, *Senegal* **100 B2** 15 4N 13 41W
Semeih, *Sudan* .... **95 E3** 12 43N 30 53 E
Semenov, *U.S.S.R.* ..... **51 C14** 56 43N 44 30 E
Semenovka, *Ukraine S.S.R., U.S.S.R.* .... **50 E8** 52 8N 32 36 E
Semenovka, *Ukraine S.S.R., U.S.S.R.* .... **52 B5** 49 37N 33 10 E
Semeru, *Indonesia* ...... **71 H15** 8 4 S 112 55 E
Semiluki, *U.S.S.R.* ..... **51 F11** 51 41N 39 2 E
Seminoe Res., *U.S.A.* .. **142 F10** 42 0N 107 0W
Seminole, *Okla., U.S.A.* **139 H6** 35 15N 96 45W
Seminole, *Tex., U.S.A.* . **139 J3** 32 41N 102 38W
Semiozernoye, *U.S.S.R.* **54 E9** 52 22N 64 8 E
Semipalatinsk, *U.S.S.R.* . **56 D9** 50 30N 80 10 E
Semirara Is., *Phil.* ...... **71 B6** 12 0N 121 20 E
Semisopochnoi, *U.S.A.* . **126 C2** 52 0N 179 40W
Semitau, *Indonesia* ..... **70 D4** 0 29N 111 57 E
Semiyarskoye, *U.S.S.R.* . **56 D8** 50 55N 78 23 E
Semmering Pass, *Austria* **30 D8** 47 41N 15 45 E
Semnān, *Iran* .... **85 C7** 35 55N 53 25 E
Semnān □, *Iran* .... **85 C7** 36 0N 54 0 E
Semois →, *Europe* ..... **21 J5** 49 53N 4 44 E
Semporna, *Malaysia* ..... **71 D5** 4 30N 118 33 E
Semuda, *Indonesia* ..... **70 E4** 2 51 S 112 58 E
Semur-en-Auxois, *France* **23 E11** 47 30N 4 20 E
Sena, *Bolivia* .... **156 C4** 11 32 S 67 11W
Senā, *Iran* .... **85 D6** 28 27N 51 36 E
Sena, *Mozam.* .... **107 F4** 17 25 S 35 0 E
Sena →, *Bolivia* .... **156 C4** 11 31 S 67 11W
Sena Madureira, *Brazil* . **156 B4** 9 5 S 68 45W
Senador Pompeu, *Brazil* **154 C4** 5 40 S 39 20W
Senaja, *Malaysia* .... **70 C5** 6 45N 117 3 E
Senanga, *Zambia* .... **104 B3** 16 2 S 23 14 E
Senatobia, *U.S.A.* **139 H10** 34 38N 89 57W
Sendafa, *Ethiopia* ...... **95 F4** 9 11N 39 3 E
Sendai, *Kagoshima, Japan* **62 F2** 31 50N 130 20 E
Sendai, *Miyagi, Japan* .. **60 E10** 38 15N 140 53 E
Sendai-Wan, *Japan* ..... **60 E10** 38 15N 141 0 E
Sendamangalam, *India* .. **83 J4** 11 17N 78 17 E
Sendenhorst, *Germany* .. **26 D3** 51 50N 7 49 E
Sendurjana, *India* ...... **82 D4** 21 32N 78 17 E
Senec, *Czech.* .... **31 C10** 48 12N 17 23 E
Seneca, *Oreg., U.S.A.* .. **142 D4** 44 10N 119 2W
Seneca, *S.C., U.S.A.* ... **135 H4** 34 43N 82 59W
Seneca Falls, *U.S.A.* **137 D8** 42 55N 76 50W
Seneca L., *U.S.A.* **136 D8** 42 40N 76 58W
Seneffe, *Belgium* .... **21 G4** 50 32N 4 16 E
Senegal ■, *W. Afr.* **100 C2** 14 30N 14 30W
Senegal →, *W. Afr.* **100 B1** 15 48N 16 32W
Senegambia, *Africa* **92 E2** 12 45N 12 0W
Senekal, *S. Africa* ...... **105 D4** 28 20 S 27 36 E
Senftenberg, *Germany* .. **26 D10** 51 30N 14 1 E
Senga Hill, *Zambia* ..... **107 D3** 9 19 S 31 11 E
Senge Khambab = Indus →, *Pakistan* ... **79 D2** 24 20N 67 47 E
Sengerema □, *Tanzania* . **106 C3** 2 10 S 32 20 E
Sengiley, *U.S.S.R.* ..... **51 E16** 53 58N 48 46 E
Sengkang, *Indonesia* .... **71 E6** 4 8 S 120 1 E
Sengua →, *Zimbabwe* ... **107 F2** 17 7 S 28 5 E
Senguerr →, *Argentina* . **160 C3** 45 35 S 68 50W
Senhor-do-Bonfim, *Brazil* **154 D3** 10 30 S 40 10W
Senica, *Czech.* .... **31 C10** 48 41N 17 25 E
Senigállia, *Italy* .... **39 E10** 43 42N 13 12 E
Seniku, *Burma* .... **78 C6** 25 32N 97 48 E
Senio →, *Italy* .... **39 D9** 44 35N 12 15 E
Senirkent, *Turkey* ...... **88 D4** 38 6N 30 33 E
Senise, *Italy* .... **41 B9** 40 6N 16 15 E
Senj, *Yugoslavia* .... **39 D11** 45 0N 14 58 E
Senja, *Norway* .... **12 B14** 69 25N 17 30 E
Senlis, *France* .... **23 C9** 49 13N 2 35 E
Senmonorom, *Cambodia* **76 F6** 12 27N 107 12 E
Sennâr, *Sudan* .... **95 E3** 13 30N 33 35 E
Senne →, *Belgium* ..... **21 G4** 50 42N 4 13 E
Senneterre, *Canada* **128 C4** 48 25N 77 15W
Senniquelle, *Liberia* **100 D3** 7 19N 8 38W
Senno, *U.S.S.R.* .... **50 D6** 54 45N 29 43 E
Sennori, *Italy* .... **40 B1** 40 49N 8 36 E
Seno, *Laos* .... **76 D5** 16 35N 104 50 E
Senonches, *France* ..... **22 D8** 48 34N 1 2 E
Senorbì, *Italy* .... **40 C2** 39 33N 9 8 E
Senožeče, *Yugoslavia* ... **39 C11** 45 43N 14 3 E

Silver Lake 265

Shëngjini, *Albania* **44 C1** 41 50N 19 35 E
Shenjingzi, *China* **67 B13** 44 40N 124 30 E
Shenmëria, *Albania* **44 B2** 42 7N 20 13 E
Shenmu, *China* **66 E6** 38 50N 110 29 E
Shennongjia, *China* **69 B8** 31 43N 110 44 E
Shenqiu, *China* **66 H8** 33 25N 115 5 E
Shenqiucheng, *China* **66 H8** 33 24N 115 2 E
Shensi = Shaanxi □, *China* **66 G5** 35 0N 109 0 E
Shenyang, *China* **67 D12** 41 48N 123 27 E
Shepetovka, *U.S.S.R.* **50 F5** 50 10N 27 10 E
Shepherd Is., *Vanuatu* **121 F6** 16 55 S 168 36 E
Shepherdsville, *U.S.A.* **141 G11** 37 59N 85 43W
Shepparton, *Australia* **117 D6** 36 23 S 145 26 E
Sheqi, *China* **66 H7** 33 12N 112 57 E
Sher Qila, *Pakistan* **81 A6** 36 7N 74 2 E
Sherborne, *U.K.* **17 G5** 50 56N 2 31W
Sherbro I., *S. Leone* **100 D2** 7 30N 12 40W
Sherbrooke, *Canada* **129 C5** 45 28N 71 57W
Sherda, *Chad* **97 D3** 20 7N 16 46 E
Shereik, *Sudan* **94 D3** 18 44N 33 47 E
Sheridan, *Ark., U.S.A.* **139 H8** 34 20N 92 25W
Sheridan, *Ill., U.S.A.* **141 C8** 41 32N 88 41W
Sheridan, *Ind., U.S.A.* **141 D10** 40 8N 86 13W
Sheridan, *Iowa, U.S.A.* **140 D2** 40 31N 94 37W
Sheridan, *Wyo., U.S.A.* **142 D10** 44 50N 107 0W
Sherkot, *India* **81 E8** 29 22N 78 35 E
Sherman, *U.S.A.* **139 J6** 33 40N 96 35W
Shërpūr, *Afghan.* **79 B3** 34 32N 69 10 E
Sherpur, *Bangla.* **78 C3** 25 0N 90 0 E
Sherridon, *Canada* **131 B8** 55 8N 101 5W
Sherwood, *N. Dak., U.S.A.* **138 A4** 48 59N 101 36W
Sherwood, *Ohio, U.S.A.* **141 C12** 41 17N 84 33W
Sherwood, *Tex., U.S.A.* **139 K4** 31 18N 100 45W
Sherwood Forest, *U.K.* **16 D6** 53 5N 1 5W
Sheslay, *Canada* **130 B2** 58 17N 131 52W
Sheslay →, *Canada* **130 B2** 58 48N 132 5W
Shethanei L., *Canada* **131 B9** 58 48N 97 50W
Shetland □, *U.K.* **18 A7** 60 30N 1 30W
Shetland Is., *U.K.* **18 A7** 60 30N 1 30W
Shevaroy Hills, *India* **83 J4** 11 58N 78 12 E
Shewa □, *Ethiopia* **95 F4** 9 33N 38 10 E
Shewa Gimira, *Ethiopia* **95 F4** 7 4N 35 51 E
Sheyenne, *U.S.A.* **138 B5** 47 52N 99 8W
Sheyenne →, *U.S.A.* **138 B6** 47 5N 96 50W
Shibām, *Yemen* **87 D5** 16 0N 48 36 E
Shibata, *Japan* **60 F9** 37 57N 139 20 E
Shibecha, *Japan* **60 C12** 43 17N 144 36 E
Shibetsu, *Japan* **60 B11** 44 10N 142 23 E
Shibîn el Kôm, *Egypt* **94 H7** 30 31N 30 55 E
Shibîn el Qanâtir, *Egypt* **94 H7** 30 19N 31 19 E
Shibing, *China* **68 D7** 27 2N 108 7 E
Shibogama L., *Canada* **128 B2** 53 35N 88 15W
Shibukawa, *Japan* **63 A11** 36 29N 139 0 E
Shibushi, *Japan* **62 F3** 31 25N 131 8 E
Shibushi-Wan, *Japan* **62 F3** 31 24N 131 8 E
Shicheng, *China* **69 D11** 26 22N 116 20 E
Shidād, *Si. Arabia* **86 B3** 21 19N 40 3 E
Shidao, *China* **67 F12** 36 50N 122 25 E
Shidian, *China* **68 E2** 24 40N 99 5 E
Shido, *Japan* **62 C6** 34 19N 134 10 E
Shiel, L., *U.K.* **18 E3** 56 48N 5 32W
Shield, C., *Australia* **114 A2** 13 20 S 136 20 E
Shiga □, *Japan* **63 B8** 35 20N 136 0 E
Shigaib, *Sudan* **97 E4** 15 5N 23 35 E
Shigaraki, *Japan* **63 C8** 34 57N 136 2 E
Shigu, *China* **68 D2** 26 51N 99 56 E
Shiguaigou, *China* **66 D6** 40 52N 110 15 E
Shihan, W. →, *Yemen* **87 C5** 17 24N 51 26 E
Shihchiachuangi = Shijiazhuang, *China* **66 E8** 38 2N 114 28 E
Shiiba, *Japan* **62 E3** 32 29N 131 4 E
Shijaku, *Albania* **44 C1** 41 21N 19 33 E
Shijiazhuang, *China* **66 E8** 38 2N 114 28 E
Shijiu Hu, *China* **69 B12** 31 25N 118 50 E
Shikarpur, *India* **80 E8** 28 17N 78 7 E
Shikarpur, *Pakistan* **79 D3** 27 57N 68 39 E
Shikine-Jima, *Japan* **63 C11** 34 19N 139 13 E
Shikoku, *Japan* **62 D5** 33 30N 133 30 E
Shikoku □, *Japan* **62 D5** 33 30N 133 30 E
Shikoku-Sanchi, *Japan* **62 D5** 33 30N 133 30 E
Shilabo, *Ethiopia* **90 F3** 6 22N 44 32 E
Shilda, *U.S.S.R.* **54 F6** 51 49N 59 47 E
Shiliguri, *India* **78 B2** 26 45N 88 25 E
Shilka, *U.S.S.R.* **57 D12** 52 0N 115 55 E
Shilka →, *U.S.S.R.* **57 D13** 53 20N 121 26 E
Shillong, *India* **78 C3** 25 35N 91 53 E
Shilo, *Jordan* **91 C4** 32 4N 35 18 E
Shilong, *China* **69 F9** 23 5N 113 52 E
Shilou, *China* **66 F6** 37 0N 110 48 E
Shilovo, *U.S.S.R.* **51 D12** 54 25N 40 57 E
Shima-Hantō, *Japan* **63 C8** 34 22N 136 45 E
Shimabara, *Japan* **62 E2** 32 48N 130 20 E
Shimada, *Japan* **63 C10** 34 49N 138 10 E
Shimane □, *Japan* **62 C4** 35 0N 132 30 E
Shimane-Hantō, *Japan* **62 B5** 35 30N 133 0 E
Shimanovsk, *U.S.S.R.* **57 D13** 52 15N 127 30 E
Shimen, *China* **69 C8** 29 35N 111 20 E
Shimenjie, *China* **69 C11** 29 29N 116 48 E
Shimian, *China* **68 C4** 29 17N 102 23 E
Shimizu, *Japan* **63 C10** 35 0N 138 30 E
Shimo-Jima, *Japan* **62 E2** 32 15N 130 7 E
Shimo-Koshiki-Jima, *Japan* **62 F1** 31 40N 129 43 E
Shimoda, *Japan* **63 C10** 34 40N 138 57 E
Shimodate, *Japan* **63 A11** 36 20N 139 55 E
Shimoga, *India* **83 H2** 13 57N 75 32 E
Shimoni, *Kenya* **106 C4** 4 38 S 39 20 E
Shimonita, *Japan* **63 A10** 36 13N 138 47 E
Shimonoseki, *Japan* **62 D2** 33 58N 130 55 E
Shimotsuma, *Japan* **63 A11** 36 11N 139 58 E
Shimpuru Rapids, *Angola* **103 F3** 17 45 S 19 55 E
Shimsha →, *India* **83 H3** 13 15N 77 10 E
Shimsk, *U.S.S.R.* **50 B7** 58 15N 30 50 E
Shin, L., *U.K.* **18 C4** 58 7N 4 30W
Shin-Tone →, *Japan* **63 B12** 35 44N 140 51 E
Shinan, *China* **68 F7** 22 44N 109 53 E
Shinano →, *Japan* **61 F9** 36 50N 138 30 E
Shīndand, *Afghan.* **79 B1** 33 12N 62 8 E
Shingbwiyang, *Burma* **78 B6** 26 41N 96 13 E
Shingleton, *U.S.A.* **128 C2** 46 25N 86 33W
Shingū, *Japan* **63 D7** 33 40N 135 55 E
Shinji, *Japan* **62 B4** 35 24N 132 54 E
Shinji Ko, *Japan* **62 B4** 35 26N 132 57 E
Shinjō, *Japan* **60 E10** 38 46N 140 18 E
Shinkafe, *Nigeria* **101 C6** 13 8N 6 29 E
Shīnkay, *Afghan.* **79 C2** 31 57N 67 26 E
Shinminato, *Japan* **63 A9** 36 47N 137 4 E
Shinonoi, *Japan* **63 A10** 36 35N 138 9 E
Shinshār, *Syria* **91 A5** 34 36N 36 43 E
Shinshiro, *Japan* **63 C9** 34 54N 137 30 E
Shinyanga, *Tanzania* **106 C3** 3 45 S 33 27 E
Shinyanga □, *Tanzania* **106 C3** 3 50 S 34 0 E
Shio-no-Misaki, *Japan* **63 D7** 33 25N 135 45 E
Shiogama, *Japan* **60 E10** 38 19N 141 1 E
Shiojiri, *Japan* **63 A9** 36 6N 137 58 E
Ship I., *U.S.A.* **139 K10** 30 16N 88 55W
Shipehenski Prokhod, *Bulgaria* **43 E10** 42 45N 25 15 E
Shiping, *China* **68 F4** 23 45N 102 23 E
Shippegan, *Canada* **129 C7** 47 45N 64 45W
Shippensburg, *U.S.A.* **136 F7** 40 4N 77 32W
Shiprock, *U.S.A.* **143 H9** 36 51N 108 45W
Shiqian, *China* **68 D7** 27 32N 108 13 E
Shiqma, N. →, *Israel* **91 D3** 31 37N 34 30 E
Shiquan, *China* **66 H5** 33 5N 108 15 E
Shīr Kūh, *Iran* **85 D7** 31 39N 54 3 E
Shirabad, *U.S.S.R.* **55 E3** 37 40N 67 1 E
Shiragami-Misaki, *Japan* **60 D10** 41 24N 140 12 E
Shirahama, *Japan* **63 D7** 33 41N 135 20 E
Shirakawa, *Fukushima, Japan* **61 F10** 37 7N 140 13 E
Shirakawa, *Gifu, Japan* **63 A8** 36 17N 136 56 E
Shirane-San, *Gumma, Japan* **63 A11** 36 48N 139 22 E
Shirane-San, *Yamanashi, Japan* **63 B10** 35 42N 138 9 E
Shiraoi, *Japan* **60 C10** 42 33N 141 21 E
Shīrāz, *Iran* **85 D7** 29 42N 52 30 E
Shirbin, *Egypt* **94 H7** 31 11N 31 32 E
Shire →, *Africa* **107 F4** 17 42 S 35 19 E
Shiretoko-Misaki, *Japan* **60 B12** 44 21N 145 20 E
Shirinab →, *Pakistan* **80 D2** 30 15N 66 28 E
Shiringushi, *U.S.S.R.* **51 E13** 53 51N 42 46 E
Shiriya-Zaki, *Japan* **60 D10** 41 25N 141 30 E
Shirley, *U.S.A.* **141 E11** 39 53N 85 35W
Shiroishi, *Japan* **60 F10** 38 0N 140 37 E
Shirol, *India* **82 F2** 16 47N 74 41 E
Shirpur, *India* **82 D2** 21 21N 74 57 E
Shīrvān, *Iran* **85 B8** 37 30N 57 50 E
Shirwa, L. = Chilwa, L., *Malawi* **107 F4** 15 15 S 35 40 E
Shishmanova, *Bulgaria* **43 E8** 42 58N 23 12 E
Shishou, *China* **69 C9** 29 38N 112 22 E
Shitai, *China* **69 B11** 30 12N 117 25 E
Shively, *U.S.A.* **141 F11** 38 12N 85 49W
Shivpuri, *India* **80 G7** 25 26N 77 42 E
Shixian, *China* **67 C15** 43 5N 129 50 E
Shixing, *China* **69 E10** 24 46N 114 5 E
Shiyan, *China* **69 A8** 32 35N 110 45 E
Shiyata, *Egypt* **94 B2** 29 25N 25 7 E
Shizhu, *China* **68 C7** 29 58N 108 7 E
Shizong, *China* **68 E5** 24 50N 104 0 E
Shizuishan, *China* **66 E4** 39 15N 106 50 E
Shizuoka, *Japan* **63 C10** 34 57N 138 24 E
Shizuoka □, *Japan* **63 B10** 35 15N 138 40 E
Shklov, *U.S.S.R.* **50 D7** 54 16N 30 15 E
Shkoder = Shkodra, *Albania* **44 B1** 42 6N 19 20 E
Shkodra, *Albania* **44 B1** 42 6N 19 20 E
Shkodra □, *Albania* **44 B1** 42 25N 19 20 E
Shkumbini →, *Albania* **44 C1** 41 5N 19 50 E
Shmidta, O., *U.S.S.R.* **57 A10** 81 0N 91 0 E
Shō-Gawa →, *Japan* **63 A9** 36 47N 137 4 E
Shoal Cr. →, *U.S.A.* **140 E3** 39 39N 93 35W
Shoal Lake, *Canada* **131 C8** 50 30N 100 35W
Shoals, *U.S.A.* **141 F10** 38 40N 86 47W
Shōbara, *Japan* **62 C5** 34 51N 133 1 E
Shōdo-Shima, *Japan* **62 C6** 34 30N 134 15 E
Shoeburyness, *U.K.* **17 F8** 51 31N 0 49 E
Shokpar, *U.S.S.R.* **55 B7** 43 49N 74 21 E
Sholapur = Solapur, *India* **82 F2** 17 43N 75 56 E
Shologontsy, *U.S.S.R.* **57 C12** 66 13N 114 0 E
Shōmrōn, *Jordan* **91 C4** 32 15N 35 13 E
Shoranur, *India* **83 J3** 10 46N 76 19 E
Shorapur, *India* **83 F3** 16 31N 76 48 E
Shortland I., *Solomon Is.* **121 L8** 7 0 S 155 45 E
Shoshone, *Calif., U.S.A.* **145 K10** 35 58N 116 16W
Shoshone, *Idaho, U.S.A.* **142 E6** 43 0N 114 27W
Shoshone L., *U.S.A.* **142 D8** 44 30N 110 40W
Shoshone Mts., *U.S.A.* **142 G5** 39 30N 117 30W
Shoshong, *Botswana* **104 C4** 22 56 S 26 31 E
Shoshoni, *U.S.A.* **142 E9** 43 13N 108 5W
Shostka, *U.S.S.R.* **50 F8** 51 57N 33 32 E
Shou Xian, *China* **69 A11** 32 37N 116 42 E
Shouchang, *China* **69 C12** 29 18N 119 12 E
Shouguang, *China* **67 F10** 37 52N 118 45 E
Shouning, *China* **69 D12** 27 27N 119 31 E
Shouyang, *China* **66 F7** 37 54N 113 8 E
Show Low, *U.S.A.* **143 J9** 34 16N 110 0W
Shpola, *U.S.S.R.* **52 B4** 49 1N 31 30 E
Shreveport, *U.S.A.* **139 J8** 32 30N 93 50W
Shrewsbury, *U.K.* **16 E5** 52 42N 2 45W
Shrirampur, *India* **81 H13** 22 44N 88 21 E
Shrirangapattana, *India* **83 H3** 12 26N 76 43 E
Shropshire □, *U.K.* **17 E5** 52 36N 2 45W
Shuangbai, *China* **68 E3** 24 42N 101 38 E
Shuangcheng, *China* **67 B14** 45 20N 126 15 E
Shuangfeng, *China* **69 D9** 27 29N 112 11 E
Shuanggou, *China* **67 G9** 34 2N 117 30 E
Shuangjiang, *China* **68 F2** 23 26N 99 58 E
Shuangliao, *China* **67 C12** 43 29N 123 30 E
Shuangshanzi, *China* **67 D10** 40 20N 119 8 E
Shuangyang, *China* **67 C13** 43 28N 125 40 E
Shuangyashan, *China* **65 B8** 46 28N 131 5 E
Shu'b, Ra's, *Yemen* **87 D6** 12 30N 53 25 E
Shucheng, *China* **69 B11** 31 28N 116 57 E
Shuguri Falls, *Tanzania* **107 D4** 8 33 S 37 22 E
Shuḩayr, *Yemen* **87 D5** 14 41N 49 23 E
Shuicheng, *China* **68 D5** 26 38N 104 48 E
Shuiji, *China* **69 D12** 27 13N 118 20 E
Shuiye, *China* **66 F8** 36 7N 114 8 E
Shujalpur, *India* **80 H7** 23 18N 76 46 E
Shukpa Kunzang, *India* **81 B8** 34 22N 78 22 E
Shulan, *China* **67 B14** 44 28N 127 0 E
Shule, *China* **64 C2** 39 25N 76 3 E
Shullsburg, *U.S.A.* **140 B6** 42 35N 90 15W
Shumagin Is., *U.S.A.* **126 C4** 55 0N 159 0W
Shumerlya, *U.S.S.R.* **51 D15** 55 30N 46 25 E
Shumikha, *U.S.S.R.* **54 D8** 55 10N 63 15 E
Shunchang, *China* **69 D11** 26 54N 117 48 E
Shunde, *China* **69 F9** 22 42N 113 14 E
Shungay, *U.S.S.R.* **53 B12** 48 30N 46 45 E
Shungnak, *U.S.A.* **126 B4** 66 55N 157 10W
Shuo Xian, *China* **66 E7** 39 20N 112 33 E
Shūr →, *Iran* **85 D7** 28 30N 55 0 E
Shūr Āb, *Iran* **85 C6** 34 23N 51 11 E
Shūr Gaz, *Iran* **85 D8** 29 10N 59 20 E
Shūrāb, *Iran* **85 C8** 33 43N 56 29 E
Shurab, *U.S.S.R.* **55 C5** 40 3N 70 33 E
Shurchi, *U.S.S.R.* **55 E3** 37 59N 67 47 E
Shūrjestān, *Iran* **85 D7** 31 24N 52 25 E
Shurkhua, *Burma* **78 D4** 22 15N 93 38 E
Shurma, *U.S.S.R.* **54 C2** 56 58N 50 21 E
Shurugwi, *Zimbabwe* **107 F3** 19 40 S 30 0 E
Shūsf, *Iran* **85 D9** 31 50N 60 5 E
Shūshtar, *Iran* **85 D6** 32 0N 48 50 E
Shuswap L., *Canada* **130 C5** 50 55N 119 3W
Shuya, *U.S.S.R.* **51 C12** 56 50N 41 28 E
Shuyang, *China* **67 G10** 34 10N 118 42 E
Shuzenji, *Japan* **63 C10** 34 58N 138 56 E
Shūzū, *Iran* **85 D7** 29 52N 54 30 E
Shwebo, *Burma* **78 D5** 22 30N 95 45 E
Shwegu, *Burma* **78 C6** 24 15N 96 26 E
Shwegun, *Burma* **78 G6** 17 9N 97 39 E
Shwenyaung, *Burma* **78 E6** 20 46N 96 57 E
Shyok, *India* **81 B8** 34 15N 78 12 E
Shyok →, *Pakistan* **81 B6** 35 13N 75 53 E
Si Chon, *Thailand* **77 H2** 9 0N 99 54 E
Si Kiang = Xi Jiang →, *China* **69 F9** 22 5N 113 20 E
Si Prachan, *Thailand* **76 E3** 14 37N 100 9 E
Si Racha, *Thailand* **76 F3** 13 10N 100 48 E
Si Xian, *China* **67 H9** 33 30N 117 50 E
Siahan Range, *Pakistan* **79 D2** 27 30N 64 40 E
Siak →, *Indonesia* **74 B2** 1 13N 102 9 E
Siaksrindrapura, *Indonesia* **70 D2** 0 51N 102 0 E
Sialkot, *Pakistan* **79 B4** 32 32N 74 30 E
Sialsuk, *India* **78 D4** 23 24N 92 45 E
Siam = Thailand ■, *Asia* **76 E4** 16 0N 102 0 E
Siam, *Australia* **116 B2** 32 35 S 136 41 E
Sian = Xi'an, *China* **66 G5** 34 15N 109 0 E
Siantan, P., *Indonesia* **77 L6** 3 10N 106 15 E
Siàpo →, *Venezuela* **152 C4** 2 7N 66 28W
Sīāreh, *Iran* **85 D9** 28 5N 60 14 E
Siargao, *Phil.* **71 C7** 9 52N 126 3 E
Siari, *Pakistan* **81 B7** 34 55N 76 40 E
Siasi, *Phil.* **71 C6** 5 34N 120 50 E
Siassi, *Papua N. G.* **120 C4** 5 40 S 147 51 E
Siátista, *Greece* **44 D3** 40 15N 21 33 E
Siau, *Indonesia* **71 D7** 2 50N 125 25 E
Siauliai, *U.S.S.R.* **50 D3** 55 56N 23 15 E
Siaya □, *Kenya* **106 C3** 0 0 34 20 E
Siazan, *U.S.S.R.* **53 F13** 41 3N 49 10 E
Sibâi, Gebel el, *Egypt* **94 B3** 25 45N 34 10 E
Sibang, *Gabon* **102 B1** 0 25N 9 31 E
Sibari, *Italy* **41 C9** 39 47N 16 27 E
Sibasa, *S. Africa* **105 C5** 22 53 S 30 33 E
Sibay, *U.S.S.R.* **54 E6** 52 42N 58 39 E
Sibayi, L., *S. Africa* **105 D5** 27 20 S 32 45 E
Šibenik, *Yugoslavia* **39 E12** 43 48N 15 54 E
Siberia, *U.S.S.R.* **58 D14** 60 0N 100 0 E
Siberut, *Indonesia* **70 E1** 1 30 S 99 0 E
Sibi, *Pakistan* **79 C2** 29 30N 67 54 E
Sibil, *Indonesia* **71 E10** 4 59 S 140 35 E
Sibiti, *Congo* **102 C2** 3 38 S 13 19 E
Sibiu, *Romania* **46 D5** 45 45N 24 9 E
Sibiu □, *Romania* **46 D5** 45 50N 24 15 E
Sibley, *Ill., U.S.A.* **141 D8** 40 35N 88 23W
Sibley, *Iowa, U.S.A.* **138 D7** 43 21N 95 43W
Sibley, *La., U.S.A.* **139 J8** 32 34N 93 16W
Sibolga, *Indonesia* **70 D1** 1 42N 98 45 E
Sibret, *Belgium* **21 J7** 49 58N 5 38 E
Sibsagar, *India* **78 B5** 27 0N 94 36 E
Sibu, *Malaysia* **70 D4** 2 18N 111 49 E
Sibuco, *Phil.* **71 C6** 7 20N 122 10 E
Sibuguey B., *Phil.* **71 C6** 7 50N 122 45 E
Sibutu, *Phil.* **71 D5** 4 45N 119 30 E
Sibutu Passage, *E. Indies* **71 D6** 4 50N 120 0 E
Sibuyan, *Phil.* **71 B6** 12 25N 122 40 E
Sibuyan Sea, *Phil.* **71 B6** 12 30N 122 20 E
Sicamous, *Canada* **130 C5** 50 49N 119 0W
Sichuan □, *China* **68 B5** 31 0N 104 0 E
Sicilia, *Italy* **41 E7** 37 30N 14 30 E
Sicilia □, *Italy* **41 E7** 37 30N 14 30 E
Sicilia, Canale di, *Italy* **40 E5** 37 25N 12 30 E
Sicilian Channel = Sicilia, Canale di, *Italy* **40 E5** 37 25N 12 30 E
Sicily = Sicilia, *Italy* **41 E7** 37 30N 14 30 E
Sicuani, *Peru* **156 C3** 14 21 S 71 10W
Šiculiana, *Italy* **40 E6** 37 20N 13 23 E
Šid, *Yugoslavia* **42 B4** 45 8N 19 14 E
Sidamo □, *Ethiopia* **95 G4** 5 0N 37 50 E
Sidaouet, *Niger* **97 E1** 18 34N 8 3 E
Sidári, *Greece* **32 A3** 39 47N 19 41 E
Siddeburen, *Neths.* **20 B9** 53 15N 6 52 E
Siddhapur, *India* **80 H5** 23 56N 72 25 E
Siddipet, *India* **82 E4** 18 5N 78 51 E
Side, *Turkey* **88 E4** 36 45N 31 23 E
Sidell, *U.S.A.* **141 E9** 39 55N 87 49W
Sidéradougou, *Burkina Faso* **100 C4** 10 42N 4 12W
Siderno Marina, *Italy* **41 D9** 38 16N 16 17 E
Sídheros, Ákra, *Greece* **32 D8** 35 19N 26 19 E
Sidhirókastron, *Greece* **44 C5** 41 13N 23 24 E
Sîdi Abd el Rahmân, *Egypt* **94 H6** 30 55N 29 44 E
Sîdi Barrâni, *Egypt* **94 A2** 31 38N 25 58 E
Sidi-bel-Abbès, *Algeria* **99 A4** 35 13N 0 39W
Sidi Bennour, *Morocco* **98 B3** 32 40N 8 25W
Sidi Haneish, *Egypt* **94 A2** 31 10N 27 35 E
Sidi Kacem, *Morocco* **98 B3** 34 11N 5 49W
Sidi Omar, *Egypt* **94 A1** 31 24N 24 57 E
Sidi Slimane, *Morocco* **98 B3** 34 16N 5 56W
Sidi Smaïl, *Morocco* **98 B3** 32 50N 8 31W
Sidi 'Uzayz, *Libya* **96 B4** 31 41N 24 55 E
Sidlaw Hills, *U.K.* **18 E5** 56 32N 3 10W
Sidley, Mt., *Antarctica* **7 D14** 77 2 S 126 2W
Sidmouth, *U.K.* **17 G4** 50 40N 3 13W
Sidmouth, C., *Australia* **114 A3** 13 25 S 143 36 E
Sidney, *Canada* **130 D4** 48 39N 123 24W
Sidney, *Mont., U.S.A.* **138 B2** 47 42N 104 7W
Sidney, *N.Y., U.S.A.* **137 D9** 42 18N 75 20W
Sidney, *Nebr., U.S.A.* **138 E3** 41 12N 103 0W
Sidney, *Ohio, U.S.A.* **141 D12** 40 18N 84 6W
Sidoarjo, *Indonesia* **71 G15** 7 27 S 112 43 E
Sidoktaya, *Burma* **78 E5** 20 27N 94 15 E
Sidon = Saydā, *Lebanon* **91 B4** 33 35N 35 25 E
Sidra, G. of = Surt, Khalīj, *Libya* **96 B3** 31 40N 18 30 E
Siedlce, *Poland* **47 C9** 52 10N 22 20 E
Siedlce □, *Poland* **47 D9** 52 0N 22 0 E
Sieg →, *Germany* **26 E3** 50 46N 7 7 E
Siegburg, *Germany* **26 E3** 50 48N 7 12 E
Siegen, *Germany* **26 E4** 50 52N 8 2 E
Siem Pang, *Cambodia* **76 E6** 14 7N 106 23 E
Siem Reap, *Cambodia* **76 F4** 13 20N 103 52 E
Siena, *Italy* **39 E8** 43 20N 11 20 E
Sieniawa, *Poland* **31 A15** 50 11N 22 38 E
Sieradź, *Poland* **47 D5** 51 37N 18 41 E
Sieraków, *Poland* **47 C3** 52 39N 16 2 E
Sierck-les-Bains, *France* **23 C13** 49 26N 6 20 E
Sierpc, *Poland* **47 C6** 52 55N 19 43 E
Sierpe, Bocas de la, *Venezuela* **153 B5** 10 0N 61 30W
Sierra Blanca, *U.S.A.* **143 L11** 31 11N 105 17W
Sierra Blanca Pk., *U.S.A.* **143 K11** 33 20N 105 54W
Sierra City, *U.S.A.* **144 F6** 39 34N 120 42W
Sierra Colorada, *Argentina* **160 B3** 40 35 S 67 50W
Sierra de Yeguas, *Spain* **37 H6** 37 7N 4 52W
Sierra Gorda, *Chile* **158 A2** 22 50 S 69 15W
Sierra Grande, *Argentina* **160 B3** 41 36 S 65 22W
Sierra Leone ■, *W. Afr.* **100 D2** 9 0N 12 0W
Sierra Madre, *Mexico* **147 D6** 16 0N 93 0W
Sierra Mojada, *Mexico* **146 B4** 27 19N 103 42W
Sierraville, *U.S.A.* **144 F6** 39 36N 120 22W
Sierre, *Switz.* **28 D5** 46 17N 7 31 E
Sif Fatima, *Algeria* **99 B6** 31 6N 8 41 E
Sífnos, *Greece* **45 H6** 37 0N 24 45 E
Sifton, *Canada* **131 C8** 51 21N 100 8W
Sifton Pass, *Canada* **130 B3** 57 52N 126 15W
Sig, *Algeria* **99 A4** 35 32N 0 12W
Sigdal, *Norway* **14 D3** 60 4N 9 38 E
Sigean, *France* **24 E6** 43 2N 2 58 E
Sighetu-Marmatiei, *Romania* **46 B4** 47 57N 23 52 E
Sighişoara, *Romania* **46 C5** 46 12N 24 50 E
Sigira, *Yemen* **87 D6** 12 37N 54 20 E
Sigli, *Indonesia* **70 C1** 5 25N 96 0 E
Siglufjörður, *Iceland* **12 C4** 66 12N 18 55W
Sigmaringen, *Germany* **27 G5** 48 5N 9 13 E
Signakhi, *U.S.S.R.* **53 F11** 41 40N 45 57 E
Signal, *U.S.A.* **145 L13** 34 30N 113 38W
Signal Pk., *U.S.A.* **145 M12** 33 25N 114 4W
Signau, *Switz.* **28 C5** 46 56N 7 45 E
Signy-l'Abbaye, *France* **23 C11** 49 40N 4 25 E
Sigourney, *U.S.A.* **140 C4** 41 20N 92 12W
Sigsig, *Ecuador* **152 D2** 3 0 S 78 50W
Sigtuna, *Sweden* **14 E11** 59 36N 17 44 E
Sigüenza, *Spain* **34 D2** 41 3N 2 40W
Siguiri, *Guinea* **100 C3** 11 31N 9 10W
Sigulda, *U.S.S.R.* **50 C4** 57 10N 24 55 E
Sigurd, *U.S.A.* **143 G8** 38 49N 112 0W
Sihanoukville = Kompong Som, *Cambodia* **77 G4** 10 38N 103 30 E
Sihaus, *Peru* **156 B2** 8 40 S 77 40W
Sihui, *China* **69 F9** 23 20N 112 40 E
Siirt, *Turkey* **89 E9** 37 57N 41 55 E
Siirt □, *Turkey* **89 E9** 37 55N 41 55 E
Sijarira Ra., *Zimbabwe* **107 F2** 17 36 S 27 45 E
Sijungjung, *Indonesia* **74 C2** 0 42 S 100 58 E
Sikao, *Thailand* **77 J2** 7 34N 99 21 E
Sikar, *India* **80 F6** 27 33N 75 10 E
Sikasso, *Mali* **100 C3** 11 18N 5 35W
Sikeston, *U.S.A.* **139 G10** 36 52N 89 35W
Sikhote Alin, Khrebet, *U.S.S.R.* **57 E14** 45 0N 136 0 E
Sikiá., *Greece* **44 D5** 40 2N 23 56 E
Síkinos, *Greece* **45 H7** 36 40N 25 8 E
Sikkani Chief →, *Canada* **130 B4** 57 47N 122 15W
Sikkim □, *India* **78 B2** 27 50N 88 30 E
Siklós, *Hungary* **31 F11** 45 50N 18 19 E
Sikotu-Ko, *Japan* **60 C10** 42 45N 141 25 E
Sil →, *Spain* **36 C3** 42 27N 7 43W
Silacayoapan, *Mexico* **147 D5** 17 30N 98 9W
Silandro, *Italy* **38 B7** 46 38N 10 48 E
Silba, *Yugoslavia* **39 D11** 44 24N 14 41 E
Silchar, *India* **78 C4** 24 49N 92 48 E
Silcox, *Canada* **131 B10** 57 12N 94 10W
Şile, *Turkey* **88 C3** 41 10N 29 37 E
Silenrieux, *Belgium* **21 H4** 50 14N 4 27 E
Siler City, *U.S.A.* **135 H6** 35 44N 79 30W
Sileru →, *India* **82 F5** 17 49N 81 24 E
Silet, *Algeria* **99 D5** 22 44N 4 37 E
Silgarhi Doti, *Nepal* **81 E9** 29 15N 81 0 E
Silghat, *India* **78 B4** 26 35N 93 0 E
Silifke, *Turkey* **88 E5** 36 22N 33 58 E
Siling Co, *China* **64 C3** 31 50N 89 20 E
Silíqua, *Italy* **40 C1** 39 20N 8 49 E
Silistra, *Bulgaria* **43 C12** 44 6N 27 19 E
Silivri, *Turkey* **88 C3** 41 4N 28 14 E
Siljan, *Sweden* **13 F13** 60 55N 14 45 E
Silkeborg, *Denmark* **15 H3** 56 10N 9 32 E
Sillajhuay, Cordillera, *Chile* **156 D4** 19 46 S 68 40W
Sillé-le-Guillaume, *France* **22 D6** 48 10N 0 8W
Sillustani, *Peru* **156 D3** 15 50 S 70 7W
Siloam Springs, *U.S.A.* **139 G7** 36 15N 94 31W
Silopi, *Turkey* **89 E10** 37 15N 42 27 E
Silsbee, *U.S.A.* **139 K7** 30 20N 94 8W
Silute, *U.S.S.R.* **50 D2** 55 21N 21 33 E
Silva Porto = Kuito, *Angola* **103 E3** 12 22 S 16 55 E
Silvan, *Turkey* **89 D9** 38 7N 41 2 E
Silvaplana, *Switz.* **29 D9** 46 28N 9 48 E
Silver City, *N. Mex., U.S.A.* **143 K9** 32 50N 108 18W
Silver City, *Nev., U.S.A.* **142 G4** 39 15N 119 48W
Silver Cr. →, *U.S.A.* **142 E4** 43 16N 119 13W
Silver Creek, *U.S.A.* **136 D5** 42 33N 79 9W
Silver Grove, *U.S.A.* **141 E12** 39 2N 84 24W
Silver L., *U.S.A.* **144 G6** 38 39N 120 6W
Silver Lake, *Calif., U.S.A.* **145 K10** 35 21N 116 7W
Silver Lake, *Ind., U.S.A.* **141 C11** 41 4N 85 53W

266 Silver Lake

Silver Lake, *Oreg., U.S.A.* **142 E3** 43 9N 121 4W
Silver Lake, *Wis., U.S.A.* **141 B8** 42 33N 88 13W
Silver Streams, *S. Africa* **104 D3** 28 20 S 23 33 E
Silverton, *Australia* **116 A4** 31 52 S 141 10 E
Silverton, *Colo., U.S.A.* **143 H10** 37 51N 107 45W
Silverton, *Tex., U.S.A.* **139 H4** 34 30N 101 16W
Silves, *Portugal* **37 H2** 37 11N 8 26W
Silvi, *Italy* **39 F11** 42 32N 14 5 E
Silvia, *Colombia* **152 C2** 2 37N 76 21W
Silvies →, *U.S.A.* **142 E4** 43 22N 118 48W
Silvolde, *Neths.* **20 E8** 51 55N 6 23 E
Silvretta-Gruppe, *Switz.* **29 C10** 46 50N 10 6 E
Silwa Bahari, *Egypt* **94 C3** 24 45N 32 55 E
Silz, *Austria* **30 D3** 47 16N 10 56 E
Sim, C., *Morocco* **98 B3** 31 26N 9 51W
Simanggang, *Malaysia* **70 D4** 1 15N 111 32 E
Simao, *China* **68 F3** 22 47N 101 5 E
Simão Dias, *Brazil* **154 D4** 10 44 S 37 49W
Simard, L., *Canada* **128 C4** 47 40N 78 40W
Sîmărtin, *Romania* **46 C6** 46 19N 25 58 E
Simav, *Turkey* **88 D3** 39 4N 28 58 E
Simba, *Tanzania* **106 C4** 2 10 S 37 36 E
Simbach, *Germany* **27 G9** 48 16N 13 3 E
Simbo, *Tanzania* **106 C2** 4 51 S 29 41 E
Simcoe, *Canada* **128 D3** 42 50N 80 20W
Simcoe, L., *Canada* **128 D4** 44 25N 79 20W
Simenga, *U.S.S.R.* **57 C11** 62 42N 108 25 E
Simeto →, *Italy* **41 E8** 37 25N 15 10 E
Simeulue, *Indonesia* **70 D1** 2 45N 95 45 E
Simferopol, *U.S.S.R.* **52 D6** 44 55N 34 3 E
Sími, *Greece* **45 H9** 36 35N 27 50 E
Simi Valley, *U.S.A.* **145 L8** 34 16N 118 47W
Simikot, *Nepal* **81 E9** 30 0N 81 50 E
Simití, *Colombia* **152 B3** 7 58N 73 57W
Simitli, *Bulgaria* **42 F8** 41 52N 23 7 E
Simla, *India* **80 D7** 31 2N 77 9 E
Şimleu-Silvaniei, *Romania* **46 B3** 47 17N 22 50 E
Simme →, *Switz.* **28 C4** 46 38N 7 25 E
Simmern, *Germany* **27 F3** 49 59N 7 32 E
Simmie, *Canada* **131 D7** 49 56N 108 6W
Simmler, *U.S.A.* **145 K7** 35 21N 119 59W
Simões, *Brazil* **154 C3** 7 36 S 40 49W
Simojärvi, *Finland* **12 C19** 66 5N 27 3 E
Simojoki →, *Finland* **12 D18** 65 35N 25 1 E
Simojovel, *Mexico* **147 D6** 17 12N 92 38W
Simonette →, *Canada* **130 B5** 55 9N 118 15W
Simonstown, *S. Africa* **104 E2** 34 14 S 18 26 E
Simontornya, *Hungary* **31 E11** 46 45N 18 33 E
Simpangkiri →, *Indonesia* **74 B1** 2 50N 97 40 E
Simplício Mendes, *Brazil* **154 C3** 7 51 S 41 54W
Simplon, *Switz.* **28 D6** 46 12N 8 4 E
Simplon Pass = Simplonpass, *Switz.* **28 D6** 46 15N 8 3 E
Simplon Tunnel, *Switz.* **28 D6** 46 15N 8 7 E
Simplonpass, *Switz.* **28 D6** 46 15N 8 3 E
Simpson Desert, *Australia* **114 D2** 25 0 S 137 0 E
Simpungdong, *N. Korea* **67 D15** 40 56N 129 29 E
Simunjan, *Malaysia* **70 D4** 1 25N 110 45 E
Simushir, Ostrov, *U.S.S.R.* **57 E16** 46 50N 152 30 E
Sina →, *India* **82 F2** 17 30N 75 55 E
Sinabang, *Indonesia* **70 D1** 2 30N 96 24 E
Sinadogo, *Somali Rep.* **90 F4** 5 50N 47 0 E
Sinai = Es Sînâ', *Egypt* **94 J8** 29 0N 34 0 E
Sinai, Mt. = Mûsa, G., *Egypt* **94 J8** 28 33N 33 59 E
Sinai Peninsula, *Egypt* **91 F3** 29 30N 34 0 E
Sinaia, *Romania* **46 D6** 45 21N 25 38 E
Sinaloa □, *Mexico* **146 C3** 25 0N 107 30W
Sinaloa de Levya, *Mexico* **146 B3** 25 50N 108 20W
Sinalunga, *Italy* **39 E8** 43 12N 11 43 E
Sinan, *China* **68 D7** 27 56N 108 13 E
Sînandrei, *Romania* **46 D2** 45 52N 21 13 E
Sinarádhes, *Greece* **32 A3** 39 34N 19 51 E
Sīnāwan, *Libya* **96 B2** 31 0N 10 37 E
Sinbaungwe, *Burma* **78 F5** 19 43N 95 10 E
Sinbo, *Burma* **78 C6** 24 46N 97 3 E
Sincé, *Colombia* **152 B2** 9 15N 75 9W
Sincelejo, *Colombia* **152 B2** 9 18N 75 24W
Sinchang, *N. Korea* **67 D15** 40 7N 128 28 E
Sinchang-ni, *N. Korea* **67 E14** 39 24N 126 8 E
Sinclair, *U.S.A.* **142 F10** 41 47N 107 10W
Sinclair Mills, *Canada* **130 C4** 54 5N 121 40W
Sincorá, Serra do, *Brazil* **155 D3** 13 30 S 41 0W
Sind, *Pakistan* **80 G3** 26 0N 68 30 E
Sind □, *Pakistan* **79 D3** 26 0N 69 0 E
Sind →, *India* **81 B6** 34 18N 74 45 E
Sind Sagar Doab, *Pakistan* **80 D4** 32 0N 71 30 E
Sindal, *Denmark* **15 G4** 57 28N 10 10 E
Sindangan, *Phil.* **71 C6** 8 10N 123 5 E
Sindangbarang, *Indonesia* **71 G12** 7 27 S 107 1 E
Sinde, *Zambia* **107 F2** 17 28 S 25 51 E
Sinegorski, *U.S.S.R.* **53 C9** 48 0N 40 52 E
Sinelnikovo, *U.S.S.R.* **52 B6** 48 25N 35 30 E
Sines, *Portugal* **37 H2** 37 56N 8 51W
Sines, C. de, *Portugal* **37 H2** 37 58N 8 53W
Sineu, *Spain* **33 B10** 39 38N 3 1 E
Sinewit, Mt., *Papua N. G.* **120 C7** 4 44 S 152 2 E
Sinfra, *Ivory C.* **100 D3** 6 35N 5 56W
Sing Buri, *Thailand* **76 E3** 14 53N 100 25 E
Singa, *Sudan* **95 E3** 13 10N 33 57 E
Singanallur, *India* **83 J3** 11 2N 77 1 E
Singapore ■, *Asia* **77 M4** 1 17N 103 51 E
Singapore, Straits of, *Asia* **77 M5** 1 15N 104 0 E
Singaraja, *Indonesia* **70 F5** 8 6 S 115 10 E
Singen, *Germany* **27 H4** 47 45N 8 50 E
Singida, *Tanzania* **106 C3** 4 49 S 34 48 E
Singida □, *Tanzania* **106 D3** 6 0 S 34 30 E
Singitikós Kólpos, *Greece* **44 D6** 40 6N 24 0 E
Singkaling Hkamti, *Burma* **78 C5** 26 0N 95 39 E
Singkawang, *Indonesia* **70 D3** 1 0N 108 57 E
Singleton, *Australia* **117 B9** 32 33 S 151 0 E
Singleton, Mt., *N. Terr., Australia* **112 D5** 22 0 S 130 46 E
Singleton, Mt., *W. Austral., Australia* **113 E2** 29 27 S 117 15 E
Singoli, *India* **80 G6** 25 0N 75 22 E
Singora = Songkhla, *Thailand* **77 J3** 7 13N 100 37 E
Singosan, *N. Korea* **67 E14** 38 52N 127 25 E
Sinhung, *N. Korea* **67 D14** 40 11N 127 34 E
Sînî □, *Egypt* **91 F3** 30 0N 34 0 E
Siniátsikon, Óros, *Greece* **44 D3** 40 25N 21 35 E
Siniscóla, *Italy* **40 B2** 40 35N 9 40 E
Sinj, *Yugoslavia* **39 E13** 43 42N 16 39 E
Sinjai, *Indonesia* **71 F6** 5 7 S 120 20 E
Sinjajevina, Planina, *Yugoslavia* **42 E4** 42 57N 19 22 E
Sinjār, *Iraq* **84 B4** 36 19N 41 52 E
Sinkat, *Sudan* **94 D4** 18 55N 36 49 E
Sinkiang Uighur = Xinjiang Uygur Zizhiqu □, *China* **64 B3** 42 0N 86 0 E
Sinmak, *N. Korea* **67 E14** 38 25N 126 14 E
Sínnai, *Italy* **40 C2** 39 18N 9 13 E
Sinnar, *India* **82 E2** 19 48N 74 0 E
Sinni →, *Italy* **41 B9** 40 9N 16 42 E
Sînnicolau Maré, *Romania* **42 A5** 46 5N 20 39 E
Sinnuris, *Egypt* **94 J7** 29 26N 30 31 E
Sinoe, L., *Romania* **46 E9** 44 35N 28 50 E
Sinop, *Turkey* **52 E6** 42 1N 35 11 E
Sinop □, *Turkey* **88 C6** 42 0N 35 0 E
Sinpo, *N. Korea* **67 E15** 40 0N 128 13 E
Sins, *Switz.* **29 B6** 47 12N 8 24 E
Sinskoye, *U.S.S.R.* **57 C13** 61 8N 126 48 E
Sint-Amandsberg, *Belgium* **21 F3** 51 4N 3 45 E
Sint Annaland, *Neths.* **21 E4** 51 36N 4 6 E
Sint Annaparoch, *Neths.* **20 B7** 53 16N 5 40 E
Sint-Denijs, *Belgium* **21 G2** 50 45N 3 23 E
Sint Eustatius, I., *Neth. Ant.* **149 C7** 17 30N 62 59W
Sint-Genesius-Rode, *Belgium* **21 G4** 50 45N 4 22 E
Sint-Gillis-Waas, *Belgium* **21 F4** 51 13N 4 6 E
Sint-Huibrechts-Lille, *Belgium* **21 F6** 51 13N 5 29 E
Sint-Katelinje-Waver, *Belgium* **21 F5** 51 5N 4 32 E
Sint-Kruis, *Belgium* **21 F2** 51 13N 3 15 E
Sint-Laureins, *Belgium* **21 F3** 51 14N 3 32 E
Sint Maarten, I., *W. Indies* **149 C7** 18 4N 63 4W
Sint-Michiels, *Belgium* **21 F2** 51 11N 3 15 E
Sint Nicolaasga, *Neths.* **20 C7** 52 55N 5 45 E
Sint Niklaas, *Belgium* **21 F4** 51 10N 4 9 E
Sint Oedenrode, *Neths.* **21 E6** 51 35N 5 29 E
Sint Pancras, *Neths.* **20 C5** 52 40N 4 48 E
Sint Philipsland, *Neths.* **21 E4** 51 37N 4 10 E
Sint Truiden, *Belgium* **21 G6** 50 48N 5 10 E
Sint Willebrord, *Neths.* **21 E5** 51 33N 4 33 E
Sîntana, *Romania* **46 C2** 46 20N 21 30 E
Sintang, *Indonesia* **70 D4** 0 5N 111 35 E
Sintjohannesga, *Neths.* **20 C7** 52 55N 5 52 E
Sinton, *U.S.A.* **139 L6** 28 1N 97 30W
Sintra, *Portugal* **37 G1** 38 47N 9 25W
Sinugif, *Somali Rep.* **108 C3** 8 33N 48 59 E
Sinŭiju, *N. Korea* **67 D13** 40 5N 124 24 E
Sinyukha →, *U.S.S.R.* **52 B4** 48 3N 30 51 E
Siocon, *Phil.* **71 C6** 7 40N 122 10 E
Siófok, *Hungary* **31 E11** 46 54N 18 3 E
Sioma, *Zambia* **104 B3** 16 25 S 23 28 E
Sion, *Switz.* **28 D4** 46 14N 7 20 E
Sioux City, *U.S.A.* **138 D6** 42 32N 96 25W
Sioux Falls, *U.S.A.* **138 D6** 43 35N 96 40W
Sioux Lookout, *Canada* **128 B1** 50 10N 91 50W
Sip Song Chau Thai, *Vietnam* **76 B4** 21 30N 103 30 E
Šipan, *Yugoslavia* **42 E2** 42 45N 17 52 E
Siping, *China* **67 C13** 43 8N 124 21 E
Sipiwesk L., *Canada* **131 B9** 55 5N 97 35W
Sipora, *Indonesia* **70 E1** 2 18 S 99 40 E
Siquia →, *Nic.* **148 D3** 12 10N 84 20W
Siquijor, *Phil.* **71 C6** 9 12N 123 35 E
Siquirres, *Costa Rica* **148 D3** 10 6N 83 30W
Siquisique, *Venezuela* **152 A4** 10 34N 69 42W
Sir Edward Pellew Group, *Australia* **114 B2** 15 40 S 137 10 E
Sir Graham Moore Is., *Australia* **112 B4** 13 53 S 126 34 E
Sira, *India* **83 H3** 13 41N 76 49 E
Siracusa, *Italy* **41 E8** 37 4N 15 17 E
Sirajganj, *Bangla.* **81 G13** 24 25N 89 47 E
Sirakoro, *Mali* **100 C3** 12 41N 9 14W
Şiran, *Turkey* **89 C8** 40 11N 39 7 E
Sirasso, *Ivory C.* **100 D3** 9 16N 6 6W
Sīrdān, *Iran* **85 B6** 36 39N 49 12 E
Sirer, *Spain* **33 C7** 38 56N 1 22 E
Siret, *Romania* **46 B7** 47 55N 26 5 E
Siret →, *Romania* **46 D9** 45 24N 28 1 E
Şiria, *Romania* **46 C2** 46 16N 21 38 E
Şirino, Monte, *Italy* **41 B8** 40 7N 15 50 E
Sirkali = Sirkazhi, *India* **83 J4** 11 15N 79 41 E
Sirkazhi, *India* **83 J4** 11 15N 79 41 E
Sírna, *Greece* **45 H8** 36 22N 26 42 E
Sirnach, *Switz.* **29 B7** 47 28N 8 59 E
Şirnak, *Turkey* **89 E10** 37 32N 42 28 E
Sirohi, *India* **80 G5** 24 52N 72 53 E
Široki Brijeg, *Yugoslavia* **42 D2** 43 21N 17 36 E
Sironj, *India* **80 G7** 24 5N 77 39 E
Síros, *Greece* **45 G6** 37 28N 24 57 E
Sirrayn, *Si. Arabia* **86 C3** 19 38N 40 36 E
Sirretta Pk., *U.S.A.* **145 K8** 35 56N 118 19W
Sirsa, *India* **80 E6** 29 33N 75 4 E
Sirsi, *India* **83 G2** 14 40N 74 49 E
Siruela, *Spain* **37 G5** 38 58N 5 3W
Sisak, *Yugoslavia* **39 C13** 45 30N 16 21 E
Sisaket, *Thailand* **76 E5** 15 8N 104 23 E
Sisante, *Spain* **35 F2** 39 25N 2 12W
Sisargas, Is., *Spain* **36 B2** 43 21N 8 50W
Sishen, *S. Africa* **104 D3** 27 47 S 22 59 E
Sishui, *Henan, China* **66 G7** 34 48N 113 15 E
Sishui, *Shandong, China* **67 G9** 35 42N 117 18 E
Sisipuk L., *Canada* **131 B8** 55 45N 101 50W
Sisophon, *Cambodia* **76 F4** 13 38N 102 59 E
Sissach, *Switz.* **28 B5** 47 27N 7 48 E
Sisseton, *U.S.A.* **138 C6** 45 43N 97 3W
Sissonne, *France* **23 C10** 49 34N 3 51 E
Sīstān va Balūchestān □, *Iran* **85 E9** 27 0N 62 0 E
Sisteron, *France* **25 D9** 44 12N 5 57 E
Sisters, *U.S.A.* **142 D3** 44 21N 121 32W
Sitamarhi, *India* **81 F11** 26 37N 85 30 E
Sitapur, *India* **81 F9** 27 38N 80 45 E
Siteki, *Swaziland* **105 D5** 26 32 S 31 58 E
Sitges, *Spain* **34 D6** 41 17N 1 47 E
Sithoniá, *Greece* **44 E5** 40 0N 23 45 E
Sitía, *Greece* **32 D8** 35 13N 26 6 E
Sítio da Abadia, *Brazil* **155 D2** 14 48 S 46 16W
Sitka, *U.S.A.* **126 C6** 57 9N 135 20W
Sitoti, *Botswana* **104 C3** 23 15 S 23 40 E
Sitra, *Egypt* **94 B2** 28 40N 26 53 E
Sittang Myit →, *Burma* **78 G6** 17 20N 96 45 E
Sittard, *Neths.* **21 G7** 51 0N 5 52 E
Sittaung, *Burma* **78 C5** 24 10N 94 35 E
Sittensen, *Germany* **26 B5** 53 17N 9 32 E
Sittona, *Ethiopia* **95 E4** 14 25N 37 23 E
Sittwe, *Burma* **78 E4** 20 18N 92 45 E
Siuna, *Nic.* **148 D3** 13 37N 84 45W
Siuri, *India* **81 H12** 23 50N 87 34 E
Sivaganga, *India* **83 K4** 9 50N 78 28 E
Sivagiri, *India* **83 K3** 9 16N 77 26 E
Sivakasi, *India* **83 K3** 9 24N 77 47 E
Sivana, *India* **80 E8** 28 37N 78 6 E
Sīvand, *Iran* **85 D7** 30 5N 52 55 E
Sivas, *Turkey* **88 D7** 39 43N 36 58 E
Sivas □, *Turkey* **88 D7** 39 45N 37 0 E
Siverek, *Turkey* **89 E8** 37 50N 39 19 E
Sivomaskinskiy, *U.S.S.R.* **48 A11** 66 40N 62 35 E
Sivrihisar, *Turkey* **88 D4** 39 30N 31 35 E
Sivry, *Belgium* **21 H4** 50 10N 4 12 E
Sīwa, *Egypt* **94 B2** 29 11N 25 31 E
Sīwa, El Wâhât es, *Egypt* **94 B2** 29 10N 25 30 E
Siwalik Range, *Nepal* **81 F10** 28 0N 83 0 E
Siwan, *India* **81 F11** 26 13N 84 21 E
Siyâl, Jazâ'ir, *Egypt* **94 C4** 22 49N 36 12 E
Sizewell, *U.K.* **17 E9** 52 13N 1 38 E
Siziwang Qi, *China* **66 D6** 41 25N 111 40 E
Sjælland, *Denmark* **15 J5** 55 30N 11 30 E
Sjællands Odde, *Denmark* **15 J5** 56 0N 11 15 E
Själevad, *Sweden* **14 A12** 63 18N 18 36 E
Sjarinska Banja, *Yugoslavia* **42 E6** 42 45N 21 38 E
Sjenica, *Yugoslavia* **42 D5** 43 16N 20 0 E
Sjoa, *Norway* **14 C3** 61 41N 9 33 E
Sjöbo, *Sweden* **15 J7** 55 37N 13 45 E
Sjösa, *Sweden* **15 F11** 58 47N 17 4 E
Sjumen = Šumen, *Bulgaria* **43 D11** 43 18N 26 55 E
Skadarsko Jezero, *Yugoslavia* **42 E4** 42 10N 19 20 E
Skadovsk, *U.S.S.R.* **52 C5** 46 17N 32 52 E
Skagafjörður, *Iceland* **12 D4** 65 54N 19 35W
Skagastølstindane, *Norway* **13 F9** 61 28N 7 52 E
Skagen, *Denmark* **15 G4** 57 43N 10 35 E
Skagerrak, *Denmark* **15 G3** 57 30N 9 0 E
Skagit →, *U.S.A.* **144 B4** 48 20N 122 25W
Skagway, *U.S.A.* **130 B1** 59 23N 135 20W
Skaidi, *Norway* **12 A18** 70 26N 24 30 E
Skala Podolskaya, *U.S.S.R.* **52 B2** 48 50N 26 15 E
Skalat, *U.S.S.R.* **50 G4** 49 23N 25 55 E
Skalbmierz, *Poland* **47 E7** 50 20N 20 25 E
Skalica, *Czech.* **31 C10** 48 50N 17 15 E
Skalni Dol = Kamenyak, *Bulgaria* **43 D11** 43 24N 26 57 E
Skals, *Denmark* **15 H3** 56 34N 9 24 E
Skanderborg, *Denmark* **15 H3** 56 2N 9 55 E
Skanör, *Sweden* **15 J6** 55 24N 12 50 E
Skantzoúra, *Greece* **45 E6** 39 5N 24 6 E
Skara, *Sweden* **13 G12** 58 25N 13 30 E
Skaraborgs län □, *Sweden* **13 G12** 58 20N 13 30 E
Skardu, *Pakistan* **81 B6** 35 20N 75 44 E
Skarrild, *Denmark* **15 J2** 55 58N 8 53 E
Skarszewy, *Poland* **47 A5** 54 4N 18 25 E
Skaryszew, *Poland* **47 D8** 51 19N 21 15 E
Skarzysko Kamienna, *Poland* **47 D7** 51 7N 20 52 E
Skebokvarn, *Sweden* **14 E10** 59 7N 16 45 E
Skeena →, *Canada* **130 C2** 54 9N 130 5W
Skeena Mts., *Canada* **130 B3** 56 40N 128 30W
Skegness, *U.K.* **16 D8** 53 9N 0 20 E
Skeldon, *Guyana* **153 B6** 5 55N 57 20W
Skellefte älv →, *Sweden* **12 D16** 64 45N 21 10 E
Skellefteå, *Sweden* **12 D16** 64 45N 20 58 E
Skelleftehamn, *Sweden* **12 D16** 64 47N 20 59 E
Skender Vakuf, *Yugoslavia* **42 C2** 44 29N 17 22 E
Skene, *Sweden* **15 G6** 57 30N 12 37 E
Skerries, The, *U.K.* **16 D3** 53 27N 4 40W
Skhíza, *Greece* **45 H3** 36 41N 21 40 E
Skhoinoúsa, *Greece* **45 H7** 36 53N 25 31 E
Ski, *Norway* **14 E4** 59 43N 10 52 E
Skíathos, *Greece* **45 E5** 39 12N 23 30 E
Skibbereen, *Ireland* **19 E2** 51 33N 9 16W
Skiddaw, *U.K.* **16 C4** 54 39N 3 9W
Skien, *Norway* **14 E3** 59 12N 9 35 E
Skierniewice, *Poland* **47 D7** 51 58N 20 10 E
Skierniewice □, *Poland* **47 D7** 52 0N 20 10 E
Skikda, *Algeria* **99 A6** 36 50N 6 58 E
Skillett Fork, Little Wabash →, *U.S.A.* **141 F8** 38 6N 88 9W
Skilloura, *Cyprus* **32 D12** 35 14N 33 10 E
Skinári, Ákra, *Greece* **45 G2** 37 56N 20 40 E
Skipton, *Australia* **116 D5** 37 39 S 143 40 E
Skipton, *U.K.* **16 D5** 53 57N 2 1W
Skirmish Pt., *Australia* **114 A1** 11 59 S 134 17 E
Skiropoúla, *Greece* **45 F6** 38 50N 24 21 E
Skíros, *Greece* **45 F6** 38 55N 24 34 E
Skivarp, *Sweden* **15 J7** 55 26N 13 34 E
Skive, *Denmark* **15 H3** 56 33N 9 2 E
Skjálfandafljót →, *Iceland* **12 D5** 65 59N 17 25W
Skjálfandi, *Iceland* **12 C5** 66 5N 17 30W
Skjeberg, *Norway* **14 E5** 59 12N 11 12 E
Skjern, *Denmark* **15 J2** 55 57N 8 30 E
Skoczów, *Poland* **31 B11** 49 49N 18 45 E
Škofja Loka, *Yugoslavia* **39 B11** 46 9N 14 19 E
Skoghall, *Sweden* **13 G12** 59 20N 13 30 E
Skoki, *Poland* **47 C4** 52 40N 17 11 E
Skokie, *U.S.A.* **141 B9** 42 3N 87 45W
Skole, *U.S.S.R.* **50 G3** 49 3N 23 30 E
Skópelos, *Greece* **45 E5** 39 9N 23 47 E
Skopí, *Greece* **32 D8** 35 11N 26 2 E
Skopin, *U.S.S.R.* **51 E11** 53 55N 39 32 E
Skopje, *Yugoslavia* **42 E6** 42 1N 21 32 E
Skórcz, *Poland* **47 B5** 53 47N 18 30 E
Skövde, *Sweden* **13 G12** 58 15N 13 59 E
Skovorodino, *U.S.S.R.* **57 D13** 54 0N 125 0 E
Skowhegan, *U.S.A.* **129 D6** 44 49N 69 40W
Skownan, *Canada* **131 C9** 51 58N 99 35W
Skradin, *Yugoslavia* **39 E12** 43 52N 15 53 E
Skreanäs, *Sweden* **15 H6** 56 52N 12 35 E
Skrwa →, *Poland* **47 C6** 52 35N 19 32 E
Skudeneshavn, *Norway* **13 G8** 59 10N 5 10 E
Skull, *Ireland* **19 E2** 51 32N 9 40W
Skultorp, *Sweden* **15 F7** 58 24N 13 51 E
Skunk →, *U.S.A.* **140 D5** 40 42N 91 7W
Skuodas, *U.S.S.R.* **50 C2** 56 21N 21 45 E
Skurup, *Sweden* **15 J7** 55 28N 13 30 E
Skutskär, *Sweden* **14 D11** 60 37N 17 25 E
Skvira, *U.S.S.R.* **52 B3** 49 44N 29 40 E
Skwierzyna, *Poland* **47 C2** 52 33N 15 30 E
Skye, *U.K.* **18 D2** 57 15N 6 10W
Skykomish, *U.S.A.* **142 C3** 47 43N 121 16W
Skyros = Skíros, *Greece* **45 F6** 38 55N 24 34 E
Slagelse, *Denmark* **15 J5** 55 23N 11 19 E
Slagharen, *Neths.* **20 C9** 52 37N 6 34 E
Slamannon, *Australia* **116 B5** 32 1 S 143 41 E
Slamet, *Indonesia* **70 F3** 7 16 S 109 8 E
Slangerup, *Denmark* **15 J6** 55 50N 12 11 E
Slânic, *Romania* **46 D6** 45 14N 25 58 E
Slankamen, *Yugoslavia* **42 B5** 45 8N 20 15 E
Slano, *Yugoslavia* **42 E2** 42 48N 17 53 E
Slantsy, *U.S.S.R.* **50 B6** 59 7N 28 5 E
Slany, *Czech.* **30 A7** 50 13N 14 6 E
Slate Is., *Canada* **128 C2** 48 40N 87 0W
Slater, *U.S.A.* **140 E3** 39 13N 93 4W
Slatina, *Romania* **46 E5** 44 28N 24 22 E
Slaton, *U.S.A.* **139 J4** 33 27N 101 38W
Slave →, *Canada* **130 A6** 61 18N 113 39W
Slave Coast, *W. Afr.* **101 D5** 6 0N 2 30 E
Slave Lake, *Canada* **130 B6** 55 17N 114 43W
Slave Pt., *Canada* **130 A5** 61 11N 115 56W
Slavgorod, *U.S.S.R.* **56 D8** 53 1N 78 37 E
Slavinja, *Yugoslavia* **42 D7** 43 9N 22 50 E
Slavkov, *Czech.* **31 B9** 49 10N 16 52 E
Slavnoye, *U.S.S.R.* **50 D6** 54 24N 29 15 E
Slavonska Požega, *Yugoslavia* **42 B2** 45 20N 17 40 E
Slavonski Brod, *Yugoslavia* **42 B3** 45 11N 18 0 E
Slavuta, *U.S.S.R.* **50 F5** 50 15N 27 2 E
Slavyanka, *U.S.S.R.* **60 C5** 42 53N 131 21 E
Slavyansk, *U.S.S.R.* **52 B7** 48 55N 37 36 E
Slavyansk-na-Kubani, *U.S.S.R.* **52 D8** 45 15N 38 11 E
Sława, *Poland* **47 D3** 51 52N 16 2 E
Sławno, *Poland* **47 A3** 54 20N 16 41 E
Sławoborze, *Poland* **47 B2** 53 55N 15 42 E
Sleaford, *U.K.* **16 E7** 53 0N 0 22W
Sleaford B., *Australia* **115 E2** 34 55 S 135 45 E
Sleat, Sd. of, *U.K.* **18 D3** 57 5N 5 47W
Sleeper Is., *Canada* **127 C11** 58 30N 81 0W
Sleepy Eye, *U.S.A.* **138 C7** 44 15N 94 45W
Sleidinge, *Belgium* **21 F3** 51 8N 3 41 E
Sleman, *Indonesia* **71 G14** 7 40 S 110 20 E
Slemon L., *Canada* **130 A5** 63 13N 116 4W
Ślesin, *Poland* **47 C5** 52 22N 18 14 E
Slidell, *U.S.A.* **139 K10** 30 20N 89 48W
Sliedrecht, *Neths.* **20 E5** 51 50N 4 45 E
Sliema, *Malta* **32 D2** 35 54N 14 30 E
Slieve Aughty, *Ireland* **19 C3** 53 4N 8 30W
Slieve Donard, *U.K.* **19 B6** 54 10N 5 57W
Slieve Gullion, *U.K.* **19 B5** 54 8N 6 26W
Slieve Mish, *Ireland* **19 D2** 52 12N 9 50W
Sligo, *Ireland* **19 B3** 54 17N 8 28W
Sligo □, *Ireland* **19 B3** 54 10N 8 35W
Sligo B., *Ireland* **19 B3** 54 20N 8 40W
Slijpe, *Belgium* **21 F1** 51 9N 2 51 E
Slikkerveer, *Neths.* **20 E5** 51 53N 4 36 E
Slite, *Sweden* **13 H15** 57 42N 18 48 E
Sliven, *Bulgaria* **43 E11** 42 42N 26 19 E
Slivnitsa, *Bulgaria* **42 E8** 42 50N 23 0 E
Sljeme, *Yugoslavia* **39 C12** 45 57N 15 58 E
Sloan, *U.S.A.* **145 K11** 35 57N 115 13W
Sloansville, *U.S.A.* **137 D10** 42 45N 74 22W
Slobodskoy, *U.S.S.R.* **54 B2** 58 40N 50 6 E
Slobozia, *Argeş, Romania* **46 E6** 44 30N 25 14 E
Slobozia, *Ialomiţa, Romania* **46 E8** 44 34N 27 23 E
Slocan, *Canada* **130 D5** 49 48N 117 28W
Slochteren, *Neths.* **20 B9** 53 12N 6 48 E
Slöinge, *Sweden* **15 H6** 56 51N 12 42 E
Słomniki, *Poland* **47 E7** 50 16N 20 4 E
Slonim, *U.S.S.R.* **50 E4** 53 4N 25 19 E
Slotermeer, *Neths.* **20 C7** 52 55N 5 38 E
Slough, *U.K.* **17 F7** 51 30N 0 35W
Sloughhouse, *U.S.A.* **144 G5** 38 26N 121 12W
Slovakian Ore Mts. = Slovenské Rudohorie, *Czech.* **31 C13** 48 45N 20 0 E
Slovenia = Slovenija □, *Yugoslavia* **39 C11** 45 58N 14 30 E
Slovenija □, *Yugoslavia* **39 C11** 45 58N 14 30 E
Slovenj Gradec, *Yugoslavia* **39 B12** 46 31N 15 5 E
Slovenska Bistrica, *Yugoslavia* **39 B12** 46 24N 15 35 E
Slovenská Republika □, *Czech.* **31 C13** 48 30N 20 0 E
Slovenské Rudohorie, *Czech.* **31 C13** 48 45N 20 0 E
Słubice, *Poland* **47 C1** 52 22N 14 35 E
Sluch →, *U.S.S.R.* **50 F5** 51 37N 26 38 E
Sluis, *Neths.* **21 F2** 51 18N 3 23 E
Slunchev Bryag, *Bulgaria* **43 E12** 42 40N 27 41 E
Slunj, *Yugoslavia* **39 C12** 45 6N 15 33 E
Słupca, *Poland* **47 C4** 52 15N 17 52 E
Słupia →, *Poland* **47 A3** 54 35N 16 51 E
Słupsk, *Poland* **47 A4** 54 30N 17 3 E
Słupsk □, *Poland* **47 A4** 54 15N 17 30 E
Slurry, *S. Africa* **104 D4** 25 49 S 25 42 E
Slutsk, *U.S.S.R.* **50 E5** 53 2N 27 31 E
Slyne Hd., *Ireland* **19 C1** 53 25N 10 10W
Slyudyanka, *U.S.S.R.* **57 D11** 51 40N 103 40 E
Smålandsfarvandet, *Denmark* **15 J5** 55 10N 11 20 E
Smålandsstenar, *Sweden* **15 G7** 57 10N 13 25 E
Small Nggela, *Solomon Is.* **121 M11** 9 0 S 160 0 E
Smalltree L., *Canada* **131 A8** 61 0N 105 0W

South Aulatsivik I. 267

Smarje, *Yugoslavia* **39 B12** 46 15N 15 34 E
Smartt Syndicate Dam,
S. Africa **104 E3** 30 45 S 23 10 E
Smartville, *U.S.A.* **144 F5** 39 13N 121 18W
Smeaton, *Canada* **131 C8** 53 30N 104 49W
Smederevo, *Yugoslavia* **42 C5** 44 40N 20 57 E
Smederevska Palanka,
Yugoslavia **42 C5** 44 22N 20 58 E
Smela, *U.S.S.R.* **52 B4** 49 15N 31 58 E
Smethport, *U.S.A.* **136 E6** 41 50N 78 28W
Smidovich, *U.S.S.R.* **57 E14** 48 36N 133 49 E
Smigiel, *Poland* **47 C3** 52 1N 16 32 E
Smilde, *Neths.* **20 C8** 52 58N 6 28 E
Smiley, *Canada* **131 C7** 51 38N 109 29W
Smilyan, *Bulgaria* **43 F9** 41 29N 24 46 E
Smith, *Canada* **130 B6** 55 10N 114 0W
Smith →, *Canada* **130 B3** 59 34N 126 30W
Smith Arm, *Canada* **126 B7** 66 15N 123 0W
Smith Center, *U.S.A.* **138 F5** 39 50N 98 50W
Smith Sund, *Greenland* **6 B4** 78 30N 74 0W
Smithburne →, *Australia* **114 B3** 17 3 S 140 57 E
Smithers, *Canada* **130 C3** 54 45N 127 10W
Smithfield, *S. Africa* **105 E4** 30 9 S 26 30 E
Smithfield, *N.C., U.S.A.* **135 H6** 35 31N 78 16W
Smithfield, *Utah, U.S.A.* **142 F8** 41 50N 111 50W
Smiths Falls, *Canada* **128 D4** 44 55N 76 0W
Smithton, *Australia* **114 G4** 40 53 S 145 6 E
Smithtown, *Australia* **117 A10** 30 58 S 152 48 E
Smithville, *Canada* **136 C5** 43 6N 79 33W
Smithville, *Mo., U.S.A.* **140 E2** 39 23N 94 35W
Smithville, *Tex., U.S.A.* **139 K6** 30 2N 97 12W
Smoky →, *Canada* **130 B5** 56 10N 117 21W
Smoky Bay, *Australia* **115 E1** 32 22 S 134 13 E
Smoky Falls, *Canada* **128 C3** 50 4N 82 10W
Smoky Hill →, *U.S.A.* **138 F6** 39 3N 96 48W
Smoky Lake, *Canada* **130 C6** 54 10N 112 30W
Smøla, *Norway* **14 A2** 63 23N 8 3 E
Smolensk, *U.S.S.R.* **50 D8** 54 45N 32 5 E
Smolikas, Óros, *Greece* **44 D2** 40 9N 20 58 E
Smolník, *Czech.* **31 C13** 48 43N 20 44 E
Smolyan, *Bulgaria* **43 F9** 41 36N 24 38 E
Smooth Rock Falls,
Canada **128 C3** 49 17N 81 37W
Smoothstone L., *Canada* **131 C7** 54 40N 106 50W
Smorgon, *U.S.S.R.* **50 D5** 54 20N 26 24 E
Smulţi, *Romania* **46 D8** 45 57N 27 44 E
Smyadovo, *Bulgaria* **43 D12** 43 2N 27 1 E
Smyrna = İzmir, *Turkey* **88 D2** 38 25N 27 8 E
Snaefell, *U.K.* **16 C3** 54 18N 4 26W
Snæfellsjökull, *Iceland* **12 D2** 64 49N 23 46W
Snake →, *U.S.A.* **142 C4** 46 12N 119 2W
Snake I., *Australia* **117 E7** 38 47 S 146 33 E
Snake L., *Canada* **131 B7** 55 32N 106 35W
Snake Ra., *U.S.A.* **142 G6** 39 0N 114 30W
Snake River Plain,
U.S.A. **142 E7** 43 13N 113 0W
Snarum, *Norway* **14 D3** 60 1N 9 54 E
Snedsted, *Denmark* **15 H2** 56 55N 8 32 E
Sneek, *Neths.* **20 B7** 53 2N 5 40 E
Sneeker-meer, *Neths.* **20 B7** 53 2N 5 45 E
Sneeuberge, *S. Africa* **104 E3** 31 46 S 24 20 E
Snejbjerg, *Denmark* **15 H2** 56 8N 8 54 E
Snelling, *U.S.A.* **144 H6** 37 31N 120 26W
Snezhnoye, *U.S.S.R.* **53 C8** 48 0N 38 58 E
Sněžka, *Europe* **30 A8** 50 41N 15 50 E
Snežnik, *Yugoslavia* **39 C11** 45 36N 14 35 E
Sniadowo, *Poland* **47 B9** 53 2N 22 0 E
Sniardwy, Jezioro, *Poland* **47 B8** 53 48N 21 50 E
Snigirevka, *U.S.S.R.* **52 C5** 47 2N 32 49 E
Snina, *Czech.* **31 C15** 48 58N 22 9 E
Snizort, L., *U.K.* **18 D2** 57 33N 6 28W
Snøhetta, *Norway* **14 B3** 62 19N 9 16 E
Snohomish, *U.S.A.* **144 C4** 47 53N 122 6W
Snoul, *Cambodia* **77 F6** 12 4N 106 26 E
Snow Hill, *U.S.A.* **134 F8** 38 10N 75 21W
Snow Lake, *Canada* **131 C8** 54 52N 100 3W
Snow Mt., *U.S.A.* **144 F4** 39 22N 122 44W
Snowbird L., *Canada* **131 A8** 60 45N 103 0W
Snowdon, *U.K.* **16 D3** 53 4N 4 8W
Snowdrift, *Canada* **131 A6** 62 24N 110 44W
Snowdrift →, *Canada* **131 A6** 62 24N 110 44W
Snowflake, *U.S.A.* **143 J8** 34 30N 110 4W
Snowshoe Pk., *U.S.A.* **142 B6** 48 13N 115 41W
Snowtown, *Australia* **116 B3** 33 46 S 138 14 E
Snowville, *U.S.A.* **142 F7** 41 59N 112 47W
Snowy →, *Australia* **117 D8** 37 46 S 148 30 E
Snowy Mts., *Australia* **117 D8** 36 30 S 148 20 E
Snug Corner, *Bahamas* **149 B5** 22 33N 73 52W
Snyatyn, *U.S.S.R.* **52 B1** 48 30N 25 50 E
Snyder, *Okla., U.S.A.* **139 H5** 34 40N 99 0W
Snyder, *Tex., U.S.A.* **139 J4** 32 45N 100 57W
Soacha, *Colombia* **152 C3** 4 35N 74 13W
Soahanina, *Madag.* **105 B7** 18 42 S 44 13 E
Soalala, *Madag.* **105 B8** 16 6 S 45 20 E
Soan →, *Pakistan* **80 C4** 33 1N 71 44 E
Soanierana-Ivongo,
Madag. **105 B8** 16 55 S 49 35 E
Soap Lake, *U.S.A.* **142 C4** 47 23N 119 31W
Sobat, Nahr →, *Sudan* **95 F3** 9 22N 31 33 E
Soběslav, *Czech.* **30 B7** 49 16N 14 45 E
Sobhapur, *India* **80 H8** 22 47N 78 17 E
Sobinka, *U.S.S.R.* **51 D12** 56 0N 40 0 E
Sobo-Yama, *Japan* **62 E3** 32 51N 131 22 E
Sobótka, *Poland* **47 E3** 50 54N 16 44 E
Sobrado, *Spain* **36 B2** 43 2N 8 2W
Sobral, *Brazil* **154 B3** 3 50 S 40 20W
Sobreira Formosa,
Portugal **37 F3** 39 46N 7 51W
Soc Giang, *Vietnam* **76 A6** 22 54N 106 1 E
Soc Trang, *Vietnam* **77 H5** 9 37N 105 50 E
Soča →, *Europe* **39 B10** 46 20N 13 40 E
Sochaczew, *Poland* **47 C7** 52 15N 20 13 E
Soch'e = Shache, *China* **64 C2** 38 20N 77 10 E
Sochi, *U.S.S.R.* **53 E8** 43 35N 39 40 E
Société, Is. de la,
Pac. Oc. **123 J12** 17 0 S 151 0W
Society Is. = Société, Is.
de la, *Pac. Oc.* **123 J12** 17 0 S 151 0W
Socompa, Portezuelo de,
Chile **158 A2** 24 27 S 68 18W
Socorro, *Colombia* **152 B3** 6 29N 73 16W
Socorro, *U.S.A.* **143 J10** 34 4N 106 54W
Socorro, I., *Mexico* **146 D2** 18 45N 110 58W
Socotra, *Ind. Oc.* **87 D6** 12 30N 54 0 E
Socúellmos, *Spain* **35 F2** 39 16N 2 47W
Soda L., *U.S.A.* **143 J5** 35 7N 116 2W
Soda Plains, *India* **81 B8** 35 30N 79 0 E
Soda Springs, *U.S.A.* **142 E8** 42 40N 111 40W
Söderhamn, *Sweden* **13 F14** 61 18N 17 10 E
Söderköping, *Sweden* **13 G14** 58 31N 16 20 E
Södermanlands län □,
Sweden **14 E10** 59 10N 16 30 E
Södertälje, *Sweden* **14 E11** 59 12N 17 39 E
Sodiri, *Sudan* **95 E2** 14 27N 29 0 E
Sodo, *Ethiopia* **95 F4** 7 0N 37 41 E
Sodražica, *Yugoslavia* **39 C11** 45 45N 14 39 E
Sodus, *U.S.A.* **136 C7** 43 13N 77 5W
Soe, *Indonesia* **72 C2** 9 52 S 124 17 E
Soekmekaar, *S. Africa* **105 C4** 23 30 S 29 55 E
Soest, *Germany* **26 D4** 51 34N 8 7 E
Soest, *Neths.* **20 D6** 52 9N 5 19 E
Soestdijk, *Neths.* **20 D6** 52 11N 5 17 E
Sofádhes, *Greece* **44 E4** 39 20N 22 4 E
Sofara, *Mali* **100 C4** 13 59N 4 9W
Sofia = Sofiya, *Bulgaria* **43 E8** 42 45N 23 20 E
Sofia →, *Madag.* **105 B8** 15 27 S 47 23 E
Sofievka, *U.S.S.R.* **52 B5** 48 6N 33 55 E
Sofiiski, *U.S.S.R.* **57 D14** 52 15N 133 59 E
Sofikón, *Greece* **45 G5** 37 47N 23 3 E
Sofiya, *Bulgaria* **43 E8** 42 45N 23 20 E
Sōfu-Gan, *Japan* **61 K10** 29 49N 140 21 E
Sogakofe, *Ghana* **101 D5** 6 2N 0 39 E
Sogamoso, *Colombia* **152 B3** 5 43N 72 56W
Sogār, *Iran* **85 E8** 25 53N 58 6 E
Sögel, *Germany* **26 C3** 52 50N 7 32 E
Sogeri, *Papua N. G.* **120 E4** 9 26 S 147 35 E
Sogn og Fjordane
fylke □, *Norway* **13 F9** 61 40N 6 0 E
Sogndalsfjøra, *Norway* **13 F9** 61 14N 7 5 E
Sognefjorden, *Norway* **13 F8** 61 10N 5 50 E
Söğüt, *Turkey* **88 C4** 40 2N 30 10 E
Söğüt Gölü, *Turkey* **88 E3** 37 3N 29 51 E
Sŏgwi-po, *S. Korea* **67 H14** 33 13N 126 34 E
Soh, *Iran* **85 C6** 33 26N 51 27 E
Sohâg, *Egypt* **94 B3** 26 33N 31 43 E
Sohano, *Papua N. G.* **120 C8** 5 22 S 154 37 E
Sŏhori, *N. Korea* **67 D15** 40 7N 128 23 E
Soignies, *Belgium* **21 G4** 50 35N 4 5 E
Soira, *Ethiopia* **95 E4** 14 45N 39 30 E
Soissons, *France* **23 C10** 49 25N 3 19 E
Sōja, *Japan* **62 C5** 34 40N 133 45 E
Sojat, *India* **80 G5** 25 55N 73 45 E
Sok →, *U.S.S.R.* **54 E2** 53 24N 50 8 E
Sokal, *U.S.S.R.* **50 F4** 50 31N 24 15 E
Söke, *Turkey* **45 G9** 37 48N 27 28 E
Sokelo, *Zaïre* **103 D4** 9 55 S 24 36 E
Sokhós, *Greece* **44 D5** 40 48N 23 22 E
Sokki, Oued In →,
Algeria **99 C5** 29 30N 3 42 E
Sokna, *Norway* **14 D3** 60 16N 9 50 E
Soknedal, *Norway* **14 B4** 62 57N 10 13 E
Soko Banja, *Yugoslavia* **42 D6** 43 40N 21 51 E
Sokodé, *Togo* **101 D5** 9 0N 1 11 E
Sokol, *U.S.S.R.* **51 B12** 59 30N 40 5 E
Sokolac, *Yugoslavia* **42 D3** 43 56N 18 48 E
Sokółka, *Poland* **47 B10** 53 25N 23 30 E
Sokolo, *Mali* **100 C3** 14 53N 6 8W
Sokolov, *Czech.* **30 A5** 50 12N 12 40 E
Sokołów Małpolski,
Poland **31 A15** 50 12N 22 7 E
Sokołów Podlaski, *Poland* **47 C9** 52 25N 22 15 E
Sokoły, *Poland* **47 C9** 52 59N 22 42 E
Sokoto, *Nigeria* **101 C6** 13 2N 5 16 E
Sokoto □, *Nigeria* **101 C6** 12 30N 5 0 E
Sokoto →, *Nigeria* **101 C5** 11 20N 4 10 E
Sokuluk, *U.S.S.R.* **55 B7** 42 52N 74 18 E
Sol Iletsk, *U.S.S.R.* **54 F4** 51 10N 55 0 E
Sola →, *Poland* **31 A12** 50 4N 19 15 E
Solai, *Kenya* **106 B4** 0 2N 36 12 E
Solander I., *N.Z.* **119 G1** 46 34 S 166 54 E
Solano, *Phil.* **71 A6** 16 31N 121 15 E
Solapur, *India* **82 F2** 17 43N 75 56 E
Solares, *Spain* **36 B7** 43 23N 3 43W
Solca, *Romania* **46 B6** 47 40N 25 50 E
Soléa □, *Cyprus* **32 D12** 35 5N 33 4 E
Solec Kujawski, *Poland* **47 B5** 53 5N 18 14 E
Soledad, *Colombia* **152 A3** 10 55N 74 46W
Soledad, *U.S.A.* **144 J5** 36 27N 121 16W
Soledad, *Venezuela* **153 B5** 8 10N 63 34W
Solent, The, *U.K.* **17 G6** 50 45N 1 25W
Solenzara, *France* **25 G13** 41 53N 9 23 E
Solesmes, *France* **23 B10** 50 10N 3 30 E
Solfonn, *Norway* **13 F9** 60 2N 6 57 E
Solhan, *Turkey* **89 D9** 38 57N 41 3 E
Soligalich, *U.S.S.R.* **51 B13** 59 5N 42 10 E
Soligorsk, *U.S.S.R.* **50 E5** 52 51N 27 27 E
Solikamsk, *U.S.S.R.* **54 B5** 59 38N 56 50 E
Solila, *Madag.* **105 C8** 21 25 S 46 37 E
Solimões =
Amazonas →,
S. Amer. **153 D8** 0 5 S 50 0W
Solingen, *Germany* **21 F10** 51 10N 7 4 E
Sollebrunn, *Sweden* **15 F6** 58 8N 12 32 E
Sollefteå, *Sweden* **14 A11** 63 12N 17 20 E
Sollentuna, *Sweden* **14 E11** 59 26N 17 56 E
Sóller, *Spain* **33 B9** 39 46N 2 43 E
Solling, *Germany* **26 D5** 51 44N 9 36 E
Solna, *Sweden* **14 E12** 59 22N 18 1 E
Solnechnogorsk, *U.S.S.R.* **51 C10** 56 10N 36 57 E
Sologne, *France* **23 E8** 47 40N 1 45 E
Solok, *Indonesia* **70 E2** 0 45 S 100 40 E
Sololá, *Guatemala* **148 D1** 14 49N 91 10W
Solomon, N. Fork →,
U.S.A. **138 F5** 39 29N 98 26W
Solomon, S. Fork →,
U.S.A. **138 F5** 39 25N 99 12W
Solomon Is. ■, *Pac. Oc.* **121 L8** 6 0 S 155 0 E
Solomon Sea,
Papua N. G. **120 D6** 7 0 S 150 0 E
Solon, *China* **65 B7** 46 32N 121 10 E
Solon Springs, *U.S.A.* **138 B9** 46 19N 91 47W
Solonópole, *Brazil* **154 C4** 5 44 S 39 1W
Solor, *Indonesia* **71 F6** 8 27 S 123 0 E
Solotcha, *U.S.S.R.* **51 D11** 54 48N 39 53 E
Solothurn, *Switz.* **28 B5** 47 13N 7 32 E
Solothurn □, *Switz.* **28 B5** 47 18N 7 40 E
Solotobe, *U.S.S.R.* **55 A3** 44 37N 66 3 E
Solsona, *Spain* **34 D6** 42 0N 1 31 E
Solt, *Hungary* **31 E12** 46 45N 19 1 E
Solta, *Yugoslavia* **39 E13** 43 24N 16 15 E
Solṭānābād, *Khorāsān,*
Iran **85 C8** 34 13N 59 58 E
Solṭānābād, *Khorāsān,*
Iran **85 B8** 36 29N 58 5 E
Solṭānābād, *Markazī, Iran* **85 C6** 35 31N 51 10 E
Soltau, *Germany* **26 C5** 52 59N 9 50 E
Soltsy, *U.S.S.R.* **50 B7** 58 10N 30 30 E
Solunska Glava,
Yugoslavia **42 F6** 41 44N 21 31 E
Solvang, *U.S.A.* **145 L6** 34 36N 120 8W
Solvay, *U.S.A.* **137 C8** 43 5N 76 17W
Solvychegodsk, *U.S.S.R.* **48 B8** 61 21N 46 56 E
Solway Firth, *U.K.* **16 C4** 54 45N 3 38W
Solwezi, *Zambia* **107 E2** 12 11 S 26 21 E
Sōma, *Japan* **60 F10** 37 40N 140 50 E
Soma, *Turkey* **88 D2** 39 10N 27 35 E
Somali Rep. ■, *Africa* **90 F4** 7 0N 47 0 E
Sombe Dzong, *Bhutan* **78 B2** 27 13N 89 8 E
Sombernon, *France* **23 E11** 47 20N 4 40 E
Sombor, *Yugoslavia* **42 B4** 45 46N 19 9 E
Sombra, *Canada* **136 D2** 42 43N 82 29W
Sombrerete, *Mexico* **146 C4** 23 40N 103 40W
Sombrero, *Anguilla* **149 C7** 18 37N 63 30W
Someren, *Neths.* **21 F7** 51 23N 5 42 E
Somers, *U.S.A.* **142 B6** 48 4N 114 18W
Somerset, *Canada* **131 D9** 49 25N 98 39W
Somerset, *Colo., U.S.A.* **143 G10** 38 55N 107 30W
Somerset, *Ky., U.S.A.* **134 G3** 37 5N 84 40W
Somerset, *Mass., U.S.A.* **137 E13** 41 45N 71 10W
Somerset, *Pa., U.S.A.* **136 F5** 40 1N 79 4W
Somerset □, *U.K.* **17 F5** 51 9N 3 0W
Somerset East, *S. Africa* **104 E4** 32 42 S 25 35 E
Somerset I., *Canada* **126 A10** 73 30N 93 0W
Somerset West, *S. Africa* **104 E2** 34 8 S 18 50 E
Somerton, *U.S.A.* **143 K6** 32 35N 114 47W
Somerville, *U.S.A.* **137 F10** 40 34N 74 36W
Someş →, *Romania* **46 B3** 47 49N 22 43 E
Someşul Mare →,
Romania **46 B5** 47 18N 24 30 E
Somma Lombardo, *Italy* **38 C5** 45 41N 8 42 E
Somma Vesuviana, *Italy* **41 B7** 40 52N 14 23 E
Sommariva, *Australia* **115 D4** 26 24 S 146 36 E
Sommatino, *Italy* **40 E6** 37 20N 14 0 E
Somme □, *France* **23 C9** 49 57N 2 20 E
Somme →, *France* **23 B8** 50 11N 1 38 E
Somme, B. de la, *France* **22 B8** 50 14N 1 33 E
Sommelsdijk, *Neths.* **20 E4** 51 46N 4 9 E
Sommepy-Tahure, *France* **23 C11** 49 15N 4 31 E
Sömmerda, *Germany* **26 D7** 51 10N 11 8 E
Sommesous, *France* **23 D11** 48 44N 4 12 E
Sommières, *France* **25 E8** 43 47N 4 6 E
Somogy □, *Hungary* **31 E10** 46 19N 17 30 E
Somogyszob, *Hungary* **31 E10** 46 18N 17 20 E
Somosomo Str., *Fiji* **121 A3** 16 0 S 180 0 E
Somoto, *Nic.* **148 D2** 13 28N 86 37W
Sompolno, *Poland* **47 C5** 52 26N 18 30 E
Somport, Paso, *Spain* **34 C4** 42 48N 0 31W
Somport, Puerto de,
Spain **34 C4** 42 48N 0 31W
Somuncurá, Meseta de,
Argentina **160 B3** 41 30 S 67 0W
Son, *Neths.* **21 E7** 51 31N 5 30 E
Son, *Norway* **14 E4** 59 32N 10 42 E
Son, *Spain* **36 C2** 42 43N 8 58W
Son Ha, *Vietnam* **76 E7** 15 3N 108 34 E
Son Hoa, *Vietnam* **76 F7** 13 2N 108 58 E
Son La, *Vietnam* **76 B4** 21 20N 103 50 E
Son Tay, *Vietnam* **76 B5** 21 8N 105 30 E
Soná, *Panama* **148 E3** 8 0N 81 20W
Sonamarg, *India* **81 B6** 34 18N 75 21 E
Sonamukhi, *India* **81 H12** 23 18N 87 27 E
Sonamura, *India* **78 D3** 23 29N 91 15 E
Sŏnchŏn, *N. Korea* **67 E13** 39 48N 124 55 E
Soncino, *Italy* **38 C6** 45 24N 9 52 E
Sondags →, *S. Africa* **104 E4** 33 44 S 25 51 E
Sóndalo, *Italy* **38 B7** 46 20N 10 20 E
Sondar, *India* **81 C6** 33 28N 75 56 E
Sønder Omme, *Denmark* **15 J2** 55 50N 8 54 E
Sønder Ternby, *Denmark* **15 G3** 57 31N 9 58 E
Sønderborg, *Denmark* **15 K3** 54 55N 9 49 E
Sønderjyllands
Amtskommune □,
Denmark **15 J3** 55 10N 9 10 E
Sondershausen, *Germany* **26 D6** 51 22N 10 50 E
Sóndrio, *Italy* **38 B6** 46 10N 9 53 E
Sone, *Mozam.* **107 F3** 17 23 S 34 55 E
Sonepur, *India* **82 D6** 20 55N 83 50 E
Song, *Thailand* **76 C3** 18 28N 100 11 E
Song Cau, *Vietnam* **76 F7** 13 27N 109 18 E
Song Xian, *China* **66 G7** 34 12N 112 8 E
Songchŏn, *N. Korea* **67 E14** 39 12N 126 15 E
Songea, *Tanzania* **107 E4** 10 40 S 35 40 E
Songea □, *Tanzania* **107 E4** 10 30 S 36 0 E
Songeons, *France* **23 C8** 49 32N 1 50 E
Songhua Hu, *China* **67 C14** 43 35N 126 50 E
Songhua Jiang →, *China* **67 A17** 47 45N 132 30 E
Songjiang, *China* **69 B13** 31 1N 121 12 E
Songjin, *N. Korea* **67 D15** 40 40N 129 10 E
Songjŏng-ni, *S. Korea* **67 G14** 35 8N 126 47 E
Songkan, *China* **68 C6** 28 35N 106 52 E
Songkhla, *Thailand* **77 J3** 7 13N 100 37 E
Songming, *China* **68 E4** 25 12N 103 2 E
Songnim, *N. Korea* **67 E13** 38 45N 125 39 E
Songo, *Angola* **103 D2** 7 22 S 14 51 E
Songololo, *Zaïre* **103 D2** 5 42 S 14 2 E
Songpan, *China* **68 A4** 32 40N 103 30 E
Songtao, *China* **68 C7** 28 11N 109 10 E
Songwe, *Zaïre* **106 C2** 3 20 S 26 16 E
Songwe →, *Africa* **107 D3** 9 44 S 33 58 E
Songxi, *China* **69 D12** 27 31N 118 44 E
Songzi, *China* **69 B8** 30 12N 111 45 E
Sonid Youqi, *China* **66 C7** 42 45N 112 48 E
Sonipat, *India* **80 E7** 29 0N 77 5 E
Sonkel, Ozero, *U.S.S.R.* **55 C7** 41 50N 75 12 E
Sonkovo, *U.S.S.R.* **51 C10** 57 50N 37 5 E
Sonmiani, *Pakistan* **79 D2** 25 25N 66 40 E
Sonnino, *Italy* **40 A6** 41 25N 13 13 E
Sono →, *Goiás, Brazil* **154 C2** 9 58 S 48 11W
Sono →, *Minas Gerais,*
Brazil **155 E2** 17 2 S 45 32W
Sonobe, *Japan* **63 B7** 35 6N 135 28 E
Sonogno, *Switz.* **29 D7** 46 22N 8 47 E
Sonora, *Calif., U.S.A.* **144 H6** 37 59N 120 27W
Sonora, *Tex., U.S.A.* **139 K4** 30 33N 100 37W
Sonora □, *Mexico* **146 B2** 29 0N 111 0W
Sonora →, *Mexico* **146 B2** 28 50N 111 33W
Sonora Desert, *U.S.A.* **145 M12** 33 40N 114 15W
Sonoyta, *Mexico* **146 A2** 31 51N 112 50W
Sŏnsan, *S. Korea* **67 F15** 36 14N 128 17 E
Sonsonate, *El Salv.* **148 D2** 13 43N 89 44W
Sonthofen, *Germany* **27 H6** 47 31N 10 16 E
Soochow = Suzhou,
China **69 B13** 31 19N 120 38 E
Sop Hao, *Laos* **76 B5** 20 33N 104 27 E
Sop Prap, *Thailand* **76 D2** 17 53N 99 20 E
Sopachuy, *Bolivia* **157 D5** 19 29 S 64 31W
Sopi, *Indonesia* **71 D7** 2 34N 128 28 E
Sopo, Nahr →, *Sudan* **95 F2** 8 40N 26 30 E
Sopot, *Poland* **47 A5** 54 27N 18 31 E
Sopot, *Yugoslavia* **42 C5** 44 29N 20 30 E
Sopotnica, *Yugoslavia* **42 F6** 41 23N 21 13 E
Sopron, *Hungary* **31 D9** 47 45N 16 32 E
Sop's Arm, *Canada* **129 C8** 49 46N 56 56W
Sopur, *India* **81 B6** 34 18N 74 27 E
Sør-Rondane, *Antarctica* **7 D4** 72 0 S 25 0 E
Sør-Trøndelag fylke □,
Norway **14 B3** 63 0N 9 30 E
Sora, *Italy* **40 A6** 41 45N 13 36 E
Sorada, *India* **82 E7** 19 45N 84 26 E
Sorah, *Pakistan* **80 F3** 27 13N 68 56 E
Söråker, *Sweden* **14 B11** 62 30N 17 32 E
Sorano, *Italy* **39 F8** 42 40N 11 42 E
Sorata, *Bolivia* **156 D4** 15 50 S 68 40W
Sorbas, *Spain* **35 H2** 37 6N 2 7W
Sorel, *Canada* **128 C5** 46 0N 73 10W
Sörenberg, *Switz.* **28 C6** 46 50N 8 2 E
Sorento, *U.S.A.* **140 F7** 39 0N 89 34W
Soreq, N. →, *Israel* **91 D3** 31 57N 34 43 E
Soresina, *Italy* **38 C6** 45 17N 9 51 E
Sorgono, *Italy* **40 B2** 40 1N 9 6 E
Sorgues, *France* **25 D8** 44 1N 4 53 E
Sorgun, *Turkey* **88 D6** 39 29N 35 22 E
Soria, *Spain* **34 D2** 41 43N 2 32W
Soria □, *Spain* **34 D2** 41 46N 2 28W
Soriano, *Uruguay* **158 C4** 33 24 S 58 19W
Soriano nel Cimino, *Italy* **39 F9** 42 25N 12 14 E
Sorkh, Kuh-e, *Iran* **85 C8** 35 40N 58 30 E
Sorø, *Denmark* **15 J5** 55 26N 11 32 E
Soro, *Guinea* **100 C3** 10 9N 9 48W
Sorocaba, *Brazil* **159 A6** 23 31 S 47 27W
Sorochinsk, *U.S.S.R.* **54 E3** 52 26N 53 10 E
Soroki, *U.S.S.R.* **52 B3** 48 8N 28 12 E
Soroksár, *Hungary* **31 D12** 47 24N 19 9 E
Soron, *India* **81 F8** 27 55N 78 45 E
Sorong, *Indonesia* **71 E8** 0 55 S 131 15 E
Soroní, *Greece* **32 C10** 36 21N 28 1 E
Soroti, *Uganda* **106 B3** 1 43N 33 35 E
Sørøya, *Norway* **12 A17** 70 40N 22 30 E
Sørøysundet, *Norway* **12 A17** 70 25N 23 0 E
Sorraia →, *Portugal* **37 G2** 38 55N 8 53W
Sorrento, *Australia* **115 F3** 38 22 S 144 47 E
Sorrento, *Italy* **41 B7** 40 38N 14 23 E
Sorsele, *Sweden* **12 D14** 65 31N 17 30 E
Sorso, *Italy* **40 B1** 40 50N 8 34 E
Sorsogon, *Phil.* **71 B6** 13 0N 124 0 E
Sortavala, *U.S.S.R.* **48 B5** 61 42N 30 41 E
Sortino, *Italy* **41 E8** 37 9N 15 1 E
Sorūbī, *Afghan.* **79 B3** 34 36N 69 43 E
Sorvizhi, *U.S.S.R.* **51 C16** 57 52N 48 32 E
Sos, *Spain* **34 C3** 42 30N 1 13W
Sŏsan, *S. Korea* **67 F14** 36 47N 126 27 E
Soscumica, L., *Canada* **128 B4** 50 15N 77 27W
Sosna →, *U.S.S.R.* **51 E11** 52 42N 38 55 E
Sosnogorsk, *U.S.S.R.* **48 B9** 63 37N 53 51 E
Sosnovka, *R.S.F.S.R.,*
U.S.S.R. **51 E12** 53 13N 41 24 E
Sosnovka, *R.S.F.S.R.,*
U.S.S.R. **57 D11** 54 9N 109 35 E
Sosnowiec, *Poland* **47 E6** 50 20N 19 10 E
Sospel, *France* **25 E11** 43 52N 7 27 E
Šoštanj, *Yugoslavia* **39 B12** 46 23N 15 4 E
Sŏsura, *N. Korea* **67 C16** 42 16N 130 36 E
Sosva, *U.S.S.R.* **54 B7** 59 10N 61 50 E
Sosva →, *U.S.S.R.* **54 B8** 59 32N 62 20 E
Soto la Marina →,
Mexico **147 C5** 23 40N 97 40W
Soto y Amío, *Spain* **36 C5** 42 46N 5 53W
Sotteville-lès-Rouen,
France **22 C8** 49 24N 1 5 E
Sotuta, *Mexico* **147 C7** 20 29N 89 43W
Souanké, *Congo* **102 B2** 2 10N 14 3 E
Soúdha, *Greece* **32 D6** 35 29N 24 4 E
Soúdhas, Kólpos, *Greece* **32 D6** 35 25N 24 10 E
Soufflay, *Congo* **102 B2** 2 1N 14 54 E
Souflíon, *Greece* **44 C8** 41 12N 26 18 E
Sougne-Remouchamps,
Belgium **21 H7** 50 29N 5 42 E
Souillac, *France* **24 D5** 44 53N 1 29 E
Souk-Ahras, *Algeria* **99 A6** 36 23N 7 57 E
Souk el Arba du Rharb,
Morocco **98 B3** 34 43N 5 59W
Soukhouma, *Laos* **76 E5** 14 38N 105 48 E
Sŏul, *S. Korea* **67 F14** 37 31N 126 58 E
Soulac-sur-Mer, *France* **24 C2** 45 30N 1 7W
Soultz-sous-Forêts, *France* **23 D14** 48 57N 7 52 E
Soumagne, *Belgium* **21 G7** 50 37N 5 44 E
Sound, The, *Denmark* **13 H12** 56 7N 12 30 E
Sound, The, *U.K.* **17 G3** 50 20N 4 10W
Soúnion, Ákra, *Greece* **45 G6** 37 37N 24 1 E
Sour el Ghozlane, *Algeria* **99 A5** 36 10N 3 45 E
Sources, Mt. aux, *Lesotho* **105 D4** 28 45 S 28 50 E
Sourdeval, *France* **22 D6** 48 43N 0 55W
Soure, *Brazil* **154 B2** 0 35 S 48 30W
Soure, *Portugal* **36 E2** 40 4N 8 38W
Souris, *Man., Canada* **131 D8** 49 40N 100 20W
Souris, *P.E.I., Canada* **129 C7** 46 21N 62 15W
Souris →, *Canada* **138 A5** 49 40N 99 34W
Soúrpi, *Greece* **45 E4** 39 6N 22 54 E
Sousa, *Brazil* **154 C4** 6 45 S 38 10W
Sousel, *Brazil* **154 B1** 2 38 S 52 29W
Sousel, *Portugal* **37 G3** 38 57N 7 40W
Souss, O. →, *Morocco* **98 B3** 30 27N 9 31W
Sousse, *Tunisia* **96 A2** 35 50N 10 38 E
Soustons, *France* **24 E2** 43 45N 1 19W
South Africa ■, *Africa* **104 E3** 32 0 S 23 0 E
South Atlantic Ocean **9 L8** 20 0 S 10 0W
South Aulatsivik I.,
Canada **129 A7** 56 45N 61 30W

268 South Australia

South Australia □, *Australia* 115 E2 32 0 S 139 0 E
South Baldy, *U.S.A.* 143 J10 34 6N 107 27W
South Beloit, *U.S.A.* 140 B7 42 29N 89 2W
South Bend, *Ind., U.S.A.* 141 C10 41 38N 86 20W
South Bend, *Wash., U.S.A.* 144 D3 46 44N 123 52W
South Boston, *U.S.A.* 135 G6 36 42N 78 58W
South Branch, *Canada* 129 C8 47 55N 59 2W
South Brook, *Canada* 129 C8 49 26N 56 5W
South Buganda □, *Uganda* 106 C3 0 15 S 31 30 E
South Carolina □, *U.S.A.* 135 J5 33 45N 81 0W
South Charleston, *U.S.A.* 134 F5 38 20N 81 40W
South China Sea, *Asia* 70 C4 10 0N 113 0 E
South Dakota □, *U.S.A.* 138 C5 45 0N 100 0W
South Downs, *U.K.* 17 G7 50 53N 0 10W
South East C., *Australia* 114 G4 43 40 S 146 50 E
South East Is., *Australia* 113 F3 34 17 S 123 30 E
South Esk →, *U.K.* 18 E5 56 44N 3 3W
South Foreland, *U.K.* 17 F9 51 7N 1 23 E
South Fork →, *U.S.A.* 142 C7 47 54N 113 15W
South Fork, American →, *U.S.A.* 144 G5 38 45N 121 5W
South Fork, Feather →, *U.S.A.* 144 F5 39 17N 121 36W
South Georgia, *Antarctica* 7 B1 54 30 S 37 0W
South Glamorgan □, *U.K.* 17 F4 51 30N 3 20W
South Grand →, *U.S.A.* 140 F3 38 17N 93 55W
South Haven, *U.S.A.* 141 B10 42 22N 86 20W
South Henik, L., *Canada* 131 A9 61 30N 97 30W
South Honshu Ridge, *Pac. Oc.* 122 E6 23 0N 143 0 E
South Horr, *Kenya* 106 B4 2 12N 36 56 E
South I., *Kenya* 106 B4 2 35N 36 35 E
South I., *N.Z.* 119 E5 44 0 S 170 0 E
South Invercargill, *N.Z.* 119 G3 46 26 S 168 23 E
South Knife →, *Canada* 131 B10 58 55N 94 37W
South Korea ■, *Asia* 67 G15 36 0N 128 0 E
South Lake Tahoe, *U.S.A.* 144 G6 38 57N 120 2W
South Loup →, *U.S.A.* 138 E5 41 4N 98 40W
South Lyon, *U.S.A.* 141 B13 42 28N 83 39W
South Magnetic Pole, *Antarctica* 7 C9 64 8 S 138 8 E
South Milwaukee, *U.S.A.* 141 B9 42 50N 87 52W
South Molton, *U.K.* 17 F4 51 1N 3 50W
South Nahanni →, *Canada* 130 A4 61 3N 123 21W
South Negril Pt., *Jamaica* 148 C4 18 14N 78 30W
South Orkney Is., *Antarctica* 7 C18 63 0 S 45 0W
South Pagai, I. = Pagai Selatan, P., *Indonesia* 70 E2 3 0 S 100 15 E
South Pass, *U.S.A.* 142 E9 42 20N 108 58W
South Pekin, *U.S.A.* 140 D7 40 30N 89 39W
South Pittsburg, *U.S.A.* 135 H3 35 1N 85 42W
South Platte →, *U.S.A.* 138 E4 41 7N 100 42W
South Pole, *Antarctica* 7 E 90 0 S 0 0 E
South Porcupine, *Canada* 128 C3 48 30N 81 12W
South River, *Canada* 128 C4 45 52N 79 23W
South River, *U.S.A.* 137 F10 40 27N 74 23W
South Ronaldsay, *U.K.* 18 C6 58 46N 2 58W
South Sandwich Is., *Antarctica* 9 P6 57 0 S 27 0W
South Saskatchewan →, *Canada* 131 C7 53 15N 105 5W
South Seal →, *Canada* 131 B9 58 48N 98 8W
South Shetland Is., *Antarctica* 7 C18 62 0 S 59 0W
South Shields, *U.K.* 16 C6 54 59N 1 26W
South Sioux City, *U.S.A.* 138 D6 42 30N 96 24W
South Taranaki Bight, *N.Z.* 118 F3 39 40 S 174 5 E
South Thompson →, *Canada* 130 C4 50 40N 120 20W
South Twin I., *Canada* 128 B4 53 7N 79 52W
South Tyne →, *U.K.* 16 C5 54 46N 2 25W
South Uist, *U.K.* 18 D1 57 20N 7 15W
South Wayne, *U.S.A.* 140 B7 42 34N 89 53W
South West Africa = Namibia ■, *Africa* 104 C2 22 0 S 18 9 E
South West C., *Australia* 114 G4 43 34 S 146 3 E
South Whitley, *U.S.A.* 141 C11 41 5N 85 38W
South Yorkshire □, *U.K.* 16 D6 53 30N 1 20W
Southampton, *Canada* 128 D3 44 30N 81 25W
Southampton, *U.K.* 17 G6 50 54N 1 23W
Southampton, *U.S.A.* 137 F12 40 54N 72 22W
Southampton I., *Canada* 127 B11 64 30N 84 0W
Southbridge, *N.Z.* 119 D7 43 48 S 172 16 E
Southbridge, *U.S.A.* 137 D12 42 4N 72 2W
Southend, *Canada* 131 B8 56 19N 103 22W
Southend-on-Sea, *U.K.* 17 F8 51 32N 0 42 E
Southern □, *Malawi* 107 F4 15 0 S 35 0 E
Southern □, *S. Leone* 100 D2 8 0N 12 30W
Southern □, *Zambia* 107 F2 16 20 S 26 20 E
Southern Alps, *N.Z.* 119 D5 43 41 S 170 11 E
Southern Cross, *Australia* 113 F2 31 12 S 119 15 E
Southern Hills, *Australia* 113 F3 32 15 S 122 40 E
Southern Indian L., *Canada* 131 B9 57 10N 98 30W
Southern Ocean, *Antarctica* 7 C6 62 0 S 60 0 E
Southern Pines, *U.S.A.* 135 H6 35 10N 79 25W
Southern Uplands, *U.K.* 18 F5 55 30N 3 3W
Southfield, *U.S.A.* 141 B13 42 29N 83 17W
Southington, *U.S.A.* 137 E12 41 37N 72 53W
Southland □, *N.Z.* 119 F3 45 51 S 168 13 E
Southold, *U.S.A.* 137 E12 41 4N 72 26W
Southport, *Australia* 115 D5 27 58 S 153 25 E
Southport, *U.K.* 16 D4 53 38N 3 1W
Southport, *U.S.A.* 135 J6 33 55N 78 5W
Southwest C., *N.Z.* 119 H2 47 17 S 167 28 E
Southwold, *U.K.* 17 E9 52 19N 1 41 E
Soutpansberg, *S. Africa* 105 C4 23 0 S 29 30 E
Souvigny, *France* 24 B7 46 33N 3 10 E
Sovata, *Romania* 46 C6 46 35N 25 3 E
Sovetsk, *Lithuania, U.S.S.R.* 50 D2 55 6N 21 50 E
Sovetsk, *R.S.F.S.R., U.S.S.R.* 51 C16 57 38N 48 53 E
Sovetskaya Gavan, *U.S.S.R.* 57 E15 48 50N 140 5 E
Sovicille, *Italy* 39 E8 43 16N 11 12 E
Soviet Union = Union of Soviet Socialist Republics ■, *Eurasia* 57 D11 60 0N 100 0 E
Sovra, *Yugoslavia* 42 E2 42 44N 17 34 E
Soweto, *S. Africa* 105 D4 26 14 S 27 54 E
Sōya-Kaikyō = La Perouse Str., *Asia* 60 B11 45 40N 142 0 E
Sōya-Misaki, *Japan* 60 B10 45 30N 141 55 E
Soyo, *Angola* 103 D2 6 13 S 12 20 E
Sozh →, *U.S.S.R.* 50 F7 51 57N 30 48 E
Sozopol, *Bulgaria* 43 E12 42 23N 27 42 E
Spa, *Belgium* 21 H7 50 29N 5 53 E
Spain ■, *Europe* 11 H5 39 0N 4 0W
Spakenburg, *Neths.* 20 D6 52 15N 5 22 E
Spalding, *Australia* 116 B3 33 30 S 138 37 E
Spalding, *U.K.* 16 E7 52 47N 0 9W
Spalding, *U.S.A.* 138 E5 41 45N 98 27W
Spangler, *U.S.A.* 136 F6 40 39N 78 48W
Spaniard's Bay, *Canada* 129 C9 47 38N 53 20W
Spanish, *Canada* 128 C3 46 12N 82 20W
Spanish Fork, *U.S.A.* 142 F8 40 10N 111 37W
Spanish Town, *Jamaica* 148 C4 18 0N 76 57W
Sparks, *U.S.A.* 144 F7 39 30N 119 45W
Sparta = Spárti, *Greece* 45 G4 37 5N 22 25 E
Sparta, *Ga., U.S.A.* 135 J4 33 18N 82 59W
Sparta, *Ill., U.S.A.* 140 F7 38 7N 89 42W
Sparta, *Mich., U.S.A.* 141 A11 43 10N 85 42W
Sparta, *Wis., U.S.A.* 138 D9 43 55N 90 47W
Spartanburg, *U.S.A.* 135 H5 35 0N 82 0W
Spartansburg, *U.S.A.* 136 E5 41 48N 79 43W
Spartel, C., *Morocco* 98 A3 35 47N 5 56W
Spárti, *Greece* 45 G4 37 5N 22 25 E
Spartivento, C., *Calabria, Italy* 41 E9 37 56N 16 4 E
Spartivento, C., *Sard., Italy* 40 D1 38 52N 8 50 E
Spas-Demensk, *U.S.S.R.* 50 D9 54 20N 34 0 E
Spas-Klepiki, *U.S.S.R.* 51 D12 55 10N 40 10 E
Spassk-Dalniy, *U.S.S.R.* 57 E14 44 40N 132 48 E
Spassk-Ryazanskiy, *U.S.S.R.* 51 D12 54 24N 40 25 E
Spátha, Ákra, *Greece* 32 D5 35 42N 23 43 E
Spatsizi →, *Canada* 130 B3 57 42N 128 7W
Spearfish, *U.S.A.* 138 C3 44 32N 103 52W
Spearman, *U.S.A.* 139 G4 36 15N 101 10W
Speed, *Australia* 116 C5 35 21 S 142 27 E
Speedway, *U.S.A.* 141 E10 39 47N 86 15W
Speer, *Switz.* 29 B8 47 12N 9 8 E
Speers, *Canada* 131 C7 52 43N 107 34W
Speightstown, *Barbados* 149 D8 13 15N 59 39W
Speke Gulf, *Tanzania* 106 C3 2 20 S 32 50 E
Spekholzerheide, *Neths.* 21 G8 50 51N 6 2 E
Spence Bay, *Canada* 126 B10 69 32N 93 32W
Spencer, *Idaho, U.S.A.* 142 D7 44 18N 112 8W
Spencer, *Ind., U.S.A.* 141 E10 39 17N 86 46W
Spencer, *Iowa, U.S.A.* 138 D7 43 5N 95 19W
Spencer, *N.Y., U.S.A.* 137 D8 42 14N 76 30W
Spencer, *Nebr., U.S.A.* 138 D5 42 52N 98 43W
Spencer, *W. Va., U.S.A.* 134 F5 38 47N 81 24W
Spencer, C., *Australia* 116 C2 35 20 S 136 53 E
Spencer B., *Namibia* 104 D1 25 30 S 14 47 E
Spencer G., *Australia* 116 C2 34 0 S 137 20 E
Spencerville, *Canada* 137 B9 44 51N 75 33W
Spencerville, *U.S.A.* 141 D12 40 43N 84 21W
Spences Bridge, *Canada* 130 C4 50 25N 121 20W
Spenser Mts., *N.Z.* 119 C7 42 15 S 172 45 E
Sperkhiós →, *Greece* 45 F4 38 57N 22 3 E
Sperrin Mts., *U.K.* 19 B5 54 50N 7 0W
Spessart, *Germany* 27 E5 50 10N 9 20 E
Spétsai, *Greece* 45 G5 37 15N 23 10 E
Spey →, *U.K.* 18 D5 57 26N 3 25W
Speyer, *Germany* 27 F4 49 19N 8 26 E
Speyer →, *Germany* 27 F4 49 19N 8 27 E
Spezzano Albanese, *Italy* 41 C9 39 41N 16 19 E
Spickard, *U.S.A.* 140 D3 40 14N 93 36W
Spiekeroog, *Germany* 26 B3 53 45N 7 42 E
Spielfeld, *Austria* 39 B12 46 43N 15 38 E
Spiez, *Switz.* 28 C5 46 40N 7 40 E
Spijk, *Neths.* 20 B9 53 24N 6 50 E
Spijkenisse, *Neths.* 20 E4 51 51N 4 20 E
Spíli, *Greece* 32 D6 35 13N 24 31 E
Spilimbergo, *Italy* 39 B9 46 7N 12 53 E
Spin Baldak = Qala-i-Jadid, *Afghan.* 80 D2 31 1N 66 25 E
Spinalónga, *Greece* 32 D7 35 18N 25 44 E
Spinazzola, *Italy* 41 B9 40 58N 16 5 E
Spineni, *Romania* 46 E5 44 43N 24 37 E
Spirit Lake, *Idaho, U.S.A.* 142 C5 47 56N 116 56W
Spirit Lake, *Wash., U.S.A.* 144 D4 46 15N 122 9W
Spirit River, *Canada* 130 B5 55 45N 118 50W
Spiritwood, *Canada* 131 C7 53 24N 107 33W
Spišská Nová Ves, *Czech.* 31 C13 48 58N 20 34 E
Spišské Podhradie, *Czech.* 31 C13 49 0N 20 48 E
Spital, *Austria* 30 D7 47 42N 14 18 E
Spithead, *U.K.* 17 G6 50 43N 1 5W
Spittal, *Austria* 30 E6 46 48N 13 31 E
Spitzbergen = Svalbard, *Arctic* 6 B8 78 0N 17 0 E
Split, *Yugoslavia* 39 E13 43 31N 16 26 E
Split L., *Canada* 131 B9 56 8N 96 15W
Splitski Kanal, *Yugoslavia* 39 E13 43 31N 16 20 E
Splügen, *Switz.* 29 C8 46 34N 9 21 E
Splügenpass, *Switz.* 29 D8 46 30N 9 20 E
Spofford, *U.S.A.* 139 L4 29 10N 100 27W
Spokane, *U.S.A.* 142 C5 47 45N 117 25W
Spoleto, *Italy* 39 F9 42 46N 12 47 E
Spoon →, *U.S.A.* 140 D6 40 19N 90 4W
Spooner, *U.S.A.* 138 C9 45 49N 91 51W
Sporádhes, *Greece* 45 F6 39 0N 24 30 E
Sporyy Navolok, Mys, *U.S.S.R.* 56 B7 75 50N 68 40 E
Spragge, *Canada* 128 C3 46 15N 82 40W
Sprague, *U.S.A.* 142 C5 47 18N 117 59W
Sprague River, *U.S.A.* 142 E3 42 28N 121 31W
Spratly I., *S. China Sea* 70 C4 8 20N 112 0 E
Spray, *U.S.A.* 142 D4 44 50N 119 46W
Spree →, *Germany* 26 C9 52 32N 13 13 E
Spremberg, *Germany* 26 D10 51 33N 14 21 E
Sprimont, *Belgium* 21 H7 50 30N 5 40 E
Spring City, *U.S.A.* 142 G8 39 31N 111 28W
Spring Garden, *U.S.A.* 144 F6 39 52N 120 47W
Spring Green, *U.S.A.* 140 A6 43 11N 90 4W
Spring Hill, *Australia* 117 B8 33 23 S 149 9 E
Spring Mts., *U.S.A.* 143 H6 36 20N 115 43W
Spring Valley, *Calif., U.S.A.* 145 N10 32 45N 117 0W
Spring Valley, *Ill., U.S.A.* 140 C7 41 20N 89 14W
Spring Valley, *Minn., U.S.A.* 138 D8 43 40N 92 23W
Springbok, *S. Africa* 104 D2 29 42 S 17 54 E
Springdale, *Canada* 129 C8 49 30N 56 6W
Springdale, *Ark., U.S.A.* 139 G7 36 10N 94 5W
Springdale, *Wash., U.S.A.* 142 B5 48 1N 117 50W
Springe, *Germany* 26 C5 52 12N 9 35 E
Springer, *U.S.A.* 139 G2 36 22N 104 36W
Springerville, *U.S.A.* 143 J9 34 10N 109 16W
Springfield, *Canada* 136 D4 42 50N 80 56W
Springfield, *N.Z.* 119 D6 43 19 S 171 56 E
Springfield, *Colo., U.S.A.* 139 G3 37 26N 102 40W
Springfield, *Ill., U.S.A.* 140 E7 39 48N 89 40W
Springfield, *Ky., U.S.A.* 141 G11 37 41N 85 13W
Springfield, *Mass., U.S.A.* 137 D12 42 8N 72 37W
Springfield, *Mo., U.S.A.* 139 G8 37 15N 93 20W
Springfield, *Ohio, U.S.A.* 141 E13 39 58N 83 48W
Springfield, *Oreg., U.S.A.* 142 D2 44 2N 123 0W
Springfield, *Tenn., U.S.A.* 135 G2 36 35N 86 55W
Springfield, *Vt., U.S.A.* 137 C12 43 20N 72 30W
Springfield, L., *U.S.A.* 140 E7 39 46N 89 36W
Springfontein, *S. Africa* 104 E4 30 15 S 25 40 E
Springhill, *Canada* 129 C7 45 40N 64 4W
Springhouse, *Canada* 130 C4 51 56N 122 7W
Springhurst, *Australia* 117 D7 36 10 S 146 31 E
Springs, *S. Africa* 105 D4 26 13 S 28 25 E
Springsure, *Australia* 114 C4 24 8 S 148 6 E
Springvale, *Queens., Australia* 114 C3 23 33 S 140 42 E
Springvale, *W. Austral., Australia* 112 C4 17 48 S 127 41 E
Springvale, *U.S.A.* 137 C14 43 28N 70 48W
Springville, *Calif., U.S.A.* 144 J8 36 8N 118 49W
Springville, *N.Y., U.S.A.* 136 D6 42 31N 78 41W
Springville, *Utah, U.S.A.* 142 F8 40 14N 111 35W
Springwater, *Canada* 131 C7 51 58N 108 23W
Spruce-Creek, *U.S.A.* 136 F6 40 36N 78 9W
Spur, *U.S.A.* 139 J4 33 28N 100 50W
Spurgeon, *U.S.A.* 141 F9 38 14N 87 15W
Spurn Hd., *U.K.* 16 D8 53 34N 0 8 E
Spuž, *Yugoslavia* 42 E4 42 32N 19 10 E
Spuzzum, *Canada* 130 D4 49 37N 121 23W
Squam L., *U.S.A.* 137 C13 43 45N 71 32W
Squamish, *Canada* 130 D4 49 45N 123 10W
Square Islands, *Canada* 129 B8 52 47N 55 47W
Squillace, G. di, *Italy* 41 D9 38 43N 16 35 E
Squinzano, *Italy* 41 B11 40 27N 18 1 E
Squires, Mt., *Australia* 113 E4 26 14 S 127 28 E
Sragen, *Indonesia* 71 G14 7 26 S 111 2 E
Srbac, *Yugoslavia* 42 B2 45 7N 17 30 E
Srbija □, *Yugoslavia* 42 D6 43 30N 21 0 E
Srbobran, *Yugoslavia* 42 B4 45 32N 19 48 E
Sre Khtum, *Cambodia* 77 F6 12 10N 106 52 E
Sre Umbell, *Cambodia* 77 G4 11 8N 103 46 E
Srebrnica, *Yugoslavia* 42 C4 44 10N 19 18 E
Sredinnyy Khrebet, *U.S.S.R.* 57 D17 57 0N 160 0 E
Sredinnyy Ra. = Sredinnyy Khrebet, *U.S.S.R.* 57 D17 57 0N 160 0 E
Središče, *Yugoslavia* 39 B13 46 24N 16 17 E
Sredna Gora, *Bulgaria* 43 E9 42 40N 24 20 E
Sredne Tambovskoye, *U.S.S.R.* 57 D14 50 55N 137 45 E
Srednekolymsk, *U.S.S.R.* 57 C16 67 27N 153 40 E
Srednevilyuysk, *U.S.S.R.* 57 C13 63 50N 123 5 E
Sredni Rodopi, *Bulgaria* 43 F9 41 40N 24 45 E
Śrem, *Poland* 47 C4 52 6N 17 2 E
Sremska Mitrovica, *Yugoslavia* 42 C4 44 59N 19 33 E
Sremski Karlovci, *Yugoslavia* 42 B4 45 12N 19 56 E
Srepok →, *Cambodia* 76 F6 13 33N 106 16 E
Sretensk, *U.S.S.R.* 57 D12 52 10N 117 40 E
Sri Kalahasti, *India* 83 H4 13 45N 79 44 E
Sri Lanka ■, *Asia* 83 L5 7 30N 80 50 E
Sriharikota I., *India* 83 H5 13 40N 80 20 E
Srikakulam, *India* 82 E6 18 14N 83 58 E
Srinagar, *India* 81 B6 34 5N 74 50 E
Sripur, *Bangla.* 78 C3 24 14N 90 30 E
Srirangam, *India* 83 J4 10 54N 78 42 E
Srivardhan, *India* 82 E1 18 4N 73 3 E
Srivilliputtur, *India* 83 K3 9 31N 77 40 E
Środa Śląska, *Poland* 47 D3 51 10N 16 36 E
Środa Wielkopolski, *Poland* 47 C4 52 15N 17 19 E
Srokowo, *Poland* 47 A8 54 13N 21 31 E
Srpska Crnja, *Yugoslavia* 42 B5 45 38N 20 44 E
Srpska Itabej, *Yugoslavia* 42 B5 45 35N 20 44 E
Staaten →, *Australia* 114 B3 16 24 S 141 17 E
Staberhuk, *Germany* 26 A7 54 23N 11 18 E
Stabroek, *Belgium* 21 F4 51 20N 4 22 E
Stad Delden, *Neths.* 20 D9 52 16N 6 43 E
Stade, *Germany* 26 B5 53 35N 9 31 E
Staden, *Belgium* 21 G2 50 59N 3 1 E
Staðarhólskirkja, *Iceland* 12 D3 65 23N 21 58W
Städjan, *Sweden* 14 C6 61 56N 12 52 E
Stadlandet, *Norway* 12 E8 62 10N 5 10 E
Stadskanaal, *Neths.* 20 B9 53 4N 6 55 E
Stadthagen, *Germany* 26 C5 52 20N 9 14 E
Stadtlohn, *Germany* 26 D2 52 0N 6 52 E
Stadtroda, *Germany* 26 E7 50 51N 11 44 E
Stäfa, *Switz.* 29 B7 47 14N 8 45 E
Stafafell, *Iceland* 12 D6 64 25N 14 52W
Staffa, *U.K.* 18 E2 56 26N 6 21W
Stafford, *U.K.* 16 E5 52 49N 2 9W
Stafford, *U.S.A.* 139 G5 38 0N 98 35W
Stafford Springs, *U.S.A.* 137 E12 41 58N 72 20W
Staffordshire □, *U.K.* 16 E5 52 53N 2 10W
Stagnone, *Italy* 40 E5 37 50N 12 28 E
Staines, *U.K.* 17 F7 51 26N 0 30W
Stainz, *Austria* 30 E8 46 53N 15 17 E
Stakhanov, *U.S.S.R.* 53 B8 48 35N 38 40 E
Stalač, *Yugoslavia* 42 D6 43 43N 21 28 E
Stalden, *Switz.* 28 D5 46 14N 7 52 E
Stalingrad = Volgograd, *U.S.S.R.* 53 B11 48 40N 44 25 E
Staliniri = Tskhinvali, *U.S.S.R.* 53 E11 42 14N 44 1 E
Stalino = Donetsk, *U.S.S.R.* 52 C7 48 0N 37 45 E
Stalinogorsk = Novomoskovsk, *U.S.S.R.* 51 D11 54 5N 38 15 E
Stalis, *Greece* 32 D7 35 17N 25 25 E
Stalowa Wola, *Poland* 47 E9 50 34N 22 3 E
Stalybridge, *U.K.* 16 D5 53 29N 2 4W
Stamford, *Australia* 114 C3 21 15 S 143 46 E
Stamford, *U.K.* 17 E7 52 39N 0 29W
Stamford, *Conn., U.S.A.* 137 E11 41 5N 73 30W
Stamford, *Tex., U.S.A.* 139 J5 32 58N 99 50W
Stamping Ground, *U.S.A.* 141 F12 38 16N 84 41W
Stamps, *U.S.A.* 139 J8 33 22N 93 30W
Stanberry, *U.S.A.* 138 E7 40 12N 94 32W
Stančevo = Kalipetrovo, *Bulgaria* 43 C12 44 5N 27 14 E
Standerton, *S. Africa* 105 D4 26 55 S 29 7 E
Standish, *U.S.A.* 134 D4 43 58N 83 57W
Stanford, *U.S.A.* 142 C8 47 11N 110 10W
Stange, *Norway* 14 D5 60 43N 11 5 E
Stanger, *S. Africa* 105 D5 29 27 S 31 14 E
Stanhope, *Australia* 117 D6 36 27 S 144 59 E
Stanhope, *U.S.A.* 140 B3 42 17N 93 48W
Stanišić, *Yugoslavia* 42 B4 45 56N 19 10 E
Stanislaus →, *U.S.A.* 144 H5 37 40N 121 15W
Stanislav = Ivano-Frankovsk, *U.S.S.R.* 50 G4 48 40N 24 40 E
Stanisławów, *Poland* 47 C8 52 18N 21 33 E
Stanke Dimitrov, *Bulgaria* 42 E8 42 17N 23 9 E
Stanley, *Australia* 114 G4 40 46 S 145 19 E
Stanley, *N.B., Canada* 129 C6 46 20N 66 44W
Stanley, *Sask., Canada* 131 B8 55 24N 104 22W
Stanley, *Falk. Is.* 160 D5 51 40 S 59 51W
Stanley, *Idaho, U.S.A.* 142 D6 44 10N 114 59W
Stanley, *N. Dak., U.S.A.* 138 A3 48 20N 102 23W
Stanley, *N.Y., U.S.A.* 136 D7 42 48N 77 6W
Stanley, *Wis., U.S.A.* 138 C9 44 57N 91 0W
Stanley Res., *India* 83 J3 11 50N 77 40 E
Stanovoy Khrebet, *U.S.S.R.* 57 D14 55 0N 130 0 E
Stanovoy Ra. = Stanovoy Khrebet, *U.S.S.R.* 57 D14 55 0N 130 0 E
Stans, *Switz.* 29 C6 46 58N 8 21 E
Stansmore Ra., *Australia* 112 D4 21 23 S 128 33 E
Stanthorpe, *Australia* 115 D5 28 36 S 151 59 E
Stanton, *U.S.A.* 139 J4 32 8N 101 45W
Stantsiya Karshi, *U.S.S.R.* 55 D2 38 49N 65 47 E
Stanwood, *U.S.A.* 144 B4 48 15N 122 23W
Staphorst, *Neths.* 20 C8 52 39N 6 12 E
Staples, *U.S.A.* 138 B7 46 21N 94 48W
Stapleton, *U.S.A.* 138 E4 41 30N 100 31W
Staporków, *Poland* 47 D7 51 9N 20 31 E
Star City, *Canada* 131 C8 52 50N 104 20W
Stara-minskaya, *U.S.S.R.* 53 C8 46 33N 39 0 E
Stara Moravica, *Yugoslavia* 42 B4 45 50N 19 30 E
Stara Pazova, *Yugoslavia* 42 C5 44 58N 20 10 E
Stara Planina, *Bulgaria* 43 D8 43 15N 23 0 E
Stara Zagora, *Bulgaria* 43 E10 42 26N 25 39 E
Starachowice, *Poland* 47 D8 51 3N 21 2 E
Starashcherbinovskaya, *U.S.S.R.* 53 C8 46 40N 38 53 E
Staraya Russa, *U.S.S.R.* 50 C7 57 58N 31 23 E
Starbuck I., *Kiribati* 123 H12 5 37 S 155 55W
Stargard Szczeciński, *Poland* 47 B2 53 20N 15 0 E
Stari Bar, *Yugoslavia* 42 E4 42 7N 19 13 E
Stari Trg, *Yugoslavia* 39 C12 45 29N 15 7 E
Staritsa, *U.S.S.R.* 50 C9 56 33N 34 55 E
Starke, *U.S.A.* 135 L4 30 0N 82 10W
Starkville, *Colo., U.S.A.* 139 G2 37 10N 104 31W
Starkville, *Miss., U.S.A.* 135 J1 33 26N 88 48W
Starnberg, *Germany* 27 H7 48 0N 11 20 E
Starnberger See, *Germany* 27 H7 47 55N 11 20 E
Starobelsk, *U.S.S.R.* 53 B8 49 16N 39 0 E
Starodub, *U.S.S.R.* 50 E8 52 30N 32 50 E
Starogard, *Poland* 47 B5 53 59N 18 30 E
Starokonstantinov, *U.S.S.R.* 52 B2 49 48N 27 10 E
Starosielce, *Poland* 47 B10 53 8N 23 5 E
Start Pt., *U.K.* 17 G4 50 13N 3 38W
Stary Sącz, *Poland* 31 B13 49 33N 20 35 E
Staryy Biryuzyak, *U.S.S.R.* 53 D12 44 46N 46 50 E
Staryy Chartoriysk, *U.S.S.R.* 50 F4 51 15N 25 54 E
Staryy Kheydzhan, *U.S.S.R.* 57 D15 60 0N 144 50 E
Staryy Krym, *U.S.S.R.* 52 D6 45 3N 35 8 E
Staryy Oskol, *U.S.S.R.* 51 F10 51 19N 37 55 E
Stassfurt, *Germany* 26 D7 51 51N 11 34 E
Staszów, *Poland* 47 E8 50 33N 21 10 E
State Center, *U.S.A.* 140 B3 42 1N 93 10W
State College, *U.S.A.* 136 F7 40 47N 77 1W
Stateline, *U.S.A.* 144 G7 38 57N 119 56W
Staten, I. = Estados, I. de Los, *Argentina* 160 D4 54 40 S 64 30W
Staten I., *U.S.A.* 137 F10 40 35N 74 10W
Statesboro, *U.S.A.* 135 J5 32 26N 81 46W
Statesville, *U.S.A.* 135 H5 35 48N 80 51W
Stauffer, *U.S.A.* 145 L7 34 45N 119 3W
Staunton, *Ill., U.S.A.* 140 F7 39 0N 89 49W
Staunton, *Va., U.S.A.* 134 F6 38 7N 79 4W
Stavanger, *Norway* 13 G8 58 57N 5 40 E
Staveley, *N.Z.* 119 D6 43 40 S 171 32 E
Stavelot, *Belgium* 21 H7 50 23N 5 55 E
Stavenhagen, *Germany* 26 B8 53 41N 12 54 E
Stavenisse, *Neths.* 21 E4 51 35N 4 1 E
Staveren, *Neths.* 20 C6 52 53N 5 22 E
Stavern, *Norway* 14 F4 59 0N 10 1 E
Stavre, *Sweden* 14 B9 62 51N 15 19 E
Stavropol, *U.S.S.R.* 53 D10 45 5N 42 0 E
Stavros, *Cyprus* 32 D11 35 1N 32 38 E
Stavrós, *Greece* 32 D6 35 12N 24 45 E
Stavros, Ákra, *Greece* 32 D6 35 26N 24 58 E
Stavroúpolis, *Greece* 44 C6 41 12N 24 45 E
Stawell, *Australia* 116 D5 37 5 S 142 47 E
Stawell →, *Australia* 114 C3 20 20 S 142 55 E
Stawiski, *Poland* 47 B9 53 22N 22 9 E

Sul, Canal do 269

Stawiszyn, Poland 47 D5 51 56N 18 4 E
Stayner, Canada 136 B4 44 25N 80 5W
Steamboat Springs, U.S.A. 142 F10 40 30N 106 50W
Stębark, Poland 47 B7 53 30N 20 10 E
Stebleva, Albania 44 C2 41 18N 20 33 E
Steckborn, Switz. 29 A7 47 44N 8 59 E
Steele, U.S.A. 138 B5 46 56N 99 52W
Steelton, U.S.A. 136 F8 40 17N 76 50W
Steelville, U.S.A. 139 G9 37 57N 91 21W
Steen River, Canada 130 B5 59 40N 117 12W
Steenbergen, Neths. 21 E4 51 35N 4 19 E
Steenkool = Bintuni, Indonesia 71 E8 2 7 S 133 32 E
Steenvoorde, France 23 B9 50 48N 2 33 E
Steenwijk, Neths. 20 C8 52 47N 6 7 E
Steep Pt., Australia 113 E1 26 8 S 113 8 E
Steep Rock, Canada 131 C9 51 30N 98 48W
Ştefăneşti, Romania 46 B8 47 44N 27 15 E
Stefanie L. = Chew Bahir, Ethiopia 95 G4 4 40N 36 50 E
Stefansson Bay, Antarctica 7 C5 67 20 S 59 8 E
Steffisburg, Switz. 28 C5 46 47N 7 38 E
Stege, Denmark 15 K6 55 0N 12 18 E
Steiermark □, Austria 30 D8 47 26N 15 0 E
Steigerwald, Germany 27 F6 49 45N 10 30 E
Steilacoom, U.S.A. 144 C4 47 10N 122 36W
Stein, Neths. 21 G7 50 58N 5 45 E
Steinbach, Canada 131 D9 49 32N 96 40W
Steinfort, Lux. 21 J7 49 39N 5 55 E
Steinfurt, Germany 26 C3 52 9N 7 23 E
Steinheim, Germany 26 D5 51 50N 9 6 E
Steinhuder Meer, Germany 26 C5 52 48N 9 20 E
Steinkjer, Norway 12 E11 63 59N 11 31 E
Steinkopf, S. Africa 104 D2 29 18 S 17 43 E
Stekene, Belgium 21 F4 51 12N 4 2 E
Stellarton, Canada 129 C7 45 32N 62 30W
Stellenbosch, S. Africa 104 E2 33 58 S 18 50 E
Stellendam, Neths. 20 E4 51 49N 4 1 E
Stelvio, Paso dello, Italy 29 C10 46 32N 10 27 E
Stemshaug, Norway 14 A2 63 19N 8 44 E
Stendal, Germany 26 C7 52 36N 11 50 E
Stene, Belgium 21 F1 51 12N 2 56 E
Stensele, Sweden 12 D14 65 3N 17 8 E
Stenstorp, Sweden 15 F7 58 17N 13 45 E
Stepanakert, U.S.S.R. 89 D12 39 40N 46 25 E
Stephan, U.S.A. 138 A6 48 30N 96 53W
Stephens, C., N.Z. 119 A8 40 42 S 173 58 E
Stephens Creek, Australia 116 A4 31 50 S 141 30 E
Stephens I., Canada 130 C2 54 10N 130 45W
Stephens I., N.Z. 119 A9 40 40 S 174 1 E
Stephenville, Canada 129 C8 48 31N 58 35W
Stephenville, U.S.A. 139 J5 32 12N 98 12W
Stepnica, Poland 47 B1 53 38N 14 36 E
Stepnoi = Elista, U.S.S.R. 53 C11 46 16N 44 14 E
Stepnoye, U.S.S.R. 54 D7 54 4N 60 26 E
Stepnyak, U.S.S.R. 56 D8 52 50N 70 50 E
Steppe, Asia 58 E9 50 0N 50 0 E
Stereá Ellas □, Greece 45 F4 38 50N 22 0 E
Sterkstroom, S. Africa 104 E4 31 32 S 26 32 E
Sterling, Colo., U.S.A. 138 E3 40 40N 103 15W
Sterling, Ill., U.S.A. 140 C7 41 45N 89 45W
Sterling, Kans., U.S.A. 138 F5 38 17N 98 13W
Sterling City, U.S.A. 139 K4 31 50N 100 59W
Sterling Heights, U.S.A. 141 B13 42 35N 83 5W
Sterling Run, U.S.A. 136 E6 41 25N 78 12W
Sterlitamak, U.S.S.R. 54 E5 53 40N 56 0 E
Sternberg, Germany 26 B7 53 42N 11 48 E
Šternberk, Czech. 31 B10 49 45N 17 15 E
Stérnes, Greece 32 D6 35 30N 24 9 E
Stettin = Szczecin, Poland 47 B1 53 27N 14 27 E
Stettiner Haff, Germany 26 B10 53 50N 14 25 E
Stettler, Canada 130 C6 52 19N 112 40W
Steubenville, U.S.A. 136 F4 40 21N 80 39W
Stevens Point, U.S.A. 138 C10 44 32N 89 34W
Stevenson, U.S.A. 144 E5 45 42N 121 53W
Stevenson L., Canada 131 C9 53 55N 96 0W
Stevns Klint, Denmark 15 J6 55 17N 12 28 E
Steward, U.S.A. 140 C7 41 51N 89 1W
Stewardson, U.S.A. 141 E8 39 16N 88 38W
Stewart, B.C., Canada 130 B3 55 56N 129 57W
Stewart, N.W.T., Canada 126 B6 63 19N 139 26W
Stewart, U.S.A. 144 F7 39 5N 119 46W
Stewart, C., Australia 114 A1 11 57 S 134 56 E
Stewart, I., Chile 160 D2 54 50 S 71 15W
Stewart I., N.Z. 119 G2 46 58 S 167 54 E
Stewarts Point, U.S.A. 144 G3 38 39N 123 20W
Stewartsville, U.S.A. 140 E2 39 45N 94 30W
Stewiacke, Canada 129 C7 45 9N 63 22W
Steynsburg, S. Africa 104 E4 31 15 S 25 49 E
Steyr, Austria 30 C7 48 3N 14 25 E
Steyr →, Austria 30 C7 48 17N 14 15 E
Steytlerville, S. Africa 104 E3 33 17 S 24 19 E
Stia, Italy 39 E8 43 48N 11 41 E
Stiens, Neths. 20 B7 53 16N 5 46 E
Stigler, U.S.A. 139 H7 35 19N 95 6W
Stigliano, Italy 41 B9 40 24N 16 13 E
Stigsnæs, Denmark 15 J5 55 13N 11 18 E
Stigtomta, Sweden 15 F10 58 47N 16 48 E
Stikine →, Canada 130 B2 56 40N 132 30W
Stilfontein, S. Africa 104 D4 26 51 S 26 50 E
Stilís, Greece 45 F4 38 55N 22 47 E
Stillwater, N.Z. 119 C6 42 27 S 171 20 E
Stillwater, Minn., U.S.A. 138 C8 45 3N 92 47W
Stillwater, N.Y., U.S.A. 137 D11 42 55N 73 41W
Stillwater, Okla., U.S.A. 139 G6 36 5N 97 3W
Stillwater Ra., U.S.A. 142 G4 39 45N 118 6W
Stilwell, U.S.A. 139 H7 35 52N 94 36W
Stimfalías, L., Greece 45 G4 37 51N 22 27 E
Štip, Yugoslavia 42 F7 41 42N 22 10 E
Stíra, Greece 45 F6 38 9N 24 14 E
Stirling, Australia 114 B3 17 12 S 141 35 E
Stirling, Canada 130 D6 49 30N 112 30W
Stirling, N.Z. 119 G4 46 14 S 169 49 E
Stirling, U.K. 18 E5 56 7N 3 57W
Stirling Ra., Australia 113 F2 34 23 S 118 0 E
Stittsville, Canada 137 A9 45 15N 75 55W
Stockach, Germany 27 H5 47 51N 9 1 E
Stockbridge, U.S.A. 141 B12 42 27N 84 11W
Stockerau, Austria 31 C9 48 24N 16 12 E
Stockett, U.S.A. 142 C8 47 23N 111 7W
Stockholm, Sweden 14 E12 59 20N 18 3 E
Stockholms län □, Sweden 14 E12 59 30N 18 20 E
Stockhorn, Switz. 28 C5 46 42N 7 33 E
Stockport, U.K. 16 D5 53 25N 2 11W
Stockton, Australia 117 B9 32 50 S 151 47 E
Stockton, Calif., U.S.A. 144 H5 37 58N 121 20W
Stockton, Ill., U.S.A. 140 B6 42 21N 90 1W
Stockton, Kans., U.S.A. 138 F5 39 30N 99 20W
Stockton, Mo., U.S.A. 139 G8 37 40N 93 48W
Stockton-on-Tees, U.K. 16 C6 54 34N 1 20W
Stockvik, Sweden 14 B11 62 17N 17 23 E
Stoczek Łukowski, Poland 47 D8 51 58N 21 58 E
Stöde, Sweden 14 B10 62 28N 16 35 E
Stogovo, Yugoslavia 42 F5 41 31N 20 38 E
Stoke, N.Z. 119 B8 41 19 S 173 14 E
Stoke on Trent, U.K. 16 D5 53 1N 2 11W
Stokes Bay, Canada 128 D3 45 0N 81 28W
Stokes Pt., Australia 114 G3 40 10 S 143 56 E
Stokes Ra., Australia 112 C5 15 50 S 130 50 E
Stokkseyri, Iceland 12 E3 63 50N 21 2W
Stokksnes, Iceland 12 D6 64 14N 14 58W
Stolac, Yugoslavia 42 D2 43 8N 17 59 E
Stolberg, Germany 26 E2 50 48N 6 13 E
Stolbovaya, R.S.F.S.R., U.S.S.R. 51 D10 55 10N 37 32 E
Stolbovaya, R.S.F.S.R., U.S.S.R. 57 C16 64 50N 153 50 E
Stolbovoy, Ostrov, U.S.S.R. 57 D17 56 44N 163 14 E
Stolbtsy, U.S.S.R. 50 E5 53 30N 26 43 E
Stolin, U.S.S.R. 50 F5 51 53N 26 50 E
Stolnici, Romania 46 E5 44 31N 24 48 E
Stolwijk, Neths. 20 E5 51 59N 4 47 E
Stomíon, Greece 32 D5 35 21N 23 32 E
Ston, Yugoslavia 42 E2 42 51N 17 43 E
Stonehaven, U.K. 18 E6 56 58N 2 11W
Stonehenge, Australia 114 C3 24 22 S 143 17 E
Stonewall, Canada 131 C9 50 10N 97 19W
Stonington, U.S.A. 140 E7 39 44N 89 12W
Stony L., Man., Canada 131 B9 58 51N 98 40W
Stony L., Ont., Canada 136 B6 44 30N 78 5W
Stony Rapids, Canada 131 B7 59 16N 105 50W
Stony Tunguska = Tunguska, Podkamennaya →, U.S.S.R. 57 C10 61 36N 90 18 E
Stonyford, U.S.A. 144 F4 39 23N 122 33W
Stopnica, Poland 47 E7 50 27N 20 57 E
Stora Lulevatten, Sweden 12 C15 67 10N 19 30 E
Stora Sjöfallet, Sweden 12 C15 67 29N 18 40 E
Storavan, Sweden 12 D15 65 45N 18 10 E
Store Bælt, Denmark 15 J5 55 20N 11 0 E
Store Creek, Australia 117 B8 32 54 S 149 6 E
Store Heddinge, Denmark 15 J6 55 18N 12 23 E
Støren, Norway 14 A4 63 3N 10 18 E
Storm B., Australia 114 G4 43 10 S 147 30 E
Storm Lake, U.S.A. 138 D7 42 35N 95 11W
Stormberge, S. Africa 104 E4 31 16 S 26 17 E
Stormsrivier, S. Africa 104 E3 33 59 S 23 52 E
Stornoway, U.K. 18 C2 58 12N 6 23W
Storozhinets, U.S.S.R. 52 B1 48 14N 25 45 E
Storsjö, Sweden 14 B7 62 49N 13 5 E
Storsjøen, Hedmark, Norway 14 D5 60 20N 11 40 E
Storsjøen, Hedmark, Norway 14 C5 61 30N 11 14 E
Storsjön, Sweden 14 B7 62 50N 13 8 E
Storstrøms Amt. □, Denmark 15 K5 54 50N 11 45 E
Storuman, Sweden 12 D14 65 5N 17 10 E
Story City, U.S.A. 140 B3 42 11N 93 36W
Stoughton, Canada 131 D8 49 40N 103 0W
Stoughton, U.S.A. 140 B8 42 55N 88 59W
Stour →, Dorset, U.K. 17 G5 50 48N 2 7W
Stour →, Here. & Worcs., U.K. 17 E5 52 25N 2 13W
Stour →, Kent, U.K. 17 F9 51 15N 1 20 E
Stour →, Suffolk, U.K. 17 F9 51 55N 1 5 E
Stourbridge, U.K. 17 E5 52 28N 2 8W
Stout, L., Canada 131 C10 52 0N 94 40W
Stove Pipe Wells Village, U.S.A. 145 J9 36 35N 117 11W
Stowmarket, U.K. 17 E9 52 11N 1 0 E
Strabane, U.K. 19 B4 54 50N 7 28W
Strabane □, U.K. 19 B4 54 45N 7 25W
Stracin, Yugoslavia 42 E7 42 13N 22 2 E
Stradella, Italy 38 C6 45 4N 9 20 E
Strahan, Australia 114 G4 42 9 S 145 20 E
Strakonice, Czech. 30 B6 49 15N 13 53 E
Straldzha, Bulgaria 43 E11 42 35N 26 40 E
Stralsund, Germany 26 A9 54 17N 13 5 E
Strand, S. Africa 104 E2 34 9 S 18 48 E
Strangford L., U.K. 19 B6 54 30N 5 37W
Strängnäs, Sweden 14 E11 59 23N 17 2 E
Strangsville, U.S.A. 136 E3 41 19N 81 50W
Stranraer, U.K. 18 G4 54 54N 5 0W
Strasbourg, Canada 131 C8 51 4N 104 55W
Strasbourg, France 23 D14 48 35N 7 42 E
Strasburg, Germany 26 B9 53 30N 13 44 E
Strasburg, U.S.A. 138 B4 46 12N 100 9W
Strassen, Lux. 21 J8 49 37N 6 4 E
Stratford, N.S.W., Australia 117 B9 32 7 S 151 55 E
Stratford, Vic., Australia 117 D7 37 59 S 147 7 E
Stratford, Canada 128 D3 43 23N 81 0W
Stratford, N.Z. 118 F3 39 20 S 174 19 E
Stratford, Calif., U.S.A. 144 J7 36 10N 119 49W
Stratford, Conn., U.S.A. 137 E11 41 13N 73 8W
Stratford, Tex., U.S.A. 139 G3 36 20N 102 3W
Stratford-upon-Avon, U.K. 17 E6 52 12N 1 42W
Strath Spey, U.K. 18 D5 57 15N 3 40W
Strathalbyn, Australia 116 C3 35 13 S 138 53 E
Strathclyde □, U.K. 18 F4 56 0N 4 50W
Strathcona Prov. Park, Canada 130 D3 49 38N 125 40W
Strathmore, Australia 114 B3 17 50 S 142 35 E
Strathmore, Canada 130 C6 51 5N 113 18W
Strathmore, U.K. 18 E5 56 40N 3 4W
Strathmore, U.S.A. 144 J7 36 9N 119 4W
Strathnaver, Canada 130 C4 53 20N 122 33W
Strathpeffer, U.K. 18 D4 57 35N 4 32W
Strathroy, Canada 128 D3 42 58N 81 38W
Strathy Pt., U.K. 18 C4 58 35N 4 3W
Stratton, U.S.A. 138 F3 39 20N 102 36W
Straubing, Germany 27 G8 48 53N 12 35 E
Straumnes, Iceland 12 C2 66 26N 23 8W
Strausberg, Germany 26 C9 52 40N 13 52 E
Strawberry Point, U.S.A. 140 B5 42 41N 91 32W
Strawberry Res., U.S.A. 142 F8 40 10N 111 7W
Strawn, U.S.A. 139 J5 32 36N 98 30W
Strážnice, Czech. 31 C10 48 54N 17 19 E
Streaky B., Australia 115 E1 32 48 S 134 13 E
Streaky Bay, Australia 115 E1 32 51 S 134 18 E
Streator, U.S.A. 138 E10 41 9N 88 52W
Středočeský □, Czech. 30 B7 49 55N 14 30 E
Středoslovenský □, Czech. 31 C12 48 30N 19 15 E
Streé, Belgium 21 H4 50 17N 4 18 E
Streeter, U.S.A. 138 B5 46 39N 99 21W
Streetsville, Canada 136 C5 43 35N 79 42W
Strehaia, Romania 46 E4 44 37N 23 10 E
Strelcha, Bulgaria 43 E9 42 30N 24 19 E
Strelka, U.S.S.R. 57 D10 58 5N 93 3 E
Streng →, Cambodia 76 F4 13 12N 103 37 E
Strésa, Italy 38 C5 45 52N 8 28 E
Strezhevoy, U.S.S.R. 56 C8 60 42N 77 34 E
Stříbro, Czech. 30 B6 49 44N 13 2 E
Strickland →, Papua N. G. 120 D1 7 35 S 141 36 E
Strijen, Neths. 20 E5 51 45N 4 33 E
Strimón →, Greece 44 D5 40 46N 23 51 E
Strimonikós Kólpos, Greece 44 D6 40 33N 24 0 E
Stroeder, Argentina 160 B4 40 12 S 62 37W
Strofádhes, Greece 45 G3 37 15N 21 0 E
Strömbacka, Sweden 14 C10 61 58N 16 44 E
Strómboli, Italy 41 D8 38 48N 15 12 E
Stromeferry, U.K. 18 D3 57 20N 5 33W
Stromness, U.K. 18 C5 58 58N 3 18W
Ströms vattudal, Sweden 12 D13 64 15N 14 55 E
Strömstad, Sweden 13 G11 58 55N 11 15 E
Strömsund, Sweden 12 E13 63 51N 15 33 E
Stronghurst, U.S.A. 140 D6 40 45N 90 55W
Stróngoli, Italy 41 C10 39 16N 17 2 E
Stronsay, U.K. 18 B6 59 8N 2 38W
Stronsburg, U.S.A. 138 E6 41 7N 97 36W
Stropkov, Czech. 31 B14 49 13N 21 39 E
Stroud, U.K. 17 F5 51 44N 2 12W
Stroud Road, Australia 117 B9 32 18 S 151 57 E
Stroudsburg, U.S.A. 137 F9 40 59N 75 15W
Stroumbi, Cyprus 32 E11 34 53N 32 29 E
Struer, Denmark 15 H2 56 30N 8 35 E
Struga, Yugoslavia 42 F5 41 13N 20 44 E
Strugi Krasnyye, U.S.S.R. 50 B6 58 21N 29 1 E
Strumica, Yugoslavia 42 F7 41 28N 22 41 E
Strumica →, Europe 42 F8 41 20N 23 22 E
Struthers, Canada 128 C2 48 41N 85 51W
Struthers, U.S.A. 136 E4 41 6N 80 38W
Stryama, Bulgaria 43 E9 42 16N 24 54 E
Stryi, U.S.S.R. 50 G3 49 16N 23 48 E
Stryker, U.S.A. 142 B6 48 40N 114 44W
Stryków, Poland 47 D6 51 55N 19 33 E
Strzegom, Poland 47 E3 50 58N 16 20 E
Strzelce Krajeńskie, Poland 47 C2 52 52N 15 33 E
Strzelce Opolskie, Poland 47 E5 50 31N 18 18 E
Strzelecki Cr. →, Australia 115 D2 29 37 S 139 59 E
Strzelin, Poland 47 E4 50 46N 17 2 E
Strzelno, Poland 47 C5 52 35N 18 9 E
Strzybnica, Poland 47 E5 50 28N 18 48 E
Strzyżów, Poland 31 B14 49 52N 21 47 E
Stuart, Fla., U.S.A. 135 M5 27 11N 80 12W
Stuart, Iowa, U.S.A. 140 C2 41 30N 94 19W
Stuart, Nebr., U.S.A. 138 D5 42 39N 99 8W
Stuart →, Canada 130 C4 54 0N 123 35W
Stuart Bluff Ra., Australia 112 D5 22 50 S 131 52 E
Stuart L., Canada 130 C4 54 30N 124 30W
Stuart Mts., N.Z. 119 F2 45 2 S 167 39 E
Stuart Ra., Australia 115 D1 29 10 S 134 56 E
Stubbekøbing, Denmark 15 K6 54 53N 12 9 E
Stuben, Austria 30 D3 47 10N 10 8 E
Studen Kladenets, Yazovir, Bulgaria 43 F10 41 37N 25 30 E
Studholme Junc., N.Z. 119 E6 44 42 S 171 9 E
Stugun, Sweden 14 A9 63 10N 15 40 E
Stull, L., Canada 128 B1 54 24N 92 34W
Stung Treng, Cambodia 76 F5 13 31N 105 58 E
Stupart →, Canada 131 B10 56 0N 93 25W
Stupino, U.S.S.R. 51 D11 54 57N 38 2 E
Sturgeon B., Canada 131 C9 52 0N 97 50W
Sturgeon Bay, U.S.A. 134 C2 44 52N 87 20W
Sturgeon Falls, Canada 128 C4 46 25N 79 57W
Sturgeon L., Alta., Canada 130 B5 55 6N 117 32W
Sturgeon L., Ont., Canada 128 C1 50 0N 90 45W
Sturgeon L., Ont., Canada 136 B6 44 28N 78 43W
Sturgis, Mich., U.S.A. 141 C11 41 50N 85 25W
Sturgis, S. Dak., U.S.A. 138 C3 44 25N 103 30W
Štúrovo, Czech. 31 D11 47 48N 18 41 E
Sturt Cr. →, Australia 112 C4 19 8 S 127 50 E
Sturt Creek, Australia 112 C4 19 12 S 128 8 E
Sturts Meadows, Australia 116 A4 31 18 S 141 42 E
Stutterheim, S. Africa 104 E4 32 33 S 27 28 E
Stuttgart, Germany 27 G5 48 46N 9 10 E
Stuttgart, U.S.A. 139 H9 34 30N 91 33W
Stuyvesant, U.S.A. 137 D11 42 23N 73 45W
Stykkishólmur, Iceland 12 D2 65 2N 22 40W
Styr →, U.S.S.R. 50 E5 52 7N 26 35 E
Styria = Steiermark □, Austria 30 D8 47 26N 15 0 E
Su-no-Saki, Japan 63 C11 34 58N 139 45 E
Su Xian, China 66 H9 33 41N 116 59 E
Suakin, Sudan 94 D4 19 8N 37 20 E
Suan, N. Korea 67 E14 38 42N 126 22 E
Suapure →, Venezuela 152 B4 6 48N 67 1W
Suaqui, Mexico 146 B3 29 12N 109 41W
Suatá →, Venezuela 153 B4 7 52N 65 22W
Subang, Indonesia 71 G12 6 34 S 107 45 E
Subansiri →, India 78 B4 26 48N 93 50 E
Subayhah, Si. Arabia 84 D3 30 2N 38 50 E
Subi, Indonesia 75 B3 2 58N 108 50 E
Subiaco, Italy 39 G10 41 56N 13 5 E
Subotica, Yugoslavia 42 A4 46 6N 19 49 E
Success, Canada 131 C7 50 28N 108 6W
Suceava, Romania 46 B7 47 38N 26 16 E
Suceava □, Romania 46 B6 47 37N 25 40 E
Suceava →, Romania 46 B7 47 38N 26 16 E
Sucha-Beskidzka, Poland 31 B12 49 44N 19 35 E
Suchan, Poland 47 B2 53 18N 15 18 E
Suchan, U.S.S.R. 60 C6 43 8N 133 9 E
Suchedniów, Poland 47 D7 51 3N 20 49 E
Suchitoto, El Salv. 148 D2 13 56N 89 0W
Suchou = Suzhou, China 69 B13 31 19N 120 38 E
Süchow = Xuzhou, China 67 G9 34 18N 117 10 E
Suchowola, Poland 47 B10 53 33N 23 3 E
Sucio →, Colombia 152 B2 7 27N 77 7W
Suck →, Ireland 19 C3 53 17N 8 18W
Suckling, Mt., Papua N. G. 120 E5 9 49 S 148 53 E
Sucre, Bolivia 157 D4 19 0 S 65 15W
Sucre, Colombia 152 B3 8 49N 74 44W
Sucre □, Colombia 152 B2 8 50N 75 40W
Sucre □, Venezuela 153 A5 10 25N 63 30W
Sucuaro, Colombia 152 C4 4 34N 68 50W
Sućuraj, Yugoslavia 39 E14 43 10N 17 8 E
Sucuriju, Brazil 154 A2 1 39N 49 57W
Sucuriú →, Brazil 157 E7 20 47 S 51 38W
Sud, Pte., Canada 129 C7 49 3N 62 14W
Sud-Ouest, Pte. du, Canada 129 C7 49 23N 63 36W
Suda →, U.S.S.R. 51 B10 59 0N 37 40 E
Sudak, U.S.S.R. 52 D6 44 51N 34 57 E
Sudan, U.S.A. 139 H3 34 4N 102 32W
Sudan ■, Africa 95 E3 15 0N 30 0 E
Suday, U.S.S.R. 51 B13 59 0N 43 0 E
Sudbury, Canada 128 C3 46 30N 81 0W
Sudbury, U.K. 17 E8 52 2N 0 44 E
Sûdd, Sudan 95 F3 8 20N 30 0 E
Suddie, Guyana 153 B6 7 8N 58 29W
Süderbrarup, Germany 26 A5 54 38N 9 47 E
Süderlügum, Germany 26 A4 54 50N 8 55 E
Süderoog-Sand, Germany 26 A4 54 27N 8 30 E
Sudeten Mts. = Sudety, Europe 31 A9 50 20N 16 45 E
Sudety, Europe 31 A9 50 20N 16 45 E
Sudi, Tanzania 107 E4 10 11 S 39 57 E
Sudirman, Pegunungan, Indonesia 71 E9 4 30 S 137 0 E
Suditi, Romania 46 E8 44 35N 27 38 E
Sudogda, U.S.S.R. 51 D12 55 55N 40 50 E
Sudr, Egypt 94 J8 29 40N 32 42 E
Sudzha, U.S.S.R. 50 F9 51 14N 35 17 E
Sueca, Spain 35 F4 39 12N 0 21W
Suedala, Sweden 15 J7 55 30N 13 15 E
Suez = El Suweis, Egypt 94 J8 29 58N 32 31 E
Suez, G. of = Suweis, Khalîg el, Egypt 94 J8 28 40N 33 0 E
Suez Canal = Suweis, Qanâl es, Egypt 94 H8 31 0N 32 20 E
Suffield, Canada 131 C6 50 12N 111 10W
Suffolk, U.S.A. 134 G7 36 47N 76 33W
Suffolk □, U.K. 17 E9 52 16N 1 0 E
Sufi-Kurgan, U.S.S.R. 55 C6 40 2N 73 30 E
Suga no-Sen, Japan 62 B6 35 25N 134 25 E
Sugag, Romania 46 D4 45 47N 23 37 E
Sugar →, Ill., U.S.A. 140 B7 42 25N 89 15W
Sugar →, Ind., U.S.A. 141 E9 39 50N 87 23W
Sugar City, U.S.A. 138 F3 38 18N 103 38W
Sugar Cr. →, U.S.A. 140 D7 40 12N 89 41W
Suğla Gölü, Turkey 88 E5 37 20N 32 0 E
Sugluk = Saglouc, Canada 127 B12 62 14N 75 38W
Sugny, Belgium 21 J5 49 49N 4 54 E
Suhaia, L., Romania 46 F6 43 45N 25 15 E
Suhār, Oman 85 E8 24 20N 56 40 E
Sühbaatar □, Mongolia 66 B8 45 30N 114 0 E
Suhl, Germany 26 E6 50 35N 10 40 E
Suhr, Switz. 28 B6 47 22N 8 5 E
Şuhut, Turkey 88 D4 38 31N 30 32 E
Sui Xian, Henan, China 66 G8 34 25N 115 2 E
Sui Xian, Henan, China 69 B9 31 42N 113 24 E
Suiá Missu →, Brazil 157 C7 11 13 S 53 15W
Suichang, China 69 C12 28 29N 119 15 E
Suichuan, China 69 D10 26 20N 114 32 E
Suide, China 66 F6 37 30N 110 12 E
Suifenhe, China 67 B16 44 25N 131 10 E
Suihua, China 65 B7 46 32N 126 55 E
Suijiang, China 68 C4 28 40N 103 59 E
Suining, Hunan, China 69 D8 26 35N 110 10 E
Suining, Jiangsu, China 67 H9 33 56N 117 58 E
Suining, Sichuan, China 68 B5 30 26N 105 35 E
Suiping, China 66 H7 33 10N 113 59 E
Suippes, France 23 C11 49 8N 4 30 E
Suita, Japan 63 C7 34 45N 135 32 E
Suixi, China 69 G8 21 19N 110 18 E
Suiyang, Guizhou, China 68 D6 27 58N 107 18 E
Suiyang, Heilongjiang, China 67 B16 44 30N 130 56 E
Suizhong, China 67 D11 40 21N 120 20 E
Sujangarh, India 80 F6 27 42N 74 31 E
Sujica, Yugoslavia 42 D2 43 52N 17 11 E
Sukabumi, Indonesia 71 G12 6 56 S 106 50 E
Sukadana, Kalimantan, Indonesia 70 E4 1 10 S 110 0 E
Sukadana, Sumatera, Indonesia 70 F3 5 5 S 105 33 E
Sukagawa, Japan 61 F10 37 17N 140 23 E
Sukaraja, Indonesia 70 E4 2 28 S 110 25 E
Sukarnapura = Jayapura, Indonesia 71 E10 2 28 S 140 38 E
Sukchŏn, N. Korea 67 E13 39 22N 125 35 E
Sukhindol, Bulgaria 43 D10 43 11N 25 10 E
Sukhinichi, U.S.S.R. 50 D9 54 8N 35 10 E
Sukhona →, U.S.S.R. 48 C6 59 40N 39 45 E
Sukhothai, Thailand 76 D2 17 1N 99 49 E
Sukhoy Log, U.S.S.R. 54 C8 56 55N 62 1 E
Sukhumi, U.S.S.R. 53 E9 43 0N 41 0 E
Sukkur, Pakistan 79 D3 27 42N 68 54 E
Sukkur Barrage, Pakistan 80 F3 27 40N 68 50 E
Sukma, India 82 E5 18 24N 81 45 E
Sukovo, Yugoslavia 42 D7 43 4N 22 37 E
Sukumo, Japan 62 E4 32 56N 132 44 E
Sukunka →, Canada 130 B4 55 45N 121 15W
Sul, Canal do, Brazil 154 B2 0 10 S 48 30W

Taninges 271

T

't Harde, *Neths.* **20 D7** 52 24N 5 54 E
't Zandt, *Neths.* **20 B9** 53 22N 6 46 E
Ta Khli Khok, *Thailand* **76 E3** 15 18N 100 20 E
Ta Lai, *Vietnam* **77 G6** 11 24N 107 23 E
Tabacal, *Argentina* **158 A3** 23 15 S 64 15W
Tabaco, *Phil.* **71 B6** 13 22N 123 44 E
Tabagné, *Ivory C.* **100 D4** 7 59N 3 4W
Ţābah, *Si. Arabia* **84 E4** 26 55N 42 38 E
Tabajara, *Brazil* **157 B5** 8 56 S 62 8W
Tabalos, *Peru* **156 B2** 6 26 S 76 37W
Tabar Is., *Papua N. G.* **120 B7** 2 50 S 152 0 E
Tabarca, I. de, *Spain* **35 G4** 38 17N 0 30W
Tabarka, *Tunisia* **96 A1** 36 56N 8 46 E
Ţabas, *Khorāsān, Iran* **85 C9** 32 48N 60 12 E
Ţabas, *Khorāsān, Iran* **85 C8** 33 35N 56 55 E
Tabasará, Serranía de, *Panama* **148 E3** 8 35N 81 40W
Tabasco □, *Mexico* **147 D6** 17 45N 93 30W
Tabatinga, Serra da, *Brazil* **154 D3** 10 30 S 44 0W
Tabayin, *Burma* **78 D5** 22 42N 95 20 E
Tabāzīn, *Iran* **85 D8** 31 12N 57 54 E
Tabelbala, Kahal de, *Algeria* **99 C4** 28 47N 2 0W
Taber, *Canada* **130 D6** 49 47N 112 8W
Tabernas, *Spain* **35 H2** 37 4N 2 26W
Tabernes de Valldigna, *Spain* **35 F4** 39 5N 0 13W
Tabi, *Angola* **103 D2** 8 10 S 13 18 E
Tabira, *Brazil* **154 C4** 7 35 S 37 33W
Tablas, *Phil.* **71 B6** 12 25N 122 2 E
Table B. = Tafelbaai, *S. Africa* **104 E2** 33 35 S 18 25 E
Table B., *Canada* **129 B8** 53 40N 56 25W
Table Grove, *U.S.A.* **140 D6** 40 20N 90 27W
Table Mt., *S. Africa* **104 E2** 34 0 S 18 22 E
Tableland, *Australia* **112 C4** 17 16 S 126 51 E
Tabletop, Mt., *Australia* **114 C4** 23 24 S 147 11 E
Tábor, *Czech.* **30 B7** 49 25N 14 39 E
Tabora, *Tanzania* **106 D3** 5 2 S 32 50 E
Tabora □, *Tanzania* **106 D3** 5 0 S 33 0 E
Tabory, *U.S.S.R.* **54 B9** 58 31N 64 33 E
Tabou, *Ivory C.* **100 E3** 4 30N 7 20W
Tabrīz, *Iran* **84 B5** 38 7N 46 20 E
Tabuaeran, *Pac. Oc.* **123 G12** 3 51N 159 22W
Tabuenca, *Spain* **34 D3** 41 42N 1 33W
Tabūk, *Si. Arabia* **84 D3** 28 23N 36 36 E
Tabwemasana, Mt., *Vanuatu* **121 E4** 15 20 S 166 44 E
Tacámbaro de Codallos, *Mexico* **146 D4** 19 14N 101 28W
Tacheng, *China* **64 B3** 46 40N 82 58 E
Tachibana-Wan, *Japan* **62 E2** 32 45N 130 7 E
Tachikawa, *Japan* **63 B11** 35 42N 139 25 E
Tach'ing Shan = Daqing Shan, *China* **66 D6** 40 40N 111 0 E
Táchira □, *Venezuela* **152 B3** 8 7N 72 15W
Tachov, *Czech.* **30 B5** 49 47N 12 39 E
Tácina →, *Italy* **41 D9** 38 57N 16 55 E
Tacloban, *Phil.* **71 B6** 11 15N 124 58 E
Tacna, *Peru* **156 D3** 18 0 S 70 20W
Tacna □, *Peru* **156 D3** 17 40 S 70 20W
Tacoma, *U.S.A.* **144 C4** 47 15N 122 30W
Tacuarembó, *Uruguay* **159 C4** 31 45 S 56 0W
Tacutu →, *Brazil* **153 C5** 3 1N 60 29W
Tademaït, Plateau du, *Algeria* **99 C5** 28 30N 2 30 E
Tadent, O. →, *Algeria* **99 D6** 22 25N 6 40 E
Tadjerdjeri, O. →, *Algeria* **99 C6** 26 0N 8 0 E
Tadjerouna, *Algeria* **99 B5** 33 31N 2 3 E
Tadjettaret, O. →, *Algeria* **99 D6** 21 20N 7 22 E
Tadjmout, *Oasis, Algeria* **99 B5** 33 52N 2 30 E
Tadjmout, *Saoura, Algeria* **99 C5** 25 37N 3 48 E
Tadjoura, *Djibouti* **90 E3** 11 50N 42 55 E
Tadjoura, Golfe de, *Djibouti* **95 E5** 11 50N 43 0 E
Tadmor, *N.Z.* **119 B7** 41 27 S 172 45 E
Tadotsu, *Japan* **62 C5** 34 16N 133 45 E
Tadoule, L., *Canada* **131 B9** 58 36N 98 20W
Tadoussac, *Canada* **129 C6** 48 11N 69 42W
Tadzhik S.S.R. □, *U.S.S.R.* **55 D5** 38 30N 70 0 E
Taechŏn-ni, *S. Korea* **67 F14** 36 21N 126 36 E
Taegu, *S. Korea* **67 G15** 35 50N 128 37 E
Taegwan, *N. Korea* **67 D13** 40 13N 125 12 E
Taejŏn, *S. Korea* **67 F14** 36 20N 127 28 E
Tafalla, *Spain* **34 C3** 42 30N 1 41W
Tafar, *Sudan* **95 F2** 6 52N 28 15 E
Tafassasset, O. →, *Algeria* **99 D6** 22 0N 9 57 E
Tafelbaai, *S. Africa* **104 E2** 33 35 S 18 25 E
Tafelney, C., *Morocco* **98 B3** 31 3N 9 51W
Tafermaar, *Indonesia* **71 F8** 6 47 S 134 10 E
Taffermit, *Morocco* **98 C3** 29 37N 9 15W
Tafí Viejo, *Argentina* **158 B2** 26 43 S 65 17W
Tafīhān, *Iran* **85 D7** 29 25N 52 39 E
Tafiré, *Ivory C.* **100 D3** 9 4N 5 4W
Tafnidilt, *Morocco* **98 C2** 28 47N 10 58W
Tafraoute, *Morocco* **98 C3** 29 50N 8 58W
Taft, *Iran* **85 D7** 31 45N 54 14 E
Taft, *Phil.* **71 B7** 11 57N 125 30 E
Taft, *Calif., U.S.A.* **145 K7** 35 9N 119 28W
Taft, *Tex., U.S.A.* **139 M6** 27 58N 97 23W
Taga, *W. Samoa* **121 W23** 13 46 S 172 28W
Taga Dzong, *Bhutan* **78 B2** 27 5N 89 55 E
Taganrog, *U.S.S.R.* **53 C8** 47 12N 38 50 E
Taganrogskiy Zaliv, *U.S.S.R.* **52 C8** 47 0N 38 30 E
Tagânt, *Mauritania* **100 B2** 18 20N 11 0W
Tagap Ga, *Burma* **78 B6** 26 56N 96 13 E
Tagbilaran, *Phil.* **71 C6** 9 39N 123 51 E
Tage, *Papua N. G.* **120 D2** 6 19 S 143 20 E
Tággia, *Italy* **38 E4** 43 52N 7 50 E
Taghrīfat, *Libya* **96 C3** 29 5N 17 26 E
Taghzout, *Morocco* **98 B4** 33 30N 4 49W
Tagish, *Canada* **130 A2** 60 19N 134 16W
Tagish L., *Canada* **130 A2** 60 10N 134 20W
Tagliacozzo, *Italy* **39 F10** 42 4N 13 13 E
Tagliamento →, *Italy* **39 C10** 45 38N 13 5 E
Táglio di Po, *Italy* **39 D9** 45 0N 12 12 E
Tagna, *Colombia* **152 D3** 2 24 S 70 37W
Tagomago, I. de, *Spain* **33 B8** 39 2N 1 39 E
Taguatinga, *Brazil* **155 D3** 12 16 S 42 26W
Tagula, *Papua N. G.* **120 F7** 11 22 S 153 15 E
Tagula I., *Papua N. G.* **120 F7** 11 30 S 153 30 E
Tagum, *Phil.* **71 C7** 7 33N 125 53 E
Tagus = Tejo →, *Europe* **37 G1** 38 40N 9 24W
Tahakopa, *N.Z.* **119 G4** 46 30 S 169 23 E
Tahala, *Morocco* **98 B4** 34 0N 4 28W
Tahan, Gunong, *Malaysia* **77 K4** 4 34N 102 17 E
Tahānah-ye sūr Gol, *Afghan.* **79 C2** 31 43N 67 53 E
Tahara, *Japan* **63 C9** 34 40N 137 16 E
Tahat, *Algeria* **99 D6** 23 18N 5 33 E
Tāherī, *Iran* **85 E7** 27 43N 52 20 E
Tahiti, *Pac. Oc.* **123 J13** 17 37 S 149 27W
Tahoe, L., *U.S.A.* **144 G6** 39 0N 120 9W
Tahoe City, *U.S.A.* **144 F6** 39 12N 120 9W
Taholah, *U.S.A.* **144 C2** 47 21N 124 17W
Tahora, *N.Z.* **118 F3** 39 2 S 174 49 E
Tahoua, *Niger* **101 C6** 14 57N 5 16 E
Tahta, *Egypt* **94 B3** 26 44N 31 32 E
Tahtali Dağlari, *Turkey* **88 D7** 38 20N 36 0 E
Tahuamanu →, *Bolivia* **156 C4** 11 6 S 67 36W
Tahulandang, *Indonesia* **71 D7** 2 27N 125 23 E
Tahuna, *Indonesia* **71 D7** 3 38N 125 30 E
Taï, *Ivory C.* **100 D3** 5 55N 7 30W
Tai Shan, *China* **67 F9** 36 25N 117 20 E
Tai Xian, *China* **69 A13** 32 30N 120 7 E
Tai'an, *China* **67 F9** 36 12N 117 8 E
Taibei, *Taiwan* **69 E13** 25 4N 121 29 E
Taibique, *Canary Is.* **33 G2** 27 42N 17 58W
Taibus Qi, *China* **66 D8** 41 54N 115 22 E
T'aichung = Taizhong, *Taiwan* **69 E13** 24 12N 120 35 E
Taidong, *Taiwan* **69 F13** 22 43N 121 9 E
Taieri →, *N.Z.* **119 G5** 46 3 S 170 12 E
Taiga Madema, *Libya* **96 D3** 23 46N 15 25 E
Taigu, *China* **66 F7** 37 28N 112 30 E
Taihang Shan, *China* **66 G7** 36 0N 113 30 E
Taihape, *N.Z.* **118 F4** 39 41 S 175 48 E
Taihe, *Anhui, China* **66 H8** 33 20N 115 42 E
Taihe, *Jiangxi, China* **69 D10** 26 47N 114 52 E
Taihu, *China* **69 B11** 30 22N 116 20 E
Taijiang, *China* **68 D7** 26 39N 108 21 E
Taikang, *China* **66 G8** 34 5N 114 50 E
Taikkyi, *Burma* **78 G6** 17 20N 96 0 E
Tailem Bend, *Australia* **116 C3** 35 12 S 139 29 E
Tailfingen, *Germany* **27 G5** 48 15N 9 1 E
Taimyr = Taymyr, Poluostrov, *U.S.S.R.* **57 B11** 75 0N 100 0 E
Taimyr, Oz., *U.S.S.R.* **57 B11** 74 20N 102 0 E
Tain, *U.K.* **18 D4** 57 49N 4 4W
Tainan, *Taiwan* **69 F13** 23 17N 120 18 E
Taínaron, Ákra, *Greece* **45 H4** 36 22N 22 27 E
Tainggyo, *Burma* **78 G5** 17 49N 94 29 E
Tainting, *China* **69 D11** 26 54N 117 9 E
Taintignies, *Belgium* **21 G2** 50 33N 3 22 E
Taiobeiras, *Brazil* **155 E3** 15 49 S 42 14W
T'aipei = Taibei, *Taiwan* **69 E13** 25 4N 121 29 E
Taiping, *China* **69 B12** 30 15N 118 6 E
Taiping, *Malaysia* **77 K3** 4 51N 100 44 E
Taipingzhen, *China* **66 H6** 33 35N 111 42 E
Taipu, *Brazil* **154 C4** 5 37 S 35 36W
Taisha, *Japan* **62 B4** 35 24N 132 40 E
Taishan, *China* **69 F9** 22 14N 112 41 E
Taishun, *China* **69 D12** 27 30N 119 42 E
Taita □, *Kenya* **106 C4** 4 0 S 38 30 E
Taita Hills, *Kenya* **106 C4** 3 25 S 38 15 E
Taitao, C., *Chile* **160 C1** 45 53 S 75 5W
Taitao, Pen. de, *Chile* **160 C2** 46 30 S 75 0W
Taivalkoski, *Finland* **12 D20** 65 33N 28 12 E
Taiwan ■, *Asia* **69 F13** 23 30N 121 0 E
Taiwan Shan, *Taiwan* **69 F13** 23 40N 121 20 E
Taixing, *China* **69 A13** 32 11N 120 0 E
Taïyetos Óros, *Greece* **45 H4** 37 0N 22 23 E
Taiyiba, *Israel* **91 C4** 32 36N 35 27 E
Taiyuan, *China* **66 F7** 37 52N 112 33 E
Taizhong, *Taiwan* **69 E13** 24 12N 120 35 E
Taizhou, *China* **69 A12** 32 28N 119 55 E
Taizhou Liedao, *China* **69 C13** 28 30N 121 55 E
Ta'izz, *Yemen* **86 D4** 13 35N 44 2 E
Tājābād, *Iran* **85 D7** 30 2N 54 24 E
Tajapuru, Furo do, *Brazil* **154 B1** 1 50 S 50 25W
Tajarḥī, *Libya* **96 D2** 24 21N 14 28 E
Tajima, *Japan* **61 F9** 37 12N 139 46 E
Tajimi, *Japan* **63 B9** 35 19N 137 8 E
Tajo = Tejo →, *Europe* **37 G1** 38 40N 9 24W
Tajrīsh, *Iran* **85 C6** 35 48N 51 25 E
Tājūrā, *Libya* **96 B2** 32 51N 13 21 E
Tak, *Thailand* **76 D2** 16 52N 99 8 E
Takāb, *Iran* **84 B5** 36 24N 47 7 E
Takachiho, *Japan* **62 E3** 32 42N 131 18 E
Takada, *Japan* **61 F9** 37 7N 138 15 E
Takahagi, *Japan* **61 F10** 36 43N 140 45 E
Takahashi, *Japan* **62 C5** 34 51N 133 39 E
Takaka, *N.Z.* **119 A7** 40 51 S 172 50 E
Takamatsu, *Japan* **62 C6** 34 20N 134 5 E
Takanabe, *Japan* **62 E3** 32 8N 131 30 E
Takaoka, *Japan* **63 A9** 36 47N 137 0 E
Takapau, *N.Z.* **118 G5** 40 2 S 176 21 E
Takapuna, *N.Z.* **118 C3** 36 47 S 174 47 E
Takasago, *Japan* **62 C6** 34 45N 134 48 E
Takasaki, *Japan* **63 A11** 36 20N 139 0 E
Takase, *Japan* **62 C5** 34 7N 133 48 E
Takatsuki, *Japan* **63 C7** 34 51N 135 37 E
Takaungu, *Kenya* **106 C4** 3 38 S 39 52 E
Takawa, *Japan* **62 D2** 33 38N 130 51 E
Takayama, *Japan* **63 A9** 36 18N 137 11 E
Takayama-Bonchi, *Japan* **63 B9** 36 0N 137 18 E
Take-Shima, *Japan* **61 J5** 30 49N 130 26 E
Takefu, *Japan* **63 B8** 35 50N 136 10 E
Takehara, *Japan* **62 C4** 34 21N 132 55 E
Takengon, *Indonesia* **70 D1** 4 45N 96 50 E
Takeo, *Cambodia* **77 G5** 10 59N 104 47 E
Takeo, *Japan* **62 D2** 33 12N 130 1 E
Tåkern, *Sweden* **15 F8** 58 22N 14 45 E
Tākestān, *Iran* **85 C6** 36 0N 49 40 E
Taketa, *Japan* **62 E3** 32 58N 131 24 E
Takh, *India* **81 C7** 33 6N 77 32 E
Takhār □, *Afghan.* **79 A3** 36 40N 70 0 E
Takhman, *Cambodia* **77 G5** 11 29N 104 57 E
Taki, *Papua N. G.* **120 D8** 6 29 S 155 52 E
Takikawa, *Japan* **60 C10** 43 33N 141 54 E
Takla L., *Canada* **130 B3** 55 15N 125 45W
Takla Landing, *Canada* **130 B3** 55 30N 125 50W
Takla Makan = Taklamakan Shamo, *China* **58 F12** 38 0N 83 0 E
Taklamakan Shamo, *China* **58 F12** 38 0N 83 0 E
Taku, *Japan* **62 D2** 33 18N 130 3 E
Taku →, *Canada* **130 B2** 58 30N 133 50W
Takum, *Nigeria* **101 D6** 7 18N 9 36 E
Takuma, *Japan* **62 C5** 34 13N 133 40 E
Takundi, *Zaïre* **103 C3** 4 45 S 16 34 E
Takutu →, *Guyana* **153 C5** 3 1N 60 29W
Tal Halāl, *Iran* **85 D7** 28 54N 55 1 E
Tala, *Uruguay* **159 C4** 34 21 S 55 46W
Talagante, *Chile* **158 C1** 33 40 S 70 50W
Talaïnt, *Morocco* **98 C3** 29 41N 9 40W
Talak, *Niger* **101 B6** 18 0N 5 0 E
Talamanca, Cordillera de, *Cent. Amer.* **148 E3** 9 20N 83 20W
Talara, *Peru* **156 A1** 4 38 S 81 18W
Talas, *Turkey* **88 D6** 38 41N 35 33 E
Talas, *U.S.S.R.* **55 B6** 42 30N 72 13 E
Talas →, *U.S.S.R.* **55 B5** 44 0N 70 20 E
Talasea, *Papua N. G.* **120 C6** 5 20 S 150 2 E
Talasskiy, Khrebet, *U.S.S.R.* **55 B6** 42 15N 72 0 E
Talâta, *Egypt* **91 E1** 30 36N 32 20 E
Talata Mafara, *Nigeria* **101 C6** 12 38N 6 4 E
Talaud, Kepulauan, *Indonesia* **71 D7** 4 30N 127 10 E
Talaud Is. = Talaud, Kepulauan, *Indonesia* **71 D7** 4 30N 127 10 E
Talavera de la Reina, *Spain* **36 F6** 39 55N 4 46W
Talawana, *Australia* **112 D3** 22 51 S 121 9 E
Talawgyi, *Burma* **78 C6** 25 4N 97 19 E
Talayan, *Phil.* **71 C6** 6 52N 124 24 E
Talbert, Sillon de, *France* **22 D3** 48 53N 3 5W
Talbot, C., *Australia* **112 B4** 13 48 S 126 43 E
Talbragar →, *Australia* **117 B8** 32 12 S 148 37 E
Talca, *Chile* **158 D1** 35 28 S 71 40W
Talca □, *Chile* **158 D1** 35 20 S 71 46W
Talcahuano, *Chile* **158 D1** 36 40 S 73 10W
Talcher, *India* **82 D7** 21 0N 85 18 E
Talcho, *Niger* **101 C5** 14 44N 3 28 E
Taldy Kurgan, *U.S.S.R.* **56 E8** 45 10N 78 45 E
Talesh, *Iran* **85 B6** 37 58N 48 58 E
Ţalesh, Kūhhā-ye, *Iran* **85 B6** 39 0N 48 30 E
Talgar, *U.S.S.R.* **55 B8** 43 19N 77 15 E
Talgar, Pic, *U.S.S.R.* **55 B8** 43 5N 77 20 E
Talguharai, *Sudan* **94 D4** 18 19N 35 56 E
Tali Post, *Sudan* **95 F3** 5 55N 30 44 E
Taliabu, *Indonesia* **71 E6** 1 45 S 124 55 E
Talibon, *Phil.* **71 B6** 10 9N 124 20 E
Talibong, Ko, *Thailand* **77 J2** 7 15N 99 23 E
Talihina, *U.S.A.* **139 H7** 34 45N 95 1W
Talikota, *India* **83 F3** 16 29N 76 17 E
Talimardzhan, *U.S.S.R.* **55 D2** 38 23N 65 37 E
Talitsa, *U.S.S.R.* **54 C8** 57 0N 63 43 E
Taliwang, *Indonesia* **70 F5** 8 50 S 116 55 E
Tall 'Asūr, *Jordan* **91 D4** 31 59N 35 17 E
Tall Kalakh, *Syria* **91 A5** 34 41N 36 15 E
Talla, *Egypt* **94 J7** 28 5N 30 43 E
Talladega, *U.S.A.* **135 J2** 33 28N 86 2W
Tallahassee, *U.S.A.* **135 K3** 30 25N 84 15W
Tallangatta, *Australia* **117 D7** 36 15 S 147 19 E
Tallarook, *Australia* **117 D6** 37 5 S 145 6 E
Tallawang, *Australia* **117 B8** 32 12 S 149 28 E
Tallering Pk., *Australia* **113 E2** 28 6 S 115 37 E
Tallinn, *U.S.S.R.* **50 B4** 59 22N 24 48 E
Tallulah, *U.S.A.* **139 J9** 32 25N 91 12W
Tălmaciu, *Romania* **46 D5** 45 38N 24 19 E
Talmest, *Morocco* **98 B3** 31 48N 9 21W
Talmont, *France* **24 B2** 46 27N 1 37W
Talnoye, *U.S.S.R.* **52 B4** 48 50N 30 44 E
Taloda, *India* **82 D2** 21 34N 74 11 E
Talodi, *Sudan* **95 E3** 10 35N 30 22 E
Talovaya, *U.S.S.R.* **51 F12** 51 6N 40 45 E
Talpa de Allende, *Mexico* **146 C4** 20 23N 104 51W
Tālqān, *Afghan.* **79 A3** 36 44N 69 33 E
Talsi, *U.S.S.R.* **50 C3** 57 10N 22 30 E
Talsinnt, *Morocco* **99 B4** 32 33N 3 27W
Taltal, *Chile* **158 B1** 25 23 S 70 33W
Taltson →, *Canada* **130 A6** 61 24N 112 46W
Talwood, *Australia* **115 D4** 28 29 S 149 29 E
Talyawalka Cr. →, *Australia* **116 B5** 32 28 S 142 22 E
Tam Chau, *Vietnam* **77 G5** 10 48N 105 12 E
Tam Ky, *Vietnam* **76 E7** 15 34N 108 29 E
Tam Quan, *Vietnam* **76 E7** 14 35N 109 3 E
Tama, *U.S.A.* **140 C4** 41 58N 92 35W
Tamala, *Australia* **113 E1** 26 42 S 113 47 E
Tamalameque, *Colombia* **152 B3** 8 52N 73 49W
Tamale, *Ghana* **101 D4** 9 22N 0 50W
Taman, *U.S.S.R.* **52 D7** 45 14N 36 41 E
Tamana, *Japan* **62 E2** 32 58N 130 32 E
Tamanar, *Morocco* **98 B3** 31 1N 9 46W
Tamano, *Japan* **62 C5** 34 29N 133 59 E
Tamanrasset, *Algeria* **99 D6** 22 50N 5 30 E
Tamanrasset, O. →, *Algeria* **99 D5** 22 0N 2 0 E
Tamanthi, *Burma* **78 C5** 25 19N 95 17 E
Tamaqua, *U.S.A.* **137 F9** 40 46N 75 58W
Tamar →, *U.K.* **17 G3** 50 33N 4 15W
Támara, *Colombia* **152 B3** 5 50N 72 10W
Tamarang, *Australia* **117 A9** 31 27 S 150 5 E
Tamarinda, *Spain* **33 B10** 39 55N 3 49 E
Tamarite de Litera, *Spain* **34 D5** 41 52N 0 25 E
Tamaroa, *U.S.A.* **140 F7** 38 8N 89 14W
Tamashima, *Japan* **62 C5** 34 32N 133 40 E
Tamási, *Hungary* **31 E11** 46 40N 18 18 E
Tamaské, *Niger* **101 C6** 14 49N 5 43 E
Tamaulipas □, *Mexico* **147 C5** 24 0N 99 0W
Tamaulipas, Sierra de, *Mexico* **147 C5** 23 30N 98 20W
Tamazula, *Mexico* **146 C3** 24 55N 106 58W
Tamazunchale, *Mexico* **147 C5** 21 16N 98 47W
Tamba-Dabatou, *Guinea* **100 C2** 11 50N 10 40W
Tambacounda, *Senegal* **100 C2** 13 45N 13 40W
Tambelan, Kepulauan, *Indonesia* **70 D3** 1 0N 107 30 E
Tambellup, *Australia* **113 F2** 34 4 S 117 37 E
Tambo, *Australia* **114 C4** 24 54 S 146 14 E
Tambo, *Peru* **156 C3** 12 57 S 74 1W
Tambo →, *Peru* **156 C3** 10 42 S 73 47W
Tambo de Mora, *Peru* **156 C2** 13 30 S 76 8W
Tambobamba, *Peru* **156 C3** 13 54 S 72 8W
Tambohorano, *Madag.* **105 B7** 17 30 S 43 58 E
Tambopata →, *Peru* **156 C4** 13 21 S 69 36W
Tambora, *Indonesia* **70 F5** 8 12 S 118 5 E
Tamboritha, Mt., *Australia* **117 D7** 37 31 S 146 40 E
Tambov, *U.S.S.R.* **51 E12** 52 45N 41 28 E
Tambre →, *Spain* **36 C2** 42 49N 8 53W
Tambuku, *Indonesia* **71 G15** 7 8 S 113 40 E
Tamburâ, *Sudan* **95 F2** 5 40N 27 25 E
Tâmchekket, *Mauritania* **100 B2** 17 25N 10 40W
Tamdybulak, *U.S.S.R.* **55 C2** 41 46N 64 36 E
Tame, *Colombia* **152 B3** 6 28N 71 44W
Tamega →, *Portugal* **36 D2** 41 5N 8 21W
Tamelelt, *Morocco* **98 B3** 31 50N 7 32W
Tamenglong, *India* **78 C4** 25 0N 93 35 E
Tamerlanovka, *U.S.S.R.* **55 B4** 42 36N 69 17 E
Tamerza, *Tunisia* **96 B1** 34 23N 7 58 E
Tamiahua, L. de, *Mexico* **147 C5** 21 30N 97 30W
Tamil Nadu □, *India* **83 J3** 11 0N 77 0 E
Tamines, *Belgium* **21 H5** 50 26N 4 36 E
Tamis →, *Yugoslavia* **46 E1** 44 51N 20 39 E
Tamluk, *India* **81 H12** 22 18N 87 58 E
Tammerfors = Tampere, *Finland* **13 F17** 61 30N 23 50 E
Tammisaari, *Finland* **13 G17** 60 0N 23 26 E
Tamo Abu, Pegunungan, *Malaysia* **70 D5** 3 10N 115 5 E
Tampa, *U.S.A.* **135 M4** 27 57N 82 38W
Tampa B., *U.S.A.* **135 M4** 27 40N 82 40W
Tampere, *Finland* **13 F17** 61 30N 23 50 E
Tampico, *Mexico* **147 C5** 22 20N 97 50W
Tampico, *U.S.A.* **140 C7** 41 38N 89 47W
Tampin, *Malaysia* **77 L4** 2 28N 102 13 E
Tamrah, *Si. Arabia* **86 B4** 20 24N 45 25 E
Tamri, *Morocco* **98 B3** 30 49N 9 50W
Tamrida = Qādib, *Yemen* **87 D6** 12 37N 53 57 E
Tamsalu, *U.S.S.R.* **50 B5** 59 11N 26 8 E
Tamsweg, *Austria* **30 D6** 47 7N 13 49 E
Tamuja →, *Spain* **37 F4** 39 38N 6 29W
Tamworth, *Australia* **117 A9** 31 7 S 150 58 E
Tamworth, *U.K.* **17 E6** 52 38N 1 41W
Tamyang, *S. Korea* **67 G14** 35 19N 126 59 E
Tan An, *Vietnam* **77 G6** 10 32N 106 25 E
Tan-tan, *Morocco* **98 C2** 28 29N 11 1W
Tana, *Norway* **12 A20** 70 26N 28 14 E
Tana →, *Kenya* **106 C5** 2 32 S 40 31 E
Tana →, *Norway* **12 A20** 70 30N 28 23 E
Tana, L., *Ethiopia* **95 E4** 13 5N 37 30 E
Tana River, *Kenya* **106 C4** 2 0 S 39 30 E
Tanabe, *Japan* **63 D7** 33 44N 135 22 E
Tanabi, *Brazil* **155 F2** 20 37 S 49 37W
Tanafjorden, *Norway* **12 A20** 70 45N 28 25 E
Tanaga, Pta., *Canary Is.* **33 G1** 27 42N 18 10W
Tanagro →, *Italy* **41 B8** 40 35N 15 25 E
Tanahbala, *Indonesia* **70 E1** 0 30 S 98 30 E
Tanahgrogot, *Indonesia* **70 E5** 1 55 S 116 15 E
Tanahjampea, *Indonesia* **71 F6** 7 10 S 120 35 E
Tanahmasa, *Indonesia* **70 E1** 0 12 S 98 39 E
Tanahmerah, *Indonesia* **71 F10** 6 5 S 140 16 E
Tanakura, *Japan* **61 F10** 37 10N 140 20 E
Tanami, *Australia* **112 C4** 19 59 S 129 43 E
Tanami Desert, *Australia* **112 C5** 18 50 S 132 0 E
Tanana, *U.S.A.* **126 B4** 65 10N 152 15W
Tanana →, *U.S.A.* **126 B4** 65 9N 151 55W
Tananarive = Antananarivo, *Madag.* **105 B8** 18 55 S 47 31 E
Tanannt, *Morocco* **98 B3** 31 54N 6 56W
Tánaro →, *Italy* **38 C5** 45 1N 8 47 E
Tanaunella, *Italy* **40 B2** 40 42N 9 45 E
Tanba-Sanchi, *Japan* **63 B7** 35 7N 135 48 E
Tanbar, *Australia* **114 D3** 25 51 S 141 55 E
Tancarville, *France* **22 C7** 49 29N 0 28 E
Tancheng, *China* **67 G10** 34 25N 118 20 E
Tanchŏn, *N. Korea* **67 D15** 40 27N 128 54 E
Tanda, *Ut. P., India* **81 F10** 26 33N 82 35 E
Tanda, *Ut. P., India* **81 E8** 28 57N 78 56 E
Tanda, *Ivory C.* **100 D4** 7 48N 3 10W
Tandag, *Phil.* **71 C7** 9 4N 126 9 E
Tandaia, *Tanzania* **107 D3** 9 25 S 34 15 E
Tăndărei, *Romania* **46 E8** 44 39N 27 40 E
Tandaué, *Angola* **103 F3** 16 58 S 18 5 E
Tandil, *Argentina* **158 D4** 37 15 S 59 6W
Tandil, Sa. del, *Argentina* **158 D4** 37 30 S 59 0W
Tandlianwala, *Pakistan* **80 D5** 31 3N 73 9 E
Tando Adam, *Pakistan* **79 D3** 25 45N 68 40 E
Tandou L., *Australia* **116 B5** 32 40 S 142 5 E
Tandsbyn, *Sweden* **14 A8** 63 3N 14 45 E
Tandur, *India* **82 E4** 19 11N 79 30 E
Tane-ga-Shima, *Japan* **61 J5** 30 30N 131 0 E
Taneatua, *N.Z.* **118 E6** 38 4 S 177 1 E
Tanen Tong Dan, *Burma* **76 D2** 16 30N 98 30 E
Tanew →, *Poland* **47 E9** 50 29N 22 16 E
Tanezrouft, *Algeria* **99 D5** 23 9N 0 11 E
Tang, Koh, *Cambodia* **77 G4** 10 16N 103 7 E
Tang Krasang, *Cambodia* **76 F5** 12 34N 105 3 E
Tanga, *Tanzania* **106 D4** 5 5 S 39 2 E
Tanga □, *Tanzania* **106 D4** 5 20 S 38 0 E
Tanga Is., *Papua N. G.* **120 B7** 3 20 S 153 15 E
Tangail, *Bangla.* **78 C2** 24 15N 89 55 E
Tanganyika, L., *Africa* **106 D3** 6 40 S 30 0 E
Tanger, *Morocco* **98 A3** 35 50N 5 49W
Tangerang, *Indonesia* **71 G12** 6 11 S 106 37 E
Tangerhütte, *Germany* **26 C7** 52 26N 11 50 E
Tangermünde, *Germany* **26 C7** 52 32N 11 57 E
Tanggu, *China* **67 E9** 39 2N 117 40 E
Tanggula Shan, *China* **64 C4** 32 40N 92 10 E
Tanghe, *China* **66 H7** 32 47N 112 50 E
Tangier = Tanger, *Morocco* **98 A3** 35 50N 5 49W
Tangkeleboke, *Indonesia* **72 B2** 3 10 S 121 30 E
Tangorin P.O., *Australia* **114 C3** 21 47 S 144 12 E
Tangshan, *China* **67 E10** 39 38N 118 10 E
Tangtou, *China* **67 G10** 35 28N 118 30 E
Tanguiéta, *Benin* **101 C5** 10 35N 1 21 E
Tangxi, *China* **69 C12** 29 3N 119 25 E
Tangyan He →, *China* **68 C7** 28 54N 108 19 E
Tanimbar, Kepulauan, *Indonesia* **71 F8** 7 30 S 131 30 E
Tanimbar Is. = Tanimbar, Kepulauan, *Indonesia* **71 F8** 7 30 S 131 30 E
Taninges, *France* **25 B10** 46 7N 6 36 E

Thomson's Falls 273

Telemark fylke □, *Norway* **14 E2** 59 25N 8 30 E
Telén, *Argentina* **158 D2** 36 15 S 65 31W
Telen →, *Indonesia* **75 C5** 0 10 S 117 20 E
Teleng, *Iran* **85 E9** 25 47N 61 3 E
Teleño, *Spain* **36 C4** 42 23N 6 22W
Teleorman □, *Romania* **46 F6** 44 0N 25 0 E
Teleorman →, *Romania* **46 E6** 44 15N 25 20 E
Teles Pires →, *Brazil* **157 B6** 7 21 S 58 3W
Telescope Peak, *U.S.A.* **145 J9** 36 6N 117 7W
Teletaye, *Mali* **101 B5** 16 31N 1 30 E
Telford, *U.K.* **16 E5** 52 42N 2 31W
Telfs, *Austria* **30 D4** 47 19N 11 4 E
Télimélé, *Guinea* **100 C2** 10 54N 13 2W
Telkwa, *Canada* **130 C3** 54 41N 127 5W
Tell City, *U.S.A.* **141 G10** 37 55N 86 44W
Tellicherry, *India* **83 J2** 11 45N 75 30 E
Tellin, *Belgium* **21 H6** 50 5N 5 13 E
Telluride, *U.S.A.* **143 H10** 37 58N 107 48W
Teloloapán, *Mexico* **147 D5** 18 21N 99 51W
Telpos Iz, *U.S.S.R.* **48 B10** 63 35N 57 30 E
Telsen, *Argentina* **160 B3** 42 30 S 66 50W
Telšiai, *U.S.S.R.* **50 D3** 55 59N 22 14 E
Teltow, *Germany* **26 C9** 52 24N 13 15 E
Teluk Anson, *Malaysia* **77 K3** 4 3N 101 0 E
Teluk Betung = Tanjungkarang Telukbetung, *Indonesia* **70 F3** 5 20 S 105 10 E
Teluk Intan = Teluk Anson, *Malaysia* **77 K3** 4 3N 101 0 E
Telukbutun, *Indonesia* **75 B3** 4 13N 108 12 E
Telukdalem, *Indonesia* **70 D1** 0 33N 97 50 E
Tema, *Ghana* **101 D5** 5 41N 0 0 E
Temanggung, *Indonesia* **71 G14** 7 18 S 110 10 E
Temapache, *Mexico* **147 C5** 21 4N 97 38W
Temax, *Mexico* **147 C7** 21 10N 88 50W
Temba, *S. Africa* **105 D4** 25 20 S 28 17 E
Tembe, *Zaïre* **106 C2** 0 16 S 28 14 E
Tembesi, *Indonesia* **74 C2** 1 43 S 103 6 E
Tembilahan, *Indonesia* **74 C2** 0 19 S 103 9 E
Temblador, *Venezuela* **153 B5** 8 59N 62 44W
Tembleque, *Spain* **34 F1** 39 41N 3 30W
Temblor Ra., *U.S.A.* **145 K7** 35 30N 120 0W
Teme →, *U.K.* **17 E5** 52 23N 2 15W
Temecula, *U.S.A.* **145 M9** 33 26N 117 6W
Temerloh, *Malaysia* **77 L4** 3 27N 102 25 E
Temir, *U.S.S.R.* **56 E6** 49 21N 57 3 E
Temirtau, *Kazakh S.S.R., U.S.S.R.* **56 D8** 50 5N 72 56 E
Temirtau, *R.S.F.S.R., U.S.S.R.* **56 D9** 53 10N 87 30 E
Témiscaming, *Canada* **128 C4** 46 44N 79 5W
Temma, *Australia* **114 G3** 41 12 S 144 48 E
Temnikov, *U.S.S.R.* **51 D13** 54 40N 43 11 E
Temo →, *Italy* **40 B1** 40 20N 8 30 E
Temora, *Australia* **117 C7** 34 30 S 147 30 E
Temosachic, *Mexico* **146 B3** 28 58N 107 50W
Tempe, *U.S.A.* **143 K8** 33 26N 111 59W
Tempe Downs, *Australia* **112 D5** 24 22 S 132 24 E
Témpio Pausania, *Italy* **40 B2** 40 53N 9 6 E
Tempiute, *U.S.A.* **144 H11** 37 39N 115 38W
Temple, *U.S.A.* **139 K6** 31 5N 97 22W
Temple B., *Australia* **114 A3** 12 15 S 143 3 E
Templemore, *Ireland* **19 D4** 52 48N 7 50W
Templeton, *U.S.A.* **144 K6** 35 33N 120 42W
Templeton →, *Australia* **114 C2** 21 0 S 138 40 E
Templeuve, *Belgium* **21 G2** 50 39N 3 17 E
Templin, *Germany* **26 B9** 53 8N 13 31 E
Tempoal, *Mexico* **147 C5** 21 31N 98 23W
Temryuk, *U.S.S.R.* **52 D7** 45 15N 37 24 E
Temse, *Belgium* **21 F4** 51 7N 4 13 E
Temska →, *Yugoslavia* **42 D7** 43 17N 22 33 E
Temuco, *Chile* **160 A2** 38 45 S 72 40W
Temuka, *N.Z.* **119 E6** 44 14 S 171 17 E
Ten Boer, *Neths.* **20 B9** 53 16N 6 42 E
Tena, *Ecuador* **152 D2** 0 59 S 77 49W
Tenabo, *Mexico* **147 C6** 20 2N 90 12W
Tenaha, *U.S.A.* **139 K7** 31 57N 94 25W
Tenali, *India* **83 F5** 16 15N 80 35 E
Tenancingo, *Mexico* **147 D5** 19 0N 99 33W
Tenango, *Mexico* **147 D5** 19 7N 99 33W
Tenasserim, *Burma* **77 F2** 12 6N 99 3 E
Tenasserim □, *Burma* **76 F2** 14 0N 98 30 E
Tenay, *France* **25 C9** 45 55N 5 31 E
Tenby, *U.K.* **17 F3** 51 40N 4 42W
Tenda, Col di, *France* **25 D11** 44 7N 7 36 E
Tendaho, *Ethiopia* **90 E3** 11 48N 40 54 E
Tende, *France* **25 D11** 44 5N 7 35 E
Tendelti, *Sudan* **95 E3** 13 1N 31 55 E
Tendjedi, Adrar, *Algeria* **99 D6** 23 41N 7 32 E
Tendrara, *Morocco* **99 B4** 33 3N 1 58W
Tendre, Mt., *Switz.* **28 C2** 46 35N 6 18 E
Teneida, *Egypt* **94 B2** 25 30N 29 19 E
Tenente Marques →, *Brazil* **157 C6** 11 10 S 59 56W
Ténéré, *Niger* **97 E2** 19 0N 10 30 E
Ténéré, Erg du, *Niger* **97 E2** 17 35N 10 55 E
Tenerife, *Canary Is.* **33 F3** 28 15N 16 35W
Tenerife, Pico, *Canary Is.* **33 G1** 27 43N 18 1W
Ténès, *Algeria* **99 A5** 36 31N 1 14 E
Teng Xian, *Guangxi Zhuangzu, China* **69 F8** 23 21N 110 56 E
Teng Xian, *Shandong, China* **67 G9** 35 5N 117 10 E
Tengah □, *Indonesia* **71 E6** 2 0 S 122 0 E
Tengah Kepulauan, *Indonesia* **70 F5** 7 5 S 118 15 E
Tengchong, *China* **68 E2** 25 0N 98 28 E
Tengchowfu = Penglai, *China* **67 F11** 37 48N 120 42 E
Tenggara □, *Indonesia* **71 E6** 3 0 S 122 0 E
Tenggarong, *Indonesia* **70 E5** 0 24 S 116 58 E
Tenggol, P., *Malaysia* **77 K4** 4 48N 103 41 E
Tengiz, Ozero, *U.S.S.R.* **56 D7** 50 30N 69 0 E
Tenigerbad, *Switz.* **29 C7** 46 42N 8 57 E
Tenino, *U.S.A.* **144 D4** 46 51N 122 51W
Tenkasi, *India* **83 K3** 8 55N 77 20 E
Tenke, *Shaba, Zaïre* **107 E2** 11 22 S 26 40 E
Tenke, *Shaba, Zaïre* **107 E2** 10 32 S 26 7 E
Tenkodogo, *Burkina Faso* **101 C4** 11 54N 0 19W
Tenna →, *Italy* **39 E10** 43 12N 13 47 E
Tennant Creek, *Australia* **114 B1** 19 30 S 134 15 E
Tennessee □, *U.S.A.* **133 C9** 36 0N 86 30W
Tennessee →, *U.S.A.* **134 G1** 37 4N 88 34W
Tenneville, *Belgium* **21 H7** 50 6N 5 32 E
Tennille, *U.S.A.* **135 J4** 32 58N 82 50W
Tennsift, Oued →, *Morocco* **98 B3** 32 3N 9 28W
Tennyson, *U.S.A.* **141 F9** 38 5N 87 7W
Teno, Pta. de, *Canary Is.* **33 F3** 28 21N 16 55W
Tenom, *Malaysia* **70 C5** 5 4N 115 57 E
Tenosique, *Mexico* **147 D6** 17 30N 91 24W
Tenri, *Japan* **63 C7** 34 39N 135 49 E
Tenryū, *Japan* **63 C9** 34 52N 137 49 E
Tenryū-Gawa →, *Japan* **63 B9** 35 39N 137 48 E
Tent L., *Canada* **131 A7** 62 25N 107 54W
Tentelomatinan, *Indonesia* **72 A2** 0 56N 121 48 E
Tenterfield, *Australia* **115 D5** 29 0 S 152 0 E
Teófilo Otoni, *Brazil* **155 E3** 17 50 S 41 30W
Teotihuacán, *Mexico* **147 D5** 19 44N 98 50W
Tepa, *Indonesia* **71 F7** 7 52 S 129 31 E
Tepalcatepec →, *Mexico* **146 D4** 18 35N 101 59W
Tepehuanes, *Mexico* **146 B3** 25 21N 105 44W
Tepelena, *Albania* **44 D2** 40 17N 20 2 E
Tepequem, Serra, *Brazil* **153 C5** 3 45N 61 45W
Tepetongo, *Mexico* **146 C4** 22 28N 103 9W
Tepic, *Mexico* **146 C4** 21 30N 104 54W
Teplice, *Czech.* **30 A6** 50 40N 13 48 E
Teploklyuchenka, *U.S.S.R.* **55 B9** 42 30N 78 30 E
Tepoca, C., *Mexico* **146 A2** 30 20N 112 25W
Tequila, *Mexico* **146 C4** 20 54N 103 47W
Ter →, *Spain* **34 C8** 42 2N 3 12 E
Ter Apel, *Neths.* **20 C10** 52 53N 7 5 E
Téra, *Niger* **101 C5** 14 0N 0 45 E
Tera →, *Spain* **36 D5** 41 54N 5 44W
Teraina, *Kiribati* **123 G11** 4 43N 160 25W
Téramo, *Italy* **39 F10** 42 40N 13 40 E
Terang, *Australia* **116 E5** 38 15 S 142 55 E
Terawhiti, C., *N.Z.* **118 H3** 41 16 S 174 38 E
Terazit, Massif de, *Niger* **97 D1** 20 2N 8 30 E
Terborg, *Neths.* **20 E8** 51 56N 6 22 E
Tercan, *Turkey* **89 D9** 39 47N 40 23 E
Tercero →, *Argentina* **158 C3** 32 58 S 61 47W
Terdal, *India* **82 F2** 16 33N 75 3 E
Terebovlya, *U.S.S.R.* **50 G4** 49 18N 25 44 E
Teregova, *Romania* **46 D3** 45 10N 22 16 E
Terek →, *U.S.S.R.* **53 E12** 44 0N 47 30 E
Terek-Say, *U.S.S.R.* **55 C5** 41 30N 71 11 E
Terenos, *Brazil* **157 E7** 20 26 S 54 50W
Tereshka →, *U.S.S.R.* **51 F15** 51 48N 46 26 E
Teresina, *Brazil* **154 C3** 5 9 S 42 45W
Teresinha, *Brazil* **153 C7** 0 58N 52 2W
Terespol, *Poland* **47 C10** 52 5N 23 37 E
Terewah, L., *Australia* **115 D4** 29 52 S 147 35 E
Terges →, *Portugal* **37 H3** 37 49N 7 41W
Tergnier, *France* **23 C10** 49 40N 3 17 E
Terhazza, *Mali* **98 D3** 23 38N 5 22W
Terheijden, *Neths.* **21 E5** 51 38N 4 45 E
Teridgerie Cr. →, *Australia* **115 E4** 30 25 S 148 50 E
Terifa, *Yemen* **86 D3** 14 24N 43 48 E
Terlizzi, *Italy* **41 A9** 41 8N 16 32 E
Terme, *Turkey* **52 F7** 41 11N 37 0 E
Termez, *U.S.S.R.* **55 E3** 37 15N 67 15 E
Términi Imerese, *Italy* **40 E6** 37 58N 13 42 E
Términos, L. de, *Mexico* **147 D6** 18 35N 91 30W
Térmoli, *Italy* **39 G12** 42 0N 15 0 E
Ternate, *Indonesia* **71 D7** 0 45N 127 25 E
Terneuzen, *Neths.* **21 F3** 51 20N 3 50 E
Terney, *U.S.S.R.* **57 E14** 45 3N 136 37 E
Terni, *Italy* **39 F9** 42 34N 12 38 E
Ternitz, *Austria* **30 D9** 47 43N 16 2 E
Ternopol, *U.S.S.R.* **52 B1** 49 30N 25 40 E
Terowie, *N.S.W., Australia* **115 E4** 32 27 S 147 52 E
Terowie, *S. Austral., Australia* **115 E2** 33 8 S 138 55 E
Terra Bella, *U.S.A.* **145 K7** 35 58N 119 3W
Terrace, *Canada* **130 C3** 54 30N 128 35W
Terrace Bay, *Canada* **128 C2** 48 47N 87 5W
Terracina, *Italy* **40 A6** 41 17N 13 12 E
Terralba, *Italy* **40 C1** 39 42N 8 38 E
Terranova = Ólbia, *Italy* **40 B2** 40 55N 9 30 E
Terranuova Bracciolini, *Italy* **39 E8** 43 31N 11 35 E
Terrasini Favarotta, *Italy* **40 D6** 38 10N 13 4 E
Terrasson-la-Villedieu, *France* **24 C5** 45 8N 1 18 E
Terre Haute, *U.S.A.* **141 E9** 39 28N 87 24W
Terrebonne B., *U.S.A.* **139 L9** 29 15N 90 28W
Terrecht, *Mali* **99 D4** 20 10N 0 10W
Terrell, *U.S.A.* **139 J6** 32 44N 96 19W
Terrenceville, *Canada* **129 C9** 47 40N 54 44W
Terrick Terrick, *Australia* **114 C4** 24 44 S 145 5 E
Terry, *U.S.A.* **138 B2** 46 47N 105 20W
Terschelling, *Neths.* **20 B6** 53 25N 5 20 E
Terskey Alatau, Khrebet, *U.S.S.R.* **55 C8** 41 50N 77 0 E
Terter →, *U.S.S.R.* **53 F12** 40 35N 47 22 E
Teruel, *Spain* **34 E3** 40 22N 1 8W
Teruel □, *Spain* **34 E4** 40 48N 1 0W
Tervel, *Bulgaria* **43 D12** 43 45N 27 28 E
Tervola, *Finland* **12 C18** 66 6N 24 49 E
Teryaweyna L., *Australia* **116 B5** 32 18 S 143 22 E
Tešanj, *Yugoslavia* **42 C2** 44 38N 17 59 E
Teseney, *Ethiopia* **95 D4** 15 5N 36 42 E
Tesha →, *U.S.S.R.* **51 D13** 55 38N 42 9 E
Teshio, *Japan* **60 B10** 44 53N 141 44 E
Teshio-Gawa →, *Japan* **60 B10** 44 53N 141 45 E
Tešica, *Yugoslavia* **42 D6** 43 27N 21 45 E
Tesiyn Gol →, *Mongolia* **64 A4** 50 40N 93 20 E
Teslić, *Yugoslavia* **42 C2** 44 37N 17 54 E
Teslin, *Canada* **130 A2** 60 10N 132 43W
Teslin →, *Canada* **130 A2** 61 34N 134 35W
Teslin L., *Canada* **130 A2** 60 15N 132 57W
Tesouro, *Brazil* **157 D7** 16 4 S 53 34W
Tessalit, *Mali* **101 A5** 20 12N 1 0 E
Tessaoua, *Niger* **97 F1** 13 47N 7 56 E
Tessenderlo, *Belgium* **21 F6** 51 4N 5 5 E
Tessin, *Germany* **26 A8** 54 2N 12 28 E
Tessit, *Mali* **101 B5** 15 13N 0 18 E
Test →, *U.K.* **17 F6** 51 7N 1 30W
Testa del Gargano, *Italy* **41 A9** 41 50N 16 10 E
Tét, *Hungary* **31 D10** 47 30N 17 33 E
Têt →, *France* **24 F7** 42 44N 3 2 E
Tetachuck L., *Canada* **130 C3** 53 18N 125 55W
Tetas, Pta., *Chile* **158 A1** 23 31 S 70 38W
Tete, *Mozam.* **107 F3** 16 13 S 33 33 E
Tete □, *Mozam.* **107 F3** 15 15 S 32 40 E
Teterev →, *U.S.S.R.* **50 F7** 51 1N 30 5 E
Teteringen, *Neths.* **21 E5** 51 37N 4 49 E
Teterow, *Germany* **26 B8** 53 45N 12 34 E
Teteven, *Bulgaria* **43 E9** 42 58N 24 17 E
Tethul →, *Canada* **130 A6** 60 35N 112 12W
Tetiyev, *U.S.S.R.* **52 B3** 49 22N 29 38 E
Teton →, *U.S.A.* **142 C8** 47 58N 111 0W
Tétouan, *Morocco* **98 A3** 35 35N 5 21W
Tetovo, *Yugoslavia* **42 E6** 42 1N 21 2 E
Tetuán = Tétouan, *Morocco* **98 A3** 35 35N 5 21W
Tetyukhe Pristan, *U.S.S.R.* **60 B7** 44 22N 135 48 E
Tetyushi, *U.S.S.R.* **51 D16** 54 55N 48 49 E
Teuco →, *Argentina* **158 B3** 25 35 S 60 11W
Teufen, *Switz.* **29 B8** 47 24N 9 23 E
Teulada, *Italy* **40 D1** 38 59N 8 47 E
Teulon, *Canada* **131 C9** 50 23N 97 16W
Teun, *Indonesia* **71 F7** 6 59 S 129 8 E
Teutoburger Wald, *Germany* **26 C4** 52 5N 8 20 E
Tevere →, *Italy* **39 G9** 41 44N 12 14 E
Teverya, *Israel* **91 C4** 32 47N 35 32 E
Teviot →, *U.K.* **18 F6** 55 21N 2 51W
Tewantin, *Australia* **115 D5** 26 27 S 153 3 E
Tewkesbury, *U.K.* **17 F5** 51 59N 2 8W
Texada I., *Canada* **130 D4** 49 40N 124 25W
Texarkana, *Ark., U.S.A.* **139 J8** 33 25N 94 0W
Texarkana, *Tex., U.S.A.* **139 J7** 33 25N 94 3W
Texas, *Australia* **115 D5** 28 49 S 151 9 E
Texas □, *U.S.A.* **139 K5** 31 40N 98 30W
Texas City, *U.S.A.* **139 L7** 29 20N 94 55W
Texel, *Neths.* **20 B5** 53 5N 4 50 E
Texhoma, *U.S.A.* **139 G4** 36 32N 101 47W
Texline, *U.S.A.* **139 G3** 36 26N 103 0W
Texoma L., *U.S.A.* **139 J6** 34 0N 96 38W
Teykovo, *U.S.S.R.* **51 C12** 56 55N 40 30 E
Teyvareh, *Afghan.* **79 B2** 33 30N 64 24 E
Teza →, *U.S.S.R.* **51 C12** 56 32N 41 53 E
Tezin, *Afghan.* **80 B3** 34 24N 69 30 E
Teziutlán, *Mexico* **147 D5** 19 50N 97 22W
Tezpur, *India* **78 B4** 26 40N 92 45 E
Tezzeron L., *Canada* **130 C4** 54 43N 124 30W
Tha-anne →, *Canada* **131 A10** 60 31N 94 37W
Tha Deua, *Laos* **76 D4** 17 57N 102 53 E
Tha Deua, *Laos* **76 C3** 19 26N 101 50 E
Tha Pla, *Thailand* **76 D3** 17 48N 100 32 E
Tha Rua, *Thailand* **76 E3** 14 34N 100 44 E
Tha Sala, *Thailand* **77 H2** 8 40N 99 56 E
Tha Song Yang, *Thailand* **76 D1** 17 34N 97 55 E
Thaba Nchu, *S. Africa* **104 D4** 29 17 S 26 52 E
Thaba Putsoa, *Lesotho* **105 D4** 29 45 S 28 0 E
Thabana Ntlenyana, *Lesotho* **105 D4** 29 30 S 29 16 E
Thabazimbi, *S. Africa* **105 C4** 24 40 S 27 21 E
Thabeikkyin, *Burma* **78 D5** 22 53N 95 59 E
Thai Binh, *Vietnam* **76 B6** 20 35N 106 1 E
Thai Hoa, *Vietnam* **76 C5** 19 20N 105 20 E
Thai Muang, *Thailand* **77 H2** 8 24N 98 16 E
Thai Nguyen, *Vietnam* **76 B5** 21 35N 105 55 E
Thailand ■, *Asia* **76 E4** 16 0N 102 0 E
Thailand, G. of, *Asia* **77 G3** 11 30N 101 0 E
Thakhek, *Laos* **76 D5** 17 25N 104 45 E
Thakurgaon, *Bangla.* **78 B2** 26 2N 88 34 E
Thal, *Pakistan* **79 B3** 33 28N 70 33 E
Thal Desert, *Pakistan* **80 D4** 31 10N 71 30 E
Thala, *Tunisia* **96 A1** 35 35N 8 40 E
Thalabarivat, *Cambodia* **76 F5** 13 33N 105 57 E
Thalkirch, *Switz.* **29 C8** 46 39N 9 17 E
Thallon, *Australia* **115 D4** 28 39 S 148 49 E
Thalwil, *Switz.* **29 B7** 47 17N 8 35 E
Thamarīt, *Oman* **87 C6** 17 39N 54 2 E
Thame →, *U.K.* **17 F6** 51 35N 1 8W
Thames, *N.Z.* **118 D4** 37 7 S 175 34 E
Thames →, *Canada* **128 D3** 42 20N 82 25W
Thames →, *U.K.* **17 F8** 51 30N 0 35 E
Thames →, *U.S.A.* **137 E12** 41 18N 72 9W
Thames, Firth of, *N.Z.* **118 D4** 37 0 S 175 25 E
Thamesford, *Canada* **136 C4** 43 4N 81 0W
Thamesville, *Canada* **136 D3** 42 33N 81 59W
Thāmit, W. →, *Libya* **96 B3** 30 51N 16 14 E
Thamūd, *Yemen* **87 C5** 17 18N 49 55 E
Than Uyen, *Vietnam* **76 B4** 22 0N 103 54 E
Thanbyuzayat, *Burma* **78 G6** 15 58N 97 44 E
Thane, *India* **82 E1** 19 12N 72 59 E
Thanesar, *India* **80 D7** 30 1N 76 52 E
Thanet, I. of, *U.K.* **17 F9** 51 21N 1 20 E
Thangoo, *Australia* **112 C3** 18 10 S 122 22 E
Thangool, *Australia* **114 C5** 24 38 S 150 42 E
Thanh Hoa, *Vietnam* **76 C5** 19 48N 105 46 E
Thanh Hung, *Vietnam* **77 H5** 9 55N 105 43 E
Thanh Pho Ho Chi Minh = Phanh Bho Ho Chi Minh, *Vietnam* **77 G6** 10 58N 106 40 E
Thanh Thuy, *Vietnam* **76 A5** 22 55N 104 51 E
Thanjavur, *India* **83 J4** 10 48N 79 12 E
Thann, *France* **23 E14** 47 48N 7 5 E
Thaon-les-Vosges, *France* **23 D13** 48 15N 6 24 E
Thap Sakae, *Thailand* **77 G2** 11 30N 99 37 E
Thap Than, *Thailand* **76 E2** 15 27N 99 54 E
Thar Desert, *India* **80 F5** 28 0N 72 0 E
Tharad, *India* **80 G4** 24 30N 71 44 E
Thargomindah, *Australia* **115 D3** 27 58 S 143 46 E
Tharrawaddy, *Burma* **78 G5** 17 38N 95 48 E
Tharrawaw, *Burma* **78 G5** 17 41N 95 28 E
Tharthar, W. →, *Iraq* **84 C4** 33 59N 43 12 E
Thasopoúla, *Greece* **44 D6** 40 49N 24 45 E
Thásos, *Greece* **44 D6** 40 40N 24 40 E
That Khe, *Vietnam* **76 A6** 22 16N 106 28 E
Thatcher, *Ariz., U.S.A.* **143 K9** 32 54N 109 46W
Thatcher, *Colo., U.S.A.* **139 G2** 37 38N 104 6W
Thaton, *Burma* **78 G6** 16 55N 97 22 E
Thau, Bassin de, *France* **24 E7** 43 23N 3 36 E
Thaungdut, *Burma* **78 C5** 24 30N 94 40 E
Thayer, *U.S.A.* **139 G9** 36 34N 91 34W
Thayetmyo, *Burma* **78 F5** 19 20N 95 10 E
Thayngen, *Switz.* **29 A7** 47 49N 8 43 E
The Alberga →, *Australia* **115 D2** 27 6 S 135 33 E
The Bight, *Bahamas* **149 B4** 24 19N 75 24W
The Brothers, *Yemen* **87 D6** 12 8N 53 10 E
The Coorong, *Australia* **116 C3** 35 50 S 139 20 E
The Dalles, *U.S.A.* **142 D3** 45 40N 121 11W
The English Company's Is., *Australia* **114 A2** 11 50 S 136 32 E
The Entrance, *Australia* **117 B9** 33 21 S 151 30 E
The Frome →, *Australia* **115 D2** 29 8 S 137 54 E
The Grampians, *Australia* **116 D5** 37 0 S 142 20 E
The Great Divide = Great Dividing Ra., *Australia* **114 C4** 23 0 S 146 0 E
The Hague = 's-Gravenhage, *Neths.* **20 D4** 52 7N 4 17 E
The Hamilton →, *Australia* **115 D2** 26 40 S 135 19 E
The Hunter Hills, *N.Z.* **119 E5** 44 26 S 170 46 E
The Macumba →, *Australia* **115 D2** 27 52 S 137 12 E
The Neales →, *Australia* **115 D2** 28 8 S 136 47 E
The Oaks, *Australia* **117 C9** 34 3 S 150 34 E
The Officer →, *Australia* **113 E5** 27 46 S 132 30 E
The Pas, *Canada* **131 C8** 53 45N 101 15W
The Range, *Zimbabwe* **107 F3** 19 2 S 31 2 E
The Remarkables, *N.Z.* **119 F3** 45 10 S 168 50 E
The Rock, *Australia* **115 F4** 35 15 S 147 2 E
The Salt L., *Australia* **115 E3** 30 6 S 142 8 E
The Stevenson →, *Australia* **115 D2** 27 6 S 135 33 E
The Warburton →, *Australia* **115 D2** 28 4 S 137 28 E
Thebes = Thívai, *Greece* **45 F5** 38 19N 23 19 E
Thebes, *Egypt* **94 B3** 25 40N 32 35 E
Thedford, *Canada* **136 C3** 43 9N 81 51W
Thedford, *U.S.A.* **138 E4** 41 59N 100 31W
Theebine, *Australia* **115 D5** 25 57 S 152 34 E
Thekulthili L., *Canada* **131 A7** 61 3N 110 0W
Thelon →, *Canada* **131 A8** 62 35N 104 3W
Thénezay, *France* **22 F6** 46 44N 0 2W
Thenia, *Algeria* **99 A5** 36 44N 3 33 E
Thenon, *France* **24 C5** 45 9N 1 4 E
Theodore, *Australia* **114 C5** 24 55 S 150 3 E
Thepha, *Thailand* **77 J3** 6 52N 100 58 E
Thérain →, *France* **23 C9** 49 15N 2 27 E
Theresa, *U.S.A.* **137 B9** 44 13N 75 50W
Thermaïkos Kólpos, *Greece* **44 D4** 40 15N 22 45 E
Thermopolis, *U.S.A.* **142 E9** 43 35N 108 10W
Thermopylae P., *Greece* **45 F4** 38 48N 22 35 E
Thesprotía □, *Greece* **44 E2** 39 27N 20 22 E
Thessalía □, *Greece* **44 E4** 38 25N 21 50 E
Thessalon, *Canada* **128 C3** 46 20N 83 30W
Thessaloníki, *Greece* **44 D4** 40 38N 22 58 E
Thessaloníki □, *Greece* **44 D5** 40 45N 23 0 E
Thessaloniki, Gulf of = Thermaïkos Kólpos, *Greece* **44 D4** 40 15N 22 45 E
Thessaly = Thessalía □, *Greece* **44 E4** 38 25N 21 50 E
Thetford, *U.K.* **17 E8** 52 25N 0 44 E
Thetford Mines, *Canada* **129 C5** 46 8N 71 18W
Theun →, *Laos* **76 C5** 18 19N 104 0 E
Theunissen, *S. Africa* **104 D4** 28 26 S 26 43 E
Theux, *Belgium* **21 G7** 50 32N 5 49 E
Thevenard, *Australia* **115 E1** 32 9 S 133 38 E
Thiámis →, *Greece* **44 E2** 39 15N 20 6 E
Thiberville, *France* **22 C7** 49 8N 0 27 E
Thibodaux, *U.S.A.* **139 L9** 29 48N 90 49W
Thicket Portage, *Canada* **131 B9** 55 19N 97 42W
Thief River Falls, *U.S.A.* **138 A6** 48 15N 96 48W
Thiel Mts., *Antarctica* **7 E16** 85 15 S 91 0W
Thiene, *Italy* **39 C8** 45 42N 11 29 E
Thiérache, *France* **23 C10** 49 51N 3 45 E
Thiers, *France* **24 C7** 45 52N 3 33 E
Thies, *Senegal* **100 C1** 14 50N 16 51W
Thiet, *Sudan* **95 F2** 7 37N 28 49 E
Thika, *Kenya* **106 C4** 1 1 S 37 5 E
Thille-Boubacar, *Senegal* **100 B1** 16 31N 15 5W
Thimphu, *Bhutan* **78 B2** 27 31N 89 45 E
þingvallavatn, *Iceland* **12 D3** 64 11N 21 9W
Thio, *N. Cal.* **121 U20** 21 37 S 166 14 E
Thionville, *France* **23 C13** 49 20N 6 10 E
Thíra, *Greece* **45 H7** 36 23N 25 27 E
Thirasía, *Greece* **45 H7** 36 26N 25 21 E
Thirsk, *U.K.* **16 C6** 54 15N 1 20W
Thiruvarur, *India* **83 J4** 10 46N 79 38 E
Thisted, *Denmark* **13 H10** 56 58N 8 40 E
Thistle I., *Australia* **116 C2** 35 0 S 136 8 E
Thitgy, *Burma* **78 F6** 18 15N 96 13 E
Thithia, *Fiji* **121 A3** 17 45 S 179 18W
Thitpokpin, *Burma* **78 F5** 19 24N 95 58 E
Thívai, *Greece* **45 F5** 38 19N 23 19 E
Thiviers, *France* **24 C4** 45 25N 0 54 E
Thizy, *France* **25 B8** 46 2N 4 18 E
þjórsá →, *Iceland* **12 E3** 63 47N 20 48W
Thlewiaza →, *Man., Canada* **131 B8** 59 43N 100 5W
Thlewiaza →, *N.W.T., Canada* **131 A10** 60 29N 94 40W
Thmar Puok, *Cambodia* **76 F4** 13 57N 103 4 E
Tho Vinh, *Vietnam* **76 C5** 19 16N 105 42 E
Thoa →, *Canada* **131 A7** 60 31N 109 47W
Thoen, *Thailand* **76 D2** 17 43N 99 12 E
Thoeng, *Thailand* **76 C3** 19 41N 100 12 E
Thoissey, *France* **25 B8** 46 12N 4 48 E
Tholdi, *Pakistan* **81 B7** 35 5N 76 6 E
Tholen, *Neths.* **21 E4** 51 32N 4 13 E
Thomas, *Okla., U.S.A.* **139 H5** 35 48N 98 48W
Thomas, *W. Va., U.S.A.* **134 F6** 39 10N 79 30W
Thomas, L., *Australia* **115 D2** 26 4 S 137 58 E
Thomas Hill Res., *U.S.A.* **140 E4** 39 34N 92 39W
Thomaston, *U.S.A.* **135 J3** 32 54N 84 20W
Thomasville, *Ala., U.S.A.* **135 K2** 31 55N 87 42W
Thomasville, *Ga., U.S.A.* **135 K4** 30 50N 84 0W
Thomasville, *N.C., U.S.A.* **135 H5** 35 55N 80 4W
Thommen, *Belgium* **21 H8** 50 14N 6 5 E
Thompson, *Canada* **131 B9** 55 45N 97 52W
Thompson, *U.S.A.* **143 G9** 39 0N 109 50W
Thompson →, *Canada* **130 C4** 50 15N 121 24W
Thompson →, *U.S.A.* **138 F8** 39 46N 93 37W
Thompson Falls, *U.S.A.* **142 C6** 47 37N 115 20W
Thompson Landing, *Canada* **131 A6** 62 56N 110 40W
Thompson Pk., *U.S.A.* **142 F2** 41 0N 123 3W
Thompson Sd., *N.Z.* **119 F1** 45 8 S 166 46 E
Thomson, *U.S.A.* **140 C6** 41 58N 90 6W
Thomson's Falls = Nyahururu, *Kenya* **106 B4** 0 2N 36 27 E

Tradate 275

Tocumwal, *Australia* **117 C6** 35 51 S 145 31 E
Tocuyo →, *Venezuela* **152 A4** 11 3N 68 23W
Tocuyo de la Costa, *Venezuela* **152 A4** 11 2N 68 23W
Todd →, *Australia* **114 C2** 24 52 S 135 48 E
Todeli, *Indonesia* **71 E6** 1 38 S 124 34 E
Todenyang, *Kenya* **106 B4** 4 35N 35 56 E
Todi, *Italy* **39 F9** 42 47N 12 24 E
Tödi, *Switz.* **29 C7** 46 48N 8 55 E
Todos los Santos, B. de, *Brazil* **155 D4** 12 48 S 38 38W
Todos Santos, *Mexico* **146 C2** 23 27N 110 13W
Todtnau, *Germany* **27 H3** 47 50N 7 56 E
Toecé, *Burkina Faso* **101 C4** 11 50N 1 16W
Toetoes B., *N.Z.* **119 G3** 46 42 S 168 41 E
Tofield, *Canada* **130 C6** 53 25N 112 40W
Tofino, *Canada* **130 D3** 49 11N 125 55W
Töfsingdalens nationalpark, *Sweden* **14 B6** 62 15N 12 44 E
Toftlund, *Denmark* **15 J3** 55 11N 9 2 E
Tofua, *Tonga* **121 P13** 19 45 S 175 5W
Toga, *Vanuatu* **121 C4** 13 26 S 166 42 E
Tōgane, *Japan* **63 B12** 35 33N 140 22 E
Togba, *Mauritania* **100 B2** 17 26N 10 12W
Togbo, *C.A.R.* **102 A3** 6 0N 17 27 E
Toggenburg, *Switz.* **29 B8** 47 16N 9 9 E
Togian, Kepulauan, *Indonesia* **71 E6** 0 20 S 121 50 E
Togliatti, *U.S.S.R.* **51 E16** 53 32N 49 24 E
Togo ■, *W. Afr.* **101 D5** 8 30N 1 35 E
Togtoh, *China* **66 D6** 40 15N 111 10 E
Toguzak →, *U.S.S.R.* **54 D8** 54 3N 62 44 E
Tohma →, *Turkey* **89 D8** 38 29N 38 23 E
Tōhoku □, *Japan* **60 E10** 39 50N 141 45 E
Toi, *Japan* **63 C10** 34 54N 138 47 E
Toinya, *Sudan* **95 F2** 6 17N 29 46 E
Tojo, *Indonesia* **71 E6** 1 20 S 121 15 E
Tōjō, *Japan* **62 C5** 34 53N 133 16 E
Tok →, *U.S.S.R.* **54 E3** 52 46N 52 22 E
Toka, *Guyana* **153 C6** 3 58N 59 17W
Tokaanu, *N.Z.* **118 E4** 38 58 S 175 46 E
Tokachi-Dake, *Japan* **60 C11** 43 17N 142 5 E
Tokachi-Gawa →, *Japan* **60 C11** 42 44N 143 42 E
Tokai, *Japan* **63 B8** 35 2N 136 55 E
Tokaj, *Hungary* **31 C14** 48 8N 21 27 E
Tokala, *Indonesia* **71 E6** 1 30 S 121 40 E
Tōkamachi, *Japan* **61 F9** 37 8N 138 43 E
Tokanui, *N.Z.* **119 G3** 46 34 S 168 56 E
Tokar, *Sudan* **94 D4** 18 27N 37 56 E
Tokara-Rettō, *Japan* **61 K4** 29 37N 129 43 E
Tokarahi, *N.Z.* **119 E5** 44 56 S 170 39 E
Tokashiki-Shima, *Japan* **61 L3** 26 11N 127 21 E
Tokat, *Turkey* **88 C7** 40 22N 36 35 E
Tokat □, *Turkey* **88 C7** 40 15N 36 30 E
Tŏkchŏn, *N. Korea* **67 E14** 39 45N 126 18 E
Tokeland, *U.S.A.* **144 D3** 46 42N 123 59W
Tokelau Is., *Pac. Oc.* **111 B16** 9 0 S 171 45W
Toki, *Japan* **63 B9** 35 18N 137 8 E
Tokmak, *U.S.S.R.* **55 B7** 42 49N 75 15 E
Toko Ra., *Australia* **114 C2** 23 5 S 138 20 E
Tokomaru Bay, *N.Z.* **118 E7** 38 8 S 178 22 E
Tokoname, *Japan* **63 C8** 34 53N 136 51 E
Tokoro-Gawa →, *Japan* **60 B12** 44 7N 144 5 E
Tokoroa, *N.Z.* **118 E4** 38 13 S 175 50 E
Tokorozawa, *Japan* **63 B11** 35 47N 139 28 E
Toktogul, *U.S.S.R.* **55 C6** 41 50N 72 50 E
Toku, *Tonga* **121 P13** 18 10 S 174 11W
Tokuji, *Japan* **62 C3** 34 11N 131 42 E
Tokuno-Shima, *Japan* **61 L4** 27 56N 128 55 E
Tokushima, *Japan* **62 C6** 34 4N 134 34 E
Tokushima □, *Japan* **62 D6** 33 55N 134 0 E
Tokuyama, *Japan* **62 C3** 34 3N 131 50 E
Tōkyō, *Japan* **63 B11** 35 45N 139 45 E
Tōkyō □, *Japan* **63 B11** 35 40N 139 30 E
Tōkyō-Wan, *Japan* **63 B11** 35 25N 139 47 E
Tokzār, *Afghan.* **79 B2** 35 52N 66 26 E
Tolaga Bay, *N.Z.* **118 E7** 38 21 S 178 20 E
Tolbukhin, *Bulgaria* **43 D12** 43 37N 27 49 E
Toledo, *Spain* **36 F6** 39 50N 4 2W
Toledo, *Ill., U.S.A.* **141 E8** 39 16N 88 15W
Toledo, *Iowa, U.S.A.* **140 C4** 42 0N 92 35W
Toledo, *Ohio, U.S.A.* **141 C13** 41 37N 83 33W
Toledo, *Oreg., U.S.A.* **142 D2** 44 40N 123 59W
Toledo, *Wash., U.S.A.* **142 C2** 46 29N 122 51W
Toledo, Montes de, *Spain* **37 F6** 39 33N 4 20W
Tolentino, *Italy* **39 E10** 43 12N 13 17 E
Tolga, *Algeria* **99 B6** 34 40N 5 22 E
Tolga, *Norway* **14 B5** 62 26N 11 1 E
Toliara, *Madag.* **105 C7** 23 21 S 43 40 E
Toliara □, *Madag.* **105 C8** 21 0 S 45 0 E
Tolima, *Colombia* **152 C2** 4 40N 75 19W
Tolima □, *Colombia* **152 C2** 3 45N 75 15W
Tolitoli, *Indonesia* **71 D6** 1 5N 120 50 E
Tolkamer, *Neths.* **20 E8** 51 52N 6 6 E
Tolkmicko, *Poland* **47 A6** 54 19N 19 31 E
Tolleson, *U.S.A.* **143 K7** 33 29N 112 10W
Tollhouse, *U.S.A.* **144 H7** 37 1N 119 24W
Tolmachevo, *U.S.S.R.* **50 B6** 58 56N 29 51 E
Tolmezzo, *Italy* **39 B10** 46 23N 13 2 E
Tolmin, *Yugoslavia* **39 B10** 46 11N 13 45 E
Tolna, *Hungary* **31 E11** 46 25N 18 48 E
Tolna □, *Hungary* **31 E11** 46 30N 18 30 E
Tolo, *Zaïre* **102 C3** 2 55 S 18 34 E
Tolo, Teluk, *Indonesia* **71 E6** 2 20 S 122 10 E
Tolochin, *U.S.S.R.* **50 D6** 54 25N 29 42 E
Tolono, *U.S.A.* **141 E8** 39 59N 88 16W
Tolosa, *Spain* **34 B2** 43 8N 2 5W
Tolox, *Spain* **37 J6** 36 41N 4 54W
Toltén, *Chile* **160 A2** 39 13 S 74 14W
Toluca, *Mexico* **147 D5** 19 20N 99 40W
Tom Burke, *S. Africa* **105 C4** 23 5 S 28 0 E
Tom Price, *Australia* **112 D2** 22 40 S 117 48 E
Tomah, *U.S.A.* **138 D9** 43 59N 90 30W
Tomahawk, *U.S.A.* **138 C10** 45 28N 89 40W
Tomakomai, *Japan* **60 C10** 42 38N 141 36 E
Tomales, *U.S.A.* **144 G4** 38 15N 122 53W
Tomales B., *U.S.A.* **144 G3** 38 15N 123 58W
Tomanlivi, *Fiji* **121 A2** 17 37 S 178 1 E
Tomar, *Portugal* **37 F2** 39 36N 8 25W
Tómaros Óros, *Greece* **44 E2** 39 29N 20 48 E
Tomarza, *Turkey* **88 D6** 38 2N 35 28 E
Tomás Barrón, *Bolivia* **156 D4** 17 35 S 67 31W
Tomaszów Mazowiecki, *Poland* **47 D6** 51 30N 19 57 E
Tomatlán, *Mexico* **146 D3** 19 56N 105 15W
Tombador, Serra do, *Brazil* **157 C6** 12 0 S 58 0W
Tombé, *Sudan* **95 F3** 5 53N 31 40 E
Tombigbee →, *U.S.A.* **135 K2** 31 4N 87 58W
Tombôco, *Angola* **103 D2** 6 48 S 13 18 E
Tombouctou, *Mali* **100 B4** 16 50N 3 0W
Tombstone, *U.S.A.* **143 L8** 31 40N 110 4W
Tombua, *Angola* **103 F2** 15 55 S 11 55 E
Tomé, *Chile* **158 D1** 36 36 S 72 57W
Tomé-Açu, *Brazil* **154 B2** 2 25 S 48 9W
Tomelilla, *Sweden* **15 J7** 55 33N 13 58 E
Tomelloso, *Spain* **35 F1** 39 10N 3 2W
Tomingley, *Australia* **117 B8** 32 26 S 148 16 E
Tomini, *Indonesia* **71 D6** 0 30N 120 30 E
Tomini, Teluk, *Indonesia* **71 E6** 0 10 S 122 0 E
Tominian, *Mali* **100 C4** 13 17N 4 35W
Tomiño, *Spain* **36 D2** 41 59N 8 46W
Tomkinson Ras., *Australia* **113 E4** 26 11 S 129 5 E
Tommot, *U.S.S.R.* **57 D13** 59 4N 126 20 E
Tomnavoulin, *U.K.* **18 D5** 57 19N 3 18W
Tomnop Ta Suos, *Cambodia* **77 G5** 11 20N 104 15 E
Tomo, *Colombia* **152 C4** 2 38N 67 32W
Tomo, *Japan* **62 C5** 34 23N 133 23 E
Tomo →, *Colombia* **152 B4** 5 20N 67 48W
Tomobe, *Japan* **63 A12** 36 20N 140 20 E
Toms Place, *U.S.A.* **144 H8** 37 34N 118 41W
Toms River, *U.S.A.* **137 G10** 39 59N 74 12W
Tomsk, *U.S.S.R.* **56 D9** 56 30N 85 5 E
Tonalá, *Mexico* **147 D6** 16 8N 93 41W
Tonale, Passo del, *Italy* **38 B7** 46 15N 10 34 E
Tonalea, *U.S.A.* **143 H8** 36 17N 110 58W
Tonami, *Japan* **63 A8** 36 40N 136 58 E
Tonantins, *Brazil* **152 D4** 2 45 S 67 45W
Tonasket, *U.S.A.* **142 B4** 48 45N 119 30W
Tonate, *Fr. Guiana* **153 C7** 5 0N 52 28W
Tonawanda, *U.S.A.* **136 D6** 43 0N 78 54W
Tonbridge, *U.K.* **17 F8** 51 12N 0 18 E
Tondano, *Indonesia* **71 D6** 1 35N 124 54 E
Tondela, *Portugal* **36 E2** 40 31N 8 5W
Tønder, *Denmark* **15 K2** 54 58N 8 50 E
Tondi, *India* **83 K4** 9 45N 79 4 E
Tondi Kiwindi, *Niger* **101 C5** 14 28N 2 2 E
Tondibi, *Mali* **101 B4** 16 39N 0 14W
Tonekābon, *Iran* **85 B6** 36 45N 51 12 E
Tong Xian, *China* **66 E9** 39 55N 116 35 E
Tonga ■, *Pac. Oc.* **121 P13** 19 50 S 174 30W
Tonga Trench, *Pac. Oc.* **122 J10** 18 0 S 175 0W
Tongaat, *S. Africa* **105 D5** 29 33 S 31 9 E
Tongala, *Australia* **117 D6** 36 14 S 144 56 E
Tong'an, *China* **69 E12** 24 37N 118 8 E
Tongareva, *Cook Is.* **123 H12** 9 0 S 158 0W
Tongatapu, *Tonga* **121 Q14** 21 10 S 174 0W
Tongatapu Group, *Tonga* **121 Q13** 21 0 S 175 0W
Tongbai, *China* **69 A9** 32 20N 113 23 E
Tongcheng, *Anhui, China* **69 B11** 31 4N 116 56 E
Tongcheng, *Hubei, China* **69 C9** 29 15N 113 50 E
Tongchŏn-ni, *N. Korea* **67 E14** 39 50N 127 25 E
Tongchuan, *China* **66 G5** 35 6N 109 3 E
Tongdao, *China* **68 D7** 26 10N 109 42 E
Tongeren, *Belgium* **21 G6** 50 47N 5 28 E
Tonggu, *China* **69 C10** 28 31N 114 20 E
Tongguan, *China* **66 G6** 34 40N 110 25 E
Tonghai, *China* **68 E4** 24 10N 102 53 E
Tonghua, *China* **67 D13** 41 42N 125 58 E
Tongjiang, *China* **68 B6** 31 58N 107 11 E
Tongjosŏn Man, *N. Korea* **67 E15** 39 30N 128 0 E
Tongking, G. of = Tonkin, G. of, *Asia* **76 C7** 20 0N 108 0 E
Tongliang, *China* **68 C6** 29 50N 106 3 E
Tongliao, *China* **67 C12** 43 38N 122 18 E
Tongling, *China* **69 B11** 30 55N 117 48 E
Tonglu, *China* **69 C12** 29 45N 119 37 E
Tongnae, *S. Korea* **67 G15** 35 12N 129 5 E
Tongnan, *China* **68 B5** 30 9N 105 50 E
Tongoa, *Vanuatu* **121 F6** 16 54 S 168 34 E
Tongobory, *Madag.* **105 C7** 23 32 S 44 20 E
Tongoy, *Chile* **158 C1** 30 16 S 71 31W
Tongren, *China* **68 D7** 27 43N 109 11 E
Tongres = Tongeren, *Belgium* **21 G6** 50 47N 5 28 E
Tongsa Dzong, *Bhutan* **78 B3** 27 31N 90 31 E
Tongue, *U.K.* **18 C4** 58 29N 4 25W
Tongue →, *U.S.A.* **138 B2** 46 24N 105 52W
Tongwei, *China* **66 G3** 35 0N 105 5 E
Tongxin, *China* **66 F3** 36 59N 105 58 E
Tongyang, *N. Korea* **67 E14** 39 9N 126 53 E
Tongyu, *China* **67 B12** 44 45N 123 4 E
Tongzi, *China* **68 C6** 28 9N 106 49 E
Tonica, *U.S.A.* **140 C7** 41 13N 89 4W
Tonj, *Sudan* **95 F2** 7 20N 28 44 E
Tonk, *India* **80 F6** 26 6N 75 54 E
Tonkawa, *U.S.A.* **139 G6** 36 44N 97 22W
Tonkin = Bac Phan, *Vietnam* **76 B5** 22 0N 105 0 E
Tonkin, G. of, *Asia* **76 C7** 20 0N 108 0 E
Tonlé Sap, *Cambodia* **76 F5** 13 0N 104 0 E
Tonnay-Charente, *France* **24 C3** 45 56N 0 55W
Tonneins, *France* **24 D4** 44 23N 0 19 E
Tonnerre, *France* **23 E10** 47 51N 3 59 E
Tönning, *Germany* **26 A4** 54 18N 8 57 E
Tono, *Japan* **60 E10** 39 19N 141 32 E
Tonopah, *U.S.A.* **143 G5** 38 4N 117 12W
Tonoshō, *Japan* **62 C6** 34 29N 134 11 E
Tonosí, *Panama* **148 E3** 7 20N 80 20W
Tønsberg, *Norway* **14 E4** 59 19N 10 25 E
Tonumea, *Tonga* **121 Q13** 20 30 S 174 30W
Tonzang, *Burma* **78 D4** 23 36N 93 42 E
Tonzi, *Burma* **78 C5** 24 39N 94 57 E
Tooele, *U.S.A.* **142 F7** 40 30N 112 20W
Toolondo, *Australia* **116 D4** 36 58 S 141 58 E
Toompine, *Australia* **115 D3** 27 15 S 144 19 E
Toongi, *Australia* **117 B8** 32 28 S 148 30 E
Toonpan, *Australia* **114 B4** 19 28 S 146 48 E
Toora, *Australia* **117 E7** 38 39 S 146 23 E
Toora-Khem, *U.S.S.R.* **57 D10** 52 28N 96 17 E
Toowoomba, *Australia* **115 D5** 27 32 S 151 56 E
Top-ozero, *U.S.S.R.* **48 A5** 65 35N 32 0 E
Topalu, *Romania* **46 E9** 44 31N 28 3 E
Topaz, *U.S.A.* **144 G7** 38 41N 119 30W
Topeka, *U.S.A.* **138 F7** 39 3N 95 40W
Topki, *U.S.S.R.* **56 D9** 55 20N 85 35 E
Topl'a →, *Czech.* **31 C14** 48 45N 21 45 E
Topley, *Canada* **130 C3** 54 49N 126 18W
Toplica →, *Yugoslavia* **42 D6** 43 15N 21 49 E
Toplița, *Romania* **46 C6** 46 55N 25 20 E
Topocalma, Pta., *Chile* **158 C1** 34 10 S 72 2W
Topock, *U.S.A.* **145 L12** 34 46N 114 29W
Topola, *Yugoslavia* **42 C5** 44 17N 20 41 E
Topolčani, *Yugoslavia* **42 F6** 41 14N 21 56 E
Topoľčany, *Czech.* **31 C11** 48 35N 18 12 E
Topoli, *U.S.S.R.* **53 C14** 47 59N 51 38 E
Topolnitsa →, *Bulgaria* **43 E9** 42 11N 24 18 E
Topolobampo, *Mexico* **146 B3** 25 40N 109 4W
Topolovgrad, *Bulgaria* **43 E11** 42 5N 26 20 E
Topolvătu Mare, *Romania* **42 B6** 45 46N 21 41 E
Toppenish, *U.S.A.* **142 C3** 46 27N 120 16W
Topusko, *Yugoslavia* **39 C12** 45 18N 15 59 E
Toquepala, *Peru* **156 D3** 17 24 S 70 25W
Torá, *Spain* **34 D6** 41 49N 1 25 E
Tora Kit, *Sudan* **95 E3** 11 2N 32 36 E
Toraka Vestale, *Madag.* **105 B7** 16 20 S 43 58 E
Torata, *Peru* **156 D3** 17 23 S 70 1W
Torbalı, *Turkey* **88 D2** 38 10N 27 21 E
Torbay, *Canada* **129 C9** 47 40N 52 42W
Torbay, *U.K.* **17 G4** 50 26N 3 31W
Tørdal, *Norway* **14 E2** 59 10N 8 45 E
Tordesillas, *Spain* **36 D6** 41 30N 5 0W
Tordoya, *Spain* **36 B2** 43 6N 8 36W
Töreboda, *Sweden* **15 F8** 58 41N 14 7 E
Torfajökull, *Iceland* **12 E4** 63 54N 19 0W
Torgau, *Germany* **26 D9** 51 32N 13 0 E
Torgelow, *Germany* **26 B9** 53 40N 13 59 E
Torhout, *Belgium* **21 F2** 51 5N 3 7 E
Tori, *Ethiopia* **95 F3** 7 53N 33 35 E
Tori-Shima, *Japan* **61 J10** 30 29N 140 19 E
Torigni-sur-Vire, *France* **22 C6** 49 3N 0 58W
Torija, *Spain* **34 E1** 40 44N 3 2W
Torin, *Mexico* **146 B2** 27 33N 110 15W
Toriñana, C., *Spain* **36 B1** 43 3N 9 17W
Torino, *Italy* **38 C4** 45 4N 7 40 E
Torit, *Sudan* **95 G3** 4 27N 32 31 E
Torkovichi, *U.S.S.R.* **50 B7** 58 51N 30 21 E
Tormac, *Romania* **42 B6** 45 30N 21 30 E
Tormes →, *Spain* **36 D4** 41 18N 6 29W
Tornado Mt., *Canada* **130 D6** 49 55N 114 40W
Torne älv →, *Sweden* **12 D18** 65 50N 24 12 E
Torneå = Tornio, *Finland* **12 D18** 65 50N 24 12 E
Torneträsk, *Sweden* **12 B15** 68 24N 19 15 E
Tornio, *Finland* **12 D18** 65 50N 24 12 E
Tornionjoki →, *Finland* **12 D18** 65 50N 24 12 E
Tornquist, *Argentina* **158 D3** 38 8 S 62 15W
Toro, *Baleares, Spain* **33 B11** 39 59N 4 8 E
Toro, *Zamora, Spain* **36 D5** 41 35N 5 24W
Torö, *Sweden* **15 F11** 58 48N 17 50 E
Toro, Cerro del, *Chile* **158 B2** 29 10 S 69 50W
Toro Pk., *U.S.A.* **145 M10** 33 34N 116 24W
Törökszentmiklós, *Hungary* **31 D13** 47 11N 20 27 E
Toroníios Kólpos, *Greece* **44 D5** 40 5N 23 30 E
Toronto, *Australia* **117 B9** 33 0 S 151 30 E
Toronto, *Canada* **128 D4** 43 39N 79 20W
Toronto, *U.S.A.* **136 F4** 40 27N 80 36W
Toropets, *U.S.S.R.* **50 C7** 56 30N 31 40 E
Tororo, *Uganda* **106 B3** 0 45N 34 12 E
Toros Dağları, *Turkey* **88 E5** 37 0N 32 30 E
Torotoro, *Bolivia* **157 D4** 18 7 S 65 46W
Torpshammar, *Sweden* **14 B10** 62 29N 16 20 E
Torquay, *Australia* **116 E6** 38 20 S 144 19 E
Torquay, *Canada* **131 D8** 49 9N 103 30W
Torquay, *U.K.* **17 G4** 50 27N 3 31W
Torquemada, *Spain* **36 C6** 42 2N 4 19W
Torralba de Calatrava, *Spain* **37 F7** 39 1N 3 44W
Torrance, *U.S.A.* **145 M8** 33 50N 118 19W
Torrão, *Portugal* **37 G2** 38 16N 8 11W
Torre Annunziata, *Italy* **41 B7** 40 45N 14 26 E
Tôrre de Moncorvo, *Portugal* **36 D3** 41 12N 7 8W
Torre del Greco, *Italy* **41 B7** 40 47N 14 22 E
Torre del Mar, *Spain* **37 J6** 36 44N 4 6W
Torre-Pacheco, *Spain* **35 H4** 37 44N 0 57W
Torre Pellice, *Italy* **38 D4** 44 49N 7 13 E
Torreblanca, *Spain* **34 E5** 40 14N 0 12 E
Torrecampo, *Spain* **37 G6** 38 29N 4 41W
Torrecilla en Cameros, *Spain* **34 C2** 42 15N 2 38W
Torredembarra, *Spain* **34 D6** 41 9N 1 24 E
Torredonjimeno, *Spain* **37 H7** 37 46N 3 57W
Torrejoncillo, *Spain* **36 F4** 39 54N 6 28W
Torrelaguna, *Spain* **34 E1** 40 50N 3 38W
Torrelavega, *Spain* **36 B6** 43 20N 4 5W
Torremaggiore, *Italy* **41 A8** 41 42N 15 17 E
Torremolinos, *Spain* **37 J6** 36 38N 4 30W
Torrens, L., *Australia* **116 A2** 31 0 S 137 50 E
Torrens Cr. →, *Australia* **114 C4** 22 23 S 145 9 E
Torrens Creek, *Australia* **114 C4** 20 48 S 145 3 E
Torrente, *Spain* **35 F4** 39 27N 0 28W
Torrenueva, *Spain* **35 G1** 38 38N 3 22W
Torreón, *Mexico* **146 B4** 25 33N 103 25W
Torreperogil, *Spain* **35 G1** 38 2N 3 17W
Torres, *Mexico* **146 B2** 28 46N 110 47W
Torres, Is., *Vanuatu* **121 C4** 13 15 S 166 37 E
Torres Novas, *Portugal* **37 F2** 39 27N 8 33W
Torres Strait, *Australia* **120 E2** 9 50 S 142 20 E
Torres Vedras, *Portugal* **37 F1** 39 5N 9 15W
Torrevieja, *Spain* **35 H4** 37 59N 0 42W
Torrey, *U.S.A.* **143 G8** 38 18N 111 25W
Torridge →, *U.K.* **17 G3** 50 51N 4 10W
Torridon, L., *U.K.* **18 D3** 57 35N 5 50W
Torrijos, *Spain* **36 F6** 39 59N 4 18W
Torrington, *Conn., U.S.A.* **137 E11** 41 50N 73 9W
Torrington, *Wyo., U.S.A.* **138 D2** 42 5N 104 8W
Torroella de Montgri, *Spain* **34 C8** 42 2N 3 8 E
Torrox, *Spain* **37 J7** 36 46N 3 57W
Torsö, *Sweden* **15 F7** 58 48N 13 45 E
Tortola, *Virgin Is.* **149 C7** 18 19N 64 45W
Tórtoles de Esgueva, *Spain* **36 D6** 41 49N 4 2W
Tortona, *Italy* **38 D5** 44 53N 8 54 E
Tortoreto, *Italy* **39 F10** 42 50N 13 55 E
Tortorici, *Italy* **41 D7** 38 2N 14 48 E
Tortosa, *Spain* **34 E5** 40 49N 0 31 E
Tortosa, C., *Spain* **34 E5** 40 41N 0 52 E
Tortosendo, *Portugal* **36 E3** 40 15N 7 31W
Tortue, I. de la, *Haiti* **149 B5** 20 5N 72 57W
Tortum, *Turkey* **89 C9** 40 19N 41 35 E
Ţorūd, *Iran* **85 C7** 35 25N 55 5 E
Torugart, Pereval, *U.S.S.R.* **55 C7** 40 32N 75 24 E
Torul, *Turkey* **89 C8** 40 34N 39 18 E
Toruń, *Poland* **47 B5** 53 2N 18 39 E
Toruń □, *Poland* **47 B6** 53 20N 19 0 E
Torup, *Denmark* **15 G3** 57 5N 9 5 E
Torup, *Sweden* **15 H7** 56 57N 13 5 E
Tory I., *Ireland* **19 A3** 55 17N 8 12W
Torysa →, *Czech.* **31 C14** 48 39N 21 21 E
Torzhok, *U.S.S.R.* **50 C9** 57 5N 34 55 E
Tosa, *Japan* **62 D5** 33 24N 133 23 E
Tosa-Shimizu, *Japan* **62 E4** 32 52N 132 58 E
Tosa-Wan, *Japan* **62 D5** 33 15N 133 30 E
Tosa-yamada, *Japan* **62 D5** 33 36N 133 38 E
Toscana, *Italy* **38 E8** 43 30N 11 5 E
Toscano, Arcipelago, *Italy* **38 F7** 42 30N 10 30 E
Tosno, *U.S.S.R.* **50 B7** 59 38N 30 46 E
Tossa, *Spain* **34 D7** 41 43N 2 56 E
Tostado, *Argentina* **158 B3** 29 15 S 61 50W
Tostedt, *Germany* **26 B5** 53 17N 9 42 E
Tostón, Pta. de, *Canary Is.* **33 F5** 28 42N 14 2W
Tosu, *Japan* **62 D2** 33 22N 130 31 E
Tosya, *Turkey* **88 C6** 41 1N 34 2 E
Toszek, *Poland* **47 E5** 50 27N 18 32 E
Totana, *Spain* **35 H3** 37 45N 1 30W
Toten, *Norway* **14 D4** 60 37N 10 53 E
Toteng, *Botswana* **104 C3** 20 22 S 22 58 E
Tôtes, *France* **22 C8** 49 41N 1 3 E
Tótkomlós, *Hungary* **31 E13** 46 24N 20 45 E
Totma, *U.S.S.R.* **51 B13** 60 0N 42 40 E
Totnes, *U.K.* **17 G4** 50 26N 3 41W
Totness, *Surinam* **153 B6** 5 53N 56 19W
Totonicapán, *Guatemala* **148 D1** 14 58N 91 12W
Totora, *Bolivia* **157 D4** 17 42 S 65 9W
Totoya, I., *Fiji* **121 B3** 18 57 S 179 50W
Totskoye, *U.S.S.R.* **54 E3** 52 32N 52 45 E
Totten Glacier, *Antarctica* **7 C8** 66 45 S 116 10 E
Tottenham, *Australia* **117 B7** 32 14 S 147 21 E
Tottenham, *Canada* **136 B5** 44 1N 79 49W
Tottori, *Japan* **62 B6** 35 30N 134 15 E
Tottori □, *Japan* **62 B6** 35 30N 134 12 E
Touat, *Algeria* **99 C5** 27 27N 0 30 E
Touba, *Ivory C.* **100 D3** 8 22N 7 40W
Toubkal, Djebel, *Morocco* **98 B3** 31 0N 8 0W
Toucy, *France* **23 E10** 47 44N 3 15 E
Tougan, *Burkina Faso* **100 C4** 13 11N 2 58W
Touggourt, *Algeria* **99 B6** 33 6N 6 4 E
Tougué, *Guinea* **100 C2** 11 25N 11 50W
Touho, *N. Cal.* **121 T19** 20 47 S 165 14 E
Toukmatine, *Algeria* **99 D6** 24 49N 7 11 E
Toul, *France* **23 D12** 48 40N 5 53 E
Toulepleu, *Ivory C.* **100 D3** 6 32N 8 24W
Toulon, *France* **25 E9** 43 10N 5 55 E
Toulon, *U.S.A.* **140 C7** 41 6N 89 52W
Toulouse, *France* **24 E5** 43 37N 1 27 E
Toummo, *Niger* **96 D2** 22 45N 14 8 E
Toummo Dhoba, *Niger* **96 D2** 22 30N 14 31 E
Toumodi, *Ivory C.* **100 D3** 6 32N 5 4W
Tounassine, Hamada, *Algeria* **98 C4** 28 48N 5 0W
Toungoo, *Burma* **78 F6** 19 0N 96 30 E
Touques →, *France* **22 C7** 49 22N 0 8 E
Touraine, *France* **22 E7** 47 20N 0 30 E
Tourane = Da Nang, *Vietnam* **76 D7** 16 4N 108 13 E
Tourcoing, *France* **23 B10** 50 42N 3 10 E
Tourine, *Mauritania* **98 D2** 22 23N 11 50W
Tournai, *Belgium* **21 G2** 50 35N 3 25 E
Tournan-en-Brie, *France* **23 D9** 48 44N 2 46 E
Tournay, *France* **24 E4** 43 13N 0 13 E
Tournon, *France* **25 C8** 45 4N 4 50 E
Tournon-St.-Martin, *France* **22 F7** 46 45N 0 58 E
Tournus, *France* **25 B8** 46 35N 4 54 E
Touros, *Brazil* **154 C4** 5 12 S 35 28W
Tours, *France* **22 E7** 47 22N 0 40 E
Touside, Pic, *Chad* **97 D3** 21 1N 16 29 E
Touwsrivier, *S. Africa* **104 E3** 33 20 S 20 2 E
Tovar, *Venezuela* **152 B3** 8 20N 71 46W
Tovarkovskiy, *U.S.S.R.* **51 E11** 53 40N 38 14 E
Tovdal, *Norway* **15 F2** 58 47N 8 10 E
Tovdalselva →, *Norway* **15 F2** 58 15N 8 5 E
Towada, *Japan* **60 D10** 40 37N 141 13 E
Towada-Ko, *Japan* **60 D10** 40 28N 140 55 E
Towamba, *Australia* **117 D8** 37 6 S 149 43 E
Towanda, *Ill., U.S.A.* **141 D8** 40 36N 88 53W
Towanda, *N.Y., U.S.A.* **137 E8** 41 46N 76 30W
Tower, *U.S.A.* **138 B8** 47 49N 92 17W
Towerhill Cr. →, *Australia* **114 C3** 22 28 S 144 35 E
Towner, *U.S.A.* **138 A4** 48 25N 100 26W
Townsend, *U.S.A.* **142 C8** 46 25N 111 32W
Townshend I., *Australia* **114 C5** 22 10 S 150 31 E
Townsville, *Australia* **114 B4** 19 15 S 146 45 E
Towson, *U.S.A.* **134 F7** 39 26N 76 34W
Toya-Ko, *Japan* **60 C10** 42 35N 140 51 E
Toyah, *U.S.A.* **139 K3** 31 20N 103 48W
Toyahvale, *U.S.A.* **139 K3** 30 58N 103 45W
Toyama, *Japan* **63 A9** 36 40N 137 15 E
Toyama □, *Japan* **63 A9** 36 45N 137 30 E
Toyama-Wan, *Japan* **61 F8** 37 0N 137 30 E
Tōyō, *Japan* **62 D6** 33 26N 134 16 E
Toyohashi, *Japan* **63 C9** 34 45N 137 25 E
Toyokawa, *Japan* **63 C9** 34 48N 137 27 E
Toyonaka, *Japan* **63 C7** 34 50N 135 28 E
Toyooka, *Japan* **62 B6** 35 35N 134 48 E
Toyota, *Japan* **63 B9** 35 3N 137 7 E
Toyoura, *Japan* **62 C2** 34 6N 130 57 E
Toytepa, *U.S.S.R.* **55 C4** 41 3N 69 20 E
Tozeur, *Tunisia* **96 B1** 33 56N 8 8 E
Tra On, *Vietnam* **77 H5** 9 58N 105 55 E
Trabancos →, *Spain* **36 D5** 41 36N 5 15W
Traben Trarbach, *Germany* **27 F3** 49 57N 7 7 E
Trabzon, *Turkey* **52 F8** 41 0N 39 45 E
Trabzon □, *Turkey* **89 C8** 41 10N 39 45 E
Tracadie, *Canada* **129 C7** 47 30N 64 55W
Tracy, *Calif., U.S.A.* **144 H5** 37 46N 121 27W
Tracy, *Minn., U.S.A.* **138 C7** 44 12N 95 38W
Tradate, *Italy* **38 C5** 45 43N 8 54 E

278 Ulubat Gölü

Ulubat Gölü, Turkey 88 C3 40 10N 28 25 E
Ulubey, Turkey 88 D3 38 25N 29 18 E
Uluborlu, Turkey 88 D4 38 4N 30 28 E
Uludağ, Turkey 88 C3 40 4N 29 13 E
Uludere, Turkey 89 E10 37 28N 42 42 E
Uluguru Mts., Tanzania 106 D4 7 15 S 37 40 E
Ulukışla, Turkey 88 E6 37 33N 34 28 E
Ulungur He →, China 64 B3 47 1N 87 24 E
Ulutau, U.S.S.R. 56 E7 48 39N 67 1 E
Ulvenhout, Neths. 21 E5 51 33N 4 48 E
Ulverston, U.K. 16 C4 54 13N 3 7W
Ulverstone, Australia 114 G4 41 11 S 146 11 E
Ulya, U.S.S.R. 57 D15 59 10N 142 0 E
Ulyanovsk, U.S.S.R. 51 D16 54 20N 48 25 E
Ulyasutay, Mongolia 64 B4 47 56N 97 28 E
Ulysses, U.S.A. 139 G4 37 39N 101 25W
Umag, Yugoslavia 39 C10 45 26N 13 31 E
Umala, Bolivia 156 D4 17 25 S 68 5W
Uman, U.S.S.R. 52 B4 48 40N 30 12 E
Umarkhed, India 82 E3 19 37N 77 46 E
Umatac, Guam 121 R15 13 18N 144 39 E
Umatilla, U.S.A. 142 D4 45 58N 119 17W
Umba, U.S.S.R. 48 A5 66 50N 34 20 E
Umbertide, Italy 39 E9 43 18N 12 20 E
Umboi I., Papua N. G. 120 C5 5 40 S 148 0 E
Umbrella Mts., N.Z. 119 F4 45 35 S 169 5 E
Umbria □, Italy 39 F9 42 53N 12 30 E
Ume älv →, Sweden 12 E16 63 45N 20 20 E
Umeå, Sweden 12 E16 63 45N 20 20 E
Umera, Indonesia 71 E7 0 12 S 129 37 E
Umfuli →, Zimbabwe 107 F2 17 30 S 29 23 E
Umgusa, Zimbabwe 107 F2 19 29 S 27 52 E
Umi, Japan 62 D2 33 34N 130 30 E
Umka, Yugoslavia 42 C5 44 40N 20 19 E
Umkomaas, S. Africa 105 E5 30 13 S 30 48 E
Umm ad Daraj, J., Jordan 91 C4 32 18N 35 48 E
Umm al Arānib, Libya 96 C2 26 10N 14 43 E
Umm al Qaywayn, U.A.E. 85 E7 25 30N 55 35 E
Umm al Qittayn, Jordan 91 C5 32 18N 36 40 E
Umm Arda, Sudan 95 D3 15 17N 32 31 E
Umm Bāb, Qatar 85 E6 25 12N 50 48 E
Umm Bel, Sudan 95 E2 13 35N 28 0 E
Umm Dubban, Sudan 95 D3 15 23N 32 52 E
Umm el Fahm, Israel 91 C4 32 31N 35 9 E
Umm Koweika, Sudan 95 E3 13 10N 32 16 E
Umm Lajj, Si. Arabia 84 E3 25 0N 37 23 E
Umm Merwa, Sudan 94 D3 18 4N 32 30 E
Umm Ruwaba, Sudan 95 E3 12 50N 31 20 E
Umm Sidr, Sudan 95 E2 14 29N 25 10 E
Umm Thalwīwah, Si. Arabia 86 B3 21 9N 40 48 E
Ummanz, Germany 26 A9 54 29N 13 9 E
Umnak, U.S.A. 126 C3 53 20N 168 20W
Umniati →, Zimbabwe 107 F2 16 49 S 28 45 E
Umpqua →, U.S.A. 142 E1 43 42N 124 3W
Umpulo, Angola 103 E3 12 38 S 17 42 E
Umred, India 82 D4 20 51N 79 18 E
Umreth, India 80 H5 22 41N 73 4 E
Umtata, S. Africa 105 E4 31 36 S 28 49 E
Umuahia, Nigeria 101 D6 5 33N 7 29 E
Umuarama, Brazil 159 A5 23 45 S 53 20W
Umvukwe Ra., Zimbabwe 107 F3 16 45 S 30 45 E
Umzimvubu = Port St. Johns, S. Africa 105 E4 31 38 S 29 33 E
Umzingwane →, Zimbabwe 107 G2 22 12 S 29 56 E
Umzinto, S. Africa 105 E5 30 15 S 30 45 E
Una, India 80 J4 20 46N 71 8 E
Una →, Yugoslavia 39 C13 45 16N 16 55 E
Unac →, Yugoslavia 39 D13 44 30N 16 9 E
Unadilla, U.S.A. 137 D9 42 20N 75 17W
Unalaska, U.S.A. 126 C3 53 40N 166 40W
Uncastillo, Spain 34 C3 42 21N 1 8W
Uncía, Bolivia 156 D4 18 25 S 66 40W
Uncompahgre Pk., U.S.A. 143 G10 38 5N 107 32W
Unden, Sweden 15 F8 58 45N 14 25 E
Underberg, S. Africa 105 D4 29 50 S 29 22 E
Underbool, Australia 116 C4 35 10 S 141 51 E
Undersaker, Sweden 14 A7 63 19N 13 21 E
Undersvik, Sweden 14 C10 61 36N 16 20 E
Unecha, U.S.S.R. 50 E8 52 50N 32 37 E
Uneiuxi →, Brazil 152 D4 0 37 S 65 34W
Ungarie, Australia 117 B7 33 38 S 146 56 E
Ungarra, Australia 116 C2 34 12 S 136 2 E
Ungava B., Canada 127 C13 59 30N 67 30W
Ungava Pen., Canada 124 D12 60 0N 74 0W
Ungeny, U.S.S.R. 52 C2 47 11N 27 51 E
Unggi, N. Korea 67 C16 42 16N 130 28 E
Ungwatiri, Sudan 95 D4 16 52N 36 10 E
Uni, U.S.S.R. 54 C2 56 44N 51 47 E
União da Vitória, Brazil 159 B5 26 13 S 51 5W
União dos Palmares, Brazil 154 C4 9 10 S 36 2W
Uniejów, Poland 47 D5 51 59N 18 46 E
Unije, Yugoslavia 39 D11 44 40N 14 15 E
Unimak, U.S.A. 126 C3 55 0N 164 0W
Unini →, Brazil 153 D5 1 41 S 61 31W
Union, Miss., U.S.A. 139 J10 32 34N 89 14W
Union, Mo., U.S.A. 140 F6 38 25N 91 0W
Union, S.C., U.S.A. 135 H5 34 43N 81 39W
Union, Mt., U.S.A. 143 J7 34 34N 112 21W
Union City, Calif., U.S.A. 144 H4 37 36N 122 1W
Union City, N.J., U.S.A. 137 F10 40 47N 74 5W
Union City, Pa., U.S.A. 136 E5 41 53N 79 50W
Union City, Tenn., U.S.A. 139 G10 36 25N 89 0W
Union Gap, U.S.A. 142 C3 46 38N 120 29W
Union Grove, U.S.A. 141 B8 42 41N 88 3W
Union of Soviet Socialist Republics ■, Eurasia 57 D11 60 0N 100 0 E
Union Springs, U.S.A. 135 J3 32 9N 85 44W
Union Star, U.S.A. 140 E2 39 59N 94 36W
Uniondale, S. Africa 104 E3 33 39 S 23 7 E
Uniontown, Ky., U.S.A. 141 G9 37 47N 87 56W
Uniontown, Pa., U.S.A. 134 F6 39 54N 79 45W
Unionville, U.S.A. 140 D3 40 29N 93 1W
Unirea, Romania 46 E8 44 15N 27 35 E
United Arab Emirates ■, Asia 85 F7 23 50N 54 0 E
United Kingdom ■, Europe 11 E5 53 0N 2 0W
United States of America ■, N. Amer. 132 C7 37 0N 96 0W
Unity, Canada 131 C7 52 30N 109 5W
Universales, Mtes., Spain 34 E3 40 18N 1 33W
University City, U.S.A. 140 F6 38 40N 90 20W
Unjha, India 80 H5 23 46N 72 24 E
Unnao, India 81 F9 26 35N 80 30 E
Uno, Ilha, Guinea-Biss. 100 C1 11 15N 16 13W
Unst, U.K. 18 A8 60 50N 0 55W
Unstrut →, Germany 26 D7 51 10N 11 48 E
Unter-engadin, Switz. 29 C10 46 48N 10 20 E
Unterägeri, Switz. 29 B7 47 8N 8 36 E
Unterkulm, Switz. 28 B6 47 18N 8 7 E
Unterseen, Switz. 28 C5 46 41N 7 50 E
Unterwaldner Alpen, Switz. 29 C6 46 55N 8 15 E
Unuk →, Canada 130 B2 56 5N 131 3W
Ünye, Turkey 52 F7 41 5N 37 15 E
Unzen-Dake, Japan 62 E2 32 45N 130 17 E
Unzha, U.S.S.R. 51 C14 58 0N 44 0 E
Unzha →, U.S.S.R. 51 C13 57 30N 43 40 E
Uors, Switz. 29 C8 46 42N 9 12 E
Uozu, Japan 63 A9 36 48N 137 24 E
Upa →, Czech. 31 A9 50 35N 16 15 E
Upata, Venezuela 153 B5 8 1N 62 24W
Upemba, L., Zaïre 107 D2 8 30 S 26 20 E
Upernavik, Greenland 6 B5 72 49N 56 20W
Upington, S. Africa 104 D3 28 25 S 21 15 E
Upleta, India 80 J4 21 46N 70 16 E
Upolu, W. Samoa 121 W24 13 58 S 172 0W
Upper Alkali Lake, U.S.A. 142 F3 41 47N 120 8W
Upper Arlington, U.S.A. 141 E13 40 0N 83 4W
Upper Arrow L., Canada 130 C5 50 30N 117 50W
Upper Austria = Oberösterreich □, Austria 30 C7 48 10N 14 0 E
Upper Foster L., Canada 131 B7 56 47N 105 20W
Upper Hutt, N.Z. 118 H4 41 8 S 175 5 E
Upper Juba, Somali Rep. 108 D2 3 0N 43 0 E
Upper Klamath L., U.S.A. 142 E3 42 16N 121 55W
Upper Lake, U.S.A. 144 F4 39 10N 122 55W
Upper Manilla, Australia 117 A9 30 38 S 150 40 E
Upper Musquodoboit, Canada 129 C7 45 10N 62 58W
Upper Red L., U.S.A. 138 A7 48 5N 95 0W
Upper Sandusky, U.S.A. 141 D13 40 50N 83 17W
Upper Sheikh, Somali Rep. 108 C3 9 56N 45 13 E
Upper Volta = Burkina Faso ■, Africa 100 C4 12 0N 1 0W
Upphärad, Sweden 15 F6 58 9N 12 19 E
Uppsala, Sweden 14 E11 59 53N 17 38 E
Uppsala län □, Sweden 13 G14 60 0N 17 30 E
Upshi, India 81 C7 33 48N 77 52 E
Upstart, C., Australia 114 B4 19 41 S 147 45 E
Upton, U.S.A. 138 C2 44 8N 104 35W
Ur, Iraq 84 D5 30 55N 46 25 E
Ura-Tyube, U.S.S.R. 55 D4 39 55N 69 1 E
Urabá, G. de, Colombia 152 B2 8 25N 76 53W
Uracara, Brazil 153 D6 2 20 S 57 50W
Urad Qianqi, China 66 D5 40 40N 108 30 E
Uraga-Suidō, Japan 63 B11 35 13N 139 45 E
Urakawa, Japan 60 C11 42 9N 142 47 E
Ural, Australia 117 B7 33 21 S 146 12 E
Ural →, U.S.S.R. 53 C14 47 0N 51 48 E
Ural Mts. = Uralskie Gory, U.S.S.R. 48 C10 60 0N 59 0 E
Uralla, Australia 117 A9 30 37 S 151 29 E
Uralsk, U.S.S.R. 54 F2 51 20N 51 20 E
Uralskie Gory, U.S.S.R. 48 C10 60 0N 59 0 E
Urambo, Tanzania 106 D3 5 4 S 32 0 E
Urambo □, Tanzania 106 D3 5 0 S 32 0 E
Urana, Australia 117 C7 35 15 S 146 21 E
Urandangi, Australia 114 C2 21 32 S 138 14 E
Uranium City, Canada 131 B7 59 34N 108 37W
Uranquinty, Australia 115 F4 35 10 S 147 12 E
Uraricaá →, Brazil 153 C5 3 20N 61 56W
Uraricuera →, Brazil 153 C5 3 2N 60 30W
Uravakonda, India 83 G3 14 57N 77 12 E
Urawa, Japan 63 B11 35 50N 139 40 E
Uray, U.S.S.R. 56 C7 60 5N 65 15 E
'Uray'irah, Si. Arabia 85 E6 25 57N 48 53 E
Urbana, Ill., U.S.A. 141 D8 40 7N 88 12W
Urbana, Mo., U.S.A. 140 G3 37 51N 93 10W
Urbana, Ohio, U.S.A. 141 D13 40 9N 83 44W
Urbandale, U.S.A. 140 C3 41 38N 93 43W
Urbánia, Italy 39 E9 43 40N 12 31 E
Urbano Santos, Brazil 154 B3 3 12 S 43 23W
Urbel →, Spain 34 C1 42 21N 3 40W
Urbino, Italy 39 E9 43 43N 12 38 E
Urbión, Picos de, Spain 34 D2 42 1N 2 52W
Urcos, Peru 156 C3 13 40 S 71 38W
Urda, Spain 37 F7 39 25N 3 43W
Urda, U.S.S.R. 53 B12 48 52N 47 23 E
Urdinarrain, Argentina 158 C4 32 37 S 58 52W
Urdos, France 24 F3 42 51N 0 35W
Urdzhar, U.S.S.R. 56 E9 47 5N 81 38 E
Ure →, U.K. 16 C6 54 20N 1 25W
Uren, U.S.S.R. 51 C14 57 35N 45 55 E
Urengoy, U.S.S.R. 56 C8 65 58N 28 25 E
Ureparapara, Vanuatu 121 C5 13 32 S 167 20 E
Ures, Mexico 146 B2 29 30N 110 30W
Ureshino, Japan 62 D1 33 6N 129 59 E
Urfa, Turkey 89 E8 37 12N 38 50 E
Urfa □, Turkey 89 E8 37 0N 39 0 E
Urfahr, Austria 30 C7 48 19N 14 17 E
Urgench, U.S.S.R. 56 E7 41 40N 60 41 E
Urgut, U.S.S.R. 55 D3 39 23N 67 15 E
Uri, India 81 B6 34 8N 74 2 E
Uri □, Switz. 29 C7 46 43N 8 35 E
Uribante →, Venezuela 152 B3 7 25N 71 50W
Uribe, Colombia 152 C3 3 13N 74 24W
Uribia, Colombia 152 A3 11 43N 72 16W
Uriondo, Bolivia 158 A3 21 41 S 64 41W
Urique, Mexico 146 B3 27 13N 107 55W
Urique →, Mexico 146 B3 26 29N 107 58W
Urirotstock, Switz. 29 C7 46 52N 8 32 E
Urk, Neths. 20 C7 52 39N 5 36 E
Urla, Turkey 88 D2 38 20N 26 47 E
Urlati, Romania 46 E7 44 59N 26 15 E
Urmia = Orūmīyeh, Iran 84 B5 37 40N 45 0 E
Urmia, L. = Orūmīyeh, Daryācheh-ye, Iran 84 B5 37 50N 45 30 E
Urner Alpen, Switz. 29 C7 46 45N 8 45 E
Uroševac, Yugoslavia 42 E6 42 23N 21 10 E
Urrao, Colombia 152 B2 6 20N 76 11W
Ursus, Poland 47 C7 52 12N 20 53 E
Uruaçu, Brazil 155 D2 14 30 S 49 10W
Uruana, Brazil 155 E2 15 30 S 49 41W
Uruapan, Mexico 146 D4 19 30N 102 0W
Uruará →, Brazil 153 D7 2 6 S 53 38W
Urubamba, Peru 156 C3 13 20 S 72 10W
Urubamba →, Peru 156 C3 10 43 S 73 48W
Urubaxi →, Brazil 153 D5 0 31 S 64 50W
Urubu →, Brazil 153 D6 2 55 S 58 25W
Uruçara, Brazil 153 D6 2 32 S 57 45W
Uruçuí, Brazil 154 C3 7 20 S 44 28W
Uruçuí, Serra do, Brazil 154 C3 9 0 S 44 45W
Uruçuí Prêto →, Brazil 154 C3 7 20 S 44 38W
Urucuia →, Brazil 155 E2 16 8 S 45 5W
Urucurituba, Brazil 153 D6 2 41 S 57 40W
Uruguai →, Brazil 159 B5 26 0 S 53 30W
Uruguaiana, Brazil 158 B4 29 50 S 57 0W
Uruguay ■, S. Amer. 158 C4 32 30 S 56 30W
Uruguay →, S. Amer. 158 C4 34 12 S 58 18W
Urumchi = Ürümqi, China 64 B3 43 45N 87 45 E
Ürümqi, China 64 B3 43 45N 87 45 E
Urup →, U.S.S.R. 53 D9 45 0N 41 10 E
Urup, Os., U.S.S.R. 57 E16 46 0N 151 0 E
Urutaí, Brazil 155 E2 17 28 S 48 12W
Uryung-Khaya, U.S.S.R. 57 B12 72 48N 113 23 E
Uryupinsk, U.S.S.R. 51 F12 50 45N 41 58 E
Urzhum, U.S.S.R. 54 C1 57 10N 49 56 E
Urziceni, Romania 46 E7 44 40N 26 42 E
Usa, Japan 62 D3 33 31N 131 21 E
Usa →, U.S.S.R. 48 A10 65 57N 56 55 E
Uşak, Turkey 88 D3 38 43N 29 28 E
Uşak □, Turkey 88 D3 38 30N 29 0 E
Usakos, Namibia 104 C2 21 54 S 15 31 E
Usborne, Mt., Falk. Is. 160 D5 51 42 S 58 50W
Ušće, Yugoslavia 42 D5 43 30N 20 39 E
Usedom, Germany 26 B9 53 50N 13 55 E
'Usfān, Si. Arabia 86 B2 21 58N 39 27 E
Ush-Tobe, U.S.S.R. 56 E8 45 16N 78 0 E
Ushakova, Os., U.S.S.R. 6 A12 82 0N 80 0 E
Ushant = Ouessant, I. d', France 22 D1 48 28N 5 6W
Ushashi, Tanzania 106 C3 1 59 S 33 57 E
Ushat, Sudan 95 F2 7 59N 29 28 E
Ushibuka, Japan 62 E2 32 11N 130 1 E
Ushuaia, Argentina 160 D3 54 50 S 68 23W
Ushumun, U.S.S.R. 57 D13 52 47N 126 32 E
Usk →, U.K. 17 F5 51 37N 2 56W
Üsküdar, Turkey 49 F4 41 0N 29 5 E
Uslar, Germany 26 D5 51 39N 9 39 E
Usman, U.S.S.R. 51 E11 52 5N 39 48 E
Usoke, Tanzania 106 D3 5 8 S 32 24 E
Usolye, U.S.S.R. 54 B5 59 28N 56 31 E
Usolye Sibirskoye, U.S.S.R. 57 D11 52 48N 103 40 E
Usoro, Nigeria 101 D6 5 33N 6 11 E
Uspallata, P. de, Argentina 158 C2 32 37 S 69 22W
Uspenskiy, U.S.S.R. 56 E8 48 41N 72 43 E
Usquert, Neths. 20 B9 53 24N 6 36 E
Ussel, France 24 C6 45 32N 2 18 E
Ussuri →, Asia 60 A7 48 27N 135 0 E
Ussuriysk, U.S.S.R. 57 E14 43 48N 131 59 E
Ussurka, U.S.S.R. 60 B6 45 12N 133 31 E
Ust-Aldan = Batamay, U.S.S.R. 57 C13 63 30N 129 15 E
Ust Amginskoye = Khandyga, U.S.S.R. 57 C14 62 42N 135 35 E
Ust-Bolsheretsk, U.S.S.R. 57 D16 52 50N 156 15 E
Ust Buzulukskaya, U.S.S.R. 51 F13 50 8N 42 11 E
Ust Chaun, U.S.S.R. 57 C18 68 47N 170 30 E
Ust-Donetskiy, U.S.S.R. 53 C9 47 35N 40 55 E
Ust'-Ilga, U.S.S.R. 57 D11 55 5N 104 55 E
Ust Ilimpeya = Yukti, U.S.S.R. 57 C11 63 26N 105 42 E
Ust-Ilimsk, U.S.S.R. 57 D11 58 3N 102 39 E
Ust Ishim, U.S.S.R. 56 D8 57 45N 71 10 E
Ust-Kamchatsk, U.S.S.R. 57 D17 56 10N 162 28 E
Ust-Kamenogorsk, U.S.S.R. 56 E9 50 0N 82 36 E
Ust-Karenga, U.S.S.R. 57 D12 54 25N 116 30 E
Ust Khayryuzova, U.S.S.R. 57 D16 57 15N 156 45 E
Ust-Kut, U.S.S.R. 57 D11 56 50N 105 42 E
Ust Kuyga, U.S.S.R. 57 B14 70 1N 135 43 E
Ust-Labinsk, U.S.S.R. 53 D8 45 15N 39 41 E
Ust Luga, U.S.S.R. 50 B6 59 35N 28 20 E
Ust Maya, U.S.S.R. 57 C14 60 30N 134 28 E
Ust-Mil, U.S.S.R. 57 D14 59 40N 133 11 E
Ust-Nera, U.S.S.R. 57 C15 64 35N 143 15 E
Ust-Nyukzha, U.S.S.R. 57 D13 56 34N 121 37 E
Ust Olenek, U.S.S.R. 57 B12 73 0N 119 48 E
Ust-Omchug, U.S.S.R. 57 C15 61 9N 149 38 E
Ust Port, U.S.S.R. 56 C9 69 40N 84 26 E
Ust Tsilma, U.S.S.R. 48 A9 65 25N 52 0 E
Ust-Tungir, U.S.S.R. 57 D13 55 25N 120 36 E
Ust Urt = Ustyurt, Plato, U.S.S.R. 56 E6 44 0N 55 0 E
Ust Usa, U.S.S.R. 48 A10 66 0N 56 30 E
Ust-Uyskoye, U.S.S.R. 54 D8 54 16N 63 54 E
Ust Vorkuta, U.S.S.R. 56 C7 67 24N 64 0 E
Ustaoset, Norway 14 D2 60 30N 8 2 E
Ustaritz, France 24 E2 43 24N 1 27W
Uste, U.S.S.R. 51 B11 59 35N 39 40 E
Uster, Switz. 29 B7 47 22N 8 43 E
Ústí nad Labem, Czech. 30 A7 50 41N 14 3 E
Ústí nad Orlicí, Czech. 31 B9 49 58N 16 24 E
Ustica, Italy 40 D6 38 42N 13 10 E
Ustinov = Izhevsk, U.S.S.R. 54 C3 56 51N 53 14 E
Ustka, Poland 47 A3 54 35N 16 55 E
Ustroń, Poland 31 B11 49 43N 18 48 E
Ustrzyki Dolne, Poland 31 B15 49 27N 22 40 E
Ustye, U.S.S.R. 57 D10 57 46N 94 37 E
Ustyurt, Plato, U.S.S.R. 56 E6 44 0N 55 0 E
Ustyuzhna, U.S.S.R. 51 B10 58 50N 36 32 E
Usu, China 64 B3 44 27N 84 40 E
Usuki, Japan 62 D3 33 8N 131 49 E
Usulután, El Salv. 148 D2 13 25N 88 28W
Usumacinta →, Mexico 147 D6 17 0N 91 0W
Usumbura = Bujumbura, Burundi 106 C2 3 16 S 29 18 E
Usure, Tanzania 106 C3 4 40 S 34 22 E
Usva, U.S.S.R. 54 B5 58 41N 57 37 E
Uta, Indonesia 71 E9 4 33 S 136 0 E
'Uta Vava'u, Tonga 121 P14 18 36 S 174 0W
Utah □, U.S.A. 142 G8 39 30N 111 30W
Utah, L., U.S.A. 142 F8 40 10N 111 58W
Ute Cr. →, U.S.A. 139 H3 35 21N 103 45W
Utena, U.S.S.R. 50 D4 55 27N 25 40 E
Ütersen, Germany 26 B5 53 40N 9 40 E
Utete, Tanzania 106 D4 8 0 S 38 45 E
Uthai Thani, Thailand 76 E3 15 22N 100 3 E
Uthal, Pakistan 80 G2 25 44N 66 40 E
Utiariti, Brazil 157 C6 13 0 S 58 10W
Utica, N.Y., U.S.A. 137 C9 43 5N 75 18W
Utica, Ohio, U.S.A. 136 F2 40 13N 82 26W
Utiel, Spain 34 F3 39 37N 1 11W
Utik L., Canada 131 B9 55 15N 96 0W
Utikuma L., Canada 130 B5 55 50N 115 30W
Utinga, Brazil 155 D3 12 6 S 41 5W
Uto, Japan 62 E2 32 41N 130 40 E
Utrecht, Neths. 20 D6 52 5N 5 8 E
Utrecht, S. Africa 105 D5 27 38 S 30 20 E
Utrecht □, Neths. 20 D6 52 6N 5 7 E
Utrera, Spain 37 H5 37 12N 5 48W
Utsjoki, Finland 12 B19 69 51N 26 59 E
Utsunomiya, Japan 63 A11 36 30N 139 50 E
Uttar Pradesh □, India 81 F9 27 0N 80 0 E
Uttaradit, Thailand 76 D3 17 36N 100 5 E
Uttoxeter, U.K. 16 E6 52 53N 1 50W
Utva →, U.S.S.R. 54 F3 51 28N 52 40 E
Ütze, Germany 26 C6 52 28N 10 11 E
Uudenmaan lääni □, Finland 13 F18 60 25N 25 0 E
Uusikaarlepyy, Finland 12 E17 63 32N 22 31 E
Uusikaupunki, Finland 13 F16 60 47N 21 25 E
Uva, U.S.S.R. 54 C3 56 59N 52 13 E
Uvá →, Colombia 152 C3 3 41N 70 3W
Uvac →, Yugoslavia 42 D4 43 35N 19 40 E
Uvalde, U.S.A. 139 L5 29 15N 99 48W
Uvarovo, U.S.S.R. 51 F13 51 59N 42 14 E
Uvat, U.S.S.R. 56 D7 59 5N 68 50 E
Uvéa, I., Vanuatu 111 E12 20 30 S 166 35 E
Uvelskiy, U.S.S.R. 54 D7 54 26N 61 22 E
Uvinza, Tanzania 106 D3 5 5 S 30 24 E
Uvira, Zaïre 106 C2 3 22 S 29 3 E
Uvs Nuur, Mongolia 64 A4 50 20N 92 30 E
Uwa, Japan 62 D4 33 22N 132 31 E
Uwajima, Japan 62 D4 33 10N 132 35 E
'Uwayfī, Oman 87 B7 22 15N 56 59 E
Uweinat, Jebel, Sudan 94 C1 21 54N 24 58 E
Uxbridge, Canada 136 B5 44 6N 79 7W
Uxin Qi, China 66 E5 38 50N 109 5 E
Uxmal, Mexico 147 C7 20 22N 89 46W
Uyandi, U.S.S.R. 57 C15 69 19N 141 0 E
Uyo, Nigeria 101 D6 5 1N 7 53 E
Uyu →, Burma 78 C5 24 51N 94 57 E
Uyuk, U.S.S.R. 55 B5 43 36N 71 16 E
Uyuni, Bolivia 156 E4 20 28 S 66 47W
Uzbek S.S.R. □, U.S.S.R. 55 C2 41 30N 65 0 E
Uzen, U.S.S.R. 49 F9 43 27N 53 10 E
Uzen, Bol. →, U.S.S.R. 51 G16 50 0N 49 30 E
Uzen, Mal. →, U.S.S.R. 51 G16 50 0N 48 30 E
Uzerche, France 24 C5 45 25N 1 34 E
Uzès, France 25 D8 44 1N 4 26 E
Uzgen, U.S.S.R. 55 C6 40 46N 73 18 E
Uzh →, U.S.S.R. 50 F7 51 15N 30 12 E
Uzhgorod, U.S.S.R. 50 G3 48 36N 22 18 E
Uzlovaya, U.S.S.R. 51 E11 54 0N 38 5 E
Uzun-Agach, U.S.S.R. 55 B8 43 35N 76 20 E
Uzunköprü, Turkey 43 F11 41 16N 26 43 E
Uzwil, Switz. 29 B8 47 26N 9 9 E

V

Vaal →, S. Africa 104 D3 29 4 S 23 38 E
Vaal Dam, S. Africa 105 D4 27 0 S 28 14 E
Vaals, Neths. 21 G8 50 46N 6 1 E
Vaalwater, S. Africa 105 C4 24 15 S 28 8 E
Vaasa, Finland 12 E16 63 6N 21 38 E
Vaasan lääni □, Finland 12 E17 63 2N 22 50 E
Vaassen, Neths. 20 D7 52 17N 5 58 E
Vabre, France 24 E6 43 42N 2 24 E
Vác, Hungary 31 D12 47 49N 19 10 E
Vacaria, Brazil 159 B5 28 31 S 50 52W
Vacaville, U.S.A. 144 G5 38 21N 122 0W
Vaccarès, Étang de, France 25 E8 43 32N 4 34 E
Vach →, U.S.S.R. 56 C8 60 45N 76 45 E
Vache, I.-à-, Haiti 149 C5 18 2N 73 35W
Vadnagar, India 80 H5 23 47N 72 40 E
Vado Lígure, Italy 38 D5 44 16N 8 26 E
Vadodara, India 80 H5 22 20N 73 10 E
Vadsø, Norway 12 A20 70 3N 29 50 E
Vadstena, Sweden 15 F8 58 28N 14 54 E
Vaduz, Liech. 29 B9 47 8N 9 31 E
Værøy, Norway 12 C12 67 40N 12 40 E
Vagnhärad, Sweden 14 F11 58 57N 17 33 E
Vagos, Portugal 36 E2 40 33N 8 42W
Váh →, Czech. 31 D11 47 43N 18 7 E
Vahsel B., Antarctica 7 D1 75 0 S 35 0W
Vaï, Greece 32 D8 35 15N 26 18 E
Vaigach, U.S.S.R. 56 B6 70 10N 59 0 E
Vaigai →, India 83 K4 9 15N 79 10 E
Vaiges, France 22 D6 48 2N 0 30W
Vaihingen, Germany 27 G4 48 55N 8 58 E
Vaijapur, India 82 E2 19 58N 74 45 E
Vaikam, India 83 K3 9 45N 76 25 E
Vailly-sur-Aisne, France 23 C10 49 24N 3 31 E
Vaippar →, India 83 K4 9 0N 78 25 E
Vaison-la-Romaine, France 25 D9 44 14N 5 4 E
Vajpur, India 82 D1 21 24N 73 17 E
Vakarel, Bulgaria 43 E8 42 35N 23 40 E
Vakfikebir, Turkey 89 C8 41 2N 39 17 E
Vakhsh →, U.S.S.R. 55 E4 37 6N 68 18 E
Vál, Hungary 31 D11 47 22N 18 40 E
Val-de-Marne □, France 23 D9 48 45N 2 28 E
Val-d'Oise □, France 23 C9 49 5N 2 10 E
Val d'Or, Canada

Vůlchedruma 281

Villard-de-Lans, France 25 C9 45 3N 5 33 E
Villarino de los Aires, Spain 36 D4 41 18N 6 23W
Villarosa, Italy 41 E7 37 36N 14 9 E
Villarramiel, Spain 36 C6 42 2N 4 55W
Villarreal, Spain 34 F4 39 55N 0 3W
Villarrica, Chile 160 A2 39 15 S 72 15W
Villarrica, Paraguay 158 B4 25 40 S 56 30W
Villarrobledo, Spain 35 F2 39 18N 2 36W
Villarroya de la Sierra, Spain 34 D3 41 27N 1 46W
Villarrubia de los Ojos, Spain 35 F1 39 14N 3 36W
Villars-les-Dombes, France 25 C9 46 0N 5 3 E
Villarta de San Juan, Spain 35 F1 39 15N 3 25W
Villasayas, Spain 34 D2 41 24N 2 39W
Villaseca de los Gamitos, Spain 36 D4 41 2N 6 7W
Villastar, Spain 34 E3 40 17N 1 9W
Villatobas, Spain 34 F1 39 54N 3 20W
Villavicencio, Argentina 158 C2 32 28 S 69 0W
Villavicencio, Colombia 152 C3 4 9N 73 37W
Villaviciosa, Spain 36 B5 43 32N 5 27W
Villazón, Bolivia 158 A2 22 0 S 65 35W
Ville-Marie, Canada 128 C4 47 20N 79 30W
Ville Platte, U.S.A. 139 K8 30 45N 92 17W
Villedieu-les-Poêlles, France 22 D5 48 50N 1 13W
Villefort, France 24 D7 44 28N 3 56 E
Villefranche-de-Lauragais, France 24 E5 43 25N 1 44 E
Villefranche-de-Rouergue, France 24 D6 44 21N 2 2 E
Villefranche-du-Périgord, France 24 D5 44 38N 1 5 E
Villefranche-sur-Cher, France 23 E8 47 18N 1 46 E
Villefranche-sur-Saône, France 25 C8 45 59N 4 43 E
Villegrande, Bolivia 157 D5 18 30 S 64 10W
Villel, Spain 34 E3 40 14N 1 12W
Villemaur-sur-Vanne, France 23 D10 48 15N 3 44 E
Villemur-sur-Tarn, France 24 E5 43 51N 1 31 E
Villena, Spain 35 G4 38 39N 0 52W
Villenauxe-la-Grande, France 23 D10 48 35N 3 33 E
Villenave-d'Ornon, France 24 D3 44 46N 0 33W
Villeneuve, Italy 38 C4 45 40N 7 10 E
Villeneuve, Switz. 28 D3 46 24N 6 56 E
Villeneuve-l'Archevêque, France 23 D10 48 14N 3 32 E
Villeneuve-lès-Avignon, France 25 E8 43 58N 4 49 E
Villeneuve-St.-Georges, France 23 D9 48 44N 2 28 E
Villeneuve-sur-Allier, France 24 B7 46 40N 3 13 E
Villeneuve-sur-Lot, France 24 D4 44 24N 0 42 E
Villeréal, France 24 D4 44 38N 0 45 E
Villers-Bocage, France 22 C6 49 3N 0 40W
Villers-Bretonneux, France 23 C9 49 50N 2 30 E
Villers-Cotterêts, France 23 C10 49 15N 3 4 E
Villers-le-Bouillet, Belgium 21 G6 50 34N 5 15 E
Villers-le-Gambon, Belgium 21 H5 50 11N 4 37 E
Villers-sur-Mer, France 22 C6 49 21N 0 2W
Villersexel, France 23 E13 47 33N 6 26 E
Villerupt, France 23 C12 49 28N 5 55 E
Villerville, France 22 C7 49 26N 0 5 E
Villiers, S. Africa 105 D4 27 2 S 28 36 E
Villingen, Germany 27 G4 48 4N 8 28 E
Villisca, U.S.A. 140 D2 40 55N 94 59W
Villupuram, India 83 J4 11 59N 79 31 E
Vilna, Canada 130 C6 54 7N 111 55W
Vilnius, U.S.S.R. 50 D4 54 38N 25 19 E
Vils →, Germany 27 G9 48 38N 13 11 E
Vilsbiburg, Germany 27 G8 48 27N 12 23 E
Vilshofen, Germany 27 G9 48 38N 13 11 E
Vilskutskogo, Proliv, U.S.S.R. 57 B11 78 0N 103 0 E
Vilusi, Yugoslavia 42 E3 42 44N 18 34 E
Vilvoorde, Belgium 21 G4 50 56N 4 26 E
Vilyuy →, U.S.S.R. 57 C13 64 24N 126 26 E
Vilyuysk, U.S.S.R. 57 C13 63 40N 121 35 E
Vimercate, Italy 38 C6 45 38N 9 25 E
Vimiosa, Portugal 36 D4 41 35N 6 31W
Vimoutiers, France 22 D7 48 57N 0 10 E
Vimperk, Czech. 30 B6 49 3N 13 46 E
Viña del Mar, Chile 158 C1 33 0 S 71 30W
Vinaroz, Spain 34 E5 40 30N 0 27 E
Vincennes, U.S.A. 141 F9 38 42N 87 29W
Vincent, U.S.A. 145 L8 34 33N 118 11W
Vinces, Ecuador 152 D2 1 32 S 79 45W
Vinchina, Argentina 158 B2 28 45 S 68 15W
Vindel älven →, Sweden 12 E15 63 55N 19 50 E
Vindeln, Sweden 12 D15 64 12N 19 43 E
Vinderup, Denmark 15 H2 56 29N 8 45 E
Vindhya Ra., India 80 H7 22 50N 77 0 E
Vine Grove, U.S.A. 141 G11 37 49N 85 59W
Vineland, U.S.A. 134 F8 39 30N 75 0W
Vinga, Romania 46 D2 46 0N 21 14 E
Vingnes, Norway 14 C4 61 7N 10 26 E
Vinh, Vietnam 76 C5 18 45N 105 38 E
Vinh Linh, Vietnam 76 D6 17 4N 107 2 E
Vinh Long, Vietnam 77 G5 10 16N 105 57 E
Vinh Yen, Vietnam 76 B5 21 21N 105 35 E
Vinhais, Portugal 36 D3 41 50N 7 5W
Vinica, Hrvatska, Yugoslavia 39 B13 46 20N 16 9 E
Vinica, Slovenija, Yugoslavia 39 C12 45 28N 15 16 E
Vinita, U.S.A. 139 G7 36 40N 95 12W
Vinkeveen, Neths. 20 D5 52 13N 4 56 E
Vinkovci, Yugoslavia 42 B3 45 19N 18 48 E
Vinnitsa, U.S.S.R. 52 B3 49 15N 28 30 E
Vinstra, Norway 14 C3 61 37N 9 44 E
Vinton, Calif., U.S.A. 144 F6 39 48N 120 10W
Vinton, Iowa, U.S.A. 140 B4 42 8N 92 1W
Vinton, La., U.S.A. 139 K8 30 13N 93 35W
Vinţu de Jos, Romania 46 D4 46 0N 23 30 E
Viöl, Germany 26 A5 54 32N 9 12 E
Viola, U.S.A. 140 C6 41 12N 90 35W
Violet Town, Australia 117 D6 36 38 S 145 42 E
Vipava, Yugoslavia 39 C10 45 51N 13 58 E
Vipiteno, Italy 39 B8 46 55N 11 25 E
Viqueque, Indonesia 71 F7 8 52 S 126 23 E
Vir, U.S.S.R. 55 E6 37 45N 72 5 E
Vir, Yugoslavia 39 D12 44 17N 15 3 E
Virac, Phil. 71 B6 13 30N 124 20 E
Virachei, Cambodia 76 F6 13 59N 106 49 E
Virago Sd., Canada 130 C2 54 0N 132 30W
Virajpet = Virarajendrapet, India 83 H2 12 10N 75 50 E
Viramgam, India 80 H5 23 5N 72 0 E
Viranşehir, Turkey 89 E8 37 13N 39 45 E
Virarajendrapet, India 83 H2 12 10N 75 50 E
Viravanallur, India 83 K3 8 40N 77 30 E
Virden, Canada 131 D8 49 50N 100 56W
Virden, U.S.A. 140 E7 39 30N 89 46W
Vire, France 22 D6 48 50N 0 53W
Vire →, France 22 C5 49 20N 1 7W
Virgem da Lapa, Brazil 155 E3 16 49 S 42 21W
Vírgenes, C., Argentina 160 D3 52 19 S 68 21W
Virgin →, Canada 131 B7 57 2N 108 17W
Virgin →, U.S.A. 143 H6 36 50N 114 10W
Virgin Gorda, Virgin Is. 149 C7 18 30N 64 26W
Virgin Is., W. Indies 149 C7 18 40N 64 30W
Virginia, S. Africa 104 D4 28 8 S 26 55 E
Virginia, Ill., U.S.A. 140 E6 39 57N 90 13W
Virginia, Minn., U.S.A. 138 B8 47 30N 92 32W
Virginia □, U.S.A. 134 G7 37 45N 78 0W
Virginia Beach, U.S.A. 134 G8 36 54N 75 58W
Virginia City, Mont., U.S.A. 142 D8 45 18N 111 58W
Virginia City, Nev., U.S.A. 144 F7 39 19N 119 39W
Virginia Falls, Canada 130 A3 61 38N 125 42W
Virginiatown, Canada 128 C4 48 9N 79 36W
Virieu-le-Grand, France 25 C9 45 51N 5 39 E
Virje, Yugoslavia 42 A1 46 4N 16 59 E
Viroqua, U.S.A. 138 D9 43 33N 90 57W
Virovitica, Yugoslavia 42 B2 45 51N 17 21 E
Virpazar, Yugoslavia 42 E4 42 14N 19 6 E
Virton, Belgium 21 J7 49 35N 5 32 E
Virtsu, U.S.S.R. 50 B3 58 32N 23 33 E
Virú, Peru 156 B2 8 25 S 78 45W
Virudunagar, India 83 K3 9 30N 77 58 E
Vis, Yugoslavia 39 E13 43 4N 16 10 E
Vis Kanal, Yugoslavia 39 E13 43 4N 16 5 E
Visalia, U.S.A. 144 J7 36 25N 119 18W
Visayan Sea, Phil. 71 B6 11 30N 123 30 E
Visby, Sweden 13 H15 57 37N 18 18 E
Viscount Melville Sd., Canada 6 B2 74 10N 108 0W
Visé, Belgium 21 G7 50 44N 5 41 E
Višegrad, Yugoslavia 42 D4 43 47N 19 17 E
Viseu, Brazil 154 B2 1 10 S 46 5W
Viseu, Portugal 36 E3 40 40N 7 55W
Viseu □, Portugal 36 E3 40 40N 7 55W
Vişeu de Sus, Romania 46 B5 47 45N 24 25 E
Vishakhapatnam, India 82 F6 17 45N 83 20 E
Vishera →, U.S.S.R. 54 B5 59 55N 56 25 E
Viskafors, Sweden 15 G6 57 37N 12 50 E
Visnagar, India 80 H5 23 45N 72 32 E
Višnja Gora, Yugoslavia 39 C11 45 58N 14 45 E
Viso, Mte., Italy 38 D4 44 38N 7 5 E
Viso del Marqués, Spain 35 G1 38 32N 3 34W
Visoko, Yugoslavia 42 D3 43 58N 18 10 E
Visokoi I., Antarctica 7 B1 56 43 S 27 15W
Visp, Switz. 28 D5 46 17N 7 52 E
Vispa →, Switz. 28 D5 46 9N 7 48 E
Visselhövede, Germany 26 C5 52 59N 9 36 E
Vissoie, Switz. 28 D5 46 13N 7 36 E
Vista, U.S.A. 145 M9 33 12N 117 14W
Vistonikos, Ormos, Greece 44 D7 41 0N 25 7 E
Vistula = Wisła →, Poland 47 A5 54 22N 18 55 E
Vit →, Bulgaria 43 D9 43 30N 24 30 E
Vitanje, Yugoslavia 39 B12 46 25N 15 18 E
Vitebsk, U.S.S.R. 50 D7 55 10N 30 15 E
Viterbo, Italy 39 F9 42 25N 12 8 E
Viti Levu, Fiji 121 A1 17 30 S 177 30 E
Vitiaz Str., Papua N. G. 120 C4 5 40 S 147 10 E
Vitigudino, Spain 36 D4 41 1N 6 26W
Vitim, U.S.S.R. 57 D12 59 28N 112 35 E
Vitim →, U.S.S.R. 57 D12 59 26N 112 34 E
Vitína, Greece 45 G4 37 40N 22 10 E
Vitina, Yugoslavia 42 D2 43 17N 17 29 E
Vitória, Brazil 155 F3 20 20 S 40 22W
Vitoria, Spain 34 C2 42 50N 2 41W
Vitória da Conquista, Brazil 155 D3 14 51 S 40 51W
Vitória de São Antão, Brazil 154 C4 8 10 S 35 20W
Vitorino Friere, Brazil 154 B2 4 4 S 45 10W
Vitré, France 22 D5 48 8N 1 12W
Vitry-le-François, France 23 D11 48 43N 4 33 E
Vitsi, Óros, Greece 44 D3 40 40N 21 25 E
Vitteaux, France 23 E11 47 24N 4 30 E
Vittel, France 23 D12 48 12N 5 57 E
Vittória, Italy 41 F7 36 58N 14 30 E
Vittório Véneto, Italy 39 C9 45 59N 12 18 E
Vitu Is., Papua N. G. 120 C5 4 50 S 149 25 E
Vivario, France 25 F13 42 10N 9 11 E
Vivegnis, Belgium 21 G7 50 42N 5 39 E
Viver, Spain 34 F4 39 55N 0 36W
Vivero, Spain 36 B3 43 39N 7 38W
Viviers, France 25 D8 44 30N 4 40 E
Vivonne, Australia 116 C2 35 59 S 137 9 E
Vivonne, France 24 B4 46 25N 0 15 E
Vivonne B., Australia 116 C2 35 59 S 137 9 E
Vizcaíno, Desierto de, Mexico 146 B2 27 40N 113 50W
Vizcaíno, Sierra, Mexico 146 B2 27 30N 114 0W
Vizcaya □, Spain 34 B2 43 15N 2 45W
Vize, Turkey 88 C2 41 34N 27 45 E
Vizianagaram, India 82 E6 18 6N 83 30 E
Vizille, France 25 C9 45 5N 5 46 E
Viziñada, Yugoslavia 39 C10 45 20N 13 46 E
Viziru, Romania 46 E8 45 0N 27 43 E
Vizovice, Czech. 31 B10 49 12N 17 56 E
Vizzini, Italy 41 E7 37 9N 14 43 E
Vjosa →, Albania 44 D1 40 37N 19 42 E
Vlaardingen, Neths. 20 E4 51 55N 4 21 E
Vlădeasa, Romania 46 C3 46 47N 22 50 E
Vladicin Han, Yugoslavia 42 E7 42 42N 22 1 E
Vladikavkaz, U.S.S.R. 53 E11 43 0N 44 35 E
Vladimir, U.S.S.R. 51 C12 56 15N 40 30 E
Vladimir Volynskiy, U.S.S.R. 50 F4 50 50N 24 18 E
Vladimirci, Yugoslavia 42 C4 44 36N 19 45 E
Vladimirovac, Yugoslavia 42 B5 45 1N 20 53 E
Vladimirovka, R.S.F.S.R., U.S.S.R. 53 B12 48 27N 46 10 E
Vladimirovka, R.S.F.S.R., U.S.S.R. 53 D11 44 45N 44 41 E
Vladimirovo, Bulgaria 43 D8 43 32N 23 22 E
Vladislavovka, U.S.S.R. 52 D6 45 15N 35 15 E
Vladivostok, U.S.S.R. 57 E14 43 10N 131 53 E
Vlamertinge, Belgium 21 G1 50 51N 2 49 E
Vlasenica, Yugoslavia 42 C3 44 11N 18 59 E
Vlašić, Yugoslavia 42 C2 44 19N 17 37 E
Vlašim, Czech. 30 B7 49 40N 14 53 E
Vlasinsko Jezero, Yugoslavia 42 E7 42 44N 22 22 E
Vlasotinci, Yugoslavia 42 E7 42 59N 22 7 E
Vleuten, Neths. 20 D6 52 6N 5 1 E
Vlieland, Neths. 20 B5 53 16N 4 55 E
Vliestroom, Neths. 20 B6 53 19N 5 8 E
Vlijmen, Neths. 21 E6 51 42N 5 14 E
Vlissingen, Neths. 21 F3 51 26N 3 34 E
Vlóra, Albania 44 D1 40 32N 19 28 E
Vlóra □, Albania 44 D2 40 12N 20 0 E
Vlorës, Gjiri i, Albania 44 D1 40 29N 19 27 E
Vltava →, Czech. 30 A7 50 21N 14 30 E
Vo Dat, Vietnam 77 G6 11 9N 107 31 E
Vobarno, Italy 38 C7 45 38N 10 30 E
Voćin, Yugoslavia 42 B2 45 37N 17 33 E
Vöcklabruck, Austria 30 C6 48 1N 13 39 E
Vodice, Yugoslavia 39 E12 43 47N 15 47 E
Vodňany, Czech. 30 B7 49 9N 14 11 E
Vodnjan, Yugoslavia 39 D10 44 59N 13 52 E
Vogelkop = Doberai, Jazirah, Indonesia 71 E8 1 25 S 133 0 E
Vogelsberg, Germany 26 E5 50 37N 9 15 E
Voghera, Italy 38 D6 44 59N 9 1 E
Voh, N. Cal. 121 T18 20 58 S 164 42 E
Vohibinany, Madag. 105 B8 18 49 S 49 4 E
Vohimarina, Madag. 105 A9 13 25 S 50 0 E
Vohimena, Tanjon' i, Madag. 105 D8 25 36 S 45 8 E
Vohipeno, Madag. 105 C8 22 22 S 47 51 E
Voi, Kenya 106 C4 3 25 S 38 32 E
Void, France 23 D12 48 40N 5 36 E
Voineşti, Iaşi, Romania 46 B8 47 5N 27 27 E
Voineşti, Prahova, Romania 46 D6 45 5N 25 14 E
Voíotía □, Greece 45 F5 38 20N 23 0 E
Voiron, France 25 C9 45 22N 5 35 E
Voisey B., Canada 129 A7 56 15N 61 50W
Voitsberg, Austria 30 D8 47 3N 15 9 E
Voïvïïs Límni, Greece 44 E4 39 30N 22 45 E
Vojens, Denmark 15 J3 55 16N 9 18 E
Vojmsjön, Sweden 12 D14 64 55N 16 40 E
Vojnik, Italy 39 B12 46 18N 15 19 E
Vojnió, Yugoslavia 39 C12 45 19N 15 43 E
Vojvodina, Auton. Pokrajina □, Yugoslavia 42 B5 45 20N 20 0 E
Vokhma, U.S.S.R. 51 B15 59 0N 46 45 E
Vokhma →, U.S.S.R. 51 C15 56 20N 46 20 E
Vokhtoga, U.S.S.R. 51 B12 58 46N 41 8 E
Volary, Czech. 30 C6 48 54N 13 52 E
Volborg, U.S.A. 138 C2 45 50N 105 44W
Volcano Is. = Kazan-Rettó, Pac. Oc. 122 E6 25 0N 141 0 E
Volchansk, U.S.S.R. 51 F10 50 17N 36 58 E
Volchayevka, U.S.S.R. 57 E14 48 40N 134 30 E
Volchya →, U.S.S.R. 52 C7 48 0N 37 0 E
Volda, Norway 12 E9 62 9N 6 5 E
Volendam, Neths. 20 D6 52 30N 5 4 E
Volga, U.S.S.R. 51 C11 57 58N 38 16 E
Volga →, U.S.S.R. 53 D13 46 0N 48 30 E
Volga Hts. = Privolzhskaya Vozvyshennost, U.S.S.R. 51 F15 51 0N 46 0 E
Volgodonsk, U.S.S.R. 53 C10 47 33N 42 5 E
Volgograd, U.S.S.R. 53 B11 48 40N 44 25 E
Volgogradskoye Vdkhr., U.S.S.R. 51 G14 50 0N 45 20 E
Volgorechensk, U.S.S.R. 51 C12 57 28N 41 14 E
Volissós, Greece 45 F7 38 29N 25 54 E
Volkach, Germany 27 F6 49 52N 10 14 E
Volkerak, Neths. 21 E4 51 39N 4 18 E
Völkermarkt, Austria 30 E7 46 39N 14 39 E
Volkhov, U.S.S.R. 50 B8 59 55N 32 15 E
Volkhov →, U.S.S.R. 50 A8 60 8N 32 20 E
Völklingen, Germany 27 F2 49 15N 6 50 E
Volkovysk, U.S.S.R. 50 E4 53 9N 24 30 E
Volksrust, S. Africa 105 D4 27 24 S 29 53 E
Vollenhove, Neths. 20 C7 52 40N 5 58 E
Vol'n'ansk, U.S.S.R. 52 C6 47 55N 35 29 E
Volnovakha, U.S.S.R. 52 C7 47 35N 37 30 E
Volochanka, U.S.S.R. 57 B10 71 0N 94 28 E
Volodarsk, U.S.S.R. 51 C13 56 12N 43 15 E
Vologda, U.S.S.R. 51 B11 59 10N 39 45 E
Volokolamsk, U.S.S.R. 51 C9 56 5N 35 57 E
Volokonovka, U.S.S.R. 51 F10 50 33N 37 52 E
Vólos, Greece 44 E4 39 24N 22 59 E
Volosovo, U.S.S.R. 50 B6 59 27N 29 32 E
Volozhin, U.S.S.R. 50 D5 54 3N 26 30 E
Volsk, U.S.S.R. 51 E15 52 5N 47 22 E
Volta →, Ghana 101 D5 5 46N 0 41 E
Volta, L., Ghana 101 D5 7 30N 0 15 E
Volta Blanche = White Volta →, Ghana 101 D4 9 10N 1 15W
Volta Redonda, Brazil 155 F3 22 31 S 44 5W
Voltaire, C., Australia 112 B4 14 16 S 125 35 E
Volterra, Italy 38 E7 43 24N 10 50 E
Voltri, Italy 38 D5 44 25N 8 43 E
Volturara Áppula, Italy 41 A8 41 30N 15 2 E
Volturno →, Italy 40 A6 41 1N 13 55 E
Volubilis, Morocco 98 B3 34 2N 5 33W
Volujak, Yugoslavia 42 D2 43 53N 17 47 E
Vólvi, L., Greece 44 D5 40 40N 23 34 E
Volvo, Australia 116 A5 31 41 S 143 57 E
Volzhsk, U.S.S.R. 51 D16 55 57N 48 23 E
Volzhskiy, U.S.S.R. 53 B11 48 56N 44 46 E
Vondrozo, Madag. 105 C8 22 49 S 47 20 E
Vónitsa, Greece 45 F2 38 53N 20 58 E
Voorburg, Neths. 20 D4 52 5N 4 24 E
Voorne Putten, Neths. 20 E4 51 52N 4 10 E
Voorst, Neths. 20 D8 52 10N 6 8 E
Voorthuizen, Neths. 20 D7 52 11N 5 36 E
Vopnafjörður, Iceland 12 D6 65 45N 14 40W
Vorarlberg □, Austria 30 D3 47 20N 10 0 E
Vóras Óros, Greece 44 D3 40 57N 21 45 E
Vorbasse, Denmark 15 J3 55 39N 9 6 E
Vorden, Neths. 20 D8 52 6N 6 19 E
Vorderrhein →, Switz. 29 C8 46 49N 9 25 E
Vordingborg, Denmark 15 K5 55 0N 11 54 E
Voreppe, France 25 C9 45 18N 5 39 E
Voríai Sporádhes, Greece 45 E5 39 15N 23 30 E
Vórios Evvoïkos Kólpos, Greece 45 F5 38 45N 23 15 E
Vorkuta, U.S.S.R. 48 A11 67 48N 64 20 E
Vorma →, Norway 14 D5 60 9N 11 27 E
Vorona →, U.S.S.R. 51 F13 51 22N 42 3 E
Voronezh, R.S.F.S.R., U.S.S.R. 51 F11 51 40N 39 10 E
Voronezh, Ukraine S.S.R., U.S.S.R. 50 F8 51 47N 33 28 E
Voronezh →, U.S.S.R. 51 F10 51 56N 37 17 E
Vorontsovo-Aleksandrovskoye = Zelenokumsk, U.S.S.R. 53 D10 44 24N 43 53 E
Voroshilovgrad = Lugansk, U.S.S.R. 53 B8 48 38N 39 15 E
Voroshilovsk = Kommunarsk, U.S.S.R. 53 B8 48 30N 38 45 E
Vorovskoye, U.S.S.R. 57 D16 54 30N 155 50 E
Vorselaar, Belgium 21 F5 51 12N 4 46 E
Vorskla →, U.S.S.R. 52 B6 48 50N 34 10 E
Võru, U.S.S.R. 50 C5 57 48N 26 54 E
Vorukh, U.S.S.R. 55 D5 39 52N 70 35 E
Vorupør, Denmark 15 H2 56 58N 8 22 E
Vosges, France 23 D14 48 20N 7 10 E
Vosges □, France 23 D13 48 12N 6 20 E
Voskopoja, Albania 44 D2 40 40N 20 33 E
Voskresensk, U.S.S.R. 51 D11 55 19N 38 43 E
Voskresenskoye, U.S.S.R. 51 C14 56 51N 45 30 E
Voss, Norway 13 F9 60 38N 6 26 E
Vosselaar, Belgium 21 F5 51 19N 4 52 E
Vostochnyy Sayan, U.S.S.R. 57 D10 54 0N 96 0 E
Vostok I., Kiribati 123 J12 10 5 S 152 23W
Votice, Czech. 30 B7 49 38N 14 39 E
Votkinsk, U.S.S.R. 54 C3 57 0N 53 55 E
Votkinskoye Vdkhr., U.S.S.R. 48 C10 57 30N 55 0 E
Vouga →, Portugal 36 E2 40 41N 8 40W
Vouillé, France 22 F7 46 38N 0 10 E
Voulou, C.A.R. 102 A4 8 33N 22 36 E
Vouvray, France 22 E7 47 25N 0 48 E
Vouvry, Switz. 28 D3 46 21N 6 51 E
Voúxa, Ákra, Greece 32 D5 35 37N 23 32 E
Vouzela, Portugal 36 E2 40 43N 8 7W
Vouziers, France 23 C11 49 22N 4 40 E
Voves, France 23 D8 48 15N 1 38 E
Voxna, Sweden 14 C9 61 20N 15 40 E
Vozhe Oz., U.S.S.R. 48 B6 60 45N 39 0 E
Vozhgaly, U.S.S.R. 51 B17 58 9N 50 11 E
Voznesenka, U.S.S.R. 57 D10 56 40N 95 3 E
Voznesensk, U.S.S.R. 52 C4 47 35N 31 21 E
Voznesenye, U.S.S.R. 48 B6 61 0N 35 45 E
Vráble, Czech. 31 C11 48 15N 18 16 E
Vraćevšnica, Yugoslavia 42 C5 44 2N 20 34 E
Vrådal, Norway 14 E2 59 20N 8 25 E
Vraka, Albania 44 B1 42 8N 19 28 E
Vrakhnéïka, Greece 45 F3 38 10N 21 40 E
Vrancea □, Romania 46 D7 45 50N 26 45 E
Vrancei, Munţii, Romania 46 D7 46 0N 26 30 E
Vrangelya, Ostrov, U.S.S.R. 57 B19 71 0N 180 0 E
Vranica, Yugoslavia 42 D2 43 55N 17 50 E
Vranje, Yugoslavia 42 E6 42 34N 21 54 E
Vranjska Banja, Yugoslavia 42 E7 42 34N 22 1 E
Vranov, Czech. 31 C14 48 53N 21 40 E
Vransko, Yugoslavia 39 B11 46 17N 14 58 E
Vratsa, Bulgaria 43 D8 43 13N 23 30 E
Vrbas, Yugoslavia 42 B4 45 40N 19 40 E
Vrbas →, Yugoslavia 42 B2 45 8N 17 29 E
Vrbnik, Yugoslavia 39 C11 45 4N 14 40 E
Vrbovec, Yugoslavia 39 C13 45 53N 16 28 E
Vrbovsko, Yugoslavia 39 C12 45 24N 15 5 E
Vrchlabí, Czech. 30 A8 50 38N 15 37 E
Vrede, S. Africa 105 D4 27 24 S 29 6 E
Vredefort, S. Africa 104 D4 27 0 S 27 22 E
Vredenburg, S. Africa 104 E2 32 56 S 18 0 E
Vredendal, S. Africa 104 E2 31 41 S 18 35 E
Vreeswijk, Neths. 20 D6 52 1N 5 6 E
Vrena, Sweden 15 F10 58 54N 16 41 E
Vrgorac, Yugoslavia 42 D2 43 12N 17 20 E
Vrhnika, Yugoslavia 39 C11 45 58N 14 15 E
Vriddhachalam, India 83 J4 11 30N 79 20 E
Vridi, Ivory C. 100 D4 5 15N 4 3W
Vries, Neths. 20 B9 53 5N 6 35 E
Vriezenveen, Neths. 20 D9 52 25N 6 38 E
Vrindavan, India 80 F7 27 37N 77 40 E
Vríses, Greece 32 D6 35 23N 24 13 E
Vrnograč, Yugoslavia 39 C12 45 10N 15 57 E
Vrondádhes, Greece 45 F8 38 25N 26 7 E
Vroomshoop, Neths. 20 D9 52 27N 6 34 E
Vrpolje, Yugoslavia 42 B3 45 13N 18 24 E
Vršac, Yugoslavia 42 B6 45 8N 21 18 E
Vrsacki Kanal, Yugoslavia 42 B6 45 15N 21 0 E
Vryburg, S. Africa 104 D3 26 55 S 24 45 E
Vryheid, S. Africa 105 D5 27 45 S 30 47 E
Vsetín, Czech. 31 B11 49 20N 18 0 E
Vu Liet, Vietnam 76 C5 18 43N 105 23 E
Vucha →, Bulgaria 43 E9 42 10N 24 26 E
Vučitrn, Yugoslavia 42 E5 42 49N 20 59 E
Vught, Neths. 21 E6 51 38N 5 20 E
Vukovar, Yugoslavia 42 B3 45 21N 19 0 E
Vulcan, Canada 130 C6 50 25N 113 15W
Vulcan, Romania 46 D4 45 23N 23 17 E
Vulcan, U.S.A. 134 C2 45 46N 87 51W
Vulcano, Italy 41 D7 38 25N 14 58 E
Vůlchedruma, Bulgaria 43 D8 43 42N 23 27 E

Xinghua Wan 285

Winnfield, U.S.A. 139 K8 31 57N 92 38W
Winnibigoshish L., U.S.A. 138 B7 47 25N 94 12W
Winning, Australia 112 D1 23 9 S 114 30 E
Winnipeg, Canada 131 D9 49 54N 97 9W
Winnipeg →, Canada 131 C9 50 38N 96 19W
Winnipeg, L., Canada 131 C9 52 0N 97 0W
Winnipeg Beach, Canada 131 C9 50 30N 96 58W
Winnipegosis, Canada 131 C9 51 39N 99 55W
Winnipegosis L., Canada 131 C9 52 30N 100 0W
Winnipesaukee, L., U.S.A. 137 C13 43 38N 71 21W
Winnsboro, La., U.S.A. 139 J9 32 10N 91 41W
Winnsboro, S.C., U.S.A. 135 H5 34 23N 81 5W
Winnsboro, Tex., U.S.A. 139 J7 32 56N 95 15W
Winokapau, L., Canada 129 B7 53 15N 62 50W
Winona, Miss., U.S.A. 139 J10 33 30N 89 42W
Winona, Wis., U.S.A. 138 C9 44 2N 91 39W
Winooski, U.S.A. 137 B11 44 31N 73 11W
Winschoten, Neths. 20 B10 53 9N 7 3 E
Winsen, Germany 26 B6 53 21N 10 11 E
Winslow, Ariz., U.S.A. 143 J8 35 2N 110 41W
Winslow, Ind., U.S.A. 141 F9 38 23N 87 13W
Winslow, Wash., U.S.A. 144 C4 47 37N 122 31W
Winsted, U.S.A. 137 E11 41 55N 73 5W
Winston-Salem, U.S.A. 135 G5 36 7N 80 15W
Winsum, Neths. 20 B9 53 20N 6 32 E
Winter Garden, U.S.A. 135 L5 28 33N 81 35W
Winter Haven, U.S.A. 135 M5 28 0N 81 42W
Winter Park, U.S.A. 135 L5 28 34N 81 19W
Winterberg, Germany 26 D4 51 12N 8 30 E
Winterhaven, U.S.A. 145 N12 32 47N 114 39W
Winters, Calif., U.S.A. 144 G5 38 32N 121 58W
Winters, Tex., U.S.A. 139 K5 31 58N 99 58W
Winterset, U.S.A. 140 C3 41 18N 94 0W
Wintersville, U.S.A. 136 F4 40 22N 80 38W
Winterswijk, Neths. 20 E9 51 58N 6 43 E
Winterthur, Switz. 29 B7 47 30N 8 44 E
Winthrop, Minn., U.S.A. 138 C7 44 31N 94 25W
Winthrop, Wash., U.S.A. 142 B3 48 27N 120 6W
Winton, Australia 114 C3 22 24 S 143 3 E
Winton, N.Z. 119 G3 46 8 S 168 20 E
Winton, U.S.A. 135 G7 36 25N 76 58W
Wintzenheim, France 23 D14 48 4N 7 17 E
Wipper →, Germany 26 D7 51 17N 11 10 E
Wirral, U.K. 16 D5 53 25N 3 0W
Wirraminna, Australia 116 A2 31 12 S 136 13 E
Wirrulla, Australia 115 E1 32 24 S 134 31 E
Wisbech, U.K. 16 E8 52 39N 0 10 E
Wisconsin □, U.S.A. 138 C10 44 30N 90 0W
Wisconsin →, U.S.A. 138 D9 43 0N 91 15W
Wisconsin Dells, U.S.A. 138 D10 43 38N 89 45W
Wisconsin Rapids, U.S.A. 138 C10 44 25N 89 50W
Wisdom, U.S.A. 142 D7 45 37N 113 27W
Wishaw, U.K. 18 F5 55 46N 3 55W
Wishek, U.S.A. 138 B5 46 20N 99 35W
Wisła, Poland 31 B11 49 38N 18 53 E
Wisła →, Poland 47 A5 54 22N 18 55 E
Wisłok →, Poland 31 A15 50 13N 22 32 E
Wisłoka →, Poland 31 A14 50 27N 21 23 E
Wismar, Germany 26 B7 53 53N 11 23 E
Wismar, Guyana 153 B6 5 59N 58 18W
Wisner, U.S.A. 138 E6 42 0N 96 46W
Wissant, France 23 B8 50 52N 1 40 E
Wissembourg, France 23 C14 49 2N 7 57 E
Wissenkerke, Neths. 21 E3 51 35N 3 45 E
Wistoka →, Poland 31 B14 49 50N 21 28 E
Wisznice, Poland 47 D10 51 48N 23 13 E
Witbank, S. Africa 105 D4 25 51 S 29 14 E
Witdraai, S. Africa 104 D3 26 58 S 20 48 E
Witham →, U.K. 16 D7 53 3N 0 8W
Withernsea, U.K. 16 D8 53 43N 0 2 E
Witkowo, Poland 47 C4 52 26N 17 45 E
Witmarsum, Neths. 20 B6 53 6N 5 28 E
Witney, U.K. 17 F6 51 47N 1 29W
Witnossob →, Namibia 104 D3 26 55 S 20 37 E
Wittdün, Germany 26 A4 54 38N 8 23 E
Witten, Germany 21 F10 51 26N 7 19 E
Wittenberg, Germany 26 D8 51 51N 12 39 E
Wittenberge, Germany 26 C7 53 0N 11 44 E
Wittenburg, Germany 26 B7 53 30N 11 4 E
Wittenoom, Australia 112 D2 22 15 S 118 20 E
Wittingen, Germany 26 C6 52 43N 10 43 E
Wittlich, Germany 27 F2 50 0N 6 54 E
Wittmund, Germany 26 B3 53 39N 7 45 E
Wittow, Germany 26 A9 54 37N 13 21 E
Wittstock, Germany 26 B8 53 10N 12 30 E
Witzenhausen, Germany 26 D5 51 19N 9 52 E
Wkra →, Poland 47 C7 52 27N 20 44 E
Władysławowo, Poland 47 A5 54 48N 18 25 E
Wlen, Poland 47 E2 51 0N 15 39 E
Wlingi, Indonesia 71 H15 8 5 S 112 25 E
Włocławek, Poland 47 C6 52 40N 19 3 E
Włocławek □, Poland 47 C6 52 50N 19 10 E
Włodawa, Poland 47 D10 51 33N 23 31 E
Włoszczowa, Poland 47 E6 50 50N 19 55 E
Woburn, U.S.A. 137 D13 42 31N 71 7W
Wodian, China 66 H7 32 50N 112 35 E
Wodonga, Australia 117 D7 36 5 S 146 50 E
Wodzisław Śląski, Poland 31 A11 50 1N 18 26 E
Woerden, Neths. 20 D5 52 5N 4 54 E
Woerth, France 23 D14 48 57N 7 45 E
Woëvre, France 23 C12 49 15N 5 45 E
Wognum, Neths. 20 C6 52 40N 5 1 E
Wohlen, Switz. 29 B6 47 21N 8 17 E
Woinbogoin, China 68 A2 32 51N 98 39 E
Wokam, Indonesia 71 F8 5 45 S 134 28 E
Wokha, India 78 B5 26 6N 94 16 E
Wolbrom, Poland 47 E6 50 24N 19 45 E
Wolcottville, U.S.A. 141 C11 41 32N 85 22W
Wołczyn, Poland 47 D5 51 1N 18 3 E
Woldegk, Germany 26 B9 53 27N 13 35 E
Wolf →, Canada 130 A2 60 17N 132 33W
Wolf Creek, U.S.A. 142 C7 47 1N 112 2W
Wolf L., Canada 130 A2 60 24N 131 40W
Wolf Point, U.S.A. 138 A2 48 6N 105 40W
Wolfe I., Canada 128 D4 44 7N 76 20W
Wolfenbüttel, Germany 26 C6 52 10N 10 33 E
Wolfheze, Neths. 20 D7 52 1N 5 48 E
Wolfsberg, Austria 30 E7 46 50N 14 52 E
Wolfsburg, Germany 26 C6 52 27N 10 49 E
Wolgast, Germany 26 A9 54 3N 13 46 E
Wolhusen, Switz. 28 B6 47 4N 8 4 E
Wolin, Poland 47 B1 53 50N 14 37 E
Wollaston, Is., Chile 160 E3 55 40 S 67 30W
Wollaston L., Canada 131 B8 58 7N 103 10W
Wollaston Pen., Canada 126 B8 69 30N 115 0W
Wollogorang, Australia 114 B2 17 13 S 137 57 E
Wollongong, Australia 117 C9 34 25 S 150 54 E
Wolmaransstad, S. Africa 104 D4 27 12 S 25 59 E
Wolmirstedt, Germany 26 C7 52 15N 11 35 E
Wołomin, Poland 47 C8 52 19N 21 15 E
Wołów, Poland 47 D3 51 20N 16 38 E
Wolseley, Australia 116 D4 36 23 S 140 54 E
Wolseley, Canada 131 C8 50 25N 103 15W
Wolseley, S. Africa 104 E2 33 26 S 19 7 E
Wolstenholme, C., Canada 124 C12 62 35N 77 30W
Wolsztyn, Poland 47 C3 52 8N 16 5 E
Wolvega, Neths. 20 C8 52 52N 6 0 E
Wolverhampton, U.K. 17 E5 52 35N 2 6W
Wommels, Neths. 20 B7 53 6N 5 36 E
Wonarah, Australia 114 B2 19 55 S 136 20 E
Wonboyn, Australia 117 D8 37 15 S 149 55 E
Wonck, Belgium 21 G7 50 46N 5 38 E
Wondai, Australia 115 D5 26 20 S 151 49 E
Wondelgem, Belgium 21 F3 51 5N 3 44 E
Wongalarroo L., Australia 116 A6 31 32 S 144 0 E
Wongan Hills, Australia 113 F2 30 51 S 116 37 E
Wongawol, Australia 113 E3 26 5 S 121 55 E
Wŏnju, S. Korea 67 F14 37 22N 127 58 E
Wonosari, Indonesia 71 G14 7 58 S 110 36 E
Wonosobo, Indonesia 75 D3 7 22 S 109 54 E
Wŏnsan, N. Korea 67 E14 39 11N 127 27 E
Wonthaggi, Australia 117 E6 38 37 S 145 37 E
Woocalla, Australia 116 A2 31 42 S 137 12 E
Wood Buffalo Nat. Park, Canada 130 B6 59 0N 113 41W
Wood Is., Australia 112 C3 16 24 S 123 19 E
Wood L., Canada 131 B8 55 17N 103 17W
Wood Lake, U.S.A. 138 D4 42 38N 100 14W
Wood River, U.S.A. 140 F6 38 52N 90 5W
Woodah I., Australia 114 A2 13 27 S 136 10 E
Woodanilling, Australia 113 F2 33 31 S 117 24 E
Woodbridge, Canada 136 C5 43 47N 79 36W
Woodburn, Australia 115 D5 29 6 S 153 23 E
Woodenbong, Australia 115 D5 28 24 S 152 39 E
Woodend, Australia 116 D6 37 20 S 144 33 E
Woodfords, U.S.A. 144 G7 38 47N 119 50W
Woodgreen, Australia 114 C1 22 26 S 134 12 E
Woodlake, U.S.A. 144 J7 36 25N 119 6W
Woodland, U.S.A. 144 G5 38 40N 121 50W
Woodlands, Australia 112 D2 24 46 S 118 8 E
Woodlark I., Papua N. G. 120 E7 9 10 S 152 50 E
Woodpecker, Canada 130 C4 53 30N 122 40W
Woodridge, Canada 131 D9 49 20N 96 9W
Woodroffe, Mt., Australia 113 E5 26 20 S 131 45 E
Woodruff, Ariz., U.S.A. 143 J8 34 51N 110 1W
Woodruff, Utah, U.S.A. 142 F8 41 30N 111 4W
Woods, L., Australia 114 B1 17 50 S 133 30 E
Woods, L., Canada 129 B6 54 30N 65 13W
Woods, L. of the, Canada 131 D10 49 15N 94 45W
Woodside, S. Austral., Australia 116 C3 34 58 S 138 52 E
Woodside, Vic., Australia 117 E7 38 31 S 146 52 E
Woodstock, N.S.W., Australia 117 B8 33 45 S 148 53 E
Woodstock, Queens., Australia 114 B4 19 35 S 146 50 E
Woodstock, W. Austral., Australia 112 D2 21 41 S 118 57 E
Woodstock, N.B., Canada 129 C6 46 11N 67 37W
Woodstock, Ont., Canada 128 D3 43 10N 80 45W
Woodstock, U.K. 17 F6 51 51N 1 20W
Woodstock, Ill., U.S.A. 138 D10 42 17N 88 30W
Woodstock, Vt., U.S.A. 137 C12 43 37N 72 31W
Woodsville, U.S.A. 137 B13 44 10N 72 0W
Woodville, N.Z. 118 G4 40 20 S 175 53 E
Woodville, Ohio, U.S.A. 141 C13 41 27N 83 22W
Woodville, Tex., U.S.A. 139 K7 30 45N 94 25W
Woodward, U.S.A. 139 G5 36 24N 99 28W
Woody, U.S.A. 145 K8 35 42N 118 50W
Woolamai, C., Australia 117 E6 38 30 S 145 23 E
Woolgoolga, Australia 115 E5 30 6 S 153 11 E
Woombye, Australia 115 D5 26 40 S 152 55 E
Woomera, Australia 116 A2 31 5 S 136 50 E
Woonona, Australia 117 C9 34 21 S 150 54 E
Woonsocket, R.I., U.S.A. 137 E13 42 0N 71 30W
Woonsocket, S. Dak., U.S.A. 138 C5 44 5N 98 15W
Wooramel, Australia 113 E1 25 45 S 114 17 E
Wooramel →, Australia 113 E1 25 47 S 114 10 E
Wooroloo, Australia 113 F2 31 48 S 116 18 E
Wooster, U.S.A. 136 F3 40 48N 81 55W
Worb, Switz. 28 C5 46 56N 7 33 E
Worcester, S. Africa 104 E2 33 39 S 19 27 E
Worcester, U.K. 17 E5 52 12N 2 12W
Worcester, Mass., U.S.A. 137 D13 42 14N 71 49W
Worcester, N.Y., U.S.A. 137 D10 42 35N 74 45W
Worden, U.S.A. 140 F7 38 56N 89 50W
Wörgl, Austria 30 D5 47 29N 12 3 E
Workington, U.K. 16 C4 54 39N 3 34W
Worksop, U.K. 16 D6 53 19N 1 9W
Workum, Neths. 20 C6 52 59N 5 26 E
Worland, U.S.A. 142 D10 44 2N 107 59W
Wormerveer, Neths. 20 D5 52 30N 4 46 E
Wormhoudt, France 23 B9 50 52N 2 28 E
Worms, Germany 27 F4 49 37N 8 21 E
Wörth, Germany 27 F8 49 1N 12 24 E
Wortham, U.S.A. 139 K6 31 48N 96 27W
Wörther See, Austria 30 E7 46 37N 14 10 E
Worthing, U.K. 17 G7 50 49N 0 21W
Worthington, Ind., U.S.A. 141 E10 39 7N 86 59W
Worthington, Minn., U.S.A. 138 D7 43 35N 95 36W
Worthington, Ohio, U.S.A. 141 D13 40 5N 83 1W
Wosi, Indonesia 71 E7 0 15 S 128 0 E
Wou-han = Wuhan, China 69 B10 30 31N 114 18 E
Woubrugge, Neths. 20 D5 52 10N 4 39 E
Woudenberg, Neths. 20 D6 52 5N 5 25 E
Woudsend, Neths. 20 C7 52 56N 5 38 E
Wour, Chad 97 D3 21 14N 16 0 E
Wouw, Neths. 21 E4 51 31N 4 23 E
Wowoni, Indonesia 71 E6 4 5 S 123 5 E
Woy Woy, Australia 117 B9 33 30 S 151 19 E
Wozniki, Poland 47 E6 50 35N 19 4 E
Wrangel I. = Vrangelya, Ostrov, U.S.S.R. 57 B19 71 0N 180 0 E
Wrangel I., U.S.S.R. 58 B22 71 0N 180 0 E
Wrangell, U.S.A. 126 C6 56 30N 132 25W
Wrangell I., U.S.A. 130 B2 56 20N 132 10W
Wrangell Mts., U.S.A. 126 B5 61 40N 143 30W
Wrath, C., U.K. 18 C4 58 38N 5 0W
Wray, U.S.A. 138 E3 40 8N 102 18W
Wrekin, The, U.K. 16 E5 52 41N 2 35W
Wrens, U.S.A. 135 J4 33 13N 82 23W
Wrexham, U.K. 16 D5 53 5N 3 0W
Wriezen, Germany 26 C10 52 43N 14 9 E
Wright, Canada 130 C4 51 52N 121 40W
Wright, Phil. 71 B7 11 42N 125 2 E
Wrightson, Mt., U.S.A. 143 L8 31 43N 110 56W
Wrightwood, U.S.A. 145 L9 34 21N 117 38W
Wrigley, Canada 126 B7 63 16N 123 37W
Wrocław, Poland 47 D4 51 5N 17 5 E
Wrocław □, Poland 47 E4 51 0N 17 0 E
Wronki, Poland 47 C3 52 41N 16 21 E
Września, Poland 47 C4 52 21N 17 36 E
Wschowa, Poland 47 D3 51 48N 16 20 E
Wu Jiang →, China 68 C6 29 40N 107 20 E
Wu'an, China 66 F8 36 40N 114 15 E
Wubin, Australia 113 F2 30 6 S 116 37 E
Wubu, China 66 F6 37 28N 110 42 E
Wuchang, China 67 B14 44 55N 127 5 E
Wucheng, China 66 F9 37 12N 116 20 E
Wuchuan, Guangdong, China 69 G8 21 33N 110 43 E
Wuchuan, Guizhou, China 68 C7 28 25N 108 3 E
Wuchuan, Nei Mongol Zizhiqu, China 66 D6 41 5N 111 28 E
Wuday'ah, Si. Arabia 86 C4 17 2N 47 7 E
Wudi, China 67 F9 37 40N 117 35 E
Wuding, China 68 E4 25 24N 102 21 E
Wuding He →, China 66 F6 37 2N 110 23 E
Wudu, China 66 H3 33 22N 104 54 E
Wufeng, China 69 B8 30 12N 110 42 E
Wugang, China 69 D8 26 44N 110 35 E
Wugong Shan, China 69 D10 27 30N 114 0 E
Wuhan, China 69 B10 30 31N 114 18 E
Wuhe, China 67 H9 33 10N 117 50 E
Wuhsi = Wuxi, China 69 B13 31 33N 120 18 E
Wuhu, China 69 B12 31 22N 118 21 E
Wujiang, China 69 B13 31 10N 120 38 E
Wukari, Nigeria 101 D6 7 51N 9 42 E
Wulajie, China 67 B14 44 6N 126 33 E
Wulanbulang, China 66 D6 41 5N 110 55 E
Wulehe, Ghana 101 D5 8 39N 0 0 E
Wulian, China 67 G10 35 40N 119 12 E
Wuliang Shan, China 68 E3 24 30N 100 40 E
Wuliaru, Indonesia 71 F8 7 27 S 131 0 E
Wuluk'omushih Ling, China 64 C3 36 25N 87 25 E
Wulumuchi = Ürümqi, China 64 B3 43 45N 87 45 E
Wum, Cameroon 101 D7 6 24N 10 2 E
Wuming, China 68 F7 23 12N 108 18 E
Wuning, China 69 C10 29 17N 115 5 E
Wunnummin L., Canada 128 B2 52 55N 89 10W
Wunsiedel, Germany 27 E8 50 2N 12 0 E
Wunstorf, Germany 26 C5 52 26N 9 29 E
Wuntho, Burma 78 D5 23 55N 95 45 E
Wuping, China 69 E11 25 5N 116 5 E
Wuppertal, Germany 26 D3 51 15N 7 8 E
Wuppertal, S. Africa 104 E2 32 13 S 19 12 E
Wuqing, China 67 E9 39 23N 117 4 E
Würenlingen, Switz. 29 A6 47 32N 8 16 E
Wurung, Australia 114 B3 19 13 S 140 38 E
Würzburg, Germany 27 F5 49 46N 9 55 E
Wurzen, Germany 26 D8 51 21N 12 45 E
Wushan, Gansu, China 66 G3 34 43N 104 53 E
Wushan, Sichuan, China 68 B7 31 7N 109 54 E
Wusuli Jiang = Ussuri →, Asia 60 A7 48 27N 135 0 E
Wutach →, Germany 27 H4 47 37N 8 15 E
Wutai, China 66 E7 38 40N 113 12 E
Wuting = Huimin, China 67 F9 37 27N 117 28 E
Wutong, China 69 E8 25 24N 110 4 E
Wutonghaolai, China 67 C11 42 50N 120 5 E
Wutongqiao, China 68 C4 29 22N 103 50 E
Wuustwezel, Belgium 21 F5 51 23N 4 36 E
Wuwei, Anhui, China 69 B11 31 18N 117 54 E
Wuwei, Gansu, China 64 C5 37 57N 102 34 E
Wuxi, Jiangsu, China 69 B13 31 33N 120 18 E
Wuxi, Sichuan, China 68 B7 31 23N 109 35 E
Wuxiang, China 66 F7 36 49N 112 50 E
Wuxing, China 69 B13 30 51N 120 8 E
Wuxuan, China 68 F7 23 34N 109 38 E
Wuyang, China 66 H7 33 25N 113 35 E
Wuyi, Hebei, China 66 F8 37 46N 115 56 E
Wuyi, Zhejiang, China 69 C12 28 52N 119 50 E
Wuyi Shan, China 69 D11 27 0N 117 0 E
Wuyo, Nigeria 101 C7 10 23N 11 50 E
Wuyuan, Jiangxi, China 69 C11 29 15N 117 50 E
Wuyuan, Nei Mongol Zizhiqu, China 66 D5 41 2N 108 20 E
Wuzhai, China 66 E6 38 54N 111 48 E
Wuzhi Shan, China 76 C7 18 45N 109 45 E
Wuzhong, China 66 E4 38 2N 106 12 E
Wuzhou, China 69 F8 23 30N 111 18 E
Wyaaba Cr. →, Australia 114 B3 16 27 S 141 35 E
Wyalkatchem, Australia 113 F2 31 8 S 117 22 E
Wyalusing, U.S.A. 137 E8 41 40N 76 16W
Wyandotte, U.S.A. 141 B13 42 14N 83 13W
Wyandra, Australia 115 D4 27 12 S 145 56 E
Wyangala Res., Australia 117 B8 33 54 S 149 0 E
Wyara, L., Australia 115 D3 28 42 S 144 14 E
Wycheproof, Australia 116 D5 36 5 S 143 17 E
Wye →, U.K. 17 F5 51 36N 2 40W
Wyemandoo, Australia 113 E2 28 28 S 118 29 E
Wyk, Germany 26 A4 54 41N 8 33 E
Wymondham, U.K. 17 E7 52 45N 0 42W
Wymore, U.S.A. 138 E6 40 10N 96 40W
Wynbring, Australia 115 E1 30 33 S 133 32 E
Wyndham, Australia 112 C4 15 33 S 128 3 E
Wyndham, N.Z. 119 G3 46 20 S 168 51 E
Wyndmere, U.S.A. 138 B6 46 23N 97 7W
Wynne, U.S.A. 139 H9 35 15N 90 50W
Wynnum, Australia 115 D5 27 27 S 153 9 E
Wynyard, Australia 114 G4 41 5 S 145 44 E
Wynyard, Canada 131 C8 51 45N 104 10W
Wyola, L., Australia 113 E5 29 8 S 130 17 E
Wyoming, Ill., U.S.A. 140 C7 41 4N 89 47W
Wyoming, Iowa, U.S.A. 140 B6 42 4N 91 0W
Wyoming, Mich., U.S.A. 141 B11 42 53N 85 42W
Wyoming □, U.S.A. 132 B5 42 48N 109 0W
Wyong, Australia 117 B9 33 14 S 151 24 E
Wyrzysk, Poland 47 B4 53 10N 17 17 E
Wysoka, Poland 47 B4 53 13N 17 2 E
Wysokie, Poland 47 E9 50 55N 22 40 E
Wysokie Mazowieckie, Poland 47 C9 52 55N 22 30 E
Wyszków, Poland 47 C8 52 36N 21 25 E
Wyszogród, Poland 47 C7 52 23N 20 9 E
Wytheville, U.S.A. 134 G5 37 0N 81 3W

X

Xa-Muteba, Angola 103 D3 9 34 S 17 50 E
Xai-Xai, Mozam. 105 D5 25 6 S 33 31 E
Xainza, China 64 C3 30 58N 88 35 E
Xambioá, Brazil 154 C2 6 25 S 48 40W
Xangongo, Angola 103 F3 16 45 S 15 5 E
Xanten, Germany 26 D2 51 40N 6 27 E
Xánthi, Greece 44 C6 41 10N 24 58 E
Xánthi □, Greece 44 C6 41 10N 24 58 E
Xanthos, Turkey 88 E3 36 19N 29 18 E
Xapuri, Brazil 156 C4 10 35 S 68 35W
Xar Moron He →, China 67 C11 43 25N 120 35 E
Xau, L., Botswana 104 C3 21 15 S 24 44 E
Xavantina, Brazil 159 A5 21 15 S 52 48W
Xenia, Ill., U.S.A. 141 F8 38 38N 88 38W
Xenia, Ohio, U.S.A. 141 E13 39 42N 83 57W
Xeropotamos →, Cyprus 32 E11 34 42N 32 33 E
Xhora, S. Africa 105 E4 31 55 S 28 38 E
Xhumo, Botswana 104 C3 21 7 S 24 35 E
Xi Jiang →, China 69 F9 22 5N 113 20 E
Xi Xian, Henan, China 69 A10 32 20N 114 43 E
Xi Xian, Shanxi, China 66 F6 36 41N 110 58 E
Xia Xian, China 66 G6 35 8N 111 12 E
Xiachengzi, China 67 B16 44 40N 130 18 E
Xiachuan Dao, China 69 G9 21 40N 112 40 E
Xiaguan, China 68 E3 25 32N 100 16 E
Xiajiang, China 69 D10 27 30N 115 10 E
Xiajin, China 66 F9 36 56N 116 0 E
Xiamen, China 69 E12 24 25N 118 4 E
Xi'an, China 66 G5 34 15N 109 0 E
Xian Xian, China 66 E9 38 12N 116 6 E
Xianfeng, China 68 C7 29 40N 109 8 E
Xiang Jiang →, China 69 C9 28 55N 112 50 E
Xiangcheng, Henan, China 66 H8 33 29N 114 52 E
Xiangcheng, Henan, China 66 H7 33 50N 113 27 E
Xiangcheng, Sichuan, China 68 C2 28 53N 99 47 E
Xiangdu, China 68 F6 23 13N 106 58 E
Xiangfan, China 69 A9 32 2N 112 8 E
Xianghuang Qi, China 66 C7 42 2N 113 50 E
Xiangning, China 66 G6 35 58N 110 50 E
Xiangquan, China 66 F7 36 30N 113 1 E
Xiangshan, China 69 C13 29 29N 121 51 E
Xiangshui, China 67 G10 34 12N 119 33 E
Xiangtan, China 69 D9 27 51N 112 54 E
Xiangxiang, China 69 D9 27 43N 112 28 E
Xiangyin, China 69 C9 28 38N 112 54 E
Xiangyun, China 68 E3 25 34N 100 35 E
Xiangzhou, China 68 F7 23 58N 109 40 E
Xianju, China 69 C13 28 51N 120 44 E
Xianning, China 69 C10 29 51N 114 16 E
Xianshui He →, China 68 B3 30 10N 100 59 E
Xianyang, China 66 G5 34 20N 108 40 E
Xianyou, China 69 E12 25 22N 118 38 E
Xiao Hinggan Ling, China 65 B7 49 0N 127 0 E
Xiao Xian, China 66 G9 34 15N 116 55 E
Xiaofeng, China 69 B12 30 35N 119 32 E
Xiaogan, China 69 B9 30 52N 113 55 E
Xiaojin, China 68 B4 30 59N 102 21 E
Xiaolan, China 69 F9 22 38N 113 13 E
Xiaoshan, China 69 B13 30 12N 120 18 E
Xiaoyi, China 66 F6 37 8N 111 48 E
Xiapu, China 69 D12 26 54N 119 59 E
Xiawa, China 67 C11 42 35N 120 38 E
Xiayi, China 66 G9 34 15N 116 10 E
Xichang, China 68 D4 27 51N 102 19 E
Xichong, China 68 B5 30 57N 105 54 E
Xichuan, China 66 H6 33 0N 111 30 E
Xiemahe, China 69 B8 31 38N 111 12 E
Xieng Khouang, Laos 76 C4 19 17N 103 25 E
Xifei He →, China 66 H9 32 45N 116 40 E
Xifeng, Guizhou, China 68 D6 27 7N 106 42 E
Xifeng, Liaoning, China 67 C13 42 42N 124 45 E
Xifengzhen, China 66 G4 35 40N 107 40 E
Xigazê, China 64 D3 29 5N 88 45 E
Xihe, China 66 G3 34 2N 105 20 E
Xihua, China 66 H8 33 45N 114 30 E
Xiliao He →, China 67 C12 43 32N 123 35 E
Xilin, China 68 E5 24 30N 105 6 E
Xilókastron, Greece 45 F4 38 4N 22 43 E
Xin Jiang →, China 69 C11 28 45N 116 35 E
Xin Xian, China 66 E7 38 22N 112 46 E
Xinavane, Mozam. 105 D5 25 2 S 32 47 E
Xinbin, China 67 D13 41 40N 125 2 E
Xincai, China 69 A10 32 43N 114 58 E
Xinchang, China 69 C13 29 28N 120 52 E
Xincheng, Guangxi Zhuangzu, China 68 E7 24 5N 108 39 E
Xincheng, Jiangxi, China 69 D10 26 48N 114 6 E
Xinfeng, Guangdong, China 69 E10 24 5N 114 16 E
Xinfeng, Jiangxi, China 69 D11 27 7N 116 11 E
Xinfeng, Jiangxi, China 69 E10 25 27N 114 58 E
Xing Xian, China 66 E6 38 27N 111 7 E
Xing'an, Guangxi Zhuangzu, China 69 E8 25 38N 110 40 E
Xingan, Jiangxi, China 69 D10 27 46N 115 20 E
Xingcheng, China 67 D11 40 40N 120 45 E
Xingguo, China 69 D10 26 21N 115 21 E
Xinghe, China 66 D7 40 55N 113 55 E
Xinghua, China 67 H10 32 58N 119 48 E
Xinghua Wan, China 69 E12 25 15N 119 20 E

286 Xinglong

Xinglong, *China* **67 D9** 40 25N 117 30 E
Xingning, *China* **69 E10** 24 3N 115 42 E
Xingping, *China* **66 G5** 34 20N 108 28 E
Xingren, *China* **68 E5** 25 24N 105 11 E
Xingshan, *China* **69 B8** 31 15N 110 45 E
Xingtai, *China* **66 F8** 37 3N 114 32 E
Xingu →, *Brazil* **153 D7** 1 30 S 51 53W
Xingyang, *China* **66 G7** 34 45N 112 52 E
Xinhe, *China* **66 F8** 37 30N 115 15 E
Xinhua, *China* **69 D8** 27 42N 111 13 E
Xinhuang, *China* **68 D7** 27 21N 109 12 E
Xinhui, *China* **69 F9** 22 25N 113 0 E
Xiniás, L., *Greece* **45 E4** 39 2N 22 12 E
Xining, *China* **64 C5** 36 34N 101 40 E
Xinjiang, *China* **66 G6** 35 34N 111 11 E
Xinjiang Uygur Zizhiqu □, *China* **64 B3** 42 0N 86 0 E
Xinjie, *China* **68 D3** 26 48N 101 15 E
Xinjin, *Liaoning, China* **67 E11** 39 25N 121 58 E
Xinjin, *Sichuan, China* **68 B4** 30 24N 103 47 E
Xinkai He →, *China* **67 C12** 43 32N 123 35 E
Xinle, *China* **66 E8** 38 25N 114 40 E
Xinlitun, *China* **67 D12** 42 0N 122 8 E
Xinlong, *China* **68 B3** 30 57N 100 12 E
Xinmin, *China* **67 D12** 41 59N 122 50 E
Xinning, *China* **69 D8** 26 28N 110 50 E
Xinping, *China* **68 E3** 24 5N 101 59 E
Xinshao, *China* **69 D8** 27 21N 111 26 E
Xintai, *China* **67 G9** 35 55N 117 45 E
Xintian, *China* **69 E9** 25 55N 112 13 E
Xinxiang, *China* **66 G7** 35 18N 113 50 E
Xinxing, *China* **69 F9** 22 35N 112 15 E
Xinyang, *China* **69 A10** 32 6N 114 3 E
Xinye, *China* **69 A9** 32 30N 112 21 E
Xinyi, *China* **69 F8** 22 25N 111 0 E
Xinyu, *China* **69 D10** 27 49N 114 58 E
Xinzhan, *China* **67 C14** 43 50N 127 18 E
Xinzheng, *China* **66 G7** 34 20N 113 45 E
Xinzhou, *China* **69 B10** 30 50N 114 48 E
Xinzhu, *Taiwan* **69 E13** 24 49N 120 57 E
Xiong Xian, *China* **66 E9** 38 59N 116 8 E
Xiongyuecheng, *China* **67 D12** 40 12N 122 5 E
Xiping, *Henan, China* **66 H8** 33 22N 114 5 E
Xiping, *Henan, China* **66 H6** 33 25N 111 8 E
Xiping, *Zhejiang, China* **69 C12** 28 16N 119 29 E
Xique-Xique, *Brazil* **154 D3** 10 50 S 42 40W
Xiruá →, *Brazil* **156 B4** 6 3 S 67 50W
Xisha Qundao = Hsisha Chuntao, *Pac. Oc.* **70 A4** 15 50N 112 0 E
Xishui, *China* **69 B10** 30 30N 115 15 E
Xituozhen, *China* **68 B7** 30 22N 108 11 E
Xiuning, *China* **69 C12** 29 45N 118 10 E
Xiuren, *China* **69 E8** 24 27N 110 12 E
Xiushan, *China* **68 C7** 28 25N 108 57 E
Xiushui, *China* **69 C10** 29 2N 114 33 E
Xiuwen, *China* **68 D6** 26 49N 106 32 E
Xiuyan, *China* **67 D12** 40 18N 123 11 E
Xixia, *China* **66 H6** 33 25N 111 29 E
Xixiang, *China* **66 H4** 33 0N 107 44 E
Xiyang, *China* **66 F7** 37 38N 113 38 E
Xizang □, *China* **64 C3** 32 0N 88 0 E
Xlendi, *Malta* **32 C1** 36 1N 14 12 E
Xu Jiang →, *China* **69 D11** 28 0N 116 25 E
Xuan Loc, *Vietnam* **77 G6** 10 56N 107 14 E
Xuancheng, *China* **69 B12** 30 56N 118 43 E
Xuan'en, *China* **68 C7** 30 0N 109 30 E
Xuanhan, *China* **68 B6** 31 18N 107 38 E
Xuanhua, *China* **66 D8** 40 40N 115 2 E
Xuchang, *China* **66 G7** 34 2N 113 48 E
Xuefeng Shan, *China* **69 D8** 27 5N 110 35 E
Xuejiaping, *China* **69 B8** 31 39N 110 16 E
Xun Jiang →, *China* **69 F8** 23 35N 111 30 E
Xun Xian, *China* **66 G8** 35 42N 114 33 E
Xundian, *China* **68 E4** 25 36N 103 15 E
Xunwu, *China* **69 E10** 24 54N 115 37 E
Xunyang, *China* **66 H5** 32 48N 109 22 E
Xunyi, *China* **66 G5** 35 8N 108 20 E
Xupu, *China* **69 D8** 27 53N 110 32 E
Xushui, *China* **66 E8** 39 2N 115 40 E
Xuwen, *China* **69 G8** 20 20N 110 10 E
Xuyen Moc, *Vietnam* **77 G6** 10 34N 107 25 E
Xuyong, *China* **68 C5** 28 10N 105 22 E
Xuzhou, *China* **67 G9** 34 18N 117 10 E
Xylophagou, *Cyprus* **32 E12** 34 54N 33 51 E

Y

Ya Xian, *China* **76 C7** 18 14N 109 29 E
Yaamba, *Australia* **114 C5** 23 8 S 150 22 E
Ya'an, *China* **68 C4** 29 58N 103 5 E
Yaapeet, *Australia* **116 C5** 35 45 S 142 3 E
Yabassi, *Cameroon* **101 E6** 4 30N 9 57 E
Yabba North, *Australia* **117 D6** 36 13 S 145 42 E
Yabelo, *Ethiopia* **95 G4** 4 50N 38 8 E
Yablanitsa, *Bulgaria* **43 D9** 43 2N 24 5 E
Yablonovy Khrebet, *U.S.S.R.* **57 D12** 53 0N 114 0 E
Yablonovy Ra. = Yablonovy Khrebet, *U.S.S.R.* **57 D12** 53 0N 114 0 E
Yabrai Shan, *China* **66 E2** 39 40N 103 0 E
Yabrūd, *Syria* **91 B5** 33 58N 36 39 E
Yacheng, *China* **65 E5** 18 22N 109 6 E
Yacuiba, *Bolivia* **158 A3** 22 0 S 63 43W
Yacuma →, *Bolivia* **157 C4** 13 38 S 65 23W
Yadgir, *India* **82 F3** 16 45N 77 5 E
Yadkin →, *U.S.A.* **135 H5** 35 23N 80 3W
Yadrin, *U.S.S.R.* **51 D15** 55 57N 46 12 E
Yagaba, *Ghana* **101 C4** 10 14N 1 20W
Yagodnoye, *U.S.S.R.* **57 C15** 62 33N 149 40 E
Yagoua, *Cameroon* **102 A3** 10 20N 15 13 E
Yaguas →, *Peru* **152 D3** 2 45 S 70 10W
Yaha, *Thailand* **77 J3** 6 29N 101 8 E
Yahila, *Zaïre* **102 B4** 0 13N 24 28 E
Yahk, *Canada* **130 D5** 49 6N 116 10W
Yahuma, *Zaïre* **102 B4** 1 0N 23 10 E
Yahyalı, *Turkey* **88 D6** 38 5N 35 2 E
Yaita, *Japan* **61 F9** 36 48N 139 56 E
Yaiza, *Canary Is.* **33 F6** 28 57N 13 46W
Yaizu, *Japan* **63 C10** 34 52N 138 20 E
Yajiang, *China* **68 B3** 30 2N 100 57 E
Yajua, *Nigeria* **101 C7** 11 27N 12 49 E
Yakage, *Japan* **62 C5** 34 37N 133 35 E
Yakamba, *Zaïre* **102 B3** 2 42N 19 38 E
Yakima, *U.S.A.* **142 C3** 46 42N 120 30W
Yakima →, *U.S.A.* **142 C3** 47 0N 120 30W
Yako, *Burkina Faso* **100 C4** 12 59N 2 15W
Yakoma, *Zaïre* **102 B4** 4 5N 22 27 E
Yakoruda, *Bulgaria* **43 E8** 42 1N 23 39 E
Yakovlevka, *U.S.S.R.* **60 B6** 44 26N 133 28 E
Yakshur Bodya, *U.S.S.R.* **54 C3** 57 11N 53 7 E
Yaku-Shima, *Japan* **61 J5** 30 20N 130 30 E
Yakut A.S.S.R. □, *U.S.S.R.* **57 C14** 62 0N 130 0 E
Yakutat, *U.S.A.* **126 C6** 59 29N 139 44W
Yakutsk, *U.S.S.R.* **57 C13** 62 5N 129 50 E
Yala, *Thailand* **77 J3** 6 33N 101 18 E
Yalbalgo, *Australia* **113 E1** 25 10 S 114 45 E
Yalboroo, *Australia* **114 C4** 20 50 S 148 40 E
Yale, *U.S.A.* **136 C2** 43 9N 82 47W
Yalgoo, *Australia* **113 E2** 28 16 S 116 39 E
Yali, *Zaïre* **102 B4** 0 4N 21 3 E
Yaligimba, *Zaïre* **102 B4** 2 13N 22 56 E
Yalinga, *C.A.R.* **102 A4** 6 33N 23 10 E
Yalkubul, Punta, *Mexico* **147 C7** 21 32N 88 37W
Yalleroi, *Australia* **114 C4** 24 3 S 145 42 E
Yalobusha →, *U.S.A.* **139 J9** 33 30N 90 12W
Yaloke, *C.A.R.* **102 A3** 5 19N 17 5 E
Yalong Jiang →, *China* **68 D3** 26 40N 101 55 E
Yalova, *Turkey* **88 C3** 40 41N 29 15 E
Yalpukh, Oz., *U.S.S.R.* **46 D9** 45 30N 28 41 E
Yalta, *U.S.S.R.* **52 D6** 44 30N 34 10 E
Yalu Jiang →, *China* **67 E13** 40 0N 124 22 E
Yalutorovsk, *U.S.S.R.* **56 D7** 56 41N 66 12 E
Yalvaç, *Turkey* **88 D4** 38 17N 31 10 E
Yam Ha Melah = Dead Sea, *Asia* **86 A1** 31 30N 35 30 E
Yam Kinneret, *Israel* **91 C4** 32 45N 35 35 E
Yamada, *Japan* **62 D2** 33 33N 130 49 E
Yamaga, *Japan* **62 D2** 33 1N 130 41 E
Yamagata, *Japan* **60 E10** 38 15N 140 15 E
Yamagata □, *Japan* **60 E10** 38 30N 140 0 E
Yamagawa, *Japan* **62 F2** 31 12N 130 39 E
Yamaguchi, *Japan* **62 C3** 34 10N 131 32 E
Yamaguchi □, *Japan* **62 C3** 34 20N 131 40 E
Yamal, Poluostrov, *U.S.S.R.* **56 B8** 71 0N 70 0 E
Yamanaka, *Japan* **63 A8** 36 15N 136 22 E
Yamanashi □, *Japan* **63 B10** 35 40N 138 40 E
Yamantau, *U.S.S.R.* **48 D10** 54 20N 57 40 E
Yamantau, Gora, *U.S.S.R.* **54 D6** 54 15N 58 6 E
Yamato, *Japan* **63 B11** 35 27N 139 25 E
Yamatotakada, *Japan* **63 C7** 34 31N 135 45 E
Yamazaki, *Japan* **62 C6** 35 0N 134 32 E
Yamba, *N.S.W., Australia* **115 D5** 29 26 S 153 23 E
Yamba, *S. Austral., Australia* **116 C4** 34 10 S 140 52 E
Yambah, *Australia* **114 C1** 23 10 S 133 50 E
Yambarran Ra., *Australia* **112 C5** 15 10 S 130 25 E
Yambata, *Zaïre* **102 B4** 2 26N 21 58 E
Yâmbiô, *Sudan* **95 G2** 4 35N 28 16 E
Yambol, *Bulgaria* **43 E11** 42 30N 26 36 E
Yamdena, *Indonesia* **71 F8** 7 45 S 131 20 E
Yame, *Japan* **62 D2** 33 13N 130 35 E
Yamethin, *Burma* **78 E6** 20 29N 96 18 E
Yamil, *Nigeria* **101 C6** 12 53N 8 4 E
Yamma-Yamma, L., *Australia* **115 D3** 26 16 S 141 20 E
Yamoussoukro, *Ivory C.* **100 D3** 6 49N 5 17W
Yampa →, *U.S.A.* **142 F9** 40 37N 108 59W
Yampi Sd., *Australia* **112 C3** 16 8 S 123 38 E
Yampol, *U.S.S.R.* **52 B3** 48 15N 28 15 E
Yamrat, *Nigeria* **101 C6** 10 11N 9 55 E
Yamrukchal, *Bulgaria* **43 E9** 42 44N 24 52 E
Yamuna →, *India* **81 G9** 25 30N 81 53 E
Yamzho Yumco, *China* **64 D4** 28 48N 90 35 E
Yan, *Nigeria* **101 C7** 10 5N 12 11 E
Yan →, *Sri Lanka* **83 K5** 9 0N 81 10 E
Yana →, *U.S.S.R.* **57 B14** 71 30N 136 0 E
Yanac, *Australia* **116 D4** 36 8 S 141 25 E
Yanagawa, *Japan* **62 D2** 33 10N 130 24 E
Yanahara, *Japan* **62 C6** 34 58N 134 2 E
Yanai, *Japan* **62 D4** 33 58N 132 7 E
Yanam, *India* **82 F6** 16 47N 82 15 E
Yan'an, *China* **66 F5** 36 35N 109 26 E
Yanaul, *U.S.S.R.* **54 C4** 56 25N 55 0 E
Yanbian, *China* **68 D3** 26 47N 101 31 E
Yanbu 'al Baḥr, *Si. Arabia* **84 F3** 24 0N 38 5 E
Yancannia, *Australia* **115 E3** 30 12 S 142 35 E
Yanchang, *China* **66 F6** 36 43N 110 1 E
Yancheng, *Henan, China* **66 H8** 33 35N 114 0 E
Yancheng, *Jiangsu, China* **67 H11** 33 23N 120 8 E
Yanchi, *China* **66 F4** 37 48N 107 20 E
Yanchuan, *China* **66 F6** 36 51N 110 10 E
Yanco, *Australia* **117 C7** 34 38 S 146 27 E
Yanco Cr. →, *Australia* **117 C6** 35 14 S 145 35 E
Yandal, *Australia* **113 E3** 27 35 S 121 10 E
Yandanooka, *Australia* **113 E2** 29 18 S 115 29 E
Yandaran, *Australia* **114 C5** 24 43 S 152 6 E
Yandé, I., *N. Cal.* **121 T17** 20 3 S 163 49 E
Yandina, *Solomon Is.* **121 M10** 9 7 S 159 13 E
Yandja, *Zaïre* **102 C3** 1 41 S 17 43 E
Yandongi, *Zaïre* **102 B4** 2 51N 22 16 E
Yandoon, *Burma* **78 G5** 17 0N 95 40 E
Yanfeng, *China* **68 E3** 25 52N 101 8 E
Yanfolila, *Mali* **100 C3** 11 11N 8 9W
Yang Xian, *China* **66 H4** 33 15N 107 30 E
Yangambi, *Zaïre* **106 B1** 0 47N 24 20 E
Yangbi, *China* **68 E2** 25 41N 99 58 E
Yangcheng, *China* **66 G7** 35 28N 112 22 E
Yangch'ü = Taiyuan, *China* **66 F7** 37 52N 112 33 E
Yangchun, *China* **69 F8** 22 11N 111 48 E
Yanggao, *China* **66 D7** 40 21N 113 55 E
Yanggu, *China* **66 F8** 36 8N 115 43 E
Yangi-Yer, *U.S.S.R.* **56 E7** 40 17N 68 48 E
Yangibazar, *U.S.S.R.* **55 C5** 41 40N 70 53 E
Yangikishlak, *U.S.S.R.* **55 C3** 40 25N 67 10 E
Yangiyul, *U.S.S.R.* **55 C4** 41 0N 69 3 E
Yangjiang, *China* **69 G8** 21 50N 111 59 E
Yangliuqing, *China* **67 E9** 39 2N 117 5 E
Yangping, *China* **69 B8** 31 12N 111 25 E
Yangpingguan, *China* **66 H4** 32 58N 106 5 E
Yangquan, *China* **66 F7** 37 58N 113 31 E
Yangshan, *China* **69 E9** 24 30N 112 40 E
Yangshuo, *China* **69 E8** 24 48N 110 29 E
Yangtze Kiang = Chang Jiang →, *China* **69 B13** 31 48N 121 10 E
Yangxin, *China* **69 C10** 29 50N 115 12 E
Yangyang, *S. Korea* **67 E15** 38 4N 128 38 E
Yangyuan, *China* **66 D8** 40 1N 114 10 E
Yangzhou, *China* **69 A12** 32 21N 119 26 E
Yanhe, *China* **68 C7** 28 31N 108 29 E
Yanji, *China* **67 C15** 42 59N 129 30 E
Yanjin, *China* **68 C5** 28 5N 104 18 E
Yanjing, *China* **68 C2** 29 7N 98 33 E
Yankton, *U.S.A.* **138 D6** 42 55N 97 25W
Yanna, *Australia* **115 D4** 26 58 S 146 0 E
Yanonge, *Zaïre* **102 B4** 0 35N 24 38 E
Yanqi, *China* **64 B3** 42 5N 86 35 E
Yanqing, *China* **66 D8** 40 30N 115 58 E
Yanshan, *Hebei, China* **67 E9** 38 4N 117 22 E
Yanshan, *Jiangxi, China* **69 C11** 28 15N 117 41 E
Yanshan, *Yunnan, China* **68 F5** 23 35N 104 20 E
Yanshou, *China* **67 B15** 45 28N 128 22 E
Yantabulla, *Australia* **115 D4** 29 21 S 145 0 E
Yantai, *China* **67 F11** 37 34N 121 22 E
Yanting, *China* **68 B5** 31 11N 105 24 E
Yantra →, *Bulgaria* **43 D10** 43 40N 25 37 E
Yanwa, *China* **68 D2** 27 35N 98 55 E
Yany Kurgan, *U.S.S.R.* **55 B3** 43 55N 67 15 E
Yanyuan, *China* **68 D3** 27 25N 101 30 E
Yanzhou, *China* **66 G9** 35 35N 116 49 E
Yao, *Chad* **97 F3** 12 56N 17 33 E
Yao, *Japan* **63 C7** 34 32N 135 36 E
Yao Xian, *China* **66 G5** 34 55N 108 59 E
Yao Yai, Ko, *Thailand* **77 J2** 8 0N 98 35 E
Yao'an, *China* **68 E3** 25 31N 101 18 E
Yaodu, *China* **68 A5** 32 45N 105 22 E
Yaoundé, *Cameroon* **101 E7** 3 50N 11 35 E
Yaowan, *China* **67 G10** 34 15N 118 3 E
Yap I., *Pac. Oc.* **122 G5** 9 30N 138 10 E
Yapen, *Indonesia* **71 E9** 1 50 S 136 0 E
Yapen, Selat, *Indonesia* **71 E9** 1 20 S 136 10 E
Yappar →, *Australia* **114 B3** 18 22 S 141 16 E
Yaqui →, *Mexico* **146 B2** 27 37N 110 39W
Yar, *U.S.S.R.* **54 B3** 58 14N 52 5 E
Yar-Sale, *U.S.S.R.* **56 C8** 66 50N 70 50 E
Yaracuy □, *Venezuela* **152 A4** 10 20N 68 45W
Yaracuy →, *Venezuela* **152 A4** 10 33N 68 15W
Yaraka, *Australia* **114 C3** 24 53 S 144 3 E
Yarangüme, *Turkey* **88 E3** 37 35N 29 8 E
Yaransk, *U.S.S.R.* **51 C15** 57 22N 47 49 E
Yaratishky, *U.S.S.R.* **50 D5** 54 3N 26 0 E
Yardea P.O., *Australia* **115 E2** 32 23 S 135 32 E
Yare →, *U.K.* **17 E9** 52 36N 1 28 E
Yarensk, *U.S.S.R.* **48 B8** 61 10N 49 8 E
Yarí →, *Colombia* **152 D3** 0 20 S 72 20W
Yaritagua, *Venezuela* **152 A4** 10 5N 69 8W
Yarkand = Shache, *China* **64 C2** 38 20N 77 10 E
Yarker, *Canada* **137 B8** 44 23N 76 46W
Yarkhun →, *Pakistan* **81 A5** 36 17N 72 30 E
Yarmouth, *Canada* **129 D6** 43 50N 66 7W
Yarmūk →, *Syria* **91 C4** 32 42N 35 40 E
Yaroslavl, *U.S.S.R.* **51 C11** 57 35N 39 55 E
Yarqa, W. →, *Egypt* **91 F2** 30 0N 33 49 E
Yarra Yarra Lakes, *Australia* **113 E2** 29 40 S 115 45 E
Yarraden, *Australia* **114 A3** 14 17 S 143 15 E
Yarraloola, *Australia* **112 D2** 21 33 S 115 52 E
Yarram, *Australia* **117 E7** 38 29 S 146 39 E
Yarraman, *Australia* **115 D5** 26 50 S 152 0 E
Yarranvale, *Australia* **115 D4** 26 50 S 145 20 E
Yarras, *Australia* **117 A10** 31 25 S 152 20 E
Yarrawonga, *Australia* **117 D7** 36 0 S 146 0 E
Yarrowmere, *Australia* **114 C4** 21 27 S 145 53 E
Yarto, *Australia* **116 C5** 35 28 S 142 16 E
Yartsevo, *R.S.F.S.R., U.S.S.R.* **50 D8** 55 6N 32 43 E
Yartsevo, *R.S.F.S.R., U.S.S.R.* **57 C10** 60 20N 90 0 E
Yarumal, *Colombia* **152 B2** 6 58N 75 24W
Yasawa, *Fiji* **121 A1** 16 47 S 177 31 E
Yasawa Group, *Fiji* **121 A1** 17 0 S 177 23 E
Yaselda →, *U.S.S.R.* **50 E5** 52 7N 26 28 E
Yashbum, *Yemen* **86 D4** 14 19N 46 56 E
Yashi, *Nigeria* **101 C6** 12 23N 7 54 E
Yashiro-Jima, *Japan* **62 D4** 33 55N 132 15 E
Yasin, *Pakistan* **81 A5** 36 24N 73 23 E
Yasinovataya, *U.S.S.R.* **52 B7** 48 7N 37 57 E
Yasinski, L., *Canada* **128 B4** 53 16N 77 35W
Yasothon, *Thailand* **76 E5** 15 50N 104 10 E
Yass, *Australia* **117 C8** 34 49 S 148 54 E
Yasugi, *Japan* **62 B5** 35 26N 133 15 E
Yata →, *Bolivia* **157 C4** 10 29 S 65 26W
Yatağan, *Turkey* **45 G10** 37 20N 28 10 E
Yates Center, *U.S.A.* **139 G7** 37 53N 95 45W
Yates Pt., *N.Z.* **119 E2** 44 29 S 167 49 E
Yathkyed L., *Canada* **131 A9** 62 40N 98 0W
Yathong, *Australia* **117 B6** 32 37 S 145 33 E
Yatsuo, *Japan* **63 A9** 36 34N 137 8 E
Yatsushiro, *Japan* **62 E2** 32 30N 130 40 E
Yatsushiro-Kai, *Japan* **62 E2** 32 30N 130 25 E
Yatta Plateau, *Kenya* **106 C4** 2 0 S 38 0 E
Yauca, *Peru* **156 D3** 15 39 S 74 35W
Yauya, *Peru* **156 B2** 8 59 S 77 17W
Yauyos, *Peru* **156 C2** 12 19 S 75 50W
Yaval, *India* **82 D2** 21 10N 75 42 E
Yavan, *U.S.S.R.* **55 D4** 38 19N 69 2 E
Yavari →, *Peru* **156 A3** 4 21 S 70 2W
Yavatmal, *India* **82 D4** 20 20N 78 15 E
Yavne, *Israel* **91 D3** 31 52N 34 45 E
Yavorov, *U.S.S.R.* **50 G3** 49 55N 23 20 E
Yavuzeli, *Turkey* **89 E7** 37 18N 37 24 E
Yawatahama, *Japan* **62 D4** 33 27N 132 24 E
Yawri B., *S. Leone* **100 D2** 8 22N 13 0W
Yaxi, *China* **68 D6** 27 33N 106 41 E
Yayama-Rettō, *Japan* **61 M1** 24 30N 123 40 E
Yazagyo, *Burma* **78 D5** 23 30N 94 6 E
Yazd, *Iran* **85 D7** 31 55N 54 27 E
Yazd □, *Iran* **85 D7** 32 0N 55 0 E
Yazdān, *Iran* **79 B1** 33 30N 60 50 E
Yazoo →, *U.S.A.* **139 J9** 32 35N 90 50W
Yazoo City, *U.S.A.* **139 J9** 32 48N 90 28W
Ybbs, *Austria* **30 C8** 48 12N 15 4 E
Ydling Skovhøj, *Denmark* **13 J10** 55 59N 9 46 E
Ydrim, *Yemen* **86 D4** 14 20N 44 22 E
Ye Xian, *Henan, China* **66 H7** 33 35N 113 25 E
Ye Xian, *Shandong, China* **67 F10** 37 8N 119 57 E
Yea, *Australia* **117 D6** 37 14 S 145 26 E
Yealering, *Australia* **113 F2** 32 36 S 117 36 E
Yearinan, *Australia* **117 A8** 31 10 S 149 11 E
Yebbi-Souma, *Chad* **97 D3** 21 7N 17 54 E
Yechŏn, *S. Korea* **67 F15** 36 39N 128 27 E
Yecla, *Spain* **35 G3** 38 35N 1 5W
Yécora, *Mexico* **146 B3** 28 20N 108 58W
Yedashe, *Burma* **78 F6** 19 10N 96 20 E
Yedintsy, *U.S.S.R.* **52 B2** 48 9N 27 18 E
Yeeda, *Australia* **112 C3** 17 31 S 123 38 E
Yeelanna, *Australia* **115 E2** 34 9 S 135 45 E
Yefremov, *U.S.S.R.* **51 E11** 53 8N 38 3 E
Yegorlyk →, *U.S.S.R.* **53 C9** 46 33N 41 40 E
Yegorlykskaya, *U.S.S.R.* **53 C9** 46 35N 40 35 E
Yegoryevsk, *U.S.S.R.* **51 D11** 55 27N 38 55 E
Yegros, *Paraguay* **158 B4** 26 20 S 56 25W
Yehuda, Midbar, *Israel* **91 D4** 31 35N 35 15 E
Yei, *Sudan* **95 G3** 4 9N 30 40 E
Yei, Nahr →, *Sudan* **95 F3** 6 15N 30 13 E
Yekumbe, *Zaïre* **102 C4** 1 2S 23 27 E
Yelabuga, *U.S.S.R.* **54 D3** 55 45N 52 4 E
Yelan, *U.S.S.R.* **51 F13** 50 55N 43 43 E
Yelan-Kolenovski, *U.S.S.R.* **51 F12** 51 16N 41 4 E
Yelandur, *India* **83 H3** 12 6N 77 0 E
Yelanskoye, *U.S.S.R.* **57 C13** 61 25N 128 0 E
Yelarbon, *Australia* **115 D5** 28 33 S 150 38 E
Yelatma, *U.S.S.R.* **51 D12** 55 0N 41 45 E
Yelcho, L., *Chile* **160 B2** 43 18 S 72 18W
Yelets, *U.S.S.R.* **51 E11** 52 40N 38 30 E
Yélimané, *Mali* **100 B2** 15 9N 10 34W
Yell, *U.K.* **18 A7** 60 35N 1 5W
Yell Sd., *U.K.* **18 A7** 60 33N 1 15W
Yellamanchilli = Elamanchili, *India* **82 F6** 17 33N 82 50 E
Yellow Sea, *China* **67 G12** 35 0N 123 0 E
Yellowhead Pass, *Canada* **130 C5** 52 53N 118 25W
Yellowknife, *Canada* **130 A6** 62 27N 114 29W
Yellowknife →, *Canada* **130 A6** 62 31N 114 19W
Yellowstone →, *U.S.A.* **138 B3** 47 58N 103 59W
Yellowstone L., *U.S.A.* **142 D8** 44 30N 110 20W
Yellowstone National Park, *U.S.A.* **142 D9** 44 35N 110 0W
Yellowtail Res., *U.S.A.* **142 D9** 45 6N 108 8W
Yelnya, *U.S.S.R.* **50 D8** 54 35N 33 15 E
Yelsk, *U.S.S.R.* **50 F6** 51 50N 29 10 E
Yelvertoft, *Australia* **114 C2** 20 13 S 138 45 E
Yelwa, *Nigeria* **101 C5** 10 49N 4 41 E
Yemanzhelinsk, *U.S.S.R.* **54 D7** 54 58N 61 18 E
Yembongo, *Zaïre* **102 B3** 3 12N 19 2 E
Yemen ■, *Asia* **86 D4** 15 0N 44 0 E
Yen Bai, *Vietnam* **76 B5** 21 42N 104 52 E
Yenakiyevo, *U.S.S.R.* **52 B8** 48 15N 38 15 E
Yenangyaung, *Burma* **78 E5** 20 30N 95 0 E
Yenanma, *Burma* **78 F5** 19 46N 94 49 E
Yenda, *Australia* **117 C7** 34 13 S 146 14 E
Yendéré, *Ivory C.* **100 C4** 10 12N 4 59W
Yendi, *Ghana* **101 D4** 9 29N 0 1W
Yengo, *Congo* **102 B3** 0 22N 15 29 E
Yenice, *Turkey* **88 D2** 39 55N 27 17 E
Yenice →, *Turkey* **88 E6** 37 37N 35 33 E
Yenisaía, *Greece* **44 C6** 41 1N 24 57 E
Yenişehir, *Turkey* **88 C3** 40 16N 29 38 E
Yenisey →, *U.S.S.R.* **56 B9** 71 50N 82 40 E
Yeniseysk, *U.S.S.R.* **57 D10** 58 27N 92 13 E
Yeniseyskiy Zaliv, *U.S.S.R.* **56 B9** 72 20N 81 0 E
Yennádhi, *Greece* **32 C9** 36 2N 27 56 E
Yenne, *France* **25 C9** 45 43N 5 44 E
Yenotayevka, *U.S.S.R.* **53 C12** 47 15N 47 0 E
Yenyuka, *U.S.S.R.* **57 D13** 57 57N 121 15 E
Yeo, L., *Australia* **113 E3** 28 0 S 124 30 E
Yeola, *India* **82 D2** 20 2N 74 30 E
Yeoryioúpolis, *Greece* **32 D6** 35 20N 24 15 E
Yeoval, *Australia* **117 B8** 32 47 S 148 40 E
Yeovil, *U.K.* **17 G5** 50 57N 2 38W
Yepes, *Spain* **34 F1** 39 55N 3 39W
Yeppoon, *Australia* **114 C5** 23 5 S 150 47 E
Yeráki, *Greece* **45 H4** 37 0N 22 42 E
Yerbent, *U.S.S.R.* **56 F6** 39 30N 58 50 E
Yerbogachen, *U.S.S.R.* **57 C11** 61 16N 108 0 E
Yerevan, *U.S.S.R.* **53 F11** 40 10N 44 31 E
Yerilla, *Australia* **113 E3** 29 24 S 121 47 E
Yerköy, *Turkey* **88 D6** 39 38N 34 28 E
Yerla →, *India* **82 F2** 16 50N 74 30 E
Yermak, *U.S.S.R.* **56 D8** 52 2N 76 55 E
Yermakovo, *U.S.S.R.* **57 D13** 52 25N 126 20 E
Yermo, *U.S.A.* **145 L10** 34 58N 116 50W
Yermolayevo, *U.S.S.R.* **54 E5** 52 58N 56 12 E
Yerofey Pavlovich, *U.S.S.R.* **57 D13** 54 0N 122 0 E
Yerólakkos, *Cyprus* **32 D12** 35 11N 33 15 E
Yeropótamos →, *Greece* **32 D6** 35 3N 24 50 E
Yeroskipos, *Cyprus* **32 E11** 34 46N 32 28 E
Yerseke, *Neths.* **21 F4** 51 29N 4 3 E
Yershov, *U.S.S.R.* **51 F16** 51 22N 48 16 E
Yerunaja, Cerro, *Peru* **156 C2** 10 16 S 76 55W
Yerushalayim = Jerusalem, *Israel* **91 D4** 31 47N 35 10 E
Yerville, *France* **22 C7** 49 40N 0 53 E
Yes Tor, *U.K.* **17 G4** 50 41N 3 59W
Yesagyo, *Burma* **78 E5** 21 38N 95 14 E
Yesan, *S. Korea* **67 F14** 36 41N 126 51 E
Yeşilhisar, *Turkey* **88 D6** 38 20N 35 5 E
Yeşilırmak →, *Turkey* **88 C7** 41 22N 36 37 E
Yesilkent, *Turkey* **88 E7** 36 57N 36 12 E
Yesnogorsk, *U.S.S.R.* **51 D10** 54 32N 37 38 E
Yeso, *U.S.A.* **139 H2** 34 29N 104 37W
Yessentuki, *U.S.S.R.* **53 D10** 44 5N 42 53 E
Yessey, *U.S.S.R.* **57 C11** 68 29N 102 10 E
Yeste, *Spain* **35 G2** 38 22N 2 19W
Yeu, I. d', *France* **22 F4** 46 42N 2 20W
Yevlakh, *U.S.S.R.* **53 F12** 40 39N 47 7 E
Yevpatoriya, *U.S.S.R.* **52 D5** 45 15N 33 20 E
Yevstratovskiy, *U.S.S.R.* **51 F11** 50 11N 39 45 E
Yeya →, *U.S.S.R.* **53 C8** 46 40N 38 40 E
Yeysk, *U.S.S.R.* **52 C8** 46 40N 38 12 E
Yezd = Yazd, *Iran* **85 D7** 31 55N 54 27 E
Yhati, *Paraguay* **158 B4** 25 45 S 56 35W
Yhú, *Paraguay* **159 B4** 25 0 S 56 0W
Yi →, *Uruguay* **158 C4** 33 7 S 57 8W
Yi 'Allaq, G., *Egypt* **91 E2** 30 22N 33 32 E
Yi He →, *China* **67 G10** 34 10N 118 8 E
Yi Xian, *Anhui, China* **69 C11** 29 55N 117 57 E
Yi Xian, *Hebei, China* **66 E8** 39 20N 115 30 E
Yi Xian, *Liaoning, China* **67 D11** 41 30N 121 22 E
Yialí, *Greece* **45 H9** 36 41N 27 11 E
Yialiás →, *Cyprus* **32 D12** 35 9N 33 44 E

Zapiga 287

Yi'allaq, G., Egypt 94 H8 30 21N 33 31 E
Yialousa, Cyprus 32 D13 35 32N 34 10 E
Yiáltra, Greece 45 F4 38 51N 22 59 E
Yianisádhes, Greece 32 D8 35 20N 26 10 E
Yiannitsa, Greece 44 D4 40 46N 22 24 E
Yibin, China 68 C5 28 45N 104 32 E
Yichang, China 69 B8 30 40N 111 20 E
Yicheng, Henan, China 69 B9 31 41N 112 12 E
Yicheng, Shanxi, China 66 G6 35 42N 111 40 E
Yichuan, China 66 F6 36 2N 110 10 E
Yichun, Heilongjiang, China 65 B7 47 44N 128 52 E
Yichun, Jiangxi, China 69 D10 27 48N 114 22 E
Yidhá, Greece 44 D4 40 35N 22 53 E
Yidu, Hubei, China 69 B8 30 25N 111 27 E
Yidu, Shandong, China 67 F10 36 43N 118 28 E
Yidun, China 68 B2 30 22N 99 21 E
Yihuang, China 69 D11 27 30N 116 12 E
Yijun, China 66 G5 35 28N 109 8 E
Yilan, Taiwan 69 E13 24 51N 121 44 E
Yıldızeli, Turkey 88 D7 39 51N 36 36 E
Yilehuli Shan, China 65 A7 51 20N 124 20 E
Yiliang, Yunnan, China 68 D5 27 38N 104 2 E
Yiliang, Yunnan, China 68 E4 24 56N 103 11 E
Yilong, China 68 B6 31 34N 106 23 E
Yimen, China 68 E4 24 40N 102 10 E
Yimianpo, China 67 B15 45 7N 128 2 E
Yinchuan, China 66 E4 38 30N 106 15 E
Yindarlgooda, L., Australia 113 F3 30 40 S 121 52 E
Ying He →, China 66 H9 32 30N 116 30 E
Ying Xian, China 66 E7 39 32N 113 10 E
Yingcheng, China 69 B9 30 56N 113 35 E
Yingde, China 69 E9 24 10N 113 25 E
Yingjiang, China 68 E1 24 41N 97 55 E
Yingjing, China 68 C4 29 41N 102 52 E
Yingkou, China 67 D12 40 37N 122 18 E
Yingshan, Henan, China 69 B9 31 35N 113 50 E
Yingshan, Hubei, China 69 B10 30 41N 115 32 E
Yingshan, Sichuan, China 68 B6 31 4N 106 35 E
Yingshang, China 69 A11 32 38N 116 12 E
Yining, China 64 B3 43 58N 81 10 E
Yinjiang, China 68 C7 28 1N 108 21 E
Yinnietharra, Australia 112 D2 24 39 S 116 12 E
Yiofiros →, Greece 32 D7 35 20N 25 6 E
Yioúra, Attikí, Greece 44 E6 39 23N 24 10 E
Yioúra, Thessalía, Greece 45 G6 37 32N 24 40 E
Yipinglang, China 68 E3 25 10N 101 52 E
Yirga Alem, Ethiopia 95 F4 6 48N 38 22 E
Yishan, China 68 E7 24 28N 108 38 E
Yishui, China 67 G10 35 47N 118 30 E
Yíthion, Greece 45 H4 36 46N 22 34 E
Yitiaoshan, China 66 F3 37 5N 104 2 E
Yitong, China 67 C13 43 13N 125 20 E
Yiwu, China 69 C13 29 20N 120 3 E
Yixing, China 69 B12 31 21N 119 48 E
Yiyang, Henan, China 66 G7 34 27N 112 10 E
Yiyang, Hunan, China 69 C9 28 35N 112 18 E
Yiyang, Jiangxi, China 69 C11 28 22N 117 20 E
Yizhang, China 69 E9 25 27N 112 57 E
Yizheng, China 69 A12 32 18N 119 10 E
Ylitornio, Finland 12 C17 66 19N 23 39 E
Ylivieska, Finland 12 D18 64 4N 24 28 E
Yngaren, Sweden 15 F10 58 50N 16 35 E
Ynykchanskiy, U.S.S.R. 57 C14 60 15N 137 35 E
Yoakum, U.S.A. 139 L6 29 20N 97 20W
Yobuko, Japan 62 D1 33 32N 129 54 E
Yog Pt., Phil. 71 B6 14 6N 124 12 E
Yogan, Togo 101 D5 6 23N 1 30 E
Yogyakarta, Indonesia 71 G14 7 49 S 110 22 E
Yogyakarta □, Indonesia 75 D4 7 48 S 110 22 E
Yoho Nat. Park, Canada 130 C5 51 25N 116 30W
Yojoa, L. de, Honduras 148 D2 14 53N 88 0W
Yŏju, S. Korea 67 F14 37 20N 127 35 E
Yokadouma, Cameroon 102 B2 3 26N 14 55 E
Yōkaichiba, Japan 63 B12 35 42N 140 33 E
Yokkaichi, Japan 63 C8 34 55N 136 38 E
Yoko, Cameroon 101 D7 5 32N 12 20 E
Yokohama, Japan 63 B11 35 27N 139 28 E
Yokosuka, Japan 63 B11 35 20N 139 40 E
Yokote, Japan 60 E10 39 20N 140 30 E
Yola, Nigeria 101 D7 9 10N 12 29 E
Yolaina, Cordillera de, Nic. 148 D3 11 30N 84 0W
Yolombo, Zaïre 102 C4 1 36 S 23 12 E
Yombi, Gabon 102 C2 1 26 S 10 37 E
Yonago, Japan 62 B5 35 25N 133 19 E
Yonaguni-Jima, Japan 61 M1 24 27N 123 0 E
Yŏnan, N. Korea 67 F14 37 55N 126 11 E
Yonezawa, Japan 60 F10 37 57N 140 4 E
Yong Peng, Malaysia 77 M4 2 0N 103 3 E
Yong Sata, Thailand 77 J2 7 8N 99 41 E
Yongampo, N. Korea 67 E13 39 56N 124 23 E
Yong'an, China 69 E11 25 59N 117 25 E
Yongcheng, China 66 H9 33 55N 116 20 E
Yŏngchŏn, S. Korea 67 G15 35 58N 128 56 E
Yongchuan, China 68 C5 29 17N 105 55 E
Yongchun, China 69 E12 25 16N 118 20 E
Yongdeng, China 66 F2 36 38N 103 25 E
Yongding, China 69 E11 24 43N 116 45 E
Yŏngdŏk, S. Korea 67 F15 36 24N 129 22 E
Yŏngdŭngpo, S. Korea 67 F14 37 31N 126 54 E
Yongfeng, China 69 D10 27 20N 115 22 E
Yongfu, China 68 E7 24 59N 109 59 E
Yonghe, China 66 F6 36 46N 110 38 E
Yŏnghŭng, N. Korea 67 E14 39 31N 127 18 E
Yongji, China 66 G6 34 52N 110 28 E
Yŏngju, S. Korea 67 F15 36 50N 128 40 E
Yongkang, Yunnan, China 68 E2 24 9N 99 20 E
Yongkang, Zhejiang, China 69 C13 28 55N 120 2 E
Yongnian, China 66 F8 36 47N 114 29 E
Yongning, Guangxi Zhuangzu, China 68 F7 22 44N 108 28 E
Yongning, Ningxia Huizu, China 66 E4 38 15N 106 14 E
Yongping, China 68 E2 25 27N 99 38 E
Yongqing, China 66 E9 39 25N 116 28 E
Yongren, China 68 D3 26 4N 101 40 E
Yongshan, China 68 C4 28 11N 103 35 E
Yongsheng, China 68 D3 26 38N 100 46 E
Yongshun, China 68 C7 29 2N 109 51 E
Yongtai, China 69 E12 25 49N 118 58 E
Yŏngwŏl, S. Korea 67 F15 37 11N 128 28 E
Yongxin, China 69 D10 26 58N 114 15 E
Yongxing, China 69 D9 26 9N 113 8 E
Yongxiu, China 69 C10 29 2N 115 42 E
Yonibana, S. Leone 100 D2 8 30N 12 19W
Yonkers, U.S.A. 137 F11 40 57N 73 51W
Yonne □, France 23 E10 47 50N 3 40 E
Yonne →, France 23 D9 48 23N 2 58 E
York, Australia 113 F2 31 52 S 116 47 E
York, U.K. 16 D6 53 58N 1 7W
York, Ala., U.S.A. 135 J1 32 30N 88 18W
York, Nebr., U.S.A. 138 E6 40 55N 97 35W
York, Pa., U.S.A. 134 F7 39 57N 76 43W
York, C., Australia 114 A3 10 42 S 142 31 E
York, Kap, Greenland 6 B4 75 55N 66 25W
York Sd., Australia 112 C4 15 0 S 125 5 E
Yorke Pen., Australia 116 C2 34 50 S 137 40 E
Yorkshire Wolds, U.K. 16 D7 54 0N 0 30W
Yorkton, Canada 131 C8 51 11N 102 28W
Yorktown, U.S.A. 139 L6 29 0N 97 29W
Yorkville, Calif., U.S.A. 144 G3 38 52N 123 13W
Yorkville, Ill., U.S.A. 141 C8 41 38N 88 27W
Yornup, Australia 113 F2 34 2 S 116 10 E
Yoro, Honduras 148 C2 15 9N 87 7W
Yoron-Jima, Japan 61 L4 27 2N 128 26 E
Yos Sudarso, Pulau, Indonesia 71 F9 8 0 S 138 30 E
Yosemite National Park, U.S.A. 144 H7 38 0N 119 30W
Yosemite Village, U.S.A. 144 H7 37 45N 119 35W
Yoshii, Japan 62 D1 33 16N 129 46 E
Yoshimatsu, Japan 62 F2 32 0N 130 47 E
Yoshkar Ola, U.S.S.R. 51 C15 56 38N 47 55 E
Yŏsu, S. Korea 67 G14 34 47N 127 45 E
Yotala, Bolivia 157 D4 19 10 S 65 17W
Yotvata, Israel 91 F4 29 55N 35 2 E
You Xian, China 69 D9 27 1N 113 17 E
Youbou, Canada 130 D4 48 53N 124 13W
Youghal, Ireland 19 E4 51 58N 7 51W
Youghal B., Ireland 19 E4 51 55N 7 50W
Youkounkoun, Guinea 100 C2 12 35N 13 11W
Young, Australia 117 C8 34 19 S 148 18 E
Young, Canada 131 C7 51 47N 105 45W
Young, Uruguay 158 C4 32 44 S 57 36W
Young Ra., N.Z. 119 E4 44 10 S 169 30 E
Younghusband, L., Australia 116 A2 30 50 S 136 5 E
Younghusband Pen., Australia 116 D3 36 0 S 139 25 E
Youngstown, Canada 131 C6 51 35N 111 10W
Youngstown, N.Y., U.S.A. 136 C5 43 16N 79 2W
Youngstown, Ohio, U.S.A. 136 E4 41 7N 80 41W
Youngsville, U.S.A. 136 E5 41 51N 79 21W
Youssoufia, Morocco 98 B3 32 16N 8 31W
Youxi, China 69 D12 26 10N 118 13 E
Youyang, China 68 C7 28 47N 108 42 E
Youyu, China 66 D7 40 10N 112 20 E
Yoweragabbie, Australia 113 E2 28 14 S 117 39 E
Yowrie, Australia 117 D8 36 17 S 149 46 E
Yozgat, Turkey 88 D6 39 51N 34 47 E
Yozgat □, Turkey 88 D6 39 30N 35 0 E
Ypané →, Paraguay 158 A4 23 29 S 57 19W
Yport, France 22 C7 49 45N 0 15 E
Ypres = Ieper, Belgium 21 G1 50 51N 2 53 E
Ypsilanti, U.S.A. 141 B13 42 18N 83 40W
Yreka, U.S.A. 142 F2 41 44N 122 40W
Ysabel Chan., Papua N. G. 120 B6 2 0 S 150 0 E
Ysleta, U.S.A. 143 L10 31 45N 106 24W
Yssingeaux, France 25 C8 45 9N 4 8 E
Ystad, Sweden 15 J7 55 26N 13 50 E
Ythan →, U.K. 18 D7 57 26N 2 0W
Ytterhogdal, Sweden 14 B8 62 12N 14 56 E
Ytyk-Kel, U.S.S.R. 57 C14 62 30N 133 45 E
Yu Jiang →, China 65 D6 23 22N 110 3 E
Yu Shan, Taiwan 69 F13 23 30N 120 58 E
Yu Xian, Hebei, China 66 E8 39 50N 114 35 E
Yu Xian, Henan, China 66 G7 34 10N 113 28 E
Yu Xian, Shanxi, China 66 E7 38 5N 113 20 E
Yuan Jiang →, Hunan, China 69 C8 28 55N 111 50 E
Yuan Jiang →, Yunnan, China 68 F4 22 20N 103 59 E
Yuan'an, China 69 B8 31 3N 111 34 E
Yuanjiang, Hunan, China 69 C9 28 47N 112 21 E
Yuanjiang, Yunnan, China 68 F4 23 32N 102 0 E
Yuanli, Taiwan 69 E13 24 29N 120 39 E
Yuanlin, Taiwan 69 F13 23 58N 120 30 E
Yuanling, China 69 C8 28 29N 110 22 E
Yuanmou, China 68 E3 25 42N 101 53 E
Yuanqu, China 66 G6 35 18N 111 40 E
Yuanyang, Henan, China 66 G7 35 3N 113 58 E
Yuanyang, Yunnan, China 68 F4 23 10N 102 43 E
Yuat →, Papua N. G. 120 C2 4 10 S 143 52 E
Yuba →, U.S.A. 144 F5 39 8N 121 36W
Yuba City, U.S.A. 144 F5 39 12N 121 37W
Yūbari, Japan 60 C10 43 4N 141 59 E
Yūbetsu, Japan 60 B11 44 13N 143 50 E
Yucatán □, Mexico 147 C7 21 30N 86 30W
Yucatán, Canal de, Caribbean 148 B2 22 0N 86 30W
Yucatan Str. = Yucatán, Canal de, Caribbean 148 B2 22 0N 86 30W
Yucca, U.S.A. 145 L12 34 56N 114 6W
Yucca Valley, U.S.A. 145 L10 34 8N 116 30W
Yucheng, China 66 F9 36 55N 116 32 E
Yuci, China 66 F7 37 42N 112 46 E
Yudino, R.S.F.S.R., U.S.S.R. 51 D16 55 51N 48 55 E
Yudino, R.S.F.S.R., U.S.S.R. 56 D7 55 10N 67 55 E
Yudu, China 69 E10 25 59N 115 30 E
Yuendumu, Australia 112 D5 22 16 S 131 49 E
Yueqing, China 69 C13 28 9N 120 59 E
Yueqing Wan, China 69 C13 28 5N 121 20 E
Yuexi, Anhui, China 69 B11 30 50N 116 20 E
Yuexi, Sichuan, China 68 C4 28 37N 102 26 E
Yueyang, China 69 C9 29 21N 113 5 E
Yufu-Dake, Japan 62 D3 33 17N 131 33 E
Yugan, China 69 C11 28 43N 116 37 E
Yugoslavia ■, Europe 42 D5 44 0N 20 0 E
Yuhuan, China 69 C13 28 9N 121 12 E
Yujiang, China 69 C11 28 10N 116 43 E
Yukhnov, U.S.S.R. 50 D9 54 44N 35 15 E
Yūki, Japan 63 A11 36 18N 139 53 E
Yukon →, N. Amer. 126 B3 62 50N 165 0W
Yukon Territory □, Canada 126 B6 63 0N 135 0W
Yüksekova, Turkey 89 E11 37 34N 44 16 E
Yukti, U.S.S.R. 57 C11 63 26N 105 42 E
Yukuhashi, Japan 62 D2 33 44N 130 59 E
Yule →, Australia 112 D2 20 41 S 118 17 E
Yuli, Nigeria 101 D7 9 44N 10 12 E
Yulin, Guangxi Zhuangzu, China 69 F8 22 40N 110 8 E
Yulin, Shaanxi, China 66 E5 38 20N 109 30 E
Yuma, Ariz., U.S.A. 145 N12 32 45N 114 37W
Yuma, Colo., U.S.A. 138 E3 40 10N 102 43W
Yuma, B. de, Dom. Rep. 149 C6 18 20N 68 35W
Yumali, Australia 116 C3 35 32 S 139 45 E
Yumbe, Uganda 106 B3 3 28N 31 15 E
Yumbi, Zaïre 106 C2 1 12 S 26 15 E
Yumbo, Colombia 152 C2 3 35N 76 28W
Yumen, China 64 C4 39 50N 97 30 E
Yumurtalık, Turkey 88 E6 36 45N 35 43 E
Yun Ho →, China 67 E9 39 10N 117 10 E
Yun Xian, Hubei, China 69 A8 32 50N 110 46 E
Yun Xian, Yunnan, China 68 E3 24 27N 100 8 E
Yunak, Turkey 88 D4 38 49N 31 43 E
Yunan, China 69 F8 23 12N 111 30 E
Yuncheng, Henan, China 66 G8 35 36N 115 57 E
Yuncheng, Shanxi, China 66 G6 35 2N 111 0 E
Yundamindra, Australia 113 E3 29 15 S 122 6 E
Yunfu, China 69 F9 22 50N 112 5 E
Yungas, Bolivia 157 D4 17 0 S 66 0W
Yungay, Chile 158 D1 37 10 S 72 5W
Yungay, Peru 156 B2 9 2 S 77 45W
Yunhe, China 69 C12 28 8N 119 33 E
Yunlin, Taiwan 69 F13 23 42N 120 30 E
Yunling, China 68 D2 27 0N 99 20 E
Yunlong, China 68 E2 25 57N 99 13 E
Yunmeng, China 69 B9 31 2N 113 43 E
Yunnan □, China 68 E4 25 0N 102 0 E
Yunomae, Japan 62 E2 32 12N 130 59 E
Yunotso, Japan 62 B4 35 5N 132 21 E
Yunquera de Henares, Spain 34 E1 40 47N 3 11W
Yunta, Australia 116 B3 32 34 S 139 36 E
Yunxi, China 66 H6 33 0N 110 22 E
Yunxiao, China 69 F11 23 59N 117 18 E
Yunyang, China 68 B7 30 58N 108 54 E
Yuping, China 68 D7 27 13N 108 56 E
Yupukarri, Guyana 153 C6 3 45N 59 20W
Yupyongdong, N. Korea 67 D15 41 49N 128 53 E
Yuqing, China 68 D6 27 13N 107 53 E
Yur, U.S.S.R. 57 D14 59 52N 137 41 E
Yurgao, U.S.S.R. 56 D9 55 42N 84 51 E
Yuria, U.S.S.R. 54 B4 59 22N 54 10 E
Yuribei, U.S.S.R. 56 B8 71 8N 76 58 E
Yurimaguas, Peru 156 B2 5 55 S 76 7W
Yurya, U.S.S.R. 51 B16 59 1N 49 13 E
Yuryev-Polskiy, U.S.S.R. 51 C11 56 30N 39 40 E
Yuryevets, U.S.S.R. 51 C13 57 25N 43 2 E
Yuryuzan, U.S.S.R. 54 D6 54 27N 58 28 E
Yuscarán, Honduras 148 D2 13 58N 86 45W
Yushanzhen, China 68 C7 29 28N 108 22 E
Yushe, China 66 F7 37 4N 112 58 E
Yushu, Jilin, China 67 B14 44 43N 126 38 E
Yushu, Qinghai, China 64 C4 33 5N 96 55 E
Yutai, China 66 G9 35 0N 116 45 E
Yutian, China 67 E9 39 53N 117 45 E
Yuxi, China 68 E4 24 30N 102 35 E
Yuyao, China 69 B13 30 3N 121 10 E
Yuzawa, Japan 60 E10 39 10N 140 30 E
Yuzha, U.S.S.R. 51 C13 56 34N 42 1 E
Yuzhno-Sakhalinsk, U.S.S.R. 57 E15 46 58N 142 45 E
Yuzhno-Surkhanskoye Vodokhranilishehe, U.S.S.R. 55 E3 37 53N 67 42 E
Yuzhno-Uralsk, U.S.S.R. 54 D7 54 26N 61 15 E
Yuzhnyy Ural, U.S.S.R. 54 E6 53 0N 58 0 E
Yvelines □, France 23 D8 48 40N 1 45 E
Yverdon, Switz. 28 C3 46 47N 6 39 E
Yvetot, France 22 C7 49 37N 0 44 E
Yvonand, Switz. 28 C3 46 48N 6 44 E

Z

Zaalayskiy Khrebet, U.S.S.R. 55 D6 39 20N 73 0 E
Zaamslag, Neths. 21 F3 51 19N 3 55 E
Zaan →, Neths. 20 D5 52 25N 4 52 E
Zaandam, Neths. 20 D5 52 26N 4 49 E
Zab, Monts du, Algeria 99 B6 34 55N 5 0 E
Žabalj, Yugoslavia 42 B5 45 21N 20 5 E
Žabari, Yugoslavia 42 C6 44 22N 21 15 E
Zabarjad, Egypt 94 C4 23 40N 36 12 E
Zabaykalskiy, U.S.S.R. 57 E12 49 40N 117 25 E
Zabid, Yemen 86 D3 14 0N 43 10 E
Zabīd, W. →, Yemen 86 D3 14 7N 43 6 E
Ząbkowice Śląskie, Poland 47 E3 50 35N 16 50 E
Žabljak, Yugoslavia 42 D4 43 18N 19 7 E
Zabłudów, Poland 47 C10 53 0N 23 19 E
Žabno, Poland 31 A13 50 9N 20 53 E
Zābol, Iran 85 D9 31 0N 61 32 E
Zābol □, Afghan. 79 C2 32 0N 67 0 E
Zābolī, Iran 85 E9 27 10N 61 35 E
Zabré, Burkina Faso 101 C4 11 12N 0 36W
Zabrze, Poland 47 E5 50 18N 18 50 E
Zacapa, Guatemala 148 D2 14 59N 89 31W
Zacapu, Mexico 146 D4 19 50N 101 43W
Zacatecas, Mexico 146 C4 22 49N 102 34W
Zacatecas □, Mexico 146 C4 23 30N 103 0W
Zacatecoluca, El Salv. 148 D2 13 29N 88 51W
Zacoalco, Mexico 146 C4 20 14N 103 33W
Zacualtipán, Mexico 147 C5 20 39N 98 36W
Zadar, Yugoslavia 39 D12 44 8N 15 14 E
Zadawa, Nigeria 101 C7 11 33N 10 19 E
Zadetkyi Kyun, Burma 77 H2 10 0N 98 25 E
Zadonsk, U.S.S.R. 51 E11 52 25N 38 56 E
Zafarqand, Iran 85 C7 33 11N 52 29 E
Zafora, Greece 45 H8 36 5N 26 24 E
Zafra, Spain 37 G4 38 26N 6 30W
Żagań, Poland 47 D2 51 39N 15 22 E
Zagazig, Egypt 94 H7 30 40N 31 30 E
Zāgheh, Iran 85 C6 33 30N 48 42 E
Zaghouan, Tunisia 96 A2 36 23N 10 10 E
Zaglivérion, Greece 44 D5 40 36N 23 15 E
Zaglou, Algeria 99 C4 27 17N 0 3W
Zagnanado, Benin 101 D5 7 18N 2 28 E
Zagorá, Greece 44 E5 39 27N 23 6 E
Zagora, Morocco 98 B3 30 22N 5 51W
Zagórów, Poland 47 C4 52 10N 17 54 E
Zagorsk, U.S.S.R. 51 C11 56 20N 38 10 E
Zagórz, Poland 31 B15 49 30N 22 14 E
Zagreb, Yugoslavia 39 C13 45 50N 16 0 E
Zāgros, Kuhhā-ye, Iran 85 C6 33 45N 48 5 E
Zagros Mts. = Zāgros, Kuhhā-ye, Iran 85 C6 33 45N 48 5 E
Žagubica, Yugoslavia 42 C6 44 15N 21 47 E
Zaguinaso, Ivory C. 100 C3 10 1N 6 14W
Zagyva →, Hungary 31 D13 47 5N 20 4 E
Zāhedān, Fārs, Iran 85 D7 28 46N 53 52 E
Zāhedān, Sīstān va Balūchestān, Iran 85 D9 29 30N 60 50 E
Zahirabad, India 82 F3 17 43N 77 37 E
Zahlah, Lebanon 91 B4 33 52N 35 50 E
Zahna, Germany 26 D8 51 54N 12 47 E
Zahrez Chergui, Algeria 99 B5 35 0N 3 30 E
Zahrez Rharbi, Algeria 99 B5 34 50N 2 55 E
Zailiyskiy Alatau, Khrebet, U.S.S.R. 55 B8 43 5N 77 0 E
Zainsk, U.S.S.R. 54 D3 55 18N 52 4 E
Zaire □, Angola 103 D2 7 0 S 14 0 E
Zaïre ■, Africa 103 C4 3 0 S 23 0 E
Zaïre →, Africa 103 D2 6 4 S 12 24 E
Zaječar, Yugoslavia 42 D7 43 53N 22 18 E
Zakamensk, U.S.S.R. 57 D11 50 23N 103 17 E
Zakani, Zaïre 102 B4 2 33N 23 16 E
Zakataly, U.S.S.R. 53 F12 41 38N 46 35 E
Zakavkazye, U.S.S.R. 53 F11 42 0N 44 0 E
Zākhū, Iraq 84 B4 37 10N 42 50 E
Zákinthos, Greece 45 G2 37 47N 20 57 E
Zaklików, Poland 47 E9 50 46N 22 7 E
Zakopane, Poland 31 B12 49 18N 19 57 E
Zakroczym, Poland 47 C7 52 26N 20 38 E
Zákros, Greece 32 D8 35 6N 26 10 E
Zala, Angola 103 D2 7 52 S 13 42 E
Zala □, Hungary 31 E9 46 42N 16 50 E
Zala →, Hungary 31 E10 46 43N 17 16 E
Zalaegerszeg, Hungary 31 E9 46 53N 16 47 E
Zalakomár, Hungary 31 E10 46 33N 17 10 E
Zalalövö, Hungary 31 E9 46 51N 16 35 E
Zalamea de la Serena, Spain 37 G5 38 40N 5 38W
Zalamea la Real, Spain 37 H4 37 41N 6 38W
Zalău, Romania 46 B4 47 12N 23 3 E
Zalazna, U.S.S.R. 54 B3 58 39N 52 31 E
Žalec, Yugoslavia 39 B12 46 16N 15 10 E
Zaleshchiki, U.S.S.R. 52 B1 48 45N 25 45 E
Zalew Wislany, Poland 47 A6 54 20N 19 50 E
Zalewo, Poland 47 B6 53 50N 19 41 E
Zalīm, Si. Arabia 86 B3 22 43N 42 10 E
Zalingei, Sudan 97 F4 12 51N 23 29 E
Zaliv Vislinskil = Zalew Wislany, Poland 47 A6 54 20N 19 50 E
Zalţan, Jabal, Libya 96 C3 28 46N 19 45 E
Zaltbommel, Neths. 20 E6 51 48N 5 15 E
Zambeke, Zaïre 106 B2 2 8N 25 17 E
Zambeze →, Africa 107 F4 18 35 S 36 20 E
Zambezi = Zambeze →, Africa 107 F4 18 35 S 36 20 E
Zambezi, Zambia 103 E4 13 30 S 23 15 E
Zambezia □, Mozam. 107 F4 16 15 S 37 30 E
Zambia ■, Africa 107 F2 15 0 S 28 0 E
Zamboanga, Phil. 71 C6 6 59N 122 3 E
Zambrano, Colombia 152 B3 9 45N 74 49W
Zambrów, Poland 47 C9 52 59N 22 14 E
Zametchino, U.S.S.R. 51 E13 53 30N 42 30 E
Zamora, Ecuador 152 D2 4 4 S 78 58W
Zamora, Mexico 146 D4 20 0N 102 21W
Zamora, Spain 36 D5 41 30N 5 45W
Zamora □, Spain 36 D5 41 30N 5 46W
Zamora-Chinchipe □, Ecuador 152 D2 4 15 S 78 50W
Zamość, Poland 47 E10 50 43N 23 15 E
Zamość □, Poland 47 E10 50 40N 23 10 E
Zamuro, Sierra del, Venezuela 153 C5 4 0N 62 30W
Zamzam, W. →, Libya 96 B2 31 0N 14 30 E
Zan, Ghana 101 D4 9 26N 0 17W
Zanaga, Congo 102 C2 2 48 S 13 48 E
Záncara →, Spain 35 F1 39 18N 3 18W
Zandijk, Neths. 20 D5 52 28N 4 49 E
Zandvoort, Neths. 20 D5 52 22N 4 32 E
Zanesville, U.S.A. 136 G2 39 56N 82 5W
Zangābād, Iran 84 B5 38 26N 46 44 E
Zangue →, Mozam. 107 F4 17 50 S 35 21 E
Zanjan, Iran 85 B6 36 40N 48 35 E
Zanjān □, Iran 85 B6 37 20N 49 30 E
Zannone, Italy 40 B6 40 58N 13 2 E
Zante = Zákinthos, Greece 45 G2 37 47N 20 57 E
Zanthus, Australia 113 F3 31 2 S 123 34 E
Zanzibar, Tanzania 106 D4 6 12 S 39 12 E
Zanzūr, Libya 96 B2 32 55N 13 1 E
Zaouiet El-Kala = Bordj Omar Driss, Algeria 99 C6 28 10N 6 40 E
Zaouiet Reggane, Algeria 99 C5 26 32N 0 3 E
Zaoyang, China 69 A9 32 10N 112 45 E
Zaozhuang, China 67 G9 34 50N 117 35 E
Zapadna Morava →, Yugoslavia 42 D6 43 38N 21 30 E
Zapadnaya Dvina, U.S.S.R. 50 C8 56 15N 32 3 E
Zapadnaya Dvina →, U.S.S.R. 50 C4 57 4N 24 3 E
Západné Beskydy, Europe 31 B12 49 30N 19 0 E
Zapadni Rodopi, Bulgaria 43 F9 41 50N 24 0 E
Zapadočeský □, Czech. 30 B6 49 35N 13 0 E
Západoslovenský □, Czech. 31 C10 48 30N 17 30 E
Zapala, Argentina 160 A2 39 0 S 70 5W
Zapaleri, Cerro, Bolivia 158 A2 22 49 S 67 11W
Zapata, U.S.A. 139 M5 26 56N 99 17W
Zapatón →, Spain 37 G4 39 0N 6 49W
Zapiga, Chile 156 D4 19 40 S 69 55W

288 Zapodnyy Sayan

Zapodnyy Sayan, *U.S.S.R.* **57 D10** 52 30N 94 0 E
Zapolyarnyy, *U.S.S.R.* **48 A5** 69 26N 30 51 E
Zaporozhye, *U.S.S.R.* **52 C6** 47 50N 35 10 E
Zapponeta, *Italy* **41 A8** 41 27N 15 57 E
Zara, *Turkey* **89 D7** 39 58N 37 43 E
Zaragoza, *Colombia* **152 B3** 7 30N 74 52W
Zaragoza, *Coahuila, Mexico* **146 B4** 28 30N 101 0W
Zaragoza, *Nuevo León, Mexico* **147 C5** 24 0N 99 46W
Zaragoza, *Spain* **34 D4** 41 39N 0 53W
Zaragoza □, *Spain* **34 D4** 41 35N 1 0W
Zarand, *Kermān, Iran* **85 D8** 30 46N 56 34 E
Zarand, *Markazī, Iran* **85 C6** 35 18N 50 25 E
Zărandului, Munţii, *Romania* **46 C3** 46 14N 22 7 E
Zaranj, *Afghan.* **79 C1** 30 55N 61 55 E
Zarasai, *U.S.S.R.* **50 D5** 55 40N 26 20 E
Zarate, *Argentina* **158 C4** 34 7S 59 0W
Zaraysk, *U.S.S.R.* **51 D11** 54 48N 38 53 E
Zaraza, *Venezuela* **153 B4** 9 21N 65 19W
Zāreh, *Iran* **85 C6** 35 7N 49 9 E
Zarembo I., *U.S.A.* **130 B2** 56 20N 132 50W
Zaria, *Nigeria* **101 C6** 11 0N 7 40 E
Zárkon, *Greece* **44 E4** 39 38N 22 6 E
Zarneh, *Iran* **84 C5** 33 55N 46 10 E
Zarós, *Greece* **32 D6** 35 8N 24 54 E
Żarów, *Poland* **47 E3** 50 56N 16 29 E
Zarqā' →, *Jordan* **91 C4** 32 10N 35 37 E
Zarrīn, *Iran* **85 C7** 32 46N 54 37 E
Zaruma, *Ecuador* **152 D2** 3 40 S 79 38W
Żary, *Poland* **47 D2** 51 37N 15 10 E
Zarza de Alange, *Spain* **37 G4** 38 49N 6 13W
Zarza de Granadilla, *Spain* **36 E4** 40 14N 6 3W
Zarzaïtine, *Algeria* **99 C6** 28 15N 9 34 E
Zarzal, *Colombia* **152 C2** 4 24N 76 4W
Zarzis, *Tunisia* **96 B2** 33 31N 11 2 E
Zas, *Spain* **36 B2** 43 4N 8 53W
Zashiversk, *U.S.S.R.* **57 C15** 67 25N 142 40 E
Zaskar →, *India* **81 B7** 34 13N 77 20 E
Zaskar Mts., *India* **81 C7** 33 15N 77 30 E
Zastron, *S. Africa* **104 E4** 30 18 S 27 7 E
Žatec, *Czech.* **30 A6** 50 20N 13 32 E
Zator, *Poland* **31 B12** 49 59N 19 28 E
Zavala, *Yugoslavia* **42 E2** 42 50N 17 59 E
Zavāreh, *Iran* **85 C7** 33 29N 52 28 E
Zaventem, *Belgium* **21 G4** 50 53N 4 28 E
Zavetnoye, *U.S.S.R.* **53 C10** 47 13N 43 50 E
Zavidovići, *Yugoslavia* **42 C3** 44 27N 18 13 E
Zavitinsk, *U.S.S.R.* **57 D13** 50 10N 129 20 E
Zavodovski, I., *Antarctica* **7 B1** 56 0 S 27 45W
Zavolzhsk, *U.S.S.R.* **51 C13** 57 30N 42 10 E
Zavolzhye, *U.S.S.R.* **51 C13** 56 37N 43 26 E
Zawadzkie, *Poland* **47 E5** 50 37N 18 28 E
Zawichost, *Poland* **47 E8** 50 48N 21 51 E
Zawidów, *Poland* **47 D2** 51 1N 15 1 E
Zawiercie, *Poland* **47 E6** 50 30N 19 24 E
Zāwiyat al Bayḍā, *Libya* **96 B4** 32 30N 21 40 E
Zāwiyat Masūs, *Libya* **96 B4** 31 35N 21 1 E
Zawyet Shammâs, *Egypt* **94 A2** 31 30N 26 37 E
Zâwyet Um el Rakham, *Egypt* **94 A2** 31 18N 27 1 E
Zâwyet Ungeîla, *Egypt* **94 A2** 31 23N 26 42 E
Zāyā, *Iraq* **84 C5** 33 33N 44 13 E
Zayarsk, *U.S.S.R.* **57 D11** 56 12N 102 55 E
Zaymah, *Si. Arabia* **86 B3** 21 37N 40 6 E
Zaysan, *U.S.S.R.* **56 E9** 47 28N 84 52 E
Zaysan, Oz., *U.S.S.R.* **56 E9** 48 0N 83 0 E
Zayü, *China* **68 C1** 28 48N 97 27 E
Zāzamt, W. →, *Libya* **96 B2** 30 29N 14 30 E
Zazir, O. →, *Algeria* **99 D6** 22 0N 5 40 E
Zázrivá, *Czech.* **31 B12** 49 16N 19 7 E
Zbarazh, *U.S.S.R.* **50 G4** 49 43N 25 44 E
Zbąszyń, *Poland* **47 C2** 52 14N 15 56 E
Zbąszynek, *Poland* **47 C2** 52 16N 15 51 E
Zblewo, *Poland* **47 B5** 53 56N 18 19 E
Zdolbunov, *U.S.S.R.* **50 F5** 50 30N 26 15 E
Ždrelo, *Yugoslavia* **42 C6** 44 16N 21 28 E
Zduńska Wola, *Poland* **47 D5** 51 37N 18 59 E
Zduny, *Poland* **47 D4** 51 39N 17 21 E
Zearing, *U.S.A.* **140 B3** 42 10N 93 20W
Zeballos, *Canada* **130 D3** 49 59N 126 50W
Zebediela, *S. Africa* **105 C4** 24 20 S 29 17 E
Zedelgem, *Belgium* **21 F2** 51 8N 3 8 E
Zeebrugge, *Belgium* **21 F2** 51 19N 3 12 E
Zeehan, *Australia* **114 G4** 41 52 S 145 25 E
Zeeland, *Neths.* **21 E7** 51 41N 5 40 E
Zeeland, *U.S.A.* **141 B10** 42 49N 86 1W
Zeeland □, *Neths.* **21 F3** 51 30N 3 50 E
Zeelst, *Neths.* **21 F6** 51 25N 5 25 E
Zeerust, *S. Africa* **104 D4** 25 31 S 26 4 E
Zefat, *Israel* **91 C4** 32 58N 35 29 E
Zegdou, *Algeria* **98 C4** 29 51N 4 45W
Zege, *Ethiopia* **95 E4** 11 43N 37 18 E
Zegelsem, *Belgium* **21 G3** 50 49N 3 43 E
Zégoua, *Mali* **100 C3** 10 32N 5 35W
Zehdenick, *Germany* **26 C9** 52 59N 13 20 E
Zeigler, *U.S.A.* **140 G7** 37 55N 89 5W
Zeil, Mt., *Australia* **112 D5** 23 30 S 132 23 E
Zeila, *Somali Rep.* **90 E3** 11 21N 43 30 E
Zeist, *Neths.* **20 D6** 52 5N 5 15 E
Zeitz, *Germany* **26 D8** 51 3N 12 9 E
Zele, *Belgium* **21 F4** 51 4N 4 2 E
Żelechów, *Poland* **47 D8** 51 49N 21 54 E
Zelee, C., *Solomon Is.* **121 M11** 9 44 S 161 34 E
Zelengora, *Yugoslavia* **42 D3** 43 22N 18 30 E
Zelenika, *Yugoslavia* **42 E3** 42 27N 18 37 E
Zelenodolsk, *U.S.S.R.* **51 D16** 55 55N 48 30 E
Zelenograd, *U.S.S.R.* **51 C10** 56 1N 37 12 E
Zelenogradsk, *U.S.S.R.* **50 D2** 54 53N 20 29 E
Zelenokumsk, *U.S.S.R.* **53 D10** 44 24N 43 53 E
Zelënyy, *U.S.S.R.* **53 B14** 48 6N 50 45 E
Zeleznik, *Yugoslavia* **42 C5** 44 43N 20 23 E
Zelhem, *Neths.* **20 D8** 52 2N 6 21 E
Zell, *Baden-W., Germany* **27 H3** 47 42N 7 50 E
Zell, *Rhld-Pfz., Germany* **27 E3** 50 2N 7 11 E
Zell am See, *Austria* **30 D5** 47 19N 12 47 E
Zella Mehlis, *Germany* **26 E6** 50 40N 10 41 E
Zelów, *Poland* **47 D6** 51 28N 19 14 E
Zelzate, *Belgium* **21 F3** 51 13N 3 47 E
Zembra, I., *Tunisia* **96 A2** 37 5N 10 56 E
Zémio, *C.A.R.* **102 A5** 5 2N 25 5 E
Zemlya Frantsa Iosifa, *Arctic* **6 A10** 81 0N 55 0 E
Zemmora, *Algeria* **99 A5** 35 44N 0 51 E
Zemmur, *W. Sahara* **98 C2** 25 5N 12 0W
Zemoul, O. →, *Algeria* **98 C3** 29 15N 7 0W
Zemst, *Belgium* **21 G4** 50 59N 4 28 E
Zemun, *Yugoslavia* **42 C5** 44 51N 20 25 E
Zendeh Jān, *Afghan.* **79 B1** 34 21N 61 45 E
Zengbe, *Cameroon* **101 D7** 5 46N 13 4 E
Zengcheng, *China* **69 F9** 23 13N 113 52 E
Zenica, *Yugoslavia* **42 C2** 44 10N 17 57 E
Zenina, *Algeria* **99 B5** 34 30N 2 37 E
Zentsūji, *Japan* **62 C5** 34 14N 133 47 E
Zenza do Itombe, *Angola* **103 D2** 9 16 S 14 13 E
Žepče, *Yugoslavia* **42 C3** 44 28N 18 2 E
Zeraf, Bahr ez →, *Sudan* **95 F3** 9 42N 30 52 E
Zeravshan, *U.S.S.R.* **55 D4** 39 10N 68 39 E
Zeravshanskiy, Khrebet, *U.S.S.R.* **55 D4** 39 20N 69 0 E
Zerbst, *Germany* **26 D8** 51 59N 12 8 E
Żerków, *Poland* **47 C4** 52 4N 17 32 E
Zermatt, *Switz.* **28 D5** 46 2N 7 46 E
Zernez, *Switz.* **29 C10** 46 42N 10 7 E
Zernograd, *U.S.S.R.* **53 C9** 46 52N 40 19 E
Zerqani, *Albania* **44 C2** 41 30N 20 20 E
Zestafoni, *U.S.S.R.* **53 E10** 42 6N 43 0 E
Zetel, *Germany* **26 B3** 53 25N 7 57 E
Zetten, *Neths.* **20 E7** 51 56N 5 44 E
Zeulenroda, *Germany* **26 E8** 50 39N 12 0 E
Zeven, *Germany* **26 B5** 53 17N 9 19 E
Zevenaar, *Neths.* **20 E8** 51 56N 6 5 E
Zevenbergen, *Neths.* **21 E5** 51 38N 4 37 E
Zévio, *Italy* **38 C8** 45 23N 11 10 E
Zeya, *U.S.S.R.* **57 D13** 53 48N 127 14 E
Zeya →, *U.S.S.R.* **57 D13** 53 13N 127 35 E
Zêzere →, *Portugal* **37 F2** 39 28N 8 20W
Zghartā, *Lebanon* **91 A4** 34 21N 35 53 E
Zgierz, *Poland* **47 D6** 51 50N 19 27 E
Zgorzelec, *Poland* **47 D2** 51 10N 15 0 E
Zhabinka, *U.S.S.R.* **50 E4** 52 13N 24 2 E
Zhailma, *U.S.S.R.* **54 F7** 51 37N 61 33 E
Zhalanash, *U.S.S.R.* **55 B9** 43 3N 78 38 E
Zhanadarya, *U.S.S.R.* **55 A2** 44 45N 64 40 E
Zhanatas, *U.S.S.R.* **55 B4** 43 35N 69 35 E
Zhangbei, *China* **66 D8** 41 10N 114 45 E
Zhangguangcai Ling, *China* **67 B15** 45 0N 129 0 E
Zhanghua, *Taiwan* **69 E13** 24 6N 120 29 E
Zhangjiakou, *China* **66 D8** 40 48N 114 55 E
Zhangping, *China* **69 E11** 25 17N 117 23 E
Zhangpu, *China* **69 E11** 24 8N 117 35 E
Zhangwu, *China* **67 C12** 42 43N 123 52 E
Zhangye, *China* **64 C5** 38 50N 100 23 E
Zhangzhou, *China* **69 E11** 24 30N 117 35 E
Zhanhua, *China* **67 F10** 37 40N 118 8 E
Zhanjiang, *China* **69 G8** 21 15N 110 20 E
Zhanyi, *China* **68 E4** 25 38N 103 48 E
Zhanyu, *China* **67 B12** 44 30N 122 30 E
Zhao Xian, *China* **66 F8** 37 43N 114 45 E
Zhao'an, *China* **69 F11** 23 41N 117 10 E
Zhaocheng, *China* **66 F6** 36 22N 111 38 E
Zhaojue, *China* **68 C4** 28 1N 102 49 E
Zhaoping, *China* **69 E8** 24 11N 110 48 E
Zhaoqing, *China* **69 F9** 23 0N 112 20 E
Zhaotong, *China* **68 D4** 27 20N 103 44 E
Zhaoyuan, *Heilongjiang, China* **67 B13** 45 27N 125 0 E
Zhaoyuan, *Shandong, China* **67 F11** 37 20N 120 23 E
Zharkol, *U.S.S.R.* **54 G9** 49 57N 64 5 E
Zharkovskiy, *U.S.S.R.* **50 D8** 55 56N 32 19 E
Zhashkov, *U.S.S.R.* **52 B4** 49 15N 30 5 E
Zhashui, *China* **66 H5** 33 40N 109 8 E
Zhdanov = Mariupol, *U.S.S.R.* **52 C7** 47 5N 37 31 E
Zhecheng, *China* **66 G8** 34 7N 115 20 E
Zhegao, *China* **69 B11** 31 46N 117 45 E
Zhejiang □, *China* **69 C13** 29 0N 120 0 E
Zheleznodorozhny, *U.S.S.R.* **48 B9** 62 35N 50 55 E
Zheleznogorsk, *U.S.S.R.* **50 E9** 52 22N 35 23 E
Zheleznogorsk-Ilimskiy, *U.S.S.R.* **57 D11** 56 34N 104 8 E
Zheltyye Vody, *U.S.S.R.* **52 B5** 48 21N 33 31 E
Zhen'an, *China* **66 H5** 33 27N 109 9 E
Zhenfeng, *China* **68 E5** 25 22N 105 40 E
Zheng'an, *China* **68 C6** 28 32N 107 27 E
Zhengding, *China* **66 E8** 38 8N 114 32 E
Zhenghe, *China* **69 D12** 27 20N 118 50 E
Zhengyang, *China* **69 A10** 32 37N 114 22 E
Zhengyangguan, *China* **69 A11** 32 30N 116 29 E
Zhengzhou, *China* **66 G7** 34 45N 113 34 E
Zhenhai, *China* **69 C13** 29 59N 121 42 E
Zhenjiang, *China* **69 A12** 32 11N 119 26 E
Zhenlai, *China* **67 B12** 45 50N 123 5 E
Zhenning, *China* **68 D5** 26 4N 105 45 E
Zhenping, *Henan, China* **66 H7** 33 10N 112 16 E
Zhenping, *Shaanxi, China* **68 B7** 31 59N 109 31 E
Zhenxiong, *China* **68 D5** 27 27N 104 50 E
Zhenyuan, *Gansu, China* **66 G4** 35 35N 107 30 E
Zhenyuan, *Guizhou, China* **68 D7** 27 4N 108 21 E
Zherdevka, *U.S.S.R.* **51 F12** 51 56N 41 29 E
Zherong, *China* **69 D12** 27 15N 119 52 E
Zhetykol, Ozero, *U.S.S.R.* **54 F7** 51 2N 60 54 E
Zhidan, *China* **66 F5** 36 48N 108 48 E
Zhigansk, *U.S.S.R.* **57 C13** 66 48N 123 27 E
Zhigulevsk, *U.S.S.R.* **51 E16** 53 28N 49 30 E
Zhijiang, *Hubei, China* **69 B8** 30 28N 111 45 E
Zhijiang, *Hunan, China* **68 D7** 27 27N 109 42 E
Zhijin, *China* **68 D5** 26 37N 105 45 E
Zhirnovsk, *U.S.S.R.* **51 F14** 50 57N 44 49 E
Zhitomir, *U.S.S.R.* **50 F6** 50 20N 28 40 E
Zhizdra, *U.S.S.R.* **50 E9** 53 45N 34 40 E
Zhlobin, *U.S.S.R.* **50 E7** 52 55N 30 0 E
Zhmerinka, *U.S.S.R.* **52 B3** 49 2N 28 2 E
Zhodino, *U.S.S.R.* **50 D6** 54 5N 28 17 E
Zhokhova, Ostrov, *U.S.S.R.* **57 B16** 76 4N 152 40 E
Zhong Xian, *China* **68 B7** 30 21N 108 1 E
Zhongdian, *China* **68 D2** 27 48N 99 42 E
Zhongdong, *China* **68 F6** 22 48N 107 47 E
Zhongdu, *China* **68 E7** 24 40N 109 40 E
Zhongning, *China* **66 F3** 37 29N 105 40 E
Zhongshan, *Guangdong, China* **69 F9** 22 26N 113 20 E
Zhongshan, *Guangxi Zhuangzu, China* **69 E8** 24 29N 111 18 E
Zhongtiao Shan, *China* **66 G6** 35 0N 111 10 E
Zhongwei, *China* **66 F3** 37 30N 105 12 E
Zhongxiang, *China* **69 B9** 31 12N 112 34 E
Zhongyang, *China* **66 F6** 37 20N 111 11 E
Zhoucun, *China* **67 F9** 36 47N 117 48 E
Zhouning, *China* **69 D12** 27 12N 119 20 E
Zhoushan Dao, *China* **69 C14** 28 5N 122 10 E
Zhouzhi, *China* **66 G5** 34 10N 108 12 E
Zhovtnevoye, *U.S.S.R.* **52 C5** 46 54N 32 3 E
Zhuanghe, *China* **67 E12** 39 40N 123 0 E
Zhuantobe, *U.S.S.R.* **55 B9** 43 43N 78 18 E
Zhucheng, *China* **67 G10** 36 0N 119 27 E
Zhugqu, *China* **66 H3** 33 40N 104 30 E
Zhuhai, *China* **69 F9** 22 15N 113 30 E
Zhuji, *China* **69 C13** 29 40N 120 10 E
Zhukovka, *U.S.S.R.* **50 E8** 53 35N 33 50 E
Zhumadian, *China* **66 H8** 32 59N 114 2 E
Zhuo Xian, *China* **66 E8** 39 28N 115 58 E
Zhuolu, *China* **66 D8** 40 20N 115 12 E
Zhuozi, *China* **66 D7** 41 0N 112 25 E
Zhupanovo, *U.S.S.R.* **57 D16** 53 40N 159 52 E
Zhushan, *China* **69 A8** 32 15N 110 13 E
Zhuxi, *China* **68 A7** 32 25N 109 40 E
Zhuzhou, *China* **69 D9** 27 49N 113 12 E
Zi Shui →, *China* **69 C9** 28 40N 112 40 E
Zīārān, *Iran* **85 B6** 36 7N 50 32 E
Ziarat, *Pakistan* **80 D2** 30 25N 67 49 E
Zibo, *China* **67 F10** 36 47N 118 3 E
Zichang, *China* **66 F5** 37 18N 109 40 E
Zichem, *Belgium* **21 F5** 51 2N 4 59 E
Zidarovo, *Bulgaria* **43 E12** 42 20N 27 24 E
Ziębice, *Poland* **47 E4** 50 37N 17 2 E
Zielona Góra, *Poland* **47 D2** 51 57N 15 31 E
Zielona Góra □, *Poland* **47 D2** 51 57N 15 30 E
Zierikzee, *Neths.* **21 E3** 51 40N 3 55 E
Ziesar, *Germany* **26 C8** 52 16N 12 19 E
Zifta, *Egypt* **94 H7** 30 43N 31 14 E
Zigazinskiy, *U.S.S.R.* **54 E5** 53 50N 57 20 E
Zigey, *Chad* **97 F3** 14 43N 15 50 E
Zigong, *China* **68 C5** 29 15N 104 48 E
Zigui, *China* **69 B8** 31 0N 110 40 E
Ziguinchor, *Senegal* **100 C1** 12 35N 16 20W
Zihuatanejo, *Mexico* **146 D4** 17 38N 101 33W
Zijin, *China* **69 F10** 23 33N 115 8 E
Zile, *Turkey* **88 C6** 40 15N 35 52 E
Žilina, *Czech.* **31 B11** 49 12N 18 42 E
Zillah, *Libya* **96 C3** 28 30N 17 33 E
Zillertaler Alpen, *Austria* **30 D4** 47 6N 11 45 E
Zima, *U.S.S.R.* **57 D11** 54 0N 102 5 E
Zimane, Adrar in, *Algeria* **99 D5** 22 10N 4 30 E
Zimapán, *Mexico* **147 C5** 20 54N 99 20W
Zimba, *Zambia* **107 F2** 17 20 S 26 11 E
Zimbabwe, *Zimbabwe* **107 G3** 20 16 S 30 54 E
Zimbabwe ■, *Africa* **107 F3** 19 0 S 30 0 E
Zimnicea, *Romania* **46 F6** 43 40N 25 22 E
Zimovniki, *U.S.S.R.* **53 C10** 47 10N 42 25 E
Zinal, *Switz.* **28 D5** 46 8N 7 38 E
Zinder, *Niger* **97 F1** 13 48N 9 0 E
Zinga, *Tanzania* **107 D4** 9 16 S 38 49 E
Zingem, *Belgium* **21 G3** 50 54N 3 40 E
Zingst, *Germany* **26 A8** 54 24N 12 45 E
Ziniaré, *Burkina Faso* **101 C4** 12 35N 1 18W
Zinkgruvan, *Sweden* **15 F9** 58 50N 15 6 E
Zinnowitz, *Germany* **26 A9** 54 5N 13 54 E
Zion, *U.S.A.* **141 B9** 42 27N 87 50W
Zion Nat. Park, *U.S.A.* **143 H7** 37 25N 112 50W
Zionsville, *U.S.A.* **141 E10** 39 57N 86 16W
Zipaquirá, *Colombia* **152 C3** 5 0N 74 0W
Zirc, *Hungary* **31 D10** 47 17N 17 42 E
Žiri, *Yugoslavia* **39 B11** 46 5N 14 5 E
Žirje, *Yugoslavia* **39 E12** 43 39N 15 42 E
Zirl, *Austria* **30 D4** 47 17N 11 14 E
Ziros, *Greece* **32 D8** 35 5N 26 8 E
Zisterdorf, *Austria* **31 C9** 48 33N 16 45 E
Zitácuaro, *Mexico* **146 D4** 19 28N 100 21W
Zitava →, *Czech.* **31 C11** 48 14N 18 21 E
Žitište, *Yugoslavia* **42 B5** 45 30N 20 32 E
Zítsa, *Greece* **44 E2** 39 47N 20 40 E
Zittau, *Germany* **26 E10** 50 54N 14 47 E
Zitundo, *Mozam.* **105 D5** 26 48 S 32 47 E
Živinice, *Yugoslavia* **42 C3** 44 27N 18 36 E
Ziway, L., *Ethiopia* **95 F4** 8 0N 38 50 E
Zixi, *China* **69 D11** 27 45N 117 4 E
Zixing, *China* **69 E9** 25 59N 113 21 E
Ziyang, *Shaanxi, China* **66 H5** 32 32N 108 31 E
Ziyang, *Sichuan, China* **68 B5** 30 6N 104 40 E
Ziyun, *China* **68 E6** 25 45N 106 5 E
Ziz, Oued →, *Morocco* **98 B4** 31 40N 4 15W
Zizhixian, *China* **69 E8** 25 0N 111 47 E
Zizhong, *China* **68 C5** 29 48N 104 47 E
Zlarin, *Yugoslavia* **39 E12** 43 42N 15 49 E
Zlatar, *Hrvatska, Yugoslavia* **39 B13** 46 5N 16 3 E
Zlatar, *Srbija, Yugoslavia* **42 D4** 43 25N 19 47 E
Zlataritsa, *Bulgaria* **43 D10** 43 2N 25 55 E
Zlatibor, *Yugoslavia* **42 D4** 43 45N 19 43 E
Zlatitsa, *Bulgaria* **43 E9** 42 41N 24 7 E
Zlatna, *Romania* **46 C4** 46 8N 23 11 E
Zlatograd, *Bulgaria* **43 F10** 41 22N 25 7 E
Zlatoust, *U.S.S.R.* **54 D6** 55 10N 59 40 E
Zletovo, *Yugoslavia* **42 F7** 41 59N 22 17 E
Zlin = Gottwaldov, *Czech.* **31 B10** 49 14N 17 40 E
Zlītan, *Libya* **96 B2** 32 32N 14 35 E
Złocieniec, *Poland* **47 B3** 53 30N 16 1 E
Złoczew, *Poland* **47 D5** 51 24N 18 35 E
Zlot, *Yugoslavia* **42 C6** 44 1N 21 58 E
Złotoryja, *Poland* **47 D2** 51 8N 15 55 E
Złotów, *Poland* **47 B4** 53 22N 17 2 E
Zloty Stok, *Poland* **47 E3** 50 27N 16 53 E
Zmeinogorsk, *U.S.S.R.* **56 D9** 51 10N 82 13 E
Żmigród, *Poland* **47 D3** 51 28N 16 53 E
Znamenka, *U.S.S.R.* **52 B5** 48 45N 32 30 E
Znamensk, *U.S.S.R.* **50 D2** 54 37N 21 17 E
Żnin, *Poland* **47 C4** 52 51N 17 44 E
Znojmo, *Czech.* **30 C9** 48 50N 16 2 E
Zoar, *S. Africa* **104 E3** 33 30 S 21 26 E
Zobeyrī, *Iran* **84 C5** 34 10N 46 40 E
Zobia, *Zaïre* **106 B2** 3 0N 25 59 E
Zoetermeer, *Neths.* **20 D5** 52 3N 4 30 E
Zofingen, *Switz.* **28 B5** 47 17N 7 56 E
Zogang, *China* **68 C1** 29 55N 97 42 E
Zogno, *Italy* **38 C6** 45 49N 9 41 E
Zogqên, *China* **68 A2** 32 13N 98 47 E
Zolder, *Belgium* **21 F6** 51 1N 5 19 E
Zollikofen, *Switz.* **28 C4** 47 0N 7 28 E
Zollikon, *Switz.* **29 B7** 47 21N 8 34 E
Zolochev, *U.S.S.R.* **50 G4** 49 45N 24 51 E
Zolotonosha, *U.S.S.R.* **52 B5** 49 39N 32 5 E
Zomba, *Malawi* **107 F4** 15 22 S 35 19 E
Zomergem, *Belgium* **21 F3** 51 7N 3 33 E
Zongo, *Zaïre* **102 B3** 4 20N 18 35 E
Zonguldak, *Turkey* **52 F4** 41 28N 31 50 E
Zonguldak □, *Turkey* **88 C4** 41 20N 31 45 E
Zonhoven, *Belgium* **21 G6** 50 59N 5 23 E
Zonqor Pt., *Malta* **32 D2** 35 51N 14 34 E
Zonza, *France* **25 G13** 41 45N 9 11 E
Zorgo, *Burkina Faso* **101 C4** 12 15N 0 35W
Zorita, *Spain* **37 F5** 39 17N 5 39W
Zorleni, *Romania* **46 C8** 46 14N 27 44 E
Zornitsa, *Bulgaria* **43 E11** 42 23N 26 58 E
Zorritos, *Peru* **156 A1** 3 43 S 80 40W
Zory, *Poland* **31 A11** 50 3N 18 44 E
Zorzor, *Liberia* **100 D3** 7 46N 9 28W
Zossen, *Germany* **26 C9** 52 13N 13 28 E
Zottegem, *Belgium* **21 G3** 50 52N 3 48 E
Zou Xiang, *China* **66 G9** 35 30N 116 58 E
Zouar, *Chad* **97 D3** 20 30N 16 32 E
Zouérate, *Mauritania* **98 D2** 22 44N 12 21W
Zousfana, O. →, *Algeria* **99 B4** 31 28N 2 17W
Zoushan Dao, *China* **69 B14** 30 5N 122 10 E
Zoutkamp, *Neths.* **20 B8** 53 20N 6 18 E
Zrenjanin, *Yugoslavia* **42 B5** 45 22N 20 23 E
Zuarungu, *Ghana* **101 C4** 10 49N 0 46W
Zuba, *Nigeria* **101 D6** 9 11N 7 12 E
Zubayr, *Yemen* **86 D3** 15 3N 42 10 E
Zubia, *Spain* **37 H7** 37 8N 3 33W
Zubtsov, *U.S.S.R.* **50 C9** 56 10N 34 34 E
Zudáñez, *Bolivia* **157 D5** 19 6 S 64 44W
Zuénoula, *Ivory C.* **100 D3** 7 34N 6 3W
Zuera, *Spain* **34 D4** 41 51N 0 49W
Zuetina, *Libya* **96 B4** 30 58N 20 7 E
Zufar, *Oman* **87 C6** 17 40N 54 0 E
Zug, *Switz.* **29 B7** 47 10N 8 31 E
Zug □, *Switz.* **29 B7** 47 9N 8 35 E
Zugdidi, *U.S.S.R.* **53 E9** 42 30N 41 55 E
Zugersee, *Switz.* **29 B7** 47 7N 8 35 E
Zugspitze, *Germany* **27 H6** 47 25N 10 59 E
Zuid-Holland □, *Neths.* **20 E5** 52 0N 4 35 E
Zuidbeveland, *Neths.* **21 F3** 51 30N 3 50 E
Zuidbroek, *Neths.* **20 B9** 53 10N 6 52 E
Zuidelijk-Flevoland, *Neths.* **20 D6** 52 22N 5 22 E
Zuidhorn, *Neths.* **20 B8** 53 15N 6 23 E
Zuidlaarder meer, *Neths.* **20 B9** 53 8N 6 42 E
Zuidlaren, *Neths.* **20 B9** 53 6N 6 42 E
Zuidwolde, *Neths.* **20 C8** 52 40N 6 26 E
Zújar, *Spain* **35 H2** 37 34N 2 50W
Zújar →, *Spain* **37 F5** 39 1N 5 47W
Zújar, Pantano del, *Spain* **37 G5** 38 55N 5 35W
Zula, *Ethiopia* **95 D4** 15 17N 39 40 E
Zulia □, *Venezuela* **152 B3** 10 0N 72 10W
Zulpich, *Germany* **26 E2** 50 41N 6 38 E
Zumaya, *Spain* **34 B2** 43 19N 2 15W
Zumbo, *Mozam.* **107 F3** 15 35 S 30 26 E
Zummo, *Nigeria* **101 D7** 9 51N 12 59 E
Zumpango, *Mexico* **147 D5** 19 48N 99 6W
Zundert, *Neths.* **21 F5** 51 28N 4 39 E
Zungeru, *Nigeria* **101 D6** 9 48N 6 8 E
Zunhua, *China* **67 D9** 40 18N 117 58 E
Zuni, *U.S.A.* **143 J9** 35 7N 108 57W
Zunyi, *China* **68 D6** 27 42N 106 53 E
Zuoquan, *China* **66 F7** 37 5N 113 22 E
Zuozhou, *China* **68 F6** 22 42N 107 27 E
Županja, *Yugoslavia* **42 B3** 45 4N 18 43 E
Žur, *Yugoslavia* **42 E5** 42 13N 20 34 E
Zura, *U.S.S.R.* **54 C3** 57 36N 53 24 E
Zurbātīyah, *Iraq* **84 C5** 33 9N 46 3 E
Zürich, *Switz.* **29 B7** 47 22N 8 32 E
Zürich □, *Switz.* **29 B7** 47 26N 8 40 E
Zürichsee, *Switz.* **29 B7** 47 18N 8 40 E
Zuromin, *Poland* **47 B6** 53 4N 19 51 E
Zuru, *Nigeria* **101 C6** 11 20N 5 11 E
Zurzach, *Switz.* **29 A6** 47 35N 8 18 E
Žut, *Yugoslavia* **39 E12** 43 52N 15 17 E
Zutendaal, *Belgium* **21 G7** 50 56N 5 35 E
Zutphen, *Neths.* **20 D8** 52 9N 6 12 E
Zuwārah, *Libya* **96 B2** 32 58N 12 1 E
Zuyevka, *U.S.S.R.* **54 B2** 58 27N 51 10 E
Zūzan, *Iran* **85 C8** 34 22N 59 53 E
Žužemberk, *Yugoslavia* **39 C11** 45 52N 14 56 E
Zvenigorodka, *U.S.S.R.* **52 B4** 49 4N 30 56 E
Zverinogolovskoye, *U.S.S.R.* **54 D9** 54 23N 64 40 E
Zvezdets, *Bulgaria* **43 E12** 42 6N 27 26 E
Zvishavane, *Zimbabwe* **107 G3** 20 17 S 30 2 E
Zvolen, *Czech.* **31 C12** 48 33N 19 10 E
Zvonce, *Yugoslavia* **42 E7** 42 57N 22 34 E
Zvornik, *Yugoslavia* **42 C4** 44 26N 19 7 E
Zwaag, *Neths.* **20 C6** 52 40N 5 4 E
Zwanenburg, *Neths.* **20 D5** 52 23N 4 45 E
Zwarte Meer, *Neths.* **20 C7** 52 38N 5 57 E
Zwarte Waler, *Neths.* **20 C8** 52 39N 6 1 E
Zwartemeer, *Neths.* **20 C10** 52 43N 7 2 E
Zwartsluis, *Neths.* **20 C8** 52 39N 6 4 E
Zwedru = Tchien, *Liberia* **100 D3** 5 59N 8 15W
Zweibrücken, *Germany* **27 F3** 49 15N 7 20 E
Zwenkau, *Germany* **26 D8** 51 13N 12 19 E
Zwettl, *Austria* **30 C8** 48 35N 15 9 E
Zwevegem, *Belgium* **21 G2** 50 48N 3 20 E
Zwickau, *Germany* **26 E8** 50 43N 12 30 E
Zwiesel, *Germany* **27 F9** 49 1N 13 14 E
Zwijnaarde, *Belgium* **21 G3** 51 0N 3 43 E
Zwijndrecht, *Belgium* **21 F4** 51 13N 4 20 E
Zwijndrecht, *Neths.* **20 E5** 51 50N 4 39 E
Zwischenahn, *Germany* **26 B4** 53 12N 8 1 E
Zwoleń, *Poland* **47 D8** 51 21N 21 36 E
Zwolle, *Neths.* **20 C8** 52 31N 6 6 E
Zwolle, *U.S.A.* **139 K8** 31 38N 93 38W
Żychlin, *Poland* **47 C6** 52 15N 19 37 E
Zymoetz →, *Canada* **130 C3** 54 33N 128 31W
Żyrardów, *Poland* **47 C7** 52 3N 20 28 E
Zyrya, *U.S.S.R.* **53 F14** 40 20N 50 15 E
Zyryanka, *U.S.S.R.* **57 C16** 65 45N 150 51 E
Zyryanovsk, *U.S.S.R.* **56 E9** 49 43N 84 20 E
Żywiec, *Poland* **31 B12** 49 42N 19 10 E
Zyyi, *Cyprus* **32 E12** 34 43N 33 20 E

NORTH
AMERICA

ARCTIC
OCEAN
6

126-127

12-13

Arctic Circle

12

14

130-131

18

19 16-17

25

142-143   138-139   134-135

22-23   20

136-137   24-25   38-39

140-141

144-
145   36-37   34-35   40

A T L A N T I C   33
                                  33
        O C E A N
                              98-99

ATLANTIC
OCEAN
8-9   33

                              33

132   148-149   Tropic of Cancer

PACIFIC
OCEAN   96-97
122-123   146-147

                        152-153

                    100-101

                        154-155   Equator

SOUTH
                                         AFRICA
AMERICA

                                         102

156-157   Tropic of Capricorn

PACIFIC   OCEAN

                        158-159

KEY TO WORLD MAP PAGES.   160